MODERN BUSINESS LAW

Second Edition

Thomas W. Dunfee
University of Pennsylvania,
The Wharton School

Frank F. Gibson
Ohio State University

John D. Blackburn
Ohio State University

Douglas Whitman
University of Kansas

F. William McCarty
Western Michigan University

Bartley A. Brennan
Bowling Green State University

 RANDOM HOUSE BUSINESS DIVISION / NEW YORK

To our students
from whom we have learned so much.

Second Edition
987654321
Copyright © 1984, 1989 by Thomas W. Dunfee, Frank F. Gibson, John D. Blackburn, Douglas Whitman, F. William McCarty, and Bartley A. Brennan

All rights reserved under International and Pan-American Copyright Conventions. No part of this book may be reproduced in any form or by any means, electronic or mechanical, including photocopying, without permission in writing from the publisher. All inquiries should be addressed to Random House, Inc., 201 East 50th Street, New York, N.Y. 10022. Published in the United States by Random House, Inc., and simultaneously in Canada by Random House of Canada Limited, Toronto.

This work was also published, in different form, in 1979.

Library of Congress Cataloging in Publication Data

Modern business law.

   Includes bibliographies and indexes.
   1. Commercial law—United States. I. Dunfee, Thomas W.
KF889.M6 1989   346.73'07   88-32373
ISBN 0-394-36538-0   347.3067

Manufactured in the United States of America

About the Authors

Thomas W. Dunfee is the Joseph Kolodny Professor of Social Responsibility at the Wharton School, University of Pennsylvania. He received the J.D. degree in 1966 and the LL.M. in 1969 from the New York University School of Law. He is Chairman of the Department of Legal Studies and also has an appointment in marketing at the Wharton School. He has served as Editor-in-Chief of *The American Business Law Journal* for three years. He is the author of many books on the subject of business law and has published widely in academic journals, including *The Northwestern Law Review* and *The American Business Law Journal.* He also has wide experience acting as consultant to corporations, government agencies, and trade associations.

Frank F. Gibson is a Professor of Business Law and Legal Environment in the College of Business of The Ohio State University, where he has taught since 1966. He also serves as Chair for the Finance Department. He was formerly Editor-in-Chief of *The American Business Law Journal,* and also served as President of the American Business Law Association.

John D. Blackburn is an Associate Professor of business law at The Ohio State University. He received his B.S. degree from Indiana State University and his J.D. degree from The University of Cincinnati. He has served on the faculties of The University of Cincinnati, Indiana University, and The Wharton School, University of Pennsylvania. He has published articles and books in the field of labor law, including *The Legal Environment of Business* with Elliot Klayman and Martin Malin; and *Labor Relations: Law, Practice, and Policy* with Julius Gettman.

Douglas Whitman is Full Professor at the School of Business Administration of the University of Kansas. He received his B.A. from Knox College, his M.B.A. from the University of Kansas, J.D. from the University of Missouri, and LL.M. from the University of Missouri at Kansas City. He has written articles on advertising law and products liability, and has published in *St. John's Law Review; Southwestern Law Journal* (at Southern Methodist Law School); *The University of California, Davis Law Review; The University of Pittsburgh Law Review Journal of Product Liability;* and *American Business Law Journal.* His articles have also been reprinted in *The Advertising Law Anthology, The Personal Injury Desk Book, The Corporate Counsel's Annual,* and by The American Trial Lawyer's Association. He has also written articles for the Advertising Compliance Service.

F. William McCarty is Chair and Professor in the Department of Finance and Commercial Law at Western Michigan University. A specialist in international business law, administrative law, and estate planning, Professor McCarty received his B.A. from De Pauw University and his J.D. degree from the University of Michigan. He also received a diploma from the Europa Institute of the University of Amsterdam. He is the author of numerous articles and books, including *Modern Business Law: Contracts, Modern Business Law: Legal Environment, Legal Environment: An Introduction to the American Legal Environment* and *Law and Business.*

Bartley A. Brennan is Chair and Professor in the Department of Legal Studies at Bowling Green State University. He is a graduate of the School of Foreign Service, Georgetown University (B.S., International Economics) and The College of Law, State University of New York at Buffalo (J.D.). He was a volunteer in the United States Peace Corps, was employed by the Office of Opinions and Review of the Federal Communications Commission, and worked in the General Counsel's office of a private corporation. He has received appointments as a visiting Associate Professor, The Wharton School, University of Pennsylvania, and as a Research Fellow, Ethics Resource Center, Washington, D.C. He is author of articles dealing with government regulation.

Preface

Modern Business Law, Second Edition, surveys the major areas of the law that have an impact on the operation of business firms. These areas include the legal environment, contracts, commercial transactions, business organizations, property, and government regulation.

Based on our combined experience as classroom teachers, active practitioners, and business consultants, *Modern Business Law,* Second Edition, features in every chapter major issues relevant to prospective business managers. Throughout the text, excerpts of court opinions from important cases are used to demonstrate the application of various rules of law to business problems.

Court opinions in every chapter are integrated into the text discussion, so that important corresponding legal issues can be analyzed as they are introduced. Cases have been selected on the basis of three criteria: (1) readability, (2) relevance to a major point or issue in the text, and (3) business context, or capacity to demonstrate the business application of a legal question. We have made an effort throughout the text to choose case excerpts that are neither too short—and therefore meaningless—nor too long—and therefore tedious for the student. In addition, case introductions, in a separate section and in a second color, are provided by the authors to help the student understand the background and impact of the cases.

In the development of the text and its supplements, attention has been given to pedagogical features helpful to both the professor and the student. A variety of review questions are provided at the end of each chapter. The first series of questions ask for information that demonstrates an understanding of the basic information provided in the chapter. The next group of questions are hypothetical problems created by the authors to test the student's ability to apply basic legal concepts. The final set of questions are problems based on actual cases to which the student is referred by specific citations. A complete glossary of legal terms and a detailed appendix are also provided. The appendix includes the Uniform Commercial Code, the Uniform Partnership Act, the Uniform Limited Partnership Act, and the 1983 Revised Model Business Corporation Act.

The second edition of *Modern Business Law* builds on the strengths of the first edition and reflects important developments in business school education. The two major developments of the past few years—increased emphasis on ethics throughout the business curriculum, and rapid internationalism of business schools as institutions—are reflected in major changes to this edition.

The second edition features a full chapter devoted to international business law (Chapter 47). Increased emphasis on business ethics has been accomplished in two ways. Material from the first edition included in the chapter on social responsibility and business ethics has been expanded into two chapters, "Business and Ethics" (Chapter 4) and "Social Responsibility of Business" (Chapter 5). In addition, throughout the text we have inserted ethics boxes that present issues related to legal material discussed in the chapter. We hope instructors will use these boxes to initiate discussion of these and related ethical issues.

We liked the idea of boxes so much that we developed them for two other areas: preventive law, and issues and trends. We believe that business managers should understand that the most effective method of reducing legal costs is to prevent legal problems from arising. Although the preventive law boxes are often legal tips, their underlying purpose is to emphasize that one of the effective uses of lawyers is to avoid legal problems. Readers are reminded that the purpose of this book is to provide general information about the legal system. The principles presented are subject to local, state, and federal laws, which vary and change frequently. This book therefore should not be used as a substitute for professional legal advice.

The issues and trends boxes are included for several reasons. Probably most important is that many students, even after a business law/legal environment course, fail to understand that the legal system is dynamic. It is characterized by constant change and conflict about what the law is and what it should be. We think that the educated person should be aware that change and conflict exist in the legal system. As with the ethics boxes, we hope that the preventive law and the issues and trends boxes will help initiate discussion.

In this edition we have expanded coverage in several other important areas. The chapter on accountant's liability (Chapter 48), available as a paperbound supplement for the first edition, has been revised and incorporated into the text. We have also added a chapter on insurance law (Chapter 42) that will allow in-

structors the opportunity for more specialized coverage of the legal aspects of insurance. Material from the first edition on competitive torts has been expanded into a complete chapter (Chapter 7) as has been the material on criminal law (Chapter 3).

Although the number of cases remains nearly the same as in the first edition, about twenty-five percent are new. We have made minor changes in case introductions to help the student better understand the history and significance of the decisions.

Modern Business Law, Second Edition, is accompanied by a complete set of supplements: an instructor's manual by the authors; a test bank by Gary Tidwell, College of Charleston, and Sebastian Rainone, Villanova University; and a study guide by Mark Phelps, University of Oregon. Both the instructor's manual and the test bank are available in computerized form.

Many persons assisted in the preparation of this edition. For their helpful comments and suggestions, we are grateful to William J. Burke, University of Lowell; Mary Jane Dundas, Arizona State University; Roy Girasa, Pace University, Pleasantville Campus; Thomas Goldman, Bucks County Community College; Howard Hammer, Ball State University; Charles Hartmann, Wright State University; Marsha Hass, College of Charleston; Robert G. Hilgerman, Santa Barbara City College; Georgia L. Holmes, Mankato State University; Percy Lambert, Borough of Manhattan Community College; Paul Lange, California State University, Fresno; Gene Marsh, University of Alabama; Jean Reid, New York University; Roger W. Reinsch, Emporia State University; Linda B. Samuels, George Mason University; Joseph Stone, Marshall University; Charles Walker, University of Mississippi; Winston Waters, St. Francis College; and Don Wiesner, University of Miami.

We also wish to thank again the reviewers of the first edition: John E. Adamson, Southwest Missouri State University; Glenn E. Droegemueller, University of Northern Colorado; Susan Grady, University of Massachusetts; Beverly Hunt, Thomas M. Cooley Law School; James Jackman, Oklahoma State University; Elliott Klayman, Ohio State University; Glen E. Laughlin, Oklahoma State University; Michael A. Mass, American University; Nicholas Ordway, University of Texas at Arlington; Lawrence E. Ross, University of Oregon; and Edwin W. Tucker, University of Connecticut-Storrs.

The staff at Random House has provided tremendous support. We thank them for their help and especially their patience and good humor. We would also like to thank Richard Merrin, an M.B.A./J.D. student at Ohio State University, who gathered much of the material for the computer crimes section of the criminal law chapter; Roy Larson, Adam Druitz, and Steve Salbu, research assistants at the University of Pennsylvania; and Lauretta Tomasco, an administrative secretary at the University of Pennsylvania, who provided substantial assistance with manuscript preparation. We acknowledge with gratitude the contribution of David B. Cohen, who wrote the original chapter on accountant's liability.

T.W.D.
F.F.G.
J.D.B.
D.W.
F.W.M.
B.A.B.

Contents in Brief

Contents in Detail

PART I

LEGAL ENVIRONMENT OF BUSINESS

The Functions and Sources of Law

One of the functions of this book is to help you understand the nature of law and how the legal system operates. In either your personal or business life, perhaps both, you probably will be involved with the legal system at some time. Often this involvement will concern a serious problem. Understanding the legal system will help you to deal with legal problems more effectively and reduce any anxiety that you might have about your involvement.

The legal system is a very important institution in our society. It is one of the principal means that society uses to solve some of the difficult problems that people face. The chapter first points out some of the specific functions of the legal system. Following this the chapter examines the sources that people must use to determine what the law is. Finally, the chapter considers some of the alternative methods of settling disputes that have become important during the last fifty years.

LEGAL SYSTEMS

Most of us would agree that human beings are social creatures and that we depend upon each other in many ways. This interdependence is the result of both biological and psychological needs; it is also the key to survival in a world in which nature grudgingly provides the requirements for subsistence. On the other hand, difficult problems arise because people live, work, and play together. Over the centuries society has attempted to solve these problems in many ways. One way that has been adopted almost universally is the development of a legal system.

A *legal system* makes the peaceful solution

3

of some of society's problems possible by establishing rules—generally called laws—that govern human conduct. In order to be effective these laws must be enforced by some social institution that has the power to control the manner in which people act. In the Western world the power that makes the enforcement of laws possible is government. In other areas of the world, institutions such as religion and the family often supply that authority.

The legal system is made up of numerous subsystems that create and enforce the law. These include the courts, legislative bodies, law enforcement agencies, and the practicing bar, as well as various types of administrative boards, commissions, and departments. As a general rule, the solution that these organizations provide for society's problems occurs in a clearly defined organizational structure. An example would be the court systems that are discussed in the next chapter. Additionally, a legal solution to a problem generally occurs in a formal and orderly fashion. Civil and criminal procedures, which are discussed in later chapters, are examples.

Because of the many different ways in which people interact, the legal system must deal with a wide range of problems. *Kelly* v. *Gwinnell*, the case that follows, illustrates the manner in which the legal system has dealt with one of the current problems facing society. The case deals with the legal liability of a person who furnishes alcoholic beverages to someone who is obviously intoxicated.

Kelly v. Gwinnell

Supreme Court of New Jersey

476 A.2d 1219 (1984)

Background: Marie E. Kelly (plaintiff-appellant) was injured in an automobile accident by an automobile driven by Donald Gwinnell. She sued Gwinnell and Joseph and Catherine Zak (defendants-appellees), who had provided liquor to Gwinnell. The Zaks moved to dismiss the case on grounds that a host is not liable for the negligence of an adult social guest. The trial court agreed and dismissed. The dismissal was affirmed by an intermediate appellate court and Kelly appealed to the New Jersey Supreme Court. Additional facts are in the opinion.

Decision: Reversed and remanded.

Wilentz, Chief Justice

This case raises the issue of whether a social host who enables an adult guest at his home to become drunk is liable to the victim of an automobile accident caused by the drunken driving of the guest.

The record . . . discloses that defendant Donald Gwinnell, after driving defendant Joseph Zak home, spent an hour or two at Zak's home before leaving to return to his own home. During that time, according to Gwinnell, Zak, and Zak's wife, Gwinnell consumed two or three drinks of scotch on the rocks. Zak accompanied Gwinnell outside to his car, chatted with him, and watched as Gwinnell then drove off to go home. About twenty-five minutes later Zak telephoned Gwinnell's home to make sure Gwinnell had arrived there safely. The phone was answered by Mrs. Gwinnell, who advised Zak that Gwinnell had been involved in a head-on collision. The collision was with an automobile operated by plaintiff, Marie Kelly, who was seriously injured as a result.

After the accident Gwinnell was subjected to a blood test, which indicated a blood alcohol concentration of 0.286 percent. Kelly's expert concluded from that reading that Gwinnell had consumed not two or three scotches but the equivalent of thirteen drinks; that while at Zak's home Gwinnell must have been showing unmistakable signs of intoxication; and that in fact he was severely intoxicated while at Zak's residence and at the time of the accident.

Under the facts here defendant provided his guest with liquor, knowing that thereafter the guest would have to drive in order to get home. Viewing the facts most favorably to plaintiff . . . one could reasonably conclude that the Zaks must have known that their provision of liquor was causing Gwinnell to become drunk, yet they continued to serve him even after he was visibly intoxicated. By the time he left, Gwinnell was in fact severely intoxicated. A reasonable person in Zak's position could foresee quite clearly that this continued provision of alcohol to Gwinnell was making it more and more likely that Gwinnell would not be able to operate his car carefully. Zak could foresee that unless he stopped providing drinks to Gwinnell, Gwinnell was likely to injure someone as a result of the negligent operation of his car. Under those circumstances the . . . question . . . is whether a duty exists to prevent such risk or, realistically, whether this Court should impose such a duty.

While the imposition of a duty here would go beyond our prior decisions, those decisions not only point clearly in that direction but do so despite the presence of social considerations similar to those involved in this case—considerations that are claimed to invest the host with immunity. In our first case on the subject, we held a licensee liable for the consequences of a customer's negligent operation of his automobile. . . .

The argument is made that the rule imposing liability on licensees is justified because licensees, unlike social hosts, derive a profit from serving liquor. We reject this analysis of the liability's foundation and emphasize that the liability proceeds from the duty of care that accompanies control of the liquor supply. Whatever the motive behind making alcohol available to those who will subsequently drive, the provider has a duty to the public not to create foreseeable, unreasonable risks by this activity.

We therefore hold that a host who serves liquor to an adult social guest, knowing both that the guest is intoxicated and will thereafter be operating a motor vehicle, is liable for injuries inflicted on a third party as a result of the negligent operation of a motor vehicle by the adult guest when such negligence is caused by the intoxication. While we recognize the concern that our ruling will interfere with accepted standards of social behavior; will intrude on and somewhat diminish the enjoyment, relaxation, and camaraderie that accompany social gatherings at which alcohol is served; and that such gatherings and social relationships are not simply tangential benefits of a civilized society but are regarded by many as important, we believe that the added assurance of just compensation to the victims of drunken driving as well as the added deterrent effect of the rule on such driving outweigh the importance of those other values.

Some fear has been expressed that the extent of the potential liability may be disproportionate to the fault of the host. A social judgment is therein implied to the effect that society does not regard as particularly serious the host's actions in causing his guests to become drunk, even though he knows they will thereafter be driving their cars. We seriously question that value judgment; indeed, we do not believe that the liability is disproportionate when the host's actions, so relatively easily corrected, may result in serious injury or death.

The goal we seek to achieve here is the fair compensation of victims who are injured as a result of drunken driving. The imposition of the duty certainly will make such fair compensation more likely. While the rule in this case will tend also to deter drunken driving, there is no assurance that it will have any significant effect. The lack of such assurance has not prevented us in the past from imposing liability on licensees. We believe the rule will make it more likely that hosts will take greater care in serving alcoholic beverages at social gatherings so as to avoid not only the moral responsibility but the economic liability that would occur if the guest were to injure someone as a result of his drunken driving.

Our ruling today will not cause a deluge of lawsuits or spawn an abundance of fraudulent and frivolous claims. Not only do we limit our holding to the situation in which a host directly serves a guest, but we impose liability solely for injuries resulting from the guest's drunken driving.

We therefore reverse the judgment in favor of the defendants Zak and remand the case to the Law Division for proceedings consistent with this opinion.

Garibaldi, Judge *(dissenting)*

Today, this Court holds that a social host who knowingly enables an adult guest to become intoxicated knowing that the guest will operate a motor vehicle is liable for damages to a third party caused by the intoxicated guest. The imposition of this liability on a social host places upon every citizen of New Jersey who pours a drink for a friend a heavy burden to monitor and regulate guests. It subjects the host to substantial potential financial liability that may be far beyond the host's resources.

I

Prior to today's decision, this Court had imposed liability only on those providers of alcoholic beverages who were licensed by the State. The Appellate Division also had expanded the liability to a social host who served liquor to a minor.

My reluctance to join the majority is not based on any exaggerated notion of judicial deference to the Legislature. Rather, it is based on my belief that before this Court plunges into this broad area of liability and imposes high duties of care on social hosts, it should carefully consider the ramifications of its actions.

A significant difference between an average citizen and a commercial licensee is the average citizen's lack of knowledge and expertise in determining levels and degrees of intoxication. Licensed commercial providers, unlike the average citizen, deal with the alcohol-consuming public every day. This experience gives them some expertise with respect to intoxication that social hosts lack. A social host will find it more difficult to determine levels and degrees of intoxication.

Whether a guest is or is not intoxicated is not a simple issue. Alcohol affects everyone differently. . . . Experts estimate that it takes alcohol twenty to thirty minutes to reach its highest level in the bloodstream. Thus, a blood alcohol concentration test demonstrating an elevated blood alcohol level after an accident may not mean that the subject was obviously intoxicated when he left the party some time earlier. "Moreover, a state of obvious intoxication is a condition that is very susceptible to after the fact interpretations, i.e., objective review of a subjective decision. Accordingly, to impose on average citizens a duty to comprehend a person's level of intoxication and the effect another drink would ultimately have on such person is to place a very heavy burden on them."

III

The most significant difference between a social host and a commercial licensee, however, is the social host's inability to spread the cost of liability. The commercial establishment spreads the cost of insurance against liability among its customers. The social host must bear the entire cost alone.

The majority cites no authority for its belief that actions against social hosts will be covered under homeowner's insurance. This new cause of action will be common and may result in large awards to third parties. Even if it is assumed that homeowner's insurance will cover this cause of action, it is unrealistic to believe that insurance companies will not raise their premiums in response to it.

Furthermore, many homeowners and apartment renters may not even have homeowner's insurance and probably cannot afford it. Other homeowners may not have sufficient insurance to cover the limitless liability that the Court seeks to impose. These people may lose everything they own if they are found liable as negligent social hosts under the Court's scheme. The individual economic cost to every New Jersey citizen should be weighed before today's result is reached.

IV

In conclusion, in trivializing these objections as "cocktail party customs" and "inconvenience," the majority misses the point. I believe that an indepth review of this problem by the Legislature will result in a solution that will further the goals of reducing injuries related to drunk driving and adequately compensating the injured party, while imposing a more limited liability on the social host.

I do not propose to fashion a legislative solution. That is for the Legislature. . . . Perhaps, after investigating all the options, the Legislature will determine that the most effective course is to impose the same civil liability on social hosts that the majority has imposed today. I would have no qualms about that legislative decision so long as it was reached after a thorough investigation of its impact on average citizens of New Jersey.

CASE NOTE

The question of whether a social host who furnishes alcoholic beverages to an intoxicated guest may be liable for death or injury caused by the guest's negligent operation of a motor vehicle has been litigated in a number of states. As the principal case indicates, traditionally, the host or hostess had no liability either to the intoxicated driver or to an injured third party. Courts justified this rule on grounds that consumption of the alcohol, and not furnishing it, was the cause of the injury. Additionally, courts held that drunk or sober individuals are responsible for their own actions.

Several state courts have modified this traditional nonliability rule. This occurred initially in states that had enacted "dram shop statutes." These statutes made liquor vendors such as bars, restaurants, taverns, and liquor stores liable for injuries to an obviously intoxicated purchaser or to a third party injured by the purchaser. Unless the dram shop statute limited liability to liquor vendors, state courts generally extended liability to social hosts as well.

A further extension of social host liability occurred in some states, like New Jersey, that did not have dram shop statutes. Beginning in the late 1960s courts in these states began to impose liability on liquor vendors on the basis of negligence if the vendor sold liquor to an obviously intoxicated person who injured another. In New Jersey and at least two other states, Washington and Ohio, liability has been extended to social hosts as well as to liquor vendors, on the basis of negligence.

SPECIFIC TASKS OF LEGAL SYSTEMS

Early in our study, we need to consider in detail some of the specific tasks of the legal system as it helps resolve some of the hard questions that society faces. At the same time, we must remember that other social institutions play important roles in solving some of these same problems. In spite of this, at least in the Western world, organized societies appear to rely most heavily upon legal systems to work out solutions to these problems.

Maintain Order

Probably the most important function of the legal system, certainly the most frequently articulated, is the maintenance of order within the community. Laws define the ramifications of relationships within a society so that people can live together with a minimum of friction and a maximum of opportunity to attain their physiological and psychological needs. The absence of order requires individuals to spend inordinate amounts of time and energy dealing with issues that might disrupt the community or groups within it. A means for orderly solution of social issues is especially important in an era such as the present when technology causes rapid and extensive changes in people's lives.

Provide a Forum for Settling Disputes

An important means by which society maintains order is by providing a forum in which individuals can settle their disputes. Without such a forum the quarrels of individuals become family, clan, or tribal problems. Frequently a group takes some form of violent action that calls forth a violent counterresponse from the individual attacked and his or her supporters. Violence continues, and in many instances no final settlement is reached until the parties and their supporters are exhausted. A principal role of the legal system even in very primitive cultures is to provide some authoritative institutional process for settling disputes.

Protect Expectations

Another task of the legal system is to ensure a measure of predictability in societal relations. For life to have meaning—in fact, for people just to survive—they must know that the agreed-upon or anticipated consequences of acting in a particular manner will generally be as expected. For example, when tenants sign a twelve-month lease for an apartment, their expectations of a place to live for at least a year are reinforced by knowledge that the legal system will provide a remedy if the owner—or anyone else—interferes with their occupancy. At the same time the owner's expectation of a certain income for the year is supported by the existence of a functioning legal system. When a consumer buys a ladder, the legal system reinforces an expectation that the user will not suffer injury because the ladder was made defectively. Of course, no law can guarantee that a person will not be injured. But the law provides compensation for injury caused by a defect and thus indirectly encourages the producer to be careful in the manufacturing process.

Maintain Established Political Authority

In almost all societies another clearly discernible function of the legal system is to maintain the dominant political authority. Laws punishing members of the society for treason are among those that have as their purpose perpetuating the established order. Authorities use to advantage the many sanctions that the legal system provides for controlling behavior. Although sanctions operate within most group relationships, the organized sanctions of the legal system, supported by political authority, are the most extensive and effective. The most potent sanctions—such as the taking of life—frequently are used to protect the existing political structure.

Bring About Social Change

Although maintaining order, providing a forum for resolving disputes, ensuring a degree of predictability, and preserving the existing political order have been important functions of even relatively primitive legal systems, legal systems also have been used to fulfill other societal needs and to help the community attain other objectives. As an important agent for accomplishing change, the legal system is effective because of the many sanctions that it can employ and because its elements ("the courts" and "the law of the land") are impersonal but respected powers that have public support. Antitrust, civil rights, and environmental protection statutes are examples of the legal system operating to accomplish social change.

SOURCES OF LAW

In trying to understand the legal environment, people need to know some of the ideas that exist about the nature of law and legal systems. Most people, however, appear more interested in determining what particular laws are and where law can be found. One of the prevailing myths accepted by many is that all laws are found in nicely indexed, officially published books of statutes. All a person has to do to learn about a law is to find the correct page in the right book, and the law will be there in clear black letters. The following sections dispel this misconception and introduce the various sources of law.

The sources of law discussed here are not the underlying sources of law such as the Judeo-Christian religious heritage or the mores and traditions of ethnic groups often reflected in the laws of a particular legal system. Instead, the sources that the individual must consult to determine what the law is are presented together with the application of these sources in particular cases.

BOX 1-1: ISSUES AND TRENDS
The Law Explosion

—

In a democratic society important social institutions such as the legal system, business, education, religion, and government are frequently subject to criticism. One criticism that has been directed against the legal system in recent years is that there is just too much of it—too much law, too much litigation, and too many lawyers.

Although no one actually knows, critics estimate that the cost of operating this system is from $20 to $40 billion a year. They note that between 1979 and 1987 the number of cases filed in the U.S. District Courts increased from 187,000 to 296,000 and that the supply of lawyers in the United States has doubled since 1960. Additionally, critics attempt to show that the United States has too much law by comparing the number of lawyers per thousand people in the major industrial nations. The fact that the United States has three times as many lawyers per thousand population as Germany, ten times the number in Sweden, and twenty times the figure in Japan is asserted as proof that the system has grown too large.

The charge that there is too much law is true to a degree; but when we consider some of the reasons for the recent explosion of the legal system, the criticism loses much of its validity. For one thing, the growth in the legal system reflects national growth. The population of the United States has more than tripled since 1900. Even more significant is the substantial increase in the concentration of population. Today, the United States is an urban nation with the attendant problems that arise when people live, work, and play in close proximity to each other.

Change, too, has led to the expansion of the legal system. During the twentieth century fundamental changes have occurred in almost all areas of American life. An agrarian society has become industrialized; sectionalism has decreased; social attitudes have altered; and new vibrant ideologies have evolved to challenge firmly held traditions and beliefs. Some of these changes have appreciably improved the quality of life for large numbers of Americans, but they have also caused significant disruption, discord, and human suffering. Industrial injury, unemployment, pollution, lack of housing, divorce, disease, stress, and a host of other problems need resolution if the fabric of social order is not to be destroyed. Yet, as these problems were arising many of the older institutions that had provided solutions such as the family, the church, and the neighborhood were losing their effectiveness. To replace them, society—for better or for worse—has turned to the legal system.

In addition to national growth and change, other factors have stimulated the expansion of the legal system. One of these is the continuing—although sometimes sporadic—quest to realize the democratic ideal in a society characterized by racial, ethnic, religious, and moral pluralism. Equality and democratic participation in this hodge-podge of ideas, beliefs, emotions, and attitudes need substantial nurturing. Some of this nurturing has been provided by a dynamic, growing legal system, albeit one that is often characterized by confusion and ineptitude as it responds to the pressures inherent in American society's quest for the democratic ideal.

ETHICS BOX
The Relationship Between Law and Ethics

Many of the issues already discussed in this chapter involve obligations among persons. The essence of ethics is concern about the impact of actions on others. Thus, law and ethics are closely related. Law defines how people should behave and sanctions those who violate legal proscriptions. Ethical theory identifies how people should behave voluntarily and provides a basis for evaluating the actions of others.

Many people mistakenly believe that law and ethics are essentially the same thing. That is not so, although legal and ethical concepts may interrelate in various ways. Merely complying with the law does not guarantee that one is ethical. Ethics goes beyond the law. The mere fact that the law requires or allows certain conduct does not make it ethical. It is possible to have an unethical law. Slavery was legal in the United States during the first half of the nineteenth century. Slavery was not sanctified as an ethical practice just because it was legal.

Ethical issues will be discussed throughout this text. Chapter 4, "Business and Ethics," will provide some general background concerning ethical theory and concepts of business ethics. Chapter 5 will apply some of these to business firms. Then, throughout the rest of the text, Ethics Boxes, similar to this one, will be used to highlight particular ethical problems and theories.

CONSTITUTIONS

Constitutions are fundamental sources of law. They establish the basic framework within which governments, both state and federal, must operate. The authority of a constitution is absolute regarding all points that it covers. In these areas, the constitution is controlling unless changed by the authority that established it. Constitutions have three major functions: (1) they guarantee individuals certain basic rights; (2) they allocate power among the legislative, judicial, and executive branches of government; and (3) they allocate power among political subdivisions.

Each state and the federal government have their own constitution. Constitutions derive their authority from the people. In the Constitution of the United States, the people, acting through state governments, grant certain powers to the federal government. In spheres where the federal government has power, its actions are supreme. On the other hand, federal action, such as a congressional enactment, is invalid unless supported by a specific constitutional provision. The Constitution also restricts actions that Congress, the President, or the federal judiciary can take. For example, Congress cannot pass a law penalizing a person for an action that was legal when committed nor can a federal agency take a person's property without providing compensation. In addition to limiting actions of government officials, the Constitution also ensures that they will not violate the rights and liberties of individuals.

State constitutions distribute the powers of government within the three branches of state government. They also provide for the distribution of power to political subdivisions. A number of state constitutions have "home rule" provisions. A provision of this nature allows municipalities the right of self-government in local affairs. Like the federal Constitution, most state constitutions declare basic rights and liberties to which people are entitled.

In the legal system operating in the United States the courts have the task of nullifying legislative or executive actions that violate a constitutional provision. In 1934 the U.S. Supreme Court declared unconstitutional the National Recovery Act, which was the cornerstone of President Roosevelt's program to end the Great Depression. When President Truman attempted to seize the steel mills in 1952 in order to end a strike that interfered with the Korean War effort, the Supreme Court determined that he did not have constitutional authority to do so.

In determining that legislative or executive actions are unconstitutional, courts have to interpret the document. Constitutional and statutory interpretation are similar, but differences do exist. Since a constitution declares fundamental principles and is intended to last

for a long time, its language may be given a broader interpretation than statutory language. Chapter 2 includes some cases in which the U.S. Supreme Court has interpreted provisions of the U.S. Constitution especially those relevant to business.

JUDICIAL LAW

A distinguishing feature of Anglo-American law is its reliance upon previously decided cases as a primary source of law. For many centuries judges and lawyers have looked for past similar cases to determine what the law is in a particular situation. Reliance upon judicial decisions, known as case law or common law, is based in part on the concept of stare decisis. *Stare decisis*, which is Latin for "to abide by or to adhere to decided cases," reflects the policy that, once a court applies a particular principle of law to a certain set of facts, that same legal principle will govern all future cases in which the facts are substantially the same.

Stare Decisis

The major problem in applying the doctrine of stare decisis arises because there are often conflicting precedents that can be analogized to the case under consideration. Opposing attorneys will argue that the facts of the present case are similar to those of cases in which different results were reached.

For example, consider a tort case involving a suit by a paying spectator at a recreation league hockey game in a municipal rink who is injured by a hockey stick flying into the stands after a player swings at a puck. Let's assume the state is one in which the statutory or common law decisions indicate that a city, as an agency of the sovereign state, is immune from suit if it is engaged in a governmental function but is not immune and can be held liable if it is engaged in a proprietary or businesslike function. The attorney for the spectator will research previous cases. He or she may find a case in which another city's operation of a municipal football stadium was found to be a businesslike operation, and thus the city could be sued and held liable for negligent operation of the stadium. On the other hand, the city attorney may find a previous case in which a city's operation of a municipal park system, including baseball diamonds, was held to be a part of the recreation program of the city, for the benefit of its citizens, and not a businesslike operation.

Which of those precedent cases would apply to the operation of a hockey rink? Would it make a difference who could use the rink? Does it matter if the city charged admission or made a profit on the operation of the rink? Is it relevant if there are privately owned rinks in or near the city? What basis for comparison or contrast would you find important?

Factual Distinction. Even if a statement in a prior case is considered to be precedent for subsequent cases, the facts of a later case may be different from those of the prior case. Even if a similar set of facts is presented in two cases, the legal issues of one case may differ from those previously considered. Thus, the problem of determining whether a hockey rink owned and operated by the city is being run as a "governmental function" or as a "business enterprise" presents different facts from the problem of determining the same question for a city baseball field, park, or football area. While the legal issues in the two cases are the same, significant future distinctions regarding the sport or recreational activity certainly could exist. For example, there might be differences in the degree of supervision exercised by the city over those using the facilities or in the existence of alternative and competing private enterprises engaged in the same activity.

When major factual distinctions exist between a case under consideration and a supposed precedent, the cases are said to be distinguished. Stare decisis does not apply to cases that can be distinguished from the relevant precedents.

Changed Conditions. On occasion courts do refuse to follow previous decisions, even though such decisions are based on similar facts, because conditions have changed significantly. The changes may involve new technology or novel economic, social, or political circumstances. An example of a change of conditions is illustrated by the case of *Flagiello* v. *Pennsylvania Hospital*. Note the comments of both the majority and the dissenting opinion as to the effect of stare decisis on their decisions. As you read the case, look for the various reasons influencing the majority decision.

Flagiello v. Pennsylvania Hospital

Supreme Court of Pennsylvania

208 A.2d 193 (1965)

Background: While Mary Flagiello (plaintiff-appellant) was a patient in Pennsylvania Hospital (defendant-appellee), she fell because of the negligence of two hospital employees. In falling she fractured her right ankle. This injury was entirely unrelated to the ailment that brought her into the hospital.

The broken ankle necessitated further hospital and medical care. As a result, Mary Flagiello and her husband brought suit against the hospital for the additional medical expense, pain, and suffering as well as impairment of earning power.

The hospital moved that their action be dismissed, asserting that under Pennsylvania

law a charitable hospital was not responsible for the negligent acts of its employees. The lower court granted the motion and plaintiffs appealed.
Decision: Reversed.

Musmanno, Judge

The hospital has not denied that its negligence caused Mrs. Flagiello's injuries. It merely announces that it is an eleemosynary institution, and, therefore, owed no duty of care to its patient. It declares in effect that it can do wrong and still not be liable in damages to the person it has wronged. It thus urges a momentous exception to the generic proposition that in law there is no wrong without a remedy.

On what basis then may a hospital, which expects and receives compensation for its services, demand of the law that it be excused from responding in damages for injuries tortiously inflicted by its employees on paying patients? The hospital . . . replies to that question with various answers, some of which are: it is an ancient rule that charitable hospitals have never been required to recompense patients who have been injured through negligence of their employees; the rule of *stare decisis* forbids that charitable hospitals be held liable . . .; if the rule of charitable immunity is to be discarded, this must be done by the State Legislature. . . .

We have seen how originally charitable hospitals devoted all their energies, resources, and time to caring for indigent patients. Today this has changed almost completely. In 1963, the fees received from patients in the still designated charitable hospitals throughout Pennsylvania constituted 90.9% of the total income of the hospitals.

But conceding that it could not operate without its paying patients the defendant hospital still objects to being categorized with business establishments because, it says, the law of charitable immunity is so deeply imbedded in our law and is of such ancient origin that it can only be extirpated by legislative enactment.

Each court which has upheld the immunity rule has relied for its authority on a previous decision or decisions, scarcely ever placing the subject for study on the table of self-asserting justice. . . .

In the early part of the twentieth century, however, some cracks began to show in the . . . edifice, and then, in 1942, Judge Rutledge (later Justice of the Supreme Court of the United States) of the United States Court of Appeals for the District of Columbia revealed in perhaps the most searching, analytical, and penetrating opinion on the subject up to that time, that the charity immunity doctrine was built on a foundation of sand. As one reads and reflects on that opinion (*Georgetown College* v. *Hughes*), he is forced to the irresistible conclusion that the immunity doctrine began in error, lifted its head in fallacy and climbed to its shaky heights only because few dared to question whether charity was really charity.

England, which is supposed to have launched the doctrine, abandoned it before it ever really set out on an authoritative voyage, and does not accept it today. Nor do Australia, Canada and New Zealand. In the United States, at least twenty-four states have wholly discarded the rule and fourteen other states have modified its application.
. . .

If havoc and financial chaos were inevitably to follow the abrogation of the immunity doctrine, as the advocates for its retention insist, this would certainly have become apparent in the states where that doctrine is no longer a defense. But neither the defendant hospital nor the Hospital Association of Pennsylvania has submitted any evidence of catastrophe in the states where charitable hospitals are tortiously liable.

The appellee and the *amicus curiae* insist that if the charity immunity doctrine is to undergo mutation, the only surgeon capable of performing the operation is the Legislature. We have seen, however, that the controverted rule is not the creation of the Legislature. This court fashioned it, and, what it put together, it can dismantle. . . .

Of course, the precedents here recalled do not justify a light and casual treatment of the doctrine of *stare decisis* but they proclaim unequivocally that where justice demands, reason dictates, equality enjoins, and fair play decrees a change in judge-made law, courts will not lack in determination to establish that change. . . .

The judgments of the Court below are reversed.

Bell, Chief Justice *(dissenting)*

I am very greatly disturbed by the virtual extirpation of the principle of stare decisis, on which the House of Law was built. In the last six years the Supreme Court of Pennsylvania has overruled cases in over forty different areas of the law which had been, prior thereto, firmly established. Today no one knows from week to week, or Court session to Court session, whenever the Supreme Court of the United States or the Supreme Court of Pennsylvania meets, what the law will be tomorrow, or what are one's rights, privileges, responsibilities and duties.

In a constitutional republican form of government such as ours, which is based upon law and order, *Certainty* and *Stability* are essential. . . . This has been the beacon light for Anglo-American Courts, for text authorities, and for law-abiding Americans ever since the foundation of our Country. In the realm of the law it is usually expressed in the principle known as Stare Decisis. Stare Decisis is one of the bed-rocks upon which the House of Law has been erected and maintained.

Scope of Precedent

Each state has its own sources of law, its own constitution, legislative enactments, administrative rulings, and judge-made precedent. As the *Flagiello* opinion notes, the courts of one state do not have to follow decisions of other states. Of course, external decisions may be consulted for reference, particularly where there are no previous decisions on the point in question in the state where a case is being heard or where, as in *Flagiello*, the reasons for adoption of new policies by another state's court may be considered applicable in the state in which the case is being heard.

Courts in each jurisdiction—federal or state—are grouped in a particular hierarchy. In this hierarchy appellate courts are generally referred to as higher courts, trial courts as lower courts. Every federal or state trial court is "under" an appellate court. Precedent flows down the hierarchy from higher to lower courts.

All courts are bound by a U.S. Supreme Court decision. In each state the lower trial and appellate courts must abide by precedent established by the highest court of the state.

Courts that are on the same level of the hierarchy are not bound to follow an opinion of a coequal court. Trial courts only need follow precedent from the appellate court covering their jurisdiction. Thus, the U.S. District Court for the Southern District of New York—a federal trial court—is not bound by a decision of the Ninth Circuit Court of Appeals, whose geographic control is limited to the West Coast.

The doctrine of stare decisis furthers the predictability of the law. If a previous case has been based upon a certain principle, that principle will be used in a subsequent case although different parties are involved in the latter case. By the principle of stare decisis, judicial decisions thus affect not only the parties to the lawsuit but also persons who are involved in a later case that is found to be similar to prior cases. People thus anticipate the legal result of their actions from a consideration of the legal results of similar actions in previous decisions. Courts are legitimately hesitant to renounce or reverse their prior decisions, preferring instead to allow any desired change to be made by the legislature.

STATUTES

Although for many years cases were the chief source of Anglo-American law, statutes were also important as a source both in England and in the United States. For many reasons, during the past 150 years statutory law has increased in importance. In addition, much of the judge-made law of previous centuries has been enacted by legislative bodies into statute. This process is called *codification.* Today, a person trying to determine the law in a particular field probably would first look for a statute covering the question. The term *statutory law* as used here encompasses not only the enactments of state and federal legislatures but also municipal ordinances, administrative rules and regulations, executive decrees, and treaties.

Distinction Between Statutory and Judicial Law

Statutory law in contrast to judicial law is usually more directly responsive to political, social, and economic considerations. While judges are clearly cognizant of societal forces that affect and are affected by their case interpretations, their written decisions are usually replete with express references to prior cases and only implicit references to the relative merits of the underlying forces involved in the case.

Statutory enactments are general and prospective, whereas judicial decisions are usually specific and retrospective. A legislative provision, for example, is usually enacted to address the problems of large numbers of people. On the other hand, the common law of judicial decisions is limited to the specific facts and legal dispute in controversy between the litigating parties. Nevertheless, a court decision not only terminates legally the dispute of the parties but, as we have seen, also has the effect of establishing principles of law that will be followed in similar situations in subsequent cases.

Conversely, statutes are prospective in nature, changing or adding to the existing law from the effective date of the statute, and thus affecting actions yet to occur as opposed to preexisting disputes. There are exceptions to these distinctions between statutory law and the common law of judicial decisions. Some statutes are so specifically drafted that only one or a small number of individuals or firms are affected by their provisions. Other judicial decisions affect many who are not parties to the particular judicial controversy.

Statutory Interpretation

The increasing use of statutes to provide solutions for social problems has not appreciably reduced the importance of cases as a source of law. Most statutes are broadly written, indicating only the outlines of legislative policy. Before the meaning of a statute is established, it often has to be interpreted or, as lawyers say, construed by the courts. Thus, in many situations when a person needs to know what the law is, he or she looks first at the statutory provision and then at cases in which it has been applied. These cases indicate what the statute actually means.

Logically, the process of judicial interpretation at first seems questionable because in effect the courts are explaining what the legislature actually meant. Upon further examination the process makes good sense, for it allows the meaning of the law to be filled in by the courts. They are better equipped than the legislature to respond to specific problems and less affected by the political pressures of the moment. Although having the courts interpret statutes is not without risk, courts in the United States have consistently stated that, in interpreting statutes, their primary function is to determine and give effect to the intention of the legislature.

As legislative bodies seldom, if ever, have specific intents, statutory interpretation is, at best, an imperfect science. To add some certainty to the process, courts have developed a number of principles, or canons of statutory interpretation, that they apply to determine legislative intent.

In applying these principles, a court must take into consideration the general purpose of the legislation. This purpose is determined from the entire act in light of its historical background, the evils at which the statute is directed, and its evident objectives. The canons of construction, which include looking at the plain meaning of terms, contextual analysis, and examination of the statute's legislative history, must yield if they conflict with clear evidence of the legislative will.

Plain Meaning. There may be words or phrases in a statute that can be interpreted in a variety of ways. A basic first step in all statutory interpretations is to look to the plain meaning of the words used to determine what the statute means. As a general rule, the words of a statute will be given their common meaning. Courts presume that the legislature intended to use them as they are used in everyday communication. In many instances the plain meaning is obvious and no further interpretative analysis is required.

On occasion, the same word may be used in different contexts by the legislature to mean different things. In some statutes *person* includes a corporation while in others, a rape statute, for example, *person* would not include a corporation. A doctor's or lawyer's practice may be a *business* for some purposes and not for others. For such words a simple dictionary definition will not suffice. Instead, the courts must consider the context in which the words are used and they must attempt to identify any relevant legislative purpose. It must be noted, however, that not all words are ambiguous. In fact, reasonable people would agree on the meanings of most words in most statutes. For example, the Uniform Partnership Act (UPA) defines a partnership as "an association of two or more persons." Section 2 of the Act defines *person* as including "individuals, partnerships, corporations, and other associations." Thus, no one could reasonably argue that *under the provisions of the UPA* a corporation could not be a partner in a partnership.

Contextual Analysis. Some legislative enactments are really segments of a larger statutory scheme. In interpreting language that is part of a larger body of legislative provisions, the courts analyze how the specific provision fits into the context of the entire legislative package. Several examples will illustrate.

In 1981 Congress passed a series of legislative enactments designed to solve pressing national economic problems. The enactments included an across-the-board reduction in personal tax rates, accelerated depreciation credits for business investment, and numerous provisions to encourage individuals to save. In interpreting a specific section of this legislation, the courts might feel constrained to analyze a provision in the context of the entire package that became law.

Similarly, one part of the Internal Revenue Code usually cannot be interpreted without reference to other sections of the Code. Thus Section 1221 of the Internal Revenue Code defines a capital asset as "property held by the taxpayer (whether or not connected with his trade or business) . . ." and then details those items which are not capital assets. . . .

(2) property used in his trade or business, of a character which is subject to the allowance for depreciation provided in section 167 . . .
(4) accounts or notes receivable acquired in the ordinary course of trade or business for services rendered or from the sale of property described in paragraph (1).

The Code's definition of capital asset is the basis for determining the tax rate to be assessed on income derived from the sale or exchange of property. If the property is not a capital asset, the gain derived is taxed at ordinary income rates instead of at capital-gains rates. Thus, the definition of a capital asset in the Internal Revenue Code would be a part of all other Code sections that directly or indirectly refer to either capital gain (or loss) or to ordinary gain (or loss) derived from the sale or exchange of property.

In reaching a decision that will reflect accurately the intent of the legislative branch, the courts seek to analyze the context in which a particular section of the Code is to be placed. Thus, the U.S. Supreme Court notes:

It would do violence to the rules of statutory construction or interpretation to single out and divorce a single phrase in a section without reference to the other portions of the Act and without reference to the manifest purpose of Congress. The legislative interest is to be determined not by taking the word or clause in question from its setting and viewing it apart, but by considering it in connection with the context, the general purposes of the statute in which it is found, the occasion and circumstance of its use, and other appropriate tests for the ascertainment of the legislative will. Helvering v. Stockholms Enskida Bank, 293 U.S. 84 (1934).

Legislative History. In seeking to interpret the meaning of statutory provisions, courts sometimes refer to committee reports, hearings, speeches from the floor of the legislature, prior drafts of the statute, failed amendments, and other aspects of the statute's legislative history. These various components of the statute's history shed light on what the legislature intended.

Dangers, however, exist when a court relies upon legislative history to determine legislative intent. Quite often legislative history is ambiguous. Legislators vote for a statute for different reasons. A statement by one senator in a committee hearing may not represent the majority view. In addition, lawmakers, aware that courts use legislative history to interpret statutes, may be tempted to make statements supporting their own views of what the legislative policy should be although they know that this is not the position of the statute's drafters. A further problem with legislative history is that many state legislatures keep few records of the deliberations and discussions upon which a statute is enacted. This problem is enlarged, for often, even when they do exist, these records are not readily available to the legal profession.

In the case that follows the court applies some of the techniques just mentioned to determine what Congress intended in enacting the Federal Arbitration Act.

Dean Witter Reynolds Inc. v. Byrd

U.S. Supreme Court
470 U.S. 213 (1985)

Background: In 1981 A. Lamar Byrd (plaintiff) sold his dental practice and invested $160,000 in securities through Dean Witter Reynolds Inc. (defendant), a securities broker-dealer. The value of the account declined and Byrd filed a complaint against Dean Witter in the U.S. District Court. He alleged violations of the Securities Exchange Act and various state law provisions.

When Byrd invested his funds with Dean Witter, he signed a Customer's Agreement providing that "[a]ny controversy between you and the undersigned arising out of . . . this contract or breach thereof, shall be settled by arbitration." Based on this agreement, Dean Witter moved to separate the state claims, to compel their arbitration pending resolution of the action in the U.S. District Court. The Securities Exchange Act claims were not subject to arbitration because of the wording of the Federal Arbitration Act. According to Dean Witter, however, the Federal Arbitration Act, which provides that arbitration agreements "shall be valid, irrevocable, and enforceable, save upon such grounds as exist at law . . . for the revocation of any contract," required the District Court to compel arbitration of the state law claims. The District Court denied Dean Witter's motion and the Court of Appeals affirmed. The U.S. Supreme Court granted certiorari.

Decision: The decisions of the District Court and the Court of Appeals not to compel arbitration were reversed.

Marshall, Justice (*delivered the opinion of the Court*)

The question presented is whether, when a complaint raises both federal securities claims and pendent state claims, a Federal District Court may deny a motion to compel arbitration of the state-law claims despite the parties' agreement to arbitrate their disputes. We granted certiorari to resolve a conflict among the Federal Courts of Appeals on this question.

Confronted with the issue we address—whether to compel arbitration of pendent state-law claims when the federal court will in any event assert jurisdiction over a federal-law claim—the Federal Courts of Appeals have adopted two different approaches. Along with the Ninth Circuit in this case, the Fifth and Eleventh Circuits have relied on the "doctrine of intertwining." When arbitrable and nonarbitrable claims arise out of the same transaction, and are sufficiently intertwined factually and legally, the district court, under this view, may in its discretion deny arbitration as to the arbitrable claims and try all the claims together in federal court. These courts acknowledge the strong federal policy in favor of enforcing arbitration agreements but offer two reasons why the district courts nevertheless should decline to compel arbitration in this situation. First, they assert that such a result is necessary to preserve what they consider to be the court's exclusive jurisdiction over the federal securities claim; otherwise, they suggest, arbitration of an "intertwined" state claim might precede the federal proceeding and the factfinding done by the arbitrator might thereby bind the federal court through collateral estoppel. The second reason they cite is efficiency; by declining to compel arbitration, the court avoids bifurcated proceedings and perhaps redundant efforts to litigate the same factual questions twice.

In contrast, the Sixth, Seventh and Eighth Circuits have held that the Federal Arbitration Act divests the district courts of any discretion regarding arbitration in cases containing both arbitrable and nonarbitrable claims, and instead requires that the courts compel arbitration of arbitrable claims, when asked to do so. These courts conclude that the Act, both through its plain meaning and the strong federal policy it reflects, requires courts to enforce the bargain of the parties to arbitrate, and "not substitute [its] own views of economy and efficiency" for those of Congress.

We agree with these latter courts that the Arbitration Act requires district courts to compel arbitration of pendent arbitrable claims when one of the parties files a motion to compel, even where the result would be the possibly inefficient maintenance of separate proceedings in different forums. Accordingly, we reverse the decision not to compel arbitration.

III

The Arbitration Act provides that written agreements to arbitrate controversies arising out of an existing contract "shall be valid, irrevocable, and enforceable, save upon such grounds as exist at law or in equity for the revocation of any contract." By its terms, the Act leaves no place for the exercise of discretion by a district court, but instead mandates that district courts *shall* direct the parties to proceed to arbitration on issues as to which an arbitration agreement has been signed. Thus, insofar as the language of the Act guides our disposition of this case, we would conclude that agreements to arbitrate must be enforced, absent a ground for revocation of the contractual agreement.

It is suggested, however, that the Act does not expressly address whether the same mandate—to enforce arbitration agreements—holds true where, as here, such a course would result in bifurcated proceedings if the arbitration agreement is enforced. Because the Act's drafters did not explicitly consider the prospect of bifurcated proceedings, we are told, the clear language of the Act might be misleading. Thus, courts that have adopted the view of the Ninth Circuit in this case have argued that the Act's goal of speedy and efficient decisionmaking is thwarted by bifurcated proceedings, and that, given the absence of clear direction on this point, the intent of Congress in passing the Act controls and compels a refusal to compel arbitration.

We turn, then, to consider whether the legislative history of the Act provides guidance on this issue. The congressional history does not expressly direct resolution of the scenario we address. We conclude, however, on consideration of Congress' intent in passing the statute, that a court must compel arbitration of otherwise arbitrable claims, when a motion to compel arbitration is made.

The legislative history of the Act establishes that the purpose behind its passage was to ensure judicial enforcement of privately made agreements to arbitrate. We therefore reject the suggestion that the overriding goal of the Arbitration Act was to promote the expeditious resolution of claims. The Act, after all, does not mandate the arbitration of all claims, but merely the enforcement—upon the motion of one of the parties—of privately negotiated arbitration agreements. The House Report accompanying the Act makes clear that its purpose was to place an arbitration agreement "upon the same footing as other contracts, where it belongs," and to overrule the judiciary's longstanding refusal to enforce agreements to arbitrate. This is not to say that Congress was blind to the potential benefit of the legislation for expedited resolution of disputes. Far from it, the House Report expressly observed:

> "It is practically appropriate that the action should be taken at this time when there is so much agitation against the costliness and delays of litigation. These matters can be largely eliminated by agreements for arbitration, if arbitration agreements are made valid and enforceable."

Nonetheless, passage of the Act was motivated, first and foremost, by a congressional desire to enforce agreements into which parties had entered, and we must not overlook this principal objective when construing the statute, or allow the fortuitous impact of the Act on efficient dispute resolution to overshadow the underlying motivation.

We therefore are not persuaded by the argument that the conflict between two goals of the Arbitration Act—enforcement of private agreements and encouragement of efficient and speedy dispute resolution—must be resolved in favor of the latter in order to realize the intent of the drafters. The preeminent concern of Congress in passing the Act was to enforce private agreements into which parties had entered, and that concern requires that we rigorously enforce agreements to arbitrate, even if the result is "piecemeal" litigation, at least absent a countervailing policy manifested in another federal statute. By compelling arbitration of state-law claims, a district court successfully protects the contractual rights of the parties and their rights under the Arbitration Act.

Finding unpersuasive the arguments advanced in support of the ruling below, we hold that the District Court erred in refusing to grant the motion of Dean Witter to compel arbitration of the pendent state claims. Accordingly, we reverse the decision of the Court of Appeals insofar as it upheld the District Court's denial of the motion to compel arbitration, and we remand for further proceedings in accordance with this opinion.

ADMINISTRATIVE RULES AND ORDERS

One of the major changes that has occurred in American political life during the past hundred years is the increasing use of administrative agencies to carry out some of the tasks of government. Agencies play important roles in local, state, and national affairs. Many but not all of them have the authority to adopt rules and regulations that have the force of law. Frequently business managers as well as private citizens must be aware of these rules when making decisions.

One example of a business in which an agency's rules and regulations are significant is the sale of securities. In 1934 Congress passed the Securities Exchange Act to insure fairness in securities transactions. This act established the Securities and Exchange Commission (SEC). On the basis of authority granted to it, the SEC has adopted numerous rules that regulate issuing and trading securities. Although the rules are not made by a legislative body, a person or firm violating them is subject to penalties such as the revocation or suspension of the privilege to market a new security or possible criminal prosecution. Other important administrative agencies with rule-making authority are the Federal Trade Commission (FTC), the National Labor Relations Board (NLRB), and the Environmental Protection Agency (EPA).

In addition to the authority to promulgate rules, administrative agencies often have the authority to hear cases and issue orders. This is referred to as administrative adjudication. When hearing cases, the agency frequently must interpret a statute that is involved. Although these agency interpretations are subject to limited review by the courts, the interpretations are an important indication of the law. The reason is that generally courts accord great deference to an agency's interpretation of the statute that it administers. Presumably the administrators have the specialized knowledge and technical skill in their area of expertise that judges do not have.

Since administrative rule-making and adjudication are undoubtedly as significant to the business manager as what courts do, the work of administrative agencies is discussed in depth in Chapter 37.

ALTERNATIVE DISPUTE RESOLUTION

As mentioned earlier in the chapter, one of the principal functions of the legal system is to provide a forum for settling disputes. During the last fifty years more and more people have turned to the courts to resolve their differences. In 1986, 255,000 civil cases were filed in federal district courts as compared to 35,000 in 1940. Most of the growth occurred in the last few years. Additionally, over 12 million cases were filed in state courts, or one lawsuit for every thirteen adults.

The cost of this litigation to the public treasury is enormous. It costs $2.2 billion each year to process civil cases and an additional $4 billion to process criminal cases. Even with this extensive use of public funds, long delays often exist in litigation. In some metropolitan areas plaintiffs must wait from two to three years before their cases are heard. Direct costs to individuals in time and money are substantial. Because of these costs and delays, both individuals and business are increasingly looking to alternative means of resolving disputes.

Alternative dispute resolution (ADR) techniques generally are intended as alternatives to the traditional court process. They usually involve impartial people who are referred to as "third parties" (no matter how many parties are involved in the dispute) or "neutrals." Some of these techniques are arbitration, mediation, fact-finding, and conciliation.

Arbitration

Arbitration is widely used in settling commercial and labor-management disputes. In many industries arbitration is the standard method of settling conflicts between firms. The use of arbitration to resolve consumer complaints recently has increased dramatically. Currently, consumers can use arbitration for complaints against automobile manufacturers, most new car dealers, appliance manufacturers, movers, and some funeral directors. In 1984 the Better Business Bureau's national arbitration program listed as participants 17,000 local businesses, ranging from carpet shops to auto repair shops. *Arbitration* involves the submission of the dispute to a third party who hears arguments, reviews evidence, and then renders a decision. Arbitration is not so formal,

BOX 1-2: ISSUES AND TRENDS
Constitutional Interpretation

In 1803 in the famous case of *Marbury* v. *Madison* the U.S. Supreme Court determined that it had the power to review the actions of other branches of government to determine their constitutionality. Within a few short years the Court established that this power of judicial review also included the power to void actions of state courts on constitutional grounds. Thomas Jefferson and many other influential statesmen of the time challenged the Court's assertion that it had this power. Over the years the existence of the Court's power of judicial review has been consistently confirmed; however, the scope of the power has been and continues to be the subject of substantial national conflict.

On one side of the debate are those who contend that the Court must interpret the Constitution with great restraint. They argue that the Supreme Court is the least democratic of the three branches of national government. Its nine members are appointed, not elected, and they serve for life. They are not directly accountable to the people as are the legislative and executive branches of government. Thus, these branches of government, not the Court, must determine public policy. Only in instances in which the other branches of government unreasonably or arbitrarily exercise their power can the Court nullify policy by holding an action unconstitutional.

On the other hand, many people argue that democracy means more than "majority rule." They contend that a truly democratic society must limit the power of the majority. In a true democracy the rights of minorities are protected and certain fundamental personal freedoms are guaranteed for everyone, not only the majority. In interpreting the Constitution, the Court must insure against potential exploitation through majority rule. Additionally, when changing social, political, and economic conditions suggest that new fundamental rights exist that are not supported by the literal words of the Constitution, the Court must go beyond the Constitution to insure that these rights are guaranteed. Since the 1950s this type of judicial activism has led to controversial decisions in cases involving legislative apportionment, civil rights, and abortion.

Decisions of this type involve matters of great national concern. Many people are deeply disturbed by them, but constitutional order requires that the Court exercise the power of judicial review. In exercising this power, the Court must not forget the lessons of history; but society must also recognize that in order to have legitimacy a constitution must reflect the needs and concerns of this time and not those of the past.

complex, or time-consuming as a court proceeding. In binding arbitration, the most common form used in commercial disputes, the parties select the arbitrator and are bound by the decision (called an "award"). In some instances, the award is binding upon the parties because of a statute. But in most instances, the parties agree to accept the award before they submit to arbitration. Agreeing on an arbitrator is sometimes difficult. One common practice is to have a panel of three arbitrators. Each party selects one of the arbitrators, and those two select the third.

In labor-management disputes, arbitration traditionally has been used to resolve grievances. Almost all collective bargaining contracts contain an arbitration clause. This clause generally outlines a grievance mechanism. If an issue cannot be resolved by the parties, the arbitration clause provides a method for selecting an arbitrator and outlines the arbitrator's authority. Generally, this authority is extensive, with the arbitrator being authorized to decide all disputes regarding the interpretation and application of the agreement.

Last offer arbitration is a relatively recent development. In last offer arbitration, the arbitrator is required to choose between the final positions of the two parties. In major league baseball, for example, last offer arbitration is used when a player and club owner cannot agree on the player's salary.

A final form of labor-management arbitration, interest arbitration, has been used when collective bargaining breaks down in the public sector, where strikes may be unlawful.

Mediation

Mediation is the involvement of a neutral third party in a dispute to help the disputing parties resolve it. Mediation is usually an informal, voluntary process that is designed to move the parties toward a mutually satisfactory agreement. Although the mediator participates in the discussion or negotiations, the mediator does not decide the dispute. Experience with mediation programs in Atlanta, Chicago, New York, San Francisco, Tulsa, Oklahoma, and Columbus, Ohio, has demonstrated that it is an effective way of resolving landlord-tenant disagreements, domestic disputes, neighbors' disputes, damages for minor theft, vandalism, and other minor criminal incidents.

Fact-Finding

Fact-finding is another alternative mechanism for dispute resolution. This process is primarily used in public sector collective bargaining. The fact finder, drawing on information provided by the interested parties and independent research, recommends a written solution to each outstanding issue. The recommended solution is never binding, but often it paves the way for further negotiation and mediation.

Conciliation

Conciliation is an informal process in which the third party tries to bring the disputing parties together in hopes of lowering tensions, improving communication, helping to interpret issues, providing technical assistance, exploring potential solutions, and bringing about a negotiated settlement, either informally or, in a subsequent step, through formal mediation. Conciliation frequently is used in volatile conflicts and in disputes where the parties are unable, unwilling, or unprepared to come to the table to negotiate their differences.

In summary, alternative dispute resolution can be characterized as the seeking of a simple but equitable form of dispute settlement with the least expenditure of money and time. It is likely that alternative dispute resolution programs will continue to grow throughout the country.

REVIEW PROBLEMS

1. What policy is reflected by the concept of stare decisis? Does this policy seem logical?
2. Compare and contrast statutory and judge-made or common law.
3. What are the functions of the legal system?
4. Explain what is meant by arbitration.
5. Briefly outline the principles that courts apply when interpreting statutes.
6. Smith was involved in litigation in California. She lost her case in the trial court. She appealed to the California appellate court, arguing that the trial court judge had incorrectly excluded certain evidence. To support her argument, she cited rulings by the Supreme Court of North Dakota and the Supreme Court of Ohio. Both the North Dakota and Ohio cases involved facts that were similar to Smith's case. Does the California court have to follow the decisions from North Dakota and Ohio? Support your answer.
7. Business in the downtown area of a large western city had expanded rapidly. As a result, the area was plagued by traffic problems during the morning rush hour. To alleviate the problem, the city council passed an ordinance that restricted traffic on certain streets to "passenger motor vehicles."

   Swenson, who worked downtown, owned a small truck that he used to drive back and forth to work. When he drove on one of the restricted streets, he was ticketed and forced to pay a substantial fine. He wishes to contest the fine and the interpretation of the ordinance and comes to you for advice. Outline a strategy that might be used to help him.
8. You are the owner of a small business and are contemplating a substantial purchase of new machinery. You are discussing the provisions of the purchase contract with your attorney. The attorney states that the contract contains an "arbitration clause." Explain what this means.
9. Madison and his adult son lived in a house owned by Madison. At the request of the son, Marshall painted the house. Madison did not authorize the work, but he knew that it was being done and raised no objection. Madison refused to pay Marshall, arguing that he had not contracted to have the house painted.

   Marshall asked his attorney if Madison was legally liable to pay him. The attorney told Marshall that in their state several appellate court opinions had established that when a homeowner allows work to be done on his home by a person who would ordinarily expect to be paid, a duty to pay exists. The attorney stated that based upon these precedents, it was advisable for Marshall to bring a suit to collect the reasonable value of the work he had done. Explain what the attorney meant by *precedent* and why the fact that precedent existed was significant.
10. Ludenia Howard was charged with violating the Federal Black Bass Act. The Act made unlawful "transportation . . . from any State . . . any black bass . . . if (1) such transportation is contrary to the law of the State . . . from which fish . . . is transported. . . ." The Florida Fish and Game Commission had a rule prohibiting the transportation of black bass out of the state. The Commission was a body authorized by the state constitution. Its members were appointed by the governor.

    Howard's attorney argued that the federal act did not apply since the Commission's rule was not a "law of the State." Discuss the validity of this defense. What are the characteristics of a law? United States v. Howard, 352 U.S. 212 (1956).

11. Butler and a number of other people organized a corporation ostensibly to assist small business firms to secure loans. They were to be compensated by a finder's fee. The firms for whom loans were to be located had to pay an initial membership charge. The firms were solicited by mail. If a firm indicated an interest, it was visited by a salesperson. The entire scheme was a fraud. The corporation retained the membership fees and did nothing to secure loans.

    The corporation, Butler, and twenty-nine others were prosecuted in a single action for mail fraud. Several of the defendants asked to have their cases severed and tried separately because combining this number of defendants in a single case was unfair. Discuss the validity of a government argument based on stare decisis and citing a number of cases in which large numbers of defendants had been tried in a single case. Is the trial court bound by these cases? Butler v. United States, 317 F2d 249 (1963).

12. Section 301(a) of the Federal Food, Drug, and Cosmetics Act prohibits the introduction into interstate commerce of any drug that is misbranded. According to Section 502(a), a product is misbranded if its "labeling is false or misleading" unless the labeling bears "adequate directions for use." The term "labeling" is defined to mean "all labels and other written, printed, or graphic matter (1) upon any article or any of its containers or (2) accompanying such article." Violation of the act is a crime.

    Kordel sells health-food products that are compounds of vitamins, minerals, and herbs. These items are sold to stores. In addition to supplying the product, Kordel separately furnishes pamphlets describing the products. Much of the literature is shipped separately from the drugs and at different times—both before and after drug shipments. Kordel is charged with violating the Food and Drug Act. Based upon the above facts, outline a defense available to him. Explain how the prosecution might overcome this defense. (Kordel v. United States, 335 U.S. 345 [1948])

Legal Systems

This chapter examines the structure of the legal system and some of the processes used to accomplish the tasks outlined in Chapter 1. In order to help you understand the framework in which the legal system operates, the chapter first discusses the relationship between state and federal governments. The discussion examines the Commerce Clause, which is the basis for much of the federal regulation of business, and the doctrine of separation of powers, a doctrine that determines the manner in which the executive, judicial, and legislative branches carry out their duties. Next, the chapter outlines the structure of the court system and considers some of the questions involving jurisdiction, which is the power of courts to hear and decide cases. Finally, the chapter introduces the process of civil litigation.

RELATIONSHIP BETWEEN FEDERAL AND STATE GOVERNMENTS

Business administrators today are often concerned and frequently puzzled by the mass of rules, regulations, directives, forms, and reports emanating from both state and federal governments. The cost to business of meeting the demands from these systems is staggering. A single 1974 data-gathering program of the Federal Trade Commission had an average cost of $56,000 for each firm required to report. One firm's reporting costs were over $1.2 million.[1] A 1979 Business Roundtable study of forty-eight companies found that in 1977 regulatory costs equaled 16 percent of the firms' after-tax profits, and in 1980 government officials estimated that business paid $100 billion a year to comply with federal regulations.

In addition to bewilderment caused by the sheer mass of government requirements, additional confusion results because federal and state laws attempting to achieve different objectives sometimes conflict. Consider the plight of firms faced with the following dilemma:

In 1980 the federal Equal Employment Opportunity Commission adopted a rule prohibiting insurers from using mortality tables differentiating between males and females. At about the same time, California and New York adopted rules requiring insurers to use mortality tables that differentiated between males and females buying annuity and life insurance contracts. What tables should the firms use?

In spite of the dissatisfaction that sometimes arises from being forced to cope with two major governmental units, the business administrator must remember that this system does have some benefits. Many matters are more effectively carried out by local authorities familiar with problems peculiar to their region. At the same time the diffusion of power between the states and the federal government reduces the authority of each. By extending the centers of power, an enduring majority becomes less possible and minority interests have some protection.

THE FEDERAL SYSTEM

The dual nature of government in the United States is attributable to *federalism.* Although the term is not mentioned in the Constitution and has seldom been defined by the judiciary, the concept is basic to understanding the American political and legal systems. In essence, American federalism is a system that allocates the powers of sovereignty between the state and federal governments.

The basis of federalism is the Constitution, which is a compact between the states and the federal government. This compact was created by the people when they ratified the Constitution. The Constitution delegates certain powers of the states—which are sovereign—to the federal government; however, it also states that all powers that are not delegated to the federal government are retained by the states. Thus, state powers are known as *retained powers* while those of the federal government are known as *delegated powers.*

The principal delegated powers are the power to tax, borrow money, regulate commerce, coin money, create a federal judicial system, declare war, and provide for an army and navy. In addition to the delegated powers, the Constitution granted Congress the power to make all laws that "shall be necessary and proper" for carrying out the delegated powers. For example, Congress under its constitutional power to regulate commerce has the power to prohibit racial discrimination in hotels, motels, and restaurants. Powers that are "necessary and proper" to carry out the delegated powers are called *implied powers.*

Article IV of the Constitution provides that when the federal government acts within the framework of its delegated powers, its actions are supreme. Similarly, the actions of each state are supreme when the state acts on the basis of a retained power. At the same time there are some powers that are *concurrent,* as they can be asserted by both state and federal governments. The power to tax is an example. Both state and federal governments have this power.

Federal Regulation of Interstate Commerce

The Commerce Clause. One of the powers that the states delegated to the federal government was the power "to regulate commerce with foreign nations, and among the several states. . . ." Over the years "the Commerce Clause," as this grant of authority is called, has been subject to varying interpretations by the U.S. Supreme Court. Today, it is largely through the use of this power that the federal government regulates many aspects of American economic life.

The different interpretations of the Commerce Clause over nearly 200 years of constitutional history provide an example of the manner in which the legal system responds to economic, political, and social change. In *Gibbons* v. *Ogden,*[2] the most famous of the early cases interpreting the clause, both *commerce* and *regulate* were given broad meanings. These insured that the national government and not the states would have authority to control navigation on public waterways, even those wholly within a state. The decision thus met the needs of expanding national economic interests for an efficient means of moving goods that could not be restricted by local pressures. At the same time the decision reflected the rise of national spirit in much of the nation at that time.

The Commerce Clause Redefined. As the nation expanded geographically and economically, there appeared to be little need for either government assistance or control. Public energies were directed primarily to the business of creating material wealth. Laissez faire based upon rugged individualism was the prevailing economic philosophy. Factors such as these led to changes in legal attitudes that were reflected in new interpretations of the commerce clause.

Decisions of the U.S. Supreme Court up to 1840 construed the Commerce Clause broadly and laid the groundwork for the extension of congressional power over the economy. But by 1870 the Commerce Clause had been reinterpreted in a manner that empowered the states to regulate many aspects of interstate commerce along with the federal government. This was accomplished when the Court permitted state regulation of local aspects of interstate commerce if no conflicting federal legislation existed. Later federal regulation was further curtailed by a series of Supreme Court decisions that limited congressional power by defining commerce very narrowly. The Court redefined commerce as transportation among the states. In this manner it excluded from federal regulation all types of manufacturing and refining as well as businesses such as insurance and advertising that were conducted within a single state.

Although this narrow interpretation of the Commerce Clause was modified gradually over the years, federal dominance in economic regulation was not reestablished until the 1930s.

Reassertion of Federal Dominance. Conditions brought about by the Great Depression resulted in a new approach to regulation by the federal government. In the 1930s, with the increase of unemployment, the collapse of industrial production, and the fall of national income, it became apparent that only solutions on a nationwide basis could solve the problems plaguing the United States. Legislation based upon the Commerce Clause was passed by Congress and with some reluctance accepted by the courts.

This legislation included the Fair Labor Standards Act, which set minimum wages for workers engaged in the production of goods for interstate commerce, the National Labor Relations Act, which established a national policy encouraging workers to join labor unions and to bargain collectively, and the 1933 and 1934 federal statutes, which regulated the sale of securities. These and many other statutes enacted during and since the 1930s have had a substantial impact upon business in the United States.

At about this time the courts also began a reevaluation of the scope of the Commerce Clause. One example of the scope of this reevaluation involves the regulation of insurance. In 1869 in *Paul* v. *Virginia*[3] the U.S. Supreme Court held that "issuing a policy of insurance is not a transaction of commerce." Consequently, federal law did not apply to insurance and any regulation of insurance was carried out by the individual states. In 1943 in *United States* v. *South-Eastern Underwriters Association*[4] the U.S. Supreme Court reevaluated *Paul* v. *Virginia* and determined that although insurance was based upon sales contracts that were local, the business of insurance was national and subject to federal regu-lation. As a result of state protests, two years later Congress enacted the McCarran-Fergu-son Act authorizing the states to continue to regulate insurance. However, Congress has the power to enact legislation regulating insurance if the states fail to regulate effectively.

The Commerce Clause Today. Since the 1930s the U.S. Supreme Court has broadened the meaning of the term "commerce" as the *South-Eastern Underwriters* case illustrates. At the same time the Court has expanded the meaning of "interstate" or, as the Constitution says, "commerce among the several states." By midcentury the Court's position was that any intrastate activity that was part of the "flow of commerce" across state lines was subject to federal control. For example, a federal statute is applicable to a contract between local sugar-beet growers and local sugar refiners as long as sugar is shipped out of state.

Federal authority based upon the Commerce Clause has also been extended to wholly local intrastate activities that in a substantial manner affect interstate commerce. This is called the "affectation doctrine." Based upon this view of the Commerce Clause, federal regulation is permissible even though the subject of the regulation never enters the stream of interstate commerce. The case that follows illustrates the extent to which the affectation doctrine has resulted in an expansion of federal power to local activities.

Hospital Building Co. v. Trustees of Rex Hospital

U.S. Supreme Court
425 U.S. 738 (1975)

Background: Mary Elizabeth Hospital (petitioner) operates a forty-nine-bed hospital in Raleigh, North Carolina. Rex Hospital (respondent) operates a nonprofit, tax-exempt hospital in the same city. Mary Elizabeth Hospital filed a complaint alleging that Rex Hospital and several co-conspirators acted to block the planned expansion of Mary Elizabeth Hospital in violation of Sections 1 and 2 of the Sherman Act. Rex Hospital moved to dismiss the complaint. The U.S. District Court dismissed, finding that Mary Elizabeth Hospital had not alleged a sufficient connection between Rex Hospital's alleged violations of the Sherman Act and interstate commerce. The Court of Appeals affirmed the judgment by dismissing the complaint. It held the provision of hospital service is only a "local" activity. Additionally, the Court of Appeals held that the complaint did not adequately allege a "substantial effect" on interstate commerce. The U.S. Supreme Court granted Mary Elizabeth's petition for certiorari.

Decision: The U.S. Supreme Court reversed and remanded the case for further proceedings.

Marshall, Justice

Since we are reviewing a dismissal on the pleadings, we must, of course, take as true the material facts alleged in petitioner's amended complaint. According to the amended complaint, respondents and their co-conspirators orchestrated a plan to delay and, if possible, prevent the issuance of the state authorization that was a necessary prerequisite to the expansion of Mary Elizabeth. After a delay of some months, the authorization was finally granted, but since then, it is alleged, respondents and their co-conspirators have employed a series of bad-faith tactics, including the bringing of frivolous litigation, to block the implementation of the expansion. . . . All these actions, it is contended, have been taken as part of an attempt by Rex to monopolize the business of providing compensated medical and surgical services in the Raleigh area.

Petitioner identifies several areas of interstate commerce in which it is involved. According to the amended complaint, petitioner purchases a substantial proportion— up to 80%—of its medicines and supplies from out-of-state sellers. In 1972, it spent $112,000 on these items. A substantial number of the patients at Mary Elizabeth Hospital, it is alleged, come from out of State. Moreover, petitioner claims that a large proportion of its revenue comes from insurance companies outside of North Carolina or from the Federal Government through the Medicaid and Medicare programs. Petitioner also pays a management service fee based on its gross receipts to its parent company, a Delaware corporation based in Georgia. Finally, petitioner has developed plans to finance a large part of the planned $4 million expansion through out-of-state lenders. All these involvements with interstate commerce, the amended complaint claims, have been and are continuing to be adversely affected by respondents' anticompetitive conduct.

B

Respondents' motion to dismiss asserted both that the District Court had no jurisdiction over the subject matter of the amended complaint, and that the amended complaint failed to state a claim upon which relief could be granted. The District Court granted the motion to dismiss, concluding that the provision of hospital and medical services "is strictly a local, intrastate business," and that "the conduct of the defendants complained of in this case directly affects only a local activity of the plaintiff, and only incidentally and insubstantially does it affect interstate commerce."

A three-judge division of the Court of Appeals . . . affirmed the ruling of the District

Court. The Court held that the allegations in the amended complaint, even if true, were inadequate to support a conclusion that the alleged anticompetitive conduct was occurring in interstate commerce, or that it had or would have a substantial effect on interstate commerce.

II

The Sherman Act prohibits every contract, combination, or conspiracy "in restraint of trade or commerce among the several States," and also prohibits monopolizing "any part of the trade or commerce among the several States." It is settled that the Act encompasses far more than restraints on trade that are motivated by a desire to limit interstate commerce or that have their sole impact on interstate commerce. "[W]holly local business restraints can produce the effects condemned by the Sherman Act." As long as the restraint in question "substantially and adversely affects interstate commerce," the interstate commerce nexus required for Sherman Act coverage is established. " 'If it is interstate commerce that feels the pinch, it does not matter how local the operation which applies the squeeze.' "

In this case, the Court of Appeals, while recognizing that Sherman Act coverage requires only that the conduct complained of have a substantial effect on interstate commerce, concluded that the conduct at issue did not meet that standard. We disagree. The complaint, fairly read, alleges that if respondents and their co-conspirators were to succeed in blocking petitioner's planned expansion, petitioner's purchases of out-of-state medicines and supplies as well as its revenues from out-of-state insurance companies would be thousands and perhaps hundreds of thousands of dollars less than they would otherwise be. Similarly, the management fees that petitioner pays to its out-of-state parent corporation would be less if the expansion were blocked. Moreover, the multimillion-dollar financing for the expansion, a large portion of which would be from out of State, would simply not take place if the respondents succeeded in their alleged scheme. This combination of factors is certainly sufficient to establish a "substantial effect" on interstate commerce under the Act.

The Court of Appeals found two considerations crucial in its refusal to find that the complaint alleged a substantial effect on interstate commerce. The Court's reliance on neither was warranted. First, the Court observed: "The effect [on interstate commerce] here seems to us the indirect and fortuitous consequence of the restraint of the intrastate Raleigh area hospital market, rather than the result of activity purposely directed toward interstate commerce." But the fact that an effect on interstate commerce might be termed "indirect" because the conduct producing it is not "purposely directed" toward interstate commerce does not lead to a conclusion that the conduct at issue is outside the scope of the Sherman Act . . . the fact that respondents in the instant case may not have had the purposeful goal of affecting interstate commerce does not lead us to exempt that conduct from coverage under the Sherman Act.

The Court of Appeals further justified its holding of "no substantial effect" by arguing that "no source of supply or insurance company or lending institution can be expected to go under if Mary Elizabeth doesn't expand, and no market price likely will be affected." While this may be true, it is not of great relevance to the issue of whether the "substantial effect" test is satisfied. An effect can be "substantial" under the Sherman Act even if its impact on interstate commerce falls far short of causing enterprises to fold or affecting market price.

The Commerce Clause and State Regulation

The Commerce Clause is a significant source of national power, but it does not prohibit the states from regulating local activity affecting interstate commerce. State regulation of interstate commerce within its borders is permissible if the regulation is essential to the health, safety, or welfare of the residents of that state and the effect on interstate commerce is incidental. For example, states may exclude articles adversely affecting the public welfare such as fruit carrying a harmful pest or livestock with an infectious disease; a state may limit the length of trains passing through it if the reason is to protect the public; and a state may ban the retail sale of milk in plastic containers if the ban is in the interest of the public.

The Constitution, however, does limit state legislation affecting interstate commerce. First, the state action must be for a valid local purpose and its effect on interstate commerce must be incidental. In addition, state regulation is prohibited when the federal government has acted in the same area and the federal action is intended to cover the field. When this occurs, the state action is said to be preempted and any state action conflicting with the federal scheme is invalid. In one case, a state required interstate pipelines to buy gas from certain suppliers. The U.S. Supreme Court determined this regulation was preempted by a federal statute regulating the interstate transportation of gas. In another case, the U.S. Supreme Court held unconstitutional a state statute that invalidated arbitration agreements that were permitted by the Federal Arbitration Act, an act through which Congress had declared a national policy favoring arbitration.

As economic, political, and social problems placed demands upon government that many felt could be solved only on a national basis, congressional legislation, supported by the expanded concept of interstate commerce, has increased markedly at the expense of the states. As the federal authority expands, the power of the states to regulate for the purpose of promoting the health, safety, and welfare of their citizens must give way. This residual power of the states, known as the police power, and federal actions based upon the Commerce Clause have over the years been recurring sources of conflict, as the following case indicates.

City of Philadelphia v. New Jersey
U.S. Supreme Court
437 U.S. 617 (1978)

Background: Chapter 363 of 1973 New Jersey Laws prohibited bringing most types of solid waste into the state. This statute prevented performance of contracts for waste disposal between operators of private landfills in New Jersey and cities in other states. These cities, led by Philadelphia (plaintiff-appellant), joined in a suit against New Jersey in the courts of that state. The plaintiffs argued that Chapter 363 was unconstitutional because it discriminated against interstate commerce. The trial court accepted this contention and awarded plaintiff cities summary judgment. Upon appeal by the state, the New Jersey Supreme Court reversed the trial court, and plaintiffs appealed to the U.S. Supreme Court.

Decision: The U.S. Supreme Court reversed.

Stewart, Justice

The purpose of ch. 363 is set out in the statute itself as follows:

> "The Legislature finds and determines that . . . the volume of solid and liquid waste continues to rapidly increase, that the treatment and disposal of these wastes continues to pose an even greater threat to the quality of the environment of New Jersey, that the available and appropriate land fill sites within the State are being diminished, that the environment continues to be threatened by the treatment and disposal of waste which originated or was collected outside the State, and that the public health, safety and welfare require that the treatment and disposal within this State of all wastes generated outside of the State be prohibited."

The New Jersey Supreme Court accepted this statement of the state legislature's purpose. The state court additionally found that New Jersey's existing landfill sites will be exhausted within a few years; that to go on using these sites or to develop new ones will take a heavy environmental toll, both from pollution and from loss of scarce open lands; that new techniques to divert waste from landfills to other methods of disposal and resource recovery processes are under development, but that these changes will require time; and finally, that "the extension of the lifespan of existing landfills, resulting from the exclusion of out-of-state waste, may be of crucial importance in preventing further virgin wetlands or other undeveloped lands from being devoted to landfill purposes." Based on these findings, the court concluded that ch. 363 was designed to protect, not the State's economy, but its environment, and that its substantial benefits outweigh its "slight" burden on interstate commerce.

The appellants strenuously contend that ch. 363, "while outwardly cloaked in the currently fashionable garb of environmental protection, . . . is actually no more than a legislative effort to suppress competition and stabilize the cost of solid waste disposal for New Jersey residents. . . ." They cite passages of legislative history suggesting that the problem addressed by ch. 363 is primarily financial: Stemming the flow of out-of-state waste into certain landfill sites will extend their lives, thus delaying the day when New Jersey cities must transport their waste to more distant and expensive sites. . . .

This dispute about ultimate legislative purpose need not be resolved, because its resolution would not be relevant to the constitutional issue to be decided in this case. Contrary to the evident assumption of the state court and the parties, the evil of protectionism can reside in legislative means as well as legislative ends. Thus, it does not matter whether the ultimate aim of ch. 363 is to reduce the waste disposal costs of New Jersey residents or to save remaining open lands from pollution, for we assume New Jersey has every right to protect its residents' pocketbooks as well as their environment. And it may be assumed as well that New Jersey may pursue those ends by slowing the flow of *all* waste into the State's remaining landfills, even though interstate commerce may incidentally be affected. But whatever New Jersey's ultimate purpose, it may not be accomplished by discriminating against articles of commerce coming from outside the State unless there is some reason, apart from their origin, to treat them differently. Both on its face and in its plain effect, ch. 363 violates this principle of nondiscrimination.

The Court has consistently found parochial legislation of this kind to be constitutionally invalid, whether the ultimate aim of the legislation was to assure a steady supply of milk by erecting barriers to allegedly ruinous outside competition; or to create jobs by keeping industry within the State; or to preserve the State's financial resources from depletion by fencing out indigent immigrants. In each of these cases, a presumably legitimate goal was sought to be achieved by the illegitimate means of isolating the State from the national economy.

Also relevant here are the Court's decisions holding that a State may not accord its own inhabitants a preferred right of access over consumers in other States to natural resources located within its borders. These cases stand for the basic principle that a "State is without power to prevent privately owned articles of trade from being shipped and sold in interstate commerce on the ground that they are required to satisfy local demands or because they are needed by the people of the State."

The New Jersey law at issue in this case falls squarely within the area that the Commerce Clause puts off limits to state regulation. On its face, it imposes on out-of-state commercial interests the full burden of conserving the State's remaining landfill space. What is crucial is the attempt by one State to isolate itself from a problem common to many by erecting a barrier against the movement of interstate trade.

Today, cities in Pennsylvania and New York find it expedient or necessary to send their waste into New Jersey for disposal, and New Jersey claims the right to close its borders to such traffic. Tomorrow, cities in New Jersey may find it expedient or necessary to send their waste into Pennsylvania or New York for disposal, and those States might then claim the right to close their borders. The Commerce Clause will protect New Jersey in the future, just as it protects her neighbors now, from efforts by one State to isolate itself in the stream of interstate commerce from a problem shared by all.

The intrusion of federal power into every aspect of American life has not gone unchallenged on the national political scene. Many commentators asserted that the 1980 and 1984 election victories of Ronald Reagan were grassroots expressions of dissatisfaction with pervasive federal regulation. This dissatisfaction has had minimal influence on the judicial interpretation of the Commerce Clause and it, along with the power to tax, continues as the basis for substantial federal regulation of business.

RELATIONSHIP OF BRANCHES OF GOVERNMENT

Government and law are not the same, but they are closely related. As a result, some of the basic principles of government appreciably influence the manner in which the legal system functions. Conversely, many legal maxims affect the operation of government. One example is the principle that government officials at all levels must act within limits prescribed by law. This principle, which is vital to the continuance of American democracy, is often referred to as the "rule of law" or "supremacy of law." Simultaneously, many of these same officials whose actions are circumscribed by law often play major roles in the development of law and in the administration of the legal system. The following material discusses actions of officials in different branches of government as these actions influence the legal system. The rule of law is reflected in the accompanying cases.

Separation of Powers

The *separation-of-powers* doctrine involves the division of the authority of government among legislative, judicial, and executive branches and contemplates that none of the three shall exercise any of the powers belonging to the others. Chief Justice John Marshall described the end result of the doctrine as follows: "The difference between the departments undoubtedly is, that the legislature makes, the executive executes, and the judiciary construes the law."[5]

Making, executing, and interpreting the law do not have to be independent of each other for a legal system to function effectively. These three services might well be performed by a single entity. Since the adoption of the Constitution, however, a cardinal principle of American political life has been to separate the three branches of government. Separation is intended to prevent the domination of one branch by another and to protect the liberties of the people by preventing the accumulation of power in a single source.

In spite of Chief Justice Marshall's statement, the business or public administrator viewing the legal environment might readily decide that the separation-of-powers principle is more honored in the breach than in the observance. It is certainly true that the American legal system has never embodied complete separation of powers. This would be inefficient even if it were possible. In fact, the checks-and-balances system, which is integral to the federal Constitution and those of most states, is based upon the concept that each of the three constituent elements of government has a substantial influence on the others. There is enough influence to ensure that power to some extent will be balanced. Although nothing requires state governments to adhere to the separation-of-powers principle, most state constitutions follow the federal pattern. Even when not especially provided for by a state constitution, the concept is usually maintained in practice or required by judicial decision.

Numerous illustrations of the intermixture of functions can be cited. Congress, if it does not violate constitutional mandates, can modify much of the jurisdiction of federal courts. Congress can restrict the power of the President to remove certain federal officials, investigate the executive departments, and remove the President from office. The judiciary can determine if legislative enactments are constitutional, and the President can veto bills passed by Congress.

During the 1970s and 1980s the separation-of-powers principle has been the subject of considerable national discussion and concern. In the early 1970s much of the legal controversy surrounding the Watergate investigation revolved around the separation of powers. In that controversy President Nixon unsuccessfully contended that the separation of powers allowed him as President to ignore requests from Congress for information and orders from federal courts that he produce certain tapes that were in his possession.

In the 1980s the separation-of-powers principle has continued to dominate legal problems involving the relationships among the branches of government. In 1983 in *INS* v. *Chada*[6] the U.S. Supreme Court held that a statutory provision allowing either house of Congress to invalidate a decision of an administrative agency violated the separation-of-powers principle. The *Chada* case effec-

tively ended congressional powers to use a "legislative veto" to control the federal administrative agencies. In 1986 separation of powers was the basis for eliminating certain provisions of major federal legislation that were designed to reduce the growing federal budget deficit. In *Bowsher* v. *Synar*, the case that follows, the U.S. Supreme Court held that a federal official who could be removed by Congress could not as required by budget-deficit legislation perform an executive function. The case illustrates the differences of opinion that exist as to the application of the separation-of-powers principle.

Bowsher v. Synar

U.S. Supreme Court

106 Sup. Ct. 3181 (1986)

Background: On December 12, 1985, President Reagan signed into law the Balanced Budget and Emergency Deficit Control Act of 1985 (Gramm-Rudman-Hollings Act). The purpose of the Act is to eliminate the federal budget deficit. The Act sets a "maximum deficit amount" for federal spending for each year from 1986 to 1991.

The Act requires automatic across-the-board cuts in federal spending to reach targeted deficit levels. The calculation of the "automatic reductions" is made by the Comptroller General after reviewing reports submitted by the Office of Management and Budget (OMB) and the Congressional Budget Office (CBO). The Comptroller General is an officer of the legislative branch who is responsible to Congress. He or she may be removed by Joint Resolution of Congress or by impeachment. Based upon the Comptroller General's calculation, the President must issue a sequestration order mandating spending reductions specified by the Comptroller General. This order becomes effective unless Congress within a specified time legislates reductions to obviate the need for it.

Shortly after the Act was signed, Congressman Synar, who had voted against it, filed a complaint asking the federal District Court to declare the Act unconstitutional. The District Court did so on grounds that the Act violated the separation-of-powers doctrine, as in the deficit reduction process the Comptroller General exercised executive functions. An appeal was taken directly to the U.S. Supreme Court as authorized by the Act. Bowsher, the Comptroller General, is the defendant and appellant.

Decision: The U.S. Supreme Court affirmed.

Burger, Chief Justice *(delivered the opinion of the Court)*

IV·

Appellants urge that the Comptroller General performs his duties independently and is not subservient to Congress. We agree with the District Court that this contention does not bear close scrutiny.

The critical factor lies in the provisions of the statute defining the Comptroller General's office relating to removability. Although the Comptroller General is nominated by the President from a list of three individuals recommended by the Speaker of the House of Representatives and the President pro tempore of the Senate, see 31 U.S.C. § 703(a)(2), and confirmed by the Senate, he is removable only at the initiative of Congress. He may be removed not only by impeachment but also by Joint Resolution of Congress "at any time" resting on any one of the following bases:

> "(i) permanent disability;
> "(ii) inefficiency;
> "(iii) neglect of duty;
> "(iv) malfeasance; or
> "(v) a felony or conduct involving moral turpitude."

The removal provision was an important part of the legislative scheme, as a number of Congressmen recognized. Representative Hawley commented: "[H]e is our officer, in a measure, getting information for us. . . . If he does not do his work properly, we, as practically his employers, ought to be able to discharge him from office." Representative Sisson observed that the removal provisions would give "[t]he Congress of the United States . . . absolute control of the man's destiny in office." The ultimate design was to "give the legislative branch of the Government control of the audit, not through the power of appointment, but through the power of removal."

It is clear that Congress has consistently viewed the Comptroller General as an officer of the Legislative Branch. The Reorganization Acts of 1945 and 1949, for example, both stated that the Comptroller General and the GAO are "a part of the legislative branch of the Government." Similarly, in the Accounting and Auditing Act of 1950, Congress required the Comptroller General to conduct audits "as an agent of the Congress."

Over the years, the Comptrollers General have also viewed themselves as part of the Legislative Branch. In one of the early Annual Reports of the Comptroller General, the official seal of his office was described as reflecting:

> "the independence of judgment to be exercised by the General Accounting Office, subject to the control of the legislative branch. . . . The combination represents an agency of the Congress independent of other authority auditing and checking the expenditures of the Government as required by law and subjecting any questions arising in that connection to quasi-judicial determination."

Against this background, we see no escape from the conclusion that, because Congress had retained removal authority over the Comptroller General, he may not be entrusted with executive powers. The remaining question is whether the Comptroller General has been assigned such powers in the Balanced Budget and Emergency Deficit Control Act of 1985.

Appellants suggest that the duties assigned to the Comptroller General in the Act are essentially ministerial and mechanical so that their performance does not constitute "execution of the law" in a meaningful sense. On the contrary, we view these functions as plainly entailing execution of the law in constitutional terms. Interpreting a law enacted by Congress to implement the legislative mandate is the very essence of "execution" of the law. Under § 251, the Comptroller General must exercise judgment concerning facts that affect the application of the Act. He must also interpret the provisions of the Act to determine precisely what budgetary calculations are required. Decisions of that kind are typically made by officers charged with executing a statute.

The executive nature of the Comptroller General's functions under the Act is revealed in § 252(a)(3) which gives the Comptroller General the ultimate authority to determine the budget cuts to be made. Indeed, the Comptroller General commands the President himself to carry out, without the slightest variation (with exceptions not relevant to the constitutional issues presented), the directive of the Comptroller General as to the budget reductions.

We noted recently that "[t]he Constitution sought to divide the delegated powers of the new Federal Government into three defined categories, Legislative, Executive, and Judicial." The declared purpose of separating and dividing the powers of government, of course, was to "diffus[e] power the better to secure liberty." Justice Jackson's words echo the famous warning of Montesquieu, quoted by James Madison in The Federalist No. 47, that " 'there can be no liberty where the legislative and executive powers are united in the same person, or body of magistrates.' . . ."

Even a cursory examination of the Constitution reveals the influence of Montesquieu's thesis that checks and balances were the foundation of a structure of government that would protect liberty. The Framers provided a vigorous legislative branch and a separate and wholly independent executive branch, with each branch responsible ultimately to the people. The Framers also provided for a judicial branch equally independent with "[t]he judicial Power . . . extend[ing] to all Cases, in Law and Equity, arising under this Constitution, and the Laws of the United States."

That this system of division and separation of powers produces conflicts, confusion, and discordance at times is inherent, but it was deliberately so structured to assure full, vigorous and open debate on the great issues affecting the people and to provide avenues for the operation of checks on the exercise of governmental power.

The Constitution does not contemplate an active role for Congress in the supervision of officers charged with the execution of the laws it enacts. The President appoints "Officers of the United States" with the "Advice and Consent of the Senate. . . ." Once the appointment has been made and confirmed, however, the Constitution explicitly provides for removal of Officers of the United States by Congress only upon impeachment by the House of Representatives and conviction by the Senate.

[The majority opinion at this point examines a number of cases in which the Court had addressed the issue of congressional power to remove an officer of the Executive Branch except by impeachment.]

In light of these precedents, we conclude that Congress cannot reserve for itself the power of removal of an officer charged with the execution of the laws except by impeachment. To permit the execution of the laws to be vested in an officer answerable only to Congress would, in practical terms, reserve in Congress control over the execution of the laws. As the District Court observed, "Once an officer is appointed, it is only the authority that can remove him, and not the authority that appointed him, that he must fear and, in the performance of his functions, obey." The structure of the Constitution does not permit Congress to execute the laws; it follows that Congress cannot grant to an officer under its control what it does not possess.

The dangers of congressional usurpation of Executive Branch functions have long been recognized. "[T]he debates of the Constitutional Convention, and the Federalist Papers, are replete with expressions of fear that the Legislative Branch of the National Government will aggrandize itself at the expense of the other two branches." Indeed, we also have observed only recently that "[t]he hydraulic pressure inherent within each of the separate Branches to exceed the outer limits of its power, even to accomplish desirable objectives, must be resisted." With these principles in mind, we turn to consideration of whether the Comptroller General is controlled by Congress.

We conclude the District Court correctly held that the powers vested in the Comptroller General under § 251 violate the command of the Constitution that the Congress play no direct role in the execution of the laws. Accordingly, the judgment and order of the District Court are affirmed.

White, Justice (dissenting)

The Court, acting in the name of separation of powers, takes upon itself to strike down the Gramm-Rudman-Hollings Act, one of the most novel and far-reaching legislative responses to a national crisis since the New Deal. The basis of the Court's action is a solitary provision of another statute that was passed over sixty years ago and has lain dormant since that time. I cannot concur in the Court's action.

The Court's decision . . . is based on a syllogism: the Act vests the Comptroller with "executive power"; such power may not be exercised by Congress or its agents; the Comptroller is an agent of Congress because he is removable by Congress; therefore the Act is invalid.

The deficiencies in the Court's reasoning are apparent. First, the Court baldly mischaracterizes the removal provision when it suggests that it allows Congress to remove the Comptroller for "executing the laws in any fashion found to be unsatisfactory"; in fact, Congress may remove the Comptroller only for one or more of five specified reasons, which "although not so narrow as to deny Congress any leeway, circumscribe Congress' power to some extent by providing a basis for judicial review of congressional removal."

The statute does not permit anyone to remove the Comptroller at will; removal is permitted only for specified cause, with the existence of cause to be determined by Congress following a hearing. Any removal under the statute would presumably be subject to post-termination judicial review to ensure that a hearing had in fact been held and that the finding of cause for removal was not arbitrary.

More importantly, the substantial role played by the President in the process of removal through joint resolution reduces to utter insignificance the possibility that the threat of removal will induce subservience to the Congress.

If the Comptroller's conduct in office is not so unsatisfactory to the President as to convince the latter that removal is required under the statutory standard, Congress will have no independent power to coerce the Comptroller unless it can muster a two-thirds majority in both Houses—a feat of bipartisanship more difficult than that required to impeach and convict. The incremental *in terrorem* effect of the possibility of congressional removal in the face of a presidential veto is therefore exceedingly unlikely to have any discernible impact on the extent of congressional influence over the Comptroller.

The practical result of the removal provision is not to render the Comptroller unduly dependent upon or subservient to Congress, but to render him one of the most independent officers in the entire federal establishment.

Realistic consideration of the nature of the Comptroller General's relation to Congress thus reveals that the threat to separation of powers conjured up by the majority is wholly chimerical. The power over removal retained by the Congress is not a power that is exercised outside the legislative process as established by the Constitution, nor does it appear likely that it is a power that adds significantly to the influence Congress may exert over executive officers through other, undoubtedly constitutional exercises of legislative power and through the constitutionally guaranteed impeachment power.

The majority's contrary conclusion rests on the rigid dogma that, outside of the impeachment process, any "direct congressional role in the removal of officers charged with the execution of the laws . . . is inconsistent with separation of powers." Reliance on such an unyielding principle to strike down a statute posing no real danger of aggrandizement of congressional power is extremely misguided and insensitive to our constitutional role.

The Act vesting budget-cutting authority in the Comptroller General represents Congress' judgment that the delegation of such authority to counteract ever-mounting deficits is "necessary and proper" to the exercise of the powers granted the Federal Government by the Constitution; and the President's approval of the statute signifies his unwillingness to reject the choice made by Congress. Under such circumstances, the role of this Court should be limited to determining whether the Act so alters the balance of authority among the branches of government as to pose a genuine threat to the basic division between the lawmaking power and the power to execute the law. Because I see no such threat, I cannot join the Court in striking down the Act.

CASE NOTE

Congress anticipated a constitutional challenge to the deficit-reduction process established by the Gramm-Rudman-Hollings Act. As a result, it included in the legislation a "fallback" deficit-reduction process to replace the procedures involving the Comptroller General if these were invalidated. In that event, the reports prepared by the Office of Management and Budget and the Congressional Budget Office are submitted directly to a specially created Temporary Joint Committee on Deficit Reduction. This committee must report in five days to both houses, setting forth the content of the two reports. Congress then must vote on the resolution under special rules, which render amendments out of order. If the resolution is passed and signed by the President, it serves as the basis for a presidential sequestration order.

THE DUAL COURT STRUCTURE

As a result of the federal system, a dual structure of courts prevails in the United States. Each person is not only subject to the laws of a particular state, which generally are interpreted by the courts of that state, but each is also subject to the laws of the United States, which are generally interpreted by the federal courts. Before examining some of the effects of the dual nature of government in the United States, a brief survey of the general structure and jurisdiction of American courts is in order.

In view of the fifty-one independent court systems that operate within the United States, this might seem an impossible task. The task, however, is simplified by a common structural pattern that exists for most states. This structure can be understood if each state system and the federal system are envisioned as pyramids with two or sometimes three levels. A typical state judicial structure and the United States judicial structure are shown in Figures 2-1 and 2-2.

Trial Courts

A court's jurisdiction is the power that it has to hear and decide cases. Trial courts are courts of *original jurisdiction*. This means that they are courts in which litigation begins. Some trial courts are also described as courts of *general jurisdiction*. They have the power to hear most types of cases. Other trial courts have *limited jurisdiction*. This is because the types of cases that these courts can hear are limited. Usually the limitation involves a monetary amount or subject matter. For example, a court might be limited to hearing cases in which the amount in dispute is less than $10,000, or it might only have the power to hear cases involving juveniles.

Federal Trial Courts. In the federal system the trial courts are called U.S. District Courts. The United States is divided into ninety-four districts, and each has a single district court. U.S. District Courts have the power to hear almost all types of federal cases except those that Congress has assigned by statute to special courts such as the U.S. Court of Claims or the U.S. Court of International Trade.

State Trial Courts. In the states the trial-court base of the structural pyramid is complicated by the existence of both courts of general jurisdiction and courts of limited jurisdiction. Each state has trial courts of general jurisdiction throughout the state. In Ohio they are called courts of common pleas; New York refers to them as supreme courts. Probably the most common designation is county court.

Although the titles differ from state to state, these general trial courts have some common characteristics. Usually they are organized on a county basis. They have the power to hear a wide variety of cases, both criminal and civil, and there are ordinarily no upper limits on their monetary jurisdiction. Their remedial powers usually include traditional remedies such as specific performance, which is a court order requiring a defendant to perform a particular act, or the injunction, which is a court order prohibiting a person from performing a

FIGURE 2–1
Ohio Judicial Structure

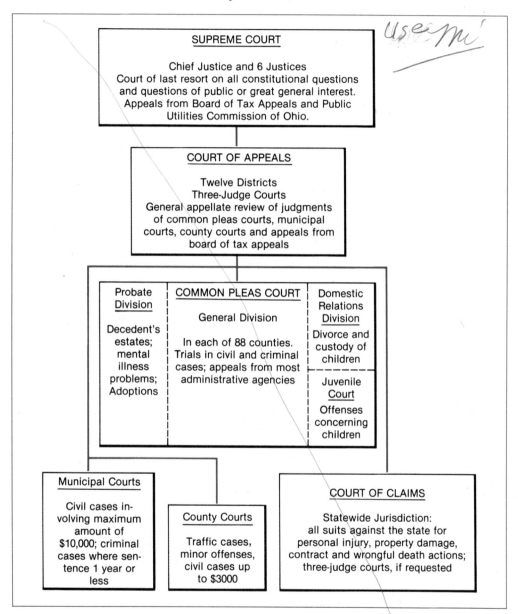

particular act. It is often only in these courts that parties have a right to jury trials in civil cases. Especially in heavily populated areas, many courts of general jurisdiction have specialized divisions to hear cases that involve domestic relations, juveniles, and decedent estates. In some states an independent probate or surrogate court handles decedent estate matters. In a number of states the specialized courts are set up independently of the state-

FIGURE 2–2
United States Judicial Structure

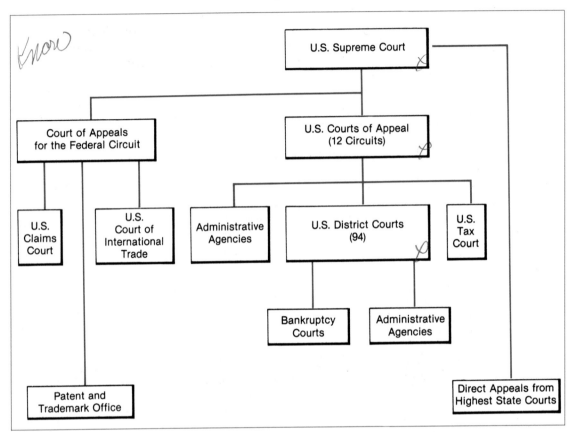

wide trial courts. It is also a common practice to separate the courts with criminal jurisdiction from those that hear civil cases.

All states have a number of trial courts of limited jurisdiction. These courts can decide only those cases in which the plaintiff is seeking monetary damages of a limited amount. Frequently they have no power to issue injunctions or to order specific performance, and their criminal jurisdiction is limited to petty offenses and minor misdemeanors. It is impossible to make general statements about these courts because of the wide variety of tasks that have been assigned to them in different states. In some areas these lower trial courts have extensive monetary jurisdiction and are manned by a number of full-time, le-

gally trained judges with large staffs. These courts often play significant roles in the administration of justice. In other places these courts hear only the most trivial cases and are presided over by part-time judges, sometimes with no legal training. Courts of this latter kind often exist only because state legislatures have failed to modernize local judicial administration.

Intermediate Appellate Courts

Federal Appellate Courts. If we consider judicial structure as a pyramid built of several levels, both the federal system and those of the heavily populated states have a second layer—

the intermediate appellate courts. The federal intermediate appellate courts are called U.S. Courts of Appeals. The United States is currently divided into twelve geographic circuits with a court of appeals for each. These courts hear appeals from the federal district courts and from actions taken by many federal administrative agencies.

Heavy Areas popul

State Intermediate Appellate Courts. State intermediate appellate courts are found only in the heavily populated states. In half the states no intermediate level of review exists. Often this is because the highest court of the state can handle all cases that are appealed. In some states a need for an intermediate level of review exists, but neither the state constitution nor the legislature has authorized the creation of this court.

The purpose of intermediate appellate courts is to improve the administration of justice by reducing the burden on the state's supreme court. This both speeds up the judicial process and allows the high court to concentrate on cases that it considers significant for the administration of the state's judicial system.

State intermediate appellate courts have broad appellate jurisdiction. They hear appeals from trial courts of general jurisdiction and, frequently, from trial courts of limited jurisdiction and/or specialized courts. In many states the intermediate appellate courts also hear appeals from administrative agency determinations. Like the trial courts, these courts have a variety of names. A number of states call them courts of appeals; superior court is also a common designation. In New York these courts are the appellate division of the supreme court.

Although these courts are not the highest appellate court, for most appeals they are the court of last resort. There are two principal reasons for this. First, an appeal is a very expensive process. Most litigants cannot afford even an initial review, much less the cost of the two appeals necessary to argue their case

before the highest appellate court. Second, in most states with an intermediate level of review the highest court has the discretion to review only those cases that it considers to be necessary. A person appealing from the intermediate level must petition the high court. Ordinarily, these petitions are rejected because the high court is satisfied that justice has been accorded by the intermediate appellate court's review.

Courts of Last Resort

The apex of the pyramid in each of the fifty states' judicial systems and the federal system is occupied by a court that makes the final determination for almost all cases appealed within the jurisdiction. This court is most frequently called the supreme court as in the federal system, but in New York the highest court is called the court of appeals. Ordinarily a party whose case is heard at this level in a state system can appeal the case no further. In some few instances, however, a case appealed to the highest court of a state can be reviewed by the U.S. Supreme Court. This is true only if the case involves a substantial federal question, such as the interpretation of the U.S. Constitution or of a federal statute, and if the U.S. Supreme Court agrees to consider the state court judgment.

Only a few cases are appealable to the U.S. Supreme Court as a matter of right. In all other circumstances the party unhappy with the federal circuit court decision must first ask the Supreme Court to hear the case by petitioning for an order of *certiorari*. If the Supreme Court wants to hear the case, it will grant the petition. Most petitions for certiorari are denied.

FEDERAL COURT JURISDICTION

The dual nature of American federalism necessitates that citizens take into account both state and federal legal systems. Because of the nature of powers retained by the states, most criminal and civil litigation is decided in state courts. Matters such as domestic relations and the administration of decedents' estates as well as matters of contract and tort law are also largely concerns of state courts. Although many more cases are tried in the state courts than in the federal, the jurisdiction of federal courts is significant to the business community because many important business regulatory statutes are federal. In order for a case to be tried in the federal system, the controversy must involve a matter over which the federal courts have jurisdiction.

Federal Questions

Federal courts have jurisdiction when the decision depends upon the interpretation of the Constitution of the United States, a federal statute, or a treaty. These cases are said to involve a *federal question.* A large percentage of federal litigation consists of federal question cases. These cases include those based upon statutes such as the Sherman Act, the Securities Exchange Act, and the National Labor Relations Act.

Diversity of Citizenship

A second important source of jurisdiction in the federal courts arises from the constitutional provision permitting Congress to grant jurisdiction to the federal courts in "controversies between citizens of different states." In the original Judiciary Act adopted in 1789 Congress granted the federal courts original jurisdiction in these kinds of cases. Although some of the conditions have changed, federal courts have had diversity jurisdiction since that time.

In order to limit the number of diversity cases that the federal courts have to decide, legislation requires that the amount in controversy must exceed $10,000. Additional limitations require that each plaintiff's claim in a multiple-party action exceed $10,000 and that

no plaintiff or defendant be a citizen of the same state. In 1958 Congress, to further limit diversity cases, adopted legislation declaring a corporation to be a citizen both of the state of incorporation and of the state in which it has its principal place of business.

The original purpose of diversity jurisdiction was to protect a citizen of one state from possible bias in favor of a party whose case was being heard in his or her home state. Today, almost no one believes that the courts of a citizen's state would favor that person over the citizen of another state. As a result, many people are critical of diversity jurisdiction. They argue that it unduly complicates litigation, increases the cost of the federal judicial system, and forces the federal courts to hear cases that might more effectively be decided by state courts since the cases involve state law.

STATE COURT JURISDICTION

The Tenth Amendment provides that each state retains the powers not delegated to the United States by the Constitution. This means that state courts have jurisdiction over all cases involving the constitution of the state, its statutes, and its common law. Federal courts cannot interfere with state courts unless a controversy involves an area in which the U.S. Constitution grants power to the federal government. For example, if a person is charged with violating a state criminal statute, a federal court is not involved unless the defendant raises a constitutional question. A similar result would follow if a business firm were being sued for breach of contract. A state court would have exclusive jurisdiction, unless the requirements for diversity jurisdiction exist or a constitutional issue was involved.

Problems of the Dual Court System

Problems critical to the administration of justice exist because of the dual court system.

One of these results from the fact that the courts of one state have no authority over the courts of the other states. Thus, a state court might ignore the valid judicial acts of another state's courts, unless compelled to recognize them by the Constitution. A second problem exists as state courts often must decide disputes that have substantial connections with other states. For example, if a contract made in Kansas is to be performed in Colorado, which state's law should apply if the contract is breached? This is called a "conflict of laws" problem.

uphold laws & judgements per states

Full Faith and Credit Clause

Imagine the problems that people in the United States would face if the judgments, public acts, and public records of each of the states could be ignored by the courts and other official bodies in another state. A business firm that won a contract case in one state might have to fight the same battle in each of the other states in which it was necessary to enforce the judgment. A person validly married in Ohio might not be recognized as married in New York. A divorce granted in California might not be recognized in any other state. The problems both to business and to the community at large would be endless and frustrating. The Framers of the Constitution fortunately anticipated these difficulties and included in the Constitution sections designed to reduce the impact of state sovereignty.

Article IV, Section 1, of the Constitution states as follows: "Full Faith and Credit shall be given in each state to the public Acts, Records and judicial Proceedings of every other State." The intention of this sentence was to prevent states from refusing to recognize the judgments, public acts, and records of a sister state. In adopting the Constitution each of the states surrendered this portion of its sovereign power.

The full faith and credit clause permits a litigant who wins a judgment in one state to take this judgment into the courts of another state, which must accept it as binding. Of course, a litigant who loses a case in the courts of one state is also denied an opportunity to bring it into another state.

As a result of the full faith and credit clause, a business firm winning a judgment for damages in Ohio can have this judgment enforced in any of the other states. This is true even though the cause of action is not recognized in the other state, the Ohio judgment is the result of legal error, or the Ohio judgment contravenes the public policy of the second state. The full faith and credit clause does not, however, require the courts of the second state to recognize a judgment rendered by a court that does not have jurisdiction. Nor does the enforcing state have to recognize a judgment obtained in violation of due process.

The full faith and credit clause is not applicable to criminal cases. A state does not have to enforce the criminal law of sister states. The criminal defendant is entitled to be tried by the courts in the state where the crime was committed. Defendants who flee to another state can be extradited and returned for trial to the state where the crime was committed.

Conflict of Laws

Today, business and most other significant human activities cut across state boundaries. Conversely, these same state boundaries are important to the structure of the American legal system. As we have seen, each state makes and enforces its own laws within its boundaries. There is no indication at this time that the legal importance of state boundaries will decrease, but it is clear that technological advances in communication and transportation will further reduce the importance of these boundaries in most other areas of American life.

The dichotomy between the limited importance of state boundaries in human activity generally and their continued importance in legal administration creates numerous problems for the business community. The following is a minute sample of the many important legal questions that the business administrator should consider if business is carried on in more than one state:

1. Are the provisions of all legal documents such as contracts, promissory notes, and bills of exchange valid in each state where used?
2. Do the same time limitations for bringing suit exist in other states where the firm is doing business?
3. If employees based in one state are assigned temporarily to jobs in another, which state's worker's compensation laws apply?
4. Is income taxable in the state where earned also taxable in the firm's home state?
5. How does the firm's responsibility for defective merchandise vary in the states where its products are marketed?

The fact that much activity, both commercial and otherwise, ignores state lines also creates a major problem for judicial administration. In many instances state courts will be called upon to settle disputes with a substantial out-of-state dimension. In these situations a question that frequently must be answered is, What state law applies?

Although we would expect that a state court would apply its own state's law in all litigation, it doesn't always do so. Many instances exist in which state courts apply the laws of a sister state instead of its own state's laws. Public-policy considerations underlie this choice. Both statutes and cases recognize that in a legal dispute the controlling law should be that which the parties reasonably would expect it to be. Results in litigation should not depend upon fortuitous circumstances that determine the forum. In addition, the U.S. Supreme Court has held that due process is violated if a state court applies its own laws to transactions that have more substantial contacts with other states. As even small businesses often operate across state lines, the business administrator must be aware of the law that applies to actions taken not only at home but in other states as well.

THE LITIGATION PROCESS

A number of different processes furnish the means by which the legal system seeks to accomplish the tasks discussed in Chapter 1. The following material examines some of these processes and, in addition, points out some general characteristics of legal dispute resolution.

A casual glance at the legal system indicates several distinct processes in operation. One is the legislative process. Another is litigation, which can be broken down by level into a trial or appellate process and by subject matter into criminal or civil litigation. The administrative process and arbitration, methods of private dispute settlement recognized by the courts, are also parts of the legal system. Sometimes the major objectives of a process are fairly clear, but in other instances a process designed to accomplish a particular objective does much more than that. For instance, compare legislation with litigation. The legislative process is a systematic series of actions to make laws for the community. Litigation is a process in which the primary objective is to settle disputes, but in doing this the actions taken also create laws. (See Figure 2-3.)

CRIMINAL AND CIVIL LITIGATION

Although the distinction between criminal and civil litigation is not always clear, criminal cases are brought by a public official against a defendant who has offended society at large by violating a statute that typically was enacted for the protection of other individuals or property. Criminal statutes provide that

FIGURE 2–3
The Litigation Process

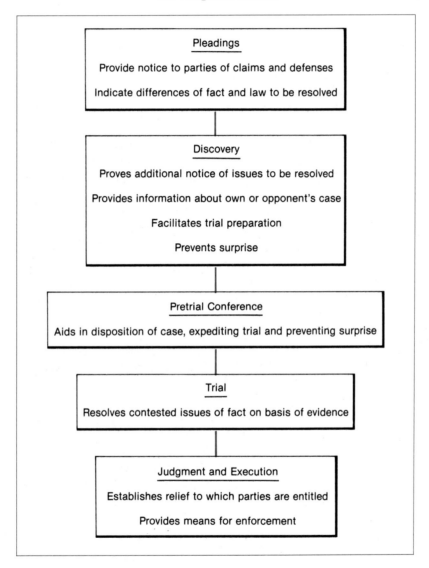

the defendant be punished in some way, usually by a fine or imprisonment. Civil cases are actions between private parties trying to resolve a question of private right or actions instituted by government in which the relief sought is not criminal—for example, an injunction prohibiting certain types of behavior.

Both civil and criminal litigation are pursued at trial and appellate levels. Initially, a trial court tries to resolve the dispute. If either or both of the parties think that the trial court has committed some type of legal error, an appeal can be taken to a higher court. Because the objectives of trial and appellate courts differ, the trial and appellate processes have different rules and procedures. In some jurisdictions the government's right to appeal in criminal cases is restricted.

THE ADVERSARY PRINCIPLE

In the United States civil and criminal litigation are characterized by the *adversary principle*. This principle places the responsibility for developing and proving cases upon the parties rather than upon some designated legal official, with the court serving primarily as a referee. Because of the complexities of litigation, ordinarily the parties hire lawyers to represent them and to argue for them.

The rationale for the adversary principle is that truth and justice will be most effectively attained by making each litigant responsible for his or her case. Those directly involved have more incentive than outsiders to see the evidence, the legal arguments, and other factors in their favor presented in the best light.

For a number of reasons, the adversary principle has been subject to considerable criticism, especially in criminal cases. Some argue that in an adversary system winning or losing often depends upon the skill of the attorneys instead of the merits of the case. Others claim that in a criminal case the resources of the state are so much greater than those of the defendant that the defendant is placed at a disadvantage. Another objection is that, because each party's primary interest is to win, each has an incentive to distort or hide facts unfavorable to his or her position.

During the past fifty years the impact of the adversary principle has been lessened as a result of several developments. The legal system has adopted a number of procedural reforms that help the individual search out information to support his or her case. Courts have become more willing to bring in witnesses and to rely upon experts. Litigants with limited resources are being furnished legal aid. And finally, new processes are being developed to substitute for traditional courtroom litigation.

BASIC CONDITIONS OF DISPUTE RESOLUTION

For the effective legal resolution of a dispute between individuals, four problems must be solved:

1. There must be machinery to enable the tribunal to find out what differences exist between the parties and to separate these from areas of agreement.
2. A means must be provided for determining what the actual facts, events, and circumstances were in the particular case. In some instances questions of this kind are the only differences between the parties.
3. As the parties often disagree about the law, some means for determining the applicable law must be provided. In litigation, disputes about events and circumstances are called "issues of fact," and disputes that involve law are called "issues of law."
4. If the legal system is to survive, its procedures must meet standards of fairness that are acceptable to the community.

PRETRIAL PROCEDURES

The mechanisms that have evolved to meet these conditions provide the framework for civil litigation. Although civil and criminal litigation are similar, major differences exist in procedures, especially in the pretrial stages.

Jurisdiction over the Person

An initial problem confronting an attorney in a civil action is to determine a court that can acquire personal jurisdiction over the defendant. Traditionally, personal jurisdiction is acquired by a court through physical control of the defendant. In a civil case this does not mean that the defendant has to be held, only that he or she be served with the proper pa-

ETHICS BOX
The Lawyer's Dilemma

The adversary principle sometimes puts lawyers into awkward situations. A lawyer is considered an officer of the court who has a general duty to see that justice is done. But a lawyer also is the advocate for his or her client and must vigorously pursue the client's best interests—within the law.

Consider the following case. An attorney is representing a client who was a bystander struck by a car as a result of a collision. The two drivers involved had insurance policies with limits of $100,000 and $50,000 for paying such claims. But one of the drivers also had an umbrella policy that would pay an additional $1,000,000 after the first policy was exhausted. The client had incurred hospital expenses of over $112,000 and the lawyer negotiated the settlement of the claim with the hospital. During the negotiation the lawyer realized that the representative of the hospital knew about the two smaller policies but did not know about the $1,000,000 policy.

What would you do? Would you mention the $1,000,000 policy?

The Code of Ethics for lawyers states that, "In his representation of a client a lawyer shall not . . . knowingly make a false statement of law or fact."

You may be surprised to learn that the lawyer who actually faced this choice and didn't tell about the policy was suspended from practicing law for six months. The failure to speak was considered the equivalent of a false statement. Nebraska State Bar Association v. Addison, 412 N.W.2d 855 (Neb. 1987).

pers within the state in which the court sits. Thus, a state court ordinarily acquires personal jurisdiction over a resident or nonresident defendant served within the state. Although the concept of control must be stretched somewhat, a court also retains jurisdiction over residents who are not in the state. As long as procedures for service are designed to give the absent resident notice of the action, he or she will be subject to the state's courts.

Long-Arm Jurisdiction. During the past sixty years the development of the automobile and the expansion of business enterprises into national markets have led to rules that extend the jurisdiction of state courts beyond state boundaries. These rules are a good example of the manner in which the legal system adapts to a changing environment. In view of the traditional requirement that the defendant be served personally, consider the difficulties of the plaintiff in each of the following situations:

1. Plaintiff is an Ohio resident injured in Ohio by a Missouri driver who returns home immediately after the accident.
2. Plaintiff is a California resident injured in California by a defective lathe manufactured by a New York firm.

In both instances the plaintiff might bring suit in the court of the state in which the defendant resides or, if the amount involved is over $10,000, in a federal court. Although these possibilities exist, very likely they would be both inconvenient and expensive, and plaintiff ordinarily would prefer to sue in his or her home state.

To permit injured plaintiffs to bring suit against nonresident drivers causing injury, a number of states in the 1920s adopted legislation that gave the local courts jurisdiction over nonresidents driving within the state based upon the fictitious appointment by the nonresident of some designated state official to receive process in the defendant's behalf. This procedure, although challenged as a violation of due process, was held constitutional by the U.S. Supreme Court.[7] During the 1930s this "long-arm" theory was extended to cover not only nonresidents driving on the state's highways but also various business-related activities carried on within the state. In 1945 the Supreme Court ruled that, as long as the defendant has certain minimal contacts with a state that make it fair for the plaintiff to sue in that state, due process is not violated and the courts of the plaintiff's state have jurisdiction.[8]

Pleadings

The first stage in a civil case is called the *pleadings*. In this stage the parties exchange legal documents in which they outline the bases of their claims and defenses. The basic pleadings are the *petition* or *complaint* and the *answer*. Copies of each document of the pleadings are filed with the court.

The Summons. A lawsuit actually begins when the defendant is served with a *summons*. The summons informs the defendant that action is being brought and that a judgment against the defendant will be entered by default if no appropriate response is made. The summons tells the defendant little or nothing about the nature of plaintiff's claim. Traditionally, the law has required that the summons be handed to the defendant, but most states today allow service by a variety of

methods, including publication, mailing, or delivery to the defendant's residence.

The Complaint. The complaint, which is the initial pleading, spells out in some detail the nature of the claim. In practice, in many jurisdictions the summons and the complaint are served together. The statements in the complaint as well as the other pleadings are statements of fact. The procedural rules of one state direct that the statements be "plain and concise" and "sufficiently particular to give the court and parties notice of the transactions, occurrences . . . intended to be proved. . . ."

The Answer. Probably the most frequent answer is that all or at least some of the allegations in the complaint are just not true. This is called a *denial*. Another possible response is that there are facts not mentioned in the complaint that constitute a defense. For example, the defendant might allege in response to a complaint for money owed that payment has been made. An answer of this kind is called an *affirmative defense*. The defendant may also counterclaim. A *counterclaim* is an assertion by the defendant that he has a claim against the plaintiff that could be the basis for an independent action. A sample complaint and answer are shown in Figures 2-4 and 2-5.

Motions. Other important responses that the defendant might make are motions. Simply stated, a *motion* is an application to the court for an order of some kind. A wide variety of motions can be made. They are important at every stage of litigation. During the trial, motions are generally made orally in open court. Motions made before or after trial, however, are generally made in writing. In most instances, a party making a motion must give notice to his or her adversary, and the court provides an opportunity for each to argue for or against the motion.

During the pleading stage many motions

FIGURE 2–4
Complaint

```
              United States District Court
           for the Southern District of Ohio

                Civil Action, File Number 85-1234


   John D. Blackburn, Plaintiff⎤
                  v.              ⎬  Complaint
   Douglas Whitman, Defendant ⎦


   1. Plaintiff is a citizen of the State of Ohio and
   defendant is a citizen of the State of Kansas. The
   matter in controversy exceeds, exclusive of interest
   and costs, the sum of ten thousand dollars.
   2. On August 31, 1985, in Mountain View, a public
   park in Portland, Oregon, defendant negligently drove
   a bicycle against plaintiff, who was jogging on a
   public way in said park. As a result plaintiff was
   thrown to the ground and had his arm and leg broken
   and was otherwise injured, was prevented from carrying
   out his business, suffered great pain in body and
   mind, and incurred expenses for medical attention and
   hospitalization in the sum of $2500.
   3. Wherefore plaintiff demands judgment against de-
   fendant in the sum of $15,000 and costs.


                          Signed: Frank F. Gibson
                          Attorney for Plaintiff
                          Address: Mulberry Building
                          Newark, Ohio 43201
```

are made. The majority of these are designed to correct defects in the pleadings. However, the *motion to dismiss* on the grounds that the complaint does not state a cause of action is of major importance to the continuation of the suit. The motion to dismiss is based upon the defendant's contention that, even if all the facts are as the plaintiff alleges, no legal recourse is available to the plaintiff. For example, the ABC Company, a small business, contracts to buy a tract of land in order to construct a plant. After the contract is signed,

FIGURE 2–5
Answer

```
            United States District Court
          for the Southern District of Ohio

                Civil Action, File Number 85-1234


John D. Blackburn, Plaintiff ⎫
             v.              ⎬  Answer
Douglas Whitman, Defendant   ⎭


1. Defendant admits the allegation contained in para-
graph 1 of the complaint.
2. Alleges that he is without knowledge or information
sufficient to form a belief as to the allegations
contained in paragraph 2 of the complaint; and denies
each and every other allegation contained in the com-
plaint.


                    Signed: Bartley A. Brennan
                    Attorney for Defendant
                    Address: 81 Main Street
                    Bowling Green, Ohio 43264
```

the firm states that it might be interested in buying the adjoining tract, which the seller also owns. The seller indicates that the company can have thirty days to decide if it wants the adjoining parcel. Within the thirty-day period, however, the seller contracts to sell to another party. In a suit brought by the ABC Company, the seller's attorney would move to dismiss, for even if all the facts are true the ABC Company would not win since no contract for the adjoining land was ever made. The motion to dismiss challenges the legal sufficiency of the plaintiff's claim. If the motion is granted, the plaintiff's case is dismissed. If the motion is denied, the plaintiff has the right to go on with the case.

Functions of Pleadings. The pleadings serve different purposes. They provide notice to the parties of the opposition's claims. In many jurisdictions this is their chief purpose. Where notice is the function of the pleadings, their purpose is to provide for fairness in the litigation. A second purpose of the pleadings is to determine what differences exist between the parties as each sees the facts and understands the law. In answering, if the defendant does not deny a statement that the plaintiff has made in the complaint, the court assumes that no dispute exists regarding that particular fact. If the defendant does deny an allegation made in the complaint, an issue of fact exists that must be resolved in some manner. Similarly, if the defendant makes a motion to dismiss on the ground of legal insufficiency, then an issue of law—a dispute as to what the law is—exists that also must be resolved.

From Pleadings to Trial

After each of the parties has responded to the claims of fact and law made by the other, the pleadings terminate. If the only difference between the parties is a legal issue, the trial court judge will resolve it. If one of the differences is a dispute as to the facts, the case must proceed to trial. From the end of the pleadings to the trial, a number of significant actions take place. These actions, like the pleadings, are designed to solve some of the basic problems of legal dispute settlement. Three of the important procedures that are often used at this stage of litigation are summary judgment, discovery, and the pretrial conference.

Summary Judgment. Either of the parties can make a motion for *summary judgment.* The party who makes the motion is contending that there really is no genuine issue of fact so litigation need proceed no further. Ordinarily, a motion for summary judgment will be based upon one party's affidavits and documentary evidence that show that the other party's factual claims have no merit. Once the motion is made, the opposing party may present his or her proof and argue against the motion. If the court is convinced that in reality no factual issue exists, it will grant the motion and the litigation terminates. The purpose of summary judgment is to terminate litigation where no genuine dispute exists. Even when a court is unable to grant summary judgment, the supporting documents often indicate that the actual dispute regarding the facts is not so

extensive as the parties believed. The procedure thus serves to narrow the factual controversy.

Discovery. The devices that the parties use to obtain further information about the case are called *discovery procedures.* Additional information tends to reduce further the facts upon which the parties disagree. Discovery procedures also tend to reduce the possibility of surprise during the trial. The use of discovery thus helps to add fairness to the litigation process. By proper use of discovery procedures either party can obtain further particulars about the opposition's case, sworn statements from hostile or friendly witnesses, and information about the prospective testimony of a particular witness. Books, papers, and items relevant to the litigation can be examined, and under certain circumstances either of the parties can be required to submit to physical or mental examination.

Pretrial Conference. Most courts throughout the United States use *pretrial conferences* to expedite litigation. The format of these conferences varies from one jurisdiction to another. In some courts the pretrial conference is a formal affair; in others, there is considerable informality. Often the parties themselves attend the conference, but in some jurisdictions only the opposing counsel and the conferring judge meet. In large metropolitan courts one or two judges will be assigned to supervise the pretrial calendar, but in rural areas the judge assigned the case will usually direct the conference.

At the conference an effort is made to narrow and simplify the factual and legal issues. If possible, admissions of fact and of documents that will avoid unnecessary proof are obtained. The parties may consider other items such as the number of expert witnesses who will testify, the need to amend the pleadings, and the date for the trial.

Exploring the issues at a pretrial conference

helps to eliminate surprise at the trial. Thus, the outcome is more likely to reflect a fair resolution of the issues between the parties. In many instances the pretrial conference is used to consider the possibility of settling the case. If the parties are not too far apart, the conferring judge may try to persuade them to reach a settlement. Under no circumstances, however, should the parties be forced to settle, since a forced settlement denies them their right to trial. In some areas the pretrial conference has been criticized as a device used by the court to force settlements in order to reduce the number of cases pending on the court dockets.

THE TRIAL

In many instances litigation results because the parties are unable to agree about what actually happened—what the facts are. The purpose of the trial is to process the information that will be used to determine the facts. For most civil litigation, the American legal system uses the *petit jury*—a group of laypersons—to decide these important questions. Parties, however, may waive their right to have a jury determine the facts. If the right is waived or the case is one in which the parties do not have the right to a jury trial, the trial judge decides the facts.

The Jury System

Although the jury system has many critics, it continues to be important in American law because of strong historic support. For many decades Americans have looked upon the jury as a bulwark of democracy. It is an institution in which citizens participate directly, and it is often seen as a protection against the power of government. These sentiments stem primarily from the use of juries in criminal cases, but parties in civil cases generally feel more satisfied when their claims are determined by ju-

ries rather than by judges. Today, the history and tradition of trial by jury are so ingrained in our legal system that many would raise strong objections to proposals to limit further the right to trial by jury.

Traditionally, the civil jury consisted of twelve persons. Over the past twenty-five years there has been a trend toward smaller trial juries, and many jurisdictions now allow juries of fewer than twelve in most civil cases. Historically, the civil jury's verdict was required to be unanimous, but here again change has taken place, and in more than half the states unanimous verdicts are no longer required. These changes have been made primarily to shorten trials and make it possible for the courts to try more cases with less delay.

One of the first steps in the jury trial is the selection of the jurors. Lists of prospective jurors are made from various sources depending upon the jurisdiction. The names should be chosen at random from these sources, and the lists should represent a fair cross section of the community.

In spite of the fact that random selection of jurors is attempted, many people chosen for jury duty will have obvious biases. These biases might influence their decisions. To insure a greater degree of fairness, the parties are given the right to exclude certain jurors by *challenge*. Each side has a limited number of *peremptory challenges* that allow a party to exclude a prospective juror without giving any reason whatsoever. In addition, any prospective juror may be challenged and excluded *for cause*.

Trial Stages

After the jury has been selected, the principal steps in the trial are the attorneys' opening statements, the presentation of evidence, the attorneys' closing statements or summations, the judge's charge or instructions to the jury, the verdict, and the judgment. The extent and manner of use of these steps are characterized by numerous procedures to insure fairness and due process of law. Parties have the right to object to any deviation from the accepted pattern of procedures that might result in an unfair determination of the issues. For example, most evidence is presented by oral testimony of witnesses in response to questions asked by attorneys. Matters such as who can be asked what or the type, form, and content of questions are governed by the rules of evidence, and parties have a right to object to questions that do not come within the framework of these rules.

After the plaintiff's witnesses have testified, the defendant frequently moves to dismiss on the grounds that the plaintiff has failed to prove all the facts necessary to establish a case. If the court agrees, it can terminate the case at this point. A similar motion is often made by one or both of the parties after all the evidence has been presented. This motion in many jurisdictions is referred to as a *motion for a directed verdict*. If granted, the case is in effect taken from the jury and determined by the judge.

Instructions to the Jury. After all the evidence has been submitted and counsel have summed up their cases, the judge explains to the jury the law that applies to the case. This process, which is called *instructing* or *charging* the jury, presents the jury with information about the essential facts that each party must prove to support its position as well as the relationships between the evidence presented and the legal issues involved.

Instructions given by the court are ordinarily based upon requests made by opposing counsel. The instructions are read to the jury in open court, and in many jurisdictions they are furnished to the jury in writing as well.

Basically, the instructions present alternatives indicating the legal result of each possible factual finding the jury might make. Suppose that in litigation involving Joe, a defendant, and Mary, a plaintiff, the single contested fact is whether Joe made a statement to Mary with the intention of deceiving her. Legally, if he did intend to deceive he will be liable; if he did not, the case against him will be dismissed. The judge might charge the jury as follows: "If you determine that the defendant made the statement with the intention of deceiving the plaintiff, you must find for the plaintiff. If, however, you determine that the defendant's statement was made with no intention of deceiving the plaintiff, you must find for the defendant."

Another important function of the judge's instructions is to explain to the jury the complex legal rules regarding which side has the burden of proof on each issue in the case. This is an especially important task, since in many situations the decision about which side has the burden of proof will determine the outcome of the case. In civil cases, for example, the plaintiff usually must prove each element of the case by a preponderance of the evidence. There may, however, be situations where the defendant will bear the burden of proof.

Although the basic concept underlying the charge to the jury is quite simple, in most cases there are numerous factual differences that can influence the outcome of the case. The result is that instructions, unless carefully drafted, can confuse the jury. In addition, determining proper instructions in many cases is a complicated, argumentative process that delays litigation and frequently results in appeal. Because of these problems, a number of jurisdictions now either encourage or require the use of standard or patterned instructions. These instructions are developed by bar associations and courts to explain the law to the jury adequately and simply.

The Verdict. A trial is usually concluded when the jury brings in a *verdict*, an answer to the questions that the court has submitted to it. In a civil action the verdict will be either general or special. A *general verdict* is one in which the jurors comprehensively determine the issues for either the plaintiff or the defendant. If the jury finds for the plaintiff, the amount of damages will also be stated. In a *special verdict* the jury will provide written answers to specific questions of fact that the court submitted to it. The court, using these answers, then applies the law and resolves the issues in dispute between the parties.

Judgment and Execution. The judgment establishes the relief to which the parties are entitled. If the jury finds for the defendant, the judgment will dismiss the plaintiff's suit. If the plaintiff wins the case, ordinarily the judgment will award him or her a sum of money. When a monetary award does not furnish the plaintiff adequate relief, the court may order relief of another sort.

If the plaintiff has won a monetary judgment, the court provides machinery for locating the defendant's assets, for preventing the defendant from disposing of these assets, and finally for selling the assets with proceeds of the sale being used to satisfy the judgment. The defendant is often referred to as a *judgment debtor.* The final step is accomplished by a sheriff who seizes and then sells the assets. If the judgment debtor's assets are in the hands of a third party, the court can order the third party to turn the property over to the plaintiff. This procedure, referred to as *garnishment,* is sometimes used to require an employer to turn over to a creditor a portion of the wages of an employee who is a judgment debtor.

Sometimes a judgment debtor has assets that are income producing. Under these circumstances the court can appoint a receiver who will operate the property and pay the proceeds to the creditor after deducting operating expenses. Often the receiver will be empowered to negotiate the sale of the property and apply the net proceeds to the debt instead of having the property seized by the sheriff and auctioned off at what might be an inopportune time.

THE APPELLATE PROCESS

The function of an appellate court is to review the legal rulings that one or both of the parties think the trial court judge made incorrectly. This is a different function from that of the trial court, which is charged primarily with deciding differences between the parties about the facts. Because of this difference in function, the appellate process differs substantially from the trial process.

In an appeal, a determination of facts is unnecessary since all factual issues have already been decided at the trial. Because the oral testimony of witnesses and other types of evidence are not needed, the direct and cross examination of witnesses and the rules of evidence, which are designed to help the finders of fact make a correct determination, are eliminated. Interim procedures such as discovery and motions for summary judgment also have no place in an appellate court, since these procedures exist to help resolve factual issues.

When deciding if a legal error has been committed, the appellate court gets considerable information. This includes a record of the trial. Additional input is supplied by the parties, who, in our adversary system, are responsible for either pointing out the errors or supporting the rulings of the lower court. In fact, if one or both of the parties does not argue that some substantial legal error has been made, the appellate court has no power to review the trial.

The input from the parties generally consists of oral arguments before the court supported by written presentations called *briefs.* The appellate court judges, especially in the higher courts, make their decisions based upon the oral arguments of the parties, the briefs, and their own research and group discussion. For many cases the appellate court decision then is supported by a published written opinion.

Another difference between the trial and

appellate process is the number of judges involved. Appeals are heard by a number of judges, whereas in a trial a single judge presides. This difference, too, is related to function.

In a trial the judge is not the important decision maker, unless the parties have waived a jury or are not entitled to one. Although the judge makes legal decisions, these are made within the context of his or her primary job, which is to see that the trial is conducted properly and with reasonable speed. A single judge can more efficiently carry out these tasks.

Appellate courts are made up of a number of judges. They are the primary decision makers, and they deal only with legal questions. As their answers to these legal questions influence the entire system, it is reasonable to have several experts deliberate and decide upon the correct decision.

In spite of fundamental differences between the appellate and trial processes, important similarities exist. These similarities give an additional inkling of some of the common characteristics of legal dispute resolution referred to earlier in the chapter.

Both trial and appellate litigation are characterized by formal, clearly articulated procedures designed to insure a solution that not only is just but appears just. Both are characterized by time-consuming deliberation with significant input from the parties, and the results of each are open to public scrutiny.

THEORY AND REALITY

A wide disparity often exists between the manner in which legal institutions are supposed to operate and the way in which they actually do. The differences between theory and reality must be recognized by business and public administrators who are trying to understand the legal system. As potential litigants, they must take these differences into account when dealing with federal and state administrative agencies, when considering proposed legislation, and when confronting a myriad of other situations in connection with the legal system.

One reality often overlooked by the layperson is the extent to which the human element often influences the system's outputs. The legal system is operated by people. Most are honest, dedicated, and hardworking, but some are not. Some are greedy, some are vain, and some are arbitrary. Some are authoritarian, while others are permissive. While many are intelligent, a fair share are not. All make mistakes. Some lie. Many work long hours and believe in what they are doing; a few do not. These, then, are the legislators, judges, lawyers, prosecutors, bailiffs, clerks, arbitrators, and mediators who play important, often critical, roles in operating the legal system. Everyone who comes into contact with the system must recognize that it is administered by ordinary people and plan accordingly.

Like the people who operate the legal system, the system's processes and procedures vary in effectiveness. Some make sense and clearly accomplish their objectives. Others are clearly a waste of time and effort.

As we look at the steps in the typical civil case, it is easy to be impressed by their orderliness and by the manner in which they appear to be directed toward solving the problems inherent in dispute settlement. For a contrasting view, ask the plaintiff who has waited three years for a case to come to trial, the executive who has lost a suit because an attorney forgot to file an important document, or the businessperson who has been hurt by the action of a judge who was biased, overworked, or just did not care. In spite of such problems, civil dispute resolution has long provided an effective means for resolving important differences between members of the community. It plays an integral part in limiting violence and self-help and in maintaining the rule of law.

BOX 2-1: ISSUES AND TRENDS
Preventive Lawyering

Lawyers perform a number of tasks as they represent business clients. The most well known is representing clients in the resolution of legal disputes. Lawyers also assist clients in situations involving complex negotiations and in drafting documents. As legal problems and costs increase, lawyers are performing an additional task of appreciable value to the business firm. That task, which is to anticipate future legal problems, is generally referred to as preventive lawyering.

Preventive lawyering involves planning to eliminate future legal problems or at least to reduce their effect on the firm. Lawyers have done this in some areas, such as estate planning and tax planning, for years, and the lawyer's contribution to many specific business deals is to prevent legal problems from arising. Until recently, however, few business firms have had comprehensive preventive law programs, yet many daily activities of a firm's employees can create serious legal problems. For example, one source of potential litigation for both large and small firms exists when the firm terminates an employee. A preventive law program would examine the firm's termination procedures and develop a plan that would keep the firm out of legal trouble. Traditionally, lawyers became involved with these types of problems only when the terminated employee sued or threatened to sue.

The firm that adopts a preventive law program can expect substantial contact with the lawyer providing the service. Although this is sometimes disconcerting to managers, in order to develop a successful program the attorney must have an in-depth understanding of the firm's operations

Lawyers obtain information about the firm's operations through a technique called the legal audit. This is a review of the client's business to determine the areas in which the firm's activities create a legal risk. To be successful the legal audit must focus on all aspects of the operation as the lawyer is looking for activities where legal difficulties would generally not be recognized. Based upon the initial audit, the lawyer develops a plan to prevent or minimize these problems. Periodic audits of the client's business are necessary to insure that new problems are recognized and dealt with as they arise.

Once potential legal problems are identified, client education programs are necessary in order to help the program succeed. Employees frequently do not realize the legal consequences of their actions. Until they do realize them and understand as well how to prevent legal problems from arising, the preventive law program is of little benefit. Additionally, in firms that are subject to substantial government regulation, preventive lawyering includes a formal regulatory compliance program together with a system for insuring that the program is carried out.

Although today many large firms have comprehensive law programs, few small firms have programs of this type. Small business managers often do not recognize that a need for this type of program exists, and even when they do recognize a need, the up-front costs involved are hard to measure against the program's benefits. This makes a decision to initiate a preventive law program difficult.

REVIEW PROBLEMS

1. Explain the purpose of the following in civil litigation: (a) pleadings, (b) long-arm statutes, (c) motion for directed verdict, (d) full faith and credit clause, and (e) peremptory challenge.

2. (a) What is the adversary principle? (b) Present arguments in support of this principle and against it.

3. What is the function of a jury in a civil trial?

4. In two or three brief paragraphs, explain the difference between civil and criminal litigation.

5. Taylor was a party to litigation involving a real estate problem. Taylor's friend Bennett testified in Taylor's behalf at the trial. Bennett's testimony was critical to the outcome of the case. Taylor lost the case and decided to appeal. When Taylor informed Bennett of his intention to appeal, Bennett told him that he could not testify a second time as the experience had drained him emotionally. Taylor told Bennett that it would not be necessary for him to testify again. Explain why.

6. Smith and Barney were involved in a dispute involving the legal meaning of a clause in their contract. Smith's attorney stated that the only difference that the parties had was a difference of law. Neither party would concede and litigation was contemplated by Barney. Would his case be brought in a court with original jurisdiction or in a court with appellate jurisdiction? Support your answer.

7. Donald Yee, who resides in Pennsylvania, enters into an agreement to construct a building for Malone Company, a New York corporation. The contract price is $125,000. The building is to be built on land owned by Malone Company in Pennsylvania. The agreement was signed in Yee's office in Philadelphia. Yee defaults and Malone sues in federal court. Does the federal court have jurisdiction? Support your answer.

8. Sam Falcone owns a house in a predominately Italian neighborhood. His neighbor, Tony Fatio, tells Falcone that the Fatios are going to sell their home. Believing that the ethnic character of the area is changing, Sam contracts to sell his home. Tony then tells Sam that the Fatios have decided not to sell. Sam is upset and hires an attorney to sue Fatio. What legal steps should Fatio's attorney take if Fatio is served with a complaint? Why?

9. Clements sued Signa Corporation for breach of warranty in the Illinois courts. Clements purchased a boat from Barney's Sporting Goods, an Illinois corporation. Signa, the manufacturer of the boat, was an Indiana corporation with no offices in Illinois. Signa advertised in boating magazines that were received by Clements, and Signa's boat was displayed at a Chicago boating show. Barney's Sporting Goods, which was located in Illinois, also displayed the boat. Barney's furnished Clements with a written warranty issued by Signa. Do the Illinois courts have jurisdiction over Signa? Support your answer.

10. The Agricultural Adjustment Act of 1938 attempted to reduce the production of certain crops by limiting the acreage that farmers could plant. Filburn received an acreage allotment of 11.1 acres for wheat. He sowed, however, 23 acres and har-

vested from his excess acreage 239 bushels, for which he was penalized $117.11. Filburn sought to enjoin enforcement of this penalty on grounds that the Agricultural Adjustment Act did not apply to him since the wheat raised on the excess acreage was not sold but used on the farm. Filburn also argued that the law was unconstitutional as applied to him because the wheat grown on the excess acreage was not part of interstate commerce. Argue against Filburn's position. What result should the court reach? Wickard v. Filburn, 317 U.S. 111 (1942).

11. Maryland has approximately 3,800 retail service stations selling over twenty different brands of gasoline. About 5 percent of these stations are owned by refiners, although no petroleum products are produced or refined within the state. Three of the refiners operate solely through company-operated stations. In 1974 Maryland adopted legislation prohibiting refiners of petroleum products from operating retail service stations within the state.

Shortly before the effective date of the statute, Exxon filed a declaratory judgment action challenging the statute on grounds that it violated the Commerce Clause. Should the declaratory judgment be granted? Discuss. Exxon Corp. of America v. Maryland, 437 U.S. 117 (1977).

12. McLain filed a class action under Section 1 of the Sherman Act, alleging that real-estate brokers, members of the Real Estate Board of New Orleans, were guilty of fixing the rate of commissions. The defendant brokers argued that the Sherman Act did not apply to them since they were not involved in interstate commerce. Considering that the function of a real-estate broker is to bring buyers and sellers together, what arguments could McLain advance to support federal jurisdiction? McLain v. Real Estate Board of New Orleans, 444 U.S. 232 (1980).

13. Robinson purchased a new Audi from Seaway Volkswagen, Inc. (Seaway) in Massena, N.Y. The following year Robinson was injured in an automobile accident while driving through Oklahoma to a new home in Arizona. The injury was caused when the Audi caught fire after being struck in the rear. Robinson claimed that her injuries resulted from defective design of the Audi's gas tank. She sued Seaway; World-Wide Volkswagen, the regional distributor in New York; and the importer, Volkswagen of America, in the Oklahoma courts. Neither Seaway nor World-Wide Volkswagen conducted business in Oklahoma. Robinson argued that it was foreseeable that an automobile purchased in New York would travel to Oklahoma and thus that the Oklahoma courts had jurisdiction. Discuss the validity of this claim from a legal and public-policy standpoint. World-Wide Volkswagen v. Woodson, 444 U.S. 286 (1980).

FOOTNOTES

[1] Bureau of National Affairs, Antitrust & Trade Regulation Report (1975), No. 721, p. a-11.
[2] 9 Wheat. 1 (1824).
[3] 8 Wall 168, 183 (1869).
[4] 322 U.S. 533 (1943).
[5] Wayman v. Southard, 10 Weat. 1 (1825).
[6] 462 U.S. 919 (1983).
[7] Hess v. Pawolski, 274 U.S. 352 (1927).
[8] International Shoe v. Washington, 326 U.S. 310 (1945).

Introduction to Criminal Law

Chapter 2 briefly mentioned differences between civil law and criminal law and discussed civil procedure. This chapter provides an overview of criminal procedure and outlines the traditional basis of criminal law. The chapter continues with an examination of the extent to which a corporation is liable for the criminal acts of its employees and summarizes some common white collar crimes. Finally, the chapter looks at the evolving problem of computer crime.

THE BASIS OF CRIMINAL LAW

Crimes are offenses against society. Local, state, and federal statutes prohibit certain acts because they are antisocial or deviate from established social norms. In some instances it is the failure to act that society considers wrong. These acts of either commission or omission are crimes.

A person who commits a crime is prosecuted by a public official, generally called a prosecuting or district attorney. The prosecution is brought on behalf of the state that is representing the interests of society. One difference between criminal and civil litigation is that in a criminal case the state is always the plaintiff.

As the state is the plaintiff in a criminal case, the victim of a criminal act recovers nothing even if the prosecution is successful. However, the victim may pursue a civil action against the wrongdoer in order to recover damages. In most cases this is not very effective as the defendant is incarcerated or is financially unable to pay damages. Therefore, some states have statutes that provide compensation for victims of criminal acts.

PUNISHMENT

Punishment is the principal means that society employs to accomplish the objectives of the criminal law. The punishments that can be imposed on those who violate the law vary widely depending upon the crime, but the punishment may be severe. It can be a fine, imprisonment, or even execution. Often the guilty person is both fined and imprisoned. Also, for many crimes conviction involves the loss of important civil rights such as the right to vote, hold public office, or serve as a juror. An additional punishment, but one that is not established by statute, is the stigma that is attached to the person convicted of a crime.

Purposes of Punishment

Two very different views exist as to the purpose of punishment. Many people believe that the purpose of punishment is deterrence. Because of punishment the criminal will not repeat the act, and the threat of punishment will deter others from doing it. Others believe that retribution is the ultimate reason for criminal punishment. They feel that because most people are capable of choosing between right and wrong, a person who violates an accepted social norm must be made to "pay" his or her debt to society. Because violating some social norms provides a greater threat to society than violating other social norms, the punishment for some criminal acts is more extensive than it is for other criminal acts.

CLASSIFICATION OF CRIMES

Crimes are commonly classified as either *felonies* or *misdemeanors*. Many state statutes define a crime as a felony if it is punishable by death or imprisonment in a state penitentiary. Federal law defines a felony as a crime that is punishable by death or imprisonment in a federal prison. The significant factor determining a felony is the punishment that is authorized by statute, not that which is imposed upon the offender.

A misdemeanor is an offense that is less serious than a felony. Some states define a misdemeanor as a crime punishable by incarceration in a place other than a state penitentiary. Some jurisdictions recognize a third classification called *petty offenses*. These are usually traffic violations and are not really considered crimes.

Both felonies and misdemeanors are divided into classes so that sentencing will be more uniform. As an illustration, the *Model Penal Code* classifies felonies as (1) felonies of the first degree, (2) felonies of the second degree, and (3) felonies of the third degree. The first- and second-degree felonies are subject to greater punishment because they apply to more serious criminal acts.

Although the distinction between felonies and misdemeanors developed at common law, in many situations it continues to be important today. For example, for most felony convictions the person who is convicted loses certain civil rights, such as the right to vote or hold public office. This is not true if the individual is convicted of a misdemeanor.

MENS REA

In order to be convicted of a crime, a person must either commit some prohibited act or fail to perform some legal duty. In addition, in most instances the state must also prove that the person had a "guilty mind." This is called the *mens rea* of the crime. For example, if A were to take a coat from a restaurant genuinely believing it to be her own, she would not be guilty of a crime. She did not have a guilty mind.

The guilty mind requirement is readily established by the state if it can prove that a person planned or intended to do a wrongful act, but lesser degrees of awareness of wrongdoing are also sufficient to establish mens rea. Consider the following situation involving bribery of a public official. The XYZ Co. needs a government license to export a product that it manufactures. The company is having difficulty obtaining the license. The company's independent sales agent states that he can get a license for $10,000 as he "knows certain people in politics." If the firm gives the agent $10,000, its conduct is such that in all probability a bribe will occur. Although the firm did not bribe anyone, the mens rea of the offense is established as it acted knowing that its actions would cause this result.

Mens rea can also be established if a person acts recklessly or negligently as the following case illustrates.

State v. Wheat

Court of Appeals of Louisiana
471 So.2d 1027 (1985)

Background: Deborah Wheat was convicted of negligent homicide under Louisiana law and was sentenced to four years imprisonment at hard labor. She appealed, arguing that the record contained no evidence proving "criminal negligence," an essential element of the crime of negligent homicide. Additional facts are in the opinion. Decision: The appellate court affirmed the trial court's judgment.

Edwards, Judge

In a non-jury trial the court found the following facts. At approximately 10:30 p.m. on April 30, 1983, Deborah Wheat was driving a 1979 Cadillac on Union Avenue, a well lighted residential area in Bogalusa, Louisiana. She made a turn at a high rate of speed onto Wilmuth Street and proceeded south. She accelerated steadily for about 180 yards with no slowing or braking, weaving all the while back and forth across the road. Farther along on Wilmuth Street, Peter Voltolina had parked his Ford automobile along the northbound lane of travel, partially in the roadway, with its headlights on. Two men were standing out in the street beside the car, speaking with Voltolina who was seated behind the wheel. The Cadillac struck both men and the Ford, killing one man and severely injuring the other.

Deborah Wheat had been seen earlier in the evening at a barroom where she was observed to be unsteady on her feet, but no one saw her actually drinking. Police at the accident scene smelled alcohol on her breath, and they found several empty beer cans in her car. No sobriety test was performed on defendant at any time. There was conflicting testimony as to whether she actually drank anything that night, since her mother and her friend, Rhonda Pierce, both testified that Deborah Wheat had remained sober.

The trial court evaluated the record and held that defendant had been drinking heavily, was drunk, had no business driving a vehicle, and consequently failed to maintain control of her automobile.

LSA-R.S. 14:32 provides in part, "[n]egligent homicide is the killing of a human being by criminal negligence." LSA-R.S. 14:12 goes on to say, "[c]riminal negligence exists when, although neither specific nor general criminal intent is present, there is such disregard of the interest of others that the offender's conduct amounts to a gross deviation below the standard of care expected to be maintained by a reasonably careful man under like circumstances."

The applicable standard for reviewing sufficiency is whether, after viewing the evidence in the light most favorable to the prosecution, any rational trier of fact could have found that the essential elements of the crime were proven beyond a reasonable doubt.

In *State v. Fontenot,* the supreme court set forth the essential elements of negligent homicide which the State must prove:

> (1) that defendant was criminally negligent, i.e., that there was such disregard of the interest of others that the offender's conduct amounted to a gross deviation below the standard of care expected to be maintained by a reasonably careful man under like circumstances; and (2) that a killing resulted from this conduct.

Defendant argues on appeal that the State proved only ordinary negligence as opposed to the required criminal negligence. She denies being drunk, citing the conflicting testimony. She argues that the speed of her vehicle was never firmly established and that the victim was negligently standing in the roadway next to a car that was improperly parked in the street. Lastly, she claims that her vehicle was weaving due to her own efforts to avoid an accident. We disagree with all of these contentions and, accordingly, we affirm the judgment of the trial court.

There is ample evidence in the record to sustain a holding that Deborah Wheat was drunk at the time of the accident. The trial judge stated that the helpful testimony on defendant's behalf by her mother and by Rhonda Pierce was actually prevarication and could not be accepted.

Likewise, the record justifies the finding that Deborah Wheat was speeding in a residential neighborhood. Several witnesses testified that they heard squealing tires as she turned onto Wilmuth Street and that the car's motor was running much too fast for moderate travel. Some witnesses saw the car approaching and noticed that its speed was too great for that particular street. Another witness seated in the parked Ford cried out in warning as the Cadillac approached on its collision course.

Defendant's contention that she was weaving to avoid an accident is hardly credible when considered in proper context. She was on an unobstructed residential street with adequate lighting and dry pavement. Even though the Ford which she struck was parked partially in the street, defendant's lane was completely open and accessible. No weaving was necessary since there was nothing for her to avoid.

This court agrees with the trial court that the test for criminal negligence was adequately met. Drunk driving at an excessive speed in a residential neighborhood constitutes a gross deviation below the standard of care expected to be maintained by a reasonable person.

REGULATORY CRIMES

There are a limited number of crimes that do not require mens rea. These are often referred to as "strict liability" crimes. Several of them are of particular importance to business. They apply to industries that are closely regulated by government. These industries involve the sale of potentially harmful products such as drugs and alcohol. Examples of strict liability offenses are actions such as the mislabeling of drugs or the sale of liquor to minors. In both of these situations many states provide that the person who committed the act will be liable even if he or she has acted in error.

When a legislature creates a regulatory crime, it has decided that the need to protect the public outweighs the traditional requirement that a person in order to be guilty of a criminal act must have a guilty mind. Because mens rea is not required, most regulatory crimes do not have punishments that are as severe as those for other crimes. Some states have made a fine the maximum penalty for regulatory crimes.

CRIMINAL PROCEDURE

Chapter 2 describes criminal and civil litigation in the United States as adversarial in nature. In an adversarial system each party is responsible for developing and proving its own case. As the state with its extensive resources seems to have an advantage in a criminal case, a fundamental goal of criminal procedure is to insure that the accused, who must defend against the state, is not convicted erroneously. Society prefers that some guilty individuals escape conviction rather than have an innocent person convicted of a crime.

Although protecting the innocent person is a primary goal of criminal procedure, other goals are also important. These other goals include minimizing the burden placed upon the person who is accused of a crime and must stand trial, maintaining the appearance as well as the reality of fairness, and achieving equality in the application of the law. The combination of these goals has played a significant role in shaping the procedures in the criminal justice system of the United States.

Procedural Protections: The Bill of Rights

A defendant in a criminal case benefits from a number of procedural protections. Several of these are contained in the Bill of Rights of the Constitution. Although the Constitution essentially dictates how the federal government is run, the U.S. Supreme Court has determined that most of the important guarantees of the Bill of Rights bind state governments as well. A brief summary of the provisions of the Bill of Rights that apply to criminal procedure follows.

The Fourth Amendment. The Fourth Amendment states, "The right of the people to be secure in their persons, houses, papers, and effects, against unreasonable searches and seizures, shall not be violated, and no Warrants shall issue, but upon probable cause, supported by Oath or affirmation, and particularly describing the place to be searched, and the persons or things to be seized." Probable cause exists when the circumstances would lead a reasonably prudent man to believe in the guilt of the arrested party. This is required before a warrant is issued. It is possible that the officer or officers believe that they were acting under a valid warrant when, in fact, they were not. The case that follows deals with that situation.

United States v. Leon

U.S. Supreme Court

468 U.S. 897 (1984)

Background: A confidential informant of unproven reliability informed the Burbank police that Armando Sanchez and Patsy Stewart (respondents) were selling large quantities of cocaine and methaqualone. On the basis of this information two experienced investigators initiated an extensive investigation. During the course of this investigation one of the people seen leaving the home of Sanchez and Stewart was established as a confidant of Albert Leon (respondent), who was under investigation on drug-related activities stemming from other information.

As a result of police observations, Officer Rombach of the Burbank police prepared an affidavit summarizing their information and applied for a warrant to search the respondents' residences and automobiles. The ensuing search turned up large quantities of drugs and the respondents were indicted for federal drug offenses.

The respondents filed motions to exclude the evidence seized on grounds that the police observations were insufficient to establish probable cause. Thus, the warrant was defective and the evidence was illegally obtained. The District Court agreed and excluded the evidence. Upon appeal the Court of Appeals affirmed. It rejected the government's argument that the Fourth Amendment exclusionary rule should not apply when evidence is seized in reasonable, good-faith reliance on a search warrant. The government appealed to the U.S. Supreme Court.

Decision: The U.S. Supreme Court reversed. It recognized a good-faith exception to the exclusionary rule.

White, Justice *(delivered the opinion of the Court)*

The Fourth Amendment contains no provision expressly precluding the use of evidence obtained in violation of its commands, and an examination of its origin and purposes makes clear that the use of fruits of a past unlawful search or seizure "work[s] no new Fourth Amendment wrong." The wrong condemned by the Amendment is "fully accomplished" by the unlawful search or seizure itself, and the exclusionary rule is neither intended nor able to "cure the invasion of the defendant's rights which he has already suffered." The rule thus operates as "a judicially created remedy designed to safeguard Fourth Amendment rights generally through its deterrent effect, rather than a personal constitutional right of the party aggrieved."

The substantial social costs exacted by the exclusionary rule for the vindication of Fourth Amendment rights have long been a source of concern. "Our cases have consistently recognized that unbending application of the exclusionary sanction to enforce ideals of governmental rectitude would impede unacceptably the truth-finding functions of judge and jury." An objectionable collateral consequence of this interference with the criminal justice system's truth-finding function is that some guilty defendants may go free or receive reduced sentences as a result of favorable plea bargains. Particularly when law enforcement officers have acted in objective good faith or their transgressions have been minor, the magnitude of the benefit conferred on such guilty defendants offends basic concepts of the criminal justice system. Indiscriminate application of the exclusionary rule, therefore, may well "generat[e] disrespect for the law and administration of justice." Accordingly, "[a]s with any remedial device, the application of the rule has been restricted to those areas where its remedial objectives are thought most efficaciously served."

To the extent that proponents of exclusion rely on its behavioral effects on judges and magistrates in these areas, their reliance is misplaced. First, the exclusionary rule is designed to deter police misconduct rather than to punish the errors of judges and magistrates. Second, there exists no evidence suggesting that judges and magistrates are inclined to ignore or subvert the Fourth Amendment or that lawlessness among these actors requires application of the extreme sanction of exclusion.

Third, and most important, we discern no basis, and are offered none, for believing that exclusion of evidence seized pursuant to a warrant will have a significant deterrent effect on the issuing judge or magistrate. Many of the factors indicating that the exclusionary rule cannot provide an effective "special" or "general" deterrent for individual offending law enforcement officers apply as well to judges or magistrates. And, to the extent that the rule is thought to operate as a "systemic" deterrent on a wider audience, it clearly can have no such effect on individuals empowered to issue search warrants. Judges and magistrates are not adjuncts to the law enforcement team; as neutral judicial officers, they have no stake in the outcome of particular criminal prosecutions. The threat of exclusion thus cannot be expected significantly to deter them. Imposition of the exclusionary sanction is not necessary meaningfully to inform judicial officers of their errors, and we cannot conclude that admitting evidence obtained pursuant to a warrant while at the same time declaring that the warrant was somehow defective will in any way reduce judicial officers' professional incentives to comply with the Fourth Amendment, encourage them to repeat their mistakes, or lead to the granting of all colorable warrant requests.

If exclusion of evidence obtained pursuant to a subsequently invalidated warrant is to have any deterrent effect, therefore, it must alter the behavior of individual law enforcement officers or the policies of their departments. One could argue that applying the exclusionary rule in cases where the police failed to demonstrate probable cause in the warrant application deters future inadequate presentations or "magistrate shopping" and thus promotes the ends of the Fourth Amendment. Suppressing evidence obtained pursuant to a technically defective warrant supported by probable cause might also encourage officers to scrutinize more closely the form of the warrant and to point out suspected judicial errors. We find such arguments speculative and conclude that suppression of evidence obtained pursuant to a warrant should be ordered only on a case-by-case basis and only in those unusual cases in which exclusion will further the purposes of the exclusionary rule.

We have frequently questioned whether the exclusionary rule can have any deterrent effect when the offending officers acted in the objectively reasonable belief that their conduct did not violate the Fourth Amendment. "No empirical researcher, proponent or opponent of the rule, has yet been able to establish with any assurance whether the rule has a deterrent effect. . . ." But even assuming that the rule effectively deters some police misconduct and provides incentives for the law enforcement profession as a whole to conduct itself in accord with the Fourth Amendment, it cannot be expected, and should not be applied, to deter objectively reasonable law enforcement activity.

As we observed in *Michigan* v. *Tucker,* and reiterated in *United States* v. *Peltier:*

> "The deterrent purpose of the exclusionary rule necessarily assumes that the police have engaged in willful, or at the very least negligent, conduct which has deprived the defendant of some right. By refusing to admit evidence gained as a result of such conduct, the courts hope to instill in those particular investigating officers, or in their future counterparts, a greater degree of care toward the rights of an accused. Where the official action was pursued in complete good faith, however, the deterrence rationale loses much of its force."

In the absence of an allegation that the magistrate abandoned his detached and neutral role, suppression is appropriate only if the officers were dishonest or reckless in preparing their affidavit or could not have harbored an objectively reasonable belief in the existence of probable cause. Only respondent Leon has contended that no reasonably well trained police officer could have believed that there existed probable cause to search his house; significantly, the other respondents advance no comparable argument. Officer Rombach's application for a warrant clearly was supported by much more than a "bare bones" affidavit. The affidavit related the results of an extensive investigation and, as the opinions of the divided panel of the Court of Appeals make clear, provided evidence sufficient to create disagreement among thoughtful and competent judges as to the existence of probable cause. Under these circumstances, the officers' reliance on the magistrate's determination of probable cause was objectively reasonable, and application of the extreme sanction of exclusion is inappropriate.

Accordingly, the judgment of the Court of Appeals is reversed.

The Fifth Amendment. No one can be deprived of "life, liberty, or property" without due process of law. *Due process* means that the procedures in litigation—either civil or criminal—must be fair. The person must have adequate notice of the charges being brought against him or her and an opportunity to defend before an impartial court. Fairness means also that the proceedings in a particular case must be the same as those in similar cases and the parties must have the same responsibilities and privileges as parties in similar cases. The due process clause is contained in the Fifth Amendment.

The prohibition against double jeopardy is also in the Fifth Amendment. *Double jeopardy* means trying someone more than once for a single offense. This may occur when more than one person is victimized in a particular crime, but only one victim is involved in the criminal suit. After the defendant is tried for that alleged crime, the victim not involved in the original court case cannot initiate another trial. Double trials and double convictions are what this restriction seeks to avoid; they are not necessarily double punishments.

The Sixth and Eighth Amendments. The Sixth Amendment states: "In all criminal prosecutions, the accused shall enjoy the right to a speedy and public trial, by an impartial jury of the State and district wherein the crime shall have been committed, which district shall have been previously ascertained by law, and to be informed of the nature and cause of the accusation; to be confronted with the witnesses against him; to have compulsory process for obtaining witnesses in his favor, and to have the Assistance of Counsel for his defence." This amendment contains many protections for the defendant in a criminal action, including the right to an impartial jury. The Eighth Amendment prohibits the use of excessive bail and fines as well as cruel and unusual punishment.

STEPS IN THE CRIMINAL JUSTICE PROCESS

The criminal justice system is complex. Criminal law involves both state and federal constitutions, state and federal legislation, and state and federal cases interpreting both constitutions and legislation. Variations in procedures for dealing with crimes exist from jurisdiction to jurisdiction. In the following paragraphs, if a substantial number of jurisdictions handle an issue one way and a substantial number handle it another way, both methods are mentioned. If only one method is mentioned, that is the manner in which the majority of states treat it.

Report of the Crime and Prearrest Investigation

The criminal justice system usually starts when the police receive information concerning the possible commission of a crime. The police may obtain this information from an outside source or through their own investigation. If it appears likely that a crime has been committed, the offense will be recorded as a "reported" crime. The officer must then determine whether the crime actually was committed and whether there is sufficient information indicating the guilt of a particular person to justify arresting and charging that person.

A variety of investigatory techniques may be used. The suspect could be questioned, potential witnesses interviewed, and the scene of the crime examined. The examination of the scene often involves collection of physical evidence.

Arrest

Arrest is taking a person into custody in a lawful manner and charging him or her with a crime. In order to make a lawful arrest, an officer must have "probable cause" indicating that a crime has been committed. *Probable cause* requires that the officer have reasonable grounds based upon more evidence for than against that an accused has committed a crime. The evidence must be such that it would convince an ordinarily prudent person.

Most arrests are made on the basis of a warrant. To obtain a warrant, a law enforcement officer must file a sworn complaint with the court alleging that a crime has been committed. If the court is convinced that probable cause exists and that a crime has been committed, it issues a warrant.

A law enforcement officer may also obtain a warrant on the basis of a grand jury indictment. A *grand jury* is a body of citizens that hears evidence from a prosecutor concerning criminal activities. The grand jury decides whether there is sufficient evidence to indict someone for the crime. It does not decide whether the person is guilty; it merely decides that there is sufficient evidence to indict. When it does decide that there is sufficient evidence, a judge issues a warrant for the person's arrest based upon the indictment.

In some situations an officer may make an arrest without a warrant. The general rule is that an officer may make a warrantless arrest for a felony if probable cause exists and the officer believes that the suspect may not easily be located again. Ordinarily warrantless arrests for misdemeanors may be made only if the misdemeanor is committed in the officer's presence.

Booking

After arrest the accused is taken to the stationhouse for recording the arrest and the offense that motivated it. This part of the process is called "booking." If the arrest is for a misdemeanor, the person arrested may be released by paying "stationhouse bail." To effect release, the accused must put up cash as security and promise to appear before a magistrate on a given day. If arrested for a more serious offense, the person will be put in a holding cell until he or she is presented before a magistrate. Before bringing the accused before a magistrate, the arresting officer must write a report as to what occurred and have it reviewed by a superior officer. The superior officer may decide that charging the individual arrested with criminal activity would not be the best way to handle the case. The officer may reduce the charges or give the accused a warning and release him or her from custody.

First Appearance

If the higher-ranking officer decides to continue the process, most states require that the arrested suspect be taken promptly before a magistrate, commissioner, or justice of the peace. This public official informs the suspect of the charges and of the suspect's constitutional rights. If the charges involve only misdemeanors, the accused may elect to plead guilty. At that time a sentence may be imposed on the accused without any further proceedings. If the accused pleads not guilty or if the charges involve a felony, the public officer will set the bail.

Preliminary Hearing. During the preliminary hearing before the magistrate the prosecutor must introduce enough evidence to convince a magistrate that there is probable cause to believe that the accused committed the crime. If the magistrate believes that the probable cause exists, he or she will "bind the case over" to the next stage in the proceedings. In some jurisdictions the case is "bound over" to a grand jury. If the grand jury agrees with the decision of the magistrate that probable cause exists, the grand jury returns an indictment. This is an instrument that charges the accused of committing a crime or crimes. Its purpose is to notify the person of the charges so that he or she can prepare a defense. Some jurisdictions do not provide a grand jury review. They have the magistrate issue an *information.* Like the indictment, an information notifies the accused of the charges against him or her so that a defense can be prepared.

Charges and Plea

Once charges have been filed with a trial court, the defendant is informed of them and asked to enter a plea. If the individual is charged with a serious crime, he or she can elect whether to have a jury trial or to be tried by a judge. A serious crime is usually defined as one for which incarceration of more than six months is possible. The defendant may enter a plea of guilty, not guilty, or nolo contendre. *Nolo contendre* is a plea in which the defendant does not admit guilt but agrees not to contest the charges. Some courts treat this the same as a guilty plea; however, the nolo contendre plea cannot be used against the defendant in a civil case.

In this stage of the judicial process *plea bargaining* often occurs. The use of plea bargaining varies from jurisdiction to jurisdiction. The purpose of plea bargaining is to get the defendant to plead guilty. This substantially reduces the prosecutor's task as a trial is no longer necessary.

In plea bargaining the prosecutor and the accused negotiate as to the particular criminal violation with which the accused will be charged. Some students of the criminal justice system are critical of plea bargaining because it allows the accused to accept responsibility for a less serious crime. Many different reasons exist for a defendant to plea bargain. Probably the most significant is to substitute a less serious offense in place of the one for which the accused is charged. This reduces uncertainty and almost always means a lesser sentence.

There are two types of plea bargains: those that reduce the seriousness of the charges and those that reduce the severity of the sentence. For example, a defendant might agree to plead guilty to a charge of manslaughter to avoid a possible conviction for murder, which in many states carries the death penalty. Although it is the prosecutor, and not the judge, who participates in plea bargaining, the recommendation of the prosecutor as to what the sentence should be usually greatly influences the sentence.

Trial: Standards of Proof

The final basic stage of the criminal judicial process, excluding appeals, is the trial. The prosecution has the entire burden of proof. The defendant does not have to prove anything. The standard of proof required to judge a person guilty in a criminal proceeding is not the probable cause standard that applied earlier in the criminal judicial process; it is proof beyond a reasonable doubt.

If convicted, the criminal will be sentenced. The punishment will vary from case to case, depending on the statutes that define the crimes and their punishment, and on the degree of latitude the judge is allowed in sentencing from one case to another.

CORPORATE CRIMINAL LIABILITY

Until the 1850s American law generally held that a corporation could not be guilty of a crime. The law rejected corporate criminal liability primarily on two grounds. First, as a corporation was not a living person, it could not have the guilty mind that the law required for a criminal conviction. In addition, as the corporation was an artificial person, it could not be physically punished. As corporations began to play a more significant role in the economy, the judicial system reexamined the reasons underlying corporate criminal immunity and rejected them.

The first successful cases against corporations involved strict liability offenses. An example would be the mislabeling of drugs. This type of offense did not require the government to prove that the defendant had a guilty mind. All it had to prove was that the defendant did the act. As the criminal law evolved, courts also began to convict corporations of crimes that required criminal intent. Courts looked at the conduct of the corporation's agents and employees to establish this necessary element. Courts also concluded that although a corporation could not be physically punished, fining a corporation that had benefited through its employees' illegal acts was an appropriate sanction.

As corporate criminal liability expanded, corporations argued that fining the organization for the illegal acts of its employees was unfair. They contended that the punishment was really being inflicted upon the shareholders who had done nothing wrong. Of course, if the board of directors authorized the employees' action, the corporation would be responsible. However, proving corporate authorization is very difficult.

Courts have usually rejected the argument that punishing the corporation for its employees' illegal acts is unfair on public-policy grounds. As the corporation benefits from the illegal acts of its employees—both legal and illegal—it should be responsible for what they do within the scope of their authority.

As the criminal liability of corporations is based upon a determination that the acts and intent of its employees are the acts of the corporation, the status of the employee who commits the act is sometimes a question in criminal litigation involving corporations. Today, the majority rule in the United States is that acts of employees at most levels will be imputed to the corporate employer as long as the employee intended to benefit the organization. Some states, however, do not impose criminal liability on a corporation for the acts of lower-level employees.

State v. Adjustment Department Credit Bureau

Supreme Court of Idaho
483 P.2d 687 (1971)

Background: Adjustment Department Credit Bureau (defendant-appellant) conducted a bill collection service. It was charged with the crime of extortion, which was alleged to have been committed through Howard Short, an employee. The corporation was convicted and fined $1,500. It appealed primarily on grounds that the particular acts of Howard Short were not authorized by the corporation. Additional facts are in the opinion.
Decision: Reversed and remanded.

McFadden, Justice

One of the defendant's customers, a pharmacy, assigned an open account owed to the pharmacy by Rodney Price to the defendant for collection. Howard Short, an agent of the defendant, handled this particular claim for the defendant company. Price had executed a promissory note to the defendant on this claim, and when the note was not paid in accord with its terms, suit was instituted in a justice court in Ada County and default judgment entered in July of 1967. Short attempted to collect on this judgment against Price, who was out of work at the time. Subsequently, Short accepted a check with the understanding it would be paid in installments. At the time of execution of this check Price told Short that there were no funds in the bank on which the check was written. After other subsequent conversations Short had Price execute another check on a different bank even though Price had told him that he had no account there, and the first check was torn up. This second check was presented for payment to the bank and returned unpaid.

Later in the summer of 1967 Price secured employment away from Boise and Short contacted Mrs. Price concerning the obligation. Price testified that on an occasion when he was in Boise, Short contacted him and advised him that Short would prosecute him for issuance of a bad check unless Price made a payment on the debt. Price then paid $20.00 to Short, which was evidenced by a receipt.

Later Price stated he believed he was going to be prosecuted for the bad check and went to see Mr. Slayton, who was the head of the collection division of the defendant corporation. Price testified "Mr. Slayton told me it was out of his hands, it was between me and Mr. Short." Mr. Slayton testified that he remembered Mr. Price came in to see him one time and was asking questions about the account. Slayton stated "I told him Mr. Short was handling the account."

On this appeal the defendant has made numerous assignments of error. The crucial issue presented by these assignments of error concerns the instruction given by the trial court to the effect that a corporation (which acts only through its agents) can be held criminally liable "for the acts of its agents who are authorized to act for it in the particular matter out of which the unlawful conduct with which it is charged grows or in the business to which it related." It is the defendant's contention that this instruction by the trial court was in error, arguing that the trial court should have instructed that the defendant corporation could have been found guilty only if the agent committed the prohibited acts, and that the agent's acts were authorized, requested or commanded by another corporate agent having responsibility for formation of corporate policy, or by a managerial agent having supervisory responsibility over the subject matter.

It is our conclusion that there is merit in the defendant's position in regard to these instructions. A corporation, being an artificial being, a creature of statute, can only act through its agents and employees. At the early common law, the fact that a corporation had no tangible, physical existence, was regarded as making it impossible for a corporation to commit a crime.

Under the modern view, however, a corporation may be found guilty of a breach of a duty imposed by law, both for acts of nonfeasance and misfeasance. A corporation is criminally responsible for statutory crimes, such as obtaining money under false pretenses, usury, illegal sale of liquor, and unlawful sale of adulterated foods.

By reason of the fact that corporations can only act through their agents, the courts have struggled with the problem of holding a corporation criminally liable in those cases involving crimes where a specific intent is required. The question is, how can a corporation, an artificial being, have the necessary *mens rea* to commit those crimes where specific intent is required. The answer is found in the relationship between the corporation and the agent that performed the acts for which the corporation is being criminally charged, and in the nature of the crime with which the corporation is being charged.

Some students of the problem of corporate criminal responsibility have drawn a distinction between those types of criminal cases where the crime is one created by statute, and where the crime is a codification of a common law offense. The conclusion of the authors in this discussion is that when a statutory offense is involved, the commission of a crime by a corporate agent within the scope of his authority is a crime of the corporation, regardless of knowledge, acquiescence, or ratification by a higher corporate officer. However, when the crime is a statutory codification of a common law crime requiring *mens rea* this reasoning as to corporate criminal liability is insufficient to bind the corporation, and more must be established to justify a conviction under this type of crime than a mere proof of an agency relationship.

Extortion is the obtaining of property from another, with his consent, induced by a wrongful force or fear or under color of official right.

I.C. § 18-2802 provides:

Fear, such as will constitute extortion, may be induced by a threat, either:
1. To do an unlawful injury to the person or property of the individual threatened or to any relative of his, or member of his family; or
2. To accuse him, or any relative of his, or member of his family of any crime; or . . .

These statutes are a codification of the common law crime of extortion or blackmail. A specific intent to extort money or other thing of value is an essential element of this crime.

The case of *Boise Dodge, Inc.* v. *Clark,* involving a fraudulent misrepresentation, and imposition of punitive damages against the corporation, is analogous to the situation here. The corporation in this case could not be bound by the actions of its agent unless that agent's acts were authorized, requested, commanded, performed or recklessly tolerated by the board of directors or by a high managerial agent acting in behalf of the corporation within the scope of his office or employment.

Corporation Law and Practice in our opinion correctly states the rule as to criminal liability as follows:

"A corporation may be convicted if (a) legislative purpose plainly appears to impose absolute liability on the corporation for the offense; or (b) the offense consists of an omission to perform an act which the corporation is required by law to perform; or (c) the commission of the offense was authorized, requested, commanded or performed (i) by the board of directors, or (ii) by an agent having responsibility for formation of corporate policy or (iii) by a 'high managerial agent' having supervisory responsibility over the subject matter of the offense and acting within the scope of his employment in behalf of the corporation. . . ."

Thus the instructions given by the trial court to the effect that the corporation could be found guilty if the jury found that the agent was acting within the scope of his authority was not a correct statement of the law under the circumstances of this case; it was not established that Short was in a managerial capacity, and no issue was submitted to the jury as to whether Short's actions were authorized, requested, or commanded by either an agent of the corporation responsible for formation of corporate policy or by a high managerial agent. This error is of a prejudicial nature and the case must be remanded.

WHITE COLLAR CRIME

White collar crime is a term commonly used to describe nonviolent criminal acts committed in a commercial context by members of the managerial or professional class. The term includes offenses committed by employees against their employers as well as offenses that business firms commit against the general public. Specific examples of white collar crime are embezzlement, employee theft, bribery, antitrust violations, income tax evasion, and securities fraud.

White collar crimes cost society billions of dollars. Criminal acts by employees may bankrupt a business, but even if they do not, they reduce profitability. The losses that are a result of criminal activity result in higher prices for goods and services as firms must cover these losses to remain in business. Criminal offenses committed by business firms are an even greater burden on society. These acts not only add to the substantial cost of crime, but they also increase distrust of both business and government.

COMMON WHITE COLLAR CRIMES

Almost all criminal acts can be committed in a commercial setting; however, some occur much more frequently in business than others. Bribery, larceny, and embezzlement are examples.

Bribery

Bribery is one of the principal crimes that cause many people to be critical of business. Incidents of bribery appear frequently in the news. People are often familiar with major bribery scandals that involve business, such as the payment of millions of dollars to the president of Honduras to eliminate an unfavorable export tax on bananas. Another well-known example is the payment that Lockheed made to the prime minister of Japan to secure government contracts. During the 1980s bribery scandals involved high public officials of both the Carter and Reagan administrations.

Legal Principles. The primary focus of the law of bribery has been on payments to public officials. The classic example of an illegal bribe would be a payment to a judge to obtain a favorable ruling in litigation. The typical stat-

ute might condemn "offering or giving or promising to give something of value with the corrupt intent to induce or influence the action, vote or opinion of a person in any public or official capacity." Although most statutes require "corrupt" intent on the part of the payor, a few do not require intent and condemn outright certain payments to judges, jurors, witnesses, etc. The reasons generally given for condemning public bribes are to protect the public interest and to insure the efficient and fair operation of governmental institutions.

Commercial bribes are treated more leniently under the law with relatively few instances resulting in legal challenges. Although several federal and state statutes apply to commercial bribes in special circumstances, few laws deal specifically or solely with commercial bribes. Some state criminal antibribery statutes apply by their literal terms to commercial bribes. The New York Penal Code is an example. It provides as follows:

A person is guilty of commercial bribing when he confers, or offers or agrees to confer any benefit upon any employee, agent, or fiduciary without the consent of the latter's employer or principal; with intent to influence his conduct in relation to his employer's or principal's affairs.

Approximately half the states condemn commercial bribery. The statutes generally require that there be an intent to influence the bribe-taker's conduct. The bribe-taker must be influenced in regard to some discretionary activity. Many statutes follow the lead of New York and condemn the soliciting of a bribe equally with the offering of one. About a dozen states condemn on a per se basis a purchasing agent receiving something of value from a seller.

Larceny

Larceny is another crime frequently associated with business. *Larceny* involves the physical taking of another's property with the wrongful intent of depriving the owner of the property or its value. Statutes generally divide larceny into two grades based upon the value of the property. *Grand larceny* involves property of substantial value and is a felony. *Petit larceny* involves less valuable property, usually less than $50, and is a misdemeanor.

In order to be larceny, the property must be taken without the owner's consent, but not by violence. If a person takes another's property by violence, the offense is *robbery.* Usually statutes make punishment for robbery more severe than punishment for larceny.

Some common law courts had difficulty applying larceny principles to a scam where the wrongdoer tricked the owner into voluntarily giving up the property. They reasoned that the property was taken with the owner's consent. As a result, many states enacted "false pretenses" statutes. These statutes made it a crime for someone to obtain another's property by a statement that intentionally deceives the victim. Computer fraud and the fraudulent use of credit cards are other forms of larceny that legislatures often treat specifically by statutes.

Embezzlement

Business firms often are the victims of embezzlement. This crime involves the misappropriation of property, usually money, by one to whom it has been entrusted. The classic examples are bank employees or accountants who take for themselves money entrusted to them as part of their jobs.

Embezzlement and larceny differ. *Embezzlement* is committed when a person who legitimately has possession of someone else's property deprives that person of the property or its value. For example, if A rents an automobile intending not to return it and does not do so, the crime is larceny. On the other hand, if after renting the automobile A decides to keep it, the offense is embezzlement. An embezzlement is committed even if a person who is entrusted with property takes it intending to restore it before the loss is discovered and even if the property is actually returned.

United States v. Coin
Court of Appeals, Ninth Circuit
753 F.2d 1510 (1985)

Background: Raymond Coin (defendant-appellant) was convicted in U.S. District Court of embezzling tribal funds. He appealed, contending that the District Court had erred in refusing to give a jury instruction which stated that restitution, while not a defense to the crime, may be considered as evidence bearing on intent.
Decision: Affirmed.

Per Curiam

Appellant Raymond Joseph Coin appeals his conviction by a jury for embezzling tribal funds in violation of 18 U.S.C. § 1163. He claims that the district court erred in refusing to give a jury instruction which stated that restitution, while not a defense to the crime, may be considered as evidence bearing on intent. We affirm.

Coin was elected vice-chairman of the Hopi Tribe in December 1981. As part of his duties, he was to run the Hopi Civic Center. In November of 1982, Coin obtained some blank requisitions, ostensibly to pay some bills for the Center. Coin's secretary subsequently picked up checks in the amount of the requisitions from the tribal treasurer's office, including one for $20,000 made out to Northern Arizona Theatre. The next day, Coin deposited the $20,000 check in a bank account he opened for Northern Arizona Theatre. From this account he made one payment of $12,258.59 to purchase movie equipment, and used the remainder for his personal benefit.

After Coin was indicted for embezzling tribal funds, but before trial, the Hopi Tribal Council demanded that he repay the embezzled funds with interest. Coin repaid the money without interest. At trial, Coin denied intending to embezzle, steal or convert funds to his own use, claiming that because the funds had been paid to his company, Northern Arizona Theatre, he could use some of the money for his own purposes. The district court refused to give Coin's restitution jury instruction, which stated that:

> You have heard evidence that the Defendant returned monies to the Hope [sic] tribe upon demand. While restitution is not a defense to the crimes with which the Defendant is charged, you may consider such payment as evidence bearing on intent.

The intent to return property is not a defense to embezzlement, nor to misapplication of funds. Such crimes are complete when the misapplication or embezzlement occurs. The victim of the crime is deprived of its right to make decisions about how its property or funds are to be used.

Some courts, however, have declared that restitution may be relevant on the issue of intent, primarily when restitution is contemporaneous with the crime.

Here, contemporaneity was lacking. Rather, Coin's offer to repay came months later, and repayment did not occur until after he was indicted. The crime occurred and was complete when funds were misapplied; whatever occurred later as to repayment was neither material nor a defense.

The district court correctly rejected Coin's proposed jury instruction. The instruction given was more favorable than was required.

NONTRADITIONAL WHITE COLLAR CRIMES

During the past seventy-five years Congress and the states have enacted numerous laws that expand the criminal liability of business firms. In some instances these acts prohibit actions that were previously lawful. Often these acts provide both criminal and civil penalties. Because of the importance of these statutes to business, several of them are discussed in later chapters. They include the Sherman Act, which is the subject of Chapter 44, the 1933 and 1934 securities acts, which are discussed in Chapter 37, and the Foreign Corrupt Practices Act, also covered in Chapter 37.

Persons convicted of violating the Sherman Act, the securities acts, or the Foreign Corrupt Practices Act, as well as numerous other federal and state acts, are subject to substantial fines and imprisonment. For example, an individual convicted of a Sherman Act violation can be fined up to $100,000 and sentenced up to three years in jail. A corporation is subject to a maximum fine of $1,000,000 for each offense. Many violations of federal securities laws are also subject to criminal prosecution.

COMPUTER CRIME

Computer crimes are not new crimes. They are the old familiar crimes except that they involve the computer. Some authorities define *computer crime* as any illegal act for which knowledge of computer technology is essential for perpetration of the crime. Computer crimes can be classified in the following categories.

1. Larceny, embezzlement, and fraud
2. Appropriation of data
3. Automatic destruction of data
4. Theft of computer services
5. Alteration and modification of data

Larceny, Embezzlement, and Fraud

Larceny, embezzlement, and fraud may involve computer equipment as it does other tangible items. A personal computer may be stolen. Or, through use of a computer, monetary funds may be transferred from a corporate to a personal account. For example, some customers of banks transfer large sums of money using magnetic tapes. Unless there is proper security, an employee of the bank's customer who participates in the preparation of the tape might embezzle these funds by directing a portion of the funds to be credited to a personal account. One difficult issue with which the courts have had to deal is whether the information stored electronically is tangible property.

State v. McGraw
Court of Appeals of Indiana
459 N.E.2d 61 (1984)

Background: McGraw (defendant) was a computer operator for the City of Indianapolis. He became involved in a private sales venture and used the city's leased computer services to keep records for his business. The use was unauthorized. Eventually, McGraw was discharged for unsatisfactory job performance and for selling his product in the office on "office time."

Following his discharge, McGraw requested a fellow employee who was also a computer operator to obtain a printout of the business records and then to erase them from the computer. Instead, the printout was turned over to McGraw's supervisor and became the basis for criminal charges of theft of computer services. Although McGraw was convicted by a jury, the trial court dismissed the charges on grounds that the unauthorized use of a computer was not theft under the Indiana statute as a matter of law. The state appealed.

Decision: The trial court was reversed and the conviction was reinstated.

Neal, Presiding Judge

Theft is defined by IND.CODE 35-43-4-2(a) as follows:

> "A person who knowingly and intentionally exerts unauthorized control over property of another person with intent to deprive the other person of any part of its value or use, commits theft, a Class D felony."

IND. CODE 35-41-1-2 defines property:

> " 'Property' means *anything of value; and includes a gain or advantage or anything that might reasonably be regarded as such by the beneficiary;* real property, personal property, money, labor, *and services;* intangibles; commercial instruments; written instruments concerning labor, services, or property; written instruments otherwise of value to the owner, such as a public record, deed, will, credit card, or letter of credit; a signature to a written instrument; extension of credit; trade secrets; contract rights, choses-in-action, and other interests in or claims to wealth; electricity, gas, oil, and water; captured or domestic animals, birds, and fish; food and drink; and human remains."

The State essentially argues that the theft statute comprehends a broad field of conduct and a wide range of activities, and is sufficiently broad to prohibit McGraw's acts here.

McGraw's initial arguments involve a close examination of the pertinent statutory language. The theft statute, he argues, is divided into a conduct portion, "knowingly and intentionally exerting unauthorized control over the property of another person," and the intent portion, "with the intent to deprive the other person of any part of its value or use." The word use does not appear in the conduct portion; therefore, the unauthorized control must be over the property itself. Further, he argues, IND.CODE 35-41-1-2, which defines property, does not include the word "use" as such, and IND.CODE 35-43-4-1(a) which defines "exert control over property," does not employ the term "use." Additionally, he contends that "services" as used in IND.CODE 35-41-1-2 is limited to the context of labor.

In addition to the above construction argument, McGraw asserts that to be guilty of the offense, a specific prohibition of his conduct must exist. He contends that he could not deprive the city of the "use" of the computer unless his data caused an overload on the computer memory banks, or that he used the computer for his private business at a time which interfered with city use. He argues that the value of the services was de minimus. He finally claims that his activities were no more than personal use of an office phone, calculator, or copy machine.

Inasmuch as the evidence clearly supports the fact that McGraw knowingly and intentionally used the city leased computer for his own monetary benefit, the only real question is whether "use" of a computer is a property subject to theft. The sufficiency question will not be discussed separately.

No Indiana case under the modern theft statute exists which addresses this question.

A search of the holdings of other jurisdictions regarding computer-related crime has turned up cases which are neither particularly helpful nor on point.

In *Hancock v. State,* a Texas Court of Criminal Appeals decision, the statutory definition of "property" applicable at the time of the decision stated in part, "[t]he term 'property' as used in relation to the crime of theft . . . provided such property possesses any ascertainable value."

The *Hancock* case concerned the theft of computer programs by an employee of a computer corporation. After examining the above definition, the court determined that computer programs are encompassed by the "property" definition and hence are subject to theft.

Similarly, in *National Surety Corporation v. Applied Systems, Inc.,* former employees of Applied Systems were charged with conversion of the company's computer programs dealing with the payroll systems of several of its clients. The employees argued that "only tangible personal property is subject to conversion". The court disagreed, noting that "there is case authority to the effect that intangible personal property can be the subject of larceny." . . .

In contrast to the above decisions, two cases discussed extensively by appellee, *People v. Weg,* and *Lund v. Commonwealth of Virginia,* reach an opposite conclusion based on more restrictive statutory interpretations.

The defendant in *Weg* was charged with misdemeanor theft of services allegedly committed by using his employer's computer for his own personal benefit. The defendant was employed by the Board of Education of the City of New York. The pertinent New York statute, as is relevant herein, provides that a person is guilty of theft of services when he "[has] control over . . . business, commercial, or industrial equipment" and uses the equipment for his personal service. The *Weg* court decided that the Board's computer did not fall into any of the three categories, and the charge was dismissed.

Similarly, in *Lund,* the defendant was convicted of grand larceny for using the time and services of a university computer without proper authorization. The applicable statute defined grand larceny, in part, as "the taking not from the person of another goods and chattels of the value of $100 or more". The court determined that the phrase "goods and chattels" does not encompass computer time; furthermore, it held that unauthorized *use* alone is insufficient to bring the act within the tenets of the grand larceny statute, since it refers to a "taking and carrying away of a certain concrete article of personal property".

Computer services, leased or owned, are a part of our market economy in huge dollar amounts. Like cable television, computer services are ". . . anything of value". Computer time is "services" for which money is paid. Such services may reasonably be regarded as valuable assets to the beneficiary. Thus, computer services are property within the meaning of the definition of property subject to theft. When a person "obtains" or "takes" those services, he has exerted control under IND.CODE 35-43-4-1(a). Taking without the other person's consent is unauthorized taking. IND.CODE 35-43-4-1(b)(1). Depriving the other person of any part of the services' use completes the offense. IND.CODE 35-43-4-2(a).

Property must be shown to have a value, however slight, but the monetary value of property is of no concern, and the jury may under proper instructions infer some value. The theft statute comprehends a broad field of conduct, and does not limit the means or methods by which unauthorized control of property may be obtained. We disagree that specific prohibition to exerting control is necessary to support the conviction theft. McGraw's reliance on *Anderson v. State,* (1981) Ind.App., 406 N.E.2d 351 for this contention is misplaced. Further, we disagree that it is a defense to exerting unauthorized control that the owner was not using the property at the time.

CASE NOTE

McGraw appealed the reinstatement of his conviction. Upon appeal the Supreme Court of Indiana agreed with the trial court that the unauthorized use of computer services was not theft under Indiana law. The appellate court was reversed and the trial court's dismissal was affirmed. State v. McGraw, 480 N.E.2d 552 (1985).

In its opinion the Supreme Court of Indiana agreed that information derived by "use" of a computer is property, but concluded that the theft statute did not apply as the city was not deprived of anything. The court stated as follows:

> Not only was there no evidence that the City was ever deprived of any part of the value or the use of the computer by reason of Defendant's conduct, the uncontradicted evidence was to the contrary. The computer was utilized for City business by means of terminals assigned to various employee-operators, including Defendant. The computer processed the data from the various terminals simultaneously, and the limit of its capacity was never reached or likely to have been. The computer service was leased to the City at a fixed charge, and the tapes or discs upon which the imparted data was stored were erasable and reusable. Defendant's unauthorized use cost the City nothing and did not interfere with its use by others. He extracted from the system only such information as he had previously put into it. He did not, for his own benefit, withdraw City data intended for its exclusive use or for sale. Thus, Defendant did not deprive the City of the "use of computers and computer services" as the information alleged that he intended to do. We find no distinction between Defendant's use of the City's computer and the use, by a mechanic, of the employer's hammer or a stenographer's use of the employer's typewriter, for other than the employer's purposes. Under traditional concepts, the transgression is in the nature of a trespass, a civil matter—and a de minimis one, at that. Defendant has likened his conduct to the use of an employer's vacant bookshelf, for the temporary storage of one's personal items, and to the use of an employer's telephone facilities for toll-free calls. The analogies appear to us to be appropriate.

A number of states have eliminated the problem of whether unauthorized use of a computer is property by statute. An example is a 1978 Virginia statute that states as follows:

> Computer time or services or data processing services or information or data stored in connection therewith is hereby defined to be property which may be the subject of larceny . . . or embezzlement . . . or false pretenses. . . . Code §18.2-98.1.

Appropriation of Data

A police officer sells cocaine in addition to her regular employment. She wants to be sure that none of her customers has a record of criminal violence. So she gains access to the U.S. Department of Justice criminal history data base.

Automatic Destruction of Data

An employee who is dismissed from his job could express annoyance with the company by programming its computer to erase a section of memory every time a file is backed up, or copied for safekeeping. A few weeks later the business has nothing in its computer memory.

This employee has caused the automatic destruction of data.

Theft of Computer Services

A microcomputer company arranges a computer class. A professor at the local university is invited as an instructor. During the instruction a salesman of the company obtains from the professor the passwords that are used for operating the university computer system. Every time that salesman demonstrates how to use the computer, he dials the university computer system to use its data and computer programs.

Alteration and Modification of Data

Three junior high school students go to the computer lab every day during study hall. One day they decide to dial up the computer system for the board of education of their district. They gain access to their own academic records, and change some of their grades.

Computer Crime Litigation

Reluctance of the Victims. Companies rarely file complaints in computer crime cases. They do not want the inadequacy of their computer system to be publicized. Directors of financial institutions fear that such unfavorable publicity will cause a run on their institutions.

Computer insurance has almost become a necessity for businesses that make extensive use of computer systems. Computer insurance may cover the cost of restoring the computer system to its condition prior to unauthorized access. It may cover extra expenses that are incurred to continue business operations until the computer system may be restored. It also may cover other financial loss directly attributable to the destruction, modification, or use of the data obtained by unauthorized access.

Corporations are even employing convicted computer hackers—people who use others' computer systems through breaking the corporate security codes—to find the weaknesses in their security systems and suggest ways of correcting those weaknesses.

Out-of-Court Settlements. Even in the rare instances where a suit is filed, the business that has been hurt will usually settle out of court. They would prefer to be repaid some of the amount requested than risk losing in court and not receiving any retribution.

Development of Computer Criminal Law

The courts and legislators have been slow to include misuse of computer technology within the scope of traditional laws. For example, larceny originally dealt with the theft of tangible property. Software is not considered tangible property, so "downloading," or copying software without permission of the owners, has not been considered larceny. Are data stored in the memory of a computer considered property for the purposes of enforcing their theft? Congress, in its Counterfeit Access Device and Computer Fraud and Abuse Act, has, in a sense, avoided this issue by making it a crime to gain unauthorized access to the computers themselves. Therefore, the operator has committed a crime even before accessing data. There is a trend for states to pass computer crime laws, thereby separating computer crime from the common law of its related counterparts of theft, larceny, and embezzlement.

Federal Government. Federal and state governments are becoming more aware of computer crime and doing something about it. In 1984 Congress passed the Counterfeit Access Device and Computer Fraud and Abuse Act. This Act creates limited federal jurisdiction over certain types of computer crimes. Among other things, the Act forbids the removal or destruction of federal records, as well as protection of federal bank and credit institution reports, entries, and transactions, and protects common carriers licensed by the Federal Commerce Commission (FCC). As stated earlier, these types of information are protected by prohibiting the access or use of computer systems that contain such information. Other federal laws apply to the misuse of computers, but no comprehensive body of law has been made by Congress.

State Governments. Most states have passed laws that deal with computer crime. Most such laws cover computer-aided credit card fraud, theft, or misappropriation of computer services, computer trespass (using computer systems without authority), damage to computers or software, and obtaining or disseminating information via computer without authority.

In the few states that have not enacted specific computer crime statutes, courts, in varying degree, apply existing criminal code sections. These sections may include arson, burglary, conspiracy, conversion, criminal mischief, embezzlement, forgery, larceny, interference with use of property, labor under false pretenses, receipt of stolen property, and theft of trade secrets.

BOX 3-1: ISSUES AND TRENDS
Criminal and Civil RICO

In 1970 Congress enacted the Racketeer Influenced and Corrupt Organizations Act (RICO). The act is one of the broadest statutes in the federal criminal code. RICO stemmed from a growing concern of Congress that gangsters were taking over legitimate business. In enacting RICO, Congress attempted to provide prosecutors with a weapon that they could use to limit the infiltration of business by organized crime. The result was a statute that made it a crime to use a "pattern of racketeering" to acquire or retain an interest in an "enterprise" affecting interstate commerce.

In interpreting the statute, the courts have broadly defined both the terms "racketeering" and "enterprise." Enterprise includes "any partnership, corporation, association, or other legal entity, and any union or group of individuals associated in fact although not a legal entity." Racketeering includes actions such as bankruptcy fraud, embezzlement from pension and union funds, mail and wire fraud, and securities law violations. Thus, if a person obtains funds through these or similar criminal activities, that person is prohibited from using them to gain control of or even investing them in a legitimate enterprise. RICO's criminal penalties are severe. In addition to a fine of up to $25,000 and a maximum jail sentence of twenty years, the key to the Act is a section providing for the forfeiture of the gains the defendant has acquired through the illegal activity. As a result, the government in a successful prosecution can seize the legitimate business interests acquired by the racketeering profits. This deprives the individual of the ability to continue to control business and weakens the hold that organized crime has over legitimate business.

Although the primary purpose of RICO is to combat organized crime, RICO is a major source of potential civil liability for legitimate business firms.

The statute contains both civil and criminal provisions. In a civil suit a plaintiff who can prove injury as a result of a "pattern of racketeering" can collect treble damages (three times the amount actually lost), court costs, and attorney's fees. As the plaintiff does not need to show that the defendant has been convicted of the acts that are the basis of the "pattern of racketeering" and these acts have been broadly interpreted, civil RICO litigation has been successfully brought against legitimate business, based upon common law fraud and breach of contract claims. Because of the threat of triple damages and the adverse public relations resulting from a charge of racketeering, business firms often settle civil RICO claims although the case against the firm is weak.

REVIEW PROBLEMS

1. People have different ideas as to why someone who violates the criminal law should be punished. What are these ideas?
2. Explain mens rea and indicate situations in which mens rea is not required as an element of criminal conduct.
3. Describe the procedural protections provided defendants in a criminal case by the Fourth, Fifth, and Sixth amendments to the U.S. Constitution.
4. List the differences that exist between civil litigation and criminal litigation.
5. Explain the difference between larceny and embezzlement.
6. White was a sheriff in a rural area. An anonymous caller informed White that Lehman, a local farmer, was promoting dog fights on his farm. Without getting a warrant, White searched several of the farm buildings. He found a number of dogs penned in a barn. Three of them were scarred and had injuries that could only have been caused by fighting. White arrested Lehman for promoting dog fights, a misdemeanor. Lehman's attorney moved that the case be dismissed on grounds that the search was illegal. Would the attorney be successful? Support your answer.
7. Carbone was a licensed electrician. One day while rewiring a residence, he decided to leave for lunch before finishing a connection. He made a temporary connection that he knew was dangerous. While he was at lunch the connection caused a short and the building caught fire. A woman who was in the building was killed. Carbone was criminally charged for her death. His attorney argued that as Carbone lacked intent, he could not be guilty. Was the attorney correct? Support your answer.
8. Lacey was killed by an automobile driven by Cantrell, who was charged and convicted of manslaughter. Lacey's estate sued Cantrell for damages. Cantrell defended on grounds that a person cannot be tried twice for the same act. Will Cantrell's defense succeed? Support your answer.
9. Ayer is the office manager for a plumbing contractor. The company receives small amounts of cash from time to time through the mail. Ayer is responsible for depositing these funds. She always does this, but often when she is short of cash she uses the funds for her personal needs and replaces them when she is paid. Has Ayer committed a crime? Discuss.

Business and Ethics

Throughout the 1980s the media has been full of stories of corruption, conflicts of interest, insider trading, environmental pollution, deadly hazards in the workplace, overbilling on defense contracts, check kiting, consumer frauds, ad infinitum. Concurrently, there has been a revival of interest in business ethics. Many basic questions are raised. How does one determine what constitutes right conduct in business? For example, is it ever acceptable to lie in a negotiation? What is the trend with business ethics? Is behavior in the business world worse than ten years ago? Are there general principles of business ethics that apply to all forms of commercial activity? This chapter will shed light on these timely and important questions.

ETHICS IN BUSINESS

Ethics involves formal consideration of the interests of others in deciding how to behave or act. All businesses impact outsiders in their operations. Consider the decision by an owner to close a small glass-blowing plant that has been vital to the well-being of a small rural community and that has always been reasonably profitable. What questions must be answered in order to determine whether the plant-closing decision is ethical? Does motive make a difference? Should the focus be solely on the outcome from the viewpoint of the decision maker? Do local attitudes and customs primarily determine the ethical course of action? Is every case unique, or are there certain fundamental principles that apply regardless of the situation?

These basic questions have been the subject of much debate and formal analysis, particularly among philosophers. However, before exploring how they might be answered, we must first deal with the fundamental issue of whether ethical analysis is even possible in business. We will first discuss the arguments that ethical analysis is not possible or legitimate in the business world, then proceed to a discussion of the fundamental theories of ethics, and finally present some principles of professional business ethics.

ARGUMENTS PURPORTING TO NEGATE BUSINESS ETHICS

Relativism

Is ethical analysis dependent upon the social-economic context in which it occurs? If so, then business can be exempted from ethics on the grounds that it must be played by different rules. In analyzing our glass-blowing plant case, a relativist would argue that closing the plant may or may not be ethical, depending upon the society in which it occurs. In a society in which ownership/property rights strongly dominate, plant closings would generally be seen as ethical. In a society recognizing significant vested interests on the part of employees stemming from the employment relationship, plant closings would be unethical unless justified by dire economic necessity.

The relativist argument lies at the heart of the current debates about the propriety of paying bribes in foreign markets, setting lower standards for plant safety overseas, or operating a branch business in South Africa. Relativists who defend such actions argue that local custom makes it mandatory that international firms follow the local rules. When in Rome, one *must* do what the Romans do. Paying bribes is justified by arguing (1) they are required by local custom and it is arrogance to impose American values upon other societies, (2) they are necessary to compete against foreign firms willing to pay bribes to get business, and (3) whatever harm results will affect only the foreign country (which after all has permitted bribery to flourish).

Similar explanations are given by those who follow different safety standards at foreign locations or who operate in South Africa. Is there anything wrong with following local practice? Certainly, there are many circumstances in which most people would defer to local preferences. Many businesspeople would not drink alcohol at a Muslim gathering, tip in an Australian restaurant, or insist on wearing shoes in a Buddhist temple.

The issue is of a different magnitude when it involves situations such as plant safety in less-developed countries. The local government may clearly prefer to have lower safety standards as a way to attract foreign investment. In Bhopal, the Union Carbide plant was producing an agricultural product that was important to India and other developing countries with chronic food shortages. The plant was partly owned by India, and therefore could also generate foreign trade earnings that were critical to the development of the Indian economy.

The fact that one might defer to local custom does not mean that local custom can *always* determine what constitutes right conduct. No one would accept bizarre local practices, such as requiring the human sacrifice of a member of the firm in order to get a license to do business, as ethical. Relativism as an ethical theory would reduce ethical analysis to nothing more than conducting a proper survey of local customs and laws.

The counterpoint to relativism is the view that there are certain universal principles that transcend local custom or practice. These universal principles may be based upon fundamental human rights such as life, liberty, and physical well-being, or upon practices that improve human welfare. Under universalism, a society as a whole can be considered to be immoral if its generally accepted practices violate universal norms.

If one accepts the notion of universal principles, then the relativism argument cannot be used to dispense with a consideration of ethical issues in business. A decision to practice apartheid in South Africa or to pay a bribe in Indonesia must be justified on ethical grounds other than local practice.

Egoism

Egoism is acting solely to maximize one's self-interest. The egoist considers the interests of others solely to determine how they affect his or her self-interest. There are two types of egoism which serve as counterpoints to formal ethical theory. The first, psychological egoism, assumes that humans are incapable of genuinely considering the interests of others. Seemingly altruistic acts such as charity and caring for the sick and disabled are dismissed as actually based upon selfish motivations. Charitable persons are considered to be getting kicks from a power trip or by having others become dependent upon them. The concept of *psychological egoism* is contrary to the basic assumptions about humankind that are found in the major religions and is counterintuitive. If psychological egoism is accepted as accurately descriptive of human nature, then there would be no point to the study of ethics.

Ethical egoism takes the normative position that everyone has the right to act in his or her own self-interest. This form has some serious defenders in the business world, who not only advocate it as a human right, but who also see it as an extension of Adam Smith's invisible hand. They claim that society is best off when people act as they selfishly desire. It is the responsibility of government to impose any necessary limits on their behavior. The "ethical" egoist will act to maximize self-interest subject only to compliance with the law. In a contract negotiation, if it is possible to lie, be undetected, and benefit, the ethical egoist will do so. The egoist would breach a contract whenever the damages to be paid are less than the benefit of the breach, so long as breaching would not produce additional offsetting costs such as the loss of reputation. Under this view the plant owner would only consider his or her own interests in deciding whether to close the plant. Society would have the responsibility for providing any necessary social safety net.

Ultimately, egoism as a theory of ethics can be criticized on the basis of its impact on society. A society made up of ethical egoists would be dominated by opportunistic behavior. Opportunistic behavior may include theft, fraud, double-dealing, treachery, and other similar actions. Negotiators anticipating opportunistic behavior enter into more costly contracts, while actual opportunism directly reduces economic efficiency. One is likely to be much more careful when contracting with someone who is considered untrustworthy, and the extra care will translate into increased costs, including greater use of elaborate contracts, monitoring, and extensive background data gathering. When these costs occur differentially among firms or industries, they may result in the misallocation of resources. Because egoism legitimizes opportunism and may sanction actions harming other human beings, it is not satisfying as an ethical theory. The argument that egoism is a basic human right is subject to challenge on grounds that it is incompatible with human nature and that most people would not choose to recognize such a right on a universal basis.

Rejection of egoism does not require adoption of a principle of ethical altruism whereby it is considered inappropriate for an individual to consider his or her own interest in evaluating the morality of a proposed course of action. That, of course, is not the case. The standard methods of ethical analysis that are relevant to business incorporate the interest of the actor in the ultimate consideration of the nature or impact of the proposed action. The actor is a member of society, and as such his or her interests do count.

THEORIES OF MORAL RESPONSIBILITY

Three theories of moral responsibility that are particularly relevant to business practice have been propounded by moral philosophers: (1) deontology, (2) utilitarianism, and (3) social justice. *Deontological theory* is founded upon concepts of duty which serve as guidelines to moral behavior. In contrast, *utilitarian theory* is outcome-oriented. *Social justice* is concerned with how rights and responsibilities are distributed among the members of society. All are relevant to the field of business ethics. In addition to these categories of theories, some philosophers have focused upon the role of "good persons."

Golden Rule

Duty-Based Ethics

Immanuel Kant (1724–1804) was a profound and influential duty-based philosopher. Kant identified several general guiding principles for moral behavior based upon the fundamental nature of human beings. The most basic of these is the categorical imperative requiring each individual to act as though his or her action would become a general rule for all society. Individuals must refrain from any action that would be problematic if everyone were to do it. One cannot make an unfair exception for him- or herself. Cutting into waiting lines or putting slugs into honor system newspaper vending machines are immoral acts. One cannot expect others to wait in line or pay fairly and then assert that one has a special privilege to violate the principle.

In addition to the categorical imperative, Kant cautioned that it is immoral to treat other human beings merely as means. The treatment of human beings as merely means is the equivalent of treating people as objects, a denial of their basic humanity.

Kant's general principles, reflecting Christ's Golden Rule, provide general guidance, but they need to be systematically applied to a business context. In that context, the disagreements are likely to begin. Is there an absolute duty not to lie in a business negotiation? Some would dispute such a concept of duty. How, then, are duties to be derived?

To begin with, it could be postulated that there are certain basic *general* duties such as acting in good faith, dealing with subordinates through fair procedures, avoiding physical harm to others, eschewing conflicts of interest, and obeying the law that apply to everyone. Such fundamental duties form the core of business ethics and are applicable to all businesspeople in all contexts.

These general duties are supplemented by specific duties that apply to certain individuals in certain contexts. Specific duties could arise from personal promises, professional codes of behavior, or role obligations. The following are examples of specific duties:

- A corporate lawyer has a duty to keep confidential the proprietary information of his or her employer.
- A real estate agent representing a seller must not purchase the property for his or her own account without notifying the seller.
- A corporate manager must not compete secretly with his or her own firm.
- An automobile engineer with responsibility for design safety must hold paramount the physical well-being of consumers.
- An arbitrator must not delegate decision making to someone else without the consent of the disputing parties.
- An accountant cannot agree to a contingent fee arrangement based upon a particular finding or result.
- Bank employees should not reveal information relating to their customers to unauthorized persons, nor should confidential information of clients be used to benefit the bank financially.

For a given individual, then, it may be possible to come up with a list of specific ethical duties that should be observed. But the task does not end at that point. One of the most difficult problems for duty-based ethical theorists arises when duties come into conflict. For example, a corporate lawyer has an obligation to maintain the confidentiality of client confidences. But suppose that the lawyer discovers a corporate plan to steal millions through computer fraud. The lawyer is aware of the implications of the plan and is certain that crimes will be committed. What should the lawyer do?

The lawyer is a member of the legal system and is charged with upholding the law. The lawyer also owes duties of confidentiality to the corporate client. Revealing the confidential information would prevent the commission of a major economic crime. In many states, the lawyers' code of professional responsibility would only provide that a lawyer *may* resign after trying various ways to blow the whistle inside the corporation.

The lawyer is thus faced with a conflict between the duty of confidentiality and the duty to uphold the law. Universalizing the action alternatives fails to provide clear-cut guidance. Widespread breaching of confidentiality may cause clients to become reluctant to disclose information to their attorneys, thus restricting their ability to provide proper representation. On the other hand, failing to disclose may result in much higher levels of crime, assisted by the passiveness of lawyers.

The case that follows presents another dimension of the problem of conflicting duties for lawyers—the client who announces that he intends to lie on the witness stand.

Nix v. Whiteside
U.S. Supreme Court
54 L.W. 4194 (1986)

Background: Whiteside (petitioner-respondent), a convicted felon, sued Nix, the warden of the state prison in which he was held, alleging that he should be released because he had been denied his constitutionally protected rights to a fair trial and representation by counsel when he was convicted.

Emanuel Whiteside fatally stabbed Calvin Love in the course of an argument over the sale of marijuana. Whiteside was charged with murder, and Gary Robinson was appointed to defend him. Whiteside told Robinson that he stabbed Love because he thought Love was reaching for a gun ("piece") hidden under a pillow. No gun was found during the police search of the premises after the stabbing. Although Whiteside had repeatedly told Robinson that he had not actually seen a gun, as the trial date drew closer, he grew nervous and told Robinson that he was going to testify that he saw something "metallic" because "if I don't say I saw a gun, I'm dead." Robinson responded by telling Whiteside that testifying to seeing something metallic would constitute perjury. Robinson further warned that if Whiteside committed perjury during the trial, Robinson would withdraw as counsel and advise the judge about the reason.

Whiteside heeded Robinson's warning and testified that he thought Love was reaching for a gun and that he acted in self-defense. He was convicted of second-degree murder. Whiteside appealed the conviction unsuccessfully through the Iowa court system, arguing that Robinson's behavior had violated the Iowa Code of Professional Responsibility for lawyers.

Whiteside then went into federal court and argued that the actions of Robinson had denied him his rights to representation by counsel and a fair trial guaranteed by the

U.S. Constitution. The federal trial court ruled against Whiteside, but the federal court of appeals reversed and found that Whiteside's constitutional rights had been violated. Decision: The Supreme Court reversed, ruling that Whiteside must remain in jail.

Burger, Chief Justice

We granted certiorari to decide whether the Sixth Amendment right of a criminal defendant to assistance of counsel is violated when an attorney refuses to cooperate with the defendant in presenting perjured testimony at his trial.

* * *

The right of an accused to testify in his defense is of relatively recent origin. Until the latter part of the preceding century, criminal defendants in this country, as at common law, were considered to be disqualified from giving sworn testimony at their own trial by reason of their interest as a party to the case. . . .

By the end of the nineteenth century, however, the disqualification was finally abolished by statute in most states and in the federal courts. Although this Court has never explicitly held that a criminal defendant has a due process right to testify in his own behalf, cases in several Circuits have so held and the right has long been assumed. . . .

In *Strickland* v. *Washington,* we held that to obtain relief by way of federal habeas corpus on a claim of a deprivation of effective assistance of counsel under the Sixth Amendment, the movant must establish both serious attorney error and prejudice. To show such error, it must be established that the assistance rendered by counsel was constitutionally deficient in that "counsel made errors so serious that counsel was not functioning as 'counsel' guaranteed the defendant by the Sixth Amendment." . . .

In *Strickland,* we acknowledged that the Sixth Amendment does not require any particular response by counsel to a problem that may arise. Rather, the Sixth Amendment inquiry is into whether the attorney's conduct was "reasonably effective." To counteract the natural tendency to fault an unsuccessful defense, a court reviewing a claim of ineffective assistance must "indulge a strong presumption that counsel's conduct falls within the wide range of reasonable professional assistance." In giving shape to the perimeters of this range of reasonable professional assistance, *Strickland* mandates that

> "Prevailing norms of practice as reflected in American Bar Association Standards and the like, . . . are guides to determining what is reasonable, but they are only guides."

Under the *Strickland* standard, breach of an ethical standard does not necessarily make out a denial of the Sixth Amendment guarantee of assistance of counsel. When examining attorney conduct, a court must be careful not to narrow the wide range of conduct acceptable under the Sixth Amendment so restrictively as to constitutionalize particular standards of professional conduct and thereby intrude into the State's proper authority to define and apply the standards of professional conduct applicable to those it admits to practice in its courts. In some future case challenging attorney conduct in the course of a state court trial, we may need to define with greater precision the weight to be given to recognized canons of ethics, the standards established by the State in statutes or professional codes, and the Sixth Amendment, in defining the proper scope and limits on that conduct.

We turn next to the question presented: the definition of the range of "reasonable professional" responses to a criminal defendant client who informs counsel that he will perjure himself on the stand. We must determine whether, in this setting, Robinson's conduct fell within the wide range of professional responses to threatened client perjury acceptable under the Sixth Amendment.

In *Strickland,* we recognized counsel's duty of loyalty and his "overarching duty to advocate the defendant's cause." Plainly, that duty is limited to legitimate, lawful conduct compatible with the very nature of a trial as a search for truth. Although counsel must take all reasonable lawful means to attain the objectives of the client, counsel is precluded from taking steps or in any way assisting the client in presenting false evidence or otherwise violating the law.

* * *

These principles have been carried through to contemporary codifications[1] of an attorney's professional responsibility. Disciplinary Rule 7-102 of the Model Code of Professional Responsibility (1980), entitled "Representing a Client Within the Bounds of the Law," provides that

"(A) In his representation of a client, a lawyer shall not:

* * *

"(4) Knowingly use perjured testimony or false evidence.

* * *

"(7) Counsel or assist his client in conduct that the lawyer knows to be illegal or fraudulent.

. . . The more recent Model Rules of Professional Conduct (1983) similarly admonish attorneys to obey all laws in the course of representing a client:

"RULE 1.2 Scope of Representation

* * *

"(d) A lawyer shall not counsel a client to engage or assist a client, in conduct that the lawyer knows is criminal or fraudulent. . . ."

These standards confirm that the legal profession has accepted that an attorney's ethical duty to advance the interests of his client is limited by an equally solemn duty

[1] There currently exist two different codifications of uniform standards of professional conduct. The Model Code of Professional Responsibility was originally adopted by the American Bar Association in 1969, and was subsequently adopted (in many cases with modification) by nearly every state. The more recent Model Rules of Professional Conduct were adopted by the American Bar Association in 1983. Since their promulgation by the American Bar Association, the Model Rules have been adopted by 11 States: Arizona, Arkansas, Delaware, Minnesota, Missouri, Montana, Nevada, New Hampshire, New Jersey, North Carolina, and Washington. Iowa is one of the states that adopted a form of the Model Code of Professional Responsibility, but has yet to adopt the Model Rules.

to comply with the law and standards of professional conduct; it specifically ensures that the client may not use false evidence. This special duty of an attorney to prevent and disclose frauds upon the court derives from the recognition that perjury is as much a crime as tampering with witnesses or jurors by way of promises and threats, and undermines the administration of justice. . . .

It is universally agreed that at a minimum the attorney's first duty when confronted with a proposal for perjurious testimony is to attempt to dissuade the client from the unlawful course of conduct. . . .

The essence of the brief *amicus* of the American Bar Association reviewing practices long accepted by ethical lawyers, is that under no circumstance may a lawyer either advocate or passively tolerate a client's giving false testimony. This, of course, is consistent with the governance of trial conduct in what we have long called "a search for truth." The suggestion sometimes made that "a lawyer must believe his client not judge him" in no sense means a lawyer can honorably be a party to or in any way give aid to presenting known perjury.

* * *

The Court of Appeals' holding that Robinson's "action deprived [Whiteside] of due process and effective assistance of counsel" is not supported by the record since Robinson's action, at most, deprived Whiteside of his contemplated perjury. Nothing counsel did in any way undermined Whiteside's claim that he believed the victim was reaching for a gun. Similarly, the record gives no support for holding that Robinson's action "also impermissibly compromised [Whiteside's] right to testify in his own defense by conditioning continued representation . . . and confidentiality upon [Whiteside's] *restricted* testimony." The record in fact shows the contrary: (a) that Whiteside did testify, and (b) he was "restricted" or restrained only from testifying falsely and was aided by Robinson in developing the basis for the fear that Love was reaching for a gun. Robinson divulged no client communications until he was compelled to do so in response to Whiteside's post-trial challenge to the quality of his performance. We see this as a case in which the attorney successfully dissuaded the client from committing the crime of perjury.

Paradoxically, even while accepting the conclusion of the Iowa trial court that Whiteside's proposed testimony would have been a criminal act, the Court of Appeals held that Robinson's efforts to persuade Whiteside not to commit that crime were improper, *first,* as forcing an impermissible choice between the right to counsel and the right to testify; and *second,* as compromising client confidences because of Robinson's threat to disclose the contemplated perjury.

Whatever the scope of a constitutional right to testify, it is elementary that such a right does not extend to testifying *falsely*. . . .

The paucity of authority on the subject of any such "right" may be explained by the fact that such a notion has never been responsibly advanced; the right to counsel includes no right to have a lawyer who will cooperate with planned perjury. A lawyer who would so cooperate would be at risk of prosecution for suborning perjury, and disciplinary proceedings, including suspension or disbarment.

Robinson's admonitions to his client can in no sense be said to have forced respondent into an *impermissible* choice between his right to counsel and his right to testify as he proposed for there was no *permissible* choice to testify falsely. For defense counsel to take steps to persuade a criminal defendant to testify truthfully, or to withdraw, deprives the defendant of neither his right to counsel nor the right to testify truthfully. . . .

Similarly, we can discern no breach of professional duty in Robinson's admonition to respondent that he would disclose respondent's perjury to the court. The crime of perjury in this setting is indistinguishable in substance from the crime of threatening or tampering with a witness or a juror. A defendant who informed his counsel that he was arranging to bribe or threaten witnesses or members of the jury would have no "right" to insist on counsel's assistance or silence. Counsel would not be limited to advising against that conduct. An attorney's duty of confidentiality, which totally covers the client's admission of guilt, does not extend to a client's announced plans to engage in future criminal conduct. In short, the responsibility of an ethical lawyer, as an officer of the court and a key component of a system of justice, dedicated to a search for truth, is essentially the same whether the client announces an intention to bribe or threaten witnesses or jurors or to commit or procure perjury. No system of justice worthy of the name can tolerate a lesser standard. . . .

We hold that, as a matter of law, counsel's conduct complained of here cannot establish the prejudice required for relief under the second strand of the *Strickland* inquiry. Although a defendant need not establish that the attorney's deficient performance more likely than not altered the outcome in order to establish prejudice under *Strickland,* a defendant must show "that there is a reasonable probability that, but for counsel's unprofessional errors, the result of the proceeding would have been different." . . .

Whether he was persuaded or compelled to desist from perjury, Whiteside has no valid claim that confidence in the result of his trial has been diminished by his desisting from the contemplated perjury. Even if we were to assume that the jury might have believed his perjury, it does not follow that Whiteside was prejudiced. . . .

The Court of Appeals was in error to direct the issuance of a writ of habeas corpus and must be reversed.

The basic concept of a mandatory duty runs into trouble when a decision maker is confronted with conflicting obligations. Some additional methodology is required to establish priorities for dealing with instances of conflicting duties. Duty-based theorists have responded to this problem by constructing hierarchical systems of duties and proposing decision techniques based upon concepts of procedural justice. The hierarchical systems never seem to eliminate completely the problem of conflicting duties; instead, they just refine the conflict to a consideration of competing comparable duties. Suggestions of following standards of procedural justice similarly beg the issue. Without some method of assigning relative weights to principles of duty, the individual businessperson is left with little guidance as to how to act in the many situations that involve conflicting duties.

The idea that a profession may set its own ethical rules is a form of relativism. Although representatives of a profession may have special insights into the daily practice and social role of the profession, they cannot be the final arbiters, in an ultimate sense, of what is "right" in professional practice. Instead, their findings must always be subject to testing under general ethical theory. Many professions over the years have developed ethical standards that limit competition among their members or that set minimum fees. This dark side of formal professional standards is reflected in the following case.

National Society of Professional Engineers v. United States

U.S. Supreme Court
435 U.S. 679 (1978)

Background: The U.S. government (plaintiff) filed a civil suit under the Sherman Antitrust Act against the National Society of Professional Engineers (defendant, Society) alleging that the provision of their code of ethics preventing competitive bidding for jobs was illegal. The Society argued that the restriction was necessary in order to insure safety. The District Court rejected that justification without even making a factual determination of the validity of the safety argument. The Court of Appeals for the District of Columbia affirmed.

Decision: The Supreme Court affirmed; a code of ethics cannot override the procompetitive principles of the Sherman Act.

Stevens, Justice

Engineering is an important and learned profession. There are over 750,000 graduate engineers in the United States, of whom about 325,000 are registered as professional engineers. Registration requirements vary from State to State, but usually require the applicant to be a graduate engineer with at least four years of practical experience and to pass a written examination. About half of those who are registered engage in consulting engineering on a fee basis. They perform services in connection with the study, design, and construction of all types of improvements to real property—bridges, office buildings, airports, and factories are examples. Engineering fees, amounting to well over $2 billion each year, constitute about 5% of total construction costs. In any given facility, approximately 50% to 80% of the cost of construction is the direct result of work performed by an engineer concerning the systems and equipment to be incorporated in the structure.

The National Society of Professional Engineers (Society) was organized in 1935 to deal with the nontechnical aspects of engineering practice, including the promotion of the professional, social, and economic interests of its members. Its present membership of 69,000 resides throughout the United States and in some foreign countries. Approximately 12,000 members are consulting engineers who offer their services to governmental, industrial, and private clients. Some Society members are principals or chief executive officers of some of the largest engineering firms in the country.

The charges of a consulting engineer may be computed in different ways. He may charge the client a percentage of the cost of the project, may set his fee at his actual cost plus overhead plus a reasonable profit, may charge fixed rates per hour for different types of work, may perform an assignment for a specific sum, or he may combine one or more of these approaches. Suggested fee schedules for particular types of services in certain areas have been promulgated from time to time by various local societies. This case does not, however, involve any claim that the National Society has tried to fix specific fees, or even a specific method of calculating fees. It involves a charge that the members of the Society have unlawfully agreed to refuse to negotiate or even to discuss the question of fees until after a prospective client has selected the engineer for a particular project. Evidence of this agreement is found in § 11(c) of the Society's Code of Ethics, adopted in July 1964.[1]

. . .

In 1972 the Government filed its complaint against the Society alleging that members had agreed to abide by canons of ethics prohibiting the submission of competitive bids for engineering services and that, in consequence, price competition among the members had been suppressed and customers had been deprived of the benefits of free and open competition. The complaint prayed for an injunction terminating the unlawful agreement.

In its answer the Society admitted the essential facts alleged by the Government and pleaded a series of affirmative defenses, only one of which remains in issue. In that defense, the Society averred that the standard set out in the Code of Ethics was reasonable because competition among professional engineers was contrary to the public interest. It was averred that it would be cheaper and easier for an engineer "to design and specify inefficient and unnecessarily expensive structures and methods of construction." Accordingly, competitive pressure to offer engineering services at the lowest possible price would adversely affect the quality of engineering. Moreover, the practice of awarding engineering contracts to the lowest bidder, regardless of quality, would be dangerous to the public health, safety, and welfare. For these reasons, the Society claimed that its Code of Ethics was not an "unreasonable restraint of interstate trade or commerce."

. . .

The Sherman Act does not require competitive bidding; it prohibits unreasonable restraints on competition. Petitioner's ban on competitive bidding prevents all customers from making price comparisons in the initial selection of an engineer, and imposes the Society's views of the costs and benefits of competition on the entire marketplace. It is this restraint that must be justified, and petitioner's attempt to do so on the basis of the potential threat that competition poses to the public safety and the ethics of its profession is nothing less than a frontal assault on the basic policy of the Sherman Act.

[1] That section, which remained in effect at the time of trial, provided:
"Section 11—The Engineer will not compete unfairly with another engineer by attempting to obtain employment or advancement or professional engagements by competitive bidding.
. . .
   "c. He shall not solicit or submit engineering proposals on the basis of competitive bidding. Competitive bidding for professional engineering services is defined as the formal or informal submission, or receipt, of verbal or written estimates of cost or proposals in terms of dollars, man days of work required, percentage of construction cost, or any other measure of compensation whereby the prospective client may compare engineering services on a price basis prior to the time that one engineer, or one engineering organization, has been selected for negotiations.

. . . The assumption that competition is the best method of allocating resources in a free market recognizes that all elements of a bargain—quality, service, safety, and durability—and not just the immediate cost, are favorably affected by the free opportunity to select among alternative offers. Even assuming occasional exceptions to the presumed consequences of competition, the statutory policy precludes inquiry into the question whether competition is good or bad.

The fact that engineers are often involved in large-scale projects significantly affecting the public safety does not alter our analysis. Exceptions to the Sherman Act for potentially dangerous goods and services would be tantamount to a repeal of the statute. In our complex economy the number of items that may cause serious harm is almost endless—automobiles, drugs, foods, aircraft components, heavy equipment, and countless others, cause serious harm to individuals or to the public at large if defectively made. The judiciary cannot indirectly protect the public against this harm by conferring monopoly privileges on the manufacturers.

. . . We adhere to the view expressed in *Goldfarb* that, by their nature, professional services may differ significantly from other business services, and, accordingly, the nature of the competition in such services may vary. Ethical norms may serve to regulate and promote this competition. . . . But the Society's argument in this case is a far cry from such a position. We are faced with a contention that a total ban on competitive bidding is necessary because otherwise engineers will be tempted to submit deceptively low bids. Certainly, the problem of professional deception is a proper subject of an ethical canon. But, once again, the equation of competition with deception, like the similar equation with safety hazards, is simply too broad; we may assume that competition is not entirely conducive to ethical behavior, but that is not a reason, cognizable under the Sherman Act, for doing away with competition.

$$\qquad \bullet \qquad \bullet \qquad \bullet$$

The Society apparently fears that the District Court's injunction, if broadly read, will block legitimate paths of expression on all ethical matters relating to bidding. But the answer to these fears is, as the Court held in *International Salt,* that the burden is upon the proved transgressor "to bring any proper claims for relief to the court's attention." In this case, the Court of Appeals specifically stated that "[i]f the Society wishes to adopt some other ethical guideline more closely confined to the legitimate objective of preventing deceptively low bids, it may move the district court for modification of the decree." This is, we believe, a proper approach, adequately protecting the Society's interests. We therefore reject petitioner's attack on the District Court's order.

Outcome-Based Ethics

Utilitarianism constitutes an alternative to a duty-based approach. Utilitarians are concerned with the ultimate impact of actions on the welfare of society as a whole. The emphasis is on the greatest good for the greatest number. Recall the example of the use of newspaper vending machines and waiting lines. A utilitarian would evaluate the practice of cutting into lines or of putting slugs into the machines on the basis of the overall effect on society. If such behaviors were common, the queuing effect of the lines would disappear, resulting in physical strength determining position in line; and the convenience of newspaper vending machines would be lost. Thus, such actions would also be found unethical under a utilitarian view.

The utilitarian calculation is made from the viewpoint of society as a whole, not just from the perspective of the actor. An individual cannot calculate what would be best for him or her and claim a utilitarian justification for the action. That would be an example of egoism.

By its emphasis on final outcomes, utilitarianism appears to avoid some of the problems encountered by the duty-based approach. Closer observation, however, reveals that utilitarians also encounter significant difficulties. A fundamental question for the utilitarian is how society's interest should be calculated. The question can be approached in very different ways. Under one approach, happiness and freedom from pain is the primary good to be used in evaluating the morality of actions. Others emphasize principles of intrinsic worth, for example, health.

A quite different approach is to evaluate an action on whether its outcome serves to maximize the preferences of individuals within society, whatever those preferences happen to be. Individuals are assumed to have very different individual preferences: some prefer the beach, some prefer the mountains, some like self-denial, others like to consume conspicuously. Advocates of maximizing personal utility argue that an action is ethical when it tends to allow other individuals the opportunity to realize their own personal preferences. Under a liberty-as-key utility approach actions that significantly interfere with the liberties of others would be characterized as unethical.

Marketplace decisions and voting are the two primary ways in which individuals indicate their preferences. Certainly any viable theory of business ethics must take into consideration the output of the market and political mechanisms. Interferences in the operation of economic and political institutions that serve to distort their output can be characterized as unethical behavior.

Pareto superiority, a principle of public choice, involves related principles and can be applied to a utilitarian analysis. An action is Pareto superior if it improves the situation of a person or group and no one else is harmed by it. Pareto superiority is concerned with outcomes and involves evaluating the impact of an action upon others, and thus is consistent with a utilitarian analysis.

The personal utility and Pareto superiority approaches share shortcomings. Both have problems with preferences that violate the principle of respect for others or are otherwise problematic. Consider the case of incest. If the individuals involved both prefer incest, then a consideration of personal utilities cannot be used to condemn the action. An analysis under Pareto superiority might condemn it, but this would require speculative analysis about the effects on others, for example, the possible offspring of such a liaison.

The major problem with Pareto superiority is that it takes the status quo as given. Major inequities may be preserved as actions are evaluated on the basis of whether they produce benefit on their own accord. Pareto superiority cannot be used to condemn the status quo. Thus, actions supporting apartheid could be characterized as ethical using a standard of Pareto superiority so long as some Afrikaners are better off and no Blacks are worse off.

There are two forms of utilitarianism: act and rule utilitarianism. *Act utilitarianism* requires an ad hoc analysis of each and every action that may have moral consequences. Once agreement is reached on the ultimate criteria to use in evaluating outcomes (happiness, health, maximization of personal utilities), the difficult task of measuring the probable impact must be faced. The problem is similar to that faced in any sort of cost-benefit-type analysis. How can the various costs and benefits be put into equivalent terms?

The second form of utilitarianism is called *rule utilitarianism.* Rule utilitarians avoid making an independent judgment for every proposed act. Instead, rules are identified that are assumed to maximize utility. A probability judgment is made that if certain behavior predominates—for example, businesspeople always try to act in good faith—then maximum utility will result. Although rule utilitarianism may seem similar to a duty-based analysis, it differs in a fundamental regard. The rule utilitarian devises the rules solely on the basis of whether they are likely to contribute to right outcomes. Further information about a rule's effectiveness or a change in patterns of behavior that alter the likely outcomes produced by a rule should result in remodeling the rule. In contrast, duty-based rules are understood as more fundamental and unchangeable, and such duties are to be observed even when they impose net costs on society.

Social Justice

Theories of *social justice* are concerned with how rights, benefits, and obligations are distributed among the members of society. They are typically based upon some principle of a social contract—an implied understanding among the members of the society that things will be done a certain way. There are many different concepts of social justice. A particular concept, demonstrably accepted by a society, will establish ethical rights and obligations.

A controversial theory of social justice that has important ramifications for business is *libertarianism*. Libertarians emphasize individual freedom based upon property rights and a minimal role for government. The wealth of society is to be distributed on the basis of market transactions. Thus, it is just for a rock star to receive much greater financial rewards than a first violinist of a symphony orchestra or a Nobel laureate scientist working on a cancer cure. The uneducated person whose talents are not in demand is justly given little. Redistribution of wealth by government fiat, seen as arbitrarily benefiting the least productive, is an infringement of the basic libertarian principle: "From each as they choose, to each as they are chosen." Of course, it is perfectly okay for one individual to freely choose to give charity to another.

As with all principles, there must be some limits imposed on libertarianism. The severely handicapped who cannot care for themselves would be treated inhumanly unless there was sufficient individual charity to provide for their needs. It is difficult to imagine characterizing a society as "just" that fails to provide for the needs of the severely disadvantaged.

This issue is picked up in American law in the context of imposing affirmative duties to act to assist those in need. The general rule of tort law has been that one cannot be sued for failing to go to the aid of another, even when the rescue would surely succeed without danger to the rescuer. An ethical obligation to attempt a rescue can be supported by both duty-based and utilitarian analyses. One would desire, as a general rule, that rescues be attempted in anticipation of a time when oneself might be in need of assistance. Under an outcome analysis, if the rescue improved the victim's position without imposing costs on society, the rescue is ethical. The case that follows provides an interesting legal dimension to this issue.

Soldano v. O'Daniels

Court of Appeals of California, Fifth District

141 Cal. App.3d 443 (1983)

Background: Soldano (plaintiff) sued O'Daniels (defendant) for denying access to a telephone in an emergency situation. The incident arose when Soldano's father got into a fight in a saloon. A witness ran across the street to the defendant's restaurant and asked to be allowed either to use the phone or that the restaurant call the police. The defendant's employee denied all help and the father was shot to death. The son filed suit alleging that the refusal to provide help contributed to the father's wrongful death. The trial court gave summary judgment against the son.

Decision: Held, reversed, summary judgment should not have been rendered in favor of the defendant.

Andreen, Judge

Does a business establishment incur liability for wrongful death if it denies use of its telephone to a good samaritan who explains an emergency situation occurring without and wishes to call the police?

* * *

This action arises out of a shooting death occurring on August 9, 1977. Plaintiff's father [Darrell Soldano] was shot and killed by one Rudolph Villanueva on that date at . . . Happy Jack's Saloon. This defendant owns and operates the Circle Inn which is an eating establishment located across the street from Happy Jack's. Plaintiff's second cause of action against this defendant is one for negligence.

Plaintiff alleges that on the date of the shooting, a patron of Happy Jack's Saloon came into the Circle Inn and informed a Circle Inn employee that a man had been threatened at Happy Jack's. He requested the employee either call the police or allow him to use the Circle Inn phone to call the police. That employee allegedly refused to call the police and allegedly refused to allow the patron to use the phone to make his own call. Plaintiff alleges that the actions of the Circle Inn employee were a breach of the legal duty that the Circle Inn owed to the decedent.

There is a distinction, well rooted in the common law, between action and nonaction. It has found its way into the prestigious Restatement Second of Torts (hereafter cited as Restatement), which provides in section 314: "The fact that the actor realizes or should realize that action on his part is necessary for another's aid or protection does not of itself impose upon him a duty to take such action." Comment c of section 314 is instructive on the basis and limits of the rule and is set forth in the footnote.[1] The distinction between malfeasance and nonfeasance, between active misconduct

[1]The rule stated in this Section is applicable irrespective of the gravity of the danger to which the other is subjected and the insignificance of the trouble, effort, or expense of giving him aid or protection.

   "The origin of the rule lay in the early common law distinction between action and inaction, or 'misfeasance' and 'nonfeasance.' . . .

   Liability for nonfeasance was slow to receive any recognition in the law. It appeared first in, and is still largely confined to, situations in which there was some special relation between the parties, on the basis of which the defendant was found to have a duty to take action for the aid or protection of the plaintiff.

   The result of the rule has been a series of older decisions to the effect that one human being, seeing a fellow man in dire peril, is under no legal obligation to aid him, but may sit on the dock, smoke his cigar, and watch the other drown. Such decisions have been condemned by legal writers as revolting to any moral sense, but thus far they remain the law. It appears inevitable that, sooner or later, such extreme cases of morally outrageous and indefensible conduct will arise that there will be further inroads upon the older rule.

working positive injury and failure to act to prevent mischief not brought on by the defendant, is founded on "that attitude of extreme individualism so typical of anglo-saxon legal thought."

Defendant argues that the request that its employee call the police is a request that it *do* something. He points to the established rule that one who has not created a peril ordinarily does not have a duty to take affirmative action to assist an imperiled person.

. . .

The refusal of the law to recognize the moral obligation of one to aid another when he is in peril and when such aid may be given without danger and at little cost in effort has been roundly criticized. Prosser describes the case law sanctioning such inaction as a "refus[al] to recognize the moral obligation of common decency and common humanity" and characterizes some of these decisions as "shocking in the extreme. . . . [¶] Such decisions are revolting to any moral sense. They have been denounced with vigor by legal writers." . . .

Francis H. Bohlen, in his article *The Moral Duty to Aid Others as a Basis of Tort Liability,* commented:

> . . . "While courts of law should not yield to every passing current of popular thought, nonetheless, it appears inevitable that unless they adopt as legal those popular standards which they themselves, as men, regard as just and socially practicable, but which, as judges, they refuse to recognize solely because they are not the standards of the past of Brian, of Rolle, of Fineux, and of Coke; they will more and more lose their distinctive common law character as part of the machinery whereby free men do justice among themselves."

As noted in *Tarasoff* v. *Regents of University of California,* the courts have increased the instances in which affirmative duties are imposed not by direct rejection of the common law rule, but by expanding the list of special relationships which will justify departure from that rule. For instance, California courts have found special relationships in *Ellis* v. *D'Angelo* (1953) (upholding a cause of action against parents who failed to warn a babysitter of the violent proclivities of their child), *Johnson* v. *State of California* (1968) (upholding suit against the state for failure to warn foster parents of the dangerous tendencies of their ward), *Morgan* v. *County of Yuba* (1964) (sustaining cause of action against a sheriff who had promised to warn decedent before releasing a dangerous prisoner, but failed to do so).

And in *Tarasoff,* a therapist was told by his patient that he intended to kill Tatiana Tarasoff. The therapist and his supervisors predicted the patient presented a serious danger of violence. In fact he did, for he carried out his threat. The court held the patient-therapist relationship was enough to create a duty to exercise reasonable care to protect others from the foreseeable result of the patient's illness.

Section 314A of the Restatement lists other special relationships which create a duty to render aid, such as that of a common carrier to its passengers, an innkeeper to his guest, possessors of land who hold it open to the public, or one who has a custodial relationship to another. A duty may be created by an undertaking to give assistance.

Here there was no special relationship between the defendant and the deceased.

It would be stretching the concept beyond recognition to assert there was a relationship between the defendant and the patron from Happy Jack's Saloon who wished to summon aid. But this does not end the matter.

It is time to reexamine the common law rule of nonliability for nonfeasance in the special circumstances of the instant case. . . .

Crime is a blight on our society and a matter of great citizen concern. The President's Commission on Law Enforcement and the Administration of Justice, Task Force Report: The police (1967) recognized the importance of citizen involvement in crime prevention: "[C]rime is not the business of the police alone. . . . The police need help from citizens, . . ." The commission identified citizen crime reporting programs in some cities. These have proliferated in recent years.

The National Advisory Commission on Criminal Justice Standards and Goals, Report on Community Crime Prevention (1973) stated: "Criminal justice professionals readily and repeatedly admit that, in the absence of citizen assistance, neither more manpower, nor improved technology, nor additional money will enable law enforcement to shoulder the monumental burden of combating crime in America."

The Legislature has recognized the importance of the telephone system in reporting crime and in summoning emergency aid. Penal Code section 384 makes it a misdemeanor to refuse to relinquish a party line when informed that it is needed to call a police department or obtain other specified emergency services. This requirement, which the Legislature has mandated to be printed in virtually every telephone book in this state, may have wider printed distribution in this state than even the Ten Commandments. It creates an affirmative duty to do something—to clear the line for another user of the party line—in certain circumstances.

* * *

We turn now to the concept of duty in a tort case. The Supreme Court has identified certain factors to be considered in determining whether a duty is owed to third persons. These factors include: "the foreseeability of harm to the plaintiff, the degree of certainty that the plaintiff suffered injury, the closeness of the connection between the defendant's conduct and the injury suffered, the moral blame attached to the defendant's conduct, the policy of preventing future harm, the extent of the burden to the defendant and consequences to the community of imposing a duty to exercise care with resulting liability for breach, and the availability, cost, and prevalence of insurance for the risk involved."

We examine those factors in reference to this case. (1) The harm to the decedent was abundantly foreseeable; it was imminent. The employee was expressly told that a man had been threatened. The employee was a bartender. As such he knew it is foreseeable that some people who drink alcohol in the milieu of a bar setting are prone to violence. (2) The certainty of decedent's injury is undisputed. (3) There is arguably a close connection between the employee's conduct and the injury: the patron wanted to use the phone to summon the police to intervene. The employee's refusal to allow the use of the phone prevented this anticipated intervention. If permitted to go to trial, the plaintiff may be able to show that the probable response time of the police would have been shorter than the time between the prohibited telephone call and the fatal shot. (4) The employee's conduct displayed a disregard for human life that can be characterized as morally wrong: he was callously indifferent to the possibility that Darrell Soldano would die as the result of his refusal to allow a person to use the telephone. Under the circumstances before us the bartender's burden was minimal and exposed him to no risk: all he had to do was allow the use of the telephone. It would have cost him or his employer nothing. It could have saved a life. (5) Finding a duty in these circumstances would promote a policy of preventing future harm. A citizen would not be required to summon the police but would be required, in circumstances such as those before us, not to impede another who has chosen to summon aid. (6) We have no information on the question of the availability, cost, and prevalence of insurance for the risk, but note that the liability which is sought to be imposed here is that of employee negligence, which is covered by many insurance policies. (7) The extent of the burden of the defendant was minimal, as noted.

* * *

As the Supreme Court has noted, the reluctance of the law to impose liability for nonfeasance, as distinguished from misfeasance, is in part due to the difficulties in setting standards and of making rules workable *Tarasoff* v. *Regents of University of California, supra.*

Many citizens simply "don't want to get involved." No rule should be adopted which would require a citizen to open up his or her house to a stranger so that the latter may use the telephone to call for emergency assistance. As Mrs. Alexander in Anthony Burgess' *A Clockwork Orange* learned to her horror, such an action may be fraught with danger. It does not follow, however, that use of a telephone in a public portion of a business should be refused for a legitimate emergency call. Imposing liability for such a refusal would not subject innocent citizens to possible attack by the "good samaritan," for it would be limited to an establishment open to the public during times when it is open to business, and to places within the establishment ordinarily accessible to the public. Nor would a stranger's mere assertion that an "emergency" situation is occurring create the duty to utilize an accessible telephone because the duty would arise if and only if it were clearly conveyed that there exists an imminent danger of physical harm.

Such a holding would not involve difficulties in proof, overburden the courts or unduly hamper self-determination or enterprise.

A business establishment such as the Circle Inn is open for profit. The owner encourages the public to enter, for his earnings depend on it. A telephone is a necessary adjunct to such a place. It is not unusual in such circumstances for patrons to use the telephone to call a taxicab or family member.

* * *

We conclude that the bartender owed a duty to the plaintiff's decedent to permit the patron from Happy Jack's to place a call to the police or to place the call himself.

• • •

In contrast to libertarianism, *equalitarianism* treats all individuals alike regardless of market preferences or even productive effort. Even though the Declaration of Independence de- clares that all men are created equal, there are obvious ways in which people differ. Some are more diligent, more intelligent, or more talented. Nonetheless, equalitarians argue that all are alike in their basic humanity. Therefore, everyone has a right to start from the same point.

An obvious problem with equalitarianism is that few would choose to work hard if everyone benefited equally from their labor. Everyone would have an incentive to be a free rider, or to try to conceal what he or she was producing. The amount of cheating that has existed with our income tax system, which has been designed to bring about limited redistributions of wealth, demonstrates that many people would not willingly accept an equalitarian system.

Some social justice systems seek to identify basic human rights. Common choices for basic rights include being adequately fed, clothed, and housed. Those unable to obtain the minimal levels of necessities would be provided for by the state, which would make the necessary redistributions through taxation. The philosopher John Rawls has proposed a theory of social justice based upon rights that seeks to overcome the widely recognized problems with libertarianism and equalitarianism. His starting point is to inquire as to the type of society that would be desired by people who could not foretell their racial, religious, social, and economic status before birth. Rawls predicts that individuals restricted by such a "veil of ignorance" would choose to live in an economically productive society (necessary for wealth) that provides for individual choice and opportunity based on merit, but that also cares for the less fortunate. Those social inequalities that are accepted would be to the benefit of the least advantaged.

Social justice theories often emphasize fair procedures. Every individual is considered entitled to basic procedural rights. Many of those are reflected in U.S. constitutional law. Typical rights would include notice prior to action being taken affecting one's status, the right to be heard, and the right to assistance by professionals.

There are many other theories of social justice, including those that are based upon need (Marxism) and effort. Our society reflects elements of many different concepts of social justice. Most theories of social justice can be used to evaluate in moral terms the actions of business firms and people.

Personal Conscience/Individual Responsibility

The prophylactic nature of rule or outcome-based analysis always seems to leave open the possibility that some theoretical justification can be offered for actions that people of judgment know to be wrong. An alternative is to consider each person an autonomous actor who is morally accountable for his or her own actions. Thus, "A morally responsible business is not one that measures its actions against some external principle but is one in which good people are making decisions."[1]

Critics of this approach claim too much is left to individual discretion. No true reference points or methods of analysis are provided the decision maker. And there is the practical problem that reason exists to believe that some people who would not qualify as "good persons" are, nonetheless, important decision makers in the business world.

Before the good-persons argument is summarily dismissed, however, its compatibility with a concept of professional ethics should be considered. Professionals may be seen as significantly autonomous actors who are required to make important judgments about a variety of difficult matters relating to their professional competence. Ethical issues involve similar kinds of appraisals, and they often are an integral part of the professional judgment. Ultimately, one cannot escape personal responsibility for exercising critical judgment.

In preparing their children for independence, parents realize that they cannot provide their children with a formal decision matrix that will handle all foreseeable problems. Instead, they try to instill in them an appreciation of general standards, accompanied by a facility for critical judgment. The same holds true for ethical judgments in business. Autonomous responsibility as a good person is an important component of a concept of business ethics.

BUSINESS ETHICS TODAY

Managers rarely explain their decisions in the language of formal ethics. An important question is whether they implicitly use particular ethical theories. If managers do, then they may be open to explanations of how their thinking can be expanded through knowledge of formal theories of ethics. Fritzshe and Becker[2] surveyed marketing managers and obtained responses to a series of vignettes posing ethical dilemmas. The managers were asked to state on a 10-point Likert scale the probability that they would engage in the particular proposed action (e.g., pay a bribe) and to provide an explanation for their response. The responses were then characterized according to whether they appeared to be act-utilitarian, rule-utilitarian, duty-based, or social justice-oriented. The managers' responses were found to be overwhelmingly utilitarian-(outcome-) oriented.

Fritzsche and Becker found that the respondents' judgments on particular vignettes varied depending on whether they used a rule- or an act-utilitarian approach. For example, the rule utilitarians were less likely to be willing to pay bribes than were the act utilitarians. Although the study was limited to marketing managers, and to a particular set of ethical dilemmas, there is corroborating evidence that managers tend to be utilitarian in their approach to ethical issues. In 1983 a *Wall Street Journal*-Gallup (*WSJ*/G) survey of ethical attitudes was published indicating that managers often consider the context and amount of a transaction in deciding whether ethical problems are involved. Thus, before concluding whether a misstatement of salary on a résumé is unethical, many managers

would like to know the extent of the overstatement.

Level of Business Behavior

There have been numerous surveys of business behavior over the years that have tended to show nontrivial levels of unethical behavior. Table 4-1 lists the percent of respondents reporting various types of behavior in the *WSJ*/G survey reported in November 1983.

These statistics are consistent with other studies of the behavior of businesspeople. A 1983 research project sponsored by the National Institute of Justice (NIJ)[3] found that a third of the employees studied had stolen property from their employer during the prior year. It was estimated that the total dollar loss due to employee theft nationally was between $5 and $10 billion. In addition, two-thirds of employees reported counterproductive behavior such as taking drugs or abusing

TABLE 4-1 PERCENTAGE OF RESPONDENTS
REPORTING BEHAVIOR

Behavior	Managers	General Public
Taken home office supplies	74%	40%
Falsely called in sick	14	31
Personal phone calls at office	78	15
Overstated tax deductions	35	13
Understated income	10	10
Driven while drunk	80	33
Seen a colleague steal and not report	7	26

Source: From R. Ricklets, "Ethics in America." A four-part series in the *Wall Street Journal*, October 31–November 3, 1983. Reprinted by permission of *The Wall Street Journal*, © Dow Jones & Company, Inc. (1983). All Rights Reserved.

sick leave, or that they engaged in "purposefully slow or sloppy workmanship." Ten percent reported instances of minor sabotage. The problem was not just at the cash register or assembly line, but instead, involved significant participation by middle-level managers. In fact, for certain types of actions, middle managers are more likely to be involved because they are better able to make use of the stolen property, for example, selling stolen software or company trade secrets.

The NIJ researchers interviewed many of the workers and discovered that often those who acted against their firms did not consider themselves unethical. Their contention was that they had been poorly treated by their firms, were underpaid, or were otherwise entitled to extra benefits. Table 4-2 summarizes the attitudes of the respondents to the *WSJ*/G survey about various questionable business practices.

There is a difference in the level of responses in the *WSJ*/G survey between managers' reported behavior and their opinion of the correctness of the behavior. Their reported behavior is generally lower than might be predicted on the basis of their opinions of whether it is ethical. This may be explained by the distinction between intended and operating attitudes. The response to a hypothetical question generally reflects an abstract assessment of how the respondent hopes to act in such a situation. The actual behavior brings all of the situational and contextual dimensions into play and often comes out at odds with the intended value or attitude.

There are interesting variances between the opinions of the managers and the general public in the *WSJ*/G survey regarding the propriety of various actions. The general public appears completely insensitive to the possible conflict of interest involved in accepting a case of liquor from a supplier. Only 29 percent of the public think that such a "gift" is problematic, whereas 75 percent of the managers see difficulties. For only one of the suggested behaviors does the general public have a

TABLE 4-2 OPINIONS OF APPROPRIATENESS OF BEHAVIORS

Statement	Managers	Public
Wrong not to declare $2500 interest income	95	75
Wrong to bill falsely cab ride to firm	76	52
Wrong for purchasing agent to take case of liquor from supplier	75	29
Wrong to make personal photocopies	20	25
Wrong to take neighbor's ashtray	99	84
Wrong to take office ashtray	90	62
Would hire someone overstating prior salary by $10,000	47	63
Would follow bosses' suggestion to pad expenses	7	25
Would dismiss employee discovered to have falsely claimed a degree on résumé	50	22

Source: From R. Ricklets, "Ethics in America." A four-part series in the *Wall Street Journal,* October 31–November 3, 1983. Reprinted by permission of *The Wall Street Journal,* © Dow Jones & Company, Inc. (1983). All Rights Reserved.

"higher" ethical standard than do managers— the question of whether or not it is appropriate to use office photocopying equipment to make personal photocopies.

It would be useful to know how levels of ethical behavior in business are shifting over time. In the *WSJ*/G survey 49 percent of the general public believed that the trend of ethics had been downward during the prior ten years. Only 9 percent of the general public thought that the level of ethics had improved. In contrast, 23 percent of managers thought that the trend of ethics had been downward, whereas 31 percent thought that the trend had been upward.

Who is right? Unfortunately, there is no really good trend data where the same questions have been asked of the same group over time. The one major attempt to study this issue was conducted by Brenner and Molander,[4] who in 1977 published a study updating an earlier survey that had been conducted by Baumhart in 1961. The same questions were asked of a group that was similar to the one surveyed by Baumhart. The results indicated that the more recently surveyed managers were more concerned about ethical issues and that the level of behavior had improved somewhat. Even so, Brenner and Molander did not find any truly dramatic changes in behavior and attitudes over the sixteen years.

Many surveys ask individuals how they behave and then ask them how they think their peers generally behave. Most of these studies indicate that individual businesspeople tend to think that they are more ethical than the average person. Stated oppositely, most managers tend to believe that the general level of ethical behavior is below the standard that they set for themselves. A persistent assumption that others are unethical should be a source of concern. If individuals misperceive that general ethical practice is lower than their own, and then conclude that they will be at a competitive disadvantage by continuing a high standard of behavior, they may shift their own behavior toward conformity with what they think others do.

Ethical Standards in Business

The basic ethical theories do not rely upon custom or practice as a primary determinant of ethical judgments. Relativism has significant limitations. Nevertheless, the opinion and practice of professionals should provide some guidance concerning the bounds of ethical behavior. This is particularly the case for a complex field such as business ethics where disagreement exists among scholars concerning how the general theories of ethical behavior should be applied.

There have been periodic surveys of managers' opinions of the ethical propriety of various actions. Table 4-2 is representative of the actions studied in these surveys. The surveys usually show a high consensus that hard-core, criminal activities are improper (e.g., providing a prostitute to a buyer in order to get business, obvious theft) and a lesser degree of consensus regarding more purely commercial activities (e.g., addressing advertising to young children, selling practices overseas, etc.). The numerous studies conducted so far do not add up to the systematic study that is required to provide useful insights concerning ethical parameters in business. The studies to date are limited in that they (1) typically survey a limited sample of managers, (2) do not treat similar topics so that they can be cross-validated, and (3) are often not particularly rigorous in concept or implementation.

PRINCIPLES OF BUSINESS ETHICS

The individual businessperson, confronted with an ethical dilemma (e.g., whether to accept a case of Scotch from a supplier), faces a daunting array of sources of information concerning the right choice. His or her firm may have a code of ethics that states either very general principles (e.g., always put the customer's interests first, be loyal to the firm) or establishes specific rules (e.g., don't accept gifts from any supplier worth $25 or more). He or she may belong to a professional society that has a suggested code (e.g., never accept anything from a supplier). His or her peers may have established practices (e.g., okay to take a gift worth more than $25 from a long-time supplier), and friends may have a different view (e.g., it's none of the firm's business if it is a holiday gift).

The general theories discussed previously seem rather abstract in such a context. How is the overall interest of society involved? Is there some fundamental human right or duty at issue? Such discussions raise the issue of whether there are any generic principles of business ethics that can serve as a foundation for everyday decision making.

Such principles would have to be consistent with the basic functions of business, would have to be defensible under general ethical theory, and would have to be meaningful. In the next section eight possible general principles will be presented. The basic concept underlying each principle can be supported by each of the ethical theories described in the preceding sections. For example, confidentiality can be expressed as a basic duty, or it can be justified on the basis of standard utilitarian and social justice theories. The parameters of the principle would differ depending upon how it is justified, but the basic concept is a useful guidepost for ethical decision making in business.

Most of the chapters in this text have Ethics Boxes that emphasize a particular ethical issue related to the legal topic covered in the chapter. The analysis in the box will often make reference to the following principles.

Honor Confidentiality. Much business information is made available with the express or implied understanding that it is to be used only for certain purposes. When a firm discloses financial information as part of a merger negotiation, it expects that the data will only be used in the context of that negotiation. A fast-food franchise which discloses its "secret recipe" to a supplier expects the supplier to keep the confidence. Many employees know proprietary information about their firm: new designs, marketing plans, competitors' weaknesses. Researchers working on new products may know critically important information. Some of the information may be of great value and could capture a high price if wrongfully disclosed. The efficiency of the business system depends upon the honoring of confidentiality. Individual privacy rights are also an important basis for confidentiality.

Avoid Even the Appearance of a Conflict of Interest. A conflict of interest arises when someone has a personal interest that contrasts with a duty owed to another, or mutually exclusive duties are owed to two or more people. A duty arises out of an obligation that comes from a promise, a contractual obligation, a role (trustee, agent, guardian . . .), a personal or family relationship, or by law. A simple example is when a purchasing agent for a corporation selects a close relative as a supplier, or an agent represents both the buyer and the seller in the same transaction.

Conflicts of interest can be resolved in several ways, so that it is not always necessary to refrain when there is a conflicting self-interest or a competing obligation. The standard ways to make sure that one has not given into a conflict of interest is to (1) disclose fully to all affected parties, (2) have a truly independent party certify the fairness of the transaction, or (3) refrain personally and have someone else from the firm, who is totally independent, make the decision. The stress on avoiding the "appearance" of a conflict is to make sure that, at the least, there is full disclosure.

Willingly Comply with the Law. Some businesspeople appear to think that they are sufficiently ethical if they just are sure to comply with the law. Although there is some relationship, ethics and the law are not the same thing. Ethics goes beyond the law; merely complying with the law does not constitute, per se, the satisfaction of all ethical obligations. Ethics involves voluntary behavior that reflects concern about others; compliance with the law may occur merely out of a fear of being caught and punished. Compliance with a law that violates universal ethical principles (e.g., a law requiring human sacrifice) is unethical behavior.

Willing compliance with the law goes beyond employing a cost-benefit analysis of complying with a particular legal rule. It also mitigates against too easy an acceptance of excuses such as (1) the law is not enforced, (2) the law is bad law, (3) the boundaries of the law are vague, or (4) the law is something different from its literal statement, for example, the speed limit is sixty-five rather than fifty-five miles per hour. Although a civil disobedience argument may be sanctioned in certain, very limited circumstances, in almost all business contexts ethical analysis supports obeying the law.

Exercise Due Care. This principle is one of professional competency. A businessperson who has special training or experience can be expected to perform at a level that reflects that training and experience. The principle of due care distinguishes professionals from lay-people. Although the principle is easily under-stood in the context of a doctor or lawyer, it has applicability to businesspeople also. A marketing manager should be expected to demonstrate special abilities in carrying out his or her job. A financial analyst would be expected to notice certain things in a financial report that might escape someone who is not trained or experienced in finance. The princi-ple constitutes an ethical duty in that others rely upon and are affected by the quality of work performed by the businessperson.

Act in Good Faith. A fundamental obliga-tion, rooted in American commercial law, is to act in good faith. Good faith incorporates a number of attributes, including honoring pro-mises, avoiding deceit, and living up to the reasonable expectations that others have con-cerning behavior. One way to think of what good faith means is to act as though you expect the business relationship to be long term. If you know that you will encounter the other person again and again, how would you act?

The essence of good faith is fairness. Treat-ing others fairly includes following just proce-dures in addition to recognizing the legitimate claims of others. Consider the case of an oil company that decides to terminate an inde-pendent dealer who has operated one of their service stations for many years. Good faith would require that the dealer's expectations based upon prior promises and actions be con-sidered, and that the dealer be given a chance to respond to the reasons for the termination. Ultimately, any termination should be for just reasons and carried out in a fair manner.

Observe Fidelity to Special Responsibilities. Businesspeople may have special responsibili-ties that derive from their position in the firm or their particular role in a transaction. Managers, directors, and corporate officers all have special responsibilities. The same is true for trustees and agents. The particulars of the special responsibilities may come from con-tracts, promises, professional codes, or directly from law. The essence of the concept is trust-worthiness. Fidelity is the basis for the con-cept of conflict of interest, but it also goes be-yond it. The trustworthy businessperson not only avoids a conflict of interest, but he or she also satisfies the full expectations that accom-pany the position.

Respect the Liberty and Rights of Others. Other humans are entitled to be treated with respect. Managers are often in a position where they can greatly influence the way in which people are treated. A common problem that younger lower-level managers report is that they perceive a conflict between their values and those of their firm. In the *WSJ*/G survey described in this chapter, 40 percent of the middle managers reported that they had been asked by a superior to do something they were sure was unethical; and 10 percent had been asked to do something illegal! Being put into a compromising position constitutes a denial of their right to respect.

Employers who consider restricting the rights of political access, privacy, and speech of their employees should consider the full consequences of the restrictions. Although it is legal to impose limits on such employee rights (not without limit), and there may be times when the greater social good requires some limitation; far-reaching limits, imposed by enough firms, may have a significantly detrimental impact on the viability of basic rights in our society. At the individual level, businesspeople should limit restrictions to those that are clearly business justified. The current debate concerning drug or AIDS testing of employees is at the heart of this principle.

Respect Human Well-Being. A fundamental ethical principle is to do no harm. The concept of harm is necessarily a relative one. Selling drugs that constitute powerful cures for serious diseases, but that also produce harmful side effects, is not per se unethical. The ethicality of the action will depend upon appropriate disclosure of the side effects and the relationship between the harm caused and the good achieved.

This principle applies to hazards in the workplace, inherently harmful substances, and hidden defects in products. It lies at the heart of much of product liability and tort law discussed in Chapters 8 and 23. This principle is very fundamental and, in many instances, can be seen as trumping the other principles. Thus, if a businessperson faces a choice between observing confidentiality and disclosing information that would prevent harm to human well-being, the information should be disclosed.

Use of Principles

The eight preceding principles are offered as general guidelines for analyzing ethical issues. They are not intended to be used as bright-line rules that can provide clear-cut, decisive resolutions to ethical dilemmas. Nevertheless, they should provide a starting point for discussing problem situations.

Consider the use of inside information in stock market transactions. (The law of insider trading is discussed in detail in Chapter 37.) Several of the principles are immediately ap-

plicable. To the extent that the practice is illegal, inside trading violates the principle of willing compliance with the law. The fact that the inside trader thinks that the securities law is a bad law, or that the law is vague in some applications, is not a sufficient excuse for violating this principle. Inside information most typically is considered confidential, so that use by the trader for his or her own benefit violates that principle. Often, when the information is misused by a law firm, brokerage firm, or investment banking house that is hired by the corporation, there is a conflict of interest. The infamous inside trader, Dennis Levine, used inside information to compete personally with his firm's own clients, a gross conflict of interest. When corporate employees use inside information about their own firm to benefit themselves, they breach the principle of fidelity to special responsibilities. Thus, insider trading, depending upon the context, may be unethical even when it is not illegal.

SPECIFIC ISSUES IN BUSINESS ETHICS

Business ethics encompasses a wide range of activities. There are numerous issues that could be explored in a text of this type. Many issues will be briefly discussed throughout the rest of the text in the Ethics Boxes that appear in many chapters. The next sections present a few specific issues of business ethics in greater detail.

Ethics in Negotiation

The process of negotiation is replete with moral issues. Many consider lying a necessary if not a sophisticated negotiating technique. Few would reveal their true price when asked at the beginning of a negotiation ("Although I'm asking $500, I'll take $350"), or volunteer information about all the shortcomings of the item they are selling ("I assume that you are aware that the prices of 1950s baseball cards have been falling and will probably continue to do so").

An ethical principle of honesty (good faith) can be based upon the premise that we all expect honesty in others and that those who are dishonest make unfair exceptions of themselves. A duty-based approach founded upon principles of strict honesty would recognize exceptions in only exceptional circumstances. An outcome-based analysis may be more flexible. If there are circumstances in which the economic system and thus society generally benefits from certain forms of falsehood (it sounds outrageous—but stay with the argument), then those forms would be considered ethical.

How might such an argument be made? Albert Carr argued such a position in 1968 in a controversial article in the *Harvard Business Review*.[5] Carr argues that business is a game, similar to sports, and that certain types of dishonesty are completely compatible with the rules of the business game. The use of deception is justified on two implicit grounds. First,

he argues that business is more efficient when appropriate dishonesty is employed. Deception is treated as an inherent element of negotiation. Carr justifies this by analogies to playing poker and military strategy. The very nature of such activities requires deception. The same would hold true for sports when a quarterback changes a play at the line of scrimmage or a baseball coach gives signals to his ball players. Both will attempt deception and the better they are at deceiving, the greater will be their chances of success in their roles.

The second justification put forward is based upon implied consent. Carr assumes that knowledgeable business practitioners realize that deception is essential in negotiation, so they anticipate that those with whom they deal will act deceptively. Those who are not aware of the standard practice have a duty to educate themselves before engaging in serious negotiations.

The following case appears to reflect the type of attitude advocated by Carr as sound business practice. Do you agree?

Vokes v. Arthur Murray, Inc.

Florida District Court of Appeals, Second District

212 So.2d 906 (1968)

Background: Vokes (plaintiff), a fifty-one-year-old widow, brought this action against Arthur Murray, Inc. (defendant), a dance-instruction corporation, to recover damages caused by the defendant's fraud. The defendant argued that there was no fraud or misrepresentation on its part, that its statements were mere "trade puffing." The trial court found for the defendant and dismissed the plaintiff's amended complaint; from that decision, the plaintiff appealed.

Decision: The Court of Appeals found the statements made by the plaintiff in her complaint could be the basis for finding that the defendant committed fraud. Accordingly, it reversed the trial court's dismissal of the plaintiff's complaint.

Pierce, Judge

This is an appeal by Audrey E. Vokes, plaintiff below, from a final order dismissing with prejudice, for failure to state a cause of action, her fourth amended complaint, hereinafter referred to as plaintiff's complaint.

Defendant Arthur Murray, Inc., a corporation, authorizes the operation throughout the nation of dancing schools under the name of "Arthur Murray School of Dancing" through local franchised operators, one of whom was defendant J. P. Davenport whose dancing establishment was in Clearwater.

Plaintiff Mrs. Audrey E. Vokes, a widow of 51 years and without family, had a yen to be "an accomplished dancer" with the hopes of finding "new interest in life." So, on February 10, 1961, a dubious fate, with the assist of a motivated acquaintance, procured her to attend a "dance party" at Davenport's "School of Dancing" where she whiled away the pleasant hours, sometimes in a private room, absorbing his accomplished sales technique, during which her grace and poise were elaborated upon and her rosy future as "an excellent dancer" was painted for her in vivid and glowing colors. As an incident to this interlude, he sold her eight ½-hour dance lessons to be utilized within one calendar month therefrom, for the sum of $14.50 cash in hand paid, obviously a baited "come-on."

Thus she embarked upon an almost endless pursuit of the terpsichorean art during which, over a period of less than sixteen months, she was sold fourteen "dance courses" totalling in the aggregate 2302 hours of dancing lessons for a total cash outlay of $31,090.45, all at Davenport's dance emporium. All of these fourteen courses were evidenced by execution of a written "Enrollment Agreement—Arthur Murray's School of Dancing" with the addendum in heavy black print, "No one will be informed that you are taking dancing lessons. Your relations with us are held in strict confidence," setting forth the number of "dancing lessons" and the "lessons in rhythm sessions" currently sold to her from time to time, and always of course accompanied by payment of cash of the realm.

These dance lesson contracts and the monetary consideration therefor of over $31,000 were procured from her by means and methods of Davenport and his associates which went beyond the unsavory, yet legally permissible, perimeter of "sales puffing" and intruded well into the forbidden area of undue influence, the suggestion of falsehood, the suppression of truth, and the free exercise of rational judgment, if what plaintiff alleged in her complaint was true. From the time of her first contact with the dancing school in February, 1961, she was influenced unwittingly by a constant and continuous barrage of flattery, false praise, excessive compliments, and panegyric encomiums, to such extent that it would be not only inequitable, but unconscionable, for a Court exercising inherent chancery power to allow such contracts to stand.

She was incessantly subjected to overreaching blandishment and cajolery. She was assured she had "grace and poise"; that she was "rapidly improving and developing in her dancing skill"; that the additional lessons would "make her a beautiful dancer, capable of dancing with the most accomplished dancers"; that she was "rapidly progressing in the development of her dancing skill and gracefulness," etc., etc. She was given "dance aptitude tests" for the ostensible purpose of "determining" the number of remaining hours instructions needed by her from time to time.

At one point she was sold 545 additional hours of dancing lessons to be entitled to award of the "Bronze Medal" signifying that she had reached "the Bronze Standard," a supposed designation of dance achievement by students of Arthur Murray, Inc.

Later she was sold an additional 926 hours in order to gain the "Silver Medal," indicating she had reached "the Silver Standard," at a cost of $12,501.35.

At one point, while she still had to her credit about 900 unused hours of instructions, she was induced to purchase an additional 24 hours of lessons to participate in a trip to Miami at her own expense, where she would be "given the opportunity to dance with members of the Miami Studio."

She was induced at another point to purchase an additional 126 hours of lessons in order to be not only eligible for the Miami trip but also to become "a life member of the Arthur Murray Studio," carrying with it certain dubious emoluments, at a further cost of $1,752.30.

At another point, while she still had over 1,000 unused hours of instruction she was induced to buy 151 additional hours at a cost of $2,049.00 to be eligible for a "Student Trip to Trinidad," at her own expense as she later learned.

Also, when she still had 1100 unused hours to her credit, she was prevailed upon to purchase an additional 347 hours at a cost of $4,235.74, to qualify her to receive a "Gold Medal" for achievement, indicating she had advanced to "the Gold Standard."

On another occasion, while she still had over 1200 unused hours, she was induced to buy an additional 175 hours of instructions at a cost of $2,472.75 to be eligible "to take a trip to Mexico."

Finally, sandwiched in between other lesser sales promotions, she was influenced to buy an additional 481 hours of instruction at a cost of $6,523.81 in order to "be classified as a Gold Bar Member, the ultimate achievement of the dancing studio."

All the foregoing sales promotions, illustrative of the entire fourteen separate contracts, were procured by defendant Davenport and Arthur Murray, Inc., by false representations to her that she was improving in her dancing ability, that she had excellent potential, that she was responding to instructions in dancing grace, and that they were developing her into a beautiful dancer, whereas in truth and in fact she did not develop in her dancing ability, she had no "dance aptitude," and in fact had difficulty in "hearing the musical beat." The complaint alleged that such representations to her "were in fact false and known by the defendant to be false and contrary to the plaintiff's true ability, the truth of plaintiff's ability being fully known to the defendants, but withheld from the plaintiff for the sole and specific intent to deceive and defraud the plaintiff and to induce her in the purchasing of additional hours of dance lessons." It was averred that the lessons were sold to her "in total disregard to the true physical, rhythm, and mental ability of the plaintiff." In other words, while she first exulted that she was entering the "spring of her life," she finally was awakened to the fact there was "spring" neither in her life nor in her feet.

It is true that "generally a misrepresentation, to be actionable, must be one of fact rather than of opinion." . . . But this rule has significant qualifications, applicable here. It does not apply where there is a fiduciary relationship between the parties, or where there has been some artifice or trick employed by the representor, or where the parties do not in general deal at "arm's length" as we understand the phrase, or where the representee does not have equal opportunity to become apprised of the truth or falsity of the fact represented.

> "... A statement of a party having ... superior knowledge may be regarded as a statement of fact although it would be considered as opinion if the parties were dealing on equal terms."

It could be reasonably supposed here that defendants had "superior knowledge" as to whether plaintiff had "dance potential" and as to whether she was noticeably improving in the art of terpsichore. And it would be a reasonable inference from the undenied averments of the complaint that the flowery eulogiums heaped upon her by defendants as a prelude to her contracting for 1944 additional hours of instruction in order to attain the rank of the Bronze Standard, thence to the bracket of the Silver Standard, thence to the class of the Gold Bar Standard, and finally to the crowning plateau of a Life Member of the Studio, proceeded as much or more from the urge to "ring the cash register" as from any honest or realistic appraisal of her dancing prowess or a factual representation of her progress.

Even in contractual situations where a party to a transaction owes no duty to disclose facts within his knowledge or to answer inquiries respecting such facts, the law is if he undertakes to do so he must disclose the *whole truth.* ... From the face of the complaint, it should have been reasonably apparent to defendants that her vast outlay of cash for the many hundreds of additional hours of instruction was not justified by her slow and awkward progress, which she would have been made well aware of if they had spoken the "whole truth."

We repeat that where parties are dealing on a contractual basis at arm's length with no inequities or inherently unfair practices employed, the Courts will in general "leave the parties where they find themselves." But (in) ... our view, from the showing made in her complaint, plaintiff is entitled to her day in Court.

It accordingly follows that the order dismissing plaintiff's last amended complaint with prejudice should be and is reversed.

As demonstrated in the *Vokes* case, one problem with Carr's analysis is that both sides may not be playing by the same rules. One side thinks that deception is understood, the other party assumes that honesty will be strictly adhered to. Carr's analysis also fails to provide any guidelines concerning what the limits are. Although a baseball manager will disguise signals and try to confuse the other team concerning whether a sacrifice bunt has been called, there are clear rules that one doesn't breach. It is not okay to bribe the umpire for favorable rulings.

The ultimate shortcoming of Carr's analysis is that it fails to consider the costs directly imposed by deception. If everyone acted completely opportunistically in negotiations by lying and refusing to honor promises, all negotiators would take steps to protect themselves. Defensive strategies that could be employed include insisting upon more elaborate and detailed contract terms and the use of monitoring or control mechanisms. These purely defensive strategies would raise the costs of negotiation and implementation and would reduce the flexibility of contracts. The cost of contracting would increase in society as a whole, and society would be worse off.

The problem is likely to be a serious one only if a significant percentage of people behave opportunistically. So long as only a few behave that way, and costs are neither high nor widespread, can opportunistic behavior be considered acceptable on moral grounds? The answer is no, because an individual can get away with deception without imposing a major cost on society only if most other people don't do it. Individuals taking advantage of this situation would be making an exception of themselves and would be violating the generally accepted ethical principles described earlier in the chapter. The case that follows demonstrates the application of the legal doctrine of good faith in the context of a common deception.

Umlas v. Acey Oldsmobile

Civil Court of the City of New York

62 Misc. 2d 819 (1970)

Background: Umlas (plaintiff) sued Acey Oldsmobile (defendants) alleging breach of contract. Umlas contracted to buy a new 1970 Oldsmobile from Acey Oldsmobile. As part of the negotiation, Umlas's 1966 Olds was valued at $650. The contract reserved to the dealer the right to reappraise a used car at the time of delivery. When Umlas's new car was ready, the dealer revalued the trade-in at $50. Upset by this, Umlas bought his new car elsewhere and sued Acey for breach of contract. Decision: The trial court found for the plaintiff.

Leonard H. Sandler, Judge

Underlying plaintiff's lawsuit is the charge that on the day he arrived to receive his new car, some months after the original order, the defendant reappraised the value of the plaintiff's used car by such a markedly reduced amount as to establish, under all the circumstances, that the reappraisal was not done in good faith. . . .

The central question here is the correct construction of that paragraph of defendant's form order sheet (undoubtedly in general use in the industry) that reserves to the dealer the right to reappraise the used car allowance at the time of actual delivery of the new car—with a correlative right in the purchaser to cancel if the new value is below the original one. . . .

I find as a fact that defendant's employee did state to plaintiff that he had reappraised plaintiff's car in the amount of $50—as testified by plaintiff—and that this valuation was not made in good faith.

The critical legal question thus becomes whether the provision of the form order, under which defendant reserved the right to reappraise the used car allowance at the time of delivery where delivery is deferred, implies that the right of reappraisal is to be exercised in good faith. I conclude as a matter of law that good faith is an essential implied condition for the exercise of the right of reappraisal. . . .

In reaching the above conclusion, I do not wish to be understood as doubting the legitimate considerations prompting the provision in question when the delivery of the car is to be deferred. Obviously, the buyer's car may suffer some deterioration during the intervening period. Arguably, although less clearly, no significant purpose would be served by driving the car at the time of original valuation, since the car must be tested again on the date of delivery.

But the fact that the clause represents a reasonable response to a practical problem does not obscure the reality that it is open to, and indeed lends itself to, serious and recurrent abuse. In the presence of a potential buyer, searching for the optimum price for his used car, a dealer may well be disposed to place a generous value on the used car, realizing that he could later renegotiate the figure when his bargaining position was immensely strengthened.

For it is surely clear that when a buyer has signed an order for a particular car of a certain color and with special accessories, has made a cash down payment, has secured a bank loan, and has arrived in his somewhat worn old car ready to receive a resplendent new vehicle, his ability to resist a new less favorable deal is at very low ebb indeed.

Surely, it is no surprise that the defendant's witness acknowledged that used car allowances are often lowered at the delivery date. And although no testimony was presented directly, it is surely a fair surmise that instances in which used cars are found to have a higher value at the delivery date would represent extraordinary phenomena in the annals of any car dealer.

In evaluating the appropriate remedy for the kind of breach presented, I have considered that the arrangement of circumstances in this very common situation presents car dealers with a powerful inducement to place high values on used cars when attempting to land the order and low values when the physical presence of the new car after an intervening period has substantially reduced the purchasers' resistance. Car dealers should be encouraged to withstand this temptation. . . .

The plaintiff, like any purchaser under the circumstances, was entitled to good faith valuation of his car on the delivery date.

In the absence of any good faith reappraisal by the defendant, the only valuation by the defendant is that fixed at the time of the original order, and I find that to be controlling.

Accordingly, I find for the plaintiff.

Misrepresentation on Résumés

The phenomenon of misrepresenting factual information on résumés provides a useful reference point for pulling together the legal and ethical dimensions of deception. There have been many reported instances of résumé fraud, and it has been estimated that as many as 80 percent of all résumés contain some misleading information. Common misrepresentations include overstating salary or responsibilities in prior jobs or misstating educational credentials.

It is not uncommon for an individual to come into the public eye because of some dishonest act and a later check then reveals that the person's résumé contains false information. David Begelman, who set up schemes at Columbia Pictures to bilk actors out of money, Janet Cook, who made up sources for a *Washington Post* story, and Ivan Boesky, the notorious inside trader, were all discovered to have used falsified résumés. In December 1984 twenty-eight students at the University of Southern California Law Center were charged with listing false class standings on their résumés. Providing false information on an application for a license to practice law may result in denial of admission to the bar. Recently, sanctions were imposed upon a lawyer who falsified class standing on an application for employment with a law firm.

Nevertheless, the legal system has very limited capacity to deal with the use of false résumés. When facts are misrepresented, for example, a false degree, it clearly constitutes fraud, and the employer who relied upon the information could use that as grounds for setting aside the employment contract. On the other hand, it would be difficult to obtain damages based upon tort or contract. It seems clear that society would not be willing to impose criminal liability for an offense of this character. Civil sanctions are hard to prove and are dependent upon a private party suing for the misuse of a résumé. The probabilities of a legal sanction being imposed are so low that it should be clear that the law will not be able to discourage effectively résumé misuse. Instead, individual responsibility based upon acceptance of ethical standards is the key.

Are there any circumstances in which misrepresentations on résumés can be considered acceptable? Justifications that could be offered include (1) lack of reliance on the part of those who receive the résumés, (2) a competitive disadvantage from not playing the generally accepted game of overstating information on résumés, and (3) countering improper discrimination in the hiring process. Upon close consideration none of these justifications is satisfying. There is strong reason for believing that enough businesses do place significant emphasis on information contained in résumés so that the chances are high that someone in fact will rely upon them. In a *WSJ-G* survey a majority of middle-level executives indicated that they would not hire someone who had overstated salary by $10,000 on their résumé. Yet surprisingly, a majority of the general public indicated that they would not

hold the misrepresentation against the applicant.[6]

The competitive disadvantage argument can be turned around to condemn résumé fraud. If most people misrepresent themselves in their résumés (the 80% figure is probably a significant overstatement of the percentage who engage in major résumé fraud, e.g., bogus degrees, falsified prior jobs, etc.), then no employer will be able to trust a résumé and résumés will become meaningless in the employment process. Or, in order to preserve the value of résumés, businesses will have to incur significant costs in double-checking the information contained on the résumés that they receive. Either way, costs rise and innocent people are harmed.

The strongest justification would appear to be using false information as a counterpoint to anticipated improper discrimination. However, unless the résumé is drafted specifically for a known discriminator, the résumé will be used generally and will affect all potential employers. Further, if there is illegal discrimination, then the most effective response would be to assert an appropriate legal remedy.

Résumé fraud is dishonest and breaches the principle of good faith.

Bribery

Bribery appears endemic in our modern world. Scanning the *Wall Street Journal* or major newspapers for articles describing incidents of bribing will produce several major stories every week. Most people are familiar with major incidents such as the payment by United Brands of millions of dollars to the president of Hondurus to eliminate an unfavorable export tax on bananas, or payments by Lockheed to the prime minister of Japan.

As widely as bribery is practiced, it is also condemned. Defenses of bribery as moral are infrequent. Those who bribe do so secretly. Few people brag publicly about successful bribes and even fewer about having been the recipient of large bribes. Yet, there are many ambiguities that must be dealt with in evaluating the ethical nature of a bribe. Consider the following situations:

1. A wealthy patron gives $20 to the maître d' of an exclusive restaurant in order to get preferred seating.
2. You tip a waitress 15 percent (or 25 percent) of the check in a restaurant where you eat once a week.
3. A banker pays $10,000 to a state legislator for a twenty-minute speech to bank employees with the expectation that the legislator will meet personally with the banker on occasion and generally support the positions of the banking industry.
4. The legislator accepts the payment and assumes that there are no strings attached, that the banker is just trying to insure general "good will," and that $10,000 is a reasonable payment for the speech. The legislator plans to consider the interests of all of his or her constituents in deciding how to vote on legislation and assumes this is understood by the banker.
5. A cola manufacturer pays $10,000 to a state government official to get a license to do business in that state. The license should be granted under state law, but the government official requires the payments in order to supplement his own income.
6. A cola manufacturer pays $10,000 to a state official in return for a promise that a competitor will be denied a license to do business in that state.
7. A salesperson gives a Christmas present of a $50 bottle of single malt Scotch to the purchasing agent of a potential buyer.
8. A salesperson gives a Christmas present of a $15,000 sports car to the purchasing agent of a potential buyer.

Numerous questions are raised by these examples. How relevant is intent? It is often stated that it takes two to have a bribe. Must both the payor and the payee be thinking "bribe" in order to consider the transaction to be one? Or, a closely related question, do certain words of expectancy have to be used in order to call an arrangement a bribe? Does it make any difference if the payor avoids stating any specific quid pro quo or if the payee avoids consenting to any requested quid pro quo? Does the status of the payee make a difference? Examples 7 and 8 involve commercial bribes rather than payments to public officials. Should commercial payments be seen as part of the market system, or are they bribes just as much as payments to public officials?

BRIBERY—ETHICAL ANALYSIS

Using as a reference the legal treatment of bribes (see Chapter 3), we can define a bribe as follows. A *bribe* is a payment or offering of something of value to another, in return for a promised or actual breach of an obligation owed to the general public or to another individual. Thus, the essence of a bribe is a conflict of interest—a payment for breaching a duty to another. This definition does not distinguish between public and commercial bribes. It includes commercial bribes because they may involve the breach of a duty that the recipient owes to an employer, partner, or business associate. A bribe need not necessarily involve the use of "magic words" or require a detailed statement of the quid pro quo required. An implied understanding of what is expected is enough. Generally, one can assume that large sums are not given in a context where current or future business dealings are involved without some expectancy of a return. Further, one can generally assume that large sums are not paid merely to ensure the normal performance of one's duty.

Trivial sums may be given as a result of custom and may not involve an expected quid pro quo (except at an equally trivial level). The relative value of the payment, its nature (concealed, purely personal to the payee, etc.), and the relative roles of the payor and payee are all important in determining whether a morally condemnable bribe has taken place.

Why condemn bribes? There are three major arguments to consider. The first is that they involve, by definition, a breach of trust or duty. There are two basic ways by which a bribe may originate—one is that the payor offers the payment to the payee for a quid pro quo; the other is that the payee solicits the payment from the payor as a form of selling his or her office or position.

The problem when the payor initiates the transaction is relatively straightforward. Assuming that the payor is acting efficiently and is paying for an outcome that would not otherwise occur, it is clear that the payee is breaching a duty to the public or to another individual. The payor is morally culpable because the payor's purpose is to induce the breach of duty.

Moral culpability is even more obvious when the payee initiates (extorts) the payment. The payee is selling his or her position or office and by requesting the payment is implying that the outcome would be otherwise if the payment is not made. By initiating the transaction, the payee is proposing a blatant breach of duty or trust.

What about the payor in a case of extortion? Is the payor excused from moral culpability because the payment is forced upon him or her by the payee? On a number of occasions businesspeople have found themselves in the awkward position of having to make a payment in order to get a vitally needed license or inspection certificate. The payment is made and then several years later there is disclosure that the particular public official had taken bribes. An investigation ensues to determine who has paid bribes to the official and at that time the businessperson's payments are discovered. The businessperson's defense is that the payments were extorted and that there

was really no choice. That argument will not constitute a legal defense if a criminal case is filed, but it will often cause the prosecutor to use discretion and decide not to prosecute. The question may reasonably be asked, If the businessperson thought that extortion was occurring, why wasn't it reported to the appropriate authorities at the time? In some unfortunate communities the answer may well be that the local law enforcement officials were part of the bribery scheme.

The second argument against bribery is that it often is a form of theft in that the payee is selling assets or resources that are not his or hers to sell. The benefit of the bribe goes to the payee who in turn directs either public or corporate assets toward the payor. Consider a typical case involving a purchasing agent. The agent in the normal performance of his or her duties would buy supplies from ABC corporation at a price of $70,000. Instead, the agent accepts a cash bribe of $5,000 from a representative of XYZ and causes his firm to buy the identical supplies from XYZ for $80,000. The agent has effectively stolen $10,000 from his company and has directly benefited in the amount of $5,000. In many circumstances involving a bribe, both the payor and the payee may be seen as stealing the object of value that is transferred to the payor (the $80,000 contract).

The final argument against bribery is that it is unfair. When a bribe is paid to a public official, that official is induced to act contrary to a politically established public policy establishing how goods and rights are to be distributed. When the payee acts contrary to that mandate, the public interest is harmed. Similarly, in a commercial bribe, the more efficient supplier is defeated, not on the merits, but because of the payment of a bribe. This outcome is both inefficient and unfair.

Justifications for Bribes. Various justifications may be offered by the parties to a bribe.

We have already discussed one common payor defense, that the bribe was extorted by the payee. Other justifications include (1) the bribe is efficient in that it overcomes irrational regulation or corruption, (2) the bribe is necessary to the survival of the firm in a competitive environment, and (3) the action is really innocent because it is impossible to determine what constitutes a bribe as distinguished from a gift.

The efficiency justification has civil disobedience overtones. Corrupt or inefficient government regulation (or corporate rules) must be overcome by a payment to a representative of the obstructionist organization. There are several defects in this argument. First, the bribery serves to foster the corruption or inefficiency, and it will not by itself correct the alleged evils. Second, civil disobedience requires a public stand to bring attention to unfair or inefficient rules. Covert bribery does not encourage public pressure or awareness and serves only to benefit the payor and/or payee. The efficiency argument is of little help in absolving the payee. If the payee recognizes impropriety and has the power to override it, the payee should not require payment in order to exercise his or her authority.

The necessity argument has been extended to the conclusion that bribes "are an essential feature of the free enterprise system and as such should be of no concern to regulatory systems."[7] The argument has often been advanced in criticism of the Foreign Corrupt Practices Act. American managers have alleged that they are at a competitive disadvantage in competing with foreign firms because of limits on their ability to bribe ascribed to the Foreign Corrupt Practices Act.

Remember, however, that our definition of a bribe involves a payment personally benefiting the payee which requires a breach of duty on the part of the payee. The efficiency of such a system is highly questionable. In contrast to the statement that the marketplace requires bribes is the following quote from a committee report on the Foreign Corrupt Practices Act, concluding that bribery ". . . short-circuits the marketplace by limiting business to those companies too inefficient to compete in terms of price, quality or service or too lazy to engage in honest salesmanship, or too intent upon unloading marginal products."[8]

The final argument justifies bribery because of the sheer uncertainty of what constitutes an illegal or immoral bribe. This "claimed uncertainty" argument is used by miscreants in many areas including the antitrust and securities laws. The accused professes that he or she didn't understand the issues and concludes that proper lines are impossible to draw. In more refined terms, the argument is that bribes are difficult to distinguish from real gifts, and that reciprocity or quid pro quo is a basic and proper component of human relationships. Reciprocity is valued in personal relationships and is a required element of an enforceable contract (the doctrine of consideration). Therefore, one should be cautious about condemning it, even in the case of a seeming bribe. The main flaw in this argument is that it fails to consider the breach of duty that is an essential part of a bribe. The reciprocity is not of something possessed by the payee personally, but instead, is of property or rights of someone else, to whom the payee owes a duty. The reciprocity is therefore not a true exchange and is not analogous to contract.

Although there are some hard "gray-area" cases in which bribes are hard to distinguish, this is also true of most other ethical issues. The ultimate question is whether or not there is a principled basis upon which to distinguish bribes. There is, and most cases will be relatively clear-cut. In the examples given at the beginning of this chapter, there should be little question that situations 3, 4, 5, 6, and 8 (p. 119) involved bribes.

REVIEW QUESTIONS*

1. Describe the difference between an egoistic and an utilitarian analysis. Explain how each might lead to the same result when employed by a drug company trying to decide whether to pull a tainted prescription drug off the market.
2. Describe the difference between a rule utilitarian and a deontological approach to business ethics. Explain how a principle of honoring confidentiality can be justified under each approach.
3. What is meant by the term "business ethics"?
4. There will be many instances in which any list of principles of business ethics will come into conflict so that it is impossible simultaneously to comply with two or more of the principles. When that happens, which of the principles are likely to be more important?
5. You are hiring a new manager for your department. You have several good applicants. Assume that the one that is most suited for the job in training and experience has also been found to have done one of the things listed here. How would that affect your decision whether to hire the individual?
   (a) The individual listed on his résumé that he had an MBA from Rutgers. In fact, he does not have an MBA.
   (b) The individual listed that his prior salary was $40,000. In fact, the prior salary was $32,000.
   (c) The individual had put in false claims on expense account forms on several occasions.
   (d) The individual had been convicted of embezzlement and put on probation.
   (e) The individual had gone to a reporter about misdealings at his prior firm. The

ensuing controversy had attracted considerable publicity and resulted in lawsuits being filed against the firm. The employee had been fired because of the whistle-blowing.

6. You have been asked to give an evaluation on an employee who is at your level and with whom you have worked. You only know the employee through work. How likely would you be to reveal the following information about the employee? Assume that there is no question at all about the truth of what you would say.
   (a) That the employee is racist.
   (b) That the employee has admitted to you about cheating on tax returns.
   (c) That the employee has admitted to you about making personal long-distance calls on company lines.
   (d) That the employee has admitted to you about double billing on expense account charges.
   (e) That the employee has admitted to you about stealing company property.
   Would it make any difference whether the party asking for your assessment was (1) your boss, (2) another supervisor in the same firm, or (3) a manager from another firm?
7. You are a purchasing manager for Alpha Corporation. You are responsible for buying two $1 million generators. Your company has a written policy prohibiting any company buyer from receiving a gratuity in excess of $50 and requiring that all gratuities be reported. The company has no policy regarding whistle-blowing. A salesperson for a generator manufacturer offers to arrange it so that you can buy a $12,000 car for $4,000. The car would be bought from a third party. You decline the offer.
   Do you now report it to your superior? To the salesperson's superior?

*Because of the nature of this chapter, different types of review questions are used.

8. You are the chief executive for River City Engineering (RCE) and on its behalf you are preparing a bid for a U.S. government contract. If you fail to secure it, you will have to close your operation and ninety employees will be out of work. The welfare rolls of Near Lost, Michigan, will more than double and many small enterprises will be forced to close. RCE is the town's leading employer and taxpayer.

Your principal competitor is Multilarge Engineering International (MEI), a company that is reported to have good political connections and is best situated to take the contract. If you can underbid its price, you can probably get the contract.

Your chief assistant proposes to discover in advance the terms of MEI's secret bid. His assistant, Bill, proposed to marry Sue, the assistant to MEI's chief executive officer's executive secretary, whom she hates. Sue would be delighted to help Bill get a promotion. She will be typing the proposal, or part of it, and is secretly planning to leave MEI anyway. She is trustworthy (Bill says) and no one would ever know. All that is needed is your okay today. The bids will be submitted in two days.

What is your reply?

9. An elderly lady who now lives in a nursing home hires you to sell her old house for her. She suggests she would take $40,000 for it. She owned the house for forty years but has not seen it for several years. She is unaware that it is now located by a new shopping center near a new expressway where similar properties have been selling for $75,000.

Assume you are a friend of the owner but are not a realtor. You know she trusts you a great deal. You also know of several possible buyers, one of whom is a close friend of yours. What would you do?

Suppose you wanted to buy the house as an investment for your church/fraternity/

social club. Would you? How much would you pay?

Suppose you face the situation described here not as a friend but as a realtor employed by the lady. Would your answers be different? What if you weren't assisting her but were a buyer who was recently transferred to the city looking for residential property. Would you take advantage of the lady's ignorance? Is this a question of law or ethics?

10. You are a lab technician for the Standard Ethical Drug Company. You run tests on animals and prepare a summary that is then doctored by your superior to make a drug appear safe when in fact it is not. Your superior determines your salary and has a significant influence on whether you retain the job. You are the sole source of support of your two children, have no close relatives to help you, and are just making it financially. Jobs equivalent to the one that you now hold are very difficult to come by. You are convinced that if the company markets the drug, the risk of cancer to the drug users will increase significantly. The drug provides significant relief for hemorrhoids.

What would you do?

11. Smith hires you to prepare his federal and state tax returns. When you have nearly completed the job, he tells you he sold a share of a business interest to a partner, incurring a capital gain of $50,000. He asks you how he can avoid or minimize the tax. After you review the law and facts you report it is not possible. He owes the tax. He tells you, "Okay, just don't report it then; they have no way of ever finding out about it."

Do you follow his instructions and sign the form as the tax preparer? If you refuse, you know you probably will not get paid and will not get any of Smith's business in the future.

Suppose you are the partner who

bought the interest. Smith asks you to keep the transaction a secret until next year so he will not have to pay the tax until then, when his rates will be lower. Do you agree?

12. Your company sells only in the state of New Wyoming. State law allows you to market your cola in "giant quarts." A quart is a standard measure, so a giant quart is the same size as an ordinary quart. A survey conducted by your firm indicates that 40 percent of cola buyers think that a giant quart is larger than a regular quart. Do you call your bottle a giant quart?

FOOTNOTES

[1] Joseph Des Jardins, "Virtues and Corporate Responsibility." In *Corporate Governance and Institutionalizing Ethics,* W. Michael Hoffman, Jennifer Mills Moore, and David A. Fedo, eds. (Lexington MA, Lexington Books, 1983), p. 139.

[2] David J. Fritzsche and Helmut Becker, "Linking Management Behavior to Ethical Philosophy— An Empirical Investigation," 27:1 *Academy of Management Journal,* 166 (1984).

[3] Richard Hollinger and John P. Clark, *Theft by Employees* (Lexington, MA: Lexington Books, 1983).

[4] Steven N. Brenner and Earl A. Molander, "Is the Ethics of Business Changing?" *Harvard Business Review* (January–February 1977).

[5] See A. Carr, "Is Business Bluffing Ethical?" 64:1 *Harvard Business Review,* 143 (1968).

[6] R. Ricklets, "Ethics in America." A four-part series in the *Wall Street Journal,* October 31–November 3, 1983.

[7] John Danley, "Toward a Theory of Bribery," 2:3 *Business and Professional Ethics Journal,* 19 (1983).

[8] Quoted in Danley, ibid., p. 33.

Social Responsibility of Business

Most major business firms at one time or another have been accused of unethical practices or have been charged with criminal offenses. The media are full of stories of controversial and irresponsible actions by corporations. Chemical plants leak toxic gases, defense contractors put in false claims or produce faulty parts, major banks launder money, brokerage houses employ fraudulent practices in dealing with banks or their customers, investment banking firms abuse client confidences, firms incur debt in fighting off corporate raiders and then have to lay off employees, firms produce dangerous products that kill or maim their customers—the list seems endless. Critics of business seize upon incidents like these and argue that business firms are irresponsible by their very nature.

This chapter summarizes the current diversity of viewpoints concerning the proper extent of business responsibility. The core question is whether business can fairly be expected to do more than just seek to maximize profits. If the answer is found to be that there are greater expectations for business, then the next question becomes, How can those additional responsibilities be determined and implemented? This chapter summarizes strategies that a business can use to implement social responsiveness, and then, consistent with the theme of the text, describes how the legal system provides incentives for responsible behavior.

125

THE MODERN DEBATE CONCERNING CORPORATE SOCIAL RESPONSIBILITY

Some readers may be surprised to learn that there has been a long-standing debate concerning the nature and extent of the social responsibility of corporations. The debate evolves from the fact that corporations are established to operate primarily to further the interests of their owners. For publicly held corporations, the *owners* are the shareholders, who expect the corporation to earn profits. *Shareholders* buy stock because they expect to benefit from some combination of an increased share price and the payment of dividends. The long-term shareholder benefits directly only when management is successful in its duty to earn profits. The debate is whether corporations should go beyond that duty and consider the interests of other parties—often referred to as *stakeholders*.

Stakeholders are those people outside the firm who are directly affected by its actions. Stakeholders may include suppliers, distributors, creditors, neighbors, local or state governments, etc. There are many ways in which stakeholders can be affected by decisions made by a firm's managers. A decision to forgo installing a device that masks noxious odors in a plant's emissions can greatly affect the quality of life of neighbors living near the plant. The decision to lay off workers or close plants can affect the infrastructure in the local community, threatening the quality of schools, medical care, and other basic community services.

In many instances, shareholders and stakeholders will have directly competing interests, making it impossible for management to serve both interests simultaneously. Installing expensive emission control equipment that goes beyond what the law requires may use funds that otherwise could be distributed to shareholders in a dividend. Keeping an unprofitable plant in operation may benefit the community while having a negative impact on the long-run profitability of the firm.

THE LIMITED VIEW: PROFIT MAKING AS SOCIAL RESPONSIBILITY

The basic challenge to the idea of social responsibility has been closely identified with Milton Friedman, the well-known conservative economist and Nobel laureate. Some of his arguments against social responsibility follow:

- There is no such thing as *corporate* social responsibility because only individuals have responsibilities.
- In an economic system based upon private property, the corporate executive is employed by the owners (shareholders) to make as much money as possible while conforming to the basic rules in society, both those embodied in law and those embodied in ethical custom.
- The corporate executive acting as an agent for the stockholders should not make decisions about social responsibilities and social investment because those represent tax decisions, and the imposition of taxes and the expenditure of tax proceeds are governmental functions.
- The doctrine of social responsibility involves the acceptance of the socialist view that political mechanisms, not market mechanisms, are the appropriate way to determine the allocation of scarce resources to alternative uses.

Milton Friedman goes so far as to characterize the concept of social responsibility as "subversive doctrine." He sees it as inconsistent with the basic tenets of a capitalistic society. Friedman fears that even when managers use claims of being responsible as a subterfuge for maximizing profits, they unwittingly encourage an environment in which social responsibility will be forced upon firms by government fiat.

There is good reason to believe that many, but not all, shareholders would agree with Friedman. Suppose that Exxon is considering giving a donation of $10 million to your university. The money would come from operating revenues. If Exxon did not give the money to your university, it could be used for capital improvements, to pay off debt, to support employee raises, or to increase dividends. If Exxon were to poll its shareholders asking whether it should give the money or increase its dividend, how do you think the majority would respond? How would you respond if a company in which you held shares asked you whether you would like an extra $10 in dividends or, instead, would prefer that they give the money to a charity that you disfavor?

Shareholders invest in companies because they expect a financial return over time. They do not expect a business corporation to be primarily involved in social activities. If they wish to distribute their wealth to others, they will do so by giving directly to an organization such as the United Way. That way, they can choose the objects of their beneficence. It is reasonable to assume that most shareholders would have a different priority for charitable contributions than the company's managers.

There are two basic types of corporate socially responsive acts: (1) actions that are designed to avoid or lessen harm to others, such as spending for safety or pollution control, and (2) actions that are designed to bring about additional social benefits, such as charitable contributions or building community day-care centers. Actions in the second category are particularly likely to involve questions of legitimacy. For example, what gives executives the right to prefer one charity over another in dispensing corporate assets? Managers of corporate philanthropic programs are often besieged by senior executives on behalf of the latters' favorite charities. Is it appropriate for a CEO (chief executive officer) to make sure that her company gives large sums of money to her alma mater and her favorite charity, particularly when, as a consequence of the gift, the CEO has a building named for her or receives a high-profile appointment to the board of the charity? It happens all the time. Many companies would defend the donation saying that it is for a worthy cause and that the recognition received by the CEO benefits the firm. Generally, the donation will be approved through standardized procedures which involve other managers in the decision process.

THE BROADER VIEW: CORPORATIONS HAVE PLURAL RESPONSIBILITIES

Many executives and commentators reject the singular purpose theory and advocate that firms engage in actions that go beyond maximizing profits. Although conceding that profits are the most important goal of a business firm, they also recognize a responsibility to respond to the critical needs of stakeholders and to play a broader role in society.

Defenders of the plural-mission concept see business as having a symbiotic relationship with its social environment. Business contributes to the material wealth of society. Business, in turn, requires a stable, structured, market-oriented environment based upon the protection of property and the rule of law. In order to insure a conducive environment in which to operate, business must respond to unmet social needs. Further, it is assumed that society desires and welcomes such responsiveness.

Professionalism

Many managers accept the concept of *professionalism* as further support for the plural concept. Professionals, such as doctors or lawyers, have well-established public service obligations. These are specified by professional bar associations or medical societies. Certainly business management is not a profession in the traditional sense of having educational requirements, licensing procedures, and enforced codes of ethical behavior. But senior managers are entrusted with the management of important resources that can affect society in dramatic ways. They are often individuals with substantial financial and technical acumen and may belong to organizations that set or endorse ethical standards, for example, the Public Affairs Council, the American Management Association, or the Business Roundtable. Although the standards or positions of these organizations may be informal, they may still have a significant effect on their members.

Corporations as Moral Agents

Another justification for plural responsibilities is based upon the claim that corporations have moral duties to give effect to the interests of stakeholders. Such claims are based upon an assumption that a corporation can be treated as a moral agent. If a corporation is a moral agent, then it is possible to point a finger of blame at the entity itself when the organization produces an immoral outcome. By investing Ford Motor Company with moral agency, one can hold the organization responsible for the defective design of the Pinto gas tanks.

But what does it mean to hold a corporation responsible for the actions of its employees? Is everyone who is associated with the corporation culpable? Such an expansive principle of guilt by association would certainly be awkward. It seems unfair to say that a maintenance employee in a business office in Los Angeles who never had any ability to influence design decisions at Ford is somehow morally accountable for the defective design. And what about an engineer who unsuccessfully protested the design but was overruled by his superiors?

Critics of the concept of *moral accountability* argue that a corporation, as a lifeless entity, cannot generate an immoral intention. A corporation can only act through human agents. It is those agents, and not the corporate entity, that should be considered responsible. Finally, the critics worry that if blame is fixed solely upon a legal entity, the human perpetrators may escape discovery and punishment. The corporate entity could thus become a shield protecting the real wrongdoers from judgment.

Advocates of the moral accountability of corporations, such as Peter French and Kenneth Goodpaster, counter that corporations are human collectives that are capable of actions attributable directly to the collective entity. Many corporations appear to have evolved policies that are the output of corporate processes which cannot be attributed to any particular individuals. This characteristic is consistent with the evolving concept of corporate culture, which posits that companies have discernible cultures resulting from company history, heroes, practices, and traditions. For example, collective attitudes regarding the treatment of minorities may become institutionalized in a firm. Senior managers desiring to change these attitudes may find the strong corporate culture nearly impossible to alter.

French would attribute to the corporate entity those actions resulting from the firm's formal policies and procedures. Thus, Ford as an entity would be held accountable for the Pinto because its design resulted from the standard processes and policies of Ford. The responsibility would attach to the entity and not to any particular Ford employees. Employees who are not involved in a direct role would not have individual responsibility. Those employees who were responsible for the design would be morally accountable on the basis of their personal actions.

The issue of *corporate moral accountability* has several ramifications in law. One is the question whether corporations can be charged with human-type crimes such as homicide or manslaughter, discussed later in this chapter. As a moral agent, a corporation is capable of the intent required to establish that a crime was committed. If not viewed as a moral agent, then the case for applying the criminal law to corporations is weakened.

The second context relates to the complex issue of *successor liability for corporations.* The problem can be demonstrated best by an example. Suppose that in 1970 Acme Space Heater produced a defective space heater that could cause fires when placed close to fabric furniture. The next year Acme changed the design of their heaters and corrected the problem. The Acme line of space heaters was quite profitable. In 1975, Conglomerate Corporation purchased the current line of space heaters from Acme by a contract that specified that Conglomerate would not assume any liability, and that Acme remained responsible for any claims. Acme tried to stay in business with some other products but failed and filed for bankruptcy in 1978. In 1980, Veronica was badly injured by one of the 1970 model heaters and sued Conglomerate Corporation. Conglomerate had made very substantial profits off the Acme line of space heaters since 1975.

Such an issue is a troublesome one for the courts. Contract law would support a conclusion that Conglomerate is not liable because of the limitation-of-liability clause in the sales contract. Nor has Conglomerate actively engaged in committing a wrong: it did not design the defective product. On the other hand, it might be possible to argue that Conglomerate should have been aware of the problems with the space heater and therefore should bear responsibility because it is profiting from the same line of products. Our moral sense might be particularly affected if it were revealed that the primary purpose of the transaction between Acme and Conglomerate was to limit potential liability by leaving behind a corporation with limited assets, which was unable to pay large claims. Ultimately, the resolution of this problem depends in part on how the corporate entity is viewed. If the entity is seen as morally accountable, then there is less justification for transferring liability to a successor corporation; when the first corporation ceases to exist, liability ends. Only Acme, the responsible entity, should be held accountable. If this situation is considered unjust to prospective plaintiffs, then state governments must find a way to set up contingency funds to deal with this common situation. The *Hamaker* case that follows provides insights into how courts handle this difficult problem.

Hamaker v. Kenwel-Jackson Machine, Inc.

Supreme Court of South Dakota

387 N.W.2d 515 (1986)

Background: Carolyn Hamaker (plaintiff) sued Kenwel-Jackson Machine, Inc. (defendant) for injuries allegedly resulting from an unreasonably dangerous notching machine.

The Kenwel Machine Company was a manufacturer of notching machines that were used to make notches in lumber stackers. The company secured a patent for model 3072, which they made for a number of years and then developed improvements, resulting in later models 3072A, 3072B, and 3072C, also patented. Kenwel sold its assets to the Jacksons for $140,000 on December 31, 1975. The agreement placed the responsibility for all liabilities on the seller. Sometime afterward, the Kenwel Machine Company was disbanded. The Jacksons formed a new company, Kenwel-Jackson Machine, Inc., which manufactured and sold notching machines. In March 1981, Carolyn Hamaker severed four fingers while using a 3072 notching machine. She sued the Kenwel-Jackson corporation, claiming that it was strictly liable for her injuries. The trial court granted summary judgment for the defendant. Decision: The Supreme Court affirmed the judgment for the defendant.

SABERS, Justice

. . .

On March 6, 1981, appellant Carolyn M. Hamaker (Hamaker) sustained injuries while operating a notcher machine incident to her employment at Dakota Pallets and Wood Products, Inc., in Alcester, South Dakota. She caught her left hand in the notcher blade and severed the second, third, fourth, and fifth fingers. She sought damages from the appellee, Kenwel-Jackson Machine, Inc. (Kenwel-Jackson), alleging various grounds of product liability including strict liability in tort, negligence, and breach of express and implied warranties.

The machine, a model 3072 notcher, was manufactured by appellee's predecessor, Kenwel Machine Company, Inc. (Kenwel).

. . .

On December 31, 1975, Kenwel sold its assets to John S. and Rosemary H. Jackson, husband and wife, for the cash sum of $140,000.00. Thereafter, Kenwel ceased business operations, and its corporate existence was terminated eighteen months later in August of 1977.

Pursuant to the purchase agreement executed between Kenwel and the Jacksons on January 30, 1976, the Jacksons bought the following assets: machinery, equipment, hand tools, furniture, fixtures, leasehold improvements, patent rights, accounts receivable, inventory, and goodwill. They did not purchase the patent for notcher model 3072. Nor did the Jacksons purchase any corporate stock from Kenwel. The purchase agreement contained the following provision:

> IV. CONDITIONS. This Offer To Purchase is expressly subject to, and conditional upon, the occurrence of each of the following conditions:
> 6. The agreement by the Seller to discharge or to provide for all liabilities of the Seller as of the date of closing, so that the Purchaser shall have no accounts payable, taxes due, or any other kind or type of current or long term liabilities incurred and unsatisfied as of the date of closing, except, however, commitments for materials ordered from suppliers.

Following the sale, the Jacksons formed the appellee corporation, Kenwel-Jackson, which began its corporate existence on February 2, 1976. No officer or director of Kenwel was ever an officer, director, stockholder, or employee of Kenwel-Jackson. Nor was there any transfer of top management personnel from the old to the new corporation. However, three craftsmen formerly employed by the predecessor corporation were retained by Kenwel-Jackson; one eventually became a vice president in charge of manufacturing.

Kenwel-Jackson was primarily interested in developing all types of board or lumber stackers. It cultivated different customers than its predecessor by marketing lumber stackers for the building component industry. Although Kenwel-Jackson continued to manufacture the model 3072A notching machine as well as its successors, models 3072B and 3072C, respectively, Kenwel-Jackson never participated in the design, manufacture, or sale of the model 3072 notcher which allegedly caused Hamaker's injuries. Kenwel-Jackson remained active in the manufacturing business until September of 1984.

ISSUE

The issue is whether Kenwel-Jackson, as the successor corporation, can be held liable for Hamaker's injuries under "continuity of enterprise" or "merger" theories, or under the "product line" theory of strict tort liability.

. . .

. . . The general rule is that a corporation which purchases the assets of another corporation does not succeed to the liabilities of the selling corporation. . . . There are, however, four exceptions to the general rule under which liability may be imposed on a purchasing corporation. They are:

(1) when the purchasing corporation expressly or impliedly agrees to assume the selling corporation's liability;
(2) when the transaction amounts to a consolidation or merger of the purchaser and seller corporations;
(3) when the purchaser corporation is merely a continuation of the seller corporation; or
(4) when the transaction is entered into fraudulently to escape liability for such obligations.

. . .

There is no language in the contract between these parties to suggest that Kenwel-Jackson impliedly assumed responsibility for future products liability actions against Kenwel. . . .

Hamaker asserts that the transaction between Kenwel-Jackson and its predecessor amounted to a "merger" of the two corporations, or that Kenwel-Jackson is a "mere continuation" of Kenwel; i.e., exceptions (2) and (3) to the general rule above. However, a merger involves the actual absorption of one corporation into another, with the former losing its existence as a separate corporate entity. When the seller corporation retains its existence while parting with its assets, a "de facto merger" may be found if the consideration given by the purchaser corporation is shares of its own stock. . . . No stock in Kenwel-Jackson was transferred as consideration for Kenwel's assets. . . .

The key element of a "continuation" is a commonality of the officers, directors, and stockholders in the predecessor and successor corporations. The top management personnel of Kenwel was not carried over to Kenwel-Jackson. Nor did any shareholder of either corporation become an owner, shareholder, director, officer, or employee of the other.

In *Turner v. Bituminous Casualty Co.* (1976), the Michigan Supreme Court deviated from the traditional requirement for a de facto merger by refusing to recognize a distinction between the purchase of assets with cash and the purchase of assets with the stock of the purchasing corporation. In *Turner,* the court held that cash consideration was sufficient to establish a prima facie case of continuation of a successor corporation's responsibility for products liability if:

(1) There was basic continuity of the enterprise of the seller corporation, including, apparently, a retention of key personnel, assets, general business operations, and the corporate name.

(2) The seller corporation ceased ordinary business operations, liquidated, and dissolved soon after distribution of consideration received from the buying corporation.

(3) The purchasing corporation assumed those liabilities and obligations of the seller ordinarily necessary for the continuation of the normal business operations of the seller corporation.

(4) The purchasing corporation held itself out to the world as the effective continuation of the seller corporation.

Many of the factors relied upon in *Turner* exist here.

The transfer included most of the assets, the business "good will," pending orders for the replacement model 3072A notching machine and the name "Kenwel" or any derivative thereof.

The name was changed simply from Kenwel Machine Company, Inc. to Kenwel-Jackson Machine, Inc. The name "Kenwel" was used because the name was known as a machinery manufacturer.

Kenwel-Jackson Machine, Inc., used the same business premises and the same tools and equipment to manufacture the same products as Kenwel Machine Company, Inc.

Kenwel-Jackson started with a work force of only three individuals, all three were previously employed as craftsmen by Kenwel. One later became vice-president in charge of manufacturing of Kenwel-Jackson and stayed in the employ of Kenwel-Jackson until operations ceased in 1984.

However, we are not persuaded to follow *Turner* in this case where none of the owners, officers or stockholders were the same, where Kenwel-Jackson expressly contracted not to assume any of Kenwel's liabilities, where Kenwel-Jackson's business developed in a different direction relative to product line and customers and especially where the notcher in question was neither designed, manufactured nor sold by the successor corporation. We find, therefore, that Kenwel-Jackson's cash purchase of Kenwel's assets does not fall within the "merger" or "continuation" exceptions to the general rule.

The fact that Hamaker's accident occurred some six years after the sale disposes of any suggestion that Kenwel-Jackson and its predecessor entered into the transaction fraudulently to escape liability. Accordingly, we hold that Kenwel-Jackson is not liable for Hamaker's injuries under any of the exceptions to the general rule in relation to successor corporate purchasers.

PRODUCT LINE LIABILITY

The general rule of corporate nonliability was developed to protect a bona fide purchaser from the unassumed debt liability of its predecessor.

However, the traditional approach has recently been attacked by a minority of jurisdictions within the context of products liability actions.

Advocates of the minority view justify the abandonment of traditional corporate analysis based on its unresponsiveness to the products liability plaintiff who seeks to place the risk of defective products on the marketing enterprise which manufactured and sold them.

Hamaker argues that Kenwel-Jackson is liable for her injuries under the "product line" theory which was created by the California Supreme Court in *Ray v. Alad Corp.* (1977), and is applicable only to tort liability for a defective product.

. . . Failing to find a basis for liability under the traditional exceptions referenced above, the court relied on public policy considerations to impose strict tort liability upon Alad, "to insure that the costs of injuries . . . are borne by the manufacturers that put such products on the market rather than the injured persons who are powerless to protect themselves." . . .

. . .

Here, Kenwel-Jackson did not acquire the patent for the model 3072 notcher when it purchased the assets of Kenwel. Moreover, Kenwel-Jackson never participated in the design, manufacture, distribution, or chain of sale of the model 3072 notcher. It is true that Kenwel-Jackson continued to manufacture the model 3072A, and subsequently, models 3072B and 3072C until the cessation of its business in 1984. However, Kenwel had already modified the model 3072 notcher by several design changes which resulted in the model 3072A, whose patent was sold to Kenwel-Jackson. Therefore, we find under the facts of this case that Kenwel-Jackson neither invited use of its predecessor's model 3072 notcher, nor represented to the public at large, and Hamaker in particular, that the notcher was safe and suitable for use.

. . .

Therefore, we hold that Kenwel-Jackson is not liable for Hamaker's injuries under any of the exceptions to the general rule of successor corporate nonliability, nor under the "product line" theory applicable to strict liability in tort. Accordingly, summary judgment is affirmed.

A corporation, considered morally accountable, becomes a candidate for reform whenever it engages in immoral actions. Reform might be achieved by changing managers, adopting new policies, formalizing ethics through company codes, or changing the composition of the board of directors. For example, E. F. Hutton pled guilty in 1985 to over 2,000 counts of mail and wire fraud based upon manipulations of financial accounts in banks that resulted in Hutton collecting interest or gaining credit on phantom money. In response, an outside study was conducted that led to changes in the board of directors and in Hutton's internal management system. By bringing outside directors into a majority position on the board and changing its internal management of financial responsibility, Hutton hoped to insure that it would never again engage in similar practices. Ultimately, Hutton underwent the most dramatic type of transformation; it was acquired by the much larger firm of Shearson Lehman Bros. There was considerable speculation at the time that one reason for the merger was that Hutton had never fully recovered from the loss of reputation associated with its various scandals.

Corporate reputations can change significantly over time, indicating public acceptance of the concept of reform. In the 1970s, Ford was plagued with a negative reputation for safety and quality problems; by the mid-1980s the Ford management had dramatically turned around the public perception of the firm.

Society's Expectations

Proponents of the limited view of profit making as social responsibility suggest that government should not expect corporations to do more than obey the law and maximize profits. That view has not been followed in practice. The probusiness Reagan administration of the 1980s explicitly called on business to increase charitable contributions and to engage in social activities under a rubric of "voluntarism." The courts have rejected shareholder suits challenging corporate contributions to charities and educational institutions, and the federal tax law allows corporations to deduct such disbursements within generous limits.

The argument that managers should only respond to the desires of the owner/shareholders is also not supported by current interpretations of corporate law. The actual, legally enforceable ownership rights given to shareholders are quite limited. Shareholders have only limited rights to corporate information and have no specific rights to any corporate buildings, equipment, or products. They do not have a right to demand that management listen to their preferences: they can only act through formal processes such as shareholder

resolutions. In fact, management often opposes shareholder proposals by which shareholder groups seek to change bylaws or otherwise make their views known. Shareholders are investors, not property owners. As investors they have a right to expect that corporate management will give primacy to their interest in financial returns. But they cannot expect that a corporation will forgo all activities that cannot demonstrably be shown to increase investor wealth. Of course, unhappy shareholders can sell their stock, and they can sue whenever management has breached its fiduciary duties to them, for example, using corporate assets for the managers' own benefit.

Ethics as Good Business

Managers often defend social responsibility as good business in the long run. They see it generally enhancing goodwill and the firm's reputation, and even may identify socially responsible actions that they believe directly benefit the firm. For example, by contributing to local education or artistic programs, a firm may help insure a better quality of life in the community which will aid them in recruiting or retaining employees and make employees happier and more productive. Although the firm's managers would be hard pressed to demonstrate empirically a real benefit to the firm, the argument seems valid on intuitive grounds. The social fabric of the society in which the firm operates must be maintained and that occurs only if the firm, in common with the other members of society, satisfies its obligation to contribute to strong social institutions.

A related argument is that by acting responsibly, the firm forestalls government regulation that would probably be less efficient than private action. This argument is based upon an assumption that private firms can perform certain social activities more efficiently than government agencies. For example, a private firm might be able to provide a day-care center that is open to the entire community and would operate with lower costs than one established by the public sector. The lower costs could be due to the fact that the firm is responding to a competitive environment, is forced to control costs, and has superior management. If the center is operated at a loss, the firm is sustaining the operation as a contribution to society from its operating revenues.

In the safety area, failure by firms to take adequate precautions may result in substantial public demand for direct regulation, or for prohibitions on the sale or advertising of certain products. Although the government can promulgate standards and set up procedures that firms must follow in new product development, there is invariably an information lag that handicaps such regulation. Often significant costs are associated with such government intervention. Progressive, responsible management can reduce the need for direct regulation by giving safety aspects considerable priority.

EVALUATION OF THE DEBATE

There are several peculiarities about the debate over the scope and nature of corporate responsibility. For one thing, it is apolitical in the sense that political Conservatives and Liberals may be found uncomfortably together supporting the same side in a particular debate. Ethics is not a particular political perspective; it is not the case that "ethics is only for Democrats" (or Republicans). Some Conservatives support private social action as a means of forestalling public action, whereas some Liberals think that corporations should stay away from a social agenda because they lack true legitimacy and will only push Conservative viewpoints.

Secondly, the debate is one-sided in that few practicing managers advocate the narrow view. Instead, most managers practice the plural concept by undertaking a wide range of socially responsive actions. For example, in 1985, corporate philanthropic contributions totaled nearly $4.4 billion. The contrary position is argued formally by only a few academics. However, much of the literature in finance and economics is based upon assumptions that firms act solely to maximize shareholder wealth.

Few firms eschew all forms of socially responsible behavior. When asked to justify socially responsive actions, managers give many explanations. The list would include all of the arguments discussed in this chapter, plus more personal responses based upon religious beliefs or individual conscience.

IMPLEMENTING SOCIAL RESPONSIBILITY

Although there are numerous supporters of the idea that business firms must be socially responsible, there is no universally agreed upon method for deciding exactly what firms should do. Managers constantly confront difficult questions in directing a firm's social agenda. Should a firm make charitable contributions in a year in which it is laying off employees or closing plants? Should a firm spend more on the safety of its products or give money to feed the homeless or sponsor medical research?

Methods of Implementation

Table 5-1 summarizes the major ways by which corporations attempt to incorporate ethical values into their cultures.

Although the use of formal codes dominates the methods used, employee training in ethics is rapidly becoming more common as firms search for ways to make ethics real for their employees. Approaches vary. Some firms have a few sessions on ethics in the general programs required for entering managerial and professional employees. Others have devel-

TABLE 5-1 IMPLEMENTING ETHICS

Ethics Strategy	Percent of Major Corporations
Codes of ethics	93.3
Employee training	44.4
Social auditing and reporting	43.9
Changes in corporate structure	20.6
Ethics committee	17.9

Source: Based upon a 1985 survey by the Center for Business Ethics reported in W. Michael Hoffman, "Developing the Ethical Corporation," 3 *Bell Atlantic Quarterly,* 31 (Summer 1986). Reprinted by permission of *Bell Atlantic Quarterly.*

oped games or problems based upon the firm's experience. In a typical game, teams of new employees are presented with case problems that have been drafted by managers of the firm. The discussions are led by corporate personnel and tied into the company code of ethics. Some programs feature senior executives of the firm who address the employees and explain the firm's ethical values, stressing the importance of ethical behavior by everyone associated with the firm.

Ethics committees, comprised of board members or senior executives, generally have responsibility for overall policy statements. Common responsibilities include setting general policies such as limits on doing business in South Africa or drafting or modifying a code of ethics. Some firms have ombudsmen or judiciary committees that are actively involved in enforcing the provisions of the code. Such officers may also hear complaints concerning the violation of employee rights and be the first contact for a potential whistleblower.

Some major firms, General Motors, for example, issue an annual report of their social activities.[1] Although critics may view such reports as public relations puffery, they can have a very positive effect upon the operations of the firm. The very process of compiling and issuing the report will likely influence management practices. When a firm publicly reports its philanthropic ventures each year, it may be unlikely to cut back without sound reasons for doing so.

Codes of Ethics

Over 90 percent of the major companies responding to a survey conducted in 1985 by the Center for Business Ethics had implemented a formal code of ethics. The widespread adoption of codes is a relatively recent phenomenon. They are usually intended as a basic code of conduct for employees and provide guidance concerning how the employee should treat the firm (for example, treat proprietary information as confidential) and deal with the firm's stakeholders (for example, no giving or receiving of business-related gifts above a certain amount). Most firms have a regularized method by which employees are informed of the code. The most formal approach is to require an annual signed statement that the employee is familiar with the provisions of the code and intends to comply. Although they vary greatly in their formality, most codes are enforced. Sanctions employed include negative performance ratings, salary reductions, and, in extreme cases, termination.

During the 1980s, the major defense contractors faced recurring allegations that they made excessive or illegal charges against government contracts, used improper political influence, produced unsatisfactory products, and otherwise abused their relationship with the government. These problems were viewed with great concern because of their potential impact on the defense readiness of the U.S. military. As a response, many of the major defense contractors (for example, General Dynamics, General Electric) signed an initiative on business ethics (see Ethics Box opposite). Note the emphasis on individual responsibility in corporate codes of conduct.

ETHICS BOX
Defense Industry Initiatives on Business Ethics and Conduct

The defense industry companies who sign this document already have, or commit to adopt and implement, a set of principles of business ethics and conduct that acknowledge and address their corporate responsibilities under federal procurement laws and to the public. Further, they accept the responsibility to create an environment in which compliance with federal procurement laws and free, open, and timely reporting of violations become the felt responsibility of every employee in the defense industry.

In addition to adopting and adhering to this set of six principles of business ethics and conduct, we will take the leadership in making the principles a standard for the entire defense industry.

I. PRINCIPLES

1. Each company will have and adhere to a written code of business ethics and conduct.
2. The company's code establishes the high values expected of its employees and the standard by which they must judge their own conduct and that of their organization; each company will train its employees concerning their personal responsibilities under the code.
3. Each company will create a free and open atmosphere that allows and encourages employees to report violations of its code to the company without fear of retribution for such reporting.
4. Each company has the obligation to self-govern by monitoring compliance with federal procurement laws and adopting procedures for voluntary disclosure of violations of federal procurement laws and corrective actions taken.
5. Each company has a responsibility to each of the other companies in the industry to live by standards of conduct that preserve the integrity of the defense industry.
6. Each company must have public accountability for its commitment to these principles.

II. IMPLEMENTATION: SUPPORTING PROGRAMS

While all companies pledge to abide by the six principles, each company agrees that it has implemented or will implement policies and programs to meet its management needs.

Principle 1: Written Code of Business Ethics and Conduct A company's code of business ethics and conduct should embody the values that it and its employees hold most important; it is the highest expression of a corporation's culture. For a defense contractor, the code represents the commitment of the company and its employees to work for its customers, shareholders, *and* the nation.

It is important, therefore, that a defense contractor's written code explicitly address that higher commitment. It must also include a statement of the standards that govern the conduct of all employees in their relationships to the company, as well as in their dealings with customers, suppliers, and consultants. The statement also must include an explanation of the consequences of violating those standards, and a clear assignment of responsibility to operating management and others for monitoring and enforcing the standards throughout the company.

Principle 2: Employees' Ethical Responsibilities   A company's code of business ethics and conduct should embody the basic values and culture of a company and should become a way of life, a form of honor system, for every employee. Only if the code is embodied in some form of honor system does it become more than mere words or abstract ideals. Adherence to the code becomes a responsibility of each employee both to the company and to fellow employees. Failure to live by the code, or to report infractions, erodes the trust essential to personal accountability and an effective corporate business ethics system.

Codes of business ethics and conduct are effective only if they are fully understood by every employee. Communication and training are critical to preparing employees to meet their ethical responsibilities. Companies can use a wide variety of methods to communicate their codes and policies and to educate their employees as to how to fulfill their obligations. Whatever methods are used—broad distribution of written codes, personnel orientation programs, group meetings, videotapes, and articles—it is critical that they ensure total coverage.

Principle 3: Corporate Responsibility to Employees   Every company must ensure that employees have the opportunity to fulfill their responsibility to preserve the integrity of the code and their honor system. Employees should be free to report suspected violations of the code to the company without fear of retribution for such reporting.

To encourage the surfacing of problems, normal management channels should be supplemented by a confidential reporting mechanism.

It is critical that companies create and maintain an environment of openness where disclosures are accepted and expected. Employees must believe that to raise a concern or report misconduct is expected, accepted, and protected behavior, not the exception. This removes any legitimate rationale for employees to delay reporting alleged violations or for former employees to allege past offenses by former employers or associates.

To receive and investigate employee allegations of violations of the corporate code of business ethics and conduct, defense contractors can use a contract review board, an ombudsman, a corporate ethics or compliance office or other similar mechanism.

In general, the companies accept the broadest responsibility to create an environment in which free, open, and timely reporting of any suspected violations becomes the felt responsibility of every employee.

Principle 4: Corporate Responsibility to the Government It is the responsibility of each company to self-govern and monitor aggressively adherence to its code and to federal procurement laws. Procedures will be established by each company for voluntarily reporting to appropriate government authorities violations of federal procurement laws and corrective actions.

In the past, major importance has been placed on whether internal company monitoring has uncovered deficiencies before discovery by governmental audit. The process will be more effective if all monitoring efforts are viewed as mutually reinforcing and the measure of performance is a timely and constructive surfacing of issues.

Corporate and government audit and control mechanisms should be used to identify and correct problems. Government and industry share this responsibility and must work together cooperatively and constructively to ensure compliance with federal procurement laws and to clarify any ambiguities that exist.

Principle 5: Corporate Responsibility to the Defense Industry Each company must understand that rigorous self-governance is the foundation of these principles of business ethics and conduct and of the public's perception of the integrity of the defense industry.

Since methods of accountability can be improved through shared experience and adaptation, companies will participate in an annual intercompany "Best Practices Forum" that will bring together operating and staff managers from across the industry to discuss ways to implement the industry's principles of accountability.

Each company's compliance with the principles will be reviewed by a board of directors committee comprised of outside directors.

Principle 6: Public Accountability The mechanism for public accountability will require each company to have its independent public accountants or similar independent organization complete and submit annually the attached questionnaire to an external independent body which will report the results for the industry as a whole and release the data simultaneously to the companies and the general public.

This annual review, which will be conducted for the next three years, is a critical element giving force to these principles and adding integrity to this defense industry initiative as a whole. Ethical accountability, as a good-faith process, should not be affirmed behind closed doors. The defense industry is confronted with a problem of public perception—a loss of confidence in its integrity—that must be addressed publicly if the results are to be both real and credible, to the government and public alike. It is in this spirit of public accountability that this initiative has been adopted and these principles have been established.

Historically, corporate codes have been criticized for emphasizing unethical behavior that might hurt the firm while paying less attention to unethical actions that might benefit the firm. Table 5-2 summarizes the typical provisions of codes of ethics in 1979. Do you see any support for the claim that codes are often self-serving?

Stakeholder Management

Stakeholder management is a relatively recent formal concept emphasizing corporate responsiveness to the external environment. The term "stakeholder" is contrasted with "stockholder" to demonstrate that management has responsibilities that transcend its obligations to the share owners of the corporation. In stakeholder management the firm's executives undertake an obligation to identify and respond to the legitimate interests of the company's stakeholders.

A stakeholder has been defined by Freeman as "any group of individuals who can affect or is affected by the achievement of an organiza-

TABLE 5-2 EMPLOYEE BEHAVIORS PROHIBITED BY COMPANY CODES, 1979

Behavior	Percent of Firms Prohibiting
1. Extortion, gifts, kickbacks	67
2. Conflicts of interest	65
3. Illegal political activities	59
4. Violation of laws	57
5. Use of insider information	43
6. Bribery	37
7. Falsification of accounts	28
8. Price-fixing, antitrust violations	25
9. Moonlighting	25
10. Foreign payments	23

tion's purpose."[2] This definition is the broadest possible and would incorporate diverse groups such as employees, shareholders, consumer activists, government regulators, and terrorist groups. For our purposes, it will help to limit the definition to those individuals or organizations that have a real economic interest in corporate decisions but are not directly subject to the authority of corporate management. A more reasonable, limited definition is more likely to be accepted as a viable management tool. The modified definition excludes employees (but not unions because they are not under management's authority); radical political groups concerned about noneconomic issues, who are themselves unaffected by the firm's operations; and those who have very minimal economic interests which would be difficult for management to incorporate, for example, the interest of a push-cart hot dog vendor in the shade provided by trees that the firm intends to transplant.

The Process of Stakeholder Management

Stakeholder management is the process by which stakeholders and their interests are identified and then incorporated into the operating and planning functions of the firm. A firm that is constantly incorporating stakeholder concerns into its management process is far more likely to anticipate developing strategic issues that represent attractive opportunities or foreboding threats. Firms that spot strategic issues as they evolve are far more likely to respond successfully.

The process of stakeholder management involves the following steps:

- Identifying present and prospective stakeholders
- Identifying stakeholder interests
- Prioritizing interests according to immediacy and likely significance
- Responding to important interests by incor-

porating them in (1) the strategic planning process, (2) ongoing business decisions, and (3) public affairs management strategy.

The first step in stakeholder management is to identify the present and prospective stakeholders of the firm. The list may vary significantly from firm to firm but will typically include governments (local, state, federal, foreign), creditors, suppliers, consumer groups, and shareholders. Depending on the nature of a firm's business, stakeholders may also include trade associations, special interest groups (for example, groups concerned about nuclear power or advertising to children), distributors, professional associations, and unions.

Figure 5-1 shows what a map of the stakeholders of a multinational consumer product company might look like.

The connecting lines between the firm and the stakeholders point both ways in order to emphasize that each of them has the power to affect the other. Stakeholders can employ a variety of strategies to influence a firm's actions that affect them, including the exercise of economic, political, and legal power.

Economic power can be exercised through employing a boycott or a strike, or by limiting the credit available to the firm. The exercise of economic power is often used in conjunction with negotiations between the firm and representatives of the stakeholder group. A well-publicized example was the consumer boycott initiated by INFACT (a consumer advocate group) to protest the marketing practices followed by Nestlé in selling infant formula in developing countries. If economic power fails, then stakeholders can turn to political or legal power. A dramatic example of

FIGURE 5–1
Stakeholder Map

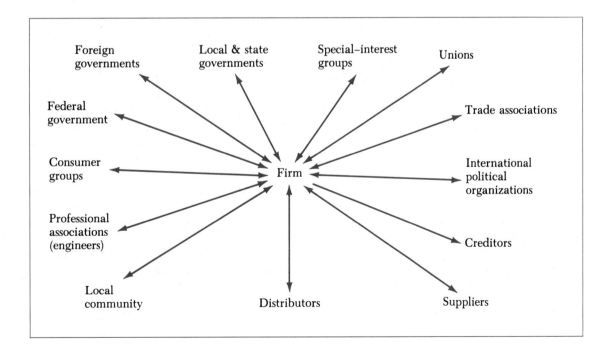

the exercise of *political power* was the successful effort of independent gasoline dealers in getting state legislation passed prohibiting oil companies from competing with them by operating company-owned stations. The dealers turned to the political arena after they were treated unfairly in the allocation of gasoline during the first OPEC (Organization of Petroleum Exporting Countries) oil crisis, and were thereafter frustrated in their attempts to work out the problem directly with their own suppliers.

Legal power would include filing suit under product liability or discrimination law, enforcing claims, or even causing the corporation to sue itself under what is known as a shareholders' derivative suit. Construction unions employed a mixed strategy of boycotts, political intervention, and lawsuits in forcing Toyota to use union labor in building an auto plant in Georgetown, Kentucky. The union boycotted the initial construction, successfully lobbied against a $32 million federal tax break for Toyota, and filed suits against the proposed plant under environmental laws.

Once the firm's stakeholders have been identified, the next step is to identify their specific claims or interests. A good starting point is to determine how the stakeholders themselves perceive their interests in the firm. Many firms employ a continuous environmental scanning system to identify emerging social issues. Corporate staff, consultants, and outside counsel monitor the media, administrative proceedings, and other activities for events that have present or future significance for the firm. One focus of such a system could be to monitor known stakeholders. Strategies for identifying stakeholder interests include (1) direct communications with representatives of stakeholder organizations (for example, setting up an organization of distributors that meets regularly), (2) employing consultants who are able to deal directly with designated stakeholders, (3) hiring new managers from the ranks of important stakeholders (for exam-

ple, former employees of a state or federal regulatory agency), and (4) regularly scanning the publications and formal statements of stakeholder organizations. Through this process, a firm can anticipate the concerns of stakeholder groups. It is often difficult for a firm's management to identify accurately stakeholder priorities without employing some formal scanning method. The values and objectives of managers and stakeholders often differ significantly regarding an appropriate strategic plan for the firm. Managers often have difficulty accepting shareholder viewpoints as valid due to the extreme variances in perspective.

The process of identifying stakeholder concerns may produce a lengthy list. The listing given in Table 5-3 opposite, which is based upon a hypothetical consumer products company, is representative.

The lengthy (although incomplete) listing of possible stakeholder issues makes it abundantly clear that a large firm may face dozens of stakeholder groups that are concerned about hundreds of issues. Multiple stakeholders may be interested in the same issue. And, on a particular issue, stakeholders may be at odds with one another. An employees' union and suppliers may wish to see a marginally profitable plant with a pollution control problem kept going, whereas lenders and state government regulators may prefer that the plant be closed. Another important stakeholder, the local community, may find its constituent parts in heated disagreement over the issue. Citizens concerned about the quality of the environment may wish to see the plant closed, whereas those dependent economically upon the plant may want to see it survive. The process by which a firm's management prioritizes issues is critical to the development of an effective response to complex multidimensional stakeholder issues.

Once stakeholder issues have been identified, they can be prioritized in terms of immediacy and likely impact on both the firm

TABLE 5-3 CONCERNS OF STAKEHOLDERS IN A MULTINATIONAL CONSUMER
PRODUCTS FIRM

Stakeholder	Interests
Federal government	Solid waste disposal
	Air pollution
	Fair employment practices
Foreign governments	Conservation of their natural resources
	Currency fluctuations
	Plant safety
	Local employment
State governments	Plant safety
	Water conservation
Unions	Runaway plants
	Plant closings
	Grievance procedures
Consumer groups	Advertising to children
	Dangerous products
	Misleading ads or advertising harmful products
Creditors	Conservation of financial resources
Suppliers	Continuity of business relationships
Distributors	Competition through dual distribution
	Promotional support
	Pricing freedom
Professional association	Observance of profession's ethical standards
Special interest groups	Advertising to children
	Trading in South Africa
Local community	Air pollution
	Plant safety
	Layoffs
	Plant closings/relocation

and the affected stakeholders. This requires a subjective judgment that is based upon prior experience with strategic issues. Line managers should be involved in the judgment process because they are likely to have direct involvement with the consequences of the strategic issues. The longer a system of stakeholder management has been in place, the greater is the likelihood of an accurate assessment of the importance of an issue because of similar prior experiences.

Once an issue is identified and prioritized, there are a variety of ways in which a firm can respond. The fundamental principle guiding response strategies is that the stakeholder in-

terest must be valued in equivalent economic terms with the firm's interests in the operating decision. If relevant, the stakeholder interest should be incorporated into the corporate planning process on a similar basis.

On many occasions, a firm's management may conclude that it should not give in to the pressures exerted by a particular stakeholder group. Strategies that can be employed to respond to opposing stakeholder groups are briefly described in Table 5-4.

Although public affairs managers often feel that they are swimming with one arm against a powerful current in trying to influence major social trends, the strategies listed in

TABLE 5-4 PUBLIC AFFAIRS MANAGEMENT STRATEGIES

Strategy	Description
Issue advertising	Develop and place ads in media advocating a particular policy position or social viewpoint
Invoke independent authority	Where creditability is at issue, involve independent authority with perceived integrity, for example, Nestlé establishing the Muskie Commission to review complaints about marketing infant formula overseas
Coalition building	Seek out and involve stakeholders having interests compatible with those of the firm
Recruitment from key stakeholders	In compliance with law, hire managers who have formerly worked for key stakeholders, for example, defense contractors hiring former military personnel (after the mandatory waiting period), regulated firms hiring former regulators
Lobbying	Sponsor and support favorable legislation; oppose harmful legislation; use company or consulting lobbyists
Establish formal communication modes	Provide access to significant stakeholders, for example, a consumer hot line for complaints
Administrative process	Scan developing regulations; comment on pending developments
Litigation	Sue as plaintiffs asserting valid causes of action (should be used as a strategy of last resort); engage in preventive legal actions to reduce exposure as a defendant
Trade associations	Join and participate actively to influence their lobbying and public positions
Political involvement	Sponsor corporate political action committees (PACs); advocate positions on referenda and other political issues
Cultivate grassroots support	Contact firm's consumers/stockholders and inform regarding the firm's position on social/public issues

Table 5-4 can have significant cumulative impacts. Faced with the boycott of its products in the United States over its marketing of infant formula in developing countries, Nestlé eventually used many of the strategies listed, and ultimately the boycott was lifted. Nestlé had some success in responding to the problems even though many religious groups had endorsed the boycott and the consumer groups were well organized. By becoming more aware of the concerns of the stakeholder groups, Nestlé came to realize that it should make some changes in its marketing strategies.

Use of some public affairs management (PAM) strategies may raise serious ethical questions. The phrase "public affairs management" carries with it overtones of manipulation. Firms should always consider the interests of stakeholders and, where relevant, the interest of society generally in employing PAM techniques. Applying these techniques without consideration of their ethical consequences may produce perverse results. PAM tools, such as issue advertising or litigation, should not be used to defeat ethically legitimate claims of stakeholders. Nor should PAM tools be used to achieve minor benefits to the firm while imposing major costs on others.

Beyond the ethical constraints on PAM, there are legal constraints. Corporations should make sure that they are not violating the legal rights of others and are acting within the permissible bounds of their authority. Many states and administrative agencies have sought to limit corporate power to engage in various public affairs strategies. Limiting regulations are often based upon a fear that corporations will come to dominate the public affairs process because of their wealth, access to media, and ability to engage the efforts of thousands of supporters.

Corporations have certain rights that must be respected by regulators. Corporations are "persons" entitled to equal protection and due process of law under the Constitution. That means, for example, that corporate property cannot be taken without appropriate notice and compensation. On the other hand, just because corporations have certain basic legal rights does not mean that they are entitled to every right that applies to human citizens. Corporations may not assert a right of privacy or the Fifth Amendment privilege against self-incrimination.

Freedom of speech and free access to government are very important rights for corporations because they pertain to very important PAM strategies, such as participating in electoral politics or engaging in advocacy advertising. In these areas, corporations have qualified rather than absolute rights. The *Bellotti* and *Consolidated Edison* cases that follow demonstrate some of the parameters of those rights.

First National Bank of Boston v. Bellotti

U.S. Supreme Court
435 U.S. 765 (1978)

Background: The First National Bank of Boston (plaintiff-appellant) sued the Massachusetts Attorney General (defendant-appellee) to prevent the enforcement of a statute limiting corporate lobbying on state referenda. The Bank wanted to spend money to publicize its opposition to a pending Massachusetts ballot question that, if successful, would permit the state legislature to impose a graduated personal income tax. A Massachusetts statute made it a crime for a corporation to spend money to influence votes on state referendum proposals pertaining to a personal income tax or other matters not materially affecting the corporation. The Bank challenged the constitutionality of the law. The Supreme Judicial Court of Massachusetts upheld the law and the Bank appealed to the U.S. Supreme Court.
Decision: The Supreme Court reversed and struck down the statute on constitutional grounds.

Powell, Justice

In sustaining a state criminal statute that forbids certain expenditures by banks and business corporations for the purpose of influencing the vote on referendum proposals, the Massachusetts Supreme Judicial Court held that the First Amendment rights of a corporation are limited to issues that materially affect its business, property, or assets. The court rejected appellants' claim that the statute abridges freedom of speech in violation of the First and Fourteenth Amendments. . . . The statute at issue . . . prohibits appellants, two national banking associations and three business corporations, from making contributions or expenditures "for the purpose of . . . influencing or affecting the vote on any question submitted to the voters, other than one materially affecting any of the property, business or assets of the corporation." The statute further specifies that "[n]o question submitted to the voters solely concerning the taxation of the income, property or transactions of individuals shall be deemed materially to affect the property, business or assets of the corporation." A corporation that violates §8 may receive a maximum fine of $50,000; a corporate officer, director, or agent who violates the section may receive a maximum fine of $10,000 or imprisonment for up to one year, or both. . . .

. . . The court below framed the principal question in this case as whether and to what extent corporations have First Amendment rights. We believe that the court posed the wrong question. The Constitution often protects interests broader than those of the party seeking their vindication. The First Amendment, in particular, serves significant societal interests. The proper question therefore is not whether corporations "have" First Amendment rights and, if so, whether they are coextensive with those of natural persons. Instead, the question must be whether §8 abridges expression that the First Amendment was meant to protect. We hold that it does.

The speech proposed by appellants is at the heart of the First Amendment's protection.

> The freedom of speech and of the press guaranteed by the Constitution embraces at the least the liberty to discuss publicly and truthfully all matters of public concern without previous restraint or fear of subsequent punishment. . . . Freedom of discussion, if it would fulfill its historic function in this nation, must embrace all issues about which information is needed or appropriate to enable the members of society to cope with the exigencies of their period. . . .

. . . If the speakers here were not corporations, no one would suggest that the State could silence their proposed speech. It is the type of speech indispensable to decision-making in a democracy, and this is no less true because the speech comes from a corporation rather than an individual. The inherent worth of the speech in terms of its capacity for informing the public does not depend upon the identity of its source, whether corporation, association, union, or individual.

. . . We thus find no support in the First or Fourteenth Amendment, or in the decisions of this Court, for the proposition that speech that otherwise would be within the protection of the First Amendment loses that protection simply because its source is a corporation that cannot prove, to the satisfaction of a court, a material effect on its business or property. The "materially affecting" requirement is not an identification of the boundaries of corporate speech etched by the Constitution itself. Rather, it amounts to an impermissible legislative prohibition of speech based on the identity of the interests that spokesmen may represent in public debate over controversial issues and a requirement that the speaker have a sufficiently great interest in the subject to justify communication.

Section 8 permits a corporation to communicate to the public its views on certain referendum subjects—those materially affecting its business—but not others. It also singles out one kind of ballot question—individual taxation—as a subject about which corporations may never make their ideas public. The legislature has drawn the line between permissible and impermissible speech according to whether there is a sufficient nexus, as defined by the legislature, between the issue presented to the voters and the business interests of the speaker.

. . . In the realm of protected speech, the legislature is constitutionally disqualified from dictating the subjects about which persons may speak and the speakers who may address a public issue. . . . If a legislature may direct business corporations to "stick to business," it also may limit other corporations—religious, charitable, or civic—to their respective "business" when addressing the public. Such power in government to channel the expression of views is unacceptable under the First Amendment. Especially where, as here, the legislature's suppression of speech suggests an attempt to give one side of a debatable public question an advantage in expressing its views to the people, the First Amendment is plainly offended. Yet the State contends that its action is necessitated by governmental interests of the highest order. We next consider these asserted interests.

. . . The constitutionality of §8's prohibition of the "exposition of ideas" by corporations turns on whether it can survive the exacting scrutiny necessitated by a state-imposed restriction of freedom of speech. Especially where, as here, a prohibition is directed at speech itself, and the speech is intimately related to the process of governing, "the State may prevail only upon showing a subordinating interest which is compelling," . . . "and the burden is on the Government to show the existence of such an interest." . . . Appellee . . . advances two principal justifications for the prohibition of corporate speech. The first is the State's interest in sustaining the active role of the individual citizen in the electoral process and thereby preventing diminution of the citizen's confidence in government. The second is the interest in protecting the rights of shareholders whose views differ from those expressed by management on behalf of the corporation. However weighty these interests may be in the context of partisan candidate elections, they either are not implicated in this case or are not served at all, or in other than a random manner, by the prohibition in §8.

. . . Preserving the integrity of the electoral process, preventing corruption, and "sustain[ing] the active, alert responsibility of the individual citizen in a democracy for the wise conduct of government" are interests of the highest importance.

. . . Preservation of the individual citizen's confidence in government is equally important. . . .

. . . Appellee advances a number of arguments in support of his view that these interests are endangered by corporate participation in discussion of a referendum issue. They hinge upon the assumption that such participation would exert an undue influence on the outcome of a referendum vote, and—in the end—destroy the confidence of the people in the democratic process and the integrity of government. According to appellee, corporations are wealthy and powerful and their views may drown out other points of view. If appellee's arguments were supported by record or legislative findings that corporate advocacy threatened imminently to undermine democratic processes, thereby denigrating rather than serving First Amendment interests, these arguments would merit our consideration. . . . But there has been no showing that the relative voice of corporations has been overwhelming or even significant in influencing referenda in Massachusetts, or that there has been any threat to the confidence of the citizenry in government. . . . To be sure, corporate advertising may influence the outcome of the vote; this would be its purpose. But the fact that advocacy may persuade the electorate is hardly a reason to suppress it: The Constitution "protects expression which is eloquent no less than that which is unconvincing." . . . Finally, appellee argues that §8 protects corporate shareholders, an interest that is both legitimate and traditionally within the province of state law. . . . The statute is said to serve this interest by preventing the use of corporate resources in furtherance of views with which some shareholders may disagree. This purpose is belied, however, by the provisions of the statute, which are both underinclusive and overinclusive.

. . . The underinclusiveness of the statute is self-evident. Corporate expenditures with respect to a referendum are prohibited, while corporate activity with respect to the passage or defeat of legislation is permitted, . . . even though corporations may engage in lobbying more often than they take positions on ballot questions submitted to the voters. Nor does §8 prohibit a corporation from expressing its views, by the expenditure of corporate funds, on any public issue until it becomes the subject of a referendum, though the displeasure of disapproving shareholders is unlikely to be any less.

The fact that a particular kind of ballot question has been singled out for special treatment undermines the likelihood of a genuine state interest in protecting shareholders. It suggests instead that the legislature may have been concerned with silencing corporations on a particular subject. Indeed, appellee has conceded that "the legislative and judicial history of the statute indicates . . . that . . . [it] was 'tailor-made' to prohibit corporate campaign contributions to oppose a graduated income tax amendment." . . .

Nor is the fact that §8 is limited to banks and business corporations without relevance. Excluded from its provisions and criminal sanctions are entities or organized groups in which numbers of persons may hold an interest or membership, and which often have resources comparable to those of large corporations. Minorities in such groups or entities may have interests with respect to institutional speech quite comparable to those of minority shareholders in a corporation. Thus the exclusion of Massachusetts business trusts, real estate investment trusts, labor unions, and other associations undermines the plausibility of the State's purported concern for the persons who happen to be shareholders in the banks and corporations covered by §8.

. . . The overinclusiveness of the statute is demonstrated by the fact that §8 would prohibit a corporation from supporting or opposing a referendum proposal even if its shareholders unanimously authorized the contribution or expenditure. Ultimately shareholders may decide, through the procedures of corporate democracy, whether their corporation should engage in debate on public issues. Acting through their power to elect the board of directors or to insist upon protective provisions in the corporation's charter, shareholders normally are presumed competent to protect their own interests. In addition to intracorporate remedies, minority shareholders generally have access to the judicial remedy of a derivative suit to challenge corporate disbursements alleged to have been made for improper corporate purposes or merely to further the personal interests of management.

Assuming, *arguendo,* that protection of shareholders is a "compelling" interest under the circumstances of this case, we find "no substantially relevant correlation between the governmental interest asserted and the State's effort" to prohibit appellants from speaking. . . .

Because that portion of §8 challenged by appellants prohibits protected speech in a manner unjustified by a compelling state interest, it must be invalidated.

Consolidated Edison Co. v. Public Service Commission of New York

U.S. Supreme Court
447 U.S. 530 (1980)

Background: Consolidated Edison (plaintiff-appellant) sued to prevent the enforcement of a Public Service Commission (defendant-appellee) regulation prohibiting bill inserts commenting on public issues. As a result of a controversy that developed when Con Ed inserted materials advocating the use of nuclear power in its monthly electric bills, the New York Public Service Commission (PSC) prohibited utilities from sending its customers bill inserts that commented upon controversial issues of public policy. Con Ed challenged the constitutionality of the PSC prohibition and won in the trial court. However, the New York intermediate appellate court and the New York Court of Appeals held that the PSC's action was constitutional.
Decision: The Supreme Court finding was that the regulation violated Consolidated Edison's right of free speech.

Powell, Justice

The question in this case is whether the First Amendment, as incorporated by the Fourteenth Amendment, is violated by an order of the Public Service Commission of the State of New York that prohibits the inclusion in monthly electric bills of inserts discussing controversial issues of public policy.

The Consolidated Edison Company of New York, appellant in this case, placed written material entitled "Independence Is Still a Goal, and Nuclear Power Is Needed To Win The Battle" in its January 1976 billing envelope. The bill insert stated Consolidated Edison's views on "the benefits of nuclear power," saying that they "far outweigh any potential risk" and that nuclear power plants are safe, economical, and clean. . . . The utility also contended that increased use of nuclear energy would further this country's independence from foreign energy sources.

In March 1976, the Natural Resources Defense Council, Inc. (NRDC) requested Consolidated Edison to enclose a rebuttal prepared by NRDC in its next billing envelope. . . . When Consolidated Edison refused, NRDC asked the Public Service Commission of the State of New York to open Consolidated Edison's billing envelopes to contrasting views on controversial issues of public importance. . . .

On February 17, 1977, the Commission, appellee here, denied NRDC's request, but prohibited "utilities from using bill inserts to discuss political matters, including the desirability of future development of nuclear power." . . . The Commission explained its decision in a Statement of Policy on Advertising and Promotion Practices of Public Utilities issued on February 25, 1977. The Commission concluded that Consolidated Edison customers who receive bills containing inserts are a captive audience of diverse views who should not be subjected to the utility's beliefs. Accordingly, the Commission barred utility companies from including bill inserts that express "their opinions or viewpoints on controversial issues of public policy." . . . The Commission did not, however, bar utilities from sending bill inserts discussing topics that are not "controversial issues of public policy." . . .

. . . The restriction on bill inserts cannot be upheld on the ground that Consolidated Edison is not entitled to freedom of speech. In *First National Bank of Boston* v. *Bellotti,* . . . we rejected the contention that a State may confine corporate speech to specified issues. . . .

. . . In the mailing that triggered the regulation at issue, Consolidated Edison advocated the use of nuclear power. The Commission has limited the means by which Consolidated Edison may participate in the public debate on this question and other controversial issues of national interest and importance. Thus, the Commission's prohibition of controversial issues strikes at the heart of the freedom to speak.

. . . The Commission's ban on bill inserts is not, of course, invalid merely because it imposes a limitation upon speech. . . . We must consider whether the State can demonstrate that its regulation is constitutionally permissible. The Commission's arguments require us to consider three theories that might justify the state action. We must determine whether the prohibition is (i) a reasonable time, place, or manner restriction, (ii) a permissible subject-matter regulation, or (iii) a narrowly tailored means of serving a compelling state interest.

. . . This Court has recognized the validity of reasonable time, place, or manner regulations that serve a significant governmental interest and leave ample alternative channels for communication. . . . But when regulation is based on the content of speech, governmental action must be scrutinized more carefully to ensure that communication has not been prohibited "merely because public officials disapprove the speaker's views."

. . . As a consequence, we have emphasized that time, place, and manner regulations must be "applicable to all speech irrespective of content." . . . Therefore, a constitutionally permissible time, place, or manner restriction may not be based upon either the content or subject matter of speech.

. . . The Commission does not pretend that its action is unrelated to the content or subject matter of bill inserts. Indeed, it has undertaken to suppress certain bill inserts precisely because they address controversial issues of public policy. The Commission allows inserts that present information to consumers on certain subjects, such as energy conservation measures, but it forbids the use of inserts that discuss public controversies. The Commission, with commendable candor, justified its ban on the ground that consumers will benefit from receiving "useful" information, but not from the prohibited information. . . . The Commission's own rationale demonstrates that its action cannot be upheld as a content-neutral time, place, or manner regulation.

The Commission next argues that its order is acceptable because it applies to all discussion of nuclear power, whether pro or con, in bill inserts. The prohibition, the Commission contends, is related to subject matter rather than to the views of a particular speaker. Because the regulation does not favor either side of a political controversy, the Commission asserts that it does not unconstitutionally suppress freedom of speech.

. . . The First Amendment's hostility to content-based regulation extends not only to restrictions on particular viewpoints, but also to prohibition of public discussion of an entire topic. As a general matter, "the First Amendment means that the government has no power to restrict expression because of its message, its ideas, its subject matter, or its content." . . .

. . . Where a government restricts the speech of a private person, the state action may be sustained only if the government can show that the regulation is a precisely drawn means of serving a compelling state interest. . . . The Commission argues finally that its prohibition is necessary (i) to avoid forcing Consolidated Edison's views on a captive audience, (ii) to allocate limited resources in the public interest, and (iii) to ensure that ratepayers do not subsidize the cost of the bill inserts.

. . . The State Court of Appeals largely based its approval of the prohibition upon its conclusion that the bill inserts intruded upon individual privacy. The court stated that the Commission could act to protect the privacy of the utility's customers because they have no choice whether to receive the insert and the views expressed in the insert may inflame their sensibilities. . . . But the Court of Appeals erred in its assessment of the seriousness of the intrusion.

. . . Even if a short exposure to Consolidated Edison's views may offend the sensibilities of some consumers, the ability of government "to shut off discourse solely to protect others from hearing it [is] dependent upon a showing that substantial privacy interests are being invaded in an essentially intolerable manner." . . . A less stringent analysis would permit a government to slight the First Amendment's role "in affording the public access to discussion, debate and the dissemination of information and ideas." . . . Where a single speaker communicates to many listeners, the First Amendment does not permit the government to prohibit speech as intrusive unless the "captive" audience cannot avoid objectional speech.

. . . Passengers on public transportation . . . or residents of a neighborhood disturbed by the raucous broadcasts from a passing soundtruck . . . may well be unable to escape an unwanted message. But customers who encounter an objectionable billing insert may "effectively avoid further bombardment of their sensibilities simply by averting their eyes." . . .

. . . The Commission contends that because a billing envelope can accommodate only a limited amount of information, political messages should not be allowed to take the place of inserts that promote energy conservation or safety, or that remind consumers of their legal rights. . . . First . . . it cannot be said that billing envelopes are a limited resource comparable to the broadcast spectrum. Second, the Commission has not shown on the record before us that the presence of the bill inserts at issue would preclude the inclusion of other inserts that Consolidated Edison might be ordered lawfully to include in the billing envelope. Unlike radio or television stations broadcasting on a single frequency, multiple bill inserts will not result in a "cacophony of competing voices." . . .

. . . Finally, the Commission urges that its prohibition would prevent ratepayers from subsidizing the costs of policy-oriented bill inserts. But the Commission did not base its order on an inability to allocate costs between the shareholders of Consolidated Edison and the ratepayers. Rather, the Commission stated "that using bill inserts to proclaim a utility's viewpoint on controversial issues *(even when the stockholder pays for it in full)* is tantamount to taking advantage of a captive audience." . . . Accordingly, there is no basis on this record to assume that the Commission could not exclude the cost of these bill inserts from the utility's rate base. Mere speculation of harm does not constitute a compelling state interest. . . .

The Commission's suppression of bill inserts that discuss controversial issues of public policy directly infringes the freedom of speech protected by the First and Fourteenth Amendments. The state action is neither a valid time, place, or manner restriction, nor a permissible subject-matter regulation, nor a narrowly drawn prohibition justified by a compelling state interest. Accordingly, the regulation is invalid. . . .

The decision of the New York Court of Appeals is reversed.

EXTERNAL INCENTIVES FOR SOCIAL RESPONSIBILITY

So far, we have considered the justifications for social responsiveness on the part of corporate management and the types of strategies used to foster an environment of responsiveness. The rationale for such actions has, up to this point, been limited to general concepts of professionalism and societal obligation and assertions of capability for enhancing profits. In this section, we encounter sources of more direct pressure on corporations to be responsible. An important, at times undervalued, incentive is the response of the market to perceived irresponsibility in the safety of products. Demand for the products can be lessened and the stock price of the company can fall in response. There are many ways by which government, at all levels, can intervene. State governments, through their chartering functions, can change the legal structure of corporations with the idea that organizational redesign will alter manager behavior. Or state legislatures and courts can modify the civil liability systems to increase their deterrence effect for irresponsible behavior. Corporations as entities and managers as individuals can be exposed to criminal liability. Or firms can be subjected to direct regulation by administrative agencies.

Market Incentives for Safety

In certain circumstances the market may provide a strong incentive for corporations to act responsibly. Even though a firm's actions may be legal, public perception that the firm has acted irresponsibly can have a strong negative impact upon the firm. This is particularly the case for dangerous consumer products, especially those bought with discretionary income and for which there are ready substitutes.

The publicity generated by product liability cases, or administrative actions such as recalls, may result in heavy costs for the firms associated with the dangerous products or services. The Great Adventure Amusement Park suffered a significant falloff in business the year after a fire in its Haunted Castle killed eight youths. The sales of Ford Pintos, Firestone 500 radials, Tylenol, and Rely tampons all fell off dramatically after publicity about potential dangers. Even more limited actions, such as compulsory product repairs, have been found to depress the sales of the brands affected.[3]

The market losses associated with negative publicity surrounding legal proceedings cannot be covered by insurance. One study of recalls of automobiles and drugs found that substantial capital market penalties, reflected in lower stock prices, are also imposed upon those producing defective products.[4] In fact, capital market losses associated with the firms studied exceeded estimates of both the direct costs of the recalls and the total social costs of the defective product. Relying on these and similar studies, some commentators conclude that the market is more effective in bringing about safe products than government regulation.[5]

There are, however, many circumstances in which government regulation should be more effective than the market. If consumers cannot discover the harms associated with products, or have no alternative even though they are aware of the risk, the market incentive for safety is substantially reduced.

Structural Change

One of the best-known advocates of structural change is Christopher Stone, who wrote *Where the Law Ends* (New York: Harper & Row, 1975). Stone argues that corporations must be encouraged to study the social and human repercussions of their proposed actions so that they can always be prepared to present justifications for their conduct. Stone proposes a number of changes in the form of corporate organization that would, he reasons, bring about positive changes in corporate behavior. He would eliminate the use of inside directors (directors who hold management positions in the firm), require that a designated percentage of directors be financially disinterested, and, most importantly, define by law the precise functions that di-

rectors must perform. A director breaching these requirements would be subjected to unindemnifiable liability and would be ineligible to serve in a major corporate post for a designated term of years.

Stone would further extend the principles applied to directors to the operating officers of the firm. He would require by law that corporations have certain designated management positions, filled by individuals who meet legally established specifications, who would be required to carry out specifically designated tasks. Thus, a steel company might be required to have a vice-president of environmental compliance who is trained in the technical aspects of pollution control, who would oversee tests of air emission, sign such reports, and see that corrective measures were implemented when necessary.

Stone has also advocated requiring corporations to gather and review certain data, such as the drug use experience of customers of a pharmaceutical firm. To insure proper review, certain internal written reports to designated officers might be required. The data in raw form would have to be retained for a designated period of time, and the government would have the right to inspect the data at any time. This would presumably open up corporations and make sure that stakeholder interests are considered at the proper points.

Stone's critics argue that his approach would increase costs and discourage competent people from entering management positions. After all, who would want to undertake a job where they might be subjected to a substantial uninsurable liability? Many problems arise with the proposals that corporate procedures and positions be determined by governmental fiat. There are many forms of corporate organization and behavior. To force all companies to fit a particular mold, even for only a small part of their operations, could produce substantial inefficiencies. Emphasis on government inspections may compromise trade secrets and product development, and might even stimulate bribery. Many of the record-keeping requirements would be difficult to enforce and might just result in higher costs.

Beyond Stone, a number of other proposals have been aimed at changing corporate behavior through structural alterations. Some have been geared to changing the role and nature of the board of directors. The argument is that a more independent board of directors will do a better job of watching over management. Some of the proposals that have been made include:

- Mandating that firms have certain "special-interest" directors, representing particular constituencies, such as customers, distributors, labor, etc.
- Establishing minimum qualifications for directors
- Limiting the number of directorships that could be held by one individual
- Requiring that directors own a certain minimum dollar value of shares or, contrariwise, that directors be entirely financially disinterested
- Requiring that the board be supported by an audit staff completely independent of management
- Mandating an Ethics Committee of the Board

Opponents of such reform proposals claim that a more independent board will be less efficient. Each director should represent the entire firm. Purposefully developing adversarial relationships can only provoke counterproductive conflict.

A second focus of reform has been to strengthen shareholders' rights. The assumption is that shareholders are a diverse lot, representative of a wide range of societal interests, and that if individual shareholders have real authority, they can effectively limit the discretionary powers of the professional managers. Various proposals to strengthen shareholder interests have included:

- Making it easier for shareholders to nominate an alternate slate of directors
- Employing cumulative voting or other methods that would increase the chances that at least one minority viewpoint director could be elected
- Making it easier for shareholders to introduce motions and resolutions pertaining to social issues
- Requiring management to distribute information prepared by supporters of shareholder motions that management opposes and restricting management's right to reply to the same size and form as the proponents' statement
- Expanding the rights of shareholders to obtain information about their firms so that they can identify and respond to problem areas

Critics of shareholder democracy are quick to note that all of the preceding proposals would increase the costs of operating the firm. They claim that the costs are not justifiable because the changes would not significantly improve businesses' response to social issues.

Incentives Through the Tort Law

A major debate today is whether the tort law, particularly in the area of product liability (discussed in Chapters 8 and 23), provides appropriate incentives for socially responsible behavior on the part of firms. Proponents of expansive tort liability argue that it is one of the most effective ways of insuring that firms consider social interests. They reason that the anticipation of potentially large judgments makes management very careful in dealing with products having the potential for harming humans. Opponents claim that the current system overdeters. In support they advance a number of arguments to the effect that the current law produces negative incentives. The potential for large claims may become so high that firms respond by holding back on product improvements, thereby causing products to be less safe than they might be. Assessing large judgments against manufacturers has the negative effect of increasing the costs of products, which tends to hurt poorer people. Opponents further argue that the system is out of control in that the large sums paid by defendants often fail to benefit the injured parties. In some cases over half of all the money paid has gone to lawyers and those responsible for administering the claims.

The awarding of punitive damages against corporations highlights the issues involved in using the court system to reform corporate behavior. The state courts in the United States have differed in their approach to the question of whether a corporation should be liable for punitive damages. Some will allow punitive damages only when the tortious act was expressly authorized (or subsequently ratified) by the corporation. Others will impose punitive damages whenever malice or recklessness is present so long as the act was committed by an employee acting within the scope of employment. Still another line of cases will impose liability when the act was authorized or committed by someone at the general management level.

As would be expected, this diversity of approaches produces inconsistent results. When Richardson-Merrell defrauded the FDA (Federal Drug Administration) in the distribution of MER/29, an anticholesterol drug, both Toole and Roginsky developed cataracts from taking the drug. Their claims were based upon the exact same actions by Richardson-Merrell, yet Toole was awarded $250,000 in punitive damages in California,[6] whereas Roginsky was denied punitive damages in New York.[7]

Which of the approaches represents better policy? Courts limiting the application of punitive damages to instances of actual authority do so for the following reasons:

1. Concern that recurring assessments of punitive damages, in which the amounts are essentially pulled out of a hat, may endanger the financial viability of the affected corporation.
2. The cost of punitive damages is ultimately borne by the shareholders, who are without fault.
3. It is unfair to impose extra damages on a company for unauthorized acts committed by its employees.

Courts imposing punitive damages more broadly find support among the following arguments:

1. The action is outrageous and is attributable to the corporation.
2. The action was undertaken for the benefit of the corporation.
3. Threats of real financial harm are necessary in order to have an impact upon the behavior of others.
4. It is unfair for an individual to receive punitive damages when an act is committed by an individual but not to be able to recover when the act is attributable to a corporation.

Punitive damage awards have been attacked by defendants as unconstitutional because they constitute "excessive fines" or "cruel and unusual punishment," which are forbidden by the Constitution. None of the attacks have been successful to date but it seems certain that more challenges will occur.

Incentives Through the Criminal Law

The imposition of criminal sanctions upon corporations or individual managers may have a significant impact upon business behavior. The prospect of jail sentences or the kind of widespread notority that accompanies criminal trials should make managers especially cautious about complying with the law. The specifics of corporate criminal liability and of various business crimes are covered in Chapter 3, "Introduction to Criminal Law."

CORPORATE OBLIGATIONS TO EMPLOYEES

An important application of the principle of business responsibility centers around how firms treat their employees. Employees may find themselves in a position where their views or interests conflict with those of the firm. An employee may not wish to donate blood or to give to the United Way, but may be put under considerable pressure to do so from the firm. An employee may oppose a referendum lowering taxes on commercial properties, while his firm publicly supports it. An employee may wish to belong to an American–Arab unity league, while his employer forbids him from joining. An employer may want to have all employees submit to drug tests or to take lie detector tests, while employees may resist them as invasive of their privacy. Some employers have dress codes, for example, that all employees wear white shirts and dark suits, which some employees may find offensive.

The important question of the extent to which a corporation has a duty to recognize the preferences of employees will be answered in part by law and in part by ethics. Employers may be seen as having an ethical duty to respect the person of their employees and not to interfere in the nonemployment-related aspects of employees' lives. Thus, if the employer seeks to control the way in which employees dress on their days off, that would clearly seem to exceed the employer's ethical rights.

The most difficult issues arise when an employer wants to restrict a job-related activity which the employee considers an important right. For example, some employers refuse to allow employee smoking on the job. The employer might argue that smoking bothers other employees, that smoke breaks reduce productivity, and that smokers have more sick days and higher medical costs. In that circumstance, the relative strength of the ethical claims is not so clear. The employer's reasons seem sound, and accommodating the employee will not eliminate the employer's concerns and will increase costs.

Assume then that the employer refuses to employ smokers, period. In order to enforce the policy, the employer requires that the employees submit to periodic respiratory or blood tests. Individuals who would forgo smoking on the job, but who want to smoke at home, would not be hired. The employer might argue that home smokers would have, on average, more sick days and that the cost of providing health insurance as an employee benefit would be higher. Although the employer does have some justification, the question becomes whether it offsets the invasion of privacy involved with the testing and the infringement of the employee's right to act as desired at home.

The law cannot go so far as an ethical analysis would require. Legal compulsion should be used only when fundamental rights are violated or clearly unsocial actions are involved. The Civil Rights Act of 1964, which prohibits employers from practicing discrimination on the basis of race, color, religion, sex, or national origin, is often the source of legal claims relating to the assertion of employee rights. When employees have claims, the law may require an analysis of the competing interests of the employer and the employee. The employer may be required to make a reasonable accommodation of the employee's rights. The *Ansonia* case that follows demonstrates how the Supreme Court analyzes the duty of accommodation and the factors that will determine whether a reasonable accommodation has been made.

Ansonia Board of Education v. Philbrook

U.S. Supreme Court

55 L.W. 4019 (1986)

Background: Philbrook (plaintiff-respondent), a teacher, sued his employer, the Ansonia Board of Education (defendant-appellant), claiming that the school's policies regarding religious leave constituted religious discrimination in violation of the Civil Rights Act of 1964.

Philbrook, a business studies and typing teacher, was a member of the Worldwide Church of God, a sect that requires its members to refrain from working during holy days. Teachers were allowed three paid days for observing religious holidays but were prohibited from using their three additional "personal business" paid days for religious purposes. Philbrook's church recognized six holy days during school days and he was forced to take unpaid absences. He requested that he either be allowed to use his personal business days for holy days or that he be allowed to hire a substitute from his own funds and receive pay for the extra religious days. The latter arrangement would save him about $100 per day. The board refused and Philbrook sued claiming religious discrimination. The District Court found for the school board, but the Second Circuit Court of Appeals reversed, remanding the case for a determination whether the arrangement proposed by Philbrook constituted an "undue hardship" on the school board.

Decision: The Supreme Court affirmed, but remanded for a different reason—to determine whether or not the board's leave policy constituted a reasonable accommodation of religious beliefs.

Rehnquist, Chief Justice

. . .

Since the 1967–1968 school year, the school board's collective-bargaining agreements with the Ansonia Federation of Teachers have granted to each teacher 18 days of leave per year for illness, cumulative to 150 and later to 180 days. Accumulated leave may be used for purposes other than illness as specified in the agreement. A teacher may accordingly use five days' leave for a death in the immediate family, one day for attendance at a wedding, three days per year for attendance as an official delegate to a national veterans organization, and the like. With the exception of the agreement covering the 1967–1968 school year, each contract has specifically provided three days' annual leave for observance of mandatory religious holidays, as defined in the contract. Unlike other categories for which leave is permitted, absences for religious holidays are not charged against the teacher's annual or accumulated leave.

The school board has also agreed that teachers may use up to three days of accumulated leave each school year for "necessary personal business." Recent contracts limited permissible personal leave to those uses not otherwise specified in the contract. This limitation dictated, for example, that an employee who wanted more than three leave days to attend the convention of a national veterans organization could not use personal leave to gain extra days for that purpose. Likewise, an employee already absent three days for mandatory religious observances could not later use personal leave for "[a]ny religious activity" or "[a]ny religious observance." . . .

The limitations on the use of personal business leave spawned this litigation. Until the 1976–1977 year, Philbrook observed mandatory holy days by using the three days granted in the contract and then taking unauthorized leave. His pay was reduced accordingly. In 1976, however, respondent stopped taking unauthorized leave for religious reasons, and began scheduling required hospital visits on church holy days. He also worked on several holy days. Dissatisfied with this arrangement, Philbrook repeatedly asked the school board to adopt one of two alternatives. His preferred alternative would allow use of personal business leave for religious observance, effectively giving him three additional days of paid leave for that purpose. Short of this arrangement, respondent suggested that he pay the cost of a substitute and receive full pay for additional days off for religious observances. Petitioner has consistently rejected both proposals.

. . . . .

We granted certiorari to consider the important questions of federal law presented by the decision of the Court of Appeals. . . . Specifically, we are asked to address whether the Court of Appeals erred in finding that Philbrook established a prima facie case of religious discrimination and in opining that an employer must accept the employee's preferred accommodation absent proof of undue hardship. . . .

. . . . .

We find no basis in either the statute or its legislative history for requiring an employer to choose any particular reasonable accommodation. By its very terms the statute directs that any reasonable accommodation by the employer is sufficient to meet its accommodation obligation. The employer violates the statute unless it "demonstrates that [it] is unable to reasonably accommodate . . . an employee's . . . religious observance or practice without undue hardship on the conduct of the employer's business." Thus, where the employer has already reasonably accommodated the employee's religious needs, the statutory inquiry is at an end. The employer need not further show that each of the employee's alternative accommodations would result in undue hardship. [T]he extent of undue hardship on the employer's business is at issue only where the employer claims that it is unable to offer any reasonable accommodation without such hardship. Once the Court of Appeals assumed that the school board had offered to Philbrook a reasonable alternative, it erred by requiring the board to nonetheless demonstrate the hardship of Philbrook's alternatives.

. . . . .

. . . We think that the school board policy in this case, requiring respondent to take unpaid leave for holy day observance that exceeded the amount allowed by the collective-bargaining agreement, would generally be a reasonable one. . . . The provision of unpaid leave eliminates the conflict between employment requirements and religious practices by allowing the individual to observe fully religious holy days and requires him only to give up compensation for a day that he did not in fact work. Generally speaking, "[t]he direct effect of [unpaid leave] is merely a loss of income for the period the employee is not at work; such an exclusion has no direct effect upon either employment opportunities or job status."

But unpaid leave is not a reasonable accommodation when paid leave is provided for all purposes *except* religious ones. A provision for paid leave "that is part and parcel of the employment relationship may not be doled out in a discriminatory fashion, even if the employer would be free . . . not to provide the benefit at all." Such an arrangement would display a discrimination against religious practices that is the antithesis of reasonableness. Whether the policy here violates this teaching turns on factual inquiry into past and present administration of the personal business leave provisions of the collective-bargaining agreement. The school board contends that the necessary personal business category in the agreement, like other leave provisions, defines a limited purpose leave. Philbrook, on the other hand, asserts that the necessary personal leave category is not so limited, operating as an open-ended leave provision that may be used for a wide range of secular purposes in addition to those specifically provided for in the contract, but not for similar religious purposes. We do not think that the record is sufficiently clear on this point for us to make the necessary factual findings, and we therefore affirm the judgment of the Court of Appeals remanding the case to the District Court. The latter court on remand should make the necessary findings as to past and existing practice in the administration of the collective-bargaining agreement.

REVIEW PROBLEMS*

1. Which of the following are stakeholders of General Motors (GM)? Ford Motor Company? The Detroit Tigers baseball team? The Goodyear tire company? The National Tire Dealers and Retreaders Association? The United Auto Workers? The City of Detroit? The GM Dealers Association?
2. What is meant by successor liability? What is the best policy regarding this issue?
3. How might stakeholder management improve a firm's profitability? Give a recent example.
4. What is the purpose in having a corporate code of ethics? How should such a code be developed?
5. In May 1984, a fire erupted in the

*Because of the nature of the subject matter in this chapter, business case-type problems are used rather than the standard format.

Haunted Castle attraction at the Great Adventure Amusement Park in central New Jersey. The fire apparently started when a young man held a cigarette lighter against the wall. Eight young people died of asphyxiation in the fire. There were no sprinklers in the Haunted Castle and it was not hooked into a central alarm system. The attraction was comprised of a series of truck trailers and people walked through it under the direction of Great Adventure employees. One or more employees, known as Rovers, constantly walked through the Castle.

The local government fire inspectors had classified the building as a temporary structure and thus had exempted it from the fire code's mandate that public buildings have sprinklers. There had been a number of studies conducted by risk consultants who had recommended, among many other things, that sprinklers be installed in the Haunted Castle. In the aftermath of the fire, the State of New Jersey brought charges of aggravated manslaughter against the corporation, Great Adventure, Inc., and against two executives, including the general manager of Great Adventure. The families of the victims also filed civil tort suits seeking damages from Great Adventure, Inc. for wrongful death. How should responsibility be allocated?

6. GOODHEALTH DRUG†

In 1980, the Goodhealth Drug Company obtained clearance from the Federal Food and Drug Administration and began marketing Colstop, a drug designed to control cholesterol levels in the blood. Colstop has been a smashing success and now accounts for 15 percent of sales and 25 percent of earnings.

Preliminary evidence from the field indicates that the drug significantly lowers cholesterol levels in 50 percent of the cases where it is used. The drug has already been used by 400,000 people and the number of users is increasing rapidly. There is no comparably effective drug on the market for treating high cholesterol, a factor in cardiovascular disease.

Eighteen cases have been reported to the company of instances in which users developed severe cataracts after prolonged use of Colstop. The most recent report came from the Mayo Clinic and involved a nine-year-old boy. Goodhealth immediately reported the cases to the FDA and to medical doctors prescribing the drug. Most doctors

†Problems 6, 7, and 8 were written by Professor Dunfee and were published as part of the 1986 report *Integrating Ethics into the MBA Curriculum,* sponsored by the Exxon Education Foundation. Samuel Davis wrote the initial draft of no. 8. © Trustees of the University of Pennsylvania.

continued to prescribe the use of Colstop on the theory that the risk of heart disease outweighs the risk of cataracts.

Goodhealth just received a report from a university researcher who claims to have tested Colstop on white rats with the result that half of them developed cataracts. In response to that report, the CEO conducted a review of the initial testing of Colstop at Goodhealth. The review uncovered the fact that the original experiments that were done at Goodhealth resulted in 5 percent of the test animals developing cataracts. The original report stated that "slightly less than 5 percent of the test mice developed cataracts after prolonged use." Dr. Merk, the project director, deleted that sentence before the report was sent to senior management and, ultimately, to the FDA. Dr. Smith had written the original report. She protested to Dr. Merk, who told her to keep quiet. Dr. Smith then protested to Dr. Chou, who was Merk's superior. Dr. Chou promised "to look into it," but nothing happened. Dr. Smith received a poor rating from Dr. Merk in her next performance review. Dr. Smith is the widowed mother of two small children and probably could not find an equivalent job with another firm.

The research director of Goodhealth has made a report on the Colstop controversy. The report indicates that there is no evidence to show a cause/effect relationship between taking the drug and developing cataracts. The report characterizes the university researcher as "unreliable and anti-drug industry" and notes that white rats are generally susceptible to cataracts. The report recommends that Goodhealth conduct research on the issue, which would take at least three months to produce definitive results.

Goodhealth is planning a major stock offering that will have a significant impact on the growth potential of the company. Sources in the field indicate that the FDA is investigating the Colstop controversy.

What should Goodhealth's managers do?

7. ABC STEEL

You have been elected as the chairman of the contributions committee at ABC Steel Company, where in addition to planning and administrating corporate contributions, you are responsible for preparing an annual contributions budget.

ABC Steel is a major producer of steel and steel products with its primary mill located in an economically depressed city in the Northeast. Unemployment due to layoffs and a low-skilled work force is running high, crime rates are higher than the national average, and living conditions in the inner city are well below national standards. Cultural activity is slowly dying.

As chairman, you may spend any amount up to 1 percent of total net income (this year's income is approximately $100 million) on corporate contributions. This year top management at ABC Steel can agree upon only seven possible areas of contribution. They are:

1. the nearby college of engineering.
2. the United Way federated drive.
3. the local cultural center for the performing arts.
4. the Harvard Business School.
5. neighborhood revitalization projects.
6. the local Unemployment Services Bureau.
7. the Worldwide Famine Relief Society.

Your job is to determine how large the corporate contributions budget should be and what amounts, if any, should be allocated among the seven alternatives.

Just a few months earlier, in a speech to the American Council for the Arts, the CEO underscored the importance of corporate philanthropy in American life and reemphasized that ABC Steel's profits were continuing to decline for the third straight year due to competition from overseas and low productivity at home. The outlook for the U.S. steel industry is not promising. ABC Steel laid off 500 employees for an indefinite period two months ago. None has been recalled to work.

As chairman, you must present your annual budget to top management with supporting arguments for your selections. You have also been asked to draft a statement to the shareholders describing the rationale behind the contributions.

8. CLASSIC CONTAINER CORPORATION

In 1974, Classic Container Corporation decided to follow the lead of Royal Cork and Seal, National Can, and Canadian Can in developing its operations in international markets. The container and packaging industry, in searching for new fields in which to grow, had sought opportunities in international markets for their canning and bottling operations. Classic, recognized as one of the top ten firms in the industry with approximately a 9 percent U.S. market share in the canning and bottling of consumer products, felt that it must follow the lead of others in the industry in the hope that new markets would bring the sales growth it so desperately needed without having to rely on technological breakthroughs.

Classic's management determined that its major competitors had overwhelming advantages in most of the European countries because of earlier entrance into those markets. Consequently, Classic's management concluded that its best strategic move would be the establishment of manufacturing and marketing operations for cans and bottles in developing countries, especially in Africa. By not having to compete with the giants of the industry on a head-to-head basis in the international markets and by maintaining its own manufacturing operation in the underdeveloped countries, it seemed reasonable that Classic could make a significant market penetration.

Responsibility for entry into African markets was assigned to the International Division of Classic. The head of that department was William Taylor, who had a reputation for exceeding performance targets, and who was considered the leading candidate eventually to succeed Thomas Hahn as CEO. The operating responsibility for Eastern Africa fell to Reginald More.

When More approached the government of East Zamia (Zamia) through diplomatic channels late in 1974, the idea of the establishment of manufacturing operations was warmly received. As negotiations proceeded with the Secretary of Commerce of Zamia, however, it became clear that Classic would not be hiring as many citizens of that country as its government desired. Because its operations were so highly mechanized, Classic required skilled American workers and managers for its operations and could employ Zamians in small numbers and only then as menial laborers. Still, the Zamian government was anxious to attract industry from the West and encouraged Classic to begin construction of a plant. All of the initial permissions were quickly granted by the appropriate Zamian officials.

By late 1976, Classic had completed the land clearing and external construction for a large plant operation in Zamia. Shipments of machinery from its U.S. operations were due to arrive by early 1977. Then, in what More considered to be a surprise move, the Commerce officials of Zamia informed More that the Classic plant operation could not begin as planned in mid-1977. The Zamian officials cited a myriad of regulations that were not previously mentioned

and the failure to hire natives as reasons for the holdup. The officials explained to More that all of these matters could be resolved immediately and operations could begin as scheduled if certain payments were made to both the officials themselves and the Secretary's staff. These payments were to be in U.S. dollars and would be a one-time payment. Unfortunately, the Zamians would not allow these "payments for administrative costs" to be publicly recorded.

More was very troubled by these developments. Delays in starting the plant operation could have a dramatic influence on its ultimate profitability. There were rumors that Royal was negotiating to build a plant in neighboring Kenya. Any significant delay would probably cause the International Division to fall short of its performance target for 1977.

On the one hand, More could not ascertain whether or not the requested payments constituted official policy of the Zamian government. Personally, More considered such payments unethical and contrary to his personal values. Classic Container had implemented a Code of Ethics in 1976. The Code had a provision that prohibited "making any payments on behalf of the Corporation that are contrary to the law of the United States or of the country in which they are made." The Code further contained a formal procedure by which an employee could whistle-blow about violations. On the other hand, the Code provided that an employee could be terminated for willful abuse of the whistle-blowing system.

More discussed the problem with Taylor. Taylor's first question was, "How much do they want?" When More mentioned the amount, Taylor said, "That sounds reasonable. Pay it." More then stated his reservations and mentioned the Code. Taylor then became somewhat irritated and said, "Look, there are big sums involved here. You can be doggoned sure that Royal will make similar payments if they go into Kenya. Pay the blankety-blank bribe!" What should More do?

FOOTNOTES

[1] Students who are not familiar with corporate social issues reports should obtain one from the library and read it, noting the types of activities that are reported upon.

[2] R. Edward Freeman, *Strategic Management: A Stakeholder Approach* (Boston: Pitman, 1984), p. 53.

[3] Crafton, Hoffer, and Reilly, "Testing the Impact of Recalls on the Demand for Automobiles," 19 *Economic Inquiry,* 694 (1981).

[4] Jarrell and Peltzman, "The Impact of Product Recalls on the Wealth of Sellers," 93:3 *Journal of Political Economy,* 512 (1985).

[5] Viscusi, "Market Incentives for Safety," *Harvard Business Review,* 133 (July–August, 1985).

[6] Toole v. Richardson-Merrell, 60 Cal.Rptr. 398 (Cal.App. 1967).

[7] Roginsky v. Richardson-Merrell, 378 F.2d 832 (2d cir. 1967).

CHAPTER 6

Intentional Torts

Torts Against the Person ————————————————————————

Torts Against Property Interests ——————————————————

The Emerging Tort of Wrongful Discharge ———————————

T ort law is that branch of the law that deals with injuries. A *tort* is an injury other than a breach of contract. A tort is not a crime, although sometimes the same conduct results in both a criminal prosecution and a civil lawsuit. For example, suppose someone drives a car into the rear of the car ahead of her on a highway. She may have committed a crime (reckless driving), and may have committed a tort (negligence). The criminal case and the civil case would be treated separately.

Torts fall into three categories: intentional torts, negligence, and strict liability. *Intentional torts* are characterized by voluntary intent on the part of the defendant to engage in conduct that interferes with the socially protected interest of the plaintiff. *Negligence* does not involve the presence of wrongful intent, but rather, the failure of the defendant to conform to a standard of reasonable conduct. *Strict liability* assesses liability without regard to either the unreasonableness of the defendant's intent or the unreasonableness of her conduct; it is liability without fault. The rest of this chapter focuses on intentional torts; Chapter 8 discusses negligence and strict liability.

Intentional torts are distinguished from other torts by the presence of voluntary intent to bring about results that the law does not sanction. The required element of intention does not necessarily mean an evil motive or desire to harm, for an actor may be liable for the consequences of a practical joke or for the consequences of an act he or she did not believe would cause injury. Rather, the actor does something knowingly, and his or her responsibility extends not only to desired consequences, such as a bloody nose from a punch in the face, but also to those that the actor believes or should believe are likely to follow. Several intentional torts are discussed briefly here. For convenience, they are classified into three categories: torts against the person, torts against property interests, and new torts that emerge as tort law evolves. (See Table 6-1.)

TABLE 6-1 INTENTIONAL TORTS

Torts Against the Person	Interference with Property Rights	New Torts
1. Assault	1. Trespass	1. Wrongful discharge
2. Battery	2. Conversion	
3. False imprisonment	3. Nuisance	
4. Defamation		
5. Invasion of privacy		
6. Intentional infliction of emotional distress		

TORTS AGAINST THE PERSON

Several torts protect an individual from intentional interference with his or her body and mind. Starting with the tort of battery, this section discusses the torts that provide redress for the intentional infliction of bodily or mental harm.

Battery

Battery is the intentional touching of another without justification and without consent. Battery also includes the unprivileged touching of another with some substance put in motion by the aggressor. Thus, shooting someone constitutes a battery. "Justification," a term of art (a word with a special meaning to a particular profession or trade—in this case, law), is usually the key to whether a battery has been committed. Obviously, minimal or social touching is not considered battery, but justification is not established merely because onlookers approve of the action. Reasonableness is the standard. Generally, courts hold that a person can meet force or the threat of force with similar force without liability. However, if the perceived threat is to a third party or if the threat is to property, the chance of establishing justification is less. Consider the following case.

Katko v. Briney

Supreme Court of Iowa
183 N.W.2d 657 (1971)

Background: Katko (plaintiff) was injured when a spring gun discharged and shot him in the leg while he was trespassing in an unoccupied farmhouse owned by the Brineys (defendants). Katko sued the Brineys for battery, and the jury returned a verdict for Katko for $20,000 actual damages and $10,000 punitive damages. The trial judge denied the Brineys' motion for a new trial. The Brineys appealed to the Supreme Court of Iowa.

Decision: The Supreme Court of Iowa affirmed the trial judge and ruled in favor of Katko.

Moore, Chief Justice

The primary issue presented here is whether an owner may protect personal property in an unoccupied boarded-up farm house against trespassers and thieves by a spring gun capable of inflicting death or serious injury.

We are not here concerned with a man's right to protect his home and members of his family. Defendants' home was several miles from the scene of the incident to which we refer infra.

Plaintiff's action is for damages resulting from serious injury caused by a shot from a 20-gauge spring shotgun set by defendants in a bedroom of an old farm house which had been uninhabited for several years. Plaintiff and his companion, Marvin McDonough, had broken and entered the house to find and steal old bottles and dated fruit jars which they considered antiques.

The main thrust of defendants' defense in the trial court and on this appeal is that "the law permits use of a spring gun in a dwelling or warehouse for the purpose of preventing the unlawful entry of a burglar or thief." They repeated this contention in their exceptions to the trial court's instructions 2, 5, and 6.

In the statement of issues the trial court stated plaintiff and his companion committed a felony when they broke and entered defendants' house. In instruction 2 the court referred to the early case history of the use of spring guns and stated under the law their use was prohibited except to prevent the commission of felonies of violence and where human life is in danger. The instruction included a statement that breaking and entering is not a felony of violence.

Instruction 5 stated: "You are hereby instructed that one may use reasonable force in the protection of his property, but such right is subject to the qualification that one may not use such means of force as will take human life or inflict great bodily injury. Such is the rule even though the injured party is a trespasser and is in violation of the law himself."

Instruction 6 stated: "An owner of premises is prohibited from wilfully or intentionally injuring a trespasser by means of force that either takes life or inflicts great bodily injury; and therefore a person owning a premises is prohibited from setting out 'spring guns' and like dangerous devices which will likely take life or inflict great bodily injury, for the purpose of harming trespassers. The fact that the trespasser may be acting in violation of the law does not change the rule. The only time when such conduct of setting a 'spring gun' or a like dangerous device is justified would be when the trespasser was committing a felony of violence or a felony punishable by death, or where the trespasser was endangering human life by his act."

The overwhelming weight of authority, both textbook and case law, supports the trial court's statement of the applicable principles of law. Prosser on Torts, third edition, pages 116–18, states:

> the law has always placed a higher value upon human safety than upon mere rights in property, it is the accepted rule that there is no privilege to use any force calculated to cause death or serious bodily injury to repeal the threat to land or chattels, unless there is also such a threat to the defendant's personal safety as to justify a self-defense. . . . Spring guns and other man-killing devices are not justifiable against a mere trespasser, or even a petty thief. They are privileged only against those upon whom the landowner, if he were present in person would be free to inflict injury of the same kind.

Restatement of Torts, section 85, page 180, states:

> The value of human life and limbs, not only to the individual concerned but also to society, so outweighs the interest of a possessor of land in excluding from it those whom he is not willing to admit thereto that a possessor of land has, as is stated in Sec. 79, no privilege to use force intended or likely to cause death or serious harm against another whom the possessor sees about to enter his premises or meddle with his chattel, unless the intrusion threatens death or serious bodily harm to the occupiers or users of the premises. . . . A possessor of land cannot do indirectly and by a mechanical device that which, were he present, he could not do immediately and in person. There-

fore, he cannot gain a privilege to install, for the purpose of protecting his land from intrusions harmless to the lives and limbs of the occupiers or users of it, a mechanical device whose only purpose is to inflict death or serious harm upon such as may intrude, by giving notice of his intention to inflict, by mechanical means and indirectly, harm which he could not, even after request, inflict directly were he present.

The legal principles stated by the trial court in instructions 2, 5, and 6 are well established and supported by the authorities cited and quoted supra. There is no merit in defendants' objections and exceptions thereto. Defendants' various motions based on the same reasons stated in exceptions to instructions were properly overruled.

Assault

Assault is the intentional act of putting someone in immediate apprehension for his or her physical safety. The victim need not necessarily be "frightened"; apprehension is used to mean "expectation." For example, words alone typically do not constitute an assault because they usually are not sufficient to put an ordinary person in apprehension of immediate harm. On the other hand, if the words are coupled with a threat of immediate physical harm—for example, a menacing gesture—an assault could be established.

It is the actor's, rather than the victim's, intention to act and the victim's, rather than the actor's, apprehensive state of mind that are relevant in cases of assault.

False Imprisonment

False imprisonment is the intentional confinement of a nonconsenting individual within boundaries fixed by the defendant for an appreciable time. The tort protects an individual's freedom of movement or liberty. The tort arises in business contexts from attempts to deal with suspected shoplifters or with employees suspected of dishonest behavior. Here the customer's or employee's interest in unrestrained movement conflicts with the storeowner's or employer's interest in protecting his or her property. At common law, a storekeeper is liable in tort for false imprisonment if he or she detains a suspected shoplifter who ultimately is found innocent. This places the storekeeper in a dilemma: if the storekeeper suspects a person of shoplifting, has the individual arrested, and then discovers that the person did not steal anything, the storekeeper is liable for false imprisonment; if the storekeeper does nothing and permits the suspected shoplifter to leave the store, all hope of proof is lost forever. The result is that, in most cases, unless he or she is absolutely sure, the storekeeper will let the suspected shoplifter go and will pass on the loss to the consuming public.

Because shoplifting is a major social problem, costing the consuming public billions of dollars through inflated prices, the law in most states resolves the conflict between the storekeeper's property interest and the consumer's liberty interest by conferring a limited or qualified privilege upon the storekeeper to reasonably detain those he or she reasonably suspects of shoplifting.

Defamation

Defamation is the communication of untrue statements about someone to a third party. The statements in question must injure the victim's reputation or character. For example, if Jack tells his friends that Mary is a prostitute, when in fact she is not, Jack has defamed Mary.

There are two categories of defamation: slander, or oral defamation, and libel, or written defamation. In most states today, plaintiffs must establish that they have been damaged, for example, by a loss of customers, business, or a particular contract.

One form of defamation, defamation per se, eliminates the necessity of establishing such damages. Four categories of defamation fall under the *per se* rule. Defamation per se exists when the plaintiff alleges that the defendant:

1. accused the plaintiff of having committed a serious crime, such as murder
2. stated that plaintiff has a loathsome disease, such as a venereal disease
3. asserted that the plaintiff was professionally incompetent, such as calling a surgeon "a butcher"
4. stated that the plaintiff was an unchaste woman

Several defenses may be asserted in a defamation case. *Truth* is an absolute defense. Thus, if Jack calls Mary a prostitute and Mary in fact is a prostitute, Jack has a good defense. It is also necessary that someone other than the person defamed hear the defamatory statement. If someone angrily shouts a defamatory remark about someone else, but no one hears it, there can be no suit for defamation. Another defense against a charge of defamation is *privilege*. If defamation occurs in a privileged context, no legal relief is available to the victim of the defamation. A privilege may be either an absolute privilege or a qualified privilege. An absolute privilege exists for judges, legislators, lawyers, and parties and witnesses acting in their official capacities or in the roles for which the privilege exists. A qualified privilege exists for communications where it is in the public interest to promote the communication. For example, if one employer asks another to comment on the character of a former employee, the former employer enjoys a qualified privilege to do so. The qualified privilege is lost if the plaintiff can establish malice on the part of the speaker.

Invasion of Privacy

A person's dignity and the right to be let alone are protected by the tort of *invasion of privacy*. The courts have recognized four types of invasion of privacy: (1) intrusion upon the plaintiff's physical solitude (for example, illegal searches of persons, eavesdropping, peering into windows); (2) appropriation of the plaintiff's name or likeness (for example, using a picture of the plaintiff in an advertisement); (3) placement of the plaintiff in a false light in the public eye (for example, falsely attributing authorship of a poem to a well-known poet); and (4) the public disclosure of private facts (for example, disclosing an employee's illness to a third party).

In the following case, the court considers whether a landlord's intrusion into a tenant's apartment constitutes the tort of invasion of privacy.

Carvajal v. Levy
Court of Appeals of Louisiana
485 So.2d 586 (1986)

Background: Mrs. Enrique Carvajal (lessor) sued Scott Levy (lessee) to cancel a written lease and evict Levy. Levy counterclaimed against Mrs. Carvajal for the tort of invasion of privacy.

Following the signing of the lease, Levy moved into the leased premises on September 15, 1981. On September 30, 1981, a neighbor told Levy that he had seen Mrs. Carvajal leaving his apartment. Levy later discovered that two burners on his stove, which had not worked since the date he had moved into the apartment, were operating. He telephoned Mrs. Carvajal and told her that he wanted to be notified before anyone went into his apartment.

Later, in November 1981, after a request by Levy, and during his absence, a switch was installed for operating the garbage disposal. Despite Levy's request to be notified in advance, no prior notice was given.

In June 1982, Levy was sleeping when he heard someone enter his front door. The person identified himself as an electrician employed by Mrs. Carvajal and stated he was there to repair a wall socket. Levy allowed the repair work but again called Mrs. Carvajal and complained that he had not been given any notice about the repair work.

In September 1982, an employee of Mrs. Carvajal was sent over at 11 A.M. to repair a door knob on the front door. The repairman knocked first and was admitted by Levy. Again, Levy complained about the lack of prior notice.

In October 1982, Mrs. Carvajal, unannounced, brought an appraiser to look at Levy's apartment. After that, Levy changed the locks. Mrs. Carvajal and a repairman were denied access because of the changed lock.

The trial court gave judgment in favor of Mrs. Carvajal. Levy appealed.

Decision: The Court of Appeals affirmed the trial court's judgment in favor of Mrs. Carvajal.

Gulotta, Judge

In considering invasion of privacy allegations, courts distinguish between actionable and non-actionable invasions. Generally, an *actionable* invasion of privacy exists only when the defendant's conduct is unreasonable and seriously interferes with plaintiff's privacy interests. The reasonableness of one's conduct is determined by balancing his interests in pursuing a course of conduct against the interest in protecting one's privacy. Where defendant's action is properly authorized or justified by circumstances, it is deemed to be reasonable and non-actionable, even though it admits to a slight invasion of the plaintiff's privacy.

In our case, all but one of the situations which lessee contends to be an invasion of privacy came about as a result of repairs to the apartment that either lessor or lessee had deemed necessary. Furthermore, although the various entries were without prior notice there is nothing in the record to indicate serious interference with lessee's privacy. Accordingly, we cannot say that lessor's conduct was unreasonable and we cannot conclude, as a matter of law, that her actions amount to an actionable invasion of privacy.

Schott, Judge *(dissenting)*

The lease permits the lessor to enter the premises for the purpose of making repairs necessary to the preservation of the property. It also permits inspection by lessor at reasonable times. The first two instances which occurred in September and November, 1981 were violations because they were unauthorized entries to make repairs which were not necessary for the preservation of the premises. The same is true of the third incident in June, 1982 although this intrusion lasted but a few moments and was acquiesced in when Levy gave the workman his permission to repair the wall socket.

The other two instances of the door knob repair and the visit by the appraiser are not actionable because Levy consented to these entries.

I do not consider it reasonable for a lessor to enter leased premises to make minor repairs without the lessee's permission, especially after the lessee has repeatedly objected to such conduct. Furthermore, any such intrusion on the privacy of one's home is, per se, a serious interference with one's right to privacy.

Intentional Infliction of Emotional Distress

A person's interest in emotional tranquility is protected as a result of a recent trend to recognize intentional infliction of emotional distress as a separate tort. The tort may be defined as the intentional causing of severe mental suffering in another by means of extreme and outrageous conduct. Liability is limited to outrageous acts that cause bona fide emotional injury. The defendant's conduct must be what the average community member would consider extremely outrageous. The plaintiff's emotional distress must in fact exist and it must be severe. Minor offenses, such as name calling, are not actionable although they may wound the feelings of the victim and cause some degree of mental upset. The plaintiff cannot recover merely because of hurt feelings; the law is not concerned with trifles and cannot provide a civil remedy for every personal conflict in a crowded world. Previously, the acts had to result in direct physical injury for there to be recovery for the mental distress. Even the more liberalized modern standard is difficult to sustain in most cases.

Consider the following case.

Goldfarb v. Baker

Supreme Court of Tennessee
547 S.W.2d 567 (1977)

Background: Mark Goldfarb (plaintiff), a Memphis State University student, was enrolled in a course taught by Professor Arthur Baker (defendant). During a class meeting, an unidentified prankster entered the classroom, threw a pie, which struck the professor, and ran away. Baker immediately accused Goldfarb of the assault. The next day, Baker forbade Goldfarb from attending class, had him ejected from the building when he attempted to take his seat, and, in the presence of others, accused Goldfarb of attempting to blackmail him.

Goldfarb sued Baker for the tort of intentional infliction of emotional distress. Goldfarb, a former state prisoner, claimed that because of this episode he was falsely portrayed as a lawless individual whose attempted rehabilitation had failed, that he lost the confidence of his associates, and was frustrated in his effort to reform his life. He claimed that Baker's actions caused him extreme mental anguish, humiliation,

ETHICS BOX
Ethical Issues and Privacy

Consider the following case. You work as an advertising manager for an airline. You go for dinner at the home of a good friend who is also a pilot for your airline. You inadvertently walk in on the pilot in his den and discover him using cocaine. You don't know his flying schedule, but you are aware that the pilot's union has resisted random drug testing. What should you do?

Disclosure to the airline would better enable the company to monitor the pilot to make sure that he is in a condition to fly. Yet disclosure also violates the pilot's privacy, particularly in view of the fact that the use was in his own home and not done purposely in front of you. If you had observed the use while on the job, it would be easy to construct a case for disclosure. This case is more difficult and may depend on other factors including knowledge of when the pilot will fly next and the company's policies both on the use of drugs off hours and on whistle-blowing.

What about the pilot? It should be easy to construct a breach of professional ethics. He is using an illegal substance, and there is a substantial possibility that his work performance will be affected.

depression, and distress. The trial judge found Baker's alleged conduct not to be sufficiently outrageous to be actionable and dismissed Goldfarb's complaint for failure to state a claim. Goldfarb appealed to the Supreme Court of Tennessee.
Decision: The Supreme Court of Tennessee affirmed the trial judge's decision in favor of Baker.

Brock, Justice

It has proven to be difficult to formulate an objective legal standard for determining whether or not particular unseemly conduct is so intolerable as to be tortious. The *Restatement (2d) of Torts* informs us that it is not enough, according to the cases, "... that the defendant has acted with an intent which is tortious or even criminal, or that he has intended to inflict emotional distress, or even that his conduct has been characterized by 'malice,' or a degree of aggravation which would entitle the plaintiff to punitive damages for another tort." It has been held that the defendant's conduct must be so outrageous in character and extreme in degree as to be beyond the pale of decency and that it must have caused serious mental injury to the plaintiff. The conduct must be "atrocious," "utterly intolerable," and "beyond all bounds of decency."

Moreover, conduct which would be intolerable if unprovoked may be excused if it results from circumstances of annoyance or stress.

This complaint shows that the defendant acted under provocation. The plaintiff claims that he was innocent of any wrongdoing in the pie-throwing episode but not that the defendant knew, or that he should have known, that he was making a false accusation. Although the accusation of blackmail was excessive, still it was the product of a sudden, unjustified, and humiliating attack by someone upon the defendant. The plaintiff was warned that he would be excluded from class because of his supposed conduct and apparently did not protest his innocence at that point. With no reason to believe he was acting against the wrong person, the defendant apparently was justified in taking measures to prevent further disorder in his classroom. We hold that the facts alleged do not state a cause of action. The facts alleged in the complaint do, indeed, constitute a misfortune for the plaintiff. However, " 'Against a large part of the frictions and irritations and clashing of temperaments incident to participating in community life, a certain toughening of the mental hide is a better protection than the law could ever be.' " The present case is among those frictions and irritations.

TORTS AGAINST PROPERTY INTERESTS

Three torts exist to redress intentional interference with an individual's interest in the possession of property: trespass, conversion, and nuisance.

Trespass

The tort of trespass is really two torts: trespass to land and trespass to personal property.

Trespass to land may be defined as intentionally entering upon another's land or causing an object or a third person to do so. Trespass to land may also occur where a person intentionally remains on another's land or fails to remove from the land an object that he or she is under a duty to remove. Liability exists for trespass to land even where no harm results from the trespass. The major defenses to trespass to land are consent and accidental intrusion.

Trespass to personal property may be defined as intentionally taking or damaging the personal property of another. An example of trespass to personal property would be a creditor, attempting to repossess a car held as collateral for a loan to a debtor, mistakenly taking someone else's car. The defenses of consent and unavoidable accident apply also to the tort of trespass to personal property.

Conversion

Conversion is the intentional exercise of control over personal property, thereby seriously interfering with another person's right of possession. The difference between the torts of trespass to personal property and conversion lies in the measure of damages for the torts. The measure of damages for trespass to personal property is the diminished value of the personal property because of any injury to it. The measure of damages for conversion is the full value of the property at the time it was converted. Because of the larger recovery, conversion is limited to serious interferences with the right of possession that justify requiring the defendant to pay its full value. Thus, in the preceding example of the creditor who repossesses the wrong car, there is no conversion if the creditor immediately returns the car. He or she would, however, be liable for trespass to personal property and could be required to pay costs such as gasoline and depreciation. If the creditor totally wrecked the car while driving it away, he or she would be liable for the full value of the car to the car's owner for the tort of conversion.

Nuisance

A *nuisance* is an unlawful interference with a person's use or enjoyment of his or her land. It includes any use of property that gives offense to or endangers life or health—for example, by unreasonably polluting the air. The interference with the landowner's interest must be substantial. The standard is similar to the test for the tort of intentional infliction of emotional distress: a definite and substantial offensiveness, inconvenience, or annoyance to the normal person in the community.

The interference must not only be substantial, it must also be unreasonable. This involves weighing the gravity and probability of harm resulting from the defendant's conduct against its social utility. Thus, a defendant may engage in a reasonable use of his or her property at the expense of the neighbors.

Although most nuisance cases are brought as intentional tort claims, the basis of liability is the nature of the interference with the plaintiff's use and enjoyment of property, not the intent of the defendant. Liability may extend to negligent interferences and, where the interference results from an abnormally offensive activity, to strict liability.

THE EMERGING TORT OF WRONGFUL DISCHARGE

As mentioned at the beginning of this chapter, tort law is not stagnant. New torts are continually being recognized by the courts. The advent of prima facie tort theory made possible the recognition of new causes of action. The *tort of wrongful discharge* is such a frontier-area tort. The development of this cause of action by the courts reflects the development of law in response to particular interests and concerns of today's society and demonstrates that tort law continues to display much ferment and change.

In states where the tort of wrongful discharge is recognized, a fired employee may recover against his or her former employer where the employer terminates the employee against public policy. That is, the employee must prove that it is in the public interest to protect the employee from termination. For example, it has been held to constitute the tort of wrongful discharge for an employer to terminate an employee for serving on a jury, because to allow such a termination would undermine the jury system.

In states that do not recognize the tort of wrongful discharge, an employment relation of indefinite duration is considered to be terminable by either the employer or the employee at will, unless there exists a contract or a statute to the contrary. An example of such a contract would be a collective bargaining contract that contains a clause prohibiting discharges except for cause. An example of a statute would be Title VII of the Civil Rights Act, which forbids discharges based on the employee's race, sex, religion, or national origin. Where no contract or statute exists to provide a different rule, an employer may discharge an employee for cause or no cause, in good faith or maliciously, for reason or no reason.

In the following case, the court recognizes the tort of wrongful discharge.

Tameny v. Atlantic Richfield Co.

Supreme Court of California
164 Cal.Rptr. 839 (1980)

Background: Gordon Tameny (plaintiff-appellant) sued his former employer, Atlantic Richfield Company (Arco) (defendant-appellee), alleging that Arco had discharged him after fifteen years of service because he refused to participate in a scheme to fix retail gasoline prices. Tameny contended that Arco's conduct in discharging him for refusing to commit a criminal act constituted a tort and subjected the employer to liability for compensatory and punitive damages under normal tort principles. Arco contended that Tameny's allegations, even if true, did not state a cause of action in tort. The trial court accepted Arco's argument and dismissed Tameny's complaint. Tameny appealed to the California Supreme Court.

Decision: The California Supreme Court reversed the trial court decision and sent the case back to the trial court for consideration of Tameny's complaint.

Tobriner, Justice

Under the traditional common law rule, codified in Labor Code section 2922, an employment contract of indefinite duration is in general terminable at "the will" of either party. Over the past several decades, however, judicial authorities in California and throughout the United States have established the rule that under both common law and the statute an employer does not enjoy an absolute or totally unfettered right to discharge even an at-will employee. In a series of cases arising out of a variety of factual settings in which a discharge clearly violated an express statutory objective or undermined a firmly established principle of public policy, courts have recognized that an employer's traditional broad authority to discharge an at-will employee "may be limited by statute . . . or by considerations of public policy."

In light of the foregoing authorities, we conclude that an employee's action for wrongful discharge subjects an employer to tort liability.

California courts have not been alone in recognizing the propriety of a tort remedy when an employer's discharge of an employee contravenes the dictates of public policy. In Nees v. Hocks (1975), for example, the Oregon Supreme Court upheld an employee's recovery of compensatory damages in tort for the emotional distress suffered when her employer discharged her for serving on a jury. Similarly, in Harless v. First Nat. Bank in Fairmont (W. Va. 1978), the Supreme Court of West Virginia upheld a wrongful discharge action by a bank employee who was terminated after attempting to persuade his employer to comply with consumer protection laws, reasoning that "where the employer's motivation for [a] discharge contravenes some substantial public policy principle, then the employer may be liable to the employee for damages occasioned by the discharge," and concluding that the employee's cause of action "is one in tort and it therefore follows that rules relating to tort damages would be applicable."

Indeed, the *Nees* and *Harless* decisions are merely illustrative of a rapidly growing number of cases throughout the country that in recent years have recognized a common law tort action for wrongful discharge in cases in which the termination contravenes public policy.

These recent decisions demonstrate a continuing judicial recognition of the fact, enunciated by this court more than 35 years ago, that "[t]he days when a servant was practically the slave of his master have long since passed." Greene v. Hawaiian Dredging Co. (1945). In the last half century the rights of employees have not only been proclaimed by a mass of legislation touching upon almost every aspect of the employer-employee relationship, but the courts have likewise evolved certain additional protections at common law. The courts have been sensitive to the need to protect the individual employee from discriminatory exclusion from the opportunity of employment whether it be by the all-powerful union or employer. This development at common law shows that the employer is not so absolute a sovereign of the job that there are not limits to his prerogative. One such limit at least is the present case. The employer cannot condition employment upon required participation in unlawful conduct by the employee.

We hold that an employer's authority over its employee does not include the right to demand that the employee commit a criminal act to further its interest, and an employer may not coerce compliance with such unlawful directions by discharging an employee who refuses to follow such an order. An employer engaging in such conduct violates a basic duty imposed by law upon all employers, and thus an employee of such discharge may maintain a tort action for wrongful discharge against the employer.

Accordingly, we conclude that the trial court erred in [dismissing] . . . plaintiff's tort action for wrongful discharge.

REVIEW PROBLEMS

1. What is a tort?
2. What are the three classifications of tort law?
3. What kind of intent is required for an intentional tort?
4. What two defenses are available for most intentional torts?
5. An employer suspected that one of ten employees had stolen company property. The employer called a meeting of the suspected employees and told them that if the guilty employee did not come forward and confess the act within five minutes, the employer would commence to fire the employees in alphabetical order during each successive minute thereafter. Employee Amy Able was the first employee fired after the initial five-minute period had elapsed. Upon being told that she was fired, Amy started crying and immediately left the employer's premises and returned home. At home, Amy's husband consoled her, saying, "Don't worry, Amy, we'll sue

the employer for all he is worth for the tort of intentional infliction of emotional distress." If Amy sues the employer, will she win? Explain.

6. A. L. Stephens and Carl Stephens had arranged to bury their brother, George Stephens, at the Goodby Cemetery, with the permission of the owners of the cemetery. At 7:30 A.M. on the day of the burial, Bud Waits came to the cemetery and informed A. L. Stephens that Stephens was trespassing on his lot. Bud Waits went home to get some papers that would prove his ownership of the lot, and he sent his wife, Ora Waits, to the cemetery to prevent the burial. At 12:30 P.M., the vault which was to be placed in the grave in which the casket was to be placed later was brought to the cemetery. Mrs. Waits seated herself on the vault, took up an iron pick and threatened to strike anyone who attempted to place the vault in the grave. From 2:30 P.M. until 3:30 P.M., funeral services were held in the

church adjoining the cemetery. When the body was brought to the grave, Ora Waits refused to allow anyone to move the vault on which she was seated or to place it in the grave. A. L. Stephens sought out a justice of the peace, who finally persuaded Ora Waits to get off the vault so that George Stephens could be put in it. A. L. and Carl Stephens sued Bud and Ora Waits, alleging that the Waitses committed the tort of intentional infliction of emotional distress. Who wins and why?

7. Dun & Bradstreet, Inc., a credit reporting agency, sent a report to five subscribers indicating that Greenmoss Builders, Inc., a construction contractor, had filed a voluntary petition for bankruptcy. The report was false and grossly misrepresented Greenmoss Builders' assets and liabilities. Thereafter Dun & Bradstreet issued a corrective notice, but Greenmoss Builders was dissatisfied with this notice and brought a defamation lawsuit against Dun & Bradstreet alleging that the report had injured its reputation and seeking damages. What must Greenmoss Builders prove in order to recover damages from Dun & Bradstreet? Explain. Does the First Amendment privilege with regard to "public figures" apply to this situation? Explain.

8. Mrs. Marion Bonkowski, accompanied by her husband, left Arlan's Department Store in Saginaw, Michigan, about 10:00 P.M. on December 18, 1962, after making several purchases. Earl Reinhardt, a private policeman on duty that night in Arlan's, called to her to stop as she was walking to her car about thirty feet away in the adjacent parking lot. Reinhardt motioned to Mrs. Bonkowski to return toward the store, and when she had done so Reinhardt said that someone in the store had told him Mrs. Bonkowski had put three pieces of jewelry into her purse without having paid for them. Mrs. Bonkowski denied she had taken anything unlawfully, but Reinhardt told her he wanted to see the contents of her purse. On a cement step in front of the store, Mrs. Bonkowski emptied the contents of her purse into her husband's hands. Mr. Bonkowski produced sales slips for the items she had purchased, and Reinhardt, satisfied that she had not committed larceny, returned to the store. Mrs. Bonkowski brought suit against Earl Reinhardt and Arlan's Department Store, claiming that, as a result of defendants' tortious acts, she suffered numerous psychosomatic symptoms, including headaches, nervousness, and depression. Who wins? Explain. Bonkowski v. Arlan's Dept. Store, 162 N.W.2d 347 (1968).

9. On leaving a restaurant, X by mistake takes Y's hat from the rack, believing it to be his own. When he reaches the sidewalk, X puts on the hat, discovers his mistake, and immediately reenters the restaurant and returns the hat to the rack. Has X committed either trespass to personal property or conversion? Blackington v. Pillsbury, 165 N.E. 895 (1927).

10. H obtained a credit card in his name only from Slick Oil Company and used it in making purchases at Slick gas stations. W, a secretary at Cow College, handled family finances. W informed H (but not Slick) that she would not make further payments on the account, and the account became delinquent in the amount of $200. Slick sent a letter to the personnel director at Cow College seeking assistance. The letter claimed W was Slick's customer and had incurred expenses, and it requested Cow College's assistance in interviewing W. Did Slick commit any intentional torts? Signal Oil & Gas Co. v. Conway, 191 S.E.2d 624 (Ga. App. 1972).

11. Morgan owned a tract of nine acres of land on which he had his dwelling, a restaurant, and accommodations for thirty-two trail-

ers. High Penn Oil Co. owned an adjacent tract on which it operated an oil refinery, at a distance of 1,000 feet from Morgan's dwelling. Morgan sued High Penn to recover damages for a nuisance and to abate such nuisance by injunction. Morgan's evidence was that for some hours on two or three different days each week the refinery emitted nauseating gases and odors in great quantities, which invaded Morgan's land and other tracts of land. High Penn failed to put an end to this atmospheric pollution after receiving notice and demand from Morgan to abate it. High Penn's evidence was that the oil refinery was a modern plant of the type approved, known, and in general use for renovating used lubricating oils; that it was not so constructed or operated as to give out noxious gases or odors in annoying quantities; and that it had not annoyed Morgan or other persons save on a single occasion when it suffered a brief mechanical breakdown. Who should win? Explain. Morgan v. High Penn Oil Co., 77 S.E.2d 682 (N.C. 1953).

12. Brents, an exasperated creditor, put a placard in the show window of his garage, on a public street, which stated that "Dr. W. R. Morgan owes an account here for $49.67. This account will be advertised as long as it remains unpaid." Morgan sued Brents for the tort of invasion of privacy. Who wins? Explain. Could Brents hold the authors of this text liable for invasion of privacy by reason of their publishing the incident in this text? Explain. Brents v. Morgan, 299 S.W. 967 (Ky. 1927).

Competitive Torts

The American economic system relies primarily upon the free market for the allocation of resources. Substantial economic and legal opinion supports the proposition that the market assures the most efficient allocation of goods and services while preserving economic, social, and political freedom. Nevertheless, limited government intervention has been deemed necessary to prevent competition from taking socially undesirable and destructive forms. In order to assure fair and honest competition, the courts have applied common law tort theory to provide redress for unfair trade practices.

This chapter focuses on some of the ways tort theory has been applied to competitive practices. Special attention is given to the torts of unfair competition, appropriation of trade values, and interference with contractual relations. Several federal statutes that provide redress for the infringement of patents, copyrights, trade names, and trademarks are also discussed.

UNFAIR COMPETITION

Because of the high value placed on competition, the law recognizes a qualified privilege to engage in business in good faith. Someone who causes loss of business to another merely by engaging in a business in good faith is not liable for the loss he or she causes. The theory is that, in the long run, competition promotes efficiency and general economic welfare and that to subject a person to liability merely for competing would prevent competition. However, the privilege is lost if a person acts in bad faith and engages in a business primarily for the purpose of causing loss of business to another and with the intention of terminating the business when that purpose is accomplished. Bad faith is usually manifested by the use of predatory business practices. Consider the following case.

Tuttle v. Buck

Supreme Court of Minnesota
119 N.W. 946 (1909)

Background: Tuttle (plaintiff-appellant) was a barber in a small town in Minnesota. He sued Buck (defendant-appellee), a banker, alleging that Buck had set up a rival barbershop for the sole purpose of driving Tuttle out of business. The trial judge overruled a motion by Buck to terminate the proceedings. Buck's motion argued that Tuttle's complaint did not make out a claim in tort. Buck appealed to the Supreme Court of Minnesota.

Decision: The Supreme Court of Minnesota ruled in favor of Tuttle and affirmed the trial judge's decision not to terminate Tuttle's lawsuit.

Elliot, Justice

For generations there has been a practical agreement upon the proposition that competition in trade and business is desirable, and this idea has found expression in the decisions of the courts as well as in statutes. But it has led to grievous and manifold wrongs to individuals, and many courts have manifested an earnest desire to protect the individuals from the evils which result from unrestrained business competition. The problem has been to so adjust matters as to preserve the principle of competition and yet guard against its abuse to the unnecessary injury to the individual. So the principle that a man may use his own property according to his own needs and desires, while true in the abstract, is subject to many limitations in the concrete. Men cannot always, in civilized society, be allowed to use their own property as their interests or desires may dictate without reference to the fact that they have neighbors whose rights are as sacred as their own. The existence and well-being of society requires that each and every person shall conduct himself consistently with the fact that he is a social and reasonable person.

To divert to one's self the customers of a business rival by the offer of goods at lower prices is in general a legitimate mode of serving one's own interest, and justifiable as fair competition. But when a man starts an opposition place of business, not for the sake of profit to himself, but regardless of loss to himself, and for the sole purpose of driving his competitor out of business, and with the intention of himself retiring upon the accomplishment of his malevolent purpose, he is guilty of a wanton wrong and an actionable tort. In such a case he would not be exercising his legal right, or doing an act which can be judged separately from the motive which actuated him. To call such conduct competition is a perversion of terms. It is simply the application of force without legal justification, which in its moral quality may be no better than highway robbery.

A majority of the Justices . . . are of the opinion that . . . the complaint states a cause of action, and the order is therefore affirmed.

INTERFERENCE WITH CONTRACTUAL RELATIONS

An individual who intentionally and without justification causes a third person not to perform a contract with another is liable for the resulting harm. The elements of the business *tort of interference with contractual relations* are: (1) an existing contract between the plaintiff and a third party; (2) the defendant's knowledge of this contract; (3) intentional and improper interference inducing or causing a breach of the contract; and (4) resulting damage. The following case considers the third element: what constitutes intentional and improper inducement to breach a contract.

Edward Vantine Studios, Inc., v. Fraternal Composite Service, Inc.

Court of Appeals of Iowa
373 N.W.2d 512 (1985)

Background: Edward Vantine Studios, Inc. (plaintiff) sued Fraternal Composite Services, Inc. (defendant) for the tort of interference with contracts. The two companies were involved in the business of photographing composites of fraternities and sororities on various campuses throughout the country. Vantine's booking agent completed signed contracts with several fraternities and sororities at Iowa State University for the 1982–1983 school year.

In the summer of 1981, a sales manager for Fraternal Composite visited all the fraternities and sororities at Iowa State, but signed no new contracts. In the spring of 1982, the sales manager visited fifteen houses on campus and again signed no new contracts. In the summer of 1982, the sales manager talked with officers at all the fraternities and sororities. He returned to many of these houses, and was told that the organizations had existing contracts with Vantine. The sales manager suggested that the houses investigate the legality of these contracts. On later visits, the sales manager signed contracts with twelve houses who had a previous contract with Vantine. All but one of those contracts contained a provision stating that Fraternal Composites would pay any legal costs or fees incurred in breaking the contracts that were already held with Vantine. (This is referred as the indemnity clause.)

Members of the fraternities and sororities expressed dissatisfaction with previous service provided by Vantine. Fraternal Composites attempted to capitalize on these objections by offering a lower price and an earlier delivery date than Vantine. However, the fraternity and sorority members indicated that they would not have terminated Vantine's contract except for the insertion of the indemnity clause in Fraternal Composite's contract. They testified that they were not subjected to any undue pressure from the actions of Fraternal Composite's sales manager. Vantine was notified that its contracts were terminated when its photographer appeared at the fraternity and sorority houses for scheduled photography sessions. Fraternal Composites later provided the desired services and all customers were satisfied.

The trial court determined that Fraternal Composites committed the tort of interference with contracts. Fraternal Composites appealed to the Iowa Court of Appeals. Decision: The Iowa Court of Appeals affirmed the trial court decision in favor of Vantine.

Hayden, Judge

Defendant's primary contention is that its actions in interfering with plaintiff's contracts were not intentional or improper and hence were not actionable. We disagree.

There can be little question but that defendant intentionally interfered with plaintiff's contracts. Defendant concedes its awareness of those contracts during the course of its attempts to obtain its own contracts with the twelve houses. Defendant advised the houses to investigate the validity of their contracts with plaintiff and then suggested or at least agreed to insert a clause in its own contracts to indemnify the houses for any legal costs or fees incurred by reason of their breach of their contracts with plaintiff. This is certainly an intentional course of conduct which induced the houses not to perform their contracts with plaintiff.

We also believe and agree with the trial court that defendant's interference was improper to the extent that it agreed to indemnify the houses for any legal costs or fees resulting from their breach of plaintiff's contracts. We concede defendant's point that the business of photographing composites for college fraternities and sororities is very competitive and that the various individual companies in that business will seek to expand their own share of the market, very often at the expense of their competitors. We do not, however, believe that this competitive factor gives defendant free rein to use whatever inducements it can think of to lure potential customers away from already existing valid and binding contracts. We adopt the trial court's language on this point:

> If the contracts had been terminated by reason of better price, better service, or better quality alone, . . . the Court would not have determined there was a tortious interference with the contracts. It may have caused some claim or cause of action between [plaintiff] and the breaching fraternity and sorority, but it would not have created an actionable tort against the Defendant herein. The Defendant, however, by the insertion, or the encouragement of the insertion, of the indemnity clause has crossed over the line of legitimate competition. It has committed an actionable tort by such activity.

Representatives from five of the fraternities involved testified that they would not have breached their agreements with plaintiff and contracted with defendant without the indemnity clause agreed to by defendant. The importance of this clause to defendant is thus obvious. Our acceptance of such a tactic would render the notion of sanctity of contract a nullity and would indicate that a contract could be breached with impunity merely by having the party inducing the breach assume the financial consequences of such breach.

The trial court correctly found defendant's conduct intentional and improper.

APPROPRIATION OF TRADE VALUES

The appropriation of trade values may be accomplished in a variety of ways. For example, an inventor's idea may be stolen by someone with whom the inventor shares the idea, or a competitor may "palm off" another's product as his or her own or steal another's trade secret. When this occurs, tort law provides remedies in the torts of misappropriation, palming off, and wrongfully obtaining a trade secret.

Misappropriation

Corporations continually receive unsolicited ideas from the general public concerning possible inventions, product innovations, or suggested advertising schemes. Difficulties arise if the suggested idea parallels the corporation's research or prior intentions. When the company later comes out with a product that is similar to the suggested product or with an advertising scheme that is similar to the one proposed, people who sent the unsolicited ideas may become aware of the corporation's product or advertisement and bring suit for the misappropriation of their ideas. *Misappropriation* is the unlawful taking of the product or idea of another and making use of it as though it were one's own. A plaintiff suing for misappropriation of unsolicited ideas will have a difficult time establishing a case, because he or she must prove: (1) that the information was presented to the company with the clear expectation that he or she was to be compensated for its use; (2) that he or she has a protected property interest in the idea described; and (3) that the company's use of the idea was wrongful vis-à-vis the plaintiff's protected property interest.

Palming Off

The tort of *palming off* involves an attempt by one producer to pass off its product as that of another manufacturer who has built up considerable goodwill. Thus, one manufacturer might make its product look similar to the well-advertised product of its competitor, hoping to confuse some of the buying public as to the source of the product. This allows the party who is palming off to take a "free ride" on its competitor's advertising. In order for such activities to constitute the tort of palming off, the courts require (1) that the original product have acquired a secondary meaning and (2) that the original product be so similar to the copied product as to cause confusion in the marketplace regarding the source of the copied product. "Secondary meaning" attaches to a product that, through long production by a particular manufacturer, has come to be recognized as its product. The consumer thus associates the product with a particular firm and draws a secondary conclusion as to the quality of the product.

Misappropriation of Trade Secrets

Someone who discloses or uses another's trade secret, without privilege to do so, may be liable to the owner of such information for the

---

PREVENTIVE LAW
Protecting Against Misappropriation
___

By and large, a plaintiff suing for misappropriation of unsolicited ideas will have a very difficult time winning his or her case. Therefore, individuals who have ideas that they think may be useful to certain businesses should clearly indicate in writing that they are disclosing their ideas in confidence and that they expect compensation. Preferably, partial disclosure should be made for the purpose of indicating the basic nature of the proposal with the understanding that complete disclosure will follow a mutually acceptable agreement concerning compensation.

Although business firms may take comfort in the fact that it is difficult for a plaintiff to win a suit for misappropriation of an unsolicited idea, they may nevertheless be faced with time-consuming and costly litigation if they fail to deal properly with unsolicited ideas. A major study found that 20 percent of the corporations whose executives were interviewed had had some problems with handling unsolicited ideas.* The study also surveyed the procedures generally followed by most companies in dealing with unsolicited information. It determined that businesses generally instruct their employees to stop reading any letter upon recognition that it involves unsolicited ideas. The employees are cautioned not to acknowledge the letter and are asked to forward the letter to corporate counsel. At this point a waiver and release form will be mailed to the letter sender asking for release of all claims except those that may arise from patent protection. In return the company would evaluate the idea. Payment for the use of a significant idea is determined by contractual negotiations.

*National Industrial Conference Board, *Patent Counsel*, p. 25.

---

damage caused. Generally, to recover for the tort of *misappropriation of trade secrets*, a plaintiff must prove the following:

1. The existence of the alleged trade secret by demonstrating that there was a degree of secrecy employed in its use, it was unknown to the public or a general industry, it gave the plaintiff a genuine competitive advantage, and it was subject to reasonably adequate safeguards against disclosure;

2. The defendant wrongfully obtained the trade secret from the plaintiff, and not merely by reverse engineering or independent discovery; and

3. Damage or the likelihood of damage will result from actual or threatened misappropriation or disclosure.

The following case considers the second element: what constitutes obtaining trade secret information in a wrongful manner.

E. I. Du Pont de Nemours & Co., Inc. v. Christopher

U.S. Court of Appeals, Fifth Circuit

431 F.2d 1012 (1970)

Background: Rolfe and Gary Christopher (defendants) were hired by a third party to take aerial photographs of a plant that was being constructed by the E. I. Du Pont de Nemours Co. (plaintiff). The plant was designed for a highly secret yet unpatented process for producing methanol. Because the plant was under construction, parts of the process were exposed to view from overhead. The pictures could be used by a skilled person to discover the process. Du Pont sued the Christophers for damages and an injunction. Du Pont claimed that one who discloses or uses another's trade secret, without a privilege to do so, is liable to the other if he discovered the secret by improper means. The Christophers contended that because they flew in public airspace and did not trespass or engage in other illegal conduct, their discovery was not by improper means. The trial judge denied the Christophers' motion to dismiss Du Pont's complaint. The Christophers appealed to the U.S. Circuit Court of Appeals for the Fifth Circuit.

Decision: The Circuit Court of Appeals ruled in favor of Du Pont and affirmed the trial judge's decision not to dismiss Du Pont's complaint.

Goldberg, Circuit Judge

This is a case of industrial espionage in which an airplane is the cloak and a camera the dagger. . . .

This is a case of first impression, for the Texas courts have not faced this precise factual issue, and . . . we must . . . divine what the Texas courts would do if such a situation were presented to them. . . . The Texas Supreme Court specifically adopted the rule found in the Restatement of Torts which provides:

> One who discloses or uses another's trade secret, without a privilege to do so, is liable to the other if
> (a) he discovered the secret by improper means, or
> (b) his disclosure or use constitutes a breach of confidence reposed in him by the other in disclosing the secret to him . . .
> Restatement of Torts Sec. 757 (1939)

The question remaining, therefore, is whether aerial photography of plant construction is an improper means of obtaining another's trade secret. We conclude that it is and that the Texas courts would so hold. The Supreme Court of that state has declared that "the undoubted tendency of the law has been to recognize and enforce higher standards of commercial morality in the business world." That court has quoted with approval articles indicating that the proper means of gaining possession of a competitor's secret process is "through inspection and analysis" of the product in order to create a duplicate.

We think, therefore, that the Texas rule is clear. One may use his competitor's secret process if he discovers the process by reverse engineering applied to the finished product, one may use a competitor's process if he discovers it by his own independent research, but one may not avoid these labors by taking the process from the discoverer without his permission at a time when he is taking reasonable precautions to maintain its secrecy. To obtain knowledge of a process without spending the time and money to discover it independently is improper unless the holder voluntarily discloses it or fails to take reasonable precautions to ensure its secrecy.

In the instant case the Christophers deliberately flew over the DuPont plant to get pictures of a process which DuPont had attempted to keep secret. The Christophers delivered their pictures to a third party who was certainly aware of the means by which they had been acquired and who may be planning to use the information contained therein to manufacture methanol by the DuPont process. The third party has a right to use this process only if he obtains this knowledge through his own research efforts, but thus far all information indicates that the third party has gained his knowledge solely by taking it from DuPont at a time when DuPont was making reasonable efforts to preserve its secrecy. In such a situation DuPont has a valid cause of action to prohibit the Christophers from improperly discovering its trade secret and to prohibit the undisclosed third party from using the improperly obtained information. In taking this position we realize that industrial espionage of the sort here perpetrated has become a popular sport in some segments of our industrial community. However, our devotion to free wheeling industrial competition must not force us into accepting the law of the jungle as the standard of morality expected in our commercial relations. Our tolerance of the espionage game must cease when the protections required to prevent another's spying cost so much that the spirit of inventiveness is dampened. Commercial privacy must be protected from espionage which could not have been reasonably anticipated or prevented. We do not mean to imply, however, that everything not in plain view is within the protected vale, nor that all information obtained through every extra optical extension is forbidden. Indeed, for our industrial competition to remain healthy there must be breathing room for observing a competing industrialist. A competitor can and must shop his competition for pricing and examine his products for quality, components, and methods of manufacture. Perhaps ordinary fences and roofs must be built to shut out incursive eyes, but we need not require the discoverer of a trade secret to guard against the unanticipated, the undetectable, or the unpreventable methods of espionage now available.

In the instant case DuPont was in the midst of constructing a plant. Although after construction the finished plant would have protected much of the process from view, during the period of construction the trade secret was exposed to view from the air. To require DuPont to put a roof over the unfinished plant to guard its secret would impose an enormous expense to prevent nothing more than a school boy's trick. We introduce here no new or radical ethic since our ethos has never given moral sanction to piracy. The market place must not deviate far from our mores. We should not require a person or corporation to take unreasonable precautions to prevent another from doing that which he ought not do in the first place. Reasonable precautions against predatory eyes we may require, but an impenetrable fortress is an unreasonable requirement, and we are not disposed to burden industrial inventors with such a duty in order to protect the fruits of their efforts. "Improper" will always be a word determined by time, place and circumstances. We therefore need not proclaim a catalogue of commercial improprieties. Clearly, however, one of its commandments does say "thou shall not appropriate a trade secret through deviousness under circumstances in which countervailing defenses are not reasonably available."

PREVENTIVE LAW
Protecting Trade Secrets

Corporations have special problems in attempting to limit the use of customer lists and other similar types of information likely to be known by a number of employees. The state courts have split on the issue of whether customer lists should be protected under trade secret law. Because of such uncertainty, many companies attempt to prevent employees from making personal use of or disclosing trade secret information. A clause in company employment contracts is inserted whereby the employees agree that, upon leaving the company, they will not compete with their former employer and will not make use of certain designated information—for example, customer lists—within a certain area and time period. The courts will enforce such restrictive clauses when they are for a reasonable business purpose and are appropriately limited in duration and geographical area of application. Thus, upon leaving a firm employees cannot necessarily take with impunity all their files, or even all of the memos, reports, and letters that they personally prepared.

TRADEMARK INFRINGEMENT

A *trademark* is an identifying mark or symbol used in conjunction with the sale of a good or service. There are five basic types of trademarks.

Types of Trademarks

Product Trademark. A *product trademark* is used to identify a particular product and to distinguish it from other similar products that are sold in the marketplace. Because of the use of such trademarks, the public is able to distinguish among the 78 different cough and cold medicines, the 22 different types of vitamins, and the 271 different brands of ready-to-eat cereals.

Trade Name. A business *trade name* is the name of a company, such as Macy's or General Electric. Trade names are used to identify particular products with the producing firm and may on occasion be the only means of identifying the product (as, for example, Campbell's soup). The use of a trade name with a wide variety of products causes the name to become intimately associated with the overall image of the particular business. Many companies devote a significant amount of advertising dollars to creation and continuance of a favorable image for their trade name. Ford's "Better Idea" advertising and "You can be sure if it's Westinghouse" are well-known examples.

Service Mark. A *service mark* relates to the sale of services rather than a product and may be used by service firms like utilities, transportation companies, and banks. Reddy Kilowatt and The Fast Flying Virginian (the name of a passenger train) are examples of service marks.

Certification Mark. A *certification mark* is used by an attesting agency or firm to indicate that certain quality standards have been met in the manufacture and testing of the product. The attesting firm strictly controls the use of the mark by other firms in conjunction with the latter's products in advertising campaigns. The Underwriters Laboratory mark and the Good Housekeeping Seal are well-known certification marks.

Collective Mark. A *collective mark* is used jointly by a related group of people or businesses for mutual purposes. For example, it might be used by an organized group of independent insurance agents in mutually sponsored advertising. Labor unions and trade associations in particular often make use of collective marks.

The law governing trademark usage derives from two basic sources: (1) the federal Lanham Act of 1946, which protects properly registered trademarks used in interstate commerce, and (2) state common law rules, which protect established trademarks and trade names within the geographic area of their active use.

The Lanham Act provides for the federal registration of trademarks by requiring the filing of a specimen and drawing of the trademark with the Patent Office. The Patent Office

checks to determine if the proposed mark cannot be registered because it is:

1. Immoral, deceptive, scandalous, or disparaging
2. The insignia of a nation
3. The name, portrait, or signature of a nonconsenting living person, or dead president with a nonconsenting living widow
5. Merely descriptive of the goods involved
6. Deceptively misdescriptive of the goods involved
7. Primarily geographically descriptive
8. Primarily merely a surname

Public notice of the proposed registration is provided for, and a proceeding in opposition to registration may be brought by individuals who believe that they may be damaged by the proposed registration. A number of challenges to trademarks may be raised, most of which pertain to the registration requirements just listed. A common objection is that the mark applied for would cause likelihood of confusion with an already registered mark. Because the test is "likelihood" of confusion, actual outright confusion need not be shown. The courts analyze the issue in terms of the similarities between the two marks in sound, meaning, and appearance. They also consider the nature of the product itself and the manner in which it is marketed.

The Lanham Act defines *trademark infringement* as the use, without the consent of the registrant, of any copy or imitation of a trademark in connection with the sale of any goods or service in a way that is likely to cause confusion or mistake or to deceive purchasers as to the origin of the goods or services. Thus, the *tort of trademark infringement* occurs when a competitor of a trademark owner uses a mark that is so similar to the registered trademark that purchasers of the competitor's goods or service are likely to be misled as to their origin.

Defenses

When a suit is brought alleging infringement of an existing well-known mark strongly associated with a particular product, commonly the defendant argues that the plaintiff's mark has become a *generic* term. A trademark that has become generic is no longer protectable regardless of the length of time it has been used and the amount spent on advertising to familiarize the public with the brand name. Companies are thus faced with a tightrope dilemma in formulating their advertising strategies. They must attempt to convince the consumer to associate their brand name with the product, but simultaneously they must make sure that the consumer does not come to think of their trademark as the product. Ironically, trade names are likely to become generic terms only by virtue of extraordinarily successful advertising campaigns. There are some penalties for being too efficient in our marketing-oriented economy. Cellophane, elevator, aspirin, cola, and shredded wheat are former brand names or parts of brand names that have become generic terms.

Companies with valuable trademarks often devote some of their advertising to instructing the public in the proper use of the trademark to prevent it from becoming generic. It is improper to use a trademark in a generic sense, as in, "Xerox a copy of this report," or, "Could you hand me a Kleenex?" when you are speaking of another brand of facial tissues. The Xerox Company sponsored a number of ads asking that the public use the word *Xerox* to identify only its products. One technique used by companies to strengthen their trademarks is to insert *brand* between their trademark and the product in advertisements (for example, Scotch Brand Cellophane Tape). Some clipping services read magazine articles and check dictionaries to make sure trademarks are not being used improperly.

An additional defense to the claim of trademark infringement is that the mark is merely *descriptive*—car starter for an automobile battery—or geographically descriptive—Columbus Moving Company or Fifth Street Deli. Trademarks may be challenged on these grounds because Congress did not want someone to be able to preempt a common word or a geographical designation by a *brief* use and then registration. However, a mark which fails because it is merely descriptive, deceptively misdescriptive, primarily geographic, deceptive, or primarily merely a surname may be registered if it "has become distinctive of the applicant's goods in commerce." The Lanham Act provides that prima facie evidence of such distinctiveness is the existing and continuous use of the trademark in interstate commerce for five years. This allows *secondary meaning* to be established in reference to the trademark, and thus permits it to be registered. When a product has secondary meaning, consumers have come to associate the product with a particular manufacturer. They make certain qualitative judgments concerning the product as a result of that association. Thus, a champagne-drinking consumer makes certain quality judgments as to taste and basic drinking quality when buying a bottle of Great Western Champagne—these judgments attach secondary meaning to the Great Western brand. Every challenge to a trademark turns on its own facts, and it is very difficult to state in general terms what constitutes being "merely descriptive" or "primarily merely a surname."

Use is critical for the maintenance of legal rights in trademarks, and failure to continue use of a mark causes it to be *abandoned* into the public domain. Some abandoned marks have carryover goodwill, and it has been occasionally profitable for small firms to pick up such a mark and to manufacture a product which enables them to obtain sales resulting solely from the prior advertising. A small company recently did this with Ipana toothpaste.

Some companies attempt to keep registration valid by having an occasional planned sale. If this is done for defensive purposes and not as a part of the regular sale of the product, it may not prevent the abandonment of the mark.

Remedies

A number of legal remedies are available to a party whose trademark has been infringed. The infringement victim may sue for an injunction which may be broadly designed by the court "to prevent the violation of any right of the registrant of a mark registered in the Patent Office." Or, if the infringement was intentional, the registrant may sue for damages which may include: (1) the defendant's profits, (2) additional direct damages sustained by the plaintiff, with the possibility of treble damages, and (3) the cost of the action.

PATENT INFRINGEMENT

A patent may be obtained for an idea involving a machine, a chemical, a design, a process, and even certain types of plants. The right granted is the *exclusive* right to make use of and sell a particular protected application of the idea. This allows the party receiving the patent, known as the patentee, to prevent others from making, using, or selling the invention and gives the patentee, in effect, a legal monopoly. Regular patents are granted for a seventeen-year period and are not renewable. A *design patent* (one involving a new, original, and ornamental design of/or accompanying a manufactured object) may be obtained for a three-and-one-half, seven-, or fourteen-year period. The duration of a design patent is determined by the amount of the fee the patentee elects to pay. The shorter, cheaper period of protection is available because designs, by their nature, are ephemeral and their economic value is often short-lived.

Requirements for Patentability

In order to be patentable the invention must be (1) new, (2) useful, and (3) nonobvious.

New means that the invention is not already generally known and that the individual applying for the patent must be the first inventor. Similarly, the invention must not have been covered by a previously granted patent.

Useful means that the invention must have some specific application and cannot be a frivolous, albeit interesting idea. Nor would it be possible to get a patent for a general idea, as, for example, one of Newton's laws of physics.

The most important requirement of patentability is that the invention must be *nonobvious*. This factor has proven to be very troublesome because there are two different ways to evaluate such a criterion. One approach is to look at the requirement of nonobviousness subjectively and to try to determine whether there exists the "spark of genius" that we associate with the efforts of brilliant inventors. The second approach is to take an objective attitude and to determine whether the idea represents an important technical advance from the viewpoint of an ordinary engineer in the field. A 1952 amendment to the patent law purported to adopt the objective "substantial degree of technical advance" test. But in spite of that provision, the courts have still tended to apply the more subjective type of test. One explanation for this is that the courts necessarily view the patented object from a position of hindsight.

The result of the often significantly different tests applied by the Patent Office and the courts is that over one-half of all patents challenged in litigation are declared invalid. The uncertainty concerning the validity of patents that results from this weakens the operation of the patent system and dilutes the value of the patent grant. The courts are able to strike down issued patents because all patents granted by the Patent Office are only prima facie valid. *Prima facie validity* means that a patent carries a presumption of validity, but that it may be declared invalid if a challenger satisfies his or her burden of proof by demonstrating that the patent has been improperly granted.

Securing the Patent

In a corporation, patent counsel have primary responsibility for the legal aspects of filing the application for a patent. In doing this, counsel work closely with the technical personnel who have developed the product or process to be patented. Individual inventors, including small businesspeople, find it mandatory to consult a patent attorney. Such advice is necessary for two reasons. First, the Patent Office has very detailed technical rules concerning patent applications which must be strictly complied with. Second, determining why a particular application has been rejected is often very difficult. The patent attorney's advice is important because most clearly unpatentable ideas are tossed out at this stage, saving prospective inventors time and money. This also accounts for the fact that a sizable percentage of patent applications are granted by the Patent Office.

Applications filed by corporate counsel or by independent patent attorneys are then reviewed by a patent examiner to determine whether the product or process is new, useful, and nonobvious. The patent application must be accompanied by a drawing along with written material extensively describing the invention. This information will be made part of the public record after a patent is granted, and the public may make direct use of it after patent protection has expired. Public disclosure of the invention assists in public dissemination of important technical information. It also serves as the basis of the Patent Office search to determine if a patent should be granted. This search often takes more than a year, a fact that

causes difficulties for those wishing to make immediate use of an important invention.

The phrase *patent pending* often found on consumer products gives notice of the fact that a patent is being applied for and that an exclusive right may be obtained. During the time that the patent application is being processed, the information disclosed about the invention is kept secret. Otherwise hopeful inventors would have to risk complete forfeiture of their ideas into the public domain in order to apply for patent protection.

Parties holding a valid patent may believe that a new patent application will infringe their registered patents. In that case they may intervene in the application process and attempt to demonstrate the potential infringement. Effective intervention, however, is difficult because of the emphasis on confidentiality in the application process.

Infringement

A patent confers on its owner a statutory right to exclude others from making, using, or selling a patented invention. Whoever violates that right is an infringer. *Infringement* of a patent occurs when someone manufactures, uses, or sells a product or process that is substantially similar to that protected by a patent. Whether or not such infringement has occurred is a question of fact that often must be resolved in a lawsuit with the assistance of technical expert testimony. To determine infringement, the court determines the meaning of the claims listed at the end of the patent and compares them with the product made, used, or sold or the process used by the defendant (called the accused product or process). If the words of any properly interpreted patent claim literally describe the accused product or process, then the patent is infringed.

Even if the accused infringer escapes the literal wording of all the patent claims, but is nevertheless using the substance of the invention, there may be infringement through the "doctrine of equivalents" if the accused product or process performs substantially the same function in substantially the same way to obtain the same results as the claimed invention.

A legal defense that is available to an alleged infringer is to challenge directly the validity of the patent itself on the grounds that it was improperly granted or that it has been used in violation of the antitrust laws. In patent infringement suits, the plaintiff/patentee has the advantage of having a statutory presumption of validity. The burden of persuasion rests with the defendant to show invalidity by clear and convincing evidence.

Patent infringement suits must be brought in federal district court. Remedies for patent infringement include injunctions and recovery of compensatory damages, which are to be not less than a "reasonable royalty."

COPYRIGHT INFRINGEMENT

A *copyright* is an exclusive right given to an author that allows him to prevent others from making copies of his or her work, and that reserves to the author the right to prepare derivative works. Published works may be protected under the federal copyright statute. Published works that are not protected by federal copyright law are considered to be in the public domain and may be freely copied by anyone. Works in the public domain include: (1) government documents, (2) uncopyrightable works, (3) copyrightable but not yet copyrighted works, and (4) works for which prior copyright protection has expired.

Federal Statutory Copyright Protection

To obtain federal protection it is necessary to:

1. Give proper notice on every copy of the date of first publication and of the fact that copyright is claimed

2. File two "best" copies of the work with the Copyright Office in the Library of Congress

3. File a copyright application form

The form accompanying the copies sent to the Library of Congress must contain the name of the copyright claimant, the title of the work, the author, the date of publication, and a statement of new matter in a later or subsequent edition, if applicable. Notice may be either by ©, the word "copyright," or the abbreviation "copr.," although some books occasionally contain lengthy explanations of the publisher's interest and specification of certain "permitted" exceptions—for example, critical reviews. Many textbooks have a series of copyright dates. The latest copyright protects only the material added at that time, which in some instances may be just a single chapter.

The federal copyright statute and the regulations of the Copyright Office specify the type of works protectable by copyright date. These specifications must take into consideration the underlying constitutional requirement that copyright may only exist in works in the nature of a writing. Books, periodicals, oral lectures for profit, musical compositions, maps, works of art, photographs, prints, and motion pictures are among the types of things that may be protected by copyright. In one instance, an unusually designed lamp base was held to be copyrightable.

The following things are generally not copyrightable: single words and short phrases, titles, ideas or plans (although one may obtain protection for the manner in which ideas are expressed), and works involving no original authorship such as a calendar or schedules of sporting events. Phonograph records have posed unique problems for Congress; special legislation has been enacted providing for compulsory licensing arrangements with specified royalty schedules. In spite of the compulsory licensing statute and the basic copyright laws, a great deal of tape and record piracy does occur.

Federal copyright protection extends for the life of the author plus fifty years. If a work is jointly authored, the term is figured from the death of the last surviving author. If a work has an anonymous author or was done for hire, the term runs for seventy-five years from publication or one hundred from creation, whichever expires first.

Copyright registration is permissible at or up to five years after publication. This is a great improvement over the prior law, which punished the author who published without a proper copyright notice by forfeiture of all property interests in the work. Prudence, however, would dictate giving notice and registering upon publication because until such actions are taken, there is no federal protection available for the work.

Infringement

Actionable copyright infringement requires an unprivileged actual copying. Wrongful copying might involve actual publication in book form, photocopying, or publicly presenting another's copyrighted musical composition or play. Because some form of copying is required, an actual independent writer of a work identical to an existing publication does not infringe the copyright of the other original writer. Two identical, independently written novels are just not likely to occur, but there are certain types of writings where it is possible that two independent parties could publish identical works. Maps, business directories, and select listing directories are ready examples. Because the copying of such a work might be hard to prove, publishers occasionally use fictitious listings to establish comparative nonsequiturs which would comprise proof that another publisher copied their work. For example, one publishing firm might place fictitious names of businesses in its directory so that if the same fictitious names were to appear in another's directory there would be overwhelming circumstantial evidence of copying. For this reason, there are fictitious names in *Who's Who in America* and other similar works.

Fair Use. One controversial and rather ill-defined defense to copying recognized by the courts is the doctrine of *fair use*. The 1976 Copyright Act provides in Section 107 as follows:

§107. Limitations on exclusive rights: Fair use

Notwithstanding the provisions of section 106, the fair use of a copyrighted work, including such use by reproduction in copies or phonorecords or by any other means specified by that section, for purposes such as criticism, comment, news reporting, teaching (including multiple copies for classroom use), scholarship, or research, is not an infringement of copyright. In determining whether the use made of a work in any particular case is a fair use the factors to be considered shall include—

(1) the purpose and character of the use, including whether such use is of a commercial nature or is for nonprofit educational purposes;
(2) the nature of the copyrighted work;
(3) the amount and substantiality of the portion used in relation to the copyrighted work as a whole; and
(4) the effect of the use upon the potential market for or value of the copyrighted work.

Examples of judicially recognized fair use would include critics' quoting several pertinent excerpts from the work they are critiquing, a comic burlesque of a work, and an academic article in which specific use of another's language is essential. Suppose, for example, that Professor Brown publishes a book that proposes substantial revisions of the Uniform Commercial Code. The specific language used is critically important to the meaning of the proposed statute. If Professor Smith wishes to write a research article analyzing Brown's proposals, it will be necessary for Smith to make use of Brown's specific language.

When infringement occurs, a number of remedies are available to the copyright holders. They may seek an injunction to prevent further copying, or they may sue for actual damages and the actual profits gleaned by the infringer from the copying. If actual damages are hard to determine—and this is generally the case—the court may assess, in its discretion, statutory damages within the limits of $250 to $10,000. A judge may also order the impounding and destruction of infringing copies and plates, molds, or other devices used to make the copies. Nevertheless, a copyright holder considering initiating an infringement action should realize that, as is the case with patents, the validity of copyrights may be directly challenged by the alleged infringer in the courts.

In the following case the court considers the issue of whether ex-Beatle George Harrison was liable for copyright infringement.

Bright Tunes Music Corp. v. Harrisongs Music, Ltd. et al.

U.S. District Court for the Southern District of New York
420 F.Supp. 177 (1976)

Background: Bright Tunes Music Corp. (plaintiff) sued Harrisongs Music, Ltd., George Harrison, Apple Records, Inc., and Apple Records, Ltd. (defendants) for copyright infringement. Bright Tunes claimed that the song "My Sweet Lord" was plagiarized from "He's So Fine."

Decision: The District Court ruled that the defendants were liable to the plaintiff for copyright infringement.

Owen, District Judge

This is an action in which it is claimed that a successful song, My Sweet Lord, listing George Harrison as the composer, is plagiarized from an earlier successful song, He's So Fine, composed by Ronald Mack, recorded by a singing group called the "Chiffons," the copyright of which is owned by plaintiff, Bright Tunes Music Corp.

He's So Fine, recorded in 1962, is a catchy tune consisting essentially of four repetitions of a very short basic musical phrase, "sol-mi-re," (hereinafter motif A),[1] altered as necessary to fit the words, followed by four repetitions of another short basic musical phrase, "sol-la-do-la-do," (hereinafter motif B).[2] While neither motif is novel, the four repetitions of A, followed by four repetitions of B, is a highly unique

pattern.[3] In addition, in the second use of the motif B series, there is a grace note inserted making the phrase go "sol-la-do-la-*re*-do."[4]

My Sweet Lord, recorded first in 1970, also uses the same motif A (modified to suit the words) four times, followed by motif B, repeated three times, not four. In place of He's So Fine's fourth repetition of motif B, My Sweet Lord has a transitional passage of musical attractiveness of the same approximate length, with the identical grace note in the identical second repetition.[5] The harmonies of both songs are identical.[6]

George Harrison, a former member of The Beatles, was aware of He's So Fine. In the United States, it was No. 1 on the billboard charts for five weeks; in England, Harrison's home country, it was No. 12 on the charts on June 1, 1963, a date on which one of the Beatle songs was, in fact, in first position. For seven weeks in 1963, He's So Fine was one of the top hits in England.

According to Harrison, the circumstances of the composition of My Sweet Lord were as follows. Harrison and his group, which included an American black gospel singer named Billy Preston,[7] were in Copenhagen, Denmark, on a singing engagement. There was a press conference involving the group going on backstage. Harrison slipped away from the press conference and went to a room upstairs and began "vamping" some guitar chords, fitting on to the chords he was playing the words, "Hallelujah" and "Hare Krishna" in various ways.[8] During the course of this vamping, he was alternating between what musicians call a Minor II chord and a Major V chord.

At some point, germinating started and he went down to meet with others of the group, asking them to listen, which they did, and everyone began to join in, taking first "Hallelujah" and then "Hare Krishna" and putting them into four part harmony. Harrison obviously started using the "Hallelujah," etc., as repeated sounds, and from there developed the lyrics, to wit, "My Sweet Lord," "Dear, Dear Lord," etc. In any event, from this very free-flowing exchange of ideas, with Harrison playing his two

---

[3] All the experts agreed on this.

[4]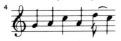

[5] This grace note, as will be seen *infra,* has a substantial significance in assessing the claims of the parties hereto.

[6] Expert witnesses for the defendants asserted crucial differences in the two songs. These claimed differences essentially stem, however, from the fact that different words and number of syllables were involved. This necessitated modest alterations in the repetitions or the places of beginning of a phrase, which had nothing to do whatsoever with the essential musical kernel that is involved.

[7] Preston recorded the first Harrison copyrighted recording of My Sweet Lord, of which more *infra,* and from his musical background was necessarily equally aware of He's So Fine.

[8] These words ended up being a "responsive" interjection between the eventually copyrighted words of My Sweet Lord. In He's So Fine, the Chiffons used the sound "dulang" in the same places to fill in and give rhythmic impetus to what would otherwise be somewhat dead spots in the music.

chords and everybody singing "Hallelujah" and "Hare Krishna," there began to emerge the My Sweet Lord text idea, which Harrison sought to develop a little bit further during the following week as he was playing it on his guitar. Thus developed motif A and its words interspersed with "Hallelujah" and "Hare Krishna."

Approximately one week after the idea first began to germinate, the entire group flew back to London because they had earlier booked time to go to a recording studio with Billy Preston to make an album. In the studio, Preston was the principal musician. Harrison did not play in the session. He had given Preston his basic motif A with the idea that it be turned into a song, and was back and forth from the studio to the engineer's recording booth, supervising the recording "takes." Under circumstances that Harrison was utterly unable to recall, while everybody was working toward a finished song, in the recording studio, somehow or other the essential three notes of motif A reached polished form.

Q. [By the Court]: . . . you feel that those three notes . . . the motif A in the record, those three notes developed somewhere in that recording session?
MR. HARRISON: I'd say those three there were finalized as beginning there.
Q. [By the Court]: Is it possible that Billy Preston hit on those [notes comprising motif A]?
MR. HARRISON: Yes, but it's possible also that I hit on that too, as far back as the dressing room, just scat singing.

Similarly, it appears that motif B emerged in some fashion at the recording session as did motif A. This is also true of the unique grace note in the second repetition of motif B.

Q. [By the Court]: All I am trying to get at, Mr. Harrison, is if you have a recollection when that [grace] note popped into existence as it ends up in the Billy Preston recording.
MR. HARRISON: . . . [Billy Preston] might have put that there on every take, but it just might have been on one take, or he might have varied it on different takes at different places.

The Billy Preston recording, listing George Harrison as the composer, was thereafter issued by Apple Records. The music was then reduced to paper by someone who prepared a "lead sheet" containing the melody, the words and the harmony for the United States copyright application.[9]

Seeking the wellsprings of musical composition—why a composer chooses the

[9] It is of interest, but not of legal significance, in my opinion, that when Harrison later recorded the song himself, he chose to omit the little grace note, not only in his musical recording but in the printed sheet music that was issued following that particular recording. The genesis of the song remains the same, however modestly Harrison may have later altered it. Harrison, it should be noted, regards his song as that which he sings at the particular moment he is singing it and not something that is written on a piece of paper.

succession of notes and the harmonies he does—whether it be George Harrison or Richard Wagner—is a fascinating inquiry. It is apparent from the extensive colloquy between the Court and Harrison covering forty pages in the transcript that neither Harrison nor Preston were conscious of the fact that they were utilizing the He's So Fine theme.[10] However, they in fact were, for it is perfectly obvious to the listener that in musical terms, the two songs are virtually identical except for one phrase. There is motif A used four times, followed by motif B, four times in one case, and three times in the other, with the same grace not in the second repetition of motif B.[11]

What happened? I conclude that the composer,[12] in seeking musical materials to clothe his thoughts, was working with various possibilities. As he tried this possibility and that, there came to the surface of his mind a particular combination that pleased him as being one he felt would be appealing to a prospective listener; in other words, that this combination of sounds would work. Why? Because his subconscious knew it already had worked in a song his conscious mind did not remember. Having arrived at this pleasing combination of sounds, the recording was made, the lead sheet prepared for copy-

---

[10] Preston may well have been the "composer" of motif B and the telltale grace note appearing in the second use of the motif during the recording session, for Harrison testified:

> THE COURT: To be as careful as I can now in summing this up, you can't really say that you or Billy Preston or somebody else didn't somewhere along the line suggest these; all you know is that when Billy Preston sang them that way at the recording session, you felt they were a successful way to sing this, and you kept it?
> THE WITNESS: Yes, I mean at that time we chose what is a good performance.
> THE COURT: And you felt it was a worthy piece of music?
> THE WITNESS: Yes. . . .

[11] Even Harrison's own expert witness, Harold Barlow, long in the field, acknowledged that although the two motifs were in the public domain, their use here was so unusual that he, in all his experience, had never come across this unique sequential use of these materials. He testified:

> THE COURT: And I think you agree with me in this, that we are talking about a basic three-note structure that composers can vary in modest ways, but we are still talking about the same heart, the same essence?
> THE WITNESS: Yes.
> THE COURT: So you say that you have not seen anywhere four A's followed by three B's or four?
> THE WITNESS: Or four A's followed by four B's.

The uniqueness is even greater when one considers the identical grace note in the identical place in each song.

[12] I treat Harrison as the composer, although it appears that Billy Preston may have been the composer as to part. (See fn. 10 *supra*). Even were Preston the composer as to part, this is immaterial.

right and the song became an enormous success. Did Harrison deliberately use the music of He's So Fine? I do not believe he did so deliberately. Nevertheless, it is clear that My Sweet Lord is the very same song as He's So Fine with different words,[13] and Harrison had access to He's So Fine. This is, under the law, infringement of copyright, and is no less so even though subconsciously accomplished.

Given the foregoing, I find for the plaintiff on the issue of plagiarism, and set the action down for trial on November 8, 1976 on the issue of damages and other relief as to which the plaintiff may be entitled. The foregoing constitutes the Court's findings of fact and conclusions of law.

[13] Harrison himself acknowledged on the stand that the two songs were substantially similar. This same conclusion was obviously reached by a recording group called the "Belmonts" who recorded "My Sweet Lord" at a later time. With "tongue in cheek" they used the words from *both* "He's So Fine" and "My Sweet Lord" interchangeably at certain points.

REVIEW PROBLEMS

1. When will competition be "unfair" for purposes of establishing the tort of unfair competition? How can the tort of unfair competition be reconciled with a national public policy that seeks to promote competition?

2. What is a trade secret? What is required for trade secret protection?

3. Why might a company decide not to patent a patentable invention and, instead, rely solely upon trade secret protection?

4. What is meant by saying that a trademark has become a generic term? Give an example of a generic word that was once a trademark. How may a business attempt to prevent a trademark from becoming generic?

5. A, a wholesaler of gasoline and motor oil who does not operate and does not intend to operate any retail stations, demands that B, the proprietor of a retail gasoline station, carry A's oil exclusively. B refuses. A thereupon determines to drive B out of business. A leases a vacant lot next to B's station for six months and daily sends a gasoline truck to park on the lot and to sell gasoline directly from the truck. Is A liable to B under any tort theory? Restatement of Torts, Section 709, Illustration 3 (1938).

6. Left Shoe, Inc., a shoe manufacturer, quarrels with Harold Hop, the owner of a local shoe store, because Harold refuses to carry Left Shoe, Inc.'s shoes. Left Shoe, Inc. rents a store in the neighborhood on a long-term lease and begins to sell its shoes there at retail. Left Shoe, Inc. desires that Harold Hop will be harmed by the competition and intends to withdraw from the retail business as soon as it can find a satisfactory purchaser for its store who will agree to carry its shoes. Is Left Shoe, Inc. subject to liability to Harold Hop? Explain. Restatement of Torts, Section 709, Illustration 4 (1938).

7. Oscar Electric Company is the sole electrical contractor in the town of Ferdinand, Indiana, a town of approximately 2,000

residents located in Dubois County, a rural county. Oscar Electric installs electrical wiring in construction projects throughout Dubois County. As such, it is the major purchaser of electrical wiring and components from several Indiana suppliers of such products. Recently, one of Oscar's employees, Meyer, quit working for Oscar Electric and opened an electrical contracting company in competition with Oscar Electric. When Oscar Electric's owner heard of this, he contacted all of the suppliers with whom he had dealt over the years and told them that if they sold electrical wiring and components to Meyer, they would no longer enjoy doing business with Oscar Electric. As a result, none of the suppliers would sell their products to Meyer, and he was forced to purchase wiring and components from other, more distant, suppliers at a higher cost. Is Oscar Electric liable to Meyer for wrongful interference with contracts? Explain.

8. Robert was employed as a route supervisor and sales manager of the Peerless Computer Company. In this position, he had sufficient opportunity to learn the customer lists of Peerless. Robert left employment with Peerless and a couple of years later started his own computer business. He solicited business from former Peerless customers, some of whom had been customers of Peerless for several years. Several of these customers became Robert's customers. Does Peerless have any recourse against Robert? Explain.

9. Sun Valley Computer Company, a computer manufacturer, hired Jim Mehling, an engineer with a Ph.D. in computer science. Mehling's job duties were to make the rounds of the various restaurants and bars that were known to be gathering places for people who worked in the Sun Valley, California, computer industry. While sitting in a booth next to another occupied by a group of programmers who worked for Magnum Computer, Inc., Mehling overheard a conversation that included detailed descriptions of Magnum's newest computer program. After dinner, Mehling rushed back to Sun Valley Computer and disclosed what he had overheard. From this information, Sun Valley Computer was able to develop a computer program that was strikingly similar to that developed by Magnum. Has Mehling or Sun Valley committed any tort against Magnum? Explain.

10. Here's Johnny Portable Toilets, Inc. rents portable toilets to those who need them. Johnny Carson, a well-known television entertainer, is introduced on his television show by the phrase "Here's Johnny." Carson also has licensed his trademark, "Here's Johnny" to a clothing manufacturer. If either Carson or the clothing manufacturer sues Here's Johnny Portable Toilets, Inc. for the tort of trademark infringement, will they succeed? Explain. Carson v. Here's Johnny Portable Toilets, Inc., 698 F.2d 831 (6th Cir. 1983).

11. Antimonopoly Inc. manufactures and sells a game entitled "Antimonopoly." Parker Brothers, Inc., manufacturer of the game "Monopoly," sues, claiming that the sale of "Antimonopoly" infringes upon its registered trademark, "Monopoly." Does Parker Brothers have a valid claim of trademark infringement against Antimonopoly? Explain. Antimonopoly v. Parker Brothers, 684 F.2d 1316.

12. Michael Smith obtained a patent on a new type of ear muff. The claim of the patent stated that the ear muff consisted of a head band:

terminating in enlarged portions, the enlarged portions being slitted with the adjacent portions of the slit lapped and secured together to form such enlarged portions in approximate cone shape, the lapped portions forming a pocket, and a securing strip for the article with its terminals secured in said pockets.

After examining the patent, Jeff Jones began making a similar ear muff. His ear muff, however, did not have a pocket and the terminals of the securing strip were not secured in any pocket. Smith sued Jones for patent infringement. Jones argued that he had designed around the patent in such a way as to avoid the literal wording of the patent claim. Who wins and why?

Negligence and Strict Liability

T his chapter considers the two remaining classifications of tort law,
both of which are concerned with
civil redress for unintentional injuries: (1) negligence and (2) strict liability.

NEGLIGENCE

Negligence is conduct that creates an unreasonable risk of harm to another.

Elements of Negligence

In order to establish a case of negligence, the
plaintiff must establish five elements. These
are:

1. That the defendant owed a *duty of care* to
   the plaintiff. The plaintiff must establish
   that the law recognized an obligation of the
   defendant to conform to a certain standard
   of conduct for the protection of the plaintiff
   against an unreasonable risk of harm.
2. That the defendant *breached this duty*.
3. That the plaintiff sustained an *injury*.
4. That the defendant caused the plaintiff's injury. This is known as *cause in fact* or *actual
   cause*.
5. That the defendant's conduct was the *proximate or legal cause* of the plaintiff's injury.

That is, the plaintiff must show a reasonably
close causal connection between the defendant's conduct and the resulting injury
to the plaintiff. Not every injury actually
caused by the defendant is compensable,
only those that are foreseeable and probable consequences of the defendant's conduct. Thus, in addition to showing that the
defendant actually caused the plaintiff's injury, the plaintiff must establish that the injury was a foreseeable consequence of the
defendant's conduct.

Each of these elements that is necessary to
a prima facie case of negligence will be examined in more detail in the discussion that follows.

Duty of Care. The first element of a plaintiff's prima facie case of negligence is the existence of a duty on the part of the defendant to
protect the plaintiff from injury resulting from
the defendant's conduct. It is not enough for
the plaintiff to show that he or she was injured
by the defendant's conduct. The plaintiff must
show that the law imposed a duty on the defendant to protect the plaintiff from the consequences of the defendant's conduct.

The determination of whether a duty of
care is to be imposed upon the defendant is a
question of law that is decided by the judge.

The judge must determine whether there is any "law" that would require the defendant to bear the risk or whether the plaintiff must bear his or her own loss.

Several factors may influence the court's decision. The factors that are considered in determining whether the law should impose a duty are the risk, foreseeability, and likelihood of injury weighed against the social utility of the actor's conduct, the extent of the burden of guarding against the injury, and the consequences of placing the burden on the actor. In the following case, the court addressed the issue of whether to recognize a duty on a manufacturer to design a "crashworthy" vehicle.

Dreisonstok v. Volkswagen of America

U.S. Court of Appeals, Fourth Circuit

489 F.2d 1066 (1974)

Background: Dreisonstok (plaintiff), a passenger in a Volkswagen microbus, sued Volkswagen (defendant) for "enhanced" injuries she received when the microbus crashed into a telephone pole. Dreisonstok claimed that because the van's front seat compartment had less "crash space" than a standard passenger car, she sustained injuries in excess of those that she would have otherwise sustained in an accident of this sort. She argued that the foreseeability of accidents required that the manufacturer be liable for specific standards of crashworthiness regardless of the type of vehicle involved. The District Court (trial court) concluded that Volkswagen had been guilty of negligence in failing to use due care in the design of its vehicle by providing "sufficient energy-absorbing materials or devices or 'crash space,' if you will, so that at 40 miles an hour the integrity of the passenger compartment would not be violated." Volkswagen appealed to the U.S. Circuit Court of Appeals for the Fourth Circuit.

Decision: The Circuit Court of Appeals ruled in favor of Volkswagen and reversed the District Court decision.

Russell, Circuit Judge

The correctness of the finding by the District Court that the defendant manufacturer was guilty of negligent design in this case depends on the determination of what extent a car manufacturer owes the duty to design and market a "crashworthy" vehicle, which, in the event of a collision, resulting accidentally or negligently from the act of another and not from any defect or malfunction in the vehicle itself, protects against unreasonable risk of injury to the occupants. The existence and nature of such a duty is a legal issue, for resolution as a matter of law. In arguing in favor of liability, the appellees stress the foreseeability in this mechanical age of automobile collisions, as affirmed in numerous authorities, and would seemingly deduce from this a duty on the car manufacturer to design its vehicle so as to guard against injury from involvement of its vehicle in any such anticipated collisions. The mere fact, however, that automobile collisions are frequent enough to be foreseeable is not sufficient in and of itself to create a duty on the part of the manufacturer to design its car to withstand such collisions under any circumstances. Foreseeability, it has been many times repeated, is not to be equated with duty; it is, after all, but one factor, albeit an important one, to be weighed in determining the issue of duty. Were foreseeability of collision the absolute litmus test for establishing a duty on the part of the car manufacturer, the obligation of the manufacturer to design a crash-proof car would be absolute. . . .

It would patently be unreasonable "to require the manufacturer to provide for every conceivable use or unuse of a car." Nader & Page, Automobile Design and the Judicial Process, 55 Cal.L.Rev. 645, 646. Liability for negligent design thus is imposed only when an unreasonable danger is created. Whether or not this has occurred should be determined by general negligence principles, which involve a balancing of the likelihood of harm, and the gravity of harm if it happens against the burden of the precautions which would be effective to avoid the harm. In short, against the likelihood and gravity of harm must be balanced in every case the utility of the type of conduct in question. The likelihood of harm is tied in with the obviousness of the danger, whether latent or patent, since it is frequently stated that a design is not unreasonably dangerous because the risk is one which anyone immediately would recognize and avoid. The purposes and intended use of the article is an even more important factor to be considered. After all, it is a commonplace that utility of design and attractiveness of the style of the car are elements which car manufacturers seek after and by which buyers are influenced in their selections. In every case, the utility and purpose of the particular type of vehicle will govern in varying degree the standards of safety to be observed in its design. Price is, also, a factor to be considered, for, if a change in design would appreciably add to cost, add little to safety, and take an article out of the price range of the market to which it was intended to appeal, it may be unreasonable as well as impractical for the courts to require the manufacturer to adopt such change. Of course, if an article can be made safer and the hazard of harm may be mitigated by an alternate design or device at no substantial increase in price, then the manufacturer has a duty to adopt such a design but a Cadillac may be expected to include more in the way of both conveniences and "crashworthiness" than the economy car. Moreover, in a "crashworthy" case it is necessary to consider the circumstances of the accident itself. In summary, every case such as this involves a delicate balancing of many factors in order to determine whether the manufacturer has used ordinary care in designing a car, which, giving consideration to the market purposes and utility of the vehicle, did not involve unreasonable risk of injury to occupants within the range of its intended use.

Applying the foregoing principles to the facts of this particular case, it is clear that there was no violation by the defendant of its duty of ordinary care in the design of its vehicle. The defendant's vehicle, described as "a van type multipurpose vehicle," was of a special type and particular design. This design was uniquely developed in order to provide the owner with the maximum amount of either cargo or passenger space in a vehicle inexpensively priced and of such dimensions as to make possible easy maneuverability. To achieve this, it advanced the driver's seat forward, bringing such seat in close proximity to the front of the vehicle, thereby adding to the cargo or passenger space. This, of course, reduced considerably the space between the exact front of the vehicle and the driver's compartment. All of this was readily discernible to anyone using the vehicle; in fact, it was, as we have said, the unique feature of the vehicle. The usefulness of the design is vouchsafed by the popularity of the type. It was of special utility as a van for the transportation of light cargo, as a family camper, as a station wagon and for use by passenger groups too large for the average passenger car. It was a design that had been adopted by other manufacturers, including American. It was a design duplicated in the construction of the large trucking tractors, where there was the same purpose of extending the cargo space without unduly lengthening the tractor-trailer coupling. There was no evidence in the record that there was any practical way of improving the "crashability" of the vehicle that would have been consistent with the peculiar purposes of its design. The plaintiff's theory of negligent design . . . was that, to meet the test of ordinary care in design so as to avoid "unreasonable risk" of injury, the vehicle of the defendant had to conform with the configuration of the standard American passenger car, . . . i.e., its motor must be in front, not in the rear; its passenger compartment must be "in the middle"; and the space in front of the passenger compartment must be approximately the same as that in a "standard American passenger car." Under this standard, any rear engine car would be "inherently dangerous"; any microbus or front-end tractor— both in wide use in 1968 and now—would be declared "inherently dangerous." To avoid liability for negligent design, no manufacturer could introduce any innovative or unique design, even though calculated to provide some special advantage such as greater roominess. Such a strait-jacket on design is not imposed. . . . It is entirely impermissible to predicate a conclusion of negligent design simply because a vehicle, having a distinctive purpose, such as the microbus, does not conform to the design of another type of vehicle, such as a standard passenger car, having a different nature and utility.

The District Court, however, seems to have accepted plaintiffs' theory, though expressing it somewhat differently from the standard stated by the plaintiffs in their brief. It stated the standard of ordinary care in design to require that a vehicle be able to withstand a "head-on" collision at 40 miles an hour without a violation of "the integrity of the passenger compartment" and held that the defendant had "violated" its duty in failing to meet their standard. Accepting the principle that a manufacturer must anticipate that its product will likely at some point in its use be involved in a collision, does ordinary care demand that, in taking precautions, it must provide against impacts at a speed of 40 miles per hour? Is this the "reasonable risk," as it has been defined in the authorities . . . against which the manufacturer must provide protection? And why "40 miles an hour" as the standard anyway? This standard was adopted, it seems clear from the District Court's order, because the plaintiffs contended that a "standard American passenger car" had sufficient "crash space" that its passenger compartment would not have been invaded in a 40 mile impact. Both the plaintiffs and the District Court employed an improper standard in determining whether the defendant had been guilty of negligent design.

Breach of Duty. The plaintiff must satisfy the judge or the jury that the defendant breached his or her duty to exercise due care. The courts have established a standard of behavior to determine breach of duty. The standard is that of the hypothetical "reasonable and prudent person under the same or similar circumstances." The judge or jury compares the defendant's conduct with the presumed conduct of the reasonably prudent person under the same or similar circumstances. If the defendant's conduct does not conform to this ideal standard of conduct, the defendant will be deemed to have breached his or her duty to exercise due care.

In the following case the court considers whether the manufacturer of an elevator breached its duty to design a reasonably safe elevator.

Westinghouse Electric Corp. v. Nutt

Court of Appeals of District of Columbia
407 A.2d 606 (1979)

Background: During lunch break at Henley Elementary School in Washington, D.C., sixth grader Dirickson Nutt (plaintiff) left the school grounds with several friends and went to a nearby apartment building. There, they boarded a self-service freight elevator that had been designed, manufactured, and installed by Westinghouse Electric Corp. (defendant). Under a service contract, Westinghouse was responsible for the maintenance and repair of the elevator.

After boarding the elevator, one of the boys pushed the fifth floor button, and the elevator ascended. At the fifth floor, the doors opened, but no one got off. As the elevator left the fifth floor, moving upward, one of the boys forced open the doors, bringing the elevator to an immediate stop between the fifth and sixth floors.

The passengers jumped out of the immobilized elevator through the door opening, landing in the hall corridor four feet below. In leaving the elevator, Dirickson Nutt slipped into the elevator shaft through the open space underneath the car. As a result of his fall, he sustained a wound to his left arm, requiring amputation above the wrist. He also suffered facial injuries requiring plastic surgery.

Dirickson Nutt, through his father, sued Westinghouse, claiming negligence in the design and maintenance of the elevator. They presented an expert witness, Mr. Frederick Foote, who suggested alternative design features that he considered feasible. The jury found in favor of the Nutts, awarding a verdict of $150,000. Westinghouse appealed to the District of Columbia Court of Appeals.

Decision: The District of Columbia Court of Appeals reversed the lower court decision and ordered the lower court to enter judgment for Westinghouse.

Gallagher, Associate Justice

Essentially, the issue is whether the Nutts established a prima facie case of negligent design. Westinghouse alleges a failure by the Nutts, as plaintiffs, to prove a departure by Westinghouse from the applicable standard of care. A breach of duty by the defendant is, of course, a prerequisite of liability; negligent conduct, by definition, "falls below the standard established by law for the protection of others against unreasonably great risk of harm."

Without question Westinghouse, as manufacturer, was under a duty to design a reasonably safe elevator.

As this court recently stated, the manufacturer of a [product] will be liable for "injuries to others expected to use the [product] when the injuries are caused by the lack of reasonable care in adopting a safe plan or design. This duty of care includes the adoption of reasonable safety devices. What constitutes "reasonable care" will vary with the circumstances, and involves "a balancing of the likelihood of harm, and the gravity of harm if it happens, against the burden of precaution which would be effective to avoid the harm."

Westinghouse points to its compliance with existing industry-wide standards as dispositive of the question of due care. Two professional engineers, experts in elevator design, testified at trial that the elevator complied with all applicable safety codes and regulations. An elevator inspector for the District of Columbia government established conformance with the local elevator code. It is axiomatic, however, that compliance with legislative or industry standards "does not prevent a finding of negligence where a reasonable man would take additional precautions."

Similarly, industry-wide custom influences, but does not conclusively determine, the applicable standard of care. As Justice Holmes put it, "What usually is done may be evidence of what ought to be done, but what ought to be done is fixed by a standard of reasonable prudence, whether it is usually complied with or not." Evidence of industry custom, however, may be conclusive when a plaintiff fails to introduce any evidence that the product was not reasonably safe for its intended use. Thus, the elevator's conformity to industry and legal standards established Westinghouse's due care unless the Nutts proffered contrary evidence that the product, as designed, created an unreasonable danger.

The sole evidence produced by the Nutts to establish a departure from the standard of care was the testimony of Mr. Foote. In effect, Mr. Foote gave his opinion that a longer toe guard or a different latch placement would have prevented the accident. However, evidence of a design alternative, by itself, is not sufficient to impose liability on the manufacturer.

It is one thing to show that the defendant might have designed a safer product; quite another to show that the product he did design was unreasonably dangerous. The defendant is not obliged to design the safest possible product, or one as safe as others make or a safer product than the one he has designed, so long as the design he has adopted is reasonably safe.

A finding of unreasonable danger most often turns on the absence of a safety device that was available at the time of manufacture. Evidence of available safety mechanisms illustrates what is feasible, and suggests a body of knowledge of which the defendant should be aware.

Here, testimony of customary safety features was not introduced. In addition, appellees' evidence failed to establish that an elongated toe guard is known to be feasible, even though not utilized by other manufacturers. This would seem to be the furthest courts have gone in imposing a duty on the manufacturer to keep abreast of recent scientific developments. Mr. Foote admitted on cross-examination that he had no knowledge of the feasibility of his suggestions.

Against Westinghouse's evidence that the equipment was reasonably safe as designed, the Nutts mustered little contrary evidence. Mr. Foote's safety suggestions were not competent evidence that Westinghouse, the manufacturer, created an unreasonable danger. Thus appellees failed to prove Westinghouse's deviation from the applicable standard of care in designing the elevator.

"Since the facts, viewed most favorably to [appellees], permit but one reasonable conclusion as to the proper judgment," the trial court erred in submitting the question of negligent design to the jury.

Injury. The plaintiff must establish that he or she sustained an injury. The injury incurred by the plaintiff is typically a physical injury to the plaintiff's person or property. The courts are reluctant to allow liability to extend to mental injuries because they are difficult to establish. In most states, the plaintiff may recover damages for negligent infliction of mental distress only if the defendant causes immediate physical injury to the plaintiff or causes mental distress that is followed by physical harm.

Actual Cause. The plaintiff must establish a causal relationship between the injury and the defendant's act. The defendant's conduct is a cause of the event if it was a material element and a substantial factor in bringing it about. If the defendant's conduct was a substantial factor in causing the plaintiff's injury, the defendant will not be absolved from liability merely because other causes contributed to the result.

Proximate Cause. Probably the most confusing element to comprehend in the prima facie case of negligence is the element of proximate cause. This is because the terms *proximate* and *cause* when used in this context are misnomers, and because the element is often discussed by courts in connection with other elements of negligence, such as duty.

Although the term *cause* is used in the label of the doctrine, it is important to separate the issue of proximate cause from the determination of actual cause or cause in fact. The determination of actual cause truly focuses on the cause-and-effect relationship between the defendant's conduct and the plaintiff's injury. Assuming such a causal connection can be shown, however, the *doctrine of proximate cause* is a policy determination of whether the defendant's legal responsibility extends to all the events that actually occurred.

The issue of proximate cause arises in situations where the defendant's original negligence, by either happenstance or intervening acts, leads to unforeseen consequences. Because one act of negligence should not subject a defendant to unlimited liability for all the consequences that could possibly result, tort law has developed the doctrine of proximate cause to limit the defendant's liability to only those events that are reasonably foreseeable. Under the doctrine of proximate cause, a defendant is liable only for the natural, probable, foreseeable, and thus avoidable consequences of his or her conduct, not for all consequences, however remote. The need for the doctrine arises because it is theoretically possible to trace the causal effects of some events through a number of ever-more-distant occurrences. In such situations, it may be theoretically possible to say that the defendant actually caused the injury by setting forth a chain of events that resulted in injury to the plaintiff. However, it is another thing to say that the defendant should be liable for the plaintiff's loss where the likelihood of injury was not foreseeable. Underlying the proximate cause requirement is recognition of the fact that a particular wrong may set off a chain of events so completely unforeseeable, and resulting in an injury so remotely related to the wrong itself, that common sense suggests that the defendant should not be liable for it. Thus, the doctrine of proximate cause should be viewed as a principle of law and policy that limits liability to foreseeable injuries. Some courts and commentators see the doctrine of proximate cause as a variant of the duty question. Consider the following case.

Kimble v. MacKintosh Hemphill Co.

Supreme Court of Pennsylvania

59 A.2d 68 (1948)

Background: Harry Kimble was killed when the roof of the MacKintosh Hemphill foundry fell upon him as he worked below. His wife, Virginia Kimble (plaintiff), sued MacKintosh Hemphill Co. (defendant) to recover the loss of her deceased husband's future earnings. The jury returned a verdict in her favor in the sum of $5,823.20. MacKintosh Hemphill moved the trial court to grant judgment in favor of MacKintosh Hemphill notwithstanding the jury verdict. The trial judge refused this request, and MacKintosh Hemphill appealed the trial judge's decision to the Supreme Court of Pennsylvania.

Decision: The Supreme Court of Pennsylvania affirmed the trial judge's decision.

Maxey, Chief Justice

Defendant's liability is predicated upon its failure to maintain the roof in a safe condition and in failing to inspect, discover and correct its faulty condition.

Defendant disclaims liability alleging (1) that the proximate cause of the fatality was a cyclonic wind of an extraordinary intensity and (2) that this relieved defendant from liability irrespective of whether or not its claimed antecedent negligence was a substantial factor in bringing about the harm.

Plaintiff's witnesses contradicted the evidence with regard to the severity of the wind on the date of the accident.

Defendant contends that the court erred in submitting the question of negligence to the jury and should have declared as a matter of law that an act of God was responsible for Kimble's death. Whether or not the fatal injury to plaintiff's decedent was due to an act of God or to defendant's negligence was a question of fact for the jury. The condition of the roof, the intensity of the wind on the date of the accident and on previous occasions at the same place were factual questions. The charge of the court was comprehensive and accurate. The trial judge charged:

> It is the law that no person is answerable for what is termed an act of Providence, that is, if some visitation of Providence comes along that in our ordinary experience we are not anticipating, then no one can be held to answer for that act, so that if the wind on this day was of such severity that it could not be reasonably anticipated by the Defendant, and that by reason of that wind, a part of the roof was blown off, then the Defendant would not be liable. However, if the storm were not of that severity, if it were only such a storm as occasionally happens, but is reasonably to be anticipated on occasions of every year or two, then that would not be an act of Providence if they were such as were reasonably to be expected to occur occasionally, then such storms should be guarded against. An act of Providence as related to cases of injurious negligence is one against which ordinary skill and foresight is not expected to provide. Whether the injury in this case is attributable to such a cause or is the consequence of negligence is a question of fact for

you to determine. Even if, with an extraordinary wind or storm there is concurring negligence, the party chargeable with it will be relieved from liability if the wind or storm is so overwhelming in character that it would of itself have produced the injury complained of, independently of negligence if there were negligence.

In the instant case, defendant by using ordinary diligence and attention could have prevented the serious consequences which resulted from its failure to inspect and correct the faulty condition of the foundry roof. We said in Fitzpatrick v. Penfield, . . . :

High winds are not of infrequent occurrence, and this particular wind was termed an ordinary wind occurring three or four times in a year. It was not an unusual one, and it was for the jury to find under all the evidence whether it was likely to have occurred, and should have been provided against. One who fails in his duty to remedy a defective or dangerous condition is liable for injuries resulting therefrom, although the immediate cause of the injury is the wind. The causal connection is not broken, and the original wrongdoer is liable for the injury sustained.

Procedural Doctrines

The plaintiff has the burden of persuading the trier of fact that he or she is entitled to a recovery. This burden of proving the defendant's negligence is placed upon the plaintiff because it is the plaintiff who is asking the court for relief. In certain cases, the plaintiff may have the burden of proof lightened by two procedural doctrines: *negligence per se* and *res ipsa loquitur.*

Negligence *Per Se.* Under the doctrine of negligence per se, a plaintiff may use the defendant's violation of a criminal statute to establish the defendant's negligence. Thus, a criminal statute may become a measure of civil liability. If a statute proscribes certain behavior and the defendant violates the statute, most states hold that the violation of the statute is negligence itself. That is, the violation of the statute creates a conclusive presumption that the defendant was negligent. In a few states, the court admits the information of the defendant's violation of the statute as evidence of negligence.

In order for the doctrine of negligence per se to apply, the statute must be relevant to the case; that is, the court must determine that the statute was intended to apply as a standard of civil liability. Thus, the court must examine the legislative purpose in enacting the statute. Since most state statutes do not contain any expression of the legislative purpose, this must be surmised by the court. Courts determine whether a statute was intended to apply in the case at hand by determining whether the plaintiff falls within the class of individuals that the statute was intended to protect and whether the injury sustained by the plaintiff was of the type that the statute was intended to prevent. If these two factors are present, the plaintiff may invoke the doctrine of negligence per se.

Res Ipsa Loquitur. The doctrine of res ipsa loquitur ("the thing speaks for itself") uses circumstantial evidence to establish a prima facie case of negligence. The doctrine is designed for cases where the plaintiff cannot know the exact negligent act. For example, if someone walking alongside a factory is hit by a crate that fell from a second-story window, the practical difficulty of proving who was at fault is obvious—yet it is just as obvious that, on its face, the act itself indicates the existence of negligence on the part of the company. Under the doctrine of res ipsa loquitur, it is inferred that the defendant's negligence caused the plaintiff's injury when (1) the event is the kind that usually does not happen without negli-

gence and (2) other responsible causes, including conduct by the plaintiff, are sufficiently eliminated by the evidence. Such proof is sufficient to support a jury verdict for the plaintiff. Because the prima facie case is based on inferences, however, the defendant is allowed to come forward with some explanation of the situation other than negligence. The doctrine of res ipsa loquitur is frequently used in cases of product liability, surgical malpractice, and negligent construction of buildings. The following case illustrates the application of the doctrine of res ipsa loquitur.

Goldstein v. Levy

Supreme Court of New York, Appellate Term
132 N.Y.S. 373 (1911)

Background: Dora Goldstein (plaintiff) purchased a ticket and went into a music hall owned and controlled by Etta Levy (defendant). Above the place where Goldstein was seated there was suspended from the dome of the hall a chandelier containing about twenty-one electric lights, which were used for lighting the hall in order that the patrons might witness the performance. A shade surrounding one of these lights broke, and a piece of it fell upon Goldstein, causing injuries to her. The accident occurred on a Thursday. Levy proved that on the previous Monday she had the chandelier and shades examined by the electrician who was employed for that purpose, that the chandelier and shade had been similarly inspected every week before the accident, that for six years before the accident no similar accident had occurred, and that the globes had never been discovered to be defective or in a dangerous condition. However, Levy offered no evidence to explain the cause of the accident.

The jury returned a verdict in favor of Goldstein, and Levy moved the trial judge to set aside the verdict. The trial judge granted Levy's motion, and Goldstein appealed. Decision: The appellate court reversed the trial judge's decision, and reinstated the jury verdict for Goldstein.

Seabury, Justice

In our opinion the facts called for the application of the rule *res ipsa loquitur,* and the burden was upon the defendant to explain the accident in such a manner as to overcome the presumption of negligence raised by the plaintiff's proof. This the defendant did not do. Evidence tending to show that inspections were carefully and regularly made is insufficient to establish that the accident itself was not caused by the defendant's negligence. The circumstances and character of the occurrence were such as to call for the application of the doctrine of *res ipsa loquitur.* The accident was unusual. The plaintiff could not be expected to define its exact cause. If the inspections which the defendant claimed were made had been carefully made, it is not inconceivable that the defect which caused the shade to fall might have been discovered. If one may be held liable for the fall of a wall upon a pedestrian or an innkeeper for the fall of plaster from a ceiling upon a guest, we can see no good reason why the same principle which was applied in those cases should not be held applicable here.

The facts proved by the plaintiff established a prima facie case, which was put in issue by the proof of care which the defendant claims she exercised. The issue was properly submitted to the jury for their determination, and in our opinion the verdict of the jury in favor of the plaintiff cannot properly be held to be contrary to the evidence or the law. In our judgment, the learned trial court erred in setting aside the verdict.

Defenses

There are two basic defenses to a negligence action: *contributory negligence* and *assumption of risk.* The burden of pleading and proving these defenses is on the defendant. Current trends with regard to these defenses have undercut their utility.

Contributory Negligence. Contributory negligence is conduct by the plaintiff that contributes as a legal cause to the harm he or she has suffered and that falls below the standard to which the plaintiff is required to conform for his or her own protection. In other words, the plaintiff's failure to exercise due care for his or her own safety constitutes a contributing cause to his or her injury. Contributory negligence, raised by the defendant, alleges that, although the defendant may have been negligent, the plaintiff was also negligent in some way directly related to the plaintiff's injury. The existence of contributory negligence is an issue of fact, governed by the same tests and rules as the negligence of the defendant. The plaintiff is required to conform to the standard of conduct of the reasonable prudent person under the same or similar circumstances.

Since the tort of negligence bases liability upon fault, proof of contributory negligence was formerly an absolute bar to recovery by the plaintiff. Because of the harshness of this rule, the concept of *comparative negligence* was developed. Comparative negligence is an alternative to contributory negligence now followed in most states. This defense weighs the relative negligence of the parties and either reduces the amount of recovery in proportion to the plaintiff's negligence or bars recovery only if the plaintiff's negligence was greater than the defendant's. In those states that follow comparative negligence, a plaintiff's contributory negligence is no longer a complete bar to recovery. Comparative negligence removes the "all or nothing" rule of contributory negligence and replaces it with a rule that allows the jury to apportion damages to reflect the relative fault of the parties.

Assumption of Risk. The defense of assumption of risk exists when the plaintiff actually had or should have had knowledge of the risk and voluntarily exposed himself or herself to it. In such a situation the defendant, although negligent, is not responsible for the resulting injury. This is similar to consent to an intentional tort, which also denies recovery.

Therefore, when the plaintiff voluntarily enters into some relationship with the defendant, with knowledge that the defendant will not protect him or her against the risk, the plaintiff is regarded as tacitly or impliedly con-

ETHICS BOX
Joint and Several Liability

A controversial doctrine in tort law is the principle of joint and several liability. Sometimes there are several parties who contribute to a plaintiff's injury. If one of the defendants is insolvent or unavailable, in most states, the plaintiff can collect the full amount from the solvent, available defendant. It is then the problem for the defendant who has paid to track down and collect from the other defendant(s).

This principle imposes liability upon individuals that goes beyond their legally assessed responsibility for the harm. A recent case dramatizes this problem at the extreme. A woman was struck from behind by her fiancé while riding on the Grand Prix car ride at Walt Disney World. She sued and the jury found that she was 14 percent at fault, her fiancé was 85 percent at fault, and Walt Disney World was 1 percent at fault. After the accident, but prior to the case, she married her fiancé. In Florida tort collections are not allowed between married individuals and therefore her husband was judgment proof. That left Walt Disney World responsible under the doctrine of joint and several liability for *all* of her assessable damages. *Walt Disney World* v. *Wood*, __ S.E. 3d __ (Fla. 1987).

The Ethics Box in Chapter 1 stated that on occasion laws could be unethical. What kind of arguments could be made that this is an unethical law? How could the law be justified?

---

senting to the possible negligence and agreeing to take a chance. For example, the plaintiff may accept employment knowing that he or she is expected to work in a dangerous area; or ride in a car with knowledge that the brakes are defective; or enter a baseball park, sit in an unscreened seat, and thereby consent that the players proceed with the game without taking any precautions to protect the plaintiff from being hit by the ball. In effect, the defendant is simply relieved of the duty that would otherwise exist.

STRICT LIABILITY

Up to this point, the discussion of tort law has focused on situations where liability is based on fault. That is, a defendant's liability depended upon either some intentional wrongdoing (discussed in Chapter 3) or on the defendant's unreasonable conduct (negligence). However, the law imposes liability in some situations even if the defendant is not guilty of intentional wrongdoing and even if the defendant has exercised reasonable care. This is known as *strict liability*. The strict liability standard has been applied in situations where the defendant's conduct creates an unusually high risk of harm even if due care is exercised. In such situations injury is highly probable, and to require the plaintiff to prove negligence is to require him or her to bear the risk inherent in the defendant's dangerous conduct. Although the law could simply prohibit such conduct on the part of the defendant, there is some hazardous conduct that is socially beneficial, such as blasting done during the construction of buildings. The strict liability standard reflects a social policy that the defendant may engage in the activity but must bear the inherent risk of loss. The result of the strict liability standard is that the injured plaintiff is compensated for his or her injury by the party who caused it, who in turn must consider such liability as a cost of undertaking that type of activity.

Strict liability was early applied to the keepers of dangerous animals. A dangerous animal is one that is known by its keeper to be likely to inflict injury, such as a lion, a tiger, or a poisonous snake. For strict liability to apply, the keeper must know or have reason to know of the animal's dangerous propensities.

Strict liability was later applied to ultrahazardous activities. Common examples are blasting operations, public fireworks, and storing gasoline in dangerous proximity to nearby property. Consider the following case.

Spano v. Perini Corp.
Court of Appeals of New York
250 N.E.2d 31 (1969)

Background: Spano (plaintiff) was the owner of a garage in Brooklyn, which was wrecked by a blast occurring on November 27, 1962. There was in that garage, then, for repairs, an automobile owned by Davis (plaintiff), which was also damaged by the blasting. Spano and Davis each sued the Perini Corp. (defendant), which was engaged in constructing a tunnel in the vicinity. The two cases were tried together, and judgments were rendered in favor of Spano and Davis. Perini appealed, and an intermediate appellate court reversed the judgment, declaring that the established rule in New York required proof of negligence. Spano and Davis appealed to the Court of Appeals of New York, which is the supreme court of that state.

Decision: The Court of Appeals of New York reversed the lower level intermediate appellate court and reinstated the trial court judgment in favor of Spano and Davis.

Fuld, Chief Judge

The principal question posed on this appeal is whether a person who has sustained property damage caused by blasting on nearby property can maintain an action for damages without showing that the blaster was negligent. Since 1893, when this court decided the case of *Booth* v. *Rome, W. & O. T. R. R. Co.,* it has been the law of this State that proof of negligence was required unless the blast was accompanied by an actual physical invasion of the damaged property—for example, by rocks or other material being cast upon the premises. We are now asked to reconsider that rule.

The Appellate Division observed that "[i]f *Booth* is to be overruled, the announcement thereof should come from the authoritative source and not in the form of interpretation or prediction by an intermediate appellate court."

In our view, the time has come for this court to make that "announcement" and declare that one who engages in blasting must assume responsibility, and be liable without fault, for any injury he causes to neighboring property.

The concept of absolute liability in blasting cases is hardly a novel one. The overwhelming majority of American jurisdictions have adopted such a rule. Indeed, this court itself, several years ago, noted that a change in our law would "conform to the more widely (indeed almost universally) approved doctrine that a blaster is absolutely liable for any damages he causes, with or without trespass."

However, the court in the *Booth* case rejected such an extension of liability for the reason that "[t]o exclude the defendant from blasting to adapt its lot to the contemplated uses, at the instance of the plaintiff, would not be a compromise between conflicting rights, but an extinguishment of the right of the one for the benefit of the other." The court expanded on this by stating, "This sacrifice, we think, the law does not exact. Public policy is sustained by the building up of towns and cities and the improvement of property. Any unnecessary restraint on freedom of action of a property owner hinders this."

This rationale cannot withstand analysis. The plaintiff in *Booth* was not seeking, as the court implied, to "exclude the defendant from blasting" and thus prevent desirable improvements to the latter's property. Rather, he was merely seeking compensation for the damage which was inflicted upon his own property as a result of that blasting. The question, in other words, was not *whether* it was lawful or proper to engage in blasting but *who* should bear the cost of any resulting damage—the person who engaged in the dangerous activity or the innocent neighbor injured thereby. Viewed in such a light, it clearly appears that *Booth* was wrongly decided and should be forthrightly overruled.

Vicarious Liability

Under the doctrine of vicarious liability, an employer is liable for the negligence committed by an employee within the scope of his or her employment. The doctrine is also known as *imputed negligence* or *respondeat superior* ("let the superior respond"). It is an application of strict liability theory, meaning that for policy reasons liability is imposed regardless of the employer's fault or blame. Unlike other applications of strict liability, however, the employer's liability is based upon some fault of the employee.

Justification. It seems odd that courts recognize a rule imposing liability upon an otherwise innocent employer for the employee's wrongdoing. Liability could be limited only to instances where the employer knowingly hires a careless agent or commands the agent's tortious conduct. Expressing his own bewilderment at the rule of respondeat superior, Justice Holmes offered this explanation for its existence:

I assume that common sense is opposed to making one man pay for another man's wrong, . . . unless . . . he has induced the immediate wrongdoer to do acts of which the wrong . . . was the natural consequence. . . . I therefore assume that common sense is opposed to the fundamental theory of agency, although I have no doubt that the possible explanations of its various rules . . . together with the fact that the most flagrant of them presents itself as a seemingly wholesome check on the indifference and negligence of great corporations, have done much to reconcile men's minds to that theory.[1]

The "possible explanations" for the doctrine's existence mentioned by Holmes show why the rule had been a legal axiom for centuries. There are many other rationales for re-

PREVENTIVE LAW

—

In an article in the *Harvard Business Review,** two researchers identified several company practices that often lead to tort liability with regard to the manufacture of products. Company practices that they found lead to trouble included the following:

- Placing a low priority on product safety
- Having the attitude that "it's the consumer's responsibility"
- Having an inadequate understanding of the consumer (for example, failing to anticipate foreseeable product misuse)
- Failure to consider total product life (for example, failing to consider product deterioration in marketing plans)
- Relying on industry or government standards, which frequently represent *minimum* standards, not state of the art research
- Insufficient communication to and from customers (for example, inadequate warning labels and user manuals, and inadequate procedures for field representatives to send information about consumer product use to upper management)

The researchers found that company strategy for dealing with product liability ranged from one they called the "cornered position" ("We're not going to let government regulate our product") to another they termed "exploitation," where the safety issue is exploited to competitive advantage.

The authors gave the following recommendations to manufacturers concerned about tort liability:

- Put organizational strength into the program. For example, designating product safety committees, staffed by employees from engineering, manufacturing, quality control, and marketing, is needed if company strategy is to be implemented.
- Establish an insurance program. In addition to providing financial protection, insurance companies often perform "safety audits" and give advice on safety measures—a valuable service to smaller companies.
- Stay in touch. Companies need to stay in touch with legal developments, consumer expectations, and technological change in order to respond effectively to the environment.
- Develop disaster plans. When disaster strikes, sound management has anticipated it and has a plan for responding to it. This may include procedures for handling a product recall, communicating with the consuming public, and dealing with lawsuits.

*L. A. and A. I. Benningson, "Product Liability, Manufacturer Beware!" 52:3 *Harvard Business Review,* 122 (May–June 1974).

spondeat superior as well. A review of them presents the thoughts of several scholars on the subject and shows why, as one of them put it, "We make men pay for faults they have not committed."[2]

The earliest rationale for the doctrine was offered by the courts in the form of a Latin maxim: *Qui facit per alium facit per se* ("he who acts through another, acts himself"). The courts thus created a legal fiction that the employer and employee were one, much in the same way the courts resolved that when two people married they became one person for legal purposes. This fictitious identification of the employee with the employer became a convenient way for courts to reach their desired result. Citing the survival of the identification fiction from ancient times, Holmes maintained that the modern rule depends upon a fiction for its present existence. Later he concluded: "I look forward to a time when the part played by history in the explanation of dogma shall be very small . . . and instead . . . we shall . . . study . . . the ends sought to be attained and the reasons for desiring them."[3]

Following Holmes's prodding, other scholars began exploring the policy justifications for respondeat superior. John Wigmore philosophized:

If . . . I employ knowingly a careless servant, here at least I should be liable, just as for imprudently keeping a dog known to be ferocious. But even this may on practical grounds be too lenient a rule, for I may still find means of evading due responsibility under that test. Public convenience then may demand that I should be liable up to still a further point, even though I select agents carefully; in other words we may say I employ a substitute more or less at my peril.[4]

Wigmore recognized a policy reason for respondeat superior that may be called the evidence theory: the difficulty of proving whether an employer exercised care in hiring the employee or knew of the employee's activities requires holding the employer liable. As another scholar succinctly stated: "It is difficult to prove exactly who directed the damage, but you can tell whose servant did it."[5]

Another justification for the doctrine is the entrepreneur or enterprise theory, which is a financial explanation based upon the best way to distribute loss. Under this theory, the risk of liability is viewed as simply a cost the employer bears for the privilege of doing business. Imposing this cost upon the employer is not viewed as unfair because the employer benefits from the employee's activities and thus acquires the means to pay for the employee's torts. Furthermore, it is maintained that the employer is in a better position to bear the risk of loss, since the employer can pass the loss on to consumers in the form of higher prices. Viewed this way, respondeat superior is seen as a form of risk spreading, with the loss ultimately falling upon the community. The leading proponent of the entrepreneur theory, Young B. Smith, gave the following example as an illustration of its operation:

A taxicab negligently runs into a pedestrian. If the injured person's sole remedy is against the negligent chauffeur, in most cases the loss will fall on the pedestrian. On the other hand, if the person carrying on the taxicab business is held responsible, the loss will not fall on him alone. . . . [I]t is feasible for him (through the medium of insurance) to spread the loss among others carrying on a similar business, and he can pass his proportionate part of slightly higher charges to the hundreds and thousands of persons who use his cabs and thus "the shock of the accident may be borne by the community."[6]

The entrepreneur theory conforms to reality. It is a financial fact of life that while many businesspeople insure their businesses against liability, few people bother to provide adequate protection against accidental harm to themselves.

Respondeat superior need not be seen simply as the application of a financial theory. It may be viewed as serving a managerial as well as a financial function. An employer who is responsible for the consequences of the employee's conduct is more apt to take precautions to prevent the injurious consequences from arising. The employer will be more careful to hire safety-conscious employees, supervise their conduct, and discipline their carelessness. Thus, respondeat superior has a preventive, or deterrent, effect. As C. Robert Morris stated: "[N]ot only could the manager insure and spread the risk, but he could also seek to minimize the loss or prevent it altogether."[7] Although the availability of insurance reduces the economic impact, to the employer faced with premium increases and possible cancellation of coverage these managerial aspects of the doctrine take on added significance.

Respondeat superior was also seen by one scholar as a reflection of a fundamental change in legal thinking. Recognizing the doctrine's managerial functions, Harold Laski interpreted its emergence as a shift away from the legal protection of individualism toward a theory of social responsibility:

It is becoming more and more clear that we may not be content with an individualistic commercial law. Just as that individualism was the natural reaction from the too strict and local paternalism of medieval policy—perhaps aided by the self-centeredness of Puritan thought—so we are compelled to turn away from every conception of the business relation which does not see the public as an effective, if silent, partner in every enterprise. . . . It is simply a legal attempt to see the individual in his social context. That at which we industrially aim is the maximum public good as we see it. In that respect the employer is himself no more than a public servant, to whom, for special purposes, a certain additional freedom of action, and therefore a greater measure of responsibility has been vouchsafed. If that employer is compelled to bear the burden of his servant's torts even when he is himself personally without fault, it is because in a social distribution of profit and loss, the balance of least disturbance seems thereby best to be obtained. . . . If we allow the master to be careless of his servant's torts we lose hold upon the most valuable check in the conduct of social life.[8]

Others have been less lofty in their rationalizations of respondeat superior. These cynics see the doctrine as a method of making the person with the money pay the price, and their theory is appropriately called the deep-pocket theory. As Thomas Baty, the originator of the idea, put it, "Servants are an impecunious race. Should we nowadays hold masters answerable for the uncommanded torts of their servants if servants were able to pay for the damages they do? In hard fact, the reason for employers' liability is . . . the damages are taken from the deep pocket."[9]

One theme is central to all of these theories: between two innocent persons, the employer and the injured person, it is the employer who should pay for the employee's torts because, for various policy reasons, the employer is in the better position to bear this burden.

Scope of Employment Limitation. While respondeat superior is recognized because society believes it desirable and expedient to make the employer responsible for injuries inflicted by the employee, the employer is not made responsible for each and every tort the employee commits. Only when the employee commits a tort in the scope of employment—that is, when the injury is caused by the employee's wrongdoing incidental to the employment purposes—is the employer liable under respondeat superior. To make the employer responsible for acts that are in no way connected with employment goals would be unfair. The employer can be expected to bear only those costs that are closely associated with the business.

This limit on the employer's liability is easier to state than to apply. Determining if the employee is acting within the scope of employment often is difficult because the employee may temporarily be performing a personal errand, or doing the employer's work while also serving a personal purpose, or performing the employer's work in a forbidden manner. No precise formula exists to solve the problem whether at a particular moment a particular employee is engaged in the employer's business. Whether the employee is inside or outside the scope of employment often is a matter of degree. Since the scope-of-employment test determines whether respondeat superior applies as a guide in close cases, reference should be made to the larger policy purposes respondeat superior is supposed to serve.

No-Fault Insurance Systems

In two areas, state-mandated insurance compensation systems have replaced the traditional tort litigation system as a means of loss allocation. These are the areas of workers' compensation and no-fault automobile insurance.

Workers' Compensation. The defenses of contributory negligence and assumption of risk, along with the fellow-servant rule (which provided that an employer was not liable for a worker's injury where the injury resulted from the negligence of a fellow worker), made it extremely unlikely that an employee could hold the employer liable for on-the-job injuries. In response to the growing number of job-related injuries and the political pressure generated by labor groups, state legislatures in the early twentieth century enacted workers' compensation statutes. By 1949, every state had some form of workers' compensation system. Although the laws vary, they have certain common features.

Workers' compensation statutes substitute a strict liability standard for negligence with regard to job-related injuries. Fault is immaterial. Employees are entitled to benefits whether or not they were negligent and whether or not their employer was free from fault.

Injuries that arise out of and during the course of employment are compensable under workers' compensation statutes. This standard is similar to the scope-of-employment test of the respondeat superior doctrine discussed previously.

Under workers' compensation, employers are required to contribute either to a state-administered workers' compensation fund or, as in most states, procure workers' compensation insurance from private insurers.

Claims for workers' compensation benefits are administered by a state agency, usually called the Industrial Commission or Workers' Compensation Bureau. If the employer contests the claim, the agency holds a hearing and determines if the injury is compensable under the statute. Because an employer's contribution to the state fund or the employer's insurance premiums depend upon the employer's experience rating, there is an economic incentive for employers to contest doubtful claims.

Workers' compensation benefits are computed according to a schedule of compensation. The schedule establishes the financial amount an injured employee is entitled to according to the type of injury or disability that the employee suffered.

No-Fault Automobile Insurance. Many negligence cases involve automobile accidents. Because of the amount of time courts devote to these cases, states have enacted statutes that, to varying degrees, remove recovery for automobile accident injuries from the courts to administrative agencies. The purpose of these statutes is to provide an injured party with an automatic but minimal amount of recovery rather than a day in court with its po-

BOX 8-1: ISSUES AND TRENDS
Tort Reform
—

Tort law, once limited to debate in the nation's courtrooms, has become a matter of intense public debate. To date, the debate has been among lawyers and representatives of the business community and insurers.

Pointing to freakish lawsuits, million-dollar damage awards, and soaring insurance costs, business groups and insurers have urged Congress and state legislatures to undertake "tort reform" by passing laws that would repudiate many court-made legal doctrines. Proponents of tort reform argue that many of these judge-made rules were made only in the last twenty years and represent judicial activism that must be rebuked by legislation.

Plaintiffs' lawyers and consumer advocates argue that what insurers and business groups want is special-interest protection. They assert that to take the few "freak" cases in the thousands of tort cases decided each year in the courts and suggest that they are typical of the mass of cases misrepresents the tort system. They argue that there is no need for radical disruption of the tort system.

Most of the reform proposals can be grouped as follows:

- *Changes in liability standards.* Business groups want to return to the negligence or fault rule rather than continue the doctrine of strict liability. They argue that liability should not exist unless the defendant is to blame. Consumer advocates counter that the fault standard permits a defendant to kill or maim as long as defendant's conduct is reasonable, and that strict liability permits efficient risk allocation.

- *Damage limits.* Citing jury awards that resemble lottery prizes, business groups want caps (typically $100,000) placed on "noneconomic damages." These damages involve awards for intangible injuries, such as pain and suffering, emotional distress, and loss of companionship. In contrast, economic damages would be awarded for quantifiable items, like lost wages and medical expenses. Business groups also seek to deny punitive damages, which are awarded to punish a wrongdoer. Consumer advocates argue that big awards are not always unjustified. They point out that under the proposed limit, a seventeen-year-old woman forced to undergo a total hysterectomy and vaginectomy because her mother took the cancer-causing drug DES would recover no more than $100,000 for her inability to have children or have normal sexual relations. Regarding punitive damages, plaintiffs' lawyers cite recent studies showing that punitive damages are awarded in only 2 percent of product liability cases, that the average award of punitive damages is less than $500,000, and that most of the cases are not simple accidents, but involve aggravating circumstances of gross negligence or recklessness.*

- *Removal of certain classes of cases from the court system.* Tort reformers argue that certain classes of cases—such as those involving product liability—should be taken from the court system so that these "special" cases can be resolved by some other tribunal or procedure, similar to the way workers' compensation operates. They assert that cases involving defective products could be more fairly, more expertly, and more efficiently resolved by an administrative process. Plaintiffs' attorneys argue that this amounts to "tossing away the courthouse keys," and taking away the victim's right to trial by jury.

*Landes and Posner, "New Light on Punitive Damages," 10:1 *Regulation,* 33 (September/October 1986).

---

tential for a greater recovery. The laws differ from state to state. Basically, they provide that the injured party need not prove negligence in the traditional way but only that the no-fault insurance statute is applicable to the case. As long as the amount claimed by the injured party is below a prescribed maximum, his or her own insurance pays the claim without regard to fault. This process is analogous to the change from the use of negligence to workers' compensation insurance for recovery by injured employees.

REVIEW PROBLEMS

1. Define negligence and describe each of its elements.
2. What procedural doctrines are available to plaintiffs in a negligence case, and what defenses are available to defendants?
3. What is strict liability, and in what types of cases has it been applied?
4. What is meant by "vicarious liability," and when is it applied?
5. A fireman developed lung cancer after some years of inhaling smoke while fighting fires and also smoking cigarettes. The fireman filed a claim for workers' compensation benefits. Will the fireman recover benefits? Explain.
6. The Kosmos Portland Cement Co. failed to clean petroleum residue out of an oil barge, which was tied to a dock. Lightning struck the barge, the vapor with which it was filled exploded, and workers on the dock were injured. Is Kosmos liable to the workers for their injuries? Explain. Johnson v. Kosmos Portland Cement Co., 64 F.2d 193 (6th Cir. 1933).
7. Breisig operated an automobile repair shop. Roberts took his car to Breisig's shop for repairs. When Roberts asked when the car would be ready, Breisig said that he hoped the repairs would be completed by the end of the day. If they were, Breisig said, he would park the car in his shop's parking lot so Roberts could pick it up that evening. About 7 P.M. Breisig finished the work and parked the car in the lot, leaving

the keys in the ignition. Soon thereafter two teenage boys stole the car and drove it around town. They picked up two friends and left the car on a street overnight. The next day one of the friends, Williams, returned to the car and, while driving negligently, struck George, who suffered serious injuries. George sued Breisig, claiming that leaving the keys in an unattended car was negligence, particularly since Breisig's shop was located in a deteriorating neighborhood. Breisig denied liability. Who wins? Explain. George v. Breisig, 477 P.2d 983 (Kan. 1970).

8. A passenger was running to catch one of the Long Island Railroad Company's trains. A railroad employee, trying to assist the passenger to board the train, dislodged a package from his arms, and it fell upon the rails. The package contained fireworks, which exploded with some violence. The concussion overturned some scales, many feet away on the platform, and they fell upon Palsgraf and injured her. Palsgraf sued the Long Island Railroad Company, claiming that it was liable for her injuries as a result of its employee's negligence. Long Island Railroad disclaimed any liability. Who wins? Explain. Palsgraf v. Long Island Railroad Co., 162 N.E. 99 (N.Y. 1928).

9. A driver for the Coca-Cola Bottling Company delivered several cases of Coca-Cola to the restaurant where Escola worked as a waitress. She placed the cases on the floor, one on top of the other, under and behind the counter, where they remained for over thirty-six hours. Escola picked up the top case and set it upon a nearby ice-cream cabinet in front of and about three feet from the refrigerator. She then proceeded to take the bottles from the case with her right hand, one at a time, and put them into the refrigerator. After she had placed three bottles in the refrigerator and had moved the fourth bottle about eighteen inches from the case, it exploded in her hand. The bottle broke into two jagged pieces and inflicted a deep five-inch cut, severing blood vessels, nerves, and muscles of the thumb and palm of her hand. Escola sued Coca-Cola, relying on the doctrines of res ipsa loquitur and strict product liability theory. Will Escola succeed under these theories? Explain. Escola v. Coca-Cola Bottling Co. of Fresno, 150 P.2d 436 (Calif. 1944).

10. A dead mouse is found baked inside a loaf of bread from the Continental Baking Co., and Doyle is injured by eating the bread. Continental introduces evidence of many witnesses who testify that all possible care was used in the bakery, and that such precautions were taken that it was impossible for mice to get into the product. Continental makes a motion for a directed verdict in its favor. Will the court grant the motion? Doyle v. Continental Baking Co., 160 N.E. 325 (1928).

11. On a stormy night the owner of a tractor truck left it parked without lights in the middle of the road. The driver of a car in which Hill was a passenger saw it in time to turn and avoid hitting it, but negligently failed to do so. Hill is injured. Who is liable to her? Hill v. Edmonds, 270 N.Y.S.2d 1020 (1966).

12. Anthony and Jeannette Luth were driving south on the Seward Highway in Alaska when their car collided with another driven by Wayne Jack. The accident occurred when Jack attempted to pass another vehicle going north. On the day of the accident and for the previous six weeks, Jack was employed by Rogers and Babler Construction Company as a flagman on a road construction project. At the time of the accident, he was returning home to Anchorage from his job site, having completed a 7-A.M.-to-5:30-P.M. workday. Since he did not live near the job site, Jack commuted approximately twenty-

five miles to work by car every day. The Master Union Agreement under which Jack worked provided for additional remuneration of $8.50 a day since the job site was located a considerable distance from Anchorage. However, all of the firm's employees on this particular construction project received the $8.50 additional remuneration whether they commuted from Anchorage or lived near the job site. The Luths sued Rogers and Babler Construction, claiming that the company was responsible under the doctrine of respondeat superior for their injuries. Is the company liable? Explain. Luth v. Rogers and Babler Construction Co., 507 P.2d 761 (Ala. 1973).

FOOTNOTES

[1] Holmes, "The History of Agency," 5 *Harvard Law Review,* 1, 14 (1891).

[2] Laski, "The Basis of Vicarious Liability," 26 *Yale Law Journal,* 105, 111 (1916).

[3] Holmes, "The Path of the Law," 10 *Harvard Law Review,* 457, 474 (1897).

[4] Wigmore, "Responsibility for Tortious Acts: Its History," 7 *Harvard Law Review,* 383, 404–405 1 (1894).

[5] Baty, *Vicarious Liability* (1916), p. 147.

[6] Smith, "Frolic and Detour," 23 *Columbia Law Review,* 444, 458 (1923).

[7] Morris, "Enterprise Liability and the Actuarial Process—The Insignificance of Foresight," 70 *Yale Law Journal,* 554 (1961).

[8] Laski, "The Basis of Vicarious Liability," 26 *Yale Law Journal,* 105, 112, 114 (1916).

[9] Baty, *Vicarious Liability* (1916), p. 154.

PART II

CONTRACTS

Introduction to the Law of Contracts

C ontracts are all-pervasive in our daily lives. Contracts govern a boarding agreement with the university, renting an apartment, buying books at the bookstore, agreeing to lend a roommate money, and buying beer at the local store. The law of contracts, which determines enforceability, defines terms and constrains use of agreements, establishes the parameters of permissible business and individual transactions.

THE UTILITY OF CONTRACTS

Contract law can be viewed in several ways. Some see the freedom of individuals and organizations to contract as fundamental to our basic free-enterprise system. Viewed in this manner, the law of supply and demand learned in economics is implemented every day by innumerable contracts between sellers and buyers. Contract law facilitates exchanges between the parties by protecting both seller and buyer against the possible bad-faith conduct of the other. Without this protection, the parties could breach contracts at will. If the law of contracts did not provide a remedy for the breach of an agreement, sellers would be forced to require deposits, or entire purchase prices, before they would sell and ship goods. This would increase transaction costs and significantly slow the flow of goods in our economy.

Another view of a contract is that it is a tool by which people—often, but not always, assisted by their lawyers—establish a private set of rules to govern a particular business or personal relationship. Under this perspective, a contract is a device by which a situation may be defined and controlled. The expectations of the contracting parties are made known and serve as guides for future behavior.

For example, by use of a real-estate purchase contract, a seller promises to sell a house and lot to a buyer. In the contract, a number of the parties' expectations are spelled out. Such expectations include: (1) when the buyer may take possession; (2) what kind of document of title the seller is to provide the buyer; (3) what articles the seller may remove from the house and yard; (4) how the taxes owing are to be split among the parties; (5) how the risk of unexpected future damage is to be allocated among the parties, etc.

By virtue of this contractual agreement, the

buyer and seller have created their own set of rules to govern the house-sale transaction. In a sense, their agreement embodies a private legal system. Not surprisingly, many of the questions that arise concerning the operation of a governmental legal system also come up in the context of private agreements. For example, what is to be done if the parties in the agreement just described fail to provide for responsibility in case of loss and the house is destroyed by an earthquake after the contract is signed but before the buyer takes possession? Or what happens if one of the parties blatantly disregards one of the clearly established private rules—for example, by refusing to provide the required evidence of title?

In the first case (loss of a house due to an earthquake) the basic expectations of at least one of the parties cannot be met. Either the buyer will be required to purchase damaged property or the seller will be required to give up a sale he or she thought was closed and final. How can this issue be resolved when the parties have not dealt with the problem themselves and insurance does not cover the loss? For commonly occurring situations of this sort, the courts and legislatures have established guidelines. In addition, general legal principles have been promulgated determining how contractual provisions should be interpreted when issues such as this arise.

The second case (refusing to provide required evidence of title) goes to the heart of contract law. From a public-policy perspective, it would not be desirable for the parties to attempt to enforce their contract by private means. Our legal system does not tolerate the use of threats or force to induce faithful observance of the terms of private agreements. (An ironic use of the term "contract" is to speak of "putting out a contract" on someone when describing the criminal procurement of violence against a designated victim.) Instead, it allows the parties to a contract to enforce its terms through civil suits.

A number of questions are immediately posed by the intervention of the legal system when private parties disagree. Should all private agreements be enforced—for example, an agreement by two bank robbers to split the proceeds of a holdup 55 percent/45 percent? What type of relief should be provided for the party injured as a result of the other's failure to observe the terms of the agreement? Could a university obtain a court order compelling a professor who has just won a million-dollar lottery to teach the last academic year of a three-year teaching contract? Should the legal system enforce only "fair" contracts? If so, what constitutes a fair contract? Should unwritten contracts be enforceable?

Because the case that follows involved actor Lee Marvin and received extensive media coverage, it provides an interesting introduction to the law of contracts. The reader should try to determine what policy issues the court considered in determining whether a private agreement should be enforced.

After the *Marvin* case, a subsequent case involving the rock star Peter Frampton is excerpted. When you read the *Frampton* opinion, note how the court distinguishes the facts from the *Marvin* case.

Marvin v. Marvin

Supreme Court of California
555 P.2d 106 (1976)

Background: Michelle Triola Marvin (plaintiff) lived with actor Lee Marvin (defendant) from October 1964 to May 1970, when he compelled her to leave. She sued Mr. Marvin, claiming that they had entered into an oral contract in 1964 in which both parties agreed they would share equally their earnings and property no matter who earned them. She claimed that they agreed to represent themselves as husband and wife and that she would be a homemaker and companion, giving up her career as an entertainer and singer. Mr. Marvin in his defense claimed that this was not an enforceable contract because it was made between nonmarital partners, involved in an illicit relationship, and thus was contrary to public policy. A lower court ruled in favor of Mr. Marvin, leaving all property accumulated by the couple with him. Ms. Marvin appealed.

Decision: The lower court decision for Lee Marvin was reversed and remanded for new trial.

Tobriner, Justice

During the past 15 years, there has been a substantial increase in the number of couples living together without marrying. Such nonmarital relationships lead to legal controversy when one partner dies or the couple separates.

We conclude: (1) The provisions of the Family Law Act do not govern the distribution of property acquired during a nonmarital relationship, such a relationship remains subject solely to judicial decision; (2) The courts should enforce express contracts between nonmarital partners except to the extent that the contract is explicitly founded on the consideration of meretricious sexual services.

Defendant first and principally relies on the contention that the alleged contract is so closely related to the supposed "immoral" character of the relationship between plaintiff and himself that the enforcement of the contract would violate public policy. He points to cases asserting that a contract between nonmarital partners is unenforceable if it is "involved in" an illicit relationship . . . or made in "contemplation" of such a relationship. A review of the numerous California decisions concerning contracts between nonmarital partners, however, reveals that the courts have not employed such broad and uncertain standards to strike down contracts. The decisions instead disclose a narrower and more precise standard: a contract between nonmarital partners is unenforceable *only to the extent* that it *explicitly* rests upon the immoral and illicit consideration of meretricious sexual services.

In *Bridges* v. *Bridges* (1954), both parties were in the process of obtaining divorces from their erstwhile respective spouses. The two parties agreed to live together, to share equally in property acquired, and to marry when their divorces became final. The man worked as a salesman and used his savings to purchase properties. The woman kept house, cared for seven children, three from each former marriage and one from the nonmarital relationship, and helped construct improvements on the properties. When they separated, without marrying, the court awarded the woman one-half the value of the property. Rejecting the man's contention that the contract was illegal, the court stated that: "Nowhere is it expressly testified to by anyone that there was anything in the agreement for the pooling of assets and the sharing of accumulations that contemplated meretricious relations as any part of the consideration or as any object of the agreement."

Defendant secondly relies upon the ground suggested by the trial court: that the 1964 contract violated public policy because it impaired the community property rights of Betty Marvin, defendant's lawful wife. Defendant points out that his earnings while living apart from his wife before rendition of the interlocutory decree were community property . . . and that defendant's agreement with plaintiff purported to transfer to her a half interest in that community property. But whether or not defendant's contract with plaintiff exceeded his authority as manager of the community property, defendant's argument fails for the reason that an improper transfer of community property is not void *ab initio,* but merely voidable at the instance of the aggrieved spouse. In the present case Betty Marvin, the aggrieved spouse, had the opportunity to assert her community property rights in the divorce action. The interlocutory and final decrees in that action fix and limit her interest. Enforcement of the contract between plaintiff and defendant against property awarded to defendant by the divorce decree will not impair any right of Betty's, and thus is not on that account violative of public policy.

Defendant's third contention is noteworthy for the lack of authority advanced in its support. He contends that enforcement of the oral agreement between plaintiff and himself is barred by Civil Code section 5134, which provides that "All contracts for marriage settlements must be in writing. . . ." A marriage settlement, however, is an agreement in contemplation of marriage in which each party agrees to release or modify the property rights which would otherwise arise from the marriage. The contract at issue here does not conceivably fall within that definition, and thus is beyond compass of section 5134.

Defendant finally argues that enforcement of the contract is barred by Civil Code section 43.5, subdivision (d), which provides that "No cause of action arises for . . . [b]reach of a promise of marriage." This rather strained contention proceeds from the premise that a promise of marriage impliedly includes a promise to support and to pool property acquired after marriage to the conclusion that pooling and support agreements not part of or accompanied by promise of marriage are barred by the section. We conclude that section 43.5 is not reasonably susceptible to the interpretation advanced by defendant, a conclusion demonstrated by the fact that since section 43.5 was enacted in 1939, numerous cases have enforced pooling agreements between nonmarital partners, and in none did court or counsel refer to section 43.5.

In summary, we base our opinion on the principle that adults who voluntarily live together and engage in sexual relations are nonetheless as competent as any other persons to contract respecting their earnings and property rights. Of course, they cannot lawfully contract to pay for the performance of sexual services, for such a contract is, in essence, an agreement for prostitution and unlawful for that reason. But they may agree to pool their earnings and to hold all property acquired during the relationship in accord with the law governing community property; conversely they may agree that each partner's earnings and the property acquired from those earnings remains the separate property of the earnings partner. So long as the agreement does not rest upon illicit meretricious consideration, the parties may order their economic affairs as they choose, and no policy precludes the courts from enforcing such agreements.

In the present instance, plaintiff alleges that the parties agreed to pool their earnings, that they contracted to share equally in all property acquired, and that defendant agreed to support plaintiff. The terms of the contract as alleged do not rest upon any unlawful consideration. We therefore conclude that the complaint furnishes a suitable basis upon which the trial court can render declaratory relief. The trial court consequently erred in granting defendant's motion for judgment on the pleadings.

CASE NOTE

The trial court, upon remand, found that the evidence did not show that Ms. Marvin gave up her career at Mr. Marvin's request or for his benefit. Further, the court found that the couple's words and conduct showed neither an express nor implied contract to share property. The court found that performance of "homemaking" services for a paramour does not of itself imply a contract to share property since such things are frequently done for other reasons, such as shared affection. Such acts do not in and of themselves show an "accumulation of property by mutual effort" under California law. Having found no expressed or implied contract, the court, in equity, awarded $104,000 to Ms. Marvin for rehabilitation purposes. It noted that this amount would be approximately equal to the highest scale she ever earned as a singer, $1,000 per week, for two years. (See Case No. C-23303, Memorandum Opinion, Superior Court of the State of California, County of Los Angeles, April 18, 1979, reprinted in 5FLR 3077, 3083–3085 [1979].)

Mr. Marvin appealed this decision, and the California Court of Appeals reversed the trial court, stating that there was no basis in equity or in law for awarding Ms. Marvin $104,000 to rehabilitate herself (122 Cal. App. 3d.871 [1981]).

McCall v. Frampton

New York Supreme Court, Westchester County

415 N.Y.S.2nd 752 (1952)

Background: McCall (plaintiff) sues Frampton (defendant) for damages and real property pursuant to the alleged breach of an oral contract. The plaintiff claims that acting on representations made by the defendant, the plaintiff left her husband, lived with the defendant, and devoted all her resources, time, and effort to the promotion and success of the defendant in his endeavors. The defendant moves herein to dismiss the plaintiff's complaint.

Decision: Frampton's motion to dismiss McCall's complaint is granted.

Gagliardi, Justice

In the first cause of action plaintiff alleges, *inter alia,* that in and prior to 1972 plaintiff "had expertise and was engaged in the business of promotion and management of musicians involved in that phase of the music business known popularly as 'Rock and Roll' or 'Rock' and, during that period, besides doing so for compensation engaged in those activities without compensation for others"; that plaintiff met defendant in 1972 when defendant was a member of the musical group known as "Humble Pie" and when plaintiff was married to the group's manager (a Mr. Brigden); that in 1973 defendant "requested that McCall *leave her then husband and her then employment . . . and that she become associated with and work with Frampton in the promotion of Frampton as a musician representing to McCall that if she did so they would be equal partners in all proceeds from his employment in that field.*"

In *Marvin v. Marvin,* the California Supreme Court . . . held that contracts between non-marital partners should be enforced to the extent that the contract was not explicitly founded on the consideration of unlawful sexual services, despite the arguments to the contrary based on public policy. That court also held that in the absence of express contract, the court should enquire into the conduct of the parties to determine whether that conduct demonstrated the existence of an implied contract, partnership or joint venture. It further held that the court may also employ the doctrine of *quantum meruit* or equitable remedies such as constructive or resulting trust. The plaintiff was held to have the right to try to establish her case at trial. It is clear however that plaintiff, Michelle Marvin, and defendant, Lee Marvin, did agree to hold themselves out as husband and wife and that she did assume his surname. It is also clear that during the time of their living together Lee Marvin was divorced from his former wife and the relationship between the parties ceased to be adulterous so that they could then have contracted a valid marriage.

This court holds that the motion to dismiss . . . is granted. In the first place, the contract between plaintiff and defendant, as pleaded in the complaint, is void and unenforceable as a matter of public policy. Taking the allegations of the complaint as true for the purposes of this motion, it is patent that plaintiff pleads as the consideration for this agreement the commission of adultery on her part, *viz,* that she leave her husband and live with defendant and become associated with him. This contract was, therefore, in derogation of her existing marriage and involved, as an integral part thereof, conduct prohibited by section 255.17 of the Penal Law: "A person is guilty of adultery when he engages in sexual intercourse with another person at a time when he has a living spouse, or the other person has a living spouse. Adultery is a class B misdemeanor." (The papers submitted on this motion leave no doubt that there was an illicit sexual relationship between the parties. There is no indication that plaintiff has ever been divorced from her husband. Apparently, defendant was divorced from his wife during the time when the parties lived together.)

. . .

. . . It is settled that agreements against public policy are unlawful and void. This rule is not based on a desire to benefit the party who breaches an illegal contract, but on a desire to protect the common weal, the general welfare of society being damaged by the very making of such a contract. By refusing to enforce such a contract and leaving the parties without a legal remedy for breach, society is protected by discouraging the making of contracts contrary to the common good. . . .

With full awareness that courts must be conscious of the difficulties which may arise in applying the doctrine of public policy and must be careful to avoid rigidity and an overdependence on individual opinions as to the demands of the common good, there being no public policy save that which is in accord with the constitution and laws of the state, it is the opinion of this court that the contract, as alleged by plaintiff, is clearly subject to the defense of illegality. It is contrary to the public policy of this state, which recognizes the state of marriage and the protection thereof as essential to the welfare of our society. It requires, in its performance, the commission of adultery, which remains a crime in this state (see Penal Law, § 255.17, *supra*). This contract as alleged, is clearly opposed to sound morality and is based on the illicit association of the parties. Thus it is void and unenforceable.

. . .

For the reasons stated above, the motion to dismiss the complaint is granted as to all three causes of action.

CONTRACT DEFINED

agreecount recog d enf.

The issues posed earlier in this chapter will be discussed in the following chapters as the basic outline of the law of contracts is presented. For now, we need to define a *contract.* The simplest, most accurate definition is: *A contract is an agreement that the courts will recognize and enforce.* What do the courts require before an agreement will be recognized and enforced? The following list represents the elements of enforceability for most types of contracts in most jurisdictions. In parentheses the reader will find the chapter in this text that discusses each element.

1. A valid offer (Chapter 10)
2. A proper acceptance (Chapter 11)
3. Sufficiency of consideration (Chapter 12)
4. Absence of fraud, force, or legally significant mistake (Chapter 13)
5. Legal capacity of parties (Chapter 14)
6. Consistency with general public policy (Chapter 15)
7. Observance of proper legal form (Chapter 16)
8. Consistency with special rules governing the type of agreement involved (throughout Part II).

The relationship among the eight requirements is dramatized in Figure 9-1. This figure, which captures the various requirements for an enforceable contract, is intended as a reference and will be more meaningful as you progress through this part of the text. We recommend that you refer back to it as you study contract law.

SOURCE OF CONTRACT LAW

General contract law has a common law basis. This means that the principles of contract law are to be found in judicial decisions of cases involving contractual disputes. Under the doctrine of precedent, or stare decisis, courts will follow their earlier decisions involving similar situations. This principle of consistency in judicial decision making produces fields of judicially made law, such as contracts, torts, and agency. With the exception of Louisiana, no state has a comprehensive statute promulgating contract law.

There are, however, a number of statutes that spell out special rules for certain types of contracts. For example, state statutes regulate the use of insurance contracts. The most important of the state statutes affecting contract law is the Uniform Commercial Code (UCC). The UCC, which has been adopted at least in part by the legislatures of all fifty states, established a series of rules dealing with all aspects of sales transactions. One part of the UCC, Article 2, contains rules governing sales contracts. (Article 2 of the UCC is included in full in the Appendix.) If the UCC does not provide a rule covering an aspect of a sales contract, the general common law of contracts controls. If there is a UCC rule, it governs sales contracts even when the common law rule is to the contrary. This relationship is spelled out in Figure 9-2.

Several basic points regarding the true nature of contracts must now be made. First, almost all contracts are voluntarily carried out by the parties to their mutual satisfaction, so that the judicial system never becomes in-

ETHICS BOX
Ethics, Morality, and the Law

As demonstrated in *Marvin* and *McCall*, court opinions often make reference to "public policy" which encompasses community morals. Consensus views of right and wrong are used to flesh out legal principles and even in some cases, to establish new rules. In contract law, morality is used to determine contracts that are illegal under the common law and therefore not judicially enforceable.

Community views of right and wrong do not determine what is ethical. Instead, as described in Chapter 5, pp. 89–90, there are formal methods for defining ethics. Ethics transcend community morality. A state legislature may respond to community morality by, for example, passing a law that prohibts certain types of business dealings on Sunday (Sunday Blue Laws) or gambling. That does not, ipso facto, make those practices unethical.

Judges often make pronouncements of community morality. But how do they determine what is public policy? They do not rely on public opinion surveys, nor are there definitive spokespeople on moral issues who can claim to represent the entire community. Instead, judges who find public policy often do so through their own conjecture. That process has the danger of (1) being biased by the judge's own cultural biases and (2) of working unfairly against certain groups.

Consider the initial policy of the common law judges not to enforce cohabitation agreements. Although probably consistent with community morality, the rule worked to the prejudice of those who wanted to participate in alternate life-styles. Ultimately, however, the flexibility of the common law was demonstrated when the courts responded to greater tolerance of relationships outside of marriage and recognized the enforceability of such arrangements.

volved. This is due in part to the fear of legal sanctions, but also results from observance of the ethical duty to act in good faith in business transactions.

Second, the mere fact that one has a legal right to sue for breach of contract does not mean that it is a sound business decision to do so. Before suit is filed, factors such as likelihood of again doing business with the other party, industry attitudes about litigious businesses, relative economic strength of the parties, and alternative private means of resolving the dispute should be considered. Third, although we will be discussing basic rules

pertaining to contracts in general, there are many specific categories of contracts that have certain individualized rules of law pertaining to them.

CLASSIFICATION OF CONTRACTS

The following classification of contracts seeks to aid the reader in analyzing problems related to contracts as they are covered in subsequent chapters. It will be assumed there that the reader is familiar with these catego-

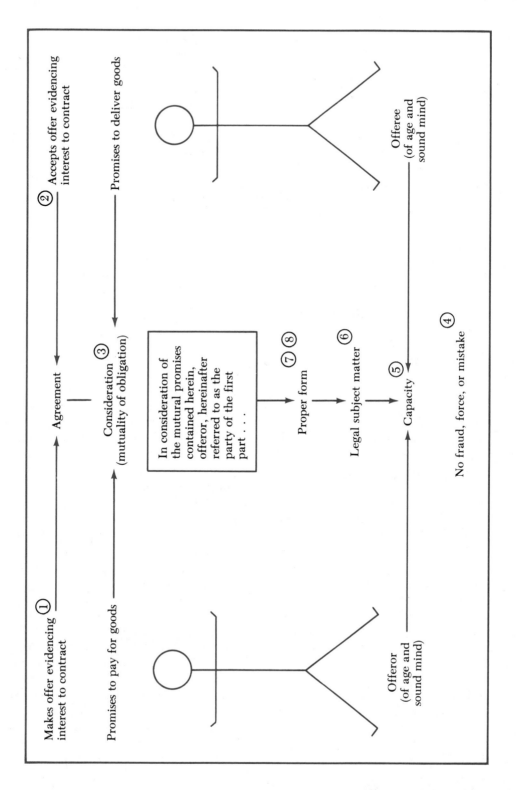

FIGURE 9–1
Forming a Binding Contract

FIGURE 9–2
Sources of Contract Law

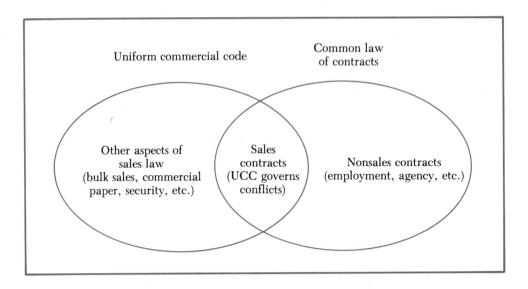

ries of contracts and the terminology involved.

Express, Implied, and Quasi Contracts

An *express* contract is one formed by the words of the parties, either oral or written. A *contract implied-in-fact* is derived from the actions of the parties. Going to a doctor, describing symptoms, and accepting treatment establishes a contract implied-in-fact. The test is whether a reasonable person would intend to contract by engaging in such actions.

A *quasi contract*, also known as a *contract implied-in-law*, differs from express and implied-in-fact contracts in that the parties did not intend to make a contract. In creating the legal fiction of a quasi contract, the courts are not trying to fathom the intentions of the parties; they are simply trying to be fair. Suppose, for example, that a doctor performed expensive and valuable services upon a patient who had suddenly become unconscious in the doctor's waiting room. There is clearly no express contract. Further, many courts would refuse

to recognize a contract implied-in-fact because no intention could be inferred regarding any actions of the patient. A quasi contract could be posited, however, that would require the patient to pay the reasonable value of the services rendered.

In order for the courts to recognize a quasi contract, there must be (1) a benefit or unjust enrichment retained by the benefited party and (2) no other legal recourse for the "victim" of the benefit. The victim is entitled to recover only the reasonable value of the benefit—not what would have been a likely contract price.

Executed and Executory Contracts

An *executed* contract is one in which all required performances have been rendered. A goes to B's garage, picks up a new tire, and pays B. The contract has been fully performed. Nothing remains to be done by either party. An *executory* contract is one in which some of the required performance remains to be done. A and B enter an agreement

BOX 9-1 ISSUES AND TRENDS
An International Comparison of Contracting

Contracting is more formal in the United States than in many other countries. The classical or formal approach to contracting involves relatively elaborate contracts which are subject to stringent tests before they will be enforced by the courts. In using formal contracts, the parties try to anticipate most of the problems that are likely to arise in the future. Thus, the contract will contain many clauses that deal with potential risks of loss, or the ability of the parties subsequently to transfer interests under the contract to someone else.

Japan is an example of a less formal system of contracting. There, a relational approach is taken. The parties form a relationship based on the mutual understanding that they will work out problems as they arise in the future. The initial agreement is less elaborate because there is no attempt to anticipate many future developments.

Many international transactions involving agreements between firms from different countries depend upon arbitration as a way of resolving disputes. The disparate legal rules and varying expectations often involved in international business produce a need for specialized expertise when disagreements occur. There is a system of international arbitration, involving even the Soviet Union, that responds to the need for dispute resolution.

Each approach has its advantages. Formal contracting reduces the chances that a party's basic expectancies under the contract will be defeated. Relational contracting is less expensive and time-consuming in the first instance because the agreement is more basic and simple. Further, the mindset of the parties may make it more likely that they can work out problems as they inevitably arise in the future.

Arbitration takes the problem out of the hands of the parties and yet can provide a quick resolution that is sensitive to the special requirements of the disputing firms.

whereby B agrees to repair A's car in two weeks and A agrees to pay B $100 upon completion. Since neither party has performed his part of the agreement, it is executory in nature. This distinction is significant, because the courts will be influenced by the performance status of an executory contract in determining the relief to be given to the victim of a breach of contract. Remedies are discussed in Chapter 18.

Valid, Void, and Voidable Contracts

A *valid* contract is one that is perfectly good and that may be enforced by all parties to it. A *void* contract, on the other hand, is not good; it is not enforceable by anyone. A void contract is a contradiction in terms in that it is not really a contract under our definition. For example, if A contracts with B to kill C, who is A's wife, the failure of B to perform will not be grounds for a suit by A because a legally enforceable contract never existed. A *voidable* contract has an in-between status. It is currently valid, but one or more of the parties has the power to render the contract unenforceable. A, a minor, contracts with B, who is of legal age, to paint B's house. The contract is voidable by A. As explained in Chapter 14, A has the right to disaffirm the agreement anytime before reaching majority and shortly thereafter.

Bilateral and Unilateral Contracts

A contract may involve an exchange of promises in which two parties agree that each will perform in a certain way in the future. Player promises to abide by the team rules and be available to play baseball for the coming season. Team promises to pay Player $85,000 for the year. At the moment the contract is signed, neither party starts performing. Instead, the agreed-upon performance will take place in the future. The exchange of a promise for a promise is known as a *bilateral contract*.

Suppose Team promises to pay Player $2,000 for every home run over thirty during the season. Player has not promised to hit more than thirty home runs and will not be in breach of contract for failing to do so. Instead, Team has made a promise that performance will be forthcoming in exchange for an act. This is an offer of a *unilateral contract* that can be accepted only by performance of the act. Most commercial contracts are bilateral.

The various definitions are diagrammed in Figure 9-3.

FIGURE 9–3
Classification of Contracts

Context	Terms	Distinctions
Manifestation of intent	Express	Formed by the words of the parties, either oral or written
	Implied–in–fact	Derived from the action of the parties. Test: Would a reasonable person intend to contract by engaging in the act?
	Implied–in–law	A legal fiction wherein contractual rights are imputed in an attempt to be fair. No actual agreement exists.
Enforceability	Valid	Enforceable by all parties.
	Void	Not enforceable by anyone.
	Voidable	Currently valid, but may be rendered unenforceable by one or more parties.
Manner of acceptance	Bilateral	Offer seeks acceptance by promise.
	Unilateral	Offer seeks acceptance by performance.

Andrews v. O'Grady

New York Supreme Court, Kings County

252 N.Y.S.2d 814 (1964)

Background: Andrews (petitioner), a bus operator for New York City, sues O'Grady (respondent), chairman of the New York Transit Authority. Andrew's religious convictions (Seventh Day Adventist) compelled that he not work between sundown Friday to after sundown Saturday, of which he advised the NYTA shortly before being hired. After being hired, he was repeatedly informed that bus "runs" were assigned as per a nondiscriminatory system, that undesirable runs could be "swapped" with other willing bus operators, but that barring such, Andrews would have to operate the bus during his Sabbath or be subject to dismissal. Andrews was assigned to work during his Sabbath, could not find a willing substitute, and failed to show up for work. Andrews was suspended without pay, and he brought suit herein to be restored to his position.

Decision: Andrew's suit is dismissed.

Pino, Justice

The first contention by petitioner is that a quasi contractual relationship arose out of the conduct of the parties, to wit: that petitioner had advised the Civil Service Commission, before taking the examination, that he was a Seventh Day Adventist and could not work during his Sabbath, but was nevertheless permitted to take the examination; that he advised respondents to the same effect, both upon his appointment and prior to the completion of his training, but nonetheless was allowed to complete his training and was assigned to a depot for work; that under these circumstances there arose an obligation on the part of respondents to assign petitioner to employment that did not violate his freedom of religion.

From the facts there can be no doubt that petitioner knew of the terms upon which he was being assigned to duty. In any event, he was necessarily charged with knowledge of the provisions of the notice of examination which in part provide: "Duties and responsibilities: To operate a bus or trolley coach in accordance with the rules and regulations of the New York City Transit Authority."

Quasi contract is an obligation which the law creates in the absence of an agreement. It is invoked by the courts in situations involving unjust enrichment.

The court can find no authority, nor has petitioner furnished any, for the imposition of a quasi contract between the parties under the facts herein presented.

Petitioner's principal contention is that his dismissal violated his right to the free exercise of his religion as guaranteed to him under the First Amendment and his right to equal protection and due process under the Fourteenth Amendment of the Constitution of the United States.

It is well settled that while in the exercise of those fundamental human rights guaranteed under the First Amendment, including the exercise of freedom of religion, *the right to believe* is absolute, the *right to act* is not; that conduct remains subject to regulation for the protection of society.

In the area of both private and public employment, in particular, the *conduct* of individuals, as it relates to their religious scruples or other basic protected freedoms, has been consistently held to be subject to the terms of such employment, as those terms are affected by lawful agreements or by laws or regulations reasonably calculated to promote the public good and safety.

Petitioner's dismissal resulted only after long and commendable efforts on the part of respondents to assist him in his unfortunate plight. His assumption, nevertheless, that respondents have the power to assign him to work which will not interfere with his religious scruples is, however, without basis.

Respondents are bound by lawful agreement to enforce the seniority rules which govern petitioner and all of his fellow employees, and to which he has chosen not to accommodate.

The respondents are charged with the proper operation of a public transportation system and are thus engaged in the performance of a governmental function. There can be no doubt, from long experience, that the seniority rules to which petitioner has refused to conform, are the only fair way to assure that every man is treated on a non-discriminatory basis with respect to work assignments. These time-honored rules are, therefore, most essential to the efficient and safe operation of the City transportation system.

The right of government, in the efficient fulfillment of its purposes, to make reasonable regulations to which *all* of its employees, regardless of their beliefs or scruples, must conform, is unquestioned.

. . .

Similarly here, since in the reasonable judgment of respondents the efficiency of the public transportation service for which they are responsible may be best obtained through inviolate seniority rules, this court can see no constitutional objection.

Respondents' rules do not deny petitioner's right to the free exercise of his religion. They do limit his choice between adherence to his scruples and employment as a surface line operator. Certainly, such limitation is not one which respondents may not properly make within the power delegated to them to provide an efficient public transportation system and thereby to promote and protect the welfare and safety of the citizens of the State.

Respondents' dismissal of petitioner from his position was proper and warranted and not arbitrary and capricious.

REVIEW PROBLEMS

1. What elements must be present before the courts will enforce a contract?
2. What is meant by the statement that contracts is a "common law field"?
3. What contracts are governed by the UCC?
4. How does a contract implied-in-law differ from one implied-in-fact?

5. Cone has a house in a development that looks very similar to his neighbor's house. The neighbor orders landscaping done. The landscaper arrives and starts working on Cone's house. Cone sees the landscaper and does nothing until the lawn has been leveled and several attractive bushes have

been planted. Landscaper sues Cone. Result?

6. Suppose that Cone had been gone all day and that Cone did not like the work done. Would that change the outcome in the case?

7. A seller "lists" a house for sale with a real estate broker, thereby promising to pay a 7 percent commission if the broker finds a buyer ready, willing, and able to buy for $75,000. What kind of contract is this?

8. John Doe requests that Jack Maverick paint his house, promising that he will pay him $1,200 when Maverick finishes. Maverick paints the house. What type of contract is this?

9. On December 20, Johnson wrote Cook and offered to pay Cook for cleaning out a drainage ditch and doing some other odd jobs. Cook replied in a letter on December 23 and promised to do the work. Meantime Johnson sold the ranch to Fink on January 22. A heavy frost prevented Cook from doing the work until April. When he finally finished the work, Cook sent a bill to Johnson for $1,790. Must Johnson pay the bill? Would it make any difference in your answer if Cook was aware of the sale to Fink before he did the job? Cook v. Johnson, 221 P.2d 525 (Sup. Ct. of Washington, 1950).

10. The Millers had several marital disputes and ultimately tried to resolve them by signing a contract among themselves. Under the contract, Mr. Miller agreed to pay Mrs. Miller $200 a year and provide for "the necessary expenses of the family." Mrs. Miller agreed to "keep her home and family in a comfortable and reasonably good condition" and both agreed to "refrain from scolding, fault-finding, and anger, insofar as relates to the future, and to use every means within their power to promote peace and harmony." Mr. Miller stopped making the payments and Mrs. Miller sued to enforce the contract. Decision? Miller v. Miller, 78 Iowa 177 (Sup. Ct. of Iowa, 1889).

11. Richardson asked the J.C. Flood Company to clear a clogged sewer line. The snake cable used in clearing the line became stuck and when the line was excavated to free the cable, it was discovered that an adjacent water line was leaking. Local laws required that a certain quality water line be used. The J.C. Flood Company replaced the water line while they had the ground opened up. Richardson had been informed of the necessity to excavate and to do additional work to clear the sewer line, and that there was a problem with the water line. When Richardson received a bill for the work done, she refused to pay for the work on the water line. Must Richardson pay the full bill? Richardson v. J.C. Flood Company, 190 A.2d 259 (App. Ct., D.C., 1963).

The Offer

I t is important for parties negotiating an agreement to know if that agreement will be enforced by the legal system. Usually, neither party envisions the need to resort to legal action to enforce their agreement (or to recover monetary damages if the other party has not performed as agreed). Yet each party wants the assurance that, if it becomes necessary, he or she can reasonably expect the law and its institutions to stand behind the agreement.

The law of contracts defines and determines which agreements will be recognized and enforced. Since contract law requires a valid offer to have been made in order for an agreement to be recognized as an enforceable contract, we begin our study of contract law with this requirement.

REQUIREMENTS FOR AN OFFER

In order for a valid offer to exist, contract law requires the offer to:

1. Manifest the intent to enter into a contract
2. Be definite and certain regarding the essential terms of the proposed contract
3. Be communicated to the party (known as the offeree) for whom the offer is intended.

Each of these requirements is discussed in detail in this chapter.

Once the existence of an offer has been determined, the question of whether the offer still exists at the time of its acceptance may arise. Has the offer terminated? How long do offers last before they expire? What brings about the termination of an offer? Questions related to the termination of an offer are discussed at the end of this chapter.

Intent to Contract

Determining Intent. How should a person's intent be determined? Consider the following situations. Suppose you are at a used-car dealer's lot. The price of a car you like is listed as $3,995. You ask the salesperson what he'd take for the car; he doesn't answer you, but responds by asking you what you would offer. If you then say, "I wouldn't pay the list price, but I might pay $3,000 if I could finance it," have you made an offer? Did you intend by that statement to commit to a contract?

An auctioneer selling home furnishings announces at the start of the auction that anyone who wants to bid on an item should simply raise his or her hand when he asks for a certain price. If you, in gesturing to a friend with whom you are talking, raise your hand while the auctioneer is asking for a $500 bid for a couch, have you offered to buy it? Are you intending to contract?

Suppose you receive an advertisement in the mail listing the prices of hundreds of items the local department store wants to sell. Have you received an offer? Did the store intend to make an offer to any person receiving or reading its advertisement? To answer these questions, we must first consider how a person's intent is ascertained.

Is intent determined by examining what a person was thinking when he or she said something? Does the law look into a person's mind to determine his or her thoughts? Do we simply ask the person what his or her intentions were? A person's actual intentions are very difficult to determine. In fact, a person's subjective state is not susceptible to discovery or verification.

Instead, the law seeks to determine intent entirely by objective standards. What would a reasonable person observing the actions and hearing the statements of the offeror conclude about the offeror's intentions of entering into a contract? The evidence of the offeror's intent is determined not by examining that person's inner feelings, but by reviewing the offeror's actions and words as perceived by a reasonable person.

Social Invitation, Excitement, or Jest. The law presumes that there is no objective manifestation of intent to contract in situations involving social invitations. Thus, an invitation to a wedding, even one requesting an RSVP, would not be considered an offer to contract. Similarly, an invitation to attend the movies or to come for dinner is not an offer to contract. Therefore, an acceptance does not impose a contractual obligation on the inviter.

Suppose that someone makes a statement in the midst of an exciting event. As I watch my favorite basketball team fall behind in the playoffs, I announce to you and to everyone else who can hear me, "I am disgusted with this team. For two cents, I'd sell my tickets to the finals." Should the law treat my statement as an offer that invites your acceptance?

If it was apparent to you that I was upset and you should have known that I did not really intend to contract, there will not be the requisite manifestation of intent. Factors to be considered in determining whether I manifested contractual intent include the correlation between the "offer" price and the value of the object, the witnessing of the precipitating incident (here, the temporary taking of the lead by the opposing basketball team), whether from an objective viewpoint I appeared excited and upset, and whether we had discussed the sale of the tickets at some previous time.

Sometimes, a statement will be made in jest; there is no manifestation of the intent to contract because the offeror was only kidding. Informal bets often fall into this category: "I'll bet you a hundred dollars you can't throw the ball through the hoop." Similarly, the prankster who says, "I'd pay a thousand dollars to anyone who gives my boss an exploding cigar," cannot be taken seriously. Yet the jester must be careful if the joke relates to a situation where the other party might take the joke seriously. The *Zehmer* case demonstrates the seriousness with which some jocular offers are taken.

Lucy v. Zehmer

Supreme Court of Appeals of Virginia
84 S.E.2d 516 (1954)

Background: This suit was instituted by W. O. Lucy and J. C. Lucy (plaintiffs) against A. H. Zehmer and Ida S. Zehmer, his wife (defendants) to have specific performance of a contract by which it was alleged the Zehmers had sold to W. O. Lucy a tract of land owned by A. H. Zehmer in Dinwiddie County containing 471.6 acres, more or less, known as the Ferguson farm, for $50,000. Defendants responded that they had considered the plaintiffs' offer to have been made in jest and that their signature to the written document was not intended by them to result in a contract. The instrument sought to be enforced was written by A. H. Zehmer on December 20, 1952, in these words: "We hereby agree to sell to W. O. Lucy the Ferguson Farm complete for $50,000.00, title satisfactory to buyer," and signed by both the defendants.

The lower court held that the plaintiffs' complaint failed to establish their right to specific performance and dismissed the case. The plaintiffs appealed the trial court's dismissal to this appellate court.

Decision: The trial court reversed the decision. A binding contract was created and the plaintiffs Lucy are entitled to specific performance.

Buchanan, Justice

W. O. Lucy, a lumberman and farmer, testified that he had known Zehmer for fifteen or twenty years and had been familiar with the Ferguson farm for ten years. Seven or eight years ago, he had offered Zehmer $20,000 for the farm which Zehmer had accepted, but the agreement was verbal and Zehmer backed out. On the night of December 20, 1952, around eight o'clock, he took an employee to McKenney, where Zehmer lived and operated a restaurant, filling station and motor court. While there he decided to see Zehmer and again try to buy the Ferguson farm. He entered the restaurant and talked to Mrs. Zehmer until Zehmer came in. On this Saturday night before Christmas, it looked like everybody and his brother came by there to have a drink. When Zehmer entered the restaurant around eight-thirty, Lucy was there and he could see that he was "pretty high." He said to Lucy, "Boy, you got some good liquor drinking, ain't you?" Lucy then offered him a drink. "I was already high as a Georgia pine, and didn't have any more better sense than to pour another great big slug out and gulp it down, and he took one too."

After they had talked awhile, Lucy asked whether he still had the Ferguson farm. He replied that he had not sold it and Lucy said, "I bet you wouldn't take $50,000 for it." Zehmer asked him if he would give $50,000 and Lucy said yes. Zehmer replied, "You haven't got $50,000 in cash." Lucy said he did and Zehmer replied that he did not believe it. They argued "pro and con for a long time," mainly about "whether he had $50,000 in cash that he could put up right then and buy that farm."

Finally, said Zehmer, Lucy told him if he didn't believe he had $50,000, "you sign that piece of paper here and say you will take $50,000 for the farm." He, Zehmer, "just grabbed the back off of a guest check there" and wrote on the back of it, "I do hereby agree to sell to W. O. Lucy the Ferguson Farm for $50,000 complete." Lucy told him he had better change it to "We" because Mrs. Zehmer would have to sign it too. Zehmer then tore up what he had written, wrote the agreement quoted above and asked Mrs. Zehmer, who was at the other end of the counter ten or twelve feet away, to sign it. She at first refused to sign, but did so after he told her that he "was just needling him (Lucy), and didn't mean a thing in the world, that I was not selling the farm." Zehmer then "took it back over there and I was still looking at the dern thing. I had the drink right there by my hand, and I reached over to get a drink, and he said, 'Let me see it.' He reached and picked it up, and when I looked back again he had it in his pocket and he dropped a five dollar bill over there, and he said, 'Here is five dollars payment on it.' I said, 'Hell no, that is beer and liquor talking. I am not going to sell you the farm. I have told you that too many times before.' "

December 20 was on Saturday. On Monday, Lucy engaged an attorney to examine the title. The attorney reported favorably on December 31 and on January 2, Lucy wrote Zehmer stating that the title was satisfactory, that he was ready to pay the purchase price in cash and asking when Zehmer would be ready to close the deal. Zehmer replied by letter, mailed on January 13, asserting that he had never agreed or intended to sell.

Zehmer testified that he bought this farm more than ten years ago for $11,000. He had had twenty-five offers, more or less, to buy it, including several from Lucy, who had never offered any specific sum of money. He had given them all the same answer, that he was not interested in selling it.

The discussion leading to the signing of the agreement, said Lucy, lasted thirty or forty minutes, during which Zehmer seemed to doubt that Lucy could raise $50,000. Lucy suggested the provision for having the title examined and Zehmer made the suggestion that he would sell it "complete, everything there," and stated that all he had on the farm was three heifers.

The defendants insist that the evidence was ample to support their contention that the writing sought to be enforced was prepared as a bluff or dare to force Lucy to admit that he did not have $50,000; that the whole matter was a joke; that the writing was not delivered to Lucy and no binding contract was ever made between the parties.

It is an unusual, if not bizarre, defense. When made to the writing admittedly prepared by one of the defendants and signed by both, clear evidence is required to sustain it.

In his testimony, Zehmer claimed that he "was high as a Georgia pine," and that the transaction "was just a bunch of two doggoned drunks bluffing to see who could talk the biggest and say the most." That claim is inconsistent with his attempt to testify in great detail as to what was said and what was done. It is contradicted by other evidence as to the condition of both parties, and rendered of no weight by the testimony of his wife that when Lucy left the restaurant she suggested that Zehmer drive him home. The record is convincing that Zehmer was not intoxicated to the extent of being unable to comprehend the nature and consequences of the instrument he executed, and hence that instrument is not to be invalidated on that ground.

The appearance of the contract, the fact that it was under discussion for forty minutes or more before it was signed; Lucy's objection to the first draft because it was written in the singular, and he wanted Mrs. Zehmer to sign it also; the rewriting to meet that objection and the signing by Mrs. Zehmer; the discussion of what was to be included in the sale, the provision for the examination of the title, the completeness of the instrument that was executed, the taking possession of it by Lucy with no request or suggestion by either of the defendants that he give it back, are facts which furnish persuasive evidence that the execution of the contract was a serious business transaction rather than a casual jesting matter as defendants now contend.

If it be assumed, contrary to what we think the evidence shows, that Zehmer was jesting about selling his farm to Lucy and that the transaction was intended by him to be a joke, nevertheless the evidence shows that Lucy did not so understand it but considered it to be a serious business transaction and the contract to be binding on the Zehmers as well as on himself. The very next day, he arranged with his brother to put up half the money and take a half interest in the land. The day after that he employed an attorney to examine the title. The next night, Tuesday, he was back at Zehmer's place, and there Zehmer told him for the first time, Lucy said, that he wasn't going to sell and he told Zehmer, "You know you sold that place fair and square." After receiving the report from his attorney that the title was good, he wrote to Zehmer that he was ready to close the deal.

Not only did Lucy actually believe, but the evidence shows he was warranted in believing, that the contract represented a serious business transaction and a good faith sale and purchase of the farm.

In the field of contracts, as generally elsewhere, we must look to the outward expression of a person as manifesting his intention rather than to his secret and unexpressed intention. The law imputes to a person an intention corresponding to the reasonable meaning of his words and acts.

The mental assent of the parties is not requisite for the formation of a contract. If the words or other acts of one of the parties have but one reasonable meaning, his undisclosed intention is immaterial except when an unreasonable meaning which he attaches to his manifestations is known to the other party. An agreement or mutual assent is, of course, essential to a valid contract, but the law imputes to a person an intention corresponding to the reasonable meaning of his words and acts. If his words and acts, judged by a reasonable standard, manifest an intention to agree, it is immaterial what may be the real but unexpressed state of his mind.

So a person cannot set up that he was merely jesting when his conduct and words would warrant a reasonable person in believing that he intended a real agreement. Whether the writing signed by the defendants and now sought to be enforced by the plaintiffs was the result of a serious offer by Lucy and a serious acceptance by the defendants, or was a serious offer by Lucy and an acceptance in secret jest by the defendants, in either event it constituted a binding contract of sale between the parties.

The plaintiffs are entitled to have specific performance of the contract sued on. The decree appealed from is therefore reversed and the cause is remanded for the entry of a proper decree requiring the defendants to perform the contract.

Advertisement of Goods for Sale. Do advertisements in the newspaper constitute offers? If they do, the reader can go into the store and say "I accept" and thereby create a contractual obligation for the store. If five people or fifty or five thousand accept, the store would have to fulfill all acceptances or else be liable for breach of contract.

Courts have interpreted the law as not imposing such an unfair burden on each business advertiser. Thus, as a general principle, advertisements do not constitute offers. However, if the advertiser uses language in the advertisement that, to the reasonable reader, expresses a commitment to contract, the courts will enforce a contract resulting from the offeree's acceptance of the seller's advertisement. While the *Lefkowitz* case is thus an illustration of the application of the exception to the general rule of law, it has become a classic involving the possible interpretation of advertisements as offers.

Lefkowitz v. Great Minneapolis Surplus Store

Supreme Court of Minnesota

86 N.W.2d 689 (1957)

Background: Lefkowitz (plaintiff) brought suit against the Great Minneapolis Surplus Store (defendant) to enforce a contract he had made to purchase a fur offered for sale by the defendant in a newspaper advertisement. The defendant responded that its advertisement was not an offer, and therefore no contract had been made between it and the plaintiff. The trial court found that a contract did exist and ordered a judgment for the plaintiff in the amount of $138.50 as damages due for the defendant's breach of contract. The defendant's request to the trial court for a new trial was denied and the defendant then appealed for review by the Minnesota Supreme Court. Decision: The trial court's decision was affirmed. Lefkowitz accepted a valid offer and Great Minneapolis must perform or pay damages.

Murphy, Justice

This case grows out of the alleged refusal of the defendant to sell to the plaintiff a certain fur piece which it had offered for sale in a newspaper advertisement. It appears from the record that on April 6, 1956, the defendant published the following advertisement in a Minneapolis newspaper:

> Saturday 9 A.M. Sharp
> 3 Brand New
> Fur
> Coats
> Worth to $100.00
> First Come
> First Served
> $1
> Each

On April 13, the defendant again published an advertisement in the same newspaper as follows:

> Saturday 9 A.M.
> 2 Brand New Pastel
> Mink 3-Skin Scarfs
> Selling for $89.50
> Out they go
> Saturday. Each. . . . $1.00
> 1 Black Lapin Stole
> Beautiful
> Worth $139.50. . . . $1.00
> First Come
> First Served

The record supports the findings of the court that on each of the Saturdays following the publication of the above-described ads the plaintiff was the first to present himself at the appropriate counter in the defendant's store and on each occasion demanded the coat and the stole so advertised and indicated his readiness to pay the sale price of $1. On both occasions, the defendant refused to sell the merchandise to the plaintiff, stating on the first occasion that by a "house rule" the offer was intended for women only and sales would not be made to men, and on the second visit that plaintiff knew defendant's house rules.

The trial court properly disallowed plaintiff's claim for the value of the fur coats since the value of these articles was speculative and uncertain. The only evidence of value was the advertisement itself to the effect that the coats were "Worth to $100.-00," how much less being speculative especially in view of the price for which they were offered for sale. With reference to the offer of the defendant on April 13, 1956, to sell the "1 Black Lapin Stole . . . worth $139.50 . . ." the trial court held that the value of this article was established and granted judgment in favor of the plaintiff for that amount less the $1 quoted purchase price.

The defendant contends that a newspaper advertisement offering items of merchandise for sale at a named price is a "unilateral offer" which may be withdrawn without notice. He relies upon authorities which hold that, where an advertiser publishes in a newspaper that he has a certain quantity or quality of goods which he wants to dispose of at certain prices and on certain terms, such advertisements are not offers which become contracts as soon as any person to whose notice they may come signifies his acceptance by notifying the other that he will take a certain quantity of them. Such advertisements instead have been construed as an invitation for an offer of sale on the terms stated, which offer, when received, may be accepted or rejected by the seller and which therefore does not become a contract of sale until such acceptance. Thus, until a contract has been so made, the seller may modify or revoke such prices or terms as it has advertised.

However, there are numerous authorities which hold that a particular advertisement in a newspaper or circular letter relating to a sale of articles may be construed by the court as constituting an offer, the acceptance of which would complete a contract. The test of whether a binding obligation may originate in advertisements addressed to the general public is whether the facts show that some performance was promised in positive terms in return for something requested. . . .

Whether in any individual instance a newspaper advertisement is an offer rather than an invitation to make an offer depends on the legal intention of the parties and the surrounding circumstances. We are of the view on the facts before us that the offer by the defendant of the sale of the Lapin fur was clear, definite, and explicit, and left nothing open for negotiation. The plaintiff having successfully managed to be the first one to appear at the seller's place of business to be served, as requested by the advertisement, and having offered the stated purchase price of the article, he was entitled to performance on the part of the defendant. We think the trial court was correct in holding that there was in the conduct of the parties a sufficient mutuality of obligation to constitute a contract of sale.

The defendant contends that the offer was modified by a "house rule" to the effect that only women were qualified to receive the bargains advertised. The advertisement contained no such restriction. This objection may be disposed of briefly by stating that, while an advertiser has the right at any time before acceptance to modify his offer, he does not have the right, after acceptance, to impose new or arbitrary conditions not contained in the published offer.

Definite and Certain Terms

The second requirement of an offer is that it be definite and certain regarding the essential terms of the proposed contract. As the court in the *Lefkowitz* case concluded, where the offeror's statement is clear, definite, and explicit and leaves nothing open for negotiation, an offer (not merely an invitation to make an offer) has been made. What terms must be expressed in order for a statement to be construed as an offer?

If I offer to sell you my 1988 Honda Accord and you agree, do we have a contract? We have omitted the most basic element of an agreement—the price. Would a court seek to complete our agreement for us? How would it do so? Reference to a standard used-car price or a trade price such as is found in a Blue Book wouldn't be of much help. My car could have been driven 5,000 miles or 50,000 miles. It could have been well cared for or poorly cared for. Thus, there is no ready reference point that a court could use to enforce this agreement. Since a court does not wish to make a contract where the parties themselves have failed to do so, it would conclude that no offer was made by me when I proposed to sell you my car. Therefore, your agreement in response was not an acceptance of an offer. Obviously, no contract resulted from our expressions.

The general legal principle requires that an offer define the essential terms of performance by both the offeror and the offeree. One of the essential terms that an offer must

contain is the subject matter of the proposed transaction. Is the offeror going to sell a car? What car? Does the sale of the car include the sale of the ski rack on top of the car? The spare tire in the trunk? The offer must reasonably identify the subject matter.

A second essential term that an offer must include is the quantity of items being offered. A farmer proposing to sell wheat to a bakery must specify how much wheat he wants to sell. A furniture dealer's agreement to sell you "bedroom furniture" for $500 would be too vague unless it specified how many items were included in the offer.

Finally, as the first example regarding the used-car sale illustrates, the price of the item offered for sale must be specified. The price is specified if it is either fixed or easily determinable. My offer to lend you $1,000 at the prime interest rate in effect at the Chase Manhattan Bank is specific. While the offer doesn't state exactly what that rate of interest actually is, the rate is determinable.

The case that follows, *Smith* v. *House of Kenton Corporation*, illustrates the need for definite terms in a contract. The case involves an agreement to lease space in premises owned by the plaintiff. Note that the agreement that the plaintiff seeks to enforce as a contract is not a document labeled by the parties a "contract." Although the court in this case found that the letters at issue did not constitute a contract, letters can in fact be contracts. So can oral expressions and conversations between the parties. Agreements do not have to be embodied in formal documents prepared by attorneys to be enforced as contracts. As long as the required elements—including the definite terms—of an offer are found to exist, a contract between the parties may result.

Smith v. House of Kenton Corporation
Court of Appeals of North Carolina
209 S.E.2d 398 (1974)

Background: This is an action brought by Smith (plaintiff) against House of Kenton Corp. (defendant), a company operated by Mrs. Shelton, for damages for breach of contract. The parties waived jury trial and the evidence tended to show that on and before May 9, 1970, the plaintiff owned certain real property located at 1601 Montford Drive in the city of Charlotte. The property was equipped for use as a beauty salon, and at that time the defendant operated a beauty salon at another location in Charlotte. On that date, the plaintiff employed Davant Realty Company (Davant) to find a tenant to lease the real estate and purchase certain equipment located thereon. Thereafter, Davant had several conversations with Mrs. Shelton, president of the defendant, and Mrs. McCormac, an employee of the defendant, with respect to the defendant leasing the premises and purchasing the equipment. Following those conversations, Davant wrote and sent to Mrs. Shelton a letter dated July 15 stating the terms discussed by the parties for leasing the premise. The letter concluded with the following paragraph: "A lease is being drawn and will be forwarded to you soon. Please execute the copy of this letter as your agreement to these terms and conditions and return to us so we can take the space off the market and hold same for you."

Mrs. Shelton signed an acceptance on the bottom of the letter and returned it to Mr. Davant on July 16. On July 31, Mr. Davant wrote a second letter to Mrs. Shelton and enclosed a lease agreement, prepared by Smith's attorney, with the letter. Subsequent differences between the parties then surfaced. The lease agreement was never signed or returned by Mrs. Shelton. The plaintiff tried to rent the premises to others but was unsuccessful for three years. Plaintiff then brought this suit for breach of contract, claiming as damages the lost rent. Plaintiff alleged that the letter which the defendant's agent, Mrs. Shelton, signed and returned on July 16, 1970, was a contract to execute a lease and was enforceable to the same extent as if the lease agreement had been signed. The trial court found for the plaintiff, and the defendant appealed to the Court of Appeals of North Carolina.

Decision: The Court of Appeals reversed the decision. No contract existed that entitled Smith to the damages sought.

Britt, Judge

The theory of plaintiff's action is that the defendant breached a contract to execute a lease. That the judgment was predicated on that theory is indicated by the following conclusion of law:

3. That the written offer of the plaintiff dated July 15, 1970, when accepted by the defendant corporation on July 16, 1970, became a contract to execute a lease and as such is enforceable to the same extent as if the parties had entered into a written lease agreement containing the terms of the said contract to execute a lease.

The question then arises, was the letter dated 15 July 1970 sufficient to constitute a binding contract to execute a lease? We answer in the negative.

Our research fails to disclose any precedent in this jurisdiction which is directly in point; however, we find in opinions of our Supreme Court numerous statements of principles which we think are applicable to the case at bar.

In *Young v. Sweet* (1966), we find: "An offer to enter into a contract in the future must, to be binding, specify all of the essential and material terms and leave nothing to be agreed upon as a result of future negotiations."

In *Dodds v. Trust* Co. (1933), the court said:

> In the formation of a contract an offer and an acceptance are essential elements; they constitute the agreement of the parties. The offer must be communicated, must be complete, and must be accepted in its exact terms. . . . In order to constitute a binding agreement to execute a lease, such agreement must be certain as to the terms of the future lease. A few points of mutual agreement are essential to a valid agreement to lease: First, the minds of the parties must have met as to the property to be included in the lease; second, the terms of the lease should be agreed upon; third, the parties should agree upon the rental; and fourth, the time and manner of payment of rent should be stated. . . .

In the case at bar, the agreement relied on by plaintiff did not specify all of the essential and material terms of the lease to be executed and left much to be agreed upon by future negotiations. The offer was not complete and the minds of the parties did not meet as to all essential terms. The agreement failed to provide for one of the specifics . . . the time and manner of payment of rent. The necessity for this provision with respect to rent is obvious. Whether the rent was payable monthly, quarterly, semi-annually, annually, or all at one time, and whether it was payable in advance, at the end of a period or otherwise, presented a major question that finds no answer in the agreement. It might be argued that the provision of "$400.00 per month" sufficiently implied that a monthly payment of rent was contemplated by the parties. The question then arises, was the rent payable in advance, in the middle of the month, or at the end of the month? A clear indication that the minds of the parties did not meet on this question is the provision in the formal lease proposed by plaintiff that defendant pay the first and last months' rent at the beginning of the five-year period.

We think there is a further reason why plaintiff was not entitled to recover. Assuming, arguendo, that the 15 July 1970 letter was sufficient to constitute a binding contract to execute a lease, plaintiff failed to show that he tendered a lease conforming to the contract. . . .

The formal lease submitted by plaintiff to defendant in the case at bar reveals a number of provisions not mentioned in the letter; we point out several of them. In addition to requiring payment of the last month's rent at the beginning of the term, it limits the lessee's right to sublet or assign without written consent of the lessor. It requires that lessee shall ". . . maintain and keep in good order and repair all heating, air conditioning, electrical and plumbing equipment located in the demised premises. . . ." It further provides that lessee will purchase and maintain, at its expense, a public liability insurance policy in the amount of $50,000 coverage for any one accident and $100,000 for any one accident involving more than one person, which policy or policies of insurance will show as named assured the lessee and the lessor as their interests may appear.

For the reasons stated, the judgment appealed from is Reversed.

The UCC and Definite Terms. The Uniform Commercial Code has substantially liberalized the definite-and-certain-terms requirement as it applies to the sale of goods. Most contracts covered by the UCC involve business transactions between experienced parties. The business world has many established reference points for value, such as organized trading exchanges and arms-length private sales transactions involving goods identical to the ones in question.

In recognition of these facts Section 2-204(3) of the UCC provides that a sales contract is valid even though it leaves open essential terms if (1) the parties nevertheless intended to make a contract *and* (2) there is a "reasonably certain basis for giving an appropriate remedy." Further, Section 2-305 provides that purposefully leaving open the price term is not fatal and that in such cases the price is to be a reasonable price. Note that under Section 2-305 we would have made a contract for the sale of my used Honda *if* we had intended to leave the price open while binding ourselves to a contract. Sections 2-308 and 309 also specify how the terms are to be filled in if nothing is said as to place of delivery or time for delivery.

Communication of the Offer

General Rule. The third requirement that must be met for a valid offer to exist is that the offer be communicated to the party for whom the offer is intended. The communication may be expressed or implied. For example, if the offeree learns of an offer from a third person who is not the offeror and the offer is a general offer susceptible of acceptance by anyone who learns of it, the offeree has the power to accept the communicated offer. Communication is usually not a problem with offers. Two recurring situations, however, present legal problems regarding the effect to be given to the communication of an offer.

The Reward Offer. The first of these is the case of a reward. A reward is an offer for a unilateral contract. It is not unusual for someone to perform the act bargained for in the reward offer without knowing about the reward. If this occurs, then under the technical rules of contract law the party performing the act is not entitled to the reward. But that does not represent sound policy when viewed in the context of the reasonable expectations of our society. Most people expect that rewards will be paid if their terms are met. As a consequence, many states provide by statute that rewards will be enforceable regardless of whether the person performing the act called for in the offer first received a communication of the offer of a reward.

The Fine-Print Offer. The second situation involves what might be called the fine-print problem. Consumers may often be asked to sign contracts that contain a myriad of fine-print provisions, many of which are quite harsh. For example, a price-adjustment clause may increase the price of a car over the contract price before delivery, or a waiver clause may surrender the consumer's rights to resist the entering of a legal judgment against him upon default of an installment payment. Most consumers signing such contracts are unaware of the existence of and/or the legal effect of such clauses. Some courts have refused to enforce them on the theory that they were not really communicated to the consumer. Consider the following case concerned with the communication of an offer.

Green's Executors v. Smith

Special Court of Appeals of Virginia
131 S.E. 845 (1926)

Background: Howard Smith (plaintiff) sued Mrs. A. D. Green (defendant) to recover damages he had been compelled to pay one John L. Moore in compensation for injuries inflicted on Moore by one of Smith's employees while the employee was driving the defendant's automobile through the streets of Richmond.

The plaintiff owned a garage where the defendant stored her car. The defendant and the plaintiff contracted for the storage of the defendant's car and for the delivery of the car by the plaintiff's employees to the defendant's residence and the car's return to the garage thereafter when requested by the defendant. After having delivered the defendant's car to her, the plaintiff's employee was in the process of returning her car to the plaintiff's garage when he collided with Mr. Moore. The plaintiff alleged the contract he had with the defendant absolved him of liability for negligence which occurred while returning the defendant's car to the garage. The defendant responded that the parties had no such contract.

Upon the trial of the case, the jury rendered a verdict in the plaintiff's favor for $2,735, for which judgment was entered by the court. Mrs. Green having died, the cause was brought to the Court of Appeals by her executors.

Decision: The trial court reversed the decision. Smith was not entitled to damages, as there was not a valid contract.

Chinn, Justice

The material facts of the case may be fairly stated to be as follows:

Defendant's automobile was first placed at plaintiff's garage some time in the early part of the year 1918 by another garage keeper who had previously kept it, and who was about to discontinue business. Mrs. Green at the time was an old lady, and her daughter, Mrs. B. R. Dunn, who resided with her at her residence on South Third Street, looked after her affairs. There was no formal contract between the parties, but plaintiff advised Mrs. Dunn of the terms and regulations then in effect at his garage for the regular monthly storage of automobiles, which were accepted by the defendant by leaving the car in his custody. According to the terms thus agreed to, in addition to certain other specified services, plaintiff contracted to deliver the car at the owner's residence and take it back to the garage once each day when requested by the owner, with the further understanding that plaintiff should not be responsible for any damage which might occur to the car while in the hands of his employees during such movements. In consideration of these services, plaintiff was to receive the sum of $37 per month, which amount was thereafter paid by Mrs. Green upon receipt of his bill. In October of that year defendant's car was damaged by a collision on the street when being driven to the garage by one of plaintiff's employees, and defendant paid the expense of the repairs without protest. In January, 1920, plaintiff had printed what he called a "folder," which bore on the title page this inscription:

"Service Rates of the Richmond Electric Garage."
"Howard M. Smith, Proprietor, 2035 W. Broad Street, Richmond, Va."
"Effective on and after January 1, 1920."

The center or inside pages of the folder contained a schedule of charges for diverse specified services performed by the garage and other printed matter, which, so far as pertinent, read as follows:

Rates by the Month.
Regular storage, lead battery, $37.
Regular storage includes car storage, delivering, cleaning, polishing, charging, and flushing battery, and oiling with oil can wherever possible upon notice from the owner.

Delivery Service.
Delivering and calling for car once each way daily (see note).
An extra charge of 25 cents each way will be made for extra trips (see note).

Note: The owner agrees to accept our employee as his or her agent and to absolve this garage from any liability whatsoever arising while his or her car is in the hands of said employee at the request of and as agent of the owner.

The back of the folder contained only a schedule of rates and terms relating to work and services in connection with automobile batteries.

The folder was mailed to all the patrons of the garage, including Mrs. Green, with the bills sent out in the early part of January, which action was repeated the following month; and copies were also placed by the employees of the garage, on several occasions, in defendant's car, as well as all other cars kept at the garage on regular storage. It also appears that the above-mentioned folder was the only document of the kind that plaintiff ever had printed and sent out to his customers. As has been noted, plaintiff seeks to recover in this action upon an alleged contract by which, it is claimed in his declaration, defendant agreed to accept plaintiff's garage employees as her agents, and to indemnify and save him harmless from any and all liability whatsoever arising from the acts of any of said employees while moving her car to and from said garage. In the absence of agreement, the defendant is in no sense liable to the plaintiff for the injuries inflicted upon Mr. Moore under the circumstances disclosed by the record. The plaintiff alone had the right to select and engage the employees of his garage, the power to discharge and control them, and he alone was responsible for the payment of their wages. The real question is, therefore, Was there a valid and subsisting contract between the plaintiff and Mrs. Green, at the time Mr. Moore received his injuries, by which the defendant bound herself to indemnify the plaintiff against the consequences of all such acts of negligence on the part of his employees?

It is elementary that mutuality of assent—the meeting of the minds of the parties—is an essential element of all contracts and, in order that this mutuality may exist, it is necessary that there be a proposal of offer on the part of one party, and an acceptance on the part of the other. It is manifest, however, that, before one can be held to have accepted the offer of another, whether such offer is made by word or act, there must have been some form of communication of the offer; otherwise there could be no assent, and in consequence no contract. In the instant case the plaintiff relies upon the ''note'' printed in the folder as constituting the terms of the proposed contract, on the fact that said folder was mailed to Mrs. Green on several occasions with her monthly bills and placed in her cars, as a communication of said terms, and on her conduct in continuing to keep her car in his garage as an implied acceptance of the terms specified in said note. The question, therefore, of whether Mrs. Green agreed to, and is bound by, the terms of the ''note'' in the main depends upon whether the means employed by the plaintiff to communicate such terms were sufficient, under the circumstances, to constitute her act in the premises as implied acceptance of the said terms. The rule as to when the delivery of a paper containing the terms of a proposed contract amounts to an acceptance, is thus stated in 13 Corpus Juris, at page 277:

> A contract may be formed by accepting a paper containing terms. If an offer is made by delivering to another a paper containing the terms of a proposed contract, and the paper is accepted, the acceptor is bound by its terms; and this is true whether he reads the paper or not. When an offer contains various terms, some of which do not appear on the face of the offer, the question whether the acceptor is bound by the terms depends on the circumstances. He is not bound as a rule by any terms which are not communicated to him. But he is bound by all the legal terms which are communicated. This question arises when a person accepts a railroad or steamboat ticket, bill of lading, warehouse receipt, or other document containing conditions. He is bound by all the conditions whether he reads them or not, if he knows that the document contains conditions. But he is not bound by conditions of which he is ignorant, even though the ticket or document contains writing, unless he knows that the writing contains terms, or unless he ought to know that it contains terms, by reason of previous dealings, or by reason of the form, size, or character of the document.

There was nothing on the face of the folder, nor in its form or character, to indicate that it contained the terms of the contract which plaintiff has attempted to establish in this case, or any other contract imposing obligations of such a nature upon the defendant. The paper only purported to contain a schedule of rates for services at plaintiff's garage, and defendant had no reason, on account of her previous dealings with the plaintiff or otherwise, to know that plaintiff proposed, by mailing the folder to her along with his monthly bill, and placing a copy of it in her car, to commit her to a new contract of such unusual terms.

Considering the circumstances under which she received the folder, she was justified in assuming it to be only what it purported to be, and, as she already knew the rates prevailing at plaintiff's garage, was justified in paying no attention to it, as she did. There is no evidence that either Mrs. Green or Mrs. Dunn, her agent, ever read the "note" or knew it was printed in the folder. . . . If plaintiff proposed to form a special contract of this kind, he should have, at the least, called Mrs. Green's attention to the terms contained in the folder as he understood to do, upon the advice of counsel, after the accident to Mr. Moore.

Under these circumstances we are of the opinion that the plaintiff has failed to establish the contract alleged in his declaration in the manner that the law requires, and is not, as a matter of law, entitled to recover over from Mrs. Green the damage he was compelled to pay Mr. Moore for the negligence of his employee.

For the foregoing reasons, the judgment complained of will be reversed and judgment entered for the defendant.

Reversed

TERMINATION OF THE OFFER

If the requirements for an offer have been met, the offeree has a chance to accept and enter into a contract with the offeror. Yet the offer may be terminated prior to its acceptance. The termination of an offer may occur in a variety of ways, as demonstrated in Table 10-1.

Lapse of Time

The offer itself may provide that it will terminate within a specified period. Once that period expires the offer is terminated. Thus an offer that states "This offer is good until May 30" would terminate after that date. It should be noted that the offeror should be specific regarding the duration of the offer. Consider the following situation. On March 1, the offeror mails a letter dated February 27 stating that "this offer expires in ten days." The offeree receives the letter on March 4. Does the offer expire ten days from February 27 or from March 4? What policy should the courts follow in interpreting this language? The

courts that have considered this problem have reached different decisions.

Even if the offeror does not provide for a specific termination date, the offer will lapse after a "reasonable time." How long is a reasonable time? The answer must vary with the circumstances surrounding the offer. An offer to sell real estate such as a home or an office building will probably last for weeks or months. An offer to buy stocks or commodities may be open for acceptance for only minutes.

Further, the definition of reasonable time is affected by the context in which an offer is made. If you seek to buy souvenir pennants to sell outside the Super Bowl, your offer to the supplier would terminate no later than the day of the game. The timing of any prior dealings between the offeror and offeree will be relevant in determining what is a reasonable time for an offer to remain open.

Revocation by the Offeror

General Rule. A revocation is a withdrawal of the offer by the offeror. The law requires

TABLE 10–1 TERMINATION OF OFFERS

Method	By	Communication Required	Limitation
Lapse of time	Expiration of stated or reasonable time	No	
Revocation	Act of offeror	Yes	Option contracts Firm offers by merchants Prior to acceptance Detrimental reliance by offeree
Rejection	Act of offeree May occur through counter-offer	Yes	
Death	Of either party	No, in most cases	Option contracts in certain cases
Destruction of subject matter	By unforeseen event	No	

that, in order to be effective, a revocation, like the original offer, must be communicated to the offeree. Generally, the revocation must be received by the offeree before the offeree has effectively accepted the offer. While an offeror generally has the power to revoke the offer at any time prior to its acceptance, there are several exceptions to this rule.

Even if the offer states that it will remain open for a specified time, the rule allowing the offeror to revoke at any time prior to acceptance usually applies. Thus, in the preceding example the offeror wrote on February 27 that the offer would expire in ten days. Suppose the offeror decides on March 2 that he wants to revoke the offer prior to the end of the ten-day period. Can he do that when he has already committed himself to holding the offer open for ten days? The general answer is "Yes" as long as no acceptance of the offer has been made by the offeree. There are, however, several situations in which the offeror is not permitted to revoke an offer.

Limitations. If someone enters into a contract with an offeror to keep an offer open for a certain time, that *option contract* will be enforced. The offer cannot be revoked for the period specified in the contract. For example, a school board offers to sell for $100,000 to Acme Development Company a school that it no longer uses. Acme is thinking of buying the school if it can interest several businesses in renting space there after the building has been remodeled. Acme might agree with the school board to enter into an option contract, by which, in consideration of a payment of $5,000, the school board gives Acme 90 days to accept or reject the offer. During those 90 days, the school board cannot sell to someone else, nor can it revoke its offer to Acme.

Second, the Uniform Commercial Code (Section 2-205) provides that if an offer to buy or sell goods contains a promise that it will be held open for a specific time, it cannot be revoked by the offeror during that time. This *firm offer* rule requires that the offeror be a merchant in the kind of goods being offered and that the offer must be in writing and signed by the offeror. Finally, the time during which the offer is irrevocable is limited to

PREVENTIVE LAW
Set Times in Offers

The situation previously described can be easily prevented by careful drafts-manship. Instead of stating that the offer expires in a certain number of days, indicate the exact time that the offer will expire—this offer is good until 3 P.M. on March 4, 1988. Otherwise, the interpretation of the time period may ultimately depend upon the state law that is applied to the case. And, if that happens, the parties may find their expectations defeated. There is, however, a downside to using a specific date. If the offer is being mailed, the offeror cannot know when the offeree will receive the offer. If the mails are substan-tially delayed, the offer may be received after the expiration. That should not be a constraint to two parties who wish to contract, so long as the offeree has enough interest to inquire whether the offer is still open.

Forethought and planning are important in using written documents. Ulti-mately, the offeror who is ambiguous has only him- or herself to blame.

three months. This rule does not apply to of-fers that are not made by merchants or that do not involve the sale of goods. Nevertheless, most commercial transactions (other than those for services or for real estate) fall within the terms of the firm offer rule.

Third, if the offer requires an act to be per-formed in order to accept the offer (i.e., the offer seeks to have the offeree enter into a unilateral contract), the law limits the offeror's power to revoke the offer while the offeree is in the process of performing the requested act of acceptance. While traditionally the of-feree's act must be fully completed before an acceptance and a contract result, in recent years the trend of many decisions has been to suspend the offeror's right of revocation until the offeree has had a reasonable time to com-plete the act called for in the offer.

Fourth, in order to avoid unfairness, courts will usually limit an offeror's right to revoke if an offer is made in such a way that the offeree reasonably expects that the offer will not be revoked. This exception to the general rule is known as the doctrine of *promissory estoppel.* It usually requires (1) that the statement of

offer is one that the offeror should anticipate would be relied on by the offeree, (2) that the offeree in fact does rely on the statement, and (3) that the offeree is harmed by relying on the offer's irrevocability.

Typical of the application of the doctrine of promissory estoppel in limiting the right to revoke an offer is in the context of the stan-dard relationship between a general building contractor and various subcontractors. The general contractor requests bids (offers) from potential subcontractors to do specialized work such as heating, plumbing, electrical, and carpentry. The general contractor relies on some of these bids in making its own bid to the building owner. Suppose that the general contractor finds that the building owner has accepted its offer to do the required work, but before the general contractor informs the sub-contractor that the subcontractor's bid (offer) is accepted, the subcontractor revokes it. The basic situation is dramatized in Figure 10-1. The use of the doctrine of promisory estoppel to constrain a subcontractor's ability to revoke is demonstrated in the Drennan case which follows Figure 10-1.

FIGURE 10–1
Bidding on Construction Jobs

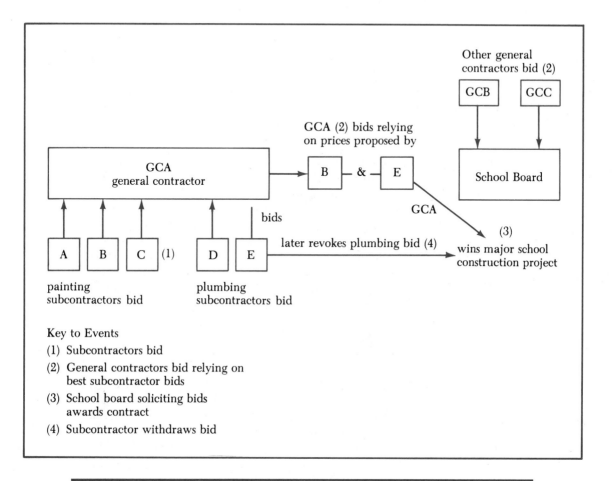

Other general
contractors bid (2)

GCB   GCC

GCA (2) bids relying
on prices proposed by

B & E

School Board

GCA
general contractor

GCA

bids

later revokes plumbing bid (4)

(3)
wins major school
construction project

A   B   C   (1)   D   E

painting
subcontractors bid

plumbing
subcontractors bid

Key to Events
(1) Subcontractors bid
(2) General contractors bid relying on
    best subcontractor bids
(3) School board soliciting bids
    awards contract
(4) Subcontractor withdraws bid

Drennan v. Star Paving Co.

Supreme Court of California
233 P.2d 757 (1958)

Background: Drennan, a general contractor (plaintiff), sued for breach of contract by
Star Paving (defendant) who allegedly had agreed to provide paving for work on a
school building. Drennan sought to win general contracting responsibilities for the
"Monte Vista School Job" in the Lancaster school district. After soliciting and receiving bids from various subcontractors, he used a bid from the defendant Star Paving
Company in computing his own bid to the school, and in that bid named the defendant
as the subcontractor for the paving work.

The plaintiff was then notified that he had been awarded the contract by the
school. When he stopped by the defendant's office, he was immediately told by the
defendant's construction engineer that a mistake had been made and that the de-

fendant could not do the work for the bid price given to the plaintiff. The plaintiff brought this suit to enforce the contract he said resulted from this transaction. The defendant claimed no contract resulted because its bid to the plaintiff was revoked before the plaintiff accepted. The trial court held for the plaintiff and the defendant appealed.

Decision: The trial court upheld the decision that Drennan was entitled to damages.

Traynor, Justice

On July 28, 1955, plaintiff, a licensed general contractor, was preparing a bid on the "Monte Vista School Job" in the Lancaster school district. Bids had to be submitted before 8:00 P.M. Plaintiff testified that it was customary in that area for general contractors to receive the bids of subcontractors by telephone on the day set for bidding and to rely on them in computing their own bids. Thus on that day plaintiff's secretary, Mrs. Johnson, received by telephone between fifty and seventy-five subcontractors' bids for various parts of the school job. As each bid came in, she wrote it on a special form, which she brought into plaintiff's office. He then posted it on a master cost sheet setting forth the names and bids of all subcontractors. His own bid had to include the names of subcontractors who were to perform one-half of one per cent or more of the construction work, and he had also to provide a bidder's bond of ten per cent of his total bid of $317,385 as a guarantee that he would perform the contract if awarded the work.

Late in the afternoon, Mrs. Johnson had a telephone conversation with Kenneth R. Hoon, an estimator for defendant. He gave his name and telephone number and stated that he was bidding for defendant for the paving work at the Monte Vista School according to plans and specifications and that his bid was $7,131.60. At Mrs. Johnson's request he repeated his bid. Plaintiff listened to the bid over an extension telephone in his office and posted it on the master sheet after receiving the bid form from Mrs. Johnson. Defendant's was the lowest bid for the paving. Plaintiff computed his own bid accordingly and submitted it with the name of defendant as the subcontractor for the paving. When the bids were opened on July 28th, plaintiff's proved to be the lowest, and he was awarded the contract.

On his way to Los Angeles the next morning plaintiff stopped at defendant's office. The first person he met was defendant's construction engineer, Mr. Oppenheimer. Plaintiff testified:

> I introduced myself and he immediately told me that they had made a mistake in their bid to me the night before, they couldn't do it for the price they had bid, and I told him I would expect him to carry through with their original bid because I had used it in compiling my bid and the job was being awarded them. And I would have to go and do the job according to my bid and I would expect them to do the same.

Defendant refused to do the paving work for less than $15,000. Plaintiff testified that he "got figures from other people" and after trying for several months to get as low a bid as possible engaged L & H Paving Company, a firm in Lancaster, to do the work for $10,948.60.

The trial court found on substantial evidence that defendant made a definite offer to do the paving on the Monte Vista job according to the plans and specifications for $7,131.60, and that plaintiff relied on defendant's bid in computing his own bid for the school job and naming defendant therein as the subcontractor for the paving work. Accordingly, it entered judgment for plaintiff in the amount of $3,817.00 (the difference between defendant's bid and the cost of the paving to plaintiff) plus costs.

Defendant contends that there was no enforceable contract between the parties on the ground that it made a revocable offer and revoked it before plaintiff communicated his acceptance to defendant.

There is no evidence that defendant offered to make its bid irrevocable in exchange for plaintiff's use of its figures in computing his bid. Nor is there evidence that would warrant interpreting plaintiff's use of defendant's bid as the acceptance thereof, binding plaintiff, on condition he received the main contract, to award the subcontract to defendant. In sum, there was neither an option supported by consideration nor a bilateral contract binding on both parties.

Plaintiff contends, however, that he relied to his detriment on defendant's offer and that defendant must therefore answer in damages for its refusal to perform. Thus the question is squarely presented: Did plaintiff's reliance make defendant's offer irrevocable? . . .

We are of the opinion that the defendants in executing the agreement made a promise which they should have reasonably expected would induce the plaintiff to submit a bid based thereon to the Government, that such promise did induce this action, and that injustice can be avoided only by enforcement of the promise. . . .

When plaintiff used defendant's offer in computing his own bid, he bound himself to perform in reliance on defendant's terms. Though defendant did not bargain for this use of its bid neither did defendant make it idly, indifferent to whether it would be used or not. On the contrary it is reasonable to suppose that defendant submitted its bid to obtain the subcontract. It was bound to realize the substantial possibility that its bid would be the lowest, and that it would be included by plaintiff in his bid. It was to its own interest that the contractor be awarded the general contract; the lower the subcontract bid, the lower the general contractor's bid was likely to be and the greater its chance of acceptance and hence the greater defendant's chance of getting the paving subcontract. Defendant had reason not only to expect plaintiff to rely on its bid but to want him to. Clearly defendant had a stake in plaintiff's reliance on its bid. Given this interest and the fact that plaintiff is bound by his own bid, it is only fair that plaintiff should have at least an opportunity to accept defendant's bid after the general contract has been awarded to him.

It bears noting that a general contractor is not free to delay acceptance after he has been awarded the general contract in the hope of getting a better price. Nor can he reopen bargaining with the subcontractor and at the same time claim a continuing right to accept the original offer. . . .

Affirmed.

Rejection by the Offeree

An offer is terminated when it is rejected by the offeree. If the offeree either states that the offer is rejected and will not be accepted or responds with a counteroffer that seeks to change the terms of the offer, the offeree has rejected it. On the other hand, an offeree who merely seeks information about the terms of the offer (Must I pay cash? What credit terms are available? Is that your lowest price?) is making an inquiry that is neither an accept- ance nor a rejection of the offer.

It is sometimes difficult to determine how to categorize the response of the offeree to an offer. If the response is an acceptance, the par- ties have made a contract. If the response is a rejection, the offer is terminated and the par- ties must begin their negotiations anew. If the response is neither an acceptance nor a rejec- tion, but instead is an inquiry, then the origi- nal offer is not terminated but remains for the offeree's review. Note that when the offeree's response is a counteroffer, the original offer is considered to have been terminated. In its place is a new offer (from the original offeree, not from the offeror) that is capable of being accepted and turned into a contract.

Death of a Party

The death of either the offeror or the offeree will terminate an ordinary offer. Assume that the offeree, not knowing about the offeror's death, accepts the offer after the offeror dies but during a reasonable time after the offer has been received. No contract will be formed. The offeree need not have notice of the offeror's death for the offer to be ter- minated; the death itself terminates the offer.

An exception to the general rule that the death of either party terminates the offer can occur with the option contract that the parties make to keep the offer irrevocable. In the case of an option contract, there is a contractual obligation to hold an offer open for a set pe-

riod. The effect of the offeror's death in this case depends upon whether the contractual obligations involved are ordinarily considered to survive the death of the offeror. This issue is discussed in Chapter 18, which deals with the discharge of contractual obligations.

Illegality

Contracts that are contrary to public policy will not be enforced. The concept of illegality as it affects contracts is discussed in detail in Chapter 15. For present purposes, it is impor- tant to note that an offer that is legal when made is terminated if it subsequently becomes illegal; the offer then cannot be accepted. If a state makes illegal the sale of a certain drug as of January 1, an offer to sell it, legally made the prior December 15, terminates on January 1 if it has not been accepted prior to that date.

Destruction of the Subject Matter

Hoper offers to sell his Porsche to Allen, who is familiar with the car. Although neither knew it, five minutes after the offer was made a landslide destroyed Hoper's garage and the car. Such destruction of the subject matter of the offer by an "act of God" will terminate the offer.

Suppose, instead, that Farmer offers to sell 10,000 bushels of apples to Processor and that Farmer's apples are subsequently destroyed by an act of God, such as a tornado. Your im- mediate reaction is very likely to be that, of course, the offer is terminated because the subject matter of the offer (Farmer's apples) has been destroyed. In fact, that is probably what a court would conclude; it is impossible for the offer to be performed. However, if Processor could prove that Farmer had of- fered to sell 10,000 bushels of apples in gen- eral rather than apples raised specifically from Farmer's property, then the offer would still be valid. In that case, Farmer could purchase the needed apples from someone else; the fact

---

PREVENTIVE LAW
Ambiguities in Negotiations

———

Many of the problems described in this chapter result from the parties using ambiguous language in their negotiations. Although ambiguity is inherent in negotiations as to the terms of an agreement, you should be very careful to make sure that you don't use language that could be interpreted as a formal offer or acceptance before you are ready to agree. Otherwise you may be stuck with terms that you didn't intend to agree to. When the contract is valuable or involves a long-term relationship, it is wise to consult with an attorney even during the preliminary stages of negotiation. Don't just wait until you are ready to have a formal document drafted. An attorney can offer important advice about terms and negotiation strategies.

Even if the importance of the contract does not justify consulting with an attorney, you should be extremely careful in the language that you use. For example, if you are responding to an offer and are seeking additional information, make very clear that you are not counteroffering and thus rejecting the offer. When you make offers be clear in your own mind whether you want the other party to promise or to act. And so on.

---

that Farmer's apples were destroyed would not mean that all apples were unavailable. Thus, it is necessary to determine whether the subject matter of Farmer's offer was 10,000 bushels of apples from his particular farm property or merely 10,000 bushels of apples. A tornado destroying Farmer's apples would terminate the offer to sell apples from his farm but would not affect the offer to sell apples in general.

REVIEW PROBLEMS

1. Tenant farmer (T), behind in his rent, explained his problem to his landlord (L), who suggested that T get more cattle to make more money. Concerned a water shortage would wipe out his stock, L told T, "Never mind the water, I will see there will be plenty of water because it never failed in Minnesota yet." Based on this representation, T purchased 107 cattle; the ensuing water shortage wiped him out. Is L liable for T's loss?

2. A defendant wrote to the plaintiff that his price for certain land was $7,500, and that he was writing this to several other interested persons. The plaintiff wired the defendant, stating that he accepted. Valid contract?

3. S wrote to B, "We quote you Hungarian flour, $5.40 per barrel, car lots only and subject to sight draft with a bill of lading. We would suggest your using wire to order as prices are so rapidly advancing that they

may be beyond reach before a letter would reach us." Is the valid offer capable of acceptance? What if the seller had written, "We *offer* you . . . "?

4. An employer issued a booklet to employees stating it had been customary for the company to make year-end bonus payments to employees, the amount of payment being dependent on earnings and at the discretion of the board of directors. An employee who read the booklet and continued working for the employer contends he has (by working) accepted the offer of the employer to pay him a year-end bonus. Do you agree?

5. Rofra, Inc., bid for plumbing work to be done for the Board of Education. The bid was sent in response to a "Solicitation for Connection of Building Sewer to the Public Sewer at Sunatsville Senior High School." Attached to that solicitation notice was a statement of "Contract General Provisions" that included a section reserving to the Board the right "to reject any and all bids, in whole or in part. . . ." Plaintiff Rofra was the second lowest bidder for the work; the lowest bidder did not have in its employ a "master plumber" as the solicitation terms required. The plaintiff sues to enforce the contract, which it claims exists as a result of the School Board's solicitation offer and its own bid, which was the lowest bid conforming to the offer. The defendant claims no contract exists. Is the plaintiff right? Rofra, Inc. v. Board of Education, Prince Georges County, Md., 346 A.2d 458 (Ct. of Special Appeals, Md., 1975).

6. Sokol made a written offer dated March 10 to purchase a house owned by Hill. At the same time, Sokol delivered to Nash, who was the real-estate broker representing Hill, a check for $500 as earnest money. The offer stated that the defendants had three days to accept. Hill signed on March 12. On the same day Sokol called Nash and orally withdrew his offer. Nash deposited

the check on March 14. On March 15, Nash hand-delivered the contract form signed by Hill and dated March 12 to Sokol. Sokol sues for the $500. What is the result? Sokol v. Hill, 310 S.W.2d 19 (Ct. App. Mo. 1958).

7. On September 16, 1964, a defendant submitted a proposal to the plaintiff to repair a pipe-bending machine owned by the plaintiff. The price for parts and labor was quoted as $1,600 plus freight costs. The defendant's letter also stated that, if the offer was accepted, the rebuilding of the machine would have to be done at a time that was convenient to both the plaintiff and the plant used by the defendant. No response was received until January 14, 1965, when the plaintiff advised the defendant its machine would be shipped that month. The plaintiff claims its response and the subsequent shipment of the machine (received by the defendant on January 20, 1965) constituted an acceptance of the defendant's offer. The defendant suggests its offer had expired and the shipment by the plaintiff was only an offer, which it later rejected. Is there a contract? Modern Pool Products, Inc. v. Rodel Machinery Co., 294 N.Y.S.2d 426 (Civ. Ct. of City of New York, 1968).

8. Scheck in writing offered to sell real estate to a specified prospective buyer and agreed to pay a percentage of the sales price as a commission to the broker. The offer fixed a six-day time limit for acceptance. Scheck then revoked the offer. On the morning of the sixth day, the broker received notice of Scheck's revocation. Later that day, the offeree accepted the offer that the broker had given to him. Does the revocation by Scheck to the offeree also revoke the broker's power to act on behalf of Scheck? If the broker had already begun to perform the offer to sell the property to the prospective purchaser, would the offer then be considered irrevocable? Marchiondo v. Scheck, 432 P2d 405 (Sup.Ct., N.M., 1967).

9. An employee brings this action against employer to enforce an alleged contract to pay the employee a bonus and commission. The agreement provided that the amount of bonus and commission would be determined three months later, after marketing operations for a new product had been commenced. However, no later agreement appears to have been made. Is there an offer capable of acceptance by the employee? Sandeman v. Sayres, 314 P.2d 428 (Sup. Ct. of Wash., 1957).

The Acceptance

 valid offer that has not been terminated creates a power of acceptance in the offeree. In order to result in a contract, the acceptance of the offer must meet certain criteria. First, like the offer itself, the acceptance must be made with the intent to contract. Second, the acceptance by the offeree must also be communicated to the offeror. Third, the acceptance must usually satisfy all the conditions and terms established by the offer. As was noted in the previous chapter, a change in the terms of an offer usually results not in an acceptance but in a rejection that terminates the offer. This chapter will discuss each of these elements required of an acceptance. Several special situations in which acceptance problems arise, and the cancellation of an acceptance, will also be discussed. Figure 11-1 demonstrates the basic process of agreement.

INTENT TO ACCEPT

The courts generally look for the same evidence of intent on the part of the offeree as is required of the offeror. Was the acceptance made with the intent to commit the offeree to enter into a contract? If the offeree replies to an offer by stating "Your offer looks good" or "I will give immediate consideration to your request," there is no manifestation of intent to enter into a contract.

The offeree must show a commitment. "I might accept your offer" leaves open the possibility that the offer will be rejected. Similarly, a response that leaves for the future the commitment of the offeree, "I'll let you know next week if the proposal is satisfactory," does not constitute an acceptance.

As with intent on the part of the offeror, it is the objective manifestation of the offeree's intent, not its subjective basis, that is critical. The law is not concerned with the offeree's state of mind; instead, it asks what the offeree's words or actions would indicate to a reasonable person about his or her intent to accept an offer.

Unless so required by the offer, the acceptance need not be expressed in words. Actions on the part of the offeree can constitute an acceptance. Thus, if a widget manufacturer sends a potential buyer five dozen widgets, with an invoice stating their purchase price, the buyer who says nothing but uses the widgets will have manifested by its action an intent to accept the manufacturer's offer to sell.

The *Crouch* case provides an example of a court determining that a person's actions can constitute an acceptance of an offer, even where the offeree argues that he did not "express" any acceptance.

FIGURE 11–1
The Process of Agreement

Offer ——— communicated ———→ Acceptance ——— communicated ———→ Contract

- Intent to offer would be apparent to reasonable person.

- Terms are definite and certain.

- Requests promise or action
  May set up required method of acceptance.

- Assent to terms of offer would be apparent to reasonable person, assent is unconditional.

- No change in terms of offer is attempted.

- Acceptance satisfies process requirements of the offer.

Note: This diagram describes the common–law process of agreement—changes have been made under the UCC for contracts for the sale of goods; for example, there may be a contract formed when the offer lacks definite terms or there are additional or different terms in the acceptance.

Crouch v. Marrs

Supreme Court of Kansas
430 P.2d 204 (1967)

Background: This was an action brought by Crouch (plaintiff) against Marrs (defendant), the current possessor of the property, seeking a determination from the court that an agreement to purchase property that Crouch made with the Purex Corporation resulted in a contract. Purex Corporation claimed it made no contract with Crouch, but instead had contracted to sell said property to Martin Asche. Asche then responded and stated he sold part of the property to Roy Marrs. When Crouch sought to take some of the property which he claimed was purchased from Purex Corporation, Marrs prevented Crouch from getting at the property. Crouch then brought this action against Marrs, seeking to prevent Marrs from interfering with the property claimed by Crouch. The other parties involved were then made parties to the suit filed by Crouch. The trial court found against Crouch and in favor of Marrs.

Decision: The trial court decision was reversed and title to the property was awarded to the plaintiff Crouch.

Hatcher, Commissioner

The facts of the controversy do not appear to be in dispute. Six miles north of Meade, Kansas, was an old silica processing plant which was owned by the Purex Corporation of Lakewood, California. The plant had not been used for many years.

On February 26, 1964, the plaintiff, Crouch, wrote to the Purex Corporation asking for their lowest price if they were interested in selling the building and its contents. The letter read in part:

> I would be interested in buying the old building that housed the plant and what other items that are still left. The items that are still left are: two crushers, furnace and the elevator is about all that is left.

On March 4, 1964, Crouch received a letter of reply from Purex Corporation signed by Frank Knox which stated:

> We will sell this building and the equipment in and about that building for a total of $500.

On March 19, 1964, Crouch wrote to Frank Knox, Purex Corporation, stating that the building was in "pretty bad condition" and asking "would you consider taking $300 for what is left?" This letter was not answered.

Later, on April 16, 1964, Crouch addressed another letter to Frank Knox, Purex Corporation, which read:

> I guess we will try the building for the amount you quoted, $500.
> I am sending you a personal check for this amount.
> It will be 2 or 3 weeks before we can get started; and I presume that we will be allowed all the time that we need to remove the material.

It is conceded that this letter constituted a new offer and was not a continuation of the previous negotiations.

The record discloses the check signed by Phillip Crouch and made payable to Frank Knox was endorsed by Knox and then was paid and cancelled by several banks, including the Piqua Bank at which Crouch maintained his checking account.

On April 17, 1964, the Purex Corporation, through Frank Knox, wrote a letter to Martin Asche which stated:

> In answer to your inquiry about our property approximately six miles north of Meade, Kansas.
> We will sell for $500 the mine building and whatever machinery and equipment which remains in or about that building. A condition of sale will require that the property purchased be removed from the premises within forty-five days.
> If this price is acceptable, we will be pleased to receive a cashier's check to cover.

On April 24, 1964, Asche wrote a letter accepting the offer of April 17, which reads:

> We are enclosing a cashier's check for $500 and the bill of sale of mine buildings with the agreement of option to purchase property.
>
> If the corporation has any other property and machinery in this area for sale, we would be pleased to deal with the corporation. It was our pleasure to deal with the Purex Corporation.

On April 27, 1964, Frank Knox sent Crouch the following telegram:

> Your counter offer received April 23 is unacceptable. Your check mistakenly deposited by Purex will be recovered and returned to you or Purex check will be issued to you if your check cannot be located.

There followed a letter dated May 16, 1964, which read:

> This is a follow-up to our telegram to you of April 27, advising you that your check which we received on April 23 was not acceptable, but that it had been deposited by mistake. Since we were unable to recover your check, we herewith enclose our check for $500 to reimburse you.
>
> We wish to explain, that the reason we could not accept your counter-offer of $500 for the mine building and machinery at Meade, Kansas was because we had received and accepted an offer from another party prior to receipt of yours on April 23.

In the meantime, Martin Asche had entered into a contract to sell the building to Roy Marrs who owned the land surrounding the building site for $500 and had entered into a contract to sell the equipment to the C. & D. Used Truck Parts for $800. Crouch commenced salvage of the building but Roy Marrs put a lock on the gate and would not allow Crouch to enter.

Appellant Crouch contends that on the basis of the prior negotiations the acceptance and endorsing appellant's check by the Purex Corporation constituted the formation of a contract of sale. The question is whether the endorsing and depositing appellant's check constituted an acceptance of his offer to buy? We think it did.

The endorsing and depositing a check constitutes an acceptance of the offer to buy which accompanies it because the act itself indicates acceptance. An offer may be accepted by performing a specified act as well as by an affirmative answer. Also, where the offeree exercised dominion over the thing offered him—in this instance the check—such exercise constitutes an acceptance of the offer. It is elementary that an offer may be accepted by performing or refraining from performing a specified act as well as by an affirmative answer.

We are forced to conclude that the acceptance and endorsement of the check accompanying the offer to purchase the property in controversy constituted an acceptance of the offer.

The judgment is reversed with instructions to the district court to quiet plaintiff's title to the building and equipment in controversy against the defendants and enjoin them from interfering with plaintiff's ingress and egress for the purpose of salvaging the property.

COMMUNICATION OF ACCEPTANCE

An acceptance must be communicated in order to be effective. What action must be taken in order to communicate an acceptance depends on whether the offeror seeks a unilateral or a bilateral contract.

Bilateral or Unilateral Agreement

If the offer is one to enter into a unilateral contract (a promise for an act or an act for a promise), the offeree must either perform the requested act or respond with the requested promise. Thus, a promise for an act ("I'll pay you $10 if you type my paper by tomorrow night") requires the offeree to perform the act (type the paper by tomorrow night) in order to accept the offer to pay $10. However, if the offer requires a promise in exchange for an act ("I'll lend you $10 right now if you promise to repay me $11 a week from tomorrow"), the offeree must make the promise to repay (either expressly by stating a promise or impliedly by taking the offered $10) in order to accept the offer. It is also clear that an offeror may seek the offeree's forbearance, an agreement to refrain from doing something that the offeree might otherwise do. Thus, the statement "I promise to pay you $100 if you don't smoke cigarettes for a year" is also an offer to enter into a unilateral contract. The offeree is asked to forbear from an act that he or she might otherwise do.

In the case where the offer requires an act from the offeree ("I'll pay you $10 if you type my paper by tomorrow night"), only the act need be performed in order to accept the offer. The offeree need not first communicate to the offeror that he or she intends to perform the requested act. On the other hand, if the offer requires a promise from the offeree ("I'll lend you $10 now if you *promise* to repay me $11 next Friday") the offeree must of course communicate that promise to the offeror.

Similarly, if the offer is one to enter into a bilateral contract, one in which each party makes a promise ("I'll promise to sell you my 1986 Ford if you promise to pay me $800 cash"), the offeree must also communicate his or her promise in order to accept the offer. In the event of uncertainty as to what the offer requires of an offeree, most courts will interpret an agreement as consisting of bilateral promises, thus requiring a communication from the offeree rather than a requested act of acceptance in exchange for the offeror's promise.

Means of Communication

Usually, any means of communication that gives the offeror notice of the offeree's intent to accept the offer is effective. However, as the third requirement of an acceptance suggests, the offeree must also comply with all the terms of the offer. Thus, if the offer dictates that the acceptance be communicated by certain means or occur at a certain time or place, the offeree generally must comply with those provisions. An acceptance made in a different manner or at a different time or place would be ineffective.

If the offer does not require the offeree to use a specific means of communication, problems can arise concerning the time at which an acceptance by an offeree would be effective. While the time of acceptance is not critical to most contracts, where the offeror has attempted a revocation or where the intended acceptance is delayed or lost, an analysis of the method or time of acceptance is necessary.

Generally, if the means of communication used by the offeree in communicating acceptance is authorized by the offer, the acceptance is effective when delivered by the offeree to the communication agency. The offeror may expressly or impliedly authorize the offeree to use a particular means of communication. Thus, if the offer states, "You may use the mail for your acceptance," the offeree's acceptance is effective at the moment a letter of acceptance is deposited with the postal service even if the letter is delayed in reaching the offeror or is lost. The offeree has effectively communicated acceptance by delivering it to the "agent" (post office) authorized by the offeror. Even if the offer does not expressly authorize the use of a particular means of communication, the law holds that an offer made by one

means of communication can be accepted by the same means. Thus, a mailed offer implies authorization to the offeree to use the mail for acceptance.

In fact, the modern rule in most jurisdictions is that the offeree may use any "reasonable means of communication" in accepting the offer. What constitutes a reasonable means of communication depends on the subject matter of the offer, the custom and usage in a particular trade or business, and the prior conduct or dealings of the parties. If, for example, it is customary in the industry or trade for acceptances to be sent by mail or if the parties in prior transactions had used the mail to enter into contracts, an acceptance would be effective when mailed. An acceptance sent by a means not recognized as an implied or express agent of the offeror will be effective only upon receipt.

The following case demonstrates the application of the rule making an acceptance effective when dispatched by an authorized means of communication.

Pribil v. Ruther

Supreme Court of Nebraska
262 N.W.2d 460 (1978)

Background: Pribil (plaintiff) brought this action against Ruther (defendant), seeking to enforce a contract whereby Pribil agreed to buy real estate owned by Ruther. The defendant claimed she verbally rejected the plaintiff's offer to purchase the property before he received her written acceptance of it. The trial court found for the plaintiff and the defendant appealed.

Decision: The trial court's decision was reversed and the Supreme Court ruled in favor of defendant Ruther.

Boslaugh, Justice

This is an appeal in an action for specific performance of a real estate contract. The defendant Bertha Ruther owns a quarter section of land in Holt County, Nebraska. The defendant listed this property for sale with John Thor, a real estate broker, on January 20, 1976.

On April 12, 1976, the plaintiff Lawrence Pribil executed a written offer to purchase the property for $68,000. The offer to purchase was on a form known as a Uniform

Purchase Agreement which included a space for a written acceptance of the offer. The defendant and her husband signed the acceptance on the same day and handed an executed copy of the agreement to Thor for delivery to the plaintiff.

Thor returned to his office in Norfolk, Nebraska, and asked an office employee, Mrs. Kasebaum, to send a copy of the agreement to the plaintiff. Mrs. Kasebaum wrote a letter to the plaintiff, dated April 14, 1976, with a copy of the agreement enclosed, which was sent to the plaintiff by certified mail. The letter was postmarked "April 15, 1976 PM." and was received by the plaintiff on April 16, 1976.

The defendant became dissatisfied with the transaction the day after she had signed the acceptance when she discovered a test well had been drilled on the property at the plaintiff's request and the driller had estimated a well would produce 500 to 800 gallons of water per minute. The defendant testified that she called the plaintiff's home at about 5 P.M. on April 13, 1976, and told the plaintiff's wife that she, the defendant, would not sell the property. The plaintiff's wife testified this conversation did not take place until some ten days later, near the end of April 1976.

The defendant further testified that she called Thor the next morning, April 14, 1976, and said that she was going to "terminate the contract," because Thor had lied to her. According to Thor this conversation took place at 11:42 A.M. on April 15, 1976. Thor testified that immediately after receiving the call from the defendant, he called the plaintiff and told the plaintiff that the defendant was not going to sell the farm.

The principal issue in this case is whether the defendant had effectively rejected the plaintiff's offer and revoked her acceptance of the offer before the acceptance had been communicated to the plaintiff. Since the plaintiff sought to enforce the contract the burden was on the plaintiff to establish that there was a contract. A party who seeks to compel specific performance of a written contract has the burden of proving the contract.

An express contract is proved by evidence of a definite offer and unconditional acceptance. Where the offer requires a promise on the part of the offeree, a communicated acceptance is essential.

The signing of the acceptance on the Uniform Purchase Agreement by the defendant did not make the contract effective. It was necessary that there be some communication of the acceptance to the plaintiff. There must be some irrevocable element such as depositing the acceptance in the mail so that it is placed beyond the power or control of the sender before the acceptance becomes effective and the contract is made. Delivery to the agent of the defendant was not delivery to the plaintiff as it did not put the acceptance beyond the control of the defendant.

The plaintiff contends that the deposit of the acceptance in the mail by Thor satisfied the requirement that the acceptance be communicated. Where transmission by mail is authorized, the deposit of the signed agreement in the mail with the proper address and postage will complete the contract. The difficulty in this case is that there is no evidence that the acceptance was deposited in the mail before Thor called the plaintiff and informed him that the defendant would not sell the property.

The evidence is that Thor handed the purchase agreement to Mrs. Kasebaum with instructions to send a copy to the plaintiff. Mrs. Kasebaum did not testify. Thor testified, "I can't testify when she mailed it, except by reading the postmarks on the envelope and the return receipts." The postmark indicates only that the postage was canceled sometime during the afternoon of April 15, 1976. The telephone call from the defendant was received at 11:42 A.M. on that same date. The call from Thor to the plaintiff was made immediately afterward.

If we assume that transmission by mail was authorized in this case, there is no evidence to show that the acceptance was deposited in the mail before the defendant's call to Thor, and Thor's call to the plaintiff notifying him that the defendant had rejected his offer. The evidence does not show that the acceptance was communicated to the plaintiff and thus became effective before the defendant changed her mind and rejected the offer. Reversed and remanded with directions to dismiss.

SATISFYING TERMS OF THE OFFER

Generally, an acceptance must mirror the terms of the offer. A variation in terms or an addition of new conditions causes the response of the offeree to be considered a rejection instead of an acceptance. There are some situations where the law or facts imply terms that may not have been expressed in the offer. In these cases, the expression of those terms by the offeree in accepting is not considered to add to or vary the terms of the offer.

For example, if you offer to sell me your house for $75,000 and in response I state, "I accept your offer, subject to my attorney checking that you have good title to the property," my response would be considered an acceptance. It is implied by law that the person offering to sell a house guarantees that he or she has a good title to it. My response has not changed the terms of your offer. Similarly, suppose it is customary in an industry (according to trade usage) that an offer to sell goods for a stated price implies that the buyer has "thirty days, same as cash" to pay for them. The buyer who expresses in an acceptance "I'll accept your offer if the normal credit terms are extended" is not varying the terms of the offer; those credit terms were a part of the original offer, even though not expressed by the offeror.

Battle of the Forms

The general rule that any response that varies the terms of an offer cannot be considered an acceptance has proved unworkable in commercial transactions where each party has form documents that it sends in response to inquiries. The problem of the "battle of the forms" arises because each party desires to be the one whose form controls the transaction.

For example, the buyer's form to the seller might say:

We offer to buy 500 widgets from you at $100 each. The goods are to be shipped to us F.O.B. our plant by June 1st. They must be packaged in cartons of 50 each. Payment will be due from us 60 days after receipt of the widgets. No arbitration. No variation in the terms of this offer can be made without our written consent.

Seller has received a definite offer. It wants to sell the widgets, but on slightly different terms, and responds with its own form:

We have received your offer to buy 500 widgets and are glad to contract with you. Our goods will be shipped to you F.O.B. your plant. They will be packaged in cartons of 100 each. Disputes will be submitted to arbitration. Payment will be due from you 30 days after receipt of the widgets. Thank you for your order.

ETHICS BOX
Honoring Agreements

Sometimes parties exchange correspondence agreeing to a contract and then the market changes dramatically and one of the parties wants out of the agreement. In such a circumstance, is it ethical for the disadvantaged party to hire a lawyer to "find a way to get out of the contract"? The lawyer may search for ambiguities in the terms or in the process of contract formation or some other defect making the contract unenforceable.

Assume that the party's sole motivation in seeking to get out of the contract is the change in circumstances. The breaching party may seek to justify his or her actions by arguing that the other party would do the same thing if the situation was reversed.

In a duty-based approach to ethics, a principle can be derived that promises carry moral force and should be honored unless there is a more compelling duty that would be served by breaching the promise. Thus, if the change in circumstances puts a manager in a position whereby he or she cannot deliver on a promise made to hundreds of employees, the duty to honor the promise made to the many employees may be more important, and may override the duty to honor the promise to the outsider.

Rule utilitarian-based ethics would focus on the net social consequences of dishonoring contracts. If most parties expect that promises will be honored and they rely on that assumption, there is a cost of defeated expectations when the promise is breached. Further, trust and good-faith behavior are a necessary foundation for business transactions. Opportunism raises transaction costs. Ad hoc utilitarians would evaluate the social consequences of breaching the particular contract in question. The net impact of the particular breach on society would determine whether breaching was ethical. Note that ethicality is not determined by looking solely at whether it is in the financial interest of the breaching party. The consideration must be from the net welfare of *all* those affected by the decision. The breach will always defeat the expectations of those that have relied upon the performance of the contract.

Although it may occasionally be all right to breach a contract and accept the consequences, most of the time such action would be found to be unethical. Thus, the ethical manager should operate on the basis of a rebuttable presumption that breaching a contract is unethical.

Do the parties have a contract? Clearly, there is an offer, but have the terms of the offer been accepted? Under common law, if the terms of the offer are not mirrored by the terms of the acceptance, no contract results. But suppose the parties act as if there is a contract, sending and accepting the goods without protest. Later a dispute arises over the terms of payment. The seller argues that the dispute must be submitted to arbitration.

Whether the seller is correct that the dispute must be submitted to arbitration depends upon how the forms are treated. Under common law, the seller's form would be considered a counteroffer that was accepted by the buyer's actions in taking the goods. This is called the *last shot doctrine,* because the last document exchanged before the parties perform controls the transaction. Under that rule, the seller's form controls, and arbitration is required.

The typical problematic exchange of forms by merchants is dramatized in Figure 11-2. Sellers typically want to restrict warranties and damages. They also tend to prefer arbitration because the system may be a familiar one to sellers who sponsor arbitration through their industry associations. Buyers, not surprisingly, want warranties and special damages and may be resistant to arbitration because they think that it may unfairly favor the sellers. Note that the crossing of forms problem is rarely a consumer problem because consumers are not very likely to use form documents.

The UCC and Acceptance

The Uniform Commercial Code has sought to deal with problems that arise because of the battle of forms. Section 2-207 provides that, in certain situations, the terms of an acceptance can add to or differ from those proposed in the offer. This provision of the UCC reads as follows:

(1) A definite and seasonable expression of acceptance or a written confirmation which is sent within a reasonable time operates as an acceptance even though it states terms additional to or different from those offered or agreed upon, unless acceptance is expressly made conditional on assent to the additional or different terms.

(2) The additional terms are to be construed as proposals for addition to the contract.

Between merchants such terms become part of the contract unless:
(a) the offer expressly limits acceptance to the terms of the offer;
(b) they materially alter it; or
(c) notification of objection to them has already been given or is given within a reasonable time after notice of them is received.

(3) Conduct by both parties which recognizes the existence of a contract is sufficient to establish a contract for sale although the writings of the parties do not otherwise establish a contract. In such case, the terms of the particular contract consist of those terms on which the writings of the parties agree, together with any supplementary terms incorporated under any other provisions of this Act.

The general approach and structure of Section 2-207 is clear. Subsection (1) determines when a contract is created as a result of an exchange of documents between the parties. In response to the realities of the modern commercial transaction, the rigid requirements of the mirror-image rule have been abolished. Under the provisions of subsection (1), the response is effective as an acceptance, creating a contract "even though it states terms additional to or different from those offered. . . ." While the response need not exactly match the offer, the response containing additional or different terms must meet two requirements to be effective as an acceptance. First, it must be stated in terms of a "definite and seasonable expression of acceptance." Second, it must not be "expressly made conditional on assent to the additional or different terms," which would be the same thing as making a counteroffer at common law. The UCC test of an operative acceptance under Section 2-207 was thus designed to bring about a closer correlation between the controlling legal principles and the commercial understanding of when a "deal" had been closed.

The contract created by the parties' ex-

FIGURE 11–2
The Crossing of Forms

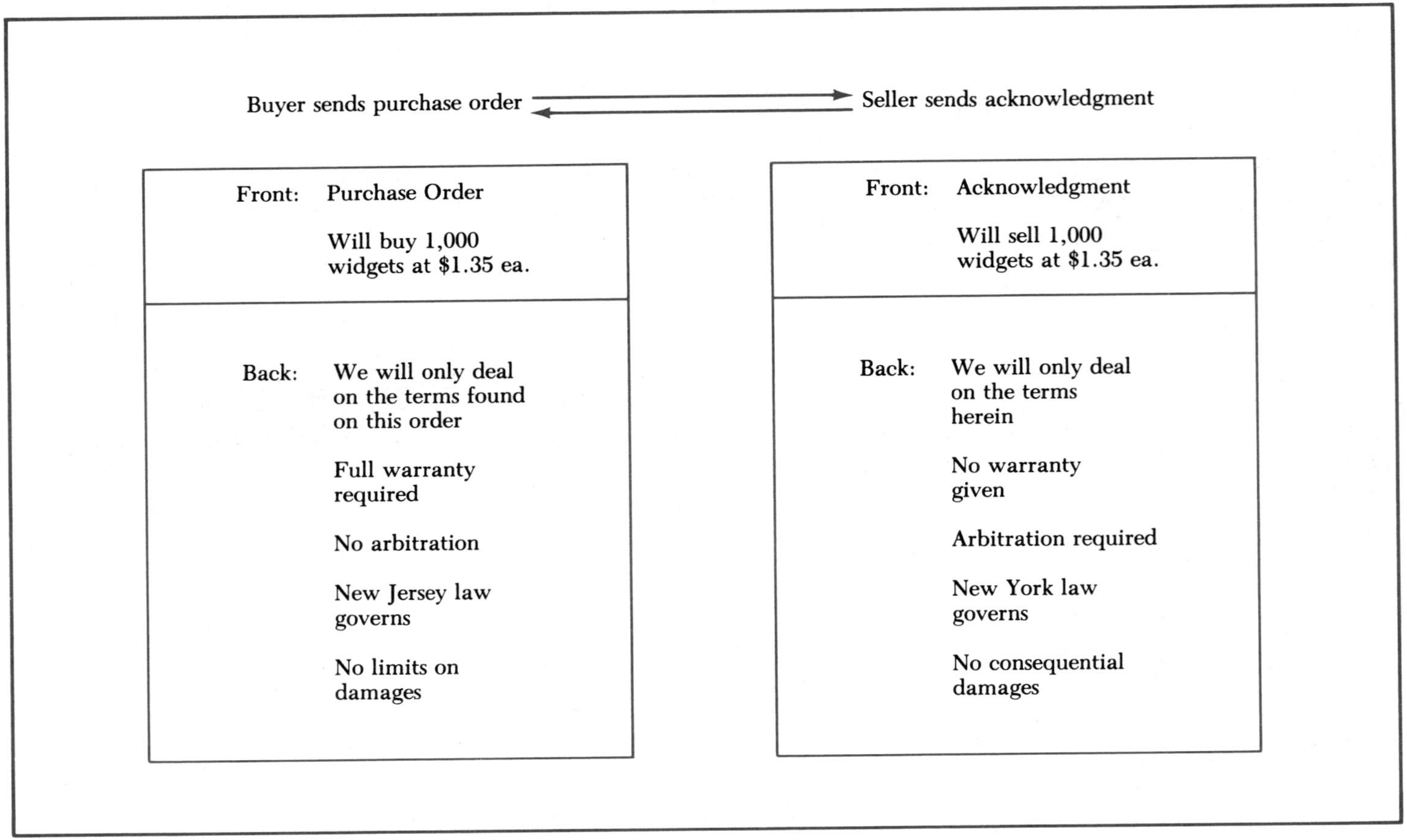

Buyer sends purchase order ⟷ Seller sends acknowledgment

Front: Purchase Order

Will buy 1,000
widgets at $1.35 ea.

Back: We will only deal
on the terms found
on this order

Full warranty
required

No arbitration

New Jersey law
governs

No limits on
damages

Front: Acknowledgment

Will sell 1,000
widgets at $1.35 ea.

Back: We will only deal
on the terms
herein

No warranty
given

Arbitration required

New York law
governs

No consequential
damages

change is based—at least insofar as its material terms are concerned—on the terms contained in the offeror's form. Subsection (2) is not concerned with the question of whether a response is in fact an acceptance. This is determined solely under subsection (1). Subsection (2) is intended only to resolve the effect of the additional and/or different terms contained in the response that subsection (1) has already deemed an acceptance. Subsection (2) establishes two separate tracks for handling these variant terms, depending on the characteristics of the parties. If the parties to the contract are not both merchants, the offeree's variant terms are "proposals for addition to the contract." The offeror can either agree to their inclusion or not, as he wishes. If the parties to the contract are both merchants, the variant terms automatically become part of the contract, unless:

1. The offeror has stated in his offer that he will agree only on the basis of his terms; or
2. The variant terms will materially alter the existing contract; or
3. The offeror has already objected or thereafter objects within a reasonable time to the variant terms.

The effect of subsection (2) is to allow changes in the contract, which is based on the offeror's terms, only if the terms are found to be nonmaterial. Even nonmaterial terms will fail to become part of the contract if the offeror objects to them generally, either in advance or after receipt.

The result of the application of subsections (1) and (2) is to form a contract at the time of the exchange between the parties that is based essentially on the offeror's terms. Thus, the inequity fostered by the common law rules, which enabled a party to withdraw easily when market conditions changed, presumably has been remedied.

Subsection (3) addresses the typical situation where, despite the fact that no contract has been created by the parties' exchange under the provisions of subsection (1), the parties nevertheless perform. When subsection (3) applies, since performance requires the finding of some contractual relationship, the contract consists of the terms on which the offer and the response agree, "together with any supplementary terms incorporated under any other provisions of [the UCC]." The effect of the application of subsection (3) is to eliminate any preference for the terms of either the offeror or the offeree in a performance situation.

Thus it would seem that the drafters of Section 2-207 attempted to cure the two basic problems that resulted when the common law rules were applied to the exchange of commercial forms. The language of Section 2-207 indicates that the offeror will be protected during the executory stage and that the contract formed on the basis of performance no longer will give a preference to the party making the last response.

Some commentators have proposed that a court should answer the following seven questions in applying Section 2-207 in actual cases:

1. Does the situation involve a response to an offer or a written confirmation? If the latter, a contract has already been formed; skip to step 4.
2. Is the response a definite and seasonable expression of acceptance?
3. Is the acceptance expressly made conditional on assent to the variant terms it contains? If a contract has been formed, continue with step 4. If no contract has been formed,
    a. Has there been conduct by both parties that recognizes the existence of a contract?
    b. Which contract terms appear in the documents of both parties?
    c. What contract terms are missing and what terms would be implied by the Code?
4. Is the transaction between merchants? If yes, then continue. If no, then the terms are

those of the offer plus any that the offeror has expressly agreed to.

5. Has the offer expressly limited acceptance to its terms?

6. Do the variant terms materially alter the contract?

7. Has an objection to the variant terms been made by the offeror?

How would you answer these questions when reviewing the Wisconsin case that follows?

Air Products & Chem., Inc. v. Fairbanks Morse, Inc.

Supreme Court of Wisconsin
206 N.W.2d 414 (1973)

Background: Air Products (plaintiff), a buyer of large electric motors, brought this action against Fairbanks (defendant), the manufacturer, alleging that the motors, which were manufactured by the defendant and sold to the plaintiff, contained defective parts unreasonably dangerous to parts of other motors that caused damage to those motors and economic loss to the plaintiff. While several issues were posed to and answered by the trial court, the issue of interest to us at this time concerns the effect to be given an acknowledgment form sent by defendant Fairbanks to the plaintiff. The trial court said the acknowledgment form could limit the plaintiff's right to recover certain damages against the defendant. The plaintiff appealed the trial court's decision.

Decision: The trial court's decision was reversed and the Supreme Court ruled in favor of plaintiff Air Products.

Hanley, Justice

As an affirmative defense to all the causes of action pleaded by . . . Air Products . . . , Fairbanks set up a provision contained in its "acknowledgments of order" which were sent by Fairbanks to Air Products with Air Products' purchase order which it had executed. The "acknowledgment of order" from Fairbanks to Air Products has the following language printed in reasonably bold face type at the bottom:

> WE THANK YOU FOR YOUR ORDER AS COPIED HEREON, WHICH WILL RECEIVE PROMPT ATTENTION AND SHALL BE GOVERNED BY THE PROVISIONS ON THE REVERSE SIDE HEREOF UNLESS YOU NOTIFY US TO THE CONTRARY WITHIN 10 DAYS OR BEFORE SHIPMENT WHICHEVER IS EARLIER. BEFORE ACCEPTING GOODS FROM TRANSPORTATION COMPANY SEE THAT EACH ARTICLE IS IN GOOD CONDITION. IF SHORTAGE OR DAMAGE IS APPARENT REFUSE SHIPMENT UNLESS AGENT NOTES DEFECT ON TRANSPORTATION BILL. ACCEPTANCE OF SHIPMENT WITHOUT COMPLYING WITH SUCH CONDITIONS IS AT YOUR OWN RISK.
>
> THIS IS NOT AN INVOICE. AN INVOICE FOR THIS MATERIAL WILL BE SENT YOU WITHIN A FEW DAYS.
>
> ACKNOWLEDGMENT OF ORDER

On the reverse side of the "acknowledgment of order" there are printed six separate provisions which are appropriately numbered and at the very beginning it is stated that:

> The following provisions form part of the order acknowledged and accepted on the face hereof, as express agreements between Fairbanks, Morse & Co. ("Company") and the Buyer governing the terms and conditions of the sale, subject to modification only in writing signed by the local manager or an executive officer of the Company:

Provision # 6 which is the subject of the dispute between the parties provides that:

> 6.—The Company nowise assumes any responsibility or liability with respect to use, purpose, or suitability, and shall not be liable for damages of any character, whether direct or consequential, for defect, delay, or otherwise, its sole liability and obligation being confined to the replacement in the manner aforesaid of defectively manufactured guaranteed parts failing within the time stated.

Fairbanks contends that provision # 6 contained on the reverse side of their "acknowledgment of order" became part of the contract between it and Air Products while Air Products contends that its right to rely on implied [warranties] . . . and consequential damages has in no way been limited because it never assented to the exclusion of any warranties or damages. Both parties are in agreement that sec. 2-207, of the Uniform Commercial Code (12A Pennsylvania Statutes Ann. sec. 2-207) is the appropriate standard by which their rights must be determined. . . .

One commentator has aptly stated the threshold questions involved in subsection (1) of 2-207:

> . . . Thus, under subsection (1), there are two instances in which a contract may not have been formed. First, if the offeror could not reasonably treat the response of the offeree as an acceptance there is no contract. Second, if the offeree's acceptance is made expressly conditional on the offeror's assent to variant provisions, the offeree has made a counter-offer. However, under section 2-207(3) either situation may result in contract formation by subsequent conduct of the parties.

Because the reverse side of Fairbanks' Acknowledgment of Order states that the provisions contained there ". . . form part of the order acknowledged and accepted on the face hereof . . ." it would seem that Air Products could have "reasonably" assumed that the parties "had a deal."

Since there is no express provision in the purchase orders making assent to different or additional terms conditioned upon Air Products' assent to them, the second requirement of coming under U.C.C. 2-207 is also met.

Once having satisfied the requirements of subsection (1), any additional matter must fall in subsection (2).

The major impact of sec. 2-207 is that it altered the common law rule which precluded an acceptance from creating a contract if it in any way varied any term of the offer. Subsection (1) expressly provides that there may be a legally binding contract even if the acceptance contains terms "different from" or "additional to" the terms of the offer.

At this point a contract does in fact exist between the parties under (1). Subsection (2) must now be resorted to to see which of the "variant" terms will actually become part of the contract.

At this juncture, Air Products . . . argue[s] that 2-207(2) only applies to "additional terms" while Fairbanks' limitation of liability provisions were "different." To this extent they contend terms are "additional" if they concern a subject matter that is not covered in the offer and "different" if the subject matter, although covered in the offer, was covered in a variant way. . . . Air Products' argument seems to expressly contradict Official U.C.C. Comment #3 which unequivocally states "Whether or not *additional or different terms* will become part of the agreement depends upon the provisions of subsection (2)." (Emphasis added.) One commentator has noted that:

> On its face, subsection (2) seems only to apply to additional and not conflicting terms, and at least one court has interpreted the language this way. However, this is an unnecessarily limited construction and, as Comment 3 to the section points out, subsection (2) should apply to both additional and different provisions.
>
>   .   .   .

Air Products . . . next contend that if the added terms of the "acknowledgment of order" were "additional" terms they still do not become part of the contract because the prerequisite to their becoming a part of the contract which are contained in subsection (2) were not satisfied. Section 2-207(2) required that:

> The additional terms are to be construed as proposals for addition to the contract. Between merchants such terms become part of the contract unless:
>   (a) the offer expressly limits acceptance to the terms of the offer;
>   (b) they materially alter it; or
>   (c) notification of objection to them has already been given or is given within a reasonable time after notice of them is received.

The language employed by Air Products in its "terms and conditions" was not express enough to bring into play the provisions of either subsection 2-207(a) or (c). The ultimate question to be determined, therefore, is whether the disclaimer contained in Fairbanks' "acknowledgment of order" materially altered the agreement between the parties pursuant to sec. 2-207(2)(b). If they materially alter what would otherwise be firmed by the acceptance of an offer, they will not become terms unless the buyer expressly agrees thereto. "If, however, they are terms which would not so change the bargain they will be incorporated unless notice of objection to them has already been given or is given within a reasonable time."
    . . . Air Products contend that the eradication of a multi-million dollar damage exposure is *per se* material. Fairbanks bases its argument on the ground that conse-

quential damages may not be recovered except in "special circumstances" or in a "proper case." 2-714(2), (3).

We agree with plaintiffs . . . Air Products and conclude that the disclaimer for consequential loss was sufficiently material to require express conversation between the parties over its inclusion or exclusion in the contract.

Affirmed in part, reversed in part.

ACCEPTANCE PROBLEMS

At the outset of the chapter, we noted the three requirements that must be met in order for an acceptance to result: there must be an intent to contract, an effective communication, and a response that generally satisfies all the terms and requirements imposed by the offer. It should be noted that, in many situations, it is generally the offeror, not the offeree, who controls the form and manner of the acceptance. This is because of the third requirement—that the acceptance conform to the terms and requirements imposed by the offer. Thus, the offeror often has the power to change the general rule applied in many of the situations this chapter has discussed. All the offeror must do is to add to the offer the requirements that it seeks to obtain from the offeree. Several unusual acceptance problems arise because of the offeror's control of the acceptance.

Silence as Acceptance

Generally, the offeree who responds silently to the offer is not considered to be accepting the offer. Mere inaction and silence are usually not regarded as manifestations of intent to agree on a contract. However, some exceptions to this rule occur, usually because of the terms suggested in the offer. Book clubs, record clubs, wine clubs, and gourmet clubs often make agreements under which the club "members" will be considered to have ac-

cepted the "monthly offer" if they are silent and do not inform the club that the merchandise offered is not desired. The exceptions recognized by the law usually occur in one of three situations:

1. If the transactions the parties have entered into in the past show their intent to regard silence as an acceptance, that intent becomes a part of their future transactions. Here, the *course of dealing* between the parties in past transactions is the basis for finding their present intent to have silence constitute acceptance.

2. The *initial agreement* between the parties constitutes the basis for treating silence by the offeree as acceptance. Thus, at the beginning of the transactions, the members of the book, record, or wine club sign a written agreement stating that they agree to pay for the items received if they do not send in the card or notice rejecting the monthly offering. The members agree that they do not have to express affirmatively their acceptance each month; silence on the part of the members is, by virtue of the initial agreement, also a method of accepting the club's monthly offering.

3. If the offeree *uses the goods* and treats them as if he had accepted them, the courts consider the offeree's actions and silence as together constituting the required acceptance. This problem occurs most often with regard to magazines or newspapers mistakenly being sent to people who didn't order them. Courts usually consider that, since

---

PREVENTIVE LAW
Use of Forms
——

Standard forms can reduce costs and simplify recurring transactions. However, they can also greatly complicate transactions if they are used carelessly. The forms should only be used for the transactions for which they have been prepared. The practice of taking a standard form and striking out or adding language to try to fit an unusual transaction is very dangerous.

Also, if a particular transaction is very important in terms of its size or duration, it is wise to review the documents that will be used and make sure that they deal with the essential aspects of the agreement. Far too often, businesspeople use forms that contain clauses that they haven't read—a practice guaranteed to cause confusion.

---

the offeror is in business and did not intend a gift, the person who receives them and reads them is assumed to have agreed to pay for them. Most states now have statutes that allow the recipient of unsolicited merchandise, particularly where sent through the mail, to treat such items as gifts. The Postal Reorganization Act provides that mailing unsolicited merchandise is an unfair method of competition unless the product is marked "sample" or is sent by a charity. The Act also provides that the recipient may treat the received merchandise as a gift. Silence and use of such products will not be construed as acceptance of an implied offer to sell.

The Auction

An auction is a sales device whereby members of the public or a designated group come together to compete, by means of bids, for the purchase of goods or realty. Auctions are usually conducted by professional auctioneers or by public officials and may be of two types. In an auction *with reserve,* the object bid for does not have to be sold if the auctioneer is dissatisfied with the level of the bidding. In an auc-

tion *without reserve,* the object must be sold to the highest bidder.

Under UCC Section 2-328, an auction is considered to be with reserve unless it is expressly stated to be without reserve. Because at least one court has held that the phrase "will sell to highest bidder" is insufficient to make an auction without reserve, the actual words "without reserve" should be used in an announcement to insure that the auction is of that type.

In an auction with reserve, each bid is considered an offer. Acceptance is signaled by the fall of the hammer or some other symbolic act that is customary for the type of auction involved. In an auction without reserve, the announcement is considered the offer and each bid is an acceptance subject to the condition that no higher bid is made. This is illustrated in Figure 11-3.

CANCELLATION OF ACCEPTANCE

We have discussed the problems that occur in determining whether there has been an acceptance of the offer. If an acceptance has been made, the offer can no longer be revoked

FIGURE 11–3
Two Types of Auctions

	Offer	Acceptance
With reserve	Each bid	Fall of the hammer following highest bid
Without reserve	Announcement that an item is up for auction	Each bid, subject to condition that no higher bid is made

by the offeror because it has now become part of a contract. Similarly, the offeree who has accepted the offer generally is not free to reject the offer subsequently. Neither party can reverse its original position. While contract law generally follows this interpretation, statutes in many states allow one of the contracting parties to cancel an acceptance (or to terminate an offer) in certain circumstances.

Typical of these statutes is Michigan's Home Solicitation Sales Act (M.C.L.A. 445.111 et. seq.). The law grants to the buyer of goods or services costing more than $25 who has made an offer or who has accepted an offer the right to revoke the offer or cancel the acceptance within three business days from the date of the transaction. The law applies only to a home solicitation sale made at the residence of the buyer and only the buyer, not the seller, is given the right to revoke the offer or cancel the acceptance. The law is intended to protect the consumer from high-pressured salespeople who force the consumer to act in a way he or she might not if given more time and less pressure. The three-day period is often referred to as a "cooling-off period" since the buyer has this time to reconsider the transaction.

REVIEW PROBLEMS

1. When can acceptance occur without some written or spoken manifestation?
2. What is the difference between a bilateral and a unilateral agreement?
3. To what extent must an acceptance match the terms of an offer under common law? Under the UCC?
4. When can silence act as acceptance of an offer?
5. What is the difference between an auction with reserve and an auction without reserve?
6. A seller offered equipment to a buyer at a specified price, stating that a 25 percent down payment was required with any order. The seller further required that the purchaser submit a signed order to be accepted by the seller. The buyer tele-

phoned the seller, stating that the offer was accepted, and asking that the seller commence delivery immediately. The seller responded, "We'll get on it immediately." Subsequently, the seller discovered an error in the price that was originally quoted. The buyer insists that a valid contract at the quoted price exists. Do you agree?

7. A purchaser, responded in writing by letter, asked a vendor to sell two railroad cars of steel products at $15 per ton. The vendor wrote back, "We can't sell at that price, but would accept a price on two cars at $17.50 per ton." The purchaser then responded in writing, "We will purchase from you two carloads at $17.50 per ton. Our inspector will inspect the shipment for parts to be accepted or rejected." The vendor replied, "We do not agree with inspection; we are not selling subject to inspection." Is there a contract? If so, does it include the right of inspection?

8. Just prior to his policy elapsing, the insured received a renewal notice from the insurer, stating that if the insured did not wish to renew, he must return the renewal notice or be liable for the renewal premium. The insured threw the notice in the trash, as he did with subsequent identical notices from the insurer. Will the insured be liable for the renewal premium?

9. A subcontractor made a contract with a general contractor that allowed the general contractor to use machines of the subcontractor for a specified time period while it was doing construction work on the landowner's property. When the time for the use of the subcontractor's machine expired, the subcontractor sent a bill to the landowner for rental due on the machine and an invoice stating the rental rate for the continued use of the machine. The landowner responded to the bill and informed the subcontractor that the equipment needs for future construction work on his property were being examined by the general contractor and that all future rental payments for the use of the subcontractor's machine would be the responsibility of the general contractor. The subcontractor's machines remained on the property of the landowner, but were not used by him or by the general contractor. Is there a contract between the landowner and the subcontractor for the rental of the subcontractor's machine? Crosby v. Paul Hardeman, Inc., 414 F2d 1 (8th Cir. 1969).

10. Westside and Hurble entered into an option agreement on April 5, 1963, wherein Hurble, for $50, was given a sixty-day option to purchase certain real estate. The option provided that the offer by Westside to sell the real estate at an agreed-upon price was irrevocable. On May 2, 1963, Hurble sent Westside a letter stating that Hurble exercised its option and also noting that "as additional inducement for Hurble to exercise its option, you have agreed that all utilities, gas, water, sewer, and electricity, will be extended to the property prior to the closing date. The contract of sale is hereby amended to provide that the seller shall extend all utility lines to the property before the closing date. Please sign this letter to indicate your acceptance of the amendment." On May 14, Hurble sent Westside another letter instructing it to disregard the proposed amendment in the letter of May 2 and that it now was exercising its option without amendment. Has Hurble accepted Westside's offer so as to create a contract? Hurble Oil & Refining Co. v. Westside Invest. Corp., 419 S.W. 2d 448 (Ct. Civ. App., Tex., 1967).

11. An antinuclear protest group, the Clamshell Alliance, sought permission to rent the National Guard armory in Portsmouth, New Hampshire, for the night of

April 29, 1978. In response to that request, the Adjutant General on March 31 mailed an offer to rent the armory and specified the terms that had to be met. The offer specified that a signed acceptance be returned to the office of the Adjutant General. Cushing, a member of the Alliance, received the offer on April 3; that same date, he signed the acceptance on behalf of the Alliance and placed the letter in the office's outbox. At 6:30 P.M. on April 4, Cushing received a telephone call from the Adjutant General revoking the offer. Cushing replied that he had already accepted the offer. The procedure followed in the Alliance office indicates that letters placed in the office outbox one day usually are put in the mailbox before 5:00 P.M. on the following day. The letter of acceptance sent by Cushing was received by the Adjutant General's office on April 6; the postmark on the letter was April 5. Was the acceptance effectively communicated before the offer was revoked? Cushing v. Thompson, 386 A.2d 805 (Sup. Ct. of N.H., 1978).

12. Farley solicited a bid from Clark whereby the latter agreed to fabricate one hundred trailers at a designated price. Farley considered other bids and decided to award the job to another firm. Farley prepared a check for the other firm and sent it by mistake to Clark. The check was for $18 less per unit than the offer. Clark deposited the check and began production. Farley sued to recover the proceeds of the check. What result? Farley v. Clark Equipment Co. 484 S.W.2d 142 (Ct. Civ. App. Tex., 1972).

13. Over a series of transactions occurring during a two-year period, the plaintiff, Carpet Mart, purchased a variety of carpeting from the defendant, Collins & Aikman. After checking that the terms agreed to in oral conversations were met, the defendant sent an acknowledgment form to the plaintiff for each of its orders. The following provision was printed on the acknowledgment form:

The acceptance of your order is subject to all of the terms and conditions on the face and reverse side hereof, including arbitration, all of which are accepted by buyer; it supersedes buyer's order form, if any. It shall become a contract either (a) when signed and delivered by buyer to seller and accepted in writing by seller, or (b) at seller's option, when buyer shall have given to seller specification of assortments, delivery dates, shipping instructions, . . . or instructions to bill and hold as to all or any part of the merchandise herein described, or when buyer has received delivery of the whole or any part thereof, or when buyer has otherwise assented to the terms and conditions hereof. . . .

Is the arbitration agreement appearing on the back of the acknowledgment form sent to the Carpet Mart by Collins & Aikman a part of the contract between them? Dorton v. Collins & Aikman Corp., 453 F.2d 1161 (6th Cir. 1972).

CHAPTER 12

Consideration

Know Well!

LEGAL DETRIMENT_____

BARGAINED EXCHANGE_____

PROMISSORY ESTOPPEL_____

No legal system enforces all promises. For example, a promise to undertake a social obligation—to come for dinner or to attend a wedding—would not be enforced by any court. The mere fact that one person promises something to another creates no legal duty and makes no remedy available if the person does not carry out the promise. The problem before the courts has been to determine which promises should be enforced and which should not.

The preceding chapters examined the requirements of a valid offer and acceptance as the essential elements of an agreement. Although agreement is essential to the formation of a contract, not all agreements are contracts. This chapter focuses on the additional element that is generally necessary if an agreement is to rise to the level of a contract. This element is the consideration.

Consideration is the exchange element of a contract. It is what induces the parties' agreement. It is what one party must give to another to make the other party legally obligated to perform its promise, the quid pro quo of the agreement. If there is no consideration there is no contract, and this is true even if there has been a valid offer and acceptance.

Consideration is the legal obligation that a person takes on. This person is a *promisee*. A promisee bargains with someone who makes a promise—the *promisor*. This bargained exchange is the consideration.

Society benefits from the fair enforcement of promises. A society that refused to enforce any promise would place people in risky positions. A promisor's word would be only as good as his or her reputation for performance. But no society can enforce all promises. Some promises are unreasonable or harmful. The existence of consideration is treated as evidence that the promisee's expectation is reasonable and that nonperformance would injure the community.

The concept of consideration can be illustrated by a simple example. John carelessly drives his car into David's. David's car is damaged and he has a right to sue John. John promises to pay David $500 and David promises that he will not sue over the car accident. The contract is supported by consideration. John has undertaken a new obligation—to pay David. David has given up a legal right—to sue John.

The following discussion examines two components of consideration: the legal detriment of the promisee and the bargained exchange for the promise.

LEGAL DETRIMENT

A person incurs *legal detriment* by voluntarily agreeing to assume a duty or to give up a right. A person must do or promise to do what he or she is not legally obligated to do, or the person must promise not to do what he or she has a right to do.

A *legal* detriment is not the same as real detriment or loss. In deciding whether someone has incurred a legal detriment, the courts do not focus on whether that person suffered economic or physical loss. The courts focus on whether the person agreed either to assume a *duty* or to relinquish a *right*. The following case illustrates the distinction between the two kinds of detriments.

Hamer v. Sidway

Court of Appeals of New York, Second Division
27 N.E. 256 (1891)

Background: In March 1869, William E. Story, Sr. promised his nephew, William E. Story, 2d, the sum of $5,000 if the nephew would refrain from drinking, smoking, swearing, and gambling until his twenty-first birthday. In January 1875, the nephew had reached his twenty-first birthday. Having satisfied all of the necessary conditions, he wrote to his uncle claiming the $5,000. The uncle replied that the nephew would get the money. But he asked to be allowed to hold it in the bank until he felt that the nephew was capable of taking care of it. In 1879, the nephew turned over his claim to the $5,000 to his wife. In turn, she turned it over to Hamer (plaintiff). When the uncle died, Hamer claimed the $5,000. But the executor of the estate, Sidway (defendant), denied the claim. The executor argued that the $5,000 was without consideration, because the nephew had benefited from the actions that were necessary to receive the reward. Hamer recovered at trial, but the judgment was reversed on appeal. Hamer then appealed to the Court of Appeals of New York, that state's highest court.

Decision: The Court of Appeals found in favor of Hamer, the plaintiff, and reversed the lower appellate court ruling and affirmed the judgment of the trial court.

Parker, Judge

The question which provoked the most discussion by counsel on this appeal, and which lies at the foundation of plaintiff's asserted right of recovery, is whether by virtue of a contract defendant's testator, William E. Story, became indebted to his nephew, William E. Story, 2d, on his twenty-first birthday in the sum of $5,000. The trial court found as a fact that "on the 20th day of March, 1869, . . . William E. Story agreed to and with William E. Story, 2d, that if he would refrain from drinking liquor, using tobacco, swearing and playing cards or billiards for money until he should become twenty-one years of age, then he, the said William E. Story, would at that time pay him, the said William E. Story, 2d, the sum of $5,000 for such refraining, to which the said William E. Story, 2d, agreed," and that he "in all things fully performed his part of said agreement." The defendant contends that the contract was without consideration to support it, and therefore invalid. He asserts that the promisee, by refraining from the use of liquor and tobacco, was not harmed, but benefited; that that which he did was best for him to do, independently of his uncle's promise—and insists that it follows that, unless the promisor was benefited, the contract was without consideration—a contention which, if well founded, would seem to leave open for controversy in many cases whether that which the promisee did or omitted to do was in fact of such benefit to him as to leave no consideration to support the enforcement of the promisor's agreement. Such a rule could not be tolerated, and is without foundation in the law. The exchequer chamber in 1875 defined "consideration" as follows: "A valuable consideration, in the sense of the law, may consist either in some right, interest, profit or benefit accruing to the one party, or some forbearance, detriment, loss, or responsibility given, suffered, or undertaken by the other." Courts "will not ask whether the thing which forms the consideration does in fact benefit the promisee or a third party, or is of any substantial value to any one. It is enough that something is promised, done, forborne, or suffered by the party to whom the promise is made as consideration for the promise made to him." Anson, Cont. 63. "In general a waiver of any legal right at the request of another party is a sufficient consideration for a promise." Pars. Cont. *444. "Any damage, or suspension, or forbearance of a right will be sufficient to sustain a promise." 2 Kent, Comm. (12th Ed.) *465. Pollock in his work on Contracts, (page 166) after citing the definition given by the exchequer chamber, already quoted, says: "The second branch of this judicial description is really the most important one. 'Consideration' means not so much that one party is profiting as that the other abandons some legal right to the present, or limits his legal freedom of action in the future, as an inducement for the promise of the first." Now, applying this rule to the facts before us, the promisee used tobacco, occasionally drank liquor, and he had a legal right to do so. That right he abandoned for a period of years upon the strength of the promise of the testator that for such forbearance he would give him $5,000. We need not speculate on the effort which may have been required to give up the use of those stimulants. It is sufficient that he restricted his lawful freedom of action within certain prescribed limits upon the faith of his uncle's agreement, and now, having fully performed the conditions imposed, it is of no moment whether such performance actually proved a benefit to the promisor, and the court will not inquire into it; but, were it a proper subject of inquiry, we see nothing in this record that would permit a determination that the uncle was not benefited in a legal sense.

Adequacy vs. Sufficiency of Consideration

When deciding whether a contract is supported by consideration, it is important to distinguish between the *adequacy* of the consideration and the *sufficiency* of the consideration. Although the semantic distinction between these terms is small, the legal distinction between them is significant. So watch your language!

The term *adequacy* refers to the quantity or value of the consideration. Courts do not generally inquire into the adequacy of the consideration; they are concerned only that there is a legally sufficient consideration, meaning that the promisee incurred a legal detriment in exchange for the promise. Thus, any legal detriment constitutes valuable consideration no matter how economically inadequate it may be.

For example, suppose that for $1 Penelope gave to Ring Telephone Company the right to install and maintain telephone wire over her land. Later Penelope finds out that other property owners have received much more money for giving the same rights to Ring. Penelope cannot later refuse to allow Ring on her land by arguing that she received an inadequate consideration for her promise to Ring. For Ring to obtain enforcement of Penelope's promise, Ring must show that Penelope received sufficient consideration for her promise. Ring would be able to obtain enforcement because, by paying $1 to Penelope, Ring relinquished the right it had to keep its money. Thus Ring incurred a legal detriment in exchange for Penelope's promise. A court would enforce her promise because the economic value of the consideration is not relevant in determining whether there is a valid consideration.

Courts do not inquire into the adequacy of consideration, because they should not be required to police the marketplace to protect people from their own imprudence. This policy of judicial self-restraint in dealing with economic matters is consistent with the common law notion that the courts do not make contracts for people. However, the rule assumes that the parties have freely entered into their agreement. Where this assumption is questioned, the courts *do* take into account the adequacy of consideration. If someone argues that a contract was made through fraud, misrepresentation, duress, undue influence, or mistake, a court will examine the adequacy of the consideration as evidence of the existence of those factors.

The only other circumstance in which a court examines the adequacy of consideration is in the equal exchange of interchangeable goods or the equal exchange of money. Goods that are *fungible* are indistinguishable and interchangeable. One carload of wheat cannot be distinguished from another; the carloads of wheat are thus fungible goods. Under the *fungible goods* doctrine, a contract calling for an exchange of equal amounts of wheat is not supported by consideration. Similarly, people who put a clause in their agreement that each has given the other $1 as consideration for the

agreement will find that they have no contract because there is no consideration.

Unlike adequacy of consideration, sufficiency of consideration is readily examined by the courts. If what was given in exchange for a promise is insufficient to constitute consideration, there is no contract. Consideration requires a legal detriment bargained for and given in exchange for a promise. When what is given is not a legal detriment, then it is not sufficient to constitute consideration, and there is no contract.

Illusory Promises

Any promise that leaves it up to the promisor whether to perform is *illusory*. A person who promises to do something "if I feel like it" has not promised anything at all and has incurred no legal detriment. Even though people use promissory language, if the person making the promise is not required to do anything, the promise is illusory. An illusory promise is not sufficient consideration because nothing has been promised.

Although the rule that an illusory promise cannot serve as sufficient consideration is logical, the result of such a rule can be harsh. Two categories of promises illustrate this problem: cancellation or termination clauses and output/requirements contracts. We turn to those now.

Cancellation or Termination Clauses. Contracts often let one or both parties cancel obligations under certain circumstances. Suppose that two enter into a contract in which one promises to buy and the other promises to sell 500 widgets a month. The buyer has the right to cancel "at any time without notice." That clause means that there is no contract. Lack of consideration makes the buyer's promise illusory. Because the buyer has the right to terminate the agreement at will and is not required to perform, the buyer has not actually assumed a duty to buy. If a cancellation clause allows a party to avoid an obligation at will, the contract is voidable. A contract that is voidable at the will of one of the parties is illusory.

However, the situation is different if the buyer is required to notify the seller that he or she is terminating the contract. Most courts hold that with a termination clause requiring notice ahead of time, the promisor incurs a legal detriment.

Additionally, many courts have held that when a termination clause contains no notice requirement, the requirement of a reasonable notice of termination is assumed. This assumption is made when it is clear that both parties intended to enter into a binding contract. This approach seeks to preserve the intent of the parties and reflects legislative and judicial reluctance to strike down an otherwise valid agreement on a technicality.

Output/Requirements Contracts. An *output contract* is an agreement to sell one's entire production of goods to a purchaser. A *requirements contract* is an agreement to purchase all one's requirements for a given product from the seller. Such contracts are useful, especially for new businesses. However, many courts once held that such agreements are illusory because they provide no specifications of how much of the product is to be sold or bought. The seller might choose not to produce all of the product that it is capable of producing, and the buyer might choose not to buy the product.

The UCC (Section 2-306) has legitimized output/requirements contracts by providing standards required for enforcement. It imposes an obligation to act in good faith on the party who determines the quantity. This good-faith obligation constitutes a sufficient consideration for any output or requirements contract.

The illusory promise problem is illustrated in the following case. Determine whether the court made the best decision in terms of both the law and business ethics. The decision predates the UCC.

Streich v. General Motors Corporation

Appellate Court of Illinois
126 N.E.2d 389 (1955)

Background: Frank Streich (plaintiff) alleged that General Motors (defendant) had entered into a contract with him to buy all of its requirements for air magnet valves between September 1948 and August 31, 1949. Streich claimed that he had originally been led to believe that 1,600 or more valves would be needed and therefore that he had spent a great deal of money, time, and effort gathering the materials needed for production of the valves. General Motors contended that it did not promise to buy 1,600 valves in its purchase order. Streich sued General Motors. The trial court ruled in favor of General Motors and dismissed the suit. Streich appealed to the Appellate Court of Illinois.

Decision: The Appellate Court affirmed the trial court decision in favor of General Motors.

McCormick, Presiding Justice

It is the contention of the plaintiff, Frank Streich, hereafter referred to as "seller," that the defendant, General Motors Corporation, hereafter referred to as the "buyer," had entered into a binding contract to purchase all the requirements of the buyer from September 1, 1948 through August 31, 1949 from the seller, and that, while the amount of the requirements was not specified, parol evidence might be properly introduced to show what the requirements were.

In order to determine whether or not the seller stated a cause of action in his complaint it is necessary to analyze the agreements between the parties.

There is no question but that under the law a contract properly entered into whereby the buyer agrees to buy all its requirements of a commodity for a certain period, and the seller agrees to sell the same as ordered, is a valid and enforceable contract and is not void for uncertainty and want of mutuality. The contract in the instant case is not such a contract. Reading and construing the two documents together, notwithstanding the detailed provisions contained on the reverse side of the purchase order, the result is an agreement on the part of the seller to sell a certain identified valve at a certain fixed price in such quantities as the buyer may designate, when and if it issues a purchase order for the same.

Here, the buyer proffers purchase order 11925, with its twenty-five or more clauses, to the seller for acceptance. In the instrument it makes no promise to do anything. On the surface it appears to be an attempt to initiate a valid bilateral contract. The seller accepts, and as by a flash of legerdemain the positions of the buyer and the seller shift. The buyer now becomes the promisee and the seller the promisor. The promise of the seller to furnish identified items at a stated price is merely an offer and cannot become a contract until the buyer issues a release or order for a designated number of items. Until this action is taken the buyer has made no promise to do anything, and either party may withdraw. The promise is illusory, and the chimerical contract vanishes. "An agreement to sell to another such of the seller's goods, wares, and merchandise as the other might from time to time desire to purchase is lacking in mutuality because it does not bind the buyer to purchase any of the goods of the seller, as such matter is left wholly at the option or pleasure of the buyer."

In Higbie v. Rust, . . . , the court says:

> Where there is no consideration for the promise of one party to furnish or sell so much of the commodity as the other may want, except the promise of the other to take and pay for so much of the commodity as he may want, and there is no agreement that he shall want any quantity whatever, and no method exists by which it can be determined whether he will want any of the commodity or, what quantity he will want, the contract is void for lack of mutuality.

In the instant case, when the seller accepted purchase order No. 11925, no contract came into being.

The agreement in question is an adaptation of what was termed an "open end contract," which was used extensively by the federal government during the late war. However, it was used only in cases where the commodities dealt with were staples and either in the possession of or easily accessible to the seller. In this case the use of the contract is shifted and extended to cover commodities which must be manufactured before they are available for sale. According to the admitted statements in the complaint, special tools had to be manufactured in order to produce the item herein involved. The seller here, misled by the many and detailed provisions contained in purchase order No. 11925 and ordinarily applicable to an enforceable bilateral contract, undoubtedly, as he alleged in his complaint, did go to considerable expense in providing tools and machines, only to find that by the accepted agreement the buyer had promised to do absolutely nothing. A statement of expectation creates no duty. Courts are not clothed with the power to make contracts for parties, nor can they, under the guise of interpretation, supply provisions actually lacking or impose obligations not actually assumed.

The agreement contained in purchase order No. 11925 was artfully prepared. It contains, in print so fine as to be scarcely legible, more than twenty-three clauses, most of which are applicable to bilateral contracts. It has all the indicia of a binding and enforceable contract, but it was not a binding and enforceable contract because the promise was defective. Behind the glittering facade is a void. This agreement was made in the higher echelons of business, overshadowed by the aura of business ethics. To say the least, the agreement was deceptive. In a more subterranean atmosphere and between persons of lower ethical standards it might, without any strain on the language, be denominated by a less deterged appellation.

Nevertheless, as the law is today, on the pleadings in the instant case, the trial court could do nothing but sustain the motion to dismiss the complaint. *why uphold?*

The Preexisting Duty Rule

When people promise to do something that they are already obligated to do, they have not incurred a legal detriment. This is known as the *preexisting duty rule.*

For example, people cannot promise not to commit crimes in return for payment because they have a preexisting duty not to commit crimes or torts. Thus, some preexisting duties are created by law. Similarly, public officials cannot collect rewards for performing their duty. If a shopkeeper offers a $5,000 reward for the arrest and conviction of the person who burglarized his or her store, the police officer who diligently pursues and jails the offender may not collect that reward. The officer is already required by law to catch criminals and therefore has incurred no new legal detriment that would entitle him or her to enforcement of the promise of reward.

A preexisting duty also may be created by contract. When the promise of one party is merely a repetition of an existing promise and no additional duties are imposed, the promise does not constitute consideration. For example, suppose that Penelope hires Julius to repair her garage door. Julius and Penelope agree that the price of the repair will be $150. However, after starting work, Julius reconsiders his costs and asks Penelope to pay him $200. She agrees. Upon completion of the repair, Julius is entitled to only $150. Because Julius was already under contract to repair Penelope's door for $150, he has incurred no legal detriment in exchange for her promise to pay $50 more. Julius has merely agreed to finish the repair, which he was under a contractual duty to do already.

The preexisting duty rule is often criticized as illogical. In the preceding example, Penelope appears able to avoid the enforcement of her promise. But the reason for the rule is the concern that enforcement of the second promise would encourage coercion. In most of the cases where the preexisting duty rule is invoked, the second bargain was coerced. For example, a contractor might threaten a homeowner that unless she pays an extra $150, he will leave her roof half fixed. Where the facts do not show coercion, the courts have stretched doctrine to reach a more desired result.

For example, if in consideration for Penelope's promise to pay $50 more, Julius had agreed to do something, however slight, that was not called for in the original contract, Julius would have incurred a legal detriment. The addition of a new duty in exchange for Penelope's promise makes the promise enforceable.

Another device for getting around the preexisting duty rule is for the parties to agree to rescind their old contract and make a new one. Contracts may be canceled and new ones made when the people involved mutually consent to the cancellation of the contracts. Furthermore, the cancellation itself is a contract and must be supported by consideration. In this case, the consideration usually takes the form of the parties' agreement to release each other from their obligations. When people rescind their earlier agreement and enter into a new one, there are actually three contracts: the original contract, the rescission contract, and the new contract.

Some courts recognize an exception to the preexisting duty rule in cases where the second promise results from substantial *unforeseen difficulties* in performance. For example, if a contractor agreed to build a house and a tornado destroyed the half-built house, some courts would hold that an owner's subsequent promise to pay the contractor more is binding, even though the contractor has not agreed to do anything more than was called for by the original contract. The suspicion of coercion by the contractor is not present, the owner might be criticized for promising to pay more to induce the contractor to continue but later disavowing the promise.

The following case illustrates some of the issues in the preexisting duty rule.

Levine v. Blumenthal

Supreme Court of New Jersey

186 A. 457 (1936)

Background: On April 16, 1931, William Levine (respondent) agreed to lease a business site to Anne Blumenthal (appellant). Rent for the first year was to be $2,100, payable in monthly installments of $175 in advance. The second year the rent was scheduled to increase to $2,400, payable in monthly installments of $200. In April 1932, approximately one year into the lease term, Blumenthal told Levine that, due to adverse business conditions generally resulting from the Great Depression, she would be unable to pay the increased rent of $200. She asserted that if Levine insisted on the extra $25 a month, she would have to leave the building and perhaps go out of business altogether. Blumenthal claimed that Levine agreed not to demand the extra $25 a month until business improved. Levine claimed that he agreed to accept the reduced rent "on account." Blumenthal paid rent of $175 for eleven months of the second year of the lease and then vacated the premises. Levine sued to recover the unpaid rent for the last month of the lease and the unpaid balance of $25 per month for the preceding eleven months. The trial court ruled in favor of Levine, and Blumenthal appealed the judgment.

Decision: The Supreme Court of New Jersey affirmed the trial court judgment in favor of Levine.

Heher, Justice

The district court judge found, as a fact, that "a subsequent oral agreement had been made to change and alter the terms of the written lease, with respect to the rent paid," but that it was not supported by "a lawful consideration," and therefore was wholly ineffective.

The insistence is that the current trade depression had disabled the lessees in respect to the payment of the full rent reserved, and a full consideration sufficient to support the secondary agreement arose out of these special circumstances; and that, in any event, the execution of the substituted performance therein provided is a defense of law, notwithstanding the want of consideration. It is said also that, "insofar as the oral agreement has become executed as to the payments which had fallen due and had been paid and accepted in full as per the oral agreement" the remission of the balance of the rent is sustainable on the theory of gift, if not of accord and satisfaction.

The point made by respondent is that the subsequent oral agreement to reduce the rent . . . created no binding obligation.

It is elementary that the subsequent agreement, to impose the obligation of a contract, must rest upon a new and independent consideration. The rule was laid down in very early times that even though a part of a matured liquidated debt or demand has been given and received in full satisfaction thereof, the creditor may yet recover the remainder. The payment of a part was not regarded in law as a satisfaction of the whole, unless it was in virtue of an agreement supported by a consideration. The principle is firmly imbedded in our jurisprudence that a promise to do what the promisor is already legally bound to do is an unreal consideration. It has been criticized, at least in some of its special applications, as "medieval" and wholly artificial—one that operates to defeat the "reasonable bargains of businessmen." But these strictures are not well grounded. They reject the basic principle that a consideration, to support a contract, consists either of a benefit to the promisor or a detriment to the promisee—a doctrine that has always been fundamental in our conception of consideration. It is a principle, almost universally accepted, that an act or forbearance required by a legal duty owing to the promisor that is neither doubtful nor the subject of honest and reasonable dispute is not a sufficient consideration.

Yet any consideration for the new undertaking, however insignificant, satisfies this rule. . . . For instance, an undertaking to pay part of the debt before maturity, or at a place other than where the obligor was legally bound to pay, or to pay in property, regardless of its value, or to effect a composition with creditors by the payment of less than the sum due, has been held to constitute a consideration sufficient in law. The test is whether there is an additional consideration adequate to support an ordinary contract, and consists of something which the debtor was not legally bound to do or give.

And there is authority for the view that, where there is no illegal preference, a payment of part of a debt, "accompanied by an agreement of the debtor to refrain from voluntary bankruptcy," is a sufficient consideration for the creditor's promise to remit the balance of the debt. But the mere fact that the creditor "fears that the debtor will go into bankruptcy, and that the debtor contemplates bankruptcy proceedings," is not enough; that alone does not prove that the creditor requested the debtor to refrain from such proceedings.

The cases to the contrary either create arbitrary exceptions to the rule, or profess to find a consideration in the form of a new undertaking which in essence was not a tangible new obligation or a duty not imposed by the lease, or, in any event, was not the price "bargained for as the exchnge for the promise," and therefore do violence to the fundamental principle. They exhibit the modern tendency, especially in the matter of rent reductions, to depart from the strictness of the basic common-law rule and give effect to what has been termed a "reasonable" modification of the primary contract.

So tested, the secondary agreement at issue is not supported by a valid consideration; and it therefore created no legal obligation. General economic adversity, however disastrous it may be in its individual consequences, is never a warrant for judicial abrogation of this primary principle of the law of contracts.

It remains to consider the second contention that, in so far as the agreement has been executed by the payment and acceptance of rent at the reduced rate, the substituted performance stands, regardless of the want of consideration. This is likewise untenable. Ordinarily, the actual performance of that which one is legally bound to do stands on the same footing as his promise to do that which he is legally compellable to do. This is a corollary of the basic principle. Of course, a different rule prevails where bona fide disputes have arisen respecting the relative rights and duties of the parties to a contract, or the debt or demand is unliquidated, or the contract is wholly executory on both sides.

It is settled in this jurisdiction that, as in the case of other contracts, a consideration is essential to the validity of an accord and satisfaction. On reason and principle, it could not be otherwise. This is the general rule. The cases cited by appellant are not in point. It results that the issue was correctly determined.

The drafters of the UCC cut through the maze of the common law and established a different rule for goods transactions. The UCC (Section 2-209) states simply: "An agreement modifying a contract within this Article needs no consideration to be binding." For example, suppose that a supplier agrees to deliver goods at $1 a unit. Later, due to market conditions, the supplier calls the buyer and asks if the buyer will agree to pay $2 a unit for the same goods. Under the preexisting duty rule, the buyer's promise to pay the higher price would not be enforceable for lack of consideration. However, under the UCC, if the buyer agrees to pay the higher price, the promise is enforceable. Note that the buyer still has to *agree* to pay the higher price. The buyer can refuse to accept the price change and hold the supplier to the original contract or recover for its breach. Once they have agreed to the modification, they cannot later disavow their promise.

Compromise of Debts. The preexisting duty rule also comes into play in agreements between debtors and creditors to compromise on payments of debts. The delinquent debtor is a perennial problem for creditors. On the theory that a bird in the hand is worth two in the bush, creditors often accept less than the amount owed on the debt. But sometimes such arrangements are not enforceable for lack of consideration. If a creditor later seeks to recover full payment on the original debt, a debtor may not be able to enforce the creditor's promise to accept only partial payment. If the creditor's promise is not supported by consideration, because the debtor has not incurred any new legal detriment, the debtor may not be able to enforce the promise.

For example, suppose that a student owes State College $1,000. State College agrees to accept $300 as full payment. State College's promise to release the student from all claims is not supported by consideration. Because the student is already under a duty to pay $300, plus an additional $700, the student has not incurred any additional legal detriment.

However, to avoid causing people severe hardship or discouraging honesty and fair dealing, the courts have tried to find new consideration of some kind to support such compromises. Thus, when a debtor gives partial payment on a loan before the loan is due, or when a debtor gives a combination of money and property as satisfaction of the debt, courts may hold that the new consideration supports a modification of the original contract.

Under bankruptcy laws, once someone is declared bankrupt, the person is no longer required to pay his or her creditors. The debts are discharged by court order. But in some circumstances, it is advantageous to the bankrupt debtor to reaffirm some old debts and keep paying them. The courts usually hold that the consideration is the refusal of the debtor to use the defense of bankruptcy to avoid the creditor. Debtor and creditor then are free to reach a settlement in which the debtor satisfies the debt with only partial payment.

A slight variation of this device involves what are called *composition agreements.* These are used when debtors are in financial difficulties and fear being unable to pay their creditors in full. To avoid bankruptcy, one creditor may call other creditors to convince them to accept less than what is owed. The expenses of declaring bankruptcy and the likelihood that some creditors may wind up with nothing sometimes are enough incentive for creditors to consent to such an agreement. For example, if Julius thinks that he can pay 40 percent of his total debts, he may seek to enter into a composition agreement with his creditors. In such a case, each creditor may agree to accept 40 percent of the amount due from Julius.

The consideration in such agreements is the promises of the creditors to forgo part of their claims, the debtor's payment to the assenting creditors in equal proportions, the debtor's securing the assent of the creditors, or the part payment made to other creditors. Courts want to encourage these agreements between creditors and debtors, because they discourage litigation.

Accord and Satisfaction. When a legitimate dispute exists about the existence or size of a debt, the preexisting duty rule gives way to the doctrine of *accord and satisfaction.*

An accord and satisfaction is the offer of something different from what was provided for in the original contract (the accord) and an agreement to accept it (the satisfaction). Partial payment of an unliquidated debt, offered as full satisfaction of the obligation, is supported by consideration and discharges the obligation.

For example, suppose that Julius hires Penelope, a marketing consultant, to advise him about where to locate his business. Penelope performs the service and delivers a bill for $10,000. Julius believes that her fee is much too high for the services rendered. He maintains that a more reasonable fee would be $3,000. Together they settle their dispute by agreeing on a fee of $4,000. Here, the debt is in dispute; the amount owed is uncertain; the

---

PREVENTIVE LAW
Accord and Satisfaction

T he precise mechanics of an accord and satisfaction vary among the states. The most common approach requires, as the first step, that the debtor notify the creditor of the disputed claim. Then, assuming that the debt is acknowledged but the amount is disputed, the debtor may write a check for the amount the debtor believes is due, indicate on the check itself that it is being tendered as payment in full, and then send it to the creditor along with a note indicating that the amount of liability is disputed. Once the creditor receives the check, the creditor has three options: (1) to cash the check, in which case the creditor accepts the debtor's offer of settlement and the debt is discharged; (2) to return the check, refusing the debtor's offer, and proceed as the creditor would in any collection case; or (3) to cash the check in defiance of the conditions upon which it was tendered, but only after first notifying the debtor that acceptance of the check is under protest. This last option is expressly allowed by Section 1-207 of the UCC. It should be noted that the accord-and-satisfaction doctrine applies only when there is a good-faith dispute. A bad-faith dispute will result in the debt being classified as a liquidated claim, in which case the preexisting duty rule would apply and the debt would not be discharged by the attempted settlement.

---

debt is unliquidated. By agreeing to pay $4,000, Julius is assuming a duty to pay $1,000 more than he in good faith believes is owed. By agreeing to take $4,000, Penelope is relinquishing her right to collect $6,000 more, which she in good faith believes is owed her. Each party has incurred a legal detriment in exchange for the other's promise. Their agreement is supported by consideration.

Forbearance to Pursue a Legal Right. If people bargain, and one side agrees to give up a legal right, that surrender is adequate consideration to support a contract. This situation arises most frequently in insurance cases, when an insurance company promises to pay an agreed upon settlement amount in return for a claimant's promise not to file suit to recover for the alleged injury. If the insurance company refuses to make the payment after it

has agreed to do so, the claimant is no longer bound by the contract and may file suit. However, the claimant may choose instead to file suit against the insurance company for breach of contract, seeking the promised settlement and any other damages.

The law in this area becomes muddied when the insurance company responds that the claimant did not have a valid claim from the outset. Because one cannot surrender what one does not have a right to in the first place, the insurance company argues that in surrendering or not asserting an invalid claim, the claimant has suffered no legal detriment and therefore any promise of settlement made in return by the insurance company is not supported by consideration.

Courts have generally not accepted this argument. Many courts have held that if the claim was made in good faith and a reasonable person could believe that the claim was well founded, surrender or forbearance would provide sufficient consideration. Other courts have held that good faith alone is sufficient. Still other courts have accepted claims when there is objective uncertainty as to the validity of the claim. The trend appears to be that if the claim is neither patently ridiculous nor corruptly asserted, then the court will view surrender or forbearance as adequate consideration.

This area of law resembles the doctrine of accord and satisfaction. Agreeing not to pursue a legal claim constitutes a legal detriment, because a person is relinquishing a right to bring suit. The requirement that the claimant believe in good faith that the claim is valid is similar to the requirement of a good-faith dispute for an accord and satisfaction.

BARGAINED EXCHANGE

A person who receives a promise can incur all kinds of legal detriment, and even much real detriment for good measure, but it will not serve as sufficient consideration unless it is the bargained exchange for the promisor's promise.

Bargain

The requirement that the parties bargain is not so much a requirement that they actually sit down and dicker over the consideration as it is a requirement that the consideration be something that the promisor requested in return for being bound by the promise. An example of an unbargained for promise is a promise to make a gift. Sometimes a person attaches conditions to making a gift, things that the promisee must do to accept the gift. For example, Jennifer promises to give her tape collection to her sister, Shannon, if Shannon will come over to pick up the tapes. Jennifer is not bargaining for Shannon to come

over, and there is no consideration for the promise to give the tapes. The critical factor in distinguishing a promise to make a gift on condition from a promise that is supported by consideration is the motive of the promisor.

Another example of a promise that is not supported by a bargained-for consideration is a promise to do something because of something the promisee has done in the past. *Past consideration* is no consideration because it was not bargained for in exchange for the promisor's promise. Past consideration cannot be used to support a new promise, because the legal detriment was neither bargained for nor given in exchange for the promise. Because every new contract requires new considerations, past consideration cannot be used to create an enforceable obligation.

The reasoning of the courts in refusing to enforce promises based upon past consideration stems not so much from a lack of legal detriment as from a lack of bargained exchange. The present promise is induced by a past consideration; the past consideration was not given in exchange for the present promise.

Likewise, a promise by one party made to another that is based on only a moral duty generally does not constitute consideration. Technically speaking, if the promisor has received a material benefit that prompts the making of a promise, there is no consideration. For example, if A pulls B from a burning building, saving B's life, and a week later B promises to give A $5,000 "in consideration for saving my life," B's promise is not enforceable because A's conduct was not induced by B's promise.

Exchange

Two parties may sign a written agreement in which one party agrees to do something in exchange for the other party's promise to pay a sum. For example, one person may promise something in exchange for "$1 in hand paid, receipt of which is acknowledged." The dollar is what is bargained for and given over in exchange for the promise.

If the stated consideration is a pretense, there is no consideration. If the stated consideration is not actually exchanged, there is no consideration. Just saying that they have agreed to a price of $1 does not constitute consideration. If the consideration is nominal, perhaps $1 in exchange for a valuable promise, courts examine whether that $1 was bargained for and given in exchange for the promise. The dollar must be both bargained for and actually exchanged for the promise to be supported by sufficient consideration. In some courts, an untrue *recital of consideration* operates as an implied promise to pay the recited sum and that this implied promise satisfies the consideration requirement.

PROMISSORY ESTOPPEL

The requirement that a contract be supported by consideration is part of classic contract law. However, many courts have criticized the results of this requirement. Legislative dissatisfaction with the doctrine has been expressed in the UCC. The courts have established a substitute for consideration, the doctrine of *promissory estoppel*.

The doctrine permits a remedy based on reliance upon a promise. Under this theory, someone who makes a promise is "estopped" (meaning "made to stop") from denying the existence of the promise in cases where the promisee has justifiably relied upon the promise and has suffered harm. Thus, a promise that induces detrimental reliance upon the part of the promisee may be sufficient to bind the promisor, even though the detriment was not bargained for and given in exchange for the promise, so long as the promisor had reason to expect some act of reliance by the promisee.

Four elements must be established by the promisee. These elements are:

1. A promise. Not just any promise will do. The promise must be the type of promise that the promisor should reasonably expect the promisee will rely upon. The promise must generally be expressed. However, silence may constitute an implied promise where the promisor is under a duty to speak.
2. The promisee must in fact rely upon the promise. The reliance must be justifiable.
3. Substantial economic detriment to the promisee is necessary.
4. Injustice can be avoided only by the enforcement of the promise.

For example, consider the case of an employer who promises to pay an employee an annuity for the rest of the employee's life. The employee resigns from a profitable job, as the employer expected the employee would. The employee receives the annuity for several years. In the meantime, the employee becomes disqualified from working. The employer's promise would be enforced under the doctrine of promissory estoppel. Now suppose that the employee had been able to work. In that event, third and fourth elements of promissory estoppel would not be met. The following case illustrates the application of promissory estoppel.

Allen M. Campbell Co. v. Virginia Metal Industries, Inc.

U.S. Court of Appeals, Fourth Circuit
708 F.2d 930 (1983)

Background: Allen M. Campbell Co. (plaintiff), in August 1981, intended to bid on a Department of Navy contract to construct housing for enlisted personnel at Camp

LeJeune, North Carolina. The deadline for submission of bids was 2:00 P.M. on August 11, 1981. At about 1:30 P.M., Virginia Metal Industries, Inc. (defendant), telephoned Campbell and quoted a price to supply all hollow metal doors and frames required by the plans and specifications. The price quoted was $193,121, plus applicable taxes. Campbell based the computation for its bid for the Navy project upon the quoted price for the hollow metal doors and frames of $193,121 and taxes. Campbell was the successful bidder and was awarded the Navy contract. Virginia Metal backed out of its promise, and as a consequence, Campbell had to obtain the items covered by the quoted price of $193,121 from another supplier, at a cost $45,562 greater than what it had been led to expect Virginia Metal would charge. Campbell sued Virginia Metal Industries, Inc. for the $45,562. The trial court dismissed Campbell's complaint, and Campbell appealed to the Fourth Circuit Court of Appeals.

Decision: Ruling for Campbell, the Fourth Circuit Court of Appeals reversed the trial court decision and sent the case back to the trial court for trial.

Murnaghan, Circuit Judge

In carrying out the functions of a judge, one comes to realize that there are very few cases indeed in which ultimately the facts do not control the outcome. Arguments impeccable in their abstract reliance upon broadly phrased principles of law tend to evaporate when the equities point to a different result. Purely linguistic considerations should not be permitted to outweigh substance.

Virginia Metal's rejoinder to Campbell's suit for the difference of $45,562 is that there had been no promise by Campbell that, should it prove the successful bidder for the Navy contract, it would purchase doors and frames from Virginia Metal. Absent the consideration that such an undertaking would have provided, the argument runs, there was no contract, Campbell was legally free to shop around and purchase from someone other than Virginia Metal, and hence there existed no obligation on Virginia Metal's part to abide by the promise to sell for $193,121 plus taxes.

As a consequence of the gigantic achievements in the field of contracts law by Samuel Williston and others, we have on rare occasions to confront situations posing some difficulty because they do not fit precisely into the patterned concepts laid down and accumulated by Williston and his followers. Nothing, not even the law of contracts, however, is altogether perfect.

We are not the first court to encounter the situation where there has been a promise unsupported by consideration which has occasioned reliance and change of position so that the promisor who backs away from his undertaking visits a real hardship on the promisee. An absence of consideration in such cases should not permit an unjust result. Rather, the law has developed the concept of promissory estoppel which allows recovery even in the absence of consideration where reliance and change of position to the detriment of the promisee make it unconscionable not to enforce the promise or to award damages for its breach.

As the case was argued to us, a great deal of attention was devoted to whether or not the doctrine of promissory estoppel applies in North Carolina. Both parties proceeded on the assumption that there was no direct authority one way or the other. However, the recent North Carolina case of *Wachovia Bank & Trust Company, N.A.* v. *Rubish* addressed the question and explicitly held that the law of North Carolina includes, and where appropriate applies, the doctrine of promissory estoppel. [T]he court stated:

> In order to prove a waiver by estoppel [a promiseee]. . . . need only prove an express or implied promise . . . and [his] detrimental reliance on that promise.

At the present stage of the case, action in reliance on the promise to sell doors and frames for $193,121 plus taxes cannot be disputed. It was alleged in the amended complaint: "Plaintiff submitted its bid for the entire project to the Government in reliance upon Defendant's quoted price for the hollow metal doors and frames."

In the case as pleaded by Campbell, the elements of a promissory estoppel are clearly present. Under the well-pleaded allegations of fact, even in the absence of consideration, there was a sufficiently binding promise by Virginia Metal.

ETHICS BOX
Policy and Ethical Considerations in Enforcing Promises

Knee deep into the study of contract law as we are, it is easy for the reader to see contract law as a web of rules to be mastered for the next exam. However, as abstract and mysterious as the material in this chapter is, it brings us face to face with the policy tensions at odds in this area of law. If you have thought of contract law as just so much doctrine, this chapter, when viewed critically, forces you to face some basic questions about contract law and policy.

The basic question that contract law seeks to answer is: When should a promise be enforced? For example, which of the following promises do you think should be enforced?

- A promise to come to dinner
- A promise by your uncle to leave you $5,000 in his will
- A promise by your uncle to leave you $5,000 in his will if you promise to take care of him in his old age
- A promise by a customer to order as much of your merchandise as the customer "chooses to order"
- A promise by your landlord to reduce your rent so long as you remain in your apartment, as you previously promised, under the existing lease.
- A seller's quoted price for supplies that you have used to compute a bid for a government contract.

The text and cases in this chapter have provided you with the answers. All but the last question can be answered by that mysterious doctrine called "consideration." In short, the doctrine represents the "bargain theory" of contracts. This may be expressed in the phrases "a deal is a deal" or "you get what you pay for." The bargain theory holds that, to be binding, a promise must be part of an exchange, a bargain.

The doctrine of consideration limits the promises that courts will enforce. Many reasons have been offered to explain the rule. One is that courts should not be bothered except to enforce socially significant promises, and the existence of a bargain shows that each party has something important at stake. Another reason is the suggestion that courts should protect only the reasonable expectations of promisees (otherwise they might do something unreasonable—like use physical force against the reluctant promisor). The required bargained-for consideration shows that the promisee's expectation of an enforceable promise is a reasonable one.

As can be seen by the judge's remarks in the *Campbell* case, the doctrine of consideration has its critics. In certain cases where the facts cry out for the enforcement of a promise, the doctrine denies enforcement because the promise was not part of a bargain. The *Campbell* court applied the doctrine of promissory estoppel to skirt the requirement of consideration. This is known as the "reliance theory." It holds that promises should be enforced when they result in detrimental reliance. It does not require a bargain.

Anyone who has ever failed to keep a promise to a small child has confronted the logic behind the theory of moral obligation. The child who screams, "But you promised!" expresses the moral outrage of promisees of all ages who confront the fact of an unkept promise. The theory of moral obligation would permit courts to enforce certain promises where it is morally imperative to do so. Under this view, a court would enforce a promise of payment to a good Samaritan by one who was materially benefited by the Samaritan. The moral obligation theory views a contract not as an obligation arising from a bargain, but as a moral obligation. A justification for this theory is that it is normally thought that morality is the arbiter of law, that the law can be justified only if it conforms to morality. However, the advocates of this theory could probably all fit into a phone booth.

Dissatisfaction with the doctrine of consideration has led to its demise in certain areas. Thus, the UCC does not require it to enforce firm offers or to modify a goods transaction. Some courts have resorted to promissory estoppel to circumvent the harshness of its rule. And a very few cases can be explained only on the basis of a moral obligation.

So, what is your opinion on the enforcement of promises? Should only market transactions be enforced? Should an unbound promisee's reliance be protected? Do you agree with the view that promises are moral commitments? If you do, does that mean that *all* promises should be kept as a matter of morality? If not, which ones should be enforced, and which should not? This brings us back to the basic queston that contract law seeks to answer: When should a promise be enforced?

REVIEW PROBLEMS

1. Explain the difference between adequacy and sufficiency of consideration.
2. List three types of situations in which the preexisting duty rule creates legal difficulties.
3. Briefly explain the two basic components of consideration.
4. Explain the doctrine of promissory estoppel.
5. Gill had performed plumbing work for Black Canyon Construction but had not been paid fully. In October 1971, the stockholders of Black Canyon sold the company and agreed to assume various liabilities that the company then had. Gill sued the stockholders in March 1972 for his accumulated debt, but he agreed to dismiss his suit in return for continued work and total payment due. Gill completed the new work and soon found himself back in court trying to collect his money. The court ruled that he was not a beneficiary of the October sale and could not collect for work done prior to then. Could he enforce the rest of the later agreement?
6. Carmichael, a shore store owner, owed International Shoe Company $5,318.92 for shoes sold to him. When his debt had earlier been $12,272.51, Carmichael had agreed to pay International Shoe $8,000 immediately and the balance at $50 a week in return for receipt on account of an additional $2,000 worth of shoes. Carmichael was making payment according to this schedule when suddenly International Shoe Company brought suit for the balance of money owed. Result?
7. Polinger pledged $200,000 to the United Jewish Appeal (UJA), a nonprofit group that raises funds for various charities. He died shortly afterward, leaving an unpaid balance of $133,500. The UJA sued to recover the unpaid balance from Polinger's estate. UJA used Polinger's announcement of his pledge to induce others to pledge large amounts, although the effect of Polinger's pledge on the decisions of other solicited contributors was not known. What additional information would you require to determine whether the UJA should recover, and how should this information affect the outcome?
8. Plaintiffs each had put down a $1,000 deposit toward the purchase of condominium units. Each receipt contained an agreement providing that the deposit was to insure the buyer the "first option" to purchase a specified unit at a specified price, and if the sales contract eventually drawn up by the seller proved unacceptable to the buyer, the deposit would be refunded with interest. The seller later notified each buyer that the units would be priced 16 percent above the agreed upon price. Plaintiffs sued for breach of contract. Were the contracts to give the buyers the option of buying their units at the original price that was supported by sufficient consideration?
9. Buyer signed an order for the purchase of three sprinklers to be installed before May 1, 1974. The sprinklers were to be paid for upon delivery. The agreement permitted the buyer to cancel by notifying the seller thirty days before the delivery date. Seller delivered only two of the three sprinklers. Buyer paid for them and sued for breach of contract for failure to deliver the third. Seller argued that buyer's option to cancel the order rendered buyer's promise to pay for the sprinklers illusory and that there was thus no consideration for the seller's promise to deliver the sprinklers. What was the result and why?
10. The Boston Redevelopment Authority (BRA) took over the buildings owned and operated by the Graphic Arts Finish Com-

pany. Graphic's president agreed with BRA that Graphic would receive its "total certified actual moving expenses" from BRA in return for leaving the premises peacefully and quickly and relocating elsewhere. Graphic alleges it performed these promises and demands the $54,069.11 still owed by BRA for moving expenses. Result? Graphic Arts Finish, Inc. v. Boston Redevelopment Authority, 225 N.E.2d 793 (Mass. 1970).

11. While Hurley worked for Marine Contractors, he accumulated $12,000 in a retirement trust plan. The plan provided that when an employee left the company for reasons other than disability or retirement at age 65, the employee's share would be held by Marine for five years before distribution to the employee. Marine's president agreed to pay Hurley his $12,000 share immediately if Hurley would not compete with Marine within one hundred miles for five years. Hurley agreed and received his money. But less than a year later Hurley was in active competition with Marine. Was the agreement valid? Marine Contractors Co., Inc. v. Hurley, 310 N.E.2d 915 (Mass. 1974).

12. Keen's mother died, leaving Keen an interest in property that the mother had owned jointly with her husband, Keen's stepfather. Keen agreed not to claim her mother's interest in return for a promise from her stepfather that he would leave the entire property to her upon his death. He died without a will, and the state claimed that it was the rightful owner as there had been inadequate consideration in the contract between Keen and her stepfather. Result? Keen v. Larson, 132 N.W.2d 350 (N.D. 1970).

13. Sons, Inc., had leased premises from W&T for over three and one-half years and wished, contrary to the terms of the lease, to leave. W&T was bound by the terms of the lease at least until April 30 of the year following its execution. It could terminate after that on ninety days' notice to Sons. Sons had no such option, and W&T intended to enforce the lease against it for the full ten-year term. Could Sons terminate? David Roth's Sons, Inc. v. Wright and Taylor, Inc., 343 S.W.2d 389 (Ky. App. 1961).

14. The Office of Milk Industry (OMI) of New Jersey established set minimum prices for gallon and half-gallon containers of milk and prohibited the giving or lending of anything of value to any customer by a retail establishment. Garden State Farms, a milk dealer, began distributing refund certificates to purchasers of milk, authorizing a small refund for each purchase payable "(o)n the day on which retail milk controls . . . are abolished in New Jersey or declared void by the court." Had Garden State violated the regulations? Hoffman v. Garden State Farms, Inc., 184 A.2d 4 (N.J. 1962).

Genuine Assent

I n the preceding chapters, the elements that are necessary for the formation of a contract were discussed. Almost all agreements that include those elements will be enforced as contracts. In some situations, however, the elements required for a valid and enforceable contract appear to be present but in reality are not. For example, if a storeowner accepts a gang leader's offer to protect his property from gang violence if he agrees to pay the gang $100 per month, the storeowner is not genuinely assenting to the terms of a contract. Similarly, if a used-car salesperson falsely states that a car has a rebuilt engine and has never been in an accident, the buyer who relies on that information and signs a purchase contract has not genuinely assented. Assent to a contract must be given voluntarily and knowingly by each of the parties; if it is not, there is no genuine assent and thus no contract between them.

This chapter discusses situations involving agreements that lack genuine assent. *Fraud, duress, undue influence,* or even *mistake* may nullify a party's assent to a contract and entitle that party to relief. The relief granted will vary with the circumstances.

FRAUD

A person who has been induced to enter into a contract as a result of fraud will be allowed to cancel or rescind the contract. In addition, since fraud is an intentional tort, the victim of the fraud can sue for damages to compensate for any loss. Punitive damages are also allowed if it can be proved that the intention to commit the fraud was malicious. It is difficult to determine exactly what actions constitute fraud. Literally thousands of acts may be fraudulent. Realizing that it would be impossible to list all possible fraudulent acts, courts have defined fraud in general terms.

The essence of fraud is misrepresentation. One party intentionally misrepresents certain facts to the second party, who, relying on the misrepresentations, changes his or her legal position in assenting to enter into a contract. If the party who misrepresents the facts clearly intends the misrepresentation and the resulting deception of the second party, fraud results. On the other hand, a misrepresentation of facts may be unintentional; in that case, there is no fraud. It is important to note, however, that a person who has assented to a contract as a result of a misrepresentation of fact, whether intentional and fraudulent or unintentional and innocent, is allowed to rescind or cancel any contract entered into as a result of the misrepresentation. The difference between the two misrepresentations is that the intentional misrepresentation constituting fraud is also a tort. The victim of such a tort may not only rescind or cancel the contract but can also sue for damages to compensate for any loss incurred. The victim of uninten-

303

tional misrepresentation has the right only to rescind or cancel the contract; no relief for loss will be granted to that party.

Since fraud requires an intentional misrepresentation of fact, it is difficult to prove. Numerous court rulings have established the elements that must be proven for fraud to exist. Fraud exists where there is:

1. a misrepresentation of a fact
2. that is material
3. that is made with knowledge of its falsity and with intent to deceive the other party
4. who reasonably relies on the misrepresented statement
5. causing injury as a consequence of the reliance.

A simple case has been diagramed in Table 13-1.

Misrepresentation of Fact

A misrepresentation is active concealment of a material fact or partial disclosure of information that is represented as the full truth. A misrepresentation may be expressed or implied; it may be made in writing, orally, or through conduct. Silence can constitute a misrepresentation in situations where the law imposes a duty to speak.

Active Concealment of Fact. An active concealment of a fact is the most obvious type of misrepresentation. If the seller of a used car turns back the odometer to conceal the number of miles the car has been driven, fraud has occurred. Of course, an express statement of fact that is a lie also constitutes fraud.

The law holds that the concept of fraud applies to a partially misleading statement as well as to an outright lie. If a company supplies a balance sheet and profit-and-loss statement to a bank from which it seeks to borrow money, and fails to disclose important information about its liabilities or the true nature of its assets, the partial disclosure of the truth constitutes a misrepresentation.

Silence and the Duty to Disclose Information. In order to find a misrepresentation the law generally requires either an affirmative act or an express statement, but on occasion silence may constitute a misrepresentation of fact leading to fraud. In order for silence to be the basis for fraud, the silence must be interpreted as an intentional misrepresentation.

Generally, mere failure to disclose information to the other party does not constitute even an unintentional and innocent misrepresentation because the law does not impose a duty of disclosure.

There are, however, a number of exceptions to this rule. Statutes such as the Truth-in-

TABLE 13–1 A CASE OF FRAUD

Intent	Jones, knowing his car has been seriously damaged in an accident and rebuilt in the auto shop,
Misrepresentation of a material fact	Tells Smith that the car has never required repairs beyond ordinary maintenance.
Reasonable reliance	Smith chooses Jones's car over another car he has considered buying because he knew the other car had once been wrecked and repaired.
Injury resulting from reliance	One week after purchase, the defect becomes obvious and Smith must spend $500 to replace the fender, which has rusted prematurely.

Lending Act require disclosure regarding finance charges in contracts where money is being lent. Similarly, many jurisdictions recognize an implied warranty, and thus a duty to disclose known defects, in the sale of a new house.

Suppose one party knows certain material facts, knows the other party does not know them, and knows that if those facts were known there would be no contract. A prospective seller of land, for example, may know of a hidden defect in the property, one that could not be observed through inspection. If the seller fails to inform the purchaser of the defect, the seller could be held liable for fraud because the silence was intended to mislead the purchaser into assuming there was no defect. The *Sorrell* v. *Young* case (on page 307) exemplifies this type of fraud.

A person in a fiduciary relationship with another must disclose all known information concerning the subject of that special relationship. An agent owes this duty to a principal, a partner owes it to another partner, and an attorney owes it to a client. The disclosure by a physician to a patient of the risk of surgery is a necessary precondition of the patient's ability to consent to the surgery. Silence and nondisclosure in the face of such a duty may be the basis for a finding of fraud.

A Fact Must Be Misrepresented. False statements that are merely opinions cannot be considered the basis for fraud since an opinion is not a fact. Whether a statement is one of fact or opinion is a matter that must be determined in each particular case. In general, an opinion is a statement of one's expectations concerning future events or one's personal beliefs, as indicated in the *Beierle* case (on page 309). A merchant who sells goods may state that the product will last "a long time" or that the "sale price is reasonable" or that the manufacturer of the goods has "an excellent reputation." Usually, such a statement is known as "puffing" and constitutes a matter of opinion. On the other hand, the car dealer's statement that a used car has been driven only 25,000 miles and was purchased by the present seller from the original owner for $3,000 are statements of fact. Such statements relate to events that either did or did not take place. Their truth or falsity can be proven.

Although statements of opinion are not generally regarded as statements of fact, the opinion of an expert is treated as a statement of fact. When an accountant states that in his or her opinion the books and records of a corporation were kept in a manner consistent with generally accepted accounting procedures, he or she speaks as an expert. If there were proof that the accountant actually did not hold that opinion, the statement would constitute a misrepresentation that could be the basis for a finding of fraud.

Materiality

The question of whether a fact is a material fact is determined on a case-by-case basis. The test usually seeks to ascertain whether the person would have entered into a contract if he or she had known of the misrepresentation. The policy of the law is to distinguish between insignificant facts and those that are significant, or material. One cannot simply review a contract with numerous complex clauses, find one minor misrepresentation of fact made by the other party, and then sue for fraud. There is a misrepresentation of a material fact only if the fact in question was one of the important reasons for entering into the contract.

Knowledge of Falsity and Intent to Deceive

The third requirement for fraud is that the misrepresentation of a material fact be made with knowledge of the falsity and with intent to deceive. Knowledge of the falsity and the intent to deceive are often referred to as *scienter,* a Latin word meaning "knowingly."

ETHICS BOX
False Opinion

Is it fair to allow someone to misstate purposely their true opinion and escape liability? Consider the following case: Sharp, a mechanic, tells Trusting that the painting that Sharp wants to sell is highly creative and is of a style that will likely increase in value. Sharp's real opinion is that the painting is most uncreative and shows no talent. As far as the ethicality of the action is concerned, it is as wrong to misstate intentionally one's opinion as it is to misstate a material fact. The other party may rely just as much on a statement of opinion based upon a mistaken trust in the party who is giving the opinion. Trusting may ultimately buy the painting because of a mistaken belief in Sharp's opinion.

Even though Sharp has acted unethically, it is impossible for the law to give relief in such cases. There is generally no effective way to determine a person's true opinion. An opinion is an amorphous thing that is often incapable of objective testing. The law cannot and should not be used to monitor all unethical behavior.

The law does not require proof that the person who committed fraud had an evil or malicious motive. The question is whether that person knew the facts and then misrepresented them. As with other areas of the law in which intent must be determined, a person is deemed to have intended the natural consequences of an action. It is no excuse for the person making a misrepresentation of a material fact to say that he or she did not intend to take advantage of the other party. Nor can a person merely say that he or she did not know the true facts if he or she recklessly disregarded those facts that were available. Knowledge of the facts will be inferred if a person makes a statement with reckless disregard for their truth.

The intent to deceive is found in the intent to create a false impression. Since fraud requires this intent, mere negligence or carelessness cannot constitute fraud. The professional accountant, lawyer, or doctor who fails to disclose certain facts or makes half-true statements is clearly negligent because he or she is not acting as a professional. In order to find fraud, however, the crucial element of scienter also must exist. There must be an active intent to deceive, essentially a cover-up of known facts.

Reliance

The fourth element to be proved in a case of fraud is that the misrepresentation of a material fact that was made knowingly and with intent to deceive was relied upon by the party to whom it was made. A person who does not pay attention to a misrepresented fact, or who conducts his or her own investigation to determine whether a fact is true, is not relying upon what the other party has said or done. In that case, even if there is a misrepresentation of a material fact, since there is no reliance there is no fraud.

Suppose a person acts foolishly in relying on a fraudulent statement. Will the law protect that person? While there is some conflict among court decisions as to what constitutes "unreasonable" reliance, where there is an intentional misrepresentation relief will generally be granted even though the defrauded party was foolish or negligent. In balancing the interests of the foolish person against those of the person intentionally misrepresenting a material fact, the law generally seeks to protect the victim of the fraud.

Injury or Damage

The fifth element required to prove fraud is that an injury occurred as a result of the fraud. The party who relied upon a misrepresentation of a material fact that was knowingly and intentionally made must prove that some damage was caused by the fraud. What loss was suffered? If the purchaser of a car relies on a statement that a car has been driven only 30,000 miles and it is later proved to have been driven 60,000 miles, what damage has the purchaser suffered? The basic standard is the difference in value between that which was promised and relied upon and that which in fact was received. If there is no difference, there is no injury; but if there is a difference, the defrauded party will be compensated for the injury suffered. If the fraudulent statement was made maliciously or with extreme carelessness or recklessness, the defrauded party can recover punitive as well as compensatory damages.

Both the cases that follow involve fraud. Analyze which of the required elements of fraud was most closely reviewed in these court decisions.

Sorrell v. Young

Court of Appeals of Washington

491 P.2d 1312 (1971)

Background: Sorrell (plaintiff) sued to rescind a land sale contract with Young (defendant) due to alleged fraudulent misrepresentations on Young's part. In May 1968, plaintiff Sorrell contracted to buy a lot owned by defendant Young. When he prepared to build a house on the property, Sorrell found that a soil test was needed before he could obtain a building permit. Sorrell's contractor testified that the soil was not stable because a great deal of fill dirt had been added to the lot. The contractor said that it would be necessary to install piling as a foundation for a house and that, even then, there was no certainty that a house could be built. No houses had been built on adjoining property that Young had sold to other purchasers, and at least one other lot owner stated that he had not built on his lot because the cost of soil testing was prohibitive.

Sorrell filed suit against Young seeking to rescind the contract and to recover the money he had already paid to Young, as well as reimbursement for taxes and other expenses. He said Young had misrepresented the property when he told Sorrell "you could build a house on the lot." Furthermore, Young did not tell Sorrell that the lots had been filled.

Young responded that he had purchased the lots in 1960 and that at that time he knew fill dirt had been added to them. He also stated that he added fill dirt himself during the next three years. However, Young did not offer to sell the lots until seven years after he had placed the fill dirt on them, when he considered the lots to be in "good saleable condition." He stated that he could not observe that the land was settling. People who wanted to buy the lots, according to Young, could look at them and then go to the building department and find out if the department considered the land to be in shape to build on.

The trial court found that it was clear that Young had not told Sorrell that the lot had been filled. Further, it was not apparent to Sorrell that the lot had been filled. Finally, the testimony showed that Sorrell had not made any inquiry concerning the existence of the fill dirt and that at the time of purchase he was unaware of it. The trial court found, however, that Sorrell had not met the burden of proving that the contract had been induced by Young's express fraudulent misrepresentation. While there was testimony that Young had stated that "a house could be built on the lot," there was no proof that a house could not in fact be built. Since there was no proof of the "falsity of the misrepresentation" made by Young, the trial court found for the defendant.

Decision: The trial court's decision was reversed and the Court of Appeals ruled in favor of plaintiff Sorrell.

James, Justice

The plaintiffs contend that the defendants misrepresented the real property in that they contend Mr. Young, the defendant, told them orally that "we could build a house on the lot." The trial court did not find that such a representation was or was not made to the plaintiffs, but found no proof had been offered showing that a house could not be built on said property. Thus, it found the defendants had not misrepresented the property to the plaintiffs.

We are satisfied that the trial judge viewed the evidence too narrowly. A failure to speak when there is a duty to do so may also be fraudulent. The controlling principle is expressed in Restatement of Contracts §472, Comment b (1932):

> A party entering into a bargain is not bound to tell everything he knows to the other party, even if he is aware that the other is ignorant of the facts; and unilateral mistake, of itself, does not make a transaction voidable (See §503). But if a fact known by one party and not the other is so vital that if the mistake were mutual the contract would be voidable, and the party knowing the fact also knows that the other does not know it, nondisclosure is not privileged and is fraudulent.

The precise question presented here—the right to rescind for nondisclosure of the fact that land was filled—has not confronted a Washington appellate court. Washington's early unqualified adherence to the doctrine of caveat emptor in real estate transactions was relatively short-lived. By the turn of the century, Washington had recognized that "the tendency of the more recent cases has been to restrict rather than extend the doctrine of *caveat emptor.*"

We are satisfied that the ruling in *Obde* v. *Schlemeyer* (1960), has aligned Washington with those jurisdictions which require a seller to disclose the fact that the apartment house he sold was infested with termites. The court noted (1) the infestation was a "manifestly . . . serious and dangerous condition," and (2) the condition was "not readily observable upon reasonable inspection." The court concluded that:

Under the circumstances, we are satisfied that "justice, equity, and fair dealing," to use Professor Keeton's language, demanded that the Schlemeyers speak—that they inform prospective purchasers, such as the Obdes, of the condition, regardless of the latter's failure to ask any questions relative to the possibility of termites.

Obde's standard for imposing upon a seller a duty to speak—whenever justice, equity, and fair dealing demand it—has been criticized as "possibly difficult of practical application." But the hazards inherent in definitional circumscription were pointed out in *American Savings Bank and Trust Co.* v. *Bremerton Gas Co.* (1917):

> Fraud is a thing to be described, rather than defined. Deception may find expression in such a variety of ways that most courts have studiously avoided reducing its elements to accurate definition. Human foresight is not sufficiently acute to anticipate the secret and covert methods of the artful and designing or those who endeavor to reap where they have not sown. Once let it be known what the courts consider fraudulent and those engaged in its perpetration will busy themselves in inventing some means of evasion. The courts, therefore, should content themselves with determining from the facts of each case whether fraud does or does not exist. While fraud is not lightly to be inferred, it does not follow that the inference of fraud cannot be gathered from surrounding circumstances, provided they are of sufficient strength and cogency to overcome the presumption of honesty and fair dealing.

We conceive the essential "elements" in proof of fraud by nondisclosure of the existence of a landfill to be: (1) a vendor, knowing that the land has been filled, fails to disclose that fact to the purchaser of the property, and (2) the purchaser is unaware of the existence of the fill because either he has had no opportunity to inspect the property, or the existence of the fill was not apparent or readily ascertainable, and (3) the value of the property is materially affected by the existence of the fill. When these three elements have been proved, a vendor's duty imposed by *Obde*'s general standard of justice, equity, and fair dealing has been violated, and a purchaser of land is entitled to rescind.

Sorrell presented substantial evidence to establish each of the three elements. . . . Young's challenge should have been denied by the trial court and therefore we reverse its decision.

Beierle v. Taylor

Supreme Court of Montana

524 P.2d 783 (1974)

Background: The Beierles (plaintiffs) sued the Taylors (defendants) for rescission of a purchase contract for a motel due to alleged misrepresentations by the Taylors. The complaint alleged fraudulent misrepresentation of the income-producing capability of the motel. The defendant seller suggested that such representations were projections of possible income and thus constituted statements of opinion and not of fact as is required for fraud. The District Court of Gallatin County granted summary judgment against the buyers, dismissing their complaint.

Decision: The Supreme Court of Montana affirmed the trial court's decision and found for defendants Taylor.

Haswell, Justice

Plaintiffs are Edwin and Agnes Beierle, husband and wife, who bought the Trail-In Motel in West Yellowstone, Montana. Defendants are the sellers, Robert A. Taylor and Wanda K. Taylor, his wife; the real estate agent, United Agencies; and the financing institution, the First National Bank of Bozeman.

Early in 1973, plaintiff Edwin Beierle was contemplating retirement. He was looking for a business he could acquire and make a living. He contacted United, who showed him several business properties.

The Beierles indicated an interest in the Trail-In Motel. United compiled and made available to them a brochure containing a description of the motel; a cost appraisal of the property; an unaudited gross income and expense statement for the years 1969, 1970, and 1971; and an analysis of projected income and expense.

The gross income and expense statements showed net operating losses of approximately $5,000 in 1969; $6,800 in 1970; and $4,600 in 1971.

The analysis of projected income and expense was based on a substantial increase in motel rates, a year-round motel operation by the owners, and an estimated future occupancy rate. The previous motel operation had been essentially a three-month summer operation by an absentee owner.

Several conversations were held between Jack Rosenthal of United and the Beierles. The failure of the motel to make money and the reasons for this were discussed. Rosenthal told Edwin Beierle that he would not be able to make it without outside work for a couple of years until the motel business was built up. The net operating loss statements were not discussed, but were available at the discussion. Copies were not furnished the Beierles.

The Beierles personally inspected the motel property. The asking price was $125,000. Eventually, Beierles purchased the motel property at this price . . . took possession of the motel on May 1, 1973, and have continued to operate it since that time. They have made no monthly installment payments on the note due to the seller.

After the Beierles' default, the entire balance of the note was declared payable. A notice of sale of the motel property was served on the Beierles. Thereafter, Beierles served notice of rescission of the purchase contract followed by a complaint seeking rescission.

The district court granted summary judgment to defendants on the ground that the alleged representations were opinion, not fact. Plaintiff appealed that judgment.

The buyers' principal claim of misrepresentation is found on the projected income figures contained in the brochure. The complaint states:

. . . Defendants falsely and fraudulently represented to plaintiffs that said property so exchanged was *capable* of producing an income of Twenty Seven Thousand Six Hundred Forty-eight Dollars. . . . (Emphasis added).

"Capable" suggests an expression of opinion rather than a statement of fact. Only under unusual circumstances, not present here, can projected future income be considered a fact. Ordinarily future income is but an estimate, subject to the vagaries of the marketplace. It is an opinion, not a guarantee.

A mere expression of opinion, however erroneous, will not warrant rescission of a contract. Although exceptions to this rule exist, none is germane here. Buyers were presented gross income figures for three years which indicated the projected future income was not based on past performance. Buyers were furnished the details of the computation.

Lincoln v. *Keane* states the controlling law here:

. . . any statement . . . as to what appellant's future income from the motel would be . . . was a matter of opinion and cannot be the basis of an action for fraud.

The trial court's summary judgment against the buyers is affirmed.

DURESS

A second factor nullifying a party's assent to a contract is duress. Few areas of the law of contracts have undergone such radical changes in the twentieth century as has the law governing duress. Relief from an agreement on the grounds of duress is clearly available if a person is deprived of liberty or property through physical force. Even the threat of physical force, although not carried out, constitutes duress. Yet duress is not limited to these situations.

The essence of duress is lack of free will or voluntary consent. Any wrongful act or threat that overcomes the free will of the consenting party constitutes duress. Economic coercion, threats to a person's family and loved ones, and other uses of moral or social force to put a person in such fear that his or her act is not voluntary constitute duress.

In determining whether a contract can be voided on account of duress, one must ascertain (1) whether the acts or threats were wrongful and (2) whether it was the acts or threats, and not the free will of the party, that induced the required contractual assent.

Duress cannot be limited to the fear that might overcome an ordinary person. If a contracting party, whether brave or timid, is actually coerced into assenting to the contract, duress has occurred. Thus, the state of mind of the person who is being threatened must be examined. Did one party involuntarily accept the terms of the other party? Were the circumstances such that there was no practicable alternative? Were those circumstances due to the coercive acts of the other party? Read carefully the *Totem Marine* case, which discusses the requirements of economic duress or business compulsion.

Totem Marine T. & B. v. Alyeska Pipeline, Etc.

Supreme Court of Alaska
584 P.2d 15 (1978)

Background: Totem (plaintiff) sued Alyeska (defendant) for accounts receivable. A contract was made between Totem and Alyeska that required Totem to transport by ship pipeline-construction materials from Texas to a designated port in Alaska. After the contract was made, numerous problems occurred that made it difficult to perform the contract by the required date. Finally, after many difficulties, Alyeska terminated the contract and took the freight off Totem's ship when it was in a California port on its way to Alaska.

Totem then sent Alyeska its invoice for the $260,000–$300,000 in costs and charges it had incurred in its attempt to perform the contract. Totem was in urgent need of cash and was close to bankruptcy. Alyeska delayed making payment and advised Totem it might have to wait months to be paid. Six or seven weeks after Alyeska had terminated the contract, it offered to pay Totem slightly less than $100,-000 in exchange for a release by Totem of all claims against Alyeska for further payment.

Totem agreed to the terms, signed the release, and six months later filed suit. It claimed its agreement to accept the partial payment due it and the release of all claims against Alyeska had been made due to the economic duress it was subjected to by Alyeska. Alyeska asserted that, as a matter of law, there was no basis for Totem's claim of economic duress and asked the court to grant a summary judgment in its favor. The trial court agreed with Alyeska and granted its request for a dismissal judgment. Totem appealed to the Alaska Supreme Court.

Decision: The court found in plaintiff Totem's favor, reversing the trial court's decision that there was no basis for economic duress asserted by Totem's complaint.

Burke, Justice

In June of 1975, Totem entered into a contract with Alyeska under which Totem was to transport pipeline construction materials from Houston, Texas, to a designated port in southern Alaska, with the possibility of one or two cargo stops along the way.

By the terms of the contract, Totem was to have completed performance by approximately August 15, 1975. From the start, however, there were numerous problems which impeded Totem's performance of the contract. For example, according to Totem, Alyeska represented that approximately 1,800 to 2,100 tons of regular uncoated pipe were to be loaded in Houston, and that perhaps another 6,000 or 7,000 tons of materials would be put on the barge at later stops along the west coast. Upon the arrival of the tug and barge in Houston, however, Totem found that about 6,700 to 7,200 tons of coated pipe, steel beams and valves, haphazardly and improperly piled, were in the yard to be loaded. This situation called for remodeling of the barge and extra cranes and stevedores, and resulted in the loading taking thirty days rather than the three days which Totem had anticipated it would take to load 2,000 tons. The lengthy loading period was also caused in part by Alyeska's delay in assuring Totem that it would pay for the additional expenses, bad weather and other administrative problems.

The difficulties continued after the tug and barge left Houston. It soon became apparent that the vessels were traveling more slowly than anticipated because of the extra load.

The vessels finally arrived in the vicinity of San Pedro, California, where Totem planned to change crews and refuel. On Alyeska's orders, however, the vessels instead pulled into port at Long Beach, California. At this point, Alyeska's agents commenced off-loading the barge, without Totem's consent, without the necessary load survey, and without a marine survey, the absence of which voided Totem's insurance. After much wrangling and some concessions by Alyeska, the freight was off-loaded. Thereafter, on or about September 14, 1975, Alyeska terminated the contract.

Following termination of the contract, Totem submitted invoices to Alyeska and began pressing the latter for payment. The invoices came to something between $260,000 and $300,000. An official from Alyeska told Totem that they would look over the invoices but that they were not sure when payment would be made—perhaps in a day or perhaps in six to eight months. Totem was in urgent need of cash as the invoices represented debts which the company had incurred on 10–30 day payment schedules. Totem's creditors were demanding payment and without immediate cash, Totem would go bankrupt. Totem then turned over the collection to its attorney, Roy Bell, directing him to advise Alyeska of Totem's financial straits. Thereafter, Bell met with Alyeska officials in Seattle, and after some negotiations, Totem received a settlement offer from Alyeska for $97,500. On November 6, 1975, Totem, through its president Stair, signed an agreement releasing Alyeska from all claims by Totem in exchange for $97,500.

On March 26, 1976, Totem filed a complaint against Alyeska seeking to rescind the settlement and release on the ground of economic duress and to recover the balance allegedly due on the original contract. Alyeska's response asserted that Totem had executed a binding release of all claims against Alyeska and that as a matter of law, Totem could not prevail on its claim of economic duress.

A court's initial task in deciding motions for summary judgment is to determine whether there exist genuine issues of material fact. In order to decide whether such issues exist in this case, we must examine the doctrine allowing avoidance of a release on grounds of economic duress.

This court has not yet decided a claim of economic duress or what is called business compulsion. At early common law, a contract could be avoided on the ground of duress only if a party could show that the agreement was entered into for fear of loss of life or limb, mayhem or imprisonment. The threat had to be such as to overcome the will of a person of ordinary firmness and courage. Subsequently, however, the concept has been broadened to include myriad forms of economic coercion which force a person to involuntarily enter into a particular transaction. The test has come to be whether the will of the person induced by the threat was overcome rather than that of a reasonably firm person.

At the outset, it is helpful to acknowledge the various policy considerations which are involved in cases involving economic duress. Typically, those claiming such coercion are attempting to avoid the consequences of a modification of an original contract or of a settlement and release agreement. On the one hand, courts are reluctant to set aside agreements because of the notion of freedom of contract and because of the desirability of having private dispute resolutions be final. On the other hand, there is an increasing recognition of the law's role in correcting inequitable or unequal exchanges between parties of disproportionate bargaining power and a greater willingness to not enforce agreements which were entered into under coercive circumstances.

Section 492(b) of the *Restatement of Contracts* defines duress as: any wrongful threat of one person by words or other conduct that induces another to enter into a transaction under the influence of such fear as precluded him from exercising free will and judgment, if the threat was intended or should reasonably have been expected to operate as an inducement.

Many courts state the test somewhat differently, eliminating use of the vague term "free will," but retaining the same basic idea. Under this standard, duress exists where: (1) one party involuntarily accepted the terms of another, (2) circumstances permitted no other alternative, and (3) such circumstances were the result of coercive acts of the other party. The third element is further explained as follows:

> In order to substantiate the allegation of economic duress or business compulsion, the plaintiff must go beyond the mere showing of reluctance to accept and of financial embarrassment. There must be a showing of acts on the part of the defendant which produced these two factors. The assertion of duress must be proven by evidence that the duress resulted from defendant's wrongful and oppressive conduct and not by the plaintiff's necessities.

. . . Economic duress does not exist merely because a person has been the victim of a wrongful act; in addition, the victim must have no choice but to agree to the other party's terms or face serious financial hardship. Thus, in order to avoid a contract, a party must also show that he had no reasonable alternative to agreeing to the other party's terms, or as it is often stated, that he had no adequate remedy if the threat were to be carried out. . . . An available alternative or remedy may not be adequate where the delay involved in pursuing that remedy would cause immediate and irreparable loss to one's economic or business interest.

Professor Dalzell, in *Duress by Economic Pressure II,* 20 N. Carolina L. Rev. 340, 370 (1942), notes the following with regard to the adequacy of legal remedies where one party refuses to pay a contract claim:

> Nowadays, a wait of even a few weeks in collecting on a contract claim is sometimes serious or fatal for an enterprise at a crisis in its history. The business of a creditor in financial straits is at the mercy of an unscrupulous debtor, who need only suggest that if the creditor does not care to settle on the debtor's own hard terms, he can sue. This situation, in which promptness in payment is vastly more important than even approximate justice in the settlement terms, is too common in modern business relations to be ignored by society and the courts.

Turning to the instant case, we believe that Totem's allegations, if proved, would support a finding that it executed a release of its contract claims against Alyeska under economic duress. Totem has alleged that Alyeska deliberately withheld payment of an acknowledged debt, knowing that Totem had no choice but to accept an inadequate sum in settlement of that debt; that Totem was faced with impending bankruptcy; that Totem was unable to meet its pressing debts other than by accepting the immediate cash payment offered by Alyeska; and that through necessity, Totem thus involuntarily accepted an inadequate settlement offer from Alyeska and executed a release of all claims under the contract. If the release was in fact executed under these circumstances, we think that under the legal principles discussed above that this would constitute the type of wrongful conduct and lack of alternatives that would render the release voidable by Totem on the ground of economic duress. . . . Therefore, we hold that the superior court erred in granting summary judgment for appellant and remand the case to the superior court for trial in accordance with the legal principles set forth above.

MAYbee Ase

Can USX (formerly U.S. Steel) rescind a contract with General Motors on grounds of economic duress? It seems fair to question whether or not a very large firm can ever be the victim of economic duress. After all, USX has well-trained managers and the resources to employ lawyers and take other steps to insure that agreements are satisfactory. Even though they may be at some disadvantage in negotiating, it seems odd to suggest that they might somehow be victimized by another firm. Courts should be cautious in rescinding contracts between parties on the basis of economic duress, because in so doing they are defeating expectations.

Also, the ambiguities that are inherent in the concept of economic duress make it possible for the courts to make the wrong decision. The concept of economic duress is similar in its approach to the idea of a "fair price" that is found in medieval religious thought. Both are prepared to set aside market outcomes on the basis of a judgment made by an official outside the transaction. Such concepts make negotiation more difficult because one must always guard against an outside intervention that sets aside the bargained outcome. This may ultimately work to the detriment of those that the law intends to protect.

Sometimes, as in the *Totem* case, one party is at a disadvantage because the legal system is costly and slow and one cannot afford to take the time and make the effort to assert legitimate legal rights. Although there may be appropriate sympathy for the party in the position that Totem found itself, the best way to deal with such a problem is to come up with more effective legal remedies for breach of contract, rather than distorting market outcomes by establishing principles that may work to set aside legitimate bargains. The old saying that "hard cases make bad law" retains its validity in the modern law of genuine assent.

The doctrine of economic duress is better limited to cases of individuals or to cases where very small firms contract with much more sophisticated larger firms. Of course, the law should always restrict the use of physical coercion, regardless of who is involved.

UNDUE INFLUENCE

Undue influence exists when one person exercises mental coercion over another. The cases frequently involve an elderly, sick, and senile person as the coerced victim of another person's undue influence. The essence of undue influence is that the influenced person's own judgment and free will are subjected to those of the dominating person. Thus, the assent given by the influenced person is not that person's genuine assent.

In examining a case involving undue influence, the courts usually follow a two-step approach. First, they seek to determine if there has been a dominant-subservient relationship between the two parties. For example, certain fiduciary relationships, such as those between attorney and client, banker and customer, and doctor and patient, involve a high degree of trust by one party in the other. Second, once the relationship is determined to have been one in which one party could by his or her influence dominate the other, the courts shift the presumption of lack of undue influence to a presumption that such undue influence did exist when a contract between the two benefited the dominant party. Unless the dominant party can then prove a lack of undue influence, the subservient party is allowed to avoid the contract. The following case raises questions that are not only about undue influence but also about fraud and duress. Note that those issues often are interrelated.

Odorizzi v. Bloomfield School District

Court of Appeals of California
54 Cal.Rptr. 533 (1966)

Background: Odorizzi (plaintiff) sued Bloomfield School District (defendant) to be reinstated as a teacher. Odorizzi was employed during 1964 as an elementary schoolteacher by the defendant Bloomfield School District and was under contract with the district to continue to teach school the following year as a permanent employee. On June 10, he was arrested on criminal charges [relating to homosexual conduct] and on June 11 he signed and delivered to his superiors his written resignation as a teacher, which the district accepted on June 13. In July, the criminal charges against Odorizzi were dismissed and in September he sought to resume his employment with the district. On the district's refusal to reinstate him, he filed suit asserting that his resignation was invalid because he lacked the capacity to make a valid contract.

Odorizzi asserted that his resignation was invalid because it was obtained through duress, fraud, mistake, and undue influence. Specifically, Odorizzi declared that he had been under such severe mental and emotional strain at the time he signed his resignation, having just completed the process of arrest, questioning by the police, booking, and release on bail, and having gone for forty hours without sleep, that he was incapable of rational thought or action.

While he was in this condition and unable to think clearly, the superintendent of the district and the principal of his school came to his apartment. They said that they were trying to help him and had his best interests at heart, that he should take their advice and immediately resign his position with the district, that there was no time to consult an attorney, that if he did not resign immediately the district would suspend and dismiss him from his position and publicize the proceedings, his "aforedescribed arrest," and cause him "to suffer extreme embarrassment and humiliation"; but that if he resigned at once, the incident would not be publicized and would not jeopardize his chances of securing employment as a teacher elsewhere. Odorizzi pleaded that because of his faith and confidence in their representations they were able to substitute their will and judgment for his own and thus obtain his signature to his purported resignation. The trial court dismissed the complaint and Odorizzi appealed.

Decision: The court found the facts were not sufficient to find duress, fraud, or mistake. However, it found the facts sufficient to allow Odorizzi to rescind his contract because of undue influence; accordingly, it reversed the trial court's judgment.

Fleming, Justice

Duress consists in unlawful confinement of another's person, or relatives, or property, which causes him to consent to a transaction through fear. Duress is often used interchangeably with menace, but in California menace is technically a threat of duress or a threat of injury to the person, property, or character of another. We agree with respondent's contention that neither duress nor menace was involved in this case, because the action is not unlawful unless the party making the threat knows the falsity of his claim. The amended complaint shows in substance that the school representatives announced their intention to initiate suspension and dismissal proceedings at a time when the filing of such proceedings was not only their legal right but their positive duty as school officials. Although the filing of such proceedings might be extremely damaging to plaintiff's reputation, the injury would remain incidental so long as the school officials acted in good faith in the performance of their duties. Neither duress nor menace was present as a ground for rescission.

Nor do we find a cause for fraud, either actual or constructive. Actual fraud involves conscious misrepresentation, or concealment, or non-disclosure of a material fact which induces the innocent party to enter the contract. A complaint for fraud must plead misrepresentation, knowledge of falsity, intent to induce reliance, justifiable reliance, and resulting damage. While the amended complaint charged misrepresentation, it failed to assert the elements of knowledge of falsity, intent to induce reliance, justifiable reliance, and resulting damage. A cause of action for actual fraud was therefore not stated.

Constructive fraud arises on a breach of duty by one in a confidential or fiduciary relationship to another which induces justifiable reliance by the latter to his prejudice. Plaintiff has attempted to bring himself within this category. . . . Plaintiff, however, sets forth no facts to support his conclusion of a confidential relationship between the representatives of the school district and himself, other than that the parties bore the relationship of employer and employee to each other. Under prevailing judicial opinion no presumption of a confidential relationship arises from the bare fact that parties to a contract are employer and employee; rather, additional ties must be brought out in order to create the presumption of a confidential relationship between the two. The absence of a confidential relationship between employer and employee is especially apparent where, as here, the parties were negotiating to bring about a termination of their relationship. In such a situation each party is expected to look after his own interests, and a lack of confidentiality is implicit in the subject matter of their dealings. We think the allegations of constructive fraud were inadequate.

However, the pleading does set out a claim that plaintiff's consent to the transaction had been obtained through the use of undue influence.

Undue influence, in the sense we are concerned with here, is a shorthand legal phrase used to describe persuasion which tends to be coercive in nature, persuasion which overcomes the will without convincing the judgment. The hallmark of such persuasion is high pressure, a pressure which works on mental, moral, or emotional weakness to such an extent that it approaches the boundaries of coercion. In this sense, undue influence has been called overpersuasion.

Misrepresentations of law or fact are not essential to the charge, for a person's will may be overborne without misrepresentation. In essence, undue influence involves the use of excessive pressure to persuade one vulnerable to such pressure, pressure applied by a dominant subject to a servient object. In combination, the elements of undue susceptibility in the servient person and excessive pressure by the dominating person makes the latter's influence undue, for it results in the apparent will of the servient person being in fact the will of the dominant person.

Undue susceptibility may consist of total weakness of mind which leaves a person entirely without understanding or, a lesser weakness which destroys the capacity of a person to make a contract even though he is not totally incapacitated; or, the first element in our equation, a still lesser weakness which provides sufficient grounds to rescind a contract for undue influence. . . . The reported cases have usually involved elderly, sick, senile persons alleged to have executed wills or deeds under pressure. In some of its aspects this lesser weakness could perhaps be called weakness of spirit. But whatever name we give it, this first element of undue influence resolves itself into a lessened capacity of the object to make a free contract.

In the present case plaintiff has pleaded that such weakness at the time he signed his resignation prevented him from freely and competently applying his judgment to the problem before him. Plaintiff declares he was under severe mental and emotional strain at the time because he had just completed the process of arrest, questioning, booking, and release on bail and had been without sleep for forty hours. It is possible that exhaustion and emotional turmoil may wholly incapacitate a person from exercising his judgment.

Undue influence in its second aspect involves an application of excessive strength by a dominant subject against a servient object. Judicial consideration of this second element in undue influence has been relatively rare, for there are few cases involving persons who persuade but do not misrepresent the benefit of their bargain. Yet logically, the same legal consequences should apply to the results of excessive strength as to the results of undue weakness. Whether from weakness on one side, or strength on the other, or a combination of the two, undue influence occurs whenever there results that kind of influence or supremacy of one mind over another by which that other is prevented from acting according to his own wish or judgment, and whereby the will of the person is overborne and he is induced to do or forbear to do an act which he would not do, or would do, if left to act freely. Undue influence involves a type of mismatch which our statute calls unfair advantage. Whether a person of subnormal capacities has been subjected to ordinary force or a person of normal capacities subjected to extraordinary force, the match is equally out of balance. If will has been overcome against judgment, consent may be rescinded.

The difficulty, of course, lies in determining when the forces of persuasion have overflowed their normal banks and become oppressive flood waters. There are second thoughts to every bargain, and hindsight is still better than foresight. Undue influence cannot be used as a pretext to avoid bad bargains or escape from bargains which refuse to come up to expectations. A woman who buys a dress on impulse, which on critical inspection by her best friend turns out to be less fashionable than she had thought, is not legally entitled to set aside the sale on the ground that the saleswoman used all her wiles to close the sale. A man who buys a tract of desert land in the expectation that it is in the immediate path of the city's growth and will become another Palm Springs, an expectation cultivated in glowing terms by the seller, cannot rescind his bargain when things turn out differently. If we are temporarily persuaded against our better judgment to do something about which we later have second thoughts, we must abide the consequences of the risks inherent in managing our own affairs.

However, overpersuasion is generally accompanied by certain characteristics which tend to create a pattern. The pattern usually involves several of the following elements: (1) discussion of the transaction at an unusual or inappropriate time, (2) consummation of the transaction in an unusual place, (3) insistent demand that the business be finished at once, (4) extreme emphasis on untoward consequences of delay, (5) the use of multiple persuaders by the dominant side against a single servient party, (6) absence of third-party advisers to the servient party, (7) statements that there is no time to consult financial advisers or attorneys. If a number of these elements are simultaneously present, the persuasion may be characterized as excessive. . . .

The difference between legitimate persuasion and excessive pressure, like the difference between seduction and rape, rests to a considerable extent in the manner in which the parties go about their business. For example, if a day or two after Odorizzi's release on bail the superintendent of the school district had called him into his office during business hours and directed his attention to those provisions of the Education Code compelling his leave of absence and authorizing his suspension on the filing of written charges, had told him that the District contemplated filing written charges against him, had pointed out the alternative of resignation available to him, had informed him he was free to consult counsel or any adviser he wished and to consider the matter overnight and return with his decision the next day, it is extremely unlikely that any complaint about the use of excessive pressure could ever have been made against the school district.

But, according to the allegations of the complaint, this is not the way it happened, and if it had happened that way, plaintiff would never have resigned. Rather, the representatives of the school board undertook to achieve their objective by overpersuasion and imposition to secure plaintiff's signature but not his consent to his resignation through a high-pressure carrot-and-stick technique—under which they assured plaintiff they were trying to assist him, he should rely on their advice, there wasn't time to consult an attorney, if he didn't resign at once the school district would suspend and dismiss him from his position and publicize the proceedings, but if he did resign the incident wouldn't jeopardize his chances of securing a teaching post elsewhere.

Plaintiff has thus pleaded both subjective and objective elements entering the undue influence equation and stated sufficient facts to put in issue the question whether his free will had been overborne by defendant's agents at a time when he was unable to function in a normal manner.

The question cannot be resolved by an analysis of pleading but requires a finding of fact.

We express no opinion on the merits of plaintiff's case, or the propriety of his continuing to teach school, or the timeliness of his rescission. We do hold that his pleading, liberally construed, states a cause of action for rescission of a transaction to which his apparent consent had been obtained through the use of undue influence.

Reversed.

MISTAKE

Mistake is generally defined as a state of mind not in accord with the facts. The term "mistake," when used in contract law, refers to a mental attitude coupled with an act having legal significance (such as the execution of a contract). There are many different kinds of mistakes that can be made by parties to a contract. They can make a mistake in the performance or execution of the contract. One party can make a mistake in judgment; another can make a mistaken assumption concerning the subject matter of the contract. Mistakes in typing a written contract can occur, as can mistakes concerning the presumed legality or tax effect of a particular transaction. In most situations in which mistakes are made, the law grants no relief to the mistaken party. If legal relief is to be given when a mistake has occurred, a number of factors must be examined.

The legal significance of any mistake must be determined by answering several questions. Among these are the following:

1. Did one or both parties have a mistaken thought?
2. Did the mistake induce a mutual expression of agreement or merely induce action by one party?
3. Should one or both parties have had reason to know of the mistake?
4. Was the fact as to which a mistake occurred of substantial importance and one that was not part of the risk assumed by either of the parties?

These questions seek to determine not only who made the mistake but also what kind of mistake was made and what effect it had on the contract. Did both parties make a mistake that induced action by only one party, or did one party make a mistake that induced action by both parties? Was it a serious mistake? If a serious mistake was made by one party, does that mean that the other party should have known of the mistake? If a mistake was made by both parties to a contract, it is referred to as a *bilateral mistake.* If only one of the parties was mistaken, then a *unilateral mistake* occurred.

Bilateral Mistake

There are several contexts in which contracting parties can make bilateral mistakes. Both parties can make a mistake concerning an important material fact on which the contract is based. Typical cases involving such mistakes are those in which the subject matter of the contract has, unknown to both parties, been destroyed prior to the agreement of the parties. Suppose you agreed to buy my lakefront summer cottage in northern Michigan and I agreed to sell it. We decided to enter into a contract for purchase and sale on our return from the cottage to the city. However, unknown to us, before we got there, a fire destroyed the cottage. Mistakenly believing the cottage was still standing, we contracted for its purchase and sale. Our mistake was a bilateral mistake of an important material fact; we both believed that the cottage still existed. When a bilateral mistake concerning the subject matter of the contract occurs, the courts grant relief to the parties and allow the contract to be rescinded. It was not the fault of either party that their assumptions were mistaken. If the parties actually had known the true facts, they would not have entered into their contract. The following case is a classic English decision involving bilateral mistakes.

Raffles v. Wichelhaus

Court of Exchequer, 1864
2 H. & C. 906, 159 Eng.Rep. 375

Background: Raffles (plaintiff) sued Wichelhaus (defendant) for breach of a contractual duty to purchase 125 bales of cotton. Defendant Wichelhaus admitted a duty to purchase cotton shipped via a sailing vessel called the "Peerless," but claimed he specifically intended to purchase cotton from the ship "Peerless" which was to set sail in October. The plaintiff, meanwhile, shipped the cotton on a different ship of the same name "Peerless," which set sail in December.
Decision: The court found in favor of defendant Wichelhaus.

Declaration. For that it was agreed between the plaintiff and the defendants, to wit, at Liverpool, that the plaintiff should sell to the defendants, and the defendants buy of the plaintiff, certain goods, to wit, 125 bales of Surat cotton, guaranteed middling fair merchant's Dhollorah, to arrive ex Peerless from Bombay; and that the cotton should be taken from the quay, and that the defendants would pay the plaintiff for the same at a certain rate, to wit, at the rate of 17¼d. per pound, within a certain time then agreed upon after the arrival of the said goods in England. Averments: that the said goods did arrive by the said ship from Bombay in England, to wit, at Liverpool, and the plaintiff was then and there ready and willing and offered to deliver the said goods to the defendants, etc. Breach: that the defendants refused to accept the said goods or pay the plaintiff for them.

Plea. That the said ship mentioned in the said agreement was meant and intended by the defendants to be the ship called the Peerless, which sailed from Bombay, to wit, in October; and that the plaintiff was not ready and willing, and did not offer, to deliver to the defendants any bales of cotton which arrived by the last-mentioned ship, but instead thereof was only ready and willing, and offered to deliver to the defendants 125 bales of Surat cotton which arrived by another and different ship, which was also called the Peerless, and which sailed from Bombay, to wit, in December.

Demurrer, and joinder therein.

MILWARD in support of the demurrer. The contract was for the sale of a number of bales of cotton of a particular description, which the plaintiff was ready to deliver. It is immaterial by what ship the cotton was to arrive, so that it was a ship called the Peerless. The words "to arrive ex Peerless," only mean that if the vessel is lost on the voyage, the contract is to be at an end. [Pollock, C.B. It would be a question for the jury whether both parties meant the same ship called the Peerless.] That would be so if the contract was for the sale of a ship called the Peerless; but it is for the sale of cotton on board a ship of that name. [Pollock, C.B. The defendant only bought that cotton which was to arrive by a particular ship. It may as well be said that if there is a contract for the purchase of certain goods in warehouse A that is satisfied by the delivery of goods of the same description in warehouse B.] In that case there would be goods in both warehouses; here it does not appear that the plaintiff had any goods on board the other Peerless. [Martin, B. It is imposing on the defendant a contract different from that which he entered into. Pollock, C.B. It is like a contract for the purchase of wine coming from a particular estate in France or Spain, where there are two estates of that name.] The defendant has no right to contradict by parol evidence a written contract good upon the face of it. He does not impute misrepresentation or fraud, but only says that he fancied the ship was a different one. Intention is of no avail, unless stated at the time of the contract. [Pollock, C.B. One vessel sailed in October and the other in December.] The time of sailing is no part of the contract.

MELLISH (Cohen with him) in support of the plea. There is nothing on the face of the contract to show that any particular ship called the Peerless was meant; but the moment it appears that two ships called the Peerless were about to sail from Bombay there is a latent ambiguity, and parol evidence may be given for the purpose of showing that the defendant meant one Peerless and the plaintiff another. That being so, there was no consensus ad idem, and therefore no binding contract. He was then stopped by the court.

PER CURIAM. Judgment for the defendants.

CASE NOTE

English cases appear in a different format from U.S. decisions. This is in part due to the fact that English appellate courts do not have a single majority opinion. Instead, each of the judges votes and writes independently. Thus, the judges may provide inconsistent explanations for their decisions. Such a system makes interpretation of the decisions more difficult.

As demonstrated in the *Raffles* case, an issue of mistake may arise in the context of the meaning of certain language. This is particularly likely to happen in international transactions in which the words used in one language may have a slightly different meaning when translated into another language. The depositive issue often becomes what constitutes a reasonable interpretation of the words used. Relevant references include industry trade usage, government regulations, statutory definitions, and even basic dictionaries. Ultimately, however, the question is one of the reasonableness of the behavior of the parties and their particular expectations. The interesting case that follows demonstrates the manner in which courts try to resolve such disputes.

Frigaliment Importing Co., Ltd. v. B.N.S.

U.S. District Court, Southern District of New York

190 F.Supp. 116 (1960)

Background: B.N.S. (defendant) entered into two contracts to sell 200,000 pounds of "U.S. Fresh Frozen Chicken, Grade A, Government Inspected, Eviscerated" of certain weight per chicken at between 33 and 37 cents a pound. Frigaliment (plaintiff) expected broiling or frying chicken and instead received stewing chicken. The plaintiff sued for breach of warranty on the grounds that the chickens did not conform to their description in the contract.

Decision: The court found in favor of defendant B.N.S.

Friendly, Circuit Judge

The issue is, what is chicken? Plaintiff says "chicken" means a young chicken, suitable for broiling and frying. Defendant says "chicken" means any bird of that genus that meets contract specifications on weight and quality, including what it calls "stewing chicken" and plaintiff pejoratively terms "fowl." Dictionaries give both meanings, as well as some others not relevant here. To support its, plaintiff sends a number of volleys over the net; defendant essays to return them and adds a few serves of its own. Assuming that both parties were acting in good faith, the case nicely illustrates Holmes' remark "that the making of a contract depends not on the agreement of two minds in one intention, but on the agreement of two sets of external signs—not on the parties' having *meant* the same thing but on their having *said* the same thing." The Path of the Law, in Collected Legal Papers, p. 178. I have concluded that plaintiff has not sustained its burden of persuasion that the contract used "chicken" in the narrower sense.

Since the word "chicken" standing alone is ambiguous, I turn first to see whether the contract itself offers any aid to its interpretation. Plaintiff says the 1½–2 lbs. birds necessarily had to be young chicken since the older birds do not come in that size, hence the 2½–3 lbs. birds must likewise be young. This is unpersuasive—a contract for "apples" of two different sizes could be filled with different kinds of apples even though only one species came in both sizes.

Plaintiff's next contention is that there was a definite trade usage that "chicken" meant "young chicken." Defendant showed that it was only beginning in the poultry trade in 1957, thereby bringing itself within the principle that "when one of the parties is not a member of the trade or other circle, his acceptance of the standard must be made to appear" by proving either that he had actual knowledge of the usage or that the usage is "so generally known in the community that his actual individual knowledge of it may be inferred." 9 Wigmore, Evidence (3d ed. 1940) § 2464. Here there was no proof of actual knowledge of the alleged usage; indeed, it is quite plain that defendant's belief was to the contrary. In order to meet the alternative requirement, the law of New York demands a showing that "the usage is of so long continuance, so well established, so notorious, so universal and so reasonable in itself, as that the presumption is violent that the parties contracted with reference to it, and made it a part of their agreement."

Defendant's witness Weininger, who operates a chicken eviscerating plant in New Jersey, testified "Chicken is everything except a goose, a duck, and a turkey. Everything is a chicken, but then you have to say, you have to specify which category you want or that you are talking about." Its witness Fox said that in the trade "chicken" would encompass all the various classifications. Sadina, who conducts a food inspection service, testified that he would consider any bird coming within the classes of "chicken" in the Department of Agriculture's regulations to be a chicken. The specifications approved by the General Services Administration include fowl as well as broilers and fryers under the classification "chickens." Statistics of the Institute of American Poultry Industries use the phrases "Young chickens" and "Mature chickens," under the general heading "Total chickens." And the Department of Agriculture's daily and weekly price reports avoid use of the word "chicken" without specification.

When all the evidence is reviewed, it is clear that defendant believed it could comply with the contracts by delivering stewing chicken in the 2½–3 lbs. size. Defendant's subjective intent would not be significant if this did not coincide with an objective meaning of "chicken." Here it did coincide with one of the dictionary meanings, with the definition in the Department of Agriculture Regulations to which the contract made at least oblique reference, with at least some usage in the trade, with the realities of the market, and with what plaintiff's spokesman had said. Plaintiff asserts it to be equally plain that plaintiff's own subjective intent was to obtain broilers and fryers; the only evidence against this is the material as to market prices and this may not have been sufficiently brought home. In any event it is unnecessary to determine that issue. For plaintiff has the burden of showing that "chicken" was used in the narrower rather than in the broader sense, and this it has not sustained.

This opinion constitutes the Court's findings of fact and conclusions of law. Judgment shall be entered dismissing the complaint with costs.

Unilateral Mistake

A unilateral mistake is a mistake made by only one of the contracting parties. If one party makes a careless or negligent mistake in negotiating or in performing a contract, the law generally will not grant that party relief from the mistake. There are, however, several exceptions to this rule. Even when a mistake is made by only one party, courts generally grant relief if refusing to do so would impose undue hardship or expense on the mistaken party. In other words, the courts seek to balance the scales of justice. In doing so, the courts examine the relative consequences to both parties of a decision to grant or deny relief for a unilateral mistake. What is the burden that will be imposed on the other party if relief is granted to the mistaken party? What is the hardship suffered by the mistaken party if no relief is granted? Either a slight burden on the innocent party or a great burden on the mistaken party generally will be grounds for granting relief even where only one party has made a mistake.

Knowledge of Mistake

If a mistake was made by only one of the contracting parties, but the other party knew or should have known of the mistake, the courts generally will not allow the other party to take advantage of the mistake by enforcing the contract. Suppose several contractors were asked to submit bids for construction work on a hospital addition and the bid submitted by one of the contractors was significantly lower than all the other bids. If the bid was lower due to the contractor's unilateral mistake in calculation and the error was so great that the hospital to which the bid was submitted had reason to know of the mistake prior to its acceptance of the contractor's bid, the contractor would be granted relief from the obligation. The *McGough* case presented below exemplifies this type of mistake.

Another type of unilateral mistake is one concerning a person's identity. We have seen in the chapters on offer and acceptance that an offer may be accepted only by the person to whom it is made. But what if the offeror receives an acceptance from one whom he mistakenly believes to be the offeree? If offeror A intends to deal only with party B, but party C accepts the offer, there is no contract between C and A even if A mistakenly believes that party C is party B. A's mistake in identifying party C as party B is a unilateral mistake about which party C knew or should have known. Party C never received an offer from A and thus must have known that A was mistaken in identifying C as a person who could accept his offer.

A mistake as to the identity of a person can also be made as a result of fraud. A person can forge identification papers and pass as someone else. Such a situation would be a combination of fraud and mistake. Consequently, there would be double reason to allow the person who was both the victim of fraud and the party who had made a unilateral mistake that was known to the other party to avoid the contract.

However, if a person makes an offer to someone who occupies a certain capacity—for example, the manager of the ABC store—any person who is in that capacity can accept it. If, unknown to the offeror, a new manager has been appointed, the offeror cannot plead mistake because he thought his friend, the former manager, was still there. In this case, the offer is made to any person in the position, not to the individual who was mistakenly thought to be there. There is no mistaken identity in this situation, only a mistaken assumption.

M. J. McGough Company v. Jane Lamb Memorial Hospital

U.S. District Court S.D. Iowa

302 F.Supp. 482 (1969)

Background: McGough (plaintiff), a contractor, sued Jane Lamb Memorial Hospital (defendant) to have his bid declared rescinded and his surety released from liability. The hospital that received the bid filed suit to recover damages for the contractor's refusal to execute the contract and other documents in accordance with the original bid. Upon a consolidated trial of the cases, the District Court held that the contractor was entitled to have its bid rescinded and its surety released from liability on bond, since because of a clerical error, the bid was low by $199,800, or approximately 10 percent of the bid.

Decision: The court found in favor of plaintiff McGough.

Stephenson, Chief Judge

This action arises out of two separate cases filed on April 11, 1968, and consolidated for trial. Jurisdiction exists by reason of diversity and requisite amount in controversy.

The controversy herein arises from the competitive bidding on a hospital improvement proposed by Jane Lamb Memorial Hospital, a nonprofit Iowa corporation. On or about January 1, 1968, the hospital published an invitation for bids on this improvement. M. J. McGough Company, a Minnesota corporation, accepted said invitation and submitted a bid along with a bid bond from the Continental Insurance Company. The bid of M. J. McGough was submitted shortly before the opening time of 2:00 P.M., on February 16, 1968. The bids were opened by the Chairman of the Board of Trustees of Jane Lamb Memorial Hospital, Mr. Clark Depue III, at 2:00 P.M., and recorded as follows:

M. J. McGough Co., St. Paul	$1,957,000
Knutson Construction Co., Minneapolis	2,123,643
Steenberg Construction Co., St. Paul	2,185,000
Rinderknecht Construction Co., Cedar Rapids	2,264,000
O. Jorgenson & Sons Construction Co., Clinton	2,322,064
Lovering Construction Co., St. Paul	2,326,380
Universal Construction Co., Kansas City, Mo.	2,500,000
Ringland-Johnson-Crowley Co., Inc., Clinton	2,577,837
Priester Construction Co., Davenport	2,611,000

These figures were relayed to Mr. J. H. McGough, President of M. J. McGough Company, by a representative present at the opening. Mr. McGough was immediately concerned over the ten percent (10%) difference between his low bid and the next lowest bid of Knutson Construction Company. (By his testimony at trial, Mr. McGough explained that Knutson Construction Company was known in the trade as a notoriously low bidder.) Feeling a serious mistake had been made in the compilation of his bid, Mr. McGough called his representative at the opening and instructed him to request that he be allowed to withdraw his bid. This request was transmitted to Mr. Depue at approximately 2:45 P.M., while the Board was still analyzing the bids received. Shortly thereafter, Mr. McGough spoke with Mr. Depue by telephone and Mr. Depue requested a letter explaining the circumstances of the mistake and a written request to withdraw. Mr. McGough and his staff then began checking the papers relating to this bid and discovered an error in the amount of $199,800. The circumstances surrounding the error were set out in a letter dated February 16, 1968, directed to Milton Holmgrain, the hospital administrator. In the letter, McGough offered to "submit to you immediately all of our records relating to this project for verification of this error." In spite of this, the Board of Trustees, without further communication with M. J. McGough Company, at its meeting on February 22, 1968, passed a "Resolution of Intent" to the effect that the Board intended to accept the bid of M. J. McGough Company subject to obtaining the approval of the Division of Hospital Services of the Iowa State Department of Health and the U. S. Public Health Service.

Thereafter, the parties communicated a number of times by telephone, letter and in person on the matter. At all times, M. J. McGough Company sought the withdrawal of its bid and offered to produce its papers to verify the error in its bid. Likewise, the representatives of Jane Lamb Memorial Hospital continuously sought to hold M. J. McGough Company to its original bid. Upon the refusal of M. J. McGough Company to execute the contract and other necessary documents, however, the contract was awarded to the next lowest bidder, Knutson Construction Company.

On April 11, 1968, M. J. McGough Company filed a complaint in this Court seeking to have its bid declared rescinded and the surety, The Continental Insurance Company, be released from liability on the bond. On that same date, Jane Lamb Memorial Hospital filed a complaint in this Court against M. J. McGough Company and the Continental Insurance Company seeking damages in the amount of $190,156.58. (Jane Lamb Memorial Hospital arrived at this amount by adding the difference ($179,393) between the M. J. McGough Company bid and the Knutson Construction Company bid, plus the amount of increased architect's fees ($10,763.58), which are based on a percentage of the total price.)

The circumstances surrounding the mistake in the bid of M. J. McGough Company are not seriously disputed. The majority of the subcontractor bids used in computing the bid of M. J. McGough Company were received on February 16, 1968, the day of the opening. It is the accepted practice and custom among subcontractors to refrain from submitting their final sub-bids until the day of the opening and, then, only within a matter of hours before the actual opening of bids. The final sub-bids were received by telephone in the offices of M. J. McGough Company in St. Paul, Minnesota, between 10:00 A.M. and 1:00 P.M. on February 16, 1968. The sub-bids were recorded as they were phoned in on a slip of paper. Mr. McGough received the sub-bid of Artcraft Interiors, Inc., during this period of frenzied activity, and although he correctly recorded it on the slip of paper as $222,000, he verbally called it to an employee who recorded it as $22,200. This erroneous figure was, subsequently, transposed by the employee on the recapitulation sheet and used in computing the final bid of M. J. McGough Company. It was not until after the opening of bids, when Mr. McGough sought to check their figures, that the mistake was discovered.

By the overwhelming weight of authority a contractor may be relieved from a unilateral mistake in his bid by rescission under the proper circumstances. The prerequisites for obtaining such relief are: (1) the mistake is of such consequence that enforcement would be unconscionable; (2) the mistake must relate to the substance of the consideration; (3) the mistake must have occurred regardless of the exercise of ordinary care; (4) it must be possible to place the other party in status quo.

Applying the criteria for rescission for a unilateral mistake to the circumstances in this case, it is clear that M. J. McGough Company and his surety, the Continental Insurance Company, are entitled to equitable relief. The notification of mistake was promptly made, and Mr. McGough made every possible effort to explain the circumstances of the mistake to the authorities of Jane Lamb Memorial Hospital. Although

Jane Lamb Memorial Hospital argues to the contrary, the Court finds that notification of the mistake was received before acceptance of the bid. The mere opening of the bids did not constitute the acceptance of the lowest bid. Likewise, the acceptance by the Board of Trustees on February 22, 1968, being conditional, was not effective. Furthermore, it is generally held that acceptance prior to notification does not bar the right to equitable relief from a mistake in the bid.

The mistake in this case was an honest error made in good faith. While a mistake in and of itself indicates some degree of lack of care or negligence, under the circumstances here there was not such a lack of care as to bar relief. The mistake here was a simple clerical error. To allow Jane Lamb Memorial Hospital to take advantage of this mistake would be unconscionable. This is especially true in light of the fact that they had actual knowledge of the mistake before the acceptance of the bid.

Nor can it be seriously contended that a $199,800 error, amounting to approximately 10% of the bid, does not relate directly to the substance of the consideration. Furthermore, Jane Lamb Memorial Hospital has suffered no actual damage by the withdrawal of the bid of M. J. McGough Company. The hospital has lost only what it sought to gain by taking advantage of M. J. McGough Company's mistake. Equitable considerations will not allow the recovery of the loss of bargain in this situation.

Under the facts before the Court, therefore, M. J. McGough Company will be allowed to rescind its bid and be relieved from any liability thereon. The Continental Insurance Company, surety on the bid bond, is likewise relieved from liability.

Judgment for McGough.

Mistake of Material Fact

Finally, in determining the legal significance of a mistake, a court seeks to evaluate the performance of the mistake. Was the fact as to which the mistake occurred of substantial importance? Would the party seeking relief from the mistake have entered into the contract even if no mistake had been made? The court must find that it was the mistaken fact that, at least in part, induced the party seeking relief to enter into the contract. The law is reluctant to undo a contract. Only the most significant and important mistakes of facts are grounds for contract rescission.

Related to the determination of the importance of the mistake is the question of the assumption of risk made by the parties. If a mistake of judgment regarding a risk assumed by either of the contracting parties has been made, the court will not grant relief. In many business situations, a contract is made conditional upon an uncertain event. Both parties exchange promises based on their assumptions concerning the likelihood of that event occurring. What is the likelihood of lightning striking your home in the next year? Do you and your insurance company have different assumptions about such an event? What is the value of property located on the outskirts of town? Do seller and purchaser have the same assumptions as to the likelihood of the proposed shopping center locating on or near the property? Certainly, if the parties disagree, one of the parties will be mistaken in its assumption; but no relief will be given if both parties have assumed the risk. The "value" of many items is by nature uncertain because of business custom, prevailing mores, social policy, and existing law.

A final summary of the basic principles of genuine assent is provided in Table 13-2.

TABLE 13–2 IN SUMMARY

There is no genuine assent if there is:

Fraud	A material fact has been misrepresented, with knowledge and intent to deceive. Reasonable reliance on the misrepresentation has caused injury to the deceived party.
Duress	A wrongful act or threat, rather than the free will of the party, has induced contractual assent.
Undue influence	A dominant–subservient relationship exists. The dominant party has induced the subservient party to enter an agreement.
Mutual mistake	When one party entered the agreement, he or she mistook some fact of substantial importance. The other party knew or should have known of this mistake.

REVIEW PROBLEMS

1. What are the essential elements of fraud?

2. Why do the courts refuse to enforce agreements made under duress?

3. How does undue influence differ from duress?

4. When does a mistake justify the rescission of an agreement?

5. Jones who had recently purchased waterfront land hired the Suntee Construction Company to build a home on his newly purchased property. The project was suspended when a county building inspector found evidence of soil slippage. The inspector issued an order suspending construction until a soil expert certified the land as sufficiently stable for construction. Jones discharged the home contractor and brought action to rescind the land sale. Will he succeed? Does Suntee have recourse?

6. A beauty salon employee's plans to open her own salon next door came to the attention of her employer. The employee was summoned to headquarters ostensibly to discuss new hair dyes. When she arrived, she was confronted with questions about her plans, which she denied. Upon management's request, she signed an employment agreement which included a clause restricting her from competing with her employer. Later, the employee brought suit to rescind the contract due to duress. What is the result?

7. Ted, aged forty-two, has been the legal guardian of Frank, aged nineteen, since Frank's childhood. Frank has always trusted Ted and relied on Ted's advice in making important decisions. When Frank inherits $100,000 from his Uncle Mortimer, Ted advises Frank to enter the following agreement: For an annual fee of $10,000, Ted will invest Frank's inheritance for him. Frank is uncertain of the wisdom of this agreement, but concurs when Ted assures him, "I am doing this solely for your welfare." Is there any way Frank can nullify the agreement?

8. Greber suffered from a weight problem. After trying a complimentary treatment at the local Slenderella Salon, she immediately agreed to take a weight-reducing course consisting of 150 treatments at a

total cost of $300. Greber also had long suffered a back ailment and informed the Slenderella Salon manager of this before signing the agreement. The manager did not discourage Greber from entering into the contract; and, she in fact thought that the treatments would do her back some good. Several days later, prior to engaging in any of the paid treatments, Greber's back hurt so much that she consulted a doctor, who advised her against taking the Slenderella program. Now Slenderella is suing for the money Greber agreed to pay, but she wants to rescind the contract. What result? Slenderella Systems, Inc. v. Greber, 163 A.2d 462 (D.C. Mun. Ct. App. 1960).

9. Oliver, and his transferee Argo, leased property and equipment to Gilreath and Johnson for use as a retail oyster and seafood business. The lease provided in pertinent part: "The lessees agree to make at their own expense, and without expense to the lessor. . . . all of the necessary and needful repairs to said premises. . . ." Soon after agreeing to take the property, Gilreath and Johnson were assured by Oliver that if the equipment needed repairs, he would have Basham fix it at no charge to them. Six months later, various refrigeration equipment broke down, causing other damage and rendering the business inoperable. Gilreath and Johnson called Basham for repairs and he refused to help them. They then vacated the building and claimed Oliver fraudulently induced them to sign the lease. Is their claim justified? Gilreath v. Argo, 219 S.E.2d 461 (Ga. Ct. App. 1975).

10. Usry leased two ice-making machines from Poag, an agent for Granite Management Services (GMS). Prior to the execution of the contract, Poag drew up a separate purchase order, signed by Usry, that contained the following: "Customer own[s] equipment at end of lease" and "free service until lease ends." The lease agreement itself contained no such language, but said: "the contract constitutes the entire agreement between the lessor and lessee and . . . no representation or statement made by any representative of lessor or the supplier not stated herein shall be binding. . . ." When the machines failed to perform properly and Usry was refused free service, he discontinued making lease payments. GMS brought suit, but Usry claimed he was induced into signing the agreement by the fraudulent misrepresentation of Poag. Will Usry be able to rescind the contract? Granite Management Services, Inc. v. Usry, 204 S.E.2d 362 (Ga. Ct. App. 1974).

11. Robinson, a young married man, was employed as the assistant manager in one of the Gallaher Drug Company stores. After eighteen months on the job, he was accused of theft and embezzlement. Robinson admitted his guilt and was discharged from employment. The following day, he was invited to corporate headquarters to discuss restitution of the funds involved. After some discussion, Robinson entered into a written agreement to pay Gallaher Drug the sum of $2,000. He thereafter made payments totaling $741.64 and then refused to continue. The company seeks to enforce the contract, but Robinson says it was procured under duress and is therefore voidable. Is Robinson's defense a good one? Gallaher Drug Company v. Robinson., 232 N.E.2d 668 (Ohio Mun. Ct. 1965).

Capacity to Contract

This chapter reviews a number of situations in which a person's contractual capacity is at issue. The capacity of the person who is allegedly incompetent is examined first. Then contracts made by persons who are minors at the time they agree to contract are discussed. A related concern, that of parental liability for the contracts of minor children, is briefly noted. Finally, contracts made by intoxicated persons are considered.

In the past, married women, convicts, corporations, and unincorporated associations were considered to lack the capacity to make certain contracts, but court decisions and statutory revisions in most states have eliminated their disabilities. Today, the defense of lack of capacity is most often raised by people who claim to have been legally incompetent, under age, or intoxicated at the time of contracting. While the law seeks to protect the person who lacks the capacity to contract, lack of capacity is not presumed. The burden of proof is on the person asserting it. Thus, a person who acts senile or who is clearly under age is presumed to be capable of making a valid contract. To void the contract, the protected party must do something to indicate that he or she wants to exercise the option that the law allows.

The test of capacity to make a contract is not whether a person's mind is impaired or unsound, and not whether that person understands all the terms of the contract, but whether that person has the ability to comprehend the nature of the transaction engaged in and to understand its consequences. If a person who lacks the capacity to contract nevertheless enters into a contract, the law will protect that person by letting him or her get out of the contract. The contract of this person is referred to as a voidable contract. It can be upheld as a valid contract, but at the election and choice of the protected party it can be made void.

CONTRACTS OF PERSONS WHO MIGHT BE INCOMPETENT

The law used to be primarily concerned with contracts made by persons who had been found legally to be lunatics or insane. Contracts made by these persons were void. Such agreements could not be enforced even if both parties regarded them as valid. As medical science came to recognize different degrees of mental illness, the courts became concerned with contracts made by persons who might be incompetent. The courts have generally refrained from declaring all contracts made by such persons to be void. The modern rule, as noted in the *Cundick* case that follows, generally treats the contracts made by a person who is suffering from mental illness as voidable instead of void.

Even where the contract is voidable due to possible incompetency, a court generally examines the fairness and equity of allowing one party to avoid his or her contract. If the result of allowing the person to avoid the contract is unfair and inequitable, no right to disaffirm the contract will be granted. Finally, as has been noted, the person who is allegedly incompetent has the burden of proving that at the time of making the contract he or she did not understand the nature and effect of the transaction that resulted in the contract.

Of course, if a person has been legally adjudged to be incompetent after a regular court hearing and a guardian or conservator of that person's property has been appointed by the court, the contracts of that person usually will be regarded as void. Without a separate and independent court determination of legal incompetency, insanity, or inability to manage one's own affairs, however, the presumption of the law is that a person has the legal capacity to enter into contracts.

Cundick v. Broadbent

U. S. Court of Appeals, Tenth Circuit

383 F.2d 157 (1967)

Background: Irma Cundick (plaintiff), guardian ad litem for her husband, Darwin Cundick, brought this diversity suit in Wyoming to set aside an agreement for the sale of (1) livestock and equipment, (2) shares of stock in a development company, and (3) base range land in Wyoming. The alleged grounds for nullification were that at the time of the transaction Cundick was mentally incompetent to execute the agreement; that Broadbent (defendant), knowing of such incompetency, fraudulently represented to Cundick that the purchase price for the property described in the agreement was fair and just; and that Cundick relied upon the false representations when he executed the agreement and transferred the property.

The court concluded that Cundick failed to sustain the burden of proving that at the time of the transaction he was mentally incapable of managing his affairs; or that Broadbent knew of any mental deficiency when they entered into the agreement; or that Broadbent knowingly overreached him. The appeal is from a judgment dismissing the action.

Decision: Affirmed. The U.S. Court of Appeals decided in favor of Broadbent.

Murrah, Chief Judge

The contentions on appeal are twofold and stated alternatively: (1) that at the time of the transaction Cundick was totally incompetent to contract; that the agreement between the parties was therefore void ab initio, hence incapable of ratification; and (2) that in any event Cundick was mentally infirm and Broadbent knowingly overreached him; that the contract was therefore voidable, was not ratified—hence rescindable.

At one time, in this country and in England, it was the law that since a lunatic or non compos mentis had no mind with which to make an agreement, his contract was wholly void and incapable of ratification. But, if his mind was merely confused or weak so that he knew what he was doing yet was incapable of fully understanding the terms and effect of his agreement, he could indeed contract, but such contract would be avoidable to his option. But in recent times courts have tended away from the concept of absolutely void contracts toward the notion that even though a contract be said to be void for lack of capacity to make it, it is nevertheless ratifiable at the instance of the incompetent party. The modern rule, and the weight of authority, seems to be . . . "the contractual act by one claiming to be mentally deficient, but not under guardianship, absent fraud, or knowledge of such asserted incapacity by the other contracting party, is not a void act but at most only voidable at the instance of the deficient party; and then only in accordance with certain equitable principles." In recognition of different degrees of mental competency the weight of authority seems to hold that mental capacity to contract depends upon whether the allegedly disabled person possessed sufficient reason to enable him to understand the nature and effect of the act in issue. Even average intelligence is not essential to a valid bargain.

From all this it may be said with reasonable assurance that if Cundick was utterly incapable of knowing the nature and effect of the transaction, the agreement is, without more, invalid, though capable of ratification by his representative or by him during lucid intervals. But, if the degree of disability was such that he was capable of contracting, yet his mental condition rendered him susceptible of being overreached by an unscrupulous superior, his complaint comes under the heading of fraud to be proved as such. The burden is, of course, on the one asserting incompetency and fraud at the crucial time of the making of the challenged agreement.

Cundick was never judicially adjudged incompetent and his guardian ad litem apparently assumes the burden and accepts, as she must, the proposition that if the court's findings are supported by the record, they are conclusively binding here. She meets the issue squarely with the emphatic contention that the findings of the court are utterly without support in the record; that the evidence is all one way to the effect that at the time of the execution of the writings Cundick was mentally incompetent to make a valid contract.

All of the physicians who examined Cundick between 1961 and 1965 testified that in their judgment he was incapable of entering into the contract. When in December, 1960, Cundick first went to his family physician his condition was diagnosed as "depressive psychosis" and he was referred to a psychiatrist in Salt Lake City. When Cundick returned to the family physician more than two years later, he was treated for sore throat and bronchitis. From that time until October, 1965, the family physician saw Cundick about 25 times and treated him for everything from a sore throat to a heart attack suffered in March, 1964, but nothing was said or done about a mental condition. Apparently after this suit was filed and upon order of the court Cundick was examined in March, 1964, by two neurosurgeons in Cheyenne. By extensive tests it was established that Cundick was suffering from an atrophy of the frontal lobes of his brain diagnosed as pre-senile or premature arteriosclerosis. Both physicians used different language to say that from their examination in March, 1964, they were of the opinion that on the date of the transaction, i.e. September 2, 1963, Cundick was a "confused and befuddled man with very poor judgment," and although there were things he could do, he was, in their opinion, unable to handle his affairs at the time of the transaction. A psychologist to whom Cundick was referred in March by the Cheyenne neurosurgeons also testified that in his judgment Cundick was incapable of transacting his important business affairs in September of 1963. There was no medical testimony to the contrary. There was also lay testimony on behalf of Cundick to the effect that he was a quiet, reserved personality changed from one of friendliness to inattentiveness and that during 1963 he was unable to make decisions with respect to the conduct of his ranching business.

This unimpeached testimony may not be disregarded and the trier of the fact is bound to honor it in the absence of countervailing evidence—expert or non-expert— upon which to rest a contrary finding. But, expert evidence does not foreclose lay testimony concerning the same matter which is within the knowledge and comprehension of the lay witness. A lay witness may tell all he knows about a matter in issue even though it may tend to impugn the conclusions of the expert.

The trial judge who heard and saw the witnesses and felt the pulse beat of the lawsuit is, to be sure, the first and best judge of the weight and value to be given to all of the evidence, both expert and non-expert.

Against the background of medical and lay evidence tending to show Cundick's incompetency on the crucial date, there is positive evidence to the effect that at the time in question he was 59 years old, married and operating a sheep ranch in Wyoming; that in previous years he had sold his lamb crop to Broadbent and on a date prior to this transaction the parties met at a midway point for the purpose of selling the current lamb crop. The meeting resulted in a one page contract signed by both parties in which Cundick agreed to sell all of his ranching properties to Broadbent. It is undisputed that Cundick and his wife thereafter took his one page contract to their lawyer in Salt Lake City who refined and amplified it into an eleven page contract providing in detail the terms by which the sale was to be consummated. The contract was signed in the lawyer's office by Cundick and Broadbent in the presence of Cundick's wife and the lawyer. The lawyer testified that the contract had been explained in detail and that all parties apparently understood it.

As we have seen Cundick was not treated nor did he consult a physician for his mental condition from the time he returned from Salt Lake City in early 1961, until he was examined apparently by order of the court in March, 1964, after this suit was commenced. The record is conspicuously silent concerning any discussion of his mental condition among his family and friends in the community where he lived and operated his ranch. Certainly, the record is barren of any discussion or comment in Broadbent's presence. It seems incredible that Cundick could have been utterly incapable of transacting his business affairs, yet such condition be unknown on this record to his family and friends, especially his wife who lived and worked with him and participated in the months-long transaction which she now contends was fraudulently conceived and perpetrated. All this record silence, together with the affirmative evidence of normal behavior during the period of the transaction speaks loudly in support of the court's finding that Cundick's acts ". . . were the acts, conduct and behavior of a person competent to manage his affairs. . . ." As applied to the critical issue of incompetency, this finding leads us to the conclusion reached by the trial judge that when the medical testimony, positive as it may be, is considered in the context of all that was said and done, it does not carry the heavy burden of proving that Cundick was incompetent, i.e. he did not know the extent and condition of his property, how he was disposing of it, to whom and upon what consideration.

CONTRACTS OF MINORS

Overview

The legal capacity to enter into contracts is not the same as the capacity to commit a crime or a tort. The law often holds a minor responsible for criminal or tortious acts, but a minor is not generally liable for contracts. The higher standard applied to contracts is due in part to the fact that contracts generally involve bargaining with another person. A minor contracting with an adult needs to be protected from making unwise or foolish contracts. Similarly, the standard of capacity is also generally higher for contracting than for making a gift or a will. Neither of those methods of disposing of property involves bargaining with other parties, as is the case with contracts.

Historically, the law has provided special protection to minors who enter into contracts. This privileged contractual status has been based on their assumed immaturity and inexperience regarding commercial transactions. Historically the common law has treated people under the age of twenty-one as minors, but since the enactment of the Twenty-sixth Amendment to the U.S. Constitution, which lowered the voting age to eighteen, most states have lowered the age of majority from twenty-one to eighteen. Accordingly, although most of the cases that follow concern individuals who are minors because they are under twenty-one, in most states now only persons under eighteen are considered minors.

The protection extended by the law allows the minor the choice of either carrying out and enforcing the contract or seeking to avoid its provisions. Avoidance of the contract is done by any act that manifests the minor's intent to no longer be bound by the contract. Since most contracts entered into by minors can be avoided, they are generally referred to as voidable contracts. The contracts are valid unless the minor, by disaffirming them, seeks to avoid their provisions. There are a number of contracts, however, that a minor is not allowed to disaffirm. Statutes in many states specify that certain contracts are not subject to disaffirmance by a minor. Contracts of this type are considered valid, not voidable. Examples of such contracts are the following:

1. A contract by a minor to enlist in the armed forces
2. A contract by a minor to borrow money from an institutional lender or the government for the purpose of financing some portion of the minor's postsecondary education
3. A contract by a minor consenting to the adoption of a child
4. A contract of a minor to participate in a professional sport
5. A contract of a minor that includes a provision where the minor as an employee or purchaser of a business agrees not to compete with the business of the employer or seller
6. A contract to borrow money from a lender which is served by a mortgage

The contracts that are not voidable by minors vary from state to state. Statutes in each state have to be examined to ascertain exactly which contracts of minors are not subject to disaffirmance.

In addition to enforcing contracts that state statutes declare not subject to disaffirmance, contracts for necessaries are also usually excepted from the general rule allowing minors to avoid their contracts. The law generally holds the minor liable for the reasonable value of the necessaries furnished to him. Thus, if a minor has contracted to pay $100 for necessary and suitable clothes whose reasonable value is only $70, the minor's liability would be $70, not $100.

Although the general presumption is that a minor's contract is subject to disaffirmance, a court deciding whether a minor is liable on his contract must determine the answers to several questions:

1. Do any statutes specify that this particular type of contract should not be subject to disaffirmance?
2. Does the law (statutes or court decisions) consider that the subject of this particular contract constitutes a necessary, so that the minor would not be liable for the contract price but only for the reasonable value of the necessary?
3. If the contract is subject to disaffirmance, has the minor done something that in fact amounts to disaffirmance?

Several other questions that must also be answered to hold a minor liable for his or her contract will be noted later in this chapter.

Fisher v. Cattani

District Court, Nassau County, Third District

278 N.Y.S. 420 (1966)

Background: This was an action brought by an employment agency, Fisher (plaintiff), to recover the amount due on a contract with an infant, Cattani (defendant), who sought to disaffirm the contract. The trial court held that the infant Cattani's disaffirmance of the contract was effective since her notice was adequate where it was promptly given and actually occurred during the defendant's minority.
Decision: The District Court ruled in favor of Cattani.

Vitale, District Judge

This action was submitted for decision by the Court, upon an agreed state of facts. In substance they are: The defendant, in September 1962, being then 19 years of age, entered into a contract with the plaintiff, a duly licensed employment agency. The plaintiff obtained employment for the defendant, who found the job unsatisfactory, and resigned after one month. By registered mail notice to the Plaintiff, in November 1962, the defendant disaffirmed the contract of September 1962. The fee due Plaintiff was $146.25. Defendant paid $45. on account. The balance due is $101.25, for which Plaintiff demands judgment.

The law takes cognizance of the infant's lack of business experience and judgment by cloaking him with an inability to contract, except as to express exceptions, created, or recognized by statute. However, infants' contracts are not thereby generally considered void, but merely voidable. The contract being valid until disaffirmed by the infant, it becomes necessary to determine, if notice of disaffirmance was sufficiently given, and if so, whether it effectively terminated the defendant's contractual liability to the Plaintiff.

The notice given to the Plaintiff by the defendant, exceeds the standards usually applied to such acts, in that it was promptly given, was actually received, and was given during the infant's minority. The question of whether or not the disaffirmance was required to be accompanied by a tender of the consideration, received by the infant from the plaintiff, need not be considered. Aside from its intangibility, and the fact that the infant does not seek affirmative relief, the defendant, before disaffirmance, left the position secured for her by the Plaintiff.

The contract between these parties, represented an agreement by the Plaintiff to secure employment for the defendant, and a promise on her part to pay for this service.

A contract of this nature has not been made the subject of a statutory exception, to the right to disaffirm inherent, generally, in infants' contracts. The legislature has seen fit to do so, in other situations wherein it is customary, under present business practices, for infants to contract. For example, an infant, over 16, may not disaffirm, upon the ground of infancy, an agreement extending credit to him for an educational loan. Similarly, he may not, on that ground, and if over 18, avoid a real property mortgage on premises occupied as a home.

Furthermore, an infant may not disaffirm contracts for necessaries. Even here, the phrase necessaries, does not possess a fixed interpretation, but must be measured against both the infant's standard of living, and the ability and willingness of his guardian, if he has one, to supply the needed services or articles. These elements are not present in the facts before the Court, and they may not be presumed.

It well may be that upon a full presentation of the facts, as to the infant's need to work, in order to support himself, and possibly his children, an employment agency contract of this nature, may be regarded as one of the necessaries contemplated by the statutory exception, but such finding cannot be made upon the stipulated facts.

Accordingly it is held that under the submitted facts, the infant properly disaffirmed the contract upon which suit is brought, by reason of her infancy.

Disaffirmance of Contracts by Minors

Contracts Subject to Disaffirmance. As has been noted, some contracts that minors make are not subject to disaffirmance. Thus, the first question that must be answered concerning the minor's act of disaffirmance is whether the contract is one that cannot be disaffirmed. Unless state statutes expressly exempt the particular contract, or its subject matter is considered a necessary, the law generally will treat any contract made by a minor as subject to disaffirmance.

Time of Disaffirmance. Generally a minor may avoid any contract that is subject to disaffirmance during the time of his minority and for a reasonable period of time after attaining the age of majority. The law thus gives the minor a period of time to review and reflect on the contractual agreements made during minority. What constitutes a reasonable time depends on the complexity of the transaction, its subject matter, and the circumstances peculiar to each agreement.

Methods of Disaffirmance. Disaffirmance occurs by the minor manifesting an unwillingness to be bound by the contract. The minor can simply inform the other party (whether an adult or minor) that he intends to disaffirm their contractual agreement. Or the minor can do some other act that clearly indicates that he or she has such an intent.

Thus, the minor who has agreed to sell goods to one purchaser but instead sells them to a third party has by such an act disaffirmed the contract made with the original purchaser. Similarly, the minor who institutes legal action to avoid responsibility for a contract's obligations manifests an intent to disaffirm the contract.

Disaffirmance and Restitution of Property by the Minor. While the law seeks to protect the minor from unwise or imprudent contracts, there is disagreement among court decisions as to the rights of the parties if a minor cannot return the property he or she received. The majority of decisions hold that the minor may disaffirm a contract and receive back any consideration given even if the minor is unable to return to the other party that which the minor has received. A minority of decisions require the minor to return the consideration received from the other party in order to be able to disaffirm the contract. If the minor is unable to return the property received (or its equivalent value), the minor will not be allowed to disaffirm the contract. Compare the decision of the *Central Bucks Aero* case to that in the *Haydocy Pontiac* case (both cases are given below). Which policy would you follow in similar situations?

Disaffirmance and Misrepresentation of Age. A minor's right to disaffirm a contract can also be influenced by misrepresentations made by the minor. When a minor misrepresents his or her age and such misrepresentation is relied on by the other party, who is then induced to enter into a contract, a conflict between legal policies results.

On the one hand, the law seeks to protect the minor and allow the minor to disaffirm contracts made while he or she was under the age of majority; thus, the law wants to insure that the minor is not victimized by a wiser and more mature adult. On the other hand, if a person is the victim of a fraudulent statement made by another person, the law generally allows the victim of the fraud to rescind or cancel the contract that resulted from the fraud. What should be done if the minor commits the fraud and the adult is the victim? The response to these questions has not been uniform; the court decisions are split.

While all three of the following cases are concerned with the right of the minor to disaffirm a contract, each addresses a distinct problem connected to that right. Can a minor who disaffirms a contract be held liable in tort for damages suffered by the other contracting party? *(Central Bucks Aero* v. *Smith)* Can the minor who misrepresented her age and is unable to return the consideration she received from the other contracting party disaffirm the contract? *(Haydocy Pontiac, Inc.* v. *Lee)* Is a minor who appears to be of legal age or who has signed a form that states he is of said age entitled to disaffirm a contract? *(Kiefer* v. *Howe Motors, Inc.)*

Central Bucks Aero, Inc. v. Smith

Superior Court of Pennsylvania
310 A.2d 283 (1973)

Background: Central Bucks Aero, Inc. (plaintiff), the lessor of an airplane, brought this action against Smith (defendant), the minor lessee, to recover for damage to the airplane occurring during landing. The Court of Common Pleas granted the minor lessee's motion for summary judgment on the ground that he had disaffirmed the lease after the accident and the lessor appealed.

Decision: Affirmed. The Superior Court ruled in favor of Smith.

Spaeth, Judge

This is an appeal from the granting of defendant-appellee's motion for summary judgment. The issue is whether we should overturn the longstanding common law doctrine that a minor by disaffirming a contract can avoid liability under the contract.

Appellee, when twenty years of age, leased an airplane from appellant. In the process of landing, appellee damaged the airplane beyond repair, and also damaged the landing field. After appellant filed suit in trespass, appellee disaffirmed the lease.

When a minor disaffirms a contract, unless the contract is for necessaries the other party cannot recover the value of any item that the minor has obtained pursuant to the contract. The only remedy the other party has is an action in replevin to recover the item itself. If the minor no longer has the item, the other party is remediless.

An action in tort which is the form of action selected by appellant, will not lie. The privilege (to avoid the contract) would be little worth if it might be eluded by fashioning the action into a particular shape. Whenever the substantive ground of an action against an infant is contract, as well where the contract is stated as incident to a supposed tort, as where it is not, the plaintiff cannot recover. In the course of his discussion of the cases in which infants may be sued in tort and those in which they cannot be, Judge Cooley said: "The distinction is this: If the wrong grows out of contract relations, and the real injury consists in the nonperformance of a contract into which the party wronged has entered with an infant, the law will not permit the former to enforce the contract indirectly by counting on the infant's neglect to perform it, or omission of duty under it as a tort. The reason is obvious: To permit this to be done would deprive the infant of that shield of protection which, in matters of contract, the law has wisely placed before him." 1 Cooley on Torts, 3d ed. 181. This principle is followed in most jurisdictions.

It may be granted that upon occasion the courts have decided to remove an immunity from legal responsibility by overruling the cases that created the immunity. In the present case, however, such a decision would be inappropriate.

A businessman may protect himself from loss incident to a minor's disaffirmance of a contract by finding out whether the person with whom he is dealing is a minor. Ordinarily this will present no difficulty. If the person is a minor, or if it is not clear that he is an adult, the businessman may decline to deal with him, or may require that someone he knows is an adult join in the contract. Inasmuch as appellant neglected such precautions, it has only itself to blame for its inability to recover for the damage to its airplane and landing field.

Haydocy Pontiac, Inc. v. Lee

Court of Appeals of Ohio
250 N.E.2d 898 (1969)

Background: Haydocy Pontiac, Inc. (plaintiff) was the seller of an automobile to Lee (defendant). At the time of the sale, Lee was twenty years of age and represented to the seller that she was twenty-one. After the sale, Lee gave the car to a friend who had repairs made on it and neither party to this suit can recover possession of the car.

Defendant asserted her infancy allowed her to avoid the contract and released her from any obligation to pay anything to plaintiff seller. The trial court agreed and rendered its judgment for the defendant. Plaintiff seller appealed.

Decision: Reversed. The Court of Appeals ruled in favor of Haydocy Pontiac, Inc.

Strausbaugh, Judge

The facts in the case are not in dispute; the defendant Jennifer J. Lee was the only witness at the time of trial. On August 22, 1967, plaintiff sold to the defendant Jennifer J. Lee a 1964 Plymouth Fury automobile; the cash price of the automobile was $1,552, which was paid by the defendant by a "trade-in" automobile of the value of $150; the balance of the purchase price was financed by the defendant executing and delivering to plaintiff a note and chattel mortgage for the unpaid purchase price plus financing charges and insurance charges; the total face amount of the note was $2,016.36. A certificate of title was issued showing that the defendant was owner of the automobile. A note and chattel mortgage were assigned by the plaintiff to a local bank which has reassigned the same back to the plaintiff.

Immediately following delivery of the automobile to the defendant, the defendant permitted one John L. Roberts to take possession of the car; the defendant never at any time thereafter had possession. John L. Roberts, subsequently, delivered the automobile to Consolidated Holdings, Inc., d.b.a. Motorland Do-It-Yourself, for repairs; neither the plaintiff nor the defendant has been able to obtain possession of it. The defendant failed to make any payments on the note and chattel mortgage. The plaintiff commenced this action to recover possession thereof and as an alternative prayer in the amended petition prayed that judgment be granted in its favor for the sum of $2,016.36, the balance due on the note and chattel mortgage, against each of the defendants.

The whereabouts of Roberts is unknown; Consolidated Holdings, Inc., is in receivership and is insolvent. The defendant filed an answer asserting as an affirmative defense to the action that she was a minor of the age of 20 years at the time of purchase, that she has not ratified the agreement to purchase the car, nor has she ratified the note or the mortgage since attaining the age of majority. It is undisputed that defendant was a minor at the time of entering into the contract and at the time of signing the note and mortgage, that the defendant has never returned the car to the plaintiff, and that at the time of the purchase the defendant represented that she was then 21 years of age. The Municipal Court found that at the time of the purchase the defendant was a minor, that she had repudiated her contact and that she, therefore, was not bound thereby, and the court entered judgment in favor of the defendant.

Careful examination of the law in Ohio discloses no case wherein the vendor has recovered from an infant who has repudiated his contract. The cases we have examined in this regard all relate to the question whether the infant can recover from the vendor the purchase price paid and the right of the vendor to counterclaim rather than the facts of this case where the vendor, in the original petition, seeks to recover the property or, in lieu thereof, the balance due on the purchase price. Many of the cases use language to the effect that when the property received by the infant is in his possession, or under his control, to permit him to rescind the contract without requiring him to return or offer to return it would be to permit him to use his privilege as a "sword rather than a shield."

At a time when we see young persons between 18 and 21 years of age demanding and assuming more responsibilities in their daily lives; when we see such persons emancipated, married, and raising families; when we see such persons charged with the responsibility for committing crimes; when we see such persons being sued in tort claims for acts of negligence; when we see such persons subject to military service; when we see such persons engaged in business and acting in almost all other respects as an adult, it seems timely to re-examine the case law pertaining to contractual rights and responsibilities of infants to see if the law as pronounced and applied by the courts should be redefined.

To allow infants to avoid a transaction without being required to restore the consideration received where the infant has used or otherwise disposed of it causes hardship on the other party. We hold that where the consideration received by the infant cannot be returned upon disaffirmance of the contract because it has been disposed of, the infant must account for the value of it, not in excess of the purchase price, where the other party is free from any fraud or bad faith and where the contract has been induced by a false representation of the age of the infant. Under this factual situation the infant is estopped from pleading infancy as a defense where the contract has been induced by a false representation that the infant was of age.

The necessity of returning the consideration as a prerequisite to obtaining equitable relief is still clearer where the infant misrepresents age and perpetrated an actual fraud on the other party. The disaffirmance of an infant's contract is to be determined by equitable principles, whether wrought in a proceeding in equity or a case at law.

The common law has bestowed upon the infant the privilege of disaffirming his contracts in conservation of his rights and interests. Where the infant, 20 years of age, through falsehood and deceit enters into a contract with another who enters therein in honesty and good faith and, thereafter, the infant seeks to disaffirm the contract without tendering back the consideration, no right or interest of the infant exists which needs protection. The privilege given the infant thereupon becomes a weapon of injustice.

Kiefer v. Howe Motors, Inc.

Supreme Court of Wisconsin
158 N.W.2d 288 (1968)

Background: On August 9, 1965, Steven Kiefer (plaintiff) entered into a contract with Fred Howe Motors, Inc. (defendant), for the purchase of a 1960 Willys station wagon. Kiefer paid the contract price of $412 and took possession of the car. At the time of the sale Kiefer was twenty years old, married, and the father of one child. Some of the testimony given in the trial court indicated that Kiefer orally stated he was an adult. Furthermore, the purchase contract he signed stated that he represented himself to be twenty-one years of age and that the dealer relied on that representation.

Kiefer had difficulty with the car that he claimed was caused by a cracked block. Kiefer contacted the dealer and asked it to take the car back. Several other attempts to secure some adjustment with the dealer failed and Kiefer contacted attorney Paul C. Konnor. The attorney wrote a letter to the dealer advising that Kiefer was under 21 at the time of the sale. The letter declared the contract void, tendered return of the automobile and demanded repayment of the purchase price. There was no response so this action was commenced to recover the $412 purchase price. After a trial a judgment for the plaintiff was entered and the defendant appealed.

Decision: Affirmed. The Supreme Court of Wisconsin ruled in favor of Kiefer.

Wilkie, Justice

Three issues are presented on this appeal. They are:

1. Should an emancipated minor over the age of eighteen be legally responsible for his contracts?
2. Was the contract effectively disaffirmed?
3. Is the plaintiff liable in tort for misrepresentation?

LEGAL RESPONSIBILITY OF EMANCIPATED MINOR

No one really questions that a line as to age must be drawn somewhere below which a legally defined minor must be able to disaffirm his contracts for nonnecessities. The law over the centuries has considered this age to be twenty-one. Legislatures in other states have lowered the age. We suggest that the appellant might better seek the change it proposes [to lower the age to eighteen] in the legislative halls rather than this court.

Undoubtedly, the infancy doctrine is an obstacle when a major purchase is involved. However, we believe that the reasons for allowing that obstacle to remain viable at this point outweigh those for casting it aside. Minors require some protection from the pitfalls of the market place. Reasonable minds will always differ on the extent of the protection that should be afforded. For this court to adopt a rule that the appellant suggests and remove the contractual disabilities from a minor simply because he becomes emancipated, which in most cases would be the result of marriage, would be to suggest that the married minor is somehow vested with more wisdom and maturity than his single counterpart. However, logic would not seem to dictate this result especially when today a youthful marriage is oftentimes indicative of a lack of wisdom and maturity.

DISAFFIRMANCE

The appellant questions whether there has been an effective disaffirmance of the contract in this case.

Williston, while discussing how a minor may disaffirm a contract, states:

> Any act which clearly shows an intent to disaffirm a contract or sale is sufficient for the purpose. Thus a notice by the infant of his purpose to disaffirm a tender or even an offer to return the consideration or its proceeds to the vendor, is sufficient.

The testimony of Steven Kiefer and the letter from his attorney to the dealer clearly establish that there was an effective disaffirmance of the contract.

MISREPRESENTATION

Appellant's last argument is that the respondent should be held liable in tort for damages because he misrepresented his age. Appellant would use these damages as a setoff against the contract price sought to be reclaimed by respondent.

The 19th-century view was that a minor's lying about his age was inconsequential because a fraudulent representation of capacity was not the equivalent of actual capacity. This rule has been altered by time. There appear to be two possible methods that now can be employed to bind the defrauding minor: He may be estopped from denying his alleged majority, in which case the contract will be enforced or contract damages will be allowed; or he may be allowed to disaffirm his contract but be liable in tort for damages. Wisconsin follows the latter approach.

Having established that there is a remedy against the defrauding minor, the question becomes whether the requisites for a tort action in misrepresentation are present in this case.

The trial produced conflicting testimony regarding whether Steven Kiefer had been asked his age or had replied that he was "twenty-one." Steven and his wife, Jacqueline, said "No," and Frank McHalsky, appellant's salesman, said "Yes." Confronted with this conflict, the question of credibility was for the trial court to decide, which it did by holding that Steven did not orally represent that he was "twenty-one." This finding is not contrary to the great weight and clear preponderance of the evidence and must be affirmed.

Even accepting the trial court's conclusion that Steven Kiefer had not orally represented his age to be over twenty-one, the appellant argues that there was still a misrepresentation. The "motor vehicle purchase contract" signed by Steven Kiefer contained the following language just above the purchaser's signature:

"I represent that I am 21 years of age or over and recognize that the dealer sells the above vehicle upon this representation."

Whether the inclusion of this sentence constitutes a misrepresentation depends on whether elements of the tort have been satisfied. They were not.

We fail to see how the dealer could be justified in the mere reliance on the fact that the plaintiff signed a contract containing a sentence that said he was twenty-one or over. The trial court observed that the plaintiff was sufficiently immature looking to arouse suspicion. The appellant never took any affirmative steps to determine whether the plaintiff was in fact over twenty-one. It never asked to see a draft card, identification card, or the most logical indicium of age under the circumstances, a driver's license. Therefore, because there was no intent to deceive, and no justifiable reliance, the appellant's action for misrepresentation must fail.

Hallows, Chief Justice *(dissenting)*

The majority opinion on the issue of whether an emancipated minor legally should be responsible for his contracts "doth protest too much." After giving very cogent reasons why the common-law rule should be abandoned, the opinion refrains from reshaping the rule to meet reality. Minors are emancipated by a valid marriage and also by entering military service. If they are mature enough to become parents and assume the responsibility of raising other minors and if they are mature enough to be drafted or volunteer to bear arms and sacrifice their life for their country, then they are mature enough to make binding contracts in the market place. The magical age limit of 21 years as an indication of contractual maturity no longer has a basis in fact or in public policy.

My second ground of the dissent is that an automobile to this respondent was a necessity and therefore the contract could not be disaffirmed. Here, we have a minor, aged 20 years and 7 months, the father of a child, and working. While the record shows there is some public transportation to his present place of work, it also shows he borrowed his mother's car to go to and from work. Automobiles for parents under 21 years of age to go to and from work in our current society may well be a necessity and I think in this case the record shows it is. An automobile as a means of transportation to earn a living should not be considered a nonnecessity because the owner is 5 months too young. I would reverse.

A Minor's Contract for Necessaries and Parent's Liability for Minor's Contracts

As we have noted, a minor is generally liable for the reasonable value of necessary items for which he or she has contracted. That liability is limited to the reasonable value of the items, which may be less than their contracted price. What constitutes necessary items varies with the needs of the individual concerned. Generally, food, clothing, and shelter, suitable to the minor's station in life, will be regarded as necessaries. The court looks to see whether the contracted items are essential to the minor's general welfare.

What about the purchase of a stereo set? A car? The contract for the payment of college tuition? Only an analysis of the needs of the individual minor can provide the answer to these questions.

Since the law often protects the minor by allowing contracts to be disaffirmed, those contracting with minors will seek to hold other parties liable for the minor's contracts. With the lowering of the age of majority in most states to eighteen, those who are minors are less likely to be emancipated, self-supporting, or totally independent from their parents or guardians. Businesspeople contracting with sixteen- or seventeen-year-olds are likely to do so only if the parent or another adult is expressly committed to perform the minor's contractual obligations. Banks will require an adult cosignor for any loan made to a minor. Merchants will check to confirm that charge cards are issued in the name of an adult and that the minor child has the express permission of that adult to make purchases. School authorities will require parental permission and approval, as well as the child's consent, prior to participation by the child in extracur-

ETHICS BOX
Fair Treatment of Minors

In *Kiefer* v. *Howe Motors, Inc.* the majority and dissenting opinions disagreed on the legal question of whether emancipated minors should legally be held responsible for their contracts. The ethical question is whether it is fair for a minor to sign a contract that says "I represent that I am twenty-one years of age or over and recognize that the dealer sells the vehicle upon this representation," and then be able to disaffirm. The question for legal policy is somewhat different—at what age is it just to hold young people accountable for their agreements, particularly when they are emancipated from their parents? Sixteen, eighteen, twenty-one?

In *Kiefer* the minor was nearly twenty-one and was even represented by a lawyer. Essentially the case involved a consumer dispute and the "minor" decided to use his minority as a sword to achieve a favorable outcome. To the extent that a minor intentionally and purposefully misrepresents his or her age with the intention of keeping options open, the minor has acted unethically.

From the viewpoint of the law, a different question is involved. The policy question is, What is the best way to protect minors overall? A rule that a few may abuse, but that protects a lot of minors who need protection, may be considered efficient, although a few people get away with acts that are inconsistent with the purpose of the law. Minors who knowingly take advantage of the law, and who intentionally act to abuse the law, are unethical even though their actions are legal.

ricular activities or special programs. Most businesses are aware of the law's desire to protect the minor; they therefore seek to make contracts with adults whose contracts are not subject to disaffirmance.

Even in situations where the merchant does not have an express contract with the parent of a minor, a merchant who furnishes necessary items to a minor may be able to hold one or both of the minor's parents liable. By statute in most states, the law requires a parent to furnish necessary items to his or her minor children. If the merchant can prove that the items the minor agreed to purchase were necessary for the minor, and were not being—but could be—furnished by a parent, the parent

can be held liable. The contract between the parent and the merchant is not an express contract, created by the parties; it is implied by the provisions of the law.

Where a merchant furnishes necessary items to a minor, the merchant may hold either the parent or the minor liable for the reasonable value (not the contract price) of those items. If the minor is emancipated and is not dependent for financial support on his or her parents, the merchant can hold the minor liable. A contract for necessaries by a minor is valid; it is not subject to disaffirmance by the minor. If the minor is dependent on one or more parents for financial support and for furnishing his or her necessaries, and if a parent is able to furnish those necessaries, then the merchant can hold the parent liable. In either case, the merchant can recover the reasonable value of necessary items furnished to a minor.

Ratification of Contracts by Minors

In general, a minor can void any contract entered into by exercising the power of disaffirmance. The effective surrender of the power of disaffirmance is known as *ratification*. Since contracts entered into by a minor are subject to disaffirmance, ratification cannot take place prior to the minor's attainment of the age of majority.

A ratification by a minor can occur in any of three ways. First, the minor may fail to make a timely disaffirmance. Since the minor has the right to disaffirm only for the period of his or her minority, plus a reasonable time after attainment of the age of majority, the minor who does not disaffirm within that time ratifies by such action (or inaction) the contract made during minority. Second, the minor can expressly state, orally or in writing, that he or she intends to ratify the contract. If the express statement is clear and unambiguous and is made after attainment of the age of majority, ratification of the contract has occurred. Once such ratification has occurred, the power and right to disaffirm terminates. Finally, the minor, after attainment of the age of majority, may by conduct manifest an intent to ratify the contract made while a minor.

Bobby Floars Toyota Inc. v. Smith

Court of Appeals of North Carolina
269 S.E.2d 320 (1980)

Background: When Charles Smith (defendant) was age seventeen years, eleven months, he bought a car from Bobby Floars Toyota (plaintiff). He signed an installment agreement to pay the balance in thirty monthly installments. Age eighteen was the year of majority for executing contracts in North Carolina. At age eighteen years, ten months, he returned the car to the plaintiff and stopped making car payments. The plaintiff sold the car at public auction, and sued Smith for the balance that was not obtained at auction. The trial court granted the defendant's motion for dismissal. The plaintiff appealed.
Decision: Reversed. The Court of Appeals ruled in favor of plaintiff Floars.

Morris, Justice

The only question is whether Smith's voluntarily relinquishing the automobile 10 months after attaining the age of majority constitutes a timely disaffirmance of his contract with Floars. The rule is that the contracts of an infant may be disaffirmed by the infant during minority or within a reasonable time after reaching majority. What is a reasonable time depends on the circumstances of each case. In the instant case, we believe that 10 months is an unreasonable time within which to elect between disaffirmance and ratification, in that this case involves an automobile, an item of personal property which is constantly depreciating in value. Modern commercial transactions require that both buyers and sellers be responsible and prompt.

We are of the further opinion that Smith waived his right to avoid the contract. The privilege of disaffirmance may be lost where the infant affirms or ratifies the contract after reaching majority. Certain affirmations or conduct evidencing ratification is sufficient to bind the infant, regardless of whether a reasonable time for disaffirmance had passed. In the present case, it is clear that Smith recognized as binding the installment note evidencing the debt owed from his purchase of an automobile. He continued to possess and operate the automobile after his 18th birthday, and he continued to make monthly installments as required by the note for 10 months after becoming 18. We hold, therefore, that Smith's acceptance of the benefits and continuance of payments under the contract constituted a ratification of the contract, precluding subsequent disaffirmance.

INTOXICATION AND CAPACITY TO CONTRACT

A person who is intoxicated may be unable to understand the nature and effects of contractual commitments made while in that condition. Generally, the law treats as voidable the contracts made by a person who doesn't know what he is doing or the effects thereof by reason of intoxication. Intoxication thus is usually treated in the same way as incompetency due to mental illness or disease. The same standard is also usually applied to a person who is under the influence of drugs.

Fairness and Fraud

There are, however, several differences in examining the capacity to contract of someone who is under the influence of drugs or alcohol and of someone who is mentally ill. Some states do not allow a person to avoid contracts made while intoxicated or under the influence of drugs unless that party can show that the person with whom his contract was made knew of the person's condition and took advantage of it. If a person is responsible for the intoxication of the other party with whom a contract is made, or if a person takes unfair advantage of the other's intoxication, whether or not responsible for causing it, the courts will often refuse to enforce the contract as a matter of fairness and equity.

Under this method of analysis, the courts are generally concerned not so much with the degree of intoxication affecting one person's capacity to contract as with the conduct of the party with whom that party contracts. In these cases, some degree of intoxication or impairment of judgment, when coupled with fraudulent action by the other contracting party, may allow the intoxicated party to avoid his contract. If one contracting party deceives the intoxicated person with whom he contracts, the court will likely allow the intoxicated person to avoid the contract on the basis of fraud, if not for lack of contract capacity.

Degree of Intoxication

While fairness and fraud are sometimes reviewed when examining the capacity to contract of the intoxicated person, the law usually is more concerned with the effect of the intoxication on the person's understanding of his contract than on who is responsible for that degree of intoxication. If a person has been legally adjudged to be incompetent because of habitual drunkenness, that person no longer has any capacity to contract; his contracts are considered void, not voidable. In the absence of a legal determination of incompetency due to intoxication, the court must determine if the degree of intoxication is sufficient to allow a person to avoid his contracts by disaffirming them.

Generally, in the absence of fraud or special circumstances, if a person is slightly under the influence of alcohol or is partially intoxicated, contracts made by that person will be considered valid. Intoxication that causes some impairment of a person's judgment or a feeling of exhilaration generally is not sufficient to render contracts voidable. Instead, as the *Olsen* case indicates, there must be intoxication to such a degree that a person is deprived of reason and unable to understand the consequences of his actions.

If a person is so intoxicated as to lack the capacity to contract, he will usually be allowed to disaffirm and avoid its obligations. If, however, the intoxicated person cannot return the consideration he has received, in the absence of fraud by the other party, he will generally not be granted the right to disaffirm the contract. Furthermore, if the contract was for necessaries, the intoxicated person, like the minor, will be held liable for the reasonable value of the furnished items.

Olsen v. Hawkins

Supreme Court of Idaho

408 P.2d 462 (1965)

Background: This case was brought by Olsen (plaintiff) to collect proceeds due him from insurance on the life of Turner, who died in 1960. Until 1957, Olsen (Turner's stepson) was Turner's beneficiary. Olsen claimed that the change of beneficiary from himself to Hawkins (defendant) made by Turner in 1957 occurred while Turner was intoxicated and therefore should not be given effect. The trial court agreed with Olsen and found the contract by which Turner changed his beneficiary to be voidable. Accordingly, it entered judgment for Olsen. Hawkins appealed to the Supreme Court of Idaho.

Decision: Reversed. The Supreme Court ruled in favor of the defendant, Hawkins.

Knudson, Justice

We approach this case with full recognition of the long established rule of this court that our province is to examine the record in the light most favorable to the judgment and that when findings of the trial court are supported by competent substantial evidence they are binding and conclusive on appeal.

The only question presented for our determination is whether respondents sustained the burden of proof in support of their charge that Turner was mentally incompetent to execute the change of beneficiary on the policy effective as of March 17, 1960.

Several rules of law are applicable to the case at bar and must be considered during our review of this record. It is a fundamental rule that the law will presume sanity rather than insanity, competency rather than incompetency; that every man is capable of managing his own affairs and responsible for his own acts. Likewise it is presumed that each man is capable of understanding the nature and effect of his contracts.

It may also be stated that as a general rule, all proceedings involving the competency of an individual to execute a valid contract start with the presumption of competency and that this presumption may be relied upon until the contrary is shown.

In the instant case Turner was described by some as being "forgetful and childish." This expression was not further defined. However, a reasonable interpretation of it would be that they did not consider Turner as possessing the mental capacity of the average man of his age. In this connection it should be noted that where a person possesses sufficient mental capacity to understand the nature of the transaction and is left to exercise his own free will, his contract will not be invalidated because he was of a less degree of intelligence than his co-contractor; because he was fearful or worried; because he was eccentric or entertained peculiar beliefs; or because he was aged or both aged and mentally weak. . . .

Clearly, a person's dissipated condition is not in itself a ground for avoiding a contract or deed, since it is well known that while habitual drunkards are, at times, mentally infirm to the same extent as an insane person or an idiot, at other times they are sober and rational. Accordingly, the rule is that in the absence of an adjudication finding a habitual drunkard to be incompetent, in order to avoid his contract or deed on the ground of his incompetency, it must be shown that his mental condition was such, at the time the contract or deed was made, that he lacked the power of reason and was unable to comprehend the nature and consequences of his act in entering into the contract or executing the deed. A deed executed in a sober interval by one who is addicted to the excessive use of liquor, but who has not been adjudicated incompetent and has not suffered a permanent impairment of mind as a result of his excessive indulgence, will stand, at least in the absence of undue influence or fraud.

The evidence submitted in support of respondents' allegations and contentions may be briefly summarized as follows:

Prior to the death of Turner's wife, they, the Turners, lived at Montpelier, Idaho, and they frequently visited respondents, who lived at Pocatello, Idaho. Mrs. Turner died in November 1956. At that time Turner was a retired railroad engineer, receiving two pensions totaling approximately $250.00 a month; that following the death of Mrs. Turner he became a "heavy drinker" and was what may be termed an alcoholic during a substantial portion of the years that followed; that on a number of occasions while he was under the influence of intoxicating liquor he was arrested for various offenses, among which were, being drunk in a public place, driving while drunk and indecent exposure, and was finally committed to the State Hospital South as an alcoholic.

The record shows that following the death of his wife Turner moved to Lava Hot Springs sometime during December 1956 and it was during 1957 when he became involved in most of the arrests hereinbefore mentioned. During May 1957 he voluntarily entered said State Hospital, at which time "he was diagnosed as a case of Chronic Alcoholism," and remained at the hospital about two weeks. Thereafter and on October 24, 1957 he was readmitted to the hospital under a judicial order and the same diagnosis was given him. On May 1, 1958, he was discharged. . . .

Following his discharge from the hospital Turner remained in the city of Blackfoot for three or four months, following which he moved to Ashton, Idaho, where he remained for several months. It was during his stay in Ashton, and on or about March 17, 1960, that the change of beneficiary here involved was accomplished.

This brings us to a consideration of one of the principal issues presented, namely, does the record disclose competent evidence in support of the court's finding that the change of beneficiary was made while Turner was incompetent and unable to transact his business or understand the nature of the transaction. . . . [A] contract by an alcoholic may not be avoided on that ground alone if at the time of its execution he was sober and in the possession of his faculties. Proofs of old age and alcoholic addiction standing alone do not constitute proof of incompetency. The evidence must show that at the time of the act his understanding was clouded or his reason dethroned by intoxication or its effects.

The only evidence regarding Turner's condition during the period of several months both before and after March 17, 1960 was submitted by appellant and three witnesses called by him. Two of said witnesses were employed by the railroad in the capacity of telegrapher-cashiers and the other as a roadmaster clerk. Their testimony may be briefly summarized as follows: They frequently saw and visited with Turner while he lived in Ashton; most of such visits were had at the railroad depot, although one testified that he had had Turner in his home, had visited him in his own apartment and on occasions had gone fishing with him; that he appeared neatly dressed and well-mannered; that he visited and conversed in a normal manner and they were not aware of any addiction he may have had for alcoholic drink. They regarded him as entirely competent; that Turner mentioned to each of them he had changed the beneficiary and to some he stated his reason for so doing. One witness testified that he was requested to and did witness the execution by Turner of the change of beneficiary form and that Turner seemed perfectly normal at that time.

Appellant also testified that at the time the assignment was made he was depot agent for the railroad at Ashton; that he had known Turner for several months prior to March 1960; that he, Turner, would come to the depot office almost each day; on a few occasions he had talked with Turner at Legion meetings and went fishing with him once; that the first time Turner mentioned anything to him about changing the beneficiary on his insurance policy was about the middle of January 1960, which occasion occurred at the depot and was described by appellant as follows:

> Q. All right. Then the two of you were present, and will you tell us as best you recall what was the conversation?
> A. Well, he showed me a letter from the railroad accounting department that said that he was about six months behind on his premiums with his group insurance, and he told me that he had tried to get his stepson to take over this policy and pay the premiums on it, and bury him. He said all he was interested in was to be buried with his wife; she was buried in Pocatello, but he said his stepson, he didn't get along good with him, and he couldn't really trust him and he wouldn't do it for him, and he wanted to know if I would accept the responsibility to pay the premiums in order to collect this insurance.

This testimony of appellant and his witnesses regarding Turner's mental and physical condition at and near the time when the assignment was accomplished is uncontradicted.

Appellant's witnesses also testified that he, Turner, had stated to them that he was not satisfied with respondents' handling of the insurance; that he refused to stop to see respondents while he was in Pocatello and did not speak very highly of them. Whether Turner felt any resentment toward his stepson for causing him to be committed to the hospital is not disclosed; however, there is no contradiction of the foregoing mentioned testimony of appellant's witnesses. It is true that appellant's evidence regarding Turner's demeanor is in contrast to that introduced by respondents. Nevertheless, it is undisputed that Turner moved to Ashton within a comparatively short time after spending approximately seven months in a hospital where no liquor was available to him.

We have not overlooked the fact that respondents also introduced substantial evidence to the effect that commencing with September 1960 and continuing to his death, Turner reverted to his former addiction. In short, we have presented to us by the evidence in this case a man whose conduct prior to and after execution of the instrument here in question, was peculiar to say the least, but the sum and substance of the testimony indicates only that his trouble was caused by intoxication.

Applying the foregoing stated rule to the facts disclosed in this case, appellant's uncontradicted evidence regarding Turner's mental condition at the time the assignment was being considered and accomplished by him cannot be disregarded. We find no substantial evidence in the record to support the finding by the court that Turner was incompetent at the time of making the assignment involved.

REVIEW PROBLEMS

(When answering these questions, assume the age of majority for entering contracts is twenty-one.)

1. What is the test of a person's capacity to make a contract?
2. Are all contracts of minors voidable? Explain.
3. Are most contracts made by people who are intoxicated voidable by them?
4. Pelham, twenty-years-old, bought a car from Howard Motors for $2,075.60, paying $500 down. In the bill of sale, Pelham certified that he was twenty-one or older, and he told the salesman he was twenty-two. Pelham took the car home but brought it back the next day for repairs. When Howard failed to correct the problems, Pelham had his attorney write the company, repudiating the contract and

demanding return of the down payment. Should Pelham prevail?
5. Horton, age nineteen, rented three furnished rooms from Johnson. He and his wife occupied the rooms for five months. When Horton moved out, Johnson brought suit for one week's rent, "one week of notice in lieu of intent to terminate tenancy," and damages to furnishings. Could Horton be held responsible?
6. Stewart and Curry were partners in a paving contracting business. Curry began to drink heavily and on one occasion was hospitalized for alcoholism. During this time, Curry contributed very little to the paving business. For several months Stewart and Curry talked about their business problems. An agreement dissolving the partnership was prepared by Stewart and given to Curry. Two weeks later Curry

returned the signed agreement. Stewart also signed. Several other documents relating to the dissolution of the partnership were also signed by both Stewart and Curry. Three months later Curry filed suit. He claimed that he was still recovering from his alcoholism, under the influence of sedatives, and therefore was entitled to avoid the dissolution agreement because he lacked the capacity to contract. Do you agree?

7. Bowling, age sixteen, bought a used car from Sperry for several hundred dollars. He paid the full amount in cash. After one week, he found the main bearing had burned out. He returned the car to Sperry and asked that it be repaired; Sperry said the repair would cost Bowling $80. Bowling said he wouldn't pay $80 and left the car with Sperry. The next week he wrote to Sperry that he wanted to disaffirm his purchase contract. He asked for his money back. Sperry refused, and Bowling sued. Can Bowling disaffirm this contract? How would you decide if this car is a necessity for Bowling?

8. Jack Jones, a sixteen-year-old high-school student, lives with his parents. He works part time but depends on his parents for most of his support. Jack buys the following items. He then notifies each of the sellers that he is a minor, was renouncing his contract, and would not return the merchandise. Further, he wanted his money back. What should happen regarding his purchase of
   (a) drugs at a drugstore that were prescribed for his asthma,
   (b) food at a local restaurant bought after school and before going to his part-time job,
   (c) a winter jacket costing $60 to keep him warm in the Michigan winter, and
   (d) $400 in photography equipment for his hobby of three years.

9. James Taylor, a minor, bought a used car

when he was one year under the age of majority and began making payments on it to the bank that financed it. Then he went into the service and made no more payments on the car. He told his father to have the bank pick up the car. It did so and sold it for salvage. When Taylor returned from the service, the bank claimed that he had not disaffirmed his contract because he did not ask for the return of his payments. Do you agree? Why?

10. Parent, a minor, made a compromise settlement with Mazurek, an adjuster representing the insurance company that underwrote Workmen's Compensation for the state. The agreement was based upon compensation due Parent for a back injury he sustained while employed at Midway Toyota. Mazurek represented Midway Toyota during the settlement negotiations and negotiated directly with Parent and his mother, who was present when he signed the agreement. Parent's mother did not object to the signing. Neither she nor any other adult cosigned the agreement. Since Parent was the sole contracting party with Mazurek while his mother was present at the agreement, is he now entitled to disaffirm the agreement? Why or why not?

11. Halbman, a minor, agreed to buy a 1968 Oldsmobile from Lemke for $1,250. Lemke was the manager of L & M Standard Station, and Halbman was an employee at L & M. At the time of the agreement, Halbman paid Lemke $1,000 cash and took possession of the car. Halbman was to pay $25 a week until the balance was paid, at which time title would be transferred. About five weeks after the purchase agreement, and after Halbman had paid $1,100, a connecting rod on the car's engine broke. Halbman sought to disaffirm his contract, but Lemke claimed that Halbman was responsible for the damage to the car. Does a minor who has

disaffirmed a contract to buy a nonessential item and who has returned the property to the seller have to make restitution for damage to the property before the disaffirmance?

12. A minor owns property that is managed for him by a legal guardian. The legal guardian filed an accounting with the court about how the property was being managed. The minor objected to that accounting and hired an attorney to represent him before the court. The attorney was successful in having some change made in the guardian's accounting. Could the contract between the minor and the attorney be disaffirmed by the minor?

13. Mrs. Schmaltz was a passenger in an automobile that was struck by a truck driven by Walder. She was injured, taken to the hospital, and treated for possible internal injuries, abrasions, and bruises. She was also given pain killers and tranquilizers. She made appointments for checkups with an internist and with her own doctor. Several days later an insurance agent, representing the truck driver, came to discuss a settlement with her. When he offered her $2,000, she discussed it with her husband, and quickly accepted. Before the agent's visit, Mrs. Schmaltz was upset, thinking constantly about how close she had come to more serious injuries. She asserts that her nervous tension and anxiety impaired her capacity to contract. Is her settlement with Walder and his insurance company voidable due to her lack of mental capacity?

14. William Schiller, a widower sixty-seven-years-old, has a gangrenous right foot, which needs to be amputated. Schiller also has organic brain damage and is considered incapable of understanding his condition or the amputation of his foot as a means of saving his life. Can the hospital operate on Schiller without his consent?

Illegality

A lthough an agreement may include all the elements necessary to constitute a valid contract, if its purpose or object is illegal the contract may not be enforced. The most obvious example of an illegal contract is an agreement to commit a crime. Television detective shows have made us all familiar with the expression "to put a contract out on someone." No one would argue that the person performing that "contract" should be aided by the courts in securing the agreed contract price.

In most jurisdictions, legislatures have declared certain transactions involving either criminal acts or tortious wrongs to be illegal. Contractual agreements that violate these statutes generally cannot be enforced. Some states prohibit the sale of firecrackers, others do not. Many states proscribe gambling, whereas a few states allow and in fact promote certain kinds of gambling.

Since the public policy of a state may be declared by the legislature or pronounced by the courts, both statutory and common law sources must be examined to determine which contractual agreements are illegal and unenforceable. While the lists of such contracts vary from state to state, this chapter examines a few of the most common regulations of illegal agreements. The first section of the chapter focuses on typical statutory provisions that make certain contracts illegal. The second section concerns court decisions based on common law principles rather than statutory language involving illegal contracts. The final section examines the effect of a statute or court decision declaring a contract to be illegal. While generally it is true that illegal contracts cannot be enforced by either party, some exceptions exist because of differences in public policy. Not all illegal contracts are totally unenforceable. Furthermore, where only a portion of a contract is illegal and unenforceable, in certain cases the remainder of the contract can be enforced. Table 15-1 summarizes the typical illegal contracts.

STATUTES AND ILLEGAL CONTRACTS

A variety of contractual agreements may be pronounced illegal by statute. Since contracts are generally regulated more by state law than by federal law, our focus here is on state stat-

TABLE 15–1 STANDARD ILLEGAL CONTRACTS

Wagering agreements
Interest rates in excess of legal maximum
Prohibited agreements made on Sunday
Agreements where party lacks required
    regulatory license
Agreements in unreasonable restraint of trade
Overreaching employee noncompetition clauses
Overreaching exculpatory clauses
Unconscionable agreements or clauses

---

utes. As has been noted, there is likely to be significant variation from state to state in areas of contract regulation. Nevertheless, there are at least four areas that are often dealt with by state statutes. These include wagering, usury, blue laws, and licensing laws.

Wagering Agreements

A wagering contract is one in which the parties promise to pay a designated sum of money or to transfer property upon the determination of an uncertain event or a fact in dispute. Bets on a horse race, football game, or roll of the dice are all wagers. The public policy regarding wagering agreements varies from state to state. While most states prohibit many wagering agreements, generally schemes such as raffles, bingo, or the awarding of door prizes are permitted under certain conditions.

A number of states have recognized that substantial revenues can be obtained from gambling and have instituted state-operated lotteries. Similarly, charitable organizations may be licensed under certain conditions to conduct raffles, to give millionaires' parties, or to sponsor bingo games. In a few states, wagering agreements that do not involve substantial amounts are permitted. Thus, a friendly bet on the local football game might be permitted in some states while prohibited in others. A poker game among senior citizens in Florida received national attention in 1982 when a local prosecutor decided to enforce the state's gambling laws. Although the enforcement of these laws is usually sporadic, it is wise to check the statutes in your state and to be aware of the possibility (if not the probability) that contracts violating these statutes could not only be unenforceable but also might result in criminal sanctions.

Not all contracts that will reward each party differently depending on a future event are wagers. An insurance policy, for example, is such a contract. Contracts for the sale or purchase of commodities that will be harvested in the future are similarly speculative. These agreements, however, involve items of value that are being sold and purchased. The parties are not merely speculating on the outcome of a future event. The insured has a substantial interest in his life or property, and the commodity purchaser agrees to accept the commodity being bargained for. Since these agreements are not wagers, they are not illegal and unenforceable.

Usury Contracts

State statutes often limit the amount of interest that may be charged by a lender. Any contract by which the lender receives more than the permitted interest is illegal. There usually are civil consequences as well as criminal penalties placed upon those who lend money at usurious rates. In most states, the lender is denied the right to collect any interest on a usurious contract. Some states also prohibit the lender from collecting the principal due on the loan as well as the interest. A few states allow the lender to collect the interest permitted by law and prohibit only the excess "illegal" interest. Lenders are usually permitted to recover expenses and fees incurred in preparing loan documents. Similarly, they may be able to assess points as a cost of obtaining a loan. These expenses, fees, or points are not generally considered interest.

There often are many different usury statutes in the same state. Some statutes apply only to small loan associations, while others are aimed at installment loans such as credit-card transactions. Loans made to businesses are often totally exempt from usury statutes. Most states permit interest rates charged by those who issue credit cards to exceed the statutory rate. Similarly, interest charged to finance a home or a car may usually exceed the basic rate. Finally, almost all states permit small loan companies to charge rates up to 36 percent. These rates are permitted so that the borrower who can't go to conventional financial institutions will have a legitimate place from which to borrow.

The primary objective of usury statutes is to protect the borrower from being forced to pay an excessive amount for the use of money. Usury has been illegal since biblical times, and the usurious lender has often been a moral outcast. Yet, frequently, the effect of usury statutes has been to penalize those persons most in need of funds. Whenever inflation pushes the market price for the use of money higher and higher, a usury statute imposing a fixed maximum interest rate forces lenders to stop making unprofitable loans. The effect of such a statute then is to reduce the consumer's options rather than to increase his or her bargaining power with the lender. Indeed, some lenders have refused to make loans in certain states. Others, including some major New York banks, have transferred some of their operations to other states because of the effect of usury laws on their business.

Blue Laws

Some states have statutes that forbid "all secular labor and business on the Sabbath." In these states, it would seem that all contracts made on Sunday are illegal and unenforceable, at least as long as they remain executory. Other states prohibit only certain types of transactions or the sale of certain goods on Sunday. Frequently, a state statute or municipal ordinance will prohibit the sale of alcoholic beverages on Sunday. The sale of automobiles or certain other consumer products on Sunday is also prohibited in some communities in order to regulate competition among sellers and to provide a day of rest from commercial activity.

In interpreting these statutes, courts typically seek to avoid the harsh effects that could result if the agreements were totally unenforceable. Instead, if some part of the agreement is made or performed on some day other than Sunday, the contract is usually enforced.

Thus, a contract that would have been illegal because it was entered into on a Sunday will be legal if the parties later negotiate or in any way approve their earlier illegal agreement. Active enforcement of these laws, however, varies significantly from state to state and even among communities within the same state.

The blue laws raise questions pertaining to both the establishment of a state religion and interference with the freedom of religion. The establishment argument is that the laws are part of an effort to legislate particular religious practices. The freedom of religion argument is based upon the impact of blue laws. If a particular businessperson is forbidden by his or her religion to work on a sabbath other than Sunday, and is forbidden by a blue law from working on Sunday, that person can only work five days a week. A competitor who is either an atheist or observes a Sunday sabbath can work six days a week. The Supreme Court has rejected these arguments, finding a secular basis for blue laws, which are seen as enhancing community life by providing for rest and quiet and protecting employees from having to work seven-day weeks.

Licensing Regulations

Statutes in all states require that licenses, certificates, permits, or registrations be obtained to perform certain acts. For example, the Michigan Department of Licensing and Regulation includes numerous boards and commissions, such as the Board of Accountancy, the Board of Registration for Architects, the Athletic Board of Control, the Board of Barber Examiners, the Builders Residential and Maintenance and Alteration Contractors Board, the Board of Chiropractic Examiners, the Professional Board of Registration for Community Planners, the Board of Dentistry, the Professional Board of Registration for Engineers, the Board of Registration for Foresters, the Board of Horology, the Boards of Regulation for

---

ETHICS BOX
Using Sunday Blue Laws as a Competitive Tool

Sunday Blue Laws are found throughout Europe and are omnipresent in Australia where few items can be bought on a weekend after noon on Saturdays. Although seemingly innocuous, such laws may have a very substantial impact on the competitive position of firms. There have been cases where blue laws have been enacted which have resulted in a firm losing 30 to 40 percent of its sales. Ironically, a moral claim is advanced in support of the statutes when, in reality, the real motivation may be commercial.

In some instances, particularly in the United States, the advocates of blue laws are merchants who have most of their sales during the week and who lose business to discounters who do a large volume weekend business. Certainly one of the most effective ways to compete is to use the power of lawmaking to have the competition declared illegal, or at least seriously constrained by law. Is it unethical for the weekday merchants to make arguments supporting blue laws based upon protecting people from having to work on weekends and providing for a day of rest when their real intent is to hamper their competitors? If their sole intent to benefit themselves is concealed and they do not believe the arguments that they put forward, they are not acting in good faith. Blue laws deny choice to consumers (who by voting with their dollars indicate that they prefer to shop on weekends) and should only be enacted when there is an overwhelming public support and valid justification for the restrictions.

Land Surveyors, and many, many more. Each board and commission is charged with regulating some activity of interest to the state, frequently by issuing licenses or permits to those persons who meet qualifications established for the regulated activity.

In some cases, state statutes merely require a fee to be paid in order to obtain the needed license. These licensing laws are known as *revenue statutes* since they are primarily concerned with raising revenue, even though there may be some application procedure that also must be completed. Usually, anyone can obtain a fishing license or a minnow and wiggler dealer license. Such licensing laws do not usually subject the licensee to any significant regulation by the state.

On the other hand, the primary purpose of *regulatory statutes* is to regulate those obtaining a license. The state wants to ensure that its nurses, doctors, real estate brokers, plumbers, lawyers, and others who serve the public are competent to engage in the profession or business being licensed. While regulatory statutes are concerned chiefly with the protection of the public, a fee is often assessed to cover administrative costs. There are several consequences for persons who do not comply with the requirements of state licensing statutes. In some cases, the violation of a state licensing law can lead to criminal charges. In other cases, a special panel, board, or professional association may be authorized to take disciplinary action against the person who has not complied with the state's licensing provisions.

Our primary concern in this chapter is not,

however, with these criminal or disciplinary consequences to the violator of a state licensing law. Instead, our focus is on the civil law consequences to the parties who have made a contract that does not comply with the licensing requirements. If a state requires you to have a license in order to be an architect, can you contract with someone to provide architectural services if you do not have the required license? Will the state enforce your contract? If you are not paid by the other contracting party, can you bring suit to recover the money you were to be paid? The answer to these questions depends on the wording of the applicable licensing statute.

Frequently, the statute itself will specify that any agreements made by persons who do not comply with its terms will be unenforceable. When the statute is silent concerning the enforceability of such agreements, the courts frequently look to the purpose of the statute. Contracts made without a license in violation of a revenue statute are usually enforceable. Thus, a farmer who should but does not have a license to sell his produce at a city market can enforce contracts with those who purchase the products. While the farmer has violated a licensing statute that is intended to raise revenue for the city, that violation does not affect contracts made by the farmer. If the purpose of the licensing statute is primarily regulatory, however, the person who performs services or delivers goods without complying with the licensing provisions will be denied the court's aid in enforcing contracts he has made with the purchasers of his goods or services. The *Silver* case exemplifies the approach of the courts to enforcement of contracts that violate these types of licensing statutes.

Silver v. A.O.C. Corporation

Court of Appeals of Michigan
187 N.W.2d 532 (1971)

Background: Silver (plaintiff), a handyman, sued A.O.C. Corporation (defendant) to collect a fee incurred when Silver replaced electrical wiring for the defendant. Plaintiff Silver was a journeyman electrician who had been employed by defendant's predecessor to repair lights at an apartment building in Detroit. He was not licensed as an electrical contractor under state law or city ordinance. Defendant A.O.C. Corporation was an apartment management company that had become the manager of the apartment building in question. When the plaintiff met the caretakers at the apartment building, he gave them his card so they could "call him in an emergency if the caretakers could not get ahold of the management company."

In 1967, the caretaker's wife called the plaintiff to repair a short circuit in the caretaker's apartment. Subsequently, he was asked by her to fix one or two hallway lights. The plaintiff found the wires in the hallway were burned by oversized bulbs and he undertook to replace all the defective wiring. His work was accomplished over a four-month period and he submitted a bill to defendant for $893. It was defendant's first notice that the work had been done.

The defendant refused to pay the plaintiff and the plaintiff sued in the common pleas court. That court found the plaintiff's work was a "minor repair" exempt from the licensing statute and awarded judgment for the plaintiff. The circuit court affirmed and the defendant was granted leave to appeal to the Court of Appeals.

Decision: The Court of Appeals found the plaintiff had violated the state's licensing requirements since his work was not merely minor repairs. The court reversed the lower court and found in favor of defendant A.O.C. Corporation.

Per Curiam

This is an appeal by leave granted from a judgment of the Wayne county circuit court which affirmed a judgment for plaintiff entered in common pleas court in a contract action for materials and services rendered.

Plaintiff is a journeyman electrician. At no time pertinent to this action was he licensed as an electrical contractor under either the state electrical administrative act, or the equivalent Detroit ordinance. Defendant is an apartment management company.

In 1966 plaintiff was employed by defendant's predecessor to repair lights at a Second boulevard apartment building in Detroit. At that time he met the caretaker, to whom he gave his card "just in case they had an emergency sometime and they couldn't get ahold of [the management company], they could call me direct."

In 1967 the caretaker's wife called plaintiff to repair a short circuit in the caretaker's apartment. After fixing the short circuit plaintiff was asked by the caretaker's wife to fix one or two hallway lights. Plaintiff discovered that the wires in the hallway fixtures were burned by oversized bulbs. He found that the same condition existed in all the lights in the building and undertook to replace and rewire all the defective wiring. The project was accomplished over a four-month period (July–October, 1967). Plaintiff spent 125 hours on the job and used $143 worth of his own materials. In October, 1967, he submitted a bill for $893 to the defendant. It was defendant's first notice that the work had been done.

Defendant refused payment and plaintiff sued. Judgment for plaintiff was given in common pleas court on findings that the work performed amounted to minor repair work which was exempted from the licensing statute and that the caretaker's wife had actual or apparent authority to contract on behalf of defendant. The circuit court affirmed, finding the characterization of the job as minor repair work not error and the finding of proper agency not against the great weight of the evidence.

Defendant claims the trial courts erred in holding that plaintiff was exempt from the licensing statute because the work done was minor repair work.

The electrical administrative act was an act "to safeguard persons and property" and "to provide for licensing of electricians and electrical contractors and the inspection of electrical wiring."

The act, in effect, is to insure that persons who do electrical work are duly licensed. Section 7 of the act provides that no person, firm, or corporation shall engage in a business of electrical contracting unless duly licensed as an electrical contractor. An exception to this section is minor repair work, Section 7(a), which is defined as "electrical wiring not in excess of a valuation of $50."

There appears to be little doubt that what plaintiff was doing would be considered to be electrical contracting. Section 1(b) defines electrical contracting as "any person, firm or corporation engaged in the business of erecting, installing, altering, repairing, servicing or maintaining electrical wiring devices, appliances or equipment." One of defendant's witnesses, a senior assistant electrical engineer and supervisor of the Detroit electrical inspection bureau, testified that the type of work done "was required to have been contracted for by a licensed electrical contractor."

Thus, unless the work fell under the "minor repair work" exception it could only be done by a licensed electrical contractor, which plaintiff wasn't.

As stated earlier, "minor repair work" is that which in value is worth $50 or less. Included in this figure must be the material as well as labor necessary to complete the repair and restore the item to good working order. It was stipulated below that the value of the work done was $893. Since this is well in excess of $50, this work would not come under the "minor repair work" exception to the licensing requirement.

Plaintiff was in violation of the licensing act when he did the work. Therefore, his action to recover on the contract should be barred from the courts. When one enters into a contract to perform services or furnish materials in violation of a statute which is enacted to protect the public health, morals, and safety, and which contains a penal provision, as this statute does, he cannot maintain an action to recover thereon.

The judgment of the circuit court affirming the judgment of the common pleas court is reversed and the case is remanded to the circuit court for entry of a judgment in favor of defendant against the plaintiff in the amount of $1,026.45, the sum recovered by plaintiff through a writ of garnishment while the appeal was pending.

Reversed.

THE COMMON LAW AND ILLEGAL CONTRACTS

In addition to contracts prohibited by statute, the courts have from time to time determined that certain agreements violate public policy and are to be considered illegal. In some instances, a court has initially declared certain classes of contracts illegal and the state legislature has subsequently endorsed that action by enacting a statute to the same effect. The contracts discussed in this section are those that the courts at common law initially condemned. But in some states they are now regulated by statute. The contracts covered in this section include those that restrain trade, relieve one party from some liability to another party, include unconscionable provisions, or involve other acts that conflict with public policy.

Agreements in Restraint of Trade

The law disfavors agreements where one person agrees not to compete with another. Such agreements impose too great a restraint on the individual and adversely affect competition within our society. Unless such agreements are incidental to other lawful contracts and are limited to reasonable terms, the courts will not enforce them.

Agreements not to compete are often found in contracts in which a business is being purchased and sold. The purchaser wants to ensure that the seller, who has built up the good will of the business, will not continue to be in competition with the purchased business. Noncompetitive agreements are also found in employer–employee contracts. An employee may be working in a vital segment of the employer's business. The employer wants to ensure that the employee does not establish a competing business based in part upon the valuable information learned from the employer.

A noncompetitive agreement will generally be examined to determine if it is reasonable to the concerned parties and to the public. Agreements that restrain trade by restricting competition between the seller and purchaser of a business are generally viewed in a favorable light by the courts. A court's inquiry will usually focus on whether a contract provision restraining the seller is reasonable in time and space. A provision restricting the seller from being employed in a similar business or opening up a new business that is competitive with the purchaser will be reasonable for several years but not for ten or twenty years. The restraint ordinarily cannot prohibit the seller from opening a similar business in the next state or in a distant community. Instead, the geographic area of the restraint must be the area in which the need for protection by the purchaser is most dominant.

Agreements made between an employer and employee that restrict the employee's right to compete with the employer are usually examined more closely by the courts than are agreements between the seller and purchaser. Unlike the purchaser of a business, the employee generally is not in an equal bargaining position with the other contracting party. In the sale of a business, there almost always is a recognized need for the purchaser to be able to protect the goodwill of the business. Frequently, the goodwill is the primary asset being purchased, and the purchaser will not be able to protect it if the seller can compete with the business being sold. The employer, on the other hand, does not have as great a need to protect the business' goodwill against the employee. Usually, an employee is less likely to be able to leave the employer's business and to take the employer's goodwill to his or her own use as the seller of a business could do. In these employment cases, the courts will examine not only the need for protection by

the employer from the employee but also the relative hardship imposed on the employee. The employee's lack of bargaining power can be a decisive factor in many cases. The public interest, served or defeated by the restraint, also will be examined, particularly when vital services or goods might be withheld from the community if the restraint is enforced.

There are, however, certain circumstances in which an employee may possess valuable information that could harm the employer if it was revealed to a competitor. Employees who are working in new product design, or drug research, or who know key client lists and confidential information relating to compensation or cost, may be in a position to damage seriously their former employer.

It is not uncommon for an employer to ask a successful employee to sign a noncompetition agreement after the employee has been working for the firm for several years. In those cases, there is an issue of sufficient consideration in addition to the question of the basic enforceability of the clause. Prior to the enactment of legislation restricting limitations on the vesting of pension plans, employers would try to tie observance of a noncompetition clause into the right to receive pension or other severance payments. If an employee went to work for a near competitor, the promised payments were cut off. Such "self-help" measures are still possible to the extent that they don't violate pension plan legislation.

Ultimately, the courts must balance these various competing equities in determining whether a restrictive clause should be enforced. A critical dimension is always the determination of the reasonableness of the restraint itself.

After the reasonableness of the restraint has been determined, the court must then decide several questions related to the agreement's enforceability. If the parties have made an unreasonable restraint, should the court rewrite the restraint so that it is reasonable and enforce it under those terms or should it leave the one party free from any restraint? Similarly, if a business sale and purchase agreement contains a provision that unreasonably restrains the seller, is that provision one that can be separated from other provisions in the agreement? Is the contract divisible into separate sections? If one part of a contract is illegal and unenforceable, can any part of the remaining contract be meaningfully enforced?

Knoebel Mercantile Company v. Siders

Supreme Court of Colorado
439 P.2d 355 (1968)

Background: Knoebel (plaintiff) sued Siders (defendant) to enforce a restrictive work covenant. Siders was employed as a salesman with Knoebel. At the time he was hired, he signed an employment contract that included a restrictive covenant providing he would not work for any of Knoebel's competitors for two years after the termination of his employment with Knoebel. Siders worked for Knoebel for several years and then took a position as a salesman with a competing company. Knoebel sued to prevent Siders from working as a salesman with the competing company. The trial court held for Siders. Knoebel appealed that decision.

Decision: The Supreme Court, finding the agreement unenforceable, affirmed the trial court's judgment in favor of the employee Siders.

Moore, Chief Justice

Knoebel brought the action against Siders, a former employee, seeking to restrain him from working as a salesman for one of its competitors. The injunctive relief sought against Siders was based on a restrictive covenant contained in a written contract of employment entered into between him and Knoebel under date of June 1, 1964. Pertinent portions of the contract are as follows:

> NOW, THEREFORE, in consideration of Employer's hiring Employee and for other good and valuable consideration, Employee promises and agrees that in the event of the termination of his said employment for any reason whatsoever, for a period of two years from and after the date of such termination he will not, directly or indirectly, either as an owner, officer, employee, agent or otherwise, engage in the institutional food, paper and supply business, bakery supply business, and janitorial supply business, or any part thereof in all or any part of the State of Colorado, Wyoming, Montana, New Mexico, Nebraska, Kansas, So. Dakota, and any other State in which Employer transacts its business at any time up to the date of such employment termination. Employee further promises and agrees that during said two-year period he will not divulge to anyone other than Employer or its officers or authorized employees or agents any of the trade secrets, methods, systems, customer or credit lists, volumes, preferences, purchasing lists and practices, standards and sources, selling and shipping practices and other methods, system records and statistics hereafter disclosed to Employee, reposed in his confidence

by Employer or otherwise acquired by Employee in the course of his employment. Failure to perform these promises by the Employee shall give the employer the right to an injunction to restrain the Employee from further violation, as well as damages. . . .

Prior to the date of the contract Siders resided in Wyoming and was working as a salesman for a candy and tobacco distributing business. After some preliminary negotiations he was advised on May 14, 1964, that his application for employment was accepted by Knoebel and he reported for work on June 1, 1964. While completing and signing documents relating to insurance, social security, withholding tax and similar matters he was presented for the first time with the restrictive agreement above quoted. He read and then signed the agreement. He was given the customary training course for salesmen, after which Knoebel assigned him to a territory consisting of Colorado Springs, Colorado, and a limited adjacent area in which about 150 customers were located. He was furnished with a price list, prospect cards, some information as to the credit ratings of the customers, their buying habits and other general information. He was also furnished with a car, order books, and other things useful to him as a salesman.

Siders terminated his employment with Knoebel on September 9, 1966, and went to work for John Sexton & Co., a competitor of Knoebel, as a salesman. Though Sexton was in competition with Knoebel there was a considerable difference in the scope of operations in the business of the two companies since it appears from the evidence that Knoebel dealt in 10,000 items of merchandise, all manufactured by others, and Sexton dealt in only 1600 items, many of which it manufactured.

The record discloses that although Siders was employed as a salesman, he was assigned to a small territory with only 150 customers, whereas if the restrictive covenant is enforced by injunction as prayed by Knoebel he will be prohibited from operating in all of Colorado, Wyoming, Montana, New Mexico, Nebraska, Kansas, South Dakota, and any other State in which Knoebel was transacting business on the date of termination of his employment.

The undisputed evidence was that Siders intended to and would, unless enjoined therefrom, solicit on behalf of John Sexton & Co. some of the customers he previously solicited on behalf of Knoebel, and the court so found. Lengthy Findings of Fact entered by the trial court included the following:

> (9) Familiarity between salesman and customer is not of primary importance. Almost all customers buy from several competitors on a continuing basis. Sales in the institutional food industry are based primarily upon product and price with time of delivery being a secondary factor. Defendant Siders is not in a position to control the business of the prior customers as a personal asset. Sales volume may either decrease or increase when the salesman in a territory is changed.
>
> (10) Siders' services for Plaintiff Knoebel were not unique in character and his place with Plaintiff Knoebel's organization has already been filled.
>
> (11) The restrictive agreement was designed to restrict Defendant Siders from doing two things. First, it prohibited the disclosure of trade secrets and confidential information acquired by Defendant Siders in the course of his

employment. Second, it prohibited Defendant Siders from competing with Plaintiff Knoebel.

(12) During the course of Defendant Siders' employment by Plaintiff Knoebel, he acquired general information regarding Plaintiff Knoebel's business. The information which Plaintiff Knoebel considered to be secret and confidential is available to Plaintiff Knoebel's competitors and is not confidential and does not involve trade secrets . . .

(14) A permanent injunction would result in Defendant Siders having to either move from the region in which he has spent most of his adult life or abandon the type of work in which he has most experience.

(15) The injury to Defendant Siders by enforcement of the agreement outweighs the benefit to Plaintiff Knoebel.

(16) There is no proof of threatened or actual irreparable damage to Plaintiff Knoebel.

The full record has been read and we find ample evidence to sustain the fact findings of the trial court. We shall not disturb those findings.

It is argued by counsel for Knoebel that the trial court erred as a matter of law in denying Knoebel's claim for injunction and, alternatively, if the restriction was unreasonable as to time and area this court should "reform" the restriction with regard thereto.

. . . The test as to whether a covenant of this kind will be enforced by injunction hinges on a determination of the reasonableness of the restriction under all the facts and circumstances of each case.

. . . If it is unfair and unreasonable in a given set of circumstances, relief by injunction will be denied. The restrictions in contracts not to engage in business in competition with another, to be valid must be reasonable, must not impose undue hardship, must be no wider than necessary to afford the required protection, and each case must stand on its own facts. In the instant case the trial court, after a lengthy and searching inquiry, determined that the restriction here involved was unreasonable under all the pertinent circumstances. We cannot say that the court erred as a matter of law in reaching this conclusion.

The judgment of the trial court is affirmed.

Contracts with Exculpatory Clauses

Exculpatory clauses in a contract relieve or limit the liability of one of the parties in the event that the party does not perform his or her part of the contract. Such clauses are viewed with disfavor by the law. The policy of the law is that damages caused by one party's nonperformance of contract terms should be recoverable by the injured party. An exculpatory clause that relieves one party of liability thus may be contrary to legal policy. While it has generally been the courts that have declared such contract provisions to be unenforceable as contrary to public policy, statutes in many states declare some of these clauses to be unenforceable and illegal. For example, in most jurisdictions there are statutes that deny the enforceability of at least some part of exculpatory clauses found in apartment leases prepared by landlords for tenants.

Exculpatory clauses that are unenforceable

PREVENTIVE LAW
Noncompetition Clauses

There are many businesses in which the enforceability of noncompetition clauses is critical to the long-run success of the business. In many high-tech fields, competitors may purposely hire away key employees to obtain information about new products and processes. Sales firms such as manufacturers' representatives and wholesalers may also be vulnerable to employees leaving and taking clients they have cultivated while working for the firm. This problem is particularly severe in the financial services industry where brokers and investment bankers often jump from one firm to another.

There is a natural tendency when drafting clauses to make them as far-reaching as possible to protect all potential interests of the firm. An aggressive strategy may backfire in this area because if the court finds that the clause is unreasonable in its reach, it may throw out the entire provision leaving the firm with no protection at all.

The noncompetition clause may be a part of an employee handbook or some other general document. As a consequence, many employees may not actually know about the clause and how it applies. New employees should check out the nature of any restrictions and be sure that they understand the rules of the game. Concurrently, the firm should make sure that employees understand what is considered trade secret material and what restrictions will be imposed upon them when they leave the firm. This will prevent unpleasant surprises later on.

---

can be classified under two main headings: (1) those limiting liability of a dealer who sells goods or services to the public and (2) those limiting an employer's liability for negligence that causes injury to an employee. As to clauses of the first type, the law notes that there rarely is equality of bargaining power between the consumer and the dealer. It is in the public interest that those people who serve the public and whose contracts with the public are usually not the subject of bargaining and negotiation not be allowed to relieve themselves of liability for their own negligence. As to clauses of the second type, the policy of the law is to discourage negligence by making wrongdoers pay damages. If an employer or its agent causes injury to anyone,

even an employee, the injured party should be able to recover damages. Furthermore, an employee too is generally not in an equal bargaining position with an employer. Thus, such clauses are not favored and will not be enforced.

Some exculpatory clauses that limit the liability of one of the contracting parties in the event of nonperformance by that party will be enforced. Some states allow contracting parties the freedom to contract under the broadest possible terms. In these states, freedom of contract outweighs concern over exculpatory clauses. Two factors are particularly important in these instances: the bargaining power of the parties and the degree to which the law otherwise regulates the concerned agreement. If both parties are business firms that have negotiated the terms of their agreement with each other, the courts are more likely to allow one of the parties to limit its liability. Similarly, if one of the businesses is already subject to significant regulatory control by the state, the rules, regulations, and policies of the state regulatory agencies may permit the business to limit its liability in certain contracts.

One of the most common situations in which one of the parties to a contract seeks to limit his or her liability concerns the bailee of property. A bailee is someone who has been given the right to possess personal property. The restaurant checkroom, the downtown parking lot, the airport baggage counter, the warehouse storing your out-of-season snowmobile are all bailees. These bailees usually have signs on their property, statements on the backs of receipts, or identification tickets that limit their liability, even for their own negligence, in the event your property is lost or damaged. While such clauses are generally enforceable, in some cases courts will not enforce them because to do so would violate public policy. While it is impossible to define what constitutes public policy, it is clear that social forces play major roles in shaping this concept. The two cases that follow demonstrate different contexts in which exculpatory clauses may be used and challenged.

Henrioulle v. Marin Ventures, Inc.

Supreme Court of California

143 Cal.Rptr. 247 (1978)

Background: Tenant Henrioulle (plaintiff-appellant) sued landlord Marin Ventures (defendant-respondent) for personal injuries sustained when plaintiff tripped on a rock on a common stairway (shared with other tenants). The defendant won at the trial court level, on the grounds of an exculpatory clause in the lease relieving defendant landlord of liability for injuries sustained on the premises "or in the common areas thereof."

Decision: The court reversed the lower court and found in favor of plaintiff Henrioulle.

Bird, Chief Justice

In *Tunkl v. Regents of the University of California,* this court held invalid a clause in a hospital admission form which released the hospital from liability for future negligence. This court noted that although courts have made "diverse" interpretations of Civil Code section 1668, which invalidates contracts which exempt one from responsibility for certain wilful or negligent acts, all the decisions were in accord that exculpatory clauses affecting the public interest are invalid.

In *Tunkl,* six criteria are used to identify the kind of agreement in which an exculpatory clause is invalid as contrary to public policy. "[1] It concerns a business of a type generally thought suitable for public regulation. [2] The party seeking exculpation is engaged in performing a service of great importance to the public, which is often a matter of practical necessity for some members of the public. [3] The party holds himself out as willing to perform this service for any member of the public who seeks it, or at least any member coming within certain established standards. [4] As a result of the essential nature of the service, in the economic setting of the transaction, the party invoking exculpation possesses a decisive advantage of bargaining strength against any member of the public who seeks his services. [5] In exercising a superior bargaining power the party confronts the public with a standardized adhesion contract of exculpation, and makes no provision whereby a purchaser may pay additional fees and obtain protection against negligence. [6] Finally, as a result of the transaction, the person or property of the purchaser is placed under the control of the seller, subject to the risk of carelessness by the seller or his agents."

The transaction before this court, a residential rental agreement, meets the *Tunkl* criteria.

However, respondent asserts that the principles discussed in *Tunkl* do not apply to private residential leases. It is true that *Tunkl* cites language in *Barkett v. Brucato* to the effect that "the relationship of landlord and tenant does not affect the public interest. . . ." In *Tunkl,* this court cited *Barkett* and other cases as examples of the uniform inquiry by courts into whether or not an exculpatory clause involved the public interest. Although this court held that an exculpatory clause could stand only if it did *not* involve the public interest, it did *not* endorse the result reached in applying that rule in each of those cases.

Furthermore, even if at the time of *Barkett* and the earlier decisions cited therein, a residential lease may have been correctly characterized as not involving the public interest, for the reasons stated above this court is convinced this is not true today. Since the residential lease transaction entered into by the parties exhibits all of the characteristics of a relationship that "affects the public interest" under *Tunkl,* the exculpatory clause cannot operate to relieve the landlord of liability in this case.

In holding that exculpatory clauses in residential leases violate public policy, this court joins an increasing number of jurisdictions. . . . Indeed, in 1975 the California Legislature enacted Civil Code section 1953, which declared invalid exculpatory clauses in residential leases executed on or after January 1, 1976.

Respondent contends that by enacting Civil Code section 1953, the Legislature impliedly sanctioned such clauses in leases executed before that date. However, this argument ignores the fact that appellant based his cause of action not on Civil Code section 1953, but on the common law as it existed prior to the passage of that section. Further, nothing in the legislative history of section 1953 suggests that the Legislature intended, in enacting that section, to expand tenants' rights prospectively while curtailing their common law rights with respect to transactions occurring before enactment of that section.

This court has consistently held that a statute should not be given retroactive effect so as to deprive an individual of a pre-existing right unless the Legislature has clearly expressed its intention to accomplish that end. Although section 1953 invalidates exculpatory clauses in leases executed after January 1, 1976, there is no indication that the Legislature intended to alter or modify the common law principles the courts applied on a case-by-case basis to leases executed before that date. Therefore, the exculpatory clause in this lease is unenforceable under the common law principles prevailing when the lease was executed. The judgment notwithstanding the verdict must be set aside.

Allright, Inc. v. Schroeder

Court of Civil Appeals of Texas
551 S.W.2d 745 (1977)

Background: Carl Schroeder (plaintiff-appellee) brought an action against Allright, Inc. (defendant-appellant), the operator of a parking lot, to recover damages sustained when the plaintiff's automobile was stolen from the lot. The defendant's defense was based on a limitation of the liability clause in the claim check given to the plaintiff. The lower court awarded damages to the plaintiff and the parking lot owner appealed. Decision: The court affirmed the lower court's ruling and found in favor of Schroeder.

Coleman, Chief Justice

On September 8, 1969, at approximately 1:30 P.M. plaintiff drove his automobile into defendant's parking lot in downtown Houston. He turned possession of the automobile over to one of the defendant's employees, who proceeded to park the automobile, and received a claim ticket from another employee. The words "We close at 6 o'clock P.M." were printed on the ticket in heavy type. . . . It can be seen that the provision limiting liability would not be so readily noticed.

Signs were located throughout the parking lot which stated that the lot closed at 6 o'clock P.M. and that anyone returning after that time could pick up their keys at another parking lot operated by defendant at a specified location. Plaintiff had parked his automobile at this lot previously. He was aware at the time he left the car at the station on the occasion in question that the signs and the claim ticket said the lot closed at 6 o'clock.

When the plaintiff returned to the lot around midnight his car was missing. He inquired at defendant's parking lot at 503 Fannin as to the whereabouts of his car. The attendant did not have his keys and knew nothing about the car. Plaintiff filed an offense report with the Houston police reporting the theft of his automobile, and the car was recovered on September 10 by the Harris County Sheriff's Department. It had been partially "stripped" and suffered other damage.

The case was tried to a jury. In answer to the special issues submitted the jury found (1) the defendant's negligence proximately caused plaintiff's automobile to be stolen; (2) there was a risk of theft to plaintiff's automobile after the lot closed for the day but this was not open and obvious to plaintiff; (3) the difference in market value of the car before and after the occurrence was $1,000.00. Judgment was rendered for the plaintiff in the amount of $1,000.00.

The defendant appeals complaining of the action of the trial court in refusing to submit the following requested issues:

1. Do you find from a preponderance of the evidence that the parking lot in question closed at or about 6 o'clock P.M. on September 8, 1969?
2. Do you find from a preponderance of the evidence that the plaintiff's automobile was stolen by an unknown third party or parties after the lot had closed for the day on September 8, 1969?

> 3. Do you find from a preponderance of the evidence that the plaintiff read the parking ticket marked in evidence as Plaintiff's Exhibit 1 prior to leaving his automobile in the lot in question on September 8, 1969?

The defendant contends that the fact issues submitted were designed to establish that the plaintiff knew the lot closed at 6 o'clock P.M. and that the plaintiff had impliedly agreed to the limitation of liability provision printed on the stub of the parking ticket. The defendant further asserts that once it is established that the defendant knew of the closing time a finding that the automobile was stolen after that time would establish a defense to the suit in that the operator of a parking lot would have no duty to protect the patron's automobile after the time of closing. The defendant also contends that where a patron of a public parking lot is aware of a statement limiting liability which appears on the parking stub given him at the time he leaves his automobile in the lot, he impliedly agrees to this limitation as a provision of the contract of bailment.

. . .

In this case the limitation provision printed on the claim check was not specifically called to the attention of the bailor at the time he left his automobile at the parking lot. Plaintiff testified that at the time he left his automobile with the defendant he knew that the claim check stated that the lot closed at 6 o'clock. The defendant asserts that this evidence also raises an issue of fact as to whether or not the plaintiff had read the provision limiting liability printed on the claim check.

There is no evidence that the plaintiff read the material appearing on the claim check which was given him on September 8. He was asked: "All right. But, you were aware that those signs read, 'Close at 6 o'clock P.M.' when you *drove up to the lot* and when you left your car on it on September 8, weren't you?" Answer: "I was aware that is what the sign read." Question: "All right. And you were aware that is what the ticket said?" Answer: "Yes." Obviously if the plaintiff was aware that the ticket said "Close at 6 o'clock P.M." when he drove up to the lot that information was obtained from tickets which he had received on previous occasions when he parked at the lot. Plaintiff was never asked if he read the ticket, nor was he asked whether or not he knew of the provision limiting the liability of the lot owner.

We find no evidence that the plaintiff read the parking ticket which was introduced into evidence as Plaintiff's Exhibit No. 1 prior to leaving his automobile in the lot on September 8, 1969. The trial court did not err in refusing to submit this issue.

Notice that a lot will "close at 6 o'clock P.M." does not give notice that cars left after such time will be at the owner's risk. Such a sign might be construed to mean that no automobiles would be accepted after 6 o'clock P.M. The fact that the closing time of the lot was posted on signs and was printed on the claim ticket does not exempt the operator of the lot from the exercise of ordinary care with respect to the safety of the property.

The evidence does not establish whether the automobile was stolen before or after the lot had closed for the day on September 8, 1969. There was testimony that on special occasions the lot stayed open to a later hour. The plaintiff testified that he knew that the lot had been open after the 6 o'clock closing time on previous occasions and that he inquired of the attendant whether or not the lot would be open later on this night. He testified that he was told that it would be open later. There was testimony that it closed at 6:00 P.M. on September 8, 1969. When his car was recovered the trunk was open, his spare tire was missing, and the keys were found in the trunk. The defendant represented that the keys to the car would be in its custody until returned to the owner.

. . .

Here the sign clearly represented to the patrons that some degree of care would be exercised for the safety of their automobiles after the closing time by reason of the notice that the car keys could be picked up after closing time at another location. No agreement that the bailment would expire at 6 o'clock P.M. will be implied from the fact that the plaintiff knew the signs stated that the lot would close at 6 o'clock P.M. under these circumstances.

The trial court did not err in refusing to submit the requested special issues since they inquired about immaterial facts.

The judgment is affirmed.

Unconscionable Contracts

Closely related to the problem of determining whether a contract is illegal and unenforceable because it contains an exculpatory clause and therefore contravenes public policy is the problem of determining whether a particular contract should not be enforced because it is unconscionable. Equity principles dictate that "he who seeks equity must do equity." If a contract is too oppressive or one-sided, the courts will not enforce it. While it is clear that a court has the power to refuse to enforce unconscionable contracts even in the absence of express legislative authority, the basis for most of the litigated cases today is the Uniform Commercial Code. Section 2-302 of the UCC provides:

1. If the court as a matter of law finds the contract or any clause of the contract to have been unconscionable at the time it was made, the court may refuse to enforce the contract, or it may enforce the remainder of the contract without the unconscionable clause, or it may so limit the application of any unconscionable clause as to avoid any unconscionable result.

2. When it is claimed or appears to the court that the contract or any clause thereof may be unconscionable, the parties shall be afforded a reasonable opportunity to present evidence as to its commercial setting, purpose and effect to aid the court in making the determination.

What makes a contract unconscionable is of course for court determination. Several factors seem important. What is the relative bargaining power of the parties? Is one party economically stronger than the other? Does each party have options? Can the seller sell to others or is there only one source of supply from which the buyer can purchase the desired goods? How reasonable are the terms which are claimed to be unconscionable?

Further guidelines are provided by the Official Comment to the UCC. Section 2-302 states: The basic test is whether, in the light of the general commercial background and the commercial needs of the particular trade or case, the clauses involved are so one-sided as to be unconscionable under the circumstances existing at the time of the making of the contract. Subsection (2) makes it clear

ETHICS BOX
Unconscionability

The test of unconsciousability comes as close to applying a principle of ethics directly as any part of our commercial law. The test is one of fairness, whether or not a practice would be seen as improper by one of good conscience.

Critics of the principle of unconscionability have argued that it produces a wild hare—an unpredictable, unstructured standard that could be used to set aside contracts willy-nilly and that would reduce certainty, make planning more difficult, and thereby increase transaction costs.

In addition, the critics claim that a principle of unconscionability is unnecessary. They note that the legal doctrines of fraud, duress, undue influence, consideration, lack of capacity and mistake all are available to deal with problems of coercion or gross unfairness. These doctrines are seen as preferable to unconscionability because they have definite parameters and can be applied without the danger of establishing a precedent for second guessing bargains. As it has turned out, however, the courts have been very reasonable in the way in which they have applied the principle and it appears clear that only the more outrageous practices have been condemned as unconscionable.

The doctrine of unconscionability can be seen as inconsistent with the concept of freedom of contract. An underlying premise of freedom of contract is that society should not act to set aside the outcomes of freely bargained agreements, regardless of how harsh (or unconscionable) they may seem to outsiders. In the *Allan* case that follows, the court discusses how the interests of fairness and of freedom of contract should be balanced in applying the doctrine of unconscionability.

that it is proper for the court to hear evidence upon these questions. The principle is one of the prevention of oppression and unfair surprise, and not of disturbance of allocation of risks because of superior bargaining power.

Allan v. Michigan Bell Telephone Company
Court of Appeals of Michigan
171 N.W.2d 689 (1969)

Background: Kenneth D. Allan (plaintiff) brought this suit for damages against Michigan Bell Telephone Company (defendant). Allan, an insurance agent, had contracted to place advertisements in the classified telephone directory but the advertisements were not included. The lower court granted summary judgment to the defendant telephone company based on the following limitation of liability clause:

>Telephone Company (a) will not be bound by any verbal agreements or (b) will not be liable to Advertiser for damages resulting from failure to include all or any of said items of advertising in the Directories or from errors in the advertising printed in the Directories, in excess of the agreed prices for such advertising for the issue in which the error or omission occurs.

Allan appealed.

Decision: The court reversed the lower court and found for plaintiff Allan.

Kavanagh, Justice

The plaintiff's appeal questions the trial court's application of this clause in granting the motion for summary judgment and, further, challenges the legality of such a clause on the grounds of public policy.

He argues that the clause in question limits the liability of the telephone company only as it pertains to damages for breach of contract, and that such a contracted disclaimer may not be read as a limitation of its liability for its own negligence.

The defendant asserts that it is not required to provide the yellow pages and therefore it is to be treated as a private party and not a public utility when soliciting and contracting advertisements. The defendant further contends, that, since this is an area of private contract, it may lawfully require those who desire to advertise in the yellow pages to agree to a limitation of liability in the event of an omission or error in the yellow pages.

We cannot properly resolve the questions presented by adopting the position of either of the parties without qualification. We cannot say with the plaintiff that all provisions for limiting one's liability for negligence are void as against public policy. Nor can we say with the defendant that public policy is not concerned with private contract, and therefore, a person is free to exculpate himself from liability as he may see fit.

The principle of freedom to contract does not carry a license to insert any provision in an agreement which a party deems advantageous. The public is concerned with the legality of contracts and limits the contractual freedom of private parties to legal undertakings. This public concern is manifest in the statutes and decisions of this state.

Nor can we say it is against public policy for the defendant to limit its liability for its own negligence in all circumstances. Such a limitation may take the form of a disclaimer of liability beyond a certain amount or it may take the form of a provision for stipulated or liquidated damages. But in all this, public policy does insist that this, as every other term of a contract, not be unconscionable.

Implicit in the principle of freedom of contract is the concept that at the time of contracting each party has a realistic alternative to acceptance of the terms offered. Where goods and services can only be obtained from one source (or several sources on noncompetitive terms) the choices of one who desired to purchase are limited to acceptance of the terms offered or doing without. Depending on the nature of the goods or services and the purchaser's needs, doing without may or may not be a realistic alternative. Where it is not, one who successfully exacts agreement to an unreasonable term cannot insist on the courts enforcing it on the ground that it was "freely" entered into, when it was not. He cannot in the name of freedom of contract be heard to insist on enforcement of an unreasonable contract term against one who on any fair appraisal was not free to accept or reject that term.

There are then two inquiries in a case such as this: (1) What is the relative bargaining power of the parties, their relative economic strength, the alternative sources of supply, in a word, what are their options?; (2) Is the challenged term substantively reasonable?

> Unconscionability has generally been recognized to include an absence of meaningful choice on the part of one of the parties together with contract terms which are unreasonably favorable to the other party.

Thus, merely because the parties have different options or bargaining power, unequal or wholly out of proportion to each other, does not mean that the agreement of one of the parties to a term of a contract will not be enforced against him; if the term is substantively reasonable it will be enforced. By like token, if the provision is substantively unreasonable, it may not be enforced without regard to the relative bargaining power of the contracting parties.

Where the contract is affected with a "public interest" a court is more likely to refuse enforcement to an exculpatory provision. Prosser has observed:

> The courts have refused to uphold such agreements, however, where one party is at such obvious disadvantage in bargaining power that the effect of the contract is to put him at the mercy of the other's negligence. Thus it is generally held that a contract exempting an employer from all liability for negligence toward his employees is void as against public policy. The same is true as to the efforts of public utilities to escape liability for negligence in the performance of their duty of public service. A carrier who transports goods or passengers for hire, or a telegraph company transmitting a message, may not contract away its public responsibility, and this is true although the agreement takes the form of a limitation of recovery to an amount less than the probable damages. It has been held, however, that the contract will be sustained where it represents an honest attempt to fix a value as liquidated damages in advance, and the carrier graduates its rates according to such value, so that full protection would be open to the plaintiff upon paying a higher rate. The same rules apply to innkeepers and public warehousemen.

It is not enough to say that "freedom of contract" is the founding principle of our economy, for freedom of contract is directly related to another basic principle of our economy—"freedom of enterprise." It must be recognized that freedom of enterprise became severely restricted as the giants in our industries and services overwhelmed their competition. It is neither rational nor just to contend that freedom of contract must remain static and immutable as freedom of enterprise inexorably recedes. Both concepts must adjust and adapt to the times.

The parties to this suit are not in positions of equal bargaining power. It is common knowledge that defendant's yellow pages is the only directory of classified telephone listings freely distributed to all the telephone subscribers in the Flint area. It is not disputed that the contract signed by the parties was a form prepared by the defendant and used by the defendant in all subscriptions for advertising in the yellow pages. Nor is it argued by the defendant that the plaintiff could have bargained for different terms in the contract. It was strictly a "take it or leave it" proposition.

Under the circumstances the plaintiff had the option of agreeing to the offered terms or doing without advertising in the yellow pages. There being no competing directory or means of communicating with the same audience of potential customers except possibly at prohibitive (and by comparison totally disproportionate) cost, doing without in this case was not a realistic alternative. Clearly the challenged term is substantively unreasonable. It relieves the defendant from all liability—its only obligation is to return the agreed contract price paid for the service it did not perform. We have concluded that this provision is unreasonable and, accordingly, we decline to enforce it.

We believe the law in Michigan to be that, where goods or services used by a significant segment of the public can be obtained from only one source, or from limited sources on no more favorable terms, an unreasonable term in a contract for such goods or services will not be enforced as a matter of public policy.

Reversed and remanded for trial on the merits. Costs to appellant.

The *Meredith* case that follows concerns several interrelated problems. The "waiver of defense clause" contained in the contract specifies that the purchaser will waive defenses against the seller (perhaps if he's unsatisfied with the quality of the product) and that any of those defenses will also be waived against the seller's assignee (in that case the Personal Finance Company) who has now stepped into the seller's place and stead. Such a clause is similar to the exculpatory clauses just noted since it limits the claims or defenses that one party can use against the other party.

The court's analysis of unconscionability thus is often affected by the same factors as would be its analysis of an exculpatory clause. While the Illinois court finds this contract and its waiver of defense clause enforceable, its opinion indicates that other courts have different policies. Again, the state law governing each agreement must be checked to determine whether it is unconscionable and thus unenforceable.

Personal Finance Company v. Meredith

Court of Appeals of Illinois
350 N.E.2d 781 (1976)

Background: Personal Finance Company (plaintiff) sued the Merediths (defendants) to collect money owed pursuant to a sales contract. The plaintiff, Personal Finance Company, was the assignee of two retail installment sales contracts under which the defendants, Bennie and Joyce Meredith, purchased a food freezer, notions, staples, and frozen meat from Tri-State Foods Company. One contract provided for the purchase by the defendants of a food freezer at a cash price of $748.00, credit life insurance of $12.91, and a finance charge of $232.69, payable in twenty-four monthly installments of $41.40. The other contract was for "notions, staples, and frozen meat" at a cash price of $552.06, credit life insurance of $1.94, and a finance charge of $43.66, payable in six monthly installments of $99.61. The contracts were assigned to the plaintiff approximately a month after their execution.

Defendants made eight payments totaling $339.63 on the food freezer contract and payments of $493.03 on the other contract. The plaintiff brought suit in Circuit Court to collect the amounts owed on the contracts in the sum of $758.60, plus attorneys' fees, totaling $253.30 and $1.31 as interest accrued since maturity of the second contract.

The defendants asserted three affirmative defenses to the plaintiff's action: (1) that the contracts were unconscionable, (2) that they failed to comply with the Truth in Lending Act and Regulation Z, and (3) that they failed to comply with the Illinois Retail Installment Sales Act. These defenses were stricken on motion by the trial court as insufficient in law. The trial court awarded judgment to plaintiff for the full amount requested, and defendant appealed to the Court of Appeals.

Decision: While the court agreed with the trial court that the terms of the contract were not unconscionable and could be enforced, it reversed and remanded the trial court's decision on other grounds

Karns, Presiding Justice

The record discloses that the defendants were induced to purchase these items by a salesman of Tri-State Foods who appeared at their home one evening while they were preparing to go bowling. They asked him to come back another night, but when he told them he was in town just that day they agreed to listen to him. The defendants testified that they agreed to purchase the food freezer and the frozen meats because the salesman made it sound "like a really good deal." They stated that at that time they did not receive a copy of the contract and the payment terms were not filled in on the contracts. Nor apparently were they furnished with a notice that they had three days to rescind the agreement as required by section 2B of the Consumer Fraud Act.

The defendants also maintained that the contract price of the food freezer ($748.00) was about $300.00 more than the price quoted them by the salesman and that they thought they were only purchasing the freezer and the meat. The salesman did not testify, as neither the assignee nor the defendants knew his whereabouts. The record discloses that when the contracts were executed defendants were both employed but at the time of the suit they were not.

[The court first determined that the plaintiffs had not violated the Consumer Fraud Act. Then it found that the trial court had erred in not admitting certain evidence related to the rights of the plaintiff as an assignee.]

Notwithstanding this prejudicial error which necessitates vacating the judgment appealed from, we must also determine whether the instant waiver of defense clauses are unconscionable. Defendants argue that the instant contracts are harsh and oppressive; that they did not know that a waiver of defense clause existed since the clause was inconspicuous; that they are persons of little formal education; that they did not "bargain for" these clauses; and, as a matter of public policy, that an assignee is better able to protect itself against losses due to sellers of shoddy merchandise and to prevent such losses. They argue this court to adopt the rationale of decisions in other jurisdictions holding waiver of defense clauses unenforceable in consumer retail installment sales contracts.

Clearly, waiver of defense clauses are not unconscionable per se, being permitted by the Commercial Code, the Retail Installment Sales Act and Illinois case law. The public policy of Illinois thus does not preclude the enforcement of such clauses in consumer transactions. This policy sharply distinguishes this case from those decisions relied upon by the defendants.

However, because these Illinois authorities do not displace the common law principle that an unconscionable contract or clause is unenforceable, that principle is applicable to the instant transaction. Courts will not permit printed, non-negotiated clauses in a seller's contract to waive the buyer's rights and eviscerate the negotiated terms of the transaction, unless the buyer is aware of these terms. Viewed in this light, unconscionability is merely a standard to determine the actual bargain of the parties, or their "agreement." Furthermore, the language of a contract is not controlling as to the parties' "agreement." Other circumstances such as course of dealing, usage of trade or course of performance are also relevant to the inquiry of the parties' bargain in fact. We believe the relevance of these considerations expresses a legislative policy in favor of courts' determining the actual agreement of the parties and against enforcing printed contract terms in a mechanical fashion. Therefore we cannot state that the instant clauses can never be unenforceable on the basis of unconscionability.

An unconscionable contract was unenforceable at common law in Illinois as were individual clauses to the extent they produced an unconscionable result. An unconscionable contract has been described as a one-sided contract or one which no man in his senses and not under delusion would make and no honest and fair man would accept. Other courts have stated that where the aggrieved party reasonably did not know that a certain clause was in the contract or had no meaningful choice but to have that clause included in the contract, that the clause is unconscionable. A clause may also be unconscionable if it purports to eliminate or limit the other party's right to assert and recover for a breach of contract or for a tort arising from the transaction.

A waiver of defense clause is similar in its effect to a disclaimer of liability clause. The latter term bars the opposite party from asserting a claim for breach of contract against the party protected by the clause, just as the former protects an assignee. Another analogous clause is a confession of judgment clause. These clauses are not void but can be useful terms to contracting parties in allocating the burdens and risks of a transaction. However, the use of these provisions can be abused.

We are well aware of the disparity of sophistication and bargaining power that frequently exists in the consumer retail installment sales market and the abuses of the mechanism of judicial enforcement which can result from automatic enforcement of these "agreements." Courts have refused to bind a person who has little education, does not speak or read English, or who has been the victim of deceptive sales techniques, resulting in lack of knowledge or notice of the contract terms. Proof of these objective indications of an aggrieved party's ignorance of the contract are exceptions to the general rule, well-established in Illinois, that a person who signs a contract has manifested his intention to be bound by the terms of that contract and cannot claim he was ignorant of those provisions.

Here the appellants claimed that they did not have an opportunity to read the contracts when they agreed to purchase the freezer and the meat. Nevertheless they signed the contracts and had them in their possession for several months before defaulting. Joyce Meredith testified that they received the contracts when the food and the freezer were delivered while Bennie Meredith stated that the contracts were not received until after that date. By either version, they paid on the contracts for more than four months after the contracts and the merchandise were delivered. While it was alleged that the appellants had little formal education, no proof of this allegation was offered. The record does not indicate that appellants were precluded from examining the contract before they signed. Although their decision to purchase the freezer and food was induced by the salesman's representations, their failure to examine the contract, by their own testimony, was not caused by the salesman's alleged unfair techniques but by their haste to get to their bowling game.

Defendants did not lack a meaningful choice since there is no indication in the record that the items purchased were necessities to defendants or that defendants could not have purchased these same items on credit without these clauses from other sources.

As discussed earlier, the contracts contained an admonition to the defendant-buyers, prominently placed on the face of the contracts above the space for defendants' signatures and in readable type, that unless the defendants notified the person to whom the contracts were assigned within five days of the date they received the merchandise of any claim they had against the seller, they could not assert a claim against the assignee later. Because from the face of the contracts we believe that the defendants should have been aware of the clauses they now challenge and have failed to demonstrate that when they signed the contracts and after they received the contracts they were precluded from reading and understanding their rights under the clause or that they could not discover defects in the merchandise or notify the assignee of their complaints within the five day period, we must conclude that the instant waiver of defense clauses are not unconscionable.

Contracts Against Public Policy

A contract or a provision in a contract may be declared contrary to public policy if it injures the interest of the public or tends to interfere with the public's general welfare, health, safety, or morals. But what constitutes public policy? The term itself is vague and uncertain. Today's public policy may be repudiated by tomorrow's generation. In *Henningsen* v. *Bloomfield Motors,* the New Jersey Supreme Court held that a provision in a printed form contract used by all large automobile companies that disclaimed all warranties express or implied except for one minor warranty in the contract was contrary to public policy. The court stated:

Public Policy is a term not easily defined. Its significance varies as the habits and needs of a people may vary. It is not static and the field of application is an ever increasing one. A contract, or a particular provision therein, valid in one era may be wholly opposed to the public policy of another.

It seems clear that public policy, while being based in constitutions, statutes, and earlier court decisions, stems from political, economic, and historical factors as well. There really is no limit as to what sources a court is permitted to use in determining public policy. An analysis of public-policy court decisions invariably will produce conflicting results among jurisdictions.

Once a contract has been found to violate public policy, the courts must then determine what sanctions are appropriate. Sometimes refusing to enforce the contract will hurt an innocent party. Yet enforcing the contract or awarding damages gives the appearance of sanctioning improper conduct. Table 15-2 dramatizes some of the problems that the courts must confront.

EFFECTS OF ILLEGALITY

The general policy of the law is to refuse to enforce an illegal agreement. But refusing to enforce an agreement is different from saying that no agreement has been made. If a contractual agreement has been made, neither party should keep what the other may have given as consideration. If an agreement that is unenforceable has been made, the party (or parties) who has done something illegal should not be able to enforce the agreement, but if one party has not done anything illegal, that party might be able to keep whatever consideration he or she was given. These parties to an illegal but unenforceable agreement have still made a contract even though the courts will usually not aid either of them by enforcing its provisions.

What about an agreement that has both legal and illegal provisions? Can the legal provisions be enforced while still denying enforcement to the illegal portions of the contract? The answer to this question depends on the degree to which the terms of and consideration paid for the contract are separate and divisible. If the essence of the entire contract is illegal, probably none of its provisions can be enforced. On the other hand, if a seller and purchaser agree to sell and buy a business and the contract terms also illegally provide that the seller will not compete with the purchaser in any business in any location for a lengthy period of time, the fact that the restraint on the seller is unreasonable and unenforceable probably would not make illegal and unenforceable the remaining terms for the transfer of the business.

There are also some other very limited circumstances in which the courts will provide relief to a party who has been caught in an illegal contract. If the public policy involved is designed to protect a class of persons and the party suing is of that class, then the courts may allow the contract to be enforced to the benefit of that party. Or, if the plaintiff is not *in pari*

TABLE 15–2 EXAMPLES OF PROBLEMS IN ENFORCING ILLEGAL CONTRACTS

How should the courts resolve the following cases?

Defendant pays judge $20,000 bribe for favorable ruling.	Judge rules for plaintiff and keeps and spends money.	Plaintiff sues for return of the $20,000.
Johnson needs to borrow $10,000 for family expenses but is a poor credit risk and cannot find a loan.	McDonald lends the $10,000 to Johnson, charging 30 percent interest. They sign a contract waiving the usury law.	Johnson refuses to pay any interest or to return the borrowed money. McDonald sues for both.
Jones contracts to deliver $100,000 worth of milk to Webster in New York City.	Jones delivers the milk that meets all federal and state standards. Jones does not have a license to sell the milk in New York City.	Webster takes the milk and then refuses to pay the $100,000. Jones sues to collect.

---

delicto (in equal fault) with the defendant, some relief may be granted. Thus, if the plaintiff is not aware that a regulatory-type license has not been obtained by the defendant, and the plaintiff would be injured if the parties are left where they are, the courts may provide some remedy.

Nevertheless, the instances in which the courts provide relief are quite limited. More typical is the view reflected in the common law decision at the turn of the century in *Woodson.* Even though one of the partners will receive a windfall from the court's unwillingness to provide a remedy, the court emphasizes its desire to take a complete hands-off approach to enforcing illegal contracts.

Woodson v. Hopkins

Supreme Court of Mississippi
37 So.Rptr. 1000 (1905)

Background: Woodson (plaintiff) and Hopkins (defendant) entered into a usurious business together. Hopkins successfully sued Woodson at the trial court level for an accounting of money allegedly due and for an injunction preventing Woodson from further participation in the business. Woodson appealed.

Decision: The court dismissed the suit and reversed the lower court on the grounds that the courts leave parties to an illegal contract in the position in which the court finds them.

Whitfield, Chief Justice

. . . We hold, without hesitation, that no such robbing contracts as this record discloses can be other than against the public policy of the state, on account of their extortionate character. "While the chief sources for determining the public policy of a nation are its constitution, laws, and judicial decisions, still, however, these are not the sole criteria, and the courts should not hesitate to declare a contract illegal merely because no statute or precedent prohibiting it can be found."

. . . "Where illegal contracts are executed by the parties, then the same principle of public policy which leads courts to refuse to act when called upon to enforce them will prevent the court from acting to relieve either party from the consequence of the illegal transactions. In such cases the defense of illegality prevails, not as a protection to the defendant, but as a disability in the plaintiff." . . . "The fact that the party seeking to enforce executory provisions of an illegal contract, though they consist only of promises to pay money, has performed the contract on his part, and that, unless the other party is compelled to perform, he will derive a benefit therefrom, will not induce the court to enforce such provisions. Nor can the party performing, on his part, the provisions of an illegal contract, recover on the ground of an implied promise on the part of the party receiving the benefits therefrom to pay therefor, as the law will imply no promise to pay for benefits received under an illegal contract by reason of the performance thereof by the other party."

. . . . .

. . . The courts leave violators of the law, as they ought to be left, in the condition where it finds them. They are repelled by the courts because of the great supervening principle of public policy involved, without reference to the attitude which one of the parties may occupy to the other, where both are in pari delicto. As pungently put in *Hoffman* v. *McMullen,* supra: "Courts are not organized to enforce the saying that 'there is honor among wrongdoers,' and the desire to punish the man that fails to observe this rule must not lead the court to a decision that such persons are entitled to the aid of courts to adjust their differences arising out of, and requiring an investigation of, their illegal transactions."

And the principle is universal that one party to an illegal contract can have no accounting from the other, where he must call in the aid, directly or indirectly, of the illegal contract to make out his case. . . .

The bill is reversed and dismissed.

REVIEW PROBLEMS

1. What is usury? Why do usury statutes exist? Would it be a good idea to enact a statute that requires that every sale be at a just price?

2. When will agreements in restraint of trade be enforced?

3. When is an exculpatory clause most likely to be enforced?

4. What is an unconscionable contract? Under the UCC, who decides what may be done with such a contract?

5. The telephone company in the region of Atlantis charges all customers a one-time hookup charge of $25 for the connection of telephone service. This charge is in addition to all itemized expenses, which are also passed on to the customer, and is labeled a "service fee." It appears on the form contracts supplied by the phone company to all customers, and phone connection is not possible without the payment of such fee. Does the service fee render the contract unconscionable?

6. Edward parked his car in a garage where the keys are left with the car. The garage had large signs at all exits stating that the garage was not liable for any damage to cars left on the premises. Edward's car disappeared. The car was worth $20,000 and had $30,000 worth of jewelry in the trunk. Edward sues the garage claiming $50,000. What is the best result?

7. Tovar, a physician practicing in the state of Kansas, wrote the Paxton Hospital in Illinois to inquire about obtaining a position as a full-time resident. In his letter and in a subsequent personal interview, Tovar fully described the nature and extent of his education, training, and licensing as a physician. The hospital assured him that his professional credentials were satisfactory and hired him. Soon thereafter Tovar, who had relocated to Illinois, was discharged by Paxton Hospital for failure to hold a license to practice medicine in Illinois as required by a state statute. Tovar claimed illegal breach of employment by the hospital. Result?

8. Weaver, a high-school dropout, signed a service-station lease with American Oil Company containing a clause in fine print that released the oil company from liability for its negligence and compelled him, as lessee, to indemnify American for any damage or loss thus incurred. Weaver never read the lease, nor was it ever explained to him. During the course of business, a visiting American Oil employee

negligently sprayed gasoline over Weaver and his assistant, causing them to be burned and injured on the leased premises. American disclaimed liability on the basis of the contract clause. Is this correct?

9. Mayfair Fabrics leased commercial premises from Natell upon the condition that Mayfair absolve Natell of all liability for loss or damage to Mayfair's property by fire, explosion, or otherwise. Natell subsequently was negligent in causing a fire that resulted in considerable damage to Mayfair's operations. Mayfair seeks to recover damages on the basis of the landlord's negligence, but Natell urges he is protected under the lease from any liability. Which way would you rule? Mayfair Fabrics v. Henley, 226 A.2d 602 (N.J. Sup. Ct. 1967).

10. Hiyanne worked as a contact lens grinder and fitter for the House of Vision from 1959 until 1964 in branch stores, several in different cities. His employment contract said that upon the termination of his relationship with the employer, he would never engage in the same or similar business anywhere within a thirty-mile radius of any of the branch stores in which he had rendered services. Hiyanne resigned his position in 1964 and began working for a competitor just 150 feet from one of those House of Vision stores. The House of Vision seeks to enforce the restrictive covenant in the original employment contract. What result? House of Vision, Inc. v. Hiyanne, 225 N.E.2d 21 (Ill. Sup. Ct. 1967).

11. The state of Ohio appropriated a portion of Schneider's farm for the relocation and improvement of several highways. The Schneider family received monetary compensation and agreed to the following condition:

Albert Schneider . . . shall have access to the Hometown Road at all points where (his) property presently abuts Hometown Road, excepting therefrom the right of way for Route 224.

The effect of this clause in the agreement was to give the Schneiders access to Route 224 from their land. Now the director of highways has filed a second appropriation action against the Schneider land to permit improvements that would make Route 224 a part of the U.S. highway system; but these changes will eliminate the Schneiders' personal access to the road. Schneider is upset and seeks to enforce the earlier agreement. What should the court do? Schneider v. Masheter, 202 N.E.2d 320 (Ohio Ct. App. 1964).

12. Sweazea, a building owner, contracted with Measday for water and gas plumbing work. A local statute requires that a permit be applied for before plumbing work is begun—the intent of the regulation being that work done for which a permit is required is to be inspected for compliance with professional standards. Measday failed to apply for a permit until he had substantially completed the job. Now Sweazea has refused to finish paying him and Measday claims a breach of their contract. Sweazea says the contract cannot be enforced because it is illegal due to the statutory violation. Does the violation make the contract illegal? Measday v. Sweazea, 438 P.2d 525 (N.M. Ct. App. 1968).

Legal Form

Many people assume that contracts must be written to be enforceable. In fact, oral contracts are also enforceable. Only a few types of contracts must be written. This chapter identifies those that must be written and then covers legal principles about the interpretation of contracts.

STATUTE OF FRAUDS

Contracts Required to Be in *Writing*

The English Parliament in 1677 enacted a Statute for the Prevention of Frauds and Perjuries. This Statute of Frauds attempted to prevent fraud about the existence of contracts by requiring that certain important contracts be written and signed before they could be enforced. Today all states in the United States have enacted similar statutes requiring that certain contracts be in writing to be enforceable. These contracts, discussed in detail later, include:

1. Contracts involving a promise by an executor to pay the debts of the deceased out of the executor's own funds

2. Contracts to pay the debt of another

3. Contracts for the sale of land or an interest in land

4. Contracts not to be performed within one year

5. Contracts for the sale of goods priced at $500 or more

6. Contracts in consideration of marriage (prenuptial agreements) *UCC*

Some states require that certain other contracts—for example, real estate brokerage agreements—be written to be enforceable.

Although the statutes were designed for the broad purpose of preventing fraud and perjury, they serve three more specific purposes.

TABLE 16–1 CONTRACTS WITHIN THE STATUTE OF FRAUDS

Nongoods	Goods
Executor's promise to pay debts of another	Sale of goods for $500 or more
Promise to pay the debt of another	
Sale of land or an interest in land	
Promises not performable in one year	

First, the presence of a written contract reduces the chance that a court and jury will be misled about the existence or terms of the contract. Second, people are more likely to think about what they are getting into if they are required to sign something. They are less likely to act rashly. Finally, requiring a writing serves as a channeling device, distinguishing between those contracts that are enforceable and those that are not.

What Constitutes a Writing?

A legal term, *within,* is used throughout this chapter. If a contract must be in writing, it is called *within the Statute.* If it does not have to be in writing, it is called "without" the Statute. Oral contracts that are required to be in writing are considered unenforceable in most states, although they are otherwise valid. Thus, if someone fails to raise the defense of the Statute of Frauds, that person is legally bound by the contract.

What must a contract that must be written include? To be enforced, such a contract must be evidenced by a document describing the basic agreement signed by the person being sued on the contract. In general, the document must identify the parties, the subject matter of the contract, and the performance obligations of the parties.

Problems with the Rule

The rule that certain contracts must be written has on occasion worked to the disadvantage of consumers. The experience of a former student provides a ready example. The student signed a contract for the purchase of a motorcycle for $1,200. The merchant then contacted the student and told him that the dealership could not sell the cycle for less than $1,350. The student produced the contract form. It had never been signed by the merchant. The student could not sue to enforce the agreement.

In similar situations, a contract may be signed by a salesperson who has not agency authority to sign. At best, there are several legal hurdles that must be overcome to enforce such an agreement. At worst, the consumer, thinking that he or she has a "deal," discovers at the end that there is no legal recourse.

The example of the student and the motorcycle also demonstrates a second problem with the Statute. The student could not sue the merchant. But could the merchant sue the student? The surprising answer is yes—because the student had signed the contract. Because of this problem of one-way enforceability, the Statute has been partially modified by the UCC in regard to agreements between merchants [2-201(2)]. Even greater strides have been made with the recent development of consumer protection laws at both state and federal levels. These laws will be discussed later in this chapter.

A final problem arises from the technical application of the rule. The purpose of the Statute is to ensure that there is in fact an underlying contract between the parties. Yet some courts have refused to enforce oral agreements that fall within the scope of the Statute and that everyone concedes were made. Modern courts have responded to this unfortunate tendency by emphasizing the rule's exceptions. When it comes to applying the Statute, it is important to recognize that the exceptions are as important as the rule.

CONTRACTS WITHIN THE STATUTE OF FRAUDS

Contracts in Consideration of Marriage

Contracts in consideration of marriage involve property settlements in exchange for a promise to marry. Such prenuptial agreements are used mainly when two well-to-do people, both with children of their own, decide to marry late in life. Mutual promises to marry do not have to be written.

Executor's Promise to Pay the Debts of Deceased

When a person dies, it is almost certain that there will be some unpaid bills. It is also certain that creditors will demand payment before any of the assets are distributed. To wind up the deceased's affairs, the executor of the estate is required to pay the debts. Generally, the executor is not personally liable for paying the debts. If the deceased has left no assets, the creditors lose. But in some situations, the executor may promise personally to satisfy the obligations of the deceased. For example, the executor who is also a family member may want to prevent creditors from seizing and selling family heirlooms, some of great sentimental value, to satisfy the debts. To be enforceable, the Statue of Frauds requires such promises to be in writing.

When you consider that a bereaved relative who is also serving as an executor may be extremely vulnerable emotionally, the rationale behind the writing requirement becomes obvious. To protect such people, any contracts by executors to satisfy personally debts of the deceased must be in writing.

Promise to Pay the Debt of Another

Promises by an executor to be personally liable for debts of a deceased and promises by one person to be liable for the debts of another are somewhat similar. The difference is that promises to pay the debts of another are not usually given in states of emotional distress, and all the parties are living.

Primary and Secondary Liability. The basic way to determine whether a person's promise to pay another's debt must be written is to ask whether the person making the promise is pri-

marily or secondarily liable. *Primary liability* exists when the creditor can proceed directly against the person making the promise. *Secondary liability* exists when the creditor must look first to the original debtor before proceeding against the promisor. Promises involving secondary liability are within the Statute and must be in writing to be enforced.

For example, Charles is the owner of a local hardware store. Martin, a recent college graduate, has gone into business for himself as a building contractor. Martin comes into Charles's store seeking building supplies because he has just landed his first building contract. Charles, however, is unwilling to let Martin have the goods on credit, essentially because Martin hasn't had time to establish a credit rating. Martin, prepared for this, has his father, Martin, Senior, a well-known local businessman, call Charles and guarantee Martin's creditworthiness. Martin, Sr. promises that if Martin, Jr. defaults, Martin, Sr. will cover Charles's losses. Martin, Sr.'s promise is covered by the Statute of Frauds. Martin, Sr. has not made an absolute promise to pay Martin, Jr.'s debts; rather, Martin, Sr. has made a *conditional* promise to pay only if Martin, Jr. defaults. Charles must *first* look to Martin, Jr., not to Martin, Sr., for payment. Martin, Sr. is secondarily liable. His promise must be in writing.

However, assume that Martin, Jr. has won the building contract from Martin, Sr., his father. This time, when Martin, Sr. calls Charles, he tells Charles to give Martin, Jr. all the supplies he needs and to send the bill to him, Martin Sr. In this case, the father is primarily liable. His oral promise is enforceable. Charles must look to the father for payment.

Main Purpose Doctrine. In addition to the primary–secondary liability distinction, the courts also limit the application of the Statute with the *main purpose doctrine*. Under this doctrine, an oral promise creating secondary liability is nonetheless enforceable if it is made mainly to benefit the person making the promise. Assume, for example, that a franchisor of a tool rental business learns that one of his franchisees in a key location is about to be evicted for not paying rent on time. Franchisor calls the landlord and says, "I'll pay the rent if Franchisee doesn't pay you what he owes you. Don't evict him right now." That oral promise would be enforceable, because Franchisor's main purpose in making the promise is his own benefit. The franchise system depends for its success upon a strong distribution system, and the franchisor usually receives direct periodic payments from each operating franchisee. Thus, Franchisor has a personal motive for promising to keep the franchised outlets operating effectively.

Sale of Land or an Interest in Land

For our purposes, land is considered earth and the things permanently attached to it. The most common real-estate transactions, such as the sale of residential or commercial property, clearly fall under this rule and must be written. But what constitutes an *interest* in land?

Assume that I promise to sell to you the right to cross my property for a particular purpose. This is known as an *easement,* and it constitutes an interest in land. Thus my promise, if only oral, is not enforceable. An option to buy is considered an interest in land, as is a lien or security interest given against the land. In many states, leases are within the Statute, although some states require that only leases for an extended term (for example, more than one year) must be in writing.

A generally recognized exception to the provision about real estate is the doctrine of *part performance.* This doctrine is used in circumstances where one party promises to sell land in return for certain actions by the buyer. For example, Owner of real property may promise to sell part of it to Tenant if Tenant improves the entire property and works it for Owner. After Tenant does the work, Owner refuses to sell and raises the Statute of Frauds as a defense. If the parties have acted as though they had entered into a contract for the sale of certain land and if failing to recognize an oral agreement would defraud Tenant, the courts enforce the oral agreement. The part performance must be substantial and in reliance on the oral promise to sell. The following case shows the application of the part-performance doctrine.

Martin v. Scholl

Supreme Court of Utah
678 P.2d 274 (1983)

Background: Rodney Martin (plaintiff) began working as a ranch laborer for George H. Chaffin in 1936. He became foreman over all of Chaffin's farm and ranch properties in 1947 and continued in that capacity beyond Chaffin's death to January of 1976. In 1947 Chaffin had orally agreed to convey to Martin 120 acres of land referred to as "the home place" if Martin would continue working as his foreman. Martin remained, receiving a salary and occasional raises. He labored long and unusual hours and, with his wife, rendered personal services to Chaffin in reliance upon the contract. In 1968, Chaffin formed the George H. Chaffin Investment Company as part of his estate plan and conveyed certain real estate to it, including the 120-acre ranch. Martin had no notice of the conveyance. Martin sued Bernice Scholl, the executrix of George H. Chaffin's estate, and the George H. Chaffin Investment Company (defendants) to obtain an order requiring the defendants to perform the contract specifically. The trial court ordered that the contract be specifically performed. Scholl and the Chaffin Investment Company appealed to the Supreme Court of Utah.

Decision: The Supreme Court of Utah ruled in favor of Scholl and the Chaffin Investment Company and reversed the trial court decision.

Howe, Justice

Ordinarily a verbal gift of land or an oral agreement to convey land is within the statute of frauds. However, the doctrine of part performance allows a court of equity to enforce an oral agreement, if it has been partially performed, notwithstanding the statute:

> Part performance to be sufficient to take a case out of the statute must consist of clear, definite, and unequivocal acts of the party relying thereon, strictly referable to the contract, and of such character that it is impossible or impracticable to place the parties in status quo, mere nonaction being insufficient.

[A]cts of part performance must be exclusively referable to the contract. . . .

[T]he requirement of exclusive referability is "an evidentiary requirement of equity that the facts speak for themselves."

In the case at bar the court found evidence to support a contract between Martin and Chaffin which was based upon the testimony of Martin's witnesses. The court also found that Martin relied upon the oral agreement. The court concluded that Martin would not have continued to work for and provided personal services to Chaffin except for the agreement between them.

[R]eviewing the court's application of our law to those findings, we can only conclude that the court erred in its holding that there was sufficient part performance. The trial court drew one conclusion from Martin's services, but that is legally insufficient since they admit of another equally valid and consonant conclusion against his claim of contract.

The fact that Martin worked for Chaffin as his foreman is not an exclusively referable act of reliance on the alleged oral agreement since it was consonant with Martin's employment. Martin's long hours, not atypical of a ranch foreman's life, were remunerated by salary. Martin's wife's driving Chaffin to various locations on occasion and asking him to stay for dinner when he was at the Martin house during mealtime were not inconsistent with good relations between an employer and an employee and his family. (At least once Mrs. Martin received compensation for her efforts.)

Martin's claim that he declined other and better offers of employment elsewhere to remain with Chaffin is also unavailing to prove reliance since, as we quoted earlier, mere nonaction is insufficient to constitute part performance.

We have no quarrel with the argument in the dissenting opinion that the statute of frauds should not be used to perpetrate a fraud upon an innocent and unsuspecting person such as an employee who renders services in good faith upon a promised expectation. Such a rule would be easy to apply if there were some magical way of determining in each case whether a contract was in fact made. There being no sure-proof method of determining whether a contract was made, the Legislature has made it the policy in this state that oral contracts for the conveyance of land will not be enforced except where there is sufficient part performance to provide a high evidentiary basis for their existence. This policy which the Legislature has translated into the statute of frauds may well result, in some cases, in the denial of a benefit to a well-deserving employee or servant. We are helpless to prevent that result where the evidence of part performance of the claimed contract falls below the high evidentiary standard required by courts of equity—regardless of the precise words which they may use in describing that standard. As unfortunate as it would be to deprive a man who had worked his life in reliance upon the expectation of receiving property, it would be equally serious to take property from an owner after his death (when he cannot be heard) on the strength of a questionable oral agreement supposedly made many years prior. If the statute of frauds is to be given any force, we cannot affirm the trial court.

Stewart, Justice *(dissenting)*

By its rigid application of the "exclusively referable test," the majority raises the standard of proof in cases such as the instant case to a level that is unnecessarily high. In cases where the existence of the contract has already been proved by independent evidence, as in the instant case, the exclusively referable test in effect requires that the plaintiff "reprove" the existence of the contract by part performance. Concededly, where there is *no* other evidence of the contract, the "exclusively referable" test is an appropriate test. However, in this case there is other evidence of the contract.

The rule should be that if clear and convincing evidence proves the existence of the contract, then it is sufficient for the plaintiff to show that the part performance is "clearly referable" to the contract, i.e., was clearly in reliance on the contract or in accordance with the terms of the contract. The opposing party should then have the burden of proving alternate explanations, if any exist, for the part performance. In fact, defendants in the instant case attempted to do this, and the trial court refused to find in their favor.

What is critical, and is clear in the record, is that the plaintiff devoted his whole life to maintaining the deceased's farm as if it were the plaintiff's own farm. The trial court's finding that plaintiff would not have spent "his lifetime but for" the existence of the contract should be dispositive.

I respectfully submit that the doctrine of part performance in this case has been construed so narrowly that it has failed to achieve its intended purpose of avoiding application of the statute of frauds with such rigor as to produce the very kind of fraud that the statute was intended to prevent.

Promises Not Performable in One Year

If a contract cannot be performed within a year, it must be put in writing. For example, a three-year contract for the services of a professional athlete must be written.

Assume that no date is set in a contract. Instead, the arrangement is to continue until some event occurs or until one of the parties cancels the agreement. Such contracts do not have to be written if the event could possibly occur within one year or if there is no limitation on the right to cancel during the first year. For example, an agreement to provide service to a person until death usually need not be written because death could occur within one year.

One final problem arises with contracts involving construction projects. Determining whether these contracts must be written becomes a question of fact. Is there any possibility that if everything goes perfectly (no strikes, good weather), the job can be completed within a year? If so, the contract need not be written.

Sale of Goods for $500 or More

The UCC Statute of Frauds [section 2-201] states:

1. Except as otherwise provided in this section a contract for the sale of goods for the price of $500 or more is not enforceable by way of action or defense unless there is some writing sufficient to indicate that a contract for sale has been made between the parties and signed by the party against whom enforcement is sought or by his authorized agent or broker. A writing is not insufficient because it omits or incorrectly states a term agreed upon but the contract is not enforceable under this paragraph beyond the quantity of goods shown in such writing.
2. Between merchants if within a reasonable time a writing in confirmation of the contract and sufficient against the sender is received and the party receiving it has reason to know its contents, it satisfies the requirements of subsection 1 against such party unless written notice of objection to its contents is given within ten days after it is received.
3. A contract which does not satisfy the requirements of subsection 1 but which is valid in other respects is enforceable
   a. if the goods are to be specially manufactured for the buyer and are not suitable for sale to others in the ordinary course of the seller's business and the seller, before notice of repudiation is received and under circumstances which reasonably indicate that the goods are for the buyer, has made either a substantial beginning of their manufacture or commitments for their procurement; or
   b. if the party against whom enforcement is sought admits in his pleading, testimony or otherwise in court that a contract for sale was made, but the contract is not enforceable under the provision beyond the quantity of goods admitted; or
   c. with respect to goods for which payment has been made and accepted or which have been received and accepted.

Subsection 1 establishes the general rule that a contract for the sale of goods for $500 or more must be evidenced by "some writing" to be enforceable. The writing must be signed by the party against whom enforcement is sought. The writing requirement may be satisfied by more than one document. One case has held that a signed memo *without* terms referring to an unsigned document with terms established an enforceable contract.

The rest of the section limits the general rule. Subsection 2 modifies the one-way enforceability result in the case of merchants. Assume that Jones and Smith, both merchants, orally agree to a contract. The next day Jones sends a signed letter to Smith detailing the terms of the agreement. Smith does not respond for ten days. The contract is enforceable against Smith on the basis of Jones's letter even though Smith has never signed anything.

The three exceptions established in Subsection 3 have a common element: in the situations defined, there is persuasive evidence that a contract has in fact been made. Under (b) there is an outright admission by the defendant that a contract exists. It would be contrary to the basic purpose of the Statute to allow a defense in such a circumstance. Under (c), one can assume that a buyer will not accept goods unless a contract is intended. Note that the contract is enforceable only in regard to the quantity of goods that has been accepted. Similarly, a seller will not accept payment unless a contract is intended. A down payment may satisfy the exception in Subsection 3, paragraph c. This is simply a version of the part-performance exception to the Statute of Frauds, which, until the UCC, applied only to contracts involving an interest in land. The specially manufactured goods in (a) must be shown to have a reasonable connection with the buyer. Again there is external evidence that a contract has been made.

The case that follows involves the application of the UCC Statute of Frauds.

Southwest Engineering Company v. Martin Tractor Company

Supreme Court of Kansas

473 P.2d 18 (1970)

Background: Southwest Engineering Company *(plaintiff)* was preparing to submit a bid to the U.S. Army Corps of Engineers for construction of runway lighting facilities. On April 28, 1966, Southwest's construction superintendent, R.E. Cloepfil, met with Ken Hurt, manager of Martin Tractor Company's *(defendant)* engine department, in the town of Springfield to negotiate the price of a standby generator and accessory equipment to be used for the project. At this meeting, the agent for Martin Tractor noted each required item and its price on a memorandum but hand-printed his name and that of his company in the upper left-hand corner. On May 24, 1966, Martin Tractor wrote to Southwest refusing to supply the generator and equipment. Southwest repeatedly tried to convince Martin Tractor to supply the equipment, until September 6, 1966, when it got the required items from another supplier at a cost of $6,041 more than the figures listed by Martin Tractor on the memorandum. Southwest sued Martin Tractor for breach of contract. The trial court entered judgment for Southwest in the amount of $6,041. Martin appealed to the Supreme Court of Kansas. Decision: The Supreme Court of Kansas affirmed the trial court judgment in favor of Southwest.

Fontron, Justice

The basic disagreement centers on whether the meeting between Hurt and Cloepfil at Springfield resulted in an agreement which was enforceable under the provisions of the Uniform Commercial Code (sometimes referred to as the Code), which was enacted by the Kansas Legislature at its 1965 session. . . .

Southwest takes the position that the memorandum prepared by Hurt at Springfield supplies the essential elements of a contract required by the foregoing statute, *i.e.,* that it is (1) a writing signed by the party sought to be charged, (2) that it is for the sale of goods and (3) that quantity is shown. In addition, the reader will have noted that the memorandum sets forth the prices of the several items listed. . . .

. . . [D]efendant . . . maintains . . . that the writing in question does not measure up to the stature of a signed memorandum within the purview of the Code; that the instrument simply sets forth verbal quotations for future consideration in continuing negotiations.

But on this point the trial court found there *was* an agreement reached between Hurt and Cloepfil at Springfield; that the formal requirements of K.S.A. 84-2-201 *were* satisfied; and that the memorandum prepared by Hurt contains the three essentials of the statute in that it evidences a sale of goods, was authenticated by Hurt and specifies quantity. . . .

We believe the record supports all the above findings. With particular reference to the preparation and sufficiency of the written memorandum, the following evidence is pertinent:

Mr. Cloepfil testified that he and Hurt sat down at a restaurant table and spread out the plans which Hurt had brought with him; that they went through the specifications item by item and Hurt wrote each item down, together with the price thereof; that while the specifications called for a D353 generator, Hurt thought the D343 model might be an acceptable substitute, so he gave prices on both of them and Southwest could take either one of the two which the Corps of Engineers would approve; that Hurt gave him (Cloepfil) the memorandum "as a record of what he had done, the agreement we had arrived at at our meeting in the restaurant at the airport."

We digress at this point to note Martin's contention that the memorandum is not signed within the meaning of 84-2-201. The sole authentication appears in hand-printed form at the top left-hand corner in these words: "Ken Hurt, Martin Tractor, Topeka, Caterpillar." The court found this sufficient, and we believe correctly so. K.S.A. 84-1-201(39) provides as follows:

> Signed includes any symbol executed or adopted by a party with present intention to authenticate a writing. . . .

It is quite true, as the trial court found, that terms of payment were not agreed upon at the Springfield meeting. Hurt testified that as the memorandum was being made out, he said they wanted 10 percent with the order, 50 percent on delivery and the balance on acceptance, but he did not recall Cloepfil's response. Cloepfil's version was somewhat different. He stated that after the two had shaken hands in the lobby preparing to leave, Hurt said their terms usually were 20 percent down and the balance on delivery; while he (Cloepfil) said the way they generally paid was 90 percent on the tenth of the month following delivery and the balance on final acceptance. It is obvious the parties reached no agreement on this point.

However, a failure on the part of Messrs. Hurt and Cloepfil to agree on terms of payment would not, of itself, defeat an otherwise valid agreement reached by them. K.S.A. 84-2-204(3) reads:

> Even though one or more terms are left open a contract for sale does not fail for indefiniteness if the parties have intended to make a contract and there is a reasonably certain basis for giving an appropriate remedy. . . .

In our view, the language of the two Code provisions is clear and positive. Considered together, we take the two sections to mean that where parties have reached an enforceable agreement for the sale of goods, but omit therefrom the terms of payment, the law will imply, as part of the agreement, that payment is to be made at time of delivery. In this respect the law does not greatly differ from the rule this court laid down years ago. . . .

We do not mean to infer that terms of payment are not of importance under many circumstances, or that parties may not condition an agreement on their being included. However, the facts before us hardly indicate that Hurt and Cloepfil considered the terms of payment to be significant, or of more than passing interest. Hurt testified that while he stated his terms he did not recall Cloepfil's response, while Cloepfil stated that as the two were on the point of leaving, each stated their usual terms and that was as far as it went. The trial court found that only a brief and casual conversation ensued as to payment, and we think that is a valid summation of what took place.

. . .

EQUITABLE ESTOPPEL AND PROMISSORY ESTOPPEL

As we have noted, courts have become increasingly sensitive to the use of the Statute of Frauds to perpetrate fraud. They have tried to minimize fraud by using the doctrines of equitable estoppel and promissory estoppel.

Equitable estoppel, a doctrine as old as the Statute itself, is used in situations where applying the Statute would result in a substantial injustice. The part-performance exception to the Statute discussed earlier in this chapter is basically an application of the doctrine of equitable estoppel.

Promissory estoppel is a more specific application of the principles of equitable estoppel. As indicated in Chapter 12, *promissory estoppel* has been used primarily to make exceptions to the rule that all contracts be supported by consideration.

If the person making the promise should have known that the promise would induce the person being promised something to rely on the promise to his or her detriment, the promisor may find that he or she is obligated to comply with the contract, even if the contract itself does not satisfy the Statute of Frauds.

For example, consider how promissory estoppel might apply to a contract governed by the Statute of Frauds in the following case. Assume that Rogers is a police captain who will be eligible for retirement in two years. The retirement package includes a pension of full salary, paid medical insurance, life insurance, and other benefits. In addition, the city's contract with the police union provides that no one, union member or not, may be discharged except for cause. Sullivan, chair of the board of a large corporation, induces Rogers to quit his job as a police officer in exchange for an extremely lucrative ten-year employment contract with Sullivan's company. Sullivan further promises to put the contract in writing when she returns from Europe. Unfortunately, Sullivan is killed while traveling, and the other board members are reluctant to honor Sullivan's promise of employment to Rogers.

Under traditional Statute of Frauds principles, the contract would be unenforceable. Because it is an offer of employment for ten years, the contract falls within the requirement that it be put in writing. Rogers, having already quit his job as a police captain, would be without a remedy and without a job. Fortunately for Rogers, most courts today do not tolerate such an inequitable result. It is apparent that Sullivan knew and intended that her promise of employment would induce Rogers to quit his current job in reliance on the prom-

PREVENTIVE LAW
Complying with the Statute of Frauds

"Get it in writing!" These four words are well worth remembering when it comes to the making of contracts. Most of the problems that have been discussed in this chapter can be avoided by observing this simple rule.

---

ise. Because he has been induced to quit his prior job, and because injustice cannot otherwise be avoided, Sullivan's fellow board members are bound by the contract. They are, in essence, "estopped" from asserting the Statute of Frauds as a defense.

The result would have been different had the policeman not yet quit his job at the time of Sullivan's death and the refusal of the other board members to honor the contract. All jurisdictions have required that the promisee be in danger of suffering "unconscionable injury" if the contract is not enforced. When people have relied to their detriment on other people's promises, and when enforcing a contract is the only way to prevent either substantial injury or injustice, the contract is to be enforced.

When deciding whether to use promissory estoppel as a means for avoiding the Statute of Frauds, it is important to consider the aspect of damages. In an action for breach of contract, a plaintiff can generally recover compensatory damages to the extent that they can be proven. However, this is not true when recovery is based upon promissory estoppel. The courts have held uniformly that when promissory estoppel is used as a means of avoiding the Statute of Frauds, only restitutional damages (i.e., out-of-pocket expenses) can be recovered. In these cases, the plaintiff generally is not entitled to the benefit of the bargain; instead, he or she will only be restored to the position he or she was in before acting in reliance on the defendant's promise.

In the following case, the court considers whether the doctrine of promissory estoppel applies to take an oral promise outside the Statute of Frauds. Excerpts of the case appeared in Chapter 12 with regard to the application of the doctrine of promissory estoppel in connection with promises that are not supported by consideration. The following is the remainder of the court's opinion.

Allen M. Campbell Co. v. Virginia Metal Industries, Inc.
U.S. Court of Appeals, Fourth Circuit
708 F.2d 930 (1983)

Background: Allen M. Campbell Co. (plaintiff), in August 1981, intended to bid on a Department of Navy contract to construct housing for enlisted personnel at Camp LeJeune, North Carolina. The deadline for submission of bids was 2:00 P.M. on August 11, 1981. At about 1:30 P.M., Virginia Metal Industries, Inc. (defendant), telephoned Campbell and quoted a price to supply all hollow metal doors and frames that were required by the plans and specifications. The price promised was $193,121, plus applicable taxes. Campbell based the computation for its bid for the Navy project upon the quoted price for the hollow metal doors and frames of $193,121 and taxes. Campbell was the successful bidder and was awarded the Navy contract. Virginia Metal backed out of its promise, and as a consequence, Campbell had to obtain the items covered by the quoted price of $193,121 from another supplier, at a cost $45,562 greater than what it had been led to expect Virginia Metal would charge. Campbell sued Virginia Metal Industries, Inc. for the $45,562. The trial court dismissed Campbell's complaint, and Campbell appealed to the Fourth Circuit Court of Appeals.

Decision: Ruling for Campbell, the Fourth Circuit Court of Appeals reversed the trial court decision and sent the case back to the trial court for trial.

Murnaghan, Circuit Judge

[W]e must next deal with the contention of Virginia Metal that it cannot be held liable since its promise was not in writing. The Uniform Commercial Code has been adopted in North Carolina and N.C.Gen.Stat. Sec. 25-2-201 requires that a contract for the sale of goods involving more than $500 must be in writing. The answer, however, lies in the language of N.C.Gen.Stat.Sec. 25-1-103:

> Unless displaced by the particular provisions of this chapter, the principles of law and equity, including . . . the law relevant to . . . estoppel . . . or other validating or invalidating cause shall supplement its provisions.

The question then becomes whether North Carolina's doctrine of promissory estoppel creates an exception to or is displaced by the statute of frauds. There is a split of authority in decisions from states other than North Carolina on the question of whether promissory estoppel is to be deemed an exception to the statute of frauds.

While North Carolina has not explicitly committed itself as to the availability of promissory estoppel as a means for overcoming the U.C.C. statute of frauds, it has expressed approval of the position taken in Restatement (Second) of Contracts, Section 139, the cornerstone of the rationale adopted by the courts which have held that promissory estoppel will, in circumstances like those here presented, render inapplicable the U.C.C. statute of frauds. Thus in the *Wachovia* case the court observed that:

> Furthermore, "[a] promise which the promisor should reasonably expect to induce action or forbearance on the part of the promisee . . . and which does induce the action or forbearance is enforceable notwithstanding the Statute of Frauds if injustice can be avoided only by enforcement of the promise. The remedy granted for breach is to be limited as justice requires." Restatement (Second) of Contracts, Section 139 (1981). This view is consistent with that found in cases in which this Court has recognized exceptions to the Statute of Frauds.

In light of the status of what we perceive to be the law that North Carolina courts would apply to the facts of this case, the fact that the promise was entirely oral would not bar recovery. Consequently, the grant to Virginia Metal of judgment on the pleadings for failure to state a claim upon which relief can be granted was erroneous.

ETHICS BOX
Raising the Defense of the Statute of Frauds

The British judge, James Stephens, wrote that "The cases in which a man of honour would condescend to avail himself of (The Statute of Frauds) must, I should think, be very rare indeed." By that he meant that most of the time that a contract is subject to the defense of the Statute of Frauds, there is little question but that a real contract has been made. Thus, the party seeking to avoid enforcement is doing so on a legal technicality, a failure of legal form, and not on the basis of a genuine claim that no contract was made.

There has been some debate whether a lawyer can act ethically to assert the claim when the lawyer believes that the underlying contract exists and is valid. In the United States, that issue has been resolved, so far, in favor of the lawyer asserting the claim, unless there is knowledge of fraud or some other disqualifying conduct.

The client has the legal right to raise the defense. The client may not appreciate the broader policies of the law. How might arguments be constructed pro and con concerning whether the client acts ethically by consenting to the defense? Who do you think is likely to be most influential concerning the decision to rely on a defense of this sort—the lawyer or the client?

THE PAROL EVIDENCE RULE

Even if people have to reduce an agreement between them to writing, and even if the writing satisfies all the requirements of the Statute of Frauds, there are bound to be some disputes over the meaning of the language in the contract or allegations that the contract has been modified or does not include *all* the terms of the agreement. To solve these problems, it is often helpful to turn to what is known as the *parol evidence rule.*

Parol evidence has nothing to do with shortening the prison terms of convicted felons. In contract situations, "parol" evidence is made up of statements or writings that do not appear in the written contract document. Parol evidence can be either written or oral.

The parol evidence rule is based upon a simple principle. The simple principle is: When contracting parties draw up a document of their agreement that appears both complete and final on its face, it is appropriate to conclude that the parties have put everything into that document. The contracting parties may not use earlier or concurrent agreements to contradict the written document.

The parol evidence rule is similar to the Statute of Frauds in that it imposes a technical, formal requirement on the way contracting parties write their agreements. Unfortunately, the parol evidence rule is also similar to the Statute of Frauds in that it often results in harm to consumers and small-business operators. The rule can make promises that were made but not written into the contract unenforceable.

Requirements

The parol evidence rule applies only to written contracts that are final and apparently complete. If the written contract is obviously incomplete or states that certain terms are to be filled in later, the rule does not apply. (The parol evidence rule does not require that the parties use a writing. Only the various Statutes of Frauds do that. Instead, the parol evidence rule affects the manner in which the contract terms may be established once a final and complete writing has been used.)

Attorneys have responded to the rule by putting clauses similar to the following in written contracts:

> This contract is the final and complete agreement between the parties. All prior negotiations and/or agreements are merged into this contract and all additions to or alterations or changes in this contract must be in writing and signed by both parties.

Such clauses are known as *integration agreements,* because they are intended to integrate all earlier agreements of the parties into the contract document. The hope is that an integration agreement will make it extremely difficult to introduce evidence of earlier agreements. Whether the final document integrates earlier documents is really a question of fact that must be resolved by considering the particular circumstances of the contract negotiations. In addition, an ambiguous provision of a written contract may be cleared up by parol evidence. But parol evidence that *contradicts* the written agreement is inadmissible.

These two issues—whether the document is a final integration and whether its terms are ambiguous—give the courts leeway to limit the application of the rule. Many courts have used this opportunity to make rulings hostile to the rule. Why such hostility? Doesn't the basic principle underlying the parol evidence rule make sense? The answer is that the principle is flawed and often produces an unfair result.

The parol evidence principle assumes a contract fully negotiated between equals or near equals. But, as we have seen, many written contracts, particularly those entered into by consumers, do not meet that standard. Instead, consumers are handed form contracts to sign. Invariably these contain a clause stating that the form represents the final agreement between the parties and that there are no other understandings between them. It is not uncommon for a salesperson to make oral statements such as, "We'll extend the warranty 30 extra days," or "Of course, we'll provide free service for a year," or "Although it's not our usual policy, we will deliver your purchase free of charge." Relying on these statements, consumers sign contracts and then are prevented by the parol evidence rule from trying to show the "other understandings" that the consumer assumed were part of the deal.

Further, form contracts are drafted for the standard or typical deal. Any customized deal causes problems with the form. Salespeople, office managers, and consumers are not likely to be familiar with the legal consequences described in legal jargon in the form. In these cases, a merchant may use the parol evidence rule as a shield against liability.

The case that follows shows how courts have tried to soften the parol evidence rule.

Masterson v. Sine

Supreme Court of California
436 P.2d 561 (1968)

Background: Rebecca Masterson and her husband, Dallas (plaintiffs), together owned a ranch. On February 25, 1958, they deeded it to Medora and Lu Sine (defendants). The deed "reserved unto grantors herein [the Mastersons] an option to purchase the above described property on or before February 25, 1968." Medora Sine was Dallas Masterson's sister. After the deed was given, Dallas became bankrupt. Rebecca and his trustee (the person in the bankruptcy proceeding who was responsible for collecting assets and paying claims) sued to enforce the option to purchase the ranch. The Sines offered evidence showing that the parties wanted the property kept in the Masterson family, and because the option was personal, it could not be exercised by the trustee in bankruptcy. The trial court found that the parol evidence rule prevented admission of the new information from the Sines and ruled that the option could be exercised. Defendants Medora and Lu Sine appealed to the Supreme Court of California.

Decision: The Supreme Court of California ruled in favor of the Sines and reversed the trial court judgment.

Traynor, Chief Justice

The trial court determined that the parol evidence rule precluded admission of extrinsic evidence offered by defendants to show that the parties wanted the property kept in the Masterson family and that the option was therefore personal to the grantors and could not be exercised by the trustee in bankruptcy. . . .

Defendants appeal. . . . The trial court properly refused to frustrate the obviously declared intention of the grantors to reserve an option to repurchase by an overly meticulous insistence on completeness and clarity of written expression. . . .

The trial court erred, however, in excluding the extrinsic evidence that the option was personal to the grantors and therefore nonassignable.

When the parties to a written contract have agreed to it as an "integration"—a complete and final embodiment of the terms of an agreement—parol evidence cannot be used to add to or vary its terms. . . . When only part of the agreement is integrated, the same rule applies to that part, but parol evidence may be used to prove elements of the agreement not reduced to writing. . . .

The crucial issue in determining whether there has been an integration is whether the parties intended their writing to serve as the exclusive embodiment of their agreement. The instrument itself may help to resolve that issue. It may state, for example, that "there are no previous understandings or agreements not contained in the writing," and thus express the parties' "intention to nullify antecedent understandings or agreements." Any such collateral agreement itself must be examined, however, to determine whether the parties intended the subjects of negotiation it deals with to be included in, excluded from, or otherwise affected by the writing. Circumstances at the time of the writing may also aid in the determination of such integration. . . .

California cases have stated that whether there was an integration is to be determined solely from the face of the instrument and that the question for the court is whether it "appears to be a complete . . . agreement." . . .

Neither of these strict formulations of the rule, however, has been consistently applied. The requirement that the writing must appear incomplete on its face has been repudiated in many cases where parol evidence was admitted "to prove the existence of a separate oral agreement as to any matter on which the document is silent and which is not inconsistent with its terms"—even though the instrument appeared to state a complete agreement. . . .

In formulating the rule governing parol evidence, several policies must be accommodated. One policy is based on the assumption that written evidence is more accurate than human memory. This policy, however, can be adequately served by excluding parol evidence of agreements that directly contradict the writing. Another policy is based on the fear that fraud or unintentional invention by witnesses interested in the outcome of the litigation will mislead the finder of facts. . . . McCormick has suggested that the party urging the spoken as against the written word is most often the economic underdog, threatened by severe hardship if the writing is enforced. In his view the parol evidence rule arose to allow the court to control the tendency of the jury to find through sympathy and without a dispassionate assessment of the probability of fraud or faulty memory that the parties made an oral agreement collateral to the written contract, or that preliminary tentative agreements were not abandoned when omitted from the writing. He recognizes, however, that if this theory were adopted in disregard of all other considerations, it would lead to the exclusion of testimony concerning oral agreements whenever there is a writing and thereby often defeat the true intent of the parties.

Evidence of oral collateral agreements should be excluded only when the fact finder is likely to be misled. The rule must therefore be based on the credibility of the evidence. One such standard, adopted by section 240(l)(b) of the Restatement of Contracts, permits proof of a collateral agreement if it "is such an agreement as might *naturally* be made as a separate agreement by parties situated as were the parties to the written contract." . . .

The option clause in the deed in the present case does not explicitly provide that it contains the complete agreement, and the deed is silent on the question of assignability. Moreover, the difficulty of accommodating the formalized structure of a deed to the insertion of collateral agreements makes it less likely that all the terms of such an agreement were included. . . . This case is one, therefore, in which it can be said that a collateral agreement such as that alleged "might naturally be made as a separate agreement." *A fortiori,* the case is not one in which the parties "would certainly" have included the collateral agreement in the deed. . . .

It is contended, however, that an option agreement is ordinarily presumed to be assignable if it contains no provisions forbidding its transfer or indicating that its performance involves elements personal to the parties. The fact that there is a written memorandum, however, does not necessarily preclude parol evidence rebutting a term that the law would otherwise presume. . . . In the present case defendants offered evidence that the parties agreed that the option was not assignable in order to keep the property in the Masterson family. The trial court erred in excluding that evidence.

Burke, Justice *(dissenting)*

I dissent. The majority opinion:

> (1) Undermines the parol evidence rule as we have known it in this state since at least 1872 by declaring that parol evidence should have been admitted

by the trial court to show that a written option, absolute and unrestricted in form, was intended to be limited and nonassignable;

(2) Renders suspect instruments of conveyance absolute on their face;

(3) Materially lessens the reliance which may be placed upon written instruments affecting the title to real estate; and

(4) Opens the door, albeit unintentionally, to a new technique for the defrauding of creditors.

The opinion permits defendants to establish by parol testimony that their grant to their brother (and brother-in-law) of a written option, absolute in terms, was nevertheless agreed to be nonassignable by the grantee (now a bankrupt), and that therefore the right to exercise it did not pass, by operation of the bankruptcy laws, to the trustee for the benefit of the grantee's creditors.

And how was this to be shown? By the proffered testimony of the bankrupt optionee himself! Thereby one of his assets (the option to purchase defendants' California ranch) would be withheld from the trustee in bankruptcy and from the bankrupt's creditors. Understandably the trial court, as required by the parol evidence rule, did not allow the bankrupt by parol evidence to so contradict the unqualified language of the written option. . . .

Exceptions

A number of logical exceptions follow directly from the basic premise of the parol evidence rule. The fact that on a particular day two people sign a formal agreement does not mean that they have intended to bind themselves forever to those particular terms. As a consequence, parol evidence is always admissible to prove a *later modification* of the contract. The major legal problem with modification, as discussed in Chapter 12, is with sufficiency of consideration.

Parol evidence is admissible to clear up an *ambiguity* in the contract terms. It is also admissible to prove fraud, alteration, mistake, illegality, duress, undue influence, or lack of capacity. If any of these things can be shown, then the document does not represent a valid contract. It would be very poor legal policy to allow the parol evidence rule to protect a defrauding party or to prevent the showing of duress or mistake. For example, fraud may be perpetrated when one party alters the document or signs it by, say, using a carbon and a second sheet with different terms. Similarly, a mistake may occur as the document is prepared. These occurrences may be proved by parol evidence.

UCC Parol Evidence Rule

The UCC (Section 2-202) has a special parol evidence rule on the sale of goods. This rule is more liberal than the common law rule. Usage of trade and course of dealing or performance are always admissible, whether or not the contract terms are found to be ambiguous. The only way by which such factors would be inadmissible would be by an express contract term to that effect.

Further, unless it is quite clear that the document represents an exclusive statement, noncontradictory *additional* terms may be admitted into evidence. There is no presumption that a written document is considered by the parties as a complete, exclusive statement of their agreement.

The Effect of Consumer Protection Statutes

Consumer protection laws can affect the use of the parol evidence rule. Most states have adopted such laws in the last few years, and they add an interesting twist to the rule. Many such laws make it illegal for suppliers to *fail* to integrate all earlier agreements, oral or otherwise, into the final contract document. Thus, if a car salesman makes a variety of performance and warranty guarantees to a car buyer, but the manufacturer's warranty that comes with the car or the bill of sale does not reflect these guarantees, the salesman has violated such consumer laws. Further, because of these laws, the salesman may not argue his guarantees should not be binding because of the parol evidence rule. Carrying this even further, once evidence of the agreements is used to prove their existence for purposes of showing violations of the consumer laws, their existence also has been proved for purposes of enforcing the guarantees themselves.

INTERPRETATION OF CONTRACTUAL PROVISIONS

When people who have made a contract dispute its terms, the courts use specific, established rules of interpretation to resolve the disputes. Problems typically arise because:

1. In using prepared form documents, the parties:
   a. add language that contradicts other provisions in the form
   b. do not intend that all of the form provisions apply to their agreement, or
   c. add contradictory or ambiguous language.

2. In using negotiated, specially prepared documents, the parties:
   a. use ambiguous language,
   b. fail to anticipate a problem that arises during performance, or
   c. compromise without coming to precise understandings of certain terms.

In interpreting the particular language used in a written contract, the courts are primarily concerned with correctly learning the intention of the contracting parties. The intentions of the parties cannot be learned by simply asking the people what they intended because, obviously, if they had agreed on such an issue they would not be in court. Consequently, the courts use the following specific rules designed to ascertain the objectively viewed intention of the parties:

1. Words are to be given their plain and ordinary meanings so long as such an interpretation does not result in a clearly unique or strange result.
   a. The meaning of words may be varied by the prior usage between the parties. The parties are governed by their course of dealing.
   b. Technical words and terms are to be given technical meanings unless it is clear that the parties intend some other definition. (This rule tends to be important in contracts for the sale of land because of the large number of technical terms used in real property law.)
   c. Trade usage may supply a basis for the interpretation of terms.
2. Writings are to be interpreted as a whole, and language is not to be taken out of context.
3. Special circumstances under which a contract was made may be used to show the actual understanding of the parties.
4. Legal and reasonable interpretations are

preferred over illegal and unreasonable alternatives.

5. Specific provisions control general provisions.

6. Generally, handwritten provisions prevail over typed provisions, and typed provisions prevail over printed provisions. In applying this rule, the courts assume that the mate-

---

PREVENTIVE LAW
Contract Law and the Written Word

T he material in this chapter should alert you to the need to give careful attention to written contracts. The Statute of Frauds, the parol evidence rule, and the rules regarding contract interpretation have all been created to carry out sound public policies. However, contracting parties that neglect to consider the impact of these rules on their contracting obligations run grave risks that their dealings will not be given their intended effect in court.

Although the Statute of Frauds requires that certain contracts be evidenced by a writing, there are occasions when this is not immediately possible. Sellers and buyers frequently do business over the phone. Under UCC 2-201, merchants can satisfy the Statute's requirements by sending confirmatory memoranda of their transactions. One common way that sellers satisfy this requirement is by sending an invoice evidencing that an order has been received from a buyer. Buyers frequently send their own purchase orders confirming their phone orders.

Often in negotiations, the parties arrive at certain preliminary understandings before they finally enter into an agreement. Later, the parties may disagree over the "intent" of their written contract. It is here that the parol evidence rule can be used to provide finality to the written word. This is particularly important for businesses that need to control the potential liability that they are exposed to by their sales agents. The use of an integration clause can serve to limit a court's treatment of a dispute to what the parties have provided in their writing.

Finally, businesspeople who are in a hurry to "close the deal" are often too quick to leave the hard task of hammering out the precise language of a contract to "the obvious intent of the document." This is often captured in expressions such as, "Well, let's not worry about all that, we know what we intend here." Such an attitude can be a lawyer's dream, since what at one time seemed "obvious" to the parties often becomes the subject of litigation. Astute businesspeople know when not to cut costs. Paying a lawyer to draft a contract that captures the parties' intent, while appearing to be an unnecessary expense, can save future costs by avoiding litigation. When memories fade and arguments arise, a carefully written contract can go a long way in settling an argument.

rial most recently added by the parties represents their true intention.

7. In commercial contracts, the UCC supplies many implied terms. Usually the UCC terms are applicable unless the parties provide otherwise in their agreement.

REVIEW PROBLEMS

1. List the types of contracts that must be in writing.
2. Explain how the doctrines of equitable estoppel and promissory estoppel minimize possibly unjust results of the Statute of Frauds.
3. Describe the general circumstances under which the parol evidence rule does *not* apply.
4. How may the Statute of Frauds and the parol evidence rule work to the detriment of consumers?
5. Cohen bought a farm jointly owned by Luca Rienzo, his eight brothers, and sisters. After the Cohen purchase, Luca, who had lived there for thirty years, made improvements on the buildings, rented part of the farm, and cultivated the rest. After eleven months Cohen asserted his interest in the property. Luca's wife claims that there was an oral agreement between her and Cohen that, after Cohen acquired the property, he would reconvey it to her. Decision?
6. Cohn advertised in the *New York Post* that his thirty-foot sloop was for sale. Fisher checked over the boat, phoned Cohn, and they agreed to the sale of the boat for $4,650. They met the next day. Fisher gave Cohn a check for $2,325 and wrote on it "deposit on sloop, *D'Arc Wind*, full amount $4,650." Fisher then contacted Cohn and said he would not close the deal. Fisher stopped payment on the check. Cohn then sold the boat for $3,000 to another and sued to enforce the contract with Fisher. Is Fisher liable for damages for breach of contract?

7. Williams entered into a home construction contract with the Johnsons. The Johnsons signed the contract that had an integration clause and further stated, "There are no verbal agreements or representations in connection therewith." Williams sought to enforce the contract against the Johnsons, and they defended that they had signed thinking that it was an estimate and that they had told Williams that their signing was contingent upon the approval of financing by their bank. Can Williams enforce the contract?
8. Pope & Cottle sold lumber to Blakely, to be used in building a garage for Wheelwright. Blakely failed to pay, and Wheelwright told Pope & Cottle that he would pay Blakely's debt "from such funds as might be in his hands due the said Blakely." Pope & Cottle then formally released Blakely and demanded payment of the $1,478.63 from Wheelwright, who refused to pay. Pope & Cottle sued Wheelwright on the promise. Decision? Pope & Cottle v. Wheelwright, 133 N.E. 106 (Mass. 1921).
9. Barney Sorrenson owed Security $1,400. Barney's mother, Ragnhild Sorrenson, wanted to borrow $200 from Security. Security agreed to make the loan if Ragnhild "would secure up the debts of Barney." Security made the loan and the question arose whether Ragnhild's estate was liable for Barney's debts. Is it? Wildung v. Secu-

rity Mortgage Co. of America, 172 N.W. 692 (Minn. 1919).

10. Draggage Co. contracted with Pacific Gas to remove and replace the cover of a steam turbine. Draggage agreed

> to idemnify Pacific against all losses, damage, expense, and liability resulting from . . . injury to property, arising out of or in any way connected with the performance of this contract.

During the work, the cover fell and damaged the turbine. Pacific sued Draggage for the $25,144.51 it spent on repairs. Draggage offered to prove by the testimony of employees of both firms that the parties had understood that the indemnity clause was meant to cover only third parties. Is such proof allowable? Pacific Gas & Electric Co. v. G. W. Thomas Draggage Co., 442 P.2d 641 (Calif. 1968).

11. Mitchell agreed by a written contract to purchase a farm from Lath. Mitchell contended that in return for her agreement to purchase the farm, Lath agreed to remove an icehouse that she found objectionable. The icehouse was not removed, and Mitchell sued to compel its removal. Decision? Mitchell v. Lath. 160 N.E. 646 (N.Y. App. 1828).

12. Harris contracted to sell cotton to Hine Cotton Co., and both signed the following document:

> This agreement is entered into this date wherein Hine Cotton Company, 103 East Third Street, Rome, Georgia agrees to buy from H. E. Harris and Sons, Route 1, Taylorsville, Georgia all the cotton produced on their 825 acres. The rate of payment shall be as follows:
>
> > 1 □ All cotton ginned prior to December 20, 1973, and meeting official U.S.D.A. Class will be paid for at 30¢ per pound. Below Grade Cotton at 24½¢ per pound.
> >
> > 2 □ All cotton ginned on or after December 20, 1973, will be paid for at the rate of 1,000 over the CCC Loan Rate with Below Grades being paid for at 24½¢ per pound. Settlement will be made on net weights on Commercial Bonded Warehouse Receipts with U.S.D.A. Class cards attached with $1 per bale being deducted from the proceeds of each bale.

During the time that the cotton was growing its market value more than doubled, and Hine Co. wrote and asked assurance of Harris that he would perform. Harris repudiated by return letter. Hine Co. sued for the $140,000 difference between the contract price and the market price. Result? Harris v. Hine, 205 S.E.2d 847 (Ga. 1974).

13. Beanblossom sold 1,000 bushels of soybeans to Lippold at $4.42 per bushel. Lippold then brought suit claiming that the 1,000-bushel transaction was partial performance of an oral contract by which Beanblossom was to sell 7,000 bushels of soybeans at $4.42 per bushel. Beanblossom denies that any oral contract was ever made. Decision? Lippold v. Beanblossom, 319 N.E.2d 548 (Ill. App. 1975).

14. A representative of Mid-South, a plastic supplier, and Fortune Furniture Manufacturing entered into an oral agreement by which Mid-South would provide Fortune with plastic needed in the latter's manufacturing process. As a consequence, the following letter was sent and received:

Mr. Sidney Whitlock, President
Fortune Furniture Manufacturers, Inc.
Okolona, Mississippi 38860

Dear Sid:

This is to confirm the agreement entered into this date between myself and Phil Stillpass on behalf of Mid-South Plastic Co. Inc. and you on behalf of Fortune Manufacturing Co. Inc.

We agree to maintain expanded and 21 oz. plastic in the warehouse of Mid-South Furniture Suppliers, Inc. in sufficient amounts to supply all of the plastic for your plant's use, and if for any reason we do not have the necessary plastic you will be at liberty to purchase the plastic from any other source and we will pay the difference in price between that paid the other source and our current price.

We also agree to pay Fortune 2% rebate on the gross sale price of our plastic as an advertisement aid to your Company which rebate to be paid at your request.

We assure you that all fabrics you need will be in our warehouse at all times and we appreciate your agreeing to buy all of your plastics from us.

Very truly yours,

W.E. Walker, President
(Mid-South)

Mid-South was unable to supply all of Fortune's needs and Fortune had to buy from other suppliers at a higher price. Does Fortune have a cause of action against Mid-South?

CHAPTER 17

Rights of Third Parties

ASSIGNMENT ————————————————————————

DELEGATION OF DUTIES ————————————————

CONTRACTS FOR THE BENEFIT OF A THIRD PARTY ———————

Originally, a plaintiff could maintain a contract action only against the party with whom the contract had been made. Over the years this limiting doctrine, which is generally referred to as privity of contract or privity, has lost most of its importance. Today, there are several situations in which a person who is not a party to a contract can use the contract as the basis for suit. The following are some examples:

1. The person suing, often called the third party, has acquired another's contract right by purchase or gift. For example, Smith agrees to sell his house to Jones. Jones decides she does not want the house. She transfers her right to Martin. In most cases, Martin would have a right to sue Smith if Smith refused to perform.
2. The original contract was made for the benefit of a noncontracting third party who is the plaintiff. For example, Brown insures his life with Capital Insurance Company. He names Green as beneficiary. If the company refuses to honor the agreement, Green ordinarily has a right to sue.

This chapter deals with these two situations.

ASSIGNMENT

In an executory contract each party acquires rights as a result of the agreement. Each party also has obligations or duties because of the agreement. An *assignment* occurs when a person who has contract rights transfers them to someone else. In example 1, Jones, who has a right to buy a house, transfers the right to Martin. Jones is said to have assigned her right to Martin.

A person or firm transferring contract rights is called an *assignor*. The recipient of these rights is the *assignee*. The party responsible for performance is the *obligor*. Consider the following example. A mill promises to deliver 1,000 bushels of wheat to a food processor for $2,000, payable in sixty days. The mill has a duty to transfer title to the wheat to the food processor. On the other hand, the food processor has a duty to pay the mill $2,000. The food processor's duty is the mill's right. Conversely, the mill's duty is the food processor's right. (See Figure 17-1.)

If the mill needed cash immediately, it might transfer its right to the $2,000 to its bank. This could be done by an assignment. The mill would be the assignor, the bank the assignee, and the food processor the obligor. Of course, the food processor could assign its

FIGURE 17–1
Rights and Duties in an Executory Contract

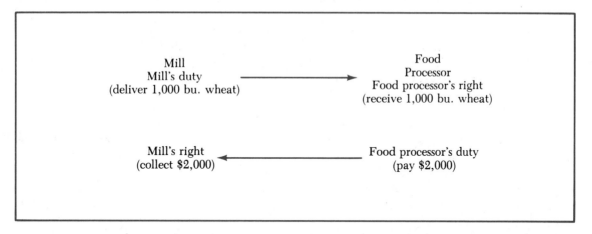

right to the wheat to someone as well. The food processor would be the assignor, the recipient of the right the assignee, and the mill the obligor. This is illustrated in Figure 17-2.

Assignment of Monetary Rights

In this credit-oriented society, the contract right most frequently assigned is the right to receive a sum of money. The transfer of rights to receive a monetary payment is an integral part of the American economic system. It is the legal basis for several types of financing. An example would be financing automobile sales. In a large percentage of cases, the buyer of a new automobile purchases on "time." The dealer, however, in order to maintain its inventory and to pay business expenses, must often have cash immediately. In order to obtain this cash, the dealer might assign its con-

FIGURE 17–2
Assignment of Food Processor's Right to Wheat

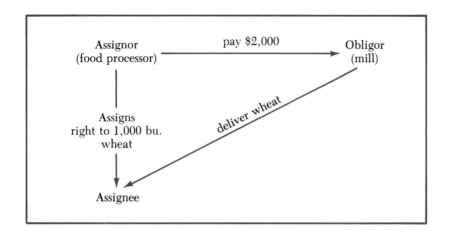

tract right to the buyer's payment to a financial institution at a small discount. The financial institution, now the owner of the right, would notify the buyer and order the buyer to make payments to it.

Accounts Receivable and Factoring. The assignment is also the basis for accounts-receivable financing and factoring. In accounts-receivable financing, a financial institution advances funds to a business that are secured by the accounts receivable of the business. In factoring, the firm advancing funds makes an absolute purchase of outstanding accounts that are assigned to it. The debtor is instructed to pay the factor directly. If the factor is unable to collect, it ordinarily suffers the loss. In accounts-receivable financing, the debtor usually continues to pay the original creditor who has guaranteed payment of the account to the financing agency.

For example, Highland Appliances sells some of its appliances on credit, allowing purchasers to make installment payments. Highland's right to receive these payments is an account receivable. If it wants the purchasers to pay the installments to Highland, it could use the accounts receivable to borrow money from First Bank. The bank would have a security interest in the accounts to insure that its loan is repaid. If Highland didn't repay the loan, the bank could order the purchasers to pay it directly. In this accounts-receivable financing, Highland owns the accounts and is paid by the purchasers. On the other hand, Highland may sell the accounts to First Bank, which would then own them. The purchaser would make payments directly to the bank, which in this case is called a factor. In factoring, the risk of nonpayment by the purchaser is on the bank, whereas in accounts-receivable financing, the risk is on Highland Appliances.

Because of the economic importance of free transferability of rights to receive money, and because the assignment of a monetary obligation does not materially alter the obligor's re-

sponsibility, few limitations have been placed upon assignment of money rights. In fact, the UCC provides that a contractual term limiting the right to assign a monetary right is ineffective.[1] However, a number of states, for public policy reasons, either prohibit or limit wage assignments.

Wage Assignments. States may regulate and restrict the assignment of wages. Legislatures hope to protect wage earners through such statutes. Some states have prohibited the assignment of future wages. In other states, statutes limit the right to make assignments of future earnings to a specific time period.

In the absence of statutes such as these, the general rule is that future earnings under an existing contract of employment may be assigned. On the other hand, if the assignor is not employed at the time of the assignment, the assignment normally is invalid at law.

Generally, an employee need not obtain the consent of his or her employer before making an assignment of wages under an existing contract of employment.

Assignment of Nonmonetary Rights

Monetary rights are almost always assignable because it really does not make much difference to whom the debtor pays the money.

In determining whether other types of rights are assignable, the guiding principle is whether the transfer materially changes the obligor's duty. The payment of money, the obligation to sell goods or land, and the obligation to do a job to a particular specification are usually freely assignable. If, however, the nature of the assignment or the circumstances are such that the obligor's responsibilities are materially changed, an assignment will be ineffective. Consider the following two examples:

1. Montgomery, an architect, has contracted to design an an office building for the ABC Co. The building is to be constructed in

New York City. The company decides not to build and assigns the contract to the XYZ Co., which plans to build an apartment house in Chicago.

2. Smith Co., a manufacturer of fine furniture, has contracted to sell a large quantity to Johnson & Sons. The buyer is a major department store with an excellent credit rating. Payment for the furniture is to be made over a twelve-month period. Johnson & Sons assigns the contract to Pepper Inc., a discount house that has been in business less than a year.

In both of these cases the assignments would probably be unenforceable as they materially change the obligor's duties under the contracts.

Prohibition of Assignment

Sometimes the parties to a contract attempt to prohibit assignment by a provision in the agreement restricting it. A number of courts have refused to recognize restrictions of this nature. Their justification is that a contract right is property and the owner should be free to transfer it if he or she wishes to do so.

On the other hand, most jurisdictions in the United States do enforce a contractual clause that restricts assignment. As one New York court stated:

[W]e think it reasonably clear that, while the courts have striven to uphold freedom of assignability, they have not failed to recognize the concept of freedom to contract. . . . When "clear language" is used, and the "plainest words . . . have been chosen," parties may limit the freedom of alienation of rights and prohibit the assignment.[2]

In the following case, the plaintiff argues that the assignment of the contract is prohibited as the assignor's duty to him cannot be effectively performed by an assignee.

Hurst v. West

Court of Appeals of North Carolina
272 S.E.2d 378 (1980)

Background: A client, William F. Hurst (plaintiff), brought an action for breach of contract against his attorneys, West and Groome (defendants). The law firm had entered into a contract with Hurst to represent him on a criminal case. In return, Hurst gave the attorneys an interest in some property he owned. The contract between the parties permitted the attorneys to sell the property and apply the proceeds against their fees. The attorneys succeeded in getting the criminal charges against Hurst dropped. Thereafter, they assigned their interest in the contract to J. D. Hurst and Hurst Distributors, Inc. William Hurst claimed it was a breach of contract for West and Groome to assign the contract. The trial court directed a verdict in favor of the attorneys.

Decision: The Court of Appeals affirmed the verdict of the trial court.

Martin, Judge

The general rule is that contracts may be assigned. The principle is firmly established in this jurisdiction that, unless expressly prohibited by statute or in contravention of some principle of public policy, all ordinary business contracts are assignable, and that a contract for money to become due in the future may be assigned.

The Supreme Court has stated:

> A valid assignment may be made by any contract between the assignor and the assignee which manifests an intention to make the assignee the present owner of the debt. The assignment operates as a binding transfer of the title to the debt as between the assignor and the assignee regardless of whether notice of the transfer is given to the debtor.

Exceptions to the rule that contracts are freely assignable are when the contract expressly provides that it is not assignable, or when performance of some term of the contract involves an element of personal skill or credit. "Whether or not a contractual duty requires personal performance by a specific individual can be determined only by interpreting the words used in the light of experience."

The contract between William F. Hurst and West and Groome contained no express prohibition against assignment. Although the duty of defendant attorneys to defend plaintiff William Hurst on the charges then pending against him involved an element of personal skill and would not have been assignable to a third party, those obligations were fulfilled and discharged when the criminal charges against Hurst were dismissed. The remaining obligation of defendants under the contract, that they sell the property at a reasonable market value if the option to purchase were not exercised, was not personal in nature, as such a performance can be rendered with equal effectiveness by an assignee of the contract. Thus it is clear that no breach occurred merely by West and Groome's assignment of the contract to J. D. Hurst and Hurst Distributors, Inc.

Traditionally the assignment of a contract did not operate to cast upon the assignee the duties and obligations or the liabilities of the contract if the assignee did not assume such liabilities. But in Rose v. Materials Co., our Supreme Court held that unless a contrary intention is apparent, an assignee under a general assignment of an executory bilateral contract becomes the delegatee of the assignor's duties and impliedly promises to perform them. The Court adopted and reaffirmed as the more reasonable rule:

> The assignment on its face indicates an intent to do more than simply to transfer the benefits assured by the contract. It purports to transfer the contract as a whole, and since the contract is made up of both benefits and burdens both must be intended to be included. It is true the assignor has power only to delegate and not to transfer the performance of duties as against the other party to the contract assigned, but this does not prevent the assignor and the assignee from shifting the burden of performance as between themselves. Moreover, common sense tells us that the assignor, after making such an assignment, usually regards himself as no longer a party to the contract. He does not and, from the nature of things, cannot easily keep in touch with what is being done in order properly to protect his interests if he alone is to be liable for non-performance. Not infrequently the assignor makes an assignment because he is unable to perform further or because he intends to disable himself for further performance. The assignee on the other hand

understands that he is to carry out the terms of the contract, as is shown by the fact that he usually does. . . .

In the present case, J. D. Hurst and Hurst Distributors, Inc. expressly agreed to assume all liabilities and responsibilities under the original contract and to hold defendants harmless "from any liability or responsibility under said contract and particularly from any liability or claim of any kind or description William Hurst may now or hereafter make against the Seller [defendants] for accounting or sale of property." J. D. Hurst and Hurst Distributors, Inc., as assignees of the contract, could take by transfer only what rights and interests the assignor had at the time of the assignment, and took subject to any setoffs and defenses available to plaintiffs against the assignor.

Because plaintiff's evidence did not establish the necessary elements of breach of contract, we hold that the directed verdict in favor of defendants was proper.

Rights of the Assignee

Defenses Good Against Assignor and Assignee Although assignment is an integral element of much business financing, the assignee, ordinarily a financial institution advancing funds, is subject to some legal risk. All that the assignee acquires are the rights possessed by the original assignor. If the obligor has defenses that can be asserted against the assignor, these same defenses can be asserted against the assignee. The axiomatic principle is spelled out clearly in both case law and the UCC.[3] For example, if the original transaction was voidable because of fraud or failure of consideration, the obligor can assert these defenses against the assignee to the same extent that it could have asserted them against the assignor. If the underlying transaction is voidable because the obligor lacked the capacity to contract, this defense can also be asserted by the obligor against the assignee. The following case illustrates the risk to a transferee who takes a contract right by assignment.

Chimney Hill Owners Association v. Antignani
Supreme Court of Vermont
392 A.2d 423 (1978)

Background: In 1966, the Chimney Hill Corporation (Corporation) developed a 900-lot tract for vacation homes known as Chimney Hill. In addition to the lots, there was a 300-to-500-acre area of common land that contained a clubhouse, pools, tennis courts, roads, and a water system. A standard deed provided that each lot was to be assessed an annual charge for use and maintenance of the common land and facilities. The Corporation and its "successors and assigns" had the right to collect the annual charge. The duty to pay the annual charge was imposed upon each lot owner.

In 1968, the Eastern Woodworking Company (defendant) acquired eleven lots. At the time the Corporation agreed in writing to charge Eastern only a single assessment on one lot rather than eleven separate assessments "until one or more of the lots have been improved.'' The same agreement was made with defendants Antignani and Keatinge, both of whom also purchased several lots.

In 1975, the Corporation conveyed the common land and facilities to the Chimney Hill Owners Association (Association) (plaintiff). The Association collectively represented all property owners in Chimney Hill. The Corporation assigned to the Association the right to collect the assessments on each lot. Subsequently, the Association billed the defendants for a separate assessment on each lot they owned. The defendants refused to pay based upon the agreement with the Corporation. The Association sued and the trial court entered judgment in favor of the defendant lot owners. The Association appealed.

Decision: The Supreme Court of Vermont affirmed the judgment of the trial court.

Hill, Justice

A Declaration of Protective Covenants, Restrictions and Reservations pertaining to Chimney Hill was executed by Chimney Hill Corporation and recorded in the Town Clerk's office in Wilmington. The Declaration was included in each purchase and sales agreement and each deed executed for lots in Chimney Hill. Paragraph 10 of the Declaration is the focus of the dispute in these actions.

Paragraph 10 states that an annual charge shall be assessed against each lot in Chimney Hill and paid ''to the grantor, its successors and assigns'' for the right to use the common lands, facilities and services maintained and provided by the ''grantor, its successors and assigns.'' The charge is made a debt collectible by suit in a court of competent jurisdiction and a lien on the lot conveyed until paid. Paragraph 10 further provides that acceptance of a deed bound by the Declaration shall be construed to be a covenant by the grantee, his heirs, successors and assigns to pay the charge to the grantor, its successors and assigns. Lastly, Paragraph 10(E) states:

> That this charge shall run with and bind the land hereby conveyed, and shall be binding upon the grantee or grantees, his, her, their, or its heirs, executors, administrators, successors and assigns, until May 31, 1988, unless earlier terminated by written release of the grantor, its successors or assigns.

The plaintiff seeks to recover the assessments, in its own right, under the assignment from Chimney Hill Corporation. In the assignment, the Corporation assigned to the plaintiff the right to collect from each owner in Chimney Hill the annual charge. As assignee, however, the plaintiff takes the right to collect subject to all defenses of the obligor against the assignor that have not been acquired or set up in fraud of the rights of the assignee after notice has been given of their existence.

As to defendant Eastern, the trial court concluded that it possessed a valid release from Chimney Hill Corporation concerning the ten unimproved lots, which was a valid defense to the plaintiff's claim. Paragraph 10(E) of the Declarations reserves to the grantor, Chimney Hill Corporation, its successors and assigns, the right to terminate the annual charge on any of the lots. Eastern's sales agreement, executed by both Eastern and Chimney Hill Corporation, provides that one annual charge only will be assessed on Eastern's eleven lots until one or more have been improved. The sales agreement contains just the release contemplated by Paragraph 10(E).

Eastern's defense based on the release is valid against the plaintiff as assignee of Chimney Hill Corporation.

Defendant Eastern has a valid written release signed by Chimney Hill Corporation, which unequivocally waives the right to annual charges on ten unimproved lots and which is binding on Chimney Hill Corporation. The court found at the time the plaintiff acquired the common lands and facilities it was aware that some multiple lot owners were being charged one assessment. The issue is whether with this knowledge the plaintiff is charged with the duty to inquire further as to when and why such single assessments were made. We think such inquiry should have been made. If such inquiry had been made of the Chimney Hill Corporation, the existence of Eastern's written release would have been revealed.

As the *Chimney Hill* case illustrates, the value of what an assignee acquires is determined by the underlying contract. This is true even when the assignee takes in good faith and has no knowledge of what took place in the underlying transaction. An assignee can protect itself from this risk to a degree by asking the obligor if it has defenses against performance. If the obligor gives assurances that no defenses exist, the obligor may not at a later time assert defenses that are inconsistent with these assurances.

Suppose that First National Bank wishes to purchase a note signed by a homeowner. The homeowner agreed to pay Acme Home Improvement $500 for work done on the home. If the bank, prior to taking the note, asks the homeowner (the obligor on the note) if Acme did the work, and the homeowner says yes, the homeowner may not assert the failure of Acme to do the work as a reason to refuse to pay the bank after it takes the note.

With and Without Recourse. An assignee can also protect itself by extracting from the assignor a commitment to repurchase a claim that is uncollectible. This is usually referred to as a *with recourse* assignment. If the assignee takes *without recourse,* it assumes the risks of collection.

Guarantees Made to Assignee. Even in situations in which an assignment is made "without recourse," the assignor by the very act of assigning makes certain warranties to the assignee. Although collection is not guaranteed, the assignor does guarantee that any document evidencing the right is genuine and that the right is not subject to any undisclosed defenses of which he or she is aware. In addition, the assignor guarantees that he will do nothing to defeat or impair the assignment. If he were to collect the debt himself, he would thus violate this last guarantee.

Notice to the Obligor

For several reasons the assignee should notify the obligor of the assignment as soon as possible.

Assignment to One Person. Suppose that Mary owes $100 to Betty. Betty then assigns her right to receive the $100 to John. Betty is thus the assignor and John the assignee of a contractual right to receive money. What if John never instructs Mary to pay him rather than Betty? In that situation because Mary is unaware of the assignment, she could pay the entire sum to Betty. This would completely discharge Mary of any obligation under the contract. John's only recourse in this situation would be against Betty. John could sue Betty for not observing the implied warranty that she would do nothing to prevent John from obtaining performance from Mary.

In most states, after proper notice is given, the person who must perform can no longer assert counterclaims or defenses against the person getting the contract rights unless these arise out of the transaction that gave rise to the assignment. Additionally, until the person who must perform gets notice of the assignment, he or she may perform to the assignor. Once the person who must perform has notice of the assignment, however, he or she can honor the contract only by performing to the assignee. If the right assigned is a debt, the debtor is discharged only by payment to the assignee. A debtor who pays the original creditor after notice of assignment would have to make a second payment to the assignee.

Assignment to Two or More People. Notice is also important if the assignor fraudulently or mistakenly assigns the same right to two different parties. For example, Mary owes $100 to Betty, and Betty assigns her right to receive the $100 to John. If John fails to notify Mary, this would give Betty the opportunity to assign this same debt to Tom. In most states, because John was the first assignee, he has the right to collect. However, in some states, if Tom notified Mary of the assignment before John did, Tom would be entitled to collect. John's only recourse in that situation would be against Betty.

Form of Assignment

Although people may validly assign rights orally, for a number of reasons they should do so in a writing and sign the document. The principal reason is to provide clear evidence that a transfer of the right has taken place. In addition, many states have statutes that require certain types of assignments to be in writing in order to be effective. One common example is the wage assignment. The UCC also requires that certain commercial assignments must be in writing in order to be effective.

The document should describe the right that is being transferred and identify who has the duty to perform. A typical assignment of a contract right might be worded as follows:

> For value received, receipt of which is hereby acknowledged, Betty Blaine does hereby assign to John Smith all her right, title, and interest in a contract between Mary Morris and Betty Blaine, dated February 28, 1988, which contract obligates Mary Morris to pay to the undersigned $10,000 on or before October 31, 1988.
>
> The undersigned further guarantees payment of and agrees that if default be made, she, Betty Blaine, will pay the full amount to John Smith upon demand.
>
> Dated July 20, 1988.
> Signed by _____
>   Betty Blaine

DELEGATION OF DUTIES

Up to this point we have been looking primarily at situations in which a person who owns a contract right wishes to transfer it. A party to a contract who has an obligation to perform may wish to transfer that obligation to another party. This is permissible as long as the obligation is not personal in nature and transferring it does not violate a public policy. A transfer of contractual duties or obligations is referred to as a *delegation*.

We have seen that when a party to a contract assigns a right, generally no guarantee is given that the new owner of the right will be able to collect. The obligor who transfers his duty makes a different commitment. He or

PREVENTIVE LAW
Assignment of Lease

A commercial or residential lease often contains a provision prohibiting the lessee from assigning the lease or subletting the premises. (The differences between assignment and subletting are discussed in Chapter 39.) Provisions limiting assignment or subletting reduce the value of the lease to the tenant, and they can cause the tenant a number of problems. For example, a business firm might need to move for a good reason. If it has signed a long-term lease with a provision limiting assignment or subletting, it might have to wait until the lease terminates in order to make this move.

Lease provisions that limit assignment or subletting are written in a variety of ways. Some of them are absolute prohibitions. Others restrict assignment or subletting without the lessor's consent. Usually these provisions provide that the lease terminates if the tenant assigns or sublets. The tenant, however, remains responsible for the rent until the lessor again leases the property. If the lessor cannot lease at the rental in the original lease, the original tenant remains liable for the difference.

Traditionally, in most states, if a lease provided that it could not be assigned without the lessor's consent, the lessor could withhold its consent without explanation or reason. Although a number of states still follow this rule, case law in some states and statute in a few states require that the lessor's consent cannot be withheld without reason.

In order to prevent misunderstanding and to limit litigation, both commercial and residential tenants should examine the lease for provisions limiting assignment or subletting. As a minimum, the tenant should insist that the provision be worded in such a way that the lessor can only withhold consent for a valid reason. Many leases are worded in this manner, and a number of states apply a rule of reason standard when the lease requires the tenant to obtain the lessor's written consent before assigning or subletting. A rule of reason standard means that the lessor can refuse its consent only upon reasonable grounds. These would include factors such as the credit rating of the proposed assignee or sublessee, its business record, and the legality of the proposed lease. In a commercial lease, both lessor and lessee would be well advised to spell out in the lease the grounds upon which the lessor can refuse to consent to an assignment or sublease.

Even in the states that follow a rule-of-reason standard, the lease may contain a provision giving the lessor absolute discretion to accept a replacement tenant. Hardship, ill-feeling, and litigation can be avoided if, when a provision of this nature is included in the lease, the tenant is aware of restrictions on the transfer of the leasehold.

she continues to be liable for performance except in those situations in which the party for whom the obligation must be performed releases the obligor from responsibility. This is called a *novation.* If a novation is carried out properly, the original obligor is released from a duty to perform, and the third party now has the entire obligation.

Delegable Duties

The delegation of a duty is an attempt to extinguish a duty in the assignor and create a similar duty in the assignee. Generally, duties are delegable, although a delegation does not extinguish the duty or relieve the assignor of the duty to perform in the event that the delegate fails to perform. The obligations incurred as a result of most business contracts can be transferred.

Construction contracts are good examples of the type of contract in which the obligor's duties are delegable. Ordinarily the parties understand that the general contractor will not perform all the work. Much will be done by subcontractors, although the general contractor is responsible for their performance. A typical delegation involving a construction contract is shown in Figure 17-3.

Nondelegable Duties

A duty may not be delegated under these conditions:

1. The performance by the person to whom the duty is delegated would be significantly different from that of the person bound by contract to perform. Johnny Cash may not honor Liza Minnelli's singing contracts.
2. The person who originally made the contract has a substantial interest in using the personal services of the other contracting party. Even though another designer or apprentice might be able to do just as good a job for me in designing a chair, if I contract with a master craftsman to do it for me, I don't want the craftsman to delegate his duty to an apprentice.

What if, in a contract between Smith and Jones, Jones delegates his duties to Brown, and informs Smith that he will no longer be responsible for the performance of the contract?

FIGURE 17–3
Delegation of Duties

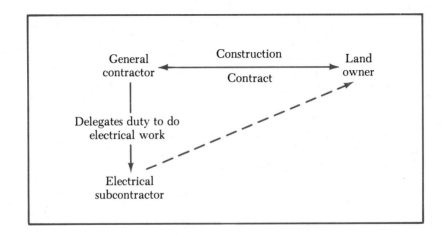

Smith may treat Jones's action as a breach of contract. However, if Brown does perform and Smith accepts Brown's performance, Jones's obligation to perform is extinguished. In this case, a novation has occurred. The person for whom the third party performs no longer has any obligation under the original contract.

In a situation such as that among Smith, Jones, and Brown, the courts disagree as to whether Jones can force such an agreement on Smith without Smith's consent. Some courts permit Smith to take Brown's services, and still sue Jones for breach of contract. Other courts treat Smith's acceptance of Brown's services as a consent by Smith to extinguish Jones's liability under the contract.

CONTRACTS FOR THE BENEFIT OF A THIRD PARTY

In many instances, a third party will benefit from the performance of a contract. In some cases, the contracting parties have actually made the agreement for the benefit of the third party. In other situations, an outsider will benefit even though the parties to the agreement did not plan to benefit the third party. A common example of a contract made primarily to benefit a third party is the life-insurance policy. Its primary purpose is to provide benefits for a third party upon the insured's death. The contract, however, is between the insured and the insuring company.

A question that the courts have frequently had to face is whether a third party who will benefit from an agreement has a right to sue if the agreement is not carried out. This question is especially troublesome when the parties to the contract did not contemplate benefiting another; or if they did, this was not their primary concern. What they were interested in doing was benefiting themselves.

Although the law varies from state to state, most jurisdictions take a positive view about allowing the third party to sue. In spite of the fact that the third party was not involved in the agreement, the legal system in general recognizes that it is both just and practical to allow an outsider to recover if it is clear that this will effectuate the intentions of the parties.[4] A third party who has a right to sue is ordinarily referred to as an *intended* beneficiary. Beneficiaries who do not have a right to sue are referred to as *incidental.*

Intended Beneficiary

As an intended beneficiary has the right to sue the promisor but an incidental beneficiary does not, determining if a person is an intended beneficiary is a critical question. The fact that a person benefits from a contract between two others is not enough. The intention of the parties to benefit the third party must be clear. This intention may be evidenced by the terms of the contract, the circumstances under which it was made, and what the parties were trying to accomplish.

The contract does not have to identify or refer to a third party by name in order for the third party to enforce it. For example, in one case, the United States sued successfully as a third-party beneficiary of a contract between two private firms. Although the United States was not named in the contract, the contract provisions indicated that certain tests were being conducted for its benefit. The laboratory conducting the tests was assured of a defense contract priority, the testing was to be witnessed by a government inspector, and the party contracting for the tests could terminate the agreement if in the best interests of the government.[5]

In the case that follows, the evidence is very clear that the parties intended to benefit a third party as well as themselves. The third party is named in the agreement as a person with whom the promisor is to undertake to conclude an agreement.

Simpson v. JOC Coal, Inc.

Supreme Court of Kentucky

677 S.W.2d 305 (1984)

Background: Simpson (plaintiff), a minority shareholder and president of Skyuka Mining Co., brought an action against JOC Companies (defendant), which had entered into an agreement with majority shareholders to purchase their stock. The trial court rendered judgment in Simpson's favor. It awarded him $907,603.92, representing the value of twenty-three shares of stock in Skyuka Mining. JOC Companies appealed. The Court of Appeals reversed and Simpson appealed.

Decision: The Kentucky Supreme Court reversed the Court of Appeals and affirmed the trial court on the third-party beneficiary issue. The case was remanded on other grounds.

Leibson, Justice

Simpson was the president of Skyuka Mining. On April 18, 1975, JOC Companies had purchased all of the assets and liabilities of Skyuka for a maximum price of $9,000,-000, of which $4,750,000 was guaranteed as a minimum and the balance of $4,250,-000 was contingent upon future production. $1,500,000 was paid down and the balance was to be paid in installments at various intervals, with the first payment due September 30, 1975.

Between April and September 1975, conditions in the coal market began to deteriorate. In addition, the JOC Companies began to complain about the assets they had purchased. They undertook renegotiations with the majority shareholders which culminated in the agreement of September 12, 1975, the effect of which was to buy out these shareholders and transfer controlling interest in Skyuka to the JOC Companies. These shareholders were paid $39,461.04 per share for sixty shares of stock.

Simpson was not a party to the modification agreement. However, his interest was recognized:

> "[T]he parties to this agreement acknowledge that two Shareholders named in the Agreement, namely James W. Simpson and [blank], are not parties to this agreement. It is, however, understood and agreed that the JOC Companies will undertake to conclude a similar arrangement with James W. Simpson under which said James W. Simpson will also consent to a similar ammending [sic] of the Agreement."

·   ·   ·

Another clause important to this transaction because it highlights the fact that Simpson had a substantial interest in the pass through of payments from JOC Companies to Skyuka which would terminate by reason of the agreement is the following:

> "The JOC Companies agree to indemnify and hold the Shareholders named herein harmless from and against any and all claims, actions, damages or

liabilities arising out of or by reason of said Shareholders entering into this agreement separate and apart from James W. Simpson."

Based on the agreement of September 12, 1975 and the testimony of record, the trial court also found that "by the same re-modified Agreement, the defendants agreed and obligated themselves, in consideration of the cancellation of the April Agreement, to enter a similar Agreement with the plaintiff, James W. Simpson." It concluded that:

> "The defendants are, as a matter of law, jointly and severally liable to the plaintiff for the fair reasonable market value of his twenty-three (23) shares of stock in SKYUKA as a third party beneficiary of the September 12, 1975 Agreement. . . . He, Simpson, is legally empowered to enforce the beneficial portions of this Agreement; he was a contemplated and intended beneficiary."

On appeal the Court of Appeals decided that Simpson had "no enforceable third-party beneficiary rights" and reversed. The Court of Appeals concluded that he was merely an incidental and not an intended beneficiary of the September 12, 1975 Agreement, citing *Long v. Reiss*. We have concluded that the record supports the trial judge's findings and conclusions that Simpson was an intended third party beneficiary and that the contract obligation of JOC Companies is sufficiently definite and certain in its terms to be enforceable. . . . We reverse the Court of Appeals and affirm the trial court on these issues.

The rule stated in *Long v. Reiss, supra,* is:

> "It is settled in this State, as well as most jurisdictions in America, that a third party for whose benefit a contract is made may maintain an action thereon; however, he must have been a party to the consideration or the contract must have been made for his benefit, and the mere fact that he will be incidentally benefited by the performance of the contract is not sufficient to entitle him to enforce it."

The *Long* opinion continues:

> "[A] third person may enforce a promise made for his benefit even though he is a stranger both to the contract and to the consideration. . . . [I]t is not necessary that any consideration move from the third party; it is enough if there is a sufficient consideration between the parties who make the agreement for the benefit of the third party."

The *Long* opinion then discusses the exception to the "American Majority Rule," which is that "the mere fact that a third person would be incidentally benefited does not give him a right to sue for its breach."

In *Long* the court would not enforce the contract because the intended beneficiary was, strictly speaking, a corporation which "was not then even in existence and did not come into existence until nearly two years after the contract was entered into. . . ."

In the present case at the time the contract in question was entered into Simpson was not only very real, but, as a practical matter, impossible to ignore. Simpson points to the fact that under the "Kentucky Business Corporation Act," enacted in 1972, he was a shareholder with a "right to dissent" from the corporate transactions involved, and the right to sue "demanding payment for his shares" if his interests were not adequately protected in the arrangements that were being made. The majority shareholders and the JOC Companies, in striking their bargain, obviously recognized his interest not only by providing in the contract for JOC Companies to make Simpson a suitable offer, but also by providing in the contract that JOC Companies would "indemnify" and "hold . . . harmless" the majority shareholder from all claims, causes of action and liabilities the shareholders could incur from "entering into this agreement separate and apart from James W. Simpson." It is hard to imagine a situation where an individual could be more of an intended beneficiary of the contract than Simpson was in these circumstances. It was necessary for the majority shareholders to provide for his interest or risk the legal consequences, and the method for so doing was expressed in the contract both in general terms and in some detail, though not in specified dollars and cents.

In short, all that is necessary is that there be consideration for the agreement flowing to the promisor and that the promisee intends to extract a promise directly benefiting the third party. The circumstances here amply justify this conclusion.

. . .

Because there were other claims of error made in the Court of Appeals which were not considered when that court decided that the contract was unenforceable, the case is remanded to the Court of Appeals to decide those issues not disposed of by this opinion.

Donee Beneficiary. If a contract is primarily for the benefit of a third party and the promisee's intent is to confer a gift upon the third party, the intended beneficiary is sometimes referred to as a *donee beneficiary.*

Life insurance is a good example of a situation involving a donee beneficiary. (See Figure 17-4.) The typical policy requires the insurance company to pay a certain amount of money in the event of the death of the insured. The insured purchased this policy with the intent to benefit the third party. If the insurance company refuses to pay, the donee beneficiary may sue the company for the amount of the insurance policy. The donee beneficiary is permitted to sue even though he or she is not in privity of contract with the company and has not given anything to the insurance company.

Creditor Beneficiary. If the purpose of the contract is to discharge an obligation that the promisee owes or believes he or she owes to the third party, the third party is sometimes called a *creditor beneficiary.* In the case of a donee beneficiary, the promisee intends to make a gift. In the case of a creditor beneficiary, the promisee wishes to discharge an obligation owed to the creditor beneficiary. Suppose that Tina owes Cindy $1,000. Tina sells her automobile to Sam, who promises to pay $1,000 to Cindy in order to discharge the debt between Tina and Cindy. Cindy is a creditor

FIGURE 17–4
Donee Beneficiary

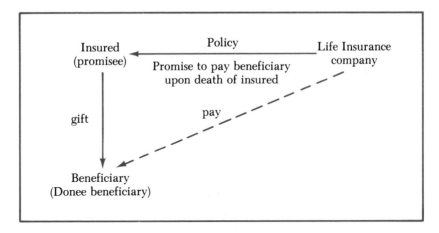

FIGURE 17–5
Creditor Beneficiary

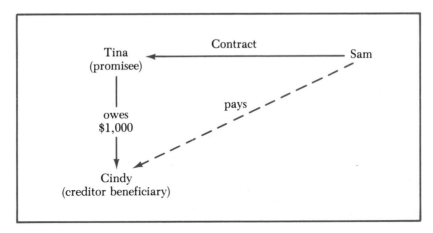

beneficiary of Sam's promise and has an enforceable claim against Sam for $1,000. (See Figure 17-5.)

Incidental Beneficiary

If a promisee neither intends to confer a gift on the third party nor is trying to discharge an obligation to the third party, the third party is called an *incidental beneficiary.* He or she has no rights under the contract. Suppose that Mc-

Donald's contracted to build a store next to Louise's dress shop. Because the McDonald's would attract many people to the area, Louise anticipated she would do more business than ever. The contract between McDonald's and the builder was not intended to benefit Louise. If the builder breaches the contract, and the McDonald's is never built, does Louise have a cause of action against the builder? No. This contract was not intended to benefit Louise in any way. She would have no cause of action against the builder even though, had the store been built, her business might have increased.

In the case that follows, the court decided that the plaintiff was an incidental beneficiary.

Bain v. Gillispie
Court of Appeals of Iowa
357 N.W.2d 47 (1984)

Background: Bain (plaintiff-appellee) refereed a basketball game between the University of Iowa and Purdue University. As the game was ending, Bain called a foul on an Iowa player. The Purdue player scored the point and Purdue won the game. John and Karen Gillispie (defendants-appellants) operate a novelty store known as Hawkeye John's Trading Post. The store specializes in University of Iowa sports memorabilia. A few days after the game, the Gillispies began marketing T-shirts showing a man with a rope around his neck and captioned "Jim Bain Fan Club."

On learning of this, Bain sought injunctive relief and damages. The Gillispies counterclaimed, alleging that Bain's conduct in officiating at the game was below the standard required of a professional referee. They asked for $175,000 in damages on grounds that Iowa's loss had deprived it of the Big Ten championship, destroying a potential market for their memorabilia. Bain moved for summary judgment on the counterclaim. The trial court sustained his motion.

The Gillispies appealed. They argued that summary judgment should not have been granted as two triable issues of fact existed. They were (1) Bain's action as a referee was negligent and (2) they were third-party beneficiaries of an employment contract between Bain and the Big Ten Athletic Conference.
Decision: The decision of the trial court was affirmed.

Snell, Presiding Judge

(The appellate court first dealt with the negligence claim. It stated that the trial court was correct when it granted summary judgment. The appellate court approved the following statement by the trial court.)

This is a case where the undisputed facts are of such a nature that a rational fact finder could only reach one conclusion—no foreseeability, no duty, no liability. Heaven knows what uncharted morass a court would find itself in if it were to hold that an athletic official subjects himself to liability every time he might make a questionable call. The possibilities are mind boggling. If there is a liability to a merchandiser like the Gillispies, why not to the thousands upon thousands of Iowa fans who bleed Hawkeye black and gold every time the whistle blows? It is bad enough when Iowa loses without transforming a loss into a litigation field day for "Monday Morning Quarterbacks." There is no tortious doctrine of athletic official's malpractice that would give credence to Gillispies' counterclaim.

The trial court also found that there was no issue of material fact on the Gillispies' claim that they were beneficiaries under Bain's contract with the Big 10. Gillispies argue that until the contract is produced, there exists a question of whether they are beneficiaries. There is some question of whether there is a contract between Bain and the Big 10. In his response to interrogatories, Bain stated that he had no written contract with the Big 10, but that there was a letter which defined "working relationship." Although this letter was never produced and ordinarily we would not decide an issue without the benefit of examining the letter's contents, we nevertheless find the issue presently capable of determination. By deposition Gillispies answered that there was no contract between them and Bain, the Big 10 Athletic Conference, the University of Iowa, the players, coaches, or with anybody regarding this issue. Thus, even if the letter were considered a contract, Gillispies would be considered third-party beneficiaries. Because Gillispies would not be privy to the contract, they must be direct beneficiaries to maintain a cause of action, and not merely incidental beneficiaries.

A direct beneficiary is either a donee beneficiary or a creditor beneficiary. In *Olney v. Hutt,* the Iowa Supreme Court defined these terms as follows:

> (1) Where performance of a promise in a contract will benefit a person other than the promisee that person is, . . . (a) a donee beneficiary if it appears from the terms of the promise in view of the accompanying circumstances that the purpose of the promisee in obtaining the promise of all or part of the performance thereof is to make a gift to the beneficiary or to confer upon him a right against the promisor to some performance neither due nor supposed or asserted to be due from the promisee to the beneficiary; (b) a creditor beneficiary if no purpose to make a gift appears from the terms of the promise in view of the accompanying circumstances and performance of the promise will satisfy an actual or supposed or asserted duty of the promisee to the beneficiary.

Gillispies make no claim that they are creditor beneficiaries of Bain, the Big 10 Athletic Conference, or the University of Iowa. "The real test is said to be whether the contracting parties intended that a third person should receive a benefit which might be enforced in the courts." It is clear that the purpose of any promise which Bain might have made was not to confer a gift on Gillispies. Likewise, the Big 10 did not owe any duty to the Gillispies such that they would have been creditor beneficiaries. If a contract did exist between Bain and the Big 10, Gillispies can be considered nothing more than incidental beneficiaries and as such are unable to maintain a cause of action.

Consequently, there was no genuine issue for trial which could result in Gillispies obtaining a judgment under a contract theory of recovery. The ruling of the trial court sustaining the summary judgment motion and dismissing the counterclaim is affirmed.

REVIEW PROBLEMS

1. Explain why it is important for an assignee to immediately notify the obligor of the assignment.

2. In situations in which an assignor has assigned the same right twice, law in some states gives priority to the assignment first made. Present arguments in support of this rule. Other states give priority to the assignee who first notifies the obligor. Present arguments in support of this rule.

3. How do you determine if an intended beneficiary is a creditor or a donee beneficiary?

4. Lenox Homes built a house for the Buengers in 1972. In 1974, the Buengers sold the house to the Coburns. The Coburns occupied the house and found that the septic system installed by Lenox was faulty. The Coburns sued Lenox and claimed that they were beneficiaries of the contract made between Lenox and the Buengers. Do you agree?

5. Mrs. Lara entered the Kern County hospital to give birth. She died shortly after her child was born, and the hospital was not paid for the medical services it provided to her child. Under state law, her husband, a part-time farmworker, was billed by the hospital. Can the hospital assign its right to receive money from Mr. Lara to a collection service?

6. Smith purchases a new automobile from the Warren Oldsmobile dealer. One of the terms of the purchase is that the dealer perform certain specified warranty work on the car for two years without further charge. A year after Smith's purchase, the chief mechanic at Warren quits, and Warren notifies Smith that all future warranty work will be performed by the Ace Garage. Warren contracts with the Ace Garage to provide this service to Smith. May Warren do this? Explain.

7. Asphalt Paving Company contracted with the city of Flint to pave certain streets. A clause in that contract provided that Asphalt would be liable for damages to any property resulting from the paving work. In moving one of its bulldozers, Asphalt struck a gas main, which exploded and seriously damaged the house of Leo Stevenson. Stevenson sued Asphalt and relied on the contract between Asphalt and the city of Flint. Can Stevenson use that contract in his case?

8. Rosier was a frequent purchaser of large quantities of oil on open account from Chanute Refining. A federal statute required inspection of oil before shipment; Chanute Refining had been doing this for Rosier, charging him an inspection fee. The statute was declared invalid and Rosier demanded a refund of the inspection fees that had been paid to Chanute Refining.

   On June 19, Rosier purchased additional oil from Chanute Refining for $3,500. On June 29, Chanute assigned Rosier's account along with several others to Sinclair Co. When Rosier refused to pay, he was sued by Sinclair. At the trial Sinclair offered to present evidence to prove that it did not know of the dispute regarding the inspection fees. Is this evidence admissible? Why or why not? Sinclair Refining Co. v. Rosier, 180 Pac. 807.

9. In the preceding case, what are Sinclair's rights, if any, against Chanute Refining?

10. Bull Dog Insurance issued a policy of insurance to D'Alassano against loss by theft of an automobile. The automobile was stolen and never recovered. D'Alassano assigned his claim under the policy to Ginsberg. The policy provided that "no assignment of interest under this policy shall be or become binding upon the association unless the written consent . . . is endorsed thereon and an additional mem-

bership fee is paid." Present arguments supporting Ginsberg's right to collect under the policy. Ginsberg v. Bull Dog Auto Fire Ins. Assn., 160 N.E. 145. (Sup. Ct. Ill. 1928)

11. Dooley contracted with Rose to provide enough stone to meet Rose's business requirements for ten years at favorable listed prices. In return, Rose promised not to compete with Dooley in the rock-crushing business. Later, Dooley assigned the contract to Vulcan Materials Co. Is Vulcan required to supply stone to Rose at the original contract prices? Rose v. Vulcan Materials Co., 194 S.E.2d 520 (Sup. Ct. N.C. 1973).

12. MGM contracted to pay Selznick royalties upon the first TV broadcast of "Gone with the Wind." Later, Selznick obtained a large loan from Haas by assigning his right to payment of the royalties to Haas as security for the loan. Selznick notified MGM of the assignment and asked that Haas be notified in advance of any royalty payments to be made to Selznick. MGM refused but neither Selznick nor Haas pursued the matter. Haas died, Selznick defaulted on the loan, and Haas's estate obtained a judgment against Selznick. When the movie was broadcast, MGM paid Selznick, but Haas did not receive notice or a payment. Haas's estate sued MGM to recover the royalty payment. Was the royalty payment effectively assigned by Selznick to Haas under the UCC? Haas Estate v. Metro-Goldwyn-Mayer, Inc., 617 F.2d 1136 (Tex. Civ. App. 1980).

13. McDonald's granted a franchise in the Omaha-Council Bluffs area to Copeland, a reputable and highly successful businessman. *In a separate agreement,* Copeland was granted a right of first refusal, that is, the right to receive the first offer of additional McDonald's franchises to be developed in the area. Subsequently, Copeland assigned his franchise contracts to Shupack, with McDonald's consent. When McDonald's later offered a new area franchise to someone else, Shupack sued, claiming that the right of first refusal was included in the assignment from Copeland so that he should have been offered the new restaurant first. McDonald's had previously written Shupack stating that the right was personal to Copeland and had not passed to Shupack. Was the right assignable? How can you determine whether it was personal to Copeland? Shupack v. McDonald's System, Inc., 264 N.W.2d 827 (Nebr. Sup. Ct. 1978).

14. Cunningham played basketball for the Cougars, a professional team owned by Southern Sports Corp. His contract prohibited assignment to another club without his consent. When Southern Sports assigned the Cougars franchise and Cunningham's contract to Munchak Corp., Cunningham protested, claiming that his contract was personal and therefore not assignable. Is the assignment of Cunningham's contract effective? Munchak Corp. v. Cunningham, 457 F.2d 721 (4th Cir. 1972).

FOOTNOTES

[1] UCC Section 9-318(4).

[2] Allhusen v. Caristo Const. Co., 303 N.Y. 446 (1952).

[3] UCC Section 9-318.

[4] Restatement (Second) of Contracts, Section 133 (1973).

[5] United States v. Ogden Technology Laboratories, 406 F.Supp. 1090 (1973).

Performance, Discharge, and Remedies

The discussion of contract law to this point has been concerned with the issue of whether or not a valid contract has been entered into by the parties. Now the focus shifts to what happens after the contract has been made: the consequences of performance and nonperformance of the contractual obligations. Some contracts are made and performed simultaneously—for example, when someone buys a newspaper from a street vendor. However, other contracts are entered into by the parties with a view to performance by one or both of them sometime in the future. Between the making of the contract and its time of performance, changed circumstances may make performance no longer desirable for one of the parties. For example, if a building contractor agrees to build a house for a buyer and the costs of supplies and labor increase significantly between the time the contract is made and the time the house is to be built, the builder may have second thoughts about the deal, particularly if another buyer is willing to pay the builder more than the current contract provides. Under these circumstances, the level of performance by the builder may

be something less than was anticipated by the first buyer. Suppose the builder uses lower-grade materials and hires other than journeymen workers to construct the building. What are the buyer's rights? Can the buyer require the contractor to fire the workers, tear down the construction made of lower-grade materials, and rebuild the house using quality materials and journeymen workers? Suppose the builder, having laid the foundation, learns of the other buyer who is willing to pay more. Can the builder negotiate a contract with the second buyer and start work on that buyer's house using workers taken off the first project with a view to finishing the first house after he has built the second? The contract may or may not deal explicitly with such possibilities. Where it does not, or if the parties disagree about their interpretations of how the contract is to resolve such issues, litigation may result. The practice of the courts is to place a commonsense construction on the intention of the parties respecting performance of a contract and to fashion a reasonable and just remedy for the breach of a duty to perform. The task of a manager is to determine what performances are due under a contract, when they will be due, and what consequences will result if the performances are not rendered at the proper time or in the proper manner.

PERFORMANCE DEPENDENT UPON CONDITIONS

Conditional Promises

Sometimes the parties to a contract will condition their respective performances upon the occurrence of an event. For example, a seller may condition its duty to deliver ordered goods upon the buyer's making a specified down payment. Similarly, the buyer may condition its obligation to pay the remainder of the price owed upon its being able to obtain financing for the purchase or upon its satisfaction with the delivered merchandise, or both. In these examples, the contract does not create a duty to perform unless and until some event occurs. Such promises are termed conditional.

Similarly, a duty of performance may be conditioned upon the nonoccurrence of an event. An example is a promise to cut a lawn if it does not rain on Saturday.

An event may create or extinguish a present duty of performance. For example, the making of the down payment by the buyer in the preceding example gives rise to a present duty in the seller to deliver the merchandise. On the other hand, in the lawn-mowing example, rain on Saturday extinguishes the mower's present duty to cut the lawn.

An event that must occur in order to give rise to a duty of performance is called a *condition precedent*. An event that extinguishes a duty of performance is called a *condition subsequent*. The nonoccurrence of a condition precedent excuses nonperformance by the party whose duty of performance was to arise only after the condition precedent materialized. The occurrence of a condition subsequent excuses the nonperformance of a party

whose duty of performance was extinguished by the condition subsequent. In both cases, the party relying upon the condition is not liable to the other party for breach of contract because the nonperformance was excused. If the condition precedent, however, happens to be the other party's performance, the nonoccurrence of the condition precedent gives the party relying upon that condition a claim against the other for breach of contract. In such a case, the party relying upon the condition has its nonperformance excused, whereas the other nonperforming party remains liable for breach of contract.

Approval or Satisfaction

Contracts sometimes contain provisions requiring that a party's performance be approved by the other party or by a person who is not a party to the contract. In such cases, the approval of the other party or the third person is a condition to the performance of one of the parties to the contract. For example, a contract for the sale of real estate may require that title be approved by an attorney. The attorney's approval is a condition precedent to the buyer's duty to purchase the property. If the attorney concludes that the seller does not have title to the property, the buyer's obligation to purchase is excused by virtue of the failure of the condition (the attorney's approval) to materialize.

A common example of a contract requiring the approval of a third party is the typical construction contract. Construction contracts frequently require outside approval of the work before the owner is obligated to pay. Usually the job must be inspected by an architect or an engineer who issues a certificate for payment if the construction is satisfactory, meaning that the construction has met the specifications contained in the architect's or engineer's building plans. Until this certificate is issued, the owner has no obligation to make payment, because the architect's or engineer's certificate is a condition precedent to performance by the owner.

Just as a party's duty of performance may be conditioned upon the other party's performance being approved by a third person, so can a party's duty to perform be conditioned upon its own satisfaction with the other party's performance. That is, one of the parties may bargain that its performance will personally satisfy the other party. Although there is considerable risk to the person or firm making this kind of commitment, it is relatively common. Contracts for the sale of goods often give the purchaser the right to return the goods if not satisfied. Employment contracts for a specific period of time sometimes allow the employer to terminate employment if the employee's service is not personally satisfactory to the employer.

Because of the potential danger of forfeiture in a contract in which one party does not have to keep its end of the bargain unless it or a third party is satisfied, courts have generally interpreted these provisions narrowly. They have consistently held that the dissatisfaction or refusal to approve must be in good faith and not left to the will or idiosyncrasies of the interested party. This means that the dissatisfaction is not to be feigned but must be based upon some valid reason.

For example, suppose that an artist agrees to paint a portrait of Penelope to her satisfaction. Any dissatisfaction expressed by Penelope must be made in good faith—that is, it must be an honest dissatisfaction. Proving Penelope's bad faith may be difficult because her dissatisfaction is a subjective state involving artistic taste and personal feeling. But suppose that the artist can show that Penelope expressed dissatisfaction with the portrait only after she had suffered severe financial reversals. The artist might succeed in arguing that Penelope was really responding to her changed financial condition rather than to the quality of the artist's work.

When performance can be measured against an objective standard—for example, if a reasonable person would be satisfied—the party to the contract must also be satisfied. Suppose that Bigdome, Inc. contracts to buy certain tools from Ace Tool that are to be satisfactory to Bigdome. If Ace can establish that the tools meet certain standards in Bigdome's industry—for example, that they have been calibrated according to industry standards—Bigdome's dissatisfaction will not excuse its nonpayment for the tools.

The following case shows a court confronting a situation involving the approval of a party as a condition to performance.

Aztec Film Productions, Inc. v. Prescott Valley, Inc.

Supreme Court of Arizona
626 P.2d 132 (1981)

Background: Aztec Film Productions, Inc. (plaintiff) contracted in May 1974 with Prescott Valley, Inc. (defendant), an Arizona land developer, to produce a film entitled *Why Arizona* to be used as a sales aid in marketing land in other states. Prescott Valley paid one-third ($6,250) of the total contract price ($18,750) upon the signing of the agreement. Their contract provided that the film was to be completed within ninety days after Prescott Valley approved the film's script. The contract further provided that such approval "shall be given expeditiously and not unreasonably withheld."

When the script was submitted, Prescott Valley refused to approve it because some of the script's factual statements were not documented as required by states where

Prescott Valley was marketing its land. Aztec argued that many of the undocumented facts did not need to be documented. The parties agreed to let a real-estate investigator for Minnesota look at the script, and this investigator stated that the script was unacceptable.

Aztec sued Prescott Valley for breach of contract, seeking payment; and Prescott Valley countersued for the return of the $6,250 paid under the contract. Aztec claimed that Prescott Valley's refusal to approve was unreasonable because the script would have satisfied a reasonable Arizona land developer. The trial judge entered judgment in favor of Prescott Valley. Aztec appealed to the Supreme Court of Arizona. Decision: The Supreme Court of Arizona affirmed the trial court judgment in favor of Prescott Valley.

Cameron, Justice

Aztec asserts that the trial court, in determining that there was no breach of contract by Prescott Valley, improperly applied a subjective test of personal satisfaction rather than the objective test, that the script would have satisfied a reasonable person in Prescott Valley's position. We agree that the objective test was the proper test to apply:

> A promise in terms conditional on the promisor's satisfaction with an agreed exchange, gives rise to no duty of immediate performance until such satisfaction; but where it is doubtful whether words mean that a promise is conditional on the promisor's personal satisfaction with an agreed exchange, or on the sufficiency of the exchange to satisfy a reasonable man in the promisor's position, the latter interpretation is adopted. Restatement of Contracts, Section 265 (1932).

In the present case, the contract provided that "approval shall be given expeditiously and not unreasonably withheld." This unreasonableness provision required Prescott Valley to be objectively dissatisfied with the shooting script. The facts support a conclusion that under the objective test of reasonableness, Prescott Valley's withholding of approval of the script was not unreasonable. We find no error.

SUBSTANTIAL PERFORMANCE AND MATERIAL BREACH

The normal manner in which the parties' contractual expectations will be satisfied is through complete and exact performance of the contract. This, of course, is the purpose of the bargain. As a factual matter, most contracts are fully performed and the relationships end. However, there may be a failure of performance, and the injured party must determine what remedy is available.

Substantial Performance

The most satisfactory manner of performance of contractual obligations is for both parties to perform exactly as promised. However, this is not always what happens. One party may perform erroneously as a result of misinterpreting the contract. Or exact performance may be prevented by circumstances that cannot be controlled. Clearly, a party is entitled to the promised performance. Just as clearly, justice dictates that the injured party should not be unjustly enriched by the penalty imposed on the defaulting party.

When one party fails to render a part of the promised performance, the following questions may arise:

1. Is the other party privileged to refuse to render a reciprocal promised performance?
2. Is the other party discharged from its contractual duty?
3. Can the other party sue for damages, regarding the breach as "total"?
4. Can the other party sue for damages for a "partial" breach?

Under the older common law, an express contract had to be completed to the last detail before a party could enforce the performance of the other party. Under the newer concept of *substantial performance,* a party who has failed to provide exact performance may nevertheless enforce the performance of the other party if (1) there was substantial performance of the contract, (2) there was an honest effort to comply fully to the contract's requirements, and (3) there was no willful or intentional departure from the terms of the contract. The rationale for what is often called the substantial-performance doctrine is that justice does not demand full, literal fulfillment of contractual obligations but only substantial fulfillment.

Where one of the contracting parties has substantially performed its contractual duties, it is entitled to enforce performance by the other party. That is, the injured party may not refuse to render a reciprocal promised performance; it is not discharged from its contractual duties. However, the party that rendered substantial performance rather than exact

performance is in breach of contract. The breach is a partial breach, not a material breach; nevertheless, it remains a breach of contract. Where there has been a breach of contract the injured party may sue and recover damages for the breach. Thus, although the injured party is not excused from its promised reciprocal performance, it is entitled to recover damages for the other party's failure to perform exactly as promised. If the injured party's promised performance is payment, it would be entitled to deduct from the contract price the amount that will compensate for the damages sustained.

Material Breach

The antithesis of substantial performance is a level of nonperformance tantamount to a material breach of contract. That is, a party who fails to perform its contractual obligation substantially is deemed to have materially breached the contract, and thereby is liable to the injured party for damages. However, a material breach carries with it a further legal consequence. The injured party is excused from rendering any reciprocal promised performance. That is, a material breach of contract by one party entitles the injured party to treat its contractual duties as discharged—any nonperformance by the innocent party is excused—and further entitles the injured party to sue and recover damages resulting from the material breach.

Whether a party's failure to perform a contractual duty exactly amounts to a material breach or substantial performance is an issue of considerable importance. The test of substantial performance is whether the performance met the essential purpose of the contract and whether the nonperformance was willful. Thus, a party who relies on the substantial-performance doctrine must show that its departure from the contract was slight and unintentional.

In the following case, the court wrestled

with the problem of balancing a policy against unjust enrichment with a policy of ensuring that a party gets what the contract promises. While reading the case, keep in mind that a business firm should never enter a contract with the intention of providing only a substantial performance. That is an unethical strategy that could easily destroy the firm's reputation.

Plante v. Jacobs

Supreme Court of Wisconsin

103 N.W.2d 296 (1960)

Background: Eugene Plante (plaintiff) contracted with Frank and Carol Jacobs (defendants) to construct a house according to plans and specifications. The specifications were standard printed forms with some modifications and additions written in by the parties. Although the house had essentially been completed, Jacobs refused to pay the full price because Plante had misplaced the wall between the kitchen and the living room, thus narrowing the living room by more than one foot. Plante sued Jacobs to recover the unpaid balance of the contract price. The trial court entered judgment for Plante in the sum of $4,152.90. The Jacobses appealed to the Supreme Court of Wisconsin.

Decision: The Supreme Court of Wisconsin affirmed the trial court judgment in favor of Plante.

Hallows, Justice

The defendants argue the plaintiff cannot recover any amount because he has failed to substantially perform the contract. The plaintiff conceded he failed to furnish the kitchen cabinets, gutters and down-spouts, sidewalk, closed clothes poles, and entrance seat amounting to $1,601.95. This amount was allowed to the defendants. The defendants claim some 20 other items of incomplete or faulty performance by the plaintiff and no substantial performance because the cost of completing the house in strict compliance with the plans and specifications would amount to 25 or 30 per cent of the contract price. The defendants especially stress the misplacing of the wall between the living room and the kitchen, which narrowed the living room in excess of one foot. The cost of tearing down this wall and rebuilding it would be approximately $4,000. The record is not clear why and when this wall was misplaced, but the wall is completely built and the house decorated and the defendants are living therein. Real estate experts testified that the smaller width of the living room would not affect the market price of the house.

The defendants rely on *Manitowoc Steam Boiler Works* v. *Manitowoc Glue Co.* for the proposition there can be no recovery on the contract unless there is substantial performance. This is undoubtedly the correct rule at common law. . . . The question here is whether there has been substantial performance. The test of what amounts to substantial performance seems to be whether the performance meets the essential purpose of the contract.

Substantial performance as applied to construction of a house does not mean that every detail must be in strict compliance with the specifications and the plans. Something less than perfection is the test of specific performance unless all details are made the essence of the contract. This was not done here. There may be situations in which features or details of construction of special or of great personal importance, which if not performed, would prevent a finding of substantial performance of the contract. In this case the plan was a stock floor plan. No detailed construction of the house was shown on the plan. There were no blueprints. The specifications were standard printed forms with some modifications and additions written in by the parties. Many of the problems that arose during the construction had to be solved on the basis of practical experience. No mathematical rule relating to the percentage of the price, of cost of completion or of completeness can be laid down to determine substantial performance of a building contract. Although the defendants received a house with which they are dissatisfied in many respects, the trial court was not in error in finding the contract was substantially performed.

The next question is what is the amount of recovery when the plaintiff has substantially, but incompletely, performed. For substantial performance the plaintiff should recover the contract price less the damages caused the defendant by the incomplete performance. Both parties agree *Venzke* v. *Magdanz* states the correct rule for damages due to faulty construction amounting to such incomplete performance, which is the difference between the value of the house [with the defects and its value] if it had been constructed in strict accordance with the plans and specifications. This is the diminished-value rule. The cost of replacement or repair is not the measure of such damage, but is an element to take into consideration in arriving at value under some circumstances. The cost of replacement or the cost to make whole the omissions may equal or be less than the difference in value in some cases and, likewise, the cost to rectify a defect may greatly exceed the added value to the structure as corrected. The defendants argue that under the *Venzke* rule their damages are $10,000. The plaintiff on review argues the defendants' damages are only $650. Both parties agree the trial court applied the wrong rule to the facts.

The trial court applied the cost-of-repair or replacement rule as to several items, relying on *Stern* v. *Schlafer,* wherein it was stated that when there are a number of small items of defect or omission which can be remedied without the reconstruction of a substantial part of the building or a great sacrifice of work or material already wrought in the building, the reasonable cost of correcting the defect should be allowed. However, in *Mohs* v. *Quarton* the court held when the separation of defects would lead to confusion, the rule of diminished value could apply to all defects.

In this case no such confusion arises in separating the defects. The trial court disallowed certain claimed defects because they were not proven. This finding was not against the great weight and clear preponderance of the evidence and will not be disturbed on appeal. Of the remaining defects claimed by the defendants, the court allowed the cost of replacement or repair except as to the misplacement of the living room wall. Whether a defect should fall under the cost-of-replacement rule or be considered under the diminished-value rule depends upon the nature and magnitude of the defect. This court has not allowed items of such magnitude under the cost-of-repair rule as the trial court did. Viewing the construction of the house as a whole and its cost we cannot say, however, that the trial court was in error in allowing the cost of repairing the plaster cracks in the ceilings, the cost of mud jacking and repairing the patio floor, and the cost of reconstructing the non-weight-bearing and nonstructural patio wall. Such reconstruction did not involve an unreasonable economic waste.

The item of misplacing the living room wall under the facts of this case was clearly under the diminished-value rule. There is no evidence that defendants requested or demanded the replacement of the wall in the place called for by the specifications during the course of construction. To tear down the wall now and rebuild it in the proper place would involve a substantial destruction of the work, if not all of it, which was put into the wall and would cause additional damage to other parts of the house and require replastering and redecorating the walls and ceilings of at least two rooms. Such economic waste is unreasonable and unjustified. The rule of diminished value contemplates the wall is not going to be moved. Expert witnesses for both parties, testifying as to the value of the house, agreed that the misplacement of the wall had no effect on the market price. The trial court properly found that the defendants suffered no legal damage, although the defendants' particular desire for specified room size was not satisfied.

Sale of Goods

In contracts for the sale of goods, the doctrine of substantial performance is not applicable. Both case law and statute require the seller to make what is often referred to as "perfect tender." In one case, a federal court stated that "there is no room in commercial contracts for the doctrine of substantial performance." Section 2-601 of the Uniform Commercial Code states that "if the goods or the tender of delivery fail in any respect to conform to the contract, the buyer may (a) reject the whole; or (b) accept the whole; or (c) accept any commercial unit or units and reject the rest."

Several other provisions of the UCC, however, ameliorate the harsh effect of the perfect-tender rule. The buyer who rejects goods as nonconforming must disclose the nature of the defect to the seller. The seller is then entitled to a reasonable time to "cure the defect." If the buyer accepts a tender of goods, it cannot revoke that acceptance if there has been substantial performance in good faith. A similar rule applies in installment contracts, where the buyer may reject any installment only "if the non-conformity substantially impairs the value of that installment and cannot be cured."

Time of Performance

Contracts often stipulate a time by which performance must be completed. A common example is a contract for goods that states the date upon which delivery will be made. Sometimes the time of performance is important to the parties. In other instances, performance by a particular time, even though stated in the agreement, really does not make much difference.

Ordinarily, unless the nature of a contract is such as to make performance by an exact date vital, failure of a party to perform on or before the agreed-upon day does not discharge the duty of the other party. This rule may be viewed as simply an application of the substantial-performance doctrine to the time-of-performance issue. Contracts for the sale of real estate usually come within this rule. If a real estate contract sets a closing date of February 15, the inability of the buyer to close because the necessary financing has not been approved does not excuse the seller from performing. The buyer would be able to enforce the contract later, but the seller would be entitled to interest on the purchase price from the originally scheduled closing date as well as actual damages, if any, that could be proved.

Some courts say that time is always of the essence in contracts for the sale of goods. This means that if a seller misses the date upon which delivery has been promised even by a day or two, the buyer has the right to refuse delivery and sue for damages. Although it is true that delay is more apt to be fatal in contracts for the sale of goods, not every delay will discharge the other party of its contractual duties. In most jurisdictions, the courts will weigh all aspects of the situation before determining whether time was of the essence even in a contract for the sale of goods.

If performance on or before a particular time is important to one or both parties, they should include a provision in the contract that clearly indicates this. Ordinarily this is indicated by the words "time is of the essence." A statement of this kind is often included in contracts. To be of any value, the statement must indicate clearly which part of the performance is of the essence of the agreement.

If the parties do not agree specifically that time is of the essence, then determining whether it is in a particular situation requires consideration of the circumstances. A wholesaler who promises delivery to a retailer before April 1 and knows that the retailer plans a major advertising campaign to begin April 1 would have to perform on or before that date even though the contract did not include a "time is of the essence" clause. If the situation, the subject matter of the contract, or a clearly written provision that time is of the essence makes time a material factor, performance by that time is essential. Late performance can be rejected even though benefit has been conferred, and the injured party can refuse to meet its own commitment as well as sue for damages.

DISCHARGE OF CONTRACTUAL OBLIGATIONS

One question that managers must frequently deal with is whether a contractual obligation has terminated. Sometimes management is concerned with this question because it believes that a performance to which the firm is entitled has not been completed. In other situations, the question is whether the firm has met its own contractual commitments.

When a contract is said to be *discharged,* one or more of the legal relations of the parties have been terminated. Most commonly this means that the legal duty of one of the parties has been terminated. A party who is under a legal duty by virtue of his or her contract may assert that the duty has been "discharged" by some event that has occurred since the making of the contract.

Seldom are all the legal relations of the contracting parties terminated at the same time. A party may be discharged from further contractual duty, by an act of the other party or some other event, and continue to retain all the rights, powers, and privileges that he or she possessed. It is indeed possible for all the contractual obligations to be terminated at once, as where contract duties are discharged by the agreement of the parties.

Contract duties may be discharged in a variety of ways. Some of these have already been discussed, although not in the context of discharge. The following discussion focuses on the primary methods of discharge.

Discharge by Complete Performance

The most obvious method of discharge of a contractual duty is by complete performance. Most contracts are discharged in this way. Complete performance means full and exact performance—not only of the character, quality, and amount required, but also within the time agreed upon.

Discharge by Occurrence of a Condition Subsequent

As mentioned earlier, a condition subsequent is an event that terminates a present duty of performance. If a condition subsequent occurs, it discharges a duty of performance. Because of their potentially harsh effect, conditions subsequent expressed in a contract are narrowly construed by the courts.

Discharge by Mutual Agreement

Rescission. A contract still executory on both sides may be discharged by an express agreement that it shall no longer bind either party. Such an agreement, called mutual *rescission,* is itself a contract to discharge a prior contract. Its purpose is to restore the parties to the positions they occupied before entering into the first contract.

Substitution of New Contract. A contract may be discharged by the substitution of a new contract. The difference between discharge by a substituted contract and discharge by rescission is that a rescission is a total obliteration of the contract, whereas a substitution provides a new contract in place of the old one. Discharge by substitution results by expressly substituting a new contract for the old one or by making a new contract inconsistent with the old one, with new terms agreed upon by both sides.

Novation. A contract duty of a party may be discharged by the substitution of a new party for one of the original parties. Such a substitution is known as a *novation.* In a novation a new contract is created whose terms are the same as the old contract's but whose parties are different. For a novation to be valid, all three parties must agree to the substitution. A novation need not be of express agreement. It may arise from the conduct of the parties indicating acquiescence in a change of liability.

Discharge by Impossibility of Performance

After a contract has been formed, but prior to full performance, an event may occur that makes performance by one of the parties difficult, unprofitable, impracticable, or impossible or that frustrates the very purpose for which one of parties entered into the contract. Given this state of affairs, the party who views its own performance as no longer desirable may be expected not to perform its contractual obligation, and the other party may be expected to sue, claiming such nonperformance to be a breach of contract. When a party is sued for nonperformance, it may defend on the basis that supervening events made its performance impossible or that the purpose for which it made the contract had become frustrated. Before examining what constitutes discharge by impossibility or frustration of purpose, it may prove helpful to view the question as one involving the issue of how the risks of loss should be distributed. That is, when some supervening event makes a party's performance impossible, the legal and policy problem that is presented is: Who should bear the risk of loss occasioned by the occurrence of the unexpected event? Thus, the role of the contract in society may be seen as an allocation of the risks of loss, and the rules regarding discharge by reason of impossibility provide an example of how the courts fashion rules allocating the risks of loss in a manner that best serves society and reflects the presumed intent of the parties where the parties have failed to state their intent precisely.

Risk of Loss. Fundamental questions of public policy are involved in many cases in which the issue of discharge of contractual obligation and its relationship to performance are considered. These policies, although often at the root of the problem as well as the solution, are generally not discussed in the opinions. A basic premise of Anglo-American contract law is that competent adults should be allowed freely to enter contracts for legitimate purposes. Connected to this premise of freedom of contract is the notion that a person should not be discharged from contractual obligations unless these commitments have been carried out exactly as promised. The emphasis given to freedom of contract and the attendant obligation to perform are reasons that contracting is used as a means of allocating many types of risks. The possibility of fluctuating price is a risk involved in many contracts. Consider a typical business agreement, tens of thousands of which are made each year. The manager of the student dining service contracts with National Dairy to have delivered to the main dining hall at the university 1,500 pints of milk each day during October at $0.08 per pint. She has accepted the risk that the market price of milk will decrease as well as numerous other risks incident to disposing of the milk. The dairy has accepted the risk of a price increase and numerous risks incident to delivery.

The bargaining underlying decisions to assume particular risks is influenced by factors such as economic power, friendship, persuasiveness, and habit. Although these and other considerations are important, the major element in arm's-length negotiations is the decision makers' anticipation and evaluation of events that might affect their ability to perform. In some transactions, however, events occur that were neither anticipated by the parties nor could reasonably have been contemplated when they made the agreement. These events often create new or different risks that materially affect the ability of a party to perform.

This can be illustrated by the oil embargo imposed by the Arabs in 1973. Manufacturers dependent upon oil found costs of production substantially increased. Many were parties to contracts made when the price of oil was low. In agreeing to sell at a particular price, they had assumed a risk under conditions that were reasonably well known. The new conditions were not only different but were also unexpected.

If performance is prevented or becomes more costly because of unexpected new conditions, what should the law's position be? Must a promise be fulfilled insofar as possible even if the result is a crushing loss to one party and a windfall profit to the other? Or should the party who will suffer because of the unexpected new conditions be allowed to avoid performance at the expense of the other who has relied upon the promised performance and given something in exchange for it? This question arises in many cases and is frequently answered only with great difficulty. The court must balance the desirability of enforcing agreements freely made against the injustice of requiring a party to suffer losses of which the risks could not have been foreseen.

Strict or Objective Impossibility. The early common law of contract disregarded unanticipated events and required a party to carry out a promised performance in spite of the fact that it was more difficult, expensive, or demanding than either party had contemplated when the agreement was made. A promise was considered absolute. If it was impossible to perform, the defaulting party was required to pay damages.

This doctrine was so harsh that in a number of common situations the courts began to excuse a promisor on grounds that performance had literally become impossible. Although this interfered with voluntarily assumed risk allocations, justice and fair play clearly supported the courts' position.

Thus, the rule developed that if, after a contract has been formed but before full performance, some unforeseeable event occurs that makes performance objectively impossible, the promisor's duty to perform is discharged. By "objectively impossible" the courts mean that no person could legally or physically perform the contract. If the event that arises makes performance impossible only for the particular promisor, it is merely a subjective impossibility and is insufficient to discharge the promisor's duty of performance. Objective impossibility has been found in the following three circumstances: (1) the death or serious illness of a promisor whose personal performance is required, (2) a change of law making the promised performance illegal, and (3) the destruction of the subject matter of the contract.

Commercial Impracticability and Frustration of Purpose.

The trend in the law is toward an enlargement of the definition of impossibility. As a result, a fourth circumstance has been frequently allowed in recent years: where impossibility is due to the existence of a certain state of affairs, the nonoccurrence of which was a basic assumption on which the contract was made. "Impossibility" is probably an inappropriate word to use in such circumstances. Thus, courts have used the terms *commercial impracticability* and *frustration of purpose* to describe such a circumstance. The two concepts are different but closely related.

The concept of commercial impracticability describes a situation where a party claims that some circumstance has made its own performance impracticable. Performance may be impracticable because extreme and unreasonable difficulty, expense, injury, or loss to one of the parties will occur. A severe shortage of raw materials or of supplies, due to war, embargo, local crop failure, unforeseen shutdown of major sources of supply, or the like, which either causes a marked increase in cost or prevents performance altogether may constitute impracticability.

The concept of frustration of purpose deals with a situation that arises when a change in circumstances makes one party's performance virtually worthless to the other, frustrating its purpose in making the contract. Frustration of purpose differs from commercial impracticability in that there is no impediment to performance by either party. For the concept of frustration of purpose to excuse a party's nonperformance, the purpose that is frustrated must have been a principal purpose of the party in making the contract, the frustration must be substantial, and the nonoccurrence of the frustrating event must have been a basic assumption on which the contract was made.

The *Second Restatement of Contracts* has endorsed both the concept of commercial impracticability (Section 261) and the concept of frustration of purpose (Section 265). The revisers of the *Restatement* were influenced by UCC Section 2-615, which excuses a seller from making timely delivery when the seller's performance has become commercially impracticable "by the occurrence of a contingency the nonoccurrence of which was a basic assumption on which the contract was made. . . ."

The following case concerns the application of UCC 2-615.

Mishara Construction Co. v. Transit Mixed Concrete Co.

Supreme Judicial Court of Massachusetts
310 N.E.2d 363 (1974)

Background: Mishara Construction Co. (plaintiff) was the general contractor for a construction project. It contracted with the Transit Mixed Concrete Co. (defendant) to supply all the ready-mixed concrete needed for the project. Under the contract, Mishara was to specify the dates and amounts of deliveries. In April 1967, a labor dispute stopped work on the project. Work resumed in June, but the workers maintained their picket line for two more years. Transit Mixed Concrete made few deliveries during the two-year period, and Mishara had to obtain concrete from other sources. Mishara sued for damages as a result of Transit's delays and the higher cost of purchasing concrete elsewhere. Transit defended on the basis of impossibility of performance. The trial court entered judgment for Transit. Mishara appealed to the Supreme Judicial Court of Massachusetts.

Decision: The Supreme Judicial Court of Massachusetts affirmed the trial court judgment for Transit.

Reardon, Justice

. . . We are asked to decide as matter of law and without reference to individual facts and circumstances that "picket lines, strikes or labor difficulties" provide no excuse for nonperformance by way of impossibility. This is too sweeping a statement of the law and we decline to adopt it.

The excuse of impossibility in contracts for the sale of goods is controlled by the appropriate section of the Uniform Commercial Code, §2-615. That section sets up two requirements before performance may be excused. First, the performance must have become "impracticable." Second, the impracticability must have been caused "by the occurrence of a contingency the non-occurrence of which was a basic assumption on which the contract was made." This section of the Uniform Commercial Code has not yet been interpreted by this court. Therefore it is appropriate to discuss briefly the significance of these two criteria.

With respect to the requirement that performance must have been impracticable, the official Code comment to the section stresses that the reference is to "commercial impracticability" as opposed to strict impossibility. This is not a radical departure from the common law of contracts as interpreted by this court. Although a strict rule was originally followed denying any excuse for accident of "inevitable necessity," it has long been assumed that circumstances drastically increasing the difficulty and expense of the contemplated performance may be within the compass of "impossibility." By adopting the term "impracticability" rather than "impossibility" the drafters of the Code appear to be in accord with Professor Williston who stated that "the essence of the modern defense of impossibility is that the promised performance was at the making of the contract, or thereafter became, impracticable owing to some extreme or unreasonable difficulty, expense, injury, or loss involved, rather than it is scientifically or actually impossible."

The second criterion of the excuse, that the intervening circumstance be one which the parties assumed would not occur, is also familiar to the law of Massachusetts. The rule is essentially aimed at the distribution of certain kinds of risks in the contractual relationship. By directing the inquiry to the time when the contract was first made, we really seek to determine whether the risk of the intervening circumstance was one which the parties may be taken to have assigned between themselves. It is, of course, the very essence of contract that it is directed at the elimination of some risks for each party in exchange for others. Each receives the certainty of price, quantity, and time, and assumes the risk of changing market prices, superior opportunity, or added costs. It is implicit in the doctrine of impossibility (and the companion rule of "frustration of purpose") that certain risks are so unusual and have such severe consequences that they must have been beyond the scope of the assignment of risks inherent in the contract, that is, beyond the agreement made by the parties. To require performance in that case would be to grant the promisee an advantage for which he could not be said to have bargained in making the contract. "The important question is whether an unanticipated circumstance has made performance of the promise vitally different from what should reasonably have been within the contemplation of both parties when they entered into the contract. If so, the risk should not fairly be thrown upon the promisor." The emphasis in contracts governed by the Uniform Commercial Code is on the commercial context in which the agreement was made. The question is, given the commercial circumstances in which the parties dealt: Was the contingency which developed one which the parties could reasonably be thought to have foreseen as a real possibility which could affect performance? Was it one of that variety of risks which the parties were tacitly assigning to the promisor by their failure to provide for it explicitly? If it were, performance will be required. If it could not be so considered, performance is excused. The contract cannot be reasonably thought to govern in these circumstances, and the parties are both thrown upon the resources of the open market without the benefit of their contract.

With this backdrop, we consider Mishara's contention that a labor dispute which makes performance more difficult never constitutes an excuse for nonperformance. We think it is evident that in some situations a labor dispute would not meet the requirements for impossibility discussed above. A picket line might constitute a mere inconvenience and hardly make performance "impracticable." Likewise, in certain industries with a long record of labor difficulties, the nonoccurrence of strikes and picket lines could not fairly be said to be a basic assumption of the agreement. Certainly, in general, labor disputes cannot be considered extraordinary in the course of modern commerce. Admitting this, however, we are still far from the proposition implicit in the plaintiff's requests. Much must depend on the facts known to the parties at the time of contracting with respect to the history of and prospects for labor difficulties during the period of performance of the contract, as well as the likely severity of the effect of such disputes on the ability to perform. From these facts it is possible to draw an inference as to whether or not the parties intended performance to be carried out even in the face of the labor difficulty. Where the probability of a labor dispute appears to be practically nil, and where the occurrence of such a dispute provides unusual difficulty, the excuse of impracticability might well be applicable. Thus in discussing the defense of impossibility, then Chief Judge Cardozo noted an excuse would be provided "conceivably in some circumstances by unavoidable strikes." The many variables which may bear on the question in individual cases were canvassed by Professor Williston in Williston, Contracts (Rev. ed.) § 1951A (1938), and he concluded that the trend of the law is toward recognizing strikes as excuses for nonperformance. We agree with the statement of the judge in Badhwar v. Colorado Fuel & Iron Corp. on the same question: "Rather than mechanically apply any fixed rule of law, where the parties themselves have not allocated responsibility, justice is better served by appraising all of the circumstances, the part the various parties played, and thereon determining liability."

PREVENTIVE LAW
Dealing with the "Impossible" Situation
——

As seen by the discussion of the defense of impossibility earlier, the trend recently has been toward a liberal definition of the term "impossibility." The concept of commercial impracticability has been recognized by many jurisdictions and is included in the Uniform Commercial Code.

Despite the trend toward expanding the situations that give rise to a discharge due to impossibility or impracticability, it is better to address this issue in a written contract than let a court determine whether a given situation will result in the discharge of a contractual duty. When a party to a contract anticipates a risk, its consequences can be limited by contractual provisions. For example, the parties might agree to excuse a late delivery if delivery is prevented by a railroad strike or by inclement weather. Many types of insurance are also used by firms to protect themselves from some of the risks incident to contract.

Discharge by Breach of Contract

A contract is breached when a party under a present duty of performance fails to perform. As already discussed, a material breach of contract by one party discharges the injured party from any further duty of performance. A partial or minor breach of contract does not operate as a discharge but does render the breaching party liable for the injuries sustained by the innocent party as a result of the breach.

Anticipatory Breach. In most instances, breach of contract occurs only after performance is due. Sometimes, however, a party to a contract repudiates a commitment to perform before the time that performance is required. This is known as an *anticipatory breach*. An anticipatory breach raises the questions whether the other party is immediately discharged from its contractual obligations and whether it can seek a remedy immediately.

Most courts allow immediate action as if the entire contract had been broken. This is justified upon the grounds that the repudiation has destroyed the good-faith relationship upon which successful performance of the contract is based and that simple justice should allow a party to take immediate action to protect its expectations.

Repudiation must be clear and unequivocal. A statement by one of the parties indicating doubt as to ability to perform or even doubt as to whether it wants to is not an anticipatory breach. Repudiation does not have to be verbal. An act is sufficient if it clearly indicates an intent not to perform in the future. A party who prevents another from performing an act that is necessary to carrying out the agreement has committed an anticipatory breach. Some courts have held that voluntary or involuntary bankruptcy is the equivalent of anticipatory breach.

When the other party to a contract has repudiated prior to performance, a firm has several options. It may treat the entire contract as broken and sue immediately for damages without complying further with its own obligations. Assume A and B have entered into an agreement in which A agrees to move a house for B. B has promised to pay A $3,000 for the job and obtain all necessary permits and road clearances. If A repudiates the agreement, it is not necessary for B to obtain the permits and clearances prior to bringing suit.

The firm may choose to ignore the repudiation and wait until performance is due before taking any action, or it may rescind the agreement and sue to recover anything it has furnished under the contract. If the contract can be specifically enforced, an immediate action requiring performance can be brought.

In goods transactions, reasonable grounds for insecurity give rise to the right to demand assurance of performance, and the failure to give such assurance is a repudiation according to Section 2-609 of the UCC. Under Section 2-610, repudiation may be treated as an immediate breach.

REMEDIES

As we noted in earlier chapters, a major function of contract law is to assure that people's expectations based upon commitments made by others are met. Businesses must be able to plan future operations effectively. Private individuals also, in our complicated world, must plan for the future if they are to live satisfactory lives. Because both business and personal planning often are based upon commitments from others, methods of inducing people to honor their agreements are of major importance to society.

Legal remedies are available to enforce legal promises. Even if the parties pay little conscious attention to what will happen if a promise is broken, the underlying threat of legal recourse has an impact. In this section, we explore some of the remedies provided by the law to induce contractual performance and list them in Table 18-1.

The courts usually do not require a party actually to perform a breached promise. They offer several reasons for this reluctance. First, because agreements often are for long periods of time, the courts feel that continuous supervision of performance would be a difficult, if not impossible, burden. Second, the courts fear that they would become involved in disputes over whether the terms of the agreement were being met. A party ordered to perform might do as little as it could get away with. The other party would raise objections to this minimal performance, with the court being required to settle recurring differences. Finally, in some cases, a court decree ordering a person to perform would verge on involuntary servitude.

Dollar Damages

As a result of judicial reluctance to order actual performance, contract law attempts to compensate the injured party by requiring monetary damages from defaulting parties. The general objective of damages is to place the injured party in the position it would have been in had the agreement been carried out. For example, if a firm has contracted to buy 1,000 units at $6 for delivery on January 15, and the units are not delivered, the buyer has a right to obtain the units elsewhere. If the market price is now $6.50, the buyer may be awarded damages of $500, the additional amount that had to be paid to obtain 1,000 units. Then the buyer is placed in the position it would have been in under the contract. In both instances, the buyer has to pay at least $6,000, so this amount is not part of its damages.

In most cases, damages cover reasonably anticipated losses and expenses as well as any gains and profits that might have been made. This rule, although easily stated, is often complex in application and leads to many legal problems.

The Reasonable Anticipation Standard. The defaulting party is responsible for those dam-

ETHICS BOX
Ethical Issues in Discharge of Contracts

In late 1982, Mesa Partners, one of the entities operating under the direction of corporate raider T. Boone Pickens, launched an attempt to acquire General American Oil (GAO). Not wishing to be acquired by Mesa, GAO sought out Phillips Petroleum as a white knight to save it from the clutches of Pickens. Eventually, Mesa backed off from acquiring GAO in return for a payment of $15 million. As part of the deal, Pickens signed a "standstill agreement" that provided:

> We hereby agree that for a period of five years from the date hereof, neither we nor any affiliate . . . of ours . . . will acquire . . . directly or indirectly . . . any voting securities of GAO.

Phillips then acquired GAO, which ceased to exist as a separate entity. In December 1984, Mesa made a tender offer to obtain control of Phillips Petroleum. The applicability of the simple standstill agreement immediately became a critical issue. Phillips argued that the agreement was valid, that it had been understood at the time that it would protect Phillips, and, further, that they could assert GAO's rights under the contract. Mesa countered by arguing that the language of the agreement was very clear—it only applied to GAO, a firm that no longer existed. The dispute was an important one that could affect the outcome of a billion-dollar transaction, not to mention thousands of jobs and even the well-being of an entire city, Bartletsville, Oklahoma. Mesa Partners v. Phillips Petroleum Co., 488 A.2d 107 (Del. Ch. 1984).

Legal arguments concerning the parties' understanding of an agreement in the context of litigation present very difficult ethical questions. There are strong temptations to overstate or misrepresent what was originally assumed. The argument can be made that the legal system should work on a principle of good faith, which would require that parties honestly believe the claims that they assert. Under that principle, if a party such as Phillips or Mesa was knowingly trying to "sell" the court on a theory that they knew was not true, they would be behaving unethically. Such unethical behavior would be very hard to discover and sanction. Very often in litigation of this type, the parties have an honest disagreement about what was intended. Surely there have been times when you have had a misunderstanding with a friend about what you had agreed to previously. The same may have been true in this case. This inability of the legal system to sanction unethical behavior is an important reason that ethics is an extralegal concept. As a matter of professional business ethics, though, you should do the right thing even though the legal system is incapable of punishing all unethical behavior.

TABLE 18–1

Contractual Remedies	When Available
Money	Generally available
Specific performance	Only if the payment of monetary damages is not an adequate remedy
Injunction	In personal service contracts, if a person agreed to exclusively serve the plaintiff and to enforce ancillary agreements
Rescission	In cases involving fraud, duress, undue influence, and mistake
Restitution	If a contract has been canceled, a party has been unjustly enriched or benefited from an unenforceable contract, and if there has been mistaken payment of money

ages that a reasonable person could foresee at the time the contract was made. In the often cited English case of *Hadley* v. *Baxendale,* a mill was shut down because of a broken shaft. The mill owner delivered the shaft to a cartage (transportation) company that promised to return it in three days. When the shaft was not returned in three days as promised, the mill owner sued for the profits lost during the additional period that the mill was closed. The appellate court refused to allow the plaintiff to recover the lost profits, contending that it was not reasonable to anticipate that a mill would be closed completely because of a broken shaft.

Although the defendant is responsible for only reasonably foreseeable losses, anticipation of a *particular* loss is unnecessary. Responsibility extends to that which a reasonable person would know in the ordinary course of events. It also extends to knowledge of special circumstances that could result in larger than ordinary loss.

Certainty. Closely related and often overlapping the rule that an injured party is entitled to compensation only for losses that could reasonably have been foreseen is the additional requirement that damages be certain, not speculative nor uncertain. The plaintiff must establish that a particular loss was caused by the breach and that the amount lost actually can be calculated.

A problem about the certainty of the relationship between breach and loss arises when the defendant can show that intervening factors might have been responsible for plaintiff's loss. Ordinarily, the relationship is a known fact. If a jury finds that the breach was the "primary" or "chief" cause of the loss, the loss is part of the damage award.

Difficult problems also arise out of the need for certainty in the actual calculation of damages. Courts generally have not equated *certainty* with *absolute exactness.* In fact, they appear to have been more concerned with the need for certainty in allowing an award of damages than they are with certainty in calculating the actual amount to be awarded. Over the years, courts in commercial cases have increasingly admitted the testimony of expert witnesses who analyze business records and market summaries to satisfy the certainty requirement. One difficult question for the courts has been whether a defaulting defendant should be responsible for the loss of future profits stemming from a particular contract. Although most jurisdictions allow an injured party to collect anticipated profits if a contract is breached with a business in operation, the rule appears to be different when the business is new or being planned. In these cases, the plaintiff is not entitled to anticipated profits.

The following case illustrates the application of the reasonable anticipation standard.

Stifft's Jewelers v. Oliver

Supreme Court of Arkansas

678 S.W.2d 372 (1984)

Background: Charles and Mary Oliver, a married couple, and their daughter Grace (plaintiffs-appellees) lived in Batesville, Arkansas; and Stifft's Jewelers (defendant-appellant) was a Little Rock company engaged in the business of selling and repairing jewelry. On June 26, 1982, Mrs. Oliver brought three rings to Stifft's to be repaired. The rings were a .70 carat marquise diamond, which was Mrs. Oliver's engagement ring; a one-third carat diamond, which Mr. Oliver's mother had willed to Grace Oliver; and a one-fourth carat garnet, which had originally belonged to Mrs. Oliver's grandmother. The value of the three rings was approximately $3,800.

On the same day, Mr. Oliver purchased a one-carat diamond ring as an anniversary gift for Mrs. Oliver. Stifft's agreed to mail all four rings after the repairs and proper cleaning were completed. The Olivers received a package in the mail from Stifft's that only contained the anniversary ring. When contacted by the Olivers, Stifft's maintained that all four rings were placed in the same box.

The Olivers sued Stifft's, seeking the replacement cost of the rings plus $50,000 in sentimental value. At trial, the jury returned a verdict in favor of the Olivers for $4,000 replacement cost and $4,000 for sentimental value. Stifft's Jewelers appealed the award of $4,000 for sentimental value to the Supreme Court of Arkansas.

Decision: The Supreme Court of Arkansas ruled in favor of Stifft's Jewelers and struck the award of $4,000 for sentimental value.

Hollingsworth, Justice

This appeal is from the judgment of $4000 in sentimental value in favor of the Olivers.

The question here is the amount of damages that can be established with reasonable certainty under the facts of this case. Since there was a market value established for the rings, we must now determine whether a special or sentimental value is greater than the market value, and what the parties understood their obligations to be. We look to our holding in *Morrow, et al* v. *First National Bank of Hot Springs,* for guidance. There we reaffirmed the adoption of the "tacit agreement test" for the recovery of special damages for a breach of contract. We stated: "By that test the plaintiff must prove more than the defendant's mere knowledge that a breach of contract will entail special damages to the plaintiff. It must also appear that the defendant at least tacitly agreed to assume responsbility."

Here the appellees have not pointed out where the appellant company was made aware of the sentimental value of the rings. Neither do they show any tacit agreement by appellant to assume responsibility.

There could be circumstances where the value of the property is primarily sentimental and the jury could determine that value, provided there was a tacit agreement by the parties. However, the circumstances do not exist here because no tacit agreement was made and the alleged sentimental value of the lost rings is so highly speculative in this case that it was not a proper element of damages for consideration by the jury. We strike that part of the judgment for sentimental value.

Mitigation of Damages. A person injured by breach of contract has a right to recover losses that are reasonably predictable and relatively certain. The injured party, however, must limit these losses as much as possible. An injured party cannot allow damages to accumulate and then collect all that has been lost. The injured party cannot continue to perform when the other party is in default and then recover the full contract price.

The obligation of the injured party to keep losses as low as possible is known as *mitigation* of damages. If opportunities to mitigate damages are available and plaintiff has not taken advantage of them, the court subtracts from any award the amount by which the plaintiff could have minimized his or her own losses.

The mitigation requirement forces the injured party to make many decisions if the contract is breached. An employee who has a contract but is fired must secure comparable employment elsewhere if possible. This requirement raises several questions. Is any employment paying the same amount comparable? Suppose a potential job involves moving to an area that the injured party does not like. Is the employment comparable?

A difficult mitigation decision for a manufacturer occurs when a buyer repudiates an agreement during the manufacturing of special items. The manufacturer-seller may have invested heavily in parts and materials necessary for the job. Managers must decide if the buyer's losses will be less if the firm immediately halts production and sells the partially completed merchandise for salvage or if it completes the contract and sells the finished merchandise on the market. The UCC allows the manufacturer to do either as long as it uses "reasonable commercial judgment."

The following case illustrates some of the possible ramifications of mitigation decisions.

Parker v. Twentieth Century Fox Film Corporation

Supreme Court of California

474 P.2d 689 (1970)

Background: Shirley MacLaine Parker (plaintiff), a well-known actress, was under contract with Twentieth Century Fox Film Corporation (defendant) to play the female lead in the film company's musical, *Bloomer Girl.* Parker was to be paid a minimum "guaranteed compensation" of $53,571.42 per week for fourteen weeks for a total of $750,000. Before beginning production, Twentieth Century Fox notified Parker of its decision not to produce the movie and offered her instead the lead role in a western, *Big Country, Big Man.* Unlike *Bloomer Girl,* which was to be filmed in California, *Big Country, Big Man* was to be filmed in Australia. Additionally, the right of approval over the director and screenplay, which was granted to Parker under her original contract, was to be omitted from any contract that she would sign to work in *Big Country, Big Man.* Parker refused the offer and sued to recover the agreed compensation. The trial court awarded judgment for Parker. Twentieth Century Fox appealed to the Supreme Court of California.

Decision: The Supreme Court of California affirmed the trial court judgment in favor of Parker.

Burke, Justice

[D]efendant's sole defense to this action which resulted from its deliberate breach of contract is that in rejecting defendant's substitute offer of employment plaintiff unreasonably refused to mitigate damages.

The general rule is that the measure of recovery by a wrongfully discharged employee is the amount of salary agreed upon for the period of service, less the amount which the employer affirmatively proves the employee has earned or with reasonable effort might have earned from other employment. However, before projected earnings from other employment opportunities not sought or accepted by the discharged employee can be applied in mitigation, the employer must show that the other employment was comparable, or substantially similar, to that of which the employee has been deprived; the employee's rejection of or failure to seek other available employment of a different or inferior kind may not be resorted to in order to mitigate damages.

In the present case defendant has raised no issue of *reasonableness of efforts* by plaintiff to obtain other employment; the sole issue is whether plaintiff's refusal of defendant's substitute offer of "Big Country" may be used in mitigation. Nor, if the "Big Country" offer was of employment different or inferior when compared with the original "Bloomer Girl" employment, is there an issue as to whether or not plaintiff acted reasonably in refusing the substitute offer. Despite defendant's arguments to the contrary, no case cited or which our research has discovered holds or suggests that reasonableness is an element of a wrongfully discharged employee's option to reject, or fail to seek, different or inferior employment lest the possible earnings therefrom be charged against him in mitigation of damages.

Applying the foregoing rules to the record in the present case, with all intendments in favor of the party opposing the summary judgment motion—here, defendant—it is clear that the trial court correctly ruled that plaintiff's failure to accept defendant's tendered substitute employment could not be applied in mitigation of damages because the offer of the "Big Country" lead was of employment both different and inferior, and that no factual dispute was presented on that issue. The mere circumstances that "Bloomer Girl" was to be a musical revue calling upon plaintiff's talents as a dancer as well as an actress, and was to be produced in the City of Los Angeles, whereas "Big Country" was a straight dramatic role in a "Western Type" story taking place in an opal mine in Australia, demonstrates the difference in kind between the two employments; the female lead as a dramatic actress in a western style motion picture can by no stretch of imagination be considered the equivalent of or substantially similar to the lead in a song-and-dance production.

Additionally, the substitute "Big Country" offer proposed to eliminate or impair the director and screenplay approvals accorded to plaintiff under the original "Bloomer Girl" contract, and thus constituted an offer of inferior employment. No expertise or judicial notice is required in order to hold that the deprivation or infringement of an employee's rights held under an original employment contract converts the available "other employment" relied upon by the employer to mitigate damages, into inferior employment which the employee need not seek or accept. . . .

Liquidated Damages. Some contracts include a provision in which the parties agree on an amount of compensation for the injured party if there is a breach. This is known as a *liquidated damages clause.* Generally, when negotiating, the parties do not concern themselves with the effects of a breach. They are primarily interested in performance and its costs and benefits. But in some instances, the results of a breach are an important part of the bargain. This consideration often is important in contracts involving large sums of money, in which the time of completion is highly important, or when the amount of loss in the event of breach is unclear.

In other cases, one of the parties may think that liquidated damages will force the other to perform. If that party has superior bargaining power, the other party might agree to pay damages that would exceed any likely loss. When liquidated damages are not reasonably related to loss, they are not damages, but rather a penalty that violates the underlying concept of damages—that is, to place the injured party in the position it would have been in had the contract been performed. Courts therefore have been unwilling to accept liquidated damage provisions that penalize the defaulting party. They do not recognize a provision that is not reasonably related to losses.

The UCC (Section 2-718) provides:

Damages for breach by either party may be liquidated in the agreement but only at an amount which is reasonable in the light of the anticipated or actual harm caused by the breach, the difficulties of proof of loss, and the inconvenience or *nonfeasibility* of otherwise obtaining an adequate remedy. A term fixing unreasonably large liquidated damages is void as a penalty.

Punitive Damages. Punitive or exemplary damages are those that exceed the injured party's loss. In tort cases, they are often a substantial portion of the plaintiff's recovery. The primary purpose of punitive damages is to deter the defendant and others from the type of act that caused the loss. Punitive damages are seldom awarded in contract cases. In those few instances in which they have been awarded, plaintiffs have been able to prove something akin to fraud, recklessness, or malice.

Recently some courts have allowed punitive awards in contract cases in which the plaintiff was a consumer, or at least a "little guy" with limited bargaining power, and the defendant, a party with greater bargaining power, acted outrageously or oppressively.

Specific Performance

Although Anglo-American law generally awards damages to a party against whom there has been a breach, under some circumstances, the courts require the defaulting party actually to perform the promised act. This remedy for breach is referred to as *specific performance.* The governing principle is that specific performance is required when payment of damages would not adequately or completely compensate the injured party. A contract promise to pay money ordinarily is not enforced specifically because the damage remedy is considered adequate.

Whether the damage remedy is adequate depends to a large extent upon the facts of the particular case. The courts generally have held that damages are inadequate in two types of cases. First are those cases in which the subject matter of the contract is unique. Unusual items of personal property, such as antiques and original paintings, clearly fall into this category. Money is not considered an adequate replacement for a prized heirloom. Second are cases involving the sale of real estate. Because of land's economic importance, the courts historically have assumed that every piece of land is unique. As a result, contracts for the sale of real estate almost inevitably can be enforced specifically. Real-estate agreements are the subject matter that is most commonly involved in actions for specific performance.

Other types of agreements that courts have considered unique pervade economic activity. They include contracts to sell a business, to issue a policy of insurance, to repurchase corporate stock, to act as a surety, to execute a written instrument, and even, in some instances, to lend money. In these and similar cases, if the defendant can show that the plaintiff has an adequate remedy at law, specific performance is not granted.

The UCC (Section 2-716) provides that in goods transactions, "Specific performance may be decreed where the goods are unique or in other proper circumstances." The Official Comment on this section states:

The present section continues in general prior policy as to specific performance. . . . However, without intending to impair in any way the exercise of the court's sound discretion in the matter, this article seeks to further a more liberal attitude than some courts have shown in connection with the specific performance of contracts of sale.

Under the UCC, if a buyer cannot readily find substitute goods in the market, the buyer is entitled to an award of specific performance, although the goods may not be "unique." The code allows a court to award specific performance "in other proper circumstances."

Injunction

An injunction is a remedy sometimes used in contract cases. But like specific performance, its use has been limited. Injunctions have been used in employment contracts to prevent a party from performing the contract service for someone else. In a leading English case, an opera singer had contracted to sing exclusively for a particular company. When she refused to do so, the court forbade her from singing for any other company. The court felt that it could not compel her specifically to perform her contractual obligation but that economic pressure might move her to honor it.

American courts generally follow a similar rule in personal service contracts where the defendant refuses to perform. If the defendant's services expressly or by clear implication have been promised exclusively to the plaintiff, the courts forbid service for anyone else. An injunction, however, is not to be granted if the injured plaintiff could be compensated adequately by damages. As a result, injunctions are granted in personal service contracts only if the individual is a person with unique skills. Professional athletes who refuse to honor their contracts with one employer are often forbidden to perform for another.

The injunction is also used to enforce *ancillary agreements* not to compete. As discussed in Chapter 15, this type of agreement is permissible under certain circumstances. These generally involve the sale of a business and its accompanying goodwill, an employment contract in which the employee agrees not to work for a competitor or compete with the employer after leaving the job, or an employment contract in which the employee has access to customer lists or trade secrets that could be used by a business rival. Injunctions are also used to enforce *covenants* that limit land use. A rental or ownership agreement may contain a provision limiting the premises to residential use. If the tenant or owner uses the property for some other purpose, someone injured by the improper use may get an injunction.

Rescission and Restitution

Many situations exist in which a party has the right to rescind or cancel a contract. Rescission (see Chapter 13) is available in cases involving fraud, duress, undue influence, and mistake. During the past decade, many laws have given consumers the right to cancel contracts under certain circumstances. One example is the home solicitation or door-to-door sales contract. Many states and a Federal Trade Commission rule allow a buyer three days to cancel certain types of agreements that have been solicited and made in the buyer's home. These laws also generally require the seller to notify the buyer in writing of this right. The three-day period does not start until notification is given. The right to cancel a home solicitation sales contract does not depend upon any wrongdoing by the seller.

When a contract is canceled, both parties must, if possible, return any benefits received under the agreement. This return is known as making *restitution*. Restitution may involve returning specific items or compensating for benefits conferred. The principle of restitution applies even for cancellation due to fraud. The defrauded plaintiff is entitled to the return of benefits conferred because of fraud; but the law requires the defrauded plaintiff, if possible, to return the wrongdoer to the *status quo*. The defrauded plaintiff may, of course, choose to enforce the contract and sue for damages.

Restitution is a remedy also available in cases in which one person has been unjustly enriched at another's expense. Unjust enrichment is a fundamental concept affecting several legal areas, the theory being that justice is violated if a person is allowed to retain benefits that enrich him or her unfairly at another's expense. As a result, the courts may order restitution of those benefits or their value. Before the courts order restitution, they must be convinced that retention of the benefits not only enriches the person but that the enrichment is unjust.

Restitution is ordered by the courts when money has been paid by mistake or when a person has benefited from a contract that turns out to be unenforceable. The restitution rule applies if one party keeps the benefits from a broken contract when these could have been returned easily.

PREVENTIVE LAW
Allocating Risk with Contracts

Perhaps no chapter better illustrates the strategic importance of a well-written contract than this chapter on performance, discharge, and remedies. In an uncertain commercial world, the contract is the tool that businesses use to allocate risks. Thus, an electric utility may enter into a long-term supply contract with a coal company in an effort to fix the cost of coal and to protect itself against future fluctuations in coal prices.

The contract rules contained in this chapter should be viewed as the legal framework surrounding a negotiated transaction. Some of the rules can serve as useful tools during contract negotiations. Most of the rules can be altered or avoided by the parties simply by addressing them in their contracts.

For example, the inclusion of conditions in a contract by a party may permit that party to avoid a contractual duty when circumstances change to make the contractual undertaking no longer attractive. Thus, during times of rising interest rates, offers to purchase real estate frequently condition the buyer's duty to purchase to the availability of a mortgage at a specified interest rate. Depending upon one's negotiating power, a contracting party could artfully draft a contract that would reduce the risk of financial loss on a contractual undertaking.

Another example of how the law discussed in this chapter can serve as a useful tool for contracting parties can be seen in the concept of liquidated damages. By including a valid liquidated damages clause in a contract, a party can limit the liability resulting from its nonperformance of a contractual duty.

The substantial-performance doctrine illustrates a rule of contract law that may be avoided by careful contract drafting. It is the substantial-performance doctrine that left the Jacobses with a dream home that was less than what they had dreamed of in the case of *Plante* v. *Jacobs.* Notice that very little was covered in the contract. The contract did not include blueprints for the house. The parties relied on "standard forms." The Jacobses could have avoided the problems they encountered by making the items that they considered important the "essence" of the contract. This, of course, would depend upon the bargaining power that they brought to the negotiation of their contract. It is the substantial-performance doctrine that also accounts for the rule that failure to comply exactly with a contract's deadline will not result in a forfeiture. This too, however, can be avoided by including a provision in the contract that "time is of the essence."

At this point in the discussion of contract law, it should not come as a surprise that a carefully written contract can serve to avoid many of the problems that parties may encounter in their business relations.

REVIEW PROBLEMS

1. What is meant by the substantial-performance doctrine? When will performance qualify as substantial under the doctrine?
2. What is meant by "impossibility of performance"?
3. What is the standard a court uses to award dollar damages when lost profits are involved?
4. Why should a party who has not breached a contract be required to mitigate the damages of the breaching party?

5. Ace contracted with Jones to do certain remodeling work on the building owned by Jones. Jones supplied the specifications for the work. The contract price was $70,000. After the work was completed, Jones was dissatisfied and had Clay, an expert, compare the work done to the specifications provided. Clay testified that the work had been done improperly by Ace and that it would cost about $6,000 to correct the mistakes of Ace. If Jones

refuses to pay any amount to Ace, what recourse, if any, does Ace have against Jones? Explain.

6. On January 4, General Contractors, Inc. entered into a contract with Julius and Penelope Jones to construct a house fit for occupancy by June 1. What is the legal consequence if General Contractors fails to complete the house by June 1, but does finish it by June 20? What would be the consequence if the contract stated that with regard to the June 1 deadline, "time is of the essence"? Suppose further that by May 10 no work has yet been started by General Contractors. When contacted by Julius, General Contractors' president states that due to other projects still pending, he is unable to build the house until late November. What legal recourse, if any, do Julius and Penelope have against General Contractors?

7. Frank and Flo Gibson enter into a contract with Ace Home Builders for the construction of a house. After construction was completed, the Gibsons discovered several cracks in the foundation which caused flooding in the basement. What recourse do the Gibsons have against Ace, if any?

8. A contractor agreed to build a skating rink for the plaintiff at a price of $180,000. The rink was to be completed by December 1 and was designed to replace a similar but older rink that the plaintiff rented for $800 per month. A clause in the contract awarded the plaintiff "$100 per day in liquidated damages" for each day after December 1 that the rink was not completed. Was this a valid liquidated damages clause? Explain.

9. On April 15, Don Construction contracted to build a house for Jessup. The contract price was $55,000. The agreement contained a provision stating that the builder would deduct $1,000 a day from the contract price for each day the house was not completed after August 15. It was not completed until September 15. Don Construction refused to deduct $30,000 from the contract price. Jessup refused to sue. Don Construction sued, claiming the $1,000 a day was a penalty clause, not a liquidated damages clause. What result? Explain.

10. Julius W. Erving ("Dr. J") entered into a four-year contract to play exclusively for the Virginia Squires of the American Basketball Association. After one year, he left the Squires to play for the Atlanta Hawks of the National Basketball Association. The contract signed with the Squires provided that the team could apply for an injunction to prohibit Erving from playing for any other team. Erving sued to have his contract set aside for fraud. The Squires counterclaimed seeking injunctive relief pending arbitration. Who won? Explain.

11. Berke entered into an employment contract with Bettinger to become a sales manager. The contract provided that if Berke terminated employment he could not work for any employment agency for at least one year within fifty miles of Philadelphia. Berke left Bettinger and opened his business immediately within a fifty-mile radius. Bettinger seeks an injunction claiming irreparable harm.

12. The Aluminum Company of America (ALCOA) sued for relief from a burdensome toll conversion contract under which it converted alumina into molten aluminum for the Essex Group, Inc. (Essex), the supplier of the raw material. ALCOA sought a declaratory judgment that its nonperformance of the contract was excused as a result of commercial impracticability and frustration of purpose. For relief, it sought a reformation or modification of the contract.

Under the terms of the contract, entered into December 26, 1967, and labeled the Molten Metal Agreement, Essex would supply ALCOA with alumina, which ALCOA would convert into molten aluminum at its Warrick, Indiana plant. Essex then would pick up the aluminum for further processing into aluminum wire products. The contract contained a complex price formula, with escalators pegged to the Wholesale Price Index–Industrial Commodities (WPI–IC), a government price index, and on the average hourly labor rates paid to ALCOA employees at the Warrick plant. The adjusted price was subject to an overall ceiling of 65 percent of the price of a specified type of aluminum sold on specified terms as published in a trade journal.

The price formula was designed to reflect changes in nonlabor and labor costs. The indexing system was evolved by ALCOA with the aid of the eminent economist Alan Greenspan. ALCOA selected the WPI–IC as a pricing element after assuring itself that the index had closely tracked ALCOA's nonlabor production costs for many years in the past and was highly likely to continue to do so in the future. The formula, however, had failed to account for burgeoning energy costs. Beginning in 1973, OPEC's actions to increase oil prices and unanticipated pollution control costs greatly increased ALCOA's electricity costs. Electrical power is the principal nonlabor cost factor in aluminum conversion, and the electrical power rates rose much more rapidly than did the WPI–IC. ALCOA complained that if it were compelled to perform the unexpired term of the sixteen-year contract, it would lose over $75 million. Essex counterclaimed for damages and specific performance of the contract, arguing that ALCOA had breached the contract. Who wins? Explain. If you decide in favor of ALCOA, should the court be allowed to reform the contract by writing a wholly new price term for the parties? If so, how would you reform the price formula? If you decide in favor of Essex, should the court award the remedy of specific performance? Aluminum Co. of America v. Essex Group, Inc., 499 F. Supp. 53 (W.D. Pa. 1980).

P A R T   I I I

COMMERCIAL TRANSACTIONS

Sales Law

ales law covers all aspects of the sale of goods that may have legal consequences. Contracts for the sale of goods, commercial paper, and sellers' security interests all come within the scope of sales law. The Uniform Commercial Code (UCC) is the primary source of law in this area, particularly Articles 2 (Sales), 3 (Commercial Paper), and 9 (Secured Transactions).

In many instances the provisions of the UCC allow the parties to agree upon a rule different from that stated in the Code. Such provisions are prefaced with phrases such as "unless otherwise agreed" and "in the absence of contrary agreement." In the interest of simplicity, in discussing such sections we have omitted reference to the fact that the provisions can be altered by agreement.

GENERAL CHARACTERISTICS OF THE UCC

The drafters of the UCC sought to update the prior sales law to achieve a balance between the law and business practice. Many very specific rules were established controlling the formation and documentation of the sales transaction. Performance obligations were specifically defined, and the remedial rights of the parties were spelled out.

In addition, the UCC is based on several important general principles, many of which represent a significant break with past law. These principles include:

1. Recognition of a general duty of good faith
2. De-emphasis of the traditional concept of title
3. Imposition of higher standards for merchants
4. Ratification of certain aspects of existing business practice

Duty of Good Faith

UCC Section 1–203 provides that "Every contract or duty within this Act imposes an obligation of good faith in its performance or enforcement."

Subsection 1–201(19) defines good faith as "honesty in fact in the conduct or transaction concerned." No direct sanction is imposed for

453

ETHICS BOX
Good Faith in Commercial Transactions
——

In Chapter 4, "Business and Ethics," good faith was identified as one of eight basic principles of business ethics. Most businesspeople can describe what is meant by "good faith" in their industry. Further, the concept of "bad faith" is coming to have a more precise meaning in contract law, where actions falling under the standard are more likely to be sanctioned by punitive damages.

Did the drafters of the Code intend to require that all sales contracts be consistent with an *ethical* standard of good faith in their formation and performance? The courts have not adopted that approach to date, and the principle of good faith has been used more as a general admonition than as a separate legal doctrine. The language is there, however, and someday the courts may use it to bring certain ethical standards into the commercial law on a more explicit basis.

---

failure to act in good faith. Instead, it is a general principle available to the courts that may be followed in dealing with other issues arising under the UCC. For example, Section 2–302 expressly provides for judicial modification or nullification of unconscionable contracts and contract terms. The good-faith provision complements the concept of unconscionability, and good faith may be used as a guideline in determining whether certain aspects of a commercial transaction may be considered unconscionable. The good-faith principle can also be used on its own—for example, to disallow an extortionate modification of a contract when the buyer has become so dependent on the seller for the supply of a commodity that the buyer cannot effectively resist the seller's demand for a higher price.

Merchant Standards

Merchants are generally held to different standards under the UCC from those of nonmerchants. The implied warranty of merchantability applies only to merchants. (Implied warranties are discussed in the chapter on warranties.) Only merchants are bound by firm offers, and only merchants may be bound, without agreement, by additional terms in an acceptance. There are other examples of the higher standards applied to merchants.

Why discriminate between merchants and nonmerchants? Several justifications can be given. Merchants can reasonably be expected to be more sophisticated regarding the legal rules pertaining to their profession. They should know when to seek the advice of counsel and are, in fact, often guided by legal advice. Many merchants enter into sales transactions day after day. A nonmerchant seller, on the other hand, may make one major sale every two or three years. If we view the special rules for merchants from a consumer perspective, it seems appropriate that consumers should be held to a less rigorous standard.

Who is a merchant? The UCC defines a merchant in three different ways. A merchant may be a person who deals in goods of the kind in question. If a person in the hardware business sells a hammer, he or she is a merchant for purposes of the sale of the hammer because a hardware store regularly deals in goods such as hammers. A second person classified by the UCC as a merchant is one who by his occupation represents himself as having knowledge or skill peculiar to the practices or goods involved in the transaction. Suppose a mechanical contracting firm installed cooling equipment; with respect to the sale of the cooling equipment, it would be regarded as a merchant. Finally, a person may be classified as a merchant if he or she employs someone who qualifies as a merchant, under the first two definitions, to act on his or her behalf. If Mary hired a jeweler to represent her in the sale of her diamonds, the UCC treats *her* as a merchant because she employed a merchant.

The *Decatur* case discusses the problem of when a farmer is a merchant. Some courts view farmers as merchants but others reject this view, as the following case illustrates.

Decatur Cooperative Association v. Urban

Supreme Court of Kansas

547 P.2d 323 (1976)

Background: Decatur Cooperative (plaintiff) sued Urban (defendant). Urban allegedly entered into an oral contract for sale of 10,000 bushels of wheat with the plaintiff, a grain elevator cooperative. The lower court ruled for Urban.

Decision: The Kansas Supreme Court affirmed. It ruled that Urban was not a merchant for purposes of the sale of the wheat.

Harman, C., Justice

Urban is a resident of Decatur County and was a member of the cooperative throughout the year 1973. He has been engaged in the wheat farming business for about twenty years. He owns about 2,000 acres of his total farmed acreage of 2,320 acres. He is engaged solely in the farming business. Decatur contends the parties entered into an oral contract by phone whereby Urban agreed to sell to the cooperative 10,000 bushels of wheat at $2.86 per bushel, to be delivered on or before September 30, 1973. Urban denies that any contract sale was made.

During the phone conversation there was discussion of a written memorandum of sale to be prepared and sent to Urban later. A confirmation was signed by Decatur's assistant manager and was binding as against Decatur. Urban received the confirmation within a reasonable time, read it, and gave no written notice of objection to its contents within ten days after it was received.

On August 13, 1973, Urban notified Decatur that he would not deliver the wheat. The price of wheat at the cooperative on that date was $4.50 per bushel.

Under Subsection (2) of 2–201 a "merchant" is deprived of the defense of the Statute of Frauds as against an oral contract with another merchant if he fails to object to the terms of a written confirmation within ten days of its receipt. The issue presently here is whether or not appellee is, under the facts, also a "merchant." If he is not, Section 2–201 acts as a bar to the enforcement of the alleged contract. Professionalism, special knowledge and commercial experience are to be used in determining whether a person in a particular situation is to be held to the standards of a merchant.

The writers of the official UCC comment virtually equate professionals with merchants—the casual or inexperienced buyer or seller is not to be held to the standard set for the professional in business. The defined term "between merchants," used in the exception proviso to the Statute of Frauds, contemplates the knowledge and skill of professionals on each side of the transaction. The transaction in question here was the sale of wheat. Urban as a farmer undoubtedly had special knowledge or skill in raising wheat but we do not think this factor, coupled with annual sales of a wheat crop and purchases of seed wheat, qualified him as a merchant in that field. The parties' stipulation states Urban has sold only the products he raised. There is no indication any of these sales were other than cash sales to local grain elevators, where conceivably an expertise reaching professional status could be said to be involved.

We think the trial court correctly ruled under the particular facts that Urban was not a merchant for the purpose of avoiding the operation of the Statute of Frauds pursuant to K.S.A. 84-2-201(1).

SCOPE OF ARTICLE 2

Article 2 of the UCC covers all transactions involving a "sale" where title passes from the seller to the buyer for a price. It also covers "contracts for sale," which include both a present sale and a contract to sell at a future time. In a *present sale* the making of the contract and the completion of the sale (passing of title) occur at the same time. In a *future sale* the making of the contract and the completion of the sale occur at different times.

Goods

Unless the sale involves the sale of "goods," the contract is not controlled by Article 2. Section 2–105(1) of the UCC defines goods as "all things . . . which are movable at the time of identification to the contract for sale . . ." In order for an item to qualify as a good, two requirements must be met: (1) the item must be tangible (have a physical existence); and (2) it must be movable.

The UCC definition of goods also includes the unborn young of animals, growing crops, and other things attached to realty that are to be severed. A contract for the sale of growing crops, timber to be cut, or other severables is a contract for the sale of goods. If the contract covers goods that are not yet existing and identified, the goods are "future goods," and the sale of future goods operates as a contract to sell.

Contracts Not Covered

Contracts that are not covered by Article 2 are those involving the sale of real property, non-goods personal property (e.g., a contract for the sale of an investment security), or services. Where a contract involves both goods and services, the court may apply Article 2 even though the contract is not a pure goods contract. The sale of mixed goods and services has created a number of complex cases. Suppose you go to a dentist; if the dentist fills one of your teeth with silver, is the transaction a sale of goods? What if a plumber comes to your house and installs a new pipe; is the transaction a sale of goods? It is most likely, in both of these examples, that a court would construe the transaction as a service contract because goods are only incidentally involved in the performance of the service contract. In other words, because the service aspect of the transaction predominates, the transaction is not covered by the UCC. Conversely, an item might be sold along with a minor service. Suppose you went to a restaurant at which a waiter or waitress brought food to the table. Courts are likely to construe this situation as predominately a sale of goods and therefore covered by the UCC. Obviously, not all situations are this clear-cut, and the mixture of goods and services gives courts some trouble in deciding whether the UCC or the common law of contracts should control a situation.

CREATION OF SALES CONTRACTS

The UCC makes it much easier for a court to find that a contract for the sale of goods has been made. If the court determines that the parties intended an agreement because of something they wrote or said, or because of their conduct, it can find that a contract for sale of goods has been made even though the moment of its making is uncertain. Section 2–204(3) states the principle pertaining to "open terms" adopted in the UCC. The contract will not be set aside for indefiniteness merely because one or more terms have been left open, as long as the parties intended to make a contract and there is a reasonably certain basis for giving an appropriate remedy. The more terms the parties have left open, the more difficult it will be for a court to conclude that the parties intended to make a binding agreement. For the court to have a reasonably certain basis for giving an appropriate remedy, the parties must specify in the contract the quantity of goods sold.

Indefiniteness

Prior to the adoption of the UCC, a court would sometimes refuse to enforce a contract because parties either intentionally or unintentionally failed to cover all the terms necessary for the contract to be considered valid and enforceable. The contract might not have

clearly specified the price to be paid or certain delivery or payment terms. Rather than fill in the missing terms for the parties, the courts simply refused to enforce the agreement. The UCC, in Part 3 of Article 2, provides a number of statutory terms that may be used by a court in the event the contract fails to specify particular terms.

Price. Section 2–304 states that the price can be made payable "in money or otherwise." Thus a contract will not fail simply because it does not make the price payable in money. The price can be paid in money, goods, realty, or "otherwise."

But what if the parties leave the price term open? Section 2–305 covers this situation. It is not necessary for the contract to include the price term. If it has not been agreed upon at the time the contract is executed, then the price will be whatever a reasonable price is at the time of delivery. Any price set at a later date must be done in "good faith." If the buyer has the right to set the price at a later time, and he sets an unreasonably low price in light of the market conditions and surrounding circumstances, then the price declared will not be controlling because the buyer acted in bad faith. If one of the parties to a contract has the duty to fix a price and he or she fails to do so, the other party may cancel the contract or may set a reasonable price.

However, a contract will fail for indefiniteness if the price term is left out and if the contract clearly states that the parties do not intend to be bound by the agreement if the price is not subsequently fixed and agreed upon. Unless the contract very clearly indicates that the parties do not wish to be bound if the price cannot be agreed upon, the court may end up setting a price for them.

Delivery. The contract may also not contain directions for the time, place, or method of delivery. Even so, the contract will not fail for indefiniteness. If the time for delivery has not been specified in the contract, subsection 2–309(1) states that the time for shipment or delivery shall be a reasonable time. What is reasonable depends on the circumstances. If the contract calls for successive performances but does not specify when the contract terminates, it is valid for a reasonable time but may be terminated at any time by either party upon reasonable notice. If the contract does not specify whether the delivery is to be in one lot or in several lots, the goods must be tendered in a single delivery and payment is due at that time.

Section 2–308 makes the seller's place of business or, if he or she has no place of business, the seller's residence the appropriate place for delivery of goods in the absence of a specified place of delivery. If the contract is for the sale of identified goods that the parties know are located at some place other than the seller's place of business or residence, the place where the goods are located is the place for delivery.

Quantity. The only term that absolutely must be stated in a contract for the sale of goods is the quantity term. Section 2–201 of the Statute of Frauds states: "a writing is not insufficient because it omits or incorrectly states a term agreed upon but the contract is not enforceable . . . beyond the quantity of goods shown in such writing." If the contract is one that must be in writing in order to be enforceable, and the writing omits the quantity term, there is no enforceable contract. If the writing incorrectly states the quantity term, there may be an enforceable contract— at least to the extent of the quantity stated in the writing.

Thus the UCC reflects the philosophy that a contract for the sale of goods should not fail, even though one or more terms have been left open, as long as the parties intended to enter into a contract and "there is a reasonably certain basis for giving an appropriate remedy" (Section 2–204[3]).

Course of Dealing, Usage of Trade, Course of Performance

In interpreting a contract, the court must take into consideration more than the literal language of the contract and the meaning that is normally associated with the words used in the contract. The UCC requires the court to examine the course of dealing, usage of trade, or course of performance between the parties.

Whenever possible, the express terms of the agreement and any course of dealing, usage of trade, and course of performance must be construed as consistent with one another. When such a construction is unreasonable, the written terms control the situation. Sections 2–208(2) and 1–205(4) make it apparent that conflicts between the express and implied terms are to be resolved in the following manner:

1. Express terms prevail over course of dealing, usage of trade, and course of performance if they cannot be reasonably construed together.
2. Course of performance prevails over both course of dealing and usage of trade.
3. Course of dealing prevails over usage of trade.

Course of Performance. Section 2–208(1) states: "Where the contract for sale involves repeated occasions for performance by either party with knowledge of the nature of the performance and opportunity for objection to it by the other, any course of performance accepted or acquiesced in without objection shall be relevant to determine the meaning of the agreement." Course of performance involves situations where more than one performance is contemplated by the contract.

Consider, for example, a contract that required the buyer to pay for sand at a certain price per ton, "truck measure." In determining the meaning of the phrase "truck measure," the court noted the seller's practice,

BOX 19-1 ISSUES AND TRENDS
Terms in an Incomplete Contract Will Be Supplied

Larry and Ralph are having lunch at a restaurant. Larry is a salesman and his company supplies Ralph's store with sunglasses. Over lunch they agreed that Ralph needed 200 pairs of sunglasses from Larry's company. The terms of the agreement such as price, time of shipment, and place of shipment were not agreed upon at that time. In order to have some written proof of the agreement, Ralph wrote on a napkin, "I order 200 pairs of sunglasses (signed) Ralph." Ralph gave the napkin to Larry.

Prior to the adoption of the Uniform Commercial Code (UCC) such a contract would have been unenforceable because of indefiniteness. The drafters of the UCC wrote the Code so that any contract would be upheld so long as there was an intent to contract. If the parties intended to contract, the UCC will assist the parties by filling in the omitted terms. The only term the UCC will not supply is the quantity term.

after entering into the contract, of determining the quantity delivered by referring to the capacity of the truck in which the sand was delivered. The buyer never objected to this practice of the seller. Thus, the behavior of the seller and the buyer *after* entering into the contract was examined in order to determine the meaning of the phrase "truck measure."

Course of Dealing. "A course of dealing is a sequence of previous conduct between the parties to a particular transaction which is fairly to be regarded as establishing a common basis of understanding for interpreting those expressions and other conduct" (Section 1–205[1]).

For example, in the past a seller may have permitted the buyer to take 5 percent off the invoice price if the buyer paid within thirty days of the billing date. By permitting the buyer to take a 5 percent discount, the seller over a period of time has created a course of dealing between the parties that would be relevant in determining whether the buyer could take a 5 percent discount in the future

for paying within thirty days of the billing date.

Course of performance relates to conduct *after* the execution of an agreement, whereas course of dealing relates to conduct between the parties *prior* to the execution of an agreement. Because the conduct that is material to a course of dealing occurs prior to the execution of an agreement, course of dealing cannot be used to modify or waive a written contract.

Usage of Trade. Section 1–205(2) states:

(2) A usage of trade is any practice or method of dealing having such regularity of observance in a place, vocation or trade as to justify an expectation that it will be observed with respect to the transaction in question. The existence and scope of such a usage are to be proved as facts. If it is established that such a usage is embodied in a written trade code or similar writing the interpretation of the writing is for the court.

Usage of trade is not the same as custom because the practice or method of dealing may be of recent origin or may be followed only in a particular part of the country. It simply must be observed with such regularity "as to justify an expectation that it will be observed with respect to the transaction in question." Like course of dealing, usage of trade can be used to give meaning to the particular language selected by the parties in their contract.

An oil company agreed to sell asphalt to a paving contractor, with the price specified as "Oil Company's posted price at time of delivery." At a later time the oil company raised its price for asphalt. The contractor contended that a usage of trade existed in the industry that sellers must deliver all asphalt at the preincrease prices if the contractor already had sold the asphalt to a third party. According to the contractor, the price increase, by trade custom, should apply only to future sales made by the contractor. This custom in the industry is a usage of trade that should be taken into consideration in determining the price the oil company could charge for its asphalt. The oil company should not be able to raise the price for asphalt delivered to the contractor that the contractor had already sold to a third party.

Filling in Terms. The UCC sets up a system to fill in the missing terms in an agreement between parties. Where a term is fully expressed in writing or by a valid oral statement, this term will control the agreement unless it conflicts with a mandatory provision of the UCC. In the absence of a particular term in a written agreement, the court will fill it in by first looking to course of performance, then to course of dealing, and finally to usage of trade to supply the missing information. If none of these enables the court to fill in a missing term, the court will examine the statutory terms in Part 3 of Article 2 of the UCC to fill in the missing information. If the UCC does not specify the term to be filled in, then the contract is enforced even though the court is unable to fill in the missing term—as long as

the contract indicates that the parties intended to be bound and there is a reasonably certain basis for giving an appropriate remedy.

ACCEPTANCE

Method of Acceptance

Several important changes from the common law rules of offer and acceptance appear in the UCC. For example, the authors of the UCC adopted subsection 2–206(1) to make it easier for offerees to determine in what manner they must accept an offer when they feel that the offer itself does not make clear how it must be accepted. The Code provides that "unless otherwise unambiguously indicated by the language or circumstances, . . . an offer to make a contract shall be construed as inviting acceptance in any manner and by any medium reasonable in the circumstances." For example, one might, when faced with an offer made by telegram, accept by mail unless the circumstances warranted a more immediate reply. If the offeror has specified a particular mode of acceptance, however, even under the UCC the offeree must accept in that manner.

Shipment. Subsection (b) of Section 2–206(1) permits a seller to accept an order or offer to buy goods "either by a prompt promise to ship or by the prompt or current shipment of conforming or nonconforming goods." This in effect allows for both bilateral and unilateral contracts. If the seller chooses to accept the offer by the prompt shipment of goods, an acceptance occurs whether conforming or nonconforming goods are shipped. This means the seller no longer can argue when the buyer receives nonconforming goods that there has been no acceptance of the offer, and therefore no breach of contract, because nonconforming goods were shipped in response to the buyer's order. When there has been a shipment of nonconforming goods in response to an order, there is both an acceptance of the offer and a breach of contract.

Accommodating Shipment. Of course, situations may arise where the seller is unable to supply the exact item ordered by the buyer but is in the position to ship something very similar and perhaps equally acceptable to the buyer. If the seller wishes to ship the goods to the buyer on the condition that the buyer may return them if he does not want them, the seller may ship nonconforming goods to accommodate a buyer. Section 2–206(1)(b) provides that "such a shipment of nonconforming goods does not constitute an acceptance if the seller seasonably notifies the buyer that the shipment is offered only as an accommodation to the buyer." If the buyer finds the goods unacceptable, he may return them, but the accommodating shipment will *not* be treated as a breach of contract.

Beginning Performance. It is also possible under the UCC to accept an offer by beginning performance. The offeree, rather than responding to an offer with an acceptance, might choose to perform the requested act. The UCC recognizes this as a method of acceptance where it is "a reasonable mode of acceptance," but it places an important limitation on the offeree's power to accept in this manner: "an offeror who is not notified of acceptance within a reasonable time may treat the offer as having lapsed before acceptance." The silence of the offeree will not be treated as an acceptance. Where the offeror in New York offers to purchase lawn mowers from a company in Los Angeles, the company in Los Angeles may begin to produce the mowers, but it must also notify the New York purchaser of its acceptance. If it fails to do so, the New York company may treat the offer as having been rejected. The Los Angeles company has only a reasonable time from the time it commences performance to notify the buyer of the acceptance. If the offeror doesn't hear from the offeree within a reasonable time, he may safely make other arrangements to obtain the lawn mowers without fear of being held to the contract.

Form of Acceptance

The common law requirement that the acceptance be a mirror image of the offer and the resulting "battle-of-forms" problem were discussed in Chapter 10. The explanation of the UCC modification of the common law rule in Section 2–207 that is supplied in Chapter 10 should be reviewed at this point.

TITLE

Modified Concept of Title

The UCC de-emphasizes the concept of title. Under prior law, title had been used as a basic determinant of other legal rights and interests, including unallocated risk of loss, security, and insurability. Thus, before these other rights could be determined, the title to the goods had to be established. This was a very indirect way of approaching the real question of who, for example, should bear the risk of any loss of the goods. The policy implications of who most appropriately should bear the risk of loss were difficult to consider. Everything was determined by the possession of title, which not only assigned risk of loss but several other important rights as well.

The UCC now has separate sections dealing with rights related to risk of loss, insurable interests, and security interests. All matters as to the rights and obligations of the parties to a contract apply irrespective of title to the goods except where a provision of the UCC specifically refers to the question of title.

Section 2–401 determines when the buyer obtains title to goods covered by a contract. Title may not pass prior to identification of the goods. When the goods are identified to the contract, the buyer acquires certain rights in them, called a special property interest in the goods. Identification means that specific goods are somehow identified (by a mark or by being set aside or described) as the object of the particular transaction. For example, a buyer agrees to purchase a color TV. When a seller selects a particular TV in the warehouse as the one that the buyer is to get, that TV becomes identified in the contract. In a sense, prior to identification of specific goods, there is nothing on which a title can be passed.

Generally, the parties are free to arrange by explicit agreement for the transfer of title to existing goods in any manner and on any conditions. If the parties fail to specify when title is to pass, it passes at the time and place when the seller has delivered the goods. The point at which the seller has completed his obligations as to delivery is discussed in the following material.

Origin Contract. If the seller intends to send the goods to the buyer, but the contract does not require the seller to deliver the goods to a destination, title to the goods passes to the buyer at the time and place of shipment. This is called an *origin contract.* It operates as follows: Suppose a buyer in Oklahoma City wishes to purchase a lawn mower from a seller in Chicago. The seller's only obligation under the contract is to put the mower on board a truck in Chicago bound for Oklahoma City. Title to the mower remains in the seller only until he or she delivers the goods to the trucking company.

Destination Contract. If the seller is obligated under the contract actually to deliver the goods to the buyer, the title to the goods does not pass to the buyer until they are tendered to the buyer at the destination specified in the contract. This is called a *destination contract.* In the example in the last paragraph, suppose the contract required the seller to ac-

tually deliver the lawn mower to the buyer in Oklahoma City, as opposed to merely delivering it to the trucking company in Chicago. In this situation, title to the mower remains in the seller until he tenders it to the buyer. This means that if the goods arrive in Oklahoma City, and the shipper, at a reasonable time, offers to deliver the mower to the buyer's place of business, a tender has been made and title passes to the buyer—whether or not the buyer actually takes delivery of the goods.

The comments on Section 2–503 make it clear that the seller is not obligated to deliver to a named destination unless he or she has specifically agreed to such a delivery. In other words, there is a presumption that the parties intended an origin, not a destination, contract. Unless the contract calls for the seller to deliver goods at a particular destination, his or her only obligation will be to deliver them to a carrier.

Documents of Title. If delivery is to be made without moving the goods, two other rules control, as set forth in subsection 2–401(3). If the seller is to deliver a document of title (explained in the introduction to commercial paper), title passes at the time and place the seller delivers the document. Suppose the lawn mower in the earlier example has been stored in a public warehouse. When the seller left the goods, the warehouseman gave the seller a document of title called a warehouse receipt. If the receipt is negotiable, anyone in possession of the receipt has the power to receive the goods from the warehouseman. This means that if the contract that is signed by the buyer and seller specifies that a delivery will take place without moving the goods from the warehouse, whenever the seller gives the buyer the negotiable warehouse receipt, title to the mower passes to the buyer.

No Documents. If the goods are already identified to the contract (the seller has specified certain goods will be given to the buyer) and no documents are to be delivered, then title to the goods passes at the time and place of contracting. In the earlier example, suppose the seller had the mower in his or her own plant. The seller intended for the buyer to pick up the mower at the seller's plant. He or she identified a certain mower as the buyer's prior to signing the contract. In this situation, title to the mower passes to the buyer at the time of contracting.

When a seller sells goods to a buyer, the seller may not retain title to the goods. Any attempt to retain title in the contract of sale will be construed by the court as a mere reservation of a security interest in the goods.

Transfer of Title to Third Persons

Section 2–401 determines when the buyer receives title to goods from the seller. Once the buyer receives goods, he or she may choose to convey them to a third party. Section 2–403 determines the title of the third person who receives goods from the original buyer.

If the buyer receives title to the goods pursuant to Section 2–401, he or she has the power to transfer the good title to goods to a third person. But what if the buyer, for example, gives the seller a bad check—does the buyer have the power to transfer good title to a third person? Section 2–403 answers this question.

Void Title. Section 2–403 gives a purchaser all title that his or her transferor had or had power to transfer. Suppose a person steals goods from someone, and the thief sells the goods to an innocent third party who knows nothing of the theft. The third party in this situation acquires a *void title*; that is, if the original owner demands the goods back from him or her, the third party must surrender the goods. The thief had no title to the goods, nor did he or she have any power to transfer title to the goods to anyone else. Figure 19-1 illustrates how a void title operates.

Voidable Title. Certain persons acquire a mere *voidable title*. As between the original owner and the buyer with a mere voidable title, the owner may reclaim his or her goods. Suppose Mary gave Alice a bad check in return for Alice's dress. As long as Mary had the dress, Alice could get it back from Mary be-

FIGURE 19–1
Void Title. In this situation the third party must return the goods to the owner.

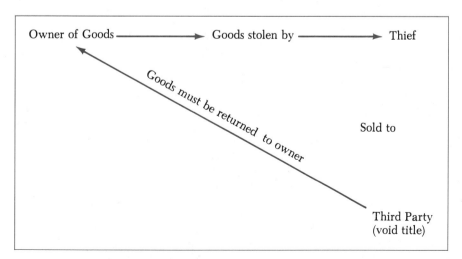

cause Mary had acquired a mere voidable title by giving a bad check.

However, if the buyer with voidable title transfers the goods to a third person, in certain instances the third person may retain possession of the goods even as against the original owner. The third person must establish several things in order to keep the goods. This person must prove that he or she was a good-faith purchaser for value. Essentially, the third person must establish that he or she acquired the goods by paying a reasonable price and that, in doing so, the person acted in good faith. Assuming the third person establishes that he or she is a good-faith purchaser for value, he or she also must establish that the person from whom the third party acquired the goods had a voidable title. Figure 19-2 illustrates how a voidable title operates.

The UCC sets out several transactions that give rise to a voidable title. If a case does not fit in one of these four transactions, the court must refer to the cases and statutes to determine whether the third person's title is voidable. The four transactions giving rise to a voidable title are:

1. When the transferor of the goods was deceived as to the identity of the purchaser
2. When the purchaser acquired the goods by giving a check that is later dishonored
3. When the transaction was one in which title was not to pass until the seller was paid
4. When the goods were procured through criminal fraud

This provision works as follows. Suppose Alfred is in the business of selling typewriters. Sam robs Alfred and takes a typewriter. Sam sells this typewriter to Alice. Alice acquires a void title. Alfred may reclaim the typewriter from Alice even if she took the typewriter in good faith, without any knowledge of the theft, and paid a reasonable price for the typewriter.

Let's change these facts somewhat so that Sam gives Alfred a check that later bounces. He sells the typewriter to Alice, who purchases it for a reasonable price and is unaware of the bad check. Alfred now demands the typewriter back from Alice. May Alice keep the typewriter? Yes, she acquired the typewriter from a person with a *voidable* title,

FIGURE 19–2
Voidable Title. In this situation the third party does not have to return
the goods to the original owner.

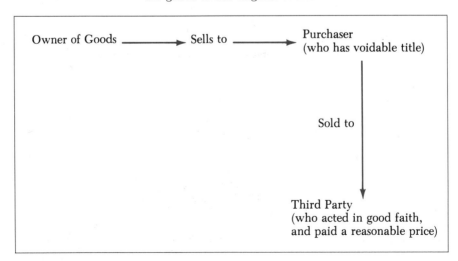

Sam. Sam acquired a voidable title because he gave Alfred a check that subsequently bounced. As between Alfred and Sam, as long as Sam kept the typewriter, Alfred was able to get it back from Sam. Once Sam transferred the typewriter to Alice, a good-faith purchaser for value, Alfred lost his right to reacquire the typewriter. The same result would occur if Sam deceives Alfred as to his identity, or if Sam agrees to pay cash for the typewriter at some later date, or if Sam acquires the typewriter through criminal fraud. If Sam acquires a voidable title by any of these devices, or any other transfer recognized as voidable by state law, Sam has the power to transfer a title good against the original seller to a good-faith purchaser for value.

Purchases from Someone with Good Title. The UCC protects anyone who purchases from a person who acquires a good title. In the case noted earlier, suppose Sam gives a check to Alfred that subsequently bounces, and Sam resells the goods to Alice, a good-faith purchaser for value. Alice now has the power to transfer all title she has. As she has a title good against even Alfred, she can transfer a good title to Linda—even if Linda knows that Sam acquired the goods from Alfred by passing a bad check! Linda cannot qualify as a good-faith purchaser, but she still acquires a good title since she takes it through Alice.

Entrustment. It is also possible for a merchant who deals in goods of the kind entrusted to him or her to transfer all title of the entruster to a buyer in the ordinary course of business. *Entrustment* is broadly defined as "any delivery and any acquiescence in retention of possession" and is covered in subsections 2–403(2) and (3).

Such a transfer might occur when a jeweler accidentally mixes a watch left with him for repair with his regular stock and sells it to a customer by mistake. Another situation in which this applies is when a manufacturer sells goods to a retailer. If the manufacturer attempts to take a security interest in the goods held by the retailer for resale, this does not prevent the retailer from cutting off the manufacturer's security interest by selling the goods to a customer. The buyer acquires a clear title if he or she qualifies as a buyer in the ordinary course of business.

To obtain a title superior to that of the previous owner of the goods, the buyer must establish several facts. The goods must have been entrusted to a merchant regularly dealing in goods of that kind. In the case of the jeweler, the jeweler regularly deals in watches so he qualifies as a merchant. (Note that the definition of merchant here is narrower than under Section 2–104.) The jeweler has the power to transfer all rights of the entruster to a buyer in the ordinary course of business. A buyer in the ordinary course of business is a person who, in good faith and without knowledge that the sale to him or her is in violation of the ownership rights or security interest of a third party, buys in ordinary course from a person in the business of selling goods of this kind. Whether a person is a buyer in the ordinary course depends on the facts and circumstances of the case. In the case of the jeweler who mixes the watch with his other stock, the jeweler has the power to transfer good title to a person who purchases the watch from him. See Figure 19-3.

RISK OF LOSS

The UCC creates several methods for allocating the risk of loss between the parties:

1. By express agreement
2. By the use of mercantile terms
3. By Sections 2–509 and 2–510
4. By Section 2–326

FIGURE 19–3

Entrustment. In this situation the third party may keep the goods because the owner entrusted the painting to a merchant who dealt in goods of this kind (paintings) and the buyer is a buyer in the ordinary course of business.

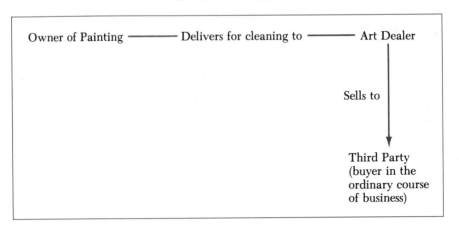

Table 19-1 illustrates who bears the risk of loss in various situations.

Terms

When contracting, merchants frequently use mercantile terms or symbols as abbreviated methods of stating the delivery duties of the seller. The UCC defines these mercantile terms in Sections 2–319 to 2–325. Unless the parties to a contract specify another meaning, the UCC definitions of these terms control.

FOB. The terms FOB (free on board a carrier, typically a truck or train) and FAS (free alongside a ship) are defined in Section 2–319. Where the contract states "FOB St. Louis" and the seller is in St. Louis, then by Section 2–319(1)(a) the seller has the expense and risk of putting the goods into the possession of a carrier and shipping the goods in accordance with the provisions of Section 2–504. This is a shipment or *origin contract.* This section requires the seller, unless otherwise agreed:

1. To put the goods in the possession of the carrier

2. To make a proper contract for transportation of the goods (e.g., meat must be refrigerated)

3. To obtain and deliver or tender to the buyer any documents necessary for the buyer to obtain possession of the goods

4. To promptly notify the buyer of the shipment

If the contract states "FOB New York" and the seller is in St. Louis and the buyer in New York, then the seller pays the freight and bears the risk of loss under Section 2–319(1)(b). This is a *destination contract.* The seller must at his or her own risk and expense transport the goods to New York and tender them to the buyer in New York. Section 2–503 requires the seller to put and hold conforming goods at the buyer's disposition and to give the buyer reasonable notification in order to enable him or her to take delivery. The tender must be at a reasonable hour and the goods must be available for a reasonable period of time.

Presumption of Origin Contract. Through an examination of the contract and the sur-

TABLE 19-1 RISK OF LOSS

Terms of Agreement	Who Bears the Loss
Written agreement	Dependent on the terms of the agreement
Terms:	
FOB Origin	On buyer when goods delivered to the carrier
FOB Destination	On buyer when goods tendered to buyer at destination
No agreement/No breach of contract 2–509	
Ship by carrier Destination contract	On buyer when goods tendered to buyer
Ship by carrier Origin contract	On buyer when goods delivered to carrier
Goods held by bailee Negotiable document of title	When buyer receives documents
Goods held by bailee Nonnegotiable document of title	When bailee acknowledges right of buyer to the goods
All other cases if merchant seller	When the goods are delivered to the buyer
All other cases if nonmerchant seller	When the goods are tendered to the buyer
No agreement/breach of contract 2–510	
Breach by seller Buyer rejects	Risk is on seller until buyer accepts
Breach by seller Buyer revokes	Risk is on seller to the extent of any deficiency in buyer's insurance
Breach by buyer	Risk is on buyer to the extent of any deficiency in seller's insurance
Sale on approval 2–326	Risk on seller until the buyer accepts the goods
Sale or return 2–236	Buyer must return goods at buyer's risk

rounding circumstances, it generally will be possible to determine whether the seller must send the goods to the buyer and whether the parties contemplated an origin or a destination contract. If the contract fails to cover this point clearly, the presumption is that the parties intended an origin contract. Suppose a contract read as follows: "Ship to ABC Corp., 1321 Redbud Lane, Mobile, Alabama." The seller's business is in Houston, Texas, and the buyer is located in Mobile. The mere fact that the label indicates where the package is to be shipped does not overcome the presumption that this is an origin contract. However, the statement "FOB ABC Corp., 1321 Redbud Lane, Mobile, Alabama" creates a destination contract. The

seller must at its own risk and expense transport the goods to Mobile and tender them to the buyer in Mobile.

If the contract specifies "FOB vessel *St. Louis*" or "FOB car or other vehicle," the seller must, in addition to bearing the expense and risk of transportation, load the goods on board.

CIF. The term CIF stands for the words cost, insurance, and freight. When this term is used, it means that the price includes the cost of the goods, the cost of insuring the goods, and freight to a named destination. The seller must at his or her own expense put the goods into the possession of a carrier at the port for shipment and obtain a negotiable bill of lading covering the entire transportation to the named destination.

C & F. According to Section 2–320(1 and 3), when a contract includes the term C & F, the price includes cost and freight to the named destination. The seller need not obtain insurance under a C & F term. The term has the same effect and imposes upon the seller the same obligations and risks as a CIF term, except for the obligation to insure. The risk of loss under CIF or C & F is on the buyer once the seller has delivered the goods to the carrier.

Ex-Ship. In a sale "ex-ship" (which means from the carrying vessel) the seller must cause the goods to be delivered to the buyer from a ship that has arrived at the port of delivery. The seller must pay freight to the named port, release the ship owner's lien, and furnish the buyer with a direction that puts the ship under a duty to deliver the goods. The risk of loss does not pass until the goods are properly unloaded from the ship.

No Arrival, No Sale. The term "no arrival, no sale" is used when the parties execute a destination contract by which the risk of loss remains on the seller during shipment. Under this term, however, the seller is not liable for breach of contract if the goods are not delivered through no fault of the seller. The parties may arrive at a different understanding, but the seller is free of liability if goods conforming to the contract fail to arrive due to the hazards of transportation. If the seller fails to ship the goods or if he ships nonconforming goods, Section 2–324 does not relieve the seller of liability.

Risk of Loss in the Absence of Terms

The Uniform Sales Act, which governed the law of sales prior to the adoption of the UCC, forced the courts to struggle with the question of who held title to the goods in order to determine which party bore the risk of loss. The UCC greatly simplifies the determination of who bears the risk of loss by treating risk of loss separately from the issue of title.

Voluntary Agreement. In general the UCC reflects the philosophy that the parties may determine the details of a contract. The parties may arrive at an agreement on risk of loss contrary to that specified in the UCC. The agreement may shift the allocation of risk of loss, or it may divide the risk between the parties. The only restraints on the modification of the risk-of-loss provisions in the UCC are that such modifications be made in good faith and are not unconscionable.

If a seller intends to shift the risk of loss to the buyer, the contract must clearly state the manner in which risk of loss will be allocated. This is especially true when the seller tries to shift the risk of loss to the buyer before he or she takes possession of the goods. In Hayward v. Postma, 188 N.W.2d 31 (1971), the seller argued that the risk of loss for a 30-foot Revel Craft Playmate Yacht worth $10,000 that was destroyed by fire while it was still at the seller's premises should fall on the buyer. Neither the seller nor the buyer had an insurance policy covering the boat. The seller claimed that he had transferred the risk of loss to the buyer by a clause in the security agreement signed by the parties. (See Chapter 28 for an explanation of security agreements.) The court acknowledged that a risk of loss could be transferred to the buyer in this fashion, but it observed that the agreement in this case was not sufficiently clear and prominent to apprise the buyer that he bore the risk of loss on the yacht. The court noted that the usual rule in such cases was for the risk of loss to fall on the merchant-seller unless he or she had physically delivered the goods to the buyer. The rationale for this rule was that the buyer had no control over the goods and that it would be extremely unlikely that the buyer would carry insurance on goods not yet in his possession. The seller might transfer this risk to the buyer only if he or she clearly brought this matter to the buyer's attention.

Risk of loss may be specifically allocated by a clause in a contract, or the parties may allocate risk of loss through the use of a mercantile term such as FOB as discussed earlier in this chapter.

No Agreement. If the contract between the buyer and the seller fails to specify how risk of loss will be allocated between the parties, Section 2–509 controls if there is a loss but no breach of contract. Section 2–510 applies if there has been a loss and a breach of contract.

The policy underlying these provisions is to place the loss on the party most likely to have insured against the loss. The person in possession of the goods normally is able to prevent a loss from occurring in the first place. For this reason the risk of loss usually falls on the party in possession of the goods.

Section 2–509 divides risk of loss into three categories: (1) goods shipped by carrier, (2) goods held by a bailee that are to be delivered without being moved, and (3) all other cases.

Identification. Risk of loss cannot pass to the buyer until the goods are identified to the contract. Section 2–501 states that, in the absence of a contrary agreement, identification occurs: when the contract is made if the goods are existing and identified; or if the goods are future goods, when the goods are shipped, marked, or otherwise designated by the seller as goods to which the contract refers.

Shipment by Carrier. When the parties enter into an origin contract and agree to delivery by carrier, risk of loss shifts to the buyer when the seller puts the goods in the possession of a carrier, makes a reasonable contract for their transportation, obtains all documents necessary for the buyer to obtain possession of the goods, and notifies the buyer of the shipment.

If a destination contract is involved, whereby the seller agrees to ship the goods to the buyer by carrier, risk passes to the buyer when the seller has put and held conforming goods at the buyer's disposition at the destination point and given the buyer any notification and documents reasonably necessary to take delivery of the goods.

Suppose a paint manufacturer sells 500 cans of paint to a retail paint store. If the parties agree for the seller to ship the goods to the buyer's store at 1011 Main, Oklahoma City, and the goods are lost in transit after the seller loads them on a common carrier (e.g., a railroad, truck, or airline), who bears the risk of loss? It must first be determined if the parties entered into an origin contract or a destination contract. Bear in mind that the UCC views an origin contract as the typical contract. The seller does not bear the risk of loss after placing the goods on the carrier unless he has specifically agreed to bear the risk of loss to the destination point. In this case the courts probably would treat the agreement as an origin contract and place the risk of loss on the buyer. The term "ship to," attached to the goods with an address, has no significance in determining who bears the risk of loss. On the other hand, language such as "FOB buyer's plant" or "Ship to buyer, risk of loss remains on seller until tender by carrier to buyer" clearly contemplates a destination contract, and the risk does not pass to the buyer until the goods are tendered to the buyer at the place of destination.

The risk of loss will not pass unless the seller makes a proper contract for transportation and ships conforming goods.

Goods Held by a Bailee. If the goods are not to be shipped by carrier but are in possession of a bailee and are to be delivered without being moved, Section 2–509(2) controls. If the bailee has issued a negotiable document of title, the risk of loss passes to the buyer when he or she receives the negotiable document of title. Risk of loss also passes to the buyer after his or her receipt of a nonnegotiable document of title, but not until the buyer has had a reasonable opportunity to present the document to the bailee. If the bailee refuses to honor the nonnegotiable document of title, risk of loss does not pass. If a nonnegotiable document of title has been issued, risk of loss passes to the buyer when the bailee acknowledges the buyer's right to the possession of the goods.

The following case discusses how risk of loss operates when goods are stored in a warehouse.

Jason's Foods, Inc. v. Peter Eckrich & Sons, Inc.

U.S. Court of Appeals, Seventh Circuit

41 UCC Rep. Serv. 1287 (1985)

Background: Jason's (plaintiff) sued Eckrich (defendant). Around December 20, 1982, Jason's Foods contracted to sell 38,000 pounds of "St. Louis style" pork ribs to Peter Eckrich & Sons, delivery to be effected by a transfer of the ribs from Jason's account in an independent warehouse to Eckrich's account in the same warehouse—a transfer on paper. Jason's notified Eckrich that the transfer would be made between January 10 and January 14, 1983. On January 13 Jason's phoned the warehouse and requested that the ribs be transferred to Eckrich's account. A clerk at the warehouse noted the transfer on its books immediately but did not mail a warehouse receipt to Eckrich until January 17 or 18, and it was not until January 24 when Eckrich received the receipt that it knew the transfer had taken place.

In the meantime, on January 17 there was a fire at the warehouse and the ribs were destroyed. Jason's sued Eckrich for the price of the ribs.

Decision: The court decided that as there had been no acknowledgment by the bailee to Eckrich, the buyer, of Eckrich's right to the ribs, risk of loss had not passed to the buyer at the time of the fire, and therefore it remained on Jason's.

Posner, Circuit Judge

Section 2–509(2) of the Uniform Commercial Code provides that where the "goods are held by a bailee to be delivered without being moved, the risk of loss passes to the buyer . . . (b) on acknowledgment by the bailee of the buyer's right to possession of the goods." We must decide whether acknowledgment to the *seller* complies with the statute.

Jason's argues that when the warehouse transferred the ribs to Eckrich's account, Jason's lost all rights over the ribs, and it should not bear the risk of loss of goods it did not own or have any right to control.

. . . Section 2–509(2) separates title from risk of loss. Title to the ribs passed to Eckrich when the warehouse made the transfer on its books from Jason's account to Eckrich's, but the risk of loss did not pass until the transfer was "acknowledged."

. . . Since whoever will be liable for the loss can insure against it, the court must determine who is liable before knowing who can insure, rather than vice versa. If acknowledgment to the seller is enough to place the risk of loss on the buyer, then Eckrich should have bought insurance against any losses that occurred afterward. If acknowledgment to the buyer is necessary (we need not decide whether acknowledgment to a third party may ever suffice), Jason's should have bought insurance against any losses occurring until then.

. . .

A related section of the Uniform Commercial Code, § 2–503(4)(a), makes acknowledgment by the bailee (the warehouse here) a method of tendering goods that are sold without being physically moved; but, like § 2–509(2)(b), it does not indicate to whom acknowledgment must be made. . . . Rules on tender have, it is true, a different function from rules on risk of loss; they determine at what point the seller has completed the performance of his side of the bargain. He may have completed performance, but if the goods are still in transit the risk of loss does not shift until the buyer receives them, if the seller is a merchant. In the case of warehouse transfers, however, the draftsmen apparently wanted risk of loss to conform to the rules for tender. And those provisions apparently require (in the case where no document of title passes) acknowledgment to the buyer. Jason's could have instructed the warehouse to call Eckrich when the transfer was complete on the warehouse books.

. . . If one party is in a better position than the other to prevent a loss, this is a reason for placing the risk of loss on him, to give him an incentive to prevent it. It would be a reason for placing liability on a seller who still had possession of the goods, even though title had passed. But between the moment of transfer of title by Jason's and the moment of receipt of the warehouse receipt by Eckrich, neither party to the sale had effective control over the ribs.

When did the risk of loss pass? Does "acknowledgment" mean receipt, as in the surrounding subsections of § 2–509(2), or mailing? Since the evidence was in conflict over whether the acknowledgment was mailed on January 17 (and at what hour), which was the day of the fire, or on January 18, this could be an important question—but in another case. Jason's waived it. The only theory it tendered to the district court, or briefed and argued in this court, was that the risk of loss passed either on January 13, when the transfer of title was made on the books of the warehouse, or at the latest on January 14, because Eckrich knew the ribs would be transferred at the warehouse sometime between January 10 and 14. We have discussed the immateriality of the passage of title on January 13; we add that the alternative argument, that Eckrich knew by January 14 that it owned the ribs, exaggerates what Eckrich knew. By the close of business on January 14 Eckrich had a well-founded expectation that the ribs had been transferred to its account; but considering the many slips that are possible between cup and lips, we do not think that this expectation should fix the point at which the risk shifts.

Other Cases. All other cases *not* involving a breach of contract are covered by Section 2–509(3). This section covers the situation where the seller intends to deliver the goods to the buyer in the seller's truck or the buyer intends to pick up the goods at the seller's place of business. Subsection (3) sets out two rules, one of which covers a merchant-seller and the other applies to a nonmerchant-seller. In the case of the merchant-seller, risk of loss remains on the seller until the buyer actually takes physical possession of the goods. If the seller is not a merchant, risk of loss passes to the buyer on tender of delivery. Tender means putting and holding conforming goods at the buyer's disposition and giving the buyer any notification reasonably necessary to enable him to take delivery. The tender must be at a reasonable hour and kept available long enough for the buyer to take possession.

Suppose Acme Glass agrees to sell fifteen panels of glass to a building contractor. Nothing is said about who bears the risk of loss in the contract. If the glass is destroyed prior to the time the contractor picks up the glass, who bears the risk of loss? As Acme Glass deals in goods of this kind, it is a merchant under Section 2–104. Acme must actually deliver physical possession of the glass to the contractor. The risk of loss is on Acme.

But suppose Elmo sells fifteen panels of glass to his next-door neighbor and tenders them to his neighbor. The neighbor fails to pick up the glass, and after a week passes a fire destroys Elmo's home and the glass. Who bears the risk of loss? Because Elmo is not a merchant, and he tendered the glass to his neighbor, the risk of loss falls on his neighbor.

Note that a merchant-seller who retains physical possession of goods after selling them retains the risk of loss. This is true even after title has passed and the seller has received his or her money for the goods, as is illustrated by the following case.

Martin v. Melland's Inc.

Supreme Court of North Dakota

283 N.W.2d 76 (1979)

Background: Israel Martin (plaintiff) purchased a haymoving machine from Melland's (defendant). Martin traded in his old haystack mover on the new one, but he retained possession of it. The old haystack mover was destroyed while in Martin's possession. Decision: The court affirmed a decision for Melland's.

Erickstad, Chief Justice

The narrow issue on this appeal is who should bear the loss of a truck and an attached haystack mover that was destroyed by fire while in the possession of the plaintiff, Israel Martin (Martin), but after the certificate of title had been delivered to the defendant, Melland's Inc. (Melland's). The destroyed haymoving unit was to be used as a trade-in for a new haymoving unit that Martin ultimately purchased from Melland's.

On June 11, 1974, Martin entered into a written agreement with Melland's, a farm implement dealer, to purchase a truck and attached haystack mover for the total purchase price of $35,389. Martin was given a trade-in allowance of $17,389 on his old unit, leaving a balance owing of $18,000 plus sales tax of $720 or a total balance of $18,720. The agreement provided that Martin "mail or bring title" to the old unit to Melland's "this week." Martin mailed the certificate of title to Melland's pursuant to the agreement, but he was allowed to retain the use and possession of the old unit "until they had the new one ready."

Fire destroyed the truck and the haymoving unit in early August, 1974, while Martin was moving hay. The parties did not have any agreement regarding insurance or risk of loss on the unit.

The district court found "that although the Plaintiff [Martin] executed the title to the . . . [haymoving unit], he did not relinquish possession of the same and therefore the Plaintiff was the owner of said truck at the time the fire occurred."

The position that the Code has taken, divorcing the question of risk of loss from a determination of title, is summed up by Professor Nordstrom in his hornbook on sales:

> No longer is the question of title of any importance in determining whether a buyer or a seller bears the risk of loss. It is true that the person with title will also (and incidentally) often bear the risk that the goods may be destroyed or lost; but the seller may have title and the buyer the risk, or the seller may have the risk and the buyer the title. In short, title is not a relevant consideration in deciding whether the risk has shifted to the buyer. R. Nordstrom, Handbook of the Law of Sales, 393 (1970).

It is clear that a barter or trade-in is considered a sale and is therefore subject to the Uniform Commercial Code. It is also clear that the party who owns the trade-in is considered the seller. Subsection 3 of Section 2–509 is applicable in this case.

Martin admits that he is not a merchant; therefore, it is necessary to determine if Martin tendered delivery of the trade-in unit to Melland's. Tender is defined in Section 2–503 UCC, as follows:

> (2–503) Manner of seller's tender of delivery.—
> 1. Tender of delivery requires that the seller put and hold conforming goods at the buyer's disposition and give the buyer any notification reasonably necessary to enable him to take delivery. The manner, time and place for tender are determined by the agreement and this chapter, and in particular
>   a. tender must be at a reasonable hour, and if it is of goods they must be kept available for the period reasonably necessary to enable the buyer to take possession; but
>   b. unless otherwise agreed the buyer must furnish facilities reasonably suited to the receipt of the goods.

It is clear that the trade-in unit was not tendered to Melland's in this case. The parties agreed that Martin would keep the old unit "until they had the new one ready."

We hold that Martin did not tender delivery of the trade-in truck and haystack mover to Melland's pursuant to Section 2–509 UCC; consequently, Martin must bear the loss.

Risk of Loss When Contract Is Breached

Section 2–510 addresses the problem of risk of loss when there has been a breach of contract by either the seller or the buyer. If for any reason the goods delivered by the seller fail to live up to the requirements of the contract, the risk of loss does not pass to the buyer.

Breach by Seller—Buyer Rejects. Section 2–510(1) covers the situation where the seller tenders or delivers goods that do not conform to the contract under circumstances that give the buyer the right to reject (refuse to accept) the goods. In this case the risk of loss remains on the seller until the buyer accepts the goods or the seller replaces the nonconforming goods with conforming goods (referred to as a "cure" by the seller).

Suppose a seller ships paper goods to the buyer. Because the goods fail to meet the standards set forth in the contract, the buyer rejects the goods. The buyer holds the goods, and while in his possession they are destroyed by fire. In this case, the seller bears the risk of loss. What if the buyer accepts the paper in spite of its nonconformity? The risk of loss is then on the buyer. Likewise, if the seller takes back the nonconforming paper and substitutes conforming paper, and then the paper is destroyed, the risk of loss is on the buyer since the seller has "cured" his or her defective performance.

Breach by Seller-Buyer Revokes. Section 2–510(2) sets forth the buyer's rights when he or she revokes an acceptance. When the buyer rightfully revokes an acceptance, the risk of loss is treated as having remained on the seller from the beginning, to the extent of any deficiency in the buyer's insurance.

Suppose a seller ships groceries, which the buyer accepts. Thereafter, the buyer finds some defect in the groceries that gives him or her grounds to revoke the acceptance. When the buyer revokes his or her acceptance, the risk of loss is treated as having been on the seller from the beginning. If the goods are destroyed while in the buyer's possession, after the buyer's revocation, the loss falls on the seller entirely if the buyer has no insurance. What if the buyer has $500 worth of insurance, but the fire destroys $2,000 worth of groceries? Five hundred dollars of the loss falls on the buyer's insurance company, and the other $1,500 falls on the seller. We are assuming in these examples that the goods are destroyed through no fault of the buyer or the seller—in a fire, for example.

Breach by Buyer. The final subsection of 2–510 puts the risk of loss on the buyer when he or she breaches the contract before the risk of loss passes to the buyer. In this case the seller may, to the extent of any deficiency in his or her insurance coverage, treat the risk of loss as resting on the buyer for a commercially reasonable time. The seller must meet several conditions to put the loss on the buyer:

1. The seller must have had conforming goods.
2. The goods must have been identified to the contract.
3. The buyer must have breached the contract before the loss passed to the buyer.
4. The loss must not have been covered, at least in part, by the seller's insurance.
5. The loss must have occurred within a commercially reasonable time.

Suppose on June 1 the parties enter into a contract for a delivery scheduled for June 15. On June 10 the seller segregates conforming goods and identifies them to the contract. Normally the risk of loss remains on a merchant-seller, assuming the buyer plans to pick up the goods at the seller's place of business, until he delivers the goods to the buyer (subsection 2–509[3]). On June 12 the buyer repudiates the contract. On June 14 the goods are destroyed while in possession of the seller. If the seller has no insurance, the whole loss falls on the buyer. What if the seller keeps the goods in storage until March of the next year, at which time they are destroyed? The buyer might argue that the loss did not occur within a commercially reasonable time. Such an argument probably would be successful.

In the following case a buyer breached the contract, and the goods were destroyed by fire.

Multiplastics, Inc. v. Arch Industries, Inc.

Supreme Court of Connecticut

328 A.2d 618 (1974)

Background: Multiplastics (plaintiff) brought an action against Arch (defendant) to recover for breach of a contract to purchase 40,000 pounds of pellets.

Decision: The Connecticut Supreme Court affirmed the ruling for Multiplastics based on Section 2–510(3).

Bogdanski, Judge

The facts may be summarized as follows: The plaintiff, a manufacturer of plastic resin pellets, agreed with the defendant on June 30, 1971, to manufacture and deliver 40,000 pounds of brown polystyrene plastic pellets for nineteen cents a pound. The pellets were specially made for the defendant, who agreed to accept delivery at the rate of 1,000 pounds per day after completion of production. The defendant's confirming order contained the notation "make and hold for release. Confirmation." The plaintiff produced the order of pellets within two weeks and requested release orders from the defendant. The defendant refused to issue the release orders, citing labor difficulties and its vacation schedule. On August 18, 1971, the plaintiff sent the defendant the following letter: "Against P.O. 0946, we produced 40,000 lbs of brown high impact styrene, and you have issued no releases. You indicated to us that you would be using 1,000 lbs. of each per day. We have warehoused these products for more than forty days, as we agreed to do. However, we cannot warehouse these products indefinitely, and request that you send us shipping instructions. We have done everything we agreed to do."

On September 22, 1971, the plaintiff's plant, containing the pellets manufactured for the defendant, was destroyed by fire. The plaintiff's fire insurance did not cover the loss of the pellets. The plaintiff brought this action against the defendant to recover the contract price.

The trial court concluded that the plaintiff made a valid tender of delivery by its letter of August 18, 1971, and by its subsequent requests for delivery instructions; that the defendant repudiated and breached the contract by refusing to accept delivery on August 20, 1971; that the period from August 20, 1971, to September 22, 1971, was not a commercially unreasonable time for the plaintiff to treat the risk of loss as resting on the defendant under section 2–510(3); and that the plaintiff was entitled to recover the contract price plus interest.

The defendant contends that section 2–510 is not applicable because its failure to issue delivery instructions did not constitute either a repudiation or a breach of the agreement. The defendant also argues that even if section 2–510 were applicable, the period from August 20, 1971, to September 22, 1971, was not a commercially reasonable period of time within which to treat the risk of loss as resting on the buyer.

The trial court's conclusion that the defendant was in breach is supported by its finding that the defendant agreed to accept delivery of the pellets at the rate of

1,000 pounds per day after completion of production. The defendant argues that since the confirming order instructed the defendant to "make and hold for release," the contract did not specify an exact delivery date. This argument fails, however, because nothing in the finding suggests that the notation in the confirming order was part of the agreement between the parties. Since, as the trial court found, the plaintiff made a proper tender of delivery, beginning with its letter of August 18, 1971, the plaintiff was entitled to acceptance of the goods and to payment according to the contract.

The remaining question is whether, under section 2–510(3), the period of time from August 20, 1971, the date of the breach, to September 22, 1971, the date of the fire, was a "commercially reasonable" period within which to treat the risk of loss as resting on the buyer. The trial court concluded that it was "not, on the facts of this case, a commercially unreasonable time," which we take to mean that it was a commercially reasonable period. The time limitation in section 2–510(3) is designed to enable the seller to obtain the additional requisite insurance coverage. The trial court's conclusion is tested by the finding. Although the finding is not detailed, it supports the conclusion that August 20 to September 22 was a commercially reasonable period within which to place the risk of loss on the defendant. As already stated, the trial court found that the defendant repeatedly agreed to transmit delivery instructions and that the pellets were specially made to fill the defendant's order. Under those circumstances, it was reasonable for the plaintiff to believe that the goods would soon be taken off its hands and so to forgo procuring the needed insurance.

There is no error.

Sale or Return and Sale on Approval

Section 2–326(1) states that if goods are delivered primarily for use and may be returned by the buyer to the seller even though they conform to the contract, the transaction is a *sale on approval.* If the goods are delivered to a buyer who is entitled to return conforming goods and the buyer intends to resell the goods, the transaction is a *sale or return.* In order to determine whether conforming goods that may be returned to the seller have been sold on sale-or-return or sale-on-approval terms, the court must examine whether the buyer intended to use the goods or to resell them.

When goods are purchased on sale on approval, the buyer may wish to try out the goods before accepting them. If he uses the goods in order to try them out, this does not constitute acceptance. The risk of loss and title remain with the seller until the buyer accepts the goods. Acceptance can occur automatically if the buyer fails to notify the seller of his election to return the goods within a reasonable time. Acceptance of any part of the goods is acceptance of the whole—if the goods conform to the contract. If the buyer elects to return the goods, the return is at the seller's risk and expense. If the buyer is a merchant, he must follow any instructions provided by the seller.

Under sale-or-return terms, the buyer can return all or part of the goods shipped to him or her as long as they are substantially in their original condition. The buyer, however, must elect to return them within a reasonable time, and he or she must return them at his or her own risk and expense.

The following case illustrates the sale-on-approval rule.

Prewitt v. Numismatic Funding Corp.

U.S. Court of Appeals, Eighth Circuit
39 UCC Rep. Serv. 797 (1984)

Background: Numismatic (Defendant) sells rare and collector coins by mail. Prewitt (Plaintiff) responded to Numismatic's advertisement in a December 1981 issue of the *Wall Street Journal* offering six Morgan silver dollars. Shortly thereafter, a salesman from Numismatic called Prewitt and Prewitt agreed to receive several coins on an "approval basis." Two weeks later, Prewitt received in the mail fifteen Morgan silver dollars. The literature enclosed with the coins stated "Everything is available to you on a fourteen-day approval basis." The invoice stated that title did not pass until the buyer paid the account in full and that the buyer had fourteen days from the date of receipt in which to settle the account. The literature gave no directions as to how to return unwanted coins.

Prewitt immediately returned the coins via Federal Express and enclosed a letter expressing his disapproval of the shipment of coins. When Numismatic contacted him again, however, he agreed to review several additional coins on an approval basis. The second shipment, containing fifty-two coins valued in excess of $20,000, was sent on the same terms as the first. Prewitt selected seven coins and returned the remaining coins via either the U.S. Postal Service or Federal Express.

On February 10, 1982 Numismatic mailed Prewitt twenty-eight gold and silver coins in two packages valued at $61,975. As with the earlier shipments, the coins were sent on a fourteen-day approval basis with no instructions for the return of unwanted coins. Prewitt instructed his wife to return them via certified mail for the maximum amount of insurance available—$400 per package. She mailed the coins February 23, 1982, but Numismatic never received them. Prewitt then brought this action seeking a declaration of his nonliability for the coins.

Decision: The court affirmed the lower court's ruling for Prewitt.

Bright, Circuit Judge

In awarding Prewitt a declaratory judgment of nonliability, the district court determined, and the parties do not dispute, that the delivery of coins between seller Numismatic and buyer Prewitt constituted a sale "on approval." Under the provisions of the Uniform Commercial Code relating to risk of loss, as adopted in Missouri, the court held that the risk of loss remained with the seller.

A. COURSE OF DEALING AND COURSE OF PERFORMANCE ARGUMENTS.

Appellant Numismatic advances two theories in which it contends that the parties impliedly agreed to shift the risk of loss to Prewitt. First, it argues that an agreement by Prewitt to assume the risk of loss arose by implication from the prior course of dealings between the parties in which Prewitt had returned coins fully insured via Federal Express.

. . . The code defines "course of dealing" as "a sequence of previous conduct between the parties to a particular transaction which is fairly to be regarded as establishing a common basis of understanding for interpreting their expressions and other conduct." Mo Rev Stat § 400.1–205(1) (1969). A court should look to course of dealing to supplement or qualify the terms of an agreement where the parties are or should be aware of that course of dealing. Mo Rev Stat § 400.1–205(3) (1969).

. . . No instructions were provided prescribing a method of return on any of the shipments. Thus, we conclude that the evidence is insufficient to show "a sequence of previous conduct" establishing a course of dealing between the parties.

Numismatic's second contention is that an agreement to shift the risk of loss from the seller to the buyer may be implied from Prewitt's conduct in obtaining some, albeit inadequate, insurance on the packages in question. Under the Missouri parol evidence rule, Mo Rev Stat § 400.2–202(a) (1969), course of performance may also be used to explain or supplement the terms of a written agreement. Course of performance is defined, and its applicability prescribed in § 400.2–208(1):

> (1) Where the contract for sale involves repeated occasions for performance by either party with knowledge of the nature of the performance and opportunity for objection to it by the other, any course of performance accepted or acquiesced in without objection shall be relevant to determine the meaning of the agreement. Mo Rev Stat § 400.2–208(1) (1969).

There is simply no basis upon which we can identify any course of performance in this case. It is undisputed that Prewitt purchased insurance on and returned the coins all in one large shipment. The official comments to § 400.2–208 note that the section has no application to cases involving only a single occasion of conduct.

B. SEASONABLE NOTIFICATION.

Numismatic also contends that the buyer assumed the risk of loss under the "sale on approval" provisions of the Uniform Commercial Code because he did not seasonably notify the seller of his election to return the goods and did not seasonably return the goods. See Mo Rev Stat § 400.2–327(1)(b)–(c) (1969).

The district court rejected Numismatic's contention because the sale on approval contract gave Prewitt fourteen days to decide whether to accept or reject the coins. Numismatic does not dispute that Prewitt placed the coins in the mail for return within the fourteen day period.

In our view of the record, we find no error in the district court's findings of fact and its conclusions of law logically follow from those findings. In sum, Numismatic failed to produce evidence sufficient to establish any basis upon which the district court could have found that the risk of loss shifted to the buyer in a "sale on approval" transaction. Accordingly, we affirm.

INSURABLE INTEREST

The UCC, in Section 2–501, specifies who has an insurable interest in goods. The buyer obtains an insurable interest in existing goods as soon as they are identified to the contract. The buyer obtains an insurable interest even though the goods identified are nonconforming.

However, if the contract is for the sale of future goods, that is, goods that are not yet in existence and identified, the buyer obtains an insurable interest in the future goods when they are shipped, mailed, or otherwise designated by the seller as goods to which the contract refers.

The seller has an insurable interest in goods so long as he or she has title to the goods or any security interest in the goods.

BULK TRANSFERS

Article 6 of the UCC covers bulk transfers. Section 6–102 defines these as "any transfer in bulk and not in the ordinary course of the transferor's business of a major part of the materials, supplies, merchandise or other inventory . . . of an enterprise." Where a substantial part of the equipment of an enterprise is transferred, it will be a bulk transfer only if it is made in connection with a bulk transfer of inventory.

All businesses whose principal business is the sale of merchandise from stock, including businesses that manufacture what they sell, are covered by Article 6. The purpose of Article 6 is to prevent a fraud on the creditors of a going business. Creditors may extend credit to a business based on its inventory. Article 6 prevents a merchant from selling his or her inventory all at once without taking care of his or her creditors.

Requirements

Inventory may be sold in bulk without violating Article 6 if the merchant adheres strictly to the provisions of the article. A bulk transfer will not be effective against any creditor of the transferor unless:

1. The buyer obtains a list of the seller's creditors
2. The parties prepare a schedule of the property to be transferred
3. The schedule of property and list of creditors are preserved for six months following the transfer and are made available to any creditor of the transferor
4. The seller signs and swears to the list of his or her creditors.

Section 6–104(3) makes the seller responsible for the completeness and accuracy of the list of the creditors. The transfer is not rendered improper because of errors and omissions unless the buyer knew of these errors or omissions.

Notice

The buyer must notify all creditors on the list of the bulk transfer or the transfer will be ineffective against those creditors not receiving notice of it. This notice must be given at least ten days before the buyer takes possession of the goods or pays for them, whichever happens first. The purchaser does not need to provide notice of the transfer when the sale is by auction. This responsibility is transferred by Section 6–108 to the auctioneer. Some states have adopted optional Section 6–106, which specifies that the proceeds of the sale are to be applied to the debts of the seller. Other states merely require notice to the creditors.

Failure to Comply

If the buyer fails to comply with the provisions of Article 6, the transfer of goods to him or her is ineffective. In other words, the creditors of the seller can reach these goods even though the buyer has paid for them. If the buyer in turn sells these goods to a bona fide purchaser for value, however, this cuts off the power of the creditors to reach the goods. Section 6–111 gives the creditors of the seller six months after the date on which the transferee took possession of the goods to take action (unless the parties concealed the transfer).

REVIEW PROBLEMS

1. Why does the UCC distinguish between "merchants" and "nonmerchants"? Explain.
2. How does the UCC define "goods"?
3. What contracts are not covered by Article 2 of the UCC?
4. Can both the seller and the buyer have an insurable interest in the same goods at the same time?
5. Define the terms "FOB," "CIF," "C & F," "Ex-ship," and "No Arrival, No Sale."
6. Weaver's contracts with Casual Slacks for the sale of teenage clothing, the order calling for delivery during "June–August." The shipment is made in August and is incomplete. Weaver's refuses to pay the full invoice price, since the shipment is received so late as to miss the major part of the preschool marketing period, making it necessary to mark the clothing from one-third to one-half off the usual retail price in order to sell it. Weaver's contends that the use of the term "June–August" has a trade meaning of delivery of a substantial portion of the goods in June, a similar delivery in July, and the balance in August. Casual Slacks, on the other hand, contends that use of the terminology "June-August" is unambiguous and means that delivery may be made at any time during the period from June 1 to August 31. Weaver's introduces parol evidence of the meaning in their trade of "June–August" at trial.

   Does the term "June–August" have a meaning given it by usage in the trade so as to explain or supplement the express terms of the written agreement, and is this testimony admissible?
7. Dravo and Key enter into an oral contract for Key to sell to Dravo up to 143,000 pounds of two-inch or smaller steel punchings. No price is specified. Key provides part of the goods under the contract but Dravo refuses to pay. Dravo now contends that the contract is invalid for lack of a specified price term. Who wins?
8. Detwiller purchases a new truck from Stevens Dodge. The truck is then shipped to Bob, a dealer closer to Detwiller's hometown, for a pickup. After Detwiller pays Stevens Dodge, documents of title are sent to Detwiller. Prior to the receipt thereof, the truck is destroyed by fire while sitting on Bob's lot. Detwiller and Stevens Dodge have no agreement regarding the risk of loss. Where does the risk of loss lie?
9. Eberhard agrees to sell and ship certain goods to Brown. The contract does not contain any FOB terms, nor is there any agreement on who bears the risk of loss.

Certain goods are placed on board a common carrier by Eberhard but are apparently lost in transit. Eberhard now sues Brown for the price of the goods. Brown contends that the risk of loss remains with Eberhard. Is Brown's contention correct?

10. Harbach, a farmer, orally contracts in February with Continental to sell 25,000 bushels of soybeans at $3.81 per bushel, delivery and payment deferred until October, November, and December. There is some question about whether Continental sent Harbach a written confirmation of the contract. Harbach contends he did not receive such a confirmation. Harbach then refuses to make delivery, contending that no contract exists and, even if there is a contract, that the Statute of Frauds prevents enforcement. Further, Harbach claims that he, as a farmer, was not a merchant at the time of the transaction and therefore the merchant exception to Section 2–201 does not apply. At trial, evidence is admitted tending to show that Harbach has been engaged in agricultural pursuits for over twenty-five years and, in particular, has raised and sold grain, primarily corn, but including some small quantities of soybeans, on the type of contract here in issue for several years. It is known that Harbach is familiar with the operations of the grain market on which both corn and soybeans are traded. Is Harbach, who is a farmer, also a merchant? See Continental Grain Co. v. Harbach, 400 F.Supp. 695 (N.D. Ill. 1975).

11. The Jetts purchased an organ from Menchey Music Service. The store attempted to retain title to the organ after delivery of it to the Jetts. Before paying for the organ, the Jetts sold the organ to another person. A criminal action was brought against the Jetts based on the theory that they had committed a crime by selling the organ. The prosecution had to prove that title was in Menchey Music Service to establish the crime of fraudulent conversion. Who had title to the organ—Menchey Music Service or the Jetts? Commonwealth v. Jett, 326 A.2d 508 (Penn. 1974).

12. Vineyard Wine Company, the buyer, bought wine from Rheinberg–Kellerei, the seller, a West German wine producer and exporter. While en route to the United States, the wine was lost at sea. The buyer did not receive prompt notice of the shipment, and in fact did not learn of the shipment until after the wine was lost at sea. Was the risk of loss on the buyer or the seller? Rheinberg–Kellerei GMBH v. Vineyard Wine Company, Inc., 281 S.E.2d 425 (1981).

Sales: Performance

The formation and interpretation of sales contracts were discussed in the preceding chapter. This chapter focuses on the performance obligations of the parties to a sales contract.

TERMS

The basic duty of the seller is to deliver or make available the goods purchased by the buyer. The buyer's basic responsibility is to pay for the goods purchased. The obligations of the seller and buyer are discussed in turn.

Delivery

Section 2–307 of the Uniform Commercial Code (UCC) makes it the duty of the seller to transfer and deliver goods in accordance with the terms of the contract. But in what manner must the seller deliver the goods? Must he or she deliver all the goods at one time? The an-

swer to this question is found in Section 2–307, which makes it clear that, unless the contract indicates a contrary agreement, all the goods must be delivered at one time. The buyer is entitled to reject a delivery that has been improperly delivered in lots—subject to the right of the seller to cure the improper tender.

Delivery in Lots. Sometimes, however, delivery in a single lot will not be possible. Suppose, for example, that the buyer does not have sufficient storage space to take delivery of the entire order at one time. Must the buyer take it anyway? Section 2–307 provides that "where the circumstances give either party the right to make or demand delivery in lots the price if it can be apportioned may be demanded for each lot." This language suggests that under certain circumstances the seller can deliver the goods in separate lots. For example, if the seller is unable to find enough trucks or railroad cars to deliver the goods in a single lot, delivery may be made in lots and the seller may demand payment for each lot.

Place for Delivery. The next question is: What is the proper place for delivery? Assuming that delivery by carrier is neither required nor authorized by the contract, Section 2–308 makes the proper place for delivery the seller's place of business or, if he or she has no place of business, the seller's residence. If the contract is for the sale of identified goods that are known by both parties to be at some other place, that place is the proper place for delivery of the goods. If the parties have agreed to delivery by carrier or have authorized delivery by carrier, the seller's duties with respect to delivery are governed by Sections 2–503 and 2–504.

Time for Delivery. If the time for shipment or delivery has not been agreed upon, the time for shipment or delivery is a reasonable time. What is reasonable depends on the nature, purpose, and circumstances of the action to be taken. Where a time has been left open for delivery, neither party may demand delivery or offer delivery at an unreasonably early time. The performance requirements of destination and shipment contracts were described in Chapter 18.

Delivery of Nonconforming Goods. What happens if the seller delivers at the proper place and time, but the goods he or she delivers do not conform to the contract? Section 2–508(1) makes it clear that, although a tender or delivery has been rejected by the buyer because it is nonconforming, the buyer does not necessarily have a right to sue for breach of contract. If the time for performance has not yet expired, the seller may seasonably notify the buyer of his intention to cure and may then make a conforming delivery within the contract time. What is seasonable notice? Section 1–204(3) states: "an action is taken 'sea-

sonably' when it is taken at or within the time agreed or if no time is agreed at or within a reasonable time." Thus if the seller is to deliver goods on December 1, and he delivers nonconforming goods that the buyer rejects on November 1, the seller may notify the buyer of his or her intention to cure and deliver conforming goods anytime up through December 1. What if the seller delivers nonconforming goods on November 29 and notifies the buyer that he or she will attempt to cure? May he or she do so at that late date? Two days is probably not seasonable notice.

What if the seller sends a nonconforming tender that he or she reasonably believes will be acceptable to the buyer? If the seller did not anticipate at the time of sending the nonconforming goods that the buyer would reject them, and if the seller lacks the time to deliver conforming goods before the time for performance elapses, the seller has a "reasonable time" to substitute performance. Suppose a seller has agreed to deliver green, red, and blue swimsuits by December 1 and, because he or she has no blue suits in stock, sends yellow, green, and red suits. The buyer may be able to reject the goods as nonconforming. If the goods arrive on November 29 the seller will not have time to cure, so he or she may try to rely on Section 2–508(2) to obtain extra time to cure after the expiration of the time for performance. Reasonable grounds to believe that the buyer will accept the goods may be found in the prior course of dealing, course of performance, or usage of trade, as well as in the circumstances surrounding the making of the contract. If the buyer has accepted a substitute color on swimsuits in the past, that is reasonable grounds for believing that the buyer will accept a substitute color now. The buyer may protect himself or herself by including a "no replacement" clause in the contract.

The following case deals with the right of the seller to cure pursuant to Section 2–508(2).

T. W. Oil, Inc. v. Consolidated Edison Co.

Court of Appeals of New York

35 UCC Rep. 12 (1982)

Background: T. W. Oil, Inc. (plaintiff) sued Con Edison (defendant) for breach of contract after Con Ed refused to accept what it claimed to be nonconforming oil and refused to allow the plaintiff to seasonably cure. The lower court awarded the plaintiff $1,385,512.83, the difference between the original price and the amount it received in the open market upon selling the oil Con Ed had refused. The Appellate Division affirmed, and the defendant appealed.

Decision: The New York Court of Appeals affirmed the judgment for T. W. Oil.

Fuchsberg, Judge

In January 1974, midst the fuel shortage produced by the oil embargo, the plaintiff purchased a cargo of fuel oil whose sulfur content was represented to it as no greater than 1%. While the oil was still at sea en route to the United States in the tanker MT Khamsin, plaintiff received a certificate from the foreign refinery at which it had been processed informing it that the sulfur content in fact was .52%. Thereafter, on January 24, the plaintiff entered into a written contract with the defendant (Con Ed) for the sale of this oil. The agreement was for delivery to take place between January 24 and January 30, payment being subject to a named independent testing agency's confirmation of quality and quantity. The contract, following a trade custom to round off specifications of sulfur content at, for instance, 1%, .5% or .3%, described that of the Khamsin oil as .5%. In the course of the negotiations, the plaintiff learned that Con Ed was then authorized to buy and burn oil with a sulfur content of up to 1% and would even mix oils containing more and less to maintain that figure.

When the vessel arrived on January 25, its cargo was discharged into Con Ed storage tanks in Bayonne, New Jersey. In due course, the independent testing people reported a sulfur content of .92%. On this basis, acting within a time frame whose reasonableness is not in question, on February 14 Con Ed rejected the shipment. Prompt negotiations to adjust the price failed; by February 20, plaintiff had offered a price reduction roughly responsive to the difference in sulfur reading, but Con Ed, though it could use the oil, rejected this proposition out of hand. It was insistent on paying no more than the latest prevailing price, which, in the volatile market that then existed, was some 25% below the level which prevailed when it agreed to buy the oil.

The very next day, February 21, plaintiff offered to cure the defect with a substitute shipment of conforming oil scheduled to arrive on the SS *Appolonian Victory* on February 28. Nevertheless, on February 22, the very day after the cure was proffered, Con Ed, adamant in its intention to avail itself of the intervening drop in prices, summarily rejected this proposal too. The two cargos were subsequently sold to third parties at the best price obtainable, first that of the Appolonian and, sometime later, after extraction from the tanks had been accomplished, that of the Khamsin.

We turn to the central issue on this appeal: Fairly interpreted, did subdivision 2 of Section 2–508 of the Uniform Commercial Code require Con Ed to accept the substitute shipment plaintiff tendered? In approaching this question, we, of course, must remember that a seller's right to cure a defective tender, as allowed by both subdivisions of Section 2–508, was intended to act as a meaningful limitation on the absolutism of the old perfect tender rule, under which no leeway was allowed for any imperfections.

Since we here confront circumstances in which the conforming tender came after the time of performance, we focus on subdivision 2–508(2). On its face, taking its conditions in the order in which they appear, for the statute to apply (1) a buyer must have rejected a nonconforming tender, (2) the seller must have had reasonable grounds to believe this tender would be acceptable (with or without money allowance) and (3) the seller must have "seasonably" notified the buyer of the intention to substitute a conforming tender within a reasonable time.

In the present case, none of these presented a problem. The first one was easily met for it is unquestioned that, at .92%, the sulfur content of the Khamsin oil did not conform to the .5% specified in the contract and that it was rejected by Con Ed. The second, the reasonableness of the seller's belief that the original tender would be acceptable, was supported not only by proof that the contract's .5% and the refinery certificate's .52% were trade equivalents, but by testimony that, by the time the contract was made, the plaintiff knew Con Ed burned fuel with a content of up to 1%, so that, with appropriate price adjustment, the Khamsin oil would have suited its needs even if, at delivery, it was, to the plaintiff's surprise, to test out at .92%. Further, the matter seems to have been put beyond dispute by the defendant's readiness to take the oil at the reduced market price on February 20.

As to the third, the conforming state of the Appolonian oil is undisputed, the offer to tender it took place on February 21, only a day after Con Ed finally had rejected the Khamsin delivery and the Appolonian substitute then already was en route to the United States. It is almost impossible, given the flexibility of the Uniform Commercial Code definitions of "seasonable" and "reasonable" to quarrel with the finding that the remaining requirements of the statute also had been met.

In dealing with the application of Section 2–508 (subd [2]), courts have been concerned with the reasonableness of the seller's belief that the goods would be acceptable rather than with the seller's pre-tender knowledge or lack of knowledge of the defect.

A seller should have recourse to the relief afforded by the Uniform Commercial Code, Section 2–508 (subd [2]) as long as it can establish that it had reasonable grounds, tested objectively, for its belief that the goods would be accepted. It goes without saying that the test of reasonableness, in this context, must encompass the concepts of "good faith" and "commercial standards of fair dealing" which permeate the Code.

The order of the Appellate Division should be affirmed, with costs.

Payment

Cash or Check. Unless the parties have agreed to the contrary or the goods are sold on credit, payment is due at the time and place at which the buyer is to receive the goods (Section 2–310[a]). Tender of payment is sufficient when it is made by any means or in any manner current in the ordinary course of business unless the seller demands payment in legal tender (Section 2–511[2]). The buyer usually may pay by check, unless the seller demands cash. If the seller demands cash, he or she must give the buyer a reasonable time to obtain the cash. The purpose of giving the buyer additional time to collect the cash is to prevent the buyer from being unprepared at the time for payment because he or she planned to pay by check or some other instrument. This provision prevents the seller from treating the buyer's inability to pay in cash at the time for payment as a breach of contract. In the event the seller accepts the buyer's check, the payment is conditional on the check being paid by the bank when it is presented for payment (Section 2–511[3]). If the bank dishonors the check, the buyer still must pay for the goods.

Right to Inspect. The buyer generally has a right before payment or acceptance to inspect the goods at any reasonable place and time and in any reasonable manner, unless the contract provides for delivery COD or for payment against documents of title. If the seller ships COD, the buyer must pay for the goods even if they do not conform to the contract unless the nonconformity appears without inspection (Section 2–512[1]). However, the buyer will have other remedies, discussed later, if the goods are nonconforming. Although the buyer must pay under these circumstances before he or she inspects the goods, the buyer still retains the right to inspect the goods after payment. The buyer is not considered to have accepted the goods until he or she has had a reasonable opportunity to inspect them. Whether or not the buyer has accepted affects the type of remedies that are available to him or her.

In the event the buyer chooses to inspect the goods the buyer must bear the cost of inspection unless he or she discovers that the goods do not conform to the contract, in which case he or she may recover expenses from the seller if he or she rejects the goods.

Where the parties have specified a particular place or method of inspection, that place or method will be presumed to be the exclusive one. If compliance becomes impossible, the buyer can inspect the goods at any reasonable time and place and in any reasonable manner, unless the place or method fixed for inspection was clearly intended as an indispensable condition, in which case the contract fails.

Delivery by Documents of Title. If delivery is authorized and made by means of documents of title, other than as specified in Section 2–310(b), payment is due at the time and place at which the buyer is to receive the documents, regardless of where the goods are to be received. The buyer must pay for the goods when he or she is tendered the appropriate documents. He or she still retains the right to inspect the goods. No acceptance occurs until the buyer has had the opportunity to inspect them. Thus if a buyer purchased the goods COD and receives the proper documents, he or she must pay for the goods even though they are still in transit. When the goods arrive, he or she may then inspect them and exercise the right to accept or reject.

Suppose a seller in Illinois ships goods to a buyer in California. The seller receives a bearer-negotiable bill of lading from the shipper. This document permits the person in possession of it to pick up the goods from the carrier. The seller gives this bill of lading to his or her bank, which in turn transfers the document to a California bank for collection. The California bank calls in the buyer, receives payment from him or her, and releases the bill of lading to the buyer. The bank then transfers the money back to the seller's bank. The buyer may now pick up the goods from the carrier when they arrive in California. If he or she inspects the goods and finds that they do not conform to the contract, the buyer may at that point reject the goods—even though the buyer has already paid for them—and demand any money paid to the seller.

ACCEPTANCE

Acceptance may occur in one of three ways under Section 2–606 of the UCC. Acceptance is unrelated to the question of who has title to the goods, which is governed by Section 2–401.

Express Statement of Acceptance

The buyer accepts the goods if, after a reasonable opportunity to inspect them, he or she indicates that the goods are conforming or that he or she will take the goods even if they are not conforming. Suppose a buyer orders 100 blue and red swimsuits. If the seller delivers 100 blue and green swimsuits, the buyer, after inspecting them, accepts the goods by indicating that he or she will take them even though they are not blue and red. Bear in mind that because this delivery was not conforming, the buyer could have rejected the swimsuits. Table 20.1 lists the consequences of an acceptance by a buyer.

Inaction

An acceptance may also occur as a result of inaction by the buyer, that is, by the buyer's failure to reject the goods effectively after he or she has had a reasonable opportunity to inspect them. Suppose the blue and green swimsuits arrive on January 1 but, rather than opening the box immediately to inspect the goods, the buyer puts the box in the storeroom. The buyer could have inspected the goods on January 1, determined that they were not conforming, and rejected them. On April 15 the buyer opens the box. The buyer now wants to reject the suits. Because of the buyer's inaction, however, it may be too late to reject them.

Act Inconsistent with Seller's Ownership

The third method of acceptance is the buyer's commission of any act that is inconsistent with the seller's ownership. Suppose the buyer receives the blue and green swimsuits, puts them on the shelves in the store, and sells a number to the public. Selling the suits amounts to an act inconsistent with the seller's ownership.

Knowledge of Defects. In considering Section 2–606(1), which provides that a buyer has accepted when he or she has done "any act inconsistent with the seller's ownership," the courts should distinguish cases where the buyer knows of a defect from those where he or she is unaware of it. In the example in the preceding paragraph the buyer knew the goods were nonconforming, made no attempt to reject them, and sold them to third parties. This is an act inconsistent with the seller's ownership. The same would be true if the buyer attempted to reject the suits but then sold them to third persons.

Sometimes it is impossible for the buyer to avoid using the product even after rejecting it. Suppose a homeowner purchases a wall-to-wall carpet that is glued to the floor. In this situation the homeowner may call the seller, reject the carpet, and continue to use it.

A more difficult case is the continued use of a car or mobile home after a rejection. Whether the continued use constitutes acceptance under Section 2–606(1)(c) is not easy for the courts to resolve. In general it is dangerous to use the goods after a rejection be-

TABLE 20-1 CONSEQUENCES OF ACCEPTANCE

1. Buyer must pay contract rate for the goods accepted.
2. Buyer forfeits the right to reject.
3. Buyer must, within a reasonable time after he or she discovers the breach, notify the seller of the breach or be barred from any remedy.
4. Burden shifts to buyer to establish the breach of contract.

PREVENTIVE LAW
Inspect Goods at Once

Johnson Fence Company receives a shipment of fencing on April 1. It places the fencing in storage and does not inspect it until August 1. At that time it determines the fencing is not in conformity with the contract. By its failure to act Johnson has probably accepted the fencing.

This situation illustrates the importance of instructing all employees to inspect immediately each shipment to make certain that it is in conformity with the buyer's order. If the fencing does not conform, the buyer should immediately notify the seller that it is rejecting the shipment.

PREVENTIVE LAW
Rejecting Goods

Payless Carpet receives a truckload of carpet. The trucker unloads the carpet in the Payless warehouse. A Payless employee immediately determines that the carpet does not conform to the contract with the seller and notifies the seller the same day of the nonconformity. In the meantime some of the Payless salesmen sell part of the carpet to customers because they did not realize Payless had rejected the carpet. By selling the carpet, Payless has accepted the goods.

Employees should be instructed to somehow mark goods that have been rejected so that other employees will not accidentally sell such goods. Everyone should also be instructed never to sell goods that have been rejected.

cause a court may construe this as an acceptance. This matter is discussed later in this chapter.

Another difficult situation arises when the buyer uses the goods prior to rejecting them although the buyer is aware of a defect. If the buyer and the seller are attempting to straighten the problem out, and this is why the buyer has delayed rejecting the goods, the use of the product at this time should not be regarded as an acceptance. The policy of the UCC is to encourage parties to work out their differences.

Similarly, the buyer's use of a product while unaware of a defect should not constitute an acceptance under Section 2–606(1)(c). Suppose the buyer purchases a car, drives it two days, and then the transmission fails. One could argue that the UCC gives the buyer the right to inspect goods and a reasonable time to reject them. Therefore use of the car for two days, prior to learning of the defect, should not constitute an acceptance.

The following case illustrates what happens to a buyer who performs an act inconsistent with the seller's ownership.

Pettibone Minnesota Corp. v. Castle

Supreme Court of Minnesota

247 N.W.2d 52 (1976)

Background: Castle (defendant) purchased a piece of machinery from Pettibone Minnesota Corporation (plaintiff). Castle originally ordered an 880 Crusher, but the plaintiff substituted a Pitmaster Crusher. The trial court found the defendant had accepted the Pitmaster Crusher and was liable for the purchase price because he did an act inconsistent with the seller's ownership. Castle appealed.

Decision: The Supreme Court of Minnesota affirmed the decision for Pettibone.

Per Curiam

This action was brought to recover the purchase price of machine used in processing gravel, namely, an 880 Crusher and washing plant. Defendant counterclaimed for damages claiming the breach of the contract to deliver the 880 Crusher. In the course of transaction between the parties, defendant accepted delivery by plaintiff of a crusher known as a Pitmaster Crusher in the fall of 1969. There was a sharp conflict in the evidence whether the Pitmaster Crusher was accepted by the defendant on a temporary basis until the 880 Crusher was reconditioned, or whether as contended by plaintiff the Pitmaster Crusher was substituted for the 880 Crusher and purchased by defendant.

The trial court found that defendant has failed to prove the allegations of the counterclaim.

We find that the trial court was correct in determining that the parties by agreement substituted the Pitmaster Crusher for the 880 Crusher originally involved in the transaction. Defendant's counterclaim was accordingly properly dismissed, as there was no breach of a contract by plaintiff to sell the 880 Crusher to defendant.

The evidence supporting that the Pitmaster Crusher was substituted for the 880 Crusher is as follows: (1) Defendant signed a purchase order for the Pitmaster Crusher, (2) defendant never attempted to return the Pitmaster Crusher, (3) defendant insured the crusher and the washing plant and named the plaintiff as the mortgagee, and (4) defendant sold the Pitmaster Crusher and washing machine to third parties.

The admitted and unexplained retention of the machinery and subsequent sale thereof by defendant of the machine to others was an act ". . . inconsistent with the seller's ownership." The evidence justifies the finding that the defendant purchased from plaintiff the machine involved.

Notice of Rejection. Assuming the buyer wants to reject a nonconforming delivery of goods, he or she must notify the seller and specify the grounds for rejection, thereby giving the seller a chance to deliver conforming goods. Should the buyer accept nonconforming goods, the buyer retains the right to sue for damages.

Suppose that Acme Lawn Equipment sends a lawn-sprinkler system on March 1 to Johnson's Lawn Supply. When the sprinkler system arrives, Johnson determines that the system fails to conform to the contract description. Johnson must reject the goods within a reasonable time after he receives them, and he must notify Acme within a reasonable time that he has done so. Suppose he receives the sprinkler system on March 5. If Johnson sends a letter to Acme on March 10 rejecting the system and specifying his reasons, he has probably complied with the requirements of Section 2–602. Since Johnson is a merchant, he must follow any instructions he receives from Acme with respect to the sprinkler system. After rejecting the goods, Johnson must be careful not to take any action inconsistent with Acme's ownership, such as selling the sprinkler to a customer. If Johnson sells the sprinkler, the courts would find he has accepted the sprinkler, even though he rejected it earlier.

Commercial Units. If the buyer chooses to accept part of a commercial unit, he or she must accept the entire unit (Section 2–606). However, the buyer does not need to accept goods that do not conform to the contract. Section 2–601 gives him or her three options if the seller tenders delivery of nonconforming goods: the buyer may (1) reject all the goods; (2) accept all the goods; or (3) accept any commercial unit or units and reject the rest. Commercial unit is defined in Section 2–105(b):

> "Commercial unit" means such a unit of goods as by commercial usage is a single whole for purposes of sale and division of which materially impairs its character or value on the market or in use. A commercial unit may be a single article (as a machine) or a set of articles (as a suite of furniture or an assortment of sizes) or a quantity (as a bale, gross, or carload) or any other unit treated in use or in the relevant market as a single whole.

Thus if the seller delivers 200 pairs of men's shoes, when the buyer ordered 100 pairs of men's shoes and 100 pairs of women's shoes, the buyer can accept all 200 pairs of shoes, reject the 100 pairs of women's shoes and accept the 100 pairs of men's shoes, or reject all the shoes. If the buyer elects to accept the 100 pairs of men's shoes, a commercial unit, he or she must pay at the contract rate for the shoes accepted. Section 2–717 allows the buyer to recover from the seller for the breach of contract or, as an alternative, to deduct damages from the purchase price.

REJECTION

Perfect-Tender Rule

Section 2–601 of the UCC gives the buyer of goods who has received an improper delivery the right to reject the goods "if the goods or the tender of delivery fail in any respect to conform to the contract." This is called the "perfect-tender" rule. It does not apply to installment contracts, which are discussed later in this chapter, and it is limited by the seller's "right to cure."

As a practical matter, the perfect-tender rule is not very significant because of the manner in which the courts interpret Section 2–601. A buyer will be able to reject goods, as a practical matter, only where the goods or tender fail in a substantial respect to conform to the contract. Trivial defects in the tender will not give the buyer a right to reject.

To Reject

As indicated earlier, failure to make an effective rejection may constitute an acceptance. To make certain that a buyer does not unintentionally accept goods, he or she must follow the provisions of Section 2–602. The goods delivered must have been nonconforming and the seller must have failed to "cure" the nonconformity. (Cure was discussed earlier in this chapter.) The buyer must then (1) reject the goods within a reasonable time after their delivery or tender and (2) seasonably notify the seller of the rejection.

Timing of Notice. Actions are taken seasonably if they are taken at or within the time agreed or, if no time is agreed, within a reasonable time (Section 1–204[3]). If the buyer acts too slowly in rejecting the goods, he or she will be deemed to have accepted them. In order to determine whether the buyer acted within a reasonable time, the court will consider the surrounding circumstances.

The court in the following case decided the buyer had properly rejected the goods sold to him.

Steinmetz v. Robertus

Supreme Court of Montana

637 P.2d 31 (1981)

Background: On May 1, 1977 Steinmetz (plaintiff) and Robertus (defendant) entered into an agreement whereby the plaintiff would sell the defendant an irrigation system. Both parties agreed that the plaintiff had the obligation to install and test the system. The pump that the defendant requested was unavailable, so the plaintiff substituted a different model. The horsepower of the substituted pump was lower and the price was higher than that of the pump originally requested. The pump was installed on June 5, 1977, with the plaintiff failing to test it. The pump never functioned properly. The defendant contacted the plaintiff several times in order to get the pump to operate properly, but he received no response. As a result of improper irrigation, the defendant's fields produced only 25% of their anticipated yield. After harvest in October 1977 the defendant told the plaintiff to pick up the pump, advising him that he would not pay for it. The defendant subsequently purchased another pump elsewhere. The plaintiff refused to take back the pump and sued for its price and installation costs. The lower court ruled for the defendant.

Decision: The Montana Supreme Court affirmed the decision for Robertus.

Weber, Justice

There was substantial evidence to support the following conclusions:

(a) The goods were non-conforming or were improperly delivered. The parties are agreed that it was part of the agreement, and a matter of common practice in the irrigation equipment trade, for the seller to supervise the installation of an irrigation system and test its performance. Here, both plaintiff and his supplier were present the day the pump was installed and yet there were a number of questionable occurrences. The screenless pump drew in sufficient debris to clog it before any water was pumped to the wheel rows. Plaintiff Steinmetz left the farm before the irrigation pump was tested. Plaintiff never returned to the farm to test the system after its "cure" and ascertain that it was functioning properly.

(b) There was a failure to cure the defects of the pump. Defendants contacted plaintiff early and emphatically, the day after the pump's installation, clearly indicating that it did not work. They made a number of unsuccessful attempts after the attempted "cure" to contact plaintiff.

(c) Finally and perhaps most importantly, defendants' ten to twelve days' "use" of the pump in June or early July was in fact a prolonged effort to determine why the pump failed to work and to cure the defect themselves in the absence of any response by the plaintiff to defendants' complaints. As such, it was never an act inconsistent with seller's ownership under Section 2–606(1)(c), but rather a reasonable and timely inspection of the pump, under Section 2–606(1)(b), to determine if it was or could be in conformity with the agreement. The Montana Power records indicate that the pump was not used for "several months," as plaintiff charges, but for no more than two weeks total. Defendants testified that, for nearly that length of time, they tried, without success, every conceivable variation to try to make the pump work as plaintiff had assured them it would work.

The Uniform Commercial Code provides ". . . acceptance does not occur until the buyer has had a reasonable opportunity to inspect [the goods]." Section 2–606(1)(b). When the goods in question can only be inspected by putting them to the use for which they are intended, a reasonable time for inspection naturally will be longer than if the goods are items whose conformity or nonconformity can be determined simply by looking at them.

A court must be realistic in appraising the sufficiency of a buyer's opportunity to inspect, and should not hold that the buyer had accepted where because of the technical or complex nature of the goods the buyer cannot determine whether they are satisfactory until he actually makes use of them. When a buyer attempts to cooperate with the seller, and "work the bugs out" of a complex piece of machinery by briefly putting the machinery to its intended use, he should not be acting at his peril. Courts should be hesitant to find that such acts are inconsistent with the seller's ownership.

Here, defendants were assured that the pump in question was designed to supply two to three wheel rows with adequate water. Defendants' use of the pump can be considered the "period of experimentation" recognized in Carl Beasley Ford, Inc. v. Burroughs Corp.

It is generally held that mere notification of poor quality is not sufficient to constitute rejection under the Uniform Commercial Code. Here we find more than mere notification. Defendants twice contacted plaintiff before the attempted "cure" of the pump's defects; defendants three times contacted Roy Bucklin, who was acting on plaintiff's behalf, after the ineffectual "cure" of those defects; and defendants, who had paid the total price of the wheel roll system within days of its installation, refused to pay any part of the pump purchase price over a period of several months.

Under the facts of this case, there was no acceptance by the defendants, no actual use inconsistent with the ownership of the plaintiff, and no delay in offering a return of non-conforming goods significant enough to justify a conclusion that defendants had accepted the pump.

Duties After Rejection. Once the buyer has given the requisite notice of rejection within a reasonable time, he or she must take care not to give the appearance of exercising ownership over the goods. If the goods are in the possession of a buyer who is not a merchant, his or her only duty is to hold them with reasonable care for a sufficient time for the seller to take possession.

If the buyer is a merchant, his or her duties with respect to rejected goods are set out in Section 2–603. If the seller has no agent or place of business at the market of rejection, the merchant-buyer who has the goods in his or her possession or control must follow any reasonable instructions received from the seller with respect to the goods.

In the absence of such instructions the merchant-buyer must make reasonable efforts to resell the goods for the seller if they are perishable or threaten to decline in value speedily. If the seller chooses to resell the goods, he or she must act in good faith. The buyer is entitled to reimbursement from the seller for caring for and selling the goods, or he or she may deduct expenses from the proceeds of the sale.

A buyer in possession or control of nonperishable goods or goods that will not decline rapidly in value has several options if the seller fails to give instructions within a reasonable time after he or she learns of the buyer's rejection. The buyer may (1) store the goods, (2) reship them to the seller, or (3) resell the goods at the seller's expense (Section 2–604).

State the Defect. It is not sufficient for the buyer merely to tell the seller that he or she rejects the goods. To be safe, the buyer must specifically state the particular defect on which he or she is basing the rejection to give the seller an opportunity to cure it. If he or she rejects the goods and fails to specify the defect, and the defect is of a nature that the seller could have cured, the buyer cannot rely on this unstated defect as a basis for rejection or to establish a breach of contract.

It is not necessary that the buyer be absolutely precise—a quick informal notice of the defects will suffice. Section 2–605(1)(b) says that a buyer must state the particular defect if both the buyer and the seller are merchants and if the seller has made a written request for a full and final written statement of all defects on which the buyer proposes to rely as justification for a rejection of the goods. If the buyer fails to list certain defects in the written statement, he or she cannot rely on these defects as grounds for rejection in a subsequent trial.

Once the buyer has accepted goods, he or she has lost the right to reject them. Whether the goods have been rejected or whether an acceptance has been revoked is important in establishing the remedies available to the buyer.

The following case discusses the question of whether a buyer who has purchased a defective mobile home may reject it after a substantial amount of time has passed and the buyer has moved it.

Jones v. Abriani *NO cure*

Court of Appeals of Indiana
350 N.E.2d 635 (1976)

Background: This suit arose as the result of the sale of a defective mobile home by the defendants, the Joneses, who were doing business as Jonesy's Mobile Home Sales, to the Abrianis (plaintiffs). The lower court rendered a judgment for the plaintiffs. Decision: The Indiana Appeals Court affirmed the judgment for the Abrianis.

Lowdermilk, Judge

An examination of the facts, viewed in the light most favorable to the trial court's judgment, reveals the following. Richard and Jayanne began shopping for a mobile home in the spring of 1971 just prior to their marriage. They viewed several models on various occasions in the Terre Haute and Indianapolis areas, and finally settled on the Spanish style Eagle mobile home that was on display at Jonesy's Mobile Home Sales because "it was fancier than most we had seen, and . . . looked to be better constructed than most we looked at for the price." Since a new mobile home could be purchased for the same price as the model home they had viewed, they decided to order a new home rather than purchasing the display unit. The new home was to be identical with the model home but for a few optional accessories and different colored sinks and carpeting.

A contract to purchase was signed by Richard. Jayanne had quickly scanned the document, but Richard himself did not read the contract, later saying "I was young, you know how everybody starts off young and I figured we could at least trust the Jones' or somebody that would watch out for us." A down payment of $1,000 was made, and the mobile home was ordered by the sellers from the manufacturer in Alabama.

When the home arrived, the Abrianis inspected the home, but were disappointed in what they found. The carpet was a different color than the one ordered, a sink was chipped, a curtain was missing, a shutter was missing, the floor plan was different from what had been ordered, the bathrooms did not have double sinks, and in general, the quality of the construction and furnishings was substantially below what they had expected. They immediately contacted Mrs. Jones to tell her that they did not want the home in that condition. She informed them that if they did not take the mobile home they would lose their down payment.

Inasmuch as the Abrianis could not afford to lose the $1,000, they decided that they had no choice but to take the mobile home on condition that the sellers would take care of their problems. Sellers installed the mobile home on a lot owned by sellers and rented to the Abrianis.

Over the next year, complaints were made to the sellers every time the rent was paid about the different problems that arose in the mobile home. Sellers eventually replaced the chipped sink, supplied the missing shutter, and connected the dryer vent free of charge. A missing curtain in the bedroom was ordered, but a correct match could not be found, so a whole new set of curtains was sent almost a year later. Although these curtains were the wrong size, the Abrianis were tired of complaining and made no further mention of the problem. Similar difficulty was experienced in gaining delivery of six missing or damaged screens, and only four were eventually received.

About four months after delivery of the home, Jayanne called Mrs. Jones to complain about a leak in the roof. Mrs. Jones informed her that the roof had to be sealed every two years, and Jayanne responded that they had only had the home for a few months, and that it should not need that kind of maintenance so soon. Mrs. Jones refused to fix the leak unless the Abrianis paid for the service. In the same call, Jayanne listed once again all of the other uncorrected problems that they had found in the home after living there for several months. They discovered that the doors were all crooked and would not shut properly. Further, the carpeting was literally falling apart and had several bald spots and a large cut. The chair was broken inside, causing the upholstery to tear. The bathtubs both leaked. All of the cabinet doors were out of alignment. The holes had been cut too large for most of the light switches. The paneling was starting to fall off, the molding was popping off, the ceiling was being damaged by the leak, there was a gas leak in the furnace, and the hot water heater element went out. There was trouble with the wiring, and a fuse was blown at least once a month. No attempt was made to remedy any of these defects.

About a year later, and after the continual assurances of repairs failed to materialize, the Abrianis wrote the Attorney General seeking help in the matter. They listed all of their complaints, including these additional problems: the bedroom windows would not raise; the window frames seemed to be out of alignment; the sliding doors on the bathtub would not fold correctly; there were no filters with the furnace; the legs on the end tables and coffee table wobbled and were about to fall off; the upholstery on the furniture was all wearing out; both mattresses were cheap and had broken springs; everytime the carpet was vacuumed the sweeper bag filled up with lint.

The only response to the letter that the Abrianis received was a printed warranty card from the manufacturer that provided that the warranty registration had to be returned within five days of purchase in order for the ninety-day warranty to be effective. Jayanne had earlier told Mrs. Jones that they had never received any information about the warranty. Since both time limits on the warranty card had long since passed, the Abrianis turned to legal counsel, and this action resulted soon thereafter.

Shortly after the Abrianis sent their letter to the Attorney General, they decided to move their home to a different lot in case any trouble arose because of the letter. At this time, the moving company pointed out a dent or bow in the A-frame hitch of the home. There was also testimony that one front panel of aluminum siding on the home "looked like it had been repaired and had buckled all up." They also discovered that the aluminum roof panel had large "wrinkles" or bulges in it, although the exact location of the leak could not be determined. . . .

We first point out that valid grounds for rejection of the mobile home existed in this case under § 2–601, the Perfect Tender Rule, which provides that "if goods or the tender of delivery fail in any respect to conform to the contract, the buyer may (a) reject the whole. . . ." While tender does not necessarily have to be "perfect," the mobile home in this case clearly failed to meet the contract requirements. The seller did have a right to cure minor defects after proper notice according to the terms of § 2–508, but the evidence demonstrates that no such cure was ever forthcoming within the contemplated time of performance, or at any time. . . .

Sellers also contend that the goods were in substantial compliance with the contract, except for the carpeting on which the manufacturer had retained an option to substitute different carpeting under the following clause:

> The manufacturer has the right to make any changes in the model or the designs or any accessories and parts of any subsequent new trailer or mobile home, at any time, without creating an obligation on the part of either the dealer or the manufacturer to make corresponding changes in the trailer or mobile home described and covered by this order either before, or subsequent to, delivery of such equipment to the purchaser.

The clear import of this provision is that the manufacturer is under no duty to provide any accessory or part other than those contained within the original contract agreement. Thus, if an improvement was made in the design of a particular mobile home model, the manufacturer is under no duty to include such new design or improvement on a mobile home that had already been contracted for on the basis of the older design. There is nothing in the clause to suggest that inferior materials may be substituted at the option of the manufacturer after an agreement on the subject matter of the contract has already been reached. Further, it is clear from the facts set out above that there were other substantial defects in the home and variances from the contract terms that would amount to imperfect tender.

We hold that the evidence was sufficient to sustain a finding that a valid rejection was made by the Abrianis and that the sellers' threats to withhold the down payment were not justified under the law.

REVOCATION

As indicated in the section on rejection, once a buyer has accepted goods, he or she has lost the right to reject them. However, it still may be possible for the buyer to revoke his or her acceptance and compel the seller to take the goods back.

A buyer cannot revoke unless he or she meets one of three conditions listed in Section 2–608:

1. The buyer knew of the defect but accepted because he or she reasonably believed the nonconformity would be cured and it was not seasonably cured
2. The buyer did not discover the defect prior to his or her acceptance because the defect was difficult to discover
3. The buyer did not discover the defect prior to his or her acceptance because the seller assured the buyer there were no defects

If any of these three conditions applies, and the nonconformity substantially impairs the value of the goods to the buyer, the buyer may revoke the acceptance. The question is not whether the seller realized at the time of contracting that the nonconformity would substantially impair the value of the goods to the buyer, but whether the nonconformity in fact caused a substantial impairment of value to the buyer even though the seller did not know of the buyer's particular circumstances. Revocation is available only under these circumstances.

The following case discusses the issue of whether there has been a substantial impairment of value to the buyer.

Colonial Dodge, Inc. v. Miller

Supreme Court of Michigan

36 UCC Rep. Serv. 2 (1984)

Background: On April 19, 1976 Clarence Miller (defendant) ordered a 1976 Dodge station wagon from Colonial Dodge (plaintiff), which included a heavy-duty trailer package with extra wide tires. On May 28, 1976 Miller picked up the car. His wife then inspected it and noticed it did not have a spare tire. The next morning Miller notified Colonial Dodge and he insisted on having the tire he ordered immediately. He was told there were no spare tires available at that time. Miller then informed the salesman that he would stop payment on the two checks that were tendered as the purchase price and that the vehicle could be picked up from in front of his home. Miller parked the car in front of his home, where it remained until the temporary ten-day registration sticker had expired, whereupon the car was towed away by the Police Department.

Colonial sued Miller for the purchase price of the car. The trial court entered a judgment for Colonial. It found that Miller had wrongfully revoked his acceptance of the vehicle.

Decision: The Michigan Supreme Court reversed and entered a judgment for Miller.

Kavanagh, Justice

This case requires the court to decide whether the failure to include a spare tire with a new automobile can constitute a substantial impairment in the value of that automobile entitling the buyer to revoke his acceptance of the vehicle under MCL 440.-2608; MSA 19.2608.

We hold it may and reverse.

Defendant argues that he never accepted the vehicle under MCL 440.2606; MSA 19.2606, claiming mere possession of the vehicle is not sufficient according to the UCC. Plaintiff contends defendant did accept the vehicle by executing an application for Michigan title and driving the vehicle away from the dealership. The trial court stated "[t]he parties agree that defendant Miller made a valid acceptance of the station wagon under § 2.606 of the Uniform Commercial Code. . . ."

Plaintiff argues the missing spare tire did not constitute a substantial impairment in the value of the automobile, within the meaning of MCL 440.2608(1); MSA 19.2608(1). Plaintiff claims a missing spare tire is a trivial defect, and a proper construction of this section of the UCC would not permit defendant to revoke under these circumstances. It maintains that since the spare tire is easy to replace and the cost of curing the nonconformity very small compared to the total contract price, there is no substantial impairment in value.

However, MCL 440.2608(1); MSA 19.2608(1) says "[t]he buyer may revoke his acceptance of a lot or commercial unit whose nonconformity substantially impairs its value *to him*. . . ." (Emphasis added.)

We cannot accept plaintiff's interpretation of MCL 440.2608(1); MSA 19.2608(1). In order to give effect to the statute, a buyer must show the nonconformity has a special devaluing effect on him and that the buyer's assessment of it is factually correct. In this case, the defendant's concern with safety is evidenced by the fact that he ordered the special package which included special tires. The defendant's occupation demanded that he travel extensively, sometimes in excess of 150 miles per day on Detroit freeways, and often in the early morning hours. Mr. Miller testified that he was afraid of a tire going flat on a Detroit freeway at 3 A.M. Without a spare, he testified, he would be helpless until morning business hours. The dangers attendant upon a stranded motorist are common knowledge, and Mr. Miller's fears are not unreasonable.

We hold that under the circumstances the failure to include the spare tire as ordered constituted a substantial impairment in value to Mr. Miller, and that he could properly revoke his acceptance under the UCC.

That defendant did not discover this nonconformity before he accepted the vehicle does not preclude his revocation. There was testimony that the space for the spare tire was under a fastened panel, concealed from view. This out-of-sight location satisfies the requirement of MCL 440.2608(1)(b); MSA 19.2608(1)(b) that the nonconformity be difficult to discover.

. . . Defendant's notice to plaintiff and holding of the car pending seller's disposition was sufficient under the statute, at least in the absence of evidence that defendant refused a request by the plaintiff to sign over title.

Plaintiff contends defendant abandoned the vehicle, denying it any opportunity to cure the nonconforming tender as prescribed in MCL 440.2508; MSA 19.2508. We find that defendant's behavior did not prevent plaintiff from curing the nonconformity. Defendant held the vehicle and gave notice to the plaintiff in a proper fashion; he had no further duties.

Reasonable Time

For the revocation of acceptance to be effective, it must occur within a reasonable time after the buyer discovers or should have discovered grounds for revocation. The buyer must act within a reasonable time to give the seller a chance to cure and to help minimize the buyer's losses. There are many cases dealing with whether the buyer's actions were taken within a reasonable time.

Substantial Change

The revocation must occur before any substantial change in the condition of the goods that is not caused by their own defects. This means that if the buyer does something to the goods to change them from their original condition, and he or she is unable to restore them to their original condition, an acceptance cannot be revoked. On the other hand, if the materials (perishable, for example) changed in condition due to their own defects, the buyer still can revoke his acceptance. In any event, a revocation of acceptance is not effective until the buyer notifies the seller of the defect.

Suppose Mrs. Smith purchased a trailer home from the Lemon Corporation. When she received the trailer on February 15, she inspected it. The carpet in the trailer was missing. When she inquired about the missing carpet, the seller told her he would see that she received a carpet at once. Mrs. Smith moved into the trailer. During the next six weeks Mrs. Smith called the seller several times about the carpet, and each time the seller assured her that he would deliver the carpet. On April 10 she sent a letter to the seller revoking her acceptance because of the failure to supply the carpet. She locked the trailer, turned the keys over to Lemon, and moved out on April 10. This revocation will probably be effective because she accepted the trailer only because the seller assured her that the nonconformity (the absence of carpet) would be cured, it was not cured within a reasonable time, and the absence of the carpet substantially impaired the value of the trailer to her. What if Mrs. Smith did not move out on April 10 but continued to occupy the trailer until December 1, at which time she attempted to revoke her acceptance? It is very likely that a court would refuse to let Mrs. Smith revoke her acceptance because she failed to revoke within a reasonable time.

Suppose Mrs. Smith inspected the trailer on February 15, failed to detect any defects, and moved in on February 16. On February 17 she realized that a hat rack in the closet was missing. She then wanted to revoke her acceptance based on the theory that the defect was difficult to discover. Mrs. Smith must keep the trailer chiefly because any nonconformity must substantially impair the value of the trailer to her. While the absence of a hat rack might lessen the value of the trailer by a few dollars, it clearly fails to constitute a substantial impairment of value. Mrs. Smith would, however, have a right to sue the seller for the value of the hat rack.

The following case discusses an attempt by purchasers of an organ to revoke their acceptance after several attempts to repair it by the seller.

Schumaker v. Ivers

Supreme Court of South Dakota
238 N.W.2d 284 (1976)

Background: The Schumakers (plaintiffs) purchased an electric organ from Ivers (defendant). After accepting the organ, the Schumakers experienced considerable difficulties with it and attempted to rescind. Although several months passed before the plaintiffs had attempted to rescind their acceptance, the trial court found the Schumakers had properly revoked their acceptance of the organ. Therefore it ruled for the plaintiffs.

Decision: The Supreme Court of South Dakota affirmed the decision for the Schumakers.

Wollman, Justice

On November 30, 1972, plaintiffs went to defendant's music store for the purpose of looking at electric organs. Plaintiffs looked at several models and discussed the matter with defendant, who recommended the organ in question, described in the testimony as a Story Clark Magi model. Defendant suggested that plaintiffs permit him to deliver the organ to their home on a trial basis. Plaintiffs agreed that defendant could do so, and the organ was delivered to plaintiffs' home on December 7, 1972. Mrs. Schumaker played the organ on the day it was delivered and noticed nothing unusual.

On December 11, 1972, Mrs. Schumaker went to defendant's store and paid in full the purchase price of the organ in the amount of $1,119.71. According to her testimony, she asked defendant about the warranty and service on the organ and was assured by defendant that it would all be taken care of and that he had a man who serviced organs.

Approximately two weeks after the organ was delivered, one of the bass pedals failed to play. Shortly thereafter another bass pedal also failed to play, as did two keys on the keyboard. Mrs. Schumaker called defendant on or about December 27, 1972, and told him about the problems she had been having with the organ. Defendant said that he would send out a serviceman. Nothing was done, however, until March 13, 1973, when defendant and his serviceman came to plaintiffs' home and worked on the organ. Following their visit—and here the record is rather vague with regard to dates—plaintiffs again experienced difficulty with the organ in that one key in every octave in both keyboards failed to play. Mrs. Schumaker called defendant on May 11, 1973, and told him that she was still having difficulty with the organ and that she was unhappy with it and wanted a refund of the purchase price. Defendant and his serviceman came to plaintiffs' home and after some discussion, during which defendant refused to accede to Mrs. Schumaker's request that he take back the organ and refund the purchase price, plaintiffs agreed to permit defendant to bring out a replacement organ on the condition that if it did not work, defendant would take it back and refund the purchase price of the first organ. On or about May 22, 1973, defendant brought out a replacement organ. Shortly thereafter the rhythm system on the second organ began to malfunction. In response to plaintiffs' call, defendant's serviceman attempted to repair the organ on several occasions during the period from May 24 to June 1, 1973, but was unable to remedy the problem. During his last service call the serviceman removed the rhythm system component from the organ. Following this visit the lower keyboard failed to play.

Sometime after June 1, 1973, defendant's employees attempted to return the original organ, which defendant claimed had been put into proper operating condition, to plaintiffs' home but were prevented from doing so by plaintiffs. Plaintiffs sought the advice of an attorney, who wrote to defendant on or about June 15, 1973, regarding the organ. On August 3, 1973, plaintiffs filed suit against defendant in the nature of a rescission action praying for the return of the purchase price of the organ.

Defendant contends that because the record reveals that he at all times stood ready to honor the one-year free parts and service warranty on the organ, plaintiffs should not have been permitted to summarily refuse him the opportunity to do so by revoking their acceptance of the organ. In view of the numerous unsuccessful attempts by defendant to satisfactorily repair the original organ, we conclude that the trial court did not err in holding that plaintiffs had rightfully revoked their acceptance.

As far as the adequacy of the notice is concerned, defendant acknowledged that Mrs. Schumaker had told him that plaintiffs wanted him to take the organ back and refund the purchase price. If this revocation of acceptance was in any way waived by plaintiffs' accepting delivery of the second organ, such waiver was clearly based upon the condition that the replacement organ would operate satisfactorily, a condition that failed to materialize. Plaintiffs moved promptly to send notice through their legal counsel shortly after the second organ became completely inoperable.

Lemon Laws

As the *Schumaker* case illustrates, consumers sometimes have a great deal of difficulty with products they purchase. This can be highly frustrating, particularly if the product in question is expensive and something a person relies on daily. Problems with automobiles have given consumers one of the greatest difficul-ties because people need some means of transportation to get to work, to buy groceries, and to do a host of other activities.

The UCC Section 2–608 gives a person a right to revoke his or her acceptance. As previously noted, however, the buyer must comply with a number of requirements before he or she can exercise his or her right to revoke.

To minimize some of the problems associated with defective vehicles, many state legislatures have passed what have popularly been dubbed "lemon laws." *Lemon laws* are laws designed to help consumers obtain replacements or refunds when they have purchased a defective vehicle. These laws require a manufacturer, its dealers, and agents to attempt to correct any vehicle problem reported by a consumer during the period the vehicle is under a warranty. If the defects are such that they cannot be repaired within a reasonable number of attempts, lemon laws generally require the manufacturer to provide either a replacement vehicle or a refund of the consumer's purchase price. Significantly, unlike the UCC, these laws define what a "reasonable number of attempts" at repairing a vehicle are. Generally, they specify that a reasonable number of attempts to repair have been made after four or more repair attempts have failed to correct the problem or after the vehicle has been out of service for a cumulative total of thirty or more working days. These laws tend to give the manufacturer, rather than the consumer, the right to choose between a replacement and a refund. This approach differs from that taken in the UCC, which does not require a person to take a replacement if he or she revokes his or her acceptance.

The threshold question in these statutes is, When does a consumer who has purchased a defective vehicle have a right to demand a refund or a replacement vehicle? Lemon laws follow the UCC Section 2–608 "substantial impairment of value" standard. Thus a fairly common requirement is that a defect must exist that substantially impairs the use and value of the vehicle to the consumer.

Assuming there is a substantial impairment of value, the consumer generally must notify the manufacturer within the warranty period or one year after delivery, whichever comes first. This means, for example, that a consumer might make a claim for a replacement or re-fund twelve months after making a purchase. If the consumer were to proceed under UCC Section 2–608 instead, there would always be the risk that a court might find the revocation did not take place "before any substantial change in the condition of the goods which is not caused by the defect." Thus the lemon laws focus on whether the consumer acted within the time specified in the statute as opposed to whether he or she acted before a substantial change in the value of the goods occurred.

The type of vehicles covered varies from state to state. Some apply to all motor vehicles, whereas others may exclude vehicles such as motorcycles or motor homes from coverage under the Act. The emphasis is generally on vehicles for personal or household use rather than for commercial use. Unlike suits filed under the UCC, consumers are permitted to recover their attorney fees.

INSTALLMENT CONTRACTS

As noted earlier, where goods are tendered to the buyer that do not conform to the contract, the buyer has three options under Section 2–601. However, a different rule applies when the parties enter into an installment contract. Section 2–612(1) defines an installment contract as "one which requires or authorizes the delivery of goods in separate lots to be separately accepted, even though the contract contains a clause, 'each delivery is a separate contract' or its equivalent." Assuming that the parties entered into an installment contract, what is the effect of a nonconforming delivery on one of the installments? Sections 2–612(2) and (3) set out the rules governing this situation. In general the standard applied when one of the parties breaches an installment contract is not so rigorous as the standard applied when there has been a breach of a contract requiring delivery to take place at one time. The reason for this is that it would be unfair if a breach on an installment could always be used as grounds for canceling the entire contract.

Rejection of an Installment

Comment 5 to Section 2–612 states that "an installment delivery must be accepted if the nonconformity is curable and if the seller gives adequate assurance of cure." However, a buyer may reject a nonconforming installment if the nonconformity substantially impairs the value of that installment and cannot be cured or if the nonconformity is a defect in the required documents. Unlike rejections, which can occur if the goods fail to conform in any respect, for both revocations and installment contracts the buyer must show that the goods are substantially nonconforming.

Cancellation of Entire Contract

In certain circumstances the nonconformity or default with respect to one or more installments may be so great that the entire contract has been impaired in value. Comment 6 to Section 2–612 makes it clear that the question is whether "the nonconformity substantially impairs the value of the whole contract." If this is the case, the entire contract may be canceled. If the aggrieved party wishes to cancel the contract, he or she must not accept a nonconforming installment without notifying the other party seasonably of the cancellation. If he or she fails to give the required notice, the contract is reinstated. Likewise, the contract is reinstated if the aggrieved party "brings an action with respect only to past installments or demands performance as to future installments."

ASSURANCE OF PERFORMANCE

What type of assurance must the seller give under Section 2–612(2) to force the buyer to accept a nonconforming installment? The standard is the same as that under Section 2–609, which deals with the right to adequate assurance of performance. Because one of the parties to a contract may become unwilling or unable to perform a contract after entering into it, this section allows the other party to demand an assurance of performance.

Comment 1 to Section 2–609 notes that the purpose of entering into a contract is to obtain actual performance of the contract rather than simply a promise to perform. Thus when a party becomes unwilling or unable to perform, the other party to the contract is threatened with the loss of what he or she bargained for—performance. The seller who faces a buyer unable to pay, or the buyer who faces uncertain deliveries by a seller, may want to avail himself or herself of this section.

Basically, Section 2–609 allows the aggrieved party to do three things:

1. Suspend his or her own performance and all preparatory action
2. Require adequate assurance of performance
3. Treat the contract as broken if the grounds for insecurity are not cleared up within a reasonable time, not to exceed thirty days

What constitutes "adequate" assurance of due performance depends on the facts. If a seller of good repute gives a promise that a defective delivery will be straightened out, this will normally be sufficient. But if an untrustworthy seller makes the same statement, the statement alone might be insufficient.

When merchants have contracted, the question of insecurity and adequacy of any assurance offered is judged by commercial standards rather than by legal standards. For example, if a reasonable merchant would believe that a buyer will not pay, this will be regarded as reasonable grounds for insecurity.

ETHICS BOX
Duty to Perform

John C. Melon, a farmer, planted a wheat crop and contracted with the local grain elevator to sell his crop at a price of $2.20 per bushel when harvested. When actually harvested the market had risen to $4.00 per bushel due to a severe drought. John had to borrow additional money from a bank, and selling his crop at $2.20 would not be enough to keep current on the loan, thus allowing the bank to take the farm and dispossess John and his family. The grain elevator contract has a liquidated damages clause that would help John come out ahead by selling to another buyer for $4.00 and paying the damages owed to the elevator.

Some people argue that contract law allows one to choose between performing and paying damages. They reason that if one is willing to pay the damages, then one is ethically entitled to breach. As seen in preceding chapters, others argue that promises have moral force and cannot be ethically broken except under special circumstances. Here two dramatic changes have occurred since the contract was formed: (1) John's financial condition has changed dramatically and (2) there has been a dramatic market upheaval. Although John's hardship seems important, we don't know the impact of his failing to pay on the operator of the grain elevator. Perhaps the operator might go bankrupt if John doesn't honor the contract. Important factors in this case could include whether the parties did or should have anticipated the volatile market, their relative financial positions, and the duties that they owe to other parties affected by the transaction.

ANTICIPATORY REPUDIATION

Rather than a situation involving uncertain ability or willingness to perform, one of the parties to a contract may be faced with a direct repudiation of the contract. If one of the parties to a contract has indicated that he or she will not perform at some date in the future, must the other party wait until that date to find out if the other party actually performs?

Suppose two persons enter into a contract to be performed on August 1. If the seller says on June 1 that he or she will not deliver on August 1, what can the buyer do? This matter is covered by Sections 2–610 and 2–611. If either party to the contract indicates that he or she will not perform at some time in the future, and the failure to perform would substantially impair the value of the contract, the aggrieved party may (1) simply wait a commercially reasonable time for performance or (2) treat the contract as broken and seek any available remedy. This is true even if the aggrieved party has urged the other party to retract his or her repudiation. In any event, his or her own performance may be suspended.

If the aggrieved party chooses the first option, Section 2–611 permits the repudiating party to retract his or her repudiation unless the aggrieved party has canceled the contract, materially changed his or her position, or indicated that he or she considers the repudiation final. Although a retraction is possible by "any method which clearly indicates to the aggrieved party that the repudiating party intends to perform," the repudiating party must give the aggrieved party whatever assurances of performance are demanded, consistent with Section 2–609.

What if two parties enter into a contract calling for delivery of goods on May 15, and on January 1 the seller tells the buyer he will not deliver the goods pursuant to the contract? The buyer may treat the contract as having been breached on January 1, acquire the goods elsewhere, and bring a suit for damages against the seller. The buyer need not wait until May 15 to see if the seller changes his or her mind. Alternatively, the buyer may wait a commercially reasonable time for the seller to perform. The question of what is a commercially reasonable time is discussed in the following case.

Whewell v. Dobson

Supreme Court of Iowa
227 N.W.2d 115 (1975)

Background: Kenneth Dobson (defendant) contracted with Donald Whewell (plaintiff) for the purchase of Christmas trees. Dobson repudiated the contract prior to the time for performance. Whewell thereafter attempted to resell the Christmas trees. The lower court found Whewell's attempted resale was within a commercially reasonable time.

Decision: The Supreme Court of Iowa affirmed the decision of the trial court for Whewell.

Mason, Justice

September 4, 1970, Donald Whewell, plaintiff-seller, and Kenneth Dobson, defendant-buyer, entered into a contract for the sale of four hundred Christmas trees.
. . .

The agreed price for the trees was $3.75 apiece, or a total of $1,500 due upon delivery on or about December 1, 1970. Sometime in the latter part of September 1970, however, plaintiff received defendant's copy of the tree order with the word "cancel" written across its face. This was followed by a letter from defendant on October 2 informing plaintiff of the desire to cancel the tree order.

The trial court found that prior to receipt of the cancelled order and the October 2 letter, plaintiff had contracted with a Michigan firm to purchase four hundred Christmas trees at $3.25 apiece. Upon receiving defendant's communications, plaintiff unsuccessfully attempted to cancel the contract with the Michigan firm, which subsequently shipped plaintiff the trees.

October 30 plaintiff's attorneys wrote defendant demanding assurances of intent to perform the contract. Defendant was given until November 6 to respond after which time plaintiff would take action to minimize his damages.

November 3 defendant's attorneys responded and advised plaintiff defendant would not be able to accept delivery, whereupon plaintiff's attorneys wrote back asking that defendant advise them if he absolutely would not accept delivery. This defendant's attorneys did November 6.

Plaintiff subsequently attempted to sell the Christmas trees and was able to dispose of 124 of them at $3.00 apiece by late December. He also sent loads to Peoria and Elgin, Illinois, but was unable to sell the trees. In these attempts, plaintiff incurred $85 in trucking expenses.

At the outset, it is agreed by both parties Christmas trees are "goods" under the Uniform Commercial Code.

Thus, Article 2 of the Uniform Commercial Code on Sales should be applied in resolving this dispute, with §554.2610 being pertinent to the instant facts. . . .

As we understand the contentions of the parties, . . . one of the questions presented for review by this appeal is whether plaintiff's effort to resell the Christmas trees was attempted within a commercially reasonable time in view of the rapid rate cut Christmas trees decline in value as shown by this record. . . .

There is substantial evidence which would support a finding a repudiation of the contract did here occur, either when defendant wrote "cancel" across the face of the instrument or when the final letter was sent stating defendant would not accept delivery of the Christmas trees. It would be more logical to conclude the repudiation came to pass at the time defendant "cancelled" the tree order as it evidenced "a clear determination not to continue with performance" or a reasonable indication of a "rejection of the continuing obligation." The trial court apparently found the repudiation occurred at the earlier date.

In fact, defendant concedes in written brief and argument he repudiated the contract before the performance date—about December 1, 1970.

Under §554.2610, ". . . when such a repudiation substantially impairs the value of the contract, the aggrieved party may at any time resort to his remedies for breach, or he may suspend performance while negotiating with, or awaiting performance by, the other party. But if the aggrieved party awaits performance beyond a commercially reasonable time he cannot recover resulting damages which he should have avoided." Uniform Commercial Code Comment 1, §554.2610.

"Generally, a seller is under a duty to resell the article of sale within a reasonable time after breach or repudiation of the contract by the buyer. If the seller acts prudently and with reasonable care and judgment, the time of resale is, to a large extent, within the seller's discretion. . . .

". . . What is such a reasonable time depends upon the nature of the goods, the condition of the market and the other circumstances of the case; its length cannot be measured by any legal yardstick or divided into degrees." (Uniform Commercial Code Comment 5, §554.2706.)

It is apparent, then, the given circumstances in a case must be taken into account in determining reasonableness. Unfortunately, there is no definite date of record indicating when plaintiff first attempted to resell. The trial transcript is singularly unhelpful. Plaintiff was asked when he began his resale attempts:

A: I am stating I did it immediately after I received the order of cancellation and the lawyer advised me—

Q: You started in October? A. After I got his cancellation.

Thus, such mitigation attempts may have commenced in October. A November 5 letter from plaintiff's attorneys indicates otherwise, however:

> Please advise us immediately if Mr. Dobson is absolutely unwilling to accept delivery of the Christmas trees he ordered. If so, we *will attempt* to either partially cancel Mr. Whewell's order with his grower or sell the trees to another retailer so that Mr. Whewell's losses will be minimized. (Emphasis supplied).

Plaintiff was the only witness called by either side in the course of the trial.

The trial court did not specifically find that plaintiff's attempted resale was within a commercially reasonable time under the circumstances, but such finding is inherent in its conclusion that plaintiff was entitled to judgment against defendant.

In the court's ruling on defendant's motion for new trial, it is stated by the time defendant notified plaintiff of his desire to cancel the contract one-third of the time had elapsed between the signing of the agreement and the delivery date. The trial judge then opined there would have been no market for the trees after the repudiation, since the date the contract was entered into indicated other wholesalers of trees would have made arrangements at the same time.

There is substantial evidence to support the trial court's findings of fact. In this court's opinion the conclusion of law drawn therefrom by the trial court was correct.

IMPOSSIBILITY

In certain instances a party to a contract may be unable to perform because the goods have been destroyed. The UCC in Section 2–613 allows both parties to escape from the contract when goods identified to the contract have been totally destroyed without fault of either party before the risk of loss passes to the buyer. If the goods have been only partially destroyed, or have deteriorated so as no longer to conform to the contract, Section 2–613(b) gives the buyer the option either to (1) treat the contract as avoided or (2) accept the goods with due allowance for the deterioration or the deficiency in quantity but without further right against the seller.

Goods Must Be Identified

For Section 2–613 to apply the goods must be identified when the contract is made. If just any goods are specified in the contract, as opposed to particular goods, then Section 2–613 does not apply. A seller who promises to deliver 100 lawn mowers to the buyer cannot rely on Section 2–613, but a seller who specifies 100 lawn mowers from his or her plant, which then burns to the ground along with all the mowers, may rely on the defense of impossibility (assuming that he or she was not responsible for the destruction). This section applies even though the goods were already destroyed at the time of contracting if neither party knew of the loss.

Impracticability

Sometimes performance will not be impossible, but will nonetheless be very difficult. Section 2–615 covers situations where performance becomes impracticable because of the occurrence of a contingency the nonoccurrence of which was a basic assumption on which the contract was made or as a result of compliance in good faith with a government regulation. This section excuses the seller from a timely delivery of goods where unforeseen supervening circumstances make performance impracticable. The mere fact that costs go up does not excuse performance; that is the type of business risk assumed in signing a contract. On the other hand, a severe shortage of raw materials or supplies due to a contingency such as war, embargo, or unforeseen shutdown of major sources of supply, which causes the goods to be significantly more expensive or impossible to obtain, is the type of situation covered.

Partial Performance

The seller is excused from the contract completely if he or she can establish that he or she is absolutely unable to perform due to the occurrence of a contingency not contemplated by the parties, but the seller must fulfill the contract to the extent possible if he or she can only partially perform. Section 2–615(b) states that when a seller can partially perform, he or she must allocate production and deliveries among the customers in a fair and reasonable manner. If the seller chooses to allocate goods, or if there will be a delay or nondelivery of goods, the seller must notify the buyer seasonably.

Section 2–616 states that a buyer, upon receipt of notification of a material or indefinite delay or of an allocation, may by written notification to the seller terminate the contract or agree to take the available allocation. The buyer must agree to this modification within a reasonable time, not to exceed thirty days, or the contract will lapse as to any deliveries affected.

Although a buyer does not have to accept the allocated goods, he or she must accept substituted performance if the agreed manner of delivery becomes commercially impossible. Likewise, if the agreed means of payment fails because of domestic or foreign government regulation, the seller under certain conditions must accept a substantially equivalent manner of payment.

REVIEW PROBLEMS

1. What must a buyer do to effectively reject nonconforming goods under the UCC?
2. Describe the difference between rejection and revocation.
3. What test of impossibility is adopted by the UCC?
4. When must the buyer pay for the goods if the contract is silent concerning the time, place, and method of payment?
5. United Airlines ordered a flight simulator from Conductron Corporation. The contract provided that the simulator would not be deemed "accepted" by United unless and until it met the specifications of United and the Federal Aviation Administration (FAA). The contract provided that title to the simulator would nonetheless pass to United upon delivery. Because of delays in the completion of the simulator, the parties modified the contract to provide for testing of the simulator at United's flight training center rather than at Conductron's plant. Before the simulator was delivered to United, United employees notified Conductron of over 600 deficiencies in the device. The modified contract entitled United to cancel the agreement if all of the deficiencies were not corrected by November 1, 1969. Conductron subsequently delivered the simulator, which

United used for training purposes. United could not use the machine as an aircraft flight simulator because it had not yet been approved by the FAA. On April 18, 1969, after the simulator had been tested for ten hours by United test pilots, it was destroyed by a fire of unknown origin. United sued Conductron for breach of contract, claiming that Conductron had failed to deliver an acceptable simulator by the agreed-upon date. Conductron claimed that United had accepted the simulator through its use and possession of it, and thus had waived its right to object to the nonconformities it had noted before delivery. What result? See UCC Sections 2–606 and 1–102.

6. In February 1980 Wickliffe Farms signed a contract with Owensboro Grain Company by which it agreed to deliver 35,000 bushels of white corn to Owensboro between December 15, 1980 and January 31, 1981. The contract said nothing about where the corn was to be grown, although there was evidence that the parties expected Wickliffe to grow the corn on its own farmland. A severe drought made it impossible for Wickliffe to grow and deliver the full 35,000 bushels. If Owensboro were to sue Wickliffe for damages resulting from the failure to deliver the full 35,000 bushels, should Wickliffe be able to raise the defense of impracticability under UCC Section 2–615?

7. Earl Gallin, who owned an electronics components business, purchased several materials from Surplus Electronics Corporation between July and September, 1977. Surplus guaranteed the usability of its products and provided that unacceptable items could be returned for full refund. Gallin had not paid for any of the aforementioned purchases by January 1978, and Surplus sued for the adjusted purchase price of $6,170. Gallin admitted to owing $2,656, but claimed that he was in

the process of testing the balance of the components for usability and would, when he was finished, return the unacceptable goods in one shipment. This testing process had apparently not been completed when the trial commenced in April 1980. What result?

8. Robertson Manufacturing brought an action against Jefferson Tile concerning payment for 13,500 tiles delivered by Robertson to Jefferson. Jefferson received the tiles and discovered they were defective. Rather than allowing the seller to attempt to correct the defect, Jefferson corrected the tiles itself and installed them on a building. Robertson now brings suit for the cost of the tiles. Jefferson argues it should be compensated for the extra expense it incurred in correcting the defects. Is Jefferson correct?

9. Harper entered into a contract with Tri-County Ford Tractor Sales to purchase a tractor. The tractor broke down a number of times. Tri-County unsuccessfully tried to repair the tractor a number of times. Harper revoked his acceptance of the tractor seventeen months after he contracted to purchase it. He seeks to cancel the contract and obtain his money back. Can Harper revoke his acceptance? Ford Motor Co. v. Harper, 671 F.2d 1117 (1982).

10. Holiday agreed to manufacture and sell to B.A.S.F. 6 million cassettes with delivery to begin April 1970 at 500,000 cassettes per month until completed. Many of the cassettes delivered were defective, but Holiday managed to correct the defects. Under what circumstances, if any, could B.A.S.F. cancel the entire contract? Holiday Mfg. Co. v. B.A.S.F. Systems, Inc., 380 F.Supp. 1096 (1974).

11. McDonald's ordered some computerized cash registers from AMF. A number of months passed and AMF was unable to deliver the cash registers. AMF was forced to

delay the date for shipment. In May McDonald's and AMF met to discuss the machines. At that time AMF did not have a working machine and could not produce one within a reasonable time because its personnel were too inexperienced. McDonald's demanded a reasonable assurance of performance, and when it did not receive one, it canceled the contract on July 29. Was McDonald's entitled to cancel the contract? AMF, Inc. v. McDonald's Corp., 536 F.2d 1167 (1976).

12. Gulf entered into a contract with Eastern for the sale of jet fuel in the early 1970s. The parties knew the price of crude oil would fluctuate so they specified West Texas Sour, a crude oil, as an indicator of the price of crude oil to Gulf. Eastern would be obligated to pay for the oil it purchased according to the price of West Texas Sour. During the period of the contract the U.S. government imposed controls on the price of West Texas Sour. Certain other oil purchased by Gulf was not controlled, especially imported oil, and Gulf felt it should be entitled to charge more for the oil delivered than the price it paid for West Texas Sour. Gulf viewed the purpose of the contract as frustrated. It argued the contract should be set aside based on the theory of commercial impracticability. Is Gulf correct? Eastern Airlines, Inc. v. Gulf Oil Corp., 415 F.Supp. 429 (1975).

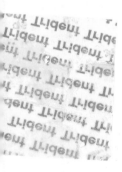

Sales: Remedies

W e now have examined some of the important principles related to the creation and performance of a contract. This chapter discusses the issue of what remedies are available to sellers and to buyers. Before discussing that question we will briefly examine the rules related to when a suit for breach of contract must be filed.

STATUTE OF LIMITATIONS

The victim of a breach in a sales transaction will often have more than one form of relief available. Some of the remedies are mutually exclusive, and others involve limiting factors such as a specific number of days within which one must act. When a breach of an important sales transaction occurs, it is imperative that the victim immediately contact a lawyer to insure that the right to seek a remedy is not inadvertently lost.

Time Limit. This is particularly true when deciding whether or not to file suit. A person who wishes to bring an action for breach of a sales contract must bring suit within four years after the cause of action has occurred—unless the parties have agreed to a shorter period of time. The statute of limitations can be reduced to not less than one year by agreement. If a party to a contract fails to bring suit within the

time stipulated in the agreement (or, if no time is stipulated, within four years), he or she is barred from ever bringing suit by the statute of limitations even though he or she may have an otherwise perfectly valid claim.

Time Statute Starts to Run. The four-year period starts to run from the date the breach of contract occurs, whether or not the aggrieved party knows of the breach, except in the case of a breach of warranty. The time limit for a breach of warranty begins to run when tender of delivery is made. If a warranty *explicitly* extends to the future performance of goods *and* discovery of the breach *must* await the time of such performance, the cause of action accrues when the breach is or should have been discovered.

Thus there are two statute-of-limitation rules that apply to warranties—the *normal warranty,* on which the time limit for filing suit begins to run when tender of delivery is made, and the *prospective warranty,* on which the time limit for filing suit begins not on delivery but when the breach is or should have been discovered.

At first blush one would suppose that most warranties are prospective in character; however, the courts *very* seldom find a warranty to be prospective.

For example, in *Voth* v. *Chrysler Motors Co.* the court dealt with a case involving a man who contracted lead poisoning. The defect in the automobile was a plugged gasoline vent that caused vapors to be gathered by the car's air conditioner. Voth inhaled gas fumes and was injured. He had purchased the automobile on August 8, 1969. He discovered the defect in the car on July 2, 1970. He filed suit June 27, 1974—four years and ten months after buying the car, and five days short of four years after discovery of the breach on July 2, 1970. Since he could not recover if this warranty was covered by the general rule, Voth argued this was a prospective warranty.

The warranty on this automobile guaranteed the buyer that if the car proved to be defective in either material or workmanship during the first twelve months or 12,000 miles, whichever occurred first, Chrysler would repair or replace any defective part without charge. The Uniform Commercial Code (UCC) requires that a warranty *explicitly* extend to future performance and discovery of the breach must await future performance. The court ruled that there was nothing concerning the discovery of the alleged defect that caused the malfunction of the air-conditioning system of an automobile sold in Kansas in August which *must* await future performance.

A careful examination of this warranty reveals that Chrysler was merely agreeing to repair defects if they were discovered. It was *not* guaranteeing the car would *not* have problems in the future, only that if problems arose, Chrysler would repair them. This is different from a situation where a seller guarantees the future performance of its goods. For example, suppose the manufacturer of a burial vault guarantees the vault "will give satisfactory service." In this case the manufacturer of the burial vault is promising more if defects are discovered; it will repair them. It is guaranteeing that the vault will be satisfactory in the future. As such a warranty is prospective, the cause of action first accrues when a breach of the warranty is or should have been discovered.

The court also, in the *Voth* case, seemed to imply that the defect could have been discovered at the time of delivery. This is different from, for example, a sale of seeds. It would be impossible to detect at the time of the sale whether the right seeds were delivered; thus a breach would not cause the statute to start to run until the seeds started to germinate—the point in time at which the buyer could determine there was a defect in the seeds sold.

As the *Voth* case did not involve a prospective warranty, the statute of limitations began to run at the time of tender of delivery. Since Voth filed suit more than four years after he picked up the car, the court ruled this suit was barred by the statute of limitations.

The *Voth* case is a typical treatment of Section 2–725(2) cases. It suggests that only in rare instances will a court permit suit to be filed more than four years after the tender of delivery of goods. Some courts have manipulated the date for delivery to circumvent this rule. However, it is probably safest to assume that suit must be filed within four years of the date of delivery in a breach-of-warranty suit.

Diligence in reporting defects is important because it permits the seller to attempt to remedy the defect and helps to minimize the buyer's damages.

SELLER'S REMEDIES

If the buyer wrongfully rejects goods, improperly revokes his or her acceptance, fails to make a payment due, or repudiates part or all of the contract, the aggrieved seller has a number of remedies.

Election of Remedies

The UCC rejects the idea that a seller must elect one remedy or another. Instead, whether one remedy bars another will depend on the circumstances of a particular case. The reader should bear in mind with respect to the UCC sections on remedies that the UCC requires the remedies to be liberally administered. The purpose of the remedies provided for in the UCC is not to punish the wrongdoer, but simply to put the aggrieved party in the position that he or she would have occupied had the contract been performed.

Remedies Available

Section 2–703 gives the aggrieved seller a number of remedies:

1. Withhold delivery of goods
2. Stop delivery of goods held by a bailee
3. Resell the goods and recover damages
4. Recover damages for nonacceptance as provided in Section 2–708
5. Recover the price
6. Cancel the contract

The aggrieved seller also has certain rights with respect to unfinished goods. When the buyer breaches the contract, the seller can identify to the contract any completed conforming goods, and he or she may either stop work on unfinished goods and sell them for their scrap or salvage value or may in the exercise of reasonable commercial judgment complete the unfinished goods and identify them to the contract. The reason the seller is allowed this option is to minimize the damages sustained by the buyer. If the seller chooses to complete the work on unfinished goods, the burden is on the buyer to show that it was unreasonable for the seller to complete the goods. The seller may then proceed to resell under Section 2–706 or, where resale is not practicable, bring an action for the price under Section 2–709.

Resale

The UCC contemplates the seller's principal remedy as resale. When the buyer has wrongfully rejected goods, revoked his acceptance improperly, failed to make a payment, or repudiated all or part of a contract, the seller may resell the goods in question. The seller is not obligated to resell the goods, but this is the usual manner of establishing damages since the seller is in the business of selling goods. If the seller resells the goods in good faith and in a commercially reasonable manner, he or she may recover the difference between the resale price and the contract price together with any incidental damages, but minus any expenses saved as a result of the buyer's breach.

Incidental Damages. Section 2–710 states that incidental damages to the seller include "any commercially reasonable charges, expenses or commissions incurred in stopping delivery, in the transportation, care and custody of the goods after the buyer's breach, in connection with return or resale of the goods or otherwise resulting from the breach." These are the typical expenses a seller might incur; however, the UCC allows for all commercially reasonable expenditures made by the seller. Suppose the seller had entered into a contract for $4,650.00, and the buyer breached. If the seller incurred $29.50 in expenses in reselling the goods, and they were sold in good faith and in a commercially reasonable manner for $3,000.00, the seller would be entitled to $1,679.50 from the buyer if he or she proceeded under Section 2–706.

Manner of Resale. To assure that the resale takes place in a fair manner, Section 2–706 sets out provisions for conducting the resale. Of course, the parties may agree between themselves as to the details of the resale, but the method of resale still must be fair. In the absence of such an agreement, the resale may be at a public or private sale, as long as every aspect of the sale is commercially reasonable. In choosing whether to have a public or private sale, the character of the goods must be considered and relevant trade practices and usages must be observed. If the seller elects a private sale, he or she must give the buyer reasonable notification of his or her intent to resell. It is not necessary to give the buyer notification of the time and place of the private sale.

At a public sale only identified goods can be sold unless the seller is able to sell them as future goods at a recognized market for public sale of future goods. These identified goods must be sold at a usual place or market for public sale if one is available. Before selling the goods, the seller must give the buyer reasonable notice of the time and place of the resale unless the goods are perishable or threaten to decline rapidly in value. This means the sale must be at a place or market where potential buyers may reasonably be expected to attend and the buyer has an opportunity to bid or notify others of the sale. In order to assure the best possible price, prospective bidders must be given an opportunity to inspect the goods. The seller is permitted to buy the goods. These measures are included to benefit the original buyer by tending to increase the resale price.

If the goods are resold improperly to a purchaser who buys in good faith at the resale, the purchaser takes title free of any rights of the original buyer.

Suppose our seller in the earlier example resold the goods for $5,000. Must he account to the buyer for the $350 above the original contract price of $4,650? The seller is not accountable to the buyer for any profit he makes. The seller in this situation may keep the profit.

The Code also requires that the resale be conducted in a timely manner. The reason for this requirement is that a resale as soon as possible after the buyer's breach is likely to bring the market price for the goods. The following case illustrates what may happen if the resale is not conducted in a timely manner.

McMillan v. Meuser Material & Equip. Co.

Supreme Court of Arkansas

541 S.W.2d 911 (1976)

Background: On December 13, 1973 McMillan (defendant) entered into an agreement with Meuser (plaintiff) for the purchase of a bulldozer. The purchase price, including a bellhousing, was $9,825, FOB Springdale. Meuser arranged transportation of the bulldozer to Greeley, Colorado, the residence of the appellant. On December 24, 1973 McMillan stopped payment on his check, asserting that since the agreed delivery date was December 21, the delivery was past due. Appellee's version is that the delivery date was January 1, 1974. After unsuccessful negotiations between the parties for about two months after the appellant-purchaser stopped payment on his check, the appellee brought this action. On March 5, 1975, or about fourteen months following the alleged breach of the purchase contract, the appellee sold the bulldozer for $7,230 at a private sale. During this fourteen-month interval the equipment remained unsheltered, although regularly serviced, on an Arkansas farm, which was its situs when the sale contract was made.

Decision: The Arkansas Supreme Court ruled for Meuser, although it indicated the resale price was not relevant in determining Meuser's damages.

Holt, Justice

We first consider appellant's assertion that the resale by appellee did not constitute the good faith and commercial reasonableness which is required by Ark. Stat. Ann.

§85-2–706. Appellee responds that this defense was not properly raised at trial. We must disagree with appellee. Appellee alleged in its complaint that it had made reasonable efforts to resell the bulldozer. The length of time between the alleged breach and the resale was joined in issue by appellee's direct testimony.

Q: Bill, at the end of a year what did you do with the bulldozer? Did you decide you wanted to keep it or did you decide to sell it?
A: No, after I kept the cat the twelve months for the man and he didn't come get it and didn't accept it, and this had all been filed and the paper work, and what-have-you, on it, I turned around and started seeking a buyer for it.

The time of the resale was again referred to, without objection, in the cross-examination of the appellee:

Q: I believe you also testified that you waited a year after the 13th of December [1973], I guess, before you started trying to sell it again; is that right?
A: That is true.
Q: Okay. So from December 13, '73, until approximately December of '74, you kept it?
A: I didn't try to sell it until after the first of the year, this year [1975].
Q: So from December 13th, 1973, until the first of this year, you just let it sit?
A: I did.
Q: You didn't try to sell it for a whole year?
A: Nope.

   We turn now to appellant's contention that the resale by appellee Meuser was not in accordance with the requirements of §85-2–706.
   In order to recover the damages prescribed in Subsection (1), Subsection (2) requires that every aspect of the resale including the method, manner, time, place, and terms must be commercially reasonable. The purpose of the resale provisions is discussed in Anderson, Uniform Commercial Code 2d, §2–706:19, at p. 385, where it is stated:

> . . . the object of the resale is simply to determine exactly the seller's damages. These damages are the difference between the contract price and the market price at the time and place when performance should have been made by the buyer. The object of the resale in such a case is to determine what the market price in fact was. Unless the resale is made at about the time when performance was due it will be of slight probative value, especially if the goods are of a kind which fluctuate rapidly in value, to show what the market price actually was at the only time which is legally important.

In Comment 5 following §85-2–706, the writers make it clear that "what is such a reasonable time depends upon the nature of the goods, the conditions of the market and the other circumstances of the case."
   Here, even though we accord a liberal interpretation to the UCC, §85-1–106,

which mandates that remedies be so administered, we are of the view that the resale of the bulldozer, in excess of fourteen months after the alleged breach, will be of "slight probative value" as an indication of the market price at the time of the breach. Appellee Meuser is in the construction business and "deal[s] in bulldozers." Meuser himself testified that he was "aware of the state of the economy in the bulldozer market" and since the time of the alleged breach in December 1973, the market for bulldozers had declined due to a recession in the construction industry and high fuel prices. As indicated, he testified he made no effort to resell the goods for in excess of a year.

Neither can we agree with appellant's contention that the measure of damages provided by §85-2–706 on resale of goods after breach by the buyer is not applicable here because of asserted noncompliance by appellee with the notice requirements. Subsection (3) of that statute requires "[W]here the resale is at private sale the seller must give the buyer reasonable notification of his intention to resell." §85-1–201(26) in pertinent part reads "[A] person 'receives' a notice or notification when (a) it comes to his attention." Appellee's complaint alleged it had made reasonable efforts to resell the goods. In answer to appellant's interrogatories, before the resale, appellee fully described his efforts to resell the bulldozer. Certainly, it must be said that the appellant received notice of appellee's intention to resell the equipment.

Failure to Comply. What happens if the seller fails to comply with the restrictions placed on the resale of goods? Does this bar him or her from any remedy? If he or she fails to comply with the provisions for resale in Section 2–706, the resale price cannot be used in calculating damages. However, the seller can still collect something. If the seller acts improperly, he or she must establish damages under Section 2–708.

Damages

Market Price. Section 2–708(1) makes the seller's damages for nonacceptance or repudiation by the buyer the "difference between the market price at the time and place for tender and the unpaid contract price. . . ." In addition to this sum, the seller may recover for any incidental damages incurred, but he or she must deduct from the damages any expenses saved as a result of the buyer's breach. A seller might utilize this section to keep the goods that the buyer has refused to accept. It

is not mandatory that the seller resell the goods in order to establish his or her damages although, as noted earlier, most sellers will attempt to resell the goods.

The market price is measured at the time and place for tender. To take an obvious case, if the buyer agreed by contract to pick up the goods at the seller's place of business on June 15 and the buyer breaches, the seller may be able to collect the difference between the contract price and the market price at which the goods are selling in the town where the seller's business is located. If the buyer agreed to pay $1,000 for the goods, and they are now selling for $800 in the seller's town, the seller collects $1,000 minus $800, or $200, plus incidental damages and minus any expenses saved. In this case the seller would receive the same amount of damages whether the seller resold the goods and sued under 2–706 or collected under 2–708(1).

Profit. In the event that the measure of damages provided by Section 2–708(1) is inadequate to put the seller in as good a position as performance would have done, the seller may collect the profit (including overhead) that he or she would have recovered had the contract been performed plus any incidental damages.

The UCC could be written more clearly on the question of when profits may be recovered. One case where the seller would not be in the same position as performance would have put him or her is that of the lost-volume seller. Suppose a retailer agrees to sell a couch for $500 to Mrs. Jones. If Mrs. Jones breaches the contract, the retailer would be entitled to the difference between the contract price ($500) and the market price ($500). This would leave the retailer with no damages as long as he or she is able to sell all the couches in stock. But what if the supply of couches exceeds the demand? In that case, because Mrs. Jones breached the contract, the seller will sell one less couch. In this situation the seller should be able to receive the profit (including overhead) that he or she would have made on Mrs. Jones's contract.

Price. The seller can recover the price of goods sold only under certain circumstances. Price actions may be maintained when resale of the goods is impracticable, when the buyer has accepted the goods, or when the goods were destroyed or lost within a reasonable time after the risk of loss had passed to the buyer. If the seller wishes to obtain the contract price, the goods that have been identified to the contract and are still in his or her possession must be held for the buyer. If the seller is able to resell them prior to collecting a judgment, he or she may do so and the proceeds will be credited to the buyer.

Once the buyer has accepted goods, the UCC permits the seller to recover the price of the goods. Whether a buyer has accepted does not depend on the passing of title or on the date set for payment. Suppose the seller delivers goods to the buyer, and the buyer states that he will take the goods. The buyer's state-

ment constitutes an acceptance and renders him liable for the price.

Likewise, if goods are lost or damaged within a commercially reasonable time after the risk of loss has passed to the buyer, the buyer is liable for the price. A seller who ships goods "FOB seller's plant" needs only to deliver the goods to the carrier. Once the goods are in the possession of the carrier, the risk of loss passes to the buyer. In the event the goods are destroyed while in possession of the carrier, the buyer is liable for the price of the goods.

If the goods have not been accepted by the buyer or destroyed after the risk of loss has passed, an action for the price can be maintained for goods identified to the contract only after a "reasonable effort to resell" them at a reasonable price. The seller need not try to resell, however, if circumstances indicate that it would not be possible to resell them at a reasonable price. Suppose a manufacturer custom designed a rolling steel door for a buyer. If the steel door does not fit any other building because it was custom designed, the buyer is liable for the price of the door. Figure 21-1 lists the remedies available to a seller.

Withhold Delivery

In the event the buyer becomes insolvent, the seller's ability to collect damages from the buyer under the sections previously discussed will be impaired. If the buyer has no money, a judgment against him or her will be of little practical value to the seller. For this reason

FIGURE 21-1
Seller's Remedies Under the UCC

2-702, 2-703	(general remedies)
or 2-706	(seller's remedy of resale)
or 2-708	(market price)
or 2-708	(profit)
or 2-709	(price of goods)
+ 2-710	(incidental damages)

the UCC provides special remedies where the buyer becomes insolvent.

When the seller discovers that a buyer has become insolvent, he or she may refuse to deliver the goods to the buyer except for cash. If the buyer owes the seller for goods delivered before the seller learned of the buyer's insolvency, the seller may also demand payment for all goods previously delivered before making any further deliveries. The mere fact that the seller withholds delivery of goods does not mean that he or she is barred from exercising any remedy available for damages.

Goods in Possession of Buyer. If the buyer received the goods on credit while he was insolvent, the seller has ten days to demand their return. Receiving goods on credit amounts to a misrepresentation of solvency by the buyer and therefore is fraudulent against the seller. If the seller learns of the buyer's insolvency and actually demands return of the goods within ten days, the seller is entitled to the goods. If the buyer misrepresented his or her solvency to the seller in writing within three months of the time the buyer received the goods, the ten-day rule does not apply. In that event the seller may claim actual fraud by the buyer and, if he or she can establish fraud, may reclaim the goods.

The following case deals with the reclamation of goods.

Montello Oil Corp. v. Marin Motor Oil, Inc.

U.S. Court of Appeals, Third Circuit

38 UCC Rep. Serv. 1425 (1984)

Background: Montello Oil Corp. (plaintiff) sued Marin Motor Oil (defendant). Montello, the seller in this case, sought to reclaim goods that it sold to Marin on credit. Marin received the goods while insolvent and subsequently filed for bankruptcy.

On March 24, 1981 Montello contracted to sell to Marin 1,054,000 gallons of regular leaded gasoline. On April 10, 1981 Marin called Montello and arranged for a commercial barge operated by a common carrier to pick up the gasoline from Montello's terminal. The barge unloaded the gasoline on April 11, 1981. On April 16, 1981 Montello's vice-president went to Marin's office and orally demanded payment, or alternatively, the return of the gasoline. On the same day Montello filed suit against Marin seeking a writ of attachment against all of Marin's assets and an injunction prohibiting Marin from reselling the gasoline. Montello's complaint and the court's temporary injunction order were served on Marin on April 20, 1981.

On April 21, 1981 Marin filed a petition for reorganization pursuant to Chapter 11 of the Bankruptcy Code. On the same day, at 11:04 P.M., Montello transmitted a demand for reclamation to Marin by telex through Western Union. The telex was physically received by Marin at approximately 9:04 A.M. on April 22, 1981, when Marin opened for business and turned on its telex machine.

Thereafter Montello instituted an adversary proceeding against Marin in bankruptcy court seeking to reclaim the gasoline. This action was unsuccessful and Montello appealed.

Decision: The Court of Appeals ruled for Montello.

Becker, Circuit Judge

This case presents several difficult questions involving the interpretation of section 546(c) of the Bankruptcy Code, 11 USC § 546(c). Section 546(c) adopts the "seller's right of reclamation" created by §2–702 of the Uniform Commercial Code, which enables a seller to reclaim its goods "upon demand made within ten days after receipt" of the goods by the buyer. Section 546(c) allows the seller to exercise this right after the buyer has filed a bankruptcy petition, but requires that the demand be made in writing.

Section 546(c) unambiguously provides that the seller may not reclaim goods from the trustee in bankruptcy unless he first "demands in writing reclamation of such goods before ten days after receipt of such goods by the debtor."

. . . We therefore agree with the bankruptcy and district courts that the state court complaint was not sufficient, in the absence of a claim for reclamation, to satisfy section 546(c)'s requirement of a written demand for reclamation.

Montello argues that Marin did not "receive" the gasoline within the meaning of section 546(c) until April 11, when the common carrier pumped the gasoline into Cities' storage terminal. Marin argues that it should be deemed to have received the gas on April 10, when Montello pumped the gas onto the common carrier barge which Marin had hired. The practical significance of this dispute is that the date of "receipt" is established by section 546(c) as the day from which to begin counting the ten-day period within which the seller must make a written demand for reclamation. If Marin is correct and "receipt" is deemed to have occurred on April 10th, then, regardless of whether the telex demand is viewed as having been made on April 21st, when it was sent, or 22nd, when it was received, it was not made within the ten-day period provided for by section 546(c).

. . . While the gasoline was in the physical possession of the common carrier, it was not in the physical possession of Marin, and Montello's remedy upon discovery of Marin's insolvency was to order the common carrier to stop delivery. Once the gasoline was delivered to Marin's bailee, i.e., Cities, Marin had constructive possession under §2–705(2) and Montello's right to stop delivery terminated and its right to reclaim the goods under UCC §2–702(2) arose.

For these reasons, we agree with the conclusion of the bankruptcy court and the district court that the date of "receipt" of the gasoline by Marin was April 11, 1981, when the common carrier pumped the gas into Cities' storage facilities.

Montello argues that Congress' purpose in enacting section 546(c) was to adopt UCC §2–702 in the situation where the buyer files for bankruptcy. Section 546(c) adopts the first half of §2–702(2) but adds the single modification that the demand must be made in writing. Montello submits that the only conceivable reason for adding the requirement of a writing is evidentiary: the writing requirement serves the purpose of documenting the seller's timely election to reclaim the goods. By requiring a writing, Congress is said to have sought to simplify the administration of bankruptcies by eliminating testimony concerning whether the seller has made a timely oral reclamation demand.

The final question we must decide is whether Montello made a "demand" within the meaning of section 546(c) on April 21st when it sent the telex at 11:04 P.M., or whether a "demand" requires receipt by the buyer, in which case the demand was not made until April 22nd when Marin turned on its telex machine and received the message.

There is, . . . , one policy that we can clearly derive from section 546(c) and its requirement of a writing: Congress favored certainty. Moreover, certainty is a generally desirable policy that should inform the interpretation of any ambiguous statute. The notion of certainty relates not only to simplification of evidentiary disputes, but also to minimizing the number and difficulty of disputes that will arise between the parties. Thus, the certainty question includes whether the disputes that will arise if we adopt a receipt rule are likely to be more or less burdensome on the courts than disputes under a dispatch rule.

. . . In view of these considerations, but primarily because it will best serve the congressional policy of certainty, we will adopt the dispatch rule for demands made pursuant to section 546(c).

In summary, we conclude that Marin "received" the gasoline within the meaning of section 546(c) of the Bankruptcy Code on April 11th, when the common carrier pumped the gas into the storage facility of Marin's bailee, Cities. We also conclude that the state court suit filed by Montello against Marin, and the temporary restraining order issued by that court against Marin, both of which were served on Marin on April 20th and therefore were timely, cannot constitute a demand for reclamation within the meaning of section 546(c) because neither mention "reclamation." However, although we concede that the question is close, we adopt a dispatch rule for demands made pursuant to section 546(c), and because we do, we conclude that the telex sent by Montello on April 21, and received by Marin on April 22 constituted a timely demand for reclamation.

Goods Held by Carrier or Bailee. If the goods have already been delivered to a carrier or other bailee, the seller may wish to stop delivery upon discovering that the buyer is insolvent. It is not necessary for the buyer to be insolvent in all cases for the seller to stop delivery; however, if the seller wishes to stop shipments of less than a carload, the buyer must be insolvent. For the seller to stop delivery when the buyer breaches the contract, the amount must be a delivery as large as a carload if the buyer is solvent. This provision was adopted because it is a burden on the carriers to stop delivery. If a seller of a smaller-than-carload lot had doubts about the buyer's capacity to pay, he or she can ship COD. There is, of course, risk in stopping any shipment because improper stoppage is a breach by the seller.

The seller can stop delivery until the buyer has received the goods, until the documents of title have been negotiated to the buyer, or until the carrier or other bailee gives notice that the goods are being held for the buyer. The seller must give notice to the bailee with sufficient time to enable the bailee by reasonable diligence to stop delivery of the goods. Assuming notice arrives in time for the bailee to act diligently, the bailee must hold and deliver the goods according to the seller's directions. If a negotiable document of title was issued, however, this must be surrendered before the bailee must obey the stop order.

BUYER'S REMEDIES

When the seller fails to make delivery or repudiates or the buyer rightfully rejects or revokes acceptance of goods, the buyer has several remedies:

1. Cancel the contract and recover any amounts paid to seller
2. Cover
3. Recover damages pursuant to Section 2–713
4. Gain possession of goods identified to the contract pursuant to Section 2–502
5. Obtain specific performance or replevy the goods pursuant to Section 2–716
6. Resell goods in his or her possession pursuant in certain circumstances

The remedy most often used is cover.

Cover

When the seller fails to make a delivery or indicates that he or she will not deliver pursuant to a contract, the buyer is faced with the situation of not having material needed to conduct business. To take care of this situation, the UCC allows the buyer to purchase goods in substitution for those covered in the contract. If the buyer acts in good faith and without unreasonable delay, he or she may establish damages as the difference between the cost of cover and the contract price.

The court will not second-guess the buyer in determining the reasonableness of his or her actions but will merely examine whether the buyer's actions were reasonable at the time and place he acted. If it later turns out that a cheaper or more effective means of cover was available, this does not automatically mean that the buyer acted unreasonably. In addition to the difference between the cover price and the contract price, the buyer is entitled to any incidental or consequential damages incurred, but he or she must deduct from the claim any expenses saved as a result of the seller's breach.

The following case deals with cover.

Dura-Wood Treating Co. v. Century Forest Industries, Inc.

U.S. Court of Appeals, Fifth Circuit
675 F.2d 745 (1982)

Background: Dura-Wood (plaintiff) sued Century (defendant). Dura-Wood contacted Century in order to get additional crossties that it (Dura-Wood) needed to complete its contractual obligations for a third party (Smith Company). An agent of Dura-Wood, Clyde Norton, spoke with Melvin Durham, an agent of Century, about Century providing Dura-Wood with 20,000 crossties. Following the conversation, Norton sent a letter dated April 5, 1978 to Century. The letter stated:

"Confirming our conversation, please enter our order of 20,000 6 × 8 -8'6" No. 3 hardwood ties at $8.60 each.

"We will send instructions just as soon as we get some releases on the job."

Later on Norton telephoned Century to relate the date that the ties would be needed. Norton was told by another agent of Century, Harry Kerr, that "due to an increase in the cost of ties, he would not be able to ship that order and would have to cancel it." Dura-Wood was forced to manufacture an additional 20,000 ties in order to meet its obligations under the contract it had with Smith Company. Dura-Wood sued Century for damages due to breach of contract by Century.

Decision: The Court of Appeals ruled for Dura-Wood.

Johnson, Circuit Judge

When a seller breaches a contract, the buyer "may 'cover' by making in good faith and without unreasonable delay any reasonable purchase of or contract to purchase goods in substitution for those due from the seller." Tex Bus & Com Code Ann § 2.712(a). "Covering" is an optional remedy for the buyer faced with securing a damage award. . . . If he chooses to cover, "The buyer may recover from the seller as damages the difference between the cost of cover and the contract price together with any incidental or consequential damages." Tex Bus & Com Code § 2.712(b).

In the case sub judice, Dura-Wood claims—and the district court found—it engaged in a valid method of cover by manufacturing the necessary ties itself. Century Forest argues this is an invalid mechanism for cover. The basis of Century Forest's argument is that the Tex Bus & Com Code does not contemplate a buyer's covering by purchasing from itself. Century Forest argues the purchase of or contract to purchase goods in substitution of those due from the seller must be made "on the market."

Comment one to § 2.712 states the "section provides the buyer with a remedy aimed at enabling him to obtain the goods he needs thus meeting his essential need." This statement essentially describes two purposes that may be fulfilled by an appropriate cover. First, it puts an aggrieved buyer in the same economic position in which it would have been had the seller actually performed. Second, it allows the buyer to achieve its prime objective, which is acquiring the needed goods.

This court acknowledges there is some language indicating the purchase of substitute goods should be "on the market."

. . . However, actually purchasing the cover goods from another source is not the exclusive means of satisfying the presumption of § 2.712. In an appropriate situation, internally producing the substitute or cover goods can satisfy the recognized underlying presumptions of § 2.712.

. . . This court determines that a buyer, at least in the case sub judice, may cover by manufacturing goods internally. The purposes and presumptions of the Tex Bus & Com Code can be, and are, fulfilled in those instances—such as in the instant case— when the buyer is already in the marketplace and can produce the goods at a price approximating or lower than the market price.

Another factual matter concerns the necessity for the aggrieved buyer to cover without "unreasonable delay" and to make a "reasonable purchase." The Tex Bus & Com Code provides only limited aid for the court attempting to determine whether a cover purchase is reasonable in the appropriate respects.

"The test of proper cover is whether at the time and place the buyer acted in good faith and in a reasonable manner, and it is immaterial that hindsight may later prove that the method of cover used was not the cheapest or most effective." At a minimum this "test" suggests a buyer has some time in which to evaluate the situation and attempt to determine what may be the best or most appropriate means to cover. . . .

Finally, there is the factual requirement that the goods be "in substitution for those due from the seller." Comment two to § 2.712 points out that "[t]he definition of 'cover' . . . envisages . . . goods not identical with those involved but commercially usable as reasonable substitutes under the circumstances of the particular case."

The price of cross-ties was high during the time Dura-Wood was evaluating the market. Consequently, Dura-Wood's waiting to determine whether a decrease in market price might occur was not unreasonable. In addition, Dura-Wood continued to urge performance, as contemplated by § 2.610 of the Tex Bus & Com Code. The record also demonstrates the internally produced cover goods were commercially usable as reasonable substitutes for those due from Century Forest.

Incidental Damages. Incidental damages include, but are not limited to, "expenses reasonably incurred in inspection, receipt, transportation and care and custody of goods rightfully rejected, any commercially reasonable charges, expenses or commissions in connection with effecting cover and any other reasonable expense incident to the delay or other breach" (Section 2–715[1]).

Consequential Damages. Consequential damages include all losses resulting from the general or particular requirements and needs of the buyer that the seller had reason to know of at the time of contracting and that could not reasonably have been prevented by cover or otherwise. It is not necessary that the buyer establish damages with mathematical precision, but the buyer does bear the burden of proving the loss. If the seller does not wish to assume liability for consequential damages, he or she should use Section 2–719(3), which states:

Consequential damages may be limited or excluded unless the limitation or exclusion is unconscionable. Limitation of consequential damages for injury to the person in the case of consumer goods is prima facie unconscionable but limitation of damages where the loss is commercial is not.

Consequential damages also include an injury to a person or property if it proximately results from a breach of warranty.

Suppose the seller agrees to deliver 10,000 bushels of wheat to the buyer on October 15.

The price per bushel is $4.50. On October 15 the seller refuses to deliver the wheat. In this situation the buyer may receive the difference between the contract price and the cover price if he or she acts in good faith and without unreasonable delay. If the buyer purchases 10,000 bushels of wheat on the open market on October 15 for $5.00 per bushel, the buyer should receive $50,000 minus $45,000, or $5,000 plus any incidental or consequential damages caused by the seller's breach but minus any expenses saved as a result of the breach.

Damages

If the seller has failed to deliver goods in accordance with a contract or has repudiated the contract, the buyer may establish damages by covering, although it is not mandatory to cover. The buyer may, instead, elect to establish damages under Section 2–713, even if other goods have been purchased. The buyer is under no duty to use the price of the goods purchased in order to establish damages. In fact, the buyer may not wish to use the damages provided for under Section 2–712 if he or she made a better deal when purchasing the goods than was made under the original contract.

Market Price. Subsection I makes the measure of damages the difference between the market price at the time the buyer learned of the breach and the contract price. The buyer also can collect any incidental and consequen-

PREVENTIVE LAW
Cover

———

The Sherwood Florist was notified by its supplier that the supplier would not honor its contract for the delivery of flowers a few days before Mother's Day, the florist's biggest day of the year. In this situation the most logical action for the florist to take is to purchase the goods on the open market from another wholesaler. The florist obviously needs flowers to sell to its customers. If the florist is forced to pay more than the original contract price, it can recover the difference from the original supplier.

tial damages incurred, but he or she must credit the seller with any expenses saved as a result of the seller's breach. The market price will be determined by examining the current market price (when the buyer learned of the breach) at the place for tender or, if the buyer rejected the goods after they arrived or revoked acceptance, by examining the current market price (when the buyer learned of the breach) at the place of arrival. Thus the UCC uses as a guideline the market in which the buyer would have obtained cover had he or she attempted to cover.

If the seller was to have tendered goods to the buyer in Los Angeles, the market price to be used would be the prevailing price in the Los Angeles market at the time the buyer learned of the breach. If the buyer had attempted to cover, presumably this would have been the price he or she would have paid.

The following case deals with market price as a measure of damages.

Allied Canners & Packers v. Victor Packing Co. of California
Court of Appeals, First District
209 Cal. Rptr. 60 (1984)

Background: Allied (plaintiff) sued Victor (defendant). Allied was a corporation engaged in the business of exporting dry, canned and frozen fruit products. Victor was engaged in the business of packing and processing fruit. On September 3, 1976, Allied entered into a contract with Victor whereby Victor was to sell and deliver five containers (each holding 37,500 pounds) of raisins during the month of October 1976. On September 8, 1976 the parties entered into a second contract whereby Victor agreed to sell and deliver an additional five containers of raisins on the same terms. The contracts provided for Victor to sell the raisins at 29.75 cents per pound with a discount of 4 percent.

On September 9, 1976 heavy rains severely damaged the raisin crop, adversely affecting Victor's supply of raisins. On September 15 Victor notified Allied that it would not deliver the raisins as required by the contracts. Allied did not cover by purchasing raisins on the open market. The earliest either party could have bought raisins was October 1976, when the price of raisins was between 80 and 87 cents per pound.

Allied had earlier contracted to export the raisins to two buyers. One of Allied's buyers agreed to rescind its contract to purchase three containers of raisins, but the other buyer demanded delivery of seven containers of raisins. However, Allied's contract with the second buyer contained a clause that relieved Allied of any liability caused by developments beyond its control. Allied sued Victor for damages due to its breach of contract.

Decision: The California Court of Appeals ruled for Allied. The court held Victor was liable for $4,462.50—not the $150,281.25 Allied had demanded.

Rouse, Judge

Allied argued at trial, and contends on appeal, that it was the buyer under its contracts with Victor and therefore entitled to damages pursuant to Commercial Code § 2713, subdivision (1). . . .

Allied contends that pursuant to § 2713, subdivision (1), it is entitled to damages in the amount of $150,281.25, representing the difference between the contract price of 29.75 cents per pound and a market price of 87 cents per pound for 262,500 pounds (seven containers) of NTS raisins.

. . . It has been recognized that the use of the market price-contract price formula under § 2-713 does not, absent pure accident, result in a damage award reflecting the buyer's actual loss.

For example, in this case it is agreed that Allied's actual lost profit on the transaction was $4,462.50, while application of the market-contract price formula would yield damages of approximately $150,000.

Viewing § 2-713 as, in effect, a statutory provision for liquidated damages, it is necessary for us to determine whether a damage award to a buyer who has not covered is ever appropriately limited to the buyer's actual economic loss which is below the damages produced by the market-contract formula, and, if so, whether the present case presents a situation in which the damages should be so limited.

We conclude that in the circumstances of this case—in which the seller knew that the buyer had a resale contract . . . the buyer has not been able to show that it will be liable in damages to the buyer on its forward contract, and there has been no finding of bad faith on the part of the seller–the policy of § 1106, subdivision (1), that the aggrieved party be put in as good a position as if the other party had performed requires that the award of damages to the buyer be limited to its actual loss, the amount it expected to make on the transaction.

Value as Warranted. When the buyer has accepted goods and the time for revocation has passed, he or she is still entitled to damages if the seller fails to perform properly. The buyer's damages are the difference between the value of the goods accepted and the value they would have had if they had been as warranted. The buyer may also collect incidental and consequential damages. For example, if the purchaser of an automobile determines that the car has a defective horn, a court might award him or her as damages the cost of repairing or replacing the defective horn.

Specific Performance/Replevin

Specific Performance. The buyer may wish to obtain the goods because of inability to find substitute goods elsewhere or because the seller is in poor financial condition. The UCC gives the buyer the right to specific performance and replevin in certain circumstances. The buyer may obtain specific performance of the contract when the goods are unique or in other proper circumstances. What is unique depends on the circumstances. In any event, if a buyer is unable to cover, this is good evidence of other proper circumstances that merit specific performance of the contract. Figure 21-2 illustrates when a person may obtain specific performance of a contract.

Replevin. The buyer has a right of replevin for goods identified to the contract if after a reasonable effort he or she is unable to find substitute goods or if the circumstances indicate that he or she will be unable to find them.

Right to Resell. If the buyer rightfully rejects goods or properly revokes acceptance of them, the buyer has a security interest in the goods in his or her possession or control. The buyer may hold and resell these goods if he or she has paid a part of the price or has incurred expenses for the inspection, receipt, transportation, care, and custody of the goods. If the buyer resells, he or she must comply with Section 2-706 and must forward the balance of the amount received (beyond what was paid on the goods and expenses) to the seller.

Liquidated Damages

Rather than leave the determination of damages to the court, the parties may agree in advance what the measure of damages will be in the event that one of the parties to the contract breaches. When damages have been specified in the contract they are referred to as *liquidated damages.* A court will enforce the amount set by the parties only if it is a reasonable amount in light of all the circumstances. If it is unreasonably large or small, it is void as a penalty. This leaves the court free to award damages as seem appropriate under the circumstances. If the buyer would normally sustain $500 a day in damages in the

FIGURE 21–2
Obtaining Specific Performance of a Contract

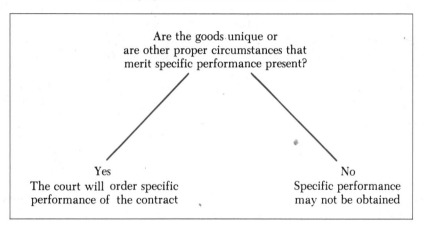

Are the goods unique or
are other proper circumstances that
merit specific performance present?

Yes
The court will order specific
performance of the contract

No
Specific performance
may not be obtained

BOX 21-1 ISSUES AND TRENDS
Computer Law—Limitation of Remedies

A problem that is becoming more widespread as more and more businesses and professionals use computer software is the failure of the software to perform as expected by the user. A user may experience very large losses when its software fails to perform properly. In such a case the purchaser may wish to sue for consequential damages. Many software sellers come with "as is" warranties. They do not even promise to correct flaws in the software. The position of the software makers has been that when a buyer opens the software, the buyer agrees to the conditions of the limited warranty.

It is quite likely this area of the law will continue to develop. In the meantime buyers should bear in mind they may be unable to collect damages for losses caused by the failure of the software to perform correctly.

event the seller fails to deliver on time, a provision awarding the buyer $10,000 a day for every day the seller is late in delivering the goods would be void as a penalty.

LIMITATION OR ALTERATION OF REMEDIES

The UCC does not require parties to a contract to follow these rules on remedies. The parties to a contract are free to shape their own remedies. They may add remedies not covered in the UCC, or they may choose to substitute different remedies for those provided in Article 2. Damages recoverable under Article 2 may be limited or altered. If the parties to a contract wish to specify one particular remedy to be employed exclusively, the contract must clearly indicate that the remedy is the sole remedy available to the aggrieved party.

All attempts to modify or eliminate the remedies provided under Article 2 are subject to the charge of unconscionability. Some minimum remedy must be available to the aggrieved party. If the remedy provisions in a contract are found to be unconscionable or to deprive either party of a substantial value of the bargain, the court may strike them and apply the remedies found in Article 2.

The following case involves a supplier of software. It should be noted that the court treated the software in this case as the sale of goods and therefore a sale covered under the UCC.

In general a computer software contract should be treated as a sale of services if a proper analysis of the design features of a program is really the predominant factor a purchaser is buying. On the other hand, prepackaged software programs ought to be treated as goods like the sale of a record or a cassette. Since the court treated this transaction as a sale of goods, it would seem that the court regarded the software here as something more like the sale of a prepackaged program than as a customized program. The court regarded any services provided as merely incidental to the sale of the goods—in this case a software program.

The court decided that the remedies provided in the contract failed of their essential purpose. Therefore, the buyer was entitled to any remedies provided to aggrieved buyers in the UCC.

RRX Industries, Inc. v. Lab-Con, Inc.

U.S. Court of Appeals, Ninth Circuit

772 F.2d 543 (1985)

Background: RRX Industries, Inc. (plaintiff) sued Lab-Con (defendant). TEKA agreed to supply RRX with a software system for use in its medical laboratories. The contract obligated TEKA to correct any malfunctions or "bugs" that arose in the system, but limited TEKA's liability to the contract price.

TEKA began installing the software system in January 1981 and completed it in June 1981. Bugs appeared in the system soon after installation. TEKA attempted to repair the bugs by instructing RRX employees, over the phone, how to correct the malfunctions. Subsequently, TEKA upgraded the system to make it more compatible with more sophisticated hardware. However, the system remained unreliable because the defects continued to exist.

Lab-Con was the successor corporation to TEKA. TEKA assigned the RRX software contract to Lab-Con. RRX sued TEKA and Lab-Con for breach of contract and fraud. The trial court concluded TEKA had materially breached the software contract. The court found that, because the exclusive remedy provided by the contract had failed of its essential purpose, it should apply the remedies found in Article 2 of the UCC.

The court found that if the supplier of the software is either unwilling or unable to provide a system that works as represented, *or* to fix the bugs in the software, then *these* limited remedies failed of their essential purpose. Because both limited remedies failed of their essential purpose, the court decided RRX was entitled to damages provided under the UCC rather than the damages provided in the contract. The trial court awarded RRX the amount paid under the contract, plus consequential damages, even though the contract limited damages to the contract price. Lab-Con appealed. Decision: The Court of Appeals affirmed the decision for RRX Industries.

Wright, Circuit Judge

In determining whether a contract is one of sale or to provide services we look to the essence of the agreement. When a sale predominates, incidental services provided do not alter the basic transaction.

Here, the sales aspect of the transaction predominates. The employee training, repair services, and system upgrading were incidental to sale of the software package and did not defeat characterization of the system as a good.

. . . Under the Code, a plaintiff may pursue all of the remedies available for breach of contract if its exclusive or limited remedy fails of its essential purpose. Appellants argue that the award of consequential damages was nevertheless improper because the contract limited damages to the amount paid.

In S.M. Wilson & Co. v. Smith Int'l., Inc., this court held that the failure of a repair remedy does not require permitting the recovery of consequential damages. . . . The court reasoned that where parties agree to a limitation of damages provision, courts should not alter the bargained-for risk allocation unless a breach of contract is so fundamental that it causes a loss which is not part of that allocation.

The district court's award of consequential damages is consistent with S.M. Wilson.

The court concluded that "since the defendants were either unwilling or unable to provide a system that worked as represented, *or* to fix the 'bugs' in the software, *these* limited remedies failed of their essential purpose. . . ." (emphasis added). This is a finding that *both* limited remedies failed of their essential purpose. The trial judge did not state that *because* the repair remedy failed, the limitation of damages provision should not be enforced.

The district court's choice of language and supporting authority creates an ambiguity. However, it properly found the default of the seller so total and fundamental that its consequential damages limitation was expunged from the contract.

. . . Neither bad faith nor procedural unconscionability is necessary under California Commercial Code § 2719(2). It provides an independent limit when circumstances render a damages limitation clause oppressive and invalid. The award of consequential damages was proper.

Norris, Judge *(concurring in part and dissenting in part)*

I concur in the majority opinion except to the extent that it affirms the award of consequential and incidental damages by the district court. Given the plain language of the contract, the applicable California law, and the district court's findings of fact, I would reverse the award of damages to the extent it exceeds the actual amount RRX paid Lab-Con for the software.

. . . Under the contract, Lab-Con undertakes to correct programming bugs, i.e. to "repair," but the parties agree that Lab-Con's liability for consequential damages for failure to correct the "bugs" shall in no event exceed the contract price. The bargain struck by the parties was that, while Lab-Con would be obligated to keep the software free of "bugs," there would be a precise "cap" on Lab-Con's liability.

In essence, § 2719 allows the parties to a contract to provide for alternative remedies, or to limit the amount of damages that may be awarded, or to do both, as was done in the contract between RRX and Lab-Con.

The uniqueness of consequential damages is reflected in the Code, which expressly contemplates that they may be limited. Limitations of consequential damages are governed by a separate subsection, § 2719(3). This subsection enables parties to limit consequential damages "unless the limitation or exclusion is unconscionable." Although the U.C.C. does not attempt to define precisely what is or is not unconscionable, "[u]nconscionability has generally been recognized to include an absence of meaningful choice on the part of one of the parties together with contract terms which are unreasonably favorable to the other party." Williams v. Walker-Thomas Furniture Co. Neither RRX nor the majority suggests that the limitation on consequential damages in this case is unconscionable in any respect.

The most pertinent authority is S.M. Wilson & Co. v. Smith International Inc., which I find extremely difficult to distinguish from the case before us. S.M. Wilson also involved the interpretation of California law with respect to an obligation to make repairs and a limitation on consequential damages. Our court enforced the limitation on damages provision notwithstanding the failure of the repair remedy. We conclude that "[t]he failure of the limited repair warranty to achieve its essential purpose makes available . . . the remedies as 'may be had as provided in this code.' [But] [t]his does not mean . . . that the bar to recovery of consequential damages should be eliminated." Thus, S.M. Wilson is clear authority that the failure of a repair remedy does not automatically result in the removal of the cap on consequential damages. The limitation was not found to be unconscionable in S.M. Wilson, and no one claims it is unconscionable in the case before us. Accordingly, I am unable to reconcile the majority's position with S.M. Wilson.

As noted in the chapter on warranties, the UCC permits consequential damages to be limited or excluded unless such an exclusion would be unconscionable. Where consumer goods are involved, however, a limitation of consequential damages for injury to a person is *prima facie* unconscionable (see Chapter 22).

REVIEW PROBLEMS

1. What is considered to be the seller's principal remedy under the UCC?
2. What is meant by "cover" as that term is used in the UCC?
3. How is the "market price" determined in a suit for breach of contract under the UCC?
4. When will a buyer be entitled to specific performance under the UCC?
5. Describe the difference between incidental and consequential damages.
6. Perry was injured while working on scaffolding. He intends to file suit for breach of warranty. The manufacturer of the scaffolding in its warranty agreed to make repairs to the equipment should they be needed. When does the statute of limitations begin to run on this equipment—on the tender of delivery or when the breach is or should have been discovered?
7. Sun Maid contracted to buy 1,800 tons of raisins from Victor Packing Company and Pyramid Packing Company. The packing companies should have been aware that Sun Maid's practice was to resell the raisins at a profit. The packers repudiated their contracts by refusing to deliver the last 610 tons of raisins. Is Sun Maid entitled to recover from the packers the profit it would have made on the resale of the 610 tons of raisins? How would these damages be characterized under the UCC? What Section, if any, grants such a remedy?
8. The Sedmaks orally contracted with Charlie's Chevrolet in Missouri to buy a certain Corvette for $15,000. The car was a limited edition manufactured by Chevrolet to commemorate the Corvette's selection as the Indianapolis 500 pace car. Six thousand such special cars were manufactured and each dealer was allotted only one. The Sedmaks ordered specific options on the car which differentiated it from most others in the limited edition. Charlie's subsequently received offers for the car of $24,000 and $28,000 from Hawaii and Florida, respectively. When the car arrived, Charlie's notified the Sedmaks that they could not have it for $15,000, but would have to bid for it. The Sedmaks, alleging that they could only acquire an identical car, if at all, at great difficulty, expense, and inconvenience, sued Charlie's for specific performance of the

contract. Do you think that the Sedmaks are entitled to specific performance under UCC Section 2–716?

9. Hays entered into an oral contract by which Wilson agreed to sell to Hays at a sale price of one cent per brick for 600,000 used uncleaned bricks. Hays paid Wilson $6,000 in advance. Wilson delivered 400,000 bricks. Hays sued for a return of the proportionate part of the sale price he did not receive—$2,000. May Hays recover $2,000? Wilson v. Hays, 544 S.W.2d 833 (Tex. Civ. App. 1976).

10. Publicker entered into a three-year requirements-type contract with Union Carbide in which Union Carbide agreed to supply Publicker with ethanol. During the three-year period Union Carbide indicated that it would no longer supply Publicker with ethanol unless Publicker agreed to pay Union Carbide an increased purchase price. Union Carbide contended that unforeseen increased costs entitled it to receive a higher price. Publicker refused and filed suit. Did Union Carbide breach the contract? If so, what damages, if any, is Publicker entitled to recover? Publicker Industries v. Union Carbide Corporation, 17 UCC Rep. Serv. 993 (E.D. Pa. 1975).

11. Thorstenon contracted to purchase a Case 730 tractor and mounted F-11 Farmland loader from Mobridge for $3,900. No delivery date was specified. In the fall of the next year Mobridge notified Thorstenon that there would be no delivery of the tractor. Thorstenon then purchased at a price of $1,000 more than the contract price the same tractor and loader. May Thorstenon recover the $1,000 extra cost? Thorstenon v. Mobridge Iron Works Co., 208 N.W.2d 715 (1973).

Warranties

When the seller of goods makes a representation as to the character, quality, or title of the goods as part of the contract of sale, and promises that certain facts are as represented, a warranty has been made. A seller who assures or guarantees the buyer that the goods will conform to certain standards may be liable for damages if the goods fail to meet those standards.

TYPES OF WARRANTIES

Table 22-1 lists how each type of warranty is created.

Express Warranties

Sometimes a seller, through words or actions, creates an *express warranty*. In a written document, or sometimes orally, the seller specifies precisely the terms of his or her guarantees to the buyer. Suppose Acme Machines states in literature provided with a lifting device that the machine will lift loads of up to 1,000 pounds. This is a representation of fact—either the machine will lift up to 1,000 pounds or it will not. A seller who makes such a state-

TABLE 22-1 TYPES OF WARRANTIES

Types	How Created
Express warranties	By affirmation of fact or promise
	By description of the goods
	By sample or model
Implied warranty of merchantability	If the seller is a merchant, automatically created by operation of law
Implied warranty of fitness for a particular purpose	Created by operation of law in certain situations
Warranty of title	Automatically created by operation of law

ment creates an express warranty that the machine will lift up to 1,000 pounds. If a buyer purchases the machine and later learns that its lifting capacity does not exceed 400 pounds, the buyer can bring an action for breach of an express warranty.

Implied Warranties of Quality

Not every warranty arises out of the words or actions of the seller. Sometimes a warranty as to the quality of the goods arises by operation of law. Two warranties arise out of a sale automatically by operation of law—the implied warranty of merchantability and the implied warranty of fitness for a particular purpose.

In the example mentioned earlier, suppose the manufacturer designed and sold the lifting device for use in loading railroad boxcars. If the machine fails to function properly when used in loading boxcars, the manufacturer has breached the implied warranty of merchantability. This warranty arose, not out of any words or actions of the seller, but merely as a result of making the sale. The machine was not merchantable because it was not fit for the purposes for which such goods are sold.

Assume instead that the purchaser of this machine told the seller what his requirements were. The buyer stated that he needed a machine capable of lifting very dense packages weighing around 2,000 pounds. The buyer relied on the seller's skill and judgment to select a suitable machine for him. These facts create an implied warranty of fitness for a particular purpose.

Implied Warranty of Title

A third warranty also automatically arises from a sale—the *warranty of title*. What if the buyer in this example learned after purchasing the lifting device that it had been stolen? In this case, by selling stolen merchandise, the seller has breached the implied warranty of title.

These warranties are discussed in greater detail in the following material.

WARRANTY LAW

Development of the Law

Warranty cases are one of the most common types of cases arising out of the sale of a product. Sometimes a person or company who purchases a product experiences problems with it. Then the question arises, Whose responsibility is it to repair the product? The buyer naturally hopes the seller will repair the product. The actual rights of the buyer are in part governed by the wording of the warranty, if any, and in part by statutes.

For many years the law favored the seller—the law followed the doctrine of *caveat emptor* (let the buyer beware). Starting with the twentieth century the law slowly moved in the direction of recognizing more rights for the buyer. More recently, really starting in the late 1960s, the consumer movement has pressed the courts and legislatures to strengthen the rights of purchasers. Certainly one cannot state that the doctrine of *caveat emptor* governs the law of sales today.

Source of Warranty Law

The law governing all aspects of sales law, including warranties, developed on a case-by-case basis. For many centuries the law of sales was found in the decisions of judges dealing with real cases.

Toward the end of the nineteenth century scholars and practitioners became increasingly dissatisfied with the case-law approach. Many people advocated more uniformity in the law. This movement gave rise to the drafting of the Uniform Sales Act (1906), which some states eventually adopted. After a number of years, the Uniform Sales Act was superseded by the Uniform Commercial Code (UCC) (1952), which has been adopted by every state except Louisiana. Louisiana has enacted some parts of the UCC, but not Article 2. Article 2 of the UCC covers the law of sales, including the rules relating to warranties.

While the UCC rules generally govern in the area of warranties, bear in mind that other statutes have been passed that have an impact on these rules. The discussion in the text is largely confined to the UCC rules.

Sale of Goods

In order to determine whether Article 2 of the UCC applies to a given case, an attorney must determine if the facts involve a sale of goods. A *sale* is defined in Section 2–106 of the UCC as "the passing of title from the seller to the buyer for a price." *Goods* are tangible (having a physical existence) property that is movable at the time of identification to the contract (Section 2–105).

Suppose Margaret agrees to sell her watch to Penelope. A watch is a tangible, movable article. If the parties intend to pass title to the watch for a price, this transaction constitutes a sale under Section 2–106.

What if Margaret *gives* the watch to Penelope? No sale is involved in such a transaction and the principles of Article 2 do not control. A gift is not a sale of property for a price.

Things Other Than Goods

The mood of the courts in the 1970s, as earlier indicated, shifted in the direction of consumer rights. Many courts were confronted with cases in which the plaintiff wished to claim some warranty protection under the UCC but had not purchased goods. Such cases often arise with leases. Technically, Article 2 does not apply to leases because the parties to the transaction do not intend a transfer of title.

Nonetheless, some courts have extended the warranty provisions of the UCC to nonsale transactions such as leases. These courts have reasoned that a lease is very much like a sale, so as a matter of public policy the warranty provisions of Article 2 should be extended to the lease transaction. In other cases courts have found warranties in the sale of homes or in personal service contracts.

The point to bear in mind is that a plaintiff should not give up on pursuing a case based on Article 2 warranties simply because the transaction does not appear to be a sale under Article 2. If a court feels there is good reason to extend the protection of the UCC beyond a pure sale of goods, it may elect to do so.

WARRANTY OF TITLE

Provisions

When a purchaser buys goods, receipt of good title to the goods is expected. This belief is reflected in the provisions of Section 2–312(1), which states that the seller of goods warrants (1) the title conveyed is good and its transfer rightful and (2) the goods are free of any security interest or other encumbrance of which the buyer at the time of contracting has no knowledge. This warranty arises automatically by operation of law.

Exposing Buyer to a Suit

The first provision—that the title conveyed is good and its transfer rightful—assures the buyer of a good title. Certainly, if a seller conveys stolen property to a buyer, the seller has breached the warranty of title. Suppose, however, that a seller, believing he owns an automobile, sells this automobile to a buyer. After the sale, a third party informs the buyer that he, the third party, is the one who lawfully holds title to the automobile. A title is not good

---

BOX 22-1 ISSUES AND TRENDS
Extension of Warranties to Leases and Bailments

—

Marsh leased a videocassette recorder from "Rent It All" for a term of one month. When she got the VCR home, Marsh plugged it in and began to watch a videotape she had rented—*Flashdance*. After about ten minutes, Marsh noticed that smoke was coming from the VCR unit. She was walking over to the machine to unplug it when the machine burst into flames. After Marsh finally succeeded in putting out the fire, she phoned the rental center to see if she could recover for her losses. The rental center refused to help her because it did not warrant the products it leased.

Is Marsh unable to obtain any relief from the rental store? In the past Marsh would have been out of luck. However, a growing number of courts are extending the Uniform Commercial Code's warranty provisions to leases and to bailments. The rationale behind the actions of the courts is that they see no difference between the way a person who buys a product uses the product and the way a person who leases a product uses the product. Therefore many courts have ruled that a person who leases a product should be entitled to the same warranty rights as a person who buys a product. Even though Marsh leased the recorder, she should be given the same warranty rights as a person who purchased such a product.

---

if it unreasonably exposes the buyer to a lawsuit. In this case the buyer may be forced to litigate the issue of title in court with the third party. Whatever the resolution of the case—that is, whether or not the third party establishes that he is the lawful owner of the automobile—if the third party's claim is not frivolous, the buyer may sue the seller for breach of the implied warranty of title. The seller's questionable title wrongfully exposed the buyer to a suit.

Free of Encumbrance

The seller also warrants to the buyer that the goods are free of any security interest or other encumbrance of which the buyer at the time of contracting has no knowledge. If the seller conveys mortgaged property to the buyer

without informing the buyer of this fact, this violates the warranty of title.

Goods Do Not Infringe

A merchant-seller also warrants that the goods sold do not infringe upon the patent, trademark, or copyright of a third party. This is true unless the seller has manufactured the goods according to the buyer's specifications.

Circumstances Indicating No Warranty of Title

There is no warranty of title in a contract for sale when the circumstances give the buyer reason to know that the person selling does not claim title in himself or herself or that he or she is purporting to sell only such right or title as he or she or a third person may have. This means that when the buyer purchases goods at a sheriff's sale, or from an executor or foreclosing creditor, the seller is not warranting the title.

Exclusion of Warranty

The warranty of title may be excluded or modified by specific language that makes the buyer aware that the seller is not claiming title in himself or herself or that the seller is selling only whatever right or title he or she or a third person may have. This is the only manner in which a warranty of title can be excluded or modified. Specific language must be included in the contract for sale beyond that specified in Section 2–316, which deals with exclusion of express and implied warranties, to make clear to the buyer that the seller does not warrant the title to the goods. The reason for this requirement is that the buyer normally may expect a seller to warrant the title even though the seller is excluding all other warranties.

EXPRESS WARRANTIES

Provisions

The UCC (Section 2–313) states that express warranties are created as follows:

(a) Any affirmation of fact or promise made by the seller to the buyer which relates to the goods and becomes part of the basis of the bargain creates an express warranty that the goods shall conform to the affirmation or promise.
(b) Any description of the goods which is made part of the basis of the bargain creates an express warranty that the goods shall conform to the description.
(c) Any sample or model which is made part of the basis of the bargain creates an express warranty that the whole of the goods shall conform to the sample or model.

Affirmation of Fact

Although a specific factual statement will create a warranty, a statement as to the value of goods or a statement of the seller's opinion or commendation of the goods does not create a warranty (Section 2–313[a]). It is reasonable to expect that a person selling goods will make favorable statements about the product being sold. For this reason statements as to value or mere opinions do not create an express warranty under the UCC.

Suppose the salesman at Al's Used Car Lot states to a person looking at a 1984 Ford, "That car is the best deal in town." Such a statement is the typical positive statement a buyer expects of a seller. No one expects a seller to run his or her products down. Because the average purchaser expects these favorable comments from a seller, a buyer may not rely upon a statement like the one here dealing with the 1984 Ford. It may not be relied upon in a breach-of-warranty case.

Basis of the Bargain. However, Comment 8 to Section 2–313 indicates that the critical question remains, What statements of the seller have in the circumstances and in objective judgment become part of the basis of the bargain? All the statements of the seller are part of the basis of the bargain unless good reason is shown to the contrary.

Exactly what is meant by the phrase "basis of the bargain"? The drafters of the UCC intended for the courts to examine what the agreement between the parties actually was. What terms did the parties agree upon in striking a deal? *Basis of the bargain* is a somewhat murky concept, but it is very much like reliance. Suppose the seller of the 1984 Ford in the earlier example states, "The tires on the

Ford are brand-new radials and cost over $500." The buyer appears to be impressed by this statement, and says, "Well, in that case, the car is a good buy. I'll take the car." If the tires turn out to be bias-belted retreads with 7,500 miles on them, has the seller breached an express warranty? Was any warranty created by this seller's statement? The answer to both questions is yes. The seller's statement is one of fact and becomes part of the deal between the buyer and seller because the buyer is apparently induced by this fact to enter into the agreement. The seller's statement will be treated by the courts as a part of the basis of the bargain.

Puffing. If the seller of a dining-room set says, "This is the best dining-room set in town," a buyer would not reasonably use this statement as part of the basis of the bargain between the parties. This type of language is commonly referred to as "puffing." To create an express warranty under the UCC more than mere puffing by the seller is required. If the seller instead says, "This table is solid oak," an express warranty that the table is solid oak is created. Either the table is oak or it is not; whether it is oak is a question of fact, not of opinion. If it turns out that the table is pine stained an oak color, and the buyer wanted an oak table, the buyer may bring an action for breach of an express warranty created by the seller's statement.

Many of the cases dealing with puffing do not cite a clear rule. The more specific the statement is, the more likely that a court will call it one of fact and not opinion. Whether the statement is oral or written is also important. The most commonly cited rule could be called the fact-opinion rule as stated by the court in Royal Business Machines v. Lorraine Corp., 633 F.2d 34 (1980):

The decisive test for whether a given representation is a warranty or merely an expression of the seller's opinion is whether the seller asserts a fact of which the buyer is ignorant or merely states an opinion or judgment on a matter of which the seller has no special knowledge and on which the buyer may be expected also to have an opinion and to exercise his judgment. . . . General statements to the effect that goods are "the best" . . . or are "of good quality," or will "last a lifetime" and be "in perfect condition" . . . are generally regarded as expressions of the seller's opinion or "the puffing of his wares" and do not create an express warranty.

Some cases following this test have failed to find an express warranty. For example, in Carpenter v. Alberto Culver Co., 184 N.W.2d 547 (Mich. App. 1970), the plaintiff brought suit because she suffered an adverse skin reaction after using a hair dye manufactured by Alberto Culver. The plaintiff argued that an express warranty was created by the City Drug Store through a clerk who stated to her that several of the clerk's friends used the dye and that her own "hair came out very nice" and the plaintiff "would get very fine results." The court found these rather vague statements were not express warranties. Other courts, however, have found such statements to be express warranties. In General Supply & Equipment Co. v. Phillips, 490 S.W.2d 913 (Tex. Civ. App. 1972), the plaintiff brought suit over some plastic paneling sold by the defendant to the plaintiff to cover the plaintiff's greenhouses as roofing material. The paneling had been advertised as follows: "Tests show no deterioration in 5 years normal use" and "It won't turn black or discolor . . . even after years of exposure." The paneling darkened and turned black about two years after it was installed. The court noted that the plaintiff had knowledge of the facts asserted in the advertising and would not have bought the paneling had he not seen the advertisement. It found that these statements appearing in the advertising constituted an express warranty. (See also *Interco v. Randustrial* later in this chapter.) Other cases in the warranty area seem to follow different tests for determining if a statement is or is not puffing.

It is sometimes difficult to distinguish between a statement of fact and a statement of opinion. In making this determination, the court examines whether the seller has used words that imply or convey an express warranty to the buyer. Predicting the outcome of a puffing defense is quite difficult.

Puffing is a major defense in express-warranty cases. Ask yourself why it should be a defense at all. If a merchant makes untrue statements about his or her products, why should he or she escape from the bargain with a defense like puffing? Generally the types of statements that are regarded as puffing are vague statements of praise not clearly relied upon by the buyer. Even so, no one can be certain about the outcome of a case.

Suppose you purchase a steak at a restaurant because an advertisement you read states, "I am sure you will find this steak to be one of the most tender and juicy steaks you have ever eaten." If you find it tough and dry, will you be able to bring a case for breach of warranty? The court would probably find such a statement by an advertiser to be mere puffing upon which you may not reasonably rely. Should this be the outcome of the case?

The following case discusses a statement that the court regarded as puffing.

Whitmer v. Schneble v. House of Hoyt, Inc.

Appellate Court of Illinois, Second District

331 N.E.2d 115 (1975)

Background: The Schnebles (plaintiffs) filed suit against House of Hoyt (defendant). On July 26, 1968 Robert and Frances Schneble bought a female Doberman pinscher from the House of Hoyt. They alleged that the dog was represented to them as a "docile dobe" appropriate for one "who is in need of a dog for companionship and friendship but wants very little aggressiveness in him." However, the bill of sale, signed by the Schnebles, described the dog as "medium aggressive," which was further described in the literature given to them as a dobe that "can love and fight with equal zeal" and was suitable "for people who want true protection."

Some two and a half years later the dog was bred and had puppies. On January 9, 1971 Sherry Whitney, a neighbor's child, was looking at the puppies when she was bitten by the mother. The parents of Sherry Whitney sued the Schnebles. The Schnebles then filed a third-party complaint against the House of Hoyt on the theory of breach of express warranty. The trial court dismissed the Schnebles' complaint against the House of Hoyt. The Schnebles appealed.

Decision: The Appellate Court affirmed the decision for House of Hoyt.

Hallett, Judge

The Schnebles contend (a) that Hoyt is liable to them because of the breach of an express warranty that the "dobe" was "docile," etc.

It is very doubtful whether any of the language alleged in Count I amounted to an express warranty. Statements merely of the seller's opinion or sales talk do not constitute express warranties. Furthermore, as we have indicated, the bill of sale and brochure, which the Schnebles concede, destroy their claim.

But even if there were an express warranty, it would not appear that there was a breach. Nowhere do the Schnebles allege that Hoyt stated that the dog would not bite. Even a docile dog is known and expected to bite under certain circumstances. And this court will not infer a warranty that the dog will never bite from the language which was used. "[T]he law will not lend itself to the creation of an implied warranty which patently runs counter to the experience of mankind or known forces of nature. It will not read into any sale or bailment a condition or proviso which is unreasonable, impossible, or absurd." Meester v. Roose (1966), 259 Iowa 357, 144 NW2d 274, 276.

In addition, the statements complained of only describe the personality of the dog at the time it was sold. There is no warranty by the seller that the dog's personality will not change in the future. Yet the plaintiff did not allege that there had been a breach of the warranty on the date of the sale or that the condition of the dog had remained unchanged during the 2½ years since the sale. Indeed, it would be difficult for the plaintiffs to so allege since the dog had new masters, gotten older and had puppies.

We therefore conclude that there is no merit to this contention.

Description

An express warranty can also be created by describing goods if the description is part of the basis of the bargain between the parties. The seller need not use the word "warranty," nor is it necessary that the buyer rely on the seller's affirmation of fact or promise in order to find that the seller made an express warranty. Comment 3 to Section 2–313 states: "In actual practice affirmations of fact made by the seller about the goods during a bargain are regarded as part of the description of those goods; hence no particular reliance on such statements need be shown in order to weave them into the fabric of the agreement." The description need not be by words. Technical specifications, blueprints, or the like, if made part of the basis of the bargain between the parties, can create an express warranty.

Sample or Model

An express warranty also can be made by a sample or model that is made part of the basis of the bargain between the parties. When the seller actually draws an item from the bulk of goods that is the subject matter of the sale, the item is referred to as a sample; when a demonstration item is offered for inspection, it is called a model.

Creation After Contracting

It is possible for an express warranty to be created after the contract has been executed by the parties. If the buyer asks the seller, for example, whether the plastic just bought will withstand freezing temperatures and the seller replies "yes," this might constitute an express warranty. Section 2–209(2) of the UCC permits modification of a contract without consideration. However, the Statute of Frauds must be complied with.

If the parties orally agree upon an express warranty, but the final executed contract fails to reflect this agreement, the party wishing to assert the warranty may encounter difficulties in establishing its existence. The parol evidence rule found in Section 2–202 prohibits any evidence that contradicts a writing intended by the parties as a final expression of their agreement.

The following facts illustrate a typical express-warranty case: A purchaser of a mobile home, John Benfer, was told that the mobile home he was interested in purchasing had quarter-inch plywood sheathing that made it better than cheaper units. A mobile home similar to the one purchased by Benfer was on the seller's lot. The seller pointed out the grade of plywood sheathing to Benfer. Among the written warranties given Benfer was one specifically warranting that his mobile home would come with quarter-inch plywood. The home delivered to Benfer did not come with this sheathing. This is a breach of express warranty by the seller.

The following case discusses the issues of puffing and reliance in express-warranty cases.

Interco, Inc. v. Randustrial Corp.

Court of Appeals of Missouri
533 S.W.2d 257 (1976)

Background: Suit was brought against Randustrial Corp. (defendant) by Interco (plaintiff) for breach of warranty. Randustrial asserted as defenses that its statements were mere puffing and that no evidence of reliance on the statements existed. Though the court rejected these defenses, the jury found for Randustrial. Interco appealed. Decision: The Appeals Court affirmed the jury verdict, although it found that the statement in question was not puffing and was relied upon by Interco.

Gunn, Judge

Interco maintains facilities consisting of 21 buildings for its International Shoe Company division in St. Louis. In 1971, Building No. 3 required floor repairs on the first story. The floor was extremely rough, rendering it difficult to move merchandise between the storage area and loading dock. Interco's Manager of Facilities Engineering read Randustrial's building maintenance supply catalogue and from it ordered a product designated as Resilihard which was designed as a floor covering to smooth rough areas. However, after a discussion with Randustrial's sales representative and upon the latter's recommendation, another of Randustrial's products, called Sylox, was selected because of its flexibility. Sylox was applied to the first floor of Building No. 3, and its use was satisfactory for Interco's purposes.

The following year—1972—a floor problem similar to that in Building No. 3 developed in Building No. 1. The second floor of Building No. 1 became rough, creating difficulty in the movement of hand-truck traffic. Because of the favorable experience with Sylox and also by reason of Randustrial's catalogue description for its use, Interco ordered and installed Sylox to the second floor of Building No. 1. The catalogue described the purpose of Sylox as "to patch or resurface old wood floors for hand-trucking or foot traffic." The order was placed and the Sylox applied without the advice of or consultation with Randustrial's representatives. The consequences were wholly undesirable, for shortly after its application, the Sylox began to deteriorate and became unserviceable; it was an impediment rather than an expedient in the movement of hand-trucking.

Interco maintains that it was entitled to judgment as a matter of law based on a breach of express warranty by Randustrial. Interco argues that the purchase of Sylox was based on the following Randustrial catalogue description of the material and asserts an express warranty thereby:

> Sylox is a hard yet malleable material which bonds firm to wood floors for smooth and easy hand-trucking. Sylox will absorb considerable flex without cracking and is not softened by spillage of oil, grease or solvents.

We have noted that Interco claims the existence of a warranty as to Sylox, and Randustrial argues the absence of a warranty. We disagree with Randustrial's contentions in this regard. Although Randustrial contends its reference to Sylox in its sales catalogue did not constitute an express warranty, if the words used in the catalogue constitute a description or an affirmation of fact or promise about Sylox and became a part of the basis of the bargain, an express warranty was created. Randustrial also asserts that there could be no breach of warranty because Interco had failed to test the material before applying it to Building No. 1 and had failed to seek advice from Randustrial on its application. The uncontradicted evidence was that the cause of the breakup of the Sylox was the movement of the floor. There was nothing vague in Interco's evidence as to the intended use of Sylox. The evidence was palpable that Interco wanted something to withstand flex without breaking. The catalogue stated that "Sylox will absorb considerable flex." Thus, there was a description or affirmation of fact or "warranty" regarding Sylox giving rise to the purpose for which it was purchased by Interco. This was not mere puffing of a product. Interco was entitled to take the catalogue description of Sylox at its face value and plain meaning. There was no need to consult Randustrial or seek its advice regarding the use of Sylox. Any suggestion that Interco was at fault for not having tested the product or sought consultation is fatuous, for the catalogue description made no such requirement. All the buyers are required to establish is that the express warranties were made and that they were false, thereby establishing a breach of the contract. Interco had no obligation to establish a defect in Sylox as Randustrial suggests. We have previously noted that there has been no contention that the Sylox was misapplied.

Randustrial's argument that Interco failed to prove reliance on any warranty is also not felicitous. There is no mention of reliance in 2-313. And the comments to that section of the UCC reveal that the concept of reliance as required in pre-UCC warranty cases was purposefully abandoned.

The fact that the language read by Interco was contained in a catalogue and was basically an advertisement does not preclude a finding that it is a warranty. A brochure, catalogue, or advertisement may constitute an express warranty. . . . However, the catalogue advertisement or brochure must have at least been read, as the UCC requires the proposed express warranty be part of the basis of the bargain. Randustrial does not dispute the fact that Interco had read the catalogue.

Randustrial relies on the pre-UCC case of *Turner* v. *Central Hardware Co.* (1964), arguing that the statement that Sylox "will absorb considerable flex" merely reflects the seller's opinion of the goods and creates no warranty. In the Central Hardware

Co. case, a ladder advertised as "mighty strong and durable" collapsed under use causing injury to the plaintiff. In discussing the use of factual information vis-a-vis mere "sales talk" in advertising, the court said:

> The seller's privilege to puff his wares, enhance their quality and recommend their value, even to the point of exaggeration, is unquestionable, so long as his salesmanship remains in the field of "dealer's talk," commendation or mere expressions of opinion. . . .

We believe that the foregoing pre-UCC law continues under 2-313, which specifically excludes a seller's mere opinion or commendation from being interpreted as an express warranty. The Central Hardware Co. case does make clear, though, that the language chosen by the seller in his advertising must be interpreted in favor of the buyer in order to restrict "untruthful puffing of wares." We believe that this is the same type of approach desired by the draftsmen of the UCC. . . . An important factor is whether the seller assumes to assert a fact of which the buyer may be expected to have an opinion and be able to express his own judgment.

Although Randustrial is pertinacious in its contention that the catalogue content regarding absorbability of considerable flex is merely a reflection of opinion, we must disagree. It is manifest that the words so used were meant to induce purchases through the assurance that considerable flex would be absorbed and were not mere opinion. The words were an affirmation of fact within the meaning of 2-313.

But having determined that an express warranty as to Sylox did exist, we reach the crux of this case—whether there was a breach of that warranty by Randustrial as a matter of fact. Ordinarily—and this case is no exception—the question of whether there has been a breach of warranty is a factual matter to be determined by the trier of fact.

The keystone of this case and the basis for Randustrial's triumph before the jury and affirmation by this court continues to be the phrase "absorb considerable flex." That phrase is too imprecise to be defined as a matter of law. It was for the jury to determine as a matter of fact whether Sylox conformed to the promise to absorb considerable flex. The jury could have reasonably found on the basis of the evidence presented to it that the flex or movement in the second floor of Building No. 1 was more than considerable and more than Sylox was designed to accommodate. The fact issue as to what amounted to considerable flex in this case was proper for the jury to determine.

Note that the plaintiff must have relied on the advertisement for it to be an express warranty. The advertisement thus must be part of the basis of the bargain between the parties for any express warranty to arise based on such advertising literature. The court in *Interco* required some evidence that Interco knew of the statement in the catalogue, "Sylex will absorb considerable flex," and that Interco relied upon the statement in making the purchase.

The absence of reliance might prevent a plaintiff from recovering. Suppose the plaintiff, Hagenbuch, purchased a cross-pen hammer from a salesman of Snap-On Tools. The plaintiff argued that the Snap-On Tools 1969 catalogue created an express warranty. The catalogue stated that the hammer was "excellent for the repair work since it has plenty of beef to handle heavy tires. Also can be used for many other jobs such as straightening frames, bumper brackets, bumpers, puller work, etc. . . ." The plaintiff was struck in the eye by a chip from the hammer. As there was no evidence that Hagenbuch had relied on the catalogue description when he purchased the hammer, Hagenbuch was not entitled to recover for breach of express warranty.

This case illustrates the importance for the plaintiff of establishing that the advertising became part of the basis of the bargain between the parties. Without evidence that the plaintiff was influenced by the advertising statement in question, it is unlikely a plaintiff will be able to establish an express warranty.

IMPLIED WARRANTY OF MERCHANTABILITY

Provisions

Section 2–314 of the UCC states:

(1) Unless excluded or modified (Section 2–316), a warranty that the goods shall be merchantable is implied in a contract for their sale if the seller is a merchant with respect to goods of that kind. Under this section the serving for value of food or drink to be consumed either on the premises or elsewhere is a sale.

(2) Goods to be merchantable must be at least such as
   (a) pass without objection in the trade under the contract description; and
   (b) in the case of fungible goods, are of fair average quality within the description; and

(c) are fit for the ordinary purposes for which such goods are used; and
   (d) run, within the variations permitted by the agreement, of even kind, quality and quantity within each unit and among all units involved; and
   (e) are adequately contained, packaged, and labeled as the agreement may require; and
   (f) conform to the promises or affirmations of fact made on the container or label if any.

(3) Unless excluded or modified (Section 2–316) other implied warranties may arise from course of dealing or usage of trade.

Thus the implied warranty of merchantability arises by operation of law—not as a result of any warranty expressly stated in the contract. The requirements stated in Section 2–314(2) are *cumulative,* but subsections (e) and (f) deal with packaging, and subsection (b) deals with fungible, or interchangeable, goods. This is not an exhaustive list of what is "merchantable" but merely states that the goods must at least comply with these requirements.

Generally the court will try to determine if the goods are fit for the ordinary purposes for which such goods are used. In making this determination, the court will consider the manner in which such goods are used. A seller who delivers shoes that come apart when the buyer walks around in them has breached the warranty of merchantability because shoes certainly should be fit for ordinary walking.

Merchants

It should be noted that Section 2–314 applies only when the seller is a merchant. If the seller is not a merchant, no such warranty arises. For example, Siemen brought suit for breach of the implied warranty of merchantability. He had purchased an old multirip saw from a man in the sawmill business. While operating the machine, Siemen was injured. Siemen cannot recover based on the implied warranty of merchantability because the defendant was not in the business of selling saws and therefore was not a merchant pursuant to Section 2–104.

If a seller is a nonmerchant, there is no implied warranty of merchantability. Nonetheless, these provisions may serve as guidelines when the nonmerchant-seller states that the goods are guaranteed.

Fungible Goods

If the sale involves fungible goods, the court will examine whether the goods are of "fair average quality." This means that the goods must be roughly of the same type as specified in the contract. Some of the lowest quality goods could be included in the delivery, but the mix must average out to be close to the standard in the contract.

Food

In determining whether or not food is merchantable, some courts follow the "foreign-natural distinction"—that is, a given food is merchantable if it contains elements that are natural to the product. A consumer who breaks his tooth on a cherry pit while eating a piece of cherry pie would be unable to recover in a jurisdiction following this test. Other jurisdictions follow the "reasonable expectation" test—that is, only those things that we reasonably expect to be in the food should be in it. In a jurisdiction following the "reasonable expectation" test the consumer who breaks a tooth on a cherry pit in a piece of pie might be able to recover.

In a famous case involving breach of the implied warranty of merchantability, Webster v. Blue Ship Tea Room, Inc., 198 N.E.2d 309 (Mass. 1964), the plaintiff brought suit because, while she was eating fish chowder at the Blue Ship Tea Room, a fish bone became lodged in her throat. This led to two esophago-scopies and the eventual extraction of the fish bone. The question in this case was whether there had been a breach of the implied warranty of merchantability. The court delved into the culinary traditions of New England and determined that fish chowder normally contains large chunks of fish in which a consumer ought to expect bones. The court ruled that the occasional presence of fish bones should be anticipated by a customer, and therefore it decided for the Tea Room.

IMPLIED WARRANTY OF FITNESS FOR A PARTICULAR PURPOSE

Particular Purpose

If the seller knows at the time of contracting the particular purpose for which the buyer wants the goods and the buyer relies on the seller's skill or judgment to select or furnish suitable goods, there is an implied warranty that the goods will be fit for the purpose the buyer specifies at the time of contracting (Section 2–315).

A particular purpose differs from the ordinary purpose for which goods are used. If a buyer wishes to purchase climbing shoes and asks the seller to select a pair for him or her, the seller breaches this warranty if he or she sells the buyer shoes used only for ordinary walking. The shoes might be suitable for walking and therefore merchantable, but they would not be suitable for the particular purpose the buyer specified. It is not necessary that the buyer state how he or she intends to use the product as long as the circumstances should make the seller aware of the needs of the buyer.

Simply because the goods are merchantable does not mean they are fit for the buyer's particular purpose. If the buyer wishes to purchase a furnace for use at home and tells the seller that he or she wants to heat a house of 2,000 square feet, the seller has breached the implied warranty of fitness for a particular purpose if the heater is inadequate to heat the buyer's house, even though it operates properly and would heat a much smaller house quite nicely.

Unlike the implied warranty of merchant- ability, this warranty applies to both merchants and nonmerchants.

Reliance

Reliance is critical under Section 2–315. If the buyer supplies specifications to the seller, there is no reliance and hence no breach of the warranty, even if the seller knows the purpose for which the goods are to be used. The following case deals with the implied warranty of fitness for a particular purpose.

Gates v. Abernathy

Court of Appeals of Oklahoma
11 UCC 491 (1972)

Background: Gates (plaintiff) brought suit against Abernathy (defendant), the owner of the shop, Penelope's. Gates purchased a dress for his wife. He was assured that the dress was suitable for his wife. It was not, and Gates sued to receive his money back. The trial court decided for Gates, and Abernathy appealed.
Decision: The Appeals Court affirmed the decision for Gates.

Neptune, Justice

One of the plaintiffs, Dr. Paul Gates, wished to purchase some clothes to give his wife (the other plaintiff) as a Christmas present. Dr. Gates had never before bought any clothing for his wife and was ignorant of what size she wore. He was aware, however, that his wife had frequently shopped at "Penelope's," a shop owned by defendant, and that she had been waited on there by the store manager, Penny. Therefore, he went to "Penelope's," spoke to Penny and explained to her that he wished to buy some clothes to give to his wife as a Christmas present. Penny showed Dr. Gates certain items in sizes that she said she was certain would be proper for Mrs. Gates. Dr. Gates picked out three pant suits in the size that Penny had recommended and purchased them. It was understood that if the suits did not fit or if there "was any problem" they could be returned.

When she received the gifts, Mrs. Gates tried them on and discovered that they were much too big. Shortly after Christmas, Dr. Gates returned the pant suits to "Penelope's" and received a credit slip. When Mrs. Gates came to the shop with the credit slip she was unable to find anything in her size. She was directed to another store owned by defendant but found nothing acceptable in her size. She demanded the money back but this was refused. Dr. and Mrs. Gates brought this action to recover the purchase price of the suits plus attorney fees.

Plaintiffs sued under section 2–315 claiming breach of an implied warranty of fitness for a particular purpose. Defendant entered a general denial. The trial court sitting without a jury entered judgment for plaintiff in the sum of $192.62 plus an attorney's fee of $50 plus $4 for costs. Defendant appeals.

Appellant asserts that this is not a situation where appellees could recover on an implied warranty of fitness. There is no merit in this contention. The statute upon which the action is based, section 2–315, states:

> Where the seller at the time of contracting has reason to know any particular purpose for which the goods are required and that the buyer is relying on the seller's skill or judgment to select or furnish suitable goods, there is unless excluded or modified under the next section an implied warranty that the goods shall be fit for such purpose.

It is hard to imagine a case which fits into the outline of the statute as well as this one. It is uncontested that the buyer here was relying on the judgment of the seller to furnish the kind of goods he wanted, nor is there any question that the seller was aware that the seller's expertise was being relied on by the buyer. Appellees did not sue on the basis that the clothes were not merchantable or useable as clothes. Rather, appellees claimed that they were not useable for the particular purpose for which they were bought, that is, for Mrs. Gates to wear.

The statute gives relief to a buyer who relies on a seller's expertise to buy a product to be used in a particular manner. Even before the statute was enacted the Oklahoma Supreme Court gave relief in analogous circumstances. In *Ransom* v. *Robinson Packer Co.* (1926), the court said:

> Where an article of personal property is sold for a definite purpose made known to the seller, and the seller represents that the article will perform that particular purpose, there is a warranty of fitness which protects the purchaser and for which the seller is liable, in the event the article fails to do what it was sold to do.

In that case, pumps sold to the buyer operated in the manner expected, but they did not perform the job that the seller had promised. In the case at bar, the clothes were good clothes but they did not fit Mrs. Gates as the seller had represented. We conclude that the instant case is controlled by section 2–315.

The judgment of $192.62 against appellant and in favor of appellees is affirmed and the case is remanded to the trial court for hearing to fix the amount of the attorney's fee.

CONFLICT OF WARRANTIES

When a purchaser buys a product, it may have only one warranty or it may have several warranties. Warranties on a product should be construed by the court in such a fashion as to give effect to every warranty. On the other hand, if it is impossible to give effect to all warranties, the intention of the parties will determine which warranty is controlling. Section 2–317 sets forth three rules to determine the intention of the parties:

(a) Exact or technical specifications displace an inconsistent sample or model or general language of description.
(b) A sample from an existing bulk displaces inconsistent general language of description.
(c) Express warranties displace inconsistent implied warranties other than an implied warranty of fitness for a particular purpose.

These rules control unless one of the parties introduces evidence indicating that the rules would lead to an unreasonable result. It should be noted that if the seller misleads the buyer by implying that all the warranties can be performed, and they cannot all be performed, the seller will be estopped from setting up the inconsistency of the warranties as a defense.

EXCLUSION OR MODIFICATION OF WARRANTIES

Express Warranties

Express warranties, as noted earlier, can be created by an affirmation of fact or promise made by the seller, or by a description, or by a sample or model that is made part of the basis of the bargain between the parties. Once an express warranty has been created, it is very difficult to disclaim. Section 2–316(1) states:

> Words or conduct relevant to the creation of an express warranty and words or conduct tending to negate or limit warranty shall be construed wherever reasonable as consistent with each other; but subject to the provisions of the Article on parol or extrinsic evidence (Section 2–202) negation or limitation is inoperative to the extent that such construction is unreasonable.

Conflict Between Warranty and Disclaimer. Once an express warranty comes into existence, any language in the contract suggesting that express warranties have been disclaimed will create a conflict between the warranty and the disclaimer. If it is possible to read the warranty and disclaimer as consistent, the court must do so, but if such a reading is unreasonable, then the express warranty prevails over the disclaimer. The drafters of the UCC were trying to protect the buyer from hidden disclaimers by making any language inconsistent with the express warranty ineffective. In this way the buyer is not misled.

Thus any contract that uses language excluding "all warranties, express or implied," but that also contains an express warranty in direct conflict with this attempted disclaimer, will not succeed in eliminating the express warranty. If the seller provides the buyer with a sample but tries to exclude all express warranties in the contract, it is unlikely that the express warranty created by the sample can be disclaimed through use of such language.

Suppose a person signs a contract for the purchase of steel pipe. The contract explicitly states that the pipe will withstand temperatures down to 30 degrees below zero. This statement is an affirmation of fact and constitutes an express warranty. The contract also attempts to exclude "all warranties, express and implied." Is such a clause effective to eliminate the warranty that the pipe will withstand temperatures at least as low as 30 degrees below zero? The court must read the warranty and disclaimer as consistent if possible. Here such a reading would not be possible. If the buyer purchases the pipe, and it fails to withstand a temperature of 30 degrees below zero, he or she has a cause of action against the seller for breach of warranty. The express warranty and the exclusion directly conflict. The express warranty has not been effectively excluded.

Problems of Proof. Subsection (1) of Section 2–316 is subject to the provisions on parol or extrinsic evidence (Section 2–202). These relate to the problem of proving an express warranty. Although the parties may have in fact agreed upon a particular express warranty, they may not have incorporated it into the final written contract. The question then becomes, Can the person asserting the existence of an express warranty introduce evidence of an oral agreement arrived at before the contract was signed (but not expressed in the contract) when the contract disclaims the existence of any express warranties? The parol evidence rule, found in Section 2–202, may prevent this evidence from being introduced at trial because it contradicts the written terms of the contract.

Suppose in our pipe example the salesman tells the purchaser orally that the pipe will withstand temperatures at least as low as 30 degrees below zero. However, the contract the buyer signs explicitly states that the seller will not guarantee the performance of the pipe in temperatures below zero. The contract states that it is intended as the final agreement of the parties and is a complete and exclusive statement of the terms of the agreement. Clearly, this contract is not silent or ambiguous on the question of the pipe's ability to withstand temperatures. The court will not permit introduction of the salesman's statement to alter or vary the explicit terms of this written contract.

Implied Warranties

Implied Warranty of Merchantability. The implied warranty of merchantability may be disclaimed if the disclaimer mentions the word "merchantability" and, in case of a writing, is conspicuous. Explicitly stating in a written contract "There is no implied warranty of merchantability," in larger type than the rest of the contract, will call the buyer's attention to the exclusion of this warranty. This may also be excluded by other language, as is discussed in the following material.

Implied Warranty of Fitness for a Particular Purpose. To exclude the implied warranty of fitness for a particular purpose, the exclusion must be in writing and conspicuous. It can be disclaimed by the language: "There are no warranties which extend beyond the description on the face hereof." Note that subsection (2) of 2–316 does not specifically require that language excluding the implied warranty of fitness must use the phrase "implied warranty of fitness." A seller might state in a written contract "There is no implied warranty of fitness." If this appears in larger type than the rest of the contract, it will call the buyer's attention to the exclusion of this warranty. This warranty may also be excluded by other language, as discussed in the next paragraph.

Language That Excludes All Implied Warranties. Excluding or modifying either of the implied warranties of quality can easily be accomplished by using the language specified in Section 2–316(2), as discussed in the two preceding paragraphs.

Phrases such as "as is" or "with all faults" can exclude all implied warranties (Section 2–316[3]). The seller need not use these exact phrases as long as the language used "in common understanding calls the buyer's attention to the exclusion of warranties and makes plain that there is no implied warranty." By using the phrases provided, a seller can be certain of protection. It should be noted that subsection (3)(a) says nothing about the phrase being conspicuous. Because there are differing court decisions on this point, a prudent seller will make such a disclaimer conspicuous.

Conspicuous Language. To make certain that disclaimer language is conspicuous, the seller probably should use bold type (type larger and darker than that of the rest of the contract) and the disclaimer should appear on the first page of the contract. An extremely careful seller might use a different color type

ETHICS BOX
Disclaimers

A. J. Ford visited Reliable Motors with the intention of purchasing a sports car. He selected a new Ferrari. Ford signed a sales contract, which was a standardized form with a sales agreement on the front and a full page of fine print on the back. The salesman never referred to or pointed out the small print on the back of the form. Ford never read it. In the middle paragraph on the reverse side of the sales contract the following clause appeared: "Warranty: It is expressly agreed that there are no warranties express or implied, made by either the dealer or the manufacturer on the automobile except the manufacturer agrees to replace defective parts. THERE IS NO IMPLIED WARRANTY OF MERCHANTABILITY."

Some courts have refused to enforce this type of disclaimer of warranty on the grounds that the consumer doesn't have bargaining power to change the language, and that the heading implies incorrectly that some additional protection is being given the buyer. In negotiations it is fair to expect parties to watch out for their own interests and to clarify points that they don't understand. However, if one party has truly superior information concerning the effect of certain clauses, and the clauses are vaguely drafted and conceal their true import, the party with superior knowledge has an ethical duty, based in good faith, to fully inform the less knowledgeable party. It violates standards of professional business ethics to draft a clause purposefully in order to mislead the other party.

---

for the disclaimer and have the buyer initial the paragraph containing the disclaimer. If this course is followed, there will be little doubt that the buyer was aware of the disclaimer of all warranties.

Examination of Goods. Section 2–316(3)(b) permits a seller to exclude the implied warranties by giving the buyer an opportunity to examine the goods or a sample or model. If a seller wishes to rely upon subsection (3)(b), he or she must demand that the buyer examine the goods and give the buyer the opportunity to inspect the goods before entering into the contract; and the buyer must have examined the goods as fully as he or she desires. The seller, by demanding that the buyer examine

the goods, puts the buyer on notice that he or she is assuming the risk of defects that an examination would reveal. Merely telling the buyer the goods are available for inspection is not sufficient; the seller must demand that the buyer examine them.

When the buyer examines the goods, a sample, or a model, the buyer's skill and method of examining will determine what defects are excluded by the examination. Defects that the buyer is unable to discover because they are latent or beyond his or her power of discovery through reasonable examination will not be excluded.

The following case illustrates the consequences of a failure to examine the goods after a demand has been made on the buyer.

Tarulli v. Birds in Paradise

Civil Court of New York, Queens County

26 UCC 872 (1979)

Background: Tarulli (plaintiff) brought suit for the death of an exotic bird he had bought from a bird dealer, called Birds in Paradise (defendant). He asserted a breach of the implied warranty of merchantability and argued that the defendant had failed to exclude this warranty. The court disagreed, saying that the defendant had asked Tarulli to have the bird examined by a veterinarian, but he had failed to do so. Because Tarulli failed to have the bird examined, the court ruled that he was bound by the agreement even though the exotic bird was ill at the time Birds in Paradise delivered it to Tarulli. Decision: The court ruled for Birds in Paradise.

Posner, Justice

This is a small claims action which involves a defendant doing business as Birds in Paradise and a plaintiff whose purchase of an exotic bird turned into a veritable Miltonian "Paradise Lost."

On Dec. 18, 1978, the plaintiff, Bart Tarulli signed an agreement with the defendant, a dealer in birds, for the sale of one Moluccan Cockatoo. The agreed upon consideration was $400 cash and one Mexican Yellow Head Parrot. The agreement of sale, specifically signed and agreed to by plaintiff, Tarulli, stated as follows:

> This bird is guaranteed to be in good health, to the best of our knowledge, at the time of sale. The customer has a health guarantee extending to close of business 12-20-78, in which to have the bird checked by a licensed veterinarian and is urged to do so. If the veterinarian finds anything seriously wrong with the bird, it will be exchanged for another bird of equal value of the customer's choice, at once or when available, provided a letter from the examining veterinarian is offered as evidence of the bird's illness, and the bird is returned within the guarantee period. No exchange will be made after this period.

Plaintiff testified during trial that he never took the cockatoo to a veterinarian during the period permitted in the agreement. On or about Jan. 12, 1979 the cockatoo showed symptoms of illness and plaintiff brought said bird to Dr. B. J. Schiller, a veterinarian. Despite the extensive care and treatment administered by Dr. Schiller, the cockatoo died that same evening.

Dr. Schiller, as an expert witness for the plaintiff, testified that a post-mortem examination revealed the cause of death as anemia which she would guess existed for more than three weeks, but wasn't sure how long.

It is the plaintiff's contention that the defendant breached the implied warranty of merchantability under the Uniform Commercial Code section 2–314, and [that plaintiff] should be entitled to the sum of $800 ($400 plus the value of the Mexican Yellow Head Parrot), and $50 for veterinary fees.

The plaintiff bolsters this contention by arguing that birds fall within the definition of "goods" as contained in UCC section 2–105(1). Furthermore, the defendant satisfied the definition of a "merchant" under the UCC section 2–104. Thus, the plaintiff maintains that he bought "goods" from a "merchant" and said goods were defective at the time of sale, thereby breaching the implied warranty of merchantability, which was not excluded or modified as per UCC section 2–316. The plaintiff emphasizes UCC section 2–316(2) that to exclude or modify the implied warranty of merchantability, there must be specific mention of the word "merchantability" and the writing must be conspicuous. The plaintiff argues that the defendant failed expressly to exclude the implied warranty of merchantability by failing to specifically mention merchantability in the conditions of sale.

However, subsection 2 of UCC section 2–316 is not the exclusive mechanism to exclude or modify the implied warranty of merchantability. Subsection (3) provides as follows:

> Notwithstanding subsection (2)
> (b) when the buyer before entering into the contract has examined the goods or the sample or model as fully as he desired or has refused to examine the goods there is no implied warranty with regard to defects which an examination ought in the circumstances to have revealed to him.

The Official Comment 8 of section 2–316 of the Code states that this subsection goes to the nature of the responsibility assumed by the seller at the time of the making of the contract.

> Of course if the buyer discovers the defect and uses the goods anyway, or if he unreasonably fails to examine the goods before he uses them, resulting injuries may be found to result from his own action, rather than proximately from a breach of warranty.
> In order to bring the transaction within the scope of "refused to examine" in paragraph (b), it is not sufficient that the goods are available for inspection. There must in addition be a demand by the seller that the buyer examine the goods fully. The seller by the demand puts the buyer on notice that he is assuming the risk of defects which the examination ought to reveal.

This court finds that the defendant did in fact make such a demand upon the plaintiff to have the cockatoo checked by a licensed veterinarian before Dec. 20, 1978, and it was specifically for the purpose of having the veterinarian determine whether there is "anything seriously wrong with the bird," which only then would entitle the plaintiff to certain relief.

Here, the defendant by the demand for an examination of the cockatoo by a veterinarian put the plaintiff on notice that he is assuming the risk of defects which the examination ought to reveal. Not only was there testimony by the plaintiff that he never took the cockatoo to a veterinarian within the designated period; in effect, bringing the transaction within the scope of a refusal to examine, as per section 2–316(3)(b). But, there is also plaintiff's expert testimony of Dr. Schiller, who on cross-examination was asked: "If the bird had been brought in during the guarantee period, could the anemia have been detected?" And in answer to that question, Dr.

Schiller stated unequivocally "yes." In other words, the burden of examination was on the plaintiff, who by not exercising his obligation which would have uncovered the anemia, forfeited any claim for damages based on discoverable defects. The plaintiff's own expert witness testified that had the cockatoo in fact been examined within the designated period the latent anemia would have been detected; and this neglect on the part of the plaintiff, in the opinion of the court, precludes any implied warranty of merchantability.

Implied Warranty of Title

Special language must be used to exclude the implied warranty of title. A buyer expects this warranty when buying goods, and a seller must comply with the provisions of Section 2–312(2), as discussed earlier, to exclude the warranty of title.

Limitation of Remedies

The reader should distinguish the attempt to exclude or modify a warranty from an attempt by the seller to limit the remedies of the buyer under Section 2–718 or 2–719. Section 2–316(4) states that remedies for breach of warranty can be limited in accordance with these two sections.

Liquidated-Damages Clauses. A liquidated-damages clause provides for the payment of a particular sum by a party if he or she breaches the contract. Section 2–718 deals with an attempt by the parties to provide for liquidated damages. Such agreements will be enforceable only if the contract provides for an amount that is reasonable in the light of the anticipated or actual harm caused by the breach, the difficulties of proving loss, and the inconvenience or nonfeasibility of otherwise obtaining an adequate remedy. A term fixing unreasonably large liquidated damages is void as a penalty. Section 2–718 allows the parties to agree in advance that the seller will pay the buyer a particular sum if there is a breach of warranty, as long as the sum is reasonable.

Limitation or Modification of Remedies. Section 2–719 allows the parties (subject to certain limitations) to modify or limit the remedies provided in Article 2. Subsection (3) is worthy of further consideration here. It recognizes the validity of clauses limiting or excluding consequential damages, unless the limitation or exclusion is unconscionable. (See the chapter on illegality of contracts for a discussion of unconscionability.)

Consequential damages include any loss resulting from general or particular requirements and needs of the buyer that the seller had reason to know about at the time of contracting and that could not reasonably have been prevented by the buyer's obtaining the goods elsewhere or otherwise, and injury to person or property proximately resulting from any breach of warranty (Section 2–715[a]).

If the seller attempts to limit consequential damages for injury to a person by consumer goods, the clause is prima facie unconscionable. Any limitation on damages when the loss is commercial is not prima facie unconscionable. Even though an attempt to limit consequential damages for injury to a person is prima facie unconscionable, the seller can still attempt to disclaim all warranties, as provided in Section 2–316. In this respect, note the limitations placed on a seller's power to disclaim as discussed in the section of this chapter on the Magnuson–Moss Act.

Consider Posttape Associates v. Eastman Kodak Co., 537 F.2d 751 (3d Cir. 1976). Posttape Associates produced a documentary film using Kodak film. Each cannister and box bore the legend:

> READ THIS NOTICE This film will be replaced if defective in manufacture, labeling or packaging, or if damaged or lost by us or any subsidiary company even though by negligence or other fault. Except for such replacement, the sale, processing, or other handling of this film for any purpose is without warranty or liability. . . .

Posttape used the film but, because it turned out to be defective, the movie had to be reshot. Posttape wished to recover consequential damages to compensate it for the cost of the second filming of the documentary.

The court noted that an agreement that limits damages in this fashion must clearly indicate that no other damages are available to the buyer other than those listed on the cannister. It remanded the case for retrial on the issue of whether the cannister provided for an exclusive remedy. In making the determination whether the remedy provided by Kodak eliminated consequential damages of this nature, the circuit court instructed the lower court to take into consideration the trade practices in the film industry and the nature of the agreements.

FEDERAL TRADE COMMISSION WARRANTY RULES

In the Magnuson–Moss Warranty–Federal Trade Commission Act, which became effective in July 1975, Congress expanded the power of the Federal Trade Commission (FTC), specified minimum disclosure standards for written consumer-product warranties, and set certain minimum standards for those warranties. The act can be enforced by the FTC, by the U.S. Attorney General, or by a private party. The act gives consumers an opportunity to learn in advance of a purchase the nature of the warranty and to provide for effective enforcement of the warranty in case of breach. However, the act does not *require* warranties on consumer products.

Products Covered

The Act applies to any consumer product accompanied by a written warranty. A consumer product is any tangible personal property normally used for personal, family, or household purposes, including personal property intended to be attached to real estate. Service contracts are also covered by the act. Goods that are purchased for commercial or industrial purposes or for resale in the ordinary course of business are not covered by the FTC warranty rules.

The FTC warranty rules require compliance only if the consumer product costs $15 or more and is accompanied by a written warranty. If a company does not wish to be bound by the act or the FTC rules, it should not offer a written warranty on its consumer products. Oral warranties are not covered by the act.

Information That Must Be Disclosed

A written warranty must be in terms easily understood by the average consumer. It must disclose to consumers before the sale of the product such information as:

1. The name and address of the warrantor
2. The products or parts covered
3. A statement of what the warrantor will do, at whose expense, and for what period of time
4. The step-by-step procedure that the consumer should follow to enforce the warranty

Full or Limited Warranty

The Act requires that a product be labeled as having either a "limited" or a "full" warranty. This labeling system allows a consumer to compare products before making a final purchase. Prior to the act, the consumer frequently did not even know what type of warranty the product carried until arriving home, opening the box, and finding the warranty.

A written full warranty must provide the following:

1. Any defects, malfunctions, or inability to conform to the terms of a written warranty must be corrected by the warrantor without charge and within a reasonable length of time.
2. The warrantor cannot limit the period within which the implied warranties will be effective with respect to the consumer product.
3. The warrantor cannot limit or exclude consequential damages on a consumer product unless noted conspicuously on the face of the warranty.
4. The warrantor must allow the consumer to choose between a refund of the purchase price or replacement of the defective product or part after a reasonable number of attempts to remedy the defect or malfunction.

A limited warranty does not give the consumer these guarantees. A product must be clearly and conspicuously labeled as having a limited warranty if a written warranty is provided and the full warranty conditions are not met. Figure 22-1 is a typical limited warranty.

Disclaimer of Implied Warranty

The provision that a warrantor cannot disclaim any implied warranty is important. The act prohibits the disclaimer or modification of an implied warranty if a written warranty is given or if a service contract is entered into with the purchaser within ninety days after the sale. A "full" warranty cannot disclaim, modify, or even limit the basic implied warranties. The purchaser of a consumer product with a "limited" warranty also is assured that the implied warranties cannot be disclaimed or modified. But the implied warranties can be limited in duration to that of the written war-

FIGURE 22-1
Acme Corporation—Limited Warranty

This product has been manufactured under the highest standards of quality and workmanship. We warrant to the CONSUMER all parts of this product against defects in material and workmanship for TEN (10) YEARS from date of purchase. Any defective part will be replaced FREE OF CHARGE, excluding labor or service charges. We will not be responsible for any product damage due to installation error, product abuse, or product misuse whether performed by a contractor, service company, or yourself. Use of other than Acme factory parts may void this warranty.

This warranty applies only TO THE CONSUMER USE of the product and any inquiries regarding warranty claims are to be directed to:

Acme Corporation
100 Main Street
Anytown, Missouri 66066

This warranty gives you specific legal rights and you may also have other rights which vary from state to state.

BOX 22-2 ISSUES AND TRENDS
Federal Trade Commission Used Car Rule
—

The Federal Trade Commission has adopted a rule designed to protect consumers who want to purchase a used automobile. In the past such people were to a great extent at the mercy of the seller.

The FTC used car rule requires dealers to place window stickers on all used cars offered for sale. This window sticker either spells out a warranty or indicates the vehicle in question is being offered "as is." If the seller does not offer a warranty, the sticker must state that the buyer is responsible for any repairs should the car fail to operate properly. The sticker must urge prospective buyers to seek an independent inspection before making a purchase. The sticker must also warn customers that since spoken promises are difficult to enforce, any promises given by the dealer should be reduced to a written form.

The FTC used car rule provides protection to persons who need protection. In the past many purchasers of used cars have ended up with a pile of repair bills. Yet these people quite often are the persons least able to afford such bills in our society. The FTC used car rule has helped such persons by informing them in advance of their rights. Such a rule helps purchasers make informed decisions whether or not to purchase used cars.

---

ranty—as long as the limitation is reasonable, conscionable, and conspicuous.

Consequential Damages

A full warranty may limit consequential damages. The Magnuson–Moss Act permits such a limitation, although UCC Section 2–719 states that the consequential damages may be limited or excluded only as long as the limitation is conscionable. The limitation of consequential damages for injury caused by consumer goods is prima facie unconscionable under Section 2–719(3).

WARRANTIES AND PERSONAL-INJURY CLAIMS

Warranties may be used by a person injured by a product to establish a personal-injury claim. If an injured party is able to establish that the defendant made a warranty, failed to live up to the warranty, and as a result of the breach of warranty the plaintiff was injured by the product, he or she may be able to collect damages based on breach of warranty. One of the major problems associated with warranties was the absence of privity of contract, as discussed in the next section.

Privity of Contract and Section 2–318

Today the trend is away from requiring the plaintiff to establish privity of contract with the defendant. *Privity* is a direct contractual relationship between the parties. Section 2–318 states the UCC's limited rule on privity. The drafters of the UCC presented three alternative sections for the states to consider adopting.

Alternative A. Many states have adopted Alternative A, which states:

A seller's warranty whether express or implied extends to any natural person who is in the family or household of his buyer or who is a guest in his home if it is reasonable to expect that such person may use, consume or be affected by the goods and who is injured in person by breach of the warranty. A seller may not exclude or limit the operation of this section.

Any natural person in the buyer's family or household, or one who is a guest in his or her home, may sue the seller directly for injuries sustained. This provision does not help all persons injured by a defective product, for example, a bystander. If a man is mowing his lawn, and the mower blade flies off and strikes his neighbor, the neighbor may not avail himself of Section 2–318 in states that have adopted only Alternative A.

Alternative B. Alternative B extends to "all natural persons who may reasonably be expected to use, consume or be affected by the goods and who are injured in person by breach of the warranty." A number of states have adopted this alternative. Both A and B limit the damages recoverable as a result of a breach of warranty to personal damages.

Alternative C. Alternative C extends the warranty protection to "any person, natural or otherwise." This would include damage to a corporation. Thus Alternative C covers injury of any type, not just personal injuries.

Suits Against Someone Other Than the Buyer's Seller. The UCC does not take a direct position on suits against someone more remote in the distributive chain than the buyer's immediate seller. If a man is injured by his defective mower, he can clearly bring suit against the retail merchant from whom he purchased the mower. The UCC does not take a position whether the man can sue the wholesaler or manufacturer of the mower. However, most courts today allow suit to be brought under Section 2–318 against the manufacturer and wholesaler, and thus privity does not pose a serious problem to an injured party who wishes to bring suit for breach of warranty. Injured parties typically try to sue the manufacturer because the manufacturer is often in a better position to pay than a local retailer.

Notice

There can be a problem under the UCC, however, if notice is not given of the breach of warranty. Section 2–607(3) clearly states that the buyer must, in a reasonable time after he or she discovers or should have discovered any breach of warranty, notify the seller of the breach or be barred from any remedy. Therefore notice must be given to the seller and everyone in the distributive chain for the injured party to sue under the UCC.

Assuming that the plaintiff establishes a warranty and a breach of that warranty, and that as a result of the breach he or she was injured, a successful case may be pursued against the seller. Today many personal-injury suits arising out of the use of a defective product are based on warranty theory. This area of law is called products liability. The other theories on which suit may be brought are discussed in the next chapter.

REVIEW PROBLEMS

1. What are the three implied warranties that automatically arise out of the sale of a good?

2. List the ways in which an express warranty may be created.

3. If you were a merchant who wanted to

exclude all implied warranties in your transaction with a consumer, what would you do to make sure the exclusion would hold up in court?

4. Autzen contracted to purchase a used 50-foot boat from Taylor for $100,000. After agreeing on the price, but during the process of negotiating, Autzen was assured that the boat was in good condition. Taylor's agent had the boat inspected for dry rot prior to Autzen's purchase, although Autzen felt it was unnecessary to do so. Upon completion of the inspection, the inspector concluded that the hull was very sound "and that the boat should be well suited for its intended purpose." Autzen then gave Taylor's agent $10,000 and took possession. Approximately two months later, Autzen discovered that parts of the boat's flying bridge had been weakened by dry rot. A further inspection of the boat revealed that there was an enormous amount of dry rot and insect infestation. Was there an express warranty made as to the condition of the boat?

5. Louis orders a quantity of enamel-lined steel pipe from Key for an Alaskan construction project. The pipe as ordered was delivered in March, a time of extremely low temperatures. In April, Louis began laying the pipe. By early May, some 5,000 feet of the pipe had been installed. An inspection of the pipe at this time revealed that portions of the interior enamel lining had cracked away from the steel outer casing and were hanging down in sheets. Louis brought suit for breach of the implied warranty of fitness for a particular purpose under Section 2–315. Was there an implied warranty of fitness for a particular purpose?

6. Christopher purchased a motor home from Larson for $16,000. Christopher was assured by Larson's salesman that the motor home would meet the requirements Christopher expressed to the salesman. This all led to Christopher's purchasing the motor home. On the backside of the contract was a disclaimer of warranties, including the implied warranty of merchantability among other fine-print provisions. This disclaimer was never called to Christopher's attention. Christopher and his family took a trip in the motor home, which proved to be defective in a number of ways. Some repairs were needed to make it back home. Was the disclaimer of warranties effective?

7. George is the owner of a 1971 Mustang, purchased from Pettigrew, a retail Ford dealer. Browder, George's mother-in-law, is injured when the right front wheel of the Mustang collapses. Ford Motor Company, the manufacturer of the Mustang, validly disclaims all implied warranties made to George. Browder sues Pettigrew and Ford for, among other things, breach of the implied warranties, alleging her status as a third-party beneficiary. Is Browder a third-party beneficiary of any implied warranties?

8. Plaintiff Cantrell was injured while using a ladder that had come in a cardboard box bearing the following message:

GOOD QUALITY; LIGHT-STRONG-SAFE; RATED LOAD 200 LBS; FOR SAFETY'S SAKE BUY ME. I'M LIGHT AND STRONG; FIVE YEAR GUARANTEE. . . . The manufacturer guarantees the ladder, under normal use and service to be free from defects in material and workmanship, for five years from the date of purchase.

Cantrell weighed only 165 pounds. The ladder had not been misused or abused, and at the time it collapsed it was being used on a clean cement floor with all braces properly extended and locked. The front legs of the ladder buckled inward, throwing the plaintiff to the cement floor.

Cantrell sued Amarillo Hardware (the wholesaler) and Werner (the manufacturer) for breach of warranty. The defendants argued that there was no evidence indicating that any component, design feature, or material used in the ladder was defective, and without product defect they were not liable. Do you agree? Cantrell v. Amarillo Hardware Co., 602 P.2d 1326 (Kan. 1979).

9. Ricklefs purchased an automobile from Clemens. Clemens gave Ricklets a certificate of title that warranted the title to be free of all liens. Ricklefs was subsequently notified by the FBI that the automobile was stolen. Has Clemens breached the warranty of title? Ricklefs v. Clemens, 531 P.2d 94 (Kan. 1975).

10. Terry Drayton was with her father while he was attempting to clear a clogged sink in the bathroom. Mr. Drayton was using a bottle of Liquid Plumr that he had purchased. After he poured half a bottle down the drain, he placed a towel over the drain. At that moment Terry screamed. She had been doused with drain cleaner. This product had been advertised as "safe." Did this create an express warranty which was breached as a result of the injury Terry sustained? Drayton v. Jiffee Chemical Corp., 395 F.Supp. 1081 (N.D. Ohio 1975).

CHAPTER 23

Products Liability

HISTORICAL BACKGROUND

NEGLIGENCE

MISREPRESENTATION

STRICT LIABILITY

P roducts liability encompasses several theories of recovery, of which the most important are negligence, strict liability, and warranty. Each theory may be used by a plaintiff who is injured as a result of a mishap involving a product. If possible, all three theories may be asserted to further the chances of recovery.

Over the past few decades there has been a trend toward increased consumer protection. Often innocent persons have been injured by products through no fault of their own. Society is faced with the question of whether a person who is injured by a dangerous product should bear the loss caused by the product or whether this loss should be sustained by the manufacturer, distributor, or seller of the product—parties arguably better able to guard against or absorb the costs of such losses. The scales appear to be tipping in favor of the consumer as responsibility for losses is increasingly imposed on manufacturers, distributors, and sellers.

In the absence of some legal liability, is there any economic incentive for a company to make a product as safe as possible? Were it not for civil damage actions, many companies might be economically pressured into marketing products that appeared to be safe to the consumer but were actually quite dangerous.

Because of the possibility of large judgments, a company can no longer safely decide that a cheap, unsafe product will bring the greatest profits.

HISTORICAL BACKGROUND

In the past absence of privity limited the power of an injured party to recover. That is, a direct contractual relationship between the injured party and the defendant was required for the injured party to recover from the defendant. A manufacturer producing a defective product was liable only to the wholesaler, the party to whom the product was sold. An injured consumer could not recover from the manufacturer. Suit generally was possible only against the retailer with whom the consumer had dealt. The requirement of privity was generally upheld throughout the nineteenth century, although some inroads were made in cases involving food, drugs, and other ultrahazardous products.

In 1916 a major departure from the requirement of privity occurred in *MacPherson* v. *Buick Motor Co.* In that case the New York Court of Appeals held a manufacturer liable for injuries resulting from the use of a product, irrespective of whether the product was "inherently dangerous," because there was evidence of negligence in the manufacture or assembly of the product. This was true even though the plaintiff was unable to establish privity of contract with the manufacturer. The *MacPherson* decision influenced the decisions of other state courts.

NEGLIGENCE

Manufacturer's Negligence

An injured party might choose to bring suit for *negligence*—that is, the breach or nonperformance of a legal duty, through neglect or carelessness, resulting in damage or injury to another. In essence, the plaintiff must establish that the defendant failed to exercise due care in the manufacturing or handling of the product. Today it is not necessary to establish privity of contract in order to make a case for negligence against the defendant. In other words, the plaintiff need not have purchased the product from the defendant. The plaintiff, however, must establish that his or her injury is a result of a breach of duty on the part of the defendant. The defendant's duty is to exercise that degree of care that would be exercised by a reasonably prudent person under the same circumstances.

The main problem with using negligence as a theory of recovery is the substantial burden of proof that falls on the plaintiff. The seller (the defendant) may be able to establish that he or she exercised all due care that was possible under the circumstances.

Negligence of Manufacturer in Assembly

Section 395 of the *Restatement of Torts Second* sets forth a standard by which the courts may judge the actions of a manufacturer. It states:

A manufacturer who fails to exercise reasonable care in the manufacture of a chattel which, unless carefully made, he should recognize as involving an unreasonable risk of causing physical harm to those who use it for a purpose for which the manufacturer should expect it to be used and those whom he should expect to be endangered by its probable use, is subject to liability for physical harm caused to them by its lawful use in a manner and for a purpose for which it is supplied.

The *Restatement* in this section covers the problem of a product that for one reason or another leaves the manufacturer's premises in an unsafe condition because reasonable care was not taken in assembling it. For example, a manufacturer of automobiles fails to inspect a vehicle carefully and so does not notice that one of two bolts necessary to the safe operation of the car is missing. As a result, while the automobile's purchaser is driving it down the highway the car veers out of control and crashes into a lamp pole.

In this case the manufacturer's failure to exercise reasonable care in manufacturing the automobile created an *unreasonable* risk of physical harm to persons using the automobile. The purchaser in this example used the car in a lawful manner and for a purpose for which automobiles are supplied—that is, driving. The manufacturer is liable to the purchaser for his or her injuries due to its negligence in the manufacture of the automobile.

Bear in mind that if the manufacturer is able to convince a court that it exercised reasonable care in manufacturing its product, no liability arises under Section 395 of the *Restatement*.

Contrast this example with one involving an automobile that should have had a second bolt but did not because the company failed to provide for it in the design. In this situation, if the vehicle ends up in an accident, the manufacturer is not liable for negligence in assembling the automobile. Instead, it may be liable for negligence in designing the automobile, as discussed in the next section.

A great number of cases today involve the issue of defective design.

Manufacturer's Negligent Design

An important aspect of the current law of product liability relates to the manufacturer's liability for a defectively designed product. Unlike negligence in production, which may affect one or a few products, defective design may affect an entire class of products and involve potential liability to thousands of individuals. Several federal agencies charged with regulating certain types of products are increasingly using mandatory recall as a corrective device.

A manufacturer can be held liable for injuries to a person caused by a product that is defective because of poor design or improper construction or assembly. The *Restatement of Torts Second* in Section 398 announces a standard for the design of products:

> A manufacturer of a chattel made under a plan or design which makes it dangerous for the uses for which it is manufactured is subject to liability to others whom he should expect to use the chattel or to be endangered by its probable use for physical harm caused by his failure to exercise reasonable care in the adoption of a safe plan or design.

This means that a manufacturer must exercise due care in the design of all products. Putting a product on the market that later is determined to be unsafe for normal use may result in liability for physical injuries caused by the product.

Suppose a manufacturer adopts a design for its product that is obviously unsafe—for example, an electric fan that does not have a screen to protect users from the rotating metal blade. A young child, unable to comprehend the danger involved, sticks his hand into the path of the blade and the blade clips off a few fingers. The manufacturer may be liable for the child's injuries because it failed to exercise reasonable care in the adoption of a safe design for the fan.

Manufacturer's Duty to Inspect, Test, and Warn

Testing and Inspecting. The manufacturer generally must exercise due care to make certain a product placed on the market is safe. This includes reasonable tests and inspections to discover present or latent defects in a product before putting it on the market. For example, the manufacturer of a chair was held liable when it failed to discover a defect that it could have ascertained by inspecting the chair.

Suppose a manufacturer of lamps exercises reasonable care with respect to the design and assembly of its lamps. Will this be sufficient to relieve it of any legal liability to someone injured by a lamp? What if the cord on the lamp was frayed when manufactured and as a result the purchaser was electrocuted when he plugged the lamp cord into a socket? One could argue that the manufacturer had failed to exercise due care in inspecting the lamp cord.

Warning. It is not sufficient for a manufacturer merely to test and inspect a product. Sometimes the manufacturer also has a duty to warn the public of the dangerous potential of a product. The *Restatement of Torts Second* in Section 388 suggests the following standard with respect to a duty to warn:

> One who supplies directly or through a third person a chattel for another to use is subject to liability to those whom the supplier should expect to use the chattel with the consent of the other or to be endangered by its probable use, for physical harm caused by the use of the chattel in the manner for which and by

a person for whose use it is supplied, if the supplier

(a) knows or has reason to know that the chattel is or is likely to be dangerous for the use for which it is supplied, and
(b) has no reason to believe that those for whose use the chattel is supplied will realize its dangerous condition, and
(c) fails to exercise reasonable care to inform them of its dangerous condition or of the facts which make it likely to be dangerous.

Suppose the manufacturer of a chemical knows that the chemical is highly caustic and that users may not be aware of that fact. In this situation the manufacturer should exercise reasonable care to inform users of the chemical of its causticity. This might be accomplished by putting a prominent warning on the containers in which the chemical is supplied. If the manufacturer fails to supply any warning, it will be liable to any person injured by the chemical who the manufacturer could expect to use or be endangered by the probable use of the product—for example, someone transferring the chemical to another container. The manufacturer must exercise reasonable care to inform such a person of the caustic nature of the chemical. If it fails to give such a warning, and the person is injured, the manufacturer will be liable for the injuries that person sustains.

The defect in the product must be the *proxi-*

FIGURE 23-1
Sample Warning from Furniture Polish

Caution: Do not use near fire or flame. Do not set or store container where temperature exceeds 120 degrees F, as container may burst. Do not puncture or incinerate. Do not spray or use on floors. Keep out of reach of children.

mate cause of the injury—that is, there must be a connection between the defect in the product and the injury sustained. If a chemical in a drum explodes when exposed to heat, but the specific injury was caused by the drum's falling on a workman's foot, it would not be possible to say that failure to warn of the chemical's flammability was the proximate cause of the worker's injury.

Subsection (a) of the *Restatement* indicates that the manufacturer must be able to *foresee* that the product may be dangerous if used improperly. Foreseeability is very important in duty-to-warn cases. The phrase "for which it is supplied" can be a problem where the injured party misuses the product. Must the manufacturer warn consumers not only of dangers inherent in the proper use of the product but also of dangers inherent in its misuse? Many courts have required this of a manufacturer.

A warning must be clear and intelligible. Even if a warning makes clear the dangers inherent in using or misusing the product, there still is the problem of to whom the warning should be given. Suppose, for example, that a warning appears in literature supplied by the manufacturer to purchasers of its products but not directly on the dangerous article itself. In Griggs v. Firestone Tire and Rubber Co., 513 F.2d 851 (8th cir. 1975), the court held that even under these circumstances the jury could have found that Firestone did not properly discharge its duty to warn because, although it provided a warning with literature that accompanied a dangerous tire rim, it could have put the warning directly on the rim. Some cases do, however, hold that adequate warning to the purchaser of the product is sufficient. The *Griggs* case illustrates the point that it is probably safer to put a warning in a place where it will be seen by all persons who might be endangered by the product. For example, if the seller of a lawn mower wants to warn purchasers not to put their hands in the mower's exhaust chute while the mower is in operation, it could put such a warning in the instructions for operating the mower. A warning decal on the exhaust chute, however, would be more likely to be seen by users of the mower.

Subsection (b) of Section 388 deals with the problem of whether the defect in the product is *obvious*. If the chattel is in an obviously dangerous condition, it may be unnecessary to warn of the danger. On the other hand, if the danger is not likely to be discovered by persons using the product (in other words, if the danger is *latent*), a duty to warn exists. The manufacturer should then exercise reasonable care to inform users of the latent danger.

In addition to Section 388 of the *Restatement of Torts Second*, a number of statutes and regulations (for example, the Food, Drug, and Cosmetic Act and the Federal Hazardous Substances Act) require warnings on certain products.

The following case discusses the duty of a seller to warn users of latent dangers associated with the use of its product.

Martin v. Bengue

Supreme Court of New Jersey
136 A.2d 626 (1957)

Background: Martin (plaintiff) sued Bengue (defendant). Martin was injured as a result of burns caused by a cigarette igniting an ointment, Ben-Gay, that he had applied to his chest. The plaintiff contends that the defendant, Bengue, is liable to him because it failed to warn him of the flammability of its product, Ben-Gay. The trial court decided for Martin. Bengue appealed.
Decision: The New Jersey Supreme Court affirmed the decision for Martin.

Jacobs, Justice

The plaintiff had a heavy cold and had been home for several days. About twice each day his wife had rubbed a medium amount of Ben-Gay on his chest, shoulders, and neck substantially in accordance with the directions for its use. On the morning of February 4, after a customary application, the plaintiff seated himself in a living room chair. He was then dressed in the same cotton pajamas which he had been wearing for several days and his pajama top had become rather greasy from its contact with the Ben-Gay. While listening to the radio and talking to his wife, who was in the kitchen, he attempted to light a cigarette. After striking the match he suddenly realized that its head had fallen off and that the lower part of his pajama top was burning. Still seated, he unsuccessfully tried to pat the fire out. He then jumped up still continuing his patting motion. The fire spread rapidly across the portions of his body which had been covered with Ben-Gay. In the plaintiff's language "it like exploded, you might say." He immediately called to his wife, who found him "completely enveloped in flames." She tore off the pajama top, applied a home remedy for his burns, called the doctor, and took him to the hospital where he remained for over a month. He suffered very severe burns, particularly about his "chest, shoulder, face and ears."

The plaintiff started to use Ben-Gay many years ago and testified that he had probably then read its accompanying literature. Similarly his wife testified that she was "an old user of Ben-Gay," had read the legend on the package, was familiar with the directions which accompanied it, and found "nothing that said it was dangerous to use." The tube which contained the Ben-Gay and the directions which accompanied it contained nothing whatever as to flammability. The directions did contemplate that the pajama top would be worn after the ointment had been applied and the plaintiff's position is that the vapors emitted by the Ben-Gay, when confined between the pajama top and the body, were flammable. In support he introduced testimony by Messrs. Bechtoldt and Kanengieser, both graduate chemists.

The testimony indicated that the methylsalicylate in Ben-Gay has a flash point (produces a puff of flame, not a fire) at about 225°F and that its vapors burn continuously at about 235°F. It also indicated that the temperature of a burning match and burning cotton is between 1200° and 2000°F. From this, coupled with the remaining evidence in the record, the Appellate Division found that it could reasonably be inferred that Ben-Gay vapors would burn at about 235°F "only when the oxygen in the air is limited in quantity, as where it is confined by some article, such as a pajama coat, so as to form with the vapors a combustible mixture . . ."

Products may not be defective but the manufacturers and suppliers may negligently fail to warn of concealed dangers with resulting foreseeable injury.

In *Tomao* v. *A. P. DeSanno & Son,* the court properly noted that "if the manufacturer owes a duty to use due care in making his products, he owes also the companion duty to warn of the latent limitations of even a perfectly made article, the use of which, however, is dangerous if the user is ignorant of those limitations and the manufacturer has no reason to believe he will recognize the danger."

While the manufacturer of a product is not an insurer of its safety, he is under a duty of care to avoid all unreasonable risks of harm from its use. When such risks are foreseeable, he must take reasonable precautions to avoid them. Within broad outer limits fixed by the court, the issue of foreseeability is properly left to the jury. Professors Harper and James havé put it this way:

> The courts, of course, set the outer boundary to what a man may reasonably be held to foresee. But a judgment upon this question, in the nature of things, may be exercised within wide limits, and this is one of the focal points where the concept of negligence is being expanded. Not only have the scientific advances noted above enlarged the scope of what a jury may find to be foreseeable, but a quickening social conscience and the general trend towards wider liability have led the courts to perceive risks in ordinary activities of men where not so long ago they ruled them out of the permissible range of what might be found. 2 Harper & James, at p. 916.

The fact that the product may have been used by many people over a considerable period of time without prior injury would not preclude the finding of foreseeability and negligence.

And the fact that the injury may have followed upon the application of an intervening force such as fire would not preclude the finding that the intervening force was itself a foreseeable risk which the defendant should have guarded against.

The totality of the evidence, viewed most favorably towards the plaintiff at this preliminary stage, was legally sufficient to enable a jury to find that when Ben-Gay is applied it emits vapors, which, when confined between the body and a pajama top, will burn with very high intensity and rapidity when ignited; that the defendant Bengue, Inc., as the manufacturer, and the defendant Thos. Leeming Co., Inc., as its sole United States distributor, had employed chemists to analyze the product and knew or should have known of the described flammability of its vapors; that the defendants knew or should have known that users of the product might indulge in smoking or otherwise incur the danger of igniting the confined Ben-Gay vapors; that in the exercise of reasonable prudence they would have warned the users of the danger; and that their failure thus to warn the users constituted actionable negligence. The defendants strenuously urge that "the risk of injury from the ignition of Ben-Gay is so far beyond the realm of probability and of normal experience as to excuse the defendants from foresight thereof." While a jury might so find, it might also reasonably find otherwise. The number of smokers has been estimated to be between 55 and 60 millions.

It seems to us that the danger of igniting the confined vapors, by a match, cigarette or otherwise, cannot fairly be said to have been so patently remote as to justify the court's withdrawal from the jury of its normal function of passing on the issue of foreseeability.

Negligence of Assemblers and Submanufacturers

Many products are composed of parts manufactured by several companies. To what extent is a company that uses the products of another company in making its own product liable if a component part malfunctions? Take the case of an airplane company. If a malfunctioning altimeter causes the plane to crash, can the manufacturer escape liability by pointing to the altimeter manufacturer?

Assemblers. An assembler generally must make reasonable tests and inspections to discover latent defects. In MacPherson v. Buick Motor Co., 111 N.E. 1050 (1916), Buick, the manufacturer, was held liable for a defective wheel used on the automobile even though Buick bought the wheel from another company. The court held Buick liable because the defect could have been discovered had Buick made a reasonable inspection of the wheel. Thus an assembler must make reasonable inspections and tests of parts to be incorporated into the finished product to protect itself from liability.

Makers of Component Parts. The manufacturer of a component part is also liable for negligence. The *Restatement of Torts Second* follows this position, indicating that the manufacturer of parts to be incorporated in a product is liable if the parts "are so negligently made as to render the product in which they are incorporated unreasonably dangerous for use" (Comment m to Section 395). Similarly, the manufacturer of materials to be used in products that would be dangerous unless the materials are carefully made is also liable if it fails to exercise reasonable care. In Schwalbach v. Antigo Electric & Gas, Inc., 135 N.W.2d 263 (1965), the manufacturer of a safety device incorporated in a furnace was held liable when the device failed to function properly and injuries resulted.

Retailer's Negligence

Design and Construction. If a plaintiff wishes to recover from the retailer for injuries sustained in using a defective product, negligence will not be an effective theory of recovery in most instances. (See, however, the discussion of strict liability.) When a retailer receives a product from a manufacturer, he or she knows very little about it beyond what the buyer may know. Quite frequently the product is packaged when the retailer receives and sells it. As the retailer actually has very little control over the product's design or fabrication, it makes sense not to hold him or her liable for negligence. The retailer's duty with regard to design or construction of products is minimal.

Inspections, Tests, Warnings. Normally a retailer does not need to inspect or test the items sold if he or she neither knows nor has reason to know that the product is dangerous. The courts tend not to impose a duty to inspect or test under these circumstances. On the other hand, if the retailer should have known that the product was dangerous and could have inspected the item or tested it, he or she may be liable. Two classes of retailers who must pay special attention to the products they sell are food retailers and druggists.

Suppose a grocery store received a shipment of frozen TV dinners. When the trucker delivered the load, he informed the manager that the truck's refrigeration unit failed to function properly during part of the trip. The truck driver believed that the dinners may have thawed although they were frozen at the time of delivery. Without inspecting them, the manager ordered the stock boys to load the dinners in the store's freezers. In such a case, although a grocery store would generally not be expected to inspect the TV dinners, here it clearly should have. If a purchaser became ill after eating one of the TV dinners, the store might be liable for its failure to inspect.

The same is true of the duty to warn. If the retailer should know that a product is dangerous, and that the danger is of a type the purchaser is not likely to discover, the retailer should warn the purchaser.

In the earlier example, the grocery store probably should warn purchasers that the

TV dinners had defrosted in transit if it sells them.

Representing Products as Own. If the retailer advertises, labels, or packages a product in such a fashion that it appears that the retailer is the manufacturer, the retailer will be held to the same standards as the manufacturer.

Many companies market under their own names products manufactured by someone else. Sears, Roebuck, for example, sells floor scrubbers manufactured by another company but labeled "Kenmore"—the Sears trade name.

The *Restatement of Torts Second*, Section 400, states: "one who puts out as his own product a chattel manufactured by another is subject to the same liability as though he were its manufacturer." Comment d indicates that when one puts his or her name or affixes his or her trade name or trademark, one puts out the product as his or her own. If the seller marks the goods as "made for" the seller, this rule still applies unless the real manufacturer is clearly indicated. In *Schwartz* v. *Macrose Lumber & Trim Co.* the court held the distributor of masonry nails liable to a person who was injured when a nail shattered. The package containing the nails indicated that they were made for the distributor but did not indicate who the manufacturer was. Conversely, where the distributor clearly indicated that a can of pineapple was manufactured by another company, the consumer was not permitted to recover from the distributor.

Statutory Violations as Proof of Negligence

Some federal and state statutes, such as the Federal Food, Drug, and Cosmetic Act, specify a certain standard of conduct. If a party injured by a product is able to point to a statute or regulation that has not been complied with, this may create a statutory right of action that is independent of the common-law action. A manufacturer who ignores safety standards promulgated by a government agency may leave the company open to liability. For this reason a company must keep well informed of governmental statutes and regulations pertaining to the products it manufactures.

Defenses Available in Negligence

Contributory Negligence. A number of defenses are available to a company in a product-liability suit. One defense frequently urged in such suits is contributory negligence. (*Contributory negligence* is any conduct on the part of the plaintiff that falls below the standard of care a reasonably prudent person would exercise in the interest of his or her own safety and that contributes to the plaintiff's injury.)

In *Tulkka* v. *Mackworth Rees, Division of Avis Industries, Inc.,* the plaintiff, injured while operating a press, had failed to use all the available safety equipment. Because of his contributory negligence, he failed to recover. The court felt that a reasonably prudent person would have used the safety equipment provided by the employer. Contributory negligence is a complete bar to recovery in a negligence suit.

Many states have replaced the doctrine of contributory negligence with that of comparative negligence, which also applies in product-liability cases. While contributory negligence bars recovery by the plaintiff, comparative negligence does not.

When a court applies the *comparative-negligence doctrine,* the court or jury weighs the relative negligence of the parties and reduces the amount of recovery in proportion to the plaintiff's negligence. It bars recovery only if the plaintiff's negligence was proportionally greater than the defendant's.

For example, suppose a jury decided that the employer was 80 percent responsible for a given injury but that the employee was 20 percent responsible. If the court followed the doctrine of contributory negligence, the plaintiff would recover nothing. If, however, the court applied the doctrine of comparative negligence, the jury would determine how much the plaintiff's injuries were worth (for example, $100,000) and then reduce this amount by 20 percent—the extent of the plaintiff's responsibility for the accident. The plaintiff would therefore receive $80,000.

Assumption of Risk. In *assumption of risk* the defendant asserts that the plaintiff acted voluntarily with full knowledge and appreciation of the risk involved. In *Goblirsch* v. *Western Land Roller Co.,* for example, a farmworker was injured by a corn-grinding machine that had to be fed by hand when the corn was wet. The court here applied the doctrine of assumption of risk and the plaintiff failed to recover.

In general, contributory negligence and assumption of risk are available to defendants in product-liability suits based on negligence. This makes negligence a less appealing doctrine for the plaintiff than other theories discussed later in this chapter.

Obvious Danger/Abnormal Use. Some courts have also denied relief to the plaintiff on the theory that the danger presented to the plaintiff was obvious, and other courts have denied recovery on the theory that the plaintiff made an abnormal use of the product.

MISREPRESENTATION

Innocent Misrepresentation

Sometimes by oral statements or through advertising, brochures, catalogues, and the like, a seller may incorrectly state something about its product. When a seller misrepresents its product, and a buyer relies upon the misrepresentation, the buyer who is injured by the product may have a cause of action based on the misrepresentation. Innocent misrepresentation is defined by the *Restatement of Torts Second,* Section 402B:

> One engaged in the business of selling chattels who, by advertising, labels or otherwise, makes to the public a misrepresentation of a material fact concerning the character or quality of a chattel sold by him is subject to liability for physical harm to a consumer of the chattel caused by justifiable reliance upon the misrepresentation, even though
> (a) it is not made fraudulently or negligently, and
> (b) the consumer has not bought the chattel from or entered into any contractual relation with the seller.

A material fact, for the misrepresentation of which the *Restatement* holds a seller accountable, is one that was taken into consideration by the buyer in deciding to purchase the product.

Many statements have been found to be misrepresentations of material facts concerning the character or quality of a product. In *Hauter* v. *Zogarts* Hauter brought suit for injuries he sustained while using a training device for golfers called the "Golfing Gizmo." On the first day of use, while practicing his golf swing, he was seriously injured by the product. He brought suit on the grounds of innocent misrepresentation—among other theories of recovery. Hauter had relied upon the manufacturer's statement "Completely Safe Ball Will Not Hit Player," which the California Supreme Court found to be a factual representation. Because the statement was false, Hauter recovered even though the manufacturer in this case believed the statement to be true.

Defenses

Two defenses frequently asserted by defendants in innocent-misrepresentation cases are puffing and absence of reliance.

Puffing. Puffing is a statement of mere opinion or loose general praise. If a statement is mere puffery, the plaintiff will not recover. For example, in *Berkebile* v. *Brantly Helicopter Corp.,* Berkebile's heirs brought suit for his death when the helicopter he was piloting crashed. Brantly had described the helicopter in an advertisement as "safe, dependable," not "tricky to operate," and one that "beginners and professional pilots alike agree . . . is easy to fly." The Pennsylvania Supreme Court characterized these statements as mere puffery and refused to allow the plaintiffs to collect damages based on innocent misrepresentation.

Determining which statements are puffing and which are not is often difficult. Courts differ in their willingness to characterize statements as puffing.

Reliance. To recover on grounds of innocent misrepresentation, not only must the manufacturer's misrepresentation of a material fact not be puffing but the buyer must prove that the misrepresentation was *justifiably relied upon* by him. If the buyer was unaware of the misrepresentation or indifferent to it, or if the statement did not influence his purchase or subsequent conduct, the buyer may not recover. The misrepresentation must have been a *substantial* factor in inducing the purchase or use of the product.

The plaintiff need not point to a specific statement of misrepresentation but may rely upon a picture. A police officer named Winkler acquired a discarded police helmet used in riot control from the department for his personal use. On the carton, the manufacturer depicted a motorcyclist wearing the helmet. Winkler was familiar with the carton and believed that the helmet was intended for motorcycle use. While riding his motorcycle, he collided with a pickup truck. He sustained head injuries because the helmet was not in fact suitable for motorcycle riding. In *Winkler* v. *American Safety Equipment Corp.*, the Colorado Court of Appeals found evidence to support a jury verdict of misrepresentation in light of Winkler's justifiable reliance on the picture on the carton.

The following case provides another example of innocent misrepresentation.

Klages v. General Ordnance Equipment Corporation

Superior Court of Pennsylvania
367 A.2d 304 (1976)

Background: Klages (plaintiff) sued General Ordnance (defendant). Plaintiff, John R. Klages, was employed as a night auditor at Conley's Motel. After once being held up by armed robbers, Klages purchased the defendant's Mace pen for protection. The promotional literature for the weapon stated in part: "Rapidly vaporizes on face of assailant effecting 'instantaneous incapacitation' . . . an attacker is 'subdued—instantly' . . . An advertisement in Time Magazine stated the Chemical Mace is '. . . a weapon that disables as effectively as a gun and yet does no permanent injury' . . ." When Klages was again held up soon thereafter, he removed the Mace pen from the cash register where it was stored. Using the cash register as a shield, he squirted the Mace, hitting the intruder right beside the nose. He immediately ducked below the register, but the intruder shot him in the head. As a result of the injury, Klages suffered complete loss of sight in his right eye. He later instituted suit against the retailer and manufacturer of the Mace pen. The lower court submitted the case to a jury based on innocent misrepresentation and the jury decided for the plaintiff. The defendant appealed.

Decision: The Superior Court affirmed the decision for Klages.

Hoffman, Judge

Having adopted section 402B of the Restatement (Second) of Torts as the law of this Commonwealth, we must determine whether the appellant misrepresented "a material fact concerning the character or quality of a chattel sold by him . . ."

The comments to section 402B are helpful in this regard. First, Comment f states that "[t]he fact misrepresented must be a material one, upon which the consumer may be expected to rely in making his purchase . . ." Comment g states that section 402B "does not apply to statements of opinion, and in particular it does not apply to the kind of *loose general praise* of wares sold which, on the part of the seller, is considered to be 'sales talk', and is commonly called 'puffing'—as, for example, a statement that an automobile is the best on the market for the price . . . In addition, the fact misrepresented must be a material one, of importance to the normal purchaser by which the ultimate buyer may justifiably be expected to be influenced in buying the chattel." (Emphasis supplied).

The facts and circumstances surrounding the purchase of a product are helpful in determining whether the representation is of a material fact. In this case, the appellant sold a product designed as a tool to deter violence. Its sole anticipated use was to protect the purchaser from harm under extremely dangerous circumstances and the appellee specifically purchased the product with these explicit purposes in mind. Specific representations about the effectiveness of the weapon under such dangerous circumstances are clearly material. The mace weapons were described as effecting as instantaneous, immediate, complete incapacitation of an assailant. This is not "loose, general praise"; rather it is specific data on the capability of a product. This situation is thus distinguishable from Berkebile v. Brantly Helicopter Corporation, where the representation that the purchaser was assured of a safe, dependable helicopter was held to be mere "puffing." The lower court, therefore, properly submitted the issue of liability under section 402B to the jury.

STRICT LIABILITY

Strict Liability in Tort Generally

The law of torts has for years recognized the doctrine of strict or absolute liability if a person or company engages in certain types of activities. For example, if a company engages in blasting as part of its business, and this blasting causes an injury to someone, the company may be held liable to the injured party under the concept of strict or absolute liability.

Strict liability in the product-liability area is different from the concept of strict liability discussed in the material on torts earlier in this book. Strict liability in the products-liability area originated only in the 1960s. Today most states have accepted the doctrine of strict liability in product liability. The doctrine does not make the seller of a defective product absolutely liable. The injured party must demonstrate that the product was defective and that it was the proximate cause of injury. The rule is set out in the *Restatement of Torts Second,* Section 402A:

(1) One who sells any product in a defective condition unreasonably dangerous to the user or consumer or to his property is subject to liability for physical harm thereby caused to the ultimate user or consumer, or to his property, if

    (a) the seller is engaged in the business of selling such a product, and

    (b) it is expected to and does reach the user or consumer without substantial change in the condition in which it is sold.

(2) The rule stated in Subsection (1) applies although

    (a) the seller has exercised all possible care in the preparation and sale of his product, and

    (b) the user or consumer has not bought the product from or entered into any contractual relation with the seller.

Caveat:

The Institute expresses no opinion as to whether the rules stated in this Section may not apply

(1) to harm to persons other than users or consumers;

(2) to the seller of a product expected to be processed or otherwise substantially changed before it reaches the user or consumer; or

(3) to the seller of a component part of a product to be assembled.

Distributors/Retailers/Lessors

Across the United States the law varies with respect to the liability of distributors under strict liability in tort. In general most jurisdictions have not held a distributor liable where he or she merely sends the product on to someone else. Strict liability in tort may, however, be applied to retailers. Some courts have applied the doctrine of strict liability in tort to lessors even though no sale is involved. In *Cintrone* v. *Hertz Truck Leasing & Rental Service*, for example, the court held a lessor subject to strict liability in tort.

The following case deals with the liability of a distributor.

Konowal v. Heinrich Baumgarden Co.

Court of Appeals, Ninth District

Slip Opinion, August 31, 1983

Background: Konowals (plaintiffs) sued Heinrich (defendant) and other companies. Vitrex was a Spanish corporation that manufactured pots and pans. Easterling Company was an Illinois corporation that purchased sets of pots and pans manufactured by Vitrex and sold them to Betsy Ross Foods. Betsy Ross Foods in turn sold the pots and pans sets to Amherst Sparkle Market. Mrs. James Camera purchased one of these sets from Amherst Sparkle Market as a gift for her daughter, Kathleen Konowal. Mrs. Konowal used one of these pots to boil water. As she picked up the pot, one of its handles came off and boiling water spilled on Mrs. Konowal's son, Jeff, who was severely burned.

The Konowals brought this suit to recover damages for Jeff's injuries. Named in the suit were Heinrich Baumgarden Company, the corporation that manufactured the handle, Vitrex, Easterling, and Amherst Sparkle Market.

The trial court dismissed the complaint against Heinrich Baumgarden and Vitrex and granted summary judgments in favor of Amherst Sparkle Market and Easterling. The plaintiffs appealed only the granting of the summary judgment in favor of Easterling.

Decision: The Appeals Court reversed the decision in favor of Easterling.

Baird, Judge

The trial court concluded that the imposition of strict tort liability upon one of the distributors would be unjust where the commodity was packaged in Spain and passed to plaintiffs through a chain of distributors which had no notice that the commodity was defective. The court found persuasive the cases cited by defendant that a middleman distributor who neither modifies nor alters a product in its original container should be held to a different standard than the manufacturer-assembler.

We are of the opinion that the determinative case on this issue is *Temple* v. *Wean United, Inc.* That opinion specifically approved Section 402(A) of the Restatement of Torts 2d.

We find Illustration 1 of the Restatement of Torts 2d particularly pertinent to the instant case:

A manufactures and packs a can of beans, which he sells to B, a wholesaler. B sells the beans to C, a jobber, who resells it to D, a retail grocer. E buys the can of beans from D, and gives it to F. F serves the beans at lunch to G, his guest. While eating the beans, G breaks a tooth, on a pebble of the size, shape, and color of a bean, which no reasonable inspection could possibly have discovered. There is satisfactory evidence that the pebble was in the can of beans when it was opened. Although there is no negligence on the part of A, B, C, or D, each of them is subject to liability to G. On the other hand E and F, who have not sold the beans, are not liable to G in the absence of some negligence on their part.

As noted in the reporter's notes to Section 402(A), public policy requires that the burden of accidental injuries caused by defective products intended for consumption be placed on those who market them, regardless of fault, so as to afford maximum protection for the consumer. We conclude, therefore, that the Supreme Court did not intend to limit the strict liability of *Temple* v. *Wean United* only to the manufacturer of products, but intended to apply strict liability to distributors and retailers as well.

To prevail on the theory of strict liability plaintiffs must prove that:

. . . (1) There was, in fact, a defect in the product manufactured and sold by the defendant; (2) such defect existed at the time the product left the hands of the defendant; and (3) the defect was the direct and proximate cause of the plaintiff's injuries or loss. . . .

A defect is considered to exist in a product which is not of good and merchantable quality, fit and safe for its ordinary intended use.

In its motion for summary judgment defendant did not provide any evidence that the pot was not defective. There is evidence, by way of depositions and affidavits, that the product was in a sealed package and remained unopened from the time it left the manufacturer until it was opened by the user. There is also evidence that the pot handle broke while being used for boiling water, an ordinary intended use, and that the handle broke the second or third time the pot was so used. Under these facts and the law as already stated, we conclude that summary judgment for Easterling was not proper and reverse the judgment of the trial court.

Manufacturers

Today many product-liability suits are brought against manufacturers on the basis of strict liability in tort.

Unlike the plaintiff in a negligence case, the plaintiff in a case of strict liability in tort does not need to concern himself or herself with whether or not the defendant's actions were reasonable. Manufacturers are liable even though they exercised all possible care in the preparation and sale of their products. Furthermore, strict liability in tort has fewer problems of proof than negligence. Contributory negligence is a good defense in a negligence case but not in a case of strict liability in tort.

As a cause of action strict liability is superior to warranty theory because warranty law is still burdened with the technical procedural requirements of the law of sales. For example, the UCC requires that notice be given to persons under certain circumstances. There is no such requirement under the *Restatement.*

It may also be superior to innocent misrepresentation because the defendant may not have misrepresented its product.

The elements that a plaintiff must establish are:

1. The defendant is in the business of selling the product.
2. The product was expected to and in fact reached the injured party without substantial change in the condition in which it was sold.
3. The product was in a defective condition.
4. This defective condition rendered the product unreasonably dangerous to the user or consumer or his property.
5. There was a causal relationship between the defect and the damage done to the plaintiff.
6. This resulted in physical harm to his person or property.

If the plaintiff succeeds in establishing all these elements, the plaintiff will prevail at trial.

The plaintiff must establish the existence of a defect in the product and prove that the defect caused his or her injuries. If there is no defect in the product, the plaintiff may not recover. Furthermore, if there is a defect but the injury sustained by the plaintiff was not related to the defect, the plaintiff will not win at trial.

The following case illustrates the application of strict liability in an automobile accident case.

Buehler v. Whalen

Court of Appeals of Illinois
355 N.E.2d 99 (1976)

Background: Buehler (plaintiff) brought an action against the driver of a vehicle, Whalen (defendant), for injuries sustained in an automobile accident. Buehler also sued Ford Motor Company, another defendant in this case, based on the contention that the design of the vehicle rendered it unreasonably dangerous to a user. The trial court decided for Buehler against Ford. Ford appealed.
Decision: The Appeals Court affirmed the judgment for Buehler.

Eberspacher, Justice

The vehicle driven by the Buehlers was a 1966 Ford Fairlane. This vehicle was one of several Ford cars that, since 1960, had been equipped with a flange mounted fuel tank. The flange mounted tank is different from strap mounted fuel tanks used on other cars in that the top of the flange mounted tank serves as the floor of the trunk whereas the strap mounted tank is placed beneath the floor of the trunk and is therefore separated from the trunk compartment. The flange mounted tank is also screwed into place and it is held rigidly to the car structure, whereas the strap mounted tank is held by metal bands which allow it to be displaced to some extent under stress.

The tank's nonflexible gas filler spout runs through the luggage compartment to a license plate bracket above the bumper. The flange of the tank is about two and one-half inches from the bumper while the rear of the tank itself is four inches from the bumper.

The flange mounted tank was not used in American cars prior to 1960. In that year

Ford began using that type of tank in some of its cars. General Motors and Chrysler stayed with the strap mounted tank. Since 1970 Ford changed back to strap mounted tanks for all its automobiles.

In the 1966 Ford Fairlane, the only shield separating the trunk compartment, where the fuel tank and filler spout are located, from the passenger compartment, is a fibreboard panel and the rear seat padding. It was undisputed that neither of these materials significantly limits the passage of fire.

After the collision, the gas cap to the Buehler auto was found near the scene of the impact. The ears to the cap, which secure it to the filler spout, were missing. Similar ears were found inside the Buehlers' fuel tank. The filler spout was found to be no longer extending through the opening in the license bracket area, but was instead below the bumper or about flush with it.

For the reasons enunciated in *Suvada* v. *White Motor Co.,* strict liability is imposed against a manufacturer in cases involving products where a defective condition makes them unreasonably dangerous to a user. Defectively designed products are unreasonably dangerous because they fail to perform in a manner reasonably to be expected in light of their nature and intended functions.

A manufacturer's duty to design a product which is reasonably fit for its intended use encompasses foreseeable ancillary consequences of normal use, which in the case of automobiles includes collisions. The environment in which an automobile is used must be taken into consideration by a manufacturer when designing its product. In an automobile dependent society, involving extensive usage, crowded highways, heavy loads, and high speeds, the statistically inevitable consequences of normal use of an auto entail the proven hazard of injury producing collisions of different kinds. Since injury producing impacts are foreseeable, the manufacturer is under a duty to design its vehicle to avoid subjecting the user to an unreasonable risk of injury in the event of a collision.

Viewing the evidence in its aspect most favorable to the plaintiffs, it appears clear that an impact to the trunk of the Buehlers' 1966 Ford Fairlane was an occurrence that was objectively reasonable to expect. In the event of such an impact it is also reasonable to expect that fire could develop in the trunk where the fuel system was located and could spread to the passenger compartment. In such a situation there would exist a high probability of serious burns or death resulting from an intense gasoline fed fire originating in the trunk. Testimony showed that Ford could have used a strap mounted tank that would have greatly reduced the risk of fire upon a rear-end impact. This type of tank was in fact used by Ford in prior as well as subsequent comparable models. Chrysler and General Motors had always used the strap mounted fuel tank. Moreover, there was testimony that the cost of placing a shield, in the 1966 Ford Fairlane, between the passenger compartment and the fuel containing system would only be one dollar plus one-half hour of labor time. Such a shield would have substantially reduced the risk of injury to the plaintiffs by providing additional time to effectuate an escape. We note that in the instant case it took less than one minute for the occupants to be removed from the burning vehicle. We are therefore of the opinion that the risks of harm to the plaintiffs were not so improbable or extraordinary as to be unforeseeable to Ford and that Ford owed the plaintiffs a duty to design its vehicles so as to reduce the probability of the injuries suffered.

We are now led to determine if the plaintiffs made a *prima facie* case that one or any design defect proximately caused the plaintiffs' injuries. Ford contends that the plaintiffs failed to sustain their burden of proof. Causation is primarily a question of fact for a jury to determine. If there was sufficient evidence from which a jury could find that an unreasonably dangerous condition existed in the Ford Fairlane by reason of its design and that the fire or the instantaneous spread of fire into the passenger compartment resulted from that condition, then the jury's verdict must be left undisturbed.

The evidence viewed in the light most favorable to the plaintiffs shows that upon impact the Buehler auto immediately burst into flame from a gasoline source in the interior of the car. Expert testimony showed that the location of the fuel tank, filler spout, and gas cap in the trunk made them extremely vulnerable in the event of a rear-end impact; that the flange mounted tank was susceptible to stress; and that the filler spout tended to be displaced into the trunk and the gas cap could break off in the event of a rear-end impact. In addition, the lack of any shielding device between the passenger compartment and the trunk permitted any fire that would develop in the trunk to spread without resistance into the passenger compartment. In the experts' opinion these conditions were unreasonably dangerous and were causally related to plaintiffs' burns. They believed that upon impact the spout was displaced into the trunk and that the configuration change of the fuel tank broke the gas cap off and forced gasoline to spray into the trunk. The fire that resulted from a spark from the impact instantly spread into the passenger compartment because no barrier protected that compartment and therefore the plaintiffs suffered serious burns, even though they were extracted in one minute or less.

We are satisfied that there was sufficient evidence to support the jury's verdict.

Privity

The privity requirement developed because the courts reasoned that a person should not be able to recover for a breach of contract unless he or she was a party to the contract. Because the warranty theory of recovery was an extension of the contractual theory of recovery, the courts for many years required the plaintiff to demonstrate that he or she was in privity of contract with the defendant. Under the tort theory, however, there is no need to establish a contractual relationship because this theory of recovery is not based in contract.

Today a plaintiff generally does not have to establish privity of contract to recover for personal injuries caused by a defective product.

There are still a few jurisdictions, however, that require it in certain cases.

Privity of contract is not an issue in strict liability in tort. Section 402A(2)(b) of the *Restatement* states that strict liability applies whether or not the user or consumer has entered into a contract with the seller. An injured party may proceed under Section 402A against retail sellers, distributors, manufacturers of component parts, and general manufacturers. The only seller an injured buyer will be unable to collect from is the seller who is not engaged in the business of selling such a product (Section 402A [1][a]). If you were to sell your lawn mower to your next-door neighbor, he or she could not sue you under this theory of liability because you would not be regarded

---

BOX 23-1 ISSUES AND TRENDS
Suits Against Successor Corporations

A corporation is a manufacturer of widgets. B corporation buys out A corporation and becomes the successor to all of A corporation's interests. Gidget was a consumer who bought widgets from A corporation. Gidget was injured by a defective widget that A corporation manufactured. Gidget wants to sue A corporation but it no longer is in business. Therefore, Gidget sues B corporation for the damages caused by the defective widget. B corporation tells Gidget that it is not responsible for the defective widgets that A corporation manufactured.

Is Gidget left without a remedy?

There is a growing number of courts that permit suits against successor corporations. This judicial approach reflects the belief that the obligation of a manufacturer should not be based solely on privity of contract but should rest on the demands of social justice. Courts have based this obligation of the successor corporation on many different theories. Some courts hold that the warranty and resulting liability run with the article like a covenant running with a piece of land. The successor corporation is thus responsible for any negligent acts of the predecessor corporation. Other courts have held that as a matter of public policy, the successor corporation should uphold the warranty and bear the liability of the company it bought. Whatever the theory of recovery employed by courts, successor corporations are more and more frequently being held responsible for acts of negligence they did not commit.

---

as a person in the business of selling lawn mowers.

General Manufacturers. Clearly, if a manufacturer sells a product in a defective condition unreasonably dangerous to the user or consumer or to his or her property, the manufacturer may be liable under strict liability in tort if the product was expected to and in fact did reach the user or consumer without substantial change in the condition in which it was sold.

Manufacturers of Component Parts. Not only may an injured party sue the manufacturer of a product under strict liability in tort, but in many jurisdictions he or she may also

sue the manufacturer of any defective part incorporated into the finished product.

Bystanders. Suppose the injured person did not purchase the product or qualify as a member of the buyer's household or a guest. Such a person is nevertheless able to collect under the theory of strict liability in tort. Section 402A of the *Restatement* makes the seller liable "to the ultimate user or consumer, or to his property." The Institute did not express an opinion on whether the rule should be extended to persons other than users or consumers, but a number of court decisions have extended strict liability to bystanders. In a Michigan case a hunter was allowed to proceed under this theory when his companion's

---

BOX 23-2 ISSUES AND TRENDS
Market Share Liability

Debbie's mother took an antinausea drug to combat morning sickness while she was pregnant. The drug had the unknown side effect of being carcinogenic to the fetus. By the time Debbie turned 20, she had developed cancer. Debbie wants to sue the drug manufacturer for selling this drug to her mother while her mother was pregnant. Unfortunately, several companies manufactured a morning sickness drug twenty years ago. As so much time has passed, Debbie is unable to prove which company actually manufactured the drug her mother took. Historically, courts have required plaintiffs to identify the precise defendant who is responsible for their injuries.

Since Debbie cannot prove exactly which manufacturer produced the drug that her mother took, is she without a remedy? Historically, the answer to this question was yes.

More recently some courts have created the concept of market share liability to address this problem. This concept creates a presumption that each manufacturer who produced the drug at the time it was prescribed is liable for its share of the market in damages. For example, if company A had a 40 percent share of the market for the drug that Debbie's mother took, then it would be liable for 40 percent of any damages awarded by the court to Debbie. The presumption may be rebutted by a showing that the particular defendant was not responsible for the injury. Therefore if company A could prove that it positively did not manufacture the drug taken by Debbie's mother, it would be relieved of liability. This presumption shifts the burden of proof from the plaintiff to the defendant. Rather than requiring Debbie to establish which drug company manufactured the drug consumed by her mother, the burden is on the manufacturers to prove that they did not manufacture the drug in question.

---

gun exploded and injured him. In a Delaware case the court held that a lease of a motor vehicle, entered into in the regular course of a truck-rental business, was subject to application of the doctrine of strict liability in tort in favor of an injured bystander.

Duty to Warn

What if a manufacturer produces a product that, although carefully manufactured, could cause injury to a person because of some latent danger? For example, suppose a drain cleaner could not safely be used with liquid bleach—two articles a person might commonly use in housecleaning—but the manufacturer failed to warn users of this fact. Under the *Restatement*, such a manufacturer could be held liable because the product was in a "defective condition unreasonably dangerous to the user or consumer."

One cannot escape liability under Section 402A by giving an incomplete or inadequate warning of the dangers inherent in using a product.

The law of product liability has for a long

BOX 23-3 ISSUES AND TRENDS
Duty to Foresee Modifications of a Product
——

Harry Fixit bought a table saw for his home woodworking shop. Harry found the blade guard on the saw made it difficult to do complex woodcuts, so Harry removed the blade guard. Several weeks later, Harry severed three fingers from his hand while making an elaborate cut. The manufacturer argued that it should not be held liable to Harry for his injuries because he removed the safety guard that was designed to protect purchasers from this very type of injury.

The manufacturer of a product has a duty to warn users of the product of any danger that is reasonably foreseeable. Many courts are now finding that in situations such as Harry's the manufacturer is liable even though the user modified the product. The rationale is that if a product has a device like a blade guard, the manufacturer should consider whether such a guard might interfere with the use of the product. If it is foreseeable that the guard would interfere with the use of the product, it is also foreseeable that the user would remove the guard to eliminate the interference—even if such an action would expose the user to a risk of injury. In this case the manufacturer is obligated either to warn the user about the danger of removing the guard or to design the product so that the guard cannot be removed.

---

time required manufacturers to warn consumers of dangers associated with their products. The following case discusses the question of whether the states can require manufacturers to disclose more information than is already required by federal law.

Cipollone v. Liggett Group, Inc.
Court of Appeals, Third Circuit
789 F.2d 181 (1986)

Background: Cipollone (plaintiff) sued Liggett (defendant). Mrs. Cipollone developed lung cancer allegedly as a result of smoking cigarettes manufactured and sold by Liggett. She began smoking in 1942 and died in October 1984. Suit was filed on August 1, 1983. Her husband continued the prosecution of the case following her death. Liggett contended that the Federal Cigarette Labeling and Advertising Act preempted her claims. Several of the claims involved the failure to provide an adequate warning of the dangers of the cigarettes sold by the defendant. The Cipollones made a motion to strike the preemption defenses. The District Court granted the Cipollones' motion to strike the defenses. The defendant appealed to the Third Circuit.

Decision: The Court of Appeals decided for Liggett.

Hunter, Circuit Judge

The Federal Cigarette Labeling and Advertising Act, originally enacted in 1965, was a response to a growing awareness among members of federal as well as state government that cigarette smoking posed a significant health threat to Americans. The original Act required the following warning label on cigarette packages: "Caution: Cigarette Smoking May Be Hazardous to Your Health." The warnings have been changed several times after that time.

The Act contains a preemption provision, which provide: that

> (a) No statement relating to smoking and health, other than the statement required by section 1333 of this title, shall be required on any cigarette package.
>
> (b) No requirement or prohibition based on smoking and health shall be imposed under State law with respect to the advertising or promotion of any cigarettes the packages of which are labeled in conformity with the provisions of this chapter.

We turn to examining whether congressional intent to preempt the Cipollones' claims may be inferred under the two general principles of implied preemption.

Under the principles of implied preemption, we must first determine whether Congress intended to occupy the field relating to cigarettes and health to the exclusion of state law product liability actions such as the Cipollones'. Our examination of the Act leads us to agree with the district court's statements that "Congress . . . intended to occupy a field" and "indicated this intent as clearly as it knew how." Not only did Congress use sweeping language in describing the preemptive effect of the Act, but it expressed its desire to establish "a comprehensive Federal program" in order to avoid "diverse, nonuniform, and confusing cigarette labeling and advertising regulations with respect to any relationship between smoking and health."

In determining the scope of this field, we observe that the Cipollones' tort action concerns rights and remedies traditionally defined solely by state law. We therefore must adopt a restrained view in evaluating whether Congress intended to supersede entirely private rights of action such as those at issue here. In light of this constraint, we cannot say that the scheme created by the Act is "so pervasive" or the federal interest involved "so dominant" as to eradicate all of the Cipollones' claims. Nor are we persuaded that the object of the Act and the character of obligations imposed by it reveal a purpose to exert exclusive control over every aspect of the relationship between cigarettes and health. Thus, we look to the extent to which the Cipollones' state law claims "actually conflict" with the Act to ascertain whether they are preempted.

The test enunciated by this court for addressing a potential conflict between state and federal law requires us to examine first the purposes of the federal law and second the effect of the operation of the state law on these purposes. The preemption provision, read together with the statement of the Act's purposes, makes clear Congress's determination that this balance would be upset by either a requirement of a warning other than that prescribed by the Act or a requirement or prohibition based on smoking and health with respect to the advertising or promotion of cigarettes.

We conclude that claims relating to smoking and health that result in liability for noncompliance with warning, advertisement and promotion obligations other than those prescribed in the Act have the effect of tipping the Act's balance of purposes and therefore actually conflict with the Act.

We hold that the Act preempts those state law damage actions relating to smoking and health that challenge either the adequacy of the warning on cigarette packages or the propriety of a party's actions with respect to the advertising and promotion of cigarettes. We further hold that where the success of a state law damage claim necessarily depends on the assertion that a party bore the duty to provide a warning to consumers in addition to the warning Congress has required on cigarette packages, such claims are preempted as conflicting with the Act.

At this stage of the litigation it is not necessary for us to identify which of the Cipollones' claims are preempted by the Act. We reverse the district court to the extent that it granted the Cipollones' motion to strike appellants' preemption defenses. We will also remand the case for further proceedings consistent with this opinion.

Defective Condition

The requirement of establishing a defect is an element in every product-liability cause of action except innocent misrepresentation. In a negligence case the plaintiff must establish that the defect was the result of the defendant's failure to exercise reasonable care. In an express warranty case the defect is established by showing that the goods did not conform to the warranties made by the seller. Evidence that the seller breached the implied warranty of merchantability or the implied warranty of fitness for a particular purpose is sufficient to establish a defect under those causes of action.

In strict-liability cases a plaintiff must establish that the product was defective, that the defect caused the injury in question, and that the defendant is the party responsible for the defect. The *Restatement of Torts Second* in comment j to Section 402A states:

The rule [of strict liability] stated in this Section applies only where the product is, at the time it leaves the seller's hands, in a condition not contemplated by the ultimate consumer, which will be unreasonably dangerous to him. The seller is not liable when he delivers the product in a safe condition, and subsequent mishandling or other causes make it harmful by the time it is consumed. The burden of proof that the product was in a defective condition at the time that it left the hands of the particular seller is upon the injured plaintiff. And unless evidence can be produced which will support the conclusion that it was then defective, the burden is not sustained.

The problem of establishing what the term "defect" means has been a difficult one for the courts. One of several tests used by the courts is to examine what the expectations of the consumer were with respect to a product, and then to determine whether the injured party was surprised by the danger associated with the product. This area is likely to continue to create problems for the courts, and other tests for what a defect is will undoubtedly be adopted by the courts in the future.

Unreasonable Danger

Not only does the *Restatement* require evidence of a defect in the product that caused injuries to a consumer, it also requires the

ETHICS BOX
Manufacture of Dangerous Products
———

Consider the following facts that raise ethical issues similar to those involved in *Cipollone*. Willie Watson acquired from an acquaintance a handgun manufactured by Charter Arms Corporation. Willie used the gun to kidnap, rob, rape, and murder Kathy Newman, who was a third-year medical student at Tulane University. Willie was tried and convicted of the crimes he committed. He is incapable of paying any monetary judgments that might be awarded against him.

Kathy Newman's mother filed suit against Charter Arms Corporation, alleging that the wrongful death of her daughter was caused by the defendant's designing, manufacturing, and marketing an unreasonably dangerous product. Mrs. Newman argued that use of the product to cause death was foreseeable, citing U.S. Justice Department estimates that 22,000 deaths, including suicides, are caused by handguns each year.

Charter Arms countered that it is legal to manufacture and sell handguns and that the corporation should not be held responsible for the criminal acts of others that could not be specifically foreseen. Charter also argued that the typical gun consumer buys a gun with full knowledge that it can be used as a murder weapon. Therefore, they reasoned, the general public does not consider the marketing of handguns to be unreasonably dangerous and would not support significant restrictions on their sale.

Difficult ethical problems are presented in the distribution of dangerous products. If the products do not have a positive utility, or are illegal, then their manufacture and distribution would be unethical. But if the products do have a positive utility, are legal, and are desired by many individuals, then the ethical duty of the manufacturer is transformed into an obligation to warn and to take reasonable steps to make the product as safe as practicable.

When a product is addictive, yet another issue is presented. Certainly distributing a product in such a way as to maximize addiction, or directing the sale of the product toward young people, is ethically problematic. Ultimately it must be the responsibility of government, reflecting the national will, to decide whether certain categories of products should be banned altogether.

plaintiff to establish that the danger posed by the product was unreasonable—that is, more dangerous than would be contemplated by an ordinary consumer.

The drafters of the *Restatement* included this requirement because some products are obviously defective but still not unreasonably dangerous. A stove that gets foods too hot may be defective but not necessarily unreasonably dangerous. A new car delivered with grease on its upholstery is defective but not dangerous.

Some courts do not require the plaintiff to establish unreasonable danger in order to recover. The California Supreme Court, for ex-

TABLE 23-1 THEORIES OF RECOVERY AND SELLER'S DEFENSES TO THESE THEORIES OF RECOVERY

Consumer's Theory of Recovery	Seller's Defense
Negligence	Contributory negligence
	Obvious danger
	Abnormal use
Innocent misrepresentation	Puffing
	No reliance
Strict liability	Assumption of the risk

ample, adopted this position in *Cronin* v. *J. B. E. Olson Corp.*, because the court thought the requirement was too similar to the concept of negligence.

Defenses

One defense available to a defendant being sued under a negligence theory is not available when suit is brought under strict liability in tort. In general, contributory negligence is not available as a defense.

Most courts recognize assumption of the risk as a valid defense in a strict-liability case.

REVIEW PROBLEMS

1. Explain the differences and similarities between a products-liability action based on negligence and one based on strict liability in tort.
2. Must a manufacturer warn of every danger associated with a product?
3. What is meant by the term "contributory negligence"?
4. What are two defenses often asserted in a misrepresentation case?
5. What elements must be established for a plaintiff to recover under strict liability in tort?
6. When Ford produced the 1966 Ford Fairlane it used a flange-mounted gasoline tank rather than a strap-mounted tank. The top of the flange-mounted tank served as the floor of the trunk. The only shield separating the trunk compartment from the passenger compartment was a fiberboard panel and the rear seat padding. Neither of these materials significantly limits the passage of fire. The cost of placing a shield between the passenger compartment and the fuel-containing system would only be one dollar plus one-half hour of labor time. Buehler was involved in a rear-end collision in which he was seriously injured. Had such a shield been in place, it would have substantially reduced the risk of injury to Buehler by having provided him additional time to escape from the accident. Should Ford be held liable to Buehler under the strict liability-in-tort theory of recovery?

7. Floyd Roysdon claimed that he suffered from severe peripheral vascular disease as a result of many years of smoking cigarettes manufactured by R.J. Reynolds Tobacco Company. He argued that the cigarettes are defective and unreasonably dangerous to the health of users and that the warnings on cigarette packages and in their advertising are inadequate to apprise users fully of the medical risks involved in smoking. Should Roysdon prevail on either argument?

8. Brown bought a helicopter from Brantly Corporation for use in his business. The promotional literature describing the helicopter described it as "safe, dependable, not tricky to operate" and one that "be-

ginners and professional pilots alike agree is easy to fly." Although Brown had his airplane pilot's license, he had never flown a helicopter. Nevertheless, he purchased the Brantly helicopter and began to use it for some of his business trips. The third time he used it he flew in fairly heavy wind. When he was unable to control it, the helicopter crashed to the ground and Brown did not survive the crash. Brown's heirs sued on the basis of the "misrepresentations made by the Brantly Corporation in its literature." Should Brown's heirs recover?

9. David Mello purchased a hydraulic jack at K-Mart. The jack bore the "K-Mart" label and its container stated "Manufactured in Taiwan, Republic of China, for K-Mart Corporation." David was injured when he was using the jack to repair an automobile. He brought suit against K-Mart alleging negligent design and manufacturing of the jack. K-Mart moved for summary judgment, stating that it did not design or manufacture the jack and that it was not designed specifically for K-Mart. Is K-Mart correct? Mello v. K-Mart Corp., 604 F.Supp. 769 (D. Mass. 1985)

10. J. B. Horne was a 300-pound furniture store employee. He injured his back when the chair he was occupying in the employees' lounge collapsed. Mr. Horne brought a strict product-liability suit against the manufacturer, alleging that the chair had been improperly glued and that the manufacturer had failed to test the chair for defects. The defendant argued that the chair was designed for home use and was not intended for use in commercial establishments and that such commercial use constituted a misuse and negated liability for injury. Does this argument relieve the defendant of liability? Horne v. Liberty Furniture Co., 452 So.2d 204 (La. App. 1984)

11. After the plaintiff had complained of mosquito bites his sister applied Union Carbide's "6–12" insect spray to his skin and clothing. Before the spray had dried, the plaintiff walked across a carpeted room and turned on a television set. As he touched the set, a spark from static electricity ignited the spray, inflicting severe burns to his upper body. The plaintiff's suit alleges that the warning label was inadequate. Does he win? Haran v. Union Carbide Corp., New York County Superior Court, No. 13541/75 (May 3, 1984).

CHAPTER 24

Commercial Paper: Introduction and Negotiability

During the latter half of the nineteenth century, the law relating to commercial transactions became very confused because the states were following different rules. This resulted in an outcry for general commercial rules that would apply everywhere in the United States.

The National Conference of Commissioners on Uniform State Laws set about drafting some suggested rules for all states to follow. One product of this effort was the Uniform Negotiable Instruments Law, which was finished in 1896. Other uniform acts soon followed. The Uniform Negotiable Instruments Law was an attempt to encourage the states to codify (put in statutory form) in a uniform manner their laws in this area. The hope was that this would simplify the conduct of business.

Unfortunately, this hope was not realized. The law was construed over a period of years in different ways in different states. Furthermore, years of experience under this and other uniform acts suggested a need for some changes in the law.

In the 1940s work was begun on a new set of rules for the commercial law area. The American Law Institute, working with the National Conference of Commissioners on Uniform State Laws, succeeded in producing a final draft of a new model act in 1952. This Act is called the Uniform Commercial Code (UCC), which has been adopted in all states except Louisiana—which has adopted part of it. Article 3 of the UCC deals with commercial paper and Article 4 covers bank deposits and collections. For the most part, the material covered in this and the following chapters on commercial paper deals with provisions of Article 3, although Article 4 is mentioned in places. Article 3 covers checks, drafts, notes, and certificates of deposit, which are called commercial paper. *Commercial paper* is a written promise or obligation to pay certain sums of money.

This chapter deals primarily with the basics of commercial paper and the law dealing with the transfer of such paper. Before examining the law as it relates to checks, drafts, notes, and certificates of deposit, we first cover another important type of document used in commercial transactions—documents of title.

DOCUMENTS OF TITLE

A *document of title* is any document that:

in the regular course of business or financing is treated as adequately evidencing that the person in possession of it is entitled to receive, hold and dispose of the document and the goods it covers. To be a document of title, a document must purport to be issued by or addressed to a bailee and purport to cover goods in the bailee's possession, which are either identified or are fungible portions of an identified mass (UCC Section 1–201 [15]).

These documents are usually issued by professional bailees who are in the business of either delivering or storing goods. A *bailee* is one who takes temporary possession of the property of another for a particular purpose.

Warehouse Receipts

Definition. If a seller wishes to store goods temporarily, he or she may deliver the goods to a "warehouseman." A warehouseman is one type of bailee. The seller receives a *warehouse receipt.* This receipt enables the seller, or any-

one to whom the seller transfers the document, to pick up the goods from the warehouseman. A seller might decide to ship goods instead of storing them. When the seller delivers the goods to a carrier (another type of bailee) for purposes of delivery, the carrier will give the seller a *bill of lading.* This document enables its possessor to receive the goods from the carrier. Warehouse receipts and bills of lading are the most familiar documents of title.

Form. A warehouse receipt need not be in any particular form, but it must contain certain information. Among other things, the warehouse receipt must contain information about the location of the warehouse, the date of issue of the receipt, to whom the goods are to be delivered, the storage or handling charges, a description of the goods or their containers, and a statement that advances have been made or liabilities incurred for which the warehouseman claims a lien or security interest.

In the event the warehouseman improperly prepares the warehouse receipt he or she may be liable—to anyone who purchases the document for value and in good faith—for any damages caused by the nonreceipt or misdescription of the goods.

Duties of Warehouseman. A warehouseman must exercise such care with respect to goods in his or her possession as a reasonably careful person would exercise under like circumstances.

Absent a contrary agreement, a warehouseman must keep separate the goods covered by each receipt so as to permit at all times identification and delivery of those goods, except that different lots of fungible goods may be commingled. *Fungible goods* are goods of which any unit is treated as the equivalent of any other like unit, such as wheat or corn.

Rights of Warehouseman. On notifying the person on whose account the goods are held

FIGURE 24–1
Warehouse Receipt

ACME WAREHOUSE
A PUBLIC WAREHOUSE

Date of Issue:

This is to certify that we have received in our warehouse located at 100 Tree Street in the city of Kansas City, Kansas for the account of _____
_____ in apparent good order except as noted hereon the following property, subject to all terms and conditions contained herein and on the reverse side hereof, such property to be delivered to the order of _____
_____ upon payment of all storage, handling and other charges and the surrender of this document bearing proper indorsement.

Lot #	Quantity	Said to Be or Contain	Storage per Month		Handling In and Out	
			Rate	Per	Rate	Per

ACME Warehouse Company claims a lien for all lawful charges for storage and preservation of the goods described above, as well as for all lawful claims for monies advanced, interest, insurance, transportation, labor, weighing, and all other charges and expenses in connection with the goods. Except as may otherwise be required by law, the ACME Warehouse Company has not insured the goods described above for the benefit of the depositor against fire or other casualty.

ACME WAREHOUSE COMPANY

By: _____

Its:

The goods listed below are hereby released from this receipt for delivery. Any unreleased balance of the goods is subject to lien for any unpaid charges and advances on the released portion, in addition to the lien as aforedescribed.

Date	Lot #	Quantity Released	Signature	Quantity Due on Receipt

[*Source:* **Douglas Whitman, F. William McCarty, Frank F. Gibson, Thomas W. Dunfee, Bartley A. Brennan, and John D. Blackburn, *Law and Business* (New York: Random House, 1987), p. 332. Copyright © 1987 by Thomas W. Dunfee, F. William McCarty, Frank F. Gibson, Douglas Whitman, John D. Blackburn, and Bartley A. Brennan.**]

and any other person known to claim an interest in the goods, a warehouseman may require payment of any charges and the removal of the goods from the warehouse at the termination of the period of storage fixed by the document. If no period is fixed in the warehouse receipt for the removal of the goods, the notice may specify their removal at a certain time after the lapse of thirty days. If the goods are not removed by such date, the warehouseman may sell the goods in accordance with UCC Section 7–210.

The warehouseman has a lien on any goods stored in his or her possession for charges for storage, transportation, insurance, labor, or other expenses relating to the goods, and for expenses necessary for preservation of the goods or reasonably incurred in their sale.

A warehouseman's lien may be enforced by public or private sale of the goods in blocks or in parcels, at any time or place and on any terms that are commercially reasonable, after notifying all persons known to claim an interest in the goods (Section 7–210).

Bills of Lading

Definition. When a shipper puts goods in the hands of a carrier, he or she receives a receipt called a bill of lading. The *bill of lading* is a document between the carrier and the shipper covering the terms and conditions of the arrangement between them. It is a document issued by the carrier to transport the goods. Thus the parties contemplate some movement of the goods from one place to another, whereas parties using a warehouse receipt plan to store the goods. UCC Section 1–201(6) defines bill of lading as follows:

"Bill of lading" means a document evidencing the receipt of goods for shipment issued by a person engaged in the business of transporting or forwarding goods and includes an airbill. "Airbill" means a document serving for air transportation as a bill of lading does for marine or rail transportation, and includes an air consignment note or air waybill.

Duties of Carrier. A carrier who issues a bill of lading must exercise the degree of care in relation to the goods that a reasonably careful person would exercise under the circumstances.

The warehouseman and carrier generally have a duty to deliver the goods to the person entitled to them under the document. Before the goods are delivered, the bailee's lien must generally be satisfied and the document of title must be surrendered for cancellation or notation of partial deliveries. A bailee has no liability if he or she delivers goods in good faith and if there has been compliance with the provisions of Article 7 of the UCC and the terms of the document. The UCC in Section 1–201(19) defines good faith as "honesty in fact in the conduct or transaction concerned."

Transferability. Section 3–103 specifically provides that Article 3 of the UCC, which deals with negotiable instruments, does not apply to documents of title. This is true even though bills of lading, warehouse receipts, and other documents of title may be negotiable. These documents are negotiable if by their terms the goods are to be delivered to the bearer or to the order of a named person. This allows documents of title to be exchanged freely between persons. Unlike a negotiable instrument, a document of title does not contain an unconditional promise or order to pay a sum of money.

A bill of lading is both a contract and a receipt and is usually transferable to another party. The person who ships goods may transfer the document to a third person. The third person may present the document to the carrier at the destination and obtain the goods.

A seller who wishes to deliver goods to a buyer in a distant location may arrange for the goods to be shipped by carrier. The carrier will deliver a bill of lading to the seller. It would be possible merely to mail the bill of lading to the purchaser. Assuming that the bill of lading is negotiable and made out to bearer, the buyer could receive delivery of the goods merely by presenting the bill of lading to the carrier. This is fine when the buyer has already paid for the goods. What if the buyer has not yet paid the seller, and the seller wants to be paid in full before he or she delivers the

FIGURE 24–2
Order Bill of Lading

ORDER BILL OF LADING
ACME TRANSPORT COMPANY

Received, subject to the classifications and tariffs in effect on the date of issue of this Bill of Lading, the property described below, in apparent good order (except as noted) marked, consigned, and destined as indicated below, which company agrees to carry to its place of delivery at said destination. It is mutually agreed that every service to be performed hereunder shall be subject to all the conditions not prohibited by law herein contained, which are hereby agreed to by the shipper and accepted for himself and his assigns. The surrender of this ORIGINAL ORDER BILL OF LADING properly indorsed shall be required before the delivery of the property.

Car Initial	Car Number	Length/Capacity of Car		Weight in Tons		Waybill Date	Waybill No.
		Ordered	Furnished	Gross	Tare		

STOP THIS CAR AT	FOR	CONSIGNEE AND ADDRESS AT STOP
AT	FOR	

ORIGIN	STATE

FULL NAME OF SHIPPER

ADDRESS:

Bill of Lading Date	Bill of Lading No.	Invoice No.

CONSIGNED TO ORDER OF:

Destination:

Shippers Special Instructions (Include Icing, Ventilation, Heating, Weighing, Etc.)

No. Pkgs.	Description of Articles	Weight	Rate	Freight	Advances	Prepaid

[*Source:* Douglas Whitman, F. William McCarty, Frank F. Gibson, Thomas W. Dunfee, Bartley A. Brennan, and John D. Blackburn, *Law and Business* (New York: Random House, 1987), p. 331. Copyright © 1987 by Thomas W. Dunfee, F. William McCarty, Frank F. Gibson, Douglas Whitman, John D. Blackburn, and Bartley A. Brennan.]

goods? The seller may deliver the bill of lading to his or her bank, along with a commercial instrument called a draft. The draft and the bill of lading are forwarded by the seller's bank to a bank in the buyer's town. The bank in the buyer's town requires the buyer to pay the draft (in essence, to pay for the goods) and then turns over the bill of lading to the buyer. The bank then sends the buyer's money to the seller's bank. In this manner a seller receives payment prior to the time the buyer receives the goods. The buyer, having paid for the

PREVENTIVE LAW
Documentary Credits

One situation in which documentary credits are very commonly used is international transactions. If the buyer is in the United States and the seller is in Europe, a buyer in this situation may have doubts about whether the seller will actually deliver the goods in question. Likewise, the seller may be concerned that if it ships the goods, the buyer might never pay for them. In order to overcome the natural reluctance on the part of parties that are far apart to enter into a contract, parties will use a documentary credit combined with a bill of lading and a draft.

Simply put, the process is as follows. The buyer goes to its bank and requests from the bank a documentary credit (in effect, a promise by the buyer's bank to pay the seller for the goods). The seller then delivers the goods to a shipper and receives a bill of lading from the shipper indicating that the goods in question are in possession of the shipper. The seller gives this document, as well as any other documents specified by the parties, to its bank. The European bank transfers these documents to the buyer's bank. The buyer may then give its bank a draft for the amount in question, and the American bank gives the buyer the bill of lading. The American bank pays the obligation and this money is forwarded to the seller in Europe.

goods and received the bill of lading, may now claim the goods from the carrier.

LETTER OF CREDIT

Another document used by businesspeople is a letter of credit. The UCC defines a *letter of credit* as an engagement by a bank or other person made at the request of a customer that the issuer will honor drafts or other demands for payment upon compliance with the conditions specified in the credit.

A buyer in one country may wish to purchase goods from a seller in another country. The seller may not be willing to extend credit to the buyer. In order to receive the goods, the buyer may arrange for a letter of credit from a bank. The bank agrees to pay the seller when the bank is presented the ap-propriate documents. This agreement makes the bank, rather than the buyer, the party obligated to pay. By using a letter of credit, the buyer may obtain goods from the seller because the seller is assured of payment from the buyer's bank.

In certain instances, the bank will be forced to pay even though the buyer is unhappy with the goods delivered under the contract. The bank's obligation to pay under the letter of credit is independent of its customer's obligations under the contract of sale.

COMMERCIAL PAPER

The law dealing with assignments, as discussed in Chapter 17, affects commercial paper. Many aspects of commercial paper are governed by the law of assignments. In particular, the law of assignments governs any instrument that fails to qualify as a negotiable instrument.

Contracts and Commercial Paper

A person may enter into a contract with another person for the payment of money. Suppose Smith agrees to pay Jones $100, and they enter into a contract that reflects Smith's obligation to pay $100 to Jones. In general, Jones's right to receive $100 may be assigned by Jones to a third person. Jones in this case is referred to as the *assignor* or *transferor,* and the person to whom he has transferred this right to receive money is referred to as the *assignee* or *transferee.* There is nothing improper about assigning a contractual right to receive money to a third party.

Rather than sign a contract to pay $100, Jones might instead ask Smith to sign a negotiable instrument in which Smith agrees to pay the $100 to Jones. Jones may then transfer the instrument to a third person. When a negotiable instrument is given by Smith to Jones, the UCC refers to the transfer as an *issuance* of the instrument. If Jones properly transfers the instrument to a third party, the UCC calls this a *negotiation.*

A right to receive money may be created by contract and *assigned* to a third party, or it may be created by a negotiable instrument and *negotiated* to a third party. In either case the third party may collect. Why would a person enter into a negotiable instrument rather than a contract to pay money?

Advantages of Negotiable Instruments

There are a number of advantages associated with a negotiable instrument as opposed to a simple contract to receive money. A person in possession of a negotiable instrument may actually be in a better legal position than the person from whom he or she took the instrument. On the other hand, an assignee of a simple contractual right to receive money is never in any better position than his or her assignor. The courts often state that the assignee "steps into the shoes" of the assignor. By this, the courts mean that the assignee is in the same position with respect to enforcing the contract as was the assignor. See Figure 24-3.

Let us take a look at how this might occur. Suppose Smith agrees to pay Jones $100. Jones then assigns his right to receive $100 to Robinson. Robinson has the same rights as her transferor or assignor, Jones. If Jones agreed to deliver a 1970 Chevrolet in return for the $100, but he never delivered it, Robinson would be subject to the defense that the car was never delivered. Because Smith could assert the failure to deliver the car against Jones, he may assert it against Robinson. But what if Smith signed a negotiable instrument and issued it to Jones instead of a contract and Jones then negotiated it to Robinson? If Robinson qualified as a holder in due course (discussed in the

FIGURE 24-3

Contractual Right to Receive Money	Negotiable Instrument

1. A agrees to pay B (assignor)
2. B assigns to C (assignee)
3. C steps into the shoes of the
    assignor, B
	1. A agrees to pay B (transferor)
	2. B negotiates to C (transferee)
	3. If C is a holder in due course,
	    C takes free of certain defenses A
	    has against B

next chapter), she would take the instrument free of the defense that Jones never delivered the automobile to Smith.

Another situation in which the holder in due course of a negotiable instrument stands in a better position than an assignee of a contractual right to receive money is when a thief transfers the instrument. Suppose in the prior example that a thief steals the negotiable instrument from Robinson. If the instrument qualifies as *bearer paper* (discussed in the next chapter), the thief has the power to transfer good title to the instrument, under certain circumstances, to an innocent third party who gives value for the instrument and is unaware that he or she is dealing with a thief. If the thief in this example transfers the instrument to Moore, Moore may receive good title to the instrument. In this case she may enforce the instrument against the original person obligated to pay, that is, Smith. Smith may not assert against Moore the defense that the instrument was stolen if Moore qualifies as a holder in due course of a bearer-negotiable instrument. Had Moore taken a contractual right to receive money from the thief, rather than a negotiable instrument, she would be subject to Smith's claim that the contract was stolen. The assignee of a contractual right to receive money steps into the shoes of the as-signor. Whatever defenses could be asserted against the assignor may be asserted against the assignee. Because the thief (the assignor) had no interest in the contract, he or she could not transfer any interest in the contract to Moore (the assignee). See Figure 24-4. The same rules apply if a finder, rather than a thief, transfers a bearer-negotiable instrument or a contractual right to receive money.

There are a number of other advantages to holding a negotiable instrument rather than a contractual right to receive money. For this reason people prefer to acquire negotiable instruments rather than take a contractual right to receive money.

Why does the law permit certain persons in possession of negotiable instruments to enforce them when their transferors could not enforce the instruments? The UCC reflects the policy that negotiable instruments should be freely transferable. By giving a holder in due course these additional rights, the UCC encourages the transfer and acceptability of negotiable instruments.

TYPES OF COMMERCIAL PAPER

Commercial paper is a document or instrument evidencing an obligation on the part of

FIGURE 24–4

Contractual Right to Receive Money	Negotiable Instrument
1. A agrees to pay B (assignor)	1. A agrees to pay B (transferor) (by bearer instrument)
2. B assigns to C (assignee)	2. B negotiates to C (transferee) (bearer instrument)
3. Stolen by D who sells it to E	3. Stolen by D who sells it to E
4. E is subject to the defense the contract was stolen	4. E is a holder in due course (if E holds bearer paper, he or she takes free of defense that instrument was stolen)

a certain party to make a designated payment in the future. There are four basic types of commercial paper: promissory notes, drafts, checks, and certificates of deposit.

Promissory Notes

A *promissory note* is a written *promise* to pay money. It must contain an unconditional promise to pay a sum certain in money. It must be payable on demand or at a definite time. It must be payable to order or to bearer. It must be signed by the person making the promise (Section 3–104).

There are two parties to the instrument: (1) the *maker,* who agrees to pay a certain sum of money, and (2) the *payee,* the person the maker promises to pay.

A demand note is one that is payable on demand. A time note is one that is payable at some definite time. If a note states that it is payable on demand, the person in possession of the instrument knows that he or she may collect on the instrument immediately by demanding payment from the maker. If the note states that it is payable ninety days after date, the person in possession of the instrument knows that the maker must pay ninety days from the date on the note.

In the note in Figure 24-5, Douglas Whitman, the maker, promises to pay a certain sum of money to Thomas Dunfee, the payee. The payee knows he will be able to demand payment on this instrument two years from January 1, 1984. Because this instrument is not payable on demand, it is a time note.

Suppose that Thomas Dunfee wishes to negotiate this instrument to Bartley Brennan. Dunfee may transfer his rights under this note to Brennan by indorsing it, usually on the back of the instrument, and delivering it to Brennan. In this case Dunfee is called the *indorser* (or transferor) and Brennan is referred to as the *indorsee* (or transferee).

Drafts

A *draft* is a written *order* to pay money. It is a written, unconditional order by one person addressed to another person, signed by the person giving the order, requiring the person to whom it is addressed to pay a sum certain in money, on demand or at some specific time, to the order of bearer or some specific person. The person giving the order is called the *drawer.* The person to whom the order is addressed is the *drawee.* The person who is to receive the money is the *payee.* The drawer may name himself or herself as the payee.

In the draft shown in Figure 24–6 John Blackburn, the drawer, orders William McCarty, the drawee, to pay a sum of money to Frank Gibson, the payee. It is an unconditional order, in writing, signed by John Blackburn (the party who gives the order), to William McCarty. It orders William McCarty to

FIGURE 24–5
Promissory Note

$100.00   Kansas City, Kansas January 1, 1984
Two (2) years after date I promise to pay to the order of Thomas Dunfee
One Hundred and no/100 -- Dollars
Payable at the First National Bank of Kansas City

Douglas Whitman
SAMPLE

FIGURE 24–6
Draft

$100.00 January 1, 1984
SAMPLE

Thirty days after date------------------------
Pay to the order of Frank Gibson
One Hundred and no/100------------------------------Dollars
To: *William McCarty* Charge the same to the
Kalamazoo, Michigan account of John Blackburn

pay a sum certain in money ($100) to the order of a specific person, Frank Gibson. The draft in this case is not payable immediately, as it would be in the case of a demand instrument. This draft is a time instrument, as opposed to a demand instrument, since it is not payable until thirty days after January 1, 1984.

While John Blackburn has ordered William McCarty to pay $100, McCarty is not obligated to pay anything until McCarty agrees to pay this draft. If he agrees to pay the draft, he becomes an *acceptor.* A drawee becomes an acceptor of a draft by signing his or her name across the face of the draft. The acceptor may also write on the instrument the date on which he or she accepted the instrument as well as the place where it will be paid. Once the drawee has accepted the draft, he or she is obligated to pay it when it becomes due.

As was the case for the note, if Frank Gibson, the payee, wants to transfer this instrument to Tom Dunfee, he may do so. Gibson may transfer his rights under this draft to Dunfee by indorsing the draft and delivering it to Dunfee. In this case Gibson is called the indorser (or transferor) and Dunfee is called the indorsee (or transferee).

Checks

A *check* is a special form of draft that is written by a depositor (drawer) directing a bank (drawee) to pay a designated sum of money on demand to a third party (payee).

The check in Figure 24-7 is payable on demand. Whenever the person named on the check presents it for payment, he or she is entitled to payment of the $100. (See Chapter 27, "Checks," for an extensive discussion of the law relating to checks.) The drawer of the check is Bartley Brennan, who signed it. The drawee is the First National Bank of Chicago. The payee is Douglas Whitman. Clearly, this check contains an unconditional order directed to the bank to pay a sum certain in money at a definite time to the order of a specific person.

A special form of check called a *cashier's check* is a check drawn by a bank on itself.

Certificates of Deposit

A *certificate of deposit* represents an acknowledgment by a bank of the receipt of a designated sum of money plus a promise to repay this sum at an agreed rate of interest.

PARTIES TO COMMERCIAL PAPER

Accommodation Party

A person may become a party to commercial paper by signing it. The signer may be the obligor of the underlying transaction, the transferor of the paper, or a surety for one of the parties to the transaction.

FIGURE 24–7
Check

SAMPLE	No. *101*
	January 1, 1984
Pay to the order of *Douglas Whitman*	*$100.00*
One Hundred and no/100------------------------Dollars	
The First National Bank of Chicago	*Bartley Brennan*

An *accommodation party* is one who signs an instrument in any capacity for the purpose of lending his or her name and credit to another party to the instrument. Special rules of suretyship apply to the obligations of an accommodation party. Thus the accommodation party is a surety for another party to the instrument.

An accommodation party is liable in the capacity in which he or she signed the instrument. An accommodation party may sign as a maker, acceptor, drawer, or indorser. If a person signs as an accommodation maker or acceptor, he or she is bound to the instrument without any resort to his or her principal. On the other hand, certain actions must be taken by the holder of the instrument (presentment, notice of dishonor, and sometimes protest) before an accommodation drawer or indorser may be liable.

Why would a person need to have an accommodation party sign an instrument? The person taking the instrument wants an assurance that he or she will be paid and refuses to accept the instrument without the signature of an accommodation party. For example, suppose a student wants to purchase a motorcycle but because he has not yet developed a satisfactory credit history, the bank refuses to lend him the money. The bank might agree to lend him the money if his parents agree to sign the note as accommodation parties. In this case the bank is assured that it will receive its money back from either the student or his parents. Obviously, there is some risk in sign-

ing as an accommodation party. The accommodation party may end up paying off someone else's debts. If that happens, however, the accommodation party is entitled to reimbursement from the party he accommodates—in this case the student's parents would have a right of reimbursement as sureties from their son (Section 3–415[5]).

Guarantor

A *guarantor* is a person who signs an instrument and agrees to pay the instrument under certain circumstances. Normally the guarantor does this by signing, in addition to his or her name, "payment guaranteed," "collection guaranteed," or similar words.

USING COMMERCIAL PAPER

Commercial paper generally is used in several ways: to borrow money, as a substitute for money, as a credit device, or to create some evidence of a debt.

To Borrow Money

If Brown goes to the bank to borrow money, the bank will probably ask Brown to sign a note in which he promises to repay the money over a certain period of time at a stated rate of interest. Suppose Brown wants to purchase an automobile with the proceeds of the loan. The bank will ask him to sign a note and a security agreement. (See Chapter 28, "Secured Transactions," for a discussion of security agreements.) The note obligates Brown to repay the money to the bank over a period of time or on a fixed maturity date. The security agreement gives the bank an interest in the automobile Brown intends to purchase. In the event Brown fails to comply with his obligations under the note, the bank will exercise its rights under the security agreement. The bank may repossess the automobile, resell it, and pay off the note with the proceeds of the sale.

To Create Evidence of a Debt

In the example discussed in the previous paragraph the note signed by Brown serves as written evidence of Brown's obligation to the bank. The fact that Brown signed a note simplifies the bank's burden of establishing that a debt exists between Brown and it. The note constitutes proof that Brown in fact owes the bank a certain amount of money, which must be repaid at a certain time.

As a Substitute for Money

Commercial paper also serves as a substitute for money. When a person goes into a store to purchase an item, she might pay for it by presenting a check to the store. If she is purchasing a very expensive item, she will probably prefer to use a check because it eliminates the need to carry a large sum of money. It also provides a record of payment.

As a Credit Device

Commercial paper may also be used as a credit device. Suppose a seller wanted to sell goods to a buyer in another part of the country. The seller could insist that the buyer send a certified check before it ships the goods. In this way the seller would be certain of payment. Alternatively, the seller might sell the goods to the buyer on credit. The seller would bill the

buyer for the goods at a later date. Of course, if the buyer does not pay at that time, the seller may have to sue. In the suit the seller would have to prove that the buyer owed him or her money. If the buyer had signed a commercial instrument, it would greatly simplify the case since the seller would have evidence of the obligation.

Another possibility open to the seller is to utilize a draft. The draft may be utilized to finance a sale. A draft is an order by the drawer to the drawee to pay a certain sum of money. Suppose an Ohio seller wishes to ship goods to a buyer in Kansas. The seller will load the goods on a carrier, such as a truck, and the trucking company will provide him or her with a bill of lading—a document giving the person holding it the power to claim the goods. The seller then ships the goods to the buyer in Kansas. At the same time the seller prepares a draft. If the seller wants to be paid at once, he or she will prepare a demand draft. The seller (the drawer of the draft) draws a draft ordering the buyer (the drawee) to pay a certain sum of money to the seller's bank (the payee). As noted earlier, at this point the buyer has no obligation on the draft. Only when he or she *accepts* the draft does the drawee incur any obligation to pay the draft. The seller will then give the draft and the bill of lading to its bank for collection. The seller's bank transfers the draft through banking channels to the buyer's bank in Kansas. The Kansas bank presents the draft to the buyer, and the buyer accepts and pays it. The buyer then receives from the bank the bill of lading, which enables the buyer to receive the goods from the carrier. The Kansas bank forwards the money back to the Ohio bank through banking channels.

When a seller uses a draft with an attached bill of lading, it is called a *documentary draft.* If a draft alone is utilized, the draft is called a *clean draft.*

The seller may also use a time draft, called a *trade acceptance.* It serves as a credit device to enable the buyer to receive the goods immediately without paying for them at once. In this instance the seller follows the same procedure outlined earlier. The seller names himself or herself on the draft as the payee and sets a time at which the draft is payable. The bank in Kansas asks the buyer to accept the draft, which he or she does by signing his or her name across the face of the instrument or in a space provided for the acceptor's signature. At this point the drawee buyer becomes an acceptor of the draft. This obligates the buyer to pay the draft at whatever date it becomes due. The bank releases the bill of lading to the buyer. It then returns the draft to the seller. The seller may retain the draft until its due date, then present the draft to the buyer for payment at that time. If the seller uses a time draft payable June 1, which the buyer signs on January 1, he or she then waits until June 1. On June 1 the seller presents the draft to the buyer for payment. Alternatively, the seller may want cash at once. In this case the seller takes the draft to a third party, such as a bank, and negotiates it to the bank. The bank pays the seller its money at once. The bank then waits until June 1 to collect the draft. On June 1 the bank presents the draft to the buyer for payment.

Drafts, notes, and checks may be used in other ways. But in general they are used as credit-extension devices, to borrow money and to create some evidence of a debt.

A *holder in due course* is a person with good title to an instrument, who took the instrument in good faith, for value, and without notice of any claims or defenses against it.

Negotiability

The UCC seeks to encourage the free transferability of negotiable instruments. The holder-in-due-course device is the basic method by which such transferability is encouraged. A holder in due course of a negotiable instrument is given preferred status.

For example, Merchant purchases goods from Manufacturer and signs a negotiable promissory note. Manufacturer negotiates the note to Financial Institution. Merchant never receives the goods and raises the fact as a defense against Financial Institution. Because Financial Institution is a holder in due course, Merchant cannot successfully raise the defense of failure of consideration and refuse to pay Financial Institution. Instead, Merchant's only recourse is to sue Manufacturer for breach of contract.

Some modifications of the rule relating to the holder-in-due-course doctrine have been made in the area of consumer transactions. Some states have adopted the Uniform Consumer Credit Code, which prohibits the use of promissory notes when consumer goods are purchased. A major modification of the holder-in-due-course device in consumer transactions was created by a Trade Regulation Rule adopted by the Federal Trade Commission. This rule is discussed in Chapter 25.

To qualify as a holder in due course, one must be (1) a holder (2) in possession of a negotiable instrument (3) that was properly negotiated.

REQUIREMENTS OF NEGOTIABLE INSTRUMENTS

The requirements of a negotiable instrument are formal, and considerable emphasis is placed upon the use of special words. The courts will look to the document itself to determine whether it is negotiable. The UCC requires that the document be (1) a signed (2) writing (3) containing a promise or order to pay (4) that is unconditional (5) relating to a sum certain (6) in money. Further, it must (7) contain no other promise or order, (8) be payable on demand or at a certain time, and (9) be payable to order or to bearer (or words of similar meaning).

The instrument must then be duly negotiated in order for the transferee to obtain the status of a holder in due course. Negotiation requires that (1) the instrument be transferred

(2) to a proper holder (3) with any required proper endorsement.

Transfer may be achieved through either physical delivery or, more rarely, a constructive delivery of the instrument. Constructive delivery occurs when the transferee, with intent to effect a transfer, performs a symbolic act representing the transfer. For example, delivery of the keys to a safe containing the instrument may constitute a constructive transfer.

Reexamine the promissory note in Figure 24–5. Does it meet all the requirements of negotiability?

1. The instrument is signed by the maker (Doug Whitman).
2. The instrument is in writing.
3. The instrument contains a promise to pay.
4. The promise is unconditional.
5. The maker promises to pay a sum certain.
6. The amount of this note is in money.
7. The instrument contains no other promise or order.
8. The instrument is payable at a certain time.
9. The instrument is payable to order.

Because all of the elements of negotiability are present, this note qualifies as a negotiable instrument.

If some of these elements are missing, the instrument could still be transferred but it would *not* be governed by the rules in Article 3 of the UCC. (However, if the only defect in the instrument is that it is not payable to either order or bearer, Article 3 still governs, but no one can be a holder in due course of the instrument [Section 3–805].) This instrument would be governed by the law of contracts as discussed earlier in this book, and in particular by the law relating to assignments. If the instrument were transferred to a third party, the maker of this instrument would be able to assert any defenses against the person holding the instrument. If this instrument qualified as a negotiable instrument, and if it were validly

negotiated to a holder in due course, the maker of the note would not be able to assert a personal defense against the holder in due course, although real defenses could be successfully raised to defeat him. (Defenses are discussed in Chapter 26.)

Even if an instrument is negotiable, so long as the instrument is in the hands of the payee, the obligor (person obligated to pay the instrument) may set up any defenses he or she has against the payee, unless the payee qualifies as a holder in due course. Whether the instrument is negotiable or nonnegotiable, the obligor may assert any defenses he or she has against the original parties to the instrument. Only when a negotiable instrument is validly negotiated to a third party who qualifies as a holder in due course are personal defenses of the obligor cut off.

Signed

To be negotiable, an instrument must be signed by the maker or drawer. It is not necessary actually to sign an instrument by handwriting; a signature may be made by printing, stamping, writing, or initialing. The question is whether the symbol on the instrument was executed or adopted by the party signing the instrument with the present intention of authenticating the writing.

Agent. It is not necessary to sign an instrument personally. The principal may designate an agent or representative to sign for him or her (subsection 3–403[1]). When an agent has authority to sign documents, he or she has the power to bind the principal.

Capacity of Signer. A person may sign an instrument in a number of capacities—as a drawer of a draft, as an acceptor of a draft, as a maker of a note, or as an indorser of an instrument. No one has any liability on an instrument unless his or her name appears on it (subsection 3–401[2]). A note to be enforceable must be signed by the maker. A draft to be enforceable must be signed by the drawer.

It is necessary to determine in what capacity a person signed an instrument. A person who signs a *note* in the lower-right-hand corner is presumed to be a maker, whereas a person who signs a *draft* in the lower-right-hand corner is presumed to be a drawer. When the drawee of an instrument signs his or her signature across the face of the draft, the signature is regarded as an acceptance. Section 3–402 adopts a presumption that, if a person's signature is ambiguous, it is deemed an indorsement. Normally an indorsement appears on the reverse side of an instrument.

Signature of a Representative. While it is true that a person's signature must appear on an instrument before he or she has any liability on the instrument, the signature may be made by someone on behalf of someone else. If an agent authorized to sign on another's behalf signs a negotiable instrument, this binds the principal. A person who is incapacitated might appoint a person to sign documents on his or her behalf. Likewise, an agent of a corporation (such as the treasurer or president) may sign commercial paper on behalf of the corporation if that agent is authorized to do so.

The power to sign for another may be an express authority granted to the agent, or it may be implied in law or in fact, or it may rest merely upon apparent authority. It is not necessary for there to be any particular form of appointment in order to establish such appointment.

An agent must sign an instrument properly, otherwise he or she may be liable under certain circumstances for the face amount of the instrument. The correct way for a person to sign an instrument in a representative capacity on behalf of another is as follows:

Peter Pringle
by Arthur Adams, agent

A signature in this manner clearly indicates to any person taking it that the agent signed on behalf of the principal and did not intend to incur any personal liability on the instrument. If an officer of the corporation is signing on behalf of the corporation, he or she should sign the instrument as follows:

Book Corporation
by Doug Whitman, President

This signature clearly indicates that Whitman signed on behalf of the corporation and intended to bind *only* the corporation and not himself. This becomes significant when a corporation is unable to pay its debts. Normally shareholders and officers are not liable for the debts of the corporation. However, when a corporation is unable to pay its debts, the holders of instruments may attempt to enforce the instruments against anyone whose signature is on them. A small corporation owned by the person who signed a note might go bankrupt. In that case the holder of the note may sue the officer who signed the note. If that person failed to sign the note in the manner suggested previously, he or she might end up paying a debt of the corporation.

A very dangerous manner of signing an instrument would be for an agent to sign but fail to name the person represented or the fact that the agent signed in a representative capacity. If Arthur Adams signs an instrument on behalf of Peter Pringle, but the only signature appearing on the instrument is "Arthur Adams," Peter Pringle is not liable on this instrument. Arthur Adams, however, is liable.

What if, rather than signing his name, Adams signs only the principal's name on the instrument: "Peter Pringle." In this case only the principal is liable. However, a signature in this manner by an agent may create problems for persons taking the instrument, who must establish that an authorized agent signed on behalf of its principal. To avoid legal problems, the agent should sign the principal's name together with his or her own name, along with some indication that the agent is signing the instrument in a representative capacity.

An agent might neglect to sign the principal's name, but he or she might sign his or her name along with some indication of the capacity in which he or she is acting, for example: "Arthur Adams, agent." So long as this instrument remains in the hands of the payee, the agent may introduce evidence that the parties were aware that the agent signed in a representative capacity. In this case the agent is not liable. However, if the instrument is transferred to a third party, the agent will be personally liable on the instrument. The agent will not be permitted to introduce evidence that he signed the instrument only in a representative capacity. In any event, the principal

will not be liable because his or her name does not appear on the instrument.

What if the agent signs the instrument as follows: "Peter Pringle, Arthur Adams"? In this case, as long as the instrument is in the possession of someone with whom the agent has dealt, the agent may introduce evidence that he or she signed in a representative capacity. But, as in the preceding example, this evidence may not be introduced against a third party. The agent must pay a third party.

The following case represents a strict interpretation of Section 3–403. The court ruled the agent should name the organization he is acting on behalf of. It rejected the notion that the printed name of the corporation on the check fulfills this obligation. It should be noted that some other courts have held that if the principal's name is printed on the check, parol evidence may be admitted to show the drawer signed in an agency capacity.

In Re Turner

U.S. Bankruptcy Court, District of Massachusetts
49 B.R. 231 (1985)

Background: A motion was made for a summary judgment for Turner (defendant), which was opposed by the petitioning creditors.

The issue presented is whether Turner is personally liable on twelve corporate checks. Each disputed check bears Turner's signature in the lower right-hand corner, without any qualification that in signing he was acting as an agent of any entity or as an officer, director, or shareholder of any corporation. The upper-middle portion of each check is imprinted with one of the following three legends:

1. THRIFTY LIQUORS, INC.
   TURNER'S PACKAGE STORE
   13 WHITE STREET
   CAMBRIDGE, MASSACHUSETTS 02140
2. THRIFTY LIQUORS
   215 ALEWIFE BROOK PARKWAY
   CAMBRIDGE, MASSACHUSETTS 02138
3. NEPONSET THRIFTY LIQUORS
   755 GALLIVAN BOULEVARD
   DORCHESTER, MASSACHUSETTS 02122

Turner claimed to have signed the eight checks imprinted with the legend "THRIFTY LIQUORS, INC., TURNER'S PACKAGE STORE, 13 WHITE STREET, CAM-

BRIDGE, MASS." as an officer of Turner's Package Store, Inc. Turner claimed to have signed the two checks imprinted with the legend "NEPONSET THRIFTY LIQUORS, 755 GALLIVAN BOULEVARD, DORCHESTER, MA 02122," as an authorized representative of John F. McCarthy, Inc. Turner claimed to have signed the two checks imprinted with the legend "THRIFTY LIQUORS, 215 ALEWIFE BROOK PARKWAY, CAMBRIDGE, MA," as an officer of Thrifty Liquors, Inc.
Decision: The court decided that Turner is liable on the checks.

Lawless, Judge

The liability of a drawer of a check is established by . . . , §3–413(2), which provides that the drawer of a check engages that upon dishonor of the draft and any necessary notice of dishonor or protest the drawer will pay the amount of the draft to the holder or to any endorser who takes it up. In the instant case, dishonor and notice of dishonor have occurred, and the drawer of these checks is primarily obligated to the petitioning creditors.

. . . Turner's defense is that he signed the checks not as an individual but as an agent or representative of certain corporations.

§3–403(2) provides the circumstances under which personal liability may be avoided by way of this defense. That statute provides in pertinent part that:

"An authorized representative who signs his own name to an instrument
"(a) is personally obligated if the instrument neither names the person represented nor shows that the representative signed in a representative capacity;
"(b) except as otherwise established between the immediate parties, is personally obligated if the instrument names the person represented but does not show that the representative signed in a representative capacity. . . ."

To make commercial paper freely negotiable without undue risk, §3–403(2) therefore incorporates the common law rule that unless something on an instrument's face or in the manner of its signature creates uncertainty as to whether the signer intended to sign in a representative capacity, parol evidence is inadmissible to alter the presumption that he is personally liable thereon. Thus, where an instrument both fails to disclose the representative capacity of the signer and also fails to name the principal, the signer's personal liability is conclusively established, and the admission of parol evidence is precluded.

In the instant case, it is undisputed that the checks fail to disclose that Turner signed in a representative capacity. Thus, the threshold issue before this court is whether the disputed checks sufficiently "name" the corporation on whose behalf Turner claimed he signed to enable extrinsic evidence to be admitted to rebut the presumption of individual liability. Although §3–403(2) clearly states that parol evidence is not allowed where the principal represented is not so named, it fails to specify what is necessary to satisfy the requirement that the principal represented by the signer be "named."

The few decisions which have addressed this issue are in conflict. The decisions fall into two categories. The majority of courts follow a strict reading of §3–403(2), while the minority view favors a more lenient approach.

The majority position requires a strict reading of the statute; parol evidence negativing the personal liability of the signer is admissible only where the name of the entity claimed to have been represented appears correctly.

In contrast with this strict view, a few courts have held that as long as there is "some indication" that the signer may have intended to sign in a representative capacity, parol evidence may be admitted on that question.

In the instant case, I feel that it is appropriate to follow the "strict" approach favored in this circuit. That is, the corporate principal must be named with specificity before parol evidence will be admitted to disestablish the signer's liability. §3–403(3) expressly provides a mechanism by which a signer of a check may put a holder on notice that he is acting in a representative capacity; the written disclosure of both the name of the organization of which he is an agent and the office he holds with the corporation. This mechanism, further, is not unduly burdensome or unusual but rather comports with standard business practice. Turner, having failed to utilize this simple mechanism, may clearly be bound individually.

Because in each case the entity claimed to be represented is not named with the specificity required by §3–403(b) (2), I conclude that the checks on their face determine Turner's liability and preclude the admission of any parol evidence to disestablish Turner's liability thereon. Turner is personally liable for the disputed checks.

Once again, the proper manner to sign an instrument, when acting in a representative capacity, is to sign the name of the principal, then sign the name of the agent with some indication that the agent is signing in a representative capacity. In signing for an organization, the name of the organization should be preceded or followed by the name and office of the individual authorized to sign on behalf of the organization—for example: "XYZ Corporation, by Douglas Whitman, President."

In the following case the president of a corporation signed some notes on behalf of the corporation without indicating that he was signing in a representative capacity.

Rotuba Extruders, Inc. v. Ceppos

Court of Appeals of New York

385 N.E.2d 1068 (1978)

Background: Rotuba (plaintiff) sued Kenneth Ceppos (defendant) to collect on seven notes he signed. Ceppos was president of Kenbert Lighting Industries, Inc. Ceppos signed these notes to enable Kenbert to receive goods. The trial court granted summary judgment in favor of plaintiff, Rotuba, on the notes. The defendant, Ceppos, appealed. The Appellate Division reversed the trial court and Rotuba appealed.

Decision: The New York Court of Appeals reversed the decision of the Appellate Division and reinstated the summary judgment on the notes for Rotuba.

Fuchsberg, Judge

This appeal, in an action between the immediate parties to a series of negotiable instruments, calls upon us to determine what measure of proof is required to free from personal liability an authorized representative who signs his own name to a series of negotiable instruments showing the name of the principal represented but that do not show that the representative signed in a representative capacity. The issue falls squarely within section 3–403.

Suit was brought against Kenneth Ceppos on seven promissory notes in the aggregate face amount of $33,898.80. These notes had been delivered to plaintiff between February and May, 1976, in payment for goods sold and delivered to Kenbert Lighting Industries, Inc., a close corporation of which Kenneth Ceppos was the chief executive officer and of which Robert Ceppos and Daniel Ceppos were the other principals. Rotuba apparently then considered Kenbert so precarious a credit risk that it was insistent that one of the three Ceppos' guarantee payment for goods sold to Kenbert. When the first notes went unpaid upon presentation for payment, Rotuba first brought an action against Kenbert. Shortly thereafter, as the due date of the remaining notes approached, Kenbert filed a voluntary petition under chapter 11 of the Federal Bankruptcy Laws. Rotuba thereupon initiated the present action against the individual defendants.

On the single printed line provided for a signature in the lower right-hand corner of each note appeared the signature of Kenneth Ceppos and, in a space immediately above this, in what is apparently a different handwriting, were the words "Kenbert Lighting Ind. Inc." No word or symbol, not even as much as "by" or "for" appeared to signify that Kenneth Ceppos was acting in a representative capacity in affixing his signature. Nor was there any designation of any office or position that Kenneth Ceppos held with Kenbert.

It is Rotuba's position that the notes indicate on their very faces that Kenneth Ceppos is personally liable on them. In opposition, Ceppos contends that a triable issue of fact exists because, as he asserts, the notes are ambiguous on their faces and his intention was only to sign them in a representative capacity.

Section 3–403 aims to foster certainty and definiteness in the law of commercial paper, requirements deriving from the "necessity for takers of negotiable instruments to tell at a glance whose obligation they hold." To make commercial paper "freely negotiable without undue risk" the basic law is that resort to extrinsic proof is impermissible when the face of the instrument itself does not serve to put its holder on notice of the limited liability of a signer.

As the statute states, the only exception has to be one that is "otherwise established between the immediate parties."

But the type of showing needed to bring the note within the "except" clause of section 3–403 must necessarily amount to more than the mere self-serving allegation of the signer's subjective intent to sign as representative. To escape personal liability, the signer has the burden to "establish" an agreement, understanding or course of dealing to the contrary. Thus, without an affirmative demonstration that the taker of the note knew or understood that the signer intended to execute the instrument in a representative status only, there can be no defense that, notwithstanding the form of the note, representative liability was "otherwise established between the parties."

Clearly, the notes in this case fall within the situation contemplated by the statute and, in factual circumstances that meet its requirements, would have permitted Ceppos to rebut the presumption of individual liability. Yet, Ceppos neither alleged nor made any evidentiary showing of the intent necessary to constitute such an agreement or understanding and, consequently, his affidavit does not serve to deny Rotuba summary judgment.

The undisclosed intention of Ceppos, without more, does not establish the understanding between the parties required by section 3–403. Ceppos' affidavit does not even disclose such elementary facts as who acted for Rotuba in accepting the notes, what disclosure was made of Ceppos' unilateral intention, or what manifestation or knowledge of such intention, if any, was made anywhere or to anyone on behalf of Rotuba.

In short, Ceppos pointed to nothing that would tend to show that the parties regarded the obligation as a corporate one alone. The nature of the transaction here gives no indication that regardless of the faces of the notes, corporate liability and none other was intended by the parties. Certainly, there was nothing unusual about it. It is common business practice to treat such an obligation as a corporate one, and creditors of small corporations often demand that officers personally obligate themselves on corporate notes.

Therefore, the order of the Appellate Division should be reversed and the order granting summary judgment on the first cause of action must be reinstated.

Unconditional Promise or Order

An instrument, in order to be negotiable, must contain an unconditional promise or order to pay. Notes and certificates of deposit must contain an unconditional *promise* to pay. Drafts and checks must include an unconditional *order* to pay. If the language in an instrument states that the obligor *promises* to pay someone, the instrument cannot be a draft or check.

Suppose John Doe wrote out the following statement on a piece of paper: "IOU $100 (signed) John Doe." This piece of paper obviously has some characteristics of a negotiable instrument. But it lacks one important element: a promise or an order to pay. While John Doe acknowledges his obligation to pay a debt of $100, he does not promise to pay it or order someone else to pay it. This missing element renders the IOU nonnegotiable. In the typical note a statement appears such as "I promise to pay." In the case of a draft some language must appear that orders someone or some institution to pay. In the draft in Figure 24-6 this requirement is fulfilled by placing the drawee's name after the word "To," or as it appears in that instrument: "To: William McCarty." On a check the name of the drawee bank will appear on the face of the check. The check illustrated in Figure 22-7 has the words "The First National Bank" in the lower left-hand corner of the check.

The negotiability of an instrument must be determinable by an examination of the face of the instrument itself. It must not be necessary for anyone who wishes to take the instrument to refer to any other document in order to determine if an instrument is negotiable.

So long as the instrument is in the possession

of the original obligee (the party the obligor must pay) or any transferee who fails to qualify as a holder in due course, an instrument may be modified or affected by any other written agreement executed as part of the same transaction. A holder in due course is not affected by any limitation of his or her rights arising out of a separate written agreement if he or she had no notice of the limitation at the time of receiving the instrument.

It is common for persons to execute several documents at the same time. Suppose a person wishes to borrow $5,000 from a bank in order to purchase a new automobile. The bank will probably ask the borrower to sign a promissory note and a security agreement. (Security agreements are covered in Chapter 28, "Secured Transactions.") The security agreement will contain information that does not appear in the note. The UCC requires that all writings executed as parts of the same transaction are to be read together as a single agreement—in this instance both the note and the security agreement. If the note is negotiated to a holder in due course who is unaware of any defense or claim arising under the terms of the security agreement, he or she will not be affected by any defense or claim arising out of the security agreement.

The negotiability of an instrument is always to be determined by what appears on the face of the instrument alone. If it is negotiable in itself, a purchaser without notice of a separate writing is not affected by the other writing (Section 3–119[2]). If the instrument states it is subject to or governed by any other agreement, it is not negotiable. If the instrument merely refers to a separate agreement or states that it arises out of such an agreement, it is negotiable.

For example, if a note contains the statement "Payment is subject to the terms of the contract entered into between the parties," it is not negotiable. In order to determine the terms of the note, a person who wishes to take it would need to examine a document other than the instrument, the contract. On the other hand, a simple notation such as "A contract was entered into at the time of executing this note" is a mere reference to the contract and does not make the note subject to the terms of the contract. A note with such a notation is negotiable.

Section 3–105 lists certain matters that may appear in an instrument without making the promise or order to pay conditional. Section 3–112 also identifies some terms and omissions that do not affect the negotiability of an instrument. The following material discusses several important points covered in Section 3–105.

To determine whether the negotiable instrument includes an unconditional promise or order to pay, one need only examine the instrument itself. Oral statements do not affect the negotiable character of an instrument. Suppose that McGrew tells Allison at the time she executes a promissory note that she will pay the note only if Allison delivers a 1959 Ford to her. This statement has no effect on the negotiable character of the instrument. A party examining the face of the instrument would be unaware of the oral condition put on the instrument by McGrew at the time she executed the note.

In the case mentioned earlier between the bank and the borrower we noted that the bank might ask its customer to sign several documents at the same time. Insofar as third persons who were not parties to the original transaction are concerned, whether the instrument is negotiable depends on what appears in the instrument. Negotiability is not influenced by what appears in a separate written document.

Take the case of Allison and McGrew. If the note McGrew signs indicates that McGrew is giving this note to Allison in consideration for the 1959 Ford, or if it indicates that the note is being transferred because Allison sold her 1959 Ford to McGrew, McGrew's promise to pay Allison is *not* rendered conditional. Such recitals only explain why the note is issued—

but the note stands regardless of the recitals. On the other hand, if McGrew writes into the note that the terms of the note are subject to or governed by the contract signed between McGrew and Allison for the sale of the 1959 Ford, the promise to pay is rendered conditional. The instrument would be nonnegotiable. This type of statement requires any person who wishes to acquire this note to examine some other document other than the note between McGrew and Allison. The negotiability of an instrument must be determinable by an examination of the face of the instrument in question.

Some instruments indicate that they are payable *only* from a particular account. Such a statement makes an instrument nonnegotiable. If language in the instrument states "Pay only out of the Acme account," the language renders the instrument nonnegotiable. However, if the instrument merely indicates a particular account to be debited, the instrument is negotiable. If a person writes on the bottom of a note "Pay out of Acme account," this would be treated as a mere reference, not a statement that conditions or limits payment of the instrument from the Acme account.

Sum Certain in Money

To be negotiable, an instrument must also contain a sum certain in money. If it is possible for a holder to determine at the time of payment the amount payable merely by examining the instrument itself, the amount payable is certain. If it is necessary to make computations in order to determine the amount payable, the sum is certain if the computation can be made from the instrument itself without reference to any outside source. The fact that the sum is payable with stated interest, or with different rates of interest before and after default, will not make the note nonnegotiable (Section 3-106[1]). All of this information can be determined from the face of the instrument. On the other hand, if the note is payable "at the current rate," the instrument is not negotiable

because the holder would not know the current rate by examining the instrument itself.

An instrument is payable in money if "the medium of exchange" in which it is payable is money at the time the instrument is made. An instrument payable in "currency" or "current funds" is payable in money (Section 3-107[1]). The promise to pay may be stated in foreign currency rather than in dollars.

Payable on Demand or at Certain Time

To be negotiable, an instrument must be payable on demand or at a definite time. An instrument is payable on demand if it is payable at sight or on presentation or if it contains no time for payment (Section 3-108). It must be paid whenever the holder presents it for payment.

An instrument payable at a definite time must state the date on which it is payable. The note in Figure 24-5 is payable two years after its date—that is, two years after January 1, 1984. If the maker of this note failed to insert a date, the note would not be negotiable because it would not be payable at a definite time. However, Section 3-115 permits a holder of an instrument to fill in the date before negotiating the instrument. Not all instruments are this simple, but they may still be payable at a definite time.

According to Section 3-109, an instrument is payable at a definite time if by its terms it is payable:

1. On or before a stated date or at a fixed period after a stated date
2. At a fixed period after sight
3. At a definite time subject to acceleration
4. At a definite time subject to extension at the option of the holder
5. At a definite time subject to extension to a further definite time at the option of the maker or acceptor or automatically upon or after a specified act or event

The instrument in Figure 24-5 is payable at a fixed period after a stated date. A draft payable "30 days after sight" is also payable at a definite time. When the holder presents it to the drawee and the drawee accepts it (thereby becoming the acceptor of the draft), the thirty-day period begins to run.

The time for payment must be determinable from the face of the instrument. An instrument may contain an *acceleration clause*, which, in an instrument payable at a definite time, permits the entire draft to become due immediately upon the option of one of the parties or the occurrence of some specified event. The option to accelerate may be exercised only if the party in good faith believes the prospect of payment or performance is impaired (Section 1–208). A clause in an instrument that reads "payable June 1, 1985, but the entire sum is due and payable immediately in the event the maker dies" is a valid acceleration clause. The payee of this instrument knows he or she will be paid on June 1, 1985, at the latest, or earlier if the maker dies before that time. An instrument can also be written in such a fashion that the holder can accelerate the time for payment. However, as noted before, the holder must reasonably believe that the prospect of payment or performance has been impaired.

The instrument also may be made payable at a definite time subject to extension at the option of the holder, or subject to extension to a further definite time at the option of the maker or acceptor, or subject to extension automatically upon the occurrence of an act or event.

If the instrument is payable only upon an act or event whose occurrence is uncertain, the instrument is not payable at a definite time even though the act or event has occurred (Section 3–109[2]). For instance, if the note is payable "upon the marriage of my daughter," and the daughter has now married, the note is still not payable at a definite time. It must be possible to determine, at the time the acceptor takes the instrument, whether the instrument is payable at a definite time or on demand. The specified event (the daughter's marriage) may never occur. She may never marry, or she may die before the note comes due. In such cases the instrument would never be payable. No one would want to take an instrument unless he or she was certain that it would be paid either immediately or at some definite time in the future.

The following case concerns a note that the court determined was not negotiable because it was not payable on demand or at a definite time.

Barton v. Hudgens Realty and Mortgage, Inc.

Court of Appeals of Georgia

222 S.E.2d 126 (1975)

Background: Hudgens Realty (plaintiff) brought suit upon what purported to be a "promissory note" signed by the Bartons (defendants) and contained the following pertinent language: "By execution of this document the undersigned hereby acknowledges and promises to pay to the order of Scott Hudgens Realty & Mortgage, Inc., a Delaware corporation, at Atlanta, Georgia, or at such other place or to such other party or parties as the holder hereof may from time to time designate, the principal sum of three thousand dollars ($3,000). This amount is due and payable upon evidence of an acceptable permanent loan of $290,000 for Barton-Ludwig Cains Hill Place Office Building, Atlanta, Georgia, from one of SHRAM's investors and upon acceptance of the commitment by the undersigned." In the answer the Bartons admitted execution of the "promissory note," and further admitted execution of the loan commitment, but denied that an acceptable permanent loan was obtained and therefore denied that the promissory note was due and payable on the date alleged. Hudgens Realty moved for judgment on the pleadings, based on the Bartons' admission of execution of the note and the loan commitment, and the motion was granted. The Bartons appealed.

Decision: The Appeals Court affirmed the decision of the trial court for Hudgens Realty.

Deen, Presiding Judge

Hudgens Realty relies upon *Freezamatic Corporation* v. *Brigadier Industries Corporation,* wherein it was held that under our Uniform Commercial Code when execution of a promissory note is admitted but an affirmative defense is not raised, judgment on the pleadings in favor of the holder is proper. While it is true that Code provides for such a circumstance, what the plaintiff (and also the defendants) overlooked is that the provisions of Code Ann. Ch. 109A-3 apply only to negotiable instruments and the "promissory note" here in issue does not so qualify. This "promissory note" by its terms was made payable "upon evidence of an acceptable permanent loan . . . and upon acceptance of the [loan] commitment"; however under Code Ann. Section 109A-3–104(1)(c) a negotiable instrument must "be payable on demand or at a definite time." The "note" here was not payable on demand under the language of section 109-A-108 and under section 109A-3–109(2) "[a]n instrument which by its terms is otherwise payable only upon an act or event uncertain as to time of occurrence is not payable on demand or at a definite time even though the act or event has occurred." The language of the "promissory note" therefore reveals that it was not payable on demand or at a definite time, was therefore not negotiable and thus the Freezamatic Corporation case is not controlling authority.

The "promissory note" is rather a *contract to pay money* when certain contingencies are satisfied—"upon evidence of an acceptable permanent loan . . . and upon acceptance of the [loan] commitment." There is no dispute that the loan commitment was accepted by the Bartons. Hudgens contends that this commitment itself, without more, wherein one of its investors agreed to make the loan in the desired amount, satisfied the requirement of evidence of an acceptable permanent loan. Barton, apparently relying on the fact that the loan was never finally consummated, denies that "an acceptable permanent loan was obtained." Thus the controversy between the parties turns upon the construction of the contract language making the amount due and payable "upon evidence of an acceptable permanent loan."

Under Code Ann. section 20–704(4) the whole contract should be looked to in arriving at the construction of any part. The contract provides specifically that it is for a loan origination fee; there is nothing which requires as a prerequisite to recovery evidence that the loan in fact be accepted. All that is required is that there be "evidence of an acceptable permanent loan." The record reveals that by their signatures, the Bartons signified their "acceptance of the terms and conditions" of the loan commitment. We agree with the Hudgens' construction of the document, that the loan commitment is evidence of a permanent loan in the desired amount and that the admission by the Bartons of its execution acknowledges its acceptability and further supplies the necessary requirement for recovery under the contract. In short, the Bartons contracted for the procurement of a loan and the signed loan commitment is "evidence of an acceptable permanent loan." The broker having successfully originated a loan, its fee was earned and the Bartons were bound by their contract.

To Order or to Bearer

To Order. To be negotiable, an instrument must also be payable to order or to bearer. "Order" and "bearer" are *words of negotiability.* "An instrument is payable to order when by its terms it is payable to the order or assigns of any person therein specified with reasonable certainty, or him or his order . . ." (Section 3–110). Thus a check payable "to the order of John Jones" is negotiable. The courts interpret this requirement strictly: a check "payable to John Jones" is not negotiable because it does not say "to the order of John Jones." The printed checks issued by banks have "to the order of" printed on them. An instrument alternatively might state "to John Jones or order" or "to John Jones or assigns."

An instrument must specify a particular person or organization so that it will be clear who is entitled to payment. It can be made payable to more than one person. For example, an instrument can be "payable to the order of John Doe and Acme Car Repair." In this case the instrument may be properly negotiated to a third party only if *both* parties to the instrument indorse it. An instrument made payable to two parties in this fashion may not be properly negotiated if only John Doe or Acme Car Repair indorses it. People often use this device when they want to make certain that all parties to whom they are obligated have been paid. On the other hand, if an instrument is made payable to the order of "John Doe *or* Acme Car Repair," the signature of *either* party as an indorser, along with a delivery of the instrument, will result in a proper negotiation.

An instrument payable to the order of "John Doe and/or Acme Car Repair" may be negotiated by the indorsement of either party along with delivery of the instrument to a third party. Suppose the instrument reads "John Doe/Acme Car Repair." In this case the instrument will be treated as payable to both of these parties, and it will require the signatures of both John Doe and Acme Car Repair.

To Bearer. Even though an instrument fails to qualify as an order instrument, it is negotiable if it is payable to bearer. An instrument is payable to bearer when by its terms it is payable to bearer or to the order of bearer, or to a specified person or bearer, or to cash or to the order of cash, so long as it does not purport to designate a specific payee. If an instrument is payable "to order of bearer" or "cash," it is bearer paper. Anyone who gets possession of this instrument has the power to negotiate it.

An instrument payable "to order of bearer," although it sounds as if it is payable to order, is treated as an instrument payable to bearer (Section 3–111[a]). An instrument that reads "pay bearer" also is treated as payable to bearer.

Under Section 3–110(3), an instrument that is made payable "to order and to bearer" is payable *to order* unless the bearer words are handwritten or typewritten. A drawer might write "Pay to the order of John Doe" and fail to note that the form has the phrase "or bearer" printed on it. In this situation the instrument is treated as payable *to order.* However, if a form contains the words "Pay to order of ————————," and the drawer writes in the blank space "John Doe or bearer," the intent of the maker or drawer to create a bearer instrument is assumed (Section 3–110, Comment 6).

Instruments containing phrases like "Pay cash," "Pay to the order of cash," "Pay bills payable," or others that do not designate a specific payee are treated as instruments payable to bearer.

Incomplete Instrument. An instrument that is incomplete because it fails to specify a payee and the space for such designation is otherwise blank (i.e., it is not payable to "cash" or the like) is payable neither to order nor to bearer. The following case illustrates what happens if the instrument fails to specify a payee.

Gray v. American Express Co.

Court of Appeals of North Carolina
239 S.E.2d 621 (1977)

Background: Gray (plaintiff) sued American Express (defendant). Joseph Faillance gave several American Express Traveler's checks to Ernie's Truck Stop, which in turn transferred the checks to Charles Gray, the plaintiff in this case. American Express refused to honor the checks on the grounds that they were incomplete because they were not payable to anyone. The trial court ruled for American Express and Gray appealed.

Decision: The Appeals Court affirmed the decision of the trial court for American Express.

Clark, Judge

Plaintiff, owner of Charles L. Gray Company, a wholesale grocery company located in Rocky Mount, received an order on 9 August 1967 from Ernie's Truck Stop for about $4,900 worth of cigarettes. He delivered the cigarettes to the manager of Ernie's. The manager gave the cigarettes over to Joseph Faillance of New York. Faillance paid the manager with $4,800 in American Express Traveler's Checks. Plaintiff saw Faillance sign and countersign the checks. Faillance did not date the checks or make them payable to anyone. The signature and countersignature were similar. The manager gave the checks to plaintiff in payment for the cigarettes. The checks remained blank as to date and payee. The manager did not indorse the checks over to plaintiff. On 10 August 1967 plaintiff turned the checks over to a local bank, still blank as to date and payee, and was refused payment on the ground that the checks were stolen. Payment was similarly refused after plaintiff forwarded the checks to Chase Manhattan Bank. Plaintiff never filled in the blanks.

A traveler's check is a negotiable instrument within the purview of Article III of the Uniform Commercial Code. 3–114 explicitly permits an instrument to be undated. Dating therefore is not a necessary element, the absence of which makes the instrument incomplete and unenforceable under 3–115. However, the name of the payee is an essential element. The payee's name is not one of the "[t]erms and omissions not affecting negotiability" under 3–112. 3–104 demands "[a]ny writing to be a negotiable instrument within this article must . . . be payable to order or to bearer" 3–104(1)(d). Under old law of commercial paper and now incorporated into the Uniform Commercial Code, a note payable neither to order nor to bearer is not negotiable. Specificity on the face of the instrument is required whether payment be to order or to bearer 3–111(b). Therefore, it is clear that the checks were legally incomplete because they lacked the name of the payee.

3–115 permits completion of an incomplete instrument if done "in accordance with authority given. . . ." *Jones* v. *Jones* (1966), construing the old law now incorporated into the Uniform Commercial Code, considered that the instrument's primary makers had the authority to complete the instrument by inserting the name of the payee. The holder had final authority. *Lawrence* v. *Mabry* (1930) held that a bill of exchange drawn and issued in blank for the name of the payee may be filled in by a bona fide holder in his own name, and will bind the drawer. It is clear that plaintiff had the authority to complete the instruments, had nine years so to do, and did not. The instruments remained incomplete and unenforceable as a matter of law.

No Other Promise, Order, Obligation, or Power

Even if an instrument is a signed writing containing an unconditional promise or order to pay a sum certain in money, payable on demand or at a definite time, and payable to order or bearer, it still may not be negotiable if the maker or drawer gives any other promise, order, obligation, or power except as authorized by Article 3.

Certain additional information may be given in an instrument without impairing its negotiability. A statement that collateral has been given to secure the obligation will not impair the negotiability of an instrument. For example, a person obtaining a loan to purchase an automobile will sign a note for the bank indicating that the maker is using the automobile as collateral—that is, if he or she fails to make the payments specified under the note, the bank may repossess the automobile. (See Chapter 28, "Secured Transactions," for a complete discussion of the use of collateral.) Merely mentioning this information does not impair the negotiability of the instrument. Similarly, the note may indicate that the maker must protect the collateral. Other information that may appear in a note without impairing its negotiability appears in UCC Section 3–112.

Section 3–112 also states that the negotiability of an instrument is not affected by the omission of the place where the instrument is drawn and payable.

Date

In most cases the negotiability of an instrument is not affected by the fact that it is undated. However, if an instrument states that it is "payable 15 days after date," the instrument will not be negotiable if it is undated. It is an incomplete instrument. Under Section 3–115 the instrument may be completed as authorized. The instrument is not negotiable until the date is filled in.

An instrument also is not rendered nonnegotiable because it is dated sometime in the past (an antedated instrument) or at some time in the future (a postdated instrument).

RULES OF CONSTRUCTION

The UCC, in Section 3–118, lists several rules of construction that apply if the writing is ambiguous or leaves out certain information. When one is in doubt as to how to interpret an instrument, these rules should be consulted.

Among other provisions, Section 3–118 provides that if there is doubt whether an instrument is a note or a draft, the holder may treat the instrument as either. It also specifies that handwritten terms control typewritten and printed terms and typewritten control printed. Words generally control figures, except that if the words are ambiguous, the figures control.

REVIEW PROBLEMS

1. What is a document of title?

2. What advantages are associated with taking a negotiable instrument as opposed to a simple contract to receive money?

3. Ross agrees to pay his cousin Mary $300. He signs a piece of paper that states: "IOU $300 (signed) Ross James." Is this a negotiable instrument?

4. Anderson signs a demand note for $200 payable to the order of Bailey. The note states that it was given in exchange for the sale of a bicycle by Bailey to Anderson. The note also states that it is governed by the terms of the contract entered into between Bailey and Anderson for the sale of the bicycle. Do either of these provisions render the note nonnegotiable?

5. Erwin enters into a contract with Singer for the purchase of some machinery. Erwin promises to pay Singer $2,000 for the machinery. Erwin signs a note that specifies, among other things, that the note will be paid by Erwin in British pounds. The note also states that it is "payable six months after sight, but the entire sum is due and payable immediately if Erwin dies." Is this instrument negotiable?

6. Prentice entered into a contract with Moore. Prentice signed the following note: "January 1, 1986, Thirty days after date, Pay to Bill Moore the sum of One Hundred and no/100 Dollars (signed) Mary Prentice." Is this instrument negotiable?

7. An instrument contains the following information: "January 1, 1986, Thirty (30) days after date I promise to pay to the order of John Frank the sum of One Hundred and no/100 Dollars (signed) Peter Graves." Identify what type of instrument this is.

8. An instrument reads as follows: "January 1, 1986, On demand, Pay to the order of Alice Smith the sum of One Hundred and no/100 Dollars (signed) Jack Jones." In the lower left-hand corner it also states "To Bill Ford, Kansas City, Missouri." What type of instrument is this? Who is liable on this instrument in its current form?

9. Michelle Clark was asked by her brother, David Clark, to act as his representative while he was out of the country. David gave Michelle the authority to sign instruments on his behalf until he returned to the United States. Michelle was asked to sign a note on behalf of David. What is the proper way for her to sign this note?

10. The president and sole stockholder of Fred Dowie Enterprises, Inc. ordered 325,000 hot dog buns from Colonial Baking. He paid for the buns with a check for $28,640. The check showed the name of the corporation and its address in the upper left-hand corner. The signature on the check was "Frederick J. Dowie." Dowie did not sign the corporation's name, nor write the word "President" after his name. Colonial sued Dowie in his personal capacity as the signer of the check. Dowie did not introduce any evidence of an agreement, understanding, or

course of dealing between the parties that when he signed he did so as a representative of the corporation. Is Dowie personally liable on this check in light of the fact that the corporation's name was imprinted on the check? Colonial Baking Co. of Des Moines v. Dowie, 35 UCC Rep. Serv. 874 (Iowa Sup. Ct 1983)

11. Cook, a corporate treasurer, signed two corporate checks, but she failed to indicate her representative capacity, that is, "Corporate Treasurer." The checks carried the imprinted name of the corporation at the top and on the lower right-hand corner just above the place for signing. Is Cook personally liable on this check? Valley National Bank, Sunnymead v. Cook, 36 UCC Rep. Serv. 578 (Ariz. App. 1983)

12. Davis Aircraft Engineering, Inc., entered into a loan agreement with Bank A. On the face of each note was printed: "This note evidences a borrowing made under, and is subject to, the terms of the loan agreement." There is nothing in the loan agreement that would impose any contingency upon the obligation to pay. Davis contends that the notes are nonnegotiable because there is not an unconditional promise to pay. Will Davis win? United States v. Farrington, 172 F.Supp. 797 (D.C. Mass. 1959).

13. Hotel Evans contracted with A. Alport & Son to construct a hotel and in return gave Alport certain promissory notes. The notes contained the notation "with interest at bank rates." At the time of payment, the bank wrote "8 ½%" above the words "bank rates." Are the notes negotiable? A. Alport & Son Inc. v. Hotel Evans, Inc., 317 N.Y.S.2d 937 (N.Y. Sup. Ct. 1970).

Transfer, Negotiation, and Holder in Due Course

As noted in the preceding chapter, several conditions must be met in order for a person to qualify as a holder in due course:

1. He or she must be in possession of a *negotiable* instrument (as explained in Chapter 24).
2. The instrument must be issued or *negotiated* to the holder.
3. The person in possession of the negotiable instrument validly issued or negotiated to him or her must also *comply with Section 3–302* of the Uniform Commercial Code (UCC).

When these three conditions are met, the person in possession of a negotiable instrument attains the preferred status of a holder in due course. This chapter examines the concepts of negotiation and holder in due course.

TRANSFER AND NEGOTIATION

Issuance

When a negotiable instrument has been drawn up and signed by the parties, one more step must take place for the instrument to become enforceable: It must be *issued* by the maker or drawer to the holder. In the typical transaction, issuance occurs when the maker or drawer of the instrument hands the instrument to the payee. This delivery of the instrument by the drawer or maker to the payee is called an *issuance* of the instrument.

The maker or drawer of an instrument is generally *not* liable on an instrument until he or she delivers or issues the instrument. Delivery of an instrument simply means the voluntary transfer of the instrument. Transfer may be achieved either by physical deliv-

612

ery or, in rare instances, by constructive delivery of the instrument. Constructive delivery occurs when the maker or drawer, with the intent to effect a transfer, performs a symbolic act representing the transfer. For example, delivery of the keys to a safe containing the instrument may constitute a constructive transfer.

In determining whether a delivery took place, the courts must examine the *intent* of the parties. However, if someone other than the assignee of the instrument has physical possession of it, there is a rebuttable presumption that delivery has occurred. If the maker or drawee still has physical possession of the instrument, there is a rebuttable presumption that delivery was not intended.

Suppose Smith signed a note payable to Jones, and he placed it on his desk. If Jones burglarized Smith's office and took the instrument, may she enforce it against Smith? No. Clearly, although he signed the instrument, Smith did not issue (voluntarily deliver) it to Jones. If a thief stole the note, however, and transferred it to a holder in due course, the holder in due course could enforce the note against Smith—even though Smith never voluntarily transferred it to Jones. This is because the absence of delivery is a *personal defense.* Personal defenses may not be asserted against a holder in due course. On the other hand, if the person in possession of the instrument did not qualify as a holder in due course, Smith could assert the personal defense of no delivery against that person. In that case Smith would not have to pay the note.

This example illustrates why it is so critical for a person to qualify as a holder in due course. Persons who attain this preferred status can then take instruments free of all *personal* defenses. (Personal defenses are discussed in the next chapter.) Anyone who is not a holder in due course takes the instrument subject to all defenses or claims by any party.

Transfer

Once the original maker or drawer of an instrument has signed and issued the instrument, the instrument may be transferred to a third party. If the transfer constitutes a *negotiation,* the person to whom the instrument is transferred becomes a *holder* of the instrument. If the transfer fails to qualify as a negotiation, the person to whom the instrument is transferred (the assignee) will never attain the status of a holder in due course. Such a person takes the instrument by *assignment* (as opposed to taking it by negotiation), and therefore may not become a holder of the instrument. A person must be a holder of an instrument in order to qualify as a holder in due course. This is true even if the instrument assigned qualifies as a negotiable instrument under Section 3–104(1).

If a person in possession of an instrument takes it by *assignment,* the transaction is governed by the law of contracts rather than Article 3 of the UCC. The person to whom the instrument is assigned is a mere *assignee* of a contractual right to receive money. The transfer gives the assignee all the rights of the *assignor* (the person who transferred the instrument to the assignee). However, the assignee also takes the instrument subject to any defenses or claims that might have been asserted against his or her assignor or any prior party to the instrument.

A person who takes a nonnegotiable instrument also is governed by the law of contracts rather than Article 3 of the UCC. Article 3 applies only to negotiable instruments.

To take an example, suppose Smith signs a note payable to Jones and issues it to her. Jones wishes to transfer the note to her daughter, Mary. If Jones fails to transfer the note properly (as discussed later in this chapter), her daughter becomes a mere assignee of a contractual right to receive money from Smith. This means that Mary acquires all the rights her mother had (the right to receive money from Smith) but takes the instrument subject to any claims or defenses Smith might have against Jones. Suppose Jones acquired the note from Smith in return for her promise to give Smith a 1959 Ford. After acquiring the note, Jones refuses to transfer the title to the Ford to Smith. So long as the note was in Jones's hands, Smith had a defense on the instrument—breach of contract. If sued by Jones on the instrument, he could refuse to pay the note because Jones failed to live up to her part of the bargain. Because Mary "steps into the shoes of her assignor," she takes the note subject to the defense of breach of contract. If Mary sues Smith on the note, Smith may assert against Mary the failure of her mother to deliver the Ford as a reason for his refusal to pay the note.

Negotiation

Section 3–202 defines a *negotiation* as "the transfer of an instrument in such form that the transferee becomes a holder." Section 1–201(20) defines a holder as a "person who is in possession of a[n] . . . instrument . . . drawn, issued, or indorsed to him or to his order or to bearer or in blank."

How does one become a holder? The person in possession of the instrument must in some cases have (1) the indorsement of the prior holder of the instrument and (2) delivery of the instrument. In other cases the delivery of the instrument alone will be sufficient to nego-

tiate the instrument. If the instrument qualifies as an *order instrument* the former is required, but a *bearer instrument* may be negotiated by delivery alone. As explained in the preceding chapter, an order instrument generally is one made payable to the order of someone. A bearer instrument is one made payable to bearer or cash.

Suppose Smith writes a note, but makes it payable to bearer as shown in Figure 25-1. Smith now physically delivers the note to Jones. The act of transferring the note to Jones is an *issuance* of the instrument. What if Jones now wants to transfer this note to her daughter, Mary? What must she do to validly negotiate the note so that Mary becomes a holder of the instrument? All Jones must do is deliver the note to Mary because this is a bearer instrument, which may be negotiated by delivery alone.

Suppose instead that this note was made payable to the order of Mrs. Jones as in Figure 25-2. If Jones merely delivers this instrument to Mary, there has not been a negotiation of the instrument. This note must be indorsed on the back by Jones and delivered to Mary to negotiate it because it is an *order instrument*.

Let us reexamine the definition of a holder in Section 1–201(20). In the two notes appearing earlier, once Jones takes delivery of either note she is a holder. The first note is "drawn to bearer." All she need do to become a holder is take delivery of the note. To become a holder of the second note, she again only

FIGURE 25–1

$100.00	Chicago, Illinois January 1, 1984

On demand I promise to pay to the order of *bearer*
One hundred and no/100 - - - - - - - - - dollars
Payable at First National Bank, Chicago, Illinois

John Smith
SAMPLE

FIGURE 25–2

$100.00	Chicago, Illinois January 1, 1984
On demand I promise to pay to the order of Grace Jones	
One hundred and no/100------------------------dollars	
Payable at First National Bank, Chicago, Illinois	*John Smith*
	SAMPLE

needs to take delivery because the second note was drawn payable to her order. Mary becomes a holder of the first note when it is delivered to her because it was "drawn to bearer." To become a holder of the second note, Mary not only must take delivery, but also must obtain her mother's indorsement, because the instrument originally was "drawn . . . to the order" of Jones. As it was not originally drawn to Mary's order, she must first obtain her mother's signature to negotiate the instrument effectively.

Because they may be negotiated by delivery alone, there is some risk in creating instruments that are payable to bearer. What if Smith signed the first note, which was payable to bearer, and a thief stole it from him? There is no delivery of the instrument to the thief because Section 1–201(14) defines a delivery as a *voluntary* transfer of possession" of the instrument. No negotiation takes place, and the thief does not acquire an interest in the note. However, the thief may transfer this instrument to a subsequent innocent purchaser. The UCC permits such a person taking bearer paper to become a holder of the instrument. In other words, while the thief may not acquire title to stolen bearer paper, the thief has the power to transfer good title to a third party. A party who is unaware of the theft may become a holder of the instrument and can enforce the instrument against the original maker.

The same rules also apply if a person *finds* a bearer instrument and transfers it to an inno-

cent third party. Bearer instruments must be handled very carefully because of the power given by the UCC to an illegitimate possessor to transfer good title to an innocent third party.

While bearer instruments expose the maker or drawer to some risks, the same is not true of order instruments. Take the note illustrated in Figure 25-2. It is payable to the order of Jones and therefore qualifies as an order instrument. Suppose a thief or finder comes into possession of this instrument. If the thief signs Jones's name and transfers the instrument to an innocent third party, Quinn, does Quinn become a holder of the instrument? No. This instrument was drawn payable to the order of Jones. To negotiate it, there must be a delivery of the instrument, and the instrument must be indorsed by Jones. The forged *indorsement by the thief* is ineffective. No title to the instrument passes to Quinn; she does not become a holder. The note has not been negotiated to Quinn because she lacks Jones's indorsement. Because Quinn holds the instrument through a forged indorsement, when she presents it to Smith for payment, Smith may refuse to pay the instrument if he detects that Jones did not sign it. Not only does Quinn not qualify as a holder of the instrument, but anyone to whom Quinn transfers the instrument also will not become a holder. Generally one may not qualify as a holder under a forged indorsement of an order instrument.

To review negotiation, (1) if the instrument is a bearer instrument, delivery alone is sufficient to negotiate the instrument and (2) if the instrument is an order instrument, to negotiate it the appropriate party must indorse and deliver it to someone.

An indorsement must be written by or on behalf of the holder. In most cases the indorsement is written on the back of the instrument. If for some reason there is no space on the reverse side of the instrument, the indorsement may appear on a paper firmly affixed to the instrument. Such a paper is called an *allonge.* It will not be sufficient to pin or clip the allonge to the instrument. The allonge must be firmly attached in such a manner that it will not become separated from the instrument—as by gluing the allonge to the instrument.

When a person transfers an order instrument for value, he or she has an obligation (absent a contrary agreement) to indorse the instrument. However, a negotiation of the instrument does not take place until the instrument has been indorsed. When a person receives an order instrument that lacks the indorsement of the transferor, the transferee may require the transferor to indorse the instrument. The transferee of an order instrument without the requisite indorsement is not a holder.

INDORSEMENTS

Negotiable instruments are indorsed for two reasons: (1) the indorsement may be necessary to negotiate the instrument and (2) the indorsement may be required to obligate the indorsee to pay the instrument under certain circumstances discussed in the next chapter.

Blank Indorsements

A *blank indorsement* specifies no particular indorsee and may consist of a mere signature.

FIGURE 25–3

Grace Jones

This is the most common type of indorsement. How would Jones indorse in blank the note in Figure 25-2 that was payable to her order? On the reverse side of the note she would sign it as shown in Figure 25-3.

When Jones signs the instrument in this fashion and delivers it to another person, there has been a negotiation of the note. The person to whom she transfers the note becomes a holder of the note. Jones has transferred title to the instrument to the third person. By indorsing the instrument in this fashion, she also promises to pay the instrument, under certain circumstances, if Smith fails to pay.

When an instrument is payable to order and it is indorsed in blank, it becomes payable to bearer and may be negotiated by delivery alone. Just as in the case of an instrument originally payable to bearer, an instrument that is indorsed in blank may be negotiated by delivery alone. This means that the same risks associated with an instrument that is originally payable to bearer also apply to an instrument that is indorsed in blank. A thief or finder has the power to negotiate the instrument indorsed in blank to an innocent third party so that the third person becomes a holder of the instrument.

Special Indorsements

A *special indorsement* specifies the person to whom or to whose order the instrument is payable. Jones could indorse the note discussed earlier as shown in Figure 25-4. The note in question was originally payable to the

FIGURE 25-4

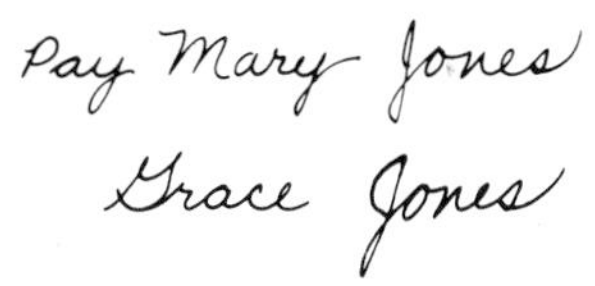

Pay Mary Jones
Grace Jones

order of Jones and therefore was an order instrument. When Jones indorsed the note in this manner it became payable to the order of the special indorsee (Mary Jones) and may be further negotiated only by Mary Jones's indorsement and delivery of the note to a third person. A note remains an order instrument when it is indorsed with a special indorsement.

Jones could also have indorsed the note with the words "Pay to the order of Mary Jones, (signed) Grace Jones" or "Pay to Mary Jones or order, (signed) Grace Jones." In other words, it is not necessary to include the words of negotiability in the special indorsement. While it is true that an instrument originally must be payable to order or to bearer for it to be negotiable, the special indorsement need not include the words of negotiability.

It is possible to convert an instrument indorsed in blank into a special indorsement by writing over the signature of the indorser in blank words such as "Pay to Mary Jones." If Mary's mother simply indorsed the note over to Mary by signing "Grace Jones" on the reverse side, Mary could convert the indorsement into a special indorsement by writing the words "Pay to Mary Jones" above her mother's signature. The instrument would then need to be indorsed by Mary Jones and delivered to someone in order for there to be a valid negotiation of the instrument.

By specially indorsing bearer paper, and thereby converting it to order paper, the person taking possession of the instrument avoids the risks associated with bearer paper. If a thief then steals the instrument, the thief must forge the signature of the special indorsee to whose order the instrument is payable. Because a forged indorsement will be ineffective, the special indorsee has protected himself or herself.

The following case illustrates the use of special indorsements.

Klomann v. Sol K. Graff & Sons
Appellate Court of Illinois
317 N.E.2d 608 (1974)

Background: Georgia Klomann (plaintiff) sued the partnership Sol K. Graff & Sons (defendant). Robert Graff executed three notes for the defendant partnership, Sol K. Graff & Sons. The notes were made payable to Fred Klomann. Klomann specially indorsed the notes to his daughter, Candace Klomann, and handed them to her. She looked at the notes, then returned them to Fred. At a later date Fred scratched out Candace's name in the special indorsement and inserted the name of his wife, Georgia Klomann, and delivered the notes to Georgia. Georgia Klomann then brought suit to enforce these notes. The lower court ruled Georgia Klomann could enforce these notes and receive payment on them from Sol K. Graff & Sons.

Decision: The Appellate Court ruled Georgia Klomann could not enforce the notes against the defendant, Sol K. Graff & Sons, because the instruments had not been properly indorsed to Georgia Klomann.

Dieringer, Justice

. . .

The defendant contends the plaintiff has no right, title or interest in the promissory notes, thereby raising an issue of fact which precluded the entry of summary judgment in favor of the plaintiff.

The plaintiff maintains the defense of whether Georgia Klomann has an interest in the notes is not available to the defendant. In support of her contention, the plaintiff relies on Section 3–306(d) of the Uniform Commercial Code which provides:

> Unless he has the rights of a holder in due course any person takes the instrument subject to (d) the defense that he or a person through whom he holds the instrument acquired it by theft or that payment or satisfaction to such holder would be inconsistent with the terms of a restrictive indorsement. *The claim of any third person to the instrument is not otherwise available as a defense to any party liable thereon unless the third person himself defends the action for such party. (Emphasis Added).*

We believe that the plaintiff has no right, title or interest in the promissory notes. Section 3–204 of the Uniform Commercial Code provides:

> (1) A special indorsement specifies the person to whom or to whose order it makes the instrument payable. Any instrument specially indorsed becomes payable to the order of the special indorsee and may be further negotiated only by his indorsement.

A review of the record in the instant case reveals Fred Klomann specially indorsed the promissory notes to his daughter, Candace, in August, 1967. The notes, therefore, could only be further negotiated by Candace. Examination of the record further reveals Candace, the special indorsee, has never negotiated the notes. Fred Klomann, in April, 1970, improperly scratched out Candace's name in the special indorsement and inserted the name of his wife Georgia. Section 3–201 of the Uniform Commercial Code provides in pertinent part:

> (1) Transfer of an instrument vests in the transferee such rights as the transferor has therein . . .

When Fred Klomann signed the notes in question to his daughter he no longer had any interest in them. His attempted assignment to Georgia approximately three years later conveyed only that interest which he had in the notes, which was nothing. Plaintiff, therefore, has no interest in the notes sued on in the instant case. We do not believe, as the plaintiff contends, that the Uniform Commercial Code intends a situation where there is an indorsement to a second party (Candace Klomann) and delivery; second party gives the note back to the payee for collection, payee subsequently strikes the name of the indorsee and puts in the name of a third party (Georgia

Klomann), to not allow the maker of the note to look into the situation and see where title really lies.

For the reasons stated herein, the judgment of the Circuit Court of Cook County is reversed and remanded.

Qualified Indorsements

The two indorsements discussed earlier, in blank and special, are also *unqualified* indorsements. This means that the in-blank or special indorser is promising to pay the holder of the instrument under certain circumstances. For example, suppose Jones received the $100 note from Smith. Jones then indorsed the note in blank and delivered it to Mary Jones. If Mary attempts to collect from Smith when the note comes due, but Smith refuses to pay, Mary could sue Jones for the $100 because Jones indorsed with an unqualified indorsement. The unqualified indorser in effect guarantees payment of the instrument if the holder is unable to collect from the maker, drawer, or acceptor when the instrument comes due.

A person who wishes to sign as a qualified indorser does so by adding "without recourse" or similar words to the indorsement as in Figures 25-5 and 25-6. The indorsement in Figure 25-5 is a qualified, in-blank indorsement. The indorsement in Figure 25-6 is a qualified, special indorsement. When Jones signs in either of these ways, she eliminates her secondary or conditional liability as an indorser. The secondary or conditional liability is the agreement of an unqualified indorser to pay the instrument if the party primarily obligated to pay fails to pay the instrument when it comes due. The concept of secondary liability is discussed in greater depth in the next chapter.

Both a qualified and an unqualified indorser, however, give certain warranties to the persons to whom they transfer their instruments.

FIGURE 25–5

Without Recourse
Grace Jones

FIGURE 25–6

Pay to the order of Mary Jones
Without Recourse
Grace Jones

This warranty liability is not excluded by signing an instrument with a qualified indorsement.

Restrictive Indorsements

In addition to in-blank, special, and qualified indorsements, the UCC also creates a category of indorsements called restrictive indorsements. The UCC creates several types of restrictive indorsements.

Conditional Restrictive. If the indorsement imposes a condition on the right of the indorsee to collect, it is a *conditional restrictive* indorsement. Suppose that Jones, when she received the note from Smith payable to her order, indorsed the note over to her daughter

Mary in the following fashion: "Pay to Mary Jones when she delivers her 1959 Ford to me, (signed) Grace Jones." This is actually a conditional restrictive indorsement. Jones then hands the note to Mary.

Why would Jones indorse the note in this manner? She wants to make certain that she receives the 1959 Ford before Mary is paid. In effect, she is putting a restriction on the ability of Mary to collect on this note. Once Mary delivers the Ford to her mother, she may collect on the note—but not before.

As with all types of restrictive indorsements, the conditional restrictive indorsement does not prevent the further transfer or negotiation of the instrument. This means that if Mary wishes to transfer the note from her mother to Smith, she may do so. This is true whether or not Mary has delivered the 1959 Ford to her mother.

However, the purpose of the conditional restrictive indorsement is to impose an obligation on the indorsee—in this case Mary's (the indorsee's) obligation is to deliver the 1959 Ford to her mother. What if Mary presents the note to Smith, and Smith pays Mary the $100 even though Mary has not yet delivered the Ford to her mother? In this situation, neither Mary nor Smith has complied with Section 3-206(3), which requires any transferee to "pay or apply any value given by him for . . . the instrument consistently with the indorsement. . . ." Because the Ford has not yet been delivered, Mary (the restrictive indorsee) and Smith (the maker) remain liable to Jones for the amount of the instrument.

Intermediary banks are not bound by conditional restrictive indorsements. An intermediary bank is any bank to which the instrument is transferred in the course of collection except the depository bank or payor bank. For example, when a check is deposited to an account for collection, the bank at which it is deposited is called the *depository* bank. The depository bank may then transfer the instrument to an *intermediary* bank, which in turn

may transfer it to the *drawee* bank. If the drawee bank pays the check, it becomes the *payor* bank.

A conditional indorsement is not the same as a conditional promise or order to pay. If the maker or drawer of an instrument writes the instrument in such a fashion that his or her promise or order is conditional, this renders the instrument nonnegotiable under Section 3-104. This is not true of a conditional indorsement. If an instrument had an unconditional promise or order to pay someone originally, it is negotiable. The conditional indorsement will not have any impact on the negotiability of the instrument.

Conditional restrictive indorsements are very uncommon.

Prohibit Further Transfer. Indorsements that attempt to prohibit further transfer of an instrument also are highly uncommon. Such an indorsement might read: "Pay to Mary Jones only." The indorser is attempting to prohibit further transfer of the instrument through such an indorsement. But such an indorsement does not prevent the further transfer or negotiation of the instrument. It is treated as if it were an unrestrictive indorsement.

For Deposit or Collection. The most common restrictive indorsement is the indorsement that includes words such as "for collection," "for deposit," "pay any bank," or like terms signifying a purpose of deposit or collection. For example, if Smith gave Jones a check for $100, Jones might indorse the check "For deposit, (signed) Grace Jones." This is an in-blank, restrictive, unqualified indorsement.

The indorsement "pay any bank" specifies that only banks are to receive the proceeds of the instrument. When a person deposits a check to his or her bank account, the bank may restrictively indorse the check in this manner. Only a bank could then become a holder of an instrument so indorsed, unless a bank specially indorsed the check to someone who is not a bank. A bank might use such an indorsement when putting a check through the collection process.

Suppose Jones takes the $100 check from Smith, indorses it "For deposit, (signed) Grace Jones," and deposits it to her account. The bank will indorse the check "for collection" or "pay any bank" and forward it to an intermediary bank for collection. The intermediary bank will present the check to the drawee bank, which, if it pays the check, becomes the payor bank. Both of these indorsements are restrictive indorsements.

To the extent that a transferee pays or applies any value given by the transferee consistently with the indorsement, he or she becomes a holder for value. If the transferee otherwise complies with Section 3–302, he or she qualifies as a holder in due course. If Jones's bank credits her account for the $100, it has applied the value consistent with the "For deposit" indorsement and therefore is a holder. When the payor bank pays the intermediary bank, it has paid the check consistent with the "For collection" or "Pay any bank" indorsement, and the payor bank qualifies as a holder.

Trust Indorsements. A restrictive indorsement that states that it is for the benefit or use of the indorser or another person is a trust indorsement. It is the fourth type of restrictive indorsement recognized under Section 3–205(d). Such an indorsement might read "Pay Lance only in trust for Mary." In this case Lance, the restrictive indorsee, is acting as a representative of Mary and holds any money paid on the instrument in trust for Mary. To the extent that Lance applies the proceeds consistent with the terms of the indorsement, he qualifies as a holder.

Trust indorsements affect only the immediate transferee—in this case Lance. A later holder for value of this instrument is neither given notice nor otherwise affected by such a restrictive indorsement unless he or she has knowledge that a fiduciary or other person has negotiated the instrument in any transaction for his or her own benefit or is otherwise in breach of duty (Section 3–206[4]).

As with the three other types of restrictive indorsements, a trust indorsement does not prevent the further transfer or negotiation of the instrument.

Restrictive Indorsements Generally. Most restrictive indorsements require the indorsee to take some action with respect to the proceeds of an instrument—such as holding it in trust for someone or depositing it to someone's account.

Unlike most transferees, intermediary banks and payor banks that are not depository banks are neither given notice nor affected by a restrictive indorsement of any person except the bank's immediate transferor or the person presenting the instrument for payment (Section 3–206[2]).

HOLDER IN DUE COURSE

In order to become a holder in due course of a negotiable instrument, a holder must take the instrument: (1) for value, (2) in good faith, and (3) without notice that the instrument is overdue or has been dishonored, or of any defense against or claim to it on the part of any person (Section 3–302).

Even assuming a person in possession of an instrument fulfills the three requirements set out in Section 3–302, he or she still may not qualify as a holder in due course. A person wishing to claim the status of a holder in due course must also establish that he or she holds a *negotiable* instrument (as defined in Section 3–104) and that he or she is a *holder* of the instrument.

As discussed in the preceding chapter, several elements must be complied with for an instrument to qualify as negotiable. It must be (1) a writing, (2) signed by the drawer or maker, (3) containing a promise or order to pay, (4) that is unconditional, (5) a sum certain, (6) in money, (7) without any other promise, (8) payable on demand or at a definite time, and (9) payable to order or bearer. An instrument that fails in any respect to fulfill these nine requirements is *not* negotiable. A person in possession of such an instrument may not qualify as a holder in due course. A person who wishes to qualify as a holder in due course will therefore examine the instrument carefully before taking it to determine if it is negotiable.

The mere fact that a person holds a non-negotiable instrument does not mean that he or she will not recover. As we noted earlier, the right to receive money is generally assignable to third persons. The only problem for the assignee is that he or she steps into the shoes of the assignor—that is, the assignee acquires only the rights the assignor had. If a defense existed between the original parties to a contract to pay money, that defense may be asserted against the assignee of the contractual right to receive money.

In the event the party originally obligated to pay has no defenses that could have been asserted against the assignor, he or she must pay the assignee. The mere fact that the assignee is in possession of a nonnegotiable instrument is not a defense. If Smith gives Jones a $100 bearer note, but it in some respect fails to comply with Section 3–104, it is nonnegotiable. Suppose that Jones transferred the note to Mary. Under these facts it appears that Smith must pay Mary when the note comes due even though the instrument is not negotiable. What if Jones defrauded Smith? Because Smith could assert the defense of fraud against Jones (the assignor), he may assert fraud to avoid paying the note against Mary (the assignee).

Instead of a nonnegotiable instrument, suppose the parties were dealing with a negotiable instrument. Smith could refuse to pay Mary, even if the instrument was negotiable, if he could establish that Mary was not a holder of the instrument. Once again, a holder is anyone in possession of an instrument drawn, issued, or indorsed to him or to his order or to bearer or in blank. If the instrument was not properly negotiated to Mary, she would not qualify as a holder of the instrument. Suppose the original note was negotiable and was payable to the order of Jones (rather than payable to bearer) and Jones delivered the note to Mary but failed to indorse it. Mary is not a holder of the note. In order to negotiate an order instrument, the holder must indorse it and deliver it to someone. Jones failed to indorse the note. (Mary may be able to require Jones to indorse the note but, until Jones indorses it, Mary may not qualify as a holder of the note.)

Assuming that the note is negotiable, and the person attempting to enforce it is a holder, that person may qualify as a holder in due course if he or she otherwise complies with Section 3–302. The following material discusses these requirements.

For Value

A holder takes an instrument for value when he or she gives a negotiable instrument for it or makes an irrevocable commitment to a third person, or to the extent that the agreed consideration has been performed, or when he or she acquires a security interest in or a lien on the instrument otherwise than by legal process, or when he or she takes the instrument in payment of or as security for an antecedent claim (Section 3–303).

Let us examine the various ways in which a person may give value.

Executory Promise. The UCC, in Section 3–303, completely separates the concepts of *value* and *consideration*. Consideration is defined as something of value given in return for a performance or a promise of performance. While a mere promise to perform is sufficient consideration to support a contract, such a promise does not amount to a giving of value under Section 3–303. An executory promise to give value is not value. Thus, if an attorney is given a note for $200,000 for $10,000 in legal services already rendered, with the rest of the services to be rendered in the future, the attorney would be a holder in due course of the note only to the extent of $10,000. The promise of the attorney to perform services could serve as consideration to support a contract, but a promise to perform services does not qualify as giving value. Had the attorney in this case already performed services worth $200,000, he or she would have given value.

Suppose that Smith executes the $100 note payable to Jones. What if Jones gives the note to Mary, who promises to pay her mother $100 in return for the note? May Mary qualify as a holder in due course? No. Mary has not given value in exchange for the note. This is a mere executory promise to give value. Until Mary pays the $100, she has not given value. If she sues Smith before she pays the $100 to her mother, Smith may assert any defense he has on the instrument against Mary because Mary is not a holder in due course.

Why does the UCC adopt this position with respect to executory promises? Comment 3 to Section 3–303 states that a person giving an executory promise does not need the protection afforded by the status of a holder in due course. When such a person learns of a defense on the instrument or of a defect in the title, the purchaser may rescind the transaction for breach of the transferor's warranty.

There are, however, instances in which an executory promise may be regarded as value. Section 3–303(c) states that a holder takes an instrument for value when he or she "gives a negotiable instrument for it or makes an irrevocable commitment to a third person." Consequently, while it may not constitute value to promise to do something, giving an instrument for an instrument constitutes value.

Suppose Jones transfers Smith's $100 note in return for Mary's check for $100. When Mary gives the check to her mother, she has given value for the note. Section 3–303 recognizes a negotiable instrument as value because it carries the possibility of negotiation to a holder in due course, after which the party who gave it cannot refuse to pay.

The same rationale applies to any irrevocable commitment by the holder to a third party. Suppose company X gives its bank a $1,000 note. In return, the bank issues a letter of credit in which it promises to pay a seller from whom X wishes to purchase goods. Because a letter of credit constitutes an irrevocable commitment by the bank to the seller, the bank has given value for the $1,000 note.

What happens if a person who gives an executory promise learns of a defense or claim to the instrument before he or she performs the promise? The person may become a holder in due course only to the extent that he or she has fulfilled the promise. In the case mentioned earlier in which Mary promises to pay her mother $100 for Smith's note, suppose Mary pays her mother $50 on June 1. On June 2 Mary learns from Smith that her mother defrauded him. May Mary enforce the note? Mary is a holder in due course only as to the amount she has already paid her mother— $50. As to the other $50, she will not be able to collect it if Smith establishes his defense of fraud by Mary's mother. What if Mary on June 3 pays her mother the other $50; could she then claim to be a holder in due course for the entire sum of $100? No. Paying off the executory promise at this point is too late because she already has learned of a defense against the instrument. Mary takes the instrument for value only to the extent the agreed consideration has been performed before she learns of any claims or defenses. As noted earlier, Mary may rescind the transaction when she learns of Smith's defense. This should be adequate protection for her.

Banks and Value. When a person receives a check from someone and deposits it to his or her account, the bank will credit the depositor's account. Probably the check was written on an account at another bank, so the depositor's bank will act as an agent for purposes of collection. Does the mere fact that a customer deposits a check to his or her account, and the bank credits the account, mean that the bank has given value for the check? No. The mere crediting of an account by a bank does not constitute the giving of value. A bank has given value to the extent that it has a security interest in an instrument (Section 4–209). A bank has a security interest in an instrument to the extent that credit given by the bank for the instrument has been withdrawn (Section 4–208[1][a]). The UCC means by this that, to the extent the depositor draws against an instrument, the bank has given value. If the bank otherwise complies with Section 3–302, it qualifies as a holder in due course of this check.

In most cases a depositor will have some money in his or her account when a check is deposited. If the bank permits the depositor to write a check on the account, how do we know whether the bank is permitting the customer to draw against the check? To simplify this matter, the UCC adopts a rule in Section 4–208 that "credits first given are first withdrawn." In other words, the UCC adopts a "first in, first out" rule.

Suppose that Alice gives Frank a check for $100. Frank takes the check to his bank and deposits it on June 1. At that time Frank already has $200 in his account. On June 2 Frank receives another $100 check from Alice, which he deposits to his account that day. On June 3 Frank withdraws $200 from his account. At this point, has the bank given value for either of Alice's checks? No. Because the UCC applies a first-in-first-out rule, the $200 is treated as a withdrawal of the $200 initially in Frank's account. On June 4 Frank withdraws another $100. In this case the bank has now given full value for Alice's first check, which was deposited to Frank's account on June 1. If the bank otherwise complies with Section 3–302, it will be treated as a holder in due course of Alice's first check, which was deposited June 1. On June 5 Alice notifies the bank of a defense on the second check. On June 6 the bank permits Frank to withdraw

the final $100 from his account. Has the bank given value for Alice's second check? No. Applying the first-in-first-out rule, Frank's final $100 withdrawal is treated as a withdrawal against Alice's second check. Because the bank gave value *after* it learned of Alice's defense, it has not given value for the second check and cannot qualify as a holder in due course of the second check.

Negotiable Instrument as Security. If a person acquires a security interest in an instrument (other than by legal process), he or she takes the instrument for value.

Suppose Jane agrees to purchase some goods from a business. The business has some doubts about Jane's capacity to pay for the goods. Jane has a note from Linda in which Linda agrees to pay her $100. If the business sells goods to Jane for $100 and takes the note from Linda to Jane as security for the debt, it has given value for Linda's note. If Jane does not pay for the goods, the business may collect the $100 from Linda since it gave value for Linda's note by taking the note as security for the debt owed by Jane.

Instrument in Payment or as Security for Antecedent Claim. The final category in which a person is treated as having given value is when the person "takes the instrument in payment of or as security for an antecedent claim against any person whether or not the claim is due" (Section 3–303[b]).

Suppose Alice purchases some goods from Jane in March for $100. Several months elapse. In May, Alice gives Jane a $100 note. Jane is treated as having given value for the note. But what if Jane merely asked for some security in May, and Alice gave Jane a $100 note executed by Tom? The UCC treats Jane as having given value for Tom's note, even though she does not extend the time in which Alice must pay her or make any other concession to Alice. If Alice fails to pay Jane, Jane might attempt to collect on the note from Tom. Jane will be treated as having

ETHICS BOX
Taking an Instrument from a Merchant

S leazy Appliances sells appliances on an installment payment basis. Sleazy has the buyer sign a sales contract and a promissory note. It then sells the promissory note to a local bank. Sleazy has a reputation for selling broken-down appliances and for being unwilling to uphold its warranties. Sleazy has just made a major sale to Acme Corp. and has brought the promissory note to National Bank. National has heard about Sleazy's poor reputation.

Is it ethical for National Bank to purchase the note from Sleazy? Will National be entitled to holder-in-due-course status?

In order to acquire the status of a holder in due course a holder must (1) give value for the note, (2) take the note in good faith, and (3) take the note without notice of claims or defenses. One might question whether the bank is acting in good faith and without notice of any claims or defenses. Notice is an objective standard. The bank could not have any prior notice as to this note unless Acme or Sleazy told it of a defense or claim. Therefore National can take it without notice. Good faith is a subjective standard that requires honesty in fact in the transaction concerned. Since National Bank knew of no problem with the contract between Acme and Sleazy, it could be said to have acted in good faith. Thus National Bank could take this note as a holder in due course even though it knew of Sleazy's poor reputation. Whether the bank acts ethically in taking such a note is another question. If National has good grounds for believing that Sleazy engages in unethical practices, then it has a professional duty to check out Sleazy before handling promissory notes from Sleazy on a regular basis. The fact that it has some information about Sleazy can be seen as triggering an ethical obligation to look further. Some cautious lawyers might advise the bank not to investigate, because if an investigation turned up specific evidence of improper practices, the bank might lose its ability to be a holder in due course in future transactions. Although some people might disagree, that concern should not be considered sufficient to eliminate the ethical duty to check things out.

---

given value for Tom's note even though she took it as security for an antecedent claim against Alice, and even though she made no additional concessions to Alice at the time she took Tom's note. If Jane otherwise has complied with Section 3–302, she will be treated as a holder in due course of Tom's note and will take the note free of certain defenses Tom might have been able to assert against Alice.

Good Faith

To be a holder in due course, the holder of the instrument must also have taken the instrument in good faith. Section 1–201(19) defines good faith to mean honesty in fact in the conduct or transaction concerned. The drafters of the UCC, in defining good faith as honesty in fact, left judges fairly wide discretion in determining what is an acceptable level of behavior. However, they clearly selected a *subjective* test as opposed to an objective test. The UCC thus does not adopt the standard of the behavior of a reasonably prudent person acting under the same circumstances. Instead, it adopts a standard that examines the actual behavior of the person taking the instrument. In order to determine if a person took an instrument in good faith, the court must determine if he or she acted honestly, even though his or her actions were not those of a reasonable person.

The UCC rejected the objective test as it developed in England under *Gill* v. *Cubitt*. This means that a person who, for example, takes an instrument under suspicious circumstances has not necessarily acted in bad faith. If this person acts honestly, although perhaps not reasonably, he or she qualifies under the UCC definition of good faith. As noted earlier, the manner in which the UCC has defined good faith gives the courts some discretion in this area.

Whether an individual took an instrument in good faith is determined at the time of taking the instrument. If a person acted in good faith at that time, and then *later* learns of facts that make him or her suspicious, he or she still is regarded as having taken the instrument in good faith.

The question of good faith is dealt with in the following case.

Money Mart Check Cashing Center, Inc. v. Epicycle Corp.

Supreme Court of Colorado

607 P.2d 1372 (1983)

Background: Money Mart (plaintiff) brought suit against Epicycle (defendant). Money Mart cashed payroll and government checks for a fee. On February 16, 1980, Epicycle issued a payroll check, payable to John Cronin, in the amount of $278.59. During the term of his employment Cronin had borrowed money from Epicycle to be offset by subsequent wages.

Cronin was fired and an Epicycle employee who was unaware of Cronin's indebtedness gave Cronin his final payroll check. Epicycle ordered payment on the check stopped. Cronin cashed the check at Money Mart on February 22, 1980. Money Mart deposited the check. The check was returned to Money Mart marked "payment stopped."

Money Mart sued for the amount of the check, claiming that as a holder in due course of the dishonored check it was entitled to recover from Epicycle. Judgment was entered in favor of Money Mart at the trial court level for $278.59. The Denver Superior Court reversed, holding that Money Mart was negligent in not verifying that the check was good prior to cashing it and therefore was not entitled to holder-in-due-course status.

Decision: The Colorado Supreme Court reversed the decision of the Denver Superior Court and entered a judgment for Money Mart.

Rovira, Justice

The question before us is whether Money Mart is a holder in due course. If it is, it takes the check free of any of Epicycle's claims to the check or defenses against Cronin. See section 4–3–305, CRS 1973. Section 4–3–302(1), CRS 1973, provides:

"(1) A holder in due course is a holder who takes the instrument:
"(a) For value; and
"(b) In good faith; and
"(c) Without notice that it is overdue or has been dishonored or of any defense against or claim to it on the part of any person."

That Money Mart took the check for value is undisputed, leaving the questions of "good faith" and "notice."

"Good faith" is defined as "honesty in fact in the conduct or transaction concerned." The drafters of the Uniform Commercial Code intended that this standard be a subjective one. Thus, the question is: "[W]as this alleged holder in due course acting in good faith, however stupid and negligent his behavior might have been?"

The only testimony on the question of good faith is that Money Mart cashed the check without knowing that a stop payment order had been issued on it. The Superior Court concluded that Money Mart was not a holder in due course because it "did not inquire as to the check itself and had no knowledge as to whether the check was stolen, incomplete, or secured by fraud." Under a subjective standard, an absence of knowledge is not equivalent to a lack of good faith. Consequently, if the Superior Court's reversal was based upon a lack of good faith on the part of Money Mart, it was in error.

We now consider whether Money Mart had "notice" of the fact that payment had been stopped on the check or that Cronin had obtained the check improperly. A person has "notice" of a fact when:

"(a) He has actual knowledge of it; or
"(b) He has received a notice or notification of it; or
"(c) From all the facts and circumstances known to him at the time in question he has reason to know that it exists."

. . . There is no allegation that Money Mart had received notification of the defenses, so we must now determine whether Money Mart had "reason to know" of them.

A determination of whether a holder has "reason to know" is based upon "all the facts and circumstances known to him." A person "knows" of a fact when he has "actual knowledge" of it. The question therefore is whether Money Mart had actual knowledge of facts giving it reason to know that a defense existed. There is nothing to distinguish the facts of this case from any other of the thousands of checks that Money Mart and others cash each year: A man came to Money Mart to cash his paycheck; Money Mart is in the business of cashing paychecks; the face of the check disclosed nothing to raise even a suspicion that there was something wrong with it.

It has often been held that where an instrument is regular on its face there is no duty to inquire as to possible defenses unless the circumstances of which the holder has knowledge are of such a nature that failure to inquire reveals a deliberate desire to evade knowledge because of a fear that investigation would disclose the existence of a defense.

Accordingly, we hold that Money Mart is a holder in due course and, as such, is not subject to the defenses Epicycle may have against Cronin. Epicycle raises other arguments concerning the question of Money Mart's entitlement to holder-in-due-course status that we find to be without merit.

Without Notice

We now know that a person, to qualify as a holder in due course, must be the holder of a negotiable instrument who took the instrument for value and in good faith. In order to qualify as a holder in due course, this person must establish one last element as set forth in Section 3–302(a)(c): that he or she took the instrument without notice that it was overdue or had been dishonored or of any defense against or claim to it on the part of any person. It therefore appears that the holder of an instrument must take it without notice of four things:

1. That the instrument is overdue
2. That the instrument has been dishonored
3. A defense by any person
4. Any claim to it by any person

Assuming the holder does not have notice of any of these four points, he or she may qualify as a holder in due course. But what did the drafters of the UCC mean when they wrote that the holder must take without notice?

Notice. The UCC defines notice in Section 1–201. Section 1–201(25) states that a person has notice of a fact when he or she has actual knowledge of it; or if he or she has received notice or notification of it; or if from all the facts and circumstances known to the person at the time in question, he or she has reason to know a fact exists.

A person knows or has knowledge of a fact when he or she has actual knowledge of the fact. If Smith takes a note knowing that the maker of the note has a valid defense against the payee, he clearly has notice and does not take the instrument as a holder in due course. However, merely because he does not qualify as a holder in due course does not mean he will not collect on the note. All we are saying is that Smith takes it subject to any defenses on the instrument. The maker still must *prove* the defense.

A person receives notice when (1) it comes to his or her attention or (2) the notice was duly delivered at the place of business through which the contract was made or at any other place held out by the person as the place for receipt of such communications. If the maker of the note previously discussed calls Smith and tells him of a defense on the instrument, Smith clearly has received notice of the defense under Section 1–201(25)(b).

By also providing that a person has notice if by the facts and circumstances known to the person he or she has reason to know a fact exists, the drafters gave the courts substantial discretion as to whether a person had notice.

When notice is received by an organization is discussed in Section 1–201(24). In general, notice must be brought to the attention of the individual in that organization conducting the transaction in question.

In any event, notice must be received at such time and in such manner as to give the person or organization a reasonable opportunity to act on the notice.

Any notice received after the person has acquired the instrument does not prevent the person from qualifying as a holder in due course. The critical issue is what the person knew at the time he or she took the instrument. Information learned at a later time is not relevant as to whether the person took with notice.

Notice of Instrument Overdue. By examining the face of an instrument, a person may learn important information. One of the most critical things revealed by the face of the instrument is whether the instrument is overdue.

Basically, there are two types of instruments: *demand instruments* and *time instruments.* The latter is payable at a specific time—for example, a note "payable June 1, 1984." A demand instrument is one that is payable "on demand," "at sight," "on presentation."

A taker of a negotiable instrument is denied status as a holder in due course if he or she takes an instrument that is overdue. The very fact that the instrument is still in circulation after it is payable should make anyone taking it suspicious. When instruments are due, one assumes that the party entitled to collect will attempt to collect.

An instrument that is payable at a definite time, such as one payable June 1, 1984, is overdue at the beginning of the day after it is due. In this case the instrument is overdue on June 2, 1984.

Section 3–304(3) lists several situations in which a person is deemed to have notice that an instrument is overdue. One of these is when he or she is taking a demand instrument after demand has been made or *more than a reasonable length of time after its issue.* The UCC sets forth a relatively clear rule as to checks: a reasonable time for presentation of a check for collection is presumed to be thirty days. Suppose Linda issues a check to Alice on September 1. This means Alice has thirty days from the date of issue (September 1) to present the check. Anyone taking the check later than thirty days after issue may not qualify as a holder in due course.

Demand instruments other than checks create more of a problem as to when they are overdue. The UCC merely states that a person has notice that such an instrument is overdue if he or she takes it more than a reasonable length of time after its issue. It is not possible to state a clear-cut rule when such an instrument is overdue.

Notice of Instrument Dishonored. In general a dishonor of an instrument occurs when a demand for payment or acceptance has been made and the party expected to pay or accept refuses to do so. Suppose a note payable September 1, 1984 is presented by the payee to the maker on that date. If the maker refuses to pay at that time, there has been a dishonor of the instrument. (See the next chapter for an in-depth discussion of the issue of dishonor.)

A person who takes an instrument knowing of such a dishonor cannot qualify as a holder in due course. In many cases a simple examination of the instrument will reveal that it has been dishonored. For example, a check that has been dishonored by a bank might be stamped "insufficient funds." Clearly, a person taking such a check would have notice of the dishonor.

However, in some cases the instrument may not indicate on its face that it has been dishonored, and the transferor may not tell the transferee of the dishonor. In such a case the court must determine whether there is any other evidence that the transferee had notice of the dishonor. If it finds that the transferee had such notice, he or she will not qualify as a holder in due course.

Notice of Claim or Defense. A purchaser has notice of a claim or defense if the instrument is incomplete; if it appears to have been forged or altered or is so irregular as to call into question its validity, terms, or ownership; if it creates an ambiguity as to the party to pay; or if the purchaser has notice that the obligation of any party is voidable or that all parties have been discharged.

A *defense* to an instrument is typically something that is asserted as a reason not to pay it. A *claim,* on the other hand, is an argument asserted by a person claiming the instrument.

Some defenses or claims are obvious from the face of the instrument, such as a crude alteration or a forgery. If such an alteration or forgery calls into question the validity, terms, or ownership of the instrument, a person holding the instrument could not qualify as a holder in due course.

It does not follow that merely because the holder knew an incomplete instrument was completed that he or she had knowledge of any defense or claim unless the holder had notice of an *improper* completion. An instrument might be blank as to some unnecessary fact, might contain minor erasures, or might even have an obvious change such as the date. For example, "January 2, 1983" could be changed to "January 2, 1984" without exciting suspicion. If a check had no date, the holder would not have notice of a defense or claim merely because the transferor filled in the date.

So long as an instrument is blank it is an incomplete instrument, and the taker may not qualify as a holder in due course. Any person taking such an incomplete instrument takes it subject to any defenses or claims. An instrument may be completed in accordance with the authority given, however, and once it is completed as authorized, it is effective as completed.

The following case illustrates the types of factors a court will consider in determining whether a holder has notice of any defense against an instrument. As you read the case, consider the relationship between the good-faith and notice requirements, and whether the court is applying an objective or subjective standard to reach a conclusion.

Kaw Valley State Bank & Trust Co. v. Riddle

Kansas Supreme Court
549 P.2d 927 (1976)

Background: The Kaw Valley State Bank & Trust Co. (plaintiff) brought suit against John H. Riddle (defendant) to collect on two notes. Kaw Valley Bank often bought discounted trade notes from Co-Mac, a construction machinery dealer. Riddle, a frequent buyer from Co-Mac, was the maker of a note payable to Co-Mac for heavy equipment in May 1971. With the machines still undelivered, Riddle and Co-Mac agreed to destroy the note and substitute a new note for a sale of some larger equipment. The larger machines were delivered and the new note executed. Instead of destroying the old note, however, Co-Mac discounted it to Kaw Valley. Co-Mac kept the note current. Riddle had no knowledge of its existence. In February of 1972 Riddle, Co-Mac, and Kaw Valley consolidated Riddle's indebtedness. No mention was made of the note that Co-Mac had not destroyed. In March 1972 Co-Mac became insolvent and a receiver was appointed. Within a week Kaw Valley informed Riddle that it held the first note. Riddle explained the situation to Kaw Valley. Sometime thereafter Riddle granted a security agreement to Planters in all of his equipment. Kaw Valley obtained possession of all the equipment by court order subsequent to this. A sale was held from which Kaw Valley received the balance due from the February 1972 consolidation ($22,000.00). Planters received $3,466.51, which was undisputed. The remainder of $21,904.64 (the amount claimed under the "destroyed" note) was left in escrow, being claimed by both Planters and Kaw Valley.

At trial, Kaw Valley was held not to be a holder in due course of the "destroyed" note and thus did not recover on grounds of a failure of consideration, because Riddle never received the equipment. The trial court ruled for Riddle. Kaw Valley appealed. Decision: The Kansas Supreme Court affirmed the decision of the trial court for Riddle.

Fromme, Justice

The primary point on appeal questions the holding of the trial court that Kaw Valley was not a holder in due course of the note and security agreement dated May 11, 1971.

.   .   .

We are confronted with the question of what is required for a holder to take an instrument "in good faith" and "without notice of defense." We will consider the two parts of the question in the order mentioned.

"Good faith" is defined in K.S.A. 84–1–201(19) as "honesty in fact in the conduct or transaction concerned." . . .

From the history of the Uniform Commercial Code it would appear that "good faith" required no actual knowledge of or participation in any material infirmity in the original transaction.

The second part of our question concerns the requirements of the UCC that a holder in due course take the instrument without notice of any defense to the instrument.

.   .   .

. . . The standard enunciated is not limited to the rigid standard of actual knowledge of the defense. Reason to know appears to be premised on the use of reasonable commercial practices. Since "good faith" and "no notice of defense" are both required of a holder to claim the status of a holder in due course it would appear that the two standards are not in conflict even though the standards of conduct may be different.

There is little or no evidence in the present case to indicate that Kaw Valley acted dishonestly or "not in good faith" when it purchased the note of May 11, 1971. However, as to "notice of defense" the court found from all the facts and circumstances known to Kaw Valley at the time in question it had reason to know a defense existed.

.   .   .

In the present case Kaw Valley had worked closely with Co-Mac in over 250 financing transactions over a period of ten years. It knew that some of these transactions were not for valuable consideration at the time the paper was delivered since the bank's money was to be used in purchasing the machinery or equipment represented in the instruments as already in possession of the maker of the note. Kaw Valley had been advised that delivery to Co-Mac's customers was sometimes delayed from 60 to 90 days. Kaw Valley continued to rely on Co-Mac to assure payment of the obligations and contacted it to collect delinquent payments. Some of these transactions, including the one in question, involved the use of coupon books to be used by the debtor in making payment on the notes. In the present case Kaw Valley did not notify Riddle that it was the holder of the note. It delivered Riddle's coupon book to Co-Mac as if it were the obligor or was authorized as its collection agent for this transaction. Throughout the period from May 11, 1971, to February 25, 1972, Kaw Valley received and credited the monthly payments knowing that payments were being made by Co-Mac and not by Riddle. Then when Riddle's loans were consolidated, the May 11, 1971 transaction was not included by Kaw Valley, either by oversight or by intention, as an obligation of Riddle. Co-Mac occupied a close relationship with Kaw Valley and with its knowledge and consent acted as its agent in collecting payments on notes held by Kaw Valley. The working relationship existing between Kaw Valley and Co-Mac was further demonstrated on February 24, 1972, when the $5,000.00 balance due on one of Riddle's notes was cancelled when it was shown that the machinery for which the note was given had previously been returned to Co-Mac with the understanding that no further payments were due.

K.S.A. 84–3–307(3) provides:

> After it is shown that a defense exists a person claiming the rights of a holder in due course has the burden of establishing that he or some person under whom he claims is in all respects a holder in due course.

In the present case the court found that the appellant, Kaw Valley, had not sustained its burden of proving that it was a holder in due course. Under the evidence in this case the holder failed to advise the maker of the note of its acquisition of the note and security agreement. It placed the payment coupon book in the hands of Co-Mac and received all monthly payments from them. A close working relationship existed between the two companies and Co-Mac was clothed with authority to collect and forward all payments due on the transaction. Agency and authority was further shown to exist by authorizing return of machinery to Co-Mac and terminating balances due on purchase money paper. We cannot say under the facts and circumstances known and participated in by Kaw Valley in this transaction it did not at the time in question have reason to know that the defense existed. This was a question of fact to be determined by the trier of fact which if supported by substantial competent evidence must stand.

Holder Through a Holder in Due Course

While a person who holds an instrument may not qualify as a holder in due course, he or she may have all the rights of a holder in due course. The so-called shelter provision of the UCC, found in Section 3–201(1), states that the "transfer of an instrument rests in the transferee such rights as the transferor had therein." The drafters of the UCC adopted this provision to encourage the free transferability of negotiable instruments. A person who for one reason or another knows that he or she cannot qualify as a holder in due course may take an instrument if the transferor is a holder in due course, or if any prior party qualified as a holder in due course. If the transferor is a holder in due course, or if any prior party qualified as a holder in due course, the transferee has the *rights* of a holder in due course.

For example, suppose on June 5 Briscoe offers to sell a note "payable on June 1" to Knott. Knott cannot qualify as a holder in due course because she knows that the instrument is overdue—it is payable June 1. She may safely take the note, however, if Briscoe is a holder in due course. In that case Knott will have all the rights of her transferor.

STATUS OF HOLDER IN DUE COURSE

A holder in due course occupies a very special position. When he or she takes an instrument, he or she takes it free of any claim of legal title or liens. Furthermore, the holder in due course generally takes the instrument free from all defenses of any party to the instrument *with whom the holder has not dealt.* This point is illustrated by the following case.

Wilmington Trust Co. v. Delaware Auto Sales

Supreme Court of Delaware

271 A.2d 41 (1970)

Background: Delaware (plaintiff) received a treasurer's check from Wilmington (defendant). When Delaware presented the check for payment, Wilmington refused to pay. It asserted the defense of failure of consideration against Delaware. Delaware claimed the status of a holder in due course and sued. The lower court found for Delaware. Wilmington appealed.

Decision: The Delaware Supreme Court reversed the judgment for Delaware because Wilmington had previously dealt with Delaware.

Carey, Justice

The facts are essentially undisputed: Robert Hoopes, of Seaford, purchased a used car from Delaware Auto Sales and paid for it with a personal check drawn on Wilmington Trust Company in the amount of $1,550. Early the next morning, due to dissatisfaction with the car, which he later returned, Hoopes called the Seaford branch of the bank and stopped payment on his check. This order was noted in the Wilmington office at 8:35 A.M. That same morning, Al Kutner, owner of Delaware Auto Sales, went to the Greenville branch of the bank between 9:00 and 9:30 A.M., and exchanged the personal check of Hoopes for a treasurer's check in the same amount. The Assistant Treasurer investigated the adequacy of Hoopes' funds, failed to discover or had not yet received notice of the stop-payment order. At 9:24 A.M., the Hoopes account was charged with a "hold" for the amount of the treasurer's check. Later, when the treasurer's check was presented for payment, the stop-payment order was noticed and the check was cancelled. Defendant below alleged want or failure of consideration and mistake. Plaintiff below contended that it was a holder in due course and therefore not subject to those defenses.

It is clear that Delaware Auto Sales cannot assert the rights of a holder in due course as against Wilmington Trust Company. The rights of a holder in due course are defined in section 3–305:

> To the extent that a holder is a holder in due course he takes the instrument free from. . . .
> (2) all defenses of any party to the instrument *with whom the holder has not dealt.* . . . (emphasis added).

In other words, personal defenses are available between immediate parties. Delaware Auto Sales dealt directly with Wilmington Trust Company; even if the auto dealer was a holder in due course, it is not immune to the defense of want or failure of consideration, as set forth in section 3–306(c).

We find that there was a failure of consideration here. Since the bank received the stop-payment order before it issued the treasurer's check, it had no right to charge the account of Hoopes, its depositor. A complete failure of consideration for the treasurer's check resulted and the bank had the right to refuse to honor it when presented by the payee.

We need not consider the defense of mistake also asserted by the bank.

FTC Modification of the Doctrine

Due to widespread abuses of the holder-in-due-course doctrine, the Federal Trade Commission (FTC) adopted a Trade Regulation Rule effective May 14, 1976, which, as far as *consumers* are concerned, virtually eliminated the problem of being forced to pay on an obligation when the seller failed to live up to his or her part of the bargain. The FTC rule provides that:

In connection with any sale or lease of goods or services to consumers, in or affecting the Federal Trade Commission Act, it is an unfair or deceptive act or practice within the meaning of Section 5 of that Act for a seller, directly or indirectly, to:

(a) take or receive a consumer credit contract which fails to contain the following provision in at least ten point, bold face, type:

NOTICE
ANY HOLDER OF THIS CONSUMER CREDIT CONTRACT IS SUBJECT TO ALL CLAIMS AND DEFENSES WHICH THE DEBTOR COULD ASSERT AGAINST THE SELLER OF GOODS OR SERVICES OBTAINED PURSUANT HERETO OR WITH THE PROCEEDS HEREOF. RECOVERY HEREUNDER BY THE DEBTOR SHALL NOT EXCEED AMOUNTS PAID BY THE DEBTOR HEREUNDER.

or, (b) accept, as full or partial payment for such sale or lease, the proceeds of any purchase money loan (as purchase money loan is defined herein), unless any consumer credit contract made in connection with such purchase money loan contains the following provision in at least ten point, bold face, type:

NOTICE
ANY HOLDER OF THIS CONSUMER CREDIT CONTRACT IS SUBJECT TO ALL CLAIMS AND DEFENSES WHICH THE DEBTOR COULD ASSERT AGAINST THE SELLER OF GOODS OR SERVICES OBTAINED WITH THE PROCEEDS HEREOF. RECOVERY HEREUNDER BY THE DEBTOR SHALL NOT EXCEED AMOUNTS PAID BY THE DEBTOR HEREUNDER.

This amendment was designed to protect the rights of consumers who purchase on credit and incur obligations to financial institutions by preserving the consumers' claims and defenses.

Note that the Act precludes *sellers* from taking a consumer-credit contract or proceeds of a purchase-money loan, unless the consumer-credit contract contains the aforementioned provision. This takes care of the situation where a seller arranges for financing a sale, or the situation where the seller refers a buyer to a finance company to obtain a loan for the goods. A *purchase-money loan* basically refers to a situation where a consumer receives a cash advance for which he or she will pay a finance charge to purchase goods and services from a seller who (1) refers the consumer to the creditor or (2) is affiliated with the creditor

BOX 25-1 ISSUES AND TRENDS
Destruction of Holder-in-Due-Course Doctrine

The abuses of the holder-in-due-course doctrine and the resulting injury to consumers have led to modification of the holder-in-due-course doctrine by the Federal Trade Commission. Another effective means of contesting the status of a holder is to utilize the provisions of the Uniform Consumer Credit Code (UCCC)—if it has been adopted in the state in question. At the present time the UCCC has been adopted in a small number of states. The scope of the act extends only to consumer-credit transactions.

In the states that have adopted the UCCC there is a virtual elimination of the holder-in-due-course doctrine as it applies to consumer-credit transactions. This is accomplished by two sections of the UCCC, Sections 3.307 and 3.404. Section 3.307 states that in consumer-credit sales or consumer leases, the seller may not take a negotiable instrument other than a check dated not later than ten days after its issuance. Section 3.404 states that an assignee of the rights of the seller or lessor is subject to all claims and defenses of the consumer against the seller, notwithstanding the fact that the assignee has the status of a holder in due course. In UCCC states a consumer's claims and defenses are not avoided by transferring the instrument to a third party who qualifies as a holder in due course.

---

by common control, contract, or business arrangement. A *consumer-credit contract* is an instrument that evidences or embodies a debt arising from a "purchase-money loan" transaction or a sale in which credit is extended to a consumer.

This rule does not apply to a person who acquires goods for use in his or her business but rather to people who purchase goods for personal, family, or household use. Such consumers now may purchase goods on credit, and if a defense, either real or personal, arises that can be asserted against the seller, this defense can be asserted against the holder of the consumer-credit contract even though the holder qualifies as a holder in due course.

What would happen if a consumer entered into a consumer-credit role, and signed a consumer-credit contract, but the FTC notice was not included in the language of the contract? At least one court has decided that, while such

a contract violates the FTC rule, in the absence of such a notice a holder in due course takes free of all personal defenses. This is true even though the contract should have included the FTC notice. Of course, this is an unfair trade practice.

The FTC rule does not apply to a credit-card transaction. However, the Fair Credit Billing Act protects buyers utilizing a credit card. There are two requirements: (1) the merchandise must cost more than $50 and (2) the consumer must live within 100 miles of the place where the original transaction took place. If both conditions are met, the consumer need only make an effort to return the item and ask for a refund or replacement. The consumer can then hold off on payment of the credit-card company's bill until the problem is ironed out with the retailer.

The following case discusses how the rule operates.

Tinker v. De Maria Porsche Audi, Inc.
District Court of Appeal of Florida
459 So.2d 487 (1984)

Background: Gerald Tinker (plaintiff) commenced this action against De Maria Porsche Audi, Inc. and Central National Bank of Miami (defendants). He alleged fraud and misrepresentation on the part of De Maria in connection with his purchase of a used Jaguar sports car. The bank counterclaimed for the unpaid balance due on the installment loan contract executed by Tinker for the purchase of the vehicle.

In 1976 Tinker purchased a 1972 Jaguar from De Maria. A salesman verbally represented to Tinker, prior to the sale, that the car was in good operating condition, was powered by its original engine, and had never been in a major collision. Tinker had problems with the car immediately after he purchased it. The car operated poorly and Tinker soon discovered that it was not powered by its original engine and had previously been "totaled" in a major collision.

In connection with the purchase of the vehicle Tinker executed a retail installment contract and note with De Maria. The Central National Bank provided financing for De Maria on a floor-plan basis and the installment contract and note were assigned to the bank pursuant to a preprinted assignment clause contained in the contract. Tinker never dealt with the bank prior to delivery of the car. The installment sales contract contained the following legend:

NOTICE
ANY HOLDER OF THIS CONSUMER CREDIT CONTRACT IS SUBJECT TO ALL CLAIMS AND DEFENSES WHICH THE DEBTOR COULD ASSERT AGAINST THE SELLER OF GOODS OR SERVICES OBTAINED PURSUANT HERETO OR WITH THE PROCEEDS HEREOF. RECOVERY HEREUNDER BY THE DEBTOR SHALL NOT EXCEED AMOUNTS PAID BY THE DEBTOR HEREUNDER.

When De Maria failed to replace or successfully repair the car after it became totally inoperable, Tinker ceased making payments to the bank and sued to recover. The trial court found for the defendants De Maria Porsche Audi and Central National Bank of Miami. Tinker appealed.

Decision: The Court of Appeal ruled for Tinker.

Ferguson, Judge

Whether the jury's finding of fraud by De Maria is, as contended by Tinker, an absolute defense to the Bank's counterclaim for the balance owed on the contract, depends on the legal efficacy of the "Notice" provision which was included. Appellant expressed some uncertainty at trial as to how the provision operates.

. . . The Notice is required by federal law in all consumer credit contracts made in connection with purchase money loans, such as installment sales contracts where the consumer executes the sales agreement together with a promissory note, both of which are, through a preprinted assignment clause, assigned to a bank which is closely affiliated with the seller. The effect of the federal rule is to defeat the holder in due course status of the assignee institutional lender, thus removing the lender's insulation from claims and defenses which could be asserted against the seller by the consumer.

Prior to the passage of the rule, consumers were caught in a "no-win" situation when the seller failed to remedy the defect either because of its unwillingness or its disappearance from the market. The institutional lenders then took advantage of protections under the holder in due course doctrine when the consumer sought to assert seller misconduct as a defense to the creditor's suit for payment on the note. The rule is expressly designed to compel creditors to either absorb seller misconduct costs or seek reimbursement of those costs from sellers.

It is clear that not only does the notice clause entitle the buyer to withhold the balance of the purchase price owed to the creditor when the seller's contractual duties are not fulfilled, but it gives the buyer a complete defense should the creditor sue for payment.

REVIEW PROBLEMS

1. What must a person do to negotiate an order-negotiable instrument? If the negotiable instrument is a bearer instrument, what must the person do to negotiate it?

2. What is a special indorsement? How does a person negotiate an instrument with a special indorsement?

3. In what respect, if any, has the FTC altered the holder-in-due-course doctrine?

4. On June 1 Morris takes a note that was payable to the order of Katz. Katz, a holder in due course of the note, indorsed and delivered the note to Morris. At that time Morris was aware that the note was overdue. Is Morris a holder in due course?

5. If a person takes an instrument under suspicious circumstances, does this mean that he cannot be a holder in due course of that instrument?

6. Talbot has $500 in his checking account at the First National Bank as of July 1. Talbot deposits a check from Smith for $250 to his account on July 2. On July 7 the bank permits Talbot to withdraw $200 from his account. On July 8 the bank allows him to withdraw $300 from his account. On July

9 it allows Talbot to withdraw the remaining $250 from his account. When, if ever, did the bank give value for Smith's check?

7. Scott Smith signed a note for $1,000 payable to the order of Yvonne Kennedy. Yvonne in turn transferred the note to Renee Clark, who gave Yvonne a check for $1,000 in return for the note. Has Renee given value for the note?

8. Christian Hughes indorsed the back of an instrument that was payable to his order as follows: "Without recourse, Christian Hughes." What type of indorsement is this, and why would a person indorse an instrument in this fashion?

9. A note was executed as follows: "Boston, Massachusetts, January 1, 1986. On demand I promise to pay to the order of Randy Davidson One Hundred and no/100 Dollars. Payable at the First National Bank of Boston (signed) Pamela Hyde." Pamela issued this note to Randy. Randy in turn indorsed the note on the back as follows: "Pay to the order of Rose Davidson (signed) Randy Davidson." He then delivered the note to his wife, Rose David-

son. Identify this indorsement and explain the consequences of using such an indorsement.

10. Yvonne Lowe signed the following note: "San Antonio, Texas, January 1, 1986. On demand I promise to pay to the order of Donna Sylvester One Hundred and no/100 Dollars. Payable at the First National Bank of San Antonio (signed) Yvonne Lowe." Yvonne issued this note to Donna. Soon thereafter a thief stole the note and sold it to an innocent purchaser. Did the thief get a good title to this instrument? Did the innocent purchaser get a good title to this instrument? Would it make any difference if the note had been payable to bearer rather than to the order of Donna Sylvester?

11. Pazol drew a check on Fulton National bank for payment to Eidson. Eidson deposited the check into his account at Sandy Springs Bank. On the same day Eidson withdrew the amount of the check from his account. On the next day Sandy Springs discovered the dishonorment of this check. Sandy Springs claims it is a holder in due course and demands payment from Pazol. Pazol claims Sandy Springs does not qualify as a holder in due course because it gave no value for the check. Is Sandy Springs a holder in due course? Pazol v. Citizen National Bank of Sandy Springs, 138 S.E.2d 442 (Ct. App. Ga. 1964)

12. Murphy gave a $15,000 check on September 27 to Brownsworth. Murphy thereafter decided Brownsworth had defrauded him, and Murphy on September 28 stopped payment on the check. Brownsworth on the morning of September 28 went to a branch bank of Manufacturers. The manager vaguely knew Brownsworth, but he still called Murphy's bank to verify that the money was in the account. This transaction took place prior to Murphy stopping payment on the check. Manufacturers cashed the check. When Manufacturers was unable to collect, because of the stop-payment order, Manufacturers brought suit on the check. Murphy argued that the bank was not a holder in due course because of a lack of good faith. By cashing the check for a person who was not a regular customer, Murphy argued, Manufacturers was not acting in good faith. Is Murphy correct? Manufacturers & Traders Trust Co. v. Murphy, 369 F.Supp. 11 (W.D. Penn. 1974).

13. Pappas purchased a carpet from Allo. Allo held up the delivery of the carpet. Allo asked Pappas to contact Jaeger. Based on the phone call, it became apparent that Allo owed Jaeger some money. In order to get the carpet released, Pappas sent a check for $6,500 to Allo, who indorsed it and forwarded the check to Jaeger. Pappas at no time stated he was placing any conditions on the check. The next day, because of a dispute with Allo, Pappas stopped payment on the check. The carpet in the meantime was released to Pappas. Pappas's check was returned to Jaeger marked "payment stopped." Pappas claimed that someone who takes a negotiable instrument cannot ignore facts which indicate the possibility of a defense good against it. Did Pappas have a good defense for stopping payment on the check? Jaeger & Branch, Inc. v. Pappas, 433 P.2d 605 (Utah 1967).

Liability of Parties and Defenses

C hapters 24 and 25 discussed the different types of commercial paper as well as the significant legal doctrines that support commercial paper as a vital component of the economy of the United States. This chapter investigates further the liability of parties who use commercial paper in business transactions and the defenses available against honoring these instruments.

TYPES OF LIABILITY

Unconditional or Primary Liability

Liability of the maker, drawer, drawee, and endorser of commercial paper differs appreciably. The liability of the maker of a promissory note is the most easily understood. A note, as indicated in Chapter 24, is a two-party in-

strument. The maker of a note assumes an unconditional responsibility based on the instrument's promise to pay. This responsibility is often referred to as primary, although the Uniform Commercial Code (UCC) does not use that term. Potentially, the drawee of a draft also assumes a similar liability, but the manner in which this arises is more complicated. Remember that a draft is a three-party instrument in which a drawer orders a drawee to pay a payee. When the drawee accepts this order, the drawee becomes the acceptor, assuming a liability comparable to that of the maker of a note.

Both the maker of a note and the acceptor of a draft contract to pay the instrument according to its terms at the time they become parties. Neither is excused from paying even if the holder presents the instrument long after it becomes due. As a primary party the maker or acceptor is bound to pay, and the holder need resort to no one else first. This obligation continues until the statute of limitations prevents the holder from recovering.

Until the drawee's acceptance—that is, his or her signed engagement to honor the draft as presented (Section 3—410[1])—the drawee has no liability on the instrument; upon acceptance, unconditional liability is established. A common example of acceptance is the certification of a check by a bank. By accepting, the drawee agrees to honor the instrument according to its terms as presented. The mechanics of acceptance were discussed in Chapter 24.

Although it is not an advisable practice, a drawee sometimes accepts an incomplete instrument. When doing so, the drawee accepts liability on the completed instrument to the extent that he or she authorized completion. If, however, the instrument is completed in an unauthorized manner and is transferred to a holder in due course, the acceptor's liability may increase if the holder in due course enforces the instrument as completed (Section 3–407[3]). In addition to becoming primarily liable by accepting, the drawee by this action admits the existence of the payee and the payee's capacity to indorse. The maker of a note also admits these same facts (Section 3–413[3]).

Secondary Liability

The liability of the drawer of a draft and of indorsers of commercial paper is not absolute. Responsibility of these parties for payment is conditioned upon certain events taking place. Accordingly, the UCC refers to indorsers and drawers as secondary parties (Section 3–102[1][d]). A secondary party is not expected to pay the instrument, whereas a primary party is.

Drawer's Commitment. Recall that a drawer initiating a draft is ordering the drawee to pay.

The drawer expects the drawee to do so. This expectation is generally based on a contractual relationship between the two. By accepting, the drawee agrees to be bound as ordered.

Indorser's Commitment. When commercial paper is transferred by indorsement, the indorser expects that the primary party, the drawee/acceptor or maker, will pay. The indorser's commitment, like that of the drawer of a draft, is to pay only if the primary party fails to do so.

Dishonor. The trigger for establishing secondary liability is dishonor. An instrument is dishonored if it is properly presented for acceptance or payment and the party upon whom presentment is made refuses to comply (Section 3–507[1][a]). A draft is dishonored by the drawee's either refusing to accept or refusing to pay, but a note is dishonored only if the maker refuses to pay.

ESTABLISHING SECONDARY LIABILITY

Generally the following events must occur to establish the secondary liability of indorsers as well as that of the drawer of a draft: (1) presentment, (2) dishonor, and (3) notice of dishonor. A fourth step called protest is required in some situations.

Presentment

Presentment is the term describing the procedure in which the holder of commercial paper or the holder's agent submits the instrument to the drawee or maker for acceptance or payment. For many drafts, presentment is made twice—once for acceptance and once for payment. A note is not presented for acceptance as the party who is liable for payment has already promised to do so.

Presentment for Acceptance. Presentment for acceptance is often a critical step in a transaction involving a draft. Initially, presentment for acceptance is necessary to establish the drawee's primary liability. Additionally, the secondary liability of the drawer and indorsers frequently depends on a proper presentment for acceptance.

According to the UCC, presentment for acceptance is required in three instances. It must be made where the draft so provides, where it is payable at some place other than the drawee's residence or place of business, or where the time of payment depends on the acceptance date (Section 3–501[1][a]). The holder may, however, present any draft payable at a stated date for acceptance. A common example would be the trade acceptance, which was discussed in Chapter 24.

Presentment for Payment. Practically, a holder of commercial paper must present the instrument to the proper party in order to collect. Presentment for payment is also a necessary step in establishing the liability of secondary parties if the instrument is dishonored. Unless presentment is accomplished correctly, all indorsers are discharged completely, and drawers to a limited extent if the drawee becomes insolvent during any delay in presentment (Section 3–502[1][b]). In the following case the drawer of a number of checks argues that he is discharged because the checks were not presented for payment for several months.

Kaiser v. Northwest Shopping Center, Inc.

Court of Civil Appeals of Texas

544 S.W.2d 785 (1976)

Background: Robert G. Kaiser (defendant-appellant) and Northwest Shopping Center, Inc. (plaintiff-appellee) were parties to a lease agreement under which Kaiser was obligated to pay $500 per month rent plus a pro rata share of property taxes, a maintenance fee, and a percentage of gross sales over $200,000.

The lease gave Kaiser the exclusive right to operate a drug store in the shopping center. The original lease term was to expire on December 31, 1973; however, a letter dated June 1, 1971, gave Kaiser an option to extend the lease on the same terms, except that his rent would be increased to $750 per month. By another letter dated January 22, 1974, Northwest Shopping Center, Inc. informed Kaiser that, since Kaiser had not elected to extend his lease, he would be considered a month-to-month tenant at a rate of $600 per month. Kaiser then took the position that he had extended the lease by tendering checks in the amount of $750 per month. Commencing in January 1974, Northwest held Kaiser's rent checks without presenting them while another tenant, a large grocery chain, was attempting to renegotiate its lease to permit it to install a pharmaceutical department, which, if permitted by Northwest, would have been contrary to a covenant in Kaiser's lease. When these negotiations collapsed, Northwest decided to acquiesce in Kaiser's lease extension. Acting on this decision, Northwest presented the accumulated checks to Kaiser's bank on October 29, 1974. The bank honored some of the checks but refused to honor others because they were stale or because the account contained insufficient funds. On October 31 Northwest again presented the dishonored checks, but payment had been stopped on them. Northwest then sued to recover the unpaid rent.

The trial court held that neither the checks nor the underlying rent obligation was discharged by the landlord's failure to make timely presentment of the checks for payment and entered judgment against Kaiser. Kaiser appealed.

Decision: The Court of Civil Appeals upheld the decision for Northwest.

Akin, Justice

Kaiser contends that because the checks were not presented within a reasonable period of time, the checks and the underlying debt are discharged [Sections 3–601 and 3–802]. These sections of the Code do not support such a contention. Section 3.802 provides:

> (a) Unless otherwise agreed, where an instrument is taken for an underlying obligation . . .
>   (2) . . . If the instrument is dishonored action may be maintained on either the instrument or the obligation; discharge of the underlying obligor on the instrument also discharges him on the obligation.

This section allows a creditor, after a check is dishonored, to choose whether he wants to sue on the check or the underlying debt. However, it goes on to provide that if the debtor's liability on the check has been discharged under another provision of the Code, then the underlying debt is also discharged. The methods by which the obligation on a check can be discharged are specified in 3.601. Kaiser apparently relies upon 3.601(b), to wit:

> Any party is also discharged from his liability on an instrument to another party by any other act or agreement with such party which would discharge his simple contract for the payment of money.

Kaiser argues that retention of the checks longer than a reasonable time is an "other act" constituting a discharge under the section. Apparently he relies on the cases holding that ". . . a creditor's retention for an unreasonable length of time of a check tendered in full payment of an unliquidated or disputed claim, without cashing or otherwise using it and without indicating a refusal to accept the check in accord and satisfaction, constitutes an acceptance of the check in settlement for payment of the claim, so as to bar any action for an alleged balance due."

The flaw in this argument is that "acceptance," as used in these cases, means that the creditor treats the check as cash, subject to payment by the bank on which it was drawn, and is bound by any conditions upon which the check was delivered. By merely holding the check, the creditor does not lose his right to be paid. If the check is not honored by the bank on which it is drawn, the debtor loses the benefit of his tender by check. Retention of the check, even beyond a reasonable time, does not discharge either the check or the underlying debt under 3.601(b) or under 3.802.

Kaiser also relies on 3.503(b)(1), which provides that instruments shall be presented for payment within a "reasonable" time, defined as thirty days from the date of issue or the date of the check, whichever is later. This section does not relieve the drawer, however, of his liability on the stale check. The only penalty the Code provides for such a delay as between the drawer and the holder is under 3.502, which provides that a drawer's liability on a stale check may be discharged if the bank on which it is drawn has become insolvent. Since no question of the bank's solvency is presented here, 3.502 and 3.503 do not assist Kaiser.

If an instrument indicates the date on which it is due, presentment for payment is due on that day. An accepted draft payable a specified number of days after sight is due at that time. If a note is payable on demand in order to fix the liability of secondary parties, presentment for payment is due within a reasonable time after the party becomes liable (Section 3–503[1][e]). A reasonable time is determined by the nature of the instrument, customs of the trade, and the facts of the particular case (Section 3–503[2]).

Presentment for either payment or acceptance must be made at a reasonable hour. If presentment is required at a bank, the presentment must be made during the banking day (Section 3–503[4]). If presentment is due on a day that is not a full business day for either party, presentment is due on the next following day that is a full business day for both parties (Section 3–503[3]). Presentment may be made by mail, through a clearinghouse, or at the place of acceptance or payment specified in the instrument. When nothing is specified, presentment may be at the place of business or residence of the party who is to accept or pay (Section 3–504[2][1]).

The party to whom presentment is made may require the presenter to (1) exhibit the instrument, (2) identify himself or herself, (3) either sign a receipt on the instrument for any partial payment, or (4) surrender the instrument upon full payment (Section 3–505[1]). If these requirements are not met, the person upon whom presentment is made may refuse to accept or pay without dishonoring.

Dishonor

Dishonor, as previously mentioned, is the refusal of a party upon whom a proper demand for payment or acceptance is made to comply within the required time. Payment of an instrument may be deferred without dishonor to provide the person upon whom demand is made an opportunity to examine it to determine if it is properly payable (Section 3–506[2]); however, payment must be made before the close of business on the day of presentment (Section 3–506[2]). Subject to any required notice of dishonor and protest, a holder has upon dishonor an immediate right of recourse against the drawers and endorsers (Section 3–507[2]).

Notice of Dishonor

In most cases the final step in establishing the liability of secondary parties is to provide notice that the instrument has been dishonored. A holder has until midnight of the third business day after dishonor to notify his or her immediate transferor of the dishonor. Prior holders are required to give notice before midnight of the third business day after they received notice of dishonor (Section 3–508[2]). A bank is required to give notice before midnight of the banking day following the banking day on which it received the item or notice of dishonor (Sections 3–508[2], 4–104[1][h]).

Although the time within which notice must be provided is relatively short, other requirements for notice are more liberal. Notice of dishonor may be given orally in a face-to-face conversation or over the telephone; however, both of these practices should be avoided because the party providing notice may have to prove later that it was given. If oral notice is given, it should be followed by a written notice within the statutory period.

The most common type of notice of dishonor is the check that has been returned through a clearinghouse because the drawer has insufficient funds or has stopped payment for some reason; but notice of dishonor is frequently given by mail or telegram. The UCC allows notice of dishonor in any reasonable manner as long as the instrument is identified and the fact of dishonor clearly indicated.

Notice of dishonor does not have to be given in any particular order. Usually the holder notifies the person who transferred the instrument to him or her. This triggers that person's liability. That person in turn would notify the individual from whom the instrument was received and so on down the line. The holder might, however, notify other transferors in order to initiate their responsibility in the event collection from the immediate transferor is not accomplished. Once a party has been notified of dishonor, no further notice need be given, for the notice operates for the benefit of all parties who have rights on the instrument (Section 3–508[8]).

Protest

Protest is an official certificate of dishonor given by a consular officer of the United States, a notary public, or other person authorized to certify dishonor by the law of the place where dishonor occurs (Section 3–509[1]). Protest is required on dishonored drafts drawn or payable outside the United States. A draft of this type is generally referred to as a *foreign bill.*

The purpose of a certificate of protest is to provide acceptable evidence of dishonor. Since a certificate of protest provides a rebuttable presumption that notice of dishonor has been given, dishonored commercial paper is often protested although no requirement exists to do so (Section 3–510[a]).

EXTENT OF SECONDARY LIABILITY

As previously indicated, an indorser's liability is secondary. This liability is conditioned upon the instrument's being dishonored when it is properly presented and notice of dishonor is provided the indorser. Unless excused, a holder's failure to meet these conditions as directed by statute discharges the indorser both completely and immediately (Section 3–502[1][a]).

The liability of the drawer of a draft is also secondary, as it depends on certain conditions being fulfilled; but a critical difference exists between the position of the drawer of a draft and that of an indorser. The drawer usually receives a consideration from the payee. This is the reason that the drawer has ordered the drawee to honor the instrument. To allow a drawer to escape liability because the holder fails to make due presentment or provide notice of dishonor would result in the drawer receiving an unjustifiable gain. As a result, in general if the drawee refuses to accept or pay, policy dictates that the drawer be liable. However, if the drawer were to suffer a loss because the holder fails to make proper presentment or provide notice of dishonor, that loss should be the holder's. Table 26-1 indicates which parties are primarily liable and which parties are secondarily liable.

TABLE 26-1 NATURE OF LIABILITY OF PARTIES TO AN INSTRUMENT

Party	Extent of Liability
Maker	Primary
Indorser of instrument	Secondary
Drawer of draft	Secondary

The drawer will suffer a loss if it leaves funds on deposit with the drawee to cover a draft and the drawee becomes insolvent. If the drawee's insolvency occurs after the draft is due, the drawer's loss is a result of the holder's failure to make the necessary presentment or give notice of dishonor in a timely manner. With this in mind, the UCC limits the drawer's liability on the draft to the extent that the drawee's insolvency deprives the drawer of funds. This result is accomplished by providing the drawer with a right to obtain a discharge of liability by assigning his or her right against the drawee to the holder (Section 3–502[1][b]).

ESTABLISHING WARRANTY LIABILITY

Whether or not a person signs an instrument when he or she transfers it to another person, he or she makes certain warranties about the instrument being transferred. The ability to recover based on these warranties is not dependent on whether there has been a proper presentment, dishonor, or protest. The following material discusses the warranty liability of unqualified indorsers, qualified indorsers, and persons who transfer an instrument without an indorsement.

Unqualified Indorsers

Section 3–417(2) of the UCC states that a person who transfers an instrument by indorsement and receives consideration makes five separate implied warranties to the indorsee and all subsequent holders. The indorser warrants:

1. He or she has good title to the instrument.
2. All signatures are genuine and authorized.
3. The instrument has not been materially altered.
4. No defense of any party is good against him.

5. He or she has no knowledge of any insolvency proceeding instituted with respect to the maker or acceptor or the drawer of an unaccepted instrument.

An indorser might breach the warranty of title in several ways, but a breach often involves a forged indorsement. Suppose Jack issues a check to Mary. A thief steals the check from Mary, forges her indorsement and transfers it to Jane. Jane in turn transfers it to Nick. When Nick presents the check to the bank, the bank refuses to pay it because Mary, who by that time had learned of the theft, had stopped payment on the check. As Mary's indorsement was forged, Nick cannot enforce the check. Even so, Nick can hold Jane liable for breach of the implied warranty of title.

The implied warranty that all signatures are genuine and authorized might be breached, for example, in the following way. Suppose in the earlier example Jack's signature was a forgery. Therefore when Nick attempted to collect on the check, the bank refused because it detected that Jack's signature had been forged. In this situation Nick can hold Jane liable for breach of her promise that all signatures were genuine.

Suppose a person acquires an instrument that has been altered and, because the person is a mere holder as opposed to a holder in due course, is unable to recover anything on the instrument. Such a person may sue his or her indorsee for breach of the implied warranty that the instrument has not been altered.

An unqualified indorser warrants absolutely that no defense of any party is good against him. As we note later, a qualified indorser makes a slightly different promise. Suppose that Mark tricks Dan into signing a negotiable instrument for $200 when in fact Dan owed Mark nothing. Mark then negotiated this instrument to Bill. When Bill attempted to recover he was unable to collect. In this case Bill can sue Mark because Mark breached the warranty that no defense existed against him.

Finally, an indorser warrants that he has no knowledge of any insolvency proceedings instituted against the maker, acceptor, or drawer of an unaccepted instrument. If when an indorser negotiates an instrument he is aware of such a proceeding, the indorser can be sued for breach of this warranty.

Qualified Indorsers

A *qualified indorser,* that is, a person who indorses an instrument with a "without recourse" indorsement, makes virtually the same warranties as an unqualified indorser. The only difference is that an *unqualified indorser* warrants absolutely that no defense of any party is good against him. The qualified indorser, however, merely warrants that he has no actual knowledge of any defense of any party that is good against him. In all other respects the implied warranties of the qualified and the unqualified indorsers are the same.

Liability of a Transferor Who Does Not Indorse

It is possible to transfer a bearer instrument without indorsing it. In such a case the person who transfers the instrument has no secondary liability on the instrument.

Such a transferor has the same warranty liability as an unqualified indorser. Therefore, while the warranties of unqualified and qualified indorsers run to all subsequent holders of an instrument, the warranties of a person who transfers an instrument without an indorsement run only to his immediate transferee.

OTHER LIABILITY RULES

As a general rule the drawer of a draft or the maker of a note does not need to pay the in-strument if the payee's indorsement has been forged. There are two important exceptions to this rule—the *imposter rule* and the *fictitious payee rule.*

Imposter Rule

The UCC, in Section 3–405(1)(a), adopts the rule that if a person pretends to be someone else and convinces a drawer or maker to issue an instrument to the person being impersonated, the imposter has the power to indorse the instrument in the name of the impersonated person.

For example, suppose a construction business owes a debt to a subcontractor, Mike Adams. Bill, after learning of this debt, goes to the construction company and represents to the bookkeeper that he is Mike Adams. The bookkeeper makes out a check to Mike Adams and gives it to Bill. Bill takes the check to a bank, indorses it on the back, "Mike Adams," and collects the amount of the check from the bank. When Bill indorsed this check with Mike Adams' name, this was an effective indorsement.

The rationale for the imposter rule is that the loss caused by this transaction should be placed on the party in the best position to avoid it in the first place, the drawer of a draft or the maker of a note. The drawer or maker is in a better position to determine the true identity of the imposter than someone who later acquires the instrument. Therefore the UCC treats the indorsement of the imposter just as if the rightful payee had indorsed the instrument.

Fictitious Payee Rule

The fictitious payee rule is similar to the imposter rule. It may arise as follows: A business gives the authority to an employee, Susan Smith, to write checks on the business account. Susan, intending to cheat the business, draws a check on the company account for

$1,000 payable to Lori Adams. The business does not owe Lori Adams anything. Susan Smith indorses the check in the name of Lori Adams and cashes it at a bank. The bank charges the company's account. Susan signed the check as the drawer, intending Lori Smith, the payee, to have no interest in the check. When she indorsed the check in Adams' name, Section 3–405(1)(b) treats this indorsement as effective.

This rule also arises in another situation. Suppose Susan Smith was not entitled to write checks on the company account, but supplied the list of persons the company owed to a person with authority to sign for the company.

Smith added Lori Adams' name to the list of legitimate creditors of the company, although the company did not owe Adams anything. After the check was signed, Smith took it, signed Lori Adams' indorsement, and cashed the check at a bank. In this case also the Code, in Section 3–405(1)(c), treats the indorsement as effective.

The UCC adopts this rule because the drafters of the Code thought that an employer is in a better position to prevent such events from occurring than persons who later deal with such instruments.

The following case discusses the fictitious payee rule.

Western Casualty & Surety Co. v. Citizens Bank of Las Cruces

U.S. Court of Appeals, Tenth Circuit

676 F.2d 1344 (1982)

Background: Western Casualty and Surety Co. (plaintiff) brought suit against the Citizens Bank of Las Cruces and the Bank of New Mexico (defendants). It alleged that these banks had failed to comply with reasonable commercial banking practices by accepting for payment a fraudulently procured and improperly indorsed warrant (check) of the state of New Mexico in the amount of $395,000. The warrant was issued to a fictitious entity, the Greater Mesilla Valley Sanitation District, which had been created by two state employees to defraud the state of money. The warrant was presented to, accepted, and processed by Citizens Bank and forwarded to the Bank of New Mexico where it was finally paid.

The trial court granted a judgment in favor of the defendant banks. Western Casualty appealed, contending that the District Court improperly applied the statutory defenses of Section 3–405 of the UCC to protect both banks from liability.

Decision: The Court of Appeals ruled for the Citizens Bank of Las Cruces and the Bank of New Mexico.

McKay, Circuit Judge

As part of an attempt to establish uniform rules governing the relationships between banks and their customers, the UCC allocates the losses caused by forged signatures on negotiable instruments based on the relative responsibilities of the parties to a transaction. As a general rule, forged indorsements are ineffective to pass title or to authorize a drawee to pay. If a drawee pays a check on which a necessary indorsement is forged, the drawer can usually require the drawee bank to recredit the drawer's account. The item is not "properly payable," UCC § 4–401, because "[a]ny unauthorized signature is wholly inoperative as that of the person whose name is signed." UCC § 3–404. The loss on an instrument containing a forged indorsement is then shifted to previous indorsers by way of an action for breach of warranty of good title. Ultimately the loss is generally borne by the person who forged the indorsement or the party who took the instrument from the forger. Therefore, as a general rule, the drawer can avoid liability on an instrument by showing an unauthorized indorsement.

Section 3–405 operates as an exception to this general rule. In certain factual situations, this section treats anyone's indorsement in the name of the payee as effective to pass title to the instrument, leaving the drawer liable on the instrument despite the forged indorsement. . . .

· · ·

The circumstances described in § 3–405(1)(c) directly apply in this case. An "employee" of the "maker or drawer," the State of New Mexico, supplied the State with the name of a "payee," the fictitious sanitation district, "intending the latter to have no . . . interest" in the instrument issued.

· · ·

Western Casualty contends that even if § 3–405 applies in this case, summary judgment was improper because factual questions concerning the banks' culpability in contributing to the loss remain to be resolved at trial. The propriety of summary judgment depends upon whether the allocation of loss to the drawer in the factual situations described in § 3–405 is absolute or whether the loss can be reshifted to the bank upon a showing that it did not follow reasonable commercial practices. Section 3–405 does not explicitly impose a standard of care on banks that assert the section as a defense, and the New Mexico courts have not yet confronted this issue. . . . While it is clear that banks must observe this standard of good faith, whether they must also be free from negligence to invoke the protection of § 3–405 is unclear. Two other sections of the Code that deal with forged signatures specifically incorporate a standard of care for banks. Under § 3–406, a drawer who has substantially contributed to the making of an unauthorized signature may not assert the lack of authority against a bank "who pays the instrument in good faith and *in accordance with . . . reasonable commercial standards.*" (Emphasis added). Section 4–406, which requires a bank customer to timely examine his bank statements and notify the bank of unauthorized signatures, nevertheless allows recovery against the bank despite failure to do so if the customer "establishes *lack of ordinary care* on the part of the bank in paying the item(s)." (Emphasis added). Under these two sections, the negligent drawer can defeat the bank's defenses to a forgery by showing that the bank acted negligently. No similar qualifying language is incorporated in § 3–405.

The interpretation that negligence is irrelevant to a § 3–405 defense is supported by the policy of placing the loss on the party in the best position to prevent it. This policy is particularly applicable in cases under § 3–405(1)(c), because

> "the wrongdoing is internal, [and] it is arguably within the drawer's ability to set up a system of controls and safeguards to prevent the embezzlement. . . . Although the bank might be expected to know or verify the signature of its drawer-customer, it is in no position to be a watchdog over the internal business procedures of its customer or to ascertain the validity of an indorsement."

We are not persuaded that the absence of language establishing a duty of care in § 3–405 was inadvertent, nor do we think a standard of care based on negligence can be implied consistent with the expressed purposes underlying that section. Therefore, we believe that the New Mexico courts would hold that the § 3–405 defense is absolute where the only allegation is one of negligence, so that a court need not consider allegations of negligence on the part of the bank in a factual situation falling within § 3–405(1)(c). The district court properly applied § 3–405 in granting summary judgment against Western Casualty on its claims that Citizens Bank of Las Cruces and the Bank of New Mexico acted negligently in accepting, processing, and making payment on the fraudulently procured warrant. Accordingly, the order of the district court is affirmed.

UNIVERSAL DEFENSES

Commercial paper is a substitute for money. Although not so acceptable generally as currency, checks, drafts, and promissory notes transfer readily in the economy. In some situations the use of commercial paper is preferable to the use of money. Individuals and business firms pay many obligations with checks because to do so is safer and more convenient than to use currency.

The doctrine of holder in due course, described in the previous chapter, is the major reason that commercial paper is readily acceptable in most transactions. Recall that the holder in due course enjoys a special position, since with limited exceptions a holder in due course takes the instrument free of defenses of any party to it with whom he or she has not dealt.

Defenses that may be asserted against a holder in due course are called *universal* or *real* defenses. Some defenses are recognized even against a holder in due course because the holder in due course never agreed to the obligation indicated by the instrument. Negotiable instruments are a form of contract. If no contractual liability has been assumed, the instrument is a nullity.

A note upon which the maker's signature is forged is an example. Even if the instrument is proper in form and duly negotiated to a holder in due course, the victim of the forgery should not be liable. A similar result follows when an instrument is materially altered after being executed. The party liable is not responsible for the instrument in its altered state, since this was not the contract to which the person agreed.

Other universal defenses exist because the public policy underlying each is considered more important to society than the public need for the ready transferability of commercial paper. Universal defenses of this kind include infancy, certain other types of incapacity, duress and illegality when these render the underlying transaction void, discharge in bankruptcy, and fraud in the execution.

Forgery

A person whose signature is used on a negotiable instrument without authority is not liable on it. If, however, the person's negligence substantially contributed to the use of the unauthorized signature, he or she is precluded from asserting the lack of authority against a holder in due course (Section 3–406).

Material Alteration

A *material alteration* is one that changes the contract of any of the parties. Changes that do not affect the agreement of the parties are not considered material. An example would be the addition of a co-maker or surety (Section 3–407, Comment 1).

A holder in due course who takes after a material alteration may enforce the instrument but only according to its original tenor (Section 3–407). If a person who is obligated on the instrument is negligent and that negligence contributes substantially to the instrument's being materially altered, the holder in due course may enforce the instrument in its altered form (Section 3–406).

In protecting the rights of a holder in due course, the UCC treats an incomplete instrument as it does one that has been materially altered. A holder in due course may enforce the instrument as it has been completed, even though it was completed in a manner that was not authorized (Section 3–407[3]). This means that a check signed by the drawer in blank and stolen or lost is enforceable by a holder in due course against the drawer as it was completed by the thief or finder.

Fraud in the Execution

The basis of this defense is similar to that underlying forgery and material alteration. A holder in due course attempting to recover on a forged instrument is not allowed to recover because the defendant never agreed to be bound. Where a material alteration has occurred, the defendant's liability is limited because he or she did not agree to the instrument's terms as they now appear. In fraud in the execution, also called fraud in the factum, the party defending escapes liability because he or she was misled as to what was being signed.

This might happen in a number of ways. Extreme cases exist in which a promissory note was cleverly hidden under another document that a person supposedly signed. Upon removal of the cover document, the signature is on the note, which the payee then negotiates. The more usual situation is one in which

a buyer signs a promissory note or some other type of commercial paper, being assured by the seller that the instrument is merely an authorization to conduct a credit investigation or a receipt. In these situations, because the signer never intended to make a promise, no liability exists. For this defense to be successful, the defendant must be able to show that no reasonable opportunity existed to discover what was actually being signed. If the defendant acted carelessly either in not reading the instrument being signed or in some other manner, the defense will fail.

Fraud in the execution differs from the false statement made to induce a person to enter into a contract. This is called fraud in the procurement or fraud in the inducement. Fraud in the inducement is not a defense against a holder in due course. Although it is a defense in a contract case, contractual defenses of this kind may be asserted only against ordinary holders. These defenses are examined in some detail later in this chapter.

Infancy

As indicated in Chapter 12, a minor has the right to rescind most contractual obligations. The extent to which this right exists depends on state law. Under the UCC a minor may raise the defense of infancy against a holder in due course to the same extent that infancy is a contractual defense according to state law governing the transaction (Section 3–305[2][a]). For example, in most states a minor purchasing a stereo is allowed to disaffirm the contract since the item is not a necessity. If the minor signs a note as payment for the stereo, the note is not enforceable even if transferred to a holder in due course who has no knowledge of the maker's minority.

Other Incapacity

Mental incapacity and incapacity as a result of intoxication can be used as defenses against a holder in due course in limited instances. Incapacity other than infancy is available against a holder in due course if applicable state laws "render the underlying obligation a nullity" (Section 3–305[1][b]). In effect this means that the underlying contract must be void, not just voidable, if incapacity is to be used successfully against a holder in due course. In most states contracts by mental incompetents are void only if the incompetent has been adjudicated insane. A similar rule applies to intoxication. If the promisor's intoxication was so extreme that he or she could not have intended to contract, the agreement is void. In a similar situation a person obligated on commercial paper has a good defense against the holder in due course.

Duress and Illegality

Duress and illegality are treated by the UCC in a manner similar to incapacity other than infancy (Section 3–305[1][b]). In both instances, if applicable state law renders the contract void, duress or illegality can be asserted against a holder in due course. In most states a contract secured by duress is voidable, not void; thus duress is generally unavailable as a defense against a holder in due course. If, however, the duress is so extreme that the agreement is void from the beginning, duress is a good defense. Illegality is treated in a comparable manner, as the following case indicates.

New Jersey Mortgage & Investment Corp. v. Berenyi

Superior Court of New Jersey, Appellate Division

356 A.2d 421 (1976)

Background: New Jersey Mortgage and Investment Corp. (plaintiff-respondent) was the holder in due course of a negotiable promissory note. Andrew and Anna Berenyi (defendants-appellants), the makers, refused to pay and the holder in due course sued on the note. Berenyi argued that no liability existed because the transaction was illegal. The trial court entered judgment for the plaintiff. Defendant appealed.

Decision: The Appellate Division ruled for New Jersey Mortgage.

Before Judges Kolovsky, Bischoff and Botter

Per Curiam

Defendant Anna Berenyi appeals from a judgment for plaintiff based on the following stipulated facts:

1. On May 25, 1964, in a proceeding brought by Arthur J. Sills, Attorney General of the State of New Jersey, against Kroyden Industries, Inc., a corporation of the State of New Jersey, in the Superior Court of New Jersey, Chancery Division, Essex County, a Consent Order was made by Honorable Ward J. Herbert, J.S.C., which Order enjoined the said Kroyden Industries, Inc. from committing certain acts or making certain representations with its customers in connection with the sale of carpeting.
2. In August, 1964, the defendants, Andrew Berenyi (now deceased) and Anna Berenyi, were referred from a participant in a sales scheme of Kroyden Industries, Inc., for the purchase of carpeting.
3. An employee of Kroyden Industries, Inc. offered, in violation of the injunc-

tion aforesaid, to give to the defendants carpeting which, if the contract price of $1,100.00 was paid, was worth $44.00 per square yard without making any payments as long as they referred prospective buyers to Kroyden Industries, Inc.

4. The defendants agreed to this plan since the carpeting would not cost them anything as long as they made the required referrals.

5. The defendants, relying upon the above offer and representations, signed a negotiable promissory note for $1,521.00. Said instrument was negotiated to the plaintiff herein.

6. The plaintiff is a holder in due course for value of the negotiable promissory note sued upon and had no knowledge or notice of the proceedings brought against Kroyden Industries, Inc.; and had no knowledge or notice of the entry of the Order in the Chancery Division by Judge Herbert; and had no knowledge or notice that Kroyden Industries, Inc., violated the aforementioned injunctive Order.

The trial judge ruled that the fact that the note was obtained as part of a transaction entered into by Kroyden Industries, Inc. (Kroyden) in violation of the injunctive order was not a defense in an action brought by plaintiff, whose status as a holder in due course, with no knowledge or notice of the injunctive order, was admitted.

The controlling issue presented is whether the defense here asserted is a "real" defense or a "personal" defense. Real defenses are available against even a holder in due course of a negotiable instrument; personal defenses are not available against such a holder. We affirm since we are satisfied that the defense presented is not a "real" defense.

Defendant argues that since the transaction which resulted in the execution and delivery of defendant's note was engaged in by Kroyden in violation of the injunctive order, the transaction was "illegal and thus a nullity under N.J.S.A. 12A:3–305," which provides in pertinent part as follows:

> To the extent that a holder is a holder in due course he takes the instrument free from . . .
> (2) all defenses of any party to the instrument with whom the holder has not dealt except . . .
> (b) such other incapacity, or duress, or illegality of the transaction, as renders the obligation of the party a nullity; and . . .

However, the fact that it was illegal for Kroyden to enter into the transaction did not by reason of that fact render defendant's obligation under the note she executed a nullity.

On the contrary, as noted in the New Jersey Study Comment on N.J.S.A. 12A:3–305(2)(b):

> In New Jersey, a holder in due course takes free and clear of the defense of illegality, unless the statute which declares the act illegal also indicates that payment thereunder is void. . . . (See e.g., N.J.S.A. 2A:40–3 which specifically

provides that notes given in payment of a gambling debt "shall be utterly void and of no effect.") . . . where no such statute is involved, it has been held that a negotiable instrument which is rooted in an illegal transaction or stems from a transaction prohibited by statute or public policy is no reason for refusing to enforce the instrument in the hands of a holder in due course.

There being no statute ordaining that a note obtained in violation of an injunction is void and unenforceable, the illegality involved is not a "real" defense; the note is enforceable in the hands of a holder in due course who had no knowledge or notice of the injunction.

The judgment is affirmed. No costs.

CASE NOTE

This case is an example of the manner in which negotiable instruments used in consumer transactions can injure unsophisticated buyers. A substantial number of states have adopted statutes requiring that notes executed in connection with a retail installment contract be labeled "Consumer Note" and additionally providing that such a note should not be negotiable. The Federal Trade Commission also has adopted a rule limiting the use of negotiable instruments in consumer transactions.

Discharge in Bankruptcy

Providing individuals and firms that are insolvent with an opportunity to make a fresh start has long been an important public policy. Where a holder in due course is a creditor of the bankrupt and for one reason or another the claim of the holder in due course is not asserted until the bankrupt is discharged, the discharge provides a good defense. Table 26-2 discusses the effectiveness of various defenses that may be asserted against a holder in due course.

LIMITED DEFENSES

An ordinary holder of commercial paper is entitled to payment unless a signature necessary to liability is missing or the obligor establishes some defense. The ordinary holder is subject to all the universal defenses as well as a wide variety of additional claims and defenses. These additional defenses are usually referred to as limited or personal defenses.

TABLE 26-2 EFFECTIVENESS OF DEFENSES AGAINST A HOLDER IN DUE COURSE

Defense	Is a Holder in Due Course Subject to It?
Breach of underlying contract	No
Infancy of the buyer	Yes
Breach of warranty	No
Fraud in the inducement	No
Forged drawer's signature	Yes
Fraud in the execution	Yes
Material alteration	Yes
Nondelivery	No
Failure of consideration	No

Limited defenses differ from universal defenses in that they are based on legally acceptable reasons for not performing a contract, whereas the universal are based generally on the idea that no contract ever existed. For example, fraud in the execution is a universal defense good even against a holder in due course because the defendant never intended to execute a negotiable instrument. On the other hand, fraud in the procurement is merely a personal defense. It is not good against a holder in due course but is good against an ordinary holder because the defendant intended to contract, although wrongfully induced to do so.

Under the UCC an ordinary holder of commercial paper is subject to all valid claims against it as well as the following defenses:

1. Breach of contract
2. Lack or failure of consideration
3. Nonperformance of a condition precedent
4. Nondelivery
5. Acquisition of the instrument through theft by any person

Although these are the chief personal defenses, other defenses may also be asserted against the ordinary holder.

The fact that numerous defenses can be raised against a holder does not limit the viability of commercial paper appreciably. In most instances the obligor has no defense and the holder collects. Additionally, as the status of holder in due course is relatively easy for the good-faith transferee of commercial paper to attain, people in the business community are generally not reluctant to use these instruments in their transactions.

REVIEW PROBLEMS

1. What events must occur to establish the secondary liability of indorsers and drawers?
2. What warranties does a person who transfers an instrument by indorsement make?
3. How does the warranty liability of a qualified indorser differ from the warranty liability of an unqualified indorser?
4. What is meant by the term "fraud in the execution"?
5. Jack wrote a check made payable to Mike Prosser. A thief stole this check and transferred it to John Collins. If the thief indorsed the check with an unqualified indorsement at the time he signed it, has the thief any warranty liability to Collins?
6. Roberson obtained Smith's checkbook. Roberson wrote out a check for $5,000 payable to himself, and he signed Smith's name as the drawer of the check. Does Smith have any liability on this instrument?
7. Martin writes a check out for $500.00. He gives this check to Mann, who skillfully alters the check to read $5,000.00. Mann negotiates the check to a holder in due course. To what extent, if any, can a holder in due course enforce this instrument?
8. Henry Jaroszewski and his wife agreed to purchase frozen food from Merit Food Corporation to be delivered in three deliveries. The note they signed authorized the bank to pay $1,850 to Merit. The purchasers became dissatisfied with the food after receiving $200 worth, and they refused to accept further deliveries. The bank in the meantime had paid Merit the $1,850. The purchasers now claim Merit's representatives fraudulently represented the nature of the forms they were signing. They also claim the bank knew of Merit's misconduct because it had dealt with Merit on similar transactions in the past. Must Jaroszewski pay the bank? Waterbury Savings Bank v. Jaroszewski, 238 A.2d 446 (4th Cir. 1967).

9. Bergfield contracted to sell Kirby a parcel of real estate for $352,560. Bergfield's attorney after the closing called Kirby's bank to learn if Kirby's $20,000 check was good. Through an error, he was informed Kirby's check was not good. Bergfield treated the contract as breached and refused to allow his attorney to deliver the deed. He also retained Kirby's deposit. Kirby now sues for specific performance. Would he be successful? Kirby v. Bergfield, 182 N.E.2d 205 (1970).

10. Evern Jones received a check from American Book Company for $432.53, payable to the order of Jones. He indorsed the check, but thereafter lost it. He called American Book Company and it stopped payment on the check.

    Between two and three o'clock that afternoon, Mrs. Tommie Davis, an employee of the White System of Jackson, Inc., took a telephone call ostensibly from Leon Ormane, at Five Point Service Station, who advised that one of their customers, with a check larger than they could handle, wished to buy some tires, and inquired if White System would cash it. She asked Mr. White, the president, what to do, and he advised that, if it was a company check, to cash it. About twenty or thirty minutes later, a man came into the office and presented the check.

    In addition to the name Jones, there purported to be an endorsement of Five Point Service Station and Leon Ormane. White System cashed the check.

    White System seeks to recover the amount of the check on which American Book Company had stopped payment. Would White System be successful? Explain. American Book Company v. White System of Jackson, 78 So.2d 582 (1955)

11. Brazil entered into a contract with the payee of a check under consideration to make improvements on his home. Brazil gave a check to the contractor based on the contractor's false representation that he had already purchased certain materials to be used in making the improvements on Brazil's home. After Brazil discovered no material had been purchased, he stopped payment on the check. By this time a holder in due course had acquired the check. Does Brazil have a defense that is good against a holder in due course? Citizens National Bank of Quitman v. Brazil, 233 S.E.2d 483 (Ga. 1977).

Checks and Electronic Fund Transfers

T his chapter discusses two important subjects dealing with the transfer of funds: checks and the electronic transfer of funds.

A check is a specialized type of draft, which is an instrument ordering one person to pay another. In the case of a check, the drawer of the check orders a bank to pay someone on the drawer's behalf. Thus a *check* is a draft drawn on a bank and payable on demand.

In the last few years, electronic fund transfers have become another method of transferring funds to take the place of checks. An *electronic fund transfer* involves the transfer of funds from one account to another account, not through the use of a piece of paper, but through an electronic transfer generated by plugging the appropriate data into a machine. This new form of transferring money poses

special problems, some of which are discussed in this chapter.

CHECKS

The Bank and Its Customers

The relationship between a bank and its customer depends on the status of the customer. Section 4–104(1)(e) of the Uniform Commercial Code (UCC) defines a customer as "any person having an account with a bank or for whom a bank has agreed to collect items and includes a bank carrying an account with another bank." Thus a customer can be someone other than a depositor. Generally, though, a customer is thought of as a depositor.

The Bank as Debtor. Ordinarily, when a person makes a deposit to his or her checking or savings account, the bank becomes a debtor of the depositor, who is then a creditor of the bank. If the depositor makes a special deposit, however, the bank will become the agent or trustee for the depositor. A deposit is general unless there is a specific agreement or understanding between the parties that the deposit is to be a special deposit. Whether a deposit is special or general depends on the bona fide contract between the depositor and the bank. For a special deposit to exist, there must be an express or clearly implied agreement that the deposit is made for some particular purpose— for example, safekeeping. Otherwise the deposit is general.

As a debtor of the general depositor, the bank is bound by an implied contract to repay the deposit, which may be money or other items, on the depositor's demand or order. The relationship between the bank and its depositor is determined by the terms of the deposit agreement, which is an express contract between the parties and is binding on them. An example of such a contract is the signature card signed by a depositor when opening his or her account at the bank. The debtor-creditor relationship attaches immediately upon the depositor's making the deposit. (Note that the provisions of Article 4 may be varied by agreement, but no agreement can disclaim a bank's responsibility for its own lack of good faith or failure to exercise ordinary care.)

The Bank as Agent. Even though the bank is a debtor, in discharging its obligations to the depositor the bank is also his or her agent and is bound by the rules of principal and agent. In this situation the bank is the agent and the customer the principal. This relationship arises, for example, when the bank pays checks drawn upon it. Thus the bank's relationship to a depositor is twofold: debtor-creditor and principal-agent.

Another situation where a principal-agent relationship arises between a bank and its depositor is when the bank seeks to obtain collection of an item for its depositor, who is the owner of the check. It should be noted that the status as agent is only a presumption and may be rebutted by evidence of a clear contrary intent.

Death or Incompetence of a Customer

In light of the principal-agent relationship between a bank and its customer, one might conclude from agency law that the bank's authority to act terminates upon the death or declaration of incompetency of the principal. Because of the large number of items handled by a bank, and the possible liability of the bank for a wrongful dishonor, the UCC instead relieves a bank of liability for payment of any instrument before it has notice of the death or incompetency of the drawer. The bank may pay (and another bank consequently may accept) an item until it knows of the death or of the adjudicated incompetence and has a reasonable opportunity to act on it.

Even if the bank knows of the death of a customer, the UCC permits the bank to pay or certify a check drawn on it for ten days after it receives notice. The bank may pay or certify a check unless a person claiming an interest in the account orders the bank to stop payment during this ten-day period. Suppose Smith writes a check on March 10 and someone presents it for payment on March 15. Even if Smith dies on March 11, and the bank knows it, the bank may honor the check. On the other hand, if an heir notifies the bank to stop payment of the check, the bank must comply.

CHECKS GENERALLY

Figure 27-1 illustrates how a check is processed in the banking system.

FIGURE 27–1
Life of a Check

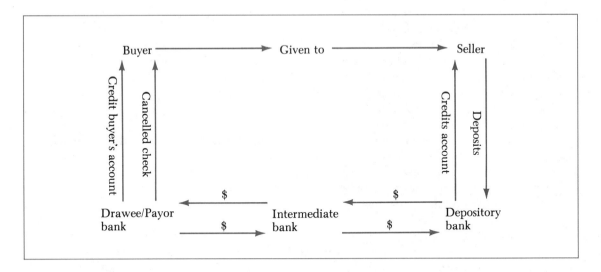

Failure to Indorse

If a customer deposits a check written by someone else, the bank will credit the customer's account for the amount of the check. The bank (called a depository bank) will then attempt to collect the check from the drawee bank (the bank on which the check was written). The customer could, of course, go directly to the drawee bank and cash the check, but this would be very time-consuming. By depositing the check, the customer authorizes the bank to collect the check for him or her.

What if the customer fails to indorse the check? Must the bank obtain the customer's signature? An order instrument must be indorsed in order for a proper negotiation to occur. Since we all make mistakes, the UCC has a special provision to speed up the collection process in this situation. Generally the depository bank may simply supply the customer's indorsement (Section 4–205[1]). This eliminates the necessity of calling the customer back to the bank to indorse the check.

Not an Assignment of Funds

Merely because one receives a check from someone else does not mean that one is entitled to the funds in the other's account. A check does not operate as an assignment of funds in the hands of the drawee (Section 3–409[1]). A bank is not liable on a check until it accepts it. As for the holder of the check, he or she has no recourse against the bank when it fails to accept a check. The holder of a check that has been dishonored must attempt to collect from the drawer of the check or from one of the indorsers.

Overdrafts

If the bank decides to honor a check, it may do so even though the charge creates an overdraft. A customer who writes a check for $550, but who has deposited only $500 in his or her account, has in effect authorized the bank to pay $550 to the payee. By implication, the customer has agreed to reimburse the bank for the other $50. The bank has no obligation to honor such a check because it creates an overdraft. At most banks the customer will soon discover that his or her check has bounced.

The following case involves an unusual situation. The bank did not bounce the check, but instead honored it even though this created an overdraft.

Pulaski State Bank v. Kalbe

Wisconsin Court of Appeals

364 N.W.2d 162 (1985)

Background: Pulaski State Bank (plaintiff) sued Kalbe (defendant). Kalbe signed a check that was later lost or stolen. The check was written for $7,260, payable in cash. Thereafter, it was stolen and cashed at a Florida bank. The Pulaski State Bank received the check on Thursday, January 8, 1982, and paid it on Monday, January 12, 1982. The check created an overdraft of $6,542.12. The bank commenced this action to recover $7,260. The trial court awarded the bank the amount of the check. Kalbe appealed. Decision: The Court of Appeals also ruled for the Pulaski State Bank.

Dean, Judge

The bank could properly pay the check even though it created an overdraft. Section 404.401(1), Stats, unambiguously states that a bank may charge a customer's account for an item otherwise properly payable even though the charge creates an overdraft. The bank's payment of an overdraft check is treated as a loan to the depositor, which may be recovered. Kalbe argues that checks creating unusually large overdrafts are not properly payable. She relies on the definition of properly payable, which "includes the availability of funds for payment at the time of decision to pay or dishonor." Section 404.104(1)(i), Stats. Section 404.104(1)(i), however, is a source of bank discretion and does not limit the bank's power to pay overdrafts. The statute gives banks the option of dishonoring checks when sufficient funds are not available. The bank may consider the check to be not properly payable and refuse to pay without risk of liability for wrongful dishonor. This does not prevent the bank from alternatively paying the overdraft check and, if it is otherwise properly payable, charging the customer's account. Section 404.401(1) places no limit on the size of the overdraft or the bank's reason for payment. Construing the statutes together, "otherwise properly payable" refers to those requirements other than availability of funds.

It is undisputed that in all other respects the check was properly payable. Kalbe does not argue that the bank honored an altered check or a check bearing a forged or unauthorized maker's signature. The check was therefore otherwise properly payable and Kalbe's liability is complete. The check creating the overdraft carried Kalbe's implied promise to reimburse the bank.

A duty of good faith, however, is imposed on the bank because it charged Kalbe's account according to the tenor of a completed item. Moreover, every contract or duty within ch 404 imposes an obligation of good faith in its performance or enforcement. For purposes of ch 404, good faith means honesty in fact.

> We cannot say that the bank's conduct evidences bad faith. The bank attempted to contact Kalbe before the midnight deadline. The bank also confirmed the check with the Florida bank. Kalbe did not report the check's loss or theft until finally contacted by the bank. . . .

Postdating

Sometimes, a customer will postdate a check—that is, he or she will issue the check before the date on the check has arrived. For example, the customer may give a check to the payee on March 1 but date it March 15. This is done when the person giving the check does not intend the check to be presented before March 15 (and very likely does not have sufficient funds in his or her account to cover the check on March 1). The UCC indicates that the negotiability of an instrument that is undated, antedated, or postdated is unaffected (Section 3–114[1]). The time such a postdated check is payable is determined by the stated date on the instrument. Thus if a customer writes a check on March 1 dated March 15, it is not payable until March 15. This is true even though a check is generally a demand instrument—that is, one payable on the demand of the payee or other holder of the instrument. The drawer hopes in this situation to pay his or her obligations on March 15. As the payee has physical possession of the instrument, the payee may run the check through on March 15. Unfortunately, this arrangement is filled with danger.

First, there is at least the argument that if the check goes through on March 15 and there are no funds to cover it, the drawer has issued an insufficient-funds check. A second possibility is that the payee will wrongfully cash the check before the date on the check. This also may result in the check's not being honored if the drawer does not have sufficient funds in his or her account. The drawer could be prosecuted in this situation. The more prudent practice is not to write checks until one has sufficient funds in the account to cover them. The Fair Debt Collection Practices Act makes it illegal for a debt collector to take a postdated check.

Failure of the Bank to Honor a Check

What if the bank fails to pay a check written by the drawer when it ought to have done so? The bank will be liable to the drawer for any damages proximately caused by a wrongful dishonor of the check. If the bank merely made a mistake, its liability is limited to actual damages proved. The UCC explicitly recognizes damages for arrest and prosecution and other consequential damages proximately caused by the wrongful dishonor. If a drawer wrote a check that the bank wrongfully failed to honor, he or she could be prosecuted. (In most states the drawer probably would not be arrested. Most states require that notice of the dishonor be given to the drawer and an opportunity to make the check good. During this period the drawer probably would be able to straighten the matter out with the bank.)

A wrongful dishonor is different from a failure to exercise ordinary care in the handling of an item. See UCC 4–103(5) for the damages stipulated when a bank fails to exercise ordinary care.

Stale Checks

A bank also has no obligation to its checking-account customers to honor uncertified checks presented more than six months after date. Such a check is referred to as a stale check (Section 4-404). On the other hand, the bank may honor such a check if it acts in good faith. If one receives a dividend check from GM on August 1 but neglects to cash it until March 1 of the following year, the check is stale. Nonetheless, it would seem reasonable to cash such a check, as GM presumably would want the check paid.

Prior to cashing a check that is more than six months old, a bank probably should consult with the drawer concerning the check. The drawer could argue that if the bank fails to check first with him or her, then a failure to make such a consultation prior to cashing the check violates the bank's obligation to act in good faith.

STOP PAYMENT

Right to Stop

Section 4-403 of the UCC gives a bank customer the right to stop payment of a check. Subsection 1 requires the customer to notify the bank in such time and manner as to give the bank a reasonable opportunity to act on the stop-payment order. The order must be received by the bank before it has paid a check in cash, accepted the check, or certified it.

Under Section 4-403(2) an oral order is effective for fourteen days; a written order is effective for six months. A written stop-payment order can be renewed for additional periods of six months. In the event a check is paid over a binding stop-payment order the burden is on the bank's customer to establish any loss incurred as a result of paying the check.

The right to stop payment is that of the drawer alone. An indorsee or payee has no right to order payment stopped on a check.

Section 4-405(2) does provide, when a bank's customer has died, that any person claiming an interest in the account of the deceased may stop payment on checks drawn on his or her account.

Defenses

Even though the drawer of the check has the right to stop payment, he or she remains liable to any holder of the instrument unless the drawer has a defense good against the holder. The drawer of a check cannot issue a check to a payee and expect to escape liability simply by stopping payment on the check. The drawer must establish a defense that can be successfully asserted against the holder of the instrument—for example, failure of consideration. If one writes a $450 check to an appliance store for a refrigerator, but the store never delivers the refrigerator, one would be able to stop payment on the check. If the store sued, one could successfully assert failure of consideration as a defense against the store. The store may not proceed against the bank for refusing to honor the check because a check is not an assignment of funds in the account of the drawer.

If the drawer of a check is so unfortunate as to write a check like the drawer in the previous example, and it is transferred to a holder in due course, or someone having the rights of a holder in due course, he or she may be liable on the check even if he or she stopped payment on it. The defense of failure of consideration is a personal defense and therefore may not be asserted successfully against a holder in due course. On the other hand, a real defense, like adjudicated insanity, may be asserted against a holder in due course.

When a bank pays a check over a stop-payment order, Section 4-407 gives the payor bank a right of subrogation. Subrogation means the bank acquires whatever rights in the check the drawer had in that instrument. This right is given to prevent unjust enrichment to the extent necessary to prevent a loss to the bank by reason of its improper payment of a check.

Payment over Stop-Payment Order

What if the bank pays a holder in due course over a stop-payment order? Section 4–407(a) gives the bank the rights of the person it pays. As the drawer has no defense against that person unless he or she has a real defense, the bank will be able to collect the amount paid from its customer, even though the check was paid over a stop-payment order. (Note that the burden of establishing a loss is on the customer under Section 4–403[3]).

Conversely, if the bank reimburses its customer when it pays a check over a stop-payment order, it receives any rights of the drawer against the payee or any other holder of the check with respect to the transaction out of which the check arose.

What if a drawer issues a check as indicated earlier for a refrigerator but the store never delivers the refrigerator? If the bank honors the check over a stop-payment order, the bank may proceed against the store for the amount it received under the check. This section does not permit, of course, a double recovery by the bank.

Comment 8 to Section 4–403 recognizes inferentially that a bank and its customer may agree under Section 4–103(1) to waive or *limit* the bank's liability for improper payment over a stop-payment order, as long as the payment is not due to a lack of ordinary care or a lack of good faith. There is a split of authority regarding the validity of these agreements. A few cases hold that such a provision is not binding because it was not supported by consideration. The general rule seems to be that these agreements are, in fact, valid.

The following case illustrates the operation of the stop-payment rule.

Thomas v. Marine Midland Tinkers National Bank

Civil Court of the City of New York

381 N.Y.S.2d 797 (1976)

Background: Thomas (plaintiff) commenced this action to recover the sum of $2,500 from the Marine Midland Tinkers National Bank (defendant), claiming that the defendant wrongfully paid a check drawn against his account after receiving a proper and timely stop-payment order.

Decision: The court ruled for Thomas.

Egeth, Judge

On Dec. 8, 1973, plaintiff entered into agreement to purchase two rugs from one Ralph Gallo for a price of $10,500. A $2500 deposit was given by delivery of a post-dated check, #221, dated Dec. 10, 1973, and drawn upon plaintiff's account at the defendant bank's 140 Broadway, New York City branch. Plaintiff agreed to pay the balance of the purchase price, to wit: $8000, by Dec. 30, 1973, and took the smaller rug home that day. At opening, on Dec. 10, 1973, plaintiff went to the branch of defendant bank where his account was maintained, spoke to an officer, Kenneth Hurley, with whom he had prior business relations, and directed that payment be stopped upon the subject check. All required information was correctly given (except the check was described as #22 rather than #221, the correct number), and a stop payment memo was issued by the bank. On the afternoon of the next day, Dec. 11, 1973, the check was presented for payment at the very same branch, and it was cashed. Thereafter, plaintiff's account was debited the $2500 paid on the check. The same day, without knowledge that the check had been cashed, plaintiff telephoned Gallo, told him the contract was rescinded, and asked him to pick up his rug. Two or three days later, the rug was picked up at plaintiff's apartment. Plaintiff had no knowledge that the check had been cashed until he received his January bank statement. He called Gallo, demanding return of the $2500. The request was refused with an indication that Gallo might seek to enforce the purchase agreement. The defendant bank rejected plaintiff's request to restore the $2500 to his account. At present plaintiff has no rug in his possession nor does he have his $2500.

UCC Sec. 4–403(1) explicitly provides:

> A customer may by order to his bank stop payment of any item payable for his account but the order must be received at such time and in such manner as to afford the bank a reasonable opportunity to act on it prior to any action by the bank with respect to the item described in Section 4–303.

It is undisputed that a detailed direction was given to the defendant to stop payment on the check in question (except for a single digit mistake on the check number), the order was confirmed in writing early in the morning, and the subject check was paid at the very same branch in the afternoon of the following day. Under these circumstances, I find that adequate notice and a reasonable opportunity was given to the bank, and that it must be held accountable for its act in making payment of the check in contravention of the stop payment order.

A day and one half is more than reasonable notice to enforce a stop order on a check presented at the very same branch, and payment of the item by the bank thereafter constitutes a breach of its obligations to honor the stop order. The normal problem of reasonable computer lag when dealing with a great number of other branches of a large bank has no relevancy to the facts at bar, where all transactions occurred in a single branch. The single digital mistake in describing the check in the stop order is deemed trivial, and insignificant. Enough information was supplied to the bank to reasonably provide it with sufficient information to comply with the stop payment order. The bank is therefore held responsible for its act of improperly making payment upon the check.

Defendant bank has virtually rested on plaintiff's case, in that no affirmative defense has been asserted or proved and no real evidence has been adduced by said defendant. The defendant contends that plaintiff has failed to prove a prima facie case in that no evidence was introduced in the plaintiff's case to negate the ultimate right of the payee of the stopped check to retain the proceeds thereof.

In this case, the defendant bank chose to try its case against the plaintiff alone without asserting any affirmative defense as to non loss, or adducing any evidence to negate the claimed loss at trial. The defendant bank chose rather to maintain a position that plaintiff was required to come forward with evidence as to the underlying transaction to negate any inference of non loss or lesser loss in order to prove plaintiff's prima facie case.

As previously stated the bank's position in this regard is in error under the law existing before and after the enactment of the Code. Therefore plaintiff has proven his prima facie case and defendant's motion to dismiss on that ground must be denied.

Plaintiff's good faith act of surrendering possession of the rug to the payee after giving defendant a stop payment order, and his assumption of compliance therewith by the defendant, is understandable and reasonable. Unless done without good faith, such surrender certainly may not defeat defendant's statutory accountability under UCC, section 4–403(1) for failure to comply with a proper stop order. The existence of defendant's subrogation right to stand in the shoes of the payee (UCC section 4–407[b]) does not negate the obligation of the subrogee bank to come forward with some evidence in support of any such claimed right. In this case defendant chose not to do so. Defendant therefore failed to produce any evidence to negate plaintiff's prima facie case. Under the circumstances, there are no issues of fact to be determined regarding plaintiff's failure to meet his burden of establishing the fact and amount of loss under UCC section 4–403(3) because of the defendant's failure to come forward with anything which controverts plaintiff's prima facie showing of loss.

Accordingly, defendant's motions are denied and plaintiff is granted judgment against the defendant in the sum of $2500 together with interest, costs, and disbursements as demanded in the complaint.

CERTIFICATION

As clearly stated in Section 3–411, certification is an acceptance. A bank has no obligation to certify a check in the absence of a specific agreement to do so. But once a bank has certified a check, it is obligated to honor it. When it certifies a check, the bank becomes primarily liable on the instrument. That being the case, there is no right as far as the drawer is concerned to stop payment of a certified check.

Certification of a check by a bank at the drawer's request does no more than affirm the genuineness of the drawer's signature and to indicate that there will be funds on deposit to meet the item when the check is presented for payment. If the drawer obtains certification of his or her check, the drawer remains secondarily liable, although the bank is primarily liable.

The holder of a check may also have the check certified. The drawer and all prior indorsers will be released from liability if the holder takes this action. Of course, a holder could present the check for payment in this situation; thus it seems reasonable to release the drawer and indorsers from liability.

It is possible for a certified check to be indorsed after the bank has certified it. In this instance the certification remains effective, and the indorser will have all the duties imposed by Section 3–414.

UNAUTHORIZED SIGNATURES AND ALTERATIONS

Customer's Duty to Discover and Report

The customer of a bank has a duty to discover and report to the bank forgeries and alterations on his or her checks. This duty arises once the bank has sent its customer both a statement of his or her account and the items honored by the bank (Section 4–406[1]). The customer must exercise "reasonable care and promptness" in examining the statement and items to discover unauthorized signatures or any alterations. If he or she discovers an improper signature or an alteration, the next step is to notify the bank "promptly." This means the customer must contact the appropriate person at the bank to enable the bank to take action on the check. Thus, after a customer receives a statement accompanied by the checks honored by the bank, he or she must review them to make certain they are proper.

If the customer fails to comply, he or she may not assert an unauthorized signature or any alteration as a defense against the bank if the bank establishes that it suffered a loss as a result of the customer's failure to comply with Section 4–406(1). The burden of proof is on the bank to establish that it suffered a loss.

Consider the following example. Pete on March 1 receives his checks and statement from the bank. Rather than examining them at that time, he throws them in his desk. After several months Pete decides to examine the checks. He discovers a forgery of a check. If the bank establishes that it suffered a loss as a result of his failure to notify it promptly, the loss falls on Pete.

Acts by the Same Wrongdoer

Once a customer has received a statement and an item on which there has been an unauthorized signature or alteration, a second rule comes into play that covers additional acts by the same wrongdoer. This rule covers indorsements as well as unauthorized signatures of the customer and alterations. A customer has a reasonable period of time not exceeding fourteen calendar days to notify the bank of any unauthorized signature or alteration. If the customer fails to notify the bank, any loss caused by an unauthorized signature or alteration by the same wrongdoer after this four-

teen-day period will be borne by the customer.

This puts the burden on the customer to police his or her account in order to prevent a wrongdoer from continuing his or her improper actions. Once a customer notifies the bank of any such unauthorized signature or alteration, the risk of loss shifts back to the bank to guard against future unauthorized signatures or alterations by the same wrongdoer.

Consider the following case. Mary receives her checks and statement on June 1. Her signature had been forged on a check that had been returned to her on June 1. Susan, an acquaintance of Mary, forged the check. Susan then forges another check on Mary's account on June 5. Mary receives the second check along with her statement and other checks on July 1. Susan then forges another check on July 18. The third check is returned to Mary on August 1.

On August 3 Mary discovers all the checks forged by Susan. She notifies the bank that day and asks the bank to recredit her account.

The UCC gives Mary fourteen days from the time she learns of the first forgery to notify the bank. The bank must recredit her account for the first two checks; however, it need not recredit her account for the third check because it was honored after the date by which Mary was obligated to notify the bank of the forgery—June 15. The bank may charge Mary's account for any check honored by the bank after June 15 up to the time it receives notice of the forgeries from Mary.

If the bank honors a forgery by Susan after Mary notifies the bank on August 3, the bank is not acting reasonably and it will not be able to charge her account for any check it honors after August 3.

Bank's Burden of Proof

Before a bank may charge its customer's account pursuant to either Section 4–406(2)(a) or (b), the bank must establish that the customer failed to exercise reasonable care and promptness in examining his or her statement and the items included with the statement and that the customer failed to notify the bank promptly. Even if the bank succeeds in establishing this, however, the risk of loss shifts back if the customer proves a lack of ordinary care on the part of the bank in paying an item (Section 4–406[3]).

If the bank loses the suit against its customer on an unauthorized drawer's signature, it may proceed against anyone who broke the presenter's warranty that he or she had no knowledge that the drawer's signature was unauthorized (Section 4–207).

The following case involves a series of forgeries by the Medford Irrigation District's bookkeeper.

Medford Irrigation District v. Western Bank

Oregon Court of Appeals

676 P.2d 329 (1984)

Background: Western Bank (defendant) appealed from a summary judgment in favor of Medford Irrigation District (plaintiff). The record showed that between September 25, 1980, and October 17, 1980, Medford's bookkeeper forged the name of its manager on several checks drawn on its account with Western. Western paid the checks and debited Medford's account.

It is conceded for purposes of the summary judgment motion that the plaintiff was negligent in not supervising the bookkeeper and in not auditing the accounts and reviewing the bank statements. It is also conceded that the plaintiff's negligence substantially contributed to the forgeries. Plaintiff argued that Western did not follow reasonable commercial banking standards and failed to exercise ordinary care in paying the forged checks.

Decision: The Court of Appeals ruled for Medford Irrigation District.

Richardson, Presiding Judge

Ordinarily the law places the risk of loss from forgeries on the bank. Any unauthorized signature is generally "wholly inoperative as that of the person whose name is signed." . . . Because a forged signature is wholly inoperative, a forged check is not "properly payable," . . . , and a bank cannot debit the depositor's account. If, however, the depositor's negligence substantially contributes to the forgery, the depositor is precluded from asserting the improper payment against a bank which pays the check in good faith and in accordance with reasonable commercial standards of the banking industry. . . . Also, if the depositor fails to exercise reasonable care in examining its bank statement and promptly reporting any unauthorized debits to the bank, the depositor is precluded from asserting the unauthorized payment unless it establishes lack of ordinary care on the part of the bank in paying the check. . . .

Western submitted affidavits and depositions in opposition to plaintiff's motion for summary judgment. It argues that there is a genuine issue of material fact as to whether it exercised ordinary care and whether its procedures comported with reasonable commercial banking standards. Western utilizes a computer check payment system.

Checks for a face amount under $5,000 are paid without human intervention or "sight review" of the signatures. Checks are received for payment at Western's data processing center in Portland, and, unless there is a "hold" or a "stop payment" order for a check, it is paid automatically by computer. The cancelled checks are ultimately forwarded to the customers along with the bank statement. The computer is programmed to "kick out" checks with a face amount of $5,000 or more. Absent specific instructions from a customer, only checks of $5,000 or more are individually reviewed for authorized signatures or alterations.

The reasonableness of commercial banking standards must be analyzed in the context of a bank's duty in relation to the depositor's account. Although a procedure may be common throughout the banking industry, it is not, by that fact alone, a reasonable procedure. Implied in the relationship between a bank and its checking account depositors is a contractual undertaking on the part of the bank that it will only discharge its obligation to a depositor on an authorized signature. ORS 73.4040 specifies that an unauthorized signature is wholly inoperative, and a check with an unauthorized signature is not properly payable by the bank. . . . The responsibility of the bank is to use ordinary care in paying only checks with authorized signatures. Thus, the procedure utilized must reasonably meet that responsibility to be considered due care or reasonable commercial banking standards in the context of ORS 73.4060 or 74.4060.

We do not hold that a bank must adopt a particular procedure, such as "sight review," in order to comply with the statutory mandate. We do hold that the procedure used must reasonably relate to the detection of unauthorized signatures in order to be considered an exercise of ordinary care or reasonable commercial banking standards. Western's approach is automatically to pay all checks under $5,000 without any procedure to detect unauthorized signatures on those items. While that approach, based on considerations of cost and efficiency, may be a prudent business decision and followed by most banks, it does not meet the bank's responsibility under the statutes.

Western contends that, if it is determined that it did not exercise due care or follow reasonable commercial practices, there remain issues of fact as to causation and damages. This argument is premised on ORS 74.1030(5):

> "The measure of damages for failure to exercise ordinary care in handling an item is the amount of the item reduced by an amount which could not have been realized by the use of ordinary care, and where there is bad faith it includes other damages, if any, suffered by the party as a proximate consequence."

Western presented the affidavit of one of its officers to the effect that he had reviewed the checks in issue and had concluded that the forgeries were so well done that they would not have been detected by individual scrutiny. Western argues that it is entitled to a fact determination whether an exercise of ordinary care would have resulted in rejection of the checks. It contends that a fact finder could conclude that some or all of the checks would have been paid even with the use of sight review and that therefore it would not be liable for those checks under ORS 74.1030(5).

The structure of the Uniform Commercial Code creates a contractual arrangement between a bank and a depositor to the effect that the bank will pay only items which are properly payable. . . . An item with an unauthorized signature is not properly payable. If the customer's negligence substantially contributes to the making of the unauthorized signature, it cannot assert that the item is not properly payable unless the bank is also negligent. If it is determined that the bank is negligent, the defense of the customer's negligence is not available, and the bank is strictly liable for improperly debiting the customer's account. There is thus no issue as to the causal relationship between the bank's lack of due care and the customer's loss if the loss is established.

We conclude that, because Western failed to exercise ordinary care or to follow reasonable commercial banking practices, it is foreclosed from asserting plaintiff's negligence and is liable for paying the face amount of the forged checks. There is no issue of fact as to Western's liability or the amount. The court did not err in granting summary judgment for plaintiff.

FORGED SIGNATURE OF THE DRAWER

Signature of Drawer Required

For an instrument to be negotiable, it must be signed by the maker or drawer. Section 3–401(1) clearly indicates that no one is liable, even to a holder in due course, on an instrument unless his or her signature appears on it. Thus where someone forges the signature of the drawer on his or her checks, the drawer is not liable. Only if a customer's authorized signature appears on a check may the bank charge his or her account.

The UCC assumes that the bank will recognize the signatures of its customers and will not honor forgeries. For example, Stan manages to steal one of Robert's checks without Robert learning of the theft. Stan makes the check payable to himself and forges Robert's signature. The bank charges Robert's account. When Robert receives his checks and statement, he discovers the forgery. Robert immediately notifies the bank. Assuming Robert was not negligent, the bank must recredit his account. If a bank honors a check that the customer alleges to be a forgery, the bank must establish that the signature is genuine. Even so, Section 3–307(1)(b) states that "the signature is presumed to be genuine or authorized" except if the signer died or has become incompetent. This means that, until evidence is introduced supporting a finding that the signature is a forgery or unauthorized, the plaintiff is not required to prove that it is authentic.

Other Persons Liable

Assuming that the bank paid a check, and the customer establishes that his or her signature was unauthorized, the bank may not charge his or her account. It may be, however, that the bank can collect from someone other than its customer.

One possibility is for the bank to bring suit based on the theory of breach of warranty. The bank might attempt to recover its loss from the party that presented the check to the bank for payment. In order to recover from such a party, the bank must establish that the party it paid *knew* of the forgery at the time it was paid on the check. However, if the party the bank paid did *not* know of the forgery of the drawer's signature, the bank will be unable to recover its loss from that party.

Another possibility is to sue the forger. Section 3–404(1) states that, even though an unauthorized signature does not bind a customer of the bank, it operates as the signature of the unauthorized signer in favor of any person who in good faith pays the instrument or takes it for value.

Of course, if a customer ratifies an unauthorized signature, the bank may charge the customer's account.

Negligence by Customer

The bank may also charge the customer's account if the customer was negligent. Section 3–406 states that if a drawer's negligence substantially contributes to a material alteration of an instrument or to the making of an unauthorized signature, he or she may not assert the lack of authority against a bank that pays the instrument in good faith and in accordance with reasonable commercial standards.

At one point in time banks examined each check to determine if the drawer's signature matched the signature the drawer had provided to the bank on the signature card. If the bank employee who examined the signature card carelessly performed his or her job, a check that might otherwise not have been paid might have ended up being honored by the bank. In such a case, even if the customer has been negligent, the bank also would have failed to observe reasonable commercial standards, and thus would not have a right to charge its customer's account for the check. Comment 7 to Section 3–406 indicates that the most obvious case of negligence is a

drawer who uses an automatic signing device and is negligent in looking after it.

Alice uses a mechanical check writer. She leaves the check writer and her checks on her desk at all times. An employee of Alice's takes a check and, by using the check writer, makes a check out to himself. Because Alice was negligent, she cannot require the bank to recredit her account if it honored the check.

Section 4–406 imposes a duty on a bank's customers to examine their checks and notify the bank promptly of any forgeries. Failure to comply with this rule may result in a customer's being unable to raise the defense of forgery against the bank, unless the customer proves a lack of ordinary care on the part of the bank in paying a check.

Today, most banks automatically process checks by some form of computerized processing. They do not do a sight review of every check because the cost of conducting such a review is quite high. This shows, however, that the banks must choose some manner of reviewing checks that reasonably relates to the detection of unauthorized signatures.

PAYMENT ON A FORGED INDORSEMENT

In order for a drawee bank to charge a drawer's account properly when it honors one of his or her checks, the bank must pay only a holder of the check. With respect to bearer paper, this does not create a problem. But what if the drawer wrote a check to a specific payee, whose indorsement was forged or unauthorized? No one who comes into possession of the check can be a holder because of the forged indorsement. (As no one could become a holder of the check, no one could become a holder in due course with respect to the check.) That being the case, it would be improper for the bank to charge its customer's account.

ETHICS BOX
The Effect of Unethical Behavior on the Law

Many of the legal rules that have been described in this part of the text are designed to anticipate problems arising from forged or stolen documents, or from a failure to honor promises to pay money. Many of the individual instances involve illegal or clear-cut, intentional unethical behavior.

The legal rules make many of the transactions more cumbersome and costly. If the level of behavior were higher it might not be necessary to have so many restrictive rules. Think of how our legal system and society might be different if unethical behavior were a rare occurrence.

In the event a bank charges its customer's account in this situation, it must recredit the customer's account for the amount of the check. In this case the bank has breached its contract with the drawer or has breached the customer–depository-bank relationship. This assumes that after the bank honors the check, the drawer discovers the forgery and notifies the bank within a reasonable time. The bank, in turn, could sue its transferors for breach of warranty of title or genuineness of signatures.

For example, Bill writes a check and makes it payable to Glenn. The check is stolen from Glenn by Richard. Richard forges Glenn's indorsement and cashes the check at Bill's bank. The bank charged Bill's account. In the meantime Glenn informs Bill the check has been stolen. When Bill receives the check from the bank, he calls Glenn who assures him the indorsement was forged. If Bill notifies his bank within a reasonable time after learning of the forged indorsement, the bank must recredit Bill's account.

In addition to a suit by the drawer against the drawee (payor) bank, there is also the possibility of a suit by the owner of the instrument when a bank has paid on a forged indorsement. Section 3–419(1)(a) stipulates that an instrument is converted when it is paid on a forged indorsement. This means that any person who pays a check bearing a forged indorsement will be liable to the true owner of the instrument. In effect, there will be a series of conversions. Section 3–419(2) indicates that if suit is brought against the drawee, the drawee's liability is the face amount of the instrument. On the other hand, a collecting bank is not liable in conversion or otherwise to the true owner beyond the amount of any proceeds remaining in its hands. The following case deals with a forged indorsement.

Levy v. First Pennsylvania Bank, N.A.
Superior Court of Pennsylvania
36 UCC Rep. Serv. 184 (1985)

Background: The Levys (plaintiffs) filed suit against First Pennsylvania Bank (defendant-appellant). The Levys were clients of the law firm of Bolger & Picker. When they sold their business, Novelty Printing, in February 1978 the Levys instructed Richard Robinson, a partner at Bolger & Picker, to open an account for them in the name of B&J Corp. at a local brokerage firm. When the treasury bills purchased by the broker matured, Robinson was directed to deposit checks sent to him by the broker into the Levys' bank accounts at Girard Bank and Industrial Valley Bank.

Robinson received three checks in the sums of $75,000, $75,000, and $72,776.87 from the broker. Instead of depositing them in the Levys' bank accounts, he deposited them in his own personal account at First Pennsylvania. Robinson accomplished this by signing the back of the checks with the names of the payees, B&J Corp. and Novelty Printing Company Profit Sharing Trust, and the notations "deposit to account No. 773–784–4." This was Robinson's personal account. He later withdrew the money and disposed of it. When the scheme was discovered, the law firm's insurer paid to the Levys the amount of the checks.

The Levys then brought this action against First Pennsylvania for conversion. The bank joined Bolger & Picker and Robinson as codefendants. At a nonjury trial the Levys were awarded $222,776.87 with interest from September 14, 1979, the date upon which the insurer reimbursed the Levys. The bank appealed.

Decision: The Pennsylvania Superior Court ruled for the Levys.

Olszewski, Justice

Appellant assigns a number of errors to the lower court's opinion; we address them seriatim. Appellant first argues that it cannot be held liable for making final payment on the instruments because Robinson's endorsements were not forgeries. The argument is rooted in the language of 13 Pa CS § 3419 (Purdon's 1984 Pamphlet), which states:

> "§ 3419. Conversion of instrument; innocent representative
> "(a) Acts constituting conversion. An instrument is converted when:
> "(1) a drawee to whom it is delivered for acceptance refuses to deliver it on demand;
> "(2) any person to whom it is delivered for payment refuses on demand either to pay or return it;
> "(3) it is paid on a forged instrument."

Appellant avers that the endorsement was not forged because Robinson had the authority to endorse the checks. If he did have the authority to endorse, appellant claims Robinson's writing of the payees' names constituted an endorsement in blank, and then the checks were properly payable to anyone under 13 Pa CS § 3204. What subsequently happened to the checks would be irrelevant to the bank's liability, in appellant's view.

The trial court found that Robinson's authority was limited to endorsing checks for deposit into the Levys' accounts at Girard and IVB. It found that neither express nor implied authority to endorse in blank existed, and that the endorsements were unauthorized.

Under Pennsylvania law, the issue of agency is for the finder of fact. Here, the court, as finder of fact, concluded that Robinson had no authority to endorse the checks as he did. When a finding of fact is adequately supported by the record, we will not overrule the trial court. The record indicates that the Levys told Robinson to deposit the checks in their accounts. Accordingly, we do not disturb the court's finding.

The question remains as to whether an *unauthorized* endorsement is the same as a *forged* instrument under 13 Pa CS § 3419. Although no court in the Commonwealth has held on this point, to our knowledge, other courts have held that "forgery" under UCC § 3–419 includes "unauthorized signature." We conclude that an unauthorized signature is the same as a forgery for purposes of an action for conversion under 13 Pa CS § 3419. The trial court properly found the bank liable for paying the checks to Robinson.

In certain instances, even though the name of the payee is forged, there can be a valid negotiation of the check (Section 3–405). In this case the preceding rules concerning forgery do not control. Also, if a customer fails to indorse a check, his or her bank may indorse the check for him or her (Section 4–205).

FULL PAYMENT CHECKS

Another problem relating to the use of checks has to do with the relationship between the Code and the contract doctrine of accord and satisfaction. As a matter of contract law, if A

TABLE 27-1 EXAMPLES OF CHECKS NOT
PROPERLY PAYABLE

Check	Is It Properly Payable?
Check without a drawer's signature	No
Check dated 1/17 and paid 1/18	Yes
Check with a forged indorsement	No
Check that would create an overdraft	Yes

owes B a debt and there is no dispute concerning the amount due, a promise of B to discharge A's debt in return for payment of an amount less than that due is unenforceable for lack of consideration. This is because by promising to pay a portion of the total debt already owed B, A is incurring no legal obligation that did not already exist. However, if the amount A owes B is subject to dispute, an agreement by B to accept a compromise sum to discharge A's indebtedness constitutes consideration for the promise to pay. An accord and satisfaction have been achieved.

Courts differ with respect to the use of an indorsement signed "under protest," when a check has been marked paid in full. Some courts treat the indorsement and deposit of a check as an accord and satisfaction. They do not give effect to the under-protest indorsement. Other courts, because of UCC Section 1–207, treat such an indorsement as a reservation of rights, and therefore do not regard the cashing of the check as an accord and satisfaction. There is substantial disagreement between the states over the effect of 1–207 with respect to full satisfaction checks.

The following case represents one court's response to the issues involved.

PREVENTIVE LAW

———

F rank visits his dentist. The dentist performs some work and two weeks later sends Frank a bill for $800. Frank thinks this amount is totally out of line. He writes the dentist a letter to that effect, and encloses a check for $500, an amount Frank believes is reasonable. On the check Frank writes, "Paid in Full." The dentist indorses the check and writes "without prejudice" on the check. The consequence of the dentist's actions depend on the state the dentist lives in. Some states permit a person to cash such a check and bring suit for the difference between what is owed and amount of the check. Other states treat cashing the check as full payment of the debt.

Rather than taking this approach, the dentist could have immediately returned the check to Frank. He could then demand payment of $800. If Frank refused to pay the full amount, the dentist could sue Frank.

Chancellor, Inc. v. Hamilton Appliance Co., Inc.

U.S. District Court, New Jersey
30 UCC Rptr. 12 (1980)

Background: Chancellor (plaintiff) sued Hamilton Appliance (defendant). The defendant retail store purchased from the plaintiff wholesale distributor twelve Pioneer stereo systems for $2785.64. As a result of quality problems, it was agreed that eight of the units would be returned to the plaintiff for full credit.

A dispute arose as to the value of the remaining four units, which the defendant attempted to resolve by forwarding to the plaintiff a check for $734.88, with a notation, "paid in full," on the front. The plaintiff endorsed the check "without prejudice" and later advised the defendant that the check was accepted without prejudice to the plaintiff's rights. The plaintiff then filed suit for the remainder of the original purchase price on the four units.

Decision: The court ruled for Hamilton Appliance.

Saunders, Judge

This contract action raises the novel issue whether the Uniform Commercial Code (NJSA 12A:1–207) has altered the common-law principle of accord and satisfaction affecting "full payment checks." More specifically, the question is whether a disputed claim is extinguished when the debtor tenders to the creditor a check marked "paid in full" and the creditor deposits the check after endorsing it "without prejudice" and notifies the debtor he is reserving his right to contend for the balance of the claim. The court finds that there was a genuine dispute between the parties as to the amount of money due from defendant to plaintiff.

The general rule in New Jersey as to the effect of the acceptance of a full payment check was announced in *Decker* v. *Smith & Co.* When a claim is unliquidated and a check is tendered in full settlement, giving the creditor notice of this condition, the creditor's retention and use of the check constitutes an accord and satisfaction.

Sixty years later the court was faced with the issue whether an explicit reservation of rights preventing an accord and satisfaction arose when the creditor obliterated a statement that the check was in full payment and substituted his own notation that it was in partial payment only. The court found that once the check was deposited by the creditor, no matter what alterations its president personally made on the reverse side, an accord and satisfaction was reached. Hence, the New Jersey rule has been that when a check is tendered as payment for an unliquidated claim on the condition that it be accepted in full payment, the creditor is deemed to have accepted this condition by depositing the check for collection notwithstanding any obliteration or alteration.

Based upon the above facts, defendant argues that an accord and satisfaction was reached between the parties at the time the check was deposited notwithstanding the fact that the plaintiff indorsed the reverse side of the check "without prejudice" and advised defendant by its attorney that the check was accepted without prejudice to plaintiff's rights.

Plaintiff argues that the Uniform Commercial Code, Section 1–207, alters the common-law accord and satisfaction principle and permits the creditor to accept and cash the check offered and to sue the debtor for the balance if the creditor explicitly reserves his rights.

Section 1–207 states:

> A party who with explicit reservation of rights performs or promises performance or assents to performance in a manner demanded or offered by the other party does not thereby prejudice the rights reserved. Such words as "without prejudice," "under protest" or the like are sufficient.

The plaintiff argues that the legislature intended Section 1–207 to redefine the law of accord and satisfaction and to restrict the use of the "full payment check." A review of the Comments to Section 1–207 and its legislative history reveals no such intent. The New Jersey Study Comment does not mention the rule on accord and satisfaction.

The Uniform Commercial Code Comments to Section 1–207 do not reflect a legislative intent to change the common-law rule. Comment One states that "This section provides machinery for the *continuation of performance along the lines contemplated by the contract* despite a pending dispute . . ." (Emphasis supplied). An accord and satisfaction involves a new contract, not the contemplated performance of the original contract. By using the "full payment check" the buyer is seeking to fulfill, not continue, its duty to pay.

Lastly, the legislative history of the Uniform Commercial Code is not supportive of the plaintiff's argument. If a change in existing law was contemplated by the adoption of Section 1–207, it must be presumed that the New Jersey Study Commission and/or the legislature would have pointed this out expressly.

The court does not find any evidence in either the legislative history or the commentaries to Section 1–207 supporting the plaintiff's position that the law of accord and satisfaction has been altered.

If the court were to conclude that a creditor could reserve his rights on a "full payment check," a convenient and informal device for the resolution of disagreements in the business community would be seriously impeded. The court is hesitant to impair such a valuable, informal settlement tool where there is no indication that the legislature intended that result. I find that the acceptance by the creditor of a check offered by the debtor in full payment of a disputed debt is an accord and satisfaction of the debt and no condition of protest or attempted reservation of rights can affect the legal quality of the action. I hold that Section 1–207 has not altered the common-law rule of accord and satisfaction.

ELECTRONIC FUND TRANSFERS

Electronic fund transfers will be of increasing importance in the future as more and more financial institutions begin to utilize this method of transferring funds. Checks and cash may someday virtually disappear. This will be both good and bad for consumers. On the one hand, it will be much easier and quicker to transact business and to transfer funds at all hours of the day. On the other hand, such systems will generate a great deal of information, much of which could conceivably be used against persons maintaining such accounts.

Types of Electronic Fund Transfers

There are several types of electronic fund transfers (EFTs) currently in use. Typically, in order to initiate a transaction on any of the machines involved, the consumer has a card that gives him or her access to the machine. Often, the consumer also has a secret number to prevent others from using the card should it fall into the wrong hands.

Point-of-Sale Terminals. In some places around the country point-of-sale (POS) terminals are utilized. Typically, these terminals are located in a business. This permits the business to transfer funds from an individual's account to the account maintained by the business. Thus a point-of-sale terminal might be found in a grocery store. When a customer purchases groceries, the terminal at the grocery store permits the customer to transfer money from his or her account to the store account.

Automated Tellers and Cash Dispensers. A second type of EFT device is the automated-teller machine (ATM) or the cash dispenser (CD). The automated-teller machine permits the user to withdraw cash, make deposits, and transfer money from one account to another without dealing with bank personnel. Automated-teller machines provide a number of benefits for consumers, the foremost of which is twenty-four-hour banking. A card-holder may make deposits or withdrawals, for example, at any time of day or night.

The cash dispenser merely dispenses cash. These machines may be either on-line or off-line. If they are on-line, the machine is connected to a central processing computer that has access to the consumer's account. Thus the entire transaction may be completed immediately. In off-line machines the machine stores the data for collection at a later time. This means that the on-line system is much more complex, but it completes all transactions at the time a consumer initiates them.

Pay-by-Phone Systems. A third EFT device is the pay-by-phone system. Here, the consumer calls his or her bank and orders the bank to pay the persons or businesses he or she specifies, thereby eliminating the need for writing a check. This system is frequently used to pay utility bills.

Preauthorized Direct Deposits and Automatic Payments. Finally, there are preauthorized direct deposits and automatic payments. An employer might enter into an agreement with its employee to deposit his or her wages periodically in the employee's account at a bank. This is a preauthorized direct deposit. Such a deposit saves a trip to the bank for the employee.

Conversely, the buyer of a product might agree with a seller to have monthly payments automatically withdrawn from the buyer's account and transferred to the seller's. Such an arrangement is frequently made between the buyer of a house and the mortgage company. The buyer need not worry about forgetting to make a payment because each payment is withdrawn from the buyer's account automatically.

The Electronic Fund Transfer Act

Congress in 1978 passed the Financial Institutions Regulatory and Interest Rate Control Act. One part of this legislation is the Electronic Fund Transfer Act (EFTA), which regulates financial institutions that offer electronic fund transfers involving an account held by a consumer. The Act, which became effective in 1980, establishes some rules by which the parties to these transactions will be governed.

Definitions. The primary objective of the Electronic Fund Transfer Act (EFTA) is to protect certain rights of consumers dealing with such electronic systems. A consumer under the act is any *natural* person. The term *electronic fund transfer* under the act means "any transfer of funds, other than a transaction originated by check, draft, or similar paper instrument, which is initiated through an electronic terminal, telephonic instrument, or computer or magnetic tape so as to order, instruct, or authorize a financial institution to debit or credit an account."

Disclosure of Terms and Conditions. The EFTA requires that the terms and conditions of electronic fund transfers be disclosed at the time a customer contracts for such services. The financial institution must disclose matters such as the consumer's liability for an unauthorized transfer, what charges may be imposed, the right of the consumer to stop payment of a preauthorized electronic fund transfer, and the liability of the institution to the consumer.

Documentation. Each time a customer initiates an electronic fund transfer, the financial institution must make available to the customer written documentation of the transfer.

The documentation must indicate the amount involved and the date of the transfer, the type of transfer, the identity of the customer's account from which or to which funds are transferred, the identity of any third party to whom or from whom funds are transferred, and the location or identification of the electronic terminal involved.

The financial institution must provide each customer with a periodic statement for each account that may be accessed by electronic means.

Preauthorized Transfers. A preauthorized electronic fund transfer is an electronic fund transfer authorized in advance to recur at substantially regular intervals.

A preauthorized electronic fund transfer

that debits a customer's account may be utilized only if the customer agrees in writing and is furnished a copy of the authorization. The customer can stop payment on such preauthorized transfers if he or she notifies the financial institution orally or in writing at any time up to three business days preceding the scheduled date of such transfer. If the financial institution requests it when the oral notice is given, the customer must provide written confirmation of the oral notice within fourteen days of an oral notification.

In the event the preauthorized transfers vary in amount the financial institution or the payee must give the customer reasonable advance notice of the amount to be transferred and the scheduled date of the transfer.

Error Resolution. Within sixty days after receiving a financial statement, a customer may notify his or her financial institution of any errors in the report. Such notice obligates the financial institution to investigate the alleged error and report the results of the investigation to the customer within ten business days. (If notice of error is given to the financial institution orally, the institution may require the customer to provide written confirmation within ten business days.)

In the event the results of the investigation reveal that an error occurred the financial institution must promptly correct the error. This must be done within one business day after such an error is discovered.

Alternatively, the financial institution may provisionally recredit the customer's account pending an investigation of the account. This must be done within ten business days after receiving notice of error. The financial institution then has forty-five days after receipt of the notice to conclude the investigation. If during this period it determines that an error did not occur, the financial institution has three business days after arriving at this conclusion to deliver or mail an explanation to the customer.

If the financial institution fails to follow this procedure, or if contrary to the evidence it knowingly and willfully concludes that the customer's account was not in error, the customer is entitled to treble damages.

Customer Liability for Unauthorized Transfers. Once the customer is in possession of means of access such as a card and a secret number, his or her liability, in the event of an unauthorized transfer, will not exceed the lesser of $50 or the amount obtained prior to the time the financial institution becomes aware that an unauthorized electronic fund transfer has been or may be effected. However, the customer must notify the financial institution of the loss or theft within two days after discovering the loss or theft of a card or other means of access.

If a bank learns on June 1 that an unauthorized transfer from a customer's account on May 31 has occurred, the maximum that the customer can lose is $50. If the transfer was for $25, the customer loses $25. But if the transfer was for $75, the customer loses only $50.

If the customer fails to report the loss or theft within two days, the customer's liability in this situation is limited to the lesser of $500 or the amount of unauthorized transfers that occur after two business days following the customer's discovery of the loss or theft but prior to his or her notifying the financial institution.

Suppose the customer loses his card on June 1 but fails to report the loss until June 10. If a thief manages to make a withdrawal from the customer's account on June 2 for $100 and another withdrawal on June 8 for $300, the customer would owe the bank $300, if the bank can establish that the customer learned of the loss on June 1.

If the customer fails to report an unauthorized use within *sixty days* of receiving a periodic statement, he or she is liable for losses resulting from *any* unauthorized transfer that appeared on the statement if the financial institution can show the loss would not have occurred but for the failure of the customer to report the loss within sixty days. This provision is similar to UCC Section 4–406, which puts the burden on customers to examine their statements in a timely fashion.

Liability of the Financial Institution. Under the EFTA a financial institution is liable to a customer for all damages proximately caused by its failure to make an electronic fund transfer, in accordance with the terms and conditions of an account, in the correct amount or in a timely manner when properly instructed to do so by the customer.

There are certain exceptions to this rule—for example, if the electronic terminal does not have sufficient cash to complete the transaction or the customer does not have sufficient funds in his or her account. If the failure was not intentional and resulted from a bona fide error, the financial institution is liable for the actual damages proved.

The financial institution is also liable for damages proximately caused by its failure to credit a deposit of funds and to fail to stop payment of a preauthorized transfer from a customer's account.

Other than the failure to stop payment, a financial institution is not liable if it shows that its failure to act resulted from an act of God or other circumstances beyond its control or from a technical malfunction that was known to the customer at the time he or she attempted to initiate an electronic fund transfer or, in the case of a preauthorized transfer, at the time such transfer should have occurred.

REVIEW PROBLEMS

1. What, if anything, should a customer do when he or she receives his or her statement and checks from the bank?
2. Under what circumstances, if any, might a person be liable for a check when his or her signature, as the drawer of the check, has been forged?
3. Under what circumstances, if any, could a bank charge its customer's account for a check it honored even though the customer had given the bank a stop-payment order on the check?
4. Must a bank certify a check presented to it? If it does certify such a check, how does this affect the drawer's obligation on the check?
5. What are the four types of electronic fund transfer services?
6. On June 1 Jones received her Zip Card in the mail from her bank. The Zip Card is utilized by her bank's automated-teller machine. Before she received the means of identifying herself (her secret number) from the bank, a bank employee stole her card on June 4. The employee somehow gained access to her account and withdrew $1,000. On these facts, does Jones have any liability? What would be the result if Jones failed to report the loss of her card until August 1? If Jones had received both the card and the means of identification, what would be her maximum liability?
7. Mark Wade wrote a check for $250 on September 30 in payment of his rent for October. The check was dated October 10. He gave the check to the manager at the Villa Apartments. The manager assured Mark that he would not deposit the check until October 10. Mark did not have enough money in his account on September 30 to cover the check, but he planned

to deposit his paycheck on October 1. Mark's employer failed to pay him on October 1. In the meantime the manager of the Villa Apartments accidentally deposited the check to the Villa account. If the check is presented to Mark's bank, could it honor the check?

8. Ron Mather wrote a check on his account on July 1, 1986. This check was presented for payment on February 1, 1987. What type of check is one that is presented so long after it was written? Can the bank honor it?

9. Amy Gardner wrote a check out and made it payable to the order of Andrew Clark. This check was stolen from Andrew, and the thief cashed the check. The thief forged Andrew Clark's signature on the back of the check. Amy's bank then honored the check and charged her account. Soon thereafter Andrew informed Amy of the theft. When Amy notified the bank of the forgery, must the bank recredit her account, if she informed the bank immediately?

10. Murphy operated a restaurant. His bookkeeper wrote a series of checks on his account by forging his name on the checks. When the checks were returned to the restaurant, the bookkeeper reviewed the checks and the statement. Several months later Murphy learned of the forgeries and notified his bank. He demanded that the bank recredit his account. The bank argued that Murphy's negligence had substantially contributed to the forgeries. What could Murphy argue even if he admitted that he had been negligent?

11. Smith, Whalley's bookkeeper, forged and cashed a series of checks, drawn on Whalley's business account with Bank. This occurred between January and May. Smith was in complete charge of Whalley's books and records. Whalley's president routinely examined the bank statements to determine the account balance but did not examine any of the canceled checks. After examining the statements, the president returned the statements and checks to Smith. No one reported the forgeries to Bank until Smith was discharged in June, when irregularities were found. Bank acted in good faith in paying the forged checks. May Whalley recover the amount of the forged checks from Bank? Was Whalley's procedure with respect to the canceled checks and bank statement an exercise of reasonable care? See George Whalley Co. v. National City Bank of Cleveland, 380 N.E.2d 742 (Ohio App. 1977).

12. Kidwell had a checking account with Exchange Bank, upon which the president of Kidwell was authorized to draw. Smith, the corporate secretary of Kidwell, forged the president's signature on sixty-five checks made payable to her. This occurred over a three-year period. These forgeries were not reported by Kidwell to Exchange Bank until after the end of the three-year period. The facts disclose that the quality of the forgeries ranged from crude to fair; that Exchange Bank handled a large volume of checks compared to other banks; and that Exchange Bank may not have compared all the signatures on the checks against the signature card bearing the signature of Kidwell's president. Will Kidwell's failure to report the forgeries to Exchange Bank excuse any liability of the bank for improper payment? Will Exchange Bank be liable at all for the improper payments? See Exchange Bank and Trust Co. v. Kidwell Construction Co., Inc., 463 S.W.2d 465 (Tex. Civ. App. 1971).

13. Zenith maintained an account with Marine Midland Bank on which either the president or vice-president of Zenith was authorized to sign checks. In 1972, between February and November, Zenith's bookkeeper drew twenty fraudulently signed checks. Marine Midland paid these

checks and charged them to Zenith's account. Each month Marine Midland sent the statements and checks from the account to Zenith for inspection. Each month, the bookkeeper received the statements and canceled checks and approved the debits. In November the subterfuge was discovered. Marine Midland was unable to recover $4,297 of the amounts paid on the checks and refused to recredit Zenith's account for this loss. Zenith sued Marine Midland to compel such action. Must Marine Midland recredit Zenith's account? Zenith Syndicate, Inc. v. Marine Midland Bank, 23 UCC Rep. Serv. 1267 (1978).

Secured Transactions

Much of the nation's economy is based on transactions involving credit. Credit is often provided to buyers by manufacturers, wholesalers, and retailers who are willing to accept payment in the future in order to market their products. In addition, institutions such as commercial banks, factors, and finance companies make loans to finance business inventories, business operations, and consumer sales.

Sometimes providing credit for individuals or business firms subjects the lender to considerable risk because of the possibility that the debt will not be paid. This risk is reduced if the lender can obtain an interest in property as assurance that the debtor will meet his or her obligation. When a creditor establishes a valid security interest and the debtor fails or refuses to pay, the creditor can take the property or have it sold and the proceeds applied against the debt. A creditor who acquires a security interest in personal property is known as a *secured creditor.* The property providing the security is called *collateral.*

This chapter discusses the nature and scope of security interests in personal property and fixtures. Chapter 40 deals with transactions in which real property is the collateral. Much of the law dealing with secured transactions in which personal property is the collateral is based on Article 9 of the Uniform Commercial Code (UCC).

ARTICLE 9

Background of Article 9

Article 9 of the UCC provides a comprehensive scheme for administering the many different types of financing using personal property as security.

One of the major objectives of the drafters of Article 9 was to provide a uniform and simple system for creditors to establish a security interest. Thus, Article 9 supersedes prior legislation dealing with such security devices as chattel mortgages, conditional sales, trust receipts, factor's liens, and assignments of accounts receivable. For these devices the drafters substituted the single term "security interest."

Terminology of Article 9

In addition to "security interest," a number of other terms have specific meanings as they are used in Article 9. The following are important for understanding how a creditor protects an interest in particular personal property or fixtures. Most of these will be discussed in greater detail as they relate to particular provisions of Article 9.

Secured Party. A lender, seller, or other person in whose favor there is a security interest, including a person to whom accounts or chattel paper have been sold (Section 9–105[m]).

Security Agreement. This is an agreement that creates or provides a security interest (Section 9–105[2]).

Financing Statement. This document gives notice to all persons searching the records that the secured party claims an interest in certain collateral owned by the debtor (Section 9–402). Subject to certain requirements to be discussed later, the security agreement may be filed instead of a separate financing statement.

Although the UCC no longer retains distinctions based on form, for purposes of filing the financing statement in the appropriate place it is extremely important to understand what type of collateral is involved. If the secured party improperly classifies the collateral, he or she may file the financing statement in the wrong place and lose whatever protection he or she might have had against other creditors of the debtor.

Goods. "Goods" are defined in Section 9–105(h) as all things that are movable at the time the security interest attaches. Goods become _fixtures_ when they become so related to particular real estate that an interest in them arises under real estate law (Section 9–313[1][a]). Goods are classified in one of four categories: _consumer goods, equipment, farm products,_ or _inventory._ The classification of goods depends on their use, but goods cannot be classified in more than one category in any single transaction.

Goods are _consumer goods_ if they are used or bought for use primarily for personal, family, or household purposes (Section 9–109[1]). A TV bought from a retail merchant for use in the home is a consumer good.

Goods are _equipment_ when they are used primarily in business if they are not inventory, farm products, or consumer goods (Section 9–102[2]). A machine used in operating a plant is considered equipment.

Goods are _farm products_ if they are crops, livestock, or supplies used or produced in farming operations, or if they are products, crops, or livestock in their unmanufactured states (for example, maple syrup), and if they are in possession of a debtor engaged in raising, fattening, grazing, or other farming operations. When crops or livestock or their products come into the hands of someone not engaged in farming operations, they cease to be farm products. Eggs in the hands of a farmer are farm products, but when the farmer sells those eggs to a dairy company, they become inventory in the hands of the dairy company.

Goods are _inventory_ if they are held by a person for sale or lease or to be furnished under service contracts or if they are raw materials, work in process, or materials used or consumed in business (Section 9–109[4]). If materials used or consumed in a business have a long life span, they are equipment; but if they are consumed in the manufacture of a product, they are inventory. For example, bolts used in manufacturing a car are inventory, but a drill used in manufacturing a car is equipment.

Purchase-Money Security Interest. A security interest taken by a seller in items sold to a buyer to secure all or part of the price is a purchase-money security interest (PMSI). This term also encompasses a security interest taken by a person who gives value to a debtor to acquire rights in or the use of collateral if the collateral is so used (Section 9–107). If a retail merchant sells goods to a purchaser and retains a security interest in these goods, it is a PMSI. Similarly, if a bank makes a loan to a man to purchase a boat and he buys a boat with the money, a PMSI in the boat may have been created. Under the UCC, purchase-money obligations often have priority over other obligations.

Instrument. According to Section 9–105(i), "instrument" means a negotiable instrument (as defined in Section 3–104, for example, a note) or a security (as defined in Section 8–102, for example, stocks) or any other writing that evidences a right to the payment of money and is not itself a security agreement or lease and is of a type that is, in the ordinary course of business, transferred by delivery with any necessary indorsement or assignment.

Document of Title. A document of title is a written instrument issued by or addressed to a person who holds goods for another. It identifies those goods unless they are fungible, that is, part of an identifiable mass (Section 1–201[15]). For example, an order from a farmer who has stored corn addressed to the storage facility to deliver 10,000 bushels of the corn to a railroad is a document of title. Other documents of title are bills of lading, dock warrants, dock receipts, and warehouse receipts.

Chattel Paper. A writing or writings that evidence both a monetary obligation and a security interest in or a lease of specific goods are chattel paper. If the transaction consists of a security agreement or a lease and an instrument or a series of instruments, the *group* of writings taken together constitutes chattel paper.

When a merchant sells goods to a consumer, the merchant may retain a security interest in the goods sold. Suppose a retail merchant sells a television set to a consumer and retains a security interest in it. The contract by which he retains a security interest in the TV is a security agreement: the merchant is the secured party; the buyer is the debtor; and the TV is the collateral. If the merchant wishes to finance his operations, he may sell a number of such contracts to a bank. With respect to the bank, these contracts are collectively referred to as *chattel paper.* The retail dealer is a debtor with respect to the bank, and the bank is the secured party. The customers are referred to as *account debtors.* Figure 28-1 illustrates a transaction involving the use of chattel paper and the creation of a purchase-money security interest.

Account. An *account* is any right to payment for goods sold or leased or for services rendered that is not evidenced by an instrument or chattel paper, whether or not it has been earned by performance (Section 9–106). Accounts are not evidenced by writing. This term covers the ordinary account receivable. If a clothing store sells clothes to customers on an open account and gives them thirty days to pay, the accounts of the customers can be sold to a financer. The financer would be a secured party, the clothing store the debtor, and the customers the account debtors.

General Intangibles. These are any personal property other than goods, accounts, chattel paper, documents, and money (Section 9–106). The term covers the various contractual rights and personal property that are used as commercial security—for example, goodwill, trademarks, and patents.

Scope of Article 9

Article 9 applies primarily to security interests in personal property and fixtures arising out of agreements. The article does not apply to statutory liens such as the mechanic's or artisan's lien. These liens are created by legislation to protect contractors and others who provide

FIGURE 28–1
A Purchase-Money Security Interest

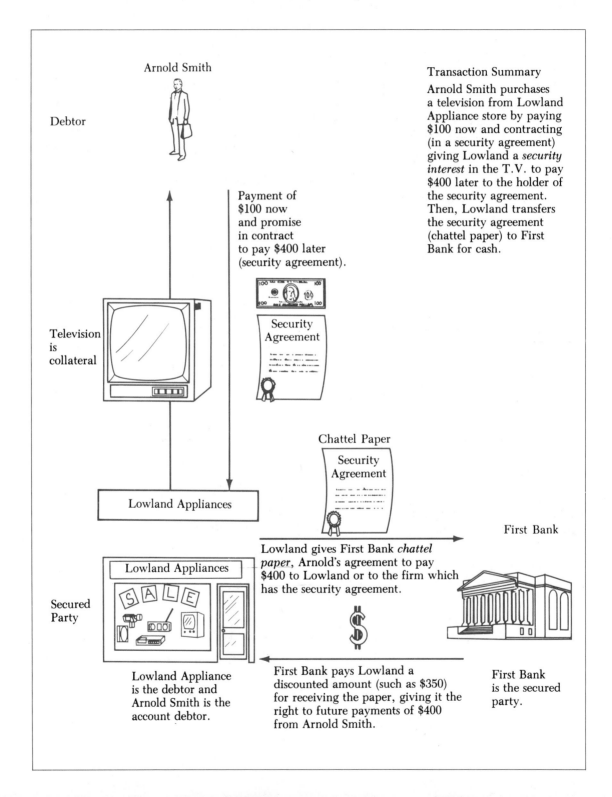

Arnold Smith

Debtor

Payment of
$100 now
and promise
in contract
to pay $400 later
(security agreement).

Television
is
collateral

Security
Agreement

Transaction Summary

Arnold Smith purchases
a television from Lowland
Appliance store by paying
$100 now and contracting
(in a security agreement)
giving Lowland a *security
interest* in the T.V. to pay
$400 later to the holder of
the security agreement.
Then, Lowland transfers
the security agreement
(chattel paper) to First
Bank for cash.

Lowland Appliances

Chattel Paper

Security
Agreement

First Bank

Lowland gives First Bank *chattel
paper*, Arnold's agreement to pay
$400 to Lowland or to the firm which
has the security agreement.

Lowland Appliances

SALE

Secured
Party

Lowland Appliance
is the debtor and
Arnold Smith is the
account debtor.

First Bank pays Lowland a
discounted amount (such as $350)
for receiving the paper, giving it the
right to future payments of $400
from Arnold Smith.

First Bank
is the secured
party.

improvements to real property. Article 9 does, however, cover priority problems between statutory liens and secured transactions (Section 9–310). Additionally, the article applies to transactions involving the sale of accounts and chattel paper.

Although Article 9 applies to consumer transactions, its provisions do not replace other state legislation such as small loan acts, retail installment sales statutes, and other regulatory measures applicable to consumer financing.

The major exclusion from Article 9 coverage is security interest in real estate. Fixtures, however, are covered, and in some circumstances real estate and Article 9 transactions are connected. For example, if Jones owns a promissory note and a real estate mortgage securing funds he has advanced to Smith, Jones may use them as collateral when borrowing from Brown. Section 9 also applies to transactions in which the collateral is minerals, standing timber, or growing crops.

Purpose of Article 9

In order to limit risk in secured financing, the creditor has two major objectives. First, he or she needs assurance that security rights in the collateral are protected if the debtor defaults. This is accomplished if the creditor obtains an enforceable security interest. Second, the creditor needs protection against third parties establishing superior rights in the collateral. To do this, the creditor must take steps in addition to those required to establish rights against the debtor. In both cases, however, the initial step is to establish a security interest.

ESTABLISHING AN ENFORCEABLE SECURITY INTEREST

Three events must take place before a creditor obtains a security interest in the collateral. These events do not have to occur simultaneously or in any particular order. Once they have occurred, the secured party's right in the collateral is said to *attach*. Attachment establishes the secured party's right to the collateral against the defaulting debtor.

The secured party's right attaches:

1. When the parties agree that the secured party has a security interest
2. The debtor receives value
3. The debtor has rights in the collateral

The Security Agreement

A *security agreement* creates or provides a security interest (Section 9–105[1]). Unless the collateral is in the possession of the secured party, the security agreement must be in writing. The agreement must contain a description of the collateral and be signed by the debtor. A description that reasonably identifies the collateral is sufficient; however, care should be taken to describe the collateral since insufficient identification can lead to litigation. In the following case, the trustee in bankruptcy argued that the bank's security agreement was invalid because it did not disclose the amount of the bank's loan or the loan's maturity date. Despite the absence of that information, the court found the security agreement did reasonably identify the collateral.

In the Matter of Charles O. Cooley, Bankrupt

U.S. Court of Appeals
624 F.2d 55 (1980)

Background: Charles O. Cooley, Jr., borrowed funds from the First National Bank of Louisville (appellee) to finance Cooley's business. To complete this transaction, Cooley and his wife executed documents giving the bank a security interest in certain collateral. When Cooley became bankrupt, Michael Clare (trustee-appellant) brought an action in the bankruptcy court asserting that the security agreement was invalid. The bankruptcy judge decided that the security agreement was enforceable; the U.S. District Court affirmed; and the trustee in bankruptcy, Clare, appealed.

Decision: The Court of Appeals affirmed.

Lively, Circuit Judge

The record contains the following written instruments: A Loan and Security Agreement dated April 9, 1974, given "to secure the payment and performance of all liabilities of the Borrower (Charles O. Cooley, Jr., dba Cooley's Lawn Service) to the Bank . . . ," a Financing Statement bearing the same date, and a promissory note from Charles O. Cooley, Jr., and Patricia E. Cooley, his wife, to the bank for $10,000 base amount plus a finance charge of $4,301.60, dated November 7, 1974. The bankruptcy judge conducted a hearing and made a finding of fact that the bankrupts executed and delivered to the bank on April 9, 1974, a promissory note for $3,000 and that the security agreement of that date granted the bank a security interest in collateral which included the personal property of Cooley's Lawn Service that is in dispute.

The trustee . . . argues that the security agreement of April 9th was insufficient because it did not disclose the amount of the loan or the maturity date. The Uniform Commercial Code (UCC), as adopted by Kentucky, sets forth the requirements of a valid security agreement. There is no requirement that the amount secured or the date of maturity be shown. These are essential contents of the underlying debt instrument (the promissory note) but not of the security instrument. The security agreement here specifically provided for future advances. The flexibility intended by the UCC would be severely limited by a requirement that a security agreement state a fixed amount and maturity date. We know of no authority for the appellant's position.

Finally, the trustee asserts that the security agreement is invalid because the description of the collateral is insufficient under Kentucky law. He relies principally upon the decision in *Mammoth Cave P.C.A.* v. *York,* where it was held that a security agreement which listed "farm equipment" as collateral and stated that it included "replacements of and additions to equipment" was not adequate to perfect a security interest in a subsequently acquired tractor.

The collateral was described in the security agreement before us as follows:

(a) All inventory of the Borrower, now owned or hereafter acquired;
(b) All contract rights of the Borrower, now existing or hereafter arising;
(c) All accounts receivable of the Borrower, now existing or hereafter arising;
(d) All goods, instruments, documents of title, policies and certificates of insurance, securities, chattel paper, deposits, cash or other property owned by the Borrower or in which it has an interest which are now or may hereafter be in the possession of the Bank or as to which the Bank may now or hereafter control possession by documents of title or otherwise;

(e) Proceeds and products of all of the foregoing; (and)

(f) All machinery and equipment, including machinery and equipment which are or will become fixtures, office supplies, furniture, office and store fixtures, raw materials, work in process, and the proceeds and products of all of the foregoing.

K.R.S. Section 355.9–110 provides that any description of property is sufficient "whether or not it is specific if it reasonably identifies what is described."

We believe *Mammoth Cave P.C.A.* v. *York* is distinguishable from the present case. Here the borrower was a going business, shown in the security agreement and the recorded financing statement as "Charles O. Cooley, Jr., DBA Cooley's Lawn Service." The listing of collateral, described by categories, included all the usual assets of a going business. It would be contrary to the purpose of the UCC to hold that lawn tending equipment of this borrower was not sufficiently described by the language used in the security agreement.

Although the formal requirements of a security agreement are minimal, most also contain references to the following items:

After-Acquired Property. After-acquired property is collateral that becomes the subject of a security interest after the parties have reached an initial agreement. One example would be a retailer's inventory purchased to replace goods subject to the original security agreement. When an after-acquired property clause is included in a security agreement, the secured party acquires a "continuing general lien" in property acquired to replace the original inventory.

Future Advances. Security agreements may include a clause covering advances of credit made by the secured party after the agreement is signed. This is necessary if the advance is to be secured by the original agreement. The clause might read: "This security agreement shall include future advances or other indebtedness that debtor may owe to secured party during the time that the security agreement is in force, whenever incurred." Rights of the debtor established by an after-acquired property clause and a future advance clause are often referred to as a *floating lien* (Section 9–204, Comment z). Combining the after-acquired property and future advances clauses facilitates the financing of inventory and accounts receivable where the collateral is goods being retailed or raw materials being manufactured.

A number of other subjects are covered in most security agreements. They include, but are not limited to, the following:

1. Amount of the debt
2. Terms of payment
3. Responsibility for care and maintenance of the collateral
4. Acceleration of payment rights
5. Right to additional collateral

Additional Requirements

In addition to a valid security agreement, two other conditions must be met before the creditor can obtain a security interest in the collateral. First, the debtor must receive value. If the secured party extends credit, makes a loan to the debtor, or provides the debtor any consideration sufficient to support a simple contract, this requirement has been fulfilled. Second, the debtor must have rights in the collateral. The debtor does not have to have title to the collateral. A purchaser acquiring property under an agreement in which the seller retains title has rights in the collateral sufficient to support a creditor's security interest.

PERFECTION OF A SECURITY INTEREST

A security interest that has attached may be enforced by the secured party against the debtor. The secured party also needs protection against claims to the collateral that others might assert arising out of their transactions with the debtor. To secure this protection, the secured party must *perfect* his or her security interest in the collateral. By perfecting the security interest, the secured party puts the world on notice that he or she claims a special interest in the collateral. Other people dealing later with the debtor may realize that the secured party has a superior interest in the property that may well be used to satisfy the debt.

Methods of Perfecting a Security Interest

The secured party may perfect a security interest by either of the following methods:

1. Filing a financing statement in the appropriate public office
2. Taking possession of the collateral

In some transactions security interests are automatically perfected when they attach to the collateral. Whether the secured party may perfect by filing, by taking possession, or by relying upon automatically obtaining a perfected security interest depends to a large extent upon the classification of the collateral involved.

In certain instances the secured party auto-matically obtains a perfected security interest without taking possession of the collateral or filing. Article 9 provides that a merchant who sells consumer goods to a buyer on credit does not need to file a financing statement or take possession of the goods to perfect interest in the items sold. With the exception of motor vehicles and fixtures, a perfected security interest arises automatically when the merchant's security interest in the collateral attaches (Section 9–302[d]). The merchant's security interest is a purchase-money security interest.

Additionally, Article 9 establishes temporary automatic security interests in two situations. The most important is a ten-day security interest in any proceeds a debtor receives from the sale of the collateral. A twenty-one-day security interest measured from the time of attachment is automatically perfected in certain negotiable interest and stocks in the debtor's possession (Sections 9–304, 9–306[3]).

Perfection by Filing

The most common method of perfecting a security interest is by filing a financing statement. This document, when properly filed, gives the public notice of the secured party's interest in the collateral. Public notice needs to be provided so other creditors or transferees of the debtor may learn of the creditor's claims to the collateral.

The Financing Statement. A financing statement must give the names of the debtor and the secured party and their respective addresses, be signed by the debtor, and contain a statement indicating the types—or describing the items—of collateral. A financing statement is effective even if it contains minor errors. When the financing statement covers crops, timber to be cut, minerals, or goods that are to become fixtures, the financing statement must describe the real estate involved. Normally a standard form is used for the financing statement (see Figure 28-2); however, under the UCC a copy of the security agreement may be used if it contains all of the preceding information and is signed by the debtor. Parties usually do not file the security agreement. If the parties wish to amend the financing statement, the UCC requires filing of a writing signed by both debtor and secured party.

FIGURE 28–2
Financing Statement
(Approved Form UCC Sec. 9–402)

This financing statement is presented to a filing officer for filing pursuant to the Uniform Commercial Code.

Name of Debtor (or Assignor) ....
Address ....
Name of Secured Party (or Assignee)..................
Address ....

1. This financing statement covers the following types (or items) of property:
   (Describe)...
2. (If collateral is crops) The above described crops are growing or are to be grown on:
   (Describe Real Estate and specify Name of Record Owner) ....
3. (If collateral is goods which are or are to become fixtures) The above described goods are affixed or to be affixed to:
   (Describe Real Estate and specify Name of Record Owner) ....
4. (If proceeds or products of collateral are claimed) Proceeds—Products of the collateral are also covered.
   Signature of Debtor (or Assignor)....................
   Signature of Secured Party (or Assignee) ......

Many financing statements are filed incorrectly because the wrong name is used for the debtor. Section 9–402(7) provides that the name on a financing statement is sufficient if it gives the individual, partnership, or corporate name of the debtor, whether or not it adds other trade names or names of partners. Suppose that Alfred Zimmer operates a business

under the name Southern Pit Barbeque. Should the statement be filed under Z or S? Here, it should be filed under the name of the debtor—Zimmer. If Zimmer changed his name, or if he were operating a corporation that changed its name, must the secured party refile its financing statement? Yes; if the filed financing statement becomes seriously misleading, it will not be effective to perfect a security interest in collateral acquired by the debtor more than four months after the name change.

Place of Filing. The place of filing depends on the type of collateral covered by the security agreement. If the secured party improperly classifies the collateral and files in the wrong office, secured status as to the described collateral does not exist.

For collateral related to land such as fixtures, goods that are to become fixtures, timber to be cut, or minerals, filing generally is required in the county where the land is located. For other types of collateral the states have different rules concerning the proper place to file. A number of states direct that filing take place in the county of the debtor's residence or, if the debtor is not a resident of the state, in the county where the goods are kept. Other states take the position that filing is most effective when centralized on a statewide basis. This reduces costs and facilitates the acquisition of credit information. These states generally require that filing, except for land-related collateral, be done in the office of the Secretary of State, located in the state capital.

Time and Duration of Filing. A financing statement can be filed at any time—even before a security agreement is made or before a security interest attaches to the collateral (Section 9–402[1]). A secured party might want to file before attachment because this may aid in getting a higher priority than other parties claiming an interest in the same collateral by filing.

A filed financing statement is effective for five years from the date of filing. To assure its continuing validity after five years, the secured party must file a *continuation statement*; otherwise, the security interest becomes unperfected. A continuation statement may be filed by the secured party within six months prior to the expiration of the five-year period. The continuation statement makes the original statement valid for an additional five years. Succeeding continuation statements may be filed. The continuation statement need be signed by only the secured party.

What if the secured party allows the financing statement to lapse at the end of five years, although the debtor is still obligated to him, and an intervening creditor files an effective financing statement? Section 9–403(2) states that the security interest "is deemed to have been unperfected as against a person who became a purchaser or lien creditor before lapse." Suppose a bank lends money to A and properly perfects a security interest in A's collateral; then four years later a finance company also lends money to A and perfects its security interest in the same equipment. If the bank allows the filing to lapse, the finance company is entitled to priority over the bank's security interest, which became unperfected by the lapse.

Once all of the obligations of the parties have been completed under the security agreement, the secured party must file a termination statement with each filing officer with whom the financing statement was filed. If consumer goods are involved, this statement must be filed within one month or, following written demand by the debtor, within ten days. If other than consumer goods are involved, and the debtor demands in writing a termination statement, the secured party must furnish a termination statement for each filing officer with whom the financing statement was filed. If the secured party fails to file as specified or to send a termination statement within ten days after a proper demand, he or she will be liable to the debtor for $100 and for any loss caused the debtor by such failure (Section 9–404).

Perfection by Possession

For most types of collateral an alternative to perfection by filing is for the secured party to take possession of the property. Article 9 permits a secured party to perfect a security interest in goods, negotiable documents, or chattel paper by taking possession of them. The secured party may choose, however, to perfect an interest in these items by filing a financial statement.

A security interest in money or in negotiable instruments, such as shares of stock, can be perfected only by the secured party's taking possession. For instance, if A borrows money from B bank with the security being 100 shares of General Motors stock, the bank must hold the stock in order to have a perfected security interest. A security interest in accounts or general intangibles must be perfected by filing.

A secured party in possession of collateral is under a duty to use reasonable care in its custody and preservation. The secured party must keep the collateral identifiable unless it is fungible, in which case it may be commingled. The secured party responsible for a loss to the collateral through failure to use reasonable care bears that loss, but the security interest is retained. Reasonable expenses incurred to preserve the collateral and insurance costs are borne by the debtor.

PRIORITY

In some situations other people besides the secured creditor claim an interest in the collateral. A secured creditor may have to compete with someone who has purchased the collateral from the debtor, holders of statutory liens, general creditors, a trustee in bankruptcy, other secured creditors, and even the government. Because of the different interests involved, numerous state and federal statutes influence the solution to these conflicts.

Article 9 of the UCC does, however, provide the rules for resolving many of them.

The Unperfected Security Interest

As a general rule, Article 9 establishes a priority for the holder of a perfected security interest against other creditors and transferees from the debtor. Although the key to the secured creditor's protection is perfection of the security interest, limited protection is afforded an unperfected security interest. The unperfected security interest does enjoy priority over general creditors of the debtor who have established no lien on the collateral.

General creditors, however, have little difficulty in overcoming this priority. The general creditor may obtain a judgment against the debtor and have the sheriff levy on the property the creditor wishes to claim, even though the creditor knew of the secured party's interest in the collateral. Because of the relative ease with which a general creditor can establish a priority over an unperfected security interest, the prudent secured creditor will always perfect to obtain maximum safety.

Conflicting Security Interests

When two or more persons claim security interests in the same collateral, the general rule of priority is stated in Section 9–312(5)(a) as follows:

a) conflicting security interests rank according to priority in time of filing or perfection– *Priority dates from the time a filing is first made covering the collateral or the time the security interest is first perfected, whichever is earlier, provided that there is no period thereafter when there is neither filing nor perfection* [emphasis added].

Under Article 9 a party may file with respect to particular collateral before it comes into existence. A security interest cannot be perfected, however, until the security interest attaches to the collateral. A secured party must take possession of the collateral or the debtor must sign a security agreement and receive value from the secured party and acquire rights in the collateral for the perfection of the security interest to occur.

Section 9–312(5)(a) specifies that priority occurs when a filing is first made covering the collateral *or* when the security interest is first perfected, whichever is earlier. This rule makes it advantageous for a secured party to file its financing statement as soon as possible. The date of the filing will control if the security interest is subsequently perfected. It is also possible to perfect by taking possession of certain types of collateral. In this case the perfection is effective from the time the secured party takes possession of the collateral.

Taking into consideration the times at which perfection is effective and the rules stated in Section 9–312(5), consider the following examples: A perfects his security agreement against collateral held by X on January 1. B perfects a security interest in the same collateral on February 1. Because A perfected his interest on January 1, A has priority (Section 9–312[5][a]). Suppose that A's security interest in X's collateral attaches on January 1 and B's security interest in X's collateral attaches on February 1, but neither secured party perfects his interest. Whichever secured party first perfects his interest (by taking possession of the collateral or by filing) takes priority, and it makes no difference whether or not he knows of the other interest at the time he perfects his own. Thus if B perfects by filing before A, his interest has priority over A's. Section 9–312(5)(b) states the rule where neither party perfects. This rule is somewhat theoretical, but if neither perfects, the first interest to attach wins—this would be A, whose interest attached on January 1.

Suppose instead that a secured party files a financing statement on June 1 but fails to perfect his or her security interest at that time because the security interest has not yet attached to the collateral. On July 1 a second secured party perfects an interest in the same collateral. On August 1 the first secured party's interest attaches to the collateral, and the security interest is thus perfected on August 1. In this situation the first secured party has priority because the filing was on June 1 and this was before the second secured party's interest became effective on July 1. Once again, there is an advantage under the UCC to filing as soon as possible.

Purchase-Money Security Interest

The UCC places the holder of a purchase-money security interest (PMSI) in a beneficial position. Article 9 provides a claimant with a PMSI priority over a conflicting security interest in the same collateral if the PMSI is perfected within ten days of the time the debtor takes possession of the collateral (Section 9–312[4]). Priority for a PMSI may be justified on grounds that the party enabling property to be purchased deserves to be protected.

A PMSI provides protection for the seller in the following situation, although a perfected security interest already exists in the collateral: First State Bank advances funds to Jones Manufacturing and perfects a security interest in all the firm's equipment. The security agreement contains a provision extending the bank's interest to any after-acquired equipment. At a later date Jones purchases a new machine on credit from Smith Machine Company. As long as Smith Machine files a financing statement within ten days of the machine's delivery, its security interest has priority over that of First State Bank.

Consumer Goods. The holder of a PMSI in most types of consumer goods has extensive protection. Perfection is automatic for the retailer who obtains a security agreement from a customer. No filing is necessary to establish the seller's priority. One exception to this rule is automobile financing. To perfect a security interest in an automobile, the secured party must file a security agreement or comply with a state's certificate of title law.

Inventory. A PMSI in inventory has priority even though another creditor has previously perfected a security interest in the debtor's inventory if the following events occur (Section 9–312[3]):

1. The PMSI is perfected at the time the debtor receives possession of the inventory.
2. The purchase-money secured party gives notification in writing to the holder of the conflicting security interest who has filed a financing statement covering the same types of inventory (i) before the date of the filing made by the purchase-money secured party or (ii) before the beginning of the twenty-one-day period where the PMSI is temporarily perfected without filing or possession.
3. The holder of the conflicting interest receives notice within five years *before* the debtor receives possession of the inventory.
4. The notification states that the person giving notice has or expects to acquire a PMSI in inventory of the debtor, describing such inventory by item or type.

It is not necessary to notify secured creditors who have not filed financing statements, even if the person claiming a PMSI has knowledge of their interests.

Problems arising under Section 9–312(3) usually involve a conflict between a secured party claiming interest in certain collateral under an after-acquired property clause and a person claiming a PMSI in the same collateral. The rationale for this section is that a secured party typically will make advances on new inventory or releases of old inventory as new inventory is received. If the inventory financer learns of the PMSI in particular inventory, he or she may not make an advance against it (Section 9–312[3][b]).

The priority of the PMSI in inventory extends only to *identifiable cash proceeds* received on or before the inventory is delivered to the buyer. If the goods are sold to a buyer on account, the PMSI priority does not extend to these proceeds. Suppose a secured party makes a loan to a retailer to finance his or her operations and retains a security interest in after-acquired accounts receivable. After this a manufacturer sells goods to the retailer and perfects a PMSI in this inventory and the proceeds from their sale. Between the two parties, whose security interest has priority if the only assets of the retailer are accounts receivable generated by the sale of merchandise sold by the manufacturer? The secured party claiming a security interest in after-acquired accounts receivable has priority because accounts are not cash proceeds.

Chattel Paper and Instruments

When chattel paper is sold by the seller to a secured party, the secured party may choose to have the retail merchant collect the accounts, or the secured party may collect the accounts. The secured party may leave the chattel paper with the dealer, or the secured party may take possession of the paper. As noted previously, an interest in chattel paper may be perfected by either filing or taking possession of it.

Leaving it in the hands of the retail merchant is dangerous: if the secured party leaves the paper in the hands of the merchant and perfects an interest by filing, a subsequent

secured party who takes possession of this chattel paper may gain priority over the secured party who merely files to perfect. Certain purchasers of chattel paper left in the debtor's possession take free of the security interest that has been perfected by filing. This is one of the limitations on the otherwise protected status of a party with a perfected security interest.

In general the rules applicable to chattel paper also apply to the purchase of instruments. Recall, however, that a security interest in instruments generally can be perfected only by possession. The only types of perfected nonpossessory security interest that can arise in an instrument are the temporary twenty-one-day perfection provided for in Section 9–304(4) and (5) or the ten-day perfection in proceeds of Section 9–306. If a security interest is temporarily perfected under either of these sections, a person taking possession of an instrument during this period without knowledge that it is subject to a security interest has priority over the conflicting security interest (Section 9–308[a]). Figure 28-3 illustrates the steps to be taken to create and perfect a security interest that will have priority over other secured creditors.

Protection of Buyers of Goods

The UCC gives some buyers of goods protection against perfected security interests. When a person in "good faith and without knowledge that the sale to him is in violation of the ownership rights or security interest of a third party in the goods buys in ordinary course from a person in the business of selling goods of that kind" (excluding pawnbrokers), he qualifies as a "buyer in ordinary course of business." Under Section 9–307(1) a buyer in the ordinary course of business takes free of a security interest created by his or her seller even if it is perfected and the buyer knows this.

This section permits the ordinary consumer

FIGURE 28-3
Creating a Valid Security Interest

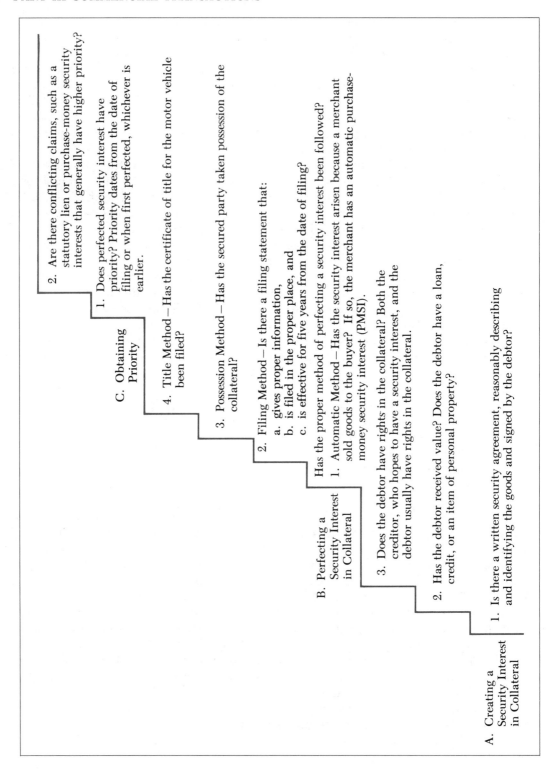

A. Creating a Security Interest in Collateral

1. Is there a written security agreement, reasonably describing and identifying the goods and signed by the debtor?

2. Has the debtor received value? Does the debtor have a loan, credit, or an item of personal property?

3. Does the debtor have rights in the collateral? Both the creditor, who hopes to have a security interest, and the debtor usually have rights in the collateral.

B. Perfecting a Security Interest in Collateral

Has the proper method of perfecting a security interest been followed?

1. Automatic Method — Has the security interest arisen because a merchant sold goods to the buyer? If so, the merchant has an automatic purchase-money security interest (PMSI).

2. Filing Method — Is there a filing statement that:
   a. gives proper information,
   b. is filed in the proper place, and
   c. is effective for five years from the date of filing?

3. Possession Method — Has the secured party taken possession of the collateral?

4. Title Method — Has the certificate of title for the motor vehicle been filed?

C. Obtaining Priority

1. Does perfected security interest have priority? Priority dates from the date of filing or when first perfected, whichever is earlier.

2. Are there conflicting claims, such as a statutory lien or purchase-money security interests that generally have higher priority?

to buy goods from a retail merchant without being liable to a secured party of the merchant who claims a security interest in the goods purchased by the buyer. Normally, of course, a security agreement permits a merchant to sell from inventory. This section therefore applies to the situation in which the security agreement between the seller and the secured party does not permit such sales.

A special rule exists for purchase of consumer goods—that is, goods used primarily for personal, family, or household purposes (Section 9–109[1]). Remember that a PMSI in consumer goods can be perfected without filing (other security interests in consumer goods must be filed). As long as the buyer buys without knowledge of the security interest for his or her own personal, family, or household purposes before a financing statement is filed, he or she takes free of even a perfected security interest (Section 9–307[2]).

If a person buys goods from someone not in the business of selling goods of that kind, he or she is *not* a buyer in ordinary course of business. This means that the buyer-in-the-ordinary-course-of-business rule stated in Section 9–307(1) does not apply. Suppose a finance company lends money to a retail merchant and obtains a perfected security interest in the merchant's equipment. Since the merchant is not in the business of selling equipment, but rather is in the business of selling inventory, someone who purchases this equipment from the merchant is *not* a buyer in the ordinary course of business. On the other hand, a person buying consumer goods, such as an automobile, from a seller who ordinarily sells those goods, when buying in good faith and without knowledge that the sale of goods to him violates an existing security interest, is a buyer in the ordinary course of business. As the following case illustrates, that buyer takes goods free of even a perfected security interest in the goods.

Cunningham v. Camelot Motors, Inc.

Superior Court of New Jersey

351 A.2d 402 (1975)

Background: Cunningham (plaintiff) and Koblentz (plaintiff) each purchased a Triumph from Camelot Motors, Inc. (defendant). Both purchasers paid in full and took possession of their automobiles, receiving temporary registration certificates. In each case Camelot promised to procure the required certificates of ownership for permanent registrations. Camelot failed to deliver these documents to either purchaser.

Three years prior to either of the preceding transactions, Camelot had entered into a floor plan financing agreement with Hudson United Bank (defendant). Under the terms of the agreement Hudson advanced moneys to Camelot and received a security interest in all motor vehicles then owned or thereafter acquired by Camelot. A UCC financing statement was filed reflecting Hudson's security interest in Camelot's inventory, and Hudson obtained possession of all of the certificates of origin issued by the manufacturer of new automobiles in Camelot's inventory. The agreement further authorized Camelot to sell any vehicles from its inventory in the regular course of its business, and Camelot was to remit to Hudson the loan balances owing to Hudson on the vehicles that Camelot sold.

Camelot failed to make the required remittance to Hudson on the automobiles that are the subject of these actions, and Hudson refused to surrender the certificates of origin to Camelot or to either of the plaintiffs. Plaintiffs sought an order directing Camelot and Hudson to surrender and indorse the certificates of origin to them. Decision: The court ordered Hudson to deliver to the plaintiffs the certificates of origin for their cars. The court found that as buyers in the ordinary course of business, they take free of a security interest created by the seller even though the security interest is perfected and even though the buyer knows of its existence.

Gelman, Justice

UCC Section 1–201(9) defines a "buyer in ordinary course of business" as

> . . . a person who in good faith and without knowledge that the sale to him is in violation of the ownership rights or security interest of a third party in the goods buys in ordinary course from a person in the business of selling goods of that kind but does not include a pawnbroker. "Buying" may be for cash or by exchange of other property or on secured or unsecured credit and includes receiving goods or documents of title under a pre-existing contract for sale but does not include a transfer in bulk or as security for or in total or partial satisfaction of a money debt.

The purpose of Section 9–307(1) is obvious: to protect bona fide purchasers for value who acquire goods in the ordinary course of business from a merchant's inventory. To meet the conditions imposed by Section 9–307(1), plaintiffs must show only that they purchased the automobiles (1) in good faith; (2) without knowledge that the sale was in violation of Hudson's security interest; (3) from a person in the business of selling goods of that kind; and (4) for present value, i.e., cash or by a present exchange of other property. The facts set forth in the moving papers establish that these conditions have been met by these plaintiffs and that under Section 9–307(1) they take free of Hudson's security interest in the automobiles.

An order will be entered directing Hudson to surrender the certificates of origin to Camelot and directing Camelot to execute and deliver the certificates to plaintiffs.

Statutory Liens

If a person furnishes services or materials in the ordinary course of his business, any lien upon goods in his or her possession given by state law for such materials or services takes priority over a perfected security interest (Section 9–310). This means that when a mechanic repairs a vehicle, if state law gives him or her a mechanic's lien on the car for services rendered, this interest is superior to that of a bank that has a security interest in the car.

Security Interests in Fixtures

Goods are *fixtures* when they become so attached to a particular piece of real estate that an interest in them arises under real-estate law (Section 9–313[1]). Article 9 recognizes three categories of goods:

1. Those that retain their *chattel* character entirely and are not part of the real estate, which should be perfected by filing in accordance with the rules on personal property

2. *Ordinary building materials* that have become an integral part of the real estate, which should be perfected by recording a real estate mortgage
3. *Fixtures* that are perfected by making a "fixture filing," a financing statement filed in the office where a <u>mortgage</u> on the real estate would be filed or recorded, covering goods that are or are to become fixtures (Section 9–313[1][b])

The financing statement covering a fixture filing must contain a description of the real estate sufficient to identify it. Applying this test, a description is adequate if a person searching the real-estate records would discover the filing. In some states the description is adequate if it sufficiently describes real estate for purposes of a mortgage.

A fixture filing gives to the fixture security interest priority as against other real estate interests based on the principle that the first to file or record prevails. This is the usual rule with respect to conflicting real estate interests. An additional requirement is that the debtor must have an interest of record in the real estate or be in possession (such as a tenant). This later requirement restricts a valid fixture filing where the creditor is a contractor.

There are three exceptions to the first-to-file rule. The first exception to the rule exists for a PMSI in a fixture. This interest has priority over previously recorded real estate interests as long as the security interest is perfected by a fixture filing before the goods become fixtures or within ten days thereafter (Section 9–314[4][a]).

Another exception to the rule covers readily removable factory or office machines or readily removable replacements of domestic appliances that are consumer goods. If an interest in these goods is perfected by any method in Article 9 before they become fixtures, the fixture filing prevails over a conflicting interest of most claims that are acquired in the real estate or the conflicting interest of the owners.

The final exception to the first-to-file rule for filing gives a perfected security interest in fixtures priority over a conflicting interest that is a lien on the real estate obtained by legal or equitable proceedings after the security interest was perfected (Section 9–313[4][c]).

Accessions and Commingled or Processed Goods

A secured party who claims an interest in goods installed or affixed to other goods ("accessions") is entitled to priority with certain exceptions over anyone else claiming an interest in the whole goods, if the security interest attaches before the goods are installed or affixed to other goods (Section 9–314[1]).

If a security interest in goods is perfected and the goods subsequently become part of a product or mass and their identity is lost in the product or goods, the security interest continues in the product or mass (Section 9–315).

As the Preventive Law Box on the next page indicates, the creditor seeking to minimize the risk of nonpayment by the debtor must, among other things, perfect the security interest in the debtor's goods.

ASSIGNMENT

A common business practice is for a seller of goods holding an installment contract with an accompanying security interest to transfer these to a finance company. In return the finance company advances funds that the seller uses in the operation of its business.

Rights of an Assignee

When an installment contract and security interest are sold to a finance company, the finance company becomes the secured party. As this transaction is usually an assignment,

PREVENTIVE LAW
Minimizing the Risk of Nonpayment by a Debtor

How can a creditor limit his or her risk of not being paid by the debtor?

- A creditor needs to make sure that he or she has an enforceable security interest in collateral of the debtor.
- A creditor needs to establish that his or her rights in the collateral are superior to the rights of other creditors.

In order to accomplish these objectives creditors should:

1. Make sure there is a written security agreement sufficiently describing the collateral and signed by the debtor.
2. Make sure the security agreement includes after-acquired property of the debtor or future advances by the creditor where this is appropriate.
3. Perfect the security interest by filing in an appropriate place and on or before the security agreement attaches to collateral or by taking possession of the collateral (such as shares of stock) if it does not occur automatically.

the finance company is often referred to as the *assignee*. The original seller, who is the assignor, is now a *debtor* since it has received an advance from the finance company. The original purchaser is referred to as an *account debtor*. In general the UCC does not permit the original purchaser to restrict the assignment of an installment contract (Section 9–318[4]). Even if the parties include a provision restricting assignment in the installment contract, the contract may be assigned.

In the absence of a contrary provision the rights of an assignee are subject to all terms of the contract between the account debtor and assignor and any defense or claim arising therefrom. The assignee takes the contract subject to any claims the account debtor has against the assignor that arise independently of the contract and accrue *before* the account

debtor receives notification of the assignment (Section 9–318[1][a] and [b]).

Waiver of Defenses

Quite often a seller, anticipating the documents will be used in financing, asks the buyer to sign an installment contract and security agreement containing words similar to the following:

Buyer hereby agrees to waive as against any assignee of this contract all claims or defenses buyer may have against secured party to the full extent permitted by law.

This clause facilitates the seller's assignment of the installment contract to a financer, for the buyer has waived its rights to sue and set up defenses against the financer (assignee). If a buyer accepts this terminology, it must settle any dispute arising over the goods with the seller, although the seller has transferred all its rights to a finance company. The UCC permits waiver-of-defense clauses as long as the assignee takes the assignment for value, in good faith, and without notice of a claim or defense.

A waiver-of-defense clause is effective against the account debtor unless his or her defense is one that could be asserted against a holder in due course of a negotiable instrument (see Chapter 21) or a statute or decision establishes a different rule for consumer goods. A Federal Trade Commission rule, discussed in Chapter 21, abolishes the use of such clauses in consumer contracts everywhere in the United States, but the clause is still effective in business transactions that do not involve sales to a consumer.

DEFAULT

When the debtor defaults under a security agreement, a secured party has the rights and remedies provided in Article 9 and whatever rights and remedies the security agreement itself gives the secured party—subject to certain limitations specified in Section 9–501(3). In general the secured party may reduce the claim to a judgment, foreclose, or otherwise enforce the security interest by any available judicial procedure. The secured party may elect to reduce the claim to a judgment and then levy on the collateral. In this case the judgment lien relates back to the date of perfection of the security interest (Section 9–501[5]). When there is a judicial sale following judgment, execution, and levy, the judicial sale is a foreclosure of the security interest, but the sale is not governed by Article 9.

Secured Party's Right to Possession After Default

In the absence of a contrary agreement, if the debtor defaults, the secured party has a right to possession of the collateral. Section 9–503 permits a secured party to take possession of the collateral if it may be done without breach of the peace. This means the secured party may go to the place where the collateral is and take possession of it. Although the UCC permits self-help repossession, the process is not without legal risk.

One problem involves the meaning of the term "breach of peace," which is used in the statute but not defined. If the secured party commits a breach of the peace in repossessing the collateral, he or she is subject to tort liability. Generally courts have construed this term in a manner that protects the debtor, as the following case indicates.

General Electric Credit Corp., et al. v. Timbrook

Supreme Court of Appeals of West Virginia

291 S.E.2d 383 (1982)

Background: Donna June Timbrook (plaintiff-appellant) purchased a mobile home from Winchester Mobile Home Sales, Inc., a Virginia corporation (defendant-appellee), on September 10, 1974, and her contract was assigned to General Electric Credit Corp. (defendant-appellee). In 1979, Timbrook became delinquent in her payments. She contacted West Virginia Legal Services Plan, Inc., which wrote several letters to Winchester trying to arrange an agreeable payment schedule; but in April 1980, Winchester sued in Mineral County Circuit Court for judgment for her indebtedness. Timbrook answered, counterclaimed, and raised a bona fide defense.

In mid-May Timbrook found a handwritten note on her door requesting that she call Winchester's collection department. The next day she purchased a new lock for her front door, but on May 29, 1980, while she was at work, representatives of the creditor broke her lock (to release a household pet) and removed her home and all her possessions from its cinder-block foundation (destroyed in the process) and carried it back to old Virginia. Timbrook sued to prevent her property from being sold. The trial court found that the credit corporation's repossession was proper because there was no breach of peace. Timbrook appealed.

Decision: The Court of Appeals reversed. Since it found the defendant had breached the peace, it remanded the case to the trial court for further proceedings consistent with its finding.

Harshbarger, Justice

A creditor's common law right to self-help repossession has been codified in the Uniform Commercial Code, Article 9, Section 503:

> Unless otherwise agreed a secured party has on default the right to take possession of the collateral. In taking possession a secured party may proceed without judicial process if this can be done *without breach of the peace* or may proceed by action. If the security agreement so provides the secured party may require the debtor to assemble the collateral and make it available to the secured party at a place to be designated by the secured party which is reasonably convenient to both parties. Without removal a secured party may render equipment unusable, and may dispose of collateral on the debtor's premises under section 9–504.

We have never defined what a breach of peace is, that would vitiate a self-help repossession. Several authorities make criminal "breach of peace" analyses, but we believe the term has a broader Uniform Commercial Code meaning.

Tortious activity incites or tends to incite breaches of the peace. The use or threat of violence impairs the tranquility to which our citizens are entitled in their homes and possessions.

White and Summers, leading scholars on the Uniform Commercial Code, have resolved:

> To determine if a breach of peace has occurred, courts inquire mainly into:
> (1) whether there was entry by the creditor upon the debtor's premises; and (2) whether the debtor or one acting on his behalf consented to the entry and repossession.
> In general, the creditor may not enter the debtor's home or garage without permission. . . .

We agree with those courts that have recognized breakings and unauthorized entries of debtors' dwellings to be breaches of the peace that deprive creditors or repossessors of self-help default remedies.

A creditor has a legitimate interest in getting collateral from a defaulting debtor. That strong interest, however, must be balanced against a person's right to be free from invasions of his home.

Creditors have other options that do not threaten rights that our laws have always jealously protected. If there can be no repossession without peace breaching, they can sue.

And, of course, if repossessions result in breaches of the peace, creditors are responsible for any torts they commit.

This record revealed that Timbrook's mobile home door was locked, evincing lack of owner consent to enter. An unauthorized entry into a debtor's dwelling is a breach of peace. . . .

The trial court erred in finding that the peace had not been breached. We remand for further proceedings consistent with this opinion.

Disposition of Collateral

After default the secured party may sell, lease, or otherwise dispose of the collateral. The disposition may be by public or private proceedings—but every aspect of the disposition, including the method, manner, time, place, and terms, must be commercially reasonable. Prior to public sale, the secured party usually must notify the debtor of the time and place of the sale or, if it is a private sale, the debtor must be notified of the time. If nonconsumer goods are involved, the secured party must also notify any other secured party from whom he or she has received written notice of a claim of an interest in the collateral. If any one aspect of the disposition is not commercially reasonable, the sale can be set aside.

The purchaser of the collateral generally takes free of any security interest or lien subordinate to that of the secured party. If the purchaser bought at a public sale, he or she must not have had knowledge of any defects in the sale and must not have bought in collusion with the secured party, other bidders, or anyone else conducting the sale. In any other case the purchaser must simply act in good faith.

As a general rule, the secured party may retain the collateral in satisfaction of the obligation. If a secured party wishes to do this, the debtor and other appropriate parties, such as those with security interests in the collateral, must be notified. In the absence of objections within twenty-one days from the date of notification, the secured party may keep the collateral. If objections are received, he or she must dispose of the collateral as directed by the UCC.

If the collateral is sold, the proceeds are distributed in the following order: The reasonable expenses incurred in repossessing and disposing of the collateral are deducted. Next, the secured party collects the unpaid debt and other lawful charges agreed to in the security agreement. Finally, if the secured party receives written demand from any subordinate security interests, these are paid. Any remaining funds go to the debtor.

For example, if the debtor owed the secured party $50,000 and put up his or her equipment as collateral for a loan, the distribution would be as follows if the secured party got $90,000 for the equipment: The secured party's reasonable administrative expenses would first be deducted (suppose they were $2,000), leaving $88,000. Then the $50,000 would be deducted, leaving $38,000. If he or she had received a written demand from a subordinate party who also claimed that the debtor owed him or her $50,000, the subordinate party would get the balance of $38,000.

In the *Gulf Homes* case, which follows, the court examines whether the sale of a mobile home was commercially reasonable. Which aspects of the disposition of the collateral most concern the court?

Gulf Homes, Inc. v. Goubeaux

Supreme Court of Arizona
602 P.2d 810 (1980)

Background: Gulf Homes (plaintiff-appellee) sold a mobile home to Goubeaux (defendant-appellant) for approximately $9,500 in Tucson, Arizona. Goubeaux made a $550 down payment but made no other payments. She subsequently abandoned the home. After the default by Goubeaux, Gulf Homes repossessed it and sought to sell it. It sent a notice to her, posted a notice on the home and in three places in Phoenix, Arizona. It also advertised the sale in a Phoenix paper. The place of the sale was at Gulf Home's Phoenix office. When no one appeared at the sale, Gulf Home purchased it for $7,000. It then sued Goubeaux for the balance due it under its sales contract. Goubeaux claimed the sale was not commercially reasonable. The trial court and Court of Appeals found for the seller.

Decision: The Supreme Court held that the seller had not established the collateral it sold had been disposed of in a commercially reasonable manner. Accordingly, it remanded the case to the trial court for further proceedings consistent with its opinion.

Holohan, Justice

The essential facts pertinent to the resolution of the issues are that appellee Gulf Homes, Inc., is in the business of selling mobile homes. Appellants, as buyers, executed in Tucson, Arizona, a contract for the purchase of one of Gulf Homes' mobile homes located on a lot in Tucson. The purchase price was $9,416 plus financing charges. The sales contract required a down payment of $550 and 132 monthly installments of $145. Appellants paid the down payment, but made no further payments and subsequently abandoned the mobile home after living in it approximately two months.

By reason of appellants' default under the contract, Gulf Homes repossessed the mobile home and sought to effect its sale. A notice of sale was sent to appellants by certified mail which was returned unclaimed. Notice of the sale was posted on the mobile home, itself, in Tucson and in three places in Phoenix, Arizona. The notice of sale was also advertised in one issue of a weekly Phoenix newspaper, the *Arizona Weekly Gazette*. The notice of sale recited the Tucson location at which the mobile home could be viewed and the time, place, and terms of sale. The place of sale was shown to be at Gulf Homes' Phoenix office.

On the day of the sale no one appeared at the sale to bid on the property. Gulf Homes purchased the mobile home for $7,000.

The repossession and disposition of the chattel in this case are governed by the provisions of the Uniform Commercial Code (UCC). A.R.S. sec. 44–3150 sets forth the requirements to be met by a secured party to dispose of collateral after a default. Subsection C in pertinent part provides:

> Disposition of the collateral may be by public or private proceedings and may be made by way of one or more contracts. Sale or other disposition may be as a unit or in parcels and at any time and place and on any terms but every aspect of the disposition including the method, manner, time, place and terms must be commercially reasonable. . . . The secured party may buy at any public sale and if the collateral is of a type customarily sold in a recognized market or is of a type which is the subject of widely distributed standard price quotations he may buy at private sale.

The first contention of appellants is that the public sale required by A.R.S. sec. 44–3150(C) must be held in the presence of the collateral.

The UCC does not define "public sale," but there is an inference in examining interrelated sections of the Code that the presence of the chattel is not required for a sale to be a "public sale." This is demonstrated by reference to A.R.S. sec. 44–3150(A) which provides that a secured party after default may sell the collateral, but any sale of the collateral is subject to the article on sales (article 2 of the UCC). . . . We conclude that the UCC does not make the presence of the collateral at a sale a necessity for a valid repossession sale.

The UCC has provided a broad, rather than a per se, rule to test the validity of a disposition. The test is whether every aspect of the disposition is commercially reasonable. . . . Some approved methods of conducting a sale of collateral are set forth in A.R.S. sec. 44–3153(B) which provides that if the secured party has "sold in conformity with reasonable commercial practices among dealers in the type of property sold he has sold in a commercially reasonable manner."

. . .

. . . We find no authority which makes it mandatory for a secured party to conduct a repossession sale in the same manner as an original sale.

The distance between the place of sale and the location of the collateral presents a more difficult issue. The sale was held approximately 125 miles from the location of the mobile home. At the time of the repossession sale, the appellee had an office in Tucson, from which the mobile home was originally sold to the appellants. In selling mobile homes in Tucson, the appellee would advertise in two major Tucson newspapers. In conducting its repossession sale, however, the appellee posted notice of the sale in Phoenix; advertised the sale in one issue of the *Arizona Weekly Gazette,* a weekly newspaper published in Phoenix; and then held the sale at its Phoenix office, while the mobile home remained on a lot in Tucson.

When suing for a deficiency, the burden of proof is upon the secured party, who must prove that disposition of the collateral was conducted in a commercially reasonable manner. . . . There was no evidence presented by appellee which showed that holding a repossession sale, as well as advertising and posting notice of such, a substantial distance from the location of the mobile home, was in conformity with reasonable commercial practices of mobile home dealers. The only evidence at trial bearing on this issue consisted of the following exchange on cross-examination of appellee's president by appellants' counsel:

Q: I believe at the time of this sale, the sale was held in your—excuse me, at the time of the repossession auction the auction itself was held in your office in Phoenix, is that correct?

A: That is correct.

Q: At that time, the mobile home itself was in a mobile home park here in Tucson, is that not correct?

A: That's correct.

Q: Could you tell me why the sale was held in your Phoenix office instead of next to the mobile home down here?

A: Well, this particular mobile home is a two-part mobile home, it's a double-wide.

Q: Yes.

A: If you tear it apart and move it, you run into a lot of expense, and of course that expense would have had to have been borne by Mr. Goubeaux; furthermore incur a lot more expense, and so for elimination of expense and convenience, that was the way it was done, probably save him—Mr. Goubeaux—probably about a thousand dollars or better.

Q: Rather than moving the mobile home to Phoenix to sell it, did you consider moving the sale to the mobile home in Tucson?

A: Well, I think this was done for convenience all the way around.

Q: That being your convenience, I take it?

A: Well, it's convenience of saving the trip, saving money, and it was properly advertised and noted and offered to people to look at, and then we didn't even have one call on it.

The decision of reasonableness is usually one of fact to be resolved by the trier of fact. No evidence was presented showing that a sale of a mobile home located a substantial distance from the place of sale was consistent with reasonable commercial practices of mobile home dealers. Absent a showing of commercial practices to the contrary, the circumstances indicate that the sale should have been advertised, noticed, and sold in Tucson where the mobile home was available for inspection. The location of the chattel was in a metropolitan area with a population in excess of 350,000 people. The area is a major trade center for the southern part of the state. Notices and advertising in Phoenix some 125 miles away would not have much efficacy in producing buyers in Tucson. As the testimony shows, any buyer in Phoenix would be faced with an additional expense of "probably about a thousand dollars or better" to move the mobile home from Tucson to Phoenix.

Right of Redemption

Although rarely done in actual practice, the collateral may be redeemed by the debtor or any other secured party any time before the secured party has disposed of it, or entered into a contract to dispose of it, or completed the process for retaining the collateral under Section 9–505(2). The party redeeming, however, must pay all money owed and perform all obligations owing at the time he or she attempts to redeem the property.

Liability of Secured Party for Noncompliance

Clearly, if the secured party is not performing as required by the UCC, he or she may be restrained from disposing of the collateral. If the disposition has already occurred, the secured party is liable for any loss caused by a failure to comply with Part 5 of Article 9. Where the disposition of the collateral is not carried out in a commercially reasonable manner, the secured party, such as the bank in the following case, cannot use the proceeds from the sale of the collateral to cover the debtor's payment deficiencies.

Citizens State Bank v. Hewitt

Court of Appeals of Georgia

279 S.E.2d 531 (1981)

Background: Citizens State Bank (plaintiff-appellant) sought a judgment against Walter C. Hewitt (defendant-appellee) for $4,225. Plaintiff alleged that the defendant had failed to make payments for a boat and automobile as agreed upon by contract and that it had exercised its right to foreclose. The defendant answered in general, denying plaintiff's claim and, as affirmative defenses, claimed that reasonable notice of foreclosure sale was not provided as required by law. The trial court directed a verdict in favor of the plaintiff on the automobile and in favor of the defendant with respect to the boat. The plaintiff appealed.

Decision: The appellate court affirmed.

McMurray, Presiding Judge

On July 24, 1975, Walter C. Hewitt executed and delivered a combination note and security agreement creating a security interest in favor of Citizens State Bank, Kingsland, Georgia, in a 1975 Dodge pickup truck. On October 7, 1976, Hewitt executed and delivered a second combination note and security agreement creating a security interest in favor of the bank in a 135 horsepower Evinrude motor, a 2000 Gator trailer, and a McKee Craft boat. Hewitt thereafter became in default in his payments on the two notes. On July 11, 1978, the bank . . . repossessed Hewitt's truck, boat, motor, and trailer, returning same to its parking lot where a "For Sale" sign was displayed on each item.

On July 12, 1978, a standard form letter correspondence was forwarded to Hewitt, titled "Notice of Intention to Pursue Deficiency Claim" with reference to the personal items secured. However, in the body of the correspondence it advised Hewitt with reference to *the automobile* [all emphases by the court] repossessed after default it would be sold "in order for Citizens State Bank to recover the amounts owed under your contract plus any expenses allowed by law." Further, if the proceeds from the sale are not sufficient to pay the entire amount owed plus any expenses, the bank intended to pursue a deficiency claim against Hewitt. The letter further advised that he had a *right to redeem the automobile* and terminate the contract by paying the bank a certain amount at any time prior to the first day on which *the automobile would be offered for sale*, "if not redeemed, or at any time thereafter until it is sold." The letter also advised him he had a *right to demand a public sale of the automobile* by so advising the bank of his demand "in writing by registered or certified mail . . . within ten . . . days of the posting of this notice." There was no mention in the body of the letter that the boat, motor and trailer had been repossessed, would thereafter be sold and a deficiency judgment sought in the event the proceeds from the sale were not sufficient to pay off the indebtedness; the right to redeem same and terminate the contract or that Hewitt had a right to demand a public sale of these items. The items were then sold at separate private sales, that is, the "Dodge pickup" to one business concern and the boat, motor and trailer to another some 6 months later.

Citizens State Bank, as plaintiff, then sought judgment against the defendant for $4,225 with interest as provided by law and reasonable attorney fees. . . .

The defendant answered in general denying the claim, admitting the execution of the two separate notes and adding other affirmative defenses that all notices were not reasonable as required by law and the private sale of the collateral was not commercially reasonable as required by Code Ann. Section 109A-9–504.

. . . At the completion of the evidence defendant moved for a directed verdict contending the plaintiff had failed to carry the burden of proof that it had "reasonably notified the debtor" that it would seek a deficiency judgment; that it intended to sell the goods at a private sale and when that sale was to take place, and that the defendant had never waived his right to notification; further, that the sale must be commercially reasonable and that plaintiff failed to prove that every aspect of the sale, including the method, manner, time, place and terms [, was] commercially reasonable and that the resale was a fair and reasonable value of the collateral at the time of the repossession, thereby precluding plaintiff from a deficiency judgment. The plaintiff in its argument and response to the motion contends that the letter was satisfactory to all purposes as to every item of personal property even though it is quite clear from the letter that *only the automobile* was mentioned. The trial court then denied the motion with respect to the Dodge motor vehicle but granted the motion with respect to the boat, motor, and trailer inasmuch as the language in the letter "your indebtedness" was insufficient under the law to supply notice as to the intentions of the secured party with reference to the boat, motor, and trailer and the notice did not notify the debtor that the plaintiff was going to dispose of them in a commercially reasonable manner in a public or private sale. The court stated to counsel that the Uniform Commercial Code, being in derogation of the common law it must be strictly construed and that the plaintiff failed to give proper notice with respect to the boat, motor, and trailer that plaintiff intended to seek a deficiency judgment after sale, either public or private.

Thereafter, plaintiff moved for a directed verdict with reference to the deficiency on the promissory note involving the motor vehicle, and the court directed a verdict in the amount of $1,666.60 (including statutory attorney fees), with reference thereto instructing the jury to eliminate plaintiff's claim for $2,731 plus statutory attorney fees, plus costs, with respect to the boat, motor and trailer, based upon the evidence in the case. A judgment was then entered reciting that the jury had been directed to render a verdict to the plaintiff with reference to the promissory note executed July 24, 1975, and in favor of the defendant with regard to the note executed October 7, 1976, and granted plaintiff judgment against the defendant for the sum of $1,666.60. Both plaintiff and defendant filed notices of appeal, but the defendant later dismissed his appeal. *Held:*

Code Ann. Section 109A-9–504 sets forth in detail the secured party's right to dispose of collateral after default. As to the effect of the disposition and its right to seek a deficiency, paragraph (3) states clearly that the disposition of the collateral may be by public or private proceedings and may be made by way of one or more contracts. Sale or other disposition may be as a unit or in parcels and at any time and place and on any terms *"but every aspect of the disposition including the method, manner, time, place and terms must be commercially reasonable . . . (and) . . . reasonable notification of the time and place of any public sale or reasonable notification of the time after which any private sale or other intended disposition is to be made shall be sent by the secured party to the debtor,"* if he has not after default signed a statement waiving, renouncing, or modifying his right to notification of the sale. Compliance with this Code section is a condition precedent to recovery of any deficiency between the sale price of the collateral and the amount of the unpaid balance. The secured party, in failing to strictly comply with the statutory law . . . cannot recover the deficiency.

The trial court did not err in directing the verdict against the plaintiff where it is clear from the notice that there was noncompliance with Code Ann. Section 109A-9–504(3).

REVIEW PROBLEMS

1. Define the following terms:
   a. purchase-money security interest
   b. financing statement
   c. chattel paper
2. Explain how goods are classified and give an example of each type of goods. Can goods become fixtures?
3. How can a retail seller be both a creditor and a debtor with respect to security interests in property once in the seller's store and then sold to a consumer or other business?
4. Why is it necessary to perfect a security interest? How does perfection of a security interest occur?

5. Stryker manufactures medical equipment for sale to medical institutions and retailers. It also sells directly to consumers in its wholly owned retail outlets. Stryker has created a subsidiary, Styk Corporation, for the purpose of financing the purchase of its products by various customers. In which of the following situations does Styk not have to file a financing statement to perfect its security interest against competing creditors in the equipment sold by Stryker?
   a. Sales made to consumers who purchase for their own personal use.
   b. Sales made to medical institutions.

   c. Sales made to retailers who in turn sell to buyers in the ordinary course of business.

   d. Sales made to any buyer who uses the equipment as a fixture.

6. Gilmore, an automobile dealer, had an inventory of forty cars and ten trucks. He financed the purchase of this inventory with First Bank under an agreement dated January 5, which gave the bank a security interest in all vehicles on Gilmore's premises, all future acquired vehicles, and the proceeds from their sale. On January 10 the bank properly filed a financing statement that identified the collateral in the same way that it was identified in the agreement. On April 1 Gilmore sold a passenger car to Todd for family use and a truck to Diamond Company for its hardware business. Does the bank have a perfected security interest? If so, when was it perfected? Does it matter whether the property being secured is inventory? Is the car subject to the security interest of the bank after it is sold?

7. Lowland Appliances, Inc., sells various brand-name appliances at discount prices. Lowland maintains a large inventory that it obtains from various manufacturers on credit. These manufacturer-creditors have all filed and taken secured interests in the appliances and proceeds therefrom that they have sold to Lowland on credit. Lowland in turn sells to hundreds of ultimate consumers; some pay cash but most pay on credit. Lowland takes a security interest but does not file a financing statement for credit. Does Lowland have a perfected security interest in the goods sold on credit? Are the appliances considered consumer goods or inventory?

8. Mary Morris is the owner of a computer store. She has borrowed money from First Bank to finance her inventory of computers. First Bank and Mary have entered into a security agreement that gives First Bank a security interest in Mary's present and after-acquired inventory and all proceeds therefrom. Suppose Mary now needs money to buy additional inventory—computers that she has never stocked before. If Second Bank were to lend Mary $25,000, could it have priority over First Bank with regard to its loan?

9. Norton bought a used tractor from Hodges for $12,500, giving Hodges a security interest in the tractor to secure the unpaid portion of the purchase price. Three months later, after paying $370, Norton defaulted and returned the tractor. Hodges then sold the tractor at a public auction for $2,500 and sued Norton for the balance.

   At the trial there was evidence that Hodges's attorney had posted a notice of the auction on the courthouse door as required by state law. This notice was posted two weeks prior to the sale. No notice of the sale was sent to Norton, nor was there any evidence of additional publicity. When returned, the tractor had been subject to ordinary wear and tear. The UCC requires that a creditor's disposition of the collateral be done in a commercially reasonable manner. Is Hodges entitled to a deficiency judgment? Discuss. Hodges v. Norton, 223 S.E.2d 848 (1976).

10. Bristol, Inc. entered into an agreement leasing a store premises to the Commonwealth of Pennsylvania. Two years later Bristol, Inc. borrowed from Girard Trust and as security assigned its interest in the lease to Girard. Girard did not record its security interest under Article 9 or make any other public record of the assignment.

   The following year Bristol, Inc. filed a petition in bankruptcy. A receiver was appointed. The receiver retained all rentals from the store and applied them to Bristol's business operations. Girard Trust thereupon filed a petition with the bankruptcy court to recover the rentals paid to the receiver under the lease that had been assigned. Should the petition be granted? Discuss. In Re Bristol Associates, Inc., 505 F.2d 1056 (1974)

11. Peco leased an electronic cutting machine to Hartbauer for thirty-six months for a rental of $26,399.96. The rental included an $8,000 "lease deposit" to be paid by work performed by Hartbauer for Peco, with the balance in regular monthly installments of $511.11 each. The lease gave Hartbauer an option to purchase the equipment anytime after the thirty-six months, if not then in default, for a purchase price of $1,000. Peco never filed a financing statement.

Within the thirty-six-month period Hartbauer, being insolvent, executed an assignment for the benefit of creditors to Dodge. Dodge intends to sell the machine leased by Peco to Hartbauer at an auction. Peco brings a suit to enjoin the sale. There is proof that at the end of the lease the value of the machine would be $10,000. Would the injunction be granted? Explain, indicating the issue involved. Peco, Inc. v. Hartbauer Tool & Die Co., 500 P.2d 708 (1972).

12. F purchased a mobile home from L, executing an installment contract and a security agreement. The security agreement gave L a purchase-money security interest in the mobile home. L eventually sold this to M. On the date that F purchased the mobile home he acquired title; however, pursuant to an understanding with L, F left the mobile home on L's lot. F would make the down payment when he later picked up the trailer.

In the meantime R, who financed L's purchase of inventory and held a security interest therein, seized all of L's inventory, including F's trailer, as L had defaulted. R eventually sold the mobile home to another. F, upon returning to L's lot, found the mobile home gone and refused to pay M. M asserts its right to the mobile home as a secured creditor of F. In order for M to prevail, the security interest under F's security agreement must have attached. Had the security interest in fact attached? Discuss. Rex Financial Corp. v. Mobile American Corp., 23 UCC Rep. 788 (Ariz. 1978)

13. A purchased a motor home from L by installment contract. The contract signed by A contained an agreement not to assert any claims or defenses A might have with respect to the contract against any assignee of the contract should L assign it. Shortly after the contract was entered into, L assigned it to Bank. Approximately one year later, A ceases to make payments under the contract, asserting that the motor home was in fact used and not new as represented by L and that L had failed to rectify defects on the motor home.

Is A bound by his agreement waiving all claims and defenses against Bank? ARE v. Barrett Bank, 300 So.2d 250 (1976)

14. R obtained a judgment against M. Upon attempting to levy execution against a herd of cattle, R discovered M's interest therein was subject to a security interest in favor of a third party. The financing statement on file in the county courthouse lacked the signature of the secured party and the addresses of both M and the secured party. R then challenged the validity of the security interest, as it otherwise had priority over the judgment lien. All parties involved are residents of the same small town—R knew M and the secured party and where they each lived.
   a. Was the failure of the secured party to sign the financing statement fatal to his or her security interest?
   b. Was the omission of the secured party's and M's addresses fatal to the security interest? Riley v. Miller, 549 S.W.2d 314 (1977)

Bankruptcy

T he use of credit for the purchase of property, goods, and services has become common for both consumers and businesses. In difficult economic times, when interest rates soar and unemployment and loss of income are experienced by consumers and businesses alike, many borrowers are forced into bankruptcy. Approximately 200,000 bankruptcies are filed each year in the United States, 85 percent of them personal bankruptcies.

Bankruptcy laws provide relief and protection to the debtor while fairly distributing the debtor's assets among creditors. Bankruptcy laws are provided for in Article I, Section 8 of the U.S. Constitution: "The Congress shall have the power . . . to establish . . . uniform laws on the subject of bankruptcies throughout the United States." Thus bankruptcy laws are entirely federal; states do not have the power to enact bankruptcy laws. State laws do, however, play a role in bankruptcy proceedings in defining the nature of liens, secured transactions, and other property interests.

BACKGROUND OF TODAY'S BANKRUPTCY LAW

There have been numerous landmark changes in bankruptcy laws in the last decade. Until recently the Bankruptcy Act of 1898 was the controlling law for bankruptcy disputes. Then, in 1978, Congress passed the Bankruptcy Reform Act. Known as the Bankruptcy Code, this law became effective on October 1, 1979. Thus, cases, including several in this chapter, which began prior to that date are governed by the 1898 law, whereas the new Bankruptcy Code governs the more recent cases.

The 1978 Act also introduced a new court structure. Bankruptcy courts were introduced into each federal district and were made adjuncts to the federal district courts. Unlike the judges of the district courts, who are given lifetime tenure, bankruptcy judges were to be appointed for a term of fourteen years. The bankruptcy courts were given broad jurisdictional powers so that they could hear and decide all cases affecting the debtor or the debtor's estate.

However, in a 1982 case, Northern Pipeline Construction Co. v. Marathon, 458 U.S. 50, the U.S. Supreme Court held that the statute's grant of broad jurisdiction to the bankruptcy courts violated Article III of the U.S. Constitution. The court made its decision prospective and stayed its judgment until near the end of that year so that changes in the law could be made by Congress. Congress was unable to reach a permanent solution to the problems raised by the Supreme Court's decision for several years. Finally, in July of 1984 the Bankruptcy Amendments and Federal Judgeship Act were passed into law.

The 1984 Act was divided into three sections or titles. Title I created a new Bankruptcy Court arrangement to replace the provisions found unconstitutional by the Supreme Court. This section, which now controls the jurisdiction of bankruptcy courts, gives original and exclusive jurisdiction of bankruptcy cases to the federal district courts. The newly created bankruptcy courts were organized as units of the district court and given only jurisdiction over proceedings arising under or related to bankruptcy laws. The bankruptcy judge's decision was also made reviewable by the district court judge.

The second section or title of the new law created additional federal district and Court of Appeals judges. The third title of the 1984 Act made several substantive changes in the 1978 Bankruptcy Code. One change, inspired by the 1984 Supreme Court case of NLRB v. Bildisco and Bildisco, 456 U.S. 513, limited the right of a debtor who filed a Chapter 11 Bankruptcy Reorganization (discussed at the end of the chapter) to reject unilaterally a collective bargaining labor contract.

A recent change in the bankruptcy laws came in October 1986. Congress added a new chapter, Chapter 12, to the bankruptcy laws to provide special treatment for the family farmer. The Bankruptcy Judges, United States Trustees, and Family Farmer Bankruptcy Act of 1986 was intended to aid the family farmer who was facing severe economic conditions. For example, the net income of family farmers in 1950 was $19 billion; by 1983 that figure had dropped to $5.4 billion. On the other hand, the farm debt in 1950 was $12.5 billion and by 1983 that amount had soared to $216.3 billion. The law was designed to be temporary in nature; it included a provision calling for the law to be repealed in October 1993. Some of the special provisions of Chapter 12 are briefly discussed at the end of the chapter.

While a bankruptcy judge has broad powers, he or she does not in fact administer the debtor's estate. That power is given to a trustee in bankruptcy. A temporary trustee is initially appointed by the bankruptcy judge; later the creditors are allowed to select a permanent trustee of their own choosing at their initial meeting. The trustee represents the debtor's estate and administers it by collecting the property, investigating the financial status of the debtor, and making reports to the court concerning the distribution of the estate.

Types of Bankruptcy Proceedings

Liquidation. The bankruptcy laws provide for three kinds of proceedings. *Liquidation* or straight bankruptcy is the most common type and will be the primary focus for our discussion.

Reorganization. A *reorganization* is a type of bankruptcy proceeding frequently used by corporate debtors. Essentially, this type of proceeding allows the debtor to stay in business rather than liquidate. In the reorganization the debtor and creditors agree on a plan that provides for the debtor to pay some portion of its debts while being discharged from paying the remaining portion. The main features of this form of bankruptcy will be noted and compared to the liquidation proceedings near the end of the chapter.

Regular Income. A third type of bankruptcy proceeding, provided for in Chapter 13 of the bankruptcy laws, permits the adjustment of debts of an individual with a *regular income.* This proceeding is often referred to as either a Chapter 13 or regular-income plan, since it provides relief for an individual who has a regular income but does not result in the debtor becoming bankrupt. The regular-income plan will be briefly discussed near the end of this chapter.

Family Farmer. A fourth type of bankruptcy proceeding is available to the family farmer. Its provisions are very similar to those in Chapter 13 for the individual with a regular income. The farmer, and his or her family, is entitled to remain in possession of the farm and prepares a plan to reorganize. Neither Chapter 12 nor Chapter 13 proceedings result in a debtor becoming bankrupt.

THE BANKRUPTCY PROCEEDING

The liquidation or straight bankruptcy proceeding is either voluntary (started by the debtor) or involuntary (started by the creditors). The debtor can be an individual, a corporation, or a partnership that has a residence, domicile, place of business, or property in the United States. Corporations that are subject to extensive regulation by administrative agencies are not subject to the bankruptcy law. The financial failures of insurance companies, banks, savings and loan associations, and similar institutions are subject to special regulatory proceedings rather than the bankruptcy laws. Railroads and municipal corporations are not subject to the liquidation or straight bank-

ruptcy proceedings. Railroads are subject to the reorganizations referred to at the end of this chapter, while municipal corporations can seek adjustment of their debts under another section of the bankruptcy laws if state laws authorize such action. A comparison of eligible and ineligible debtors for the different types of bankruptcy proceedings is depicted in Figure 29-1.

Commencement of the Proceeding

Voluntary Proceeding. The filing of a voluntary proceeding automatically subjects the debtor and its property to the jurisdiction and supervision of the bankruptcy court. Once the petition is filed, creditors cannot start a suit or seek the enforcement of an existing judgment against the debtor. The filing of the petition for a voluntary bankruptcy by the debtor acts as a *stay* upon other proceedings. However, some actions such as criminal proceedings and the collection of alimony or child support are excluded from the effect of the stay.

Involuntary Proceeding. Creditors can file an involuntary proceeding against any debtor who could have filed a voluntary proceeding, with two exceptions: an involuntary proceeding cannot be filed against farmers or nonprofit corporations. If the debtor has twelve or more creditors, at least three of the creditors must join in filing the petition. If there are fewer than twelve creditors, any one of them can file the petition. Regardless of how many creditors file, their unsecured claims against the debtor must total at least $5,000. Thus two irate creditors, with claims against a debtor totaling $3,000, cannot force the debtor into involuntary bankruptcy; neither can 200 such creditors having a total of less than $5,000 in claims.

If the debtor does not challenge the creditors' petition, the debtor's property is sub-

FIGURE 29-1

Types of Bankruptcy Proceedings and Eligible Debtors

	Chapter 7 Liquidation	Chapter 11 Reorganization	Chapter 12 Family Farmer	Chapter 13 Regular Income
Eligible Debtors	Individual Partnership Corporation	Individual Partnership Corporation	Individual (and spouse) Partnership Corporation	Individual
Ineligible Debtors	Municipalities Railroads Insurance co. Banks, Savings & Loan, & credit unions	Stockbrokers Commodity Brokers Insurance co. Banks, Savings & Loan, & credit unions	Debtor has less than 50% of gross income from farming Debtor has more than $1.5 million in debts. Corporate debtor with less than 50% of stock held by family, or some stock has been publicly issued	Stockbrokers Commodity brokers
	Farmers, non-profit corporations and municipalities are not eligible for involuntary cases			There can be no involuntary Chapter 13 cases

jected to the jurisdiction and supervision of the bankruptcy court. However, if the debtor does challenge the petition, the creditors must prove that the debtor has not been paying his debts as they become due or that the debtor's property has been placed in receivership or assignment for the benefit of the creditors within 120 days before the petition was filed. Once the creditors prove either requirement, the debtor's property is subjected to the court's supervision. But if neither requirement is proven, the creditors' petition is dismissed.

The Role of Creditors

Within a reasonable time after a petition in bankruptcy has been filed, the debtor must file with the court a schedule of assets and liabilities, a statement of financial affairs, and a list of creditors. The creditors listed by the debtor are then notified of the bankruptcy petition. Those who have claims against the debtor file proofs of claims with the court. The court generally allows the claims unless they are objected to by the debtor or other creditors. The creditors who are claimants in the bankruptcy proceeding are generally unsecured creditors.

If a creditor has a claim secured by a security interest or other lien on specific property of the debtor, that creditor, and only that creditor, can use the property to pay off the debt. If the value of that property is equal to the value of the debt, he need not be concerned with the debtor's remaining assets and liabilities. An unsecured creditor is a person whose claim must be paid from the general property of the debtor; this creditor has no right or legal interest to any specific property of the debtor. It is this creditor who usually is most affected by the debtor's bankruptcy.

After the claims of the creditors have been filed and allowed, the court calls a meeting of the unsecured creditors. The judge cannot ap-

pear at the creditors' meeting, but a temporary trustee appointed by the judge does attend. At their first meeting the creditors normally do several things. First, they usually elect a permanent trustee. The permanent trustee may be the person appointed by the court to serve on a temporary basis or it may be someone else. At least 20 percent of the total amount of unsecured claims that have been filed and allowed must be represented at the meeting. The vote of creditors holding more than half of the total value of the unsecured claims represented at the meeting elects the trustee.

The second function performed by the creditors at their first meeting is the examination of the debtor. The debtor is placed under oath and is asked questions by the creditors and the trustee. The questions usually concern the nature of the debtor's assets and matters relevant to the potential discharge of the debts listed by the debtor.

THE DEBTOR'S ESTATE

Property in the Estate

The trustee is responsible for administering the debtor's estate. He or she collects all the property in the estate, reduces the property to money, and closes the estate after distributing the money according to the priorities established by the bankruptcy law. The debtor's estate consists of all property owned by or on behalf of the debtor as of the date of the filing of the bankruptcy petition. While the Johns-Manville Corporation case that follows concerns a reorganization proceeding instead of a liquidation proceeding, the court is asked to determine whether insurance policies of the debtor corporation constitute property of the estate. Note too the court's interpretation as to the effect of the "stay" order on pending litigation.

In Re Johns-Manville Corporation

U.S. District Court, S.D. New York
40 B.R. 219 (1984)

Background: Johns-Manville Corporation filed a Chapter 11 reorganization petition because claims and lawsuits filed against it for injuries caused by the asbestos it manufactured totaled more than the company's net worth. Since Johns-Manville's petition stayed the cases brought against it, Lake, a Quebec company that was also a defendant in many of those cases, sought to determine the effect of that stay on its defense in those cases. GAF, the insurance company for Johns-Manville, also sought a ruling regarding the effect of the stay order on cases brought against it.

Decision: The Bankruptcy Court held that the stay order against Johns-Manville also applied to Lake's attempt to obtain from Johns-Manville information that would be useful to Lake in its own defense. The court also determined that the insurance policies of Johns-Manville constituted property of the bankrupt's estate. For this reason the stay order also affected claims brought against GAF as the insurer of Johns-Manville.

MEMORANDUM AND ORDER

Brieant, Judge

Three separate appeals from decisions and orders of the Honorable Burton Lifland, Bankruptcy Judge, are before this Court for determination. They arise out of the proceedings pursuant to Chapter 11 of the Bankruptcy Code, initiated by Johns-Manville Corporation ("Manville"). Since these are related matters, we consider them together.

After more than a century of use of asbestos containing products, in residences, schools, ships, automobiles, factories, and in a vast number of applications, it was suddenly discovered that asbestos is dangerous and that inhalation of the dust is carcinogenic and debilitating. A litigation explosion ensued with a vast number of cases brought by persons claiming injury in plants where the product was used, or otherwise. The financial threat and the disruption of its business flowing from the litigation caused the Debtor Manville, a large manufacturer of asbestos, to seek the protection of the Bankruptcy Court in this district, which it did on August 26, 1982, treating those claiming to have been injured as its contingent creditors in the amounts set forth in their pleadings, making a total of claims in excess of Two Billion Dollars, more than the net worth of the Debtor.

As of 1982, appellant Lac D'Amiante du Quebec, Ltee. (hereinafter "Lake") was an original or impleaded defendant in several hundred asbestos-related tort cases pending in various jurisdictions throughout the United States. Manville was also a defendant in many of these suits. Among the proceedings against Manville which were stayed under the Bankruptcy Code following the filing of its Chapter 11 proceedings on August 26, 1982 are approximately 80 cases (the "plantworker cases") pending in New Jersey relating to claims arising from exposure to asbestos suffered at a Manville plant located at Manville, New Jersey. Lake is one of Manville's co-defendants in these cases.

In November 1982 Lake applied for an order clarifying the extent of the stays issued by the Bankruptcy Court pursuant to §§ 105 and 362 of the Bankruptcy Code. Lake sought a ruling from Judge Lifland that neither the statutory stay nor the accompanying stay order issued by the Bankruptcy Court prohibit it from obtaining pretrial discovery of documents and by deposition, as well as trial testimony from Manville, for its own use in those suits from which Manville has been severed.

On January 10, 1983 Judge Lifland issued two decisions determining the Lake application, the Manville proceeding, and several additional consolidated proceedings involving interpretation of the stay and stay order. . . . Appellants contend that the automatic stay provision simply does not apply to the testimony or discovery sought here. They argue that since they do not seek discovery by Manville as a party opponent, discovery from its employees as non-party witnesses cannot be construed as "proceedings against the debtor" which are subject to stay. . . .

This Court recognizes, as does the Bankruptcy Court, that stays of proceedings of the sort present here are not intended to be permanent. They must be reasonable as to scope and duration. Eventually, as a part of some plan of reorganization, and by some judicial process, either in this Court or in the Bankruptcy Court, or in the many state and federal courts where asbestos related cases are now pending, the liability of the Debtor's estate to respond to these claims and cross-claims must be adjudicated in accordance with due process, as must be its obligations for indemnification or contribution to other possible joint tort-feasors. Thereafter, whatever Manville owes, it must pay, either as part of its plan of reorganization pursuant to Chapter 11 of the Code, or as a disposition of its assets to claimants in order of their priority pursuant to Chapter 7 of the Code, or as a judgment debtor if these proceedings be dismissed.

Notwithstanding any impressions to the contrary, neither the reorganization proceedings nor the stay can last forever.

At least as of the present, which is the only time as of which this Court may speak, the determination of the Bankruptcy Court to continue the stay is entirely reasonable, and absolutely necessary if there shall be any hope of reorganizing the Debtor in accordance with the statutory goal. Manville cannot be reorganized while its management is chasing around the country preparing for pre-trial discovery and protecting its legitimate interests in the scope and conduct of deposition testimony. To suggest otherwise, as noted above, would be to ignore the realities of modern litigation.

In light of the statutory purpose of the stay in bankruptcy, which "does more than prevent claims against the assets of the debtor," but gives "the debtor a breathing period in which to organize his or her affairs," the court below was fully justified in protecting the debtor for a reasonable time from the attempts to remove the stay.

The second issue, one raised independently by GAF, concerns the Court's authority to enjoin direct actions arising under state law against the Debtor's insurance carriers. Initially, in Decision No. 2, the Bankruptcy Court refused to enjoin suits against Manville's insurers and sureties.

Following that decision, Judge Lifland revised his earlier rulings on the propriety of staying direct action suits. The Court ruled that insurance policies and their proceeds and the claims or causes of action which are or may be asserted by Manville against its insurance carriers in pending suits, constituted "substantial property of the Manville estate which will be diminished if and to the extent that third party direct actions against the insurance carriers result in plaintiffs' judgments."

· · · ·

GAF contends that § 362 operates solely to stay proceedings against the Debtor and his property, and is insufficiently broad to encompass independent claims against the Debtor's insurers. Essentially, GAF contends . . . that Manville's insurance is not "property" of its estate under that section, and hence is not subject to the automatic stay provision which operates to stay "any act to obtain possession of property of the estate or of property from the estate." That insurance falls within the scope of the Debtor's "property" is suggested by the expansive fashion in which property has been defined generally under the Code:

> "The scope of this paragraph [§ 541(a)(1)] is broad. It includes all kinds of property, including tangible or intangible property, causes of action . . . and all other forms of property specified in Section 70a of the Bankruptcy Act."

That Manville's insurance is property of its estate is supported as well by decisional law holding that insurance constitutes property of the estate.

The court concluded that:

> "Resolution by one forum, preferably this Court, of the many issues relating to Manville's insurance coverage and the liability of its insurance carriers . . . will be in the best interest of all parties in the reorganization proceedings. . . . Fragmenting these relevant issues by permitting various forums to decide the issues will *frustrate prompt and effective formulation of a plan of reorganization.*" (emphasis added).

Because the Court has determined that Manville's insurance is property of the estate under the Code and that actions by third parties against the bankrupt's insurers are automatically stayed upon the filing of the petition, we need not address [another issued raised by one of the insurers]. . . .

CONCLUSION

The Bankruptcy Court's order of April 14, 1983 pertaining to the automatic stay, and its order of May 23, 1983 granting the Debtor's motion to dismiss Lake's April 20, 1983 complaint, are affirmed.

Property Added to the Estate

After-Acquired Property. Certain property acquired by the debtor after the petition has been filed will be added to the debtor's estate. Specifically, property acquired within 180 days after the date of the filing of the petition is added to the estate if the debtor acquired the property by inheritance, as a result of a property settlement or divorce decree with the debtor's spouse, or as a beneficiary on a life-insurance policy.

Preference Property. The trustee has the right under some circumstances to void or recall certain transfers of property made by the debtor. If the debtor transferred property to one creditor in prejudice to other creditors at a time when the debtor was insolvent, the property transferred may, under certain circumstances, be recovered and added to the debtor's estate. The transfer must have been made by the debtor within ninety days prior to the filing of the bankruptcy petition. It must have been made at a time when the debtor was insolvent, that is, when his debts were greater than his assets. The transfer must have given the creditor more than the creditor would have received through the bankruptcy proceeding in order to constitute a preference. Thus not all transfers of property to creditors prior to the filing of the petition constitute preferences; however, if the transfer does constitute a preference, it can be added to the debtor's estate.

Lien Creditor's Property. A third type of property that may be added to the debtor's estate is the property obtained by the trustee acting as a lien creditor. Thus if the debtor had given to a creditor a lien on certain property

and if that lien had not been perfected or had not become effective as of the date of the filing of the petition, the trustee could add that property to the debtor's estate. The trustee, as of the date of the filing of the petition, has the status of a lien creditor, and if that status gives the trustee a better claim on certain property than the claims of other creditors, the property that those creditors thought they had an interest in can be added to the debtor's estate. Those creditors would then not have any preference on the specific property added to the debtor's estate. Instead, they would become unsecured creditors who would file a claim and receive whatever portion of their debt that is eventually distributed to them by the trustee. In the *Hurst* case that follows the court addresses the conflict between the trustee of the debtor's estate and the interest of the debtor's former wife in real property owned by the debtor.

In Re Hurst

U.S. Bankruptcy Court, E.D. Tennessee
27 B.R. 740 (1983)

Background: This case presents a contest between the the debtor's former wife, Betty Hurst (defendant), and the trustee in bankruptcy (plaintiff) of the estate of the debtor, George Hurst. The trustee claims that the property occupied by the defendant is owned by the debtor and that as a lien creditor the trustee has rights in that property that are entitled to priority over the rights of the defendant. The defendant admits that the property she occupies is owned by her former husband, but she asserts the trustee's rights are subject to her right, granted in the decree of divorce between her and the defendant, to occupy the property rent free for as long as she remains unmarried.

Decision: The Bankruptcy Court found that since the divorce decree giving the defendant the right to occupy the property could have been, but was not recorded, the defendant had not perfected her interest in the property. Thus the court decided the trustee, as a hypothetical lien creditor, had priority in the debtor's property over that of his former wife.

Bare, Judge

The facts are generally undisputed. From their marriage date until the entry of a final decree of divorce on August 9, 1972, George Washington Hurst and the defendant

Betty Jean Kitts Hurst were husband and wife. The divorce decree incorporates the parties' agreement that Betty Jean Kitts Hurst should be allowed to occupy the property at issue, which is admittedly owned by George Washington Hurst, "rent free so long as she does not remarry, and so long as she uses said house for the care of the said minor daughter and properly cares for said daughter." The divorce decree was entered upon the minutes of the Jefferson County Chancery Court on August 11, 1972, but it was not registered with the office of the register of deeds. . . .

On March 2, 1981, nearly ten years after his divorce from the defendant, George Washington Hurst and his present wife, Catheline Hurst, filed their joint chapter 11 petition. Their case was converted to chapter 7 on October 27, 1981.

In his complaint, filed on December 23, 1981, the plaintiff trustee asserts there is considerable equity in the property at issue. The trustee . . . (asks the court) . . . to determine the rights of the defendant, if any, in the property and to enter a decree requiring the defendant to immediately vacate the property if her interest is inferior to that of the trustee. . . .

The defendant contends the trustee's interest in the residential property is subject to her right to occupy the premises under the terms of the divorce decree, which she interprets to authorize her occupancy rent free so long as she does not remarry.

II

. . . Bankruptcy Code § 544 (Trustee as lien creditor and as successor to certain creditors and purchasers) enacts in part:

> (a) The trustee shall have, as of the commencement of the case, and without regard to any knowledge of the trustee or of any creditor, the rights and powers of, or may avoid any transfer of property of the debtor or any obligation incurred by the debtor that is voidable by—
>
> (1) a creditor that extends credit to the debtor at the time of the commencement of the case, and that obtains, at such time and with respect to such credit, a judicial lien on all property on which a creditor on a simple contract could have obtained a judicial lien, whether or not such a creditor exists;
>
> (2) a creditor that extends credit to the debtor at the time of the commencement of the case, and obtains, at such time and with respect to such credit, an execution against the debtor that is returned unsatisfied at such time, whether or not such a creditor exists; and
>
> (3) a bona fide purchaser of real property from the debtor, against whom applicable law permits such transfer to be perfected, that obtains the status of a bona fide purchaser at the time of the commencement of the case, whether or not such a purchaser exists. 11 U.S.C.A. § 544(a)(1979).

Commonly referred to as the "strong arm clause," this subsection is derived from section 70c of the former Bankruptcy Act. The status which it confers upon the trustee in bankruptcy is that of "the ideal creditor, irreproachable and without notice, armed with every right and power which is conferred by the law of the state upon its most favored creditor who has acquired a lien by legal or equitable proceedings." Section 544(a) bestows upon the trustee in bankruptcy all of the powers and rights available under the applicable state law to a "hypothetical creditor of the debtor who, as of the commencement of the case, had completed the legal (or equitable) processes for perfection of a lien upon all the property available for the satisfaction of his claim against the debtor." Thus, the plaintiff trustee in this case is empowered with the rights of a judicial lien creditor, a creditor holding an execution returned unsatisfied, and a bona fide purchaser of real property from the debtor.

The trustee questions whether the defendant has taken the necessary steps under Tennessee law to perfect her occupancy interest, arising under the divorce decree, in the property at issue. Defendant contends it was not incumbent upon her to register the final decree of divorce to perfect her interest because the decree is not among those writings eligible for registration listed in Tenn.Code Ann. § 66–24–101(a) (1982).

. . . Clearly, a creditor or a transferee of the debtor is not required to perform the impossible in order to perfect an interest. Therefore, neither the lien creditor test of § 544(a)(1) nor the bona fide purchase test of § 544(a)(3) requires perfection, vis-a-vis the bankruptcy trustee, of a transfer if the applicable law does not permit perfection. However, the court must disagree with defendant's assertion that the divorce decree was ineligible for registration. The statute recites in part: "The following writings may be registered: . . . (14) All instruments in writing transferring or conveying any right of . . . occupancy. . . ." Tenn.Code Ann. § 66–24–101(a) (1982). The divorce decree irrefragably provides for occupancy of the contested premises by the defendant, under certain conditions.

III

The question of the eligibility of the divorce decree for registration is quite significant considering the Tennessee Code provisions pertaining to the registration of those documents enumerated in Tenn.Code Ann. § 66–24–101 (1982). Tenn.Code Ann. § 66–26–101 (1982) enacts:

> *Effect of instruments with or without registration.* —All of the instruments mentioned in § 66–24–101 shall have effect between the parties to the same, and their heirs and representatives, without registration; but as to other persons, not having actual notice of them, only from the noting thereof for registration on the books of the register, unless otherwise expressly provided.

Tenn.Code Ann. § 66–26–102 (1982) provides that the registration of a document or writing eligible for registration is effective to give notice "to all the world" from the time of noting for registration. Most significantly, Tenn.Code Ann. § 66–26–103 (1982) recites:

> *Unregistered instruments void as to creditors and bona fide purchasers.* — Any of said instruments not so proved, or acknowledged and registered, or

noted for registration, shall be null and void as to existing or subsequent creditors of, or bona fide purchasers from, the makers without notice.

. . .

The distinction between the effect of an unregistered conveyance upon a purchaser or creditor affected with notice, which was recognized and maintained under the various registration acts preceding the one now involved, is a distinction preserved most distinctly by section 2890, [Now Tenn.Code Ann. § 66–26–103 (1982)]. . . . By the very unambiguous language of that section, unregistered instruments are expressly declared to be "null and void as to existing or subsequent creditors of, or bona fide purchasers from, the makers without notice." "Without notice" qualifies bona fide purchasers, and is not grammatically a qualification of the words preceding. . . .

. . . Assuming *arguendo* the trustee in bankruptcy is charged with notice of the defendant's possession of the premises and thus prohibited from attaining the status of a bona fide purchaser, the trustee still retains the rights of a judicial lien creditor and a creditor with an execution returned unsatisfied. Notice of an unregistered instrument eligible for registration does not impair the rights of a creditor of the maker of the instrument in Tennessee. . . .

A determination by this court that the defendant's right to occupy the contested premises is paramount to the trustee's rights under § 544(a) would ignore the provisions of Tenn.Code Ann. § 66–26–103 (1982) and numerous decisions interpreting the precursors of that statute. It was incumbent upon the defendant to register the divorce decree to perfect her occupancy interest against creditors of her former husband. . . . Such unrecorded conveyances, at least insofar as they affect the rights of creditors, are void.

. . .

Although the Tennessee decisions mandate a conclusion by this court that the trustee is entitled to the controverted premises, the trustee's request for judgment for payment of rent while this controversy was in litigation is denied on the basis of equitable considerations.

This Memorandum constitutes findings of fact and conclusions of law.

Voidable Transfers. The trustee also has the power to restore to the debtor's estate certain property transferred by or on behalf of the debtor to third parties. First, any transfer made *after* the filing of the bankruptcy petition, whether by or on behalf of the debtor, can be voided by the trustee within two years after the transfer or before the bankruptcy case is concluded, whichever occurs first. Second, the trustee may void any transfer made by the debtor within one year prior to the filing of the petition if the transfer was a fraudulent transfer or was made with the intent of hindering, delaying, or defrauding a creditor. Finally, since the trustee administers the property of the debtor, any property that can be returned to the debtor due to someone else's fraud, mistake, duress, or undue influence can be reached by the trustee and added to the estate.

Exemptions from the Estate

An individual debtor can claim certain exemptions that are not available to corporations or partnerships. While the exempt property is brought into the estate when the bankruptcy petition is filed, if the debtor properly claims an exemption the exempt property will be removed from the estate. Thus it will not be subject to distribution to the creditors, but can be retained by the debtor. He or she is allowed to keep the exempt property and still be discharged from listed debts and liabilities.

The Bankruptcy Reform Act of 1978 made available to all debtors a list of properties exempt under federal bankruptcy laws. However, the debtor need not rely on that list if he or she desires instead to select the exemptions available under the law of the state where the debtor lives. Furthermore, the bankruptcy laws permit a state to require that the debtor use the exemptions listed under the state law. Thus the debtor has the choice of following either the state or the federal exemption list unless the law of the state where the debtor lives requires the debtor to follow the state list. Over one-half of the states require debtors in those states to follow the state's exemption laws.

Federal Exemptions. The list of properties exempted by federal law from the debtor's estate in bankruptcy includes:

1. The debtor's residence, up to a value of $7,500
2. The debtor's interest in a motor vehicle, up to $1,200 in value
3. The debtor's interest in household furnishings, wearing apparel, appliances, books, musical instruments, animals, or crops held for personal, family, or household use up to $200 in value for each item
4. Up to $500 in jewelry

5. The debtor's interest in any property, up to $400, plus up to $3,750 of any amount unused under Section 1 (residence)
6. The debtor's interest, up to $750, in implements, tools of the trade, or professional books
7. Any unmatured life insurance policy owned by the debtor, except for credit life policies
8. The debtor's interest, not exceeding $4,000, in the accrued interest or dividends from life insurance policies
9. Prescribed health aids
10. The debtor's right to certain public benefits, including unemployment compensation, social security, veteran's benefits, and disability benefits
11. The debtor's interest in any other kind of property, up to a value of $400, plus any amount not used under the first exemption listed (thus if a debtor does not own a residence, he or she can exempt $7,900 of the property under this exemption).

State Exemptions. The properties exempt for a debtor under state law vary, depending on the state of the debtor's residence. Some state laws do not place a dollar limit on the amount of certain exemptions. Such a law exists in Kansas and is discussed in the *Belcher* v. *Turner* case. Other states do limit the amount of their exemptions. In the *Rizzo* case a New York court had to interpret whether the $10,000 limit on its homestead exemption could be doubled for joint debtors, such as a husband and wife, if each of them filed for bankruptcy and each claimed an exemption in the same residential property.

Belcher v. Turner

U.S. Court of Appeals, Tenth Circuit

579 F.2d 73 (1978)

Background: Carl and Esther Belcher (appellants) filed a voluntary petition for bankruptcy. They claimed that the duplex in which they lived was exempt property under the Kansas homestead exemption law. Turner, the trustee in bankruptcy, argued that only one-half of their duplex was exempt.

The bankruptcy judge accepted the trustee's argument and, upon appeal, the District Court agreed.

Decision: The Court of Appeals affirmed the judgment of the District Court. Note that under present law, if the debtor elects to use state exemptions rather than federal exemptions, the law of the state where the debtor resided for the greater part of the preceding six months would be considered.

Lewis, Circuit Judge

This appeal arises out of bankruptcy proceedings in the district court for the District of Kansas. Appellants Carl and Esther Belcher filed a voluntary petition for bankruptcy in which they claimed as exempt property a side-by-side duplex which they own. The claim was made under the homestead exemption set out in the Kansas Constitution, art. 15, § 9 and Kan.Stat.Ann. §60-2301.[a]

In a memorandum decision the bankruptcy judge found that each unit in the duplex has a separate entrance, driveway, garage, and address. There is no common entrance except through an unfinished attic. The Belchers had resided in one unit since purchasing the property and had always leased the other unit. After finding the above facts the bankruptcy judge discussed the applicable law and determined that only the half occupied by the Belchers was exempt. The district court affirmed.

. . . (T)he Bankruptcy Act makes available to bankrupts those exemptions prescribed by state law. The scope and application of such exemptions are defined by the state courts and we are bound by their interpretations.

The Kansas cases which are most analogous on their facts are those considering an application of the exemption to property used by an owner partly as a residence and partly for business purposes. The most recent statement of the general rule [is] that

> [t]he test for determining whether a structure is a homestead is determined by its use or occupancy as a residence, and an incidental departure for business purposes does not deprive it of its homestead character. . . .

Of course, if [the building] should practically become a business house rather than a home, it would then cease to be exempt.

Appellants argue the overriding purpose of this duplex was to provide them with a home. They suggest the rental of half the building was consistent with this purpose because the rent was used to pay the mortgage on the entire property. We believe these arguments ignore the underlying fact that half of the duplex has always been rented out and was never intended or expected to serve as appellants' residence. The unit was intended to produce income. Reduced to its essential, appellants' claim of

[a]Kan.Stat.Ann. §60-2301 provides in pertinent part:
  A homestead to the extent of one hundred and sixty (160) acres of farming land, or of one acre within the limits of an incorporated town or city, occupied as a residence by the family of the owner, together with all the improvements on the same, shall be exempted from forced sale under any process of law. . . .
The above exemption is made applicable to bankruptcy proceedings by 11 U.S.C. § 24.

exemption is based only on the fact that the two units are part of the same physical structure. This one factor is not and should not be dispositive. The Kansas cases cited by appellants which inferentially support exempting the entire duplex did not involve bankruptcy. The purpose and intent of the Bankruptcy Act and its allowance of the homestead exemption counsel a different result. The aim is to protect and preserve the residence of the debtor; exempting the half of the duplex in which appellants reside will fully achieve that purpose.

In Re Rizzo

U.S. Bankruptcy Court, W.D. New York
21 B.R. 913 (1982)

Background: There were actually two cases heard as one. In each case the debtor filed for bankruptcy in 1979 and his list of property included a residence, owned by himself and his nondebtor wife as tenants by the entirety. The residence was valued at approximately $50,000 and the debtor claimed a $10,000 homestead exemption pursuant to New York law. The trustee claims that under New York law, the $10,000 exemption applies to the entire homestead. Thus he asserts, because the debtor owned only one-half of the homestead, his exemption should be $5,000, not $10,000.

Decision: The bankruptcy judge disagreed with the trustee in bankruptcy. He determined that "each" debtor, whether or not married, was entitled to a $10,000 homestead exemption. Thus if there were joint debtors, they would be entitled to have a total of $20,000 exempted from their residence.

MEMORANDUM AND DECISION

Hayes, Judge

These two cases brought under Chapter 7 of the 1978 Bankruptcy Code are being considered together because they contain similar factual situations and legal questions. Each of these debtors are individual debtors, whose residences are held by the entirety with their respective non-debtor wives. In each case, their trustee is the same, and he has moved for an Order authorizing him to sell both the interest of the bankruptcy estate and the interest of the co-owner in the residences pursuant to 11 U.S.C. §363(h). The debtors oppose the sale of the property and their respective spouses have offered to pay for the non-exempt portion of their estates. The problem arising is how much of the bankrupt estates are non-exempt. In each case, the debtor has claimed the New York State exemption of $10,000. The trustee argues that the debtors be permitted to claim only half of the exemption, since their wives are entitled to the other half of the exemption. . . .

. . . The wording of CPLR 5206, which provides the $10,000 homestead exemption in New York State, has posed interpretive problems for bankruptcy courts seeking to apply the exemption provisions of 11 U.S.C. §522.

The cases at bar have in common a single issue which is at the heart of the interpretation problem. When a tenant by the entireties files in bankruptcy and elects the State homestead exemption, can that debtor elect only one-half the $10,000 exemption or the full $10,000 exemption against the debtor's equity in the property and can tenants by the entirety have available to them in the bankruptcy context a total of $20,000 in homestead exemptions.

CPLR 5206 reads in part as follows:

> (a) Exemption of homestead. Property of one of the following types, not exceeding ten thousand dollars in value above liens and encumbrances, owned and occupied as a principal residence, is exempt from application to the satisfaction of a money judgment, unless the judgment was recovered wholly for the purchase price thereof.

It then proceeds to spell out various ways of owning property, none of which affects the problem at hand.

11 U.S.C. § 522(m) reads as follows:

> (m) This section shall apply separately with respect to each debtor in a joint case.

The clear meaning of this provision is that in a joint case, the husband and the wife may each claim the exemption that State or Federal law grants to either of them. The question then becomes would a New York Court in a non-bankruptcy case grant a judgment debtor a full $10,000 against the creditor seeking to levy on his home.

. . .

The New York Courts have in a number of cases granted a judgment debtor a full homestead exemption against the efforts of judgment creditors to levy on the debtor's interest in the entirety. Furthermore, only the debtor's interest in property may be levied upon under N.Y.Law. Therefore, the $10,000 exemption applies only to the debtor's interest in the property. However, it is not so clear as to whether a New York Court would grant both the husband and wife the full exemption, if one creditor got a judgment against both. But the answer to that question is not material to the case at bar, since in the bankruptcy context 11 U.S.C. § 522(m) provides the answer and is paramount to State law. New York law permits a $10,000 exemption to a debtor against his creditors. Therefore, 11 U.S.C. § 522(m) permits joint debtors to each claim a $10,000 exemption on their own estate, for an aggregate of $20,000 against the whole of their combined equity.

It would achieve little good to force married debtors to file separately to achieve the "fresh start" manifested in 11 U.S.C. § 522(m). Numerous cases have held that the Supremacy Clause of the Constitution and 11 U.S.C. § 522(m) require double exemptions even where State exemption law would prohibit it.

In the cases at bar, the exemptions for the value of the property in the estates should be figured as follows: in the Rizzo case, the value of the property is $53,000; deduct the cost of sale or $3,180; deduct the mortgage of $17,900 and this would leave equity of $31,920 which is divided equally between the husband and the wife. The amount of $15,960 goes into the husband's estate in bankruptcy. From this he is permitted to claim a $10,000 exemption leaving the value of the estate's interest at $5,960. . . .

In the LeMon case, the real property is worth $48,500. The cost of sale is $2,910. The mortgages are worth $20,000 which leaves the husband and wife an equity of $25,590. Splitting this between the two of them, the debtor would have $12,795 in his estate. From this, the debtor, Mr. LeMon, is permitted to deduct $10,000 leaving a value to the bankruptcy estate of $2,795. . . .

If the debtors' spouses do not wish to purchase the property, then the trustee, to get the value for the estate, should be permitted to sell the property under 11 U.S.C. § 363(h) and it is so ordered.

DISTRIBUTION OF DEBTOR'S ESTATE

Priority Claims

After the trustee has collected all the debtor's property and reduced it to money, the money is distributed to the creditors. (Secured creditors can proceed against the property with which their debt is secured. If any portion of their debt is unsecured, that portion must be considered along with other unsecured claims.) Some claims are given a higher priority than others. Claims are paid in order of their priority. Thus each class of claims is paid in full before any payment is made of claims of lower priority. If there is not enough money to pay fully all claims in any class, the money available is prorated among the creditors in that class.

The highest priority is assigned to the costs and expenses involved in administering the bankruptcy proceeding. These include legal fees, accountants' fees, trustee fees, and court costs. The next class of claims pertains only to involuntary proceedings: expenses occurring in the ordinary course of the debtor's business or financial affairs after filing of the case but prior to the appointment of the trustee make up the second class of claims. The third class consists of claims for wages, salaries, or commissions earned by employees within ninety days before the filing of the petition or the cessation of the debtor's business, whichever occurs first. Claims in this class are given priority up to $2,000 per individual.

Three other categories of claims have some priority over general claims. The fourth class consists of claims for contributions to an employee benefit plan arising from services rendered within 180 days before the filing of the petition or the cessation of the debtor's business. The limit per claimant in this category is also $2,000, and no individual can receive more than $2,000 from a combination of claims falling in the third and fourth priority classes. The fifth class is for claims for deposits made on consumer goods or services that were not received; the limit for claims in this class is $900. The sixth and last class consists of tax claims submitted by governmental units.

General Claims

If a claim exceeds the amount allowed as a priority, the excess becomes a general claim. After all classes of priority have been paid, any remaining property is distributed on a pro rata basis to all unsecured creditors with general claims against the debtor's estate. Often, as Figure 29-2 illustrates, there will be little, if any, distribution to creditors who have only a general claim against the debtor. Thus it is important to creditors who can do so to have their claims classified as priority claims.

FIGURE 29–2
Collection and Distribution of Debtor's Estate for a Chapter 7 Liquidation Proceeding

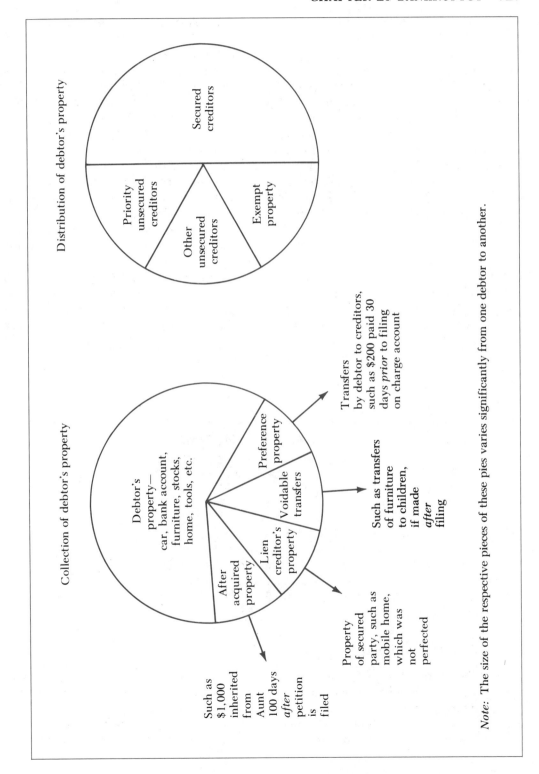

Distribution of debtor's property

Collection of debtor's property

Note: The size of the respective pieces of these pies varies significantly from one debtor to another.

DISCHARGE OF DEBTS

After the debtor's estate has been liquidated and distributed among the creditors, the bankruptcy court conducts a hearing to determine if the debtor should be discharged from the remaining debts. A discharge can be granted to an individual petitioner, but a partnership or a corporation cannot be discharged from its debts under the bankruptcy laws. Those business entities may seek to reorganize under Chapter 11 of the federal bankruptcy laws or they may seek liquidation under state laws.

Exceptions to Discharge

Under certain circumstances the court will deny a discharge to a debtor. If this occurs, the debtor remains liable for the unpaid portion of the creditors' claims. A debtor will be denied a discharge if a prior discharge was granted within six years of the filing of the petition. A discharge will not be granted if the debtor, within one year before the filing of the petition, or at any time thereafter, intentionally concealed or transferred assets with the intent to hinder, delay, or defraud creditors.

Other reasons for refusing a discharge to a debtor include the debtor's concealment, destruction, falsification, or failure to keep records related to the debtor's financial condition or business transactions. A debtor who fails to explain the loss of assets adequately or who refuses to obey a lawful order of the bankruptcy court or who makes any fraudulent statement or claim in connection with the bankruptcy case can be denied the discharge of unpaid debts, as the *Horton* case indicates. Since the new bankruptcy law has virtually the same provisions as those of the old law referred to in the *Horton* case, the determination made in *Horton* would probably be followed by courts reviewing the new law.

Matter of Horton

U.S. Court of Appeals, Ninth Circuit

621 F.2d 968 (1980)

Background: Horton, the defendant debtor, filed a bankruptcy petition but was denied a discharge by the bankruptcy judge because the debtor failed to keep adequate records or accounts from which his financial condition and business transactions could be determined. The debtor dealt in cash in all his business transactions and kept few records. The bankruptcy judge's decision was affirmed by the District Court and Horton appealed to the Court of Appeals.

Decision: The Court of Appeals affirmed the District Court judgment denying a discharge to Horton.

Grant, District Judge

The defendant, Robert Jackson Horton, sought a discharge of his debts in bankruptcy. This was refused by the bankruptcy judge in December 1974. The reason for refusing discharge was "Horton's unjustified failure to keep adequate books of accounts or records from which his financial condition and business transactions could be discerned." Maintaining such records is required. This decision was affirmed by the district court which entered judgment against Horton after a consideration of the merits of his claim. Horton now appeals to this court, contending that the lower courts erred in not granting him relief.

Horton is no stranger to the Bankruptcy Court. He has made his appearance there like clockwork every seven years. He was first granted a discharge in 1960 and again in 1967. This latest petition in bankruptcy was filed in 1973. At that time the case was routinely assigned to Judge Downey. The judge immediately disqualified himself, however, since he had presided over the previous discharges and felt he did not have the requisite impartiality in Horton's latest cause. The case was accordingly assigned to Judge Hughes.

The Bankruptcy Act provides that a discharge cannot be granted if the bankrupt has failed to keep sufficient records of his financial transactions. Although this failure may be deemed justifiable under the particular circumstances of the bankrupt, in this case the failure was found unjustified. Horton alleges that the findings of fact and law were insufficient under the requirements of Bankruptcy Rule 752(a).

The record reveals that the bankruptcy judge filed a five-page memorandum in which he reduced a convoluted and often contradictory factual record into findings of law and fact. This memorandum assessed (1) the records Horton kept, (2) the sufficiency of those records, and (3) once the records were found to be insufficient, whether the keeping of insufficient records was excusable in this particular case. The memorandum is more than sufficient to satisfy the requirements of Rule 752(a).

Horton's essential disagreement is not with the sufficiency of the findings, but with their correctness and the appropriateness of the legal standard applied. Therefore, we turn our attention to determining whether these findings are supported by the record. Unless they are clearly erroneous, they will not be disturbed on appeal.

Using these standards, we have assessed the record in this case. It shows that Horton dealt almost exclusively in cash during all his business transactions, keeping little or no verifiable records. He was unable to show where his salary was spent. As the bankruptcy judge and the district court concluded, his dislike of banks did not absolve him from keeping records. These fact findings are not clearly erroneous.

Against this general backdrop of scanty record keeping, we have examined Horton's contention that certain of his daughter's records provide the information Horton cannot supply. Horton built a house for his daughter, acting as a general contractor and paying suppliers and builders over Twenty Thousand Dollars in cash payments, without keeping any financial records of these dealings. Horton alleges that his daughter's records should be substituted for his own, to satisfy the provisions of Section 14(c)(2).

Legally, however, Horton had a duty to maintain his own records of such a transaction, even if his daughter's records were complete.

Even if we accepted the dubious contention that Horton could rely upon his daughter's records, they are not sufficient for that purpose. The transcript reveals that these records do not differentiate between payments made to Horton to reimburse him and those which were made directly to suppliers for the materials. Therefore, even if they are considered, they do not clarify Horton's financial position. Furthermore, the testimony of Horton and his daughter and her roommate [was] found to be "incredible" and replete with inconsistencies and contradictions.

Once the Trustee has shown that the bankrupt's records are inadequate, the burden shifts to the bankrupt to justify the nonexistence of these records. The record explicitly and implicitly indicates that the bankruptcy judge correctly applied these presumptions and burden of proof. Horton's argument to the contrary is without merit.

Nondischargeable Claims

If none of the exceptions applies, the discharge relieves the debtor from any obligation for the payment of the debts that arose prior to the filing of the petition. A judgment entered by a court on a debt that is discharged becomes void; no action can be taken to collect that debt. Nevertheless, there are some claims for which the debtor continues to be liable; these are known as *nondischargeable claims.* Claims that are not dischargeable include:

1. Claims for back taxes accrued within three years prior to the bankruptcy
2. Claims arising out of the debtor's embezzlement, fraud, or larceny
3. Claims based on the debtor's willful or malicious torts
4. Claims for alimony or child support
5. Unscheduled claims
6. Certain fines and penalties payable to governmental units
7. Educational loans that became due and payable less than five years prior to the filing of the bankruptcy petition

Reaffirmations

While the discharge of debts owed by the debtor to creditors relieves the debtor of any legal obligation to pay those debts, the debtor may agree to reaffirm or reassume the debts after the bankruptcy proceeding. However, since the debtor may be under a great deal of pressure from former creditors to reaffirm the discharged debts, the bankruptcy laws make the reaffirmation of debts somewhat difficult.

A simple promise by the debtor, even in writing, is not sufficient for a valid reaffirmation. First, the court must conduct a hearing at which the debtor is informed of the consequences of such action. Second, the debt must usually be approved by the court as not imposing an undue hardship on the debtor and being in the debtor's best interest. If these conditions are not met, the reaffirmation of the debt is not valid and its discharge is effective.

BUSINESS REORGANIZATION

Instead of filing a petition for liquidation, an individual or business may elect to file for reorganization under Chapter 11 of the Bankruptcy Act. As in a liquidation proceeding, a petition for reorganization may also be filed by the creditors. Most of the rules that apply to the liquidation proceeding also apply to the reorganization. Railroads, however, are not subject to liquidation because of the public's dependence on their services. Reorganization allows a financially troubled firm or railroad to continue to operate while its financial resources and obligations are put in order.

Under Chapter 11 reorganizations the court must appoint a creditors committee. This committee usually consists of the seven largest unsecured creditors and is appointed as soon as practicable after the order for relief has been entered by the court. The task of the creditors committee is to examine the affairs of the business and decide whether the business should continue in operation. The committee also usually determines whether to re-

---

ETHICS BOX
Any Ethical Obligation After Discharge?

Lauretta T. goes th   'ankruptcy proceeding and is fully discharged from all remaining debt.   'nsecured creditors are paid 25 cents on the dollar. Several of the credit.   '' businesspeople who are hurt by their inability to collect 100 percent o.   'v Lauretta owes them. One month after the discharge Lauretta wins $5 .   'n the state lottery.

Under the law Lauretta does not have to pay hu   'er creditors, but does she have an ethical obligation? If there had been a vo   'v resolution of the debts between Lauretta and her creditors, then one mig.   'lude that Lauretta has no obligation to go back and make good her forme.   ' However, if the transaction was involuntary, had a negative impact upon   'editors, and now can be paid with little cost, Lauretta should pay the deb.

---

quest of the court that a trustee should take over the management of the business. If necessary, the committee may employ attorneys, accountants, and other agents to assist it in performing these tasks. Generally, the debtor or any other interested party may file a plan for reorganization. While only the debtor may file a plan during the first 120 days after the petition has been filed (unless a trustee has been appointed), the debtor's plan is usually developed in consultation with the creditors. A debtor who files a plan within the 120 days has an additional 60 days to have the plan approved by the creditors. The court can extend or reduce these time periods for good cause. If the debtor does not meet the deadline or is unable to obtain the consent of the creditors, any party in interest (a creditor or the trustee) may propose a plan.

The plan that is proposed must classify claims and ownership interests. It must specify the treatment of each class of claims and must provide for the same treatment for all persons in the same class unless the holder of a particular claim agrees to less favorable treatment. The plan must also provide adequate means for carrying out the plan's payment terms. If the debtor is a corporation, the plan must also protect stockholder voting rights, ensure that nonvoting stock will not be issued, and provide that in the selection of officers and directors the interests of creditors and stockholders will be protected.

The plan may modify the rights of some of the creditors. It may specify that some property be transferred to other creditors, that some creditors be partially paid over an extended time, and even that some creditors not be paid. The only requirement is that all the debtor's claimants must receive as much as they would have received in a liquidation proceeding.

Those who hold claims or interests in the debtor's property are allowed to vote on the proposed plan. If creditors representing more than one-half of the number of claimants and at least two-thirds of the value of the claims in a class vote in favor of the plan, that class of creditors has accepted the plan.

Normally a plan will not be approved unless all those whose claims or interests have been impaired—those whose rights have been altered or who are to receive less than the full value of their claims or interests—have agreed

PREVENTIVE LAW
Actions to Be Taken by a Creditor of a Chapter 11 Bankruptcy Reorganization

What can creditors do if a business firm they deal with is considering a Chapter 11 reorganization?

1. First and foremost, make critical decisions before a filing occurs.
   a. Monitor accounts closely. If a debtor falls behind on payments, seek additional collateral for your account. You are in a stronger position if your claim is secured.
   b. Review the debtor's business. If you think you will not receive much under a reorganization, consider making a deal to cancel the debt for immediate but partial payment. (Bankruptcy laws do allow the trustee to set aside such deals if they are made just prior to the filing.)
2. Once a petition is filed, your first step should be to file a proof of claim—find out the date by which all claims must be filed and be sure all your claims are filed before that date.
3. You may be able to reclaim property—you have until ten days after the filing to reclaim any goods supplied up to ten days before the filing.
4. Talk to other creditors—the more information you have about the debtor's assets, the better position you can be in. Obtain the list of creditors and amount owed from the bankruptcy clerk.
5. Keep tabs on what is happening.
   a. Consider filing a notice of appearance. Unless your claim is for a small amount and there are many other large claims, you probably will want to receive notice of the proceedings.
   b. Make a personal visit to court to help establish contact and to find out whom to call if you need quick information.
   c. Look after your own interest. If the debtor doesn't file a plan within 120 days, the creditors can file their own plan, although this doesn't often occur.

to it. The court, however, may possibly confirm a plan even when those with impaired claims don't consent if the court determines that all persons in a particular class are treated fairly and equitably. Confirmation of the plan binds debtor and creditors. The property of the debtor is released from the claims of the creditors, and the debtor is given a Chapter 11 discharge. The process followed in a Chapter 11 reorganization proceeding is illustrated in Figure 29-3 while Figure 29-4 depicts a court's order for a recent reorganization.

FIGURE 29-3
The Chapter 11 Reorganization Process

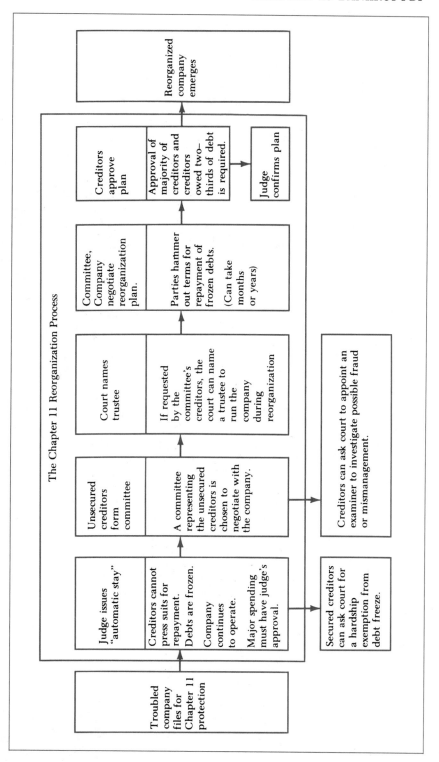

The Chapter 11 Reorganization Process

Troubled company files for Chapter 11 protection

Judge issues "automatic stay"
Creditors cannot press suits for repayment.
Debts are frozen.
Company continues to operate.
Major spending must have judge's approval.

Unsecured creditors form committee
A committee representing the unsecured creditors is chosen to negotiate with the company.

Court names trustee
If requested by the committee's creditors, the court can name a trustee to run the company during reorganization

Committee, Company negotiate reorganization plan.
Parties hammer out terms for repayment of frozen debts.
(Can take months or years)

Creditors approve plan
Approval of majority of creditors and creditors owed two-thirds of debt is required.

Judge confirms plan

Reorganized company emerges

Secured creditors can ask court for a hardship exemption from debt freeze.

Creditors can ask court to appoint an examiner to investigate possible fraud or mismanagement.

FIGURE 29–4
Confirmation of Chapter 11 Reorganization Plan

**UNITED STATES BANKRUPTCY COURT
FOR THE WESTERN DISTRICT OF LOUISIANA
SHREVEPORT DIVISION**

IN RE:

CRYSTAL OIL COMPANY,   CASE NO. 586-02834

DEBTOR   CHAPTER 11 PROCEEDING

**NOTICE OF ENTRY OF ORDER CONFIRMING
PLAN OF REORGANIZATION OF CRYSTAL OIL COMPANY**

TO: The Creditors and Shareholders of Crystal Oil Company and all Other Parties in Interest.

PLEASE TAKE NOTICE that on December 31, 1986, the Second Amended and Restated Plan of Reorganization (the "Plan") of Crystal Oil Company, debtor and debtor-in-possession in the above referenced case (the "Company"), was confirmed by the United States Bankruptcy Court for the Western District of Louisiana, Shreveport Division, and an Order Confirming Plan (the "Confirmation Order") was entered on the docket by the Clerk of the Bankruptcy Court which, among other things, provided:

(1) that the provisions of the Plan shall bind all the Company's creditors and interest holders, whether or not they have accepted the Plan, and shall discharge the Company from all debts that arose before October 1, 1986, the petition date, and that the distributions provided for under the Plan shall be in exchange for and in complete satisfaction, discharge, and release of all claims against and interest in the Company or any of its assets or properties, including any claim or interest accruing after October 1, 1986, and prior to the Effective Date (as defined herein);

(2) that the property of the Company's estate shall revest in the Company on the Effective Date and after the Effective Date, except as provided in the Plan, the Company may operate its business and buy, use, acquire, and dispose of its property, free of any restrictions contained in the Bankruptcy Code;

(3) that as of the Effective Date, all property of the Company shall be free and clear of all claims and interest of creditors and equity security holders, except for the obligations that are imposed in the Plan; and

(4) that as a condition to the receipt of the distributions to be provided under the Plan, all creditors and interest holders of the Company shall be required to surrender such creditor's or interest holder's securities and related documents as required under the Plan.

PLEASE TAKE FURTHER NOTICE that the New Securities (as defined in the Plan) that are to be issued to the holders of the 15% Senior Notes, the Debentures and the Common Stock (as such terms are defined in the Plan) shall be deemed to have been issued as of December 31, 1986, and the sole and exclusive right of such holders against the Company with respect to such securities shall be to exchange such securities for the New Securities to be issued to them pursuant to the Plan.

PLEASE TAKE FURTHER NOTICE that the Plan shall become effective (i) on January 30, 1987, if the Confirmation Order has not been stayed on appeal by a court of competent jurisdiction, and (ii) if the Confirmation Order is stayed on appeal by a court of competent jurisdiction. 15 days after such stay is resolved by final order (the "Effective Date").

December 31, 1986.

BY ORDER OF STEPHEN V. CALLAWAY,
UNITED STATES BANKRUPTCY JUDGE

FULBRIGHT & JAWORSKI
51st Floor
1301 McKinney Street
Houston, TX 77010
(713) 651-5350

COOK, YANCEY, KING & GALLOWAY
Suite 400, American Tower
401 Market Street
Shreveport, LA 71101
(318) 221-6277
COUNSEL FOR CRYSTAL OIL COMPANY

[*Source: The Wall Street Journal*, January 9, 1987, page 31. Reprinted with permission.]

CHAPTER 13—REGULAR INCOME PLANS

Chapter 13 proceedings are used by individuals with regular incomes who owe debts and want to pay them without harassment by creditors. While the prior law made this bankruptcy proceeding available only to wage earners, under the present law any individual (except a stockbroker or commodity broker) who has a regular income (whether from wages, investments, social security, or pensions) and unsecured debts of less than $100,000 and secured debts of less than $350,000 may use Chapter 13. Unlike liquidation or reorganization, Chapter 13 proceedings can be begun only by a voluntary petition filed by the debtor.

Upon the filing by the debtor of a Chapter 13 proceeding, an automatic stay stops creditors from taking action against the debtor. The debtor then proposes a plan providing for the use of future income for the payment of creditors. That income will be subject to control by a trustee, and the plan must ensure that all claims entitled to priority are paid in full. Unsecured claims may be divided into classes, but all claims within any class must be treated the same. Claimants may be paid in full or paid an amount not less than what they would receive in a liquidation proceeding. Usually, the plan provides for the payment of creditors over three years or less; however, the court may extend the period of payment to five years.

In order for the plan to be confirmed by the court, priority claimants must be paid in full, to the extent that money is available, unless they agree to accept less than the full amounts of their claims. Secured creditors vote on whether to accept the plan. If these creditors do not accept the plan, but either retain their liens or receive the properties securing their claims, the court will still confirm the plan. Unsecured creditors do not vote on the plan, but they must receive at least the amounts they would have received in a liquidation proceeding. A comparison of Chapter 13 with Chapter 7's straight bankruptcy provisions, particularly as they relate to secured claims, is included in the *Whitman* case that follows. Note that the case also discusses the "good-faith" requirement which must be met before a Chapter 13 plan is confirmed.

Memphis Bank & Trust Co. v. Whitman

U.S. Court of Appeals, Sixth Circuit

692 F.2d 427 (1982)

Background: An automobile dealer sold a car to the defendant debtor. Plaintiff bank financed the purchase of the car by lending her $5,659. The loan was secured by the automobile and the bank's security interest in the car was noted on the certificate of title. The defendant made no payments on the car and filed a Chapter 13 case two months after purchasing the car. The plan proposed reducing the monthly payments on the car and extending the time for repayment of the balance. The bankruptcy judge found that the defendant's conduct in securing the loan and immediately filing for Chapter 13 indicated her plan was not in good faith and refused to confirm the plan unless the original payment provisions were continued in force. The defendant agreed to the change and her plan was then confirmed. The District Court upheld the bankruptcy judge's confirmation and the plaintiff bank appealed to the Court of Appeals. Decision: The Court of Appeals set aside the confirmation of the defendant's plan. It reviewed the treatment of the secured creditor (bank) in a Chapter 13 proceeding and the good-faith requirement and then remanded the case so that the court could follow its opinion.

Merritt, Circuit Judge

This secured claim case arises under the newly revised Chapter 13 of the Bankruptcy Code which sets out principles for courts to follow in composing the debts of distressed wage earners. It is a case of first impression under the new Code. The "confused state of the law concerning the treatment of secured claims" caused major problems under the old Chapter XIII, and led to a radical revision of the treatment of wage earner plans in the new Code. We first explain the legal framework in which the case arises and then deal with the facts and applicable law.

I. THE STATUTORY CONCEPT UNDERLYING TREATMENT OF SECURED CLAIMS

Chapter 13 of the new Code is considerably more helpful to debtors than either the old Chapter XIII or the old or new straight bankruptcy provisions under Chapter 7. Creditors no longer have to agree to the Chapter 13 plan; it is court imposed. Business debtors are eligible to file now. Creditors may not file an involuntary proceeding as in Chapter 7 cases. Creditors are not necessarily entitled to full but delayed payment as under the old Chapter XIII but only to an amount equal to what they would have received in a straight bankruptcy. The stay and retention of property provisions are more protective than Chapter 7; and Chapter 13 also provides more favorable treatment of liens, defaults and taxes than Chapter 7.

On the question of discharge, under section 1328(a) of the new Chapter 13, the only debts excepted from discharge are alimony and child support, claims not included in the plan and certain long-term obligations voluntarily excepted from the plan. Thus except for alimony and child support the nine exceptions to discharge, including fraud, applicable to Chapter 7 are not applicable to Chapter 13. A debtor who obtains credit by fraud or other dishonesty receives a discharge under Chapter 13 but not under Chapter 7.

The concept behind the treatment of secured claims under the new Chapter 13 is fairly simple. The total claim of the secured creditor which is to be allowed is divided into two parts, the secured portion of the claim and the unsecured portion. These two are called in section 1325 the "allowed secured claim" and the "allowed unsecured claim." The secured portion of the total claim represents the present value of the collateral and the unsecured portion is the remainder, i.e., the amount the allowed claim exceeds the value of the collateral. The House Report on the new Code explains the reason for this division:

> Most often in a consumer case, a secured creditor has a security interest in property that is virtually worthless to anyone but the debtor. The creditor obtains a security interest in all of the debtor's furniture, clothes, cooking utensils, and other personal effects. These items have little or no resale value. They do, however, have a high replacement cost. The mere threat of re-

possession operates as pressure on the debtor to repay the secured creditor more than he would receive were he actually to repossess and sell the goods.

Current Chapter XIII does little to recognize the differences between the true value of the goods and their value as leverage. Proposed Chapter 13 instead views the secured creditor-debtor relationship as a financial relationship, and not one where extraneous, non-financial pressures would enter. The bill requires the court to value the secured creditor's interest. To the extent of the value of the security interest, he is treated as having a secured claim, entitled to be paid in full under the plan, unless, of course, he accepts less than full payment. To the extent that his claim against the debtor exceeds the value of his collateral, he is treated as having an unsecured claim, and he will receive payment along with all other general unsecured creditors.

Section 1325(a)(5)(B) seems to require the Bankruptcy Court to assess interest on the secured claim for the present value of the collateral (if it is not to be paid immediately) in order not to dilute the value of that claim through delay in payment. In effect the law requires the creditor to make a new loan in the amount of the value of the collateral rather than repossess it, and the creditor is entitled to interest on his loan.

II. THE FACTS OF THE INSTANT CASE

The instant case involves an automobile loan in the principal amount of $5,659, which was to have been paid over 42 months at $233 per month, making a total debt of $9,799, consisting of interest at 21% in the amount of $2,922 and insurance and other charges of $1,217. Having made no payments under the contract, the debtor, a divorced woman with three children, filed a Chapter 13 complaint two months after incurring the debt. The judge found that although the debtor "puffed" her income somewhat on her loan application, the basic reason for her default was a reduction in wages. He declined to find that she acted dishonestly in securing the loan. She filed a payment plan asking to reduce the monthly payment on the automobile from $233 to $157 and to extend the time to 60 months. The judge at the confirmation hearing found that her conduct in securing the loan and immediately filing under Chapter 13 for a reduction in payments made the proposed plan lack good faith. He indicated he would approve a plan that continued monthly payments at $233 until the contract debt was paid in full, and the debtor amended her plan to embody this proposal. . . .

· · ·

III. THE APPROPRIATE PROCEDURE TO FOLLOW IN A SECURED CLAIM CASE

Although there are as yet few court of appeals and district court cases touching on the new Chapter 13, there are already many bankruptcy court cases. A reading of those cases suggests a composite set of procedures followed implicitly by most bankruptcy courts in secured claim cases:

1. Determine the present value of the collateral under the secured claim provisions of 1325.
2. Determine the amount allowable under applicable law to the creditor by virtue of the debtor's default including unpaid principal, finance charges, interest earned prior to filing but unpaid, etc.
3. Subtract the amount of the secured claim determined in Step 1 from the amount calculated in Step 2. This represents the unsecured claim.
4. Determine the appropriate interest rate to be applied to the secured claim, as more fully discussed below. Add the secured claim and the interest to be paid.
5. Determine based on the debtor's ability to pay and his conduct how much of the "allowed unsecured claim" should be paid, provided this amount is not less than the value the creditor would receive in straight bankruptcy.
6. Determine whether the debtor's proposed plan, based on his ability to pay and conduct, is reasonable and in good faith.
7. Confirm, deny confirmation or suggest modifications in the plan depending on the outcome of Step 6.

This procedure seems to fit well with the statutory framework and statutory purpose in Chapter 13 cases. It eliminates the confusion under the old law and had the Bankruptcy Court followed it, we would not have the present confusion about what it intended to do in this case. We reverse and remand the case to the Bankruptcy Court with instructions to follow this procedure.

. . .

V. THE "GOOD FAITH" REQUIREMENT

We cannot tell exactly what the Bankruptcy Court did on the issue of whether "the plan has been proposed in good faith" under Section 1325(a)(3) of Chapter 13. . . .

. . .

The "good faith" requirement is neither defined in the Bankruptcy Code nor discussed in the legislative history. The phrase should, therefore, be interpreted in light of the structure and general purpose of Chapter 13. Obviously the liberal provisions of the new Chapter 13 are subject to abuse, and courts must look closely at the debtor's conduct before confirming a plan. We should not allow a debtor to obtain money, services or products from a seller by larceny, fraud or other forms of dishonesty and then keep his gain by filing a Chapter 13 petition within a few days of the wrong. . . .

One way to refuse to sanction the use of the bankruptcy court to carry out a basically dishonest scheme under Chapter 13 is to deny confirmation to the proposed plan. When the debtor's conduct is dishonest, the plan simply should not be confirmed. Unless courts enforce this requirement, the debtor will be able to thwart the statutory policy denying discharge in Chapter 7 cases for dishonesty.

Another way to deal with the problem when the conduct is questionable but is not shown to be dishonest, as the Bankruptcy Court found it to be in the instant case, is to require full payment in accordance with the contract. This is the position the Bankruptcy Court apparently intended to take until it wrote the last paragraph of its

FIGURE 29–5
Summary of Four Types of Bankruptcy Proceedings

	Chapter 7 Liquidation	Chapter 11 Reorganization	Chapter 12 Family Farmer	Chapter 13 Regular Income Plan
Who initiates the case?	Debtor–voluntary or creditor–involuntary	Debtor	Debtor	Debtor
What happens to debtor's property?	It is liquidated to pay creditors (except for exempt property of individual)	It is preserved	It is preserved	It is preserved
How are creditors paid?	From property of debtor	From debtor's future income	From debtor's future income	From debtor's future income
What happens to unpaid debts?	They are eliminated by the discharge	They may be reduced but not below amount creditor would have received under Chapter 7 liquidation	Priority claimants are paid in full; others may be reduced or eliminated	Priority claimants are paid in full; others may be reduced or eliminated

opinion. On remand the Bankruptcy Court should make clear whether it is, in fact, taking this position and state on the record its reasons for its decision on the good faith issue.

Accordingly, the judgment of the District Court is reversed and the case remanded for further proceedings consistent with this opinion.

CHAPTER 12—RELIEF FOR THE FAMILY FARMER

As noted at the beginning of the chapter, this recent section of the bankruptcy law was intended to provide relief for family farmers who had been and were facing some very difficult economic conditions. Only a family farmer with regular annual income can be a debtor under Chapter 12. Over 50 percent of the annual gross income of the debtor must be from farming operations.

Essentially, Chapter 12 allows a debtor to reorganize, much like the small businesses and individuals who can use the provisions of Chapter 13. The farmer is allowed to remain in possession of the property and is required to file a plan for reorganization within ninety days (the time can be extended by the court). The plan is quite similar to plans that are to be filed in Chapter 13 proceedings. The farmer's future income is to be subject to control by the trustee. All priority claims are to be paid in full and the repayment period is to be no longer than three years (the court can extend it to five years). Finally, the plan is to provide for the same treatment for all claims and interests within a particular class, unless the holder agrees to accept less (this is a little different from the comparable Chapter 13 provision).

A summary of the four types of bankruptcy proceedings is provided in Figure 29-5. Note the similarity between the Chapter 12 and 13 procedures.

REVIEW PROBLEMS

1. Compare and contrast the uses and consequences of the three kinds of bankruptcy proceedings.
2. What is the purpose of the bankruptcy law?
3. What are exemptions? Give several examples of exemptions in bankruptcy.
4. Who receives the property of the debtor that is not exempt?
5. Assume that an individual debtor has a regular income, owns a small ($20,000) business; and has $30,000 of property, $75,000 of unsecured debts, and $225,000 of secured debts. The debtor wants to stay in business but cannot pay her debts. Which of the bankruptcy proceedings is available for and might help this debtor?
6. Review the federal exemptions in bankruptcy listed on page 722. Assume Belcher's duplex is valued at $75,000—$40,000 for the portion he resides in and $35,000 for the rental portion (it is not maintained as well as his residence). If the court followed federal law rather than

state law in the debtor's use of exemptions, how would the court's decision in this case differ from the version presented in the text?

7. Brenda purchases a refrigerator, stove, and air conditioner from Freddie's Appliance Store. She paid Freddie $1,000 and signed a contract to take delivery of the appliances in two weeks. One week after her purchase of the appliances, Freddie filed a straight bankruptcy. What will be Brenda's status as a claimant? Is she entitled to any priority?

8. Nancy is a debtor considering bankruptcy. She does not own a home but does own a car (valued at $5,000, on which she still owes $4,000), jewelry valued at $1,000, six items of household goods, three of which are valued at $400 each and three of which are valued at $200 each, and $8,000 in the bank. How much of this property would be exempt under the federal exemptions?

9. Bob Smith filed a petition for a Chapter 13 regular income adjustment. His plan proposed paying $6,000 to the unsecured creditors, who were owed $20,000. The trustee determined that the sale of the debtor's nonexempt property in a Chapter 7 proceeding would provide $12,000 for the unsecured creditors. Should Smith's plan be confirmed?

10. The two defendants, Kapela and Brovenick, were the sole shareholders of a corporation that borrowed money from a bank. Each personally guaranteed to the bank the loan made to the corporation. Later the corporation lent money to Brovenick, one of the shareholders; he gave the corporation a promissory note for that loan. The corporation assigned that note to the bank.

One week prior to the corporation's filing for bankruptcy, Brovenick paid money to the bank; he claimed that payment reduced his debt to the corporation and also reduced his guarantor obligation to the bank. Five months after the bankruptcy petition was filed by the corporation, Newman, the corporation's trustee in bankruptcy, brought suit against both shareholders and sought to recover for the corporation the money paid by Brovenick to the bank. The trustee claimed the payment constituted a voidable preference, benefiting the shareholder/guarantors at the expense of other creditors of the same class. Do you agree? Kapela v. Newman, 649 F.2d 887 (1st Cir. 1981).

11. Keidel, borrowed $3,500 from the bank to finance the purchase of a mobile home she was buying from its seller, Mitchell. She signed a security agreement with the bank and gave it her promissory note. The bank gave her a check, issued to her and to Olin Employees' Credit Union, the prior lienholder. The bankrupt was advised to get a new certificate of title showing that she, instead of the seller Mitchell, had the title to the mobile home.

Keidel began to apply for a certificate of title, but didn't complete her application. Five months later she filed a petition in bankruptcy. One month after that date the bank applied for and obtained a new certificate of title, showing Keidel's ownership of the mobile home and the bank's lien interest. Under the state law the bank had a security interest in the mobile home as of the date of its loan to Keidel, but that security interest was not perfected until the date the bank applied for the new certificate of title. Does the trustee in bankruptcy, standing in the position of a lien creditor, prevail over the bank that had a security interest created prior to the date of the petition in bankruptcy, but perfected after that date? Matter of Keidel, 613 F.2d 172 (7th Cir. 1980)

12. Emily Westhem's original engagement ring had belonged to Andrew Westhem's grandmother. A number of years ago it

was stolen and the insurance proceeds were used to purchase the ring here in question. The present ring is a diamond ring having a fair market value of more than $3,000 and described as one emerald-cut diamond of approximately four carats with two side diamonds.

The present California Code of Civil Procedure exempts "[n]ecessary household furnishings and appliances and wearing apparel, ordinarily and reasonably necessary to, and personally used by, the debtor and his resident family." The bankrupt claims the ring is exempt as wearing apparel, reasonably necessary to and personally used by his wife. The trustee claims it is not exempt. Who is correct? In re Westhem, 642 F.2d 1139 (9th Cir. 1981)

13. The defendant filed a voluntary proceeding in bankruptcy. Six weeks later his mother died and he became entitled to money from a trust fund that had been created by the defendant's father. After his mother's death, the debtor filed a disclaimer, which under state law disclaimed his interest in that money and passed it instead to his children. The trustee in bankruptcy claims that the property that the debtor was entitled to was part of his estate and that the state law allowing him to disclaim it is inconsistent with and subject to the federal bankruptcy law. Is the trustee correct? Mickelson v. Detlefsen, 466 F.Supp 161 (D. Minn. 1979)

14. The debtor, Dennis Mazzola, a builder and contractor who owned his own construction company, filed a voluntary petition in bankruptcy. The plaintiffs claimed that, since some of the statements made by Mazzola on the debtor's schedule and statement of affairs were false, the debtor's discharge should be denied. Mazzola conceded that false statements existed, but said that they were mere mistakes and not fraudulent, as is necessary to bar his discharge.

The debtor was asked if he had transferred any property during the year preceding the filing of the petition. The debtor answered no, saying that he had interpreted the question to ask if he currently owned property. In fact he had transferred property to his corporation. The debtor also failed to disclose his ownership of the stock of the construction company because he didn't believe the stock to be of any value. Should the discharge be denied to Mazzola? In re Mazzola, 4 B.R. 179 (D. Mass. 1980)

15. Petitioners are claims adjusters and attorneys who provided professional services to an insurance company that has been liquidated under state law. The statutory scheme for distributing assets of an insolvent insurance company gives priority status, after expenses of administration are paid, to claims owed to employees. The language of the state law is very similar to that in the federal bankruptcy statutory provision. The other general creditors claim that the attorneys and claims adjusters are not employees, but rather, are independent contractors. Thus amounts owed to them are not due as "wages" and are not entitled to priority status. Assume that this provision in the state law is interpreted in the same way as is the provision in the federal bankruptcy laws. Should the claims adjusters' and attorneys' claims, or a part of them, be granted priority status? White v. State ex Rel Block, 597 P.2d 172 (1979)

PART IV

BUSINESS ORGANIZATIONS

The Agency Relationship

T he purpose of an agency is to allow one person to accomplish results through another person's activities. Despite modern advances in communication and transportation, a person has only one pair of hands to work with, one mouth to speak from, and can be in only one place at a time. When the time arrives that more hands and mouths are needed, or when it becomes necessary to transact business at the same time in various and remote places, the businessperson must turn to someone for assistance and representation. That someone is the agent.

AGENCY DEFINED

Agency is the legal relationship created when two people agree that one of them, called the *agent,* is to represent the other, called the *principal,* subject to the principal's right to control the agent's conduct in the delegated activity. Agency relates to commercial or business transactions conducted between the principal and third parties through the agent. In agency relations the principal confides to the agent the management of some business that the principal may lawfully do in person. The result is to bind the principal legally to third persons as though the principal personally transacted the business. The agent is merely the medium. When the dealings are completed and the dust finally clears, it is the principal and the third person who are legally bound to each other. It is the agent who ties the bond.

Types of Agents

Agents are classified as either general agents or special agents. The *general* agent is more or less continuously employed by the principal to conduct a series of transactions. He or she may be the manager of the principal's business or the lowliest of clerks. The *special* agent is hired for one particular transaction or occasion. There is no continuity in the special agent's employment. He or she is hired on a one-shot basis. Realtors and investment brokers are examples of special agents. The distinction between general and special agents is primarily a matter of degree, depending on the agent's continuity of employment.

Types of Principals

Principals are classified as either disclosed or undisclosed. In the usual agency transaction the third person knows that the agent is acting for a principal and the principal's identity.

The principal's identity may be important because the third person may be relying on the principal's credit and reputation. The agent's identity is unimportant because the transaction is between the principal and the third person, and the agent is not a party to the deal. When the third person knows the principal's identity, the principal is referred to as a *disclosed principal*.

Sometimes a principal may not wish to reveal his or her identity and the existence of the agency relation to the third person. When the third person has no knowledge that the agent is working for the particular principal, the principal is called an *undisclosed principal*. In these situations the agent's identity becomes more important than the principal's identity. Because the agent purports to be acting on his or her own, the agent is a party to the contract along with the principal. Undisclosed principals really are not sinister. People frequently have honest reasons for not wishing their connection with a transaction known. In some dealings the principal's identity simply is unimportant. For example, buyers and sellers of stock usually are unaware of the identity of the other, each knowing only his or her broker in the deal.

Agency Distinguished

There are many relationships in which one person acts for the benefit of another that are distinguished from agency. It is important to distinguish an agency relationship from something else. If it is an agency, certain legal consequences attach. If it is some other relation, significantly different legal consequences may attach.

In determining whether a relationship is an agency, the name the parties give it is not controlling. The *substance* of the relationship is controlling. Whether a relationship is an agency does not depend on clever draftsmanship. Otherwise people could label their relationships to avoid liability.

What distinguishes agency from other similar relations is the power of control retained by the principal over the agent's activities. Relations usually distinguished from agency may become agency relations if this power of control is present. Frequently called the "power of control" test, the concept is more a useful tool than an acid test for the existence of agency.

Because they render services while pursuing independent occupations, *independent contractors* usually are not agents. When working for employers, these contractors agree only to accomplish certain results and are responsible only for their final products. Employers hire them by the job and do not control the details of performance. This relationship differs from the principal-agent relationships, because principals control their agents' contractual dealings. Because independent contractors usually are not agents, their employers are not liable to the contractors' creditors nor to persons harmed by the contractors' negligence. But an individual contractor may become an agent or servant if the employer retains control over the details of performance. Whether an independent contractor becomes an agent depends on the degree and character of the control retained by the employer over the work done, and no absolute dividing line can be drawn between the two. An employer who hires an independent contractor to perform dangerous work or to take on duties which by law cannot be delegated to others remains liable for injuries caused by the contractor.

CREATION OF AGENCY RELATIONS

Capacity

Any person having capacity to consent can become a principal or an agent. A principal only has capacity to appoint an agent to perform activities that the principal may lawfully perform. A person is not allowed to accomplish through an agent what he or she is not allowed to accomplish alone. A statute may restrict a person's capacity to be an agent. Licensing statutes may limit the capacity of someone to act as an agent by requiring a license to engage in a particular business. For example, most states require real-estate brokers to be licensed before they may lawfully engage in the practice of buying and selling real estate for others.

Formalities

Generally, no formalities are required to create an agency. Payment need not be promised or made to the agent for representing the principal. Uncompensated agents are called *gratuitous* agents. The transactions they conduct are as binding on their principals as dealings conducted by *paid* agents. For example, if Penelope, knowing that her roommate is going by the bookstore after classes, asks her roommate to stop and buy a book on Penelope's account, the bookstore is entitled to payment from Penelope.

Usually it is not necessary to create an agency relation in writing. But written authorization often is desirable. Prudent businesspeople spell out their agency relations in carefully drafted written instruments. Written authorization, sometimes called a *power of attorney*, is necessary in a few situations. (For more on power of attorney, see Chapter 31.)

RIGHTS AND DUTIES BETWEEN PRINCIPAL AND AGENT

Agent's Right to Compensation

Unless it appears that the agent's services are intended to be gratuitous, the agent is entitled to compensation for the general value of his or her services. The agent's right to compensa-

tion usually is provided by contract, with matters of interpretation determined according to the ordinary rules of contract law.

In the absence of an agreement, there is an implied obligation on a principal to pay for services rendered by the agent when the services are customarily paid for. If the agency contract does not provide compensation, a promise to pay is inferred from the fact that the agent's services are rendered at the principal's request or have been accepted by the principal.

When customary and practical, the principal is obligated to keep and render accounts of the compensation owed to the agent. This allows the agent to know what he or she is entitled to and serves to implement the agent's right to compensation. Like the right to compensation, this right to an accounting depends on custom and usage. For example, principals employing traveling sales agents whose compensation is based on completed sales are in the better position to maintain sales records. Therefore they customarily keep the accounts. When this custom exists, an individual principal is required to maintain the records. But agents such as real-estate brokers and lawyers, who own their own businesses and have complete knowledge of all transactions, ordinarily keep their own accounts. Principals employing them are relieved of accounting responsibilities. But principals may be required to maintain certain records for tax purposes. The parties also may state in their agency contract who is to maintain and render accounts.

As another incident of the principal's obligation to compensate the agent, the principal is obligated to assist and cooperate with the agent and to do nothing that unreasonably prevents the agent's performance. This duty of the principal to refrain from unreasonably interfering with the agent's work allows the agent to render performance and be compensated. If the principal unreasonably interferes with the agent's performance, the agent is entitled to the compensation that would have

PREVENTIVE LAW

It is in the interests of both agent and principal to have the terms of their relationship in writing. A written agency or employment contract reduces the likelihood of a future misunderstanding. Not everything can be included in a contract, but the more important issues should be covered.

Potentially the most troublesome issue involves the agent's compensation. Frequently, sales and other agents enter into an agency relationship with one understanding of when and how they are to be paid, only to become embroiled in a dispute with their employer when the hoped-for paycheck is not in the mail. Disputes about compensation often involve disagreements between employer and agent over whether the agent performed the services specified in the contract.

The matters to be considered with respect to compensation will vary with each agency, but parties to most agencies ordinarily should consider the amount and the basis of compensation. For example, whether the compensation is to be by salary, wages, commission, a share of profits, bonuses, or in a form other than money should be expressly provided in writing. The agent also should consider including some provision to compensate for extra services and to reimburse expenses. The principal should consider including conditions governing the right of compensation. For example, he or she may wish to provide that the agent is to achieve certain results or render specified services before becoming entitled to compensation. Both parties should consider providing for compensation in the form of liquidated damages—that is, damages that are specified in the contract—in the event of a breach of the agency contract or other misconduct.

been earned if he or she had been permitted to perform as originally requested. Only the principal's unreasonable interference is prohibited, and what is "unreasonable" depends on the circumstances. Unreasonable interference may be improper commands to the agent or the principal's conduct toward third persons. The parties also may specify what constitutes an unreasonable interference. For example, ordinarily nothing is said by the parties about competition by the principal, and the principal is allowed to compete with the agent because competition is not considered unreasonable. But if the parties provide that

the principal is not to compete either directly or by hiring other agents, competition by the principal is an unreasonable interference and constitutes a material breach of the agency agreement. An example of this type of agency contract is an exclusive real-estate listing contract between a homeowner and a real-estate broker, providing that the owner not compete against the broker by attempting to sell the property through his or her own efforts or by listing the property with other brokers.

In addition to compensating the agent for services rendered, the principal is obligated to indemnify or reimburse the agent for any authorized expenses or losses suffered by the agent while acting for the principal. An *indemnity* is an obligation or duty resting on one person to make good any loss or damage incurred by another while acting for his or her benefit. It is simply the shifting of an economic loss to the person primarily responsible for it. The guiding principle is that the true benefactor should bear the burden of payment. In agency relations the agent customarily has expenses for the principal. The agent is exposed to claims as a result of being designated an agent by the principal. Because the principal originally put the agent in this position, the principal bears the financial burden.

The agent's right to indemnity usually is provided in the agency agreement, and the parties may provide that the agent bears the risk of loss and the expenses of performance of his or her duties. But if no provision is made for indemnity, the right is inferred when the agent incurs an expense, suffers a loss, or assumes a liability while acting in an authorized manner. For example, the agent is entitled to reimbursement from the principal for any authorized payment that is necessary to the agent's performance. This right to reimbursement does not arise until payment is made.

When the principal is liable to the agent for compensation, reimbursement, or indemnity, the agent is permitted a lien or security interest in the principal's goods or money lawfully possessed by the agent. This lien only extends to the amount of the agent's compensation or indemnity and entitles the agent to retain possession of the property or the proceeds from its sale until the agent is paid what is owed.

Agent's Fiduciary Duty of Loyalty

Because the agent acts solely for the principal's benefit in all matters connected with the agency, the principal-agent relation is called a *fiduciary relationship,* and the agent is referred to as the principal's fiduciary. A *fiduciary* is simply someone who acts for someone else or holds property for the benefit of another. An agency relation is just one form of fiduciary relation. Other examples are executors and administrators of estates as well as trustees.

The important element of the fiduciary relation is that the fiduciary acts for another person. Because someone else puts trust and confidence in the fiduciary, the fiduciary is held to very high standards of conduct. Certain fiduciary duties are imposed for the protection of the other person's property and interests, and the courts do not tolerate any change of these duties without the consent of the other person. A fiduciary is under a general duty to act for the other person's benefit on matters within the relationship. The agent, therefore, is under a fiduciary obligation to act solely for the principal's benefit in all matters affecting the agency relation.

As part of the fiduciary duty, the agent must give undivided loyalty to the principal. Such fidelity is fundamental to the agency relation, because without it there would be no assurance that the principal's interests would be promoted. The agent must act with the utmost good faith solely for the principal's benefit with no adverse or competing interests on his or her part. The agent must not allow his or her personal interests to conflict with the principal's. He or she may not compete directly with the principal without permission or indirectly by working for the principal's competition without the principal's consent.

Because the agent is bound to act solely for the principal, the agent must forward all agency profits to the principal. All benefits resulting from the agency relation belong to the principal. The agent may not secretly profit from his or her performance. All profits belong to the principal. The agent may not use the principal's property for his or her own benefit without the principal's consent. Furthermore, the agent may not take advantage of an opportunity rightfully belonging to the principal. For example, a purchasing agent, authorized to buy property for the principal, cannot buy for himself or herself any property that the principal would be interested in buying. Any such property bought belongs to the principal even though held by the agent.

It follows that the agent cannot deal with the principal as an adverse party, unless the principal consents to such a transaction. For example, a sales agent authorized to sell the principal's property to third persons cannot buy the property for himself or herself without the principal's consent. Even if the agent pays a fair price, the principal may cancel the sale and recover the property or obtain any profits made by the agent in any resale of the property to an innocent purchaser.

Because the agent cannot deal with the principal as an adverse party, the agent also cannot represent an adverse party in a transaction with the principal unless both parties are fully informed and agree to the arrangement. Such dual agencies, involving the agent representing two adverse parties, have a great potential for fraud. Any transaction negotiated by a double agent is voidable at the option of the party having no knowledge of the agency.

The agent's duty of loyalty also extends to the use of confidential information, such as the principal's trade secrets and customer lists. The agent may not use or communicate information confidentially given to him or her by the principal.

The following case illustrates the application of an agent's fiduciary duty of loyalty to the principal.

Douglas v. Aztec Petroleum Corp.

Court of Appeals of Texas
695 S.W.2d 312 (1985)

Background: In February 1980 Richard Seib, president of Aztec Petroleum Corporation (defendant-appellee), engaged Donnie Douglas (plaintiff-appellant) to buy a 4,900-acre block of oil and gas leases for Aztec in Anderson County, Texas. For his services Douglas was to receive $5,000, together with an assignment of an overriding royalty interest in the leases obtained.

On February 23, 1980 Aztec sent Douglas a $5,000 payment in advance for buying the leases and two other checks totaling $124,180 to pay for leases. Douglas immediately went to work getting the block together. By the end of March all but a few tracts had been leased.

Douglas had a $60 personal checkbook balance when he made the agreement with Aztec. As soon as Aztec's money arrived, Douglas put it in his own account and embarked on a spending spree. He bought two cars and a boat, paid numerous personal expenses and retired two bank notes out of the account recently filled with Aztec money. Later a photocopy of each check was sent to Aztec with the payee altered to show that a lessor had received the money actually spent on personal items.

Douglas did not put all of Aztec's money in the bank. During the acquisition period Aztec sent Douglas $343,557.36. Forty-two thousand dollars was kept as cash by Douglas and never deposited. When he made the final accounting to Aztec in June 1980, Douglas sent bogus receipts to show that the cash went to lessors. He later admitted at trial that he did not really obtain receipts for cash payments but that his wife had forged all of those sent to Aztec by transposing signatures of lessors from other documents.

Once most of the leases were obtained, Douglas became very anxious to receive his override royalty. However, Seib kept badgering Douglas for an accounting. Douglas concocted a false account by using forged receipts and altering the amount and payee of the checks to plug in whatever figure was necessary to come to $338,557.35, the amount committed to his charge. He then took the false account, together with the forged receipts and altered checks supporting it, to Aztec's Dallas headquarters.

Upon receipt of the account, Seib contacted some of the lessors and discovered several who were not paid the amounts reported. With this knowledge he refused to convey the override royalty to Douglas.

Douglas sued Aztec for the override royalty. Aztec denied liability and counterclaimed for actual and exemplary damages. A jury verdict resulted in a judgment denying Douglas the override royalty and awarding Aztec $107,834.57 in actual damages and $100,000 in exemplary damages. Douglas appealed to the Texas Court of Appeals.

Decision: The Texas Court of Appeals affirmed the trial court judgment against Douglas.

Bass, Justice

[B]oth Aztec's defensive pleadings and counterclaim state facts sufficient to allege Douglas' breach of fiduciary duty. Breach of fiduciary duty is a tort.

It is uncontroverted that Douglas was Aztec's agent. An agency is a fiduciary relationship. The law requires more of a fiduciary than arms-length marketplace ethics. He owes his principal loyalty and good faith; integrity of the strictest kind; fair, honest dealing; and the duty not to conceal matters which might influence his actions to his principal's prejudice. He is obligated to exercise a high degree of care to conserve his principal's money and to pay it only to those entitled to receive it. He must keep his principal's funds as a separate and identifiable account. The agent must make an accounting to his principal of any money that has come into his possession because of his agency. "A fiduciary has no right to make merchandise of the confidence reposed in him."

Douglas' own testimony is a startling catalogue of violations of almost every fiduciary duty.

The evidence in this case overwhelmingly and conclusively demonstrates Douglas' breach of trust. Douglas' own testimony establishes it. We therefore conclude that Douglas' breach of fiduciary duty is established as a matter of law. It is a fundamental principle of our law that an agent who acts adversely to his principal or otherwise breaches his fiduciary obligation is not entitled to compensation for his services. In *Jackson* v. *Williams,* the court cited with approval sec. 469 Restatement of Agency which states:

> An agent is entitled to no compensation for conduct which is disobedient or which is a breach of his duty of loyalty; if such conduct constitutes a wilful and deliberate breach of his contract of service, he is not entitled to compensation even for properly performed services for which no compensation is apportioned.

The override represented compensation due Douglas for "honest and forthright" performance of his agency, a duty imposed on every fiduciary. The court's judgment that Douglas is not entitled to the overriding royalty interest is based upon conclusive evidence of his willful breach of fiduciary duty. The court's denial of the override to Douglas is a proper legal consequence of his established infidelity.

Honest and forthright performance is a covenant implied in every contract. But the fiduciary relationship imposes an even more rigorous standard on the agent—"loyalty, good faith and integrity of the strictest kind." Douglas admits diverting large amounts of Aztec money to his personal use. He acknowledges preparing a bogus account. Aztec's accountant testified that, excluding Douglas' $5,000 compensation and $2,903.34 legitimate leasing expense, $107,874.57 out of the $343,557.36 did not go for the purchase of oil leases. There is ample legally sufficient evidence from which the jury could decide that Douglas willfully misappropriated that sum. The evidence is uncontroverted that he failed to account for it.

Douglas seeks to set aside the jury's award of exemplary damages arguing that exemplary damages are not recoverable for breach of contract. However, punitive damages are proper when a coincident tort is pleaded and proven. "We should not say to defaulting fiduciaries that the most for which they can be held accountable in equity are the profits which would have remained theirs had they not been called to account."

Aztec alleged and conclusively proved breach of fiduciary duty, a tort justifying the award of exemplary damages. Therefore we hold the trial court did not err in awarding exemplary damages as found by the jury.

Agent's Duty to Obey

Because the principal's control over the agent's activity is an important element of the agency relation, the agent must obey any reasonable instruction from the principal regarding the agent's performance. The "reasonableness" of an instruction depends on ethical and legal considerations. For example, a sales agent need not obey an order to misrepresent the quality of merchandise, for such an order is illegal and unethical.

If the principal issues an ambiguous instruction, the agent should seek clarification while giving it a reasonable interpretation consistent with trade practice and prior dealings. Reasonable instructions that are clear, precise, and imperative must be strictly followed, or the agent is liable for any losses resulting from disobedience. Any violation of such a clear directive is not excused by custom or usage in the business. Furthermore, the agent's motives are immaterial to his or her liability. The fact that the agent disobeys in good faith, intending to benefit the principal, does not relieve the agent of liability for any resulting loss. But the agent may disobey instructions to respond to an emergency that the agent did not create, if communication with the principal is impractical.

Agent's Duty to Use Skill and Care

The agent must use whatever skill and care is required to perform the principal's business. If the agent fails to exercise reasonable skill and care, the principal may recover for any loss or damage resulting from the agent's negligence. The principal is permitted to rely on the agent to perform the assigned responsibilities properly, and the agent is in the better position to know whether he or she possesses the qualifications to perform the job. The duty of skill and care arises from what is commonly accepted as the customs and experience in everyday living. If someone hires another to perform a job, he or she usually expects that the job will be done skillfully and carefully. Thus the agent should possess and exercise the necessary skill and care to perform the principal's business. For example, an insurance broker should know something of the trade, the form of policy, the nature of the risk, the solvency of the underwriter, and all general matters affecting the contract, or the broker is liable for negligently failing to provide adequate insurance protection for the insured.

The agent is only required to exercise reasonable and ordinary skill and care in the performance of the agency objectives. He or she is held to a standard of skill and care ordinarily possessed by persons engaged in the same business or occupation. However, if the agent claims certain special skills, he or she is held to a higher standard of care that is commensurate with the claimed specialization.

The following case shows the duty of diligence in a contemporary setting.

Bucholtz v. Sirotkin Travel Limited

U.S. District Court of New York, Nassau County

343 N.Y.S.2d 438 (1973)

Background: Bucholtz (claimant) engaged Sirotkin Travel (defendant) to arrange a trip for herself and her husband to Las Vegas. The agency advised her that they would stay at the Aladdin Hotel. Changes were made in the arrival and departure time of their flight from that originally stated. At the airport tags on Bucholtz's baggage were switched so that the baggage was not directed to the Aladdin Hotel. They were required to take alternative accommodations at a motel. The motel was located a half mile out of town. This created additional expense and inconvenience for Bucholtz and her husband in traveling to the places of interest in the town. Bucholtz sued Sirotkin for $106 for damages resulting from the Bucholtzs' inconvenience and discomfort. Decision: The trial court entered judgment in favor of Bucholtz.

Donovan, Judge

The law presently lacks clarity with respect to the relationship between the travel agency and its clients. Obviously the travel agency is an agent, but the question comes, whose agent? Is it the agent of a hotel or other innkeeper with whom, or for whom, the agency transacts business? Or the steamship line or airline with whom it does business? Generally the travel agency is neither an agent nor an employee of the common carriers and innkeepers with whom it may do business. Nor do we see any justification for holding the travel agent to be the agent of any intermediate wholesaler who may put together a "package" of accommodations.

The travel agent deals directly with the traveler. He must be charged with the duty of exercising reasonable care in securing passage on the appropriate carrier and lodging with an innkeeper. The money was paid over by the traveler to the defendant agency for that specific purpose.

News reports are constantly appearing with stories of travelers—many of them quite young—being stranded far from home or having vacation plans ruined because passage or lodging for which they have paid has not been provided. Who is to bear the responsibility? Is it some remote "wholesaler" who is unknown to the traveler, or the traveler himself, or the travel agency in whom the traveler has reposed his confidence?

In this case nothing was done by the travel agency to verify or confirm either the plane reservations or the hotel reservations. If this duty is the responsibility of the travel agency, then the travel agency is liable in negligence for its failure to exercise reasonable care in making the reservations.

It may be urged that the default in this respect is that of the remote "wholesaler."

Where, as here, the agent is selected because he is supposed to have some special fitness for the performance of the duties to be undertaken, the traveler is entitled to rely on the judgment and discretion of that agent as well as his honesty and financial responsibility. The agent may not evade responsibility by delegating to a subagent the carrying out of the task which has been committed to him. Travel agencies may find it convenient in the course of transacting their business, to deal with wholesalers. The news reports are so voluminous that we may take judicial notice of the vice inherent in conducting business in so loose a fashion. The wholesaler may fail to pay for accommodations or may even fail to book the accommodations and the traveler is left in a helpless situation. He either has no recourse because of financial insufficiency or he may be required to travel to a distant jurisdiction in order to maintain a suit.

Unless the principal, here the traveler, has expressly or impliedly authorized the travel agency to delegate responsibility to a second agency or "wholesaler," the responsibility must remain on the defendant travel agency. In an area so fraught with danger to the traveler, public policy demands that the travel agency be held responsible to: (a) verify or confirm the reservations and (b) use reasonable diligence in ascertaining the responsibility of any intervening "wholesaler" or tour organizer.

This duty parallels, or is analogous to, the duty of an insurance broker in obtaining insurance coverage for his client.

Claimant here did not consent to any delegation of the duty owed to her by the defendant travel agency.

The defendant is liable to the claimant for the breach of its fiduciary responsibility in failing to use reasonable care to confirm the reservations.

Agent's Duty to Inform and Account

It makes sense that parties in agency relations should communicate with each other. Therefore a duty is imposed on the agent to communicate to the principal on anything affecting the principal's interests. The agent must make a reasonable attempt to inform the principal of matters relating to any agency transaction about which the agent should realize the principal would want to know. For example, a real-estate agent who is authorized to sell the principal's property at a specified price and on specified terms should inform the principal if he or she knows of someone who will pay a higher price or agree to better terms. Furthermore, the agent should disclose any information that disqualifies the agent from effectively promoting the principal's interests. If the agent is unable to undertake the principal's interests, he or she must inform the principal. Even if the agent is merely ill for a day, the agent's duty to inform requires the agent to notify the principal of the fact so that the principal may make other arrangements.

It follows that if the agent must communicate with the principal, he or she also must keep and render an account of money or other property that the agent receives. This account includes anything received from the principal as well as anything obtained from third persons for the principal. The agent is liable to the principal if he or she does not properly account for all funds coming into the agent's possession during the agency relation. Although it is ordinarily the principal's duty to keep his or her own accounts, the duty shifts to the agent if the agent is entrusted with funds or property or is required to make collections and expenditures. The manner of accounting need not be formal or meet technical accounting

requirements. The method of bookkeeping depends on what is normally done in the business or is accepted by the principal.

Implicit in the duty to account is the agent's duty not to mix the principal's money or property with his or her own. The reason for this requirement is to make any accounting more accurate. Thus the agent may not put the principal's money in his or her own bank account or in a joint account unless the principal agrees to such an arrangement. To allow otherwise would make it difficult to determine whether it was the principal's or the agent's money that was deposited.

The following case illustrates the judicial approach to disclosure within the context of the broker-investor relationship. The case is also included because it brings together many of the agent's fiduciary duties.

McKeehan v. Wittels
Court of Appeals of Missouri
508 S.W.2d 277 (1977)

Background: Dorothy McKeehan (plaintiff), looking for investment opportunities, dealt directly with Malcolm and Jacob Wittels of Wittels Investment Company (defendants). In response to the Wittelses' urging, McKeehan entrusted $28,813 to them. The Wittelses invested this money in a type of investment security known as a deed of trust in property. After the investments matured, McKeehan repeatedly demanded that her funds be returned. The Wittelses, who knew of McKeehan's instructions, disregarded them. The Wittelses renewed the investments without her consent and against her expressed wishes. Additionally, tax liens existed on all properties in the investments, and there was strong evidence that the Wittelses were aware of these tax liens. McKeehan sued the Wittelses for damages, alleging that they breached their fiduciary duties to her. The trial court entered judgment in favor of McKeehan in the amount of $29,942.65 actual damages and $25,000 punitive damages. The Wittelses appealed to the Missouri Court of Appeals.

Decision: The Missouri Court of Appeals ruled in favor of McKeehan and affirmed the trial court judgment.

McMillian, Judge

[P]laintiff pleads that defendants breached their fiduciary duty by deliberately failing to follow her instructions, failing to disclose essential information affecting the security of her investments, and misrepresenting certain facts for the purpose of furthering their own financial position.

> Loyalty to their trust is firmly exacted of all agents by law, and when one uses his position for his own ends, regardless of the welfare of his principal, he becomes responsible for a resultant loss, as if he unscrupulously handles money or property confided to him to benefit himself. An agent cannot ignore the directions given to him as to how the business put into his hands shall be transacted, and cannot use his agency for his own advantage, to the detriment of the principal.

Likewise, a fiduciary relationship between principal and agent obligates the agent to fully disclose all material facts to the principal, to strictly avoid misrepresentation and in all respects to act with utmost good faith.

[The] evidence is sufficient to sustain a finding that defendants Malcolm Wittels and Wittels Investment Co., knowingly failed to follow plaintiff's explicit instructions regarding the handling of her investments.

We also find ample evidence to sustain a finding that Malcolm and Jacob Wittels and Wittels Investment Co. breached their fiduciary duty to plaintiff by failing to disclose material facts regarding her investments. It is the established law in this jurisdiction that the existence of a confidential or fiduciary relationship between principal and agent obligates the agent to make a complete and full disclosure of all material facts concerning the transaction which might affect the principal's decision regarding his or her investments. Similarly, it is a breach of fiduciary duty for an agent to occupy a position antagonistic to his principal.

Plaintiff's evidence strongly supports the trial court's finding that the defendants Malcom and Jacob Wittels and Wittels Investment Company did occupy a position antagonistic to plaintiff and consequently failed to disclose all necessary facts to plaintiff regarding her investments. The record is clear that as to certain parcels of property, defendants sold the first deed of trust to plaintiff and held on to the more profitable second deed themselves. Plaintiff also introduced exhibits and testimony that tax liens existed on all of the parcels of property held under the deeds of trust purchased from defendants. Malcolm Wittels testified that he knew that a tax lien was considered to be a first lien on the property. There is strong evidence that Malcolm and Jacob Wittels were aware of the existence and accrual of tax liens on the properties at the time plaintiff purchased and held the deeds of trust. When the deeds of trust were given to Dorothy McKeehan under the circumstances shown in the evidence, she was justified in believing she was purchasing a first deed of trust constituting a first lien on the property and not subject to any prior tax liens. The record clearly reflects the extreme unlikelihood that defendants Malcolm and Jacob Wittels were unaware of these tax liens. Their failure to disclose the tax liens to plaintiff at the time of sale and the failure to disclose the accrual of these tax liens is more than sufficient evidence to sustain the trial court's finding and judgment with respect to these defendants.

We have carefully read the record and have concluded that there is substantial evidence to support the trial court's finding that defendants Malcolm and Jacob Wittels and Wittels Investment Company breached their fiduciary duty to plaintiff.

ETHICS BOX
The Opportunistic Agent

There is a growing literature in management and finance that stresses certain inherent problems in the agency relationship. The agent is expected to act on behalf of the principal, but the agent may have certain expertise or possess certain exclusive information that will make it hard for the principal to monitor the agent's activities. Knowing this, the unethical agent may take advantage of the principal and either shirk on the job, if the agent is being paid by the hour, or divert resources to his or her own use.

The agent who shirks or diverts is giving in to an actual conflict of interest. The agent owes a duty to the principal to put the principal's interests first. But the agent may have a personal financial interest that is at odds with the obligation to the principal. The agent who gives in to this temptation violates standards of professional business ethics.

REVIEW PROBLEMS

1. What is an agency relationship? Who is the principal and who is the agent?
2. What distinguishes an agent from an independent contractor?
3. Why is an agency relationship a fiduciary relationship?
4. What duties does a principal owe an agent? What duties does an agent owe a principal?
5. Penelope had inspected equipment to be sold at an auction. She planned to go to the auction and try to buy three pieces of equipment. On the day of the auction her friend Andrew gratuitously offered to go to the auction for Penelope and to bid on the equipment for her. Penelope authorized Andrew to bid up to $10,000 for each of the three pieces she wanted. Andrew acquired the first piece for Penelope for $9,000. He bid on the second piece on his own behalf and bought it for $9,500. Andrew left the auction before the third piece was offered. It was sold for $7,000. Is

Andrew the agent of Penelope? Explain. If so, has Andrew violated any of the duties that an agent owes a principal? Explain.

6. Owner orally authorized Agent to sell his house. Agent completed a sale of the house to Buyer. When Buyer attempted to enforce the contract against Owner, Buyer was told that the contract was not enforceable because Owner's agency relation with Agent was not in writing. Must Owner have given Agent written authorization?

7. Owner listed his house with Penelope, a real-estate broker, granting Penelope an exclusive right to sell Owner's house. Penelope entered negotiations with Buyer, who seemed interested in purchasing the property. Buyer found the price agreeable. But he insisted on including a clause in the sales contract giving him the right to cancel the contract if he could not get a loan to finance his purchase. At the closing, Buyer exercised his right to cancel,

giving as his reason the inability to procure a loan. Penelope turned to Owner and claimed that she was entitled to her commission even though the sale did not go through. Must Owner pay Penelope a commission?

8. Peter authorized Arnon, a grain broker, to buy for Peter at the market 20,000 bushels of wheat. Arnon had in storage at the time 5,000 bushels belonging to John, who had authorized Arnon to sell for him. Arnon also had 15,000 bushels which she owned. Arnon transferred these 20,000 bushels to Peter's name and charged Peter the current market price. Shortly thereafter and before Peter had used or sold the wheat, the market price declined sharply. Peter refused to pay for the wheat and tried to cancel the contract. Can Peter do this? Explain.

9. The Hagertys decided to spend a week in Hawaii. They went to the Ace Travel Agency, secured reservations at the Ritz Hotel, and were issued round trip tickets on Kamikaze Airline to and from Hawaii. When they arrived at the airport on the date of departure, they found that an airline employee had failed to record their reservation properly. They could not be accommodated on the assigned flight. The Hagertys managed to secure a reservation on a flight that left several hours later. They arrived later that day at the Ritz Hotel and checked in. Two days before their scheduled checkout date, the Hagertys were asked by the management to leave the hotel to make room for a convention checking in that day. When they refused to comply with the request, the hotel authorized its employees to enter their room and remove their belongings. When Mr. Hagerty resisted eviction, he was knocked to the floor and suffered a broken arm. The Hagertys left the hotel, spent the remaining two days of their vacation at a nearby motel, and then re-turned home on the assigned flight. Worn and harassed by the preceding events, the Hagertys sued the Ace Travel Agency for medical expenses incurred by Mr. Hagerty, for mental anguish, and for the additional expenses resulting from these occurrences. The Hagertys claim that Ace breached its fiduciary duties as the Hagertys' agent. Ace claims that it was not Hagertys' agent. Who is right?

10. Porter had been employed by the Brinn & Jensen Company for many years as a traveling salesman and had been assigned to cover a definite territory. Porter used his own automobile as a means of transportation and covered his territory once every five weeks. He worked on commissions but had a drawing account with the company, which was treated as an advance on commissions earned. He also made collections for the company and performed other services when so directed by the home office. The company could discharge Porter any time it became dissatisfied with the manner in which he was doing his work. The company required Porter to furnish an automobile to be used in covering his territory, and he would not have been retained if he could not provide one. It was generally left to Porter to determine the route to be used in covering his territory, but the company retained the right to direct him to go elsewhere within the territory if it desired to do so. Porter was required to make personal calls on customers and to send in his orders daily. The company instructed him about the merchandise to be pushed. He was required to devote all of his time to company business. While driving on company business, Porter was killed when his automobile crashed into another automobile driven by Peterson, who was seriously injured. At the time of the accident Porter had with him a sample case, forms, catalogues, and a number of orders signed by

customers. Peterson sued the company, claiming that Porter was its agent. The company claimed it had no liability, because it did not control the physical movements of the automobile being driven by Porter. Who is right? Peterson v. Brinn & Jensen Co., 280 N.W.171 (1938)

11. Arthur Murray, Incorporated, licenses people to operate dancing studios using its registered trade name and its method of dancing. Burkin, Inc., obtained such a license for a dancing school in San Diego. The agreement between Arthur Murray and Burkin provided that Arthur Murray would:

   (a) fix minimum tuition rates;
   (b) designate the school's location and layout;
   (c) make pupil refunds and charge the amounts to Burkin; and
   (d) collect 5 percent of the school's weekly gross receipts to be used to pay any suits against Arthur Murray's.

   The agreement also provided that Burkin would:

   (a) obey Arthur Murray's rules regarding the qualifications and conduct of instructors and discharge any employee found unacceptable to Arthur Murray;
   (b) submit advertising for Arthur Murray's approval;
   (c) maintain and manage the school according to Arthur Murray's general policies; and
   (d) submit weekly financial records to Arthur Murray.

   Gertrude Nichols entered into several contracts with the San Diego school and made prepayments for lessons that were never furnished because Burkin discontinued its operations. Nichols brought suit against Arthur Murray, Inc., claiming that the San Diego school was its agent. Is she right? Nichols v. Arthur Murray, Inc., 56 Cal. Rptr. 728 (1967)

12. Julius and Olga Sylvester owned an unimproved piece of land near King of Prussia, Pennsylvania. They were approached by Beck, a real-estate broker, who asked if they were willing to sell their land, stating that an oil company was interested in buying, renting, or leasing the property. The Sylvesters said that they were only interested in selling, and they authorized Beck to sell the property for $15,000. Several weeks later Beck phoned the Sylvesters and offered to buy the property for himself for $14,000. Olga asked, "What happened to the oil company?" and Beck responded, "They are not interested. You want too much money for it." The Sylvesters sold the property to Beck. A month later Beck sold the property to Epstein for $25,000. When the Sylvesters learned that Beck had realized a huge profit in a quick resale of the property, they sued Beck, claiming that he owed them the $9,000 profit. Does Beck owe the Sylvesters the money? Sylvester v. Beck, 178 A.2d 755 (1962)

The Effect of Agency Relations

C hapter 30 examined the nature of the principal-agent relation by focusing on how the two parties create their relation and the rights and duties they owe each other. But there is more to the agency relation. The principal hires the agent to interact with others as the principal's representative. This interaction is the essence of the agency. It is the reason the agent is hired. The agent interacts with others in two ways: (1) by making contracts for the principal with third persons and (2) by committing torts during the agent's employment that harm others. When the agent acts in these ways, the legal picture adds a third dimension. The legal consequences of this interaction attach not only to the principal and the agent, but to the third person, affecting the rights and duties of each person toward the others. This chapter explores how these legal consequences affect all three individuals. The chapter also examines the ending of the agency relation and how it affects the rights of the parties.

CONTRACTUAL DEALINGS: PRINCIPAL AND THIRD PARTIES

The contracts made by an authorized agent for a principal are as binding on the principal as they would have been had the principal entered into them in person.

An agent's authority is conferred by various methods. The principal may expressly authorize the agent's action. The principal may indicate to the agent by conduct that the agent has authority to undertake certain transactions. Authority is established also if others can reasonably infer from the principal's conduct that the principal authorizes the agent's activity. Even when the principal does not authorize someone to act as an agent, a third party may establish authority if the principal later authorizes transactions done for him or her.

Actual Authority

Actual authority is the power of an agent to affect the principal's legal relations by acts

FIGURE 31-1
Scope of Authority

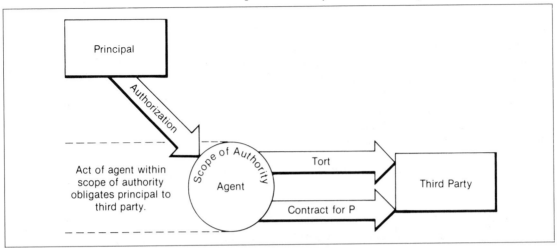

[*Source:* Douglas Whitman, F. William McCarty, Frank F. Gibson, Thomas W. Dunfee, Bartley A. Brennan, and John D. Blackburn, *Law and Business* (New York: Random House, 1987), p. 468. Copyright © 1987 by Thomas W. Dunfee, F. William McCarty, Frank F. Gibson, Douglas Whitman, John D. Blackburn, and Bartley A. Brennan.]

done according to the principal's show of consent to the agent. The principal may consent by any means that causes the agent to understand what the principal wants the agent to do. If the agent's actual authority is stated in words, it is referred to as *express* authority. If the agent's actual authority is communicated by the principal's conduct toward the agent, it is called *implied* authority. The legal effect of the two is the same: the agent is empowered to change the principal's legal relations with third persons (see Figure 31-1). For example, if a businessperson tells a secretary to accept customer payments, the secretary has express authority to collect payments as instructed. If the secretary also buys office supplies and the principal pays without objection, the secretary or the seller may reasonably infer that the principal authorizes continued purchases of office supplies. In both situations the principal is obligated to others by the secretary's actions.

Express Authority. The clearest example of express authority is the *power of attorney.* A power of attorney is a formal written instrument conferring authority upon an agent. Powers of attorney often are used because a third person entering into a specific, major transaction with an agent may require evidence of the agent's authority. In these situations the authority may be set forth in a form that is familiar and convenient to people in the business. The acts authorized usually require the execution of specifically described documents. For example, banks and other professional lenders that deal regularly with borrowers' agents have standard forms for the purpose of assuring themselves of the authority of agents to borrow on their principals' credit. Because of absence, sickness, age, or lack of interest, people widely delegate the management of their affairs to others. Interpretation of the activities included in these powers often is a problem.

Informal written expressions of authority

often are included in standard form contracts that the agent negotiates with third persons. Known as merger, integration, or *exculpatory clauses,* these statements serve explicitly to limit an agent's authority to make only those agreements contained in the standard form contract. A typical merger clause is:

It is hereby further agreed that there are no prior writings, verbal negotiations, understandings, representations or agreements between the parties not herein expressed, and no agent of Seller is authorized to make or enter into on Seller's behalf any writings, verbal negotiations, understandings, representations or agreements not here expressed.

Unauthorized transactions made by the agent with a third person who has notice of this limitation on the agent's authority are not binding on the principal. Obligations undertaken in violation of this express limitation of authority are the agent's.

The following case illustrates the rules governing limitations on an agent's authority.

Dembrowski v. Central Construction Company

Supreme Court of Nebraska

185 N.W.2d 461 (1971)

Background: Central Construction Company (defendant) was in the home improvement business. It sold materials and furnished labor for that purpose. It also employed a number of sales agents on a commission basis. One of Central's sales agents called on the Dembrowskis (plaintiffs) and induced them to sign a contract for the purchase and installation of new siding, aluminum doors, and windows on their home. The contract provided:

> There are no representations, guarantees, or warranties except such as may herein be incorporated. Contractor does not make, and no agent of Contractor is authorized to make, any agreement with Owner(s) either concerning the use of the Owner(s) premises as a "model home" or concerning any payments, credits or commissions to be received by Owner(s) for referrals of prospective customers.

The Dembrowskis were aware of this provision, objected to it to the agent, but nevertheless executed the contract in reliance upon the agent's representations that they would not have to pay anything on the contract because their house was to be used as a model home, and a percentage of other sales made on the strength of it would be credited to them in sufficient amounts to pay the contract in full. The agent told them that the contract provision mentioned did not apply to them and would be disregarded. The Central Construction Company had no knowledge of the fraudulent conduct of its agent until after the materials and labor called for in the contract had been furnished by the company.

The Dembrowskis sued Central Construction Company to have the contract "reformed" to include the sales agent's statements regarding payment. The trial court granted judgment in favor of the Dembrowskis. Central Construction appealed to the Supreme Court of Nebraska.

Decision: Ruling in favor of Central Construction Company, the Supreme Court of Nebraska reversed the trial court decision and returned the case back to the trial court with directions to dismiss the case.

Newton, Justice

The issue presented is the responsibility of the defendant principal for the fraud of its agent.

As noted, plaintiff and his wife were aware of the contract provisions limiting the agent's authority to enter into what would be a most unusual contract. Ordinarily, "a person with notice of a limitation of an agent's authority cannot subject the principal to liability upon a transaction with the agent if he should know that the agent is acting improperly."

The evidence fails to establish that the defendant principal had knowledge of its agent's fraudulent conduct until after the contract had been entered into and fully performed by defendant.

> (1) An innocent principal can, by contract with another, relieve himself of liability for deceit because of unauthorized fraud by a servant or other agent upon the other party.
>
> (2) A contract with, or a conveyance to, the principal obtained by his agent through misrepresentations can be rescinded by the other party to the contract or conveyance prior to a change of position by the principal, even though the contract provides for "it shall not be affected by misrepresentations not contained therein" and includes a statement that the agent has made no representations.
>
> One seeking to recover from a principal, for an unauthorized act of an agent, must establish that the principal obtained knowledge of such act before it had changed its position.

Implied Authority. In most agency relations it is impossible to express every detail of the agent's authority. For example, if a storeowner hires someone to manage the business, it is impossible to describe every single management function. For the sake of flexibility the agent is allowed additional implied authority to perform activities that he or she or a third party might reasonably infer are incidental or necessary to carry out the principal's instructions.

Several factors determine whether implied authority exists. The circumstances generally considered by courts are customary trade usages, the principal's practices with other agents in similar situations, and earlier experiences of the principal and the particular agent. For example, a question of whether a particular salesperson has the implied authority to extend warranties on merchandise sold to third persons may be answered by examining what similar salespeople in the trade usu-

PREVENTIVE LAW
Exculpatory Clauses

Merger or exculpatory clauses of the type discussed on page 762 and in the *Dembrowski* case have enormous implications, especially in this era of increasing emphasis on consumer protection. From a company's viewpoint these clauses are often the only practical way in which the company can control against liability that might otherwise result from the promises of a too-eager sales agent. The merger or exculpatory clause effectively limits a sales agent's actual authority to make any additional representations than the ones contained in the sales contract. Not having authorized the sales agent's statements, the principal-seller is not liable to honor them. However, consumers frequently do not appreciate the legal effect of these clauses.

The crucial facts in situations involving merger or exculpatory clauses often are whether the purchaser reads the clause and complains before the seller fully performs its part of the bargain. If the purchaser reads the clause, the purchaser is put on notice of the agent's limited authority. If the purchaser does not read the clause, and if the clause is prominently placed in the contract, a court usually will reach the same result, because it is not unreasonable to expect people to read, understand, and be bound by their contracts. Courts even entertain the presumption that parties to contracts knowingly read the agreements they sign. If, however, the clause is not prominently displayed in the contract, a court may not enforce it against the purchaser. In home-solicitation sales situations—where the sales agent solicits sales in the purchaser's home—the consumer may feel obliged to sign a contract just to assure the sales agent's departure. Most states have enacted statutes permitting purchasers in these situations to cancel the contract within three days of its making.

Companies that use merger or exculpatory clauses in their sales contracts should train their sales agents as to the effect of such clauses. The sales agents should be advised not to exceed their authority. Even though such statements will not be legally binding on the company, they will not help the company's reputation. A good practice would be to require the sales agent to point out the clause to the consumer, explain its significance, and have a place on the contract for the consumer to sign or initial, indicating that the consumer has read the clause and understands its significance.

ally do, what other salespeople employed by the principal usually do, and what the principal has permitted that particular salesperson to do in the past.

Although the principal implicitly authorizes the agent to do whatever is ordinarily required to accomplish the job, sometimes as the job progresses the agent confronts an emergency. In such an emergency the agent can reasonably infer that the principal consents to the agent's undertaking whatever is required to protect the principal's interests. Authorization of the agent's activity is implied in these situations. This implied authority exists only when the threat to the principal's business is sudden and unexpected and when contact with the principal or superior officer is impractical. It extends only to activities that the emergency makes necessary.

Apparent Authority

Authority also exists if the principal's conduct causes third persons reasonably to believe that the agent is authorized. This rule permits third parties to rely on the principal's manifestation in dealing with an agent. This type of authority is called *apparent authority*. Its effect on the principal's liability to third persons is the same as actual authority, because both types empower the agent to affect the principal's legal relations with others. The adjectives "actual" and "apparent" denote only the viewpoints used in interpreting the principal's conduct. Actual authority is determined from the agent's viewpoint. Apparent authority is determined from the third person's viewpoint.

The agent's apparent authority may arise in various ways. It may result from the principal's statement to a third person or from the principal's allowance of the agent's activities. It may be established from the principal's permission to the agent to do something under circumstances creating a reputation of authority in the area in which the agent acts. Earlier dealings between the agent and third persons might lead a third person reasonably to infer that the agent is authorized. For example, a customer might reasonably believe that a salesperson in a department store is authorized to transact business in an adjacent department. But apparent authority cannot be established by the agent's statements alone. If it could, anyone might confer upon himself or herself authority to obligate others simply by acting and talking like an agent.

Ratification of Unauthorized Activity

Authorization of the agent need not occur before the agent transacts the principal's business. If the principal earlier has not authorized someone to act as an agent, the principal may supply the authority later by ratifying the transaction. Ratification is the later approval by the principal of an earlier, unauthorized act by someone claiming to act as an agent. Ratification may occur when the agent exceeds his or her original authority and enters into unauthorized transactions or when a stranger supposedly acts as another's agent. The difference between the principal's liability created by ratification rather than earlier authorization is the timing of the principal's consent to be bound. In actual or apparent authority the principal shows consent before the agent conducts any business. In ratification the principal's consent comes after the business is conducted.

Because ratification treats the transaction as if it had been originally authorized, only those acts that could have been authorized originally may later be ratified. For this reason the ratifier must have been competent to be a principal at the time the transaction took place. Only those acts undertaken for the principal may be ratified. No ratification can occur for acts done by someone acting on his or her own.

Any act of a principal that shows complete, knowledgeable affirmation of the agent's acts can constitute a ratification. Any acts, words, or conduct reasonably indicating an intent to ratify may constitute a ratification. For example, a principal who benefits by an agent's unauthorized bargain or sues to enforce a contract made by a false agent may constitute a ratification. But the principal's affirmation must be complete. He or she cannot affirm part of a transaction but disaffirm the rest. The following case shows a court applying the concepts of express authority, implied authority, apparent authority, and ratification.

Pailet v. Guillory
Louisiana Court of Appeals
315 S.2d 893 (1975)

Background: Cenla Equipment Company entered into a five-year lease with Rae Abramson and her sister, Ruth Pailet (appellee), for the lease of office space. Ruth and Rae had inherited the property from their mother's estate. In the lease Richard Michel and Twyman Guillory (appellants) personally guaranteed Cenla's rental payments. Later the lease was assigned (transferred) to Twyman Guillory with the lessors' approval.

All matters concerning the leased property were handled for the lessors by Rae Abramson's husband, Dr. Albert Abramson. Michel and Guillory first contacted Dr. Abramson about leasing the property. They sent Dr. Abramson the rent checks made out to the lessors. And Dr. Abramson handled minor repairs on the property. Michel and Guillory never had any direct contact with the lessors; their only contact was with Dr. Abramson. Dr. Abramson made it clear to Michel and Guillory that he did not own the leased property and that in certain matters he could act only with the permission of the lessors. For instance, he made it clear that he did not have authority to lease the property. The lease was made only after Ruth and Rae had approved the lease terms and signed the lease themselves. Also, the assignment of the lease from Cenla to Guillory was approved in writing by the lessors.

In March of 1973 Guillory and Michel approached Dr. Abramson and asked that the lease be canceled. Dr. Abramson told them that he would have to check with the lessors, because he did not have authority to cancel. A few days later Dr. Abramson notified Guillory that the lessors had agreed to cancel the lease. Later Rae admitted that she had consented to the cancellation, but Ruth vigorously denied that she had been contacted by Dr. Abramson and denied that she had agreed to the cancellation.

Guillory vacated the property in 1973, and the building was not rented until after 1974. In 1975 Pailet sued Guillory and Michel for her half of the rents due to her, which she claimed was $82.50 per month for twenty-four months for a total of $1,980. The trial court entered judgment for Pailet. Guillory and Michel appealed to the Louisiana Court of Appeals.

Decision: The Louisiana Court of Appeals ruled in favor of Pailet and affirmed the trial court decision in her favor.

Fruge, Judge

Appellants contend that even if Mrs. Pailet did not agree to cancellation of the lease, she is bound by the act of Dr. Abramson who was vested with the implied authority to cancel the lease.

An agency relationship may be created through either express or implied authority. Like an express agency, an implied agency is an actual agency. Apparent authority, on the other hand, creates no actual agency relationship. However, where the principal clothes an agent with apparent authority to perform certain acts and a third party who has no knowledge of or reason to believe that there are limitations on that authority, deals with the agent, then the principal is bound by the acts of the agent, which although beyond the actual power delegated to him, are within his apparent authority.

In the case before us, although there was never any express agency relationship between Mrs. Pailet and Dr. Abramson, he clearly had the authority to act as her agent in some matters concerning the leased property. Dr. Abramson was given the authority to collect rents, to make minor repairs, and to represent the lessors in preliminary negotiations regarding the lease.

However, the question before us is whether he had the implied authority to cancel the lease. Implied authority is actual authority which is inferred from the circumstances and nature of the agency itself. "An agent is vested with the implied authority to do all of those things necessary or incidental to the agency assignment." In this case, Dr. Abramson's agency authority included collecting the rent and making minor repairs. Certainly the authority to cancel the lease is not incidental or necessary to his authority to collect rent and make minor repairs. No such authority can be inferred in these circumstances, particularly where the authority to lease or permit assignment was not given.

We turn now to the issue of apparent authority. The concern here is whether the principal did anything to clothe the agent with apparent authority to perform the act though no actual authority was given. Because third persons are not privy to the actual terms of the agency agreement, they may rely upon the indicia of authority with which the agent is vested.

We do not find that the lessors in this case clothed Dr. Abramson with the apparent authority to cancel the lease. Dr. Abramson himself denied that he had any authority to do so. The lease agreement and permission for the assignment to Twyman Guillory were signed by the lessors and not by Dr. Abramson. Thus all the indications were that Dr. Abramson did not have authority to cancel.

Appellants rely on the fact that all of their communications with the lessors concerning the leased property were through Dr. Abramson. This alone is not enough. The fact that Dr. Abramson failed to secure cancellation of the lease from Mrs. Pailet is not imputable to her, but rather to the appellants since they relied on Dr. Abramson to secure cancellation.

Appellants' final argument is that because Mrs. Pailet waited nine months before making any claim to the rent, she ratified the cancellation made by Dr. Abramson. However, for ratification to occur the facts must indicate a clear and absolute intent to ratify the act. In this case, there is no evidence that Mrs. Pailet even had any knowledge that Dr. Abramson told the defendants that the lease was cancelled. In these circumstances there could be no intent to ratify.

Effect of Agent's Knowledge

An important consequence of the agency relation is that the principal is charged with knowing everything about the agency that the agent knows. The agent must communicate to the principal information about agency matters. Presumably the agent tells the principal everything relating to the agent's performance. Whether this actually is done is unimportant, because the reason for imputing the agent's knowledge to the principal is to protect innocent third persons. When determining the principal's liability to innocent third persons, the principal and not the third person bears the risk of the agent's failure to inform.

Notification is the act of informing an agent, which has the same legal effect as if the principal had received it. For example, filing a claim with an insurance company's claims agent is a form of notification to the company. To be effective, notification must be made to an agent authorized to receive it. Frequently the terms of a contract specify the person authorized to receive notice, but the agent also may be implicitly or apparently authorized to receive notification. Notice to an agent who is not authorized to receive it is not effective notification to the principal unless the principal later ratifies its receipt.

A principal is not assumed to know what an agent knows when the agent and a third party conspire to cheat or defraud the principal or when the agent otherwise acts against the principal's interests. In these situations the principal's knowledge is not assured because it cannot be presumed that the agent communicates the information to the principal. For example, an insurance company may rescind an insurance contract when there is collusion between the insured and the company's agent to defraud the company.

CONTRACTUAL DEALINGS: AGENTS AND THIRD PARTIES

Contractual liability depends on whether a person is a party to the contract. Generally an agent who negotiates an authorized contract for a principal is not a party to the agreement and therefore is neither liable on the contract nor able to enforce it against the third person. The agent may agree to become a party, but in most situations the agent acts only for the principal. But even if not a party to the agreement, an agent is responsible for unauthorized dealings, based on an implied warranty of authorization to act for the principal.

Undisclosed Agency

When the agent acts for an undisclosed principal, the third person has no notice of the agency relation or the principal's identity. From the third person's viewpoint the person negotiating the contract is the party to the contract. For this reason an agent purporting to act alone, but in fact acting for an undisclosed principal, becomes a party to the contract, along with the principal. However, while outwardly appearing to be a party, in reality the agent is still acting for another. This relationship transforms the agent into a peculiar form of contracting party with special rights and duties. For example, if the agent enforces the contract against the third person, the principal is entitled to any proceeds or performance, because that is what the principal and agent originally agreed. Once the undisclosed principal's identity is revealed, the agent may force the third person to choose which party is responsible for performance. If the agent is forced to perform, he or she is entitled to reimbursement from the principal.

Disclosed Agency

The agent who contracts in the name of a disclosed principal does not become a party to the contract unless he or she personally agrees to do so. The principal and third person are directly liable to each other, and the agent is not involved. An agent seeking to avoid personal liability under a contract must fully disclose the principal's identity.

The following case illustrates the need for agents to disclose their agency relationship to avoid liability on the contracts that they negotiate.

Bio-Chem Medical Laboratories, Inc. v. Harvey

Louisiana Court of Appeals
310 S.2d 173 (1973)

Background: From May 17, 1973 to June 1973 Bob Harvey (defendant) was employed by the Magnolia Health Center as a laboratory technician. While at Magnolia, Harvey ordered laboratory testing services from Bio-Chem Medical Laboratories (plaintiff). Harvey left Magnolia on June 13, 1973 to assume an administrative position with another clinic. Later that month he received a bill from Bio-Chem for the testing services he ordered while at Magnolia. Harvey claimed that he contracted for these services in a representative capacity for his employer and therefore was not obligated to pay the bill.

Bio-Chem sued Harvey to recover the amount owed for the lab testing services, and the trial court entered judgment against Harvey. Harvey appealed to the Louisiana Court of Appeals.

Decision: The Louisiana Court of Appeals ruled in favor of Bio-Chem and affirmed the trial court judgment against Harvey.

Lemmon, Judge

[T]he only remaining issue is whether Harvey is personally liable for the services he ordered while employed by Magnolia.

A person contracting for services in a representative capacity must disclose that fact in order to avoid personal liability under the contract. This disclosure, however, is unnecessary if the circumstances surrounding the contract reasonably informed the creditor he was dealing with the person in a representative capacity.

In the present case Harvey ordered the testing and failed to disclose he was merely an employee of the contracting party. For all Bio-Chem knew at the time the services were ordered, Harvey could have operated a sole proprietorship under the trade name of Magnolia Health Center. Furthermore, the record does not divulge any circumstances to indicate Bio-Chem would be unreasonable in so believing.

We therefore conclude from the record Harvey was the contracting party and became personally liable for the cost of the services. Perhaps his employer, Magnolia (whether a proprietorship, partnership, corporation or whatever), received the benefits of the services and is also liable for the charges, but this does not affect a creditor's right to recover from the agent of the undisclosed principal.

Agent's Warranty Liability

The agent for a disclosed principal may be liable to a third person even without becoming a party to the contract. If the agent purports to act with authority but actually exceeds this authorization, the principal is not bound on the transaction unless it is ratified. However, the agent is not a party to the contract because he or she purported to contract for someone else. While not liable as a contracting party, the agent is responsible for

PREVENTIVE LAW
Signing on Behalf of a Principal

The agent for a disclosed principal must exercise care when a negotiated agreement is put in writing. When the names of both the principal and the agent appear on the written contract, to avoid liability the agent should make certain that his or her signature indicates the agency relation and identifies the principal. For example, "Peter Principal by Arthur Adams, his agent" is sufficient.

In court evidence other than the document may be used to explain an ambiguous signature. Currently the courts do not uniformly interpret a signature in the form of "Arthur Adams, agent." The trend is to treat the signature as sufficiently ambiguous to permit evidence to explain whether the agent was intended to become a party. However, some states still prohibit any explanation and hold the signer personally liable.

damages to the third person for breach of an implied warranty of authority. The agent is better able to know the limits of his or her authorization, and a third person is permitted reasonably to rely on the agent's representation of authority. The agent may avoid liability by informing the third person that he or she makes no warranty or is unsure of his or her authority.

AGENT'S TORTIOUS ACTIVITY

Besides performing contract negotiations, the agent's activity may involve a tort against others. This tort may be intentional or negligent. Either way, the innocent victim may recover damages for the resulting injury. Damages may be recovered from the agent, because every person is responsible for his or her own torts unless acting under a cloak of government immunity. The principal also is sometimes financially responsible for the agent's torts. The result is that the victim gets a windfall in the form of an additional responsible party.

Doctrine of Respondeat Superior

The principal is liable for any torts the agent commits during the agent's employment. This concept, called the doctrine of *respondeat superior* ("let the superior respond"), is imposed regardless of the principal's fault or blame. Strict liability is used in other areas of tort law where significant policy reasons require discarding traditional fault ideas in favor of no-fault liability. However, unlike other applications of strict liability, the principal's liability is based on some original fault of the agent. Thus the principal's responsibility is often referred to as *vicarious*.

Scope of Vicarious Liability

While respondeat superior is recognized because it is believed desirable and expedient to make the principal responsible for injuries inflicted by the agent, the principal is not made responsible for every tort the agent commits. Only when the agent commits a tort in the scope of employment is the principal liable under respondeat superior. The phrase "scope of employment" indicates the limits of the principal's liability for another's wrongdoing. The principal is liable only for accidents that are incidental to agency purposes. To make the principal responsible for acts that are in no way connected with agency goals would be unfair. The principal can be expected to bear only those costs that are closely associated with the business.

This limit on the principal's liability is easier to state than to apply. Determining if the agent is acting within the scope of employment often is difficult because the agent may temporarily be performing a personal errand or doing the principal's work while also serving a personal purpose, or the agent may be performing the principal's work in a forbidden manner. No precise formula exists to determine whether at a particular moment a particular agent is engaged in the principal's business. Whether the agent is inside or outside the scope of employment is often a matter of degree. Since the scope-of-employment test determines whether respondeat superior applies, as a guide courts often refer to the policy purposes that respondeat superior is supposed to serve.

The following case shows just how far an agent's scope of employment may extend.

Mauk v. Wright

U.S. District Court, Middle District of Pennsylvania
367 F.Supp. 961 (1973)

Background: Denise Mauk (plaintiff) was driving her 1969 Volkswagen shortly after midnight on July 21, 1971, when she was involved in an accident with a 1968 Lincoln Continental driven by Stephen Wright (defendant), a professional football player for the Washington Redskins (defendant). Wright had just picked up a girlfriend to give her a ride from her place of work to her home in Carlisle, Pennsylvania. Carlisle was the site of the Redskins' annual training camp, operated from July 10 until Labor Day.

Wright had spent the day before the accident in football training exercises. After dinner the team viewed training films until midevening. Then they watched the annual College All Star football game, which began at 9:00 P.M. on July 20. That night the players were given a curfew of thirty minutes after the end of the televised game.

Wright watched the game at a local "beer joint," then went to a local cocktail lounge where his girlfriend worked. Several minutes after midnight, Wright and his girlfriend left the cocktail lounge and were shortly thereafter involved in the collision.

Mauk sued the Washington Redskins as well as Wright, seeking compensation for her injuries. In the federal District Court (trial court) the defendant Washington Redskins requested that the trial judge grant a summary judgment in its favor. The Washington Redskins argued that Wright's leisure time activity fell outside the scope of his employment with the Redskins.

Decision: The District Court judge refused to grant the Washington Redskins' request for a summary judgment in its favor.

Herman, District Judge

The entire National Football League provides a unique backdrop to the employment situation. The standard player contract has clauses which if violated effectively bar the player from joining any other team. As a general provision of employment, the Redskins' rules for training camp provide: "The Club reserves the right to impose and require observance of reasonable standards of personal conduct, regardless of whether these situations are directly connected with the team."

According to Coach Allen, the players average two free hours per day between the end of the evening meetings and curfew. The issue is whether that recreation time, in the context of training camp, comes within the course and scope of employment.

In order to establish the Redskins' liability via *respondeat superior* the plaintiff must establish that Wright was acting within the scope of his employment. The concept requires that the employee's actions benefit the employer in his business relation.

[T]his court sees the primary potential benefit to be the morale of the players during a time when the club must build "players mentally and physically ready to play in the NFL season." The training camp, albeit brief, is all-important to establishing a cohesive mental unity amongst the team members, a unity apparently not possible were the players free of close contact and scrutiny.

This court finds the employment relationship between Wright and the Redskins to be so unique as to be without parallel. For the fixed period of the football training camp the players' time is accounted for seven days per week and all but two or three hours per day. During the limited "free time" the conduct, dress and associates of the players are circumscribed to the extent that the player can be barred from employment for improper conduct "regardless of whether [it is] . . . directly connected with the team."

Although the fact of employment is not seriously at issue, the nature of that relationship is. The parties have not agreed on the type nor import of any "free time" controls which might exist over the players. The tone, temper and character of training camp, though in dispute, are such that a jury could find recreation beneficial to player and team alike. Taking plaintiff's evidence at face value, there is sufficient evidence that the Redskins did "control" the players during free time to deny the Redskins' motion for summary judgment and require a complete exposition of evidence from all sides. Given the jury's role and the disputed facts, this court is of the view that summary judgment would be inappropriate at this juncture.

Agent's Liability to Third Parties

In conducting the principal's business, the agent may, of course, harm third persons. The fact that the agent acts in a representative capacity does not make the agent immune from tort liability to third persons. Although the doctrine of respondeat superior extends the principal's liability by making the principal liable to third persons for the agent's torts, the doctrine does not affect the agent's liability. An agent's tort liability to another is the same as if the agent were not employed. The doctrine of respondeat superior does not repeal the law of torts, which makes individuals liable for the torts they commit. Respondeat superior makes both the principal and the agent liable to the victim. Thus the agent's tort liability differs from the agent's liability in contract. Because the agent for a disclosed principal usually is not a party to the agreement, the agent is not liable on the contract.

TERMINATION OF AGENCY

Probably a majority of agencies end when the objective for which the agency was created is met or when the time allotted for completing performance expires. But the agency can end in many other ways. It may be ended by events or conditions that destroy the agent's power to act for the principal. An example is the bankruptcy of the principal or of the agent, if the agent's financial status is important to the relationship. Another example is the destruction of the subject matter. In addition, because the agency relationship is consensual, either party may end the agency at any time by withdrawing his or her consent. The death or incompetence of the principal also ends the agency. But some states permit the relationship to continue after the principal's incompetence if a power of attorney expressly so provides or if the power of attorney is approved by the court.

Notifying Agent of Termination

Before an attempted termination is effective, the other party to the relation ordinarily must be notified of the termination. Thus if the principal wishes to fire the agent, notice to the agent of the termination is required to revoke the agent's authority. Notification may be made in any way that tells the agent that his or her services are no longer desired. For example, if a realtor who has been hired by a homeowner to sell the owner's house hears that the owner has sold the house on his or her own, the realtor should realize the agency relation has been terminated. In this way revocation of an agent's authority is like revocation of an offeror's contract offer. Actual notice is needed, but no particular form of notice is required. All that is needed is for the agent to realize that the agency is over.

Notifying Third Parties of Termination

Although revocation of the agent's real authority may be accomplished by notifying the agent, third parties also must be notified. If they do not know of the termination, they may think that the agency still exists and continue to transact business with the agent and hold the principal responsible. To revoke the agent's apparent authority, the principal must give suitable notice of the agent's termination to third parties.

What constitutes "suitable" notice depends on the circumstances. In some cases no notice need be given at all. Generally no notice need be given to third parties when the principal ends the employment of a special agent, such as a realtor, because this type of agency gives notice to third parties of its limited authority. People dealing with special agents should seek assurance of the agent's continued authority. Usually this may be done by seeking written authorization. Principals giving their agents written authority should invalidate the writing upon ending the agency.

When the principal ends a general agency, the principal generally must actually notify everyone whom the principal has dealt with through the agent. This may require consulting appropriate records for determining the agent's customers, although sometimes it is impossible to notify every person who has dealt with the agent. Others who might rely upon the agency relationship deserve to know that the agency has ended. In these situations reasonable notice requires some compromise between the principal's duty to notify third parties and the difficulty of doing so. Suitable notice is any means reasonably designed to reach all third parties. Publication in a newspaper is a typical method. After publication, all persons except those who dealt with the agent on a regular basis are considered to have been notified of the termination.

A number of changes in circumstances automatically terminate the agent's authority. These include events such as the loss or destruction of the subject matter, the bankruptcy of the principal or, under some circumstances, the bankruptcy of the agent, and the death or incompetence of the principal. When the agency is terminated because of changes of this nature, generally neither the agent nor the third party need be notified of the termination. The courts entertain the fiction that these events are facts known to all. Because everybody in the world knows about the event all at once, its occurrence automatically revokes the agent's authority. This results in excusing the principal from liability to anyone and in making the agent liable to the third party for breach of the agent's warranty of authority.

A sizable minority of states allow the agent's authority to continue after the principal dies or is declared incompetent until the agent or the third party learns of the death or incompetence. In these states the agent can bind the estate of a dead or incompetent principal and can avoid any warranty liability. In the case of banks the Uniform Commercial Code (UCC) provides that neither the death nor the incompetence of the customer revokes a bank's authority to accept, pay, or collect an item until the bank knows of the death or the judgment

of incompetency and has a reasonable opportunity to act on it.

Irrevocable Agency

In some agency relations the principal cannot revoke the agent's authority because the agent has an interest in continuing the relation. Courts sometimes say the agent possesses a property right in the relation or has an *agency coupled with an interest.* Actually these are not true agencies. Usually an agency exists to allow the principal to accomplish something through the agent. An *irrevocable agency* is designed to allow the agent to do something for himself or herself.

An irrevocable agency is like a contract that must be specifically performed. Someone breaching a contract must perform the agreed undertaking if money is no substitute for performance. Similarly, if the agent must continue performing as an agent to protect an interest because money will not pay for the principal's breach of a promise not to revoke, the agency is irrevocable. An example of an irrevocable agency is when a debtor borrows money, giving property as collateral by granting the creditor authority to sell the property in the event of default. The creditor is the debtor's agent. Money cannot substitute for continuing the agency relation because the agency has been created to protect the creditor against the debtor's financial default.

The following case discusses some of the issues involved in termination of an agency relation as a result of the death of the principal.

Charles Webster Real Estate v. Rickard

Court of Appeals of California
98 Cal. Rptr. 559 (1971)

Background: On May 26, 1967 Dr. Moore and his wife executed an exclusive listing contract with Warde D. Watson Realty Company, giving the broker an exclusive and irrevocable right to sell a 156-acre vineyard at a stated price of $234,000 for a term ending December 31, 1968. The agreed commission was to be 5 percent of the selling price, to be paid to the broker if the property was sold during the term of the listing by the broker, by the owner, or through any other source. The agreement also provided that if the owner withdrew the property from sale or if it was transferred or leased during the term, he would pay the specified commission to the broker.

On March 18, 1968, the listing was transferred from Warde D. Watson Realty to Webster Real Estate (plaintiff). Dr. Moore and his wife consented in writing to the transfer. The stated price was reduced to $187,200. Dr. Moore died on June 19, 1968, and the probate court appointed H. E. Rickard (defendant) as executor of Dr. Moore's estate. (An executor is someone who manages the affairs of a dead person's estate in order to carry out, or "execute," the terms of the will.) In November 1968 Rickard sold the vineyard for $152,000 independently of any efforts by Webster Real Estate. Upon learning of the sale, Webster Real Estate demanded $7,600, representing a 5 percent commission on the sale price of $152,000. When payment was not made, Webster Real Estate sued Rickard for the $7,600. After a trial before a judge without a jury, judgment was entered in favor of Webster Real Estate. Rickard appealed to the California Court of Appeals.

Decision: The California Court of Appeals reversed the trial court judgment and found in favor of Rickard, Dr. Moore's executor.

Franson, Judge

A real estate listing creates an agency between the broker and the owner.

Because of its personal and fiduciary character, the agency is terminated by the death of or renunciation by the agent or by the death of or revocation by the principal, unless the agent has an interest in the subject of the agency. Respondent concedes that under the listing he was not vested with an interest in the agency. Upon termination of the agency, the authority of the agent ceases except as to bona fide transactions entered into with third parties prior to actual notice of termination.

Death is a fortuitous event beyond the control of the decedent. It cannot be deemed to be a wrongful act and ordinarily is not even a breach of contract by the deceased. Death terminates the agency by operation of law, and the authority of the broker to represent the owner in seeking a buyer for the property is ended.

In the *Restatement Second of Agency,* section 120, "Death of Principal," Comment a, the following is stated:

> *Rationale.* Agency is a personal relation, necessarily ending with the death of the principal; the former principal is no longer a legal person with whom there can be legal relations. One cannot act on behalf of a non-existent person. Further, to the extent that agency is a consensual relation, it cannot exist after the death or incapacity of the principal or the agent . . . an agreement that an agency should continue after death is a legal impossibility.

The *Restatement* gives the following example: P employs A as a salesman at a specified commission, the agreement stating that the employment is to continue for one year and is not to terminate if P dies. P dies—the authority ends.

The owner-broker relationship is a personal one based on mutual confidence and requires not only diligence by the broker in seeking a buyer but, necessarily, the cooperation of the owner in giving the broker information concerning the property, in showing the property, and in negotiating the terms of sale to a prospective buyer. We believe that it is reasonable to assume that both the broker and the owner intended that the listing would terminate on the death of either party. In the absence of an expression of intention to the contrary, the continued life of both reasonably must be deemed an implied condition of the contract. In such a case the death of either renders impossible the performance contemplated and the contract is discharged.

We recognize that there may be situations where a representative may be liable for a commission to a broker if he has ratified or affirmed the contract of his decedent. Also, where the representative has accepted the benefit of the efforts of the broker he may be liable for the reasonable value of the services; for example, if he sells the property to a buyer procured by the broker. Neither of these situations is before us. The record shows that respondent never procured a buyer at the price stated in the listing, nor was he responsible for securing the buyer for the ultimate sale.

We conclude that the contractual obligation of Dr. Moore under the listing terminated on his death rather than devolving upon his executor, and that the judgment for a commission based upon the contract cannot stand.

REVIEW PROBLEMS

1. How can an agent affect a principal's liability to third parties in contractual transactions?

2. How can an agent affect the principal's tort liability to third parties?

3. When does an agent who negotiates contracts on behalf of a principal become liable to the third party?

4. Why is notification important in ending agency relations?

5. Profit Corporation authorized Anderson, an employee, to find a buyer for used equipment that Profit intended to sell. Anderson believed that he had authority to contract for the sale of the equipment, but in fact he did not have such authority. Anderson found a prospective buyer, Caveat Corporation, and contracted with Caveat on behalf of Profit for the sale of the equipment to Caveat. In this contract Anderson warranted that the equipment was fit for Caveat's particular needs. A responsible officer of Profit read the contract and directed that the equipment be shipped to Caveat. The equipment did not meet the special needs of Caveat, and Caveat refused to pay for it. Profit sued Caveat for the contract price. Who wins and why?

6. Mrs. Terry, dealing with Alice, a clerk in Peters Department Store, sees a cashmere sweater she likes, but she notices that it is slightly soiled. Alice, pushing for a sale, agrees to mark it down from $55 to $40, which she has no authority to do. Mrs. Terry consents, asks that the sweater be delivered, and promises to pay COD. The manager of Peters sees the item being wrapped, corrects the bill, and sends it out to Mrs. Terry. On seeing her sweater accompanied by a bill for $55, Mrs. Terry calls and is told by Peters that Alice had no authority to knock down the price. Mrs.

Terry is told that she should either pay the bill or return the sweater. Is Mrs. Terry entitled to the bargain? Why or why not?

7. Anderson and Boyd planned to form Capable Corporation to market a new product. Anderson told Portaro that he was president of Capable Corporation and contracted with Portaro to lease a retail store building. Anderson signed the lease as follows: "Capable Corporation by Anderson, President." When Capable Corporation was chartered (given legal existence), it did not ratify the contract. Portaro sued Capable Corporation, Anderson, and Boyd for breach of the contract to lease. What result and why?

8. Principal Corporation owns a chain of jewelry stores. All stores are owned completely by Principal, but each store is operated under the name of the person who is the store manager. Ambrose manages one of Principal's stores. Xenia sold merchandise to Ambrose for sale in the store. The merchandise was to be delivered within ten days, and payment was to be made thirty days after delivery. Ambrose signed the contract in his own name. Xenia did not know of the agency relationship between Principal and Ambrose. If Xenia fails to perform the contract, what are the rights and liabilities of Principal, Ambrose, and Xenia among themselves? Explain. If Xenia delivers the merchandise and is not paid within thirty days, what are the rights and liabilities of Principal, Ambrose, and Xenia among themselves? Explain.

9. Harold, the owner of Harold's Department Store, directed Julius, his stock handler, to arrange a display containing light bulbs. Julius arranged the display in a negligent manner. Penelope, a purchaser, was injured when the display fell over, causing the light bulbs to explode. Penelope brought suit against both Harold and Julius for damages. Harold went bankrupt before the case went to court. Julius claimed that he should not be liable because he had acted under Harold's direction. Is Julius right? Explain.

10. Paul, the sole owner of a small manufacturing plant producing special equipment, employed Arnon as a traveling sales representative. On March 1 Paul's plant was damaged by fire. On March 2 Arnon contracted with Terry for the sale of certain equipment to be manufactured at Paul's plant. Neither Arnon nor Terry knew of the fire. On March 3 Paul died of a heart attack. On March 4 Arnon contracted with Frank for the sale of equipment to be manufactured at Paul's plant. Neither Arnon nor Frank knew of the fire or Paul's death. What are the rights and liabilities of Paul, Arnon, Terry, and Frank among themselves? Explain.

11. All-Pro Reps, Inc., is engaged in the business of representing professional athletes in contractual dealings and in providing financial-management services to athletes. John Jones contacted Nate Archibald to make a one-day appearance at Jones's boys' camp and was told by Archibald to contact All-Pro. All-Pro informed Jones that Archibald would appear at the camp on August 15, 1973. A timely payment of the agreed compensation was made by Jones. On August 10, five days before the scheduled appearance, All-Pro, which had been notified by Archibald on the night of August 9 that circumstances prevented him from making the appearance, sent this information by mail to Jones and refunded the consideration paid by Jones. This letter was received by Jones on August 14. Jones filed suit against All-Pro. His complaint alleged that All-Pro was Archibald's authorized agent in the transaction, that Archibald willfully breached the contract, that All-Pro knew or should have known that Archibald would not appear, that All-Pro knew or should have known

that its method of communication would not allow sufficient time to secure a replacement, that All-Pro breached its duty to supply to Jones a replacement of a person of equal stature and reputation as Archibald and to give timely notice of Archibald's nonappearance, and that the consequence of all this was that Jones incurred damages in the amount of $200,000 for loss of reputation. Who wins and why? Jones v. Archibald, 360 N.Y.S.2d 119 (1974)

CHAPTER 32

Nature and Formation of Partnerships

NATURE OF PARTNERSHIPS

K nown to the ancients, the partnership is the oldest form of business association. The partnership concept is traceable from Babylonian sharecropping through classical Greece and Rome to the enterprise of the Renaissance. Today the partnership still is an important form of business organization, especially in areas outside manufacturing.

Sources of Partnership Law

The primary sources of partnership law are two statutes, the Uniform Partnership Act (UPA) and the Uniform Limited Partnership Act of 1985 (ULPA). The UPA has been enacted in virtually every state. The ULPA was originally drafted in 1916 and revised in 1976 and 1985. Virtually every state has enacted one of these versions of the ULPA. The three versions of the ULPA vary greatly from one another. For purposes of this and the following chapter this text refers to the 1985 version of the ULPA.

Partnership Defined

The UPA defines a partnership as "an association of two or more persons to carry on as co-owners a business for profit" (Section 6[1]). This statutory definition governs whether a partnership exists. Anyone entering a relation satisfying this definition incurs the liability of a partner to the firm's creditors.

Types of Partnerships. Partnerships are either general or limited. A *general* partnership is the ordinary partnership governed by the UPA. To constitute a general partnership, nothing more is needed than to satisfy the definition of a partnership provided by Section 6(1). All the participants in a general partnership incur unlimited personal liability to partnership creditors.

A *limited* partnership carries many characteristics of a general partnership except that the liability of some members is limited. Governed by the ULPA, it offers some of the benefits of both partnerships and corporations and may be used to attract investors willing to put up money but unwilling to risk personal liability. A limited partnership protects a special partner by exempting him or her from personal liability. It consists of one or more general partners who conduct the business and are personally liable to creditors, as in an ordinary partnership. It also includes one or more limited partners who contribute capital and share in profits but who do not participate in the control of the business and who assume no liability for the obligations of the limited partnership.

Aggregate and Entity Nature of Partnerships

There are two conceptions of partnerships: (1) it is an aggregate of people who associate to share its profits and losses, owning its property and liable for its debts and (2) it is an artificial being, a distinct entity, separate in rights and responsibility from the partners who compose it. The first conception is referred to as the aggregate theory of partnership, and the second is called the entity theory.

Aggregate Theory

The *aggregate theory* considers the partners to be co-owners of the enterprise and the property used in it, each owning an individual interest in the partnership. The consequence of this is to hold each partner personally liable for partnership debts. Creditors can reach each partner's personal assets if partnership assets are insufficient to discharge a debt.

Entity Theory. The *entity theory* treats the partnership as a separate legal entity, distinct from the individual partners. This theory holds that the partnership is a "person" for legal purposes. Because the partnership is a separate legal person, individual partners may enter into transactions with the firm, such as lending it money or equipment. Accountants and businesspeople generally regard and treat a partnership as a business, separate and distinct from its individual partners.

UPA Approach. The UPA strikes a balance between the two theories. Generally speaking, under the UPA a partnership is an aggregate, but in certain limited circumstances it is treated as an entity. For example, the UPA recognizes the partnership as an entity for owning its own property by authorizing conveyances of real estate to or by the partnership in the partnership name and by creating the presumption that all property acquired with partnership funds is partnership property. Thus the UPA adopts both the aggregate and entity theories of partnership, depending upon the particular problem involved.

In the following case the court considers whether a partnership is to be treated as an entity or as an aggregate.

McKinney v. Truck Insurance Company

Court of Appeals of Missouri

324 S.W.2d 773 (1959)

Background: Truck Insurance Company (defendant) issued a workers' compensation policy to "Ralph McKinney & Paul McKinney dba Acme Glass Co.," which was described in the policy as a "co-partnership" whose "operations" were classified as "glass merchants." Davis, a man employed by Paul McKinney (plaintiff) in connection with McKinney's 167-acre farm, was injured while working on activities wholly unrelated to the business conducted by Acme Glass. Davis filed a claim for benefits against McKinney, as employer, and Truck Insurance, as his insurer. After successfully defending against Davis's claim, Paul sued Truck Insurance to recoup his expenses incurred in the defense. Paul theorized that "a partnership cannot be considered as a separate entity." It is an aggregate of individuals, and the effect of the policy was to insure fully all workers' compensation obligations of the two individuals named.

The trial court rendered a judgment against Paul McKinney and he appealed. Decision: The Court of Appeals affirmed the trial court judgment against Paul McKinney.

Stone, Presiding Judge

Cut to the quick by the indignity inflicted upon him, a bull calf being castrated by one Davis, "sort of an expert" at such matters, rebelled and grievously injured his tormentor, by reason of which Davis filed a claim for benefits under the Missouri Workmen's Compensation Law against Paul McKinney, as employer, and Truck Insurance Exchange (hereinafter referred to as the Exchange), his alleged insurer. The Exchange theretofore had issued a "standard workmen's compensation and employers' liability policy" to "Ralph McKinney & Paul McKinney dba Acme Glass Co., 1647 St. Louis, Springfield, Missouri," as "employer," described in the policy declarations as a "co-partnership"; but, claimant Davis having been employed by Paul in connection with operation of a 167-acre farm in another county owned by Paul and his wife and Davis' castration of the calf having been wholly unrelated to the business conducted by Acme Glass Company (even though the castrated calf had wreaked as much havoc as the proverbial bull in a china closet), the Exchange insisted that its policy issued to Acme afforded no coverage to Paul with respect to his farm operation and refused to defend him in the compensation proceeding instituted by Davis, although Davis' joinder of the Exchange as a party to the proceeding necessitated a defense on its own behalf. After counsel employed by Paul personally and counsel for the Exchange, presenting a united front against their common antagonist, had concluded upon appeal to this court a successful defense of Davis' claim . . . and thus had put out of the way (if not out of mind) the castrated calf and the contentious claimant, Paul turned on the Exchange and brought the instant suit to recoup the expenses (primarily attorneys' fees) incurred by him personally in such defense. Cast in the trial court on the Exchange's motion to dismiss his petition, Paul appeals from the adverse judgment.

. . . Although other jurisdictions reflect a sharp conflict of authority as to whether or not a partnership is a legal or juristic entity separate and distinct from the individuals who compose it . . . , the courts of this state usually have regarded a partnership as a mere ideal entity with no legal existence apart from its members, and have followed the so-called aggregate or common-law theory of partnership rather than the entity theory. There may be a judicial tendency toward the entity theory . . . ; and, as counsel for the Exchange assert, the Uniform Partnership Act adopted in Missouri in 1949 . . . may have "wrought decided changes in the common-law conception" of a partnership. However, the persuasive opinion of informed scholars is that the Uniform Partnership Act does not transform a partnership into a separate legal or juristic entity . . . but "adopts the common-law approach with 'modifications' relating to partnership property" so that the Act "is consistent with the entity approach for the purposes of facilitating transfers of property, marshalling assets, and protecting the business operation against the immediate impact of personal involvements of the partners." Mazzu-chelli v. Silberberg, 1959. Accordingly, we cannot agree with counsel for the Exchange that the Uniform Partnership Act "makes a partnership a legal entity."

But, grave danger lurks in unquestioning acceptance and unguarded application of potentially deceptive generalities; and, although our Missouri courts usually follow the aggregate or common-law theory as to partnerships, we think that it should not and cannot be announced, as an arbitrary, absolute, unqualified and unyielding rule, that under no circumstances and for no purposes may a partnership be considered and treated as an entity. We read that the partnership entity sometimes is recognized with reference to its contracts with third persons . . . ; and we like and adopt the logical, forthright, common-sense reasoning of the Supreme Court of Tennessee in United States Fidelity & Guaranty Co. v. Booth, a case involving a workmen's compensation policy, where it was said that, in construing and giving effect to contracts made by and with partnerships, it may appear from the subject-matter or otherwise that the parties dealt with and treated the partnership as if it were an entity, separate and distinct from the individuals composing it; and, to the extent that this is so, the intention of the parties can only be given effect, in the enforcement of the contract, by judicial recognition of the partnership entity as contemplated by the parties.

Thus, in jurisdictions where, as in Missouri, the aggregate or common-law theory as to partnerships usually is followed, the courts have given effect to the intention of contracting parties by treating a partnership as an entity in determining and delimiting the coverage afforded by insurance policies issued to the partnership. . . .

Since the unambiguous provisions of the policy contract establish beyond room for reasonable doubt that the parties thereto intended and undertook to provide workmen's compensation coverage for Acme Glass Company, and since nothing in the policy suggests that thereby such coverage would be provided for any employee of either individual partner engaged in work wholly unrelated to the partnership operation, we believe that we should recognize the partnership entity of Acme Glass Company as the employer with whom the Exchange contracted, thereby giving effect to the plain intent of the contracting parties and following the general rule that an insurer may afford workmen's compensation coverage for a partnership and its business activities without exposing itself to liability for all of the unrelated business operations of each individual partner.

PARTNERSHIP FORMATION

No particular steps are required to form a general partnership. Although customarily each partner's rights and responsibilities are established in an instrument called the *partnership agreement* or the *articles of partnership*, usually this is not required. A partnership may result from any arrangement of facts fulfilling UPA Section 6(1)'s definition of a partnership.

Factors Establishing Partnership Existence

To understand how the UPA (Section 6[1]) determines partnership existence, the meaning of each phrase of the definition must be examined. The following paragraphs dissect the definition of a partnership and explain the reasons for the words used.

"An Association." *Association* denotes the voluntary nature of the partnership arrangement. Because a partnership is a voluntary association, the participants must intend to enter into a partnership. Whether or not a partnership is created depends on the intent of the participants to create one. Their intent is the primary test of partnership existence. This intent may be expressed by either a written or an oral agreement, or it may be inferred from conduct. As with contractual intent, partnership intent is measured objectively. Subjective intent is not material.

"Of Two or More Persons." One person alone cannot form a partnership. A sole proprietor cannot convert his or her sole proprietorship into a partnership by drafting articles of partnership or otherwise conducting the business as a partnership. It takes two to tango, and it takes at least two to partner. Although a minimum number of two is required, the UPA imposes no maximum limit on the number of people who may form a partnership. A thousand people may create a partnership.

The intention of one person alone cannot create a partnership. When someone wishes to join an existing partnership, all the partners must consent to the new member's admission.

Section 2 states that a *person* "includes individuals, partnerships, corporations, and other associations." Thus the definition of a partnership provides that any of these entities may form a partnership. Any individual having contractual capacity may become a partner. By including partnerships as persons in Section 2, the UPA permits one partnership to be a member of another partnership. Similarly, two corporations ought to be able to form a partnership. But there is some disagreement on this point. The courts are divided on whether a corporation may become a partner. The prevailing view is that without some statutory authorization by a state corporation code, a corporation may not become a partner. The trend recently has been for such codes to permit this. Many contemporary corporation codes allow corporations to become partners. Some states permit a corporation to become a partner only if it is allowed to do so by the corporation's charter or articles of incorporation.

"To Carry On." It is often said that "the carrying on" of a business, not an agreement to carry on business at a future date, is the test of partnership existence. The official comment to UPA Section 6 indicates that this is not the intended meaning of the phrase "to carry on." Section 6(1) does not provide that persons are not partners until they participate in the carrying on of the business. The words "to carry on," not "carrying on," are used.

"As Co-Owners." To form a partnership, the associates must *co-own* the business. Co-ownership distinguishes partnership from nonpartnership relations such as employment. For example, if a general manager is not a co-owner of the enterprise, he or she is an employee, not a partner.

Co-ownership describes the community of interest each partner shares in the firm's operations. It includes the power of ultimate control each partner possesses in the firm's management. For an association to consist of co-owners, the associates must have equal rights in the decision-making process. Section 18(e) of the UPA states that "all partners have equal rights in the management and conduct of the partnership business." Factors reflecting co-ownership include giving instructions, hiring and firing employees, and determining how money is spent. But Section 18 permits partners to agree to delegate their managerial rights to a managing partner.

"A Business." Co-ownership of property by itself does not establish a partnership. The co-ownership required by Section 6(1) is co-ownership of a *business*. A partnership must be formed as a business. Section 2 states that a business includes "every trade, occupation, or profession." If two people together inherit real estate that remains unimproved and idle, they are co-owners, but not of a business. However, if they improve the property by erecting an apartment complex, their actions constitute a business.

"For Profit." A partnership must be formed as a business *for profit*. Nonprofit organizations cannot be formed as partnerships under the UPA. Courts require only an expectation, not the actual making, of profit for the existence of a partnership. Profit motive, not profit making, is the test.

The importance of profit sharing to the determination of partnership existence is reflected in UPA Section 7(4)'s declaration:

The receipt by a person of a share of the profits of a business is prima facie evidence that he is a partner in the business.

Protected Relations

While providing that profit sharing presumes partnership existence, Section 7(4) enumerates certain situations in which profit sharing does not create a partnership. These include situations in which profits are:

1. Received to discharge a debt
2. Received as wages or rent
3. Paid to a widow or an estate as an annuity
4. Paid for the purchase of a partnership asset

This protection against the risk of unwanted partnership formation can be lost if the protected party becomes too involved in the firm's operation. In the following case the court considers whether the parties created a partnership.

Lupien v. Malsbenden

Supreme Court of Maine
477 A.2d 749 (1984)

Background: On March 5, 1980 Robert Lupien (plaintiff) entered into a written agreement with Stephen Cragin, doing business in the town of York, Maine, as York Motor Mart, for the construction of a Bradley automobile. (A Bradley automobile is a "kit car" constructed on a Volkswagen chassis.) Lupien made a deposit of $500 toward the purchase price of $8,020 upon signing the contract, and made a further payment of $3,950 one week later on March 12. Both the purchase order of March 5, 1980, and a later bill of sale, although signed by Cragin, identified the seller as York Motor Mart. After he signed the contract, Lupien visited York Motor Mart on an average of once or twice a week to check on the progress being made on his car. During those visits he dealt with Frederick Malsbenden (defendant) because Cragin was seldom present. On one visit in April, Malsbenden told Lupien that it was necessary for Lupien to sign over ownership of his pickup truck, which would constitute the balance of the payment due under the contract, so that the proceeds from the sale of the truck could be used to complete construction of the Bradley. When Lupien complied, Malsbenden provided him with a rental car, and later with a "demo" model of the Bradley, for his use pending the completion of the vehicle he had ordered. When it was discovered that the demo actually belonged to a third party who had entrusted it to York Motor Mart for resale, Malsbenden purchased the vehicle for Lupien's use. Lupien never received the Bradley he had contracted to purchase.

Lupien sued both Cragin and Malsbenden, claiming that they were liable as partners for the breach of contract. Because Cragin had "disappeared" several months before the lawsuit, Cragin was never served with process, and the trial judge dismissed Lupien's claim against him. However, the trial judge entered judgment against Malsbenden, holding him to partnership liability on the contract with Lupien. Malsbenden appealed to the Supreme Court of Maine.

Decision: The Supreme Court of Maine affirmed the trial court's decision against Malsbenden.

McKusick, Chief Justice

The sole issue asserted on appeal is whether the Superior Court erred in its finding that Malsbenden and Cragin were partners in the pertinent part of York Motor Mart's business.

In his trial testimony, defendant Malsbenden asserted that his interest in the Bradley operation of York Motor Mart was only that of a banker. He stated that he had loaned $85,000 to Cragin, without interest, to finance the Bradley portion of York Motor Mart's business. The loan was to be repaid from the proceeds of each car sold. Malsbenden acknowledged that Bradley kits were purchased with his personal checks and that he had also purchased equipment for York Motor Mart. He also stated that after Cragin disappeared sometime late in May 1980, he had physical control of the premises of York Motor Mart and that he continued to dispose of assets there even to the time of trial in 1983.

The Uniform Partnership Act, adopted in Maine, defines a partnership as "an association of 2 or more persons . . . to carry on as co-owners a business for profit." Whether a partnership exists is an inference of law based on established facts. A finding that the relationship between two persons constitutes a partnership may be based upon evidence of an agreement, either express or implied, to place their money, effects, labor, and skill, or some or all of them, in lawful commerce or business with the understanding that a community of profits will be shared. No one factor is alone determinative of the existence of a partnership. If the arrangement between the parties otherwise qualifies as a partnership, it is of no matter that the parties did not expressly agree to form a partnership or did not even intend to form one. It is possible for parties to intend no partnership and yet to form one. If they agree upon an arrangement which is a partnership in fact, it is of no importance that they call it something else, or that they even expressly declare that they are not to be partners. The law must declare what is the legal import of their agreements, and names go for nothing when the substance of the arrangement shows them to be inapplicable.

Here the trial justice concluded that, notwithstanding Malsbenden's assertion that he was only a "banker," his "total involvement" in the Bradley operation was that of a partner. The testimony at trial, both respecting Malsbenden's financial interest in the enterprise and his involvement in day-to-day business operations, amply supported the Superior Court's conclusion. Malsbenden had a financial interest of $85,000 in the Bradley portion of York Motor Mart's operations. Although Malsbenden termed the investment a loan, significantly he conceded that the "loan" was not made in the form of a fixed payment or payments, but was made to the business, at least in substantial part, in the form of day-to-day purchases of Bradley kits, other parts and equipment, and in the payment of wages. Furthermore, the "loan" was not to be repaid in fixed amounts or at fixed times, but rather only upon the sale of Bradley automobiles.

The evidence also showed that, unlike a banker, Malsbenden had the right to participate in control of the business and in fact did so on a day-to-day basis. According to Urbin Savaria, who worked at York Motor Mart from late April through June 1980, Malsbenden during that time opened the business establishment each morning, remained present through part of every day, had final say on the ordering of parts, paid for parts and equipment, and paid Savaria's salary. On plaintiff's frequent visits to York Motor Mart, he generally dealt with Malsbenden because Cragin was not present. It was Malsbenden who insisted that plaintiff trade in his truck prior to the completion of the Bradley because the proceeds from the sale of the truck were needed to complete the Bradley. When it was discovered that the demo Bradley [had] given to plaintiff while he awaited completion of his car actually belonged to a third party, it was Malsbenden who bought the car for plaintiff's use. As of three years after the making of the contract now in litigation, Malsbenden was still doing business at York Motor Mart, "just disposing of property."

Malsbenden and Cragin may well have viewed their relationship to be that of creditor-borrower, rather than a partnership. [W]hatever the intent of these two men as to their respective involvements in the business of making and selling Bradley cars, there is no clear error in the Superior Court's finding that the Bradley car operation represented a pooling of Malsbenden's capital and Cragin's automotive skills, with joint control over the business and intent to share the fruits of the enterprise. As a matter of law, that arrangement amounted to a partnership under [section 6 of the UPA].

Partnership Established by Representation

The existence of a true partnership depends on the intent of the parties to associate as partners. But in certain situations people who actually are not partners are liable to third parties as though they were. People who represent themselves to be partners or consent to others' representing them as partners are liable as partners to third parties who rely upon those representations in their dealings with the purported partnership. This arrangement is called partnership by *estoppel.* Represented partners are called *partners by estoppel* or *ostensible partners.* The statutory basis for this doctrine is provided by UPA Section 4(2), and Section 16's more detailed declaration that:

When a person . . . represents himself or consents to another representing him to any one as a partner . . . he is liable to any such person to whom such representation has been made, who has, on the faith of such representation, given credit to the apparent partnership.

PREVENTIVE LAW
Controlling Against Unintended Partnership Status

Frequently an uneasy creditor or landlord, unsatisfied with simply a share of the profits of a business, seeks to protect his or her interests by controlling the firm's operations. If the control reserved over business operations is merely that which is necessary to protect the creditor's or landlord's interests, the relation remains protected from becoming a partnership. But if the control goes beyond what is necessary to protect the creditor's or landlord's interest, the risk of unwanted partnership formation increases. No clear-cut rule exists for determining when protected status is lost and partnership status is gained. A sliding scale, not a rigid rule, is the measure. The greater the participation in the business is and the greater the degree of unnecessary control is, the greater will be the risk of partnership formation.

Liability is imposed on the represented partner in these situations, because he or she is in a better position to avoid injury to others by correcting the misconception. Liability rests on the person most capable of preventing any loss from occurring. Two elements are the essence of estoppel: representation and reliance.

Representation. Partnership by estoppel results either from someone representing himself or herself as a partner or from consenting to such a representation by another. A signature on a letter or check can constitute a representation. Liability resulting from someone's own representation simply is another application of the principle, well established in contract law, that a person is responsible for the apparent or objective manifestations of intent. Someone behaving like a partner is liable as a partner. It is not material that a person may secretly deny all connection with the partnership or even be unaware of the significance of the behavior.

Liability also results from someone consenting to being represented as a partner by another. But it is not enough that a person knows that he or she is being portrayed as a partner. UPA Section 16 imposes liability only where there is some consent to the other person's representation.

Reliance. Someone seeking to hold another liable as a partner by estoppel must have extended credit in reliance upon the representation of that person as a partner. UPA Section 16 requires that the duped person must have "on the faith of such representation, given credit to the actual or apparent partnership." Thus not every creditor of the purported partnership relation may hold the false partner responsible as a partner by estoppel. Only creditors who have suffered economic loss by relying on the represented partnership may require payment from the ostensible partner.

A creditor's reliance must be reasonable under the circumstances. This requirement of reasonable reliance may impose upon a creditor a duty to investigate the relationship before assuming the existence of a partnership. In certain circumstances a creditor may have no obligation to inquire further, such as when the representations of partnership are made

directly to the creditor by one of the purported partners.

The following case illustrates the nature of
the consent requirement.

Cox Enterprises, Inc. v. Filip

Court of Civil Appeals of Texas
538 S.W. 2d 836 (1976)

Background: A newspaper publisher, Cox Enterprises, Inc. (plaintiff-appellant), doing
business as the *Austin American Statesman,* sued two individuals, Richard Filip and
Jack Elliott (defendant-appellee), doing business as Trans Texas Properties. Cox Enterprises sued to recover payment for newspaper advertising services furnished to Trans
Texas Properties. Elliott defended on the ground that he had no financial interest in
Trans Texas Properties and was not liable for the debts of that business. The evidence
showed that to obtain credit for Trans Texas, its employee, Tracey Peoples, represented to Cox Enterprises that Elliott was an owner of the business. Peoples had no
authority to make that representation, and Cox Enterprises made no effort to verify
it. As for Elliott, he did not hold himself out as having an ownership interest in Trans
Texas. The trial court rendered judgment against Filip for $622.78 but in favor of
Elliott. Cox Enterprises appealed to the Texas Court of Civil Appeals.
Decision: The Texas Court of Civil Appeals affirmed the trial court judgment in favor
of Elliott.

Shannon, Justice

Prior to the enactment of the Texas Uniform Partnership Act, the rule in Texas was
that for liability to be based upon partnership by estoppel, it must be established that
the person held out as a partner knew of, and consented in fact to the holding out.
. . .

Section 16(1) codifies and enlarges upon the common law of partnership by estoppel. That section imposes a duty on a person to deny that he is a partner once he
knows that third persons are relying on representations that he is a partner. We do
not read section 16(1) as creating an affirmative duty upon one to seek out all those
who may represent to others that he is a partner.

Appellant argues that §16(1) means that one who negligently holds himself out or
permits himself to be held out as a member of a partnership relationship is estopped
to deny such partnership relationship as against third persons who in good faith relied
on the existence of such apparent partnership and extended credit thereon. Branscome v. Schoneweis, 361 F. 2d 717 (7th Cir. 1966). In *Branscome,* the Seventh
Circuit construed Ill.Rev.Stat. ch. 106½, §16(1) (1952), which is identical to the
Uniform Partnership Act and Tex.Rev.Civ.Stat.Ann. art. 6132b, §16(1)(1970). The
court held Schoneweis personally liable for debts of the company because *he* negligently held *himself* out to be a partner.

In the case at bar, and in the terms of §16(1), appellant's factual theory was that
appellee consented to Peoples' representation to appellant that appellee was a partner

in Trans Texas Properties. Appellant, however, failed in its burden to convince the trier of fact that appellee consented for Peoples to represent that appellee was a partner in Trans Texas Properties.

Formalities

Although under the UPA no formalities are required to create a general partnership, some may be required by other statutes. Certificates, licenses, and permits may have to be obtained. A name should be selected and in some cases must be registered. Although not usually required, the execution of a partnership agreement often is advisable. Technical formalities do accompany the formation of limited partnerships.

License, Permit, and Certificate Requirements. Partnerships engaging in certain types of activity usually do need to obtain state or local licenses to do business. Occupational licensing is a well-known fact of professional life among doctors and lawyers. License requirements also fall on those in other callings. Certified public accountants, real-estate brokers, and construction contractors are only a few of the many businesspeople required to obtain licenses. Failure to obtain the necessary licenses and permits may deprive a partnership of the ability to enforce its contracts. Here is another application of the rule of contract law to the nonenforcement of illegal agreements.

Name Selection and Registration. It is customary, but not necessary, to use a firm name for a partnership. A partnership should have a business name because of the good will that may develop from its use. As a practical matter, a name may be required for the opening of the partnership's bank account.

Unless prohibited by statute, the partners may use any name they desire so long as fraud, trade name infringement, and unfair competition are not involved. Thus the partnership cannot use a name that is deceptively similar to the name of another business.

Most businesses operate under fictitious names. A fictitious name is one that does not disclose the surnames of all the firm's owners. For example, if Julius Jones and Penelope Smith operate a cafe under the name of "The Bottoms Up Bar," their business name is fictitious. By statute in most states, fictitious names must be registered so that creditors of the partnership can enforce their rights against all the firm's members. A nonfictitious name is one containing the surnames of all the partners and does not have to be registered. Any form of expression may be used for the fictitious name. But some states prohibit use of the word "Company" or any other word that might confuse the partnership with a corporation.

Registration provides public notice of the names and addresses of all partners. It usually involves the filing of a certificate with the county recorder where the partnership is located and, in some states, in each county in which partnership real estate is situated. A few states, such as California, require the information supplied on the certificate to be published in a local newspaper for a designated period. A new certificate or amendments to the old certificate must be filed for every change in the firm's composition.

Noncompliance usually results in the partnership's inability to sue on its contracts until the registration requirement is satisfied. Registration is easily done and does not usually result in hardship to the partnership. Fines and penalties are also authorized but seldom levied because prosecutors and police usually

PREVENTIVE LAW
Drafting Partnership Agreements

Although not required for most partnerships, entering into a written partnership agreement when forming a partnership is still a good idea. There are advantages to a writing. A written partnership agreement avoids the problems of later proving that the agreement to enter into partnership was actually made. Drafting articles of partnership with the guidance of good legal counsel can focus the parties' attention on potential problem areas in their relationship. The written agreement also helps avoid future disagreements by clarifying the parties' relationship for future reference.

The partnership agreement usually takes the form of a series of numbered paragraphs addressing important aspects of the parties' relationship. Partnership agreements range from fairly simple instruments to rather complex documents, depending on the nature of the business and the number and character of the associates. The following items may be considered when drafting the partnership agreement. The list is not exhaustive, but it provides a good start.

1. Name of the partnership
2. Names of the partners
3. Date of the agreement
4. Purpose of the partnership
5. Location of the business
6. Duration of the enterprise
7. Investment of each partner, whether capital, realty, services, and so on
8. Any loans to the partnership of assets or cash
9. Sharing of profits and losses
10. Whether there will be any remuneration to the partners for services rendered to the partnership
11. Management and voting powers of each partner
12. Whether there will be arbitration for the disposition of disagreements
13. Whether there will be voluntary or involuntary retirement
14. The method of disposing of any dead partner's share in the partnership, and the method of evaluation
15. Cross-insurance of the partners
16. Respective duties of the partners
17. How books of account are to be established and maintained, and what the period of accounting will be
18. What the banking arrangements will be
19. Who has the authority to borrow money
20. Method of hiring and firing—who does it, and who determines pay

have more important matters to look after than pursuing nonregistered partnerships.

Partnership Articles. Although not usually required, it is customary to define the rights and duties of the members of a partnership in an instrument called *the partnership agreement* or *articles of partnership.* Written partnership articles are necessary if the partnership agreement qualifies as a contract coming under the Statute of Frauds, which requires a written memorandum signed by the party against whom enforcement is sought for certain contracts. If a partnership is to continue for longer than one year or involves the transfer of an interest in real estate to or by the partnership, written partnership articles must be executed.

Limited Partnerships. The UPA does not require formalities to form general partnerships, but technical formalities do accompany the formation of limited partnerships. Under the Uniform Limited Partnership Act of 1985 (ULPA), in order to form a limited partnership, a certificate of limited partnership must be executed and filed in the office of the Secretary of State. The certificate must set forth the names and addresses of the general and limited partners, the date when the partnership is to dissolve, and any other matters the general partners determine to include in the certificate. A limited partnership is formed at the time of the filing of the certificate of limited partnership or at any later time specified in the certificate. The certificate must be amended whenever a general partner is admitted or withdraws from the firm.

The name of the limited partnership, as set forth in its certificate of limited partnership, must contain the words "limited partnership." The name may not contain the name of a limited partner unless it is also the name of a general partner or the business had been carried on under that name before the admission of that limited partner. Further, the name may not be the same or deceptively similar to the name of any corporation or limited partnership organized or registered in the state. To make it easy to choose a name, the ULPA provides for the reservation of the intended partnership name.

REVIEW PROBLEMS

1. What is a partnership? How is the general partnership different from the limited partnership?
2. What is meant by treating the partnership as an entity? As an "aggregate"? When is a partnership treated as an entity? When is it treated as an aggregate?
3. What are the essential elements of partnership existence under Section 6 of the Uniform Partnership Act? What test of partnership existence is provided in Section 7 of the Uniform Partnership Act?
4. What is required to establish partnership by estoppel (under Section 16 of the Uniform Partnership Act)?
5. Seller operates a store in a building he rents from Owner. Creditor, who dealt with Seller, wants to hold Owner liable for the debt as Seller's partner. May Owner ignore the obligation on the basis that both Seller and Owner had mutually agreed that their relationship was not a partnership? Suppose Owner and Seller had an agreement that reads: "The parties do not intend by this agreement to form a partnership of any kind, but rather a landlord-

tenant relationship." Is this language conclusive on the issue of partnership liability?

6. Can-Do Corporation and Cannot Corporation wish to form a partnership. Can they?

7. Penelope and Julius inherit joint ownership rights in a house. Are they partners? Suppose they decide to lease the house to Renter. Are they then partners?

8. Penelope and Julius decide to go into the business of making widgets, but instead of making profits they lose money. Are they liable to creditors as partners?

9. United Foods, a food broker, was an authorized buyer of produce from Minute Maid. It realized profits by purchasing Minute Maid inventories at bargain prices. United entered into an agreement with Cold Storage as follows: Cold Storage would lend money to United to purchase produce. The produce would be collateral for the loans. A special account would be established and managed by Cold Storage. The books were to be credited with advances by Cold Storage and debited by advances made by Minute Maid. At the year's end the books were to be closed and the profits divided. Over the year United became overextended and indebted to Minute Maid, which sued Cold Storage rather than United because it was a more attractive defendant, alleging that Cold Storage was United's partner. What result? Minute Maid Corp. v. United Foods, Inc., 291 F.2d 577 (5th Cir. 1961)

10. Ralph Presutti approached his father, Claude, in April 1969, saying, "Dad, if you put up the money, we'll go partners in a gas station." However, because the oil company whose station they were to operate frowned on partnership stations, Ralph explained that Claude could not sign any dealer agreements or leases or any other partnership documents, such as tax returns. Claude agreed to the arrangement. He withdrew $8,000 from his bank account, which he and Ralph used to open a joint account under the service station's trade name. From time to time Claude drew checks upon the account for payment of merchandise at the station. In July, Ralph returned $2,000 to Claude. In September, Claude began working at the station and continued for one year. For these services Claude drew a salary of $125 each week. Occasionally he received additional sums that were from partnership profits, as well as free gas, tires, and automobile accessories. During his one-year tenure Claude managed the station whenever Ralph was away and participated in policy decisions such as whether they should buy a truck and whether they should distribute trading stamps. After a year Ralph still refused to sign a written partnership agreement, so Claude stopped working at the station. Despite this, he continued to receive payments of money and car repairs from the station until January 1972. As of January 1972, Claude had received approximately $17,000 as salary, partial return of his capital contribution, and distribution of profits. When Ralph finally refused to affirm the partnership's existence, Claude filed suit for an accounting of his share of the partnership profits. What result? Presutti v. Presutti, 310 A.2d 791 (Md.App. 1973)

11. A barbershop owner executed two separate but similar partnership agreements with two barbers in his shop. Under the agreements the owner provided the barber chair, supplies, and licenses while the others provided the tools of their trade. Upon dissolution, ownership of these items was to revert to the party providing them. Income was divided 30–70 percent between the owner and one barber and 20–80 percent between the owner and the other barber. The agreements further required the owner to hold and distribute all receipts and stated the work hours and

holidays of the two barbers. The agreements provided that all policy was to be decided by the shop owner, and it also forbade any assignment of the agreement without the owner's permission. By state law, employers are to file an assessment report with the state employment commission and to make unemployment compensation contributions. But partnerships are not subject to unemployment compensation assessment when no nonpartner employees are involved. Must the barbershop owner file the forms and make the assessed contributions? Chaiken v. Employment Security Comm., 274 A.2d 707 (Del. 1971)

12. Francis and Thelma Gosman were an ambitious and industrious young couple, married in 1945 when he was 21 and she was 18. He drove a milk truck and she was a clerk-typist. After several years of marriage, when their first child was expected and Thelma could no longer keep her job, she began to raise chickens at home and planted a garden to supplement the family income—selling chickens, eggs, and garden produce from the house. The sale proceeds were deposited in the Gosmans' joint bank account, which was subject to the order of either of them. Ultimately Francis gave up his milk route, and his participation in the family business increased while Thelma's decreased. This was followed by the removal of the business from their home to a business complex, where the business ultimately became a grocery store, a liquor store, a restaurant, and a night club, which grossed almost $500,000 in 1969, close to $600,000 in 1970, and over $600,000 in 1971. Francis managed the enterprise and, although Thelma's duties were less onerous, she continued stocking grocery shelves, waiting tables in the restaurant and night club, bartending, counting money and making bank deposits, managing the club when Francis was sick or out of town, decorating the building interior, and running errands. In 1972 Francis filed for divorce against Thelma, and she counterclaimed, seeking a divorce and alleging that, because she was a "partner" with Francis in the family business, her property rights should be determined pursuant to the Uniform Partnership Act, awarding her 50 percent of the partnership's fair market value and 50 percent of the balance of the checking account. What result? Gosman v. Gosman, 318 A.2d 821 (Md. 1974)

Operation and Dissolution of Partnerships

T his chapter explores the rights and duties resulting from the operation and dissolution of partnerships. First it focuses on the property rights created by the partnership relation. Next, it examines the rules governing the relations among partners and their relations with persons dealing with the partnership. The chapter concludes with an explanation of how partnerships are dissolved and wound up.

PROPERTY RIGHTS IN PARTNERSHIPS

The Uniform Partnership Act (Section 24) defines the property rights of partners as:

1. Their rights in a specific partnership property
2. Their interest in the partnership and
3. Their right to participate in the management

The following paragraphs discuss the first two types of property rights. The partner's right to participate in the firm's management is discussed in the material or the rules about a partner's managerial rights and responsibilities.

Property rights in partnerships pose two problems:

1. Distinguishing partnership property from an individual partner's personal assets and
2. Distinguishing partnership property from the related type of property known as the partner's interest in the partnership.

Partnership property is property that the partners agree belongs to the partnership and must be used for partnership purposes. It differs from a partner's personal assets because it belongs to all the partners as tenants in partnership. Partnership property differs from a partner's interest in the partnership, which is the partner's share of the profits and surplus. In ordinary language, a partner's interest is commonly called a *partner's share.*

Partnership Property

Most partnerships require property for their operation. This property may be either *real property* (land) or *personal property* (movable items). Usually the partnership acquires its original property from individual partners as their capital contributions. The partners may contribute specific assets to the firm, such as land, equipment, or patents, or they may contribute money used to purchase assets. These assets, including money, usually become partnership property.

Partners may have property that is not partnership property. This property may remain the sole property of an individual partner even though it is used by the firm. For example, an individual partner's real estate may be used by the firm for its business premises without becoming the partnership's property if the partner providing it intends only to lend it to the firm. Similarly, nothing prevents a partner from lending equipment to the firm while retaining ownership of it.

What Constitutes Partnership Property. Although a partner's personal assets may be vulnerable to partnership obligations, distinguishing partnership property from a partner's personal assets is essential for several reasons. If property belongs to the partnership, its use by individual partners is restricted. If it is sold, any *capital gain or loss* is distributed to each partner in the same proportion as profits, unless otherwise agreed. If the property must be applied to satisfy creditor claims, partnership creditors have priority over an individual partner's personal creditors. But if the property is an individual partner's personal asset, his or her use of it is unrestricted. The entire capital gain or loss from its sale belongs to the partner and is subject to personal income taxes. If the partner dies, the property belongs to his or her estate.

The controlling criterion for deciding if certain property is the partnership's is the partners' *intent* that it belong to the firm and be devoted to its purposes. The partners' intent is the primary consideration. They may decide among themselves what will be owned by all as partnership property and what will be retained by each as his or her own.

One measure of the partners' intent is the way the property is acquired. Property bought with the firm's money is considered the partnership's. If it is bought with individual funds, it is considered that individual's property. Additional factors may strengthen this presumption. Repairing and improving the property at partnership expense, paying insurance premiums from partnership accounts, or listing the property on partnership financial statements may reinforce this presumption. But the presumption can be explained away if an intention of individual ownership appears.

Tenancy in Partnership. Assuming that certain property belongs to the partnership, the UPA describes the nature of a partner's ownership rights in it. "A partner is a co-owner with his [or her] partner of specific partnership property as a tenant in partnership." This tenancy in partnership is a unique property concept created by the UPA especially for partnerships. It recognizes that a partner's co-ownership rights in specific partnership property differ from other types of co-ownership. For example, many of the details of land ownership do not fit the needs of partnerships. The UPA's tenancy in partnership recognizes that the rights of a partner as a co-owner of specific partnership property should depend on the needs of the partnership relation.

The special needs of the partnership relation require that an individual partner's ownership rights in specific partnership property be restricted. Although the partners are co-owners of partnership property, they have limited ownership rights. Generally a partner cannot sell specific partnership property or

PREVENTIVE LAW
Partnership Property

The UPA creates the presumption that property bought with partnership funds is partnership property. On occasion this may not be what the individual partners intend. One way for the partners to explain away the presumption is to establish their intent at the outset in their partnership agreement. The partnership agreement generally governs, because it is the clearest indication of intent. Usually the statement describes the partnership property and its agreed-upon value in a separate schedule incorporated by reference into the agreement. Property used by the firm but owned by an individual partner also may be identified in this way. When an individual partner's property is loaned to the partnership, a copy of the lease may be attached to the agreement and incorporated by reference. The partnership agreement can provide that acquired property be recorded as partnership property in the partnership accounts. A well kept set of books will identify the partnership's assets, and the property listed there will be considered partnership property.

dispose of it by will. The theory is that the partnership property is to remain intact. It reflects recognition of the business primacy of the partnership relation.

Under the UPA

> A partner . . . has an equal right with his partners to possess specific partnership property for partnership purposes, but he has no right to possess such property for any other purpose without the consent of his partners.

A partner's use of partnership property is limited to partnership purposes. He or she may not use partnership property for personal or other nonpartnership purposes unless all the other partners agree. Their agreement may be implied by continued acceptance of the individual partner's personal use of partnership property, or the partners may expressly provide their consent in their partnership agreement.

Because a partner cannot possess partnership property for personal purposes, he or she cannot claim that specific partnership property as part of his or her home and thereby free it from seizure by creditors in a bankruptcy proceeding.

The UPA further restricts a partner's power to assign his or her rights in specific partnership property. A partner cannot assign his or her rights in partnership property unless it is an assignment of the rights of all the partners in the same property. For example, a partner cannot *mortgage* specific partnership property for a personal obligation. This aspect of the tenancy in partnership is necessary because partnerships are voluntary, personal relations. If the law recognized the possibility of individual assignments, the assignee would become a partner in the firm with the rights to possess the property for partnership purposes. But partnerships are voluntary relations, and people cannot have partners forced on them.

Creditors may not force an involuntary assignment through a judicial seizure of the property. Thus a partner's rights to partnership property are not subject to creditor claims, except upon a claim against the partnership.

When a partner dies, his or her ownership of specific partnership property passes to the surviving partners. It is not included in the deceased partner's estate. This is called the right of *survivorship*. It fits nicely the needs of the partnership, because it permits the partnership to be dissolved without interference from the dead partner's estate. Because a deceased partner's ownership rights in specific partnership property is not distributed to the heirs or beneficiaries, a partner may not include it in a will.

Partner's Interest in the Partnership

The UPA states that "a partner's interest in the partnership is his [or her] share of the profits and surplus, and the same is personal property." This interest is an intangible economic right. Its value appears on the partnership's balance sheet as each partner's capital account. Unlike specific partnership property, which belongs to the firm and is collectively held by the partners, each partner's interest belongs to him or her individually. Because it is each partner's individual property, a partner's interest has most of the ownership qualities that are denied to a partner in specific partnership property: it is assignable; it may be seized by creditors; and, when a partner dies, it becomes a part of the estate.

Assignment of Partner's Interest. Partners may convey their interest to another. An attempted assignment by a partner of his or her ownership in specific partnership property is regarded as valid. The person to whom the partner transfers the interest does not become a partner in the firm but only receives a right to share in the firm's profits. The assignee does not enjoy the usual rights and privileges of partners. He or she may not interfere with the firm's management, require information about the firm's transactions, or inspect the partnership books. But if the partnership is dissolved, the assignee may require an accounting of the interest from the date it was acquired. These restrictions place the assignee of a partner's interest in an insecure position and effectively make it difficult to find a buyer.

Creditor's Rights. Unlike specific partnership property, which is shielded from attack by a partner's personal creditors, a partner's interest in the partnership may be seized by his or her individual creditors to satisfy a debt resulting from a transaction outside the firm's business. In that a partner may voluntarily assign his or her interest to creditors, it follows that the partner's personal creditors should be able to force an involuntary assignment by a judicial seizure of the interest. The creditors may accomplish this by seeking a *charging order*, which is similar to the garnishment of someone's wages. Under the charging order, a personal creditor may reach the partner's interest without interfering with the firm's business.

The charging order attaching the partner's interest is the exclusive remedy for a partner's personal creditors. It is available only to a partner's personal creditors, those who have obtained a judgment against the partner. UPA (Section 28) provides that a court "may charge the interest of the debtor partner with payment of the unsatisfied amount of such judgment debt."

A creditor also may ask a court to appoint a receiver, an independent person who receives the partner's share of profits for the creditor. The receiver enters into the partnership and acts as a partner. The receiver may make:

orders, directions, accounts and inquiries which the debtor partner might have made, or which the circumstances of the case may require.

From the other partners' perspective the appointment of a receiver is not desirable. They may redeem the charged interest and get rid of the receiver by paying off the judgment creditor. They also can use partnership property to do this, provided there is approval among all the partners whose interests are not subject to the charging order.

Inheritance. When a partner dies, his or her interest in the partnership passes to the heirs or beneficiaries of his or her estate. Because a partner individually owned the partnership interest while living, it follows that it should become a part of the estate upon death. A partner may convey the interest by will. This may be done by a specific *bequest* of the interest to a particular beneficiary. But because a partner's interest is personal property, a bequest of all a partner's personal property includes a transfer of the partnership interest.

In addition to transfers by will, a partner may provide in the partnership agreement that his or her interest in the partnership will pass to one or more surviving partners. Usually this is done by a buy-sell provision in the partnership agreement. Under a *buy-sell agreement,* the partners agree that the survivors will buy the deceased partner's interest by paying the representative of the deceased partner the value of the deceased's interest in the firm. This payment may be either in a lump sum or in installments, and it may be backed by insurance. The partnership agreement may state that partnership proceeds be used to purchase life insurance for each partner covering the value of each partner's interest. The insurance proceeds then are used to pay the value of the deceased partner's interest to the deceased's representative.

Limited Partnerships

A limited partner's property rights are similar to a general partner's, except there is no right to participate in the control of the limited partnership. Distinguishing partnership property from a limited partner's individual property is seldom a problem. The nature of a limited partner's interest in a limited partnership is similar to the general partner's.

Partnership Property. Confusion over the distinction between partnership property and a limited partner's personal assets is not likely because the Uniform Limited Partnership Act of 1985 (ULPA) requires that each limited partnership keep a written record describing and stating the agreed value of any property that each limited partner contributes to the firm. This written record can take the form of the limited partnership agreement.

Limited Partner's Interest. A limited partner's interest in a limited partnership is the same as a general partner's interest—the partner's share of the profits and losses of the limited partnership and the right to receive distributions of partnership assets. Like the interest in a general partnership, it is personal property, assignable and subject to a charging order. When the limited partner dies, the interest is included in the estate.

Except as provided in the limited partnership agreement, a partner in a limited partnership can assign all or part of a limited partnership interest. An assignment entitles the assignee to receive only the distribution to which the assignor would have been entitled. Except where the partnership provides a different rule, a partner ceases to be a partner upon assignment.

RELATIONS AMONG PARTNERS

The UPA contains rules governing the relations of the partners to each other. These rules reflect the partners' presumed intent regarding their relationship. In providing general rules for determining the rights and obligations of the partners, the UPA states:

The rights and duties of the partners in relation to the partnership shall be determined, *subject to any agreement between them,* by the following rules [emphasis added].

The phrase *subject to any agreement between them* lets the partners alter or waive the rules governing their relationship when that is their actual intent. They usually make these changes in the partnership agreement, in that its function is to express the intentions of the partners about law and tax considerations. When no partnership agreement exists, or when an existing agreement is silent, the UPA provisions are implied. Thus the UPA serves as a backdrop and as a point of departure for the drafting of the partnership agreement.

As we have noted earlier, smart businesspeople appreciate the advantages of a written partnership agreement. Because a partnership is an intimate relationship, perhaps the greatest potential problem is the risk of future disagreement among those who start out with the highest mutual regard. This risk may be diminished by reducing the partners' relation to a written instrument. By focusing attention on potential trouble spots, a carefully drafted partnership agreement may avoid future disagreements and litigation. Because the UPA provides the basic rules governing the partners' relation to each other and also provides that these rules may be varied by the partners, the following paragraphs discuss these rules and the extent to which they may be altered by agreement. In short, the UPA defines: the fiduciary duties of partners, their rights to compensation, their management rights, and their right to information. Special rules exist for limited partners, reflecting the differences between the limited and general partnership relations.

Partners' Fiduciary Duties

The UPA provides that partners owe a fiduciary duty to each other. The fiduciary duties of agents were discussed in Chapter 30. In that the UPA provides that "every partner is an agent of the partnership for purposes of its business" and further states that "the law of agency shall apply under this act," it follows that partners share fiduciary duties similar to those of agents. A partnership is just a special type of agency, and partnership law is simply the application of agency principles to partnerships.

The intimate nature of the partnership also makes the application of the fiduciary rule to partnerships appropriate. Someone should not have to deal with his or her partners as if they were opposing parties. A partner should be able to trust his or her partners, to expect that they are pursuing a common goal and not working at cross purposes.

The partner's fiduciary duty requires loyalty to his or her partners. In a partnership, each partner is the confidential agent of his or her other partners. Therefore, no one may act at his or her partners' expense. The fiduciary relation prohibits all forms of trickery, secret dealings and selfishness in matters relating to the partnership. For example, a secret profit may not be made to the exclusion of other partners.

The duty of loyalty resulting from a partner's fiduciary position is such that the severity of a partner's breach is not questioned. The question is whether there has been any breach at all. The required degree of loyalty must be maintained at all times. From the first exploratory discussions, through formal association in partnership, to final severance of the relationship, partners are required to exercise scrupulous loyalty and good faith. A partner's duty of loyalty usually operates in two areas:

1. Instances in which a partner engages in transactions with other partners and the firm and
2. Instances in which partnership opportunities are presented to a partner

Nothing prohibits partners from dealing with each other at arm's length, as ordinary businesspeople, when negotiating a nonpartnership transaction. But when a transaction concerns any aspect of the partnership relation, the requisite degree of loyalty must be maintained. Transactions of this type include one partner's purchase of the partnership share of another and one partner's sale of personal property to the partnership.

Whenever a person buys the partnership share of another partner, the purchasing partner must inform the selling partner fully of any information he or she has that would affect the value of the partnership share. The purchaser may not conceal or fraudulently represent material facts to his or her partner. Similarly, when a partner sells his or her own property to the partnership, there must be no misrepresentation to the firm nor concealment of the seller's identity.

The same high standards of loyalty apply when partners are presented with a partnership opportunity. Occasionally third parties refuse to deal with the partnership and offer a partnership opportunity to a partner in his or her individual capacity. A partner may not accept such an offer while still a member of the firm, unless his or her partners grant permission.

When partners learn of or are offered any opportunity in their capacity as a member of a partnership, they may not appropriate this opportunity for personal benefit without first offering it to the firm. A partner may not, for example, purchase the rights to manufacture a product that would fit into the firm's product line. When the firm is presented with a business opportunity, a partner may take the opportunity for himself or herself if the partnership does not have enough money to take advantage of the opportunity or simply fails to take action on it. Otherwise, a partner may take advantage of a partnership opportunity only when it has been completely abandoned by the firm.

Because a partner is a fiduciary, he or she is held accountable for profits made in competition with the business. But a partner may engage in additional enterprises for personal benefit so long as they are not within the scope of the partnership and are undertaken in good faith. When litigation develops, it is not always easy to determine what the partners intended as the scope of the business. For example, partners in real estate may intend to retain some freedom to deal on their own accounts. Failure to delineate the scope of the partnership business in a partnership agreement invites quarrels. This problem is usually avoided by the inclusion of a purpose clause in the partnership agreement. A closely allied problem is the amount of time each partner must spend on firm business. If outside interests of one or more partners are to be permitted, a partnership agreement can provide for this.

The classic case of *Meinhard* v. *Salmon* demonstrates the high degree of loyalty required from a partner.

Meinhard v. Salmon
Court of Appeals of New York
164 N.E. 545 (1928)

Background: Walter Salmon (defendant) secured a twenty-year lease to the Hotel Bristol, at 42nd Street and Fifth Avenue, in New York City. The lease provided that he alter the hotel to make it suitable for shops and offices. Needing capital for the work, he enlisted the financial help of Meinhard (plaintiff). Under a joint venture agreement, Meinhard was to furnish one-half of the cost of alteration, upkeep, and repair in return for one-half of the profits. Losses were to be shared equally. Salmon retained sole management responsibility and authority. The project was highly successful. Four months before the end of the twenty-year term, the lessor, Mr. Gerry, made a new lease, having renewal provisions up to eighty years, with the Midpoint Realty Company, which was owned by Salmon. Salmon, as Midpoint Realty Company, was to develop the hotel property and adjoining lots on both streets and to construct a larger $3 million building. About one month later Meinhard learned of the project and demanded that the lease be held in trust for the joint venture, which had not yet expired. When Salmon refused, Meinhard sued. The trial court found for Meinhard, limiting his interest in the new lease to 25 percent, the proportion that his interest under the joint venture bore to the new project. An appellate court enlarged Meinhard's interest to 50 percent. Salmon then appealed to the Court of Appeals of New York, that state's highest court.

Decision: The New York Court of Appeals affirmed the lower court judgments in favor of Meinhard, except to modify the judgment to give Salmon 51 percent interest in the new project.

Cardozo, Chief Justice

Joint adventurers like copartners, owe to one another, while the enterprise continues, the duty of the finest loyalty. Many forms of conduct permissible in a workaday world for those acting at arm's length, are forbidden to those bound by fiduciary ties. A trustee is held to something stricter than the morals of the market place. Not honesty alone, but the punctilio of an honor the most sensitive, is then the standard of behavior. As to this there has developed a tradition that is unbending and inveterate. Uncompromising rigidity has been the attitude of courts of equity when petitioned to undermine the rule of undivided loyalty by the "disintegrating erosion" of particular exceptions. . . . Only thus has the level of conduct for fiduciaries been kept at a level higher than that trodden by the crowd. It will not consciously be lowered by any judgment of this court.

The owner of the reversion, Mr. Gerry, had vainly striven to find a tenant who would favor his ambitious scheme of demolition and construction. Baffled in the search, he turned to the defendant Salmon in possession of the Bristol, the keystone of the project. He figured to himself beyond a doubt that the man in possession would prove a likely customer. To the eye of an observer, Salmon held the lease as owner in his own right, for himself and no one else. In fact he held it as a fiduciary, for himself and another, shares in a common venture. If this fact had been proclaimed, if the lease by its terms had run in favor of a partnership, Mr. Gerry, we may fairly assume, would have laid before the partners, and not merely before one of them, his plan of reconstruction. The pre-emptive privilege, or, better, the pre-emptive opportunity, that was thus an incident of the enterprise, Salmon appropriated to himself in secrecy and silence. He might have warned Meinhard that the plan had been submitted, and that either would be free to compete for the award. If he had done this, we do not need to say whether he would have been under a duty, if successful in the competition, to hold the lease so acquired for the benefit of a venture then about to end, and thus prolong by indirection its responsibilities and duties. The trouble about his conduct is that he excluded his coadventurer from any chance to compete, from any chance to enjoy the opportunity for benefit that had come to him alone by virtue of his agency. This chance, if nothing more, he was under a duty to concede. The price of its denial is an extension of the trust at the option and for the benefit of the one whom he excluded.

No answer is it to say that the chance would have been of little value even if seasonably offered. Such a calculus of probabilities is beyond the science of the chancery.

We have no thought to hold that Salmon was guilty of a conscious purpose to defraud. Very likely he assumed in all good faith that with the approaching end of the venture he might ignore his coadventurer and take the extension for himself. He had given to the enterprise time and labor as well as money. He had made it a success. Meinhard, who had given money, but neither time nor labor, had already been richly paid. There might seem to be something grasping in his insistence upon more. Such recriminations are not unusual when coadventurers fall out. They are not without their force if conduct is to be judged by the common standards of competitors. That is not to say that they have pertinency here. Salmon had put himself in a position in which thought of self was to be renounced, however hard the abnegation. He was much more than a coadventurer. He was a managing coadventurer. For him and for those like him the rule of undivided loyalty is relentless and supreme. . . . A different question would be here if there were lacking any nexus of relation between the business conducted by the manager and the opportunity brought to him as an incident of management. . . . For this problem, as for most, there are distinctions of degree. If Salmon had received from Gerry a proposition to lease a building at a location far removed, he might have held for himself the privilege thus acquired, or so we shall assume. Here the subject-matter of the new lease was an extension and enlargement of the subject-matter of the old one. A managing coadventurer appropriating the benefit of such a lease without warning to his partner might fairly expect to be reproached with conduct that was underhand, or lacking, to say the least, in reasonable candor, if the partner were to surprise him in the act of signing the new instrument. Conduct subject to that reproach does not receive from equity a healing benediction.

A question remains as to the form and extent of the equitable interest to be allotted to the plaintiff. The trust as declared has been held to attach to the lease which was in the name of the defendant corporation. We think it ought to attach at the option of the defendant Salmon to the shares of stock which were owned by him or were under his control. The difference may be important if the lessee shall wish to execute an assignment of the lease, as it ought to be free with the consent of the lessor. On the other hand, an equal division of the shares might lead to other hardships. It might take away from Salmon the power of control and management which under the plan of the joint venture he has to have from first to last. The number of shares to be allotted to the plaintiff should, therefore, be reduced to such an extent as may be necessary to preserve to the defendant Salmon the expected measure of dominion. To that end an extra share should be added to his half.

Profits and Compensation

Unless there is an agreement to the contrary, under the UPA partners share equally in the profits. This equal sharing in profits results regardless of unequal contributions of capital, skills, or services by the partners.

Without an agreement stating otherwise, a partner is not entitled to compensation for services rendered for the firm's business. What a partner does for the firm's business is presumed to be in his or her own interest. It is ordinarily expected that each partner will devote himself or herself to the promotion of the firm's business without compensation. This expectation holds even when one partner performs more than the others. This rule rests on the presumed intent of the partners. If a provision for compensation is included in the partnership agreement, it is enforced.

From an economic perspective, the rules governing profits and compensation are sound when partners have contributed equally to the venture. To the extent that contributions are unequal, different rules are needed. For example, the senior partner in an accounting firm may demand more of the earnings than the other partners on the basis of his or her experience and reputation. Contributions to a manufacturing enterprise may vary widely in terms of equipment, good will, and time. By fixing the percentages of each partner's share of the profits in the partnership agreement, some of these differences may be taken into account. If the chief variation in contribution is the amount of capital, the proportion of capital contributed may determine the proportion of the profits received. But in many situations it is wise to base salaries on economic contributions, as for example, when one partner contributed managerial talent. The important point is that, unless the partners want the UPA's rules governing equal sharing of profits and no compensation to apply, the partnership agreement should specify the partners' intent.

Management

Under the UPA all partners have equal rights in the management and conduct of the partnership business. From this concept of equality it follows that a majority of the partners may decide ordinary partnership matters, provided that no agreement between them makes a different rule. A majority of the partners may determine the firm's action in ordinary affairs regardless of each partner's comparative investment in the firm. A majority governs over a minority in such matters as borrowing money, hiring and firing employees, collecting debts, and determining when and how profits are to be divided.

Individual partners and those in a minority are protected from majority oppression by two exceptions to the general principle of majority rule in management matters:

1. No partner may be excluded from participating in the firm's management.
2. The majority must act in good faith for the firm's interest and not out of self-interest.

Because each partner has an equal right to take part in the management of the firm's business, it makes sense that one partner may not exclude another partner from his or her full share in the management of the partnership. The requirement that the majority act in good faith and not for private advantage springs from the fiduciary duty of loyalty each partner owes to the other. Practically speaking, fairness requires consulting with the minority before taking action.

Individual partners and minorities are also protected by the requirement of unanimous approval on extraordinary matters, admission of incoming partners, and changes in the partnership agreement. Because the UPA permits

---

PREVENTIVE LAW
Partnership Agreement

——

Because either majority or unanimous approval usually governs the partnership's operations regardless of each partner's contribution, the partners may prefer to specify a different rule in the partnership agreement. For example, majority rule may be replaced by a provision in the partnership agreement leaving ordinary business decisions to a "majority in interest" of either the earnings or the capital contributions of the partners. The partners who together are entitled to more than half of the profits or who together contributed more than half the capital would make ordinary business decisions under this provision. A major contributor may insist on complete control, and the partnership agreement may allow it. When the partners contemplate that one of them will assume most of the managerial duties, the partnership agreement may designate a "managing partner," specifying the responsibilities entrusted to him or her. When a firm has many partners, such as a large, national accounting firm, provisions for centralizing management in an executive committee may be considered. If there is an even number of partners, the agreement may provide for arbitration to resolve deadlocks.

---

majority rule regarding *ordinary matters* connected with the partnership business, majority control does not extend to unusual or extraordinary transactions. These require unanimous approval. For example, a majority cannot engage the firm in a different business nor change the firm's location if any partner objects.

The UPA provides that no one may become a member of a partnership without the consent of all the partners. This rule reflects the intimate nature of partnership. No person should have a partner forced on him or her. Each partner may choose his or her associates.

Nothing contradicting the partnership agreement may be undertaken without unanimous approval. This rule is just another application of contract law, in that an act contravening the partnership agreement constitutes a breach of contract, and any modification of a contract requires agreement among all parties. Both majority and unanimous actions

may be taken with complete informality, such as an exchange of letters or a telephone call.

Information

The UPA provides:

> Partners shall render on demand true and full information of all things affecting the partnership to any partner or to the legal representative of any deceased partner or any partner under legal disability.

Thus each partner has the right to all information concerning partnership affairs. Although the UPA conditions the duty to render information on a demand, the courts hold that partners must perform a duty of disclosure regardless of demand. The duty to inform springs from the partners' fiduciary duty of loyalty. As part of this duty, partners must not conceal information from each other.

A partner's right to information continues even if a partner lets others manage the firm. To protect his or her investment and to guard against exposure to potential liability, a partner needs access to all partnership information whether or not the partner actively participates in the firm's management.

The UPA requires:

The partnership books shall be kept, subject to any agreement between the partners, at the principal place of business of the partnership, and every partner shall *at all times* have access to and may inspect and copy *any* of them [emphasis added].

Although the UPA does not specify what type of books and records are to be kept, federal income tax regulations require a detailed balance sheet, statements of partnership income and each partner's share of income and deductions, and a reconciliation of the partners' capital accounts. A partner need not be a bookkeeper or an accountant to maintain the records, nor need he or she follow standard accounting practice. But partners may be wise to hire a competent accountant or bookkeeper when they lack these skills themselves. If keeping partnership records at the principal place of business and making them available at all times seems inconvenient, the partnership agreement may provide for a different location and specify times when records may be inspected.

To protect a partner's right to partnership information further, the UPA gives each partner the right to a formal accounting of partnership affairs. A formal accounting is a comprehensive, court-ordered investigation of partnership transactions by a court-appointed investigator. The UPA gives the right to an accounting when specific circumstances justify it even though there is no dissolution of the partnership. Under the UPA a partner may seek an accounting without dissolving the partnership when:

1. He or she is wrongfully excluded from partnership business
2. A partner withholds profits from a secret transaction
3. It is provided for in the partnership agreement
4. Other circumstances render it just and reasonable

Except in these situations one partner does not have a right to an accounting from his or her partners unless the partnership is dissolved. The partner already has access to the firm's books and property.

A partner's only recourse against his or her partners for breaching a duty owed under either the UPA or the partnership agreement is to bring an action for an accounting. A partner cannot otherwise sue his or her partners or the partnership for claims arising out of the partnership's affairs because the partner would be both plaintiff and defendant in the case. Outside of an action for an accounting, a partner can sue his or her partners only when the problems at issue have nothing to do with partnership affairs or when an accounting has already taken place and the partner's share has been determined.

Limited Partners

Limited partners are not subject to the same rules as general partners. Limited partners owe no fiduciary duties, have different rights to compensation, and may not participate in the control of the partnership. But generally they have the same rights to information as general partners.

Unlike a general partner, a limited partner owes no duty of loyalty and may, for example, operate a business in competition with the partnership.

Under the Uniform Limited Partnership Act of 1985 (ULPA) a limited partner may receive any profits or compensation stipulated in the limited partnership agreement. In the absence of an agreement, profits are allocated according to the value of each partner's contribution to the partnership.

The limited partner's management rights are less than those of a general partner. The trade-off for obtaining limited liability is the surrender of any right to participate in the control of the partnership. This arrangement prevents a creditor from mistaking a limited partner for one of the general partners with full liability. Under the ULPA, if a limited partner participates in the control of the business, he or she is liable to persons who transact business with the limited partnership reasonably believing, based upon the limited partner's conduct, that the limited partner is a general partner. The ULPA lists certain activities—such as consulting or being a contractor, employee, or an agent of the firm—that a limited partner may perform without being considered to take part in the control of the business.

Although limited partners may not participate in the control of the partnership as fully as general partners without risking loss of their limited liability, their passive position requires that they have access to information to protect their investment. Under the ULPA a limited partner may obtain from the general partners relevant partnership records.

RELATIONS WITH THIRD PARTIES

Because partnerships exist to do business, partners need to interact with third parties who deal with the partnership. This interaction may be in making contracts or committing torts. The problem is to what extent a partner's conduct binds the firm and fellow partners.

As mentioned earlier, partnership law is a particular application of agency law. A partner's power to bind the firm in dealings with third parties is determined by the general rules of agency law as provided in the UPA. Because each partner is an agent of the partnership for the purpose of its business, his or her acts may result in the firm's being:

1. liable for contracts made and torts committed by a partner
2. bound by a partner's admissions
3. charged with the knowledge of or notice to a partner.

Agency rules provided in the UPA also apply for determining the liability of incoming and withdrawing partners for obligations incurred by the partnership. A limited partner is not an agent of the partnership and therefore has no authority to act for the firm and bind it to third parties.

Contracts

The power of a partner to bind the partnership to contracts with third parties may be either actual or apparent. The partner may have actual authority as expressly provided in the partnership agreement. If no actual or express authority is provided there, the partner may have apparent authority. When a partner's acts are unauthorized, they may be ratified by a majority of the partners and made binding on the firm. Thus the power of a partner to bind the firm by contract to third parties may be found either in the partnership agreement or, by implication, in his or her conduct or the conduct of the partners.

The UPA provides that any act of a partner is binding on the partnership if it is "for apparently carrying on in the usual way the business of the partnership." This is just a restatement of the agency rule regarding apparent authority. Partners have apparent authority consistent with the nature of the partnership business. The usual authority possessed by partners in similar businesses is the measure of a particular partner's apparent authority. The UPA further provides that any:

act of a partner which is not apparently for the carrying on of the business of the partnership in the usual way does not bind the partnership unless authorized by the other partners.

For acts unrelated to the partnership's business, a partner needs actual authority, whether informal or given in the partnership agreement.

Sometimes a partnership agreement restricts a partner's authority to bind the partnership. For example, a partnership agreement may provide that no partner shall incur any debt for the firm of over $500. What effect should this have on third parties? Under the UPA third parties are not limited nor bound by secret restrictions of a partner's authority or by restrictions in a partnership agreement, unless they know of them. Thus any contracts made by a partner for the firm and related to its business are binding on the partnership despite any secret restrictions on the partner's authority if they are unknown to the third party.

In the following case the court examines to what extent a partnership is liable on the contracts entered into by the partners.

National Biscuit Company v. Stroud

Supreme Court of North Carolina

106 S.E.2d 692 (1959)

Background: In March 1953 C. N. Stroud (defendant) and Earl Freeman entered into a general partnership to sell groceries under the name of Stroud's Food Center. Thereafter the National Biscuit Company (Nabisco) (plaintiff) sold bread regularly to the partnership. In October 1955 Stroud advised an agent of Nabisco that he personally would not be responsible for any additional bread sold by Nabisco to Stroud's Food Center. From February 6, 1956, to February 25, 1956, Nabisco, through this same agent, at the request of Freeman, sold and delivered bread in the amount of $171.04 to Stroud's Food Center. Stroud and Freeman by agreement dissolved the partnership at the close of business on February 25, 1956. Stroud paid all of the partnership obligations, amounting to $12,014.45, except the amount of $171.04 claimed by Nabisco. To pay the partnership obligations, Stroud exhausted all the partnership assets. Nabisco sued both Stroud and Freeman seeking to recover the $171.04. Stroud claimed that he was not liable to Nabisco. The trial court awarded judgment for Nabisco, and Stroud appealed to the Supreme Court of North Carolina. Decision: The Supreme Court of North Carolina affirmed the trial court judgment in favor of Nabisco.

Parker, Justice

In *Johnson* v. *Bernheim,* this Court said: "A and B are general partners to do some given business; the partnership is by operation of law, a power to each to bind the partnership in any manner legitimate to the business. If one partner goes to a third person to buy an article on time for the partnership, the other partner cannot prevent it by writing to the third not to sell to him on time; or, if one party attempts to buy for cash, the other has no right to require that it shall be on time. And what is true in regard to buying is true in regard to selling. What either partner does with a third person is binding on the partnership. It is otherwise where the partnership is not general, but is upon special terms, as that purchases and sales must be with and for cash. There the power to each is special, in regard to all dealings with third persons at least who have notice of the terms." There is contrary authority: 68 C.J.S., Partnership, pp. 578–579. However, this text of C.J.S. does not mention the effect of the provisions of the Uniform Partnership Act.

The General Assembly of North Carolina in 1941 enacted a Uniform Partnership Act, which became effective 15 March 1941. [The court then quoted the applicable sections of the UPA.]

Freeman as a general partner with Stroud, with no restrictions on his authority to act within the scope of the partnership business so far as the agreed statement of facts shows, had under the Uniform Partnership Act "equal rights in the management and conduct of the partnership business." Under [the UPA] Stroud, his co-partner, could not restrict the power and authority of Freeman to buy bread for the partnership as a going concern, for such a purchase was an "ordinary matter connected with the partnership business." . . . Therefore Freeman's purchases of bread from plaintiff for Stroud's Food Center as a going concern bound the partnership and his co-partner Stroud. The quoted provisions of our Uniform Partnership Act, in respect to the particular facts here, are in accord with the principle of law stated in *Johnson* v. *Bernheim.*

In Crane on Partnership, 2nd Ed., p. 277, it is said:

> In cases of an even division of the partners as to whether or not an act within the scope of the business should be done, of which disagreement a third person has knowledge, it seems that logically no restriction can be placed upon the power to act. The partnership being a going concern, activities within the scope of the business should not be limited, save by the expressed will of the majority deciding a disputed question; half of the members are not a majority.

Torts

Under the UPA the partnership is liable for the torts of any partner acting in the ordinary course of the business of the partnership or with the authority of his or her partners. All members of a partnership are liable for a partner's torts committed within the scope and course of the partnership business. This liability also extends to absent partners who did not participate in, ratify, or know about the tort.

The determining factor for invoking partnership liability is whether the tort was committed within the reasonable scope of and on behalf of the partnership business. If the wrongful conduct was clearly outside the scope of the partnership business, the nonparticipating partners may still be liable if they authorize, ratify, or consent to the tort. Consent, scope, and course of business provide the principal channels through which liability attaches to a partnership for a partner's torts.

Liability usually attaches when a partner's negligence injures a third party. In comparison to negligent conduct, a willful and malicious tort is generally held not to be within the scope of an ordinary partnership, and the partnership is not liable unless the nonparticipating partners authorize, ratify, or consent to their partner's willful tort. For example, if a partner in a tavern assaults a customer without provocation, liability would not extend to the absent partner who had neither consented to nor authorized the attack.

The following case demonstrates the potential tort liability of partners.

Kelsey-Seybold Clinic v. Maclay

Supreme Court of Texas
466 S.W.2d 716 (1971)

Background: For several years John Dale Maclay (plaintiff) and his wife and children had been under the medical care of the Kelsey-Seybold Clinic (defendant), including treatment by a pediatrician, Dr. Brewer, who was a partner in the clinic. Claiming that Dr. Brewer was engaging in conduct designed to alienate the affections of his wife, Maclay notified Dr. Kelsey, a senior partner at the clinic, of the alleged tortious relationship. Maclay claimed that despite such notice, the physician's relationship with Maclay's wife continued. Maclay brought suit against Dr. Brewer and the clinic for the tort of alienation of affection. The trial court awarded summary judgment in favor of the clinic. Maclay appealed to the Texas Court of Civil Appeals, which ruled in favor of Maclay and reversed the trial court decision. The clinic then appealed to the Texas Supreme Court.

Decision: The Texas Supreme Court affirmed the appellate court decision in favor of Maclay and ordered the case to be sent back to the trial court for a trial.

Walker, Justice

We are unwilling to believe that plaintiff seriously expects to prove in a conventional trial that the acts alleged to have been committed by Dr. Brewer were in the course and scope of the partnership business or were either authorized or ratified by the Clinic. . . . [W]e assume for the purpose of this opinion that Dr. Brewer was not acting in the ordinary course of the Clinic's business and that his conduct was neither authorized nor ratified by the partnership. This will enable us to reach questions that may well arise at the trial of the case.

The Court of Civil Appeals reasoned that the summary judgment was improper because the Clinic had not conclusively negated consent on its part of the alleged wrongful conduct of Dr. Brewer. In reaching this conclusion, it relied on our opinion in *K & G Oil Tool & Service Co. v. G & G Fishing Tool Service,* where it was stated that:

> A non-participating partner is ordinarily not personally liable for the wrongful, tortious or criminal acts of the acting partner unless such acts are within the scope of the partnership's business or were consented to, authorized, ratified or adopted by the non-participating partner.

There was no question of consent in *K & G,* and it was held that the non-participating partner was not liable.

Where a partner proposed to do, in the name or for the benefit of the partnership, some act that is not in the ordinary course of the business, consent by the other partners may constitute his authority to do the act for the partnership. We also recognize that even a wilful or malicious act outside the ordinary scope of the partnership business may be so related to the business that tacit consent of the other partners could fairly be regarded as a grant of authority. In this instance, however, Dr. Brewer was acting solely for his own personal gratification. His conduct could not benefit the Clinic in any way, and no one would have supposed that he was acting for the partnership. It is our opinion that in these circumstances the "consent" that might be inferred from the silence or inaction of the Clinic after learning of his conduct does not render the Clinic vicariously liable for the damages claimed by plaintiff.

On the basis of the present record and the facts we are assuming in this case, the liability of the Clinic must rest, if at all, upon some theory akin to that recognized by the court in *Williams.* [Williams v. F. & W. Grand Five, Ten and Twenty-five Cent Stores, 273 Pa. 131, 116 A. 652]. The Clinic was under a duty, of course, to exercise ordinary care to protect its patients from harm resulting from tortious conduct of persons upon the premises. A negligent breach of that duty could subject the Clinic to liability without regard to whether the tortious conduct immediately causing the harm was that of an agent or servant or was in the ordinary scope of the partnership business. For example, it might become liable, as a result of its own negligence, for damage done by a vicious employee while acting beyond the scope of his authority.

. . .

We are also of the opinion that the Clinic owed a duty to the families of its patients to exercise ordinary care to prevent a tortious interference with family relations. It was not required to maintain constant surveillance over personnel on duty or to inquire into and regulate the personal conduct of partners and employees while engaged in their private affairs. But if and when the partnership received information from which it knew or should have known that there might be a need to take action, it was under a duty to use reasonable means at its disposal to prevent any partner or employee from improperly using his position with the Clinic to work a tortious invasion of legally protected family interests. This duty relates only to conduct of a partner or employee on the premises of the Clinic or while purportedly acting as a representative of the Clinic elsewhere. Failure to exercise ordinary care in discharging that duty would subject the Clinic to liability for damages proximately caused by its negligence.

The rather meager information in the present record does not necessarily indicate that the Clinic was under a duty to act or that it could have done anything to prevent the damage when Dr. Kelsey first learned of the situation. On the other hand, it does not affirmatively and clearly appear that the Clinic could or should have done nothing. Mrs. Maclay's affections may have been alienated from her husband before anyone talked with Dr. Kelsey, but the facts in that respect are not fully developed. There is not proof as to when, where or under what circumstances the misconduct, if any, on Dr. Brewer's part occurred. Dr. Kelsey testified that he did not believe anything improper occurred at the Clinic, but the proofs do not establish as a matter of law that he was justified in not making further inquiry after his conversations with plaintiff and

Mr. Maclay's uncle. The record does not show whether there is a partnership agreement that might have a bearing on the case, and we have no way of knowing the extent to which the Clinic might have determined which patients were to be seen by Dr. Brewer or controlled his actions while on duty. Dr. Kelsey's testimony suggests that the partners might have been in a position to prevent improper conduct by one of their number on the premises of the Clinic. In our opinion the Clinic has failed to discharge the heavy, and in a case of this character virtually impossible, burden of establishing as a matter of law at the summary judgment stage that it is not liable under any theory fairly presented by the allegations.

Greenhill, Justice *(dissenting)*

I am unable to agree that the partners of Dr. Brewer or the Kelsey Clinic are even potentially liable.

This suit was brought by a husband for the alienation of his wife's affections. The acts alleged to have occurred were not any sort of assault or battery as in the Williams case from Pennsylvania relied upon by the majority opinion. The alleged acts involved here between Dr. Brewer and the plaintiff's wife were between consenting adults; and obviously, they were committed in secret. The majority opinion correctly finds that Dr. Brewer was acting solely for his own personal gratification; that his conduct could not benefit the clinic in any way; and it assumes that his conduct was neither authorized nor ratified by the partnership. The Uniform Partnership Act provides for liability of the partnership for wrongful acts of a partner "acting in the ordinary course of the business of the partnership." Article 6132b, §13, Vernon's Annotated Civil Statutes. I find no such action here. [The rest of Justice Greenhill's opinion regarding the tort of alienation of affections is omitted.]

Admissions, Knowledge, and Notice

Agency rules make the partnership responsible for the admissions or representations of any partner about partnership affairs within the scope of his or her authority. As in agency law, knowledge or notice to any partner of matters relating to partnership affairs is assumed to extend to all the partnership. Thus notice to a partner about a matter of firm business—for example, a prior mortgage on property acquired by the firm—is notice to the partnership and all its members. But knowledge or notice is not assumed when the partner acquires it while acting fraudulently, adversely to the firm, or when the knowledge was acquired by the partner before joining the firm.

Withdrawing and Incoming Partners

Partners often withdraw or retire from firms and are replaced by incoming partners. Partners must take care to consider how the change in membership will affect the liabilities of each. A retiring partner remains liable to third parties unless he or she notifies third parties who know of the partnership and have extended credit to it. This notice may be given informally by letter or phone, or by a novation, substituting the incoming partner for the retiring partner as responsible to the partnership's creditors. Constructive notice, such as publication in a newspaper, is essential to notify third parties adequately who know about the partnership but never extended credit to it.

An incoming partner is liable for all partnership obligations arising before his or her admission, just as if the incoming partner had been a partner when such obligations were incurred. But this liability may be satisfied only out of the partnership property. A judgment for such an obligation may not be satisfied out of the incoming partner's individual property. An incoming partner may promise the partners that old creditors will be paid. When this happens, the promise can be enforced by the creditors as third-party beneficiaries to the contract and may subject the incoming partner's individual property to satisfy the debt. Another way to accomplish the same result is for the creditors to enter into a novation, substituting the incoming partner for any withdrawing partner.

PARTNERSHIP DISSOLUTION

The day may come when the partnership is dissolved. The partners may wish to withdraw from the firm or simply to change to the corporate form. The partnership may be bankrupt. There are many reasons for *partnership dissolution.* Unlike corporations, partnerships lack continued existence. Like humankind, they are mortal. But with a little wizardry, the partnership business may be born again and continue its commercial course in a new guise. We now visit the deathbed of the partnership, view its "dissolution," and witness its "winding up." However, this discussion concludes on a happier note, with how the business may be continued.

Dissolution, Winding Up, and Termination

The UPA distinguishes among a partnership's dissolution, winding up, and termination, which are the three phases of ending a partnership. The first phase, the partnership's dissolution, occurs when the partners cease being

associated with one another as partners. It has nothing to do with the discontinuation of the partnership *business* but refers only to a change of *relation* among the partners. The partnership does not automatically stop doing business upon dissolution. A partnership continues after dissolution until the business is liquidated and the partnership terminated, unless continued by agreement or pursuant to the UPA. The second phase is the winding up of partnership affairs. *Winding up* is the process of bringing the partnership business to an end. The third phase is the partnership's termination. Upon termination the partnership is legally and functionally dead.

Dissolution. The UPA defines dissolution as the change in the relation of the partners caused by any partner's ceasing to be associated in the carrying on, as distinguished from the winding up, of the business. Dissolution is a legal event, a point in time when partners stop doing business together. The partnership has technically dissolved.

Winding Up and Termination

The UPA cautions that "on dissolution the partnership is not terminated, but continues until the winding up is completed." The winding up, otherwise called by businesspeople *liquidation,* is the process of ending partnership affairs. It is the process through which termination is reached. It is the administration of assets to discharge the firm's obligations to its creditors and members. When that process is complete, the partnership is terminated.

Causes of Dissolution

Partnership dissolution is caused by the acts of the partners or by operation of law.

Acts of the Partners. Any partner may dissolve the partnership at any time, and each partner has the power to dissolve the partnership. But the distinction between the *power* to dissolve and the *right* to dissolve should be carefully noted. A power is the ability to affect the legal status of another—for example, a partner's ability to alter his or her associates' status as members of a partnership by dissolving the firm. A person may incur a liability for exercising a power wrongfully. But with a right to do something, there is no liability for its exercise. A partner may have the power to dissolve but not the right. Although a partner can cause a dissolution of the partnership at any time, if the dissolution is wrongful, the guilty partner may be liable to his or her partners for the misconduct.

Whether the partner has the right to dissolve is determined by the agreement among the partners. It may show consent to future dissolution. It may confer the right to dissolve the firm upon a partner, or it may withhold the right under certain circumstances. Any act by a partner that causes the firm's dissolution is rightful if it complies with the agreement. Any act by a partner that causes the firm's dissolution is wrongful if it contradicts the agreement. Under the UPA dissolution is caused without violating the agreement between the partners:

1. When the partnership term expires, which may be upon the completion of a specified time period or a particular project
2. If no definite time or particular undertaking is specified, at the express will of any partners
3. By agreement of all the partners or by less than all when one or more of the partners has assigned his or her interest or it has been subjected to a *charging order*
4. By expelling a partner according to the terms of the partnership agreement

When a dissolution contradicts the partnership agreement, the remaining partners may recover damages from the guilty partner. This provision is another application of the con-

tract law principles regarding the rights of contracting parties in the event of a breach. The UPA also protects the remaining partners from wrongful dissolution by permitting them to continue the partnership without the errant partner. To do so, the remaining partners must pay to the dissolving partner the value of his or her interest in the partnership, less damages, and must *indemnify* (repay) him or her against all partnership liabilities.

Operation of Law. Dissolution of a partnership also may be caused by operation of law. Under the UPA dissolution is caused by operation of law in the following ways:

1. By any event that makes it unlawful to carry on the partnership business
2. By the death of any partner
3. By the bankruptcy of any partner or the partnership
4. By court decree under the UPA

The UPA allows dissolution by a court when a partner applies for it on one of the following grounds:

1. When a partner is incapable of performing as a partner
2. When improper conduct of a partner is detrimental to the business, such as continual breaches of the partnership agreement
3. When the business can only be carried on at a loss
4. When circumstances and equities show that dissolution is necessary

Limited Partnerships. The causes of dissolution are fewer in number for limited partnerships, according to the Uniform Limited Partnership Act of 1985. For example, although in a general partnership the ceasing of a partner to carry on the business may bring about dissolution, this is not true with limited partnerships. The death, incapacity, bankruptcy, or withdrawal of one of the limited partners does not dissolve a limited partnership. Further, the withdrawal of a general partner does not dissolve a limited partnership if there is at least one other general partner and the partnership agreement permits the business to be carried on by the remaining general partners. Even where the agreement is silent on the issue, or the only general partner withdraws from the firm, the limited partnership will not be dissolved if the remaining partners appoint the necessary additional partners and agree in writing to continue the business. A limited partnership is dissolved, however, by the completion of its term or the occurrence of events specified in the partnership agreement or upon the written consent of all the partners. Under the ULPA a partner may obtain a court-ordered dissolution of a limited partnership if it is not reasonably practical to carry on the business in conformity with the partnership agreement.

Winding Up the Partnership Business

The winding up is the process by which the partnership business is brought to an end. After the partnership relation has dissolved, the partnership's affairs must be wound up if business is to be terminated. This winding up of firm affairs is the process of reducing assets to pay creditors and members of the partnership. During winding up all uncompleted transactions are finished, debts are settled or paid, claims and accounts owed are collected or settled, and the remaining assets are either sold or distributed along with any surplus to the partners. During this process the partnership continues for the limited purpose of liquidation, and the partners retain only those powers that are incidental to winding up the business.

Right to Wind Up. The surviving partners who are not bankrupt and who have not wrongfully dissolved the partnership have the right to wind up the affairs of the partnership. When the partners agree to a dissolution, or when the partnership's term expires, all the partners have the right to wind up the firm's affairs. Partners often designate a fellow partner to be in charge of winding up the business. This person is usually called the *liquidating partner* or liquidator. The partners may appoint the liquidating partner by agreement in the articles of partnership.

If the partnership is dissolved because of the bankruptcy or death of a partner, the remaining or surviving partners are entitled to wind up the partnership. Under the UPA a surviving partner is entitled to reasonable compensation for winding up the business. Only if the last surviving partner dies before the business is wound up does the legal representative of a deceased partner have the right to participate in the winding up. If dissolution is by court order, a court-appointed receiver winds up the firm.

Partners' Powers During Winding Up. Two needs arise upon dissolution of the partnership:

1. The need to wind up the firm affairs and
2. The need to protect third parties who do business with the firm without knowing of its dissolution.

Both needs are satisfied by two agency law concepts: actual and apparent authority.

To prevent partners from engaging in any new business that might delay winding up, a partner's actual authority upon dissolution is limited to what needs to be done to end the business. A partner may do only what is necessary and incidental to winding up the firm's affairs.

Whether a transaction is necessary and incidental to winding up the partnership depends on the circumstances. Generally the partners who are winding up the partnership may sell partnership property to liquidate firm assets, take payment for obligations owed to the partnership, and enter into compromises with creditors to release the partnership from its obligations. Actions that at first seem inappropriate actually may be appropriate if they are necessary and incidental to the partnership's winding up.

The concept of apparent authority protects third parties who deal with a partner without knowing about the partnership's dissolution and winding up. A partner's apparent authority may serve to bind the firm to a transaction that would have been binding before dissolution when a third party deals with a partner without knowledge or notice of the dissolution. The UPA incorporates the concept of apparent authority by providing that after dissolution a partner may still bind the partnership to transactions with those who formerly extended credit to the firm if the former creditors have no notice of the dissolution. People who never extended credit to the firm are considered to have notice of the dissolution if the fact of dissolution has been advertised in a newspaper of general circulation.

In the following case the court considers what constitutes the winding up of partnership affairs and the extent of a surviving partner's authority.

King v. Stoddard

Court of Appeals of California
104 Cal. Rptr. 903 (1972)

Background: Lyman Stoddard, Sr., his wife, Alda, and their son, Lyman, Jr., operated a partnership that published a newspaper, the *Walnut Kernel*. After Lyman, Sr., and Alda died, Lyman, Jr., continued operating the paper as the sole surviving partner. King and White, an accounting firm, had been accountants for the *Walnut Kernel* for about ten years before the deaths of Lyman, Sr., and Alda and continued to render accounting services after Lyman, Sr. and Alda died. When King and White (plaintiffs) were not paid, they sued Lyman, Jr., and the estates of Lyman, Sr., and Alda (defendants). The agents of the estates argued that the estates were not liable because the son lacked the authority to employ an accounting firm and only had the authority to wind up the partnership business. King and White argued that Lyman, Jr., had the authority to hire them on behalf of the partnership because the newspaper had continued to preserve its asset value as a going business so that it could be sold and that this was part of the winding up of the business. The trial court found the estates liable to King and White, and the estates appealed.

Decision: The California Court of Appeals reversed the trial court decision and ruled that the estates were not liable to the accounting firm.

Brown, Justice

The partnership was dissolved by operation of law upon the deaths of Alda and Lyman E. Stoddard, Sr. [The UPA] provides that dissolution of a partnership is ". . . caused by any partner ceasing to be associated in the carrying on as distinguished from the winding up of the business." Death is one of the causes of dissolution. Dissolution, however, does not terminate the partnership which ". . . continues until the winding up of partnership affairs is completed." Although the general rule is that a partner has no authority to bind his copartners to new obligations after dissolution, [the UPA] provides that "[a]fter dissolution a partner can bind the partnership . . . (a) By any act appropriate for winding up partnership affairs. . . ."

It is this latter provision upon which the court based its decision that the estates of the deceased partners were liable for the accounting services performed after dissolution. The court found that "LYMAN STODDARD JR.'S continuation of the WALNUT KERNEL business was an appropriate act for winding up the partnership, since the assets of the business would have substantial value only if it was a going business. It was to the advantage of the partnership that the business be maintained as a going business."

Respondents, as accountants, had performed services both before and after the dissolution. The services, however, were a continuation of the accounting services pursuant to the ordinary course of the operation of the business. Respondent King testified that he was ". . . doing work for the activity of the newspaper, the financial activity of the newspaper" and that he was doing the same type of work as he had always performed for the Walnut Kernel. The exhibits which support his bill for services indicate that he did not, or was not able to, break down his services into categories which would separate ordinary accounting services from those related to the winding up of the partnership. The court, however, found that the continuation of the business itself was an "act appropriate for winding up partnership affairs."

We disagree with this finding. It is probably true that there might have been advantages to the partnership to sell the business as a going business, but the indefinite continuation of the partnership business is contrary to the requirement for winding up of the affairs upon dissolution.

Even if we assume that a situation might exist where continuation of the business for a period would be appropriate to winding up the partnership interest, such a situation did not exist here. The record reflects the fact that the surviving partner was not taking action to wind up the partnership as was his duty, nor did the estates consent in any way to a delay. Rather, their insistence on winding up took the form of an effort to sell the business and a suit to require an accounting. There is nothing in the record upon which to base the argument made by respondents that appellants consented to their continued employment. The fact that they did not object is of no relevance. They had no right to direct and did not participate in the operation of the business. Therefore, the determination that the acts of the accountants were rendered during a winding up process is not based upon substantial evidence.

Distribution of Assets

Order of Claims. After partnership assets are liquidated the proceeds are distributed to pay any claims against the firm. Claims against the partnership are paid in the following order:

1. Claims of partnership creditors
2. Claims of partners for loans or advances

3. Partners' capital contributions
4. Remaining assets distributed as profits and surplus to the partners

If the partnership is solvent, no problems are presented because everyone gets paid. But if the partnership assets are insufficient to pay its debts, the partners must make up the loss in the same proportion as they shared profits. If some of the partners are insolvent but others are able to pay, the firm's creditors are paid by the solvent partners.

Upon the winding up of a limited partnership, according to the Uniform Limited Partnership Act of 1985, the assets are to be distributed as follows:

1. Creditors, including limited partners who are creditors (This does not include the return of a limited partner's capital contribution.)
2. Withdrawing partners' return of their contributions to the partnership, except where the partnership agreement provides otherwise
3. Remaining partners receive first the return of their contributions and secondly, their partnership interest, in the proportions in which they share distributions, except where the partnership agreement provides otherwise

Marshaling of Assets. A partnership creditor has a claim against partnership assets. When partnership assets are insufficient to pay the claim, the creditor has a claim against the individual partners' property. A problem arises when there are both individual and partnership creditors. What are their relative rights to a partner's partnership and individual property? Individual creditors have priority to the partner's individual property, but partnership creditors have priority to partnership property. Under the doctrine called *marshaling of assets* a partnership creditor must pursue a claim against partnership property before pursuing a partner's individual property. By compelling partnership creditors to exhaust partnership property before pursuing a partner's individual property, the doctrine lets both individual and partnership creditors satisfy their claims if there are substantial assets.

Continuing the Partnership Business

Depending on the particular business involved, dissolution and subsequent liquidation without the right to continue the partnership business can be economically disastrous to the remaining partners. Consequently, one of the major reasons for having a partnership agreement is to provide for the firm's continuation by the remaining partners despite dissolution. In large accounting and brokerage firms, for example, partners are continually joining and withdrawing from the firm. Technically, these comings and goings dissolve the partnership. But through carefully considered provisions in their partnership agreements, they avoid any termination of activities. A continuation provision in a partnership agreement may allow remaining partners to carry on the partnership by buying out a withdrawing partner. Although this arrangement technically is a dissolution of the partnership, the partnership *business* continues.

Right to Continue. Partners may have the right to continue the partnership business although their agreement contains no continuation provision. As we mentioned earlier, when dissolution is caused by an act that contradicts the agreement, the innocent partners may continue the business by

1. Paying the dissolving partner the value of his or her interest minus an amount attributable to any damages resulting from the breach and

PREVENTIVE LAW
Dissolution of Partnership

A dissolved partnership may be continued by an agreement between the withdrawing and remaining partners at the time of dissolution. It may be provided for in advance by a provision in the partnership agreement. For example, a clause in the partnership agreement may provide:

> In the event of dissolution caused by the retirement of a partner, the remaining partners shall have the right to continue the partnership business under the same name by themselves or with any other persons they may choose; however, they shall pay to the retiring partner the value of his or her interest as of the date of dissolution.

When the dissolution occurs, liquidation will consist of bookkeeping and buying out the withdrawing partner.

Providing for the firm's continuation in the partnership agreement requires foresight and care by the partners. They should determine:

1. Which events, such as death, retirement, bankruptcy, and so on, that cause dissolution may also give rise to the right to continue
2. Which partners have the right to continue
3. The method of disposing of the withdrawing partner's interest—for example, purchase by the remaining partners or by an incoming partner
4. The method of paying for the withdrawing partner's interest, such as cash, insurance proceeds, or payments out of future earnings
5. The method of allocating the price of the withdrawing partner's interest

On the last point the partners should agree on a valuation method. For example, an appraisal may be good for a real-estate partnership but not for a service or professional partnership. The valuation method must be fair. An agreed dollar value, even with periodic adjustments, is not considered fair. Using book value is unfair, unless provisions require periodic reappraisal of assets, such as real estate and inventories.

The partnership provision calling for the purchase of a withdrawing partner's interest is usually referred to as a buy-sell agreement. When the death of a partner is contemplated, the buy-sell agreement usually provides for the purchase of a deceased partner's interest at death and is frequently funded by insurance. In a growing business where the partners have reinvested their profits the surviving partners may be without immediate funds to pay the deceased partner's interest. The only source of funds for the deceased partner's interest may be the future profits of the business, which then will not be available for reinvestment. In such a situation the buy-sell provision in the partnership agreement may provide for the funding of the purchase price with insurance. The insurance premiums may be paid by the partners or the partnership. On the death of a partner the insurance policy proceeds are then used to pay the deceased partner's interest.

2. Repaying the wrongful partner for all partnership liabilities.

The value of the partner's interest is generally determined by its market value at dissolution rather than its book value.

The UPA grants the innocent partners the right to continue when there is a wrongful dissolution, but the partners still should provide for the situation in their partnership agreement. Their continuation agreement should include at least:

1. A method for placing a value on the guilty partner's interest
2. An agreed method of reimbursement
3. An agreed method of payment if other than cash

Continuation's Effect on Existing Liabilities. When a partnership continues, creditors of the former partnership remain as creditors of the continuing partnership. The creditors may enforce their claims against a withdrawing partner, who remains liable for any obligations incurred by the partnership before he or she withdrew from the firm. The remaining partners may relieve the withdrawing partner of existing liabilities, but third parties are not bound by the arrangement unless they agree to the change through a novation.

Continuation's Effect on Later Liabilities. Just as it is important to notify third parties of the partnership's dissolution when it is terminated, it is equally important to provide notice when the business continues. Failure to notify third parties of the dissolution when the business continues may increase the liability of the continuing and former partners. If the continuing partners fail to notify third parties of the partnership's dissolution when a partner withdraws from the firm, the continuing partners may be bound by later acts of their former partner. Conversely, if the business is continued as a corporation, failure to notify former creditors may result in the former partners being held personally liable for new obligations as if they were still partners.

REVIEW PROBLEMS

1. What is the difference between partnership property and a partner's interest in a partnership?
2. In the absence of a partnership agreement, how are ordinary partnership matters to be decided by the partners?
3. Compare what is meant by partnership dissolution and to winding up of partnership business.
4. What are the rights and powers of the partners during the winding up of the partnership business?
5. Julius and Penelope formed a partnership to operate under the name, The Swish Toi-

let Company, which would manufacture and sell contour toilet fixtures. Julius applied for a personal loan at the Hard Luck Loan Company. The intended purpose of the loan, as disclosed by Julius to Hard Luck, was to purchase a new car for his wife, Fifi. Hard Luck refused to lend Julius the money unless the firm signed as guarantor, guaranteeing Julius's repayment. Julius signed his name on the loan contract and then signed the Swish Toilet Company name, as guarantor. All this was done in the presence of the Hard Luck agent. If Julius fails to pay back the loan and is insolvent, can Hard Luck holds the Swish Toilet Company liable as guarantor of the loan? Explain. Can Hard Luck obtain Julius's partnership interest in the Swish Toilet Company? Explain. Suppose the same facts, except that Julius has died. What are Penelope's and Fifi's rights with regard to the partnership property? Explain.

6. Doug Whitman, Bill McCarty, and Bartley Brennan formed a partnership, the Ace Cosmetic Company, which manufactured cosmetics for women. They did not enter into either a written or an oral partnership agreement. Whitman and McCarty each contributed $200,000 to the capital of the partnership. Brennan contributed $50,000. For the first year of operation Brennan managed the business. Profits for the first year amounted to $300,000. How should the profits be distributed among the three partners? Explain. Assume that Brennan now wants the partnership to bring out a new line of cosmetics for the older woman. Whitman and McCarty think that this is a bad idea. How should the issue be decided if the partners maintain their positions? Explain.

7. Julius owned and operated a sawmill. One day his daughter, Penelope, introduced him to Frank, who had recently moved into the area and who had met Penelope at a social function. Frank had previously managed a sawmill in another state. Julius asked Frank if he would be interested in going into the mill business as his partner. Frank looked the sawmill over and agreed to go into partnership with Julius. It was agreed that Frank would pay $60,000 for a half interest. He would pay $20,000 down, $10,000 in thirty days, and the rest at $1,000 a month. Things went smoothly for a month, but the mill was forced to close down when loggers refused to deliver logs due to the failure of the mill to pay on past accounts. It was then that Frank took his first look at the mill's books. There he discovered that the mill's liabilities exceeded its assets. The only cash in the bank was the money Frank had contributed. The mill owed over $300,000 to creditors. Its chief assets were its premises and its equipment. But Frank discovered that the First National Bank held mortgages on the land, the building, and the equipment. What are Frank's rights and liabilities with regard to the mill's creditors and Julius? Explain.

8. Curtis Cyrus wrote to his brother Cecil in North Dakota asking him to come to Minnesota to form a partnership in a resort venture. Curtis had recently bought sixty acres of land in Minnesota with his own money and in his own name. Cecil, a skilled carpenter, agreed. He moved his family to Minnesota, built a cabin on the property, and moved his family into it. Cecil built six other cabins on the property and operated them as a resort. Each year the brothers divided the profits equally between them. When Cecil died several years later, his wife decided to move back to North Dakota. She asked Curtis to pay her one-half of the value of the resort, including the fair market value of the land. Curtis claimed that the land was his. What are the rights of the parties? Explain.

9. Anderson, Baker, and Chase were partners. Anderson contributed $50,000 in cap-

ital and loaned the partnership $40,000. Baker contributed $30,000 in capital. Chase contributed his services. Five years after the partnership was formed, the three partners agreed to dissolve the partnership and wind up the business. The partnership creditors, other than Anderson, have claims of $130,000. After all profits and losses have been recorded, there are $176,000 of assets to be distributed to creditors and partners. How are the proceeds of the partnership to be distributed upon dissolution? Explain.

10. Baker and Corbin were partners doing business as Ace Photographers. When Corbin indicated that she wanted to withdraw from the business, the partners entered into a written dissolution agreement whereby Baker was allowed to continue the business. No notice was given to the firm's creditors. Photo Film, Incorporated, had sold film to Ace Photographers before the dissolution and continued to do so for several years after the dissolution. Baker ran into financial trouble. He terminated the business and filed for personal bankruptcy. Photo Film had a claim against Ace Photographers for $5,000 for film sold to Ace after the dissolution date. Photo Film, Inc. sued Corbin, claiming that she was liable on the claim. Who wins and why?

11. McCarty and Brennan are partners. Recently McCarty has noticed that Brennan's memory is slipping more than usual and that he rambles and annoys customers. McCarty has been thinking of dissolving the partnership and continuing the business as a sole proprietor. The partnership agreement still has several years to go before its termination. What should McCarty do? Explain.

12. Hugo and Charles were brothers who did business as partners. After several years Hugo died, and Charles was appointed administrator of his estate. Tax returns disclosed that the partnership business was continued just as it had been before Hugo's death. Hugo's estate received the profits and was charged with the losses of the business. Did Charles have the authority to continue the partnership business after the dissolution of the partnership brought on by Hugo's death, and are the assets of Hugo's estate chargeable with the liabilities of the partnership incurred after Hugo's death? Blomer Brewing Co. v. Mayer, 223 Wis. 540 (1936)

Nature and Formation of Corporations

One of the most important tools of modern business is the corporate form of organization. For some businesses the corporate structure is ideal. That is because corporations offer two major benefits: (1) the corporation has an identity of its own, separate and distinct from its human operatives, who are not held personally liable; and (2) it may continue to function regardless of the death or departure of its management. If limited liability and business continuity are not important objectives for a firm, however, the corporate form may be inefficient. Corporations are more administratively complex than other types of business organization, they are often expensive to set up, and they are frequently taxed at higher rates than individuals.

This chapter and the three that follow complete our discussion of the law of business associations begun in Chapter 30 with agency law. A functional approach to corporate law is developed here. The present chapter examines the formation of a corporation; the following chapters discuss corporate financing (Chapter 35) and corporate operations (Chapter 36). Examination of the law of corporations is completed with a chapter on how the Securities and Exchange Commission regulates some corporations (Chapter 37). The Model Business Corporation Act as revised in 1984 will be the basis for discussion of materials set forth here.

HISTORICAL PERSPECTIVE

The corporation as a form of business organization was well known to the Romans. It was Elizabethan England, however, that gave birth to the modern business corporation. Two forerunners of contemporary corporations were the overseas trading company and the joint stock company. (Recall from high-school history the role that joint stock companies like the British East India Company played in colonizing America.) Even in their infancy corporations had their critics. In 1720 a panic-stricken British Parliament passed the "Bubble Act," establishing as criminal the "acting or presuming to act as a corporate body or bodies" without being incorporated, which at that time was an expensive and cumbersome process. The act did not stem the corporate tide, however, as imaginative lawyers created new forms of business organization to circumvent the law. It was not until 1825 that Parliament officially recognized the reality of corporate existence and repealed its anticorporate law.

The United States has evolved from a mid-nineteenth-century nation of farmers, shopkeepers, and small manufacturers into a highly industrialized society dominated by corporations. During the twentieth century several changes have occurred in the nature of corporations and corporate law. As corporate size has increased, so has the need for capitalization, usually obtained through the sale of securities to investors. The focus of the law in recent decades has been to provide investors with protection in the securities market. At the same time, legislatures have sought to attract corporations to their states by adopting corporate codes that give management more and shareholders less control over corporate activities. Currently the focus of attention is on the problems of small, privately owned corporations (called close corporations), which have different needs from those addressed by state laws directed toward large corporations. For example, one recent change has been the modification of state corporate law to permit the creation of single-shareholder corporations.

NATURE OF CORPORATIONS

As the discussion of partnership law made clear, partnerships have two distinct disadvantages: (1) the partners share unlimited personal liability for partnership obligations and (2) a technical dissolution of the partnership results from any change in the partnership relation, such as the retirement or death of one of the partners. These features of personal liability and lack of business continuity add risks to partnership ventures that potential investors may be unwilling to assume. This is particularly true when the potential investors do not wish to participate in the management of the business.

Even a limited partnership may be unattractive to such investors, since limited partnership statutes require the filing of information revealing the involvement of each limited partner; thus a publicity-shy investor may have information regarding his or her financial support become part of the public record. Further, a limited partner runs some risk of losing his or her limited liability if there is not strict compliance with the statutory prohibitions concerning participating in the control of the firm.

The corporation was conceived as a means of avoiding the risks and discontinuities of partnership and of achieving business objectives beyond the reach of individuals. When capital needs are great, risks are high, and the enterprise's duration is long, the corporation is the preferred form of business organization. The corporation is the legal institution that can hold over a period of time the aggregated capital of many people, unaffected by the death or withdrawal of individuals. (See Table 34-1.)

Corporate Characteristics

The chief attributes of a corporation are (1) its entity status, sometimes called juristic or corporate personality; (2) the limited liability of its owners; (3) its continued existence, meaning that a corporation may be established in perpetuity; (4) the transferability of its ownership; and (5) the centralization of its management in its officers and directors rather than in its shareholders/owners. These corporate characteristics are descriptive only. They are not generally "tests" of corporate existence and are not necessarily found in all corporations.

TABLE 34-1 COMPARISON OF PARTNERSHIPS AND CORPORATION

Partnership	Corporation
Controlled by partners each with equal vote, unless partnership agreement directs otherwise	Controlled indirectly by shareholders, who elect directors, who appoint managers, who have centralized operational control
Unlimited liability except in case of limited partnerships, where only general partners have unlimited liability	Limited liability of shareholders for debts of corporation as well as managers and directors, unless corporate veil is "pierced"
Interest of partnership can be assigned but not partnership rights unless approved by partners	Shares of stock in a corporation can be transferred
Partners pay pro rata share of income taxes on net profits of partnership, whether or not distributed. Does not pay federal income tax, but some states levy taxes	Corporation income tax paid at federal and state levels; dividends of shareholders taxed at federal and state levels
Not a separate legal entity in most states, dissolved upon death of a partner unless partnership agreement states otherwise	A separate legal entity with perpetual existence in the event of death of a shareholder, officer, or director

However, most corporations share these characteristics. Furthermore, for federal income tax purposes the presence or absence of these characteristics determines whether an enterprise is taxed as a corporation.

Juristic Personality. The principal characteristic of a corporation that distinguishes it from all other business organizations is its status as a legal entity. Because of that status, the law treats the corporation as a person. This convenient fiction permits the corporation to enter into and execute contracts, own and convey property, and sue and be sued as a separate entity distinct from its owners and managers.

To the uninitiated the concept of the corporation as a legal person separate from its members may seem mysterious. But in fact it is a very practical solution to an important societal problem. Because human beings must be the subjects of the law's commands, it is necessary for the law to personify the corporation—treat it like a person—in order to regulate it for beneficial social and economic purposes. One such purpose is to permit the efficient conduct of business. To imagine life without the concept of the corporation as a legal entity, imagine a transaction between the Ford Motor Company and B.F. Goodrich. Treating the transaction as involving two partnerships would involve millions of people as "partners" with hundreds changing every day. Keeping track of the potentially liable people would be a burdensome task even in a computer society.

Limited Liability. A major consequence of the corporation's entity status is the limited liability it accords to its shareholders. Corporate rights and liabilities are not to be confused with those of its owners. Generally shareholders are not liable for corporate debts beyond the amount of their investment, and the corporation is not liable for the debts of its shareholders. The limited liability includes tort and criminal as well as contractual liability. This is a major business incentive for investors because they can avoid personal liability for corporate activities. Similarly, personal creditors of shareholders cannot reach the corporate property, although they may reach the shares of the debtor shareholder.

Continued Existence. Another key advantage of the corporation that stems from its separateness from the shareholders is its capacity for continuous life, sometimes called perpetual succession. In his *Commentaries,* Blackstone described corporations as "artificial persons who enjoy a kind of legal immortality," and compared them to the River Thames that flows with constantly changing water but continues as the same stream. Similarly, shareholders may come and go with no effect upon the corporate entity. A corporation such as the Ford Motor Company can continue long after its founder and major stockholder has died. As Peter Drucker wrote, "The corporation is permanent, the shareholder is transitory."

Although in most states corporations enjoy continuous existence, a few jurisdictions, such as Mississippi and Oklahoma, limit the life of a corporation to a certain number of years. Furthermore, the corporation's articles of incorporation and bylaws, which are its governing instruments, may limit its duration if that is deemed desirable by its incorporators. Thus the Revised Model Business Corporation Act (RMBCA) provides, "Unless its articles of incorporation provided otherwise every corporation . . . has without limitation power to have perpetual duration and succession in its corporate name."

Transferability of Ownership. Ownership interest in a corporation, which generally takes the form of shares of corporate stock, can be traded readily. This permits investors to place a value on their investment and to liquidate it if their investment objectives change. Because ownership interest in a corporation may be transferred by a shareholder while living, upon his or her death it is possible to distribute the interest to the shareholder's beneficiaries or heirs. Thus a shareholder may convey by will his corporate stock to another just as he or she could have given that stock away while alive. When the stockholder dies without leav-

ing a will, the shares pass to the heirs as a part of the estate.

Restrictions on the transferability of shares provided in the corporate governing instruments are permitted if they are reasonable. This usually occurs in corporations having only a few shareholders who wish to limit the corporation's ownership to themselves. Generally this takes the form of a right of first refusal being conferred upon the corporation or the other shareholders in the event of any sale of the corporate stock. A right of first refusal generally means that before any stock may be sold it must first be offered to the corporation or other stockholders who have the right to purchase the stock for fair value, thereby preventing outsiders from obtaining an ownership interest in the corporation.

Centralized Management and Control. The final characteristic of a corporation is the separation of its management from its ownership. Shareholders have no direct control over the daily business of the corporation. While this may not be as true of those corporations that have only a few shareholders, individual shareholders are generally powerless to affect corporate affairs in the case of large organizations where the ownership of stock is dispersed. This is because shareholder control is generally limited to electing the corporation's directors and approving major changes in the corporation's structure and operation.

The corporation's management rests with its officers and directors. By statute in most states the management function is centralized in the board of directors. The board of directors often delegates its duties to several officers, such as a president and vice-presidents, whom the board appoints to manage the daily corporate business and to report to the directors for guidance. The only control usually possessed by the shareholders is the power to elect and remove the directors. Shareholders, of course, can achieve power if they join together, but in many large corporations this is often difficult and involves large-scale organization.

There are obvious efficiencies in centralized management since direct participation of shareholders in management decision making is likely to create more problems than it solves. Thus the centralized management promotes large-scale organization, not individual rights. The result has been the emergence in recent years of an increasingly professionalized and frequently self-perpetuating class of corporate managers who merely go through the formalities of accounting to shareholders. It would not be unfair to characterize the government of a large corporation as "oligarchical" in the sense that the small group running it accounts only to itself or to a few large shareholders. Considering, however, that management selection is often meritocratic and that there is a community of interest and outlook in most instances between management and shareholders, the virtual disenfranchisement of the shareholder is not so oppressive as it appears. In partial recognition of these realities corporate law in recent times has sought to protect the shareholder—viewed primarily as investor rather than owner—against fraud and has substantially strengthened the obligations of management to act honestly and to disclose all material facts.

Corporations and the Constitution

The legal personification of the corporation raises questions as to whether and how the rights and protections that the U.S. Constitution extends to "persons," "people," and "citizens" apply to corporations. For example, the Fifth and Fourteenth Amendments provide that no "person" shall be "deprived of life, liberty or property, without due process of law," and the Fourteenth Amendment prohibits any state to "deny to any person within its jurisdiction the equal protection of the laws." The Fifth Amendment also provides that no person "shall be compelled in any

criminal case to be a witness against himself . . ." and the Fourth Amendment guarantees "the right of the people to be secure in their persons, houses, papers, and effects against unreasonable searches and seizures. . . ." Furthermore, Article IV and the Fourteenth Amendment secure the privileges and immunities of the "citizens" of each state and the United States.

Are corporations "persons" and "citizens" under these constitutional provisions? Is a corporation one of "the people" entitled to the Fourth Amendment's protection against unreasonable searches and seizures? The answer to these questions depends not on semantics but on the purposes underlying these various constitutional provisions.

The U.S. Supreme Court has specifically held that a corporation is a "person," entitled to the equal protection of the law, whose property cannot be taken without legal due process. However, a corporation is not a "person" entitled to the Fifth Amendment's privilege against self-incrimination, although it is considered one of the "people" entitled to the Fourth Amendment's protection against unreasonable searches.

This apparent inconsistency rests on the different purposes underlying these constitutional guarantees. The constitutional provision against self-incrimination is considered essentially a personal one, applying only to natural persons. It is not applicable to corporations because its original purpose was to protect individuals against the use of legal process to obtain self-incriminating testimony. Thus a corporation cannot oppose the subpoenaing of its books and records by asserting the privilege. Further, an officer or employee of a corporation cannot withhold testimony or documents on the ground that the corporation would be incriminated, although it would be permissible for such an officer or employee to refuse such evidence on the ground that he or she might be incriminated by its production.

Unlike the privilege against self-incrimination, the Fourth Amendment's protection against unreasonable searches and seizures applies to corporations as well as to individuals. However, the protection is not absolute; only *unreasonable* governmental searches are prohibited. Hence the protection yields in the face of a valid search warrant or subpoena.

Thus under the Fourth and Fifth Amendments the books and records of a corporation cannot be insulated from governmental inspection unless the scope of the governmental intrusion is unreasonable under the Fourth. The determination of which governmental intrusions are reasonable and which are not is a judicial function. In appraising the reasonableness of an intrusion, the courts attempt to balance the expectation of privacy with the government's need for information before issuing warrants or subpoenas.

Although the word "person" impliedly includes "citizen," a corporation is not considered to be a citizen entitled to the protection of the privileges and immunities clauses of the federal Constitution since these also apply only to natural persons. The consequence of a corporation not being a citizen under these clauses is that it may be compelled to comply with the corporation laws of a state in which it intends to do business but in which it is not incorporated. It may even be kept out of the state entirely if the state so wishes, unless the corporation is an interstate business. A state's "doing business" requirements cannot burden interstate commerce because of overriding provisions in the federal Constitution. Thus a state may usually require out-of-state corporations to register and pay fees for the privilege of doing business within the state or to designate an agent within the state for the acceptance of service of legal process.

The U.S. Supreme Court in the case that follows resolved the question of whether the corporation possesses freedom of expression under the First Amendment.

First National Bank of Boston v. Bellotti

U.S. Supreme Court

435 U.S. 765 (1978)

Background: First National Bank and other corporations (appellants) brought suit against Bellotti, attorney-general of the Commonwealth of Massachusetts (appellee), to have Section 8 of the state's criminal statute declared unconstitutional. Section 8 forbade expenditures by banks and business corporations for purposes of influencing or affecting the vote on any question submitted to the voters other than one materially affecting any of the property, business, or assets of the corporation. Further, the statute specifically stated that "questions submitted to the voters solely concerning taxation of income, property or transaction of individuals shall not be considered to materially affect the property, business or assets of corporation." Violations of the statute were punishable by a maximum fine of $50,000 to be levied against each corporation, and a fine of $10,000 and/or one year in prison for corporate officers, directors, or agents of the corporation.

When First National Bank and other corporations sought to spend money to publicize their opposition to a referendum proposed to amend Massachusetts' constitution to authorize the legislature to enact a graduated personal income tax, the appellee, Attorney-General Bellotti, informed appellants that he intended to enforce the statute. The Massachusetts courts held Section 8 to be constitutional. First National and other corporations appealed to the U.S. Supreme Court.

Decision: The Supreme Court ruled in favor of First National Bank and other corporations.

Powell, Justice

The court below framed the principal question in this case as whether and to what extent corporations have First Amendment rights. We believe that the court posed the wrong question. The Constitution often protects interests broader than those of the party seeking their vindication. The First Amendment, in particular, serves significant societal interests. The proper question therefore is not whether corporations "have" First Amendment rights and, if so, whether they are coextensive with those of natural persons. Instead, the question must be whether § 8 abridges expression that the First Amendment was meant to protect. We hold that it does.

The speech proposed by appellants is at the heart of the First Amendment protection. In appellants' view, the enactment of a graduated personal income tax, as proposed to be authorized by constitutional amendment, would have a seriously adverse effect on the economy of the State. The importance of the referendum issue to the people and government of Massachusetts is not disputed. Its merits, however, are the subject of sharp disagreement.

As the Court said in *Mills* v. *Alabama*, "there is practically universal agreement that a major purpose of [the First] Amendment was to protect the free discussion of governmental affairs." If the speakers here were not corporations, no one would suggest that the State could silence their proposed speech. It is the type of speech indispensable to decision making in a democracy, and this is no less true because the speech comes from a corporation rather than an individual. The inherent worth of the speech in terms of its capacity for informing the public does not depend upon the identity of its source, whether corporation, association, union, or individual.

The court below nevertheless held that corporate speech is protected by the First Amendment only when it pertains directly to the corporation's business interests. In deciding whether this novel and restrictive gloss on the First Amendment comports with the Constitution and the precedents of this Court, we need not survey the outer boundaries of the Amendment's protection of corporate speech, or address the abstract question whether corporations have the full measure of rights that individuals enjoy under the First Amendment. The question in this case, simply put, is whether the corporate identity of the speaker deprives this proposed speech of what otherwise would be its clear entitlement to protection. We turn now to that question.

We (thus) find no support in the First or Fourteenth Amendments, or in the decisions of this Court, for the proposition that speech that otherwise would be within the protection of the First Amendment loses that protection simply because its source is a corporation that cannot prove, to the satisfaction of a court, a material effect on its business or property. The "materially affecting" requirement is not an identification of the boundaries of corporate speech etched by the Constitution itself. Rather, it amounts to an impermissible legislative prohibition of speech based on the identity of the interests that spokesmen may represent in public debate over controversial issues and a requirement that the speaker have a sufficiently great interest in the subject to justify communication.

Section 8 permits a corporation to communicate to the public its views on certain referendum subjects—those materially affecting its business—but not others. It also singles out one kind of ballot question—individual taxation—as a subject about which corporations may never make their ideas public. The legislature has drawn the line between permissible and impermissible speech according to whether there is a sufficient nexus, as defined by the legislature, between the issue presented to the voters and the business interests of the speaker.

In the realm of protected speech, the legislature is constitutionally disqualified from dictating the subjects about which persons may speak and the speakers who may address a public issue. If a legislature may direct business corporations to "stick to business," it also may limit other corporations—religious, charitable, or civic—to their respective "business" when addressing the public. Such power in government to channel the expression of views is unacceptable under the First Amendment. Especially where, as here, the legislature's suppression of speech suggests an attempt to give one side of a debatable public question an advantage in expressing its views to the people, the First Amendment is plainly offended. Yet the State contends that its action is necessitated by governmental interests of the highest order. We next consider these asserted interests.

Appellees (nevertheless) advance two principal justifications for the prohibition of corporation speech. The first is the State's interest in sustaining the active role of the individual citizen in the electoral process and thereby preventing diminution of the citizen's confidence in government. The second is the interest in protecting the rights of shareholders whose views differ from those expressed by management on behalf of the corporation. However weighty these interests may be in the context of partisan candidate elections, they either are not implicated in this case or are not served at all, or in other than a random manner, by the prohibition in § 8.

Appellee advances a number of arguments in support of his view that these interests are endangered by corporate participation in discussion of a referendum issue. They hinge upon the assumption that such participation would exert an undue influence on the outcome of a referendum vote, and—in the end—destroy the confidence of the people in the democratic process and the integrity of government. According to appellee, corporations are wealthy and powerful and their views may drown out other points of view. If appellee's arguments were supported by record or legislative findings that corporate advocacy threatened imminently to undermine democratic processes, thereby denigrating rather than serving First Amendment interests, these arguments would merit our consideration. But there has been no showing that the relative voice of corporations has been overwhelming or even significant in influencing referenda in Massachusetts, or that there has been any threat to the confidence of the citizenry in government.

Finally, the State argues that Section 8 protects corporate shareholders, an interest that is both legitimate and traditionally within the province of state law. The statute is said to serve this interest by preventing the use of corporate resources in furtherance of views with which some shareholders may disagree. This purpose is belied, however, by the provisions of the statute, which are both under- and over-inclusive.

The under-inclusiveness of the statute is self-evident. Corporate expenditures with respect to a referendum are prohibited, while corporate activity with respect to the passage or defeat of legislation is permitted, even though corporations may engage in lobbying more often than they take positions on ballot questions submitted to the voters. Nor does § 8 prohibit a corporation from expressing its views, by the expenditure of corporate funds, on any public issue until it becomes the subject of a referendum, though the displeasure of disapproving shareholders is unlikely to be any less.

The fact that a particular kind of ballot question has been singled out for special treatment undermines the likelihood of a genuine state interest in protecting shareholders. It suggests instead that the legislature may have been concerned with silencing corporations on a particular subject. Indeed, appellee has conceded that "the legislative and judicial history of the statute indicates . . . that the second crime was 'tailor-made' to prohibit corporate campaign contributions to oppose a graduated income tax amendment."

Nor is the fact that § 8 is limited to banks and business corporations without relevance. Excluded from its provisions and criminal sanctions are entities or organized groups in which numbers of persons may hold an interest or membership, and which often have resources comparable to those of large corporations. Minorities in such groups or entities may have interests with respect to institutional speech quite comparable to those of minority shareholders in a corporation. Thus the exclusion of Massachusetts business trusts, real estate investment trusts, labor unions, and other associations undermines the plausibility of the State's purported concern for the persons who happen to be shareholders in the banks and corporations covered by § 8.

The over-inclusiveness of the statute is demonstrated by the fact that § 8 would prohibit a corporation from supporting or opposing a referendum proposal even if its shareholders unanimously authorized the contribution or expenditure. Ultimately shareholders may decide, through the procedures of corporate democracy, whether their corporation should engage in debate on public issues. Acting through their power to elect the board of directors or to insist upon protective provisions in the corporation's charter, shareholders normally are presumed competent to protect their own interests. In addition to intra-corporate remedies, minority shareholders generally have access to the judicial remedy of a derivative suit to challenge corporate disbursements alleged to have been made for improper corporate purposes or merely to further the personal interests of management.

Assuming, *arguendo,* that protection of shareholders is a "compelling" interest under the circumstances of this case, we find "no substantially relevant correlation between the governmental interest asserted and the State's effort" to prohibit appellants from speaking.

Because § 8 prohibits protected speech in a manner unjustified by a compelling state interest, it must be invalidated.

Classes of Corporations

The corporate form of organization has many dimensions. A corporation may be either public or private, profit or nonprofit, publicly issued or closely held, professional or nonprofessional, and foreign or domestic. Thus there are many different kinds of corporations, each bearing a generally accepted label. Because a court may refer to a corporation by its label, familiarity with the common types of corporations and the terminology used to describe

---

ETHICS BOX
Moral Accountability of Corporations

Can a corporation be unethical? If one says that a corporation is unethical, what does that mean? There are various answers. It could mean that the abstract entity of the corporation is somehow unethical. Or that the senior managers, or directors, or shareholders, or some combination are unethical. If you worked for Beech-Nut and they were found to have sold a synthetic substance as apple juice, would that mean that you were unethical? Would your answer be influenced by whether you were a truck driver or a quality control manager for juice?

Those that argue that a corporation cannot be unethical note that a corporation can't think and can't have an unethical intent. Further, they accuse those who attribute morality to the corporate entity of assessing guilt by association on corporate members. Advocates of the moral accountability of corporations point out that corporations do have distinct cultures that influence employee behaviors. They reason that if the corporation, or the law, recognizes something as an "official", corporate act, then the corporation should bear full responsibility for its consequences.

The issue is not merely an abstraction. The concept of moral accountability supports the idea of liability of the corporate entity for specific-intent crimes such as homicide.

---

them is useful. Moreover, comparison of various kinds of corporations that at first appear to be dissimilar often reveals certain commonly shared characteristics.

Public and Private Corporations. A corporation may be broadly classified as either public or private. The distinction refers to its purposes and powers. A public corporation is created and funded by the government to act as its instrumentality for the carrying out of some public purpose. Examples of public corporations include municipal, school, and water districts and various public-benefit corporations such as the U.S. Legal Services Corporation. Many state colleges and universities are organized as public corporations.

Private corporations are all corporations other than those that are public. They are created for private rather than public purposes. The General Motors Corporation is an example of a private corporation.

Profit and Nonprofit Corporations. A corporation for profit is primarily a business corporation, one engaged in commercial enterprises. Thus a corporation for profit is organized to conduct a business with a view to realizing gains to be distributed as dividends among its shareholders. A nonprofit corporation is not organized to make a profit for its members and does not conduct a business. Because they are not organized with a view to distributing gains, nonprofit corporations are usually expressly forbidden by statute to issue certificates of shares. They may issue membership certificates, if they so desire. Thus they are sometimes characterized as membership rather than shareholder corporations. Social, philanthropic, religious, and cultural corporations are examples of nonprofit corporations.

Public-Issue and Closely Held Corporations. A public-issue corporation is one whose stock ownership is diffused and whose management is divorced from its owners. "Going public" is a phrase frequently used to describe the process by which a privately owned firm issues stock to the public. This process is usually accompanied by increased governmental regulation, most notably from the Securities and Exchange Commission (SEC), which administers federal legislation regulating the issuance and trading of corporate securities.

In contrast to a public-issue corporation, in which stock is often widely held and management is normally unrelated to stock ownership, a "close" or "closely held" corporation is one whose stock is not publicly traded and whose stock ownership and management usually intertwine. A close corporation usually has only a few shareholders, most or all of whom participate in its management. Thus there is a striking resemblance to a partnership.

Many corporate concepts and principles created with public-issue corporations primarily in mind are ill-adapted to close corporations. Although the nature and methods of operation of the two kinds of corporations are different, in the past, and especially before 1960, state corporate codes generally established the same rules for governing both corporations. Great Britain and some countries of continental Europe have long had special statutes governing the "private company." Since

World War II, strong pleas have been made to enact in this country similar comprehensive statutes to govern close corporations. Since 1960 a legislative breakthrough has occurred, with many states adding to their corporation statutes provisions designed to meet the problems of close corporations. Even now, however, only a handful of states, most notably Florida, Delaware, and Maryland, have adopted separate statutes for close corporations.

Professional Corporations. Until recently every state prohibited professionals, such as accountants, architects, doctors, and lawyers, from incorporating their professional practices. A recent trend in some states has been to authorize professionals to practice their professions in the corporate form of organization. An individual or group of persons licensed in some kind of professional service may now organize as a corporation in these states. However, restrictions are imposed to protect the public. Thus stock may usually be issued only to duly licensed professionals engaged in the service for which the corporation has been organized.

Foreign and Domestic Corporations. A corporation is domestic to the state where it is created. It is considered foreign in all other states and countries where it does business. Thus a corporation incorporated in Delaware is considered a "foreign" corporation in Ohio. This is true even if the corporation's principal place of business is in Ohio.

Reisman v. Martori, Meyer, Hendricks and Victor

Court of Appeals of Georgia

271 S.E.2d 685 (1980)

Background: A law firm incorporated in Arizona (plaintiff), sued Reisman (defendant), a surgeon practicing in Georgia, for the balance of a debt owed for professional service in the amount of $6,438.14. The defendant hired a member of the plaintiff law firm,

Hendricks, in order to represent him in a dispute with a Georgia hospital. Hendricks flew to Atlanta, and with local counsel brought about a negotiated compromise with the hospital. The defendant argued that the plaintiff's action should have been dismissed because the Arizona law firm failed to register as a foreign corporation under Georgia corporation laws. The trial court ruled in favor of the law firm. Dr. Reisman appealed.

Decision: The Court of Appeals ruled in favor of the plaintiff law firm.

Banke, Judge

Assuming, without deciding, that the appellee professional association was required under Code Ann. § 22–1421(a) to procure a certificate of authority from the Secretary of State in order to transact business in Georgia, its activities in this state have not been sufficiently extensive to invoke the statute here. "In most jurisdictions it has been held that single or isolated transactions do not constitute doing business within the meaning of such statutes, although they are a part of the very business for [sic] which the corporation is organized to transact, if the action of the corporation in engaging therein indicated no purpose of continuity of conduct in that respect." *(Winston Corp.* v. *Park Elec. Co.)*

Winston held that "the question of 'doing business' is to be considered a matter of fact to be resolved on an ad hoc or case-by-case basis . . . and . . . the meaning of 'isolated transaction' in our corporation code is to be determined in the same way as the term 'doing business.' " Winston also makes it clear that the purpose of Code Ann. § 22–1401 is to require registration of foreign corporations which intend to conduct business in Georgia on a continuous basis, not as a temporary matter. Activity related to a single transaction or contract is thus not contemplated.

The evidence here showed that the law firm's activities were concentrated in Arizona, although various attorneys in the firm had handled litigation (or "transacted business") outside the state of incorporation. Hendricks had represented clients in Georgia on two prior occasions, but these had nothing to do with his representation of Dr. Reisman. Under these circumstances, there is ample basis for the court's conclusion that the law firm had neither extended its business into Georgia on a continuous basis nor engaged "in the course of a number of repeated transactions of like nature" within the state. The trial court correctly held that the law firm's representation of Dr. Reisman amounted to an isolated transaction and therefore properly denied the motion for directed verdict.

REGULATION OF CORPORATIONS

Since the beginning of the Republic the activities of corporations have been enmeshed in government regulation. Before the middle of the nineteenth century corporations were generally created pursuant to the granting of a corporate charter or franchise by the state in the form of special legislation. However, as the corporate form of organization became popular, the states enacted general corporate codes that governed the creation and operation of corporations.

Although the commerce clause and the necessary and proper clause of the federal Constitution empower the U.S. government to grant corporate charters, the federal government has no corporate code. On occasion, however, the federal government has chartered certain corporations, such as the Postal Service Corporation, by the enactment of special legislation. Virtually all corporations are the creations of the states. Various federal laws, such as the securities and exchange laws, the tax code, the labor statutes, and the antitrust laws, are noteworthy for their impact upon corporations. These may be viewed as constituting a "federal law of corporations" even though there is no single comprehensive federal corporate code.

State Corporation Codes

Corporate law is basically statutory. Each state has its own corporation statutes, usually consisting of a general corporation statute for commercial corporations and several supplemental or special statutes governing certain specific corporations, such as banks, insurance companies, nonprofit corporations, and other categories of corporations. Although there is no uniformity among the various state general corporation laws, the Model Business Corporation Act (MBCA) has served as the basic guideline for the majority of states, and the corporate law principles employed in the remaining state statutes are sufficiently similar to permit a degree of generalized discussion.

Because it has affected the majority of state statutes, the MBCA will provide the primary statutory basis for discussion. Drafted by the American Bar Association in 1946 and substantially revised in 1969, the MBCA has widely influenced recent statutory revisions. Because it is a "model" statute, states are not discouraged from adopting it with modifications, as opposed to a "uniform" statute such

as the UCC (Uniform Commercial Code), which, in the interests of uniformity, is encouraged by its drafters to be adopted by the states in its completed form with only a few suggested alternative provisions. A major revision of the MBCA was set forth in 1983 by the Bar Association. It is entitled the "Revised Model Business Corporation Act" (RMBCA). It will be the primary statutory basis for discussion in this chapter and the two that follow.[1]

Federal Regulation of Corporations

State corporate codes are having diminishing effects on corporate management as various federal regulatory laws increasingly impact upon the corporation. Although there is no federal corporate code, there has been a tremendous upsurge of federal law affecting corporate activities in such areas as antitrust, labor-management relations, taxation, the securities markets, civil rights, and consumer protection. The Sherman Antitrust Act has been in existence since the late nineteenth century, but most federal regulation of corporations has occurred since 1933 when the Securities Act was enacted as one response to the Great Depression. Taken together, these various federal regulatory laws constitute a federal corporation law.

Proposals for federal chartering of corporations date from the creation of the Republic. Federal chartering was advocated early in this century by Louis Brandeis in his book *Other People's Money*. The main contemporary support for the proposal derives from those who most vocally criticize the social performance of corporations, the foremost of whom is Ralph Nader. In his book *Taming the Giant Corporation*, Nader argues that sweeping federal legislation is needed rather than piecemeal reforms of the existing regulatory framework in response to particular problems. Federal chartering proposals vary from proposals for the federal licensing of large corporations to a full-scale federal corporate code complete with an "employee bill of rights." The serious proponents of federal chartering so far have limited their proposals for the most part to large interstate corporations.

Taxation of Corporations

Unlike the partnership, which is merely a tax-reporting entity under the federal income tax law, the corporation is a taxpayer. It is required to file returns and pay income taxes in a manner similar to that required of individual taxpayers. This produces what is known as a "double tax effect"; income is taxed to the corporation as earned and taxed again to the shareholders when distributed.

An exception to this double-tax treatment is the Subchapter S corporation, which is not taxed. Subchapter S of the Internal Revenue Code allows certain corporations to elect special tax treatment and thereby avoid any income tax at the corporate level. As long as it remains qualified, the Subchapter S corporation may elect to pay virtually no federal income tax and have its income included in the personal incomes of its shareholders and taxed directly to them. However, a Subchapter S corporation is heavily restricted as to the number and kind of shareholders. To qualify as a Subchapter S corporation, the corporation must (1) have only thirty-five or fewer individual shareholders, (2) limit its stock to a single class, and (3) obtain from every shareholder a written consent, which is filed with the Internal Revenue Service. Although there is a limit on the number of shareholders of a Subchapter S corporation, there is no limit on the size of corporate assets; even large corporations may qualify for Subchapter S treatment although the provisions of the tax law were designed to allow certain small businesses to be treated as tax conduits in which income flows through the corporation to the shareholders in much the same way as income to a partnership passes through it to the partners and is not taxed to the firm. Because shareholders of Subchapter S corporations must be individuals, partnerships and corporations are excluded from holding stock in such a corporation.

CORPORATE FORMATION

Modern incorporation procedures are not nearly as cumbersome and time-consuming as they were when incorporators had to shepherd special corporate charters through state legislatures. Today thousands of corporations are formed each year without much intellectual effort on the part of the incorporators and without raising any significant legal issues.

Preincorporation Activity

Corporation formation starts with certain preincorporation activity on the part of those who are promoting the yet-to-be-formed corporation. Before the corporation is formally launched, contracts must sometimes be made, legal relations created, and business activities undertaken with a view to creation of the corporation. Preincorporation problems are not as common as they once were, because modern corporation laws making incorporation relatively easy have all but eliminated the need for much work to be done in advance of actual incorporation. The preincorporation problems that do arise result from the activities of promoters.

The Promoter. A promoter is someone who undertakes to form a corporation. Corporations do not spring into existence spontaneously. They result from planning and preliminary work by promoters. It is the promoter who transforms an idea into a business. The promoter plans the development of a corporate business venture, brings together people who are interested in the projected enterprise, effectuates its organization and incorporation, and establishes the newly formed corporation as a fully functioning business.

Although promoters are sometimes called "preincorporators," their activities often reach beyond the point of formal incorporation.

The promoter's efforts are largely devoted to making contracts on behalf of the proposed corporation. Sometimes these contracts are self-serving—for instance, when the promoter conveys property to the corporation in exchange for shares of the corporation's stock. Frequently the contracts are with third persons for materials and services that are necessary to launch the enterprise. Problems arising from these promoter contracts involve (1) the duties of promoters toward the unborn corporation and (2) the contractual liabilities of both the promoter and the newborn corporation to third parties.

Promoter's Duties to the Corporation. Since at the time of the promoter's activities no corporation is yet in being, the promoter is not the corporation's agent. No agency can be said to exist because there is no principal. Furthermore, someone cannot serve another as a self-appointed agent. Nevertheless, a promoter is under certain obligations.

Because they are joint venturers in forming the corporation, all promoters occupy a fiduciary relationship with any other co-promoters. Promoters also occupy a fiduciary relationship to the corporation they form. This fiduciary relationship casts upon the promoter an affirmative duty of full disclosure to the corporation regarding any dealings with the corporation in which the promoter has a personal interest and, further, a duty to enter any transactions with the corporation in good faith. Thus the promoter may not obtain any secret profits out of transactions with or on behalf of the corporation to be formed.

A typical case of promoter liability for failing to disclose material information fully to the corporation occurs when, after organizing the new corporation, the promoter sells to it his or her own property. If the promoter conveys property to the corporation, he or she must fully disclose any personal interest, the extent of any profit on the transaction, and any other material factors that might affect the corporation's decision whether to purchase. This disclosure must be made to either an independent board of directors, meaning a board that is not controlled by the promoter, or to all existing shareholders.

The usual case of promoter liability for failing to deal in good faith with the corporation is when "watered stock" has been issued to the promoter. The term *watered stock* refers to stock issued by a corporation in excess of any fair and adequate consideration received in exchange for it. This results in a diminution of the value of the stock held by other shareholders and further damages creditors of the corporation who may have relied on the belief that the corporation had received assets equivalent in value to the value of the issued shares. Stock watering occurs when promoters cause the overvaluation of their contribution to the corporation, resulting in the issuance of stock by the corporation for less than fair consideration. When there is stock watering innocent shareholders whose stock has been devalued by the issuance of the watered stock may bring suit on behalf of the corporation to recover the lost value. Further, any injured creditors may force the promoter to pay to the corporation the unpaid value of the shares.

Preincorporation Contracts. A contract made by the promoter with a third party on behalf of the proposed corporation raises the question of whether the promoter, the corporation, or both are contractually liable. Generally the promoter remains liable as a party to the contract unless relieved of the liability by the corporation. On the other hand, the corporation generally is not bound by the contract of the promoter until the corporation affirmatively assents to the contractual obligation.

The usual case of promoter liability on

preincorporation contracts occurs when the proposed corporation never comes into existence or the corporation completely disavows the contract. In such a situation the other party to the contract will usually attempt to hold the promoter liable. Because the promoter acts for the corporation before its organization, under the general rules of agency law he or she is the principal on the contract. Under agency law an agent for an undisclosed or, more aptly, a nonexistent principal becomes a party to any contracts made with third parties. Similarly, the promoter is held bound by his or her contracts. If this were not so, any agreement made by the promoter on behalf of the future corporation would be inoperative until after the corporation was formally organized, thereby depriving the third party of any remedy until that time. Personal liability for the promoters on preincorporation contracts is not unfair since the promoter is in the best position to bring about incorporation and the adoption of the contract by the corporation. Thus it is only fair that the risk that the corporation may not be formed should be the promoter's and not the third party's, even if the third party is advised of the exact state of affairs.

Nevertheless, it is possible that those dealing with the promoter may be said to be looking to the corporation and not the promoter for performance of the contractual obligation. If the promoter clearly negates liability, the agreement is considered to be a continuing offer to the corporation rather than a contract. Thus, if the promoter specifically states that he or she is contracting in the name of the proposed corporation and not individually, the other party must rely entirely on the credit of the proposed corporation and has no claim against the promoter. This is simply a matter of recognizing the intention of the parties.

Generally a corporation is not liable on a contract made by the promoter for its benefit unless it takes some affirmative action to adopt the contract when it formally comes into existence. Mere incorporation does not of itself render the promoter's contracts binding on the company; there must be some action by the corporation indicating its assent. This adoption may be by express words or writing or may be inferred from the corporation's knowingly accepting the contract's benefits. Thus adoption of the contract need not be express but may be implied. The rationale for this rule of corporation nonliability on preincorporation contracts, unless the circumstances indicate an intent to be bound, is to avoid any injustice to the corporation's shareholders and subsequent creditors that would result if the corporation were forced to come into existence burdened with the obligation to perform its promoters' promises. The case that follows illustrates this general rule of corporate nonliability with regard to promoters' contracts.

Solomon v. Cedar Acres East, Inc.

Supreme Court of Pennsylvania

317 A.2d 283 (1974)

Background: Jerome Solomon (plaintiff-appellant) is an architect who sought specific performance of a contract for architectural services against Cedar Acres East, Inc. (defendant-appellee). The corporation joined Frank Millmond, promoter of the corporation, as an additional defendant. On August 3, 1966 the promoter signed an option to buy a fifty-two-acre tract of land for a corporation primarily controlled and owned by the promoter (this corporation is not the corporate defendant involved in this case). Soon thereafter the promoter engaged the appellant, who did certain preliminary architectural work for the site during August, September, and October of 1966. The defendant corporation was not contemplated and was not in existence at that time.

On November 13, 1966, the promoter entered into an agreement with four other men for the creation of the defendant corporation. The agreement provided for the issuance of 100 percent of the stock of the proposed corporation. Two days later, on November 15, 1966, the appellant and the promoter entered into a contract whereby the appellant was to perform architectural services as required for the development of the tract of land. The appellant was to be a 5-percent owner of any corporation formed for the development of the tract, was to receive 5 percent of the profits of any corporation formed, and was to receive $50 for each one-family living unit erected on the tract. The agreement did not make any reference to the defendant corporation. The appellant performed additional services after the signing of his agreement, but performed no services after December 8, 1966.

On December 21, 1966, the promoter assigned to the defendant corporation the option to buy the fifty-two-acre tract.

On June 30, 1967 the appellant sent an itemized bill for architectural services to the defendant corporation stating "Amount due as of this invoice . . . $1,500." A second notice of the $1,500 billing was sent to the defendant corporation on August 10, 1967. A letter followed on December 7, 1967, in which the appellant requested payment of the $1,500 in "complete settlement." This letter referred to the terms of the agreement that the appellant had entered into with the promoter on November 15, 1966. This letter was the first notice that the defendant corporation had received concerning the appellant's agreement with the promoter. The defendant corporation refused to honor the agreement or to pay for the architectural services that had been rendered by the appellant at the promoter's request. The appellant then filed this equity action for specific performance requesting 5 percent of the stock in defendant corporation and damages. The trial court denied specific performance of the contract against both the corporate defendant and the promoter, but ordered the defendants to pay $2,000 in quantum meruit for architectural services. The architect, Solomon, appealed.

Decision: Reversed. The Supreme Court of Pennsylvania ruled in favor of Solomon.

Manderino, Justice

We shall first discuss the issue raised concerning the corporate defendant. The trial court concluded that the corporate defendant was not bound by the contract entered into on November 15, 1966, between the appellant and the promoter. . . . The trial court did find, however, that the corporate defendant had received some benefit from the architectural services rendered by the appellant and, therefore, held that the corporate defendant was liable in quantum meruit.

The sole claim in this appeal, concerning the corporate defendant, is that the record does not support the trial court's conclusion that the corporate defendant did not ratify the November 15, 1966 agreement. The appellant admits that no express ratification ever occurred. He argues, however, that ratification can be inferred because the corporate defendant benefited from the use of architectural plans knowing that such plans were prepared by the appellant. The corporate defendant had no knowledge of the agreement or that it provided for the issuance of stock to the appellant and for profit sharing by the appellant. These material facts were unknown to anyone except the promoter and the appellant. Ratification of a contract by one not a party to the contract requires that the ratifying party be in possession of all the material facts and act with such knowledge. . . . The only shareholder of the corporate defendant who had knowledge of all of the material facts concerning the November 15, 1966 agreement was the promoter. His knowledge, however, cannot be imputed to the corporate defendant. Knowledge possessed by a single promoter having only a minority interest cannot bind the corporate defendant.

In this case, the promoter was not a majority stockholder. His stock interest was only twenty-five per cent. In *Beltz* v. *Garrison,* cited by the appellant, a ratification was inferred because the corporation received benefits from a contract signed by four persons who, after the signing of the contract, became members of the corporation's board of directors and constituted eighty per cent of the directors and owned all of the stock of the corporation. *Beltz* is of no help to the appellant.

The other issue raised by the appellant concerns the promoter defendant. Although the trial court found that the promoter had entered into the November 15, 1966 agreement with the appellant, the trial court did not award damages based on that agreement. Instead, the trial court awarded damages only in quantum meruit. The trial court further granted to the appellant, "without prejudice, the right to pursue any claim he may have with regard to these shares or compensation therefrom against [the promoter] in a separate proceeding."

Appellant contends that the trial court erred in its refusal to allow full recovery against the promoter. We agree. The trial court concluded that the appellant and the promoter entered into an agreement on November 15, 1966. That conclusion was fully supported by the record. In fact, the promoter admitted that he entered into that agreement with the appellant and said that it was a personal contract. Under these circumstances, the trial court should have determined the amount of damages to which the appellant was entitled under the agreement. . . . Complete relief should have thus been given to the appellant against the promoter in the same manner as though the promoter had been the original defendant.

Since the promoter was no longer a shareholder in the corporate defendant, the trial court could not direct specific performance. Full recovery, however, could have been awarded in the form of money damages. Although such recovery is a legal remedy rather than an equitable remedy, such relief would have been proper. Once equity has assumed jurisdiction of an action, money damages may be awarded to insure a just result. . . . There is no reason why this dispute should not be settled in the present action.

Incorporation Procedure

The modern mechanics of incorporation are much more streamlined than they once were. However, because corporate existence continues to be a privilege conferred by the state, the proper papers must be filed and certain formalities attended to in order to bring about incorporation. Businesspeople will continue to require the assistance of an attorney during this process.

The first step taken in incorporating a business is the selection of the state of incorporation. Once that has been decided the incorporators must prepare and file the articles of incorporation, along with any fees and taxes, with the secretary of state. If all is in order, the secretary issues a certificate of incorporation, sometimes called the corporate charter. After the issuance of the certificate, an organizational meeting must be held to adopt the corporate bylaws, elect officers, and transact any initial corporate business.

Selecting the State of Incorporation. After determining to incorporate the first decision to be made is where to incorporate. Most small corporations usually incorporate in the state where they are to be located. If the business is of an interstate nature, consideration is sometimes given to other states if the local state corporation and tax laws have restrictions. Delaware is often the first state considered because the climate of opinion prevalent in its legislature and courts is generally favorable to corporate management and unfavorable to dissident minority shareholders. Delaware's corporation statute is considered "liberal" because of its flexibility, which enables management to conduct corporate business with few restrictions.

Delaware is not the only state that may be attractive to incorporators. Although early state corporation codes were hostile to the corporation, states later encouraged corporations by enacting unrestrictive legislation. New Jersey and New York competed with Delaware by offering liberal corporation codes. Today many corporations are incorporated in these states even though their principal places of business are elsewhere. Thus the official state residences of many Delaware corporations are mailboxes. This practice has led to the characterization of some state corporation laws as "for export only." On the other hand, California has a corporate code that attempts to limit the discretion of corporate management.

One disadvantage of out-of-state incorporation is that the corporation will incur double taxation in the form of a franchise tax for doing business in the state where its business is done. Out-of-state incorporation also subjects the corporation to liability for suits in a jurisdiction removed from its principal place of business. Furthermore, in the event of litigation, there may be an issue of which state's law applies. The general rule is that the law of the incorporating state will be applied to issues relating to the internal affairs of the corporation. However, there is a trend toward making this determination on the basis of whether the state of incorporation has an interest in having its law applied.

Articles of Incorporation. After the state of incorporation is selected the incorporators must prepare and file the articles of incorporation, which are to be submitted, along with any fees, to the secretary of state (Figure 34-1). Among the items to be included in the articles is the corporation's name. This name must include the word "corporation," "company," "incorporated," or "limited" or an abbreviation of one of those words. The RMBCA prohibits using any word or phrase that indicates that the corporation is organized for any purpose other than the one stated in its articles. It requires a corporate name to be distinguishable upon the records of the secretary of state from that of other corporations authorized to transact business. If a name is available, the RMBCA permits incorporators to apply to the secretary of state in advance to reserve the name for 120 days while the corporation is being organized.

Additional information regarding the corporation's capital structure must also be provided, such as the number and classes of authorized shares. Although many states require a minimum stated capital for starting the business, the RMBCA does not.

The articles must also state the name and address of the corporation's initial registered agent and initial office and the names and addresses of all incorporators. Although many

FIGURE 34–1
Articles of Incorporation of XYZ Corporation

ARTICLE I
Name

The name of this corporation is **XYZ Corporation.**

ARTICLE II
Registered Office and Resident Agent

The registered office of the corporation is **15 Main Street, Kansas City, Kansas.**

The resident agent at that address is **John Doe.**

ARTICLE III
Nature of Business

The nature of the business or purposes to be conducted or promoted are:

To engage in any lawful conduct or activity for which corporations may be organized under the Kansas Corporation Code.

ARTICLE IV
Capital Stock

This corporation is authorized to issue Ten Thousand (10,000) shares of common stock without par value.

ARTICLE V
Incorporators

The names and mailing addresses of the incorporators are as follows:

Dennis Jones — 100 Main Street, Kansas City, Kansas
Mary Jones — 100 Main Street, Kansas City, Kansas

ARTICLE VI
Initial Directors

The powers of the incorporators are to terminate upon the filing of these Articles of Incorporation, and the names and mailing address of the persons who are to serve as directors until the first annual meeting of stockholders or until their successors are elected and qualified are:

Dennis Jones — 100 Main Street, Kansas City, Kansas
Mary Jones — 100 Main Street, Kansas City, Kansas

ARTICLE VII
Bylaws

The power to adopt, repeal and amend the bylaws of this corporation shall reside in the Board of Directors of this corporation.

IN TESTIMONY WHEREOF, we have hereunto set our names this

_____ day of _____ ,

Source: Douglas Whitman, F. William McCarty, Frank F. Gibson, Thomas W. Dunfee, Bartley A. Brennan, and John D. Blackburn, *Law and Business* (New York, Random House, 1987), p. 555. Copyright © 1987 by Thomas W. Dunfee, F. William McCarty, Frank F. Gibson, Douglas Whitman, John D. Blackburn, and Bartley A. Brennan.

states still require that there be three incorporators and three directors, the RMBCA permits the corporation to have only one incorporator and one director, thus enabling sole proprietors to incorporate their businesses without needlessly involving others.

Organizational Meeting. After issuance of the certificate of incorporation by the secretary of state (see Figure 34-2), an organizational meeting of the board of directors must be held for the purpose of adopting the bylaws, electing officers, and transacting ini-

FIGURE 34–2
Certificate of Incorporation

1467645

STATE OF KANSAS

OFFICE OF SECRETARY OF STATE
JACK H. BRIER • SECRETARY OF STATE

To all to whom these presents shall come, Greeting:

I, JACK H. BRIER, Secretary of State of the State of Kansas, do hereby certify that the following and hereto attached is a true copy of

**ARTICLES OF INCORPORATION
OF
XYZ CORPORATION**

STATE OF KANSAS
COUNTY OF JOHNSON } SS
FILED FOR RECORD

RUBIE M. SCOTT
REGISTER OF RECORDS
BY _____ REP.

Filed:

the original of which is now on file and a matter of record in this office.

IN TESTIMONY WHEREOF:

I hereto set my hand and cause to be affixed my official seal.

Done at the City of Topeka, this _____Thirtieth_____ day of

January   A.D.   1982

JACK H. BRIER
SECRETARY OF STATE

BY ASSISTANT SECRETARY OF STATE
Willa M. Roe

VOL 2002 PAGE 533

Source: Douglas Whitman, F. William McCarty, Frank F. Gibson, Thomas W. Dunfee, Bartley A. Brennan, and John D. Blackburn, *Law and Business* (New York, Random House, 1987), p. 556. Copyright © 1987 by Thomas W. Dunfee, F. William McCarty, Frank F. Gibson, Douglas Whitman, John D. Blackburn, and Bartley A. Brennan.

tial corporate business, such as the adoption of any preincorporation contracts. The corporate bylaws provide private legislation for the regulation and management of corporate affairs and must not be inconsistent with the articles or state law. Unless the articles provide otherwise, adoption of the initial bylaws as well as any later amendments rests with the board of directors. Many states permit shareholder adoption and amendment of the bylaws.

Incomplete Incorporation

Problems may arise when there has been some defect in the incorporation process, such as a failure by one of the incorporators to sign the articles or a failure to provide sufficient information in the articles as required by statute. Streamlined incorporation procedures make this less of a problem. When it does occur, however, it raises the possibility of personal liability for the shareholders. Because the consequences of failing to comply with the technical requirement of incorporation are potentially so dire, three mitigating doctrines have been developed by the courts to shield shareholders from being treated as partners. These doctrines are (1) de jure incorporation, (2) de facto incorporation, and (3) corporation by estoppel.

De Jure Incorporation. In construing the requirements of incorporation statutes, courts have generally held that no useful purpose will be served by a strict technical interpretation that converts every detailed requirement into a prerequisite of corporate existence. Thus, if there has been substantial compliance with the provisions of a statute authorizing the formation of a corporation—that is, if the noncompliance is slight—a "de jure" corporation results. A de jure corporation is recognized as a corporation for all purposes and as to all parties, including the state of incorporation. No

one, not even the state, may challenge the organization's corporate status, notwithstanding a technical noncompliance with the incorporation procedures.

To obtain de jure status there must be literal compliance with all mandatory requirements of incorporation and substantial compliance with all directive requirements. What constitutes a mandatory as opposed to a directive requirement is a matter of statutory construction and depends on the nature of the incorporation defect. Requirements that are merely formalities, such as the requirement that a seal be affixed on the articles, are considered directive only. Their absence is not sufficient to defeat corporate existence. However, the more important a requirement is, the more likely it will be considered a mandatory requirement. Thus the requirement that the articles be filed would be mandatory; failure to file the articles could not result in de jure corporate status.

De Facto Incorporation. Where there are significant defects in the incorporation to prevent a de jure existence, courts may nevertheless recognize the organization as a de facto corporation. In the case of a de facto corporation third persons cannot take advantage of the defects to charge the shareholders with unlimited liability or to void contracts with them. The state, however, can maintain proceedings to attack the corporate existence directly to have its charter revoked. This is because the defect is significant enough that the law cannot ignore it, and the state is permitted to take any necessary steps to remedy the situation. Thus, whereas a de jure corporation cannot be challenged by anyone, a de facto corporation can be challenged by the state.

Generally a de facto corporation results if there is a law in the state under which a corporation might be formed, there has been a colorable or apparent attempt in good faith to incorporate under such law, and the organization has conducted business as a corporation. An example of de facto corporate existence might be when articles are drafted in due form and turned over to an attorney who neglects to file them through no fault of the incorporators. Although there is not sufficient compliance for de jure existence, the de facto corporate status thus achieved will nevertheless shield the shareholders from personal liability to third parties.

The statutory trend is to eliminate the de facto doctrine because it is believed that modern incorporation statutes are sufficiently streamlined to justify stricter compliance than the doctrine requires. Further, it is believed that the continued viability of the de facto doctrine at a time when it is not needed only encourages noncompliance with incorporation procedures. Thus the RMBCA has eliminated the doctrine.

Incorporation by Estoppel. Where a third person deals with a defectively organized corporation as if it were in fact incorporated, he or she may be estopped to challenge the corporate status of the organization upon later learning of the defective incorporation. It is generally considered to be unfair to allow the third party to hold the shareholders personally liable when he or she originally dealt with the organization as though it were a corporation, knowing that a corporation is an entity of limited liability. Unlike the de facto doctrine, however, which recognizes a corporate status as to all third parties, the estoppel theory recognizes the corporation only for the particular third-party transaction. The following case illustrates a court's use of de facto and estoppel theories of incorporation, as well as the RMBCA's most recent statements as to when de jure incorporation takes place.

Timberline Equipment Co., Inc. v. Davenport, Bennett et al.

Supreme Court of Oregon
514 P.2d 1109 (1973)

Background: Timberline (plaintiff-appellee) brought this complaint to recover rentals on equipment leased to Bennett and others (defendant-appellant). In addition to making general denial, Bennett alleged as a defense that the rentals were to a de facto corporation, Aero-Fabb Corp., of which Bennett was an incorporator, director, and shareholder. He also alleged that plaintiff was estopped from denying the corporate character of the organization to whom plaintiff rented the equipment.

On January 22, 1970, Bennett signed articles of incorporation for Aero-Fabb Co. The original articles were not in accord with the statutes and, therefore, no certificate of incorporation was issued for the corporation until June 12, 1970, after new articles were filed. The leases were entered into and rentals earned during the period between January 22 and June 12, 1970. The lower court ruled in favor of the plaintiff. Bennett appealed.

Decision: Affirmed. The Supreme Court of Oregon ruled in favor of Timberline.

Denecke, Justice

Prior to 1953 Oregon had adopted the common-law doctrine that prohibited a collateral attack on the legality of a defectively organized corporation which had achieved the status of a de facto corporation.

In 1953 the legislature adopted the Oregon Business Corporation Act. Oregon Laws

1953, ch. 549. The Model Business Corporation Act was used as a working model for the Oregon Act.

ORS 57.321 of the Oregon Business Corporation Act provides:

> Upon the issuance of the certificate of incorporation, the corporate existence shall begin, and such certificate of incorporation shall be conclusive evidence that all conditions precedent required to be performed by the incorporators have been complied with and that the corporation has been incorporated under the Oregon Business Corporation Act, except as against that state in a proceeding to cancel or revoke the certificate of incorporation or for involuntary dissolution of the corporation.

This selection is virtually identical to § 56 of the Model Act. The Comment to the Model, prepared as a research project by the American Bar Foundation and edited by the American Bar Association Committee on Corporate Laws, states:

> Under the Model Act, de jure incorporation is complete upon the issuance of the certificate of incorporation, except as against the state in certain proceedings challenging the corporate existence. In this respect, the Model Act provisions are the same as those in many states, although in a number of them some further action is required before the corporation has legal existence, such as local filing or recording or publication.
>
> Under the unequivocal provisions of the Model Act, any steps short of securing a certificate of incorporation would not constitute apparent compliance. Therefore a de facto corporation cannot exist under the Model Act.
>
> Like provisions are made throughout the Model Act in respect of the conclusiveness of the issuance by the secretary of state of the appropriate certificate in connection with filings made in his office. . . .
>
> In some states, however, issuance of the certificate of incorporation and compliance with any additional requirements for filing, recording or publication is not conclusive evidence of incorporation.
>
> In those states, such action is stated to be only prima facie evidence of incorporation, and in others the effect is merely one of estoppel preventing any question of due incorporation being raised in legal actions by or against the corporation. Model Business Corporation Act annotated § 56, p. 305 (2nd ed. 1971).

ORS 57.793 provides:

> All persons who assume to act as a corporation without the authority of a certificate of incorporation issued by the Corporation Commissioner, shall be jointly and severally liable for all debts and liabilities incurred or arising as a result thereof.

This is merely an elaboration of § 146 of the Model Act. The Comment states:

> This section is designed to prohibit the application of any theory of de facto incorporation. The only authority to act as a corporation under the Model Act

arises from completion of the procedures prescribed in sections 53 to 55 inclusive. The consequences of those procedures are specified in section 56 as being the creation of a corporation. No other means being authorized, the effect of section 146 is to negate the possibility of a de facto corporation.

Abolition of the concept of de facto incorporation, which at best was fuzzy, is a sound result. No reason exists for its continuance under general corporate laws, where the process of acquiring de jure incorporation is both simple and clear. The vestigial appendage should be removed. 2 Model Business Corporation Act Annoted § 146, pp. 908–909 (2nd ed. 1971)

We hold the principle of de facto corporation no longer exists in Oregon.

The defendant also contends that the plaintiff is estopped to deny that it contracted with a corporation. . . . Corporation by estoppel is a difficult concept to grasp and courts and writers have "gone all over the lot" in attempting to define and apply the doctrine. One of the better explanations of the problem and the varied solutions is contained in Ballentine, Manual of Corporation Law and Practice §§§§28–30 (193):

> The so-called estoppel that arises to deny corporate capacity does not depend on the presence of the technical elements of equitable estoppel, viz. misrepresentations and change of position in reliance thereon, but on the nature of the relations contemplated, that one who has recognized the organization as a corporation in business dealings should not be allowed to quibble or raise immaterial issues on matters which do not concern him in the slightest degree or affect his substantial rights. Ballentine, supra, at 92.

We need not decide whether the doctrine of corporation by estoppel would apply in such a case as this. The trial court found that if this doctrine was still available under the Business Corporation Act defendants did not prove all the elements necessary for its application, and, moreover, it would be inequitable to apply the doctrine.

Under the explanation stated above for the application of the doctrine of estoppel in this kind of case, it is necessary that the plaintiff believe that it was contracting with a corporate entity. The evidence on this point is contradictory and the trial court apparently found against defendants.

A final question remains: Can the plaintiff recover against Dr. Bennett individually?

In the first third of this century the liability of persons associated with defectively organized corporations was a controversial and well-documented legal issue. The orthodox view was that if an organization had not achieved de facto status and the plaintiff was not estopped to attack the validity of the corporate status of the corporation, all shareholders were liable as partners. This court, however, rejected the orthodox rule. In *Rutherford* v. *Hill* we held that a person could not be held liable as a partner merely because he signed the articles of incorporation though the corporation was so defectively formed as to fall short of de facto status. The court stated that under this rule a mere passive stockholder would not be held liable as a partner. We went on to observe, however, that if the party actively participated in the business he might be held liable as a partner.

This controversy subsided 30 or 40 years ago probably because the procedure to achieve de jure corporate status was made simpler; so the problem did not arise.

The Model Act and the Oregon Business Corporation Act, ORS 57.793, solve the problem as follows:

> All persons who assume to act as a corporation without the authority of a certificate of incorporation issued by the Corporation Commissioner, shall be jointly and severally liable for all debts and liabilities incurred or arising as a result thereof.

We have found no decisions, comments to the Model Act, or literature attempting to explain the intent of this section.

We find the language ambiguous. Liability is imposed on "[a]ll persons who assume to act as a corporation." Such persons shall be liable "for all debts and liabilities incurred or arising as a result thereof."

We are of the opinion that the phrase, "persons who assume to act as a corporation" should be interpreted to include those persons who have an investment in the organization and who actively participate in the policy and operational decisions of the organization. Liability should not necessarily be restricted to the person who personally incurred the obligation.

The trial court found that Dr. Bennett "acted in the business venture which was subsequently incorporated on June 12, 1970."

The proposed business of the corporation which was to be formed was to sell airplanes, recondition airplanes and give flying lessons. Land was leased for this purpose. Equipment was rented from plaintiff to level and clear for access and for other construction.

There is evidence from which the trial court could have found that while Drs. Bennett and Gorman, another defendant, entrusted the details of management to Davenport, they endeavored to and did retain some control over his management. All checks required one of their signatures. Dr. Bennett frequently visited the site and observed the activity and the presence of the equipment rented by plaintiff. He met with the organization's employees to discuss the operation of the business. Shortly after the equipment was rented and before most of the rent had accrued, Dr. Bennett was informed of the rentals and given an opinion that they were unnecessary and ill-advised. Drs. Bennett and Gorman thought they had Davenport and his management "under control."

This evidence all supports the finding that Dr. Bennett was a person who assumed to act for the organization and the conclusion of the trial court that Dr. Bennett is personally liable.

DISREGARDING CORPORATE PERSONALITY

Once incorporation is complete shareholders reasonably expect to be insulated from liability for the corporation's debts. One of the main purposes of incorporating is to enable the stockholders to engage in a business without incurring any personal liability beyond the loss of their investments. However, if the recognition of the corporate entity will result in some injustice, such as defrauding creditors, evading statutory obligations, or defeating the interest of the public, the corporate entity will be disregarded. In such a case personal liability will be imposed on the stockholders.

The rapid growth of closely held corporations and diversified corporate organization consisting of a single parent and several subsidiaries has compelled the courts recently to reexamine the entity status of some corporations. Like most statutes the RMBCA confers liability on the corporation for corporate debts. As a legal entity the corporation normally bears sole liability for debts created in its name. However, limited liability protection is a privilege granted to shareholders for the convenience of conducting business in the corporate form. It is a privilege that must be used to promote decent and fair objectives. The corporate entity will be disregarded, resulting in a loss of limited liability, when the privilege is abused. Shareholders will be held personally liable for corporate debts when such a solution is necessary to avoid an injustice.

Courts have used colorful language in holding shareholders liable. The most common phrase is "piercing the corporate veil," meaning that the corporate entity, which is normally an effective veil shielding shareholders from liability on corporate debts, will be "pierced" to reach the shareholders and hold them liable. Another phrase frequently found is that the corporate entity is merely the "alter ego" or "instrumentality" of the shareholder, meaning that there is in reality no distinction between the corporation's and the shareholder's legal personalities. Stripped of this verbiage, and irrespective of any enunciated formulas, the end result is that shareholder liability will be imposed to reach an equitable result.

The question of the status of a corporation often arises when a liability has been incurred in the name of the corporation but the corporation has become insolvent. The creditor, seeking to find a solvent defendant, may sue all or some of the shareholders, arguing that for some reason they should be called upon to pay the corporation's debts. The issue presented is whether the loss should be imposed on third persons or shareholders. A blind application of the entity approach would mean that the creditor inevitably suffers the loss. In most cases this is a reasonable result since the creditor extended credit to a corporation, which he or she should realize is a creature of limited liability. However, this result often does not occur when it would be unjust to the creditor. This is more likely to be true in cases of involuntary creditors, such as tort victims. Creditors who made contracts with the corporation have greater difficulty in obtaining shareholder liability because they presumably dealt with the corporation voluntarily and should have known whether the corporation lacked substance.

Significant considerations in deciding whether to disregard the corporate entity are whether there has been a lack of observance of corporate formalities resulting in a commingling of shareholder and corporate assets and whether there has been inadequate capitalization of the corporation. When control by the stockholders or a parent corporation is carried out in a normal manner, with due regard for all necessary formalities and for the rights of creditors, separate entity status will normally be sustained. However, when the corporation is totally without any voice in its own affairs, when there is a manipulation of the assets of the corporation and the shareholders, and when corporate and personal activities are so intertwined that no separation is discernible, then the courts will look behind the façade and consider the identities as one. In doing this, the courts sometimes say that the corporate entity is merely a "sham" or a mere shadow of the shareholder's personality. Closely held and parent-subsidiary corporations are particularly vulnerable to this attack because frequently close corporations fail to follow the formalities of corporate existence and parent-subsidiaries often share the same directors. Undercapitalized corporations are also targets for piercing litigation, because a grossly undercapitalized corporation may be considered a fraud upon creditors. The case that follows illustrates this point.

DeWitt Truck Brokers, Inc. v. W. Ray Flemming Fruit Company

U.S. Court of Appeals, Fourth Circuit

540 F.2d 681 (1976)

Background: DeWitt Trucking Company (plaintiff) seeks to recover transportation charges from Flemming (defendant), who is the president of a fruit company for which plaintiff hauled produce. The plaintiff seeks to pierce the corporate veil and hold defendant personally liable. Flemming owned approximately 90 percent of the corporation's stock. It began in 1962 with a capitalization of 5,000 shares issued for a consideration of $1 each. Approximately 2,000 shares were retired. The corporation has one director other than Flemming. The corporation engaged in the business of a commission agent selling fruit for growers in the South Carolina area. It would additionally arrange for and pay the transportation from the grower's warehouse to the purchaser. The failure to pay such charges owed to the plaintiff led to this suit. The District Court ruled in favor of the plaintiff.

Decision: Affirmed. The U.S. Court of Appeals ruled in favor of the DeWitt Trucking Company.

Russell, Justice

At the outset, it is recognized that a corporation is an entity, separate and distinct from its officers and stockholders, and that its debts are not the individual indebtedness of its stockholders. This is expressed in the presumption that the corporation and its stockholders are separate and distinct. . . . And this oft-stated principle is equally applicable, whether the corporation has many or only one stockholder. But this concept of separate entity is merely a legal theory, "introduced for purposes of convenience and to subserve the ends of justice," and the courts "decline to recognize [it] whenever recognition of the corporate form would extend the principle of incorporation 'beyond its legitimate purposes and [could] produce injustices or inequitable consequences.'" *Krivo Industrial Supp. Co.* v. *National Distill. & Chem. Corp.* Accordingly, "in an appropriate case and in furtherance of the ends of justice," the corporate veil will be pierced and the corporation and its stockholders "will be treated as identifiable."

The circumstances which have been considered significant by the courts in actions to disregard the corporate fiction have been "rarely articulated with any clarity." Perhaps this is true because the circumstances "necessarily vary according to the circumstances of each case," and every case where the issue is raised is to be regarded as *"sui generis* [to] . . . be decided in accordance with its own underlying facts."

Contrary to the basic contention of the defendant, however, proof of plain fraud is not a necessary element in a finding to disregard the corporate entity. This was made clear in *Anderson* v. *Abbott* where the Court, after stating that "fraud" has often been found to be a ground for disregarding the principle of limited liability based on the corporate fiction, declared:

". . . The cases of fraud make up part of that exception [which allows the corporate veil to be pierced, citing cases]. *But they do not exhaust it.* An obvious inadequacy of capital, measured by the nature and magnitude of the corporate undertaking, has frequently been an important factor in cases denying stockholders their defenses of limited liability."

On the other hand, equally as well settled as is the principle that plain fraud is not a necessary prerequisite for piercing the corporate veil is the rule that the mere fact that all or almost all of the corporate stock is owned by one individual, or a few individuals, will not afford sufficient grounds for disregarding corporateness. But when substantial ownership of all the stock of a corporation in a single individual is combined with other factors clearly supporting disregard of the corporate fiction on grounds of fundamental equity and fairness, courts have experienced "little difficulty" and have shown no hesitancy in applying what is described as the "alter ego" or "instrumentality" theory in order to cast aside the corporate shield and to fasten liability on the individual stockholder.

But, in applying the "instrumentality" or "alter ego" doctrine, the courts are concerned with reality and not form, with how the corporation operated and the individual defendant's relationship to that operation. . . . And the authorities have indicated certain facts which are to be given substantial weight in this connection. One fact which all the authorities consider significant in the inquiry, and particularly so in the case of the one-man or close-held corporation is whether the corporation was grossly undercapitalized for the purposes of the corporate undertaking. . . . Other factors that are emphasized in the application of the doctrine are failure to observe corporate formalities, nonpayment of dividends, the insolvency of the debtor corporation at the time, siphoning of funds of the corporation by the dominant stockholder, nonfunctioning of other officers or directors, absence of corporate records, and the fact that the corporation is merely a façade for the operations of the dominant stockholder or stockholders. The conclusion to disregard the corporate entity may not, however, rest on a single factor, whether undercapitalization, disregard of corporation's formalities, or what-not, but must involve a number of such factors; in addition, it must present an element of injustice or fundamental unfairness. But undercapitalization, coupled with disregard of corporate formalities, lack of participation on the part of the other stockholders, and the failure to pay dividends while paying substantial sums, whether by way of salary or otherwise, to the dominant stockholder, all fitting into a picture of basic unfairness, has been regarded fairly uniformly to constitute a basis for an imposition of individual liability under the doctrine.

If these factors, which were deemed significant in other cases concerned with this same issue, are given consideration here, the finding of the District Court that the corporate entity should be disregarded was not clearly erroneous. Certainly the corporation was, in practice at least, a close, one-man corporation from the very beginning. Its incorporators were the defendant Flemming, his wife and his attorney. It began in 1962 with a capitalization of 5,000 shares, issued for a consideration of one dollar each. In some manner which Flemming never made entirely clear, approximately 2,000 shares were retired. At the times involved here, Flemming owned approximately 90% of the corporation's outstanding stock, according to his own testimony, though this was not verified by any stock records. Flemming was obscure on who the other stockholders were and how much stock these other stockholders owned, giving at different times conflicting statements as to who owned stock and how much. His testimony on who were the officers and directors was hardly more direct. He testified that the corporation did have one other director, Ed Bernstein, a resident of New York. It is significant, however, that whether Bernstein was nominally a director or not, there were no corporate records of a real directors' meeting in all the years of the corporation's existence and Flemming conceded this to be true. Flemming countered this by testifying that Bernstein traveled a great deal and that his contacts with Bernstein were generally by telephone. The evidence indicates rather clearly that Bernstein was, like the directors in *G. M. Leasing,* "nothing more than [a] figurehead[s]," who had "attended no directors meeting," and even more crucial, never received any fee or reimbursement of expenses or salary of any kind from the corporation.

The District Court found, also, that the corporation never had a stockholders' meeting. . . . It is thus clear that corporate formalities, even rudimentary formalities, were not observed by the defendant.

Beyond the absence of any observance of corporate formalities is the purely personal manner in which the corporation was operated. No stockholder or officer of the corporation other than Flemming ever received any salary, dividend, or fee from the corporation, or, for that matter, apparently exercised any voice in its operation or decisions. In all the years of the corporation's existence, Flemming was the sole beneficiary of its operations, and its continued existence was for his exclusive benefit. During these years he was receiving from $15,000 to $25,000 each year from a corporation, which, during most of the time, was showing no profit and apparently had no working capital. Moreover, the payments to Flemming were authorized under no resolution of the board of directors of the corporation, as recorded in any minutes of a board meeting. Actually, it would seem that Flemming's withdrawals varied with what could be taken out of the corporation at the moment: If this amount were $15,000, that was Flemming's withdrawal; if it were $25,000, that was his withdrawal.

Under the arrangement with the growers, it was to remit to the grower the full sale price, less any transportation costs incurred in transporting the products from the growers' farm or warehouse to the purchaser and its sales commission. An integral part of these collections was represented by the plaintiff's transportation charges. Accordingly, during the period involved here, the corporation had as operating funds seemingly only its commissions and the amount of the plaintiff's transportation charges, for which the corporation had claimed credit in its settlement with its growers. At the time, however, Flemming was withdrawing funds from the corporation at the rate of at least $15,000 per year; and doing this, even though he must have known that the corporation could only do this by withholding payment of the transportation charges due the plaintiff, which in the accounting with the growers Flemming represented had been paid the plaintiff. And, it is of some interest that the amount due the plaintiff for transportation costs was approximately the same as the $15,000 minimum annual salary the defendant testified he was paid by the corporation. Were the opinion of the District Court herein to be reversed, Flemming would be permitted to retain substantial sums from the operations of the corporation without having any real capital in the undertaking, risking nothing of his own and using as operating capital what he had collected as due to the plaintiff.

Finally, . . . Flemming stated to the plaintiff, according to the latter's testimony as credit by the District Court, that "he (i.e., Flemming) would take care of [the charges] personally, if the corporation failed to do so. . . ." When one, who is the sole beneficiary of a corporation's operations and who dominates it, as did Flemming in this case, induces a creditor to extend credit to the corporation such an assurance as given here, that fact has been considered by many authorities sufficient basis for piercing the corporate veil.

REVIEW PROBLEMS

1. What are the chief characteristics of a corporation? List.
2. Is the corporation a "person" entitled to the Fifth Amendment privilege against self-incrimination? Does it possess freedom of expression under the First Amendment to the U.S. Constitution? Explain.
3. What is the distinction between a public and private corporation? Explain.
4. Are all states required to have the same incorporation law?
5. A, a promoter of a real-estate corporation, B, that was not yet formed, entered into a contract with C for real-estate services in buying land. Corporation B was later formed. C sued A for a breach of contract when A refused to pay a commission to C. A's defense was that C knew that the corporation had not been formed at the time the contract was entered into. What result?
6. A, an armored truck company, was charged with maintaining a gambling room in violation of a Florida criminal statute carrying a term of imprisonment up to three years or a fine not exceeding $5,000. B, the president of the corporation, sought an injunction to prevent the case from going to trial because he claimed the cor-

poration was not a natural person, therefore it was not subject to the state gambling law. Who won? Explain.
7. A, a cemetery company, owned a cemetery of approximately sixty acres. Part of the cemetery was for stone monuments and part for bronze. A seldom sold stone monuments but did sell a number of bronze markers to customers purchasing burial places. B, a competitor, sued claiming that A's charter did not provide for the sale of bronze markers. A's charter did not expressly mention the bronze markers but did provide that it could "enter into any or all contracts" "proper" to the "conduct of its business." Who won? Explain.
8. A, B, and C signed articles of incorporation in New Jersey whereby the corporation was to engage in the trucking business. Before filing the articles with the secretary of state, one of the association's trucks injured Frawley. At the time of the accident was the company a corporation and liable on that basis, or is there individual liability?
9. The Illinois incorporation statute provided that people wishing to form a corporation must "sign, send, and acknowledge" the articles of incorporation before

a notary public. Ford and Fisher signed and filed articles of incorporation with the secretary of state but failed to affix any seal to the document. Later the Illinois attorney general brought legal proceedings against the two men, claiming that they were doing business under an illegal corporate certificate and attempting to revoke the corporate status. What result? State ex re. Carlton v. Triplett, 517 P.2d 135 (Kan. 1973)

10. Carlton owned the stock of ten taxi corporations, each owning two cabs and carrying the minimum insurance required by state law. Walkovszky was injured in an accident as a result of the negligence of one of the drivers of the cabs. Can Walkovszky successfully sue Carlton and hold him personally liable for his injuries, or must he satisfy any claim he has against the assets of the particular two-cab corporation involved in the accident? Walkovszky v. Carlton 18 N.Y.2d. 414 (1966)

11. Seller entered into a contract for the sale of plants to the Denver Memorial Nursery, Inc. The contract was signed by Parr as Denver's president. Seller knew that the corporation was not yet formed, and the contract recited this fact, but Seller insisted that the contract be executed this way rather than wait until the corporation was organized. The corporation was never formed. Seller sued Parr to hold him personally liable on the contract. What result? Quaker Hill v. Parr, 148 Colo. 45 (1961)

12. Helen Joplin owned a liquor store as a sole proprietorship. Later she sold 25 percent to Henderson. They agreed that a new corporation would be formed with Henderson purchasing 25 percent of the stock, becoming an officer, and drawing a salary of $700. The business was incorporated and operated successfully for three years. Then Henderson proposed a buyout. Joplin refused and fired Henderson. Henderson sued based on a breach of contract.

Joplin defended, claiming that preincorporation agreements between directors or shareholders are contrary to public policy and thus void. What result? Henderson v. Joplin, 217 N.W.2d. 924 (1974)

13. Before the Bolshevik Revolution in 1917 in Russia, a Russian bank held a balance outstanding to its credit of $66,749.45 in a U.S. bank. When the revolution took place all its assets in the Soviet Union were confiscated by the Bolsheviks, and its stock was canceled. Years later the Russian bank through its shareholders sued a New York bank for the balance outstanding. The defense of the New York bank was that the corporation had been dissolved under Russian law, and thus there existed no legal person or corporation under U.S. law. It refused to pay the credit balance. What result? Konnerchesky v. National City Bank of New York 170 N.E. 479 (1930)

14. A restaurant owner, Zechery, entered into a security agreement for a loan of $11,000 on July 24, 1975. A certificate of incorporation for the restaurant, Roseberry Inn, Inc., was executed on July 24 but was not filed with the secretary of state until July 30, 1975. When the restaurant failed the bank sued Roseberry Inn, Inc. and Zechery for repossession of the restaurant equipment, which was security for the loan. Zechery, the defendant, and one of the owners of the Inn argued that the bank could not have acquired a security interest in the equipment because the restaurant was not incorporated, and thus did not exist (de jure) at the time the security agreement was executed. What result? Bankers Trust Company v. Zechery, 426 N.Y.S.2d 960 (1980)

15. Cranson invested in a new corporation, Real Estate Service Bureau, which was about to be created. Cranson would become an officer and director. He was advised by an attorney that the corporation

was conducted through corporate bank accounts, and auditors kept corporate books. Cranson was later elected president of the corporation and as an officer of the corporation had dealings with IBM. Due to an oversight on the part of the attorney, the certificate of incorporation was not filed until after the transactions for typewriters with IBM took place. IBM sued Cranson personally for a balance of $4,334 owed on the typewriters. Cranson claimed that a de facto corporation existed at the time the typewriters were purchased, and thus he was not personally liable. What result? IBM v. Cranson, 200 A.2d (1964)

16. A suffered an on-the-job injury. She sued the Heritage Building Company to recover workmen's compensation benefits at a time when the company's liabilities exceeded its debts. Shortly after she sued all the company's assets were transferred to B, the president and sole stockholder, in consideration of the company's indebtedness to him. He, in turn, on the same day transferred these assets to another of his corporations, Heritage Corporation. A won a judgment against Heritage Building Company, but the company had no assets from which to satisfy a judgment. A then filed a suit against B and the Heritage Corporation. What result? Will B be held personally liable? Tigrett v. Pointer, 580 W.2d 375 (1979)

Financing the Corporation

I n most states before a corporation can begin conducting business it must have money to finance its operations. *Financing,* or capitalizing, a corporation is the process of assembling funds in exchange for issued shares of stock. These funds are collectively called the corporation's capital. Although capitalization is an accounting term, it is used by courts to refer to the financing of the corporate enterprise. In addition to funds raised from issued shares, courts often consider loans to a corporation from its shareholders, or even accumulated earnings that are not withdrawn from the corporation, as capital. The reader should be aware of the imprecise use of this term.

Financing may occur initially during the launching of the corporation, or it may occur later when the corporation needs more capital for expansion, resuscitation, or operation. The process has two components: (1) short-term financing and (2) long-term financing. Short-term funds are assembled largely by use of promissory notes and mortgages. The common source is the commercial bank, which will extend lines of credit. Long-term funds are raised by the selling of securities (stocks and bonds). If the financing is public, the securities are sold in the formal capital market.

This chapter focuses primarily on the legal problems involved in the assembling of long-term funds. The material falls roughly into three parts: (1) the kinds of securities and their provisions, (2) the method of acquiring initial capital through subscription contracts, and (3) the method of acquiring capital following incorporation.

KINDS OF SECURITIES

The sale of securities is the usual method of corporate financing. Most financing comes from investors who receive securities in return for their investments. The security is usually represented by a certificate, such as a share of stock or a bond, that evidences the security holder's rights in the corporate business. However, a security need not necessarily involve this type of formal paper. The two main types of securities are (1) debt securities and (2) equity securities. (See Table 35-1.)

Debt Securities

The Revised Model Business Corporation Act (RMBCA) authorizes corporations to borrow money, incur liabilities, and issue bonds; none of these expedients needs shareholder approval. The funds generated by this borrowing must be used only for corporate purposes. Debt securities evidence a debt of the corporation and become corporate liabilities.

TABLE 35-1 CHARACTERISTICS OF STOCKS AND BONDS

Stocks	Bonds
1. Those holding stocks elect the board of directors which hire and control management.	1. In general those holding bonds have no control over the board of directors or management, except in bankruptcy situations.
2. No maturity date exists for repayment of owners of stock, although corporations can buy back their stock from stockholders.	2. Bonds have a maturity date for repayment to holders of the value of the bond at that time.
3. Returns (dividends) are paid on stocks at the option of the board of directors depending on the profit level of the corporation.	3. Returns (interest) on bonds must be paid whether or not profit level expectations are met.
4. Upon dissolution of a corporation, stockholders' claims against the assets of the corporation are secondary to all creditors including bondholders.	4. Upon dissolution of a corporation, bondholders have a claim against the assets of the corporation prior to shareholders.

Types of Debt Securities. Debt securities include *notes, debentures,* and *bonds.* Notes usually represent short-term borrowing of the corporation. They are payable upon order to a bank or person. Interest payments are due periodically. Debentures are unsecured corporate obligations backed by the general credit of the corporation and its assets. If the corporation defaults, creditors will attempt to seize the assets. A bond (used interchangeably with debentures) is usually a long-term debt security secured by a lien or mortgage on corporate property. Bonds are bearer instruments. Interest payments are made periodically upon submission of coupons by the bondholders.

Debt securities have two important characteristics. They are subject to *redemption* and *conversion.* Redemption means the corporation reserves the right to call in and pay off its obligations at any time before they are due, usually at a premium over face value. Debt securities may also be convertible—that is, they may be converted into equity securities (for example, common stock) at a certain ratio.

Tax Advantages of Debt Securities. Debt securities offer significant tax advantages for the corporation that issues them. Interest payments on bonds or notes are tax deductible for the corporation, whereas dividend payments on equity securities (such as common stock) are not. Payments of a debt by a corporation may be considered a nontaxable return on capital for the investor, whereas a redemption of equity securities from a shareholder by the corporation may be taxed as ordinary income. The Internal Revenue Service (IRS) has often investigated corporations' debt structures to determine if they are excessive. If the IRS finds that a debt structure is excessive, it attempts to treat the excessive debt as a form of corporate equity for tax purposes. Thus the substantial advantages associated with corporate debt financing have led to considerable litigation. Because the courts have treated each situation as unique, no overriding legal principle has evolved to determine when a corporation's debt is excessive. Courts have considered the ratio of debt to equity as relevant but have rejected a purely quantitative approach.

Equity Securities

Every business corporation must issue equity securities, usually called shares or stock (Fig-

BOX 35-1 ISSUES AND TRENDS

/ / "Junk" bonds are issues of corporate debt judged by credit agencies such as Moody's to be lower than investment grade; that is, the bond is seen to be very risky for the purchaser, usually mutual funds, banks, or insurance companies. They are used extensively by corporations or individuals (often called "raiders") seeking to finance the acquisition or takeover of another corporation (see Chapter 44 for a discussion of the antitrust statutes and the process of acquisition). Those in favor of junk bonds argue that the premiums (or returns) earned by investors compensate them for the added risk they take. Typically junk bonds earn 4 to 6 percentage points more than risk-free U.S. Treasury bonds. The default rate for junk bonds as of September 1987 was approximately 1.6 percent. However, because many have been issued in times of economic expansion (1982–1987), it is difficult to say if this percentage would hold up in the event of a downturn in the economy.

Junk bonds represent $50 billion of $8 trillion U.S. debt or 0.5 percent of the country's total debt. Of the $50 billion, $30 billion has been used to finance the takeovers of companies.

ure 35-1). Stockholders (shareholders) own the corporation. Authorization for the issuance of equity is contained in the corporation's articles of incorporation. Unless authorized, the sale of shares is void.

The money raised by the corporation from the sale of stock is the fund out of which the corporation may meet its obligations to creditors; it represents the corporation's stated capital. The corporation is not bound to return to the shareholders their investment before liquidation of the enterprise. The shares usually have no maturity date. Return on the shareholders' investment takes two forms: dividends, which are dependent on the availability of profits and the discretion of the board of directors, and capital gains, which result from the shareholders' ability to sell their stock for a higher price than was originally paid. Shareholders' claims are subordinate to the claims of debt-security holders because debt holders stand as creditors of the corporation, not as its

owners. Upon corporate liquidation following dissolution, shareholders receive only those funds available after all corporate creditors have been paid.

Common and Preferred Stock. Most states authorize the issuance of more than one class of corporate stock and permit the corporation to vary the rights, preferences, and restrictions among the different classes. The two classes most frequently issued are (1) common stock and (2) preferred stock.

If the corporation issues only one class of stock, that stock will be common stock. Because common stockholders assume the most risk and have the most to gain from the corporate venture, they receive none of the preferences that the holders of other classes of stock may receive. Common stockholders stand behind bondholders and holders of other classes of stock when corporate distributions are made. However, common stockholders are

FIGURE 35–1
Stock Certificate

Source: Douglas Whitman, F. William McCarty, Frank F. Gibson, Thomas W. Dunfee, Bartley A. Brennan, and John D. Blackburn, *Law and Business* (New York, Random House, 1987), p. 568. Copyright © 1987 by Thomas W. Dunfee, F. William McCarty, Frank F. Gibson, Douglas Whitman, John D. Blackburn, and Bartley A. Brennan.

able to participate in the corporate management. (See Chapter 33 for a discussion of the shareholders' role in management.)

Preferred stock is given special rights and preferences when corporate distributions are made. Because of these preferences, preferred shareholders assume less risk than common shareholders. They do not usually participate in corporate management.

Under the RMBCA the preferences of any class of stock must be stated in the articles of incorporation. Thus the extent that preferred stock differs from common stock depends on the provisions of the articles of incorporation.

However, Section 6.03 permits the articles to authorize the board of directors to issue preferred stock in series and to determine the relative rights and preferences of the shares of each series regarding:

1. The dividend rate
2. The amount payable to shareholders upon liquidation
3. Any redemption rights along with any provisions for sinking funds for redeeming preferred shares
4. The conditions for convertible shares
5. Any voting rights

As a practical matter, the special rights and preferences accorded preferred shareholders by either the articles or the board will be printed on the preferred stock certificates.

Preferred stock usually has a stated dividend rate. Although it is not mandatory that a corporation pay a dividend in any given year, if it does declare a dividend, the preferred shareholders will receive the rate stipulated by the articles and will be paid before the common shareholders. Preferred shareholders also have superior standing in the distributions of corporate assets upon the corporation's liquidation.

Preferred stock may be made redeemable. The RMBCA permits the articles to provide that preferred stock may be redeemed by the corporation at the price fixed by the articles. This is usually done by establishing a sinking fund for the redemption of preferred stock.

Preferred stock may also be convertible into shares of another class or into another type of security, such as a bond. However, the RMBCA provides that the shares of one class of stock may not be converted into those of another class that has superior or prior rights and preferences regarding corporate distributions. Thus preferred stock may be converted into common stock, but not vice versa.

As noted earlier, preferred shareholders generally participate less in corporate management than common shareholders. This balances the lower risk assumed by preferred shareholders. Thus preferred stock is generally nonvoting. The RMBCA permits the elimination of voting rights for particular classes of stock.

Stock Options and Warrants. In addition to common and preferred stock, the RMBCA authorizes the issuance of stock options and rights. These securities entitle their holders to purchase from the corporation shares of the corporation's stock. If the option is a negotiable instrument giving the owner the right to purchase stock of the corporation at a specified price, it is called a *warrant.* Warrants are usually issued to make the issue of some other security more attractive. The owner of the warrant is not only guaranteed the right to buy a number of shares but also is permitted to trade it freely. Often warrants are issued to present shareholders to prevent a dilution of ownership. Shareholders are able to buy a new issue in the form of warrants and thus get an opportunity to buy the stock at a price lower than its market price.

Stock options are often issued by a corporation to an officer or employee to compensate him or her for work done or to provide an incentive for further effort. Under the RMBCA, if options or warrants are to be issued to the directors, officers, or employees of the corporation, shareholder approval is not required. The following is a well-reasoned decision illustrating the law as applied to stock options granted to executives as part of a compensation package.

Lieberman v. Koppers Co., Inc.

Court of Chancery of Delaware.
149 A.2d 756, affd. sub. nom. Lieberman v. Becker, 155 A.2d 596 (1959)

Background: Lieberman (plaintiff), a stockholder of Koppers Co., Inc. (defendant), brought a derivative action against the company to have declared invalid a deferred-compensation unit plan approved by the stockholders. The purpose of the plan was to attract and retain persons of outstanding competence and to give key employees a stockholder's point of view of the company. The plan provided for the issuance of units in lieu of options to purchase stocks. The value of each unit on the date of issue was that of one share of common stock on the same date. Each unit was subject to being increased in value by the crediting to it of dividends paid on a share of stock as well as any increase in the market value of a single share before a participant's right to a unit occurred. As a condition to the award of units, each participant agreed to remain in the company's employ for five years from the date of his award or until retirement and to be available for consultation for a ten-year period after retirement, during which time a participant might not compete with Koppers. The plan was administered by three or more board members declared ineligible to participate. Both parties moved for summary judgment.

Decision: The court ruled in favor of Koppers Co., Inc.

Marvel, Vice Chancellor

The complaint alleges that as of December 31, 1957, 89,800 units had been awarded under the plan to various employees and that to the extent that the plan provides for awards to participants based on the increased market value of common stock of the defendant corporation it is invalid for the reason that such awards bear no reasonable relation to the value of services rendered by a participant, and that such awards thus constitute a waste and gift of corporate assets. No complaint, however, is made concerning the provisions of the plan dealing with dividend credits. It is further alleged that since the adoption of the plan the stock of Koppers has fluctuated widely, that such fluctuations bear little or no relation to the services to the corporation and its stockholders and so are invalid.

In addition to the enjoining of the operation of the plan the complaint seeks an accounting for all payments made by Koppers under the plan and for general equitable relief, but admittedly those persons who have become eligible for and received payments under the plan by reason of severance of employment are not before the Court, and no accounting is presently sought.

The answer admits the pleaded facts as to the adoption of the plan, sets forth the vote on stockholder approval and concludes that the plan was adopted and given effect by directors of Koppers in the exercise of their best business judgment as directors and was approved by substantially all of the stockholders who voted thereon in the belief the plan is a fair, reasonable, appropriate and valid plan in furtherance of the welfare and success of Koppers and for the advantage of all its shareholders.

There being no doubt but that the plan here under attack is reasonably calculated to insure the receipt of services by the corporation, it is not subject to the Kerbs ruling (Kerbs v. California Eastern Airways).

Furthermore, while it is alleged that certain directors are beneficiaries of the plan, no real attack is made nor could such be made on the basis of director self-dealing in view of the existence of an impartial committee and stockholder approval.

In short, it is my considered opinion that the plan is reasonably and fairly designed to achieve a legitimate business purpose, namely to retain or obtain qualified executive personnel through the medium of deferring compensation until retirement. While a substantial block of stock has been reserved for financing the plan, corporate reserves, if any, may be allocated to the payment of deferred compensation, thereby probably reducing what would have been the stock demands of a comparable stock option plan. Furthermore, while moneys are not paid out by participants for units, there is no reason advanced why a reasonable and impartial committee may not be expected to take this factor into consideration in the award of units, and when need be, in the reduction of units already awarded. Plaintiff also declines to give proper recognition to the dividend credit provision, the most tangible and perhaps the most attractive feature of the plan in the eyes of participants. Finally, the so-called speculative or capital gains features of the plan are by no means absent from conventional option plans and certain types of incentive plans based on earnings, and it would be unrealistic not to recognize that the plan, if fairly operated, will add to job satisfaction and induce added effort on the part of participants with resulting benefits to the corporation.

Admittedly, the market value of stock of any substantial corporation cannot be isolated from broad economic trends, wars, rumours and many other factors both direct and indirect which affect stock prices. However, earnings are the mark of corporate success and the main factor in stock appreciation, and I do not believe it can be dogmatically said that the services of employees given in response to an incentive plan based in substantial part on the appreciation in the market value of their employer's common stock bear no reasonable relation to such appreciation, and I decline to strike down the plan as per se unreasonable and invalid.

While it may be established in the future that the award of specific units under the plan may in an individual case ultimately pose the threat of payment of illegally excessive compensation, such a case is not now before me.

STOCK SUBSCRIPTIONS

A method of corporate financing more common with small corporations than with large corporations is the stock subscription. A *stock subscription* is an agreement between a corporation and a prospective shareholder whereby the corporation agrees to issue shares and the subscriber agrees to pay for them. In a majority of states an offer by the prospective shareholder and an acceptance by the corporation must exist in order to bring the stock subscription contract into existence. Stock subscriptions may be executed either before or after incorporation. The issue raised by both preincorporation and postincorporation subscriptions is whether the subscriber attains shareholder status in the corporation. If the subscriber does, he or she will be liable for whatever consideration was promised under the subscription agreement in payment for the shares.

Preincorporation Subscriptions

Persons interested in the formation of a business corporation frequently desire to begin the process of financing the proposed enterprise before the formal steps resulting in the formation of the corporation are complete. One of the devices employed in this process of assembling funds is the *preincorporation subscription,* by which one or more investors make known to the promoter their intention to purchase shares of a designated class and number in the proposed corporation at an agreed-upon sum.

A preincorporation subscription may take

many forms. Although a few states, such as Delaware and Kansas, require that stock subscriptions be in writing and signed by the subscriber, most states do not require that a subscription be written. A preincorporation subscription may be an individual transaction or it may be a class of transactions by a number of persons, as when a "subscription list" is signed. The word "subscriber" need not appear, and other language such as "I hereby purchase, etc." may be employed. The agreement may include definite provisions as to the time and manner of payment of the agreed amount, the time when the subscriber is to become entitled to a stock certificate, and the legal relations between the subscriber and other shareholders; but usually it gives little or no indication of the intent of the parties with respect to these matters.

Authorities disagree whether a subscriber may withdraw his or her subscription before the corporation comes into existence. The older rule, which still prevails in many jurisdictions, is that a preincorporation subscription may be withdrawn at any time prior to acceptance by the corporation, which cannot occur until the corporation comes into existence. Because there is no corporation in existence at the time the subscription is executed, the subscription is merely an expression of intent to purchase shares and has no legal effect. Furthermore, under general contract law the subscriber's death, insanity, or bankruptcy will terminate the subscription offer in accordance with the usual rules relating to an unaccepted offer. Newer statutes, including the RMBCA, make preincorporation subscriptions irrevocable for a stated period of time, typically six months, unless the subscription agreement provides otherwise or all the subscribers consent to the revocation. Although by statute in some states acceptance of the subscription offer is deemed to occur upon incorporation, most statutes, including the RMBCA, require that the corporation act affirmatively to accept the preincorporation subscription offers. Thus, to make a binding

subscription contract under these statutes, not only must the corporation be completely organized but there must be an acceptance by the corporation after coming into existence, either expressly by issuing shares to the subscribers or impliedly by recognizing the subscriber as a stockholder.

The realities of corporate finance require an exception to the general principles of contract law. The function of preincorporation subscriptions is to raise capital with which to finance the future corporation. The status of preincorporation subscriptions is of great concern to the incipient corporation. A practical disadvantage of preincorporation subscriptions presented by the revocable-offer rule is that such subscription agreements may be illusory before incorporation. The practical consequences of subscribers' right to revoke is not only uncertainty as to the amount of funds a proposed corporation will have available upon incorporation, but even the possibility that there will not be sufficient funds to permit its formal organization. If a subscriber who happens to be one of the major contributors to the proposed corporation revokes his or her subscription, the whole venture may collapse even before it gets started.

The RMBCA recognizes that some corporations must be financed before actual incorporation and that preincorporation subscribers should therefore be bound for a limited time so that the articles may be filed, unless the agreement provides otherwise. The effect of the RMBCA's approach is that the ultimate receipt of capital by the corporation is better assured, since each potential investor is obligated to put up a specific amount of money for a specific number of shares as soon as the corporation is formed and the subscriptions are accepted.

Postincorporation Subscriptions

When the subscription agreement is made between the subscriber and a corporation already in existence, there exists a binding obligation for the subscriber to purchase, and the corporation to sell, shares of the corporate stock. Ordinary contract principles of offer and acceptance are determinative. Thus a stock subscription made with a corporation already in existence is a contract between the subscriber and the corporation. The contract may result either from an offer made by the corporation and accepted by the subscriber or from an offer made by the subscriber and accepted by the corporation.

A *postincorporation subscription* agreement must be distinguished from an executory contract to purchase stock. A subscription agreement confers shareholder status instantly on the subscriber even though no stock certificate has yet been issued. Under an executory contract for the purchase of shares, shareholder status is suspended until the contract is fully executed—that is, until a stock certificate has been issued to the purchaser.

Shareholder status under a stock subscription contract does not depend on the issuance of a stock certificate. Under a subscription contract, the subscriber is liable for the subscription payment even though the corporation has not delivered the stock certificate. When the subscription is made, the subscriber is instantly vested with all the rights and obligations of a shareholder, even though some shareholder rights, such as voting and receiving dividends, may be suspended until full payment of the subscription price is made.

However, when the agreement is an executory contract for the purchase of stock, the purchaser does not become a stockholder until the purchase price is fully paid and the stock certificate has been issued. Thus an executory purchaser of shares is relieved of the duty to pay in the event of the corporation's bankruptcy because the corporation cannot perform its duty to deliver shares in a going concern. This is simply an application of the contract law principle that a material breach of an executory contract will discharge the nonbreaching party of any obligation of performance under the contract.

The problem presented by postincorporation subscriptions and by executory contracts to purchase stock is to distinguish between the two transactions. Because both are contracts, the intent of the parties is controlling. Although not conclusive, calling the contract a "subscription agreement" or a "purchase contract" will be highly persuasive. Beyond this, courts look to the nature of the transaction and the rights conferred by the corporation.

Consideration to Be Paid by Subscriber

The issuance of shares by a corporation implies that it has received consideration equal in value to the stated value of the shares. Once the corporation has set a formal valuation on its shares, it cannot sell them below that price. Stockholders who have been issued shares for consideration below the fixed value are liable for any unpaid consideration.

The value of shares to be received as consideration by the corporation is determined by the Board of Directors. Under the RMBCA the board may set a minimum price or establish a formula or any other method to determine price. Although the RMBCA eliminates the distinction between *par* and *no par* stock and the use of the term *stated capital* (Official Comment), most state statutes continue to use such terms. Traditionally, Boards of Directors have designated the value of shares as the par value or stated value of the stock. The total of the par and stated values of the corporation's issued shares constitutes the stated capital of the corporation.

Par value is the price established by either the articles or the directors below which a share may not be originally issued by the corporation. The dollar value is usually quite low—$1 is typical—but the par value has little practical effect on the issuance of shares. Shareholders who do not contribute an amount at least equal to the par value of the stock issued are liable to creditors for the balance. The extent of liability is the difference between the par value and the amount actually contributed. Creditors, including bond-holders, can seek to have this amount paid to the corporate treasury or, sometimes in the event of dissolution and a deficiency, paid to them to satisfy their claims.

The RMBCA provides that payment for shares may be made with money or other property of any description actually transferred to the corporation or with labor or other services actually rendered to the corporation. Also, the RMBCA allows promissory notes and agreements to provide future services to constitute payment for shares (Section 6.21). Most state statutes presently will not allow these latter items to serve as consideration. Because shares may be issued for a consideration other than cash, a question sometimes arises over whether the corporation received full value for its stock.

Authorities disagree regarding the valuation of property or services transferred to the corporation in consideration for its shares. A few states follow the "true value" rule. Under this rule, whether a shareholder is liable for any unpaid value depends on whether the assets given in consideration for the shares were actually worth the price of the stock. The shareholder is held liable for any substantial variance between the fair market value of the property or service transferred to the corporation and the price of the stock.

Most states (including those that adopt the RMBCA), follow the "good-faith" rule, which is based on the assumption that people may honestly differ about the value of property and service rendered to a corporation in consideration for its stock. Under this rule the valuation made by the corporation will be upheld as long as it was honestly made, no fraud or bad faith exists on the part of the directors, and they have exercised the degree of care that an ordinary, prudent person in their position would exercise. The case that follows is the landmark opinion of the U.S. Supreme Court that originally set forth the good-faith rule.

Coit v. Amalgamating Company

U.S. Supreme Court
119 U.S. 343 (1886)

Background: Coit (plaintiff), holder of a judgment for $5,489 against Gold (defendant), brought this suit to compel the stockholders to pay what he claimed to be due and unpaid on the shares of the capital stock held by them. Coit was unable to obtain execution of his judgment against the corporation itself because it was insolvent. The defendant, the North Carolina Gold Amalgamating Company, was incorporated under the laws of North Carolina, on January 30, 1874, for the purpose, among other things, of working, milling, smelting, reducing, and assaying ores and metals, with the power to purchase such property, real and personal, as might be necessary in its business and to mortgage or sell the same. By its charter the minimum capital stock was fixed at $100,000, divided into 1,000 shares of $100 each; the corporation was empowered to increase it from time to time, by a majority vote of the stockholders, to $2.5 million. The charter provided that the subscription to the capital stock might be paid "in such installments, in such manner and in such property, real and personal," as a majority of the corporators might determine, and that the stockholders should not be liable for any loss or damages or be responsible beyond the assets of the company. Previously to the charter, the corporators had been engaged in mining operations, conducting their business under the name and title which they took as a corporation.

When the charter was obtained, the capital stock was paid by the property of the former association, which was estimated to be of the value of $100,000, the shares being divided among the stockholders in proportion to their respective interests in the property. Each stockholder placed his estimate upon the property; and the average estimate amounted to $137,500. This sum they reduced to $100,000, inasmuch as the capital stock was to be of that amount. The lower courts ruled in favor of the defendant, and it is from these decisions that plaintiff appealed.

Decision: Affirmed. The U.S. Supreme Court ruled in favor of Amalgamating Company

Field, Justice

The plaintiff contends, and it is the principal basis of his suit, that the valuation thus put upon the property was illegally and fraudulently made at an amount far above its actual value, averring that the property consisted only of a machine for crushing ores, the right to use a patent called the Crosby process, and the charter of the proposed organization; that the articles had no market or actual value, and, therefore, that the capital stock issued thereon was not fully paid, or paid to any substantial extent, and that the holders thereof were still liable to the corporation and its creditors for the unpaid subscription. If it were proved that actual fraud was committed in the payment of the stock, and that the complainant had given credit to the company from a belief that its stock was fully paid, there would undoubtedly be substantial ground for the relief asked. But where the charter authorizes capital stock to be paid in property, and the shareholders honestly and in good faith put in property instead of money in payment of their subscriptions, third parties have no ground of complaint. The case is very different from that in which subscriptions to stock are payable in cash, and where only a part of the instalments has been paid. In that case there is still a debt due to the corporation, which, if it becomes insolvent, may be sequestered in equity by the creditors, as a trust fund liable to the payment of their debts. But where full paid stock is issued for property received, there must be actual fraud in the transaction to enable creditors of the corporation to call the stockholders to account. A gross and obvious overvaluation of property would be strong evidence of fraud.

But the allegation of intentional and fraudulent undervaluation of the property is not sustained by the evidence. The patent and the machinery had been used by the corporators in their business, which was continued under the charter. They were immediately serviceable, and therefore had to the company a present value. The corporators may have placed too high an estimate upon the property, but the court below finds that its valuation was honestly and fairly made; and there is only one item, the value of the chartered privileges, which is at all liable to any legal objection. But if that were deducted, the remaining amount would be so near to the aggregate capital, that no implication could be raised against the entire good faith of the parties in the transaction. In May, 1874, the company increased its stock, as it was authorized to do by its charter, to $1,000,000 or 10,000 shares of $100 each. This increase was made pursuant to an agreement with one Howes, by which the company was to give him 2000 shares of the increased stock for certain lands purchased from him. Of the balance of the increased shares, 4000 were divided among the holders of the original stock upon the return and delivery to the company of the original certificates—they thus receiving four shares of the increased capital stock for one of the original shares returned. The other 4000 shares were retained by the company. The land purchased was subject to three mortgages, of which the plaintiff held the third; and the agreement was that, under the first mortgage, a sale should be made of the property, and that mortgages for a like amount should be given to the parties according to their several and respective amounts, and in their respective positions and priorities. The plaintiff was to be placed by the company, after the release of his mortgage, in the same position. Accordingly he made a deed to it of all his interest and title under the mortgage held by him, the trustee joining with him, in which deed the agreement was recited. The company, thereupon, gave him its mortgage upon the same and other property, which was payable in installments. The plaintiff also received at the same time an accepted draft of Howe's on the company for $1000. When the first instalment on the mortgage became due, the company being unable to pay it, he took its draft for the amount, $3000, payable in December following. It is upon these drafts that the judgment was recovered in the Court of Common Pleas of Philadelphia, which is the foundation of the present suit. It is in evidence that the plaintiff was fully aware, at the time, of the increase in the stock of the company, and of its object. Six months afterwards, the increase was cancelled, the outstanding shares were called in, and the capital stock reduced to its original limit of $100,000. Nothing was done after the increase to enlarge the liabilities of the company. The draft of the Howes was passed to the plaintiff and received by him at the time the agreement was carried out upon which the increase of the stock was made; and the draft for $3000 was for an instalment upon the mortgage then executed. The plaintiff had placed no reliance upon the supposed paid-up capital of the company on the increased shares, and, therefore, has no cause of complaint by reason of their subsequent recall. Had a new indebtedness been created by the company after the issue of the stock and before its recall, a different question would have arisen. The creditor in that case, relying on the faith of the stock being fully paid, might have insisted upon its full payment. But no such new indebtedness was created, and we think, therefore, that the stockholders cannot be called upon, at the suit of the plaintiff, to pay in the amount of the stock, which, though issued, was soon afterwards recalled and cancelled.

TRANSFER OF SECURITIES

Transfer

The transfer of stocks and bonds is governed by Article 8 of the Uniform Commercial Code (UCC). Generally investors upon receipt of title of securities have a right to transfer by sale, gift, or one's will. Less complex is a bearer bond (no name appears on the certificate but "pay to bearer") which is transferred upon delivery. When a stock or bond is "registered" the name of the owner appears on the security, and it is recorded on the corporate books. These securities require *delivery* and *indorsement* to the new owner (UCC 8–309). Generally stocks are endorsed on an assignment form on the back of the stock certificate, or on a "stock power" document separate from the certificate. Indorsement often does not provide as difficult a problem as does delivery. The case set out here illustrates the legal difficulties involved in delivery of stocks.

Bankwest v. Williams

Supreme Court of South Dakota

347 N.W.2d 163 (1974)

Background: Bankwest (plaintiff) attempted to levy on the surplus of a stock sale in order to collect on two unsecured loans defaulted on by Williams (defendant). Williams had been divorced from his wife Pamela. He transferred by a written assignment 317 shares of stock, which were not delivered to Pamela because Williams had delivered them to Bankwest as collateral for a loan outstanding. Pamela did not notify the Bank of the assignment of stock to her. When Williams, her ex-husband, defaulted on the loan, the bank sold the shares at a private sale following proper notice. The surplus was paid into the court for distribution. When the bank attempted to claim the surplus for two other unsecured notes, Pamela objected, claiming she had the sole right to the surplus. The lower court ruled in favor of Bankwest. Pamela appealed. Decision: Affirmed. The Supreme Court of South Dakota ruled in favor of Bankwest.

Henderson, Justice

(1) Delivery to a purchaser occurs when
   (a) He or a person designated by him acquires possession of a security; or . . .
   (d) With respect to an identified security to be delivered while still in the possession of a third person when that person acknowledges that he holds for the purchaser; or
   (e) Appropriate entries on the books of a clearing corporation are made under 8–320 . . . 8–313(1)(a, d, e).

Pamela did not acquire possession of the security, for it was being held by [the bank]; thus there was no delivery under item (a). Neither did the bank acknowledge it was holding the certificates for Pamela. In point of fact, it was never notified of the agreement transferring the stock. Pamela also testified that she did not notify [the corporation] of the agreement, nor did she request a change of name on its books. There was, then, no delivery under provisions (d) and (e).

Without delivery, the agreement, in itself, could not act to validly transfer ownership of the stock. When a transfer is by separate document, Section 8–309 specifically states: "An endorsement of a security whether in special or in blank does not constitute a transfer until delivery of the security on which it appears or if the endorsement is on a separate document until delivery of both the document and the security."

The execution of the . . . 1981 agreement between Williams and Pamela did not constitute an effective delivery transferring ownership of the 317 shares of stock. The stock remained in the name of Williams. Bankwest, having a valid judgment against Williams, could lawfully execute upon the proceeds arising from the sale of the stock to satisfy its claim.

CASE NOTE

The corporation has a duty to transfer any registered security presented to it by an owner provided it has been endorsed and delivered properly, and is not subject to any restrictions. Failure to do so makes it liable to the new owner. Each state corporation law will treat such situations with different remedies. Some will allow the new owner to collect the cash value of the stock, whereas others will grant specific performance.

REVIEW PROBLEMS

1. Define stock options and warrants.
2. What is the prevailing rule as to whether a preincorporation subscriber to shares of a corporation may withdraw his or her subscription before the corporation comes into existence?
3. Who determines the value of shares to be received as consideration when a corporation issues stocks?
4. Define the "true value" and "good-faith" rules governing the valuation of property or services transferred to the corporation in consideration for its shares.
5. The transfer of stocks and bonds is governed by what article and statute?
6. D Corporation was organized by S, who transferred property for preferred stock and then caused $1.5 million in par value common stock to be issued. D and S agreed that there would be no consideration paid for the common stock. D subsequently incurred liabilities, became insolvent, and entered receivership. P, a corporation organized to purchase the assets of D and to carry on the business, bought the claims of creditors and sued to collect from S the par value of the common stock. What will be the result?
7. Henry Molina attended a meeting with Rudy Largosa to discuss the formation of a corporation to engage in selling stereo equipment. At the meeting Molina signed a subscription form for the purchase of forty shares at $50 per share for a total investment of $2,000 in the proposed corporation. The subscription form did not set forth the capital of the proposed corporation or the extent of Molina's proportionate interest in it. Molina later paid Largosa $2,000, which was deposited in a bank account under the name of the proposed corporation. Shortly after the corporation was officially organized, it failed. Molina sued Largosa to recover his $2,000, contending that because the subscription form did not set forth the total capital of the proposed corporation and his proportionate interest in it, there was no valid subscription contract. What result would you expect? Molina v. Largosa, 456 P.2d 293 (1970)
8. The Columbia Straw Paper Company purchased thirty-nine paper mills from Emanuel Stein for $5 million, for which it issued to Stein $1 million of the corporation's bonds, $1 million worth of its preferred stock, and $3 million worth of common stock. The value of the mills was arrived at by analyzing the expected profits to be derived from the property. Columbia later became insolvent, and creditors of the company sued Stein, claiming that the mills he sold to the corporation were not worth $5 million; that

the directors acted in bad faith by basing the value of the mills on an extravagant estimation of prospective profits rather than on the appraised value of the mills' property. May a corporation make an exchange for its stock on the basis of an estimation of prospective profits to be derived from that property? See v. Heppenheimer, 61 A.843 (1905)

9. Citizens of Schuyler, Nebraska, sought to form a corporation for the processing of chicory. Lednicky signed a subscription agreement to purchase five shares of stock, par value $50, in the proposed company. Articles of incorporation were obtained. Lednicky agreed to pay for his five shares at the rate of $10 a month. After paying $80 he refused to continue payment, and the corporation sued for the balance. The defense was that the subscription agreement was not an enforceable contract. What will be the result? Nebraska Chicory Co. of Schuyler, Nebraska v. Lednicky, 113 N.W. 245 (1941)

10. The Clifton Coal Co. was organized with 1,200 shares, par value $100, with power to increase the shares to 2,000 by a majority vote of the stockholders. This increase was later voted, but the corporation was unable to sell the additional 800 shares. The corporation then issued $50,000 worth of bonds and was able to dispose of them by offering the buyers $50,000 worth of stock as a bonus; the remaining $30,000 worth of stock was given to the original stockholders of the corporation. The stock certificates bore the statement that the shares were "fully paid and nonassessable." Stutz and other creditors of the corporation brought an action to compel an assessment on the 800 shares. What should the result be? Handley v. Stutz, 139 U.S. 417 (1891)

11. Sherman, to whom certain creditors of the Oleum Development Co. had assigned their judgments, sued the stockholders of Oleum to recover amounts alleged due on unpaid subscriptions to the capital stock of the corporation. The stock had a par value of $1 a share and was issued as fully paid-up stock, but in no instance was it actually fully paid for, and in some cases the corporation had received no more than 10 cents a share. These facts were fully known to the creditors when they extended credit to the corporation. What will be the result? Sherman v. Harley et al. 174 P.901 (1921)

Operating the Corporation

O nce the corporation has been formed and financed, it is ready to commence the operation of its business. Just what that business may be depends on the purpose of the corporation as reflected by its charter and articles of incorporation. Thus, in discussing corporate operation, this chapter focuses first on the subject of permissible corporate activity as circumscribed by the corporation's purposes and powers. Then it turns to the three groups who participate in operating the corporation: the shareholders, the board of directors, and the corporate officers or executives. These three groups are examined separately, but their roles are closely interrelated. Generally speaking, those who comprise the corporation's management (the board of directors and the corporate executives) are permitted much flexibility in operating the corporation, and are protected from shareholder involvement in management affairs. This protection against shareholder interference is offset by certain fiduciary obligations imposed upon corporate management for the protection of shareholder interests. This chapter also examines management's fiduciary duties. The chapter concludes with a discussion of how the corporation's existence is terminated.

CORPORATE PURPOSES AND POWERS

Both business and legal theory hold that a corporation must have a purpose. Business theorists speak of corporate purpose in terms of "strategy," which is defined as the determination of fundamental long-term goals for the company and the adoption of courses of action and the allocation of resources necessary to achieve them. Strategy includes selecting target markets, defining products or services to address these markets, and determining the distribution system in a manner that is within the corporation's resources and capabilities.

Legal theorists view corporate purpose differently. A corporation's purpose is defined in the articles of incorporation and state statutory law under which the corporation is formed.

Closely related to the subject of proper purposes is the subject of proper powers. State law often sets forth the acts that a corporation may legally perform. These acts should be consistent with proper corporate purposes. If the corporation engages in an improper purpose or exercises an improper power, the purpose or act is declared to be "ultra vires" (beyond the corporation's power) and unenforceable. This is known as the *ultra vires* doctrine. Recent legislative developments have attached a declining role to this doctrine.

Corporate Purposes

The corporation's purpose is the reason for which the corporation is organized. This establishes the nature of its business and circumscribes the range of permissible corporate activities. Corporations need not be formed for a single purpose only; they may be organized to undertake as many purposes as the incorporators deem desirable. Section 3.01 of the Revised Model Business Corporation Act (RMBCA) provides that "Every corporation incorporated under this Act has the purpose of engaging in *any* lawful business unless a narrower purpose is set forth in the articles of incorporation." Implicit in this statement also is the requirement that a corporation formed under the general corporate law must have a profit-making purpose, since nonprofit corporations are usually organized under a separate statute.

Earlier in the evolution of corporation law, detailed descriptions of corporate purposes were required to be included in the articles of incorporation. This reflected the general mistrust of unchecked corporate activity. Under modern corporate codes, including the RMBCA, a generally worded purpose clause may be provided in the articles.

Sometimes incorporators desire to limit the activities of the corporation to the furtherance of a particular purpose. When this is the case a narrower purpose clause may be included in the articles, or a specific prohibition against certain activities may be stated. Because most modern corporate codes permit a "full purpose" clause to be included in the articles, the subject of what is a proper corporate purpose is of diminishing importance.

Corporate Powers

Closely related to the subject of corporate purposes is that of corporate powers. Corporate powers are those powers granted to the corporation by articles and statute to implement its overall objectives. Because corporate purposes and powers are to be compatible, the corporation's powers must be consistent with the corporation's stated purpose.

A corporation's powers may be express or implied. A corporation has express power to perform those acts authorized by the general corporation law of the state of incorporation and those acts authorized by its articles. Most states have express statutory provisions allowing corporations to sue and be sued, own property, borrow money, etc. Corporations also have implied powers to do whatever is reasonably necessary to promote their express powers, unless such acts are expressly prohibited by law. The trend is to construe broadly what is meant by reasonably necessary. Two current issues involving proper corporate powers are whether a corporation may join a partnership and whether a corporation may guarantee the debt of another—for example, one of its key employees.

The RMBCA codifies most of the permissible powers of a corporation. Two additional powers—the ability to indemnify directors, officers, and other employees, and the ability to purchase and dispose of its own shares—are provided. Many of the powers included in these sections were provided to remove doubt that existed with regard to certain activities. For example, Section 3.02(9) empowers the corporation to lend money and invest its funds. By statute the RMBCA also expands the scope of a corporation's implied powers. As mentioned, a corporation's implied powers usually include whatever is reasonably necessary to effectuate the corporation's express powers. Under RMBCA Section 3.02(16) the corporation is allowed "to ... do any other act not inconsistent with law, that furthers the business and affairs of the corporation."

The Ultra Vires Doctrine. Corporate transactions outside the corporation's purposes and powers are ultra vires (beyond the power). Under the doctrine of ultra vires the corporation is not responsible for transactions that were not authorized by its charter, the articles of incorporation, or the law of the state of incorporation. The older view was that ultra vires acts were void for lack of legal capacity, the reason being that the state had not given the corporation the power to do the particular act. Under this view the shareholders could not subsequently ratify the unauthorized corporate act because the transaction was void. The present view is that ultra vires transactions are voidable. If completely unperformed on both sides, neither party can bring an action on the contract. However, if the ultra vires transaction has been fully performed or executed on both sides, either party can bring an action on the contract. The doctrine does not apply to tortious or criminal conduct, because the lack of authorization is not considered an excuse for such conduct.

Two legal consequences *attach* to an ultra vires transaction: (1) the doctrine may serve as a *basis of liability* asserted by the state or shareholders to enjoin or set aside a corporate act and (2) the doctrine may serve as a *defense to liability* by the corporation arising from an unauthorized transaction, much in the same manner as a minor can defend against a contract claim by raising the defense of lack of contractual capacity. This second consequence has been criticized because it permits a corporation to reap the benefits from an ultra vires transaction while avoiding any of its burdens by raising the doctrine as a defense.

Because the use of the doctrine as a defense threatens the security of commercial transactions, the doctrine is in decline. Most statutes, including the RMBCA, severely limit the ultra

vires doctrine by stating that "corporate action may not be challenged on the ground that the corporation lacks power or lacked power to act" (Section 3.04[a]). The RMBCA limits challenges to the corporation's power to act to suits brought by the state Attorney General, suits by the corporation against officers or directors for previously authorizing an ultra vires act, and shareholder suits to enjoin ultra vires acts (Section 3.04[b]).

Additional Areas of Ultra Vires Vitality. As seen earlier, two legislative developments have resulted in the decline of the doctrine of ultra vires: (1) the elimination of the doctrine as a defense to creditor claims and (2) the expansion of permissible corporate powers. The doctrine retains vitality where the general corporation statute is silent on the subject. For example, the corporation's right to make charitable contributions is still uncertain in some states. According to the older view, corporations existed solely for the economic benefit of the shareholders; thus corporate charitable contributions were considered ultra vires unless a benefit to the corporation could be shown. Under this "corporate benefit rule" a corporate contribution to a business college, for example, would have to be supported by showing that the act was intended to create goodwill between the corporation and the college, which might provide the corporation with a pool of potential employees. Some state corporation codes are still silent on the subject of corporate charitable contributions, thus necessitating this type of analysis. However, present provisions in the federal income tax law allowing deductions for charitable contributions, along with the current concern for corporate social responsibility, have resulted in the amendment of three-quarters of states' corporation statutes to allow gifts for "the public welfare or for charitable, scientific or educational purposes."

Another area where the doctrine of ultra vires is presently applicable is that of corporate political activity. Although federal legislation currently regulates this kind of corporate activity, the courts have held that shareholders are not permitted to bring private suits under the federal law, thus relegating shareholders to state law and the doctrine of ultra vires. Presently the power to make political contributions is not specifically included in the RMBCA or most corporate statutes. The following case illustrates the application of the doctrine of ultra vires in the area of corporate political activity.

Marsili v. Pacific Gas and Electric Company

Court of Appeals of California
124 Cal. Rptr. 313 (1975)

Background: Marsili and two other stockholders (plaintiffs) initiated a derivative suit challenging the propriety of a $10,000 contribution made by Pacific Gas and Electric Company (PG&E) (defendants) to Citizens for San Francisco, an unincorporated association that advocated the defeat of Proposition T appearing on the ballot in the November 2, 1971 election for the city and county of San Francisco. (Proposition T was a nonpartisan initiative proposal that, if adopted, would have prohibited construction in San Francisco of any building more than 72 feet high without prior approval of the voters.) Plaintiffs argued that the contribution was ultra vires because neither PG&E's articles of incorporation nor the law of California permitted PG&E to make political contributions. They argued that the individual members of the board of directors of PG&E should be compelled to restore the $10,000 contribution to the Corporation. The lower court granted a motion for summary judgment made by the defendants and dismissed the complaint.

Decision: The California Court of Appeals ruled in favor of Pacific Gas and Electric Co.

Kane, Associate Justice

By definition adopted by plaintiffs themselves, "ultra vires" refers to an act which is beyond the powers conferred upon a corporation by its charter or by the laws of the state of incorporation.

The parties are in agreement that the powers conferred upon a corporation include both express powers, granted by charter or statute, and implied powers to do acts reasonably necessary to carry out the express powers. In California, the express powers which a corporation enjoys include the power to "do any acts incidental to the transaction of its business . . . or expedient for the attainment of its corporate purposes."

The articles of PG&E are manifestly consistent with this statutory imprimatur. Thus, for example, they authorize all activities and endeavors incidental or useful to the manufacturing, buying, selling, and distributing of gas and electric power, including the construction of buildings and other facilities convenient to the achievement of its corporate purposes, and the performance of "all things whatsoever that shall be necessary or proper for the full and complete execution of the purposes for which

. . . [the] corporation is formed, and for the exercise and enjoyment of all its powers and franchises."

In addition to the exercise of such express powers, the generally recognized rule is that the management of a corporation, "in the absence of express restrictions, has discretionary authority to enter into contracts and transactions which may be deemed reasonably incidental to its business purposes." In short, "a corporation has authority to do what will legitimately tend to effectuate . . . [its] express purposes and objects." California is in accord with this general rule also: " 'Whatever transactions are fairly incidental or auxiliary to the main business of the corporation and necessary or expedient in the protection, care and management of its property may be undertaken by the corporation and be within the scope of its corporated [sic] powers.' "

No restriction appears in the articles of PG&E which would limit the authority of its board of directors to act upon initiative or referendum proposals affecting the affairs of the company or to engage in activities related to any other legislative or political matter in which the corporation has a legitimate concern. Furthermore, there are no statutory prohibitions in California which preclude a corporation from participating in any type of political activity. In these circumstances, the contribution by PG&E to Citizens for San Francisco was proper if it can fairly be said to fall within the express or implied powers of the corporation.

The crux of the controversy at bench, therefore, is whether a contribution toward the defeat of a local ballot proposition can ever be said to be convenient or expedient to the achievement of legitimate corporate purposes. Appellants take the flat position that in the absence of express statutory authority, corporate political contributions are illegal. This contention cannot be sustained. We believe that where, as here, the board of directors reasonably concludes that the adoption of a ballot proposition would have a direct, adverse effect upon the business of the corporation, the board of directors has abundant statutory and charter authority to oppose it.

The law is clear that those to whom the management of the corporation has been entrusted are primarily responsible for judging whether a particular act or transaction is one which is helpful to the conduct of corporate affairs or expedient for the attainment of corporate purposes. . . . Indeed, a court cannot determine that a particular transaction is beyond the powers of a corporation unless it clearly appears to be so as a matter of law. With respect to the means which the corporation may adopt to further its objects and promote its business, its managers are not limited in law to the use of such means as are usual or necessary to the objects contemplated by their organization, but where not restricted by law, may choose such means as are convenient and adapted to the end, though they be neither the usual means, nor absolutely necessary for the purpose intended. . . .

Neither the court nor minority shareholders can substitute their judgment for that of the corporation "where its board has acted in good faith and used its best business judgment in behalf of the corporation."

Plaintiffs, as mentioned earlier, do not contend that the individual defendants acted in bad faith, or that they acted unreasonably or for an improper purpose. Accordingly, the judgment of the board of directors cannot be disturbed by the court unless it is held, as a matter of law, that the contribution could not be construed as incidental or expedient for the attainment of corporate purposes. For several reasons which we shall set forth, such a holding would simply not be reasonable in the light of the uncontradicted record below.

First, the Executive Committee of PG&E based its decision to authorize the contribution upon its judgment that the adoption of Proposition T would have an adverse impact upon the corporation and, in particular, would increase the tax rate applicable to the company's facilities and interfere with present and future building plans of the company, including the construction of the Embarcadero Substation.

Second, the Executive Committee considered the adoption of Proposition T to be detrimental to the City and County of San Francisco: specifically, by increasing taxes, it would have depressed business growth and, by imposing an immutable proscription on building heights, it would have rendered the Urban Design Plan ineffective.

Third, by requiring voter approval for the construction of any building more than 72 feet in height, the decision to construct necessary corporate facilities would depend upon the mood of the electorate rather than upon relevant business considerations. The corporation would thereby become embroiled in a contested political campaign every time it determined that it was in the corporation's interest to construct a building more than 72 feet in height.

Not only would the business judgment of the board of directors be subservient to the vagaries of an election campaign, but the cost of submitting such a proposal to the voters would undoubtedly be considerable. This is demonstrated by the very case at bench where in excess of $68,000 was spent by the supporters of Proposition T, and an even greater sum was spent by its opponents. These figures attest to the high cost of submitting a proposal to the voters and demonstrate the severe economic burden that the proposition would have imposed upon those seeking to comply with its terms.

The members of the Executive Committee of PG&E reasonably sought to avoid these consequences. Their judgment was not arbitrary or capricious but was based upon pertinent business considerations that were of direct and immediate concern to the corporation.

CORPORATE MANAGEMENT

Three groups participate in operating the corporation: the shareholders, the board of directors, and the corporate officers and executives. The following pages examine the management role of each of these groups. The material begins with a discussion of the role of shareholders, whose involvement in corporate management is indirect and therefore minimal. It proceeds to a discussion of the role of the board of directors, which is charged with the responsibility of setting corporation policy, and concludes with a look at the function of corporate officers and executives, to whom the day-to-day management of the corporation is delegated.

The Role of Shareholders

Shareholders have no direct control over corporate operations. They cannot command the board of directors or the corporate executives to undertake an activity or decide a matter in a particular way. Although ultimate control resides with the shareholders, they usually do not participate actively in corporate affairs. They can take action only by voting during a shareholders meeting. Shareholder suffrage at these meetings is usually confined to selecting the membership of the board of directors and approving certain extraordinary transactions. Little more than this minimal involvement is permitted of investors. If they are dissatisfied with their investment, they may sell their stock. However, if the corporate management has violated the corporate documents or otherwise incurred a liability toward the investors, the shareholders may bring suit against the responsible parties to recover any loss on behalf of the corporation or to recoup any loss to their investment.

Areas of Shareholder Involvement. There are usually two areas of shareholder involvement in corporate affairs: (1) the election of members of the board of directors and (2) the approval of certain extraordinary corporate transactions. Thus under the RMBCA shareholder participation is restricted to the annual election or removal of corporate directors, loans to employees and directors, sale of the corporation's assets outside the usual course of corporate business, any plan of merger or share exchange, and a voluntary dissolution of the corporation. Although some statutes require shareholder approval of bylaw amendments, the RMBCA does not. Of course, it is always permissible to increase the areas of shareholder involvement by appropriate provisions in the corporate articles and bylaws.

Shareholders Meetings. Because they are not agents of the corporation, shareholders cannot act individually; they can act only collectively at shareholders meetings. The RMBCA requires that an annual shareholders meeting be held at the times specified in the corporate bylaws. Sometimes it is necessary to have a special meeting of the shareholders for a particular purpose. The RMBCA further permits special meetings to be called by the board of directors, by the holders of more than 5 percent of the shares entitled to vote at the meeting, or by any person authorized to do so in the articles or bylaws.

Most statutes, including the RMBCA, require that notice of any shareholders meeting be provided to each shareholder of record entitled to vote at such a meeting. The RMBCA stipulates that the notice be in writing, stating the place, day, and hour of the meeting. In the case of a special meeting the notice must also include the purpose or purposes for which the meeting is called (Figure 36-1). The notice must be delivered not less than ten days or more than fifty days before the date of the meeting.

Unless the required notice is waived, failure to provide it voids any action taken at the meeting. A waiver may be made by a signed writing or evidenced by conduct, such as attending the meeting without objecting to the lack of notice. The RMBCA permits action to be taken without a shareholders meeting if written consent specifying the action to be taken is signed by all the shareholders entitled to vote on the matter.

A quorum of the shares entitled to vote, represented in person or by proxy, must be present before any action can take place at the shareholders meeting. Section 7.25 of the RMBCA provides that a majority of the voting shares shall constitute a quorum, unless the articles provide otherwise. However, the articles cannot provide for a quorum consisting of less than one-third of the voting shares.

The shareholders meeting is usually conducted according to the provisions of the corporate articles or bylaws, which generally provide that the board chairman or corporate president preside. Minutes of the meeting are customarily recorded by the corporate secretary. Shareholders are entitled to submit and speak upon proposals and resolutions during

FIGURE 36–1
Notice of Special Meeting of Shareowners

October 4, 1985

To the Common Stock Shareowners of
The Toledo Edison Company:

A special meeting of the Shareowners of The Toledo Edison Company ("Toledo Edison") will be held at the principal office of Toledo Edison, Edison Plaza, 300 Madison Avenue, Toledo, Ohio, on November 26, 1985 at 10:00 a.m., Toledo time, for the purpose of acting on the following matters:

1. To consider and vote upon a proposal to approve and adopt an Agreement and Plan of Reorganization between Toledo Edison and The Cleveland Electric Illuminating Company ("CEI") dated June 25, 1985, as amended, which agreement provides for simultaneous mergers of two subsidiaries of Centerior Energy Corporation (the "Holding Company") into Toledo Edison and CEI, respectively, with the result that Toledo Edison and CEI each will become subsidiaries of the Holding Company as described in the accompanying Joint Proxy Statement/Prospectus and the common stock shareowners of Toledo Edison and CEI will become common stock shareowners of the Holding Company; and to approve and adopt an Agreement of Merger among the Holding Company, Toledo Edison and the West Merger Company, a wholly-owned subsidiary of the Holding Company.

2. Any other matters which may properly come before the meeting.

Holders of record of Common Stock at the close of business on September 30, 1985 will be entitled to vote at the meeting.

By order of the Board of Directors,

STRATMAN COOKE, *Secretary*

Source: Douglas Whitman, F. William McCarty, Frank F. Gibson, Thomas W. Dunfee, Bartley A. Brennan, and John D. Blackburn, *Law and Business* (New York), Random House, 1987), p. 589. Copyright © 1987 by Thomas W. Dunfee, F. William McCarty, Frank F. Gibson, Douglas Whitman, John D. Blackburn, and Bartley A. Brennan.

the meeting. Recently shareholders who are concerned about social issues and politically active have used the shareholders meeting to submit proposals to limit the involvement of their corporations in certain activities, such as investing in countries that violate human rights or practice apartheid.

Because most voting at shareholders meetings is done by proxy and therefore the result is normally a foregone conclusion, the typical shareholders meeting is a well-orchestrated occasion designed to fulfill the formalities of corporate law. For this reason some scholars seriously question the continued practice of requiring an annual shareholders meeting. In what may very well be a harbinger of future development, Delaware no longer requires an annual meeting.

Voting. Shareholders function by voting on matters at the shareholders meeting. Each share of stock entitles its holder to one vote on each matter submitted to a vote, unless the corporate articles provide for more or less than one vote per share. Thus the holder of fifty shares is generally entitled to cast fifty votes. The RMBCA also authorizes the issuance of nonvoting shares. For example, preferred stock generally has no voting rights. However, even nonvoting stock is entitled to vote on certain extraordinary transactions, such as amendments to the corporate articles, mergers and consolidations, and dissolution of the corporation. To determine who is entitled to vote, the directors may set a date of record, and the person having legal title to the stock on the record date is entitled to vote the shares. A person acquiring legal title to the shares after the record date must obtain the proxy of the record title holder in order to vote them at the shareholders meeting.

Because a shareholder is entitled to one vote for each share held, the holder of 51 percent of the voting shares will have complete control over corporate operations. To assure minority shareholders some voice in corporate affairs, most statutes permit a shareholder to cumulate his or her votes for directors, meaning that the shareholder can cast as many votes for one candidate for director as there are directors to be elected, multiplied by the shareholder's number of shares. This form of proportional representation usually applies only to the election of directors. In some states cumulative voting is required by statute and cannot be refused in any election or eliminated in the corporate articles or bylaws. In other states it is permissive, meaning that cumulative voting can be eliminated in the corporate documents. Under the RMBCA cumulative voting is permissive.

Cumulative voting for directors is controversial. Proponents claim that it is necessary to assure a minority voice in corporate affairs. Opponents claim that minority representation means dissent in the boardroom.

A device for diluting the effect of cumulative voting is the staggered election of directors, because the fewer directors there are to be elected, the greater the number of shares that will be necessary to assure representation. This is allowed by the RMBCA, which permits boards consisting of nine or more directors to be divided into two or three classes, with each class being elected to a staggered three-year term. Since the RMBCA is permissive on the subject of cumulative voting, requiring the staggered election of directors in classes poses no problems. However, in states where cumulative voting is mandatory, the staggered election of directors is often prohibited.

A shareholder may vote either in person or by proxy. A proxy is a delegation of authority given by a shareholder to another person to vote his or her stock. A proxy is basically a special type of principal-agent relationship and therefore is subject to the rules of agency law as modified by special state statutes or by federal regulations under Section 14 of the Securities Exchange Act of 1934.

The RMBCA requires that a proxy be in writing. A telegram or cablegram should be sufficient. Some states, like California, require that the proxy be filed with the corporation before or at the shareholders meeting. A few states allow oral proxies.

Because the proxy is an agency, every appointment of a proxy is revocable. One way a shareholder may revoke a proxy is to attend and vote at the shareholders meeting. A proxy is not revocable if it is coupled with an interest, meaning that some consideration has been received by the shareholder for his or her delegation of voting rights—for example, an option or pledge to purchase the stock.

Even when proxies are irrevocable, statutes generally limit their duration. The RMBCA provides that the appointment of a proxy is valid for only eleven months after it is made unless otherwise provided in the proxy. Thus a proxy can extend beyond eleven months only if the writing specifies the date on which it is to expire or the length of time it is to continue in force.

Proxy solicitation by corporate management, insurgent shareholder groups, competing shareholder factions, or even outsiders has become a common and effective method of establishing or maintaining control over a corporation without actually purchasing enough stock to exert control. Section 14 of the Securities Exchange Act of 1934 and Rule 14a of the Securities and Exchange Commission (SEC) regulate proxy solicitation. Their purpose is to protect shareholders from misleading or concealed information in the solicitation of proxies. These proxy rules apply to corporations having more than 500 shareholders and assets of more than $1 million. They are discussed in detail in Chapter 37.

Because proxies are revocable, other devices for combining votes for control of the corporation are frequently used. Two such devices are the pooling agreement and the voting trust. A pooling agreement, sometimes called a voting agreement, is a contract entered into by several shareholders who mutually promise to vote their shares in a certain manner. In most states such agreements are specifically enforceable. Section 7.31 of the RMBCA provides that "a voting agreement under this section is specifically enforceable."

A voting trust is an agreement among shareholders to transfer their voting rights to a trustee, who is permitted to vote the shares in a block at the shareholders meeting according to the terms of the trust instrument. Courts are divided as to the legality of voting trusts at common law, but most statutes, including the RMBCA, provide for and limit them. Under the RMBCA a voting trust must be in writing. This writing, termed the "voting trust agreement," must specify the terms and conditions of the voting trust, and a copy of it must be deposited with the corporation. The shareholders must transfer their shares to the trustee and receive in return trust certificates, sometimes called certificates of beneficial ownership. The RMBCA also limits the life of a voting trust to ten years.

Inspection Rights. For a shareholder to exercise his or her voting rights intelligently, it may be necessary to have access to certain corporate information. Most statutes, including the RMBCA, recognize that the opposition to corporate management must be able to obtain a list of existing shareholders if it is ever to be successful in ousting management; therefore they grant shareholders an absolute right to examine and copy shareholder lists. Under the RMBCA the shareholder list must be available at the shareholders meeting.

The shareholder may also be able to obtain information contained in the corporate records. The RMBCA provides that a shareholder has a qualified right to certain corporate information. Section 16.01 requires that the corporate records of account, the minutes of shareholders and directors meetings, and a shareholders list are to be kept, usually at the corporation's principal place of business. Upon written demand five business days before the date on which a shareholder wishes to inspect, he or she may examine any of the relevant corporate records during reasonable working hours. The RMBCA permits an attorney or an agent, who could be an accountant, to accompany the shareholder or to make the inspection for the shareholder if the shareholder so wishes. The written demand must be in good faith and for a proper purpose. The right of inspection is limited to three classes of corporate records: minutes of meetings of the board and committees of the board, accounting records, and a record of shareholders.

What is a "proper purpose" or a request made in good faith is an issue left for the courts to decide. The following case illustrates the judicial approach to defining these terms.

National Consumers Union v. National Tea Company

Appellate Court of Illinois

302 N.E.2d 118 (1973)

Background: Jan Schakowsky and the National Consumers Union (NCU) (plaintiffs), shareholders of National Tea Company (National) (defendant), filed a petition for a writ of mandamus to compel National to permit them to examine the books and records of the corporation. Schakowsky was the owner of one share of the corporation for more than six months. NCU also owned one share but for less than six months. Plaintiffs argued that demands for records, minutes, books, and records of account were made in a reasonable manner, in good faith, and for a proper purpose. Defendant argued that NCU was seeking to "sensitize" National to NCU's brand of "consumer" demands by their own admission in a discovery deposition. The defendants argued that their motion for summary judgment should be granted as NCU expressed no proper purpose for inspecting the documents they wished to examine. The trial court granted defendants' motion for summary judgment.

Decision: Affirmed. The Appellate Court of Illinois ruled in favor of the defendant.

Lorenz, Justice

Plaintiffs first contend that the trial court erred in holding that N.C.U. had no rights of its own to examine defendants' books and records. Section 45 of the Business Corporation Act . . . gives shareholders the right to examine a corporation's books and records of account, its minutes, and its record of shareholders, if they hold their shares of record for at least six months preceding their demand or if they hold at least five percent of the corporation's outstanding shares. Furthermore, the books and records must be examined at a reasonble time and for a proper purpose. Shareholders may examine the books and records in person or through an agent or attorney. Section 45 also gives courts of competent jurisdiction discretion, upon a showing of proper purpose, to compel a corporation to allow shareholders, who do not otherwise meet the requirements of the section, to examine the books and records. Since the complaint does not allege that N.C.U. held its single share of stock for more than six months, it is clear that it had no right of its own to examine defendant's books and records.

The claim then made by both plaintiffs is that they showed a proper purpose for examining National's books and records, namely—to solicit proxies and that the court abused its discretion in denying them this right. We recognize that soliciting proxies is a proper purpose for examining shareholders lists and for examining a corporation's books and records.

We also agree with plaintiffs and the trial court that a single proper purpose is sufficient to satisfy the requirements of the statute. However, we also recognize that shareholders no longer have an absolute right to examine shareholders lists or corporate books and records. Now, the rights of minority stockholders must be balanced with the needs of the corporation upon the facts of each case.

In the instant case, the trial court determined that the evidence before it showed that plaintiffs had a speculative purpose at best. Although plaintiffs assert that they wanted to examine the books and records because they desired to solicit proxies, the evidence clearly showed that N.C.U. and Schakowsky had actually engaged in a course of conduct inimical to National's interest. Schakowsky admitted that they had urged shoppers not to frequent National's stores. On the basis of single shares of stock, the plaintiffs desire to go on a fishing expedition through National's books and records apparently searching for further ammunition to "sensitize" National to N.C.U.'s brand of "consumer" demands. Numerous cases . . . relied on by the trial court, indicate that such speculative purposes do not satisfy the requirements of having a proper purpose. On these facts we cannot say that the trial court erred in holding that plaintiffs had no proper purpose for examining National's books. Furthermore, although plaintiffs contend that they satisfied the statutory requirements for examining National's books, it is clear that they cannot satisfy those requirements without having a proper purpose.

Dividends. A dividend is a distribution paid to shareholders because of their stock ownership. It may be in cash, property (including the stock of other corporations), or the stock of the corporation itself. This latter type of dividend is referred to as a "stock dividend."

The RMBCA prohibits the declaration or payment of a dividend when the corporation is insolvent or when such a payment would render the corporation insolvent, meaning that the corporation is unable to pay its debts as they become due. Dividends can be lawfully declared and paid only out of the corporation's earned surplus under the traditional approach now used in most states. Earned surplus represents the profits realized on operations and investments. However, the RMBCA would permit dividends to be paid out by the board of directors based on financial statements prepared on the basis of accounting principles and practice that are "reasonable" under the circumstances, or on a fair evalua-

tion, or other method that is reasonable under the circumstances (Section 6.40[d]). The RMBCA retains an equity insolvency test but allows directors wider discretion in making judgments as to the future ability of the corporation to generate funds and remain solvent.

The directors have wide discretion concerning whether or not to declare a dividend. The shareholders ordinarily have no right to a dividend. The directors alone determine the amount of dividends and when they are to be distributed. A shareholder's "right" to a dividend normally materializes only after a dividend has been declared by the board.

Although courts usually do not disturb the discretion of directors with regard to a dividend declaration, there is an exception to this general rule. When there is a bad-faith refusal by the board of directors to declare a dividend, a court may use its equitable powers to compel a distribution. However, courts do not possess any equitable power to require a board of directors to declare dividends out of abundant earnings in the absence of fraud or abuse of discretion.

Preemptive Rights. If the articles of incorporation so provide, a shareholder has an option called a preemptive right that entitles the shareholder to subscribe to a newly authorized issue of shares in the same proportion that his or her present shares bear to all outstanding shares before new shares are offered to the public. Preemptive rights are aimed at preventing the dilution of the shareholder's equity in the corporation against his or her wishes. Under most state statutes presently on the books preemptive rights usually do not apply to treasury shares (meaning shares previously issued and reacquired by the corporation), previously authorized but unsold and unissued shares, or shares that are issued or agreed to be issued upon the conversion of convertible shares. Preemptive rights do not apply to these shares because such shares are not new issues but are part of previous offerings.

Since preemptive rights often interfere with the disposition of large issues of shares, many corporations restrict or eliminate this right. How preemptive rights may be restricted or eliminated depends on the particular statutory provision governing their application. Some statutes provide that preemptive rights exist unless otherwise provided in the articles. Under these statutes preemptive rights can be eliminated or limited only by an appropriate provision in the corporate articles. Other statutes provide that preemptive rights do not exist unless otherwise provided in the corporate articles. Under this approach for shareholders to have preemptive rights such rights must be expressly included in the articles of incorporation. The RMBCA adopts this latter approach.

Transfer of Shares. Generally a shareholder who is dissatisfied with corporate operations may freely transfer his or her shares to some-

one else. Such transfers traditionally have been governed by Article 8 of the Uniform Commercial Code (UCC) as adopted by most states today.

Under Article 8 a stock certificate can be validly transferred only by the delivery of the certificate and its indorsement by the registered owner. The indorsement may be on either the certificate itself or a separate instrument called a "stock power." The signature of the registered owner on the back of the certificate constitutes a valid indorsement. An indorsement of the certificate on a stock power alone does not transfer any rights unless the certificate is also delivered to the transferee. When a certificate has been delivered to a purchaser without the necessary indorsement, a transfer has been completed and the purchaser has a specifically enforceable right to compel any necessary indorsement. The effect of a valid transfer is to make the transferee the complete legal and equitable owner of the shares, and the corporation must register the transfer and recognize the transferee as the rightful owner.

Because it is considered to be sound public policy to promote the free transfer of property, a shareholder may freely transfer his or her shares. This is known as the doctrine of free alienability of property, or the doctrine of free alienation. Under this doctrine free alienability is considered an inherent attribute of corporate securities, and unreasonable restraints on alienation are invalid. However, the doctrine invalidates only unreasonable restraints on transfer; reasonable restrictions are permitted. To be valid, any such reasonable restriction must be noted conspicuously on the certificate.

Most jurisdictions recognize the right of corporations to impose restrictions giving the corporation or other shareholders the option to purchase the shares at an agreed-upon price before they are offered to third parties. This type of restriction is known as a "right of first refusal" and is most commonly imposed by close corporations in an attempt to restrict control if not total membership to a homogeneous shareholder group. However, restrictions giving the directors an option to purchase the shares at a price to be fixed at the directors' sole discretion are generally considered to be unreasonable restraints and therefore invalid.

Transfer restrictions are increasingly being resorted to today to police enforcement of the registration requirements of the Securities Act of 1933 against persons purchasing their securities in a transaction exempt from that act's registration requirements as one "not involving a public offering." Under the Securities Act shares issued pursuant to this private offering exemption must be held by the issuee as an investment and not for resale or public distribution. A subsequent sale may render the seller liable as an underwriter under the act and destroy the private offering exemption and render the issuer liable as well. To protect themselves, corporate issuers often require the issuee to sign a letter indicating his or her investment intent. Stock sold in this fashion is known as "lettered stock," but the letter alone is not an effective transfer restriction, because the restriction is not conspicuously included on the certificate pursuant to UCC Section 8–204. As additional protection, corporate issuers must print a legend on the face of the certificate stating that the shares are not transferred until registered, thus notifying potential purchasers that the corporation may refuse to recognize any transfer that will impair the exemption.

The RMBCA has added a provision seeking to codify court decisions that have ruled both for and against transfer restrictions. It authorizes transfer restrictions when imposed by the articles of incorporation, bylaws, and agreements among shareholders. Transfer restrictions are authorized to maintain the corporation's identity, to preserve exemptions under federal or state securities laws, and "for any other reasonable purpose."

Appraisal and Buy-Out Rights of Dissenting Shareholders. Certain kinds of extraordinary transactions, even though lawfully authorized and validly effected, entitle dissenting shareholders to have their shares purchased by the corporation at a fair cash value. This is referred to as the shareholder's appraisal and buy-out right. Its purpose is to effect a compromise between the overwhelming majority who desire a fundamental change in the corporate venture and the insistence of a dissenter not to be forced into a position different from that bargained for when he or she bought the stock.

The RMBCA recognizes five extraordinary transactions that give rise to an appraisal and buy-out right:

1. A merger or consolidation
2. A sale or exchange of all or substantially all of the corporate property and assets not in the regular course of business
3. The acquisition of the corporation by another through the exchange of the corporate stock
4. An amendment to the articles of incorporation that materially and adversely affects rights of a dissenter's shares
5. Any other corporate action that by virtue of the articles of incorporation, bylaws, or board resolution entitles shareholders to dissent, and be paid for their shares

However, the right does not apply to the shareholders of a surviving corporation in a merger if a vote of that corporation's shareholders is not necessary to authorize the merger. The right also does not apply when the corporation's shares are registered on a national securities exchange. Some states, such as Ohio, additionally grant appraisal rights when certain amendments to the corporate articles change the purpose of the corporation or adversely affect the class of shares owned by the dissenter.

Under the RMBCA the shareholder must

take certain procedural steps to effectuate an appraisal and buy-out remedy. If one of the transactions noted here is to be voted on, and dissenter rights are created, the dissenting shareholder must notify the corporation prior to the shareholders meeting that he or she intends to demand payment if the proposed action of management is approved. Then the shareholder must vote against the proposed action at the meeting. After majority approval has been obtained the dissenting shareholder must be notified how to demand payment and then make a written demand on the corporation for payment of the fair value of the shares. The corporation must respond with an offer to the shareholder of what it considers to be the fair value of the shares plus interest. If no agreement is reached, either party may petition the court in the county where the registered office of the corporation is located for an appraisal of the fair value of the shares. All dissenting shareholders will be made parties to the proceeding and will be bound by any judgment. In such a case the court may appoint one or more appraisers to recommend a fair value of the shares. The costs of the proceeding, including the expenses of the appraisers, will be assessed against the corporation unless the court determines that the shareholders' failure to accept the corporation's offer was arbitrary, vexatious, or not in good faith, in which case the cost and expenses will be apportioned among the dissenting shareholders.

When mergers or consolidations involve proxy offers or tender offers, they are subject to federal and state securities regulations discussed in Chapter 37. When merger combinations of sales or acquisitions of a corporation are contemplated, state and federal antitrust laws discussed in Chapter 44 may become important.

Shareholder Suits. Sometimes in order to enforce a right or to protect his or her investment, a shareholder must resort to legal action in the form of a lawsuit. Although the procedural aspects of shareholder litigation are of more concern to lawyers than to businesspeople, some awareness of the fundamentals of shareholder litigation is appropriate.

Shareholder litigation falls into two broad categories: (1) direct suits by shareholders on their own behalf and (2) derivative suits on behalf of the corporation. Direct actions by shareholders on their own behalf may be further subdivided into two additional categories: (a) individual actions and (b) class actions.

Direct suits by shareholders on their own behalf are limited to the enforcement of claims belonging to the shareholder based on his or her share ownership. When the injury is primarily to the shareholder, the shareholder may bring an action on his or her own behalf. If the injury is peculiar to the shareholder, the action will be an individual one. If the injury affects several shareholders or a class of shares, a class action may be pursued, with the shareholder initiating the action representing the entire class. In a shareholder class action the representative of the class brings suit on behalf of himself or herself individually and on behalf of all other shareholders who are similarly situated. Some examples of shareholder suits that may be brought individually or by way of class action are suits:

1. To enforce the right to vote
2. To sue for breach of a shareholder agreement
3. To enforce the right to inspect corporate books and records
4. To compel the payment of lawfully declared dividends
5. To protect preemptive rights
6. To compel corporate dissolution

When the injury to the shareholder's investment results from a wrong to the corporation rather than a wrong directed against the shareholder, a shareholder cannot bring a direct suit on his or her own behalf but must bring a derivative action on behalf of the corporation to enforce a right belonging to the corporation. Any judgment will go directly to the corporation, not to the shareholder who brings the action. The reason for this restriction is to avoid a multiplicity of litigation that might otherwise occur if all shareholders were permitted to bring direct actions on their own behalf for wrongs committed against the corporate entity. The restriction also is consistent with the separateness of corporate and shareholder interests recognized by the courts when the corporation is sued as a defendant. Although any remedy belongs to the corporation, theoretically the shareholder will also benefit from the judgment because any corporate remedy should also enhance the shareholder's investment.

The shareholder's derivative suit involves the assertion by a shareholder of a corporate cause of action against persons either in or out of the corporation who have allegedly wronged it. Such suits are brought where the corporation has failed to enforce such claims itself. Some examples of derivative suits would be actions:

1. To recover damages resulting from a consummated ultra vires act
2. To enjoin corporate officials from breaching their fiduciary duty to the corporation
3. To recover improperly paid dividends
4. To enjoin outsiders from wronging the corporation or to recover from such a wrong

Certain procedural prerequisites must be met in a shareholder's derivative suit. The plaintiff must have been a shareholder at the time the wrong was committed against the corporation or have acquired the shares by operation of law (such as through the distribution of a decedent's estate) from someone who was a holder of record at that time. The shareholder must also show that he or she has exhausted internal corporate remedies, describing with particularity the efforts, if any, made to obtain the desired action from the directors and, if necessary, from the shareholders, and providing the reasons for any failure to obtain the action or for not making the effort. A derivative proceeding, once begun, cannot be discontinued or settled without court approval.

The Role of the Board of Directors

Although the shareholders are the owners of the corporation, the board of directors is the supreme power in the management of the corporation. The following pages examine the nature of the board's authority, the appointment of directors to the board, and the formalities of board functions.

Nature of Board Authority. Although the board of directors is charged by statute with the duty of managing the corporation, it is generally recognized that the purpose of the board is only to establish policy and to provide direction to the corporation. Recent legislative developments reflect a trend toward recognizing this reality.

Most state statutes say that the business affairs of the corporation "shall be managed by a board of directors." Recently many commentators have voiced concern that such language may be interpreted to mean that the directors must become involved in the detailed administration of the corporation's affairs. Although requiring such involvement is reasonable in closely held corporations, recent developments make such an expectation unreasonable in today's complex corporations. Noteworthy among these developments is the advent of outside directors, who are individuals from outside the corporate management and not otherwise involved with the corporation. The RMBCA seeks to clarify board responsibility and bring it into accord with the realities of today's corporations, particularly the large diversified enterprise. Section 8.01

ETHICS BOX
Ethics and Boards of Directors

In recent years Delaware and New York courts, two trend-setting states in the area of corporate law, have ruled that they will accept the findings of litigation committees of boards of directors when a company is sued by shareholders. Usually, but not always, these committees are made up of outside directors. Those in favor of litigation committees argue that they represent the most efficient way for both the company and the shareholders to handle a suit; otherwise both may be faced with several years of discovery proceedings before getting to trial. Those who oppose such committees raise ethical questions posed here:

1. If the members of a litigation committee are picked by the board of directors of the corporation that is being sued, will they be able to make an objective decision?
2. If "outside directors" are picked for a committee, will they be truly independent in light of the fact that they tend to belong to the same clubs, travel in the same professional circles, have similar attitudes, and are chosen by inside management to sit on boards initially?
3. Do members of the litigation committees of a board of directors have conflicting ethical and legal obligations? Is there fiduciary obligation to the majority shareholders of the corporation, or is there a higher obligation to render an independent judgment on a suit brought by shareholders while a member of a litigation committee?

---

now provides that the business and affairs of the corporation shall be managed *"under the direction"* of a board of directors. The RMBCA eliminates any ambiguity regarding the role of the board of directors in formulating major management policy as opposed to direct day-to-day management. Only a few state statutes, such as Delaware's and California's, have similar provisions, although a trend exists toward adopting such language.

Generally the board's responsibility may be broadly described as establishing basic corporate objectives, selecting competent senior executives, monitoring personnel policies and procedures with a view to assuring that the corporation is provided with other competent managers in the future, reviewing the performance of senior executives, and monitoring the corporation's performance. Typical matters over which the board has control include dividends, financing, and corporate policy as to the prices of its products, expansion, and labor relations. More specifically, the board of directors is also required or authorized to: call special shareholders meetings, elect corporate officers, declare dividends, recommend dissolution, approve any merger or consolidation, change the registered office or registered agent, allocate to capital surplus consideration received for shares having no par value, cancel reacquired shares, and approve amendments to the corporate bylaws.

Appointment of Directors. Under the RMBCA the initial directors may be named in the articles of incorporation. These directors may be "dummy directors" who serve only until the first shareholders meeting and then resign. The RMBCA does not require that the number and names of the directors constituting the initial board be stated in the articles. Except for the first board, the number of directors may be established by either the corporate articles or the bylaws. The effect of this is to permit the directors to retain for themselves the power to change the number of directors without seeking shareholder approval. This is because under Section 2.06 of the RMBCA, the power to amend the bylaws is vested solely in the board unless reserved to the shareholders by the articles, whereas amendments to the articles require shareholder approval. Thus, by providing for the number of directors only in the bylaws, the directors may reserve for themselves the power to determine their number.

Until recently most state statutes required a minimum of three directors. However, the trend, as illustrated by Section 8.03 of the RMBCA, is to allow for only one director. This eliminates the need for single-shareholder corporations to enlist superfluous directors.

Although traditionally shareholders elect the directors from among their ranks, most statutes specifically provide that directors need not be shareholders of the corporation. Furthermore, few statutes impose age and residency requirements upon directors. For example, the RMBCA specifically states that "directors need not be residents of this State . . ." (Section 8.02). However, these and other requirements may be prescribed in the corporate articles. Thus, if it is felt that a real financial stake in the success of the enterprise will likely increase both vigilance and diligence, the articles may provide a requirement of substantial stock ownership by directors. Such stock is generally called a director's qualifying stock.

Federal legislation affecting board composition may disqualify some individuals from becoming directors. Interlocking directorates of competing corporations are restricted by Section 8 of the Clayton Act. This statute forbids someone from serving as a director of two or more competing corporations if one corporation has capital, surplus, and undivided profits aggregating more than $1 million and if the elimination of competition between them would constitute a violation of federal antitrust laws.

Aside from the members of the initial board, directors are elected at the annual shareholders meeting and usually hold office until the next annual meeting. Section 8.03 of the RMBCA provides, "Directors are elected at the first annual meeting of shareholders and at each annual meeting thereafter. . . ." However, under the RMBCA directors may serve staggered terms in corporations having nine or more directors if the articles authorize the classification of directors. When there is a classification of directors the terms of the classes into which the directors are divided will expire serially and will be longer than one year. For example, a board of nine directors may be divided into three classes with three directors in each class. After the first two years each director will serve for three years, and three directors will be elected each year.

Vacancies may occur on the board as the result of the resignation, death, or removal of an incumbent director or as the result of an increase in the number of directors. Many statutes provide that any vacancy on the board must be filled by a vote of the shareholders. The RMBCA allows the shareholders or the remaining directors to fill the vacancy. Under the RMBCA a director elected to fill a vacancy created by an incumbent is elected until the next shareholders meeting at which directors are elected. Any director elected to fill a vacancy created by an increase in the number of directors serves only until the next election of directors by shareholders.

Although directors may be removed from the board by failure to obtain reelection at the annual shareholders meeting, a stickier question is presented when the removal is to occur during the director's term of office. In the absence of a statute or a provision in the articles the courts do not permit shareholders to remove a director without cause. Thus, at common law, directors can be removed during their terms only for cause. Exactly what constitutes cause is often unclear. Today most statutes permit a majority of the voting shareholders to remove a director or the entire board "with or without cause" before the end of his or her term at a special shareholders meeting called expressly for that purpose.

Formalities of Board Functions. The general common-law rule is that a director can act as a part of the board of directors only at a proper meeting of the board. Under this approach the board cannot act unless it is formally convened. Informal action is insufficient; the directors have to be physically present at the meeting and cannot vote by proxy. The reason for this is to encourage consultation among board members as a body. Today most statutes establish a contrary rule and allow board members to act informally without a meeting upon the written consent of all board members. The RMBCA also allows board members to participate in board meetings via a telephone conference call.

Board meetings may be held either in or outside the state of incorporation. The time for board meetings is included in the corporate bylaws; therefore, a director is considered to have constructive notice of all regular board meetings. Many statutes provide that if there is no provision to the contrary in the bylaws, the directors must be given notice of the time and topic of all specially called meetings. The RMBCA provides only that such notice as required by the bylaws must be given, and it also states that neither the business to be trans-

acted nor the purpose of any special meeting must be specified in the notice unless required by the bylaws. When notice is required by the bylaws the RMBCA states that a director's attendance at the meeting constitutes a waiver of the required notice, unless the director attends to object to the meeting.

Under the RMBCA, unless the articles or bylaws provide a greater number, a majority of the board members constitutes a quorum for a meeting of the directors. A majority vote of the quorum constitutes a binding act of the board.

The RMBCA permits the articles or bylaws to authorize the board to designate an executive committee or other committees composed of board members to exercise all the authority of the board except in extraordinary matters, such as article amendments, mergers, and so on. Executive committees function between board meetings and are especially useful when the board of directors is large and when consideration of specific matters by the smaller group will facilitate decision making. Finance and audit committees, with duties relating to corporate finance and the selection of auditors, are less common.

The Role of Officers and Executives

It is generally recognized that the board of directors is not expected to operate the corporate business. The board delegates the day-to-day management to the corporate officers and executives, who are elected by the board and serve at the board's discretion. The RMBCA provides that "A corporation has the officers described in its bylaws or appointed by the board of directors . . ." (Section 8.40). Unlike most state statutes today, the RMBCA does not require that there be a president, vice-president, and treasurer, but leaves the number and titles of officers to the bylaws or the board. This is especially important for small corporations. The officers are regarded as agents of the corporation, having such authority as is conferred by the bylaws or by a board resolution.

MANAGEMENT'S FIDUCIARY OBLIGATIONS

As already observed, those who control and manage modern corporations are protected against interference from shareholders in the handling of corporate affairs. Thus individual shareholders are generally powerless to affect corporate affairs in the case of large-scale organizations. However, this virtual disenfranchisement of the shareholder is not so oppressive as it appears. In partial recognition of these realities, corporate and securities law in recent times have substantially strengthened the fiduciary obligations of management and of other controlling persons to both the corporation and to the shareholder.

Fiduciary Duty to the Corporation

Directors and officers owe fiduciary duties to the corporation similar to the fiduciary duties that agents owe their principals. These fiduciary duties fall broadly into two categories: (1) the duty of loyalty and (2) the duty of care.

Duty of Loyalty. Corporate directors and officers occupy a fiduciary relationship with the corporation, which requires the exercise of good faith and loyalty in any dealings with and for the corporation. The basic principle is that corporate directors and officers should not use their positions to make personal profits or to gain other personal advantages. In principle, this duty of loyalty is similar to the duty of loyalty exercised by agents and partners; however, this duty is owed to the corporate entity, not to the shareholders. The duty arises most frequently in transactions between the corporation and the corporate official involving possible conflict of interest or when a corporate opportunity comes to the attention of the corporate official.

Conflicts of interest between officers and directors and their corporations can occur whenever a transaction takes place between the corporation and them. The RMBCA does not prohibit a transaction between a director and the corporation in which the director has a financial interest as long as the transaction was fair when authorized, or was ratified by the board of directors. When a transaction is contested the burden of proof to establish fairness falls on the person charged with having a conflict. The person charged has the burden to show there was full disclosure of the conflict and approval by disinterested directors or shareholders.

The general rule is that a corporation has a prior claim to opportunities for business and profits that may be regarded as incidental to its business. Such an opportunity is called a "corporate opportunity," and directors and officers cannot acquire this business opportunity to the detriment of the corporation. Usurpation of a corporate opportunity is normally dealt with by imposing a constructive trust on the wrongful director or officer, meaning that he or she is deemed to hold the benefits of the bargain for the corporation. When an opportunity that is relevant to the corporation's present or prospective business activities comes to the attention of a corporate director or officer, he or she must first offer it to the corporation. Only after a disinterested board determines that the corporation should not pursue the opportunity may the corporate officer or director pursue the matter for his or her own account. However, if the corporation is financially unable to take advantage of the opportunity, the officer or director need not present it to the corporation. The following case clearly illustrates the corporate opportunity doctrine.

Guth v. Loft, Inc.

Supreme Court of Delaware

5 A.2d 503 (1939)

Background: Loft (plaintiff) filed a complaint in the Court of Chancery against Charles Guth, Grace Company, and Pepsi-Cola Company (defendants) seeking to impress a trust in favor of Loft upon all shares of capital stock of Pepsi-Cola registered in the name of Guth and Grace (approximately 91 percent of the capital stock).

Guth became the president and general manager of Loft in 1931. Loft manufactured and sold candies, syrups, and beverages in 115 retail stores along the Middle Atlantic seaboard and had wholesale activities amounting to $800,000 in sales. Its total assets exceeded $9,000,000 in 1931. When Coca-Cola refused to give Guth a jobber's discount based on volume of purchases made by Loft, Guth found out that Pepsi-Cola could be purchased for considerably less. When Pepsi-Cola was adjudicated bankrupt in 1931, one Megargel, an officer and major stockholder of that company, and Guth entered into an agreement whereby 50 percent of the stock of Pepsi-Cola went to Grace, a corporation owned by Guth's family that made syrups for soft drinks and that sold some syrup to Loft. Through several other transactions with Megargel, Guth came to own another 41 percent of Pepsi-Cola stock. During this period 1931–35, Guth borrowed heavily from Loft, and Grace became insolvent. Additionally, without the knowledge of the board of directors, Guth used Loft's facilities, materials, credit, executives, and employees at will. Some reimbursement was made for wages to workers. Loft suffered a loss of profits in its retail stores estimated at $300,000. Guth had discarded Coca-Cola and spent $20,000 advertising Pepsi-Cola.

Guth claimed that in 1931 he had offered Loft's board of directors the opportunity to take over Pepsi-Cola but they had declined for the following reasons: Pepsi-Cola was a failure, they did not wish to compete with Coca-Cola, the proposition was not in line with Loft's business, and it was not equipped to carry on such a business on the extensive scale needed. Guth also claimed that the board in August, 1933 consented to Loft's extending to Guth its facilities and resources without limit upon Guth's guarantee of all advances and upon Guth's contract to furnish Loft a supply of syrup at a favorable price. No record of these actions was found in contract form or in the minutes of meetings of Loft's board of directors. The lower court found in favor of Loft.

Decision: Affirmed. The Supreme Court of Delaware ruled in favor of Loft.

Layton, Chief Justice

Corporate officers and directors are not permitted to use their position of trust and confidence to further their private interests. While technically not trustees, they stand in a fiduciary relation to the corporation and its stockholders. A public policy, existing through the years, and derived from a profound knowledge of human characteristics and motives, has established a rule that demands of a corporate officer or director, peremptorily and inexorably, the most scrupulous observance of his duty, not only affirmatively to protect the interests of the corporation committed to his charge, but also to refrain from doing anything that would work injury to the corporation, or to deprive it of profit or advantage which his skill and ability might properly bring to it, or to enable it to make in the reasonable and lawful exercise of its powers. The rule that requires an undivided and unselfish loyalty to the corporation demands that there shall be no conflict between duty and self-interest. The occasions for the determination of honesty, good faith and loyal conduct are many and varied, and no hard and fast rule can be formulated. The standard of loyalty is measured by no fixed scale.

If an officer or director of a corporation, in violation of his duty as such, acquires gain or advantage for himself, the law charges the interest so acquired with a trust for the benefit of the corporation, at its election, while it denies to the betrayer all benefit and profit. The rule, inveterate and uncompromising in its rigidity, does not rest upon the narrow ground of injury or damage to the corporation resulting from a betrayal of confidence, but upon a broader foundation of a wise public policy that, for the purpose of removing all temptation, extinguishes all possibility of profit flowing from a breach of the confidence imposed by the fiduciary relation. Given the relation between the parties, a certain result follows; and a constructive trust is the remedial device through which precedence of self is compelled to give way to the stern demands of loyalty.

The rule, referred to briefly as the rule of corporate opportunity, is merely one of the manifestations of the general rule that demands of an officer or director the utmost good faith in his relation to the corporation which he represents.

The real issue is whether the opportunity to secure a very substantial stock interest in a corporation to be formed for the purpose of exploiting a cola beverage on a wholesale scale was so closely associated with the existing business activities of Loft, and so essential thereto, as to bring the transaction within that class of cases where the acquisition of the property would throw the corporate officer purchasing it into competition with his company. This is a factual question to be decided by reasonable inferences from objective facts.

The facts and circumstances demonstrate that Guth's appropriation of the Pepsi-Cola opportunity to himself placed him in a competitive position with Loft with respect to a commodity essential to it, thereby rendering his personal interest incompatible with the superior interests of his corporation; and this situation was accomplished, not openly and with his own resources, but secretly and with the money and facilities of the corporation which was committed to his protection.

Although the facts and circumstances disclosed by the voluminous record clearly show gross violations of legal and moral duties by Guth in his dealings with Loft, the appellants make bold to say that no duty was cast upon Guth, hence he was guilty of no disloyalty. The fiduciary relation demands something more than the morals of the market place. Guth's abstractions of Loft's money and materials are complacently referred to as borrowings. Whether his acts are to be deemed properly cognizable in a civil court at all, we need not inquire, but certain it is that borrowing is not descriptive of them. A borrower presumes a lender acting freely. Guth took without limit or stint from a helpless corporation, in violation of a statute enacted for the protection of corporations against such abuses, and without the knowledge or authority of the corporation's Board of Directors. Cunning and craft supplanted sincerity. Frankness gave way to concealment. He did not offer the Pepsi-Cola opportunity to Loft, but captured it for himself. He invested little or no money of his own in the venture, but commandeered for his own benefit and advantage the money, resources and facilities of his corporation and the services of its officials. He thrust upon Loft the hazard, while he reaped the benefit. His time was paid for by Loft. The use of the Grace plant was not essential to the enterprise. In such manner he acquired for himself and Grace ninety-one percent of the capital stock of Pepsi, now worth many millions. A genius in his line he may be, but the law makes no distinction between the wrongdoing genius and the one less endowed.

Upon a consideration of all the facts and circumstances as disclosed we are convinced that the opportunity to acquire the Pepsi-Cola trademark and formula, goodwill and business belonged to the complainant, and that Guth, as its President, had no right to appropriate the opportunity to himself.

Duty of Care. Corporate officers and directors are charged with affirmative duties concerning the management and control of the business of their corporations, and they are liable for any corporate losses resulting from their negligence. As recently amended, the RMBCA sets forth the duty of care for corporate directors as follows:

[a] A director shall discharge his duties as a director, including his duties as a member of a committee:

1. in good faith;
2. with the care an ordinary prudent person in a like position would exercise; and
3. when exercising his business judgment with the belief, premised on a rational basis, that his decision is in the "best interests of the corporation" Section 8.30

The drafters' comment explains the applications of this standard as follows:

By combining the requirement of good faith with the statement that a director must act (1) "with such care as an ordinary prudent person in a like position would use under similar circumstances" and (2) "when exercising his business judgment . . .," Section 8.30(a) incorporates the familiar concept that a director should not be held liable for an honest mistake of business judgment if these criteria are satisfied (Official Comment).

This is known as the "business judgment rule."

Section 8.30 further permits a director to rely on information, opinions, and statements prepared by corporate officials and consultants whom the director reasonably believes are reliable and competent, and any board committees on which he or she does not serve regarding matters within their designated authority.

The following case illustrates an application of the business judgment rule, where directors and officers were held personally liable.

Smith v. Van Gorkom

Supreme Court of Delaware

488 A.2d 858 (1985)

Background: Smith (plaintiff) initiated a class action suit on behalf of the shareholders of Trans Union Corporation ("Trans Union" or "the Company") against Van Gorkom, the Chief Executive Officer (CEO), members of the Board of Directors ("Board"), and others (defendants) seeking a rescission of a cash buy-out merger of Trans Union into a new corporation. Alternatively, money damages were sought against the board of directors of Trans Union, and the newly merged corporation. Van Gorkom, a certified public accountant and lawyer, had been CEO for seventeen years and chairman of the board for two years prior to the transaction described here. He was approaching 65 years of age and mandatory retirement. He was familiar with acquisition procedures, valuation methods, and negotiations in merger situations. Beginning September 5, 1980, he held several private meetings with one Jay Pritzker, a well-known acquirer of corporations, and convinced the latter that he should make a cash-buy-out merger offer for Trans Union at $55 per share. On September 18 Pritzker advised his attorney, a merger and acquisition specialist, to begin drafting merger documents. Pritzker insisted on September 19 that Trans Union's Board of Directors act by September 21 on his proposal. After obtaining financing from Trans Union's lead bank on September 19 Van Gorkom called for a meeting of senior management and scheduled a Board meeting the next day. Trans Union's investment bankers (Solomon Brothers) were not present at the Senior Management meeting. Donald Romans, Chief Financial Officer of Trans Union, reported that a study he prepared showed the price range of a leveraged buyout by management would be between $55 and $65 per share. Van Gorkom never saw the study and did not make it available to the Board. Senior management's reaction to the Pritzker proposal was negative based on the $55 price, the adverse tax consequences to many shareholders, and the closing out of potential higher bids if an auction took place. Nevertheless, the Board met the following day to discuss the proposal. After a 20-minute oral presentation by Van Gorkom of his understanding of the Pritzker offer, and a brief statement by the Chief Financial Officer on his preliminary study of the buyout (without his evaluation of Trans Union's worth or whether $55 per share was a fair price), the directors approved the proposed merger agreement. Neither Van Gorkom nor any member of the Board had seen copies of the merger agreement prior to voting as they were delivered too late. The total length of the meeting was two hours. The Board claimed that several conditions were attached to its acceptance among which was the fact that Trans Union reserved the right to accept any better offer during a ninety-day period following its acceptance. The minutes of the Board meeting do not reflect this. Nonetheless, after amending the merger agreement with Pritzker, Solomon Brothers solicited offers from October 21, 1980 to January 21, 1981 producing only one serious suitor, General Electric Credit Corporation, which was unwilling to make an offer unless Trans Union rescinded the agreement it had with Pritzker. Shareholder approval took place on February 10, 1981. The Delaware Court of Chancery found that the Board's approval of the Pritzker merger proposal fell within the protection of the business judgment rule, and that the Board was not reckless or imprudent, but informed.

Decision: Reversed. The Supreme Court of Delaware ruled in favor of the plaintiffs, Smith and other shareholders.

Horsey, Justice

The plaintiffs contend that the Court of Chancery erred as a matter of law by exonerating the defendant directors under the business judgment rule without first determining whether the rule's threshold condition of "due care and prudence" was satisfied. The plaintiffs assert that the Trial Court found the defendant directors to have reached an informed business judgment on the basis of "extraneous considerations and events that occurred after September 20, 1980." The defendants deny that the Trial Court committed legal error in relying upon post–September 20, 1980 events and the directors' later acquired knowledge. The defendants further submit that their decision to accept $55 per share was informed because: (1) they were "highly qualified"; (2) they were "well-informed"; and (3) they deliberated over the "proposal" not once but three times.

The standard of care applicable to a director's duty of care has been recently restated by this Court. In *Aronson,* we stated:

> While the Delaware cases use a variety of terms to describe the applicable standard of care, our analysis satisfies us that under the business judgment rule director liability is predicated upon concepts of gross negligence. (footnote omitted)

We again confirm that view. We think the concept of gross negligence is also the proper standard for determining whether a business judgment reached by a board of directors was an informed one.

On the record before us, we must conclude that the Board of Directors did not reach an informed business judgment on September 20, 1980 in voting to "sell" the Company for $55 per share pursuant to the Pritzker cash-out merger proposal. Our reasons, in summary, are as follows:

The directors (1) did not adequately inform themselves as to Van Gorkom's role in forcing the "sale" of the Company and in establishing the per share purchase price; (2) were uninformed as to the intrinsic value of the Company; and (3) given these circumstances, at a minimum, were grossly negligent in approving the "sale" of the Company upon two hours' consideration, without prior notice, and without the exigency of a crisis or emergency.

As has been noted, the Board based its September 20 decision to approve the cash-out merger primarily on Van Gorkom's representations. None of the directors, other than Van Gorkom and Chelberg, had any prior knowledge that the purpose of the meeting was to propose a cash-out merger of Trans Union. No members of Senior Management were present, other than Chelberg, Romans and Peterson; and the latter two had only learned of the proposed sale an hour earlier. Both general counsel Moore and former general counsel Browder attended the meeting, but were equally uninformed as to the purpose of the meeting and the documents to be acted upon.

Without any documents before them concerning the proposed transaction, the members of the Board were required to rely entirely upon Van Gorkom's 20-minute oral presentation of the proposal. No written summary of the terms of the merger was presented; the directors were given no documentation to support the adequacy of $55 price per share for sale of the Company; and the Board had before it nothing more than Van Gorkom's statement of his understanding of the substance of an agreement which he admittedly had never read, nor which any member of the Board had ever seen.

Under 8 Del.C. Sec. 141(e), "directors are fully protected in relying in good faith on reports made by officers." The term "report" has been liberally construed to include reports of informal personal investigations by corporate officers. However, there is no evidence that any "report," as defined under Sec. 141(e), concerning the Pritzker proposal, was presented to the Board on September 20. Van Gorkom's oral presentation of his understanding of the terms of the proposed Merger Agreement, which he had not seen, and Romans' brief oral statement of his preliminary study regarding the feasibility of a leveraged buy-out of Trans Union do not qualify as Sec. 141(e) "reports" for these reasons: the former lacked substance because Van Gorkom was basically uninformed as to the essential provisions of the very document about which he was talking. Romans' statement was irrelevant to the issues before the Board since it did not purport to be a valuation study. At a minimum for a report to enjoy the status conferred by Sec. 141(e), it must be pertinent to the subject matter upon which a board is called to act, and otherwise be entitled to good faith, not blind, reliance. Considering all of the surrounding circumstances—hastily calling the meeting without prior notice of its subject matter, the proposed sale of the Company without any prior consideration of the issue or necessity therefore, the urgent time constraints imposed by Pritzker, and the total absence of any documentation whatsoever—the directors were duty bound to make reasonable inquiry of Van Gorkom and Romans, and if they had done so, the inadequacy of that upon which they now claim to have relied would have been apparent.

We do not imply that an outside valuation study is essential to support an informed business judgment; nor do we state that fairness opinions by independent investment bankers are required as a matter of law. Often insiders familiar with the business of a going concern are in a better position than are outsiders to gather relevant information; and under appropriate circumstances, such directors may be fully protected in relying in good faith upon the valuation reports of their management.

Here, the record establishes that the Board did not request its Chief Financial Officer, Romans, to make any valuation study or review of the proposal to determine the adequacy of $55 per share for sale of the Company. On the record before us: The Board rested on Romans' elicited response that the $55 figure was within a "fair price range" within the context of a leveraged buy-out. No director sought any further information from Romans. No director asked him why he put $55 at the bottom of his range. No director asked Romans for any details as to his study, the reason why it had been undertaken or its depth. No director asked to see the study; and no director asked Romans whether Trans Union's finance department could do a fairness study within the remaining 36-hour period available under the Pritzker offer.

Had the Board, or any member, made an inquiry of Romans, he presumably would have responded as he testified: that his calculations were rough and preliminary; and that the study was not designed to determine the fair value of the Company, but rather to assess the feasibility of a leveraged buy-out financed by the Company's projected cash flow, making certain assumptions as to the purchaser's borrowing needs. Romans would have presumably also informed the Board of his view, and the widespread view of Senior Management, that the timing of the offer was wrong and the offer inadequate.

The record also establishes that the Board accepted without scrutiny Van Gorkom's representation as to the fairness of the $55 price per share for sale of the Company—a subject that the Board had never previously considered. The Board thereby failed to discover that Van Gorkom had suggested the $55 price to Pritzker and, most crucially, that Van Gorkom had arrived at the $55 figure based on calculations designed solely to determine the feasibility of a leveraged buy-out. No questions were raised either as to the tax implications of a cash-out merger or how the price for the one million share option granted Pritzker was calculated.

We do not say that the Board of Directors was not entitled to give some credence to Van Gorkom's representation that $55 was an adequate or fair price. Under Sec. 141(e), the directors were entitled to rely upon their chairman's opinion of value and adequacy, provided that such opinion was reached on a sound basis. Here, the issue is whether the directors informed themselves as to all information that was reasonably available to them. Had they done so, they would have learned of the source and derivation of the $55 price and could not reasonably have relied thereupon in good faith.

None of the directors, Management or outside, were investment bankers or financial analysts. Yet the Board did not consider recessing the meeting until a later hour that day (or requesting an extension of Pritzker's Sunday evening deadline) to give it time to elicit more information as to the sufficiency of the offer, either from inside Management (in particular Romans) or from Trans Union's own investment banker, Solomon Brothers, whose Chicago specialist in merger and acquisitions was known to the Board and familiar with Trans Union's affairs.

Thus, the record compels the conclusion that on September 20 the Board lacked valuation information adequate to reach an informed business judgment as to the fairness of $55 per share for sale of the Company.

We conclude that Trans Union's Board was grossly negligent in that it failed to act with informed reasonable deliberation in agreeing to the Pritzker merger proposal on September 20; and we further conclude that the Trial Court erred as a matter of law in failing to address that question before determining whether the directors' later conduct was sufficient to cure its initial error.

Fiduciary Duty to Shareholders

In early court decisions the directors and officers of a corporation were said to have no fiduciary duty to existing or potential stockholders but solely to the corporation. More recently there has been a trend in decisions finding a duty on the part of officers, directors, employees of the corporation, as well as employees of investment banking firms retained by the corporation, to disclose information obtained as a result of being insiders. At the federal level, the Securities Exchange Act addressed itself to disclosure requirements for officers and directors and to what constitutes insider trading. Chapter 37 on the Securities and Exchange Commission will discuss these and other topics in detail.

While the "business judgment" rule has given officers and directors wide latitude in managing a corporation, minority shareholders have recently been filing suits alleging that

BOX 36-1 ISSUES AND TRENDS

Following *Smith* v. *Van Gorkom* examined here, the Delaware Supreme Court and the federal courts have scrutinized carefully board of directors' decisions in what are referred to as "control" situations; that is, where control of the corporation is threatened by investors outside the corporation such as in *Smith*, or when officers of the corporation seek to gain control by a leveraged buyout (using the assets of the corporation to finance a buyout and take the company private). With the number of mergers and leveraged buyouts taking place in the 1980s, the courts in these situations no longer presume boards of directors have correctly applied the business judgment rule. The courts have offered guidelines for directors, officers, and shareholders to follow in "control" situations:

1. The board of directors should have a preponderance of outside directors, or at minimum a committee of outside directors that weighs a takeover or leveraged buyout proposal and any defensive measures that are to be taken.
2. Defensive measures should generally be enacted only when there is a specific pending threat, or the industry environment is such that takeovers are frequent.
3. When a board of directors is involved in the takeover process it should seek advice from in-house counsel, as well as retained counsel, investment bankers, and others who can show that they have some expertise in valuating the assets of the corporation. A valuating report should be prepared by the board taking into consideration the definition of a "report" in *Smith*.
4. Boards of directors should plan on being sued when making decisions in control situations, and thus develop a legal and management strategy that is perceived by courts of law as having the interests of shareholders as its primary goal.

they have been "frozen out" of the corporation. Minority shareholders often seek injunctions or damages in cases where corporate boards have ratified high salaries for majority or controlling shareholders who are also officers of the corporation. A minority shareholder suit may also result when the board fails to declare dividends and it can be shown that there was not a "good-faith" reason. For example, if the controlling shareholders seek to force the minority to sell their stock by not declaring a dividend, or to depress the price of the stock to serve the interest of officers or directors, the courts will see a wrongful purpose and a violation of the "business judgment" rule.

Other circumstances in which minority shareholders have charged "oppression" involve mergers and amendments to the corporate charter altering voting rights of a class of stock.

DISSOLUTION AND TERMINATION OF THE CORPORATION

In Chapter 32 it was noted that one of the advantages of a corporate form of doing business was that the corporation lived on in perpetuity despite the death of a member of management, a member of the board of directors, or a shareholder. However, perpetual existence does not prevent *dissolution* and *termination*. A corporation *dissolves* itself when it stops doing business, winds up its affairs, and liquidates its business. *Termination* occurs when all assets have been liquidated and creditors and shareholders have received the proceeds. The RMBCA provides for voluntary and involuntary dissolutions, which are discussed here.

Voluntary Dissolution

The RMBCA (Section 14) provides for dissolution *before* and *after* a corporation begins business. A vote of a majority of its incorporators or initial members of the board of directors dissolves a corporation *before* it commences business. *After* business has been commenced the RMBCA allows a corporation to be dissolved by adoption of a dissolution resolution by a board of directors and its approval by holders of a majority of the shares *outstanding* at a shareholders' meeting. In order for the dissolution to be effective, the corporation must file *articles* of *dissolution* with the secretary of state of the state where the corporation is incorporated. *Articles* of *dissolution* should include the date of approval of dissolution and the number of voters in favor of and opposed to dissolution.

Voluntary dissolution also takes place when the time of existence provided for in the corporation's certificate of incorporation expires. Also, when all shareholders of all existing shares of a corporation decide to dissolve the corporation dissolution may take place.

Involuntary Dissolution

Involuntary dissolution of a corporation takes place under the RMBCA through court action (judicial dissolution) or administrative decree. Sections 14.20 and 14.30 are the basis for involuntary dissolution of a corporation and for the discussion that follows.

The RMBCA allows the *secretary of state* of the corporation's state of incorporation, *shareholders,* and *creditors* to institute involuntary dissolution proceedings in a court of law having jurisdiction.

The *secretary of state* may file for a dissolution, and obtain such, if it can be proven that the corporation's articles of incorporation were obtained through fraud, or the corporation exceeded or abused its authority under law. In some states a corporation found guilty of an antitrust violation may be subject to dissolution.

Shareholders, under Section 14.30, may obtain a court-ordered dissolution when the directors are deadlocked and such is harmful to the corporation, or when the shareholders are deadlocked and cannot elect directors, or when directors are acting contrary to the best interests of the corporation.

Creditors may obtain a judicial order for dissolution of the corporation if it is proven that the company is *insolvent.*

Termination

Upon dissolution the *winding up* and *liquidation* process must take place. The assets of the dissolved corporation are liquidated by the orderly collection, sale, and distribution of the assets. When an *involuntary* dissolution occurs the board of directors of a corporation or someone appointed by the board carries out this process. The board serves as trustees of the corporate assets for creditors and shareholders. In the case of an *involuntary dissolution* a court-appointed *receiver* carries out the liquidation of the corporate assets and other windup activities.

The proceeds from the sale of assets are paid in the following order of claims: (1) creditors, (2) preferred shareholders, and (3) common shareholders. *Termination* of the corporation's existence occurs following these winding-up and liquidation activities.

REVIEW PROBLEMS

1. What is the business judgment rule?
2. What is the purpose of a corporation as set out in the RMBCA?
3. What is meant by the ultra vires doctrine?
4. What rights do shareholders of a corporation have?
5. For what reasons do minority shareholders in a corporation bring suits against the corporation, its board of directors, and officers?
6. X Corporation was organized with an authorization of 1,000 shares of stock. The adopted bylaws of the corporation contained provisions limiting the number of shares available to each stockholder and restricting stock transfers during both the life of the stockholder and in case of death. According to the bylaws, if a stockholder wanted to sell or transfer shares, he or she had to give the corporation or other stockbrokers the chance to purchase the stock from the stockholder at the price paid when the stock was originally purchased. If the option was not exercised within ninety days, the stockholder then was free to sell the stock. Y had purchased shares with restrictions of sale and transfer, as detailed previously, printed on the stock certificates. When Y died the board of directors of X voted to exercise its option to repurchase the shares from Y's es-

tate and agreed to pay a sum greater than Y paid for the stock. Those administering the estate declined to sell and wanted the stock transferred to the estate. They brought a lawsuit to compel the corporation to transfer the stock according to the estate's wishes, claiming that the limitation on sale and transfer was an unreasonable restraint. The corporation argued that due to the restriction of sale and transfer of the stock, it was not prohibiting the transfer of stock, but merely putting a reasonable restriction on the transfer. Does the provision in the corporate bylaws, giving the corporation a right or first option to purchase the stock at the price that it originally received for it, amount to an unreasonable restraint on the transfer of the stock?

7. A, who owned stock in a gold mining company, B, made a contract with the company to sell his stock. For financial reasons A later refused to sell and breached his contract. The bylaws of the corporation allowed the executive committee to "conduct the corporation's business." When B sued A, the latter's defense was that the contract was invalid because B's articles of incorporation did not expressly allow the company to purchase its stock from stockholders. Was A's defense valid? Explain.

8. A, president of B company, made a contract with an employee, C, by which C was promised certain retirement benefits. A owned 80 percent of the stock of B and had managed the company independent of the board of directors. When C retired, the board refused to pay the benefits promised him. C sued based on a breach of contract. B company's defense was that the contract was invalid because it was not approved by the board of directors. What result? Explain.

9. Gilbert, the owner of record of seventeen shares of Transamerica Corporation, wrote the management of the company and submitted four proposals that he wanted to be presented for action by shareholders at the next annual stockholders meeting. The Securities and Exchange Commission (SEC) demanded that Transamerica comply with Gilbert's request, but the company refused. The SEC brought an action to forbid Transamerica from making use of any proxy solicited by it for use at the annual meeting, from making use of the mails or any instrumentality of interstate commerce to solicit proxies, or from making use of any soliciting material without complying with the SEC's demands. Transamerica claimed that the shareholder may interest himself only in a subject in respect to which he is entitled to vote at a stockholders meeting when every requirement of state law and of the provisions of the charter and bylaws has been fulfilled. State law states that a certificate of incorporation may set forth provisions that limit, regulate, and define the powers and functions of the directors and stockholders.

A bylaw of Transamerica vested in the board of directors the power to decide whether any proposal should be voted on at an annual meeting of stockholders. Three of Gilbert's proposals were: (1) to have independent public auditors of the books of Transamerica elected by the stockholders, (2) to eliminate from a bylaw the requirement that notice of any proposed alteration or amendment of the bylaws be contained in the notice of meetings, (3) to require an account or a report of the proceedings at the annual meetings to be sent to all stockholders. Is Gilbert entitled to make such demands? What are the reasons for and against the proposals made by Gilbert? Will the power of shareholders go to an extreme if small shareholders like Gilbert can exert so much pressure? Securities and Exchange Commission v. Transamerica Corp., 163 F.2d 511 (3d Cir. 1947), *cert. denied,* 332 U.S. 847 (1948)

10. The directors of Acoustic Products Company concluded that it was essential for the success of the company to purchase the rights to manufacture under certain patents held by the DeForest Radio Company. Acoustic was already involved in the manufacture of phonographs and radios. A contract was entered into between an agent of Acoustic and the major shareholder of DeForest providing that Acoustic could purchase one-third of the DeForest stock. This would increase the possibility for Acoustic to obtain the needed patent rights. The directors of Acoustic were not able to acquire enough funds for Acoustic to perform the contract. Thus they personally purchased the DeForest stock. When Acoustic later went bankrupt, the trustee in bankruptcy brought this action against the directors, claiming that by purchasing the DeForest shares they had violated the fiduciary duty owed to the corporation. The parties agreed that the acquisition of the rights under the DeForest patents was essential for Acoustic's success. Conceding that there existed a close relation between Acoustic and DeForest, the directors argued that since the company did not have

the money to purchase the shares, the directors had violated no duty by purchasing the shares themselves. Who should win? Should the directors suffer financially even though they made their effort to help Acoustic? Or is this possibility for suffering by the directors part of the game in order to prompt directors to use their best efforts in uncovering financial resources to be used by their companies in acquiring an attractive opportunity? Irving Trust Co. v. Deutsch, 73 F.2d 121 (2d Cir. 1934), *cert. denied,* 274 U.S. 708 (1935)

11. Emerson Electric Company acquired 13.2 percent of the outstanding common stock of Dodge Manufacturing Company through a tender offer made in an unsuccessful attempt to take over Dodge. Shortly thereafter, the shareholders of Dodge approved a merger with Reliance Electric Company. Emerson decided to dispose of enough of its shares to bring its holdings below 10 percent in order to immunize the disposal of the remainder of its shares from liability under Section 16(b) of the Securities Exchange Act of 1934. Section 16(b) provides that a corporation may recover for itself the profits realized by an owner of more than 10 percent of its shares from a purchase and sale of its stock within any six-month period, provided the owner held more than 10 percent at the time of both purchase and sale. Emerson sold some shares of Dodge, reducing its holdings in Dodge to 9.96 percent of the outstanding shares. Several weeks later Emerson sold the remainder of the Dodge shares to Dodge. Reliance demanded the profits realized on both sales, since the purchase and two sales all occurred within a three-month period. Emerson does not dispute the fact that the profits from the first sale should now be turned over. It contends that after the first sale it no longer held more than 10 percent and should not be treated as an "insider" but

like any other investor, and consequently, should be able to keep its profit. Who should prevail? If Emerson should lose, is there any time it can keep its profit, or will it always be penalized since it once held more than 10 percent of Dodge's stock? Reliance Electric Co. v. Emerson Electric Co., 404 U.S. 418 (1972)

12. Pillsbury had long opposed the Vietnam War. He learned that Honeywell, Inc. had a substantial part of its business in the production of munitions used in the war and also that Honeywell had a large government contract to produce antipersonnel fragmentation bombs. Pillsbury was determined to stop this production. He bought one share of Honeywell in his name in order to get himself a voice in Honeywell's affairs so he could persuade the company to cease producing munitions. Pillsbury submitted demands to Honeywell requesting that it produce its original shareholder ledger, current shareholder ledger, and all corporate records dealing with weapons and munitions manufacture. Honeywell refused. Pillsbury brought suit to compel Honeywell to let him inspect the requested records. Pillsbury claimed that he wished to inspect the records in order to correspond with other shareholders, with the hope of electing to the board one or more directors who represented his particular viewpoint. Should the court let Pillsbury inspect the records? Does Pillsbury have a proper purpose germane to his interest as a shareholder? Should a shareholder be allowed to persuade a company to adopt his social and political views? State ex rel. Pillsbury v. Honeywell, Inc., 291 Minn. 322, 191 N.W.2d 406 (1971)

13. Cole Real Estate Corporation was a closely held corporation that owned, managed, and rented residential apartment properties. Mrs. Helen Cole was the majority stockholder, owning all but 86 of the 4,120

outstanding shares of common stock. Peoples Bank & Trust Company of Indianapolis held the remaining 86 shares in a trustee capacity. Mrs. Cole had been a director, the president, and treasurer of the corporation since its organization in 1935. Cole Corporation was a "one-woman corporation," and little evidence of corporate identity was maintained. The most recent board of directors meeting was held in 1954, when the corporation was reorganized. At that meeting the last stock dividend was declared on previously outstanding preferred shares. Mrs. Cole testified that a shareholder meeting had not been held due to lack of interest, even though she knew Indiana law required annual shareholder meetings. As the corporation's sole employee, Mrs. Cole lived in a home owned and operated by the corporation. The home also was the corporate office, and she paid no rent or utilities. Two automobiles—owned, operated, and maintained by the corporation—provided Mrs. Cole with her only means of transportation. She set her own salary during the years 1964–1970 without consulting the board of directors. Peoples Bank & Trust, as minority shareholder, brought a lawsuit for an accounting, recovery of corporate assets, and a declaration of dividends. Mrs. Cole argues that a close corporation should be justifiably distinguished from a public corporation when questions of corporate formality and internal operations are at issue. Peoples Bank contends that corporate law prevents an officer and a director of a corporation from using the assets of a corporate entity for their personal gain. Who should win? Was there excessive compensation and/or converted corporate assets? Should a dividend be declared? Cole Real Estate Corp. v. Peoples Bank & Trust Co., 310 N.E. 2d 275 (Ct App. Ind. 1974)

14. Wiberg, a director of Gulf Coast Land and Development Company, and another director contracted with the corporation to devote their full time to selling a new line of its stock, for which they were to receive a commission on sales. The corporate resolution creating this contract was passed by the votes of these two directors and by a third director. The resolution was later ratified by holders of a majority of the shares at a special meeting in which the three directors, who were the majority shareholders, voted to ratify their action as directors. After two years the corporation terminated the contract and refused to pay Wiberg his commission. Wiberg sued to recover his commission. The defendant contends that the contract was void as against public policy because two of the three directors who had voted for it had personal interest in the transaction and because it had not been ratified by 100 percent of the shareholders. Wiberg argues that the contract is enforceable even when the corporation makes a contract with a director; that the director's vote is necessary to authorize the contract if the contract appears to be fair, just, and beneficial to the corporation; and that the director personally made a full disclosure and the contract was then ratified by a majority of the stockholders. Assuming that the contract is what Wiberg contends it is—that is, fair, just, and beneficial to the corporation—should Wiberg prevail? Even though Wiberg has a personal interest in the contract, do you think he will act fairly and honestly in the corporation's interests? Wiberg v. Gulf Coast Land and Development Company, 360 S.W.2d 563 (Tex. Civ. App. 1962)

CHAPTER 37

Securities Regulation

THE SECURITIES ACT OF 1933 —————————

THE SECURITIES ACT OF 1934 —————————

THE FOREIGN CORRUPT PRACTICES ACT OF 1977 —————

STATE SECURITIES LAWS ——————————

I n Chapter 35 two types of securities (stocks and bonds) were described and their roles in raising capital for corporate financing were analyzed. The importance of securities to our society cannot be overemphasized. Not only are they a means of raising capital for corporate expansion, but they also serve as instruments by which individual citizens accumulate wealth through interest received on bonds and dividends paid on stocks. This wealth is often passed on to heirs or contributed to nonprofit organizations such as universities to be used for student scholarship funds and faculty research. Additionally, securities are an integral part of the private sector of our economy with its emphasis on individual decision making in the marketplace. Individual investors, by themselves or through their pension and mutual funds, determine which segments of the economy and which industries within segments will grow. For example, if investors believe that solar power rather than nuclear power will be the energy source of the future, they will move their capital in that direction, stimulating the growth of the solar industry. Further, security holders are the owners of corporations. Through their election of boards of directors they determine which officers will govern and what direction the corporations

will take. For example, stockholders through derivative suits may force officers and directors to personally return to the corporation funds illegally spent or wasted. When over 400 corporations in the mid–1970s confessed to the Securities and Exchange Commission that they had made questionable payments overseas and illegal political contributions in this country, many stockholder derivative suits were filed.

This chapter discusses the role of government in regulating securities. Initially the Securities Act of 1933 (1933 Act) is examined. It sets forth rules governing the *issuance* of securities and their registration. While the 1933 Act prescribes requirements for registration, it does not seek to evaluate the worth of a particular stock or bond offering made to the investing public. Its primary purpose is to force publicly held corporations to disclose all material information to potential investors so the latter can make prudent judgments on whether or not to invest. Second, the chapter examines the 1934 Securities Exchange Act (Exchange Act). This act sets forth rules governing the *trading* in securities once issued. With the Exchange Act, Congress established the Securities and Exchange Commission (SEC) to protect the securities market from fraudulent conduct and to ensure full disclo-

FIGURE 37-1
Securities and Exchange Commission

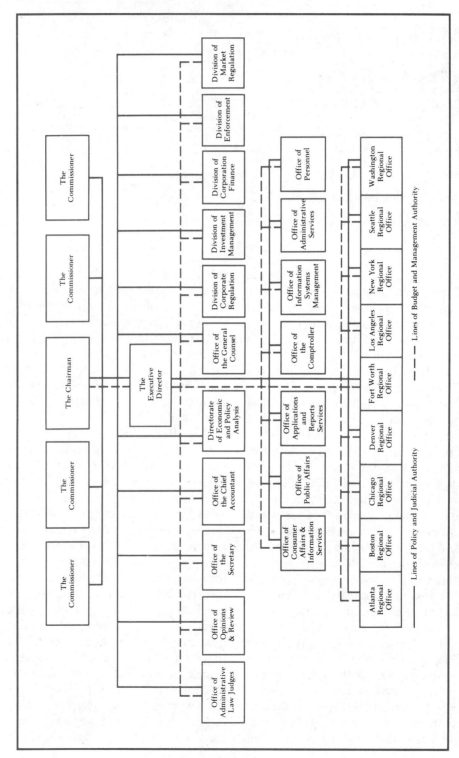

Source: U.S. Government Manual 1985–1986 (Washington, DC: U.S. Government Printing Office).

sure for investors trading in securities. *(see Figure 37-1)*. The 1933 Act and the Exchange Act are often referred to as the "Securities Acts." While they are the most significant federal legislation regulating securities, Congress has passed additional specialized security statutes.[1] This chapter concludes with an analysis of the role of state legislation in regulating securities issued and traded in intrastate commerce.

THE SECURITIES ACT OF 1933

Definition of a Security

Section 2(1) of the 1933 Act defines a security as

> any note, stock, treasury stock, bond, debenture, evidence of indebtedness, certificate of interest or participation in any profit-sharing agreement, collateral-trust certificate, preorganization certificate or subscription, transferable share, investment contract, voting-trust certificate, certificate of deposit for a security, fractional undivided interest in oil, gas, or other mineral rights, or, in general, any interest or instrument commonly known as a "security," or any certificate of interest or participation in, temporary or interim certificate for, receipt for, guarantee of, or warrant or right to subscribe to or purchase, any of the foregoing.

The interpretation of this definition has been left to the SEC, through its rule-making power and advisory releases, as well as to the courts in individual decisions. In a landmark case, *SEC v. W. J. Howey Co.*,[2] the U.S. Supreme Court outlined a test that is presently used in determining whether a particular instrument or transaction can be termed a "security" and thus falls within the federal security statutes. The Court stated that:

1. A contract or scheme must exist where a person invests money in a common enterprise.
2. The investors must have some expectation of profits.
3. The profits must be derived *solely* from the efforts of a promoter or third party but not the investors themselves.

The third element in this test has been the focus of further court concern. It has been interpreted to mean that notes formalizing a debt incurred in a business[3] or shares of stock entitling a purchaser to lease an apartment in a state-subsidized nonprofit housing cooperative[4] are *not* securities. More recently the courts have modified their interpretation of the words "solely from the efforts of those other than investors." This is particularly true when the efforts made by noninvestors are the significant ones. The following case involving a fraudulent pyramid sales scheme illustrates this trend.

SEC v. Glenn W. Turner Enterprises
U.S. Court of Appeals, Ninth Circuit
474 F.2d. 476 (1973)

Background: This is an action by the Securities and Exchange Commission (plaintiff) to enjoin Glenn W. Turner (defendant) from violating the securities law by selling securities that were not registered. Dare To Be Great (Dare) was a subsidiary of Glenn W. Turner Enterprises, Inc. It offered courses in self-motivation that were entitled Adventures I, II, III. The initial course (Adventure I) included a portable tape recorder, twelve tape-recorded lessons, and some printed material. The purchaser also was entitled to attend a twelve-to-sixteen-hour series of group meetings. The initial cost was $300. For Adventure II, which included more tapes and an additional eighty hours of meetings, the purchaser paid $700. If he or she paid $2,000 more, Adventure III was made available with more tape recordings, more group sessions, and a notebook called "The Fun of Selling." The purchaser of Adventure III could also become an "independent sales trainee" for the purpose of selling Adventures I, II, and III. For an additional $5,000, he or she also received Adventure IV and the right to sell Adventure IV. The purchaser also had the option of selling a $1,000-plan that was similar to Adventure II. The SEC claimed that all these plans were "securities" within the meaning of the 1933 and 1934 Securities Acts. The federal district court decided in favor of the SEC. Defendant, Turner Enterprises, Inc. appealed.

Decision: Affirmed. The Court of Appeals ruled in favor of the SEC.

Duniway, Justice

The trial court's findings, which are fully supported by the record, demonstrate that Turner Enterprises' scheme is a gigantic and successful fraud. The question presented is whether the "Adventures" or "Plans" enjoined are "securities" within the meaning of the federal securities laws.

It is apparent from the record that what is sold is not of the usual "business motivation" type of courses. Rather, the purchaser is really buying the possibility of deriving money from the sale of the plans by Dare to individuals whom the purchaser has brought to Dare. The promotional aspects of the Plans, such as seminars, films, and records, are aimed at interesting others in the Plans. Their value for any other purpose is, to put it mildly, minimal.

Once an individual has purchased a Plan, he turns his efforts toward bringing others into the organization, for which he will receive a part of what they pay. His task is to bring prospective purchasers to "Adventure Meetings."

These meetings are like an old-time revival meeting, but directed toward the joys of making easy money rather than salvation. Their purpose is to convince prospective purchasers, or "prospects," that Dare is a sure route to great riches. Films are shown, usually involving the "rags-to-riches" story of Dare founder, Glenn W. Turner. The goal of all this is to persuade the prospect to purchase a plan, especially Adventure IV, so that he may become a "salesman," and thus grow wealthy as part of the Dare organization. It is intimated that as Glenn W. Turner Enterprises, Inc., expands, high positions in the organization, as well as lucrative opportunities to purchase stock, will be available. After the meeting, pressure is applied to the prospect by Dare people, in an effort to induce him to purchase one of the Adventures or the Plan. In *SEC* v. *W. J. Howey Co.*, the Supreme Court set out its by now familiar definition of an investment contract: "The test is whether the scheme involves an investment of money in a common enterprise with profits to come solely from the efforts of others."

In *Howey* the Court held that a land sales contract for units of a citrus grove, together with a service contract for cultivating and marketing the crops, was an investment contract and hence a security. The Court held that what was in essence being offered was "an opportunity to contribute money and to share in the profits of a large citrus-fruit enterprise managed and partly owned by respondents." The purchasers had no intention themselves of either occupying the land or developing it; they were attracted only "by the prospects of a return on their investment." It was clear that the profits were to come "solely" from the efforts of others.

For purposes of the present case, the sticking point in the *Howey* definition is the word "solely," a qualification which of course exactly fitted the circumstances in *Howey*. All the other elements of the *Howey* test have been met here. There is an investment of money, a common enterprise, and the expectation of profits to come from the efforts of others. Here, however, the investor, or purchaser, must himself exert some efforts if he is to realize a return on his initial cash outlay. He must find prospects and persuade them to attend Dare Adventure Meetings, and at least some of them must then purchase a plan if he is to realize that return. Thus it can be said that the returns or profits are not coming "solely" from the efforts of others.

We hold, however, that in light of the remedial nature of the legislation, the statutory policy of affording broad protection to the public, and the Supreme Court's admonitions that the definition of securities should be a flexible one, the word "solely" should not be read as a strict or literal limitation on the definition of an investment contract, but rather must be construed realistically, so as to include within the definition those schemes which involve in substance, if not form, securities. Within this context, we hold that Adventures III and IV and the $1,000 Plan are investment contracts within the meaning of the 1933 and 1934 Acts.

Securities Markets

Securities markets are not easily defined because, unlike goods (for example, clothes) that are manufactured, distributed, and consumed by the public, securities as defined earlier are not consumed directly by the purchaser/investor. Securities become a form of currency in which an initial investor may trade for other securities in what are known as "securities markets." These may have a physical location, such as the New York Stock Exchange (NYSE) with its trading floor, or none, such as the over-the-counter (OTC) market. There is a marked contrast to their operations. The NYSE acts in a very formal manner, determining who will be allowed to trade on the exchange (who has a "seat") and the function of each member. Until 1975 it prescribed the commissions to be charged. In a NYSE transaction a buyer or seller goes to an investment firm, which acts as a broker. The broker transmits the customer's order to the exchange floor, where only a registered specialist may buy or sell as a dealer in the security. The broker's firm charges the customer a commission.

In contrast, the OTC market has no physical facilities and no specialists. Most work is done by a computer network or phone, and anyone can act as a dealer. If a customer orders a particular stock on the OTC market and the firm is not a dealer in the stock, it will purchase it as a broker from another dealer, making a market in the stock.

With satellite communication and data-transmission networks, some have argued that there is no longer a need for physical facilities like the NYSE. In effect they argue that computerized national and international marketing systems for securities will soon be in place and that stock exchanges will be outmoded.

Registration of Securities

The 1933 Act forbids the public offer or sale through the mail or other means of interstate

---

BOX 37-1 ISSUES AND TRENDS
International

In 1986 the British government opened its securities markets to foreign securities firms and investors. This brought to world attention the deregulated and self-regulatory system used to police the securities markets in Great Britain. A new Securities and Investment Board (SIB) came into being in 1987. It is totally financed by the securities firms it regulates, and has many contrasting functions to the SEC as shown here:

Securities and Exchange Commission	Securities and Investments Board
Regulation limited to securities	Covers securities, commodities, insurance policies—anything sold for investment purposes in Britain
Government financed	Industry financed
Substantial enforcement division, which often acts first against ill-doers	Enforcement division will be small, with reliance on exchanges and other self-regulatory organizations to initiate most actions
Acts as primary disclosure agency for U.S. corporations	Will collect no corporate information
Has primary responsibility for setting capital adequacy standards for investment firms	Relies on capital adequacy standards set by industry self-regulators
Primary investigator of insider trading	Leaves insider trading investigation and prosecution to stock exchange and another government department
Commissioners appointed by the president	Directors appointed by governor of Bank of England and cabinet minister for trade and industry
Has internal judicial system to hear SEC cases against firms	No substantial internal judicial system

Source: Wall Street Journal, October 24, 1986, p. 12.

---

commerce of any instrument or transaction defined as a security unless it has been registered with the SEC or meets one of the exemptions set out in Section 3 or 4 of the Act. When a corporation wishes to issue securities (issuer or issuing corporation), it files a registration statement with the SEC that contains a prospectus (Figure 37–2) and additional exhibits and information. A copy of the prospec-

tus must be provided to every purchaser. The additional exhibits and information are kept on file. The SEC staff examines the prospectus and exhibits to see if they include such information as the nature of the registrant's business, properties held, the management, control, and operation of the business, the securities to be offered for sale, and certified financial statements. The SEC has authority to

FIGURE 37–2
Insider Traders

Wall Street's Army of Insider Traders

THE INSIDERS
As part of their jobs, hundreds of people help to arrange mergers and buybacks that will push up stock prices once the deals become public. The process often begins in the executive suite, when chairmen talk merger and bring in their top associates.

Vice Chairmen   General Counsel   Boards of Directors

INVESTMENT BANKS ·Any company involved in a merger hires a Wall Street bank, with its numerous specialists.

Financial Experts   Research Analysts   Merger and Acquisition Teams

THE SUPPORTING CAST

Law Firms   Public Relations Advisers   Banks, Bond Dealers, Lenders

ON THE EDGE
Many others get insider information from the key players. These are the friends and relatives of the deal makers. Arbitragers, who speculate on mergers, can end up as well-informed as the key players through constant sleuthing.

Proxy Solicitors   Printers   Secretaries

Source: New York Times, **May 18, 1986, Section 3, p. F-1. (Reprinted with permission of *The New York Times*.)**

request additional information or to issue a "refusal order" not permitting a registration to become effective if it contains serious deficiencies. Usually a letter of comment ("deficiency letter") by the SEC staff is sufficient to correct deficiencies. If no action is taken by the staff, registration automatically becomes effective twenty days after a registration statement has been filed. As noted previously in this chapter, the purpose of the 1933 Act is to provide public disclosure of material information to potential investors so they will have an adequate basis for determining whether to invest in an issuer's securities offering. The registration statement is a vehicle for implementing this goal. The SEC does not evaluate the merit or worth of the securities registered and to be issued.

After the securities are registered and the effective date for issuance has arrived, the issuer, usually through underwriters and dealers, sells its securities to individual and institutional investors. It should be noted that after filing but before the effective date ("waiting period") oral offers by underwriters to dealers and the public are permitted, but no written offers or sales are allowed until the effective date. During this waiting period the SEC allows notices to appear in newspapers of potential offerings by the issuer as long as such notices clearly specify that they are not offers to sell. It should be emphasized that the SEC can shorten the time between registration and effectiveness to forty-eight hours. This has become common, especially with volatile markets.

Traditionally, corporations that issue securities have worked through investment-banking firms (underwriters), which buy or offer to buy securities and in turn employ dealers as agents to sell securities to the public. In an attempt to cut red tape and help issuers raise capital at opportune moments, the SEC adopted Rule 415. The rule allows over 2,000 large publicly traded corporations to file single "shelf registration" statements with the SEC, designating

the amount of bonds and stocks they want to put on the "shelf" for a two-year period. This statement covers all potential sales of securities, so the individual company does not have to publish a new, detailed prospectus each time it wants to raise capital. It can simply refer investors to data published in its annual or quarterly reports and enter the market with its "shelf securities" at an opportune time. Corporations such as American Telephone and Telegraph applauded the new rule for the flexibility it provides, especially in a period of fluctuating market conditions. Large investment banking firms and regional underwriters opposed Rule 415, claiming that the investor will have little opportunity to learn of new offerings before issued. Regional securities firms fear that they will be squeezed out of the underwriting business. Historically the regional underwriters have relied on big investment firms such as Morgan Stanley to include them in large syndicates selling securities for an issuer. In May 1982, under Rule 415, AT&T sold its entire offering of $110.8 million in stock to an investment-banking firm, Morgan Stanley, which in turn sold the securities to institutional investors. The rule has added impetus to the merging of regional firms with financial giants like American Express and Prudential Insurance. This trend, combined with large corporations like Phillip Morris doing their own in-house underwriting, has led to a different marketing style and greater concentration in the investment-banking industry.

Exempted Securities

Section 3 of the 1933 Act, and regulations implementing it, exempt from the registration provision certain types of securities. It should be noted that the Section 3 securities discussed here are *not* exempted from the antifraud provisions of either the 1933 or 1934 Securities Acts.

Section 3(a) exempts from registration commercial paper such as drafts, notes, and bankers' acceptance provided they arise out of current transactions, have maturity dates of not more than nine months, and are not advertised for sale to the public.

Section 3(b) authorizes the SEC to exempt relatively small offerings of securities that do not exceed $5 million. Also, Section 3(b) exempts small public offerings of securities that do not exceed $1.5 million over a twelve-month period. The issuing company must file a notification and offering circular with a regional SEC office ten days before each proposed offering of securities. The SEC may follow with some informal comments similar to the regular registration process.

Section 3(b) also provides an exemption for a public offering of "any security which is part of an issue sold only *within the border of a single state* and to residents of that state." The issuer must be a resident or a corporation incorporated or doing business in that state. The courts and the SEC under Rule 147 have emphasized that *all* purchasers must be residents of the state. If one is not, the securities offering will not be exempted. Additionally, Rule 147 requires that 80 percent of the gross revenues of the issuer must come from operations within the state.

Certain other securities are also exempt from registration by virtue of Section 3 of the 1933 Act and SEC interpretations of that section—for example, securities issued by the U.S. government, nonprofit organizations, and domestic banks, as well as securities regulated by agencies other than the SEC. Securities are exempted if issued pursuant to mergers or reorganizations where no cash is involved and the issuer offers securities solely in exchange for other securities.

Exempted Transactions

Section 4(1) of the 1933 Act exempts transactions by persons other than an issuer, underwriter, or dealer. Sections 4(3) and 4(4) allow qualified exemptions for dealers and brokers. In reality, underwriters are the only ones not exempted. Rule 144 promulgated by the SEC sets forth the conditions that determine when a person is not an underwriter and not involved in selling restricted securities and is therefore exempt.

Section 4(2) involves transactions that are exempt because they do *not* involve any public offering of securities. Approximately 25 percent of all corporate securities fall under this exemption. As noted in the case that follows, there are several factors that the courts and the SEC consider in determining whether one qualifies for a private-placement exemption.

Hill York Corp. et al. v. Gurn H. Freeman et al. and American International Franchises, Inc. et al.

U.S. Court of Appeals, Fifth Circuit
448 F.2d 680 (1971)

Background: Freeman and Browne (defendants) had developed a franchise promotion scheme designed to funnel funds from the sale of stock in certain franchise sales centers to themselves as stockholders of American International Franchises, Inc. (American). The Freemans formed American in Springfield, Mo., in July 1967; Browne joined one month later as executive vice-president. These three individuals comprised all the officers and stockholders of American.

The franchising concept conceived by the Freemans involved the marketing of two restaurant franchises called Hickory Corral and Italian Den. The chairman of the board of directors of Hickory Corral was Gurn Freeman, and the chairman of the board of Italian Den was Jack Freeman. The only restaurant of either type to be operated was one Hickory Corral, which opened in Springfield, Mo., and closed shortly thereafter. Under the plan commonly used American would seek out local investors to incorporate a statewide or regional franchise sales center. The payment of a franchise fee to American conferred upon the purchaser the exclusive right to sell Hickory Corral and Italian Den franchises within the state or region. The local investors who formed the franchise sales center corporation would sell stock in the corporation to a small number of persons who would be most likely to furnish supplies and services to the restaurants—for instance, a real-estate firm, an air-conditioning company, a builder. American was also in the franchise consulting business and was to assist the local investors in organizing and developing the business of the sales center. During the first year of operation the defendants formed six state franchising systems, one of which involved a plaintiff in this case, Florida Franchise Systems, Inc. As in other transactions, Browne, the defendant, sought out the plaintiff, solicited capital from it, and provided sales brochures designed by the defendants to secure additional capital. American International advised the franchisees on every step, purchasing $10,000 worth of stock out of the $70,000 available. Additionally, two of the five directors were required by the agreement with Florida Franchise to be representatives of American. On October 4, 1968 American and Florida Franchise entered into a franchise agreement, utilizing a form agreement drafted by American. The price to Florida Franchise for this exclusive right to sell was $25,000. Subsequent to the payment of the $25,000, on October 22, American insisted that Florida Franchise enter into a new agreement that provided for an additional franchise fee of $1,000 per month.

Plaintiffs, Hill York Corporation and others, alleging that these activities amounted to a pyramiding scheme to funnel money to American, brought this suit for rescission of the stock sales and the return of their investments. A jury in the lower court awarded rescission of the agreement and a return of the monies paid. Punitive damages of $85,000 were assessed against the defendants individually. They appealed.

Decision: Affirmed. The U.S. Court of Appeals ruled in favor of Hill York Corporation and other investors.

Clark, Judge

It is conceded that no registration statement had been filed with the SEC in connection with this offering of securities. The defendants contend, however, that the transactions come within the exemptions to registration found in 15 U.S.C.A. § 77d(2) (commonly known as Section 4(2)). Specifically, they contend that the offering of securities was not a public offering.

At the threshold of this contention we deem it appropriate to consider the instructions under which the public offering phase of the exemption was decided.

The SEC has stated that the question of public offering is one of fact and must depend upon the circumstances of each case. We agree with this approach. It is of course apparent that presenting an issue of fact to SEC analysts is totally different from presenting a question of fact to a jury unsophisticated and untrained in the niceties of securities law. Although courts accord a marked deference to the expertise of such an agency which is charged with broad regulation of a specific field when reviewing their regulatory action, we do not intimate that their procedures are binding precedent. However, to be consistent—which is the constant aim if not the invariable result of the law—and, most vitally, because we find SEC criteria both legally accurate and meaningfully sufficient for testing the issue, we hold that a jury should consider the factors enumerated below which the SEC considers, together with the policies embodied in the Act.

The following specific factors are relevant:

1. The number of offerees and their relationship to each other and to the issuer.

In the past the SEC has utilized the arbitrary figure of twenty-five offerees as a litmus test of whether an offering was public. A leading commentator in the field has noted, however, that in recent years the SEC has increasingly disavowed any safe numerical test. Initially, the figure of twenty-five was probably no more than a rule of administrative convenience. In any case, such an arbitrary figure is inappropriate as an absolute in a private civil lawsuit. The Supreme Court has put it thus: "No particular numbers are prescribed. Anything from two to infinity may serve: perhaps even one." SEC v. Ralston Purina Co., 346 U.S. 119, 73 S. Ct. 981, 97 L.Ed.2d 1494 (1953). Obviously, however, the more offerees, the more likelihood that the offering is public. The relationship between the offerees and the issuer is most significant. If the offerees know the issuer and have special knowledge as to its business affairs, such as high executive officers of the issuer would possess, then the offering is apt to be private. The Supreme Court laid special stress on this consideration in *Ralston Purina* by stating that "[t]he focus of the inquiry should be on the need of the offerees for the protections afforded by registration. The employees here were not shown to have access to the kind of information which registration would disclose." Also to be considered is the relationship between the offerees and their knowledge of each other. For example, if the offering is being made to a diverse and unrelated group, i.e. lawyers, grocers, plumbers, etc., then the offering would have the appearance of being public; but an offering to a select group of high executive officers of the issuer who know each other and of course have similar interests and knowledge of the offering would more likely be characterized as a private offering.

2. The number of units offered.

Here again there is no fixed magic number. Of course, the smaller the number of units offered, the greater the likelihood the offering will be considered private.

3. The size of the offering.

The smaller the size of the offering, the more probability it is private.

4. The manner of offering.

A private offering is more likely to arise when the offer is made directly to the offerees rather than through the facilities of public distribution such as investment bankers or the securities exchanges. In addition, public advertising is incompatible with the claim of private offering.

Even an objective testing of these factors without determining whether a more comprehensive and generalized prerequisite has been met, is insufficient. "The natural way to interpret the private offering exemption is in light of the statutory purpose. The design of the statute is to protect investors by promoting full disclosure of information thought necessary to informed investment decisions." Thus the ultimate test is whether " 'the particular class of persons affected need the protection of the Act'." *SEC* v. *Ralston Purina Co.* The Act is remedial legislation entitled to a broad construction. Conversely, its exemptions must be narrowly viewed. Thus, only where the practical need for the enforcement of the safeguards afforded by the Act or the public benefit derived from such enforcement can confidently be said to be remote with respect to the transactions is the private offering exemption met.

It is well-settled law that the defendants have the burden of proving their affirmative defense of private offering. *SEC* v. *Ralston Purina Co.* The defendants, however, adduced no evidence on this issue, relying instead on the evidence introduced by the plaintiffs to prove these sales were exempt from registration. The evidence indicates that this offering was limited to sophisticated businessmen and attorneys who planned to do business with the new firm. The thirteen actual purchasers paid 5,000 dollars each for their stock. In order to be exempt from the Florida Blue Sky Law, the total number of purchasers in the first year of stock sales was deliberately kept below fifteen and the number of original subscribers below five, pursuant to advice these plaintiff-purchasers obtained from independent legal counsel who they retained to render advice on the Blue Sky and SEC laws. Finally, the defendants assert that the plaintiffs had access to all the information they desired. We take this to mean that the plaintiffs had access to all information concerning Florida Franchise. We also interpret it to mean that the plaintiffs could have obtained any information they desired concerning American and the background of the individual defendants if they had just asked.

The defendants rely most strongly on the fact that the offering was made only to sophisticated businessmen and lawyers and not the average man in the street. Although this evidence is certainly favorable to the defendants, the level of sophistication will not carry the point. In this context, the relationship between the promoters and the purchasers and the "access to the kind of information which registration would disclose" become highly relevant factors. Relying specifically upon the words just quoted from *Ralston Purina,* the SEC has rejected the position which the defendants posit here, stating: " 'The Supreme Court's language does not support the view that the availability of an exemption depends on the sophistication of the offerees or buyers, rather than their possession of, or access to, information regarding the issuer.' " Obviously if the plaintiffs did not possess the information requisite for a registration statement, they could not bring their sophisticated knowledge of business affairs to bear in deciding whether or not to invest in this franchise sales center. There is abundant evidence to support the conclusion that the plaintiffs did not in fact possess the requisite information. The plaintiffs were given:

1. a brochure representing that the defendants had just left the very successful firm of Nationwide, but without disclosing the fact that Nationwide was then under investigation by the SEC;
2. a brochure representing Browne as an expert in capitalization consulting, when in fact he had no expertise in such consulting;
3. a brochure stating that the franchise fee would be 25,000 dollars, when

in fact the franchise fee turned out to be 25,000 dollars plus a 1,000 dollar per month royalty;

4. a brochure representing that the existing sales centers were successfully operating, without disclosure of the fact that most of them were under investigation by various state securities commissions.

No reasonable mind could conclude that the plaintiffs had access to accurate information on the foregoing points since the only persons who reasonably could have relieved their ignorance were the ones that told them the untruths in the first instance. This proof, as an *a priori* matter, inexorably leads to the conclusion that even the most sanguine of the purchasers would have entertained serious, if not fatal, doubts about investing in this scheme if completely accurate information had been furnished.

Following this case, and a decision against granting a private placement exemption in the *Continental Tobacco Company* case,[5] the SEC has sought to clarify standards for obtaining a private placement exemption. The SEC has promulgated Regulation D, composed of Rules 501–506 summarized here:

Rule 501 defines the terms used in Regulation D. Of most significance is the definition of "accredited investors," which are generally investors that do not need the protection afforded by the 1933 Act registration process. They include banks; insurance companies; investment companies; employee benefit plans; business development companies; charitable or educational institutions with assets of more than $5 million; individuals with a net worth of over $1 million, or with an annual income of over $200,000 for 3 years; or a person who buys $150,000 of securities at one time.

Under Rule 504 an issuer can sell an aggregate of up to $500,000 of securities in any twelve-month period to accredited or nonaccredited purchasers with no requirement for the furnishing of any information to such purchasers. This exemption is available to any issuer except an investment company or an issuer disqualified by Rule 252 from using Regulation A.

Under Rule 505 an issuer can sell up to $5 million of securities in a twelve-month period to any number of accredited investors and up to thirty-five other nonaccredited investors. However, the $5 million will be reduced by amounts sold and exempted under other provisions. Investment companies are not eligible for this exemption.

Rule 506 seeks to clarify Section 4(2) dealing with the private placement exemptions (text page 911). It allows an issuer to sell an unlimited amount of securities to any number of accredited investors and up to thirty-five nonaccredited investors. However, the rule states that an issuer must believe, prior to sale, that each nonaccredited investor or "purchaser representative" (as defined by Rule 501) has enough knowledge or experience in business or financial matters to evaluate the merits and risks of the investment.

Rule 502 sets forth certain conditions and information that must be given nonaccredited investors when purchasing pursuant to Rules 505 and 504.

Integration

In cases where companies may seek to qualify for a small business exemption of dividing a large issuance of securities into smaller units, the SEC has adopted *integration* and *aggregation* rules. These rules prohibit companies from making two or more exempt offerings of similar shares at approximately the same times. The SEC will integrate and aggregate otherwise exempt offerings if:

1. The offerings are part of a unitary plan of financing by an issuing company
2. The offerings concern the same class of securities
3. The offerings are made for the same general purpose, and about the same level of pricing

Additionally, the SEC has adopted a "safe harbor rule," which in effect states that any offering made six months before or six months after an offering will not be integrated.

Liability Under the 1933 Act

The 1933 Act seeks to assure full disclosure for potential investors. The registration process, as noted previously, is the major tool for carrying out this statutory policy. Congress provided civil liability for the failure of issuing corporations to meet the provisions of the 1933 Act in Sections 11, 12, and 17. It should be noted that both private and public remedies are provided.

Section 11 provides for a statutory cause of action allowing purchasers who have relied on material misstatements or incorrect data in the registration statement to sue and obtain civil damages. Since Section 11 was promulgated, case law has pointed to certain individuals as most likely to be held liable. For example, losses have been recouped from

1. The issuer
2. All who signed the registration statement
3. Lawyers, engineers, and accountants who participated in the preparation of the registration statement

4. Every director
5. Every underwriter

The issuing corporation and all those involved in the preparation of a registration statement should therefore exercise great care. It should be noted that all but the issuer are allowed a due-diligence defense. This defense requires the individual defendant to show that he or she had reasonable grounds to believe that there were no misstatements or material omissions. In the landmark case *Escott* v. *Bar Chris Corp.,*[6] the court treated each of the defendants' pleas of due diligence individually, considering their relationships to the issuing corporation and their areas of expertise. Based on *Bar Chris,* an "inside" director of a corporation who is also a lawyer will have greater difficulty establishing a "due-diligence" defense than will an outside director, especially if he or she is a nonlawyer.

Section 12(1) imposes liability for the sale of an unregistered security that fails to meet any of the Section 3 or 4 exemptions. The sale of securities prior to the filing of a registration statement or before the effective date subjects the issuer to liability from the person who purchased the securities. The standard for recovery set out by the courts is the purchase price paid for the security, plus interest, less income received. The purchaser must return the security to the seller.

Section 17 imposes liability on all those who aid and abet any fraud in connection with the offer or sale of securities. It is a general fraud section, bolstered by Section 24, which imposes criminal sanctions where it can be shown that there were any *willful* violations of any provision of the 1933 Act or rules and regulations made by the SEC pursuant to that statute. An individual convicted can be imprisoned for up to five years and/or fined up to $10,000. The reach of Section 17 is illustrated in the case that follows.

United States v. Naftalin

Supreme Court of the United States

441 U.S. 768 (1979)

Background: Naftalin (defendant) was president of a registered broker-dealer firm. In July and August 1969, he selected stocks that had peaked in price and were entering declines. He placed five broker orders to sell shares of these stocks, although he did not own the shares he pretended to sell. Gambling that the price of securities would decline before he was requested to deliver them to the broker, he planned to make offsetting purchases through other brokers at lower prices. His profit would be the difference between the price at which he sold and the price at which he covered. Naftalin was aware, however, that had the brokers who executed his sell orders known that he did not own the securities, they would either not have accepted the orders or would have required a margin deposit. He therefore falsely represented that he owned the shares he directed them to sell.

Unfortunately for Naftalin, the market prices of the securities he "sold" did not fall prior to the delivery date but instead rose sharply. Naftalin was unable to make covering purchases and never delivered the promised securities. Consequently, the five brokers were unable to deliver the stock they had "sold" to investors and were forced to borrow stock to keep their delivery promises. Then, in order to return the borrowed stock, the brokers had to purchase replacement shares in the open market at the now-higher prices. The five brokers suffered substantial losses, although the persons to whom the stocks were sold suffered no losses.

The brokers reported the scheme to the SEC, which in turn reported it to the Department of Justice. The Justice Department instituted criminal proceedings against Naftalin for violating Section 17 of the Securities Act of 1933. Naftalin was found guilty, but the Court of Appeals reversed, citing that the act was designed to protect investors rather than brokers. The government appealed to the Supreme Court.

Decision: Reversed. The Supreme Court of the United States ruled in favor of the United States.

Brennan, Justice

Section 17 of the Securities Act of 1933 states: "It shall be unlawful for any person in the offer or sale of any security by the use of any means or instruments of transportation or communication in interstate commerce or by the use of the mails, directly or indirectly:

(1) to employ any device, scheme, or artifice to defraud, or

(2) to obtain money or property by means of any untrue statement of a material fact or any omission to state a material fact necessary in order to make the statements made in the light of the circumstances under which they were made not misleading, or

(3) to engage in any transaction, practice or course of business which operates or would operate as a fraud or deceit upon the purchaser."

Naftalin claims he did commit fraud but the fraud was against the brokers, not the investors who purchased the securities. He claims brokers are not investors under the Act. Nothing in the Act supports this view. Subsection (1) makes it unlawful for any person in the offer or sale of any securities directly or indirectly to employ any device to defraud. This language does not require that the victim of the fraud be an investor— only that the fraud occur in an offer or sale.

An offer and sale occurred here. Naftalin placed orders to sell with the brokers, the brokers acted as his agent and executed the orders and the results were contracts of sale. The fraud can occur at any stage of the selling transaction. Section 17 of the Act applies not only to the issuance of new securities but to the subsequent resale of those securities. This section was intended to cover any fraudulent scheme in an offer or sale of securities, whether in the course of an initial distribution or in the course of ordinary market trading.

THE SECURITIES ACT OF 1934

Purpose and Scope

As stated in the introduction to this chapter, the Securities Exchange Act of 1934 established the SEC to ensure fair trading practices for investors and others in the securities market. It sets forth rules governing the trading of securities, not initial offerings, that are governed by the 1933 Act. Following enactment of the Exchange Act, congressional and SEC investigations continued to reveal abuses in the marketplace. The Exchange Act was amended in major ways in 1964, 1968, 1975, and 1977. Aspects of the act discussed here include:

1. Requirements for detailed registration and reporting
2. Rules governing the use of proxies
3. Provisions governing tender offers
4. Provisions relating to short swing profits
5. Provisions relating to securities fraud in the marketplace
6. Provisions governing corrupt practices of American-based corporations abroad (included in the Foreign Corrupt Practices Act of 1977)

Registration and Reporting Requirements

Section 12 of the Exchange Act requires all publicly held companies regulated by the SEC to register two classes of securities: debt and equity. This requirement pertains to all companies with assets of $1 million or more and a class of equity securities having at least 500 shareholders of record. Such securities must be registered or they will not be allowed to be traded on a national securities exchange. Registration of a class of securities under the Exchange Act should not be confused with the registration of an initial offering of nonexempt securities within a class under the 1933 Act. A company registering a class of securities under the Exchange Act will always have to meet the requirements of the 1933 Act when making an initial public offering that does not meet any of the exemptions noted previously in this chapter. The 1933 Act regulates the initial sale of securities, whereas the Exchange Act governs its trading on national exchanges.

Over the years since 1934 the SEC has promulgated rules and prescribed forms for registering classes of securities. Much of the information requested is similar to that required by the 1933 Act. The Exchange Act registration requirements supplement and extend the requirements of the 1933 Act.

The SEC through its rule-making power has also devised periodic refiling requirements for corporate registrants to ensure that the potential investor has continuing access to information about securities that are being traded on the exchanges. Annual reports (Form 10-K) and quarterly reports (Form 10-Q) have been updated to provide increasing amounts of information for potential investors. Additionally, current reports (Form 8-K) can be requested and must be filed by the registering company within fifteen days if the SEC perceives that a material event has taken place that a reasonably prudent investor should know about in order to make an investment decision. A significant change in a company's assets or a potential merger have been considered material events.

Section 18 of the Exchange Act makes a registering company liable for civil damages to anyone who buys or sells securities and relies on misleading statements contained in the registration statement or any of the reports noted earlier.

Proxy Solicitations

A *proxy* is best defined as a writing whereby a holder of registered securities gives permission to another person to vote the stockholder's shares at a stockholders meeting. In many cases inside management seeks proxies from its shareholders to defeat a particular issue that has been placed before the board by dissident shareholders. Proxies are also given by shareholders who will not be present for the purpose of electing new directors or preventing a takeover of a company. Since the proxy solicitation process often involves the future direction of the corporation, full disclosure is required by the Exchange Act and the SEC. Ten days prior to mailing a proxy statement to shareholders, the issuing company must file it with the SEC. The Commission

often issues informal letters of comment requiring some changes before proxies are mailed. SEC rules require the solicitor of proxies to furnish shareholders with all material information concerning the matter being submitted to them for their vote. A form by which shareholders may indicate their agreement or disagreement must be provided as well. In the case of proxies solicited for the purpose of voting for directors, shareholders must be furnished an annual report.

Often shareholders will request that a certain proposal be placed on the agenda at an annual meeting. Under the Exchange Act and SEC rules, if timely notice is given by the shareholder(s), management must include such proposals in its proxy statement and allow shareholders to vote for or against it. If management opposes the proposal, it must include a statement in support of the shareholder's proposal, not to exceed 200 words, along with its statement of opposition. This shareholder prerogative has been used to oppose the making of napalm, to force companies to deal with forms of discrimination, and to deal with company-caused environmental problems. SEC rules allow management to exclude shareholder proposals for the following reasons:

1. The matter is moot.
2. The matter is not significantly related to the issuing company's business.
3. The matter relates to ordinary business operations.
4. The matter would violate state or federal law if included in a proxy proposal passed by the board of directors.[7]

Any issuing company that supplies a proxy statement that is misleading to its shareholders may be held civilly liable under Section 18 of the Exchange Act to any person who relies on such statements in the buying or selling of registered securities. The SEC is authorized to force compliance with proxy rules by invoking injunctive relief. Additionally, the U.S. Supreme Court had held that a private right of action exists for damages and other relief under Section 14 in light of Section 27, which grants federal district courts jurisdiction over actions "to enforce any liability or duty rendered by the Exchange Act."[8]

Tender Offers

A *tender offer* is an offer by an individual or a corporation to the shareholder of another corporation to purchase a number of shares at a specified price. Tender offers are sometimes referred to as "takeover bids" and are usually communicated through newspaper advertising.

In the 1960s, following a large number of conglomerate mergers, many of which involved bitter struggles between acquiring and targeted corporations, Congress became concerned with charges of fraud, insider trading, and manipulation of markets. As a result, it passed the Williams Act, which amended the Exchange Act by adding provisions giving the SEC authority over tender offers, particularly those involving cash. The three most important provisions governing tender offers are set out in Sections 13(d), 14(d), and 14(e).

Under Section 13(d) any person or group that acquires more than 5 percent of a class of securities registered under the Exchange Act is required to file a statement with the SEC and the issuing company within ten days. It must include:

1. The person or group background and the number of share owners
2. Its purpose in acquiring the stock
3. The source of funds used to acquire the securities
4. Its plans for the targeted company
5. Any contracts or understandings with individuals or groups relevant to the targeted company

It should be noted that if there is a hostile tender offer or takeover bid, the targeted company must also file a statement in its attempt to defeat the takeover.

Section 14(d) sets forth procedural and substantive requirements that must be met in making a tender offer. For example, no tender offer that would result in the ownership of 5 percent or more of a class of securities may be made unless the offeror furnishes each offeree a statement concerning the information required by Section 13(d). Certain substantive requirements dealing with the term of the tender offer are also provided for, as well as such matters as the right of withdrawal of a tender offer, terms of its acceptance, and payment of consideration.

Section 14(e) makes it a criminal offense for any person to misstate or omit a material fact or to engage in fraudulent or deceptive practice in connection with a tender offer. Both civil action by shareholders who have relied on such statements and can show injury as well as SEC-initiated administrative proceedings can be brought. The following case interpreted the meaning of Section 14(e).[9]

Short Swing Profits

Section 16(b) of the Exchange Act seeks to further the goal of full disclosure for potential investors by preventing certain insiders from realizing profits solely by virtue of their access to material information. It prevents directors, officers, and owners of 10 percent of the securities of an issuing corporation that has securities registered with the SEC or a national exchange from realizing profits on stocks by buying and selling within a six-month period. Any such profits must be returned to the corporation. If the corporation fails to sue for recovery of profits, shareholders may file on behalf of the corporation. The SEC seeks to monitor insider short swing profits by requiring officers, directors, and 10-percent owners to file forms with the SEC within ten days of a sale or purchase. It should be noted that major newspapers such as the *Wall Street Journal* also report such buying or selling by insiders.

Securities Fraud

Section 10(b) and Rule 10b–5. As stated in the introduction to this chapter, the Securities Act seeks to ensure full disclosure of material information for potential investors. Therefore, it is important that any form of fraudulent conduct that would distort the free flow of infor-

mation to investors in the securities market be made unlawful.

Section 10(b) of the Exchange Act is referred to as a "catchall" provision to deal with securities fraud. It makes illegal the use of the mails or other facilities of interstate commerce to do the following:

To use or employ, in connection with the purchase or sale of any security, any manipulative or deceptive device or contrivance in contravention of such rules and regulations as the Commission may prescribe as necessary or appropriate in the public interest or for the protection of investors.

Barbara Schreiber v. Burlington Northern, Inc.

U.S. Supreme Court
472 U.S. 1 (1985)

Background: Schreiber (petitioner) on behalf of herself and other shareholders of El Paso Gas Company sued Burlington Northern (respondent) claiming that the company violated 14(e) of the Securities Exchange Act of 1934. In December 1982 Burlington issued a hostile tender offer for El Paso Gas Company. Burlington did not accept the shares traded by a majority of shareholders of El Paso, but rather, rescinded the December tender offer and substituted a January offer for El Paso. The rescission of the first tender offer caused a lesser payment per share to shareholders who retendered following the January offer. The petitioners claims that Burlington's withdrawal of the December tender offer, and the substitution of the January offer, was a "manipulative" distortion of the market for El Paso Stock and a violation of 14(e). The respondent argued that "manipulative" acts under 14(e) require misrepresentation or nondisclosure. They argued that no such acts took place in this case, and moved for dismissal of the case based on a failure to state a cause of action. The federal District Court granted the motion for dismissal. The Court of Appeals affirmed. Schreiber appealed.

Decision: The U.S. Supreme Court affirmed.

Burger, Justice

We are asked in this case to interpret §14(e) of the Securities Exchange Act. The starting point is the language of the statute. Section 14(e) provides:

> It shall be unlawful for any person to make any untrue statement of a material fact or omit to state any material fact necessary in order to make the statements made, in the light of the circumstances under which they are made,

not misleading, or to engage in any fraudulent, deceptive or manipulative acts or practices, in connection with any tender offer or request or invitation for tenders, or any solicitation of security holders in opposition to or in favor of any such offer, request, or invitation. The Commission shall, for the purposes of this subsection, by rules and regulations define, and prescribe means reasonably designed to prevent, such acts and practices as are fraudulent, deceptive, or manipulative.

Our conclusion that "manipulative" acts under §14(e) require misrepresentation or nondisclosure is buttressed by the purpose and legislative history of the provision. Section 14(e) was originally added to the Securities Exchange Act as part of the Williams Act.

It is clear that Congress relied primarily on disclosure to implement the purpose of the Williams Act. Senator Williams, the Bill's Senate sponsor, stated in the debate:

Today, the public shareholder in deciding whether to accept or reject a tender offer possesses limited information. No matter what he does, he acts without adequate knowledge to enable him to decide rationally what is the best course of action. This is precisely the dilemma which our securities laws are designed to prevent. 113 Cong. Rec. 24664 (1967) (Remarks of Sen. Williams).

The expressed legislative intent was to preserve a neutral setting in which the contenders could fully present their arguments. To implement this objective, the Williams Act added §§13(d), 13(e), 14(e), and 14(f) to the Securities Exchange Act. Some relate to disclosure; §§13(d), 14(d), and 14(f) all add specific registration and disclosure provisions. Others—§§13(e) and 14(d)—require or prohibit certain acts so that investors will possess additional time within which to take advantage of the disclosed information.

To adopt the reading of the term "manipulative" urged by petitioner would not only be unwarranted in light of the legislative purpose but would be at odds with it. Inviting judges to read the term "manipulative" with their own sense of what constitutes "unfair" or "artificial" conduct would inject uncertainty into the tender offer process. An essential piece of information—whether the court would deem the fully disclosed actions of one side or the other to be "manipulative"—would not be available until after the tender offer had closed. This uncertainty would directly contradict the expressed congressional desire to give investors full information.

Congress' consistent emphasis on disclosure persuades us that it intended takeover contests to be addressed to shareholders. In pursuit of this goal, Congress, consistent with the core mechanism of the Securities Exchange Act, created sweeping disclosure requirements and narrow substantive safeguards. The same Congress that placed such emphasis on shareholder choice would not at the same time have required judges to oversee tender offers for substantive fairness.

We hold that the term "manipulative" as used in §14(e) requires misrepresentation or nondisclosure. It connotes "conduct designed to deceive or defraud investors by controlling or artificially affecting the price of securities." Without misrepresentation of nondisclosure, §14(e) has not been violated.

Applying that definition to this case, we hold that the actions of respondents were not manipulative. The amended complaint fails to allege that the cancellation of the first tender offer was accompanied by any misrepresentation, nondisclosure or deception.

Defensive Strategies

The *business judgment rule* is based principally on the fifty states' case law and the Revised Model Business Corporations Act. It has traditionally allowed management in targeted companies wide latitude, as long as they act in good faith in the best interests of the shareholders, do not waste the corporate assets, or enter into conflict of interest situations. Defensive tactics to prevent hostile takeovers include (1) awarding large compensation packages ("golden parachutes") to target company management when there is a rumored takeover, (2) issuing new classes of securities before or during a takeover battle that require a tender offerer to pay much more than the market rate ("poison pill"), or (3) buying out a "hostile" shareholder at a price far above the current market price of the target company's stock in exchange for the "hostile shareholders" agreement not to buy more shares for a long time ("greenmail").

Other defensive strategies include (1) writing supermajority requirements into the bylaws and corporation articles for merger approval ("porcupine provisions"), (2) issuing treasury shares (stock repurchased by the issuing corporation) to friendly parties, (3) moving to states with strong antitakeover ("shark repellent") laws, (4) bankrupting a company ("scorched earth" policy), and (5) attempting by target companies to find a "white knight." This statutory provision's broad language encompasses all possible forms of fraud that the Commission may proscribe using its rule-making powers. In 1942 the Commission set forth Rule 10b–5, which has been the foundation for most SEC and private enforcement action dealing with fraudulent conduct. It states:

It shall be unlawful for any person, directly or indirectly, by the use of any means or instrumentality of interstate commerce, or of the mails, or of any facility of any national securities exchange,

(1) to employ any device, scheme, or artifice to defraud,
(2) to make any untrue statement of a material fact necessary in order to make the statements made, in the light of circumstances under which they were made, not misleading, or
(3) to engage in any act, practice, or course of business which operates or would operate as a fraud or deceit upon any person, in connection with the purchase or sale of any security.

The reader should be aware that the rule applies to *any* purchase or sale by *any* person of *any* securities in interstate commerce. Whether or not a company is registered under the Exchange Act is unimportant. Thus all the exempted securities and transactions previously set forth in this chapter are *not* exempted from Rule 10b–5. Privately held corporations, as well as those publicly held, can be held liable under the rule. It should be noted that the conduct of the purchaser as well as the seller is covered by Rule 10b–5. Further, there must be a misrepresentation or deceptive omission of a material fact with intent shown.

The rule is basically an antifraud provision designed to prohibit manipulative or deceptive practices. Both the SEC and private parties alleged to have been injured may bring actions because no specific standards for determining fraud under Rule 10b–5 were set out by the Commission. It was left to the federal courts to develop criteria. In the 1960s and early 1970s federal district and appellate courts developed a broad interpretation of fraud under 10b–5, imposing liability for negligent conduct as well as for intended or deliberate acts. With a change in the makeup of the Supreme Court in the mid–1970s, private and SEC actions alleging fraud were held to a narrower *intent* (scienter) standard, with some federal courts imposing liability for knowing or reckless behavior.[10] An illustration of the present standard of liability for fraud under Rule 10b–5 is provided by the following case. This case has special importance for the accounting profession.

Ernst & Ernst v. Hochfelder

Supreme Court of the United States
425 U.S. 185 (1976)

Background: Ernst & Ernst (defendant-appellant) is a "big eight" accounting firm retained by First Securities Company (First Securities), a small brokerage firm, to audit its books and records, to prepare annual reports for SEC filing, and to respond to questionnaires from the Midwest Stock Exchange.

Plaintiff-respondents were customers of First Securities who invested in a fraudulent securities scheme perpetrated by Leston B. Nay, president of the firm and owner of 92 percent of its stock. Nay induced the respondents to invest funds in "escrow" accounts that he represented would yield a high rate of return. Respondents did so from 1942 through 1966, with the majority of the transactions occurring in the 1950s. In fact, there were no escrow accounts since Nay converted respondents' funds to his own use immediately upon receipt. These transactions were not in the customary form of dealings between First Securities and its customers. The respondents drew their personal checks payable to Nay or a designated bank for his account. No such escrow accounts were reflected on the books and records of First Securities, and none was shown on its periodic accounting to respondents in connection with their other investments. Nor were they included in First Securities' filings with the SEC or the Exchange.

The fraud came to light in 1968 when Nay committed suicide, leaving a note that described First Securities as bankrupt and the escrow accounts as "spurious." Respondents subsequently filed this action for damages against Ernst & Ernst in the U.S. District Court for the Northern District of Illinois under Section 10(b) of the 1934 Act. The complaint charged that Nay's escrow scheme violated Section 10(b) and Commission Rule 10b–5, and that Ernst & Ernst had "aided and abetted" Nay's violations by its "failure" to conduct proper audits of First Securities. As revealed through discovery, respondents' cause of action rested on a theory of negligent nonfeasance. The premise was that Ernst & Ernst had failed to utilize "appropriate auditing procedures" in its audits of First Securities, thereby failing to discover internal practices of the firm said to prevent an effective audit. The practice principally referred to was Nay's rule that only he could open mail addressed to him at First Securities or addressed to First Securities to his attention, even if it arrived in his absence. Respondents contended that if Ernst & Ernst had conducted a proper audit, it would have discovered this "mail rule." The existence of the rule then would have been disclosed in reports to the Exchange and to the SEC by Ernst & Ernst as an irregular procedure that prevented an effective audit. This would have led to an investigation of Nay that would have revealed the fraudulent scheme. Respondents specifically disclaimed the existence of fraud or intentional misconduct on the part of Ernst & Ernst.

The District Court granted Ernst & Ernst's motion for summary judgment and dismissed the action. The Court of Appeals for the Seventh Circuit reversed and remanded, holding that one who breaches a duty of inquiry and disclosure owed another is liable in damages for aiding and abetting a third party's violation of Rule 10b–5 if the fraud would have been discovered or prevented but for the breach. The Court stated in its reasoning that Ernst & Ernst had both a common law and statutory duty of inquiry into the adequacy of First Securities' internal control system by virtue of its contractual duties to audit and prepare filings with the SEC.

Decision: Reversed. The U.S. Supreme Court ruled in favor of Ernst & Ernst.

Powell, Justice

We granted certiorari to resolve the question whether a private cause of action for damages will lie under §10(b) and Rule 10b–5 in the absence of any allegation of "scienter"—intent to deceive, manipulate, or defraud. We conclude that it will not and therefore we reverse.

Section 10(b) makes unlawful the use or employment of "any manipulative or deceptive device or contrivance" in contravention of Commission rules. The words "manipulative or deceptive" used in conjunction with "device or contrivance" strongly suggest that §10(b) was intended to proscribe knowing or intentional misconduct.

In its "amicus curiae" brief, however, the Commission contends that nothing in the language "manipulative or deceptive device or contrivance" limits its operation to knowing or intentional practices. In support of its view, the Commission cites the overall congressional purpose in the 1933 and 1934 Acts to protect investors against false and deceptive practices that might injure them.

The Commission then reasons that since the effect upon investors of given conduct is the same regardless of whether the conduct is negligent or intentional, Congress must have intended to bar all such practices, not just those done knowingly or intentionally.

In addition to relying upon the Commission's argument with respect to the operative language of the statute, respondents contend that since we are dealing with "remedial legislation," it must be construed " 'not technically and restrictively, but flexibly to effectuate its remedial purposes.' " They argue that the "remedial purposes" of the Acts demand a construction of §10(b) that embraces negligence as a standard of liability.

Although the extensive legislative history of the 1934 Act is bereft of any explicit explanation of Congress' intent, we think the relevant portions of that history support our conclusion that §10(b) was addressed to practices that involve some element of scienter and cannot be read to impose liability for negligent conduct alone.

The section was described rightly as a "catch all" clause to enable the Commission "to deal with new manipulative (or cunning) devices." It is difficult to believe that any lawyer, legislative draftsman, or legislator would use these words if the intent was to create liability for merely negligent acts or omissions. Neither the legislative history nor the briefs supporting respondents identify any usage or authority for construing "manipulative (or cunning) devices" to include negligence.

We have addressed to this point, primarily the language and history of §10(b). The Commission contends, however, that subsections (b) and (c) of Rule 10b–5 are cast in language which—if standing alone—could encompass *both intentional* and *negligent* behavior. These subsections respectively provide that it is unlawful "[t]o make any untrue statement of a material fact or to omit to state a material fact necessary in order to make the statements made, in the light of the circumstances under which they were made, not misleading . . ." and "[t]o engage in any act, practice, or course of business which operates or would operate as a fraud or deceit upon any person . . ." Viewed in isolation the language of subsection (b), and arguably that of subsection (c), could be read as proscribing, respectively, any type of material misstatement or omission, and any course of conduct, that has the effect of defrauding investors, whether the wrongdoing was intentional or not.

We note first that such a reading cannot be harmonized with the administrative history of the Rule, a history making clear that when the Commission adopted the Rule, it was intended to apply only to activities that involved scienter. More importantly, Rule 10b–5 was adopted pursuant to authority granted the Commission under §10(b). The rule-making power granted to an administrative agency charged with the administration of a federal statute is not the power to make law. Rather, it is " 'the power to adopt regulations to carry into effect the will of Congress as expressed by the statute.' " Thus, despite the broad view of the Rule advanced by the Commission in this case, its scope cannot exceed the power granted the Commission by Congress under §10(b). For the reasons stated above, we think the Commission's original interpretation of Rule 10b–5 was compelled by the language and history of §10(b) and related sections of the Acts. When a statute speaks so specifically in terms of manipulation and deception, and of implementing devices and contrivances—the commonly understood terminology of intentional wrongdoing—and when its history reflects no more expansive intent, we are quite unwilling to extend the scope of the statute to negligent conduct.

Over the past forty years Rule 10B–5 has been most frequently applied to three forms of conduct: (1) insider trading, (2) corporate misstatements, (3) corporate mismanagement.

Insider Trading. *Insider trading* may be defined as the buying or selling of securities of a corporation by individuals who have access to nonpublic material information and have a fiduciary obligation to shareholders and potential investors. In most cases the courts have also required a showing that the insider or a tippee to whom the nonpublic material information was given benefited from trading on that information. The SEC and courts originally defined "insiders" as corporate officers, directors, and major stockholders. Over the years Rule 10b–5 has been interpreted to include anyone who receives nonpublic material information from a corporate source. Courts have found insider trading by partners in a brokerage firm,[11] broker-dealers acting as underwriters,[12] and even an employee of a financial printing firm who worked on documents that in-volved a contemplated tender offer.[13] (See Table 37-1)

In the financial printing firm case, which is set out here the U.S. Supreme Court appeared to limit the scope of the rule by defining "insiders" as those who "have a relationship of trust and confidence with shareholders."

Vincent F. Chiarella v. United States

Supreme Court of the United States

445 U.S. 222 (1980)

Background: In 1975 and 1976, Chiarella (defendant), a printer, worked as a "markup man" in the composing room of Pandick Press, a New York financial printer. Among documents that the defendant handled were five announcements of corporate take-over bids. When these documents were delivered to the printer, the identities of the acquiring and target corporations were concealed by blank spaces or false names. The true names were sent to the printer on the night of the final printing.

The defendant, however, was able to deduce the names of the target companies before the final printing from other information contained in the documents. Without disclosing his knowledge, the defendant purchased stock in the target companies and sold the shares immediately after the takeover attempts were made public. By this method, the defendant realized a gain of slightly more than $30,000 in the course of fourteen months. Subsequently, the SEC began an investigation of his trading activities. In May 1977 the defendant entered into a consent decree with the Commission in which he agreed to return his profits to the sellers of the shares. On the same day he was discharged by Pandick Press.

In January 1978 the defendant was indicted on seventeen counts of violating Section 10(b) of the Securities Exchange Act of 1934 (1934 Act) and SEC Rule 10b–5. After the defendant unsuccessfully moved to dismiss the indictment, he was brought to trial and convicted on all counts. The Court of Appeals affirmed his conviction. Decision: Reversed. The Supreme Court of the United States ruled in favor of Chia-rella.

Powell, Justice

The question in this case is whether a person who learns from the confidential documents of one corporation that it is planning an attempt to secure control of a second corporation violates §10(b) of the Securities Exchange Act of 1934 if he fails to disclose the impending takeover before trading in the target company's securities.

In this case, the defendant was convicted of violating §10(b) although he was not a corporate insider and he received no confidential information from the target company. Moreover, the "market information" upon which he relied did not concern the earning power or operations of the target company, but only the plans of the acquiring company. Defendant's use of that information was not a fraud under §10(b) unless

TABLE 37-1 INSIDER TRADING CRIMINAL CASES

A LINE UP OF INSIDERS

A SAMPLER OF MAJOR CRIMINAL CASES BROUGHT BY THE U.S. ATTORNEY'S OFFICE RELATED TO INSIDER TRADING

Defendant	Title	Company	Sentence
Adrian Antoniu	Associate	Morgan Stanley; Kuhn Loeb	Thirty-nine months probation, $5,000 fine[a]
Peter N. Brant	Stockbroker	Kidder, Peabody	Awaiting sentence[a]
E. Jacques Courtois	VP mergers and acquisitions	Morgan Stanley	Six months imprisonment
Steven M. Crow	Word processor	Skadden, Arps	Three years probation, restitution, 150 hours of community service each year of probation[a]
Michael David	Attorney	Paul Weiss	Arrested, awaiting trial
Howard L. Davidowitz	Accountant	Ernst & Whinney	Thirty-nine weekends imprisonment, $10,000 fine, five years probation
Kenneth P. Felis	Stockbroker	Kidder, Peabody	Six months imprisonment, $25,000 fine, 500 hours community service
Carlo Florentino	Attorney	Wachtell, Lipton; Davis Polk	Two years imprisonment
Alan Ihne	Manager, office services	Sullivan & Cromwell	Three and one-half years imprisonment and five years probation
Darius N. Keaton	Director	Santa Fe International	Indicted, awaiting trial
Dennis B. Levine	Managing director	Drexel Burnham	Awaiting sentence
Kenneth Petricig and Alfred Salvatore	Proofreaders	Skadden, Arps	Three years probation, restitution, 150 hours of community service each year of probation
Kenneth Rubinstein	Attorney	Fried, Frank	Thirty months probation
W. Paul Thayer	Former chairman	LTV Corporation	Four years imprisonment, $5,000 fine
Giuseppe Tome	Branch manager	Baird-Patrick & Company	Indicted, currently a fugitive in Europe
R. Foster Winans	Reporter	*Wall Street Journal*	Eighteen months imprisonment, $5,000 fine, five years probation, 400 hours community service

[a]Defendant pleaded guilty and cooperated with the investigation.
Source: U.S. Attorney, Southern District of New York. (Reprinted in *New York Times*, May 18, 1986, Section 3, p. F-8.)

he was subject to an affirmative duty to disclose it before trading. In this case, the jury instructions failed to specify any such duty. In effect, the trial court instructed the jury that defendant owed a duty to everyone; to all sellers, indeed, to the market as a whole. The jury simply was told to decide whether defendant used material nonpublic information at a time when "he knew other people trading in the securities market did not have access to the same information."

The Court of Appeals affirmed the conviction by holding that "anyone—corporate insider or not—who regularly received material nonpublic information may not use that information to trade in securities without incurring an affirmative duty to disclose." Although the court said that its test would include only persons who regularly receive material, nonpublic information, its rationale for that limitation is unrelated to the existence of a duty to disclose. The Court of Appeals, like the trial court, failed to identify a relationship between defendant and the sellers that could give rise to a duty. Its decision thus rested solely upon its belief that the federal securities laws have "created a system providing equal access to information necessary for reasoned and intelligent investment decisions." The use by anyone of material information not generally available is fraudulent, this theory suggests, because such information gives certain buyers or sellers an unfair advantage over less informed buyers and sellers.

This reasoning suffers from two defects. First, not every instance of financial unfairness constitutes fraudulent activity under §10(b). Second, the element required to make silence fraudulent—a duty to disclose—is absent in this case. No duty could arise from petitioner's relationship with the seller of the target company's securities, for petitioner had no prior dealings with them. He was not their agent, he was not a fiduciary, he was not a person in whom the sellers had placed their trust and confidence. He was in fact, a complete stranger who dealt with the sellers only through impersonal market transactions.

In this case, as we have emphasized before, the 1934 Act cannot be read " 'more broadly than its language and the statutory scheme reasonably permits.' " Section 10(b) is aptly described as a catch-all provision, but what it catches must be fraud. When an allegation of fraud is based upon nondisclosure, there can be no fraud absent a duty to speak. We hold that a duty to disclose under §10(b) does not arise from the mere possession of nonpublic market information. The contrary result is without support in the legislative history of §10(b) and would be inconsistent with the careful plan that Congress has enacted for regulation of the securities markets.

Following this decision the SEC adopted Rule 14e-3, which makes it illegal for "any person to purchase or sell a security while in possession of material nonpublic information about a prospective tender offer, if he or she knows or has reason to know that such information emanates from either the offering person or the issuer or person acting on their behalf."

In September 1982 the SEC extended its enforcement scope with regard to insider trading in American stocks to individuals who use Swiss bank accounts to trade in stocks illegally. In a memorandum of understanding negotiated with Swiss officials, a system was established in Switzerland to process SEC requests for information about bank clients suspected of insider trading. A special three-member Swiss commission was set up to review these inquiries. Upon receipt of a SEC request for information the Swiss bank involved freezes assets in a client's account equal to his or her alleged trading profits, studies the SEC allegations, and reports to the Swiss special commission. That panel then makes a decision as to whether the bank should honor the SEC request. If the SEC loses, it may appeal to the Swiss Federal Banking Commission. Prior to this agreement, bank secrecy legislation in Switzerland provided insiders with a shield against disclosure of trading in American stocks based on nonpublic information. The SEC sees this agreement as a model for future understandings with countries like the Bahamas, Panama, Bermuda, and the Cayman Islands that also have bank secrecy laws.

Corporate Misstatements. In addition to disclosure required by the Securities Act of 1933 (Sections 13 and 14) when dealing with proxies and other documents filed with the SEC, Rule 10b–5 prohibits misstatements in the form of overoptimistic profit reports or press releases as to earnings if they would affect the prudent judgment of potential investors. In the landmark case of *SEC* v. *Texas Gulf Sulfur,*[14] executives were held liable for releasing pessimistic, not overoptimistic, statements concerning the possible success of Texas Gulf's (TGS) exploration for ore. After denying the company's success in its Timmens, Ontario, operation, executives purchased stock, or calls on the stock, knowing of a potential ore discovery. The same information was undisclosed to the investing public, to sellers, the stock option committee of TGS, or the TGS board of directors. TGS argued that the press release denying ore discoveries was not issued "in connection with the purchase or sale of securities." Since the company was not engaged in buying or selling securities at the time of the release, there was no violation of Rule 10b–5. The Second Circuit Court of Appeals rejected this argument, stating that prices of TGS stock had been artificially held down by the pessimistic press release, enabling the executives and their tippees, acting on information not available to potential investors, to purchase stock and options at low prices. The court, basing its decision on the legislative history of 10(b), found that the SEC was correct in stating that there was a connection between the press release and the investing public's transactions if it "would cause reasonable investors to rely thereon, and in connection therewith, so relying, cause them to purchase or sell a corporation's security." In that case the court deemed that a misleading statement needed a "wrongful purpose" for it to be a violation of Section 10(b) and Rule 10b–5.

Corporate Mismanagement The *Hochfelder* case previously set out in this chapter is an obvious illustration of corporate mismanagement and fraud upon shareholders. Shareholder derivative suits or minority stockholders' actions have become common in attacking transactions dealing with mergers and reorganizations, and sales and purchases of corporations of their own securities. State incorporation laws provide for a fiduciary duty between shareholders and a corporation's officers and directors. Suits have been based on breaches of this duty. When attempts have been made by shareholders to avoid state corporation law and to sue on the basis of fraud under Section 10(b), the Supreme Court has been reluctant to "federalize" state corporate law.[15] The courts have refused to allow actions for mismanagement under Rule 10b–5 unless the plaintiffs (shareholders) have bought or sold securities in the transactions under question and there exists some connection between the alleged fraud and the transactions.

Insider Trader Sanctions Act. Following this decision and *Dirks* v. *United States,*[16] where the SEC was unable to persuade the U.S. Supreme Court to broaden its definition of insider trading, Congress enacted the *Insider Trader Sanctions* Act of 1984. The Act leaves the definition of insider trading to the courts. It does, however, provide for treble damages ("three times the profits gained or avoided") to be levied against "any person who has violated any provision [of the 1934 Act] or rules or regulations while in possession of material nonpublic information. . . ." The treble damage provision does not apply to aiders and abettors, but other provisions of the Act do. The Act increases criminal penalties for insider trading and other violations of the Exchange Act from $10,000 to $100,000 per violation. The Act also expressly allows the SEC to bring administrative proceedings against individuals within an organization who are responsible for its violation. Previously the Commission had to use an "aid and abet" theory. Before this Act the sole enforcement remedies available to the SEC had been an injunction against future violations and disgorgement of profits. Using its new administrative enforcement power, the SEC General Counsel has proposed that members of boards of directors who are continually found guilty of insider trading be barred from serving as officers or members of the boards of any U.S. registered corporations. However, the Act leaves three important issues unresolved: (1) definition of insider trading, (2) the availability of treble damages to injured private plaintiffs, (3) who are "aiders" and "abettors" under the statute.

THE FOREIGN CORRUPT PRACTICES ACT OF 1977

Background

In 1973, during the Watergate hearings, Americans learned for the first time about illegal domestic political contributions made by corporations to President Nixon's 1972 reelection campaign. The SEC undertook a study in 1974 of these secret payments, viewing the companies' failures to disclose as violations of the Exchange Act of 1934. The SEC found upon further investigation that corporations had made questionable payments overseas as well. The Commission's staff concluded that there were clear patterns of illegal or questionable payments both domestically and overseas. The SEC considered these payments *material* information under the Securities Acts because they affected the integrity of both management and the record-keeping procedures of the companies involved. This undisclosed information, in the eyes of the Commission, would in all likelihood have altered the judgment of a reasonably prudent investor. The corporations argued that disclosure was not required because the amounts involved were small compared to sales or earnings and thus not material. The SEC interpretation of materiality was accepted by the Supreme Court in 1976. The Court defined "material information" as that which a "reasonable investor would consider important in deciding how to vote, or whether to buy, sell or hold securities."[17] The SEC brought thirty-nine enforcement actions prior to passage of the Foreign Corrupt Practices Act, alleging violations of the Exchange Act. The Commission also set up in 1975 a volunteer disclosure program whereby companies were encouraged to conduct investigations of their operations and, upon finding questionable payments, to discuss appropriate disclosure methods with the SEC staff. More than 450 companies admitted making questionable or illegal payments totaling more than $300 million; 117 of the *Fortune* 500 were involved.[18] Payments had been made to high-level officials for the purpose of obtaining contracts. In the enforcement actions, as well as in the voluntary disclosure program, corporate officials testified that these "bribes" or "commissions" were a means of doing business. They were "facilitating" or "grease" payments that were often necessary to meet the competition of

---

ETHICS BOX
Ethics and International Issues

—

Many have argued that insider trading should not be illegal and is not unethical. They argue that insiders' ability to trade on nonpublic information is good for the marketplace in that it shows that an officer or director has confidence in his or her firm because they trade in their own stocks and that others will then follow. Others argue that it is part of the "perks" of being an officer or director. It is an incentive device particularly when applied to stock options awarded managers as compensation. Still others believe the cost of enforcing insider trading rules far outweighs benefits. They argue that insider trading is simply so far-reaching and indefinable that no particular government agency can regulate it.

Some of these arguments are supported by looking at Japanese and European markets where little effort is made to control insider trading. When the Tokyo Stock Exchange does discover insider trading it issues warnings to violators that remain confidential, thus denying investors the chance to know who are the "bad guys." In thirty-eight years Japan has prosecuted only five securities law violations. This may be explained in some part by Japanese cultural aversion to adversary processes and to court systems in general. Only in late 1986 after a major scandal has Great Britain shown some concern over insider trading. Prior to that time, of the 100 cases the London Stock Exchange turned over to the British government, only a handful were prosecuted. In Germany trading on nonpublic material information is not illegal.

Of course, the fact that some argue insider trading should not be criminally sanctioned and that some foreign countries do not have strictly enforced laws cannot justify engaging in insider trading. So long as it is illegal in the United States insider trading is unethical to engage in. The arguments that the law is inefficient or erratically enforced do not make a sufficient case, on ethical grounds, for disobeying the law.

---

other American firms as well as of foreign multinationals. In many cases it was learned that the payments were treated by corporate accountants as expense items and illegally deducted as business expenses on income-tax returns filed with the Internal Revenue Service.

Although the Justice Department was able to prosecute some payments under currency-transaction regulations and mail-wire fraud statutes, statutory authority to reach questionable payments overseas for foreign political bribery was only indirect. The SEC had forced disclosure under Exchange Act provisions, but by 1977 Congress felt a need to take further action.

Provisions

The Foreign Corrupt Practices Act was enacted because Congress considered corporate bribes to foreign officials to be (1) unethical, (2) harmful to our relations with foreign governments (Korean and Japanese officials were forced to resign after disclosure of payments from American-based multinational corporations), and (3) unnecessary to American companies doing business overseas.

Passed in 1977, the act applies to all "domestic concerns" whether or not doing business overseas and whether or not registered with the SEC. Examined here are its antibribery and accounting provisions.

The act's antibribery provisions[20] prohibit all domestic concerns, whether or not registered with SEC, from offering or authorizing corrupt payments to:

1. A foreign official (or someone acting in an official capacity for a foreign government)
2. A foreign political party official or a foreign political party
3. A candidate for political office in a foreign country

A payment is "corrupt" if its purpose is to get the recipient to act or refrain from acting so the American firm can retain or get business. The standard that corporate officials are held to is "knowing" or "has reason to know." If he or she knows or should know that a payment violates the provisions of the act, the official and the company will be held liable.

Officers, directors, stockholders, employees, and U.S. agents who act on behalf of the company and willfully violate the act's antibribery provisions can be fined up to $10,000 per violation and imprisoned for not more than five years. Companies cannot directly or indirectly pay fines for convicted officers or employees.

The Foreign Corrupt Practices Act (FCPA) prohibits the "offer" or "promise" of a bribe even if it is not consummated. It prohibits the payment of "anything of value." The *Congressional Record* indicates that small gifts and tokens of hospitality that are customarily given in a foreign country do not fall within the prohibitions of the FCPA, even if made to officials. Only "political" payments are prohib-

ited. This raises the question of whether a bribe paid to a company owned by a foreign official is illegal. "Foreign officials" are not clerical or ministerial employees. Thus payments to a clerk in order to get goods through customs *may* not be prohibited by the act. There is no maximum set on these "grease payments" as long as the recipient is merely "clerical or ministerial." The "reason to know" standard of liability for directors and officers of corporations indicates that all domestic companies must be aggressive in setting and enforcing strict ethical standards for doing business.

The accounting provisions of the act apply only to companies subject to the Securities Acts—that is, only public nonexempt companies. The SEC, in its report to Congress on illegal and questionable payments,[21] requested some reforms. Congress enacted record-keeping and internal-control provisions. The accounting provisions were enacted as amendments to the Exchange Act, Sections 13(b)2(A) and 13(b)2(B).

Section 13(B)2(A) requires that all publicly held, registered companies "make and keep books, records and accounts in reasonable detail" that "accurately and fairly" reflect transactions and disposition of assets. Concern has been expressed whether inaccuracies involving small amounts would violate the FCPA.

Section 13(b)(2)B requires publicly held companies to maintain systems of internal controls sufficient to provide "reasonable assurances" that transactions are executed in accordance with management's authorization, that transactions are recorded to permit preparation of financial statements in accordance with generally accepted accounting principles, and that at regular intervals management compares records with the actual assets available. There exists no particular definition of "reasonable assurances," although the *Congressional Record* indicates that Congress intended that the cost of maintaining the system should not exceed its benefits.[22]

The penalties for willful violation of the accounting provisions are those imposed by the Exchange Act. They include fines of up to $10,000 and imprisonment up to five years. In all cases brought by the SEC for violations of the accounting provisions only civil remedies have been sought.

Enforcement

The SEC and the Justice Department share responsibility for enforcing the Foreign Corrupt Practices Act. SEC is charged with investigating suspected violations of the bribery and accounting provisions. The SEC can bring only civil actions, but it may recommend criminal enforcement to the Justice Department. The Justice Department has authority to proceed civilly and criminally against domestic concerns alleged to have violated the antibribery provisions.

STATE SECURITIES LAWS

State regulation of securities began in 1911 when Kansas enacted a securities statute. The U.S. Supreme Court in 1917 called such regulations of securities "blue-sky" laws, describing their purpose as "the prevention of speculative schemes which have no more basis than so many feet of blue sky."[23] In enacting the 1933 Securities Act, Congress specifically preserved the power of the states to regulate securities transactions of an *intrastate* nature. All fifty states, the District of Columbia, and Puerto Rico have enacted securities statutes. A corporation issuing securities in interstate commerce must meet the registration requirements of each of the states in which its securities are sold as well as the federal requirements. The cost and time involved in meeting various state requirements has led to the adoption of the Uniform Securities Act (USA), in whole or in part, by some thirty states.

Common Provisions

Almost all state statutes contain provisions covering: registration of securities, broker-dealer registration, and fraud in issuance and trading of securities.

Registration of Securities. The 1933 Securities Act has served as a model for state statutes with regard to types of information required for registration. There are generally three methods of registration: notification, qualification, and coordination. Unlike the federal securities acts, state laws provide that securities may be registered by notification when the issuing corporation meets certain tests of reliability and earnings. In most states notification is effective if the state administrator of the securities law does not take action within a number of days after filing. When an issuing company registers in a "coordination" state the same procedure is followed except that generally a prospectus is all that is required. In "qualification" states, following the filing of information, registration of the securities is not effective until the state administrator has approved. It should be noted that this power is in sharp contrast to that of the SEC under the 1933 Act. The SEC has no power to determine the worth of a particular filing. The sole purpose of the federal securities acts is to provide full disclosure of material information for potential investors. State administrators, however, may evaluate the securities being issued as well as the issuing corporation. Most states exempt from registration those securities exempted by the 1933 Securities Act—for example, governmental securities and securities issued by institutions subject to different federal regulatory statutes. Additionally, state securities legislation exempts securities listed on major stock exchanges.

Broker-Dealer Registration and Fraud. Almost every state statute requires registration by brokers and agents. Some establish licensing requirements and reserve the right to deny or revoke licenses. Issuers or broker-dealers must post surety bonds in many states.

Most states have adopted antifraud provisions similar to those set forth in Section 10–b of the Exchange Act and Rule 10b–5. States generally use some form of injunctive relief as a remedy for fraud, but many also have criminal provisions in their statute. The USA would permit individual investors to recover money damages.

Conflict Between Federal and State Security Statutes

As noted earlier, fifty-two separate jurisdictions in addition to the federal government have statutes governing securities registration and trading. Often securities statutes apply to any offer or sale of securities in a state, but many transactions involve a seller or securities-issuing company incorporated or doing business in one state and a buyer located in another state. Besides the question of which state law governs the particular sale of a security, serious federal-state constitutional questions have arisen. For example, at what point do state statutes interfere with federal securities laws and become a burden on interstate commerce? In a landmark case that follows the U.S. Supreme Court for the first time fully discussed this question. The reader should examine the importance the Court attaches to the Commerce Clause first discussed in Chapter 2 of this text. Also, the Court refers to the *MITE Corp.* case (Edgar V. Mite Corporation 457 U.S. 624 (1982)). In that case the court struck down an Illinois statute that required the secretary of state to review all tender offers made to Illinois corporations in order to determine their fairness. When the secretary determined that a tender offer was not fair, and was about to issue a cease and desist order, the tender offeror went to federal district court and obtained an injunctive order. The Court of Appeals and the U.S. Supreme Court affirmed stating that the Illinois statute violated the Commerce Clause of the U.S. Constitution, and that the federal Williams Act preempted the statute.

CTS Corporation v. Dynamics Corporation of America

U.S. Supreme Court

— U.S. — (1987)

Background: The federal Williams Act and implementing regulations govern hostile corporate stock tender offers by requiring, *inter alia,* that offers remain open for at least twenty business days. An Indiana Act applies to certain business corporations chartered in Indiana that have specified levels of shares or shareholders within the State. The Indiana Act provides that the acquisition of "control shares" in such a corporation—shares that, but for the Act, would bring the acquiring entity's voting power to or above certain threshold levels—does not include voting rights unless a majority of all preexisting disinterested shareholders so agree at their next regularly scheduled meeting. However, the stock acquirer can require a special meeting within fifty days by following specified procedures. The appellee, Dynamics Corporation, announced a tender offer that would have raised its ownership interest in CTS Corporation above the Indiana Act's threshold. Dynamics also filed suit in federal District Court alleging federal securities violations by CTS. After CTS opted into the Indiana Act, Dynamics amended its complaint to challenge the Act's validity. The District Court granted Dynamics' motion for declaratory relief, ruling that the Act is preempted

by the Williams Act and violates the Commerce Clause. The Court of Appeals affirmed, adopting the holding of the plurality opinion in *Edgar* v. *MITE Corp.,* that the
Williams Act preempts state statutes that upset the balance between target company
management and a tender offeror. The court based its preemption finding on the view
that the Indiana Act, in effect, imposes at least a fifty-day delay on the consummation
of tender offers and that this conflicts with the minimum twenty-day hold-open period
under the Williams Act. The court also held that the state Act violates the Commerce
Clause since it deprives nonresidents of the valued opportunity to accept tender offers
from other nonresidents.

Decision: Reversed. The Supreme Court of the United States ruled in favor of the CTS
Corporation.

Powell, Justice

Our discussion begins with a brief summary of the structure and purposes of the
Williams Act. Congress passed the Williams Act in 1968 in response to the increasing
number of hostile tender offers. Before its passage, these transactions were not covered by the disclosure requirements of the federal securities laws. The Williams Act,
backed by regulations of the Securities and Exchange Commission (SEC), imposes
requirements in two basic areas. First, it requires the offeror to file a statement
disclosing information about the offer, including: the offeror's background and identity; the source and amount of the funds to be used in making the purchase; the
purpose of the purchase, including any plans to liquidate the company or make major
changes in its corporate structure; and the extent of the offeror's holdings in the target
company.

Second, the Williams Act, and the regulations that accompany it, establish procedural rules to govern tender offers. For example, stockholders who tender their shares
may withdraw them during the first 15 business days of the tender offer and, if the
offeror has not purchased their shares, any time after 60 days from commencement
of the offer. The offer must remain open for at least 20 business days. If more shares
are tendered than the offeror sought to purchase, purchases must be made on a pro
rata basis from each tendering shareholder. Finally, the offeror must pay the same
price for all purchases; if the offering price is increased before the end of the offer,
those who already have tendered must receive the benefit of the increased price.

The Indiana Act operates on the assumption, implicit in the Williams Act, that
independent shareholders faced with tender offers often are at a disadvantage. By
allowing such shareholders to vote as a group, the Act protects them from the coercive
aspects of some tender offers. If, for example, shareholders believe that a successful
tender offer will be followed by a purchase of nontendering shares at a depressed
price, individual shareholders may tender their shares—even if they doubt the tender
offer is in the corporation's best interest—to protect themselves from being forced to
sell their shares at a depressed price. In such a situation under the Indiana Act the
shareholders as a group, acting in the corporation's best interest, could reject the offer.
The desire of the Indiana Legislature to protect shareholders of Indiana corporations
from this type of coercive offer does not conflict with the Williams Act. Rather, it
furthers the federal policy of investor protection.

In implementing its goal, the Indiana Act avoids the problems the plurality discussed in MITE. Unlike the MITE statute, the Indiana Act does not give either management or the offeror an advantage in communicating with the shareholders about the impending offer. The Act also does not impose an indefinite delay on tender offers. Nothing in the Act prohibits an offeror from consummating an offer on the 20th business day, the earliest day permitted under applicable federal regulations. Nor does the Act allow the state government to interpose its views of fairness between willing buyers and sellers of shares of the target company. Rather, the Act allows *shareholders* to evaluate the fairness of the offer collectively.

The principal objects of dormant Commerce Clause scrutiny are statutes that discriminate against interstate commerce.

Dynamics nevertheless contends that the statute is discriminatory because it will apply most often to out-of-state entities. This argument rests on the contention that, as a practical matter, most hostile tender offers are launched by fearers outside Indiana. But this argument avails Dynamics little. "The fact that the burden of a state regulation falls on some interstate companies does not, by itself, establish a claim of discrimination against interstate commerce." Because nothing in the Indiana Act imposes a greater burden on out-of-state fearers than it does on similarly situated Indiana fearers, we reject the contention that the Act discriminates against interstate commerce.

This Court's recent Commerce Clause cases also have invalidated statutes that adversely may affect interstate commerce by subjecting activities to inconsistent regulations. The Indiana Act poses no such problem. So long as each State regulates voting rights only in the corporations it has created, each corporation will be subject to the law of only one State. No principle of corporation law and practice is more firmly established than a State's authority to regulate domestic corporations, including the authority to define the voting rights of shareholders. Accordingly, we conclude that the Indiana Act does not create an impermissible risk of inconsistent regulation by different States.

The Court of Appeals did not find the Act unconstitutional for either of these threshold reasons. Rather, its decision rested on its view of the Act's potential to hinder tender offers. We think the Court of Appeals failed to appreciate the significance for Commerce Clause analysis of the fact that state regulation of corporate governance is regulation of entities whose very existence and attributes are a product of state law. Every State in this country has enacted laws regulating corporate governance. By prohibiting certain transactions, and regulating others, such laws necessarily affect certain aspects of interstate commerce. This necessarily is true with respect to corporations with shareholders in States other than the State of incorporation. Large corporations that are listed on national exchanges, or even regional exchanges, will have shareholders in many States and shares that are traded frequently. The markets that facilitate this national and international participation in ownership of corporations are essential for providing capital not only for new enterprises but also for established companies that need to expand their businesses. This beneficial free market system depends at its core upon the fact that a corporation—except in the rarest situations—is organized under, and governed by, the law of a single jurisdiction, traditionally the corporate law of the State of its incorporation.

These regulatory laws may affect directly a variety of corporate transactions. Mergers are a typical example. In view of the substantial effect that a merger may have on the shareholders' interests in a corporation, many States require supermajority votes to approve mergers. By requiring a greater vote for mergers than is required for other transactions, these laws make it more difficult for corporations to merge. State laws also may provide for "dissenters' rights" under which minority shareholders who disagree with corporate decisions to take particular actions are entitled to sell their shares to the corporation at fair market value. By requiring the corporation to purchase the shares of dissenting shareholders, these laws may inhibit a corporation from engaging in the specified transactions.

It thus is an accepted part of the business landscape in this country for States to create corporations, to prescribe their powers, and to define the rights that are acquired by purchasing their shares. A State has an interest in promoting stable relationships among parties involved in the corporations it charters, as well as in ensuring that investors in such corporations have an effective voice in corporate affairs.

There can be no doubt that the Act reflects these concerns. The primary purpose of the Act is to protect the shareholders of Indiana corporations. It does this by affording shareholders, when a takeover offer is made, an opportunity to decide collectively whether the resulting change in voting control of the corporation, as they perceive it, would be desirable. A change of management may have important effects on the shareholders' interests; it is well within the State's role as overseer of corporate governance to offer this opportunity. The autonomy provided by allowing shareholders collectively to determine whether the takeover is advantageous to their interests may be especially beneficial where a hostile tender offer may coerce shareholders into tendering their shares.

Appellee Dynamics responds to this concern by arguing that the prospect of coercive tender offers is illusory, and that tender offers generally should be favored because they reallocate corporate assets into the hands of management who can use them most effectively. As indicated *supra* Indiana's concern with tender offers is not groundless. Indeed, the potentially coercive aspects of tender offers have been recognized by the Securities and Exchange Commission. The Constitution does not require the States to subscribe to any particular economic theory. We are not inclined "to second-guess the empirical judgments of lawmakers concerning the utility of legislation." In our view, the possibility of coercion in some takeover bids offers additional justification for Indiana's decision to promote the autonomy of independent shareholders.

Dynamics argues in any event that the State has " 'no legitimate interest in protecting the nonresident shareholders.' " Dynamics relies heavily on the statement by the *MITE* Court that "[i]nsofar as the . . . law burdens out-of-state transactions, there is nothing to be weighed in the balance to sustain the law." But that comment was made in reference to an Illinois law that applied as well to out-of-state corporations as to instate corporations. We agree that Indiana has no interest in protecting nonresident shareholders *of nonresident corporations.* But this Act applies only to corporations incorporated in Indiana. We reject the contention that Indiana has no interest in providing for the shareholders of its corporations the voting autonomy granted by the

Act. Indiana has a substantial interest in preventing the corporate form from becoming a shield for unfair business dealing. Moreover, like the Illinois statute invalidated in MITE, the Indiana Act applies only to corporations that have a substantial number of shareholders in Indiana. Thus, every application of the Indiana Act will affect a substantial number of Indiana residents, whom Indiana indisputably has an interest in protecting.

Dynamics' argument that the Act is unconstitutional ultimately rests on its contention that the Act will limit the number of successful tender offers. There is little evidence that this will occur. But even if true, this result would not substantially affect our Commerce Clause analysis. We reiterate that this Act does not prohibit any entity—resident or nonresident—from offering to purchase, or from purchasing, shares in Indiana corporations, or from attempting thereby to gain control. It only provides regulatory procedures designed for the better protection of the corporations' shareholders. We have rejected the "notion that the Commerce Clause protects the particular structure or methods of operation in a . . . market." The very commodity that is traded in the securities market is one whose characteristics are defined by state law. Similarly, the very commodity that is traded in the "market for corporate control"—the corporation—is one that owes its existence and attributes to state law. Indiana need not define these commodities as other States do; it need only provide that residents and nonresidents have equal access to them. This Indiana has done. Accordingly even if the Act should decrease the number of successful tender offers for Indiana corporations this will not offend the Commerce Clause.

On its face, the Indiana Control Share Acquisitions Chapter evenhandedly determines the voting rights of shares of Indiana corporations. The Act does not conflict with the provisions or purposes of the Williams Act. To the limited extent that the Act affects interstate commerce, this is justified by the State's interests in defining the attributes of shares in its corporations and in protecting shareholders. Congress has never questioned the need for state regulation of these matters. Nor do we think such regulation offends the Constitution. Accordingly, we reverse the judgment of the Court of Appeals.

REVIEW PROBLEMS

1. What is the major difference in purpose between the Securities Act of 1933 and the Securities Exchange Act of 1934?

2. What criteria are used by the courts to determine whether an instrument or transaction is a "security" within the meaning of the 1933 Act?

3. Which securities are exempt from registration under the 1933 Act?

4. Define insider trading under the 1934 Exchange Act.

5. What defenses may be used by target companies in an effort to prevent a hostile takeover?

6. How do state securities statutes differ from the federal securities laws?

7. A owned oil and gas leases in Ohio. Because he needed cash he sought to sell in-

terests in the leases. He organized three separate corporations for this purpose, and each sold $1 million in securities over a twelve-month period. Do the corporations need to register under the 1933 Securities Act, or are they exempt? Explain.

8. A was a journalist for the *Wall Street Journal*. He wrote a column telling of rumors on Wall Street about various companies' health or lack of it. His roommate, B, traded on this information before it was published, because he found drafts of A's columns in the wastebasket in the room where A wrote. B also passed information on to C. The SEC charged A with being a tipper under Section 10(b) of the Exchange Act and B and C with being tippees. Should A, B, and C be found guilty of insider trading under Section 10(b)(5) of the 1934 Exchange Act? Explain.

9. Maresh, a geologist, owned some oil and gas leases on land in Nebraska. He entered into an oral agreement with Garfield whereby the latter would provide some investment funds for Maresh to drill for oil. Garfield, a businessman, knew a great deal about oil stocks and the securities market. He promised to wire the money to Maresh, who began drilling immediately. Maresh found out that the land was dry before he received Garfield's money. Garfield refused to invest as he had promised, claiming that the offered lease investment was a "security" within the meaning of the Securities Act of 1933 and that it had not been registered. What result? Garfield v. Strain, 320 F.2d 116 (10th Cir. 1963)

10. Continental Tobacco Company, a manufacturer of cigarettes, sold some unregistered five-year debentures, paying 6 percent common stock, to thirty-eight persons between June 1969 and October 1970. All investors prior to purchase signed an agreement with Continental

that acknowledged receipt of unaudited financial statements, other information about the corporation, access to officers of the company, knowledge of the risk involved, and that they were experienced investors. Purchasers went to meetings in a room where telephones were manned and orders for securities continually came in. One investor called the meetings a "boiler plate operation" where high-pressure tactics were used to sell the securities. The SEC brought suit against Continental claiming that it was selling unregistered securities. The company claimed that its sale of securities was a private offering and thus was exempt from registration under the 1933 Act. SEC v. Continental Tobacco Co., 463 F.2d 137 (5th Cir. 1972)

11. Truckee Showboat, a California corporation, offered to sell its common stock to residents of California through the use of the U.S. mail. Its offer to sell was advertised in the *Los Angeles Times* on June 18, 1957, and the offer was made exclusively to residents of the State of California. The proceeds of the sale of the stock, minus commission, were to be used to acquire the El Cortez Hotel in Las Vegas, Nevada. Truckee Showboat, Inc. was incorporated and kept all its records in California. All its directors and officers were Californians. The SEC charged the company with issuing unregistered nonexempt securities under the 1933 Act. Truckee Showboat claimed an intrastate exemption. What result? SEC v. Truckee Showboat, Inc., 157 F.Supp. 824 (S.D. Calif. 1957)

12. Livingston was a twenty-year employee of Merrill Lynch, a large securities investment firm. Livingston was a securities salesman who was given the title "account executive." In January 1972 the company gave Livingston and forty-seven other account executives the title "vice-president" as a reward for outstanding sales records.

All of their duties and responsibilities were the same as before this recognition. Livingston never acquired any executive duties and never attended board of directors meetings. In November and December 1972 Livingston sold 1,000 shares of Merrill Lynch stock. In March 1973 he repurchased the same number of shares, making a profit of $14,836.37. The company sued for the profits, claiming that Livingston by virtue of his inside information made short swing profits in violation of Section 16(b) of the Securities Exchange Act of 1934. The defendant denied this charge. What result? Merrill Lynch, Pierce, Fenner, Smith v. Livingston, 566 F.2d 1119 (9th Cir. 1978)

13. Mills was a minority shareholder of Electric Auto-Lite Company. Prior to the merger of Auto-Lite and Mergenthaler into the Mergenthaler Linotype Co., Mergenthaler owned 50 percent of Auto-Lite and dominated its board of directors. American Manufacturing Company in turn had control of Mergenthaler and through it controlled Auto-Lite. Auto-Lite's management at the time of the merger sent out a proxy statement to shareholders of Auto-Lite telling them that their board of directors recommended that they vote for approval of the merger. They failed to include in the proxy statement information concerning the fact that Morgenthaler dominated the board and that American Manufacturing through Morgenthaler controlled Auto-Lite. Mills and other minority shareholders filed a class-action and derivative suit claiming that management had sent out a misleading proxy in violation of Section 14 of the Exchange Act of 1934 and that the merger should be set aside. Management and the board of directors of the merged company claimed that there was no material omission in the proxy statement. What result? Mills v. Auto-Lite, 396 U.S. 375 (1970)

14. Lakeside Plastics and Engraving Company (LPE) was a closed corporation incorporated in the State of Minnesota in 1946. It suffered losses until 1952, when it showed a yearly profit but still a large overall deficit. Fields and King in 1946 had each purchased thirty shares, which they held. Myzel, a relative of the Levine family, founders of the company, advised Fields and King in 1954 that the company stock was not worth anything and the company was going out of business. Both sold their shares to Myzel, who sold them to the Levine family at a substantial profit. Myzel failed to disclose before purchasing the shares that there were increased sales in 1953, a new Blatz contract, and profits of $30,000, along with the potential of 1954 sales. Fields, King, and others in separate actions sought damage for violation of 10(b) of the Exchange Act of 1934. What result? Myzel v. Fields, 386 F.2d 718 (8th Cir. 1967)

NOTES

[1] Statutes affecting securities that are not discussed in this chapter include The Public Utility Holding Company Act of 1935, The Trust Indenture Act of 1939, The Investment Company Act of 1940, Bankruptcy Reform Act of 1978 (Chapter 11), The Securities Investor Protection Act of 1970.

[2] 328 U.S. 293 (1946).

[3] Exchange National Bank v. Touche Ross & Co., 544 F.2d 1126 (2d Cir. 1976).

[4] United Housing Foundation v. Foreman, Inc., 421 U.S. 837 (1975).

[5] SEC v. Continental Tobacco, 463 F.2d 137 (5th Cir. 1972).

[6] 283 F.Supp. 643 (S.D. N.Y. 1968).

[7] In August 1983 the SEC amended Regulation 14a to define for the first time "matters not significantly related to business" as those accounting for more than 5 percent of the assets, earnings, and sales of a company. Shareholder proposals can now be excluded if a stockholder does not own more than $1,000 worth of stock, or 17 percent of the shares outstanding, for a period of one year or more. Also, a proposal can be excluded when it has been previously submitted, and has received less than 5 percent of the vote. Shareholders are limited to one proposal per company per annual meeting.

[8] See J.I. Case Co. v. Berak, 377 U.S. 426 (1964).

[9] See Electronic Speciality Co. v. International Controls Corp., 409 F.2d 937 (2d Cir. 1969).

[10] See Santa Fe Industries v. Green, 430 U.S. 462 (1977); Aaron v. SEC 446 U.S. 680 (1980).

[11] Cady Roberts and Co., 40 S.E.C. 907 (1961).

[12] Investors Management Co., 44 S.E.C. 633 (1971).

[13] Chiarella v. U.S., 45 U.S. 222 (1980).

[14] 401 F.2d 833 (2d Cir. 1968).

[15] See Santa Fe Industries v. Green, 430 U.S. 462, 467 (1977).

[16] See Superintendent of Insurance v. Bunkers Life and Casualty Co., 404 U.S. 6 (1971), Blue Chip Stumps v. Manor Drugstore, 421 U.S. 723 (1976).

[17] TSC Industries, Inc. v. Northway, 426 U.S. 438, 449 (1976).

[18] See U.S. Congress, House Committee on Interstate and Foreign Commerce, *Unlawful Corporate Payments Act of 1977,* H.R. Rep 640, 95th Congress, 1st Session, 1977, p. 4.

[19] 463 U.S. 646 (1983).

[20] 15 U.S.C., 78 dd-1, 78 dd-2, 78 ff.

[21] Securities and Exchange Commission, *Report on Questionable and Illegal Corporate Payments and Practices,* May 12, 1976. SEC Release 34-15570.

[22] Senate Report on S. 3664, 94th Congress, 2d Session, 1977, p. 12.

[23] Hall v. Geiger Jones Co., 24 U.S. 539 (1917).

PART V

PROPERTY AND RELATED TOPICS

Personal Property

W hen a person speaks of property he or she usually refers to something he or she owns—a piano, an automobile, a house. From a legal standpoint, however, the things themselves are not significant. What is important are the rights the individual has in them. Traditional legal usage defines *property* as the bundle or aggregate of rights that people have in things they own. These include the right to use, sell, or even destroy the thing if the person wishes to do so.

PROPERTY AND GOVERNMENT

The very existence of property depends on government. State and federal laws create and maintain the "bundle of rights" that the legal system refers to as property. A trademark, for example, has value because the government establishes certain guarantees and protections for its owner. The mutual promises of a contract have economic significance because courts will award damages if a promise is not kept. A patent is property because society, through law, supports the owner's capacity to control the actions of others through it.

Conversely, although a person's right to travel is important, it is not property. The state establishes no bundle of rights relating to one's passport. All that an individual can do is travel or refrain from traveling. This can also be said of other civil rights, such as the right to vote. Figure 38-1 illustrates some of the rights that an owner of property can have in things.

Whether something is considered as property is important because both federal and state constitutions prohibit the government from taking "property" without due process of law. More will be said about this in Chapter 39.

REAL AND PERSONAL PROPERTY

One of the points stressed throughout this book is that legal institutions often reflect dominant economic, political, and social values. Property law illustrates this point.

Until about 150 years ago land was the most

FIGURE 38–1
Property: A Bundle or Package of Rights

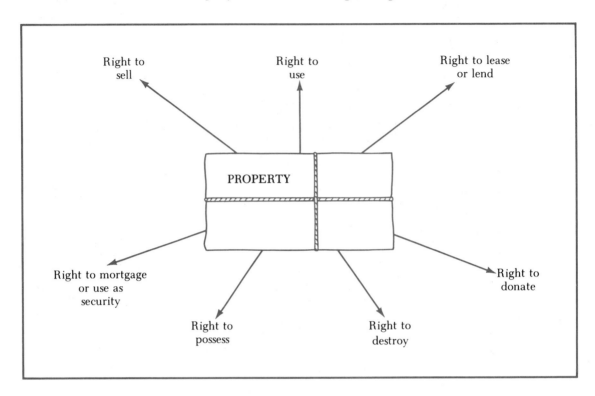

important source of wealth and a major determinant of social position in both England and the United States. Ownership of land also had important political significance, since often only landowners were permitted to vote. Today items of personal property, particularly intangibles, often are more important sources of individual wealth than is land.

Real Property

One result of the historic importance of land is a distinction in Anglo-American law between it and other forms of wealth. Because of land's economic significance, the early common law provided extensive protection to landowners. A landowner ousted from possession could immediately bring an action to recover the land. This was known as a real ac-

tion, and it is the reason that land is called *real property* or real estate. However, a person who lost control of something of economic value other than land, usually a movable item, initially could sue only for money. This was known as a personal action and the item involved was thus considered *personal property*. In modern law the distinction between real and personal property continues to be recognized.

Personal Property

Personal property generally is characterized as movable. Historically, personal property consisted of items that had substance. These items were often referred to as *goods or chattels*. In the farm economy that existed in the United States until this century, livestock, farm equipment, and the tools of a person's trade were common examples. Along with land, these items were major forms of wealth. As the nature of the American economy changed, new forms of wealth were created. Today a significant amount of wealth is in the form of *intangible property* (for example, bank accounts, corporate stock or bonds). It consists of rights that a person has that represent value. An intangible right, often referred to as a chose (French, "thing") in action, is also personal property.

Intangible Personal Property

Consider the intangible personal property of a stock certificate. The certificate is evidence of value, although it has no worth itself. The owner of the stock can sell it, use it as security, or give it away. He or she also has numerous rights in relation to the firm, other owners, and creditors. Intangible property figures in many business transactions. In addition to corporate stocks and bonds, intangible personal property also includes patents, trademarks, copyrights, and trade secrets. These types of intangible property are generally referred to as intellectual property. Table 38-1 provides examples of property within different classifications; Cases discussing the different types of property are also noted.

Intellectual Property

Intellectual property is intangible property that is generally created by mental rather than physical efforts. Four types of intellectual property are discussed here: patents, trademarks, copyrights, and trade secrets. The first three are governed primarily by federal law, whereas trade secrets are mostly regulated by state laws.

Patents

A *patent* protects inventions by giving to its owner the right to make, sell, and use the product or process. New drugs, ballpoint pens and sewing machines are all products that have been patented. A patent is issued by the Patent Office for products that are original, novel, useful, and nonobvious. If the product is not new, has no usefulness, or is obvious to a person of ordinary skill in a particular field, it will not be patentable. Unlike most of the other types of intellectual property, the pro-

TABLE 38-1 CLASSIFICATION OF PROPERTY

Type	Example	Case Reference
Real property Real estate	Forty acres of farmland; house and garage in city	—
Real property Fixtures	Built-in-oven	*George* v. *Commercial Credit Corp.*
Trade fixtures	Machines	In Re *Park Corrugated Box Corp.*
Personal Property Goods or chattels	Chairs, typewriters, and other movable items	*Barron* v. *Edwards*
Intangible property Economic assets	Stock certificate, bank account	—
Intangible property Intellectual property	Patent, trademark, copyright	—
Intangible property Emerging rights	Right to employment, license to practice law, status and reputation	*Memphis Development Foundation* v. *Factors*

cess for obtaining a patent is often time-consuming and expensive. In the United States most patents are granted for a period of seventeen years. In exchange for the novel and useful invention of the inventor the government gives the patent owner an exclusive monopoly for a limited time.

While patents are issued to the person inventing the product or process, the patent holder may assign his or her rights to others. Thus an inventor may, in exchange for royalty payments, assign a patent to a firm that agrees to manufacture and market the new product. Frequently corporations will require as a condition of employment that scientists or engineers employed by it agree that any patents developed within the scope of the employee's job belong to the corporation. In such cases the patent will be issued to the corporation instead of to the employees who worked on the invention.

During this period anyone who uses the patented product without the consent of the patent holder may be committing patent infringement. A person who infringes a patent can be held liable for damages caused to the patent holder and stopped from committing future infringements. After the term of the patent has expired, other firms or individuals are free to use the information about the patented product to make and sell their own products.

Trademarks

A *trademark* is a mark on goods that distinguishes those goods from goods of competitors. The mark may be a picture, a word, or a design. The golden arches of McDonald's are trademarked; they are used on packages and in advertisements to show the consumer that the products originate from that firm instead of from competitors. Although most people refer to all marks as trademarks, in fact there are four types of marks that are protected by federal law:

1. Trademarks—IBM and Coca-Cola are trademarks used to identify goods originating from a specific company.
2. Service marks—Holiday Inn and McDonald's are service marks because the mark identifies the user's services.
3. Certification marks—Napa Valley wines or Grade A meats are certification marks because they certify that goods come from a particular region or that certain standards have been met by the manufacturer of the goods.
4. Collective marks—Girl Scouts of America is a collective mark used by an association to identify and distinguish its goods, such as cookies, or services from those offered by nonmembers.

The Lanham Act establishes a system of federal registration for all such marks (we refer to them hereafter as trademarks). Registered trademarks are valid for twenty years and if the mark is still in use in commerce after that period, it can be renewed for an additional twenty years. The Act also makes unauthorized use of that mark illegal. Both Pepsi and Coke are registered trademarks of competing soft drink manufacturers. Thus, if you order a "Coke" in a restaurant that serves only" Pepsi," you will likely be asked if Pepsi is okay. If the restaurant does not ask, it could be accused of trying to pass off another product when you have ordered one from a certain source.

In order to have a valid trademark, the public must associate the mark with the firm or source from which it comes. If everyone were to associate Coke with any cola drink, it no longer could be trademarked. The name then would be available to anyone wanting to use it. This happened with the names Kleenex and the LITE beer; those names once were valid trade names, but they became associated in the minds of the public with generic products rather than products from one particular producer. A similar problem seems to be occurring with several products, such as the copy machines manufactured by the Xerox Corporation or the cola from Coca-Cola, which are very popular today. The Xerox Corporation, which has placed advertisements, such as the one illustrated in Figure 38-2, in numerous newspapers and magazines, is seeking to call the public's attention to the proper usage of its tradename.

Copyrights

A *copyright* protects the original work of authors, painters, and musicians who produce original works of artistic or intellectual merit. This book is copyrighted, so it is illegal for anyone to take the words used by the authors and treat them as their own words. Like the owner of the patent who assigns the patent to a firm that agrees to manufacture and market a novel product, the writer or artist frequently assigns the copyright for his or her work to the publisher that agrees to produce the work for sale. A copyright is effective for the life of the creator plus an additional fifty years. If there is more than one creator, as is true of this book, the copyright lasts for fifty years beyond the life of the longest surviving creator.

A common-law copyright exists once a work is created. However, if the work is widely distributed without statutory copyright protection, it becomes part of the public domain and is no longer protected by copyright law. Statutory protection is available if the work is published and distributed with a copyright notice. The notice can take the form of the word, "copyright," the abbreviation, "copr," or a symbol "©," followed by the year and the name of the copyright holder. The copyright for this text is located on the back side of the title page.

While the words or tune used by an author or composer are copyrightable, an idea is not subject to copyright. Thus you can read portions of this text and use ideas from it to create your own book. However, as the term "copyright" suggests, the creator of this text or a particular song has the right to determine who can copy his or her creation. Some use of copyrighted material is permitted under the fair use doctrine.

You can quote a paragraph or two from the text and use it in a report or a review you are writing about the book. It is fair use, for example, that allows you to copy for your own use a song played on the radio onto your tape or compact disk. Similarly, you can copy a television show onto your VCR for later personal enjoyment by you. However, as the broadcasters of baseball games and other televised athletic contests remind us, "no rebroadcast or other use of the copyrighted game and the play-by-play announcement of it is permissible without the written consent of major league baseball and the competing teams."

Trade Secrets

Trade secrets are valuable formulas, patterns, or information used in a business that are not known to competitors. Thus two elements must be present in order to have a trade secret. First, there must be some valuable information such as a customer list, a process for making a certain product, or a special recipe. Second, the information must be kept secret. If the information is widely known to other competitors or to the public in general, it cannot be a trade secret.

Employees working in sensitive positions are often asked to sign agreements to keep certain information confidential. Although employees with access to such information have that duty anyway, since as Chapter 30 notes they are agents of the employer, a written agreement may help to ensure that the information is intended to be kept secret. Unlike the other types of intellectual property, trade secrets are not protected for a specific period of time. Instead, it is the duration of the information as being valuable and secret that

FIGURE 38–2
Trademark Protection: The Xerox Corporation

There are two R's in Xerox.

One is right in the middle.

But the really important one is the one you probably never notice.

It's the little R in a circle—like the one you see at the bottom of this ad—that tells you that Xerox is a registered trademark.

And it reminds you that our name —which is also our trademark—should only be used in connection with the products and services of our corporation.

Including everything from Xerox copiers to information processors to electronic printers.

So as you can see, our trademark is a very valuable one.

To us. And to you, too.

Because it ensures that when you ask for something you can be sure of what you're going to get.

Of course, we don't expect you to use the second R every time you use our name.

But we do hope you'll give it a second thought.

XEROX

XEROX® is a trademark of XEROX CORPORATION.

TABLE 38-2 INTELLECTUAL PROPERTY

Type of Property	What Is Protected	Period of Protection
Patent	Right to make, sell, and use product	Seventeen years
Trademark	Use of mark by other manufacturers or sellers of similar products or services	Twenty years plus twenty years if still in use
Copyright	Unauthorized copying of words, music, or artistic work of creator	Life of creator plus fifty years
Trade secret	Wrongful appropriation of valuable and secret information such as customer list, special manufacturing process, or unique recipe	As long as information is secret

determines the period of protection granted to its owner.

The owner of a trade secret is protected from its wrongful appropriation. If someone reverse engineers a product or figures out through trial and error your secret recipe, no wrongful appropriation has occurred. On the other hand, if an employee of your firm is bribed to give the customer list or unique manufacturing process wrongfully to a competitor, a wrongful appropriation of your trade secret has occurred.

Patents and trade secrets can both protect ideas. If the inventor of the idea believes he or she can keep the idea secret for longer than the term for which a patent is granted, he or she may want to make it into a trade secret rather than patent it. This is what the owners of the Coca-Cola syrup formula have done; they have kept secret their method of making the syrup and have never patented that process. Conversely, the patent guaran-

tees protection for an established time period, and even if others were about to discover the same idea you discovered when you patented its use on a particular type of product, your protection continues for seventeen years after the patent is applied for. Table 38-2 portrays the different types of intellectual property and the protection available to owners.

As new forms of wealth have been created, personal property has become more like real property in economic significance. This trend has led to a narrowing of the legal distinction between the two, but differences continue to exist and to influence decisions that businesspeople must make. The distinction between real and personal property raises numerous insurance, tax, financing, and inheritance questions. In the case that follows the distinction between the two types of property influenced the outcome of the litigation.

Barron v. Edwards

Court of Appeals of Michigan
206 N.W.2d 508 (1973)

Background: Barron (plaintiff-appellee) entered into an oral agreement to sell sod to Edwards (defendant-appellant). The land on which the sod was growing was then condemned by the State Highway Department. Barron sued to stop Edwards from removing the sod. He claimed the sod was a part of the realty that had been condemned by the State Highway Department. Barron also asserted that since the agreement concerned real estate, the agreement was unenforceable because it was not in writing as required by the Statute of Frauds.

Edwards argued that since the sod was a growing crop, it was to be treated as goods under the law and could be removed by him. He also claimed the written confirmation of the sale that he received from Barron satisfied the Statute of Frauds requirements.

The trial court decided in favor of Barron. It held that the contract was for the sale of an interest in land and was unenforceable because it was not in writing. Edwards appealed to the Court of Appeals.

Decision: The Court of Appeals reversed.

Bashara, Judge

Plaintiff owned and operated a sod farm in Wayne County. Defendant was in the business of selling sod and had purchased sod from plaintiff on several prior occasions. Defendant alleges that on November 10, 1969, he entered into an oral contract with plaintiff whereby he agreed to purchase the plaintiff's entire crop of sod, consisting of approximately 30 acres, for $350.00 per acre. Defendant paid $700.00 in 1969 and removed approximately 1½ acres of sod. His answer alleged that the understanding between the parties was that he would remove the remaining 28 acres in the spring of 1970.

On April 9, 1970, plaintiff notified defendant that the State Highway Department had condemned and taken title to the entire farm. He offered to return the $700.00 and reimburse the defendant for any funds expended on maintaining the sod. This payment was refused by defendant.

The statutory provisions applicable to the solution of this problem are M.C.L.A. Section 440.2105(1); M.S.A. Section 19.2105(1), and M.C.L.A. Section 440.2107(2); M.S.A. Section 19.2107(2), which provide:

> Sec. 2105. (1) "Goods" means all things (including specially manufactured goods) which are moveable at the time of identification to the contract for sale other than the money in which the price is to be paid, investment securities and things in action. "Goods" also includes the unborn young of animals and *growing crops and other identified things attached to realty as described in the section on goods to be severed from realty.* [Emphasis supplied by the court.]

> Sec. 2107. (2) A contract for the sale apart from the land of growing crops or other things attached to realty and capable of severance without material harm thereto but not described in subsection (1) is a contract for the sale of goods within this article whether the subject matter is to be severed by the buyer or by the seller even though it forms part of the realty at the time of contracting, and the parties can by identification effect a present sale before severance.

Although these provisions do not specifically state what is to be included within the meaning of growing crops, the Official Comment to 2–105 of the Uniform Commercial Code contains the following statement:

Growing crops are included within the definition of goods since they are frequently intended for sale. The concept of "industrial" growing crops has been abandoned, for under modern practices fruit, perennial hay, nursery stock and the like must be brought within the scope of this Article.

Thus, if sod can be considered a crop rather than a part of the realty, it is within the above-cited statutory provisions. The factors used in determining this issue are stated in 21 Am. Jur.2d, Crops, Sec. 3, pp. 581–582:

> The primary and most easily recognizable distinction is that between fructus naturales and fructus industriales. Apart from statutes or peculiar circumstances requiring a contrary conclusion, it is stated in many cases that those products of the earth which are annual, raised by yearly manurance and labor, and which owe their annual existence to cultivation by man, may be treated as personal chattels, for some purposes at least, even while still annexed to the soil and irrespective of their maturity. Conversely, and also in the absence of statutory provisions or peculiar circumstances requiring a contrary conclusion, fructus naturales—grasses growing from perennial roots and, according to some courts, the fruit or other products of trees, bushes, and plants growing from perennial roots—are regarded as realty while they are unsevered from the soil.

Here the sod owed its existence to yearly fertilizing and cultivation by man. It is also significant that plaintiff raised this sod on several prior occasions and apparently treated it as a commercial product. Thus, this sod cannot be considered "growing grass" as the plaintiff contends. We therefore hold that the sod in the instant case was personalty.

This result is supported by recent decisions which have interpreted the above-cited statutory provisions. In *Groth* v. *Stillson,* this Court held that Christmas trees were growing crops. Our Court relied on the fact that the trees required annual care, and that such trees were a fruit of industry. Likewise, in the instant case, the sod owed its existence to annual maintenance and fertilization.

Plaintiff further argues that even if this Court finds that the sod in question is personalty, the contract is nevertheless unenforceable due to M.C.L.A. Sec. 440.–2201; M.S.A. Sec. 19.2201, which provides in relevant part:

> Sec. 2201. (1) Except as otherwise provided in this section a contract for the sale of goods for the price of $500.00 or more is not enforceable by way of action or defense unless there is some writing sufficient to indicate that a contract for sale has been made between the parties and signed by the party against whom enforcement is sought or by his authorized agent or broker. A writing is not insufficient because it omits or incorrectly states a term agreed upon but the contract is not enforceable under this paragraph beyond the quantity of goods shown in such writing.
>
> (2) Between merchants if within a reasonable time a writing in confirmation of the contract and sufficient against the sender is received and the party receiving it has reason to know its contents, it satisfies the requirements of

subsection (1) against such party unless written notice of objection to its contents is given within 10 days after it is received.

Defendant does not dispute the fact that the contract was for the sale of goods valued at more than $500.00 but contends that subsection (2) controls the instant case. We agree.

The record indicates that both parties were merchants. Defendant was in the business of selling and installing sod and the plaintiff had sold sod on numerous occasions. The record further indicates that a confirmatory memorandum was sent by the defendant to the plaintiff and that the plaintiff did not send a written notice of objection until the 10-day period had elapsed.

The appellee counters that this provision is not controlling of the instant case since the confirmatory memorandum was not delivered within a reasonable time as required by statute.

As to what constitutes a reasonable time, M.C.L.A. Sec. 440.1204(2); M.S.A. Sec. 19.1204(2), states:

What is a reasonable time for taking any action depends on the nature, purpose and circumstances of such action.

We agree that, under the circumstances present in the instant case, there is a factual question as to whether the defendant sent the memorandum within a reasonable time. Since an accelerated judgment was granted, there was no testimony with regard to this question. We remand so as to allow the trier of fact to determine this issue. Reversed and remanded. Costs to defendant.

FIXTURES

As the previous case indicates, the classification of property as real or personal has important legal consequences. In many situations conflicting arguments exist for classifying property one way or the other. Naturally, individuals and firms wish to have property classified in the manner most beneficial to them. This classification problem is further complicated by the fact that the property's designation can change, depending on how it is used.

A common example is items used in home construction, such as a built-in oven. The oven would be personal property when part of a building supplier's inventory. But as part of a dwelling, the built-in oven becomes real property. As we mentioned in Chapter 23, personal property that becomes real property through attachment to land or a building is called a *fixture.*

In some instances real property is transformed into personal property. This change is often referred to as severance. Trees growing in a forest are real property, but if a tree is cut to be milled into lumber or stacked as firewood it becomes personal property. In some states courts recognize the doctrine of constructive severance. In these states trees standing in a forest are considered personal property as soon as a contract is made selling them to be logged.

Determination of Fixtures

The chief test in determining whether personal property has become a fixture is the intention of the party who attached the item to real property. This intention is not the secret intention of that person, but the intention determined by how the person acted. Other factors that courts consider are how the item is attached and its application and use as a permanent part of the realty. Often attachment and use are considered only as evidence of what was intended. The *George* case that follows indicates the importance of intention. In a case that appears later in this chapter, *In Re Park Corrugated Box Corporation*, alternative approaches to determining fixtures are discussed.

George v. Commercial Credit Corp.

U.S. Court of Appeals

440 F.2d 551 (7th Cir. 1971)

Background: George (petitioner-appellant), a trustee in bankruptcy for Foskett, claimed an interest in a mobile home owned by the bankrupt, Foskett. Commercial Credit Corp. (respondent-appellee) was the assignee of a mortgage that Foskett had taken out on the property. George claimed the mobile home was an item of personalty and thus not a part of the real estate on which the mortgage had been given. Commercial Credit argued that the mobile home was a fixture, attached to the realty, and thus had become a part of it.

The bankruptcy referee found the mobile home to be a fixture and rejected George's claim for the property. George appealed to the Court of Appeals.

Decision: The Court of Appeals affirmed the referee's decision.

Duffy, Senior Circuit Judge

Foskett owned five acres of land in Jefferson County, Wisconsin. On December 6, 1968, he purchased a Marshfield Mobile Home, No. 9090, from Highway Mobile Home Sales, Inc. He signed an installment contract and paid $880 on the purchase price of $8,800. Added was a sales tax and interest covering a ten-year period.

Sometime in December 1968, Foskett executed a real estate mortgage to Highway Mobile Home Sales, Inc. The mortgage recites the sum of $14,227.70 and described the real estate in metes and bounds. The mortgage was assigned to Commercial Credit Corporation, the respondent-appellee herein.

The mobile home here in question could not move under its own power. It was delivered to Foskett's real estate property by Mobile Sales. This mobile home was never again operated on or over the highways as a motor vehicle.

The mobile home here in question was 68 feet in length, 14 feet in width, and 12 feet in height. It contained six rooms and weighed 15,000 pounds.

The bankrupt owned no other home and he and his wife occupied the mobile home continuously from December 6, 1968 until forced to vacate same by order of the Trustee in Bankruptcy.

The home was set on cement cinder blocks three courses high. It was connected with a well. It was hooked up to a septic tank. It also was connected with electric power lines.

The bankrupt never applied for a certificate of title from the Wisconsin Motor Vehicle Department. However, he did apply for a homeowner's insurance policy and he asked the seller to remove the wheels from his home. He also applied for a building permit and was told he had to construct a permanent foundation for the home. The permit was granted upon condition that the foundation be constructed within one year. However, within that period, the petition for bankruptcy was filed.

The issue before us can be thus stated: Commercial Credit Corporation argues that the mobile home was a fixture under applicable law and is not personalty. The trustee insists that the mobile home was and still is a "motor vehicle" and is personalty.

The mobile homes industry has grown rapidly in the last few years. There has been a great demand for relatively inexpensive housing by middle income families. In Wisconsin, a distinction is now recognized between mobile homes (those used as homes) and motor homes (those often used as vehicles).

In the recent case of *Beaulieu* v. *Minnehoma Insurance Company,* the Wisconsin Supreme Court pointed out the unique character of mobile homes: "As indicated by the plaintiff, a mobile home has a dual nature. It is designed as a house; yet, unlike a house, it is also capable of being easily transported. In the instant case, it was employed solely as an economical means of housing. It was never moved, nor was moving contemplated at the time the insurance coverage was procured."

We look to state law to determine the applicable standards for determining when personalty becomes affixed to real property.

The Wisconsin law on the question is found in *Auto Acceptance and Loan Corp.* v. *Kelm,* where the Wisconsin Supreme Court reaffirmed its decision in *Standard Oil Co.* v. *LaCrosse Super Auto Service, Inc.* That case held that the three tests for determining whether facilities remain personalty or are to be considered part of the realty are (1) actual physical annexation to the realty; (2) application or adaptation to the use or purpose to which the realty is devoted, and (3) intention of the person making annexation to make a permanent accession to the freehold.

In the *Standard Oil Company* case, the Court pointed out that "physical annexation" is relatively unimportant and "intention" of the parties is the principal consideration.

In *Premonstratensian Fathers* v. *Badger Mutual Insurance Co.,* the Court reaffirmed its adherence to the three-fold test saying, "It is the application of these tests to the facts of a particular case which will lead to a determination of whether or not an article, otherwise considered personal property, constitutes a common-law fixture, and hence takes on the nature of real property."

Viewed in light of these Wisconsin tests, the finding of the referee and the District Court that this mobile home had become a fixture must clearly stand. The bankrupt's actual intention pointed definitely toward affixing the mobile home to the land as a permanent residence, as seen in his application for a building permit (which, by law, required him to erect a concrete slab as a permanent foundation within one year), his purchase of a homeowner's insurance policy, and his requests made to the seller to have the wheels of the home removed. Moreover, the home was clearly adapted to use as the permanent residence of the bankrupt and was never moved off of his five-acre plot.

The fact that it may have been physically possible for this mobile home to have been more securely attached to the ground should not alter our position. Physical attachment did occur by means of cinder blocks and a "C" clamp, while connections for electricity, sewage and natural gas were provided as well. Finally, we note that the very size and difficulty in transporting this mobile home further highlight the fact that this was a vehicle which was intended primarily to be placed in one position for a long period of time and to be used as an intended permanent home.

Trade Fixtures

The rule that once personal property is permanently annexed to real estate it becomes a part of it has serious consequences to tenants. Unless the tenant and owner agree, a tenant making permanent additions to real property may not remove a fixture at the end of the term. This greatly hampers a business from leasing a building if the firm needs to add items—such as display cases or machinery—to operate effectively. Because of this, the legal system differentiates between fixtures and personalty attached to real estate to carry on a trade or business.

Items of this latter nature are called *trade fixtures* and generally may be taken by the tenant at the end of the term. Agricultural fixtures are treated in a similar manner. To remove a trade or agricultural fixture, the tenant must restore the premises to its original condition and must remove the item while in possession.

Allowing tenants to remove trade fixtures has social benefits. It encourages both the use of land and efficiency in business. Tenants are more likely to invest in new and improved equipment if they can remove these items. In a number of states, statutes establish tenants' rights to remove trade fixtures.

Because the doctrine of trade fixtures is important to tenants, parties to a commercial lease should include provisions clearly expressing their intentions. They might agree that the tenant shall not remove items that ordinarily would be trade fixtures. On the other hand, a lease provision stating the tenant's right to remove items added to carry out its business or trade would clearly show the intention of the parties and would lessen possibilities of disagreement.

The case that follows illustrates the trade fixture doctrine and discusses an additional approach to determining when an item is a fixture.

In Re Park Corrugated Box Corp.

U.S. District Court

249 F.Supp 56 (D.N.J. 1966)

Background: Manufacturers Leasing Corporation (Manufacturers) petitioned a referee in bankruptcy for an order allowing it to reclaim a machine from Park Corrugated Box Corp. (Park). It claimed it had a security interest in the machine that it had perfected by filing its interest against the machine as a fixture attached to real estate.

The Trustee in Bankruptcy argued that the machine was not a fixture. As a result, Manufacturers had not perfected its interest because it did not file its interest against the machine as goods.

The referee in bankruptcy held that the machine had not become a fixture and as such, Manufacturers had not perfected its interest in it. Manufacturers appealed that decision.

Decision: The District Court affirmed the decision and the determination that the machine in question had not become a fixture.

Augelli, District Judge

On February 8, 1965 Park filed a petition for an arrangement under Chapter XI of the Bankruptcy Act. Manufacturers was listed in Park's schedules as a security-holding creditor in the amount of $34,952.60. On March 8, Manufacturers filed its petition to reclaim from Park the machine above mentioned, which was used in the manufacture of corrugated boxes, and known as a "Hooper Combined Printer Slotter, Model WSG2P-200-E, size 50 × 103½ inches."

On September 4, 1963, Manufacturers and Park entered into a "Conditional Sale and Security Agreement," whereby Park purchased the subject machine from Manufacturers for the sum of $47,405.00. The agreement stated that Manufacturers was to have a purchase money security interest in the collateral to secure the balance due, that Manufacturers was to have all the rights of a secured party under applicable state law, and that Manufacturers was to retain title to the collateral until the balance was paid in full.

The agreement between Manufacturers and Park was filed twice with the Register of Deeds of Passaic County, on September 10, 1963 and again on October 10, 1963. It had not been filed with the Secretary of State in Trenton, New Jersey.

Under the Uniform Commercial Code as adopted in New Jersey, N.J.S.A. 12A:9–401(1) provides that:

> The proper place to file in order to perfect a security interest is as follows:
> (a) . . . (not applicable);
> (b) when the collateral is goods which at the time the security interest attaches are or are to become fixtures, then in the office where a mortgage on the real estate concerned would be filed or recorded;
> (c) In all other cases, in the office of the Secretary of State.

Manufacturers contends that the machine was a fixture, that the agreement was properly filed in the County Register's Office, and that therefore Manufacturers has a perfected security interest in the machine prior to the rights of the Trustee. The Trustee argues, as the Referee has found, that the machine was not a fixture, that the agreement should have been filed in the office of the Secretary of State, and that therefore Manufacturers' security interest was not perfected. The issue in this case is thus simply whether the machine in question is or is not a fixture within the meaning of N.J.S.A. 12A:9–401(1)(b).

N.J.S.A. 12A:9–313(1) provides that the law of New Jersey determines whether and when goods become fixtures. The law in New Jersey concerning fixtures has most recently been reviewed in the case of *Fahmie* v. *Nyman.* In that case, the court discussed the two tests used in New Jersey to determine whether and when a chattel becomes a fixture. They are known as the "traditional test" and the "institutional doctrine."

Under the "traditional test," intention is the dominant factor. A chattel becomes a fixture when the party making the annexation intends a permanent accession to the freehold. This intention may be "inferred from the nature of the article affixed, the relation and situation of the party making the annexation, the structure and mode of annexation, and the purpose or use for which the annexation was made."

The testimony before the Referee . . . shows that there was no intention to annex the machine permanently to the freehold. A witness for Manufacturers testified that although the machine was annexed to the building, it could easily be removed in one hour without material physical damage to the building. He described the machine as being about 125 inches wide by 8 feet long, weighing 45,000 pounds, anchored by two or three leg screws on each side, and connected to a 220 volt electric line. This same witness testified that a rigger could remove the machine quite easily by merely unbolting the screws, disconnecting the 220 volt line, jacking it up, putting it on rollers and taking it out. Park's president testified that the machine had been moved two or three times to other sections of the plant by employees of Park during the time it was located in the plant.

Under the "institutional doctrine," the test is whether the chattel is permanently essential to the completeness of the structure or its use. A chattel is a fixture if its severance from the structure would cause material damage to the structure or "prevent the structure from being used for the purposes for which it was erected or for which it has been adapted." Thus, in *Temple Co.* v. *Penn. Mutual Life Ins. Co.,* the Court stated, in holding lighting equipment and seats to be fixtures under the "institutional doctrine," that "[t]he building was erected and used as a theatre, and whatever was incorporated with the building to fit it for use as a theatre became part of the realty."

Again, the testimony before the Referee shows that the machine in question was not essential to the structure or its use, and that the severance of the machine would not prevent the structure from being used for the purposes for which it was erected or could be adapted. There was testimony that after the machine was removed from the building, the structure could be used for industrial uses generally; also testimony that different prior uses had been made of the structure. Thus, both before the machine was installed and after it was removed, the structure was and could be used for any number of different purposes. Finally, there was attached to the agreement between the parties a statement by Manufacturers that the machine is "to be affixed to real property . . . by removable screw joints or otherwise, so as to be severable from the realty without material injury to the freehold."

While the machine in question does not appear to be a fixture under either the "traditional test" or the "institutional doctrine," Manufacturers makes the further contention that the machine is a "trade fixture" under New Jersey law, and therefore a "fixture" pursuant to N.J.S.A. 12A:9–401(1)(b). However, the term "trade fixture" is generally applied only in landlord and tenant cases to describe a chattel which the tenant has installed on the landlord's premises for trade purposes, and which the tenant is allowed to remove if it can be severed without material injury to the freehold. Otherwise, the chattel would be a fixture and belong to the landlord. Thus, a "fixture" is just the opposite of a "trade fixture" under landlord and tenant law; the latter can be removed by the tenant without material injury to the freehold. A "trade fixture" is not a fixture within the meaning of N.J.S.A. 12A:9–401(1)(b).

> Since the machine here involved was not a fixture under N.J.S.A. 12A:9–401(1)(b), and the agreement between Manufacturers and Park was not filed in the office of the Secretary of State pursuant to N.J.S.A. 12A:9–401(1)(c), Manufacturers' security interest was not perfected prior to the filing of the Chapter XI petition. Therefore the Trustee's rights to the machine take priority over the rights of Manufacturers.
>
> Under the circumstances, and for the reasons so well stated in the Referee's opinion, the order denying reclamation in this case will be affirmed.

BAILMENTS

As we have seen, the determination as to whether personal property has become a fixture causes problems in some business transactions. Other legal problems may arise when one person holds an item of property that is owned by another. This practice is common in many business relationships. Generally if an owner places an item of personal property in the holder's control to accomplish something about which both have agreed, a legal relationship called *bailment* exists. The owner who has surrendered the property is called the bailor; the person who holds and controls it is called the bailee.

Examples of bailment in commercial transactions include leasing an automobile or equipment, storing goods in a warehouse, or delivering goods to a trucker for shipment. On a personal basis, a bailment also exists when a person takes an automobile to a garage for repairs, checks a coat in a restaurant, or borrows a friend's golf clubs.

Since bailments are important in business, the business manager must know the rights and duties of the parties to a bailment and be able to distinguish bailments from other transactions.

Essential Elements

The essential elements of the relationship are as follows:

1. A bailment's subject matter is personal property.
2. The bailee must have possession of the property.
3. There must be an agreement, either express or implied, to create a bailment.
4. The property must be returned or accounted for when the bailment is completed.

Personal Property. The subject matter of a bailment must be personal property. The property can be either tangible or intangible, but it must be in existence at the time the bailment is created. The promise of a company to deliver stock to an employee is not a bailment if that stock does not exist. However, if the stock has been issued, but the company retains the certificates until the employee obtains the money to pay for it, the relationship is a bailment.

Possession. Possession of the property by the bailee is a major element in any bailment. Possession is generally determined by the control that the bailee exercises over the property. In most bailments the property is actually in the bailee's possession. However, constructive possession is also sufficient. For example, a bank that supplies safe-deposit facilities generally is considered as a bailee in spite of the fact that the bank as bailee does not have actual control of the bailor's property. The bank's control of admission to the vault where the property is stored is the basis for considering the bank to be in control of the property.

Agreement

A bailment may be created by an express agreement (such as an agreement I make with a business firm that agrees to store my boat in their winter storage sheds) or by actions indicating that the parties intended to make such an agreement (I leave my boat in my neighbor's garage again this year as I have done for the last three years).

Return of Property

Ordinarily the item bailed, or a substitute for it, usually money, is to be returned or accounted for by the bailee. This aspect of the bailment clearly distinguishes it from a sale or a gift. In both a sale and a gift the title to the personal property in question passes to the recipient. That is not true with the bailment. As a result of this important distinction, the legal rights and obligations of the bailee are significantly different from those of the buyer of property. For this reason the business manager should be able to determine clearly if a given transaction is a bailment or a sale.

Consider the conditional sale and the consignment. If an item of property is delivered to another, who is to pay for the item over a period of time, with title to the property passing to the recipient once the item is paid for, the transaction is considered a conditional sale, not a bailment. This transaction is a sale rather than a bailment because the parties do intend for the title to the property to be transferred, even though that transfer generally comes well after the transfer of the possession of the property.

On the other hand, if an item of property is delivered to another and the recipient has the option of purchasing the property or selling it to others, no sale has yet taken place. Instead, the transaction, known as a consignment, is a type of bailment. All that is being transferred at the present time is the possession of the property. At the time of the consignment the parties do not intend for title to pass to the recipient. In fact, in most consignments, the title to the property never passes to the bailee-recipient, but passes from the seller only after the bailee has found a buyer to purchase the property. Gasoline is often consigned to service stations by the major gasoline producers, and works of art are frequently consigned to art galleries for sale from the artist or owner to the purchaser.

Legal Principles

Before discussing some common legal problems involving bailors and bailees, two fundamental legal principles need to be reviewed. First, as in other legal relationships, a bailment results from the way in which the parties act. A bailment is not created merely because the parties label their transaction as a bailment. If the essential elements we have discussed exist, a bailment is created, regardless of the name given by the parties to their transaction. If those elements are not present, no bailment exists.

Second, subject to a few specific statutory provisions, the rights and duties of a bailor and a bailee are determined by their agreement. The parties can settle on almost any terms they find desirable. Courts will first look to the agreement of the parties to determine their respective rights and duties. Of course, as noted in Chapter 15, any agreement that violates public policy will not be enforced.

Classification

In many bailments the parties fail to indicate how their duties and obligations will be divided adequately between them. In such cases courts have to determine how to equitably divide the duties between the parties. One method that has been used to assist in making that determination is based on looking at the benefits received by both the bailor and the bailee.

A threefold method of classification of bailments has developed. The most common type of bailment in business is one in which both parties benefit. This is referred to as a mutual-benefit bailment. A bailment in which the bailee furnishes no consideration for the property he or she possesses is referred to as a bailment for the sole benefit of the bailee or a gratuitous bailment. In this situation someone lends an item to another, expecting no payment in return. If only the owner of the property benefits, the bailment is said to be for the sole benefit of the bailor. This type of bailment exists if someone who is not paid holds another's property for safekeeping. Not all courts look to these classifications to assist them in solving problems involving bailments, but they are helpful in some cases.

Bailor's Responsibility for Defective Goods

In bailments for the sole benefit of the bailee, the gratuitous bailment, courts traditionally have required only that the bailor warn the bailee of known dangers that expose the borrower to an unreasonable risk of harm. In a mutual benefit bailment or a bailment for the sole benefit of the bailor the bailor's responsibility for defects in the property is more extensive.

The law in most states is that the bailor must use reasonable care in inspecting the property and seeing that it is safe for the purposes for which it is being used. For example, if Hertz does not conduct a reasonable inspection of the cars and trucks it rents after they have been used by one of its bailees, it would be liable if the vehicle had defective brakes and that defect caused injury to a subsequent user of that same item.

Some states go even further and impose an implied warranty of fitness for goods that are rented to or loaned by a bailor. These courts reason that the bailee is relying on the bailor's expertise and in such cases liability can occur even if the bailor was reasonable. Suppose that Hertz does conduct a reasonable inspection of all its cars and trucks after they are returned by one of the bailees. Even though it acted reasonably and was not negligent, if one of their vehicles is found to have defective brakes, Hertz as the bailor would be liable due to its implied warranty that its property was fit for use by the next bailee. Like the seller of goods warranted to be fit for a particular purpose, the bailor generally is allowed to disclaim this specific warranty.

Cintrone v. Hertz Truck Leasing, Etc.

Supreme Court of New Jersey

212 A.2d 769 (1965)

Background: Cintrone (plaintiff) was injured while a passenger in a truck leased by his employer from Hertz (defendant). His suit against Hertz claims his injury resulted from the defendant's negligent inspection or maintenance of the leased vehicle or from a breach of warranty that the vehicle was fit and safe for use. The trial court dismissed the warranty claim and submitted the negligence claim to the jury; it found in favor of defendant Hertz and Cintrone appealed.

Decision: The Supreme Court accepted the case for review before the Court of Appeals decision was made. It found that even though there was a lease and not a sale, the rental firm had an obligation to inspect the vehicle and to warrant it as fit for use. Accordingly, it reversed the trial court's judgment and remanded the case for a new trial.

Francis, Justice

Defendant Hertz Truck Leasing & Rental Service (Hertz) is in the business of leasing and renting various types of motor vehicles to the public. Plaintiff's employer, Contract Packers, Inc., had leased nine trucks from defendant for use in its business. One of them was a 1959 Ford, 22 feet long and 11 feet high. The leasing of the trucks was on a long-term basis.

Under the lease the trucks were kept at Contract Packers' premises but Hertz agreed to service, repair and maintain them. The arrangement was that once a year or every 18,000 miles, whichever came first, Hertz was to provide "preventive maintenance." This meant that the vehicle was taken from the lessee (who was given a replacement) and brought to Hertz' garage. There the entire vehicle was examined and serviced; . . . In addition, every 14 days a Hertz mechanic was sent to Contract Packers' premises to inspect the trucks.

Moreover, under the arrangement between the parties, at the end of each day's use the Contract Packers driver who had driven one of the trucks that day brought it to the Hertz garage where it would be "gassed up" for the next day. While this was being done, the procedure was for each driver to report any trouble he had or complaint he wished to make in connection with the operation of his truck. If a complaint related to some minor difficulty that could be corrected quickly, it would be taken care of immediately and after the gassing operation was completed, the driver would be allowed to drive the vehicle back to his employer's place of business.

Whenever a needed repair which a driver had brought to Hertz' attention could not be made during gassing up, or on the lessee's lot at night, the truck would be removed from service and replaced by another. Then on completion of the work, the vehicle would be returned to the lessee and the substitute recalled. If a complaint related to allegedly defective brakes, the truck would be replaced.

The plaintiff Cintrone had been in the employ of Contract Packers as a driver-helper for three years before the accident in question which occurred on Monday, April 3, 1961. On Wednesday, Thursday and Friday of the previous week he had driven the leased truck. He testified that at the end of the run on each of those days he reported the brakes were not working and needed adjustment. . . .

On April 3, 1961 the Ford truck was scheduled for a delivery trip. Cintrone was to be the helper that day and one Robert Sottilare, another Contract Packers employee, the driver.

Sottilare testified that up until the time of the accident he had no difficulty with the brakes; they were in operating condition; they did not fail in any way; "they wasn't perfect"; "they were a little low but they held."

Sottilare was going along Route 202, apparently within the limits of Suffern, when he came around a bend in the road and saw an overhead bridge or trestle a hundred feet or so ahead of him. It was a low bridge, the clearance only 9 feet, 6 inches. Sottilare applied his brakes; they failed. The truck "just kept going" forward until the peak of its body hit the overhead structure. As Cintrone put it, he saw the driver pumping the brakes. And he never stopped the truck because the brakes didn't work.

Both men were injured. They were removed to a hospital in Suffern, Sottilare by ambulance, Cintrone by police car. Cintrone was examined, given some pills and released; Sottilare remained there.

Schipper v. *Levitt & Sons, Inc.* and *Henningsen* v. *Bloomfield Motors, Inc.* have made it plain that if the relationship in the present case between Contract Packers and Hertz were manufacturer or dealer and purchaser, an implied warranty of fitness for operation on the public highway would have come into existence at the time of the sale. Moreover, under those cases, breach of the warranty which caused personal injury to an employee of the purchaser would be actionable by the employee. It must be recognized, however, that the occasions have been relatively few when the courts have been asked to imply warranties in personal injury cases as an incident of transactions other than sales of chattels. Certainly in New Jersey there is no case precisely like this one involving the contention that a bailment for hire of a motor vehicle by a bailor or lessor engaged in such rental business carries with it an implied warranty that the rented vehicle is fit and will continue to be fit for the rental period for the ordinary and expected purposes of the rental.

There is no good reason for restricting such warranties to sales. Warranties of fitness are regarded by law as an incident of a transaction because one party to the relationship is in a better position than the other to know and control the condition of the chattel transferred and to distribute the losses which may occur because of a dangerous condition the chattel possesses. These factors make it likely that the party acquiring possession of the article will assume it is in a safe condition for use and therefore refrain from taking precautionary measures himself.

. . . (I)t may be observed also that the comment to the warranty section of the Uniform Commercial Code speaks out against confining warranties to sales transactions. The comment says:

> Although this section is limited in its scope and direct purpose to warranties made by the seller to the buyer as part of a contract of sale, the warranty sections of this Article are not designed in any way to disturb those lines of case law growth which have recognized that warranties need not be confined either to sales contracts or to the direct parties to such a contract. They may arise in other appropriate circumstances such as in the case of bailments for hire, whether such bailment is itself the main contract or is merely a supplying of containers under a contract for the sale of their contents.

A sale transfers ownership and possession of the article in exchange for the price; a bailment for hire transfers possession in exchange for the rental and contemplates eventual return of the article to the owner. By means of a bailment parties can often reach the same business ends that can be achieved by selling and buying. The goods come to the user for the time being and he benefits by their use and enjoyment without the burdens of becoming and remaining the owner. The owner-lessor benefits by receiving the rent for the temporary use.

We may take judicial notice of the growth of the business of renting motor vehicles, trucks and pleasure cars.

The nature of the U-drive-it enterprise is such that a heavy burden of responsibility for the safety of lessees and for members of the public must be imposed upon it. The courts have long accepted the fact that defective trucks and cars are dangerous instrumentalities on highways. They present great potentiality for harm to other highway users as well as to their own drivers and passengers. Therefore the offering to the public of trucks and pleasure vehicles for hire necessarily carries with it a representation that they are fit for operation. This representation is of major significance because both new and used cars and trucks are rented. In fact, as we were advised at oral argument, the rental rates are the same whether a new or used vehicle is supplied. In other words, the lessor in effect says to the customer that the representation of fitness for use is the same whether the vehicle supplied is new or old. From the standpoint of service to the customer, therefore, the law cannot justly accept any distinction between the obligation assumed by a U-drive-it company whether the vehicle is new or old when rented. The nature of the business is such that the customer is expected to, and in fact must, rely ordinarily on the express or implied representation of fitness for immediate use.

In the case before us, it is just as obvious that when a company like Contract Packers rents trucks for limited or extended periods for use in its occupation of transportation of goods, it too relies on the express or implied representation of the person in the business of supplying vehicles for hire, that they are fit for such use.

A bailor for hire, such as a person in the U-drive-it business, puts motor vehicles in the stream of commerce in a fashion not unlike a manufacturer or retailer. In fact such a bailor puts the vehicle he buys and then rents to the public to more sustained use on the highways than most ordinary car purchasers. The very nature of the business is such that the bailee, his employees, passengers and the traveling public are exposed to a greater quantum of potential danger of harm from defective vehicles than usually arises out of sales by the manufacturer.

The operator of the rental business must be regarded as possessing expertise with respect to the service life and fitness of his vehicles for use. That expertise ought to put him in a better position than the bailee to detect or to anticipate flaws or defects or fatigue in his vehicles. Moreover, as between bailor for hire and bailee the liability for flaws or defects not discoverable by ordinary care in inspecting or testing ought to rest with the bailor just as it rests with a manufacturer who buys components containing latent defects from another maker, and installs them in the completed product, or just as it rests with a retailer at the point of sale to the consumer. And, with respect to failure of a rented vehicle from fatigue, since control of the length of the lease is in the lessor, such risk is one which in the interest of the consuming public as well as of the members of the public traveling the highways, ought to be imposed on the rental business.

In this developing area of the law we perceive no sound reason why a distinction in principle should be made between the sale of a truck to plaintiff's employer by a manufacturer, and a lease for hire of the character established by the evidence.

For the reasons stated, the trial judge should have submitted the issue of breach of implied warranty of fitness to the jury for determination. His refusal to do so constituted reversible error.

Defendant contends that since there is no privity of contract between plaintiff and Hertz, plaintiff has no cause of action for breach of an implied warranty of fitness arising from the bailment relationship created thereby. Obviously Hertz knew when the leasing took place that Contract Packers' employees would be using the trucks as drivers or helpers. In such a situation absence of privity between plaintiff and Hertz is of no legal consequence.

Bailee's Responsibility for Care and Use

Although the bailee is in possession of the bailor's property, the bailee does not guarantee the safety of the property against loss or injury. Almost all courts have stated that a bailee is not an insurer. A bailee is, however, responsible for any loss caused by its negligence, but traditionally the courts have measured the degree of care that must be exercised by the type of bailment.

In a mutual-benefit bailment the general rule requires the bailee to take ordinary and reasonable care of the subject of the bailment. Liability occurs if the bailee does not exercise the same degree of care that an ordinarily prudent person would use in caring for his or her own property.

Some jurisdictions allow the bailee to escape or limit its liability by agreement with the bailor; however, in a number of states an agreement of this nature is against public policy and not enforceable. These kinds of agreements are especially apt to be unenforceable if the bargaining power of the bailee is substantially greater than that of the bailor. As it is possible for the bailee to limit its liability by agreement, the bailor, too, can increase the bailee's responsibility by contract. A common example would be a requirement that the bailee insure the property for the bailor's benefit.

Negligence or the absence of due care is also the standard in a bailment for the sole benefit of the bailor or one that solely benefits the bailee. In each case, however, the degree of care that the bailee must exercise in order to escape liability differs. In a situation where only the bailor benefits, the bailee needs to exercise only slight diligence. Thus the bailee is liable only if its neglect of duty amounts to willfulness and evidences a reckless disregard for the rights of others. Conversely, if the bailment is for the sole benefit of the bailee, slight negligence is enough to establish the bailee's responsibility for injury or loss. Courts feel that it is reasonable to expect that a person who borrows another's property will take extraordinary care to protect it. This degree of care has been defined as that which the prudent person would exercise in his or her own affairs of great importance.

Although classification of bailments based on benefit has traditionally aided courts in determining liability, the current trend is to consider the type of bailment as only one factor in measuring whether conduct is reasonable under the circumstances. Whether a bailee has exercised the proper degree of care is determined by this and factors such as the type of property, the reason for the bailment, custom of the trade, and prior dealings between the parties.

Bailee's Use of Property

A bailee who treats the property in a manner not authorized by the agreement becomes absolutely liable for any loss or damage. This

PREVENTIVE LAW
A Checklist for Both the Potential Bailor and Bailee

Is this a bailment? Bailment transactions include:

- Renting a car from Hertz
- Storing skis in a self-store warehouse during the summer
- Parking the car at a parking garage while attending a concert
- Giving a watch to a jeweler to repair
- Dropping off film for development at the drug store

Steps a Bailor Should Take When Entering into a Bailment Relationship:

1. Identify the transaction as bailment instead of sale or gift
2. Classify bailment as to whether it benefits one party or both parties
3. Determine if bailee is relying on your special expertise (as in *Hertz* case)
4. Establish in writing standard of care to be exercised by bailee.
5. Expressly state special duties to be performed by bailee

Questions a Bailee Should Ask and Answer When Entering into a Bailment Relationship:

1. Is the transaction a bailment instead of a gift or conditional sale?
2. Are all terms of bailment, including specific duties of bailee, spelled out in a written agreement?
3. Is this transaction one that allows the bailee to rely on special expertise of the bailor?
4. Is the bailor responsible for the warranty with regard to the condition of the subject property?
5. What duty of care is placed on the bailee?
6. Will the law allow the bailee to escape or limit its liability?

responsibility exists in spite of the bailee's exercise of due care or of a result that actually benefits the bailor. A bailee who uses the property in an unauthorized manner, stores it some place other than that agreed upon, or fails to return it according to the contract is liable to the bailor even though injury or loss is caused by an accident or act of God.

In many transactions the bailee's authority to deal with the property is not clearly expressed by the parties. In these cases the court usually considers the following factors to determine the bailee's liability:

1. The purpose of the transaction
2. The type of property
3. The relationship between the parties
4. The custom of the business

TRANSFER OF TITLE TO PROPERTY

Sale

Sale is the most important method of transferring title to property. Although the methods of selling both real and personal property have developed along somewhat different lines, both are governed extensively by statute and case law. The sale of goods is the subject of Article 2 of the Uniform Commercial Code, which is discussed in detail in Chapters 19 and 20. Some of the legal problems inherent in the transfer of title to real property by sale are discussed in Chapter 40.

In general the process involved in selling real property is much more formal than that involved in the sale of goods. Statutes in all states require public recording of the transfer of title to real property if the owner's title is to be valid against claims of third parties who might acquire an interest in that property.

Gift

Title to property frequently is transferred by gift. In dollar value the vast majority of gifts are made through the testamentary disposition of a deceased person. Gifts by living persons, however, are very important. A gift by a living person is usually an *inter vivos* gift. If a living person makes a gift in expectation of impending death, the gift is said to be *causa mortis.* In an inter vivos gift the recipient or donee receives an irrevocable title. In a causa mortis gift the gift may be revoked if the donor does not die.

For a gift by a living person to be valid the donor must intend to make a gift, and delivery of the item must take place. In addition, the donee must be willing to accept the gift. While this last requirement causes few problems, the other essential elements of a gift sometimes result in litigation, as the following case illustrates. The role of joint property in estate planning is discussed in Chapter 41.

In Re the Estate of Alfred V. Sipe, Deceased

Supreme Court of Pennsylvania

422 A.2d 826 (1980)

Background: Eleanor Sipe (petitioner-appellee), executrix of the estate of Alfred V. Sipe, petitioned the Court for an order directing Mary Drabik (respondent-appellant) to turn over to the estate the money she withdrew after the decedent's death from a joint savings account opened by the decedent in his name and her name. The trial court found that since Ms. Drabik had never signed the card opening the savings account the decedent had not made an effective gift to her during his lifetime.

Ms. Drabik appealed, claiming the requirements for a valid gift had been met. Decision: The Court of Appeals agreed, and reversed the trial court's decision.

Flaherty, Justice

The trial court concluded that a gift had not been made because the decedent, when he opened the account, filled out the entire signature card himself by signing both his name and the appellant's name and their Social Security numbers on the card. Appellant's failure to sign the joint signature card was "fatal to her case" according to the trial court. We do not agree.

Although this Court has held on numerous occasions that the "[e]xecution of a signature card creating a joint savings account with a right of survivorship is *sufficient* to establish an inter vivos gift to the joint tenant by the depositor of the funds" . . . , it is not the law and we have never held that such proof is the only proof which can establish a gift. All of the circumstances must be considered in determining whether a gift was made or whether the joint account was established for some other purpose.

Sometime prior to September 17, 1975, decedent opened a savings account in his own name at a branch of the Union National Bank. On the above date, decedent went to the bank and told an employee of the bank that he wanted to close the account in his own name and open a new account in his name and the name of the appellant into which was deposited approximately $8,000.00, which included the $3,000.00 balance in his old account. Decedent signed a temporary signature card for the account and was given a permanent signature card to be signed by himself and the appellant and returned to the bank. The court found that decedent, not appellant, signed appellant's name on the signature card.

About eighteen months later, on February 20, 1977, decedent, who was about to enter the hospital for surgery, gave the passbook for the joint account to appellant. After his discharge from the hospital about a month later, decedent, who needed care, went to the residence of his nephew Vernon Sipe, which was next door. Decedent died about six weeks later on April 30, 1977. After his discharge from the hospital, decedent was not confined to bed. Although he could not drive himself, he visited the hospital for treatments, went shopping on various occasions and was in the bank where the joint account existed sometime in early April, although he did not transact any business, but was there in the company of his nephew Vernon Sipe, who had business at the bank.

The requirements for a gift are intent, delivery and acceptance in all cases. This is so whether we are concerned with monies, a bank account, a stock certificate, or a horse. Accepting the trial judge's conclusion that the appellant did not sign the signature card herself, the issue remains whether or not a valid gift was established.

As to the first requirement for a valid gift—intent—there is no question that the evidence satisfies that requirement. Decedent was not opening a savings account for the first time. He specifically asked that that account be closed and a new joint account be opened in his name and the name of appellant. He was given an explanation of the account and a signature card which he signed and returned to the bank. That signature card clearly states that a joint account is being established with the right of either party to withdraw and with the right of survivorship. The only conclusion possible is that the decedent intended to make a gift.

Appellee seems to attach great significance to the lower court's finding that appellant did not sign the signature card. . . . Signing the card would have shifted the burden of proof to the challenger that joint ownership was not created. Not signing the card merely means that we must consider all the circumstances in determining whether a joint account was intended to exist, whether the requirements of the law pertaining to the creation of gifts have been met. . . .

In addition to donative intent, the law of gifts also requires acceptance of the gift, but acceptance is presumed. The acceptance requirement was met when appellant received the passbook from decedent. It has never been required that a donee sign a document acknowledging acceptance, which is what appellee's position would dictate.

Finally, the law of gifts also requires a delivery. Without reaching the question of whether a delivery was effected when decedent gave the signature card to the bank, it is clear that delivery was made when decedent gave the passbook to appellant.

The only conclusion warranted on the basis of the undisputed facts, coupled with the facts as found by the trial court, is that the decedent made a valid gift to the appellant.

The decree of the trial court is reversed and a decree entered in favor of appellant.

In addition to sale or gift, title to property is transferred in several other ways. Some of these, such as adverse possession and eminent domain, are more commonly associated with real property and are discussed in Chapter 40.

Judicial Sale

Most courts have the power to order the sale of a defendant's real or personal property in order to satisfy a judgment. Sometimes the court's order is based on an agreement in which one of the parties has used specific property as a security. Usually the property secures a loan or is used to finance the purchase of the property. A real-estate mortgage (See Ch 39) or a security agreement (See Chapter 28) executed by the purchaser of goods are examples. In addition, many states allow designated officials to seize various assets of a defendant and to sell them to satisfy a money judgment. As has been noted in Chapter 29, state statutes usually exempt from seizure the property which is necessary to earn a livelihood or sustain life. Table 38-3 depicts the different requirements for transferring real and personal property by sale, gift, or judicial sale.

Abandoned property is that which the owner has voluntarily given up with the intention of surrendering any interest that he or she has. In the event of litigation over supposedly abandoned property, the person claiming title must be able to prove that the owner intended to abandon the property. Merely not using property even for an extended time is not abandonment, although nonuse may be used as evidence showing an intention to abandon. The first person to acquire abandoned property gets title to it.

Lost property and abandoned property are not the same. Lost property is that which the owner had no intention of giving up but has parted with through carelessness or accident. Loss of a diamond that falls out of a ring setting would be an example.

Acquisition of title to lost property differs from the acquisition of title to abandoned property. In most cases the person who finds lost property acquires an interest that is good against everyone but the true owner. But before the finder acquires title, certain conditions must be met. These conditions vary from state to state.

Some states continue to follow the common-law rule. At common law, before the finder of lost property acquired title, he or she was required to make a reasonable search for the true owner. Most states by statute require a

TABLE 38-3 TRANSFERRING TITLE TO PROPERTY

	Real Property	Personal Property
Sale	Transfer by deed and public recording (for a house or a vacant lot) (See Chapter 40)	Transfer by: Bill of sale (stereo); certificate of title (auto); possession (textbook) (See Chapters 19 and 20)
Gift	Transfer by deed and public recording (See Chapter 40)	During life (inter vivos)—Intent and delivery (savings account); at death (testamentary) by valid will or according to intestate law (See Chapter 41)
Judicial sale	Transfer of property used as security (purchaser of home gives mortgage to lender; if purchaser doesn't pay, home can be sold at judicial sale and proceeds used to pay lender)	Transfer of property used as security (if car is used as security for loan, nonpayment by buyer may lead to transfer of car to lender)

finder to notify a designated public official of the finding. If the property is not claimed within a specified period of time—usually six months to a year—the finder acquires the property.

The law considers mislaid property and lost property differently. *Mislaid property* is property that an owner has intentionally placed somewhere and then forgotten. Supposedly when the owner remembers the item, he or she knows where to look for it. As a result, the owner of the place where the property is found and not the finder has the right to the property if it is not claimed by the rightful owner. The law assumes that the owner will return to the place where the item was mislaid. Entrusting the owner of that place with property makes it easier for the true owner to recover his or her property.

For example, Sam, a customer of First Bank, finds a woman's purse on a counter in the lobby. If unclaimed, the purse and its contents become the property of the bank, because the purse apparently was mislaid. If the property had been lost and not mislaid, the result probably would differ. Assume that Sam found the purse on the floor of the lobby and not on the counter. In that event, Sam would acquire title if he took the proper steps, because the purse apparently was lost. But if Sam were an employee of the bank, the bank would be entitled to the purse. An employee who finds lost property while on the job has no right to it as long as the employer has a policy of accepting responsibility for it.

CHANGING CONCEPTS OF PROPERTY

Property is a dynamic concept continually being reshaped by society to meet new economic and social needs. In the United States today two movements modifying traditional rights associated with property are worth noting. One of these involves the restructuring of property rights in their relationship to civil rights. This is illustrated by legislation and cases that attempt to ensure the fundamental interests of minorities. In most instances, where traditional property rights conflict with basic civil rights, property rights have been limited.

The 1948 U.S. Supreme Court opinion in *Shelly* v. *Kramer,* discussed in Chapter 1, exemplifies this trend. This case involved an agreement by certain owners of real estate not to sell or lease their homes to "any person not of the Caucasian race." When Shelly, a black, purchased a parcel covered by this restriction, Kramer and others sued to restrain him from taking possession. The Supreme Court held that state courts could not enforce a private agreement depriving a person of a constitutional right. In effect, the Supreme Court limited the right of Kramer and the others to restrict the use of their real estate in this manner.

A second direction that the law is taking is to extend property rights to a person's employment or to the degrees and licenses that are necessary to practice. Although the movement in this direction is slow, the trend is clear. Recently courts have been urged to treat status and reputation as property, as the following case illustrates.

Memphis Development Foundation v. Factors Etc., Inc.

U.S. Court of Appeals, Sixth Circuit

616 F.2d 956 (1980)

Background: Memphis Development Foundation (Foundation) (plaintiff-appellant) sued in U.S. District Court to enjoin Factors Etc. Inc. (defendant-appellee) from interfering with Foundation's attempt to erect a large bronze statue of Elvis Presley in downtown Memphis. Foundation solicited public contributions to pay for the sculpture. Donors of $25 or more received an eight-inch pewter replica of the proposed statue.

During his lifetime Presley had conveyed the exclusive right to exploit the commercial value of his name to Boxcar Enterprises in exchange for royalties. These rights had been assigned to Factors Etc., Inc. (Factors) two days after Presley's death. Factors by counterclaim sought damages and an injunction against distribution of the replicas by Foundation.

The District Court granted Foundation's injunction prohibiting interference with its efforts to erect the statue but prohibited it from distributing any statue bearing the image or likeness of Elvis Presley. Foundation appealed.

Decision: The Court of Appeals reversed.

Merritt, Circuit Judge

This appeal raises the interesting question: Who is the heir of fame? The famous have an exclusive legal right during life to control and profit from the commercial use of their name and personality. We are called upon in this diversity case to determine whether, under Tennessee law, the exclusive right to publicity survives a celebrity's death. We hold that the right is not inheritable. After death the opportunity for gain shifts to the public domain, where it is equally open to all.

At common law, there is a right of action for the appropriation or unauthorized commercial use of the name or likeness of another. An individual is entitled to control the commercial use of these personal attributes during life. But the common law has not heretofore widely recognized this right to control commercial publicity as a property right which may be inherited.

Tennessee courts have not addressed this issue directly or indirectly, and we have no way to assess their predisposition. Since the case is one of first impression, we are left to review the question in the light of practical and policy considerations, the treatment of other similar rights in our legal system, the relative weight of the conflicting interests of the parties, and certain moral presuppositions concerning death, privacy, inheritability and economic opportunity. These considerations lead us to conclude that the right of publicity should not be given the status of a devisable right, even where as here a person exploits the right by contract during life.

Recognition of a post-mortem right of publicity would vindicate two possible interests: the encouragement of effort and creativity, and the hopes and expectations of the decedent and those with whom he contracts that they are creating a valuable capital asset. Although fame and stardom may be ends in themselves, they are normally by-products of one's activities and personal attributes, as well as luck and promotion. The basic motivations are the desire to achieve success or excellence in a chosen field, the desire to contribute to the happiness or improvement of one's fellows and the desire to receive the psychic and financial rewards of achievement.

. . .

The desire to exploit fame for the commercial advantage of one's heirs is by contrast a weak principle of motivation. It seems apparent that making the right of publicity inheritable would not significantly inspire the creative endeavors of individuals in our society.

On the other hand, there are strong reasons for declining to recognize the inheritability of the right. A whole set of practical problems of judicial line-drawing would arise should the courts recognize such an inheritable right. How long would the "property" interest last? In perpetuity? For a term of years? Is the right of publicity taxable? At what point does the right collide with the right of free expression guaranteed by the first amendment? Does the right apply to elected officials and military heroes whose fame was gained on the public payroll, as well as to movie stars, singers and athletes? Does the right cover posters or engraved likenesses of, for example, Farah Fawcett Majors or Mahatma Gandhi, kitchen utensils ("Revere Ware"), insurance ("John Hancock"), electric utilities ("Edison"), a football stadium ("RFK"), a pastry ("Napoleon"), or the innumerable urban subdivisions and apartment complexes named after famous people? Our legal system normally does not pass on to heirs other similar personal attributes even though the attributes may be shared during life by others or have some commercial value. Titles, offices and reputation are not inheritable. Neither are trust or distrust and friendship or enmity descendible. An employment contract during life does not create the right for heirs to take over the job. Fame falls in the same category as reputation; it is an attribute from which others may benefit but may not own.

The law of defamation, designed to protect against the destruction of reputation including the loss of earning capacity associated with it, provides an analogy. There is no right of action for defamation after death. The two interests that support the inheritability of the right of publicity, namely, the "effort and creativity" and the "hopes and expectations" of the decedent, would also support an action for libel or slander for destruction of name and reputation after death. Neither of these reasons, however, is sufficient to overcome the common law policy terminating the action for defamation upon death. . . .

Heretofore, the law has always thought that leaving a good name to one's children is sufficient reward in itself for the individual, whether famous or not. Commercialization of this virtue after death in the hands of heirs is contrary to our legal tradition and somehow seems contrary to the moral presuppositions of our culture.

There is no indication that changing the traditional common law rule against allowing heirs the exclusive control of the commercial use of their ancestor's name will increase the efficiency or productivity of our economic system. It does not seem reasonable to expect that such a change would enlarge the stock or quality of the goods, services, artistic creativity, information, invention or entertainment available. Nor will it enhance the fairness of our political and economic system. It seems fairer and more efficient for the commercial, aesthetic, and political use of the name, memory and image of the famous to be open to all rather than to be monopolized by a few. An equal distribution of the opportunity to use the name of the dead seems preferable. The memory, name and pictures of famous individuals should be regarded as a common asset to be shared, an economic opportunity available in the free market system.

These same considerations also apply to the Presley assigns' more narrow argument based on the fact that Presley entered into contracts during his life for the commercial use of his image. It is true that the assignment of the right of publicity during life shows that Presley was aware of the value of the asset and intended to use it. The assignment also suggests that he intended to convert a mere opportunity or potential for profit into a tangible possession and consciously worked to create the asset with, perhaps, the hope of devising it.

The question is whether the specific identification and use of the opportunity during life is sufficient to convert it into an inheritable right after death. We do not think that whatever minimal benefit to society may result from the added motivation and extra creativity supposedly encouraged by allowing a person to pass on his fame for the commercial use of his heirs or assigns outweighs the considerations discussed above.

Accordingly, the judgment of the District Court is reversed and the case is remanded for further proceedings consistent with the principles announced above.

REVIEW PROBLEMS

1. Explain the difference between real and personal property, and indicate some of the legal consequences of this difference.

2. Define intangible personal property and provide some examples of it.

3. Indicate the tests courts use to determine if an item is a fixture.

4. What are the essential elements necessary for making a valid gift?

5. Explain the different legal consequences of classifying an item as a trade fixture as compared with a fixture.

6. Tillotson purchased a drying bin from the B. C. Manufacturing Company. The bin was erected on property owned by the Newman Grove Grain Company. The bin was anchored to a concrete base and became an integral part of the grain corpora-

tion's elevator, to which it was attached with loading and unloading ducts, electrical wiring, and so on. The Newman Grove Grain Company mortgaged the real estate to the Battle Creek State Bank. Is the bin a fixture? What difference does this make? Explain.

7. Anne P. Graham and Dennis J. Graham were husband and wife. During their six-year marriage Anne Graham was employed full time. Her husband worked part time, although his main pursuit was his education. He attended school for approximately three and one half years, acquiring a bachelor of science degree and a master's degree in business. Approximately 70 percent of the family funds were supplied by the wife.

   The Grahams filed a petition for dissolution of marriage. As part of this action, Anne Graham claimed that the master's degree was marital property and subject to division by the court. She asked for $33,-134 as her share of this property. Should the degree be treated as property? Discuss.

8. Health Clubs, Inc., contracted to purchase an indoor swimming pool from Stanton. The pool was heated and had a large filtering unit. The heater and filter were easily removable once disconnected. Before Health Clubs, Inc., took possession, Stanton removed both units. When sued, Stanton contended that the units were personal property. Health Clubs, Inc., argued that the units were fixtures. Who is correct? Support your answer.

9. Fishbien purchased a small motel from January. He was to take possession in thirty days. The day after he received a deed to the property, he noticed that January was removing all the furniture. Fishbien sued for a court order to prevent this. He argued that the motel was worthless without the furniture. Would he be successful? Discuss.

10. Milligan owned a farm in Iowa, which he sold to Meyers. Milligan moved into town from the farm, but he left a well drilling rig on the property with the permission of Meyers. The rig was in poor condition, and two of its tires were flat. Milligan told Meyers that the rig was for sale. Several people did come to examine the rig in the weeks following the sale. But the rig was never moved. About two years later Meyers learned that Milligan had moved to California. The following year Meyers repaired the rig and began to use it. Has Meyers acquired title to the rig? Discuss.

11. Cogliano owned a nursery business on land taken by the state to build a highway. The nursery stock consisted principally of young trees of varying ages and heights, some shrubbery, rose bushes, and perennials. The value of the land apart from the stock was $10,000. The value of the nursery stock was $40,000. The state Department of Public Works awarded Cogliano $10,000 for the land. This award did not include the nursery stock, which Cogliano was given thirty days to remove.
   (a) Indicate the legal basis that the Department of Public Works might use in support of the limited award.
   (b) On what grounds might Cogliano argue that he was entitled to $50,000?
   (c) Who has the best argument? Why? Cogliano v. Commonwealth of Massachusetts, 135 N.E.2d 648 (1956)

12. Amerson wished to borrow an electric drill from Howell. Howell was aware that the drill had previously shocked three people, none of whom was injured. This information was conveyed to Amerson. In addition, before giving the drill to Amerson, Howell changed the plug and tested the drill, receiving no shock. When Amerson used the drill, he suffered a fatal shock. Would Amerson's estate be able to recover from Howell? Discuss. Howell v. Amerson, 156 S.E.2d 371 (1967)

13. Boyd entered State University on a one-year football scholarship that was renewable at the University's option. State University offered to renew Boyd's scholarship for the next year, but he decided to transfer to Central College which played in the same football conference with State University. The conference, Gulf South Conference, had a rule that prohibited a player who had received a scholarship to play from one college in the conference from playing for another college unless the first college did not offer to renew that player's scholarship and the player waited two years after his first college scholarship was not renewed. Boyd claims the rules of Gulf South Conference deprive him of a property right, the right to play football, with a possible scholarship for him if he did so, at Central College. Do you agree with Boyd? Gulf South Conference v. Boyd, Supreme Court of Alabama, 369 So.2d 553 (1979)

14. Evans rented a safe deposit box and stored his valuables in it. When he went in the hospital, Evans gave the keys to the box to his niece whom he had been close to for many years. Just before he died, Evans told his minister he was giving the church $10,000 and the rest of his things to his niece.

The executor of Evans's estate claims Evans did not make a gift of the contents of the safe deposit box (worth about $80,000) to his niece because he didn't give her the things in the box and he didn't put her name on the box. Evans did visit the safe deposit box about a month before his death. Even though his niece had the keys to the box, the bank would not let her have access to it after Evans's death because her name was not on it. Has Evans made a valid gift to his niece? Why? In Re Estate of Evans, Supreme Court of Pennsylvania, 356 A.2d 778 (1976)

Interests in Real Property

R eal property law deals with ownership of land and those things permanently attached to it. Because land is an unusual commodity and for centuries has been of great economic importance in the Western world, the legal relationships involving real property are extensive and complicated. This chapter discusses some of the many interests that exist in real estate.

SCOPE OF REAL PROPERTY

As traditionally defined by courts and commentators, land ownership encompasses the surface of the earth, and everything above and below the surface. The space over which the surface owner has dominion is compared to a pyramid extending upward indefinitely into space and downward to the center of the earth. As air travel became an important means of transportation, the traditional rule gradually has been modified. Today the general rule is that the surface owner's air rights are limited to the space that can be reasonably used and enjoyed.

Both the air space above and the natural resources such as oil or minerals below the surface of the land can be separated from the land and treated as independent commodities. In cities some landowners retain ownership of the land's surface, and sell the air space above it for the construction of commercial buildings. In mining regions the right to extract natural resources is frequently separated from ownership of the surface and leased or sold. In the arid areas of the West water rights are very often separated from surface ownership of land.

ESTATES IN LAND

Interests in land may be divided in many different ways. One way, as the previous section indicates, is to divide use and enjoyment of the land itself horizontally in relation to space. Another way is to separate the land from possible rights in it and allow numerous interests to exist simultaneously. This is the basis of the doctrine of estates. This doctrine was important in the historic development of English

---

ETHICS BOX
Spying on Property

DuPont built a new plant in Beaumont, Texas, incorporating a novel technique for manufacturing methanol. Before the plant's roof was installed, a plane—presumably hired by a competitor—flew over the plant and took pictures. It would be possible for a chemical engineer to figure out the new manufacturing process by looking at the pictures of the partially constructed plant.

This case of industrial spying for hire raises numerous ethical and legal questions. Was the flying over the property a trespass? Does it depend on the height of the plane or the intent of the pilot? If DuPont claimed a trade secret in the process, did it take adequate care to make sure that the secret process was not discoverable?

In the era of spy satellites it might be argued that a company in the position of DuPont should take care to protect its innovations from being viewed from above. If the property was out of the way and unlikely to be flown over in the normal course of activity, then that might change the situation.

The better view is that the actions of the competitor went beyond the bounds of proper competition. It might be very expensive for DuPont to protect its properties from viewing from above, and if all firms have to incur such costs, society is worse off. The actions in this case vary little from hiring someone to find a way to be invited into the plant and then surreptitiously take pictures from within.

---

and American land law and continues to influence real property law today.

The word "estate" as used in real property law indicates the nature, quantity, and quality of an ownership interest. As an estate refers to an ownership interest, it is or must have the potential for becoming possessory. The extent of an estate is determined by the duration of the interest and the time when the right to possess and enjoy the land begins.

For example, a wife might provide by will that her real property go to her husband for the duration of his life and then to her daughter. Upon the wife's death, both husband and daughter would have existing estates. The husband's estate would be measured by the duration of his life; the daughter's estate could last forever, but it does not begin until her father dies.

Fee Simple Estates

A *fee simple estate,* also called a fee simple absolute or simply a fee, is the most extensive interest that a person can have in land. This is the type of estate held by most owners of real property. The estate is potentially infinite in duration. It may be transferred to others during the lifetime of the owner. Upon the owner's death, his or her interest does not end but passes by will or the laws of intestate succession, if the owner dies without leaving a will. This is the type of estate held by the wife in the previous example. In most states, the only restrictions or conditions that can be imposed on this estate are those imposed by government. If a question exists as to the type of estate that is transferred, the courts presume that a fee simple is intended.

Fee Simple Defeasible

A defeasible fee is less extensive than a fee simple, since the *defeasible fee* terminates if certain events occur. Until these events occur, however, the owner of a defeasible fee possesses essentially the same interests as those possessed by the owner of a fee simple. For example, a defeasible fee might be used if a person wished to give land to a municipality for recreational purposes. The grantor might execute a deed with the following language: "to the City of Columbus, Georgia, and its successors and assigns so long as the property is used for recreational purposes."

If the land is not used for the stated purpose, the city's interest terminates automatically and reverts to the grantor or the grantor's heirs. Not all defeasible fees terminate automatically. Some require the grantor or the grantor's successors to take steps to terminate them. Although the defeasible fee is not used extensively today, it has played a significant role historically in property law.

Life Estates

A *life estate* is one whose duration is measured by the life of a person, typically the owner but possibly some other person. This latter type of estate is called an estate *pur autre vie*. Life estates may be created by deed or will. They are also created by statute and case law. A life estate may be sold or mortgaged, but the acquiring party's interest is terminated by the life tenant's death. The following case illustrates one of the limitations placed on a life tenant. While the life tenant has a recognizable interest in real property, that tenant's rights are limited because others (usually referred to as remaindermen) also have rights in that same property.

Sauls v. Crosby

District Court of Appeals of Florida
258 So.2d 326 (1972)

Background: Sauls (plaintiff-appellant) sold real property she owned in Florida to Crosby (defendant-appellee), retaining for herself a life estate in that property. After she cut some of the timber from the land, Crosby objected. He claimed that as a life tenant, Sauls had no right to cut the timber. Sauls sued to enforce her right to cut the timber from the land she had sold to Crosby.

The trial court determined that because Sauls had only a life estate in the Florida property, she had no right to cut timber from that land unless the proceeds were used for the benefit of the remaindermen (such as Crosby). Sauls appealed to the Court of Appeals.

Decision: The Court of Appeals affirmed the judgment of the trial court.

Rawls, Judge

On the 9th day of October 1968, appellant (Sauls) conveyed to appellees (Crosby) certain lands situated in Hamilton County, Florida, with the following reservation set forth in said conveyance: "The Grantor herein, reserves a life Estate in said property."

By this appeal appellant now contends that the trial court erred in denying her, as a life tenant, the right to cut merchantable timber and enjoy the proceeds.

The English common law, which was transplanted on this continent, holds that it is waste for an ordinary life tenant to cut timber upon his estate when the sole purpose is to clear the woodlands. American courts today as a general rule recognize that an ordinary life tenant may cut timber and not be liable for waste if he uses the timber for fuel; for repairing fences and buildings on the estate; for fitting the land for cultivation; or for use as pasture if the inheritance is not damaged and the acts are conformable to good husbandry; and for thinning or other purposes which are necessary for the enjoyment of the estate and are in conformity with good husbandry.

In this jurisdiction a tenant for life or a person vested with an ordinary life estate is entitled to the use and enjoyment of his estate during its existence. The only restriction on the life tenant's use and enjoyment is that he not permanently diminish or change the value of the future estate of the remainderman. This limitation places on the "ordinary life tenant" the responsibility for all waste of whatever character.

An instrument creating a life tenancy may absolve the tenant of responsibility for waste, unless it is wanton or malicious, by stating that the life tenant has the power to consume or that the life tenant is without impeachment for waste. Thus, there is a sharp distinction in the rights of an ordinary life tenant or life tenant without impeachment for waste or life tenant who has the power to consume. An ordinary life tenant has no right to cut the timber from an estate for purely commercial reasons and so to do is tortious conduct for which the remainderman may sue immediately.

. . . In the cause sub judice (under review), the trial court was concerned with the rights of an ordinary life tenant and correctly concluded that appellant "does not have the right to cut merchantable timber from the land involved in this suit unless the proceeds of such cutting and sale are held in trust for the use and benefit of the remaindermen. . . ."

Legal Life Estates

Despite potential legal problems, life estates have been used to provide financial security for one spouse upon the death of the other. At common law, dower and curtesy were estates that widows and widowers enjoyed in their spouse's real property by virtue of the marriage.

At common law, a *dower* interest gave to a wife, upon the death of her husband, a one-third life interest in land that he had owned during the marriage. Although most states have abolished dower, it continues to exist in a few of them.

Similarly, at common law, the concept of *curtesy* gave to a widower a life interest in all his wife's real property if a child had been born of the marriage. While curtesy has been abolished in most states, a few still allow the surviving husband a life interest in his deceased wife's realty.

Statutes modifying common-law dower and curtesy have been enacted in many states. Typically these statutes give to a surviving spouse a distributive share in the assets, both real and personal property, of the decedent. Thus the interest of the surviving spouse in the real property owned by the decedent is not limited to a life estate. Instead, full title to a fixed share of the personal and real property is provided by law. If the decedent leaves property to the surviving spouse by a will, the survivor may choose between taking the property passing by the will or the *elective share,* which the statutory law provides. It is likely that these statutory reforms will completely abolish the common-law concepts of dower and curtesy.

LEASEHOLD ESTATES

Leasehold estates are among the most significant interests that exist today in real property. In business, the lease provides a method for obtaining an interest in land with far less capital than fee simple ownership requires. In housing, a lease requires less immediate money to be paid than does the purchase of a fee simple ownership. Further, since the lessee's interest terminates once the lease expires, he or she can easily select a different type of housing without concern about recouping the original housing investment.

A leasehold interest is created when the owner of real property, usually referred to as the landlord or *lessor,* conveys possession and control of property to another, called the tenant or *lessee,* in exchange for a payment known as *rent.* The possessory right granted by the owner is temporary. Upon termination of the leasehold interest, possession and control revert to the owner.

Both real property and contract law apply to leases. In the past courts generally applied real property principles to the lease, treating it primarily as a transfer of land ownership. That treatment generally favored the owner of the property. However, as the country became more urbanized, the condition of the building or unit rented took on more importance to the lessee than the land on which the building rested.

Thus, by the middle of this century, the balance of power began to shift in favor of the tenant instead of the landlord. The form leases prepared for the owner no longer were automatically enforced. Legislative statutes and court decisions began to emphasize the contractual and warranty terms implied in a lease in order to provide increased protection for the tenant. The following case illustrates this trend.

Javins v. First National Realty Corp.

U.S. Court of Appeals, D.C. Circuit

428 F.2d 1071 (1970)

Background: First National Realty Corp. (plaintiff-appellee) sued the Javins (defendants-appellants) seeking possession of rented apartments because the defendants had defaulted in payment of rent due for April. The defendants admitted they had not paid rent for the month in question, but defended on grounds that approximately 1,500 violations of the District of Columbia housing regulations affected their apartment either directly or indirectly.

The Landlord and Tenant Branch of the District of Columbia Court and the District of Columbia Court of Appeals refused to consider these violations and found for the plaintiff. The defendants appealed to the U.S. Court of Appeals.

Decision: The Court of Appeals found the housing regulations constituted an implied warranty of habitability by the lessor. Accordingly, it reversed the lower court's decisions.

Wright, Circuit Judge

Because of the importance of the question presented, we granted appellants' petitions for leave to appeal. We now reverse and hold that a warranty of habitability, measured by the standards set out in the Housing Regulations for the District of Columbia, is implied by operation of law into leases of urban dwelling units covered by those Regulations and that breach of this warranty gives rise to the usual remedies for breach of contract.

Since, in traditional analysis, a lease was the conveyance of an interest in land, courts have usually utilized the special rules governing real property transactions to resolve controversies involving leases. . . .

The assumption of landlord-tenant law, derived from feudal property law, that a lease primarily conveyed to the tenant an interest in land may have been reasonable in a rural, agrarian society; it may continue to be reasonable in some leasing involving farming or commercial land. In these cases, the value of the lease to the tenant is the land itself. But in the case of the modern apartment dweller, the value of the lease is that it gives him a place to live. The city dweller who seeks to lease an apartment on the third floor of a tenement has little interest in the land 30 or 40 feet below, or even in the bare right to possession within the four walls of his apartment. When American city dwellers, both rich and poor, seek "shelter" today, they seek a well known package of goods and services—a package which includes not merely walls and ceilings, but also adequate heat, light and ventilation, serviceable plumbing facilities, secure windows and doors, proper sanitation, and proper maintenance.

Some courts have realized that certain of the old rules of property law governing leases are inappropriate for today's transactions. In order to reach results more in accord with the legitimate expectations of the parties and the standards of the community, courts have been gradually introducing more modern precepts of contract law in interpreting leases.

In our judgment the trend toward treating leases as contracts is wise and well considered. Our holding in this case reflects a belief that leases of urban dwelling units should be interpreted and construed like any other contract.

Modern contract law has recognized that the buyer of goods and services in an industrialized society must rely upon the skill and honesty of the supplier to assure that goods and services purchased are of adequate quality. In interpreting most contracts, courts have sought to protect the legitimate expectations of the buyer and have steadily widened the seller's responsibility for the quality of goods and services through implied warranties of fitness and merchantability. Thus without any special agreement a merchant will be held to warrant that his goods are fit for the ordinary purposes for which such goods are used and that they are at least of reasonably average quality. Moreover, if the supplier has been notified that goods are required for a specific purpose, he will be held to warrant that any goods sold are fit for that purpose. These implied warranties have become widely accepted and well established features of the common law, supported by the overwhelming body of case law. Today most states as well as the District of Columbia have codified and enacted these warranties into statute, as to the sale of goods, in the Uniform Commercial Code.

Implied warranties of quality have not been limited to cases involving sales. The consumer renting a chattel, paying for services, or buying a combination of goods and services must rely upon the skill and honesty of the supplier to at least the same extent as a purchaser of goods. Courts have not hesitated to find implied warranties of fitness and merchantability in such situations. In most areas product liability law has moved far beyond "mere" implied warranties running between two parties in privity with each other.

The rigid doctrines of real property law have tended to inhibit the application of implied warranties to transactions involving real estate. Now, however, courts have begun to hold sellers and developers of real property responsible for the quality of their product. For example, builders of new homes have recently been held liable to purchasers for improper construction on the ground that the builders had breached an implied warranty of fitness. In other cases courts have held builders of new homes liable for breach of an implied warranty that all local building regulations had been complied with.

In our judgment the common law itself must recognize the landlord's obligation to keep his premises in a habitable condition. This conclusion is compelled by three separate considerations. First, we believe that the old rule was based on certain factual assumptions which are no longer true; on its own terms, it can no longer be justified. Second, we believe that the consumer protection cases discussed above require that the old rule be abandoned in order to bring residential landlord-tenant law into harmony with the principles on which those cases rest. Third, we think that the nature of today's urban housing market also dictates the abandonment of the old rule.

Since a lease contract specifies a particular period of time during which the tenant has a right to use his apartment for shelter, he may legitimately expect that the apartment will be fit for habitation for the time period for which it is rented.

Even beyond the rationale of traditional products liability law, the relationship of landlord and tenant suggests further compelling reasons for the law's protection of the tenants' legitimate expectations of quality. The inequality in bargaining power between landlord and tenant has been well documented. Tenants have very little leverage to enforce demands for better housing. Various impediments to competition in the rental housing market, such as racial and class discrimination and standardized form leases, mean that landlords place tenants in a take it or leave it situation. The increasingly severe shortage of adequate housing further increases the landlord's bargaining power and escalates the need for maintaining and improving the existing stock. Finally, the findings by various studies of the social impact of bad housing has led to the realization that poor housing is detrimental to the whole society, not merely to the unlucky ones who must suffer the daily indignity of living in a slum.

Thus we are led by our inspection of the relevant legal principles and precedents to the conclusion that the old common law rule imposing an obligation upon the lessee to repair during the lease term was really never intended to apply to residential urban leaseholds. Contract principles established in other areas of the law provide a more rational framework for the apportionment of landlord-tenant responsibilities; they strongly suggest that a warranty of habitability be implied into all contracts for urban dwellings.

We believe, in any event, that the District's housing code requires that a warranty of habitability be implied in the leases of all housing that it covers. The housing

code—formally designated the Housing Regulations of the District of Columbia
. . . provide[s] a comprehensive regulatory scheme setting forth in some detail: (a) the
standards which housing in the District of Columbia must meet; (b) which party, the
lessor or the lessee, must meet each standard; and (c) a system of inspections,
notifications and criminal penalties.

We therefore hold that the Housing Regulations imply a warranty of habitability,
measured by the standards which they set out, into leases of all housing that they
cover.

The judgment of the District of Columbia Court of Appeals is reversed and the cases
are remanded for further proceedings consistent with this opinion.

Classification by Duration of Term

Leased estates are classified in several different ways. A traditional classification is by the duration of the term. Major legal differences exist between leases that are for fixed terms and those that are of indefinite duration. A second method of classifying leases is by how rent is determined; thus commercial or income-producing leases are differentiated from residential leases.

Term Tenancy. A *term tenancy,* sometimes called an estate for years, exists for a fixed period of time. The agreement creating the term establishes particular beginning and ending dates. A lease beginning on February 1, 1990, and terminating on January 31, 1991, would be a term tenancy. The term may be as short as a week or a month, but most are for a year or more. Some in common leases are written with terms of ninety-nine years.

A term tenancy ends automatically at the time designated in the agreement. The owner is not required to notify the tenant of the termination of the lease. Generally in the United States a term tenancy for more than a year must be in writing to be enforceable.

Periodic Tenancy. A *periodic tenancy,* also referred to as a tenancy from month to month or year to year, is a rental agreement that continues to successive periods until terminated by proper notice from either party. A periodic tenancy, which is usually oral rather than in writing, may be created in several ways. If a tenant is in possession under a term tenancy that is unenforceable because it is not in writing, courts generally hold that a periodic tenancy exists. More commonly the periodic tenancy is created by the express agreement of the parties to enter into an agreement of this type. Periodic tenancies are also created when a tenant holds over after a term tenancy. The *holdover tenancy* is discussed later in the chapter. The major factor distinguishing the periodic tenancy from the term tenancy is that the periodic tenancy continues until one of the parties gives proper notice of its termination.

The determination of the time period for proper notice varies considerably from state to state. In the United States today over one-quarter of the states have adopted the Uniform Residential Landlord and Tenant Act. This Act requires a written notice of ten days for a week-to-week tenancy and sixty days for a month-to-month tenancy. While year-to-year tenancies are not mentioned in the Act, the prevailing rule for year-to-year tenancies is the requirement of six months notice.

Tenancy at Will. A *tenancy at will* is created when the owner of property gives someone permission to occupy it for an unspecified period of time. This type of tenancy may be created by express agreement or by implication. The key factors are that the tenant is lawfully in possession of the property but the duration of possession is uncertain. An example of a tenancy at will would be a situation in which the landlord allows a tenant to remain in possession of space in a building scheduled to be torn down until the actual demolition begins.

A tenancy at will ends when either party indicates he or she no longer wishes to continue the tenancy. A number of states have passed legislation requiring the person wishing to terminate the tenancy to give proper notification to the other party. Generally the time required for notification is thirty days. The death of either party or the sale or lease of the property also terminates a tenancy at will.

Tenancy at Sufferance. A *tenancy at sufferance* exists when someone who was once a lawful occupant unlawfully occupies another's property. The landlord owes this tenant no duties other than not to injure him or her wantonly or willfully. The most common example of the tenancy at sufferance is when a person holds over after the expiration of his or her term. This person becomes a holdover tenant if the landlord elects to treat him as such; however, until this decision is made and acted upon, the tenancy is at sufferance.

Holding Over. When a term tenant remains on the premises at the expiration of the term without the owner's consent, the owner has the option of either evicting the tenant or treating the tenant as a holdover. If the owner decides to treat the tenant as a holdover, in most states a periodic tenancy is created. If the original tenancy was for a year or more, almost all states treat the new term as a periodic tenancy for a year. If the original term was for less than a year, the term of holdover tenancy is for a similar period. For example, a month-to-month tenancy is created if the original term tenancy was for a month. When a tenant holds over after being notified of a rent increase, most states will hold the tenant responsible for the increased rent.

Classification by Method of Determining Rent

A wide range of methods exists for determining the amount of the rent the tenant must pay. In residential leases the rent is usually a fixed amount, but in commercial leases different arrangements are often used to establish the tenant's obligation. These arrangements are primarily the result of the lessor's desire to shift as many economic risks as possible to the tenant. A lessor leasing property for a long term naturally wishes to limit the effect of inflation on rental income. If the rent is a fixed amount and property expenses increase, the owner's income from the property can be drastically reduced. Rental payments can be negotiated that protect the owners from this possibility. In other situations an owner might wish to share in the increased productive use of a parcel of real estate without assuming the risk of investing in a building or a business to utilize the property.

This objective too can be attained through various types of rental payments. A few of the more common methods for determining rent in commercial leases to accomplish the objectives are the percentage lease, the net lease, and the revaluation or appraisal lease. Many variations and combinations of these basic patterns are also frequently used.

Percentage Leases. A *percentage lease* provides the lessor with a rent determined by a fixed percentage of the gross sales or net profits from a business operated on the leased premises. Some percentage leases are written with a fixed minimum rental. Percentage leases protect the lessor against inflation and also provide him or her with a share in the productive use of the property.

Net Leases. A *net lease* is a lease in which the tenant pays a fixed rent and in addition agrees to pay the taxes, insurance, and maintenance expenses. A variation of the net lease is the net-net lease. In the net-net lease the tenant agrees to pay all costs attributed to the property. The net lease protects the lessor against inflation.

Revaluation or Appraisal Leases. Some long-term leases provide for adjustment of rental payments based on periodic revaluation of the property. Several different methods of revaluation are used. Revaluation allows the lessor to share in any increase in the value of the land.

Rights and Duties of the Parties

Most problems that arise in a tenancy can be solved by the parties if they have a well-drafted lease. In the lease, landlord and tenant may allocate rights and duties in any manner that they choose as long as what they do is not illegal or against public policy (see Chapter 15). Sometimes parties who enter into a lease do not anticipate a problem that occurs during the term. If a dispute arises that is not settled by the lease, the solution must be found in state statutory or case law.

Understanding how the law allocates the rights and duties of the parties absent agreement in the lease is complicated by the dual nature of the lease and by developments in landlord–tenant law during the past fifty years. The case of *Javins* v. *First National Realty Corp.,* earlier, illustrates a trend in American law to provide residential tenants with rights that are not generally available to commercial tenants. This increased protection for residential tenants is also reflected in the statutory law, since many states have expanded the duties of landlords of residential property.

Duty to Repair and Maintain. The allocation of the duty to repair and maintain the premises illustrates the different treatment states sometimes afford commercial and residential leases. At common law, in the absence of agreement, the landlord had a limited duty to repair and maintain the property. If he or she knew of a latent defect, this had to be corrected before the lease began. No duty existed to maintain the premises except for the common areas of multiunit buildings. A number of states retain the common-law rule for commercial leases, but in most states the rule has been modified for residential property. In these states, if residential property is not maintained in habitable condition, tenants have various remedies against landlords. These remedies can include revoking the lease or not paying the rent as it becomes due. In a few states, tenants are permitted to make necessary repairs and deduct the cost from the rent.

Use of the Premises. Because a lease is a transfer of property as well as a contract, during the term the lessee has the right to possession and control of the property. Generally this means the lessor may not enter the premises unless the parties have agreed to the contrary. Thus, at common law the landlord's right of access to inspect, to make alterations or repairs, or to show the premises is limited.

Three principal exceptions exist to the rule limiting the landlord's right of access. First, he or she may enter to collect the rent if the lease fails to state where rent shall be paid. Next, the Uniform Residential Landlord–Tenant Act and similar state statutes extend the landlord's right of access to inspect the condition of the property and to make necessary repairs in emergencies. Inspection requires notice to the tenant and must be done at reasonable times and intervals. Finally, the landlord has a right of access to prevent material damage or loss to the property resulting from the tenant's negligence or misconduct.

The tenant may use the property for any reasonable purpose in view of the surrounding circumstances. But the tenant cannot use the property for an illegal purpose, for a purpose that violates public policy, or in a manner that would result in substantial or permanent damage to the property. Most commercial leases limit the use that the tenant can make of the property.

Rent Control Laws

Rent control laws were enacted at the federal and state levels during World War I and World War II. While many of these controls were removed in the late 1940s, some rent control laws still exist. The best known law is the rent control laws that are applicable to selected real property in the city of New York. In 1962 the state of New York transferred to the city of New York the authority to impose and administer rent controls in the city. The city was also permitted to adopt and amend local laws regarding rent control.

The basis of the protection granted to the tenant by the New York law is the statutory provision restricting the right of the landlord to remove the tenant from possession. If the tenant continues to pay the rent, only specified acts of the tenant (for example, negligently damaging the property, using the property for illegal purposes, or committing a nuisance) will justify an eviction of the tenant. The second critical provision in the rent control law is the limitation on the maximum statutory rent. The rent established March 1, 1950, pursuant to federal law, was adopted by the state of New York, and applied by the city after the transfer of power to it from the state, as the maximum statutory rent. Increases are permitted only if the landlord falls within one of the contemplated situations justifying an increase. These situations include an increase in service, an increase in rental value due to substantial rehabilitation of the building, a voluntary agreement between lessor and lessee, and the maximum rent being substantially lower than prevailing rents in the same area.

Transfer of Leased Premises

A tenant transfers his or her interest in leased property by assignment or sublease. Because the legal consequences of the two types of transfer differ, the parties to a transfer should be certain that their documents clearly indicate which type they intend.

A transfer is an *assignment* if the tenant conveys all of his or her remaining interest. If this is the case, both the new tenant and the landlord are liable to each other according to the terms of the original lease. The original tenant becomes a guarantor that the provisions of the lease will be carried out.

A transfer is a *sublease* if the tenant transfers less than his or her remaining interest. An example would be a tenant with a lease running from January 1 to December 31. If that tenant wants to allow someone else (a subtenant) to lease the premises during June and July, the transfer is a sublease. As the following case indicates, if the original lessee keeps any interest in the property itself, its transfers will be a sublease not an assignment. Neither the subtenant nor landlord can sue the other directly for breach of the original lease. If the landlord breaches a lease provision, the subtenant must seek relief by bringing an action against the original tenant on the sublease. If the rent is not paid, the landlord must look to the original tenant with whom the lease was made. The court in the *Bostonian Shoe Co.* case indicates the distinction between an assignment and a sublease.

Bostonian Shoe Co. v. Wulwick Associates

Supreme Court, Appellate Division

501 N.Y.S.2d 393 Supreme Court, Appellate Division (1986)

Background: Bostonian Shoe Co. (plaintiff) was a tenant in premises it leased in Brooklyn for fifteen years ending July 31, 1986. Its lease with Wulwick Associates (defendant) as landlord included a provision that the tenant could not assign its lease without prior approval from the landlord. In 1983 Bostonian entered into an agreement with Genesco subletting the leased premises to it until July 30, 1986, one day prior to the expiration of Bostonian's lease with Wulwick.

Bostonian sued to have the court declare its sublease with Genesco valid and the trial court found in its favor. Landlord Wulwick appealed, claiming the nonassignment provision prohibited Bostonian's sublease of the premises for all but one day of its tenancy.

Decision: The Appellate Division held the sublease agreement valid and affirmed the trial court's decision.

Memorandum by the Court

The instant appeal involves a written lease between the plaintiff, as tenant, and the defendant, as landlord, which provides for the lease of the premises located at 453 Fulton Street, Brooklyn, for a 15-year period ending July 31, 1986. The lease specifically prohibits the assignment of the lease by the plaintiff without the defendant's prior approval. The lease does not, however, restrict in any way the plaintiff's right to sublet the premises.

On or about April 18, 1983 the plaintiff entered into an agreement with one Genesco, Inc. (hereinafter Genesco), whereby the latter agreed to rent the demised premises for the period beginning May 1, 1983 and ending July 30, 1986, one day prior to the expiration of the lease between the parties hereto. Under that agreement, the plaintiff retained the right of re-entry upon Genesco's default, and Genesco was precluded from assigning or subletting the premises without the prior written approval of the plaintiff.

Shortly after the plaintiff entered into the agreement with Genesco, the defendant contacted the plaintiff through a series of notices, stating that the agreement with Genesco constituted an invalid assignment of the parties' lease. As a result, the defendant declared the lease terminated and demanded that the plaintiff cure the breach or vacate the premises and remove Genesco therefrom.

The plaintiff subsequently commenced the instant action seeking declaratory and injunctive relief. Special Term declared, that the agreement between the plaintiff and Genesco constituted a valid sublease, and, that as a result, the plaintiff was not in breach of the provision of the lease which prohibited its assignment without the defendant's consent. We affirm.

"The essential distinction between an assignment and a sublease is simply this: If a lessee, by any instrument whatever, whether reserving conditions or not, parts with his entire interest, he has made a complete assignment, . . . If he retains a reversion in himself, he has made a sublease."

Significantly, the retained reversionary interest need not be for a substantial period of time in order for an agreement to be considered a sublease. Thus, agreements calling for the surrender of possession one day or, in one case, 12 hours short of the expiration of the term of the main lease, have been held to be a sublease rather than an assignment.

Judged by these standards, it is clear that the plaintiff's agreement with Genesco is a sublease rather than an assignment. By the terms of that agreement, Genesco is required to surrender possession of the demised premises to the plaintiff on July 30, 1986, one day prior to the expiration of the plaintiff's lease with the defendant. Thus, since the plaintiff retained a reversionary interest in the demised premises, albeit one short in duration, the subject agreement is a valid sublease. Moreover, given the absence of any provision in the parties' lease restricting the plaintiff's ability to sublease the premises, the plaintiff's actions did not constitute a breach of the provision thereof regarding assignment.

Termination of Lease

Most leases end at a certain time or by agreement of the parties. Many leases contain provisions providing for their termination under certain conditions. A common example is a provision terminating the lease if the premises are destroyed. In the absence of that type of provision the tenant remains responsible for the rent. Another example would be a provision terminating the lease if the tenant files for bankruptcy. Without this provision the tenant remains responsible for the rent until a judgment is entered.

A lease is also terminated by condemnation, the acquiring of private property for a public purpose by the government. In some instances statutes provide for the termination of a lease. Generally death does not terminate the obligations of either party, but a few states allow the estate of a decedent to cancel a lease covering the deceased's residence.

NONPOSSESSORY INTERESTS IN REAL PROPERTY

Easements

An easement is an example of a nonpossessory interest in land. An *easement* is an interest in land possessed by another party. The easement grants a limited use or enjoyment of that land to its owner. The requirement that the land on which the easement exists, the servi-

ent tenement, be in possession of someone other than the owner of the easement frequently occurs in situations in which there is an easement appurtenant.

An *easement appurtenant* involves two parcels of land, usually, but not necessarily, adjoining. The easement allows the possessor of one parcel to benefit by using the other parcel of land. The parcel that benefits is referred to as the dominant tenement, whereas the property that is subject to the easement is known as the servient tenement. If an easement is appurtenant, any transfer of the dominant tenement includes the easement. The easement cannot be separated and transferred independently of the dominant estate. Further, the use of the servient tenement is limited to the terms of the easement. Easements appurtenant run with the land. The easement, allowing the owner of the dominant property to make a limited use of the servient property, passes automatically to the succeeding owner of that dominant property.

Unless the document creating the easement indicates that the easement is exclusive, the owner of the servient property may also use the land upon which the easement has been dedicated. The servient owner's use must not conflict with the purpose and character of the easement. The cost of maintenance is a problem that sometimes arises when an easement has been created without the parties' agreement as to how this burden should be allocated. The following case deals with this problem.

Island Improvement Association of Upper Greenwood Lake v. Ford

Superior Court of New Jersey, Appellate Division
383 A.2d 133 (1978)

Background: The plaintiff-appellant, Island Improvement Association of Upper Greenwood Lake (hereinafter Association), owned and developed property around Greenwood Lake. It retained title to common property, such as the roads in the development, and sold lots to individual homeowners. The owners of the lots were granted express easements to use the roads owned by the Association. The Association then sought to have the lot owners contribute funds to repair and maintain the roads. One of the homeowners, defendant-appellee Ford, objected and the Association filed suit to force him to pay his share of the road repair costs.

The trial court found that because there was no contract between Ford and the Association, Ford did not have to contribute a share of the funds needed to maintain the roads. The Association appealed.

Decision: The Superior Court decided in the Association's favor. It held that because Ford as a lot owner (a dominant tenement) benefited from the easement in the roads (the servient tenement), he had the burden of contributing to the cost of repairing and maintaining them.

Fritz, Presiding Justice

There seems to be no factual question but that (1) title to the roads is in a private association, the grantor of the deeds to the individual purchasers, (2) an express easement to use the roads was conveyed to each property owner and (3) none of the deeds to the individual owners imposes any contractual obligation on the owners to maintain the roads.

At the end of the plaintiff's case the trial judge granted defendants' motions to dismiss. He came to this conclusion with respect to the individual owners on the ground that there was no contractual obligation imposed on or assumed by those owners and he lacked the authority to "clothe the (plaintiff) association with quasi municipal authority."

No contractual obligation having been undertaken by the individual owners, we look to see if any obligation is imposed on the dominant tenement by law. While *Ingling* v. *Public Service Elec. & Gas Co.* concerns itself with a different type easement and with problems of a somewhat different nature, we are satisfied that it correctly imposes upon the owner (or owners) of a dominant tenement—in the case before us an easement over lands of another—the duty of maintenance and repair. The *right* [sic] of the dominant tenant to maintain and repair has been recognized as an incident to the beneficial use of the easement. Convinced that with the benefit ought to come the burden, absent agreement to the contrary, we hold that the *obligation* to maintain devolves upon the dominant tenant. This is certainly the rule where the easement is solely for the benefit of the dominant estate. In our judgment there are compelling equitable reasons to apply the rule to the situation before us even though there may well be incidental use of these roads by others than the individual landowners.

We make it abundantly clear that by the enunciation of this rule we are not establishing plaintiff-appellant as a "*quasi*-municipal" agency. As a matter of fact we do not even suggest what the relationship or obligations, administrative or otherwise, of the appellant association should be in the scheme of things. Further we are not mandating [a joining] of the association by those of the individual owners who are not members. We are merely declaring the obligation of all the individual owners to contribute to the repair and maintenance of the easement in question.

Affirmed. The matter is remanded to the Chancery Division for further proceedings consistent with the foregoing, including the fashioning of a remedy.

Easement in Gross. An *easement in gross* exists independently of a dominant tenement. The privileges given by the easement belong to an individual or firm independently of ownership or possession of any specific land. Telephone and electric transmission lines are examples of easements in gross. The right of access over property in such cases does not benefit any particular piece of property.

Easements, such as those granted to gas and electric utility companies, are used extensively in the development of land. The easement of the utility company typically gives it the right to lay cable in a part of the land of a homeowner. In this case the property owner's land is the servient tenement, because the easement allows another to use a portion of its property, and there is no dominant tenement.

Because of the personal nature of the easement in gross, many American jurisdictions do not allow a noncommercial easement in gross to be transferred. However, commercial easements in gross, because of their importance to the public, are transferable.

Creation of Easements

Easements can be created by express agreement or implied by law. An easement may arise because of an agreement between the developer of property and the utilities that provide hookups to the lots being developed. Similarly, in the absence of an express agreement the law will declare an easement exists if a purchaser of land acquires land that has no access to public roads, except over lands retained by the seller. Courts will imply that the seller meant to grant an easement over the retained land to the purchaser. This type of easement is known as a "way of necessity."

Profit à Prendre and License

Other important nonpossessory interests are the profit *à prendre*, the license, and the lien.

A *profit à prendre* or profit is an interest in real property similar in many ways to an easement in gross. The distinguishing difference is that the owner of a profit has the right to take something of supposed value from the land. The right to cut and remove timber or to quarry and take gravel are examples of a profit. The profit carries with it the right to enter upon the land. Since a profit is an interest in land, it is irrevocable.

A *license* differs from a profit in that the license is merely a personal privilege to enter upon the land of another for a particular purpose. A license is not an interest in real property. Holding a ticket to an athletic event or occupying a motel room are examples of license. Most licenses are revocable at the will of the owner of the property on which the license is exercised; however, if a license is coupled with an interest in the land, license may not be revoked.

Liens

A *lien* is a very important nonpossessory interest in land. It is a right existing in the property of another to secure payment of a debt or performance of some obligation. Some liens are created by statute, others by agreement of the parties. Liens can exist in both real and personal property. One real property lien with which most people are familiar is the mortgage. Mortgages are discussed in the following chapter. Each of the nonpossessory interests in land are portrayed here.

1. *Easement Appurtenant.* Allows an owner of a dominant tenement (A) to use a part of a servient tenement (B) for a specific purpose, for example, to have access to the lake.

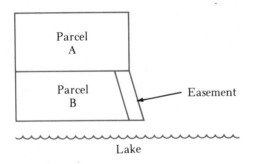

2. *Easement in Gross.* Allows an independent owner, ABC utilities, to use the land of another owner (servient tenement—parcel C) for specific purpose, for example, to place telephone transmission lines. Here, the owner of the easement does not have a dominant tenement.

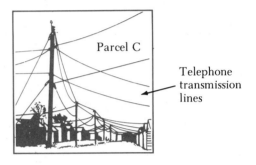

3. *License.* This is the privilege to enter the land of another owner for a particular purpose, for example, attending an athletic event or occupying a motel room.

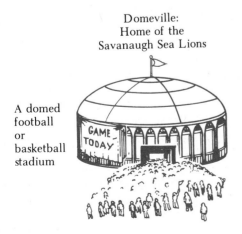

A domed football or basketball stadium

Domeville:
Home of the
Savanaugh Sea Lions

GAME TODAY

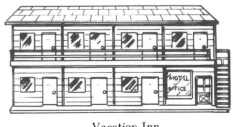

Vacation Inn
Budget Motel

4. *Profit* à Prendre. The owner of the profit, XYZ lumber company, has a right to come on the land of another owner, owner of Parcel D, and to remove something of value, for example, to cut and remove timber.

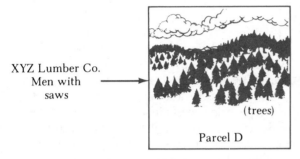

XYZ Lumber Co.
Men with
saws

(trees)

Parcel D

5. *Lien.* This is a right existing in the property of another to secure payment of a debt, such as a mortgage.

Mortgage
to ABC Bank

House

CO-OWNERSHIP

A third method of dividing rights in land exists when several people own undivided interests in a parcel of land at the same time. Generally in this type of ownership each person is entitled to a specific fraction of the parcel but also shares with others a single right to possession and profits from the land. This is generally referred to as concurrent ownership or *co-ownership.* Co-ownership is often used for holding investment real estate.

Co-ownership was important to the common law, and the various concurrent estates that developed at common law remain important today. A number of legal problems are associated with these common-law concurrent estates. These problems are reduced or eliminated if multiple owners use a partnership, corporation, or other arrangement (such as a trust, discussed later in this chapter) to hold title to the property. These devices are becoming increasingly important in real estate, replacing the common-law forms of multiple ownership.

Joint Tenancy

The principal feature of a joint tenancy is the right of survivorship. This means that upon the death of one of the co-owners, that person's interest passes automatically to the surviving joint owners.

Many people today own both personal property (automobiles and bank accounts) and real property as joint tenants. While some states prohibit the creation of a joint tenancy with the right of survivorship, most states permit it. Still the person establishing a joint tenancy should clearly indicate that this is the form of co-ownership that he or she intended to create.

Rights of Joint Tenants. Each co-owner who holds a joint tenancy has an equal right to possession of the entire property. This is referred to as an undivided interest. Although a joint tenant may not exclude other joint tenants from possession, the law considers occupancy by one as occupancy by all. If each tenant is to benefit, all must agree to share the property. Where agreement cannot be reached, the tenancy must be terminated.

Termination of Joint Tenancy. A joint tenancy is terminated if one of the owners sells his or her interest. In some states a joint tenancy is terminated if an owner's interest is mortgaged. The joint tenancy is also terminated if the interest of a joint tenant is sold to satisfy a debt. In any case a person who acquires the interest of a joint tenant becomes a tenant in common with the remaining co-owners.

Tenancy in Common

A tenancy in common is a form of co-ownership in which each owner possesses an individual interest in a parcel of land, but other than that, each owner's rights are the same as those possessed by a sole owner. In almost all states where co-ownership of property is concerned, a tenancy in common is implied unless a joint tenancy is clearly indicated by the instrument creating the concurrent estate.

Rights of Tenants in Common. Like joint tenants, each tenant in common has an undivided right to possession of the entire parcel. Normally a tenant in common will not be responsible to the co-owners for any benefits obtained through exclusive occupancy. At the same time no tenant in common is entitled to the exclusive use of any part of the land. The result is that problems arise when one co-tenant wrongfully excludes the others or when the property can be practically occupied only by a single tenant. Under these circumstances, in a number of states, the co-tenants not in occupancy will be entitled to a fair compensation for the use of the property. Similar problems arise where a co-tenant not in possession receives benefits from the property exceeding those of his or her co-owners. These types of problems can best be solved by agreement among the parties, as can problems involving liability of co-tenants for upkeep and improvements. When agreement cannot be reached, *partition* of property may be the only solution.

Partition. By partition a co-owner divides property and ends any interest of other co-owners in the divided portion. Although courts traditionally ordered partition even when no statute authorized them to do so, today partition exists in some form by statute in every state. In a few states the wording of the statute is broad enough to include partition when owners are divorced. Many states also make partition available to certain holders of future interests. Under the law of almost all states co-owners of personal property enjoy the right to partition to the same degree as do co-owners of realty.

In the *Milian* case that follows the court first had to determine if a man and woman who each contributed to the purchase of a house were co-owners. Since it determined they were, it ordered a partition of their property through sale so that they could equally divide the proceeds.

Milian v. Deleon

Court of Appeal, Fourth District

226 Cal.Rptr. 831 (1986)

Background: Arthur Milian (plaintiff) and Sylvia Sanchez Deleon (defendant, hereafter Sanchez) began dating in 1970. In late 1977 they purchased a house as joint tenants. Sanchez claims Milian and she bought the house with plans to marry in a year or two. Milian asked Sanchez to move into the house with him but she refused. The couple separated in late 1978 and Milian sued to have the property declared his. Sanchez, claiming she owned one-half of the house, sought a partition of the property. The trial court agreed with her.

Milian appealed, saying the trial court wrongly relied on the *Marvin* v. *Marvin* case concerning the division of property by two people who lived together.

Decision: The appellate court disagreed. It held that since the two parties were co-owners of the property, each was entitled to one-half of the proceeds on its sale.

Kaufman, Associate Justice

Milian and Sanchez began dating in 1970. Their relationship continued for eight years but ended without marriage. Sanchez testified the two became engaged in 1976 and set a marriage date for approximately one year later.

Sanchez stated repeatedly at trial that the couple's sharing of financial resources during their dating relationship proceeded upon the shared contemplation that the two would eventually marry. Milian denied ever proposing marriage or otherwise discussing plans to get married. Milian stated he asked Sanchez to live with him in order to discover whether the relationship was "going to work out or not." Sanchez, however, refused to live with him outside of marriage.

In late 1977, the couple jointly purchased a house which is the subject real property in the partition action. . . . Milian paid the $500 deposit required to reserve the vacant lot upon which the house was to be constructed and testified he made the loan application in his own name. Sanchez was on vacation at the time of the $500 payment, but she testified both parties provided financial statements to obtain the loan. Both parties' names appear signed to the offer and both parties signed escrow instructions. The eventual grant deed was taken in the names of both parties as joint tenants. Sanchez testified that to her "joint tenancy" meant the two would be partners in the property prior to marriage, while Milian testified he did not understand the significance of such designation and believed only that Sanchez would live with him and share expenses.

Only Milian occupied the house after its purchase. Although Sanchez fully participated in furnishing, decorating and landscaping the house and provided funds for these purposes, she refused to move in without marriage and never did occupy the house as a full-time resident. She had a key to the house and was there almost every weekend until the couple separated in late 1978.

Most of the couple's testimony concerned numerous exhibits which showed the extent to which they had commingled their property and collectively incurred expenses on the house and otherwise. Sanchez testified to providing $700 to Milian to help purchase a $7,000 bank money order for the down payment on the property; Milian apparently obtained most of the balance for the down payment from his father. The monthly mortgage payments were paid by Milian out of his savings account. However, Sanchez also testified that over eight months in 1978 she deposited to that savings account at least $4,300, including a $2,100 annual bonus from her employer and an $1,100 tax refund.

In respect to other decoration and improvement, Sanchez paid $560 on drapes and incurred a $900 charge on her credit card for upgrading the quality of carpet for the house. . . . Sanchez also made considerable nonfinancial contribution to the decoration of the house, spending many weekends landscaping and weeding, shopping with Milian for various home improvements, and purchasing the large patio slab for behind the house. Sanchez frequently stated at trial that the couple's extensive financial entanglement was based upon an agreement that the two would be equal partners in owning the home, sharing all of their property and resources, and preparing for marriage.

The couple stopped dating in late 1978. Milian filed an action to quiet title in the subject property and for declaratory relief. Sanchez answered seeking a declaration that she owned an undivided one-half interest in the property, a partition by sale granting her half the proceeds, compensation for Milian's use of the real and personal property in dispute, and a fair division of the personal property acquired by the parties during their relationship. . . .

The court . . . rendered judgment of partition by sale of the real property, ordering the proceeds of sale to be divided equally between the parties without any accounting, reimbursement or contribution. The court stated:

> It appears that both ARTHUR and SYLVIA spent money jointly to accomplish all of the following purposes: purchase real property and build a house, improve the exterior of the home, landscape the property, purchase books for schooling for each other, cash transfers made to each other, Christmas party, vacation expenses for each other's family and insurance on the real property, each other's car payments, repair of each other's vehicles, credit purchases made to benefit each other and the real property, equipping the home with linen, pictures and other accoutrements. In short, these parties treated both each other and the property in which they had a mutual interest in a fashion far different than the average real property owner or owners. There was, in fact, an implied contract by and between ARTHUR and SYLVIA to treat their property equally and to divide the same equally. Accordingly, it is the intent of the Court to divide the real property in question in conformity with the instructions of Marvin v. Marvin, (1976) [see Chapter 9]. . . . The property is ordered sold and the proceeds divided equally by and between the parties after payment of costs of sale.

Milian's initial contention is: "The Marvin decision has no applicability to this case, in that the present does not concern two cohabiting adults who were living in a meretricious relationship." Whether or not this contention is correct, it is of no consequence.

The effect of Marvin was simply to place parties involved in such a situation in the same position as "any other unmarried persons." The court explained that "adults who voluntarily live together and engage in sexual relations are nonetheless as competent as any other persons to contract respecting their earnings and property rights. . . ."

It is of course true that cohabitation and the rendition of housekeeping and similar services may be an important factor in the determination as to whether or not an implied agreement or "tacit understanding" (Marvin, 134 Cal.Rptr. 815, 557 P.2d 106) exists. However the only limitation upon the right of unmarried persons to contract with response to their property and financial arrangements is that the contract must not be illegal or against public policy. As stated repeatedly by the court in Marvin: "Agreements between nonmarital partners fail only to the extent that they rest upon a consideration of meretricious sexual services"; "a contract between nonmarital partners is unenforceable only to the extent that it explicitly rests upon the immoral and illicit consideration of meretricious sexual services."

It is of course correct that a cotenant who pays taxes, trust deed payments or other charges against the property or expends money for the preservation of the property or who, with the assent of his cotenant, makes improvements to the property is entitled to contribution from the cotenant, and on partition by sale is entitled to reimbursement for those expenditures before division of the proceeds among the property owners. However, what Milian fails to deal with is that the court ultimately declined to make an accounting and order reimbursement in this case because it found an agreement between the parties to own and divide the property equally irrespective of the exact dollar contributions of each party to the purchase price or to the subsequent improvement, maintenance, or preservation of the property. The parties were perfectly competent to make such an agreement and the critical question on appeal is whether the court's finding of such an agreement is supported by substantial evidence. . . .

(I)t appears to us that once the court in a partition action has determined that a true joint tenancy exists, it may not order reimbursement or contribution on account of differences in the amounts the parties have paid toward the initial acquisition of the property. Of course, if one joint tenant has advanced funds on behalf of the other and there is an agreement between them for reimbursement in the event of sale of the property, that agreement can be enforced by the court. However, by definition joint tenancy ownership means equal ownership, and in the absence of an agreement for reimbursement we are unaware of any authority which authorizes reimbursement on account of unequal contributions to the down payment.

If a tenancy in common rather than a joint tenancy is found, the court may either order reimbursement or determine the ownership interests in the property in proportion to the amounts contributed. It appears to be otherwise in respect to true joint tenancies, however, where by definition ownership of the property is equal.

The burden of all this is twofold; first, there is no inconsistency in the court's finding of joint tenancy and its ordering equal division of the property. Secondly, when the contributions to the down payment on the property are disregarded, the disparity in the potentially reimbursable contributions of these parties is not nearly so great as Milian contends.

We come then to the question whether the court's finding that the parties agreed to own and divide the property equally irrespective of the exact dollar amounts each contributed to the acquisition, improvement, maintenance and preservation of the property is supported by substantial evidence. We conclude it is. . . .

Tenancy by the Entirety

Nearly half the states recognize tenancy by the entirety, a type of co-ownership existing only between husband and wife. This type of co-ownership is based on an ancient legal fiction by which the common law regarded husband and wife as a single legal person. One result was that if the two acquired equal interests in real estate by the same instrument, the property was considered owned as an indivisible legal unit. Upon the death of either, the survivor remained as the parcel's sole owner. This result has also been accepted by modern law. Today a right of survivorship exists for the tenancy by the entirety similar to that existing for the joint tenancy.

A tenancy by the entirety is a more stable type of co-ownership than the joint tenancy. Because the marital partners are considered as a single unit, neither husband nor wife can break the tenancy without the other's consent. Unlike the joint tenancy, a sale by either husband or wife does not terminate the tenancy nor end the right of survivorship.

In many jurisdictions a tenancy by the entirety cannot be terminated by the forced sale of the husband's or wife's interest. If either spouse refuses to pay an individually incurred debt, the creditor cannot attach his or her interest in the property. This rule has been criticized for permitting the debtor to escape responsibility while owning an interest in a valuable asset. In a few states creditors of the husband, but not of the wife, may reach the income, profits, and title of the property. Other states permit the separate creditors of either spouse to sell the share of the debtor, whether husband or wife. If the creditor holds a joint judgment against both spouses, the creditor can attach the estate held by the entirety.

Tenancies by the entireties are terminated primarily by divorce, when the parties become tenants in common.

Community Property

Community property is a form of co-ownership between husband and wife in which each has a half interest in property acquired by the labor or skill of either spouse during marriage. A number of jurisdictions in the United States apply the doctrine of community property to property owned by a husband or wife, including Arizona, California, Idaho, Louisiana, Nevada, New Mexico, Texas, and Washington. Since community property ownership is statutory, each state varies the characteristics of the system to fit its own needs.

Community property is based on the marital relationship. In community property jurisdictions the husband and wife are regarded as partners. Each becomes a co-owner with the other in all property acquired by the labor or skill of either while the two are married.

This rule applies even though title to the property is individually held by the husband or wife.

Property owned by the husband or wife prior to marriage and property acquired during marriage by gift, inheritance, or will does not become community property. In addition, any real property purchased with the separate property of one spouse who takes title in his or her name remains separate property.

Table 39-1 depicts the distinctive features of the forms by which property is commonly co-owned.

Tenancy in Partnership

Most states have adopted the Uniform Partnership Act, which creates the *tenancy in partnership.* This act permits a partnership to buy, hold, and sell real estate in the partnership name. Individual partners share ownership in particular property only as members of the firm. Spouses, heirs, and creditors of individual partners have no rights in partnership property. Although an individual partner can transfer partnership real property, any transfer is made only as an agent for the firm. Upon the death of any partner, that person's share passes to surviving partners.

Condominiums and Cooperatives

Condominiums and cooperatives are forms of co-ownership that have become significant factors in the real-estate market since World War II. In both cooperatives and condominiums owners enjoy individual control over designated units in a facility, usually an apartment or office building, while sharing portions of the facility with other owners. This type of ownership is generally found in urban and resort areas where land values have increased because of the concentration of population. Condominium and cooperative ownership is based on statutes, which vary considerably from state to state.

TABLE 39-1 TYPES OF CO-OWNERSHIP

Type	Distinctive Features	Example
Joint tenancy	Rights of survivorship, equal right of each tenant to possess entire property	Bill and Susan own a farm together. If Bill dies, Susan automatically owns the farm. While both live, each has the right to live on the farm. If Bill sells his interest to Doug, the joint tenancy between Bill and Susan terminates.
Tenancy in common	Each tenant's share is transferred on death to that tenant's heirs. Each tenant has a right to possess entire property.	Bill and Susan own a farm as tenants in common. If Bill dies, Bill's heirs own his share of the property and Susan still owns her share. While both live, each has the right to live on the farm. If Bill sells his interest to Doug, Doug and Susan will be cotenants if Susan agrees. Otherwise, the property will be partitioned.
Tenancy by the entirety	This co-ownership of property between husband and wife is recognized in approximately twenty-five states. Upon death of one tenant, survivor is owner of property. The property is owned by the two people as if they were one person.	If Bill and Susan are married, they can own the farm as tenants by the entirety. If Bill dies, Susan automatically owns the farm. While both live, the farm is neither Bill's nor Susan's separate property, but it is owned by the two of them (as one person).
Community property	This co-ownership of property is recognized in approximately ten states. Both a husband and wife have a half interest in property acquired by either spouse during marriage.	If Bill and Susan are married and living in a community property state, when they decide to purchase a farm, it will become their community property. Even if Susan's money is used and the title to the farm is only in Bill's name, it is community property, not the separate property of either spouse. If Bill dies, the property is automatically owned by Susan.

Condominiums. In condominium ownership a person individually owns part of a building. At the same time he or she has ownership rights as a tenant in common with other condominium owners in elements of the real estate necessary for effective use of the entire structure. This includes land, walls, halls, lobbies, and service

PREVENTIVE LAW
Co-Ownership of Real Property

There are several common methods by which a person can own joint property with another person. If you refer to property merely as joint property, you are not clearly indicating the way in which you want the ownership, rights, and duties regarding that property to be shared between the owners. Thus when you are contemplating sharing the ownership of a vacant lot, residence, or business building jointly, be sure you are clear in indicating whether the parties are: (1) joint tenants with the right of survivorship, (2) tenants in common, (3) tenants by the entirety, or (4) owners of community property. In most states a joint ownership of land between parties who are not spouses is presumed to be shared as tenants in common. Consult the preceding table for characteristics of each of the major methods by which real property can be "jointly" owned.

facilities such as elevators and heating and plumbing systems. Because each unit is owned separately and the owner possesses an undivided interest in the common elements, a person may sell, mortgage, or lease an individual unit.

The condominium is created by a *declaration*, a document describing the parcel, units in the structure, and the rights and duties of condominium owners. A set of bylaws regulates the operation and maintenance of the building. Owners of the units share in the costs of maintaining the common elements of the real estate. The case that follows illustrates one type of problem that arises in condominium ownership.

Ritchey v. Villa Nueva Condominium Association

Court of Appeals of California
146 Cal.Rptr. 695 (1978)

Background: Joe B. Ritchey (plaintiff-appellant) purchased a two-bedroom unit in the Villa Nueva condominium project. He rented the unit to Dorothy Westphal, a woman with two young children. This violated a bylaw of the condominium restricting occupancy to persons 18 years of age and older. The Villa Nueva Condominium Association (defendant-respondent) sued to remove Westphal, who moved out before an answer could be filed. Ritchey then sued seeking an injunction and declaratory relief, as well as damages.

The trial court found the Association's regulation reasonable and decided in its favor. Ritchey appealed.

Decision: The Court of Appeals affirmed the trial court's judgment in favor of the Association.

Caldecott, Justice

Appellant challenges the validity of an amendment to the bylaws of the Villa Nueva Condominium project which restricts occupancy in the high-rise portion of the project to persons 18 years of age and older. . . .

Appellant urges that an age restriction is patently unreasonable in that it discriminates against families with children. Age restrictions in condominium documents have not been specifically tested in our courts. Nevertheless, we conclude on the basis of statutory and case authority that such restrictions are not per se unreasonable.

In *Flowers* v. *John Burnham & Co.,* an apartment house restriction limiting tenancy to adults, female children of all ages, and male children under the age of five was held not to violate the Unruh Act guaranteeing equal access to "accommodations, advantages, facilities, privileges, or services in all business establishments of every kind whatsoever." The court noted that arbitrary discrimination by a landlord is prohibited by the act, but held: "Because the independence, mischievousness, boisterousness and rowdyism of children vary by age and sex . . . [the defendant], as landlord, seeks to limit the children in its apartments to girls of all ages and boys under five. Regulating tenants' ages and sex to that extent is not unreasonable or arbitrary."

Similarly, in *Riley* v. *Stoves,* the Arizona Court of Appeals upheld a covenant in a deed restricting occupancy of a subdivision to persons 21 years of age or older: "The restriction flatly prevents children from living in the mobile home subdivision. The obvious purpose is to create a quiet, peaceful neighborhood by eliminating noise associated with children at play or otherwise. . . .

"We do not think the restriction is in any way arbitrary. It effectively insures that only working or retired adults will reside on the lots. It does much to eliminate the noise and distractions caused by children. We find it reasonably related to a legitimate purpose and therefore decline to hold that its enforcement violated defendants' rights to equal protection."

It should also be noted that the United States Congress has adopted several programs to provide housing for the elderly, setting an age minimum of 62 years for occupancy. As the Riley court observed, "These sections represent an implicit legislative finding that not only do older adults need inexpensive housing, but also that their housing interests and needs differ from families with children."

Under Civil Code section 1355, reasonable amendments to restrictions relating to a condominium project are binding upon every owner and every condominium in that project "whether the burdens thereon are increased or decreased thereby, and whether the owner of each and every condominium consents thereto or not." Whether an amendment is reasonable depends upon the circumstances of the particular case.

The amendment of the bylaws here in issue operates both as a restraint upon the owner's right of alienation, and as a limitation upon his right of occupancy. However, for the reasons hereinafter discussed, we conclude that under the facts of this case the amendment is reasonable. For the sake of simplicity, we will address each of these aspects of the amendment independently.

Title 10 of the Administrative Code provides that restrictions in the bylaws may limit the right of an owner to sell or lease his condominium unit so long as the standards are uniform and objective, and are not based upon the race, creed, color, national origin or sex of the purchaser or lessee. It thus appears that a restriction upon alienation can be based upon the age of the vendee or lessee, or his family.

THE LIMITATION UPON OCCUPANCY

Appellant purchased his condominium unit approximately 16 months prior to the [amendment] of the bylaws. At that time, the enabling declaration establishing a plan for condominium ownership, the model form of subscription and purchase agreement, and the report issued to the public by HUD, consistently referred to units in the condominium project as "family home units" or "family units" located in "multi-family structures," and emphasized their suitability for families with children. Appellant states that he relied upon these representations when he purchased his unit.

Appellant, however, does not claim that any of these representations were false or were made to mislead him. As far as the record shows, appellant, at the time of his purchase and for several months thereafter, could lease the premises to a person with children under 18 years of age. Furthermore, appellant does not contend that it was represented to him that the conditions of occupancy would not be changed. In fact, at the time of his purchase, the enabling declaration specifically provided that the bylaws could be amended, and that he would be subject to any reasonable amendment that was properly adopted. Thus, the amendment is reasonable.

Appellant contends that the association exceeded the scope of its authority in enacting an age restriction on occupancy. He argues that the association was established for the sole purpose of operating and maintaining the common areas and facilities of the condominium project, and that any attempt to limit or prescribe the use of the individually owned units was ultra vires [beyond its authority]. This argument is without merit.

The authority of a condominium association necessarily includes the power to issue reasonable regulations governing an owner's use of his unit in order to prevent activities which might prove annoying to the general residents. Thus, an owners' association can prohibit any activity or conduct that could constitute a nuisance, regulate the disposition of refuse, provide for the maintenance and repair of interiors of apartments as well as exteriors, and prohibit or regulate the keeping of pets.

Therefore, a reasonable restriction upon occupancy of the individually owned units of a condominium project is not beyond the scope of authority of the owners' association.

Cooperatives. In *cooperative* (often called a co-op) ownership, an individual controls a unit in a building, but the land and building itself are owned by some type of association, often a corporation. The corporation's shareholders are the building's tenants. An individual's right to a particular unit is based on a lease from the association, available only because he or she is a shareholder. The bylaws of the corporation detail the rights and duties of the tenants. Although the building is maintained by the association, maintenance expenses are shared by the shareholder-tenants. Because the individual does not own the unit to which he or she is entitled, individual financing is not available. Most bylaws restrict the individual's right to transfer his or her lease.

Real-Estate Investment Trusts

The trust is a device that has been used in the United States and England for centuries. In a trust one person or an institution has the legal title to specific property that is to be managed for the benefit of others. The property may be real or personal. The trust has been an important instrument for law reform and the legal basis for some significant economic innovations. One trust that is frequently used for real property is the real-estate investment trust (REIT).

A REIT is an organization in which the trustees own real estate, or loans secured by real estate, that is managed for beneficiaries (at least 100 persons must be beneficial owners of the trust) who hold transferable shares representing their respective interests. REITs developed in the 1960s because they enjoy tax advantage over the corporate form of business organization. Income earned by the trust is not taxable to the trust as long as it is distributed to the beneficiaries. Of course, the income from the trust that is distributed is taxable to each of the trust beneficiaries. On the contrary, income earned by a corporation is taxable both to the corporation, when earned, and to shareholders when distributed to them. Thus the REIT escapes the double taxation (at the corporate and shareholder level) associated with the corporate form. REITs are regulated by both federal and state laws. They exist as a form of business organization that differs from the partnership or corporation referred to in Chapters 32 and 34. The REIT is generally regarded as a Massachusetts business trust specializing in a particular field of operations.

LAND AND THE LAW

The variety of interests that can exist in real property illustrates the interrelationships among legal, economic, and social systems. Land always has been a critical factor in economic and social life in the Western world. Its importance is reflected in real-estate law. Innovative use of air rights, the use of REITs, and the creation of condominium and cooperative methods of ownership exemplify the dynamism of the legal system. At the same time the historic interests in real property that continue to be useful to society—such as the concept of estates—are links that join the past and present.

REVIEW PROBLEMS

1. Explain the difference between a fee simple absolute and a fee simple defeasible. How are they similar?

2. What is the principal difference between a term tenancy and a periodic tenancy?

3. Define co-ownership. Compare and con-

trast a joint tenancy and a tenancy in common.

4. Explain the differences between an easement in gross and an easement appurtenant.

5. What is the difference between a sublease and an assignment of the lease?

6. Tom owned a unit in a condominium. Red occupied a unit in a cooperative. The apartments were very similar. Red argued that he had a better deal because he did not have to pay real-estate taxes but Tom did. Do you agree with Red? Support your answer.

7. Pete Brangs and his son, Al, owned real estate as joint tenants. Pete had been involved in a business deal and accumulated a large debt, which he refused to pay because he felt that the creditor had defrauded him. The creditor threatened to attach the real estate if the debt was not paid. Pete believed the creditor could not attach the property because Al had had nothing to do with Pete's business and he and Al were co-owners of the real estate. Was Pete correct? Discuss.

8. Jim and Lucy Monroe, a married couple, lived in a community property state. Jim had not worked for many years because he hated to get up in the morning. Lucy was the sole support of the family. Lucy bought a house and took title in her own name. Six years later, she died, leaving the house to her son. What rights, if any, did Jim have in the property? Support your answer.

9. Anne Crowley purchased a house from Alex Baldwin. The house adjoined an apartment complex that Baldwin was developing. Baldwin promised Crowley that she and future owners of the property would have the use of the pool. Crowley lived in the house for several years. During this period she used the pool each summer. When she sold the property, she told the new owners of Baldwin's promise. But Baldwin would not allow them to use the pool. Describe Crowley's interest in the use of the pool. Could Baldwin prevent the new owners from using the pool? Support your answer.

10. May conveyed to Tenneco, Inc., an easement crossing a portion of his land. Using this easement, Tenneco constructed and put into service an underground natural gas pipeline. Several years later May constructed a road over a portion of Tenneco's easement. Federal regulations require installation of a protective encasement around pipe where it passes under a street. Tenneco installed the encasement at a cost of $4,903.39 and billed May for this amount. May refuses to pay and Tenneco sues. Will Tenneco be successful? Discuss. Tenneco, Inc. v. May, 512 F.2d 1381 (1975)

11. Cushman is developing Blackacre as a residential subdivision. Prior to Cushman's acquisition of the property, Blackacre had been an apricot orchard. A roadway based on an easement ran from the orchard to a public street. This property subject to the roadway easement was owned by Davis. The road had existed for many years. Its primary use was to move spraying and picking equipment into the orchard. This was done about ten times each year. Davis also used the road for access to his home and to a water tank. From time to time others used the road to reach the orchard. Cushman seeks to quiet title to the easement for access to the subdivision and Davis strenuously objects. Will Cushman be successful in his quiet title action? Discuss. Cushman v. Davis, 145 Cal.Rptr. 791 (1978)

12. The will of Alma H. Rand contained the following provision: "3rd. That the share of the Estate of Henry Rand of the town of Southport, Lincoln County, State of Maine, shall be left to John Freeman Rand in fee simple *with the proviso that he shall*

never deny access or occupation to the several heirs hereinafter named during their lifetime." What kind of estate did John Rand have as a result of this provision? Explain. Babb v. Rand, 345 A.2d 496 (1974)

13. The Chelsea Yacht Club owned a clubhouse that had been erected on piles driven into the bed of the Mystic River. The land was owned by the state, but the club had secured a license to construct the building. The only access to the clubhouse was over the Chelsea North Bridge. Both clubhouse and bridge were over sixty years old. Because of the age of the bridge, the state constructed a new bridge several miles away. The old bridge was removed. This left the clubhouse surrounded by water. The club sued the bridge authority for damages occasioned by the loss of access over the bridge. On what theory might the club sue the bridge authority? Would the club be successful? Discuss. Chelsea Yacht Club v. Mystic River Bridge Authority, 116 N.E.2d 153 (1953)

14. Luithle and his wife owned real estate as joint tenants. Luithle purchased cattle from Schlichenmayer, paying for the cattle with a worthless check. Luithle immediately sold the cattle. Part of the proceeds were used to make a $1,100 mortgage payment on the real property that the couple owned. A short time later Luithle died and Schlichenmayer sued the wife to recover the $1,100 on grounds that she was unjustly enriched. Would Luithle be successful? Discuss. Schlichenmayer v. Luithle, 221 N.W.2d 77 (1974)

CHAPTER 40

Acquisition, Financing, and Control of Real Property

T he previous chapter explained interests that can exist in real property. This chapter discusses the acquisition, financing, and control of real property.

Title or ownership of real property may be acquired in a number of ways. While purchase is the most common, individuals and sometimes business firms become owners of real property by gift or by inheritance. (Acquisition of real property as a result of the death of the owner is treated in Chapter 41. Gifts are discussed in Chapter 38.) A government or those persons or firms it authorizes can acquire title to real property by exercising the power of eminent domain. In certain instances a person or firm can obtain title to property by adverse possession or unauthorized occupancy.

ADVERSE POSSESSION

Obtaining title by adverse possession is a legal oddity. A person occupying land as a trespasser can defeat the rights of the true owner. The justification for this unusual policy is that society benefits when idle land is put to use. The legal system encourages the use of land by providing a trespasser with a means to establish clear title to the property he or she is using.

Balanced against the policy of encouraging land use is concern with the protection of private property rights. Because of the importance of protecting private property, a trespasser acquires title only if prescribed conditions are met and certain acts occur. These acts and conditions exist to ensure that the owner has an opportunity to discover challenges to his or her title and a reasonable chance to protect it.

Statutes of Limitations

Basic to all adverse possession claims are state *statutes of limitations.* These statutes establish a period of time during which the rightful owner of land must bring an action to oust the trespasser.

At common law the owner had to bring suit within twenty years; several states have adopted this as the limitation period. Although only a handful of states allow the owner more than twenty years to act, a substantial number apply shorter periods, ranging from five to eighteen years. Many of the states with short limitation periods are in the sparsely populated western United States. This reflects the public policy underlying adverse possession, which is to encourage land use. In some states the limitation period is reduced if the adverse possessor has paid taxes or occupies the land on the basis of a document such as an invalid deed or will.

Elements of Adverse Possession

Generally five elements must exist for title to be acquired by adverse possession. The claimant must prove his or her possession is: (1) continuous for the statutory period, (2) open and notorious, (3) hostile, (4) actual, and (5) exclusive.

A number of states allow occupancy of two or more successive adverse possessors to be added together to establish possession for the necessary period. This is called *tacking,* since the periods are "tacked" together. Although tacking is probably permitted in a majority of

states, some jurisdictions limit it to cases involving heirs, spouses, or blood relatives.

Continuous. A person seeking title to property must prove that his or her possession has been continuous for the statutory period.

Open and Notorious. Open and notorious acts are those that will alert the true owner to claims that are adverse to his or her rights. Although the true owner does not have to know what is taking place, the acts must be such that a diligent owner would become aware of them.

Hostile. Facts that are open and notorious are often hostile. The requirement that possession be hostile does not require ill will or evil intent but merely that the person in possession of the property claims to occupy it as the owner. Most state courts accept that possession is hostile for purposes of adverse possession if the occupant claims ownership either by mistake or willfully. A person who enters into property with the owner's permission cannot claim title by adverse possession unless he or she later repudiates the owner's title.

Actual Possession. Actual possession consists of exercising dominion over land, making ordinary use of it, and taking the ordinary profit the land is capable of yielding. Courts determine actual possession by looking at the character of the land that is involved. Residing on the property is not necessary unless that use would be expected. In a few states the adverse possessor must enclose the land to establish a claim.

Exclusive Use. Exclusive use means that the claimant possesses the land for his or her own use. Total exclusion of others is not required, but the adverse possessor must exclude others as would be expected of an owner under the circumstances. Occasional use by others, even the rightful owner, does not negate exclusiveness if the use permitted by the adverse possessor is consistent with his or her claims of ownership. The following case involves the element of exclusive use and several other aspects of adverse possession.

Porter v. Posey

Missouri Court of Appeals

592 S.W.2d 844 (1979)

Background: The Porters (plaintiffs) purchased property from the Engelmeyers. In addition to the property conveyed to them by deed, the plaintiffs also took possession of a 0.18 acre tract of land that had been maintained and used by the Engelmeyers but that was owned by the Poseys (defendants). The parcel in question was used by the Engelmeyers for twenty years; they built a graveled turnaround on it and used the property for parking and for access by them to other adjoining property they owned. At all times the Engelmeyers believed they owned the disputed parcel.

Just prior to the Porters' purchase from the Engelmeyers, the Poseys had the property surveyed. They then discovered that the turnaround was on their land. They threatened Mr. Engelmeyer and told him to get off the property and blocked the access to the turnaround. The Porters sued to clear title to the land; they claimed the Engelmeyers had title through adverse possession. The trial court found the possession by the Engelmeyers of the disputed parcel satisfied the requirements for adverse possession. Accordingly, it found the plaintiffs, who purchased from them, had title to the parcel. The defendants appealed to the Court of Appeals.

Decision: The Court of Appeals affirmed the trial court's decision.

Satz, Judge

The crucial questions in this case are: (1) was title to the tract in dispute vested in the Englemeyers; (2) if so, was their title subsequently extinguished or divested; and (3) if not divested or extinguished, was their title properly transferred to plaintiffs.

In order for the trial court to have vested title in plaintiffs on the present record, it must have found that title first vested in the Englemeyers by adverse possession. Thus, implicit in the court's ultimate decision is a finding that the Englemeyers occupied the tract in dispute intending to possess it as their own, or, more specifically, that the Engelmeyers occupied or used the tract and their occupation or use of the tract was (1) actual (2) open and notorious (3) hostile (4) exclusive and (5) continuous for ten years. Defendants limit their attack on these implicit findings to an attack on the open and notorious, hostile and exclusive elements of the Engelmeyers' adverse possession.

Open and notorious occupancy or possession is an essential element of adverse possession because the openness and notoriety of the occupancy or possession gives the owner cause to know that an adverse claim of ownership is being made by another. . . . The element of open and notorious is satisfied by a showing that the occupancy or possession manifested a claim of ownership and was conspicuous, widely recognized and commonly known.

In the instant case, the Engelmeyers entered the disputed tract with a bulldozer, cleared the land, built the turnaround, then maintained it and the land surrounding it. The family also played volleyball and parked on this land. In addition, a neighbor testified that he believed the Engelmeyers to be the owners of this tract of land because they were the only ones who maintained it and used it with any regularity for a period of 18 years. Changing the physical structure of the land by clearing it, building a turnaround and then using and maintaining the turnaround was sufficient evidence to support the court's finding that the Engelmeyers' acts were acts of ownership, sufficient to give the then existing owner notice of this claim and were commonly known so as to constitute open and notorious occupancy or possession.

· · ·

Defendants next argue that the Engelmeyers' use and possession was not hostile. Hostility of possession does not imply ill will or acrimony. . . . Hostile possession is simply an assertion of ownership adverse to that of the true owner and all others; i.e., "the claimant must occupy the land with the intent to possess it as his own and not in subservience to a recognized, superior claim of another." Thus, as with other elements of adverse possession, the element of hostility is founded upon the intent with which the claimant held possession and, since the elements of adverse possession are not mutually exclusive, acts which are open and notorious, supporting a claim of ownership, may and often do logically satisfy the element that the claim be hostile.

In the present case, as we have previously noted, there was sufficient evidence for the trial court to find that the Engelmeyers occupied and used the disputed tract with the intent to possess it as their own and, thus, clearly their use and occupancy was hostile.

Defendants' next attack on adverse possession is that the Engelmeyers' possession was not exclusive because others occasionally used the turnaround and, thus, defendants contend, plaintiffs' evidence, at best, merely established a common easement by prescription. . . .

. . . Possession or use is exclusive when the claimant occupies or uses the land for his own use and not for that of another. The present record reveals that the Engelmeyers built the turnaround believing it to be on their property. The fact that travelers occasionally also used this roadway to turn around does not imply nor indicate that the Engelmeyers occupied the land for the benefit of these travelers. Indeed, even occasional use of disputed property by the record owner will not of itself negate the exclusive use by an adverse claimant, if the record owner's knowledge or notice of the adverse claim is not otherwise altered. For these reasons, defendants' argument against exclusivity is not persuasive.

The remaining question, then, is whether the Engelmeyers properly transferred title to plaintiffs. As noted, the principle urged by plaintiffs to support the Engelmeyers' transfer of title to plaintiffs, in effect, permits title to property acquired by adverse possession to be transferred without a written conveyance, and simply requires the title owner to intend to transfer the property so acquired and the transferee to receive or take possession of that property.

In the present case, Mrs. Engelmeyer's unrefuted testimony was that she and her husband intended to convey the disputed tract to plaintiffs. Moreover, this was plaintiffs' understanding, and the fact that plaintiff Eugene Porter sought legal advice to carry out that intention merely enforces the weight to be given to Mrs. Engelmeyer's testimony. Further, there was sufficient explicit testimony and inferential evidence for the trial court to find that, after the transfer, plaintiffs took possession of the disputed tract. Thus, the Engelmeyers transferred their title to the disputed tract to plaintiffs.

Prescription

The previous chapter described the easement, a nonpossessory right to use the land of another for a particular purpose. Most easements are created by written instruments; however, an easement may be created by *prescription*, a legal doctrine similar in several ways to adverse possession. Both are based on wrongful invasion of the property rights of the true owner, but prescription is based on adverse use, not occupancy. As a result, a person acquiring a prescriptive easement merely acquires a *right to use another's land*, while the successful adverse possessor actually acquires title. Another common difference between the two is that the time necessary to acquire an easement by prescription is frequently less than the time required to acquire title by adverse possession.

EMINENT DOMAIN

Eminent domain is the power of the government to acquire private property without the owner's consent. Both the United States and the individual states may delegate the power of eminent domain. They often delegate this power to cities, counties, state colleges and universities, and public service corporations. The federal and state constitutions limit the government's power by requiring that:

- The property must be taken for a public purpose.
- The owner must be adequately compensated.

- The property cannot be taken without due process of law.

There can be problems with each of these requirements. The first problem—concerned with taking for a public purpose—occurs in situations where private owners benefit from the government-taking. Clearly, if the taking is for the purpose of building an interstate highway, a state prison, or local civic center, a public purpose is involved. However, where private property is taken for urban development, condemned private property is taken by the government and then generally resold to a private developer. In these cases the public purpose—to improve and develop the city—seems less clear when the property is ultimately returned to private ownership.

The second problem concerns when a "taking of property" occurs. Government regulation of private property is permitted even when that regulation interferes with the owner's use of the property. For example, if the state or local government through the exercise of its police power regulates the use of property but does not take it, there is no obligation to compensate the owner. On the other hand, if there has been a "taking" of property, the government is obligated to compensate the owner. *Inverse condemnation* occurs if there is a significant interference with the private property owner's use and enjoyment of his or her property. Many recent cases have discussed this aspect of the government's use of its power of eminent domain. The *Burrows* case that follows illustrates the application of this concept.

The third problem concerns the process

used by the government exercising its eminent domain power. The owner of the property is guaranteed the opportunity to have a trial focusing on public use being made of the property and on the amount of compensation to be paid. The owner of the property is entitled to the fair market value of the property. Is that determined by the current use of the property or the highest and most expensive use to which the property could be put? Should the amount of compensation reflect the emotional attachment of a person who has long occupied the property as a home? These and other related questions concern the process surrounding the government's eminent domain power.

Burrows v. City of Keene

Supreme Court of New Hampshire
432 A.2d 15 (1981)

Background: Burrows, the plaintiff, was a real-estate developer, who, along with a partner, owned undeveloped woodlands on the side of a pond in the city of Keene. He presented a plan to the defendant city to subdivide and develop the property. However, the city wished to preserve the land as open space and therefore negotiated with Burrows to sell it to the city. Because the parties could not reach agreement on the price to be paid for the property, the plaintiff again submitted a development plan to the city. When the planning board rejected the plaintiff's proposal, the plaintiff brought suit. The city then amended its zoning ordinance to include most of the plaintiff's property in a conservation zone. The trial court found the inclusion of the plaintiff's lands in the city's conservation zone constituted an inverse condemnation of his property.

The city appealed the trial court decision to the Supreme Court of New Hampshire. Decision: The Supreme Court of New Hampshire agreed with the trial court's decision that there had been a taking of the plaintiff's property, and accordingly remanded the case for a determination of damages due the plaintiff as compensation.

Grimes, Chief Justice

The issue in this case is whether an amendment to the Keene zoning ordinance, which had the effect of including a substantial part of the plaintiffs' land in a conservation district, resulted in a taking of the plaintiffs' property entitling them to damages for inverse condemnation. We hold that it did.

On October 15, 1973, the plaintiffs, John P. Burrows and George Whitham, purchased approximately 124 acres of undeveloped woodland on the southern side of Goose Pond Road in Keene for $45,000. Plaintiff Burrows is, and has been for many years, a real estate developer, and the property was purchased for the purpose of subdivision development, which was a permitted use in the rural zone in which it was located. . . .

In January 1975, the plaintiffs went to the Keene Planning Board and presented three plans for subdividing the property. The planning board indicated that the prospects of subdivision approval were not favorable because the city was trying to preserve as open space the area in which the plaintiffs' land was located. Accordingly, the board advised the plaintiffs to consult the city conservation commission concerning the possibility of selling the land to the conservation commission as an alternative to development. The conservation commission expressed a desire to purchase the property and requested a delay so that it could obtain federal funding to make the purchase. The plaintiffs agreed. . . .

Because the parties could not reach agreement on price, the plaintiffs went forward with their subdivision plans.

After various studies and meetings, a public hearing was held on September 27, 1976, following which the board denied the plaintiffs' application for subdivision approval and adopted a resolution favoring acquisition of the plaintiffs' land.

The plaintiffs did not appeal from the planning board's denial of their subdivision plan but instead brought this action for equitable relief in the superior court. In December 1977, the city amended its zoning ordinance. The effect of this amendment was to include 109 acres of the plaintiffs' land in a conservation zone and the balance in a rural zone. Thereafter, the plaintiffs amended their petition in the superior court to include a claim that the amendment to the zoning ordinance had deprived them of all reasonable use of that portion of their property which was included in the conservation zone and, in effect, sought damages for inverse condemnation.

· · ·

The Trial Court considered the claim based on inverse condemnation, ruled that the inclusion of the land in the conservation zone did constitute inverse condemnation and ordered that damages be determined by a jury if no appeal was taken from its ruling. The city appealed. . . .

The substantive issue raised in this case involves a principle that lies at the very foundation of civilized society as we know it. The principle that no man's property may be taken from him without just compensation reaches at least as far back as 1215, when on "the meadow which is called Runnymede" the Barons of England exacted from King John the Magna Carta, which contains at least three references to this fundamental truth. . . .

Our own constitution provides that "no part of a man's property shall be taken from him, or applied to public uses, without his consent. . . ." N.H.Const. pt. I, art. 12. Early on, this clause was held to require just compensation. . . .

The same principle was embodied in the Fifth Amendment to the Constitution of the United States at the insistence of a majority of the states, including New Hampshire, in ratifying the Constitution. It has now been made binding on the states through the Fourteenth Amendment.

It should be noted that the New Hampshire Constitution makes explicit what is implicit in the Fifth Amendment to the Federal Constitution, namely, that "no *part* of a man's property shall be taken from him . . . without his consent. . . ." N.H.Const. pt. I, art. 12. (Emphasis added.) Furthermore, our New Hampshire Bill of Rights provides that among the "natural, essential and inherent rights" of all men is the right of "acquiring, possessing, and protecting property; and, in a word, of seeking and obtaining happiness." N.H.Const. pt. I, art. . . . .

The rights mentioned in N.H.Const. pt. I, art. 2 are not bestowed by that constitutional provision but rather are recognized to be among the natural and inherent rights of all humankind. This provision of our Bill of Rights "has been held to be so specific that it 'necessarily limits all subsequent grants of power to deal adversely with it.' " . . .

Because it limits all subsequent express grants of power, it necessarily limits the so-called police power, which is only an implied power. "The right to just compensation is [likewise] a constitutional restriction on the police power and is therefore superior to it." . . .

Because the constitution prohibits any taking of private property by whatever means without compensation, the just compensation requirement applies whenever the exercise of the so-called police power results in a "taking of property." . . .

The question in the case before us is whether the action of the city constituted a taking of the plaintiffs' property. "Property," in the constitutional sense, is not the physical thing itself but is rather the group of rights which the owner of the thing has with respect to it. The term refers to a person's right to "possess, use, enjoy and dispose of a thing and is not limited to the thing itself."

The property owner's right of "indefinite user (or of using indefinitely) . . . necessarily includes the right . . ." to exclude others from using the property, whether it be land or anything else. "From the very nature of these rights of user and of exclusion, it is evident that they cannot be materially abridged without, . . . taking the owner's 'property.' " "The principle must be the same whether the owner is wholly deprived of the use of his land, or only partially deprived of it. . . ."

"Police power regulations such as zoning ordinances and other land-use restrictions can destroy the use and enjoyment of property in order to promote the public good just as effectively as formal condemnation or physical invasion of property." *San Diego Gas & Elec.* v. *City of San Diego,* 101 S.Ct. at 1304 (Brennan, J., dissenting). It matters not to the owner whether the use of his land is taken from him by actual physical invasion or condemnation or whether he is prevented from using it by regulation.

On the other hand, the benefits resulting to the public from the taking may be equally great whether the taking is accomplished by regulation or actual condemnation.

This is not to say that every regulation of private property through the police power constitutes a taking. Reasonable regulations that prevent an owner from using his land in such a way that it causes injury to others or deprives them of the reasonable use of their land may not require compensation. . . . But arbitrary or unreasonable restrictions which substantially deprive the owner of the "economically viable use of his land" in order to benefit the public in some way constitute a taking within the meaning of our New Hampshire Constitution requiring the payment of just compensation.

. . . The owner need not be deprived of all valuable use of his property. If the denial of use is substantial and is especially onerous, a taking occurs. There can be no set test to determine when regulation goes too far and becomes a taking. Each case must be determined under its own circumstances. The purpose of the regulation is an element to be considered.

Turning now to the zoning amendment involved in this case, we have already stated that it does not come anywhere near the line dividing constitutional and unconstitutional regulation.

From the outset, it was plain that the city wished that the plaintiffs' land be devoted to open space. The city's comprehensive plan sets out a goal of having fifty per cent of the city remain as open space, and the Goose Pond area is one of those designated for preservation. The planning board and the conservation commission both took positions opposed to subdivision and in favor of acquisition of the plaintiffs' land by the city. The city, however, would not pay a reasonable price for the property, electing instead to offer to purchase the property for a sum representing the land's value based on the city's intended use of the land rather than the price to which the plaintiffs were entitled, which was one reflecting the land's highest and best use. . . .

Instead of acquiring the plaintiffs' land by paying just compensation as required by our constitution, however, the city, when it found that it was unable to acquire it for little more than half its value, elected to accomplish its purpose by regulating the use of the property so as to prohibit all "normal private development." It is plain that the city and its officials were attempting to obtain for the public the benefit of having this land remain undeveloped as open space without paying for that benefit in the constitutional manner. The city sought to enjoy that public benefit by forcing the plaintiffs to devote their land to a particular purpose and prohibiting all other economically feasible uses of the land, thus placing the entire burden of preserving the land as open space upon the plaintiffs. . . .

The purpose of the regulation is clearly to give the public the benefit of preserving the plaintiffs' land as open space. Its purpose is not to restrain an injurious use of the property. Although there may undoubtedly be some uses of the land which are sufficiently injurious to others that their use may be prohibited, the normal development of the land for residential purposes is not one of them. . . .

We hold that the creation of the "conservation district" in Keene constituted a taking with respect to all of the plaintiffs' land which falls within it, entitling the plaintiffs to compensation for inverse condemnation in an amount equal to the diminution in the value of the result from the taking.

PURCHASE AND SALE OF REAL PROPERTY

The purchase and sale of real property should be of special interest to business students because they will probably participate in several such transactions during their lifetime. The large amounts of money, long-term financial commitments, and technical legal procedures that are a part of most real-estate sales make knowledge of these transactions particularly important. Buying and selling real estate involves several legal areas. Agency and contract law are especially important. Many real-estate sales are negotiated by brokers who are agents. Brokers are also involved in leasing, property management, and real-estate appraisal. The contract is the critical document in a real-estate sale; it governs the relationship between brokers and clients and also between landlords and tenants.

Anatomy of a Real-Estate Sale

The typical real-estate sale in the United States is usually the result of negotiations between the buyer and seller, often with the help of a real-estate broker. In some areas, especially for residential real estate, a person desiring to buy property will submit a purchase offer to the seller. Buyers should realize that this document's terms become the contract if the seller accepts the offer. However, the seller can reject or make a counteroffer if he or she is not satisfied with the purchase offer terms. In this case the negotiations often continue and a contract on different terms may result.

Another procedure, more frequently used in commercial transactions, is for the parties to negotiate until an agreement appears to have been reached. Then the parties will have a document drafted; they will then review and sign it as their agreement. Whatever procedure is used, all states require that a contract for the sale of real property be in writing to be enforceable.

Equitable Title. When a contract for the sale of real estate is completed, the buyer acquires *equitable title.* This gives the buyer the right to sue for damages or specific performance if the seller refuses to perform. Simultaneously, the seller acquires a right to enforce the contract.

During the interval between the making of the contract and its performance the buyer completes the necessary arrangements for financing and examines the seller's title. If the title is defective, the seller has an opportunity to cure defects before the date set for title closing. At that time the buyer obtains legal title by a deed and the seller gets the purchase price.

Risk of Loss. As the buyer has equitable title during the period between the contract signing and title closing, in some states the buyer bears the risk of loss or damage to the property. Thus if the property is damaged by fire, the buyer still must complete the transaction as agreed. Other states reject this rule as unfair, especially when the buyer is not in posses-

sion. These states allow the buyer an adjustment in the price to compensate for loss. Parties to a real-estate contract need not leave the allocation of the risk of loss to state law. Instead, this problem can and should be settled by the parties in their contract.

Title Closing. Two types of title closing are common in the United States. In most areas the parties involved in the transaction meet as a group and exchange the funds and documents required to complete the transfer. Ordinarily the buyer, the seller, brokers, a representative of the institution financing the sale, and attorneys for each party are present.

In some areas real-estate sales close through a third party, called an escrow agent. In an *escrow closing,* the buyer and seller submit the necessary documents and funds to the escrow agent, who is responsible for seeing that the transaction closes on the terms agreed upon in the contract. When the seller delivers a properly executed deed to the escrow agent and the agent is assured that the seller is passing a good title, the funds and mortgage documents are turned over to the proper parties, and the transaction is completed.

Deeds

Ownership of real property is transfered by an instrument called *a deed.* A deed is a two-party instrument; the person conveying the property is called the grantor and the person to whom the property is conveyed, the grantee. Several types of deeds are in common use in the United States. Generally the type of deed a seller will use is agreed upon in the sales contract.

Warranty Deed. The most common type of deed used in a real-estate transaction is the *warranty deed.* A warranty deed conveys title and warrants that the title is good and free of liens and encumbrances. The warranties are also referred to as covenants. They provide the purchaser with some protection against claims that might interfere with ownership.

Although the use and wording of particular covenants vary from one jurisdiction to another, four covenants are common in the United States. One of these is called the *covenant of seisin* or *covenant of right to convey*. By this covenant the seller guarantees that he or she has a good title and the right to transfer it. A second covenant used in many jurisdictions is the *covenant against encumbrances*. In making this covenant, the seller affirms that no encumbrances exist against the property. The *covenant of quiet enjoyment* and the *covenant of general warranty* are guarantees that the buyer will not be evicted from the property by someone with a title superior to the seller's. As a result of these two covenants, the seller agrees to defend the buyer's title against all lawful claims.

Warranty deed covenants do not assure the buyer that the seller has title, but they do provide a right to sue if a covenant is broken. This is a valuable right if the seller is solvent and still within the jurisdiction.

Bargain and Sale Deed. A *bargain and sale deed* conveys title but contains no warranties. Although no formal guarantees of title are made, the bargain and sale deed is by nature contractual, and the seller implies that he or she has a title to convey. It will sometimes contain covenants against the seller's acts. If so, the seller guarantees that he or she has done nothing that might adversely affect the title.

Quitclaim Deed. A *quitclaim deed* merely releases whatever interest the grantor has. Unlike the warranty deed and bargain and sale deed, the transferor by a quitclaim does not purport to convey title. But if the grantor has title, this interest is conveyed as effectively as it would be by a warranty or bargain and sale deed. Quitclaim deeds are commonly used to correct defective titles.

Essential Elements of a Deed

A *deed* is a complicated legal instrument that should be drafted by an attorney. To be valid, a deed must contain words of conveyance that indicate an intention to convey title. The deed also must identify a competent grantor and grantee, contain a legal description, and be properly signed and executed. A final requirement is a valid delivery and acceptance. Most legal problems involving deeds arise because someone claims the deed has not been properly delivered. The case that follows is an example.

Bennett v. Mings
Court of Civil Appeals
535 S.W.2d 408 (1976)

Background: Nellie Mings (plaintiff-appellee), a 91-year-old woman, signed a warranty deed conveying land on which her home was located to her nephew, Cyril Bennett (defendant-appellant). Both parties agreed the deed was not to be recorded until Mrs. Mings's death. A year later the nephew returned the deed to Mrs. Mings. A few days thereafter, Bennett regained possession of the deed and recorded it. He claimed she then gave him permission to record it, but she claimed he was only to use it for security.

Mrs. Mings sued, claiming she did not validly deliver the deed to him, and the trial court found in her favor. Bennett appealed.

Decision: The Court of Civil Appeals affirmed the trial court's judgment for Mrs. Mings.

Ray, Justice

Appellant Bennett contends that the appellee failed to introduce any evidence to support the jury finding that Mrs. Mings did not intend for the deed to become operative as a conveyance. . . .

The evidence shows that on September 7, 1972, Nellie Mings, a lady ninety-one years of age at that time, signed a warranty deed conveying a tract of land with her home and furnishings located thereon, to her nephew, Cyril C. Bennett. Manual delivery of the deed was made to appellant and he put it in his safety deposit box. In December of 1973, appellee requested the return of the deed and appellant Bennett returned it to Mrs. Mings. A few days later, Bennett regained possession of the deed and recorded it. Upon learning of this, Mrs. Mings again demanded return of her deed, and upon Bennett's refusal, she brought this suit. The evidence is undisputed that originally both parties agreed that the deed would not be recorded until Mrs. Mings's death and that "delivery" was not then complete. Appellant stated that the deed still belonged to Mrs. Mings though he had it in his safety deposit box. Bennett testified that he got the deed the second time with the permission of Mrs. Mings because she wanted things cleared up before her death. Mrs. Mings testified that she surrendered the deed to Bennett only with the permission that he could use the deed for security, but that under no circumstances was the deed to be recorded. She further testified that she gave up the deed under Bennett's insistent demand and that she was put in fear.

Appellant contends that once there has been a complete and effective delivery of a deed, the delivery is absolute and unconditional and is operative immediately.

The jury found that Mrs. Mings signed the deed, but that Mrs. Mings did not intend the deed to become operative as a conveyance of her land, home and furnishings when it was delivered to Bennett and further, the jury found that no consideration was paid to Mrs. Mings.

Whether a deed has been delivered is a question for the jury's determination, . . . and the question is primarily one of the grantor's intent. . . .

In order to constitute delivery, a deed of conveyance must be placed in the hands of the grantee, or within his control, with the intention that it is to become presently operative as a conveyance. Without such intention manual delivery to the grantee is insufficient to pass title. . . .

The issue in the present case is whether or not at either time Bennett obtained possession of the deed that Mrs. Mings intended that the deed become immediately operative as a conveyance. The evidence is clear that when Bennett obtained possession of the deed the first time neither he nor Mrs. Mings felt that the deed constituted such delivery as to become immediately operative as a conveyance and Bennett so testified. However, when Bennett obtained the deed the second time he testified that she gave him the deed with permission to record it. Her testimony is in direct conflict with his and the jury could have properly inferred that Mrs. Mings gave Bennett the deed out of fear or that she let Bennett use the deed as security, but with no present intent that it become immediately operative as a conveyance. We conclude that it was the duty of the jury to weigh the conflicting evidence as it did, and to determine whether the requisite intent was present for the conveyance to be effective when Bennett obtained possession of the deed the second time. We have reviewed the evidence and hold that the jury was justified in finding that Mrs. Mings did not intend the deed to become operative as a conveyance of her land, home and furnishings.

The judgment of the trial court is affirmed.

Recording Statutes

All states have statutes requiring that important instruments affecting the title to real property be entered into the public record. In addition to deeds and mortgages, the statutes generally require that long-term leases, easements, assignments, and other similar instruments be recorded. The purpose of these statutes is to notify third parties of interests that might exist in a particular piece of land. This notice protects the third party from loss that might occur if he or she were to acquire an interest in land subject to unknown claims of others.

Recording statutes are based on the idea that if a real property interest is not recorded, a person acquiring a conflicting interest will have superior rights in the land. For example, if X conveys real property to Y, Y is required to record the deed. If Y does not and X fraudulently conveys to Z, Z may acquire an ownership interest superior to Y's. In order for this to occur, Z must be a good-faith purchaser. This means that Z must not have knowledge of the sale to Y and must give value for the property. The person who has recorded an interest in property is favored by the law over others who later acquire some interest in that same property.

Constructive Notice. Constructive notice is knowledge that the law implies a person has. Constructive notice exists if a person without actual knowledge is in a position to have acquired that knowledge by reasonably investigating available sources. If a person acquiring an interest in realty knows something that would induce a reasonable person to make further inquiry, and none is made, the law presumes actual knowledge exists. In addition, any information that might be discovered by a careful check of the record is presumed known. A person with actual or constructive knowledge of a prior conflicting interest does not acquire his or her interest in good faith. Thus the result is that a person who does not examine the record is penalized and the recording statutes operate effectively. Since several documents granting interests to different parties may be recorded for the same property, the time of recording can affect the priority given to the owner of the interest being recorded. In the following case the Supreme Court of Kansas had to determine whether higher priority should be given to the person holding a mechanic's lien, an interest given for labor performed or materials furnished in the construction or improvements made to real property, or to the holder of a valid mortgage on the property.

Davis-Wellcome Mortgage Co. v. Long Bell Lumber Co.

Supreme Court of Kansas

336 P.2d. 463 (1959)

Background: Durham owned several parcels of land in the city of Newton on which he intended to build homes that would then be sold. On June 28, 1955 he obtained a loan from the plaintiff, Davis-Wellcome Mortgage Co. (Davis) and delivered to it his promissory note and mortgage. On June 30, 1955 the mortgage was recorded. On June 29, 1955 the defendant Long-Bell Lumber Company (Long-Bell) agreed to furnish lumber to Durham for use in the construction of the homes.

Durham failed to pay the amount due to either Long-Bell or to Davis. Plaintiff Davis then sued to foreclose on its loan to Durham. The trial court, having found that defendant Long-Bell commenced work on June 29, 1955, rendered judgment in favor of both Davis and Long-Bell against Durham. It also determined that because the statutory lien of Long-Bell arose before the mortgage of Davis, that lien was entitled to priority over the mortgage interest of Davis.

Davis appealed the trial court's decision granting Long-Bell's lien priority over its mortgage interest.

Decision: The Supreme Court of Kansas, finding that the mortgage interest of Davis was not valid as to Long-Bell until the date of its recording, affirmed the trial court's decision.

Fatzer, Justice

The principal question presented is the priority of liens of a mortgagee and a mechanic's lien holder where construction of houses on real estate covered by the mortgage was begun the day after the mortgage was executed and delivered, but the day before it was recorded.

Floyd L. Durham and his wife were the owners of eight unimproved lots in Eastview Heights subdivision in the city of Newton. On June 28, 1955, they obtained a loan from plaintiff and executed and delivered their promissory note and mortgage. . . .

Two days later, June 30, 1955, the mortgage was filed of record in Harvey county, and funds were first advanced thereunder on July 7, 1955. . . .

On June 29, 1955, Long-Bell Lumber Company, hereafter referred to as Long-Bell, entered into an oral contract with Floyd L. Durham whereby it agreed to furnish lumber and other building materials for the construction of a house upon each of the eight lots described in the mortgage. Pursuant to the oral contract and between June 29, 1955, and September 15, 1955, Long-Bell sold to Durham and delivered to the building sites lumber and materials which were used in the construction of the houses. Durham failed to pay any part of the amount due and Long-Bell timely filed its verified mechanic's lien statement in the office of the clerk of the district court.

The Durhams defaulted in the payment of principal and interest due under the mortgage and plaintiff commenced the instant action to foreclose.

. . . The trial court found that plaintiff's mortgage was not a purchase money mortgage, and that construction of the houses had commenced on June 29, 1955, the day after plaintiff's note and mortgage were executed and delivered but the day before the mortgage was filed of record. In accordance with its findings, the trial court rendered judgment that the various lien holders have judgment against the Durhams for the amounts due and payable and that the liens of plaintiff and Long-Bell be foreclosed. With respect to the priority of the liens, the court, in conformity with its findings, entered judgment that Long-Bell's mechanic's lien was prior in right to plaintiff's mortgage lien. Plaintiff appealed from the judgment granting priority of Long-Bell's lien over its mortgage lien. . . .

Plaintiff . . . contends that if it is determined construction began on June 29, 1955, there is a basic and compelling reason why the trial court's judgment must be reversed. That reason is best stated by quoting from plaintiff's brief:

> ". . . it is the contention of the appellant . . . that its lien attached and became operative against the real estate above described as of the date of execution and delivery to it of the above mentioned note and mortgage—that is to say, on June 28, 1955. It is appellant's further contention that the lack of recording thereof does not in any way lessen the force and effect of said mortgage as a lien, or destroy its priority as against a mechanic's lien, for the reason that a mechanic's lien holder or a material-man's lien holder is not a *subsequent purchaser or mortgagee for value* within the meaning of the recording statutes of the State of Kansas. That, therefore, such material-man's or mechanic's lien holder cannot look to, nor rely on the records of the Register of Deeds for protection of its lien priority."

As preliminary to discussing this contention, we refer to well-settled rules of this court pertaining to a mechanic's lien established pursuant to G.S.1949, 60–1401: First, that such a lien for labor performed or material furnished in the construction or erection of improvements attaches from the date work or construction commences which, in the instant case, was found to be June 29, 1955; second, that the excavation for foundation walls of a house (pushouts) is regarded as the commencement of the building in determining when such lien attaches; third, that where construction is commenced prior to the execution and delivery of a mortgage, such a lien is prior in right to a later executed delivered and recorded mortgage; and fourth, a mortgage executed, delivered and *recorded* prior to commencement of work is superior and paramount to such a lien for materials furnished. . . .

In support of its second contention plaintiff asserts the trial court erred in holding that the recording of plaintiff's mortgage on June 30, 1955, determined the date on which its lien became effective as against the lien of Long-Bell. The assertion requires an examination of our so-called recording statutes. G.S.1957 Supp. 67–221 provides in effect that every instrument in writing that conveys real estate or whereby any real estate may be affected, proved or acknowledged, may be recorded in the office of the register of deeds of the county in which such real estate is situated. It is elementary that a real estate mortgage is a written instrument affecting real estate and subject to recordation. The following sections of General Statutes 1949 provide:

> "67–222. Every such instrument in writing, certified and recorded in the manner hereinbefore prescribed, shall, from the time of filing the same with the register of deeds for record, impart notice to all persons of the contents thereof; and all subsequent purchasers and mortgagees shall be deemed to purchase with notice.
> "67–223. *No such instrument in writing shall be valid,* except between the parties thereto, and such as have actual notice thereof, *until the same shall be deposited with the register of deeds for record.*" (Emphasis supplied.)

There is nothing in the record which suggests that Long-Bell had actual notice of plaintiff's mortgage prior to its recordation on June 30, 1955, and the clear and unambiguous language of 67–223 would seem to decide this controversy. But, plaintiff contends it does not, and, as previously noted, argues that the sections above quoted have application to and protect only subsequent purchasers and mortgagees in good faith; further, that a judgment creditor is not a subsequent purchaser or mortgagee in good faith and for a valuable consideration. . . .

There is a basic distinction between a judgment creditor and a mechanic's lien holder. A judgment creditor is not a bona fide purchaser and parts with nothing to acquire his lien which is subject to the equities of all other persons in the property of the judgment debtor.

On the other hand, a mechanic's lien holder parts with a valuable consideration in the form of labor or materials for which the statute gives a lien upon the property improved; it is not acquired by an adverse proceeding after the debt has been incurred but it accrues as the debt accrues, being incident to the improvements, and the owner of the land to which it is attached consents to it when he consents to the improvements.

We can see no fundamental difference between a statutory lien and a lien created by a mortgage. Each arises as a result of a contract with the owner of the property. Under G.S.1949, 60–1401 a mechanic's lien is security for a debt and is an encumbrance in the nature of a statutory mortgage founded upon consent, under which the holder parts with a valuable consideration. In the language of the statute, the lien for materials and labor furnished or performed in the erection or improvement of land,

> "shall be preferred to all other liens or encumbrances which may attach to or upon said land, building, or improvement, or either of them, subsequent to the commencement of such building, the furnishing or putting up of such fixtures, or machinery, the planting of trees, vines, plants or hedge, the building of such fence, footwalk, as sidewalk, or the making of any such repairs or improvements." (Emphasis supplied.)

Although plaintiff's mortgage was executed and delivered prior to the commencement of work and created a valid lien upon the property as between the parties, it was invalid under the clear and unambiguous terms of G.S.1949, 67–223 as to Long-Bell's statutory mortgage which attached upon the real estate on June 29, 1955, the day before plaintiff's mortgage was recorded. Thus, being subsequent in time to the statutory mortgage . . ., the trial court did not err in holding that Long-Bell's lien was prior in right to the lien of plaintiff's mortgage. . . .

Under the facts in this case Long-Bell perfected and filed its mechanic's lien in accordance with the terms of the statute which was protected by the recording statutes. Long-Bell was a stranger to the mortgage, and the trial court did not err in holding that its statutory mortgage was prior in right to the mortgage lien of the plaintiff.

PREVENTIVE LAW
Purchase of Real Property—Points for Purchasers

Because the purchase of a home is generally the largest monetary transaction a person makes, it is important for that purchaser to be sure that his or her legal rights in the property are protected. In most cases the best advice is to hire a real-estate attorney who will look after your interests. The points noted here are general comments and should not be regarded as complete or appropriate for every purchase.

1. Have you inspected the property for obvious problems with the land (sewer, water drainage) or the building's roof, furnace, cracking walls, and so on?
2. Before having a purchase offer prepared, have you:
   a. Discussed what personal property is to be included?
   b. Made inquiries with financial institutions to determine if you are likely to obtain financing?
   c. Established a tentative time for possession and closing?
   d. Included any special terms and conditions in your offer?
   e. Limited the time for the offer to be accepted?
   f. Specified you want a warranty deed?
3. After agreeing on the terms of purchase, do you know what you have to do and what the seller must do before closing?
   a. Seller—provide survey, deed, discharge of existing mortgage, evidence of tax payments, evidence of title.
   b. Purchaser—obtain financing, review seller's evidence of title, tax payments and other documents, make plans for taking possession.
4. At closing, transfer documents and money based on closing statement, obtain documents (deed and bill of sale) showing title to real and personal property, and plan for recording of deed and safekeeping of title policy.

REAL PROPERTY AS SECURITY

People often must borrow money for their purchases of a home or commercial real estate. When people have to borrow money the loan ordinarily is secured by an interest in the property. This security interest gives the lender the right to sell the property and apply the proceeds against the debt if the borrower defaults. Security interests in real estate are established by mortgages and deeds of trust.

The Mortgage Transaction

Financing based on a mortgage involves two instruments—the mortgage and a note or bond. The mortgage provides the lender with a security interest in the real estate; the note or bond contains the terms of the loan and establishes the borrower's personal obligation to pay.

The mortgage and promissory note give the lender alternative remedies in the event of default. Suit may be brought on the note and a personal judgment obtained against the debtor, or the real property may be sold and the proceeds applied against the debt. The latter remedy is called *foreclosure.*

If the lender wins a judgment on the note, the judgment may be collected by attaching other property or by garnishing the debtor's wages. If the security when sold does not bring enough to pay the debt, the lender may sue for the difference, using the note. A few states require the lender to choose either to foreclose against the collateral to pay the debt or to sue on the note.

Lien and Title Theories of Mortgages

Modern mortgage law can be traced to the early use of the mortgage in England. At common law a borrower who mortgaged real property as security actually transferred title to the lender. The lender obtained a deed just as if he had purchased the property. As the mortgage was given as security, the title that the lender acquired was not absolute. A provision in the mortgage, called the defeasance clause, provided that if the debt was paid when due, transfer of title to the lender was voided. Title reverted to the borrower.

The historical theory that the mortgage conveys title to the mortgagee continues to be used in some states, referred to as *title theory* states. Even in these states, however, although the lender acquires title, the lender does not acquire the right of possession unless the mortgagor defaults.

Most states recognize that in reality a mortgage is a lien. It is a device used by debtors and creditors to secure a debt. The creditor is primarily interested in having the security sold and the proceeds applied to the debt if the debtor fails to pay or violates some other mortgage provision. States taking this position are called *lien theory* states.

Deed of Trust

In a number of states the typical real-estate security instrument involves three parties and is based on the law of trusts. Instead of executing a mortgage, the borrower transfers title to a trustee by a deed of trust. The important difference between a mortgage and a deed of trust is that in the latter, legal title to the real estate passes to the trustee.

The trustee holds the property for the benefit of both the borrower and the lender. When the debt secured by the deed of trust is repaid the trustee must reconvey title to the borrower.

The trustee may sell the property if the borrower fails to pay or breaches some other condition of the loan agreement. The power-of-sale provision makes foreclosure unnecessary (although the trustee usually can elect that procedure). Because foreclosure can be avoided, applying the security to a defaulted debt is more rapid and economical than through the judicial procedure. Lawyers in states where the deed of trust is common argue that the ability to sell the security efficiently is the deed of trust's major advantage over the mortgage.

Mortgage Provisions

Interest Payments. Although many mortgages establish a fixed annual rate of interest to be paid by the borrower over the life of the mortgage, in recent years variable rate mortgages have also become available. In a variable rate mortgage the note and mortgage documents provide for interest payments at a rate that fluctuates based on prevailing interest rates at the time the payments are being made. Frequently the prime rate, the interest rate charged by a lender to its prime or best corporate customers, is the benchmark against which the interest rate due on the mortgage loan is to be tied. Thus a variable rate mortgage may provide for an interest rate that is "two per cent above the prime rate charged by this institution."

Usually variable rate mortgages also provide some limit to the amount of annual increase in the interest rate. For example, assume that a variable mortgage that is set at 2 percent above the prime rate also has a 2 percent annual cap. Now let's assume that in one year the prime lending rate increases from 9 to 13 percent. Would the mortgage rate, which was 11 percent the year before jump to 15 percent the next year? No, the 2 percent cap would hold the rate for that year to 13 percent. Of course, if the prime interest rate for the following year was still 13 percent, the mortgage interest rate for that year would then rise to 15 percent.

Due-on-Sale Clause. Because the term of mortgage is typically fifteen, twenty, or thirty years, the lender will seek some protection against rising interest rates. The variable rate mortgage was devised to provide such protection for the lender. Another form of protection is available through the use of the due-on-sale clause.

A *due-on-sale clause* in a mortgage provides that when the property that is the security for the loan is sold, the full amount of the loan made by the mortgage lender is due. Suppose a purchaser of a $65,000 home borrows $50,000 from a mortgage lender. Let's assume the mortgage and note is for twenty years and it provides that annual interest at the fixed rate of 10 percent will be due with each payment. Even though the loan is for twenty years, let's assume that four years later the purchaser decides to sell the original home and move into another one. Because the note and mortgage has a due-on-sale clause in it, the purchaser now owes the mortgage lender the full amount that is unpaid on the loan (probably about $48,000).

If during those four years the prevailing interest rate on fixed-rate mortgages has increased from 10 to 13 percent, the lender will receive the $48,000, which was lent out at 10 percent, and will be able to lend it out to another borrower at the higher 13 percent rate. The homeowner will find that he or she will not be able to borrow money for the new home at the 10 percent rate in effect four years ago. Thus the homeowner, who borrowed at a time when interest rates were lower than they are at the time his or her home is being sold, does not want the due-on-sale clause to be enforced. Lenders, of course, do want such clauses to be enforced. The *Occidental* case that follows illustrates the decisions reached by many states regarding the enforceability of such due-on-sale clauses.

Occidental Savings and Loan Association v. Venco Partnership

Supreme Court of Nebraska
293 N.W.2d 843 (1980)

Background: Venco Partnership (defendant-appellant) sought to sell real property it owned to a buyer without having to pay off the balance it owed to Occidental Savings and Loan Association (Occidental, plaintiff-appellee), the holder of a mortgage on the property. Occidental noted that the mortgage provided that upon sale of the property used as security for its loan, the entire balance of the loan became due.

When Venco sold the subject property without the consent of Occidental, Occidental sued and sought to foreclose on the property. It claimed Venco was in default on its obligation because it had not paid the balance due to it. Venco argued that the due-on-sale clause was unenforceable.

The trial court found the due-on-sale clause enforceable and directed the foreclosure to proceed. Venco appealed.

Decision: The Supreme Court of Nebraska affirmed the decision that the due-on-sale clause was enforceable.

Krivosha, Chief Justice

The instant appeal presents the court with its first opportunity to consider the validity and enforceability of what is commonly referred to as a "due on sale" clause frequently found in a real estate mortgage. . . .

While "due on sale" clauses take a number of forms, essentially they are, in form, similar to the clause involved in the instant case, which provided "[I]n the event of a sale of said premises without the written approval of said [lender], then the whole indebtedness hereby secured shall, at the option of said [lender], immediately become due and collectible without further notice, and this mortgage may then be foreclosed to recover the amount due on said note or obligation. . . ." Another variation on this theme is what is commonly referred to as a "due on encumbrance" clause, which is essentially the same as a "due on sale" clause, except that the triggering mechanism is the placing of a subsequent lien or encumbrance upon the mortgaged property. We concern ourselves here only with the "due on sale" clause.

While this is our first opportunity to examine the validity of "due on sale" clauses, many other courts have already made such an examination and reached varying results. The clause has also been the subject of numerous articles.

. . . The questioned clause in no manner precludes the owner-mortgagor from conveying his property. The owner is free to convey without legal restraint and the conveyance does not cause a forfeiture of the title, but only an acceleration of the debt.

It is true that the possibility of acceleration may impede the ability of an owner to sell his property as he wishes; nonetheless, not every impediment to a sale is a restraint on alienation, let alone contrary to public policy. It is a fact that zoning restrictions, building restrictions, or public improvements may impede the sale and substantially affect the ability of an owner to realize a maximum price. Yet no one suggests that such restrictions or covenants, as a class, are invalid simply because they affect the ease with which one may dispose of one's property. We are somewhat at a loss to understand how or why so many courts have been willing to describe a "due on sale" clause as a restraint on alienation and we are unwilling to do so. Therefore, we begin our analysis by holding that "due on sale" clauses are not direct restraints on alienation within the meaning of the law.

Appellants next argue that, if a "due on sale" clause is not a direct restraint on alienation and, therefore, void, it is, at least, an unreasonable *indirect* restraint on alienation which should be declared invalid and unenforceable as a matter of public policy unless a mortgagee pleads and proves that his security is in jeopardy.

. . . Nothing better demonstrates that a "due on sale" clause, in and of itself, is not a practical restraint on alienation than the facts in the instant case. The land in question was unimproved urban land subject to a 30-year mortgage. Unless the owner intended to construct a building for cash (an unlikely event), the property would have to be remortgaged in order to grant to the mortgagee of the improvement a first mortgage on not only the improvement, but on the land as well. It is not realistic to argue that the owner here intended the mortgage to remain in effect for the entire mortgage term, nor is it realistic to argue that the lender could not reasonably expect the mortgage to be prepaid well in advance of its due date.

The facts of the instant case further establish that the clause did not restrain the alienation. The transfer of title was made without any obvious difficulty resulting from the terms of the mortgage. The seller-mortgagor did not even answer the petition to foreclose the mortgage and was declared in default by the court. Moreover, the seller-mortgagor has not appeared in this court and apparently is completely unconcerned with the outcome of this case. How does one argue in light of those facts that the "due on sale" clause was a practical restraint on the alienation of title in this case? . . . The rights and needs of the seller, as seen by the court, are detailed and balanced against the rights and needs of the lender, as seen by the court. The court concludes that the rights and needs of the seller outweigh those of the lender, notwithstanding the fact that the parties have freely entered into a contract to the contrary.

The difficulty with determining that a "due on sale" clause is an indirect restraint on alienation is that it requires investigations by the court of many different types of conditions and people unrelated to the mortgage document itself. A legal concept should not be established on that basis. . . .

A further inequity of declaring all "due on sale" clauses invalid occurs when, as in the instant case, the note and mortgage contain no prepayment penalty. In the event that the market should decline below the established mortgage rate, the seller and his subsequent buyer are at liberty to pay off the lender without penalty and adjust their loan by seeking another, lower interest, mortgage. A "due on sale" clause allows a lender to adjust its portfolio in a rising market. The effect of a rising interest market and an invalid "due on sale" clause would be to permit a seller to obtain a premium for the sale of its property at the expense of the lender. We know of no principle in law or equity which would sustain such a position. We must find, as a matter of law, that "due on sale" clauses are neither direct nor indirect restraints on alienation and, therefore, are not void as such.

The only remaining basis for declaring the questioned clauses invalid would be a finding that they are repugnant to public policy. This should not be done lightly or without sufficient compelling reason. . . .

Not only are we convinced that a "due on sale" clause is not repugnant to public policy but, to the contrary, we recognize that, under certain economic circumstances, they may favor the public interest and, therefore, be supportive of public policy. On the one hand, the assets of savings and loan associations are principally invested in long-term mortgages, while, on the other hand, the funds necessary to make such loans are obtained from short-term and demand savings accounts and certificates. As the cost of obtaining deposits rises, the spread widens between what the association must pay for funds by way of interest and what the association receives from borrowers. Once the spread gets too great, the association will be unable to meet the standards set by government regulations and will fail. The potential failure of savings and loan associations and the loss of their depositors' funds should be of no less a concern to the courts than the inability of a property owner to transfer its mortgage at a premium when selling its property. Balancing portfolio return with cost of money is an important factor in the survival of lending associations. The "due on sale" clause is an important device in maintaining that balance. . . .

. . .

We are cited to no authority, nor are we able to find any, which would legally justify declaring a contract provision such as the one in the instant case, generally referred to as a "due on sale" clause, to be contrary to public policy and void. Generally, a "due on sale" clause contained in a mortgage contract is not contrary to the public policy of this jurisdiction and is, therefore, valid and enforceable. Accordingly, we affirm the judgment of the trial court directing the foreclosure of the instant mortgage.

Installment Land Contracts

An alternative to using mortgages or deeds of trust is the *installment land contract.* In this agreement the buyer contracts to purchase the property and to pay for it over a period of time. Until the buyer makes all the required payments the title to the property remains with the seller. The buyer, however, has the right to possess the property and to collect rents and profits from it.

Installment land contracts are often used by a buyer who cannot acquire the mortgage financing needed to purchase property. Such a buyer can agree to make a down payment and have the seller receive periodic payments over a period of time. While the seller who sells the property does not receive the full purchase price until all contractual payments are made, the buyer has agreed to buy the property and the seller still retains title if the buyer defaults. Statutes in many states regulate the use of land contracts. A maximum interest rate that can be charged is specified and provisions requiring the seller to give a defaulting buyer a certain time to make up missed payments are common features in such laws.

FORECLOSURE

A *foreclosure* occurs when a lender, who has advanced funds with real property as security,

recovers in the event of default. A foreclosure may lead to the sale of the property with the sale proceeds applied to pay the debt. Any balance remaining after paying the expenses of the sale and the debt is turned over to the borrower. If the sale does not bring enough to pay the debt, in most states the lender can sue for the remainder.

Judicial Foreclosure

In the United States foreclosure generally is accomplished by a judicial decree ordering the mortgaged real estate sold to pay the debt. This process is known as judicial foreclosure and is what most people have in mind when they use the term "foreclosure." Judicial foreclosure requires a complicated and costly legal action. Because the procedure results in a court order, the procedural requirements of litigation designed to protect the parties must be observed. In obtaining the court order and selling the premises, the lender must strictly follow the law.

Power-of-Sale Foreclosure

Legal complications, expenses, and delays associated with judicial foreclosure have encouraged alternative methods of foreclosure. Many mortgages contain provisions granting a mortgagee or third party power to sell the real estate without resorting to judicial foreclosure if the mortgagor defaults. The deed of trust, also, normally is enforced by a nonjudicial sale since the deed empowers the trustee to sell the security if the borrower defaults.

Statutes in most states provide some protection for the mortgagor whose property is subject to a power-of-sale foreclosure. These statutes require a public sale, notice of the action to be taken, usually by advertisement, and a sale that is fairly conducted in order to produce the best price. Trustees are subject to the same statutory regulations in carrying out a power-of-sale provision. In addition, the trustee must conform to an extensive body of law that regulates fiduciaries generally.

CONTROL OF LAND USE

An owner's rights in real property are not absolute. Often these rights are subject to restrictions imposed by government and/or by private agreements. The most common type of public control of land use *is zoning.* Private agreements limiting land use are called *restrictive covenants.*

Restrictive Covenants

Restrictive covenants are usually placed in a deed by the seller when conveying land to a buyer. The buyer, of course, must have agreed to accept these limitations on the use of the land. Restrictive covenants can be made part of a plan for the development of real property. Such covenants are included in the plot plan, which must be filed with the proper authorities.

In developing real property restrictive covenants are used to ensure that property owners do not suffer a loss in property value because of a neighbor's activity. Restrictive covenants in a residential development might limit the use of land to single family dwellings or require houses to exceed a minimum square footage. Restrictive covenants also are used when an individual sells a portion of his or her property to ensure that the buyer will not use the land in a way that the seller, who remains a neighbor, finds objectionable.

Restrictive covenants run with the land. This means that the limitations on the use of the land are not dependent on the continued ownership of the buyer who originally agreed to the restriction. In general, enforcement of restrictive covenants has not been favored by courts because they interfere with the free transferability of property. In order for a restrictive covenant to run with the land it must have been the intention of the original grantor and grantee, and the covenant must substantially affect the essential nature of the land. The idea that property, both real and personal, should be freely transferable is an important concept in Anglo-American law.

Restrictive covenants can be terminated in several ways. All concerned parties may agree in writing to the termination. This method of termination is very difficult if the number involved is large. Covenants can also be terminated by condemnation or by not being enforced when they are violated. The longer violations of covenants are ignored, the less likely a court is to enforce them.

Zoning

Zoning is the division of an area, usually a municipality, into districts to control land use. Zoning ordinances regulate such things as the structure and design of buildings, lot size, setback requirements, and uses to which land may be put. Limitations on the use of land through zoning are of recent vintage. Comprehensive control of land use is a product of the twentieth century. The notion of comprehensive zoning was first approved by the U.S. Supreme Court in 1926.

Today zoning is based on the states' police power. On the basis of this power, land use can be regulated to protect the health, safety, and welfare of the public. Like all regulation based on police power, zoning ordinances to be valid must not be unreasonable or arbitrary.

Traditional zoning ordinances divide the municipality into districts for residential, commercial, and industrial uses. Over the years these basic zoning classifications have expanded considerably. As a result, many localities now have fifteen to twenty or more zones. Because use within these zones is restricted, multiplication of zones promotes inflexibility in land use and gives rise to criticism of the traditional zoning process. In response to criticism of the zoning process, other techniques for controlling land use have developed since World War II.

Planned Unit Developments (PUDs) are an example of innovative use of the zoning power. In a PUD zoning regulations are applied to an area larger than the traditional subdivision. The objective of a PUD is to permit mixed use of an area within a development while providing a maximum amount of land for open space. Various types of housing such as townhouses, apartments, and single family dwellings are permitted within the same tract. In some instances the zoning plan permits commercial as well as residential use. In addition, the plan provides for extensive open areas. A major advantage of the PUD is the flexibility it provides in planning for community growth.

The extension of public control of real property through zoning is illustrative of major changes that have occurred in real property law. Other changes include the development of new forms of ownership such as condominiums and cooperatives, major modifications in financing and investing techniques, and limits on the rights of owners to deal with their property in a manner interfering with the civil rights of others. In spite of such changes, traditional legal concepts and terminology remain important factors in the real property field.

REVIEW PROBLEMS

1. Explain the difference between a warranty deed and a bargain and sale deed.
2. What is constructive notice? Explain how constructive notice is related to the operation of the recording statutes.
3. Compare and contrast the lien and title theories of mortgages.
4. What is the difference between a judicial foreclosure and a power of sale foreclosure? How are they similar?
5. List some of the uses of restrictive covenants.
6. McNaughten's deed contained a restrictive covenant barring the use of the land for purposes such as a "bar, tavern, alehouse, or the like." McNaughten wants to open a restaurant that serves alcoholic beverages. Will he be prohibited from doing so by the restrictive covenant? Support your answer.
7. Fox bought a $90,000 home in a newly developed area. To finance the purchase, he borrowed $80,000 from Central Savings, executing the customary note and mortgage in Central's favor. Some time later a major highway was proposed for the area, and real-estate values fell sharply. At about this time Fox accepted a job in another state. Unable to sell the house or keep up payments, Fox defaulted on the loan. Central Savings then foreclosed. Discuss Fox's potential liability if the home sells at the foreclosure sale for $60,000, with $72,000 remaining on the debt.
8. Cordes, who died in 1946, owned a 420-

acre farm in western Illinois. His will divided the farm between his sons, Isaac and James. James built a home on his portion. Isaac's portion contained the family residence. The easiest way to reach James's home was over a lane along the edge of a field belonging to Isaac. This lane was used until 1975, when Isaac died. Isaac's farm was sold to Von Schied, who blocked the lane. James contended that he had an easement by prescription over the land. Do you agree? Discuss.

9. General Motors wished to expand its Detroit plant. The economy of the area was depressed, and the city wanted to help GM get the properties necessary to expand. The city council used the power of eminent domain to acquire several pieces of property in the neighborhood. Local landowners who did not want the plant expanded tried to prevent the transfer of title to GM on grounds that the city did not have the right to acquire this land by eminent domain. Explain on what basis this argument might be made. Do you agree? Discuss.

10. In 1935 Malone gave an easement to his brother Ted. The easement allowed Ted to cross a corner of Malone's land so that Ted could make repairs to a windmill. The easement was recorded, but little use was made of it, and both parties forgot that it existed. In 1972 Malone sold the property to Cudy. Title was transferred by warranty deed. What warranty, if any, has Malone breached? Support your answer.

11. Eva Corley and other heirs of George Johns sued the estate of J. W. Johns and legatees under J. W.'s will. They sought to have title to forty acres willed by J. W. to these legatees declared in them. George Johns had deeded the forty acres to J. W. in 1924. Corley alleged that the deed was invalid because there was no proof of delivery; the deed, never recorded, had been found in a trunk belonging to J. W.

after his death in 1972. Would an argument that J. W. did not have title because the deed was never recorded be effective? Explain. Corley v. Parson, 223 S.E.2d 708 (1976)

12. Linmont purchased a corner lot from Amoco in order to construct and operate a filling station. At the time of the purchase, Linmont and Amoco entered into an agreement by which Linmont agreed to take all its requirements of gas and oil from Amoco. The agreement also obligated subsequent owners and tenants of the station to purchase all requirements of petroleum products from Amoco. This agreement and the deed were properly recorded in the office of the County Clerk. Linmont sold the property to Chock Full of Power, which refused to comply with the agreement. Amoco sues. Would Amoco be successful? Discuss. Bill Wolf Petroleum Corp. v. Chock Full of Power, 333 N.Y.S.2d 472 (1972)

13. Smith owned one of three contiguous parcels of wetlands situated in low-lying and partially submerged peninsuly in upper Tampa Bay known as Cooper's Point. The city had zoned the land in a general business district, permitting single family or multiple dwelling uses with limited residental use. In 1974, development plans for the parcel, which was to be combined with others in the same area, were submitted. The following year, the city applied its "aquatic lands" zone, which limited property use to recreational purposes, to over 50% of Smith's property. Smith claims the rezoning of its property to aquatic lands constitutes a taking. Do you agree? *Smith* v. *City of Clearwater* 388 So. 2d 681 (Florida Court of Appeals, 1980)

14. Stephens and his wife had two sons. They quarreled with the older son and as a result wished to deny him any interest in a farm they owned. In order to accomplish

this, they conveyed the farm to their younger son, retaining a life estate for themselves. The younger son gave no consideration for the farm. A few months later Stephens and his wife wished to vacate the deed to the younger son because they believed he had conspired against them with his brother. They brought an action to cancel the deed on grounds that no consideration had been paid. Would they be successful? Discuss. Stephens v. Stephens, 193 So.2d 755 (1967)

15. The Village of Northbrook approved a zoning ordinance permitting the construction of a large shopping center in an area along its boundary with Highland Park. Residents of Highland Park and the municipality of Highland Park sued to block construction of the shopping center on grounds that it would cause massive congestion in the area, destroying the quiet residential character of their community. They argued that this violated the equal protection clause of the Constitution since the shopping center actually protected much of the residential character of Northbrook. The reason for this was that the chief highway leading to the site ran through Highland Park. Would the suit be successful? Support your answer. City of Highland Park v. Train, 519 F.2d 681 (1975)

Wills, Trusts, and Estates

I n this chapter we are concerned with the laws affecting the disposition of property when the owner of that property dies. The word "estate" means the interest a person has in property, both real and personal property. Thus estate planning occurs during a person's life when he or she arranges for the future distribution of the estate. It concerns the distribution of a person's property not only after death, but also during his or her lifetime.

This chapter first focuses on the state laws that govern the descent and distribution of a decedent's property. Those laws determine who is entitled to receive that property if the decedent did not make a valid will. However, since by making a valid will a person can specify, with certain limitations, who shall inherit his or her property, the laws governing wills are also examined.

The chapter then briefly describes the process, known as *estate administration,* by which property is transferred from the decedent to those entitled to receive it. Finally, some of the techniques used in estate planning—such as the creating of a trust or the transfer of property to children, parents, or a charity during a person's lifetime—are discussed.

STATE INTESTACY LAWS

Two sets of state laws govern the inheritance of property. The first set comes into effect if the person did not make a valid will and is referred to as the *intestacy* laws. The second set of laws, those affecting the *testate* distribution of property, comes into effect when a person makes a valid "last will and testament."

There are significant differences in state inheritance laws, particularly as they relate to community property of married persons. There are no federal laws governing the inheritance of property (of course, federal tax laws certainly affect estate planning). A uniform law, the Uniform Probate Code, governing the descent and distribution of property has been adopted in a number of states. Our discussion of intestacy laws focuses on the general provisions found in most state statutes.

State intestacy laws govern the disposition of the decedent's real and personal property. Since real property descends to a person's heirs while personal property is distributed according to state statutes, these laws are generally referred to as *statutes of descent and distribution.*

The law of the state where the decedent's

real estate is located determines the heirs to whom the real estate descends. Consequently, if an Indiana decedent owned a Michigan summer cottage, the statutory descent and distribution laws of Michigan will determine who inherits that real estate. But since the decedent's personal property is distributed according to the laws of the state where the decedent was domiciled, the furniture in that summer cottage will be distributed according to the Indiana descent and distribution statutes.

As a general rule, state intestacy laws provide that a decedent's estate, both real and personal property, shall be shared by the surviving spouse and children. The spouse's share will typically be from one-third to one-half if there are descendants of the decedent, such as children or grandchildren. If no children or grandchildren survive the decedent, the surviving spouse usually takes the entire estate.

If children and grandchildren survive the decedent, the question arises as to how each of them will share in the decedent's estate. If there is no surviving spouse, the entire estate will usually be split among the lineal descendants (children and grandchildren) of the decedent. In determining a descendant's share, the law provides that any children of a deceased child generally will take the share that the deceased child would have been entitled to inherit. This method of dividing property is known as *per stirpes* distribution. Consider the following example. John Adams is married to Jane Adams and they have three children, Al(A), Bonnie(B) and Carl(C). If Carl dies before his father John, then Carl's children (George, Harold, and Irene) would inherit Carl's share of John Adams's estate. According to typical intestacy laws, John Adams's estate would be distributed as follows (see Figure 41-1 for illustration):

1. Jane Adams as the surviving spouse would receive a certain share, usually one-third.

2. The remaining two-thirds would be split among John's descendants. In a per stirpes distribution a share is given to each child and the children of any child who did not survive the decedent take that child's share.
   a. Thus, Al and Bonnie each would receive one-third of the remaining two-thirds (two-ninths).
   b. Carl's three children (George, Harold, and Irene) would split a similar share. Thus each of these grandchildren would receive two-twenty-sevenths of John's estate.

Another method by which property may be divided is on a *per capita* basis. This means that each person who is to receive a share of the estate as a descendant of the deceased would receive a similar amount. Usually the per capita distribution system, if followed, is used for persons of the same generation rather than for persons of different generations. Thus it would probably not be used in dividing John Adams's property among his children and grandchildren.

However, if neither Jane Adams nor any children survived John Adams, his estate would then be distributed to his grandchildren. Assume there are six grandchildren, two who are Al's children, one who is Bonnie's child, and the three who are Carl's children. In this case, as Figure 41-2 indicates, a grandchild's share under a per stirpes system of distribution could vary from $33,333 to $11,111. This can be contrasted with a per capita system of distribution, which would provide each grandchild with the same amount, $16,667. Table 41-1 provides a summary comparison of how the per stirpes and per capita systems of distribution could affect our hypothetical situation.

In most states, if the decedent leaves neither a spouse nor descendants, the estate will be divided in some way among the decedent's

FIGURE 41–1
Intestacy Laws—Per Stirpes Distribution

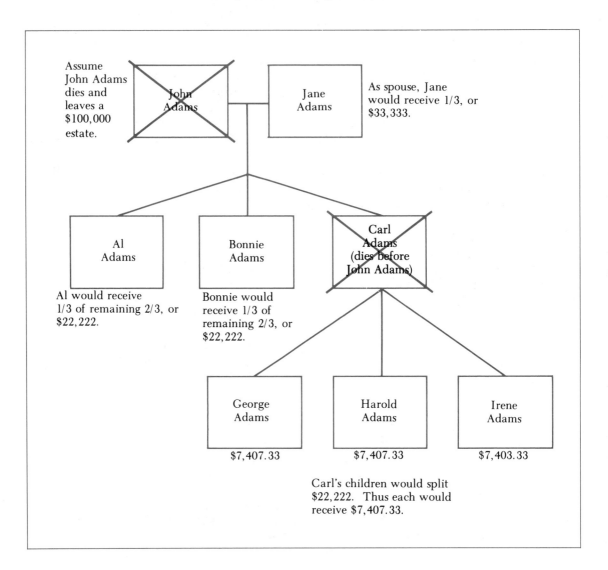

parents, if living (known as ascendants), and surviving brothers and sisters, whereas in other states one or more parents may take the entire estate. If there are no people in these categories, the estate will usually be distributed to nephews and nieces since they are blood relatives of the decedent. It should also be noted that most statutes of descent and distribution make no provision for relatives by marriage. The spouse of a child, brother, or parent who is not a blood relative of the decedent usually takes no share of a decedent's estate. Similarly, stepchildren, unless they have been legally adopted, are usually

FIGURE 41–2

Intestacy Laws—Per Capita Distribution

Assume Jane Adams predeceases John Adams and that all of their children, Al, Bonnie, and Carl, have died. On John's death, if a *per stirpes* distribution is used, John's $100,000 would be divided as follows. If a *per capita* distribution is used, each of the grandchildren would receive the same amount, $16,667.

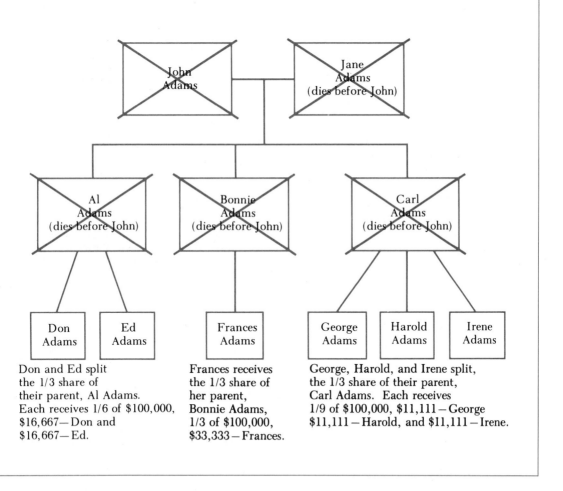

Don and Ed split
the 1/3 share of
their parent, Al Adams.
Each receives 1/6 of $100,000,
$16,667—Don and
$16,667—Ed.

Frances receives
the 1/3 share of
her parent,
Bonnie Adams,
1/3 of $100,000,
$33,333—Frances.

George, Harold, and Irene split,
the 1/3 share of their parent,
Carl Adams. Each receives
1/9 of $100,000, $11,111—George
$11,111—Harold, and $11,111—Irene.

TABLE 41-1

	Per Stirpes	Per Capita
Grandchild		
D	⅙ share (½ of A's ⅓)	⅙ share
E	⅙ share (½ of A's ⅓)	⅙ share
F	⅓ share (all of B's ⅓)	⅙ share
G	⅑ share (⅓ of C's ⅓)	⅙ share
H	⅑ share (⅓ of C's ⅓)	⅙ share
I	⅑ share (⅓ of C's ⅓)	⅙ share

excluded as heirs since they are not blood relatives. Adopted children are generally regarded as children and heirs of a decedent.

Finally, if there are no descendants, ascendants, or collateral relatives of the decedent, the intestacy laws provide that the property goes to the state. This provision, known as *escheat,* is rarely applied.

Interpretation of the intestacy laws is exemplified by the *Warpool* case.

Warpool v. Floyd

Supreme Court of Tennessee
524 S.W.2d 247 (1975)

Background: The decedent, Warpool, was one of three children. He was predeceased by his parents and his brother and sister. His sister left no children, whereas his brother's sole surviving child, James Warpool, is the administrator of the estate and the defendant-appellant.

Warpool's father had children and grandchildren of a previous marriage, and one of those surviving grandchildren, plaintiff-appellee, Ida Mae Floyd, asked the trial court to rule that the children of half-brothers and half-sisters were to share with the child of a brother of the whole blood in Warpool's estate.

The trial court held that Floyd and the other children of the decedent's half-brothers and half-sisters were entitled to share equally with the children of the decedent's brother of the whole blood. James Warpool appealed.

Decision: The trial court's decision was affirmed by the Supreme Court of Tennessee.

Harbinson, Judge

The decedent, Warpool, had one full brother and sister, both of whom predeceased him. His sister died without issue (children or grandchildren) but the brother left one child surviving as the full nephew by blood of the decedent.

Decedent, who never married, was predeceased by both parents. His father, however, by a previous marriage had ten children, all of whom had predeceased the decedent. Eight of these, however, left surviving children, representatives of whom were named as defendants in the court below. There are some twenty-eight of these nephews and nieces of the half blood.

Under the law of intestate distribution in this state, . . . children of brothers and sisters, however, do take by representation, and it has been held that they take the intestate's personal property *per stirpes,* rather than *per capita.*

The statutes governing distribution of intestate personal property give priority to the surviving spouse and/or children of a decedent. Where there are no persons in these categories, however, the parents are preferred. The statutes then provide as follows:

> If no father or mother, to brothers and sisters, or the children of such brothers and sisters representing them, equally.

The statutes provide that if there are neither brothers, sisters, nieces nor nephews, then the personal estate is distributed "to every of the next of kin of the intestate who are in equal degree, equally."

In the case of Kyle v. Moore, 35 Tenn. 183 (1855), this Court expressly held that brothers and sisters of half blood shared equally in intestate personal property with brothers and sisters of the whole blood.

The Court noted that in the computation of the degrees of kinship, there was no distinction between the half blood and the whole blood. The Court said:

> There is no law giving any preference to the half blood on the side of the transmitting ancestor, to the exclusion of the other line, in the distribution of personality. 35 Tenn. at 185.

The Court in that case took note of express provisions in the statutes governing the descent of real property, which had altered the feudal policy of earlier English law, excluding persons of the half blood entirely. Statutes in effect at the time of the decision of the Kyle case, and still in effect today, do make certain distinctions between acquired and inherited realty, insofar as inheritance by half-brothers or half-sisters are concerned.

These "ancestral property" provisions were not part of the law of distribution of personal property when the Kyle case was decided, nor have they since been included therein.

The Kyle case has not been overruled or modified by any subsequent decision of this Court, and appellant concedes that it would be controlling here except for certain changes in the statutes of distribution which occurred in the revision and codification of the state law, resulting in the Code of 1858. For the first time, in that code, there were included provisions for inheritance by brothers and sisters and their children, if the decedent did not leave a surviving spouse, child or parent.

It is insisted that because the words "brothers and sisters" were used in the Code of 1858, without qualification and without reference to relatives of the half blood, the Legislature intended to prefer brothers and sisters of the whole blood to those of the half blood.

This Court is unable to find such a legislative intent in the Code of 1858. It is true that the "ancestral property" statutes governing real estate were then in force, and that they contained explicit reference to half-brothers and half-sisters. The argument before us is that if the legislature had intended for siblings of the half blood to share fully with those of the whole blood, the legislature would have so provided.

It is equally plausible to assume, however, that if the legislature had intended to exclude half-brothers and half-sisters or to put them in a less-preferred category than full siblings, it could easily have so provided. Since it did not do so, it is the opinion of the Court that the legislature did not so intend, and that the holdings in the Kyle and Deadrick cases, supra, were not intended to be modified.

Finding no legislative history which would lead us to believe that the General

Assembly intended to prefer siblings of the whole blood over those of the half blood, we hold that half-brothers and half-sisters share equally with full brothers and sisters in the distribution of intestate personalty, and that their children, taking by representation, take equally with the children of full brothers and sisters.

WILLS AND TESTAMENTARY LAWS

If a person does not make a will expressing his or her own desires regarding the distribution at death, state intestacy laws determine who inherits the property and how it will be divided. Thus the basic reason for preparing a will is to establish one's own plan for the distribution of property owned at death.

A will is also used to indicate to the courts the decedent's choice of the person who will care for and look after one's children and estate. The naming of a guardian for minor children and of a personal representative for administrating one's property accomplish this purpose. Gifts to charities or the creation of trusts to split the use of property among several people also can be provided for when a will is used. Finally, a will usually clarifies the rights of possible claimants to the decedent's property, thereby making possible the settlement of the estate. For these reasons it is sound business practice for a person to prepare a will and review its provisions periodically throughout his or her lifetime.

Requirements for a Valid Will

The requirements for a valid will are established by a state's testamentary statutes. Some states have *statutory wills.* These are wills that can be filled in by any person choosing to use them. Statutory wills provide a person who does not want to consult an attorney with a model or sample that can be used and that will be given effect if completed according to the requirements of the statute. The require-

ments that must be met for statutory wills to be valid generally are the same as those for wills that are drafted by a person or his or her attorney.

The statutory requirements of the state where a person lives or is a legal resident at the time of death must be met in order to dispose of personal property by will. The statutes of the state where a person's real property is located must be complied with to dispose of it by a will. Since statutes vary from state to state, the person who drafts a will must be familiar with the law of the state where the will is to be effective. If the statutory requirements are not complied with, the will is usually not valid and the person's property then passes according to the intestacy laws.

Terminology. A *will* is a written declaration stating its maker's desires for the disposition of his or her property or estate after death. The person making a will is called a *testator* if male and a *testatrix* if female; in this chapter the term testator refers to both a testator and a testatrix. The person named by the testator to look after and administer the estate of the decedent is referred to as the *executor, administrator,* or *personal representative;* this chapter uses the term personal representative. Finally, the term *probate* refers to the process by which the will is legally approved as valid and through which the estate is administered until all its property is distributed. If a will is found to be invalid, it will be denied probate; in that case it has no legal effect and does not control the distribution of the testator's estate.

In the *Kenney* case the court looks at the decedent's will to see what he intended to do with his property. Where, as in *Kenney*, the court is unable to determine what the decedent intended with regard to some of his property, the will does not control who is to receive that property. Instead, the laws of intestacy govern.

Kenney v. Pasieka

Appellate Court of Illinois

260 N.E.2d 766 (1970)

Background: Frank Pasieka, the decedent, lived in Tonica, Illinois. Two other relatives of the decedent were also named Frank Pasieka; one was a cousin of the decedent, living in Chicago and referred to as Chicago Frank, and the other a nephew living in Peoria, and referred to as Peoria Frank. The decedent's will left a share of his estate to the children of "Frank Pasieka." Kenney, the executor of the decedent's estate, sought to have the will admitted to probate and asked the court to determine who was the decedent referred to as Frank Pasieka. Mary Pasieka, the surviving wife of the decedent, claimed that since the will was ambiguous, it was ineffective.

The trial court admitted the will to probate and determined that the decedent was referring to himself when his will referred to the children of "Frank Pasieka." Mary Pasieka appealed that decision to the Court of Appeals.

Decision: The Appellate Court found the phrase ambiguous and ineffective and reversed the trial court's decision. Thus the property that was to be distributed under the will to the children of Frank Pasieka would have to be distributed according to the intestacy laws.

Moran, Justice

This case involves three men with the same name—Frank Pasieka. The first is the deceased testator who lived at Tonica, Illinois and was, in the argument before this Court, called "Tonica Frank"; the second, a nephew of the testator, who resided in Peoria and was called "Peoria Frank"; and the third, a cousin of the testator, who resided in Chicago and was called "Chicago Frank."

Tonica Frank died on October 5, 1966, leaving a last will which was executed November 24, 1962. Tonica Frank was twice married and left surviving him his second wife. He had one child by his first marriage, Theodore Pasieka, and none by his second marriage. Theodore died on October 11, 1964, after the making of the will in question but before the death of his father.

During his lifetime, Tonica Frank took into his home two boys, Walter and Joseph, both of whom changed their last name to his and lived with him as his sons. Walter never married and has no children. Joseph, on the other hand, is married and is the father of three children.

Tonica Frank's will is relatively simple but the problems it creates are substantial. After providing for the payment of his debts and funeral expenses, he bequeathed all of his personal property to his second wife. He then devised all of his real estate to his son, Theodore, for life and provided that, upon the death of Theodore, the real estate would become part of the residue of his estate. The residue was then devised "one-third thereof to the children of Walter Pasieka, share and share alike; one-third thereof to the children of Joseph Pasieka, share and share alike; and one-third thereof to the children of Frank Pasieka, share and share alike." The will then provided, "In the event any child shall not be living at the time of the death of my son, Theodore Pasieka, but shall leave brothers and sisters him surviving, said brothers and sisters shall take the share of such deceased child."

. . . The executor filed suit for a proper construction. There is no dispute as to the one-third share to the children of Joseph Pasieka. They do exist and are entitled to that portion. The difficulty, however, arises in determining which "Frank Pasieka" the testator intended, since there were three, and what happens to the share devised to the children of Walter Pasieka, since he has no children.

The trial court, after considerable deliberation and effort, wrote a memorandum of decision which concluded that the testator meant himself when he devised a one-third share to the children of "Frank Pasieka" and, therefore, this share was to be divided equally between Joseph and Walter, and finally that the one-third share to the children of Walter did not fail but passed one-half to the children of Joseph and one-fourth each to Joseph and to Walter.

This appeal followed raising the issues that the trial court erred in ruling that the testator meant himself and that the disposition of the one-third interest to the children of Walter was erroneous since there were no such children.

Both the plaintiffs and the trial court agree that the will before us presents latent ambiguities. Even though the language is clear and suggests a single meaning, extrinsic facts show the clear necessity for an interpretation.

In construing a will the guiding principle is the intention of the testator, and the question for our determination is not what the testator meant to say by the language employed, but rather what he meant by what he did say.

Therefore, in construing this will it was proper for the trial court, and it is proper for us, to consider the surrounding circumstances. The evidence presented clearly indicates that the decedent treated his own son, Theodore, and Joseph and Walter exactly the same. Joseph and Walter were never legally adopted but they were brought into the decedent's home, they took his name and he treated them as his sons. He never indicated any desire to have one receive more than another. It was really on this basis that the trial court reached its conclusion.

While that evidence is clear, it is not very helpful in construing the decedent's will. There, he did not treat the three boys alike because he gave his son, Theodore, all of his property for life and he gave nothing to Walter or Joseph, since the devise is to their children and not to them.

In determining who is the right "Frank Pasieka" it appears clear to us that it cannot be Peoria Frank. Peoria Frank had not seen the decedent for twenty-eight years before his death and they had no communication.

Similarly, it would seem clear that the Frank in question cannot be Chicago Frank because they were not close and saw each other only about once each year.

We are hard pressed to find that the decedent referred to himself because the gift, of course, is not to himself but to his children and he had already provided for his only natural child by giving him a life estate in all of his property.

Likewise, we cannot determine what the decedent meant by the gift to the "children" of Walter, since Walter never had and does not now have any children.

The sad thing about this case is that the decedent went to an attorney and made an attempt to write a will. Unfortunately, he did not make a will which completely disposed of his property and the only way there can be a complete disposition is for this Court to write his will for him or for the property to be administered as though the decedent had no will. While there is a presumption against intestacy and the Court should make an effort to construe the will if that is possible, this Court has no power to write a new will for a decedent if it cannot determine his intention. As our Supreme Court said in Hampton v. Dill, the testator's "intention must be determined by the language of the will itself and not from any surmise that he used the language to express an intention or meaning he had in his mind which he failed to express. If he has overlooked a condition which he probably would have provided against had he thought of it, the court cannot guess which provision he would have made and read it into his will on the presumption that he would naturally have made such a provision if he had thought of it." Where a testator in disposing of his property overlooks a particular event, which, had it occurred to him, he would have in all probability provided against, the court will not supply a provision by intendment, on a presumption of what the testator would naturally have done.

. . .

We conclude that the two-thirds of the residue of the decedent's estate which were devised to the children of "Frank Pasieka" and to the children of Walter Pasieka, go as intestate under the statute.

The case is, therefore, reversed and remanded to the trial court with instructions to enter an order consistent with this opinion.

General Requirements. There are three different kinds of requirements that must be met according to the statutes in most states for a will to be valid. First, the person making the will must have proper testamentary capacity. A person's capacity to make valid contracts was discussed in Chapter 14. The testamentary capacity required by inheritance laws, while similar to contractual capacity, differs from it in several important respects. Second, testamentary intent is required to make a valid will. The testator must clearly intend that the document offered as a will be effective to transfer property at death. Thus, if a person intends to transfer property during his or her lifetime and writes a statement giving stock, jewelry, or personal property to another, that statement cannot be a will; it does not indicate the intent to transfer the property effective only with the testator's death. Third, the testator must comply with the statutory requirements relating to the execution or signing of the will. Certain formalities in writing, signing, and witnessing a will must be complied with for the will to be valid. If these requirements are not strictly adhered to, the proposed will is not valid and legally effective.

Testamentary Capacity. There are two elements of the requirement of testamentary capacity. The statutes require that the person making a will have attained a certain age (usually eighteen) before signing the will. A person who has not attained that age cannot leave his or her property to another by a will. A will executed or signed by a person who is under the statutory age is invalid for lack of testamentary capacity.

The second element of testamentary capacity is the testator's being of "sound mind." The test of a "sound mind" is expressed by courts in different terms, but usually it requires that the testator be aware of three different matters. The testator must know who are the "natural objects of his or her bounty." Usually this means the testator's family members, but it could also include close friends for whom the testator has special concerns. Second, the testator must realize the kind and extent of

property that he or she is proposing to distribute by the will. Finally, the testator must be able to plan for the disposition of that property.

Each of these requirements is generally reviewed in a case where the testator's testamentary capacity is questioned. Usually, less mental capacity is required to make a valid will than is necessary to manage business affairs or enter into contracts. A person may be feeble, aged, or of low intelligence and still have the required testamentary capacity. In the *Lockwood* case the court is asked to determine whether a codicil (an addition to or alteration of an existing will) is valid. The claim is that it is not valid because the testatrix, Mrs. Lockwood, lacked testamentary capacity at the time she signed the codicil.

In re Estate of Lockwood

California Court of Appeals
62 Cal. Rptr. 230 (1967)

Background: The decedent, Annie Lockwood, executed a valid will in 1958. Then four days before her death in 1964 when she was 89 years of age, she executed a codicil (an addition or amendment to an existing will) to that will. The codicil was executed eight days after the decedent entered the hospital and during the time she was suffering her last illness.

The decedent's heirs at law who were to receive most of her estate under the provisions of the codicil sought to admit it to probate, but the probate court held the decedent lacked testamentary capacity at the time it was executed.

The heirs at law appealed the decision of the probate court to the Court of Appeals. Decision: The Court of Appeals affirmed the Probate Court's decision denying probate to the codicil.

Salsman, Associate Justice

This is an appeal from a judgment entered on a jury verdict denying probate of a codicil to the will of Annie L. Lockwood on the ground that the testatrix lacked testamentary capacity on February 28, 1964 when the codicil was executed, four days before her death. The will itself was admitted to probate, there being no question of Mrs. Lockwood's testamentary capacity on July 28, 1958 when it was executed.

The codicil revoked the testatrix's gift of her entire estate to William and Irene Rolfe, close friends for many years, who had rendered personal services to her at various times, and substituted a gift of $5,000 to May Delaney and gave the remainder of her estate to her heirs at law, Alan, Audrie and Sharon Swanson, who are appellants here.

The sole issue on appeal is whether there is any substantial evidence to support the verdict of the jury, which found . . . that the testatrix was not mentally competent at the time she executed the codicil. In order to resolve this issue it is necessary to set forth the facts in detail.

The testatrix was 89 years of age at the time of her death on March 3, 1964. An autopsy report gave the cause of death as cardiac failure due to arteriosclerotic heart disease, but the report also catalogued the many physical miseries from which the testatrix suffered at the end of her life. . . .

The testatrix was brought to the hospital on February 20, 1964, eight days before the execution of the codicil. Up to that date there was no serious question as to her mental competency. Her condition while in the hospital, that is, from February 20th to the date of her death on March 3rd, is described by numerous witnesses, and as will appear, their testimony is in conflict as to the mental competency of the testatrix during that interval.

Dr. Challen examined the testatrix on the 27th and again on the 28th and found her alert. Dr. Sharp saw her on the 21st, 25th and 29th and also found her alert. This witness also stated that the testatrix remained alert until the day of her death. The subscribing witnesses to the codicil, who of course were with the testatrix on the 28th when the codicil was executed, also testified that the testatrix was mentally alert, knew what she was doing, and answered questions logically and understandably at that time.

Nurse Ludwig, who attended the testatrix as her day nurse from February 20th to the 26th, testified that the testatrix was a very sick person. She described her many and grave physical ailments. As to her mental condition the witness said the testatrix was at times in a stupor or coma, and would be coherent for a few moments and then become incoherent for a period of three or four hours.

Frank Crouse, an intimate friend of the testatrix, visited her at the hospital on the 25th. He found her in a semi-coma, hardly able to communicate with him. She asked his name, was told, and a few minutes later repeated the inquiry. He visited her again on March 1st, and on this date the testatrix could not communicate at all.

Annie L. Crouse, also a close friend of the testatrix, visited her daily from the 20th to the 27th, and March 1st. She testified that on the 23rd the testatrix became progressively worse and less communicative, giving only momentary recognition to her friend, then saying, "Who are you?" On the 27th she found the testatrix in a deep coma, eyes and mouth open, unable to recognize her visitor.

Nurse Madeiros attended the testatrix from the 22nd to the 27th. She testified that the testatrix was noisy and confused. Asked her opinion of the mental competency of the testatrix she replied: "At no time did I ever see any evidence that Mrs. Lockwood was—mentally clear. She always—appeared confused and disorientated. At no time was I ever able to carry on a conversation with Mrs. Lockwood. I don't remember there was ever anything understandable from her."

. . .

Dr. Burton W. Adams, a psychiatrist, testified from medical records, including the autopsy report. His opinion was that on February 28th, when the codicil was executed, the testatrix was suffering from a hardening of the arteries, in the brain as well as the body, and that she was also suffering a severe impairment of her mental faculties as well as her physical health. Although the doctor admitted the possibility of periods of lucidity on February 28th he felt such an event unlikely because of her arteriosclerosis, infection and fever that prevailed throughout her hospital stay.

The trial court gave accurate, full and complete instructions to the jury.

They were instructed that the contestants had the burden of proving that the testatrix was not mentally competent to execute her codicil on the 28th of February, and that proof had to be by a preponderance of the evidence. . . . The court then gave the jury the test by which it was to measure mental competency.

The instruction declared that: "The determinants of testamentary capacity are whether or not the decedent had sufficient mental capacity to be able to understand the nature of the act she was doing, and to understand and recollect the nature and situation of her property, and to remember and understand her relations to the persons who have claim upon her bounty and whose interests are affected by the provisions of the instrument." The jury was further instructed that the contestants were required to prove testamentary incapacity at the very moment of the execution of the will, and that a contestant must prove that the will was not made at a lucid interval. The court also instructed that: "Not every weakness and impairment of the faculties of a testatrix will invalidate a will or codicil. Even where a testatrix is feeble in health, suffering from disease and aged and infirm, yet if she was sufficiently of sound mind to be capable of understanding the nature and situation of her property, and disposing thereof intelligently, without any delusions affecting her actions, she had sufficient capacity to make a will or codicil." . . .

Upon submission, as we have related, the jury found the testatrix mentally incompetent to execute the codicil to her will. . . .

The proponents of the codicil did produce evidence through the testimony of the subscribing witnesses to the instrument to show that at the time it was executed the testatrix was of sound mind. But there was contrary evidence. Thus Mrs. King, one of the hospital nurses who cared for the testatrix from the 25th of February to the 29th, including the day upon which the codicil was executed, testified that Mrs. Lockwood showed no recognition or understanding during that period of time, and did not realize or understand her surroundings. Other witnesses, however, were able only to testify as to Mrs. Lockwood's testamentary capacity before and after the date the codicil was executed. There was testimony that both before and after February 28th the testatrix was often in deep coma, unable to be aroused, unable to recognize old friends or to remember who such friends were even for brief moments after being told. Several witnesses testified that conversation and communication with the testatrix while she was in the hospital was virtually impossible. Thus the evidence shows that both before and after the 28th the testatrix, overcome both physically and mentally by the extremities of age and her many physical ailments, was unable to communicate with her nurses and old friends and was often, if not continuously, in a semi-coma from which she could not be aroused. It may be inferred from this evidence that, before the codicil was executed, and afterwards to the time of her death a few days later, the condition of the testatrix remained the same.

It has been held that, once it is shown that testamentary incapacity exists, and that it is caused by a mental disorder of a general and continuous nature, the inference is reasonable that the incompetency continues to exist.

Whether a testator has testamentary capacity at the time of the making of his will depends upon the facts found by the trier of fact. Thus, in every case, the fact finder must weigh and evaluate all of the evidence, and from it find whether the testator had sufficient mental capacity to understand his act, to recollect the nature and situation of his property, to remember and understand his relationship to persons who have claims upon his bounty and whose interests may be affected by the instrument he is about to execute. . . .

We think the jury by its verdict, and the trial judge by denying the motion for judgment notwithstanding the verdict, and also in denying appellants' motion for a new trial, were justified in concluding that the decedent, weakened by age, illness and disease, lacked testamentary capacity both before and after she executed the codicil to her will, and in inferring that such lack of capacity existed at the very moment the codicil was executed. . . .

Testamentary Intent. The testator must (1) intend to transfer the property and (2) intend that the transfer occur only upon his or her death. Thus a document that does not clearly show the testator's intent to transfer property will be lacking in testamentary intent. Suppose I have a valuable diamond ring in an envelope and write on the envelope "This ring is for my sister Susan Sleaford." If the other requirements for a valid will are met, would this document indicate my intent to transfer the property and to have the property transferred at my death? Review the *Brown* case that follows as it relates to this question.

A second problem with finding proper testamentary intent relates to influences upon the testator that may replace his intent with that of another. Chapter 13 discussed several problems related to the *genuine assent* required for entering into valid contracts. Similar problems can occur with a testamentary document such as a will. Did fraud, duress, undue influence, or mistake distort the testator's true intent? While each of these enemies of genuine assent or of valid testamentary intent can invalidate a will, most problems with testamentary intent concern undue influence: Did someone so influence the testator that the testator made a disposition of property contrary to what he would have done had he followed his own judgment? The *Franco* case, following *Brown*, concerns this problem of testamentary intent.

In re Estate of Brown
Court of Civil Appeals of Texas
507 S.W.2d 801 (1974)

Background: The decedent, Ada Brown, wrote a short note to Josephine May Benton on an envelope containing a certificate of deposit. Ms. Benton filed in the County Court to have the note declared to be a valid holographic codicil (a *holographic document* is one that is wholly written in the handwriting of the person) to a will the decedent had made several years before her death. Josephine Brown, a beneficiary under the will of the decedent, contested the probate of the note as a codicil to the decedent's will.

The County Court ordered the note to be probated as a codicil and on appeal the District Court agreed with the county court. That court's decision was appealed to the Court of Civil Appeals.

Decision: The Court of Civil Appeals affirmed the admission to probate of the note as a codicil to the decedent's will.

Claude Williams, Chief Justice

This appeal is from a judgment admitting to probate a writing offered as a codicil to the will of Ada B. Brown, deceased. Miss Brown executed a formal and witnessed will in 1965. Following Miss Brown's death in 1970 this will was duly probated by the County Court of Collin County, Texas, without contest. Thereafter Josephine May Benton filed her application in the County Court of Collin County to probate a written instrument as a codicil to Miss Brown's will. The writing tendered as a codicil was a cryptic note written on an envelope. The envelope contained a certificate of deposit dated July 2, 1968, from the First Savings and Loan Association of McKinney, Texas, in the principal sum of $10,000 payable to Ada B. Brown and reciting that the holder thereof would be paid earnings at the rate of five and one-half percent interest per annum. The writing on the envelope was as follows:

> This certafice [sic] from
> Ada B. Brown—
> Goes to Josephine May Benton

Josephine Brown, a beneficiary under the 1965 will, filed a contest to the probate of the alleged codicil. The County Court ordered the tendered codicil to be probated. Appeal from this judgment was timely made to the District Court.

Trial was had before the court, without a jury. The proponent of the codicil offered in evidence the writing on the envelope, together with its contents. Two witnesses testified that the writing was entirely in the handwriting of Ada B. Brown. Sally Lou Brown Benton, the mother of Josephine May Benton and the other beneficiary under the original will, testified that in July 1968 she took Ada B. Brown to the First Savings and Loan Association in McKinney where she transacted some business. Mrs. Benton testified that at that time she saw the envelope and that Ada B. Brown said to her: "This is for Josephine if anything happens to me, and I don't need it." The witness said that she did not see the envelope again until Miss Brown died in 1970. At that time she gathered up all of Miss Brown's papers which the deceased had given her to keep at the time the deceased went to the hospital, and took these instruments, including the envelope with the writing thereon, to the office of Miss Brown's attorney, Mr. Truett, who is executor under the original will. On cross-examination the witness testified that the envelope, together with its writing, was not attached to the original will in any way; that Mr. Truett had possession of the will in his office.

Based upon this evidence the District Judge decided that the writing tendered was a valid holographic codicil to the 1965 will and decreed that it be admitted to probate. It is from this order that appellant-contestant appeals.

The principal question to be resolved is whether the instrument in question is testamentary in character. . . .

The right of a person who owns property in this state to give, bequeath or devise it to another at his death is purely statutory. Tex.Prob.Code Ann. § 59 (1956) V.A.T.S., provides that every last will and testament, except when otherwise provided by law, shall be in writing and signed by the testator in person or by another person for him by his direction and shall, if not wholly in the handwriting of the testator, be attested by two or more credible witnesses above the age of fourteen years. Section 63 of the Probate Code provides that no will in writing shall be revoked, except by a subsequent will, codicil, or declaration in writing, executed with like formalities, or by the testator destroying or canceling the same.

Our statutes do not define in so many words what form an instrument shall take before it becomes a will. A will is generally defined as an instrument by which a person makes a disposition of his property, to take effect after his death, and which by its own nature is ambulatory and revocable during his lifetime.

If a writing in substance embodies the factors above enumerated the particular phraseology adopted by the draftsman is of no consequence.

It is established law in Texas that whether there was testamentary intent on the part of the maker is a proper question in a proceeding to probate or in a contest of an application to probate. . . . While the actual words utilized by the maker of an instrument are the primary subject of inquiry to resolve the question of testamentary intent the rule concerning the admissibility of extrinsic evidence to resolve any doubt created by the actual words used seems to be well settled. This rule is but a refinement of the long-followed principle of Texas law that the extrinsic evidence is inadmissible to supply something necessary in, but totally missing from, the instrument itself.
. . .

Applying the rule announced to the factual situation presented to the trial court we conclude that it was not error for the trial court to receive and consider extrinsic evidence relating to the circumstances which surrounded the preparation of the writing in question as well as declarations on the part of the writer of the instrument wherein she definitely clarified the meaning of the words "from" and "goes to." These words could possibly express the intent of the writer to make a gift *inter vivos* of the certificate. Clearly the statement of the decedent to the effect that she wanted Josephine to have the certificate "if anything happens to me and I don't need it" clearly negates any intention on the part of the writer to give the certificate to Josephine prior to the time that "anything happens to me." The words "if I don't need it" clearly indicate the revocability of the instrument during the lifetime of the writer. The words "goes to" have been held to indicate testamentary intent, i.e., to give property upon death, especially when there are no findings of fact and conclusions of law. These words of the writer, when taken in connection with the fact that the writer did not deliver the certificate to Josephine but kept the same in her private papers where it remained until after her death, constitute adequate evidence of testamentary intent to support the trial court's findings and judgment ordering probate of the instrument.

• • •

An instrument which is totally in the handwriting of the deceased, which includes the signature somewhere in the writing, satisfies the statutory requirements for a holographic codicil. It is not necessary that the signature appear at the bottom or end of the instrument in question.

All of appellant-contestant's points of error are overruled. The judgment of the trial court is affirmed.

In re Estate of Franco

Court of Appeals of California
122 Cal.Rptr. 661 (1975)

Background: Carlo Franco, the decedent, died on May 30, 1970 at the age of 76. He was survived by two sisters and one brother. Carlo executed his will on November 29, 1969 after being taken to an attorney's office by his brother John Franco. That will left almost all of Carlo's property to John's children. The decedent's sister, Caterina (plaintiff) filed a petition alleging that Carlo's will was obtained by undue influence and fraud. The executor of the estate, John LeRoy Franco (defendant), claimed the will to be valid.

Because there was only circumstantial evidence of undue influence, the trial court admitted the will to probate. The plaintiff appealed.

Decision: The California Court of Appeals reversed the Trial Court's decision and denied the admission to probate of Carlo's will.

Gargano, Associate Justice

. . .

The decedent was born in Genoa, Italy; he migrated to this country in his youth and died in Tuolumne County on May 30, 1970, at the age of 76. He was survived by his brother John, his sister Caterina and his sister Rosetta Vassello, who was living in Italy. A second brother, Joseph Franco, had died about two years earlier in Calistoga, California.

After settling in California, Carlo worked for many years as a farm hand on a ranch owned by Sal Ferretis near Groveland.

On May 28, 1968, Joseph Franco died intestate, leaving an estate valued at $40,-000; John Franco was appointed administrator of the estate. In the meanwhile, Caterina Armario went to Calistoga and made funeral arrangements for her deceased brother. She also took care of some other matters that needed attention, expending some of her own money in the process. Then, when Caterina's son asked John Franco about presenting a claim in Joseph's estate for reimbursement for his mother, John told the son to "pad" the claim; John Franco and his sister Rosetta Vassello had been feuding over the distribution of an estate in Italy, and John told Caterina's son to double Caterina's expenses so the "son-of-a-bitch in Italy [would] get as little as possible." Later, John Franco showed the padded claim to Carlo and told his brother that Caterina was trying to cheat them out of their share of Joseph Franco's estate; Carlo became very angry over the incident.

On November 29, 1969, John Franco and his wife, Mary C. Franco, took Carlo to John's attorney in Merced where Carlo executed his will; with the exception of a $300 gift to Caterina, the will bequeathed all of Carlo's estate to John Franco's two sons, John Leroy Franco and James Carlo Franco, to be divided equally between them; John Leroy was named executor of the estate. . . .

On May 10, 1970, Carlo died alone in his small cabin. Thereafter, his will was admitted to probate, and John Leroy Franco was appointed the executor of the estate.

On November 2, 1970, Caterina filed a petition for revocation of probate; the petition alleged that the will which was admitted to probate was obtained by undue influence and fraud.

At the trial, it was established that Carlo Franco was illiterate; that he could write his name but he could not read or write English or his native Italian; that he had the mental maturity of a 14 to 16-year-old boy, was very naive in business matters and trusted anyone who was friendly with him; and that he was bashful, honest and very frugal.

It also was established that Caterina Armario was illiterate in the English language and almost illiterate in the Italian language and that she had no understanding of business affairs. There was testimony that she would sign anything that was put before her, that she could be influenced easily and that she and her brother Carlo trusted each other implicitly.

At the conclusion of the trial . . . the court entered an order in the probate action refusing to revoke the probate of the will. . . . and Caterina appealed that order.

THE WILL CONTEST

We turn to Caterina's appeal in the probate action; she contends that the court erred in . . . holding as a matter of law that the will was not obtained by undue influence.

Undue influence consists of conduct which subjugates the will of the testator to the will of another and constrains the testator to make a disposition of his property contrary to and different from that he would have done had he been permitted to follow his own inclination or judgment.

In *Estate of Lingenfelter,* the California Supreme Court stated:

> The indicia of undue influence have been stated as follows: '(1) The provisions of the will were unnatural . . . (2) the dispositions of the will were at variance with the intentions of the decedent, expressed both before and after its execution; (3) the relations existing between the chief beneficiaries and the decedent afforded to the former an opportunity to control the testamentary act; (4) the decedent's mental and physical condition was such as to permit a subversion of his freedom of will; and (5) the chief beneficiaries under the will were active in procuring the instrument to be executed.' These, coupled with a confidential relationship between at least one of the chief beneficiaries

and the testator, altogether were held 'sufficient to shift the burden to the proponents of the will to establish an absence of undue influence and coercion and to require the issues to be determined by the jury.'

In the case at bench, there was sufficient evidence to support a jury finding that decedent's mental condition was such as to permit a subversion of his freedom of will; Carlo had the mental maturity of a 14 to 16-year-old boy, and there was testimony that he was bashful and trusted anyone who was friendly to him.

There was also sufficient evidence to support a jury finding that the testamentary dispositions of Carlo's will were at variance with his intentions expressed both before and after its execution; before Carlo made his will, he never expressed a desire to make one; at different times he told his sister that she would inherit all of his American Telephone and Telegraph stock if he predeceased her. After he made the will, he became disenchanted with his nephews and before his death expressed a desire to change the will.

Next, there was substantial evidence for the jury to find that the will was unnatural; decedent in 1969 suddenly left almost his entire estate to two nephews he had only seen on five or six occasions during his lifetime, even though he not only had an older brother, two sisters and other nieces and nephews living, but for many years had been in rapport with his sister Caterina, and had been visiting another relative almost daily. Clearly, a will in which the decedent has left his entire estate to two nephews he had hardly known and seldom seen, to the exclusion of a sister with whom he had a long, close relationship and other close relatives, is unnatural. . . .

The question narrows to whether the third and fifth factors mentioned in *Estate of Lingenfelter, supra,* are present in this case. More specifically, the crucial question is whether John Leroy Franco, a chief beneficiary in decedent's will, had the opportunity to control his uncle's testamentary act and, if so, whether he actually participated in the preparation and execution of the will.

We have concluded that the circumstantial evidence allows for the inference that John Franco schemed to have his brother Carlo leave the bulk of his estate to John's two sons and that John Leroy Franco and his wife Reva were aware of the scheme and actively participated in its execution. In other words, we believe that the circumstantial evidence, when viewed as a whole, shows that at the very minimum the Francos from Merced not only induced Carlo to make his will but that it was John, John Leroy and Reva who must have suggested its provisions.

In summary, the evidence presented by Caterina in this case raises more than a mere suspicion that Carlo Franco's will was the product of undue influence. It paints a vivid picture of connivance, scheming and the application of undue pressure on the part of clever relatives which culminated in their becoming the objects of a not so clever testator's bounty.

A confidential relationship between the testator and beneficiary is not an essential factor in the indicia of undue influence mentioned in the *Lingenfelter* opinion; all that is required once the other factors enumerated in the opinion are present is circumstantial evidence giving rise to the inference that the relationship existing between the chief beneficiary and decedent offered the former the opportunity to control the testamentary act and that the chief beneficiary was active in procuring the instrument to be executed, at least in the sense that he discussed the terms of the will with the testator and suggested some of its provisions.

The order of the Tuolumne County Superior Court . . . is reversed.

Execution of a Will. Most states require that a will be written, signed, and witnessed. A written document is usually required, although in some states there are by statute certain instances in which oral wills are valid. The writing usually does not need to be on a particular kind of material nor made by particular instruments. A will can be written on a paper bag, a scrap of paper, or a piece of wallpaper. It can be typed or written in ink or crayon. No particular language is required as long as the testator's intentions can be determined.

A will must be signed by the testator. In some states, statutes specify that the signature be at the end of the will in order to assure that no pages are later added to the document that was signed. In most states the statute specifies only that the will be signed but does not state where the signature is to appear.

Similarly, each state by statute and court decision indicates the type of signature that will be effective. Use of nicknames ("Junior"), marks ("X"), or other designations ("Mom") usually will be acceptable. As long as the testator has indicated by some mark or sign on the document that he approves and intends it to dispose of property at his death, the signature will be valid. A person who is unable to sign his name or make a mark may by state statute usually have another person, at the testator's request and in his presence, place the testator's signature on the document.

Finally, a will must be witnessed in order to be valid. Most states require two witnesses, but a few states require three. Witnesses are there to verify that the testator actually signed the document and that, according to the witnesses, he or she had the required testamentary intent and capacity at that time. A witness does not have to read the will in order to witness it.

Some states require that the witnesses actually see the testator sign the document; others require only that the testator in some way acknowledge to the witnesses that the signature is his or her signature. Some states also require that the witnesses sign their names to the document in the presence of the testator and in the presence of the other witnesses. The statutes may also require that the will be published, which means that the witnesses must be told that the paper they are signing is a will.

The witnesses to a will usually need not be of legal age as long as they can understand that they are witnessing a signature. If a witness is an interested person who will receive some property by the will (a beneficiary), some statutes require an additional witness to verify the testator's signature or limit the witness's legacy to the amount he or she would have received had there been no valid will.

While other requirements may be imposed by some statutes, the writing, signing, and witnessing of the will are usually the only formalities that must be met to make a valid will. While a will does not have to be prepared by an attorney, the preparation of a simple will by an attorney usually is not very costly. The will does not generally have to be notarized, although a notary can be a witness. The will does not have to be filed in a specific place in the county of a person's residence or handed over to an attorney. Each of those alternatives exists in some states but usually they are not requirements. Whoever has the will of a person at the time that person dies is required by law to file it with a court (usually the probate court). Once the will or wills of a person are on file, admission to probate and the validation of the document as the last will and testament of the decedent can be sought.

Revocation of a Will

Since a will is without legal effect until the testator dies, a testator may revoke a will at any time prior to death. A person usually revokes a will when he or she desires to make a different distribution of the estate. The new will generally includes a clause stating that all prior wills made by the testator are revoked. In other situations the testator may simply tear up or burn an existing will, leaving property to be distributed under the intestacy laws. In addition to these methods of revoking a will by the act of the testator, the law specifies several circumstances under which revocation of an existing will occurs.

If a person subsequently executes a new will or a codicil but does not state that the new revokes the old, the law generally presumes there was the intent to revoke the old will if the new one is totally inconsistent with it. If the new will and the old will are not totally inconsistent, both are read together.

If a person who has written a will changes his or her marital status, some state statutes provide that the will is automatically revoked. In these states the marriage of a person who was single or the divorce of a person who was married automatically revokes that person's will.

In most states a divorce does not revoke the entire will. It only cancels that portion of the will providing for the former spouse. Most states also provide that a person cannot totally disinherit a spouse. By common law a wife (and less frequently also a husband) had an interest in the real property acquired during the marriage by her spouse. This interest, known as dower (which is discussed in Chapter 39), gives the wife a life estate in her spouse's land. Today most states have replaced dower with an elective share. Under these laws a surviving spouse can elect the portion of the total assets of the decedent's estate provided by law, often one-third of the estate, if she or he prefers them to the assets left to that spouse by the decedent's will.

The birth of a child usually does not revoke a will, but most states provide that a child born after a will has been executed will receive that portion of the estate of the testator that he or she would have received had no will been made. However, if it appears from the terms of a will that a person does not want that child (or other children born before execution of the will) to inherit property, the testator's intentions will be honored. Statutes usually do not provide for a forced share for the children of a decedent in the same way they provide for the surviving spouse.

ESTATE ADMINISTRATION

Whether or not the decedent makes a valid will, there still must be some method by which the decedent's property can be collected, debts and taxes paid, and the estate distributed among those people who are entitled to receive it. The rules and procedures for administering or probating a decedent's estate determine what happens to the property from the moment of the decedent's death until the property and title to it are distributed according to law.

Probate of an Estate

Estates are usually administered according to statutory law and rules of procedure developed and overseen by probate courts. The first step in the administration or probate of a decedent's estate is to determine if the decedent had a valid will. If there is a will, the will should contain the name of the person who the decedent desired to be responsible for administering the estate—the *personal representative*. If there is no will, one of the decedent's heirs, usually a surviving spouse or child, will petition the probate court to be named the personal representative. The court will usually appoint such a close heir as personal representative although in some states the person appointed to administer the estate must live within the state where the court being petitioned is located.

If there is a will, the will must be admitted to probate before it is considered valid. Persons interested in the will or in the decedent's estate must be notified that there is a petition to admit the will to probate. At the court hearing proof that the will was executed according to the statutory requirements will be given. If anyone questions the execution of the will or either the testamentary intent or the capacity of the decedent, a will contest may develop. In extraordinary cases such as occurred when billionaire Howard Hughes died the will contests may take years to resolve. In the usual case the hearing of the court to probate the will and appoint the personal representative (whether or not there is a will) will be simple, uncontested, and quick. If more than one person seeks to be the personal representative, statutory provisions giving preference to close relatives will have to be consulted and interpreted by the court.

Once the personal representative has been appointed, the actual administration of the estate begins. Creditors of the decedent are notified, usually by publication in a local newspaper, that they must present their claims against the estate of the decedent within a specified time period (generally six months or less). A monetary award for the support of a surviving spouse while the estate is being administered is then made; this temporary support or allowance paid to the spouse generally takes precedence over all other claims.

Next, the personal representative must inventory all the assets in the estate and establish the value of the property. If there are sufficient assets, the funeral and burial expenses, expenses of the decedent's last illness, estate administration costs, and debts of the decedent are then paid.

Taxes that may be due the state or the federal government must be determined and paid. Estate taxes due to the federal government are assessed against the estate based on its value. Sizable exemptions from the estate taxes are incorporated in the estate tax laws. Additionally, transfers from one spouse to the other are generally deductible. Accordingly, most estates today do not have significant estate tax liability.

Inheritance taxes due to the state government are assessed on the property received from the decedent. The amount of tax depends not only on the value of the property received but also on the relationship between the decedent and the inheritor; the closer the relationship is, the lower the rate of inheritance tax will be. These taxes are then due not from the decedent giver, but rather, from the living recipient. However, since the testator may have provided by will that the estate was to pay the inheritance tax, it can become liable for this tax. In any event the taxing authorities can ensure that their taxes are paid before the title to any property is transferred from the estate.

After all administration expenses, taxes, and valid claims or debts have been paid, the personal representative furnishes an accounting to the court and, once it is approved, distributes the remaining property and money to the beneficiaries.

Alternative Methods of Estate Administration

Statutes in a number of states provide several alternatives to administering an estate through the probate procedure. A very simple procedure can usually be used for small estates that do not contain unusual amounts or types of property. Often these estates are exempt from the normal probate procedures. Other statutes provide for a probate procedure that can be used if the persons interested in the estate have no objections to it. Usually, the beneficiaries and heirs of the decedent are allowed to administer the estate independently with only minimal review by probate court authorities.

Finally, there are a number of estate planning techniques that can be used to minimize the need for estate administration under the probate court. Trusts, life insurance policies, custodial accounts, and joint tenancy agreements are often used. These techniques are discussed in the concluding pages of this chapter. Not every method is suitable in every situation, but alternatives to the formalized probate method of estate administration exist and should be considered in formulating an estate plan.

ESTATE PLANNING

Estate planning is the process of planning for the future distribution of a person's estate. The distribution of property during a person's life as well as after death can be planned to achieve various objectives. An estate plan cannot be simply chosen and then put aside; it requires periodic review and revision as a person's assets increase, marital status changes, and expenses such as those related to rearing and educating children or caring for elderly parents fluctuate.

There are often numerous objectives around which the estate must be planned. Generally the primary objective is to ensure that the testator's property is distributed to those persons he or she wants to provide for, at the time and in the portion and manner most desirable to the testator. The estate plan also seeks to minimize the taxes and fees that will have to be paid from the estate. The payment of substantial taxes not only would interfere with the primary objective, but also could force the sale of valuable property, such as a business, that the testator may prefer to pass along intact to the chosen beneficiaries.

Estate Planning and Taxation

The desire to avoid or minimize taxes due at one's death should not be the primary purpose of estate planning. A person's estate plan should seek instead to meet objectives regarding the distribution of the estate and the care and support of those who are to benefit from it. Only after the objectives of the plan have been determined and the means for attaining them have been examined should attention be focused on the taxation of the estate.

There are several taxes that affect an estate plan. The two that are of central concern are usually the federal estate tax and the state inheritance tax. Both must be paid before the decedent's property can be transferred to heirs or named beneficiaries.

Income taxes also must be paid from the estate for income received by the decedent prior to death. If the estate receives income while it is being administered, further income taxes may be due. The federal income tax on estates is set at rates that are comparable to the income tax rates for a married couple.

Estate Planning and Trusts

Under a trust a person has legal title to property but must use that property for the benefit of other people (the beneficiaries). The person who is given legal title to the property (the trustee) is generally instructed how the property is to be used in a written document referred to as a trust agreement or trust deed. If a person enters into a trust agreement and transfers property to someone else while living, the trust is referred to as a living or *inter vivos* trust. If the trust is established by the terms of a person's will, it is referred to as a *testamentary trust.*

A person (the settlor) who creates a *living trust* may want to retain the power to change the trust agreement to name a new trustee or totally revoke the trust. This type of living trust is a *revocable trust,* and since the creator of the trust can change it, the property in trust will usually be taxed as part of the estate of its creator. On the other hand, since the property has been transferred during the settlor's lifetime, it would not be property that is transferred at the settlor's death. Accordingly, the assets in the trust will usually not be subject to probate on the settlor's death.

If a person creates an *irrevocable trust* during his lifetime, the property in the trust is legally owned by the trustee. The trust, not the person who created it, now must pay taxes on income earned by the trust property. If the creator of the trust dies after having transferred property to the trustee, generally no estate taxes are assessed against that property and no probate fees are due for its administration. The property is not in the estate of the decedent at his death since he earlier transferred it to another person (the trustee). However, since the trust property is managed and administered by the trustee from the date the trust is established, fees are usually charged for those services. Most major banks have trust departments staffed by a variety of people who provide professional service to the property that the bank holds as trustee.

A testamentary trust found in a will does not become effective until the death of the testator. This means of course that the testamentary trust can be revoked or modified at any time during its creator's lifetime. Since the trust assets are in the control of the testator until death, the trust is actually created by transfer from the executor or personal representative of the decedent's estate to the person named as trustee. In many cases the creator of a testamentary trust will name a bank to act as both the personal representative of the estate and as trustee of the trust. Its powers and directions are those specified by the will creating the trust (as well as some statutory and common-law provisions).

One of the benefits of a trust is that it provides for professional property management by the trustee instead of by the person for whom the property is to be used. Another benefit is that the income from property can be given to one person for a limited time (ten years, twenty years, or a lifetime) with instructions that after that time another person is to become owner of the property. In this way a trust can "skip" a generation, and the person in the skipped generation, who never owned the property, would not have that property subject to estate taxes or probate fees at his or her death.

In the following example George's children, Alice and Bill, are the skipped generation:

George Smith has $500,000 that he wants to give to his children and grandchildren. Since George's children are adults and have good jobs and reasonable incomes, George, by means of a trust, will primarily provide for his grandchildren. Assume that George has two children, Alice and Bill, and that each of them has two children; George then has four grandchildren. His inter vivos trust agreement would:

1. Give $500,000 to the First National Bank as trustee of the George Smith Trust
2. Provide that the income from the trust be paid annually in equal amounts to his children, Alice and Bill
3. Provide that on the death of either Alice or Bill, their share of the trust (one-half for each) should be kept in trust for the benefit of their children (grandchildren 1, 2, 3, and 4) until the youngest grandchild attains age 30 and then given to the grandchildren as their own property. (If one of the grandchildren dies before attaining age 30, that share could go to that grandchild's brothers or sisters. If both grandchildren of the same parent die before reaching age 30, their shares would go to the surviving grandchildren.)

Review the *Estate of Hart* case to see how one court interpreted an inter vivos irrevocable trust agreement.

Connecticut Bank & Trust Co. (Estate of Hart) v. Hills

Supreme Court of Connecticut

254 A.2d 453 (1969)

Background: The bank was the trustee of a trust established by Helen Hart. It provided for payment of the trust income to Lotta Kirkpatrick for her life and upon her death, provided that the income was to be paid to her brothers, Charles and Thomas Hills. At the death of either brother, his share of the income was to be paid to his descendants. One of the brothers, Charles, had adopted his wife's son, defendant William Hills, from a prior marriage. As trustee, the plaintiff's bank brought this case to determine if the defendant William Hills was a descendant of Charles Hills.

The trial court held the term "descendant" did not include an adopted son. Defendant William Hills appealed to the Supreme Court.

Decision: The Supreme Court affirmed the trial court's decision denying him a right to income from the Hart trust.

King, Chief Justice

The plaintiff bank is the trustee of an irrevocable, inter vivos trust established by Helen Hart, of Hartford, on January 27, 1949. The provisions of the trust which are material to a disposition of this proceeding may be stated in simplified form as follows: The trust, the validity and interpretation of which was to be governed by the laws of Connecticut, provided that the income is to be paid to Lotta J. Kirkpatrick during her lifetime; that at her death the income should be paid equally to Charles I. Hills and Thomas K. Hills, who were brothers; that, at the death of either, his share of the income should continue to be paid "per stirpes, to his descendants living at the time of each regular income payment . . . during the period of the Trust and, if all descendants of such deceased cousin should die during such period the Trustee shall pay over the entire net income from this Trust to the survivor of said two cousins during his life". The father of Charles and Thomas Hills was the brother of Miss Hart's mother, and thus Charles and Thomas were Miss Hart's cousins.

Lotta J. Kirkpatrick died on May 26, 1962, and thereafter the income was paid to Charles and Thomas Hills until January 26, 1966, when Charles Hills died.

Charles Hills had no children of his own, but his wife had a son, William, born May 22, 1922, of a prior marriage, whom Charles adopted on March 19, 1936, and who thereafter had the name of William S. Hills and continued to live with his mother and adoptive father until his own marriage in 1944.

The basic question in this proceeding is whether William S. Hills is entitled to receive his adoptive father's share of the income of the trust and this question in turn depends on whether, as an adopted son, he is embraced in the term "descendants" of Charles Hills as used in the trust.

The present action was instituted by the trustee seeking advice as to the proper interpretation of the trust with respect to William's rights, if any, under it.

The words "descendant" or "issue" in their ordinary and primary meaning connote lineal relationship by blood, and they will be so construed unless it clearly appears that they were used in a more extended sense.

The court concluded that it did not clearly appear that Miss Hart used the word "descendants" with other than its primary meaning, and, so, it refused to find that William was embraced in the term "descendants" and answered the questions accordingly. From that decision William took this appeal.

William claims that under our cases words such as "descendant" or "issue" include an adopted child where (1) the adoption occurred prior to the execution of the instrument to be construed, (2) the testator or settlor regarded the adopted person as the son or daughter of the adoptive parent, and (3) the testator or settlor never expressed opposition to the adoption.

Our cases do not support any such mechanical rule of construction.

Moreover, precedents in the construction of wills or trusts are seldom of persuasive force, since the surrounding circumstances in each case, as well as the precise words employed, usually differ significantly.

Second, the quest in each case is the expressed intent of the testator or settlor in the light of the circumstances surrounding him at the time the instrument was executed.

Miss Hart was an educated woman, and there was much justification for the conclusion of the court that, had she intended to include William, she would not have chosen, in expressing such an intention, an inapt word primarily signifying lineal blood relationship. . . .

It is true, as William claims, that the fact that the adoption took place about thirteen years prior to the execution of the trust is an important factor. This is because it is seldom that any clear expression of an intention to include an adopted child in the use of a word such as "descendant" can be found if the adoption took place subsequent to the execution of the instrument and if the settlor, when the instrument was executed, did not know that any adoption was even contemplated. But the converse of William's claim does not follow. Thus, neither the fact that the adoption preceded the execution of the trust instrument nor the fact that, as the court found from circumstantial evidence, Miss Hart probably knew of the adoption when she established the trust would, even together, suffice to require the court to conclude that, in using the term "descendants" of Charles, she intended to include his adopted son William.

William makes much of the fact that there is nothing to indicate that Miss Hart disapproved of his adoption and that this added element is sufficient to prove that she intended to include him. This argument has little weight. It would have been rather bad manners and rather bad taste if Miss Hart had taken it upon herself to express to William, to his parents, or to anyone else, her disapproval of the adoption. . . . Whatever might have been the case had Miss Hart expressed disapproval of the adoption, we attach no controlling significance to her failure so to do.

William claims that, since Thomas and Charles were in their late forties when the trust was executed and since neither had had natural children, it is necessary to conclude that the word "descendants" included an adopted child since there was no natural child to which the term "descendants" could apply. This is a circumstance to be considered, but many men of fifty or over become fathers, and we do not find this claim of William of controlling weight. It must also be remembered that the inter vivos trust was irrevocable and could not have been subsequently altered by Miss Hart, even had she so desired, to the prejudice of nonconsenting beneficiaries.

. . .

Obviously, under a broad type of adoption statute such as ours, the use of the word "child" or "children" as intentionally inclusive of an adopted child is not unlikely. If the testator or settlor is the adopting parent, the term "child" or "children" is ordinarily held inclusive of an adopted child. But the same cannot be said of the term "descendants," which was the term used here, since that word, much more than the word "child" or "children," distinctly and emphatically connotes a lineal blood relationship.

The trial court concluded that there was nothing clearly to indicate that Miss Hart used the word "descendants" in other than its primary sense and that when so used it would not include William. We find no justification for disturbing either conclusion.

Estate Planning and Joint Property

Joint property is used in estate planning to transfer property from one person to another by an agreement made during a person's life. Thus joint property is usually not in the *probate estate* of the first of the two persons to die; that property has been transferred by agreement prior to that person's death to the second person. However, joint property is usually a part of the *taxable estate* of the first person to die.

There are several ways in which the ownership of property can be shared by two or more people. The first method is to establish the two or more persons as joint tenants with rights of survivorship; the second is to establish them as joint tenants in common. The first method is probably the most common; most states have statutes that provide that bank accounts or securities held in two names are usually held as joint tenants with the right of survivorship. For example, Tom and Jane have a $1,000 savings account in their joint names. If Tom dies before Jane, the $1,000 is owned by Jane. It is not transferred to her by Tom's will or by the intestacy laws but by the agreement they made while they were both alive.

If Tom and Jane instead hold the savings account as tenants in common, both of them own one-half or $500. When Tom dies, $500 is transferred by his will or by the intestacy laws to his heirs or beneficiaries. Thus Jane would still have her $500, but the $500 owned by Tom might be transferred to her or to someone else.

If Tom and Jane are husband and wife, their joint property is sometimes referred to as being owned by them as "tenants in the entirety." This is simply a special term for joint tenants who are spouses and who want the survivor by virtue of the agreement they made (or which the law assumes they made) to inherit all their jointly held property.

A husband and wife often hold title to property jointly. This allows each access to the property during his or her lifetime and automatically provides that the property passes to the survivor on the death of either. Property that is held by joint tenants with right of survivorship (or by tenants in the entirety) avoids probate fees but usually not estate taxes. Often, because of the size of the estate and the marital deduction that the estate tax laws allow for transfers at death to one's spouse, estate taxes are not a consideration in the estate plan. Thus joint property is a viable estate planning device for many people.

Estate Planning and Insurance

Life insurance can be used in a variety of ways in estate planning. Ownership of an insurance policy may be established in such a way that the proceeds from the policy at the insured's death will not be subject to federal estate taxes. Life insurance is usually not subject to probate expenses since the benefits are due pursuant to the policy and not by virtue of any provision in a will or the intestacy laws. In many states some of the proceeds from insurance policies on the decedent's life are also exempt from state inheritance taxes.

Life insurance is thus often used as a means of providing security for the average person. A variety of policies—whole life, term, endowment, annuity—are available to serve different needs and desires. Persons who have significant assets in a business often use insurance as a means for transferring those assets to the surviving business associates. The business owns the insurance policy on the partner or key employee, and on that person's death the proceeds from the policy are used by the surviving business associates to purchase the decedent's share and to compensate the estate of the deceased for the decedent's ownership interest in the business.

Estate Planning and Custodial Accounts

A *custodial account* is a type of trust account. One person, the custodian, holds money that belongs to someone else, the beneficiary. While the custodian oversees the money, he or she can use it only for the benefit of the beneficiary to whom it belongs. Many custodial accounts are established by parents for their minor children. When a custodial account is used, once the child attains the age of majority (usually 18), the money in the account then belongs to the child and no longer is administered by the parent.

The 1986 Tax Reform Act made several significant changes in the tax treatment for money held in a custodial account by a parent custodian for a child as beneficiary. The law now provides that when the child who is the beneficiary of the custodial account is under the age of 14, the income derived from that money (except for the first $1,000) will be taxed at the parent's tax rates, not at the child's tax rates. Thus the parent is no longer able to set aside money for a child's education in a separate custodial account and have the tax liability for the income from the property in the account shift from the parent to the child.

Tax planners have noted, however, that the Tax Reform Act does not apply to custodial accounts that are not established by the parent for a child. Thus a grandparent or a relative of a child could set aside money for the child in a custodial account and have the income derived from that money taxed at the rates applicable to the child rather than to the donor. Obviously, the Internal Revenue Service will carefully examine the source of such donations to ensure that they are not traceable back to the parent.

Furthermore, the Tax Reform Act does not alter the tax treatment for the income derived from property in a custodial account established for children who are 14 years of age. The income from such an account is taxable at the tax rate applicable for the child, not the tax rate of the parent.

Finally, custodial accounts that are established for young minor children would still remove the property transferred from the parent's estate. Since the property in a custodial account is owned by the beneficiary (child), not the custodian, any estate or inheritance tax due on property owned by the custodian (parent) would not affect property owned by the beneficiary.

Tax laws allow a parent to transfer $10,000

PREVENTIVE LAW
Estate Planning for Younger Individuals

Estate Planning concerns the planning for the future distribution of an estate. The answers to several common questions may provide some guidance regarding the appropriate degree of estate planning for younger individuals.

1. Do I need to be concerned with Estate Planning?
   This depends on several things. First, what is the size of your "estate"? Total the value of your assets—both real and personal property, insurance policies, and pension benefits. If this value is significant to you or exceeds $100,000, you need an estate plan. Second, who are you concerned about if you were to die? Do you have parents, children, brothers, or sisters whom you want to inherit your property? Both the number of people and the intensity of your concern about providing for them, as well as the value of your estate, affect the need for an estate plan.

2. Do I have to be concerned with wills, trusts, custodial accounts, and taxes? It sounds too complicated and expensive.
   Not necessarily. If you have a normal sized estate and are concerned about providing for several people, you probably need a will. The other items referred to only affect those people with sizable estates. A simple will usually can be prepared for less than $100 dollars and a review of your overall estate may not be much more expensive.

3. If I make a will and prepare an Estate Plan when I'm 25 or 30 years old, how long will it be good for?
   Again, there is not one answer. If your situation does not change a lot, it could be good for a decade or more. However, if you get married, have children, buy a house, purchase life insurance policies, and begin to acquire such stocks or inherit money from someone, a review should occur. A good rule of thumb would be to review your estate plan yourself every five years and note what is different in your life. If there are major differences in your circumstances or in your estate, you probably want to schedule a meeting with an estate planning attorney.

per year to any recipient (including their children) without any gift tax liability. Thus if George and Mary Smith have three children, each year George can give $30,000 to them and Mary can give $30,000 to them. While such gifts made to minor children under the age of 14 will not save George or Mary income taxes due on the income from the transferred property, the property given will not incur the estate tax or inheritance tax due if they were transferred at their death. Thus the transfer of property from parent to child during the parent's lifetime can still minimize the tax burden due on that property.

REVIEW PROBLEMS

1. Which basic laws govern the inheritance of property?
2. Which requirements must be met for a will to be valid?
3. What does the term *probate* mean?
4. Is there more to estate planning than the drafting of a valid will? Explain.
5. The Hunts, a married couple, were both admitted to a nursing home on June 4, 1979. A few days later, Mrs. Hunt died. Mr. Hunt, who was terminally ill with cancer, was hospitalized on July 5, 1979. Two days later, on July 7, he executed a will. He died the next day, July 8, 1979. Mr. Hunt had been taking a variety of medication since his cancer had been discovered in October 1978. He had pain medicine available to him every four hours, if needed. He had taken the medicine several times on the day he executed his will. Usually after taking this medicine, Mr. Hunt was incoherent for several hours. Mr. Hunt's doctor saw him several times on the day he died. He testified that at 9:00 A.M. Mr. Hunt was very ill but that by noon he had improved. When he saw him at 5:00 P.M., one hour before the will was signed, he was sitting up in a chair. Did Mr. Hunt have the testamentary capacity needed to make a valid will?
6. Bass died in March 1975, leaving a will dated May 2, 1974, in which he gave all his property to the local Baptist Church, to the exclusion of his wife. His widow objected to the probate of his will, claiming that he lacked testamentary capacity due to his use of drugs and alcohol. The testa-

tor had been a heavy drinker for several years and was known in the community as a habitual drunkard. Does the testimony on Bass's alcoholism prove that he lacked testamentary capacity to make a valid will?
7. Ritcheson died in July 1971, in Arkansas. In January of that year he asked his close friend, Peevy, to help him make his will. But Peevy refused and suggested that Ritcheson see a lawyer. In March 1971 Ritcheson was involved in an automobile accident. He remained in poor health from that time until his death. Ritcheson went to Peevy about a week before his death and asked Peevy to call his attorney so that he could have his will made. Ritcheson made some notes on a yellow legal pad for the proposed will. When Peevy found the lawyer out of the office, Ritcheson left the yellow pad of notes with Peevy. These notes were never again found. A week later, Peevy found Ritcheson dead at his home. On the table beside him, Peevy found a note, entirely in Ritcheson's handwriting, which claimed to dispose of all of Ritcheson's property. In fact, the note did not dispose of some of Ritcheson's property. The note was not signed at the end, nor was it dated. But it did include the decedent's name in the body of the note. Does the document qualify as a holographic will?
8. Ruth Evans claims that her father's will is valid. Other relatives assert that it is not, because Ruth used undue influence over her father. Ruth did arrange for her father

to make a will, found an attorney, and accompanied him to the attorney's office for its signing. But the attorney testified that she did not participate in any discussion regarding the terms of the will. The father was found to have acted "senile" at times, but he was also referred to as "stubborn." He insisted on driving his own car and managing some of his own affairs. He confided in his daughter Ruth and frequently followed her suggestions on things he should do. Should the will of Ruth Evans's father be voided due to her undue influence?

9. On January 12, 1962, Thomas Jackson, an attorney, wrote to several of his clients, "As I am rather ill, I am discontinuing my active practice." Four months later Jackson signed a will that his attorney had prepared for him. The will left Jackson's property to his wife and nothing to his two sons by a prior marriage. The two sons contended that the letter and other evidence showed that during the period just prior to the date on which their father signed the will Jackson was forgetful, less talkative and communicative, unable to drive a car, and prone to sit and stare for long periods of time. The decedent was 72 when he died on July 9, 1962. Do you think the decedent lacked testamentary capacity to make a will? Jackson v. Jackson 238 A.2d 852 (Ct. App. Md. 1968)

10. Charles Jones and Mary Jones entered into a separation agreement that stipulated, among other things, that Charles execute a will providing that Mary and their daughter Betty would each receive a portion of his property and that such will would not be revoked. Charles executed a will that conformed to the agreement; however, ten years later he executed another will. The second will expressly revoked the first and named Charles's second wife, Helen, as his sole beneficiary. Is

the second will valid? Jones v. Jones 200 S.E.2d 725 (Sup. Ct. Ga. 1973)

11. William Birkeland died in 1972. In 1970 he had a document stated to be a will drafted by an attorney. However, contrary to the attorney's instructions, he did not sign it in the attorney's office. He had it sent to him and he signed it alone. Then, on separate occasions, it was witnessed by two witnesses. Birkeland did not tell either witness that the document was a will, and neither saw him sign his name. One witness said Birkeland had already signed it, and the other said he didn't recall if there was any other signature on it. The state statute requires that a will (1) be signed by the testator (2) in the presence of two attesting witnesses and (3) be acknowledged by the testator to the witnesses as his will. Is this will validly executed? In re Estate of Birkeland 519 P.2d 154 (Sup. Ct. Mont. 1974)

12. A father wrote a letter to his son containing the following language: "I want to inform you that I bequeathed to you by my last Will the farm in Converville, Virginia, after my wife's death and my own death. I have the Will in my safe here and it nullifies the one which is in the bank. Be sure and keep this letter." The son says the letter is a valid holographic will. The state statute says a will totally in the handwriting of the testator and signed by him can be given effect even if it is not witnessed. Does the letter constitute a will? Can it revoke a prior will (the one in the bank)? Mumaw v. Mumaw 203 S.E.2d 136 (Sup. Ct. Va. 1974)

13. The decedent executed a will approximately one year before death. In the will she expressly excluded her husband because "he is financially well off" and her daughter because "she is financially well off and has not visited me for many years." The decedent was 82 when she died. To-

ward the end of her life she expressed hostility toward her husband and voiced delusions about his attempts to poison her (which the facts show he did not do). The husband claims the decedent was unduly influenced by her son, who: (1) took his mother to a lawyer's office to arrange for her to make a will; (2) asked the family doctor to witness his mother's will, but when the doctor refused unless the mother was examined by a psychiatrist, declined to take his mother to a psychiatrist; (3) was present with his mother in the lawyer's office when she conferred about the will and also when she signed it. Do you think these facts constitute undue influence sufficient to set aside the will? In re Estate of Goetz 61 Cal.Rptr. 181 (Calif. Ct. App. 1967)

14. Decedent died intestate in Buffalo, New York. Surviving him were six brothers and sisters. Also surviving him was a person who claimed to be his daughter. She claimed that the decedent had lived with her mother in Florida, where she now resided, for fifteen years prior to the decedent's move to Buffalo three years before his death. The person who claimed to be his daughter said that under Florida law she would be considered the decedent's daughter and as such should be chosen to be the personal representative of his estate. Under New York law she would not be considered his daughter and would not have a claim to be his personal representative. Should the laws of Florida be referred to in order to determine her legal status and claim to be his personal representative? In re Estate of Thomas 367 N.Y.S.2d 182 (Sur.Ct., 1975)

Insurance Law

T he term *insurance* is used to refer to a variety of contracts, each of which involves an *insurer* who agrees to pay a sum of money or to give something of value to another person, the *insured* or the *beneficiary,* upon the happening of a contingency or fortuitous event that is beyond the control of the contracting parties. Insurance sales and contracts are regulated by state law pursuant to the terms of the McCarran Act, a federal law enacted in 1945.

Each state has its own statutes and administrative regulations establishing standards that both its own domestic and foreign (those that are situated either in other states in the United States or in foreign countries) insurance companies must meet in order to do business in the state. Most of the state laws are concerned with the solvency of the firms that can be incorporated or licensed in the state. Other provisions specify the conditions under which insurance agents and brokers can be licensed to conduct business.

Because the insurance relationship arises from a contract between the insurer and the insured, insurance law is best viewed as a subpart of contract law. Thus the concepts of offer and acceptance as well as the other rules relating to contracts generally apply to the insurance contract. Of course, since there are special terms, conditions, and practices that affect insurance contracts, this chapter highlights some of the unique aspects of this important field of law.

KINDS OF INSURANCE

There are many kinds of insurance and the listing that follows is not necessarily comprehensive. Nevertheless, the descriptions found in this section refer to those insurance agreements that are most frequently encountered by the individual business person, in either a personal or a business capacity.

Life Insurance

A *life insurance policy* is one in which the insurer agrees to pay a specific sum of money upon the death of the insured, provided that the premiums due to keep the policy in force have been paid. The insurer pays the money to the person designated by the insured, *the beneficiary,* or, if no such person is named, to the estate of the insured. As long as the insured is alive, he or she generally retains the right to change the beneficiary on the insurance policy. There are several different types of life insurance policies; the most common are the ordinary life, the term life, and the universal life policies.

Ordinary Life Policies

Ordinary life insurance generally requires the insured to pay premiums throughout his or her life. In addition to the death benefit that is payable to the insured's beneficiary, this policy gives the insured the right to borrow against the policy during his or her lifetime. Thus ordinary life policies combine a form of investment or savings with the benefits due at death to the named beneficiary. The amount that can be borrowed is limited to the savings portion of the policy, referred to as the *cash surrender value* of the policy. As premiums are paid, this amount generally increases throughout the life of the policy.

Some life insurance policies require premium payments only for a limited period, rather than for the life of the insured. Further, full prepayment of the premium due for the policy to remain in effect throughout the life of the insured is possible by the purchase of a single-premium life insurance policy. Finally, if the insured is unable to continue to pay the premiums due on the ordinary life insurance policy, it is generally possible, without any further payment being made, to convert the policy to an extended term insurance policy or to have a smaller amount of ordinary life insurance. This sum is referred to as the *paid-up amount.*

Term Insurance

Term insurance is issued for a limited number of years or terms; beyond that date it provides no insurance or benefits for the insured or for the named beneficiary. *Term insurance* is the least expensive form of insurance because it grants no loan or cash surrender value to the insured. Thus it provides protection but no savings. Some term insurance policies have provisions allowing the owner to convert at some later date to ordinary life or endowment insurance. Term insurance is a popular alternative for people who want to separate the investment portion of ordinary life insurance from its death benefits or who cannot afford the equivalent protection provided by an ordinary life plan. Frequently this type of insurance may be provided by an employer to a group of employees for the term of each individual employee's employment.

Universal Life

A *universal life* insurance policy combines the benefits of the term and the ordinary life insurance policies. Essentially these policies give the insured an opportunity to receive market rate increases in the cash value, rather than in the smaller guaranteed company rate. Only the portion of premium necessary to support death benefits is withheld from the investment program; the remainder is available for cash value growth. It is also possible to vary the premium and in so doing to vary the amount of death protection provided by the policy.

Endowment and Annuity Contracts

Endowment and annuity contracts are similar to the ordinary life insurance contract. They generally obligate the insurer to pay either a lump sum of money or a fixed sum for a period of time to the insured. The payments are to be made when the insured reaches a specified age or after a set period of time. If the insured dies prior to the date established in the policy, the insured's beneficiary receives the sum of money. The *endowment policy* generally pays the insured a lump sum of money at a specified date, whereas the *annuity contract* pays specific sums to the insured at periodic intervals after the insured reaches a specified age. These policies are often used to fund a child's education or to provide some additional security during a person's retirement years.

Although annuity contracts are not technically regarded as pure insurance agreements, they are similar and therefore are subject to regulation by state insurance departments. Under a *fixed annuity* the insured or his beneficiary receives a set sum of money for a set term or for life of the insured. A *variable annuity* obligates the insurer to pay a variable sum of money to the insured. The amount to be paid varies with the rate of inflation or with the rate of return on the insurance company's investments. The assumption is that investment return will parallel the cost of living so that the varying payment will provide the insured with a stable amount of purchasing power.

Accident and Health Insurance

Accident and health insurance protects the insured against losses suffered due to accidents or sickness. These policies provide for the payment of benefits or the reimbursement of specified expenses if the insured becomes ill from an accident or illness. These policies generally limit the amount of benefits to be paid. Furthermore, certain health problems or illnesses may be either excluded by the terms of a health insurance policy or covered only after a waiting period. This type of insurance is also referred to as *medical insurance*, since it provides the insured with benefits for medical expenses, hospital fees, and doctor bills.

Employers often provide some group-based health or accident insurance to employees. In group insurance the insurer offers one master contract for the employer. Further, since many group policies base some of the premium cost on previous claims experience of the group, its cost per person may be at significantly lower rates than would be true for similar individually based contracts.

Disability Insurance

Disability insurance provides income to those who become too ill to continue work in their occupation. While medical insurance covers a person's hospital and medical expenses during an illness, disability insurance provides a source of income for the person during the time of the disability. Generally, disability insurance does not completely replace a person's former income. Because disability insurance benefits are not taxable, a smaller amount of income usually allows the person to continue to meet normal household and living expenses.

Casualty and Fire Insurance

Casualty insurance protects the insured from loss due to the damage or destruction of personal property by causes other than fire or the elements. This type of insurance is frequently applied to loss or injury due to accident. Fire insurance protects the policyholder against loss of insured real or personal property from fire. While the terms of fire insurance policies are standardized by law, additional coverage is generally available for other forms of damage or to benefit the insured in ways that are not provided by the standard policy.

Liability Insurance

Liability insurance provides the insured with money to cover losses suffered by others, whether for personal or property damages, for which the insured is held liable. Liability insurance is commonly carried by owners of automobiles and by people who own or lease real property. A related type of insurance covers a professional person who could be held liable for injuries caused to his or her clients, patients, or students. The insurance company agrees to indemnify or repay the insured for the amount of his or her liability up to an amount specified in the policy. In many cases a *deductible amount* will first have to be paid by the insured before the insurance company pays for the damages for which the insured is liable.

No-Fault Insurance

No-fault insurance is available in states that have laws aimed at compensating victims of automobile or other motor vehicle accidents regardless of the fault or liability of the parties. Generally the policy provides coverage to the insured, to members of his or her household, to authorized drivers, passengers, and pedestrians who are injured as a result of an accident involving an insured vehicle.

Credit Insurance

Credit insurance protects both the creditor and the debtor by providing for the payment of an indebtedness of the insured in the event of death before the indebtedness has been paid. It is most commonly used to cover a mortgage indebtedness on a home or for a debt due by a business that might be forced out of business to pay creditors if a key officer or partner dies.

Title Insurance

Title insurance repays the insured for a loss arising from defects in the title to real estate. Title policies for an owner of a home generally are written to cover the purchase price of the property. Similar policies for the amount of a mortgage are written for the mortgagee's benefit (usually the mortgagee is a bank or

other financial institution). If the seller of the property does not provide a clear title to the property, the purchaser has a right to recover damages either from the seller, or from the title insurance company.

Business Interruption Insurance

A *business interruption insurance* policy provides benefits to cover losses due to interruptions in business operations caused by an insured peril. An interruption might be caused by a strike, fire, or storm or because of construction near the place of business that prevents customers from reaching the business.

Worker's Compensation Insurance

State laws generally require employers to compensate workers who are accidentally injured while on the job. Even if an employee was injured because of an act of another employee, the employer must compensate the injured employee. These laws are not based on negligence or fault by the employer. Instead, they hold the employer strictly liable for injuries occurring in the workplace. Thus it is employers who are the purchasers of workers compensation policies. In most states policies can be purchased either from a state fund or from private insurance companies. Sometimes, rather than purchase an insurance policy, an employer uses company assets to pay for any claims. This method of providing insurance coverage is called *self-insurance* and is used in a variety of situations.

NATURE OF INSURANCE CONTRACTS

Because insurance companies generally deal in volume and in spreading their covered risks among a pool of people, their contracts, of necessity, must be standardized. In fact, laws in many states require substantial standardization in policies covering the same risk for different people. For this reason insurance contracts are not subject to the same bargaining between parties as are most other contracts.

Offer and Acceptance

While insurance agents frequently contact customers to try to sell insurance policies, by law it is the customer, not the insurance agent, who makes the offer. Thus the contract occurs only after the company accepts the offer, not after the customer has signed approval of the policy terms.

If a customer seeks health insurance, the company may condition its acceptance on the results of an up-to-date physical examination. If the examination reveals a history of disease or other physical problems, the company may reject the offer. It could, of course, make a

counteroffer and agree to write a different or more expensive policy.

Many insurance problems relate to the authority of the agent to bind the company. If the customer signs an offer, can the agent sign and accept that offer on behalf of the company or must someone else in the company's home office accept any offers made to the company? An agent generally has authority to bind the company that issues fire or casualty insurance through offering a *binder* that commits the company even before a person in the home office issues the actual policy. However, that same agent does not have similar authority to bind the company to issue most life insurance policies. Because the agent represents the company, the agent's statements can and do affect the terms of the insurance contract made between the company and the insured. The *Phillips* case raises issues about the effect of an agent's statement on the terms of an insurance policy.

Ranger Insurance Company v. Phillips

Arizona Court of Appeals
544 P.2d 250 (1976)

Background: Boyle was a passenger in a small plane owned by Phillips (defendant-appellee) that crashed while being piloted by Bruner, a student pilot. Ranger (plaintiff-appellant) had issued a liability insurance policy to Phillips that contained a standard clause, as specified by FAA (Federal Aviation Administration) regulations, limiting those who were qualified to pilot the insured aircraft. The policy did not cover student pilots. In fact Bruner had a note affixed to his student pilot's license that expressly prohibited him from carrying passengers.

However, Phillips proved that he told Ranger's agent that he wanted insurance coverage that covered student pilots. The agent assured Phillips of the requested coverage and sent Phillips a handwritten note to that effect. Later, the coverage for the student pilot was deleted from the policy by the agent without informing Phillips of the change. The actual policy was not delivered to Phillips until after the crash causing Boyle's death.

The insurance company argues that the written insurance policy, not the oral or written statement of its agents, specifies the terms of its coverage. Further, it notes that the premium charged to Phillips was not based on the higher cost associated with student pilot coverage. Thus Ranger claims it is not obligated to pay claims for the accident involving the student pilot. The trial court found for Phillips and the insurance company appealed.

Decision: The Court of Appeals affirmed the trial court's decision.

Froeb, Judge

This suit was filed by appellant Ranger Insurance Company (Ranger) to obtain a judicial declaration of the extent of its duties and obligations under a contract of aircraft insurance. After a non-jury trial, the trial court found the company had a duty to defend appellees Robert W. Phillips (Phillips) and Ivadelle Bruner, administratrix of the estate of Marvin L. Bruner, deceased, against a claim asserted by Inez Boyle, individually and as executrix of the estate of Gayle Boyle, deceased, and to indemnify them against any judgment not exceeding $100,000.

Gayle Boyle was a passenger in a small two-seat aircraft (known as a Lark 95) when he died in a crash near Willcox, Arizona, on April 20, 1967. The plane was piloted by Marvin L. Bruner (Bruner), student pilot, whose total experience and flight time consisted of approximately 70 hours. Phillips, the owner of the plane, conducted a flight service business at Falcon Field in Mesa, Arizona, from which the fatal flight originated. As this case involves only the question of insurance coverage, we are not here concerned with the cause of the crash.

Ranger issued a liability policy covering the aircraft (referred to as Lark 9502) in which the two men were killed. Both Phillips and Ivadelle Bruner claim liability coverage for the wrongful death claim arising out of the crash. . . .

As written, the policy does not cover a student pilot. "Student pilot" is a separate category of pilot under Federal Air Regulations, and flight conducted by a "student pilot" is authorized only after the issuance of a student pilot "certificate." . . .

The trial court could reasonably have found that there was an oral contract between Phillips and Ranger (through its agents) by which a student pilot was insured. The general rule is that a parol contract of insurance is valid and enforceable. This is true where there is a showing that the parties have agreed on all the essential terms of the contract, including the subject matter, the risk insured against, the time of commencement and duration of the risk, the amount of insurance and the amount of the premium. . . .

Turning now to the evidence in the case, Phillips testified that student instruction was one of the services he provided and that he would not have considered insurance without such coverage. Initially he contacted his own insurance agent, Sabatelli Insurance Agency. Not being familiar with aircraft insurance, Sabatelli contacted John Sanderson who was employed by American Underwriters Agencies, Inc. (American). . . .

The product of these communications was a written "set-up" sheet in Alderman's handwriting, whereby coverage was arranged for "student, private or commercial pilots" on five aircraft, including Lark 9502, the one which crashed. The words "student, private or commercial pilots" where thereafter crossed out on the "set-up" sheet by Alderman without Phillips' knowledge or consent. The written policy, absent an endorsement for student pilot coverage, was thereafter issued on February 27, 1967, but, as has been pointed out, the policy was not delivered to Phillips until after

April 20, 1967, the date of the accident, nor was Phillips informed that the written policy did not provide student pilot coverage. We find that this evidence was sufficient for the trial court to find that student pilot coverage had been sought by Phillips and contracted for by Ranger through its agents.

Appellant argues that Phillips was neither charged nor did he pay a premium for student pilot coverage. This is not, however, controlling as to the issue of whether coverage was provided by Ranger. If by not charging the higher premium Ranger intended not to cover student pilots, contrary to the mutual understanding of the parties, that fact was never communicated to Phillips. No policy had ever been delivered which would have indicated to Phillips the extent of coverage provided and a breakdown of premiums charged. . . .

In conclusion, the true contract of insurance in this case was found by the trial court to be that which arose out of the oral agreement between the parties and not that as evidenced by the written policy. . . .

A second argument raised by Ranger is that the insurance contract did not provide coverage against liability for death or injury to a passenger carried on a student flight. . . .

Ranger argues that since Bruner was not holding the proper pilot certificate for carrying passengers, passenger liability coverage is excluded under the policy.

In construing insurance policy provisions, any ambiguity is to be construed against the insurer.

This rule is particularly applicable where a policy exclusion is concerned.

Turning to the language of the contract, we find that the pilot clause provisions are ambiguous as to the issue of passenger coverage. Bruner had a valid student license at the time of the accident. Although Federal Air Regulations impose a restriction against a student pilot carrying passengers, a violation of this regulation does not mean that Bruner's license was not "proper" or that it was thereby invalidated. . . .

For the foregoing reasons, we conclude that the judgment of the trial court is correct and it is therefore affirmed.

Insurable Interest

To eliminate gambling and immoral activities, the law allows only certain people to obtain insurance covering specific risks. If anyone could purchase a large life insurance policy on a stranger's life or personal property, people might be tempted to purchase such insurance and cause that death or property damage just to collect the insurance benefits. Thus the law requires a person to have an *insurable interest*, such that another person's loss or injury would result in a direct loss or injury to that person.

If you own property or even lease property, you have an insurable interest in it. Shareholders in a closely held corporation would have such an interest in the property of the corporation. In life insurance a close relative, business associate, or creditor of another person would have an insurable interest enabling him or her to take out life insurance on that person's life. For the purchase of life insurance the insurable interest must exist at the time the policy is taken out. For other forms of insurance the insurable interest must exist at the time of the loss.

An insured may take out a life insurance

policy on his own life and assign the benefits due under the policy to any person, even if that person does not have an insurable interest in the insured's life. Fire and casualty insurance policies can be assigned only with the approval of the insurer.

The concept of an insurable interest is discussed in the following case.

Gendron v. Pawtucket Mutual Insurance Company

Supreme Judicial Court of Maine

384 A.2d 694 (1978)

Background: On August 15, 1969 Gendron (plaintiff) purchased a fire insurance policy from Pawtucket Mutual Insurance Company (defendant). The policy, effective for three years, insured a gasoline service station in the town of Lewiston. The plaintiff then leased the property to Shell Oil Co. for a period of fifteen years. In the lease the buildings were declared to be Shell's property and it was obligated to insure the property. Shell also agreed to destroy the existing buildings and construct new ones.

A fire destroyed the service station in 1971 and Gendron sued for payment according to its insurance policy. Pawtucket refused, claiming the lease of the property to Shell transferred all of Gendron's interest in the property so that Gendron no longer had an insurable interest. The trial court found for Pawtucket and Gendron appealed. Decision: The Supreme Judicial Court reversed the judgment for the defendant and remanded the case to the lower court.

Wernick, Justice

We address, first, the . . . conclusion that plaintiffs' insurable interest was terminated by the clause of the lease obligating, and exclusively entitling, Shell to insure the property covered by plaintiffs' fire insurance policy with defendant. We disagree with this conclusion because we disagree with the premise which underlies it:—that defendant insurance company may avail itself of the terms of a collateral contract between plaintiffs and a third person to destroy plaintiffs' insurable interest in property insured under a contract of insurance between plaintiffs and defendant.

The existence of an insured's insurable interest in property covered by a contract of insurance is determined by the relationship between the insured and the property insured—more specifically, by whether there is a relationship such that injury to the property will, as a natural consequence, result in a loss to the insured.

Since the question of insurable interest thus necessarily involves the insured's relationship to the property insured, we conclude that even if plaintiffs had purported by an executory contract to give a third person exclusive entitlement to place insurance on property already insured by plaintiffs, that fact is not by itself sufficient to terminate plaintiffs' insurable interest in the insured property. Plaintiffs had not, here, made an actual transfer of such of their rights in the insured property as would destroy their insurable interest; the mere leasing of property is not such an alienation of it as destroys insurable interest. . . . The insurer simply cannot thus benefit from collateral contractual relations between the insured and a third person so long as the insured retains legal title to the property.

We turn to the . . . other rationale of decision: that plaintiffs lacked insurable interest because the fire caused them no actual loss.

We take as settled principles of law in Maine that (1) insurable interest signifies such a relationship to property "as will necessarily entail a pecuniary loss in case of its injury or destruction," and (2) the term "actual cash value" in the fire insurance policy signifies the fair market value of the insured property, as measured by the usual test of what a willing buyer would offer and a willing seller accept in a cash sale on an open and free market.

Under the plain language of the instant policy (in accordance with Maine's standard form of fire insurance policy), the actual cash value of the insured property is its fair market value as *of the time of its destruction by fire.* True, particular circumstances might render a building utterly worthless by the time fire consumes it; for example, if the process of demolition has been commenced, or if the owner has abandoned the building. . . .

. . . And the mere existence of an executory contract for demolition does not destroy the value of the building or deprive the owner of an insurable interest.

These principles have . . . application, here. Plaintiffs continued to have legal title to the property they had insured with defendant and thus had rights to recover damages in the event Shell should commit a breach of the lease and demolition agreement. Moreover, special circumstances existed here tending to show affirmatively that the building was not worthless at the time of the fire. Plaintiff . . . Gendron was still operating the gasoline service station as a sub-lessee, and under a separate contract with Shell plaintiffs had retained rights to the salvage value of the old station, potentially valued at approximately $10,000.00, intending to use the materials to build another garage at another location.

Lastly, that plaintiffs had the benefit of Shell's contractual obligation to build a new service station to replace the old structure cannot support defendant's assertion that thereby plaintiffs lost an insurable interest. An insured's entitlement to be compensated for the value of insured property from sources other than the insurance does not destroy insurable interest of the insured in the insured property.

The decision that plaintiffs lacked an insurable interest was error.

· · ·

Premiums

Premiums (payments) for life insurance coverage generally are paid by the insured over a long time period, whereas payments for casualty, fire insurance, health, and accident insurance are usually paid over short time periods. The premiums charged on a life insurance policy are determined on the basis of mortality rates, guaranteed interest, and expenses. The mortality rates are based on the experience of insurance companies in the past with the rate of death. Premiums also reflect the rate of interest the company expects to earn on the money it receives in premiums and the expenses it incurs for medical examinations, commission payments to its agents, and operating expenses.

The premiums charged for many kinds of business and casualty insurance are based primarily on the company's evaluation of the risks it is assuming. Rates charged for certain kinds of casualty and business insurance are regulated by state law. The regulating authority seeks to allow the company to charge rates that are high enough to provide the company with a reasonable return on its assets and low enough so that people and businesses desiring insurance will not find its cost prohibitive.

DEFENSES OF THE INSURER

People who purchase insurance may believe that the insurance contract is filled with fine print and that thousands of different defenses are asserted by companies refusing to pay claims against the policy. In fact, in addition to the ordinary defenses used in contract cases, only three defenses are generally used by insurance companies seeking to avoid paying an otherwise valid claim. The three defenses commonly asserted by the insurer are concealment, misrepresentation, and breach of warranty.

Concealment

Concealment is the intentional failure of the insured to disclose a material fact to the insurer that would affect the insurer's willingness to accept the risk. For example, a driver who fails to reveal convictions for drunken driving when applying for an automobile insurance policy is committing concealment. The essence of concealment is the intentional nondisclosure of a material fact. However, if an insurance application specifically asks the applicant for information and the applicant provides false information, misrepresentation, not concealment, occurs.

Misrepresentation

Misrepresentation occurs when a prospective insured intentionally or innocently misrepresents a material fact that leads an insurer to enter into an insurance contract. The misrepresentation may be oral or written. It may be made on the insurance application form or in written or oral statements made while discussing the possible insurance contract. A person who states that she or he is in perfect health when in fact she or he has been under recent treatment for a heart condition makes a misrepresentation.

Only a material misrepresentation provides the insurer with a defense. Further, if the insurer investigates and learns the truth before issuing the insurance policy, it cannot rely on the representation made by the applicant. In that case, because the applicant's statement did not induce the insurer to enter into the contract (the insurer knew the statement to be false), the insurer would not have a valid defense to payment of the insurance benefits.

Finally, whether the misrepresentation is innocent or intentional, the insurer would have a defense. The principal difference between the innocent and intentional misrepresentation concerns the effect of the misrepresentation on the remedy available to the insurer. The principal remedy available to the insurer is rescission, but damages are available if the misrepresentation was intentional instead of innocent. Rescission returns the parties to their places prior to the making of the contract. Thus the insurer must return all unused premiums and the insured is without the insurance coverage that the policy provided.

To be effective, the rescission by the insurer must be made as soon as the misrepresentation is discovered. Statutes generally require that life insurance contracts include an *incontestability clause*. Typically, this clause provides that after the passage of a set period of time (usually one or two years) the insurer may not contest the representations of the insured. One exception to the incontestability clause exists for a life insurance applicant who misrepresents his or her age. Even if the two-year period of incontestability has passed, a contract provision usually limits the amount of benefits payable on the insured's death to the amount that the paid premiums would have purchased for a person of the insured's actual age. The *Smirlock* case illustrates the misrepresentation defense.

Smirlock Realty Corp. v. Title Guarantee Co.

Court of Appeals of New York

418 N.E.2d 650 (1982)

Background: Smirlock Realty (plaintiff) purchased property from the Bass Rock corporation. At the time of the purchase Bass Rock knew it soon would be entitled to some money from the city that was condemning the adjoining property and condemnation affected part of the Bass property. In the contract between Smirlock and Bass Rock, Bass Rock agreed to turn over to Smirlock any proceeds it might receive from the condemnation of any of its property.

Smirlock then contracted with Title Guarantee (defendant) to issue a title insurance policy for the property. Smirlock did not tell Title Guarantee that it knew a portion of the property was being condemned, but the pending condemnation was a matter of public record. When Smirlock leased the property to a tenant who wanted to enlarge the warehouse on it, the tenant and Smirlock both discovered that the condemnation had affected more of their property than they thought. Smirlock then sued the title insurance company, which had insured his title to the property. The insurance company defended by seeking to cancel the contract due to Smirlock's misrepresentation in failing to tell it about the condemnation. The trial court concluded that the policy was nullified and the appellate division affirmed. Smirlock appealed.

Decision: The Court of Appeals reversed and remanded the case to the trial court for a trial on the issue of damages.

Jasen, Judge

This appeal presents a question of first impression for our court. At issue is whether a policy of title insurance will be rendered void pursuant to a standard misrepresentation clause found therein as a result of the insured's failure to disclose a material fact which was a matter of public record at the time the policy was issued.

In November, 1967, the Town of Hempstead condemned and thereby acquired title to certain property on and adjacent to the premises known as 31–39 Carvel Place, which is located in Inwood, Long Island. At that time, the premises were owned by Bass Rock Holding, Inc. (Bass Rock), a corporation controlled by Helen and Anthony De Giulio. The Bass Rock property was improved by a warehouse and access to and from the property was over three public streets: Carvel Place to the north of the premises and St. George Street and Jeanette Avenue to its east. The principal loading docks for the warehouse were located at the easterly end of the building with direct access from St. George Street and Jeanette Avenue. . . .

. . . The Bass Rock property was heavily indebted and in 1968 there was a default in mortgage payments. A foreclosure proceeding was instituted in the early part of 1969. It was at about this time that Gerald Tucker, general counsel for one of the mortgagees in the foreclosure proceeding, indicated an interest in the property and negotiations were commenced with the De Giulios with a view toward the eventual purchase of the Bass Rock property. Soon thereafter, the plaintiff corporation was formed by Tucker and a group of associated investors.

It was also around this time that Lee (a town official) telephoned Tucker to inform him that a portion of the Bass Rock property had been condemned by the town and should be excluded from the foreclosure proceeding. . . .

. . . Sometime after Tucker spoke with Lee, Tucker and Joseph Tiefenbrun, the attorney retained by plaintiff, met with the Bass Rock attorney to discuss the details of the sales contract. At this meeting, Tucker was informed that, although the exact location of the property involved was uncertain, Bass Rock was entitled to a $5,000 to $6,000 condemnation award from the Town of Hempstead. As a result of this discussion, the contract was amended to include a clause assigning "any condemnation award affecting the premises then due or to be due in the future" to the plaintiff. It was agreed that the necessary information concerning this condemnation would be provided at the title closing. On April 25, 1969, the sales contract was executed by Bass Rock and the plaintiff. The purchase price was set at $600,000.

On May 14, 1969, title was closed. During the closing, and in the presence of defendant's title closer, Tucker and Mrs. De Giulio discussed the condemnation award referred to in the sales contract. . . .

After title closed, defendant issued plaintiff a title policy covering the warehouse property. The policy contained the following clause insuring access to public streets: "Notwithstanding any provisions in this paragraph to the contrary, this policy, unless otherwise excepted, insures the ordinary rights of access and egress belonging to abutting owners." It should be noted that no exception was listed in the policy for any condemnation affecting Carvel Place, St. George Street or Jeanette Avenue.

At the time the property was purchased, plaintiff leased the entire premises to Pan American World Airways, Inc. In addition, plaintiff had spent an additional $95,000 above the purchase price in order to improve the premises for its new tenant. Unfortunately, it was soon discovered that the title search had failed to reveal that the roadbeds of St. George Street and Jeanette Avenue and a portion of the property along Carvel Place had been condemned by the Town of Hempstead two years prior to plaintiff's acquisition of the property. It was apparent that the defendant's title searchers simply failed to check the master card on file at the Nassau County Clerk's office covering the applicable section and block which would have revealed these condemnations.

By 1971, plans for urban development in the Town of Hempstead required the closing down of the warehouse access routes at St. George Street and Jeanette Avenue, thereby rendering the property valueless. As a result, Pan American quit the premises and plaintiff eventually lost 31–39 Carvel Place in a foreclosure sale. Plaintiff then commenced the present action against the defendant seeking to recover $600,-000 in damages pursuant to its title insurance policy based on the defendant's failure to discover the condemned roadbed property.

In its answer, defendant pleaded an affirmative defense based on the following standard provision in its policy:

> "MISREPRESENTATION
>
> "Any untrue statement made by the insured, with respect to any material fact, or any suppression of or failure to disclose any material fact, or any untrue answer by the insured, to material inquiries before the issuance of this policy, shall void this policy."

According to defendant, plaintiff, through its agent Tucker, had knowledge prior to the closing of the town's condemnation as a result of his conversation with Lee. Defendant asserted that plaintiff's failure to divulge this knowledge to the defendant was a "failure to disclose [a] material fact" which rendered the title policy void.
. . .

Trial Term concluded that the policy was nullified.

On appeal, a unanimous Appellate Division, affirmed. . . . We reverse.

At the outset, we note our agreement with the court below that information concerning the condemnations of damage parcel 8–6 adjacent to Carvel Place and the St. George Street and Jeanette Avenue roadbeds was material. It is manifest that revelation of this information certainly would have affected defendant's choice of insuring the risk covered by the policy issued to plaintiff. . . .

However, contrary to the view expressed by the Appellate Division, the mere existence of knowledge of a material fact on plaintiff's part does not end the analysis. Rather, in order to ascertain whether the policy has been voided, a further determination must be made as to whether plaintiff was under a duty to disclose this information to defendant.

In order to make that determination, we first must examine the nature of the agreement entered into by the parties and the respective expectations and obligations of the insured and insurer which arise out of a policy of title insurance. . . .

Essentially, therefore, a policy of title insurance is a contract by which the title insurer agrees to indemnify its insured for loss occasioned by a defect in title.

Beyond its purely contractual aspects, however, the unique nature of a title insurance transaction was quickly recognized by the courts. . . . Rather than being treated merely as a contract of indemnity, title insurance was viewed as being more in the nature of a covenant of warranty against encumbrances under which "mere knowledge of a defect [in title] by the insuring owner would not constitute a defense."

Interestingly, in response to the decision in the *Empire Dev. Co.* case, title companies adopted as a standard provision in their policies the very misrepresentation clause at issue on this appeal.

To date, however, this court has not been presented with an opportunity to examine the effect to be given to this clause in terms of imposing an obligation on the insured to disclose information to the insurer.

One Federal court, addressing a provision identical to that found in the defendant's policy, stated that the clause "must be given a common sense application and, considering the nature of title insurance transactions, a duty to speak could be found only if the insurance applicant had actual knowledge of certain defects or encumbrances. Further, misrepresentation could be found only if one charged with such a duty to speak intentionally failed to disclose the information."

In a like manner, other jurisdictions which have addressed similar clauses have required a showing that the insured had actual knowledge of the title defect which was intentionally concealed from the insurer. Moreover, these cases indicated, either expressly or by implication, that the title policy would only be voided in instances where the undisclosed information was not discoverable by the insurer by reference to publicly filed records. . . .

We agree with the view expressed by these cases. Therefore, we hold that a policy of title insurance will not be rendered void pursuant to a misrepresentation clause absent some showing of intentional concealment on the part of the insured tantamount to fraud. Moreover, because record information of a title defect is available to the title insurer and because the title insurer is presumed to have made itself aware of such information, we hold that an insured under a policy of title insurance such as is involved herein is under no duty to disclose to the insurer a fact which is readily ascertainable by reference to the public records. Thus, even an intentional failure to disclose a matter of public record will not result in a loss of title insurance protection.

In so holding, we merely recognize the practical realities of the transaction involved. As mentioned earlier, title insurance is procured in order to protect against the risk that the property purchased may have some defect in title. The emphasis in securing these policies is on the expertise of the title company to search the public records and discover possible defects in title. Thus, unlike other types of insurance, the insured under a title policy provides little, if any, information to the title company other than the lot and block of the premises and the name of the prospective grantor. . . .

Of course, an intentional failure by the insured to disclose material information not readily discernible from the public records will render the policy void. . . .

In this case, there was no showing that plaintiff's agent, Tucker, intentionally failed to disclose the information concerning the Carvel Place condemnation. In fact, it would appear that defendant was at least put on notice as to the existence of condemnations affecting the Bass Rock property by the recital in the sales contract assigning all condemnation awards to plaintiff and by the discussion of the condemnation of the small southwest parcel which took place at the closing. In any event, it is undisputed that the existence of the St. George Street and Jeanette Avenue condemnations was readily ascertainable from the public records available at the Nassau County Clerk's office. Defendant, having failed to avail itself of this information, now attempts to avoid its obligation under the policy by claiming that plaintiff failed to disclose material information concerning title to the property. However, because plaintiff was under no duty to disclose this publicly available information to defendant, the policy will not be rendered void pursuant to the misrepresentation provision found therein . . . .

> Accordingly, the order of the Appellate Division should be modified, with costs to plaintiff, to the extent of reversing the dismissal of plaintiff's first cause of action and remitting the case to Supreme Court, Nassau County, for a trial on the issue of plaintiff's damages. As so modified, the order should be affirmed.

Warranties

Warranties are important in insurance contracts because they concern representations within the insurance policy itself. These representations operate as conditions that must exist before the policy is effective or before the insurer's promise to pay benefits is enforceable. If the condition specified fails to occur, the insurer is not obligated to pay. A condition may express the limits of the insurer's liability. For example, the following clause specifies the time period and the locations of accidents that are or are not covered by an automobile insurance policy:

> This automobile policy applies only to accidents occurring during the policy period while the automobile is within the United States, its territories, or Canada.

Similarly, a liability policy may provide time limits affecting the insurer's obligation to pay policy claims. A common clause is one that states:

> The insurer shall not be liable unless suit is brought within 12 months from the date of the occurrence of the loss or of the event giving rise to a claim.

Generally the trend is away from allowing an insurer to avoid liability on the policy for any breach of a warranty made by the insured. Instead, as in the case of misrepresentation, the breach of warranty must be regarded as material to be given effect. Statutes in some states provide that all statements made by an applicant for life insurance will be considered to be representations and not warranties. Thus

the materiality requirement must be met for the insurer's defense to be valid.

INTERPRETATION OF INSURANCE CONTRACTS

Waiver, Estoppel, and Unconscionability

Sometimes, even though an insurer might be able to assert a defense to paying a claim under a policy, because of other factors the insurer is not permitted to use the defense. A *waiver* is the voluntary relinquishment of a known right. Actions by an insurance agent that waive, on behalf of the company, some factual concealment by the applicant exemplify the waiver.

Estoppel, as we have noted in earlier chapters, is the prevention of a person from asserting a position that is inconsistent with his or her actions or conduct when those actions or conduct have been justifiably relied on by the other party. Thus a company that periodically accepts premium payments from an insured that are late by several weeks is estopped later from asserting that a similar late payment of premiums is a defense to its obligation to continue the insurance coverage. The prior conduct of accepting the payments in earlier months estops the company from asserting the warranty defense (payments must be made before the policy is in effect) for similar subsequent late payments.

Both waiver and estoppel are specific legal concepts that prevent an insurance company from assessing a defense to the payment of benefits. However, the general concept of unconscionability also affects the defenses available to the insured. *Unconscionability* is the quality of being shocked to the conscience. As we noted in Chapter 15, when one party has little bargaining power and is faced with a standard contract that cannot be altered and that has been prepared by the other party, the courts may declare the contract or particular parts of it unconscionable and unenforceable.

Performance and Termination

As with contracts generally, most insurance contracts are performed according to their terms. The payment of premiums by the insured and the payment of benefits due by the insurer usually constitute performance of the insurance contract. Performance terminates the obligations of both the insured and the insurer under the contract. A policy of insurance may also provide that the insurer has the option to cancel the policy after the happening of an insured event. If cancellation occurs before the end of the effective date for which premiums have been paid, the unearned premiums must be returned by the insurer.

Thus cancellation is another way of terminating the insurance contract. The *Spindle* case at the end of this section shows how a cancellation clause in an insurance contract may be interpreted.

The nonperformance by one party of material terms of a contract generally excuses the other party's duty to perform. Clearly, nonpayment of premiums terminates any performance obligation of the insurer. On the other hand, many insurance contracts have notice clauses that require the insured to notify the insurer within a specified time of a claim that the insurer is obligated to pay. If the insured does not give this notice, the obligation to perform by the insurer may be discharged or excused. But these notice provisions usually are not strictly enforced. Instead, a reasonable time requirement is imposed. Of course, because the notice provision allows the insurance company to begin its investigation regarding its liability in a timely manner, such provisions benefit both the insurer and the insured. In the *Milam* case the court is faced with interpreting the notice provisions found in an automobile policy.

Spindle v. Travelers Insurance Cos.

Court of Appeals of California

136 Cal.Rptr. 404 (1977)

Background: Spindle, a neurosurgeon in California, had malpractice liability insurance coverage by virtue of the agreement between Travelers (along with Phoenix Insurance Co., hereinafter the insurer) and the Southern California Physicians Council, a nonprofit association of 7,000 physicians and surgeons (including Spindle) in Southern California. Spindle claims the insurer agreed to provide liability insurance for the Council members beginning in January 1974 and continuing as long as those members did not have excessive claims filed against them. Despite that agreement, and even though no malpractice claims were filed against Spindle, the insurer notified Spindle of its intent to cancel his insurance as of August 1975.

Spindle (plaintiff) sued Travelers and Phoenix (defendants) for breaching their agreement and warranty not to cancel his insurance except for excessive claims. Defendant insurers claimed their insurance policy clearly gave them the right to cancel plaintiff's malpractice liability insurance simply by providing thirty days notice

of the cancellation. The trial court found for the insurers and the plaintiff Spindle appealed.
Decision: The Court of Appeals reversed.

Jefferson, Associate Judge

It is plaintiff's contention that defendant was seeking a premium increase of 141 percent while members of the Council were resisting this percentage increase and contending that the Master Contract between the Council and defendant Phoenix limited such increase during the period from January 2, 1975 to January 1, 1976, to 15 percent. In effect, plaintiff alleges that his malpractice insurance policy was cancelled to serve as an example to other members so they would agree to the greater premium increase sought by defendant, the only insurer in a position to insure them.

Plaintiff alleges that he was informed by Norman Aronson, head of the Professional Claims Department of defendant Travelers, that his insurance would not have been cancelled had the Council agreed to the 141 percent premium increase.

Plaintiff further alleges that, at the time of cancellation, defendant Phoenix was aware that plaintiff would be unable to practice medicine and surgery in hospitals without malpractice insurance. He also states that the wrongful cancellation of his insurance was "intended as a threat and a warning" to every member of the Council, *i.e.,* that the members could each expect similar treatment if they opposed the premium increase. . . .

In asserting by their demurrer that plaintiff's amended complaint fails to state a cause of action, defendants rely on what they regard as their "absolute" right, set forth in the contract with the Council and in the contract with plaintiff, to cancel the policy of insurance for any reason upon which they chose to act. We note that the Master Contract, exhibit A to the amended complaint, provides: "No provision of this Agreement [dealing with the circumstances under which the Council and the defendant Phoenix could terminate it] shall restrict the rights of cancellation specified in the policies of insurance issued pursuant to this Agreement." We note also that plaintiff's particular policy provides: "This policy may be cancelled by the *named insured* by surrender thereof to the Company or any of its authorized agents or by mailing to the Company written notice stating when thereafter the cancellation shall be effective. This policy may be cancelled by the *Company* by *mailing* to the *named insured* at the address shown in this policy, written *notice stating when,* not less than 30 days thereafter, such *cancellation shall be effective.* The mailing of notice as aforesaid shall be sufficient proof of notice. The time of surrender or the effective date and hour of cancellation stated in the notice shall become the end of the policy period. Delivery of such written notice either by the *named insured* or by the Company shall be equivalent to mailing." (Emphasis added except for "named insured.") . . .

It is plaintiff's contention that public policy requires the rule of law that precludes an insurance carrier from possessing the right to cancel a policy for a malicious reason such as the wrongful objective of making an "example" of plaintiff, the insured, during the struggle between the Council and its members and defendant Phoenix over the problem of premium increases. Defendants reject the notion that public policy requires, as plaintiff contends, that the legal principle of good faith and fair dealing between an insurer and its insured be extended to include a limitation on an insurer's right to cancel malpractice insurance policies issued to its insured.

We have not discovered any California decisional-law authority expressing a rule of law relative to a bad-faith cancellation of a policy of medical malpractice insurance. Plaintiff has formulated his theory of a right to recover damages on the principle that public policy does—or should—dictate a legal remedy when such a cancellation occurs. . . .

Despite the absence of an expressed "public policy" basis pursuant to existing California decisional law, it is clear that the right of insurers to cancel insurance policies is not absolute in this state. Sections 660 through 679.73 of the Insurance Code deal with the subjects of cancellation and failure to renew particular kinds of insurance policies such as automobile liability policies and property loss policies. Section 661 sets forth and limits specifically the grounds upon which an automobile liability or collision policy may be cancelled, and section 676 specifies and limits the grounds for cancellation of property loss policies. In addition, section 679.71 declares that real or personal property loss insurance policies may not be cancelled because of the insured's marital status, sex, race, color, religion, national origin, or ancestry. These sections reflect legislative policy limiting the "absolute" right of insurance policy cancellation.

In addition, there is the area of developed case law in California which pertains to the matter of bad faith in carrying out the terms of a contract. While defendants term plaintiff's allegations of bad faith as "absurd," we note again that in a demurrer situation, we are compelled to accept plaintiff's allegation as true for the purpose of weighing the sufficiency of the amended complaint against a demurrer thereto, and need not concern ourselves with any problems of proof that plaintiff Spindle may encounter in a trial.

"There is an implied covenant of good faith and fair dealing in *every contract* that neither party will do anything which will injure the right of the other to receive the benefits of the agreement.

"This principle is applicable to policies of insurance." . . .

We are unable to discern any logical basis for distinguishing between an insurer's conduct in settling a claim made pursuant to the policy and that involved in an insurer's cancelling a policy if bad-faith conduct is the basis for the cancellation. The situations are similar in that the ultimate result of the conduct of the insurer effectively deprives the insured of the benefit of his bargain, *i.e.,* the coverage for the period for which he paid a premium. Cancellation provisions of a contract are subject to the covenant of good faith and fair dealing just as are other provisions of a contract. No plausible reason exists why cancellation provisions of a contract should be treated differently from other contractual provisions insofar as application of the implied covenant of good faith and fair dealing is concerned. . . .

In the instant case, the deprivation to the insured of the benefit of his bargain is greater than average due to the lack of competition in the field of malpractice insurance alleged in the amended complaint.

Conspiratorial conduct on the part of insurers to avoid the contractual liability they undertake is not countenanced in California, and the evolvement of the doctrine of the implied covenant of good faith and fair dealing *is* an expression of *public policy* in our state. We hold that this same doctrine is applicable to subject an insurer to liability to its insured for a malpractice insurance policy in accordance with permissible terms of the cancellation provisions of the policy, if the reasons for such cancellation are such as to make the cancellation a violation of the implied covenant of good faith and fair dealing. Plaintiff's amended complaint, therefore, has stated a cause of action against defendants.

The judgment (order of dismissal) appealed from is reversed.

State Farm Mutual Automobile Insurance Company v. Milam

U.S. District Court, S.D. West Virginia
438 F.Supp. 227 (1977)

Background: Carlos Milam (defendant) was the insured on a policy of automobile liability insurance issued by State Farm (plaintiff). On June 17, 1973 Andrew Milam, Carlos's 19-year-old son, was driving a truck owned by Jarrell. The truck veered off the road and struck three pedestrians, killing one and injuring two others.

Andrew Milam was arrested and charged with negligent homicide while under the influence of drugs. He pleaded guilty and was sentenced to a year in jail and a $100.00 fine. On January 29, 1974 a civil case was filed against both Andrew and Carlos Milam by one of the persons who was injured. Soon after the suit was filed, Carlos learned that Andrew perhaps was covered by the insurance policy issued by State Farm. He then notified State Farm of the accident and asked it to defend Andrew in the civil case. State Farm refused, claiming it first learned of the January 17, 1973 accident and the January 29, 1974 civil suit on April 29, 1974. State Farm sought a declaratory judgment. It argued that Milam's failure to give it timely and adequate notice of the accident, as required by its insurance policy, was grounds for it to refuse to defend Andrew Milam in the civil suit brought against him.

Decision: The U.S. District Court found for the defendants.

MEMORANDUM OPINION

Knapp, Chief Judge

State Farm Mutual Automobile Insurance Company (State Farm) instituted this declaratory judgment action seeking a determination by this court that a certain policy of automobile liability insurance issued by State Farm to Carlos Milam does not afford coverage to Andrew Milam for any damages for which he may become liable arising from an accident which occurred on June 17, 1973. State Farm's contention that coverage does not exist is based solely on the fact that it had no notice of the accident until nearly 10 months after the accident occurred, including a three months' period subsequent to a civil action having been instituted against Andrew Milam on behalf of one of the persons injured in the accident. The facts germane to the issues in this action are not, for the most part, in serious dispute.

Carlos Milam, Andrew's father, was the named insured on a policy of automobile liability insurance issued by State Farm, . . . which afforded liability coverage on vehicles owned by him. On June 17, 1973, Andrew, then 19 years of age and a member of his father's household, was driving a 1971 Ford pick-up truck owned by Jarrell when the vehicle, in which Jarrell and Sharon Wingo were riding as passengers, veered left off the paved portion of West Virginia State Route 3 in Raleigh County, West Virginia, and struck three pedestrians, killing James Ferrell Pettry, age 15, and injuring Billy Ray Akers and Johnny Boggess, ages 16 and 15, respectively. . . .

Trooper W. W. Walker of the West Virginia State Police was the investigating officer of the tragic occurrence. By all accounts, including that of State Farm, Trooper Walker made a very thorough investigation of all the ascertainable circumstances surrounding the accident. . . . (He) Trooper Walker obtained the following statement from Andrew Milam:

"I was going toward Sundial on Route 3. All of a sudden the vehicle went to my left, I could not cut it back, I went down over the hill and hit 2 boys. As soon as the vehicle stopped, I heard them yelling for help. I could not find them, so I got back up on the road and stopped a truck and people started stopping and helping.

Q. How many cigarettes did you smoke with Marihuana before the accident?
A. 5 or 6.
Q. How long before the accident did you smoke them?
A. 7 hours.
Q. Do you feel as if you are under the influence now?
A. Yes sir, drowsy and sleepy.
Q. Did you take or smoke anything just prior to the accident?
A. No sir.
/S/ Andrew J. Milam

/W/ Trooper W. W. Walker"

Trooper Walker arrested Andrew at the scene of the accident, charging him with negligent homicide and driving while under the influence of drugs. Andrew thereafter pleaded guilty to the negligent homicide charge and was sentenced to one year in jail and fined $100.00.

On January 29, 1974, a civil action was commenced in state court on behalf of Billy Ray Akers against Andrew and Jarrell for damages resulting from the accident. Andrew was served with the summons and complaint on February 1, 1974. Carlos retained the services of Leo Bridi, an attorney practicing in Beckley, West Virginia, to represent his son. On February 10, 1974, Bridi filed an answer on behalf of Andrew to the Akers complaint.

After having been advised by a person referred to at trial as being from an "uninsured motorist" insurance company that Andrew perhaps was covered under the insurance policy State Farm issued to Carlos, Mrs. Milam immediately telephoned State Farm's agent, W. R. Straub, and informed him of the accident. The following day, April 30, 1974, Straub, Andrew and Carlos met at the Milam home and discussed the events up to that time. On May 1, 1974, a representative of the claims department of State Farm interviewed Andrew Milam and obtained his statement regarding the events surrounding the occurrence of the accident. Carlos also gave the claims representative a written statement to the effect that no report of the accident was given State Farm prior to Mrs. Milam's telephoning Straub. In addition, the representative obtained a copy of Trooper Walker's report and inspected the scene of the accident. . . .

This declaratory action was commenced on January 17, 1975. In paragraph 12 of the complaint, State Farm states that it has never denied coverage to Andrew Milam but has refused to defend him. On October 14, 1976, State Farm filed a motion for summary judgment. . . .

Affidavits of Carlos and Andrew Milam were filed in opposition to the summary judgment motion. These counter-affidavits were to the effect that the Milams were not aware that the accident should be reported to State Farm inasmuch as no State Farm insured vehicle was involved in the accident; that notice was given State Farm within a reasonable time and that in any event, State Farm suffered no prejudice in receiving notice of the accident when it did. . . .

Andrew Milam, Sharon Wingo and Johnny Boggess testified on their own behalf as to events surrounding the accident itself, as hereinbefore set forth. In addition, Andrew testified that he was unaware that he could have been afforded coverage under his father's insurance policy.

Carlos Milam's testimony was that he too was unaware that his State Farm policy would provide Andrew with coverage and that no one even suggested this to him until April 29, 1974. . . .

. . .

The State Farm policy contained the following provision:

> "1. Notice. In the event of an accident or loss, written notice containing particulars sufficient to identify the insured and also reasonably obtainable information respecting the time, place and circumstances of the accident, and the names and addresses of injured *persons* and available witnesses, shall be given by or on behalf of the *insured* to the company or any of its authorized agents as soon as practicable. If claim is made or suit is brought against the *insured,* he shall immediately forward to the company every demand, notice, summons or other process received by him or his representative." (Emphasis in original).

The purpose of a notice provision in policies of automobile liability insurance is to give the insurer an opportunity to make a timely and adequate investigation of the circumstances *surrounding the event* which resulted in the claim being made against an insured. . . .

In *Republic Mutual* we held. . . . that under West Virginia law the question of lack of prejudice was material as to issues involving the question of delay in giving notice of an accident or loss so as to relieve the insurer from his obligation under the terms of an automobile liability policy for a particular occurrence. [The court's discussion of other case holdings is omitted.] . . .

In the instant case, State Farm would distinguish *Republic Mutual, Higginbotham* and *Willey* on the basis that in each of those cases the insurer had actual notice of the accident, claim or loss. While this is certainly true, the distinction is actually one without a difference. At best, it is a matter of degree. . . .

. . . In the case at bar we feel that whether or not State Farm was prejudiced by the 10 months' delay is a question of fact that the trier of the facts must decide.

It must be remembered, too, that in all of these "lack of notice" cases, the insurer, sooner or later, does receive notice of the occurrence. In order then for the insurer to successfully avail itself of the "lack of notice" defense, it must show that it was prejudiced by reason thereof. The test to apply is whether the insurer would be in a better position with regard to the investigation of the circumstances surrounding the event which resulted in the claim being made either against it or its insured had it been furnished notice within a reasonable time of the occurrence which gave rise to such claim.

Thus, the focal point of the test is with regard to how the accident occurred, or, more simply stated, "what happened?" In the instant case, State Farm does not seriously contend that the circumstances surrounding the accident were other than as set forth in Trooper Walker's report. That report, included in which was the statement of Andrew regarding the use of marijuana and how he felt as a result therefrom and a finding of lack of mechanical failure of the vehicle involved, taken together with Andrew's plea of guilty to the negligent homicide charge (i.e., an admission of such negligence), constitute beyond any peradventure as to "what happened."

Furthermore, there was no evidence adduced at the trial which showed or even tended to show that additional salient facts as to the events surrounding the accident could have been uncovered if notice had been received even at the earliest possible moment after the accident. There were no skid marks to observe, thus making a view of the scene of the accident a perfunctory act. . . .

The contention of State Farm regarding its not knowing whether Jarrell had insurance and its not being able to settle the claims early are of no moment in determining the prejudice issue in view of the stated purpose of the notice provision in the policy of insurance.

In view of all of the foregoing, the Court, as trier of the facts in the case, accordingly finds as a fact that State Farm's rights were not prejudiced by the delay in receiving notice of the June 17, 1973 accident.

As quoted, supra, the "notice" provision of the State Farm policy required that written notice of an accident or loss be given "as soon as practicable." The West Virginia courts have interpreted the phrase "as soon as practicable" to mean "within a reasonable time, having regard to all of the circumstances." . . .

The explanation or excuse of the Milams for not reporting the accident was that neither had any idea that Carlos Milam's State Farm policy would afford coverage to Andrew while the latter was driving the Jarrell vehicle. We think that as a result of that tendered explanation, the issue of the timeliness of the notice is one of fact. Considering all of the circumstances in this case, we resolve this issue in favor of the defendants. Thus, we find and hold that notice was given "as soon as practicable."

In view of the foregoing, this Court declares, concludes and holds that the policy of insurance issued by State Farm to Carlos Milam does afford coverage to Andrew Milam with respect to the June 17, 1973, accident, in accordance with the applicable limits of liability as stated in the policy.

Accordingly, judgment will be for the defendants.

INSURANCE FIRMS

Forms of Organization

There are two major types of insurance organizations: stock companies and mutual companies. A *stock insurance company* is a corporation that is established to sell insurance for a profit. The corporation is organized like other businesses. It generally has a board of directors, officers, employees, and shareholders. The shareholders may receive corporate profits in the form of dividends declared by the corporation's board of directors. The shareholders are not necessarily customers of the corporation.

A *mutual insurance company* is owned by the policyholders. By purchasing insurance from the company, the policyholders obtain the right to elect the directors and they in turn select the officers. Only policyholders may have an ownership interest in a mutual insurance company. A mutual insurance company does not have shareholders, and therefore it does not distribute any profit in the form of dividends.

Agents and Brokers

Because both the agent and the broker are agents of other parties in sales of insurance,

you may find it helpful to review Chapter 30. Under the law of agency, an agent is a person who represents another person, the principal, and who is subject to control by the principal.

The insurance *agent* represents the insurance company (the insurer) that acts as the principal in the selling of insurance to third persons (the insured). The insurance agent who contracts with an applicant for insurance does so on behalf of the principal and not in his or her own right. The agent for an insurance company must be appointed by the company he or she represents and must be licensed as a sales agent by the state. An independent agent represents more than one insurer and thus can select from those companies for the insurance needs of the insured.

An *insurance broker* represents the buyer of insurance, by placing an order with an insurance company on behalf of that buyer. The broker is the representative or agent for the insured, and, like the insurance agent, generally is compensated through commissions paid by the insurance companies. Unlike an agent, the broker does not represent one insurance company but chooses the company to write policies needed by the insured. The state licensing requirements imposed on brokers are generally higher than those on insurance agents. Some states allow only agents, not brokers, to write insurance within their boundaries.

REVIEW PROBLEMS

1. Describe the primary features and typical uses for whole life insurance, term life insurance, and endowment or annuity life insurance.

2. What type of coverage is generally provided in a health insurance policy? How does a group health insurance policy differ from an individual policy?

3. Why are the rules of offer and acceptance especially important in insurance contracts?

4. Describe the insurer's defenses of breach of warranty. What is the significance of an insurance policy's incontestability clause?

5. Explain how the insurer can use the defenses of concealment, misrepresentation,

ETHICS BOX
An Ethical Problem for an Insurance Agent or Broker

An insurance agent is negotiating products liability coverage for a manufacturing firm with an insurance company underwriter. The agent knows that the Consumer Product Safety Commission (CPSC) is considering investigating the safety of one of the firm's products. If the Commission does conduct such an investigation and recommends the client recall its product, the recall expenses of the client would be covered by the products liability insurance policy. The insurance company underwriter does not ask the insurance agent about any possible Commission action against the firm. Does the agent have an ethical obligation to divulge the information he knows about the firm and its products to the insurance underwriter? Would the ethical obligation be the same for a broker?

Based on the Code of Professional Ethics of the American Institute for Property and Liability Underwriters, there appears to be no ethical obligation for an agent to volunteer information in his or her possession except when the information is specifically requested in the application, or by the underwriter, or if the agent knows the information is material to insurers and the agent has good reason to believe the insurer cannot readily discover the information. Here, the latter of these exceptions is applicable. The agent must have known that an investigation by the CPSC is material to insurers whose insurance covers recall expenses. Thus ethically the agent is concealing a material fact, one that the insurer cannot readily discover. This is ethically wrong, and perhaps also illegal (if the omission was intentional, there might be fraud).

Legally the agent is a representative of the insurer, whereas the broker is a representative of the insured. While the legal obligations of the two differ, both have ethical obligations to their clients and to the public interest. The agent who represents the insurer (insurance company), of course, has the clearest obligation to divulge the information to his or her principal. However, even the broker, who represents the insured (manufacturing firm), has an ethical obligation not to conceal knowingly material information from an insurer.

---

and breach of warranty against paying claims.

6. Jim Johnson just purchased an office building. He informs his agent at 10:00 A.M. that he wants the building insured immediately. The agent represents only one company and tells him, "no problem, you are covered." The agent intends to begin processing the paperwork but is interrupted several times and decides to do the paperwork after lunch and relay the information to the insurer. When the insurance agent returns from lunch, he is informed that the building caught on fire at 11:00 A.M. Is there an enforceable contract?

7. An application for property insurance ex-

plicitly stated that the building was to be used only as a center for teenagers. This was reiterated in the terms of the policy, giving it the effect of a warranty. The center for teenagers was a front for a legal, but unpopular dissident group. The group was subject to threats of violence and the building was burned down by a rival group. Can the insurer be allowed to avoid the terms of the policy?

8. The general agent of an insurer learned that an insured materially lied on an insurance application. The agent collects premiums on the policy, but doesn't report the discrepancy. The company has "knowledge" as imputed by the general agent. Does the insurer have a right to rescission when it accepts the premium and has knowledge of the discrepancy?

9. Sarah has been named in the will of her uncle, as he willed his mansion to "my daughter Joan for life, and then to Sarah in fee simple." The uncle had several operations before he died, and the hospital obtained a $40,000 judgment against him for bills due from his last illness. The savings and loan held a mortgage on the mansion and rented it to an attorney on a two-year lease. Who would suffer a pecuniary (legally recognized) loss if the mansion was damaged or destroyed?

10. Cook purchased a life insurance policy from plaintiff, New York Life Insurance Co., and named as beneficiary defendant Baum, who was an agent of the plaintiff, and had lent Cook money for Cook's business. Some of the money had been lent before Cook purchased insurance from plaintiff, but most of it was lent after the policy went into effect. When New York Life found Baum was Cook's beneficiary, it required Cook to designate another beneficiary because its corporate policy prohibited one of its agents (such as Baum) from being a beneficiary. Cook named a corporation, which was to be created solely for that purpose. The corporation was not completely created. After Cook died, Baum claimed to be the legitimate beneficiary of the policy. New York Life claimed he did not have an insurable interest. Do you agree? *New York Life Insurance Co.* v. *Brown* 700 F. 2d 928 (5th Cir., 1983).

11. Armstrong purchased a fire insurance policy from the Travelers Insurance Co. The policy promised to pay the insured "the actual cash value" if the property being insured, a farmhouse, was totally destroyed by fire. After a fire destroyed Armstrong's farmhouse, Travelers asserted that the "actual cash value" as used in the policy meant the replacement cost of the farmhouse, less depreciation. Armstrong claims that since the policy provides it will indemnify him from loss, the actual cash value means the replacement cost, unaffected by depreciation. Who is correct? *Traveler's Indemnity Co.* v. *Armstrong*, 384 N.E. 2d 607 (Ind. Ct. App. 1979).

12. In August, Mrs. Englert applied for automobile insurance with the American Family Insurance Co. A policy was issued effective August 9. Then, on September 1, Mrs. Englert received notice that due to the poor driving record of her husband, who would be a potential driver of the car being insured, her policy would be cancelled effective September 16. After Mrs. Englert was involved in an accident on September 3, the insurer discovered that Mrs. Englert's application contained misrepresentations regarding her own and her husband's driving record. Has the insurer waived the right to cancel her policy effective August 9, instead of September 16? *American Family Mutual Insurance Co. v. Kimela,* 408 N.E. 2d 805 (Ind. App. 1980).

PART VI

GOVERNMENT REGULATION

CHAPTER 43

Government Regulation of Business and the Role of Administrative Agencies

Part VI of this text deals with the impact of government regulatory agencies on business decision making. It was noted in Chapter 2 that recent court decisions interpreting the commerce clause of the U.S. Constitution have extended federal government influence over business activities affecting interstate commerce. Parallel to this trend in court decisions, Congress has created numerous administrative agencies to regulate business activities. This trend has stimulated the present national debate over whether government regulates business too much or not enough. Those who argue that there is too much regulation say that the President and Congress should get government "off the back" of business and let the laws of supply and demand dictate prices and production. They urge deregulation of business and elimination of some federal and state regulatory agencies. Those who argue in favor of government regulation note that it is the role of Congress, and of the regulatory agencies it has established, to protect the wider public interest. Pointing out that corporations are created to serve only the narrow interests of their stockholders, they argue that without government regulation the public interest would not be served in many instances where business activity impacts upon a community, a state, or the nation as a whole. This debate should be kept in mind while reading the chapters in Part VI.

The present chapter discusses the historical background of government regulation, the reasons for the creation of administrative agencies, and their role in regulating the commerce of this nation. Chapter 44 considers the types of business behavior that administrative agencies and courts have traditionally scrutinized under the antitrust laws. Chapters 45 and 46 examine several agencies that have been at the center of the debate over government regulation: the Federal Trade Commission (FTC), the Equal Employment Opportunity Commission, and the Office of Contract Compliance in the U.S. Department of Labor.

HISTORY OF GOVERNMENT REGULATION

In the eighteenth century the royal governments of Europe regulated and sometimes monopolized all forms of commerce. Their fear of such centralized government and economic regulation led the founders of the United States to espouse private property concepts and a laissez-faire theory of government. Eventually, however, the need to preserve competition and prevent corporate bad conduct made regulation a government interest. The Interstate Commerce Act (1887) was passed in response to farmers' complaints that the railroads were charging discriminatory rates. The Sherman Antitrust Act (1890) was passed in response to the growth of combinations or trusts in oil, whisky, sugar, lead, and beef. Federal regulation grew with the passage of the Clayton Act (1914) and the Federal Trade Commission Act (1914). Despite the

passage of new legislation, the courts generally accepted the arguments of lawyers representing business, resisting many attempts by federal agencies to regulate business activities.

This came to an end in the 1930s when a breakdown of the free enterprise system necessitated vastly increased government intervention in the nation's economic life. The creation of such agencies as the Federal Communications Commission (FCC), the National Labor Relations Board (NLRB), the Civil Aeronautics Board (CAB), and the Securities and Exchange Commission (SEC) initiated unprecedented federal regulation of business. The acceptance by the courts of regulation was based in large part on their interpretation of congressional authority under the Commerce Clause. With the advent of civil rights and worker safety legislation in the 1960s and 1970s, new areas of regulation, along with new administrative agencies, came into being. In the federal government today we have over 150 regulatory agencies that affect all aspects of individual and business activity.[1]

ADMINISTRATIVE AGENCIES

Definition and Nature

As previously noted, every type of business enterprise in the United States falls within the area of concern of one or more administrative agencies. Our political system operates so extensively through administrative agencies that they have been called a "fourth branch of government" and the United States has been described as an "administrative state." Administrative agencies can be defined as governmental bodies, other than the courts and legislatures, that carry out the administrative tasks of government and affect the rights of private parties through adjudication or rule making.[2]

Administrative agencies are found at every

ETHICS BOX
Balancing Competing Interests

———

The Reserve Mining Company operates an iron ore processing plant at Silver Bay, Minnesota. For many years the plant discharged massive amounts of effluent, which contained asbestos, into Lake Superior. Traces of the effluent were found in the drinking water of Duluth, Minnesota.

Reserve was sued by the Department of Justice and several other parties for violating federal and state water quality laws. The trial court found that Reserve had violated those laws and enjoined it from discharging effluent into Lake Superior. The injunction effectively shut down the plant because alternative means of disposal would require time to develop.

On appeal, the injunction was overturned and the court was ordered to fashion a remedy "which will serve the ultimate public weal by insuring clean air, clean water, and continued jobs in an industry vital to the nation's welfare."

The plant employed 3,300 people, and at least one analysis indicated that its contribution to the economy of the region was $422 million over three years. There was uncertainty concerning the effects of the plant's discharge. Protecting the physical well-being of humans is a prime ethical obligation for all businesses. Satisfying this duty requires research into the dangers of products and taking reasonable steps to mitigate against harmful effects. Yet the firm can only do so much. There are physical and financial limits to achieving absolute safety. The key is that a firm should act vigorously, in good faith, to maximize human physical welfare, and disclose potential dangers.

level of government. Often they are called boards, commissions, or agencies; but the terms department, bureau, division, office, or authority also frequently designate an administrative agency. A municipal health board, a county zoning commission, a state public utilities commission, and federal organizations such as the NLRB and the Internal Revenue Service are but a few of the many agencies that directly influence American life.

Administrative agencies differ considerably in size. In general federal agencies are highly structured and staffed with hundreds or thousands of employees; state and local agencies tend to be smaller and more loosely organized. As a result, state and local agencies are more informal, and much important business is carried out behind the scenes by people who are personally acquainted with the problems and the parties or their representatives. People in state and local agencies are also usually acquainted with others in government and can interact with them informally. Frequently they work in the same office building, share other facilities, and have a background of common participation in state and local party politics.

Administrative agencies affect the rights of private parties in many ways. Some, such as parole boards or the Immigration and Naturalization Service of the U.S. Department of Justice, are concerned with matters involving rights as basic as liberty itself. Others, such as state worker's compensation boards, make determinations that involve substantial monetary claims. The Interstate Commerce Commission (ICC) and state public utility commissions fix rates that influence profits in sizable segments of the economy. A principal function of other agencies is to police certain types of activities, such as the sale of liquor, by granting licenses and permits. Many of these same agencies also attempt to protect the public by prohibiting certain actions under threat of fine or suspension of license.

Sometimes an agency has the power to bring criminal actions against those who violate a statute that the agency has been authorized to enforce. The fields in which agencies operate are extensive and their influence in our society is far-reaching.

Reasons for Growth

With the growth of federal legislation noted previously, Congress found it necessary to set up agencies to carry out the details of the statutes enacted. Congress is composed of 435 members of the House of Representatives and 100 senators. Collectively they could not realistically regulate the radio and television industry, for example, on a daily basis. Thus when passing the Federal Communications Act of 1933, they created the FCC. A second reason for creating the agencies was the need for expertise to deal with complex and technical details that demand attention. For example, imagine a new senator or representative attempting to deal with the daily regulation of satellite communications. Members of the FCC staff have the training and experience to perform that task. A third reason Congress created administrative agencies was to keep a large number of complex cases out of the already overcrowded federal courts. To the extent that the ICC can settle disputes over trucking routes, for example, it keeps trucking cases out of court. Fourth, as one legal scholar notes, the desire of Congress to make legislative changes that will not be interpreted or

construed away by conservative courts may be one of "the prime reasons for the growth of the administrative process."[3] For example, when Congress enacted the 1964 and 1965 Civil Rights acts it also created the Equal Employment Opportunity Commission. Congress was changing social policy with these statutes, and it wanted an administrative agency that would implement the legislation as Congress intended.

ADMINISTRATIVE AGENCIES AND CONSTITUTIONAL SEPARATION OF POWERS

Historically our government has been viewed as composed of three independent branches: the executive, the legislative, and the judicial. Each possesses certain powers that enable it to restrain, but not entirely control, the actions of the others. The relationships between administrative agencies and the traditional branches of government influence to a large degree what agencies can accomplish. A working knowledge of these relationships is important to businesspeople, for they can use this knowledge to modify the impact of agency activity.

Before examining the relationships, we need to consider an important difference in the lines of authority between certain agencies and the executive branch. Several of the largest and most influential federal agencies are not part of any department of the executive branch. The ICC, FTC, SEC, and NLRB are examples of *independent agencies* that are very important to the business community. In some states major administrative agencies are independent of the chief executive. Many state constitutions provide for the election of important administrative officers, such as the attorney general and the state treasurer, and deny the governor the right to remove even appointive department heads except for cause.

On the other hand, some well-known federal agencies are parts of *executive departments.* For example, both the Food and Drug Administration and the Social Security Administration are parts of the U.S. Department of Health and Human Services. The Federal Aviation Administration (FAA) is a part of the U.S. Department of Transportation. Most local agencies and a majority of state agencies are also organized within larger executive departments. On a day-to-day basis this does not make much difference because the agencies operate without interference from the other components of the executive branch, but when agencies are organized within the executive branch greater potential for direct control exists. Many major policy decisions within the jurisdictional power of the agencies may be influenced by the chief executive and his staff. (See Table 43-1.)

Executive Branch and Independent Agencies

Although many federal agencies are structurally independent of the executive branch, the President, with the advice and consent of the Senate, does appoint the chief agency officials. Once the appointment is confirmed, however, the President has no direct control over the appointee. He cannot remove the individual from office. In addition, the enabling act that creates a commission generally requires that

the commission itself be politically balanced within practical limits. The Federal Trade Commission Act, for example, provides as follows:

[A] commission is hereby created and established, to be known as The Federal Trade Commission, which shall be composed of five commissioners, who shall be appointed by the President by and with the advice and consent of the Senate. Not more than three of the commissioners shall be members of the same political party.[4]

The terms of commissioners tend to be quite lengthy—seven years is typical—and thus considerable time may elapse before a newly elected President is able to put his personal "stamp" on one of the commissions. In addition, the length of the terms tends to make even a President's own appointees somewhat independent. But in spite of this and of their structural independence from the executive branch, the major regulatory agencies are in reality subject to considerable executive influence. A member of the presidential staff sometimes attempts directly to persuade a commissioner to adopt the President's position. Because the independent regulatory agencies presumably make their decisions without interference from the executive branch, this type of influence is generally viewed with disapproval. More frequently a

TABLE 43-1 ILLUSTRATIVE INDEPENDENT AND EXECUTIVE FEDERAL ADMINISTRATIVE AGENCIES

Independent	Executive
Interstate Commerce Commission (ICC)	Small Business Administration (SBA)
Federal Trade Commission (FTC)	Occupational Safety and Health Administration (OSHA)
Securities and Exchange Commission (SEC)	National Science Foundation (NSA)
National Labor Relations Board (NLRB)	Office of Personnel Management (OPM)
Commodities Futures Trading Commission (CFTC)	Federal Aviation Administration (FAA)
Federal Reserve Board (FRB)	Department of Transportation (DOT)

presidential memorandum or the report of a presidential task force studying the matter also being investigated by a commission may be released to the public in a manner designed to sway the commission. Finally, executive influence may be asserted through the budgetary process. Agency requests for funds go through the Office of Management and Budget (OMB) and so are subject to executive surveillance . . . Executive orders 12291 and 12498 issued in 1980 and 1985 require all agencies located in the executive branch to provide a yearly agenda to OMB of all proposed rule making. A cost-benefit analysis for all proposed rules must be included when published in the *Federal Register.*

Judicial Review and Administrative Agencies

Although the scope of judicial review of particular administrative agency decisions is limited, most state and federal administrative agency decisions are subject to review by the courts. The logic underlying the limitations on judicial review is that the agency, rather than the court, is the expert in those fields in which it has been empowered to act. Clearly the courts can reverse any action taken by an agency that is outside the scope of the agency's jurisdiction.

As will be discussed later, administrative agencies may perform two separate functions: (1) to issue rules and regulations and (2) to adjudicate cases. The criteria used by the courts in reviewing the actions of an agency may vary according to the functions involved. When an agency acts in a *legislative manner* the courts will review the agency action to make sure that:

1. The congressional delegation of legislative authority to the agency is constitutional in that Congress sufficiently limited the area within which the agency can act

2. The action of the agency was within the powers granted it by Congress
3. The agency action did not violate another constitutional limitation or disregard a prohibitory provision of an applicable federal statute

When an administrative agency acts in an *adjudicative context,* the courts review its procedures to ensure that

1. They are constitutionally valid
2. The agency had proper jurisdiction
3. The statutory rules controlling procedures have been observed

The courts may also review the agency's interpretation of substantive law in its adjudication, but they exercise substantial restraint in this area and their powers are limited.

Generally courts have accepted agency determinations of fact as final, provided that substantial evidence supporting the findings is shown by the record. Substantial evidence has been described as "the kind of evidence on which responsible persons are accustomed to rely in serious affairs"[5] and as "more than a mere scintilla. It means such relevant evidence as a reasonable mind might accept to support a conclusion."[6] Courts also have refused to consider suits brought by those who question the wisdom of the agency's discretionary decisions. If an administrative agency decides to apply a greater portion of its resources, such as funds and personnel, to a particular segment of the industry over which it has jurisdiction than it has previously done, an individual adversely affected by this new policy is not entitled to judicial review. Businesspeople should object, however, to those discretionary agency decisions that appear to be clearly arbitrary or capricious, for courts will not allow these to stand even though the agency is the expert.

In spite of its limitations, judicial review of administrative agency actions is important to the business community. It provides a safeguard against administrative excesses and the unfair or arbitrary actions of overzealous officials. A court will be most likely to set aside an agency ruling when the agency has erred in the interpretation of a statute, has acted outside the scope of its authority, or appears to have denied due process by unfair agency procedures. The following case illustrates the significance of judicial review for the business community. It reveals how an overzealous administrative agency can sometimes act outside the scope of its authority and endanger a total industry's control over a service it provides.

Federal Communications Commission v. Midwest Video Corporation

United States Supreme Court
440 U.S. 689 (1979)

Background: Midwest Video Corporation (respondent) petitioned the Court of Appeals to review certain rules promulgated by the Federal Communications Commission (FCC) (appellant) affecting the development of access channels of cable television operations through the country. The FCC promulgated rules requiring cable television systems that had 3,500 or more subscribers and carried broadcast signals to develop, at a minimum, a twenty-channel capacity by 1986, to make available certain channels for access by public, educational, local governmental, and leased-access users, and to furnish equipment and facilities for access purposes. Under the rules, cable operators were deprived of all discretion regarding who might exploit their access channels and what might be transmitted over such channels. During the rule-making proceedings the FCC rejected a challenge to the rules on jurisdictional grounds, maintaining that the rules would promote "the achievement of long-standing communications regulatory objectives by increasing outlets for local self-expression and augmenting the public's choice of program." On petition for review, the Court of Appeals set aside the FCC's rules as beyond the agency's jurisdiction. The court was of the view that the rules amounted to an attempt to impose common-carrier obligations on cable operators and thus ran counter to the command of Section 3(h) of the Communications Act of 1934 that "a person engaged in . . . broadcasting shall not . . . be deemed a common carrier." The FCC was granted a petition for review.
Decision: Affirmed. The United States Supreme Court ruled in favor of Midwest Video.

White, Justice

The Commission derives its regulatory authority from the Communications Act of 1934. The Act preceded the advent of cable television and understandably does not expressly provide for the regulation of that medium. But it is clear that Congress meant to confer "broad authority" on the Commission, so as "to maintain, through appropriate administrative control, a grip on the dynamic aspects of radio transmission." To that end, Congress subjected to regulation "all interstate and foreign communication by wire or radio." Communications Act of 1934, §2(a), 47 U.S.C. §152(a). In *United States* v. *Southwestern Cable Co.,* we construed §2(a) as conferring on the Commission a circumscribed range of power to regulate cable television, and we reaffirmed that determination in *United States* v. *Midwest Video Corp.* The question now before us is whether the Act, as construed in these two cases, authorizes the capacity and access regulations that are here under challenge. [The Court then reviewed *U.S.* v. *Southwestern Cable* and *U.S.* v. *Midwest Video.* The *Midwest Video* case was ruled on in 1972 and should not be confused with the present case involving the same corporation.]

Because its access and capacity rules promote the long-established regulatory goals of maximization of outlets for local expression and diversification of programming—the objectives promoted by the rule sustained in *Midwest Video*—the Commission maintains that it plainly had jurisdiction to promulgate them. Respondents, in opposition, view the access regulations as an intrusion on cable system operations that is qualitatively different from the impact of the rule upheld in *Midwest Video.* Specifically, it is urged that by requiring the allocation of access channels to categories of users specified by the regulations and by depriving the cable operator of the power to select individual users or to control the programming on such channels, the regulations wrest a considerable degree of editorial control from the cable operator and in effect compel the cable system to provide a kind of common-carrier service. Respondents contend, therefore, that the regulations are not only qualitatively different from those heretofore approved by the courts but also contravene statutory limitations designed to safeguard the journalistic freedom of broadcasters, particularly the command of §3(h) of the Act that "a person engaged in . . . broadcasting shall not . . . be deemed a common carrier."

We agree with respondents that recognition of agency jurisdiction to promulgate the access rules would require an extension of this Court's prior decisions. Our holding in Midwest Video sustained the Commission's authority to regulate cable television with a purpose affirmatively to promote goals pursued in the regulation of television broadcasting; and the plurality's analysis of the origination requirement stressed the requirement's nexus to such goals. But the origination rule did not abrogate the cable operators' control over the composition of their programming, as do the access rules. It compelled operators only to assume a more positive role in that regard, one comparable to that fulfilled by television broadcasters. Cable operators had become enmeshed in the field of television broadcasting, and, by requiring them to engage in the functional equivalent of broadcasting, the Commission had sought "only to ensure that [they] satisfactorily [met] community needs within the context of their undertaking."

With its access rule, however, the Commission has transferred control of the content of access cable channels from cable operators to members of the public who wish to communicate by the cable medium. Effectively, the Commission has relegated cable systems, pro tanto, to common-carrier status. The Commission is directed explicitly by §3(h) of the Act not to treat persons engaged in broadcasting as common carriers. In determining, then, whether the Commission's assertion of jurisdiction is "reasonably ancillary to the effective performance of [its] responsibilities for the regulation of television broadcasting," we are unable to ignore Congress' stern disapproval—evidenced in §3(h)—of negation of the editorial discretion otherwise enjoyed by broadcasters and cable operators alike. Though the lack of congressional guidance has in the past led us to defer—albeit cautiously—to the Commission's judgment regarding the scope of its authority, here there are strong indications that agency flexibility was to be sharply delimited.

In light of the hesitancy with which Congress approached the access issue in the broadcast area, and in view of its outright rejection of a broad right of public access on a common-carrier basis, we are constrained to hold that the Commission exceeded those limits in promulgating its access rules. The Commission may not regulate cable systems as common carriers, just as it may not impose such obligations on television broadcasters. We think authority to compel cable operators to provide common carriage of public-originated transmissions must come specifically from Congress.

Legislatures and Administrative Agencies

Agencies acquire their authority to act from the legislature. For a legislative grant of authority to be constitutional, it must set standards to guide the agency's actions because the legislature is either delegating some of its power to a nonelected body or authorizing it to perform a judicial function. The legislation creating an agency is called an enabling act. Since the 1930s very few respondents have successfully challenged the action of either state or federal agencies on the constitutional grounds that the act creating the agency did not include sufficient standards. Most modern enabling acts that allow an agency considerable discretion to act have been approved by the courts. Thus very broad and general standards may be constitutional. The Federal Trade Commission Act authorized the FTC to commence an action in a deceptive practice or false advertising case "if it shall appear to the Commission that a proceeding . . . would be in the interest of the public." The only standard is the Commission's own belief that an action is in the public interest.

Administrative agencies that have been created by the legislature can also be terminated by the legislature; however, the threat of termination has not been taken seriously in the past. Most legislative influence on agencies is the result of the agencies' dependence on the legislature for financial support. For example, much of the early history of the FTC was dominated by congressional refusal to finance the agency adequately. This was especially true in the early 1920s when the Commission planned an aggressive attack against the structure of American industry. Adverse congressional reaction to the Commission's investigation of the meat-packing industry led to a reduction in funds for the agency. Agency personnel had to be discharged, and Congress transferred jurisdiction over meat-packing to the U.S. Department of Agriculture. In addition, the agency was denied appropriations for other investigations that it had planned.[7] More recently, after receiving harsh criticism in the late 1960s and early 1970s for being a "do nothing" agency, the FTC became active on behalf of consumers in such areas as deceptive advertising and antitrust. By 1980 the FTC, with its aggressive investigations and rule making, had alienated a large number of businesses, which then lobbied Congress for a cutback in the authority of the agency as well as in its level of funding. In response to this lobbying effort Congress enacted the FTC Improvement Act of 1980.[8] The Act provided for some clear restraints on FTC operations and much closer scrutiny by Congress through the House and Senate commerce committees, which are responsible for overseeing the agency. For example, one provision forced the FTC to reconsider any order previously issued upon the request of the corporation or person involved if it can be shown that changed conditions of law or fact require an altering, modifying, or setting aside of the order. Additionally, the Act subjected any new FTC rule to a veto by a concurrent resolution of the House and Senate.[9] The FTC was required to submit advance notice of rule making to the oversight committees in both the House and Senate thirty days prior to publishing the rule in the *Federal Register*. In its notice the FTC had to provide an explanation of the need for the new rule and its potential benefits and adverse effects. The Commission was barred from using any funds to issue or propose a regulation affecting the funeral industry similar to ones it had previously drafted. The 1980 Act forbade the use of funds for initiating or conducting an investigation of the insurance industry. It also put a three-year moratorium on existing FTC authority to promulgate rules for unfair commercial advertising. When one reviews the 1980 Act it is clear that Congress intended the FTC to be a less activist agency. It also explains why all administrative agencies tend to be solicitous of congressmen's views before launching investigations or proposing new rules.

WORK OF ADMINISTRATIVE AGENCIES

Administrative agencies do much of the day-to-day work of government. As a consequence, they make many significant policy decisions. Businesspeople who fail to recognize this will lose an opportunity to influence governmental changes that might benefit them and society. Some businesspeople find that the record-keeping requirements of the various agencies that directly affect their business operations add significantly to costs and even adversely affect their competitive positions. Nevertheless, regulatory agencies perform many needed services and assist businesspeople by working to control potentially harmful market conditions.

The work done by a single administrative agency may encompass a broad range of activities. In addition, the general nature and scope of operations often vary significantly from agency to agency. Thus a broad generalization regarding the work of administrative agencies is almost impossible. Some agencies, such as draft boards, were created to accomplish very limited objectives; others have very extensive assignments. The FTC, for example, (see Figure 43-1), has a primary responsibility for enforcing the antitrust provisions of the Clayton Act and the unfair business practices sections of the Federal Trade Commission Act. The Commission also has responsibility for carrying out all or some of the provisions of several other federal statutes.[10] An additional complication exists because agencies operate at all levels of government. As a result, they focus on problems and needs that are very different. In fact arms of government sometimes appear to be working in opposition to each other. For example, at a time when the FCC was attempting to limit the sale of cigarettes by restricting television advertising, the U.S. Department of Agriculture continued to encourage the production of tobacco by paying price-supporting subsidies to tobacco growers.

The powers of those agencies that have the greatest impact on the business community are broad. Those agencies, which include the ICC, FTC, SEC, NLRB, and FCC, generally have the authority to make rules that have the force of law. Many agencies also function like courts. They settle disputes and hear and decide on violations of statutes or of their own rules. Finally, much of the work of agencies is administrative in nature. This covers a wide variety of duties: investigating firms in the regulated industry, determining if formal action should be brought, and negotiating settlements. A substantial number of agencies have

FIGURE 43–1
The Federal Trade Commission

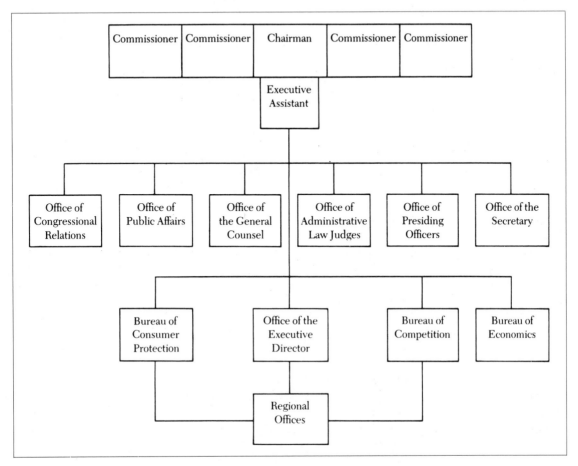

Source: U.S. Government Manual, 1984–1985 (Washington, DC: U.S. Government Printing Office).

administrative responsibilities but do not have adjudicatory or rule-making powers.

Adjudication

Probably the best-known function of administrative agencies is judicial in nature. In many instances both state and federal agencies find facts and apply rules and regulations to these facts just as a court would. In carrying out this adjudicatory function, the federal agencies generally employ procedures similar to those used by the courts. This is probably due to the influence of the large number of legally trained people who are involved in some way with agency adjudication. In addition, the Administrative Procedure Act requires almost all federal agencies to meet certain standards in their procedures. As a result of these factors, generally there is considerable similarity in the enforcement procedures of federal agencies, and state agencies frequently follow similar patterns. Thus we can examine the procedures of an agency such as the FTC and obtain an idea how the adjudicatory function is performed in agencies in general.

In adjudication proceedings the FTC, like most administrative agencies, follows a procedure of "investigation-complaint-hearing-order." However, because of limited resources, the Commission makes a determined effort to prevent disputes from reaching the hearing stage; as a result, more than 90 percent of the investigations of violations do not result in hearings.

Many cases are administratively "closed" by the Commission because investigation fails to turn up sufficient evidence to substantiate a violation or because the public interest does not warrant the lengthy and costly investigation needed to develop the facts necessary to establish a prima facie case. In a substantial number of cases where evidence of a violation does exist, the Commission is able to dispose of the case before a hearing by a consent order procedure.

Both the Commission and the respondent (corporation, partnership, or individual) benefit from the consent order procedure. The Commission obtains a binding cease-and-desist order with minimal cost and without having to worry about appeal. Respondents benefit because the agreement is for settlement purposes only and does not constitute an admission of guilt. As a result, the order cannot be used in a triple-damage action brought against them, and they avoid the cost of litigation and the possible public disclosures that would stem from a formal hearing.[11]

If settlement attempts are unsuccessful, an initial hearing is conducted by an administrative law judge.[12] The procedures used are similar to those used by the federal courts, although the rules of evidence are relaxed. The parties have the rights of due notice, cross-examination, presentation of evidence, objections, motions, argument, and any other right essential to a fair trial. This does not include, however, the right to a jury, and factual questions as well as legal issues are resolved by the administrative law judge. In most instances the respondent will be represented by an attorney who ordinarily will be a specialist in the law related to the particular agency.

Within ninety days after the completion of the hearing, the administrative law judge files an initial decision, which becomes the decision of the Commission unless appealed. Any party to the proceeding, but not everyone who might be interested, may appeal the administrative law judge's decision to the Commission; or the Commission may review the decision of its administrative law judge upon its own motion. In the event of appeal or review, briefs are generally submitted by the parties and oral arguments are heard unless the Commission feels they are not necessary. In rendering its decision, the Commission has broad power to modify the administrative law judge's decision, including his or her findings of fact.

As stated earlier in this chapter, limited judicial review of the Commission's order to cease and desist is permitted in the Court of Appeals. The facts as found by the Commission are conclusive if supported by evidence. Most appeals are taken on questions of law, although the Administrative Procedure Act allows review of agency decisions that are arbitrary, capricious, or an abuse of the agency's discretion, as well as those decisions or procedures that violate the Constitution or exceed the agency's statutory authority.[13] A final review may be requested of the Supreme Court, but the Supreme Court does not have to consider the case.

The case that follows is an example of a typical adjudication proceeding within an administrative agency. This is an SEC proceeding, although we have described procedures in the FTC. There is no dearth of FTC cases. The SEC case was selected to indicate the similarity between the adjudication machinery in these two agencies.

In the Matter of Paine, Webber, Jackson & Curtis

The Federal Securities and Exchange Commission

Securities Exchange Act Release No. 8500. January 22, 1969

Background: A charge was filed with the SEC (Securities and Exchange Commission) against Ralph M. Klopp (defendant) a salesman for Paine, Webber, Jackson & Curtis, claiming that he had induced excessive trading by customers by using false representations concerning the trading activities of another customer. In addition, his employer and William P. Cowden, a former office manager, were charged with failure to supervise Klopp reasonably.

Following hearings, a hearing examiner for the SEC filed an initial decision, in which he concluded that Klopp should be suspended from association with any brokers or dealers for a period of four months but that proceedings against Paine, Webber, Jackson, & Curtis and William P. Cowden should be dismissed.

Klopp petitioned for review of the examiner's decision and the Commission ordered a reconsideration of all issues. Briefs were filed by both the respondents and the Commission's Division of Trading and Marketing before the full Commission.

Decision: Affirmed. The SEC ruled in favor of the Commission's Division of Trading and Marketing with some modification.

By the Commission (Chairman Cohen, Commissioners Owens, Budge, and Smith. Commissioner Wheat, not participating.)

The examiner found that during the period from about May, 1962 through October, 1963, Klopp made certain false representations to two of his customers, J. and R. Those customers, who were close friends, opened accounts with Klopp in the spring of 1961 and effected a number of transactions through him during the ensuing year, relying largely on the recommendations of an investment service to which they had subscribed at his suggestion. The examiner found that in May and June, 1962, Klopp told those customers that another customer had made substantial trading profits and that he would inform them of the trading by that customer so that they could duplicate his transactions. The examiner further found that as a result of the customers' reliance on false information concerning such trading given them by Klopp, Klopp in effect obtained discretionary power over their accounts and induced them to engage in excessive trading.

The two customers testified as follows: On May 29, 1962, while R. was at registrant's office, Klopp told him that one of his customers had a "huge" account, used the services of an investment adviser and had made large profits by selling his portfolio and selling additional stock short just before a sharp market drop on the preceding day and covering the short sales and purchasing stock just prior to the market rally on May 29. R. told J. of this conversation and Klopp himself made essentially the same representations to J. He also advised both customers that the other customer was a doctor, although he did not identify him by name; and used the services of a "Chinese chartist." When Klopp and J., in June, 1962, reviewed the latter's portfolio, consisting mostly of low priced over-the-counter securities which had depreciated, Klopp stated that he would inform J. about the doctor's transactions after they were executed. In July, 1962, Klopp informed J. that the doctor had just sold stock of Cinerama, Inc. short, and J. instructed Klopp to effect a short sale of stock for his account. This was followed by a series of further transactions, extending to September, 1963, which were effected by J. on the basis of Klopp's statements regarding transactions by the doctor. R.'s first transaction, based on a transaction reported to have been effected by the doctor, took place in August, 1962. In about November, 1962, R., based on Klopp's statement that it "might be a good idea to follow the doctor," sold many of the securities in his portfolio in order to obtain additional funds to follow the doctor's transactions. He continued to follow those transactions until October, 1963, when he ceased dealing with Klopp.

Klopp denied making any representations concerning the nature of, and transactions in, another account, and testified that, far from inducing J. and R. to increase their trading activity, he advised them to reduce such activity and instead to buy and hold high quality stocks, but that they disregarded his advice.

CREDIBILITY ISSUE

The examiner, in resolving the credibility issue against Klopp, noted that the probative effect of the testimony of J. and R. was weakened by a lack of specificity and consistency and some contradictory evidence in the record, but concluded that "in sum their testimony on salient aspects of the issues involved remains credible and must be accepted." His conclusion, in this respect, is entitled to considerable weight and is supported by various facts shown by the record which provide strong corroboration for the customers' testimony.

There is a significant correlation between certain of the information which they testified was given to them and the actual activity in the account of a Dr. R., which was also serviced by Klopp and was a large and active one. The record shows that Dr. R. effected a substantial number of sales and short sales shortly prior to May 28, 1962, and the day before Klopp told J. that the "doctor" had sold Cinerama stock short, Dr. R. had effected a short sale of that stock. In addition, in October, 1962, the last month in which there was substantial activity in Dr. R.'s account, J. had eight transactions in stock of International Business Machines, Inc. ("IBM") which were identical in nature and date with transactions effected by Dr. R. These circumstances suggest that Klopp's representations had their genesis in Dr. R.'s account. Klopp testified, however, that as far as he knew Dr. R. did not have an investment adviser or a chartist. Further corroboration of the customers' testimony is provided by the fact that in November, 1962, J. had four transactions and R. three transactions in IBM stock which were identical as to nature and date with transactions in the account of Klopp's wife.

EXAMINER'S CONCLUSION ACCEPTED

We accordingly accept the examiner's conclusion on the credibility issue and concur with his findings as to the misrepresentations made by Klopp. We also agree with his finding that Klopp induced excessive trading in the accounts of the two customers.

In view of the foregoing, we find, as did the examiner, that Klopp willfully violated Section 10(b) of the Act and Rule 10b–5 thereunder, and Section 17(a) of the Securities Act of 1933.

PUBLIC INTEREST

We cannot agree with the conclusion of the examiner that, despite the serious nature of Klopp's violations, a four-month suspension is appropriate in the public interest. We conclude that notwithstanding the mitigating factors noted by the examiner, including Klopp's previously good record and his public service in civilian life and with the armed forces, his misconduct was such as to require in the public interest that a more substantial sanction be imposed. In our opinion, it is appropriate that he be barred from association with any broker or dealer, with the proviso that such bar shall not preclude his association, after a period of one year, with a broker or dealer in a nonsupervisory capacity upon a showing that he will be adequately supervised. . . .

An appropriate order will issue.

Rule Making

When a pronouncement affecting the rights and duties of a number of people is made by an agency, the agency acts in the same manner as a legislature. The power to make rules and regulations of this kind, which may be as binding as laws passed by legislative bodies, has been delegated to the agency by the legislature. The only important difference between an agency rule and a "law" enacted by a legislative body is that the former may be slightly more susceptible to attack in the courts because the rule was not made by elected officials. Let us consider examples of the rule-making authority that some administrative agencies possess.

There are two major types of rule making

carried on by administrative agencies: (1) formal and (2) informal. (See Table 43-2.)

Formal Rule Making. Section 553(c) of the Administrative Procedure Act (APA) requires formal rule making when an enabling statute or other legislation requires that all regulations or rules be enacted by an agency as part of a formal hearing process that includes a complete transcript. This procedure provides for (1) a notice of proposed rule making to the public by the agency in the *Federal Register;* (2) a public hearing at which witnesses give testimony on the pros and cons of the proposed rule, cross-examination of each witness takes place, and formal rules of evidence are applied; (3) formal findings are made and pub-

TABLE 43-2 FORMAL AND INFORMAL RULE
MAKING

Formal	Informal
1. Notice of proposed rule in *Federal Register*	1. Notice of proposed rule in *Federal Register*
2. Public hearing, at which there are witnesses, cross-examination of witnesses, and formal rules of evidence	2. All interested parties may submit written comments
3. Formal findings are made and published with final rule in the *Federal Register*	3. Publication of final rule with statement of its basis and purpose in *Federal Register*

lished by the agency; and (4) based on these findings, an agency may or may not promulgate a regulation. Because of the expense and time involved in obtaining a formal transcript and record, most enabling statutes do not require a formal rule-making procedure when promulgating regulations.

Informal Rule Making It is provided in Section 553 of the APA and applies in all situations where the agency's enabling legislation or other congressional directives do not require another form. The APA requires that the agency (1) give prior notice of the proposed rule by publishing it in the *Federal Register;* (2) provide an opportunity for all interested parties to submit written comments; and (3) publish the final rule, with a statement of its basis and purpose, in the *Federal Register.* This type of rule making is most often used because it is more efficient in terms of time and cost to the agency. No formal public hearing is required and no formal record need be established as in formal rule making. Parties opposing a particular rule arrived at after informal rule making often seek to persuade the courts to enjoin an agency from enforcing the rule or regulation by showing that provisions of the APA were violated by the agency in the process. The case excerpted here illustrates such an attempt.

Dow Chemical, USA v. Consumer Product Safety Commission

U.S. District Court
459 Fed.Supp. 378 (1978)

Background: Following an informal rule-making exercise, the Consumer Product Safety Commission (defendant) issued regulations classifying certain substances in consumer products that were suspected of causing cancer. The regulations were published in the *Federal Register* under the heading "Interim Policy and Procedures for Classifying, Evaluating and Regulating Carcinogens in Consumer Products." Dow Chemical (plaintiff) and fifty-eight other chemical companies sought to enjoin the agency from enforcing the regulation by seeking a preliminary injunction.
Decision: The Federal District Court granted the preliminary injunction.

Veron, Justice

The court preliminarily finds that the Consumer Product Safety Commission (CPSC), in promulgating the interim regulations without prior notice and an opportunity for public comment, violated the Administrative Procedure Act (APA). In essence, the

CPSC has placed the proverbial cart before the horse. Specifically, the APA requires an agency engaged in "informal rulemaking" to provide notice of proposed rules in the *Federal Register* and to solicit comments from interested parties.

However, "statements of policy" are specifically exempt from the notice and comment procedures. The CPSC relies on this exemption to justify its failure to comply with the APA's procedural requirements.

The APA mandates quite clearly that, in reviewing agency action, a court "shall hold unlawful and set aside agency action . . . found to be without observance of procedure required by law." Numerous cases have held that an administrative rule which is not issued in accordance with the prior notice and opportunity for public comment procedures of Section 553 of the APA is void.

Informal rulemaking has been heralded as one of the most successful innovations of administrative law. It is a truly democratic procedure and provides the agency with channels of information. It is fair to all parties and produces a record by which the courts and Congress can efficiently supervise agency action.

Solicitation of comments is the basis of informal rulemaking, because it is the means by which the public participates in the rulemaking process. It is also an efficient channel through which experts in the field and those affected by the proposed rules can provide information which may have been overlooked by the agency. Additionally, it can point out the abstruse effects of the proposed rules, and can suggest alternatives. The solicitation of comments serves another important function. Judicial review of informal rulemaking must be based on the record kept by the agency of its rulemaking procedure. One of the essential elements of that record is the comments solicited from interested parties.

When the fourth branch of the government ignores the Congressional dictates of the APA it opens itself to harsh criticism. While this reprobation surely is not always valid or justified, it is clear that the independent regulatory commissions sometimes have or are perceived to have "failed to discharge their respective mandates to protect the interests of the public in given fields of administration."

The CPSC does not profess to have complied with the notice and comment requirements here. The Commission states in the preamble to these interim regulations that it considers the regulations to be "a general statement of policy, . . . exempt from the notice, public procedure and delayed effective date provisions of the Administrative Procedure Act." This court in determining whether the CPSC complied with the procedural requirements of the APA is not bound by the delineation the Commission has attached to its action. Rather, the court has the responsibility to examine the substance of what has been done affording appropriate respect for the agency's characterization.

The Administrative Procedure Act defines a "rule" to mean:

> the whole or a part of an agency statement of general or particular applicability and future effect designed to implement, interpret, or prescribe law or policy . . . and includes the approval or prescription for the future of . . . valuations, costs, or accounting, or practices bearing on any of the foregoing. . . . The APA does not define the term "general statements of policy."

The court, in resolving whether these regulations are statements of policy or rules, will not abandon common sense and equitable principles, but rather will recollect the basic purpose of the statutorily imposed requirements of notice and comment. The APA's rulemaking procedures "were designed to assure fairness and mature consideration of rules of general application."

Additionally, this court, in determining the legal issue presented herein, is guided by a substantial body of jurisprudence which announces several general principles to be utilized in distinguishing a policy statement from a rule:

1. Is the announcement subject to change prior to its implementation?
2. Does the announcement focus the agency's attention on a fixed set of criteria that might have been formulated differently if there had been an opportunity for public comment?
3. Will the inquiry in subsequent rulemakings be whether the facts fit the alleged policy or will the policy itself be subject to challenge in such proceedings?
4. Does the announcement have a substantial impact on regulated parties so as to make the process of public comment an important requirement?

We find that the June 13, 1978 regulations are not subject to change prior to their implementation. Although these announcements are ostensibly labeled in the defense brief as "temporary policy and procedure," there is language employed in the *Federal Register* announcement itself which dispositively indicates that these regulations are made effective immediately upon publication and will be followed in subsequent proceedings. The "Summary" paragraph of the preamble to these interim regulations states that "the purpose of this document is to *establish* on an interim basis" the Commission's policy for the regulation of carcinogens in consumer products. This same paragraph further states that the CPSC action establishes "(1) [t]he standards CPSC *will apply* in classifying substances suspected of causing cancer, and evaluating products containing such substances, and (2) the regulatory *action likely to be taken* by the CPSC following classification and evaluation." The *Federal Register* notice also indicates how regulatory action will be taken as to particular products or classes of products in the future. Such determinations "will continue to be made in individual proceedings, in accordance with the applicable statutory provisions and *the terms of this policy statement.*"

The Commission's action will additionally have an immediate adverse impact on plaintiffs. Experience and common sense indicate that the implementation of this interim policy in proceedings involving individual consumer products will result in substantial loss of business for the plaintiffs as verified by the numerous affidavits filed herein.

Finally in evaluating whether an agency's action has a substantial impact, and is thus subject to the rulemaking provisions of the APA, an appropriate consideration is "whether there is such genuine ground for difference of opinion on the wisdom of the policy embodied in the rule as to make the hearing process a meaningful and important requirement." In the scientific community there presently exists a vigorous debate as to the classification of carcinogens, risk evaluation and the appropriate regulatory response.

The court, without communicating any opinion on the merits of the relative scientific positions, confidently concludes that these examples demonstrate that the interim rules should have been announced only after the informed reflection and genuine dialogue contemplated by the APA.

Administrative Activities

The acts of administrative agencies of most interest from the legal standpoint are those that involve rule making or adjudication. Agencies, however, act in many ways that are neither judicial nor legislative in nature. They carry out a myriad of statutory directives and have countless functions that defy classification. Many of these acts are purely administrative, although they may involve the rights and duties of many citizens, thousands of transactions, and millions of dollars. In many cases these acts are informal in nature and are usually not reviewed by a court.

Even when the possibility of judicial review of intra-agency actions exists, the person affected often does not, for many reasons, believe that review is practical, and the agency's action is accepted without formal protest.

Many examples of administrative acts of this nature can readily be cited. Agencies are often responsible for the allocation of funds and the granting of licenses; they make tests, manage government property, and supervise inmates in institutions. Different agencies carry out tasks as varied as clearing vessels to leave port and classifying grain. Agencies grant patents, collect taxes, and oversee educational institutions. Agencies frequently conduct investigations. Sometimes this is done at the request of the executive or the legislature, but many agencies have the power to initiate their own investigations. Some agencies are responsible for the business of law enforcement and prosecution. The principal function of others is to plan or to approve or disapprove the plans of others. Most of the countless jobs that are necessary in the administration of government are done by people in administrative agencies.

Many of these administrative acts are politically, economically, and socially significant and clearly relate to important issues of public policy. The SEC decision in the late 1960s to investigate the selling of mutual funds was an administrative act of this type. As a result of this investigation, the Commission proposed sweeping legislation curtailing certain practices in the industry. When the FTC decided in 1972 to bring a legal action against the major sellers of ready-to-eat cereals, alleging that they were involved in an illegal "shared monopoly," the decision to file suit, although administrative in nature, had a potentially substantial impact on many other areas of the economy. This suit was dropped by the Commission in 1981, ostensibly for failure to find anticompetitive conduct. Many believe it was a political decision made by appointees of a new administration that favored less regulation.

In carrying out its administrative activities the agency involved employs many people who have frequent informal contacts with businesses and individuals whom they are supposed to regulate. These informal agency activities do not fall within the rule-making and adjudicative models for decision making discussed in this chapter. They often involve *ex parte* (with only one side present) communications between agency decision makers or representatives of decision makers when only one interested party is present. Some would do away with all *ex parte* communication, claiming they bias decisions in favor of one party over the other. The Administrative Conference, which sets forth procedural rules for administrative agencies, disagrees, noting that flexibility is needed to help rule-making procedures and *ex parte* contacts are needed by the agencies. It does, however, believe that such contacts should be banned when agencies are involved in adjudication of a specific dispute. One court's approach to this question is shown here.

Home Box Office Inc. v. Federal Communications Commission

U.S. Court of Appeals

567 F.2d 9 (D.C. Cir. 1977)

Background: In March 1975 the Federal Communications Commission (defendant-respondent) adopted amendments to its rules governing the programs that could be shown by paid television services. If contemporary films on sports could be shown over these services, the networks were afraid they would be at a disadvantage, and viewers who could not afford the cost of paid television would be injured. The informal rule-making process resulted in neither the paid television carriers nor the commercial networks being satisfied. There were many *ex parte* contacts in the informal rule-making process, all of which formed one of the bases for parties on both sides to appeal.

Decision: The U.S. Court of Appeals remanded the case to the FCC with instructions that it appoint a hearing examiner to determine the nature and source of all *ex parte* approaches to the Commission and its employees during the informal rule-making process.

Per Curiam

. . . In an attempt to clarify the facts this court ordered the Commission to provide "a list of all of the *ex parte* presentations, together with the details of each, made to it, or to any of its members or representatives, during the rulemaking proceedings." In response to this order the Commission filed a document over 60 pages long which revealed, albeit imprecisely, widespread *ex parte* communications involving virtually every party before this court. It is apparently uncontested that a number of participants before the Commission sought out individual commissioners or Commission employees for the purpose of discussing *ex parte* and in confidence the merits of the rules under review here. In fact, the Commission itself solicited such communications in its notices of proposed rulemaking.

Unfortunately, the document filed with this court does not allow an assessment of what was said to the Commission by the various persons who engaged in *ex parte* contacts. To give a flavor of the effect of these contacts, however, we think it useful to quote at length from the brief of *amicus* Geller:

> [*Ex parte*] presentations have in fact been made at crucial stages of the proceeding. Thus, in early 1974, then-Chairman Burch sought to complete action in this proceeding. Because the Commission was "leaning" in its deliberations towards relaxing the existing rules "with 'wildcard' rights for 'blockbuster' movies," American Broadcasting Company's representatives contacted "key members of Congress," who in turn successfully pressured

the Commission not to take such action. Further, in the final crucial decisional period, the tentative course to be taken by the Commission would leak after each non-public meeting, and industry representatives would rush to make *ex parte* presentations to the Commissioners and staff. On March 10, 1975, the trade journals state that "word of last week's changes . . . got out during the week, and both broadcast and cable lobbyists rushed to the Commission, unhappy with some facets"—that broadcast representatives ". . . were calling on commissioners on Friday . . ." to oppose the changes. The following week the trade press again reported that "various [industry] groups lobbied the Commission, pressing for changes in the tentative decision"—that National Association of Broadcasters ". . . staff members met with [FCC] Broadcast Bureau staffers to present data backing up [an] asserted need for [a more restrictive] standard.

It is important to note that many contacts occurred in the crucial period between the close of oral argument on October 25, 1974 and the adoption of the *First Report and Order* on March 20, 1975, when the rulemaking record should have been closed while the Commission was deciding what rules to promulgate. The information submitted to this court by the Commission indicates that during this period broadcast interests met some 18 times with Commission personnel, cable interests some nine times, motion picture and sports interests five times each, and "public interest" intervenors not at all.

[T]he possibility that there is here one administrative record for the public and this court and another for the Commission and those "in the know" is intolerable.

As a practical matter, . . . the public record must reflect what representations were made to an agency so that relevant information supporting or refuting those representations may be brought to the attention of the reviewing courts by persons participating in agency proceedings. This course is obviously foreclosed if communications are made to the agency in secret and the agency itself does not disclose the information presented. Moreover, where, as here, an agency justifies its actions by reference only to information in the public file while failing to disclose the substance of other relevant information that has been presented to it, a reviewing court cannot presume that the agency has acted properly, . . . but must treat the agency's justifications as a fictional account of the actual decisionmaking process and must perforce find its actions arbitrary.

The failure of the public record in this proceeding to disclose all the information made available to the Commission is not the only inadequacy we find here. Even if the Commission had disclosed to this court the substance of what was said to it *ex parte*, it would still be difficult to judge the truth of what the Commission asserted it knew about the television industry because we would not have the benefit of an adversaries discussion among the parties. The importance of such discussion to the proper functioning of the agency decisionmaking and judicial review processes is evident in our cases. We have insisted, for example, that information in agency files or consultants' reports which the agency has identified as relevant to the proceeding be disclosed to the parties for adversaries comment. Similarly, we have required agencies to set out their thinking in notices of proposed rulemaking. This requirement not only allows adversaries critique of the agency but is perhaps one of the few ways that the public may be apprised of what the agency thinks it knows in its capacity as a repository of expert opinion. From a functional standpoint, we see no difference between assertions of fact and expert opinion tendered by the public, as here, and that generated internally in an agency: each may be biased, inaccurate, or incomplete—failings which adversary comment may illuminate.

Equally important is the inconsistency of secrecy with fundamental notions of fairness implicit in due process and with the ideal of reasoned decisionmaking on the merits which undergirds all of our administrative law. . . . In the Government in the Sunshine Act, for example, Congress has declared it to be "the policy of the United States that the public is entitled to the fullest practicable information regarding the decisionmaking processes of the Federal Government," . . . and has taken steps to guard against *ex parte* contacts in formal agency proceedings. . . .

From what has been said above, it should be clear that information gathered *ex parte* from the public which becomes relevant to a rulemaking will have to be disclosed at some time. On the other hand, we recognize that informal contacts between agencies and the public are the "bread and butter" of the process of administration and are completely appropriate so long as they do not frustrate judicial review or raise serious questions of fairness. Reconciliation of these considerations in a manner which will reduce procedural uncertainty leads us to conclude that communications which are received prior to issuance of a formal notice of rulemaking do not, in general, have to be put in a public file. Of course, if the information contained in such a communication forms the basis for agency action, then, under well established principles, that information must be disclosed to the public in some form. Once a notice of proposed rulemaking has been issued, however, any agency official or employee who is or may reasonably be expected to be involved in the decisional process of the rulemaking proceeding, should "refus[e] to discuss matters relating to the disposition of a [rulemaking proceeding] with any interested private party, or an attorney or agent for any such party, prior to the [agency's] decision." If *ex parte* contacts nonetheless occur, we think that any written document or a summary of any oral communication must be placed in the public file established for each rulemaking docket immediately after the communication is received so that interested parties may comment.

GOVERNMENT REGULATION AND ADMINISTRATIVE AGENCIES: AN EVALUATION

As stated at the beginning of this chapter, there exists a debate between those who advocate deregulation and the abolition of administrative agencies and those who argue that the wider public interest would suffer if there were no regulation. The work of administrative agencies in carrying out the statutory responsibilities that Congress and the President have given them is subject to criticism by industry, consumer, environmentalist, and other groups. Over the past fifty years, administrative agencies have probably been sub-

ETHICS BOX
Ethics and Government Regulation

———

The vice-president for Government Relations (Jones) of Dunfee Communications, Inc., the second largest communications common carrier in the United States, frequently plays golf with a commissioner (Abbott) of the Federal Communications Commission (FCC) on Saturday mornings at a posh country club. They are also neighbors and talk over FCC business at social functions. The agency forbids all *ex parte* communications during business hours and requires that each office log in the name of any individual who is not an employee and engages in such communications, and the subject matter discussed. While playing golf one Saturday morning Jones indicates to Abbott that a present rule-making procedure that would deregulate all long-distance telephone rates would drive his company into bankruptcy. He notes that the company cannot show this in its financial statement or the capital markets will dry up immediately for the company. If the FCC turns down this proposal the company will be able to stay in business and prosper. He shows Jones financial statements that have not been made public to any administrative agency inclusive of the FCC. In a 4 to 3 vote turning down the proposal for complete deregulation of long-distance telephone rates, Abbott is the swing vote. He does not mention his conversation with Jones or the fact that he has seen the true financial statements of Dunfee Communications Inc. Later, he fails to disclose that his club dues have been paid anonymously for the next five years shortly after this decision.

The Ethics in Government Act of 1978, as well as FCC rules, forbid Abbott from participating in the FCC vote, and require disclosure of all information received by Abbott from Jones. Abbott must disclose the payment of his country club dues even if he does not know the source. A potential bribery and statute violation exists for Jones and Dunfee Communications, Inc. if the paying of Abbott's dues can be traced to either.

---

ject to more criticism than praise. One frequently expressed charge is that there is just too much regulation. The result is that the individual, the economy, in fact society as a whole, is stifled. Often this general condemnation is given added weight because critics are able to point to specific instances in which agencies have not performed well. Many times agencies, which supposedly are the experts, have erred in major decisions that have hurt both the regulated business and the general public. For example, long after it became clear in the 1930s that the nineteenth-century concept of the common-carrier responsibility of the railroads to provide a complete transportation service to every locality along every mile of track had become obsolete, the ICC only reluctantly allowed railroads to abandon unprofitable passenger service. This policy forced the railroads to continue passenger service, often when losing money, to the detriment of their competitive position. This eventually led to a deterioration in the ability of the railroads to provide the type of transportation that the economy actually needed.

Although some critics charge that agencies regulate too much, others claim that regulation is either insufficient or frequently oriented to the needs of the industry rather than to the needs of the public. Because most agencies operate in only one field, their members often acquire a sympathetic knowledge of the industry they are supposed to regulate. As a result, they forget their duty to regulate for the public welfare. This condemnation has been made by groups initiated by consumer advocate Ralph Nader that have reviewed the operations of the ICC and the FTC.

Industry Influence

The close ties that develop between the agencies and industry stem from a natural tendency of people to be interested in the problems of others with whom they share a common background. Few deliberate instances of industry-agency collusion can be supported. Commissioners and other agency executives frequently receive their appointments because they have employment backgrounds in the industry regulated by their agency. Often they intend to return to the industry after government service. Personnel who have not been hired from the industry may regard the industry as a potential employer; agency lawyers may think of it as a source of future fees. As a result of these and other considerations, regulators perhaps unconsciously curtail their activities.

Legislative Influence

Administrative agencies have also been accused of being overly susceptible to legislative as well as executive influence. Pressures that would never be countenanced by the courts

are part of the everyday experience of many federal and state regulatory authorities. Pressures from legislative sources are highly effective because the legislatures control agency funds. Almost every state can point to at least one scandal in which legislative leverage has influenced a state agency. At the federal level, congressmen and members of their immediate staffs have been exposed as sources of influence peddling. The power that some agencies have to grant the right to engage in certain types of highly profitable business makes them particularly susceptible to attempts to influence them. For a long time the right to operate a television station was so valuable that the granting of such licenses by the FCC was thought to be similar to the granting of licenses to print money.

Other criticisms of a more esoteric nature have been directed against agencies. In several agencies rule making and adjudicatory functions are not separated. In other instances not only do agency personnel establish the rules and serve as the judges, but the decision to bring an action is also made within the agency. One of the highly esteemed American political traditions is the separation of legislative, judicial, and executive powers; this tradition would seem to be violated when the decision to bring an action is not separated from adjudication. During the 1940s the NLRB was subjected to considerable criticism because its general counsel was controlled by the Board. Eventually, as a result of public pressure, Congress adopted legislation separating the office of the general counsel for the NLRB from the Board, which was responsible for deciding cases initiated by the general counsel. At the present time staff personnel of the FTC adjudicate cases that are brought by the agency and that involve, in many instances, purported violations of agency rules.

Another charge against some agencies, including several of the most important federal agencies, is that the commissioners, who make the ultimate decisions in many cases, are removed from the actual fact finding. Thus, the critics argue, the commissioners never really know what is going on because they see only a record when they make their decisions. They act on the basis of facts found by an administrative law judge, and they do not hear the actual testimony themselves.

Many of these criticisms are partially valid, and most authorities agree that steps should be taken to improve the performance of the administrative agencies. In spite of their problems, they have performed an important function in our system of government, and they have unquestionably taken much of the burden from courts and legislatures, as noted earlier in this chapter. Without them in this age of rapidly increasing population, expanding technology, and specialization, the traditional branches of government would long ago have come to a standstill. Agencies appear to be the most practical method of administering the complex statutes necessary to regulate activities effectively in our society. If some form of government regulation is desired by society, institutions of this type are inevitable. They have developed in all the heavily industrialized nations of the West and will continue to be important as technology expands and our economy becomes more complex.

Administrative Agency Reform

Recently a number of proposals have been made to improve the effectiveness of administrative agencies. These proposals range widely in nature and in the extent to which they advocate change. The modifications suggested include changes in the alignment of responsibilities of several agencies as well as in their internal structures and processes.

During recent administrations a number of proposals to reorganize major federal agencies responsible to the President were carried out. These changes were the outcome of broad authority granted by Congress to the President to reorganize the executive branch. This au-

thority allows the Chief Executive to submit proposals for reorganization of executive agencies to Congress. If Congress does not veto a proposal within sixty days, it automatically goes into effect *(see footnote 9)*. The presidential authority to modify agency organization and responsibility does not apply to the independent federal regulatory agencies.

Over the years numerous presidential, congressional, and private committees have studied the federal regulatory agencies and made suggestions for change. The most recent detailed proposal was submitted in 1971 by the President's Advisory Council on Executive Reorganization. This Council recommended major realignment of responsibility within the independent agencies. One proposal would have combined the ICC, the CAB, and the Federal Maritime Commission into a single transportation agency. The chief argument for this proposal was that the nation's transportation systems increasingly are becoming an integrated network, and overall regulation of all elements of the system is necessary for effective control.

A second proposal recommended dividing the FTC into two agencies. One would concentrate on antitrust matters, the other on consumer protection. The Council also considered combining the Justice Department's antitrust function with those recommended for separation from the present FTC. Antitrust activities would then be carried out either within the Justice Department or a new separate agency. A Reagan administration proposal to do away with FTC antitrust authority met with opposition from Congress.

In addition to proposals realigning agency responsibility, the Council recommended modifications in internal organization and functions for some agencies. The most far-reaching proposal suggested replacing boards or commissions with single administrators. The rationale struck at the heart of the concept of having several governmental functions included in a single organization.

Council members felt that a number of agencies would operate more effectively if policy or rule making were separated from adjudication. A single administrator would have final responsibility in these agencies as in the vast majority of executive department agencies. This person would be more accountable to Congress than to the Board or Commission. Administrative courts would be created to carry out the current adjudicatory functions of the agency.

Opinions vary as to what is necessary to improve the regulatory system. On the one hand, there are numerous authorities who propose the creation of new, powerful independent agencies to solve society's problems. Congress has considered bills creating an independent Consumer Protection Agency, an independent Federal Elections Committee, an independent public prosecutor, and even an independent commission to review classified material. On the other hand, both in Congress and in many of the states, proposed legislation calls for the automatic termination of agencies after they have been in operation for a number of years. In some industries deregulation will lighten the work load of agencies.

A different approach to agency reform has been "sunshine" or "open government" legislation. Several states have adopted laws requiring governmental bodies to meet regularly in announced sessions open to the public. Bills introduced in Congress would require all agencies headed by two or more persons, a majority of whom were appointed by the President and confirmed by the Senate, to open all meetings to the public unless a majority voted to close. These bills also specifically set the types of meetings that could be closed by vote. These include meetings dealing with national defense, foreign policy, company trade secrets, and reviews of agency personnel rules and practices. This type of legislation may force administrative agencies to be more aware of the needs of the public.

Congress enacted the Regulatory Flexibility Act of 1980,[14] which seeks to force all agencies to fit regulations and information requirements made by the agency to the size of the business. This act was a result of agencies making regulations for an industry that burdened small businesses with high costs. Whereas large businesses were able to pass on the costs of regulation to consumers, small businesses often could not. Under the act, an agency must show each October and April the areas of regulation it will be concerned with. The agency must present its agenda to the Small Business Administration, which will publish it for small businesses. Each agency must solicit comments from small businesses and periodically review all rules in order to assess their impact on small companies.

Additional reforms of administrative agencies have been making their way through both houses of Congress.

REVIEW PROBLEMS

1. For what reasons have administrative agencies grown?
2. Explain how the executive branch controls administrative agencies.
3. What are the grounds for a court to review an administrative agency action when it acts in an adjudicative context?
4. What broad standard of delegation of power does Congress use when it authorizes an administrative agency to act in a regulatory manner?
5. What are the two most important functions performed by administrative agencies? Explain each.

6. In September 1969 the State of Tennessee, following agreement with local Memphis city officials, acquired a right-of-way inside Overton Park. The right-of-way was to be used to extend Interstate 40 into Memphis. If this was done, the park would have been cut in two, with the zoo on one side of the highway and all other facilities on the other. The U.S. Secretary of Transportation (Volpe), after consulting with state and local officials, approved the plan without indicating whether a "feasible" alternative existed. A citizens' group sued to enjoin the U.S. Department of Transportation from financing this extension of Interstate 40, claiming that Congress, in creating the Department of Transportation, prohibited the use of funds for highway construction through a park if "feasible" alternatives existed. The Citizens to Preserve Overton Park claimed that the Secretary of Transportation had failed to show that he had investigated and considered "feasible" alternatives or design changes that might have brought less harm to the park, with the result that his order approving the new route was invalid. What standards would a court have used in determining whether Secretary Volpe had met the statutory requirement? Who would win? Citizens to Preserve Overton Park v. Volpe, 401 U.S. 402 (1971)

7. The Federal Communications Commission set forth rules prohibiting cable television systems from broadcasting first-run feature films (shown on over-the-air television) that were less than three but more than ten years old. Home Box Office (HBO) appealed this rule and other restrictions to the District of Columbia Circuit Court of Appeals, claiming that this exercise of the Commission's rule-making authority was arbitrary and capricious and that it restricted competition. The Commission claimed that the regulations were needed to prevent siphoning by cable companies of copyrighted material broadcast over the air. Were the regulations arbitrary and capricious? Who wins? HBO v. Federal Communications Commission, 567 F.2d. 9 (D.C. Cir. 1977)

8. The Endangered Species Act of 1973 invested the Secretary of the Interior with exclusive authority to determine whether a species is "endangered" or "threatened" and to ascertain the factors that have led to the problem. The Secretary is also commanded by Congress under the 1973 act to issue regulations to provide for the conservation of the endangered species. The Secretary of the Interior set forth regulations that declared the snail darter as an endangered species whose habitat would have been destroyed by the creation of the Tellico Reservoir on the Little Tennessee River. The dam creating the reservoir was almost completed ($100 million having been spent) when environmental groups and others brought suit under the 1973 act to enjoin the Tennessee Valley Authority from completing the dam. Would the court be usurping the power of the Secretary of the Interior and Congress if it failed to enforce the 1973 act? What about the $100 million spent on the dam? Is it significant in terms of the court's decision? Who wins? Tennessee Valley Authority v. Hill, 437 U.S. 153 (1978)

9. The Emergency Price Control Act established an Office of Price Administration with authority to promulgate rules and orders fixing maximum prices of commodities and rents during World War II. The Administrator of the OPA was given two standards by Congress to fix prices: (a) he had to consult with the industries and promulgate regulations that were "fair and equitable" and (b) due consideration had to be given to prices prevailing between October 1 and October 15, 1941. When Yakus and other defendants

sold beef in excess of the wholesale price set by the regulations, they were prosecuted under a criminal section of the act and sentenced to six months in jail and fined $1,000 each. The defendants argued that the standards set by Congress for the Administrator were so broad that they failed to give adequate notice and thus violated the Fifth Amendment's due process requirements. Were they too broad? Who wins?

10. The National Highway Traffic Safety Administration in 1972 issued a standard requiring that all pneumatic passenger tires retreaded after February 1974 contain information (permanently molded into one side of the tire) as to size, inflation pressure, load, and whether they were bias-belted or radial. This rule was promulgated pursuant to the National Traffic and Motor Safety Vehicle Act of 1966, which required that rules be "practical" and "meet the need for motor vehicle safety." The National Tire Dealers and Retreaders Association opposed the rule, claiming that it was arbitrary and capricious in that it was not "practicable" and that the Administrator had failed to show that the information required by the rule met "the need for vehicle safety" only if it was permanently molded onto a tire. The Administrator of Traffic Safety argued that safety could be provided only through perma-nent labeling because tires are often transferred from wheel to wheel or car to car. Was the rule economically "feasible" and did it "meet the need for vehicle safety"? Who wins?

11. An association of fishermen represented by the National Resources Defense Council sued U.S. Secretary of the Interior Morton, challenging the Secretary's decision to open a large part of the outer continental shelf off the Louisiana Coast to oil and gas exploration. Under the National Environmental Policy Act of 1969, Congress directed all governmental agencies to file environmental impact statements (EISs) noting "any adverse environmental effects of the proposed action" and "alternatives to the proposed action." The Secretary filed an EIS but failed to consider in any detailed way alternative methods for meeting the energy needs of the nation. The Secretary argued that he failed to consider alternatives (for example, removal of oil import quotas, development of oil shale, coal liquefaction) because they were outside his statutory duty or had no prospect for increasing energy in 1970. The fishermen argued that the Secretary had failed to meet the statutory mandate and that his decision should be overturned. Who wins? National Resources Defense Council v. Morton, 458 F.2d 827 (D.C. Cir. 1972)

FOOTNOTES

[1] General Index, Code of Federal Regulations, Office of the Register, Revised January 1, 1982 (Washington: National Archives and Record Service, General Services Administration).

[2] Kenneth Culp Davis, *Administrative Law Text* (St. Paul, Minn: West Publishing, 1959), p. 1.

[3] Id., p. 15.

[4] 15 United States Code Annotated, Section 41.

[5] National Labor Relations Board (NLRB) v. Remington Rand, Inc., 92 F.2d 862 (1938).

[6] Consolidated Edison v. NLRB, 305 U.S. 197 (1938).

[7] Susan Wagner, *The Federal Trade Commission* (New York: Praeger, 1971), p. 24.

[8] 15 United States Code Annotated, Section 41 *et seq.* as amended by Publ L. 96–239.

[9] The constitutionality of a legislative veto of a specific rule was called into question by a 1983 Supreme Court Decision: Immigration and Naturalization Service v. Chadha, 462 U.S. 919 (1983).

[10] See S. Wagner, *The Federal Trade Commission* (New York: Praeger, 1971), p. 233.

[11] See O.L. Reid, "Advertising and the FTC," in *Business Law: Key Issues and Concepts,* eds., T. Dunfee and J.D. Reitzel, p. 104.

[12] In 1972 the Civil Service Commission approved the title of "administrative law judge" for hearing examiners throughout the federal government.

[13] Administrative Procedure Act-5, United States Code 701–706.

[14] See Regulatory Flexibility Act Pub. L. 96–354.

Antitrust Laws: Enforcement and Content

This chapter addresses forms of business behavior that are considered to be anticompetitive and thus regulated by federal and state governments under the antitrust laws.

Historically this nation's economy was founded on the concept of laissez-faire—that is, government would not interfere in the activities of individual sellers freely competing in the marketplace. Underlying this classical economic theory was the assumption that there would be many sellers in the marketplace and a free flow of information between sellers and buyers. In the latter half of the nineteenth and the early twentieth century business power in several industries (particularly oil) became concentrated in one or two companies. Public demand to break up these "trusts" resulted in the passage of federal antitrust laws and some state statutes. (See Table 44-1 for a summary of these statutes and the business behavior they regulate. They will frequently be referred to throughout the chapter.) While concentrating on such business conduct as price fixing, conspiracies to restrain trade, and other anticompetitive behavior, this chapter also looks at how industry structure affects competition. When industry structure is mentioned, the reader should know that the concern of antitrust enforcement agencies will generally be with the number and size of sellers. If the industry has only four domestic sellers, like the auto industry, is it more or less competitive? Should we look further and include Volkswagen and Nissan when we talk about the number of sellers and how competitive the industry may be?

In some industries (including many of our most important national industries) a few firms account for all or sizable portions of production. A presidential task force reported in 1969 that:

industries in which four or fewer firms account for more than 70 percent of output produce nearly ten percent of the total value of [all American] manufactured products; industries in which four or fewer firms account for more than 50 percent of output produce nearly 24 percent.[1]

TABLE 44-1 SUMMARY OF SELECTED FEDERAL ANTITRUST STATUTES

Structurally Oriented	Behaviorally Oriented
Sherman Act (1890). Sec. 2 prohibits monopolies and attempts or conspiracies to monopolize. Applies to interstate and foreign commerce.	Sherman Act (1890). Sec. 1 condemns combinations and conspiracies in restraint of trade including vertical and horizontal price fixing, group boycotts, division of markets. Applies to interstate or foreign commerce.
Clayton Act (1914). Sec. 7 prohibits mergers, the effect of which may be substantially to lessen competition or to tend to create a monopoly. *Amended (1950). Celler–Kefauver Act* clarified application of Sec. 7 to acquisitions of assets.	Clayton Act (1914). Sec 2 prohibits price discriminations, substantially lessening sellers' level competition (primary line violations). *Amended (1936). Robinson–Patman Act* prohibits price discriminations, substantially lessening buyers' (and below) level competition (secondary line violations). Clayton Act (1914). Sec. 3 prohibits exclusive dealing and tying arrangements, the effect of which may be to lessen competition substantially.

Other industries are composed of a large number of relatively small firms with no single firm having a significant share of the market.

A matter of concern to those charged with enforcing the antitrust laws is the relationship between differing industry structures and specific business behaviors, particularly pricing. For example, is there less competitive pricing (resulting in higher prices for consumers) in industries with just a few sizable firms? The importance of this question stems from the widespread belief that the pricing mechanism is a central component of viable competition. Thus, if proof exists that certain types of industry structure hamper the operation of the price mechanism, there is strong justification for government restriction of the formation of such structures and for affirmative action to break up firms. The reader will constantly be made aware of the relationship between industry structure (monopolistic, oligopolistic, and competitive) and company behavior (price fixing, customer and territorial restrictions).

This chapter identifies important federal antitrust statutes, describes their enforcement, and explains certain exemptions. It then discusses business behaviors regulated under these acts, with particular emphasis on monopolies, mergers, and price discrimination.

LAW AND ECONOMICS IN SETTING ANTITRUST POLICY

In examining the enforcement and content of antitrust statutes, we need to know that two major schools of thought have arisen in the last twenty-five years. They analyze antitrust statutes believing that Congress had distinctly different goals in mind when enacting these laws.

The Chicago School approach believes that all antitrust decisions by courts should be based on the sole criterion of economic efficiency; that is, the decision should promote the maximization of consumer welfare. Consumer welfare is defined as an improvement in the allocation of resources without an impairment to productive efficiencies. Reagan administration Justice Department officials argued successfully in many cases that by encouraging the efficient allocation of resources, antitrust enforcement can make sure consumers are provided goods at the lowest possible prices. Also, efficiency criteria when used in antitrust decision making helps U.S. firms to compete with large state-subsidized and privately owned foreign multinational corporations. This approach to antitrust enforcement will become evident to the reader when analyzing the present merger guidelines as well as the vertical restraint cases, such as *GTE Sylvania, Inc.* and *Jefferson Hospital,* that are set out in this chapter.

In contrast, the Harvard School approach to setting antitrust policy would emphasize goals such as:

1. The preservation of small businesses and an economy where many sellers compete with each other
2. The prevention of the concentration of economic and political power in the hands of a few large industries
3. The prevention of labor dislocation by keeping control of businesses in the hands of local people.

This approach calls for the breakup of large corporations such as General Motors, the nonparticipation of large corporations in the political process, and the prevention of economic concentration through strict enforcement of our antitrust statutes. Adherents to this approach also advocate plant closing legislation that would mandate that companies give six months or more notice before they close a plant, as well as the return of all tax abatements previously received from the state or local community where the plant is located.

An approach that emphasizes these criteria is set forth for the reader in this chapter in *United States* v. *Du Pont & Co.* and *Brown Shoe Co.* v. *United States.*

ENFORCEMENT OF THE ANTITRUST LAWS

The major antitrust statutes are set forth in Table 44-1. As we examine several forms of business conduct prohibited by these laws, it should be remembered that their major purpose is to preserve a competitive industry structure and economy.

Actions under the antitrust laws may be initiated in one of the following three ways:

1. By the Department of Justice in the regular court system
2. By administrative agencies through specially established procedures
3. By private citizens to obtain compensation for injuries they have suffered as a result of violations of the antitrust laws

The Department of Justice has a special Antitrust Division, headed by an Assistant Attorney General, responsible for enforcing the Sherman Act and, together with the Federal Trade Commission (FTC), for enforcing the Clayton Act. In addition, the Antitrust Division has special powers relating to the antitrust actions of federal administrative agencies. The FTC is the most important agency in this field. It has exclusive jurisdiction to enforce the Federal Trade Commission Act and has concurrent jurisdiction with the Department of Justice to enforce the Clayton Act. In addition, the FTC has authority to enforce a number of other statutes relating to labeling and export trade. In jointly enforcing the Clayton Act, the Department of Justice and the FTC attempt to coordinate their efforts to prevent wasteful duplication. For example, the FTC has taken primary responsibility for enforcing the Robinson–Patman Act; the Department of Justice rarely litigates under that statute.

These public agencies make use of three basic remedies:

1. Injunctions
2. Criminal sanctions
3. Fines

An *injunction* is a court order prohibiting a specified action (for example, dissemination of pricing information by a trade association) or requiring affirmative action on the part of the party against whom the order applies (for example, the divestiture of certain designated assets).

Violation of the Sherman Act is a felony and may result in imprisonment for up to three years. Although the imposition of jail terms in Sherman Act proceedings has received considerable publicity when it has occurred, the number of instances in which jail terms have actually been imposed on businesspeople is relatively small. The Sherman Act also provides for fines of $100,000 per count for an individual and $1 million per count for a corporation.

Both the Clayton and Sherman acts provide for civil treble-damage suits by private citizens. Although victims of an electrical equipment price-fixing conspiracy in the 1950s were able to recover hundreds of millions of dollars, private plaintiffs found that antitrust litigation was costly and time consuming. In addition, there is often an imbalance of economic interest in the lawsuit. An extreme example will emphasize the latter point. Suppose the manufacturers of a mass-distributed product such as legal pads were to engage in a price-fixing conspiracy unlawfully raising the price five cents per pad. Even the most prolific purchasers of legal pads would find it hardly worth their while to bring suit. If they were to bring suit, they would find that the outcome of the case would be substantially more important to the manufacturers than it would be to them. There are two possible solutions to this dilemma. A state government might bring suit on behalf of all of its citizens and then spend whatever monies it obtained in the public interest. Or a *class action* might

be allowed, whereby a sufficiently homogeneous group, having substantially the same claim, would bring action as though it were a single person. The courts may allow a class action in an antitrust suit if they are convinced that it is practicable and that there are no other realistic alternatives available to the plaintiffs comprising the class. The courts determine whether class actions will be allowed on a case-by-case basis.

The decision of the U.S. Supreme Court in Eisen v. Carlisle & Jacquelin, 417 U.S. 156 (1974), has had the effect of limiting the use of class actions under the federal antitrust laws. In *Eisen* the Court held that the plaintiff must bear the costs of notifying all the members of the class of their rights during the progress of the suit. The costs of notifying a large class that may involve tens of thousands (or, in some cases, even millions) are prohibitively high (postage alone would be staggering) and operate as a practical matter to discourage the very large class action.

In 1972 the Supreme Court had held in *Hawaii* v. *Standard Oil of California* that a state could not bring a civil antitrust action for damages against a defendant on behalf of all the citizens of the state. Ironically, in the *Hawaii* decision the Supreme Court suggested that a class action was the better way to deal with this problem. Hawaii had tried to bring an action as *parens patriae* (legal guardian) on behalf of its citizens.

In reaction to the *Eisen* and *Hawaii* decisions Congress passed the Antitrust Improvements Act (1976), which established a statutory *parens patriae* right of action that would allow state attorneys general to bring civil treble-damage suits on behalf of all natural persons within the state against defendants who had committed violations of the antitrust laws. At the direction of the federal court the proceeds of a successful suit would either be distributed to injured citizens or added to the state's general revenues. Damages would be calculated from the losses suffered by the natural citizens of the state. Sampling and aggregation techniques could be used to make the calculation if price fixing was involved.

In *Illinois Brick* v. *Illinois* (1977) the Supreme Court refused to allow Illinois and some 700 Illinois government entities to recover treble damages as indirect purchasers. The state had alleged that it and others had been overcharged $3 million for concrete blocks sold by Illinois Brick and other manufacturers who had engaged in price fixing. The manufacturers sold blocks to masonry contractors who in turn passed on the extra costs to general contractors who passed them on to the state when building office buildings. Illinois taxpayers were the injured citizens. To support its refusal, the Court cited the evidentiary complexity involved in analyzing price and output decisions based on economic models; it also pointed to problems associated with apportionment of damages. This decision has been criticized by Congress, the federal courts, and legal scholars. This decision, the easing of Justice Department merger guidelines in 1982 and 1984, and a probusiness Supreme Court may be reasons for a decline in private antitrust actions as shown in Table 44-2.

Historically a high percentage of the antitrust cases initiated by the Department of Justice have been settled by agreement between the government and the defendants. This is an impressive fact because it is more difficult for the government to settle a case than for a private litigant. Before a settlement may be judicially approved, the government must publish the terms of the proposed agreement along with a Competitive Impact Statement that details its likely economic effect. This is done to ensure that the interests of the public are served by the settlement. If the judge approves, a consent decree is filed with the court. Violation of the terms of the decree puts the violating party in contempt of court. If a criminal action has been filed, the same basic process is followed to obtain a decree of nolo contendere.

Settling of cases saves the government time

TABLE 44-2 PRIVATE ANTITRUST CASES

Fiscal Year When Filed	Number Filed
1960	228
1961	341
1962	266
1963	283
1964	317
1965	443
1966	444
1967	536
1968	659
1969	740
1970	877
1971	1,003
1972	1,203
1973	1,089
1974	1,162
1975	1,334
1976	1,416
1977	1,528
1978	1,321
1979	1,208
1980	1,457
1981	1,292
1982	1,037
1983	1,192
1984	1,100

Source: 1984 Annual Report of the Director of the Administrative Office of the United States Courts, *Official Reports* (1984).

and money and allows the Department of Justice to deal with more antitrust violations. Nevertheless, the settlement of antitrust cases has several drawbacks. For example, if the government litigates and wins, that victory constitutes prima facie evidence of the antitrust violation and may be used by a private plaintiff in a civil treble-damages suit. It is then only necessary for the private plaintiff to prove the injuries that he or she suffered and that they resulted from the proven antitrust violation. On the other hand, a consent settlement entered into and accepted prior to the taking of any testimony carries no implications for a private suit. The private litigant will have

BOX 44-1 ISSUES AND TRENDS

Sections 1 and 2 of the Sherman Act apply to "trade or commerce, . . . with foreign nations" as indicated in Table 44-1. The courts on a case-by-case basis have interpreted the language of these statutes to determine what activities of U.S. companies operating abroad come within this jurisdiction of the Sherman Act. The general principle that has evolved on a case-by-case basis has been that if United States or foreign private companies enter into an *agreement* forbidden by Section 1, and it *affects* the foreign commerce of the United States, American courts have jurisdiction. The Department of Justice has issued foreign antitrust enforcement guidelines in which it requires business practices to have a "substantial and foreseeable effect" on U.S. commerce. The business practices must have a direct and intended effect. For example, if two companies based in the United States were able to fix the prices of widgets in three Eastern European countries because they were the sole licensed producers there, and then use the profits to force out competitors in the United States, the Justice Department might be willing to step in.

Another issue is whether nations that do not have a competitive model of private entrepreneurs are subject to the jurisdiction of U.S. courts. For example, when the International Association of Machinists sued the Organization of Petroleum Exporting Countries (OPEC) for price fixing under Section 1 of the Sherman Act, the federal court said it lacked jurisdiction under the Act of State doctrine which states that U.S. courts will not evaluate the lawfulness of acts of nation-states or state-owned companies performed within their own territory even if the foreign commerce of the United States is affected.

---

to prove both the fact of the antitrust violation and his or her injuries resulting therefrom. In addition, it may be questioned whether an "I'll promise not to do it again if you won't prosecute" approach effectively deters others from engaging in similar practices.

EXEMPTIONS FROM THE ANTITRUST LAWS

Certain types of businesses and certain business and labor-union activities are specifically exempted from the antitrust laws. In some instances exemptions are based on recognition of the fact that competition is not desirable in all market situations. Other exemptions, like the exempt status of professional baseball, are based on nothing more than historical legal quirks. Two of the most important exemptions—regulated industries and labor unions—are briefly discussed here. In addition to these two, there are other important exemptions (see Table 44-3). In spite of the number of exemptions, the percentage of total goods produced by both *unregulated* and *exempted* industries is quite small.[2]

Regulated Industries

A number of important industries are closely regulated by federal and state agencies to protect the public interest. These include trans-

TABLE 44-3 ACTIVITIES WHOLLY OR PARTIALLY EXEMPT FROM THE FEDERAL ANTITRUST STATUTES

Activities	Examples and/or Bases for Exemptions
Regulated industries	Transportation, electric, gas, and telephone.
Labor union activities	Collective bargaining.
Intrastate activities	Intrastate telephone calls are regulated by state public utility commissions.
Agricultural activities	Farmers may belong to cooperatives that legally set prices.
Baseball	The U.S. Supreme Court declared baseball a sport, not a trade. No other professional sport has been exempted by the Congress or courts.
Activities falling within the "State Action" doctrine	In *Parker* v. *Brown* [317 U.S. 341 (1943)] the U.S. Supreme Court held a state marketing program that was clearly anticompetitive to be exempt from the federal antitrust statutes because it obtained its authority from a "clearly articulated legislative command of the state." The Court looks at the degree of involvement before exempting any *activity* under this doctrine.
Cities', towns', and villages' activities	The *Local Government Antitrust Act of 1984* prohibits monetary recovery under the federal antitrust laws from any of these local subdivisions or from local officials, agents, or employees.
Export activities	The *Webb–Pommerce Act of 1918* and the *Export Trading Act of 1982* made the formation of selling cooperatives of U.S. exporters exempt.
	Also, the *Joint Venture Trading Act of 1983* exempted certain joint ventures of competing companies when seeking to compete with foreign companies that are private and/or state controlled. Approval of the Justice Department is required. *The Shipping Act of 1984* allows shippinglines to enter into joint ventures and to participate in international shipping conferences that set worldwide rates and divide routes and shipments.

portation, electricity, gas, telephone service, and broadcasting. Because intervention by antitrust enforcement agencies would be redundant, these industries enjoy a qualified exemption from direct application of the antitrust laws. In addition, some of these industries are thought to involve so-called natural monopolies, thus making competitive considerations irrelevant. The exemptions, however, are not absolute, and the Justice Department has the authority to review antitrust-related decisions by federal regulatory agencies.

Labor Unions

Over the years Congress has exempted the organizational and operational activities of labor unions from the antitrust laws. Today labor unions retain their exempt status so long as they do not combine with nonlabor groups to effect restraints of trade. Thus, if a firm enters into a conspiracy with a labor union for the purpose of economically handicapping a competing firm, the antitrust laws will apply. There have been few examples of such outright labor–nonlabor conspiracies. Instead, the courts have had to deal with the question of the applicability of the antitrust laws to more ordinary and more subtle labor–management relationships. For example, labor in a sense combines with a nonlabor group every time a collective-bargaining agreement is signed. Yet the peaceful resolution of labor disputes through collective bargaining is encouraged by federal labor law. In view of these countervailing policies, can an anticompetitive provision contained in a collective-bargaining agreement in and of itself be considered a conspiracy in restraint of trade? The courts have yet to effectively resolve this difficult question.

SHERMAN ACT

Price Fixing and Conspiracies in Restraint of Trade

Section 1 of the Sherman Act (summarized in Table 44-1) prohibits contracts, combinations, or conspiracies that restrain interstate trade. The U.S. Supreme Court has used two standards to determine what acts violate Section 1. In a landmark case, *Chicago Board of Trade* v. *United States* (1918),[3] the Court set out a *rule of reason* standard, noting that only *unreasonable* restraints of trade are illegal. The Court instructed lower courts and regulatory agencies to weigh the procompetitive effects of a particular business restraint against the anticompetitive effects to determine its reasonableness. Such factors as the nature of the business, the history of the restraint, the reason why businesses adopted it, and other factors peculiar to the business were to be considered.[4] Certain other business activities or restraints are treated as *per se* (in and of themselves) illegal. Once shown to exist, they are illegal, and no balancing of the pro- and anticompetitive effects will be allowed into evidence to prove their reasonableness. In *Northern Pacific Railway Co.* v. *United States* (1958) the Supreme Court defined a per se standard, noting that there are certain business practices or agreements "which because of their pernicious effect on competition . . . lack any redeeming virtue and are conclusively presumed to be unreasonable and therefore illegal without elaborate inquiry as to the precise harm they have caused or the business excuse for their use."[5]

The courts with few exceptions have applied a per se standard to horizontal price fixing. Agreements fixing prices have always appealed to businesspeople because they reduce, even eliminate, the risks of economic loss. Suppose competitors A, B, and C, the major manufacturers of generators, agree to take turns offering low bids. Each is assured a portion of the available market, and each knows that price competition with its attendant potential for monetary losses will be eliminated. Artificially high prices can safely be charged and greater profits made because those who buy generators will pay more than they would in a competitive market. Similar results would follow in a broader-based industry if the majority of firms were to agree to charge the same price, or at least that no one would charge less than a specified price. Price fixing of this kind—among competitors operating on the same level of the marketing structure—is referred to as *horizontal price fixing*.

Price fixing also occurs—in fact it is probably more easily achieved—between firms at different levels of the distribution system for particular goods. Price agreements between wholesalers and retailers, manufacturers and dealers, franchisors and franchisees are examples of *vertical price fixing*. The parties to price-fixing agreements of this type are not competitors, but what they do affects competition.

The U.S. Supreme Court in *Monsanto* v. *Spray-Rite Service Corporation* 465 U.S. 752 (1984) continued to adhere to a per se approach to vertical price fixing despite a Justice Department *amicus curiae* brief, which urged a *rule of reason* standard in order to promote economic efficiencies. In its 1985 *Vertical Restraint Guidelines* the Justice Department stated that it would hold vertical price restraints per se illegal only when "there is direct or circumstantial evidence of an explicit agreement to establish specific resale prices."

The judicial rationalization for treating horizontal price fixing as a per se violation of the antitrust laws is provided by the following quotation from a 1927 case:

The aim and result of every price-fixing agreement, if effective, is the elimination of one form of competition. The power to fix prices, whether reasonably exercised or not, involves power to control the market and to fix arbitrary and unreasonable prices. The reasonable price fixed today may through economic and business changes become the unreasonable price of tomorrow. Once established, it may be maintained unchanged because of the absence of competition secured by the agreement for a price reasonable when fixed.[6]

In the important case that follows the Supreme Court emphasized the significance it continues to attach to the per se rule as it is applied to horizontal price-fixing arrangements whether entered into by individuals or by corporations.

Arizona v. Maricopa County Medical Society

United States Supreme Court
457 U.S. 332 (1982)

Background: Respondent-defendant foundations for medical care were organized by respondent, Maricopa County Medical Society, and another medical society to promote fee-for-service medicine and to provide the community with a competitive alternative to existing health insurance plans. The foundations, by agreement of their member doctors, established the maximum fees the doctors could claim in full payment for health services provided to policyholders of specified insurance plans. Petitioner State of Arizona filed a complaint against respondents in federal District Court, alleging that they were engaged in an illegal price-fixing conspiracy in violation of Section 1 of the Sherman Act. The Court of Appeals affirmed the lower court's denial of the motion for partial summary judgment and held that the certified question could not be answered without evaluating the purpose and effect of the agreements at a full trial.

Decision: Reversed. The United States Supreme Court ruled in favor of the state of Arizona.

Stevens, Justice

The question presented is whether §1 of the Sherman Act has been violated by an agreement among competing physicians setting, by majority vote, the maximum fees that they may claim in full payment for health services provided to policyholders of specified insurance plans.

The respondents recognize that our decisions establish that price fixing agreements are unlawful on their face. But they argue that the *per se* rule does not govern this case because the agreements at issue are horizontal and fix maximum prices, are among members of a profession, are in an industry with which the judiciary has little antitrust experience, and are alleged to have procompetitive justifications.

Our decisions foreclose the argument that the agreements at issue escape *per se* condemnation because they are horizontal and fix maximum prices. *Keifer-Stewart* and *Albrecht* place horizontal agreements to fix maximum prices on the same legal—even if not economic—footing as agreements to fix minimum or uniform prices. The *per se* rule "is grounded on faith in price competition as a market force [and not] on a policy of low selling prices at the price of eliminating competition." Rahl, Price Competition and the Price Fixing Rule—Preface and Perspective, 57 Nw. U. L. Rev. 137, 142 (1962). In this case the rule is violated by a price restraint that tends to provide the same economic rewards to all practitioners regardless of their skill, their experience, their training, or their willingness to employ innovative and difficult procedures in individual cases. Such a restraint also may discourage entry into the market and may deter experimentation and new developments by individual entrepreneurs. It may be a masquerade for an agreement to fix uniform prices, or it may in the future take on that character.

Nor does the fact that doctors—rather than nonprofessionals—are the parties to the price fixing agreements support the respondents' position. In *Goldfarb* v. *Virginia State Bar,* we stated that the "public service aspect, and other features of the professions, may require that a particular practice, which could properly be viewed as a violation of the Sherman Act in another context, be treated differently." See *National Society of Professional Engineers* v. *United States.* The price fixing agreements in this case, however, are not premised on public service or ethical norms. The respondents do not argue, as did the defendants in *Goldfarb* and *Professional Engineers,* that the quality of the professional service that their members provide is enhanced by the price restraint. The respondents' claim for relief from the *per se* rule is simply that the doctors' agreement not to charge certain insureds more than a fixed price facilitates the successful marketing of an attractive insurance plan. But the claim that the price restraint will make it easier for customers to pay does not distinguish the medical profession from any other provider of goods or services.

We are equally unpersuaded by the argument that we should not apply the *per se* rule in this case because the judiciary has little antitrust experience in the health care industry. The argument quite obviously is inconsistent with *Socony-Vacuum.* In unequivocal terms, we stated that, "[w]hatever may be its peculiar problems and characteristics, the Sherman Act, so far as price-fixing agreements are concerned, establishes one uniform rule applicable to all industries alike." We also stated that "[t]he elimination of so-called competitive evils [in an industry] is no legal justification" for price fixing agreements, yet the Court of Appeals refused to apply the *per se* rule in this case in part because the health care industry was so far removed from the competitive model. Consistent with our prediction in *Socony-Vacuum,* the result of this reasoning was the adoption by the Court of Appeals of a legal standard based on the reasonableness of the fixed prices, an inquiry we have so often condemned. Finally, the argument that the *per se* rule must be rejustified for every industry that has not been subject to significant antitrust litigation ignores the rationale for *per se* rules, which in part is to avoid the "necessity for an incredibly complicated and prolonged economic investigation into the entire history of the industry involved, as well as related industries, in an effort to determine at large whether a particular restraint has been unreasonable—an inquiry so often wholly fruitless when undertaken."

The respondents' principal argument is that the *per se* rule is inapplicable because their agreements are alleged to have procompetitive justifications. The argument indicates a misunderstanding of the *per se* concept. The anticompetitive potential inherent in all price fixing agreements justifies their facial invalidation even if procompetitive justifications are offered for some. Those claims of enhanced competition are so unlikely to prove significant in any particular case that we adhere to the rule of law that is justified in its general application. Even when the respondents are given every benefit of the doubt, the limited record in this case is not inconsistent with the presumption that the respondents' agreements will not significantly enhance competition.

The respondents contend that their fee schedules are procompetitive because they make it possible to provide consumers of health care with a uniquely desirable form of insurance coverage that could not otherwise exist. The features of the foundation-endorsed insurance plans that they stress are a choice of doctors, complete insurance coverage, and lower premiums. The first two characteristics, however, are hardly unique to these plans. Since only about 70% of the doctors in the relevant market are members of either foundation, the guarantee of complete coverage only applies when an insured chooses a physician in that 70%. If he elects to go to a nonfoundation doctor, he may be required to pay a portion of the doctor's fee. It is fair to presume, however, that at least 70% of the doctors in other markets charge no more than the "usual, customary, and reasonable" fee that typical insurers are willing to reimburse in full. Thus, in Maricopa and Pima Counties as well as in most parts of the country, if an insured asks his doctor if the insurance coverage is complete, presumably in about 70% of the cases the doctor will say yes and in about 30% of the cases he will say no.

It is true that a binding assurance of complete insurance coverage—as well as most of the respondents' potential for lower insurance premiums—can be obtained only if the insurer and the doctor agree in advance on the maximum fee that the doctor will accept as full payment for a particular service. Even if a fee schedule is therefore desirable, it is not necessary that the doctors do the price fixing. The record indicates that the Arizona Comprehensive Medical/Dental Program for Foster Children is administered by the Maricopa foundation pursuant to a contract under which the maximum fee schedule is prescribed by a state agency rather than by the doctors. This program and the Blue Shield plan challenged in *Group Life & Health Insurance Co. v. Royal Drug Co.* indicate that insurers are capable not only of fixing maximum reimbursable prices but also of obtaining binding agreements with providers guaranteeing the insured full reimbursement of a participating provider's fee. In light of these examples, it is not surprising that nothing in the record even arguably supports the conclusion that this type of insurance program could not function if the fee schedules were set in a different way.

The most that can be said for having doctors fix the maximum prices is that doctors may be able to do it more efficiently than insurers. The validity of that assumption is far from obvious, but in any event there is no reason to believe that any savings that might accrue from this arrangement would be sufficiently great to affect the competitiveness of these kinds of insurance plans. It is entirely possible that the potential or actual power of the foundations to dictate the terms of such insurance plans may more than offset the theoretical efficiencies upon which the respondents' defense ultimately rests.

Our adherence to the *per se* rule is grounded not only on economic prediction, judicial convenience, and business certainty, but also on a recognition of the respective roles of the Judiciary and the Congress in regulating the economy. Given its generality, our enforcement of the Sherman Act has required the Court to provide much of its substantive content. By articulating the rules of law with some clarity and by adhering to rules that are justified in their general application, however, we enhance the legislative prerogative to amend the law. The respondents' arguments against application of the *per se* rule in this case therefore are better directed to the legislature. Congress may consider the exception that we are not free to read into the statute.

Horizontal Territorial Limitation and Customer Allocation

One device for reducing competition is an agreement between business rivals to divide markets on a geographic basis. Each of two or more competitors agrees not to sell in a designated territory. Courts have frequently referred to these agreements as *horizontal territorial limitations.* Similarly, business competitors sometimes agree to allocate customers. Where horizontal territorial limitations and/or customer allocations are carried out, the seller who is left in the market can generally obtain higher prices and provide less service because of its monopoly position. As territorial sales restrictions and customer allocation have few redeeming features, they have consistently been held to be per se violations of antitrust laws. In *United States* v. *Topco Associates, Inc.* (1972) the Supreme Court ruled that market allocations were per se illegal even when a group of small- and medium-sized grocery chains with 6 percent of the market created a joint subsidiary to market private-label products in competition with large supermarket chains such as A&P and Safeway. The Topco participants divided markets for the sale of Topco brand products so they could compete more efficiently with large rival chains. Competition among sellers of Topco private-label products in the same market was eliminated following the market division. This decision has been criticized in light of the *Sylvania* case cited later in this chapter. The critics argue that Topco had so little market power (6 percent) that it could not adversely affect interbrand competition— that is, between A&P and Topco or Safeway and Topco. Second, it is often argued that if Topco did not allocate exclusive territories to the participants, they would have no incentive to compete with A&P or Safeway. Sellers of Topco labels in adjoining areas would undercut a participant's prices and also have a "free ride" on their promotions or advertising. Critics suggest that some joint ventures may be procompetitive and thus horizontal/vertical restraints might be best judged by a rule of reason. In *NCAA* v. *Board of Regents of the University of Oklahoma* the United States Su- preme Court rejected the per se approach in determining whether the NCAA was the ex- clusive agent to sell all college football games to the television networks and to fix prices for those broadcasts. This case is excerpted here.

National Collegiate Athletic Association, Petitioner v. Board of Regents of the University of Oklahoma and University of Georgia Athletic Association

U.S. Supreme Court
468 U.S. 85 (1984)

Background: In 1981 petitioner-defendant National Collegiate Athletic Association (NCAA) adopted a plan for the televising of college football games of its member institutions for the 1982–1985 football seasons. The plan stated that its purpose was to reduce the adverse effects of live television on football game attendance. The plan limited the total amount of televised intercollegiate football games and the number of games that any one college might televise. No member of the NCAA was permitted to make any sale of television rights except in accordance with the plan. The NCAA had separate agreements with the two carrying networks, ABC and CBS, granting each network the right to telecast the live "exposures" described in the plan. Each network agreed to pay a specified "minimum aggregate compensation" to the participating NCAA members, and was authorized to negotiate directly with the members for the right to televise their games. Respondent-plaintiff universities, in addition to being NCAA members, were members of the College Football Association (CFA), which was originally organized to promote the interests of major football-playing colleges within the NCAA structure, but whose members eventually claimed that they should have a greater voice in the formulation of football television policy than they had in the NCAA. The CFA negotiated a contract with NBC that would have allowed a more liberal number of television appearances for each member college and increased the revenues realized by CFA members. In response, the NCAA announced that it would take disciplinary action against any CFA member that complied with the CFA–NBC contract. Respondents then commenced an action in federal District Court, which, after an extended trial, held that the controls exercised by the NCAA over televising college football games violated Section 1 of the Sherman Act and, accordingly, granted injunctive relief. The Court of Appeals affirmed. The NCAA appealed.

Decision: The United States Supreme Court ruled in favor of the University of Okla- homa and University of Georgia.

Stevens, Justice

The plan adopted in 1981 for the 1982–85 seasons is at issue in this case. This plan recites that it is intended to reduce, insofar as possible, the adverse effects of live television upon football game attendance. It provides that "all forms of television of the football games of NCAA member institutions during the Plan control periods shall be in accordance with this Plan.''

There can be no doubt that the challenged practices of the NCAA constitute a "restraint of trade" in the sense that they limit members' freedom to negotiate and enter into their own television contracts. In that sense, however, every contract is a restraint of trade, and as we have repeatedly recognized, the Sherman Act was intended to prohibit only unreasonable restraints of trade.

It is also undeniable that these practices share characteristics of restraints we have previously held unreasonable. The NCAA is an association of schools which compete against each other to attract television revenues, not to mention fans and athletes. As the District Court found, the policies of the NCAA with respect to television rights are ultimately controlled by the vote of member institutions. By participating in an association which prevents member institutions from competing against each other on the basis of price or kind of television rights that can be offered to broadcasters, the NCAA member institutions have created a horizontal restraint—an agreement among competitors on the way in which they will compete with one another. A restraint of this type has often been held to be unreasonable as a matter of law *(per se)*. Because it places a ceiling on the number of games member institutions may televise, the horizontal agreement places an artificial limit on the quantity of televised football that is available to broadcasters and consumers. By restraining the quantity of television rights available for sale, the challenged practices create a limitation on output; our cases have held that such limitations are unreasonable restraints of trade. Moreover, the District Court found that the minimum aggregate price, in fact, operates to preclude any price negotiation between broadcasters and institutions, thereby constituting horizontal price fixing, perhaps the paradigm of an unreasonable restraint of trade.

Horizontal price-fixing and output limitation are ordinarily condemned as a matter of law under an "illegal *per se*" approach because the probability that these practices are anticompetitive is so high; a *per se* rule is applied when "the practice facially appears to be one that would always or almost always tend to restrict competition and decrease output." In such circumstances a restraint is presumed unreasonable without inquiry into the particular market context in which it is found. Nevertheless, we have decided that it would be inappropriate to apply a *per se* rule to this case.

Our decision not to apply a *per se* rule rests in large part on our recognition that a certain degree of cooperation is necessary if the type of competition that petitioner and its member institutions seek to market is to be preserved. It is reasonable to assume that most of the regulatory controls of the NCAA are justifiable means of fostering competition among amateur athletic teams and therefore procompetitive because they enhance public interest in intercollegiate athletics. The specific restraints on football telecasts that are challenged in this case do not, however, fit into the same mold as do rules defining the conditions of the contest, the eligibility of participants, or the manner in which members of a joint enterprise shall share the responsibilities and the benefits of the total venture.

The interest in maintaining a competitive balance that is asserted by the NCAA as a justification for regulating all television of intercollegiate football is not related to any neutral standard or to any readily identifiable group of competitors. The television plan is not even arguably tailored to serve such an interest. There is no evidence that this restriction produces any greater measure of equality throughout the NCAA than would a restriction on alumni donations, tuition rates, or any other revenue producing activity.

Perhaps the most important reason for rejecting the argument that the interest in competitive balance is served by the television plan is the District Court's unambiguous and well supported finding that many more games would be televised in a free market than under the NCAA plan. The hypothesis that legitimates the maintenance of competitive balance as a procompetitive justification under the Rule of Reason is that equal competition will maximize consumer demand for the product. The finding that consumption will materially increase if the controls are removed is a compelling demonstration that they do not in fact serve any such legitimate purpose.

Today we hold only that the record supports the District Court's conclusion that by curtailing output and blunting the ability of member institutions to respond to consumer preference, the NCAA has restricted rather than enhanced the place of intercollegiate athletics in the nation's life.

Vertical Territorial Limitation and Customer Allocation

Agreements that limit territories in which sales can be made are frequently entered into by manufacturers and dealers or by distributors who sell the manufacturer's product. These *vertical territorial limitations* generally provide an exclusive territory for a single or small number of dealers in a particular product. Both the manufacturer and the dealer-distributor benefit from these territorial restraints. Many argue that limitations of this kind benefit society as well because they increase *interbrand* competition even though they clearly curtail *intrabrand* competition. For example, franchises frequently contain provisions limiting the territory in which the franchisee can operate.

Because under certain circumstances benefits can be shown as a result of market divisions of this nature, the Supreme Court has generally examined each case individually and weighed the reasons for the restrictions against the value of the general policy of fostering competition. Territorial restraints are important to successful quality merchandising. A manufacturer who wishes to keep deal-

ers who are financially sound and able to provide high-grade distribution and service facilities frequently has to guarantee that the dealer will enjoy an exclusive right to market the product in a particular territory. Without such assurances some dealers might be reluctant to invest the capital necessary to develop and maintain quality facilities.

Another argument used to support the imposition of territorial restraints by a manufacturer on a distributor is that these restraints facilitate the distributor's ability to compete with other brands because he is not forced to spend his resources competing with others who sell the same brand. This, the argument goes, is one reason that small businesses sometimes survive in highly competitive markets. Preventing intrabrand competition also has social utility in a market in which a company competes with a much stronger rival as well as for enterprises that depend for their success on personal relationships between the buyer and seller.

Territorial restraints that eliminate intrabrand competition, however, are not always in the best interests of the public. Many generically similar products sold under different brand names may be highly differentiated in the buyer's mind. Thus the buyer might consider purchasing only one brand and would look for price competition among different dealers in that brand. Much competition in the automobile industry is actually intrabrand. Were the antitrust laws to permit territorial arrangements that allocated exclusive territories to dealers in a particular brand, the ability of automobile buyers to compare prices among different dealers in that brand would be eliminated and a substantial reduction in competition would result. Another argument against intrabrand territorial restrictions is that the elimination of competitors often increases concentration in markets in which far too little competition already exists.

A corollary of the agreement that allots a specific territory to a seller is the agreement allocating customers. These two often go hand in hand because a territorial restriction prohibiting sales outside a specified area limits the customers with whom the seller may deal. Sometimes, however, customer restrictions go beyond territorial allocations. It is not unusual for a manufacturer to reserve a particular buyer for direct sales, prohibiting distributors and dealers from selling to that buyer. Most of the arguments for and against vertical territorial restrictions apply to vertical agreements dividing customers. In the case that follows the manufacturer attempted to maintain control over territory by limiting locations from which retailers sold. Here the U.S. Supreme Court overrules a previous case where it had used a per se standard to judge nonprice vertical restrictions illegal. Using a rule of reason standard, it comes to a different conclusion as to the legality of vertical territorial restraints.

Continental T.V., Inc. v. GTE Sylvania
United States Supreme Court
433 U.S. 36 (1977)

Background: GTE Sylvania (plaintiff-respondent) manufactures and sells television sets. Prior to 1962 Sylvania sold its televisions to independent or company-owned distributors, who resold to a large and diverse group of retailers. Prompted by a decline in its market share to 1 to 2 percent of the national market, Sylvania adopted a franchise plan.

Sylvania phased out its wholesale distributors and sold directly to a smaller and more select group of franchised retailers. In order to attract aggressive, competent retailers, Sylvania limited the number of franchises in any area and required each franchisee to sell only from the location at which he was franchised. A franchise did not constitute an exclusive territory. Sylvania retained the right to modify the number of franchises in an area.

The revised marketing strategy was successful, and by 1965 Sylvania's share of national television set sales had increased to approximately 5 percent. Dissatisfied with its sales in the city of San Francisco, Sylvania decided to establish an additional San Francisco retailer (Young Brothers), who would be in competition with Continental (defendant-petitioner-appellant in this case) since the proposed new franchisee would be only one mile away. Continental protested that the location of the new franchise violated Sylvania's marketing policy, but Sylvania persisted in its plan. Continental then canceled a large Sylvania order and placed an order with Phillips, one of Sylvania's competitors.

During this same period Continental expressed a desire to open a store in Sacramento, a desire Sylvania attributed at least in part to Continental's displeasure over the Young Brothers decision. Sylvania believed that the Sacramento market was adequately served by existing Sylvania retailers and denied the request. In the face of this denial, Continental advised Sylvania in September 1965 that it was moving Sylvania merchandise from its San Jose warehouse to a new retail location that it had leased in Sacramento. Two weeks later, allegedly for unrelated reasons, Sylvania's credit department reduced Continental's credit line from $300,000 to $50,000. In response to the reduction in credit and the generally deteriorating relations with Sylvania, Continental withheld all payments owed to John P. Maguire & Co., Inc. (Maguire), the finance company that handled the credit arrangements between Sylvania and its retailers. Shortly thereafter, Sylvania terminated Continental's franchise, and Maguire filed this diversity action in the U.S. District Court seeking recovery of money owed and of secured merchandise held by Continental. Continental filed cross claims against Sylvania and Maguire, claiming that Sylvania had violated Section 1 of the Sherman Act by entering into and enforcing franchise agreements that prohibited sale of Sylvania products by Continental and other franchises except from specific locations. At the District Court level the jury found in favor of Continental, awarding treble (triple) damages totaling $1,774,515 for violations of Section 1 of the Sherman Act. The Court of Appeals reversed in favor of Sylvania.

Decision: Affirmed. The United States Supreme Court ruled in favor of Sylvania.

Powell, Justice

We turn first to Continental's contention that Sylvania's restriction on retail locations is a *per se* violation of §1 of the Sherman Act as interpreted in *Schwinn.* (United States v. Arnold Schwinn, 338 U.S. 365(1967)).

Schwinn came to this Court on appeal by the United States from the District Court's decision. . . . [T]he Court (in *Schwinn*) proceeded to articulate the following "bright line" *per se* rule of illegality for vertical restrictions: "Under the Sherman Act, it is unreasonable without more for a manufacturer to seek to restrict and confine areas or persons with whom an article may be traded after the manufacturer has parted with dominion over it." But the Court expressly stated that the rule of reason governs when "the manufacturer retains title, dominion, and risk with respect to the product and the position and function of the dealer in question are, in fact, indistinguishable from those of an agent or salesman of the manufacturer."

In the present case, it is undisputed that title to the televisions passed from Sylvania to Continental. Thus, the *Schwinn per se* rule applies unless Sylvania's restriction on locations falls outside *Schwinn's* prohibition against a manufacturer attempting to restrict a "retailer's freedom as to where and to whom it will resell the products."

Sylvania argues that if *Schwinn* cannot be distinguished, it should be reconsidered. Although *Schwinn* is supported by the principle of *stare decisis,* we are convinced that the need for clarification of the law in this area justifies reconsideration. *Schwinn* itself was an abrupt and largely unexplained departure from *White Motor Co.* v. *United States,* where only four years earlier the Court had refused to endorse a *per se* rule for vertical restrictions. Since its announcement, *Schwinn* has been the subject of continuing controversy and confusion, both in the scholarly journals and in the federal courts. The great weight of scholarly opinion has been critical of the decision, and a number of the federal courts confronted with analogous vertical restrictions have sought to limit its reach. In our view, the experience of the past 10 years should be brought to bear on this subject of considerable commercial importance.

In essence, the issue before us is whether *Schwinn's per se* rule can be justified under the demanding standards of *Northern Pac. R. Co.* The Court's refusal to endorse a *per se* rule in *White Motor Co.* was based on its uncertainty as to whether vertical restrictions satisfied those standards. Addressing this question for the first time, the Court stated:

> We need to know more than we do about the actual impact of these arrangements on competition to decide whether they have such a 'pernicious effect on competition and lack . . . any redeeming virtue' and therefore should be classified as *per se* violations of the Sherman Act.

Only four years later the Court in *Schwinn* announced its sweeping *per se* rule without even a reference to *Northern Pac. R. Co.* and with no explanation of its sudden change in position. We turn now to consider *Schwinn* in light of *Northern Pac. R. Co.*

The question remains whether the *per se* rule stated in *Schwinn* should be expanded to include nonsale transactions or abandoned in favor of a return to the rule of reason. We have found no persuasive support for expanding the rule. As noted above, the *Schwinn* Court recognized the undesirability of "prohibit[ing] all vertical restrictions of territory and all franchising. . . ." And even Continental does not urge us to hold that all such restrictions are *per se* illegal.

We revert to the standard articulated in *Northern Pac. R. Co.,* and reiterated in *White Motor,* for determining whether vertical restriction must be "conclusively presumed to be unreasonable and therefore illegal without elaborate inquiry as to the precise harm they have caused or the business excuse for their use." Such restrictions, in varying forms, are widely used in our free market economy. As indicated above, there is substantial scholarly and judicial authority supporting their economic utility. There is relatively little authority to the contrary. Certainly, there has been no showing in this case, either generally or with respect to Sylvania's agreements, that vertical restrictions have or are likely to have a "pernicious effect on competition" or that they "lack . . . any redeeming virtue." Accordingly, we conclude that the *per se* rule stated in *Schwinn* must be overruled. In so holding we do not foreclose the possibility that particular applications of vertical restrictions might justify *per se* prohibition under *Northern Pac. R. Co.* But we do make clear that departure from the rule of reason standard must be based upon demonstrable economic effect rather than—as in *Schwinn*—upon formalistic line drawing.

In sum, we conclude that the appropriate decision is to return to the rule of reason that governed vertical restrictions prior to *Schwinn.* When competitive effects are shown to result from particular vertical restrictions they can be adequately policed under the rule of reason, the standard traditionally applied for the majority of anticompetitive practices challenged under §1 of the Act.

Trade Associations

A *trade association* is a loosely knit combination of business firms operating in the same industry. Frequently the members are either competitors or potential competitors. Most associations are supported by dues and governed by directors elected by members. The relationship is often an informal one, and members can usually resign at will. Daily operations of the association generally are the responsibility of a paid executive director and his staff. In most instances the purpose of the association is to promote the common interests of the members by providing services, supplying information, and engaging in promotional activities such as institutional advertising. Many activities of trade associations are beneficial not only to the members but also to the economic system.

Trade associations sometimes promote more effective competition. When participants in a particular industry have some idea of industrywide inventories, sales, and costs of production, they can plan more efficiently. This reduces costs, prevents waste, and improves services to the public. Trade associations have often been leaders in the standardization and development of products. In addition, they may establish general rules for the industry, carry out market surveys, provide a means for exchanging credit information, and supply arbitrators to aid in settling disputes. Some trade associations have also been instrumental in developing and improving ethical standards within their industry.

The opportunity provided competitors by trade-association contacts, however, sometimes leads to activities that may violate the antitrust statutes. Activities that have resulted in antitrust prosecutions usually have involved some covert effort to control prices. When members report prices to their association, pressures can be used to force those firms charging lower prices (who are now clearly identified) to get into line with the industry. In several cases trade associations have been used by dominant members to enforce desired price levels by denying certain benefits of the association to recalcitrants. These activities have reduced competition and increased profit levels for association members at the expense of the buying public.

In general the courts attempt to distinguish between legitimate and illegitimate activities of trade associations. Price reports by members for the use of the membership are usually permitted if the association does not identify the prices with the names of the reporting firms and if the information is also available to nonmembers, customers, and the government. Just as knowledge of prices charged by competitors can be used to attain common industrywide prices, so other types of data sometimes supplied by members of a trade association may be used to restrict competition. Nevertheless, the compilation of cost data and the circulation of information about inventories, unused production capacity, unfilled orders, and sales can also encourage more realistic competition. As long as this type of information is disclosed in general terms, it is not subject to government restraints. If, however, such information is used solely by the membership and is not available to the public, the courts will closely scrutinize those activities.

Boycotts

Another business practice that is permissible if done individually but illegal if done in collusion is the *boycott.* A single business firm may withhold its patronage or refuse to sell in order to accomplish some self-serving end, but a concerted group refusal to deal has been held to violate Section 1 of the Sherman Act. Courts have generally applied a per se prohibition to this type of activity when carried out in a commercial context. Boycotts unrelated to the profits of the group refusing to deal have generally not been held violations of Section 1 of the Sherman Act. For example, when the National Organization of Women (NOW) organized a boycott of states that refused to endorse the proposed Equal Rights Amendment, Missouri sued NOW, claiming a violation of Section 1 of the Sherman Act. The Eighth Circuit Court of Appeals termed the Sherman Act inapplicable to this situation, and the Supreme Court denied Missouri's petition for review.[7]

Tying Agreements

Business managers who control the sale of a product in limited supply because of some natural advantage, or possibly because of a patent, have sometimes tried to increase the sale of another product by tying purchase of the two together. The buyer is not permitted to purchase one item without also purchasing the other. Arrangements of this kind are called *tie-in* or *tying agreements.* In one well-known case, the International Salt Company, which had patents on two salt-dispensing machines, leased the machines (the *tying* product) only if the lessee would agree to buy all the salt (the *tied* product) to be used in the machines from International Salt. The Supreme Court held this to be an unlawful restraint of trade.[8] Tying agreements have also been used by sellers who, for one reason or another, are convinced that the "leverage" of one of their products will enable them to sell another, less marketable product.

Tying agreements have been used extensively in sales to consumers, but most litigation has arisen out of transactions at the producer level. Economically the device is objectionable because it limits other sellers of the tied product (the second good or service) from competing in that particular market. This is considered an artificial barrier to competition and has been the subject of considerable judicial censure.

At one time the Supreme Court argued that the effects of a tie-in were so pernicious that mere proof of the agreement established a violation of the antitrust laws (Section 1 of the Sherman Act, Section 3 of the Clayton Act). That is, such agreements were to be condemned per se. This, however, does not appear to be the present state of the law. Tie-in agreements will almost invariably be struck down if the tying product is either a natural or a legal monopoly, such as a patented product. Even when the seller of the tying product does not have monopoly control, tying contracts will be unenforceable (1) if control of the tying product has given the seller sufficient economic power to lessen competition in the market where the tied product is sold and (2) if a substantial amount of interstate commerce is affected. This is true even if no actual injury to competition can be proved.

On the other hand, tying agreements have been allowed by the courts using a rule of reason, where the seller was able to prove that the tied product or service was necessary to maintain the utility and reputation of the desired product. Sellers have successfully defended also by showing that the tying product is only of minor importance in the market and that the buyer was not forced by economic pressures to accept the tied product. In addition, tie-ins are economically beneficial when used by new competitors to facilitate entry into markets dominated by established sellers. The case excerpted here illustrates a rule of reason approach.

Jefferson Parish Hospital District No. 2 v. Edwin G. Hyde

U.S. Supreme Court
468 U.S. 2 (1984)

Background: Jefferson Parish Hospital (petitioner-defendant) was sued by Hyde, an anesthesiologist (plaintiff-respondent) who claimed that the hospital violated Section

1 of the Sherman Act. The defendant entered into an exclusive contract between itself and a firm of anesthesiologists (Roux & Associates), whereby the firm would provide all the anesthesiological services required by the hospital's patients. When the plaintiff applied for admission to the hospital staff the credentials committee and the medical staff's executive committee recommended approval of his application. The hospital board denied the application because of its exclusive contract with Roux & Associates. There are about twenty hospitals in the New Orleans area. About 70 percent of the patients living in Jefferson Parish go to hospitals other than East Jefferson. The District Court held for the defendants. The Court of Appeals held for the plaintiff. The hospital appealed.

Decision: Reversed. The Supreme Court of the United States ruled in favor of Jefferson Parish Hospital.

Stevens, Justice

At issue in this case is the validity of an exclusive contract between a hospital and a firm of anesthesiologists. We must decide whether the contract gives rise to a *per se* violation of §1 of the Sherman Act because every patient undergoing surgery at the hospital must use the services of one firm of anesthesiologists, and, if not, whether the contract is nevertheless illegal because it unreasonably restrains competition among anesthesiologists.

Certain types of contractual arrangements are deemed unreasonable as a matter of law. The character of the restraint produced by such an arrangement is considered a sufficient basis for presuming unreasonableness, without the necessity of any analysis of the market context in which the arrangement may be found. A price fixing agreement between competitors is the classic example of such an arrangement. It is far too late in the history of our antitrust jurisprudence to question the proposition that certain tying arrangements pose an unacceptable risk of stifling competition and therefore are unreasonable "per se."

Any inquiry into the validity of a tying arrangement must focus on the market or markets in which the two products are sold, for that is where the anticompetitive forcing has its impact. Thus, in this case our analysis of the tying issue must focus on the hospital's sale of services to its patients, rather than its contractual arrangements with the providers of anesthesiological services. In making that analysis, we must consider whether petitioners are selling two separate products that may be tied together, and, if so, whether they have used their market power to force their patients to accept the tying arrangement.

The hospital has provided its patients with a package that includes the range of facilities and services required for a variety of surgical operations. At East Jefferson Hospital the package includes the services of the anesthesiologist. Petitioners argue that the package does not involve a tying arrangement at all—that they are merely providing a functionally integrated package of services. Therefore, petitioners contend that it is inappropriate to apply principles concerning tying arrangements to this case.

Our cases indicate, however, that the answer to the question whether one or two products are involved, turns not on the functional relation between them, but rather on the character of the demand for the two items. Thus, in this case no tying arrangement can exist unless there is a sufficient demand for the purchase of anesthesiological services separate from hospital services to identify a distinct product market in which it is efficient to offer anesthesiological services separately from hospital services.

Unquestionably, the anesthesiological component of the package offered by the hospital could be provided separately and could be selected either by the individual patient or by one of the patient's doctors if the hospital did not insist on including anesthesiological services in the package it offers to its customers. As a matter of actual practice, anesthesiological services are billed separately from the hospital services petitioners provide. There is ample and uncontroverted testimony that patients or surgeons often request specific anesthesiologists to come to a hospital and provide anesthesia, and that the choice of an individual anesthesiologist separate from the choice of a hospital is particularly frequent in respondent's specialty, obstetric anesthesiology. The record amply supports the conclusion that consumers differentiate between anesthesiological services and the other hospital services provided by petitioners.

The question remains whether this arrangement involves the use of market power to force patients to buy services they would not otherwise purchase.

Seventy percent of the patients residing in Jefferson Parish enter hospitals other than East Jefferson. Thus East Jefferson's "dominance" over persons residing in Jefferson Parish is far from overwhelming. The fact that a substantial majority of the parish's residents elect not to enter East Jefferson means that the geographic data does not establish the kind of dominant market position that obviates the need for further inquiry into actual competitive conditions. The Court of Appeals acknowledged as much; it recognized that East Jefferson's market share alone was insufficient as a basis to infer market power, and buttressed its conclusion by relying on "market imperfections" that permit petitioners to charge noncompetitive prices for hospital services: the prevalence of third party payment for health care costs reduces price competition, and a lack of adequate information renders consumers unable to evaluate the quality of the medical care provided by competing hospitals. While these factors may generate "market power" in some abstract sense, they do not generate the kind of market power that justifies condemnation of tying. The record therefore does not provide a basis for applying the *per se* rule against tying to this arrangement.

In order to prevail in the absence of *per se* liability, respondent has the burden of proving that the Roux contract violated the Sherman Act because it unreasonably restrained competition. That burden necessarily involves an inquiry into the actual effect of the exclusive contract on competition among anesthesiologists.

Petitioners' closed policy may raise questions of medical ethics, and may have inconvenienced some patients who would prefer to have their anesthesia administered by someone other than a member of Roux & Associates, but it does not have the obviously unreasonable impact on purchasers that has characterized the tying arrangements that this Court has branded unlawful. There is no evidence that the price, the quality, or the supply or demand for either the "tying product" or the "tied product" involved in this case has been adversely affected by the exclusive contract between Roux and the hospital. It may well be true that the contract made it necessary for Dr. Hyde and others to practice elsewhere, rather than at East Jefferson. But there has been no showing that the market as a whole has been affected at all by the contract. There is simply no showing here of the kind of restraint on competition that is prohibited by the Sherman Act.

Monopoly Behavior

Monopoly in its purest economic sense involves a single firm without any effective competition. This means that not only is no other firm producing the same product, but that no other firm produces a product that consumers could switch to if the monopolist's prices are too high. The foregoing definition is far too restrictive for an antimonopoly statute because a firm could have the ability to act unilaterally and create market restraints without falling within the economic definition of a monopoly. Consequently, a legal definition of monopoly has been developed by the courts as they have interpreted the language of Section 2 of the Sherman Act. Section 2, summarized in Table 44-1, reads as follows:

Every person who shall monopolize, or attempt to monopolize, or combine or conspire with any other person or persons, to monopolize any part of the trade or commerce among the several States, or with foreign nations, shall be deemed guilty of a felony, and, on conviction thereof, shall be punished by fine not exceeding one-million dollars, if a corporation, or, if any other person, one-hundred thousand dollars, or by imprisonment not exceeding three years. . . .

As its language clearly indicates, Section 2 prohibits three types of activities: (1) monopolization, (2) attempts to monopolize, and (3) combinations or conspiracies to monopolize. Most actions under Section 2 have been against single firms charged with monopolization. Suits based on attempts or conspiracies to monopolize are much more difficult to win because they require proof of a specific intent to achieve the unlawful result of monopoly power.

The most difficult problem arising from the language of Section 2 is how the term *monopolize* should be legally defined. A variety of definitions is available to the courts. The courts could determine, for example, that only firms in single-firm industries are monopolies. They might alternatively decide that any firm capable of realizing specified "excess" profits by its pricing ability is a monopoly. They could take yet another approach and conclude that any firm controlling a certain percentage of an industry's total sales or assets is a monopoly. Unfortunately, the actual words of the statute provide little guidance in choosing among alternative definitions.

In analyzing monopoly cases, the courts have set out the guidelines discussed subsequently as a basis for decision making. They include a determination of (1) the relevant product market, (2) the relevant geographic market, (3) whether overwhelming market power exists, and (4) whether intent to monopolize exists.

Relevant Product Market

To judge accurately whether a particular firm has overwhelming market power, we need to determine the specific industry (market) in respect to which the firm's market power is to be judged. Thus a relevant competitive market must be delineated in terms of geography and product-line. First it is generally necessary to determine the relevant product market, because the relevant geographic market will ordinarily be defined in terms of the product. The following well-known case established the basic test of cross-elasticity or interchangeability that the courts use in defining relevant markets.

United States v. Du Pont & Co.
Supreme Court of the United States
351 U.S. 377 (1956)

Background: The government instituted suit under Section 2 of the Sherman Act alleging that Du Pont (defendant) had monopolized and attempted and conspired to monopolize the cellophane market. The government asked the court to issue an injunction to prevent further monopolization and to order the divestiture of plants and assets, if necessary. At the time of the suit Du Pont produced approximately 75 percent of all cellophane sold in the United States. This in turn represented 17.9 percent of all flexible wrapping material. The District Court found that the relevant product market was all flexible wrapping materials and entered a judgment for Du Pont on all counts. The government appealed directly to the Supreme Court. Decision: Affirmed. The United States Supreme Court ruled in favor of Du Pont.

Reed, Justice

During the period that is relevant to this action, du Pont produced almost 75 percent of the cellophane sold in the United States, and cellophane constituted less than 20 percent of all "flexible packaging materials" sales. Du Pont . . . contends that the prohibition of §2 against monopolization is not violated because it does not have the power to control the price of cellophane or to exclude competitors from the market in which cellophane is sold. The court below found that the "relevant market for determining the extent of du Pont's market control is the market for flexible packaging materials," and that competition from those other materials prevented du Pont from possessing monopoly powers in its sales of cellophane.

The Government asserts that cellophane and other wrapping materials are neither substantially fungible nor like priced. For these reasons, it argues that the market for other wrappings is distinct from the market for cellophane and that the competition afforded cellophane by other wrappings is not strong enough to be considered in determining whether du Pont has monopoly powers. . . . Every manufacturer is the sole producer of the particular commodity it makes, but its control, in the above sense of the relevant market, depends upon the availability of alternative commodities for buyers: i.e., whether there is a cross-elasticity of demand between cellophane and the other wrappings. This interchangeability is largely gauged by the purchase of competing products for similar uses considering the price, characteristics and adaptability of the competing commodities. The court below found that the flexible wrappings afforded such alternatives.

If cellophane is the "market" that du Pont is found to dominate, it may be assumed it does have monopoly power over that "market." Monopoly power is the power to control prices or exclude competition. It seems apparent that du Pont's power to set the price of cellophane has been limited only by the competition afforded by other flexible packaging materials. Moreover, it may be practically impossible for anyone to commence manufacturing cellophane without full access to du Pont's technique. However, du Pont has no power to prevent competition from other wrapping materials. It is inconceivable that price could be controlled without power over competition or vice versa. . . .

Determination of the competitive market for commodities depends on how different from one another are the offered commodities in character or use, how far buyers will go to substitute one commodity for another. For example, one can think of building materials as in commodity competition, but one could hardly say that brick competed with steel or wood or cement or stone in the meaning of Sherman Act litigation; the products are too different . . . [T]here are certain differences in the formulae for soft drinks but one can hardly say that each one is an illegal monopoly.

Cellophane costs more than many competing products and less than a few.

Cellophane differs from other flexible packaging materials. From some, it differs more than from others.

It may be admitted that cellophane combines the desirable elements of transparency, strength and cheapness more definitely than any of the others. . . .

But, despite cellophane's advantages, it has to meet competition from other materials in every one of its uses. The Government makes no challenge to Finding 283 that cellophane furnishes less than seven percent of wrappings for bakery products, 25 percent for candy, 32 percent for snacks, 35 percent for meats and poultry, 27 percent for crackers and biscuits, 47 percent for fresh produce, and 34 percent for frozen foods. 75 to 80 percent of cigarettes are wrapped in cellophane. Finding 292. Thus, cellophane shares the packaging market with others. The overall result is that cellophane accounts for 17.9 percent of flexible wrapping materials, measured by the wrapping surface.

An element for consideration as to cross-elasticity of demand between products is the responsiveness of the sales of one product to price changes of the other. . . . The court below held that the "[g]reat sensitivity of customers in the flexible packaging markets to price or quality changes" prevented du Pont from possessing monopoly control over price. . . .

We conclude that cellophane's interchangeability with the other materials mentioned suffices to make it a part of this flexible packaging material market.

Relevant Geographic Market

Once the relevant product market has been defined, it is necessary to determine the relevant geographic market. Basically the courts define the relevant geographic market in terms of the area of the defendant firm's effective competitive presence in regard to sales of the relevant product. This determination has not represented an important issue in Section 2 proceedings because generally only national producers have been challenged as monopolies. However, the *Grinnell* case, appearing later in this chapter, did involve the issue of whether the national relevant geographic market found to exist by a lower court should be broken down into local markets.

Overwhelming Market Power

The development of a legally practical and economically meaningful test of monopoly power within a particular relevant competitive market has been a major task of the federal judiciary. The difficulties encountered by the federal courts in their search for an appropriate test have been due, in part, to the fact that a variety of tests could be considered consistent with the very general language of Section 2. Reasonable alternative approaches might include basing the determination of illegality on

1. The achievement of a particular absolute or relative size
2. The existence of a specified "monopolistic" intent
3. The actual commission of specified anticompetitive acts

The question of the competitive effect of sheer physical size is central to determining which alternative test is most appropriate for application by the courts in Section 2 cases. We often hear the term "big business" used in a derogatory sense. Noted judges have written that "bigness is bad." Unfortunately, economic theorists have yet to answer definitively, by empirical findings, the question of whether large firm size is necessary to realize productive efficiencies from the viewpoint of the economy as a whole.

Proponents of large firm size argue that large firms are more efficient by virtue of their ability to realize economies of scale in production and promotion, attract top talent, obtain capital market advantages, effectively conduct research, and introduce advanced technology. Opponents of large firm size argue that many firms become unmanageable beyond an optimum size, economies of scale are often not effectively realized, large size (which is likely to result in just a few firms in a particular industry) encourages collusive pricing and other harmful market practices, and the resulting lack of competition deters research. Opponents further argue that the promotion economies and capital-market power of large firms permit these less efficient firms to survive and even dominate their industries.

In applying Section 2 of the Sherman Act,

the courts have been unable to rely directly on the economic model of monopoly, which posits a single firm in its market protected from entry of new firms and from the competition of substitute products. Because this is an exceedingly rare phenomenon in our modern economy, it does not afford a practical *legal* standard. The *Grinnell* case that follows dramatizes the generally analytical, nontechnical approach that the courts have used in determining the presence of the overwhelming market power necessary to violate the statute.

The first major monopoly case was the famous *Standard Oil of New Jersey* v. *United States* (1911).[9] That decision, which broke up the Standard Oil of New Jersey holding company, established a rule of reason approach—the Court looked for an intent to monopolize and actual instances of conduct manifesting that intent. Thus, if such elements were present, an illegal monopoly would be found to exist. That case was quickly followed by the *United States Steel Corporation* case in 1920, in which the Supreme Court stated that "the law does not make mere size an offense, or the existence of unexerted power an offense."[10] The Court found that United States Steel did not have the power to control prices, even though at times it had controlled 50 percent of the market, and refused to break up the company. This resulted in the so-called abuse theory under which the courts for the next twenty years looked for specific abuses and analyzed the actions of alleged monopolists to determine whether they were "good" or "bad" trusts. During this period the courts applied essentially behavioral criteria to determine whether Section 2 had been violated.

The case establishing the modern interpretation of Section 2, and perhaps the most important monopoly case decided to date, is the circuit court opinion of Judge Learned Hand in *United States* v. *Aluminum Co. of America* (Alcoa) (1945). In *Alcoa* the court used a structuralist approach and focused mainly on the percentage of the market controlled by Alcoa. Judge Hand found that Alcoa had 90 percent of the relevant competitive market and concluded that "that percentage is enough to constitute a monopoly; it is doubtful whether 60 or 64 percent would be enough; and certainly 33 percent is not." On the basis of the monopolization cases decided to date, it can be said that when a firm controls more than 80 percent of a relevant competitive market it is likely to be found in violation of Section 2 of the Sherman Act. This "big is bad" approach by Judge Hand has been severely criticized because the monopoly position of a firm could have been gained by patents or internal efficiencies. Are innovative and efficient firms to be punished because they have obtained more than 80 percent of their market? Will a firm fail to expand and meet buyer demand for fear of obtaining too large a share of its market and becoming a "monopoly"? What effect does this have on production, output, and employment? An equity standard that opposes "big-ness" seems to be in conflict with an efficiency standard that is concerned with consumer welfare. The meaning of *Alcoa* is still debated.

Intent to Monopolize

The existence of market power by itself does not constitute monopolization. The defendant must be shown to have a *general intent* to exercise that power. General intent exists if acts are performed leading to the prohibited result regardless of whether that particular result was actually desired. It is not necessary to show specific intent—that is, the defendant wanted to monopolize. Often general intent to monopolize can be inferred from common and usual methods of doing business.

The case that follows outlines the elements of monopoly and identifies conduct that may show an intent to monopolize. Additionally, the Court defines what constitutes a relevant product market.

United States v. Grinnell Corp.

United States Supreme Court

384 U.S. 563 (1966)

Background: The United States (plaintiff) charged Grinnell (defendant) with monopolizing the accredited central-station protection business by using its subsidiaries (identified in the opinion) to obtain a dominant market position. Grinnell manufactured plumbing supplies and fire-sprinkler systems. It also owned 76 percent of the stock of ADT, 89 percent of the stock of AFA, and 100 percent of the stock of Holmes. ADT provided both burglary and fire-protection services; Holmes provided burglary services alone; AFA supplied only fire-protection service. Each offered a central-station service under which hazard-detecting devices installed on the protected premises automatically transmitted an electric signal to a central station. The three companies that Grinnell controlled had over 87 percent of the business. The District Court found for the government and ordered Grinnell to prepare a plan for divestiture of certain of its subsidiaries. The government felt that the relief granted was inadequate, and both parties appealed to the Supreme Court.

Decision: Affirmed. The United States Supreme Court ruled in favor of the United States.

Douglas, Justice

The offense of monopoly under §2 of the Sherman Act has two elements: (1) the possession of monopoly power in the relevant market and (2) the willful acquisition or maintenance of that power as distinguished from growth or development as a consequence of a superior product, business acumen, or historic accident. In the present case, 87 percent of the accredited central station service business leaves no doubt that the congeries of these defendants have monopoly power—power which, as our discussion of the record indicates, they did not hesitate to wield—if that business is the relevant market. The only remaining question therefore is, what is the relevant market?

In case of a product, it may be of such a character that substitute products must also be considered, as customers may turn to them if there is a slight increase in the price of the main product. That is the teaching of the *du Pont* case . . . viz., that commodities reasonably interchangeable make up that "part" of trade or commerce which §2 protects against monopoly power.

The District Court treated the entire accredited central station service business as a single market and we think it was justified in so doing. Defendants argue that the different central station services offered are so diverse that they cannot, under *du Pont,* be lumped together to make up the relevant market. For example, burglar alarm services are not interchangeable with fire alarm services. They further urge that *du Pont* requires that protective services other than those of the central station variety be included in the market definition.

But there is here a single use, *i.e.,* the protection of property, through a central station that receives signals. It is that service, accredited, that is unique and that competes with all the other forms of property protection. . . .

[W]e deal with services, not with products; and . . . we conclude that the accredited central station is a type of service that makes up a relevant market and that domination or control of it makes out a monopoly and a "part" of trade or commerce within the meaning of §2 of the Sherman Act. The defendants have not made out a case for fragmentizing the types of services into lesser units.

There are, to be sure, substitutes for the accredited central station service. But none of them appears to operate on the same level as the central station service so as to meet the interchangeability test of the *du Pont* case.

Watchman service is far more costly and less reliable. Systems that set off an audible alarm at the site of a fire or burglary are cheaper but often less reliable. They may be inoperable without anyone's knowing it. Moreover, there is a risk that the local ringing of an alarm will not attract the needed attention and help. Proprietary systems that a customer purchases and operates are available; but they can be used only by a very large business or by government and are not realistic alternatives for most concerns.

The accredited, as distinguished from nonaccredited service, is a relevant part of commerce. Virtually, the only central station companies in the status of the nonaccredited are those that have not yet been able to meet the standards of the rating bureau. The accredited ones are indeed those that have achieved, in the eyes of underwriters, superiorities that other central stations do not have. These standards are important, as insurance carriers often require accredited central station service as a condition to writing insurance. There is indeed evidence that customers consider the unaccredited service as inferior.

As the District Court found, the relevant market for determining whether the defendants have monopoly power is not the several local areas which the individual stations serve, but the broader national market that reflects the reality of the way in which they build and conduct their businesses.

Grinnell was ordered to file, not later than April 1, 1966, a plan of divestiture of its stock in each of the other defendant companies. It was given the option either to sell the stock or distribute it to its stockholders or combine or vary those methods.

The defendants object to the requirements that Grinnell divest itself of its holdings in the three alarm company defendants, but we think that provision is wholly justified. Dissolution of the combination is essential as indicated by many of our cases, starting with *Standard Oil Co.* v. *United States.*

The few large American firms that control 40 to 60 percent of their identifiable relevant competitive markets react with extreme caution to changes in their market shares to make sure they will not be charged with monopolization. The restraint exercised by such firms directly affects their marketing and advertising strategies. These strategies often emphasize maintaining rather than increasing *relative* market shares, and steps are taken to make sure that the company does not have even the appearance of engaging in anticompetitive activities. Following the *Grinnell* case, one can imagine the reaction of the board of directors and top officers at General Motors to a proposal by a young marketing vice-president for an aggressive long-run marketing strategy whose aim would be to obtain an 85 percent share of domestic auto sales within ten years. On occasion the dominant firm in an industry has even provided marketing and research assistance to weak or marginal competitors to keep them in business.

Two important monopolization cases were settled in January 1982. If one or the other had been carried to the U.S. Supreme Court, we might have had a redefinition of the law of monopolization. The Justice Department suits against American Telephone and Telegraph

(AT&T) and International Business Machines (IBM) charged both firms with monopolizing and attempting to monopolize services and equipment in the telecommunications and computer industries, respectively. After the cases were filed (in the early 1970s) more competitors entered both fields, domestically and abroad, and technology revolutionized the two industries. Also, congressional pressure, in the form of proposed legislation, was brought to bear on the companies and the Justice Department. All these factors led to an agreed modification of a 1956 consent decree (AT&T case) and a stipulated dismissal (IBM case).

From these cases and several cases reaching federal courts of appeal,[11] it has become clear that some monopolistic conduct will be considered permissible. When a monopolist seeks to protect its position against rivals entering the market with new products, aggressive pricing policies and innovative products, these actions will be considered legitimate as long as the monopolist does not subsidize one product with revenue from others. In addition to the intent to monopolize, it now appears that efficiency and consumer-welfare criteria will be considered by some federal courts in examining Section 2 monopoly charges against firms that have large shares of a market.

Attempts to Monopolize

Section 2 of the Sherman Act forbids *attempts* to monopolize as well as monopolization. In other words, a company does not have to be successful in monopolizing a market. Conduct that brought a corporation close to monopolization and showed an intent to monopolize was all that was required by the Supreme Court in early cases. Today most authorities agree that an attempt to monopolize requires

1. Specific intent
2. Predatory or anticompetitive conduct to attain the purpose
3. A dangerous probability of success

A "dangerous probability of success" is usually shown through direct proof of the market power that the firm has attained. "Predatory pricing" has been the focus of much academic and case analysis of monopoly and price-discrimination situations. Courts have generally agreed that pricing above marginal or variable costs will obviously not be predatory, and thus no specific intent can be shown to support charges that a firm attempted to monopolize. The question is at what point in a firm's pricing policy do prices become predatory? In light of the fact that an attempt to monopolize is punishable as a felony, with heavy criminal penalties, the answer to this question has some significance for businesspeople. The Areeda–Turner standard[12] (most popular with the courts) states that when a firm sets its price below marginal cost (or average variable cost used as a substitute) it is engaged in predatory pricing because it no longer seeks to maximize profits, but rather, to eliminate an economically viable competitor. Critics of this standard argue that those not trained in economic analysis have a difficult time understanding terms such as marginal, variable, and fixed costs. They point out that accountants and economists who regularly use these terms define them differently. Because of the imprecision

of economic analysis (particularly in a litigation context), critics argue that definitions of predatory pricing that include economic-cost terminology should be received with some skepticism by the courts.

CLAYTON ACT

Mergers

A *merger* is the acquisition by one corporation of the assets or stock of another independent corporation wherein the acquired corporation comes to be controlled by the acquirer. Mergers have had an important effect on the nature of industrial organization. They have accounted for a substantial degree of the current concentration in many industries. Numerous mergers take place in the United States each year. In the fiscal year 1981, 2,314 mergers took place in the United States, up 53 percent over the previous year. Du Pont's acquisition of Conoco and Sohio's of Kennecott Copper were the most prominent.[13] The increase in mergers in 1981 was largely due to the Reagan Administration's more relaxed approach to enforcement of Section 7 of the Clayton Act. Also, undervalued stocks, particularly in the oil industry, led companies to believe that it was cheaper to acquire a company than to finance internal expansion, especially at high interest rates. Finally, a number of companies divested themselves of subsidiaries purchased in the late 1950s and early 1960s that were no longer viable profit centers.

On the basis of the economic interrelationships between the firms involved, mergers may be classified into three basic types—horizontal, vertical, and conglomerate. A *horizontal merger* involves two competing firms at the same level of the distribution structure. A *vertical merger* involves two firms at different levels of the distribution structure that deal with the same basic product or process. A *con-*

glomerate merger results when noncompeting, nonrelated firms merge. The acquisition by RCA of the Hertz Rental Car Company is an example of a conglomerate merger and the acquisition of RCA by General Electric.

Relevant Competitive Market. To evaluate the effect of a merger for regulatory purposes, we need to define the product and geographic dimensions of a relevant competitive market. This is mandated by amended Section 7 of the Clayton Act, which provides:

No person engaged in commerce or in any activity affecting commerce shall acquire, directly or indirectly, the whole or any part of the stock or other share capital and no person subject to the jurisdiction of the Federal Trade Commission shall acquire the whole or any part of the assets of another person engaged also in commerce or in any activity affecting commerce, where *in any line of commerce* or *in any activity affecting commerce in any section of the country,* the effect of such acquisition may be substantially to lessen competition, or to tend to create a monopoly.

The determination of the relevant competitive market in a merger case often establishes whether the postmerger firm is relatively a whale or a minnow. It often is *the* critical factor in the lawsuit's ultimate outcome.

In defining "line of commerce"—that is, the relevant product market—the courts have used the same basic standards of cross-elasticity of demand and marketplace treatment discussed earlier in reference to monopoly. When considering mergers, the courts are concerned with the treatment accorded products by consumers and industry representatives. They have shown a willingness to break product lines into submarkets or to combine product lines into aggregate markets whenever the circumstances in a particular case justified either approach.

After having defined the relevant product market, the court must determine the relevant geographic market. Section 7 condemns mergers whose effects may be to lessen competition substantially "in any section of the country." On its face that language raises an important question. If a lessening of competition can be found to exist in any single market area, is it then necessary to define a relevant geographic market? For example, could an acquisition by American Motors of a small custom-car manufacturer in Maine (who sells interstate) be found to violate Section 7 because of its combined market share in Bangor? The implications of this question are particularly bothersome if we assume that in no other city of the United States would its combined market share represent a violative figure. To date, with one confusing exception, all the cases have involved delineation of a relevant geographic market even if that were only a single metropolitan or commercial area.

As should be apparent, the determination of the boundaries of the relevant geographic market may significantly influence the final outcome of a particular case. For example, assume that a twenty-five-store discount chain selling throughout Ohio were to acquire an even smaller discount chain selling only in southern Ohio. For jurisdictional purposes, further assume that both are interstate firms. If the relevant geographic market were found to be the nation as a whole, there would be little chance that the merger would be in violation of Section 7. If, on the other hand, the state of Ohio were found to comprise the relevant geographic market, the chances of the merger's being set aside would be substantially increased. In general the smaller the relevant geographic market is, the more likely the government will prevail. The larger the geographic market is, the more likely the defendant firm will prevail.

In defining a relevant geographic market, the courts have sought to determine the boundaries of the geographic area of effective competition of the business involved in terms of the relevant product(s). When mergers at the manufacturing level are involved, the relevant geographic market is likely to be the nation as a whole, or at least several contiguous states. Retailing presents more complex questions, and a single large city (for supermarket retailing) or a contiguous four-county area (for commercial banking) may constitute the relevant geographic market. In the *Brown Shoe* case, excerpted later in this chapter, the court found the relevant geographic market to consist of those cities with populations of 10,000 or more in which both merging firms (Brown Shoe and Kinney Shoe) had outlets. Thus the courts have not required that the geographic market be defined as one unitary, contiguous area.

Department of Justice Merger Guidelines. The Department of Justice has issued merger guidelines outlining the standards the department will apply in defining relevant competitive markets and in evaluating the legality of acquisitions. The guidelines do not have the force of a court decision and do not represent a legally binding interpretation of Section 7. In fact each new administration of the Department of Justice is free to ignore or change the guidelines. In spite of this, the guidelines are of considerable value to businesspeople because the guidelines give them and their attorneys a basis for estimating whether a proposed acquisition is likely to be challenged by the government. The merger guidelines indicate that a relevant geographic market will be determined for each product market of each merging firm. Depending on the nature of the product, the geographic market may be a city, a state, or the country. Taking the location of the merging firm (or of each plant for a multiplant firm) as a starting point, the Department of Justice first establishes a provisional geographic market based on the shipment patterns of the merging firm and its closest competitors. As a first approximation, the department tests the market by hypothesizing a small price increase (5 percent) and asks how many sellers could sell the product to customers included in the provisional market. If the relevant product can be obtained from sellers outside the provisional market in sufficient quantity at a comparable price, the relevant geographic market is expanded to include those firms that can make "significant sales" to customers within the new market boundaries. This expanded area is then defined as the relevant geographic market.

Potential Effect on Competition. Once a court has defined the boundaries of the relevant competitive market and has thereby implicitly determined the type of merger involved, it must then evaluate the potential effect of the proposed merger on competition within that market. Section 7 indicates, in general terms, the anticompetitive effect necessary in order to condemn a merger. The language "effect of such acquisition *may be* substantially to lessen competition" and "tend to create a monopoly" seems to indicate that it is not necessary for the government to prove an actual, existing competitive restraint. Instead, the language is concerned with future probabilities. Thus in the past the government was required to demonstrate only that a proposed merger would probably result in prohibited anticompetitive effects in order to obtain a judgment striking down the merger. More recently (as discussed at the end of this section) the courts have required stricter proof of anticompetitive effects by the government.

In developing the criteria by which to apply the general language of Section 7 to actual mergers, the courts have found it necessary to distinguish between the different types of mergers. Such distinctions are proper and logical because horizontal, vertical, and conglomerate mergers may have significantly different economic effects. Thus, even though the same language of the same statute is applied to each type of merger, the specific questions to be answered in applying the statute will vary. These distinctions will become evident in the following discussion.

HORIZONTAL MERGERS. Of the three types of mergers, a horizontal merger involves the most direct and immediate competitive effect. Unless a firm's acquisition of a competitor is offset by a new entry into the industry, an immediate result of the merger will be increased concentration. Because horizontally merging firms already have identifiable market shares in their industry, the courts have specific, objective criteria from which to draw initial conclusions concerning the competitive effect of the merger. Consequently, the courts have had to resolve the following two questions concerning the use of market-share information:

1. What postacquisition market shares, if any, are so insignificant that the merger may be found to be clearly legal without further questions?
2. What market shares, if any, are probably so anticompetitive that the merger may be found to be illegal without further investigation?

In *United States* v. *Philadelphia National Bank* (1963) the Supreme Court determined that a postacquisition market share of 30 percent or more was prima facie illegal and thus resolved the second question. Note that the *Philadelphia Bank* opinion indicated that a share smaller than 30 percent could be prima facie illegal, but no lower limit has yet been established by the Supreme Court.

The question of whether an identifiable minimum postacquisition market share could be clearly legal was faced by the Supreme Court in the first important merger case reaching it under Section 7. *Brown Shoe* v. *United States,* set out subsequently, is particularly instructive because it clearly outlines the relevant product and geographic markets as well as the merger's potential effect on competition.

VERTICAL MERGERS. Vertical mergers are more difficult to evaluate because they do not involve combinations of direct competitors. Thus the courts cannot avail themselves of easily applied criteria such as market share or percentage of total productive assets controlled. Instead, the courts must analyze the resulting market structure and the probable market behavior of the postacquisition firm to determine if an actual or potential competitor is likely to be foreclosed from important markets. Ordinarily, the exclusion is of a direct competitor of one of the merging firms. For example, in *Brown Shoe* the reader will see the Supreme Court's concern that independent shoe manufacturers should not be denied access to retail outlets because of the number of retail stores that Brown-Kinney would control after the acquisition; and because of the established tendency of retail stores acquired by Brown to sell a much higher percentage of Brown's shoes after acquisition. Typically, the foreclosure is of a manufacturer from retail outlets or from a needed source of supply. As in this case, it is most likely to occur in an industry in which a few large firms are vertically integrated and a large number of smaller competitors are not.

Brown Shoe Co. v. United States

Supreme Court of the United States

370 U.S. 294 (1962)

Background: The government challenged the acquisition of the G. R. Kinney Company by Brown Shoe (defendant) on the grounds that the merger violated Section 7 of the Clayton Act. Brown was the third largest retail shoe seller (over 1,230 outlets) and the fourth largest shoe manufacturer, whereas Kinney was the eighth largest seller (over 350 outlets) and the twelfth largest manufacturer. The District Court found for the government and Brown appealed to the Supreme Court.

Decision: Affirmed for the United States.

Warren, Chief Justice

This case is one of the first to come before us in which the Government's complaint is based upon allegations that the applicants have violated Section 7 of the Clayton Act, as that section was amended in 1950.

The dominant theme pervading congressional consideration of the 1950 amendments was a fear of what was considered to be a rising tide of economic concentration in the American economy. Other considerations cited in support of the bill were the desirability of retaining "local control" over industry and the protection of small businesses. Throughout the recorded discussion may be found examples of Congress' fear, not only of accelerated concentration of economic power on economic grounds, but also of the threat to other values a trend toward concentration was thought to pose.

Congress neither adopted nor rejected specifically any particular tests for measuring the relevant markets, either as defined in terms of product or in terms of geographic locus of competition, within which the anticompetitive effects of a merger were to be judged. Nor did it adopt a definition of the word "substantially," whether in quantitative terms of sales or assets or market shares or in designated qualitative terms, by which a merger's effects on competition were to be measured.

Congress used the words *"may* tend substantially to lessen competition" (emphasis supplied), to indicate that its common concern was with probabilities, not certainties. Statutes existed for dealing with clear-cut menaces to competition; no statute was sought for dealing with ephemeral possibilities. Mergers with a probable anticompetitive effect were to be proscribed by this Act.

THE VERTICAL ASPECTS OF THE MERGER

Economic arrangements between companies standing in a supplier-customer relationship are characterized as "vertical." The primary vice of a vertical merger or other arrangement tying a customer to a supplier is that, by foreclosing the competitors of either party from a segment of the market otherwise open to them, the arrangement may act as a "clog on competition," . . . which "deprive(s) . . . rivals of a fair opportunity to compete."

The "area of effective competition" must be determined by reference to a product market (the "line of commerce") and a geographic market (the "section of the country").

The Product Market

The outer boundaries of a product market are determined by the reasonable interchangeability of use or the cross-elasticity of demand between the product itself and substitutes for it. However, within this broad market, well-defined submarkets may exist which, in themselves, constitute product markets for antitrust purposes. The boundaries of such a submarket may be determined by examining such practical indicia as industry or public recognition of the submarket as a separate economic entity, the product's peculiar characteristics and uses, unique production facilities, distinct customers, distinct prices, sensitivity to price changes, and specialized vendors.

Applying these considerations to the present case, we conclude that the record supports the District Court's finding that the relevant lines of commerce are men's, women's, and children's shoes. The product lines are recognized by the public; each line is manufactured in separate plants; each has characteristics peculiar to itself rendering it generally noncompetitive with the others; and each is, of course, directed toward a distinct class of customers.

Appellant, however, contends that the District Court's definitions fail to recognize sufficiently "price/quality" distinctions in shoes. Brown argues that the predominantly medium-priced shoes which it manufactures occupy a product market different from the predominantly low-priced shoes which Kinney sells. But agreement with that argument would be equivalent to holding that medium-priced shoes do not compete with low-priced shoes. We think the District Court properly found the facts to be otherwise.

The Geographic Market

We agree with the parties and District Court that insofar as the vertical aspect of this merger is concerned, the relevant geographic market is the entire Nation.

The Probable Effect of the Merger

. . . (I)t is apparent from both past behavior of Brown and from testimony of Brown's president, that Brown would see its ownership of Kinney to force Brown shoes into Kinney stores.

Another important factor to consider is the trend toward concentration in the industry.

. . . The necessary corollary of these trends is the foreclosure of independent manufacturers from markets otherwise open to them. And because these trends are not the product of accident but are rather the result of deliberate policies of Brown and other leading shoe manufacturers, account must be taken of these facts in order to predict the probable future consequences of this merger.

THE HORIZONTAL ASPECTS OF THE MERGER

An economic arrangement between companies performing similar functions in the production or sale of comparable goods or services is characterized as "horizontal." Where the arrangement effects a horizontal merger between companies occupying the same product and geographic market, whatever competition previously may have existed in that market between the parties to the merger is eliminated. The 1950 amendments made plain Congress' intent that the validity of such combinations was to be gauged on a broader scale: Their effect on competition generally in an economically significant market.

Thus, again, the proper definition of the market is a "necessary predicate" to an examination of the competition that may be affected by the horizontal aspects of the merger. The acquisition of Kinney by Brown resulted in a horizontal combination at both the manufacturing and retailing levels of their businesses. (T)he District Court found that the merger of Brown's and Kinney's *manufacturing* facilities was economically too insignificant to come within the prohibition of the Clayton Act.

The Product Market

Shoes are sold in the United States in retail shoe stores and in shoe departments of general stores. These outlets sell: (1) Men's shoes, (2) women's shoes, (3) women's or children's shoes, or (4) men's, women's and children's shoes.

The Geographic Market

The criteria to be used in determining the appropriate geographic market are essentially similar to those used to determine the relevant product market. Moreover, just as a product submarket may have Section 7 significance as the proper "line of commerce," so may a geographic submarket be considered the appropriate "section of the country." . . . Congress prescribed a pragmatic, factual approach to the definition of the relevant market and not a formal, legalistic one. The geographic market selected must, therefore, both "correspond to the commercial realities" of the industry and be economically significant. Thus, although the geographic market in some instances may encompass the entire Nation, under other circumstances it may be as small as a single metropolitan area.

We believe, however, that the record fully supports the District Court's findings that shoe stores in the outskirts of cities compete effectively with stores in central downtown areas, and that while there is undoubtedly some commercial intercourse between smaller communities within a single "standard metropolitan area," the most intense and important competition in retail sales will be confined to stores within the particular communities in such an area and their immediate environs.

We therefore agree that the District Court properly defined the relevant geographic markets in which to analyze this merger as those cities with a population exceeding 10,000 and their environs in which both Brown and Kinney retailed shoes through their own outlets.

The Probable Effect of the Merger

Having delineated the product and geographic markets within which the effects of this merger are to be measured, we turn to an examination of the District Court's finding that, as a result of the merger, competition in the retailing of men's, women's, and children's shoes may be lessened substantially in those cities in which both Brown and Kinney stores are located.

In 118 separate cities, the combined shares of the market of Brown and Kinney in the sale of one of the relevant lines of commerce exceeded 5%. In 47 cities, their share exceeded 5% in all three lines.

The market share which companies may control by merging is one of the most important factors to be considered when determining the probable effects of the combination on effective competition in the relevant market. In an industry as fragmented as shoe retailing, the control of substantial shares of the trade in a city may have important effects on competition. If a merger achieving 5% control were now approved, we might be required to approve future merger efforts by Brown's competitors seeking similar market shares. The oligopoly Congress sought to avoid would then be furthered and it would be difficult to dissolve the combinations previously approved. Furthermore, in this fragmented industry, even if the combination controls but a small share of a particular market, the fact that this share is held by a large national chain can adversely affect competition. It is competition, not competitors, which the Act protects. But we cannot fail to recognize Congress' desire to promote competition through the protection of viable, small, locally owned businesses. Congress appreciated that occasional higher costs and prices might result from the maintenance of fragmented industries and markets. It resolved these competing considerations in favor of decentralization. We must give effect to that decision.

Other factors to be considered in evaluating the probable effects of a merger in the relevant market lend additional support to the District Court's conclusion that this merger may substantially lessen competition. One such factor is the history of tendency toward concentration in the industry. As we have previously pointed out, the shoe industry has, in recent years, been a prime example of such a trend.

On the basis of the record before us, we believe the Government sustained its burden of proof. We hold that the District Court was correct in concluding that this merger may tend to lessen competition substantially in the retail sale of men's, women's, and children's shoes in the overwhelming majority of those cities and their environs in which both Brown and Kinney sell through owned or controlled outlets.

Trends in Horizontal and Vertical Mergers. Since *United States* v. *General Dynamics* (1974) the Supreme Court has moved away from the aggregate numbers/relative percentage approach and begun to evidence a willingness to consider the competitive consequences or the specific economic characteristics of the market involved. The Court has looked not only at the conduct of the merging firms and the structure of their market but at the economic consequences of the merger for their industry. For example, the Court refused to allow the Justice Department to claim that the potential effect of a merger of one national bank and a bank in the Seattle area would be to decrease competition because the acquired bank would have expanded internally or merged with smaller banks if it were not acquired. The Court also rejected the claim that the acquiring bank was seeking to eliminate a "potential competitor." After examining the regulated nature of the banking industry and its effect on ease of entry into the Seattle banking market, the Court approved the merger.[14] Following this decision, the federal courts have required the Justice Department and FTC to show the actual anticompetitive effects of a merger they oppose. The government must demonstrate by objective facts that the acquiring firm would enter the market via internal expansion if the merger were disallowed. How near the firm was to entering the market on its own prior to the merger is a question that must be answered by the plaintiffs. Contentions based on subjective intent, or looking into the company's mind, are not acceptable.[15]

Conglomerate mergers are generally mergers between two firms in unrelated industries. For example, General Electric's acquisition of RCA could be considered a conglomerate merger. They have been considered illegal under Section 7 of the Clayton Act if the acquiring firm is a perceived potential entrant into the market. For example, if antitrust enforcers had perceived that General Electric had some special incentive to enter the broadcasting market, and this market was an "extension" of its own, they might have objected. Also, if General Electric had been on the "edge" of the broadcast market itself, and could have entered without acquiring, the antitrust enforcement agencies might have taken a closer look. Presently, the Justice Department antitrust merger guidelines indicate little interest in stopping conglomerate mergers, rationalizing that such mergers are economically efficient and necessary in order to allow United States based companies to compete abroad.

Price Discrimination

In an economy based on freedom and competition, neophyte business managers, not unnaturally, might expect that they would be permitted to price their products as the economics of production, distribution, and profit dictate. This, however, is not the case. Management responsible for determining prices must make its decisions within the framework of extensive federal and state regulations that restrict choices.

One of the most important statutory provisions influencing pricing decisions is Section 2 of the Clayton Act as amended by the Robinson–Patman Act. This legislation attempts to foster competition by prohibiting price discrimination in certain instances. Selling physically identical products at different prices can be anticompetitive in many situations. To be found illegal, price discrimination must occur in *interstate commerce* between a seller and different purchasers of commodities of *like*

grade and quality, and the effect of such discrimination by the seller must be to *substantially lessen competition* or *tend* to create a monopoly. Congress enacted the law in 1936 to protect small businesses from huge sellers coming into a market and cutting prices on a product below cost for the sole purpose of driving out small sellers.

One situation, frequently referred to as "primary" or "seller's level" competition, involves competition between sellers and their rivals. The primary-seller's-level competitive strategy that is likely to violate Section 2 of the Clayton Act is *whip-sawing.* When, for example, the price-cutting seller operates in several geographic markets, it can cut prices in one while maintaining its prices in another. This gives it an unfair advantage when competing with a seller that operates only in a single geographic market. Unable to maintain its price, the latter has no way of keeping up its profits; the former, however, can make up at least a portion of its losses by profits earned in other areas. After eliminating one regional competitor by selective price-cutting, the firm functioning in several regions can then turn its attention to another region and so on until all regional competitors have been eliminated.

Cases of blatant whip-sawing are rare, and selective price cutting can be done for legitimate economic motives—for example, when a firm wishes to secure a market share in a new geographic market area. The courts have had some difficulty balancing legitimate economic interests with the price-discrimination laws in the situation where a national firm invades a market area that is dominated by a regional firm.

The major defenses of large sellers for their selective price cutting or discrimination among purchasers are (1) cost justification, (2) changing conditions in the market, and (3) meeting the competition. The "meeting the competition" defense is most controversial. Those who view the act as being noncompetitive in nature argue that this defense should be widened by the courts to allow the marketplace to dictate price. They argue that many inefficient small businesses are kept in existence if this defense is narrowed, and consumers lose in the form of higher prices.

The case that follows illustrates the Supreme Court's most recent attempt to widen the "meeting-the-competition" defense.

Falls City Industries, Inc. v. Vanco Beverage, Inc.
United States Supreme Court
460 U.S. 428 (1983)

Background: During a certain period of time from 1972 through 1978 the petitioner (Falls City Industries, Inc.) sold its beer to respondent, the sole wholesale distributor for petitioner's beer in Vanderburgh County, Indiana, at a higher price than petitioner charged its only wholesale distributor in Henderson County, Kentucky. The two counties form a single metropolitan area extending across the state line. Under Indiana law, brewers were required to sell to all Indiana wholesalers at a single price, Indiana wholesalers were prohibited from selling to out-of-state retailers, and Indiana retailers were not permitted to purchase beer from out-of-state wholesalers. Vanco Beverage, Inc. (respondent) filed suit in federal District Court, alleging that petitioner's price discrimination violated Section 2(a) of the Clayton Act, as amended by the Robinson–Patman Act. After trial the court held that the respondent had established a prima facie case of price discrimination, finding that although the respondent and petitioner's Kentucky wholesaler did not sell to the same retailers, they competed for the sale of the petitioner's beer to consumers of beer from retailers in the market area; that the petitioner's pricing policy resulted in lower retail prices for its beer in Kentucky than in Indiana; that many customers living in the Indiana portion of the market ignored Indiana law to purchase petitioner's beer more cheaply from Kentucky retailers; and that the petitioner's pricing policy thus prevented the respondent from competing effectively with the petitioner's Kentucky wholesaler and caused the respondent to sell less beer to Indiana retailers. The court rejected the petitioner's "meeting the competition" defense under Section 2(b) of the Clayton Act, which provides that a defendant may rebut a prima facie showing of illegal price discrimination by establishing that its lower price to any purchaser or purchasers "was made in good faith to meet an equally low price of a competitor." The court reasoned that instead of reducing its prices to meet those of a competitor, the petitioner had created the price disparity by raising its prices to Indiana wholesalers more than it had raised its Kentucky prices; that instead of adjusting prices on a customer-by-customer basis to meet competition from other brewers, the petitioner charged a single price throughout each state; and that the higher Indiana price was not set in good faith, but instead, was raised solely to allow the petitioner to follow other brewers to enhance its profits. The Court of Appeals affirmed. Falls City Industries appealed.

Decision: The U.S. Supreme Court ruled in favor of Fall Cities Industries. The case was remanded to the lower court.

CHAPTER 44 ANTITRUST LAWS: ENFORCEMENT AND CONTENT 1159

Blackmun, Justice

Section 2(b) of the Clayton Act, as amended by the Robinson–Patman Act, provides that a defendant may rebut a prima facie showing of illegal price discrimination by establishing that its lower price to any purchaser or purchasers "was made in good faith to meet an equally low price of a competitor." The United States Court of Appeals for the Seventh Circuit has concluded that the "meeting-competition" defense of §2(b) is available only if the defendant sets its lower price on a customer-by-customer basis and creates the price discrimination by lowering rather than by raising prices. We conclude that §2(b) is not so inflexible.

When proved, the meeting-competition defense of §2(b) exonerates a seller from Robinson–Patman Act liability. This Court consistently has held that the meeting-competition defense at least requires the seller, who has knowingly discriminated in price, to show the existence of facts which would lead a reasonable and prudent person to believe that the granting of a lower price would in fact meet the equally low price of a competitor. The seller must show that under the circumstances it was reasonable to believe that the quoted price or a lower one was available to the favored purchaser or purchasers from the seller's competitors. Neither the District Court nor the Court of Appeals addressed the question whether Falls City had shown information that would have led a reasonable and prudent person to believe that its lower Kentucky price would meet competitors' equally low prices there; indeed, no findings whatever were made regarding competitors' Kentucky prices, or the information available to Falls City about its competitors' Kentucky prices.

On its face, §2(b) requires more than a showing of facts that would have led a reasonable person to believe that a lower price was available to the favored purchaser from a competitor. The showing required is that the "lower price . . . was made in good faith to meet" the competitor's low price. Thus, the defense requires that the seller offer the lower price in good faith for the purpose of meeting the competitor's price, that is, the lower price must actually have been a good faith response to that competing low price. In most situations, a showing of facts giving rise to a reasonable belief that equally low prices were available to the favored purchaser from a competitor will be sufficient to establish that price. In others, however, despite the availability from other sellers of a low price, it may be apparent that the defendant's low offer was not a good faith response.

Almost 20 years ago, the FTC set forth the standard that governs the requirement of a "good faith response":

> At the heart of Section 2(b) is the concept of "good faith." This is a flexible and pragmatic, not a technical or doctrinaire, concept. The standard of the prudent businessman responding fairly to what he reasonably believes is a situation of competitive necessity. Continental Baking Co., 63 FTC. 2071, 2163 (1963).

Although the District Court characterized the Indiana prices charged by Falls City and its competitors as "artificially high," there is no evidence that Falls City's lower prices in Kentucky were set as part of a plan to obtain artificially high profits in Indiana rather than in response to competitive conditions in Kentucky. Falls City did not adopt an illegal system of prices maintained by its competitors. The District Court found that Falls City's prices rose in Indiana in response to competitors' price increases there; it did not address the crucial question whether Falls City's Kentucky prices remained lower in response to competitors' prices in that State.

Vanco attempts to argue that the existence of industry-wide price discrimination within the single geographic retail market itself indicates "tacit or explicit collusion, or . . . market power" inconsistent with a good faith response.

The collusion argument founders on a complete lack of proof. Persistent, industry-wide price discrimination within a geographic market should certainly alert a court to a substantial possibility of collusion. Here, however, the persistent interstate price difference could well have been attributable, not to Falls City, but to extensive state regulation of the sale of beer. Indiana required each brewer to charge a single price for its beer throughout the State, and barred direct competition between Indiana and Kentucky distributors for sales to retailers. In these unusual circumstances, the prices charged to Vanco and other wholesalers in Vanderburgh County may have been influenced more by market conditions in distant Gary and Fort Wayne than by conditions in nearby Henderson County, Kentucky. Moreover, wholesalers in Henderson County competed directly, and attempted to price competitively, with wholesalers in neighboring Kentucky counties. A separate pricing structure might well have evolved in the two States without collusion, notwithstanding the existence of a common retail market along the border. Thus, the sustained price discrimination does not itself demonstrate that Falls City's Kentucky prices were not a good faith response to competitors' prices there.

The Court of Appeals explicitly relied on two other factors in rejecting Falls City's meeting-competition defense: the price discrimination was created by raising rather than lowering prices, and Falls City raised its prices in order to increase its profits. Neither of these factors is controlling. Nothing in §2(b) requires a seller to lower its price in order to meet competition. On the contrary, §2(b) requires the defendant to show only that its "lower price . . . was made in good faith to meet an equally low price of a competitor." A seller is required to justify a price difference by showing that it reasonably believed that an equally low price was available to the purchaser and that it offered the lower price for that reason; the seller is not required to show that the difference resulted from subtraction rather than addition.

A different rule would not only be contrary to the language of the statute, but also might stifle the only kind of legitimate price competition reasonably available in particular industries. In a period of generally rising prices, vigorous price competition for a particular customer or customers may take the form of smaller price increases rather than price cuts. Thus, a price discrimination created by selective price increases can result from a good faith effort to meet a competitor's low price.

Nor is the good faith with which the lower price is offered impugned if the prices raised, like those kept lower, respond to competitors' prices and are set with the goal of increasing the seller's profits. A seller need not choose between ruinously cutting its prices to all its customers to match the price offered to one, [and] refusing to meet the competition and then ruinously raising its prices to its remaining customers to cover increased unit costs. Nor need a seller choose between keeping all its prices ruinously low to meet the price offered to one, and ruinously raising its prices to all customers to a level significantly above that charged by its competitors. A seller is permitted "to retain a customer by realistically meeting in good faith the price offered to that customer, without necessarily changing the seller's price to its other customers." The plain language of §2(b) also permits a seller to retain a customer by realistically meeting in good faith the price offered to that customer, without necessarily freezing his price to his other customers.

Section 2(b) does not require a seller, meeting in good faith a competitor's lower price to certain customers, to forgo the profits that otherwise would be available in sales to its remaining customers. The very purpose of the defense is to permit a seller to treat different competitive situations differently. The prudent businessman responding fairly to what he believes in good faith is a situation of competitive necessity might well raise his prices to some customers to increase his profits, while meeting competitors' prices by keeping his prices to other customers low.

Vanco also contends that Falls City did not satisfy §2(b) because its price discrimination "was not a defensive response to competition." According to Vanco, the Robinson–Patman Act permits price discrimination only if its purpose is to retain a customer. We agree that a seller's response must be defensive, in the sense that the lower price must be calculated and offered in good faith to "meet not beat" the competitor's low price. Section 2(b), however, does not distinguish between one who meets a competitor's lower price to retain an old customer and one who meets a competitor's lower price in an attempt to gain new customers. Such a distinction would be inconsistent with that section's language and logic.

The Court of Appeals relied on *FTC* v. *Staley* for the proposition that the meeting-competition defense "places emphasis on individual [competitive] situations, rather than upon a general system of competition," 654 F.2d, at 1230 (quoting Staley, 324 U.S., at 753), and "does not justify the maintenance of discriminatory pricing among classes of customers that results merely from the adoption of a competitor's discriminatory pricing structure." The Court of Appeals was apparently invoking the District Court's findings that Falls City set prices statewide rather than on a "customer to customer basis," and the District Court's conclusion that this practice disqualified Falls City from asserting the meeting-competition defense.

There is no evidence that Congress intended to limit the availability of §2(b) to customer-specific responses. Section 2(b)'s predecessor, §2(b) of the original Clayton Act, stated that "nothing herein contained shall prevent . . . discrimination in price in the same or different communities made in good faith to meet competition."

Section 2(b) specifically allows a "lower price . . . to any purchaser or purchasers" made in good faith to meet a competitor's equally low price. A single low price surely may be extended to numerous purchasers if the seller has a reasonable basis for believing that the competitor's lower price is available to them. Beyond the requirement that the lower price be reasonably calculated to "meet not beat" the competition, Congress intended to leave it a "question of fact . . . whether the way in which the competition was met lies within the latitude allowed." 80 Cong. Rec. 9418 (1936) (remarks of Rep. Utterback). Once again, this inquiry is guided by the standard of the prudent businessman responding fairly to what he reasonably believes are the competitive necessities.

A seller may have good reason to believe that a competitor or competitors are charging lower prices throughout a particular region. In such circumstances, customer-by-customer negotiations would be unlikely to result in prices different from those set according to information relating to competitors' territorial prices. A customer-by-customer requirement might also make meaningful price competition unrealistically expensive for smaller firms such as Falls City, which was attempting to compete with larger national breweries in 13 separate States. Territorial pricing can be a perfectly reasonable method—sometimes the most reasonable method—of responding to rivals' low prices. We choose not to read into §2(b) a restriction that would deny the meeting-competition defense to one whose area-wide price is a well tailored response to competitors' low prices.

In summary, the meeting-competition defense requires the seller at least to show the existence of facts that would lead a reasonable and prudent person to believe that the seller's lower price would meet the equally low price of a competitor; it also requires the seller to demonstrate that its lower price was a good faith response to a competitor's lower price.

Falls City contends that it has established its meeting-competition defense as a matter of law. In the absence of further findings, we do not agree. The District Court and the Court of Appeals did not decide whether Falls City had shown facts that would have led a reasonable and prudent person to conclude that its lower price would meet the equally low price of its competitors in Kentucky throughout the period at issue in this suit. Nor did they apply the proper standards to the question whether Falls City's decision to set a single statewide price in Kentucky was a good faith, well-tailored response to the competitive circumstances prevailing there. The absence of allegations to the contrary is not controlling; the statute places the burden of establishing the defense on Falls City, not Vanco. There is evidence in the record that might support an inference that these requirements were met, but whether to draw that inference is a question for the trier of fact, not this Court.

REVIEW PROBLEMS

1. What three remedies does the Justice Department make use of most in enforcing the antitrust laws? Explain.

2. What is the difference between horizontal and vertical price fixing? Explain.

3. Do the courts use a rule of reason or *per se* standard when determining the legality of nonprice vertical territorial restraints? Explain.

4. What guidelines do the courts use in analyzing monopoly cases under Section 2 of the Sherman Act?

5. Explain the importance of the Department of Justice's merger guidelines to the business community.

6. Define price discrimination, and list the three defenses that companies most commonly use when charged with such behavior.

7. Beginning in 1959 four major distributors of stainless steel pipe and tubing who sold in Washington, Oregon, California, Idaho, and Utah began to experience substantial price competition from eastern mills and from small local jobbers who sold but did not stock pipe and tubing. Upon the invitation of Tubesales Corporation, the dominant and largest distributor, a series of meetings was held to discuss mutual problems.

The government claimed that at these meetings the parties agreed to reduce discounts to nonstocking jobbers from 10 to 5 percent and to reduce the freight factor in their prices; as a result, new price lists embracing lower freight rates were drawn up by Tubesales and hand delivered to the others. All four distributors were charged with violations of Section 1 of the Sherman Act. What result?

8. In 1864 and 1870 Congress granted the Northern Pacific Railway Company approximately 40 million acres of land to facilitate financing and constructing a railroad to the northwest. The grant consisted of alternate sections of land in a belt 20 miles wide on each side of the track. The granted lands were of various kinds.

By 1949 the railroad had sold about 37 million acres of its holdings and leased most of the rest. In a large number of sales and leases the railroad had inserted "preferential routing" clauses that compelled the owner or lessee to ship over Northern Pacific lines all commodities produced on the land. The preferential routing clause applied only if Northern Pacific's rates were equal to those of competing carriers.

In 1949 the government sued under Section 1 of the Sherman Act seeking a declaration that the preferential routing clauses were unlawful as unreasonable restraints of trade because they constituted tying arrangements. What result?

9. A group of Carvel franchisees operating stores selling soft ice cream products sued Carvel Corporation for treble damages. They alleged that Carvel engaged in illegal exclusive dealing and tying arrangements by requiring the franchisees (1) to refrain from selling non-Carvel products, (2) to purchase from Carvel or its designatees certain supplies that ultimately would be part of the final product sold (the franchisees were allowed to purchase equipment and paper goods from other sources subject to quality-control specifications), and (3) to follow "suggested" resale prices. What result? Susser v. Carvel Corporation, 322 F.2d 505 (1964)

10. From 1958 until 1961 Utah Pie Company, a local producer, was the leading seller of frozen pies in the Salt Lake City market. Because of the advantage of its location, the company usually was able to maintain the lowest prices in a market in which the major competitive weapon was price. During a four-year period Utah Pie was challenged at one time or another by each of three major competitors, all of whom operated in several other markets. Evidence showed that each of these competitors sold frozen pies in the Salt Lake market at prices lower than they charged for pies of like grade and quality in other markets considerably closer to their plants. Evidence also indicated that in several instances one or more of them had sold at prices below actual cost and that one of the competitors had sent an industrial spy into Utah's plant.

During the period price levels deteriorated substantially. In 1958 Utah had been selling pies for $4.15 per dozen. Some forty-four months later Utah was selling similar pies for $2.75 per dozen. As a result of the actions of Pet Milk, Carnation, and Continental, the three major competitors, Utah Pie brought an action for treble damages charging each with a violation of Section 2(a) of the Clayton Act as amended by the Robinson–Patman Act. What result? Utah Pie Company v. Continental Baking Company, 386 U.S. 685 (1967)

11. The Philadelphia National Bank and Girard Trust Bank were the second and third largest of the forty-two commercial banks with head offices in the metropolitan area consisting of the city of Philadelphia and three adjoining counties. Philadelphia National had assets over $1 billion; Girard had assets of over $750 million. The boards of directors of the banks approved a merger. If they merged, the resulting bank would be the largest in the four-county Philadelphia area. The two banks viewed the merger as strengthening their hand in competing with other large banks in the northeastern United States. The government filed suit alleging that the proposed merger was in violation of Section 7 of the Clayton Act and asking that the court enjoin it. What result? United States v. Philadelphia National Bank, 374 U.S. 321 (1963)

12. Reynolds Metal Company was the largest producer of aluminum foil in the world. In 1956 it acquired Arrow Brands, Inc., then engaged in converting aluminum and selling it nationally to wholesale florist-supply houses. Arrow purchased its "raw" aluminum from Reynolds, converted it, and, prior to its acquisition by Reynolds, accounted for 33 percent of the converted foil sold to the florist industry. Eight other firms also supplied converted aluminum to the florist industry, and some bought from Reynolds. The FTC sued under Section 7, claiming that aluminum foil in the florist trade was the relevant market. Reynolds argued that all trades that require specialized use of aluminum are the relevant product market. What result? Reynolds Metal Company v. Federal Trade Commission, 309 F.2d. 223 (1962)

13. Kennecott Copper Corporation, holding 33 percent of the copper market, acquired Peabody Coal Company, which held 10 percent of the coal market. Both were leaders in their respective markets. Kennecott also owned a small coal company. There were high barriers to entry in the coal industry, and copper supplies were dwindling for Kennecott at the time of purchase. The FTC charged Kennecott with a violation of Section 7 of the Clayton Act, noting that Kennecott would have entered the coal industry on its own due to dwindling copper reserves. The FTC charged that a potential entrant into the coal industry was eliminated when this acquisition took place. What result? FTC v. Kennecott Copper Corporation, 298 U.S. 451 (1958)

14. United Shoe Machinery Corporation produced 75 percent of all shoe machines. The company *leased* these machines for ten-year periods and provided free maintenance and repair. It refused to *sell* machines and required all its lessees to operate the leased machines at full capacity. The Justice Department sued United Shoe, charging that it monopolized the shoe machinery market in violation of Section 2 of the Sherman Act. The company claimed that its market share was gained from its superior business acumen and attempts to protect its patents and reputation. What result? United Shoe Machine Corp. v. United States, 258 U.S. 451 (1922)

FOOTNOTES

[1] *The White House Task Force Report on Antitrust Policy* (Washington, D.C.: Bureau of National Affairs, 1969), p. 3.

[2] Clair Wilcox, *Public Policies Toward Business,* 4th Ed. (Homewood, Ill.: Richard D. Irwin, 1971), p. 690.

[3] 246 U.S. 231 (1918).

[4] Id., at p. 237.

[5] Northern Pacific Railway Co. v. United States, 345 U.S. 1 (1958).

[6] United States v. Trenton Potteries Co., 273 U.S. 392 (1972).

[7] Missouri v. National Organization of Women, 620 F.2d. 1301 (8th Cir. 1980), cert. denied (101 S. Ct. 122).

[8] International Salt Co. v. United States, 332 U.S. 392 (1947).

[9] 221 U.S. 1 (1911).

[10] 251 U.S. 417 (1920).

[11] See Telex v. IBM, 510 F.2d 894 (10th Cir. 1975), Berkey Photo Inc. v. Eastman Kodak (2d Cir. 1979).

[12] See Phillip Areeda and Donald Turner, "Predatory Pricing and Related Practices Under Section 2 of the Sherman Act," 88 *Harvard Law Review* 697 (1975).

[13] *Merger and Acquisitions Quarterly,* Vol. 16 (4), Fall–Winter, 1981, p. 60.

[14] United States v. Marine Bancorporation, Inc., 418 U.S. 602 (1974).

[15] See FTC v. Atlantic Richfield Co., 549 F.2d 289 (4th Cir. 1977) and United States v. Siemens Corp., 621 F.2d 499 (2d. Cir. 1980).

CHAPTER 45

The Federal Trade Commission and Consumer Protection

THE FEDERAL TRADE COMMISSION AS AN ADMINISTRATIVE

AGENCY

THE FEDERAL TRADE COMMISSION AND UNFAIR TRADE

PRACTICES

THE FEDERAL TRADE COMMISSION AND CONSUMER-PROTECTION

LAWS

A s previously discussed in Chapter 43, a national debate exists between those who favor increased government regulation of the private sector as a means of protecting the public interest and those who wish to get government agencies "off the back" of business. This debate has nowhere been more vigorously pursued by politicians, businesspeople, consumerists, and scholars than in their discussion of the role of the Federal Trade Commission (FTC or Commission) as an enforcer of consumer-protection laws.

In the late 1960s diverse parties such as the American Bar Association[1] and a Ralph Nader study group[2] accused the FTC of being a "do nothing" agency and called for its reorganiza-tion and a more activist stance in carrying out its duties under the antitrust statutes and the Federal Trade Commission Act of 1914. The Commission responded to these criticisms by upgrading its staff and organizing its bureaus by functions. Major procedural changes, granting the Commission specific authority to prescribe enforceable rules for the first time, were initiated by Congress with passage of the Magnuson-Moss Warranty–Federal Trade Commission Improvement Act of 1975[3] (Magnuson-Moss Act). Subsequent to the passage of this legislation, the Commission, using its rule-making authority, eliminated the "holder-in-due course" doctrine in consumer transactions and issued rules governing the advertisement of eyeglasses. It also proposed rules to regulate diverse areas such as the funeral industry, vocational schools, and children's advertising. Additionally, a proconsumerist environment in the 1970s led Congress to pass numerous consumer-oriented statutes delegating regulatory authority and enforcement duties to the FTC. This increased authority and responsibility ultimately led to calls from affected private-sector interests for limits on the FTC. After being criticized for being a "do nothing" agency in the late 1960s, an activist Commission, ten years later, was "reined in" by Congress with passage of the 1980 Federal Trade Commission Improvement Act, which limited the FTC's rule-making authority and made it more accountable to Congress.

This chapter focuses on the role of the FTC in protecting consumers. First, the FTC's structure, membership, jurisdiction, and operations are examined. Second, Section 5 of the Federal Trade Commission Act of 1914, which prohibits unfair and deceptive practices, is discussed, particularly as it relates to commercial advertising. The chapter concludes with a discussion of the FTC's role in regulating consumer credit and debt collection.[4]

THE FEDERAL TRADE COMMISSION AS AN ADMINISTRATIVE AGENCY

History, Purpose, Jurisdiction

The Federal Trade Commission Act of 1914[5] created a five-member bipartisan Commission to enforce the antitrust laws discussed in Chapter 44. The Commission was particularly charged with enforcement of Sections 2, 3, 7, and 8 of the Clayton Act and Section 5 of the Federal Trade Commission Act. Section 5 forbids "unfair methods of competition." Congress sought to use this broad language to reach anticompetitive practices not covered by the Sherman and Clayton acts. Only civil

remedies may be sought and no private treble-damage suits can be brought under Section 5 of the Federal Trade Commission Act. In 1938 the Wheeler–Lea amendment to Section 5 added the words "unfair or deceptive acts or practices," providing the Commission with broad authority to regulate business practices that may not violate the antitrust statutes but that are considered "unfair" or "deceptive." With this statutory language and a congressional mandate, the FTC ventured into the marketplace as a consumer protector.

Following the growth of a proconsumerist environment in the late 1960s and 1970s, Congress passed additional statutes delegating administrative and enforcement authority to the FTC beyond the original antitrust laws and the Federal Trade Commission Act of 1914. Some of these statutes are the Export Trade Act, Packers and Stockyard Act, Wool Products Labeling Act, Lanham Trade Mark Act, Fur Products Labeling Act, Textile Fiber Product Identification Act, Federal Cigarette and Advertising Act, Fair Packaging and Labeling Act, Truth-in-Lending Act, Fair Credit Reporting Act, Fair Credit Billing Act, Equal Credit Opportunity Act, Hobby Protection Act, Magnuson-Moss Warranty–Federal Trade Improvement Act, Energy Policy and Conservation Act, Hart-Scott-Rodino Antitrust Improvement Act, and the Federal Drug and Cosmetic Act. It should be noted that Congress has given the FTC exclusive authority under some statutes, whereas in other instances the Commission shares authority with other agencies. For example, it shares enforcement authority with the Food and Drug Administration under the Federal Drug and Cosmetic Act.

Structure and Functions

The structure of the FTC is diagramed in Figure 45-1. The chairman and four commissioners are appointed for five-year terms by the President of the United States with the advice

FIGURE 45–1
Federal Trade Commission

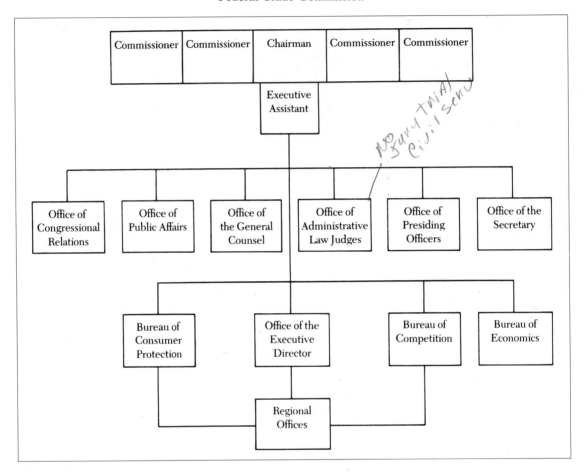

Source: U.S. Government Manual, 1984–1985 (Washington, DC: U.S. Government Printing Office).

and consent of the Senate. No more than three of the five may be from a single political party. The chairman is the executive and administrative head of the agency. He or she presides at Commission meetings and hearings conducted by the Commission.

Other officers of the Commission include the executive director, who supervises regional offices and coordinates bureaus, and the general counsel, who is the chief law officer and adviser to the Commission, and who represents the Commission in federal and state courts. An important role played by the general counsel is to assist businesspeople in obtaining advice from the Commission as to the legal propriety of a proposed course of action.

Three bureaus carry out the FTC's mandated functions. The Bureau of Competition investigates potentially unfair or deceptive acts or practices under Section 5 of the FTCA and prosecutes cases before administrative law judges after issuance of a formal complaint. These adjudicatory proceedings are described in Chapter 43. As an alternative to adjudication, it may obtain negotiated consent orders, which must be approved by the full Commission. The Bureau also conducts rule-making proceedings in order to define specific acts that may be violations of statutes enforced by the FTC. The Bureau of Consumer Protection is significant to the business community and consumers because it is the initiator of litigation in specific cases as well as the source of proposed rules that may affect an entire industry. Also, it makes public efforts to educate all parties as to the laws that it is charged with enforcing. The Bureau of Economics advises the Commission on the economic aspects of all its functions. Its work has become more important as the Commission has begun to rely on cost-benefit analyses in proposing new rules and evaluating present regulations.

Functions

Adjudication. The FTC has used its authority under Section 5 to investigate various types of unfair or deceptive business practices. The FTC staff seeks to bring about a voluntary admission of wrongdoing or a consent order from the firm involved in a questionable practice before issuing a formal complaint. If this negotiating procedure fails, the FTC initiates litigation before an administrative-law judge. Following a hearing and initial decision of the judge, either the staff of the FTC or the corporation may appeal. On appeal the case is heard by the full Commission. The Commission's decision becomes final if not appealed to a federal court of appeals within sixty days. The Commission issues cease-and-desist orders.

Advisory Opinions. Additionally, the Commission, when asked, issues advisory opinions on the legality of a firm's proposed activity, assuming that such activity falls under one of the statutes enforced by the FTC. Advisory opinions are *not* binding on the Commission.

Rule Making. As discussed earlier, the FTC can also issue rules for an entire industry. For example, the FTC has proposed rules that would require the funeral industry to publish its rates. If proposed rules become final, they can be enforced against a violator by fines on individuals or firms of up to $10,-000 per day per violation. The FTC can also obtain temporary restraining orders or preliminary injunctions from courts in order to prevent violations or threatened violations of Commission-administered laws. The Magnuson-Moss Act provides that the Commission may bring civil actions in federal or state courts upon behalf of consumers if they have been injured by unfair or deceptive practices that violate Commission regulations.

The FTC's rule-making authority has come under closer scrutiny by Congress since passage of the 1980 Federal Trade Commission Improvement Act.[6] The act provided Congress with the power to override an FTC rule by majority votes of the Senate and the House. This "legislative veto" was applied in 1982 to an FTC regulation that required used-car dealers to list a car's major defects on the car before it was sold. Of the 286 House members who voted to kill the FTC regulation, 242 had received contributions to their 1980 campaigns totaling $675,000 from the Used Car Dealers Association's political action committees.[7] A federal Court of Appeals in October 1982 unanimously overturned the "legislative veto" of the FTC used-car regulation, claiming that such a veto of regulatory action violated the constitutional principle of separation of powers. As stated in Chapter 42, the U.S. Supreme Court in June 1983 declared legislative veto provisions within all federal acts to be unconstitutional.

THE FEDERAL TRADE COMMISSION AND UNFAIR TRADE PRACTICES

Section 5 of the Federal Trade Commission Act

As previously noted, Section 5 of the Federal Trade Commission Act allocates broad consumer-protection powers to the FTC because it forbids "unfair or deceptive acts or practices." While deceptive practices have a long history of common-law definition, court and FTC interpretations of the word "unfair" now permit the FTC to investigate a practice that is neither deceptive nor a violation of the antitrust statutes under Section 5 if it (1) offends public policy, (2) is immoral, unethical, or unscrupulous, and (3) causes material or substantial harm to the consumer. The Commission has investigated false or misleading labeling, palming off, misleading product names, disparagement of competition, violations of warranties (see Chapter 17 for the FTC role), and many other practices using these standards; however, few practices affecting the consuming public have been so closely monitored by the FTC as deceptive and unfair advertising and product labeling.

The FTC and Deceptive Advertising

As previously stated, the Wheeler–Lea Act amended Section 5 of the Federal Trade Commission Act to include "unfair or deceptive trade practices." In passing the amendment, Congress made it clear that the FTC had broad power to "cover every form of advertisement deception over which it would be humanly practical to exercise governmental control." It was to reach every case, from inadvertent or uninformed to the most subtle or vicious advertising. Through a case approach to enforcement the FTC prior to 1983 evolved a standard by which the advertiser did not have to *intend* deception as in the common-law definition of deceit to be guilty of unfair or deceptive practices. All that was required was a misrepresentation and a tendency to deceive an ordinary purchaser at whom the advertisement was directed or by whom it was expected to be read or viewed. The FTC did not have to demonstrate that specific consumers relied on or believed the advertisement.

Following a change in makeup of the Commission, the FTC by a 3 to 2 vote issued a policy statement in October 1983[8] offering guidelines as to what it would consider to be "deceptive" advertising under Section 5 for the future:

1. The advertising would have to contain a *material* misrepresentation or omission
2. that would *likely mislead* a consumer acting *reasonably* under the circumstances.

In the *Cliffdale Associates* case that follows the Commission seemed to follow its policy statement.

In re Cliffdale Associates, Inc.

46 Antitrust & Trade Reg. Rep. 703 (1984)

Background: The FTC staff (plaintiff) issued a complaint against Cliffdale Associates (defendant) before an administrative law judge (ALJ) claiming Cliffdale, a mail order company, misrepresented the value and performance of an automobile engine attachment known as the "Ball-Matic-6." The advertisements claimed that the Ball-Matic, a device designed to allow additional air to enter a car engine and thus improve gas, was "the most significant automotive breakthrough in the last ten years" and that "every car needs one," and owners could "save up to 20 percent on gasoline costs." Several advertisements showed "test results" claiming gasoline savings of 8 to 40 percent. The ALJ found Cliffdale's claims to be both unfair and deceptive under Section 5 of the Federal Trade Commission Act, and ordered the company to cease and desist from making such claims. Cliffdale appealed to the full Commission. Decision: Affirmed. The Federal Trade Commission ruled in favor of the FTC staff.

Federal Trade Commission

At trial, the charge of *unfair* competition was not specifically addressed. The record does not contain sufficient evidence to support liability on this charge. Accordingly, we reverse those portions of the ALJ's decision that relate to unfair methods of competition. Deception was the standard under which the claims were actually tried, and this was the appropriate approach.

The ALJ concluded that "any advertising representation that has the tendency and capacity to mislead or deceive a prospective consumer is an unfair and deceptive practice." We find this approach inadequate to provide guidance on how a deception claim should be analyzed. Consistent with the Policy Statement on Deception, issued on October 14, 1983, the Commission will find an act or practice deceptive if, first, there is a representation, omission, or practice that, second, is likely to mislead consumers acting reasonably under the circumstances, and, third, the representation, omission, or practice is material.

The requirement that an act or practice be "likely to mislead" reflects the established principle that the Commission need not find *actual* deception to hold that a violation of section 5 has occurred. Similarly, the requirement that an act or practice be considered from the perspective of a "consumer acting reasonably in the circumstances" is not new. Virtually all representations can be misunderstood by some consumers. The third element is materiality. A material representation, omission, act, or practice involves information that is important to consumers and, hence, likely to affect their choice of, or conduct regarding, a product. Consumers are thus likely to suffer injury from a material misrepresentation.

The first step in analyzing whether a claim is deceptive is to determine what claim has been made. When the advertisement contains an express claim, the representation itself establishes its meaning. When the claim is implied, the Commission will often be able to determine the meaning through an examination of the representation, including an evaluation of the entire document, the juxtaposition of various phrases, the nature of the claim, and the nature of the transaction. In other situations, the Commission will require extrinsic evidence that reasonable consumers interpret the implied claims in a certain way. The evidence can consist of expert opinion, consumer testimony, copy tests, surveys, or any other reliable evidence of consumer interpretation.

1. *The Descriptive Claims.* Cliffdale's advertisements refer to the Ball-Matic as an "amazing automobile discovery" [and] as "the most significant automotive breakthrough in the last ten years." These advertisements expressly claim that the Ball-Matic is an important, significant, and unique new invention. Further, Cliffdale expressly

claimed that under normal driving conditions a typical driver could usually obtain a fuel economy improvement of 20 percent (or more). A consumer would be reasonable in expecting the average savings from the Ball-Matic to be within the stated range.

The Ball-Matic is a simple air-bleed device. Air-bleed devices have been around a long time, and are considered to be of little use by the automobile industry. The claim that the Ball-Matic was a new invention was expressly made. Having found such a claim to have been made, and that the claim is false, the Commission may infer that it is material. This claim was deceptive. The representation that the Ball-Matic would significantly improve fuel economy [is] false. The fuel savings do not approach those claimed by Cliffdale. Claims about enhanced fuel efficiency are clearly material to consumers, and were therefore deceptive.

2. *Representation that Competent Scientific Tests Prove the Fuel Economy Claims.* Some advertisements state that the Ball-Matic was tested and proven to yield up to a 20 percent increase in fuel economy. At trial, Cliffdale introduced a number of tests with varying evaluations of the Ball-Matic. The tests did not prove the fuel economy claims. First, none revealed improvement even close to that claimed. Moreover, the FTC counsel's expert witness testified that, given the basic theory of engineering and combustion, the Ball-Matic could never result in any significant improvement in fuel economy. The ALJ further noted a 1978 article in *Consumer Reports* magazine disclosing that there is no statistically significant effect on gasoline mileage from the use of air-bleed devices. The ALJ also noted an EPA test which gave similar results.

With respect to materiality, the performance of the Ball-Matic is difficult for consumers to evaluate for themselves. Accordingly, consumers will tend to rely more heavily on the scientific support claims made by Cliffdale. Clearly these false claims injured consumers by misleading them on a material point.

3. *Representations Based on Consumer Endorsements.* Numerous advertisements contained a black bordered box with statements by users about their fuel saving experiences. Consumers could reasonably interpret these advertisements as claiming that the Ball-Matic would produce significant fuel economy improvement, and that the testimonials were unrestrained and unbiased.

By printing the testimonials, Cliffdale implicitly made claims similar to those express claims already found to be false and deceptive. Thus, Cliffdale's use of the testimonials was, itself, deceptive. A good number of the testimonials were by business associates of the marketers of the product. Whenever there exists a connection between the endorser and the seller which might materially affect the weight or credibility of the endorsement, it should be disclosed. In a case such as this, where it is difficult for a consumer to evaluate the effectiveness of the product, the consumer is likely to rely more heavily on endorsements by other users, particularly if the consumer believes such endorsements are independent and unbiased.

Deceptive Price Advertising. Some examples of deceptive advertising are false price comparisons (if the advertisement claims a price is reduced, it must be reduced from the regular price), bait and switch, and offers of a free good or service to a customer who buys one. The case that follows illustrates the "free good" type of deceptive price advertising.

Federal Trade Commission v. Mary Carter Paint Co., et al.

Supreme Court of the United States

382 U.S. 46 (1965)

Background: Mary Carter Paint Company (respondent) manufactured and sold paint and related products. The FTC ordered the respondent to cease and desist from the use of certain representations found by the Commission to be deceptive and in violation of Section 5 of the Federal Trade Commission Act. The representations appeared in advertisements that stated in various ways that, for every can of respondent's paint purchased by a buyer, the respondent would give the buyer a "free" can of equal quality and quantity. The Court of Appeals for the Fifth Circuit set aside the Commission's order.

Decision: Reversed. The Supreme Court of the United States ruled in favor of the FTC.

Brennan, Justice

Although there is some ambiguity in the Commission's opinion, we cannot say that its holding constituted a departure from Commission policy regarding the use of the commercially exploitable word "free." Initial efforts to define the term in decisions were followed by "Guides Against Deceptive Pricing." These informed businessmen that they might advertise an article as "free," even though purchase of another article was required, so long as the terms of the offer were clearly stated, the price of the article required to be purchased was not increased, and its quality and quantity were not diminished. With specific reference to two-for-the-price-of-one offers, the Guides required that either the sales price for the two be "the advertiser's usual and customary retail price for the single article in the recent, regular course of his business," or where the advertiser has not previously sold the article, the price for the two be the "usual and customary" price for one in the relevant trade areas. These, of course, were guides, not fixed rules as such, and were designed to inform businessmen of the factors which would guide Commission decisions. Although Mary Carter seems to have attempted to tailor its offer to come within these terms, the Commission found that it failed; the offer complied in appearance only.

The gist of the Commission's reasoning is in the hearing examiner's finding, which it adopted, that "the usual and customary retail price of each can of Mary Carter paint was not, and is not now, the price designated in the advertisement [$6.98] but was, and is now, substantially less than such price. The second can of paint was not, and is not now, 'free,' that is, was not, and is not now, given as a gift or gratuity. The offer is, on the contrary, an offer of two cans of paint for the price advertised as or purporting to be the list price or customary and usual price of one can." In sum, the Commission found that Mary Carter had no history of selling single cans of paint; it was marketing twins, and in allocating what is in fact the price of two cans to one can, yet calling one "free," Mary Carter misrepresented. It is true that respondent was not permitted to show that the quality of its paint matched those paints which usually and customarily sell in the $6.98 range, or that purchasers of paint estimate quality by the price they are charged. If both claims were established, it is arguable that any deception was limited to a representation that Mary Carter has a usual and customary price for single cans of paint, when it has no such price. However, it is not for courts to say whether this violates the Act. "[T]he Commission is often in a better position than are courts to determine when a practice is 'deceptive' within the meaning of the Act."

The Commission advises us in its brief that it believes it would be appropriate here "to remand the case to it for clarification of its order." The judgment of the Court of Appeals is therefore reversed and the case is remanded to that court with directions to remand to the Commission for clarification of its order.

Advertising and Product Quality and Quantity. There is often a fine line between "puffing" and deception. The FTC and the courts have recognized that certain types of claims by advertisers do not violate Section 5 of the Federal Trade Commission Act. A car salesman's claim that "this car is the best that ever came out of Detroit" is an example of "puffing," but when an advertisement claims that "this car will run for 50,000 miles without a mechanical breakdown" it goes beyond puffing and approaches deception. A famous example of deception arose in the case of a Firestone Tire and Rubber Company ad that stated: "When you buy a Firestone tire—no matter how much or little you pay—you get a safe tire."[9] It should be noted that a claim does not have to be expressly deceptive; it may deceive by implication. The FTC must also show that there was no basis for the claim. The Commission argued that the Firestone ad could have been interpreted to mean that, regardless of road conditions or usage, the tire was absolutely safe. This would obviously be false. In this case the FTC was found to be correct in its position. The Commission requires that an advertiser keep data on file to support its claims as to quality, performance, and comparative price. During the Reagan administration the FTC chairman and the head of its Consumer Protection Bureau have argued that requirements of immense amount of data to support advertising claims are an unjustified burden on advertisers and hurtful to consumers because the cost of such substantiation is passed on to the consumer in the form of higher prices. The chief of the FTC Consumer Protection Bureau believes that criteria should be developed for the amount of substantiation of ads that is required. He argues that consumers who act reasonably "do not expect subjective claims to be backed up by substantiation." Consumer advocates do not agree; they argue that a loosening of FTC requirements established in the early 1970s would lead to increased unsubstantiated claims in advertising.

Sometimes advertisers are accused of deception by their competitors. Seven-Up, for example, accused Pepsi-Cola of false, misleading, and deceptive ads because Pepsi did not say clearly in its television ads that regular, sugared Pepsi Free wasn't completely caffeine free—only 99 percent. In two cases brought under the Lanham Act, Section 43(a), which forbids "false description or representation," McDonald's and Wendy's accused Burger King of falsely portraying its hamburger as superior on the basis of an alleged "taste test." Both plaintiffs challenged the method and results of the taste test and sought injunctions and corrective advertising.[10] The cases were settled out of court. The FTC can receive complaints from competitors as well as consumers, but it is not required to act on the complaints. The FTC generally takes the position that the government should not be involved when two or more private parties want to fight it out as to comparative advertising claims dealing with quality and quantity.

Deceptive Advertising and Testimonials. The FTC forbids endorsement of products by well-known personalities who either don't use the product or don't actually prefer it over another product. The Bureau of Consumer Protection also monitors claims by well-known personalities that they have superior knowledge of a product. In a negotiated consent order entertainer Pat Boone agreed to pay damages to purchasers of Acne Stain. Boone represented the product as a cure for acne when in fact there was no scientific basis for such a claim. Boone also failed to reveal that he had a commercial interest in Acne Stain. A review of the *Cliffdale* opinion set out earlier in this chapter gives the reader another illustration of the FTC's view of using testimonials in advertising.

The FTC and Unfair Advertising

Section 5 forbids "unfair" as well as deceptive advertising. As discussed earlier in this chapter, advertising is considered "unfair" if it (1) offends public policy; (2) is immoral, unethical, or unscrupulous; and (3) causes material or substantial harm to the consumer.

The basis of FTC-proposed rules banning certain types of advertising for children is not that the ads are deceptive but that the particular group they are addressed to is incapable of judging their truthfulness. The ads are unfair also, according to the FTC, because the group they are addressed to is susceptible to a type of "brainwashing."

The failure of the Commission to provide a precise definition of the word "unfair" has led to calls by some at the FTC for more specificity from Congress. As an alternative others have argued that "unfair and deceptive practices" should be deleted from Section 5 of the Federal Trade Commission Act. Others have used the vagueness of definition as grounds for requesting an exemption from FTC authority under Section 5.

Remedies for Deceptive and Unfair Advertising

In adjudicative proceedings the FTC has the power to issue cease-and-desist orders. It has also ordered firms to disclose their deceptive or unfair advertising to the public through corrective advertising. The firm is usually ordered to allocate a portion of its advertising budget under this remedy to correct the long-held impression it has created in the public mind. In the following case corrective advertising was approved by a federal appeals court.

Warner Lambert v. Federal Trade Commission

U.S. Court of Appeals, D.C. Circuit

562 F.2d. 49 (1977)

Background: Warner Lambert (petitioner) advertised that the product Listerine prevented, cured, or alleviated the common cold. Listerine had been on the market since 1879, and its formula and advertising (begun in 1921) had never changed. The FTC ordered the company to cease and desist advertising this claim and to devote $10 million to corrective advertising that included the following: "Contrary to prior advertising Listerine will not help prevent colds or sore throats or lessen their severity." The petitioner challenged this order. The administrative law judge (ALJ) ruled in favor of the FTC staff. Petitioner appealed to the full Commission. The Commission affirmed essentially all the findings of the ALJ. Petitioner appealed to the Court of Appeals. Decision: The U.S. Court of Appeals ruled in favor of the FTC with modifications.

ETHICS BOX
Ethics and Advertising

P, a cereal company, spends one-third of its annual budget on television advertising. One-half of that amount is spent on sponsoring Saturday morning children's television programming. Critics contend that this is unfair advertising because it "brainwashes" children who cannot distinguish between the claims that are made in the advertising and reality. P has recently commissioned a study by a marketing research professor in a college of business administration to determine what ill effects, if any, its advertising has on children who watch television programs on Saturday morning. The marketing research professor (who was paid $50,000) found that the study did influence children between the ages of 4 and 10, and this age group was not able to differentiate between the claims made in ads and reality. For example, the professor pointed out that one of P's advertisements claimed that its cereal provided extra protein and children grew to be healthier, faster. P was able to substantiate its claim of more protein, but not that children grew faster as visually shown in the advertisement. The professor under previous agreement with P is about to publish his results, which are based on scientific research:

1. What ethical problems, if any, does P face?
2. What ethical problems, if any, do the television networks that carry the Saturday morning ads have?
3. What ethical problems, if any, does the marketing professor have?
4. What ethical problems, if any, do the parents of the children watching the ads have?

Wright, Judge

The first issue on appeal is whether the Commission's conclusion that Listerine is not beneficial for colds or sore throats is supported by the evidence. The Commission's findings must be sustained if they are supported by substantial evidence on the record viewed as a whole. We conclude that they are.

Both the ALJ and the Commission carefully analyzed the evidence. They gave full consideration to the studies submitted by petitioner. The ultimate conclusion that Listerine is not an effective cold remedy was based on six specific findings of fact.

First, the Commission found that the ingredients of Listerine are not present in sufficient quantities to have any therapeutic effect. This was the testimony of two leading pharmacologists called by Commission counsel. The Commission was justified in concluding that the testimony of Listerine's experts was not sufficiently persuasive to counter this testimony.

Second, the Commission found that in the process of gargling it is impossible for

Listerine to reach the critical areas of the body in medically significant concentration. The liquid is confined to the mouth chamber. Such vapors as might reach the nasal passage would not be in therapeutic concentration. Petitioner did not offer any evidence that vapors reached the affected areas in significant concentration.

Third, the Commission found that even if significant quantities of the active ingredients of Listerine were to reach the critical sites where cold viruses enter and infect the body, they could not interfere with the activities of the virus because they could not penetrate the tissue cells.

Fourth, the Commission discounted the results of a clinical study conducted by petitioner on which petitioner heavily relies. Petitioner contends that in a four-year study school children who gargled with Listerine had fewer colds and cold symptoms than those who did not gargle with Listerine. The Commission found that the design and execution of the "St. Barnabas study" made its results unreliable. For the first two years of the four-year test no placebo was given to the control group. For the last two years the placebo was inadequate: the control group was given colored water which did not resemble Listerine in smell or taste. There was also evidence that the physician who examined the test subjects was not blinded from knowing which children were using Listerine and which were not, that his evaluation of the cold symptoms of each child each day may have been imprecise, and that he necessarily relied on the non-blinded child's subjective reporting. Both the ALJ and the Commission analyzed the St. Barnabas study and the expert testimony about it in depth and were justified in concluding that its results are unreliable.

Fifth, the Commission found that the ability of Listerine to kill germs by millions on contact is of no medical significance in the treatment of colds or sore throats. Expert testimony showed that bacteria in the oral cavity, the "germs" which Listerine purports to kill, do not cause colds and play no role in cold symptoms. Colds are caused by viruses. Further, "while Listerine kills millions of bacteria in the mouth, it also leaves millions. It is impossible to sterilize any area of the mouth, let alone the entire mouth."

Sixth, the Commission found that Listerine has no significant beneficial effect on the symptoms of sore throat. The Commission recognized that gargling with Listerine could provide temporary relief from a sore throat by removing accumulated debris irritating the throat. But this type of relief can also be obtained by gargling with salt water or even warm water. The Commission found that this is not the significant relief promised by petitioner's advertisements. It was reasonable to conclude that "such temporary relief does not 'lessen the severity' of a sore throat any more than expectorating or blowing one's nose 'lessens the severity' of a cold."

Petitioner contends that even if its advertising claims in the past were false, the portion of the Commission's order requiring "corrective advertising" exceeds the Commission's statutory power. The argument is based upon a literal reading of Section 5 of the Federal Trade Commission Act, which authorizes the Commission to issue "cease and desist" orders against violators and does not expressly mention any other remedies. The Commission's position, on the other hand, is that the affirmative disclosure that Listerine will not prevent colds or lessen their severity is absolutely necessary to give effect to the prospective cease and desist order; a hundred years of false cold claims have built up a large reservoir of erroneous consumer belief which would persist, unless corrected, long after petitioner ceased making the claims.

The need for the corrective advertising remedy and its appropriateness in this case are important issues. But the threshold question is whether the Commission has the authority to issue such an order. We hold that it does [based on the legislative history of the Federal Trade Commission Act of 1914, the Wheeler–Lea Act Amendments of 1938, and the 1975 amendments, along with case precedents interpreting the Act].

Having established that the Commission does have the power to order corrective advertising in appropriate cases, it remains to consider whether use of the remedy against Listerine is warranted and equitable. We have concluded that part 3 of the order should be modified to delete the phrase "Contrary to prior advertising." With that modification, we approve the order.

Our role in reviewing the remedy is limited. The Supreme Court has set forth the standard:

> The Commission is the expert body to determine what remedy is necessary to eliminate the unfair or deceptive trade practices which have been disclosed. It has wide latitude for judgment and the courts will not interfere except where the remedy selected has no reasonable relation to the unlawful practices found to exist.

The Commission has adopted the following standard for the imposition of corrective advertising:

> [I]f a deceptive advertisement has played a substantial role in creating or reinforcing in the public's mind a false and material belief which lives on after the false advertising ceases, there is clear and continuing injury to competition and to the consuming public as consumers continue to make purchasing decisions based on the false belief. Since this injury cannot be averted by merely requiring respondent to cease disseminating the advertisement, we may appropriately order respondent to take affirmative action designed to terminate the otherwise continuing ill effects of the advertisement.

We think this standard is entirely reasonable. It dictates two factual inquiries: (1) Did Listerine's advertisements play a substantial role in creating or reinforcing in the public's mind a false belief about the product? and (2) Would this belief linger on after the false advertising ceases? It strikes us that if the answer to both questions is not yes, companies everywhere may be wasting their massive advertising budgets. Indeed, it is more than a little peculiar to hear petitioner assert that its commercials really have no effect on consumer belief.

The FTC and Deceptive Packaging and Labeling

Closely related to the problems associated with advertising are questions involved in packaging and labeling. Studies have in-dicated that consumers tend to rely more heavily on labeling than other forms of advertising. Labeling and packaging came under fire when a study by the Food and Drug Administration (1965) indicated that it was not uncommon to find packages with as little as 20 percent of the inner container filled with a food product.

Against this background Congress in 1966 passed the Fair Packaging and Labeling Act.[11] Congress ordered the Secretary of Health, Education and Welfare (HEW, now Health and Human Services) and the FTC to develop mandatory and discretionary rules governing the labeling and packaging of products. HEW was authorized to regulate packaging of foods, drugs, and cosmetics, whereas the FTC was given jurisdiction over other consumer commodities.

The rules require that a packaged or labeled consumer commodity must bear the following information:

1. The name and address of the manufacturer, packer, or distributor of the product
2. The net quantity, which must be conspicuously placed on the package front
3. An accurate description of the contents

These requirements were intended to enable consumers to compare prices of competing products on the basis of uniform measures. This seemed necessary because of the wide variety of package weights and volumes used by manufacturers.

In passing the Fair Packaging and Labeling Act, Congress authorized discretionary regulations to:

1. Set up standards for size characterization (for example, "small," "medium," "large")
2. Control "cents off" promotions
3. Regulate additional ingredient information on containers of drugs and cosmetics
4. Prevent nonfunctional slack fill of packages

The Fair Packaging and Labeling Act provides that any violation of the act is also a violation of Section 5 of the Federal Trade Commission Act. Thus the FTC has used the same enforcement measures for violations of both acts.

Criticisms of the Fair Packaging and Labeling Act have focused on the amount of disclosure required, the cost involved for companies, and the failure of Congress to define what products constitute "consumer commodities" under the Act. There are several statutory omissions, such as uniform pricing per unit, that still make it difficult for consumers to compare prices. Some argue that the Act is unwieldy and should be scrapped. Others argue that it provides some benefits for consumers in terms of their ability to do comparison shopping and should be retained.

THE FEDERAL TRADE COMMISSION AND CONSUMER-PROTECTION LAWS

In 1968 Congress passed the Consumer Credit Protection Act,[12] which addresses problems associated with consumer buying on credit. This comprehensive act comprises the Truth-in-Lending Act (Title I), the Fair Credit Reporting Act (Title IV), the Equal Credit Opportunity Act (Title VI), and the Fair Debt Collection Practices Act. Basically the act requires disclosure of information concerning the cost of credit transactions and prohibits unfair treatment of consumers in credit applications and debt collections.

Those who support consumer protection in the area of credit point to the fact that consumers owe over $1.5 trillion in debts and use credit cards frequently. They argue that prior to 1969 many abuses existed in the issuance and reporting of credit terms by the consumer-finance industry. Often a consumer-debtor did not know the dollar amount or the percentage rate that he or she was being charged for credit. A consumer might be paying 25 percent rather than the 8 percent he or she thought because the industry had no uniform way of quoting rates. Because the consumer was not able to compare rates, there was little competition among lenders. Also, there were abuses in the use of credit information. A consumer would be denied credit on the basis of outdated or inaccurate credit bureau files. Another common abuse was discrimination against women and nonwhites. Moreover, collection agencies sometimes harassed debtors by telephone at all hours of the night.

Those who oppose the Consumer Credit Protection Act argue that complete disclosure of credit information and attempts to impose honest conduct in the consumer-finance marketplace fail to pass a cost-benefit analysis. For example, it is argued that the Truth-in-Lending Act, which requires uniform disclosure of credit terms and conditions (interest rates or finance charges) to consumers, does little to help the lower-income and uneducated people for whose protection it was passed. Lower-income people, it is argued, do not buy on installments or borrow from a bank because they cannot meet credit standards. They do not need uniform guidelines as to interest rates and finance charges because they do not compare the credit charges. It is the rich and educated who benefit from such legislation, and presumably they can protect themselves or hire lawyers to speak for them. The unregulated consumer-finance industry would normally supply most information now mandated by statute. Over the long run, it is argued, those in the consumer-finance industry who engage in unfair or deceptive practices will be exposed by the free-market mechanism. Traditional statutory-law punishments should be imposed at the state and local levels, where most illegal practices take place.[13] Opponents argue that consumers in fact "pay" twice for consumer-protection legislation: once through higher taxes and again through higher prices for credit. Initially they pay taxes to cover the operating costs of the FTC and other agencies that implement the consumer protection statutes by passing regulations. Then consumer-finance and other private-sector companies pass on their compliance costs to the consumer in the form of higher finance charges, interest rates, or additional annual fees. For example, the applicant for a VISA or Mastercharge card pays the cost of his or her own consumer protection in increased annual fees. These fees in large part cover the administrative costs associated with doing the paperwork to comply with federal regulations.

Opponents of consumer legislation argue further that the FTC and other agencies would be more effective in combating misinformation and fraud in the consumer-credit markets if they could award reparations to injured consumers, invoke criminal sanctions against "bad actors," and force convicted companies to pay the costs of prosecution.

These arguments for and against consumer-protection legislation should be weighed carefully by readers as they examine the four consumer-protection statutes set out here.

The Truth-in-Lending Act

Title I of the Consumer Credit Protection Act is commonly known as the Truth-in-Lending Act. It was amended by the Truth-in-Lending Simplification and Reform Act, which became effective April 1, 1982.

The main thrust of the Truth-in-Lending Act is to require disclosure by creditors of the terms and conditions of consumer credit before extending such credit to consumer-debtors. In theory, as a result of these disclosures, the creditor and the consumer-debtor should have equal knowledge of the terms of the transaction, and the consumer should be able to shop for the cheapest price (interest rate or finance charge) in the credit marketplace. Competition in the consumer-credit markets should thus be enhanced.

Under the Truth-in-Lending Act the board of governors of the Federal Reserve Board is given the power to prescribe regulations. Regulation Z and its interpretations are given def-

all chgs to credit be paid for credit

erence by the courts and thus are important in daily business transactions. The eight agencies responsible for enforcing the law and the bodies they regulate are the Comptroller of the Currency (national banks), the Federal Reserve Board (member banks that are not national banks), the Federal Deposit Insurance Corporation (insured banks, not members of the Federal Reserve system), the Federal Home Loan Board (savings institutions not insured by the FDIC), the Bureau of Federal Credit Unions (federal credit unions), the Civil Aeronautics Board (creditors subject to the CAB), the Interstate Commerce Commission (creditors subject to the ICC), and the Packers and Stockyards Administration (creditors subject to the Packers and Stockyards Act). All truth-in-lending activities not regulated by these agencies are administered by the FTC. Thus the largest amount of enforcement activity against commercial lenders, other than banks and retailers who sell on credit, is left to the Commission. It is estimated that the number of creditors subject to FTC truth-in-lending enforcement exceeds 1.5 million. A violation of the Truth-in-Lending Act is also a violation of Regulation Z. Uniformity of enforcement was enhanced through adoption of the Uniform Guidelines for Enforcement of Regulation Z in 1978. Aimed primarily at violations resulting in overcharges to consumer-debtors, they require uniform corrective actions by all agencies enforcing the Truth-in-Lending Act. Most important, they allow a consumer to be reimbursed for disclosure errors with regard to finance or other charges by creditors, when these result from a clear and consistent pattern of negligence or a willful violation intended to mislead. Additionally, the Department of Justice, upon referral from an enforcement agency, can bring criminal actions under the Truth-in-Lending Act against creditors who "willfully and knowingly" give false information or fail to make proper disclosures as required by the act. If convicted, a creditor is subject to a fine of not more than $5,000 or imprisonment for not more than one year or both.

A consumer has a right to bring an individual action for damages if he or she can show that the transaction comes within the Truth-in-Lending Act and that the creditor failed to comply with the requirements of Regulation Z. It is *not* necessary for the consumer to show that the creditor's noncompliance was substantial, that it was relied on, or that any injury resulted. The measure of damages is actual damages plus a statutory penalty, usually twice the amount of the finance charges imposed when dealing with open-end transactions (for example, installment credit where one can pay in full or partially, as in the case of VISA or department store accounts). The statutory penalty cannot exceed $1,000. Closed-end transactions (for example, mortgages) limit creditors' liability for a statutory penalty to certain types of nondisclosure.

Scope of the Truth-in-Lending Act. The Truth-in-Lending Act affects a substantial number of credit transactions. Under the act those who in the ordinary course of business regularly extend consumer credit must make proper disclosures. Basically consumer-credit transactions are those in which credit of less than $25,000 is extended to a natural person for personal, family, or household use. Natural persons borrowing for business or commercial purposes, or those borrowing over $25,000 for any purpose, are not entitled to the Truth-in-Lending disclosures. Congress reasoned that people in these categories should be able to protect themselves. Disclosures also do not have to be made to organizations such as corporations, partnerships, trusts, estates, and associations, nor do the required disclosures have to be made to governments or units of government. Institutional debtors are not protected because they, like the businessperson and the wealthy individual, are assumed to be sophisticated borrowers with sufficient economic and legal resources to protect their interests. Transactions in real property exceeding $25,000 in which security interests are acquired are also exempt. Items of personal property used or expected to be used at the principal dwelling place of a consumer to which a security interest attaches are also excluded if their value exceeds $25,000. Finally, the consumer credit granted must involve a finance charge or be payable in four or more installments.

Finance Charges. For disclosure of the costs of credit to be meaningful each offer or extension of credit to a consumer should include all of the charges to be paid for the credit. If one potential lender includes in the cost of credit the premium on credit life insurance and a second does not (even though the latter also requires credit life insurance), the quoted costs to the consumer in the second instance will be misleading. The Truth-in-Lending Act and Regulation Z require all who extend credit to include certain costs if they are charged the consumer.

The Truth-in-Lending Act and Regulation Z use the term "finance charge" when referring to dollar charges that make up the cost of credit. Basically, any charge paid by a debtor that he or she would not have had to pay except for the grant of credit is to be included in the finance charge. Many of these charges are obvious, but in some instances the creditor must look to both Regulation Z and the Federal Reserve Board's interpretations to determine if a particular amount must be included in the finance charge.

Annual Percentage Rate. The "annual percentage rate" (APR) is similar to "simple annual interest." The requirement that the APR be disclosed allows consumers to compare finance charges on a common basis. The importance of this is illustrated by the following example.

Suppose that a consumer is interested in buying a combination stereo and color television unit that costs $500. The consumer's account with a large retail store allows him or her to pay all the bill or a specified minimum portion of it based on the size of the balance. He or she may also pay any sum in between and may have a number of days within which to pay without incurring a finance charge. If the consumer does not pay the entire account, monthly carrying charges are 1½ percent on the average daily balance. The APR that the retailer must disclose is 18 percent.

A second alternative open to this consumer is to borrow the $500 from a bank, which may charge 7 percent if the loan is repaid in twenty-four monthly installments. The consumer is also required to pay $6, which includes charges for a credit report and credit life insurance. The bank would have to show finance charges of $76 and an APR of 14 percent. Without knowing the APR, this consumer would have difficulty comparing the two sources of credit.

General Disclosure Provisions. It should be emphasized that the Truth-in-Lending Act is solely a disclosure statute. It does not prescribe interest rates or finance charges. What must be disclosed will depend on whether the consumer-credit transaction is classified as open-end or closed-end. However, there are some general requirements imposed by the Act and Regulation Z, including the following:

1. All disclosure of terms and conditions of credit must be made "clearly and conspicuously in meaningful sequence."
2. Additional nonrequired information may be disclosed if it does not confuse customers.
3. A creditor must furnish the consumer with a copy of the disclosure requirements at the time of disclosure.

The case that follows addresses the "meaningful disclosure" requirement.

Bussey v. Georgia Bank Americard

U.S. Court of Appeals

516 F.2d 452 (1975)

Background: Bussey (plaintiff) was a credit-card customer of Georgia Bank Americard (defendant), which was a trade style of the First National Bank of Atlanta. Plaintiff claims that the terms "annual percentage rate" and "finance charge" were not disclosed as conspicuously as required by law on her periodic statement, that the disclosures relating to the finance charge were not made in terminology required by the Act, and the information disclosed on the statement was not in meaningful sequence. The open-end credit arrangement provided an account by which the First National Bank of Atlanta, doing business as its trade style, Georgia Bank Americard, made advances on behalf of the plaintiff upon presentation to the bank of appropriate merchants' sales drafts or made cash advances to the plaintiff upon his application. The bank charged a monthly finance charge respecting the account and a fixed percentage on cash advances at the time of an advance. The plaintiff and defendant filed opposing motions for summary judgment in the U.S. District Court. The court assigned the case to a special master for findings and a recommendation. The special master recommended that summary judgment be granted in favor of the defendant. The District Court adopted the master's recommendation and granted the defendant's motion for summary judgment.

Decision: Affirmed. The Court of Appeals ruled for Georgia Bank Americard.

Before Justices Coleman, Hinsworth, and Simpson: Per Curiam

Rather than rephrase that which has already been decided and with which we agree, we incorporate, as our opinion, the applicable portions of the special master's report and the District Court Order "RECOMMENDATION OF BANKRUPTCY JUDGE W. HOMER DRAKE, JR. SITTING AS SPECIAL MASTER."

The plaintiff contends that the periodic statement which the defendant utilized with respect to plaintiff was deficient in that the terms "annual percentage rate" and "finance charge" were not disclosed more conspicuously than other disclosures required by the Act and Regulation; that the disclosures relating to the finance charge were not made in the terminology required by the Act and Regulation; that the "periodic rate" was not disclosed; and that the information disclosed on the periodic statement was not in a meaningful sequence.

The defendant filed a motion for summary judgment on August 6, 1974, and the plaintiff thereafter also filed a motion for summary judgment, and opposed defendant's motion for summary judgment.

The periodic statement of defendant utilizes a color-coordinated scheme to emphasize the disclosures required by the Regulation and the Act to be more "conspicuous." Attached to the motion for summary judgment of defendant and in support thereof is an affidavit which includes a periodic statement in its original form showing the colors as they appear on the statement as sent to customers of Bank Americard. The disclosures required to be "more conspicuous," that is, disclosures of "annual percentage rate'' and ''finance charge'' are offset on a yellow background, which contrasts with the blue background, for all the remaining disclosures required by the Act and Regulation. This Court finds that such color offset system of disclosure does cause these disclosures to be ''more conspicuous'' than the other disclosures required by the Act and Regulation. Plaintiff contends further, however, that even though this color contrast exists that, since not only is the total finance charge disclosed in this manner, but also the itemized portions of the finance charge are so disclosed, a violation of the Act and Regulation results. This Court finds this contention to be without merit.

The controlling regulation is Regulation ''Z,'' which requires a periodic statement setting forth:

> (4) The amount of any finance charge, using the term ''finance charge,'' debited to the account during the billing cycle, itemized and identified to show the amounts, if any, due to the application of periodic rates and the amount of any other charge included in the finance charge, such as a minimum fixed, check service, transaction, activity, or similar charge, using appropriate descriptive terminology.

This Court finds that the periodic statement used by defendant complies with this Regulation. The statement applies the appropriate descriptive terminology to the finance charge disclosure in all its aspects. It does so with respect to the required itemization of the components of the finance charge by using appropriate descriptive terminology of ''periodic finance charge at 1½%'' and ''cash advance finance charge at 4%,'' and it does so with respect to the entire finance charge with the appropriate descriptive terminology of ''total'' finance charge.

This is in accord with the purpose of the Act and Regulation to assure ''meaningful information'' to consumers. The method used by defendant provides the consumer in a meaningful way, information concerning those items which make up the entire finance charge, and the entire finance charge as a ''total.''

The periodic statement, therefore, complies with both the ''conspicuity'' requirements of Regulation Z, and the finance charge disclosure requirements respecting periodic statements of Regulation Z.

Plaintiff also contends that defendant failed to disclose the ''periodic rate'' pursuant to Regulation Z. This Court finds that defendant has complied with this Regulation by the statement at the lower, left-hand corner on the face of the periodic statement, describing that ''the monthly periodic rate of 1½% results in a corresponding nominal annual percentage rate of 18%.''

Plaintiff has contended that the disclosures made by defendant are not in ''meaningful sequence'' as required by Regulation Z. This contention is without merit. The disclosures of defendant are itemized in an arithmetical sequence which this Court finds to be understandable, clear, and in accordance with the requirements of the Act and Regulation.

In accordance with the foregoing, this Court does hereby:

. . .

2) deny the motion for summary judgment of plaintiff; and

3) grant the motion for summary judgment of defendant.
This 23 day of September, 1974.

Closed-End Credit. Closed-end credit includes both loans to consumers and sales made on credit, where the credit is for a specific period of time and the total amount, number of payments, and due dates are agreed upon by the buyer and seller. Typically closed-end credit is used in buying or financing "big ticket" items like an automobile, washing machine, television set, or other major appliance. Closed-end credit also includes a single-payment loan.

If the credit is closed-end, in addition to an explanation of the "finance charge" and the "APR" the consumer is entitled upon written request to an itemization of the "amount financed." The creditor must affirmatively disclose this right to the consumer. Also, such terms as "total of payments" and "total sale price" must be described by the creditor. The Federal Reserve Board has prepared forms for creditors' use.

Open-End Credit. Regulation Z defines open-end credit as credit extended on an account pursuant to a plan under which

1. The creditor may permit the customer to make purchases or obtain loans from time to time.
2. The customer has the privilege of paying the balance in full or in installments.
3. A finance charge may be computed from time to time on an outstanding unpaid balance.

An open-end credit plan as defined by the Reform Act includes a requirement that the creditor "reasonably contemplated repeated transactions." Common examples of this type of consumer credit are revolving charge accounts of retail stores, oil company and bank credit cards, and bank plans that permit limited overdrafts with finance charges periodically imposed on any unpaid balances.

For consumer credit of this type an initial statement by the creditor must be given at the time the account is opened. It must indicate the conditions under which the finance charge may be imposed, the method of computing it, and the means of determining the balance subject to the finance charge. The periodic rates as well as the corresponding annual percentage rates must also be disclosed in the initial statement.

At the end of each billing period the creditor must provide the customer with a statement if the customer's account has an outstanding balance of over $1. Regulation Z requires certain disclosures to appear on the face of the periodic statement.

Credit Advertising. The Truth-in-Lending Act requires that terms be disclosed before credit is granted. This provides some protection for the consumer. However, because the act does not require any specific time interval between the disclosures and the consummation of the credit transaction, the benefits of disclosure are frequently illusory in practice.

The act and Regulation Z impose restrictions on advertising as it relates to credit terms. The definition of advertising in Regulation Z is very broad. All of the usual channels—newspapers, radio, television, and direct mail—are specifically mentioned. The provisions also cover almost any "commercial message" made available to the public if the message "aids, promotes, or assists" an extension of consumer credit. Although a statement made by a salesman to a particular client is not considered to be an advertisement, a similar statement promoting a sale or loan posted in writing at the store or delivered over a store's public-address system would be an advertisement.

Both the act and Regulation Z prohibit lenders and sellers from advertising terms of credit that are not usually or regularly extended to customers. For example, a creditor who advertises "No down payment" or a seller who advertises "$5 down, $5 per month" must regularly extend credit on those terms. This provision helps to eliminate the practice of enticing customers by advertising generous credit terms that are seldom, if ever, granted. It does not require that every customer be offered the advertised terms, only that the terms be "usually and customarily" those upon which credit is granted.

The basic philosophy of the credit-advertising section of the Truth-in-Lending Act is *if* creditors advertise credit terms they must make disclosures. Following the 1982 amendments to the act, disclosures were limited to: (1) down payment, if any, (2) terms of repayment, and (3) finance charges expressed as an annual percentage rate. Additionally, the act requires that an advertisement of consumer credit payable in four installments without a finance charge must clearly and conspicuously state: "THE COST OF CREDIT IS INCLUDED IN THE PRICE QUOTED FOR THE GOODS AND SERVICES."

Although credit advertising may merit regulation, the provisions of Truth-in-Lending do not effectively deal with the problems. First, the Act provides only for criminal prosecution; civil suits are not authorized. Unfortunately, white-collar crime of this type traditionally has not been given a high priority by law-enforcement authorities. In addition, the prosecution has difficulty establishing a case because it must prove that the Act was willfully and knowingly violated. "Intent" has been almost impossible to prove under other consumer-protection statutes. Finally, the philosophy of requiring disclosure of *all* information if *any* specific information is given might, as a practical matter, result in less information. Creditors might decide to say nothing or to use very vague and general terms to avoid the necessity of making full disclosure. If this happens, consumers have less information than they had prior to Truth-in-Lending. The case that follows includes an FTC and federal court of appeals interpretation of Truth-in-Lending's provisions relating to credit disclosures and credit advertising.

Leon A. Tashoff v. Federal Trade Commission

U.S. Court of Appeals (D.C. Circuit)

473 F.2d 707 (1970)

Background: Tashoff (appellant) was the owner of New York Jewelry Company (NYJC), which advertised and sold jewelry in a low-income area of New York City. Not many NYJC customers had bank or charge accounts; thus 85 percent of all sales were made on credit. The staff of the FTC filed a complaint charging NYJC with engaging in deceptive credit practices and misrepresenting easy credit terms in its advertising (in addition to other unfair trade practices). The hearing examiner dismissed the staff's charges. The full Commission found in favor of the FTC staff. The appellant claimed the evidence was insufficient to support the Commission's findings, and in any event the order was not justified.

Decision: Affirmed. The Court of Appeals ruled in favor of the FTC.

Bazelon, Judge

FAILURE TO DISCLOSE CREDIT CHARGES

Nearly all the evidence regarding NYJC's failure to inform its customers fully and adequately of all credit charges was documentary. It showed that NYJC used three different contract forms during the time in question. All three were materially deficient in one respect or another. The first form failed to disclose the annual percentage charge on the unpaid balance, the dollar amount of the credit charge, and the cash price of the item. The second form failed to show either a monthly or annual percentage interest rate. The third form failed to reveal the total obligation, the finance charge in dollars, and the annual percentage interest rate. Moreover, there was substantial evidence that NYJC often failed even to provide all the information contemplated by the contract form. Also, the evidence revealed unexplained discrepancies among NYJC's contract forms, its own internal records, and the "customer cards" it handed to credit clients.

We think the record amply supports the Commission's finding that NYJC's credit practices were deceptive. The offer of credit without disclosure of the charges therefor in an understandable fashion is, of course, likely to prevent the customer from learning about the cost of credit. This is particularly true for NYJC's customers, many of whom both lack the sophistication to make the complex calculation of credit costs for themselves, and must depend to a large extent on credit for their purchases.

FALSE REPRESENTATION OF "EASY CREDIT"

NYJC's advertising was permeated with references to "easy credit." The complaint charged that the credit was not easy for two reasons: first, because NYJC sought "often with success, to obtain garnishments against (customer's) wages," after having extended credit "without determining (the customer's) credit rating or financial ability to meet payments"; and second, because NYJC sold goods "at unconscionably high prices that greatly exceeded the prices charged for like or similar merchandise by other retail establishments." We hold that the record supports the Commission's finding that NYJC's representations of easy credit were misleading because of its rigorous collection policy. Consequently, there is no need to decide whether the Commission's finding that the representations were misleading because of the store's "greatly excessive prices" is adequately supported.

1. *Rigorous Collection Policy*—The Commission found that NYJC's collection policies were rigorous indeed, and therefore its representation of easy credit was misleading. The record supports this finding.

We have no doubt that the Commission was within its discretion in interpreting "easy credit" to refer not only to easy availability but also to easy terms and leniency with respect to repayment and collection. The Commission noted the oppressive effect of wage garnishments on persons who, like many of NYJC's customers, have low-paying jobs, and found that NYJC regularly garnished its customers' wages. In one year, for example, it sued some 1600 customers—about one out of every three. Firms with many more customers than NYJC used the garnishment process much less often. NYJC, which possessed all the relevant facts, offered nothing to negate the Commission's finding that it pursued a rigorous collection program, and, indeed, in this court did not challenge the Commission's opinion on this point.

NYJC does claim, however, that the complaint did not fairly apprise it of the charge that its easy credit representations might be found misleading on the basis of its collection policy. Although the complaint is hardly a model of clarity, we think that a fair reading provides sufficient notice. It is clear that the main charge is misrepresentation by use of the term "easy credit," not, as NYJC has urged throughout the course of proceedings, unconscionably high prices *per se*. High prices were but one of the two independent grounds said to make the representation deceptive. The other was NYJC's collection policies. Moreover, NYJC has claimed no prejudice from the alleged vagueness of the complaint. It has pointed to no evidence it might have introduced if it had been given clearer notice of the charge. And by the time of the hearing it must have known that its collection policies were under attack, for it agreed to a stipulation about the number of garnishments it, and other stores, filed each year.

2. *Greatly Excessive Prices*—The other ground for the Commission's ultimate conclusion that NYJC's representations of "easy credit" were misleading was its finding that NYJC charged "greatly excessive prices." We need not decide whether this finding is adequately supported, however, for, even if it is not, we have no "substantial doubt [that] the administrative agency would have made the same ultimate finding [i.e., that NYJC's representations of "easy credit" were misleading] with the erroneous findings or inferences out of the picture." In this case it is clear from the structure of the Commission's opinion and the reasons it gave in support of its order that NYJC's representations of "easy credit" were considered misleading on two separate grounds, to wit, the store's rigorous collection practices and its greatly excessive prices.

ENFORCEMENT

To combat NYJC's failure to reveal its credit terms, the Commission ordered it to disclose, both orally and in writing, a variety of factors relating to credit charges in its installment contracts. NYJC argues that the enactment of the new Truth-in-Lending Act shows that the Commission had theretofore lacked the power to order affirmative disclosures of credit information. The argument is without merit. The Act establishes minimum standards of disclosure which the Commission may enforce without proving unfairness and deception on a case-by-case basis. It was not intended to cure a previous deficiency in Commission power to deal with individual cases, and to shape its remedies to the facts of these cases.

Equally unpersuasive is NYJC's contention that the Truth-in-Lending Act sets the bounds of an affirmative disclosure order. NYJC has pointed to nothing in the terms of the Act or its legislative history which supports this view. The sole question for us is whether the remedy chosen by the Commission bears a reasonable relationship to

ETHICS BOX
Ethics and Bank Lending

———

Jones and Mary Smith earn together approximately $70,000 as elementary school teachers. Their monthly disposable income after mortgage payments, credit cards, utilities, and so on is $600 per month. They have a one-year-old house with $10,000 equity. An ad from a local bank urged them to use their home equity for a loan to consolidate their debts on "easy terms." In asterisk form at the bottom of the ad all the terms were outlined as required by the Truth-in-Lending Act. They were disclosed again to Mr. and Mrs. Smith by First National Bank's lending officer when they borrowed $7,000 at a variable rate of 14 percent, with no cap, which was based on the monthly Treasury bill rate. No lawyer was present when this loan was taken out to advise the Smiths and the bank's lawyers drafted the documents they signed. Two years later they cannot make the monthly payments when the variable rate has risen to 22 percent. The Bank forecloses.

There are several ethical issues involved in this case. The bank has more experience and information about the capacity of individuals to handle mortgage payments than the schoolteachers. The bank should gather this information in the course of the application and inform the borrowers about the risks. Further, when there is a new financial mechanism, as in the case of the variable-rate home equity loan, the bank has an obligation to make sure that the borrowers understand how this arrangement differs from the more traditional forms.

Advertising performs many useful and important functions. It reduces consumer search costs for significant information about products and can inform prospective buyers about new products. As is true of many things, advertising can also have a dark side. Providing incorrect or misleading information is a major problem. There may also be a question of advertising being manipulative, when it is designed to overcome critical judgment and induce people to act in a manner that they later regret. So long as the Smiths accurately understood the basic facts and risks of the transaction, no ethical principles have been breached.

———

the violations uncovered. Viewed in this light, NYJC's attacks on the disclosure order are unavailing. The Commission's demand that NYJC disclose credit terms in all transactions, for example, is reasonably related to its finding that many of NYJC's sales involved a small dollar credit charge, but a high percentage rate, and that credit information is crucial to NYJC's low income customers. Thus, the fact that the Truth-in-Lending Act exempts sales involving minimal dollar charges is not controlling. Similarly, the Commission's order that NYJC disclose its credit terms orally is reasonably related to the finding that many of NYJC's customers are unsophisticated consumers who would not benefit from written disclosure alone. That the Truth-in-Lending Act has no such requirement does not invalidate this portion of the order.

The Fair Credit Reporting Act

Purpose. The Fair Credit Reporting Act of 1970[14] was enacted by Congress to require consumer-credit-reporting agencies to adopt reasonable procedures for meeting the needs of lenders while maintaining the confidentiality, accuracy, and relevancy of their records. This legislation was aimed at several problems:

1. Inaccurate and sometimes misleading information in the files of credit-reporting agencies
2. Irrelevant information in such files (for example, the name of a credit applicant's dog)
3. Lack of standards to maintain the confidentiality of credit files

Scope. The Fair Credit Reporting Act regulates the "consumer reporting agency," which is defined as any entity that "regularly" engages in the practice of assembling or evaluating consumer credit or other information on consumers for the purpose of furnishing "consumer reports to third parties." A business can escape the coverage of the act if it disseminates information *infrequently* or if it collects it solely for its own use and does not transmit it to third parties. The act's provisions contain:

1. Requirements for consumer reporting agencies
2. Requirements for users of consumer reports
3. Rights of consumers
4. Remedies for violations

The requirements for consumer-reporting agencies include a directive that all agencies must maintain "reasonable procedures" to avoid making a consumer report that contains obsolete information. Such information is "obsolete" under the act if it is older than seven years (ten years in the case of information relating to bankruptcy). These time limitations are inapplicable if the report is to be used in conjunction with a credit or life-insurance transaction involving $50,000 or more. If the consumer-reporting agency is reporting to a prospective employer, it cannot use materials that are not up-to-date. Further, the act requires that consumer-reporting agencies maintain "reasonable" procedures to assure that its reports will be furnished only to those designated or qualified under the Act. They include:

1. A consumer who requests the reporting agency to furnish information
2. A court of law, or someone authorized by a valid court order
3. A person or entity whom the credit-reporting agency has "reason to believe" intends to use such information to determine if a consumer is eligible for credit, employment, government license, or other business purposes

The Fair Credit Reporting Act also prescribes certain regulations for users of reports received from credit-reporting agencies. Among the obligations users have is to notify a consumer in advance if they intend to order an investigative report from a reporting agency. They must also notify the consumer of the probable content of the report. If the user relies "wholly or partly" on the report in rejecting a consumer for credit, insurance, or employment, it must notify the consumer and provide the name and address of the reporting agency. If a consumer-reporting agency as defined by the act is *not* involved, the user of a report that is the basis for the denial of credit must make all such information available upon request and must advise the consumer of his or her right to make that request.

Consumers have rights under the act as noted earlier. Inaccurate and obsolete information cannot be used in their credit reports. They have a right to be notified of a reporting agency's reliance on adverse information when denied credit. The act gives the consumer a right of disclosure upon request. The reporting agency must disclose:

1. Nature and substance of all information (except medical)
2. Source of all information (except when it is used solely in preparing "investigative reports")
3. Names of any users of the report who have received the consumer's file in the last two years when employment was involved, the last six months for all other reasons

The consumer has a right to correct information in his or her file once it is received. Following notification of errors, the reporting agency must investigate the matter in the file that the consumer disputes, assuming that the correction is not frivolous or irrelevant. The agency must note the dispute and provide a consumer statement for the file or a summary of the consumer's views. Upon request, the reporting agency must notify any users of the file of the disputed information.

Remedies. The FTC has the principal responsibility for administering the act, and does so through cease-and-desist orders. Other agencies share enforcement authority when applicable to matters subject to their regulatory jurisdictions. Some of the same agencies are involved in enforcement of both the Fair Credit Reporting Act and the Truth-in-Lending Act. Criminal liability is involved if a user obtains information from a consumer-report-ing agency "knowingly and willfully" under false pretenses. Officers and employees of an agency are also subject to a penalty of up to $5,000 and one year imprisonment for willfully providing information from an agency file to unauthorized persons. Civil liability is also provided for if there is a *willful* violation of the Act by the reporting agency or user. Compensatory (actual) and punitive damages can be awarded to a consumer, along with attorney's fees and court costs. In case of *negligence* by a reporting agency or user, only compensatory damages are available. The major defense for a reporting agency in a civil suit is that "reasonable procedures" were used as required by the Act.

The Equal Credit Opportunity Act

Purpose. Following a study by the National Commission on Consumer Finance, which showed blatant discrimination against women in the granting of credit, Congress in 1974 enacted the Equal Credit Opportunity Act[15] to prohibit discrimination against a person applying for credit based on sex or marital status. In 1976 Congress amended the Act to include age, race, color, national origin, recipients of public-assistance, and those who exercise their rights under any section of the Consumer Credit Protection Act. The Act empowers the Federal Reserve Board to prescribe regulations and allows the Board to exempt "any classes of transaction not primarily for personal, family or household purposes." Regulation B has been issued by the board as a basis for interpreting and enforcing the act. Several administrative agencies share enforcement authority depending on the type of credit involved. Overall enforcement is entrusted to the FTC.

Scope. The Equal Credit Opportunity Act covers all phases of a credit transaction and all groups noted previously. A creditor may not ask for information about race, age, sex, religion, or national origin. The act prohibits asking for information about marital status, alimony, child support, use of birth-control pills, and former spouses. A model application form has been issued by the Federal Reserve Board. Use of this form by the creditor offers a presumption of compliance with these provisions.

The Act requires that a creditor give an applicant notification of action it has taken on his or her completed application for credit within thirty days. If the application is incomplete, a ninety-day notice period is required if the application is denied. The notification must include:

1. A statement of the action taken
2. Basic provisions of ECOA
3. Name and address of compliance agency
4. A statement of the specific reasons for the action taken, or a disclosure of the applicant's right to receive a statement of reason

Remedies. The FTC, as well as individuals, may sue to enforce the Act. A person injured may recover actual and punitive damages. In individual actions such punitive damages may not exceed $10,000, whereas in class actions $500,000 or 1 percent of the net worth of the creditors (whichever is less) is the maximum.

The Fair Debt Collection Practices Act

Purpose. Up to this point discussion has centered on federal laws that seek to protect consumers in obtaining credit. A consumer-debtor may be financially unable to pay his or her bills or may simply not pay them. Approximately 5,000 debt-collection agencies

seek collection of approximately $5 billion in debts from 8 million consumers each year. These figures grow during times of recession. Collection agencies use computer calls and sophisticated WATS telephone lines to make 25 to 50 percent commissions on what they collect. Because of abusive practices, including threats of violence, obscene language, and anonymous phone calls in the middle of the night, Congress in 1977 passed the Fair Debt Collection Practices Act.[16] As noted previously, this and other pieces of consumer-protection legislation are included as separate titles under the Consumer Credit Protection Act. The FTC is charged with its administration and enforcement. A violation of this Act is considered to be an unfair or deceptive practice under Section 5 of the Federal Trade Commission Act.

Scope. Because laws preventing abuses in debt collection have been passed in many states, the Fair Debt Collection Practices Act allows exemptions for states that meet federal standards. Also, the Act covers only those debt collectors who collect for someone other than themselves. Large companies that do their own debt collecting are not covered by the Act but may be covered by state legislation. The Act forbids the following practices:

1. A debt collector may contact someone other than the consumer debtor, his or her family, or his or her attorney only for purposes of finding the debtor. This section seeks to prevent a collector from ruining the good name of a debtor with his employer or neighbors.
2. Debt collectors may not contact a debtor at inconvenient times (9 P.M.–8 A.M.), or at all if the collector is aware that the consumer is represented by an attorney.

3. Any conduct by debt collectors that is abusive, deceptive, misleading, or unfair is forbidden. Posing as lawyers or police officers to collect debts, for example, is forbidden.

4. Collections that require liens on real property may be brought only where the property is located. Other collection actions must be brought where the debtor resides.

Attorneys and law firms that participate in debt collection also fall within the Act, as a result of a 1986 amendment passed by Congress.

Remedies. Action can be brought by the FTC and individuals. Any violator of the Act is liable for actual damages and "additional damages" up to $1,000. Attorneys' fees and court costs also may be assessed.

REVIEW PROBLEMS

1. What three areas of deceptive price advertising does the FTC most concern itself with?

2. When does the court consider advertising to be "unfair"?

3. What remedies can the FTC invoke against deceptive and unfair advertising?

4. What is the main purpose of the Truth-in-Lending Act?

5. What is the scope of the Truth-in-Lending Act?

6. Distinguish between open-end and closed-end credit.

7. What is the purpose of the Fair Credit Reporting Act?

8. What is the purpose of the Equal Credit Opportunity Act?

9. The Campbell Soup Company ran ads showing pictures of a bowl of soup in a ready-to-eat situation. Solid ingredients were shown at the top of the bowl. The Federal Trade Commission charged that this picture was a misrepresentation because the bowl of soup as shown was a "mockup" display. The company had placed marbles in the bottom of the soup bowl. The FTC charged that the marbles forced the solid ingredients to the top, making them visible to the viewer. The Commission argued that the solids would not have been visible at the top of the bowl but for the marbles and that therefore the picture was misleading. Is Campbell Soup in violation of Section 5 of the Federal Trade Commission Act? FTC v. Campbell Soup Company, Inc., FTC-DKT C-1741 (May 25, 1970)

10. *Reader's Digest* magazine tested seven leading cigarettes in order to find out which was lowest in tar and nicotine. It published the results, stating that the cigarette "whose smoke was lowest in nicotine" was Old Gold. The report went on to say that the differences between the brands were small and that no single brand was so superior to its competitors as to justify its selection as less harmful. Lorillard Company, manufacturer of Old Gold cigarettes, advertised: "Old Golds Found Lowest in Nicotine. Old Golds Found Lowest in Throat Irritating Tars and Resins. See Impartial Test by *Reader's Digest,* July issue." Was this deceptive advertising under Section 5 of the Federal Trade Commission Act? P. Lorillard Company v. Federal Trade Commission, 186 F.2d 52 (1970)

11. The Colgate-Palmolive Company, manu-

facturer of a shaving cream, "Rapid Shave," sought to test the effectiveness of its cream on men's beards. In an advertisement broadcast on television, Colgate sought to show that its product could soften even sandpaper. However, when the advertisement was run, a sheet of Plexiglas with sand sprinkled on it was used in place of sandpaper. The FTC claimed that the commercial was deceptive and violated Section 5 of the FTC Act. Colgate claimed there was no deception because the viewer was simply being given a visual presentation of the test on sandpaper that had actually been made. Was there a violation of Section 5? FTC v. Colgate-Palmolive Company, 380 U.S. 374 (1965)

12. Kathleen Carroll, a single working woman, applied for an Exxon credit card in August 1976 and was advised by mail shortly thereafter that her application for credit was denied. No reason for the denial was given. Fourteen days after the denial she asked to be advised of the specific reasons. In an undated letter she was told by Exxon that a local reporting agency had not been able to supply sufficient information. The name of the credit bureau used by Exxon was not included in any of their communications. Upon filing the present lawsuit, Carroll was given the name and address of the credit bureau. Carroll did not have a major credit card, nor a savings account, and had been employed for one year. Would Carroll win the suit? If so, based on what consumer protection statute(s)? Carroll v. Exxon, 434 F.Supp. 557 E.D. La. (1977)

13. For the price of $408 Linda Glaire obtained a seven-year membership in a health club owned and operated by LaLanne. The $408 was paid by Glaire over a two-year period at the rate of $17 monthly. The installment contract stated that there were no finance charges. The contract was sold to Universal Guidance Acceptance Corporation. LaLanne and Universal are in reality owned by the same shareholders, with Universal assisting LaLanne in financing. Glaire filed suit against LaLanne alleging violation of the Truth-in-Lending Act. Is there a violation of the Truth-in-Lending Act? Glaire v. LaLanne–Paris Health Spa, Inc., 528 P.2d 357 (1974)

14. Rutyna was a 60-year-old widow and Social Security retiree, suffering from high blood pressure and epilepsy. In late December 1976 and early 1977 she incurred a debt for services performed by a doctor that were not covered by Medicare or private insurance. Rutyna assumed it had been paid or would be paid by her insurance. When the defendant, a collection agency, notified her of $56 that remained unpaid to a medical group, she denied the existence of the debt. Rutyna claimed that she received telephone calls and a letter from the collection agency (defendant) notifying her of a neighborhood investigation that was to be undertaken. The letter, with the defendant's return address on it, required immediate payment or a visit by her to the defendant's office to prevent any further embarrassment. Upon receipt of this communication, Rutyna claimed she became very nervous and upset because of the embarrassment that might be caused by the defendant. The defendant claimed a lack of knowledge concerning Rutyna's reaction to their letter, denied the phone calls, and insisted that the plaintiff called many times. What consumer protection statute is the basis for Rutyna's claim? Will she win? Rutyna v. Collection Accounts Terminal, Inc., 478 F.Supp. 980 (N.D. Ill. 1979)

FOOTNOTES

[1] American Bar Association, *Report of the Commission to Study the Federal Trade Commission.*

[2] R. Fellmet & E. Cox, *Nader Report on the Federal Trade Commission* (1969).

[3] Pub.L. 96–637 (codified in various sections of 15 U.S.C.). This Act and the role of the FTC in enforcing warranties is discussed in Chapter 22 of this text.

[4] This chapter deals with consumer protection statutes enforced by the FTC. However, the reader should know that each of the fifty states, the District of Columbia, and Puerto Rico have state consumer protection statutes, and local ordinances dealing with consumer problems. Additionally, the Uniform Consumer Credit Code, a model piece of legislation, has been adopted by some states.

[5] 15 U.S.C. 41–58.

[6] 15 U.S.C. 45 *et seq.*

[7] See E. Drew, "Politics and Money," *New Yorker* magazine, December 6, 1982, pp. 54–149, for an in-depth analysis of the impact of political action committees on the legislative and regulating process. See p. 131 for reference to their impact on the FTC.

[8] 745 *Antitrust and Trade Regulation Report* 689 (October 27, 1983).

[9] Firestone Tire & Rubber Co. v. FTC, 481 F.2d 246 (6th Cir. 1973).

[10] McDonald's v. Burger King, 82-2005 (S.D. Fla. 1982); Wendy's International, Inc. v. Burger King, C-2-82-1175 (S.D. Ohio 1982).

[11] 15 U.S.C. 1451.

[12] 15 U.S.C. 1601 *et seq.*

[13] See R. Posner, *Economic Analysis of Law,* 2nd Ed. (1977), pp. 272–275, for additional thoughts on the value of mandated disclosure of credit terms.

[14] 15 U.S.C. 1681, *et seq.*

[15] 15 U.S.C. 1691, *et seq.*

[16] 15 U.S.C. 1692, *et seq.*

Fair Employment Practices

ince passage of the Civil Rights Act of 1964, employment discrimination has been one of the major policy concerns of business and industry. This federal statute, coupled with related federal and state regulations, affects the daily operation of business firms of all types. It is important not only to business executives but to employees, union leaders, and, because it deals with questions of fundamental fairness and economic opportunity, to all citizens. This chapter examines the boundaries and prohibitions of discrimination in employment on the basis of race, sex, national origin, and religion. It also explores the requirements and legal bases of affirmative-action programs.

STATUTES AND REGULATIONS

Fair-employment-practices law is primarily statutory. Although a body of case law is devel-oping, the cases have been generally concerned with interpreting statutes that provide the framework for preventing discrimination in employment. (See Table 46-1.)

Title VII of the 1964 Civil Rights Act

Basic to an understanding of fair-employment-practices law is Title VII of the 1964 Civil Rights Act, which was strengthened by the Equal Employment Opportunity Act of 1972. Title VII was enacted as part of a broad civil rights program dealing with discrimination in restaurants and hotels (public accommodations), educational institutions, and federal programs as well as employment. It was one congressional response to the civil rights movement and resulting strife of the 1950s and 1960s.[1]

Title VII makes it unlawful for employers, unions, or employment agencies to make any decision concerning the employment or work

TABLE 46-1 SELECTED CIVIL RIGHTS STATUTES AND REGULATIONS

Statute or Regulation	Purpose
Title VII of the Civil Rights Act of 1964	Makes it unlawful for employers, unions, or employment agencies to make any decision concerning the employment or work status of an individual based on race, sex, religion, or national origin
Executive Order 11246	Prohibits contractors from discriminating against employees or applicants because of race, sex, religion, or national origin. Also requires affirmative action by employers to ensure that applicants are employed without regard to race, sex, religion, or national origin
Equal Pay Act of 1963	Prohibits unequal pay for equal work regardless of sex at managerial levels in state and local government as well as most private industries
National Labor Relations Act	Prohibits employers from refusing to engage in collective bargaining with a union selected by its employees
Age Discrimination in Employment Act of 1967	Prohibits discrimination in employment based on age of people
Vocational Rehabilitation Act of 1973	Prohibits discrimination against handicapped individuals by the federal government, private employers having government contracts, and those firms receiving federal government financial assistance.

status of an individual on the basis of race, sex, religion, or national origin. This prohibition covers private and public employers who have at least fifteen employees. One of the few defenses available under Title VII is the bona fide occupational qualification (bfoq). This provision allows an employer to hire and employ (or a union and employment agency to classify) on the basis of sex, religion, or national origin in limited circumstances where the sex, religion, or national origin of the individual is reasonably relevant to the employment. This defense or exception has been narrowly construed by the courts and is discussed more fully later. The bfoq provision does not mention race; discrimination on the basis of race, if proven, cannot be justified by this exception.

Executive Order 11246

In 1965 President Johnson issued Executive Order 11246, and in 1968 President Nixon issued another executive order to amend and strengthen it. Order 11246 prohibits federal contractors who receive more than $10,000 from the federal government from discriminating against any employee or applicant on the basis of race, sex, religion, or national origin. The executive order also requires employers to take "affirmative action" to ensure that applicants are employed, and that employees are treated during employment, without regard to their race, sex, religion, or national origin. Specifics of affirmative-action requirements are discussed later in the chapter.

Other Statutes

The Equal Pay Act. The Equal Pay Act of 1963 is an amendment to the Fair Labor Standards Act of 1938, the federal minimum-wage and maximum-hour law. Amendments to the Equal Pay Act in 1972 and 1974 broadened its coverage so that it mandates equal pay for equal work regardless of sex at professional and managerial levels, in state and local government, as well as in most private industries. The most difficult questions raised under the Equal Pay Act are determining whether male and female workers are actually doing substantially the same work and, if so, whether the pay differential is based on a factor other than sex. In most instances the nature of this inquiry demands a case-by-case analysis.

The National Labor Relations Act. The National Labor Relations Act of 1936 deals specifically with the right of employees to engage in or to refrain from collective-bargaining activities. Because once selected a union becomes the exclusive bargaining representative of the employees, the union has a duty of fair representation. To enforce this duty, the National Labor Relations Board has held that failures of fair representation, including acts of racial and gender-based discrimination, are unfair labor practices and subject to the usual remedies.[2] Since passage of the 1964 Civil Rights Act (Title VII), the use of this theory has been limited.

State and Local Law. Most states and many communities have their own fair-employment-practices laws and enforcement agencies that parallel the Title VII provisions. Title VII allows for, and in some instances mandates, deferral to these local agencies where the procedures are adequate and the responsibilities are similar.

Statutory Purpose and Constitutionality

The policies expressed by these statutes and regulations are both general and specific. Primarily, they reflect the judgment that the most effective way to end physical or economic segregation of women and minority-group members is to bring them fully into the business environment. Specifically, the statutes reject employment decisions based on group stereotypes. An applicant's or an employee's race, sex, religion, or national origin is irrelevant except in a few narrowly defined situations. Moreover, employment standards must be job-related or justified by business necessity if they have an unequal impact on any protected group. Implicitly, the fair-employment-practices laws pursue the traditional "work ethic" principle—that is, artificial barriers should not keep men or women from jobs they can perform.

The policies of the regulations as well as their specific mandates are constitutionally based. For example, the federal statutes are enacted under Congress's power to regulate interstate commerce and under Section 5 of the Fourteenth Amendment; state statutes are enacted under each state's police powers. The authority for the Executive Order is found in the constitutional command that the President "take care that the laws be faithfully executed"[3] and the Fifth Amendment's due-process clause, which requires equal protection of citizens by the federal government.

Administration and Enforcement

Each statute typically creates an administrative agency for enforcement. Most also encourage and rely on informal means of settling disputes. Title VII created the Equal Employment Opportunity Commission (EEOC), which presently is empowered to receive and investigate complaints, pursue informal conciliation, and bring suit in its own name against a respondent. The complainant also has the right to sue in federal district court after exhausting his or her administrative remedies. Additionally, the EEOC has the power to issue and to publish interpretations of Title VII. Although these guidelines do not have the force of law, they indicate the legal position of the EEOC, which is also likely to be its position in any future litigation. Statutory remedies include reinstatement, back-pay awards, injunctions, and other appropriate equitable relief.

A parallel structure has evolved to effectuate the mandates of the Executive Order. Primary responsibility is assigned to the Secretary of Labor and the Office of Federal Contract Compliance Programs (OFCCP). However, the secretary may delegate this authority to other agencies and has done so in cases such as schools and hospitals (Health and Human Services) and banks (Treasury). The OFCCP also publishes regulations and interpretive guidelines and seeks informal resolutions of disputes. The typical enforcement technique is an administrative compliance hearing resulting in the withdrawal of federal monies by the government.

State agencies often possess the preceding powers with the further authority to issue cease-and-desist orders enforceable through appropriate court action.

RACE DISCRIMINATION

The U.S. Constitution protects individual rights and sets the outer limits of permissible government activity. It is also the basis for suits by individuals against the government (or others if they are closely connected with the government). Specifically, individuals alleging unlawful discrimination challenge a particular action as a violation of the Fourteenth Amendment's equal protection clause, applicable to the states, or the Fifth Amendment's due-process clause, applicable to the federal government. Unlike the statutes discussed earlier, the equal protection clause is not limited to race or sex discrimination but applies to any sort of irrational discrimination. However, race and sex discrimination issues are tested by different standards. While in general discriminations are valid if they rest on any rational ground, distinctions on the basis of race or sex are not valid unless they rest on "compelling" grounds, in the case of race, or on "substantial" grounds, in the case of sex.

Neutral Standards

Since 1965, the effective date of Title VII, overt disparate treatment on the basis of race, sex, religion, or national origin has been increasingly rare. On the other hand, covert and unintentional discrimination remain problems that are often difficult to detect or remedy. Much of the litigation following the enactment of Title VII has been in the area of apparently neutral standards for hiring, promotion, and other conditions of employment that, when applied, have disproportionately adverse effects on protected groups. In such cases the burden of proof is on the plaintiff to show the disparate impact of applying the standard. When that has been established the burden then shifts to the defendant to show that the standard in question is job-related or justified by business necessity. For example, suppose a state requires all its police officers to meet a 5'9" minimum height requirement. A woman presents evidence that approximately 95 percent of the female labor pool are disqualified by the standard. It is then the duty of the defendant to prove that the standard is job-related. That is, given the specific duties of a police officer, is the job performed more effectively by someone at least 5'9" tall? In the case of guards at maximum-security prisons in

Alabama, the U.S. Supreme Court answered no.[4]

Particular problems are raised by testing and educational requirements. In an era when many people seek legitimation through objective measures, more employers are using the results of tests to make employment decisions, either in initial hiring, in promotion decisions, or in terminations. Title VII, Section 703(h), provides that it is not unlawful for an employer:

> to give and to act upon the result of any professionally developed ability test, provided that such test, its administration or action upon the results is not designed, intended or used to discriminate because of race, color, religion, sex or national origin.

However, in many instances minority-group members score disproportionately lower in often-used standardized tests. Some experts argue that these tests are culturally biased.[5] Thus even a "professionally developed test" may have a discriminatory impact, inconsistent with the primary policies of the equal-employment-opportunity statute. In the courts' view, if the complainant can prove that a test has a disparate impact on a protected group, it is then the responsibility of the employer to show that the test is valid in both a legal and a psychological sense. For a test to be valid, it must be able to predict with some degree of accuracy whether an applicant will be successful on the particular job for which the test was used. To measure the chances of success on a particular job, one must know what the job requires, what "success" is for the job, and what qualities need to be examined.

Similar issues are raised concerning educational requirements for employment. On the one hand, Americans have great faith in their educational system. Education is mandatory for a certain number of years and involves a sizable percentage of governmental expenditures. On the other hand, significant segments of the population get less education, either in quality or quantity, than the majority. Therefore the requirement of a diploma for employment may have a disparate impact on members of a protected group. If such an effect is shown, the employer must establish the job-relatedness of the requirement. Often the defendant's burden is not so great when the requirement is for a college degree, postgraduate education, or professional training as it is when the requirement is for passing grades on scored tests.

The dimensions of the job-relatedness standard are presently unclear. It appears to be a test of specificity, since notions of simply a "more intelligent" work force have been rejected by the courts. Job-relatedness also has been used to invalidate consideration of arrest records in an employment decision. On the other hand, the defendant's burden of proof is difficult to assess since there have been few cases where the attempt has even been made. Moreover, the distinction between the concepts of job-relatedness and business necessity remains unclear. At least one court[6] has held that an employment criterion having a disparate impact can be justified only by a showing that the criterion relates to job performance and not by a broader notion of business necessity. Other courts have said that similar criteria may be justified with reference to business-related factors such as employee morale and efficiency or the integrity and security of the business.

The inquiry does not necessarily end when the employer proves job-relatedness or business necessity. The court must still determine whether other tests or selection criteria would serve the employer's interest without the undesirable impact. The EEOC places this burden on the employer; the U.S. Supreme Court indicated, in a case it remanded for further proceedings, that the burden falls on the plaintiff.

Griggs v. Duke Power Co.

Supreme Court of the United States

401 U.S. 424 (1971)

Background: A group of black employees (plaintiffs) brought a suit against Duke Power Co. (defendant) alleging violations of Title VII, Section 703(a), in requiring a high-school diploma and a passing score on a standardized general-intelligence test for employment or transfer between departments. The District Court found for Duke Power Co. and the Court of Appeals affirmed.

Decision: Reversed. The U.S. Supreme Court ruled in favor of Griggs and other black employees.

Burger, Chief Justice

The District Court found that prior to July 2, 1965, the effective date of the Civil Rights Act of 1964, the Company openly discriminated on the basis of race in the hiring and assigning of employees at its Dan River plant. The plant was organized into five operating departments: (1) Labor, (2) Coal Handling, (3) Operations, (4) Maintenance, and (5) Laboratory and Test. Negroes were employed only in the Labor Department where the highest paying jobs paid less than the lowest paying jobs in the other four "operating" departments in which only whites were employed. Promotions were normally made within each department on the basis of job seniority. Transferees into a department usually began in the lowest position.

In 1955 the Company instituted a policy of requiring a high school education for initial assignment to any department except Labor, and for transfer from the Coal Handling to any "inside" department (Operations, Maintenance, or Laboratory). When the Company abandoned its policy of restricting Negroes to the Labor Department in 1965, completion of high school also was made a prerequisite to transfer from Labor to any other department. . . .

The Company added a further requirement for new employees on July 2, 1965, the date on which Title VII became effective. To qualify for placement in any but the Labor Department it became necessary to register satisfactory scores on two professionally prepared aptitude tests, as well as to have a high school education. Completion of high school alone continued to render employees eligible for transfer to the four desirable departments from which Negroes had been excluded if the incumbent had been employed prior to the time of the new requirement. In September 1965 the Company began to permit incumbent employees who lacked a high school education to qualify for transfer from Labor or Coal Handling to an "inside" job by passing two tests—the Wonderlic Personnel Test, which purports to measure general intelligence, and the Bennett Mechanical Comprehension Test. Neither was directed or intended to measure the ability to learn to perform a particular job or category of jobs. The requisite scores used for both initial hiring and transfer approximated the national median for high school graduates.

The objective of Congress in the enactment of Title VII is plain from the language of the statute. It was to achieve equality of employment opportunities and remove barriers that have operated in the past to favor an identifiable group of white employees over other employees. Under the Act, practices, procedures, or tests neutral on their face, and even neutral in terms of intent, cannot be maintained if they operate to "freeze" the status quo of prior discriminatory employment practices. . . .

The Act describes not only overt discrimination but also practices that are fair in form, but discriminatory in operation. The touchstone is business necessity. If an employment practice which operates to exclude Negroes cannot be shown to be related to job performance, the practice is prohibited.

On the record before us, neither the high school completion requirement nor the general intelligence test is shown to bear a demonstrable relationship to successful performance of the jobs for which it was used. Both were adopted, as the Court of Appeals noted, without meaningful study of their relationship to job-performance ability. Rather, a vice president of the Company testified, the requirements were instituted on the Company's judgment that they generally would improve the overall quality of the work force.

The evidence, however, shows that employees who have not completed high school or taken the tests have continued to perform satisfactorily and make progress in departments for which the high school and test criteria are now used. . . .

The Company's lack of discriminatory intent is suggested by special efforts to help the undereducated employees through Company financing of two-thirds the cost of tuition for high school training. But Congress directed the thrust of the Act to the *consequences* of employment practices, not simply the motivation. More than that, Congress has placed on the employer the burden of showing that any given requirement must have a manifest relationship to the employment in question.

Present Effects of Past Discrimination

Another form of discrimination that fair-employment-practices laws attempt to rectify is exclusion resulting from past discriminatory treatment or the continuing effects of prior exclusion. For example, previous experience on particular jobs is often a selection criterion. If blacks have been excluded from these particular jobs so that they were denied the opportunity to gain the requisite experience, the apparently neutral criterion has a disparate impact. Such criteria are difficult to justify in the face of the additional burden of showing that there is no less onerous alternative. An example of this perpetuation of past discrimination is provided in *Griggs*, discussed previously.

The issue of present effects of past discrimination is particularly important in connection with seniority systems, which affect, among other things, promotions and layoffs. Past exclusions were, according to the standards of the day, often legal. However, the present effects of these systems operate adversely on at least a generation of "locked-in" employees.

Seniority systems are among the major achievements of the labor movement in the United States. For the unions there are several advantages to using seniority to determine issues of promotion and layoff. First, it prevents total domination and favoritism on the part of the employer. Second, seniority adds order and objectivity to dispute resolution. Third, seniority discourages rapid turnover both internally and externally and protects the employee's expectations. There are, however, important disadvantages to seniority systems in direct conflict with Title VII principles. Seniority as a determinant of promotions may or may not be job- or ability-related. More important, a seniority system may have serious present-day consequences for those who were treated unfairly before the enactment of Title VII.

For example, one problem under seniority systems is promotional opportunities for minority-group members hired in limited and segregated positions. Typically minorities were limited in the past to jobs in only one department segregated from white employees. Seniority was department-based, and transfer to other departments was restricted, if not entirely prohibited. Under Title VII transfer to other departments may still be limited or prohibited, but all departments are open to new employees. Complaints of discrimination come primarily from the minority-group members who were hired before enactment of Title VII or implementation of the company's nondiscrimination policy and who are now frozen into their department. Although the seniority system is neutral on its face, it has a disparate impact on such a group.

Congress's compromise solution to the problems presented by the present operation of seniority systems is another special section, 703(h), which allows:

different terms, conditions, or privileges of employment pursuant to a bona fide seniority system . . . provided that such differences are not the result of an intention to discriminate because of race, color, religion, sex or national origin. . . .

Lower federal courts have interpreted this section to require a balance between the protection of existing seniority rights and the need for a realistic remedy for past discrimination. The courts used "bona fide" and "the result of an intention to discriminate" to invalidate seniority systems that perpetuated pre-Act discrimination. As a remedy, courts granted blacks artificial seniority, called constructive seniority, so that they would be able to obtain future positions that would have been open to them but for the previous discrimination.

In 1977 the U.S. Supreme Court in *International Brotherhood of Teamsters* v. *United States,* excerpted on page 1204, rejected previous interpretations of Section 703(h) and held that the section immunized seniority systems that did not originate in racial discrimination even if such systems perpetuated previous discrimination. At the same time the Court reaffirmed the validity of a 1976 decision holding that Section 703(h) allows the award of constructive seniority as a remedy for unlawful employment practices unrelated to the seniority system.

Another problem, critical in times of economic decline, is layoffs. The traditional rule of seniority systems is that the last person hired is the first person fired. In companies where minorities and women were previously excluded but are hired today, the effect of the "last hired–first fired" rule falls heavily on the recently employed minority and female employees. Here again a neutral rule has an adverse impact on protected groups, but the solution is not clear. Minor adjustments in the seniority system do not effect a remedy. While deferring the promotion of a white male may be less onerous than a layoff, to lay off more senior white males in order not to lay off a woman or minority-group member would seem to violate the antipreference clause of Title VII, Section 703(j), and to be another form of discrimination in violation of the basic Title VII provision, Section 703(a). No adequate remedy has been found.

Teamsters v. United States

Supreme Court of the United States

431 U.S. 324 (1977)

Background: The United States (plaintiff-respondent) brought suit against T.I.M.E.D.C. Inc. and the International Brotherhood of Teamsters (defendants-petitioners) alleging that the company and the union had engaged in a pattern or practice of discriminating against minorities in hiring line drivers. The District Court and the Court of Appeals found for the plaintiff.

Decision: Reversed in part. The Supreme Court ruled in favor of the company and Teamsters Union on the finding of discrimination due to the seniority system.

Stewart, Justice

The District Court and the Court of Appeals also found that the seniority system contained in the collective-bargaining agreements between the company and the union operated to violate Title VII of the Act.

For purposes of calculating benefits, such as vacations, pensions, and other fringe benefits, an employee's seniority under this system runs from the date he joins the company and takes into account his total service in all jobs and bargaining units. For competitive purposes, however, such as determining the order in which employees may bid for particular jobs, are laid off, or are recalled from layoff, it is bargaining-unit seniority that controls. Thus, a line driver's seniority, for purposes of bidding for particular runs and protection against layoff, takes into account only the length of time he has been a line driver at a particular terminal. The practical effect is that a city driver or serviceman who transfers to a line-drive job must forfeit all the competitive seniority he has accumulated in his previous bargaining unit and start at the bottom of the line drivers' "board."

The vice of this arrangement, as found by the District Court and the Court of Appeals, was that it "locked" minority workers into inferior jobs and perpetuated prior discrimination by discouraging transfers to jobs as line drivers. While the disincentive applied to all workers, including whites, it was Negroes and Spanish-surnamed persons who, those courts found, suffered the most because many of them had been denied the equal opportunity to become line drivers when they were initially hired, whereas whites either had not sought or were refused line-driver positions for reasons unrelated to their race or national origin.

The linchpin of the theory embraced by the District Court and the Court of Appeals was that a discriminatee who must forfeit his competitive seniority in order finally to obtain a line-driver job will never be able to "catch up" to the seniority level of his contemporary who was not subject to discrimination. Accordingly, this continued, built-in disadvantage to the prior discriminatee who transfers to a line-driver job was held to constitute a continuing violation of Title VII, for which both the employer and the union who jointly create and maintain the seniority system were liable.

The union, while acknowledging that the seniority system may in some sense perpetuate the effects of prior discrimination, asserts that the system is immunized from a finding of illegality by reason of §703(h) of Title VII, 42 U.S.C. §2000e–2(h).

It argues that the seniority system in this case is "bona fide" within the meaning of §703(h) when judged in light of its history, intent, application, and all of the circumstances under which it was created and is maintained. More specifically, the union claims that the central purpose of §703(h) is to ensure that mere perpetuation of *pre-Act* discrimination is not unlawful under Title VII. And, whether or not §703(h) immunizes the perpetuation of *post-Act* discrimination, the union claims that the seniority system in this litigation has no such effect. Its position in this Court, as has been its position throughout this litigation, is that the seniority system presents no hurdle to post-Act discriminatees who seek retroactive seniority to the date they would have become line drivers but for the company's discrimination. Indeed, the union asserts that under its collective-bargaining agreements the union will itself take up the cause of the post-Act victim and attempt, through grievance procedures, to gain for him full "make whole" relief, including appropriate seniority.

The Government responds that a seniority system that perpetuates the effects of prior discrimination—pre-Act or post-Act—can never be "bona fide" under §703(h); at a minimum Title VII prohibits those applications of a seniority system that perpetuate the effects on incumbent employees of prior discriminatory job assignments.

The issues thus joined are open ones in this Court. We considered §703(h) in Franks v. Bowman Transportation Co., 424 U.S. 747, but there decided only that §703(h) does not bar the award of retroactive seniority to job applicants who seek relief from an employer's post-Act hiring discrimination.

Because the company discriminated both before and after the enactment of Title VII, the seniority system is said to have operated to perpetuate the effects of both pre- and post-Act discrimination. Post-Act discriminatees, however, may obtain full "make whole" relief, including retroactive seniority under *Franks* v. *Bowman, supra,* without attacking the legality of the seniority system as applied to them. *Franks* made clear and the union acknowledges that retroactive seniority may be awarded as relief from an employer's discriminatory hiring and assignment policies even if the seniority system agreement itself makes no provision for such relief. Here the Government has proved that the company engaged in a post-Act pattern of discriminatory hiring, assignment, transfer and promotion policies. Any Negro or Spanish-surnamed American injured by those policies may receive all appropriate relief as a direct remedy for this discrimination. What remains for review is the judgment that the seniority system unlawfully perpetuated the effects of *pre-Act* discrimination. We must decide, in short, whether §703(h) validates otherwise bona fide seniority systems that afford no constructive seniority to victims discriminated against prior to the effective date of Title VII, and it is to that issue that we now turn.

Were it not for §703(h), the seniority system in this case would seem to fall under the *Griggs* rationale. The heart of the system is its allocation of the choicest jobs, the greatest protection against layoffs, and other advantages to those employees who have been line drivers for the longest time. Where, because of the employer's prior intentional discrimination, the line drivers with the longest tenure are without exception white, the advantages of the seniority system flow disproportionately to them and away from Negro and Spanish-surnamed employees who might by now have enjoyed these advantages had not the employer discriminated before the passage of the Act. This disproportionate distribution of advantages does in a very real sense "operate to 'freeze' the status quo of prior discriminatory employment practices." Both the literal terms of §703(h) and the legislative history of Title VII demonstrate that Congress considered this very effect of many seniority systems and extended a measure of immunity to them.

Throughout the initial consideration of H.R. 7152, later enacted as the Civil Rights Act of 1964, critics of the bill charged that it would destroy existing seniority rights. The consistent response of Title VII's congressional proponents and of the Justice Department was that seniority rights would not be affected even where the employer had discriminated prior to the Act.

In sum, the unmistakable purpose of §703(h) was to make clear that the routine application of a bona fide seniority system would not be unlawful under Title VII. As the legislative history shows, this was the intended result even where the employer's pre-Act discrimination resulted in whites having greater seniority rights than Negroes. Although a seniority system inevitably tends to perpetuate the effects of pre-Act discrimination in such cases, the congressional judgment was that Title VII should not outlaw the use of existing seniority lists and thereby destroy or water down the vested seniority rights of employees simply because their employer had engaged in discrimination prior to the passage of the Act.

To be sure, §703(h) does not immunize all seniority systems. It refers only to "bona fide" systems, and a proviso requires that any differences in treatment not be "the result of an intention to discriminate because of race . . . or national origin. . . ." But our reading of the legislative history compels us to reject the Government's broad argument that no seniority system that tends to perpetuate pre-Act discrimination can be "bona fide." To accept the argument would require us to hold that a seniority system becomes illegal simply because it allows the full exercise of the pre-Act seniority rights of employees of a company that discriminated before Title VII was enacted. It would place an affirmative obligation on the parties to the seniority agreement to subordinate those rights in favor of the claims of pre-Act discriminatees without seniority. The consequence would be a perversion of the congressional purpose. We cannot accept the invitation to disembowel §703(h) by reading the words "bona fide" as the Government would have us do. Accordingly, we hold that an otherwise neutral, legitimate seniority system does not become unlawful under Title VII simply because it may perpetuate pre-Act discrimination. Congress did not intend to make it illegal for employees with vested seniority rights to continue to exercise those rights, even at the expense of pre-Act discriminatees.

Because the seniority system was protected by §703(h), the union's conduct in agreeing to and maintaining the system did not violate Title VII. On remand, the District Court's injunction against the union must be vacated.

SEX DISCRIMINATION

Although sex discrimination is prohibited by the same statutes that prohibit racial, religious, and national-origin discrimination, there are some fundamental differences in the problems women face. Women constitute 40 percent of the labor force and more than 40 percent of white collar workers. Women accounted for nearly three-fifths of the increase in the labor force in the last decade. Some legislation that is today considered discriminatory against women was actually enacted, in the belief of the legislators, for their protection. And all of us can recite basic cultural and biological distinctions between men and women. However, many of these protective laws and cultural and biological distinctions are used to deny women equal employment opportunity even though the distinctions are irrelevant or the laws unduly restrictive.

In 1978 the median salary for full-time, year-round work was $16,360 for white men; $12,530 for black men; $9,732 for white women; and $9,020 for black women.[7] The unemployment rates for persons aged 20 and over for 1979 are also significant: white men, 3.6 percent; black men, 8.4 percent; white women, 5.2 percent; and black women, 10.1 percent.[8] Moreover, even though women constitute more than 40 percent of all white collar workers, only one-fifth of managers and administrators are women. Women constitute two-fifths of all professional and technical workers, but most of these women are teachers; in fact women account for 72 percent of all teachers.

One purpose of fair-employment-practices legislation is to change this statistical picture by questioning widely accepted myths about women workers. One myth is that women as a group are too emotional for leadership positions. Another is that women are physically weak and morally delicate. Women, furthermore, are believed to be less committed than men to careers and therefore unreliable. Finally, there is a belief that women do not need to work, although the evidence contradicts this. In 1972 two-thirds of all women workers were single, widowed, divorced, separated, or married to men who made less than $7,000 a year. In 1974, 46 percent of all families with incomes below the poverty level were headed by women. Moreover, the "need" standard is not applied universally to disqualify other workers. Psychological fulfillment, ego-gratification, and the desire to succeed are generally acceptable reasons for working.

To counter these myths, fair-employment-practices legislation encourages employment decisions to be made on an individual basis, not according to perceived group characteristics. Too, the bona-fide-occupational-qualification provision of Title VII and parallel laws provide an opportunity to test the validity of these myths. (See Table 46-2.)

Bona Fide Occupational Qualification (bfoq)

Section 703(e) of Title VII states:

> Notwithstanding any other provision of this title, (1) it shall not be an unlawful employment practice for an employer to hire and employ employees . . . on the basis of his . . . sex . . . in those certain instances where

TABLE 46-2 EXEMPTIONS FROM CIVIL RIGHTS LAWS

1. Bona fide occupational qualifications
2. National security reasons
3. Objective ability tests
4. Statutes giving preferential status to veterans and Indians
5. Private educational or religious institutions giving preference to people of a certain religion or sex

... sex ... is a bona fide occupational qualification reasonably necessary to the normal
operation of that particular business. . . .

The bfoq exception also applies to discrimination on the basis of religion and national
origin but not to discrimination based on race.
(See Table 46-2.) This section reflects Congress's belief that in certain situations the sex
of an applicant is relevant to job performance.
Through its guidelines, the EEOC has narrowly defined these exceptions to include authenticity (model or actor) and sex-function
(sperm donor or wet nurse).

Much sex-discrimination litigation has involved testing the scope of these exceptions.
For example, many states have laws dealing
with employment conditions for women.
These laws restrict the number of hours per
day or per week women can work, limit by
weight the number of pounds women can lift
or carry, exclude women from certain occupations, and provide certain minimal benefits
(pay, rest periods, seats) that women must
have. Under the supremacy clause of the U.S.
Constitution, if these state statutes are in conflict with Title VII the federal law prevails.
Consequently, courts first must decide
whether a state law conflicts with Title VII and
then determine the effect on state laws.

The EEOC's guidelines take the position
that benefits provided to women by state laws
should be extended to men in order to eliminate discriminatory treatment. Arguably, such
action by a court is proper since it avoids holding a statute unconstitutional and is consistent
with the legislative intent to protect workers
from various hazards. Other state laws that
limit or foreclose opportunities should be considered superseded by Title VII, according to
the guidelines. In these cases extension of the
law's application to both sexes would be unworkable, leaving no one legally allowed to do
certain work. Here new laws could be passed
providing necessary protections for all workers but no outright prohibitions by sex. A more

difficult problem is a third group of laws whose
protections may not be perceived as beneficial—for example, maximum-hours laws. On
the one hand, maximum-hours laws protect
workers from compulsory overtime. On the
other hand, such laws limit workers' opportunities to take advantage of the premium pay
offered for overtime. It is clear, however, that
the mere existence of a relevant state law does
not provide an automatic basis for the bfoq
exception.

A second issue raised by the bfoq provision
is its relevance to customer preference. For
example, can the fact that a particular business
caters to male clients be the basis for hiring
only men (or only women) to deal with these
clients? What of the accounting firm that believes its clients will not take advice from a
woman? Whether founded on fact or supposi-
tion, these beliefs, according to the EEOC's
guidelines, should not be the basis for a bfoq
exception. There are still unanswered questions concerning advertising tactics, maintenance of atmosphere and propriety, privacy,
and the need for role models, as well as the
practical implications of dictating this standard to employers. In one sense the role of the
EEOC can best be understood as educational
as well as remedial. In another sense a narrow
functional definition of the bfoq provision
would indicate that customer or co-worker
preference as to the sex of an employee is irrelevant.

The burden of proof in establishing a bfoq
exception falls on the employer. In *Weeks* v.
Southern Bell Telephone (1969)[9] a federal
court of appeals held that the defendant-em-
ployer could not exclude women as a class
from a particularly strenuous job without establishing that "all or substantially all women"
could not perform it. However, even this standard may be objectionable, since the "substantially all" language allows decisions to be
based on group rather than on individual characteristics. In *Diaz* v. *Pan American World
Airways, Inc.* (1971)[10] the court held that the

employer must prove that gender was essential to the job or business before establishing that all or substantially all men could not perform. Other courts have imposed a more stringent burden of proof, imposing a functional definition on bfoqs.

Rosenfeld v. Southern Pacific Co.
U.S. Court of Appeals
444 F. 2d 1219 (1971)

mgnt couple bel.
rock hoid

Background: Leah Rosenfeld (plaintiff) brought an action against Southern Pacific Co. (defendant) under Title VII, Section 703(a), alleging that, in filling the position of agent-telegrapher, Southern Pacific discriminated against her solely because of her sex by assigning the position to a junior male employee. The District Court entered a summary judgment in favor of the plaintiff. Southern Pacific and the State of California (intervenor to defend validity of the state's labor laws) appealed.
Decision: Affirmed. The U.S. Court of Appeals ruled in favor of Rosenfeld.

Hamley, Circuit Judge

On the merits, Southern Pacific argues that it is the company's policy to exclude women, generically, from certain positions. The company restricts these job opportunities to men for two basic reasons: (1) the arduous nature of the work-related activity renders women physically unsuited for the jobs; (2) appointing a woman to the position would result in a violation of California labor laws and regulations which limit hours of work for women and restrict the weight they are permitted to lift. Positions such as that of agent-telegrapher at Thermal fall within the ambit of this policy. The company concludes that effectuation of this policy is not proscribed by Title VII of the Civil Rights Act due to the exception created by the Act for those situations where sex is a "bona fide occupational qualification."

While the agent-telegrapher position at Thermal is no longer in existence, the work requirements which that position entailed are illustrative of the kind of positions which are denied to female employees under the company's labor policy described above. During the harvesting season, the position may require work in excess of ten hours a day and eighty hours a week. The position requires the heavy physical effort involved in climbing over and around boxcars to adjust their vents, collapse their bunkers and close and seal their doors. In addition, the employee must lift various objects weighing more than twenty-five pounds and, in some instances, more than fifty pounds. . . .

In the case before us, there is no contention that the sexual characteristics of the employee are crucial to the successful performance of the job, as they would be for the position of a wet-nurse, nor is there a need for authenticity or genuineness, as in the case of an actor or actress, 29 C.F.R. §1604.1(a)(2). Rather, on the basis of a general assumption regarding the physical capabilities of female employees, the company attempts to raise a commonly accepted characterization of women as the "weaker sex" to the level of a BFOQ. The personnel policy of Southern Pacific here in question is based on "characteristics generally attributed to the group" of exactly the same type that the Commission has announced should not be the basis of an employment decision. 29 C.F.R. §1604.1(a)(1)(ii). Based on the legislative intent and on the Commission's interpretation, sexual characteristics, rather than characteristics that might, to one degree or another, correlate with a particular sex, must be the basis for the application of the BFOQ exception. *See* Developments in the Law—Title VII, 84 Harv. L. Rev. 1109, 1178–1179 (1971). Southern Pacific has not, and could not allege such a basis here, and section 703(e) thus could not exempt its policy from the impact of Title VII. There was no error in the granting of summary judgment on this issue. . . .

But the company points out that, apart from its intrinsic merit, its policy is compelled by California labor laws. One of the reasons Mrs. Rosenfeld was refused assignment to the Thermal position, and would presumably be refused assignment to like positions, is that she could not perform the tasks of such a position without placing the company in violation of California laws. Not only would the repeated lifting of weights in excess of twenty-five pounds violate the state's Industrial Welfare Order No. 9–63, but for her to lift more than fifty pounds as required by the job would violate section 1251 of the California Labor Code. Likewise, the peak-season days of over ten hours would violate section 1350 of the California Labor Code.

It would appear that these state law limitations upon female labor run contrary to the general objectives of Title VII of the Civil Rights Act of 1964, as reviewed above, and are therefore, by virtue of the Supremacy Clause, supplanted by Title VII. However, appellants again rely on section 703(e) and argue that since positions such as the Thermal agent-telegrapher required weight-lifting and maximum hours in excess of those permitted under the California statutes, being a man was indeed a bona fide occupational qualification. This argument assumes that Congress, having established by Title VII the policy that individuals must be judged as individuals, and not on the basis of characteristics generally attributed to racial, religious, or sex groups, was willing for this policy to be thwarted by state legislation to the contrary.

We find no basis in the statute or its legislative history for such an assumption. . . .

We have considered the meaning which appellants would ascribe to BFOQ, as provided for in the Act. We conclude, however, that the Commission is correct in determining that BFOQ establishes a narrow exception inapplicable where, as here, employment opportunities are denied on the basis of characterizations of the physical capabilities and endurance of women, even when those characteristics are recognized in state legislation.

Sexual Harassment

Another form of sex discrimination that the courts have recognized as a basis for recovery under Title VII is sexual harassment. EEOC guidelines define *sexual harassment* as "unwelcome sexual advances, requests for sexual favors, and other verbal or physical conduct of a sexual nature" that: (1) involves submission explicitly or implicitly as a term or condition of employment; (2) makes employment decisions relating to the individual dependent on submission or rejection of such conduct; or (3) has the purpose or effect of creating an intimidating, hostile, or offensive environment. It should be noted that both men and women may file claims of sexual harassment. In a landmark decision excerpted here the U.S. Supreme Court for the first time agreed with the EEOC definition of sexual harassment, while at the same time refusing to hold an employer liable in all cases for a supervisor who sexually harassed an employee.

Meritor Savings Bank, FSB et al. v. Michelle Vinson et al.
U.S. Supreme Court
106 Sp. Ct. 2399 (1986)

Background: Vinson (plaintiff-respondent) brought suit for an injunction and damages against Meritor Savings Bank (Bank) and her supervisor, Taylor (defendant-petitioners) claiming that during her four years of employment at the Bank she had been subject to sexual harassment in violation of Title VII of the Civil Rights Act of 1964. Respondent alleges that Taylor invited her out to dinner and during the meal suggested they have sexual relations following the completion of her teller-trainee period. Because she feared the loss of her job she agreed to accompany him to her hotel. She alleged that Taylor (a vice-president and manager of a branch office) made repeated demands on her both during and after business hours, and over several years she had sexual intercourse with him forty or fifty times. The respondent testified at the trial court level that Taylor touched and fondled other women employees of the Bank. Further, she testified that because she was afraid of Taylor, she never reported his harassment, and never attempted to use the Bank's complaint procedure. Taylor denied these allegations of sexual activity. He contended that they were made in response to a business-related dispute. The Bank denied the allegations also, and asserted that any sexual harassment by Taylor was unknown to it, and engaged in without its consent or approval. The District Court ruled in favor of the defendants. The Court of Appeals reversed in favor of the plaintiff, holding Taylor and the Bank liable; the latter absolutely liable for supervisory personnel whether it knew or should have known about the sexual harassment.

Decision: Affirmed. The Supreme Court of the United States ruled in favor of Michelle Vinson.

Rehnquist, Justice

Title VII of the Civil Rights Act of 1964 makes it "an unlawful employment practice for an employer . . . to discriminate against any individual with respect to his compensation, terms, conditions, or privileges of employment, because of such individual's race, color, religion, sex, or national origin." The prohibition against discrimination based on sex was added to Title VII at the last minute on the floor of the House of Representatives. The principal argument in opposition to the amendment was that "sex discrimination" was sufficiently different from other types of discrimination that it ought to receive separate legislative treatment. (Statement of Rep. Celler quoting letter from U.S. Department of Labor). This argument was defeated, the bill quickly passed as amended, and we are left with little legislative history to guide us in interpreting the Act's prohibition against discrimination based on "sex."

Respondent argues, and the Court of Appeals held, that unwelcome sexual advances that create an offensive or hostile working environment violate Title VII. Without question, when a supervisor sexually harasses a subordinate because of the subordinate's sex, that supervisor "discriminate[s]" on the basis of sex. Petitioner apparently does not challenge this proposition. It contends instead that in prohibiting discrimination with respect to "compensation, terms, conditions, or privileges" of employment, Congress was concerned with what petitioner describes as "tangible loss" of "an economic character," not "purely psychological aspects of the workplace environment." In support of this claim petitioner observes that in both the legislative history of Title VII and this Court's Title VII decisions, the focus has been on tangible, economic barriers erected by discrimination.

We reject petitioner's view. First, the language of Title VII is not limited to "economic" or "tangible" discrimination. The phrase "terms, conditions, or privileges of employment" evinces a congressional intent " 'to strike at the entire spectrum of disparate treatment of men and women' " in employment. Petitioner has pointed to nothing in the Act to suggest that Congress contemplated the limitation urged here.

Second, in 1980 the EEOC issued guidelines specifying that "sexual harassment" as there defined, is a form of sex discrimination prohibited by Title VII. As an "administrative interpretation of the Act by the enforcing agency," these guidelines, while not controlling upon the courts by reason of their authority, do constitute a body of experience and informed judgment to which courts and litigants may properly resort for guidance. The EEOC guidelines fully support the view that harassment leading to non-economic injury can violate Title VII.

In defining "sexual harassment," the guidelines first describe the kinds of workplace conduct that may be actionable under Title VII. These include "[u]nwelcome sexual advances, requests for sexual favors, and other verbal or physical conduct of a sexual nature." Relevant to the charges at issue in this case, the guidelines provide that such sexual misconduct constitutes prohibited "sexual harassment," whether or not it is directly linked to the grant or denial of an economic *quid pro quo,* where "such conduct has the purpose or effect of unreasonably interfering with an individual's work performance or creating an intimidating, hostile, or offensive working environment."

Since the guidelines were issued, courts have uniformly held, and we agree, that a plaintiff may establish a violation of Title VII by proving that discrimination based on sex has created a hostile or abusive work environment. As the Court of Appeals for the Eleventh Circuit wrote in *Henson* v. *Dundee,* 682 F.2d 897, 902 (1982):

> Sexual harassment which creates a hostile or offensive environment for members of one sex is every bit the arbitrary barrier to sexual equality at the workplace that racial harassment is to racial equality. Surely, a requirement that a man or woman run a gauntlet of sexual abuse in return for the privilege of being allowed to work and make a living can be as demeaning and disconcerting as the harshest of racial epithets.

The question remains, however, whether the District Court's ultimate finding that respondent "was not the victim of sexual harassment," effectively disposed of respondent's claim. The Court of Appeals recognized, we think correctly, that this ultimate finding was likely based on one or both of two erroneous views of the law. First, the District Court apparently believed that a claim for sexual harassment will not lie absent an *economic* effect on the complainant's employment. . . . Since it appears that the District Court made its findings without ever considering the "hostile environment" theory of sexual harassment, the Court of Appeals' decision to remand was correct.

Second, the District Court's conclusion that no actionable harassment occurred might have rested on its earlier "finding" that "[i]f [respondent] and Taylor did engage in an intimate or sexual relationship . . ., that relationship was voluntary one." But the fact that sex-related conduct was "voluntary," in the sense that the complainant was not forced to participate against her will, is not a defense to a sexual harassment suit brought under Title VII. The graveman of any sexual harassment claim is that the alleged sexual advances were "unwelcome." While the question whether particular conduct was indeed unwelcome presents difficult problems of proof and turns largely on credibility determinations committed to the trier of fact, the District Court in this case erroneously focused on the "voluntariness" of respondent's participation in the claimed sexual episodes. The correct inquiry is whether respondent by her conduct indicated that the alleged sexual advances were unwelcome, not whether her actual participation in sexual intercourse was voluntary.

Petitioner contends that even if this case must be remanded to the District Court, the Court of Appeals erred in one of the terms of its remand. Specifically, the Court of Appeals stated that testimony about respondent's "dress and personal fantasies," which the District Court apparently admitted into evidence, "had no place in this litigation." The apparent ground for this conclusion was that respondent's voluntariness *vel non* in submitting to Taylor's advances was immaterial to her sexual harassment claim. While "voluntariness" in the sense of consent is not a defense to such a claim, it does not follow that a complainant's sexually provocative speech or dress is irrelevant as a matter of law in determining whether he or she found particular sexual advances unwelcome. To the contrary, such evidence is obviously relevant. The EEOC guidelines emphasize that the trier of fact must determine the existence of sexual harassment in light of "the record as a whole" and "the totality of circumstances, such as the nature of the sexual advances and the context in which the alleged incidents occurred." Respondent's claim that any marginal relevance of the evidence in question was outweighed by the potential for unfair prejudice is the sort of argument properly addressed to the District Court. In this case the District Court concluded that the evidence should be admitted, and the Court of Appeals' contrary conclusion was based upon the erroneous, categorical view that testimony about provocative dress and publicly expressed sexual fantasies "had no place in this litigation." While the District Court must carefully weigh the applicable considerations in deciding whether to admit evidence of this kind, there is no *per se* rule against its admissibility.

Although the District Court concluded that respondent had not proved a violation of Title VII, it nevertheless went on to consider the question of the bank's liability. Finding that "the bank was without notice" of Taylor's alleged conduct, and that notice to Taylor was not the equivalent of notice to the bank, the court concluded that the bank therefore could not be held liable for Taylor's alleged actions. The Court of Appeals took the opposite view, holding that an employer is strictly liable for a hostile environment created by a supervisor's sexual advances, even though the employer neither knew nor reasonably could have known of the alleged misconduct. The court held that a supervisor, whether or not he possesses the authority to hire, fire, or promote, is necessarily an "agent" of his employer for all Title VII purposes, since "even the appearance" of such authority may enable him to impose himself on his subordinates.

We decline the parties' invitation to issue a definitive rule on employer liability, but we do agree with the EEOC that Congress wanted courts to look to agency principles for guidance in this area. While such common-law principles may not be transferable in all their particulars to Title VII, Congress' decision to define "employer" to include any "agent" of an employer, surely evinces an intent to place some limits on the acts of employees for which employers under Title VII are to be held responsible. For this reason, we hold that the Court of Appeals erred in concluding that employers are always automatically liable for sexual harassment by their supervisors. See generally Restatement (Second) of Agency, Sections 219–237 (1958). For the same reason, absence of notice to an employer does not necessarily insulate that employer from liability.

Finally, we reject petitioner's view that the mere existence of a grievance procedure and a policy against discrimination, coupled with respondent's failure to invoke that procedure, must insulate petitioner from liability. While those facts are plainly relevant, the situation before us demonstrates why they are not necessarily dispositive. Petitioner's general nondiscrimination policy did not address sexual harassment in particular, and thus did not alert employees to their employer's interest in correcting that form of discrimination. Moreover, the bank's grievance procedure apparently required an employee to complain first to her supervisor, in this case Taylor. Since Taylor was the alleged perpetrator, it is not altogether surprising that respondent failed to invoke the procedure and report her grievance to him. Petitioner's contention that respondent's failure should insulate it from liability might be substantially stronger if its procedures were better calculated to encourage victims of harassment to come forward.

In sum, we hold that a claim of "hostile environment" sex discrimination is actionable under Title VII, that the District Court's findings were insufficient to dispose of respondent's hostile environment claim, and that the District Court did not err in admitting testimony about respondent's sexually provocative speech and dress. As to employer liability, we conclude that the Court of Appeals was wrong to entirely disregard agency principles and impose absolute liability on employers for the acts of their supervisors, regardless of the circumstances of a particular case.

Pregnancy

Congress amended the 1964 Civil Rights Act in 1978 with the addition of the following language:

The terms "because of sex" or "on the basis of sex" include, but are not limited to, because of or on the basis of pregnancy, child-birth or related medical conditions; and women affected by pregnancy, childbirth, or related medical conditions shall be treated the same for all employment-related purposes, including receipt of benefits under fringe benefit programs, as other persons not so affected but similar in their ability or inability to work, and nothing in Section 703(h) of this title shall be interpreted to permit otherwise. This subsection shall not require an employer to pay for health insurance benefits for abortion, except where the life of the mother would be endangered if the fetus were carried to term, or except where medical complications have arisen from an abortion: *Provided,* That nothing herein shall preclude an employer from providing abortion benefits or otherwise effect bargaining agreements in regard to abortion.

In amending Title VII Congress indicated that pregnancy should be treated by employers similar to any other disability. For example, a company cannot discharge a woman for the sole reason that she became pregnant, nor can she lose her seniority. The amendment makes it clear, however, that medical plans of companies may exclude coverage of abortion unless an abortion is necessary to save the mother's life.

In 1987 the U.S. Supreme Court ruled that a California state law that requires unpaid leave for four months for pregnant women, and reinstatement of the employee following birth is constitutional, although the state law required neither for other disabilities. The Court said that the intent of such laws is to make women equal in the workplace rather than to give them favored treatment, and thus they are not in conflict with the Civil Rights Act of 1964, which prohibits discrimination in employment. Excerpts from this landmark decision are set out here.

California Federal Savings and Loan Association, et al. v. Department of Fair Employment and Housing et al.

U.S. Supreme Court
_____ U.S. _____ (1987)

Background: California Federal Savings and Loan Association (Cal Fed), Merchants and Manufacturers Association, and the California Chamber of Commerce (petitioners) brought an action in the U.S. District Court against the California Department of Fair Employment and Housing (respondent) seeking a declaration that a section of the Fair Employment and Housing Act (Sec. 12945b(2)) requiring employers to provide leave and reinstatement for employees disabled by pregnancy was inconsistent with and preempted by Title VII of the Civil Rights Act of 1964. The petitioners further sought an injunction to prevent its enforcement.

Title VII of the Civil Rights Act of 1964, which prohibits employment discrimination on the basis of sex, as amended by the Pregnancy Discrimination Act (PDA), specifies that sex discrimination includes discrimination on the basis of pregnancy. A woman employed as a receptionist by petitioner California Federal Savings and Loan Association took a pregnancy disability leave in 1982, but when she notified Cal Fed that she was able to return to work she was informed that her job had been filled and there were no similar positions available. She then filed a complaint with the respondent Department of Fair Employment and Housing, which charged Cal Fed with violating Sec. 12945(b)(2). Before a hearing was held on the complaint, Cal Fed, joined by the other petitioners, brought this action in federal District Court. The Court granted summary judgment for the petitioners. The U.S. Court of Appeals reversed and ruled in favor of the respondent. Cal Fed appealed.

Decision: Affirmed. The U.S. Supreme Court ruled in favor of the California Department of Fair Employment and Housing.

Marshall, Justice

The question presented is whether Title VII of the Civil Rights Act of 1964, as amended by the Pregnancy Discrimination Act of 1978, pre-empts a state statute that requires employers to provide leave and reinstatement to employees disabled by pregnancy.

California's Fair Employment and Housing Act (FEHA) is a comprehensive statute that prohibits discrimination in employment and housing. In September 1978, California amended the FEHA to proscribe certain forms of employment discrimination on the basis of pregnancy. Subdivision (b)(2)—the provision at issue here—is the only portion of the statute that applied to employers subject to Title VII. It requires these employers to provide female employees an unpaid pregnancy disability leave of up to four months. Respondent Fair Employment and Housing Commission, the state agency authorized to interpret the FEHA, has construed Sec. 12945(b)(2) to require California employers to reinstate an employee returning from such pregnancy leave to the job she previously held, unless it is no longer available due to business necessity. In the latter case, the employer must make a reasonable, good faith effort to place the employee in a substantially similar job. The statute does not compel employers to provide *paid* leave to pregnant employees. Accordingly, the only benefit pregnant workers actually derive from Sec. 12945(b)(2) is a qualified right to reinstatement.

Title VII of the Civil Rights Act of 1964 also prohibits various forms of employment discrimination, including discrimination on the basis of sex. However, in *General Electric Co.* v. *Gilbert,* 429 U.S. 125 (1976), this Court ruled that discrimination on the basis of pregnancy was not sex discrimination under Title VII. In response to the *Gilbert* decision, Congress passed the Pregnancy Discrimination Act of 1978 (PDA). The PDA specifies that sex discrimination includes discrimination on the basis of pregnancy.

In determining whether a state statute is pre-empted by federal law and therefore invalid under the Supremacy Clause of the Constitution, our sole task is to ascertain the intent of Congress. Federal law may supersede state law in several different ways.

First, when acting within constitutional limits, Congress is empowered to pre-empt state law by so stating in express terms. Second, congressional intent to pre-empt state law in a particular area may be inferred where the scheme of federal regulation is sufficiently comprehensive to make reasonable the inference that Congress "left no room" for supplementary state regulation. Neither of these bases for pre-emption exists in this case. Congress has explicitly disclaimed any intent categorically to pre-empt state law or to "occupy the field" of employment discrimination law.

As a third alternative, in those areas where Congress has not completely displaced state regulation, federal law may nonetheless pre-empt state law to the extent it actually conflicts with federal law. Such a conflict occurs either because "compliance with both federal and state regulations is a physical impossibility," or because the state law stands "as an obstacle to the accomplishment and execution of the full purposes and objectives of Congress."

This third basis for pre-emption is at issue in this case. In two sections of the 1964 Civil Rights Act, Sections 708 and 1104, Congress has indicated that state laws will be pre-empted only if they actually conflict with federal law. Section 708 of Title VII provides:

> Nothing in this title shall be deemed to exempt or relieve any person from any liability, duty, penalty, or punishment provided by any present or future law of any State or political subdivision of a State, other than any such law which purports to require or permit the doing of any act which would be an unlawful employment practice under this title.

Section 1104 of Title XI, applicable to all titles of the Civil Rights Act, establishes the following standard for pre-emption:

> Nothing contained in any title of this Act shall be construed as indicating an intent on the part of Congress to occupy the field in which any such title operates to the exclusion of State laws on the same subject matter, nor shall any provision of this Act be construed as invalidating any provision of State law unless such provision is inconsistent with any of the purposes of this Act, or any provision thereof.

Accordingly, there is no need to infer congressional intent to pre-empt state laws from the substantive provisions of Title VII; these two sections provide a "reliable indicium of congressional intent with respect to state authority" to regulate employment practice.

Sections 708 and 1104 severely limit Title VII's pre-emptive effect. Instead of pre-empting state fair employment laws, Sec. 708 " 'simply left them where they were before the enactment of Title VII.' " Similarly, Sec. 1104 was intended primarily to assert the intention of Congress to preserve existing civil rights laws. The narrow scope of pre-emption available under Sections 708 and 1104 reflects the importance Congress attached to state antidiscrimination laws in achieving Title VII's goal of equal employment opportunity.

In order to decide whether the California statute requires or permits employers to violate Title VII, as amended by the PDA, or is inconsistent with the purposes of the statute, we must determine whether the PDA prohibits the States from requiring employers to provide reinstatement to pregnant workers, regardless of their policy for disabled workers generally.

Petitioners argue that the language of the federal statute itself unambiguously rejects California's "special treatment" approach to pregnancy discrimination, thus rendering any resort to the legislative history unnecessary. They contend that the second clause of the PDA forbids an employer to treat pregnant employees any differently than other disabled employees. However, we must examine the PDA's language against the background of its legislative history and historical context. As to the language of the PDA, "[i]t is a 'familiar rule, that a thing may be within the letter of the statute and yet not within the statute, because not within its spirit, nor within the intention of its makers.' "

It is well established that the PDA was passed in reaction to this Court's decision in *General Electric Co.* v. *Gilbert,* 429 U.S. 125 (1976). When Congress amended Title VII in 1978, it unambiguously expressed its disapproval of both the holding and the reasoning of the Court in the *Gilbert* decision. By adding pregnancy to the definition of sex discrimination prohibited by Title VII, the first clause of the PDA reflects Congress' disapproval of the reasoning in *Gilbert*. Rather than imposing a limitation on the remedial purpose of the PDA, we believe that the second clause was intended to overrule the holding in *Gilbert* and to illustrate how discrimination against pregnancy is to be remedied. Accordingly, subject to certain limitations, we agree with the Court of Appeals' conclusion that Congress intended the PDA to be "a floor beneath which pregnancy disability benefits may not drop—not a ceiling above which they may not rise."

The context in which Congress considered the issue of pregnancy discrimination supports this view of the PDA. Congress had before it extensive evidence of (sic) *against* pregnancy, particularly in disability and health insurance programs like those challenged in *Gilbert* and *Nashville Gas Co.* v. *Satty,* 434 U.S. 136 (1977). The reports, debates, and hearings make abundantly clear that Congress intended the PDA to provide relief for working women and to end discrimination against pregnant workers. In contrast to the thorough account of discrimination against pregnant workers, the legislative history is devoid of any discussion of preferential treatment of pregnancy, beyond acknowledgments of the existence of state statutes providing for such preferential treatment. Opposition to the PDA came from those concerned with the cost of including pregnancy in health and disability benefit plans and the application of the bill to abortion, not from those who favored special accommodation of pregnancy.

In support of their argument that the PDA prohibits employment practices that favor pregnant women, petitioners and several *amici* cite statements in the legislative history to the effect that the PDA does not *require* employers to extend any benefits to pregnant women that they do not already provide to other disabled employees. For example, the House Report explained that the proposed legislation "does not require employers to treat pregnant employees in any particular manner. . . . H.R. 6075 in no way requires the institution of any new programs where none currently exist." We do not interpret these references to support petitioners' construction of the statute. On the contrary, if Congress had intended to *prohibit* preferential treatment, it would have been the height of understatement to say only that the legislation would not *require* such conduct. It is hardly conceivable that Congress would have extensively discussed only its intent not to require preferential treatment if in fact it had intended to prohibit such treatment.

We also find it significant that Congress was aware of state laws similar to California's but apparently did not consider them inconsistent with the PDA. In the debates and reports on the bill, Congress repeatedly acknowledged the existence of state antidiscrimination laws that prohibit sex discrimination on the basis of pregnancy. Two of the states mentioned then required employers to provide reasonable leave to pregnant workers. After citing these state laws, Congress failed to evince the requisite "clear and manifest purpose" to supersede them. To the contrary, both the House and Senate Reports suggest that these laws would continue to have effect under the PDA.

Title VII, as amended by the PDA, and the California pregnancy disability leave statute share a common goal. The purpose of Title VII is to achieve equality of employment opportunities and remove barriers that have operated in the past to favor an identifiable group of . . . employees over other employees. Rather than limiting existing Title VII principles and objectives, the PDA extends them to cover pregnancy.

As Senator Williams, a sponsor of the Act, stated: "The entire thrust . . . behind this legislation is to guarantee women the basic right to participate fully and equally in the work force, without denying them the fundamental right to full participation in family life."

Section 12945(b)(2) also promotes equal employment opportunity. By requiring employers to reinstate women after a reasonable pregnancy disability leave, Sec. 12945(b)(2) ensures that they will not lose their jobs on account of pregnancy disability. By "taking pregnancy into account," California's pregnancy disability leave statute allows women, as well as men, to have families without losing their jobs.

We emphasize the limited nature of the benefits Sec. 12945(b)(2) provides. The statute is narrowly drawn to cover only the period of *actual physical disability* on account of pregnancy, childbirth, or related medical conditions. Accordingly, unlike the protective labor legislation prevalent earlier in this century, Sec. 12945(b)(2) does not reflect archaic or stereotypical notions about pregnancy and the abilities of pregnant workers. A statute based on such stereotypical assumptions would, of course, be inconsistent with Title VII's goal of equal employment opportunity.

Moreover, even if we agreed with petitioners' construction of the PDA, we would nonetheless reject their argument that the California statute requires employers to violate Title VII. Section 12945(b)(2) does not prevent employers from complying with both the federal law (as petitioners construe it) and the state law. This is not a case where compliance with both federal and state regulations is a physical impossibility, or where there is an inevitable collision between the two schemes of regulation. Section 12945(b)(2) does not compel California employers to treat pregnant workers *better* than other disabled employees; it merely establishes benefits that employers must, at a minimum, provide to pregnant workers. Employers are free to give comparable benefits to other disabled employees, thereby treating "women affected by pregnancy" no better than "other persons not so affected but similar in their ability or inability to work." Indeed, at oral argument, petitioners conceded that compliance with both statutes "is theoretically possible."

Petitioners argue that "extension" of the state statute to cover other employees would be inappropriate in the absence of a clear indication that this is what the California Legislature intended. They cite cases in which this Court has declined to rewrite underinclusive state statutes found to violate the Equal Protection Clause.

This argument is beside the point. Extension is a remedial option to be exercised by a court once a statute is found to be invalid.

Thus, petitioners' facial challenge to Sec. 12945(b)(2) fails. The statute is not preempted by Title VII, as amended by the PDA, because it is not inconsistent with the purposes of the federal statute, nor does it require the doing of an act which is unlawful under Title VII.

CASE NOTE

Following this decision, all states were free to join California, Massachusetts, and Connecticut in enacting such laws. Two bills in Congress would not leave it up to the states but would require by federal law "parental leave" up to twenty-six weeks for both men and women, as well as guaranteed reinstatement for both.

DISCRIMINATION BASED ON RELIGION AND NATIONAL ORIGIN

Fair-employment-practices law specifically prohibits discrimination on the basis of religion or national origin. Under Title VII these prohibitions are subject to the bfoq exceptions. In the area of religion or national origin, race or sex discrimination, though, a case raising racial discrimination often includes national origin issues or complaints. There are, however, several crucial problems in this area of fair employment.

Religious Discrimination

Overt discrimination on the basis of an applicant's or an employer's religion is illegal unless a bfoq exception is established by the employer. As with sex as a bfoq, group stereotypes or characteristics commonly associated with a particular religion cannot be the basis of a bfoq exception unless factually established by the employer.

Typically the issue of religious discrimination is raised because the religious beliefs of applicants or employees prohibit them from working on a particular day or during a particular time. Thus an employer might refuse to hire an applicant not because he or she was a Seventh Day Adventist but because that religion forbids its members to work from sundown Friday to sundown Saturday. Until 1972 the cases dealing with this issue were divided as to whether such a refusal to hire was discrimination on the basis of religion and, if so, what kind of accommodation must be made by the employer. The position of the EEOC, through its guidelines, was that a refusal to hire and to accommodate was religious discrimination and that the duty not to discriminate included the obligation to make reasonable accommodations to the religious needs of the employee or applicant. Courts with contrary views held that such a denial was not based on religion but on the nonavailability of the employee or applicant at a particular time. Further, these courts held that employers had no obligation to accommodate religious beliefs, usually on the theory that such an accommodation would discriminate against other applicants or employees.

When Congress amended Title VII in 1972, it added to Section 701 subsection (j), which states:

The term "religion" includes all aspects of religious observances and practices, as well as belief, unless an employer demonstrates that he is unable to reasonably accommodate to an employee's or prospective employee's religious observance or practice without undue hardship on the conduct of the employer's business.

The extent to which an employer must reasonably accommodate and what constitutes undue hardship are not defined by the statute. In 1977 the Supreme Court took up these issues in *Trans World Airlines, Inc.* v. *Hardison.* The case has been criticized for its failure to address the constitutionality of Section 701(j) and its extremely narrow reading of Congress's intent in enacting the 1972 amendment.

Religious discrimination may be an issue in other situations. For example, an employer may require all employees to attend weekly sermonettes, to donate blood, or to contribute money to a union in violation of an employee's religious convictions. It is unclear whether or in what way *Hardison* is applicable to these situations.

The implications of the other 1972 action by Congress relating to religious discrimination are also not straightforward. The 1972 amendment broadened the exemption for religious institutions (Section 702) by exempting them from the religious-discrimination prohibitions of Title VII with respect to all employees.

Previously Section 702 had exempted only those positions that involved participating in the religious activities of the institution. The impetus for the more pervasive exclusion probably resulted from another Title VII amendment—one that removed the exemption of educational institutions. However, Section 702 raises a significant constitutional question because the exemption treats religious institutions differently from nonreligious institutions and thus may violate the First Amendment's clause prohibiting governmental establishment of religion. The case excerpted below illustrates how the United States Supreme Court has dealt with discrimination based on religion.

Trans World Airlines, Inc. v. Hardison

Supreme Court of the United States

432 U.S. 63 (1977)

Background: Hardison (plaintiff-respondent) brought suit against Trans World Airlines and the International Association of Machinists (defendants-petitioners) alleging that the defendants' failure to accommodate his religious practices and his subsequent discharge constituted religious discrimination in violation of Title VII. The District Court found for the defendants; the Court of Appeals reversed.

Decision: The U.S. Supreme Court ruled in favor of Trans World Airlines.

White, Justice

The issue in this case is the extent of the employer's obligation under Title VII to accommodate an employee whose religious beliefs prohibit him from working on Saturdays.

Petitioner Trans World Airlines (TWA) operates a large maintenance and overhaul base in Kansas City, Mo. On June 5, 1967, respondent Larry G. Hardison was hired by TWA to work as a clerk in the Stores Department at its Kansas City base. Because of its essential role in the Kansas City operation, the Stores Department must operate 24 hours per day, 365 days per year, and whenever an employee's job in that department is not filled, an employee must be shifted from another department, or a supervisor must cover the job, even if the work in other areas may suffer.

Hardison, like other employees at the Kansas City base, was subject to a seniority system contained in a collective-bargaining agreement that TWA maintains with petitioner International Association of Machinists and Aerospace Workers (IAM). The seniority system is implemented by the union steward through a system of bidding by employees for particular shift assignments, and the most junior employees are required to work when the union steward is unable to find enough people willing to work at a particular time or in a particular job to fill TWA's needs.

In the spring of 1968 Hardison began to study the religion known as the Worldwide Church of God. One of the tenets of that religion is that one must observe the Sabbath by refraining from performing any work from sunset on Friday until sunset on Saturday. The religion also prohibits work on certain specified religious holidays.

When Hardison informed Everett Kussman, the manager of the Stores Department, of his religious conviction regarding observance of the Sabbath, Kussman agreed that the union steward should seek a job swap for Hardison or a change of days off; that Hardison would have his religious holidays off whenever possible if Hardison agreed to work the traditional holidays when asked; and that Kussman would try to find Hardison another job that would be more compatible with his religious beliefs. The problem was temporarily solved when Hardison transferred to the 11 P.M.–7 A.M. shift. Working this shift permitted Hardison to observe his Sabbath.

The problem soon reappeared when Hardison bid for and received a transfer from Building 1, where he had been employed, to Building 2, where he would work the day shift. The two buildings had entirely separate seniority lists; and while in Building 1 Hardison had sufficient seniority to observe the Sabbath regularly, he was second from the bottom on the Building 2 seniority list.

In Building 2 Hardison was asked to work Saturdays when a fellow employee went on vacation. TWA agreed to permit the union to seek a change of work assignments for Hardison, but the union was not willing to violate the seniority provisions set out in the collective-bargaining contract, and Hardison had insufficient seniority to bid for a shift having Saturdays off.

A proposal that Hardison work only four days a week was rejected by the company. Hardison's job was essential and on weekends he was the only available person on his shift to perform it. To leave the position empty would have impaired Supply Shop functions, which were critical to airline operations; to fill Hardison's position with a supervisor or an employee from another area would simply have undermanned another operation; and to employ someone not regularly assigned to work Saturdays would have required TWA to pay premium wages.

When an accommodation was not reached, Hardison refused to report for work on Saturdays. A transfer to the twilight shift proved unavailing since that schedule still required Hardison to work past sundown on Fridays. After a hearing, Hardison was discharged on grounds of insubordination for refusing to work during his designated shift.

The Court of Appeals held that TWA had not made reasonable efforts to accommodate Hardison's religious needs under the 1967 EEOC guidelines in effect at the time the relevant events occurred. In its view, TWA had rejected three reasonable alternatives, any one of which would have satisfied its obligation without undue hardship. First, within the framework of the seniority system, TWA could have permitted Hardison to work a four-day week, utilizing in his place a supervisor or another worker on duty elsewhere. That this would have caused other shop functions to suffer was insufficient to amount to undue hardship in the opinion of the Court of Appeals. Second—according to the Court of Appeals, also within the bounds of the collective-bargaining contract—the company could have filled Hardison's Saturday shift from other available personnel competent to do the job, of which the court said there were at least 200. That this would have involved premium overtime pay was not deemed an undue hardship. Third, TWA could have arranged a "swap between Hardison and another employee either for another shift or for the Sabbath days." In response to the assertion that this would have involved a breach of the seniority provisions of the contract, the court noted that it had not been settled in the courts whether the required statutory accommodation to religious needs stopped short of transgressing seniority rules, but found it unnecessary to decide the issue because, as the Court of Appeals saw the record, TWA had not sought, and the union had therefore not declined to entertain, a possible variable from the seniority provisions of the collective-bargaining agreement. The company had simply left the entire matter to the union steward who the Court of Appeals said "likewise did nothing."

We disagree with the Court of Appeals in all relevant respects. It is our view that TWA made reasonable efforts to accommodate and that each of the Court of Appeals' suggested alternatives would have been an undue hardship within the meaning of the statute as construed by the EEOC guidelines.

A

It might be inferred from the Court of Appeals' opinion and from the brief of the EEOC in this Court that TWA's efforts to accommodate were no more than negligible. The findings of the District Court, supported by the record, are to the contrary. In summarizing its more detailed findings, the District Court observed:

> TWA established as a matter of fact that it did take appropriate action to accommodate as required by Title VII. It held several meetings with plaintiff at which it attempted to find a solution to plaintiff's problems. It did accommodate plaintiff's observance of his special religious holidays. It authorized the union steward to search for someone who would swap shifts, which apparently was normal procedure. 375 F.Supp. at 890–891.

It is also true that TWA itself attempted without success to find Hardison another job. The District Court's view was that TWA had done all that could reasonably be expected within the bounds of the seniority system.

The Court of Appeals observed, however, that the possibility of a variance from the seniority system was never really posed to the union. This is contrary to the District Court's findings and to the record. As the record shows, Hardison himself testified that Kussman was willing, but the union was not, to work out a shift or job trade with another employee.

As will become apparent, the seniority system represents a neutral way of minimizing the number of occasions when an employee must work on a day that he would prefer to have off. Additionally, recognizing that weekend work schedules are the least popular, the company made further accommodation by reducing its work force to bare minimum on those days.

B

We are also convinced, contrary to the Court of Appeals, that TWA cannot be faulted for having failed itself to work out a shift or job swap for Hardison. Both the union and TWA had agreed to the seniority system; the union was unwilling to entertain a variance over the objections of men senior to Hardison; and for TWA to have arranged unilaterally for a swap would have amounted to a breach of the collective-bargaining agreement.

(1)

Hardison and the EEOC insist that the statutory obligation to accommodate religious needs take precedence over both the collective-bargaining contract and the seniority rights of TWA's other employees. We agree that neither a collective-bargaining contract nor a seniority system may be employed to violate the statute, but we do not believe that the duty to accommodate requires TWA to take steps inconsistent with the otherwise valid agreement. Collective bargaining, aimed at effecting workable and enforceable agreements between management and labor, lies at the core of our national labor policy, and seniority provisions are universally included in these contracts. Without a clear and express indication from Congress, we cannot agree with Hardison and EEOC that an agreed-upon seniority system must give way when necessary to accommodate religious observances. The issue is important and warrants some discussion.

It was essential to TWA's business to require Saturday and Sunday work from at least a few employees even though most employees preferred those days off. Allocating the burdens of weekend work was a matter for collective bargaining. In considering criteria to govern this allocation, TWA and the union had two alternatives: adopt a neutral system, such as seniority, a lottery, or rotating shifts; or allocate days off in accordance with the religious needs of its employees. TWA would have had to adopt the latter in order to assure Hardison and others like him of getting the days off necessary for strict observance of their religion, but it could have done so only at the expense of others who had strong, but perhaps nonreligious reasons for not working on weekends. There were no volunteers to relieve Hardison on Saturdays, and to give Hardison Saturdays off, TWA would have had to deprive another employee of his shift preference at least in part because he did not adhere to a religion that observed the Saturday Sabbath.

(2)

Our conclusion is supported by the fact that seniority systems are afforded special treatment under Title VII itself. [Discussion of *Teamsters* omitted.]

C

The Court of Appeals also suggested that TWA could have permitted Hardison to work a four-day week if necessary in order to avoid working on his Sabbath. Recognizing that this might have left TWA shorthanded on the one shift each week that Hardison did not work, the court still concluded that TWA would suffer no undue hardship if it were required to replace Hardison, either with supervisory personnel or with qualified personnel from other departments. Alternatively, the Court of Appeals suggested that TWA could have replaced Hardison on his Saturday shift with other available employees through the payment of premium wages. Both of these alternatives would involve costs to TWA, either in the form of lost efficiency in other jobs or as higher wages.

To require TWA to bear more than a *de minimus* cost in order to give Hardison Saturdays off is an undue hardship. Like abandonment of the seniority system, to require TWA to bear additional costs when no such costs are incurred to give other employees the days off that they want would involve unequal treatment of employees on the basis of their religion. By suggesting that TWA should incur certain costs in order to give Hardison Saturdays off the Court of Appeals would in effect require TWA to finance an additional Saturday off and then to choose the employee who will enjoy it on the basis of his religious beliefs. While incurring extra costs to secure a replacement for Hardison might remove the necessity of compelling another employee to work involuntarily in Hardison's place, it would not change the fact that the privilege of having Saturdays off would be allocated according to religious beliefs.

National Origin Discrimination

Issues of discrimination on the basis of national origin are often combined with cases involving racial discrimination. Similar problems arise as to the validity of tests and educational requirements. Specifically national origin discrimination cases often raise such questions as the validity of an English-language test or of height and weight standards.

The particular problem raised in national origin cases is whether discrimination on the basis of citizenship is in fact discrimination on the basis of national origin, and thus in violation of the fair employment practices laws. In 1973 the U.S. Supreme Court, in *Espinoza* v. *Farah Manufacturing*,[11] held that although Congress may have the power to prohibit discrimination on the basis of citizenship, it had not exercised such power in prohibiting discrimination on the basis of national origin. Specifically the Court stated that a resident alien who was denied employment because she was not a U.S. citizen was not discriminated against on the basis of national origin (which the Court interpreted as ancestry) but rather on the basis of citizenship. However, the dissenting opinion by Justice Douglas in *Espinoza* argued that U.S. citizenship is directly related to ancestry. The dissenting opinion also urged the Court to examine this charge in terms of the disparate-effect analysis used effectively in other areas.

EEOC's guidelines were amended in response to the *Espinoza* decision. At present they state:

[W]here discrimination on the basis of citizenship has the purpose or effect of discrimination on the basis of national origin, a lawfully immigrated alien who is domiciled or residing in this country may not be discriminated against on the basis of his (her) citizenship. . . .

Thus these guidelines may be the compromise necessary between the majority and dissenting opinions in *Espinoza*.

The *Espinoza* decision has been criticized on two other grounds. First, the majority opinion found significance in the fact that approximately 95 percent of the relevant work force consisted of people of Mexican ancestry. However, that fact relates to the employer's purpose or overall intention and does not deal with the specific allegations of the particular complainant. Second, the Court relied on the analogy with federal and state governments' requirements of citizenship to compete for civil-service jobs. There have been several recent cases that have held that such an employment rule if imposed by the states violates the Fourteenth Amendment's due-process and equal-protection clauses.[12] Since alienage is considered a "suspect classification," the courts have stated that the state must have a "compelling" reason to treat aliens differently from others in order to meet the courts' "strict scrutiny" standard of review. In these cases the state did not sustain that burden.

Further, it can be argued that the citizenship rule is unconstitutional because it is overbroad in that it may be sensible and permissible to limit some civil-service jobs to citizens but not to limit all jobs. On the other hand, it is possible that the constitutional citizenship cases and the *Espinoza* decision are consistent if the relevant distinction is the difference between treatment of public and private employees.

AGE DISCRIMINATION

In 1967 Congress enacted the Age Discrimination in Employment Act (ADEA) outlawing employment discrimination on the basis of age, between the ages 40 and 65. The ADEA applies to the federal government, states, and their political subdivision and to employers with at least twenty workers. A recent amendment removed any upper limit, except for certain occupations, such as firefighters, law enforcement officers, and tenured university faculty members. The exceptions are temporary in nature, scheduled to end in 1993. The act is administered by the EEOC, and its scope, coverage, and procedures are similar to those of the Equal Pay Act. The purpose of the statute is to encourage the making of employment decisions on individual characteristics rather than on stereotypic notions of the effect of age on ability. The statute provides four defenses:

1. Age is a bona fide occupational qualification (bfoq) reasonably necessary to the normal operation of the particular business
2. The differentiation is based on reasonable factors other than age
3. The terms of a bona fide seniority system or any bona fide employee benefit plan (retirement, pension, or insurance) that is not a subterfuge
4. Discharge or discipline for good cause

Although the substantive and procedural provisions of the act are nearly identical to those of Title VII, the federal courts appear to apply different standards of proof and liability. The courts have found age discrimination justified by one of the defenses on the basis of less evidence than would satisfy the burden in a Title VII case. Probably the reasons for the distinction lie in the fact that age, at some point, is related to individual ability and that the basis for age discrimination is not hostility but inaccurate perceptions or miscalculated costs. Thus the test formulated by many courts is whether there is a generalization other than age that more accurately predicts ability or whether the employer can adequately test individually without a substantial increase in cost.

The case excerpted here illustrates how the United States Supreme Court has acted on the test for age discrimination.

Trans World Airlines, Inc. v. Thurston et al.

U.S. Supreme Court
469 U.S. 111 (1985)

Background: Three pilots (plaintiffs-respondents) were forced to retire at age 60 under rules negotiated with their union by Trans World Airlines, their employer (defendants-petitioners).

In 1977 TWA and the pilots' union concluded a collective-bargaining agreement stating that every employee in a cockpit position had to retire at age 60. At the time the agreement was lawful under the ADEA's "bona fide seniority system" defense.

In 1978, however, the Act was amended to make most involuntary retirements based on a seniority system illegal. Because an FAA regulation declared that pilots and copilots had to retire at 60, TWA was mainly concerned with the amendment's effect on the rule regarding compulsory retirement of flight engineers. Thus after seeking legal advice and consulting with the union, TWA adopted a new rule. Under this plan flight engineers were allowed to continue working in that job past the age of 60. Captains who reached the age of 60 could remain with TWA only if they were able to obtain flight engineer status through certain bidding procedures. Under these procedures captains who wished to remain with TWA had to submit a "standing bid" for a flight engineer position before they reached 60. If there were no vacant flight engineer slots before a captain reached 60, or if he had insufficient seniority to outbid other captains trying for vacant slots before he reached 60, he was involuntarily retired. Under the agreement with the union, however, captains who had to leave that job for any reason other than age (for example, illness) did not have to follow the "standing bid" procedure. Instead, they were allowed to "bump" less senior flight engineers even if no vacancies existed. This meant that TWA treated captains who had to leave that position because of age differently from captains who had to leave the position for other reasons. The District Court held in favor of TWA. The Court of Appeals held in favor of the plaintiffs, awarding each a double back-pay award because it claimed TWA willfully violated the ADEA.

Decision: The U.S. Supreme Court affirmed the award.

Powell, Justice

The ADEA broadly prohibits arbitrary discrimination in the workplace based on age. Section 4(a)(1) of the Act proscribes differential treatment of older workers "with respect to [a] privileg[e] of employment." Under TWA's transfer policy, 60-year-old captains are denied a privilege of employment on the basis of age. Captains who become disqualified from serving in that position for reasons other than age automatically are able to displace less senior flight engineers. Captains disqualified because of age are not automatically able to displace less senior flight engineers. Captains disqualified because of age are not afforded this same "bumping" privilege. Instead, they are forced to resort to the bidding procedures set forth in the collective-bargaining agreement. If there is no vacancy prior to a bidding captain's 60th birthday, he must retire. The Act does not require TWA to grant transfer privileges to disqualified captains. Nevertheless, if TWA does grant qualified captains the "privilege" of "bumping" less senior flight engineers, it may not deny this opportunity to others because of their age.

Although we find that TWA's transfer policy discriminates against disqualified captains on the basis of age, our inquiry cannot end here. Petitioners contend that the age-based transfer policy is justified by two of the ADEA's five affirmative defenses. Petitioners first argue that the discharge of respondents was lawful because age is a "bona fide occupational qualification" (BFOQ) for the position of captain. Furthermore, TWA claims that its retirement policy is part of a "bona fide seniority system," and thus exempt from the Act's coverage.

Section 4(f)(1) of the ADEA provides that an employer may take "any action otherwise prohibited" where age is a "bona fide occupational qualification." In order to be permissible under section 4(f)(1), however, the age-based discrimination must relate to a "particular business." Every court to consider the issue has assumed that the "particular business" to which the statute refers is the job from which the protected individual is excluded.

TWA's discriminatory transfer policy is not permissible under section 4(f)(1) because age is not a BFOQ for the "particular" position of flight engineer. It is necessary to recognize that the airline has two aged-based policies: (i) captains are not allowed to serve in that capacity after reaching the age of 60; and (ii) age-disqualified captains are not given the transfer privileges afforded captains disqualified for other reasons. The first policy, which precludes individuals from serving as captains, is not challenged by respondents. The second practice does not operate to exclude protected individuals from the position of captain; rather it prevents qualified 60-year-olds from working as flight engineers. Thus, it is the "particular" job of flight engineer from which the respondents were excluded by the discriminatory transfer policy. Because age under 60 is not a BFOQ argument, it is supported by the legislative history of the amendments to the ADEA. In 1978, Congress amended ADEA section 4(f)(2), to prohibit the involuntary retirement of protected individuals on the basis of age. Some Members of Congress were concerned that this amendment might be construed as limiting the employer's ability to terminate workers subject to a valid BFOQ. The Senate proposed an amendment to section 4(f)(1) providing that an employer could establish a mandatory retirement age where age is a BFOQ. In the Conference Committee, however, the proposed amendment was withdrawn because "the [Senate] conferees agreed that . . . [it] neither added to nor worked any change upon present law." The House Committee Report also indicated that an individual could be compelled to retire from a position for which age was a BFOQ.

The legislative history of the 1978 Amendments does not support petitioners' position. The history shows only that the ADEA does not prohibit TWA from retiring all disqualified captains, including those who are incapacitated because of age. This does not mean, however, that TWA can make dependent upon the age of the individual the availability of a transfer to a position for which age is not a BFOQ. Nothing in the legislative history cited by petitioners indicates a congressional intention to allow an employer to discriminate against an older worker seeking to transfer to another position, on the ground that age was a BFOQ for his former job.

TWA also contends that its discriminatory transfer policy is lawful under the Act because it is part of a "bona fide seniority system." The Court of Appeals held that the airline's retirement policy is not mandated by the negotiated seniority plan. We need not address this finding; any seniority system that includes the challenged practice is not "bona fide" under the statute. The Act provides that a seniority system may not "require or permit" the involuntary retirement of a protected individual because of his age. Although the FAA "age 60 rule" may have caused respondents' retirement, TWA's seniority plan certainly "permitted" it within the meaning of the ADEA. Moreover, because captains disqualified for reasons other than age are allowed to "bump" less senior flight engineers, the mandatory retirement was age-based. Therefore, the "bona fide seniority system" defense is unavailable to the petitioners.

In summary, TWA's transfer policy discriminates against protected individuals on the basis of age, and thereby violates the Act. The two statutory defenses raised by petitioners do not support the argument that this discrimination is justified. The BFOQ defense is meritless because age is not a bona fide occupational qualification for the position of flight engineer, the job from which the respondents were excluded. Nor can TWA's policy be viewed as part of a bona fide seniority system. A system that includes this discriminatory transfer policy permits the forced retirement of captains on the basis of age.

DISCRIMINATION IN PUBLIC EMPLOYMENT

Today most public employees are protected from discrimination on the basis of race, sex, religion, or national origin by fair-employment-practices laws, particularly Title VII of the Civil Rights Act of 1964. Before 1972, public employees' rights were protected, if at all, by separate legislation and constitutional doctrines. The Constitution remains an important source of law in employment decisions, although its protections are broader in some respects and narrower in others than Title VII or other fair-employment-practices laws.

It is essential to understand that the Constitution and its protections apply to public employees, although the precise effect of its applicability changes from case to case. Therefore it is impossible to list in detail what the Constitution prohibits or allows in the employment field. What an individual may do, however, is to acquaint himself or herself with basic constitutional principles and study cases to discover the ways in which courts modify the principles in order to deal with the unique employer–employee relationship. A full discussion of these principles is not included in this chapter but is left to other courses where the underlying theories of the Constitution are studied.

AFFIRMATIVE-ACTION PROGRAMS

Affirmative-action programs are designed to effectuate equal employment opportunity laws. Such programs reduce reliance on case-by-case enforcement, provide faster, more effective relief, and generally tend to make equal employment opportunity a reality, not merely rhetoric. The key to affirmative-action programs is the employers' mandatory self-evaluation as to all terms and conditions of employment.

Affirmative-action obligations are twofold. First, employers must eliminate all present discriminatory practices and conditions—that is, they must comply with equal opportunity laws. More specifically, employers must eliminate discriminatory tests, non-job-related employment requirements, and other apparently neutral standards that, although nondiscriminatory on their face, have discriminatory effects when applied. Second, employers must take further affirmative steps to increase female and minority-group participation in their work forces. This latter obligation is a remedy for the present effects of past discrimination.

Authority for affirmative-action programs derives from two primary sources—Executive Order 11246 as amended and Title VII of the 1964 Civil Rights Act as amended. The executive order is administered by the Secretary of Labor, who may (and does) delegate the authority to require and review affirmative-action plans to other federal agencies. Title VII (like similar state laws) gives the courts broad equitable powers to remedy discrimination, with the result that a court may order a particular defendant to engage in affirmative action. Additionally, the EEOC often requires an affirmative-action plan as part of its conciliation efforts.

The constitutionality of present-day affirmative-action plans has not been specifically

ETHICS BOX

Professor William Smith is a tenured faculty member at a state university in its Department of Management. In 1994 he will be 70 years old and does not have to retire at any future age under the ADEA. He lectures to his class by reading from his coauthored textbook, which covers materials outlined in the college catalog. The chairman of the Management Department receives complaints each semester from a number of students who enroll in his class. The complaints systematically indicate that Professor Smith is often forgetful, is an arbitrary and capricious grader, continually tells about his experiences thirty years ago, treats women students "different" from men, and does not disguise his contempt for students. He holds two hours a week of office hours. If students come to consult with him, he lectures them on their inadequacies and refuses to answer their questions. The university hiring manual that is incorporated in Professor Smith's contract requires that he attend classes and hold office hours. The state statute covering his employment, as interpreted by the courts, indicates that he can be fired only for reasons of "moral turpitude." The chairman of the department has discussed this matter with Professor Smith frequently. The chairman has been told to find a way to fire Professor Smith by the Dean of the College of Business and the Provost of the University.

1. What ethical question(s), if any, face Professor Smith?
2. What ethical question(s), if any, face the chairman of the Management Department?
3. What ethical question(s), if any, face the Dean and Provost?

Answers to these questions should be sought by referring to Chapter 4.

---

decided by the Supreme Court. Lower courts have upheld more dubious plans (where the government imposed goals), and the various opinions in *Regents of the University of California* v. *Bakke* (1979)[13] provide some indication of the acceptable boundaries of such plans. *Bakke,* decided by an extremely divided court, dealt specifically with the legality of a special minority admissions program for medical school. The Court did not rule on affirmative-action plans under the executive order or on the legality of preferential treatment as a remedy following a judicially determined violation of Title VII.

When applied to specific situations, affirmative-action rules and regulations can be quite complex. Basically, affirmative-action programs require employers to evaluate their present work force to see if women and minority-group members are present in all positions in appropriate numbers. Appropriateness is determined by the number of women and minorities available and seeking work within the recruitment area. Specifically, there must be:

1. An evaluation of the employer's present work force—how many women, men,

ETHICS BOX

John Smith, a supervisor of a plant making widgets, is told by one of his employees that William White, a twenty-year employee who has recently received the Outstanding Employee Award for 1987, is a carrier of AIDS, and his three children are afflicted by the disease. He has received bomb threats over the phone and told to "get out of town." Several employees have refused to work with Mr. White, and rumors continue to spread among the 4,000-person work force at the plant. Mr. Smith has been told by the vice-president of operations to fire Mr. White immediately.

  1. What ethical issue(s), if any, does Mr. Smith face?
  2. What ethical issue(s), if any, does Mr. White face?
  3. What ethical issue(s), if any, does the vice-president of operations face?

These questions can best be answered by turning to Chapter 4.

whites, and minority-group members at all levels
2. An analysis of all recruitment and selection procedures
3. An analysis of those people applying for employment, accepting employment, applying for promotion, receiving promotion, and terminating
4. Data to determine the hiring community's labor-force characteristics—total population, work-force population, training, unemployment

Once collected, these data can detail areas of disproportionate employment. It is then the obligation of the employer to examine these areas to determine if the employment of women or minorities is inhibited by any internal or external factor and, if so, to remedy the situation. With these data, goals and timetables can be set by the employer. Goals reflect employers' decisions concerning how many women and minority-group members are necessary for adequate balance, and time-tables reflect employers' predictions of when these goals will be attained. An essential characteristic of affirmative-action plans is the employers' determination of goals and timetables and relativeness of these goals and timetables to local work forces.

There are several common criticisms of affirmative-action programs. Some argue that "goal" is a euphemism for "quota," and some employers act as if the distinction were only a semantic one. However, legally there is a difference in that a good-faith effort to meet affirmative-action responsibility is a defense to nonattainment of a goal. Additionally, "goal" takes into account the availability of qualified workers.

A second criticism is that affirmative action results in lower quality among employees. However, if an employer takes into account valid qualifications, such a prediction is not true. Affirmative action may actually raise the quality of a particular work force since there is an expanded pool of applicants and expanded perceptions of women and minorities.

A third criticism is that affirmative action is in fact unfair to white males, dictating reverse discrimination. This is the question that divided the Court in *Bakke*. In that case the Court held the particular program unlawful because it was unfair but was careful to reserve judgment as to other, less restrictive programs. In the landmark case excerpted here the court approved a *voluntary, nongovernment-ordered* affirmative-action program agreed to by a company and the union that represented some of its workers despite the fact that it discriminated against whites.

Steelworkers of America v. Weber

U.S. Supreme Court
443 U.S. 193 (1979)

Background: Weber (plaintiff-respondent), a white employee, sued defendants-appellants, the United Steelworkers of America (USWA) and Kaiser Aluminum Company (Kaiser), challenging the legality of an affirmative-action plan that was collectively bargained for by them, and requesting that the program be enjoined. The plan preserved 50 percent of all openings in a craft training program solely for blacks until blacks in the training program were commensurate with blacks in the labor force. The District Court enjoined the program. The Court of Appeals affirmed.

Decision: Reversed. The U.S. Supreme Court ruled in favor of the United Steelworkers of America and Kaiser Aluminum Company.

Brennan, Justice

The only question before us is the narrow statutory issue of whether Title VII *forbids* private employers and unions from voluntarily agreeing upon bona fide affirmative action plans that accord racial preferences in the manner and for the purpose provided in the Kaiser–USWA plan.

Respondent argues that Congress intended in Title VII to prohibit all race-conscious affirmative action plans. Respondent's argument rests upon a literal interpretation of Sections 703(a) and (d) of the Act.

Respondent's argument is not without force. But it overlooks the significance of the fact that the Kaiser–USWA plan is an affirmative action plan voluntarily adopted by private parties to eliminate traditional patterns of racial segregation. In this context respondent's reliance upon a literal construction of Sections 703(a) and (d) and upon *McDonald* is misplaced. It is a "familiar rule that a thing may be within the letter of the statute and yet not within the statute, because not within its spirit nor within the intention of its makers." The prohibition against racial discrimination in Sections 703(a) and (d) of Title VII must therefore be read against the background of the legislative history of Title VII and the historical context from which the Act arose. Examination of those sources makes clear that an interpretation of the sections that forbade all race-conscious affirmative action would "bring about an end completely at variance with the purpose of the statute" and must be rejected.

Congress' primary concern in enacting the prohibition against racial discrimination in Title VII of the Civil Rights Act of 1964 was with "the plight of the Negro in our economy."

Congress feared that the goals of the Civil Rights Act—the integration of blacks into the mainstream of American society—could not be achieved unless this trend were reversed. And Congress recognized that that would not be possible unless blacks were able to secure jobs "which have a future." Accordingly, it was clear to Congress that "[t]he crux of the problem [was] to open employment opportunities for Negroes in occupations which have been traditionally closed to them," and it was to this problem that Title VII's prohibition against racial discrimination in employment was primarily addressed.

It plainly appears from the House Report accompanying the Civil Rights Act that Congress did not intend wholly to prohibit private and voluntary affirmative action efforts as one method of solving this problem. The Report provides:

> No bill can or should lay claim to eliminating all of the causes and consequences of racial and other types of discrimination against minorities. There is reason to believe, however, that national leadership provided by the enactment of Federal legislation dealing with the most troublesome problems *will create an atmosphere conducive to voluntary or local resolution of other forms of discrimination.*

Given this legislative history, we cannot agree with respondent that Congress intended to prohibit the private sector from taking effective steps to accomplish the goal that Congress designed Title VII to achieve. The very statutory words intended as a spur or catalyst to cause "employers and unions to self-examine and to self-evaluate their employment practices and to endeavor to eliminate, so far as possible, the last vestiges of an unfortunate and ignominious page in this country's history," cannot be interpreted as an absolute prohibition against all private, voluntary, race-conscious affirmative action efforts to hasten the elimination of such vestiges. It would be ironic indeed if a law triggered by a Nation's concern over centuries of racial injustice and intended to improve the lot of those who had "been excluded from the American dream for so long," constituted the first legislative prohibition of all voluntary, private, race-conscious efforts to abolish traditional patterns of racial segregation and hierarchy.

Our conclusion is further reinforced by examination of the language and legislative history of Section 703(j) of Title VII. . . . Had Congress meant to prohibit all race-conscious affirmative action, as respondent urges, it easily could have answered both objections by providing that Title VII would not require or *permit* racially preferential integration efforts. But Congress did not choose such a course. Rather, Congress added Section 703(j) which addresses only the first objection. The section provides that nothing contained in Title VII "shall be interpreted to *require* any employer . . . to grant preferential treatment . . . to any group because of the race . . . of such . . . group on account of" a *de facto* racial imbalance in the employer's work force. The section does *not* state that "nothing in Title VII shall be interpreted to *permit*" voluntary affirmative efforts to correct racial imbalances. The natural inference is that Congress chose not to forbid all voluntary race-conscious affirmative action.

The reasons for this choice are evident from the legislative record. Title VII could not have been enacted into law without substantial support from legislators in both Houses who traditionally resisted federal regulation of private business. Those legislators demanded as a price for their support that "management prerogatives, and union freedoms . . . be left undisturbed to the greatest extent possible." Section 703(j) was proposed by Senator Dirksen to allay any fears that the Act might be interpreted in such a way as to upset this compromise. The section was designed to prevent Section 703 of Title VII from being interpreted in such a way as to lead to undue "Federal Government interference with private businesses because of some Federal employee's ideas about racial balance or racial imbalance." . . . Clearly, a prohibition against all voluntary, race-conscious, affirmative action efforts would deserve these ends. Such a prohibition would augment the powers of the Federal Government and diminish traditional management prerogatives while at the same time impeding attainment of the ultimate statutory goals. In view of this legislative history and in view of Congress' desire to avoid undue federal regulation of private businesses, use of the word "require" rather than the phrase "require or permit" in Section 703(j) fortifies the conclusion that Congress did not intend to limit traditional business freedom to such a degree as to prohibit all voluntary, race-conscious affirmative action.

We therefore hold that Title VII's prohibition in Sections 703(a) and (d) against racial discrimination does not condemn all private, voluntary, race-conscious affirmative action plans. . . . the challenged Kaiser–USWA affirmative action plan falls on the permissible side of the line. The purposes of the plan mirror those of the statute. Both were designed to break down old patterns of racial segregation and hierarchy. Both were structured to "open employment opportunities for Negroes in occupations which have been traditionally closed to them."

At the same time, the plan does not unnecessarily trammel the interests of the white employees. The plan does not require the discharge of white workers and their replacement with new black hirees. Nor does the plan create an absolute bar to the advancement of white employees; half of those trained in the program will be white. Moreover, the plan is a temporary measure; it is not intended to maintain racial balance, but simply to eliminate a manifest racial imbalance. Preferential selection of craft trainees at the Gramercy plant will end as soon as the percentage of black skilled craftworkers in the Gramercy plant approximates the percentage of blacks in the local labor force.

CASE NOTE

In *Johnson* v. *Transportation Agency, Santa Clara County, California* (55 *Law Week* 4379, March 24, 1987) the U.S. Supreme Court, relying on the *Weber* case, approved the Transportation Agency's voluntary plan to achieve a statistical yearly improvement in hiring and promoting minorities and women in job classifications where they were underrepresented. There were no specific set-aside quotas but short-range goals were established and adjusted annually. When the Agency announced a vacancy in the position of road dispatcher, none of the positions in that classification was held by a woman. A female was promoted and Johnson, a male, was passed over. He sued pursuant to Title VII of the Civil Rights Act of 1964, and the Federal District Court held in his favor. The Court of Appeals reversed and held in favor of the Agency. The U.S. Supreme Court, as noted here, affirmed. Relying on *Weber,* the Court noted that there was a "manifest imbalance" that reflected underrepresentation of women; the imbalance need *not* be such that it would support a prima facie case against the employer under Title VII. The Court feared that a prima facie standard would discourage *public* or *private* employers from adopting voluntary plans. The court stressed the fact that the Agency's goal was long-term and temporary in nature; that is, to redress an imbalance gradually, and that there was minimal intrusion on the expectations of other employees. It further stressed that this voluntary plan posed no danger that personnel decisions would be made by adherence to numerical standards. This case indicates that the same standards will be applied for voluntary affirmative-action plans in the public sector as in the private sector. It should be noted that Chief Justice Rehnquist, Justice Scalia, and Justice White dissented from the majority opinion.

Sanctions

The sanctions for either not having an affirmative-action plan when required or not putting into effect an existing program can be quite severe; they may include withdrawal of all federal funds. Such a sanction can be imposed only after an administrative hearing on the merits. Arguably, fund termination is necessary since at least one line of thought reasons that it would be a violation of the Fifth Amendment's due-process clause for the federal government to continue financial assistance to a person or an organization that discriminates.

Vocational Rehabilitation Act of 1973

Congress passed the Vocational Rehabilitation Act of 1973 (Act) in order to broaden the coverage of individuals protected against discrimination in employment. A handicapped individual under the Act is defined as one who has a "physical or mental impairment which substantially limits one or more of such person's major life activities" and has a record of such impairment. The Equal Opportunity Employment Commission, the Department of Labor's Office of Contract Compliance, and the courts have determined that individuals suffering from cancer, epilepsy, heart disease, blindness, and deafness are covered by this definition. Additionally, recovering alcoholics and drug addicts are covered by the Act, as well as individuals who have been successfully treated for emotional disturbances. These people are not protected unless they are qualified for the job. Employers must make "reasonable accommodations" to adjust to the employee's handicap.

Section 501 of the Act covers federal employees and requires each federal agency or department to implement an affirmative-action plan for hiring and promoting the handicapped. Section 503 covers private employers and is enforced by the Labor Department's Office of Contract Compliance. It states employers having federal contracts exceeding $2,500 must take affirmative-action steps to hire and promote the handicapped. Section 504 forbids discrimination against the handicapped in all programs receiving financial assistance. Welfare programs, training programs, and universities are covered by this section. Acquired immune deficiency syndrome (AIDS) has increased rapidly in recent years, with its mortality rate at nearly 100 percent. It has raised serious sociological, political, economic, and legal issues. One of the legal issues has been whether a contagious disease such as AIDS is covered by the Section 504 of the Act.[14] On March 3, 1987 in a tuberculosis case set out here the U.S. Supreme Court decided that persons afflicted with contagious diseases do fall within the protection of Section 504. By implication a person physically impaired by AIDS would seem to be covered. In a footnote to its decision, however, the Court noted that the facts of the case did not require it to reach the legal questions of whether a *carrier* of a contagious disease such as AIDS could be considered to have a "physical impairment," and thus covered by the Act, or whether that person could be considered a "handicapped person" as defined by the Act solely on the basis of being a *carrier*. The importance of this footnote from a policy perspective is that 1 to 2 million Americans are thought to be carriers of AIDS. In reading this case, one should be careful to note that it is a tuberculosis case in which the plaintiff has been *afflicted* by a contagious disease. The Court is ruling only on the factual situation presented it, and not on the related *carrier* issue.

School Board of Nassau County, Florida et al. v. Arline et al.

U.S. Supreme Court
107 Sp. Ct. 1123 (1987)

Background: Arline (plaintiff-respondent), an elementary schoolteacher, alleged that the school board of Nassau County (defendant-appellant) was in violation of Section 504 of the Rehabilitation Act of 1973 when they fired her because of a continuing recurrence of tuberculosis. Arline was hospitalized for tuberculosis in 1957 at age 14. The disease went into remission for the next twenty years during which time she began teaching elementary school. In 1977 and 1978 she had three long relapses. In November 1978 after the last relapse she was suspended from school with pay for the rest of the year. At the end of the 1978–1979 school year she was discharged without pay because of the continuing recurrence of the disease. Following denial of relief in state administrative proceedings, she brought suit in federal District Court, which held that she was not a "handicapped person" under the Act. The Court of Appeals reversed holding that persons with contagious diseases are within the Act's coverage. The Nassau County Board of Education appealed.
Decision: The U.S. Supreme Court ruled in favor of Arline.

Brennan, Justice

Section 504 of the Rehabilitation Act of 1973 prohibits a federally funded state program from discriminating against a handicapped individual solely by reason of his or her handicap. This case presents the questions whether a person afflicted with tuberculosis, a contagious disease, may be considered a "handicapped individual" within the meaning of Section 504 of the Act, and, if so, whether such an individual is "otherwise qualified" to teach elementary school.

In enacting and amending the Act, Congress enlisted all programs receiving federal funds in an effort "to share with handicapped Americans the opportunities for an education, transportation, housing, health care, and jobs that other Americans take for granted." To that end, Congress not only increased federal support for vocational rehabilitation, but also addressed the broader problem of discrimination against the handicapped by including Section 504, an antidiscrimination provision patterned after

Title VI of the Civil Rights of 1964. Section 504 of the Rehabilitation Act reads in pertinent part:

> No otherwise qualified handicapped individual in the United States, as defined in Section 706(7) of this title, shall, solely by reason of his handicap, be excluded from participation in, be denied the benefits of, or be subjected to discrimination under any program or activity receiving Federal financial assistance. . . .

In 1974 Congress expanded the definition of "handicapped individual" for use in Section 504 to read as follows:

> [A]ny person who (i) has a physical or mental impairment which substantially limits one or more of such person's major life activities, (ii) has a record of such an impairment, or (iii) is regarded as having such an impairment.

In determining whether a particular individual is handicapped as defined by the Act, the regulations promulgated by the Department of Health and Human Services are of significant assistance. As we have previously recognized, these regulations were drafted with the oversight and approval of Congress; they provide "an important source of guidance on the meaning of Section 504." The regulations are particularly significant here because they define two critical terms used in the statutory definition of handicapped individual. "Physical impairment" is defined as follows:

> [A]ny physiological disorder or condition, cosmetic disfigurement, or anatomical loss affecting one or more of the following body systems: neurological; musculoskeletal; special sense organs; respiratory, including speech organs; cardiovascular; reproductive, digestive, genito-urinary; hemic and lymphatic; skin; and endocrine.

In addition, the regulations define "major life activities" as:

> functions such as caring for one's self, performing manual tasks, walking, seeing, hearing, speaking, breathing, learning, and working.

Within this statutory and regulatory framework, then, we must consider whether Arline can be considered a handicapped individual. According to the testimony of Dr. McEuen, Arline suffered tuberculosis "in an acute form in such a degree that it affected her respiratory system," and was hospitalized for this condition. Arline thus had a physical impairment as that term is defined by the regulations, since she had a "physiological disorder or condition . . . affecting [her] . . . respiratory [system.]" This impairment was serious enough to require hospitalization, a fact more than sufficient to establish that one or more of her major life activities were substantially limited by her impairment. Thus, Arline's hospitalization for tuberculosis in 1957 suffices to establish that she has a "record of . . . impairment" within the meaning of and is therefore a handicapped individual.

Petitioners concede that a contagious disease may constitute a handicapping condition to the extent that it leaves a person with "diminished physical or mental capabilities," and concede that Arline's hospitalization for tuberculosis in 1957 demonstrates that she has a record of a physical impairment. Petitioners maintain, however, Arline's record of impairment is irrelevant in this case, since the school board dismissed Arline not because of her diminished physical capabilities, but because of the threat that her relapses of tuberculosis posed to the health of others.

We do not agree with petitioners that, in defining a handicapped individual under Section 504, the contagious effects of a disease can be meaningfully distinguished from the disease's physical effects on a claimant in a case such as this. Arline's contagiousness and her physical impairment each resulted from the same underlying condition, tuberculosis. It would be unfair to allow an employer to seize upon the distinction between the effects of a disease on others and the effects of a disease on a patient and use that distinction to justify discriminatory treatment.

Allowing discrimination based on the contagious effects of a physical impairment would be inconsistent with the basic purpose of Section 504, which is to ensure that handicapped individuals are not denied jobs or other benefits because of the prejudiced attitudes or the ignorance of others. By amending the definition of "handicapped individual" to include not only those who are actually physically impaired, but also those who are regarded as impaired and who, as a result, are substantially limited in a major life activity, Congress acknowledged that society's accumulated myths and fears about disability and disease are as handicapping as are the physical limitations that flow from actual impairment. Few aspects of a handicap give rise to the same level of public fear and misapprehension as contagiousness. Even those who suffer or have recovered from such noninfectious diseases as epilepsy or cancer have faced discrimination based on the irrational fear that they might be contagious. The Act is carefully structured to replace such reflexive reactions to actual or perceived handicaps with actions based on reasoned and medically sound judgments; the definition of a "handicapped individual" is broad, but only those individuals who are both handicapped *and* otherwise qualified are eligible for relief. The fact that *some* persons who have contagious diseases may pose a serious health threat to others under certain circumstances does not justify excluding from the coverage of the Act *all* persons with actual or perceived contagious diseases. Such exclusion would mean that those accused of being contagious would never have the opportunity to have their condition evaluated in light of medical evidence, and a determination made as to whether they were "otherwise qualified." Rather, they would be vulnerable to discrimination on the basis of mythology—precisely the type of injury Congress sought to prevent. We conclude that the fact that a person with a record of a physical impairment is also contagious does not suffice to remove that person from coverage under Section 504.

The remaining question is whether Arline is otherwise qualified for the job of elementary schoolteacher. To answer this question in most cases, the District Court will need to conduct an individualized inquiry and make appropriate findings of fact. Such an inquiry is essential if Section 504 is to achieve its goal of protecting handicapped individuals from deprivations based on prejudice, stereotypes, or unfounded fear, while giving appropriate weight to such legitimate concerns of grantees as avoiding exposing others to significant health and safety risks. The basic factors to be considered in conducting this inquiry are well established. In the context of the employment of a person handicapped with a contagious disease, we agree with *amicus* American Medical Association that this inquiry should include:

> [findings of] facts, based on reasonable medical judgments given the state of medical knowledge, about (a) the nature of the risk (how the disease is transmitted), (b) the duration of the risk (how long is the carrier infectious), (c) the severity of the risk (what is the potential harm to third parties) and (d) the probabilities the disease will be transmitted and will cause varying degrees of harm.

In making these findings, courts normally should defer to the reasonable medical judgments of public health officials. The next step in the "otherwise-qualified" inquiry is for the court to evaluate, in light of these medical findings, whether the employer could reasonably accommodate the employee under the established standards for that inquiry.

We hold that a person suffering from the contagious disease of tuberculosis can be a handicapped person within the meaning of the Section 504 of the Rehabilitation Act of 1973, and that respondent Arline is such a person. We remand the case to the District Court to determine whether Arline is otherwise qualified for her position.

Sanctions

Following a complaint and hearing process, in addition to time for conciliation, private contractors determined to be in violation of the Act are subject to immediate withholding of payments due on federal government contracts, and cancellation of such. This decision by a government agency is subject to judicial review.

REVIEW PROBLEMS

1. Title VII of the 1964 Civil Rights Act forbids discrimination based on race and sex. Explain the standards used by the courts in deciding whether discrimination exists in each case.
2. Define a bfoq.
3. What is the purpose of the Age Discrimination in Employment Act?
4. What do affirmative-action programs require employers to do?
5. Handy Dan's Barber Shop employed fifteen barbers, eleven of whom were Span-ish-surnamed Americans, two were black, and two were white. Handy Dan's maintained a longstanding rule forbidding its Spanish-surnamed American barbers from speaking Spanish to each other in the presence of English-speaking patrons. Three Spanish-surnamed barbers were discharged pursuant to this policy. Did Handy Dan's violate Title VII? What additional information would be helpful for determining whether a violation existed? If Handy Dan's had employed only fourteen

barbers, would it have been in violation of Title VII?

6. Sanchez is a 50-year-old black female worker in a large department store. She is a fitter in the women's wear department. She earns $150 a week. Cranchford, a white male, worked as a fitter in the men's wear department for $200 a week. Both Sanchez and Cranchford joined the company on the same day. Cranchford was fired for refusing on religious grounds to work on Saturdays. Sanchez requested a transfer to Cranchford's vacant position. Sanchez was the worker with the most experience, which under company rules governed who received a transfer. Sanchez was denied the transfer. List the legal issues involved in this case.

7. Jelleff Associates is a women's specialty store that catered to mature women. It began reducing personnel because of poor business conditions and excessive payroll expenses. By discharging its older employees (those over 40) and expanding its product line, the company hoped to appeal to a younger market. In terminating one employee, the company gave as its reason the fact that "business was falling off." Another was terminated after being advised that "business was slow." The terminated employees sued Jelleff Associates, claiming that it had violated the Age Discrimination in Employment Act. What result? Bishop v. Jelleff Associates, 398 F.Supp. 579 (D.C.C. 1974)

8. Weiner, a disgruntled taxpayer, filed suit to set aside the award of a contract to the second lowest bidder. The contract was for the installation of heating and air-conditioning equipment in classrooms being constructed by the Cuyahoga Community College with federal funding. The college contended that the lowest bid was not acceptable because the contractor would not promise to refrain from discriminatory hiring practices. The lowest bid had been submitted by a contractor who would make a reasonable effort to hire blacks. The bidder who was awarded the contract promised the college that blacks would be represented in all crafts employed on the project. It was the taxpayer's contention that the promise made by the lowest bidder was consistent with state and federal law and that it was an unlawful and unconstitutional abuse of discretion for the college to reject the bid. Who won? Explain. Weiner v. Cuyahoga Community College, 249 N.E.2d 907 (Ohio 1969)

9. Phillips applied for a job as assembly trainee with Martin Marietta Corporation. She was denied the position because the company was not hiring women with preschool children. At the time that she applied 70 to 75 percent of those applying were women, and 75 to 80 percent of those hired were women. The company employed men with preschool children. Has Martin Marietta violated Title VII? Discuss. Phillips v. Martin Marietta Corporation, 400 U.S. 542 (1971)

10. Six firefighters challenged a Baltimore provision that established retirement age at lower than 70. They claimed that these provisions violated provisions of the Age Discrimination in Employment Act. The city argued that age is a bfoq for the position of firefighters, and the city's retirement provisions were valid. It argued that Congress by statute had selected age 55 as the retirement age for most federal firefighters, and thus as a matter of law it constitutes a bfoq for state and local firefighters. Who won? Explain. Johnson v. Mayor and City Council of Baltimore, 53 *Law Week* 4754 (June 18, 1985)

11. Western Airlines required that its flight engineers, who are members of the cockpit crew but do not operate flight controls unless the pilot and co-pilot are incapacitated, retire at age 60. A Federal Aviation Administration (FAA) regulation

prohibits pilots and co-pilots from serving after age 60. A group of flight engineers forced to retire at age 60 and pilots who at age 60 were denied reassignment as flight engineers brought suit against Western Airlines, contending that the age 60 retirement requirement for flight engineers was in violation of the Age Discrimination in Employment Act. The airline defended, arguing that a bfoq existed because its age 60 retirement requirement was "reasonably necessary" for the safe operation of the airline. Who won? Explain. Western Airlines v. Criswell, 53 *Law Week* 4766 (June 18, 1985)

12. Marie Fernandez was employed by the Wynn Oil Company from February 1968 to February 4, 1977. During that time she held various positions, including that of administrative assistant to the executive vice-president reporting directly to Wynn's director of worldwide marketing. Wynn has extensive operations outside the United States. Much of its business, in fact, takes place in Latin America and Southeast Asia. Fernandez applied for and was denied a promotion to the position of director of international marketing. She sued Wynn, alleging that it discriminated against her on the basis of sex in violation of Title VII. Wynn defended by claiming that it was legally entitled to discriminate on the basis of sex in hiring for the position of director of international marketing because sex is a bona fide occupational qualification for the position. It argued that it would not consider any woman for the position because of the feeling among Wynn's customers and distributors that it would be undesirable to deal with a woman in a high management position. It contended that many of Wynn's South American distributors and customers, for instance, would be offended by a woman conducting business meetings in her hotel room. The offensive nature of this conduct stems from prevailing cultural customs and mores in Latin America. Will Wynn be successful in establishing sex as a bfoq for the position of director of international marketing? Explain. Fernandez v. Wynn Oil Company, 20 F.E.P. Cases 1162 (C.D. Calif. 1979)

13. Buck Green, who is black, applied for employment as a clerk at the Missouri Pacific Railroad Company's personnel office in the corporate headquarters in St. Louis, Missouri. In response to a question on the application form, Green disclosed that he had been convicted in December 1967 for refusing military induction. He stated that he had served twenty-one months in prison until paroled in 1970. After reviewing the application form, Missouri Pacific's personnel officer informed Green that he was not qualified for employment at Missouri Pacific because of his conviction and prison record. Missouri Pacific followed an absolute policy of refusing consideration to any person convicted of a crime other than a minor traffic offense. Green sued Missouri Pacific, seeking relief under Title VII. At trial, Green introduced statistical evidence showing that Missouri Pacific's policy operated automatically to exclude from employment 53 of every 1,000 black applicants but only 22 of every 1,000 white applicants. The rejection rate for blacks was two and one-half times that of whites under Missouri Pacific's policy. At trial, Missouri Pacific proffered the following reasons for following its policy:

a. Fear of cargo theft

b. Employees' handling of company funds

c. Bonding qualifications

d. Possible impeachment of an employee as a witness

e. Possible liability for hiring people with known violent tendencies

f. Employment disruption caused by recidivism and

g. A lack of moral character of persons
  with convictions

Will Green be successful in his suit against

Missouri Pacific? Explain. Green v. Missouri Pacific R.R. Co., 523 F.2d 1296 (8th Cir. 1975)

FOOTNOTES

[1] Other congressional responses included the Voting Rights Act of 1965, the Fair Housing Act of 1968, and other educational amendments (for example, Title IX) in 1972.

[2] Local Union No. 12, United Rubber, Cork, Linoleum and Plastic Workers of America v. NLRB, 368 F.2d 12 (5th Cir. 1966); United Packinghouse Food and Allied Workers International Union v. NLRB, 416 F.2d 1126 (D.C. Cir. 1969).

[3] U.S. Constitution Art. 2, §3.

[4] Dothard v. Rawlinson, 433 U.S. 321 (1977).

[5] In Plaintiff's Memorandum of Law, Hicks v. Crown Zellerbach, reprinted in *Sovern, Racial Discrimination in Employment,* pp. 439–440 (1969); Note, *Legal Implications of the Use of Standardized Ability Tests in Employment and Education,* 68 *Coumm. Law Review* 691, pp. 701–703 (1968).

[6] Johnson v. Pike Corporation of America, 332 F.Supp. 490 (C.D. Cal 1971).

[7] 1981 *World Almanac and Book of Facts* 271 (Newspaper Enterprise Assoc., Inc.).

[8] Id. at 177.

[9] 408 F.2d 228 (5th Cir. 1969).

[10] 442 F.2d 385 (5th Cir. 1971).

[11] 414 U.S. 86 (1973).

[12] See Sugarman v. Dougall, 414 U.S. 86 (1973); Graham v. Richardson, 403 U.S. 365 (1971). In *Sugarman* the Court held unconstitutional a New York statute that provided that only U.S. citizens may hold permanent positions in the competitive class of the state civil service. The Court stated that the statute swept indiscriminately and was not narrowly limited to the accomplishment of substantial state interests.

In *Graham* the Court held unconstitutional Arizona and Pennsylvania statutes that denied welfare benefits to resident aliens and to aliens who had not resided in the United States for a specified number of years. The Court rejected the states' justification that they could prefer their own citizens over aliens in the distribution of limited resources. 13.98 5. Ct. 2733 (1978).

[13] 438 U.S. 265 (1979).

[14] See Schneiderman and Perkins, "Contagious Diseases Deemed 'Handicaps' Under Federal Law," *Legal Times,* May 11, 1987, p. 18, Col. 1.

CHAPTER 47

International Business

THE INTERNATIONAL ENVIRONMENT _____

SOURCES OF LAW _____

INTERNATIONAL BUSINESS: TRADE _____

INTERNATIONAL BUSINESS: INVESTMENTS _____

THE INTERNATIONAL ENVIRONMENT

Because international business has become so important both to the nation as a whole and to the business firms that manufacture products or provide services, some study of its scope and character is essential for today's business student. This chapter examines the laws and legal environment affecting both international trade and international investing.

After briefly noting the current status of foreign trade and investment in and by the United States, we review the different sources of law affecting the conduct of international business. The chapter then discusses in detail the laws affecting both international trade, such as export controls and licensing restrictions, and international investing, whether conducted through joint ventures or direct investing.

International Trade

Despite a great deal of talk about national protectionism, the most recent figures show that the value of world trade continues to increase. As Figure 47–1 depicts, according to the Inter-

national Monetary Fund, global exports reached their highest level in 1986, some 1.992 trillion, more than twice the amount of trade recorded ten years earlier. The dollar value of world trade from 1980 to 1982 was higher than other years due to the very high oil prices during that period. Note too that the industrial countries have consistently accounted for approximately 75 percent of the dollar value of the world's trade.

Even though the United States remains the world's largest exporter, its role in the world's trade is significantly different from what it was several decades ago. In 1960 the United States accounted for approximately 18 percent of world exports and 12.5 percent of world imports. Twenty-five years later, in 1985, the U.S. percentage of world trade had flip-flopped. In 1985 it accounted for 12.5 percent of world exports and 18 percent of world imports.

Figure 47-2 depicts the change in trade between the United States and its trading partners over a period of twenty years. Since the late 1960s, the share of trade between the United States and the nations of the Pacific Rim has almost doubled. The countries of the Pacific Rim, stretching from New Zealand and Australia on the south through Singapore, Malaysia, and Thailand to Hong Kong, China,

FIGURE 47–1
Trends in World Trade

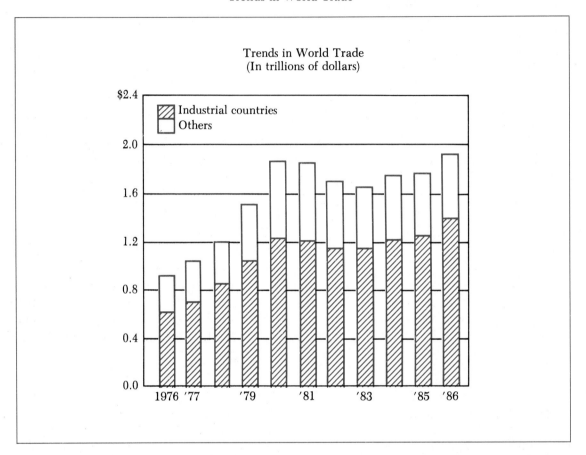

Source: *Direction of Trade Statistics Yearbooks, 1980–1987* (Washington, DC: International Monetary Fund).

South Korea, and Japan in the north, accounted for over 35 percent of the total U.S. trade in 1987.

International Investment

While there are continuing opportunities to conduct international business through trade, in recent years many businesses have focused on investments rather than on trade. These firms do so for several reasons. First, there is a more or less logical progression from trade to investment. Once a firm does enough trade volume, it may find that investment in the new market area has become more economical than export trade. Second, once enough sales are made in a market to obtain a competitive position with local firms, a foreign firm may find that to keep its market share, it needs to be continually present in that market. Finally, investing inside a country or region may be a way of avoiding protectionist measures aimed at those whose products originate outside a country's borders.

Foreign investment can include both portfolio investment and direct investment. *Port-*

FIGURE 47–2
U.S. Trading Partners: 1967 and 1987

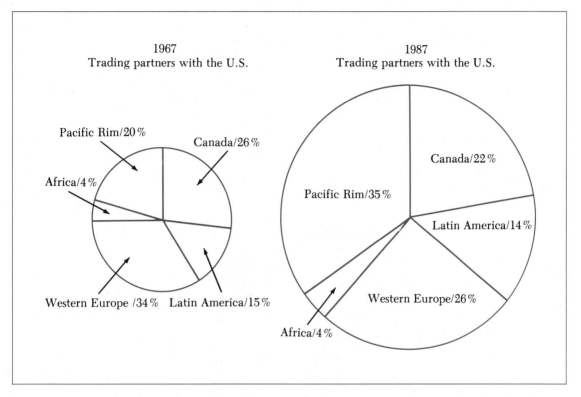

1967
Trading partners with the U.S.

Pacific Rim/20%
Canada/26%
Africa/4%
Western Europe /34%   Latin America/15%

1987
Trading partners with the U.S.

Canada/22%
Pacific Rim/35%
Latin America/14%
Western Europe/26%
Africa/4%

Source: **U.S. Department of Commerce (Washington, DC: U.S. Government Printing Office).**

folio investment is the purchase of stocks, bonds, and notes for the purpose of obtaining a return on the investment. Portfolio investment in the United States by individuals, corporations, and governments from outside the United States provides a very significant source of funds flowing into the country.

Direct investment occurs when an investor not only invests funds, but also participates in the management of the firm in which the investment has been made. Further, when an investment in the stock of a particular firm reaches the stage where it accounts for at least 25 percent of that firm's total stock, most scholars would characterize the investment as a direct investment rather than as a portfolio investment. Our focus in this chapter is on direct investments rather than on portfolio investments.

Although figures on the total amount of worldwide foreign direct investment are difficult to determine, one source found the total to be over $600 billion in 1985. Investment by U.S.-based corporations accounted for nearly 40 percent of that total, some $232 billion. While most of the foreign direct investment is placed in the industrialized countries, there is increasing direct investment in Mexico, Central America, and the countries of the Pacific Rim.

Twenty-five of the 500 largest U.S. corporations derive at least half of their total profits from outside the United States. Coca-Cola, IBM, American Standard, and International

Harvester exemplify this group of multinational corporations with significant foreign investments.

In recent years the United States has also become an attractive place for foreign-based corporations to expand their operations. In 1985 over $17.5 billion poured into the United States as foreign investments. According to *Forbes* magazine (July 25, 1988), the top ten sources of foreign investment in the United States are headed by the Seagram Co. of Canada (which owns 23 percent of DuPont as well as 100 percent of the Seagrams distillers), the Dutch/English Shell and the English/British

Petroleum oil companies. Another Canadian firm (Compeau, which owns the Allied and Federated Department stores) and a German firm, (The Tengelmann Group, owners of A&P supermarkets) rank fourth and fifth. Firms from England (B.A.T. Industries, owners of Peoples Drugs, and Hanson, owner of Hanson and Kidde), the Netherlands (Unilever, owner of Lever Brothers, Chesebrough-Pond's and Lipton), Switzerland (Nestlé, owner of Nestlé and Carnation), and Venezuela (Petroleos de Venezuela, owner of Citgo) round out the list of the top ten foreign investors in the United States. Figure 47-3 il-

FIGURE 47–3
Source of Foreign Direct Investment in the United States: 1970 and 1985

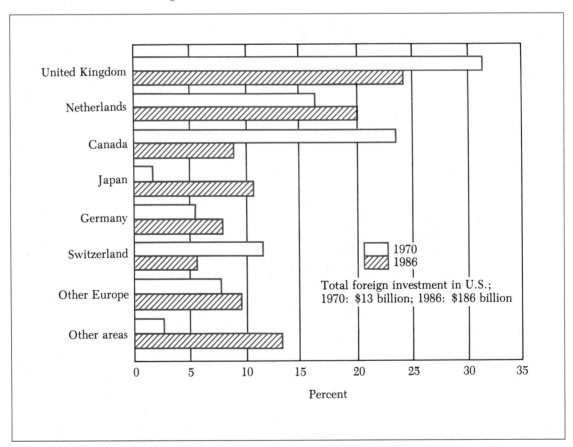

Source: Chart prepared by U.S. Bureau of the Census. *Statistical Abstract of the United States: 1985,* 105th ed. (Washington, DC: U.S. Bureau of the Census).

lustrates the changing composition of that investment. Note that the dollar value of the investment in the United States in the period of fifteen years has multiplied fourteen times, from $13 billion in 1970 to $183 billion in 1985.

We know that significant legal, financing, and marketing problems are encountered by firms engaged in international business. Why do businesses go into other countries? Comments made over a decade ago by the then Chairman of the Board of the RCA Corporation provide both a glimpse of the degree to which a company can be internationalized and some reasons why the conduct of international business has become so important:

RCA is stepping up its activities in the Far East in a number of significant ways and is also evaluating business opportunities in Eastern Europe and the Middle East. Among the solid reasons for seeking to expand abroad is our conviction that it would be unwise not to do so. Except in rare instances, national economics tend to grow at different rates and fluctuate at different frequencies. In seeking sustained growth and profitability, geographical diversification can be just as important as product diversification to a company like RCA.

Moreover, there are no natural boundaries for such RCA businesses as electronics, communications, car rentals, and prepared foods. Competition is worldwide. We must face our competitors abroad as well as at home if we expect to remain a leader. Finally, we increase our competence by operating internationally. This country is by no means the sole repository of technological skill or business capability. There is a constant exchange of ideas and experience with associates and customers abroad. We benefit from this give-and-take by gaining greater insight to apply to our operations elsewhere, including domestic market. Beyond considerations of self-interest, your management is committed to liberalized trade and international cooperation. Companies like ours can play a constructive part in furthering these objectives.

They serve as vehicle for the free flow of goods and capital, the evolution of living standards, and the wider distribution of managerial skills and advanced technology. . . .*

Nations and International Business Firms

The increasing role of foreign firms in the economic life of a nation has led to a loss of power for the host national government. As early as the 1950s governments began to realize that local businesses that were subsidiaries of foreign corporations could pursue objectives that were in conflict with those of the governments. This realization led to the imposition of a variety of laws, administrative rules, and investment codes by some national governments. Other national governments wanted to welcome the foreign investors who held out the promise of additional jobs and improved economic conditions. These nations modified their tax laws, currency exchange regulations, and administrative regulations to attract the multinational enterprise.

Thus different nations have different policies and laws that affect the conduct of business in their country by foreign-based firms. Countries also seek to regulate how firms in their own country conduct international business activities. At times exports are encouraged, whereas at other times they are restricted. Foreign investment may be promoted or subjected to significant legal controls. Even within one country, some laws may promote international business, whereas others seek to control it. Some countries have banded together in regional associations, granting to those regional authorities some of their law-making authority. A few international organizations, such as the IMF or the

*Comment of Robert W. Sarnoff, Chairman of the Board of Directors, RCA Corporation, *1974 Annual Meeting of Shareholders* (p. 4), May 7, 1974, New York.

United Nations (UN) also can have significant effect on the legal environment affecting firms conducting international business.

SOURCES OF LAW

Whenever a firm engages in international business, that firm's activity is regulated by international, regional, and national laws. International laws are developed by international organizations such as the IMF, the General Agreement on Tariffs and Trade, or the World Bank. Regional laws, on the other hand, are developed by a specific group of nations (such as the EEC), whereas national laws emanate from lawmakers within one nation. On the international level, recent international conferences on the law of the sea, environmental problems, and monetary matters provide examples of the continuing international development of new rules, regulations, and laws that affect the transaction of international business.

International laws also are based in the customers and practices agreed to by countries of the world. The following quotas about international law, and its role in the U.S. legal system, are taken from a federal District Court's decision in Zenith Radio Corporation v. Matsushita Electric Industries Company. 404 F.Supp. 1161, 1178–79 (1980):

Essentially, international law is a body of consensual principles which have evolved from the customs and practices civilized nations utilize in regulating their relationships. These customs have great moral force, and are often cited approvingly by domestic courts. The United States, for example, adheres to the frequently quoted view that "[i]nternational law is part of our law." However, international law must give way when it conflicts with or is superseded by a federal statute or treaty, made supreme under Article VI of the Constitution, to the extent permitted by the due process clause of the Fifth Amendment. It is therefore possible that the United States might find it necessary, in order to enforce domestic law, to violate international principles. In order to avoid such conflict to the extent possible, it has been said that "an act of Congress ought never to be construed to violate the law of nations, if any other possible construction remains."

Much of international law is concerned with delineating the respective jurisdictional spheres of nations. Five principles govern the exercise of jurisdiction by a nation: the territorial principle, by which jurisdiction is based on the place where the offense was committed; the nationality principle, based on the nationality of the offender; the protective principle, which covers conduct which threatens the national security or operation of governmental functions, such as counterfeiting and falsification of official documents; the universality principle, under which the custody of a perpetrator of a crime of universal interest, such as piracy, provides jurisdiction; and the passive personality principle, based on the nationality of the victim. As to jurisdiction over economic regulatory matters, only the territorial principle is applicable. That principle, however, admits of two interpretations. Viewed subjectively, a state may extend its jurisdiction over persons found within its borders who violate its laws there. Under what the law styles an "objective interpretation," however, a state has jurisdiction over acts which take effect within its borders, regardless of the location of the actor.

On a regional level, we find an increasing number of regional institutions with legal authority in or affecting that region. Smaller nations, seeking to have a greater impact on world problems and their solutions, turn to regional associations to solve particular problems, such as investments by foreigners (the significant concern of the Andean Common Market members), or to formulate common export policies for the same or similar products (as the oil-exporting countries have exemplified). Thus, while the regional organizations provide a larger forum than the nation-state institutions, they are also more manageable and cohesive than international bodies.

The business enterprise conducting an international venture soon realizes that instead of dealing with the laws of one nation, there are perhaps several overlapping and conflicting national laws that may attempt to control or regulate a transaction. Thus the expansion of business abroad is accompanied by increasingly complex legal problems. The transition from doing business domestically to doing business internationally involves a change from dealing with sources of law that are generally quite stable and well known (the national and state or local rules of one county) to dealing with legal sources that may be ever-changing and unfamiliar. These sources include the national laws of a foreign country, regional rules enforced in several countries in specified geographical areas, and international standards from international organizations and institutions.

National and International Problems

A national legal problem is approached by attempting to fit the facts into a known legal framework. While doing business within the United States, a business manager assumes the existence of rules and principles established by a legislature or an administrative body and interpreted by a court with the power to resolve disputes. The international community has few such institutions that are organized for solving business disputes. The national (and perhaps regional) rules and principles that govern a transaction occurring in a foreign country may be based on social, political, and economic values with which the U.S. businessperson is unfamiliar. The role of law and the legal system itself may be totally different from that of the domestic environment with which the business is familiar.

Nowhere are the rules of doing business more different than in Eastern and Western countries. The increases in trade between East and West in the last decade have been accompanied by accommodations in the legal, economic, and political systems of both blocs. Many Eastern bloc countries recently have abandoned the principle that foreign capital should be prohibited from direct participation in domestic economic ventures in their countries. In the Western countries businesspeople have accepted the fact that foreign trade with the Eastern bloc countries involves direct dealings with state enterprises, instead of with their business counterparts. Current East–West relations are not tied to the legal systems of either socialistic or capitalistic doctrines, but rather, they are based on what can only be described as an amalgamation of both legal systems.

Classification of World's National Legal Systems

The national laws of the country in which a firm does business usually have the greatest impact on that firm's activities. While there are variations among the laws of many countries, most laws can be considered to belong to one of three major legal systems:

1. The Romano–Germanic system (the civil law or code law found in countries such as France and West Germany)
2. The socialistic system (found in the USSR and most East European countries)
3. The common-law system (found in countries such as the United States, England, and Australia).

It should be noted that many authorities also regard Islamic laws as a separate legal system, since it is so influential in many Middle Eastern countries.

Despite the different legal systems found throughout the world, most laws are found in custom, judicial decisions, or legislative sources. Although similar sources of law are found in the different legal systems, there are significant differences in how each legal system makes use of those sources. In the common-law legal system found in the United States the judicial decisions are clearly recognized as a source of law. Further, the courts are vested with the power to interpret acts of the legislative branch and to declare them to be null and void if they conflict with the Constitution. In a civil law or code law legal system, such as that found in France, the role of the courts in interpreting legislation is much more restrictive. There, it is the administrators, not the court judges, who initially interpret legislative enactments. Additionally, the court decisions are not given the same status as are the legislative enactments that are based on provisions in the code.

There are also important differences in many of the basic substantive law fields. In most of the civil and common-law legal systems international business contracts generally are made by privately owned business firms, not by the government. Consequently, public-law concepts such as sovereign immunity and the act of state doctrine (both discussed near the end of the chapter) do not intrude into contract law. That is not the case in the socialistic legal systems where the government, not the individual or business firm, owns most of the property and the means of production in the society. Some types of laws found in one legal system do not have any counterpart in other legal systems. Consumer protection laws and civil rights laws, for example, are practically nonexistent in the countries that have a socialistic legal system.

In a common-law legal system, such as that found in the United States, means are available to change the law as conditions change. New legislation amends outdated statutes and courts generally are flexible in following or rejecting prior cases that do not apply to current problems. By contrast, in a country with a legal system based primarily on a code or on religious teachings found in a specific source (such as the Koran in the Islamic law or the Talmud in Jewish law), existing laws may be more rigid and less adaptable to change. Finally, the legal institutions in different countries may have varying degrees of independence and authority. The courts may be subservient to the head of the country's government. The legislative body may be composed of people from different political parties or it may be packed with loyal supporters of the government. Even where the letter of the law seems to be similar from country to country, its interpretation, application, and enforceability can differ greatly from a similar law in another country.

National Laws and Extraterritoriality

In addition to encountering national laws that originate in a different legal system from that with which the domestic business is familiar, in some cases more than one nation may have laws that seek to regulate the same transaction. This conflict between laws of different nations usually occurs when the laws of one of the nations seek to have some effect beyond its own territory or boundary; for this reason these laws are referred to as *extraterritorial laws.* Two examples of the extraterritorial reach of national laws are found in provisions of the U.S. income tax laws and antitrust laws.

For example, if a corporation incorporated in a state in the United States derives income from:

1. Export sales to West Germany,
2. License royalties from Brazil, and
3. Dividend income from a branch operation in Japan,

all three sources of income will be subject to taxation by the United States. This occurs because the United States asserts worldwide (extraterritorial) jurisdiction over the income earned by corporations located within its territory. Thus the U.S. position is that the income earned by these corporations is subject to U.S. taxation, even if the income was earned outside its territory.

Of course, the country where the income is earned, known as the country of source, generally also seeks to tax this same income. The result is that the income of U.S. corporations can be subject to double taxation, once from the United States and once from the country of source. There are, however, credit provisions in the U.S. tax laws and bilateral treaty agreements between the United States and many other countries that are designed to reduce or eliminate this possible double taxation.

Another example of an extraterritorial law is found in the Sherman Act, which is the keystone of the U.S. antitrust laws. Section 1 of the Sherman Act reads:

Every contract, combination or conspiracy in restraint of trade or commerce . . . with foreign nations is declared to be illegal.

In 1945 Judge Learned Hand made it clear that the Sherman Act applied to restrictive business practices of non–U.S. firms acting abroad if their practices were intended to and did affect imports into the United States, "It is settled law . . . that any state may impose liabilities, even upon persons not within its allegiance for conduct outside its borders which the state reprehends." United States v. Aluminum Co. of America, 148 F.2d 416, 419 (2d Cir. 1945). The *Timberlane* case that follows illustrates the application of the U.S. antitrust laws to actions taking place outside the territory of the United States.

Timberlane Lumber Co. v. Bank of America

U.S. Court of Appeals, Ninth Circuit

749 F.2d 1378 (1984)

Background: Timberlane Lumber Co. (plaintiff) claimed that soon after it began lumber operations in Honduras, a competing lumber business in Honduras and Bank of America (defendants) conspired to disrupt its efforts. Since Timberlane's business in Honduras was operated in part to export lumber from there to the East Coast of the United States, it claimed that the defendants violated the U.S. antitrust law by interfering with the foreign commerce of the United States. The court had to determine whether the antitrust laws prohibiting acts and conspiracies that restrain foreign commerce applied to conduct occurring outside U.S. borders.

The District Court dismissed the plaintiff's claim because it determined that the actions of the defendants, which took place in Honduras, did not have sufficient effect on the foreign commerce of the United States for its antitrust laws to apply. Timberlane appealed and the Court of Appeals (Timberlane I) vacated the dismissal of the lower court and remanded the case back to it. The District Court again dismissed the case and Timberlane again appealed.

Decision: In this opinion the Court of Appeals upheld the dismissal of the plaintiff's claim.

Sneed, Judge

FACTS AND PROCEEDINGS BELOW

Timberlane, an Oregon partnership whose primary business is the purchase and distribution of lumber in the United States, formed a partnership with two Honduran corporations (Danli Industrial, S.A. and Maya Lumber Company, S. de R.L.) that were incorporated and principally owned by the general partners of Timberlane. The partnership sought to develop alternative sources of lumber for delivery to the United States from Honduras. It eventually purchased an interest in an existing but financially unstable lumber mill owned by the Lima family.

Before the Timberlane purchase, ownership of the Lima enterprise had been transferred to a group of Lima employees, Bank of America, and another competing lumber mill, Casanova. Timberlane purchased its interest from the Lima employees, who had priority over the other claims. The other two owners refused to sell their interests to Timberlane. Bank of America's actions in connection with these interests form the basis for the alleged illegal antitrust conduct.

Timberlane alleges that Bank of America refused to sell its share in the Lima enterprise because it wanted to protect its interests in other competing lumber mills by driving Timberlane out of the Honduran lumber market.

Timberlane filed this antitrust action seeking more than $5,000,000 in damages from Bank of America and its Honduran subsidiaries. . . . The district court, . . . dismissed the antitrust action on the ground that the act of state doctrine [which is discussed in the OPEC case which follows] prevented the federal courts from entertaining suit. . . .

In *Timberlane I,* we vacated the district court's act of state holding and announced a tripartite test for determining the extent of federal jurisdiction over claims alleging illegal antitrust behavior abroad.

On remand, Timberlane appeals the . . . district court's judgment.

II. APPLICATION OF TIMBERLANE I'S JURISDICTIONAL RULE OF REASON

Timberlane I's test undertakes three separate inquiries: (1) the effect or intended effect on the foreign commerce of the United States; (2) the type and magnitude of the alleged illegal behavior; and (3) the appropriateness of exercising extraterritorial jurisdiction in light of considerations of international comity and fairness.

B. *Timberlane I's "jurisdictional rule of reason."*

. . . The district court applied *Timberlane*'s analysis and, on the basis of its third part, concluded that jurisdiction should not be exercised in this case. Although we agree with the district court's conclusion regarding each part of the *Timberlane I* test, we do not expressly approve all of its analysis. Therefore, we discuss each part of the inquiry as set forth in *Timberlane I.*

   1. *Does the alleged restraint affect, or was it intended to affect, the foreign commerce of the United States?*

The first part of *Timberlane I*'s analysis requires "that there be *some* effect—actual or intended—on American foreign commerce before the federal courts may legitimately exercise subject matter jurisdiction under [the antitrust] statutes." On appeal, Bank of America does not deny that Timberlane has met this requirement. "[B]y alleging the ability and willingness to supply cognizable markets with lumber that they allege would have been competitive with that already in the marketplace, they have satisfied this prong of the Circuit's test."

2. *Is it of such a type and magnitude so as to be cognizable as a violation of the Sherman Act?*

Under the second part of *Timberlane I*'s analysis, "a greater showing of burden or restraint may be necessary to demonstrate that the effect is sufficiently large to present a cognizable injury to the plaintiffs and, therefore, a civil *violation* of the antitrust laws." The only issue under the second part of the inquiry is whether the magnitude of the effect identified in the first part of the test rises to the level of a civil antitrust violation, i.e., conduct that has a direct and substantial anticompetitive effect.

In this case Timberlane alleges that Bank of America conspired with its Honduran subsidiaries to prevent Timberlane from milling lumber in Honduras and exporting it to the United States. Our review of the complaint reveals that Timberlane has alleged an injury that would state a claim under the antitrust laws against Bank of America. Thus, it satisfies the second part of the analysis.

3. *As a matter of international comity and fairness, should the extraterritorial jurisdiction of the United States be asserted to cover it?*

Under the third part of *Timberlane I*'s analysis, the district court must determine "whether the interests of, and links to, the United States—including the magnitude of the effect on American foreign commerce—are sufficiently strong, vis-a-vis those of other nations, to justify an assertion of extraterritorial authority." This determination requires that a district court consider seven factors. The district court here found that the undisputed facts required that jurisdiction not be exercised in this case. We agree. To support our conclusion each factor will be examined.

a. *The degree of conflict with foreign law or policy*

We must determine whether the extraterritorial enforcement of United States antitrust laws creates an actual or potential conflict with the laws and policies of other nations. Timberlane argues that no conflict exists between United States and Honduran law. We disagree. The application of United States antitrust law in this case creates a potential conflict with the Honduran government's effort to foster a particular type of business climate.

Although Honduras does not have antitrust laws as such, it does have definite policies concerning the character of its commercial climate. To promote economic development and efficiency within its relatively undeveloped economy, the Honduran Constitution and Commercial Code guarantee freedom of action. The Code specifically condemns any laws prohibiting agreements (even among competitors) to restrict or divide commercial activity. Under Honduran law, competitors may agree to allocate geographic or market territories, to restrict price or output, to cut off the source of raw materials, or to limit credit financing to obtain enterprises as long as the contracting parties are not de facto monopolists.

On balance, we believe that the enforcement of United States antitrust laws in this case would lead to a significant conflict with Honduran law and policy. This conflict, unless outweighed by other factors in the comity analysis, is itself a sufficient reason to decline the exercise of jurisdiction over this dispute.

b. *The nationality or allegiance of the parties and the locations of principal places of business of corporations*

Next we should consider the citizenship of the parties and witnesses involved in the alleged illegal conduct. In this case, with only one exception, all of the named parties are United States citizens or nationals. But it is also true that "[a]ll of the crucial percipient witnesses to the incidents were either Honduran citizens or residents." We believe, therefore, that the citizenship of the parties weighs slightly in favor of the exercise of jurisdiction.

c. *The extent to which enforcement by either state can be expected to achieve compliance*

The weighing of this factor yields no clear answer. Of course, any judgment against Bank of America could easily be enforced in a United States court. Whether such a judgment could be enforced as easily in Honduras is less certain. We believe that the enforcement factor tips slightly in favor of the assertion of jurisdiction in this case.

d. *The relative significance of effects on the United States as compared with those elsewhere*

A more definitive answer emerges when we compare the effect of the alleged illegal conduct on the foreign commerce of the United States with its effect abroad. The insignificance of the effect on the foreign commerce of the United States when compared with the substantial effect in Honduras suggests federal jurisdiction should not be exercised.

A comparison of Honduran lumber imports to both United States imports and total United States lumber consumption is instructive.

. . .

The actual effect of Timberlane's potential operations on United States foreign commerce is insubstantial, even in the narrow pine lumber market. In comparison, the effects of its activity on the considerably smaller Honduran lumber markets would have been much greater. . . . We believe that the relative significance of effects in this case weighs strongly against the exercise of jurisdiction.

e. *The extent to which there is explicit purpose to harm or affect American commerce*

Timberlane has not demonstrated that Bank of America had any particular interest in affecting United States commerce.

f. *The foreseeability of such effect*

A court should also consider whether, at the time of the alleged illegal behavior, the defendant should have foreseen an effect on the foreign commerce of the United States. Aside from the fact that American commerce has not been substantially affected, Timberlane has not shown that Bank of America should have foreseen the consequences of its actions. We do not believe that a reasonable investor would have foreseen the minimal effect that has occurred here. This weighs against the exercise of jurisdiction.

g. *The relative importance to the violations charged of conduct within the United States as compared with conduct abroad*

Finally, a court should consider the location of the alleged illegal conduct in order to assess the appropriateness of the exercise of extraterritorial jurisdiction. In this case both parties agree that virtually all of the illegal activity occurred in Honduras. This factor clearly weighs against the exercise of jurisdiction.

h. *Resolving the Seven Factor Test*

It follows that all but two of the factors in *Timberlane I*'s comity analysis indicate that we should refuse to exercise jurisdiction over this antitrust case. The potential for conflict with Honduran economic policy and commercial law is great. The effect on the foreign commerce of the United States is minimal. The evidence of intent to harm American commerce is altogether lacking. The foreseeability of the anticompetitive consequences of the allegedly illegal actions is slight. Most of the conduct that must be examined occurred abroad. The factors that favor jurisdiction are the citizenship of the parties and, to a slight extent, the enforcement effectiveness of United States law. We do not believe that this is enough to justify the exercise of federal jurisdiction over this case.

In this case, we find no abuse of discretion in the district court's application of the doctrine.

Legal Problems in Doing Business with Foreign Governments

In the United States most domestic and international business activities are conducted primarily by private corporations. These corporations, owned by institutional and individual shareholders and managed by company officers and directors, are recognized as legally separate from the government. In other countries of the world, particularly those with so-cialistic or communistic governments, most international business transactions are per-formed by the governments or by separate corporations that are totally owned and oper-ated by the government.

Thus the U.S. business manager often finds that the "business manager" with whom he or she deals in conducting international business is a representative of a foreign government.

Several unique legal problems occur when one or more of the parties to an international business transaction are agents or representa-tives of a government. Two of these problems, the *sovereign immunity* of the foreign gov-ernment and the application by the U.S. courts of the *Act of State* doctrine are dis-cussed in the *Machinists* case brought against the Organization of Petroleum Exporting Countries (OPEC).

International Association of Machinists, Etc. v. OPEC

U.S. Court of Appeals, Ninth Circuit

649 F.2d 1354 (1981)

Background: The International Association of Machinists and Aerospace Workers (IAM) was disturbed by the high price of petroleum in the United States. Believing the high prices were caused by the price-fixing activities of the Organization of Petroleum Exporting Countries (OPEC), the IAM as plaintiffs brought suit against OPEC (defen-dants), alleging that the price-fixing activities violated U.S. antitrust laws. Even though the defendants did not appear in court or recognize its jurisdiction to hear the case, the District Court ordered various parties to provide it with information and to argue the case on behalf of OPEC. At the close of the trial the District Court granted judgment in favor of the defendants and the plaintiffs appealed.

Decision: The Court of Appeals affirmed the judgment of the District Court in favor of OPEC. It found the OPEC countries immune from suit due to their sovereign immunity, and also indicated that the Act of State doctrine would lead the court to decline to exercise any jurisdiction it might have against OPEC.

Choy, Circuit Judge

IAM is a non-profit labor association. Its members work in petroleum-using industries, and like most Americans, they are consumers of gasoline and other petroleum-derived products. They object to the high and rising cost of such products.

OPEC is an organization of the petroleum-producing and exporting nations. . . . The OPEC nations have organized to obtain the greatest possible economic returns for a special resource which they hope will remove them from the ranks of the under-developed and the poverty-plagued. OPEC was formed in 1960 by the defendants Iran, Iraq, Kuwait, Saudi Arabia, and Venezuela. The other defendants, Algeria, Ecua-dor, Gabon, Indonesia, Libya, Nigeria, Qatar, and the United Arab Emirates, joined thereafter.

The OPEC nations produce and export oil either through government-owned com-panies or through government participation in private companies. Prior to the forma-tion of OPEC, these diverse and sometimes antagonistic countries were plagued with fluctuating oil prices. Without coordination among them, oil was often in oversupply on the world market resulting in low prices.

After formation of OPEC, it is alleged, the price of crude oil increased tenfold and more. Whether or not a causal relation exists, there is no doubt that the price of oil has risen dramatically in recent years, and that this has become of international concern.

Supporters of OPEC argue that its actions result in fair world prices for oil, and allow OPEC members to achieve a measure of economic and political independence. Without OPEC, they say, in the rush to the marketplace these nations would rapidly deplete their only valuable resource for ridiculously low prices.

Detractors accuse OPEC of price-fixing and worse in its deliberate manipulation of the world market and withholding of a resource which many world citizens have not learned to do without.

In December 1978, IAM brought suit against OPEC and its member nations. IAM's complaint alleged price fixing in violation of the Sherman Act, and requested treble damages and injunctive relief under the Clayton Act.

The defendants refused to recognize the jurisdiction of the district court, and they did not appear in the proceedings below. Their cause was argued by various amici friends with additional information provided by court-appointed experts. The district court ordered a full hearing, noting that the Foreign Sovereign Immunities Act (FSIA) prohibits the entry of a default judgment against a foreign sovereignty "unless the claimant establishes his claim or right to relief by evidence satisfactory to the court."

The testimony was extensive. Experts in economics and international relations were examined and cross-examined. Exhibits, including masses of statistical and technical data, were received. A full day of legal argument concluded the proceedings below.

The record reflects an outstanding effort on the part of the district judge to amass the information necessary to understand the international politics and economy of oil and to marshal the legal arguments for and against IAM's requested relief.

At the close of the trial, the district judge granted judgment in favor of the defendants. The court held, first, that it lacked jurisdiction over the defendant nations under the Foreign Sovereign Immunities Act. The court also decided that default judgment could not properly lie against the non-appearing defendants, and that the defendants had not waived their immunity.

DISCUSSION

A. Sovereign Immunity

In the international sphere each state is viewed as an independent sovereign, equal in sovereignty to all other states. It is said that an equal holds no power of sovereignty over an equal. Thus the doctrine of sovereign immunity: the courts of one state generally have no jurisdiction to entertain suits against another state. This rule of international law developed by custom among nations. Also by custom, an exception developed for the commercial activities of a state. The former concept of absolute sovereign immunity gave way to a restrictive view. Under the restrictive theory of sovereign immunity, immunity did not exist for commercial activities since they were seen as non-sovereign.

The court below defined OPEC's activity as follows:

> [I]t is clear that the nature of the activity engaged in by each of these OPEC member countries is the establishment by a sovereign state of the terms and conditions for the removal of a prime natural resource—to wit, crude oil— from its territory.

. . . The trial judge reasoned that, according to international law, the development and control of natural resources is a prime governmental function. . . . The opinion cites several resolutions of the United Nations' General Assembly, which the United States supported, and the United States Constitution, Art. 4, §3, cl. 2, which treat the control of natural resources as governmental acts.

B. The Act of State Doctrine

The act of state doctrine declares that a United States court will not adjudicate a politically sensitive dispute which would require the court to judge the legality of the sovereign act of a foreign state. This doctrine was expressed by the Supreme Court in *Underhill* v. *Hernandez,* 168 U.S. 250, 252 (1897):

> Every sovereign State is bound to respect the independence of every other sovereign State, and the courts of one country will not sit in judgment on the acts of the government of another done within its own territory.

The doctrine recognizes the institutional limitations of the courts and the peculiar requirements of successful foreign relations. To participate adeptly in the global community, the United States must speak with one voice and pursue a careful and deliberate foreign policy. The political branches of our government are able to consider the competing economic and political considerations and respond to the public will in order to carry on foreign relations in accordance with the best interests of the country as a whole. . . .

When the courts engage in piecemeal adjudication of the legality of the sovereign acts of states, they risk disruption of our country's international diplomacy.

The act of state doctrine is similar to the political question doctrine in domestic law. It requires that the courts defer to the legislative and executive branches when those branches are better equipped to resolve a politically sensitive question. . . .

The Supreme Court has stated that the act of state doctrine arises out of the basic relationships between branches of government in a system of separation of powers. . . . The doctrine as formulated in past decisions expresses the strong sense of the Judicial Branch that its engagement in the task of passing on the validity of foreign acts of state may hinder rather than further this country's pursuit of goals both for itself and for the community of nations as a whole in the international sphere. . . .

The doctrine of sovereign immunity is similar to the act of state doctrine in that it also represents the need to respect the sovereignty of foreign states. The two doctrines differ, however, in significant respects. The law of sovereign immunity goes to the jurisdiction of the court. The act of state doctrine is not jurisdictional. Rather, it is a prudential doctrine designed to avoid judicial action in sensitive areas. Sovereign immunity is a principle of international law, recognized in the United States by statute. It is the states themselves, as defendants, who may claim sovereign immunity. The act of state doctrine is a domestic legal principle, arising from the peculiar role of American courts. It recognizes not only the sovereignty of foreign states, but also the spheres of power of the co-equal branches of our government. . . . The record in this case contains extensive documentation of the involvement of our executive and legislative branches with the oil question. IAM does not dispute that the United States has a grave interest in the petro-politics of the Middle East, or that the foreign policy arms of the executive and legislative branches are intimately involved in this sensitive area. It is clear that OPEC and its activities are carefully considered in the formulation of American foreign policy.

The remedy IAM seeks is an injunction against the OPEC nations. The possibility of insult to the OPEC states and of interference with the efforts of the political branches to seek favorable relations with them is apparent from the very nature of this action and the remedy sought. . . .

A further consideration is the availability of internationally-accepted legal principles which would render the issues appropriate for judicial disposition. . . .

While conspiracies in restraint of trade are clearly illegal under domestic law, the record reveals no international consensus condemning cartels, royalties, and production agreements. The United States and other nations have supported the principle of supreme state sovereignty over natural resources. The OPEC nations themselves obviously will not agree that their actions are illegal. We are reluctant to allow judicial interference in an area so void of international consensus.

CONCLUSION

The act of state doctrine is applicable in this case. The courts should not enter at the will of litigants into a delicate area of foreign policy which the executive and legislative branches have chosen to approach with restraint.

INTERNATIONAL BUSINESS: TRADE

While there are several methods of conducting international business, the least complex method is *exporting* (or importing)—the selling (or buying) of a product manufactured in one country and purchased by a firm in another country. Different laws affect both the export and import of the product and each will be dealt with subsequently. A second method commonly used in conducting international business is licensing. A *license* permits a foreign manufacturer or distributor to make or distribute a product in a certain territory or country. The basic legal framework of licensing agreements is briefly examined. The more complex international direct investments are discussed in the next section. We look at both the laws affecting a firm deciding to enter into a joint venture with a foreign firm and the laws governing the establishment of a wholly owned office or manufacturing plant in a foreign country.

Laws Affecting Exports

Laws affecting exports may be directed at either encouraging or discouraging such exports; this section examines some legal provisions of each type. Those laws that are directed at discouraging exports may be imposed because of the scarcity of the products domestically (U.S. export quotas have been imposed on wheat and soybean commodities during periods of crop shortages) or as a result of the concern over the use of the product by the importer (such as is true for military equipment and technologically advanced computer hardware). On the other hand, exports are often stimulated and encouraged to take markets away from foreign competitors and to ease the balance of trade problems. Our analysis of the laws affecting exports first focus on laws seeking to control, restrict, or regulate exports.

License Regulations for Exports. Each nation's government is usually careful about what it exports, particularly during wartime or periods of economic crisis. Thus it is important that a business attempting to export should investigate its own laws to see if the goods in question require prior approval before they are allowed to leave the country. Sometimes a law restricts particular goods from being sent to another country, whereas in other cases a law may restrict certain products from some countries while allowing them to be shipped to other destinations.

A U.S. exporter may determine whether a commodity requires a license by consulting the U.S. Department of Commerce. All commodities to be exported carry a designation number known as a Schedule B number. These numbers, published by the Bureau of the Census, make it possible to record the dollar value and volume of all commodities leaving the country. A typical Schedule B listing would be: steel sheets, galvanized, 60340.

The Export Administration Act provides for three types of licenses: (1) the *general license,* which authorizes the export without any application by the exporter—no specific documentary approval is required for the export of goods under this license; (2) a *validated license,* which authorizes a specific export and is issued pursuant to an application by the exporter; and (3) a *qualified license,* which authorizes multiple exports and is also issued pursuant to the exporter's application.

The export of certain goods, technology, or industrial techniques developed in part, directly or indirectly, from federally financed research and development must be approved by the Secretary of Defense. If the Secretary of Defense determines that the export of such goods, technology, or techniques would significantly increase the present or potential military capacity of a controlled country, he can recommend that the application for the validated or qualified license be denied. Controlled countries include the USSR, Poland, Romania, Hungary, Bulgaria, Czechoslovakia, East Germany, and other countries such as may be designated by the Secretary of Defense.

Any individual, corporation, or partnership acting as an exporter under the jurisdiction of the United States may apply for an export license. The license requires information such as the quantity of the commodity, the description, the Schedule B number, the processing code, the unit price, the total value, the end use of the material, and the identity of the foreign importer.

Governmental Assistance for Exports. A variety of governmental programs are designed to assist the exporter. Since tax incentives, credits, and rebates are often a pivotal part of such governmental assistance, those laws will be examined separately in the next section of this chapter. In addition to providing tax assistance, a government frequently provides valuable information to the potential exporter.

In the United States the Department of Commerce has several publications available that are of significant value to any potential exporter. In addition to providing brochures and pamphlets, the Department of Commerce conducts searches for agents to represent a U.S. firm in foreign countries. The Department also organizes various exhibits and trade fairs in U.S.-owned trade centers located throughout the world so that U.S. goods can be shown to potential foreign purchasers.

Another type of assistance given to U.S. firms is provided by the Export Trading Company Act of 1982. This law is designed to assure exporting firms that they will not be prosecuted for violations of U.S. antitrust laws. Essentially the company files information regarding its activities and applies for a certificate of antitrust immunity. If the firm meets appropriate conditions and does in fact perform according to the terms outlined in the certificate, the company will be immune from antitrust prosecution by the government. Another section of this law also permits U.S. banks to invest capital in and make loans to export trading companies.

Financial assistance is available for the exporter from several governmental organizations. For example, the Export–Import Bank (Eximbank) offers both medium- and long-term loans and credit guarantees for the exporter. While some direct loans are made by Eximbank, it primarily provides credit guarantees to commercial banks that in turn lend money to the exporting business.

Tax Assistance for Exports. Although exports are frequently encouraged because of the jobs they provide to a nation's employees and the money added to its economy, when a country experiences serious balance of trade prob-

lems, additional tax assistance to exporters is frequently also made available. The U.S. Congress took such steps in the early 1970s when it passed the Revenue Act of 1971. That law provided tax benefits when U.S. products were marketed overseas through a Domestic International Sales Corporation (DISC). Over a decade later, after some of the trading partners of the United States claimed that law violated the international General Agreement on Tariffs and Trade, the DISC provisions of the U.S. tax laws were replaced in 1984 by the Foreign Sales Corporation (FSC) rules.

A Foreign Sales Corporation must be located outside the United States, either in a U.S. possession or in a foreign country that has a tax information exchange agreement with the United States. Meetings of the corporation's shareholders and board of directors also must be maintained outside the United States. The principal benefit of the FSC is the exemption from U.S. taxation of about 15 percent of the corporation's income that is derived from qualified export transactions. Thus if a corporation has one million dollars of income from qualified export transactions, only $850,000 of it will be subject to U.S. income taxes.

Laws Affecting Imports

In international trade a business may encounter legal controls imposed on products by the country into which a product is imported, as well as by the country from which it is exported. The country from which the product is exported may not want to lose the resource to governments or consumers of other nations. A country into which a product is imported may not want foreign products to compete with products manufactured by local firms, or it simply may lack the capital necessary to pay for the import. There are a number of means by which a country seeks to prohibit, restrict, or regulate imports into it from outside its borders.

Such legal restrictions could range from a

prohibition (declaring no such products could be imported), to a *quota* (limiting the number of products imported), to a *tariff* (imposing a tax on the product to be imported), to various forms of discriminating against foreign goods or in favor of domestic items (nontariff barriers). While each nation can and does adopt its own import policy, international institutions, such as the General Agreement on Tariffs and Trade and the IMF, limit some policies that member countries may impose. While different nations use various means of restricting or encouraging imports, an examination of some U.S. laws affecting imports should illustrate the type of legal measures often used.

Prohibitions on Imports The United States has enacted several *prohibition* laws aimed at prohibiting importation of certain products. Among these are laws prohibiting the import of undesirable products (drugs and guns) or agricultural items that could cause disease. The Trading with the Enemy Act also grants to the President the power to restrict all imports from the countries considered to be enemies.

Many developing nations also prohibit imports on goods that otherwise might overwhelm their own infant industries. Brazil prohibits the import of small computers and light passenger airplanes, whereas Taiwan keeps out chemicals used in making drugs if those chemicals can be produced domestically. Japan's import laws are frequently cited as being among the most restrictive among industrialized countries.

Quotas. A *quota* limits the number of items that may be imported. While a quota is less restrictive than an outright prohibition, it generally is more restrictive than a policy that merely taxes the product to be imported. Since 1964 the United States has had a quota on the import of meat products.

Quotas are widely regarded as one of the most effective forms of laws restricting imports. Quotas are frequently disguised as "voluntary" agreements between trading partners. The EEC has pressured Japan to limit its shipments of quartz watches, stereo equipment, and computer-controlled machine tools. The United States has similar promises from steel-exporting countries in Europe and in South America.

Tariffs. *Tariffs* are taxes assessed on imported goods but not on domestic goods; thus such taxes are invariably discriminatory. Usually these taxes are levied to protect infant industries against the industrial force possessed by foreign competitors. The tariffs may be levied on an ad valorem basis (the tariff represents a percent of the value or price of the item imported) or on a flat rate basis (the tariff being levied on each barrel of oil, foot of pipe, or pound of nails). An examination of customs duties would disclose page after page of tariff rates applicable to various classifications of goods. As the next case indicates, the placing of goods within a particular classification is often a critical factor in determining whether importing an item is economically feasible.

Childcraft Education Corp. v. United States
U.S. Court of International Trade
572 F.Supp. 1275 (1983)

Background: Childcraft (plaintiff) imported from Japan a Teaching Typewriter and Touch to Learn machine, which were made for use by children. The United States (defendant) classified the items as toys, subject to a 21 percent ad valorem tariff, instead of educational machines, subject to a 6 or 6.5 percent tariff. The plaintiff claims that since the chief use of the merchandise was for the education of children, the items should not have been classified as toys.

Decision: The Court of International Trade upheld the classification of the plaintiff's imported items as toys. Items that are primarily for the amusement of children, even though also educational in nature, are considered to be toys.

Landis, Judge

This action involves merchandise known as "Teaching Typewriters," "Touch to Learn," and "Touch to Match," manufactured in Japan and entered at the port of New York between May 28, 1971 and October 1, 1971.

The pertinent statutory provisions are as follows:

Classified
Schedule 7, Part 5, Subpart E
Subpart E headnotes:

. . .

2. For the purposes of the tariff schedules, a "toy" is any article chiefly used for the amusement of children or adults.

. . .

Item	Articles	Rate of Duty
	Toys, and parts of toys, not specifically provided for:	
	. . .	
737.90	Other	21% ad val.

Claimed:

Schedule 6, Part 4, Subpart H

678.50	Machines not specially provided for, and parts thereof	6% ad val.

Alternatively Claimed:

Schedule 6, Part 5

688.40	Electrical articles and electrical parts of articles, not specifically provided for	6.5% ad val.

The primary issue is whether the merchandise in issue is chiefly used for the *education* of pre-school children or whether it is used chiefly for the *amusement* of adults or children and thereby classifiable as a "toy."

At the trial, plaintiff introduced eight exhibits and called one witness. One joint exhibit was introduced by the parties. Defendant called no witnesses nor solely introduced any exhibits.

Plaintiff's witness, Mr. Saul Cohen, was at the time of the trial Senior Vice-President of Merchandising for plaintiff corporation. His testimony indicated that he has been employed by plaintiff for twenty-eight (28) years. According to the witness, approximately eighty (80) percent of plaintiff's business is generated by sales to schools and other educational systems (R–7).

Mr. Cohen's testimony and actual demonstration indicated that the merchandise known as "Teaching Typewriter" (Exhibit 1A) and the related programmed cards (Exhibit 1B) were designed for educational purposes. According to the witness, the machine functions by introducing a programmed card containing a mathematical, spelling or other educational type problem. The merchandise user then presses one of the typewriter keys that completes a word or answers a mathematical problem. If the user engages the wrong key the programmed card is immobilized and new problems are not presented to the user. If the user selects a correct answer the programmed card advances presenting a new problem. This process is repeated each time the user gives a correct answer.

Subsequently, the witness described and illustrated the "Touch to Learn" merchandise and its related cassette.

According to the witness, "Touch to Learn" operates in the same manner as the "Teaching Typewriter," except that it uses programmed cassettes instead of programmed cards. Basically, when the user engages the machine it presents a problem. If the correct response is made, the cassette automatically moves to the next problem. If the wrong answer is made, the cassette will not present a subsequent problem. The problems on the cassette are in different combinations to teach the child, for example, that two and one equal three, etc. The sequence of problems increases in degree of difficulty as the cassette progresses. The principles behind the "Touch to Learn" and the "Teaching Typewriter" are the same.

Mr. Cohen's testimony further indicates that the imported machines could not function without a programmed card or cassette and that the particular programs were progressive in degree of learning difficulty.

Plaintiff sells programmed cards other than those included at the initial purchase for the "Teaching Typewriter" and the "Touch to Learn."

The witness stated that the articles in question were merchandised through a school catalog and through a force of sales representatives who conducted workshops in schools and with teachers to demonstrate the merchandise. Additionally, Childcraft attempted to sell these articles through its stores, a consumer catalog, and by public distribution through retail stores.

A review of the evidence of record, including trial testimony and illustrative samples, indicates that defendant should have judgment in this action.

Plaintiff has failed to demonstrate by the evidence of record that the imported merchandise is chiefly used for educational purposes and not chiefly used for the amusement of children.

Under TSUS, a "toy" for the purposes of the tariff schedules is any article chiefly used for the amusement of children or adults (schedule 7, part 5, subpart E, headnote 2 (1971)). Thus, plaintiff's burden is to prove that the chief purpose of the merchandise in issue is not amusement.

Plaintiff's case ultimately relies upon the theory that the chief utilitarian purpose of the imported merchandise is that of education of children and that any amusement derived therefrom is merely incidental to its chief use. When amusement and utility become locked in controversy, the question becomes one of determining whether the amusement is incidental to the utilitarian purpose, or the utilitarian purpose incidental to the amusement.

Plaintiff's only witness at the trial did not have a background as an educator or in educational psychology although he did indicate that he worked with teachers and educational consultants as well as people who are engaged in the field of education of pre-school children.

While the testimony of the witness indicated that in his belief the main purpose of the merchandise in issue was to teach children he also stated that he had observed children using the merchandise in school and that the children were enjoying themselves.

Thus, the witness admitted that the basis of the merchandise was amusement of a young child with the hopeful purpose that the child would learn something while being amused. An article that has some incidental educational value or is used in school does not remove it from the toy category.

Moreover, in toy cases especially, a sample is a potent witness. The court in viewing a demonstration of the merchandise at trial and reviewing the exhibits in chambers is of the solid conclusion that the main effect thereof is the amusement of children and any educational value is merely incidental thereto. Moreover, if plaintiff's position were sustained then almost any toy could be deemed educational in nature as most experiences are new to the young child's receptive mind and he learns by the new experiences.

Exhibit 5 is a copy of plaintiff's 1971 catalog which is entitled "Christmas Catalogue Toys that Teach." A review of this forty-seven (47) page catalog indicates that it is essentially a toy catalog the like of which is sent to retail outlets such as Gimbels and F.A.O. Schwarz Co., famous toy stores. Articles listed in this catalog appear to be only for the basic purpose of the amusement of children. The fact that the articles were marketed as toys, while not determinative, is of obvious probative value.

In conclusion, the court in reviewing the testimony given at trial and the samples submitted therein finds that plaintiff has failed to sustain its burden of proving that the defendant's classification is in error and that its own claimed classification is correct.

Nontariff Barriers

It is impracticable, if not impossible, to attempt to enumerate even the dominant forms of nontariff barriers. They would include import licensing controls, foreign exchange controls, deposits required of importers, and fees other than tariffs levied by custom officials. The definition of *nontariff barriers* generally includes all references to import restrictions of any kind, except for tariffs.

Our discussion of nontariff barriers first focuses on those that affect the goods as they come into a country; these are known as *nontariff barriers effective upon entry*. The second category consists of programs, practices, and policies within a country that discriminate against imported goods, but that are not effective on the entry of goods into a country. These practices are referred to as *nontariff barriers effective subsequent to the entry* of the goods.

Effective upon Entry. Import licensing controls require importers to obtain a license through a governmental agency. The license may require payment of a fee, completion of extensive documentation, or approval by several different agencies. An import license may be available only if a business also has certain export "credits" with which to purchase the imported goods. In some Latin American countries the required license may take months to process; often almost complete discretion as to the approval of the license is given to chosen officials.

Standards, procedures, and guidelines for determining the likelihood of receiving a license may be nonexistent. In most Communist countries import licenses are granted only if the imported item is required pursuant to governmental plans. Imports that do not fit into the plan are effectively, although perhaps not expressly, prohibited.

Foreign exchange controls are measures that are adopted to regulate payments in or transfers of local or foreign currencies or both. Usually these controls restrict the conversion of local currency into foreign currency and the movement of local or foreign currencies into or out of the country. France imposed exchange controls in 1983 limiting the amount of French francs that individuals could take out of the country.

Laws may specify through what institutions and under what circumstances exchanges between local and foreign currency take place. While different schemes can become extremely complex, all such controls seek to restrict the import or export of some commodities, goods, or services or limit the possibility of acquiring certain foreign currencies. In extreme cases the only currency that can be used to pay for imported goods is the local currency. Thus, in East Germany, where the currency is not freely traded on the world market, a foreign seller would have difficulty in converting East German marks into a marketable currency.

Effective Subsequent to Entry. These non-tariff barriers include governmental procurement policies, internal tax policies, subsidy programs, and other practices that accord an advantage to domestic industries. The "Buy America" Act prohibits the purchase by federal agencies of foreign goods when domestic equivalents are available at comparable prices or when national security interests are involved.

Since late in the nineteenth century the United States has required all imported items to be marked with a legend identifying the foreign country from which it originated. The purpose of the requirement is to insure that the consumer or user of the item in the United States knows the item is a product of a particular foreign country. If there is no marking, no import is permitted. As a result, this law is effective on the entry of an imported item. However, if there is a marking, given the choice, the consumer may choose the American-made product. Thus the law imposing the "country of origin" requirement is also a nonentry barrier.

A section of the applicable statute follows:

(a) Except as herein provided, every article of foreign origin (or its container, as provided in subsection (b) hereof) imported into the United States, shall be marked in a conspicuous place as legibly, indelibly, and permanently as the nature of the article (or container) will permit in such manner as to indicate to an ultimate purchaser in the United States the English name of the country of origin of the article.

Licenses

A second method of conducting international business trade is by licensing agreements. A *license* is a certificate or document that gives permission. Thus a *patent license* gives written authority from the owner of a patent to another person to make or use the patented article for a limited time in a designated territory. License arrangements are particularly advantageous in providing an entry into foreign markets without direct investment. A company may be able to add income to its balance sheet without incurring added research or development expenditures. Some companies that are not willing or able to commit large amounts of capital abroad in fact seem to specialize in licensing.

Usefulness of Licenses

Licensing arrangements may be entered into for patents, copyrights, trademarks, or know-how and technical assistance. A license usually grants to the licensee the right to use, lease, or sell a product that the licensor manufactures domestically. Anyone who has traveled abroad is aware of the franchise type of license agreements used in the hotel (Hilton or Holiday Inns), fast food (McDonald's), and soft drink (Coca-Cola) industries.

Property rights that can be licensed arise from statutory or nonstatutory sources. Statutory sources include patents, trademarks, designs, and copyrights, whereas nonstatutory examples include know-how, technical data, and nonpatentable inventions. Usually more protection is available for the licensing of property rights based on statutory sources, such as patents, than for nonstatutory products or services.

Special Legal Concerns with Licensing Agreements

In addition to a concern with taxation, discussed in the next section, international licensing agreements should be particularly concerned with the governing law, the resolution of disputes, and the effect of the licensing agreement on competition.

The rules for determining the law that will govern the licensing agreement vary from country to country. Frequently the choice of the governing law depends on the place in which any legal action is brought. Most countries enforce a contract provision in which the parties specify in their licensing agreement the law governing any contract dispute.

Disputes between the licensor and licensee may arise regarding the obligation to disclose new techniques affecting the manufacture of a product or the need to maintain quality production standards. Differences regarding the level of support in advertising or expertise given by the licensor to the licensee may occur. While we might expect such differences between parties to a contract to be resolved in courts, most parties to international licensing agreements instead prefer the use of arbitration. *Arbitration* is the voluntary reference of a dispute to one or more arbitrators for final resolution.

The effect of the licensing agreement on competition may be of concern to both the country of the licensor and the country of the licensee. For example, if a U.S. licensor grants to a foreign licensee an exclusive right to manufacture a product that is protected by patent or trademark laws, the licensor should be concerned with U.S. antitrust laws and the effect the agreement has on the foreign commerce of the United States. Conversely, the laws where the licensee is located may prohibit certain provisions in a licensing agreement. Provisions that restrict the flow of technology into the country or that impose on the licensee the obligation to share with the licensor new technologies learned by the licensee are among those that might be prohibited by the country of the licensee.

Taxation of Licenses

The tax effect of a licensing agreement is of significant concern to both the licensor and licensee. The country in which the licensor has a place of business and the country in which the licensee manufactures, uses, or sells the licensed product both will try to obtain a share of the royalty payments provided for by the licensing agreement. In the absence of tax treaties, royalties for licenses are usually subject to income tax in the country of the licensee since the income came from the manufacture, use, or sale of the product in that country (known as the country of source). The tax authorities of the country of source normally require that the licensee withhold the tax due to it prior to any payment of the royalty to the licensor.

After the royalties have been received by the licensor, the royalty income generally is taxed in the country in which the licensor resides (the country of origin since the product or process licensed and for which a royalty is paid originates there). Some countries have sought to avoid such double taxation by concluding tax treaties that either exempt royalty payments from taxation in one of the two countries involved or at least give credit for the tax paid in the country of source. Generally if the licensor is doing business in the country of source or origin by way of permanent establishment (branch, office, factory, warehouse, or other fixed place of business), the royalty is taxed only in the country of source.

INTERNATIONAL BUSINESS: INVESTMENTS

While exporting and licensing arrangements allow a company to derive income from foreign trade without substantial investment, critical legal restraints on those methods of operation may tend to make international investment a more desirable means of conducting international business. Thus in the face of severe import restrictions or local laws that discriminate against foreign products, the only way in which a product may be sold is by directly establishing plants and equipment in those countries.

Similarly, critical business factors affect the need for direct investment as opposed to the international trade options of exporting or licensing. Many U.S. enterprises began direct investment in European countries not only to get inside the tariff walls of the EEC, but also to be able to market their goods more effectively through onsite locations. Transportation expenses often make trade arrangements prohibitively costly; thus investment becomes the most profitable means of selling internationally.

Joint Ventures

For whatever reason, international investments through joint ventures and direct participation are significant methods by which businesses engage in international transactions.

Joint venture investments are those investments with two or more active participants; *direct investments* are those undertaken by a single firm. In the joint venture there is a sharing of contributions by each party as well as a sharing of ownership. For example, a foreign firm may contribute capital and management experience, whereas a local firm may contribute raw material resources and local marketing expertise.

Particular legal problems accompany all such international investments. The laws of the countries in which the operations are conducted, as well as certain aspects of international law, must be closely examined to determine the benefits of international investment.

Whether investing through direct investment or via a joint venture, the laws of the country in which the investment is made are of crucial importance in the organization and operation of the business enterprise.

Other legal sources are superimposed on those national laws. Certain rules of international law, extraterritorial aspects of the laws of the business's country of origin, treaty obligations between the two nations, and relevant rules of international institutions also affect the international investment ventures. Our analysis of some of the laws affecting international investments begins with a review of some of the unique legal problems associated with investing in a joint venture.

A joint venture is a common form used by

companies engaged in international business. It involves a sharing of the ownership of a business enterprise among two or more parties. Unlike the joint venture the direct investment generally places all of the control and management of the new investment operations with one business enterprise. Even if the direct investment involves less than 100 percent ownership of another firm, if the effective manage-

ment and control of the subsidiary is vested in one parent firm, it can be regarded as a direct investment rather than a joint venture. A comparison of these two methods of investment is shown in Figure 47-4.

A joint venture can be compared to a partnership. Each of the parties to the business agrees to cooperate with the other in pursuit of a profitable business that will benefit both par-

FIGURE 47–4
Comparison of Joint Venture and Direct Investment

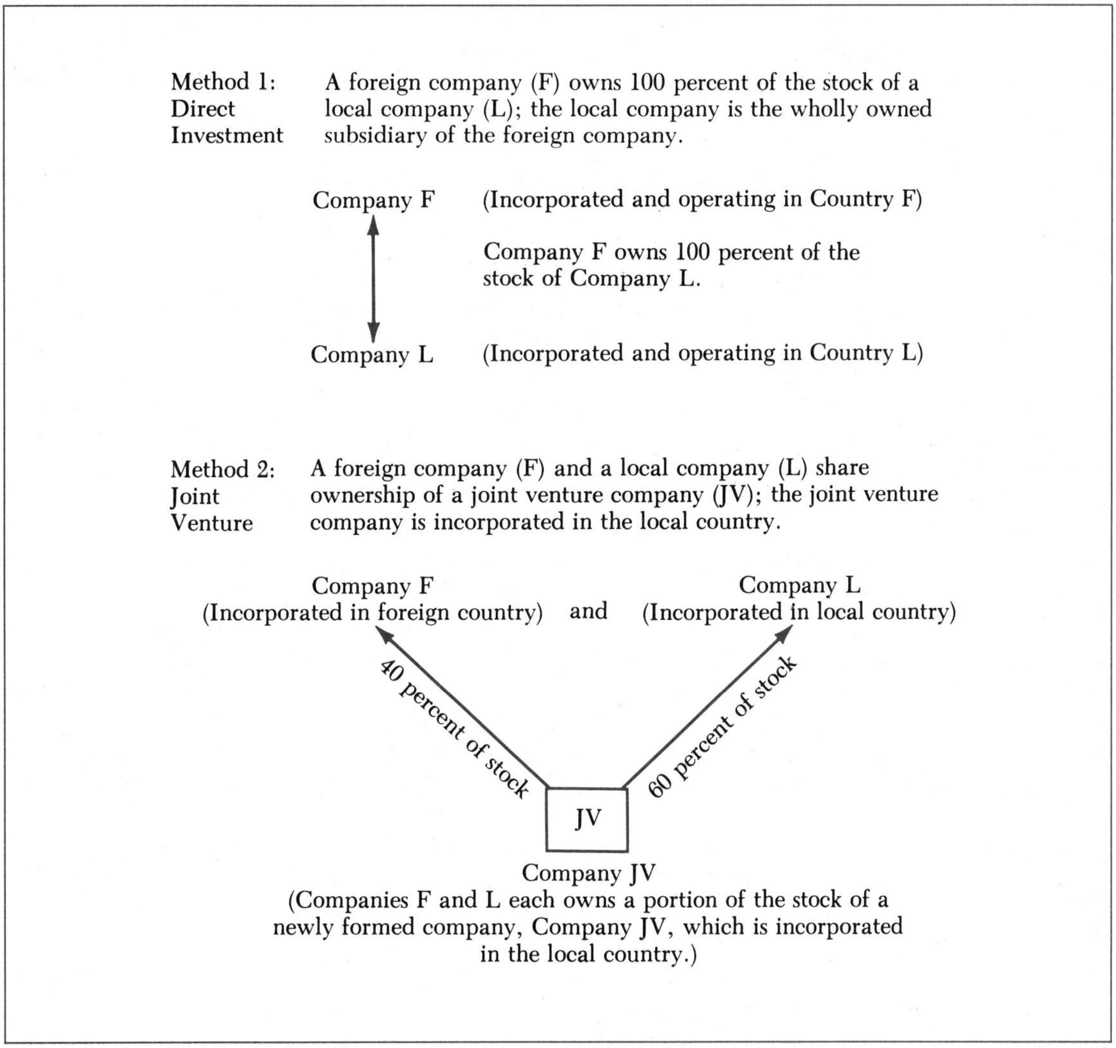

Method 1: Direct Investment — A foreign company (F) owns 100 percent of the stock of a local company (L); the local company is the wholly owned subsidiary of the foreign company.

Company F (Incorporated and operating in Country F)

Company F owns 100 percent of the stock of Company L.

Company L (Incorporated and operating in Country L)

Method 2: Joint Venture — A foreign company (F) and a local company (L) share ownership of a joint venture company (JV); the joint venture company is incorporated in the local country.

Company F (Incorporated in foreign country) and Company L (Incorporated in local country)

40 percent of stock

60 percent of stock

JV

Company JV (Companies F and L each owns a portion of the stock of a newly formed company, Company JV, which is incorporated in the local country.)

ties. However, unlike a partnership, a joint venture is generally limited in scope. The parties are not agreeing to merge all of their activities and ventures into one combined business. Instead, each agrees to do certain things and to cooperate in some areas while still competing as separate firms in other activities.

The General Motors–Toyota agreement to produce cars in California is a joint venture. It is neither a direct investment nor a partnership. If Toyota was purchasing the California plant and running it as a branch or as a subsidiary of Toyota, it would be a direct investment. On the other hand, if Toyota and General Motors agreed to drop their other activities and to work together not only in building these cars, but as partners on other products, they could form a partnership or merge their corporations into one. This venture is more limited in scope. They are to produce one type of car in one plant; the other operations of both Toyota and General Motors are to be kept separate.

While direct investment into wholly owned subsidiaries once was the prevalent method for establishing manufacturing facilities in a foreign country, today rising nationalism has brought about legal restrictions that often prohibit such direct investments. This trend away from participation by direct investment and toward joint ventures with foreign enterprises is not limited to countries in the Communist bloc or to those in Latin America. In recent years investment laws in Mexico, Canada, France, and even to some extent in England have made joint ventures the normal mode for foreign investments in those countries. Conducting international business through joint ventures allows the foreign firm some of the advantages of direct investment without acceptance of all the risks that such direct participation may bring.

Many countries have an investment code that details rather extensively the type of investments welcomed or permitted. Such an investment code generally establishes the degree of capital participation allowed and specifies the required training of local personnel that must accompany any approved investment. In these instances the joint venture is the only permitted form of investment by foreign enterprises in many countries.

Even in the absence of legal restraints that have the effect of forcing the foreign investor to use joint ventures, this method of international investing may be selected. More involved participation by the firm may be too expensive. The political or business risk may be so great, it can only be accepted if shared with some other business. There may be some critical ingredient or assistance that only a partner can provide, such as access to local capital, political contacts, easier recruitment of personnel, broader access to local suppliers, or faster penetration of local or regional markets.

The organization of a joint venture usually requires the parties to prepare and exchange a number of legal documents. A typical list of the documents that might be used would include:

1. A contract between the parties entering into the joint venture
2. Documents necessary to establish a joint corporation, such as the articles of incorporation, bylaws, and shareholder agreements
3. A loan agreement to provide for payment of funds lent by one party to the other to establish the joint venture
4. Patent, trademark, or know-how licensing agreements
5. Management assistance or know-how agreements
6. An export agreement for one party to export supplies, machinery, or parts the venture may need

In some countries, particularly in the Socialist or Communist bloc countries, the government itself must be an owner of any joint venture. There are both advantages and disadvantages to having a foreign government as a joint venture partner. A clear advantage is that the venture is now very likely to obtain the needed licenses and necessary regulatory approval from the governmental agencies that must approve certain of the venture's actions. Disadvantages are found when the governmental participants lack business experience or are subject to being replaced simply because they fall out of favor with the ruling government.

The unique legal problems associated with the international joint venture are primarily those that affect the venture's organization and the relations with the firms that have created it. Whether investing by joint venture or by direct investment, a number of legal sources must be consulted to determine the profitability of the venture. The most prominent legal sources are the laws of the country in which the venture is to operate (the country of source). Since a review of the laws of the country of source is also important to the firm engaged in direct investments, the next section of the text highlights some of the concerns with such laws for both the joint venture and the direct investment in international business.

Direct Investments

The most involved method of conducting international business is by direct investment. Nations have mixed views about granting to foreign firms the right to participate directly in economic activities within their borders. The attitudes toward private foreign investment vary from country to country. The policies adopted are shaped by and reflective of political and economic considerations. A country's historical experiences with foreign investors, the relative state of development of its economy, its need for foreign capital and technology, as well as its political ideology are important considerations in the formation of a country's national policy toward foreign in-

vestment. Significant segments of a country's legal system are relevant to a firm's judgment as to the desirability of engaging in international business through either a joint venture or direct foreign investment.

Of course, economic regulations are a primary consideration. What is the taxation policy of the source country? Are there different labor laws requiring worker representation on a company's board of directors or demanding a certain percentage of the labor force to be from that country? What are the antitrust policies and how are they developing? In direct investment possibilities the entire legal climate must be evaluated. Is expropriation or nationalization a possibility? Are the courts independent of the political framework of the government? Highlights from several legal areas that particularly affect international direct investments will be examined to illustrate the overall concern with the legal system in the source country.

Investment Laws and Policies. Probably the first area for investigation when contemplating international investment is the controlling foreign investment law. In many countries legislation has been enacted to attract foreign investors. Incentives to invest in particular industries, in stipulated depressed geographical locales, or in special programs are common in numerous countries. The devices used are often tax incentives such as tax holidays, increased depreciation, or other benefits aimed at making the tax rate of the country favorable for foreign investors. The DeLorean automobile manufacturing operation located in Ireland due largely to the existence of such tax incentives.

Form of Business Organization. Corporations, rather than partnerships or proprietorships, are the dominant form of business organization for international investments. While state laws in the United States generally do not distinguish between a closely held corporation (with only a few shareholders) and a publicly held corporation (with many shareholders), laws in many other countries have different requirements for those seeking to organize such corporations. In France and Germany, for example, only the limited liability company (the closely held corporation) can impose restrictions on the transfer of shares by corporate shareholders.

Before any final decision is made concerning the specific corporate form to use, the firm seeking to organize such a corporation needs to consider the relationship between the organization used for conducting international activities and the organizing firm itself. This choice normally involves some comparison of the advantages and disadvantages of the branch and subsidiary relationships. One choice would be to organize a separate foreign corporation. When this choice is selected, the foreign corporation is generally established as a subsidiary of the parent firm since the parent firm will own all or most of the shares of stock of the foreign firm.

A second choice would be to forgo the establishment of a separate foreign corporation. If this choice is selected, the foreign operations are treated like the domestic operations and all are performed by and on behalf of the parent corporation. Since the foreign activities are conducted in a different location from that for the corporation's domestic activities, the foreign activities are generally seen as a branch of the domestic ones. Unlike the subsidiary, the branch is not an independent legal entity. Instead, like a branch bank, it is a part of the overall activities of the parent corporation. It will have its own managers and different operations than the parent firm, but is legally seen as a part of the parent corporation.

Figure 47-5 provides a comparison of these two basic methods by which corporate units can be organized.

Exchange Controls. An investment decision is not only concerned with applicable legal provisions regarding investing money in a foreign country, but also with exchange controls that may seek to limit the right to withdraw profits, interest, dividends, or portions of the invested capital. The IMF's Twenty-third Annual Report on exchange restrictions lists 123 countries that have exchange controls and regulations of varying kinds and intensities. Some protection against the most severe restrictions is available to U.S. corporations through treaty provisions and through insurance protection that generally protects business in certain countries against the risk of inability to convert investment receipts from the local currency into dollars.

Tax Considerations. As we have noted, the tax laws in the context of the investment incentives or the form in which to organize a firm should be reviewed. A comprehensive review of both foreign and U.S. tax laws affecting the business's operations, as well as its initial organization, is also necessary. In reviewing the foreign tax laws, the investor must examine not only direct taxes but also indirect taxes. In many countries the indirect taxes, such as the sales tax, turnover tax, or excise tax, account for most of the country's income. Indirect taxes are easier to collect and are not so dependent on a high level of per capita income of the taxpayers as are direct taxes. For example, 67 percent of France's income from taxes is from indirect taxes (turnover tax, tobacco, gas, liquor, and customs).

Municipal or state taxes, as well as national taxes, must be taken into account to determine the real tax burden; in Switzerland, for example, the municipal tax on corporate income is far more significant than is the federal tax. Finally, tax treaties often play an important role in determining the tax burden in effect for a particular transaction. Often such treaties do much to alleviate double taxation that each country might otherwise impose and to simplify conflicting or overlapping tax provisions of the country of source (the country where the income will be produced) and the country of

FIGURE 47–5

Comparison of a Branch and a Foreign Subsidiary of a U.S. Corporation

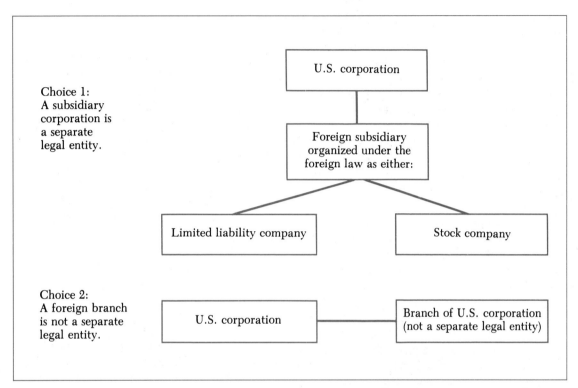

Choice 1:
A subsidiary
corporation is
a separate
legal entity.

U.S. corporation

Foreign subsidiary
organized under the
foreign law as either:

Limited liability company

Stock company

Choice 2:
A foreign branch
is not a separate
legal entity.

U.S. corporation

Branch of U.S. corporation
(not a separate legal entity)

origin (the country that invested the capital to make the income possible).

Labor Laws. Labor laws influence any foreign investment, as they affected the decision of some domestic companies once operating in northern states to move into southern states that had fewer labor unions and lower wage rates. The labor laws that affect the investment deal not only with any minimum or prevailing wage laws, but also with provisions regarding hours of work, workmen's compensation, retirement benefits, and vacation bonuses. Bonuses of one month or less are required by legislation or practice in most European countries for both salaried and hourly workers. In Japan, bonuses of one month or more are awarded to most Japanese workers in July and December and are usually as much as two to six months in pay. Severance pay-

ments required to accompany notice of termination are expected or legislated in many countries.

A worker may have a vested right to his or her job; Mexican and Colombian laws restrict the right of an employer to discharge a worker except for carefully prescribed conditions. Local laws often require all foreign workers to obtain work permits. Further, a minimum percentage of the labor force may be required to be local nationals. Saudi Arabian law requires all foreigners working in the country to obtain work permits; the law also requires all companies employing foreigners to employ 75 percent Saudi nationals, with a total of 51 percent of the total payroll being paid to nationals.

Safety of Investment from Expropriation or Nationalization. Expropriation or nationalization occurs when a country takes over the ownership and management of private firms. While the terms are often used interchangeably, *nationalization* is often used in situations where the government pays compensation to the former owner, whereas *expropriation* occurs where no such compensation is paid. In 1982 France nationalized many banks operating in France, both foreign and domestically owned, whereas in the 1960s and 1970s Cuba expropriated many banks operating in Cuba.

Available legal protection against risk of expropriation may be a consideration where a sizable investment is contemplated. Such protection may be available from a variety of sources. The local investment code may have express nonexpropriation guarantees. Treaties signed by some foreign countries and by the United States indicate agreement as to the standard for "reasonable compensation." Certainly insurance protection offered through U.S. agencies such as the Export–Import Bank, the Foreign Credit Insurance Association, and the Office of Private Investment Controls should be examined if there is any danger regarding the safety of one's investment from expropriation or nationalization.

Antitrust Laws. Firms operating in the United States, whether of domestic or foreign origin, have long been aware of the possible effect of antitrust laws on their business operations. Antitrust laws aim at preserving a relatively free system of competition by controlling anticompetitive practices and attempting to regulate the growth and use of economic power. The basic provisions of the key U.S. statute, the Sherman Act, are as follows:

Section 1: Every contract, combination in the form of trust or otherwise, or conspiracy, in restraint of trade or commerce among the several states, or *with foreign* nations, is declared to be illegal. . . .

Section 2: Every person who shall monopolize, or attempt to monopolize, or combine or conspire with any other person or persons, to monopolize any part of the trade or commerce among the several States, or *with foreign* nations, shall be deemed guilty of a felony. . . .

It is clear from the italicized references both in Sections 1 and 2 that the U.S. antitrust law has an extraterritorial reach; that is, it applies not only to transactions taking place within the United States but also to contracts ". . . in restraint of trade or commerce . . . with foreign nations." Most of the cases, such as the *Timberlane* Case found on page 1251, which have applied U.S. antitrust law in international transactions, have involved allegations of restraints on competition occurring, at least in part, outside the United States. Those activities violate U.S. law if they have had an adverse effect on competition and commerce in the United States.

Although U.S. antitrust law has had the most influence on international business transactions, antitrust laws were enacted in most major European countries after World War II. Those national laws subsequently have been supplemented and to some extent replaced by Article 85–90 of the Rome Treaty creating the EEC. Article 85 of the Treaty of Rome prohibits practices and agreements that restrict or distort competition within the EEC between member states. Furthermore, the EEC has clearly indicated that the Article also applies to extraterritorial activities that affect trade or commerce in the member states even if one of the parties is outside the EEC.

Trademarks and Patents. Intimately connected with antitrust provisions is the legal protection afforded trademarks and patents. It is not surprising that these legal areas often overlap. Whereas antitrust law is antimonopolistic, patent law gives a limited monopoly to a certain process, product, or design, and trademark law gives a limited monopoly to a symbol or word.

Trademarks designate the source or origin of a product, whereas patents give to the owner a monopoly over its manufacture, sale, or use. The consumer of trademarked goods often does not know the name of the manufacturer of a trademarked item; the mark merely identifies that all goods with that mark have come from the same source. The golden arches, Ronald McDonald, the "Big Mac," and other names and symbols are all trademarks and trade names used by one producer. Obviously with the expansion of international business operations, an owner of a trademarked item (McDonald's, Coca-Cola, Hilton Hotel) or of a patent will seek to have that legal protection extended internationally. A *patent* confers rights that are protected only within the boundaries of the country issuing the patent. Thus a U.S. and a Canadian patent, even when granted for the same invention, create separate and distinct rights that may differ in scope and effect in each country.

In the same manner, U.S. courts have held that a foreign patent confers upon its owner no rights or protection with respect to acts done in the United States. Today every country has its own distinct set of patent laws and regulations.

Some of these differences can be noted briefly. Under U.S. patent laws, inventors are not required to use or permit others to use their patent; they do not have to pay taxes to maintain it; they are not compelled to grant licenses to others unless they misuse their patents. In some other nations many of these obligations must be performed to maintain a patent's validity.

As in the United States, Britain, Germany, and Holland, a thorough examination as to novelty and patentability is required. In Belgium, France, Italy, Austria, Switzerland, and Spain, there is little or no examination and the validity is left for the courts to determine. In Japan, in order to be patentable, an invention must be capable of being used in industry; thus patents are available for typical methods of doing business, such as methods of advertising. In the United States no taxes are imposed to maintain the patent. In many nations a tax or annuity fee must be paid to maintain the patent. If the taxes are not paid when due, the patent is considered abandoned.

The principal international agreement relating to patents is the International Convention for the Protection of Industrial Property (Paris Union). Over ninety nations, including the United States, are members of the International Convention. The Paris Union contains no provisions that directly affect the substantive aspects of national patent law. Instead, it creates uniformity by allowing applicants in one country to apply subsequently for protection in other countries. If a person in one nation files an application in another country, within twelve months of the original filing that person is entitled to priority based on the original filing date. Such protection is granted to any person domiciled in one country or any firm having a place of business in a member country.

REVIEW PROBLEMS

1. Describe the four methods of conducting international business and explain how each method differs from the others.
2. Discuss the various methods by which imports can be discouraged.
3. Give an example of a U.S. law, other than the antitrust laws, that can be applied to conduct occurring outside the United States.
4. Why would a company sometimes prefer

ETHICS BOX
International Ethics

——

Do ethical standards vary between nations? Italians take a different approach to paying taxes. Does that mean that while in Italy behaving as the Italians behave constitutes ethical behavior? The issue is one of ethical relativism. To what extent can each society define for itself what is ethical?

Certainly it makes sense to follow local customs such as removing shoes when entering a house, or not serving alcoholic beverages at business gatherings. But, as discussed in Chapter 4, if the local practice violates universal or fundamental ethical principles, then it can be condemned as unethical even though it is accepted by the society. Thus apartheid can be condemned because it violates fundamental principles.

Complying with Italian tax law presents a very difficult question. Here the law on the books says that the tax must be paid. But the actual practice is not to report all of the income and thus not to pay the full amount owing. Legal realists might support not paying the full tax on the grounds that the actual law is determined by the way in which it is enforced. Under that approach, having accurate information about what constitutes acceptable practice becomes critically important.

---

to invest in a foreign operation through a joint venture rather than through direct investment?

5. Assume your company manufactures parts for certain industrial machinery and you are considering establishing a manufacturing plant in West Germany. What specific German laws would you examine before you committed to make such an investment?

6. If you were to consider a joint venture with a Czechoslovakian company rather than a direct investment in West Germany, what special legal concerns other than those mentioned in your answer in Problem 5 would you want to examine?

7. What considerations lead a company to organize its foreign business activities into either a branch or subsidiary form?

8. Explain the differences and similarities in the Act of State and the doctrine of Sovereign Immunity. Give one example of the possible application of each concept.

9. Eurim is a small West German firm that distributes worldwide brand name drugs manufactured by multinational pharmaceutical manufacturers. Pfizer is a multinational pharmaceutical corporation headquartered in the United States. It had a patent on one of the drugs it manufactured and after its patent expired, Pfizer granted an exclusive license to several manufacturers in each of its major foreign markets to produce that drug.

The manufacturers agreed to restrict their sales to specific geographic areas assigned by Pfizer and to sell the drug at prices Pfizer established. Eurim claims

Pfizer's practices have increased the worldwide price of its drug and made it difficult for Eurim to sell that drug either in Germany or in the United States. Eurim claims Pfizer's price-fixing agreements violate U.S. antitrust law. Do you think Eurim can prove the antitrust case against Pfizer? Eurim v. Pfizer, 593 F.Supp. 1102 (N.Y. 1984)

10. The United States has entered into a tax treaty with Switzerland that provides that an individual resident of Switzerland is exempt from U.S. tax on compensation received for labor or personal services performed in the United States if he or she is temporarily present in the United States for less than 183 days and received compensation for labor or services performed as an employee or agent of a corporation or other entity of Switzerland.

Ingemar Johansson, a Swedish citizen, fought Floyd Patterson three times for the heavyweight championship of the world, each time in the United States. All three fights occurred between December 1, 1959 and March 1, 1961. When the IRS claimed Johansson owed it approximately one million dollars in tax payments, Johansson claimed he was a resident of Switzerland and thus was exempt from U.S. taxes. Johansson argues:

a. Switzerland has classified him as a resident.
b. He entered into a contract on December 1, 1959 with a Swiss corporation and was employed by it for the entire period through March 1961.

The IRS argues:

a. Johansson resided in Switzerland only 80 days compared to the 120 days he spent in Sweden and 217 days he spent in the United States during this period.
b. Johansson was the sole employee of the Swiss corporation and his revenue was its sole source of income.

Who is correct and why? Johansson v. United States, 336 F.2d 809 (5th Cir. 1964)

11. Taca International Airlines, a San Salvador corporation, sued Rolls-Royce of England, Ltd., a British corporation, for negligence causing damage to its airplanes. Taca brought suit against the English corporation in New York by serving a summons on Rolls-Royce, Inc., a U.S. subsidiary corporation incorporated in and doing business in the United States. Rolls-Royce Ltd. maintains that the New York court does not have jurisdiction over it since its products in the United States, including the engine sold to Taca, are sold and serviced only by its subsidiary, R.R. Inc. Do you agree? Taca International Airlines v. Rolls-Royce of England, Ltd. 204 N.E.2d 329. (N.Y. 1965)

12. What relationship or activities performed by a U.S.-based multinational chemical corporation, such as Union Carbide Inc., would make it liable for damages to persons killed or seriously injured from an explosion in a foreign country from a factory owned by one of its foreign subsidiary corporations? In Re Union Carbide Corporation Gas Plant Disaster 6347. F.Supp. 842 (1986)

CHAPTER 48

Accountant's Liability

THE ROLE OF GAAP AND GAAS

An accountant's potential liability to third parties, once tightly restricted by the privity-of-contract requirement, has been expanded in recent years. An accountant's exposure to criminal liability has also expanded. This chapter traces the legal developments affecting accountants and their profession.

Accountant's liability is an important topic in business law today. Increasingly accounting firms are sued when there have been financial misdealings resulting in bankruptcy or violations of the securities laws. It is important that both certified public accountants (CPAs) and managers understand the legal principles that govern the accountant–client relationship.

There are several ways in which public accountants can incur liability in the practice of their profession. Failure to meet the standards of an employment contract will expose an accountant to contract liability (see the general discussion of contractual liability in Part II of

this text). Theories of intentional tort and negligence (discussed in Chapters 3 and 4) can also provide the basis for a suit against an accountant who has performed improperly. In addition to common-law actions, there are various federal and state statutes that impose both civil and criminal liability on accountants. Table 48-1 summarizes the basic sources of accountants' liability.

The American Institute of Certified Public Accountants (AICPA), the professional association of CPAs, has promulgated principles and standards to guide accountants in their practice. Accountants are expected to comply with generally accepted accounting principles (GAAP) and generally accepted auditing standards (GAAS). Evidence of compliance or noncompliance with these principles can be used to determine whether the accountant exercised the degree of skill and care required.

While compliance with GAAP and GAAS can substantially reduce the likelihood that an accountant will be subject to liability, compliance is not in itself a complete defense. Thus

TABLE 48-1 SOURCES OF ACCOUNTANT'S LIABILITY

Source	Liability To	
Common law	Client	Third party/public
Contract	Yes	No
Fraud	Yes	Yes
Negligence	Yes	In some states, to foreseen users
Gross negligence	Yes	In some states, to foreseen or foreseeable users
Statutory law (civil liability)		
Securities Act of 1933		Buyers and sellers of securities
Securities Exchange Act of 1934		Buyers and sellers of securities
Statutory law (criminal liability)		Federal government
Both Securities Acts		Federal government enforces these criminal statutes.
Internal Revenue Code		
False Statements Act		
Mail Fraud Act		
Conspiracy Statute		

the court in *U.S.* v. *Simon* (excerpted later in this chapter), in affirming the convictions of accountants who had apparently adhered to GAAP, stated:

> Generally accepted accounting principles instruct an accountant what to do in the usual case where he has no reason to doubt that the affairs of the corporation are being honestly conducted. Once he has reason to believe that this basic assumption is false, an entirely different situation confronts him.

Accountants' common-law civil liability to clients can be grounded in contract or in tort. The choice of theories on which to sue can be especially important when the statute of limitations for contract actions differs from that for tort actions. In many contract suits and in all tort actions the plaintiff will be required to show that the defendant accountant failed to satisfy a required standard of care. Accountants are expected to exercise "reasonable care and competence." In *Kemmerlin* v. *Wingate*, the Supreme Court defined this standard as the care and competence normally exercised by accountants in the particular locality, ac-

cording to accepted professional standards. Since lay persons generally do not possess knowledge of this standard, a plaintiff must produce expert testimony to establish the standard of care allegedly breached.

CONTRACT LIABILITY

An accountant's liability to a client is usually based in some way on the contract with the client. Violation of the agreement's terms can give rise to an action for breach of contract. A breach-of-contract action can be based on violations of either the express or implied terms of the contract.

If an accountant expressly agrees to prepare and file a client's tax returns by April 15 and then misses the deadline, an express term of the agreement has been violated. The accountant can be held liable to the client for any penalties resulting from the late filing.

If the accountant commits careless errors that cause the client to suffer losses, the client again has an action in breach of contract. This is true even though the contract is silent regarding the standard of care to which the accountant must adhere. Every accountant is impliedly bound, in the performance of a contract, to exercise that degree of skill and competence commonly exercised by members of the profession.

An accountant is also, of course, impliedly bound to perform his or her services without fraud. In the following case an accounting firm was held liable for breach of contract because its employee had helped defraud its client.

In the Matter of F. W. Koenecke and Sons, Inc.

U.S. Court of Appeals, Seventh Circuit
605 F.2d 924 (1979)

Background: Heyman (plaintiff) sued Wilkes, Birnie, Kahler, and Koenecke (defendants), alleging attempt to defraud Heyman as creditor of a bankrupt firm. F. W. Koenecke and Sons, a cigarette distributor, ceased operations in February 1969 after declaring bankruptcy. Shortly before the firm shut down, company president Robert Koenecke caused $315,000 in checks to be drawn on the corporation's account. The checks were payable to Koenecke and to Clifford Kahler, the sales manager. Glenn Heyman, the company's trustee in bankruptcy, retained the accounting firm of James T. Wilkes and Company to complete the company's books for February and March. Wilkes put staff accountant Alex Birnie in charge of the matter. Apparently unbeknown to Wilkes, Birnie was also employed by Koenecke. Birnie made false entries into the books in order to conceal the fact that $315,000 had been paid to Koenecke and Kahler.

After discovering the fraud two years later, Heyman sued Wilkes, Birnie, Kahler, and Koenecke in bankruptcy court. The case excerpt focuses on the liability of the Wilkes accounting firm.

Decision: Bankruptcy court judgment against Wilkes was initially reversed by the federal District Court. The U.S. Court of Appeals for the Seventh Circuit reaffirmed the bankruptcy court's original finding that Wilkes was in fact liable for breach of contract.

Bauer, Circuit Judge

The first major issue in this appeal is whether the district court correctly concluded that the Wilkes accounting group is not liable to the trustee for breach of contract. In reversing the bankruptcy judge on this issue, the lower court relied on several findings, the most significant of which are: (1) the fraudulent entries were made by Birnie before Wilkes was hired by the trustee; (2) Wilkes did not have a contractual duty to check the accuracy of pre-existing entries since it was hired only to "update" the records; and (3) Birnie's conduct cannot be imputed to Wilkes since he was acting for his own purposes when he made the fraudulent entries.

We see no significance, however, in the date of the fraudulent entries, for it is clear that Birnie not only failed to disclose the false entries *after* Wilkes was hired, but indeed committed two specific acts in furtherance of the fraud. On April 10, 1969, he personally caused the $200,000 check to be endorsed over to Kahler, and on May 6, 1969, he deposited the proceeds of that check in his "nominee" account at the First National Bank of Chicago Heights.

If this conduct can be imputed to Wilkes, it would constitute, in our view, a breach of Wilkes' contractual obligations to the trustees. We think it clear that the terms of the contract contemplated that Wilkes would complete or correct any entries in the Koenecke books that were known to be incorrect—or, at the very least, that Wilkes would commit no acts in furtherance of a fraud on the estate. Accordingly, the key issue is whether liability for Birnie's conduct can be imputed to Wilkes under the applicable law of agency.

On this point, we held in *Securities Exchange Commission v. First Securities Co. of Chicago* (1972), that the Illinois courts would follow Section 261 of the Restatement of the Law of Agency, Second (1958), which provides:

> "A principal who puts a servant or other agent in a position which enables the agent, while apparently acting within his authority, to commit fraud upon third persons is subject to liability to such third persons for the fraud."

It is our view that Section 261 is controlling in this case, for Wilkes clearly authorized Birnie to discharge its contractual obligations and thereby placed him in a position that enabled him to continue the fraud while apparently acting within his authority. We therefore hold that Wilkes is liable to the trustee for breach of contract.

Wilkes argues, however, that even if it did breach a contractual duty, the damages claimed by the trustee did not result from that breach. It is apparently Wilkes' position that it did not cause the loss of the $315,000 since the money was taken by Kahler and Koenecke before it was hired to update the books. But if Birnie had properly discharged Wilkes' contractual duties and disclosed the fraudulent entries to the trustee, the court could have easily placed the funds under its control before they were dissipated. We thus find no merit in Wilkes' claim that its breach of contract did not result in the loss of the $315,000. Accordingly, we reverse the district court's judgment on this issue, and in addition, find Wilkes liable for pre-judgment interest from the date the action was filed.

TORT LIABILITY

In a contract action against an accountant the parties' rights and obligations are primarily determined by their own agreement. The parties' rights and liabilities in a tort action are determined by the common law or by statute. Recall from Chapter 4 that tort liability is founded upon the breach of duties imposed by society. The breach can be unintentional, as in the case of negligence, or deliberate, as with fraud. We will consider accountants' liability for both unintentional and intentional torts.

Negligence

As in other negligence actions, a client suing an accountant for negligence must establish (1) that the accountant owed the client a *duty of care*; (2) that the accountant *breached this duty*; (3) that the client suffered an *injury*; and (4) that the accountant's breach was the *proximate cause* of the client's injury.

The accountant's duty of care to a client generally originates in the contract between them. The accountant's obligations in tort law are thus organically linked to obligations in contract law. As with other professionals, accountants have a general duty to perform services with the level of "skill, care, knowledge and judgment usually possessed and exercised by members of that profession in the particular locality, in accordance with accepted professional standards and in good faith. . . ."

Other Torts

Accountants can also be held liable to their clients for intentional torts. Perhaps the most common action is one alleging fraud. Recall from Chapter 13 that fraud involves a material misrepresentation of fact, made with knowledge of its falsity and with intent to deceive. To collect damages for fraud, a plaintiff must prove personal reliance on the misrepresentation and that the reliance caused injury. Since accountants' opinions are representations, they can be used as the basis for fraud actions.

THE EFFECT OF ACCOUNTANTS' OPINIONS

After auditing a company's financial statements, an accountant will issue an *opinion.* An accountant's opinion is a representation to those who can reasonably be expected to rely on the financial statements.

By expressing an *unqualified opinion,* an accountant represents that the company's financial statements fairly reflect the company's financial picture; that is, the balance sheet properly presents the firm's financial position, the income statement fairly represents the results of the firm's operations, and changes in financial position are accurately depicted. An unqualified opinion requires that the financial statements reflect the consistent application of GAAP.

An accountant who is unable to express an unqualified opinion is required to issue either a *qualified opinion,* which can be necessitated by material uncertainty or deviations from GAAP; an *adverse opinion,* which states that the financial statements do not fairly present the firm's position in conformance with the GAAP; or a *disclaimer of opinion,* which is issued when the accountant lacks sufficient information to form an opinion on the accuracy of the audited statements.

Accountants may sometimes prepare or analyze financial documents without conducting a full-blown audit. In such circumstances accountants rely on the client's financial records without investigating their accuracy. The AICPA has developed the concepts of *compilations* and *reviews* to protect accountants from unwarranted reliance on such documents. In a *compilation* the accountant puts information supplied by the client into the form of financial statements. The compilation should be accompanied by a report explaining that no audit has been performed and that the accuracy of the information cannot be assured. Each page of the compiled financial statements should contain a printed reference directing the reader to the disclaiming report. A *review* involves a limited analysis of financial statements that have been prepared by the client. In a review the accountant expresses limited assurance that the financial statements are not materially misleading. In an accompanying report, which must be referred to on each page of the statements, the accountant states that the analysis conducted in the review was substantially less than that for a proper audit.

Although qualifications and disclaimers can limit an accountant's liability in certain tort actions, they will not in themselves relieve the accountant of contractual obligations.

LIABILITY OF TAX PREPARERS

Accountants can expose themselves to contract or tort liability in the preparation of cli-

ETHICS BOX
Accountants' Professional Responsibility

———

The practice of accountancy is a recognized profession. Entry into the accounting field is controlled through educational requirements and an exam. Standards are developed and enforced by the profession and the license to practice may be revoked under certain circumstances.

As with all professions, the question may be raised whether the minimal levels for professional conduct should be determined primarily by the profession itself. On the pro side is the argument that the professionals themselves better understand the technical intricacies of their field and have greater depth of knowledge. They also have a strong incentive to self-regulate because the public is often unable to judge the quality of individual practitioners, and incompetents and wrong-doers must be weeded out in order to maintain the reputation of the accounting profession.

On the other hand, the practice of a profession is a business and the professionals may often be accused of looking out for themselves in assuming all the power of regulation of their practice. Critics of professional self-regulation point to "ethics" rules that formerly prohibited competition in fees (these have been struck down by antitrust actions brought against the profession itself) and still do restrict advertising.

As emphasized in this chapter, the law poses an outer bound on the actions of accountants. Yet the law is not entirely independent in that many cases make reference to and rely on the self-created standards of the profession in deciding to impose liability. At times the courts have been handicapped by a "conspiracy of silence" in which the most qualified professionals refused to step forward and testify against colleagues.

———

ents' tax returns. Accountants can be held liable for damages resulting from the late filing of clients' returns, from negligent misstatement of tax liability, and from erroneous tax advice. In *Whitlock* v. *PKW Supply* Co. [269 S.E.2d 36 (Ga. Ct. App. 1980)] an accountant was held liable for breach of contract for refusing to either file or return the client's tax returns until the bill was paid. The court noted that the accountant could also have been held liable for the tort of nonfeasance, for failing to attempt to perform as promised.

In preparing taxes, as in an accountant's other duties, an accountant is required to exercise the degree of care, skill, and competence exercised by others in the profession. Breach of this duty can leave the accountant liable for compensatory damages, which are commonly penalties and interest assessed against the client because of the tax preparer's mistake. Tax preparers are sometimes also required to compensate clients for fees paid to attorneys and/or other accountants to straighten out the tax preparer's error.

A tax preparer can also be subject to civil and criminal liability under the provisions of the Internal Revenue Code. This will be discussed later in the chapter.

GOVERNMENT ACCESS TO ACCOUNTANTS' RECORDS

The Supreme Court has upheld the right of an authorized government agency to obtain an accountant's records in the investigation of a client. The Court has thus held that the accountant–client relationship, unlike the attorney–client relationship, is not a privileged one. It is now settled that requiring delivery of an accountant's records to an appropriate government agency does not violate the client's constitutional right against compulsory self-incrimination. This doctrine is set forth in the *Couch* case, which follows.

Couch v. United States

U.S. Supreme Court
409 U.S. 322 (1973)

Background: In a tax investigation of a restaurant owner (petitioner) the IRS summoned the records of her accountant. The restaurant owner had been giving the records to her accountant over the years for the purpose of preparing her tax returns. After the summons was issued, she sought to prevent the records from being turned over to the IRS, claiming that enforcing the summons would violate her Fifth Amendment right against compulsory self-incrimination. She also argued that the accountant–client relationship has the privilege of confidentiality. The U.S. District Court and the Court of Appeals rejected those claims, holding that the summons was valid.
Decision: The Supreme Court affirmed.

Powell, Justice

It is important to reiterate that the Fifth Amendment privilege is a *personal* privilege: it adheres basically to the person, not to information that may incriminate him. As Mr. Justice Holmes put it: "A party is privileged from producing the evidence but not from its production." The Constitution explicitly prohibits compelling an accused to bear witness "against himself"; it necessarily does not proscribe incriminating statements elicited from another. Compulsion upon the person asserting it is an important element of the privilege, and "prohibition of compelling a man . . . to be witness against himself is a prohibition of the use of physical or moral compulsion to extort communications from *him.*" It is extortion of information from the accused himself that offends our sense of justice.

In the case before us the ingredient of personal compulsion against an accused is lacking. The summons and the order of the District Court enforcing it are directed against the accountant. He, not the taxpayer, is the only one compelled to do anything. And the accountant makes no claim that he may tend to be incriminated by the production. Inquisitorial pressure or coercion against a potentially accused person, compelling her, against her will, to utter self-condemning words or produce incriminating documents is absent.

The divulgence of potentially incriminating evidence against petitioner is naturally unwelcome. But the petitioner's distress would be no less if the divulgence came not from her accountant but from some other third party with whom she was connected and who possessed substantially equivalent knowledge of her business affairs. The basic complaint of petitioner stems from the fact of divulgence of the possibly incriminating information, not from the manner in which or the person from whom it was extracted. Yet such divulgence, where it does not result from coercion of the suspect herself, is a necessary part of the process of law enforcement and tax investigation.

. . .

Petitioner further argues that the confidential nature of the accountant–client relationship and her resulting expectation of privacy in delivering the records protect her, under the Fourth and Fifth Amendments, from their production. Although not itself controlling, we note that no confidential accountant–client privilege has been recognized in federal cases. Nor is there justification for such a privilege where records relevant to income tax returns are involved in a criminal investigation or prosecution . . . there can be little expectation of privacy where records are handed to an accountant, knowing that mandatory disclosure of much of the information therein is required in an income tax return. What information is not disclosed is largely in the accountant's discretion, not petitioner's. Indeed, the accountant himself risks criminal prosecution if he willfully assists in the preparation of a false return. His own need for self-protection would often require the right to disclose the information given him. Petitioner seeks extensions of constitutional protections against self-incrimination in the very situation where obligations of disclosure exist and under a system largely dependent upon honest self-reporting even to survive. Accordingly, petitioner here cannot reasonably claim, either for Fourth or Fifth Amendment purposes, an expectation of protected privacy or confidentiality.

We hold today that no Fourth or Fifth Amendment claim can prevail where, as in this case, there exists no legitimate expectation of privacy and no semblance of governmental compulsion against the person of the accused.

The *Couch* case upheld the right of the IRS to summon from an accountant records owned by a client. It would seem to follow from that holding that the IRS would have similar access to the workpapers an accountant uses to evaluate a client's tax liability.

Despite the *Couch* ruling, however, the U.S. Court of Appeals for the Second Circuit devised a doctrine of accountant's work-product immunity from disclosure. In the 1982 case of *U.S.* v. *Arthur Young and Co.* [677 F.2d 211 (2d Cir. 1982)] the Second Circuit held that protecting the confidentiality of accountants' work was necessary to promote full disclosure by clients to accountants. This disclosure, the court reasoned, was necessary to protect the integrity of the securities markets, which depended on complete and accurate information from their participants. The court thus developed a doctrine for accountants similar to the work-product immunity that applies to attorneys.

But the doctrine of accountants' work-product immunity had a short life. In 1982 the Supreme Court granted the government's petition for certiorari. In its opinion, which follows, the Court relied on the *Couch* decision to reject the doctrine of work-product immunity.

United States v. Arthur Young and Co.

U.S. Supreme Court

465 U.S. 805 (1984)

Background: The IRS sued the accounting firm of Arthur Young and Co. (respondent), an independent auditor for the Amerada Hess Corporation, to obtain files and work-papers relating to Amerada's tax returns. One of Young's functions was to evaluate the adequacy of Amerada's reserve account for contingent tax liabilities. The reserve account was required to cover tax liabilities that might later be assessed by the IRS over and above those reflected on the corporation's return.

After a routine IRS audit revealed questionable financial practices on the part of the corporation, the IRS initiated a criminal investigation of its tax returns. The IRS issued a summons to Young commanding that it hand over its Amerada files, including workpapers. At Amerada's request, Young refused to honor the summons. The IRS sued in federal District Court to enforce the summons.

The District Court ruled in favor of the IRS. The Court of Appeals for the Second Circuit, in reversing the lower court's decision with regard to the workpapers, fashioned a doctrine of work-product immunity for accountants.

Decision: The Supreme Court ruled that the summons was enforceable.

Burger, Chief Justice

[The Court's review of the facts is omitted.]

The Court of Appeals . . . concluded that "substantial countervailing policies" required the fashioning of a work-product immunity for an independent auditor's tax accrual workpapers. To the extent that the Court of Appeals, in its concern for the "chilling effect" of the disclosure of tax accrual workpapers, sought to facilitate communication between independent auditors and their clients, its remedy more closely resembles a testimonial accountant–client privilege than a work-product immunity for accountants' workpapers. But as this Court stated in *Couch* v. *United States,* "no confidential accountant–client privilege exists under federal law, and no state-created privilege has been recognized in federal cases." In light of *Couch,* the Court of Appeals' effort to foster candid communication between accountant and client by creating a self-styled work-product privilege was misplaced, and conflicts with what we see as the clear intent of Congress.

Nor do we find persuasive the argument that a work-product immunity for accountants' tax accrual workpapers is a fitting analogue to the attorney work-product doctrine established in *Hickman* v. *Taylor.* The *Hickman* work-product doctrine was founded upon the private attorney's role as the client's confidential advisor and advocate, a loyal representative whose duty it is to present the client's case in the most favorable possible light. An independent certified public accountant performs a different role. By certifying the public reports that collectively depict a corporation's financial status, the independent auditor assumes a *public* responsibility transcending any employment relationship with the client. The independent public accountant performing this special function owes ultimate allegiance to the corporation's creditors and stockholders, as well as to investing public. This "public watchdog" function demands that the accountant maintain total independence from the client at all times and requires complete fidelity to the public trust. To insulate from disclosure a certified public accountant's interpretations of the client's financial statements would be to ignore the significance of the accountant's role as a disinterested analyst charged with public obligations.

We cannot accept the view that the integrity of the securities markets will suffer absent some protection for accountants' tax accrual workpapers. The Court of Appeals apparently feared that, were the IRS to have access to tax accrual workpapers, a corporation might be tempted to withhold from its auditor certain information relevant and material to the proper evaluation of its financial statements. But the independent certified public accountant cannot be content with the corporation's representations that its tax accrual reserves are adequate; the auditor is ethically and professionally obligated to ascertain for himself as far as possible whether the corporation's contingent tax liabilities have been accurately stated. If the auditor were convinced that the scope of the examination had been limited by management's reluctance to disclose matters relating to the tax accrual reserves, the auditor would be unable to issue an unqualified opinion as to the accuracy of the corporation's financial statements. Instead, the auditor would be required to issue a qualified opinion, an adverse opinion, or a disclaimer of opinion, thereby notifying the investing public of possible potential problems inherent in the corporation's financial reports. Responsible corporate management would not risk a qualified evaluation of a corporate taxpayer's financial posture to afford cover for questionable positions reflected in a prior tax return. Thus, the independent auditor's obligation to serve the public interest assures that the integrity of the securities markets will be preserved, without the need for a work-product immunity for accountants' tax accrual workpapers.

Congress has granted to the IRS "broad latitude to adopt enforcement techniques helpful in the performance of [its] tax collection and assessment responsibilities." Recognizing the intrusiveness of demands for the production of tax accrual workpapers, the IRS has demonstrated administrative sensitivity to the concerns expressed by the accounting profession by tightening its internal requirements for the issuance of such summonses.

Beyond question it is desirable and in the public interest to encourage full disclosures by corporate clients to their independent accountants; if it is necessary to balance competing interests, however, the need of the Government for full disclosure of all information relevant to tax liability must also weigh in that balance. This kind of policy choice is best left to the Legislative Branch. Accordingly, the judgment of the Court of Appeals is reversed in part, and the case is remanded.

LIABILITY TO THIRD PARTIES

Clients are not the only parties that rely on accountants' work. A potential creditor will rely on a company's financial statements to evaluate the riskiness of a contemplated loan. A potential purchaser of a firm will examine its balance sheet to determine the value of the assets and the extent of the liabilities that would be assumed. A potential buyer of a

FIGURE 48–1
Open-Ended Scope of Accountants' Potential Liability

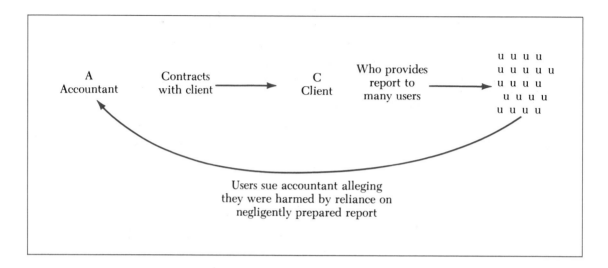

firm's securities will use the firm's prospectus and other financial data to make the purchase decision. A potential assignee of a debt will want to determine the collectibility of that debt before exchanging something of value for the assignment.

In deciding how far to extend an accountant's liability to third parties, the law must reconcile conflicting policy interests. On the one hand, it would appear that the efficient operation of credit markets, securities markets, and other markets would require that participants be entitled to rely on the relevant information available to them. If participants in these markets are forced to assume the risks associated with inaccurate information, they will demand compensation for that risk in the marketplace. An economist would argue that it is most efficient to place the risk on the party with the power to control the risk. In our case the accountant would be one of the parties best able to control the risks to third parties of inaccurate information.

On the other hand, the accountant might not be able to bear the risk of liability to every third party that could conceivably be hurt by reliance on a financial document prepared by the accountant. For one thing there is no clear way to control the number of people who rely on particular financial documents since clients are the ones that distribute the documents. If a negligent mistake could leave an accountant liable to thousands of unknown third parties, the accountant would clearly be assuming an unreasonable risk. Accountants could, of course, insure against such risk, but the cost of such extensive coverage—whether borne by accountants or their clients—might be prohibitive.

For many years the law placed more emphasis on the need to limit accountants' liability to third parties than on the need to protect third parties from the negligent mistakes of accountants. Thus an accountant's liability for negligence was limited to those with contractual relationships with the accountant—those in *privity of contract* with the accountant. Over the last several decades the privity requirement has been steadily eroded in most areas of law. Since the 1960s the privity doctrine has been weakened with regard to accountants. The scope of potential liability is dramatized in Figure 48-1.

Privity and the Ultramares Doctrine

The proposition that an accountant's negligence liability is limited to those in privity with the accountant was set forth in the classic case of *Ultramares Corporation* v. *Touche*. In an often-quoted phrase from his opinion, Chief Justice Cardozo stated that an accountant's negligent error should not result in exposure to liability ". . . in an indeterminate amount for an indeterminate time to an indeterminate class." Cardozo's opinion is excerpted here.

Ultramares Corporation v. Touche

Court of Appeals of New York
174 N.E. 441 (1931)

Background: Ultramares Corporation (plaintiff) sued Touche, Niven & Company (defendant) for losses sustained in lending money to a Touche client whose Touche-certified balance sheet misrepresented its solvency. Touche performed accounting services for Fred Stern and Co., a rubber dealer. In February 1924 Touche issued a balance sheet that showed Stern's net worth to be over a million dollars. Touche certified that the balance sheet presented "a true and correct view" of Stern's financial position as of December 31, 1923. In reality, Stern was insolvent. The firm's net worth was misrepresented by falsified entries in Stern's books. The Ultramares Corporation loaned a large amount of money to Stern, relying on the balance sheet. Although Touche was not specifically aware that Ultramares would rely on the balance sheet, it was aware that Stern would use the balance sheet for the purpose of securing credit. Stern went bankrupt in January 1925. Ultramares sued Touche for both fraud and negligence in the preparation of Stern's balance sheet.

The trial court judge dismissed the fraud action and sent the negligence action to the jury. After the jury returned a verdict for Ultramares for $187,576.32 on the negligence action, the trial judge dismissed the cause of action for negligence. The case was appealed to the Supreme Court, Appellate Division (an intermediate appeals court in New York), which affirmed the dismissal of the fraud action but restored the jury verdict with regard to the negligence action.

Decision: The Court of Appeals, New York's highest court, refused to allow a recovery based on negligence, but granted a new trial with regard to the allegation of fraud.

Cardozo, Chief Justice

We are brought to the question of duty, its origin and measure.

The defendants owed to their employer a duty imposed by law to make their certificate without fraud, and a duty growing out of contract to make it with the care and caution proper to their calling. Fraud includes the pretense of knowledge when knowledge there is none. To creditors and investors to whom the employer exhibited the certificate, the defendants owed a like duty to make it without fraud, since there was notice in the circumstances of its making that the employer did not intend to keep it to himself. A different question develops when we ask whether they owed a duty to these to make it without negligence. If liability for negligence exists, a thoughtless slip or blunder, the failure to detect a theft or forgery beneath the cover of deceptive entries, may expose accountants to a liability in an indeterminate amount for an indeterminate time to an indeterminate class. The hazards of a business conducted on these terms are so extreme as to enkindle doubt whether a flaw may not exist in the implication of a duty that exposes to these consequences.

. . .

The assault upon the citadel of privity is proceeding these days apace. How far the inroads shall extend is now a favorite subject of judicial discussion. [The court then reviewed case law dealing with privity of contract.]

. . .

Liability for negligence if adjudged in this case will extend to many callings other than an auditor's. Lawyers who certify their opinion as to the validity of municipal or corporate bonds, with knowledge that the opinion will be brought to the notice of the public, will become liable to the investors, if they have overlooked a statute or a decision, to the same extent as if the controversy were one between client and adviser. Title companies insuring titles to a tract of land, with knowledge that at an approaching auction the fact that they have insured will be stated to the bidders, will become liable to purchasers who may wish the benefit of a policy without payment of a premium. These illustrations may seem to be extreme, but they go little, if any, farther than we are invited to go now. Negligence, moreover, will have one standard when viewed in relation to the employer, and another and at times a stricter standard when viewed in relation to the public. Explanations that might seem plausible, omissions that might be reasonable, if the duty is confined to the employer, conducting a business that presumably at least is not a fraud upon his creditors, might wear another aspect if an independent duty to be suspicious even of one's principal is owing to investors. "Every one making a promise having the quality of a contract will be under a duty to the promisee by virtue of the promise, but under another duty, apart from contract, to an indefinite number of potential beneficiaries when performance has begun. The assumption of one relation will mean the involuntary assumption of a series of new relations, inescapably hooked together."

Our holding does not emancipate accountants from the consequences of fraud. It does not relieve them if their audit has been so negligent as to justify a finding that they had no genuine belief in its adequacy, for this again is fraud. It does no more than say that, if less than this is proved, if there has been neither reckless misstatement nor insincere profession of an opinion, but only honest blunder, the ensuing liability for negligence is one that is bounded by the contract, and is to be enforced between the parties by whom the contract has been made. We doubt whether the average business man receiving a certificate without paying for it, and receiving it merely as one among a multitude of possible investors, would look for anything more.

Gross Negligence and Fraud

In the second part of his *Ultramares* opinion, Cardozo noted that the lack of privity was no defense to a fraud action. As for the relationship between negligence and fraud, Cardozo wrote: ". . . negligence or blindness, even when not equivalent to fraud, is none the less evidence to sustain an inference of fraud. At least this is so if the negligence is gross."

Since the *Ultramares* opinion many courts have used gross negligence theories to circumvent the privity requirement. Although the accepted legal doctrine allows gross negligence to raise only an inference of fraud, many courts have treated it as being tantamount to fraud. Courts have thus allowed recovery against accountants to third parties who have established gross negligence, without requiring any other evidence to support the inference of fraud. Some of these courts have not made it clear that the recovery is based on fraud and not on gross negligence. This manipulation of the relationship between fraud and gross negligence has been harshly criticized by legal scholars.

The Erosion of the Privity Requirement

Since the late 1960s the "assault on the citadel of privity" has spread into the area of accountant's liability. Courts in many jurisdictions will now allow a third-party plaintiff to recover against an accountant for ordinary negligence.

Such recoveries are limited to circumstances where the plaintiff's reliance on the accountant's work was actually foreseen by the accountant. Through the requirement that the reliance be foreseen, the courts limit liability to a small, well-defined group. An example of such an extension of liability occurred in *Rusch Factors, Inc.* v. *Levin,* where a federal court in Rhode Island upheld an action by a financier who relied on financial statements prepared by an accountant for a corporation seeking a loan. The credit application required the financial statements and the accountant understood the purpose of the statements. The *Rusch* court, in support of its argument for broader accountants' liability to third parties, cited tentative drafts of the Restatement (Second) of Torts. This Restatement has since been finalized. Section 552, dealing with information negligently supplied for the guidance of others, provides:

(1) One who, in the course of his business, profession or employment, or in any other transaction in which he has a pecuniary interest, supplies false information for the guidance of others in their business transactions, is subject to liability for pecuniary loss caused to them by their justifiable reliance upon the information, if he fails to exercise reasonable care or competence in obtaining or communicating the information.

(2) Except as stated in Subsection (3), the liability stated in Subsection (1) is limited to loss suffered
  (a) by the person or one of a limited group of persons for whose benefit and guidance he intends to supply the information or knows that the recipient intends to supply it; and
  (b) through reliance upon it in a transaction that he intends the information to influence or knows that the recipient so intends or in a substantially similar transaction.

(3) The liability of one who is under a public duty to give the information extends to loss suffered by any of the class of persons for whose benefit the duty is created, in any of the transactions in which it is intended to protect them.

The current question is whether or not liability should extend to circumstances where the accountant should have foreseen that the statements could be used in a certain manner but failed to foresee the actual third party. For example, an accountant may prepare documents for filing with the (SEC) Securities and Exchange Commission and those documents may be subsequently relied on by a third party in dealing with the accountant's client. Should liability be imposed on the accountant in favor of the relying third party?

Several cases are now pending and there is some limited, although growing, legal precedent for extended liability. But as the following 1985 case indicates, there is still considera- ble judicial reluctance to extend accountants' liability for ordinary negligence beyond the bounds of privity or actual foreseeability.

Credit Alliance Corporation v. Arthur Andersen & Co.

Court of Appeals of New York

493 N.Y.S.2d 435 (1985)

Background: Credit Alliance Corporation (plaintiff) sued Arthur Andersen and Company (defendant), asserting negligence and fraud. The plaintiff lent funds to L. B. Smith, Inc., in reliance on the defendant's audit statement that vouched for Smith's financial statements. The plaintiff claimed that the defendant failed to conduct investigations that would have uncovered Smith's financial problems, which later led to bankruptcy and default on the plaintiff's loans. The defendant countered that there was no privity between itself and the plaintiff, and thus there was no liability.

Decision: The Court of Appeals, reversing the Appellate Division, dismissed both of plaintiff's causes of action.

Jasen, Judge

Plaintiffs are major financial service companies engaged primarily in financing the purchase of capital equipment through installment sales or leasing agreements. Defendant, Arthur Andersen & Co. ("Andersen"), is a national accounting firm. Plaintiffs' complaint and affidavit allege that prior to 1978, plaintiffs had provided financing to L.B. Smith, Inc. of Virginia ("Smith"), a capital intensive enterprise that regularly required financing. During 1978, plaintiffs advised Smith that as a condition to extending additional major financing, they would insist upon examining an audited financial statement. Accordingly, Smith provided plaintiffs with its consolidated financial statements, covering both itself and its subsidiaries, "For The Years Ended December 31, 1977 and 1976" (the "1977 statements"). These statements contained an auditor's report prepared by Andersen stating that it had examined the statements in accordance with generally accepted auditing standards ("GAAS") and found them to reflect fairly the financial position of Smith in conformity with generally accepted accounting principles ("GAAP"). In reliance upon the 1977 statements, plaintiffs provided substantial amounts in financing to Smith through various extensions of credit. Thereafter, in 1979, as a precondition to continued financing, plaintiffs requested and received from Smith the consolidated financial statements "For The Years Ended February 28, 1979 and December 31, 1977" (the "1979 statements"). Again, Andersen's report vouched for its examination of the financial statements and the financial position of Smith reflected therein. Relying upon these certified statements, plaintiffs provided additional substantial financing to Smith.

It is alleged that both statements overstated Smith's assets, net worth and general financial health, and that Andersen failed to conduct investigations in accordance with proper auditing standards, thereby failing to discover Smith's precarious financial condition and the serious possibility that Smith would be unable to survive as a going concern. Indeed, in 1980, Smith filed a petition for bankruptcy. By that time, Smith had already defaulted on several millions of dollars of obligations to plaintiffs.

In August 1981, plaintiffs commenced this suit for damages lost on its outstanding loans to Smith, claiming both negligence and fraud by Andersen in the preparation of its audit reports. The complaint alleges that Andersen knew, should have known or was on notice that the 1977 and 1979 certified statements were being utilized by Smith to induce companies such as plaintiffs to make credit available to Smith. The complaint further states that Andersen knew, should have known or was on notice that the certified statements were being shown to plaintiffs for such a purpose. It is also alleged that Andersen knew or recklessly disregarded facts which indicated that the 1977 and 1979 statements were misleading.

In the seminal case of *Ultramares Corp.* v. *Touche,* this court, speaking through the opinion of Chief Judge Cardozo more than 50 years ago, disallowed a cause of action in negligence against a public accounting firm for inaccurately prepared financial statements which were relied upon by a plaintiff having no contractual privity with the accountants. [The court in *Ultramares* noted] that the "assault upon the citadel of privity is proceeding in these days apace." We acknowledged that inroads had been made, for example, where third-party beneficiaries or dangerous instrumentalities were involved. Indeed, we referred to this court's holding in *MacPherson* v. *Buick Motor Co.,* where it was decided that the manufacturer of a defective chattel—there an automobile—may be liable in negligence for the resulting injuries sustained by a user regardless of the absence of privity. [In a professional certification case, imposing liability on a party certifying weights, *Glanzer* v. *Shepard,* the certification at issue] *. . . recites that it was made by order of the former for the use of the latter.* . . . Here was a case where *the transmission of the certificate to another was* not merely one possibility among many, but the *'end and aim of the transaction,'* as certain and immediate and deliberately willed as if a husband were to order a gown to be delivered to his wife, or a telegraph company, contracting with the sender of a message, were to telegraph it wrongly to the damage of the person expected to receive it. . . . The *intimacy of the resulting nexus* is attested by the fact that after stating the case in terms of legal duty, we went on to point out that . . . we could reach the same result by stating it in terms of contract. . . . The bond was *so close as to approach that of privity, if not completely one with it.* . . . In a word, the service rendered by the defendant in *Glanzer* v. *Shepard* was primarily for the information of a third person, *in effect, if not in name, a party to the contract,* and only incidentally for that of the formal promisee."

[T]he facts as alleged by plaintiffs [in this Case.] fail to demonstrate the existence of a relationship between the parties sufficiently approaching privity. Though the complaint and supporting affidavit do allege that Andersen specifically knew, should have known or was on notice that plaintiffs were being shown the reports by Smith, Andersen's client, in order to induce their reliance thereon, nevertheless, there is no adequate allegation of either a particular purpose for the reports' preparation or the prerequisite conduct on the part of the accountants. While the allegations state that Smith sought to induce plaintiffs to extend credit, no claim is made that Andersen was being employed to prepare the reports with that particular purpose in mind. Moreover, there is no allegation that Andersen had any direct dealings with plaintiffs, had specifically agreed with Smith to prepare the report for plaintiffs' use or according to plaintiffs' requirements, or had specifically agreed with Smith to provide plaintiffs with a copy or actually did so. Indeed, there is simply no allegation of any word or action on the part of Andersen directed to plaintiffs, or anything contained in Andersen's retainer agreement with Smith which provided the necessary link between them.

Accordingly, both causes of action should be dismissed.

STATUTORY LIABILITY

In addition to common-law theories of liability, there are various federal and state statutes that can provide the basis for accountants' liability. We confine our discussion to the federal statutes.

The statutes with the greatest effect on accountants are the Securities Act of 1933 and the Securities and Exchange Act of 1934, both of which were discussed in detail in Chapter 31. Accountants can be brought under the jurisdiction of these acts through their work on financial statements, annual reports, registration statements, and proxy statements.

Recall that Section 11 of the 1933 Act provides a civil remedy for securities buyers who have been injured by their reliance on misinformation in the registration statement. Accountants can be held liable under this section for materials that they prepare or certify. Accountants who aid and abet a securities fraud are subject to liability under Section 17.

Accountants who make misstatements in proxy statements can be held liable under Section 14(a) of the 1934 Act or under SEC Rule 14a–9. Accountants who make false statements in tender offers can be held liable under Section 14(e) of the 1934 Act. Courts have held that *scienter*—knowledge of falsity with intent to deceive—is required to hold an accountant liable under both sections.

Accountants' liability under the 1934 Act is typically founded on Section 10(b), which grants an implied civil remedy to buyers or sellers of securities who have been damaged by fraud. In the landmark case of *Ernst and Ernst* v. *Hochfelder,* excerpted in Chapter 35, the Supreme Court ruled that a plaintiff would have to establish that the defendant acted with scienter in order to prevail in a Section 10(b) action. This standard also applies to SEC Rule 10b–5, which fills in gaps left open by Section 10(b). In the absence of guidance from the Supreme Court many circuits have held that reckless conduct is sufficient to satisfy the scienter requirement of *Ernst.*

In *Ernst* the Court did not rule on whether a party could be held liable for aiding and abetting violations of Section 10(b) or Rule 10b–5. Aiding and abetting, along with other potential sources of liability under the securities laws, is discussed in the *Resnick* case.

Resnick v. Touche Ross and Co.

U.S. District Court, Southern District of New York

470 F.Supp. 1020 (1979)

Background: A group of investors (plaintiffs) sued the accounting firm Touche Ross (defendant) for securities law violations after their investments in Touche Ross's client went sour. The plaintiffs purchased securities of Weis Securities, Inc., before the latter's collapse in 1973. The plaintiffs claimed that in purchasing the securities they relied on misinformation in the financial statements. The statements were certified by Touche Ross and Co., the defendant accounting firm. The plaintiffs sued Touche Ross on a number of grounds, including violations of Section 10(b) of the Securities and Exchange Act of 1934, aiding and abetting violations of Section 10(b) and Rule 10b–5, and violations of the antifraud provisions of Section 17 of the Securities Act of 1933. The federal District Court denied the defendant accountant's motion to dismiss the aforementioned claims.

Decision: The court ruled that the plaintiffs had stated claims for which relief could be granted, but did not rule on the substance of those claims.

Knopp, District Judge

SCIENTER AND THE 10(B) AND 17(A) CLAIMS:

Defendants argue that plaintiffs' claims under 10(b) and 17(a) should be dismissed because they fail to satisfy the *scienter* standard enunciated by the Supreme Court in *Ernst & Ernst* v. *Hochfelder* (1976). Although that decision held that negligent action or inaction was not sufficient to support a 10b–5 claim, in a footnote the Court left open the question of whether recklessness would suffice. Prior to *Hochfelder,* it was established in this Circuit that the standard of *scienter* required in an action under Rule 10b–5 was "willful or reckless disregard for the truth." Several recent cases have confirmed that, in the absence of further word from the Supreme Court, reckless conduct will continue to meet the requirements of *scienter* for 10b–5 actions. Thus, the *scienter* standard we will apply is one of recklessness.

The amended complaint alleges that the statements certified by defendant were "materially false and misleading" in twenty-four specified respects, and that "defendant knew, should have known or was on notice of or recklessly disregarded" facts relating to these misstatements. The amended complaint further alleges that "the defendant obtained actual knowledge of the materially false and misleading entries . . . or, in the alternative conducted its examination and audit with reckless disregard for the truth." Finally, the amended complaint sets forth the circumstances, with respect to each alleged misstatement, that are said to constitute "defendant's knowing and/or reckless conduct."

Defendant argues, with some force, that the amended complaint in essence alleges no more than several instances of negligent conduct. However, we cannot say as a matter of law that if plaintiffs prove all their allegations the recklessness standard will not be met. As we thus cannot say as a matter of law that the *scienter* requirement has not been satisfied, plaintiff's claim under Rule 10b–5 must survive this motion to dismiss.

AIDING AND ABETTING

In addition to their allegations of primary violations under the securities laws by defendant, plaintiffs argue that the defendant is secondarily liable as an aider and abettor of the violations of Weis. In this Circuit, Section 10(b) and Rule 10b–5 may give rise to aiding and abetting liability.

Three elements must be established in order to impose such liability. First, it must be shown that the primary party (Weis), as distinguished from the alleged aider and abettor (Touche Ross), violated the securities laws. Second, it must be established that the aider and abettor knew of the violation. Third, the aider and abettor must have rendered substantial assistance in effecting the violation.

As to the first element, the parties do not dispute that Weis engaged in violations of the securities laws. Knowledge of the violation, the second element, has been pleaded by the plaintiffs. Once again, the *Rolf* court indicates that the *scienter* element will be satisfied by a showing of recklessness. We cannot say, as a matter of law, that plaintiffs would be unable to meet that standard at trial. Finally, the plaintiffs allege that defendant gave substantial assistance in effecting the primary securities laws violation. While it is not clear what sort of conduct is included within the term "substantial assistance," plaintiffs' allegations are sufficient for purposes of this motion. Therefore plaintiffs' cause of action for aiding and abetting under Section 10(b) and Rule 10b–5 survives this motion to dismiss.

The Internal Revenue Code

The Internal Revenue Code (IRC) is an important source of liability for accountants who prepare their clients' tax returns. Section 6694 of the IRC imposes a $100 fine on preparers who negligently understate a client's tax liability and a $500 fine on preparers who willfully make such a misstatement. Section 6695 provides penalties for tax preparers who fail to furnish a copy of the return to the client, who fail to sign the return, or who fail to retain the return (or a proper listing of it) for a period of three years after the return is due.

Section 7407 of the IRC authorizes the federal government to seek injunctions to prevent violations of Sections 6694 and 6695. Injunctions are also available to prevent tax preparers from engaging in other types of conduct, such as guaranteeing to clients the payment of any tax refund or the allowance of any tax credit. Tax preparers who have repeatedly violated the IRC can be enjoined from preparing taxes.

The IRC and the securities acts also contain criminal provisions, which will be discussed in the next section.

Criminal Liability

The federal securities statutes contain criminal as well as civil sanctions. Section 24 of the 1933 Act, as amended, provides for a maximum $10,000 fine or five-year jail sentence, or both, for persons who willfully violate any section of the act. The penalties also apply to anyone who willfully makes an untrue statement of material fact—or omits pertinent information—in a registration statement. Section 32(a) of the 1934 Act prescribes identical sanctions for willful violators of the statute. Criminal liability for accountants can derive from their preparation and filing of annual reports, quarterly reports, and proxy statements.

Accountants can also be subject to criminal liability under the Internal Revenue Code, the Federal False Statements Act, the Federal Mail Fraud Act, and the Conspiracy statute.

Accountants who assist in the fraudulent preparation of a tax return can be subject to a

$100,000 fine under Section 7206(2) of the Internal Revenue Code. The section also provides for a maximum prison term of three years.

The Federal False Statements Act makes it a crime to make false statements knowingly and willfully to any federal department or agency. Violators can be subject to a $10,000 fine, five years in jail, or both. An accountant's liability under the act would commonly be based on work on documents filed with the SEC. Audit reports for the financial statements in annual reports, quarterly reports, registration statements, and proxy statements are prime examples; the financial statements themselves are representations of the audited company, but statements in the audit reports are attributed to the accountant.

The Federal Mail Fraud Statute makes it a crime to use the postal service to perpetrate a fraudulent scheme. The law carries a maximum $1,000 fine, five-year prison sentence, or both. Courts have interpreted the statute to allow for each mailing to constitute a separate offense. An accountant can be exposed to liability under this statute by certifying financial statements that he or she knows (or should know) to be false and when he or she knows that the statements will be mailed for the purpose of fraud.

Conspiracy liability can be incurred when parties agree to violate any of the preceding statutes. To be convicted of conspiracy, one need only be party to a criminal agreement in which one of the parties overtly acts to further the crime. The crime need not have been successful nor have been completed by the time it was discovered. A convicted conspirator can face a fine of up to $10,000, a jail term of up to five years, or both.

Intent

To be convicted of crimes, defendants have traditionally had to manifest *mens rea*—criminal intent. This requirement has been somewhat weakened by the operation of certain statutes, but most crimes still require some specified level of culpable intent.

The criminal statutes discussed in this section all require that the prohibited act be committed willfully. Courts have convicted accountants for violations of these statutes without direct evidence that the accountants acted with a guilty state of mind. Courts have ruled that evidence of the accountant's actions can be sufficient to infer *mens rea.*

Courts have further ruled that the willfulness requirement does not have to entail some wicked purpose on the part of the defendant. An accountant can thus be found criminally liable for passive compliance with a violation that provided the accountant with no personal benefit. The *Simon* case that follows illustrates this principle.

United States v. Simon
U.S. Court of Appeals, Second Circuit
425 F.2d 796 (1970)

Background: The United States brought criminal actions against Simon (defendant) and other accountants for securities and mail fraud violations stemming from their preparation of certified financial statements for Continental Vending. This case stems from the financial collapse of the Continental Vending Machine Company in 1963. Harold Roth, Continental's president, also supervised the operations of the Valley Commercial Corporation, a Continental affiliate. Valley's business was to lend money to Continental and other vending machine companies. In addition to the loans made by Valley to Continental, several cash loans were made by Continental to Valley. The bulk of these loans were in turn "borrowed" by Roth to support his personal investments. The cash payments from Continental to Valley were recorded in Continental's "Valley Receivable" account, which rose as high as $3.9 million. In 1962 it became apparent that the "Valley Receivable" account would not be collectible because Roth was unable to repay the money he had taken from Valley. Carl Simon and other defendant accountants, members of the firm of Lybrand, Ross Bros. and Montgomery, arranged with Roth to secure the receivable so that it could be properly treated as an asset on the balance sheet. Continental's financial situation was dire; its very solvency depended on the collectibility of the "Valley Receivable." Roth offered to secure the "Valley Receivable" by offering his own securities as collateral. The securities were actually inadequate to secure the account, then valued at $3.6 million. This was because 80 percent of the securities were in Continental, the same shaky concern that the collateral was designed to prop up. Also, the securities were subject to the liens of creditors. The accountants prepared financial statements for Continental in February 1963. The certified balance sheet indicated that the large "Valley Receivable" account was properly secured. In fact the value of the collateral securities plunged to about one-tenth of the value of the uncollectible "Valley Receivable" five days after the financial statements were mailed to the SEC. Continental went bankrupt soon after. The accountants were tried and convicted for mail fraud and for conspiracy to violate the Federal False Statements Statute, Section 32 of the Securities and Exchange Act of 1934, and the Federal Mail Fraud Statute. The accountants had argued that the necessary criminal motive could not be proven, since the accountants had not stood to profit from the falsity of the financial statements.

Decision: The Court of Appeals affirmed the accountants' conviction.

Friendly, Circuit Judge

Defendants properly make much of the alleged absence of proof of motivation. They say that even if the Government is not bound to show evil motive, and we think it is not, see *Pointer* v. *United States,* lack of evidence of motive makes the burden of proving criminal intent peculiarly heavy and the Government did not discharge this.

It is quite true that there was no proof of motive in the form usual in fraud cases. None of the defendants made or could make a penny from Continental's putting out false financial statements. Neither was there evidence of motive in the sense of fear that telling the truth would lose a valuable account. Continental was not the kind of client whose size would give it leverage to bully a great accounting firm, nor was it important to the defendants personally in the sense of their having brought in the business. One would suppose rather that the Continental account had become a considerable headache to the Lybrand firm generally and to the defendants in particular; they could hardly have been unaware of the likelihood that the many hours the firm had devoted to the 1962 audit would not be compensated and that another might never occur. Ordinary commercial motivation is thus wholly absent.

The Government finds motive in defendants' desire to preserve Lybrand's reputation and conceal the alleged dereliction of their predecessors and themselves in former years—the failure to advise Continental's board of directors of Roth's role in creating the Valley receivable, the failure to expand the scope of the audit for those years to determine the nature and collectibility of the Valley receivable, despite the injunction in a well-known text originally authored by one of the founders of the Lybrand firm, that receivables from affiliates must be scrutinized carefully to determine they "are what they purport to be"; and the certification of the 1961 statements despite Simon's warning to Roth that a further increase in the receivable would necessitate an examination of Valley's books. The apparent failure of the defendants to consult with the Lybrand executive committee, or with the partner in the firm to whom "problems" in audits were supposed to be referred, on what would seem highly important policy questions concerning the 1962 audit adds force to these arguments.

The main response is that if the defendants had wanted to cover up any past delinquencies they would not have insisted on financial statements so dismal in other respects. It is alleged that defendants demanded certain adjustments which good accounting practice permitted but did not require. It is said also that defendants must have known the statements were so unfavorable, even with the limited disclosure in Note 2, that Continental was bound to fold and a full investigation would follow. The argument is impressive but not dispositive. Defendants may have harbored the illusion that the dexterity of Continental's treasurer in "juggling cash" would enable it to survive. Moreover, men who find themselves in a bad situation of their own making do not always act with full rationality.

Even if there were no satisfactory showing of motive, we think the Government produced sufficient evidence of criminal intent. Its burden was not to show that defendants were wicked men with designs on anyone's purse, which they obviously were not, but rather that they had certified a statement knowing it to be false. As Judge Hough said for us long ago, "while there is no allowable inference of knowledge from the mere fact of falsity, there are many cases where from the actor's special situation and continuity of conduct an inference that he did know the untruth of what he said or wrote may legitimately be drawn." Moreover, so far as criminal intent is concerned, the various deficiencies in the footnote should not be considered in isolation. Evidence that defendants knowingly suppressed one fact permitted, although it surely did not compel, an inference that their suppression of another was likewise knowing and willful.

CASE NOTE

The defendants were subsequently pardoned by President Richard Nixon.

REVIEW PROBLEMS

1. What different types of opinions can an accountant express?
2. To whom besides clients can an accountant be held liable? Under what circumstances?
3. What is the privity requirement in regard to accountant liability? How has the requirement been altered in recent years?
4. What acts can expose an accountant to criminal liability?
5. Accountants prepared and certified a fi-

ETHICS BOX
Ethical Dilemmas Facing Professionals

All types of professional practitioners face similar ethical dilemmas. Doctors, engineers, lawyers, and accountants encounter problems concerning determining who is the real client, how much should be disclosed to clients, who should make certain decisions, and what information should be kept confidential. For example, all of these professionals may encounter clients who are engaged in wrongdoing where the professional possesses key information relating to the wrongful acts. Under what circumstances should a professional blow the whistle using confidential information?

Consider the following short case problems.

- An accountant conducts an audit for a client. In the process of the audit the accountant discovers that the client is using unsafe procedures in pasteurizing its product. There have been several recent outbreaks of salmonella poisoning in the area, but they have not been associated with the client. The accountant reports the information to the client, but no action is taken. What should the accountant do?
- An accounting firm provides a full range of services for both the Alpha Brokerage Company and the Modern Industrial Bank. In the process of auditing Alpha, the firm discovers that Alpha is engaged in money mobilizing practices that have the effect of creating negative balances in their checking accounts with Modern Industrial. From their work for Modern Industrial the accounting firm realizes that the bank is not aware of Alpha's practices. The legality of Alpha's action is ambiguous, but it clearly breaches the implied understanding with the bank concerning the operation of the checking accounts. Should the firm notify the bank of what is going on?
- An accountant discovers that a manager at one of its clients is embezzling large sums. The accountant discloses this and the manager is removed from all financial responsibility. The accountant then discovers that the manager is being hired by another client having received a strong positive recommendation from the first client. What, if anything, should the accountant do?

---

nancial statement for their client, who used the statement to induce a bank to lend it money. The accountants made several major errors in the statement. In addition, they delayed sending out an explanatory letter—which they believed should

be read by anyone using the statement—for about thirty days. The bank, which was not in privity of contract with the accountants, claimed to have suffered damages as a result of the accountants' negligence. Assume that you have been hired to represent the bank in a lawsuit against the accountants. If your jurisdiction recognizes the lack of privity as a bar to accountants' negligence actions, what theory should you pursue?

6. Your tax accountant has agreed to file your income tax return and supporting documents by April 15 of this year. In October you receive notice that the tax payment sent is insufficient, because the return did not arrive at IRS headquarters until July, and interest payments are due. In addition, you discover in going over the forms filed by the accountant that he failed to minimize your tax burden through taking certain deductions for which you are eligible. Is your accountant liable to you? Under what theory of law? How might the accountant defend himself against your claim?

7. In preparing Ann's tax return, accountant intentionally inflated the value of certain real estate listed in order to minimize income realized upon sale of the land in the future. Ann provided these inflated documents to Herbert Finance, which gave Ann a loan based on an assumption that collateral of the inflated value existed. Ann defaulted on the loan and moved to South America. Herbert Finance sued Ann's tax accountant for the amount of the unpaid debt. What decision should the court reach? What legal doctrines should be used to reach this decision?

8. Herzfeld purchased securities issued by FGL, a real estate dealer, after reading its financial statements for the period ending November 30, 1969. Those statements, audited by Laventhol, presented FGL as a very profitable company. Crucial to that impression was Laventhol's treatment of two contemplated transactions: FGL's purchase of nursing homes from Monterey for $13.4 million and the resale of those properties to Continental for $15.4 million. FGL had paid $5,000 down to Mon-

terey before November 30, 1969. Continental had apparently paid $25,000 down to FGL before November 30. FGL wanted the expected profit of over $2 million to be reflected on its financial statements for the period ending November 30, 1969. It threatened to fire and/or sue Laventhol if it didn't comply. Laventhol knew that Continental's net worth was only $100,-000; that the purchase and resale of the nursing homes had been recorded neither in FGL's books nor in the minutes of its corporate meetings; that FGL had yet to acquire title to the homes; and that recognizing the revenue would turn a loss of almost $800,000 to a gain of over $1.2 million. Nonetheless, Laventhol recorded the balance of the expected profit in the income statement as "deferred gross profit." Laventhol qualified the opinion letter accompanying the report, stating that the financial statements represented FGL's position "subject to the collectibility of the balance receivable on the contract to sell the homes." FGL's contracts to purchase and resell the homes both fell through. About a year later FGL went bankrupt. Assuming that he can show injury, does Herzfeld have a cause of action against Laventhol? Herzfeld v. Laventhol, Krekstein, Horwath and Horwath, 540 F.2d 27 (U.S. Ct. App., 2nd Cir. 1975).

9. Guarante-Harrington Associates was a limited partnership engaged in trading securities. According to the partnership agreement, partners could withdraw portions of their interest only at the end of a fiscal year upon thirty days' notice. Guarante and Harrington, the general partners, withdrew $2 million of their capital investment in violation of the agreement. From examining the partnership's audit report and tax returns, which were prepared by Anderson, one could not discover that the $2 million withdrawal was

made in violation of the agreement. White, a limited partner, claimed to have suffered damages resulting from his use of the partnership's negligently prepared tax returns to prepare his own tax returns. He sued Anderson. Can Anderson avoid liability by claiming that it did not foresee that White would rely on the partnership's tax returns to prepare his own? White v. Guarante, 372 N.E. 2d 315 (Ct. of App. of N.Y. 1977).

10. The accounting partnership of James, Guinn and Head audited the financial statements of Buddy Paschal, who owned various automobile glass businesses. James knew that the Shatterproof Glass Corporation would rely on the audited statements in deciding whether to loan money to Paschal's enterprises. James issued an unqualified opinion that the financial statements, which showed Paschal's businesses to be solvent, were accurate. The businesses were actually insolvent. Shatterproof loaned money to Paschal and lost $400,000. How do you think the court in *Rusch Factors, Inc.* v. *Levin* would have ruled if Shatterproof sued James? Do you think the court in *Ultramares Corp.* v. *Touche* would have ruled differently? Shatterproof Glass Corporation v. James, 466 S.W.2d 873 (Tex. Ct. Civ. App. 1971).

APPENDIX A
UNIFORM COMMERCIAL CODE
Selected Sections

ARTICLE ONE — GENERAL PROVISIONS

PART 1

Short Title, Construction, Application and Subject Matter of the Act

§ 1-101. Short Title.—This Act shall be known and may be cited as Uniform Commercial Code.

§ 1-102. Purposes; Rules of Construction; Variation by Agreement.—

(1) This Act shall be liberally construed and applied to promote its underlying purposes and policies.

(2) Underlying purposes and policies of this Act are

(a) to simplify, clarify and modernize the law governing commercial transactions;

(b) to permit the continued expansion of commercial practices through custom, usage and agreement of the parties;

(c) to make uniform the law among the various jurisdictions.

(3) The effect of provisions of this Act may be varied by agreement, except as otherwise provided in this Act and except that the obligations of good faith, diligence, reasonableness and care prescribed by this Act may not be disclaimed by agreement but the parties may by agreement determine the standards by which the performance of such obligations is to be measured if such standards are not manifestly unreasonable.

(4) The presence in certain provisions of this Act of the words "unless otherwise agreed" or words of similar import does not imply that the effect of other provisions may not be varied by agreement under subsection (3).

(5) In this Act unless the context otherwise requires

(a) words in the singular number include the plural, and in the plural include the singular.

(b) words of the masculine gender include the feminine and the neuter, and when the sense so indicates words of the neuter gender may refer to any gender.

§ 1-103. Supplementary General Principles of Law Applicable.—Unless displaced by the particular provisions of this Act, the principles of law and equity, including the law merchant and the law relative to capacity to contract, principal and agent, estoppel, fraud, misrepresentation, duress, coercion, mistake, bankruptcy, or other validating or invalidating cause shall supplement its provisions.

§ 1-104. Construction Against Implicit Repeal.—This Act being a general act intended as a unified coverage of its subject matter, no part of it shall be deemed to be impliedly repealed by subsequent legislation if such construction can reasonably be avoided.

§ 1-105. Territorial Application of the Act; Parties' Power to Choose Applicable Law.—

(1) Except as provided hereafter in this section, when a transaction bears a reasonable relation to this state and also to another state or nation the parties may agree that the law either of this state or of such other state or nation shall govern their rights and duties. Failing such agreement this Act applies to transactions bearing an appropriate relation to this state.

(2) Where one of the following provisions of this Act specifies the applicable law, that provision governs and a contrary agreement is effective only to the extent permitted by the law (including the conflict of laws rules) so specified:

Rights of creditors against sold goods. Section 2-402.

Applicability of the Article on Bank Deposits and Collections. Section 4-102.

Bulk transfers subject to the Article on Bulk Transfers. Section 6-102.

Applicability of the Article on Investment Securities. Section 8-106.

Perfection provisions of the Article on Secured Transactions. Section 9-103.

§ 1-106. Remedies to Be Liberally Administered.—

(1) The remedies provided by this Act shall be liberally administered to the end that the aggrieved party may be put in as good a position as if the other party had fully performed but neither consequential or special nor penal damages may be had except as specifically provided in this Act or by other rule of law.

(2) Any right or obligation declared by this Act is enforceable by action unless the provision declaring it specifies a different and limited effect.

§ 1-107. Waiver or Renunciation of Claim or Right After Breach.—Any claim or right arising out of an alleged breach can be discharged in whole or in part without consideration by a written waiver or renunciation signed and delivered by the aggrieved party.

§ 1-108. **Severability.**—If any provision or clause of this Act or application thereof to any person or circumstances is held invalid, such invalidity shall not affect other provisions or applications of the Act which can be given effect without the invalid provision or application, and to this end the provisions of this Act are declared to be severable.

§ 1-109. **Section Captions.**—Section captions are parts of this Act.

PART 2

General Definitions and Principles of Interpretation

§ 1-201. **General Definitions.**—Subject to additional definitions contained in the subsequent Articles of this Act which are applicable to specific Articles or Parts thereof, and unless the context otherwise requires, in this Act:

(1) "Action" in the sense of a judicial proceeding includes recoupment, counter-claim, set-off, suit in equity and any other proceedings in which rights are determined.

(2) "Aggrieved party" means a party entitled to resort to a remedy.

(3) "Agreement" means the bargain of the parties in fact as found in their language or by implication from other circumstances including course of dealing or usage of trade or course of performance as provided in this Act (Sections 1-205 and 2-208). Whether an agreement has legal consequences is determined by the provisions of this Act, if applicable; otherwise by the law of contracts (Section 1-103). (Compare "Contract".)

(4) "Bank" means any person engaged in the business of banking.

(5) "Bearer" means the person in possession of an instrument, document of title, or certificated security payable to bearer or indorsed in blank.

(6) "Bill of lading" means a document evidencing the receipt of goods for shipment issued by a person engaged in the business of transporting or forwarding goods, and includes an airbill. "Airbill" means a document serving for air transportation as a bill of lading does for marine or rail transportation, and includes an air consignment note or air waybill.

(7) "Branch" includes a separately incorporated foreign branch of a bank.

(8) "Burden of establishing" a fact means the burden of persuading the triers of fact that the existence of the fact is more probable than its non-existence.

(9) "Buyer in ordinary course of business" means a person who in good faith and without knowledge that the sale to him is in violation of the ownership rights or security interest of a third party in the goods buys in ordinary course from a person in the business of selling goods of that kind but does not include a pawnbroker. [All persons who sell minerals or the like (including oil and gas) at wellhead or minehead shall be deemed to be persons in the business of selling goods of that kind.] "Buying" may be for cash or by exchange of other property or on secured or unsecured credit and includes receiving goods or documents of title under a pre-existing contract for sale but does not include a transfer in bulk or as security for or in total or partial satisfaction of a money debt.

(10) "Conspicuous": A term or clause is conspicuous when it is so written that a reasonable person against whom it is to operate ought to have noticed it. A printed heading in capitals (as NON-NEGOTIABLE BILL OF LADING) is conspicuous. Language in the body of a form is "conspicuous" if it is in larger or other contrasting type or color. But in a telegram any stated term is "conspicuous". Whether a term or clause is "conspicuous" or not is for decision by the court.

(11) "Contract" means the total legal obligation which results from the parties' agreement as affected by this Act and any other applicable rules or law. (Compare "Agreement".)

(12) "Creditor" includes a general creditor, a secured creditor, a lien creditor and any representative of creditors, including an assignee for the benefit of creditors, a trustee in bankruptcy, a receiver in equity and an executor or administrator of an insolvent debtor's or assignor's estate.

(13) "Defendant" includes a person in the position of defendant in a cross-action or counterclaim.

(14) "Delivery" with respect to instruments, documents of title, chattel paper, or certificated securities means voluntary transfer of possession.

(15) "Document of title" includes a bill of lading, dock warrant, dock receipt, warehouse receipt or order for the delivery of goods, and also any other document which in the regular course of business or financing is treated as adequately evidencing that the person in possession of it is entitled to receive, hold and dispose of the document and the goods it covers. To be a document of title a document must purport to be issued by or addressed to a bailee and purport to cover goods in the bailee's possession which are either identified or are fungible portions of an identified mass.

(16) "Fault" means wrongful act, omission or breach.

(17) "Fungible" with respect to goods or securities means goods or securities of which any unit is, by nature or usage of trade, the equivalent of any other like unit. Goods which are not fungible shall be deemed fungible for the purposes of this Act to the extent that under a particular agreement or document unlike units are treated as equivalents.

(18) "Genuine" means free of forgery or counterfeiting.

(19) "Good faith" means honesty in fact in the conduct or transaction concerned.

(20) "Holder" means a person who is in possession of a document of title or an instrument or a certificated investment security drawn, issued, or indorsed to him or his order or to bearer or in blank.

(21) To "honor" is to pay or to accept and pay, or where a credit so engages to purchase or discount a draft complying with the terms of the credit.

(22) "Insolvency proceedings" includes any assignment for the benefit of creditors or other proceedings intended to liquidate or rehabilitate the estate of the person involved.

(23) A person is "insolvent" who either has ceased to pay his debts in the ordinary course of business or cannot pay his debts as they become due or is insolvent within the meaning of the federal bankruptcy law.

(24) "Money" means a medium of exchange authorized or adopted by a domestic or foreign government as a part of its currency.

(25) A person has "notice" of a fact when

    (a) he has actual knowledge of it; or

    (b) he has received a notice of notification of it; or

    (c) from all the facts and circumstances known to him at the time in question he has reason to know that it exists.

A person "knows" or has "knowledge" of a fact when he has actual knowledge of it. "Discover" or "learn" or a word or phrase of similar import refers to knowledge rather than to reason to know. The time and circumstances under which a notice or notification may cease to be effective are not determined by this Act.

(26) A person "notifies" or "gives" a notice or notification to another by taking such steps as may be reasonably required to inform the other in ordinary course whether or not such other actually comes to know of it. A person "receives" a notice or notification when

    (a) it comes to his attention; or

    (b) it is duly delivered at the place of business through which the contract was made or at any other place held out by him as the place for receipt of such communications.

(27) Notice, knowledge or a notice or notification received by an organization is effective for a particular transaction from the time when it is brought to the attention of the individual conducting that transaction, and in any event from the time when it would have been brought to his attention if the organization had exercised due diligence.

(28) "Organization" includes a corporation, government or governmental subdivision or agency, business trust, estate, trust, partnership or association, two or more persons having a joint or common interest, or any other legal or commercial entity.

(29) "Party", as distinct from "third party", means a person who has engaged in a transaction or made an agreement within this Act.

(30) "Person" includes an individual or an organization (See Section 1-102).

(31) "Presumption" or "presumed" means that the trier of fact must find the existence of the fact presumed unless and until evidence is introduced which would support a finding of its nonexistence.

(32) "Purchase" includes taking by sale, discount, negotiation, mortgage, pledge, lien, issue or re-issue, gift or any other voluntary transaction creating an interest in property.

(33) "Purchaser" means a person who takes by purchase.

(34) "Remedy" means any remedial right to which an aggrieved party is entitled with or without resort to a tribunal.

(35) "Representative" includes an agent, an officer of a corporation or association, and a trustee, executor or administrator of an estate, or any other person empowered to act for another.

(36) "Rights" includes remedies.

(37) "Security interest" means an interest in personal property or fixtures which secures payment or performance of an obligation. The retention or reservation of title by a seller of goods notwithstanding shipment or delivery to the buyer (Section 2-401) is limited in effect to a reservation of a "security interest". The term also includes any interest of a buyer of accounts [or] chattel paper which is subject to Article 9. The special property interest of a buyer of goods on identification of such goods to a contract for sale under Section 2-401 is not a "security interest", but a buyer may also acquire a "security interest" by complying with Article 9. Unless a lease or consignment is intended as security, reservation of title thereunder is not a "security interest" but a consignment is in any event subject to the provisions on consignment sales (Section 2-326). Whether a lease is intended as security is to be determined by the facts of each case; however,

    (a) the inclusion of an option to purchase does not of itself make the lease one intended for security, and

    (b) an agreement that upon compliance with the terms of the lease the lessee shall become or has the option to become the owner of the property for no additional consideration or for a nominal consideration does make the lease one intended for security.

(38) "Send" in connection with any writing or notice means to deposit in the mail or deliver for transmission by any other usual means of communication with postage or cost of transmission provided for and properly addressed and in the case of an instrument to an address specified thereon or otherwise agreed, or if there be none to any address specified thereon or otherwise agreed, or if there be none to any address reasonable under the circumstances. The receipt of any writing or notice within the time at which it would have arrived if properly sent has the effect of a proper sending.

(39) "Signed" includes any symbol executed or adopted by a party with present intention to authenticate a writing.

(40) "Surety" includes guarantor.

(41) "Telegram" includes a message transmitted by radio, teletype, cable, any mechanical method of transmission, or the like.

(42) "Term" means that portion of an agreement which relates to a particular matter.

(43) "Unauthorized" signature or indorsement means one made without actual implied or apparent authority and includes a forgery.

(44) "Value". Except as otherwise provided with respect to negotiable instruments and bank collections (Sections 3-303, 4-208 and 4-209) a person gives "value" for rights if he acquires them

    (a) in return for a binding commitment to extend credit or for the extension of immediately available credit whether or not drawn upon and whether or not a charge-back is provided for in the event of difficulties in collection; or

    (b) as security for or in total or partial satisfaction of a pre-existing claim; or

    (c) by accepting delivery pursuant to a pre-existing claim; or

    (d) generally, in return for any consideration sufficient to support a simple contract.

(45) "Warehouse receipt" means a receipt issued by a person engaged in the business of storing goods for hire.

(46) "Written" or "writing" includes printing, typewriting or any other intentional reduction to tangible form.

§ 1-202. Prima Facie Evidence by Third Party Documents.—A document in due form purporting to be a bill of lading, policy or certificate of insurance, official weigher's or inspector's certificate, consular invoice, or any other document authorized or required by the contract to be issued by a third party shall be prima facie evidence of its own authenticity and genuineness and of the facts stated in the document by the third party.

§ 1-203. Obligation of Good Faith—Every contract or duty within this Act imposes an obligation of good faith in its performance or enforcement.

§ 1-204. Time; Reasonable Time; "Seasonably".—

(1) Whenever this Act requires any action to be taken within a reasonable time, any time which is not manifestly unreasonable may be fixed by agreement.

(2) What is a reasonable time for taking any action depends on the nature, purpose and circumstances of such action.

(3) An action is taken "seasonably" when it is taken at or within the time agreed or no time agreed at or within a reasonable time.

§ 1-205. Course of Dealing and Usage of Trade.—

(1) A course of dealing is a sequence of previous conduct between the parties to a particular transaction which is fairly to be regarded as establishing a common basis of understanding for interpreting their expressions and other conduct.

(2) A usage of trade is any practice or method of dealing having such regularity of observance in a place, vocation or trade as to justify an expectation that it will be observed with respect to the transaction in question. If it is established that such usage is embodied in a written trade code or similar writing the interpretation of the writing is for the court.

(3) A course of dealing between parties and any usage of trade in the vocation of trade in which they are engaged or of which they are or should be aware give particular meaning to and supplement or qualify terms of an agreement.

(4) The express terms of an agreement and an applicable course of dealing or usage of trade shall be construed wherever reasonable as consistent with each other; but when such construction is unreasonable express terms control both course of dealing and usage of trade and course of dealing controls usage of trade.

(5) An applicable usage of trade in the place where any part of performance is to occur shall be used in interpreting the agreement as to that part of the performance.

(6) Evidence of a relevant usage of trade offered by one party is not admissible unless and until he has given the other party such notice as the court finds sufficient to prevent unfair surprise to the latter.

§ 1-206. Statute of Frauds for Kinds of Personal Property Not Otherwise Covered.—

(1) Except in the cases described in subsection (2) of this section a contract for the sale of personal property is not enforceable by way of action or defense beyond five thousand dollars in amount or value of remedy unless there is some writing which indicates that a contract for sale has been made between the parties at a defined or stated price, reasonably identifies the subject matter, and is signed by the party against whom enforcement is sought or by his authorized agent.

(2) Subsection (1) of this section does not apply to contracts for the sale of goods (Section 2-201) nor of securities (Section 8-319) nor to security agreements (Section 9-203).

§ 1-207. Performance or Acceptance Under Reservation of Rights.—A party who with explicit reservation of rights performs or promises performance or assents to performance in a manner demanded or offered by the other party does not thereby prejudice the rights reserved. Such words as "without prejudice", "under protest" or the like are sufficient.

§ 1-208. Option to Accelerate at Will.—A term providing that one party or his successor in interest may accelerate payment or performance or require collateral or additional collateral "at will" or "when he deems himself insecure" or in words of similar import shall be construed to mean that he shall have power to do so only if he in good faith believes that the prospect of payment or performance is impaired. The burden of establishing lack of good faith is on the party against whom the power has been exercised.

ARTICLE TWO — SALES

PART 1

Short Title, General Construction and Subject Matter

§ 2-101. Short Title.—This Article shall be known and may be cited as Uniform Commercial Code—Sales.

§ 2-102. Scope; Certain Security and Other Transactions Excluded From This Article.—Unless the context otherwise requires, this Article applies to transactions in goods; it does not apply to any transaction which although in the form of an unconditional contract to sell or present sale is intended to operate only as a security transaction nor does this Article impair or repeal any statute regulating sales to consumers, farmers or other specified classes of buyers.

§ 2-103. Definitions and Index of Definitions.—
(1) In this Article unless the context otherwise requires
    (a) "Buyer" means a person who buys or contracts to buy goods.
    (b) "Good faith" in the case of a merchant means honesty in fact and the observance of reasonable commercial standards of fair dealing in the trade.
    (c) "Receipt" of goods means taking physical possession of them.
    (d) "Seller" means a person who sells or contracts to sell goods. . . .

§ 2-104. Definitions: "Merchant"; "Between Merchants"; "Financing Agency."—
(1) "Merchant" means a person who deals in goods of the kind or otherwise by his occupation holds himself out as having knowledge or skill peculiar to the practices or goods involved in the transaction or to whom such knowledge or skill may be attributed by his employment of an agent or broker or other intermediary who by his occupation holds himself out as having such knowledge or skill.
(2) "Financing agency" means a bank, finance company or other person who in the ordinary course of business makes advances against goods or documents of title or who by arrangement with either the seller or the buyer intervenes in ordinary course to make or collect payment due or claimed under the contract for sale, as by purchasing or paying the seller's draft or making advances against it or by merely taking it for collection whether or not documents of title accompany the draft. "Financing agency" includes also a bank or other person who similarly intervenes between persons who are in the position of seller and buyer in respect to the goods (Section 2-707).
(3) "Between merchants" means in any transaction with respect to which both parties are chargeable with the knowledge or skill of merchants.

§ 2-105. Definitions: Transferability; "Goods"; "Future" Goods; "Lot"; "Commercial Unit".—
(1) "Goods means all things (including specially manufactured goods) which are movable at the time of identification to the contract for sale other than the money in which the price is to be paid, investment securities (Article 8) and things in action. "Goods" also includes the unborn young of animals and growing crops and other identified things attached to realty as described in the section on goods to be severed from realty (Section 2-107.)
(2) Goods must be both existing and identified before any interest in them can pass. Goods which are not both existing and identified are "future" goods. A purported present sale of future goods or of any interest therein operates as a contract to sell.
(3) There may be a sale of a part interest in existing identified goods.
(4) An undivided share in an identified bulk of fungible goods is sufficiently identified to be sold although the quantity of the bulk is not determined. Any agreed proportion of such a bulk or any quantity thereof agreed upon by number, weight or other measure may to the extent of the seller's interest in the bulk be sold to the buyer who then becomes an owner in common.
(5) "Lot" means a parcel or a single article which is the subject matter of a separate sale or delivery, whether or not it is sufficient to perform the contract.
(6) "Commercial unit" means such a unit of goods as by commercial usage is a single whole for purposes of sale and division of which materially impairs its character or value on the market or in use. A commercial unit may be a single article (as a machine) or a set of articles (as a suite of furniture or an assortment of sizes) or a quantity (as a bale, gross, or carload) or any other unit treated in use of in the relevant market as a single whole.

§ 2-106. Definitions: "Contract"; "Agreement"; "Contract for Sale"; "Sale"; "Present Sale"; "Conforming" to Contract; "Termination"; "Cancellation".—
(1) In This Article unless the context otherwise requires "contract" and "agreement" are limited to those relating to the present or future sale of goods. "Contract for sale" includes both a present sale of goods and a contract to sell goods at a future time. A "sale" consists in the passing of title from the seller to the buyer for a price (Section 2-401). A "present sale" means a sale which is accomplished by the marking of the contract.
(2) Goods or conduct including any part of a performance are "conforming" or conform to the contract when they are in accordance with the obligations under the contract.
(3) "Termination" occurs when either party pursuant to a power created by agreement or law puts an end to the contract otherwise than for its breach. On "termination" all obligations which are still executory on both sides are discharged but any right based on prior breach or performance survives.
(4) "Cancellation" occurs when either party puts an end to the contract for breach by the other and its effect is the same as that of "termination" except that the cancelling party also retains any remedy for breach of the whole contract or any unperformed balance.

§ 2-107. Goods to Be Severed From Realty: Recording.—
(1) A contract for the sale of minerals or the like [(including oil and gas)] or a structure or its materials to be removed from realty is a contract for the sale of goods within this Article if they are to be severed by the seller but until severance a purported present sale thereof which is not effective as a transfer of an interest in land is effective only as a contract to sell.
(2) A contract for the sale apart from the land of growing crops or other things attached to realty and capable of severance without material harm thereto but not described in subsection (1) [or of timber to be

cut] is a contract for the sale of goods within this Article whether the subject matter is to be severed by the buyer or by the seller even though it forms part of the realty at the time of contracting, and the parties can by identification effect a present sale before severance.

(3) The provision of this section are subject to any third party rights provided by the law relating to realty records, and the contract for sale may be executed and recorded as a document transferring an interest in land and shall then constitute notice to third parties of the buyer's rights under the contract for sale.

PART 2

Form, Formation and Readjustment of Contract

§ 2-201. Formal Requirements; Statute of Frauds.—

(1) Except as otherwise provided in this section a contract for the sale of goods for the price of $500 or more is not enforceable by way of action or defense unless there is some writing sufficient to indicate that a contract for sale has been made between the parties and signed by the party against whom enforcement is sought or by his authorized agent or broker. A writing is not insufficient because it omits or incorrectly states a term agreed upon but the contract is not enforceable under this paragraph beyond the quantity of goods shown in such writing.

(2) Between merchants if within a reasonable time a writing in confirmation of the contract and sufficient against the sender is received and the party receiving it has reason to know its contents, it satisfies the requirements of subsection (1) against such party unless written notice of objection to its contents is given within ten days after it is received.

(3) A contract which does not satisfy the requirements of subsection (1) but which is valid in other respects is enforceable

(a) if the goods are to be specially manufactured for the buyer and are not suitable for sale to others in the ordinary course of the seller's business and the seller, before notice of repudiation is received and under circumstances which reasonably indicate that the goods are for the buyer, has made either a substantial beginning of their manufacture or commitments for their procurement; or

(b) if the party against whom enforcement is sought admits in his pleading, testimony or otherwise in court that a contract for sale was made, but the contract is not enforceable under this provision beyond the quantity of goods admitted; or

(c) with respect to goods for which payment has been made and accepted or which have been received and accepted (Sec. 2-606).

§ 2-202. Final Written Expression: Part or Extrinsic Evidence.—

Terms with respect to which the confirmatory memoranda of the parties agree or which are otherwise set forth in a writing intended by the parties as a final expression of their agreement with respect to such terms as are included therein may not be contradicted by evidence of any prior agreement or of a contemporaneous oral agreement but may be explained or supplemented

(a) by course of dealing or usage of trade (Section 1-205) or by course of performance (Section 2-208); and

(b) by evidence of consistent additional terms unless the court finds the writing to have been intended also as a complete and exclusive statement of the terms of the agreement.

§ 2-203. Seals Inoperative.—

The affixing of a seal to a writing evidencing a contract for sale or an offer to buy or sell goods does not constitute the writing a sealed instrument and the law with respect to sealed instruments does not apply to such a contract or offer.

§ 2-204. Formation in General.—

(1) A contract for sale of goods may be made in any manner sufficient to show agreement, including conduct by both parties which recognizes the existence of such a contract.

(2) An agreement sufficient to constitute a contract for sale may be found even though the moment of its making is undetermined.

(3) Even though one or more terms are left open a contract for sale does not fail for indefiniteness if the parties have intended to make a contract and there is a reasonably certain basis for giving an appropriate remedy.

§ 2-205. Firm Offers.—

An offer by a merchant to buy or sell goods in a signed writing which by its terms gives assurance that it will be held open is not revocable, for lack of consideration, during the time stated or if no time is stated for a reasonable time, but in no event may such period of irrevocability exceed three months; but any such term of assurance on a form supplied by the offeree must be separately signed by the offeror.

§ 2-206. Offer and Acceptance in Formation of Contract.—

(1) Unless otherwise unambiguously indicated by the language or circumstances

(a) an offer to make a contract shall be construed as inviting acceptance in any manner and by any medium reasonable in the circumstances.

(b) an order or other offer to buy goods for prompt or current shipment shall be construed as inviting acceptance either by a prompt promise to ship or by the prompt or current shipment of conforming or non-conforming goods, but such a shipment of non-conforming goods does not constitute an acceptance if the seller seasonably notifies the buyer that the shipment is offered only as an accommodation to the buyer.

(2) Where the beginning of a requested performance is a reasonable mode of acceptance an offeror who is not notified of acceptance within a reasonable time may treat the offer as having lapsed before acceptance.

§ 2-207.   Additional Terms in Acceptance or Confirmation.—

(1) A definite and seasonable expression of acceptance or a written confirmation which is sent within a reasonable time operates as an acceptance even though it states terms additional to or different from those offered or agreed upon, unless acceptance is expressly made conditional on assent to the additional or different terms.

(2) The additional terms are to be construed as proposals for addition to the contract. Between merchants such terms become part of the contract unless:

    (a) the offer expressly limits acceptance to the terms of the offer;

    (b) they materially alter it; or

    (c) notification of objection to them has already been given or is given within a reasonable time after notice of them is received.

(3) Conduct by both parties which recognizes the existence of a contract is sufficient to establish a contract for sale although the writings of the parties do not otherwise establish a contract. In such case the terms of the particular contract consist of those terms on which the writings of the parties agree, together with any supplementary terms incorporated under any other provisions of this Act.

§ 2-208.   Course of Performance or Practical Construction.—

(1) Where the contract for sale involves repeated occasions for performance by either party with knowledge of the nature of the performance and opportunity for objection to it by the other, any course of performance accepted or acquiesced in without objection shall be relevant to determine the meaning of the agreement.

(2) The express terms of the agreement and any such course of performance, as well as any course of dealing and usage of trade, shall be construed whenever reasonable as consistent with each other; but when such construction is unreasonable, express terms shall control course of performance and course of performance shall control both course of dealing and usage of trade (Section 1-205).

(3) Subject to the provisions of the next section on modification and waiver, such course of performance shall be relevant to show a waiver or modification of any term inconsistent with such course of performance.

§ 2-209.   Modification, Rescission and Waiver.—

(1) An agreement modifying a contract within this Article needs no consideration to be binding.

(2) A signed agreement which excludes modification or rescission except by a signed writing cannot be otherwise modified or rescinded, but except as between merchants such a requirement on a form supplied by the merchant must be separately signed by the other party.

(3) The requirements of the statute of frauds section of this Article (Section 2-201) must be satisfied if the contract as modified is within its provisions.

(4) Although an attempt at modification or rescission does not satisfy the requirements of subsection (2) or (3) it can operate as a waiver.

(5) A party who has made a waiver affecting an executory portion of the contract may retract the waiver by reasonable notification received by the other party that strict performance will be required of any term waived, unless the retraction would be unjust in view of a material change of position in reliance on the waiver.

§ 2-210.   Delegation of Performance; Assignment of Rights.—

(1) A party may perform his duty through a delegate unless otherwise agreed or unless the other party has a substantial interest in having his original promisor perform or control the acts required by the contract. No delegation of performance relieves the party delegating of any duty to perform or any liability for breach.

(2) Unless otherwise agreed all rights of either seller or buyer can be assigned except where the assignment would materially change the duty of the other party, or increase materially the burden or risk imposed on him by his contract, or impair materially his chance of obtaining return performance. A right to damages for breach of the whole contract or a right arising out of the assignor's due performance of his entire obligation can be assigned despite agreement otherwise.

(3) Unless the circumstances indicate the contrary a prohibition of assignment of "the contract" is to be construed as barring only the delegation to the assignee of the assignor's performance.

(4) An assignment of "the contract" or of "all my rights under the contract" or an assignment in similar general terms is an assignment of rights and unless the language or the circumstances (as in an assignment for security) indicate the contrary, it is a delegation of performance of the duties of the assignor and its acceptance by the assignee constitutes a promise by him to perform those duties. This promise is enforceable by either the assignor or the other party to the original contract.

(5) The other party may treat any assignment which delegates performance as creating reasonable grounds for insecurity and may without prejudice to his rights against the assignor demand assurances from the assignee (Section 2-609).

PART 3

General Obligation and Construction of Contract

§ 2-301.   General Obligations of Parties.—The obligation of the seller is to transfer and deliver and that of the buyer is to accept and pay in accordance with the contract.

§ 2-302. Unconscionable Contract or Clause.—

(1) If the court as a matter of law finds the contract or any clause of the contract to have been unconscionable at the time it was made the court may refuse to enforce the contract, or it may enforce the remainder of the contract without the unconscionable clause, or it may so limit the application of any unconscionable clause as to avoid any unconscionable result.

(2) When it is claimed or appears to the court that the contract or any clause thereof may be unconscionable the parties shall be afforded a reasonable opportunity to present evidence as to its commercial setting, purpose and effect to aid the court in making the determination.

§ 2-303. Allocation or Division of Risks.—Where this Article allocates a risk or a burden as between the parties "unless otherwise agreed," the agreement may not only shift the allocation but may also divide the risk or burden.

§ 2-304. Price Payable in Money, Goods, Realty, or Otherwise.—

(1) The price can be made payable in money or otherwise. If it is payable in whole or in part in goods each party is a seller of the goods which he is to transfer.

(2) Even though all or part of the price is payable in an interest in realty the transfer of the goods and the seller's obligations with reference to them are subject to this Article, but not the transfer of the interest in realty or the transferor's obligations in connection therewith.

§ 2-305. Open Price Term.—

(1) The parties if they so intend can conclude a contract for sale even though the price is not settled. In such a case the price is a reasonable price at the time for delivery if:

(a) nothing is said as to price; or

(b) the price is left to be agreed by the parties and they fail to agree; or

(c) the price is to be fixed in terms of some agreed market or other standard as set or recorded by a third person or agency and it is not so set or recorded.

(2) A price to be fixed by the seller or by the buyer means a price for him to fix in good faith.

(3) When a price left to be fixed otherwise than by agreement of the parties fails to be fixed through fault of one party the other may at his option treat the contract as cancelled or himself fix a reasonable price.

(4) Where, however, the parties intend not to be bound unless the price be fixed or agreed and it is not fixed or agreed there is no contract. In such a case the buyer must return any goods already received or if unable so to do must pay their reasonable value at the time of delivery and the seller must return any portion of the price paid on account.

§ 2-306. Output, Requirements and Exclusive Dealings.—

(1) A term which measures the quantity by the output of the seller or the requirements of the buyer means such actual output or requirements as may occur in good faith, except that no quantity unreasonably disproportionate to any stated estimate or in the absence of a stated estimate to any normal or otherwise comparable prior output or requirements may be tendered or demanded.

(2) A lawful agreement by either the seller or the buyer for exclusive dealing in the kind of goods concerned imposes unless otherwise agreed an obligation by the seller to use best efforts to supply the goods and by the buyer to use best efforts to promote their sale.

§ 2-307. Delivery in Single Lot or Several Lots.—Unless otherwise agreed all goods called for by a contract for sale must be tendered in a single delivery and payment is due only on such tender but where the circumstances give either party the right to make or demand delivery in lots the price if it can be apportioned may be demanded for each lot.

§ 2-308. Absence of Specified Place for Delivery.—Unless otherwise agreed

(a) the place for delivery of goods is the seller's place of business or if he has none his residence; but

(b) in a contract for sale of identified goods which to the knowledge of the parties at the time of contracting are in some other place, that place is the place for their delivery; and

(c) documents of title may be delivered through customary banking channels.

§ 2-309. Absence of Specific Time Provisions; Notice of Termination.—

(1) The time for shipment or delivery of any other action under a contract if not provided in this Article or agreed upon shall be a reasonable time.

(2) Where the contract provides for successive performances but is indefinite in duration it is valid for a reasonable time but unless otherwise agreed may be terminated at any time by either party.

(3) Termination of a contract by one party except on the happening of an agreed event requires that reasonable notification be received by the other party and an agreement dispensing with notification is invalid if its operation would be unconscionable.

§ 2-310. Open Time for Payment or Running of Credit; Authority to Ship Under Reservation.—Unless otherwise agreed

(a) payment is due at the time and place at which the buyer is to receive the goods even though the place of shipment is the place of delivery; and

(b) if the seller is authorized to send the goods he may ship them under reservation, and may tender the documents of title, but the buyer may inspect the goods after their arrival before payment is due unless such inspection is inconsistent with the terms of the contract (Section 2-513); and

(c) if delivery is authorized and made by way of documents of title otherwise than by subsection (b) then payment is due at the time and place at which the buyer is to receive the documents regardless of where the goods are to be received; and

(d) where the seller is required or authorized to ship the goods on credit the credit period runs from the time of shipment but post-dating the invoice or delaying its dispatch will correspondingly delay the starting of the credit period.

§ 2-311. Options and Cooperation Respecting Performance.—

(1) An agreement for sale which is otherwise sufficiently definite (subsection (3) of Section 2-204) to be a contract is not made invalid by the fact that it leaves particulars of performance to be specified by one of the parties. Any such specification must be made in good faith and within limits set by commercial reasonableness.

(2) Unless otherwise agreed specifications relating to assortment of the goods are at the buyer's option and except as otherwise provided in subsections (1) (c) and (3) of Section 2-319 specifications or arrangements relating to shipment are at the seller's option.

(3) Where such specification would materially affect the other party's performance but is not seasonably made or where one party's cooperation is necessary to the agreed performance of the other but is not seasonably forthcoming, the other party in addition to all other remedies

    (a) is excused for any resulting delay in his own performance; and

    (b) may also either proceed to perform in any reasonable manner or after the time for a material part of his own performance treat the failure to specify or to cooperate as a breach by failure to deliver or accept the goods.

§ 2-312. Warranty of Title and Against Infringement; Buyer's Obligation Against Infringement.—

(1) Subject to subsection (2) there is in a contract for sale a warranty by the seller that

    (a) the title conveyed shall be good, and its transfer rightful; and

    (b) the goods shall be delivered free from any security interest or other lien or encumbrance of which the buyer at the time of contracting has no knowledge.

(2) A warranty under subsection (1) will be excluded or modified only by specific language or by circumstances which give the buyer reason to know that the person selling does not claim title in himself or that he is purporting to sell only such right or title as he or a third person may have.

(3) Unless otherwise agreed a seller who is a merchant regularly dealing in goods of the kind warrants that the goods shall be delivered free of the rightful claim of any third person by way of infringement or the like but a buyer who furnishes specifications to the seller must hold the seller harmless against any such claim which arises out of compliance with the specifications.

§ 2-313. Express Warranties by Affirmation, Promise, Description, Sample.—

(1) Express warranties by the seller are created as follows:

    (a) Any affirmation of fact or promise made by the seller to the buyer which relates to the goods and becomes part of the basis of the bargain creates an express warranty that the goods shall conform to the affirmation or promise.

    (b) Any description of the goods which is made part of the basis of the bargain creates an express warranty that the goods shall conform to the description.

    (c) Any sample or model which is made part of the basis of the bargain creates an express warranty that the whole of the goods shall conform to the sample or model.

(2) It is not necessary to the creation of an express warranty that the seller use formal words such as "warrant" or "guarantee" or that he have a specific intention to make a warranty, but an affirmation merely of the value of the goods or a statement purporting to be merely the seller's opinion or commendation of the goods does not create a warranty.

§ 2-314. Implied Warranty: Merchantability; Usage of Trade.—

(1) Unless excluded or modified (Section 2-316), a warranty that the goods shall be merchantable is implied in a contract for their sale if the seller is a merchant with respect to goods of that kind. Under this section the serving for value of food or drink to be consumed either on the premises or elsewhere is a sale.

(2) Goods to be merchantable must be at least such as

    (a) pass without objection in the trade under the contract description; and

    (b) in the case of fungible goods, are of fair average quality within the description; and

    (c) are fit for the ordinary purposes for which such goods are used; and

    (d) run, within the variations permitted by the agreement, of even kind, quality and quantity within each unit and among all units involved; and

    (e) are adequately contained, packaged, and labeled as the agreement may require; and

    (f) conform to the promises or affirmations of fact made on the container or label if any.

(3) Unless excluded or modified (Section 2-316) other implied warranties may arise from course of dealing or usage of trade.

§ 2-315. Implied Warranty: Fitness for Particular Purpose.—Where the seller at the time of contracting has reason to know any particular purpose for which the goods are required and that the buyer is relying on the seller's skill or judgment to select or furnish suitable goods, there is unless excluded or modified under the next section an implied warranty that the goods shall be fit for such purpose.

§ 2-316. Exclusion or Modification of Warranties.—

(1) Words or conduct relevant to the creation of an express warranty and words or conduct tending to negate or limit warranty shall be construed wherever reasonable as consistent with each other; but subject to the provisions of this Article on parol or extrinsic evidence (Section 2-202) negation or limitation is inoperative to the extent that such construction is unreasonable.

(2) Subject to subsection (3), to exclude or modify the implied warranty of merchantability or any part of it the language must mention merchantability and in case of a writing must be conspicuous, and to exclude or modify any implied warranty of fitness the exclusion must be by a writing and conspicuous. Language to exclude all implied warranties of fitness is sufficient if it states, for example, that "There are no warranties which extend beyond the description on the face hereof."

(3) Notwithstanding subsection (2)

    (a) unless the circumstances indicate otherwise, all implied warranties are excluded by expressions like "as is," "with all faults" or other language which in common understanding calls the buyer's attention to the exclusion of warranties and makes plain that there is no implied warranty; and

    (b) when the buyer before entering into the contract has examined the goods or the sample or model as fully as he desired or has refused to examine the goods there is no implied warranty with regard to defects which an examination ought in the circumstances to have revealed to him; and

    (c) an implied warranty can also be excluded or modified by course of dealing or course of performance or usage of trade.

(4) Remedies for breach of warranty can be limited in accordance with the provisions of this Article on liquidation or limitation of damages and on contractual modification of remedy (Sections 2-718 and 2-719).

§ 2-317. Cumulation and Conflict of Warranties Express or Implied.—Warranties whether express or implied shall be construed as consistent with each other and as cumulative, but if such construction is unreasonable the intention of the parties shall determine which warranty is dominant. In ascertaining that intention the following rules apply:

    (a) Exact or technical specifications displace an inconsistent sample or model or general language of description.

    (b) A sample from an existing bulk displaces inconsistent general language of description.

    (c) Express warranties displace inconsistent implied warranties other than an implied warranty of fitness for a particular purpose.

§ 2-318. Third Party Beneficiaries of Warranties Express or Implied.—A seller's warranty whether express or implied extends to any natural person who is in the family or household of his buyer or who is a guest in his home if it is reasonable to expect that such person may use, consume or be affected by the goods and who is injured in person by breach of the warranty. A seller may not exclude or limit the operation of this section.

§ 2-319. F.O.B. and F.A.S. Terms.—

(1) Unless otherwise agreed the term F.O.B. (which means "free on board") at a named place, even though used only in connection with the stated price, is a delivery term under which

    (a) when the term is F.O.B. the place of shipment, the seller must at that place ship the goods in the manner provided in this Article (Section 2-504; and bear the expense and risk of putting them into the possession of the carrier; or

    (b) when the term is F.O.B. the place of destination, the seller must at his own expense and risk transport the goods to that place and there tender delivery of them in the manner provided in this Article (Section 2-503);

    (c) when under either (a) or (b) the term is also F.O.B. vessel, car or other vehicle, the seller must in addition at his own expense and risk load the goods on board. If the term is F.O.B. vessel the buyer must name the vessel and in an appropriate case the seller must comply with the provisions of this Article on the form of bill of lading (Section 2-323).

(2) Unless otherwise agreed the term F.A.S. vessel (which means "free alongside") at a named port, even though used only in connection with the stated price, is a delivery term under which the seller must

    (a) at his own expense and risk deliver the goods alongside the vessel in the manner usual in that port or on a dock designated and provided by the buyer; and

    (b) obtain and tender a receipt for the goods in exchange for which the carrier is under a duty to issue a bill of lading.

(3) Unless otherwise agreed in any case falling within subsection (1) (a) or (c) or subsection (2) the buyer must seasonably give any needed instructions for making delivery, including when the term is F.A.S. or F.O.B. the loading berth of the vessel and in an appropriate case its name and sailing date. The seller may treat the failure of needed instructions as a failure of cooperation under this Article (Section 2-311). He may also at his option move the goods in any reasonable manner preparatory to delivery or shipment.

(4) Under the term F.O.B. vessel or F.A.S. unless otherwise agreed the buyer must make payment against tender of the required documents and the seller may not tender nor the buyer demand delivery, of the goods in substitution for the documents.

§ 2-320. C.I.F. and C. & F. Terms.—

(1) The term C.I.F. means that the price includes in a lump sum the cost of the goods and the insurance and freight to the named destination.

(2) Unless otherwise agreed and even though used only in connection with the stated price and destination, the term C.I.F. destination or its equivalent requires the seller at his own expense and risk to

    (a) put the goods into the possession of a carrier at the port for shipment and obtain a negotiable bill or bills of lading covering the entire transportation to the named destination; and

    (b) load the goods and obtain a receipt from the carrier (which may be contained in the bill of lading) showing that the freight has been paid or provided for; and

    (c) obtain a policy or certificate of insurance, including any war risk insurance, of a kind and on terms then current at the port of shipment in the usual amount, in the currency of the contract, shown to cover the same goods covered by the bill of lading and providing for payment of loss to the order of the buyer or for the account of whom it may concern; but the seller may add to the price the amount of the premium for any such war risk insurance; and

    (d) prepare an invoice of the goods and procure any other documents required to effect shipment or to comply with the contract; and

    (e) forward and tender with commercial promptness all the documents in due form and with any indorsement necessary to perfect the buyer's rights.

(3) Unless otherwise agreed the term C. & F. or its equivalent has the same effect and imposes upon the seller the same obligations and risks as a C.I.F. term except the obligation as to insurance.

(4) Under the term C.I.F. or C. & F. unless otherwise agreed the buyer must make payment against tender of the required documents and the seller may not tender nor the buyer demand delivery of the goods in substitution for the documents.

§ 2-321.   C.I.F. or C. & F.: "Net Landed Weights"; "Payment on Arrival"; Warranty of Condition on Arrival.—Under a contract containing a term C.I.F. or C. & F.

(1) Where the price is based on or is to be adjusted according to "net landed weights," "delivered weights," "out turn" quantity or quality or the like, unless otherwise agreed the seller must reasonably estimate the price. The payment due on tender of the documents called for by the contract is the amount so estimated but after final adjustment of the price a settlement must be made with commercial promptness.

(2) An agreement described in subsection (1) or any warranty of quality or condition of the goods on arrival places upon the seller the risk of ordinary deterioration, shrinkage and the like in transportation but has no effect on the place or time of identification to the contract for sale or delivery or on the passing of the risk of loss.

(3) Unless otherwise agreed where the contract provides for payment on or after arrival of the goods the seller must before payment allow such preliminary inspection as is feasible; but if the goods are lost delivery of the documents and payment are due when the goods should have arrived.

§ 2-322.   Delivery "Ex-Ship".—
(1) Unless otherwise agreed a term for delivery of goods "ex-ship" (which means from the carrying vessel) or in equivalent language is not restricted to a particular ship and requires delivery from a ship which has reached a place at the named port of destination where goods of the kind are usually discharged.

(2) Under such a term unless otherwise agreed
(a) the seller must discharge all liens arising out of the carriage and furnish the buyer with a direction which puts the carrier under a duty to deliver the goods; and
(b) the risk of loss does not pass to the buyer until the goods leave the ship's tackle or are otherwise properly unloaded.

§ 2-323.   Form of Bill of Lading Required in Overseas Shipments; "Overseas."—
(1) Where the contract contemplates overseas shipment and contains a term C.I.F. or C. & F. or F.O.B. vessel, the seller unless otherwise agreed must obtain a negotiable bill of lading stating that the goods have been loaded on board or, in the case of a term C.I.F. or C. & F., received for shipment.

(2) Where in a case within subsection (1) a bill of lading has been issued in a set of parts, unless otherwise agreed if the documents are not to be sent from abroad the buyer may demand tender of the full set; otherwise only one part of the bill of lading need be tendered. Even if the agreement expressly requires a full set
(a) due tender of a single part is acceptable within the provisions of this Article on cure of improper delivery (subsection (1) of Section 2-508); and
(b) even though the full set is demanded, if the documents are sent from abroad the person tendering an incomplete set may nevertheless require payment upon furnishing an indemnity which the buyer in good faith deems adequate.

(3) A shipment by water or by air or a contrct contemplating such shipment is "overseas" insofar as by usage of trade or agreement it is subject to the commercial, financing or shipping practices characteristic of international deep water commerce.

§ 2-324.   "No Arrival, No Sale" Term.—Under a term "no arrival, no sale" or terms of the like meaning, unless otherwise agreed
(a) the seller must properly ship conforming goods and if they arrive by any means he must tender them on arrival but he assures no obligation that the goods will arrive unless he has caused the non-arrival; and
(b) where without fault of the seller the goods are in part lost or have so deteriorated as no longer to conform to the contract or arrive after the contract time, the buyer may proceed as if there had been casualty to identified goods (Section 2-613).

§ 2-325.   "Letter of Credit" Term; "Confirmed Credit."—
(1) Failure of the buyer seasonably to furnish an agreed letter of credit is a breach of the contract for sale.

(2) The delivery to seller of a proper letter of credit suspends the buyer's obligation to pay. If the letter of credit is dishonored, the seller may on seasonable notification to the buyer require payment directly from him.

(3) Unless otherwise agreed the term "letter of credit" or "banker's credit" in a contract for sale means an irrevocable credit issued by a financing agency of good repute and, where the shipment is overseas, of good international repute. The term "confirmed credit" means that the credit must also carry the direct obligation of such an agency which does business in the seller's financial market.

§ 2-326.   Sale on Approval and Sale or Return; Consignment Sales and Rights of Creditors.—
(1) Unless otherwise agreed, if delivered goods may be returned by the buyer even though they conform to the contract, the transaction is
(a) a "sale on approval" if the goods are delivered primarily for use, and
(b) a "sale or return" if the goods are delivered primarily for resale.

(2) Except as provided in subsection (3), goods held on approval are not subject to the claims of the

buyer's creditors until acceptance; goods held on sale or return are subject to such claims while in the buyer's possession.

(3) Where goods are delivered to a person for sale and such person maintains a place of business at which he deals in goods of the kind involved, under a name other than the name of the person making delivery, then with respect to claims of creditors of the person conducting the business the goods are deemed to be on sale or return. The provisions of this subsection are applicable even though an agreement purports to reserve title to the person making delivery until payment or resale or uses such words as "on consignment" or "on memorandum." However, this subsection is not applicable if the person making delivery

(a) complies with an applicable law providing for a consignor's interest or the like to be evidenced by a sign, or

(b) establishes that the person conducting the business is generally known by his creditors to be substantially engaged in selling the goods of others, or

(c) complies with the filing provisions of the Article on Secured Transactions (Article 9).

(4) Any "or return" term of a contract for sale is to be treated as a separate contract for sale within the statute of frauds section of this Article (Section 2-201) and as contradicting the sale aspect of the contract within the provisions of this Article on parol or extrinsic evidence (Section 2-202).

§ 2-327. Special Incidents of Sale on Approval and Sale or Return.—

(1) Under a sale on approval unless otherwise agreed

(a) although the goods are identified to the contract the risk of loss and the title do not pass to the buyer until acceptance; and

(b) use of goods consistent with the purpose of trial is not acceptance but failure seasonably to notify the seller of election to return the goods is acceptance, and if the goods conform to the contract acceptance of any part is acceptance of the whole; and

(c) after due notification of election to return, the return is at the seller's risk and expense but a merchant buyer must follow any reasonable instructions.

(2) Under a sale or return unless otherwise agreed

(a) the option to return extends to the whole or any commercial unit of the goods while in substantially their original condition, but must be exercised seasonably; and

(b) the return is at the buyer's risk and expense.

§ 2-328. Sale by Auction.—

(1) In a sale by auction if goods are put up in lots each lot is the subject of a separate sale.

(2) A sale by auction is complete when the auctioneer so announces by the fall of the hammer or in other customary manner. Where a bid is made while the hammer is falling in acceptance of a prior bid the auctioneer may in his discretion reopen the bidding or declare the goods sold under the bid on which the hammer was falling.

(3) Such a sale is with reserve unless the goods are in explicit terms put up without reserve. In an auction with reserve the auctioneer may withdraw the goods at any time until he announces completion of the sale. In an auction without reserve, after the auctioneer calls for bids on an article or lot, that article or lot cannot be withdrawn unless no bid is made within a reasonable time. In either case a bidder may retract his bid until the auctioneer's announcement of completion of the sale, but a bidder's retraction does not revive any previous bid.

(4) If the auctioneer knowingly receives a bid on the seller's behalf or the seller makes or procures such a bid, and notice has not been given that liberty for such bidding is reserved, the buyer may at his option avoid the sale or take the goods at the price of the last good faith bid prior to the completion of the sale. This subsection shall not apply to any bid at a forced sale.

PART 4

Title, Creditors and Good Faith Purchasers

§ 2-401. Passing of Title; Reservation for Security; Limited Application of This Section.—Each provision of this Article with regard to the rights, obligations and remedies of the seller, the buyer, purchasers or other third parties applies irrespective of title to the goods except where the provision refers to such title. Insofar as situations are not covered by the other provisions of this Article and matters concerning title become material the following rules apply:

(1) Title to goods cannot pass under a contract for sale prior to their identification to the contract (Section 2-501), and unless otherwise explicitly agreed the buyer acquires by their identification a special property as limited by this Act. Any retention or reservation by the seller of the title (property) in goods shipped or delivered to the buyer is limited in effect to a reservation of a security interest. Subject to these provisions and to the provisions of the Article on Secured Transactions (Article 9), title to goods passes from the seller to the buyer in any manner and on any conditions explicitly agreed on by the parties.

(2) Unless otherwise explicitly agreed title passes to the buyer at the time and place at which the seller completes his performance with reference to the physical delivery of the goods, despite any reservation of a security interest and even though a document of title is to be delivered at a different time or place; and in particular and despite any reservation of a security interest by the bill of lading.

(a) if the contract requires or authorizes the seller to send the goods to the buyer but does not require him to deliver them at destination, title passes to the buyer at the time and place of shipment; but

(b) if the contract requires delivery at destination, title passes on tender there.

(3) Unless otherwise explicitly agreed where delivery is to be made without moving the goods,

(a) if the seller is to deliver a document of title, title passes at the time when and the place where he delivers such documents; or

(b) if the goods are at the time of contracting already identified and no documents are to be delivered, title passes at the time and place of contracting.

(4) A rejection or other refusal by the buyer to receive or retain the goods, whether or not justified, or a justified revocation of acceptance revests title to the goods in the seller. Such revesting occurs by operation of law and is not a "sale."

§ 2-402. Rights of Seller's Creditors Against Sold Goods.—

(1) Except as provided in subsections (2) and (3), rights of unsecured creditors of the seller with respect to goods which have been identified to a contract for sale are subject to the buyer's rights to recover the goods under this Article (Sections 2-502 and 2-716).

(2) A creditor of the seller may treat a sale or an identification of goods to a contract for sale as void if as against him a retention of possession by the seller is fraudulent under any rule of law of the state where the goods are situated, except that retention of possession in good faith and current course of trade by a merchant-seller for a commercially reasonable time after a sale or identification is not fraudulent.

(3) Nothing in this Article shall be deemed to impair the rights of creditors of the seller

(a) under the provisions of the Article on Secured Transactions (Article 9); or

(b) where identification to the contract or delivery is made not in current course of trade but in satisfaction of or as security for a preexisting claim for money, security or the like and is made under circumstances which under any rule of law of the state where the goods are situated would apart from this Article constitute the transaction a fraudulent transfer or voidable preference.

§ 2-403. Power to Transfer; Good Faith Purchase of Goods; "Entrusting."—

(1) A purchaser of goods acquires all title which his transferor had or had power to transfer except that a purchaser of a limited interest acquires rights only to the extent of the interest purchased. A person with voidable title has power to transfer a good title to a good faith purchaser for value. When goods have been delivered under a transaction of purchase the purchaser has such power even though

(a) the transferor was deceived as to the identity of the purchaser, or

(b) the delivery was in exchange for a check which is later dishonored, or

(c) it was agreed that the transaction was to be a "cash sale," or

(d) the delivery was procured through fraud punishable as larcenous under the criminal law.

(2) Any entrusting of possession of goods to a merchant who deals in goods of that kind gives him power to transfer all rights of the entruster to a buyer in ordinary course of business.

(3) "Entrusting" includes any delivery and any acquiescence in retention of possession regardless of any condition expressed between the parties to the delivery or acquiescence and regardless of whether the procurement of the entrusting or the possessor's disposition of the goods have been such as to be larcenous under the criminal law.

(4) The rights of other purchasers of goods and of lien creditors are governed by the Articles on Secured Transactions (Article 9), Bulk Transfers (Article 6) and Documents of Title (Article 7).

PART 5

Performance

§ 2-501. Insurable Interest in Goods; Manner of Identification of Goods.—

(1) The buyer obtains a special property and an insurable interest in goods by identification of existing goods as goods to which the contract refers even though the goods so identified are non-conforming and he has an option to return or reject them. Such identification can be made at any time and in any manner explicitly agreed to by the parties. In the absence of explicit agreement identification occurs

(a) when the contract is made if it is for the sale of goods already existing and identified;

(b) if the contract is for the sale of future goods other than those described in paragraph (c), when goods are shipped, marked or otherwise designated by the seller as goods to which the contract refers;

(c) when the crops are planted or otherwise become growing crops or the young are conceived if the contract is for the sale of unborn young to be born within twelve months after contracting or for the sale of crops to be harvested within twelve months or the next normal harvest season after contracting whichever is longer.

(2) The seller retains an insurable interest in goods so long as title to or any security interest in the goods remains in him and where the identification is by the seller alone he may until default or insolvency or notification to the buyer that the identification is final substitute other goods for those identified.

(3) Nothing in this section impairs any insurable interest recognized under any other statute or rule of law.

§ 2-502. Buyer's Right to Goods on Seller's Insolvency.—

(1) Subject to subsection (2) and even though the goods have not been shipped a buyer who has paid a part or all of the price of goods in which he has a special property under the provisions of the immediately preceding section may on making and keeping good a tender of any unpaid portion of their price recover them from the seller if the seller becomes insolvent within ten days after receipt of the first installment on their price.

(2) If the identification creating his special property has been made by the buyer he acquires the right to recover the goods only if they conform to the contract for sale.

§ 2-503. Manner of Seller's Tender of Delivery.—

(1) Tender of delivery requires that the seller put and hold conforming goods at the buyer's disposition and give the buyer any notification reasonably necessary to enable him to take delivery. The manner, time and place for tender are determined by the agreement and this Article, and in particular

(a) tender must be at a reasonable hour, and if it is of goods they must be kept available for the period reasonably necessary to enable the buyer to take possession; but

(b) unless otherwise agreed the buyer must furnish facilities reasonably suited to the receipt of the goods.

(2) Where the case is within the next section respecting shipment tender requires that the seller comply with its provisions.

(3) Where the seller is required to deliver at a particular destination tender requires that he comply with subsection (1) and also in any appropriate case tender documents as described in subsections (4) and (5) of this section.

(4) Where goods are in the possession of a bailee and are to be delivered without being moved

(a) tender requires that the seller either tender a negotiable document of title covering such goods or procure acknowledgment by the bailee of the buyer's right to possession of the goods; but

(b) tender to the buyer of a nonnegotiable document of title or of a written direction to the bailee to deliver is sufficient tender unless the buyer seasonably objects, and receipt by the bailee of notification of the buyer's rights fixes those rights as against the bailee to honor the non-negotiable document of title or to obey the direction remains on the seller until the buyer has had a reasonable time to present the document or direction, and a refusal by the bailee to honor the document or to obey the direction defeats the tender.

(5) Where the contract requires the seller to deliver documents

(a) he must tender all such documents in correct form, except as provided in this Article with respect to bills of lading in a set (subsection (2) of Section 2-323); and

(b) tender through customary banking channels is sufficient and dishonor of a draft accompanying the documents constitutes non-acceptance or rejection.

§ 2-504. Shipment by Seller.—

Where the seller is required or authorized to send the goods to the buyer and the contract does not require him to deliver them at a particular destination, then unless otherwise agreed he must

(a) put the goods in the possession of such a carrier and make such a contract for their transportation as may be reasonable having regard to the nature of the goods and other circumstances of the case; and

(b) obtain and promptly deliver or tender in due form any document necessary to enable the buyer to obtain possession of the goods or otherwise required by the agreement or by usage of trade; and

(c) promptly notify the buyer of the shipment.

Failure to notify the buyer under paragraph (c) or to make a proper contract under paragraph (a) is a ground for rejection only if material delay or loss ensues.

§ 2-505. Seller's Shipment Under Reservation.—

(1) Where the seller has identified goods to the contract by or before shipment:

(a) his procurement of a negotiable bill of lading to his own order or otherwise reserves in him a security interest in the goods. His procurement of the bill to the order of a financing agency or of the buyer indicates in addition only the seller's expectation of transferring that interest to the person named.

(b) a non-negotiable bill of lading to himself or his nominee reserves possession of the goods as security but except in a case of conditional delivery (subsection (2) of Section 2-507) a non-negotiable bill of lading naming the buyer as consignee reserves no security interest even though the seller retains possession of the bill of lading.

(2) When shipment by the seller with reservation of a security interest is in violation of the contract for sale it constitutes an improper contract for transportation within the preceding section but impairs neither the rights given to the buyer by shipment and identification of the goods to the contract nor the seller's powers as a holder of a negotiable document.

§ 2-506. Rights of Financing Agency.—

(1) A financing agency by paying or purchasing for value a draft which relates to a shipment of goods acquires to the extent of the payment or purchase and in addition to its own rights under the draft and any document of title securing it any rights of the shipper in the goods including the right to stop delivery and the shipper's right to have the draft honored by the buyer.

(2) The right to reimbursement of a financing agency which has in good faith honored or purchased the draft under commitment to or authority from the buyer is not impaired by subsequent discovery of defects with reference to any relevant document which was apparently regular on its face.

§ 2-507. Effect of Seller's Tender; Delivery on Condition.—

(1) Tender of delivery is a condition to the buyer's duty to accept the goods and, unless otherwise agreed, to his duty to pay for them. Tender entitles the seller to acceptance of the goods and to payment according to the contract.

(2) Where payment is due and demanded on the delivery to the buyer of goods or documents of title, his right as against the seller to retain or dispose of them is conditional upon his making the payment due.

§ 2-508. Cure by Seller of Improper Tender or Delivery; Replacement.—

(1) Where any tender or delivery by the seller is rejected because non-conforming and the time for performance has not yet expired, the seller may seasonably notify the buyer of his intention to cure and may then within the contract time make a conforming delivery.

(2) Where the buyer rejects a non-conforming tender which the seller had reasonable grounds to believe would be acceptable with or without money allowance the seller may if he seasonably notifies the buyer have a further reasonable time to substitute a conforming tender.

§ 2-509. Risk of Loss in the Absence of Breach.—

(1) Where the contract requires or authorizes the seller to ship the goods by carrier

(a) if it does not require him to deliver them at a particular destination, the risk of loss passes to the buyer when the goods are duly delivered to the carrier even though the shipment is under reservation (Section 2-505); but

(b) if it does require him to deliver them at a particular destination and the goods are there duly tendered while in the possession of the carrier, the risk of loss passes to the buyer when the goods are there duly so tendered as to enable the buyer to take delivery.

(2) Where the goods are held by a bailee to be delivered without being moved, the risk of loss passes to the buyer

(a) on his receipt of a negotiable document of title covering the goods; or

(b) on acknowledgment by the bailee of the buyer's right to possession of the goods; or

(c) after his receipt of a non-negotiable document of title or other written direction to deliver, as provided in subsection (4) (b) of Section 2-503.

(3) In any case not within subsection (1) or (2), the risk of loss passes to the buyer on his receipt of the goods if the seller is a merchant; otherwise the risk passes to the buyer on tender of delivery.

(4) The provisions of this section are subject to contrary agreement of the parties and to the provisions of this Article on sale on approval (Section 2-327) and on effect of breach on risk of loss (Section 2-510).

§ 2-510. Effect of Breach on Risk of Loss.—

(1) Where a tender or delivery of goods so fails to conform to the contract as to give a right of rejection the risk of their loss remains on the seller until cure or acceptance.

(2) Where the buyer rightfully revokes acceptance he may to the extent of any deficiency in his effective insurance coverage treat the risk of loss as having rested on the seller from the beginning.

(3) Where the buyer as to conforming goods already identified to the contract for sale repudiates or is otherwise in breach before risk of their loss has passed to him, the seller may to the extent of any deficiency in his effective insurance coverage treat the risk of loss as resting on the buyer for a commercially reasonable time.

§ 2-511. Tender of Payment by Buyer; Payment by Check.—

(1) Unless otherwise agreed tender of payment is a condition to the seller's duty to tender and complete any delivery.

(2) Tender of payment is sufficient when made by any means or in any manner current in the ordinary course of business unless the seller demands payment in legal tender and gives any extension of time reasonably necessary to procure it.

(3) Subject to the provisions of this Act on the effect of an instrument on an obligation (Section 3-802), payment by check is conditional and is defeated as between the parties by dishonor of the check on due presentment.

§ 2-512. Payment by Buyer Before Inspection.—

(1) Where the contract requires payment before inspection non-conformity of the goods does not excuse the buyer from so making payment unless

(a) the non-conformity appears without inspection; or

(b) despite tender of the required documents the circumstances would justify injunction against honor under the provisions of this Act (Section 5-114).

(2) Payment pursuant to subsection (1) does not constitute an acceptance of goods or impair the buyer's right to inspect or any of his remedies.

§ 2-513. Buyer's Right to Inspection of Goods.—

(1) Unless otherwise agreed and subject to subsection (3), where goods are tendered or delivered or identified to the contract for sale, the buyer has a right before payment or acceptance to inspect them at any reasonable place and time and in any reasonable manner. When the seller is required or authorized to send the goods to the buyer, the inspection may be after their arrival.

(2) Expenses of inspection must be borne by the buyer but may be recovered from the seller if the goods do not conform and are rejected.

(3) Unless otherwise agreed and subject to the provisions of this Article on C.I.F. contracts (subsection (3) of Section 2-321), the buyer is not entitled to inspect the goods before payment of the price when the contract provides

(a) for delivery "C.O.D." or on other like terms; or

(b) for payment against documents of title, except where such payment is due only after the goods are to become available for inspection.

(4) A place or method of inpspection fixed by the parties is presumed to be exclusive but unless otherwise expressly agreed it does not postpone identification or shift the place for delivery or for passing the risk of loss. If compliance becomes impossible, inspection shall be as provided in this section unless the place or method fixed was clearly intended as an indispensable condition failure of which avoids the contract.

§ 2-514. When Documents Deliverable on Acceptance; When on Payment.—Unless otherwise agreed documents against which a draft is drawn are to be delivered to the drawee on acceptance of the draft if it is payable more than three days after presentment; otherwise, only on payment.

§ 2-515. Preserving Evidence of Goods in Dispute.—In furtherance of the adjustment of any claim or dispute

(a) either party on reasonable notification to the other and for the purpose of ascertaining the facts and preserving evidence has the right to inspect, test and sample the goods including such of them as may be in the possession or control of the other; and

(b) the parties may agree to a third party inspection or survey to determine the conformity or condition of the goods and may agree that the findings shall be binding upon them in any subsequent litigation or adjustment.

PART 6

Breach, Repudiation and Excuse

§ 2-601. Buyer's Rights on Improper Delivery.—Subject to the provisions of this Article on breach in installment contract (Section 2-612) and unless otherwise agreed under the sections on contractual limitations of remedy (Sections 2-718 and 2-719), if the goods or the tender of delivery fail in any respect to conform to the contract, the buyer may

(a) reject the whole; or

(b) accept the whole; or

(c) accept any commercial unit or units and reject the rest.

§ 2-602. Manner and Effect of Rightful Rejection.—

(1) Rejection of goods must be within a reasonable time after their delivery or tender. It is ineffective unless the buyer seasonably notifies the seller.

(2) Subject to the provisions of the two following sections on rejected goods (Sections 2-603 and 2-604)

(a) after rejection any exercise of ownership by the buyer with respect to any commercial unit is wrongful as against the seller; and

(b) if the buyer has before rejection taken physical possession of goods in which he does not have a security interest under the provisions of this Article (subsection (3) of Section 2-711), he is under a duty after rejection to hold them with reasonable care at the seller's disposition for a time sufficient to permit the seller to remove them; but

(c) the buyer has no further obligations with regard to goods rightfully rejected.

(3) The seller's rights with respect to goods wrongfully rejected are governed by the provisions of this Article on Seller's remedies in general (Section 2-703).

§ 2-603. Merchant Buyer's Duties as to Rightfully Rejected Goods.—

(1) Subject to any security interest in the buyer (subsection (3) of Section 2-711), when the seller has no agent or place of business at the market or rejection a merchant buyer is under a duty after rejection of goods in his possession or control to follow any reasonable instructions received from the seller with respect to the goods and in the absence of such instructions to make reasonable efforts to sell them for the seller's account if they are perishable or threaten to decline in value speedily. Instructions are not reasonable if on demand indemnity for expenses is not forthcoming.

(2) When the buyer sells goods under subsection (1), he is entitled to reimbursement from the seller or out of the proceeds for reasonable expenses of caring for and selling them, and if the expenses include no selling commission then to such commission as is usual in the trade or if there is none to a reasonable sum not exceeding ten per cent on the gross proceeds.

(3) In complying with this section the buyer is held only to good faith and good faith conduct hereunder is neither acceptance nor conversion nor the basis of an action for damages.

§ 2-604. Buyer's Options as to Salvage of Rightfully Rejected Goods.—Subject to the provisions of the immediately preceding section on perishables if the seller gives no instructions within a reasonable time after notification of rejection the buyer may store the rejected goods for the seller's account or reship them to him or resell them for the seller's account with reimbursement as provided in the preceding section. Such action is not acceptance or conversion.

§ 2-605. Waiver of Buyer's Objections by Failure to Particularize.—

(1) The buyer's failure to state in connection with rejection a particular defect which is ascertainable by reasonable inspection precludes him from relying on the unstated defect to justify rejection or to establish breach

(a) where the seller could have cured it if stated seasonably; or

(b) between merchants when the seller has after rejection made a request in writing for a full and final written statement of all defects on which the buyer proposes to rely.

(2) Payment against documents made without reservation of rights precludes recovery of the payment for defects apparent on the face of the documents.

§ 2-606. What Constitutes Acceptance of Goods.—

(1) Acceptance of goods occurs when the buyer

(a) after a reasonable opportunity to inspect the goods signifies to the seller that the goods are conforming or that he will take or retain them in spite of their non-conformity; or

(b) fails to make an effective rejection (subsection (1) of Section 2-602), but such acceptance does not occur until the buyer has had a reasonable opportunity to inspect them; or

(c) does any act inconsistent with the seller's ownership; but if such act is wrongful as against the seller it is an acceptance only if ratified by him.

(2) Acceptance of a part of any commercial unit is acceptance of that entire unit.

§ 2-607. Effect of Acceptance; Notice of Breach; Burden of Establishing Breach After Acceptance; Notice of Claim or Litigation to Person Answerable Over.—

(1) The buyer must pay at the contract rate for any goods accepted.

(2) Acceptance of goods by the buyer precludes rejection of the goods accepted and if made with knowledge of a nonconformity cannot be revoked because of it unless the acceptance was on the reasonable assumption that the non-conformity would be seasonably cured but acceptance does not of itself impair any other remedy provided by this Article for non-conformity.

(3) Where a tender has been accepted

(a) the buyer must within a reasonable time after he discovers or should have discovered any breach notify the seller of breach or be barred from any remedy; and

(b) if the claim is one for infringement or the like (subsection (3) of Section 2-312) and the buyer is sued as a result of such a breach he must so notify the seller within a reasonable time after he receives notice of the litigation or be barred from any remedy over for liability established by the litigation.

(4) The burden is on the buyer to establish any breach with respect to the goods accepted.

(5) Where the buyer is sued for breach of a warranty or other obligation for which his seller is answerable over

(a) he may give his seller written notice of the litigation. If the notice states that the seller may come in and defend and that if the seller does not do so he will be bound in any action against him by his buyer by any determination of fact common to the two litigations, then unless the seller after seasonable receipt of the notice does come in and defend he is so bound.

(b) if the claim is one for infringement or the like (subsection (3) of Section 2-312) the original seller may demand in writing that his buyer turn over to him control of the litigation including settlement or else be barred from any remedy over and if he also agrees to bear all expense and to satisfy any adverse judgment, then unless the buyer after seasonable receipt of the demand does turn over control the buyer is so barred.

(6) The provisions of subsections (3), (4) and (5) apply to any obligation of a buyer to hold the seller harmless against infringement or the like (subsection (3) of Section 2-312).

§ 2-608. Revocation of Acceptance in Whole or in Part.—

(1) The buyer may revoke his acceptance of a lot or commercial unit whose non-conformity substantially impairs its value to him if he has accepted it

(a) on the reasonable assumption that its non-conformity would be cured and it has not been seasonably cured; or

(b) without discovery of such nonconformity if his acceptance was reasonably induced either by the difficulty of discovery before acceptance or by the seller's assurances.

(2) Revocation of acceptance must occur within a reasonable time after the buyer discovers or should have discovered the ground for it and before any substantial change in condition of the goods which is not caused by their own defects. It is not effective until the buyer notifies the seller of it.

(3) A buyer who so revokes has the same rights and duties with regard to the goods involved as if he had rejected them.

§ 2-609. Right to Adequate Assurance of Performance.—

(1) A contract for sale imposes an obligation on each party that the other's expectation of receiving due performance will not be impaired. When reasonable grounds for insecurity arise with respect to the performance of either party the other may in writing demand adequate assurance of due performance and until he receives such assurance may if commercially reasonable suspend any performance for which he has not already received the agreed return.

(2) Between merchants the reasonableness of grounds for insecurity and the adequacy of any assurance offered shall be determined according to commercial standards.

(3) Acceptance of any improper delivery or payment does not prejudice the aggrieved party's right to demand adequate assurance of future performance.

(4) After receipt of a justified demand failure to provide within a reasonable time not exceeding thirty days such assurance of due performance as is adequate under the circumstances of the particular case is a repudiation of the contract.

§ 2-610. Anticipatory Repudiation.—When either party repudiates the contract with respect to a performance not yet due the loss of which will substantially impair the value of the contract to the other, the aggrieved party may

(a) for a commercially reasonable time await performance by the repudiating party; or

(b) resort to any remedy for breach (Section 2-703 or Section 2-711), even though he has notified the repudiating party that he would await the latter's performance and has urged retraction; and

(c) in either case suspend his own performance or proceed in accordance with the provisions of this Article on the seller's right to identify goods to the contract nonwithstanding breach or to salvage unfinished goods (Section 2-704).

§ 2-611. Retraction of Anticipatory Repudiation.—

(1) Until the repudiating party's next performance is due he can retract his repudiation unless the aggrieved party has since the repudiation cancelled or materially changed his position or otherwise indicated that he considers the repudiation final.

(2) Retraction may be by any method which clearly indicates to the aggrieved party that the repudiating party intends to perform, but must include any assurance justifiably demanded under the provisions of this Article (Section 2-609).

(3) Retraction reinstates the repudiating party's rights under the contract with due excuse and allowance to the aggrieved party for any delay occasioned by the repudiation.

§ 2-612. "Installment Contract"; Breach.—

(1) An "installment contract" is one which requires or authorizes the delivery of goods in separate lots to be separately accepted, even though the contract contains a clause "each delivery is a separate contract" or its equivalent.

(2) The buyer may reject any installment which is non-conforming if the nonconformity substantially impairs the value of that installment and cannot be cured or if the non-conformity is a defect in the required documents; but if the non-conformity does not fall within subsection (3) and the seller gives adequate assurance of its cure the buyer must accept that installment.

(3) Whenever non-conformity or default with respect to one or more installments substantially impairs the value of the whole contract there is a breach of the whole. But the aggrieved party reinstates the contract if he accepts a non-conforming installment without seasonably notifying of cancellation or if he brings an action with respect only to past installments or demands performance as to future installments.

§ 2-613. Casualty to Identified Goods.—

Where the contract requires for its performance goods identified when the contract is made, and the goods suffer casualty without fault of either party before the risk of loss passes to the buyer, or in a proper case under a "no arrival, no sale" term (Section 2-324) then

(a) if the loss is total the contract is avoided; and

(b) if the loss is partial or the goods have so deteriorated as no longer to conform to the contract the buyer may nevertheless demand inspection and at his option either treat the contract as avoided or accept the goods with due allowance from the contract price for the deterioration or the deficiency in quantity but without further right against the seller.

§ 2-614. Substituted Performance.—

(1) Where without fault of either party the agreed berthing, loading, or unloading facilities fail or an agreed type of carrier becomes unavailable or the agreed manner of delivery otherwise becomes commercially impracticable but a commercially reasonable substitute is available, such substitute performance must be tendered and accepted.

(2) If the agreed means or manner of payment fails because of domestic or foreign governmental regulation, the seller may withhold or stop delivery unless the buyer provides a means or manner of payment which is commercially a substantial equivalent. If delivery has already been taken, payment by the means or in the manner provided by the regulation discharges the buyer's obligation unless the regulation is discriminatory, oppressive or predatory.

§ 2-615. Excuse by Failure of Presupposed Conditions.—

Except so far as a seller may have assumed a greater obligation and subject to the preceeding section on substituted performance:

(a) Delay in delivery or non-delivery in whole or in part by a seller who complies with paragraphs (b) and (c) is not a breach of his duty under a contract for sale if performance as agreed has been made impracticable by the occurrence of a contingency the non-occurrence of which was a basic assumption on which the contract was made or by compliance in good faith with any applicable foreign or domestic governmental regulation or order whether or not it later proves to be invalid.

(b) Where the causes mentioned in paragraph (a) affect only a part of the seller's capacity to perform, he must allocate production and deliveries among his customers but may at his option include regular customers not then under contract as well as his own requirements for further manufacture. He may so allocate in any manner which is fair and reasonable.

(c) The seller must notify the buyer seasonably that there will be delay or non-delivery and, when allocation is required under paragraph (b), of the estimated quota this made available for the buyer.

§ 2-616. Procedure on Notice Claiming Excuse.—

(1) Where the buyer receives notification of a material or indefinite delay or an allocation justified under the preceding section he may by written notification to the seller as to any delivery concerned, and where the prospective deficiency substantially impairs the value of the whole contract under the provisions of this Article relating to breach of installment contracts (Section 2-612), then also as to the whole,

(a) terminate and thereby discharge any unexecuted portion of the contract; or

(b) modify the contract by agreeing to take his available quota in substitution.

(2) If after receipt of such notification from the seller the buyer fails so to modify the contract within a reasonable time not exceeding thirty days the contract lapses with respect to any deliveries affected.

(3) The provisions of this section may not be negated by agreement except in so far as the seller has assumed a greater obligation under the preceding section.

PART 7

Remedies

§ 2-701. Remedies for Breach of Collateral Contracts Not Impaired.—

Remedies for breach of any obligation or promise collateral or ancillary to a contract for sale are not impaired by the provisions of this Article.

§ 2-702. Seller's Remedies on Discovery of Buyer's Insolvency.—

(1) Where the seller discovers the buyer to be insolvent he may refuse delivery except for cash including payment for all goods theretofore delivered under the contract, and stop delivery under this Article (Section 2-705).

(2) Where the seller discovers that the buyer has received goods on credit while insolvent he may reclaim the goods upon demand made within ten days after the receipt, but if misrepresentation of solvency has been made to the particular seller in writing within three months before delivery the ten day limitation does not apply. Except as provided in this subsection the seller may not base a right to reclaim goods on the buyer's fraudulent or innocent misrepresentation of solvency or of intent to pay.

(3) The seller's right to reclaim under subsection (2) is subject to the rights of a buyer in ordinary course or other good faith purchaser or lien creditor under this Article (Section 2-403). Successful reclamation of goods excludes all other remedies with respect to them.

§ 2-703. Seller's Remedies in General.—Where the buyer wrongfully rejects or revokes acceptance of goods or fails to make a payment due on or before delivery or repudiates with respect to a part or the whole, then with respect to any goods directly affected and, if the breach is of the whole contract (Section 2-612), then also with respect to the whole undelivered balance, the aggrieved seller may

(a) withhold delivery of such goods;

(b) stop delivery by any bailee as hereafter provided (Section 2-705);

(c) proceed under the next section respecting goods still unidentified to the contract;

(d) resell and recover damages as hereafter provided (Section 2-706);

(e) recover damages for non-acceptance (Section 2-708) or in a proper case the price (Section 2-709);

(f) cancel.

§ 2-704. Seller's Right to Identify Goods to the Contract Notwithstanding Breach or to Salvage Unfinished Goods.—

(1) An aggrieved seller under the preceding section may

(a) identify to the contract conforming goods not already identified if at the time he learned of the breach they are in his possession or control;

(b) treat as the subject of resale goods which have demonstrably been intended for the particular contract even though those goods are unfinished.

(2) Where the goods are unfinished an aggrieved seller may in the exercise of reasonable commercial judgment for the purposes of avoiding loss and of effective realization either complete the manufacture and wholly identify the goods to the contract or cease manufacture and resell for scrap or salvage value or proceed in any other reasonable manner.

§ 2-705. Seller's Stoppage of Delivery in Transit or Otherwise.—

(1) The seller may stop delivery of goods in the possession of a carrier or other bailee when he discovers the buyer to be insolvent (Section 2-702) and may stop delivery of carload, truckload, planeload or larger shipments of express or freight when the buyer repudiates or fails to make a payment due before delivery or if for any other reason the seller has a right to withhold or reclaim the goods.

(2) As against such buyer the seller may stop delivery until

(a) receipt of the goods by the buyer; or

(b) acknowledgment to the buyer by any bailee of the goods except a carrier that the bailee holds the goods by the buyer; or

(c) such acknowledgment to the buyer by a carrier by reshipment or as warehouseman; or

(d) negotiation to the buyer of any negotiable document of title covering the goods.

(3) (a) To stop delivery the seller must so notify as to enable the bailee by reasonable diligence to prevent delivery of the goods.

(b) After such notification the bailee must hold and deliver the goods according to the directions of the seller but the seller is liable to the bailee for any ensuing charges or damages.

(c) If a negotiable document of title has been issued for goods the bailee is not obliged to obey a notification to stop until surrender of the document.

(d) A carrier who has issued a non-negotiable bill of lading is not obliged to obey a notification to stop received from a person other than the consignor.

§ 2-706. Seller's Resale Including Contract for Resale.—

(1) Under the conditions stated in Section 2-703 on seller's remedies, the seller may resell the goods concerned or the undelivered balance thereof. Where the resale is made in good faith and in a commercially reasonable manner the seller may recover the difference between the resale price and the contract price together with any incidental damages allowed under the provisions of this Article (Section 2-710), but less expenses saved in consequence of the buyer's breach.

(2) Except as otherwise provided in subsection (3) or unless otherwise agreed resale may be at public or private sale including sale by way of one or more contracts to sell or of identification to an existing contract of the seller. Sale may be as a unit or in parcels and at any time and place and on any terms but every aspect of the sale including the method, manner, time, place and terms must be commercially reasonable. The resale must be reasonably identified as referring to the broken contract, but it is not necessary that the goods be in existence or that any or all of them have been identified to the contract before the breach.

(3) Where the resale is at private sale the seller must give the buyer reasonable notification of his intention to resell.

(4) Where the resale is at public sale

(a) only identified goods can be sold except where there is a recognized market for a public sale of futures in goods of the kind; and

(b) it must be made at a usual place or market for public sale if one is reasonably available and except in the case of goods which are perishable or threaten to decline in value speedily the seller must give the buyer reasonable notice of the time and place of the resale; and

(c) if the goods are not to be within the view of those attending the sale the notification of sale must state the place where the goods are located and provide for their reasonable inspection by prospective bidders; and

(d) the seller may buy.

(5) A purchaser who buys in good faith at a resale takes the goods free of any rights of the original buyer even though the seller fails to comply with one or more of the requirements of this section.

(6) The seller is not accountable to the buyer for any profit made on any resale. A person in the position of a seller (Section 2-707) or a buyer who has rightfully rejected or justifiably revoked acceptance must account for any excess over the amount of his security interest, as hereinafter defined (subsection (3) of Section 2-711).

§ 2-707. "Person in the Position of a Seller."—

(1) A "person in the position of a seller" includes as against a principal an agent who has paid or become responsible for the price of goods on behalf of his principal or anyone who otherwise holds a security interest or other right in goods similar to that of a seller.

(2) A person in the position of a seller may as provided in this Article withhold or stop delivery (Section 2-705) and resell (Section 2-706) and recover incidental damages (Section 2-710).

§ 2-708. Seller's Damages for Nonacceptance or Repudiation.—

(1) Subject to subsection (2) and to the provisions of this Article with respect to proof of market price (Section 2-723), the measure of damages for non-acceptance or repudiation by the buyer is the difference between the market price at the time and place for tender and the unpaid contract price together with any incidental damages provided in this Article (Section 2-710), but less expenses saved in consequence of the buyer's breach.

(2) If the measure of damages provided in subsection (1) is inadequate to put the seller in as good a position as performance would have done then the measure of damages is the profit (including reasonable overhead) which the seller would have made from full performance by the buyer, together with any incidental damages provided in this Article (Section 2-710), due allowance for costs reasonably incurred and due credit for payments or proceeds of resale.

§ 2-709. Action for the Price.—

(1) When the buyer fails to pay the price as it becomes due the seller may recover, together with any incidental damages under the next section, the price

(a) of goods accepted or of conforming goods lost or damaged within a commercially reasonable time after risk of their loss has passed to the buyer; and

(b) of goods identified to the contract if the seller is unable after reasonable effort to resell them at a reasonable price or the circumstances reasonably indicate that such effort will be unavailing.

(2) Where the seller sues for the price he must hold for the buyer any goods which have been identified to the contract and are still in his control except that if resale becomes possible he may resell them at any time prior to the collection of the judgment. The net proceeds of any such resale must be credited to the buyer and payment of the judgment entitles him to any goods not resold.

(3) After the buyer has wrongfully rejected or revoked acceptance of the goods or has failed to make a payment due or has repudiated (Section 2-610), a seller who is held and entitled to the price under this section shall nevertheless be awarded damages for non-acceptance under the preceding section.

§ 2-710. Seller's Incidental Damages.—

Incidental damages to an aggrieved seller include any commercially reasonable charges, expenses or commissions incurred in stopping delivery, in the transportation, care and custody of goods after the buyer's breach, in connection with return or resale of the goods or otherwise resulting from the breach.

§ 2-711. Buyer's Remedies in General, Buyer's Security Interest in Rejected Goods.—

(1) Where the seller fails to make delivery or repudiates or the buyer rightfully rejects or justifiably revokes acceptance then with respect to any goods involved, and with respect to the whole if the breach goes to the whole contract (Section 2-612), the buyer may cancel and whether or not he has done so may in addition to recovering so much of the price as has been paid

(a) "cover" and have damages under the next section as to all the goods affected whether or not they have been identified to the contract; or

(b) recover damages for non-delivery as provided in this Article (Section 2-713).

(2) Where the seller fails to deliver or repudiates the buyer may also

(a) if the goods have been identified recover them as provided in this Article (Section 2-502); or

(b) in a proper case obtain specific performance or replevy the goods as provided in this Article (Section 2-716).

(3) On rightful rejection or justifiable revocation of acceptance a buyer has a security interest in goods in his possession or control for any payments made on their price and any expenses reasonably incurred in their inspection, receipt, transportation, care and custody and may hold such goods and resell them in like manner as an aggrieved seller (Section 2-706).

§ 2-712. "Cover"; Buyer's Procurement of Substitute Goods.—

(1) After a breach within the preceding section the buyer may "cover" by making in good faith and without unreasonable delay any reasonable purchase of or contract to purchase goods in substitution for those due from the seller.

(2) The buyer may recover from the seller as damages the difference between the cost of cover and the contract price together with any incidental or consequential damages as hereinafter defined (Section 2-715), but less expenses saved in consequence of the seller's breach.

(3) Failure of the buyer to effect cover within this section does not bar him from any other remedy.

§ 2-713. Buyer's Damages for Non-Delivery or Repudiation.—

(1) Subject to the provisions of this Article with respect to proof of market price (Section 2-723), the measure of damages for non-delivery or repudiation by the seller is the difference between the market price at the time when the buyer learned of the breach and the contract price together with any incidental and consequential damages provided in this Article (Section 2-715), but less expenses saved in consequence of the seller's breach.

(2) Market price is to be determined as of the place for tender or, in cases of rejection after arrival or revocation of acceptance, as of the place of arrival.

§ 2-714. Buyer's Damages for Breach in Regard to Accepted Goods.—

(1) Where the buyer has accepted goods and given notification (subsection (3) of Section 2-607) he may recover as damages for any non-conformity of tender the loss resulting in the ordinary course of events from the seller's breach as determined in any manner which is reasonable.

(2) The measure of damages for breach of warranty is the difference at the time and place of acceptance between the value of the goods accepted and the value they would have had if they had been as warranted, unless special circumstances show proximate damages of a different amount.

(3) In a proper case any incidental and consequential damages under the next section may also be recovered.

§ 2-715. Buyer's Incidental and Consequential Damages.—

(1) Incidental damages resulting from the seller's breach include expenses reasonably incurred in inspection, receipt, transportation and care and custody of goods rightfully rejected, and any commercially reasonable charges, expenses or commissions in connection with effecting cover and any other reasonable expense incident to the delay or other breach.

(2) Consequential damages resulting from the seller's breach include

(a) any loss resulting from general or particular requirements and needs of which the seller at the time of contracting had reason to know and which could not reasonably be prevented by cover or otherwise; and

(b) injury to person or property proximately resulting from any breach of warranty.

§ 2-716. Buyer's Right to Specific Performance or Replevin.—

(1) Specific performance may be decreed where the goods are unique or in other proper circumstances.

(2) The decree for specific performance may include such terms and conditions as to payment of the price, damages, or other relief as the court may deem just.

§ 2-717. Deduction of Damages From the Price.—

The buyer on notifying the seller of his intention to do so may deduct all or any part of the damages resulting from any breach of the contract from any part of the price still due under the same contract.

§ 2-718. Liquidation or Limitation of Damages; Deposits.—

(1) Damages for breach by either party may be liquidated in the agreement but only at an amount which is reasonable in the light of the anticipated or actual harm caused by the breach, the difficulties of proof of loss, and the inconvenience or nonfeasibility of otherwise obtaining an adequate remedy. A term fixing unreasonably large liquidated damages is void as a penalty.

(2) Where the seller justifiably withholds delivery of goods because of the buyer's breach, the buyer is entitled to restitution of any amount by which the sum of his payments exceeds

(a) The amount to which the seller is entitled by virtue of terms liquidating the seller's damages in accordance with subsection (1), or

(b) in the absence of such terms, twenty per cent of the value of the total performance for which the buyer is obligated under the contract or $500, whichever is smaller.

(3) The buyer's right to restitution under subsection (2) is subject to offset to the extent that the seller establishes

(a) a right to recover damages under the provisions of this Article other than subsection (1), and

(b) the amount or value of any benefits received by the buyer directly or indirectly by reason of the contract.

(4) Where a seller has received payment in goods their reasonable value or the proceeds of their resale shall be treated as payments for the purposes of subsection (2); but if the seller has notice of the buyer's breach before reselling goods received in part performance, his resale is subject to the conditions laid down in this Article on resale by an aggrieved seller (Section 2-706).

§ 2-719. Contractual Modification or Limitation of Remedy.—

(1) Subject to the provisions of subsections (2) and (3) of this section and of the preceding section on liquidation and limitation of damages,

(a) the agreement may provide for remedies in addition to or in substitution for those provided in this Article and may limit or alter the measure of damages recoverable under this Article, as by limiting the buyer's remedies to return of the goods and repayment of the price or to repair and replacement of nonconforming goods or parts; and

(b) resort to a remedy as provided is optional unless the remedy is expressly agreed to be exclusive, in which case it is the sole remedy.

(2) Where circumstances cause an exclusive or limited remedy to fail of its essential purpose, remedy may be had as provided in this Act.

(3) Consequential damages may be limited or excluded unless the limitation or exclusion is unconscionable. Limitation of consequential damages for injury to the person in the case of consumer goods is prima facie unconscionable but limitation of damages where the loss is commercial is not.

§ 2-720. **Effect of "Cancellation" or "Rescission" on Claims for Antecedent Breach.**—Unless the contrary intention clearly appears, expressions of "cancellation" or "rescission" of the contract or the like shall not be construed as a renunciation or discharge of any claim in damages for an antecedent breach.

§ 2-721. **Remedies for Fraud.**—Remedies for material misrepresentation or fraud include all remedies available under this Article for non-fraudulent breach. Neither rescission or a claim for rescission of the contract for sale nor rejection or return of the goods shall bar or be deemed inconsistent with a claim for damages or other remedy.

§ 2-722. **Who Can Sue Third Parties for Injury to Goods.**—Where a third party so deals with goods which have been identified to a contract for sale as to cause actionable injury to a party to that contract

(a) a right of action against the third party is in either party to the contract for sale who has title to or a security interest or a special property or an insurable interest in the goods; and if the goods have been destroyed or converted a right of action is also in the party who either bore the risk of loss under the contract for sale or has since the injury assumed that risk as against the other;

(b) if at the time of the injury the party plaintiff did not bear the risk of loss as against the other party to the contract for sale and there is no arrangement between them for disposition of the recovery, his suit or settlement is, subject to his own interest, as a fiduciary for the other party to the contract;

(c) either party may with the consent of the other sue for the benefit of whom it may concern.

§ 2-723. **Proof of Market Price: Time and Place.**—

(1) If an action based on anticipatory repudiation comes to trial before the time for performance with respect to some or all of the goods, any damages based on market price (Section 2-708 or Section 2-713) shall be determined according to the price of such goods prevailing at the time when the aggrieved party learned of the repudiation.

(2) If evidence of a price prevailing at the times or places described in this Article is not readily available the price prevailing within any reasonable time before or after the time described or at any other place which in commercial judgment or under usage of trade would serve as a reasonable substitute for the one described may be used, making any proper allowance for the cost of transporting the goods to or from such other place.

(3) Evidence of a relevant price prevailing at a time or place other than the one described in this Article offered by one party is not admissible unless and until he has given the other party such notice as the court finds sufficient to prevent unfair surprise.

§ 2-724. **Admissibility of Market Quotations.**—Whenever the prevailing price or value of any goods regularly bought and sold in any established commodity market is in issue, reports in official publications or trade journals or in newspapers or periodicals of general circulation published as the reports of such market shall be admissible in evidence. The circumstances of the preparation of such a report may be shown to affect its weight but not its admissibility.

§ 2-725. **Statute of Limitations in Contracts for Sale.**—

(1) An action for breach of any contract for sale must be commenced within four years after the cause of action has accrued. By the original agreement the parties may reduce the period of limitation to not less than one year but may not extend it.

(2) A cause of action accrues when the breach occurs, regardless of the aggrieved party's lack of knowledge of the breach. A breach of warranty occurs when tender of delivery is made, except that where a warranty explicitly extends to future performance of the goods and discovery of the breach must await the time of such performance the cause of action accrues when the breach is or should have been discovered.

(3) Where an action commenced within the time limited by subsection (1) is so terminated as to leave available a remedy by another action for the same breach such other action may be commenced after the expiration of the time limited and within six months after the termination of the first action unless the termination resulted from voluntary discontinuance or from dismissal for failure or neglect to prosecute.

(4) This section does not alter the law on tolling of the statute of limitations nor does it apply to causes of action which have accrued before this Act becomes effective.

ARTICLE THREE — COMMERCIAL PAPER

PART 1

Short Title, Form and Interpretation

§ 3-101. **Short Title.**—This Article shall be known and may be cited as Uniform Commercial Code—Commercial Paper.

§ 3-102. **Definitions and Index of Definitions.**—

(1) In this Article unless the context otherwise requires

(a) "Issue" means the first delivery of an instrument to a holder or a remitter.

(b) An "order" is a direction to pay and must be more than an authorization or request. It must identify the person to pay with reasonable certainty. It may be addressed to one or more such persons jointly or in the alternative but not in succession.

(c) A "promise" is an undertaking to pay and must be more than an acknowledgment of an obligation.

(d) "Secondary party" means a drawer or endorser.

(e) "Instrument" means a negotiable instrument. . . .

§ 3-103. Limitations on Scope of Article.—

(1) This Article does not apply to money, documents of title or investment securities.

(2) The provisions of this Article are subject to the provisions of the Article on Bank Deposits and Collections (Article 4) and Secured Transactions (Article 9).

§ 3-104. Form of Negotiable Instruments; "Draft"; "Check"; "Certificate of Deposit"; "Note."—

(1) Any writing to be a negotiable instrument within this Article must

(a) be signed by the maker or drawer; and

(b) contain an unconditional promise or order to pay a sum certain in money and no other promise, order, obligation or power given by the maker or drawer except as authorized by this Article; and

(c) be payable on demand or at a definite time; and

(d) be payable to order or to bearer.

(2) A writing which complies with the requirements of this section is

(a) a "draft" ("bill of exchange") if it is an order;

(b) a "check" if it is a draft drawn on a bank and payable on demand;

(c) a "certificate of deposit" if it is an acknowledgment by a bank of receipt of money with an engagement to repay it;

(d) a "note" if it is a promise other than a certificate of deposit.

(3) As used in other Articles of this Act, and as the context may require, the terms "draft", "check", "certificate of deposit" and "note" may refer to instruments which are not negotiable within this Article as well as to instruments which are so negotiable.

§ 3-105. When Promise or Order Unconditional.—

(1) A promise or order otherwise unconditional is not made conditional by the fact that the instrument

(a) is subject to implied or constructive conditions; or

(b) states its consideration, whether performed or promised, or the transaction which gave rise to the instrument, or that the promise or order is made or the instrument matures in accordance with or "as per" such transaction; or

(c) refers to or states that it arises out of a separate agreement; or

(d) states that it is drawn under a letter of credit; or

(e) states that it is secured, whether by mortgage, reservation of title or otherwise; or

(f) indicates a particular account to be debited or any other fund or source from which reimbursement is expected; or

(g) is limited to payment out of a particular fund or the proceeds of a particular source, if the instrument is issued by a government or governmental agency or unit; or

(h) is limited to payment out of the entire assets of a partnership, unincorporated association, trust or estate by or on behalf of which the instrument is issued.

(2) A promise or order is not unconditional if the instrument

(a) states that it is subject to or governed by any other agreement; or

(b) states that it is to be paid only out of a particular fund or source except as provided in this Section.

§ 3-106. Sum Certain.—

(1) The sum payable is a sum certain even though it is to be paid

(a) with stated interest or by stated installments; or

(b) with stated different rates of interest before and after default or a specified date; or

(c) with a stated discount or addition if paid before or after the date fixed for payment; or

(d) with exchange or less exchange, whether at a fixed rate or at the current rate; or

(e) with costs of collection or an attorney's fee or both upon default.

(2) Nothing in this Section shall validate any term which is otherwise illegal.

§ 3-107. Money.—

(1) An instrument is payable in money if the medium of exchange in which it is payable is money at the time the instrument is made. An instrument payable in "currency" or "current funds" is payable in money.

(2) A promise or order to pay a sum stated in a foreign currency is for a sum certain in money and, unless a different medium of payment is specified in the instrument, may be satisfied by payment of that number of dollars which the stated foreign currency will purchase at the buying sight rate for that currency on the day on which the instrument is payable or, if payable on demand, on the date of demand. If such an instrument specifies a foreign currency as the medium of payment the instrument is payable in that currency.

§ 3-108. Payable on Demand.—Instruments payable on demand include those payable at sight or on presentation and those in which no time for payment is stated.

§ 3-109. Definite Time.—

(1) An instrument is payable at a definite time if by its terms it is payable

(a) on or before a stated date or at a fixed period after a stated date; or

(b) at a fixed period after sight; or

(c) at a definite time subject to any acceleration; or

(d) at a definite time subject to extension at the option of the holder, or to extension to a further definite time at the option of the maker or acceptor or automatically upon or after a specified act or event.

(2) An instrument which by its terms is otherwise payable only upon an act or event uncertain as to time of occurrence is not payable at a definite time even though the act or event has occurred.

§ 3-110. Payable to Order.—

(1) An instrument is payable to order when by its terms it is payable to the order or assigns of any person therein specified with reasonable certainty, or to him or his order, or when it is conspicuously designated on its face as "exchange" or the like and names a payee. It may be payable to the order of

(a) the maker or drawer; or

(b) the drawee; or

(c) A payee who is not maker, drawer or drawee; or

(d) two or more payees together or in the alternative; or

(e) an estate, trust or fund, in which case it is payable to the order of the representative of such estate, trust or fund or his successors; or

(f) an office, or an officer by his title as such in which case it is payable to the principal but the incumbent of the office or his successors may act as if he or they were the holder; or

(g) a partnership or unincorporated association, in which case it is payable to the partnership or association and may be indorsed or transferred by any person thereto authorized.

(2) An instrument not payable to order is not made so payable by such words as "payable upon return of this instrument properly indorsed."

(3) An instrument made payable both to order and to bearer is payable to order unless the bearer words are handwritten or typewritten.

§ 3-111. Payable to Bearer.—An instrument is payable to bearer when by its terms it is payable to

(a) bearer or the order of bearer; or

(b) a specified person or bearer; or

(c) "cash" or the order of "cash", or any other indication which does not purport to designate a specific payee.

§ 3-112. Terms and Omissions Not Affecting Negotiability.—

(1) The negotiability of an instrument is not affected by

(a) the omission of a statement of any consideration or of the place where the instrument is drawn or payable; or

(b) a statement that collateral has been given for the instrument or in case of default on the instrument the collateral may be sold; or

(c) a promise or power to maintain or protect collateral or to give additional collateral; or

(d) a term authorizing a confession of judgment on the instrument if it is not paid when due; or

(e) a term purporting to waive the benefit of any law intended for the advantage or protection of any obligor; or

(f) a term in a draft providing that the payee by indorsing or cashing it acknowledges full satisfaction of an obligation of the drawer; or

(g) a statement in a draft drawn in a set of parts (Section 3-801) to the effect that the order is effective only if no other part has been honored.

(2) Nothing in this Section shall validate any term which is otherwise illegal.

§ 3-113. Seal.—An instrument otherwise negotiable is within this Article even though it is under a seal.

§ 3-114. Date, Antedating, Postdating.—

(1) The negotiability of an instrument is not affected by the fact that it is undated, antedated or post-dated.

(2) Where an instrument is antedated or postdated the time when it is payable is determined by the stated date if the instrument is payable on demand or at a fixed period after date.

(3) Where the instrument or any signature thereon is dated, the date is presumed to be correct.

§ 3-115. Incomplete Instruments.—

(1) When a paper whose contents at the time of signing show that it is intended to become an instrument is signed while still incomplete in any necessary respect it cannot be enforced until completed, but when it is completed in accordance with authority given it is effective as completed.

(2) If the completion is unauthorized the rules as to material alteration apply (Section 3-407), even though the paper was not delivered by the maker or drawer; but the burden of establishing that any completion is unauthorized is on the party so asserting.

§ 3-116. Instruments Payable to Two or More Persons.—An instrument payable to the order of two or more persons

(a) if in the alternative is payable to any one of them and may be negotiated, discharged or enforced by any of them who has possession of it;

(b) if not in the alternative is payable to all of them and may be negotiated, discharged or enforced only by all of them.

§ 3-117. Instruments Payable With Words of Description.—An instrument made payable to a named person with the addition of words describing him

(a) as agent or officer of a specified person is payable to his principal but the agent or officer may act as if he were the holder;

(b) as any other fiduciary for a specified person or purpose is payable to the payee and may be negotiated, discharged or enforced by him;

(c) in any other manner is payable to the payee unconditionally and the additional words are without effect on subsequent parties.

§ 3-118. Ambiguous Terms and Rules of Construction.—The following rules apply to every instrument:

(a) Where there is doubt whether the instrument is a draft or a note the holder may treat it as either. A draft drawn on the drawer is effective as a note.

(b) Handwritten terms control typewritten and printed terms, and typewritten control printed.

(c) Words control figures except that if the words are ambiguous figures control.

(d) Unless otherwise specified a provision for interest means interest at the judgment rate at the place of payment from the date of the instrument, or if it is undated from the date of issue.

(e) Unless the instrument otherwise specifies two or more persons who sign as maker, acceptor or drawer or indorser and as a part of the same transaction are jointly and severally liable even though the instrument contains such words as "I promise to pay."

(f) Unless otherwise specified consent to extension authorizes a single extension for not longer than the original period. A consent to extension, expressed in the instrument, is binding on secondary parties and accommodation makers. A holder may not exercise his option to extend an instrument over the objection of a maker or acceptor or other party who in accordance with Section 3-604 tenders full payment when the instrument is due.

§ 3-119. Other Writings Affecting Instrument.—

(1) As between the obligor and his immediate obligee or any transferee the terms of an instrument may be modified or affected by any other written agreement executed as a part of the same transaction, except that a holder in due course is not affected by any limitation of his rights arising out of the separate written agreement if he had no notice of the limitation when he took the instrument.

(2) A separate agreement does not affect the negotiability of an instrument.

§ 3-120. Instruments "Payable Through" Bank.—An instrument which states that it is "payable through" a bank or the like designates that bank as a collecting bank to make presentment but does not of itself authorize the bank to pay the instrument.

§ 3-121. Instruments Payable at Bank.—A note or acceptance which states that it is payable at a bank is not of itself an order or authorization to the bank to pay it.

§ 3-122. Accrual of Cause of Action.—

(1) A cause of action against a maker or an acceptor accrues

(a) in the case of a time instrument on the day after maturity;

(b) in the case of a demand instrument upon its date or, if no date is stated, on the date of issue.

(2) A cause of action against the obligor of a demand or time certificate of deposit accrues upon demand, but demand on a time certificate may not be made until on or after the date of maturity.

(3) A cause of action against a drawer of a draft or an indorser of any instrument accrues upon demand following dishonor of the instrument. Notice of dishonor is a demand.

(4) Unless an instrument provides otherwise, interest runs at the rate provided by law for a judgment

(a) in the case of a maker acceptor or other primary obligor of a demand instrument, from the date of demand;

(b) in all other cases from the date of accrual of the cause of action.

PART 2

Transfer and Negotiation

§ 3-201. Transfer: Right to Indorsement.—

(1) Transfer of an instrument vests in the transferee such rights as the transferor has therein, except that a transferee who has himself been a party to any fraud or illegality affecting the instrument or who as a prior holder had notice of a defense or claim against it cannot improve his position by taking from a later holder in due course.

(2) A transfer of a security interest in an instrument vests the foregoing rights in the transferee to the extent of the interest transferred.

(3) Unless otherwise agreed any transfer for value of an instrument not then payable to bearer gives the transferee the specifically enforceable right to have the unqualified indorsement of the transferor. Negotiation takes effect only when the indorsement is made and until that time there is no presumption that the transferee is the owner.

§ 3-202. Negotiation.—

(1) Negotiation is the transfer of an instrument in such form that the transferee becomes a holder. If the instrument is payable to order it is negotiated by delivery with any necessary indorsement; if payable to bearer it is negotiated by delivery.

(2) An indorsement must be written by or on behalf of the holder and on the instrument or on a paper so firmly affixed thereto as to become a part thereof.

(3) An indorsement is effective for negotiation only when it conveys the entire instrument or any unpaid residue. If it purports to be of less it operates only as a partial assignment.

(4) Words of assignment, condition, waiver, guaranty, limitation or disclaimer of liability and the like accompanying an indorsement do not affect its character as an indorsement.

§ 3-203. Wrong or Misspelled Name.—Where an instrument is made payable to a person under a misspelled name or one other than his own he may indorse in that name or his own or both; but signature in both names may be required by a person paying or giving value for the instrument.

§ 3-204. Special Indorsement; Blank Indorsement.—

(1) A special indorsement specifies the person to whom or to whose order it makes the instrument payable. Any instrument specially indorsed becomes payable to the order of the special indorsee and may be further negotiated only by his indorsement.

(2) An indorsement in blank specifies no particular indorsee and may consist of a mere signature. An instrument payable to order and indorsed in blank becomes payable to bearer and may be negotiated by delivery alone until specially indorsed.

(3) The holder may convert a blank indorsement into a special indorsement by writing over the signature of the indorser in blank any contract consistent with the character of the indorsement.

§ 3-205. Restrictive Indorsements.—an indorsement is restrictive which either

    (a) is conditional; or

    (b) purports to prohibit further transfer of the instrument; or

    (c) includes the words "for collection", "for deposit", "pay any bank", or like terms signifying a purpose of deposit or collection; or

    (d) otherwise states that it is for the benefit or use of the indorser or of another person.

§ 3-206. Effect of Restrictive Indorsement.—

(1) No restrictive indorsement prevents further transfer or negotiation of the instrument.

(2) An intermediary bank, or a payor bank which is not the depositary bank, is neither given notice nor otherwise affected by a restrictive indorsement of any person except the bank's immediate transferor or the person presenting for payment.

(3) Except for an intermediary bank, any transferee under an indorsement which is conditional or includes the words "for collection", "for deposit", "pay any bank", or like terms (subparagraphs (a) and (c) of Section 3-205) must pay or apply any value given by him for or on the security of the instrument consistently with the indorsement and to the extent that he does so he becomes a holder for value. In addition such transferee is a holder in due course if he otherwise complies with the requirements of Section 3-302 on what constitutes a holder in due course.

(4) The first taker under an indorsement for the benefit of the indorser or another person (subparagraph (d) of Section 3-205) must pay or apply any value given by him for or on the security of the instrument consistently with the indorsement and to the extent that he does so he becomes a holder for value. In addition such taker is a holder in due course if he otherwise complies with the requirements of Section 3-302 on what constitutes a holder in due course. A later holder for value is neither given notice nor otherwise affected by such restrictive indorsement unless he has knowledge that a fiduciary or other person has negotiated the instrument in any transaction for his own benefit or otherwise in breach of duty (subsection (2) of Section 3-304).

§ 3-207. Negotiation Effective Although It May Be Rescinded.—

(1) Negotiation is effective to transfer the instrument although the negotiation is

    (a) made by an infant, a corporation exceeding its powers, or any other person without capacity; or

    (b) obtained by fraud, duress or mistake of any kind; or

    (c) part of an illegal transaction; or

    (d) made in breach of duty.

(2) Except as against a subsequent holder in due course such negotiation is in an appropriate case subject to rescission, the declaration of a constructive trust or any other remedy permitted by law.

§ 3-208. Reacquisition.—Where an instrument is returned to or required by a prior party he may cancel any indorsement which is not necessary to his title and reissue or further negotiate the instrument, but any intervening party is discharged as against the reacquiring party and subsequent holders not in due course and if his indorsement has been cancelled is discharged as against subsequent holders in due course as well.

PART 3

Rights of a Holder

§ 3-301. Rights of a Holder.—The holder of an instrument whether or not he is the owner may transfer or negotiate it and, except as otherwise provided in Section 3-603 on payment or satisfaction, discharge it or enforce payment in his own name.

§ 3-302. Holder in Due Course.—

(1) A holder in due course is a holder who takes the instrument

    (a) for value; and

    (b) in good faith; and

    (c) without notice that it is overdue or has been dishonored or of any defense against or claim to it on the part of any person.

(2) A payee may be a holder in due course.

(3) A holder does not become a holder in due course of an instrument:

(a) by purchase of it at judicial sale or by taking it under legal process; or

(b) by acquiring it in taking over an estate; or

(c) by purchasing it as part of a bulk transaction not in regular course of business of the transferor.

(4) A purchaser of a limited interest can be a holder in due course only to the extent of the interest purchased.

§ 3-303.   Taking for Value.—A holder takes the instrument for value

(a) to the extent that the agreed consideration has been performed or that he acquires a security interest in or a lien on the instrument otherwise than by legal process; or

(b) when he takes the instrument in payment of or as security for an antecedent claim against any person whether or not the claim is due; or

(c) when he gives a negotiable instrument for it or makes an irrevocable commitment to a third person.

§ 3-304.   Notice to Purchaser.—

(1) The purchaser has notice of a claim or defense if

(a) the instrument is so incomplete, bears such visible evidence of forgery or alteration, or is otherwise so irregular as to call into question its validity, terms or ownership or to create an ambiguity as to the party to pay; or

(b) the purchaser has notice that the obligation of any party is voidable in whole or in part, or that all parties have been discharged.

(2) The purchaser has notice of a claim against the instrument when he has knowledge that a fiduciary has negotiated the instrument in payment of or as security for his own debt or in any transaction for his own benefit or otherwise in breach of duty.

(3) The purchaser has notice that an instrument is overdue if he has reason to know

(a) that any part of the principal amount is overdue or that there is an uncured default in payment of another instrument of the same series; or

(b) that acceleration of the instrument has been made; or

(c) that he is taking a demand instrument after demand has been made or more than a reasonable length of time after its issue. A reasonable time for a check drawn and payable within the states and territories of the United States and the District of Columbia is presumed to be thirty days.

(4) Knowledge of the following facts does not of itself give the purchaser notice of a defense or claim

(a) That the instrument is antedated or postdated;

(b) that it was issued or negotiated in return for an executory promise or accompanied by a separate agreement, unless the purchaser has notice that a defense or claim has arisen from the terms thereof;

(c) that any party has signed for accommodation;

(d) that an incomplete instrument has been completed, unless the purchaser has notice of any improper completion;

(e) that any person negotiating the instrument is or was a fiduciary;

(f) that there has been default in payment of interest on the instrument or in payment of any other instrument, except one of the same series.

(5) The filing or recording of a document does not of itself constitute notice within the provisions of this Article to a person who would otherwise be a holder in due course.

(6) To be effective notice must be received at such time and in such manner as to give a reasonable opportunity to act on it.

§ 3-305.   Rights of Holder in Due Course.—To the extent that a holder is a holder in due course he takes the instrument free from

(1) all claims to it on the part of any person; and

(2) all defenses of any party to the instrument with whom the holder has not dealt except

(a) infancy, to the extent that it is a defense to a simple contract; and

(b) such other incapacity, or duress, or illegality of the transaction, as renders the obligation of the party a nullity; and

(c) such misrepresentation as has induced the party to sign the instrument with neither knowledge nor reasonable opportunity to obtain knowledge of its character or its essential terms; and

(d) discharge in insolvency proceedings; and

(e) any other discharge of which the holder has notice when he takes the instrument.

§ 3-306.   Rights of One Not Holder in Due Course.—Unless he has the rights of a holder in due course any person takes the instrument subject to

(a) all valid claims to it on the part of any person; and

(b) all defenses of any party which would be available in an action on a simple contract; and

(c) the defenses of want or failure of consideration, non-performance of any condition precedent, non-delivery, or delivery for a special purpose (Section 3-408); and

(d) the defense that he or a person through whom he holds the instrument acquired it by theft, or that payment or satisfaction to such holder would be inconsistent with the terms of a restrictive indorsement. The claim of any third person to the instrument is not otherwise available as a defense to any party liable thereon unless the third person himself defends the action for such party.

§ 3-307.   Burden of Establishing Signatures, Defenses and Due Course.—

(1) Unless specifically denied in the pleadings each signature on an instrument is admitted. When the

effectiveness of a signature is put in issue

(a) the burden of establishing it is on the party claiming under the signature; and

(b) the signature is presumed to be genuine or authorized except where the action is to enforce the obligation of a purported signer who has died or become incompetent before proof is required.

(2) When signatures are admitted or established, production of the instrument entitles a holder to recover on it unless the defendant establishes a defense.

(3) After it is shown that a defense exists a person claiming the rights of a holder in due course has the burden of establishing that he or some person under whom he claims is in all respects a holder in due course.

PART 4

Liability of Parties

§ 3-401. Signature.—

(1) No person is liable on an instrument unless his signature appears thereon.

(2) A signature is made by use of any name, including any trade or assumed name, upon an instrument, or by any word or mark used in lieu of a written signature.

§ 3-402. Signature in Ambiguous Capacity.—Unless the instrument clearly indicates that a signature is made in some other capacity it is an indorsement.

§ 3-403. Signature by Authorized Representative.—

(1) A signature may be made by an agent or other representative, and his authority to make it may be established as in other cases of representation. No particular form of appointment is necessary to establish such authority.

(2) An authorized representative who signs his own name to an instrument

(a) is personally obligated if the instrument neither names the person represented nor shows that the representative signed in a representative capacity;

(b) except as otherwise established between the immediate parties, is personally obligated if instrument names the person represented but does not show that the representative signed in a representative capacity, or if the instrument does not name the person represented but does show that the representative signed in a representative capacity.

(3) Except as otherwise established the name of an organization preceded or followed by the name and office of an authorized individual is a signature made in a representative capacity.

§ 3-404. Unauthorized Signatures.—

(1) Any unauthorized signature is wholly inoperative as that of the person whose name is signed unless he ratifies it or is precluded from denying it; but it operates as the signature of the unauthorized signer in favor of any person who in good faith pays the instrument or takes it for value.

(2) Any unauthorized signature may be ratified for all purposes of this Article. Such ratification does not of itself affect any rights of the person ratifying against the actual signer.

§ 3-405. Imposters; Signature in Name of Payee.—

(1) An indorsement by any person in the name of a named payee is effective if

(a) an imposter by use of the mails or otherwise has induced the maker or drawer to issue the instrument to him or his confederate in the name of the payee; or

(b) a person signing as or on behalf of a maker or drawer intends the payee to have no interest in the instrument; or

(c) an agent or employee of the maker or drawer has supplied him with the name of the payee intending the latter to have no such interest.

(2) Nothing in this Section shall affect the criminal or civil liability of the person to indorsing.

§ 3-406. Negligence Contributing to Alteration or Unauthorized Signature.—Any person who by his negligence substantially contributes to a material alteration of the instrument or to the making of an unauthorized signature is precluded from asserting the alteration or lack of authority against a holder in due course or against a drawee or other payor who pays the instrument in good faith and in accordance with the reasonable commercial standards of the drawee's or payor's business.

§ 3-407. Alteration.—

(1) Any alteration of an instrument is material which changes the contract of any party thereto in any respect, including any such change in

(a) the number of relations of the parties; or

(b) an incomplete instrument, by completing it otherwise than as authorized; or

(c) the writing as signed, by adding to it or by removing any part of it.

(2) As against any person other than a subsequent holder in due course

(a) alteration by the holder which is both fraudulent and material discharges any party whose contract is thereby changed unless that party assents or is precluded from asserting the defense;

(b) no other alteration discharges any party and the instrument may be enforced according to its original tenor, or as to incomplete instruments according to the authority given.

(3) A subsequent holder in due course may in all cases enforce the instrument according to its original tenor, and when an incomplete instrument has been completed, he may enforce it as completed.

§ 3-408. Consideration.—Want or failure of consideration is a defense as against any person not having the rights of a holder in due course (Section 3-305), except that no consideration is necessary for an instrument or obligation thereon given in payment of or as security for an antecedent obligation of any kind. Nothing in this Section shall be taken to displace any statute outside this Act under which a promise is enforceable notwithstanding lack or failure of consideration. Partial failure of consideration is a defense pro tanto whether or not the failure is in an ascertained or liquidated amount.

§ 3-409. Draft Not an Assignment.—

(1) A check or other draft does not of itself operate as an assignment of any funds in the hands of the drawee available for its payment, and the drawee is not liable on the instrument until he accepts it.

(2) Nothing in this Section shall affect any liability in contract, tort or otherwise arising from any letter of credit or other obligation or representation which is not an acceptance.

§ 3-410. Definition and Operation of Acceptance.—

(1) Acceptance is the drawee's signed engagement to honor the draft as presented. It must be written on the draft, and may consist of his signature alone. It becomes operative when completed by delivery or notification.

(2) A draft may be accepted although it has not been signed by the drawer or is otherwise incomplete or is overdue or has been dishonored.

(3) Where the draft is payable at a fixed period after sight and the acceptor fails to date his acceptance the holder may complete it by supplying a date in good faith.

§ 3-411. Certification of a Check.—

(1) Certification of a check is acceptance. Where a holder procures certification the drawer and all prior indorsers are discharged.

(2) Unless otherwise agreed a bank has no obligation to certify a check.

(3) A bank may certify a check before returning it for lack of proper indorsement. If it does so the drawer is discharged.

§ 3-412. Acceptance Varying Draft.—

(1) Where the drawee's proffered acceptance in any manner varies the draft as presented the holder may refuse the acceptance and treat the draft as dishonored in which case the drawee is entitled to have his acceptance cancelled.

(2) The terms of the draft are not varied by an acceptance to pay at any particular bank or place in the continental United States, unless the acceptance states that the draft is to be paid only at such bank or place.

(3) Where the holder assents to an acceptance varying the terms of the draft each drawer and indorser who does not affirmatively assent is discharged.

§ 3-413. Contract of Maker, Drawer and Acceptor.—

(1) The maker or acceptor engages that he will pay the instrument according to its tenor at the time of his engagement or as completed pursuant to Section 3-115 on incomplete instruments.

(2) The drawer engages that upon dishonor of the draft and any necessary notice of dishonor or protest he will pay the amount of the draft to the holder or to any indorser who takes it up. The drawer may disclaim this liability by drawing without recourse.

(3) By making, drawing or accepting the party admits as against all subsequent parties including the drawee the existence of the payee and his then capacity to indorse.

§ 3-414. Contract of Indorser; Order of Liability.—

(1) Unless the indorsement otherwise specifies (as by such words as "without recourse") every indorser engages that upon dishonor and any necessary notice of dishonor and protest he will pay the instrument according to its tenor at the time of his indorsement to the holder or to any subsequent indorser who takes it up, even though the indorser who takes it up was not obligated to do so.

(2) Unless they otherwise agree indorsers are liable to one another in the order in which they indorse, which is presumed to be the order in which their signatures appear on the instrument.

§ 3-415. Contract of Accommodation Party.—

(1) An accommodation party is one who signs the instrument in any capacity for the purpose of lending his name to another party to it.

(2) When the instrument has been taken for value before it is due the accommodation party is liable in the capacity in which he has signed even though the taker knows of the accommodation.

(3) As against a holder in due course and without notice of the accommodation oral proof of the accommodation is not admissible to give the accommodation party the benefit of discharges dependent on his character as such. In other cases the accommodation character may be shown by oral proof.

(4) An indorsement which shows that it is not in the chain of title is notice of its accommodation character.

(5) An accommodation party is not liable to the party accommodated, and if he pays the instrument has a right of recourse on the instrument against such party.

§ 3-416. Contract of Guarantor.—

(1) "Payment guaranteed" or equivalent words added to a signature mean that the signer engages that if the instrument is not paid when due he will pay it according to its tenor without resort by the holder to any other party.

(2) "Collection guaranteed" or equivalent words added to a signature mean that the signer engages that if the instrument is not paid when due he will pay it according to its tenor, but only after the holder has reduced his claim against the maker or acceptor to judgment and execution has been returned unsatisfied, or

after the maker or acceptor has become insolvent or it is otherwise apparent that it is useless to proceed against him.

(3) Words of guaranty which do not otherwise specify guarantee payment.

(4) No words of guaranty added to the signature of a sole maker or acceptor affect his liability on the instrument. Such words added to the signature of one of two or more makers or acceptors create a presumption that the signature is for the accommodation of the others.

(5) When words of guaranty are used presentment, notice of dishonor and protest are not necessary to charge the user.

(6) Any guaranty written on the instrument is enforceable notwithstanding any statute of frauds.

§ 3-417. Warranties on Presentment and Transfer.—

(1) Any person who obtains payment or acceptance and any prior transferor warrants to a person who in good faith pays or accepts that

(a) he has a good title to the instrument or is authorized to obtain payment of acceptance on behalf of one who has a good title; and

(b) he has no knowledge that the signature of the maker or drawer is unauthorized, except that this warranty is not given by a holder in due course acting in good faith

(i) To a maker with respect to the maker's own signature; or

(ii) To a drawer with respect to the drawer's own signature, whether or not the drawer is also the drawee; or

(iii) to an acceptor of a draft if the holder in due course took the draft after the acceptance or obtained the acceptance without knowledge that the drawer's signature was unauthorized; and

(c) the instrument has not been materially altered, except that this warranty is not given by a holder in due course acting in good faith

(i) to the maker of a note; or

(ii) To the drawer of a draft whether or not the drawer is also the drawee; or

(iii) to the acceptor of a draft with respect to an alteration made prior to the acceptance if the holder in due course took the draft after the acceptance, even though the acceptance provided "payable as originally drawn" or equivalent terms; or

(iv) to the acceptor of a draft with respect to an alteration made after the acceptance.

(2) Any person who transfers an instrument and receives consideration warrants to his transferee and if the transfer is by indorsement to any subsequent holder who takes the instrument in good faith that

(a) he has a good title to the instrument or is authorized to obtain payment or acceptance on behalf of one who has a good title and the transfer is otherwise rightful; and

(b) all signatures are genuine or authorized; and

(c) the instrument has not been materially altered; and

(d) no defense of any party is good against him; and

(e) he has no knowledge of any insolvency proceeding instituted with respect to the maker or acceptor or the drawer of an unaccepted instrument.

(3) By transferring "without recourse" the transferor limits the obligation stated in subsection (2) (d) to a warranty that he has no knowledge of such a defense.

(4) A selling agent or broker who does not disclose the fact that he is acting only as such gives the warranties provided in this Section, but if he makes such disclosure warrants only his good faith and authority.

§ 3-418. Finality of Payment or Acceptance.—Except for recovery of bank payments as provided in the Article on Bank Deposits and Collections (Article 4) and except for liability for breach of warranty on presentment under the preceding section, payment or acceptance of any instrument is final in favor of a holder in due course, or a person who has in good faith changed his position in reliance on the payment.

§ 3-419. Conversion of Instrument; Innocent Representative.—

(1) An instrument is converted when

(a) a drawee to whom it is delivered for acceptance refuses to return it on demand; or

(b) any person to whom it is delivered for payment refuses on demand either to pay or to return it; or

(c) it is paid on a forged indorsement.

(2) In an action against a drawee under subsection (1) the measure of the drawee's liability is the face amount of the instrument. In any other action under subsection (1) the measure of liability is presumed to be the face amount of the instrument.

(3) Subject to the provisions of this Act concerning restrictive indorsements a representative, including a depositary or collecting bank, who has in good faith and in accordance with the reasonable commercial standards applicable to the business of such representative dealt with an instrument or its proceeds on behalf of one who was not the true owner is not liable in conversion or otherwise to the true owner beyond the amount of any proceeds remaining in his hands.

(4) An intermediary bank or payor bank which is not a depositary bank is not liable in conversion solely by reason of the fact that proceeds of an item indorsed restrictively (Section 3-205 and 3-206) are not paid or applied consistently with the restrictive indorsement of an indorser other than its immediate transferor.

PART 5

Presentment, Notice of Dishonor and Protest

§ 3-501. When Presentment, Notice of Dishonor, and Protest Necessary or Permissible.—

(1) Unless excused (Section 3-511) presentment is necessary to charge secondary parties as follows:

(a) presentment for acceptance is necessary to charge the drawer and indorsers of a draft where the draft so provides, or is payable elsewhere than at the residence or place of business of the drawee, or its date of payment depends upon such presentment. The holder may at his option present for acceptance any other draft payable at a stated date;

(b) presentment for payment is necessary to charge any indorser;

(c) in the case of any drawer, the acceptor of a draft payable at a bank or the maker of a note payable at a bank, presentment for payment is necessary, but failure to make presentment discharges such drawer, acceptor or maker only as stated in Section 3-502 (1) (b).

(2) Unless excused (Section 3-511)

(a) notice of any dishonor is necessary to charge any indorser;

(b) in the case of any drawer, the acceptor of a draft payable at a bank or the maker of a note payable at a bank notice of any dishonor is necessary, but failure to give such notice discharges such drawer, acceptor or maker only as stated in Section 3-502 (1) (b).

(3) Unless excused (Section 3-511) protest of any dishonor is necessary to charge the drawer and indorsers of any draft which on its face appears to be drawn or payable outside of the states and territories of the United States and the District of Columbia. The holder may at his option make protest of any dishonor of any other instrument and in the case of a foreign draft may on insolvency of the acceptor before maturity make protest for better security.

(4) Notwithstanding any provision of this Section, neither presentment nor notice of dishonor nor protest is necessary to charge an indorser who has indorsed an instrument after maturity.

§ 3-502. Unexcused Delay; Discharge.—

(1) Where without excuse any necessary presentment or notice of dishonor is delayed beyond the time when it is due

(a) Any indorser is discharged; and

(b) any drawer or the acceptor of a draft payable at a bank or the maker of a note payable at a bank who because the drawee or payor bank becomes insolvent during the delay is deprived of funds maintained with the drawee or payor bank to cover the instrument may discharge his liability by written assignment to the holder of his rights against the drawee or payor bank in respect of such funds, but such drawer, acceptor or maker is not otherwise discharged.

(2) Where without excuse a necessary protest is delayed beyond the time when it is due any drawer or indorser is discharged.

§ 3-503. Time of Presentment.—

(1) Unless a different time is expressed in the instrument the time for any presentment is determined as follows:

(a) where an instrument is payable at or a fixed period after a stated date any presentment for acceptance must be made on or before the date it is payable;

(b) where an instrument is payable after sight it must either be presented for acceptance or negotiated within a reasonable time after date or issue whichever is later;

(c) where an instrument shows the date on which it is payable presentment for payment is due on that date;

(d) where an instrument is accelerated presentment for payment is due within a reasonable time after the acceleration;

(e) with respect to the liability of any secondary party presentment for acceptance or payment of any other instrument is due within a reasonable time after such party becomes liable thereon.

(2) A reasonable time for presentment is determined by the nature of the instrument, any usage of banking or trade and the facts of the particular case. In the case of an uncertified check which is drawn and payable within the United States and which is not a draft drawn by a bank the following are presumed to be reasonable periods within which to present for payment or to initiate bank collection:

(a) with respect to the liability of the drawer, thirty days after date or issue whichever is later; and

(b) with respect to the liability of an endorser, seven days after his indorsement.

(3) Where any presentment is due on a day which is not a full business day for either the person making presentment or the party to pay or accept, presentment is due on the next following day which is a full business day for both parties.

(4) Presentment to be sufficient must be made at a reasonable hour, and if at a bank during its banking day.

§ 3-504. How Presentment Made.—

(1) Presentment is a demand for acceptance or payment made upon the maker, acceptor, drawee or other payor by or on behalf of the holder.

(2) Presentment may be made

(a) by mail, in which event the time of presentment is determined by the time of receipt of the mail; or

(b) through a clearing house; or

(c) at the place of acceptance or payment specified in the instrument or if there be none at the place of business or residence of the party to accept or pay. If neither the party to accept or pay nor anyone authorized to act for him is present or accessible at such place presentment is excused.

(3) It may be made

(a) to any one of two or more makers, acceptors, drawees or other payors; or

(b) to any person who has authority to make or refuse the acceptance or payment.

(4) A draft accepted or a note made payable at a bank in the continental United States must be presented at such bank.

(5) In the cases described in Section 4-210 presentment may be made in the manner and with the result stated in that section.

§ 3-505. Rights of Party to Whom Presentment is Made.—

(1) The party to whom presentment is made may without dishonor require

    (a) exhibition of the instrument; and

    (b) reasonable identification of the person making presentment and evidence of his authority to make it if made for another; and

    (c) that the instrument be produced for acceptance or payment at a place specified in it, or if there be none at any place reasonable in the circumstances; and

    (d) a signed receipt on the instrument for any partial or full payment and its surrender upon full payment.

(2) Failure to comply with any such requirements invalidates the presentment but the person presenting has a reasonable time in which to comply and the time for acceptance or payment runs from the time of compliance.

§ 3-506. Time Allowed for Acceptance or Payment.—

(1) Acceptance may be deferred without dishonor until the close of the next business day following presentment. The holder may also in a good faith effort to obtain acceptance and without either dishonor of the instrument or discharge of secondary parties allow postponement of acceptance for an additional business day.

(2) Except as longer time is allowed in the case of documentary drafts drawn under a letter of credit, and unless an earlier time is agreed to by the party to pay, payment of an instrument may be deferred without dishonor pending reasonable examination to determine whether it is properly payable, but payment must be made in any event before the close of business on the day of presentment.

§ 3-507. Dishonor; Holder's Right of Recourse; Term Allowing Re-Presentment.—

(1) An instrument is dishonored when

    (a) a necessary or optional presentment is duly made and due acceptance or payment is refused or cannot be obtained within the prescribed time or in case of bank collections the instrument is seasonably returned by the midnight deadline (Section 4-301); or

    (b) presentment is excused and the instrument is not duly accepted or paid.

(2) Subject to any necessary notice of dishonor and protest, the holder has upon dishonor an immediate right of recourse against the drawers and indorsers.

(3) Return of an instrument for lack of proper indorsement is not dishonor.

(4) A term in a draft or an indorsement thereof allowing a stated time for representment in the event of any dishonor of the draft by nonacceptance if a time draft or by nonpayment if a sight draft gives the holder as against any secondary party bound by the term an option to waive the dishonor without affecting the liability of the secondary party and he may present again up to the end of the stated time.

§ 3-508. Notice of Dishonor.—

(1) Notice of dishonor may be given to any person who may be liable on the instrument by or on behalf of the holder or any party who has himself received notice, or any other party who can be compelled to pay the instrument. In addition an agent or bank in whose hands the instrument is dishonored may give notice to his principal or customer or to another agent or bank from which the instrument was received.

(2) Any necessary notice must be given by a bank before its midnight deadline and by any other person before midnight of the third business day after dishonor or receipt of notice of dishonor.

(3) Notice may be given in any reasonable manner. It may be oral or written and in any terms which identify the instrument and state that it has been dishonored. A misdescription which does not mislead the party notified does not vitiate the notice. Sending the instrument bearing a stamp, ticket or writing stating that acceptance or payment has been refused or sending a notice of debit with respect to the instrument is sufficient.

(4) Written notice is given when sent although it is not received.

(5) Notice to one partner is notice to each although the firm has been dissolved.

(6) When any party is in insolvency proceedings instituted after the issue of the instrument notice may be given either to the party or to the representative of his estate.

(7) When any party is dead or incompetent notice may be sent to his last known address or given to his personal representative.

(8) Notice operates for the benefit of all parties who have rights on the instrument against the party notified.

§ 3-509. Protest; Noting for Protest.—

(1) A protest is a certificate of dishonor made under the hand and seal of a United States consul or vice consul or a notary public or other person authorized to certify dishonor by the law of the place where dishonor occurs. It may be made upon information satisfactory to such person.

(2) The protest must identify the instrument and certify either that due presentment has been made or the reason why it is excused and that the instrument has been dishonored by non-acceptance or nonpayment.

(3) The protest may also certify that notice of dishonor has been given to all parties or to specified parties.

(4) Subject to subsection (5) any necessary protest is due by the time that notice of dishonor is due.

(5) If, before protest is due, an instrument has been noted for protest by the officer to make protest, the protest may be made at any time thereafter as of the date of the noting.

§ 3-510. Evidence of Dishonor and Notice of Dishonor.—The following are admissable as evidence and create a presumption of dishonor and of any notice of dishonor therein shown:

    (a) a document regular in form as provided in the preceding section which purports to be a protest;

(b) the purported stamp or writing of the drawee, payor bank or presenting bank on the instrument or accompanying it stating that acceptance or payment has been refused for reasons consistent with dishonor;

(c) any book or record of the drawee, payor bank, or any collecting bank kept in the usual course of business which shows dishonor, even though there is no evidence of who made the entry.

§ 3-511.   Waived or Excused Presentment, Protest or Notice of Dishonor or Delay Therein.—

(1) Delay in presentment, protest or notice of dishonor is excused when the party is without notice that it is due or when the delay is caused by circumstances beyond his control and he exercises reasonable diligence after the cause of the delay ceases to operate.

(2) Presentment or notice or protest as the case may be is entirely excused when

(a) the party to be charged has waived it expressly or by implication either before or after it is due; or

(b) such party has himself dishonored the instrument or has countermanded payment or otherwise has no reason to expect or right to require that the instrument be accepted or paid; or

(c) by reasonable diligence the presentment or protest cannot be made of the notice given.

(3) Presentment is also entirely excused when

(a) the maker, acceptor or drawee of any instrument except a documentary draft is dead or in insolvency proceedings instituted after the issue of the instrument; or

(b) acceptance or payment is refused but not for want of proper presentment

(4) Where a draft has been dishonored by nonacceptance a later presentment for payment and any notice of dishonor and protest for nonpayment are excused unless in the meantime the instrument has been accepted.

(5) A waiver of protest is also a waiver of presentment and of notice of dishonor even though protest is not required.

(6) Where a waiver of presentment or notice of protest is embodied in the instrument itself it is binding upon all parties; but where it is written above the signature of an indorser it binds him only.

PART 6

Discharge

§ 3-601.   Discharge of Parties.—

The extent of the discharge of any party from liability on an instrument is governed by the sections on

(a) payment or satisfaction (Section 3-603); or

(b) tender of payment (Section 3-604); or

(c) cancellation or renunciation (Section 3-605); or

(d) impairment of right of recourse or of collateral (Section 3-606); or

(e) reacquisition of the instrument by a prior party (Seciton 3-208); or

(f) fraudulent and material alteration (Section 3-407); or

(g) certification of a check (Section 3-411); or

(h) acceptance varying a draft (Section 3-412); or

(i) unexcused delay in presentment or notice of dishonor or protest (Section 3-502).

(2) Any party is also discharged from his liability on an instrument to another party by any other act or agreement with such a party which would discharge his simple contract for the payment of money.

(3) The liability of all parties is discharged when any party who has himself no right of action or recourse on the instrument

(a) reacquires the instrument in his own right; or

(b) is discharged under any provisions of this Article, except as otherwise provided with respect to discharge for impairment of recourse or of collateral (Section 3-606).

§ 3-602.   Effects of Discharge Against Holder in Due Course.—No discharge of any party provided by this Article is effective against a subsequent holder in due course unless he has notice thereof when he takes the instrument.

§ 3-603.   Payment or Satisfaction.—

(1) The liability of any party is discharged to the extent of his payment or satisfaction to the holder even though it is made with knowledge of a claim of another person to the instrument unless prior to such payment or satisfaction the person making the claim either supplies indemnity deemed adequate by the party seeking the discharge or enjoins payment or satisfaction by order of a court of competent jurisdiction in an action in which the adverse claimant and the holder are parties. This subsection does not, however, result in the discharge of the liability

(a) of a party who in bad faith pays or satisfies a holder who acquired the instrument by theft or who (unless having the rights of a holder in due course) holds through one who so acquired it; or

(b) of a party (other than an intermediary bank or a payor bank which is not a depositary bank) who pays or satisfies the holder of an instrument which has been restrictively indorsed in a manner not consistent with the terms of such restrictive indorsement.

(2) Payment of satisfaction may be made with the consent of the holder by any person including a stranger to the instrument. Surrender of the instrument to such a person gives him the rights of a transferee (Section 3-201).

§ 3-604.   Tender of Payment.—

(1) Any party making tender of full payment to a holder when or after it is due is discharged to the extent

of all subsequent liability for interest, costs and attorney's fees.

(2) The holder's refusal of such tender wholly discharges any party who has a right of recourse against the party making the tender.

(3) Where the maker or acceptor of an instrument payable otherwise than on demand is able and ready to pay at every place of payment specified in the instrument when it is due, it is equivalent to tender.

§ 3-605. Cancellation and Renunciation.—

The holder of an instrument may even without consideration discharge any party

(a) in any manner apparent on the face of the instrument or the indorsement, as by intentially cancelling the instrument or the party's signature by destruction or mutilation, or by striking out the party's signature; or

(b) by renouncing his rights by a writing signed and delivered or by surrender of the instrument to the party to be discharged.

(2) Neither cancellation nor renunciation without surrender of the instrument affects the title thereto.

§ 3-606. Impairment of Recourse or of Collateral.—

(1) The holder discharges any party to the instrument to the extent that without such party's consent the holder

(a) without express reservation of rights releases or agrees not to sue any person against whom the party has to the knowledge of the holder a right of recourse or agrees to suspend the right to enforce against such person the instrument or collateral or otherwise discharges such person, except that failure or delay in effecting any required presentment, protest or notice of dishonor with respect to any such person does not discharge any party as to whom presentment, protest or notice of dishonor is effective or unnecessary; or

(b) unjustifiably impairs any collateral for the instrument given by or on behalf of the party or any person against whom he has a right of recourse.

(2) By express reservation of rights against a party with a right of recourse the holder preserves

(a) all his rights against such party as of the time when the instrument was originally due; and

(b) the right of the party to pay the instrument as of that time; and

(c) all rights of such party to recourse against others.

PART 7

Advice of International Sight Draft (omitted)

PART 8

Miscellaneous

§ 3-801. omitted.

§ 3-802. Effect of Instrument on Obligation for Which It Is Given.—

(1) Unless otherwise agreed where an instrument is taken for an underlying obligation

(a) the obligation is pro tanto discharged if a bank is drawer, maker or acceptor of an instrument and there is no recourse on the instrument against the underlying obligor; and

(b) in any other case the obligation is suspended pro tanto until the instrument is due or if it is payable on demand until its presentment. If the instrument is dishonored action may be maintained on either the instrument or the obligation; discharge of the underlying obligor on the instrument also discharges him on the obligation.

(2) The taking in good faith of a check which is not postdated does not of itself so extend the time on the original obligation as to discharge a surety.

§ 3-803. Notice to Third Party.—

Where a defendant is sued for breach of an obligation for which a third person is answerable over under this Article he may give the third person written notice of the litigation, and the person notified may then give similar notice to any other person who is answerable over to him under this Article. If the notice states that the person notified may come in and defend and that if the person notified does not do so he will in any action against him by the person giving the notice be bound by any determination of fact common to the two litigations, then unless after seasonable receipt of the notice the person notified does come in and defend he is so bound.

§ 3-804. Lost, Destroyed or Stolen Investments.—

The owner of an instrument which is lost, whether by destruction, theft or otherwise, may maintain an action in his own name and recover from any party liable thereon upon due proof of his ownership, the facts which prevent his production of the instrument and its terms. The court may require security indemnifying defendant against loss by reason of further claims on the instrument.

§ 3-805. Instruments Not Payable to Order or to Bearer.—

This Article applies to any instrument whose terms do not preclude transfer and which is otherwise negotiable within this Article but which is not payable to order or to bearer, except that there can be no holder in due course of such an instrument.

ARTICLE FOUR — BANK DEPOSITS AND COLLECTIONS

PART I

General Provisions and Definitions

§ 4-101.   Short Title.—This Article shall be known and may be cited as Uniform Commercial Code—Bank Deposits and Collections.

§ 4-102.   Applicability.—

(1) To the extent that items within this Article are also within the scope of Articles 3 and 8, they are subject to the provisions of those Articles. In the event of conflict the provisions of this Article govern those of Article 3 but the provisions of Article 8 govern those of this Article.

(2) The liability of a bank for action or non-action with respect to any item handled by it for purposes of presentment, payment or collection is governed by the law of the place where the bank is located. In the case of action or non-action by or at a branch or separate office of a bank, its liability is governed by the law of the place where the branch or separate office is located.

§ 4-103.   Variation by Agreement; Measure of Damages; Certain Action Constituting Ordinary Care.—

(1) the effect of the provisions of this Article may be varied by agreement except that no agreement can disclaim a bank's responsibility for its own lack of good faith or failure to exercise ordinary care or can limit the measure of damages for such lack or failure; but the parties may by agreement determine the standards by which such responsibility is to be measured if such standards are not manifestly unreasonable.

(2) Federal reserve regulations and operating letters, clearing house rules, and the like, have the effect of agreements under subsection (1), whether or not specifically assented to by all parties interested in items handled.

(3) Action or non-action approved by this Article or pursuant to Federal Reserve regulations or operating letters constitutes the exercise of ordinary care and, in the absence of special instructions, action or non-action consistent with clearing house rules and the like or with a general banking usage not disapproved by this Article, prima facie constitutes the exercise of ordinary care.

(4) The specification or approval of certain procedures by this Article does not constitute disapproval of other procedures which may be reasonable under the circumstances.

(5) The measure of damages for failure to exercise ordinary care in handling an item is the amount of the item reduced by an amount which could not have been realized by the use of ordinary care, and where there is bad faith it includes other damages, if any, suffered by the party as a proximate consequence.

§ 4-104.   Definitions and Index of Definitions.—

(1) In this Article unless the context otherwise requires

(a) "Account" means any account with a bank and includes a checking, time, interest or savings account;

(b) "Afternoon" means the period of a day between noon and midnight.

(c) "Banking day" means that part of any day on which a bank is open to the public for carrying on substantially all of its banking functions;

(d) "Clearing house" means any association of banks or other payors regularly clearing items;

(e) "Customer" means any person having an account with a bank or for whom a bank has agreed to collect items and includes a bank carrying an account with another bank;

(f) "Documentary draft" means any negotiable or non-negotiable draft with accompanying documents, securities or other papers to be delivered against honor of the draft;

(g) "Item" means any instrument for the payment of money even though it is not negotiable but does not include money;

(h) "Midnight deadline" with respect to a bank is midnight on its next banking day following the banking day on which it receives the relevant item or notice or from which the time for taking action commences to run, whichever is later;

(i) "Property payable" includes the availability of funds for payment at the time of decision to pay or dishonor;

(j) "Settle" means to pay in cash, by clearing house settlement, in a charge or credit or by remittance, or otherwise as instructed. A settlement may be either provisional or final.

(k) "Suspends payments" with respect to bank means that it has been closed by order of the supervisory authorities, that a public officer has been appointed to take it over or that it ceases or refuses to make payments in the ordinary course of business.

(2) Other definitions applying to this Article and the sections in which they appear are:

"Collecting bank"	Section 4-105.
"Depositary bank"	Section 4-105.
"Intermediary bank"	Section 4-105.
"Payor bank"	Section 4-105.
"Presenting bank"	Section 4-105.
"Remitting bank"	Section 4-105.

(3) The following definitions in other Articles apply to this Article:

"Acceptance"	Section 3-410.
"Certificate of deposit"	Section 3-104.

"Certification"	Section 3-411.
"Check"	Section 3-104.
"Draft"	Section 3-104.
"Holder in due course"	Section 3-302.
"Notice of dishonor"	Section 3-508.
"Presentment"	Section 3-504.
"Protest"	Section 3-509.
"Secondary party"	Section 3-102.

(4) In addition Article 1 contains general definitions and principles of construction and interpretation applicable throughout this Article.

§ 4-105. "Depositary Bank"; "Intermediary Bank"; "Collecting Bank"; "Payor Bank"; "Presenting Bank"; "Remitting Bank"—In this Article unless the context otherwise requires:

(a) "Depositary bank" means the first bank to which an item is transferred for collection even though it is also the payor bank.

(b) "Payor bank" means a bank by which an item is payable as drawn or accepted;

(c) "Intermediary bank" means any bank to which an item is transferred in course of collection except the depositary or payor bank;

(d) "Collecting bank" means any bank handling the item for collection except the payor bank;

(e) "Presenting bank" means any bank presenting an item except a payor bank;

(f) "Remitting bank" means any payor or intermediary bank remitting for an item.

§ 4-106. Separate Office of a Bank.—A branch or separate office of a bank [maintaining its own deposit ledgers] is a separate bank for the purpose of computing the time within which and the place at or to which action may be taken or notices or orders shall be given under this Article.

Note: The brackets are to make it optional with the several states whether to require a branch to maintain its own deposit ledgers in order to be considered to be a separate bank for certain purposes under Article 4. In some states "maintaining its own deposit ledgers" is a satisfactory test. In others branch banking practices are such that this test would not be suitable.

§ 4-107. Time of Receipt of Items.—

(1) For the purpose of allowing time to process items, prove balances and make the necessary entries on its books to determine its position for the day, a bank may fix an afternoon hour of two P.M. or later as a cut-off hour for the handling of money and items and the making of entries on its books.

(2) Any item or deposit of money received on any day after a cut-off hour so fixed or after the close of the banking day may be treated as being received at the opening of the next banking day.

§ 4-108. Delays.—

(1) Unless otherwise instructed, a collecting bank in a good faith effort to secure payment may, in the case of specific items and with or without the approval of any person involved, waive, modify or extend time limits imposed or permitted by this Act for a period not in excess of an additional banking day without discharge of secondary parties and without liability to its transferor or any prior party.

(2) Delay by a collecting bank or payor bank beyond time limits prescribed or permitted by this Act or by instructions is excused if caused by interruption of communication facilities, suspension of payments by another bank, war, emergency conditions or other circumstances beyond the control of the bank provided it exercises such diligence as the circumstances require.

PART 2

Collection of Items: Depositary and Collecting Banks

§ 4-201. Presumption and Duration of Agency Status of Collecting Banks and Provisional Status of Credits; Applicability of Article; Item Indorsed "Pay Any Bank".—

(1) Unless a contrary intent clearly appears and prior to the time that a settlement given by a collecting bank for an item is or becomes final (subsection (3) of Section 4-211 and Section 4-212 and 4-213) the bank is an agent or sub-agent of the owner of the item and any settlement given for the item is provisional. This provision applies regardless of the form of indorsement or lack of indorsement and even though credit given for the item is subject to immediate withdrawal as of right or is in fact withdrawn; but the continuance of ownership of an item by its owner and any rights of the owner to proceeds of the item are subject to rights of a collecting bank such as those resulting from outstanding advances on the item and valid rights of setoff. When an item is handled by banks for purposes of presentment, payment and collection, the relevant provisions of this Article apply even though action of parties clearly establishes that a particular bank has purchased the item and is the owner of it.

(2) After an item has been indorsed with the words "pay any bank" or the like, only a bank may acquire the rights of a holder

(a) until the item has been returned to the customer initiating collection; or

(b) until the item has been specially endorsed by a bank to a person who is not a bank.

§ 4-202. Responsibility for Collection; When Action Seasonable.—

(1) A collecting bank must use ordinary care in

(a) presenting an item or sending it for presentment; and

(b) sending notice of dishonor or non-payment or returning an item other than a documentary draft to the bank's transferor [or directly to the depositary bank under subsection (2) of Section 4-212] *(see note to Section 4-212)* after learning that the item has not been paid or accepted, as the case may be; and

    (c) settling for an item when the bank receives final settlement; and

    (d) making or providing for any necessary protest; and

    (e) notifying its transferor of any loss or delay in transit within a reasonable time after discovery thereof.

(2) A collecting bank taking proper action before its midnight deadline following receipt of an item, notice or payment acts seasonably; taking proper action within a reasonably longer time may be seasonable but the bank has the burden of so establishing.

(3) Subject to subjection (1) (a), a bank is not liable for the insolvency, neglect, misconduct, mistake or default of another bank or person or for loss or destruction of an item in transit or in the possession of others.

§ 4-203. Effect of Instructions.—Subject to the provisions of Article 3 concerning conversion of instruments (Section 3-419) and the provisions of both Article 3 and this Article concerning restrictive indorsements only a collecting bank's transferor can give instructions which affect the bank or constitute notice to it and a collecting bank is not liable to prior parties for any action taken pursuant to such instructions or in accordance with any agreement with its transferor.

§ 4-204. Methods of Sending and Presenting; Sending Direct to Payor Bank—

(1) A collecting bank must send items by reasonably prompt method taking into consideration any relevant instructions, the nature of the item, the number of such items on hand, and the cost of collection involved and the method generally used by it or others to present such items.

(2) A collecting bank may send

    (a) any item direct to the payor bank;

    (b) any item to any non-bank payor if authorized by its transferor; and

    (c) any item other than documentary drafts to any non-bank payor, if authorized by Federal Reserve regulation or operating letter, clearing house rule or the like.

§ 4-205. Supplying Missing Indorsement; No Notice From Prior Indorsement.—

(1) A depositary bank which has taken an item for collection may supply any indorsement of the customer which is necessary to title unless the item contains the words "payee's indorsement required" or the like. In the absence of such a requirement a statement placed on the item by the depositary bank to the effect that the item was deposited by a customer or credited to his account is effective as the customer's indorsement.

(2) An intermediary bank, or payor bank which is not a depositary bank, is neither given notice nor otherwise affected by a restrictive indorsement of any person except the bank's immediate transferor.

§ 4-206. Transfer Between Banks—Any agreed method which identifies the transferor bank is sufficient for the item's further transfer to another bank.

§ 4-207. Warranties of Customer and Collecting Bank on Transfer or Presentment of Items; Time for Claims.—

(1) Each customer or collecting bank who obtains payment or acceptance of an item and each prior customer and collecting bank warrants to the payor bank or other payor who in good faith pays or accepts the item that

    (a) he has a good title to the item or is authorized to obtain payment or acceptance on behalf of one who has a good title; and

    (b) he has no knowledge that the signature of the maker or drawer is unauthorized, except that this warranty is not given by any customer or collecting bank that is a holder in due course and acts in good faith

        (i) to a maker with respect to the maker's own signature; or

        (ii) to a drawer with respect to the drawer's own signature, whether or not the drawer is also the drawee; or

        (iii) to an acceptor of an item if the holder in due course took the item after the acceptance or obtained the acceptance without knowledge that the drawer's signature was unauthorized; and

    (c) the item has not been materially altered, except that this warranty is not given by any customer or collecting bank that is a holder in due course and acts in good faith

        (i) to the maker of a note; or

        (ii) to the drawer of a draft whether or not the drawer is also the drawee; or

        (iii) to the acceptor of an item with respect to an alteration made prior to the acceptance if the holder in due course took the item after the acceptance, even though the acceptance provided "payable as originally drawn" equivalent terms; or

        (iv) to the acceptor of an item with respect to an alteration made after the acceptance.

(2) Each customer and collecting bank who transfers an item and receives a settlement or other consideration for it warrants to his transferee and to any subsequent collecting bank who takes the item in good faith and

    (a) he has a good title to the item or is authorized to obtain payment or acceptance on behalf of one who has a good title and the transfer is otherwise rightful; and

    (b) all signatures are genuine or authorized; and

    (c) the item has not been materially altered; and

    (d) no defense of any party is good against him; and

    (e) he has no knowledge of any insolvency proceeding instituted with respect to the maker or acceptor or the drawer of an unaccepted item.

In addition each customer and collecting bank so transferring an item and receiving a settlement or other consideration engages that upon dishonor and any necessary notice of dishonor and protest he will take up the item.

(3) The warranties and the engagement to honor set forth in the two preceding subsections arise notwithstanding the absence of endorsement or words of guaranty or warranty in the transfer or presentment and a collecting bank remains liable for their breach despite remittance to its transferor. Damages for breach of such warranties or engagement to honor shall not exceed the consideration received by the customer or collecting bank responsible plus finance changes and expenses related to the item, if any.

(4) Unless a claim for breach of warranty under this section is made within a reasonable time after the person claiming learns of the breach, the person liable is discharged to the extent of any loss caused by the delay in making claim.

§ 4-208.   Security Interest of Collecting Bank in Items, Accompanying Documents and Proceeds.—

(1) A bank has a security interest in an item and any accompanying documents or the proceeds of either

(a) in case of an item deposited in an account to the extent to which credit given for the item has been withdrawn or applied;

(b) in case of an item for which it has given credit available for withdrawal as of right, to the extent of the credit given whether or not the credit is drawn upon and whether or not there is a right of charge-back; or

(c) if it makes an advance on or against the item.

(2) When credit which has been given for several items received at one time or pursuant to a single agreement is withdrawn or applied in part the security interest remains upon all the items, any accompanying documents or the proceeds of either. For the purpose of this section, credits first given are first withdrawn.

(3) Receipt by a collecting bank of a final settlement for an item is a realization on its security interest in the item, accompanying documents and proceeds. To the extent and so long as the bank does not receive final settlement for the item or give up possession of the item or accompanying documents for purposes other than collection, the security interest continues and is subject to provisions of Article 9 except that

(a) no security agreement is necessary to make the security interest enforceable (subsection (1)(b) of Section 9-203); and

(b) no filing is required to perfect the security interest; and

(c) the security interest has priority over conflicting perfected security interests in the item, accompanying documents or proceeds.

§ 4-209.   When Bank Gives Value for Purposes of Holder in Due Course.—For purposes of determining its status as a holder in due course, the bank has given value to the extent that it has a security interest in an item provided that the bank otherwise complies with the requirements of Section 3-302 on what constitutes a holder in due course.

§ 4-210.   Presentment by Notice of Item Not Payable by, Through or at a Bank; Liability of Secondary Parties.—

(1) Unless otherwise instructed, a collecting bank may present an item not payable by, through or at a bank by sending to the party to accept or pay a written notice that the bank holds the item for acceptance or payment. The notice must be sent in time to be received on or before the day when presentment is due and the bank must meet any requirement of the party to accept or pay under Section 3-505 by the close of the bank's next banking day after it knows of the requirement.

(2) Where presentment is made by notice and neither honor nor request for compliance with a requirement under Section 3-505 is received by the close of business on the day after maturity or in the case of demand items by the close of business on the third banking day after notice was sent, the presenting bank may treat the item as dishonored and charge any secondary party by sending him notice of the facts.

§ 4-211.   Media of Remittance; Provisional and Final Settlement in Remittance Cases.—

(1) A collecting bank may take in settlement of an item

(a) a check of the remitting bank or of another bank on any bank except the remitting bank; or

(b) a cashier's check or similar primary obligation of a remitting bank which is a member of or clears through a member of the same clearing house or group as the collecting bank; or

(c) appropriate authority to charge an account of the remitting bank or of another bank with the collecting bank; or

(d) if the item is drawn upon or payable by a person other than a bank, a cashier's check, certified check or other bank check or obligation.

(2) If before its midnight deadline the collecting bank properly dishonors a remittance check or authorization to charge on itself or presents or forwards for collection a remittance instrument or of on another bank which is of a kind approved by subsection (1) or has not been authorized by it, the collecting bank is not liable to prior parties in the event of the dishonor of such check, instrument or authorization.

(3) A settlement for an item by means of a remittance instrument or authorization to charge is or becomes a final settlement as to both the person making and the person receiving the settlement

(a) if the remittance instrument or authorization to charge is of a kind approved by subsection (1) or has not been authorized by the person receiving the settlement and in either case the person receiving the settlement acts seasonably before its midnight deadline in presenting, forwarding for collection or paying the instrument or authorization,—at the time the remittance instrument or authorization is finally paid by the payor by which it is payable;

(b) if the person receiving the settlement has authorized remittance by a non-bank check or obligation or by a cashier's check or similar primary obligation of or a check upon the payor or other remitting bank which is not of a kind approved by subsection (1)(b),—at the time of the receipt of such remittance check or obligation; or

    (c) if in a case not covered by subparagraphs (a) or (b) the person receiving the settlement fails to seasonably present, forward for collection, pay or return a remittance instrument or authorization to it to charge before its midnight deadline,—at such midnight deadline.

§ 4-212. Right of Charge-Back or Refund.—

(1) If a collecting bank has made provisional settlement with its customer for an item and itself fails by reason of dishonor, suspension of payments by a bank or otherwise to receive a settlement for the item which is or becomes final, the bank may revoke the settlement given by it, charge back the amount of any credit given for the item to its customer's account or obtain refund from its customer whether or not it is able to return the items if by its midnight deadline or within a longer reasonable time after it learns the facts it returns the item or sends notification of the facts. These rights to revoke, chargeback and obtain refund terminate if and when a settlement for the item received by the bank is or becomes final (subsection (3) of Section 4-211 and subsections (2) and (3) of Section 4-213).

[(2) Within the time and manner prescribed by this section and Section 4-301, an intermediary or payor bank, as the case may be, may return an unpaid item directly to the depositary bank and may send for collection a draft on the depositary bank and obtain reimbursement. In such case, if the depositary bank has received provisional settlement for the item, it must reimburse the bank drawing the draft and any provisional credits for the item between banks shall become and remain final.]

    Note: *Direct return is recognized as an innovation that is not yet established bank practice, and therefore, Paragraph 2 has been bracketed. Some lawyers have doubts whether it should be included in legislation or left to development by agreement.*

(3) A depositary bank which is also the payor may charge-back the amount of an item to its customer's account or obtain refund in accordance with the section governing return of an item received by a payor bank for credit on its books (Section 4-301).

(4) The right to charge-back is not affected by

    (a) prior use of the credit given for the item; or

    (b) failure by any bank to exercise ordinary care with respect to the item but any bank so failing remains liable.

(5) A failure to charge-back or claim refund does not affect other rights of the bank against the customer or any other party.

(6) If credit is given in dollars as the equivalent of the value of an item payable in a foreign currency the dollar amount of any charge-back or refund shall be calculated on the basis of the buying sight rate for the foreign currency prevailing on the day when the person entitled to the charge-back or refund learns that it will not receive payment in ordinary course.

§ 4-213. Final Payment of Item by Payor Bank; When Provisional Debits and Credits Become Final; When Certain Credits Become Available for Withdrawal.—

(1) An item is finally paid by a payor bank when the bank has done any of the following, whichever happens first:

    (a) paid the item in cash; or

    (b) settled for the item without reserving a right to revoke the settlement and without having such right under statute, clearing house rule or agreement; or

    (c) completed the process of posting the item to the indicated account of the drawer, maker or other person to be charged therewith; or

    (d) made a provisional settlement for the item and failed to revoke the settlement in the time and manner permitted by statute, clearing house rule or agreement.

Upon a final payment under subparagraphs (b), (c) or (d) the payor bank shall be accountable for the amount of the item.

(2) If provisional settlement for an item between the presenting and payor banks is made through a clearing house or by debits or credits in an account between them, then to the extent that provisional debits or credits for the item are entered in accounts between the presenting and payor banks or between the presenting and successive prior collecting banks seriatim, they become final upon final payment of the item by the payor bank.

(3) If a collecting bank receives a settlement for an item which is or becomes final (subsection (3) of Section 4-211, subsection (2) of Section 4-213) the bank is accountable to its customer for the amount of the item and any provisional credit given for the item in an account with its customer becomes final.

(4) Subject to any right of the bank to apply the credit to an obligation of the customer, credit given by a bank for an item in an account with its customer becomes available for withdrawal as of right.

    (a) in any case where the bank has received a provisional settlement for the item,—when such settlement becomes final and the bank has had a reasonable time to learn that the settlement is final;

    (b) in any case where the bank is both a depositary bank and a payor bank and the item is finally paid,—at the opening of the bank's second banking day following receipt of the item.

(5) A deposit of money in a bank is final when made but, subject to any right of the bank to apply the deposit to an obligation of the customer, the deposit becomes available for withdrawal as of right at the opening of the bank's next banking day following receipt of the deposit.

§ 4-214. Insolvency and Preference.—

(1) Any item in or coming into the possession of a payor or collecting bank which suspends payment and which item is not finally paid shall be returned by the receiver, trustee or agent in charge of the closed bank to the presenting bank or the closed bank's customer.

(2) If a payor bank finally pays an item and suspends payments without making a settlement for the item with its customer or the presenting bank which settlement is or becomes final, the owner of the item has a preferred claim against the payor bank.

(3) If a payor bank gives or a collecting bank gives or receives a provisional settlement for an item and thereafter suspends payments, the suspension does not prevent or interfere with the settlement becoming final if such finality occurs automatically upon the lapse of certain time or the happening of certain events (subsection (3) of Section 4-211, subsections (1) (d), (2) and (3) of Section 4-213).

(4) If a collecting bank receives from subsequent parties settlement for an item which settlement is or becomes final and suspends payments without making a settlement for the item with its customer which is or becomes final, the owner of the item has a preferred claim against such collecting bank.

PART 3

Collection of Items: Payor Banks

§ 4-301. Deferred Posting; Recovery of Payment by Return of Items; Time of Dishonor.—
(1) Where an authorized settlement for a demand item (other than a documentary draft) received by a payor bank otherwise than for immediate payment over the counter has been made before midnight of the banking day of receipt the payor bank may revoke the settlement and recover any payment if before it has made final payment (subsection (1) of Section 4-213) and before its midnight deadline it

(a) returns the item; or

(b) sends written notice of dishonor or nonpayment if the item is held for protest or is otherwise unavailable for return.

(2) If a demand item is received by a payor bank for credit on its books it may return such item or send notice of dishonor and may revoke any credit given or recover the amount thereof withdrawn by its customer, if it acts within the time limit and in the manner specified in the preceding subsection.

(3) Unless previous notice of dishonor has been sent an item is dishonored at the time when for purposes of dishonor it is returned or notice sent in accordance with this section.

(4) An item is returned:

(a) as to an item received through a clearing house, when it is delivered to the presenting or last collecting bank or the clearing house or is sent or delivered in accordance with its rules; or

(b) in all other cases, when it is sent or delivered to the bank's customer or transferor or pursuant to his instructions.

§ 4-302. Payor Bank's Responsibility for Late Return of Item.—In the absence of a valid defense such as breach of a presentment warranty (subsection (1) of Section 4-207), settlement effected or the like, if an item is presented on and received by a payor bank the bank is accountable for the amount of

(a) a demand item other than a documentary draft whether properly payable or not if the bank, in any case where it is not also the depositary bank, retains the item beyond midnight of the banking day of receipt without settling for it or, regardless of whether it is also the depositary bank, does not pay or return the item or send notice of dishonor until after its midnight deadline; or

(b) any other properly payable item unless within the time allowed for acceptance or payment of that item the bank either accepts or pays the item or returns it and accompanying documents.

§ 4-303. When Item Subject to Notice, Stop-Order, Legal Process or Setoff; Order in Which Items May Be Charged or Certified.—
(1) Any knowledge, notice or stop-order received by, legal process served upon or setoff exercised by a payor bank, whether or not effective under other rules of law to terminate, suspend or modify the bank's right or duty to pay an item or to charge its customer's account for the item, comes too late to so terminate, suspend or modify such right or duty if the knowledge, notice, stop-order or legal process is received or served and a reasonable time for the bank to act thereon expires or the setoff is exercised after the bank has done any of the following;

(a) accepted or certified the item;

(b) paid the item in cash;

(c) settled for the item without reserving a right to revoke the settlement and without having such right under statute, clearing house rule or agreement;

(d) completed the process of posting the item to the indicated account of the drawer, maker or other person to be charged therewith or otherwise has evidenced by examination of such indicated account and by action its decision to pay the item; or

(e) become accountable for the amount of the item under subsection (1) (d) of Section 4-213 and Section 4-302 dealing with the payor bank's responsibility for late return of items.

(2) Subject to the provisions of subsection (1) items may be accepted, paid, certified or charged to the indicated account of its customer in any order convenient to the bank.

PART 4

Relationship Between Payor Bank and Its Customer

§ 4-401. When Bank May Charge Customer's Account.—

(1) As against its customer, a bank may charge against his account any item which is otherwise properly payable from that account even though the charge creates an overdraft.

(2) A bank which in good faith makes payment to a holder may charge the indicated account of its customer according to

(a) the original tenor of his altered item; or

(b) the tenor of his completed item, even though the bank knows the item has been completed unless the bank has notice that the completion was improper.

§ 4-402. **Bank's Liability to Customer for Wrongful Dishonor.**—A payor bank is liable to its customer for damages proximately caused by the wrongful dishonor of an item. When the dishonor occurs through mistake liability is limited to actual damages proved. If so proximately caused and proved damages may include damages for an arrest or prosecution of the customer or other consequential damages. Whether any consequential damages are proximately caused by the wrongful dishonor is a question of fact to be determined in each case.

§ 4-403. **Customer's Right to Stop Payment; Burden of Proof of Loss.**—

(1) A customer may by order to his bank stop payment of any item payable for his account but the order must be received at such time and in such manner as to afford the bank a reasonable opportunity to act on it prior to any action by the bank with respect to the item described in Section 4-303.

(2) An oral order is binding upon the bank only for fourteen calendar days unless confirmed in writing within that period. A written order is effective for only six months unless renewed in writing.

(3) The burden of establishing the fact and amount of loss resulting from the payment of an item contrary to a binding stop payment order is on the customer.

§ 4-404. **Bank Not Obligated to Pay Check More Than Six Months Old.**—A bank is under no obligation to a customer having a checking account to pay a check, other than a certified check, which is presented more than six months after its date, but it may charge its customer's account for a payment made thereafter in good faith.

§ 4-405. **Death or Incompetence of Customer.**—

(1) A payor or collecting bank's authority to accept, pay or collect an item or to account for proceeds of its collection if otherwise effective is not rendered ineffective by incompetence of a customer of either bank existing at the time the item is issued or its collection undertaken if the bank does not know of an adjudication of incompetence. Neither death nor incompetence of a customer revokes such authority to accept, pay, collect or account until the bank knows of the fact of death or of an adjudication of incompetence and has reasonable opportunity to act on it.

(2) Even with knowledge a bank may for ten days after the date of death pay or certify checks drawn on or prior to that date unless ordered to stop payment by a person claiming an interest in the account.

§ 4-406. **Customer's Duty to Discover and Report Unauthorized Signature or Alteration.**—

(1) When a bank sends to its customer a statement of account accompanied by items paid in good faith in support of the debit entries or holds the statement and items pursuant to a request or instructions of its customer or otherwise in a reasonable manner makes the statement and items available to the customer, the customer must exercise reasonable care and promptness to examine the statement and items to discover his unauthorized signature or any alteration on an item and must notify the bank promptly after discovery thereof.

(2) If the bank establishes that the customer failed with respect to an item to comply with the duties imposed on the customer by subsection (1) the customer is precluded from asserting against the bank

(a) his unauthorized signature or any alteration on the item if the bank also establishes that it suffered a loss by reason of such failure; and

(b) an unauthorized signature or alteration by the same wrongdoer on any other item paid in good faith by the bank after the first item and statement was available to the customer for a reasonable period not exceeding fourteen calendar days and before the bank receives notification from the customer of any such unauthorized signature or alteration.

(3) The preclusion under subsection (2) does not apply if the customer establishes lack of ordinary care on the part of the bank in paying the item(s).

(4) Without regard to care or lack of care of either the customer or the bank a customer who does not within one year from the time the statement and items are made available to the customer (subsection (1)) discover and report his unauthorized signature or any alteration on the face or back of the item or does not within three years from that time discover and report any unauthorized indorsement is precluded from asserting against the bank such unauthorized signature or endorsement or such alteration.

(5) If under this section a payor bank has a valid defense against a claim of a customer upon or resulting from payment of an item and waives or fails upon request to assert the defense the bank may not assert against any collecting bank or other prior party presenting or transferring the item a claim based upon the unauthorized signature or alteration giving rise to the customer's claim.

§ 4-407. **Payor Bank's Right to Subrogation on Improper Payment.**—If a payor bank has paid an item over the stop payment order of the drawer or maker or otherwise under circumstances giving a basis for objection by the drawer or maker, to prevent unjust enrichment and only to the extent necessary to prevent loss to the bank by reason of its payment of the item, the payor bank shall be subrogated to the rights

(a) of any holder in due course on the item against the drawer or maker; and

(b) of the payee or any other holder of the item against the drawer or maker either on the item or under the transaction out of which the item arose; and

(c) of the drawer or maker against the payee or any other holder of the item with respect to the transaction out of which the item arose.

PART 5

Collection of Documentary Drafts

§ 4-501. Handling of Documentary Drafts; Duty to Send for Presentment and to Notify Customer of Dishonor.—A bank which takes a documentary draft for collection must present or send the draft and accompanying documents for presentment and upon learning that the draft has not been paid or accepted in due course must seasonably notify its customer of such fact even though it may have discounted or bought the draft or extended credit available for withdrawal as of right.

§ 4-502. Presentment of "On Arrival" Drafts.—When a draft or the relevant instructions require presentment "on arrival", "when goods arrive" or the like, the collection bank need not present until in its judgment a reasonable time for arrival of the goods has expired. Refusal to pay or accept because the goods have not arrived is not dishonor; the bank must notify its transferor of such refusal but need not present the draft again until it is instructed to do so or learns of the arrival of the goods.

§ 4-503. Responsibility of Presenting Bank for Documents and Goods; Report of Reasons for Dishonor; Referee in Case of Need.—Unless otherwise instructed and except as provided in Article 5 a bank presenting a documentary draft

(a) must deliver the documents to the drawee on acceptance of the draft if it is payable more than three days after presentment; otherwise, only on payment; and

(b) upon dishonor, either in the case of presentment for acceptance or presentment for payment, may seek and follow instructions from any referee in case of need designated in the draft or if the presenting bank does not choose to utilize his services it must use diligence and good faith to ascertain the reason for dishonor, must notify its transferor of the dishonor and of the results of its effort to ascertain the reasons therefor and must request instructions.

But the presenting bank is under no obligation with respect to goods represented by the documents except to follow any reasonable instructions seasonably received; it has a right to reimbursement for any expense incurred in following instructions and to prepayment of or indemnity for such expenses.

§ 4-504. Privilege of Presenting Bank to Deal With Goods; Security Interest for Expenses.—
(1) A presenting bank which, following the dishonor of a documentary draft, has seasonably requested instructions but does not receive them within a reasonable time may store, sell, or otherwise deal with the goods in any reasonable manner.

(2) For its reasonable expenses incurred by action under subsection (1) the presenting bank has a lien upon the goods or their proceeds, which may be forclosed in the same manner as an unpaid seller's lien.

ARTICLE FIVE—LETTERS OF CREDIT

§ 5-101. Short Title.—This Article shall be known and may be cited as Uniform Commercial Code—Letters of Credit.

§ 5-102. Scope.—
(1) This Article applies

(a) to a credit issued by a bank if the credit requires a documentary draft or a documentary demand for payment; and

(b) to a credit issued by a person other than a bank if the credit requires that the draft or demand for payment be accompanied by a document of title; and

(c) to a credit issued by a bank or other person if the credit is not within subparagraphs (a) or (b) but conspicuously states that it is a letter of credit or is conspicuously so entitled.

. . . [The remaining portion of this article omitted as it contains materials not usually covered in Business Law.]

ARTICLE SIX—BULK TRANSFERS

§ 6-101. Short Title.—This Article shall be known and may be cited as Uniform Commercial Code—Bulk Transfers.

§ 6-102. "Bulk Transfer"; Transfers of Equipment; Enterprises Subject to This Article; Bulk Transfers Subject to This Article.—
(1) A "bulk transfer" is any transfer in bulk and not in the ordinary course of the transferor's business of a major part of the materials, supplies, merchandise or other inventory (Section 9-109) of an enterprise subject to this Article.

(2) A transfer of a substantial part of the equipment (Section 9-109) of such an enterprise is a bulk transfer if it is made in connection with a bulk transfer of inventory, but not otherwise.

(3) The enterprises subject to this Article are all those whose principal business is the sale of merchandise from stock, including those who manufacture what they sell.

(4) Except as limited by the following section all bulk transfers of goods located within this State are subject to this Article.

§ 6-103. Transfers Excepted From This Article.—The following transfers are not subject to this Article:

(1) Those made to give security for the performance of an obligation;

(2) General assignments for the benefit of all the creditors of the transferor, and subsequent transfers by the assignee thereunder;

(3) Transfers in settlement or realization of alien or other security interests;

(4) Sales by executors, administrators, receivers, trustees in bankruptcy, or any public offer under judicial process;

(5) Sales made in the course of judicial or administrative proceedings for the dissolution or reorganization of a corporation and of which notice is sent to the creditors of the corporation pursuant to order of the court or administrative agency;

(6) Transfers to a person maintaining a known place of business in this State who becomes bound to pay the debts of the transferor in full and gives public notice of that fact, and who is solvent after becoming so bound;

(7) A transfer to a new business enterprise organized to take over and continue the business, if public notice of the transaction is given and the new enterprise assumes the debts of the transferor and he receives nothing from the transaction except an interest in the new enterprise junior to the claims of creditors;

(8) Transfers of property which is exempt from execution.

§ 6-104. Schedule of Property, List of Creditors.—

(1) Except as provided with respect to auction sales (Section 6-108), a bulk transfer subject to this Article is ineffective against any creditor of the transferor unless:

(a) The transferee requires the transferor to furnish a list of his existing creditors prepared as stated in this section; and

(b) The parties prepare a schedule of the property transferred sufficient to identify it; and

(c) The transferee preserves the list and schedule for six months next following the transfer and permits inspection of either or both and copying therefrom at all reasonable hours by any creditor of the transferor, or files the list and schedule in *(a public office to be here identified)*.

(2) The list of creditors must be signed and sworn to or affirmed by the transferor or his agent. It must contain the names and business addresses of all creditors of the transferor, with the amounts when known, and also the names of all persons who are known to the transferor to assert claims against him even though such claims are disputed.

(3) Responsibility for the completeness and accuracy of the list of creditors rests on the transferor, and the transfer is not rendered ineffective by errors or omissions therein unless the transferee is shown to have had knowledge.

§ 6-105. Notice to Creditors.—In addition to the requirements of the preceding section, any bulk transfer subject to this Article except one made by auction sale (Section 6-108) is ineffective against any creditor of the transferor unless at least ten days before he takes possession of the goods or pays for them, whichever happens first, the transferee gives notice of the transfer in the manner and to the persons hereafter provided (Section 6-107).

[§ 6-106. Application of the Proceeds.—In addition to the requirements of the two preceding sections:

(1) Upon every bulk transfer subject to this Article for which new consideration becomes payable except those made by sale at auction it is the duty of the transferee to assure that such consideration is applied so far as necessary to pay those debts of the transferor which are either shown on the list furnished by the transferor (Section 6-104) or filed in writing in the place stated in the notice (Section 6-107) within thirty days after the mailing of such notice. This duty of the transferee runs to all the holders of such debts, and may be enforced by any of them for the benefit of all.

(2) If any of said debts are in dispute the necessary sum may be withheld from distribution until the dispute is settled or adjudicated.

(3) If the consideration payable is not enough to pay all of the said debts in full distribution shall be made pro rata.]

> **Note:** *This section is bracketed to indicate division of opinion as to whether or not it is a wise provision, and to suggest that this is a point on which State enactments may differ without serious damage to the principle of uniformity.*
>
> *In any State where this section is omitted, the following parts of sections, also bracketed in the text, should also be omitted, namely:*
> *Section 6-107(2)(e).*
> *6-108(3)(c).*
> *6-109(2).*
> *In any State where this section is enacted, these other provisions should be also.*

§ 6-107. The Notice.—

(1) The notice to creditors (Section 6-105) shall state:

(a) that a bulk transfer is about to be made; and

(b) the names and business addresses of the transferor and transferee, and all other business names and addresses used by the transferor within three years last past so far as known to the transferee; and

(c) whether or not all the debts of the transferor are to be paid in full as they fall due as a result of the transaction, and if so, the address to which creditors should send their bills.

(2) If the debts of the transferor are not to be paid in full as they fall due or if the transferee is in doubt on that point then the notice shall state further:

(a) the location and general description of the property to be transferred and the estimated total of the transferor's debts;

(b) the address where the schedule of property and list of creditors (Section 6-104) may be inspected;

(c) whether the transfer is to pay existing debts and if so the amount of such debts and to whom owing;

(d) whether the transfer is for new consideration and if so the amount of such consideration and the time and place of payment; and

[(e) if for new consideration the time and place where creditors of the transferor are to file their claims.]

(3) The notice in any case shall be delivered personally or sent by registered mail to all the persons shown on the list of creditors furnished by the transferor (Section 6-104) and to all other persons who are known to the transferee to hold or assert claims against the transferor.

§ 6-108. Auction Sales; "Auctioneer".—

(1) A bulk transfer is subject to this Article even though it is by sale at auction, but only in the manner and with the results stated in this section.

(2) The transferor shall furnish a list of his creditors and assist in the preparation of a schedule of the property to be sold, both prepared as before stated (Section 6-104).

(3) The person or persons other than the transferor who direct, control or are responsible for the auction are collectively called the "auctioneer". The auctioneer shall:

(a) receive and retain the list of creditors and prepare and retain the schedule of property for the period stated in this Article (Section 6-104);

(b) give notice of the auction personally or by registered mail at least ten days before it occurs to all persons shown on the list of creditors and to all other persons who are known to him to hold or assert claims against the transferor; [and]

[(c) assure that the net proceeds of the auction are applied as provided in this Article (Section 6-106).]

(4) Failure of the auctioneer to perform any of these duties does not affect the validity of the sale or the title of the purchasers, but if the auctioneer knows that the auction constitutes a bulk transfer such failure renders the auctioneer liable to the creditors of the transferor as a class for the sums owing to them from the transferor up to but not exceeding the net proceeds of the auction. If the auctioneer consists of several persons their liability is joint and several.

§ 6-109. What Creditors Protected.—

(1) The creditors of the transferor mentioned in this Article are those holding claims based on transactions occurring before the bulk transfer, but creditors who become such after notice to creditors is given (Sections 6-105 and 6-107) are not entitled to notice.

[(2) Against the aggregate obligation imposed by the provisions of this Article concerning the application of the proceeds (Section 6-106 and subsection (3)(c) of 6-108) the transferee or auctioneer is entitled to credit for sums paid to particular creditors of the transferor, not exceeding the sums believed in good faith at the time of the payment to be properly payable to such creditors.]

§ 6-110. Subsequent Transfers.—When the title of a transferee to property is subject to a defect by reason of his noncompliance with the requirements of this Article, then:

(1) a purchaser of any such property from such transferee who pays no value or who takes with notice of such noncompliance takes subject to such defect, but

(2) a purchaser for value in good faith and without such notice takes free of such defect.

§ 6-111. Limitation of Actions and Levies.—No action under this article shall be brought nor levy made more than six months after the date on which the transferee took possession of the goods unless the transfer has been concealed. If the transfer has been concealed, actions may be brought or levies made within six months after its discovery.

Note to Article 6: *Section 6-106 is bracketed to indicate division of opinion as to whether or not it is a wise provision and to suggest that this is a point on which State enactments may differ without serious damage to the principal of uniformity.*

In any State where Section 6-106 is not enacted, the following parts of sections, also bracketed in the text, should also be omitted, namely:

Sec. 6-107(2)(e)

6-108(3)(c)

6-109(2).

In any State where Section 6-106 is enacted, these other provisions should be also.

ARTICLE SEVEN—WAREHOUSE RECEIPTS, BILLS OF LADING AND OTHER DOCUMENTS OF TITLE

PART 1

General

§ 7-101. **Short Title.**—This Article shall be known and may be cited as Uniform Commercial Code—Documents of Title.

. . . [The remaining portion of this article omitted as it contains material not usually covered in Business Law.]

ARTICLE EIGHT—INVESTMENT SECURITIES

PART 1

Short Title and General Matters

§ 8—101. **Short Title.**—This Article shall be known and may be cited as Uniform Commercial Code—Investment Securities.

§ 8—102. **Definitions and Index of Definitions.**

(1) In this Article, unless the context otherwise requires:

(a) A "certificated security" is a share, participation, or other interest in property of or an enterprise of the issuer or an obligation of the issuer which is

(i) represented by an instrument issued in bearer or registered form;

(ii) of a type commonly dealt in on securities exchanges or markets or commonly recognized in any area in which it is issued or dealt in as a medium for investment; and

(iii) either one of a class or series or by its terms divisible into a class or series of shares, participations, interests, or obligations.

(b) An "uncertificated security" is a share, participation, or other interest in property or an enterprise of the issuer or an obligation of the issuer which is

(i) not represented by an instrument and the transfer of which is registered upon books maintained for that purpose by or on behalf of the issuer;

(ii) of a type commonly dealt in on securities exchanges or markets; and

(iii) either one of a class or series or by its terms divisible into a class or series of shares, participations, interests, or obligations.

(c) A "security" is either a certificated or an uncertificated security. If a security is certificated, the terms "security" and "certificated security" may mean either the intangible interest, the instrument representing that interest, or both, as the context requires. A writing that is a certificated security is governed by this Article and not by Article 3, even though it also meets the requirements of that Article. This Article does not apply to money. If a certificated security has been retained by or surrendered to the issuer or its transfer agent for reasons other than registration of transfer, other temporary purpose, payment, exchange, or acquisition by the issuer, that security shall be treated as an uncertificated security for purposes of this Article.

(d) A certificated security is in "registered form" if

(i) it specifies a person entitled to the security or the rights it represents; and

(ii) its transfer may be registered upon books maintained for that purpose by or on behalf of the issuer, or the security so states.

(e) A certificated security is in "bearer form" if it runs to bearer according to its terms and not by reason of any indorsement.

(2) A "subsequent purchaser" is a person who takes other than by original issue.

(3) A "clearing corporation" is a corporation registered as a "clearing agency" under the federal securities laws or a corporation:

(a) at least 90 percent of whose capital stock is held by or for one or more organizations, none of which, other than a national securities exchange or association, holds in excess of 20 percent of the capital stock of the corporation, and each of which is

(i) subject to supervision or regulation pursuant to the provisions of federal or state banking laws or state insurance laws,

(ii) a broker or dealer or investment company registered under the federal securities laws, or

(iii) a national securities exchange or association registered under the federal securities laws; and

(b) any remaining capital stock of which is held by individuals who have purchased it at or prior to the time of their taking office as directors of the corporation and who have purchased only so much of the capital stock as is necessary to permit them to qualify as directors.

(4) A "custodian bank" is a bank or trust company that is supervised and examined by state or federal authority having supervision over banks and is acting as custodian for a clearing corporation.

(5) Other definitions applying to this Article or to specified Parts thereof and the sections in which they appear are:
"Adverse claim". Section 8—302.
"Bona fide purchaser". Section 8—302.
"Broker". Section 8—303.
"Debtor". Section 9—105.
"Financial intermediary". Section 8—313.
"Guarantee of the signature". Section 8—402.
"Initial transaction statement". Section 8—408.
"Instruction". Section 8—308.
"Intermediary bank". Section 4—105.
"Issuer". Section 8—201.
"Overissue". Section 8—104.
"Secured Party". Section 9—105.
"Security Agreement". Section 9—105.

(6) In addition, Article 1 contains general definitions and principles of construction and interpretation applicable throughout this Article.

§ 8—103. Issuer's Lien.—A lien upon a security in favor of an issuer thereof is valid against a purchaser only if:
(a) the security is certificated and the right of the issuer to the lien is noted conspicuously thereon; or
(b) the security is uncertificated and a notation of the right of the issuer to the lien is contained in the initial transaction statement sent to the purchaser or, if his interest is transferred to him other than by registration of transfer, pledge, or release, the initial transaction statement sent to the registered owner or the registered pledgee.

§ 8—104. Effect of Overissue; "Overissue".
(1) The provisions of this Article which validate a security or compel its issue or reissue do not apply to the extent that validation, issue, or reissue would result in overissue; but if:
(a) an identical security which does not constitute an overissue is reasonably available for purchase, the person entitled to issue or validation may compel the issuer to purchase the security for him and either to deliver a certificated security or to register the transfer of an uncertificated security to him, against surrender of any certificated security he holds; or
(b) a security is not so available for purchase, the person entitled to issue or validation may recover from the issuer the price he or the last purchaser for value paid for it with interest from the date of his demand.
(2) "Overissue" means the issue of securities in excess of the amount the issuer has corporate power to issue.

§ 8—105. Certificated Securities Negotiable; Statements and Instructions Not Negotiable; Presumptions.
(1) Certificated securities governed by this Article are negotiable instruments.
(2) Statements (Section 8—408), notices, or the like, sent by the issuer of uncertificated securities and instructions (Section 8—308) are neither negotiable instruments nor certificated securities.
(3) In any action on a security:
(a) unless specifically denied in the pleadings, each signature on a certificated security, in a necessary indorsement, on an initial transaction statement, or on an instruction, is admitted;
(b) if the effectiveness of a signature is put in issue, the burden of establishing it is on the party claiming under the signature, but the signature is presumed to be genuine or authorized;
(c) if signatures on a certificated security are admitted or established, production of the security entitles a holder to recover on it unless the defendant establishes a defense or a defect going to the validity of the security;
(d) if signatures on an initial transaction statement are admitted or established, the facts stated in the statement are presumed to be true as of the time of its issuance; and
(e) after it is shown that a defense or defect exists, the plaintiff has the burden of establishing that he or some person under whom he claims is a person against whom the defense or defect is ineffective (Section 8—202).

§ 8—106. Applicability.—The law (including the conflict of laws rules) of the jurisdiction of organization of the issuer governs the validity of a security, the effectiveness of registration by the issuer, and the rights and duties of the issuer with respect to:
(a) registration of transfer of a certificated security;
(b) registration of transfer, pledge, or release of an uncertificated security; and
(c) sending of statements of uncertificated securities.

§ 8—107. Securities Transferable; Action for Price.
(1) Unless otherwise agreed and subject to any applicable law or regulation respecting short sales, a person obligated to transfer securities may transfer any certificated security of the specified issue in bearer form or registered in the name of the transferee, or indorsed to him or in blank, or he may transfer an equivalent uncertificated security to the transferee or a person designated by the transferee.
(2) If the buyer fails to pay the price as it comes due under a contract of sale, the seller may recover the price of:
(a) certificated securities accepted by the buyer;
(b) uncertificated securities that have been transferred to the buyer or a person designated by the buyer; and
(c) other securities if efforts at their resale would be unduly burdensome or if there is no readily available market for their resale.

§ 8—108. Registration of Pledge and Release of Uncertificated Securities.—A security interest in an uncertificated security may be evidenced by the registration of pledge to the secured party or a person designated by him. There can be no more than one registered pledge of an uncertificated security at any time. The registered owner of an uncertificated security is the person in whose name the security is registered, even if the security is subject to a registered pledge. The rights of a registered pledgee of an uncertificated security under this Article are terminated by the registration of release.

PART 2

Issue—Issuer

§ 8—201. "Issuer."

(1) With respect to obligations on or defenses to a security, "issuer" includes a person who:

(a) places or authorizes the placing of his name on a certificated security (otherwise than as authenticating trustee, registrar, transfer agent, or the like) to evidence that it represents a share, participation, or other interest in his property or in an enterprise, or to evidence his duty to perform an obligation represented by the certificated security;

(b) creates shares, participations, or other interests in his property or in an enterprise or undertakes obligations, which shares, participations, interests, or obligations are uncertificated securities;

(c) directly or indirectly creates fractional interests in his rights or property, which fractional interests are represented by certificated securities; or

(d) becomes responsible for or in place of any other person described as an issuer in this section.

(2) With respect to obligations on or defenses to a security, a guarantor is an issuer to the extent of his guaranty, whether or not his obligation is noted on a certificated security or on statements of uncertificated securities sent pursuant to Section 8—408.

(3) With respect to registration of transfer, pledge, or release (Part 4 of this Article), "issuer" means a person on whose behalf transfer books are maintained.

§ 8—202. Issuer's Responsibility and Defenses; Notice of Defect or Defense.

(1) Even against a purchaser for value and without notice, the terms of a security include:

(a) if the security is certificated, those stated on the security;

(b) if the security is uncertificated, those contained in the initial transaction statement sent to such purchaser or, if his interest is transferred to him other than by registration of transfer, pledge, or release, the initial transaction statement sent to the registered owner or registered pledgee; and

(c) those made part of the security by reference, on the certificated security or in the initial transaction statement, to another instrument, indenture, or document or to a constitution, statute, ordinance, rule, regulation, order or the like, to the extent that the terms referred to do not conflict with the terms stated on the certificated security or contained in the statement. A reference under this paragraph does not of itself charge a purchaser for value with notice of a defect going to the validity of the security, even though the certificated security or statement expressly states that a person accepting it admits notice.

(2) A certificated security in the hands of a purchaser for value or an uncertificated security as to which an initial transaction statement has been sent to a purchaser for value, other than a security issued by a government or governmental agency or unit, even though issued with a defect going to its validity, is valid with respect to the purchaser if he is without notice of the particular defect unless the defect involves a violation of constitutional provisions, in which case the security is valid with respect to a subsequent purchaser for value and without notice of the defect. This subsection applies to an issuer that is a government or governmental agency or unit only if either there has been substantial compliance with the legal requirements governing the issue or the issuer has received a substantial consideration for the issue as a whole or for the particular security and a stated purpose of the issue is one for which the issuer has power to borrow money or issue the security.

(3) Except as provided in the case of certain unauthorized signatures (Section 8—205), lack of genuineness of a certificated security or an initial transaction statement is a complete defense, even against a purchaser for value and without notice.

(4) All other defenses of the issuer of a certificated or uncertificated security, including nondelivery and conditional delivery of a certificated security, are ineffective against a purchaser for value who has taken without notice of the particular defense.

(5) Nothing in this section shall be construed to affect the right of a party to a "when, as and if issued" or a "when distributed" contract to cancel the contract in the event of a material change in the character of the security that is the subject of the contract or in the plan or arrangement pursuant to which the security is to be issued or distributed.

§ 8—203. Staleness as Notice of Defects or Defenses.

(1) After an act or event creating a right to immediate performance of the principal obligation represented by a certificated security or that sets a date on or after which the security is to be presented or surrendered for redemption or exchange, a purchaser is charged with notice of any defect in its issue or defense of the issuer if:

(a) the act or event is one requiring the payment of money, the delivery of certificated securities, the registration of transfer of uncertificated securities, or any of these on presentation or surrender of the certificated security, the funds or securities are available on the date set for payment or exchange, and he takes the security more than one year after that date; and

(b) the act or event is not covered by paragraph (a) and he takes the security more than 2 years after the date set for surrender or presentation or the date on which performance became due.

(2) A call that has been revoked is not within subsection (1).

§ 8—204. Effect of Issuer's Restrictions on Transfer.—A restriction on transfer of a security imposed by the issuer, even if otherwise lawful, is ineffective against any person without actual knowledge of it unless:

(a) the security is certificated and the restriction is noted conspicuously thereon; or

(b) the security is uncertificated and a notation of the restriction is contained in the initial transaction statement sent to the person or, if his interest is transferred to him other than by registration of transfer, pledge, or release, the initial transaction statement sent to the registered owner or the registered pledgee.

§ 8—205. Effect of Unauthorized Signature on Certificated Security or Initial Transaction Statement.—An unauthorized signature placed on a certificated security prior to or in the course of issue or placed on an initial transaction statement is ineffective, but the signature is effective in favor of a purchaser for value of the certificated security or a purchaser for value of an uncertificated security to whom the initial transaction statement has been sent, if the purchaser is without notice of the lack of authority and the signing has been done by:

(a) an authenticating trustee, registrar, transfer agent, or other person entrusted by the issuer with the signing of the security, of similar securities, or of initial transaction statements or the immediate preparation for signing of any of them; or

(b) an employee of the issuer, or of any of the foregoing, entrusted with responsible handling of the security or initial transaction statement.

§ 8—206. Completion or Alteration of Certificated Security or Initial Transaction Statement.

(1) If a certificated security contains the signatures necessary to its issue or transfer but is incomplete in any other respect:

(a) any person may complete it by filling in the blanks as authorized; and

(b) even though the blanks are incorrectly filled in, the security as completed is enforceable by a purchaser who took it for value and without notice of the incorrectness.

(2) A complete certificated security that has been improperly altered, even though fraudulently, remains enforceable, but only according to its original terms.

(3) If an initial transaction statement contains the signatures necessary to its validity, but is incomplete in any other respect:

(a) any person may complete it by filling in the blanks as authorized; and

(b) even though the blanks are incorrectly filled in, the statement as completed is effective in favor of the person to whom it is sent if he purchased the security referred to therein for value and without notice of the incorrectness.

(4) A complete initial transaction statement that has been improperly altered, even though fraudulently, is effective in favor of a purchaser to whom it has been sent, but only according to its original terms.

§ 8—207. Rights and Duties of Issuer With Respect to Registered Owners and Registered Pledgees.

(1) Prior to due presentment for registration of transfer of a certificated security in registered form, the issuer or indenture trustee may treat the registered owner as the person exclusively entitled to vote, to receive notifications, and otherwise to exercise all the rights and powers of an owner.

(2) Subject to the provisions of subsections (3), (4), and (6), the issuer or indenture trustee may treat the registered owner of an uncertificated security as the person exclusively entitled to vote, to receive notifications, and otherwise to exercise all the rights and powers of an owner.

(3) The registered owner of an uncertificated security that is subject to a registered pledge is not entitled to registration of transfer prior to the due presentment to the issuer of a release instruction. The exercise of conversion rights with respect to a convertible uncertificated security is a transfer within the meaning of this section.

(4) Upon due presentment of a transfer instruction from the registered pledgee of an uncertificated security, the issuer shall:

(a) register the transfer of the security to the new owner free of pledge, if the instruction specifies a new owner (who may be the registered pledgee) and does not specify a pledgee;

(b) register the transfer of the security to the new owner subject to the interest of the existing pledgee, if the instruction specifies a new owner and the existing pledgee; or

(c) register the release of the security from the existing pledge and register the pledge of the security to the other pledgee, if the instruction specifies the existing owner and another pledgee.

(5) Continuity of perfection of a security interest is not broken by registration of transfer under subsection (4)(b) or by registration of release and pledge under subsection (4)(c), if the security interest is assigned.

(6) If an uncertificated security is subject to a registered pledge:

(a) any uncertificated securities issued in exchange for or distributed with respect to the pledged security shall be registered subject to the pledge;

(b) any certificated securities issued in exchange for or distributed with respect to the pledged security shall be delivered to the registered pledgee; and

(c) any money paid in exchange for or in redemption of part or all of the security shall be paid to the registered pledgee.

(7) Nothing in this Article shall be construed to affect the liability of the registered owner of a security for calls, assessments, or the like.

§ 8—208. Effect of Signature of Authenticating Trustee, Registrar, or Transfer Agent.

(1) A person placing his signature upon a certificated security or an initial transaction statement as authenticating trustee, registrar, transfer agent, or the like, warrants to a purchaser for value of the certificated security or a purchaser for value of an uncertificated security to whom the initial transaction statement has been sent, if the purchaser is without notice of the particular defect, that:

(a) the certificated security or initial transaction statement is genuine;

(b) his own participation in the issue or registration of the transfer, pledge, or release of the security is within his capacity and within the scope of the authority received by him from the issuer; and

(c) he has reasonable grounds to believe the security is in the form and within the amount the issuer is authorized to issue.

(2) Unless otherwise agreed, a person by so placing his signature does not assume responsibility for the validity of the security in other respects.

PART 3

Transfer

§ 8—301. Rights Acquired by Purchaser.

(1) Upon transfer of a security to a purchaser (Section 8—313), the purchaser acquires the rights in the security which his transferor had or had actual authority to convey unless the purchaser's rights are limited by Section 8—302(4).

(2) A transferee of a limited interest acquires rights only to the extent of the interest transferred. The creation or release of a security interest in a security is the transfer of a limited interest in that security.

§ 8—302. "Bona Fide Purchaser"; "Adverse Claim"; Title Acquired by Bona Fide Purchaser.

(1) A "bona fide purchaser" is a purchaser for value in good faith and without notice of any adverse claim:

(a) who takes delivery of a certificated security in bearer form or in registered form, issued or indorsed to him or in blank;

(b) to whom the transfer, pledge, or release of an uncertificated security is registered on the books of the issuer; or

(c) to whom a security is transferred under the provisions of paragraph (c), (d)(i), or (g) of Section 8—313(1).

§ 8—303. "Broker".—"Broker" means a person engaged for all or part of his time in the business of buying and selling securities, who in the transaction concerned acts for, buys a security from, or sells a security to, a customer. Nothing in this Article determines the capacity in which a person acts for purposes of any other statute or rule to which the person is subject.

§ 8—304. Notice to Purchaser of Adverse Claims.

(1) A purchaser (including a broker for the seller or buyer, but excluding an intermediary bank) of a certificated security is charged with notice of adverse claims if:

(a) the security, whether in bearer or registered form, has been indorsed "for collection" or "for surrender" or for some other purpose not involving transfer; or

(b) the security is in bearer form and has on it an unambiguous statement that it is the property of a person other than the transferor. The mere writing of a name on a security is not such a statement.

(2) A purchaser (including a broker for the seller or buyer, but excluding an intermediary bank) to whom the transfer, pledge, or release of an uncertificated security is registered is charged with notice of adverse claims as to which the issuer has a duty under Section 8—403(4) at the time of registration and which are noted in the initial transaction statement sent to the purchaser or, if his interest is transferred to him other than by registration of transfer, pledge, or release, the initial transaction statement sent to the registered owner or the registered pledgee.

(3) The fact that the purchaser (including a broker for the seller or buyer) of a certificated or uncertificated security has notice that the security is held for a third person or is registered in the name of or indorsed by a fiduciary does not create a duty of inquiry into the rightfulness of the transfer or constitute constructive notice of adverse claims. However, if the purchaser (excluding an intermediary bank) has knowledge that the proceeds are being used or the transaction is for the individual benefit of the fiduciary or otherwise in breach of duty, the purchaser is charged with notice of adverse claims.

§ 8—305. Staleness as Notice of Adverse Claims.—An act or event that creates a right to immediate performance of the principal obligation represented by a certificated security or sets a date on or after which a certificated security is to be presented or surrendered for redemption or exchange does not itself constitute any notice of adverse claims except in the case of a transfer:

(a) after one year from any date set for presentment or surrender for redemption or exchange; or

(b) after 6 months from any date set for payment of money against presentation or surrender of the security if funds are available for payment on that date.

§ 8—306. Warranties on Presentment and Transfer of Certificated Securities; Warranties of Originators of Instructions.

(1) A person who presents a certificated security for registration of transfer or for payment or exchange warrants to the issuer that he is entitled to the registration, payment, or exchange. But, a purchaser for value and without notice of adverse claims who receives a new, reissued, or re-registered certificated security on registration of transfer or receives an initial transaction statement confirming the registration of transfer of an equivalent uncertificated security to him warrants only that he has no knowledge of any unauthorized signature (Section 8—311) in a necessary indorsement.

(2) A person by transferring a certificated security to a purchaser for value warrants only that:

(a) his transfer is effective and rightful;

(b) the security is genuine and has not been materially altered; and

(c) he knows of no fact which might impair the validity of the security.

(3) If a certificated security is delivered by an intermediary known to be entrusted with delivery of the security on behalf of another or with collection of a draft or other claim against delivery, the intermediary by delivery warrants only his own good faith and authority, even though he has purchased or made advances against the claim to be collected against the delivery.

(4) A pledgee or other holder for security who redelivers a certificated security received, or after payment and on order of the debtor delivers that security to a third person, makes only the warranties of an intermediary under subsection (3).

(5) A person who originates an instruction warrants to the issuer that:

(a) he is an appropriate person to originate the instruction; and

(b) at the time the instruction is presented to the issuer he will be entitled to the registration of transfer, pledge, or release.

(6) A person who originates an instruction warrants to any person specially guaranteeing his signature (subsection 8—312(3)) that:

(a) he is an appropriate person to originate the instruction; and

(b) at the time the instruction is presented to the issuer

(i) he will be entitled to the registration of transfer, pledge, or release; and

(ii) the transfer, pledge, or release requested in the instruction will be registered by the issuer free from all liens, security interests, restrictions, and claims other than those specified in the instruction.

(7) A person who originates an instruction warrants to a purchaser for value and to any person guaranteeing the instruction (Section 8—312(6)) that:

(a) he is an appropriate person to originate the instruction;

(b) the uncertificated security referred to therein is valid; and

(c) at the time the instruction is presented to the issuer

(i) the transferor will be entitled to the registration of transfer, pledge, or release;

(ii) the transfer, pledge, or release requested in the instruction will be registered by the issuer free from all liens, security interests, restrictions, and claims other than those specified in the instruction; and

(iii) the requested transfer, pledge, or release will be rightful.

(8) If a secured party is the registered pledgee or the registered owner of an uncertificated security, a person who originates an instruction of release or transfer to the debtor or, after payment and on order of the debtor, a transfer instruction to a third person, warrants to the debtor or the third person only that he is an appropriate person to originate the instruction and, at the time the instruction is presented to the issuer, the transferor will be entitled to the registration of release or transfer. If a transfer instruction to a third person who is a purchaser for value is originated on order of the debtor, the debtor makes to the purchaser the warranties of paragraphs (b), (c)(ii) and (c)(iii) of subsection (7).

(9) A person who transfers an uncertificated security to a purchaser for value and does not originate an instruction in connection with the transfer warrants only that:

(a) his transfer is effective and rightful; and

(b) the uncertificated security is valid.

(10) A broker gives to his customer and to the issuer and a purchaser the applicable warranties provided in this section and has the rights and privileges of a purchaser under this section. The warranties of and in favor of the broker, acting as an agent are in addition to applicable warranties given by and in favor of his customer.

§ 8—307. Effect of Delivery Without Indorsement; Right to Compel Indorsement.—If a certificated security in registered form has been delivered to a purchaser without a necessary indorsement he may become a bona fide purchaser only as of the time the indorsement is supplied; but against the transferor, the transfer is complete upon delivery and the purchaser has a specifically enforceable right to have any necessary indorsement supplied.

§ 8—308. Indorsements; Instructions.

(1) An indorsement of a certificated security in registered form is made when an appropriate person signs on it or on a separate document an assignment or transfer of the security or a power to assign or transfer it or his signature is written without more upon the back of the security.

(2) An indorsement may be in blank or special. An indorsement in blank includes an indorsement to bearer. A special indorsement specifies to whom the security is to be transferred, or who has power to transfer it. A holder may convert a blank indorsement into a special indorsement.

(3) An indorsement purporting to be only of part of a certificated security representing units intended by the issuer to be separately transferable is effective to the extent of the indorsement.

(4) An "instruction" is an order to the issuer of an uncertificated security requesting that the transfer, pledge, or release from pledge of the uncertificated security specified therein be registered.

(5) An instruction originated by an appropriate person is:

(a) a writing signed by an appropriate person; or

(b) a communication to the issuer in any form agreed upon in a writing signed by the issuer and an appropriate person.

If an instruction has been originated by an appropriate person but is incomplete in any other respect, any person may complete it as authorized and the issuer may rely on it as completed even though it has been completed incorrectly.

(6) "An appropriate person" in subsection (1) means the person specified by the certificated security or by special indorsement to be entitled to the security.

(7) "An appropriate person" in subsection (5) means:

(a) for an instruction to transfer or pledge an uncertificated security which is then not subject to a registered pledge, the registered owner; or

(b) for an instruction to transfer or release an uncertificated security which is then subject to a registered pledge, the registered pledgee.

(8) In addition to the persons designated in subsections (6) and (7), "an appropriate person" in subsections (1) and (5) includes:

(a) if the person designated is described as a fiduciary but is no longer serving in the described capacity, either that person or his successor;

(b) if the persons designated are described as more than one person as fiduciaries and one or more are no longer serving in the described capacity, the remaining fiduciary or fiduciaries, whether or not a successor has been appointed or qualified;

(c) if the person designated is an individual and is without capacity to act by virtue of death, incompetence, infancy, or otherwise, his executor, administrator, guardian, or like fiduciary;

(d) if the persons designated are described as more than one person as tenants by the entirety or with right of survivorship and by reason of death all cannot sign, the survivor or survivors;

(e) a person having power to sign under applicable law or controlling instrument; and

(f) to the extent that the person designated or any of the foregoing persons may act through an agent, his authorized agent.

(9) Unless otherwise agreed, the indorser of a certificated security by his indorsement or the originator of an instruction by his origination assumes no obligation that the security will be honored by the issuer but only the obligations provided in Section 8—306.

(10) Whether the person signing is appropriate is determined as of the date of signing and an indorsement made by or an instruction originated by him does not become unauthorized for the purposes of this Article by virtue of any subsequent change of circumstances.

(11) Failure of a fiduciary to comply with a controlling instrument or with the law of the state having jurisdiction of the fiduciary relationship, including any law requiring the fiduciary to obtain court approval of the transfer, pledge, or release, does not render his indorsement or an instruction originated by him unauthorized for the purposes of this Article.

§ 8—309. Effect of Indorsement Without Delivery.—An indorsement of a certificated security, whether special or in blank, does not constitute a transfer until delivery of the certificated security on which it appears or, if the indorsement is on a separate document, until delivery of both the document and the certificated security.

§ 8—310. Indorsement of Certificated Security in Bearer Form.—An indorsement of a certificated security in bearer form may give notice of adverse claims (Section 8—304) but does not otherwise affect any right to registration the holder possesses.

§ 8—311. Effect of Unauthorized Indorsement or Instruction.—Unless the owner or pledgee has ratified an unauthorized indorsement or instruction or is otherwise precluded from asserting its ineffectiveness:

(a) he may assert its ineffectiveness against the issuer or any purchaser, other than a purchaser for value and without notice of adverse claims, who has in good faith received a new, reissued, or re-registered certificated security on registration of transfer or received an initial transaction statement confirming the registration of transfer, pledge, or release of an equivalent uncertificated security to him; and

(b) an issuer who registers the transfer of a certificated security upon the unauthorized indorsement or who registers the transfer, pledge, or release of an uncertificated security upon the unauthorized instruction is subject to liability for improper registration (Section 8—404).

§ 8—312. Effect of Guaranteeing Signature, Indorsement or Instruction.

(1) Any person guaranteeing a signature of an indorser of a certificated security warrants that at the time of signing:

(a) the signature was genuine;

(b) the signer was an appropriate person to indorse (Section 8—308); and

(c) the signer had legal capacity to sign.

(2) Any person guaranteeing a signature of the originator of an instruction warrants that at the time of signing:

(a) the signature was genuine;

(b) the signer was an appropriate person to originate the instruction (Section 8—308) if the person specified in the instruction as the registered owner or registered pledgee of the uncertificated security was, in fact, the registered owner or registered pledgee of the security, as to which fact the signature guarantor makes no warranty;

(c) the signer had legal capacity to sign; and

(d) the taxpayer identification number, if any, appearing on the instruction as that of the registered owner or registered pledgee was the taxpayer identification number of the signer or of the owner or pledgee for whom the signer was acting.

(3) Any person specially guaranteeing the signature of the originator of an instruction makes not only the warranties of a signature guarantor (subsection (2)) but also warrants that at the time the instruction is presented to the issuer:

(a) the person specified in the instruction as the registered owner or registered pledgee of the uncertificated security will be the registered owner or registered pledgee; and

(b) the transfer, pledge, or release of the uncertificated security requested in the instruction will be registered by the issuer free from all liens, security interests, restrictions, and claims other than those specified in the instruction.

(4) The guarantor under subsections (1) and (2) or the special guarantor under subsection (3) does not otherwise warrant the rightfulness of the particular transfer, pledge, or release.

(5) Any person guaranteeing an indorsement of a certificated security makes not only the warranties of a signature guarantor under subsection (1) but also warrants the rightfulness of the particular transfer in all respects.

(6) Any person guaranteeing an instruction requesting the transfer, pledge, or release of an uncertificated security makes not only the warranties of a special signature guarantor under subsection (3) but also warrants the rightfulness of the particular transfer, pledge, or release in all respects.

(7) No issuer may require a special guarantee of signature (subsection (3)), a guarantee of indorsement (subsection (5)), or a guarantee of instruction (subsection (6)) as a condition to registration of transfer, pledge, or release.

(8) The foregoing warranties are made to any person taking or dealing with the security in reliance on the guarantee, and the guarantor is liable to the person for any loss resulting from breach of the warranties.

§ 8—313. When Transfer to Purchaser Occurs; Financial Intermediary as Bona Fide Purchaser; "Financial Intermediary".

(1) Transfer of a security or a limited interest (including a security interest) therein to a purchaser occurs only:

(a) at the time he or a person designated by him acquires possession of a certificated security;

(b) at the time the transfer, pledge, or release of an uncertificated security is registered to him or a person designated by him;

(c) at the time his financial intermediary acquires possession of a certificated security specially indorsed to or issued in the name of the purchaser;

(d) at the time a financial intermediary, not a clearing corporation, sends him confirmation of the purchase and also by book entry or otherwise identifies as belonging to the purchaser

(i) a specific certificated security in the financial intermediary's possession;

(ii) a quantity of securities that constitute or are part of a fungible bulk of certificated securities in the financial intermediary's possession or of uncertificated securities registered in the name of the financial intermediary; or

(iii) a quantity of securities that constitute or are part of a fungible bulk of securities shown on the account of the financial intermediary on the books of another financial intermediary;

(e) with respect to an identified certificated security to be delivered while still in the possession of a third person, not a financial intermediary, at the time that person acknowledges that he holds for the purchaser;

(f) with respect to a specific uncertificated security the pledge or transfer of which has been registered to a third person, not a financial intermediary, at the time that person acknowledges that he holds for the purchaser;

(g) at the time appropriate entries to the account of the purchaser or a person designated by him on the books of a clearing corporation are made under Section 8—320;

(h) with respect to the transfer of a security interest where the debtor has signed a security agreement containing a description of the security, at the time a written notification, which, in the case of the creation of the security interest, is signed by the debtor (which may be a copy of the security agreement) or which, in the case of the release or assignment of the security interest created pursuant to this paragraph, is signed by the secured party, is received by

(i) a financial intermediary on whose books the interest of the transferor in the security appears;

(ii) a third person, not a financial intermediary, in possession of the security, if it is certificated;

(iii) a third person, not a financial intermediary, who is the registered owner of the security, if it is uncertificated and not subject to a registered pledge; or

(iv) a third person, not a financial intermediary, who is the registered pledgee of the security, if it is uncertificated and subject to a registered pledge;

(i) with respect to the transfer of a security interest where the transferor has signed a security agreement containing a description of the security, at the time new value is given by the secured party; or

(j) with respect to the transfer of a security interest where the secured party is a financial intermediary and the security has already been transferred to the financial intermediary under paragraphs (a), (b), (c), (d), or (g), at the time the transferor has signed a security agreement containing a description of the security and value is given by the secured party.

(2) The purchaser is the owner of a security held for him by a financial intermediary, but cannot be a bona fide purchaser of a security so held except in the circumstances specified in paragraphs (c), (d)(i), and (g) of subsection (1). If a security so held is part of a fungible bulk, as in the circumstances specified in paragraphs (d)(ii) and (d)(iii) of subsection (1), the purchaser is the owner of a proportionate property interest in the fungible bulk.

(3) Notice of an adverse claim received by the financial intermediary or by the purchaser after the financial intermediary takes delivery of a certificated security as a holder for value or after the transfer, pledge, or release of an uncertificated security has been registered free of the claim to a financial intermediary who has given value is not effective either as to the financial intermediary or as to the purchaser. However, as between the financial intermediary and the purchaser the purchaser may demand transfer of an equivalent security as to which no notice of adverse claim has been received.

(4) A "financial intermediary" is a bank, broker, clearing corporation, or other person (or the nominee of any of them) which in the ordinary course of its business maintains security accounts for its customers and is acting in that capacity. A financial intermediary may have a security interest in securities held in account for its customer.

§ 8—314. Duty to Transfer, When Completed.

(1) Unless otherwise agreed, if a sale of a security is made on an exchange or otherwise through brokers:

(a) the selling customer fulfills his duty to transfer at the time he:

(i) places a certificated security in the possession of the selling broker or a person designated by the broker;

(ii) causes an uncertificated security to be registered in the name of the selling broker or a person designated by the broker;

(iii) if requested, causes an acknowledgment to be made to the selling broker that a certificated or uncertificated security is held for the broker; or

(iv) places in the possession of the selling broker or of a person designated by the broker a transfer instruction for an uncertificated security, providing the issuer does not refuse to register the requested transfer if the instruction is presented to the issuer for registration within 30 days thereafter; and

(b) the selling broker, including a correspondent broker acting for a selling customer, fulfills his duty to transfer at the time he:

(i) places a certificated security in the possession of the buying broker or a person designated by the buying broker;

(ii) causes an uncertificated security to be registered in the name of the buying broker or a person designated by the buying broker;

(iii) places in the possession of the buying broker or of a person designated by the buying broker a transfer instruction for an uncertificated security, providing the issuer does not refuse to register the requested transfer if the instruction is presented to the issuer for registration within 30 days thereafter; or

(iv) effects clearance of the sale in accordance with the rules of the exchange on which the transaction took place.

(2) Except as provided in this section or unless otherwise agreed, a transferor's duty to transfer a security under a contract of purchase is not fulfilled until he:

(a) places a certificated security in form to be negotiated by the purchaser in the possession of the purchaser or of a person designated by the purchaser;

(b) causes an uncertificated security to be registered in the name of the purchaser or a person designated by the purchaser; or

(c) if the purchaser requests, causes an acknowledgment to be made to the purchaser that a certificated or uncertificated security is held for the purchaser.

(3) Unless made on an exchange, a sale to a broker purchasing for his own account is within subsection (2) and not within subsection (1).

§ 8—315. Action Against Transferee Based Upon Wrongful Transfer

(1) Any person against whom the transfer of a security is wrongful for any reason, including his incapacity, as against anyone except a bona fide purchaser, may:

(a) reclaim possession of the certificated security wrongfully transferred;

(b) obtain possession of any new certificated security representing all or part of the same rights;

(c) compel the origination of an instruction to transfer to him or a person designated by him an uncertificated security constituting all or part of the same rights; or

(d) have damages.

(2) If the transfer is wrongful because of an unauthorized indorsement of a certificated security, the owner may also reclaim or obtain possession of the security or a new certificated security, even from a bona fide purchaser, if the ineffectiveness of the purported indorsement can be asserted against him under the provisions of this Article on unauthorized indorsements (Section 8—311).

(3) The right to obtain or reclaim possession of a certificated security or to compel the origination of a transfer instruction may be specifically enforced and the transfer of a certificated or uncertificated security enjoined and a certificated security impounded pending the litigation.

§ 8—316. Purchaser's Right to Requisites for Registration of Transfer, Pledge, or Release on Books—Unless otherwise agreed, the transferor of a certificated security or the transferor, pledgor, or pledgee of an uncertificated security on due demand must supply his purchaser with any proof of his authority to transfer, pledge, or release or with any other requisite necessary to obtain registration of the transfer, pledge, or release of the security; but if the transfer, pledge, or release is not for value, a transferor, pledgor, or pledgee need not do so unless the purchaser furnishes the necessary expenses. Failure within a reasonable time to comply with a demand made gives the purchaser the right to reject or rescind the transfer, pledge, or release.

§ 8—317. Creditors' Rights

(1) Subject to the exceptions in subsections (3) and (4), no attachment or levy upon a certificated security or any share or other interest represented thereby which is outstanding is valid until the security is actually seized by the officer making the attachment or levy, but a certificated security which has been surrendered to the issuer may be reached by a creditor by legal process at the issuer's chief executive office in the United States.

(2) An uncertificated security registered in the name of the debtor may not be reached by a creditor except by legal process at the issuer's chief executive office in the United States.

(3) The interest of a debtor in a certificated security that is in the possession of a secured party not a financial intermediary or in an uncertificated security registered in the name of a secured party not a financial intermediary (or in the name of a nominee of the secured party) may be reached by a creditor by legal process upon the secured party.

(4) The interest of a debtor in a certificated security that is in the possession of or registered in the name of a financial intermediary or in an uncertificated security registered in the name of a financial intermediary may be reached by a creditor by legal process upon the financial intermediary on whose books the interest of the debtor appears.

(5) Unless otherwise provided by law, a creditor's lien upon the interest of a debtor in a security obtained pursuant to subsection (3) or (4) is not a restraint on the transfer of the security, free of the lien, to a third party for new value; but in the event of a transfer, the lien applies to the proceeds of the transfer in the hands of the secured party or financial intermediary, subject to any claims having priority.

(6) A creditor whose debtor is the owner of a security is entitled to aid from courts of appropriate jurisdiction, by injunction or otherwise, in reaching the security or in satisfying the claim by means allowed at law or in equity in regard to property that cannot readily be reached by ordinary legal process.

§ 8—318. No Conversion by Good Faith Conduct—An agent or bailee who in good faith (including observance of reasonable commercial standards if he is in the business of buying, selling, or otherwise dealing with securities) has received certificated securities and sold, pledged, or delivered them or has sold or caused the transfer or pledge of uncertificated securities over which he had control according to the instructions of his principal, is not liable for conversion or for participation in breach of fiduciary duty although the principal had no right so to deal with the securities.

§ 8—319. Statute of Frauds—A contract for the sale of securities is not enforceable by way of action or defense unless:

(a) there is some writing signed by the party against whom enforcement is sought or by his authorized agent or broker, sufficient to indicate that a contract has been made for sale of a stated quantity of described securities at a defined or stated price;

(b) delivery of a certificated security or transfer instruction has been accepted, or transfer of an uncertificated security has been registered and the transferee has failed to send written objection to the issuer within 10 days after receipt of the initial transaction statement confirming the registration, or payment has been made, but the contract is enforceable under this provision only to the extent of the delivery, registration, or payment;

(c) within a reasonable time a writing in confirmation of the sale or purchase and sufficient against the sender under paragraph (a) has been received by the party against whom enforcement is sought and he has failed to send written objection to its contents within 10 days after its receipt; or

(d) the party against whom enforcement is sought admits in his pleading, testimony, or otherwise in court that a contract was made for the sale of a stated quantity of described securities at a defined or stated price.

§ 8—320. Transfer or Pledge Within Central Depository System

(1) In addition to other methods, a transfer, pledge, or release of a security or any interest therein may be effected by the making of appropriate entries on the books of a clearing corporation reducing the account of the transferor, pledgor, or pledgee and increasing the account of the transferee, pledgee, or pledgor by the amount of the obligation or the number of shares or rights transferred, pledged, or released, if the security is shown on the account of a transferor, pledgor, or pledgee on the books of the clearing corporation; is subject to the control of the clearing corporation; and

(a) if certificated,

(i) is in the custody of the clearing corporation, another clearing corporation, a custodian bank, or a nominee of any of them; and

(ii) is in bearer form or indorsed in blank by an appropriate person or registered in the name of the clearing corporation, a custodian bank, or a nominee of any of them; or

(b) if uncertificated, is registered in the name of the clearing corporation, another clearing corporation, a custodian bank, or a nominee of any of them.

(2) Under this section entries may be made with respect to like securities or interests therein as a part of a fungible bulk and may refer merely to a quantity of a particular security without reference to the name of the registered owner, certificate or bond number, or the like, and, in appropriate cases, may be on a net basis taking into account other transfers, pledges, or releases of the same security.

(3) A transfer under this section is effective (Section 8—313) and the purchaser acquires the rights of the transferor (Section 8—301). A pledge or release under this section is the transfer of a limited interest. If a pledge or the creation of a security interest is intended, the security interest is perfected at the time when both value is given by the pledgee and the appropriate entries are made (Section 8—321). A transferee or pledgee under this section may be a bona fide purchaser (Section 8—302).

(4) A transfer or pledge under this section is not a registration of transfer under Part 4.

(5) That entries made on the books of the clearing corporation as provided in subsection (1) are not appropriate does not affect the validity or effect of the entries or the liabilities or obligations of the clearing corporation to any person adversely affected thereby.

§ 8—321. Enforceability, Attachment, Perfection and Termination of Security Interests

(1) A security interest in a security is enforceable and can attach only if it is transferred to the secured party or a person designated by him pursuant to a provision of Section 8—313(1).

(2) A security interest so transferred pursuant to agreement by a transferor who has rights in the security to a transferee who has given value is a perfected security interest, but a security interest that has been transferred solely under paragraph (i) of Section 8—313(1) becomes unperfected after 21 days unless, within that time, the requirements for transfer under any other provision of Section 8—313(1) are satisfied.

(3) A security interest in a security is subject to the provisions of Article 9, but:

(a) no filing is required to perfect the security interest; and

(b) no written security agreement signed by the debtor is necessary to make the security interest enforceable, except as provided in paragraph (h), (i), or (j) of Section 8—313(1). The secured party has the rights and duties provided under Section 9—207, to the extent they are applicable, whether or not the security is certificated, and, if certificated, whether or not it is in his possession.

(4) Unless otherwise agreed, a security interest in a security is terminated by transfer to the debtor or a person designated by him pursuant to a provision of Section 8—313(1). If a security is thus transferred, the security interest, if not terminated, becomes unperfected unless the security is certificated and is delivered to the debtor for the purpose of ultimate sale or exchange or presentation, collection, renewal, or registration of transfer. In that case, the security interest becomes unperfected after 21 days unless, within that time, the security (or securities for which it has been exchanged) is transferred to the secured party or a person designated by him pursuant to a provision of Section 8—313(1).

PART 4

Registration

§ 8—401. Duty of Issuer to Register Transfer, Pledge, or Release

(1) If a certificated security in registered form is presented to the issuer with a request to register transfer or an instruction is presented to the issuer with a request to register transfer, pledge, or release, the issuer shall register the transfer, pledge, or release as requested if:

(a) the security is indorsed or the instruction was originated by the appropriate person or persons (Section 8—308);

(b) reasonable assurance is given that those indorsements or instructions are genuine and effective (Section 8—402);

(c) the issuer has no duty as to adverse claims or has discharged the duty (Section 8—403);

(d) any applicable law relating to the collection of taxes has been complied with; and

(e) the transfer, pledge, or release is in fact rightful or is to a bona fide purchaser.

(2) If an issuer is under a duty to register a transfer, pledge, or release of a security, the issuer is also liable to the person presenting a certificated security or an instruction for registration or his principal for loss resulting from any unreasonable delay in registration or from failure or refusal to register the transfer, pledge, or release.

§ 8—402. Assurance that Indorsements and Instructions Are Effective

(1) The issuer may require the following assurance that each necessary indorsement of a certificated security or each instruction (Section 8—308) is genuine and effective:

(a) in all cases, a guarantee of the signature (Section 8—312(1) or (2)) of the person indorsing a certificated security or originating an instruction including, in the case of an instruction, a warranty of the taxpayer identification number or, in the absence thereof, other reasonable assurance of identity;

(b) if the indorsement is made or the instruction is originated by an agent, appropriate assurance of authority to sign;

(c) if the indorsement is made or the instruction is originated by a fiduciary, appropriate evidence of appointment or incumbency;

(d) if there is more than one fiduciary, reasonable assurance that all who are required to sign have done so; and

(e) if the indorsement is made or the instruction is originated by a person not covered by any of the foregoing, assurance appropriate to the case corresponding as nearly as may be to the foregoing.

(2) A "guarantee of the signature" in subsection (1) means a guarantee signed by or on behalf of a person reasonably believed by the issuer to be responsible. The issuer may adopt standards with respect to responsibility if they are not manifestly unreasonable.

(3) "Appropriate evidence of appointment or incumbency" in subsection (1) means:

(a) in the case of a fiduciary appointed or qualified by a court, a certificate issued by or under the direction or supervision of that court or an officer thereof and dated within 60 days before the date of presentation for transfer, pledge, or release; or

(b) in any other case, a copy of a document showing the appointment or a certificate issued by or on behalf of a person reasonably believed by the issuer to be responsible or, in the absence of that document or certificate, other evidence reasonably deemed by the issuer to be appropriate. The issuer may adopt standards with respect to the evidence if they are not manifestly unreasonable. The issuer is not charged with notice of the contents of any document obtained pursuant to this paragraph (b) except to the extent that the contents relate directly to the appointment or incumbency.

(4) The issuer may elect to require reasonable assurance beyond that specified in this section, but if it does so and, for a purpose other than that specified in subsection (3)(b), both requires and obtains a copy of a will, trust, indenture, articles of co-partnership, by-laws, or other controlling instrument, it is charged with notice of all matters contained therein affecting the transfer, pledge, or release.

§ 8—403. Issuer's Duty as to Adverse Claims

(1) An issuer to whom a certificated security is presented for registration shall inquire into adverse claims if:

(a) a written notification of an adverse claim is received at a time and in a manner affording the issuer a reasonable opportunity to act on it prior to the issuance of a new, reissued, or re-registered certificated security, and the notification identifies the claimant, the registered owner, and the issue of which the security is a part, and provides an address for communications directed to the claimant; or

(b) the issuer is charged with notice of an adverse claim from a controlling instrument it has elected to require under Section 8—402(4).

(2) The issuer may discharge any duty of inquiry by any reasonable means, including notifying an adverse claimant by registered or certified mail at the address furnished by him or, if there be no such address, at his residence or regular place of business that the certificated security has been presented for registration of transfer by a named person, and that the transfer will be registered unless within 30 days from the date of mailing the notification, either:

(a) an appropriate restraining order, injunction, or other process issues from a court of competent jurisdiction; or

(b) there is filed with the issuer an indemnity bond, sufficient in the issuer's judgment to protect the issuer and any transfer agent, registrar, or other agent of the issuer involved from any loss it or they may suffer by complying with the adverse claim.

(3) Unless an issuer is charged with notice of an adverse claim from a controlling instrument which it has elected to require under Section 8—402(4) or receives notification of an adverse claim under subsection (1), if a certificated security presented for registration is indorsed by the appropriate person or persons the issuer is under no duty to inquire into adverse claims. In particular:

(a) an issuer registering a certificated security in the name of a person who is a fiduciary or who is described as a fiduciary is not bound to inquire into the existence, extent, or correct description of the fiduciary relationship; and thereafter the issuer may assume without inquiry that the newly registered owner continues to be the fiduciary until the issuer receives written notice that the fiduciary is no longer acting as such with respect to the particular security;

(b) an issuer registering transfer on an indorsement by a fiduciary is not bound to inquire whether the transfer is made in compliance with a controlling instrument or with the law of the state having jurisdiction of the fiduciary relationship, including any law requiring the fiduciary to obtain court approval of the transfer; and

(c) the issuer is not charged with notice of the contents of any court record or file or other recorded or unrecorded document even though the document is in its possession and even though the transfer is made on the indorsement of a fiduciary to the fiduciary himself or to his nominee.

(4) An issuer is under no duty as to adverse claims with respect to an uncertificated security except:

(a) claims embodied in a restraining order, injunction, or other legal process served upon the issuer if the process was served at a time and in a manner affording the issuer a reasonable opportunity to act on it in accordance with the requirements of subsection (5);

(b) claims of which the issuer has received a written notification from the registered owner or the registered pledgee if the notification was received at a time and in a manner affording the issuer a reasonable opportunity to act on it in accordance with the requirements of subsection (5);

(c) claims (including restrictions on transfer not imposed by the issuer) to which the registration of transfer to the present registered owner was subject and were so noted in the initial transaction statement sent to him; and

(d) claims as to which an issuer is charged with notice from a controlling instrument it has elected to require under Section 8—402(4).

(5) If the issuer of an uncertificated security is under a duty as to an adverse claim, he discharges that duty by:

(a) including a notation of the claim in any statements sent with respect to the security under Sections 8—408(3), (6), and (7); and

(b) refusing to register the transfer or pledge of the security unless the nature of the claim does not preclude transfer or pledge subject thereto.

(6) If the transfer or pledge of the security is registered subject to an adverse claim, a notation of the claim must be included in the initial transaction statement and all subsequent statements sent to the transferee and pledgee under Section 8—408.

(7) Notwithstanding subsections (4) and (5), if an uncertificated security was subject to a registered pledge at the time the issuer first came under a duty as to a particular adverse claim, the issuer has no duty as to that claim if transfer of the security is requested by the registered pledgee or an appropriate person acting for the registered pledgee unless:

(a) the claim was embodied in legal process which expressly provides otherwise;

(b) the claim was asserted in a written notification from the registered pledgee;

(c) the claim was one as to which the issuer was charged with notice from a controlling instrument it required under Section 8—402(4) in connection with the pledgee's request for transfer; or

(d) the transfer requested is to the registered owner.

§ 8—404. Liability and Non-Liability for Registration

(1) Except as provided in any law relating to the collection of taxes, the issuer is not liable to the owner, pledgee, or any other person suffering loss as a result of the registration of a transfer, pledge, or release of a security if:

(a) there were on or with a certificated security the necessary indorsements or the issuer had received an instruction originated by an appropriate person (Section 8—308); and

(b) the issuer had no duty as to adverse claims or has discharged the duty (Section 8—403).

(2) If an issuer has registered a transfer of a certificated security to a person not entitled to it, the issuer on demand shall deliver a like security to the true owner unless:

(a) the registration was pursuant to subsection (1);

(b) the owner is precluded from asserting any claim for registering the transfer under Section 8—405(1); or

(c) the delivery would result in overissue, in which case the issuer's liability is governed by Section 8—104.

(3) If an issuer has improperly registered a transfer, pledge, or release of an uncertificated security, the issuer on demand from the injured party shall restore the records as to the injured party to the condition that would have obtained if the improper registration had not been made unless:

(a) the registration was pursuant to subsection (1); or

(b) the registration would result in overissue, in which case the issuer's liability is governed by Section 8—104.

§ 8—405. Lost, Destroyed, and Stolen Certificated Securities

(1) If a certificated security has been lost, apparently destroyed, or wrongfully taken, and the owner fails to notify the issuer of that fact within a reasonable time after he has notice of it and the issuer registers a transfer of the security before receiving notification, the owner is precluded from asserting against the issuer any claim for registering the transfer under Section 8—404 or any claim to a new security under this section.

(2) If the owner of a certificated security claims that the security has been lost, destroyed, or wrongfully taken, the issuer shall issue a new certificated security or, at the option of the issuer, an equivalent uncertificated security in place of the original security if the owner:

(a) so requests before the issuer has notice that the security has been acquired by a bona fide purchaser;

(b) files with the issuer a sufficient indemnity bond· and

(c) satisfies any other reasonable requirements imposed by the issuer.

(3) If, after the issue of a new certificated or uncertificated security, a bona fide purchaser of the original certificated security presents it for registration of transfer, the issuer shall register the transfer unless registration would result in overissue, in which event the issuer's liability is governed by Section 8—104. In addition to any rights on the indemnity bond, the issuer may recover the new certificated security from the person to whom it was issued or any person taking under him except a bona fide purchaser or may cancel the uncertificated security unless a bona fide purchaser or any person taking under a bona fide purchaser is then the registered owner or registered pledgee thereof.

§ 8—406. Duty of Authenticating Trustee, Transfer Agent, or Registrar

(1) If a person acts as authenticating trustee, transfer agent, registrar, or other agent for an issuer in the registration of transfers of its certificated securities or in the registration of transfers, pledges, and releases of its uncertificated securities, in the issue of new securities, or in the cancellation of surrendered securities:

(a) he is under a duty to the issuer to exercise good faith and due diligence in performing his functions; and

(b) with regard to the particular functions he performs, he has the same obligation to the holder or owner of a certificated security or to the owner or pledgee of an uncertificated security and has the same rights and privileges as the issuer has in regard to those functions.

(2) Notice to an authenticating trustee, transfer agent, registrar or other agent is notice to the issuer with respect to the functions performed by the agent.

§ 8—407. Exchangeability of Securities

(1) No issuer is subject to the requirements of this section unless it regularly maintains a system for issuing the class of securities involved under which both certificated and uncertificated securities are regularly issued to the category of owners, which includes the person in whose name the new security is to be registered.

(2) Upon surrender of a certificated security with all necessary indorsements and presentation of a written request by the person surrendering the security, the issuer, if he has no duty as to adverse claims or has discharged the duty

(Section 8—403), shall issue to the person or a person designated by him an equivalent uncertificated security subject to all liens, restrictions, and claims that were noted on the certificated security.

(3) Upon receipt of a transfer instruction originated by an appropriate person who so requests, the issuer of an uncertificated security shall cancel the uncertificated security and issue an equivalent certificated security on which must be noted conspicuously any liens and restrictions of the issuer and any adverse claims (as to which the issuer has a duty under Section 8—403(4)) to which the uncertificated security was subject. The certificated security shall be registered in the name of and delivered to:

    (a) the registered owner, if the uncertificated security was not subject to a registered pledge; or

    (b) the registered pledgee, if the uncertificated security was subject to a registered pledge.

§ 8—408. Statements of Uncertificated Securities

(1) Within 2 business days after the transfer of an uncertificated security has been registered, the issuer shall send to the new registered owner and, if the security has been transferred subject to a registered pledge, to the registered pledgee a written statement containing:

    (a) a description of the issue of which the uncertificated security is a part;

    (b) the number of shares or units transferred;

    (c) the name and address and any taxpayer identification number of the new registered owner and, if the security has been transferred subject to a registered pledge, the name and address and any taxpayer identification number of the registered pledgee;

    (d) a notation of any liens and restrictions of the issuer and any adverse claims (as to which the issuer has a duty under Section 8—403(4)) to which the uncertificated security is or may be subject at the time of registration or a statement that there are none of those liens, restrictions, or adverse claims; and

    (e) the date the transfer was registered.

(2) Within 2 business days after the pledge of an uncertificated security has been registered, the issuer shall send to the registered owner and the registered pledgee a written statement containing:

    (a) a description of the issue of which the uncertificated security is a part;

    (b) the number of shares or units pledged;

    (c) the name and address and any taxpayer identification number of the registered owner and the registered pledgee;

    (d) a notation of any liens and restrictions of the issuer and any adverse claims (as to which the issuer has a duty under Section 8—403(4)) to which the uncertificated security is or may be subject at the time of registration or a statement that there are none of those liens, restrictions, or adverse claims; and

    (e) the date the pledge was registered.

(3) Within 2 business days after the release from pledge of an uncertificated security has been registered, the issuer shall send to the registered owner and the pledgee whose interest was released a written statement containing:

    (a) a description of the issue of which the uncertificated security is a part;

    (b) the number of shares or units released from pledge;

    (c) the name and address and any taxpayer identification number of the registered owner and the pledgee whose interest was released;

    (d) a notation of any liens and restrictions of the issuer and any adverse claims (as to which the issuer has a duty under Section 8—403(4)) to which the uncertificated security is or may be subject at the time of registration or a statement that there are none of those liens, restrictions, or adverse claims; and

    (e) the date the release was registered.

(4) An "initial transaction statement" is the statement sent to:

    (a) the new registered owner and, if applicable, to the registered pledgee pursuant to subsection (1);

    (b) the registered pledgee pursuant to subsection (2); or

    (c) the registered owner pursuant to subsection (3).

Each initial transaction statement shall be signed by or on behalf of the issuer and must be identified as "Initial Transaction Statement".

(5) Within 2 business days after the transfer of an uncertificated security has been registered, the issuer shall send to the former registered owner and the former registered pledgee, if any, a written statement containing:

    (a) a description of the issue of which the uncertificated security is a part;

    (b) the number of shares or units transferred;

    (c) the name and address and any taxpayer identification number of the former registered owner and of any former registered pledgee; and

    (d) the date the transfer was registered.

(6) At periodic intervals no less frequent than annually and at any time upon the reasonable written request of the registered owner, the issuer shall send to the registered owner of each uncertificated security a dated written statement containing:

    (a) a description of the issue of which the uncertificated security is a part;

    (b) the name and address and any taxpayer identification number of the registered owner;

    (c) the number of shares or units of the uncertificated security registered in the name of the registered owner on the date of the statement;

    (d) the name and address and any taxpayer identification number of any registered pledgee and the number of shares or units subject to the pledge; and

    (e) a notation of any liens and restrictions of the issuer and any adverse claims (as to which the issuer has a duty under Section 8—403(4)) to which the uncertificated security is or may be subject or a statement that there are none of those liens, restrictions, or adverse claims.

(7) At periodic intervals no less frequent than annually and at any time upon the reasonable written request of the registered pledgee, the issuer shall send to the registered pledgee of each uncertificated security a dated written statement containing:

(a) a description of the issue of which the uncertificated security is a part;

(b) the name and address and any taxpayer identification number of the registered owner;

(c) the name and address and any taxpayer identification number of the registered pledgee;

(d) the number of shares or units subject to the pledge; and

(e) a notation of any liens and restrictions of the issuer and any adverse claims (as to which the issuer has a duty under Section 8—403(4)) to which the uncertificated security is or may be subject or a statement that there are none of those liens, restrictions, or adverse claims.

(8) If the issuer sends the statements described in subsections (6) and (7) at periodic intervals no less frequent than quarterly, the issuer is not obliged to send additional statements upon request unless the owner or pledgee requesting them pays to the issuer the reasonable cost of furnishing them.

(9) Each statement sent pursuant to this section must bear a conspicuous legend reading substantially as follows: "This statement is merely a record of the rights of the addressee as of the time of its issuance. Delivery of this statement, of itself, confers no rights on the recipient. This statement is neither a negotiable instrument nor a security."

ARTICLE NINE—SECURED TRANSACTIONS

PART 1

Short Title, Applicability and Definitions

§ 9-101. Short Title.—This Article shall be known and may be cited as Uniform Commercial Code—Secured Transactions.

§ 9-102. Policy and [Subject Matter] of Article.—

(1) Except as otherwise provided in Section 9-103 on multiple state transactions and in Section 9-104 on excluded transactions, this Article applies so far as concerns any personal property and fixtures within the jurisdiction of this State

(a) to any transaction (regardless of its form) which is intended to create a security interest in personal property or fixtures including goods, documents, instruments, general intangibles, chattel paper of accounts and also

(b) to any sale [or] accounts or chattel paper.

(2) This Article applies to security interests created by contract including pledge, assignment, chattel mortgage, chattel trust, trust deed, factor's lien, equipment trust, conditional sale, trust receipt, other lien or title retention contract and lease or consignment intended as security. This Article does not apply to statutory liens except as provided in Section 9-310.

(3) The application of this Article to a security interest in a secured obligation is not affected by the fact that the obligation is itself secured by a transaction or interest to which this Article does not apply.

§ 9-103* [Perfection of Security Interests in Multiple State Transactions—

(1) Documents, instruments and ordinary goods.

(a) This subsection applies to documents and instruments and to goods other than those covered by a certificate of title described in subsection (2), mobile goods described in subsection (3), and minerals described in subsection (5).

(b) Except as otherwise provided in this subsection, perfection and the effect of perfection or nonperfection of a security interest in collateral are governed by the law of the jurisdiction where the collateral is when the last event occurs on which is based the assertion that the security interest is perfected or unperfected.

(c) If the parties to a transaction creating a purchase money security interest in goods in one jurisdiction understand at the time that the security interest attaches that the goods will be kept in another jurisdiction, then the law of the other jurisdiction governs the perfection and the effect of perfection or non-perfection of the security interest from the time it attaches until thirty days after the debtor receives possession of the goods and thereafter if the goods are taken to the other jurisdiction before the end of the thirty-day period.

(d) When collateral is brought into and kept in this state while subject to a security interest perfected under the law of the jurisdiction from which the collateral was removed, the security interest remains perfected, but if action is required by Part 3 of this Article to perfect the security interest,

(i) if the action is not taken before the expiration of the period of perfection in the other jurisdiction or the end of four months after the collateral is brought into this state, whichever period first expires, the security interest becomes unperfected at the end of that period and is thereafter deemed to have been unperfected as against a person who became a purchaser after removal;

(ii) if the action is taken before the expiration of the period specified in sub-paragraph (i), the security interest continues perfected thereafter;

(iii) for the purpose of priority over a buyer of consumer goods (subsection (2) of Section 9-307), the period of the effectiveness of a filing in the jurisdiction from which the collateral is removed is governed by the rules with respect to perfection in subparagraphs (i) and (ii).

(2) Certificate of title.

(a) This subsection applies to goods covered by a certificate of title issued under a statute of this state or of another jurisdiction under the law of which indication of a security interest on the certificate is required as a condition of perfection.

(b) Except as otherwise provided in this subsection, perfection and the effect of perfection or nonperfection of the security interest are governed by the law (including the conflict of laws rules) of the jurisdiction issuing the certificate until four months after the goods are removed from that jurisdiction and thereafter until the goods are registered in another jurisdiction, but in any event not beyond surrender of the certificate. After the expiration of that period, the goods are not covered by the certificate of title within the meaning of this section.

(c) Except with respect to the rights of a buyer described in the next paragraph, a security interest, perfected in another jurisdiction otherwise than by notation on a certificate of title, in goods brought into this state and thereafter covered by a certificate of title issued by this state is subject to the rules stated in paragraph (d) of subsection (1).

(d) If goods are brought into this state while a security interest therein is perfected in any manner under the law of the jurisdiction from which the goods are removed and a certificate of title is issued by this state and the certificate does not show that the goods are subject to the security interest or that they may be subject to security interests not shown on the certificate, the security interest is subordinate to the rights of a buyer of the goods who is not in the business of selling goods of that kind to the extent that he gives value and receives delivery of the goods after issuance of the certificate and without knowledge of the security interest.

(3) Accounts, general intangibles and mobile goods.

(a) This subsection applies to accounts (other than an account described in subsection (5) on minerals) and general intangibles and to goods which are mobile and which are of a type normally used in more than one jurisdiction, such as motor vehicles, trailers, rolling stock, airplanes, shipping containers, road building and construction machinery and commercial harvesting machinery and the like, if the goods are equipment or are inventory leased or held for lease by the debtor to others, and are not covered by a certificate of title described in subsection (2).

(b) The law (including the conflict of laws rules) of the jurisdiction in which the debtor is located governs the perfection and the effect of perfection or non-perfection of the security interest.

(c) If, however, the debtor is located in a jurisdiction which is not a part of the United States, and which does not provide for perfection of the security interest by filing or recording in that jurisdiction, the law of the jurisdiction in the United States in which the debtor has its major executive office in the United States governs the perfection and the effect of perfection or non-perfection of the security interest through filing. In the alternative, if the debtor is located in a jurisdiction which is not a part of the United States or Canada and the collateral is accounts or general intangibles for money due or to become due, the security interest may be perfected by notification to the account debtor. As used in this paragraph, "United States" includes its territories and possessions and the Commonwealth of Puerto Rico.

(d) A debtor shall be deemed located at his place of business if he has one, at his chief executive office if he has more than one place of business, otherwise at his residence. If, however, the debtor is a foreign air carrier under the Federal Aviation Act of 1958, as amended, it shall be deemed located at the designated office of the agent upon whom service of process may be made on behalf of the foreign air carrier.

(e) A security interest perfected under the law of the jurisdiction of the location of the debtor is perfected until the expiration of four months after a change of the debtor's location to another jurisdiction, or until perfection would have ceased by the law of the first jurisdiction, whichever period first expires. Unless perfected in the new jurisdiction before the end of that period, it becomes unperfected thereafter and is deemed to have been unperfected as against a person who became a purchaser after the change.

(4) Chattel paper. The rules stated for goods in subsection (1) apply to a possessory security interest in chattel paper. The rules stated for accounts in subsection (3) apply to a non-possessory security interest in chattel paper, but the security interest may not be perfected by notification to the account debtor.

(5) Minerals. Perfection and the effect of perfection or non-perfection of a security interest which is created by a debtor who has an interest in minerals or the like (including oil and gas) before extraction and which attaches thereto as extracted, or which attaches to an account resulting from the sale thereof at the wellhead or minehead are governed by the law (including the conflict of laws rules) of the jurisdiction where in the well head or minehead is located.

(6) Uncertificated securities. The law (including the conflict of laws rules) of the jurisdiction of organization of the issuer governs the perfection and the effect of perfection or nonperfection of a security interest in uncertificated securities.

*[This section 9-103 has been completely rewritten]

§ 9-104. **Transactions Excluded From Article.**—This Article does not apply

(a) to a security interest subject to any statute of the United States such as the Ship Mortgage Act, 1920, to the extent that such statute governs the rights of parties to and third parties affected by transactions in particular types of property; or

(b) to a landlord's lien; or

(c) to a lien given by statute or other rule of law for services or materials except as provided in Section 9-310 on priority of such liens; or

(d) to a transfer of a claim for wages, salary or other compensation of an employee, or

(e) to a transfer by a government or governmental subdivision or agency; or

(f) to a sale of accounts or chattel paper as part of a sale of the business out of which they arose, or an assignment of accounts or chattel paper which is for the purpose of a collection only, or a transfer of a right to payment under a contract to an assignee who is also to do the performance under the contract or a transfer of a single account to an assignee in whole or partial satisfaction of a preexisting indebtedness; or

(g) to a transfer of an interest or claim in or under any policy of insurance, except as provided with respect to proceeds (Section 9-306) and priorities in proceeds (Section 9-312); or

(h) to a right represented by a judgment; (other than a judgment taken on a right to payment which was collateral); or

(i) to any right of set-off; or

(j) except to the extent that provision is made for fixtures in Section 9-313, to the creation or transfer of an interest in or lien on real estate, including a lease or rents thereunder; or

(k) to a transfer in whole or in part of any claim arising out of tort; or

(l) to a transfer of an interest in any deposit account (Subsection (1) of Section 9-105), except as provided with respect to proceeds (Section 9-106) and priorities in proceeds (Section 9-312).

§ 9-105. Definitions and Index of Definitions.—

(1) In this Article unless the context otherwise requires:

(a) "Account debtor" means the person who is obligated on an account, chattel paper, contract right or general intangible;

(b) "Chattel paper" means a writing or writings which evidence both a monetary obligation and a security interest in or a lease of specific goods. When a transaction is evidenced both by such a security agreement or a lease and by an instrument or a series of instruments, the group of writings taken together constitutes chattel paper;

(c) "Collateral" means the property subject to a security interest, and includes accounts, contract rights and chattel paper which have been sold;

(d) "Debtor" means the person who owes payment or other performance of the obligation secured, whether or not he owns or has rights in the collateral, and includes the seller of accounts, contract rights or chattel paper. Where the debtor and the owner of the collateral are not the same person, the term "debtor" means the owner of the collateral in any provision of the Article dealing with the collateral, the obligor in any provision dealing with the obligation, and may include both where the context so requires;

[(e) "Deposit account" means a demand, time, savings, passbook or like account maintained with a bank, savings and loan association, credit union or like organization, other than an account evidenced by a certificate of deposit;]

[(f)] "Document" means document of title as defined in the general definitions of Article 1 (Section 1-201), [and a receipt of the kind described in subsection (2) of Section 7-201;]

[(g) "Encumbrance" includes real estate mortgages and other liens on real estate and all other rights in real estate that are not ownership interests.]

[(h)] "Goods" includes all things which are movable at the time the security interest attaches or which are fixtures (Section 9-313), but does not include money, documents, instruments, accounts, chattel paper, general intangibles, or minerals or the like (including oil and gas) before extraction. "Goods" also includes standing timber which is to be cut and removed under a conveyance or contract for sale, the unborn young of animals, and growing crops.

[(i)] "Instrument" means a negotiable instrument (defined in Section 3-104), or a certificated security (defined in Section 8-102) or any other writing which evidences a right to the payment of money and is not itself a security agreement or lease and is of a type which is in ordinary course of business transferred by delivery with any necessary indorsement or assignment;

[(j)] "Mortgage" means a consensual interest created by a real estate mortgage, a trust deed on real estate, or the like;]

[(k) An advance is made "pursuant to commitment" if the secured party has bound himself to make it, whether or not a subsequent event of default or other event not within his control has relieved or may relieve him from his obligation.]

[(l)] ["Security agreement" means an agreement which] creates or provides for a security interest;

[(m)] "Secured party" means a lender, seller or other person in whose favor there is a security interest, including a person to whom accounts, (contract rights) or chattel paper have been sold. When the holders of obligations issued under an indenture of trust, equipment trust agreement or the like are represented by a trustee or other person, the representative is the secured party;

[(n) "Transmitting utility" means any person primarily engaged in the railroad, street railway or trolley bus business, the electric or electronics communications transmission business, the transmission of goods by pipeline, or the transmission or the production and transmission of electricity, steam, gas or water, or the provision of sewer service.]

(2) Other definitions applying to this Article and the sections in which they appear are: . . .

§ 9-106. Definitions: "Account"; "Contract Right"; "General Intangibles."—"Account" means any right to payment for goods sold or leased or for services rendered which is not evidenced by an instrument or chattel paper [whether or not it has been earned by performance.] "General intangibles" means any personal property (including things in action) other than goods, accounts, chattel paper, documents, instruments [and money] . . .

§ 9-107. Definitions: "Purchase Money Security Interest."—A security interest is a "purchase money security interest" to the extent that it is

(a) taken or retained by the seller of the collateral to secure all or part of its price; or

(b) taken by a person who by making advances or incurring an obligation gives value to enable the debtor to acquire rights in or the use of collateral if such value is in fact so used.

§ 9-108. When After-Acquired Collateral Not Security for Antecedent Debt.—Where a secured party makes an advance, incurs an obligation, releases a perfected security interest, or otherwise gives new value which is to be secured in whole or in part by after-acquired property his security interest in the after-acquired collateral shall be deemed to be taken for new value and not as security for an antecedent debt if the debtor acquires his rights in such collateral either in the ordinary course of his business or under a contract of purchase made pursuant to the security agreement within a reasonable time after new value is given.

§ 9-109. **Classification of Goods; "Consumer Goods"; "Equipment"; "Farm Products"; "Inventory."**—Goods are

(1) "consumer goods" if they are used or brought for use primarily for personal, family or household purposes;

(2) "equipment" if they are used or bought for use primarily in business (including farming or a profession) or by a debtor who is a non-profit organization or a governmental subdivision or agency or if the goods are not included in the definitions of inventory, farm products or consumer goods;

(3) "farm products" if they are crops or livestock or supplies used or produced in farming operations or if they are products of crops or livestock in their unmanufactured states (such as ginned cotton, woolclip, maple syrup, milk and eggs), and if they are in the possession of a debtor engaged in raising, fattening, grazing or other farming operations. If goods are farm products they are neither equipment nor inventory;

(4) "inventory" if they are held by a person who holds them for sale or lease or to be furnished under contracts of service or if he has so furnished them, or if they are raw materials, work in process or materials used or consumed in a business. Inventory of a person is not to be classified as his equipment.

§ 9-110. **Sufficiency of Description.**—For the purposes of this Article any description of personal property or real estate is sufficient whether or not it is specific if it reasonably identifies what is described.

§ 9-111. **Applicability of Bulk Transfer Laws.**—The creation of a security interest is not a bulk transfer under Article 6 (see Section 6-103).

§ 9-112. **Where Collateral Is Not Owned by Debtor.**—Unless otherwise agreed, when a secured party knows that collateral is owned by a person who is not the debtor, the owner of the collateral is entitled to receive from the secured party any surplus under Section 9-502(2) or under Section 9-504(1), and is not liable for the debt or for any deficiency after resale, and he has the same right as the debtor

(a) to receive statements under Section 9-208;

(b) to receive notice of and to object to a secured party's proposal to retain the collateral in satisfaction of the indebtedness under Secton 9-505;

(c) to redeem the collateral under Section 9-506;

(d) to obtain injunctive or other relief under Section 9-507(1) Section 9-507 (1); and

(e) to recover losses caused to him under Section 9-208(2).

§ 9-113. **Security Interests Arising Under Article on Sales.**—A security interest arising solely under the Article on Sales (Article 2) is subject to the provisions of this Article except that to the extent that and so long as the debtor does not have or does not lawfully obtain possession of the goods

(a) no security agreement is necessary to make the security interest enforceable; and

(b) no filing is required to perfect the security interest; and

(c) the rights of the secured party on default by the debtor are governed by the Article on Sales (Article 2).

§ 9-114. **Consignment—**

(1) A person who delivers goods under a consignment which is not a security interest and who would be required to file under this Article by paragraph (3) (c) of Section 2-326 has priority over a secured party who is or becomes a creditor of the consignee and who would have a perfected security interest in the goods if they were the property of the consignee, and also has priority with respect to identifiable cash proceeds received on or before delivery of the goods to a buyer, if

(a) the consignor complies with the filing provision of the Article on Sales with respect to consignments (paragraph (3) (c) of Section 2-326) before the consignee receives possession of the goods; and

(b) the consignor gives notification in writing to the holder of the security interest if the holder has filed a financing statement covering the same types of goods before the date of the filing made by the consignor; and

(c) the holder of the security interest receives the notification within five years before the consignee receives possession of the goods; and

(d) the notification states that the consignor expects to deliver goods on consignment to the consignee, describing the goods by item or type.

(2) In the case of a consignment which is not a security interest and in which the requirements of the preceding subsection have not been met, a person who delivers goods to another is subordinate to a person who would have a perfected security interest in the goods if they were the property of the debtor.]*

*This section new in 1972.

PART 2

Validity of Security Agreement and Rights of Parties Thereto

§ 9-201. **General Validity of Security Agreement.**—Except as otherwise provided by this Act a security agreement is effective according to its terms between the parties, against purchasers of the collateral and against creditors. Nothing in this Article validates any charge or practice illegal under any statute or regulation thereunder governing usury, small loans, retail installment sales, or the like or extends the application of any such statute or regulation to any transaction not otherwise subject thereto.

§ 9-202. Title to Collateral Immaterial.—Each provision of this Article with regard to rights, obligations and remedies applies whether title to collateral is in the secured party or in the debtor.

§ 9-203. [Attachment and] Enforceability of Security Interest; Proceeds; Formal Requisites.—

[(1) Subject to the provisions of Section 4-208 on the security interest of a collecting bank, Section 8-321 on security interests in securities and Section 9-113 on a security interest arising under the Article on Sales, a security interest is not enforceable against the debtor or third parties with respect to the collateral and does not attach unless

(a) the collateral is in the possession of the secured party pursuant to agreement, or the debtor has signed a security agreement which contains a description of the collateral and in addition, when the security interest covers crops growing or to be grown or timber to be cut, a description of the land concerned; and

(b) value has been given; and

(c) the debtor has rights in the collateral.

(2) A security interest attaches when it becomes enforceable against the debtor with respect to the collateral. Attachment occurs as soon as all of the events specified in subsection (1) have taken place unless explicit agreement postpones the time of attaching.

(3) Unless otherwise agreed a security agreement gives the secured party the rights to proceeds provided by Section 9-306.]

[(4)] A transaction, although subject to this Article, is also subject to the "Consumer Finance Act" . . . "The Retail Installment Sales Act" . . . and in the case of conflict between the provisions of this Article and any such statute, the provisions of such statute control. Failure to comply with any applicable statute has only the effect which is specified therein.

§ 9-204. When Security Attaches; After-Acquired Property; Future Advances.—

[(1) Except as provided in subsection (2), a security agreement may provide that any or all obligations covered by the security agreement are to be secured by after-acquired collateral.

(2) No security interest attaches under an after-acquired property clause to consumer goods other than accessions (Section 9-314) when given as additional security unless the debtor acquires rights in them within ten days after the secured party gives value.]

[(3)] Obligations covered by a security agreement may include future advances or other value whether or not the advances or value are given pursuant to commitment [subsection (k) of Section (1) of Section 9-105).]

§ 9-205. Use or Disposition of Collateral Without Accounting Permissible.—A security interest is not invalid or fraudulent against creditors by reason of liberty in the debtor to use, commingle or dispose of all or part of the collateral (including returned or repossessed goods) or to collect or compromise accounts, contract rights or chattel paper, or to accept the return of goods or make repossessions, or to use, commingle or dispose of proceeds, or by reason of the failure of the secured party to require the debtor to account for proceeds or replace collateral. This Section does not relax the requirements of possession where perfection of a security interest depends upon possession of the collateral by the secured party or by a bailee.

§ 9-206. Agreement Not to Assert Defenses Against Assignee; Modification of Sales Warranties Where Security Agreement Exists.—

(1) Subject to any statute or decision which establishes a different rule for buyers of consumer goods, an agreement by a buyer that he will not assert against an assignee any claim or defense which he may have against the seller is enforceable by an assignee who takes his assignment for value, in good faith and without notice of a claim or defense, except as to defenses of a type which may be asserted against a holder in due course of a negotiable instrument under the Article on Commercial Paper (Article 3). A buyer who as part of one transaction signs both a negotiable instrument and a security agreement makes such an agreement.

(2) When a seller retains a purchase money security interest in goods the Article on Sales (Article 2) governs the sale and any disclaimer, limitation or modification of the seller's warranties.

§ 9-207. Rights and Duties When Collateral Is in Secured Party's Possession.—

(1) A secured party must use reasonable care in the custody and preservation of collateral in his possession. In the case of an instrument or chattel paper reasonable care includes taking necessary steps to preserve rights against prior parties unless otherwise agreed.

(2) Unless otherwise agreed, when collateral is in the secured party's possession

(a) reasonable expenses (including the cost of any insurance and payment of taxes or other charges) incurred in the custody, preservation, use or operation of the collateral are chargeable to the debtor and are secured by the collateral;

(b) the risk of accidental loss or damage is on the debtor to the extent of any deficiency in any effective insurance coverage;

(c) the secured party may hold as additional security any increase or profits (except money) received from the collateral, but money so received, unless remitted to the debtor, shall be applied in reduction of the secured obligation;

(d) the secured party must keep the collateral identifiable but fungible collateral may be commingled;

(e) the secured party may repledge the collateral upon terms which do not impair the debtor's right to redeem it.

(3) A secured party is liable for any loss caused by his failure to meet any obligation imposed by the preceding subsections but does not lose his security interest.

(4) A secured party may use or operate the collateral for the purpose of preserving the collateral or its value or pursuant to the order of a court of appropriate jurisdiction or, except in the case of consumer goods, in the manner and to the extent provided in the security agreement.

§ 9-208.   Request for Statement of Account or List of Collateral.—

(1) A debtor may sign a statement indicating what he believes to be the aggregate amount of unpaid indebtedness as of a specified date and may send it to the secured party with a request that the statement be approved or corrected and returned to the debtor. When the security agreement or any other record kept by the secured party identifies the collateral a debtor may similarly request the secured party to approve or correct a list of the collateral.

(2) The secured party must comply with such a request within two weeks after receipt by sending a written correction or approval. If the secured party claims a security interest in all of a particular type of collateral owned by the debtor he may indicate that fact in his reply and need not approve or correct an itemized list of such collateral. If the secured party without reasonable excuse fails to comply he is liable for any loss caused to the debtor thereby; and if the debtor has properly included in his request a good faith statement of the obligation or a list of the collateral or both, the secured party may claim a security interest only as shown in the statement against persons misled by his failure to comply. If he no longer has an interest in the obligation or collateral at the time the request is received he must disclose the name and address of any successor in interest known to him and he is liable for any loss caused to the debtor as a result or failure to disclose. A successor in interest is not subject to this Section until a request is received by him.

(3) A debtor is entitled to such a statement once every 6 months without charge. The secured party may require payment of a charge not exceeding $10 for each additional statement furnished.

PART 3

Rights of Third Parties; Perfected and Unperfected

Security Interests; Rules of Priority

§ 9-301.   Persons Who Take Priority Over Unperfected Security Interests; [Rights of] "Lien Creditor".—

(1) Except as otherwise provided in subsection (2), an unperfected security interest is subordinate to the rights of

(a) persons entitled to priority under Section 9-312;

(b) a person who becomes a lien creditor before [the security interest] is perfected;

(c) in the case of goods, instruments, documents, and chattel paper, a person who is not a secured party and who is a transferee in bulk or other buyer not in ordinary course of business, [or is a buyer of farm products in the ordinary course of business] to the extent that he gives value and receives delivery of the collateral without knowledge of the security interest and before it is perfected;

(d) in the case of accounts, contract rights, and general intangibles, a person who is not a secured party and who is a transferee to the extent that he gives value without knowledge of the security interest and before it is perfected.

(2) If the secured party files with respect to a purchase money security interest before or within ten days after the [debtor receives possession of the] collateral, he takes priority over the rights of a transferee in bulk or of a lien creditor which arise between the time the security interest attaches and the time of filing.

(3) A "lien creditor" means a creditor who has acquired a lien on the property involved by attachment, levy or the like and includes as assignee for benefit of creditors from the time of assignment, and a trustee in bankruptcy from the date of the filing of the petition or a receiver in equity from the time of appointment. Unless all the creditors represented had knowledge of the security interests such a representative of creditors is a lien creditor without knowledge even though he personally has knowledge of the security interest.

[(4) A person who becomes a lien creditor while a security interest is perfected takes subject to the security interest only to the extent that it secures advances made before he becomes a lien creditor or within 45 days thereafter or made without knowledge of the lien or pursuant to a commitment entered into without knowledge of the lien.]

§ 9-302.   When Filing is Required to Perfect Security Interest; Security Interests to Which Filing Provisions of This Article Do Not Apply.—

(1) A financing statement must be filed to perfect all security interests except the following:

(a) a security interest in collateral in possession of the secured party under Section 9-305;

(b) a security interest temporarily perfected in instruments or documents without delivery under Section 9-034 or in proceeds for a 10 day period under Section 9-306;

[(c) a security interest created by an assignment of a beneficial interest in a trust of a decedent's estate;]

(d) a purchase money security interest in consumer goods; but filing is required [for a motor vehicle required to be registered; and fixture filing is required for priority over conflicting interests in fixtures to the extent provided in Section 9-313;]

(e) an assignment of accounts or contract rights which does not alone or in conjunction with other assignments to the same assignee transfer a significant part of the outstanding accounts or contract rights of the assignor;

(f) a security interest of a collecting bank (Section 4-208) or in securities (Section 8-321) or arising under the Article on Sales (see Section 9-113) or covered in subsection (3) of this section;

[(g) an assignment for the benefit of all the creditors of the transferor, and subsequent transfers by the assignee thereunder.]

(2) If a secured party assigns a perfected security interest, no filing under this Article is required in order to continue the perfected status of the security interest against creditors of and transferees from the original debtor.

[(3) The filing of a financing statement otherwise required by this Article is not necessary or effective to perfect a security interest in property subject to

(a) a statute or treaty of the United States which provides for a national or international registration or a national or international certificate of title or which specifies a place of filing different from that specified in this Article for filing of the security interest; or

(b) the following statutes of this state: [[list any certificate of title statute covering automobiles, trailers, mobile homes, boats, farm tractors, or the like, and any central filing statute*.]]; but during any period in which collateral is inventory held for sale by a person who is in the business of selling goods of that kind, the filing provisions of this Article (Part 4) apply to a security interest in that collateral created by him as debtor; or

(c) a certificate of title statute of another jurisdiction under the law of which indication of a security interest on the certificate is required as a condition of perfection (subsection (2) of Section 9-103).

(4) Compliance with a statute or treaty described in subsection (3) is equivalent to the filing of a financing statement under this Article, and a security interest in property subject to the statute or treaty can be perfected only by compliance therewith except as provided in Section 9-103 on multiple state transactions. Duration and renewal of perfection of a security interest perfected by compliance with the statute or treaty are governed by the provisions of the statute or treaty; in other respects the security interest is subject to this Article.

*Note: *It is recommended that the provisions of certificate of title acts for perfection of security interests by notation on the certificates should be amended to exclude coverage of inventory held for sale.*]

§ 9-303. When Security Interest Is Perfected; Continuity of Perfection.—

(1) A security interest is perfected when it has attached and when all of the applicable steps required for perfection have been taken. Such steps are specified in Sections 9-302, 9-304, 9-306. If such steps are taken before the security interest attaches, it is perfected at the time when it attaches.

(2) If a security interest is originally perfected in any way permitted under this Article and is subsequently perfected in some other way under this Article, without an intermediate period when it was unperfected, the security interest shall be deemed to be perfected continuously for the purposes of this Article.

§ 9-304. Perfection of Security Interest in Instruments, Documents and Goods Covered by Documents; Perfection by Permissive Filing; Temporary Perfection Without Filing or Transfer of Possession.—

(1) A security interest in chattel paper or negotiable documents may be perfected by filing. A security interest in money or instruments (other than certificated securities or instruments which constitute part of chattel paper) can be perfected only by the secured party's taking possession, except as provided in subsections (4) and (5) of this section and subsections (2) and (3) of Section 9—306 on proceeds.

(2) During the period that goods are in the possession of the issuer of a negotiable document therefor, a security interest in the goods is perfected by perfecting a security interest in the document, and any security interest in the goods otherwise perfected during such period is subject thereto.

(3) A security interest in goods in the possession of a bailee other than one who has issued a negotiable document therefor is perfected by issuance of a document in the name of the secured party or by the bailee's receipt of notification of the secured party's interest or by filing as to the goods.

(4) A security interest in instruments (other than certificated securities) or negotiable documents is perfected without filing or the taking of possession for a period of 21 days from the time it attaches to the extent that it arises for new value given under a written security agreement.

(5) A security interest remains perfected for a period of 21 days without filing where a secured party having a perfected security interest in an instrument (other than a certificated security), a negotiable document or goods in possession of a bailee other than one who has issued a negotiable document therefor

(a) makes available to the debtor the goods or documents representing the goods for the purpose of ultimate sale or exchange or for the purpose of loading, unloading, storing, shipping, transshipping, manufacturing, processing or otherwise dealing with them in a manner preliminary to their sale or exchange, but priority between conflicting security interests in the goods is subject to subsection (3) of Section 9—312; or

(b) delivers the instrument to the debtor for the purpose of ultimate sale or exchange or of presentation, collection, renewal or registration of transfer.

(6) After the 21 day period in subsections (4) and (5) perfection depends upon compliance with applicable provisions of this Article.

§ 9—305. When Possession by Secured Party Perfects Security Interest Without Filing—A security interest in letters of credit and advices of credit (subsection (2)(a) of Section 5—116), goods, instruments (other than certificated securities), money, negotiable documents, or chattel paper may be perfected by the secured party's taking possession of the collateral. If such collateral other than goods covered by a negotiable document is held by a bailee, the secured party is deemed to have possession from the time the bailee receives notification of the secured party's interest. A security interest is perfected by possession from the time possession is taken without a relation back and continues only so long as possession is retained, unless otherwise specified in this Article. The security

interest may be otherwise perfected as provided in this Article before or after the period of possession by the secured party.

§ 9-306. "Proceeds"; Secured Party's Rights on Disposition of Collateral

(1) ["Proceeds" includes whatever is received upon the sale, exchange, collection or other disposition of collateral or proceeds. Insurance payable by reason of loss or damage to the collateral is proceeds, except to the extent that it is payable to a person other than a party to the security agreement.] Money, checks, [deposit accounts,] and the like are "cash proceeds". All other proceeds are "non-cash proceeds".

(2) Except where this Article otherwise provides, a security interest continues in collateral notwithstanding sale, exchange or other disposition thereof unless [the disposition was] authorized by the secured party in the security agreement or otherwise, and also continues in any identifiable proceeds including collections received by the debtor.

(3) The security interest in proceeds is a continuously perfected security interest if the interest in the original collateral was perfected but it ceases to be a perfected security interest and becomes unperfected ten days after receipt of the proceeds by the debtor unless

[(a) a filed financing statement covers the original collateral and the proceeds are collateral in which a security interest may be perfected by filing in the office or offices where the financing statement has been filed and, if the proceeds are acquired with cash proceeds, the description of collateral in the financing statement indicates the types of property constituting the proceeds; or]

[(b) a filed financing statement covers the original collateral and the proceeds are identifiable cash proceeds; or]

[(c)] the security interest in the proceeds is perfected before the expiration of the ten day period. [Except as provided in this section, a security interest in proceeds can be perfected only by the methods or under the circumstances permitted in this Article for original collateral of the same type.]

(4) In the event of insolvency proceeding instituted by or against a debtor, a secured party with a perfected security interest in proceeds has a perfected security interest [only in the following proceeds:]

(a) in identifiable non-cash proceeds[,] [and in separate deposit accounts containing only proceeds;]

(b) in identifiable cash proceeds in the form of money which is [neither] commingled with other money [nor] deposited in a [deposit] account prior to the insolvency proceedings;

(c) in identifiable cash proceeds in the form of checks and the like which are not deposited in a [deposit] account prior to the insolvency proceedings; and

(d) in all cash and [deposit] accounts of the debtor [in which] proceeds have been commingled [with other funds,] but the perfected security interest under this paragraph (d) is

(i) subject to any right of set-off; and

(ii) limited to an amount not greater than the amount of any cash proceeds received by the debtor within ten days before the institution of the insolvency proceedings [less the sum of (I) the payments to the secured party on account of cash proceeds received by the debtor during such period and (II) the cash proceeds received by the debtor during such period to which the secured party is entitled under paragraphs (a) through (c) of this subsection (4).]

(5) If a sale of goods results in an account or chattel paper which is transferred by the seller to a secured party, and if the goods are returned to or are repossessed by the seller or the secured party, the following rules determine priorities:

(a) If the goods were collateral at the time of sale for an indebtedness of the seller which is still unpaid, the original security interest attaches again to the goods and continues as a perfected security interest if it was perfected at the time when the goods were sold. If the security interest was originally perfected by a filing which is still effective, nothing further is required to continue the perfected status; in any other case, the secured party must take possession of the returned or repossessed goods or must file.

(b) An unpaid transferee of the chattel paper has a security interest in the goods against the transferor. Such security interest is prior to a security interest asserted under paragraph (a) to the extent that the transferee of the chattel paper was entitled to priority under Section 9-308.

(c) An unpaid transferee of the account has a security interest in the goods against the transferor. Such security interest is subordinate to a security interest asserted under paragraph (a).

(d) A security interest of an unpaid transferee asserted under paragraph (b) or (c) must be perfected for protection against creditors of the transferor and purchasers of the returned or repossessed goods.

§ 9-306.01. Debtor Disposing of Collateral and Failing to Pay Secured Party Amount Due under Security Agreement; Penalties for Violation.—

(1) It is unlawful for a debtor under the terms of a security agreement (a) who has no right of sale or other disposition of the collateral or (b) who has a right of sale or other disposition of the collateral and is to account to the secured party for the proceeds of any sale or other disposition of the collateral, to sell or otherwise dispose of the collateral and willfully and wrongfully to fail to pay the secured party the amount of said proceeds due under the security agreement.

(2) An individual convicted of a violation of this Section shall be punished by imprisonment in the penitentiary for not less than one year nor more than ten years.

(3) A corporation convicted of a violation of this Section shall be punished by a fine of not less than two thousand dollars nor more than ten thousand dollars.

(4) In the event the debtor under the terms of a security agreement is a corporation or a partnership, any officer, director, manager, or managerial agent of the debtor who violates this Section or causes the debtor to violate this Section shall, upon conviction thereof, be punished by imprisonment in the penitentiary for not less than one year nor more than ten years.

§ 9-307. Protection of Buyers of Goods.—

(1) A buyer in ordinary course of business (subsection (9) of Section 1-201) other than a person buying farm products from a person engaged in farming operations takes free of a security interest created by his seller even though the security interest is perfected and even though the buyer knows of its existence.

(2) In the case of consumer goods, a buyer takes free of a security interest even though perfected if he buys without knowledge of the security interest, for value and for his own personal, family or household purposes or his own farming operations unless prior to the purchase the secured party has filed a financing statement covering such goods.

[(3) A buyer other than a buyer in ordinary course of business (subsection (1) of this section) takes free of a security interest to the extent that it secures future advances made after the secured party acquires knowledge of the purchase, or more than 45 days after the purchase, whichever first occurs, unless made pursuant to a commitment entered into without knowledge of the purchase and before the expiration of the 45 day period.]

§ 9-308.* Purchase of Chattel Paper and Instruments—[A purchaser of chattel paper or an instrument who gives

new value and takes possession of it in the ordinary course of his business has priority over a security interest in the chattel paper or instrument

(a) which is perfected under Section 9-304 (permissive filing and temporary perfection) or under Section 9-306 (perfection as to proceeds) if he acts without knowledge that the specific paper or instrument is subject to a security interest; or

(b) which is claimed merely as proceeds of inventory subject to a security interest (Section 9-306) even though he knows that the specific paper or instrument is subject to the security interest.]

*This section was redrafted in 1972.

§ 9—309. Protection of Purchasers of Instruments, Documents and Securities—Nothing in this Article limits the

rights of a holder in due course of a negotiable instrument (Section 3-302) or a holder to whom a negotiable document of title has been duly negotiated (Section 7—501) or a bona fide purchaser of a security (Section 8—302) and the holders or purchasers take priority over an earlier security interest even though perfected. Filing under this Article does not constitute notice of the security interest to such holders or purchasers.

§ 9-310. Priority of Certain Liens Arising by Operation of Law.—When a person in the ordinary course of his

business furnishes services or materials with respect to goods subject to a security interest, a lien upon goods in the possession of such person given by statute or rule of law for such materials or services takes priority over a perfected security interest unless the lien is statutory and the statute expressly provides otherwise.

§ 9-311. Alienability of Debtor's Rights: Judicial Process.—The debtor's rights in collateral may be voluntarily or

involuntarily transferred (by way of sale, creation of a security interest, attachment, levy, garnishment or other judicial process) notwithstanding a provision in the security agreement prohibiting any transfer or making the transfer constitute a default.

§ 9-312. Priorities Among Conflicting Security Interests in the Same Collateral.—

[(1) The rules of priority stated in other sections of this Part and in the following sections shall govern when applicable: Section 4-208 with respect to the security interests of collecting banks in items being collected, accompanying documents and proceeds; Section 9-103 on security interests related to other jurisdictions; Section 9-114 on consignments.]

(2) A perfected security interest in crops for new value given to enable the debtor to produce the crops during the production season and given not more than three months before the crops become growing crops by planting or otherwise takes priority over an earlier perfected security interest to the extent that such earlier interest secures obligations due more than six months before the crops become growing crops by planting or otherwise, even though the person giving new value had knowledge of the earlier security interest.

[(3) A perfected purchase money security interest in inventory has priority over a conflicting security interest in the same inventory and also has priority in identifiable cash proceeds received on or before the delivery of the inventory to a buyer if

(a) the purchase money security interest is perfected at the time the debtor receives possession of the inventory; and

(b) the purchase money secured party gives notification in writing to the holder of the conflicting security interest if the holder had filed a financing statement covering the same types of inventory (i) before the date of the filing made by the purchase money secured party, or (ii) before the beginning of the 21 day period where the purchase money security interest is temporarily perfected without filing or possession (subsection (5) of Section 9-304); and

(c) the holder of the conflicting security interest receives the notification within five years before the debtor receives possession of the inventory; and

(d) the notification states that the person giving the notice has or expects to acquire a purchase money security interest in inventory of the debtor, describing such inventory by item or type.]

(4) A purchase money security interest in collateral other than inventory has priority over a conflicting security interest in the same collateral [or its proceeds] if the purchase money security interest is perfected at the time the debtor receives possession of the collateral or within 10 days thereafter.

(5) In all cases not governed by other rules stated in this section (including cases of purchase money security interests which do not qualify for the special priorities set forth in subsections (3) and (4) of this section), priority between conflicting security interests in the same collateral shall be determined [according to the following rules:

(a) Conflicting security interests rank according to priority in time of filing or perfection. Priority dates from the time a filing is first made covering the collateral or the time the security interest is first perfected, whichever is earlier, provided that there is no period thereafter when there is neither filing nor perfection.

(b) So long as conflicting security interests are unperfected, the first to attach has priority.]

[(6) For the purposes of subsection (5) a date of filing or perfection as to collateral is also a date of filing or perfection as to proceeds.

(7) If future advances are made while a security interest is perfected by filing, the taking of possession, or under Section 8—321 on securities, the security interest has the same priority for the purposes of subsection (5) with respect to the future advances as it does with respect to the first advance. If a commitment is made before or while the security interest is so perfected, the security interest has the same priority with respect to advances made pursuant thereto. In other cases a perfected security interest has priority from the date the advance is made.

§ 9-313. Priority of Security Interests in Fixtures.—

[(1) In this section and in the provisions of Part 4 of this Article referring to fixture filing, unless the context otherwise requires

(a) goods are "fixtures" when they become so related to particular real estate that an interest in them arises under real estate law

(b) a "fixture filing" is the filing in the office where a mortgage on the real estate would be filed or recorded of a financing statement covering goods which are or are to become fixtures and conforming to the requirements of subsection (5) of Section 9-402

(c) a mortgage is a "construction mortgage" to the extent that it secures an obligation incurred for the construction of an improvement on land including the acquisition cost of the land, if the recorded writing so indicates.

(2) A security interest under this Article may be created in goods which are fixtures or may continue in goods which become fixtures, but no security interest exists under this Article in ordinary building materials incorporated into an improvement on land.

(3) This Article does not prevent creation of an encumbrance upon fixtures pursuant to real estate law.

(4) A perfected security interest in fixtures has priority over the conflicting interest of an encumbrancer or owner of the real estate where

(a) the security interest is a purchase money security interest, the interest of the encumbrancer or owner arises before the goods become fixtures, the security interest is perfected by a fixture filing before the goods become fixtures or within ten days thereafter, and the debtor has an interest of record in the real estate or is in possession of the real estate; or

(b) the security interest is perfected by a fixture filing before the interest of the encumbrancer or owner is of record, the security interest has priority over any conflicting interest of a predecessor in title of the encumbrancer or owner, and the debtor has an interest of record in the real estate or is in possession of the real estate; or

(c) the fixtures are readily removable factory or office machines or readily removable replacements of domestic appliances which are consumer goods, and before the goods become fixtures the security interest is perfected by any method permitted by this Article; or

(d) the conflicting interest is a lien on the real estate obtained by legal or equitable proceedings after the security interest was perfected by any method permitted by this Article.

(5) A security interest in fixtures, whether or not perfected, has priority over the conflicting interest of an encumbrancer or owner of the real estate where

(a) the encumbrancer or owner has consented in writing to the security interest or has disclaimed an interest in the goods as fixtures; or

(b) the debtor has a right to remove the goods as against the encumbrancer or owner. If the debtor's right terminates, the priority of the security interest continues for a reasonable time.

(6) Notwithstanding paragraph (a) of subsection (4) but otherwise subject to subsections (4) and (5), a security interest in fixtures is subordinate to a construction mortgage recorded before the goods become fixtures if the goods become fixtures before the completion of the construction. To the extent that it is given to refinance a construction mortgage, a mortgage has this priority to the same extent as the construction mortgage.

(7) In cases not within the preceding subsections, a security interest in fixtures is subordinate to the conflicting interest of an encumbrancer or owner of the related real estate who is not the debtor.]

[(8)] When the secured party has priority over all owners and encumbrancers of the real estate, he may, on default, subject to the provisions of Part 5, remove his collateral from the real estate but he must reimburse any encumbrancer or owner of the real estate who is not the debtor and who has not otherwise agreed for the cost of repair of any physical injury, but not for any diminution in value of the real estate caused by the absence of the goods removed or by any necessity for replacing them. A person entitled to reimbursement may refuse permission to remove until the secured party gives adequate security for the performance of this obligation.

§ 9-314. Accessions.—

(1) A security interest in goods which attaches before they are installed in or affixed to other goods takes priority as to the goods installed or affixed (called in this section "accessions") over the claims of all persons to the whole except as stated in subsection (3) and subject to Section 9-315(1).

(2) A security interest which attaches to goods after they become part of a whole is valid against all persons subsequently acquiring interests in the whole except as stated in subsection (3) but is invalid against any person with an interest in the whole at the time the security interest attaches to the goods who has not in writing consented to the security interest or disclaimed an interest in the goods as part of the whole.

(3) The security interests described in subsections (1) and (2) do not take priority over

(a) a subsequent purchaser for value of any interest in the whole; or

(b) a creditor with a lien on the whole subsequently obtained by judicial proceedings; or

(c) a creditor with a prior perfected security interest in the whole to the extent that he makes subsequent advances

if the subsequent purchase is made, the lien by judicial proceedings obtained or the subsequent advance under the prior perfected security interest is made or contracted for without knowledge of the security interest and before it is perfected. A purchaser of the whole at a foreclosure sale other than the holder of a perfected security interest purchasing at his own foreclosure sale is a subsequent purchaser within this Section.

(4) When under subsections (1) or (2) and (3) a secured party has an interest in accessions which has priority over the claims of all persons who have interests in the whole, he may on default subject to the provisions of Part 5 remove his collateral from the whole but he must reimburse any encumbrancer or owner of the whole who is not the debtor and who has not otherwise agreed for the cost of repair of any physical injury but not for any diminution in value of the whole caused by the absence of the goods removed or by any necessity for replacing them. A person entitled to reimbursement may refuse permission to remove until the secured party gives adequate security for the performance of this obligation.

§ 9-315. Priority When Goods Are Commingled or Processed.—

(1) If a security interest in goods was perfected and subsequently the goods or a part thereof have become part of a product or mass, the security interest continues in the product or mass if

(a) the goods are so manufactured, processed, assembled or commingled that their identity is lost in the product or mass; or

(b) a financing statement covering the original goods also covers the product into which the goods have been manufactured, processed or assembled.

In a case to which paragraph (b) applies, no separate security interest in that part of the original goods which has been manufactured, processed or assembled into the product may be claimed under Section 9-314.

(2) When under subsection (1) more than one security interest attaches to the product or mass, they rank equally according to the ratio that the cost of the goods to which each interest originally attached bears to the cost of the total product or mass.

§ 9-316. Priority Subject to Subordination.—Nothing in this Article prevents subordination by agreement by any person entitled to priority.

§ 9-317. Secured Party Not Obligated on Contract of Debtor.—The mere existence of a security interest or authority given to the debtor to dispose of or use collateral does not impose contract or tort liability upon the secured party for the debtor's acts or omissions.

§ 9-318. Defenses Against Assignee; Modification of Contract After Notification of Assignment; Term Prohibiting Assignment Ineffective; Identification and Proof of Assignment.—

(1) Unless an account debtor has made an enforceable agreement not to assert defenses or claims arising out of a sale as provided in Section 9-206 the rights of an assignee are subject to

(a) all the terms of the contract between the account debtor and assignor and any defense or claim arising therefrom; and

(b) any other defense or claim of the account debtor against the assignor which accrues before the account debtor receives notification of the assignment.

(2) So far as the right to payment [or a part thereof] under an assigned contract [has not been fully earned by performance,] and notwithstanding notification of the assignment, any modification of or substitution for the contract made in good faith and in accordance with reasonable commercial standards is effective against an assignee unless the account debtor has otherwise agreed but the assignee acquires corresponding rights under the modified or substituted contract. The assignment may provide that such modification or substitution is a breach by the assignor.

(3) The account debtor is authorized to pay the assignor until the account debtor receives notification that the [amount due or to become due] has been assigned and that payment is to be made to the assignee. A notification which does not reasonably identify the rights assigned is ineffective. If requested by the account debtor, the assignee must seasonably furnish reasonable proof that the assignment has been made and unless he does so the account debtor may pay the assignor.

(4) A term in any contract between an account debtor and an assignor [is ineffective if it] prohibits assignment of an account [or prohibits creation of a security interest in a general intangible for money due or to become due or requires the account debtor's consent to such assignment or security interest.]

PART 4

FILING

§ 9-401. Place of Filing; Erroneous Filing; Removal of Collateral

First Alternative Subsection (1)

(1) The proper place to file in order to perfect a security interest is as follows:

[(a) when the collateral is timber to be cut or is minerals or the like (including oil and gas) or accounts subject to subsection (5) of Section 9-103, or when the financing statement is filed as a fixture filing

(Section 9-313) and] the collateral is goods which are or are to become fixtures, then in the office where a mortgage on the real estate would be filed or recorded;

  (b) in all other cases, in the office of the Secretary of State.

Second Alternative Subsection (1)

(1) The proper place to file in order to perfect a security interest is as follows:

  (a) when the collateral is equipment used in farming operations, or farm products, or accounts, [contract rights] or general intangibles arising from or relating to the sale of farm products by a farmer, or consumer goods, then in the office of the........in the county of the debtor's residence or if the debtor is not a resident of this state then in the office of the........in the county where the goods are kept, and in addition when the collateral is crops [growing or to be grown] in the office of the........in the county where the land [on which the crops are growing or to be grown] is located;

  (b) when the collateral is [timber to be cut or is minerals or the like (including oil and gas) or accounts subject to subsection (5) of Section 9-103, or when the financing statement is filed as a fixture filing (Section 9-313) and the collateral is goods which are or are to become fixtures,] then in the office where a mortgage on the real estate would be filed or recorded;

  (c) in all other cases, in the office of the Secretary of State.

Third Alternative Subsection (1)

(1) The proper place to file in order to perfect a security interest is as follows:

  (a) when the collateral is equipment used in farming operations, or farm products, or accounts, [contract rights] or general intangibles arising from or relating to the sale of farm products by a farmer, or consumer goods, then in the office of the........in the county of the debtor's residence or if the debtor is not a resident of this state then in the office of the........in the county where the goods are kept, and in addition when the collateral is crops growing or to be grown in the office of the........in the county where the land [on which the crops are growing or to be grown] is located;

  (b) when the collateral is [goods which at the time the security interest attaches are or are to become fixtures] timber to be cut or is minerals or the like (including oil and gas) or accounts subject to subsection (5) of Section 9-103, or when the financing statement is filed as a fixture filing (Section 9-313) and the collateral is goods which are or are to become fixtures, then in the office where a mortgage on the real estate [concerned] would be filed or recorded;

  (c) in all other cases, in the office of the Secretary of State and in addition, if the debtor has a place of business in only one county of this state, also in the office of........of such county, or, if the debtor has no place of business in this state, but resides in the state, also in the office of........of the county in which he resides.

Note: *One of the three alternatives should be selected as subsection (1).*

(2) A filing which is made in good faith in an improper place or not in all of the places required by this section is nevertheless effective with regard to any collateral as to which the filing complied with the requirements of this Article and is also effective with regard to collateral covered by the financing statement against any person who has knowledge of the contents of such financing statement.

(3) A filing which is made in the proper place in this State continues effective even though the debtor's residence or place of business or the location of the collateral or its use, whichever controlled the original filing, is thereafter changed.

(4) [The] rules stated in Section 9-103 determine whether filing is necessary in this State.

[(5) Notwithstanding the preceding subsections, and subject to subsection (3) of Section 9-302, the proper place to file in order to perfect a security interest in collateral, including fixtures, of a transmitting utility is the office of the Secretary of State. This filing constitutes a fixture filing (Section 9-313) as to the collateral described therein which is or is to become fixtures.

(6) For the purposes of this section, the residence of an organization is its place of business if it has one or its chief executive office if it has more than one place of business.]

Note: *Subsection (6) should be used only if the state chooses the Second or Third Alternative Subsection (1).*

§ 9-402. Formal Requisites of Financing Statement; Amendments; Mortgage as Financing Statement.—

(1) A financing statement is sufficient if it [gives the names of the debtor and the secured party,] is signed by the debtor, gives an address of the secured party from which information concerning the security interest may be obtained, gives a mailing address of the debtor and contains a statement indicating the types, or describing the items, of collateral. A financing statement may be filed before a security agreement is made or a security interest otherwise attaches. When the financing statement covers crops growing or to be grown [or goods which are or are to become fixtures,] the statement must also contain a description of the real estate concerned. [When the financing statement covers timber to be cut or covers minerals or the like (including oil and gas) or accounts subject to subsection (5) of Section 9-103, or when the financing statement is filed as a fixture filing (Section 9-313) and the collateral is goods which are or are to become fixtures, the statement must also comply with subsection (5).] A copy of the security agreement is sufficient as a financing statement if it contains the above information and is signed by [the debtor. A carbon, photographic or other reproduction of a security agreement or a financing statement is sufficient as a financing statement if the security agreement so provides or if the original has been filed in this state.]

(2) A financing statement which otherwise complies with subsection (1) is sufficient [when] it is signed by the secured party [instead of the debtor] if it is filed to perfect a security interest in

(a) collateral already subject to a security interest in another jurisdiction when it is brouight into this state, [or when the debtor's location is changed to this state.] Such a financing statement must state that the collateral was brought into this state [or that the debtor's location was changed to this state] under such circumstances; [or]

(b) proceeds under Section 9-306 if the security interest in the original collateral was perfected. Such a financing statement must describe the original collateral; [or

(c) collateral as to which the filing has lapsed; or

(d) collateral acquired after a change of name, identity or corporate structure of the debtor (subsection (7).]

(3) A form substantially as follows is sufficient to comply with subsection (1):

Name of debtor (or assignor) ....

Address ....

Name of secured party or assignee) ....

Address ....

1. This financing statement covers the following types (or items) of property:
   (Describe) ....

2. (If collateral is crops) The above described crops are growing or are to be grown on:
   (Describe Real Estate) ....

[3. (If applicable) The above goods are to become fixtures on*]

*Where appropriate substitute either "The above timber is standing on...." or "The above minerals or the like (including oil and gas) or accounts will be financed at the wellhead or minehead of the well or mine located on...."

   [(Describe Real Estate) ....
   and this financing statement is to be filed [for record] in the real estate records. (If the debtor does not have an interest of record) The name of a record owner is] ....

4. (If [proceeds or] products of collateral are claimed) Products of the collateral are also covered.

(use   ....
whichever   Signature of Debtor (or Assignor)
is   ....
applicable) Signature of Secured Party (or Assignee)

(4) [A financing statement may be amended by filing a writing signed by both the debtor and the secured party. An amendment does not extend the period of effectiveness of a financing statement.] If any amendment adds collateral, it is effective as to the added collateral only from the filing date of the amendment. [In this Article, unless the context otherwise requires, the term "financing statement" means the original financing statement and any amendments.

(5) A financing statement covering timber to be cut or covering minerals or the like (including oil and gas) or accounts subject to subsection (5) of Section 9-103, or a financing statement filed as a fixture filing (Section 9-313) where the debtor is not a transmitting utility, must show that it covers this type of collateral, must recite that it is to be filed [for record] in the real estate records, and the financing statement must contain a description of the real estate [sufficient if it were contained in a mortgage of the real estate to give constructive notice of the mortgage under the law of this state.] If the debtor does not have an interest of record in the real estate, the financing statement must show the name of a record owner.

(6) A mortgage is effective as a financing statement filed as a fixture filing from the date of its recording if (a) the goods are described in the mortgage by item or type, (b) the goods are or are to become fixtures related to the real estate described in the mortgage, (c) the mortgage complies with the requirements for a financing statement in this section other than a recital that it is to be filed in the real estate records, and (d) the mortgage is duly recorded. No fee with reference to the financing statement is required other than the regular recording and satisfaction fees with respect to the mortgage.

(7) A financing statement sufficiently shows the name of the debtor if it gives the individual, partnership or corporate name of the debtor, whether or not it adds other trade names or the names of partners. Where the debtor so changes his name or in the case of an organization its name, identity or corporate structure that a filed financing statement becomes seriously misleading, the filing is not effective to perfect a security interest in collateral acquired by the debtor more than four months after the change; unless a new appropriate financing statement is filed before the expiration of that time. A filed financing statement remains effective with respect to collateral transferred by the debtor even though the secured party knows of or consents to the transfer.]

[(8)] A financing statement substantially complying with the requirements of this section is effective even though it contains minor errors which are not seriously misleading.

§ 9-403. What Constitutes Filing; Duration of Filing; Effect of Lapsed Filing; Duties of Filing Officer.—

(1) Presentation for filing of a financing statement and tender of the filing fee or acceptance of the statement by the filing officer constitutes filing under this Article.

[(2) Except as provided in Subsection (6)] a filed financing statement is effective for a period of five years from the date of filing. The effectiveness of a filed financing statement lapses on the expiration of [the five] year period unless a continuation statement is filed prior to the lapse. [If a security interest perfected by filing exists at the time insolvency proceedings are commenced by or against the debtor, the security interest remains perfected until termination of the insolvency proceedings and thereafter for a period of sixty days or until expiration of the five year period, whichever occurs later.] Upon lapse the security interest becomes unperfected, [unless it is perfected without filing. If the security interest becomes unperfected upon lapse, it is deemed to have been unperfected as against a person who became a purchaser or lien creditor before lapse.]

(3) A continuation statement may be filed by the secured party [(i) within six months before and sixty days after a stated maturity date of five years or less, and (ii) otherwise] within six months prior to the expiration of the five year period specified in subsection (2). Any such continuation statement must be signed by the secured party, identify the original statement by file number and state that the original statement is still effective. [A continuation statement signed by a person other than the secured party of record must be accompanied by a separate written statement of assignment signed by the secured party of record and complying with subsection (2) of Section 9-405, including payment of the required fee.] Upon timely filing of the continuation statement, the effectiveness of the original statement is continued for five years after the last date to which the filing was effective whereupon it lapses in the same manner as provided in subsection (2) unless another continuation statement is filed prior to such lapse. Succeeding continuation statements may be filed in the same manner to continue the effectiveness of the original statement. Unless a statute on disposition of public records provides otherwise, the filing officer may remove a lapsed statement from the files and destroy it [immediately if he has retained a microfilm or other photographic record, or in other cases after one year after the lapse. The filing officer shall so arrange matters by physical annexation of financing statements to continuation statements or other related filings, or by other means, that if he physically destroys the financing statements of a period more than five years past, those which have been continued by a continuation statement or which are still effective under subsection (6) shall be retained.]

[(4) Except as provided in subsection (7) a] filing officer shall mark each statement with a [consecutive] file number and with the date and hour of filing and shall hold the statement [or a microfilm or other photographic copy thereof] for public inspection. In addition the filing officer shall index the statements according to the name of the debtor and shall note in the index the file number and the address of the debtor given in the statement.

[(5) The uniform fee for filing and indexing and for stamping a copy furnished by the secured party to show the date and place of filing for an original financing statement or for a continuation statement shall be $........if the statement is in the standard form prescribed by the [Secretary of State] and otherwise shall be $........, plus in each case, if the financing statement is subject to subsection (5) of Section 9-402, $........The uniform fee for each name more than one required to be indexed shall be $........The secured party may at his option show a trade name for any person and an extra uniform indexing fee of $........shall be paid with respect thereto.

(6) If the debtor is a transmitting utility (subsection (5) of Section 9-401) and a filed financing statement so states, it is effective until a termination statement is filed. A real estate mortgage which is effective as a fixture filing under subsection (6) of Section 9-402 remains effective as a fixture filing until the mortgage is released or satisfied of record or its effectiveness otherwise terminates as to the real estate.

(7) When a financing statement covers timber to be cut or covers minerals or the like (including oil and gas) or accounts subject to subsection (5) of Section 9-103, or is filed as a fixture filing, [it shall be filed for record and] the filing officer shall index it under the names of the debtor and any owner of record shown on the financing statement in the same fashion as if they were the mortgagors in a mortgage of the real estate described, and, to the extent that the law of this state provides for indexing of mortgages under the name of the mortgagee, under the name of the secured party as if he were the mortgagee thereunder, or where indexing is by description in the same fashion as if the financing statement were a mortgage of the real estate described.]

§ 9-404. Termination Statement.—

[(1) If a financing statement covering consumer goods is filed on or after........, then within one month or within ten days following written demand by the debtor after there is no outstanding secured obligation and no commitment to make advances, incur obligations or otherwise give value, the secured party must file with each filing officer with whom the financing statement was filed, a termination statement to the effect that he no longer claims a security interest under the financing statement, which shall be identified by file number. In other cases whenever there is no outstanding] secured obligation and no commitment to make advances, incur obligations or otherwise give value, the secured party must on written demand by the debtor send the debtor, [for each filing officer with whom the financing statement was filed,] a [termination] statement [to the effect] that he no longer claims a security interest under the financing statement, which shall be identified by file number. A termination statement signed by a person other than the secured party of record must be accompanied by a [separate written] statement [of assignment signed] by the secured party of record [complying with subsection (2) of Section 9-405, including payment of the required fee.] If the affected secured party fails to [file such a termination statement as required by this subsection, or to] send such a termination statement within ten days after proper demand therefor he shall be liable to the debtor for one hundred dollars, and in addition for any loss caused to the debtor by such failure.

(2) On presentation to the filing officer of such a termination statement he must note it in the index. [If he has received the termination statement in duplicate, he shall return one copy of the termination statement to the secured party stamped to show the time of receipt thereof. If the filing officer has a microfilm or other photographic record of the financing statement, and of any related continuation statement, statement of assignment and statement of release, he may remove the originals from the files at any time after receipt of the termination statement, or if he has no such record, he may remove them from the files at any time after one year after receipt of the termination statement.]

[(3) If the termination statement is in the standard form prescribed by the Secretary of State,] the uniform fee for filing and indexing [the] termination statement shall be $........, [and otherwise shall be $........, plus in each case an additional fee of $........for each name more than one against which the termination statement is required to be indexed.]

Note: *The date to be inserted should be the effective date of the revised Article 9.*

§ 9-405.   Assignment of Security Interest; Duties of Filing Officer; Fees.—

(1) A financing statement may disclose an assignment of a security interest in the collateral described in the [financing] statement by indication in the [financing] statement of the name and address of the assignee or by an assignment itself or a copy thereof on the face or back of the statement. On presentation to the filing officer of such a financing statement the filing officer shall mark the same as provided in Section 9-403(4). The uniform fee for filing, indexing and furnishing filing data for a financing standard form prescribed by the Secretary of State and otherwise shall be $........, plus an additional fee of $........for each name more than one against which the financing statement is required to be indexed.

(2) A secured party may assign of record all or a part of his rights under a financing statement by the filing [in the place where the original financing statement was filed] of a separate written statement of assignment signed by the secured party of record and setting forth the name of the secured party of record and the debtor, the file number and the date of filing of the financing statement and the name and address of the assignee and containing a description of the collateral assigned. A copy of the assignment is sufficient as a separate statement if it complies with the preceding sentence. On presentation to the filing officer of such a separate statement, the filing officer shall mark such separate statement with the date and hour of the filing. He shall note the assignment on the index of the financing statement [or in the case of a fixture filing, or a filing covering timber to be cut, or covering minerals or the like (including oil and gas) or accounts subject to subsection (5) of Section 9-103, he shall index the assignment under the name of the assignor as grantor and, to the extent that the law of this state provides for indexing the assignment of a mortgage under the name of the assignee. The uniform fee for filing, indexing and furnishing filing data about such a separate statement of assignment shall be $........if the statement is in the standard form prescribed by the Secretary of State and otherwise shall be $........, plus in each case an additional fee of $........for each name more than one against which the statement of assignment is required to be indexed. Notwithstanding the provisions of this subsection, an assignment of record of a security interest in a fixture contained in a mortgage effective as a fixture filing (subsection (6) of Section 9-402) may be made only by an assignment of the mortgage in the manner provided by the law of this state other than this Act.]

(3) After the disclosure or filing of an assignment under this section, the assignee is the secured party of record.

§ 9-406.   Release of Collateral; Duties of Filing Officer; Fees.—

A secured party of record may by his signed statement release all or a part of a collateral described in a filed financing statement. The statement of release is sufficient if it contains a description of the collateral being released, the name and address of the debtor, the name and address of the secured party, and the file number of the financing statement. [A statement of release signed by a person other than the secured party of record must be accompanied by a separate written statement of assignment signed by the secured party of record and complying with subsection (2) of Section 9-405, including payment of the required fee.] Upon presentation of such a statement [of release] to the filing officer he shall mark the statement with the hour and date of filing and shall note the same upon the margin of the index of the filing of the financing statement. The uniform fee for filing and noting such a statement of release shall be $........[if the statement is in the standard form prescribed by the [Secretary of State] and otherwise shall be $........,plus in each case an additional fee of $........for each name more than one against which the statement of release is required to be indexed.

[§ 9-407.   Information From Filing Officer.]*—

[(1) If the person filing any financing statement, termination statement, statement of assignment, or statement release, furnishes the filing officer a copy thereof, the filing officer shall upon request note upon the copy the file number and date and hour of the filing of the original and deliver or send the copy to such person.]

[(2) Upon request of any person, the filing officer shall issue his certificate showing whether there is on file on the date and hour stated therein, any presently effective financing statement naming a particular debtor and any statement of assignment thereof and if there is, giving the date and hour of filing of each such statement and the names and addresses of each secured party therein. The uniform fee for such a certificate shall be $........if the request for the certificate is in the standard form prescribed by the [Secretary of State] and otherwise shall be $........ Upon request the filing officer shall furnish a copy of any filed financing statement or statement of assignment for a uniform fee of $........per page.]

*This section optional.

§ 9-408.   Financing Statements Covering Consigned or Leased Goods.—

*A consignor or lessor of goods may file a financing statement using the terms "consignor," "consignee," "lessor," "lessee" or the like instead of the terms specified in Section 9-402. The provisions of this Part shall apply as appropriate to such a financing statement but its filing shall not of itself be a factor in determining whether or not the consignment or lease is intended as security (Section 1-201(37)). However, if it is determined for other reasons that the consignment or lease is so intended, a security interest of the consignor or lessor which attaches to the consigned or leased goods is perfected by such filing.

*This section new in 1972.

PART 5

Default

§ 9-501.   Default; Procedure When Security Agreement Covers Both Real and Personal Property.—

(1) When a debtor is in default under a security agreement, a secured party has the rights and remedies provided in this Part and except as limited by subsection (3) those provided in the security agreement. He may reduce his claim to judgment, foreclose or otherwise enforce the security interest by any available judicial procedure. If the collateral is documents the secured party may proceed either as to the documents or as to the goods covered thereby. A secured party in possession has the rights, remedies and duties provided in Section 9-207. The rights and remedies referred to in this subsection are cumulative.

(2) After default, the debtor has the rights and remedies provided in this Part, those provided in the security agreement and those provided in Section 9-207.

(3) To the extent that they give rights to the debtor and impose duties on the secured party, the rules stated in the subsections referred to below may not be waived or varied except as provided with respect to compulsory disposition of collateral [(subsection (3) of Section 9-504 and] Section 9-505) and with respect to redemption of collateral (Section 9-506) but the parties may by agreement determine the standards by which the fulfillment of these rights and duties is to be measured if such standards are not manifestly unreasonable:

(a) subsection (2) of Section 9-502 and subsection (2) of Section 9-504 insofar as they require accounting for surplus proceeds of collateral;

(b) subsection (3) of Section 9-504 and subsection (1) of Section 9-505 which deal with disposition of collateral;

(c) subsection (2) of Section 9-505 which deals with acceptance of collateral as discharge of obligation;

(d) Section 9-506 which deals with redemption of collateral; and

(e) subsection (1) of Section 9-507 which deals with the secured party's liability for failure to comply with this Part.

(4) If the security agreement covers both real and personal property, the secured party may proceed under this Part as to the personal property or he may proceed as to both the real and the personal property in accordance with his rights and remedies in respect to the real property in which case the provisions of this Part do not apply.

(5) When a secured party has reduced his claim to judgment the lien of any levy which may be made upon his collateral by virtue of any execution based upon the judgment shall relate back to the date of the perfection of the security interest in such collateral. A judicial sale, pursuant to such execution, is a foreclosure of the security interest by judicial procedure within the meaning of this Section, and the secured party may purchase at the sale and thereafter hold the collateral free of any other requirements of this Article.

§ 9-502.   Collection Rights of Secured Party.—

(1) When so agreed and in any event on default the secured party is entitled to notify an account debtor or the obligor on an instrument to make payment to him whether or not the assignor was theretofore making collections on the collateral, and also to take control of any proceeds to which he is entitled under Section 9-306.

(2) A secured party who by agreement is entitled to charge back uncollected collateral or otherwise to full or limited recourse against the debtor and who undertakes to collect from the account debtors or obligors must proceed in a commercially reasonable manner and may deduct his reasonable expenses of realization from the collections. If the security agreement secures an indebtedness, the secured party must account to the debtor for any surplus, and unless otherwise agreed, the debtor is liable for any deficiency. But, if the underlying transaction was a sale of accounts or chattel paper, the debtor is entitled to any surplus or is liable for any deficiency only if the security agreement so provides.

§ 9-503.   Secured Party's Right to Take Possession After Default.—Unless otherwise agreed a secured party has on default the right to take possession of the collateral. In taking possession a secured party may proceed without judicial process if this can be done without breach of the peace or may proceed by action.

If the security agreement so provides the secured party may require the debtor to assemble the collateral and make it available to the secured party at a place to be designated by the secured party which is reasonably convenient to both parties. Without removal a secured party may render equipment unusable, and may dispose of collateral on the debtor's premises under Section 9-504.

§ 9-504.   Secured Party's Right to Dispose of Collateral After Default; Effect of Disposition.—

(1) A secured party after default may sell, lease or otherwise dispose of any or all of the collateral in its then condition or following any commercially reasonable preparation or processing. Any sale of goods is subject to the Article on Sales (Article 2). The proceeds of disposition shall be applied in the order following to

(a) the reasonable expenses of retaking, holding, preparing for sale [or lease,] selling, [leasing] and the like and, to the extent provided for in the agreement and not prohibited by law, the reasonable attorneys' fees and legal expenses incurred by the secured party;

(b) the satisfaction of indebtedness secured by the security interest under which the disposition is made;

(c) the satisfaction of indebtedness secured by any subordinate security interest in the collateral if written notification of demand therefor is received before distribution of the proceeds is completed. If requested by the secured party, the holder of a subordinate security interest must seasonably furnish reasonable proof of his interest, and unless he does so, the secured party need not comply with his demand.

(2) If the security interest secures an indebtedness, the secured party must account to the debtor for any surplus, and, unless otherwise agreed, the debtor is liable for any deficiency. But if the underlying transaction was a sale of accounts or chattel paper, the debtor is entitled to any surplus or is liable for any deficiency only if the security agreement so provides.

(3) Disposition of the collateral may be by public or private proceedings and may be made by way of one or more contracts. Sale or other disposition may be as a unit or in parcels and at any time and place and on any terms but every aspect of the disposition including the method, manner, time, place and terms must be commercially reasonable. Unless collateral is perishable or threatens to decline speedily in value or is of a type customarily sold on a recognized market, reasonable notification of the time and place of any public sale or reasonable notification of the time after which any private sale or other intended disposition is to be made shall be sent by the secured party to the debtor, if he has not signed after default a statement renouncing or modifying his right to notification of sale. In the case of consumer goods no other notification need be sent. In other cases notification shall be sent to any other secured party from whom the secured party has received (before sending his notification to the debtor or before the debtor's renunciation of his rights) written notice of a claim of an interest in the collateral. The secured party may buy at any public sale and if the collateral is of a type customarily sold in a recognized market or is of a type which is the subject of widely distributed standard price quotations he may buy at private sale.

(4) When collateral is disposed of by a secured party after default, the disposition transfers to a purchaser for value all of the debtor's rights therein, discharges the security interest under which it is made and any security interest or lien subordinate thereto. The purchaser takes free of all such rights and interests even though the secured party fails to comply with the requirements of this Part or of any judicial proceedings

(a) in the case of a public sale, if the purchaser has no knowledge of any defects in the sale and if he does not buy in collusion with the secured party, other bidders or the person conducting the sale; or

(b) in any other case, if the purchaser acts in good faith.

(5) A person who is liable to a secured party under a guaranty, indorsement, repurchase agreement or the like and who receives a transfer of collateral from the secured party or is subrogated to his rights has thereafter the rights and duties of the secured party. Such a transfer of collateral is not a sale or disposition of the collateral under this Article.

§ 9-505. Compulsory Disposition of Collateral; Acceptance of the Collateral as Discharge of Obligation.—

(1) If the debtor has paid 60 percent of the cash price in the case of a purchase money security interest in consumer goods or 60 percent of the loan in the case of another security interest in consumer goods, and has not signed after default a statement renouncing or modifying his rights under this Part a secured party who has taken possession of collateral must dispose of it under Section 9-504 and if he fails to do so within ninety days after he takes possession the debtor at his option may recover in conversion or under Section 9-507(1) on secured party's liability.

(2) In any other case involving consumer goods or any other collateral a secured party in possession may, after default, propose to retain the collateral in satisfaction of the obligation. Written notice of such proposal shall be sent to the debtor [if he has not signed after default a statement renouncing or modifying his rights under this subsection. In the case of consumer goods no other notice need be given. In other cases notice shall be sent to any other secured party from whom the secured party has received (before sending his notice to the debtor or before the debtor's renunciation of his rights) written notice of a claim of an interest in the collateral. If the secured party receives objection in writing from a person entitled to receive notification within twenty-one days after the notice was sent, the secured party must dispose of the collateral under Section 9-504.] In the absence of such written objection the secured party may retain the collateral in satisfaction of the debtor's obligation.

§ 9-506. Debtor's Right to Redeem Collateral.—

At any time before the secured party has disposed of collateral or entered into a contract for its disposition under Section 9-504 or before the obligation has been discharged under Section 9-505(2) the debtor or any other secured party may unless otherwise agreed in writing after default redeem the collateral by tendering fulfillment of all obligations secured by the collateral as well as the expenses reasonably incurred by the secured party in retaking, holding, and preparing the collateral for disposition, in arranging for the sale, and to the extent provided in the agreement and not prohibited by law, his reasonable attorneys' fees and legal expenses.

§ 9-507. Secured Party's Liability for Failure to Comply With This Part.—

(1) If it is established that the secured party is not proceeding in accordance with the provisions of this Part disposition may be ordered or restrained on appropriate terms and conditions. If the disposition has occurred the debtor or any person entitled to notification or whose security interest has been made known to the secured party prior to the disposition has a right to recover from the secured party any loss caused by a failure to comply with the provisions of this Part. If the collateral is consumer goods, the debtor has a right to recover in any event an amount not less than the credit service charge plus 10 percent of the principal amount of the debt or the time price differential plus 10 percent of the cash price.

(2) The fact that a better price could have been obtained by a sale at a different time or in a different method from that selected by the secured party is not of itself sufficient to establish that the sale was not

made in a commercially reasonable manner. If the secured party either sells the collateral in the usual manner in any recognized market therefor or if he sells at the price current in such market at the time of his sale or if he has otherwise sold in conformity with reasonable commercial practices among dealers in the type of property sold he has sold in a commercially reasonable manner. The principles stated in the two preceding sentences with respect to sales also apply as may be appropriate to other types of disposition. A disposition which has been approved in any judicial proceeding or by any bona fide creditors' committee or representative of creditors shall conclusively be deemed to be commercially reasonable, but this sentence does not indicate that any such approval must be obtained in any case nor does it indicate that any disposition not so approved is not commercially reasonable.

Part I

Preliminary Provisions

§ 1. **Name of Act.**—This Act may be cited as Uniform Partnership Act.

§ 2. **Definition of Terms.**—In this Act, "Court" includes every court and judge having jurisdiction in the case.

"Business" includes every trade, occupation, or profession.

"Person" includes individuals, partnerships, corporations, and other associations.

"Bankrupt" includes bankrupt under the Federal Bankruptcy Act or insolvent under any state insolvent act.

"Conveyance" includes every assignment, lease, mortgage, or encumbrance.

"Real property" includes land and any interest or estate in land.

§ 3. **Interpretation of Knowledge and Notice.**—(1) A person has "knowledge" of a fact within the meaning of this Act not only when he has actual knowledge thereof, but also when he has knowledge of such other facts as in the circumstances shows bad faith.

(2) A person has "notice" of a fact within the meaning of this Act when the person who claims the benefit of the notice:

(a) States the fact to such person, or

(b) Delivers through the mail, or by other means of communication, a written statement of the fact to such person or to a proper person at his place of business or residence.

§ 4. **Rules of Construction.**—(1) The rule that statutes in derogation of the common law are to be strictly construed shall have no application to this Act.

(2) The law of estoppel shall apply under this Act.

(3) The law of agency shall apply under this Act.

(4) This Act shall be so interpreted and construed as to effect its general purpose to make uniform the law of those states which enact it.

(5) This Act shall not be construed so as to impair the obligations of any contract existing when the Act goes into effect, nor to affect any action or proceedings begun or right accrued before this Act takes effect.

§ 5. **Rules for Cases not Provided for in this Act.**—In any case not provided for in this Act the rules of law and equity, including the law merchant, shall govern.

Part II

Nature of a Partnership

§ 6. **Partnership Defined.**—(1) A partnership is an association of two or more persons to carry on as co-owners a business for profit.

(2) But any association formed under any other statute of this state, or any statute adopted by authority, other than the authority of this state, is not a partnership under this act, unless such association would have been a partnership in this state prior to the adoption of this act; but this act shall apply to limited partnerships except in so far as the statutes relating to such partnerships are inconsistent herewith.

§ 7. **Rules for Determining the Existence of a Partnership.**—In determining whether a partnership exists, these rules shall apply:

(1) Except as provided by § 16 persons who are not partners as to each other are not partners as to third persons

(2) Joint tenancy, tenancy in common, tenancy by the entireties, joint property, common property, or part ownership does not of itself establish a partnership, whether such co-owners do or do not share any profits made by the use of the property.

(3) The sharing of gross returns does not of itself establish a partnership, whether or not the persons sharing them have a joint or common right or interest in any property from which the returns are derived.

(4) The receipt by a person of a share of the profits of a business is prima facie evidence that he is a partner in the business, but no such inference shall be drawn if such profits were received in payment:

(a) As a debt by installments or otherwise.

(b) As wages of an employee or rent to a landlord,

(c) As an annuity to a widow or representative of a deceased partner,

(d) As interest on a loan, though the amount of payment vary with the profits of the business.

(e) As the consideration for the sale of a good-will of a business or other property by installments or otherwise.

§ 8. **Partnership Property.**—(1) All property originally brought into the partnership stock or subsequently acquired by purchase or otherwise, on account of the partnership, is partnership property.

(2) Unless the contrary intention appears, property acquired with partnership funds is partnership property.

(3) Any estate in real property may be acquired in the partnership name. Title so acquired can be conveyed only in the partnership name.

(4) A conveyance to a partnership in the partnership name, though without words of inheritance, passes the entire estate of the grantor unless a contrary intent appears.

Part III

Relations of Partners to Persons Dealing With the Partnership

§ 9. **Partner Agent of Partnership as to Partnership Business.**—(1) Every partner is an agent of the partnership for the purpose of its business, and the act of every partner, including the execution in the partnership name of any instrument, for apparently carrying on in the usual way the business of the partnership of which he is a member binds the partnership, unless the partner so acting has in fact no authority to act for the partnership in the particular matter, and the person with whom he is dealing has knowledge of the fact that he has no such authority.

(2) An act of a partner which is not apparently for the carrying on of the business of the partnership in the usual way does not bind the partnership unless authorized by the other partners.

(3) Unless authorized by the other partners or unless they have abandoned the business, one or more but less than all the partners have no authority to:

(a) Assign the partnership property in trust for creditors or on the assignee's promise to pay the debts of the partnership,

(b) Dispose of the good-will of the business,

(c) Do any other act which would make it impossible to carry on the ordinary business of a partnership,

(d) Confess a judgment,

(e) Submit a partnership claim or liability in arbitration or reference.

(4) No act of a partner in contravention of a restriction on authority shall bind the partnership to persons having knowledge of the restriction.

§ 10. **Conveyance of Real Property of the Partnership.**—(1) Where title to real property is in the partnership name, any partner may convey title to such property by a conveyance executed in the partnership name; but the partnership may recover such property unless the partner's act binds the partnership under the provisions of paragraph (1) of §9 or unless such property has been conveyed by the grantee or a person claiming through such grantee to a holder for value without knowledge that the partner, in making the conveyance, has exceeded his authority.

(2) Where title to real property is in the name of the partnership, a conveyance executed by a partner, in his own name, passes the equitable interest of the partnership, provided the act is one within the authority of the partner under the provisions of paragraph (1) of §9.

(3) Where the title to real property is in the name of one or more but not all the partners, and the record does not disclose the right of the partnership, the partners in whose name the title stands may convey title to such property, but the partnership may recover such property if the partners' act does not bind the partnership under the provisions of paragraph (1) of §9, unless the purchaser or his assignee, is a holder for value, without knowledge.

(4) Where the title to real property is in the name of one or more or all the partners, or in a third person in trust for the partnership, a conveyance executed by a partner in the partnership name, or in his own name, passes the equitable interest of the partnership, provided the act is one within the authority of the partner under the provisions of paragraph (1) of §9.

(5) Where the title to real property is in the names of all the partners a conveyance executed by all the partners passes all their rights in such property.

§ 11. **Partnership Bound by Admission of Partner.**—An admission or representation made by any partner concerning partnership affairs within the scope of his authority as conferred by this Act is evidence against the partnership.

§ 12. **Partnership Charged with Knowledge of or Notice to Partner.**—Notice to any partner of any matter relating to partnership affairs, and the knowledge of the partner acting in the particular matter, acquired while a partner or then present to his mind, and the knowledge of any other partner who reasonably could and should have communicated it to the acting partner, operate as notice to or knowledge of the partnership, except in the case of a fraud on the partnership committed by or with the consent of that partner.

§ 13. **Partnership Bound by Partner's Wrongful Act.**—Where, by any wrongful act or omission of any partner acting in the ordinary course of the business of the partnership or with the authority of his co-partners, loss or injury is caused to any person, not being a partner in the partnership, or any penalty is incurred, the partnership is liable therefor to the same extent as the partner so acting or omitting to act.

§ 14. **Partnership Bound by Partner's Breach of Trust.**—The partnership is bound to make good the loss:

(a) Where one partner acting within the scope of his apparent authority receives money or property of a third person and misapplies it; and

(b) Where the partnership in the course of its business receives money or property of a third person and the money or property so received is misapplied by any partner while it is in the custody of the partnership.

§ 15. **Nature of Partner's Liability.**—All partners are liable:

(a) Jointly and severally for everything chargeable to the partnership under §§13 and 14.

(b) Jointly for all other debts and obligations of the partnership; but any partner may enter into a separate obligation to perform a partnership contract.

§ 16. **Partner by Estoppel.**—(1) When a person, by words spoken or written or by conduct, represents himself, or consents to another representing him to any one, as a partner in an existing partnership or with one or more persons not actual partners, he is liable to any such person to whom such representation has been made, who has, on the faith of such representation, given credit to the actual or apparent partnership, and if he has made such representation or consented to its being made in a public manner he is liable to such person, whether the representation has or has not been made or communicated to such person so giving credit by or with the knowledge of the apparent partner making the representation or consenting to its being made:

(a) When a partnership liability results, he is liable as though he were an actual member of the partnership.

(b) When no partnership liability results, he is liable jointly with the other persons, if any, so consenting to the contract or representation as to incur liability, otherwise separately.

(2) When a person has been thus represented to be a partner in an existing partnership, or with one or more persons not actual partners, he is an agent of the persons consenting to such representation to bind them to the same extent and in the same manner as though he were a partner in fact, with respect to persons who rely upon the representation. Where all the members of the existing partnership consent to the representation, a partnership act or obligation results; but in all other cases it is the joint act or obligation of the person acting and the persons consenting to the representation.

§ 17. **Liability of Incoming Partner.**—A person admitted as a partner into an existing partnership is liable for all the obligations of the partnership arising before his admission as though he had been a partner when such obligations were incurred, except that this liability shall be satisfied only out of partnership property.

Part IV

Relations of Partners to One Another

§ 18. **Rules Determining Rights and Duties of Partners.**—The rights and duties of the partners in relation to the partnership shall be determined, subject to any agreement between them, by the following rules:

(a) Each partner shall be repaid his contributions, whether by way of capital or advances to the partnership property and share equally in the profits and surplus remaining after all liabilities, including those to partners, are satisfied; and must contribute towards the losses, whether of capital or otherwise, sustained by the partnership according to his share in the profits.

(b) The partnership must indemnify every partner in respect of payments made and personal liabilities reasonably incurred by him in the ordinary and proper conduct of its business, or for the preservation of its business or property.

(c) A partner, who in aid of the partnership makes any

payment or advance beyond the amount of capital which he agreed to contribute, shall be paid interest from the date of the payment or advance.

(d) A partner shall receive interest on the capital contributed by him only from the date when repayment should be made.

(e) All partners have equal rights in the management and conduct of the partnership business.

(f) No partner is entitled to remuneration for acting in the partnership business, except that a surviving partner is entitled to reasonable compensation for his services in winding up the partnership affairs.

(g) No person can become a member of a partnership without the consent of all the partners.

(h) Any difference arising as to ordinary matters connected with the partnership business may be decided by a majority of the partners; but no act in contravention of any agreement between the partners may be done rightfully without the consent of all the partners.

§ 19. **Partnership Books.**—The partnership books shall be kept, subject to any agreement between the partners, at the principal place of business of the partnership, and every partner shall at all times have access to and may inspect and copy any of them.

§ 20. **Duty of Partners to Render Information.**—Partners shall render on demand true and full information of all things affecting the partnership to any partner or the legal representative of any deceased partner or partner under legal disability.

§ 21. **Partner Accountable as a Fiduciary.**—(1) Every partner must account to the partnership for any benefit, and hold as trustee for it any profits derived by him without the consent of the other partners from any transaction connected with the formation, conduct, or liquidation of the partnership or from any use by him of its property.

(2) This section applies also to the representatives of a deceased partner engaged in the liquidation of the affairs of the partnership as the personal representatives of the last surviving partner.

§ 22. **Right to an Account.**—Any partner shall have the right to a formal account as to partnership affairs:

(a) If he is wrongfully excluded from the partnership business or possession of its property by his co-partners.

(b) If the right exists under the terms of any agreement,

(c) As provided by §21,

(d) Whenever other circumstances render it just and reasonable.

§ 23. **Continuation of Partnership Beyond Fixed Term.**—(1) When a partnership for a fixed term or particular undertaking is continued after the termination of such term or particular undertaking without any express agreement, the rights and duties of the partners remain the same as they were at such termination, so far as is consistent with a partnership at will.

(2) A continuation of the business by the partners or such of them as habitually acted therein during the term, without any settlement or liquidation of the partnership affairs, is prima facie evidence of a continuation of the partnership.

Part V

Property Rights of a Partner

§ 24. **Extent of Property Rights of a Partner.**—The property rights of a partner are (1) his rights in specific partnership property, (2) his interest in the partnership, and (3) his right to participate in the management.

§ 25. **Nature of a Partner's Right in Specific Partnership Property.**—(1) A partner is co-owner with his partners of specific partnership property holding as a tenant in partnership.

(2) The incidents of this tenancy are such that:

(a) A partner, subject to the provisions of this Act and to any agreement between the partners, has an equal right with his partners to possess specific partnership property for partnership purposes; but he has no right to possess such property for any other purpose without the consent of his partners.

(b) A partner's right in specific partnership property is not assignable except in connection with the assignment of rights of all the partners in the same property.

(c) A partner's right in specific partnership property is not subject to attachment or execution, except on a claim against the partnership. When partnership property is attached for a partnership debt the partners, or any of them, or the representatives of a deceased partner, cannot claim any right under the homestead or exemption laws.

(d) On the death of a partner his right in specific partnership property vests in the surviving partner or partners, except where the deceased was the last surviving partner, when his right in such property vests in his legal representative. Such surviving partner or partners, or the legal representative of the last surviving partner, has no right to possess the partnership property for any but a partnership purpose.

(e) A partner's right in specific partnership property is not subject to dower, curtesy, or allowances to widows, heirs, or next of kin.

§ 26. **Nature of Partner's Interest in the Partnership.**—A partner's interest in the partnership is his share of the profits and surplus, and the same is personal property.

§ 27. **Assignment of Partner's Interest.**—(1) A conveyance by a partner of his interest in the partnership does not of itself dissolve the partnership, nor, as against the other partners in the absence of agreement, entitle the assignee, during the continuance of the partnership to interfere in the management or administration of the partnership business or affairs, or to require any information or account of partnership transactions, or to inspect the partnership books; but it merely entitles the assignee to receive in accordance with his contract the profits to which the assigning partner would otherwise be entitled.

(2) In case of a dissolution of the partnership, the assignee is entitled to receive his assignor's interest and may require an account from the date only of the last account agreed to by all the partners.

§ 28. **Partner's Interest Subject to Charging Order.**—(1) On due application to a competent court by any judgment creditor of a partner, the court which entered the judgment, order, or decree, or any other court, may charge the interest of the debtor partner with payment of the unsatisfied amount of such judgment debt with interest thereon; and may then or later appoint a receiver of his share of the profits, and of any other money due or to fall due to him in respect of the partnership, and make all other orders, directions, accounts and inquiries which the debtor partner might have made, or which the circumstances of the case may require.

(2) The interest charged may be redeemed at any time before foreclosure, or in case of a sale being directed by the court may be purchased without thereby causing a dissolution:

(a) With separate property, by any one or more of the partners, or

(b) With partnership property, by any one or more of the partners with the consent of all the partners whose interests are not so charged or sold.

(3) Nothing in this Act shall be held to deprive a partner of his right, if any, under the exemption laws, as regards his interest in the partnership.

Part VI

Dissolution and Winding Up

§ 29. Dissolution Defined.—The dissolution of a partnership is the change in the relation of the partners caused by any partner ceasing to be associated in the carrying on as distinguished from the winding up of the business.

§ 30. Partnership Not Terminated by Dissolution.—On dissolution the partnership is not terminated, but continues until the winding up of partnership affairs is completed.

§ 31. Causes of Dissolution.—Dissolution is caused:
(1) Without violation of the agreement between the partners:
    (a) By the termination of the definite term or particular undertaking specified in the agreement,
    (b) By the express will of any partner when no definite term or particular undertaking is specified,
    (c) By the express will of all the partners who have not assigned their interests or suffered them to be charged for their separate debts, either before or after the termination of any specified term or particular undertaking,
    (d) By the explusion of any partner from the business bona fide in accordance with such a power conferred by the agreement between the partners;
(2) In contravention of the agreement between the partners, where the circumstances do not permit a dissolution under any other provision of this section, by the express will of any partner at any time;
(3) By any event which makes it unlawful for the business of the partnership to be carried on or for the members to carry it on in partnership;
(4) By the death of any partner;
(5) By the bankruptcy of any partner or the partnership;
(6) By decree of court under §32.

§ 32. Dissolution by Decree of Court.—(1) On application by or for a partner the court shall decree a dissolution whenever:
    (a) A partner has been declared a lunatic in any judicial proceeding or is shown to be of unsound mind,
    (b) A partner becomes in any other way incapable of performing his part of the partnership contract,
    (c) A partner has been guilty of such conduct as tends to affect prejudicially the carrying on of the business,
    (d) A partner wilfully or persistently commits a breach of the partnership agreement, or otherwise so conducts himself in matters relating to the partnership business that it is not reasonably practicable to carry on the business in partnership with him.
    (e) The business of the partnership can only be carried on at a loss,
    (f) Other circumstances render a dissolution equitable.
(2) On the application of the purchaser of a partner's interest under §§27 or 28:
    (a) After the termination of the specified term or particular undertaking,
    (b) At any time if the partnership was a partnership at will when the interest was assigned or when the charging order was issued.

§ 33. General Effect of Dissolution on Authority of Partner.—Except so far as may be necessary to wind up partnership affairs or to complete transactions begun but not then finished, dissolution terminates all authority of any partner to act for the partnership,
(1) With respect to the partners,
    (a) When the dissolution is not by the act, bankruptcy or death of a partner; or
    (b) When the dissolution is by such act, bankruptcy or

death of a partner, in cases where §34 so requires.
(2) With respect to persons not partners, as declared in §35.

§ 34. Right of Partner to Contribution From Co-partners After Dissolution.—Where the dissolution is caused by the act, death or bankruptcy of a partner, each partner is liable to his co-partners for his share of any liability created by any partner acting for the partnership as if the partnership had not been dissolved unless:
    (a) The dissolution being by act of any partner, the partner acting for the partnership had knowledge of the dissolution, or
    (b) The dissolution being by the death or bankruptcy of a partner, the partner acting for the partnership had knowledge or notice of the death or bankruptcy.

§ 35. Power of Partner to Bind Partnership to Third Persons After Dissolution.—(1) After dissolution a partner can bind the partnership except as provided in Paragraph (3)
    (a) By any act appropriate for winding up partnership affairs or completing transactions unfinished at dissolution;
    (b) By any transaction which would bind the partnership if dissolution had not taken place, provided the other party to the transaction:
        (I) Had extended credit to the partnership prior to dissolution and had no knowledge or notice of the dissolution; or
        (II) Though he had not so extended credit, had nevertheless known of the partnership prior to dissolution, and, having no knowledge or notice of dissolution, the fact of dissolution had not been advertised in a newspaper of general circulation in the place (or in each place if more than one) at which the partnership business was regularly carried on.
(2) The liability of a partner under paragraph (1b) shall be satisfied out of partnership assets alone when such partner had been prior to dissolution:
    (a) Unknown as a partner to the person with whom the contract is made; and
    (b) So far unknown and inactive in partnership affairs that the business reputation of the partnership could not be said to have been in any degree due to his connection with it.
(3) The partnership is in no case bound by any act of a partner after dissolution:
    (a) Where the partnership is dissolved because it is unlawful to carry on the business, unless the act is appropriate for winding up partnership affairs; or
    (b) Where the partner has become bankrupt; or
    (c) Where the partner has no authority to wind up partnership affairs; except by a transaction with one who:
        (I) Had extended credit to the partnership prior to dissolution and had no knowledge or notice of his want of authority; or
        (II) Had not extended credit to the partnership prior to dissolution, and, having no knowledge or notice of his want of authority, the fact of his want of authority has not been advertised in the manner provided for advertising the fact of dissolution in paragraph (1bII).
(4) Nothing in this section shall affect the liability under §16 of any person who after dissolution represents himself or consents to another representing him as a partner in a partnership engaged in carrying on business.

§ 36. Effect of Dissolution on Partner's Existing Liability.—(1) The dissolution of the partnership does not of itself discharge the existing liability of any partner.
(2) A partner is discharged from any existing liability upon dissolution of the partnership by an agreement to that effect between himself, the partnership creditor and the person or partnership continuing the business; and such agreement may be inferred from the course of dealing between the creditor having knowledge of the dissolution and the person or partnership continuing the business.

(3) Where a person agrees to assume the existing obligations of a dissolved partnership, the partners whose obligations have been assumed shall be discharged from any liability to any creditor of the partnership who, knowing of the agreement, consents to a material alteration in the nature or time of payment of such obligations.

(4) The individual property of a deceased partner shall be liable for all obligations of the partnership incurred while he was a partner but subject to the prior payment of his separate debts.

§ 37. **Right to Wind Up.**—Unless otherwise agreed the partners who have not wrongfully dissolved the partnership or the legal representative of the last surviving partner, not bankrupt, has the right to wind up the partnership affairs; provided, however, that any partner, his legal representative or his assignee, upon cause shown, may obtain winding up by the court.

§ 38. **Rights of Partners to Application of Partnership Property.** —(1) When dissolution is caused in any way, except in contravention of the partnership agreement, each partner as against his co-partners and all persons claiming through them in respect of their interests in the partnership, unless otherwise agreed, may have the partnership property applied to discharge its liabilities, and the surplus applied to pay in cash the net amount owing to the respective partners. But if dissolution is caused by expulsion of a partner, bona fide under the partnership agreement and if the expelled partner is discharged from all partnership liabilities, either by payment or agreement under §36 (2), he shall receive in cash only the net amount due him from the partnership.

(2) When dissolution is caused in contravention of the partnership agreement the rights of the partners shall be as follows:

(a) Each partner who has not caused dissolution wrongfully shall have:

(I) All the rights specified in paragraph (1) of this section, and

(II) The right, as against each partner who has caused the dissolution wrongfully, to damages for breach of the agreement.

(b) The partners who have not caused the dissolution wrongfully, if they all desire to continue the business in the same name, either by themselves or jointly with others, may do so, during the agreed term for the partnership and for that purpose may possess the partnership property, provided they secure the payment by bond approved by the court, or pay to any partner who has caused the dissolution wrongfully, the value of his interest in the partnership at the dissolution, less any damages recoverable under clause (2aII) of the section, and in like manner indemnify him against all present or future partnership liabilities.

(c) A partner who has caused the dissolution wrongfully shall have:

(I) If the business is not continued under the provisions of paragraph (2b) all the rights of a partner under paragraph (1), subject to clause (2aII), of this section,

(II) If the business is continued under paragraph (2b) of this section the right as against his co-partners and all claiming through them in respect of their interests in the partnership, to have the value of his interest in the partnership, less any damages caused to his co-partners by the dissolution, ascertained and paid him in cash, or the payment secured by bond approved by the court, and to be released from all existing liabilities of the partnership; but in ascertaining the value of the partner's interest the value of the good-will of the business shall not be considered.

§ 39. **Rights Where Partnership is Dissolved for Fraud or Misrepresentation.**—Where a partnership contract is rescinded on the ground of the fraud or misrepresentation of one of the parties thereto, the party entitled to rescind is, without prejudice to any other right, entitled:

(a) To a lien on, or right of retention of, the surplus of the partnership property after satisfying the partnership liabilities to third persons for any sum of money paid by him for the purchase of an interest in the partnership and for any capital or advances contributed by him; and

(b) To stand, after all liabilities to third persons have been satisfied, in the place of the creditors of the partnership for any payments made by him in respect of the partnership liabilities; and

(c) To be indemnified by the person guilty of the fraud or making the representation against all debts and liabilities of the partnership.

§ 40. **Rules for Distribution.**—In settling accounts between the partners after dissolution, the following rules shall be observed, subject to any agreement to the contrary:

(a) The assets of the partnership are:

(I) The partnership property,

(II) The contributions of the partners necessary for the payment of all the liabilities specified in clause (b) of this paragraph.

(b) The liabilities of the partnership shall rank in order of payment, as follows:

(I) Those owing to creditors other than partners,

(II) Those owing to partners other than for capital and profits,

(III) Those owing to partners in respect of capital,

(IV) Those owing to partners in respect of profits.

(c) The assets shall be applied in the order of their declaration in clause (a) of this paragraph to the satisfaction of the liabilities.

(d) The partners shall contribute, as provided by §18 (a) the amount necessary to satisfy the liabilities; but if any, but not all, of the partners are insolvent, or, not being subject to process, refuse to contribute, the other partners shall contribute their share of the liabilities, and, in the relative proportions in which they share the profits, the additional amount necessary to pay the liabilities.

(e) An assignee for the benefit of creditors or any person appointed by the court shall have the right to enforce the contributions specified in clause (d) of this paragraph.

(f) Any partner or his legal representative shall have the right to enforce the contributions specified in clause (d) of this paragraph, to the extent of the amount which he has paid in excess of his share of the liability.

(g) The individual property of a deceased partner shall be liable for the contributions specified in clause (d) of this paragraph.

(h) When partnership property and the individual properties of the partners are in possession of a court for distribution, partnership creditors shall have priority on partnership property and separate creditors on individual property, saving the rights of lien or secured creditors as heretofore.

(i) Where a partner has become bankrupt or his estate is insolvent the claims against his separate property shall rank in the following order:

(I) Those owing to separate creditors,

(II) Those owing to partnership creditors,

(III) Those owing to partners by way of contribution.

§ 41. **Liability of Persons Continuing the Business in Certain Cases.**—(1) When any new partner is admitted into an existing partnership, or when any partner retires and assigns (or the representative of the deceased partner assigns) his rights in partnership property to two or more of the partners, or to one or more of the partners and one or more third persons, if the business is continued without liquidation of the partnership affairs, creditors of the first or dissolved partnership are also creditors of the partnership so continuing the business.

(2) When all but one partner retire and assign (or the representative of a deceased partner assigns) their rights in partnership property to the remaining partner, who continues the business without liquidation of partnership affairs, either alone or with others, creditors of the dissolved partnership are also creditors of the person or partnership so continuing the business.

(3) When any partner retires or dies and the business of the dissolved partnership is continued as set forth in paragraphs (1) and (2) of this section, with the consent of the retired partners or the representative of the deceased partner, but without any assignment of his right in partnership property, rights of creditors of the dissolved partnership and of the creditors of the person or partnership continuing the business shall be as if such assignment had been made.

(4) When all the partners or their representatives assign their rights in partnership property to one or more third persons who promise to pay the debts and who continue the business of the dissolved partnership, creditors of the dissolved partnership are also creditors of the person or partnership continuing the business.

(5) When any partner wrongfully causes a dissolution and the remaining partners continue the business under the provisions of §38 (2b), either alone or with others, and without liquidation of the partnership affairs, creditors of the dissolved partnership are also creditors of the person or partnership continuing the business.

(6) When a partner is expelled and the remaining partners continue the business either alone or with others, without liquidation of the partnership affairs, creditors of the dissolved partnership are also creditors of the person or partnership continuing the business.

(7) The liability of a third person becoming a partner in the partnership continuing the business, under this section, to the creditors of the dissolved partnership shall be satisfied out of partnership property only.

(8) When the business of a partnership after dissolution is continued under any conditions set forth in this section the creditors of the dissolved partnership, as against the separate creditors of the retiring or deceased partner or the representative of the deceased partner, have a prior right to any claim of the retired partner or the representative of the deceased partner against the person or partnership continuing the business, on account of the retired or deceased partner's interest in the dissolved partnership

or on account of any consideration promised for such interest or for his right in partnership property.

(9) Nothing in this section shall be held to modify any right of creditors to set aside any assignment on the ground of fraud.

(10) The use by the person or partnership continuing the business of the partnership name, or the name of a deceased partner as part thereof, shall not of itself make the individual property of the deceased partner liable for any debts contracted by such person or partnership.

§ 42. Rights of Retiring or Estate of Deceased Partner When the Business is Continued.—When any partner retires or dies, and the business is continued under any of the conditions set forth in §41 (1, 2, 3, 5, 6), or §38 (2b), without any settlement of accounts as between him or his estate and the person or partnership continuing the business, unless otherwise agreed, he or his legal representative as against such persons or partnership may have the value of his interest at the date of dissolution ascertained, and shall receive as an ordinary creditor an amount equal to the value of his interest in the dissolved partnership with interest, or, at his option or at the option of his legal representative, in lieu of interest, the profits attributable to the use of his right in the property of the dissolved partnership; provided that the creditors of the dissolved partnership as against the separate creditors, or the representative of the retired or deceased partner, shall have priority on any claim arising under this section, as provided by §41 (8) of this Act.

§ 43. Accrual of Actions.—The right to an account of his interest shall accrue to any partner, or his legal representative, as against the winding up partners or the surviving partners or the person or partnership continuing the business, at the date of dissolution, in the absence of any agreement to the contrary.

Part VII

Miscellaneous Provisions

§ 44. When Act Takes Effect.—This Act shall take effect on the . . . . . . day of . . . . . . one thousand nine hundred and . . . . .

§ 45. Legislation Repealed.—All Acts or parts of Acts inconsistent with this Act are hereby repealed.

Appendix C
UNIFORM LIMITED PARTNERSHIP ACT (1976)

Article 1

General Provisions

§ 101. Definitions.—As used in this Act, unless the context otherwise requires:

(1) "Certificate of limited partnership" means the certificate referred to in Section 201, and the certificate as amended.

(2) "Contribution" means any cash, property, services rendered, or a promissory note or other binding obligation to contribute cash or property or to perform services, which a partner contributes to a limited partnership in his capacity as a partner.

(3) "Event of withdrawal of a general partner" means an event that causes a person to cease to be a general partner as provided in Section 402.

(4) "Foreign limited partnership" means a partnership formed under the laws of any State other than this State and having as partners one or more general partners and one or more limited partners.

(5) "General partner" means a person who has been admitted to a limited partnership as a general partner in accordance with the partnership agreement and named in the certificate of limited partnership as a general partner.

(6) "Limited partner" means a person who has been admitted to a limited partnership as a limited partner in accordance with the partnership agreement and named in the certificate of limited partnership as a limited partner.

(7) "Limited partnership" and "domestic limited partnership" mean a partnership formed by 2 or more persons under the laws of this State and having one or more general partners and one or more limited partners.

(8) "Partner" means a limited or general partner.

(9) "Partnership agreement" means any valid agreement, written or oral, of the partners as to the affairs of a limited partnership and the conduct of its business.

(10) "Partnership interest" means a partner's share of the profits and losses of a limited partnership and the right to receive distributions of a partnership assets.

(11) "Person" means a natural person, partnership, limited partnership (domestic or foreign), trust, estate, association, or corporation.

(12) "State" means a state, territory, or possession of the United States, the District of Columbia, or the Commonwealth of Puerto Rico.

§ 102. Name.—The name of each limited partnership as set forth in its certificate of limited partnership:

(1) shall contain without abbreviation the words "limited partnership";

(2) may not contain the name of a limited partner unless (i) it is also the name of a general partner or the corporate name of a corporate general partner, or (ii) the business of the limited partnership had been carried on under that name before the admission of that limited partner;

(3) may not contain any word or phrase indicating or implying that it is organized other than for a purpose stated in its certificate of limited partnership;

(4) may not be the same as, or deceptively similar to, the name of any corporation or limited partnership organized under the laws of this State or licensed or registered as a foreign corporation or limited partnership in this State; and

(5) may not contain the following words [here insert prohibited words].

§ 103. Reservation of Name.—

(a) The exclusive right to the use of a name may be reserved by:

(1) any person intending to organize a limited partnership under this Act and to adopt that name;

(2) any domestic limited partnership or any foreign limited partnership registered in this State which, in either case, intends to adopt that name;

(3) any foreign limited partnership intending to register in this State and adopt that name; and

(4) any person intending to organize a foreign limited partnership and intending to have it register in this State and adopt that name.

(b) The reservation shall be made by filing with the Secretary of State an application, executed by the applicant, to reserve a specified name. If the Secretary of State finds that the name is available for use by a domestic or foreign limited partnership, he shall reserve the name for the exclusive use of the applicant for a period of 120 days. Once having so reserved a name, the same applicant may not again reserve the same name until more than 60 days after the expiration of the last 120-day period for which that applicant reserved that name. The right to the exclusive use of a reserved name may be transferred to any other person by filing in the office of the Secretary of State a notice of the transfer, executed by the applicant for whom the name was reserved and specifying the name and address of the transferee.

§ 104. Specified Office and Agent.—Each limited partnership shall continuously maintain in this State:

(1) an office, which may but need not be a place of its business in this State, at which shall be kept the records required by Section 105 to be maintained; and

(2) an agent for service of process on the limited partnership, which agent must be an individual resident of this State, a domestic corporation, or a foreign corporation authorized to do business in this State.

§ 105. Records to be Kept.—Each limited partnership shall keep at the office referred to in Section 104(1) the following: (1) a current list of the full name and last known business address of each partner set forth in alphabetical order, (2) a copy of the certificate of limited partnership and all certificates of amendment thereto, together with executed copies of any powers of attorney pursuant to which any certificate has been executed, (3) copies of the limited partnership's federal, state and local income tax returns and reports, if any, for the 3 most recent years, and (4) copies of any then effective written partnership agreements and of any financial statements of the limited partnership for the 3 most recent years. Those records are subject to inspection and copying at the reasonable request, and at the expense, of any partner during ordinary business hours.

§ 106. Nature of Business.—A limited partnership may carry on any business that a partnership without limited partners may carry on except [here designate prohibited activities].

§ 107. Business Transactions of Partner with Partnership.—Except as provided in the partnership agreement, a partner may lend money to and transact other business with the limited partnership and, subject to other applicable law, has the same rights and obligations with respect thereto as a person who is not a partner.

Article 2

Formation: Certificate of Limited Partnership

§ 201. Certificate of Limited Partnership.—
(a) In order to form a limited partnership two or more persons must execute a certificate of limited partnership. The certificate shall be filed in the office of the Secretary of State and set forth:

(1) the name of the limited partnership;

(2) the general character of its business;

(3) the address of the office and the name and address of the agent for service of process required to be maintained by Section 104;

(4) the name and the business address of each partner (specifying separately the general partners and limited partners);

(5) the amount of cash and a description and statement of the agreed value of the other property or services contributed by each partner and which each partner has agreed to contribute in the future;

(6) the times at which or events on the happening of which any additional contributions agreed to be made by each partner are to be made;

(7) any power of a limited partner to grant the right to become a limited partner to an assignee of any part of his partnership interest, and the terms and conditions of the power;

(8) if agreed upon, the time at which or the events on the happening of which a partner may terminate his membership in the limited partnership and the amount of, or the method of determining, the distribution to which he may be entitled respecting his partnership interest, and the terms and conditions of the termination and distribution;

(9) any right of a partner to receive distributions of property, including cash from the limited partnership;

(10) any right of a partner to receive, or of a general partner to make, distributions to a partner which include a return of all or any part of the partner's contribution;

(11) any time at which or events upon the happening of which the limited partnership is to be dissolved and its affairs wound up;

(12) any right of the remaining general partners to continue the business on the happening of an event of withdrawal of a general partner; and

(13) any other matters the partners determine to include therein.

(b) A limited partnership is formed at the time of the filing of the certificate of limited partnership in the office of the Secretary of State or at any later time specified in the certificate of limited partnership if, in either case, there has been substantial compliance with the requirements of this section.

§ 202. Amendment to Certificate.—(a) A certificate of limited partnership is amended by filing a certificate of amendment thereto in the office of the Secretary of State. The certificate shall set forth:

(1) the name of the limited partnership;

(2) the date of filing the certificate; and

(3) the amendment to the certificate.

(b) Within 30 days after the happening of any of the following events, an amendment to a certificate of limited partnership reflecting the occurrence of the event or events shall be filed:

(1) a change in the amount or character of the contribution of any partner, or in any partner's obligation to make a contribution:

(2) the admission of a new partner;

(3) the withdrawal of a partner; or

(4) the continuation of the business under Section 801 after an event of withdrawal of a general partner.

(c) A general partner who becomes aware that any statement in a certificate of limited partnership was false when made or that any arrangements or other facts described have changed, making the certificate inaccurate in any respect, shall promptly amend the certificate, but an amendment to show a change of address of a limited partner need be filed only once every 12 months.

(d) A certificate of limited partnership may be amended at any time for any other proper purpose the general partners determine.

(e) No person has any liability because an amendment to a certificate of limited partnership has not been filed to reflect the occurrence of any event referred to in subsection (b) of this Section if the amendment is filed within the 30-day period specified in subsection (b).

§ 203. Cancellation of Certificate.—A certificate of limited partnership shall be cancelled upon the dissolution and the commencement of winding up of the partnership or at any other time there are no limited partners. A certificate of cancellation shall be filed in the office of the Secretary of State and set forth:

(1) the name of the limited partnership;

(2) the date of filing of its certificate of limited partnership;

(3) the reason for filing the certificate of cancellation;

(4) the effective date (which shall be a date certain) of cancellation if it is not to be effective upon the filing of the certificate; and

(5) any other information the general partners filing the certificate determine.

§ 204. Execution of Certificates.—
(a) Each certificate required by this Article to be filed in the office of the Secretary of State shall be executed in the following manner:

(1) an original certificate of limited partnership must be signed by all partners named therein;

(2) a certificate of amendment must be signed by at least one general partner and by each other partner designated in the certificate as a new partner or whose contribution is described as having been increased; and

(3) a certificate of cancellation must be signed by all general partners;

(b) Any person may sign a certificate by an attorney-in-fact, but a power of attorney to sign a certificate relating to the admission, or increased contribution, of a partner must specifically describe the admission or increase.

(c) The execution of a certificate by a general partner constitutes an affirmation under the penalties of perjury that the facts stated therein are true.

§ 205. Amendment or Cancellation by Judicial Act.—If a person required by Section 204 to execute a certificate of amendment or cancellation fails or refuses to do so, any other partner, and any assignee of a partnership interest, who is adversely affected by the failure or refusal, may petition the [here designate the proper court] to direct the amendment or cancellation. If the court finds that the amendment or cancellation is proper and that any person so designated has failed or refused to execute the certificate, it shall order the Secretary of State to record an appropriate certificate of amendment or cancellation.

§ 206. Filing in Office of Secretary of State.—
(a) Two signed copies of the certificate of limited partnership and of any certificates of amendment or cancellation (or of any judicial decree of amendment or cancellation) shall be delivered to the Secretary of State. A person who executes a certificate as an agent or fiduciary need not exhibit evidence of his authority as a prerequisite to filing. Unless the Secretary of State finds that any certificate does not conform to law, upon receipt of all filing fees required by law he shall:

(1) endorse on each duplicate original the word "Filed" and the day, month and year of the filing thereof;

(2) file one duplicate original in his office; and

(3) return the other duplicate original to the person who filed it or his representative.

(b) Upon the filing of a certificate of amendment (or judicial decree of amendment) in the office of the Secretary of State, the certificate of limited partnership shall be amended as set forth therein, and upon the effective date of a certificate of cancellation (or a judicial decree thereof), the certificate of limited partnership is cancelled.

§ 207. Liability for False Statement in Certificate.—If any certificate of limited partnership or certificate of amendment or cancellation contains a false statement, one who suffers loss by reliance on the statement may recover damages for the loss from:

(1) any person who executes the certificate, or causes another to execute it on his behalf, and knew, and any general partner who knew or should have known, the statement to be false at the time the certificate was executed; and

(2) any general partner who thereafter knows or should have known that any arrangement or other fact described in the certificate has changed, making the statement inaccurate in any respect within a sufficient time before the statement was relied upon reasonably to have enabled that general partner to cancel or amend the certificate, or to file a petition for its cancellation or amendment under Section 205.

§ 208. Notice.—The fact that a certificate of limited partnership is on file in the office of the Secretary of State is notice that the partnership is a limited partnership and the persons designated therein as limited partners are limited partners, but it is not notice of any other fact.

§ 209. Delivery of Certificates to Limited Partners.—Upon the return by the Secretary of State pursuant to Section 206 of a certificate marked "Filed", the general partners shall promptly deliver or mail a copy of the certificate of limited partnership and each certificate to each limited partner unless the partnership agreement provides otherwise.

Article 3

Limited Partners

§ 301. Admission of Additional Limited Partners.—(a) After the filing of a limited partnership's original certificate of limited partnership, a person may be admitted as an additional limited partner:

(1) in the case of a person acquiring a partnership interest directly from the limited partnership, upon the compliance with the partnership agreement or, if the partnership-agreement does not so provide, upon the written consent of all partners; and

(2) in the case of an assignee of a partnership interest of a partner who has the power, as provided in Section 704, to grant the assignee the right to become a limited partner, upon the exercise of that power and compliance with any conditions limiting the grant or exercise of the power.

(b) In each case under subsection (a), the person acquiring the partnership interest becomes a limited partner only upon amendment of the certificate of limited partnership reflecting that fact.

§ 302. Voting.—Subject to Section 303, the partnership agreement may grant to all or a specified group of the limited partners the right to vote (on a per capita or other basis) upon any matter.

§ 303. Liability to Third Parties.—(a) Except as provided in subsection (d), a limited partner is not liable for the obligations of a limited partnership unless he is also a general partner or, in addition to the exercise of his rights and powers as a limited partner, he takes part in the control of the business. However, if the limited partner's participation in the control of the business is not substantially the same as the exercise of the powers of a general partner, he is liable only to persons who transact business with the limited partnership with actual knowledge of his participation in control.

(b) A limited partner does not participate in the control of the

business within the meaning of subsection (a) solely by doing one or more of the following:

(1) being a contractor for or an agent or employee of the limited partnership or of a general partner;

(2) consulting with and advising a general partner with respect to the business of the limited partnership;

(3) acting as surety for the limited partnership;

(4) approving or disapproving an amendment to the partnership agreement; or

(5) voting on one or more of the following matters:

(i) the dissolution and winding up of the limited partnership;

(ii) the sale, exchange, lease, mortgage, pledge, or other transfer of all or substantially all of the assets of the limited partnership other than in the ordinary course of its business;

(iii) the incurrence of indebtedness by the limited partnership other than in the ordinary course of its business;

(iv) a change in the nature of the business; or

(v) the removal of a general partner.

(c) the enumeration in subsection (b) does not mean that the possession or exercise of any other powers by a limited partner constitutes participation by him in the business of the limited partnership.

(d) A limited partner who knowingly permits his name to be used in the name of the limited partnership, except under circumstances permitted by Section 102(2)(i), is liable to creditors who extend credit to the limited partnership without actual knowledge that the limited partner is not a general partner.

§ 304. Person Erroneously Believing Himself Limited Partner.—(a) Except as provided in subsection (b), a person who makes a contribution to a business enterprise and erroneously but in good faith believes that he has become a limited partner in the enterprise is not a general partner in the enterprise and is not bound by its obligations by reason of making the contribution, receiving distributions from the enterprise, or exercising any rights of a limited partner, if, on ascertaining the mistake, he:

(1) causes an appropriate certificate of limited partnership or a certificate of amendment to be executed and filed; or

(2) withdraws from future equity participation in the enterprise.

(b) A person who makes a contribution of the kind described in subsection (a) is liable as a general partner to any third party who transacts business with the enterprise (i) before the person withdraws and an appropriate certificate is filed to show withdrawal, or (ii) before an appropriate certificate is filed to show his status as a limited partner and, in the case of an amendment, after expiration of the 30-day period for filing an amendment relating to the person as a limited partner under Section 202, but in either case only if the third party actually believed in good faith that the person was a general partner at the time of the transaction.

§ 305. Information.—Each limited partner has the right to:

(1) inspect and copy any of the partnership records required to be maintained by Section 105; and

(2) obtain from the general partners from time to time upon reasonable demand (i) true and full information regarding the state of the business and financial condition of the limited partnership, (ii) promptly after becoming available, a copy of the limited partnership's federal, state and local income tax returns for each year, and (iii) other information regarding the affairs of the limited partnership as is just and reasonable.

Article 4

General Partners

§ 401. Admission of Additional General Partners.—After the filing of a limited partnership's original certificate of limited partnership, additional general partners may be admitted only with the specific written consent of each partner.

§ 402. Events of Withdrawal.—Except as approved by the specific written consent of all partners at the time, a person ceases to be a general partner of a limited partnership upon the happening of any of the following events:

(1) the general partner withdraws from the limited partnership as provided in Section 602;

(2) the general partner ceases to be a member of the limited partnership as provided in Section 702;

(3) the general partner is removed as a general partner in accordance with the partnership agreement;

(4) unless otherwise provided in the certificate of limited partnership, the general partner: (i) makes an assignment for the benefit of creditors; (ii) files a voluntary petition in bankruptcy; (iii) is adjudicated a bankrupt or insolvent; (iv) files a petition or answer seeking for himself any reorganization, arrangement, composition, readjustment, liquidation, dissolution or similar relief under any statute, law, or regulation; (v) files an answer or other pleading admitting or failing to contest the material allegations of a petition filed against him in any proceeding of this nature; or (vi) seeks, consents to, or acquiesces in the appointment of a trustee, receiver, or liquidator of the general partner or of all or any substantial part of his properties;

(5) unless otherwise provided in the certificate of limited partnership, [120] days after the commencement of any proceeding against the general partner seeking reorganization, arrangement, composition, readjustment, liquidation, dissolution or similar relief under any statute, law, or regulation, the proceeding has not been dismissed, or if within [90] days after the appointment without his consent or acquiescence of a trustee, receiver, or liquidator of the general partner or of all or any substantial part of his properties, the appointment is not vacated or stayed or within [90] days after the expiration of any such stay, the appointment is not vacated;

(6) in the case of a general partner who is a natural person,

(i) his death; or

(ii) the entry by a court of competent jurisdiction adjudicating him incompetent to manage his person or his estate;

(7) in the case of a general partner who is acting as a general partner by virtue of being a trustee of a trust, the termination of the trust (but not merely the substitution of a new trustee);

(8) in the case of a general partner that is a separate partnership, the dissolution and commencement of winding up of the separate partnership;

(9) in the case of a general partner that is a corporation, the filing of a certificate of dissolution, or its equivalent, for the corporation or the revocation of its charter; or

(10) in the case of an estate, the distribution by the fiduciary of the estate's entire interest in the partnership.

§ 403. General Powers and Liabilities.—Except as provided in this Act or in the partnership agreement, a general partner of a limited partnership has the rights andpowers and is subject to the restrictions and liabilities of a partner in a partnership without limited partners.

§ 404. Contributions by General Partner.—A general partner of a limited partnership may make contributions to the partnership and share in the profits and losses of, and in distributions from, the limited partnership as a general partner. A general partner also may make contributions to and share in profits, losses, and distributions as a limited partner. A person who is both a general partner and a limited partner has the rights and powers, and is subject to the restrictions and liabilities, of a general partner and, except as provided in the partnership agreement, also has the powers, and is subject to the restrictions, of a limited partner to the extent of his participation in the partnership as a limited partner.

§ 405. Voting.—The partnership agreement may grant to all or certain identified general partners the right to vote (on a per capita or any other basis), separately or with all or any class of the limited partners, on any matter.

Article 5

Finance

§ 501. Form of Contribution.—The contribution of a partner may be in cash, property, or services rendered, or a promissory note or other obligation to contribute cash or property or to perform services.

§ 502. Liability for Contribution.—(a) Except as provided in the certificate of limited partnership, a partner is obligated to the limited partnership to perform any promise to contribute cash or property or to perform services, even if he is unable to perform because of death, disability or any other reason. If a partner does not make the required contribution of property or services, he is obligated at the option of the limited partnership to contribute cash equal to that portion of the value (as stated in the certificate of limited partnership) of the stated contribution that has not been made.

(b) Unless otherwise provided in the partnership agreement, the obligation of a partner to make a contribution or return money or other property paid or distributed in violation of this Act may be compromised only by consent of all the partners. Notwithstanding the compromise, a creditor of a limited partnership who extends credit, or whose claim arises, after the filing of the certificate of limited partnership or an amendment thereto which, in either case, reflects the obligation, and before the amendment or cancellation thereof to reflect the compromise, may enforce the original obligation.

§ 503. Sharing of Profits and Losses.—The profits and losses of a limited partnership shall be allocated among the partners, and among classes of partners, in the manner provided in the partnership agreement. If the partnership agreement does not so provide, profits and losses shall be allocated on the basis of the value (as stated in the certificate of limited partnership) of the contributions made by each partner to the extent they have been received by the partnership and have not been returned.

§ 504. Sharing of Distributions.—Distributions of cash or other assets of a limited partnership shall be allocated among the partners, and among classes of partners, in the manner provided in the partnership agreement. If the partnership agreement does not so provide, distributions shall be made on the basis of the value (as stated in the certificate of limited partnership) of the contributions made by each partner to the extent they have been received by the partnership and have not been returned.

Article 6

Distribution and Withdrawal

§ 601. Interim Distributions.—Except as provided in this Article, a partner is entitled to receive distributions from a limited partnership before his withdrawal from the limited partnership and before the dissolution and winding up thereof:

(1) to the extent and at the times or upon the happening of the events specified in the partnership agreement; and

(2) if any distribution constitutes a return of any part of his contribution under Section 608(c), to the extent and at the times or upon the happening of the events specified in the certificate of limited partnership.

§ 602. Withdrawal of General Partner.—A general partner may withdraw from a limited partnership at any time by giving written notice to the other partners, but if the withdrawal violates the partnership agreement, the limited partnership may recover from the withdrawing general partner damages for breach of the partnership agreement and offset the damages against the amount otherwise distributable to him.

§ 603. Withdrawal of Limited Partner.—A limited partner may withdraw from a limited partnership at the time or upon the happening of events specified in the certificate of limited partnership and in accordance with the partnership agreement. If the certificate does not specify the time or the events upon the happening of which a limited partner may withdraw or a definite time for the dissolution and winding up of the limited partnership, a limited partner may withdraw upon not less than 6 months' prior written notice to each general partner at his address on the books of the limited partnership at its office in this State.

§ 604. Distribution Upon Withdrawal.—Except as provided in this Article, upon withdrawal any withdrawing partner is entitled to receive any distribution to which he is entitled under the partnership agreement and, if not otherwise provided in the agreement, he is entitled to receive, within a reasonable time after withdrawal, the fair value of his interest in the limited partnership as of the date of withdrawal based upon his right to share in distributions from the limited partnership.

§ 605. Distribution in Kind.—Except as provided in the certificate of limited partnership, a partner, regardless of the nature of his contribution, has no right to demand and receive any distribution from a limited partnership in any form other than cash. Except as provided in the partnership agreement, a partner may not be compelled to accept a distribution of any asset in kind from a limited partnership to the extent that the percentage of the asset distributed to him exceeds a percentage of that asset which is equal to the percentage in which he shares in distributions from the limited partnership.

§ 606. Right to Distribution.—At the time a partner becomes entitled to receive a distribution, he has the status of, and is entitled to all remedies available to, a creditor of the limited partnership with respect to the distribution.

§ 607. Limitations on Distribution.—A partner may not receive a distribution from a limited partnership to the extent that, after giving effect to the distribution, all liabilities of the limited partnership, other than liabilities to partners on account of their partnership interests, exceed the fair value of the partnership assets.

§ 608. Liability Upon Return of Contribution.—(a) If a partner has received the return of any part of his contribution without violation of the partnership agreement or this Act, he is liable to the limited partnership for a period of one year thereafter for the amount of the returned contribution, but only to the extent necessary to discharge the limited partnership's liabilities to creditors who extended credit to the limited partnership during the period the contribution was held by the partnership.

(b) If a partner has received the return of any part of his contribution in violation of the partnership agreement or this Act, he is liable to the limited partnership for a period of 6 years thereafter for the amount of the contribution wrongfully returned.

(c) A partner receives a return of his contribution to the extent that a distribution to him reduces his share of the fair value of the net assets of the limited partnership below the value (as set forth in the certificate of limited partnership) of his contribution which has not been distributed to him.

Article 7

Assignment of Partnership Interests

§ 701. Nature of Partnership Interest.—A partnership interest is personal property.

§ 702. Assignment of Partnership Interest.—Except as provided in the partnership agreement, a partnership interest is assignable in whole or in part. An assignment of a partnership interest does not dissolve a limited partnership or entitle the assignee to become or to exercise any rights of a partner. An assignment entitles the assignee to receive, to the extent assigned, only the distribution to which the assignor would be entitled. Except as provided in the partnership agreement, a partner ceases to be a partner upon assignment of all his partnership interest.

§ 703. Rights of Creditor.—On application to a court of competent jurisdiction by any judgment creditor of a partner, the court may charge the partnership interest of the partner with payment of the unsatisfied amount of the judgment with interest. To the extent so charged, the judgment creditor has only the rights of an assignee of the partnership interest. This Act does not deprive any partner of the benefit of any exemption laws applicable to his partnership interest.

§ 704. Right of Assignee to Become Limited Partner.—(a) An assignee of a partnership interest, including an assignee of a general partner, may become a limited partner if and to the extent that (1) the assignor gives the assignee that right in accordance with authority described in the certificate of limited partnership, or (2) all other partners consent.

(b) An assignee who has become a limited partner has, to the extent assigned, the rights and powers, and is subject to the restrictions and liabilities, of a limited partner under the partnership agreement and this Act. An assignee who becomes a limited partner also is liable for the obligations of his assignor to make and return contributions as provided in Article 6. However, the assignee is not obligated for liabilities unknown to the assignee at the time he became a limited partner and which could not be ascertained from the certificate of limited partnership.

(c) If an assignee of a partnership interest becomes a limited partner, the assignor is not released from his liability to the limited partnership under Sections 207 and 502.

§ 705. Power of Estate of Deceased or Incompetent Partner.—If a partner who is an individual dies or a court of competent jurisdiction adjudges him to be incompetent to manage his person or his property, the partner's executor, administrator guardian, conservator, or other legal representative may exercise all the partner's rights for the purpose of settling his estate or administering his property, including any power the partner had to give an assignee the right to become a limited partner. If a partner is a corporation, trust, or other entity and is dissolved or terminated, the powers of that partner may be exercised by its legal representative or successor.

Article 8

Dissolution

§ 801. Nonjudicial Dissolution.—A limited partnership is dissolved and its affairs shall be wound up upon the happening of the first to occur of the following:

(1) at the time or upon the happening of events specified in the certificate of limited partnership;

(2) written consent of all partners;

(3) an event of withdrawal of a general partner unless at the time there is at least one other general partner and the certificate of limited partnership permits the business of the limited partnership to be carried on by the remaining general partner and that partner does so, but the limited partnership is not dissolved and is not required to be wound up by reason of any event of withdrawal, if, within 90 days after the withdrawal, all partners agree in writing to continue the business of the limited partnership and to the appointment of one or more additional partners if necessary or desired; or

(4) entry of a decree of judicial dissolution under Section 802.

§ 802. **Judicial Dissolution.**—On application by or for a partner the [here designate the proper court] court may decree dissolution of a limited partnership whenever it is not reasonably practicable to carry on the business in conformity with the partnership agreement.

§ 803. **Winding Up.**—Except as provided in the partnership agreement, the general partners who have not wrongfully dissolved a limited partnership or, if none, the limited partners, may wind up the limited partnership's affairs; but the [here designate the proper court] court may wind up the limited partnership's affairs upon application of any partner, his legal representative, or assignee.

§ 804. **Distribution of Assets.**—Upon the winding up of a limited partnership, the assets shall be distributed as follows:

(1) to creditors, including partners who are creditors, to the extent permitted by law, in satisfaction of liabilities of the limited partnership other than liabilities for distributions to partners under Section 601 or 604;

(2) except as provided in the partnership agreement, to partners and former partners in satisfaction of liabilities for distributions under Section 601 or 604; and

(3) except as provided in the partnership agreement, to partners *first* for the return of their contributions and *secondly* respecting their partnership interests, in the proportions in which the partners share in distributions.

Article 9

Foreign Limited Partnerships

§ 901. **Law Governing.**—Subject to the Constitution of this State, (1) the laws of the state under which a foreign limited partnership is organized govern its organization and internal affairs and the liability of its limited partners, and (2) a foreign limited partnership may not be denied registration by reason of any difference between those laws and the laws of this State.

§ 902. **Registration.**—Before transacting business in this State, a foreign limited partnership shall register with the Secretary of State. In order to register, a foreign limited partnership shall submit to the Secretary of State, in duplicate, an application for registration as a foreign limited partnership, signed and sworn to by a general partner and setting forth:

(1) the name of the foreign limited partnership and, if different, the name under which it proposes to register and transact business in this State;

(2) the state and date of its formation;

(3) the general character of the business it proposes to transact in this State;

(4) the name and address of any agent for service of process on the foreign limited partnership whom the foreign limited partnership elects to appoint; the agent must be an individual resident of this state, a domestic corporation, or a foreign corporation having a place of business in, and authorized to do business in, this State;

(5) a statement that the Secretary of State is appointed the agent of the foreign limited partnership for service of process if no agent has been appointed under paragraph (4) or, if appointed, the agent's authority has been revoked or if the agent cannot be found or served with the exercise of reasonable diligence;

(6) the address of the office required to be maintained in the State of its organization by the laws of that State or, if not so required, of the principal office of the foreign limited partnership; and

(7) if the certificate of limited partnership filed in the foreign limited partnership's state of organization is not required to include the names and business addresses of the partners, a list of the names and addresses.

§ 903. **Issuance of Registration.**—

(a) If the Secretary of State finds that an application for registration conforms to law and all requisite fees have been paid, he shall:

(1) endorse on the application the word "Filed", and the month, day and year of the filing thereof;

(2) file in his office a duplicate original of the application; and

(3) issue a certificate of registration to transact business in this State.

(b) The certificate of registration, together with a duplicate original of the application, shall be returned to the person who filed the application or his representative.

§ 904. **Name.**—A foreign limited partnership may register with the Secretary of State under any name (whether or not it is the name under which it is registered in its state of organization) that includes without abbreviation the words "limited partnership" and that could be registered by a domestic limited partnership.

§ 905. **Changes and Amendments.**—If any statement in the application for registration of a foreign limited partnership was false when made or any arrangements or other facts described have changed, making the application inaccurate in any respect, the foreign limited partnership shall promptly file in the office of the Secretary of State a certificate, signed and sworn to by a general partner, correcting such statement.

§ 906. **Cancellation of Registration.**—A foreign limited partnership may cancel its registration by filing with the Secretary of State a certificate of cancellation signed and sworn to by a general partner. A cancellation does not terminate the authority of the Secretary of State to accept service of process on the foreign limited partnership with respect to [claims for relief] [causes of action] arising out of the transactions of business in this State.

§ 907. **Transaction of Business Without Registration.**—(a) A foreign limited partnership transacting business in this State may not maintain any action, suit, or proceeding in any court of this State until it has registered in this State.

(b) The failure of a foreign limited partnership to register in this State does not impair the validity of any contract or act of the foreign limited partnership or prevent the foreign limited partnership from defending any action, suit, or proceeding in any court of this State.

(c) A limited partner of a foreign limited partnership is not liable as a general partner of the foreign limited partnership solely by reason of having transacted business in this State without registration.

(d) A foreign limited partnership, by transacting business in this State without registration, appoints the Secretary of State as its agent for service of process with respect to [claims for relief] [causes of action] arising out of the transaction of business in this State.

§ 908. **Action by [Appropriate Official.]**—The [appropriate official] may bring an action to restrain a foreign limited partnership from transacting business in this State in violation of the Article.

Article 10

Derivative Actions

§ 1001. **Right of Action.**—A limited partner may bring an action in the right of a limited partnership to recover a judgment in its favor if general partners with authority to do so have refused to bring the action or if an effort to cause those general partners to bring the action is not likely to succeed.

§ 1002. **Proper Plaintiff.**—In a derivative action, the plaintiff must be a partner at the time of bringing the action and (1) at the time of the transaction of which the complains or (2) his status as a partner had devolved upon him by operation of law or pursuant to the terms of the partnership agreement from a person who was a partner at the time of the transaction.

§ 1003. Pleading.—In a derivative action, the complaint shall set forth with particularity the effort of the plaintiff to secure initiation of the action by a general partner or the reasons for not making the effort.

§ 1004. Expenses.—If a derivative action is successful, in whole or in part, or if anything is received by the plaintiff as a result of a judgment, compromise or settlement of an action or claim, the court may award the plaintiff reasonable expenses, including reasonable attorney's fees, and shall direct him to remit to the limited partnership the remainder of those proceeds received by him.

Article 11

Miscellaneous

§ 1101. Construction and Application.—This Act shall be so applied and construed to effectuate its general purpose to make uniform the law with respect to the subject of this Act among states enacting it.

§ 1102. Short Title.—This Act may be cited as the Uniform Limited Partnership Act.

§ 1103. Severability.—If any provision of this Act or its application to any person or circumstance is held invalid, the invalidity does not affect other provisions or applications of the Act which can be given effect without the invalid provision or application, and to this end the provisions of this Act are severable.

§ 1104. Effective Date, Extended Effective Date and Repeal.— Except as set forth below, the effective date of this Act is   and the following Acts [list prior limited partnership acts] are hereby repealed:

(1) The existing provisions for execution and filing of certificates of limited partnerships and amendments thereunder and cancellations thereof continue in effect until [specify time required to create central filing system], the extended effective date, and Sections 102, 103, 104, 105, 201, 202, 203, 204 and 206 are not effective until the extended effective date.

(2) Section 402, specifying the conditions under which a general partner ceases to be a member of a limited partnership, is not effective until the extended effective date, and the applicable provisions of existing law continue to govern until the extended effective date.

(3) Sections 501, 502, and 608 apply only to contributions and distributions made after the effective date of this Act.

(4) Section 704 applies only to assignments made after the effective date of this Act.

(5) Article 9, dealing with registration of foreign limited partnerships, is not effective until the extended effective date.

§ 1105. Rules for Cases Not Provided for in This Act.—In any case not provided for in this Act the provisions of the Uniform Partnership Act govern.

APPENDIX D
1983 REVISED MODEL BUSINESS CORPORATION ACT
Contents of 1983 Revised Model Business Corporation Act Cross-Referenced to Contents of 1969 Model Business Corporation Act
(Sections marked with an * are not included in this appendix)

Section No. in 1983 Act	Section Title	Section No. in 1969 Act
	Chapter 1. General provisions	
	Subchapter A. Short title and reservation of power	
1.01	Short title	1
1.02*	Reservation of power to amend or repeal	149
	Subchapter B. Filing documents	
1.20*	Filing requirements	new
1.21*	Forms	142
1.22*	Filing, service, and copying fees	128, 129
1.23*	Effective date of filing	new
1.24*	Correcting filed document	new
1.25*	Filing duty of secretary of state	new
1.26*	Appeal from secretary of state's refusal to file document	140
1.27*	Evidentiary effect of copy of filed document	141
1.28*	Certificate of good standing	new
1.29*	Penalty for signing false document	136
	Subchapter C. Secretary of State	
1.30*	Powers	139
	Subchapter D. Definitions	
1.40*	Act definitions	2
1.41*	Notice	new
1.42*	Number of shareholders	new
	Chapter 2. Incorporation	
2.01	Incorporators	53
2.02	Articles of incorporation	54
2.03*	Incorporation	55, 56
2.04*	Liability for preincorporation transactions	146
2.05	Organization of corporation	57
2.06	Bylaws	27 sent. 1, 3
2.07	Emergency bylaws	27A part
	Chapter 3. Purposes and powers	
3.01	Purposes	3
3.02	General powers	4
3.03*	Emergency powers	27A part
3.04	Ulta vires	7
	Chapter 4. Name	
4.01	Corporate name	8
4.02	Reserved name	9
4.03*	Registered name	10, 11
	Chapter 5. Office and agent	
5.01*	Registered office and registered agent	12
5.02*	Change of registered office or registered agent	13 part
5.03*	Resignation of registered agent	13 part
5.04*	Service on corporation	14

Section No. in 1983 Act	Section Title	Section No. in 1969 Act
	Chapter 6. Shares and distributions	
	Subchapter A. Types of shares	
6.01	Authorization generally	15
6.02	Classes of preferred shares	15
6.03	Series within a class	16
6.04*	Fractional shares	24
	Subchapter B. Issuance of shares	
6.20	Subscription for shares	17
6.21	Issuance of shares	18(a), 19
6.22	Liability of subscribers and shareholders	25
6.23	Share exchanges, dividends, and splits	18(b)
6.24	Share rights and options	20
6.25*	Form and content of certificates	23
6.26*	Shares without certificates	23
6.27	Restriction on transfer or registration of shares or other securities	new
6.28*	Expense of issue	22
	Subchapter C. Acquisition of shares by shareholders and corporation	
6.30	Shareholders' preemptive rights	26, 26A
6.31	Corporation's power to acquire own shares	6
	Subchapter D. Distributions	
6.40	Distributions to shareholders	45
	Chapter 7. Shareholders	
	Subchapter A. Meetings	
7.01	Annual Meeting	28
7.02	Special Meeting	28
7.03*	Court-ordered meeting	new
7.04	Action without meeting	145
7.05	Notice of meeting	29
7.06	Waiver of notice	144
7.07	Record date	30
	Subchapter B. Voting	
7.20	Shareholders' list for meeting	31
7.21	Voting entitlement of shares	33
7.22	Proxies	33
7.23*	Shares held by nominees	2(f)
7.24	Corporation's acceptance of votes	33
7.25*	Normal quorum and voting requirements	32
7.26*	Class voting	new
7.27*	Greater quorum or voting requirements	143
7.28*	Cumulative voting for directors	33
	Subchapter C. Voting trusts and agreements	
7.30	Voting trusts	34
7.31	Voting agreements	34
	Subchapter D. Derivative proceedings	
7.40	Procedure in derivative proceedings	49
	Chapter 8. Directors and officers	
	Subchapter A. Board of directors	
8.01	Requirement for and duties of board	35
8.02	Qualifications of directors	35
8.03	Number and election of directors	36 part
8.04*	Election of directors by certain classes of shareholders	new

Section No. in 1983 Act	Section Title	Section No. in 1969 Act
8.05	Terms of directors generally	36 part, 38 part
8.06	Staggered terms for directors	37
8.07*	Resignation of directors	new
8.08	Removal of directors by shareholders	39
8.09*	Removal of directors by judicial proceeding	new
8.10	Vacancy on board	38 part
8.11*	Compensation of directors	35

Subchapter B. Meetings and action of board

8.20	Meetings	43
8.21	Action without meeting	44
8.22	Notice of meeting	43
8.23	Waiver of notice	144, 43
8.24	Quorum and voting	40
8.25	Committees	42

Subchapter C. Standards of conduct

8.30	General standards for directors	35
8.31	Director or officer conflict of interest	41
8.32	Loans to directors	47
8.33*	Liability for unlawful distributions	48

Subchapter D. Officers

8.40	Required officers	50
8.41	Duties of officers	50
8.42	Standards of conduct for officers	new
8.43	Resignation and removal of officers	51 part
8.44*	Contract rights of officers	51 part

Subchapter E. Indemnification

8.50	Subchapter definitions	5(a), (b)(3) part
8.51*	Authority to indemnify	5(b), (c), (h) part
8.52*	Mandatory indemnification	5 (d)(1)
8.53*	Advance for expenses	5(f)
8.54*	Court-ordered indemnification	5(d) (2)
8.55*	Determination and authorization of indemnification	5(e)
8.56*	Indemnification of officers, employees, and agents	5(i)
8.57*	Insurance	5(k)
8.58*	Application of subchapter	5(g)

Chapter 10. Amendment of articles of incorporation and bylaws

Subchapter A. Amendment of articles of incorporation

10.01*	Authority to amend	58
10.02	Amendment by directors	59(a) sent. 3
10.03	Amendment by directors and shareholders	59(a) sent. 1, (b)
10.04	Shareholder class voting on amendments	60
10.05*	Amendment before issuance of shares	59(a) sent. 2
10.06*	Articles of amendment	61, 62
10.07*	Restated articles of incorporation	64
10.08*	Amendment pursuant to reorganization	65
10.09*	Effect of amendment and restatement	63

Subchapter B. Amendment of bylaws

10.20	Amendment by directors or shareholders	27 sent. 2

Chapter 11. Merger and share exchange

11.01*	Merger	71
11.02*	Share exchange	72A
11.03	Action on plan by shareholders	73
11.04*	Merger of subsidiary	75
11.05*	Articles of merger or share exchange	74, 75

Section No. in 1983 Act	Section Title	Section No. in 1969 Act
11.06*	Effect of merger or share exchange	76
11.07*	Merger or share exchange with foreign corporation	77
	Chapter 12. Sale of assets	
12.01	Sale of assets in regular course of business and mortgage of assets	78
12.02	Sale of assets other than in regular course of business	79
	Chapter 13. Dissenters' rights	
	Subchapter A. Right to dissent and obtain payment for shares	
13.01	Definitions	81(a)
13.02	Right to dissent	80(a), (c), (d)
13.03*	Dissent by nominees and beneficial owners	80(b)
	Subchapter B. Procedure for exercise of dissenters' rights	
13.20	Notice of dissenters' rights	81(b), (d) sent. 2
13.21*	Notice of intent to demand payment	81(c)
13.22	Notice of how to demand payment	81(d) sents. 1, 3, 4
13.23	Duty to demand payment	81(e) sent. 1
13.24	Share restrictions	81(e) sent. 2, 3
13.25	Payment	81(f) (3)
13.26*	Failure to make payment	81(f) (1), (2)
13.27*	After-acquired shares	81(j) (1)
13.28	Procedure if shareholder dissatisfied with payment or offer	81(g), (j) (2)
	Subchapter C. Judicial appraisal of shares	
13.30	Court action	81(j)(3), (h)
13.31	Court costs and counsel fees	81(i)
	Chapter 14. Dissolution	
	Subchapter A. Voluntary dissolution	
14.01*	Dissolution by incorporators or initial directors	82
14.02	Dissolution by directors and shareholders	84(a)–(c)
14.03*	Articles of dissolution	83, 84(d), 92, 93
14.04*	Revocation of dissolution	88–91
14.05*	Effect of dissolution	87
14.06*	Known claims against dissolved corporation	87(a)
14.07*	Unknown claims against dissolved corporation	105
	Subchapter B. Administrative dissolution	
14.20*	Grounds for administrative dissolution	95
14.21*	Procedure for administrative dissolution	new
14.22*	Reinstatement following administrative dissolution	new
14.23*	Appeal from denial of reinstatement	new
	Subchapter C. Judicial dissolution	
14.30*	Grounds for judicial dissolution	94(b), (c), 97(a)–(d)
14.31*	Procedure for judicial dissolution	96, 97, 98
14.32*	Receivership or custodianship	98, 99, 101
14.33*	Decree of dissolution	100, 102, 103
	Subchapter D. Miscellaneous	
14.40*	Deposit with state treasurer	104
	Chapter 15. Foreign corporations	
	Subchapter A. Certificate of authority	
15.01*	Authority to transact business required	106
15.02*	Consequences of transacting business without authority	124
15.03*	Application for certificate of authority	110, 111
15.04*	Amended certificate of authority	118

§ 1.01. Short Title

This Act shall be known and may be cited as the "[name of state] Business Corporation Act."

§ 2.01. Incorporators

One or more persons may act as the incorporator or incorporators of a corporation by delivering to the secretary of state articles of incorporation.

§ 2.02. Articles of Incorporation

(a) The articles of incorporation must set forth:

(1) a corporate name for the corporation that satisfies the requirements of section 4.01;

(2) the number of shares the corporation is authorized to issue;

(3) the address of the corporation's initial registered office and the name of its initial registered agent at that office; and

(4) the name and address of each incorporator.

(b) The articles of incorporation may set forth:

(1) the names and addresses of the individuals who are to serve as the initial directors;

(2) provisions not inconsistent with law regarding:

(i) the purpose or purposes for which the corporation is organized;

(ii) managing the business and regulating the affairs of the corporation;

(iii) defining, limiting, and regulating the powers of the corporation, its directors, and shareholders;

(iv) a par value for authorized shares or classes of shares; and

(3) any provision that under this Act is required or permitted to be set forth in the bylaws.

(c) The articles of incorporation need not set forth any of the corporate powers enumerated in this Act.

§ 2.05. Organization of Corporation

(a) After incorporation:

(1) if initial directors are named in the articles of incorporation, the initial directors shall hold an organizational meeting, at the call of a majority of the directors, to complete the organization of the corporation by appointing officers, adopting bylaws, and carrying on any other business brought before the meeting;

(2) if initial directors are not named in the articles, the incorporator or incorporators shall hold an organizational meeting at the call of a majority of the incorporators:

(i) to complete the organization of the corporation; or

(ii) to elect directors who shall complete the organization of the corporation.

(b) Action required or permitted by this Act to be taken by incorporators at an organizational meeting may be taken without a meeting if the action taken is evidenced by one or more written consents describing the action taken and signed by each incorporator.

(c) An organizational meeting may be held in or out of this state.

§ 2.06. Bylaws

(a) The incorporators or initial directors of a corporation shall adopt initial bylaws for the corporation.

(b) The bylaws of a corporation may contain any provision for managing the business and regulating the affairs of the corporation that is not inconsistent with law or the articles of incorporation.

§ 2.07. Emergency Bylaws

(a) Unless the articles of incorporation provide otherwise, the directors of a corporation may adopt bylaws to be effective only in an emergency defined in subsection (d). The emergency bylaws, which are subject to amendment or repeal by the shareholders, may make all provisions necessary for managing the corporation during the emergency, including:

(1) procedures for calling a meeting of the board;

(2) quorum requirements for the meeting; and

(3) designation of additional or substitute directors.

(b) All provisions of the regular bylaws consistent with the emergency bylaws remain effective during the emergency. The emergency bylaws are not effective after the emergency ends.

(c) Corporate action taken in good faith in accordance with the emergency bylaws:

(1) binds the corporation; and

(2) may not be used to impose liability on a corporate director, officer, employee, or agent.

(d) An emergency exists for purposes of this section if a quorum of the corporation's directors cannot readily be assembled:

(1) because of attack on the United States or on the location where the corporation conducts its business or where its directors or shareholders customarily meet;

(2) because of nuclear disaster; or

(3) because of some other catastrophic event.

§ 3.01. Purposes

(a) Every corporation incorporated under this Act has the purpose of engaging in any lawful business unless a narrower purpose is set forth in the articles of incorporation.

(b) A corporation engaging in a business that is subject to regulation under another statute of this state may incorporate under this Act only if permitted by, and subject to all limitations of, the other statute.

§ 3.02. General Powers

Unless its articles of incorporation provide otherwise, every corporation has the same powers as an individual to do all things necessary or convenient to carry out its business and affairs, including without limitation power:

(1) to have perpetual duration and succession in its corporate name;

(2) to sue and be sued, complain and defend in its corporate name;

(3) to have a corporate seal, which may be altered at will, and to use it, or a facsimile of it, by impressing or affixing it or in any other manner reproducing it;

(4) to make and amend bylaws, not inconsistent with its articles of incorporation or with the laws of this state, for managing the business and regulating the affairs of the corporation;

(5) to purchase, receive, lease, or otherwise acquire, and own, hold, improve, use, and otherwise deal with, real or personal property, or any legal or equitable interest in property, wherever located;

(6) to sell, convey, mortgage, pledge, lease, exchange, and otherwise dispose of all or any part of its property;

(7) to purchase, receive, subscribe for, or otherwise acquire; own, hold, vote, use, sell, mortgage, lend, pledge, or otherwise dispose of; and deal in and with shares or other interests in, or

obligations of, other domestic or foreign corporations, associations, partnerships (without regard to their purpose or purposes), and individuals, the United States, a state, or a foreign government;

(8) to make contracts and guarantees, incur liabilities, borrow money, issue its notes, bonds, and other obligations, and secure any of its obligations by mortgage or pledge of any of its property, franchises, or income;

(9) to lend money, invest and reinvest its funds, and receive and hold real and personal property as security for repayment;

(10) to be a promoter, partner, member, associate, or manager of any partnership, joint venture, trust, or other entity;

(11) to conduct its business, locate offices, and exercise the powers granted by this Act within or without this state;

(12) to elect directors and appoint officers, employees, and agents of the corporation, define their duties, fix their compensation, and lend them money and credit;

(13) to pay pensions and establish pension plans, pension trusts, profit sharing plans, share bonus plans, share option plans, and benefit and incentive plans for any or all of its current or former directors, officers, employees, and agents;

(14) to make donations for the public welfare or for charitable, scientific, or educational purposes;

(15) to transact any lawful business that will aid governmental policy;

(16) to make payments or donations, or do any other act, not inconsistent with law, that furthers the business and affairs of the corporation.

§ 3.04. Ultra Vires

(a) Except as provided in subsection (b), the validity of corporate action may not be challenged on the ground that the corporation lacks or lacked power to act.

(b) A corporation's lack of power to act may be challenged:

(1) in a proceeding by a shareholder against the corporation to enjoin the act;

(2) in a proceeding by the corporation, directly, derivatively, or through a receiver, trustee, or other legal representative, against an incumbent or former director, officer, employee, or agent of the corporation; or

(3) in a proceeding by the Attorney General under section 14.30.

(c) In a shareholder's proceeding under subsection (b)(1) to enjoin an unauthorized corporate act, the court may enjoin or set aside the act, if equitable and if all affected persons are parties to the proceeding, and may award damages for loss (other than anticipated profits) suffered by the corporation or another party because of enjoining the unauthorized act.

§ 4.01. Corporate Name

(a) A corporate name:

(1) must contain the word "corporation," "incorporated," "company," or "limited," or the abbreviation "corp.," "inc.," "co.," or "ltd."; and

(2) may not contain language stating or implying that the corporation is organized for a purpose other than that permitted by section 3.01 and its articles of incorporation.

(b) Except as authorized by subsections (c) and (d), a corporate name must be distinguishable upon the records of the secretary of state from:

(1) the corporate name of a corporation incorporated or authorized to transact business in this state;

(2) a corporate name reserved or registered under section 4.02 or 4.03; and

(3) the fictitious name adopted by a foreign corporation authorized to transact business in this state because its real name is unavailable.

(c) A corporation may apply to the secretary of state for authorization to use a name that is not distinguishable upon his records from one or more of the names described in subsection (b). The

Secretary of State shall authorize use of the name applied for if:

(1) the other corporation consents to the use in writing and submits an undertaking in form satisfactory to the secretary of state to change its name to a name that is distinguishable upon the records of the secretary of state from the name of the applying corporation; or

(2) the applicant delivers to the secretary of state a certified copy of the final judgment of a court of competent jurisdiction establishing the applicant's right to use the name applied for in this state.

(d) A corporation may use the name (including the fictitious name) of another domestic or foreign corporation that is used in this state if the other corporation is incorporated or authorized to transact business in this state and the proposed user corporation:

(1) has merged with the other corporation;

(2) has been formed by reorganization of the other corporation; or

(3) has acquired all or substantially all of the assets, including the corporate name, of the other corporation.

§ 4.02. Reserved Name

(a) A person may apply to the secretary of state to reserve the exclusive use of a corporate name, including a fictitious name for a foreign corporation whose corporate name is not available. If the secretary of state finds that the corporate name applied for is available, he shall reserve the name for the applicant's exclusive use for a nonrenewable 120-day period.

(b) The owner of a reserved corporate name may transfer the reservation to another person by delivering to the secretary of state a signed notice of the transfer that states the name and address of the transferee.

§ 6.01. Authorization Generally

(a) Each corporation may create and issue the number of shares of each class stated in its articles of incorporation.

(b) If classes of shares are authorized, the articles of incorporation must describe the designations, preferences, limitations, and relative rights of each class.

(c) The articles of incorporation may limit or deny the voting rights of or provide special voting rights for the shares of any class except to the extent prohibited by this Act.

(d) The articles of incorporation may authorize:

(1) the redemption at the option of the corporation or shareholder of:

(i) classes of preferred shares that have a preference over any other class of shares in the assets of the corporation upon liquidation; and

(ii) classes of common shares, whether or not they have a preference over other classes of common shares, if there exists at least one class of voting common shares not subject to redemption;

(2) the redemption at the option of the shareholder of shares of an investment corporation regulated under federal law; and

(3) the redemption at the option of the corporation of common shares issued by:

(i) a corporation that is subject to governmental regulation or regulation by a national securities exchange, if the regulation requires some or all of the shareholders to possess prescribed qualifications or limits the permissible holdings of shareholders and redemption is necessary to prevent loss or allow reinstatement of benefits or entitlements;

(ii) a professional corporation, if the redemption complies with [section 23 of the Model Professional Corporation Supplement].

§ 6.02. Classes of Preferred Shares

(a) If the articles of incorporation so provide, a corporation may issue classes of preferred shares:

(1) subject to the right or duty of the corporation to redeem the shares under section 6.01(d) at a price fixed in accordance with the articles of incorporation;

(2) entitling the holders of the shares to cumulative, noncumulative, or partially cumulative dividends;

(3) having preference over any other class of shares in the payment of dividends;

(4) having preference over any other class of shares in the assets of the corporation upon liquidation;

(5) convertible into shares of any other class or into shares of any series of the same or any other class, except a class having a prior or superior right to the payment of dividends or in the assets upon liquidation.

(b) Subsection (a)'s description of the designations, preferences, limitations, and relative rights of share classes is not exhaustive.

§ 6.03. Series Within a Class

(a) If the articles of incorporation so provide, a corporation may issue the shares of any preferred class in series.

(b) The articles may authorize the board of directors to create one or more series within a preferred class of shares and determine the designation, relative rights, preferences, and limitations of each series in accordance with the requirements of this section and the articles of incorporation.

(c) Each series of a class must be given a unique designation.

(d) All shares of the same class must provide identical relative rights, preferences, and limitations except with respect to:

(1) dividend rates;

(2) redeemability, including the redemption price, terms, and conditions;

(3) repurchase obligations of the corporation for all or part of a series at the option of the holders of another class;

(4) the amount payable per share upon liquidation;

(5) sinking fund provisions for the redemption or repurchase of shares;

(6) convertibility, including the terms and conditions of conversion;

(7) voting rights.

(e) Before issuing any shares of a series created under subsection (b), the corporation must deliver to the secretary of state articles of amendment, which are effective without shareholder action, that set forth:

(1) the name of the corporation;

(2) a copy of the resolution creating the series showing the date it was adopted; and

(3) a statement that the resolution was duly adopted by the board.

§ 6.20. Subscription for Shares

(a) A subscription for shares entered into before incorporation is irrevocable for six months unless the subscription agreement provides a longer or shorter period or all the subscribers agree to revocation.

(b) A subscription agreement entered into after incorporation is a contract between the subscriber and corporation.

(c) The board of directors may determine the payment terms of subscriptions for shares, whether entered into before or after incorporation, unless the subscription agreement specifies them. The board's call for payment on subscriptions must be uniform as to all shares of the same class or series.

(d) If a subscriber defaults in payment under the agreement, the corporation may collect the amount owed as any other debt. The bylaws may prescribe other penalties for nonpayment but a subscription and the installments already paid on it may not be forfeited unless the corporation demands the amount due by written notice to the subscriber and it remains unpaid for at least 20 days after the effective date of the notice.

(e) If a subscription for unissued shares is forfeited for nonpayment, the corporation may sell the shares subscribed for. If the shares are sold for more than the amount due on the subscription, the corporation shall pay the excess, after deducting the expense of sale, to the subscriber or his representative.

§ 6.21. Issuance of Shares

(a) The powers granted in this section are subject to restriction by the articles of incorporation.

(b) Shares may be issued at a price determined by the board of directors, or the board may set a minimum price or establish a formula or method by which the price may be determined.

(c) Consideration for shares may consist of cash, promissory notes, services performed, contracts for services to be performed, or any other tangible or intangible property. If shares are issued for other than cash, the board of directors shall determine the value of the consideration received as of the time the shares are issued.

(d) Shares issued when the corporation receives the consideration determined by the board are validly issued, fully paid, and nonassessable.

(e) A good faith judgment of the board of directors as to the value of the consideration received for shares is conclusive.

(f) The corporation may place shares issued for a contract for future services or a promissory note in escrow, or make other arrangements to restrict the transfer of the shares, and may credit distributions in respect of the shares against their purchase price, until the services are performed or the note is paid. If the services are not performed or the note is not paid, the shares escrowed or restricted and the distributions credited may be cancelled in whole or part.

§ 6.22. Liability of Subscribers and Shareholders

(a) A subscriber for or holder of shares of a corporation is not liable to the corporation or its creditors with respect to the shares except to pay the subscription price or the consideration determined for them under section 6.21.

(b) If shares are issued for promissory notes, for contracts for services to be performed, or before subscriptions are fully paid, a transferee of the shares is not liable to the corporation or its creditors for the unpaid balance but the transferor remains liable.

§ 6.23. Share Exchanges, Dividends, and Splits

(a) The powers granted in this section are subject to restriction by the articles of incorporation.

(b) If authorized by its board of directors, and subject to the limitation of subsection (c), a corporation may, without requiring consideration:

(1) issue its own shares to its shareholders in exchange for or in conversion of its outstanding shares; or

(2) issue its own shares pro rata to its shareholders or to the shareholders of one or more classes or series to effectuate share dividends or splits.

(c) Shares of one class or series may not be issued to the shareholders of another class or series unless (1) the articles of incorporation so authorize, (2) the holders of at least a majority of the outstanding votes of the class or series to be issued consent in writing to or vote affirmatively for the issue, or (3) there are no holders of the class or series to be issued.

§ 6.24. Share Rights and Options

(a) The powers granted in this section are subject to restriction by the articles of incorporation.

(b) A corporation may create and issue rights or options entitling their holders to purchase shares of any class, or any series within a class, in forms, on terms, at times, and for prices prescribed by the corporation's board of directors. Rights or options may be issued together with or independently of the corporation's issue and sale of its shares or other securities and may be issued as incentives to directors, officers, or employees of the corporation or any of its subsidiaries.

(c) A good faith judgment of the board of directors as to the value of the consideration received for rights or options entitling their holders to purchase shares is conclusive.

§ 6.27. Restriction on Transfer or Registration of Shares and Other Securities

(a) The articles of incorporation, bylaws, an agreement among shareholders, or an agreement between shareholders and the corporation may impose restrictions on the transfer or registration of transfer of shares of the corporation. A restriction does not affect shares issued before the restriction was adopted unless the holders of the shares are parties to the restriction agreement or voted in favor of the restriction.

(b) A restriction on the transfer or registration of transfer of shares is valid and enforceable against the holder or a transferee of the holder if the restriction is authorized by this section and is noted conspicuously on the front or back of the certificate or is contained in the information statement required by section 6.26(b). Unless so noted, a restriction is not enforceable against a person without knowledge of the restriction.

(c) A restriction on the transfer or registration of transfer of shares is authorized:

(1) to maintain the corporation's status when it is dependent on the number or identity of its shareholders;

(2) to preserve exemptions under federal or state securities law;

(3) for any other reasonable purpose.

(d) A restriction on the transfer or registration of transfer of shares may:

(1) obligate the shareholder first to offer the corporation or other persons (separately, consecutively, or simultaneously) an opportunity to acquire the restricted shares;

(2) obligate the corporation or other persons (separately, consecutively, or simultaneously) to acquire the restricted shares;

(3) require the corporation, the holders of any class of its shares, or another person to approve the transfer of the restricted shares, if the requirement is not manifestly unreasonable;

(4) prohibit the transfer of the restricted shares to designated persons or classes of persons, if the prohibition is not manifestly unreasonable.

(e) For purposes of this section, "shares" includes a security convertible into or carrying a right to subscribe for or acquire shares.

§ 6.30. Shareholders' Preemptive Rights

(a) The shareholders of a corporation do not have a preemptive right to acquire the corporation's unissued shares except to the extent the articles of incorporation so provide.

(b) A statement included in the articles of incorporation that "the corporation elects to have preemptive rights" (or words of similar import) means that subsections (c) through (f) apply except to the extent the articles of incorporation expressly provide otherwise.

(c) If the articles of incorporation provide for preemptive rights, the shareholders of a corporation have a preemptive right, granted on uniform terms and conditions prescribed by the board of directors to provide a fair and reasonable opportunity to exercise the right, to acquire proportional amounts of the corporation's unissued shares upon the decision of the board of directors to issue them.

(d) A shareholder may waive his preemptive right. A waiver evidenced by a writing is irrevocable even though it is not supported by consideration.

(e) There is no preemptive right:

(1) to acquire shares issued as incentives to directors, officers, or employees under section 6.24;

(2) to acquire shares issued to satisfy conversion or option rights;

(3) to acquire shares authorized in articles of incorporation that are issued within six months from the effective date of incorporation;

(4) to acquire shares sold otherwise than for money;

(5) for holders of shares of any class preferred or limited as to entitlement to dividends or assets;

(6) for holders of common shares to acquire shares of any class preferred or limited as to obligations or entitlement to dividends or assets unless the shares are convertible into common shares or carry a right to subscribe for or acquire common shares.

(f) Shares subject to preemptive rights that are not acquired by shareholders may be issued to any person for a period of one year after being offered to shareholders at a consideration set by the board of directors that is not lower than the consideration set for the exercise of preemptive rights. An offer at a lower consideration or after the expiration of one year is subject to the shareholders' premptive rights.

§ 6.31. Corporation's Power to Acquire Own Shares

(a) A corporation may acquire its own shares.

(b) If a corporation acquires its own shares, they constitute authorized but unissued shares unless the articles of incorporation prevent reissue, in which event the acquired shares are cancelled and the number of authorized shares is reduced by the number of shares acquired.

(c) If the number of authorized shares is reduced by an acquisition, the corporation must deliver to the secretary of state, not later than the due date of its next annual report, articles of amendment, which are effective without shareholder action, that set forth:

(1) the name of the corporation;

(2) the number of acquired shares cancelled, itemized by class and series; and

(3) the total number of authorized shares, itemized by class and series, remaining after cancellation of the acquired shares.

§ 6.40. Distributions to Shareholders

(a) Subject to restriction by the articles of incorporation and the limitation in subsection (c), a board of directors may authorize and the corporation may make distributions to its shareholders.

(b) If the directors do not fix the record date for determining shareholders entitled to a distribution (other than one involving a repurchase or reacquisition of shares), it is the date the board authorizes the distribution.

(c) No distribution may be made if, after giving it effect:

(1) the corporation would not be able to pay its debts as they become due in the usual course of business; or

(2) the corporation's total assets would be less than the sum of its total liabilities plus (unless the articles of incorporation permit otherwise) the maximum amount payable at the time of distribution to shareholders having preferential rights in liquidation.

(d) A board may base a determination that a distribution may be made under subsection (c) either on financial statements prepared on the basis of accounting practices and principles that are reasonable in the circumstances or on a fair valuation or other method that is reasonable in the circumstances.

(e) The effect of a distribution under subsection (c) is measured:

(1) in the case of distribution by purchase, redemption, or other acquisition of the corporation's shares, as of the earlier of (i) the date money or other property is transferred or debt incurred by the corporation or (ii) the date the shareholder ceases to be a shareholder with respect to the acquired shares;

(2) in all other cases, as of (i) the date of its authorization if payment occurs within 120 days after the date of authorization or (ii) the date of payment if payment occurs more than 120 days after the date of authorization.

(f) A corporation's indebtedness to a shareholder incurred by reason of a distribution made in accordance with this section is at parity with the corporation's indebtedness to its general, unsecured creditors except to the extent subordinated by agreement.

§ 7.01. Annual Meeting

(a) A corporation shall hold a shareholders' meeting annually at a time stated in or fixed in accordance with the bylaws.

(b) Annual shareholders' meetings may be held in or out of this state at the place stated in or fixed in accordance with the bylaws. If no place is stated in or fixed in accordance with the bylaws, annual meetings shall be held at the corporation's principal office.

(c) The failure to hold an annual meeting at the time stated in or fixed in accordance with a corporation's bylaws does not affect the validity of any corporate action.

§ 7.02. Special Meeting

(a) A corporation shall hold a special shareholders' meeting:

(1) on call of its board of directors or the individual or individuals authorized to do so by the articles of incorporation or bylaws; or

(2) if the holders of at least five percent of all the votes entitled to be cast at a proposed special meeting sign and deliver to the corporation's secretary one or more written demands for the meeting describing the purpose or purposes for which it is to be held.

(b) If not otherwise fixed under section 7.07, the record date for determining shareholders entitled to demand a special meeting is the date the first shareholder signs the demand.

(c) Special shareholders' meetings may be held in or out of this state at the place stated in or fixed in accordance with the bylaws. If no place is stated or fixed in accordance with the bylaws, special meetings shall be held at the corporation's principal office.

(d) Only business within the purpose or purposes described in the meeting notice required by section 7.05 (c) may be conducted at a special shareholders' meeting.

§ 7.04. Action Without Meeting

(a) Action required or permitted by this Act to be taken at a shareholders' meeting may be taken without a meeting and without action by the directors if the action is taken by all the shareholders entitled to vote on the action. The action must be evidenced by one or more written consents describing the action taken, signed by all the shareholders entitled to vote on the action, and delivered to the secretary of the corporation for inclusion in the minutes or filing with the corporate records.

(b) If not otherwise determined under section 7.07, the record date for determining shareholders entitled to take action without a meeting is the date the first shareholder signs the consent under subsection (a).

(c) A consent signed under this section has the effect of a meeting vote and may be described as such in any document.

(d) If this Act requires that notice of proposed action be given to nonvoting shareholders and the action is to be taken by unanimous consent of the voting shareholders, the corporation must give its nonvoting shareholders written notice of the proposed action at least 10 days before it is to be taken. The written consent or consents must recite that this notice was given.

§ 7.05. Notice of Meeting

(a) An officer of the corporation shall notify its shareholders of the date, time, and place of each annual and special shareholders' meeting no fewer than 10 nor more than 50 days before the meeting date. Unless this Act or the articles of incorporation require otherwise, the corporation is required to give notice only to shareholders entitled to vote at the meeting.

(b) Unless this Act or the articles of incorporation require otherwise, notice of an annual meeting need not include a description of the purpose or purposes for which the meeting is called.

(c) Notice of a special meeting must include a description of the purpose or purposes for which the meeting is called.

(d) If not otherwise fixed under section 7.07, the record date for determining shareholders entitled to notice of and to vote at an annual or special shareholders' meeting is the close of business on the day before the notice is mailed to the shareholders.

(e) Unless the bylaws require otherwise, if an annual or special shareholders' meeting is adjourned to a different date, time, or place, notice need not be given of the new date, time, or place if the new date, time, or place is announced at the meeting before adjournment. If a new record date for the adjourned meeting is or must be fixed under section 7.07, however, notice of the adjourned meeting must be given under this section to the shareholders of record on the new record date.

§ 7.06. Waiver of Notice

(a) A shareholder may waive any notice required by this Act, the articles of incorpⅰration, or bylaws before or after the date and time stated in the notice. The waiver must be in writing, be signed by the shareholder entitled to the notice, and be delivered to the secretary of the corporation for inclusion in the minutes or filing with the corporate records.

(b) A shareholder's attendance at a meeting:

(1) waives objection to lack of notice or defective notice of the meeting, unless the shareholder at the beginning of the meeting objects to holding the meeting or transacting business at the meeting;

(2) waives objection to consideration of a particular matter at the meeting that is not within the purpose or purposes described in the meeting notice, unless the shareholder objects to considering the matter when it is presented.

§ 7.07. Record Date

(a) The bylaws may fix or provide the manner of fixing the record date for determining the shareholders entitled to notice of a shareholders' meeting, to demand a special meeting, to vote, or to take any other action. If the bylaws do not fix or provide for fixing a record date, the directors of the corporation may fix a future date as the record date.

(b) A record date fixed under this section may not be more than 60 days before the meeting or action requiring a determination of shareholders.

(c) A determination of shareholders entitled to notice of or to vote at a shareholders' meeting is effective for any adjournment of the meeting unless the board fixes a new record date, which it must do if the meeting is adjourned to a date more than 120 days after the record date fixed for the original meeting.

(d) If a court orders a meeting adjourned to a date more than 120 days after the record date, it may provide that the original record date continues in effect or it may fix a new record date.

§ 7.20. Shareholders' List for Meeting

(a) After fixing a record date for a meeting, a corporation shall prepare an alphabetical list of the names of all its shareholders who are entitled to notice of a shareholders' meeting. The list must be arranged by class of shares and showing the address of and number of shares held by each shareholder.

(b) The shareholders' list must be available for inspection by any shareholder, beginning two business days after notice of the meeting for which the list was prepared is given and continuing through the meeting, at the corporation's principal office or at a place identified in the meeting notice in the city where the meeting will be held. A shareholder, his agent, or attorney is entitled on written demand to inspect and copy the list, during regular business hours and at his expense, during the period it is available for inspection.

(c) The corporation shall make the shareholders' list available at the meeting, and any shareholder, his agent, or attorney is entitled to inspect and copy the list at any time during the meeting or any adjournment.

(d) If the corporation refuses to allow a shareholder, his agent, or attorney to inspect and copy the shareholders' list before or at the meeting, the [name or describe] court in the county where the corporation's principal office (or if none in this state its registered office) is located, on application of the shareholder, may summarily order the inspection and copying at the corporation's expense and may postpone the meeting for which the list was prepared until the inspection and copying are complete.

(e) Refusal or failure to prepare or make available the shareholders' list does not affect the validity of action taken at the meeting.

§ 7.21. Voting Entitlement of Shares

(a) Except as provided in subsections (b) and (c) or unless the articles of incorporation provide otherwise, each outstanding share, regardless of class, is entitled to one vote on each matter voted on at a shareholders' meeting. Only shares are entitled to vote.

(b) Absent special circumstances, the shares of a corporation are not entitled to vote if they are owned, directly or indirectly, by a second corporation, domestic or foreign, and the first corporation owns, directly or indirectly, a majority of the shares entitled to vote for directors of the second corporation.

(c) Redeemable shares are not entitled to vote after notice of redemption is mailed to the holders and a sum sufficient to redeem the shares has been deposited with a bank, trust company, or other financial institution under an irrevocable obligation to pay the holders the redemption price on surrender of the shares.

§ 7.22. Proxies

(a) A shareholder may vote his shares in person or by proxy.

(b) A shareholder may appoint a proxy to vote or otherwise act for him by signing an appointment form, either personally or by his attorney-in-fact.

(c) An appointment of a proxy is effective when received by the secretary or other officer or agent authorized to tabulate votes. An appointment is valid for 11 months unless a longer period is expressly provided in the appointment form.

(d) An appointment of a proxy is revocable by the shareholder unless the appointment form conspicuously states that it is irrevocable and the appointment is coupled with an interest. Appointments coupled with an interest include the appointment of:

(1) a pledgee;

(2) a person who purchased or agreed to purchase the shares;

(3) a creditor of the corporation who extended it credit under terms requiring the appointment;

(4) an employee of the corporation whose employment contract requires the appointment; or

(5) a party to a voting agreement created under section 7.31.

(e) The death or incapacity of the shareholder appointing a proxy does not affect the right of the corporation to accept the proxy's authority unless notice of the death or incapacity is received by the secretary or other officer or agent authorized to tabulate proxy votes before the proxy exercises his authority under the appointment.

(f) An appointment made irrevocable under subsection (d) is revoked when the interest with which it is coupled is extinguished.

(g) A transferee for value of shares subject to an irrevocable appointment may revoke the appointment if he did not know of its existence when he acquired the shares and the existence of the irrevocable appointment was not noted conspicuously on the certificate representing the shares or on the information statement for shares without certificates.

(h) Subject to section 7.24 and to any express limitation on the proxy's authority appearing on the face of the appointment form, a corporation is entitled to accept the proxy's vote or other action as that of the shareholder making the appointment.

§ 7.24. Corporation's Acceptance of Votes

(a) If the name signed on a vote, consent, waiver, or proxy appointment corresponds to the name of a shareholder, the corporation if acting in good faith is entitled to accept the vote, consent, waiver, or proxy appointment and give it effect as the act of the shareholder.

(b) If the name signed on a vote, consent, waiver, or proxy appointment does not correspond to the name of its shareholder, the corporation if acting in good faith is nevertheless entitled to accept the vote, consent, waiver, or proxy appointment and give it effect as the act of the shareholder if:

(1) the shareholder is an entity and the name signed purports

to be that of an officer or agent of the entity;

(2) the name signed purports to be that of an administrator, executor, guardian, or conservator representing the shareholder and, if the corporation requests, evidence of fiduciary status acceptable to the corporation has been presented with respect to the vote, consent, waiver, or proxy appointment;

(3) the name signed purports to be that of a receiver or trustee in bankruptcy of the shareholder and, if the corporation requests, evidence of this status acceptable to the corporation has been presented with respect to the vote, consent, waiver, or proxy appointment;

(4) the name signed purports to be that of a pledgee, beneficial owner, or attorney-in-fact of the shareholder and, if the corporation requests, evidence acceptable to the corporation of the signatory's authority to sign for the shareholder has been presented with respect to the vote, consent, waiver, or proxy appointment;

(5) two or more persons are the shareholder as cotenants or fiduciaries and the name signed purports to be the name of at least one of the coowners and the person signing appears to be acting on behalf of all the coowners.

(c) The corporation is entitled to reject a vote, consent, waiver, or proxy appointment if the secretary or other officer or agent authorized to tabulate votes, acting in good faith, has reasonable basis for doubt about the validity of the signature on it or about the signatory's authority to sign for the shareholder.

(d) The corporation and its officer or agent who accepts or rejects a vote, consent, waiver, or proxy appointment in good faith and in accordance with the standards of this section are not liable in damages to the shareholder for the consequences of the acceptance or rejection.

(e) Corporate action based on the acceptance or rejection of a vote, consent, waiver, or proxy appointment under this section is valid unless a court of competent jurisdiction determines otherwise.

§ 7.30. Voting Trusts

(a) Shareholders may create a voting trust, conferring on a trustee the right to vote or otherwise act for them, by signing an agreement setting out the provisions of the trust (which may include anything consistent with its purpose) and transferring their shares to the trustee. When a voting trust agreement is signed, the trustee shall prepare a list of the names and addresses of all owners of beneficial interests in the trust, together with the number and class of shares each transferred to the trust, and deliver copies of the list and agreement to the corporation's principal office.

(b) A voting trust becomes effective on the date the shares subject to the trust are registered in the trustee's name. A voting trust is valid for not more than 10 years after its effective date unless extended under subsection (c).

(c) All or some of the parties to a voting trust may extend it for additional terms of not more than 10 years each by signing an extension agreement and obtaining the voting trustee's written consent to the extension. An extension agreement must be executed during the 12-month period immediately preceding expiration of the voting trust it is intended to extend. The voting trustee must deliver copies of the extension agreement and list of beneficial owners to the corporation's principal office. An extension agreement binds only those parties signing it.

§ 7.31. Voting Agreements

(a) Two or more shareholders may provide for the manner in which they will vote their shares by signing an agreement for that purpose. A voting agreement created under this section is not subject to the provisions of section 7.30.

(b) A voting agreement created under this section is specifically enforceable.

§ 7.40. Procedure in Derivative Proceedings

(a) A person may not commence a proceeding in the right of a domestic or foreign corporation unless he was a shareholder of the corporation when the transaction complained of occurred or unless he became a shareholder through transfer by operation of law from one who was a shareholder at that time.

(b) A complaint in a proceeding brought in the right of a corporation must be verified and allege with particularity the demand made, if any, to obtain action by the directors and either that the demand was refused or ignored or why he did not make the demand. Whether or not a demand for action was made, if the corporation commences an investigation of the changes made in the demand or complaint, the court may stay any proceeding until the investigation is completed.

(c) A proceeding commenced under this section may not be discontinued or settled without the court's approval. If the court determines that a proposed discontinuance or settlement will substantially affect the interest of the corporation's shareholders or a class of shareholders, the court shall direct that notice be given the shareholders affected.

(d) On termination of the proceeding the court may require the plaintiff to pay any defendant's reasonable expenses (including counsel fees) incurred in defending the proceeding if it finds that the proceeding was commenced without reasonable cause.

(e) For purposes of this section, "shareholder" includes a beneficial owner whose shares are held in a voting trust or held by a nominee on his behalf.

§ 8.01. Requirement for and Duties of Board

(a) Except as provided in subsection (c), each corporation must have a board of directors.

(b) All corporate powers shall be exercised by or under the authority of, and the business and affairs of the corporation managed under the direction of, its board.

(c) A corporation having 50 or fewer shareholders may dispense with or limit the authority of a board of directors by describing in its articles of incorporation who will perform some or all of the duties of a board.

§ 8.02. Qualifications of Directors

The articles of incorporation or bylaws may prescribe qualifications for directors. A director need not be a resident of this state or a shareholder of the corporation unless the articles of incorporation or bylaws so prescribe.

§ 8.03. Number and Election of Directors

(a) A board of directors must consist of one or more individuals, with the number specified in or fixed in accordance with the articles of incorporation or bylaws.

(b) If a board of directors has power to fix or change the number of directors, the board may increase or decrease by 30 percent or less the number of directors last approved by the shareholders, but only the shareholders may increase or decrease by more than 30 percent the number of directors last approved by the shareholders.

(c) The bylaws may establish a variable range for the size of the board by fixing a minimum and maximum number of directors. If a variable range is established, the number of directors may be fixed or changed from time to time, within the minimum and maximum, by the shareholders or the board. After shares are issued, only the shareholders may change a variable-range board size or change from a fixed to a variable-range board size or vice versa.

(d) Directors are elected at the first annual shareholders' meeting and at each annual meeting thereafter unless their terms are staggered under section 8.06.

§ 8.05. Terms of Directors Generally

(a) The terms of the initial directors of a corporation expire at the first annual shareholders' meeting.

(b) The terms of all other directors expire at the next annual shareholders' meeting following their election unless their terms are staggered under section 8.06.

(c) A decrease in the number of directors does not shorten an incumbent director's term.

(d) The term of a director elected to fill a vacancy expires at the next shareholders' meeting at which directors are elected.

(e) Despite the expiration of a director's term, he continues to serve until his successor is elected and qualifies or until there is a decrease in the number of directors.

§ 8.06. Staggered Terms for Directors

If there are nine or more directors, the articles of incorporation may provide for staggering their terms by dividing the total number of directors into two or three groups, with each group containing one-half or one-third of the total, as near as may be, and specifying that the terms of directors in the first group expire at the first annual shareholders' meeting after their election, that the terms of the second group expire at the second annual shareholders' meeting after their election, and that the terms of the third group, if any, expire at the third annual shareholders' meeting after their election.

§ 8.08. Removal of Directors by Shareholders

(a) The shareholders may remove a director with or without cause unless the articles of incorporation provide that directors may be removed only for cause.

(b) If a director is elected by a class of shareholders, he may be removed only by the shareholders of that class.

(c) If cumulative voting is authorized, a director may not be removed if the number of votes, or if he was elected by a class of shareholders the number of votes of that class, sufficient to elect him under cumulative voting is voted against his removal.

(d) A director may be removed by the shareholders only at a meeting called for the purpose of removing him and the meeting notice must state that the purpose, or one of the purposes, of the meeting is removal of the director. Except as provided in subsection (c), a director may be removed only if the number of votes cast to remove him would be sufficient to elect him at a meeting to elect directors.

(e) An entire board of directors may be removed under this section.

§ 8.10. Vacancy on Board

(a) Unless the articles of incorporation provide otherwise, if a vacancy occurs on a board of directors, including a vacancy resulting from an increase in the number of directors:

(1) the board of directors may fill the vacancy; or

(2) if the directors remaining in office constitute fewer than a quorum of the board, they may fill the vacancy by the affirmative vote of a majority of all the directors remaining in office.

(b) If the vacant office was held by a director elected by a class of shareholders, only the holders of that class of shares are entitled to vote to fill the vacancy if it is filled by the shareholders.

(c) A vacancy that will occur at a specific future date (by reason of a resignation effective at a future date under section 8.07(b) or otherwise) may be filled before the vacancy occurs if the new director does not take office until the vacancy occurs.

§ 8.20. Meetings

(a) A board of directors may hold regular or special meetings in or out of this state.

(b) Unless the articles of incorporation or bylaws provide otherwise, a board may permit one or more directors to participate in a regular or special meeting by, or conduct the meeting through the use of, any means of communication by which all directors participating may simultaneously hear each other during the meeting. A director participating in a meeting by this means is deemed to be present in person at the meeting.

§ 8.21 Action Without Meeting

(a) Unless the articles of incorporation or bylaws provide otherwise, action required or permitted by this Act to be taken at a board of directors' meeting may be taken without a meeting if the action is taken by all members of the board. The action must be evidenced by one or more written consents describing the action taken, signed by each director, and delivered to the secretary of the board for inclusion in the minutes or filing with the corporate records.

(b) Action taken under this section is effective when the last director signs the consent, unless the consent specifies a different effective date.

(c) A consent signed under this section has the effect of a meeting vote and may be described as such in any document.

§ 8.22. Notice of Meeting

(a) Unless the articles of incorporation or bylaws provide otherwise, regular meetings of the board may be held without notice of the date, time, place, or purpose of the meeting.

(b) Unless the articles of incorporation or bylaws provide for a longer or shorter period, special meetings of the board must be preceded by at least two days' notice of the date, time, and place of the meeting. The notice need not describe the purpose of the special meeting unless required by the articles of incorporation or bylaws.

§ 8.23. Waiver of Notice

(a) A director may waive any notice required by this Act, the articles of incorporation, or bylaws before or after the date and time stated in the notice. The waiver must be in writing, signed by the director entitled to the notice, and delivered to the secretary of the corporation for inclusion in the minutes or filing with the corporate records.

(b) A director's attendance at or participation in a regular or special meeting waives any required notice of the meeting unless the director at the beginning of the meeting objects to holding the meeting or transacting business at the meeting and does not thereafter vote for or assent to action taken at the meeting.

§ 8.24. Quorum and Voting

(a) Unless the articles of incorporation or bylaws require a greater number, a quorum of a board of directors consists of:

(1) a majority of the fixed number of directors if the corporation has a fixed board size; or

(2) a majority of the number of directors prescribed, or if no number is prescribed the number in office immediately before the meeting begins, if the corporation has a variable-range board size.

(b) The articles of incorporation may authorize a quorum of a board of directors to consist of no fewer than one-third of the fixed or prescribed number of directors determined under subsection (a).

(c) If a quorum is present when a vote is taken, the affirmative vote of a majority of directors present is the act of the board unless the articles of incorporation or bylaws require the vote of a greater number of directors.

(d) A director who is present at a meeting of the board or a committee of the board when corporate action is taken is deemed to have assented to the action taken unless: (1) he objects at the beginning of the meeting to holding it or transacting business at the meeting; (2) he requests that his dissent from the action taken be entered in the minutes of the meeting; or (3) he gives written notice of his dissent to the presiding officer of the meeting before its adjournment or to the secretary of the corporation immediately after adjournment of the meeting. The right of dissent is not available to a director who votes in favor of the action taken.

§ 8.25. Committees

(a) If the articles of incorporation or bylaws so provide, a board of directors may create one or more committees and appoint members of the board to serve on them. Each committee may have two or more members, who serve at the pleasure of the board.

(b) The creation of a committee and appointment of members to it must be approved by the greater of (1) a majority of all the directors in office when the action is taken or (2) the number of directors required by the articles of incorporation or bylaws to take action under section 8.24.

(c) Sections 8.20 through 8.24, which govern meetings, action without meetings, notice and waiver of notice, and quorum and voting requirements of the board of directors, apply to committees and their members as well.

(d) To the extent specified by the board of directors or in the articles of incorporation or bylaws, each committee may exercise the board's authority under section 8.01.

(e) A committee may not, however:

(1) authorize distributions;

(2) approve or recommend to shareholders action that this Act requires to be approved by shareholders;

(3) fill vacancies on the board or on any of its committees;

(4) adopt, amend, or repeal the bylaws;

(5) approve a plan of merger not requiring shareholder approval;

(6) authorize or approve reacquisition of shares, except according to a general formula or method prescribed by the board; or

(7) authorize or approve the issuance or sale or contract for sale of shares, or determine the designation and relative rights, preferences, and limitations of a series of shares, except that the board may direct a committee (or another person or persons) to fix the specific terms of the issuance or sale or contract for sale.

(f) The creation of, delegation of authority to, or action by a committee does not alone constitute compliance by a director with the standards of conduct described in section 8.30.

§ 8.30. General Standards for Directors

(a) A director shall discharge his duties as a director, including his duties as a member of a committee:

(1) in good faith;

(2) with the care an ordinarily prudent person in a like position would exercise under similar circumstances; and

(3) when exercising his business judgment, with the belief, premised on a rational basis, that his decision is in the best interests of the corporation.

(b) In discharging his duties a director is entitled to rely on information, opinions, reports, or statements, including financial statements and other financial data, if prepared or presented by:

(1) one or more officers or employees of the corporation whom the director reasonably believes to be reliable and competent in the matters presented;

(2) legal counsel, public accountants, or other persons as to matters the director reasonably believes are within the person's professional or expert competence; or

(3) a committee of the board of which he is not a member, as to matters within its jurisdiction, if the director reasonably believes the committee merits confidence.

(c) A director is not acting in good faith if he has knowledge concerning the matter in question that makes reliance otherwise permitted by subsection (b) unwarranted.

(d) Subject to compliance with section 8.31 if a director has an interest in a transaction:

(1) the director is not liable for the performance of the duties of his office if he acted in compliance with this section; and

(2) a person alleging a violation of this section has the burden of proving the violation.

(e) Subject to compliance with other provisions of this Act and other applicable law, a proceeding to enjoin, modify, rescind, or reverse a business decision, based on an alleged violation of this section, may not prevail if the directors who made the decision discharged their duties in compliance with this section.

§ 8.31. Director or Officer Conflict of Interest

(a) If a transaction is fair to a corporation at the time it is authorized, approved, or ratified, the fact that a director or officer of the corporation has a direct or indirect interest in the transaction is not a ground for invalidating the transaction or for imposing liability on that director or officer.

(b) In a proceeding contesting the validity of a transaction in which a director or officer has an interest, the person asserting validity has the burden of proving fairness unless:

(1) the material facts of the transaction and the director's or officer's interest were disclosed or known to the board of directors or a committee of the board and the board or committee authorized, approved, or ratified the transaction by the vote of a requisite quorum of directors who had no interest in the transaction; or

(2) the material facts of the transaction and the director's or officer's interest were disclosed to the shareholders entitled to vote and they authorized, approved, or ratified the transaction by the vote of a requisite quorum of shareholders who had no interest in the transaction.

(c) The presence of, or votes entitled to be cast by, the director or officer who has a direct or indirect interest in the transaction may be counted in determining whether a quorum is present but may not be counted when the board of directors, a committee of the board, or the shareholders vote on the transaction.

(d) For purposes of this section, a director or officer has an indirect interest in a transaction if an entity in which he has a material financial interest or in which he is an officer, director, or general partner is a party to the transaction. A vote or consent of that entity is deemed to be a vote or consent of the director or officer for purposes of subsection (c).

§ 8.32. Loans to Directors

(a) Except as provided by subsection (c), a corporation may not lend money to or guarantee the obligation of a director of the corporation unless:

(1) the particular loan or guarantee is approved by vote of the holders of at least a majority of the votes represented by the outstanding voting shares of all classes, except the votes of the benefited director; or

(2) the corporation's board of directors determines that the loan or guarantee benefits the corporation and either approves the specific loan or guarantee or a general plan authorizing loans and guarantees.

(b) The fact that a loan or guarantee is made in violation of this section does not affect the borrower's liability on the loan.

(c) This section does not apply to loans and guarantees authorized by statute regulating any special class of corporations.

§ 8.40. Required Officers

(a) A corporation has the officers described in its bylaws or appointed by the board of directors in accordance with the bylaws.

(b) A duly appointed officer may appoint one or more assistant officers if authorized by the board of directors.

(c) The board shall delegate to one of the officers responsibility for preparing minutes of the directors' and shareholders' meetings and for authenticating records of the corporation. The officer with this responsibility is deemed to be the secretary of the corporation for purposes of this Act.

(d) The same individual may simultaneously hold more than one office in a corporation.

§ 8.41. Duties of Officers

Each officer has the authority and shall perform the duties set forth in the bylaws or, to the extent consistent with the bylaws, the duties prescribed in a resolution of the board of directors or by direction of an officer authorized by the board to prescribe the duties of other officers.

§ 8.42. Standards of Conduct for Officers

(a) An officer with discretionary authority shall discharge his duties under that authority:

(1) in good faith;

(2) with the care an ordinarily prudent person in a like position would exercise under similar circumstances; and

(3) when exercising his business judgment, with the belief, premised on a rational basis, that his decision is in the best interests of the corporation.

(b) In discharging his duties an officer is entitled to rely on information, opinions, reports, or statements, including financial statements and other financial data, if prepared or presented by:

(1) one or more officers or employees of the corporation whom the officer reasonably believes to be reliable and competent in the matters presented; or

(2) legal counsel, public accountants, or other persons as to matters the officer reasonably believes are within the person's professional or expert competence.

(c) An officer is not acting in good faith if he has knowledge concerning the matter in question that makes reliance otherwise permitted by subsection (b) unwarranted.

(d) Subject to compliance with section 8.31 if an officer has an interest in a transaction:

(1) an officer is not liable for the performance of the duties of his office if he acted in compliance with this section; and

(2) a person alleging a violation of this section has the burden of proving the violation.

(e) Subject to compliance with other provisions of this Act and other applicable law, a proceeding to enjoin, modify, rescind, or reverse a business decision, based on an alleged violation of this section, may not prevail if the officer who made the decision discharged his duty in compliance with this section.

§ 8.43. Resignation and Removal of Officers

(a) An officer may resign at any time by giving written notice to the corporation. A resignation is effective when the notice is given unless the notice specifies a future effective date. If a resignation is made effective at a future date and the corporation accepts the future effective date, its board of directors may fill the pending vacancy before the effective date if the board provides that the successor does not take office until the effective date.

(b) A board of directors may remove any officer at any time with or without cause.

§ 8.50. Subchapter Definitions

In this subchapter:

(1) "Corporation" includes any domestic or foreign predecessor entity of a corporation in a merger or other transaction in which the predecessor's existence ceased upon consummation of the transaction.

(2) "Director" means an individual who is or was a director of a corporation or an individual who, while a director of a corporation, is or was serving at the corporation's request as a director, officer, partner, trustee, employee, or agent of another foreign or domestic corporation, partnership, joint venture, trust, employee benefit plan, or other enterprise. A director is considered to be serving an employee benefit plan at the corporation's request if his duties to the corporation also impose duties on, or otherwise involve services by, him to the plan or to participants in or beneficiaries of the plan.

(3) "Expenses" include counsel fees.

(4) "Liability" means the obligation to pay a judgment, settlement, penalty, fine (including an excise tax assessed with respect to an employee benefit plan), or reasonable expenses incurred with respect to a proceeding.

(5) "Official capacity" means: (i) when used with respect to a director, the office of director in a corporation; and (ii) when used with respect to an individual other than a director, as contemplated in section 8.56, the office in a corporation held by the officer or the employment or agency relationship undertaken by the employee or agent on behalf of the corporation. "Official capacity" does not include service for any other foreign or domestic corporation or any partnership, joint venture, trust, employee benefit plan, or other enterprise.

(6) "Party" includes an individual who was, is, or is threatened to be made a named defendant or respondent in a proceeding.

(7) "Proceeding" means any threatened, pending, or completed action, suit, or proceeding, whether civil, criminal, administrative, or investigative and whether formal or informal.

§ 10.02. Amendment by Directors

Unless the articles of incorporation provide otherwise, a corporation's board of directors may adopt one or more amendments to the corporation's articles of incorporation without shareholder action:

(1) to extend the duration of the corporation if it was incorporated at a time when limited duration was required by law;

(2) to delete the names and addresses of the initial directors;

(3) to delete the name and address of the initial registered agent or registered office, if a statement of change is on file with the secretary of state;

(4) to split the issued and unissued authorized shares if the corporation has only one class of shares and, if the shares have a par value, to reduce proportionately the par value;

(5) to change the corporate name by substituting the word "corporation," "incorporated," "company," "limited," or the abbreviation "corp.," "inc.," "co.," or "ltd.," for a similar word or abbreviation in the name, or by adding, deleting, or changing a geographical attribution for the name; or

(6) to make any other change expressly permitted by this Act to be made without shareholder action.

§ 10.03. Amendment by Directors and Shareholders

(a) A corporation's board of directors may propose one or more amendments to the articles of incorporation for action by the shareholders.

(b) To be adopted:

(1) the board must recommend the amendment to the shareholders unless the board determines that because of conflict of interest or other special circumstances it should make no recommendation and communicates the basis for its determination to the shareholders with the amendment; and

(2) the shareholders must approve the amendment.

(c) The board may condition its submission of the proposed amendment on any basis.

(d) The corporation shall notify each shareholder, whether or not entitled to vote, of the proposed shareholders' meeting in accordance with section 7.05. The notice must also state that the purpose, or one of the purposes, of the meeting is to consider the proposed amendment and contain or be accompanied by a copy or summary of the amendment.

(e) Unless this Act or the articles of incorporation require a greater vote:

(1) if the amendment would create dissenters' rights, the amendment to be adopted must be approved by a majority of all votes entitled to be cast on the amendment;

(2) all other amendments to be adopted must be approved by the holders of a majority of all votes cast on the amendment.

§ 10.04. Shareholder Class Voting on Amendments

(a) The holders of the outstanding shares of a class are entitled to vote as a class (if shareholder voting is otherwise required) on a proposed amendment if the amendment would:

(1) increase or decrease the aggregate number of authorized shares of the class;

(2) effect an exchange or reclassification of all or part of the shares of the class;

(3) effect an exchange, or create the right of exchange, of all or part of the shares of the class into the shares of another class;

(4) change the designation, relative rights, voting rights, preferences, or limitations of all or part of the shares of the class;

(5) change the shares of all or part of the class into the same or a different number of shares of the same class or another class;

(6) create a new class of shares having rights or preferences prior, superior, or substantially equal to the shares of the class, or increase the rights, preferences, or number of authorized shares of any class having rights or preferences prior, superior, or substantially equal to the shares of the class;

(7) in the case of a preferred class of shares, divide the shares

into a series, designate the series, and determine (or authorize the board of directors to determine) variations in the relative rights and preferences between the shares of the series;

(8) limit or deny an existing preemptive right of all or part of the shares of the class; or

(9) cancel or otherwise affect dividends on all or part of the shares of the class that have accumulated but not yet been declared.

(b) If a proposed amendment would affect a series of a class of shares in one or more of the ways described in subsection (a), the holders of that series are entitled to vote as a separate class on the proposed amendment.

(c) If a proposed amendment that entitles two or more series to vote as separate classes under subsection (b) would affect two or more series of a class of shares in the same or a substantially similar way, the holders of the shares of all the series so affected must vote as a single class on the proposed amendment.

(d) A class or series of shares is entitled to the voting rights granted by this section although the articles of incorporation provide that the shares are nonvoting shares.

§ 10.20. Amendment by Directors or Shareholders

(a) A corporation's board of directors may amend or repeal the corporation's bylaws unless:

(1) the articles of incorporation reserve this power exclusively to the shareholders in whole or part; or

(2) the shareholders in amending or repealing a particular bylaw provide expressly that the directors may not amend or repeal that bylaw.

(b) A corporation's shareholders may amend or repeal the corporation's bylaws even though the bylaws may also be amended or repealed by its board of directors.

11.03. Action on Plan by Shareholders

(a) After adopting a plan of merger or share exchange, the board of directors of each corporation party to the merger, and the board of directors of the corporation whose shares will be acquired in the share exchange, shall submit the plan of merger (except as provided in subsection (g)) or share exchange for action by its shareholders.

(b) To be authorized:

(1) the board must recommend the plan of merger or share exchange to the shareholders unless the board determines that because of conflict of interest or other special circumstances it should make no recommendation and communicates the basis for its determination to the shareholders with the plan; and

(2) the shareholders must approve the plan.

(c) The board may condition its submission of the proposed merger or share exchange on any basis.

(d) The corporation shall notify each shareholder, whether or not entitled to vote, of the proposed shareholders' meeting in accordance with section 7.05. The notice must also state that the purpose, or one of the purposes, of the meeting is to consider the plan of merger or share exchange and contain or be accompanied by a copy or summary of the plan.

(e) Unless this Act, the articles of incorporation, or the board require a greater vote, the plan of merger or share exchange to be authorized must be approved by the holders of a majority of all the votes entitled to be cast on the plan.

(f) Voting by a class or series of shares is required:

(1) on a plan of merger if the plan contains a provision that, if contained in a proposed amendment to articles of incorporation, would entitle the class or series to vote as a class or series on the proposed amendment under section 10.04;

(2) on a plan of share exchange if the class or series is included in the exchange.

(g) Action by the shareholders of the surviving corporation on a plan of merger is not required if:

(1) the articles of incorporation of the surviving corporation will not differ (except in name) from its articles before the merger;

(2) each shareholder of the surviving corporation whose shares were outstanding immediately before the effective date of the merger will hold the same number of shares, with identical designations, preferences, limitations, and relative rights, immediately after;

(3) the number of voting shares outstanding immediately after the merger, plus the number of voting shares issuable on conversion of other securities or on exercise of rights and warrants issued pursuant to the merger, will not exceed by more than 20 percent the total number of voting shares of the surviving corporation outstanding immediately before the merger; and

(4) the number of participating shares outstanding immediately after the merger, plus the number of participating shares issuable on conversion of other securities or on exercise of rights and warrants issued pursuant to the merger, will not exceed by more than 20 percent the total number of participating shares outstanding immediately before the merger.

(h) As used in subsection (g):

(1) "Participating shares" means shares that entitle their holders to participate without limitation in distributions.

(2) "Voting shares" means shares that entitle their holders to vote unconditionally in elections of directors.

(i) After a merger or share exchange is authorized, and at any time before articles of merger or share exchange are filed, the planned merger or share exchange may be abandoned, subject to any contractual rights, without further shareholder action.

§ 12.01. Sale of Assets in Regular Course of Business and Mortgage of Assets

(a) A corporation may sell, lease, exchange, or otherwise dispose of all, or substantially all, of its property in the usual and regular course of business, or mortgage, pledge, or dedicate to the repayment of indebtedness (whether with or without recourse) any or all of its property whether or not in the usual and regular course of business, on the terms and conditions and for the consideration determined by the board of directors.

(b) Unless the articles of incorporation require it, approval by the shareholders of a transaction described in subsection (a) is not required.

§ 12.02. Sale of Assets Other Than in Regular Course of Business

(a) A corporation may sell, lease, exchange, or otherwise dispose of all, or substantially all, of its property (with or without the good will), otherwise than in the usual and regular course of business, on the terms and conditions and for the consideration determined by the corporation's board of directors, if the board adopts and its shareholders approve the proposed transaction.

(b) To be authorized:

(1) the board must recommend the proposed transaction to the shareholders unless the board determines that because of conflict of interest or other special circumstances it should make no recommendation and communicates the basis for its determination to the shareholders with the proposed transaction; and

(2) the shareholders must approve the transaction.

(c) The board may condition its submission of the proposed transaction on any basis.

(d) The corporation shall notify each shareholder, whether or not entitled to vote, of the proposed shareholders' meeting in accordance with section 7.05. The notice must also state that the purpose, or one of the purposes, of the meeting is to consider the sale, lease, exchange, or other disposition of all, or substantially all, the property of the corporation and contain or be accompanied by a description of the transaction.

(e) Unless the articles of incorporation or the board require a greater vote, the transaction to be authorized must be approved by the holders of a majority of all the votes entitled to be cast on the transaction.

(f) After a sale, lease, exchange, or other disposition of property is authorized, the transaction may be abandoned, subject to any contractual rights, without further shareholder action.

(g) A transaction that constitutes a distribution is governed by section 6.40 and not by this section.

§ 13.01. Definitions

In this chapter:

(1) "Corporation" means the issuer of the shares held by a dissenter before the corporate action, or the surviving or acquiring corporation by merger or share exchange of that issuer.

(2) "Dissenter" means a shareholder who is entitled to dissent from corporate action under section 13.02 and who exercises that right when and in the manner required by sections 13.20 through 13.28.

(3) "Fair value," with respect to a dissenter's shares, means the value of the shares immediately before the effectuation of the corporate action to which the dissenter objects, excluding any appreciation or depreciation in anticipation of the corporate action unless exclusion would be inequitable.

(4) "Interest" means interest from the effective date of the corporate action until the date of payment, at the average rate currently paid by the corporation on its principal bank loans or, if none, at a rate that is fair and equitable under all the circumstances.

(5) "Shareholder" includes a beneficial owner of shares held by a nominee.

§ 13.02. Right to Dissent

(a) A shareholder of a corporation is entitled to dissent from, and obtain payment for his shares in the event of, any of the following corporate actions:

(1) consummation of a plan of merger to which the corporation is a party if (i) shareholder approval is required for the merger by section 11.03 or the articles of incorporation or (ii) the corporation is a subsidiary that is merged with its parent under section 11.04;

(2) consummation of a plan of share exchange to which the corporation is a party as the corporation whose shares will be acquired;

(3) consummation of a sale or exchange of all, or substantially all, of the property of the corporation other than in the usual and regular course of business, including a sale in dissolution, but not including a sale pursuant to court order or a sale for cash pursuant to a plan by which all or substantially all of the net proceeds of the sale will be distributed to the shareholders within one year after the date of sale;

(4) an amendment of the articles of incorporation that materially and adversely affects rights in respect of a dissenter's shares because it:

(i) alters or abolishes a preferential right of the shares;

(ii) creates, alters, or abolishes a right in respect of redemption, including a provision respecting a sinking fund for the redemption or repurchase, of the shares;

(iii) alters or abolishes a preemptive right to acquire shares or other securities;

(iv) excludes or limits the right to vote on any matter, or to cumulate votes, other than a limitation by dilution through issuance of shares or other securities with similar voting rights; or

(5) any other corporate action taken pursuant to a shareholder vote if the articles of incorporation, bylaws, or a resolution of the board of directors provides that shareholders are entitled to dissent and obtain payment for their shares.

(b) A shareholder entitled to dissent and obtain payment for his shares under this chapter may not challenge the corporate action creating his entitlement unless the action is unlawful or fraudulent with respect to the shareholder or the corporation.

§ 13.20. Notice of Dissenters' Rights

(a) If proposed corporate action creating dissenters' rights under section 13.02 is submitted to a vote at a shareholders' meeting, the meeting notice must state that shareholders are or may be entitled to assert dissenters' rights under this chapter and be accompanied

by a copy of this chapter.

(b) If proposed corporate action creating dissenters' rights under section 13.02 is taken without a vote of shareholders, the corporation shall notify in writing all shareholders entitled to assert dissenters' rights that the action was taken and send them the notice described in section 13.22.

§ 13.22. Notice of How to Demand Payment

(a) If proposed corporate action creating dissenters' rights under section 13.02 is authorized at a shareholders' meeting, the corporation shall notify in writing all shareholders who satisfied the requirements of section 13.21 how to demand payment for their shares.

(b) The subsection (a) notice must:

(1) state where the payment demand must be sent and where and when certificates for certificated shares must be deposited;

(2) inform holders of uncertificated shares to what extent transfer of the shares will be restricted after the payment demand is received;

(3) supply a form for demanding payment that includes the date of the first announcement to news media or to shareholders of the terms of the proposed corporate action and requires that the person asserting dissenters' rights certify whether he acquired beneficial ownership of the shares before or after that date;

(4) set a date by which the corporation must receive the payment demand, which date may not be fewer than 30 nor more than 60 days after the effective date of the subsection (a) notice; and

(5) be accompanied by a copy of this chapter.

§ 13.23. Duty to Demand Payment

(a) A shareholder notified of how to demand payment for his shares under section 13.22 must demand payment, certify that he acquired beneficial ownership of the shares either before or after the first announcement date, and deposit his certificates in accordance with the terms of the notice.

(b) A shareholder who does not demand payment or deposit his share certificates where required, each by the date set in the demand notice, is not entitled to payment for his shares under this chapter.

§ 13.24. Share Restrictions

(a) The corporation may restrict the transfer of uncertificated shares from the date the demand for their payment is received until the proposed corporate action is effectuated or the restrictions released under section 13.26.

(b) The person for whom dissenters' rights are asserted as to uncertificated shares retains all other rights of a shareholder until these rights are modified by effectuation of the proposed corporate action.

§ 13.25. Payment

(a) As soon as the proposed corporate action is effectuated, or upon receipt of a payment demand if the action has already been effectuated, the corporation shall pay each dissenter who complied with section 13.23 the amount the corporation estimates to be the fair value of his shares, plus accrued interest.

(b) The payment must be accompanied by:

(1) the corporation's balance sheet as of the end of a fiscal year ending not more than 16 months before the date of payment, an income statement for that year, a statement of changes in shareholders' equity for that year, and the latest available interim financial statements, if any;

(2) a statement of the corporation's estimate of the fair value of the shares;

(3) a statement of the dissenter's right to demand payment under section 13.28; and

(4) a copy of this chapter.

§ 13.28. Procedure if Shareholder Dissatisfied with Payment or Offer

(a) A dissenter may notify the corporation in writing of his own estimate of the fair value of his shares and amount of interest due, and demand payment of the difference between his estimate and the corporation's payment under section 13.25, or reject the corporation's offer under section 13.27 and demand payment of the fair value of his shares and interest due, if:

(1) the dissenter believes that the amount paid under section 13.25 or offered under section 13.27 is less than the fair value of his shares or that the interest due is incorrectly calculated; or

(2) the corporation does not make payment and does not return the deposited certificates or release the transfer restrictions imposed on uncertificated shares within 60 days after the date set for demanding payment.

(b) A dissenter waives his right to demand payment under this section unless he notifies the corporation of his demand in writing under subsection (a) within 30 days after the corporation made or offered payment for his shares.

§ 13.30. Court Action

(a) If a demand for payment under section 13.28 remains unsettled, the corporation shall commence a proceeding within 60 days after receiving the payment demand and petition the [name or describe] court to determine the fair value of the shares and accrued interest. If the corporation does not commence the proceeding within the 60-day period, it shall pay each dissenter whose demand remains unsettled the amount demanded.

(b) The corporation shall commence the proceeding in the county where its principal office, or if none in this state its registered office, is located. If the corporation is a foreign corporation without a registered office in this state, it shall commence the proceeding in the county in this state where the registered office of the domestic corporation merged with or whose shares were acquired by the foreign corporation was located.

(c) The corporation shall make all dissenters (whether or not residents of this state) whose demands remain unsettled parties to the proceeding as in an action against their shares and all parties must be served with a copy of the petition. Nonresidents may be served by registered or certified mail or by publication as provided by law.

(d) The jurisdiction of the court in which the proceeding is commenced under subsection (b) is plenary and exclusive. The court may appoint one or more persons as appraisers to receive evidence and recommend decision on the question of fair value. The appraisers have the powers described in the order appointing them, or in any amendment to it. The dissenters are entitled to the same discovery rights as parties in other civil proceedings.

(e) Each dissenter made a party to the proceeding is entitled to judgment (1) for the amount, if any, by which the court finds the fair value of his shares, plus interest, exceeds the amount paid by the corporation or (2) for the fair value, plus accrued interest, of his after-acquired shares for which the corporation elected to withhold payment under section 13.27.

§ 13.31. Court Costs and Counsel Fees

(a) The court in an appraisal proceeding commenced under section 13.30 shall determine all costs of the proceeding, including the reasonable compensation and expenses of appraisers appointed by the court, and shall assess the costs against the corporation. The court may assess costs against all or some of the dissenters, in amounts the court finds equitable, to the extent the court finds the dissenters acted arbitrarily, vexatiously, or not in good faith in demanding payment under section 13.28.

(b) The court may also assess the fees and expenses of counsel and experts for the respective parties, in amounts the court finds equitable:

(1) against the corporation and in favor of any or all dissenters if the court finds the corporation did not substantially comply with the requirements of sections 13.20 through 13.28; or

(2) against either the corporation or a dissenter, in favor of any other party, if the court finds that the party against whom the fees and expenses are assessed acted arbitrarily, vexatiously, or not in good faith with respect to the rights provided by this chapter.

(c) If the court finds that the services of counsel for any dissenter were of substantial benefit to other dissenters similarly situated, and that the fees for those services should not be assessed against the corporation, the court may award to these counsel reasonable fees to be paid out of the amounts awarded the dissenters who were benefited.

§ 14.02. Dissolution by Directors and Shareholders

(a) A corporation's board of directors may propose dissolution for action by the shareholders.

(b) To be authorized:

(1) the board must recommend dissolution to the shareholders unless the board determines that because of conflict of interest or other special circumstances it should make no recommendation and communicates the basis for its determination to the shareholders; and

(2) the shareholders must approve dissolution.

(c) The board may condition its submission of the proposal for dissolution on any basis.

(d) The corporation shall notify each shareholder, whether or not entitled to vote, of the proposed shareholders' meeting in accordance with section 7.05. The notice must also state that the purpose, or one of the purposes, of the meeting is to consider dissolving the corporation.

(e) Unless the articles of incorporation or the board require a greater vote, dissolution is authorized if approved by the holders of a majority of all votes entitled to be cast at the meeting.

§ 16.01. Corporate Records

(a) A corporation shall keep as permanent records minutes of all meetings of its shareholders and board of directors, a record of all actions taken by the shareholders or directors without a meeting, and a record of all actions taken by a committee of the board of directors in place of the board on behalf of the corporation.

(b) A corporation shall maintain appropriate accounting records.

(c) A corporation or its agent shall maintain a record of its shareholders, in a form that permits preparation of a list of the names and addresses of all shareholders, in alphabetical order by class of shares showing the number and class of shares held by each.

(d) A corporation shall maintain its records in written form or in another form capable of conversion into written form within a reasonable time.

(e) A corporation shall keep the following records at its principal office:

(1) its articles or restated articles of incorporation and all amendments to them currently in effect;

(2) its bylaws or restated bylaws and all amendments to them currently in effect;

(3) resolutions adopted by its board of directors creating one or more series of shares, and fixing their relative rights, preferences, and limitations, if shares issued pursuant to those resolutions are outstanding;

(4) the minutes of all shareholders' meetings, and records of all action taken by shareholders without a meeting, for the past three years;

(5) all written communications to shareholders generally within the past three years, including the financial statements furnished for the past three years under section 16.20;

(6) a list of the names and business addresses of its current directors and officers; and

(7) a copy of its most recent annual report supplied the secretary of state under section 16.22.

§ 16.02. Inspection of Records by Shareholders

(a) Subject to section 16.03 (c), a shareholder of a corporation is entitled to inspect and copy, during regular business hours at the corporation's principal office, any of the records of the corporation described in section 16.01 (e) if he gives the corporation written notice of his demand at least five business days before the date on which he wishes to inspect and copy.

(b) A shareholder of a corporation is entitled to inspect and copy, during regular business hours at a reasonable location specified by the corporation, any of the following records of the corporation if the shareholder meets the requirements of subsection (c) and gives the corporation written notice of his demand at least five business days before the date on which he wishes to inspect and copy:

(1) excerpts from minutes of any meeting of the board of directors, records of any action of a committee of the board while acting in place of the board on behalf of the corporation, minutes of any meeting of the shareholders, and records of action taken by the shareholders or directors without a meeting, to the extent not subject to inspection under section 16.02(a);

(2) accounting records of the corporation; and

(3) the record of shareholders.

(c) A shareholder may inspect and copy the records identified in subsection (b) only if:

(1) his demand is made in good faith and for a proper purpose;

(2) he describes with reasonable particularity his purpose and the records he desires to inspect; and

(3) the records are directly connected with his purpose.

(d) The right of inspection granted by this section may not be abolished or limited by a corporation's articles of incorporation or bylaws.

(e) This section does not affect:

(1) the right of a shareholder to inspect records under section 7.20 or, if the shareholder is in litigation with the corporation, to the same extent as any other litigant;

(2) the power of a court, independently of this Act, to compel the production of corporate records for examination.

§ 16.03. Scope of Inspection Right

(a) A shareholder's agent or attorney has the same inspection and copying rights as the shareholder he represents.

(b) The right to copy records includes, if reasonable, the right to receive copies made by photographic, xerographic, or other means.

(c) The corporation may impose a reasonable charge, covering the costs of labor and material, for providing copies of any documents the shareholder is entitled to inspect. The charge may not exceed the estimated cost of production or reproduction of the records.

(d) The corporation may comply with a shareholder's demand to inspect the record of shareholders under section 16.02 (b)(3) by providing him with a list of its shareholders that was compiled no earlier than the date of the shareholder's demand.

§ 16.04 Court-Ordered Inspection

(a) If a corporation does not allow a shareholder who complies with section 16.02 (a) to inspect and copy any records required by that subsection to be available for inspection, the [name or describe court] in the county where the corporation's principal office, or if none in this state its registered office, is located may summarily order inspection and copying of the records demanded at the corporation's expense upon application of the shareholder.

(b) If a corporation does not within a reasonable time allow a shareholder to inspect and copy any other record, the shareholder who complies with section 16.02(b) and (c) may apply to the [name or describe court] in the county where the corporation's principal office, or if none in this state its registered office, is located for an order to permit inspection and copying of the records demanded. The court shall dispose of an application under this subsection on an expedited basis.

(c) If the court orders inspection and copying of the records demanded, it shall also order the corporation to pay the shareholder's costs (including reasonable counsel fees) incurred to obtain the order unless the corporation proves that it refused inspection in good faith because it had a reasonable basis for doubt about the right of the shareholder to inspect the records demanded.

(d) If the court orders inspection and copying of the records demanded, it may impose reasonable restrictions on the use or distribution of the records by the demanding shareholder.

Glossary

A fortiori—With a stronger reason; much more (Latin). A term used to emphasize that because one fact exists, another must logically be true.

A priori—A method of reasoning that starts with general principles and attempts to find specific facts that will flow from them (Latin).

Acceleration clause—A statement in a time instrument that permits the instrument to become due immediately upon the occurrence of some specified event.

Acceptance—The receipt and retention of that which is offered; the assent to a legal offer that is a prerequisite to the formation of a contract.

Acceptor—A person who has agreed to accept a draft.

Accession—The obtaining of a right or an office; the acquisition of property by its addition or incorporation with other property already owned.

Accommodation paper—A note signed by another as a favor without consideration passing between the individuals.

Accommodation party—A person who signs an instrument in any capacity for the purpose of lending his or her name and credit to another party to the instrument.

Acknowledgment—A declaration before a notary that the executor of a document executed such of his or her own free will.

Act of state doctrine—A policy whereby a court agrees to recognize the act of a foreign government, taken in its territory, as valid and causing the court (of another country) not to question the validity of that foreign government's action.

Actionable—Furnishing a basis or legal reason for a lawsuit.

Ad valorem—According to its value (Latin). For example, an *ad valorem* tax will generate revenues based on the percentage value of the item taxed as opposed to a fixed or specific tax, which is imposed regardless of value.

Adjudication—The pronouncing of a formal judgment by a court for one party or the other in a lawsuit.

Administrative agency—Governmental department created by Congress or executive order to regulate some specialized aspect of interstate commerce (e.g., Federal Trade Commission).

Administrative law judge (Hearing examiner)—Officer who presides at initial hearing on matters litigated before a federal agency. He or she is chosen by civil service exam and is independent of the agency staff.

Administrative Procedure Act—A statute setting forth the procedural rules for U.S. regulatory agencies and for parties appearing before such agencies.

Adversary principle—The principle that places the responsibility for developing or defending a case upon the parties and not on some designated legal official.

Adverse possession—Method of acquiring title to real property by occupying property in an open and notorious manner for a statutory period, thus denying title or ownership to anyone else.

Advisory opinion—A formal opinion rendered by a judge or a court on a question of law submitted by the legislative or executive branch; such an opinion will not usually arise out of an adversary proceeding or lawsuit.

Affidavit—A written statement of facts that a person has sworn to before someone qualified to take an oath.

Affirm—To confirm or agree with. A higher court affirms a lower court decision when it declares the decision valid.

Affirmative action—A process by which the public and private sectors are required by executive orders, regulations, and court decisions to take steps to remedy past discrimination in the hiring and promotion of minorities and women.

Affirmative defense—A part of defendant's answer to plaintiff's complaint; sets out new arguments showing why defendant should win even if everything in the complaint is true.

After-acquired property—Property that becomes the subject of a security interest after the parties have made a security agreement.

Agency—A legal relationship in which one person is authorized to act for another, who is called a principal.

Agent—A person authorized to act for another in a legal relationship.

Allonge—A paper firmly attached to an instrument on which indorsements are written.

Altruism, ethical—Giving primacy

to the interests of others in one's decisions. The opposite of egoism.

Amend—To revise or correct. For example, the proposed equal rights amendment (ERA) is an attempt to correct past discriminatory patterns against women.

Amicus curiae—Friend of the court (Latin). A person who is not a direct party to the proceeding but, with the permission of the court, is allowed to file a brief and often participate in oral argument on appeal.

Ancilliary—A subordinate or attendant to the main proceeding or process. For example, *ancilliary* administration is a proceeding in a state where a deceased person may have property but did not live there, and thus his or her main estate is not administered there.

Annual percentage—The actual cost of borrowing money for a stated period expressed in yearly terms. Required by federal statute to make it easier for people to understand the terms of a credit agreement and compare rates charged by financial institutions.

Annuity contract—A contract that pays a specific sum to the insured at periodic intervals after the insured reaches a specified age.

Anticipatory breach—A breach of an agreement prior to the duty of performance. Words or actions showing an intention to refuse performance in the future are grounds for immediate suit by a party without waiting for the time of performance.

Apparent authority—The authority of an agent that seems superficially true to a third party because of the words or conduct of such agent in representing his or her principal, and the latter's acquiescence in these representations.

Appeal—A process by which a party asks a higher court to review alleged errors of law made by a lower court or federal–state agency. In the case of new facts that develop following a lower court decision, an appellate court may also be requested to review the decision with the purpose of obtaining a new trial. Appeals from regulatory agencies may also

be based on abuse of discretion or arbitrary judgment.

Appellant—The party to a suit who appeals a case to a higher court. Usually the party who loses in a lower court is the one who will appeal. The party who wins below will sometimes appeal, asking for a greater recovery or modification of a court order.

Appellee—The party to a suit against whom an appeal may be brought. This person is usually, but not always, the winner in the court below.

Appurtenance—Something adjoined or attached to a principal. For example, a house or barn is an *appurtenance* to land.

Arbitration—The process of submitting a dispute to an independent expert for decision. This takes place outside the formal court system and is based on an agreement between the parties to the dispute that they will accept the outcome of the process.

Arguendi—"In the course of argument" (Latin). Usually applies to a statement made by a judge, referee, or arbitrator as a matter of illustration but having no direct bearing on the case in dispute.

Assault—An intentional *tort* or *crime* in which force or movement could put the person approached in reasonable fear of bodily harm or contact.

Assignee—A person to whom an assignment has been made. Also called a *grantee.*

Assignment—The process of transferring rights in real or personal property to another person. Such rights are commonly called *choses in action.* For example, *A* sells and assigns his contract right to *C,* to be paid money by *B. A* is the assignor, *C* is the assignee.

Assignor—A person who makes an assignment. Also referred to as a *grantor.*

Attachment—The process of bringing property or persons within the jurisdiction of the court by seizing one or both. For example, one may *attach* a bank account in order to be sure that a person pays a debt owed.

Attest—To bear witness to a fact; to act as a witness to a fact.

Automated teller machine—A machine that enables the user to withdraw cash, make deposits, transfer money from one account to another, and carry on other similar transactions with a bank.

Bailee—The person to whom personal property is delivered by a bailor under a contract of bailment.

Bailment—The delivery of personal property by owner to bailee in trust for a specific purpose. Delivery takes place as a result of an expressed or implied agreement between the parties.

Bailor—The person who initiates a contract of bailment and delivers the personal property to the bailee.

Bankruptcy—The process by which a person who is unable to pay his, her, or its (corporation) debts is declared a bankrupt, has its nonexempt debts distributed by a bankruptcy court, and thereafter is released from claims on any balance due to creditors. Bankruptcy is not *insolvency.*

Bargain and sale deed—A deed that conveys title but makes no warranties.

Battery—An intentional physical contact by one individual (or through a thing in the control of that person) with another individual. Can be a basis for criminal and/or tort action.

Bearer—A person possessing a negotiable instrument (e.g., a check) that is payable to any individual and does not specifically designate a payee. The instrument may be made "payable to bearer" or indorsed in blank.

Bearer paper—An instrument that is payable to bearer.

Beneficiary—A person who receives benefit from an insurance policy as a payee, who benefits from a trust, or who inherits under a will. *Creditor beneficiary* is one who is not a direct party to an agreement between a promisor and promisee but receives performance because the promisee wishes to discharge a debt to him or her. A *donee beneficiary* is one who is also not a party to the original agreement but receives benefit from the agreement as a gift (e.g., life insurance policy designated for a child upon the death of parents).

Bequeath—To give personal property to another by a will.

Bid—A legal offer for property at an auction.

Bilateral contract—An agreement in which the oral or written promises of the parties serve as consideration for each other's promises.

Bill of complaints—A formal written declaration of bases for a plaintiff's action against a defendant in a court proceeding.

Bill of lading—A document of title or acknowledgment evidencing receipt of particular goods on board a ship (or by whoever is transporting the goods); the bill of lading also serves to note that the goods were in good order and fit for shipment.

Binder—A document that commits an insurance company prior to a policy being issued.

Blank indorsement—An indorsement that does not specify a particular payee.

"Blue Sky" laws—A common or popular term for state and federal statutes that regulate the sale of securities. These laws seek to protect investors from fraudulent or unethical promoters of investment schemes.

Boiler plate—A standard form contract, or clause in a contract, that is not drafted for the particular client but is generally issued (e.g., insurance contracts and clauses therein).

Bona fide—In good faith (Latin).

Boycott—A conspiracy on the part of individuals, unions, or firms to refuse to do business with someone else, or to prevent others from doing business with, or employing, others.

Bribe—Payment or offer of payment of something of value in return for a breach of duty.

Brief—A written summary for an appellate court setting forth facts, issues, and points of law argued by counsel in a lower court. Also students use a *brief* of a case as a way of summarizing a long published case and thus preparing for class.

Broker—1. A person who carries on negotiations and makes contracts for a principal. 2. A person who buys and sells securities on behalf of a third party.

Bulk transfer—A sale or transfer of major inventory of a business at one particular time, such sale not ordinarily carried on in daily business.

Burden of proof—The process in a lawsuit by which one party has the duty of proving the facts in dispute.

Bylaws—The internal self-made regulations of a corporation adopted for the purpose of governing the company's internal management. Nonprofit organizations and other business associations also have bylaws.

C.I.F.—Shipping agreement in which seller agrees to pay insurance and freight as well as cost of goods.

C.O.D.—Cash on delivery. The buyer must pay for the goods upon receipt before opening goods.

Capacity—The ability or competency to do something at law. For example, a child is capable of entering a contract depending on his or her age; a person is capable of committing a crime depending on his or her state of mind at the time of commission.

Cash dispenser—A machine that dispenses cash.

Cash surrender value—The amount of money that a whole life insurance is worth if surrendered to the company prior to the death of the insured.

Casualty insurance—Insurance that protects the insured from loss due to damage or destruction of personal property by causes other than fire or elements.

Causa mortis gift—A gift given by a living person in contemplation of approaching death.

Cause of action—When a person's legal rights have been invaded, the facts showing that invasion constitute a *cause of action* and are usually set out in a complaint.

The failure to set out these facts by the plaintiff will lead to a motion for dismissal of the case by the defendant, alleging that the plaintiff has failed to state a cause of action.

Caveat emptor—Let the buyer beware (Latin). This idea at common law expressed the view that the buyer could not depend on the seller for any warranties after sale and thus should be careful in making his or her purchase.

Caveat venditor—Let the seller beware (Latin). Present-day maxim that, considering the amount of consumer action legislation and the number of proconsumer court decisions, it is the seller who should be careful to whom he, she, or it sells.

Cease and desist order—An order by a court or administrative agency requiring an individual or a corporation to stop carrying on a particular act.

Certificate of title—A written opinion by a lawyer that a title to property is valid.

Certification—An acceptance by a bank of a check; it guarantees that the bank will pay the check when it is presented.

Certiorari—The process by which an appellate court exercises discretionary authority to hear appeals.

Chattel mortgage—A transfer of a right in personal property or a lien on such that serves as security for payment of a debt or performance of a promised act.

Chattels—Personal property.

Check—A bank draft that is payable on demand.

Chose in action—A personal right of an owner to recover in a legal action things owned by him or her but not in his or her possession.

Code of Professional Responsibility—Rules governing the practice of law; drafted by the American Bar Association and adopted by the chief governing authority of each state bar.

Codicil—An addition to a person's will modifying, altering, or revoking provisions.

Collateral action—An attempt to avoid or evade a judicial proceeding or order by instituting a pro ceeding in another court attacking such.

Common carrier—One who transports goods (e.g., train) or services (e.g., telephone) for hire to the public and is regulated by federal and/or state agencies who insure that the public convenience and necessity is served.

Common law—A law derived from the published opinions of appellate courts as contrasted with law derived from statute.

Compensatory damages—A term used to denote damages that compensate the injured party for the injury suffered and nothing more.

Competent—Describes one who is capable at law. *See* capacity.

Complainant—A person who asks a court of law for redress of an injury allegedly suffered.

Composition—A legal agreement made between a debtor and several creditors whereby the latter agree to accept less from the debtor on a *pro rata* basis in satisfaction of all debts.

Conciliation—An informal method of bringing together parties to a dispute to settle differences before going to court.

Concur—To agree. With reference to appellate court decisions a "concurring opinion" is often written by a judge who may agree with the majority opinion's conclusion, but for differing reasons; thus he or she writes a separate opinion.

Conditional acceptance—A statement by the offeree to a bargain that he or she will enter into an agreement that differs from the original offer. In effect a *conditional acceptance* constitutes a counteroffer as to personal and real property. Often used to qualify or limit offeree's liability on bills of exchange.

Conditional sale—The sale of goods in which buyer obtains possession but seller retains title until the purchase price is paid.

Confession of judgment—The process by which a debtor agrees to submit to the jurisdiction of a court, and the judgment of such court, without extended legal proceedings, in the event that he or she breaches an agreement.

Conflict of interest—When one has a personal interest that contrasts with a duty owed to another; mutually exclusive duties to two or more entities.

Consequential damages—Damages that do not flow directly from the acts of a party (e.g., breach of contract) but only indirectly.

Consignment—1. The delivery of goods to a seller to be sold for the owner's account. 2. Delivery of goods to a common carrier to be shipped as directed by the owner.

Constructive fraud—Acts or omissions that, though having no intent to deceive, by their nature mislead an individual, corporation, or the public at large.

Constructive notice—A legal presumption that a person has knowledge of certain facts.

Consumer-credit contract—A contract for the sale of consumer goods on an installment basis.

Contempt citation—An order issued by a judge holding a person for incarceration following the individual's affront to the judge or his or her attempts to obstruct the court processes.

Conversion—The taking and keeping of personal property or goods without an owner's consent.

Corporate moral accountability—The concept that a corporation, as an independent entity, can be morally accountable for its actions.

Cost-benefit analysis—A measurement technique by which one adds up the total cost of implementation of a regulation(s), then compares it to the benefits accrued to both private and public parties.

Counterclaim—A claim by the defendant in opposition to plaintiff's claim that, if proved true would tend to diminish, alter, or defeat plaintiff's action.

Counteroffer—An offer made by the offeree to the offeror that would materially alter the original offer and thus demand acceptance by the offeror.

Cover—A remedy for buyer under the Uniform Commercial Code that allows the buyer in good faith to purchase, or make a contract to purchase, goods in substitution for

those seller has not been able to deliver.

Credit insurance—Protects both the creditor and the debtor by providing for the payment of an indebtedness of the insured in the event of death before the indebtedness has been paid.

Cross-appeal—A term used to denote a situation where both parties appeal from a lower court decision. Their appeals are said to "cross" each other.

Cross-examination—The examination of a witness provided by the opposition in a civil or criminal trial.

Curtesy—The estate at common law that a husband has in the estate of his wife upon her death.

Custodial account—An account in which one person holds property and uses it for the benefit of another; the person for whom the property is to be used is generally regarded as its owner for tax purposes.

De facto—What has happened *in fact* as opposed to what was ordered or may be ordered at law (Latin).

De jure—An action is taken by *right* or by *law* (Latin).

Debenture—An instrument issued as evidence of unsecured debt. A debenture is usually made payable to bearer with interest to be paid (e.g., a corporate bond).

Debtor—One who is under an obligation to pay a sum of money to another.

Decedent—A deceased person.

Deceit—A fraudulent mispresentation, or device by which one person tricks another who is ignorant of or does not have full knowledge of the facts.

Declaratory judgment—An order of the court that renders an opinion on a question of law but does not order the parties to do any specific act.

Decree—An order of a court in equity determining the rights of both parties.

Deed—An instrument that transfers title to real estate.

Deed of trust—An instrument that conveys title to real estate to a trustee, who holds title as security for a debt owed to a lender who is the beneficiary of the trust.

Default—A failure on the part of a party to perform a legal obligation. For example, the failure of a party to appear to defend against a claim brought against him may result in a *default judgment.*

Defeasible—A term that refers to the capability of title for real property being defeated or revoked.

Defendant—A party who is being sued in a civil action or accused of a crime in a criminal matter.

Defendant in error—A party who receives a favorable judgment in a lower court, which *plaintiff in error* now seeks to reverse.

Delegable duties—Contractual obligations that may be performed by a person who was not a party to the original contract.

Delegatee—A person to whom a *delegator* transfers rights and duties.

Delegation—The process of transferring or assigning authority from one person to another.

Delegator—The person who is responsible for transferring rights and duties.

Demurrer—The equivalent of a motion by defendant to dismiss, because even admitting the facts stated in plaintiff's complaint, they are insufficient for plaintiff to proceed on, and serve as no basis for defendant to form an answer.

Deontology—Concepts of duty that serve as guidelines for moral behavior.

Deposition—The process by which testimony of witnesses is taken in writing prior to a trial for use in the actual court action. The basis for this process may be by court order or statutory rules of procedure.

Depository bank—The bank in which an instrument is first deposited for purpose of collection.

Derivative action—A suit by shareholder(s) of a corporation to force the corporation to enforce shareholders' rights against a third party (often an officer of the company).

Descent—A term used to denote a receiving of real property by inheritance.

Detriment (legal)—A term used to show a loss or harm suffered to real or personal property or the giving up of a right to take action.

Direct investment—Situation in which an investor participates in the management of a firm in which investment has been made.

Directed verdict—A verdict that the court instructs the jury to bring back, such as a verdict in favor of one party because reasonable minds could not differ as to the facts. This verdict usually results from a motion on the part of counsel for either party in a trial but can be granted by the judge alone as well.

Disability insurance—Provides income to persons too ill or injured to continue to work.

Disaffirm—To revoke or repudiate. For example, an infant may *disaffirm* a contract prior to reaching the age of majority, or within a reasonable time thereafter.

Discharge—To release a party from obligations set forth in a contract. Also, a term used in bankruptcy to denote a release from all obligations. Used after a person is adjudicated a bankrupt.

Disclaimer—A refusal or rejection. For example a *disclaimer* clause in a contract notes the promises or warranties that will be given and disclaims all other responsibilities or warranties.

Discovery—The pretrial process by which parties to a suit disclose to each other relevant facts that are necessary for framing the issues, correcting them, and expediting trial procedure.

Dishonor—The refusal to pay or accept a negotiable instrument upon presentation for acceptance.

Dismiss—A term used to show a discharge of a cause of action. A *motion* for *dismissal* can be made by either party and will be ruled on by the judge.

Disparagement—The act of discrediting. For example, the tort of *disparagement* is a basis for a claim for damages when a business can show that a competitor has with intent injured the reputation and product of the business.

Dissolution—A cancellation or breaking up by mutual agreement. For example, the dissolution of a marriage contract.

Distribution—The division of personal property of a person who dies without a will; often also applied to the division of real property of a person who dies without a will.

Diversity of citizenship—One of the bases of jurisdiction for the federal courts; that is, when parties to a suit are citizens from different states.

Document of title to personal property—Any document that in the regular course of business financing is treated as adequately evidencing that the person in possession of it is entitled to receive, hold, and dispose of the document and the goods it covers. To be a document of title, the document must purport to be issued by or addressed to a bailee and purport to cover goods in the bailee's possession, which are either identified or are fungible portions of an identified mass.

Documentary draft—A draft used with an attached bill of lading.

Domain—The absolute and complete ownership of real property. For example, the right of *eminent domain* relates to the primary power of the legislature to control private property when it uses such for public purposes and compensates the owners.

Dominion—The perfect ownership or power over something.

Dower—The right of a wife to the real property of her husband as set forth by state statute.

Draft—A written order to pay money to another on demand or at a stated date.

Drawee—The individual to whom a bill of exchange is addressed and to whom a request for payment is made by a *drawer.*

Drawee bank—A bank that a check or draft is drawn on and that is ordered to pay the instrument when it is presented.

Drawer—The person who draws a bill of exchange.

Due-on-sale clause—A clause in a mortgage allowing the lender to treat sale of the property by the owner as a default.

Due process—Fundamental fairness in the administration of justice.

Duress—An unlawful restraint placed on an individual by another. It does not have to be the use of physical force; it may be any form of coercion that leads an individual to an act contrary to his or her free will.

Duty based ethics—Ethical theories based on principles of duty derived through religion, logic, or some conception of natural law.

Easement—The right of an individual to use the land of another for a limited purpose without obtaining possession or title.

Egoism—Acting solely to maximize one's self-interest.

Egoism, ethical—The idea that everyone has the right to act in his or her own self-interest and that it is the job of the government to place any restrictions on behavior.

Egoism, psychological—The idea that humans are incapable of considering the interests of others in their decisions.

Electronic fund transfer—Any transfer of funds, other than a transaction originated by check draft or similar paper instrument, that is initiated through an electronic terminal, telephonic instrument, computer, or magnetic tape so as to order, instruct, or authorize a financial institution to debit or credit an account.

Embezzlement—Fraudulently taking money or property of another by a person to whom it has been entrusted.

Endorsement—*See* Indorsement

Entrustment—Leaving goods temporarily in the hands of a third party.

Equalitarism—A theory of social justice based on the premise that everyone should be treated equally.

Equitable estoppel—A term that refers to the inability of an individual based on justice and fairness (equity) to assert legal rights, especially when another individual has been induced to act based on conduct or silence of the former's representation.

Equity—A legal system that developed in England. Today *equity* is used to denote fairness and justice as opposed to statutory or case law as a basis for decisions.

Error of law—Drawing incorrect conclusions of law from known and existing facts. Refers to the basis for appeals from lower courts to appellate courts.

Escheat—A reversion of property rights to the state when there is no individual competent to inherit.

Estate—The interest that anyone has in land. An *estate for life* denotes an interest in land that an individual has for his or her life or the life of another.

Estate administration—The process by which property is transferred from a decedent's estate to those entitled to receive it.

Estate planning—The process of planning for the future distribution of a person's property or estate.

Estate taxes—Taxes due to the government for the transfer of property at death; calculated on the value of the decedent's estate minus applicable exemptions.

Ethics—Standards of behavior based on personal values and external standards. Ethics are principles reflecting what is good or bad and what is acceptable to one's self and to others.

Ex delicto—From a tort or fault (Latin). Refers to a legal action arising out of fault, misconduct, or malfeasance.

Exculpatory—Clearing someone from guilt or excusing a party to a contract from doing something. For example, an *exculpatory clause* may excuse the seller from some warranties on the product sold.

Executed—Denoting a form of contract that has been completely performed and is now in effect.

Execution—The process of completing or carrying out something.

Executor—A man appointed by the deceased to carry out his or her directions as set out in a will.

Executory—Not yet completed because acts are incomplete.

Executrix—A woman appointed by a testator to carry out the terms of his or her will.

Exemplary damages—Damages granted to an injured party to compensate her or him for mental anguish and shame when there is shown that wrong was done with malice or wanton conduct. Often called *punitive damages*.

Exhaustion of administrative remedies—A legal doctrine that requires a party to seek all remedies within an administrative agency or entity if provided for by statute before requesting assistance from a court of law.

Express warranty—A guarantee created by a seller by an affirmation of fact, a description, a sample, or a model.

Expressed authority—Authority given in writing or by words, as opposed to that given by implication from a principal to an agent.

Expropriation—The taking of another's property, by a private party or for public use by the right of eminent domain.

Extortion—Taking property from another by wrongful threat of force or violence.

Extraterritorial laws—Laws of a nation that have effect beyond its own territory or boundary.

Extrinsic evidence—Those facts obtained from things outside an agreement. For example, the fact that an individual was or was not competent to sign an agreement is *extrinsic* to the terms of the agreement itself.

F.A.S.—The abbreviation for "free alongside ship." Denotes that seller must deliver goods to the correctly designated dock where ship is waiting to be loaded and must assume all expenses and risks up to that point.

FOB—The abbreviation for "free on board." Denotes that seller must ship and bear expenses to the point designated for delivery.

Fair market value—The price at which a willing seller and buyer will trade.

Fee simple—An estate in real property that is limited to an individual and heirs and assigns forever without any limitations on title or ownership.

Felony—A crime that is of a graver nature than misdemeanor and is punishable by incarceration in a state or federal prison. A *felony* will always be set out by statute.

Fiduciary—A person holding a relationship of trust in which he or she acts primarily for the benefit of another in certain matters.

First instance—A trial court in which a case is first tried, as opposed to an appellate court.

Fixture—A chattel attached to real property. Generally refers to something attached to real property and intended to be permanent.

Forbearance—The giving up of a right by one party to a contract in exchange for a promise by the other.

Foreclosure—The termination of all interests or rights of the mortgagor in property covered by a mortgage.

Fraud—An intentional misrepresentation of facts relied on by another, leading to legal injury.

Full faith and credit rule—Article IV, Section 1, in the United States Constitution, which requires that each state treat as valid and enforceable where appropriate the laws of other states.

Fungible—Describing goods that are equivalent to each other in general mercantile usage; for example, wines and liquors; used in the UCC.

Future interests—The present interest in real or personal property that gives the right to future use.

Futures contract—A contract for future delivery of goods.

Garnishee—A person holding money or property of a debtor that a creditor is trying to reach. A garnishee is served with a garnishment order.

Garnishment—The process by which a creditor obtains money or property of a debtor that is in the possession of another (garnishee).

General creditor—A creditor whose debt or claim is not secured by a lien on particular property; that is, it must be paid from the debtor's assets or estate.

General license—A license that authorizes export without application by the exporter.

Good faith—In Uniform Commercial Code transactions, honesty in fact in the conduct or transaction concerned.

Grand jury—A jury that hears evidence presented by the state and determines if sufficient evidence exists to indict a person for a specific crime.

Grantee—An individual to whom a grant is given. Usually refers to the deeding of land or the assignment of real property.

Grantor—An individual who is assigning or granting something.

Gratuitous promise—Promise made as part of an agreement without consideration for such promise being expected.

Guarantor—A person who signs an instrument agreeing to pay the instrument under certain circumstances.

Guaranty—A promise by an individual to answer for the debt of another in the event that the latter cannot pay.

Habeas corpus—Generally refers to any of the common law writs that bring a prisoner before a court (Latin). Used today to determine whether a prisoner was incarcerated in accordance with due process procedure.

Hearing examiner—An individual who is the chief fact finder in most federal administrative agency hearings.

Hearsay—The evidence coming not from a primary source but from an individual who has obtained such information from others, or a secondary source.

Hold harmless—A clause in an agreement in which an individual agrees to hold another party not liable and pay all claims against that party.

Holder—Anyone in possession of an instrument drawn, issued, or indorsed to him or her, to his or her order, to bearer, or in blank.

Holder in due course—An individual holder of a negotiable instrument who has taken it in good faith, for value, complete on its face, without knowledge of the instrument's being dishonored or overdue, and without notice of defect in the title.

Holding company—A corporation that owns other companies' stock but is not responsible for their day-to-day operations.

Illusory contract—An agreement that on its face appears to be binding but in reality lacks mutuality of obligation.

Implied agency rule—A rule in contract law that implies the proper form of communication by offeree in transmitting an acceptance to an offeror, although it may not be clear from words or writings.

Implied authority—A form of authority of an agent inferred from his or her position and conduct in representing a principal. The principal will be bound in contract to a third party based on this authority unless he or she renounces such authority and communicates such to the third party.

Implied warranty—A guarantee automatically created by operation of law when goods are sold.

Impossibility—A doctrine in contract law that allows for a rescission when a contract becomes legally impossible to perform. For example, if the subject matter of an agreement is destroyed by an unforeseen tornado, the defendant will plead impossibility of performance.

Impracticability—A doctrine that may allow for rescission of a contract when it becomes commercially impracticable to perform. This excuse for performance has been adopted by the Uniform Commercial Code in the event that a contingency occurs that was not planned for and that affects the complete capacity of the seller to perform.

In camera—In chambers (Latin). A court hearing that is closed to public scrutiny. Often used in cases where matters under consideration affect the national security of the country.

In pari delicto—In equal fault (Latin). Often used as a basis in tort law for joining two parties as defendants in a legal action.

In personam—Against a person (Latin). Basis for jurisdiction in a legal action to enforce rights against a specific person. For example, a suit brought against another person for injuries suffered in an automobile accident is *in personam* because it is against the driver or owner only.

In re—In the matter of (Latin). Often used in the heading of a case to denote that the suit is concerned with a thing rather than a lawsuit between two individuals directly. For example, "In re Brennan's Estate" refers to a title of a legal proceeding to dispose of property of a dead person.

In rem—Against a thing (Latin). Basis for jurisdiction in a legal action against the whole world, as opposed to in personam jurisdiction. For example, a suit to establish title to land. The winner has title against all other possible claimants, or the whole world.

Incontestability—A term used to denote the fact that for the life of an agreement or patent it is not open to any contesting claims.

Incontestability clause—A clause providing that after the passage of a set period of time (usually one or two years) the insurer may not contest representations made by the insured.

Incorporate—To create a formal corporate entity.

Independent contractor—An individual who contracts with a principal to do work by his or her own methods, unsupervised, and not subject to any control of the principal. He or she is solely responsible for the finished work product.

Indictment—Charge by a group of sitting jurors that an individual has committed some crime punishable by incarceration in a prison.

Indorsement—The signing of the back of a negotiable instrument by a drawee, thus assigning such property to another.

Infringement—An encroachment on others' rights in violation of law. For example, the unauthorized use for profit of a patented invention is a basis for a legal action for an *infringement of patent.*

Inheritance taxes—Taxes due a state government assessed on property received from a person who has died. The amount of the tax depends on the relationship between the decedent and the inheritor and on the value of the property inherited.

Injunction—An equitable writ or order directing the defendant to stop doing an act or preventing him or her from continuing a course of conduct.

Insolvency—The inability of an individual legal entity to pay its, his, or her debts at the time they become due.

Insurable interest—An interest in property protected that would lead to a benefit from property owned, or a loss in case of destruction. Such an interest is usually protected by an insurance policy covering a risk.

Integrated—Describing legal writings that are considered to be final and complete to all parties having a direct interest.

Inter alia—Among other things (Latin). Often used in pleadings and other legal documents to show that only a portion of a statute or a line of cases is cited.

Inter vivos gift—A gift given by a living person to another living person.

Inter vivos trust—A trust that is established by a person while he or she is alive and that transfers property to the trustee prior to the death of the person establishing it.

Interlocutory—Denoting decisions made by a court during a pending lawsuit; not final as to the substance of the litigation.

Intermediary bank—Any bank to which an instrument is transferred in the course of collection except the depository bank or payor bank.

Interpleader—The process by which a third party having no ownership in held property brings two adversary claimants into court and asks the judge to decide which claimant is entitled to the property.

Interpretation—The process by which a statute or written document is given meaning.

Intestate—A legal state in which a person dies without a will.

Ipso facto—By the fact itself (Latin).

Irreparable harm—An injury that cannot be measured and for which a court remedy would be insufficient or which a court would be incapable of redressing.

Issue—The voluntary delivery of an instrument by the maker or drawer to the payee.

Joint and several—Referring to a situation in which two parties having a related obligation can be sued jointly or individually.

Joint property—Property owned by two or more persons.

Joint tenancy—An estate in which two co-owners have undivided interests; upon death of one owner his or her interest passes to the other.

Joint venture investments—Investments with two or more active participants.

Judgment debtor—A defendant who has not satisfied a judgment that has been entered against him or her.

Judicial law—Law derived from the opinions of appellate courts; also referred to as common law or case law.

Jurisdiction—The geographic area, persons, and subject matter over which a particular court has the power to make decisions.

Jurisprudence—The philosophy of law. Schools of jurisprudence include positivist, sociological, existential, and natural law.

Larceny—Taking property of another intending to deprive that person of the property or its value.

Legacy—A gift or bequest of personal property.

Legislative veto—The method by which Congress reserves to itself the right to prevent a proposed agency regulation from becoming law.

Lemon laws—State laws designed to protect the purchasers of motor vehicles.

Letter of credit—An instrument issued by a bank that requests payment to bearer or guarantees payment of financial obligation for goods sold on credit.

Levy—To collect, or to seize goods by an officer of the law.

Liability insurance—Insurance that covers losses suffered by others for which the insured is legally responsible.

Libel—A written defamation in which an individual is held up to public contempt and ridicule that injures his or her reputation.

Libertarianism—Theory of social justice that emphasizes individual freedom based on property rights and a minimal role for government.

Lien creditor—A creditor whose debt or claim is secured by a lien on particular property.

Life estate—An estate whose duration is measured by the life of the holder or some other person.

Limited partnership—A partnership of one or more general partners who manage the business and are personally responsible for partnership debts, and one or more limited partners who contribute capital, share in profits, but take no part in running the business and incur no liability for partnership obligations beyond their contribution.

Liquidated damages—A form of damages fixed as part of a contractual relationship. For example, a general contractor agrees with an owner that for every day's delay in completion of a commercial building beyond an agreed date the contractor will pay the owner $1,000 a day.

Litigant—A party to a legal action.

Litigation—A lawsuit.

Maker—A person who makes or first executes a negotiable instrument.

Mandamus—We command (Latin). A term that denotes a court order directing an officer of a private or public corporation to carry out a specified act that is within his or her power by virtue of the office held.

Material—A term describing something essential or significant. For example, a *material* alteration in a contract might be a six-month delay in delivery when the parties agree on a specific date that both knew was important to the buyer.

Material alteration—In commercial paper, any alteration of the instrument that changes the contract of any party to the instrument.

Mechanic's lien—A claim on real property that seeks to secure priority of payment on debts owed for value of work completed and materials supplied in constructing or making improvements on debtor-owned building.

Mediation—A method of settling a dispute by bringing in a neutral third party to help resolve differences between the parties.

Mens rea—A guilty mind (Latin). A term used to show criminal intent; an essential element of a crime.

Merchantability—A term used to show the goods sold are fit for the purpose for which they are sold.

Merger guidelines—Specific U.S. Justice Department guidelines for private sector corporate mergers set forth as a warning that the Department *may* challenge companies that violate or plan to violate them. The guidelines are *not* law.

Misappropriation—The act of taking something one does not own and using it for a wrongful purpose. For example, in some states a banker may be accused of *misappropriation* of funds if he or she deals fraudulently with money entrusted to him or her.

Misdemeanor—A crime considered less serious than a felony and punishable by a fine or incarceration in an institution other than a state penitentiary for less than one year.

Misrepresentation—Words or conduct that misleads others as to the material facts of a situation. If such acts or conduct are unintentional, *innocent misrepresentation* has taken place. If done with intent and relied on by a party, and injury can be proven, fraud has been committed.

Mistake—An unintentional act or omission of law or fact. A *bilateral* or *mutual mistake* is an error made by both parties; if material to a contract, it will be grounds for rescission or reformation. A *unilateral mistake* is an error made by a single party and is not usually grounds for rescission.

Mistrial—A fundamental error in procedure that causes a trial judge to end and cancel out the proceedings of a trial. This is done usually without prejudice to a new trial's taking place. For example, an error in selection of jurors may be a basis for *mistrial.*

Mitigation of damages—A lowering or abatement of injury from a wrongful act.

Monopoly—A market structure in which a single seller (monopolist) has virtually complete control over the source of goods as well as the means of production. The monopolist is the sole influence on the price variable in this market.

Mortgage—A contract or conveyance of a lien on real property by a debtor to a creditor to secure the payment of an obligation by the debtor.

Mortgagee—An individual who receives or takes a mortgage, for example, a financial institution.

Mortgagor—The debtor who gives a mortgage for purpose of securing a debt owed by mortgagee.

Mutual insurance company—A company owned by policyholders.

Nationalization—The taking of private property by government, which pays compensation.

Necessaries—Goods and services that are reasonably proper for the maintenance of a minor in light of his or her family's income and position in the community. For example, food, clothing, shelter, and education through high school.

Negligence—A theory of tort law where damages are awarded based on the failure of an individual to exercise reasonable care when there existed such a duty toward another individual. This failure must be the proximate cause of damage to that individual.

Negotiable instrument—A written instrument that is executed containing an unconditional promise to pay a certain amount of money on demand or at an agreed time to order or to bearer.

Negotiation—The transfer of a negotiable instrument in a manner that makes the transferee a holder in due course. *See* Holder in due course.

No-fault insurance—Insurance that compensates victims of motor vehicle accidents regardless of fault or liability of the parties.

No-par value stock—The stock issued with no value amount on its certificate. A subscriber will pay that value as set by the board of directors of the corporation.

Nolo contendere—I will not contest it (Latin). A plea in a criminal action; it is treated by most courts as the equivalent of a guilty plea. It allows the defendant freedom from liability in a civil suit based on the same cause of action.

Nominal consideration—Consideration passing between parties may be *nominal*, thus inflating a portion of the exchange. For example, *A* deeds two acres of land to his son in exchange for one dollar.

Nominal damages—A small sum of money awarded to a plaintiff who is unable to prove substantial loss.

Nonfeasance—The failure of one party to attempt performance. Often referred to in agency law when an agent fails to begin performance of agreed upon duties.

Nonsuit—A term used for judgment entered by a court when a plaintiff fails to carry the burden of proof or proceed with a case.

Nontariff barriers—Any factor adversely affecting imports, except for tariffs.

Note—A written promise to pay money to another on demand or at a stated date.

Novation—An agreement to substitute one party for another in a contract.

Nuisance—A legal action in which plaintiff attempts to show that someone is interfering with the use and enjoyment of his or her property.

Obligee—A creditor or promisee.

Obligor—A debtor or promisor.

Offeree—One who accepts an offer or acts upon a legal offer in some manner.

Offeror—One who initiates or makes an offer.

Option contract—A contract in which one party has exchanged consideration for the sole purpose of having the right to buy certain real property or goods at a time of his or her choosing, at a price stated in the option agreement.

Order paper—An instrument that is payable to the order of a specific person.

Ostensible authority—Such authority in agency law that is allowed by a principal to his or her agent as seen from the perspective of a third party dealing with the agent.

Overdraft—A withdrawal of money by a depositor in excess of that which he or she has on account. Can also be used to mean a form of loan to depositor.

Pareto superiority—The condition of welfare maximization in which no action may be taken that will make someone better off without making others less well off.

Parol evidence—Evidence extrinsic or external to that set out in writing.

Partition—Proceedings by which a court divides lands usually held by joint tenants or tenants in common so that parties can hold such real property separately.

Patents—A document that protects inventors by giving the patent owner the exclusive right to make, sell, and use the product or process.

Payee—An individual who is paid, or to whom an instrument is made payable.

Payor bank—A bank on which an instrument is drawn.

Per capita distribution—The distribution of property among a person's descendants whereby each descendant's share is determined pro rata based on the number of beneficiaries.

Per curiam—By the court (Latin). Generally refers to a short statement of decision by the whole court as distinguished from a decision with reasoning written by an individual judge.

Per se—By himself or itself (Latin). A term referring to something forbidden in and of itself because of its pernicious nature, with the court not allowing an argument for the reasonableness of conduct. For example, price fixing in the antitrust area is *per se* illegal.

Per stirpes—The distribution of property among a person's descendants whereby equal shares are granted to the first generation of beneficiaries. If a beneficiary predeceases the testator, the beneficiary's descendants must share his or her portion.

Perfect tender rule—A rule of the law of sale of goods stating that the seller must tender the goods exactly as specified by the contract.

Perjury—The giving of willful false statements under oath in a court of law or in depositions material to such proceeding. One can also *perjure* oneself before legislative bodies.

Personal representative—The person named by the testator to look after and administer his or her estate after death.

Petit jury—A jury, traditionally of 12 people, used in a civil or criminal trial.

Petitioner—A party that files an appeal with a higher court after losing in a lower court.

Plaintiff-in-error—Generally, a party who is appealing from a lower court decision that has gone against him or her.

Planned unit development—A form of zoning that allows various uses of a site in order to provide maximum land for open space.

Pmsi (Purchase money security interest)—A security interest taken by a seller in items sold to a buyer securing all or a part of the price.

Point-of-sale terminal—A machine that permits the transfer of funds from an individual's account directly into an account maintained by the business in payment for goods or services.

Possession—The dominion or control over property.

Power of attorney—An executed instrument authorizing an agent to represent the individual signing in a general manner or only with reference to a particular transaction or proceeding.

Precedent—A previous decision relied upon by a court for authority in making a current decision.

Prescription—The method of obtaining a right to use another's land through wrongful use for a period of time established by statute.

Presentment—The act of presenting a negotiable instrument to a party for acceptance or payment.

Prima facie—"At first sight" (Latin). Denoting a fact that appears true and will stand as such in the eyes of the court until contradicted.

Principal—In agency law an individual who delegates authority to an agent to represent him or her either generally or only for a specific transaction.

Privileged communication—A term used to denote the right of counsel to refuse disclosure of any communication between the attorney and his or her client to any individual or court of law.

Privity—A contractual relation between parties to a contract as opposed to those affected by the agreement but not parties to it.

Pro rata—"Proportionately, or by share" (Latin).

Probable cause—The existence of sufficient circumstances leading a reasonable person to believe that a person accused of a crime had committed the act.

Probate—A legal process by which a will is proven valid and conflicting claims on the estate are settled. This process takes place in a *probate* court.

Procure—To initiate a proceeding.

Promisee—An individual who receives a promise.

Promisor—An individual who initiates and makes a promise to promisee.

Promissory estoppel—An equitable doctrine often used as a substitute when consideration is not present in a contract and a grave injustice will result if the agreement is not enforced. The doctrine will be specifically invoked when a promise is made by one party that induces justifiable reliance by the other and causes a change in position on the part of the injured party.

Promissory note—A written promise to pay a certain sum to order or bearer within a specific period or at a stated time.

Proximate cause—Used in tort law

and negligence theory to denote the direct and natural sequence between the breach of a duty and the injury to an individual.

Proxy—The process by which a shareholder gives another the right to vote his or her stock.

Public affairs management—Techniques that firms use to influence the external environment, for example, lobbying, issues advertising.

Puffing—The favorable statements a seller makes about his or her product.

Punitive damages—Those nonquantifiable damages that do not flow directly from a cause of action but are awarded by the court because of the willful and malicious nature of conduct of the defendant. The court sees such damages as a deterrent to future wrongful conduct.

Qualified indorsement—Indorsement that eliminates the secondary liability of an indorser on the instrument.

Qualified privilege—In tort actions, an exemption for a speaker from liability on a charge of libel or slander unless the defendant can be shown to have had actual malice and knowledge of the falsity of the statement.

Quantum meruit—"As much as he deserved" (Latin). An old common law pleading requesting recovery for materials and services rendered.

Quasi contract—A court-imposed agreement designed to provide equitable relief when one party has received a benefit at the expense of the other. The court imposes a legal relationship on the parties even though all the elements of a contract are not present.

Quid pro quo—Something in exchange for something else.

Quitclaim deed—An instrument of conveyance of the grantor. It passes rights and interest in real property but does not warrant title.

Quota—A legal restriction on the number of items of a particular

type that may be imported into a given country.

Ratification—The process by which one adopts the terms of an agreement by silence or affirmative conduct. For example, a minor ratifies agreements made in his or her minority by continuous adherence to the terms for a reasonable period after reaching legal majority.

Rebuttal—An introduction of evidence in a trial that attempts to show that a previous witness's testimony is not credible.

Recoupment—A holding back of an amount of money by a defendant that is owed plaintiff for damages. Defendant may argue that, although he or she breached, plaintiff also failed to comply with obligations arising out of the same agreement.

Regulation Z—A group of rules set forth by the Federal Reserve Board that requires lenders to disclose a number of items to borrowers.

Relativism—Belief that ethical analysis depends on social and economic context in which it occurs and is not universal.

Release—The giving up of a claim or right on the part of one party in exchange for some consideration.

Replevin—A common law term referring to the legal process of obtaining, or taking back, of personal property that is in the hands of another.

Res—A thing or object (Latin).

Res ipsa loquitur—The thing speaks for itself (Latin). Presumption in tort law that defendant is negligent because instrument was in sole control of him or her, and accident would not have happened but for defendant's negligence.

Res judicata—A thing decided (Latin). A legal doctrine that a decision by a court in a suit is final as to future suits on the same cause of action and between the same parties.

Rescission—A remedy in contract law that cancels or abrogates an agreement.

Respondeat superior—The doctrine that the employer is responsible for acts of an employee who is acting within the scope of his or her employment.

Respondent—An appellee or a person who usually has won a verdict in a lower court, and against whom an appeal is being taken.

Restatement of agency—A scholarly work prepared by the American Law Institute summarizing the law of agency; the model the authors recommend be followed for the future.

Restatement of contracts—A scholarly work prepared by the American Law Institute summarizing present contract law; the model the authors recommend be followed for the future.

Restitution—A remedy for breach of a contract in which the court seeks to restore both parties to their original position following rescission of the agreement.

Restrictive indorsement—An indorsement that is conditional, or purports to prohibit the further transfer of the instrument, or includes words that signify a purpose of deposit or collection, or otherwise states that it is for the benefit or use of the indorsee or another person.

Reversion—The returning of an estate left to a grantor after the termination of an estate granted by him or her to another individual.

Revocation—Recall of an offer by an offeror prior to acceptance by offeree.

Rule making—A function of most federal agencies; allows interested parties to comment on proposed binding rules prior to their enactment.

Sale on approval—A sale on terms that allow the buyer to reject the goods after inspecting them.

Satisfaction—The discharge of a debt by payment in full or in part, with agreement of the parties.

Scienter—"Knowingly" (Latin). Generally refers to need for knowledge as an essential element in a tort action for deceit or fraud.

Security interest—A pledge by debtor of property or other matters of value, to make his or her

promise of payment under a contract enforceable by creditor in the event of a breach.

Severable—Capable of being divided and existing independently. For example, a severable contract is one that can be enforced in part, since performance can be divided and apportioned.

Social justice—Manner in which rights and responsibilities are distributed among members of society.

Sovereign immunity—The doctrine that holds that courts of one country have no jurisdiction over suits brought against another country. The doctrine is generally restricted to noncommercial activities of a country.

Special indorsement—An indorsement that specifies the person to whom or to whose order the instrument is payable.

Stakeholder—A person affected by corporate actions who has a claim that the corporation should consider his or her interests.

Stale check—An uncertified check that is presented for payment more than six months after date of issue.

Stare decisis—A legal doctrine stating that decisions of a court should serve as precedent for future legal actions dealing with similar factual situations and points of law.

Statute of frauds—State laws that require certain forms of contracts to be in writing. For example, a promise in consideration of marriage in some states is required to be in writing.

Stay order—A court judgment that prevents a lower court order from being enforced pending an appeal by one of the parties.

Stop-payment order—An order by a customer to the drawee not to pay a check when it is presented for payment.

Strict liability—A concept applied in both civil and criminal law. In criminal law it imposes criminal penalty without proof of intent. In civil law it imposes liability without fault.

Subpoena—The process by which a court orders an individual to appear and testify at a time stated.

Subpoena duces tecum—The process by which, at the request of a party to a suit, the court orders a witness to appear with a relevant document in his or her possession.

Substantial performance—In contract law, the term indicates that all material terms of an agreement have been met, and only insignificant matters remain.

Substantive—Pertaining to essential or basic law that sets out rights. Procedural law is concerned with the legal procedures necessary to obtain these rights in courts or administrative agencies.

Sui generis—One of a kind (Latin).

Supra—Above (Latin). The term refers the reader to a previous part of a book.

Surety—An individual who is originally bound on a debtor–creditor contract to assume primary liability for his or her principal (debtor) in case of a failure of the latter to perform.

Takeover—A process by which an individual or a corporation seeks to obtain control of the management of a corporation by purchasing controlling shares of the stock.

Tariff—A tax assessed on imported goods. The tariff may be based on the value of the goods (ad valorem) or on the number of goods (flat rate) being imported.

Tenancy at will—A leased estate created when the owner of real property allows someone to occupy it for an unspecified period of time.

Tenants in common—The method of holding title to property in which each person owns a certain amount of the property; on the death of one of the parties, that person's property goes to his or her heirs, not to the other tenant.

Tenant by the entirety—Joint tenants who are spouses and who provide that the survivor of them will automatically become the owner of the property held as joint tenants.

Tender—An offer to pay a sum of money without conditions attached.

Testamentary trust—A trust created by a person's will; comes into effect only on that person's death.

Testator—An individual who has died leaving a will.

Title insurance—Insurance that repays the insured for a loss arising from defects in the title to real estate.

Tort-feasor—In law of torts, a wrong-doer, or one guilty of a tort.

Trade acceptance—Time draft drawn by a seller naming the seller as payee and the purchaser of goods as drawee; obligates the buyer to pay the draft upon acceptance of the goods.

Trade fixtures—Articles a tenant attaches to land or buildings to be used in the tenant's trade or business.

Trade secrets—Valuable formulas, patterns, or information used by a business but unknown to competitors.

Transferability—An instrument's assignability or negotiability.

Transferee—An individual to whom a transfer is made.

Transferor—A person who initiates or makes a transfer.

Treasury shares—Generally refers to stock issued by a corporation to shareholders and subsequently acquired by the issuing corporation.

Treble damages—Refers to triple the amount of damages awarded by a jury. The purpose of such is to discourage similar conduct in the future. Such statutory damages are usually awarded by the court on motion of the plaintiff following a jury award.

Trespass—Unlawful violation of another's person or property.

Trust—1. An interest or right in real or personal property by one party for the benefit of another. 2. In antitrust law an unlawful combination seeking to do an act in contravention of federal or state statute.

Trust endorsement—An indorsement that indicates that the proceeds of an instrument should be held in trust for a third party.

Trustee in bankruptcy—An individual who holds title to a bankrupt's property at the direction of the court. His or her function is to defend all assets in suits and to provide an accounting to the court of moneys for distribution to creditors.

Tying agreements—In antitrust law, a refusal by a manufacturer to sell a primary product (tying) unless the retailer or franchisee agrees to buy a secondary product (tied).

Ultra vires—"Beyond its power" (Latin). Pertaining to a corporation's acting beyond the scope of the power set out in its charter or articles of incorporation.

Unconscionable—Denoting a contract that is grossly unfair and shocking to the conscience. For example, the use of small print and technical language in a contract for necessaries with poor, illiterate people while charging prices that are far above normal market prices. The court will generally not enforce such agreement and will order a rescission.

Underwriter—Usually, a firm that markets securities for a corporate registrant. It sells corporate securities as an agent and receives a commission for such work.

Undue influence—The pressure exerted on an individual to sign an agreement. Generally it refers to the misuse of a position of confidential communication (e.g., doctor-patient) to influence an individual.

Unilateral—Pertaining to one side, or to only one party. For example, a *unilateral* mistake by a party to a contract is a misunderstanding of the terms of an agreement by one party but not the other.

Universalism—The view that there are universal principles that transcend local custom or practice.

Utilitarianism—The theory that the morality of actions is determined by their outcome, with an emphasis on the greatest number. It is an example of outcome based ethics.

Utilitarianism, act—Requires an individual analysis of any action that may have moral consequences.

Utilitarianism, rule—The practice of identifying rules that are assumed to maximize utility instead of making an individual assessment of each action's moral consequences.

Unliquidated debt—A debt the exact amount of which cannot be determined by the terms of the obligation.

Usage of trade—Well-known manner of conducting transactions in a particular industry or trade.

Usury—The loan of money at an interest rate in excess of that allowed by law.

Valid—Containing all the elements of a contract and thus is operative at law.

Vendee—A purchaser of property.

Vendor—A seller of property.

Vest—To give an immediate fixed right of possession in an estate of real property.

Vicarious liability—Indirect liability. Used in agency law to describe a principal's liability to third party for the acts of an agent.

Void—Having no legal force in the eyes of the law at its inception. A *void* agreement can never be cured of its defect and will always be inoperative.

Voidable—Pertaining to an agreement that becomes inoperative when the parties treat it as effective and binding.

Waive—To relinquish intentionally a legal right that could be exercised.

Warehouse receipt—A receipt, issued by a warehouse supervisor, that enables the person in possession of it to pick up goods from the warehouse.

Warrant—In criminal law a written order directing a law enforcement officer to arrest a person.

Warranty—An undertaking by a seller to guarantee a product against defects. The scope of such warranty as to goods is usually set out in writing. Implied warranties are those established from the nature of goods and their intended purpose.

Warranty deed—A deed that conveys title and warrants that the seller's title to the real estate is marketable.

Watered stock—The issued stock that is represented as fully paid but in fact is not paid up.

Whistle blowing—Reporting the

wrongdoing of another person to someone in authority; a type of ethical problem that places one person in a position of telling his or her supervisors that the actions of someone else are illegal, wrongful or unethical.

White collar crime—The term used to describe nonviolent criminal acts committed in a commercial context by a member of the management or professional class.

Will—A written declaration stating its maker's desires as to the disposition of his or her property or estate after death.

Workable competition—A term used to denote industrial organization economists' yardstick for measuring the effect a merger will have on an industry's competitive framework. Conduct, structure, and performance criteria are used to judge the effectiveness of competition in a market.

Zoning—The division of an area, usually a municipality, into districts to control land use.

Subject Index

Case Index

Italic page references indicate Cases that are excerpted in the text.